American Literature

VOLUME ONE

American Literature
A Prentice Hall Anthology

EMORY ELLIOTT, General Editor
University of California, Riverside

LINDA K. KERBER
University of Iowa

A. WALTON LITZ
Princeton University

TERENCE MARTIN
Indiana University

 Prentice Hall, Englewood Cliffs, New Jersey 07632

Library of Congress Cataloging-in-Publication Data

American literature: a Prentice Hall anthology / Emory Elliott,
  general editor, . . . [et al.].
    p.   ch.
   Includes bibliographical references and index.
   ISBN 0-13-027244-2 (v. 1)
   1. American literature. I. Elliott, Emory, (date)
PS507.A5757 1990
810.8--dc20

90-7875
CIP
Rev.

Editorial/production supervision and
  interior design: Hilda Tauber
Development editor: Karen S. Karlin
Manufacturing buyers: Herb Klein, Dave Dickey
Photo research: Barbara Schultz
Photo editor: Lorinda Morris-Nantz
Design director: Florence Dara Silverman
Art preparation: Maria Piper
Cover design: Lydia Gershey
Cover art: Hannah Foote, *Baltimore Album Applique Quilt*
  (detail), 1850. Baltimore. Cotton, 104 × 104".
  Collection America Hurrah Antiques, New York City.
  (Photograph by Schecter Lee)

Printed in the United States of America
10 9 8 7 6 5 4 3 2 1

ISBN   0-13-027244-2

Prentice-Hall International (UK) Limited, *London*
Prentice-Hall of Australia Pty. Limited, *Sydney*
Prentice-Hall Canada Inc., *Toronto*
Prentice-Hall Hispanoamericana, S.A., *Mexico*
Prentice-Hall of India Private Limited, *New Delhi*
Prentice-Hall of Japan, Inc., *Tokyo*
Simon & Schuster Asia Pte. Ltd., *Singapore*
Editora Prentice-Hall do Brasil, Ltda., *Rio de Janeiro*

Contents

PART TWO

The Age of the Democratic Revolution: The Late 18th Century 415

LATE 18TH-CENTURY NONFICTION PROSE *425*

PART THREE

Progress and Crisis: The Early to Middle 19th Century 695

EARLY TO MIDDLE 19TH-CENTURY FICTION *703*

Preface

During the past twenty years, the field of American literature has been going through one of the most exciting periods in its development as a discipline. Of the many changes in literary theory and in critical methods, the most significant advance affecting the teaching of American writing—and thereby anthologies of American literature—has been the discovery and rediscovery of important works that had received little critical attention in the past. For the most part, these newly valued texts are by women writers and members of ethnic and racial minority groups whose works had been misunderstood, overlooked, or consciously rejected by the professors who were in positions to make such decisions, most of whom were themselves male and primarily interested in the English heritage of American literature. Thus, for example, anthologies always used to begin with the writings of the English Puritans who came to what was referred to as a "new world." One recent shift has been the recognition that long before the English arrived in the land now called America, that land had been inhabited for centuries by peoples who possessed rich and complex literary cultures that form part of American literature. Before the English arrived, explorers from Spain, Italy, and other parts of the world had also left a literary record of their encounters with this land and its peoples. Today's literature courses and anthologies present these earlier writings as more accurate beginnings of American literature.

Whereas the list of writers and texts in American literature has grown substantially as a result of these new attitudes, the number of weeks in each semester and the number of courses in college curricula allotted for the teaching of the subject have not expanded. Teachers in the field would like more time to do justice to the established writers such as Emerson, Melville, James, and Faulkner, whose works have long been studied. Concurrently, they want to introduce students to the many rewarding texts by writers such as Kate Chopin, Charlotte Perkins Gilman, Constance Fenimore Woolson, Mary E. Wilkins Freeman, Emma Lazarus, Charles W. Chesnutt, Paul Laurence Dunbar, Booker T. Washington, and W. E. B. Du Bois, to note a few examples from the 1880s and 1890s alone. To accommodate these desires, anthology editors have been producing longer and longer texts. In 1974 a standard collection of this kind was about 1700 pages per volume; the most recent anthologies have been approaching 3000 pages per volume. Teachers lament that they are overwhelmed by the huge number of choices to be made and frustrated by the hundreds of pages to be covered in a given year. The large physical size of the books has even become an inconvenience, and in some cases the efforts of publishers to produce smaller books has led to the use of very thin paper and a reduced typeface that makes reading the texts difficult.

Balancing the Canon

Before beginning this anthology, Prentice Hall conducted an extensive survey of American literature teachers at a wide range of institutions of higher learning. The results demonstrated that most teachers want an anthology that is more concise and, at the same time, provides a balance of works by the long-established authors and by those receiving recognition and attention long overdue. Therefore, the editors of *American Literature: A Prentice Hall Anthology* have attempted to produce a text that is complete and contemporary in its inclusion of the widest representation of American writing and yet is more concise than other available texts. In every decision about the table of contents, the format, and the critical apparatus of this anthology, we have kept the needs of teachers and students in the forefront. By making the difficult decision to exclude some texts by established authors that are not frequently taught, we have been able to make room for ample selections by writers excluded in the past. We believe that this anthology provides teachers and students with a practical and useable text that fully reflects the cultural diversity of our national literature.

Indeed, teachers will find many authors and selections that either have not been included in previous anthologies or have only very recently been acknowledged as part of the canon. Robert Calef is placed next to Cotton Mather to demonstrate a rationalist Puritan response to the Salem witchcraft trials. Judith Sargent Murray is included with Mercy Otis Warren, Hannah Webster Foster, and Susanna Haswell Rowson, thus expanding the coverage of female authors of the late eighteenth century. Henry Clay Lewis appears with Augustus Baldwin Longstreet, George Washington Harris, and Thomas Bangs Thorpe as increased interest in regionalism has led to new attention to the Southwest Humorists. Fanny Fern joins Lydia Maria Child, Margaret Fuller, Louisa May Alcott, Rebecca Harding Davis, and Frances E. W. Harper in the antebellum period, and the Declaration of Sentiments, issued at the Seneca Falls Women's Rights Convention, provides readers with a chorus of voices for women's rights in the 1840s. In the twentieth-century sections, Maya Angelou, Paula Gunn Allen, Lawson Inada, Maxine Kumin, Yvor Winters, and Stanley Kunitz are included with T. S. Eliot, William Faulkner, and Flannery O'Connor. In addition to offering the complete texts of *The Contrast, The Scarlet Letter*, "Benito Cereno," *Billy Budd, Nature, Walden, Huckleberry Finn, The Awakening, Daisy Miller, Maggie*, "Red Wind," "Hugh Selwyn Mauberley," "The Waste Land," and *Seize the Day*, we have included in their entirety the *Narrative of the Life of Frederick Douglass*, Lorraine Hansberry's *A Raisin in the Sun* and N. Scott Momaday's *The Way to Rainy Mountain*. These are only a few examples of the newly recognized and established authors and texts that readers will find here. Because some survey courses cover Whitman in the first term and others cover him in the second, we duplicate the entire Whitman section in each volume. In addition, we are proud of our extraordinarily full list of complete plays. The limited number of selections by Hemingway, Fitzgerald, and Faulkner are the result of restrictions their publishers have placed upon reprinting their works.

Placing Works in Contexts

This anthology focuses strongly upon the connections between American literature and its various contexts: historical, political, economic, religious, intellectual, and international. Because teachers report that students are often daunted by extremely long period introductions that attempt to cover too much history and literature at once, we have provided shorter introductory background segments and placed them closer to the appropriate texts. We have avoided overly long introductions and designed a combination of historical background essays by editor-historian Linda K. Kerber and essays on the various literary genres. This separation enables readers to perceive the literary matters in relation to—but separate from—the political and social contexts at the time of writing. The repeated juxtaposition of literary text with historical material reminds the readers of the connections between them as well. The historical introductions engage controversial issues of American history and examine the conflicts and failures as well as the victories of America's past. Genre introductions discuss the development and complexities of the literary forms and styles in relation to the intellectual movements of the time periods.

Along with the emphasis upon linking texts and contexts more closely, we have placed in each section several "Contexts" boxes, which present relevant historical and critical statements or examples of other pertinent literature. In some cases, the "Contexts" boxes present special developments: a series of boxes in the twentieth-century sections traces the chronological development of different schools of literary criticism and theory. Throughout both volumes, boxes help to define and illustrate key terms such as "neoclassicism," "romanticism," and "modernism." Significant nonliterary documents also appear, including portions of the "I Have a Dream" speech by Dr. Martin Luther King, Jr.

Adding the Visual Element

With the strong emphasis upon the visual in our society, it is surprising how few illustrations appear in literature anthologies. The Prentice Hall anthology has portraits of one hundred authors and one hundred additional illustrations that capture the feel of the historical periods, the action and events that surrounded the writing of the literature, and the associations between writing and other arts. For example, students using this text will be able to see the domes and columns of neoclassical architecture and thus better grasp the relationship between the balance and form of eighteenth-century writing and the style of neoclassical buildings. The illustrations add an exciting feature to the Prentice Hall anthology that distinguishes it sharply from others.

With the daily experiences of teachers and students in mind, we have sought to make an anthology that people will truly enjoy using. Avoiding overly long biographical essays, we have made the headnotes more concise. In addition to historical period introductions, we have provided illustrated, eye-catching time lines that integrate key historical and literary events and their dates. Readers will obtain a clear picture of the chronology and the interconnection of texts and contexts. A glossary at the end of each volume serves to underscore and define literary terms that arise in the historical and genre introductions and headnotes as well as those that naturally come up in classroom discussions. An appendix, "Writing About Literature," discusses the student's special problems involved in writing an essay about literature and outlines procedures for meeting the challenge successfully. We have tried to annotate the texts sensibly in order to provide in a concise form the essential information students need. Dates for the initial publication of works are listed at the end of each selection; when known, dates of composition precede the publication dates. Whenever possible, we have used the approved, definitive editions of the texts. For ease of reading we have modernized archaic punctuation and spelling of some works in the early period. Readers should note that within excerpts of works, three centered asterisks indicate an omission of a paragraph or more, whereas run-in ellipses marks indicate the omission of less than a paragraph. Finally, each volume is accompanied by an instructor's manual with questions for study and discussion, suggested topics for student papers, and guidelines for teaching American literature.

ACKNOWLEDGMENTS

Many scholars provided various forms of assistance in the preparation of this anthology. We are grateful to Anne Agee, Anne Arundel Community College; Steven Gould Axelrod, University of California, Riverside; David Arnold, University of California, Riverside; David Austin; Lea Baechler, Columbia University; Rosemarie Battaglia, Michigan State University; Ronald Bosco, State University of New York, Albany; Jack Branscomb, East Tennessee State University; Brian Bremen, University of Texas; Mark Busby, Texas A & M University; James Buzzard, Harvard University; Bruce Coad, Mountain View College; Joan Corcoran, Columbia University; Gwen Crane, Princeton University; Keith Cushman, University of North Carolina, Greensboro; Allan Emery, Bowling Green State University; Joseph Essid, Indiana University; Virginia Feury-Gagnon; Thomas Fick, Southeastern Louisiana University; Joan Frederick, James Madison University; Sam Girgus, Vanderbilt University; Sonja Freiland, Indiana University; Maureen Goldman, Bentley College; Consuela Golden; Janet Gray, Princeton University; Jennifer M. Ginn, North Carolina State University; June Chase Hankins, Southwest Texas State University; Joseph Heininger, University of Michigan; Wendy Hirsh, Columbia University; Anne Hiemstra, Columbia University; Michael J. Hoffman, University of California, Davis; Joonok Huh, Northern Colorado University; Mary Hunter, University of California, Riverside; Claudia Johnson, University of Alabama; Emory D. Jones, Northeast Mississippi Community College; Alan Kaufman, Bergen Community College; Margot Kelley, Indiana University; Katherine Kinney, University of California, Riverside; James A. Levernier, University of Arkansas, Little Rock; Ina Lipkowitz, Columbia University; Michael Lofaro, University of Tennessee; Mason Lowance, University of Massachusetts; Robert Lynch, University of Nebraska; John McCammon, Indiana University; John H. McElroy, University of Arizona; June J. McManus, San Antonio College; Marilyn Miller; Randall Moon, University of California, Riverside; Nancy A. Mower, University of Hawaii; Anne C. Myers, DeVry Institute of Technology, Phoenix; Louis Owens, University of New Mexico; Jay Parini, Middlebury College; Mark Patterson, University of Washington; Timothy Redman, Ohio State University; Mary Margaret Richards, University of Texas, Permian Basin; Judith M. Riggin, Northern Virginia Community College; Michael Robertson, Lafayette College; James K. Ruppert, University of Alaska; Ramón Saldivar, University of Texas, Austin; Rosalind Sackoff; William J. Scheick, University of Texas; James Scrimgeour; Thomas E. Shields, East Carolina University; Frank Shuffelton, Rochester University; William Shurr, University of Tennessee; Nancy Craig Simmons, Virginia Polytechnic Institute and State University; Pat Skantze, Columbia University; Diane Stevens, Indiana University; Gordon Tapper, Columbia University; John Timmerman, Calvin College; David Van Leer, University of California, Davis; Edward Watts, Indiana University; Lori J. Williams, Indiana University; Ann Woodlief, Virginia Commonwealth University; and David Wyatt, University of Maryland. We also thank Josephine Koster Tarvers of Rutgers University, New Brunswick, for composing the essay "Writing About Literature."

Several students, secretaries, family members, and friends have provided various forms of editorial assistance. We wish to thank Deborah Barker, Sara Lynn Bowers, Marcia Hack, Bruce Hagood, Carla Latteri, Kandi Leonard, Barbara Burke Martin, Elizabeth Patton, Marsha Rosh, Maggi Schuman, Estelle Shapiro-Childers, and Holly Whitten. The staffs of the following libraries have been quite helpful: the University of California, Riverside; the University of California, Los Angeles; the Huntington Library; Princeton University; the University of Iowa; and Indiana University, especially Anthony Shipps.

Finally, we wish to thank the following people at Prentice Hall who worked closely with us: our development editor, Karen Karlin, whose endurance, patience, and editorial skills have been remarkable; Hilda Tauber, our production editor and designer, for her imaginative work and flexible planning; and editor in chief Phil Miller and senior English editor Kate Morgan for directing the project with wisdom and good cheer. Others who contributed in important ways are supplements editor Ann Knitel, photo editor Lorinda Morris-Nantz, design director Florence Silverman, permissions researcher Mary Helen Fitzgerald, marketing managers Tracy Augustine and Gina Sluss, and assistants Fran Falk, Heidi Moore, Page Poore, and Kathy Hursch.

EMORY ELLIOTT
General Editor

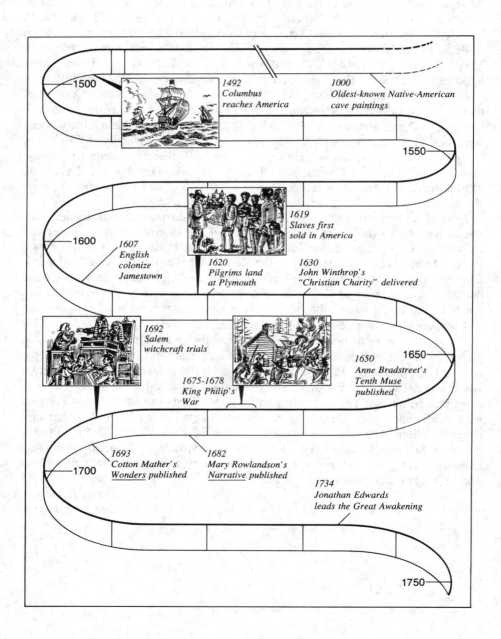

1492
*Columbus
reaches America*

1000
*Oldest-known Native-American
cave paintings*

1550

1619
*Slaves first
sold in America*

1600

1607
*English
colonize
Jamestown*

1620
*Pilgrims land
at Plymouth*

1630
*John Winthrop's
"Christian Charity" delivered*

1692
*Salem
witchcraft trials*

1675-1678
*King Philip's
War*

1650
*Anne Bradstreet's
Tenth Muse
published*

1650

1693
*Cotton Mather's
Wonders published*

1682
*Mary Rowlandson's
Narrative published*

1700

1734
*Jonathan Edwards
leads the Great Awakening*

1750

The European Colonization of the Americas

Through the Middle 18th Century

> *Historians . . . believe that the meaning of an event is perpetually open to revision, that its meaning for successive generations will differ from its contemporary meaning or its causes.*
>
> —JAMES AXTELL, The European and the Indian, 1981

We are so used to the terms "Old World" and "New World" that we can easily fall into the habit of thinking that, somehow, the Western Hemisphere is literally new. As late as the eighteenth century, a French scientist explained that Florida is swampy because it had not quite dried out from the Flood. We inherit these terms from European explorers, who worked the concept of old and new into their rationalization for conquest and destruction. Their conquest myth—that America was virgin land, empty wilderness, inhabited by savages incapable of civilization—is still resonant in the twentieth century. This myth began in Columbus's own lifetime and received an early and powerful literary formulation in William Shakespeare's final play, *The Tempest* (1611). In that play European civilization is embodied in a wise philosopher/scientist who is shipwrecked with his beautiful daughter, Miranda, on an island in the "brave new world." There he uses his knowledge to subdue an evil witch, who is native to the island, and her crude and hostile son, Caliban.

The peoples of the Americas were not witches. They were descendants of the several hundred Asians who had moved across the now-submerged land bridge between Siberia and Alaska as early as twenty-five thousand years ago, over the course of hundreds of centuries. When Christopher Columbus stepped out on a gleaming beach of white coral on October 12, 1492, he in effect reconstituted the land bridge. The land he claimed was no empty wilderness; it was inhabited by some 100 million people speaking over 850 languages. The earliest Americans had developed a stunning range of societies. Many, such as the Algonquins of the Northeast, were hunting and gathering clans; others, including the Mayas and Aztecs of the central regions and the Incas of the South, had developed highly complex, sophisticated societies characterized by major engineering feats, precise mathematical calculation, astronomy, and written languages.

1

Columbus came as explorer and scientist but also as conqueror. Historians traditionally distinguish between his expedition and those of the "conquistadores"—his successors, including Hernando Cortés and Francisco Pizarro, who came explicitly as military men and intended to conquer the region by means of military power. However, Columbus was commissioned by Queen Isabella of Spain as part of a great celebration of the defeat of the Muslim kings of Grenada in 1492, of the unification of the territories held by the crowns of Aragon and Castille, and of the expulsion from Spain of the last Moslems and of the Jews. His expedition celebrated the extirpation of a great multiracial, multicultural society. Columbus's expedition was delayed three days because the harbor at Cádiz, Spain was blocked by the boats of desperate Jewish refugees. As the historian Samuel Eliot Morison wrote (*Admiral of the Ocean Sea,* 1942), Columbus could see weeping women and children on board.

==CONTEXTS==

Impressions of the New World

The very first American literatures, oral narratives and poems of the Native American, may have been produced contemporaneously with similar expressions in Europe as early as 1000 B.C. A literary record written in stone dating about A.D. 1000 still exists in narrative cave paintings in what is now the southwestern United States. The written literature of the first 130 years after the arrival of Europeans in the Americas consist of travel narratives, personal accounts and letters, histories, and propaganda encouraging migration to the New World.

The journals and letters of Columbus, Giovanni da Verrazzano, Alvar Núñez Cabeza de Vaca, Amerigo Vespucci, Richard Hakluyt, Pedro de Casteñeda, Thomas Harriot, and Samuel de Champlain testify to the awe and confusion with which European minds confronted very different cultures and peoples. In Europe important Renaissance authors drew upon these accounts in creating influential images. William Shakespeare created a clearly negative image of the New World's natives through his grotesque character Caliban in *The Tempest*. In contrast, the Elizabethan poet Michael Drayton created a glowingly positive image of the New World's natural resources in his poem "To the Virginian Voyage" (1619). The poem was written in response to Richard Hakluyt's accounts of early explorations of the New World and in anticipation of the Virginia Company's expedition to colonize the land in 1607.

To the Virginian Voyage

Virginia,
Earth's only paradise,

Where nature hath in store
Fowl, venison, and fish,
    And the fruitful'st soil
    Without your toil
Three harvests more,
All greater than your wish.
                MICHAEL DRAYTON, 1606, 1619

The era of the invasion of America, from the fifteenth century through the eighteenth, was characterized from the start by a complex mixture of courage, scientific quest, and display of imperial power. The invasion was accompanied by major dislocations. First, Europeans disrupted Native-American societies on a scale that was truly genocidal. Second, Europeans who had already begun to subject black Africans to forced labor in the sugar plantations of the Azores developed an extensive transatlantic slave trade, which affected the African societies that sold captives and the communities to which captive labor was sold as well as the men and women forced into lifelong captivity. Third, the era of settlement was shaped by major dislocations within European society, notably the Protestant Reformation, both a religious and social revolution, and by the commercial revolution engendered by the importation of wealth from the Americas. Fourth and last, the encounter with the Americas posed an extraordinary intellectual challenge to Europeans, who struggled to understand the world they had encountered and to express this understanding in political theory, law, scientific description and prediction, and imaginative literature. All writing, however mundane, is an act of the imagination; nowhere is that principle easier to discern than in the fiction and nonfiction of the American colonies and early republic. In those genres, men and women struggled for words and narrative structures to describe experiences for which their contemporaries in Europe had no parallel, sometimes no appropriate words.

From the start, Columbus found the American lands strange and troubling. "The trees were as different from ours as day from night, and so the fruits, the herbage, the rocks, and all things," Columbus wrote (as quoted in Alfred W. Crosby, Jr., *The Columbian Exchange* [1972]). One sixteenth-century explorer in Brazil complained that he found only three familiar plants—purslane, basil, and a certain fern. Animals, too, were unfamiliar. Explorers noted that the animals tended to be smaller than their Asian and African counterparts: for example, the American jaguar was considerably smaller than the African lion. The explorers were amazed at the iguana, at electric eels, and at catfish (Crosby, 1972).

The intellectual system brought by Columbus and his successors had no room for what they saw. Christians believed that the book of Genesis was definitive in that "there was one God, and there had been one Creation . . . . [But] if God had created all of the life forms in one week in one place and they had then spread out . . . over the whole world, then why are life forms in the eastern and western hemispheres so different?" (Crosby, 1972). Indeed, what could be made of the people found in America? They looked very different from any people Europeans had encountered. Europeans "knew" that individual possession was the "proper" way to handle property; what could they think of the Carib people, who shared what they possessed? Christians "knew" that heterosexual monogamy was the way to handle sex; what could they think when they encountered people happily practicing promiscuity, polygamy, and homosexuality (Francis Jennings, *The Invasion of America* 1975)?

Faced with the challenge of the unknown and the inexplicable, Europeans could either invoke cultural toleration or condemn Native Americans as allies of the Devil. Virtually all Europeans did the latter. The Devil's true allies were the germs the European conquerors carried to the New World. Since antiquity,

Asians, Africans, and Europeans were in contact through trade and had built up some immunity to each others' diseases. However, the peoples of America had been isolated from Europe. As descendants of the original inhabitants who had crossed the land bridge, they shared a limited gene pool that lessened the range of their resistance (Crosby, 1972).

The most deadly of the early epidemics were fevers—smallpox, measles, typhus. "Not even the most brutally depraved of the conquistadors was able purposely to slaughter Indians on the scale that the gentle priest unwittingly accomplished by going from his sickbed ministrations to lay his hands in blessing on his Indian converts" (Jennings, 1975). In an unvaccinated population, smallpox can infect virtually everyone, killing thirty percent of those infected. According to one Spanish historian, a million Native Americans lived in the Antilles when the Spanish arrived in 1492; by 1548 no more than five hundred were left. Virtually the entire Arawak people, the first to greet Columbus, died (Crosby, 1972). Central Mexico's population plummeted from 25 million to 2 million within less than a century.

The pattern was repeated in North America, where, well before the Pilgrims landed, English explorers and fishing parties brought typhus and smallpox. While the Pilgrims were buying their ships in Leiden, the Netherlands, in 1616 and 1617, a pestilence swept through New England, nearly exterminating the Massachuset Indians and depopulating the area. Years later Cotton Mather, a famous Puritan minister and historian, discerned the hand of God, who had cleared the land "of those pernicious creatures, to make room for better growth." The settlement of America was a resettlement; nearly every European settlement—Mexico City, Quebec, Montreal, Plymouth, Salem, Boston, New Amsterdam, Philadelphia, Detroit, Chicago—had previously been a Native-American town (Jennings, 1975).

The devastation of European illness had important imaginative effects as well as the obvious demographic ones. By undermining the natives' confidence in their gods, the destruction also undermined the natives' psychological resistance to European power. The ability of Europeans to survive when so many Native Americans were dying added to the myth of the Europeans' strength. Not understanding the physiology of immunity, they truly believed and told the natives that disease was sent as punishment and that the Europeans' ability to survive was a mark of divine favor (Crosby, 1972).

Thus, if the encounter between Europeans and Native Americans was a matter of empire and of demography, it was also a matter of understanding and imagination. This point was marked from the moment that Columbus, setting foot on the first island he encountered, undertook to name it rather than to learn the existing name from the inhabitants. This insistence that the lands were for Europeans to name and to define freely, without constraints set by the natives, permanently characterized the European encounter with the New World.

In general, most Europeans understood the Native Americans to be cruel savages, only marginally human, agents of the Devil, and best served by enforced acculturation in European plantations or townships. Others understood that they had encountered people who lived together harmoniously, their needs simple and their lives cooperative. The Americas seemed a golden world that had escaped expulsion from the Garden of Eden and had never known Original Sin. The concept that the lands in the West somehow had a special life-sustaining power has haunted the European imagination ever since and continues to be embedded in American political rhetoric. In the seventeenth century, when Europeans began to theorize about the origins of human society and of inequality, they found a point of departure in the conditions of "natural" equality and shared property that the first European adventurers had found.

European Forms on the American Land

The Europe from which Columbus sailed was rigidly hierarchical, not only in power relationships, but in the very concepts of self. There was, for example, strict division by gender: the nature of men and women was considered to be fundamentally different. "Male" was associated with heat and dryness and was symbolized by the sun. "Female" was associated with coolness and wetness and was symbolized by the moon, whose waxing and waning phases symbolized women's changeable, fluid nature. Conception was understood to involve a man implanting a miniature person in a woman's womb, implying that the source of life is male.

Deriving their status through fathers and husbands, women were placed in society differently than were men. Rituals of knighthood and institutions such as the courts and universities were strictly organized along gender lines. Among the upper classes, knowledge of Latin and of the written vernacular language was so generally confined to men that the two sexes literally used different languages. In a society in which perhaps one out of five men could read, the literacy of women hovered at half that of men, a relationship that continued through the eighteenth century, even as literacy of both sexes slowly improved. This gender system began to come under direct attack as being illogical and an inequitable ascription of power to one sex over the other.

Columbus's contemporaries, already living in a gendered hierarchy, also lived in a world rigidly divided by class. The political world was strictly divided into estates, each with its own hierarchical alignments. Thus, the "First Estate," the church, was ordered by popes, bishops, priests, abbots and monks, and abbesses and nuns. The "Second Estate," the nobility, was aligned from kings, to dukes and counts, to knights. Among the commoners, landowners and bourgeois (city-property owners) were superior to artisans, who in turn were superior to unskilled workers in the cities or peasants in the countryside, many of whom owed labor service to the large landowners. The hierarchical system was rigidly Christian. The last European Moslems were expelled from southern Europe by Ferdinand and Isabella; Jews throughout Europe were strictly controlled as to where they could live and what work they could pursue (and typically what they could wear) both by law and by custom.

With few exceptions the Europeans who ventured to the Americas expected to replicate there the class hierarchies with which they were familiar. They commonly succeeded, especially in Central and South America, where the Spanish came with sufficient military strength to force Native Americans into service on plantations. In New England churches, pews were allocated by rank. However, the conditions that sustained hierarchy generally did not exist in North America. Moreover, some elements of traditional class structure were already breaking down within Europe. The rigidity of the church was shattered by the challenge of the Reformation. Only twenty-five years after Columbus's voyage, Martin Luther called for the priesthood of all believers and for the recognition that God could be served in any calling, not just a religious vocation. Luther demanded that all believers be literate enough to read the Bible. "A priesthood of all believers" eventually disrupted secular intellectual hierarchies as well as religious ones. People who learned to question their religious superiors could conceive of questioning their political superiors.

The Reformation also affected the relationships among the nations of Europe. In 1533, when the pope rejected Henry VIII's efforts to divorce his Spanish wife for not producing a male heir, the king broke with the Catholic church. In effect, he proclaimed his own reformation, creating a Protestant church of England. Those who came to England's North American colonies during the following century embodied elements of the religious upheavals at home: Anglicans moved to Virginia; a wide range of Protestant dissenters traveled to New England, New York, New Jersey, and Pennsylvania; and Catholic refugees fled to Maryland. Furthermore, the religious break with the church sealed an enmity between England and Spain when an already overextended Spanish empire sent its great armada against England in 1588, only to be defeated. The power to control North Atlantic shipping routes—and thus North America—passed to England.

New sources of wealth, American mines and trade with the Americas, recast European economies in the sixteenth and seventeenth centuries. The old hereditary nobilities were uprooted, engendering a capitalist revolution that encouraged commercial growth, wider markets, pride in personal profit, and greatly expanded credit facilities in the form of banks and joint-stock companies. Merchants and traders, not titled nobility, then led the various efforts to settle North America. The privileged nobility was always a minor element in North American society and was easily erased during the Revolution. Also, the economic revolution destabilized old peasant and artisan relationships. Working people who were insecure, even desperate, found the promise of North America appealing. Nearly one-half of all immigrants came as indentured servants, bound to work for the costs of their passage.

Over the course of two centuries, the English established and maintained some seventeen colonial settlements in America. The sugar produced in Jamaica and Barbados made those settlements by far the most profitable ones. As late as 1776, guide books published in London paid much more attention to West Indian possessions than to the mainland colonies, then on the brink of rebellion. Only hindsight draws historians of the United States to the mainland colonies.

British settlements sorted into three economic/cultural groups. A historical scenario in which three nations could have formed after the Revolution can easily be imagined: a racially divided nation stretching from Virginia to the West Indies; New England, which was ethnically English, religiously derived from Puritan sects, and marked by widespread land ownership and political participation; and the middle colonies, with an ethnically diverse society.

After a number of attempts by individual entrepreneurs to establish trading settlements in North America failed, those who wished to venture across the Atlantic experimented with joint-stock companies. These companies were chartered by the Crown and permitted to sell shares. The resources of a large number of small investors were pooled, thereby raising money and spreading the risk. This type of organization was used both by the Virginia Company that settled Jamestown in 1607 and the Virginia Company of London, which established the Massachusetts Bay Colony in 1620. The use of joint-stock companies as a method of settlement had crucial political implications. Men who brought their families and paid their own passage became stockholders of the company and could claim a voice in the settlement's affairs.

Landholders in Virginia were defined as "burgesses," equivalent to urban voters in England, and beginning in 1619 were permitted to elect representatives to a House of Burgesses. Within a few years of settlement, the freemen of the Massachusetts Bay Colony demanded to see their charter and deduced that they had the right to a representative assembly to determine the affairs of the corporation. Because the economic aspects of the corporation were impossible to disentangle from the political ones, those who had an economic relationship to the joint-stock company could also claim a political voice. Men who had not been able to vote in England because they would not meet high property requirements could easily meet traditional minimal property requirements in America, where land seemed "empty." Almost from the beginning, the settlements were the scene of an inadvertent but far-reaching political revolution.

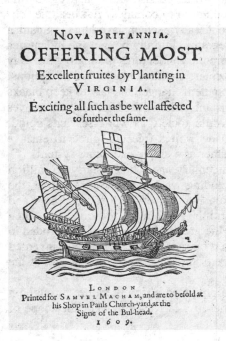

Nova Britannia.

OFFERING MOST

Excellent fruites by Planting in
Virginia.

Exciting all such as be well affected
to further the same.

London
Printed for Samvel Macham, and are to besold at
his Shop in Pauls Church-yard, at the
Signe of the Bul-head.
1609.

An advertisement to encourage immigration to the New World.

The South

The Virginia Colony was the scene of a far-reaching social revolution as well. The earliest settlers were largely single men who had come, they thought, to make their fortunes; they were ill-prepared to deal with malaria and other fevers endemic to the swampy shores on which they found themselves. Starvation was prevalent throughout the first years, as wave after wave of adventurers met disaster. Only thirteen hundred of the first eight thousand are estimated to have survived. As tobacco became established as a reliable and profitable crop, the population stabilized, but deaths outnumbered births in the Chesapeake until well into the seventeenth century. Most who came were male indentured servants, who could form families only after they had worked out the terms of their bondage and who typically died young.

This demographic instability had important social implications. For example, in a society in which the death rate was high and men outnumbered women, even poor women seemed to have a wider range of marriage choices than they had in England. The control of fathers over daughters eroded; the father who came with his daughter to America or who, if she were born here, lived to see her to maturity, was rare. Workmen could fairly easily establish themselves on their own land after their indentures were complete. The appeal of the Chesapeake was that a person would not have to work for a master.

The very prosperity of the southern colonies meant that laborers were at a premium. Forcing Native Americans to work as bound laborers was almost impossible; they were familiar with the terrain and could easily escape. Because the English economy had improved (due in part to the transatlantic trade), fewer people were desperate enough to indenture themselves as bondservants, and those who did as the seventeenth century progressed could go to colonies with healthier climates than Virginia had. Black Africans had already been enslaved by the Spanish and Portuguese. Planters, who had white servants, initially bought the indentures of blacks for limited periods of time, but temporary indentures gradually gave way to permanent bondage. Unlike indentured whites, captured blacks had no options. They were not in a position to resist when planters changed the law to keep blacks in service for life. Slavery provided a constant, cheap labor supply, and slaves could not easily assimilate with the free, white society as white servants could. Ironically, the same market forces that made whites free conspired to enslave blacks: slavery and freedom developed together as a single economic system.

From the 1670s on, over the course of a century and a half, nearly 10 million Africans—largely from the West coast, including what is now Sierra Leone, the Ivory Coast, Benin, and Biafra—were taken into slavery. Most were men and were taken to South and Central America and the Caribbean; 300,000 were taken to the mainland colonies. Although English hierarchies had softened and eroded in the Americas, a new kind of hierarchy, based on race, was energetically invented and maintained. It came to infuse the culture of the American colonies and of the new republic.

The English culture in southern America produced a rich literature throughout the seventeenth and early eighteenth centuries. As in New England, the scope of religious literature was considerable, consisting of sermons, theological tracts, personal diaries, and spiritual autobiographies—such as Thomas Cradock's "Sermon on the Governance of Maryland's Established Church" (1753) and Samuel Davies' *The State of Religion Among the Protestant Dissenters in Virginia* (1751). The South supported a large body of secular writing as well. Produced mostly by aristocratic men of classical training, such texts as *The History of the Dividing Line* (first published in 1841) by Virginia's William Byrd II, are witty, sophisticated, and richly detailed accounts of life on southern plantations. Works of satire and comedy followed the classical and Renaissance English traditions. Robert Beverley's *The History of the Present State of Virginia* (1705) is a serious account of Virginia's exploration and settlement but contains satiric observations of social follies. Ebenezer Cook's comic poem *The Sot-Weed Factor* (1708) is a mock-epic satire of Maryland colonial life and the exchanges and conflicts between the new Americans and their English competitors in the marketplace.

New England

The early settlements of New England were established by people who, although Protestant, dissented from the Church of England and merged religious motives with economic ones for their departure from England. Pilgrims, who wished to separate completely from the Church of England, and Puritans, who planned to purify it from within, understood themselves to be founding a godly community in which religious leaders and secular leaders would be allies. Intensely committed to their faith and to examining their souls for evidence of salvation, they encouraged confessional diaries and journals detailing their experiences on the road to salvation. Especially in the early years of settlement, Puritans were particularly worried about dissent in a godly community; though they had left England to live their own way, they did not tolerate Quakers, Baptists, or atheists. Captain John Smith, one of the most important promotional writers of the early seventeenth century, whose *A Description of New England* (1616) helped entice the Puritans to America in 1630, had himself been turned down as an undesirable person in his offer to guide the Puritans to America.

In the South, people claimed their lands individually. In New England, land was granted first to a group of town leaders, who then allocated it to the original settlers, taking social position into account. Thus, ministers, lawyers, and men who had been elite in England received the largest and most central allotments. Compact towns were understood to nurture a godly community in which traditional leadership patterns could be maintained. The dream of "peaceable kingdoms" could not be sustained indefinitely, especially as seaport towns (including Boston and Newport, Rhode Island) became small metropolises into which international trade and thousands of immigrants poured annually.

In the 1630s the Puritans had little difficulty expelling religious dissenters, such as Roger Williams and Anne Hutchinson, from the Massachusetts Bay Colony. However, by the mid-eighteenth century Boston had itself become an urban center of some twenty thousand residents, the hub of a trade in which New England shippers sold fish, livestock, and lumber to the West Indies and fish, furs, and lumber to England. From the West Indies, ships returned with slaves for sale in the southern colonies and with molasses, to be distilled into rum, for sale in the northern colonies and in Africa, where the rum would be traded for more slaves. Thus, even the regions in which slavery was not a major source of labor were economically dependent on the institution of slavery, a pattern that persisted until the Civil War.

=CONTEXTS=

Anne Hutchinson's Puritan Challenge

An early challenge to the authority of the Puritan ministers and magistrates came from Anne Hutchinson. A devout parishioner of Rev. John Cotton in Boston, England, Hutchinson and her family followed Cotton to New England. There she raised twelve children and served the community as a midwife and nurse. An intelligent reader of the Scriptures, she regularly held meetings in her home for as many as eighty people to discuss theology. Her view, which she attributed to Cotton's sermons, that saved Christians could interpret the Bible without the help of clerics (a position called antinomianism) was controversial. For her beliefs she was tried for heresy and banished from Massachusetts in 1637. Even Cotton abandoned her cause. During her trial she defended herself with learning, grace, and courage that has made her a champion of independent thought. Below is an excerpt from the court record of her trial:

Mrs. H. [Hutchinson]. Now if you do condemn me for speaking what in my conscience I know to be truth I must commit myself unto the Lord.

Mr. Nowell [a magistrate]. How do you know that that was the spirit?

Mrs. H. How did Abraham know that it was God that bid him offer his son, being a breach of the sixth commandment?

Dep. Gov. [Deputy Governor]. By an immediate voice.

Mrs. H. So to me by an immediate revelation.

Dep. Gov. How! an immediate revelation.

Mrs. H. By the voice of his own spirit to my soul . . . I have been confident of what he hath revealed unto me . . . . I was then much troubled concerning the ministry under which I lived, and then that place in the 30th of Isaiah [Isaiah 30:20] was brought to my mind. "Though the Lord give thee bread of adversity and water of affliction yet shall not thy teachers be removed into corners any more, but thine eyes shall see thy teachers." The Lord giving me this promise and they being gone there was none then left that I was able to hear, and I could not be at rest but I must come hither. Yet that place of Isaiah did much follow me, though the Lord give thee the bread of adversity and water of affliction. This place lying I say upon me then this place in Daniel [Daniel 6:4–5] was brought unto me and did shew me that though I should meet with affliction yet I am the same God that delivered Daniel out of the lion's den, I will also deliver thee.

Court record of Anne Hutchinson's trial, 1637

Puritan Writing. Puritan literature consisted mostly of various forms of religious writing: sermons, theological treatises, spiritual autobiographies, spiritualized histories, diaries, and religious poetry. Because the Puritans believed that the

Bible should serve as the source of all knowledge and inspiration, they wondered whether the writings of human beings are not merely presumptuous efforts to compete with God's sacred words. Despite this reservation, the Puritans produced an extraordinary volume of writings while attempting to explain and understand the Scriptures and their plans, efforts, and failures.

During the two decades after the settlement of New England in 1630, ties between England and the American colonies remained strong: many Massachusetts Puritans planned to return to England if Puritans there gained control of the government. The learned continued to purchase books from abroad and studied the classics and Renaissance literature as well as the works of Puritan theologians. Because of their commitment to the pursuit of God's word, the Puritans put great stock in education and literacy. As soon as the basics for sustaining life were established, the leaders set about creating the first college in America, established in 1636 and named after John Harvard. Exhibiting the "plaine style" that was to

The clothing in this anonymous 1674 portrait of Elizabeth Freake and her baby, Mary, shows that the Puritans appreciated rich adornment despite their religious purity and simplicity. The Puritans viewed children as small adults and dressed them as such. (Worcester Art Museum)

appeal to reason and not to the emotions, Puritan writing is direct and highly controlled. Nevertheless, because the Puritan venture was dramatic and culturally important to America in subsequent years, many of these works remain engaging today.

As the century progressed, Puritan writers developed new genres and styles. The clergy of the second and third generations after settlement redefined or abandoned the plain style in favor of figurative language, classical references, and a liberalized use of biblical typology—a language system for drawing parallels between biblical history and Puritan experience. The Puritan imagination was characterized by two strong tendencies. One, the Puritans were much inclined to read meaning out of natural events, biblical passages, and history and always tried to discern the plan behind happenings that might to the untrained mind seem to be random. Two, to discover if they were saved or damned, the Puritans constantly searched their own minds and hearts, worrying that self-delusion might damn them as hypocrites who would be exposed on Judgment Day. Thus, Puritan writings are packed with emotion, as individual souls struggled through language for truths of immense importance and as writers of the communal experience tried to determine if God supported the Puritans in their errand into the wilderness.

Those themes run through the sermons and histories and make such poems as Michael Wigglesworth's *The Day of Doom* (1662) unmistakably Puritan. Still, even within what would seem to be a very limited literary frame, poets such as Anne Bradstreet and Edward Taylor composed moving expressions of universal human experiences. Samuel Sewall's eloquent description of Plum Island, from his *Phaenomena Quaedam Apocalyptica* (1697), and his impassioned repudiation of slavery, *The Selling of Joseph* (1700), put into perspective his fretting over theological fine points that appear in his *Diary* (1673–1729, first published 1878–1882).

By the beginning of the eighteenth century, many of the original doctrines and social controls of the first Puritans had eroded, and Anglicans, Quakers, and others had settled among the saints. Imposed by the English Crown, religious toleration drastically changed the character of Boston and other New England towns. The writings of such thinkers as John Locke, Sir Isaac Newton, and René Descartes had begun to affect European thought in ways that would usher in the Enlightenment, with its stress on reason and science.

Before the demise of the Enlightenment, the American Puritan theologian Jonathan Edwards produced a major body of writing. Young Edwards observed the decline of the religion of his father and grandfathers and concurrently studied Newton and Locke. By his early twenties, Edwards was working to create a philosophical and theological synthesis of traditional Puritan doctrines regarding free will and God's sovereignty with the Enlightenment philosophy of Locke and of others. As Edwards labored at this stunning intellectual feat in the 1730s, he preached at a church in Northampton, Massachusetts. Beginning then and sweeping the colonies in the 1740s was a remarkable religious revival that became known as the first Great Awakening. The writings that Edwards produced during the next two decades, while he struggled to reconcile the Bible with philosophy and human experience, stand as eloquent expressions of a brilliant literary imagination.

The Middle Colonies

Historians are only now beginning to appreciate the continuities of the societies that were established in the region between New England and the Chesapeake, although that region is still known by the vague term "the middle colonies." With no established churches and a wide range of ethnic and religious groups, this region possessed less sense of community than New England had and less permanent class division than the Chesapeake had. The middle colonies set the model for the cultural pluralism that continues to characterize American life.

Dutch settlement of New Amsterdam (now Manhattan) was once understood by historians to be largely a failure: an expected fortune in the fur trade never materialized, the Dutch failed to establish lasting legislatures, and the English were easily able to capture the colony in 1664. Fewer of the Dutch were willing to migrate than were the English, thousands of whom were dislocated subjects with no other options. Yet, from another perspective, the Dutch experience is exemplary. While the English were deeply embroiled in civil war and were hesitant to tolerate dissenters, the Dutch, having recently concluded their civil and religious wars, had created a stable society at home and tolerated religious diversity (including the refugee Jews expelled by Ferdinand and Isabella).

In New Amsterdam, the Dutch were receptive to many cultures: eighteen languages are said to have been spoken there in the seventeenth century, and dissenters from the Massachusetts Bay Colony were welcome in Dutch settlements on Long Island. Dutch family law was much more concerned with women's and children's rights than was English law. For example, married women in their own right could inherit real estate. When New Netherland became New York, married women's property rights declined sharply.

William Penn was a Quaker who had managed to claim a charter from the Crown in 1681. He governed his colony (now Pennsylvania) as though he were a private proprietor with the right to design its government. Penn defined his colony as a refuge for Quakers and other victims of religious persecution. "Any government is free where the laws rule," he wrote in the introduction to the first Frame of Government (1682), "and the people are a party to those laws . . . . Governments, like clocks, go from the motion men give them, and as governments are made and moved by men, so by turn are they ruined too."

Migration to Pennsylvania in the 1680s was as phenomenal as the great migration to the Massachusetts Bay Colony in the 1630s had been. Within six years of its founding in 1682, Pennsylvania had twelve thousand settlers. The deep radicalism of English Quakers infused the early settlement. Custom respected the Quaker refusal to take oaths and to remove hats as a sign of deference and the Quaker insistence that all—men and women, rich and poor—could speak in meeting and achieve salvation. Penn's first Frame of Government explicitly guaranteed freedom of worship to all religious groups. All Christian men could vote and hold office. As pacifists the Quakers avoided warfare with Native Americans: Penn did not allocate land until he had first purchased it. In fact, no major Native-American war occurred in Pennsylvania until the 1750s. Quakers were skeptical of slavery, as were Mennonites, who published the first public protest against "Traffic in Men's Bodies" (1688).

Pennsylvania quickly became a magnet. Not long after settlement, representatives of a wide variety of religions were found in that colony: Quakers, Anglicans, Lutherans, Mennonites, Catholics, Moravians. Fertile lands meant rapid economic prosperity, and within a few years of settlement, Philadelphia became a seaport rivaling Boston. The Pennsylvania experience reveals the tensions of a political society composed of distinct ethnic and religious groups. By the mid-eighteenth century, Pennsylvania politics were sharply divided along ethnic/cultural lines, as politics continue to be in the United States.

In addition to being lively in social and political activity, Pennsylvania, especially Philadelphia, developed into the colonies' leading cultural center. Whereas the Puritan temper continued to impose restraint upon the development of imaginative literature in New England, the more liberal spirit of the city of Friends, as the Quakers were called, encouraged the arts. The leading literary figure of Philadelphia was Benjamin Franklin, who founded the first circulating library in 1831, among his many other accomplishments. With his graceful style and wit, Franklin typified the cosmopolitan ideal in both his life and his writing.

Whereas Franklin made a mark for American letters abroad by his verbal skills and personality, the Quaker author John Woolman combined the traditions of religious writing and a sophisticated Enlightenment style to preach, lecture, and write about the social ills in America. Woolman's *Some Considerations on the Keeping of Negroes* (1754) powerfully argues for the abolition of slavery. His *A Plea for the Poor or a Word of Remembrance and Caution to the Rich* (written in 1763 but not published until 1793) is directed to issues of class division and social injustice.

William Smith, the energetic provost of the College of Philadelphia (now the University of Pennsylvania), was himself an important writer. He inspired young authors such as Thomas Godfrey, whose *The Prince of Parthia* (1767) may have been the first play genuinely written by an American and produced in America. By the time of the American Revolution, Philadelphia was a major publishing center of the small literary world that was taking shape in the colonies.

Traditional Native-American Literary Expression

When European explorers began to visit the Americas, they found more than three hundred cultural groups speaking some two hundred languages from several major language families in North America alone. These tribes varied widely in political organization, economic structure, and cultural values, but they all had in common a rich oral literature, developed over centuries and perfectly responsive to cultural needs and social relations. However, the oral nature of traditional Native-American literary expression, the violent political struggle between the colonists and native tribes, and their differing social systems made it difficult for the colonists to appreciate native creativity.

There are significant differences between the written and oral modes of expression, even without considerations of translation or divergent cultural expectations. But all literature presents verbal creation rising from negotiations between individual talent and a supporting tradition regardless of the format. A vibrant oral tradition was central to most Native-American societies and continues to be so today. Through the oral tradition, people pass on their wisdom, their understanding of how to survive, their cultural values, and their sense of identity. Native-American societies clarify their relationship to the world around them, to both seen and unseen powers, as exemplified by the Trickster myth of Wisconsin's Winnebago tribe. They formally encode a world view and make sacred their paths through life in a way that requires the older generations to encourage and guide the younger ones. In the oral tradition communities are bound together, and individuals find their place in society. Over centuries, an expressive body of literature has matured. That literature may be divided into oral narratives, oratory, song/poetry, and religious expression. However, these categories are not exclusive and may overlap.

Oral narratives might consist of sacred or secular stories. Most often they were told by an elder in a storytelling session with young people and adults in attendance, as were the myths of the Cherokees. Some narratives were told in religious circumstances as part of a larger ritual. Others deal with more historical material, as does the Tlingit tribe's story of their first contact with white people—and with the experience of one person or ancestor.

Europeans expressed fascination with the Native Americans in painting as well as in writing. John White painted this watercolor, The Flyer, *after arriving in Roanoke, Virginia, with Sir Walter Raleigh.*

Native-American orators perfected their rhetorical skills during such events as council meetings, religious presentations, welcomings, petitions, and meetings with other tribes. The highly personal and transitory nature of this form has made it difficult to record, but some traditions have been documented by tribal and nontribal scholars. Many of the speeches of noted orators and chiefs, such as the Seneca chief known as Red-jacket, were recorded at official meetings between natives and whites.

Native-American song may also be of a religious or personal nature. Most often it has been written in English with the appearance of poetry, as have the war song of the Papagos of the Southeast and the transcribed hieroglyphs of the Mayas of Central America. The oral context of a song or chant makes it something quite different from poetry of the western tradition; the importance that poetry places on appreciating each word and pause is similar to the appreciation of Native-American song traditions. The reader must supply much of the music, gesture, and social context that informs the expression.

The forms of Native-American religious expression may vary from dance dramas staged as public ritual to personal vision songs, depending on the individual tribal tradition and religious activity. Religious expression may take the form of a highly formalized series of chants that take years to learn or a personal rite evoking an animal spirit protector. Expressions from any of the other categories might also be religious, but some literary works, such as Zuni prayers, fit most conveniently into this category.

Because oral literature is a performance literature, written texts of oral expression can present only one dimension of a multifaceted experience. In Native-American oral performance the audience plays a crucial role in shaping the total expression. An intense interactive context is built up, extending into a tradition of previous performances and a web of shared cultural expectations and references. In reading written translations of verbal acts, we may be unaware of aesthetic norms and cultural expectations unique to Native Americans or to a specific tribal group. Even the best of translations must struggle to give the reader of English some sense of the texture of the language used—which might include its formality, voice, word choice—and of the dramatic sense of performance and religious ramifications of the verbal event. But from these translations we gain deeper insight into the native peoples of the Americas and into the fascinating variety of literary expression illuminating the human experience.

Suggested Readings: W. Apes, *The Experiences of Five Christian Indians: Or, the Indian's Looking Glass for the White Men,* 1833. M. Austin, *The American Rhythm: Studies and Reexpressions of Amerindian Songs,* 1930. Black Hawk, *Black Hawk: An Autobiography,* ed. D. Jackson, 1955. M. Astrov, ed., *The Winged Serpent: An Anthology of American Indian Prose and Poetry,* 1973. R. Slotkin, *Regeneration Through Violence: The Mythology of the American Frontier, 1600–1860,* 1973. M. Castro, *Interpreting the Indian: Twentieth-Century Poets and the Native American,* 1983. H. D. Brumble, *American Indian Autobiography,* 1988. J. M. Dent, *Savagism and Civilization: A Study of the Indian and the American Mind,* 1988. A. Krupat, *The Voice in the Margin: Native American Literature and the Canon,* 1989.

Texts Used: "How the World Was Made" and "The First Fire": *Nineteenth Annual Report of the Bureau of American Ethnology, 1897–1898,* Pt. I, ed. J. W. Powell, 1900. "The Winnebago Trickster Cycle": *The Trickster: A Study in American Indian Mythology,* ed. P. Radin, 1956. A Zuni Prayer and "An Offering of Prayer Sticks at the Winter Solstice": *Forty-Seventh Annual Report of the Bureau of American Ethnology, 1929–1930,* 1932. "They Came From the East": *The Book of Chilam Balam of Chumayel,* trans. R. L. Roys. 1967. "The Coming of the First White Man": told by G. R. Betts, *Haa Shuka, Our Ancestors: Tlingit Oral Narratives,* ed. N. M. Dauenhauer and R. Dauenhauer, 1987. Song of the Papago War Orator: *Singing for Power,* ed. R. Underhill, 1938. Speech of Chief Red-jacket: Sagoyewatha, *Biography and History of the Indians of North America,* ed. S. E. Drake, 1834.

CHEROKEE MYTH

How the World Was Made*

The earth is a great island floating in a sea of water, and suspended at each of the four cardinal points by a cord hanging down from the sky vault, which is of solid rock. When the world grows old and worn out, the people will die and the cords will break and let the earth sink down into the ocean, and all will be water again. The Indians are afraid of this.

When all was water, the animals were above in Gălûñ'lătĭ,[1] beyond the arch; but it was very much crowded, and they were wanting more room. They wondered what was below the water, and at last Dâyuni'sĭ, "Beaver's Grandchild," the little Water-beetle, offered to go and see if it could learn. It darted in every direction over the surface of the water, but could find no firm place to rest. Then it dived to the bottom and came up with some soft mud, which began to grow and spread on every side until it became the island which we call the earth. It was afterward fastened to the sky with four cords, but no one remembers who did this.

At first the earth was flat and very soft and wet. The animals were anxious to get down, and sent out different birds to see if it was yet dry, but they found no place to alight and came back again to Gălûñ'lătĭ. At last it seemed to be time, and they sent out the Buzzard and told him to go and make ready for them. This was the Great Buzzard, the father of all the buzzards we see now. He flew all over the earth, low down near the ground, and it was still soft. When he reached the Cherokee country, he was very tired, and his wings began to flap and strike the ground, and wherever they struck the earth there was a valley, and where they turned up again there was a mountain. When the animals above saw this, they were afraid that the whole world would be mountains, so they called him back, but the Cherokee country remains full of mountains to this day.

When the earth was dry and the animals came down, it was still dark, so they got the sun and set it in a track to go every day across the island from east to west, just overhead. It was too hot this way, and Tsiska'gĭlĭ', the Red Crawfish, had his shell scorched a bright red, so that his meat was spoiled: and the Cherokee do not eat it. The conjurers put the sun another hand-breadth higher in the air, but it was still too hot. They raised it another time, and another, until it was seven hand-breadths high and just under the sky arch. Then it was right, and they left it so. This is why the conjurers call the highest place Gûlkwâ'gine Di'gălûñ'lătiyûn', "the seventh height," because it is seven hand-breadths above the earth. Every day the sun goes along under this arch, and returns at night on the upper side to the starting place.

There is another world under this, and it is like ours in everything—animals,

---

* This Cherokee story (and the one that follows) was collected in North Carolina, where some Cherokee communities survived dissolution and removal. Such creation stories are told to explain the origin of the world, but more importantly they establish the nature of the processes that have influenced the world and continue to do so. This story reflects a type of Native-American creation story known as the "earthdiver motif," but it is only one of the many different creation stories of Native-American communities.

[1] The Cherokees believed the world consists of various levels: the earth, an underworld, a heaven, and this level between heaven and earth.

plants, and people—save that the seasons are different. The streams that come down from the mountains are the trails by which we reach this underworld, and the springs at their heads are the doorways by which we enter it, but to do this one must fast and go to water and have one of the underground people for a guide. We know that the seasons in the underworld are different from ours, because the water in the springs is always warmer in winter and cooler in summer than the outer air.

When the animals and plants were first made—we do not know by whom—they were told to watch and keep awake for seven nights, just as young men now fast and keep awake when they pray to their medicine. They tried to do this, and nearly all were awake through the first night, but the next night several dropped off to sleep, and the third night others were asleep, and then others, until, on the seventh night, of all the animals only the owl, the panther, and one or two more were still awake. To these were given the power to see and to go about in the dark, and to make prey of the birds and animals which must sleep at night. Of the trees only the cedar, the pine, the spruce, the holly, and the laurel were awake to the end, and to them it was given to be always green and to be greatest for medicine, but to the others it was said: "Because you have not endured to the end you shall lose your hair every winter."

Men came after the animals and plants. At first there were only a brother and sister until he struck her with a fish and told her to multiply, and so it was. In seven days a child was born to her, and thereafter every seven days another, and they increased very fast until there was danger that the world could not keep them. Then it was made that a woman should have only one child in a year, and it has been so ever since.

1900

The First Fire

In the beginning there was no fire, and the world was cold, until the Thunders (Anï'-Hyûñ'tïkwălâ'skĭ), who lived up in Gălûñ'lătĭ,[1] sent their lightning and put fire into the bottom of a hollow sycamore tree which grew on an island. The animals knew it was there, because they could see the smoke coming out at the top, but they could not get to it on account of the water, so they held a council to decide what to do. This was a long time ago.

Every animal that could fly or swim was anxious to go after the fire. The Raven offered, and because he was so large and strong they thought he could surely do the work, so he was sent first. He flew high and far across the water and alighted on the sycamore tree, but while he was wondering what to do next, the heat had scorched all his feathers black, and he was frightened and came back without the fire. The little Screech-owl *(Wa'huhu')* volunteered to go, and reached the place safely, but while he was looking down into the hollow tree a blast of hot air came up and nearly burned out his eyes. He managed to fly home as best he could, but it was a long time before he could see well, and his eyes are red to this day. Then the Hooting Owl *(U'guku')* and the Horned Owl *(Tskĭlĭ)* went, but by the time they got to the hollow tree the fire was burning so fiercely that the smoke nearly blinded them, and the ashes carried up by the wind made white rings about their

---

[1] According to Cherokee myth, a level between heaven and earth.

eyes. They had to come home again without the fire, but with all their rubbing they were never able to get rid of the white rings.

Now no more of the birds would venture, and so the little Uksu'hĭ snake, the black racer, said he would go through the water and bring back some fire. He swam across to the island and crawled through the grass to the tree, and went in by a small hole at the bottom. The heat and smoke were too much for him, too, and after dodging about blindly over the hot ashes until he was almost on fire himself he managed by good luck to get out again at the same hole, but his body had been scorched black, and he has ever since had the habit of darting and doubling on his track as if trying to escape from close quarters. He came back, and the great blacksnake, Gûle'gĭ, "The Climber," offered to go for fire. He swam over to the island and climbed up the tree on the outside, as the blacksnake always does, but when he put his head down into the hole the smoke choked him so that he fell into the burning stump, and before he could climb out again he was as black as the Uksu'hĭ.

Now they held another council, for still there was no fire, and the world was cold, but birds, snakes, and four-footed animals, all had some excuse for not going, because they were all afraid to venture near the burning sycamore, until at last Kănăne'skĭ Amai'yĕhĭ (the Water Spider) said she would go. This is not the water spider that looks like a mosquito, but the other one, with black downy hair and red stripes on her body. She can run on top of the water or dive to the bottom, so there would be no trouble to get over to the island, but the question was, How could she bring back the fire? "I'll manage that," said the Water Spider; so she spun a thread from her body and wove it into a *tusti* bowl, which she fastened on her back. Then she crossed over to the island and through the grass to where the fire was still burning. She put one little coal of fire into her bowl, and came back with it, and ever since we have had fire, and the Water Spider still keeps her tusti bowl.

1900

WINNEBAGO TRICKSTER MYTH

from   THE WINNEBAGO TRICKSTER CYCLE[*]

I I

Again he wandered aimlessly about the world. On one occasion he came in sight of the shore of a lake. To his surprise, he noticed that, right near the edge of the lake, a person was standing. So he walked rapidly in that direction to see who it was. It was someone with a black shirt on. When Trickster came nearer to the lake, he saw that this individual was on the other side of the lake and that he was pointing at him. He called to him, "Say, my younger brother, what are you pointing at?" But he received no answer. Then, for the second time, he called, "Say,

---

[*] Trickster stories are extremely common throughout North America. The Winnebago Trickster Cycle portrays an intriguing figure from the oral tradition of the Upper Midwest tribe. Trickster can act as a hero or a self-centered fool; however, it is through his actions that the textures of the natural and human worlds become established. His paradoxical actions reveal a wide variety of psychological processes, social mores, and cultural values.

my younger brother, what is it you are pointing at?" Again he received no answer. Then, for the third time, he addressed him, again receiving no answer. There across the lake the man still stood, pointing. "Well, if that's the way it's going to be, I, too, shall do that. I, too, can stand pointing just as long as he does. I, too, can put a black shirt on." Thus Trickster spoke.

Then he put on his black shirt and stepped quickly in the direction of this individual and pointed his finger at him just as the other one was doing. A long time he stood there. After a while Trickster's arm got tired so he addressed the other person and said, "My younger brother, let us stop this." Still there was no answer. Then, for the second time, when he was hardly able to endure it any longer, he spoke, "Younger brother, let us stop this. My arm is very tired." Again he received no answer. Then, again he spoke, "Younger brother, I am hungry! Let us eat now and then we can begin again afterward. I will kill a fine animal for you, the very kind you like best, that kind I will kill for you. So let us stop." But still he received no answer. "Well, why am I saying all this? That man has no heart at all. I am just doing what he is doing." Then he walked away and when he looked around, to his astonishment, he saw a tree-stump from which a branch was protruding. This is what he had taken for a man pointing at him. "Indeed, it is on this account that the people call me the Foolish One. They are right." Then he walked away.

12

As he was walking along suddenly he came to a lake, and there in the lake he saw numerous ducks. Immediately he ran back quietly before they could see him and sought out a spot where there was a swamp. From it he gathered a large quantity of reedgrass and made himself a big pack. This he put on his back and carried it to the lake. He walked along the shore of the lake carrying it ostentatiously. Soon the ducks saw him and said, "Look, that is Trickster walking over there. I wonder what he is doing? Let us call and ask him." So they called to him. "Trickster, what are you carrying?" Thus they shouted at him, but he did not answer. Then, again they called to him. But it was only after the fourth call that he replied and said, "Well, are you calling me?" "What are you carrying on your back?" they asked. "My younger brothers, surely you do not know what it is you are asking. What am I carrying? Why, I am carrying songs. My stomach is full of bad songs. Some of these my stomach could not hold and that is why I am carrying them on my back. It is a long time since I sang any of them. Just now there are a large number in me. I have met no people on my journey who would dance for me and let me sing some for them. And I have, in consequence, not sung any for a long time." Then the ducks spoke to each other and said, "Come, what if we ask him to sing? Then we could dance, couldn't we?" So one of them called out, "Well, let it be so. I enjoy dancing very much and it has been a very long time since I last danced."

So they spoke to Trickster, "Older brother, yes, if you will sing to us we will dance. We have been yearning to dance for some time but could not do so because we had no songs." Thus spoke the ducks. "My younger brothers," replied Trickster, "you have spoken well and you shall have your desire granted. First, however, I will erect a dancing-lodge." In this they helped him and soon they had put up a dancing-lodge, a grass-lodge. Then they made a drum. When this was finished he invited them all to come in and they did so. When he was ready to sing he said, "My younger brothers, this is the way in which you must act. When I sing, when I have people dance for me, the dancers must, from the very beginning, never open their eyes." "Good," they answered. Then when he began to sing he said, "Now remember, younger brothers, you are not to open your eyes. If you do they will become red." So, as soon as he began to sing, the ducks closed their eyes and danced.

After a while one of the ducks was heard to flap his wings as he came back to the entrance of the lodge, and cry, "Quack!" Again and again this happened. Sometimes it sounded as if the particular duck had somehow tightened its throat. Whenever any of the ducks cried out then Trickster would tell the other ducks to dance faster and faster. Finally a duck whose name was Little-Red-Eyed-Duck secretly opened its eyes, just the least little bit it opened them. To its surprise, Trickster was wringing the necks of his fellows ducks! He would also bite them as he twisted their necks. It was while he was doing this that the noise which sounded like the tightening of the throat was heard. In this fashion Trickster killed as many as he could reach.

Little-Red-Eyed-Duck shouted. "Alas! He is killing us! Let those who can save themselves." He himself flew out quickly through the opening above. All the others likewise crowded toward this opening. They struck Trickster with their wings and scratched him with their feet. He went among them with his eyes closed and stuck out his hands to grab them. He grabbed one in each hand and choked them to death. His eyes were closed tightly. Then suddenly all of them escaped except the two he had in his grasp.

When he looked at these, to his annoyance, he was holding in each hand a scabby-mouthed duck. In no way perturbed, however, he shouted, "Ha, ha, this is the way a man acts! Indeed these ducks will make fine soup to drink!" Then he made a fire and cut some sharp-pointed sticks with which to roast them. Some he roasted in this manner, while others he roasted by covering them with ashes. "I will wait for them to be cooked," he said to himself. "I had, however, better go to sleep now. By the time I awake they will unquestionably be thoroughly done. Now, you, my younger brother, must keep watch for me while I go to sleep. If you notice any people, drive them off." He was talking to his anus. Then, turning his anus toward the fire, he went to sleep.

13

When he was sleeping some small foxes approached and, as they ran along, they scented something that seemed like fire. "Well, there must be something around here," they said. So they turned their noses toward the wind and looked and, after a while, truly enough, they saw the smoke of a fire. So they peered around carefully and soon noticed many sharp-pointed sticks arranged around a fire with meat on them. Stealthily they approached nearer and nearer and, scrutinizing everything carefully, they noticed someone asleep there. "It is Trickster and he is asleep! Let us eat this meat. But we must be very careful not to wake him up. Come, let us eat," they said to one another. When they came close, much to their surprise, however, gas was expelled from somewhere. "Pooh!" such was the sound made. "Be careful! He must be awake," So they ran back. After a while one of them said, "Well, I guess he is asleep now. That was only a bluff. He is always up to some tricks." So again they approached the fire. Again gas was expelled and again they ran back. Three times this happened. When they approached the fourth time gas was again expelled. However, they did not run away. So Trickster's anus, in rapid succession, began to expel more and more gas. Still they did not run away. Once, twice, three times, it expelled gas in rapid succession. "Pooh! Pooh!" Such was the sound it made. Yet they did not run away. Then louder, still louder, was the sound of the gas expelled. "Pooh! Pooh! Pooh!" Yet they did not run away. On the contrary, they now began to eat the roasted pieces of duck. As they were eating, the Trickster's anus continued its "Pooh" incessantly. There the foxes stayed until they had eaten up all the pieces of duck roasted on sticks. Then they came to those pieces that were being roasted under ashes and, in spite of the fact that the anus was expelling gas, "Pooh! Pooh! Pooh! Pooh!" continuously, they ate these all up too. Then they replaced the pieces with the meat eaten off, nicely under the ashes. Only after that did they go away.

14

After a while Trickster awoke, "My, O my!" he exclaimed joyfully, "the things I had put on to roast must be cooked crisp by now." So he went over, felt around, and pulled out a leg. To his dismay it was but a bare bone, completely devoid of meat. "How terrible! But this is the way they generally are when they are cooked too much! So he felt around again and pulled out another one. But this leg also had nothing on it. "How terrible! These, likewise, must have been roasted too much! However, I told my younger brother, anus, to watch the meat roasting. He is a good cook indeed!" He pulled out one piece after the other. They were all the same. Finally he sat up and looked around. To his astonishment, the pieces of meat on the roasting sticks were gone! "Ah, ha, now I understand! It must have been those covetous friends of mine who have done me this injury!" he exclaimed. Then he poked around the fire again and again but found only bones. "Alas! Alas! They have caused my appetite to be disappointed, those covetous fellows! And you, too, you despicable object, what about your behavior? Did I not tell you to watch this fire? You shall remember this! As a punishment for your remissness, I will burn your mouth so that you will not be able to use it!"

Thereupon he took a burning piece of wood and burnt the mouth of his anus. He was, of course, burning himself and, as he applied the fire, he exclaimed, "Ouch! Ouch! This is too much! I have made my skin smart. Is it not for such things that they call me Trickster? They have indeed talked me into doing this just as if I had been doing something wrong!"

Trickster had burnt his anus. He had applied a burning piece of wood to it. Then he went away.

As he walked along the road he felt certain that someone must have passed along it before for he was on what appeared to be a trail. Indeed, suddenly, he came upon a piece of fat that must have come from someone's body. "Someone has been packing an animal he had killed," he thought to himself. Then he picked up a piece of fat and ate it. It had a delicious taste. "My, my, how delicious it is to eat this!" As he proceeded however, much to his surprise, he discovered that it was a part of himself, part of his own intestines, that he was eating. After burning his anus, his intestines had contracted and fallen off, piece by piece, and these pieces were the things he was picking up. "My, my! Correctly, indeed, am I named Foolish One, Trickster! By their calling me thus, they have at last actually turned me into a Foolish One, a Trickster!" Then he tied his intestines together. A large part, however, had been lost. In tying it, he pulled it together so that wrinkles and ridges were formed. That is the reason why the anus of human beings has its present shape.

1956

ZUNI RITUAL POETRY*

A ZUNI PRAYER

This many are the days
Since our moon mother
Yonder in the west[1]
Appeared, still small;
When but a short space yet remained
Till she was fully grown,
Then out daylight father,[2]
Pekwin of the Dogwood clan,
For his sun father
Told off the days.   10
This many days we have waited.
We have come to the appointed time.
My children,
All my children,
Will make plume wands.
My child,
My father,[3] sun,

My mother, moon,
All my children will clothe you with prayer plumes.
When you have arrayed yourselves in these,   20
With your waters,
Your seeds
You will bless all my children.
All your good fortune
You will grant to them all.
To this end, my father,
My mother:
May I finish my road;
May I grow old;
May you bless me with life.   30

1932

AN OFFERING OF PRAYER STICKS AT THE WINTER SOLSTICE

This many are the days
Since at the new year
For those who are our fathers,

---

* The Zunis of what is now New Mexico chanted prayers over prayer sticks before they planted their crops (and the sticks) in the spring. The prayer sticks honor the powers of life, especially the ancestors who have become masked gods who bring rain.
[1] The new moon, which first appears at sunset in the West.
[2] Our human father; "father" applied to all supernaturals or men of high office.
[3] "My father, my child" is the most intimate, affectionate form of address.

Ḳä′eto·we,
Tcu′eto·we,[1]
The days[2] were made.
From all the wooded places
Breaking off the young straight shoots
Of the male willow, female willow,
In our hands we held them fast,   10
With them we gave our plume wands human form.[3]
With the striped cloud wing
The one who is our father,
Male turkey,
We gave our plume wands human form.
With the flesh of our mother,
Cotton woman,
Even a poorly made cotton thread.
With this four times encircling the plume wands,
And tying it about their bodies,   20
We finished our plume wands.
Having finished our plume wands.
And offering our fathers their plume wands
We make their days.[4]
Anxiously awaiting their days.
We have passed the days.
After a little while
Your massed clouds,
Your rains,
We shall desire.   30
We have given you plume wands.
That with your waters,
Your seeds,
Your riches,[5]
Your long life,
Your old age,
You may bless us—
For this I have given you plume wands.
To this end, my fathers,
May our roads reach to dawn lake;[6]   40
May our roads be fulfilled;
May we grow old;
To where the road of our sun father goes
May our roads reach;
May our roads be fulfilled;
May we grow old;
May we be blessed with life.

1932

---

[1] The priests' rain-bringing and corn-growing fetishes, or objects believed to have magical powers.
[2] The priests' retreat.
[3] The stick forms the body; the feathers, robes, and cotton cord, the belt; and the paint, the flesh.
[4] To observe the taboo period.   [5] Clothing and ornaments.
[6] The water on the eastern rim of the world, from which the sun was thought to arise.

MAYAN HISTORICAL POETRY

THEY CAME FROM THE EAST*

They came from the east when they arrived.
Then Christianity also began.
The fulfillment of its prophecy is ascribed to the east . . .
Then with the true God, the true *Dios,*
came the beginning of our misery.
It was the beginning of tribute,
the beginning of church dues,
the beginning of strife with purse-snatching,
the beginning of strife with blow-guns;
the beginning of strife by trampling on people,   10
the beginning of robbery with violence,
the beginning of forced debts,
the beginning of debts enforced by false testimony,
the beginning of individual strife,
a beginning of vexation.

1542?, 1933

TLINGIT ORAL HISTORY

THE COMING OF THE FIRST WHITE MAN†

People lived in Lituya Bay[1]
loooong ago.
Smoke houses and other houses were there.
There was a deserted place called Lituya Bay before the white man
      migrated in from the sea.
At one point one morning
a person went outside.
Then there was a white object that could be seen way out on the sea
bouncing on the waves
and rocked by the waves.
At one point it was coming closer to the people.   10
"What's that?"

---

* This poem was transcribed from Mayan hieroglyphs shortly after the Spanish conquest of the Central American peoples in 1541. It was preserved in *The Book of Chilam Balam of Chumayel*, translated in 1933 by Ralph L. Roys.

† Variations of this first contact narrative have been told for centuries all over the Tlingit country of Southeast Alaska. Some traditions specify the white men as Russians; others signify only Europeans. These stories are thought to refer either to the visit by Compte de La Pérouse (1741–1788) in 1786 or Izmailov and Bocharov in 1788. This version was told by George R. Betts and translated by Nora Dauenhauer.

[1] In southeastern Alaska.

"What's that, what's that?"
"It's something different!"
"It's something different!"
"Is it Raven?"
"Maybe that's what it is."
"I think that's what it is—
Raven who created the world.
He said he would come back again."
Some dangerous thing was happening.   20
(Lituya Bay
lay like a lake.
There was a current;
salt water flowed in when the tide was coming in.
But when the tide was going out
the sea water would also drain out.)
So the thing went right on in with the flood tide.
Then the people of the village ran scared right into the forest,
all of them;
the children too,   30
were taken to the forest.
They watched from the forest.
At one point
they heard strange sounds.
Actually it was the anchor that was thrown in the water.
"Don't look at it!"
they told the children.
"Don't anybody look at it.
If you look at it, you'll turn to stone.
That's Raven, he's come by boat."   40
"Oh! People are running around on it!"
Things are moving around on it.
Actually it was the sailors climbing around the mast.
At one point after they had watched for a loooong time,
they took blue hellebore[2]
and broke the stalks,
blue hellebore.
They poked holes though them
so that they wouldn't turn to stone;
they watched through them.   50
When no one turned to stone while watching,
someone said,
"Let's go out there.
We'll go out there."
"What's that?"
Then there were two young men;
from the woods
a canoe
(the kind of canoe called "seet")
was pulled down to the beach.   60

---

[2] A poisonous plant.

They quickly went aboard.
They quickly went out to it, paddled out to it.
When they got out to it,
a rope ladder was lowered.
Then they were beckoned to go aboard,
they were beckoned over by the crewmen's fingers,
the crewmen's fingers.
Then they went up there.
They examined it; they had not seen anything like it.
Actually it was a huge sail boat.   70
When the crew took them inside the cabin,
they saw—
they saw themselves.
Actually it was a huge mirror inside there,
a huge mirror.
They gave this name then,
to the thing an image of people could be seen on.
Then they were taken to the cook's galley.
There they were given food.
Worms were cooked for them,   80
worms.
They stared at it.
White sand also.
White sand
was put in front of them.
Then they spooned this white sand into the rice.
Actually it was sugar.
What they thought were worms, was rice.
This was what they had just been staring at.
At what point was it one of them took a spoonful?   90
"Hey! Look!
Go ahead! Taste it!"
"It might be good."
So the other took a spoonful.
Just as he did, he said "This is good food,
these worms,
maggots,
this is good food."
After they were fed all kinds of food,
then they were given alcohol   100
alcohol
perhaps it was brandy.
Then they began to feel very strange.
Never before . . . . . .
"Why am I beginning to feel this way?
Look! I'm beginning to feel strange!"
And "I'm beginning to feel happiness settling through my body too,"
they said.
After they had taken them through the whole ship,
they took them to the railing.   110
They gave them some things.

Rice
and sugar
and pilot bread
were given to them to take along.
They were told how to cook them.
Now I wonder what it was cooked on.
You know, people didn't have pots then . . . .
There was no cooking pot for it.
When they got ashore   120
they told everyone:
"There are many people in there.
Strange things are in there too.
A box of our images,
this looking glass,
a box of our images;
we could just see ourselves.
Next
they cooked maggots for us to eat."
They told everything.   130
After that,
they all went out on their canoes.
This was the very first time the white man came ashore,
through Lituya Bay;
Ltu.àa is called Lituya Bay
in Alaska.
Well! This is all of my story.

1987

PAPAGO SONG

SONG OF THE PAPAGO WAR ORATOR*

Is it for me to eat what food I have
And all day sit idle?
Is it for me to drink the sweet water poured out
And all day sit idle?
Is it for me to hold my child in my arms
And all day sit idle?

My desire was uncontrollable.
It was the dizziness [of battle];   10
I ground it to powder and therewith I painted my face.
It was the drunkenness [of battle];
I ground it to powder and therewith I tied my hair in a war knot.
Then did I hold firm my well-covering shield and my hard-striking club.

* This text is chanted by a knowledgeable warrior of the Papago tribe (of what is now Arizona) to
encourage other warriors as they prepare for battle. The songs focus on the rain, kinship, and growth
reveal their central importance to the desert-dwelling Papagos.

Then did I hold firm my well-strung bow and my smooth, straight-flying
   arrows.
To me did I draw my far-striding sandals, and fast I tied them.

Over the flat land did I then go striding,
Over the embedded stones did I then go stumbling,
Under the trees in the ditches did I go stooping,
Through the trees on the high ground did I go hurtling,   20
Through the mountain gullies did I go brushing quickly.

In four halts did I reach the shining white eagle, my guardian,
And I asked power.
Then favorable to me he felt
And did bring forth his shining white stone.
Our enemy's mountains he made white as with moonlight
And brought them close,
And across them I went striding.

In four halts did I reach the blue hawk, my guardian,
And I asked power.   30
Then favorable to me he felt
And did bring forth his blue stone.
Our enemy waters he made white as with moonlight.
And around them I went striding.
There did I seize and pull up and make into a bundle
Those things which were my enemy's,
All kinds of seeds and beautiful clouds and beautiful winds.
Then came forth a thick stalk and a thick tassel,
And the undying seed did ripen.

This I did on behalf of my people.   40
Thus should you also think and desire,
All you my kinsmen.

1938

SENECA ORATORY

from   THE SPEECH OF CHIEF RED-JACKET[*]

"*Friend and brother,* it was the will of the Great Spirit that we should meet together this day. He orders all things, and he has given us a fine day for our council. He has taken his garment from before the sun, and caused it to shine with

[*] This speech was given by a well-respected chief of the Senecas, Sagoyewatha (1758?–1830), or
Red-jacket (because of the British coat he often wore). It was given to a council in Buffalo in 1805,
called at the request of a missionary from Massachusetts, Mr.Cram, who had come seeking permission to convert the tribes under Iroquois influence in northern New York state. Red-jacket was one of
the greatest Indian orators. His eloquence and vision affected the relationship between the European
settlers and the Iroquois for many years.

brightness upon us; our eyes are opened, that we see clearly; our ears are un-stopped, that we have been able to hear distinctly the words that you have spoken; for all these favors we thank the Great Spirit, and him only.

"*Brother,* this council fire was kindled by you; it was at your request that we came together at this time; we have listened with attention to what you have said; you requested us to speak our minds freely; this gives us great joy, for we now consider that we stand upright before you, and can speak what we think; all have heard your voice, and all speak to you as one man; our minds are agreed.

"*Brother,* you say you want an answer to your talk before you leave this place. It is right you should have one, as you are a great distance from home, and we do not wish to detain you; but we will first look back a little, and tell you what our fathers have told us, and what we have heard from the white people.

"*Brother, listen to what we say.* There was a time when our forefathers owned this great island.[1] Their seats extended from the rising to the setting sun. The Great Spirit had made it for the use of Indians. He had created the buffalo, the deer, and other animals for food. He made the bear, and the beaver, and their skins served us for clothing. He had scattered them over the country, and taught us how to take them. He had caused the earth to produce corn for bread. All this he had done for his red children because he loved them. If we had any disputes about hunting grounds, they were generally settled without the shedding of much blood: but an evil day came upon us; your forefathers crossed the great waters, and landed on this island. Their numbers were small; they found friends, and not enemies; they told us they had fled from their own country for fear of wicked men, and come here to enjoy their religion. They asked for a small seat; we took pity on them, granted their request, and they sat down amongst us; we gave them corn and meat; they gave us poison[2] in return. The white people had now found our country, tidings were carried back, and more came amongst us; yet we did not fear them, we took them to be friends; they called us brothers; we believed them, and gave them a larger seat. At length, their numbers had greatly increased; they wanted more land; they wanted our country. Our eyes were opened, and our minds became uneasy. Wars took place; Indians were hired to fight against Indians, and many of our people were destroyed. They also brought strong liquors among us: it was strong and powerful, and has slain thousands.

"*Brother,* our seats were once large, and yours were very small; you have now become a great people, and we have scarcely a place left to spread our blankets; you have got our country, but are not satisfied; *you want to force your religion upon us.*

"*Brother, continue to listen.* You say that you are sent to instruct us how to worship the *Great Spirit* agreeably to his mind, and if we do not take hold of the religion which you white people teach, we shall be unhappy hereafter; you say that you are right, and we are lost; how do we know this to be true? We understand that your religion is written in a book; if it was intended for us as well as you, why has not the Great Spirit given it to us, and not only to us, but why did he not give to our forefathers the knowledge of that book, with the means of understanding it rightly? We only know what you tell us about it; how shall we know when to believe, being so often deceived by the white people?

"*Brother,* you say there is but one way to worship and serve the Great Spirit; if

---

[1] Native Americans tended to believe that America is an island.   [2] Probably liquor.

there is but one religion, why do you white people differ so much about it? why not all agree, as you can all read the book?

"*Brother*, we do not understand these things; we are told that your religion was given to your forefathers, and has been handed down from father to son. We also have a religion which was given to our forefathers, and has been handed down to us their children. We worship that way. *It teacheth us to be thankful for all the favors we receive; to love each other, and to be united; we never quarrel about religion.*

"*Brother*, the Great Spirit has made us all; but he has made a great difference between his white and red children; he has given us a different complexion, and different customs; to you he has given the arts; to these he has not opened our eyes; we know these things to be true. Since he has made so great a difference between us in other things, why may we not conclude that he has given us a different religion according to our understanding; the Great Spirit does right; he knows what is best for his children; we are satisfied.

"*Brother*, we do not wish to destroy your religion, or take it from you; we only want to enjoy our own.

"*Brother*, you say you have not come to get our land or our money, but to enlighten our minds. I will now tell you that I have been at your meetings, and saw you collecting money from the meeting. I cannot tell what this money was intended for, but suppose it was for your minister, and if we should conform to your way of thinking, perhaps you may want some from us.

"*Brother*, we are told that you have been preaching to white people in this place; these people are our neighbors; we are acquainted with them, we will wait a little while and see what effect your preaching has upon them. If we find it does them good, makes them honest, and less disposed to cheat Indians, we will then consider again what you have said.

"*Brother*, you have now heard our answer to your talk, and this is all we have to say at present. As we are going to part, we will come and take you by the hand, and hope the Great Spirit will protect you on your journey, and return you safe to your friends."

1805, 1834

The Literature of Exploration
(Late 15th–17th Centuries)

The literature of the early European explorers of North America is characterized by the conflicts between the explorers' preconceptions and the realities of the Western Hemisphere. The first Europeans to investigate what they perceived as a "new world"—including Christopher Columbus, an Italian whose voyages were financed by Spain—were initially convinced that they had reached Asia. This conclusion was based on classical calculations of the earth's size and on biblical prophecies; the Europeans were not aware that the North and South American continents existed. With the 1501 voyage to Brazil by

Amerigo Vespucci, which he described in a letter after returning to Portugal in 1502, it was acknowledged that the continent we know as North America was a region previously unknown to Europeans. (That region was named for Vespucci, a Florentine navigator, at the suggestion of Martin Waldseemüller, a German geographer.) Although European interest in establishing trade routes to the Orient persisted through the sixteenth century, the immediate focus shifted to exploitation, and later to colonization, of the "newly discovered" continent.

Deeper exploration of the Americas bred further ambivalence. Early accounts, many designed to generate funding for further exploration, described the region as an earthly paradise, a fertile garden where food falls from the trees and fish leap from the oceans. European interest was also inflamed by reports of alleged "cities of gold" in South America and in what is now southwestern America. However, other tales of the harsh realities of existence in the Americas tempered the optimism engendered by these fabulous reports. One such sobering story is *The Narrative of the Expedition of Coranado* (1896), the account by Pedro de Casteñeda of Francisco Vásquez de Coronado's ill-fated search from 1540 to 1542 for the Seven Golden Cities of Cíbola. Casteñeda, a native of northern Spain, was a colonist at San Miguel Culiacan in northwestern Mexico when Coronado's expedition moved through that area. Casteñeda joined the expedition as a private soldier. Though he admits that he is no great rhetorician, his narrative remains one of the most important documents of this expedition and vividly portrays the dangers and hardships attendant upon the pursuit of easy wealth in the Americas.

Europeans' struggles for survival gave shape to many early forms of exploration literature. Narratives of hardship, captivity, and survival stressed the kinds of traits and skills uniquely suited to life in the wilderness. Strength, endurance, a measure of cunning, and an understanding of nature became the prime elements of the literature of exploration. Works such as the *Relation of Núñez Cabeza de Vaca* (1542), by Alvar Núñez Cabeza de Vaca, in which four shipwrecked Europeans wander for eight years in the Gulf Coast region, emphasize the skills necessary for adaptation and survival. After his rescue in 1536 Cabeza de Vaca was appointed governor and captain-general of the South American province Paraguay, but political intrigue led to his arrest and return to Spain. Though he was eventually acquitted, he found it difficult to realign himself with European society, and his experiences can be seen as representative of the problems early explorers and colonists faced in reconciling a European set of intellectual paradigms with American realities.

Another narrative indicative of the conflicts Europeans encountered in their early investigations of the Americas is *Voyages of Samuel de Champlain, 1604–1618* (1907). A native of Brouage, a small French port on the Bay of Biscay, Samuel de Champlain displayed early in life an aptitude for sea travel and for administration. In 1608, on his third trip to Canada, he founded Quebec and explored the New England coast and the Great Lakes region, documenting in the *Voyages* his disputes with the Iroquois Indians. Those disputes initiated long-standing hostility between the French and the Iroquois.

For Europeans the existence of two enormous continents between Europe and Asia was a cultural shock. When the trans-Atlantic contact was first made, many Europeans had already begun to doubt the received authority of popes, kings, and traditionally educated scholars in all aspects of life. The explorers of the Americas provided new facts about the nature and shape of the world and thus fed a growing skepticism among European thinkers. This skepticism, which characterized the Renaissance and the Reformation, intensified the desire to investigate the American continents and report the facts—yet, every new account inflamed imaginations and produced new myths and mysteries. The ambivalence to the Americas expressed by the early explorers reflects the questioning nature of the Renaissance-era European mind, and their literature gives shape to the paradoxes of American experience that would become the foundation of classic American literature.

Suggested Readings: D. B. Quinn, ed., *North American Discovery, ca. 1000–1612,* 1971. W. P. Cumming, R. A. Eston, and D. B. Quinn, *The Discovery of North America,* 1972. F. Chiappelli, ed., *First Images of America,* 1976. D. B. Quinn, ed., *North America From Earliest Discovery to First Settlements: The Norse Voyages to 1612,* 1977. D. B. Quinn, ed., *New American World: A Documentary History of North America to 1612,* 5 vols., 1979. S. E. Morison, *Admiral of the Ocean Sea: A Life of Christopher Columbus,* 1983. F. W. Hodge and T. H. Lewis, *Spanish Explorers in the Southern United States, 1528–1543,* 1984. S. H. Palmer and D. Reinhartz, eds., *Essays on the History of North American Discovery and Exploration,* 1988.

Texts Used: *The Journal of the First Voyage of Christopher Columbus: Journals and Other Documents on the Life and Voyages of Christopher Columbus,* ed. S. E. Morison, 1963. Letter of Vespucci's First Brazilian Voyage: *The European Discovery of America: The Southern Voyages,* A.D. *1492–1616,* trans. S. E. Morison, 1974. *Relations of Núñez Cabeza de Vaca: Original Narratives of Early American History: Spanish Explorers in the Southern United States, 1528–1543,* ed. J. F. Jameson, 1925. *The Narrative of the Expedition of Coronado: Original Narratives of Early American History. Voyages of Samuel de Champlain: Original Narratives of Early American History: Voyages of Samuel de Champlain, 1604–1618,* ed. W. L. Grant, 1907.

from   THE JOURNAL OF THE FIRST VOYAGE OF
CHRISTOPHER COLUMBUS[*]

by   CHRISTOPHER COLUMBUS (1451–1506)

The Discovery of the West Indies, 12 October 1492–15 January 1493

[*Friday, 12 October*]

At two hours after midnight appeared the land,[1] at a distance of 2 leagues. They handed[2] all sails and set the *treo,* which is the mainsail without bonnets,[3] and lay-to waiting for daylight Friday, when they arrived at an island of the Bahamas that was called in the Indians' tongue *Guanahani.* Presently they saw naked people, and the Admiral went ashore in his barge, and Martin Alonso Pinzón and Vicente Yáñez, his brother, who was captain of the Niña, followed. The Admiral broke out the royal standard, and the captains [displayed] two banners of the Green Cross, which the Admiral flew on all the vessels as a signal, with an F and a Y,[4] one at one arm of the cross and the other on the other, and over each letter his or her crown.

Once ashore they saw very green trees, many streams, and fruits of different kinds. The Admiral called to the two captains and to the others who jumped ashore and to Rodrigo de Escobedo, secretary of the whole fleet, and to Rodrigo Sánchez of Segovia, and said that they should bear faith and witness how he before them all was taking, as in fact he took, possession of the said island for the King and Queen, their Lord and Lady, making the declarations that are required, as is set forth at length in the testimonies which were there taken down in writing.

---

[*] Columbus's journal was first translated into English in 1827.
[1] San Salvador, an island in the Bahamas.   [2] Lowered.
[3] Canvas strips fastened to sails to increase the sails' area.
[4] Ferdinand V (1452–1516) and Isabella I (1451–1504), king and queen of Spain, who together ruled Castile and Aragon from 1479 to 1504 and financed Columbus's voyage.

Presently there gathered many people of the island. What follows are the formal words of the Admiral, in his Book of the First Navigation and Discovery of these Indies:[5]

"I," says he, "in order that they might develop a very friendly disposition towards us, because I knew that they were a people who could better be freed and converted to our Holy Faith by love than by force, gave to some of them red caps and to others glass beads, which they hung on their necks, and many other things of slight value, in which they took much pleasure. They remained so much our [friends] that it was a marvel, later they came swimming to the ships' boats in which we were, and brought us parrots and cotton thread in skeins and darts and many other things, and we swopped them for other things that we gave them, such as little glass beads and hawks' bells.[6] Finally they traded and gave everything they had, with good will; but it appeared to me that these people were very poor in everything. They all go quite naked as their mothers bore them; and also the women, although I didn't see more than one really young girl. All that I saw were young men, none of them more than 30 years old, very well built, of very handsome bodies and very fine faces; the hair coarse, almost like the hair of a horse's tail, and short, the hair they wear over their eyebrows, except for a hank behind that they wear long and never cut. Some of them paint themselves black (and they are of the color of the Canary Islanders, neither black nor white), and others paint themselves white, and some red, and others with what they find. And some paint their faces, others the body, some the eyes only, others only the nose. They bear no arms, nor know thereof; for I showed them swords and they grasped them by the blade and cut themselves through ignorance. They have no iron. Their darts are a kind of rod without iron, and some have at the end a fish's tooth and others, other things. They are generally fairly tall and good looking, well built. I saw some who had marks of wounds on their bodies, and made signs to them to ask what it was, and they showed me that people of other islands which are near came there and wished to capture them, and they defended themselves. And I believed and now believe that people do come here from the mainland to take them as slaves. They ought to be good servants and of good skill, for I see that they repeat very quickly whatever was said to them. I believe that they would easily be made Christians, because it seemed to me that they belonged to no religion. I, please Our Lord, will carry off six of them at my departure to Your Highnesses, that they may learn to speak. I saw no animal of any king in this island, except parrots." All these are the words of the Admiral.

[*Saturday, 13 October*]

At the time of daybreak there came to the beach many of these men, all young men, as I have said, and all of good stature, very handsome people. Their hair is not kinky but straight and coarse like horsehair; the whole forehead and head is very broad, more so than [in] any other race that I have yet seen, and the eyes very handsome and not small. They themselves are not at all black, but of the color of the Canary Islanders; nor should anything else be expected, because this is on the same latitude as the island of Ferro in the Canaries. The legs of all, without exception, are very straight and [they have] no paunch, but are very well proportioned.

---

[5] The formal title of Columbus's journal.　　[6] Small, round bells used in falconry.

They came to the ship in dugouts[7] which are fashioned like a long boat from the trunck of a tree, and all in one piece, and wonderfully made (considering the country), and so big that in some came 40 or 50 men, and others smaller, down to some in which but a single man came. They row with a thing like a baker's peel[8] and go wonderfully, and if they capsize all begin to swim and right it and bail it out with calabashes[9] that they carry. They brought skeins of spun cotton, and parrots, and darts, and other trifles that would be tedious to describe, and give all for whatever is given to them. And I was attentive and worked hard to know if there was any gold, and saw that some of them wore a little piece hanging from a thing like a needle case which they have in the nose; and by signs I could understand that, going to the S, or doubling the island to the S, there was a king there who had great vessels of it and possessed a lot. I urged them to go there, and later saw that they were not inclined to the journey. I decided to wait until tomorrow afternoon and then depart to the SW, since, as many of them informed me, there should be land to the S, SW, and NW, and that they of the NW used to come to fight them many times; and so also to go to the SW to search for gold and precious stones. This island is very big[10] and very level; and the trees very green, and many bodies of water, and a very big lake in the middle, but no mountain, and the whole of it so green that it is a pleasure to gaze upon, and this people are very docile, and from their longing to have some of our things, and thinking that they will get nothing unless they give something, and not having it, they take what they can, and soon swim off. But all that they have, they give for whatever is given to them, even bartering for pieces of broken crockery and glass. I even saw 16 skeins of cotton given for three *ceitis* of Portugal, which is [equivalent to] a *blanca* of Castile,[11] and in them there was more than an *arroba*[12] of spun cotton. This I should have forbidden and would not have allowed anyone to take anything, except that I had ordered it all taken for Your Highnesses if there was any there in abundance. It is grown in this island; but from the short time I couldn't say for sure; and also here is found the gold that they wear hanging from the nose. But, to lose no time, I intend to go and see if I can find the Island of *Cipango*.[13] Now, as it was night, all went ashore in their dugouts.

[*Sunday, 14 October*]

"When day was breaking I ordered the ship's gig and the caravels' barges[14] to be readied, and I went along the coast of the island to the NNE, to see the other side, which was the eastern side, what there was there, and also to see the villages; and soon I saw two or three, and the people who all came to the beach, shouting and giving thanks to God. Some brought us water, others, other things to eat. Others, when they saw that I didn't care to go ashore, plunged into the sea swimming, and came out, and we understood that they asked us if we had come from the sky. And one old man got into the boat, and others shouted in loud voices to all, men and women, 'Come and see the men who come from the sky, bring them food and drink.' Many came and many women, each with something, giving

---

[7] Canoes.   [8] A long, shovel-like board used for moving bread into and out of ovens.
[9] Gourds.   [10] Roughly sixteen nautical miles long, seven wide.
[11] Worth a fraction of a cent.   [12] About twenty-five pounds.
[13] Japan, which Marco Polo (1254–1324) indicated to be 1500 miles from Asia.
[14] The small, secondary boat (typically reserved for the captain's use) and the large, primary boat.

thanks to God, throwing themselves on the ground, they raised their hands to the sky, and then shouted to us to come ashore; but I was afraid to, from seeing a great reef of rocks which surrounded the whole of this island, and inside it was deep water and a harbor[15] to hold all the ships in Christendom, and the entrance of it very narrow. It's true that inside this reef there are some shoal spots, but the sea moves no more than within a well. In order to see all this I kept going this morning, that I might give an account of all to Your Highnesses, and also [to see] where there might be a fortress; and I saw a piece of land which is formed like an island,[16] although it isn't one (and on it there are six houses), the which could in two days be made an island, although I don't see that it would be necessary, because these people are very unskilled in arms, as Your Highnesses will see from the seven that I caused to be taken to carry them off to learn our language and return; unless Your Highnesses should order them all to be taken to Castile or held captive in the same island, for with 50 men they could all be subjected and made to do all that one wished. And, moreover, next to said islet are groves of trees the most beautiful that I have seen, and as green and leafy as those of Castile in the months of April and May; and much water. I inspected all that harbor, and then returned to the ship and made sail, and saw so many islands that I could not decide where to go first; and those men whom I had captured made signs to me that they were so many that they could not be counted, and called by their names more than a hundred. Finally I looked for the biggest,[17] and decided to go there, and so I did, and it is probably distant from this island of San Salvador 5 leagues, and some of them more, some less. All are very level, without mountains, and very fertile, and all inhabited, and they make war on one another, although these are very simple people and very fine figures of men."

[*Monday, 15–Tuesday, 16 October*]

"I had lain-to[18] this night for fear of approaching the shore and anchoring before morning, not knowing whether the coast was clear of reefs, and at dawn made sail. And as the island was more than 5 leagues distant and nearer 7, and the current detained me, it was about midday when I arrived at the said island, and I found that the coast which lies over against the island of San Salvador ran N and S and for 5 leagues; and that the other which I followed ran E and W for more than 10 leagues. And when from this island I saw another bigger one to the W, I made sail to navigate all that day until nightfall, because otherwise I would not have been able to reach the western cape, to which I gave the name, The Island of *Sancta Maria de la Conçepçión,* and just about sunset I anchored near the said cape to find out if there was any gold there, because those whom I had captured on the Island of San Salvador told me that there they wore very big bracelets of gold on their legs and arms. I well believed that all they said was humbug in order to escape. However, it was my wish to bypass no island without taking possession, although having taken one you can claim all; and I anchored and remained until

---

[15] Graham's Harbor.

[16] Rocky Point, which then stretched off San Salvador into Graham's Harbor but has since been broken off into an island.

[17] Rum Cay, about twenty-five nautical miles from San Salvador; Columbus named the island Sancta María de la Concepción.

[18] Lain stationary.

today Tuesday, when at break of day I went ashore in the armed boats, and landed, and the people who were numerous and also naked and of the same condition as they of the other island of San Salvador, let us go over the island and gave us what we asked. And because the wind veered to the SE quarter I did not care to stay and departed for the ship, and a big dugout came aboard[19] the caravel *Niña,* and one of the men of the island of San Salvador, who was aboard, leaped into the sea and went away in it, and the night previously, about midnight, the other [had fled] and went after the dugout, which then escaped because there never was a boat that could catch up with her, even though we had great advantage over her. However they reached the land and abandoned the dugout and some of my company went ashore after them, and they all fled like chickens, and the dugout that they had abandoned we brought aboard the caravel *Niña,* to which already came from another cape a little dugout with a man who came to trade a skein of cotton; and some sailors jumped into the sea because he wouldn't come aboard the caravel, and seized him. And I who was on the poop of the ship seeing everything, sent for him and gave him a red cap and some little beads of green glass which I placed on his arm, and two hawk's bells which I placed on his ears, and I ordered him to be given back his dugout, which they also had on the ship's boat, and sent him ashore. And I made sail to go to the other big island[20] which I saw to the westward, and I ordered the other dugout which the caravel *Niña* was towing astern to be cast off, and later saw it ashore at the time of the arrival of the other man to whom I had given the aforesaid things; and I had not wished to take the skein of cotton, although he wished to give it to me, and all the others surrounded him and held it a great marvel, and well it appeared to him that we were good people, and that the other man who had fled had done us some harm, "[and that]" for that account we were carrying him along. For this reason I used him thus, and gave him the aforesaid articles, in order that they might hold us in such esteem that on another occasion when your Highnesses send men back here again, they may not make bad company, and all that I gave him was not worth four maravedis.[21]

"And so I departed,[22] it would be at 10 o'clock with the wind SE veering to the S, to go to the other island, which is very big, and where all those men that I am taking from San Salvador make signs that there is a lot of gold and that they wear it in the form of bracelets on the arms, legs, ears, nose and neck. And there was from this island of Santa Maria to that other [Long Island] 9 leagues on a parallel, and all this part of the island runs NW-SE, and it appears that there is certainly on this coast more than 28 leagues on this side, very level without any mountains like those of San Salvador and Santa Maria, and all beach without boulders, except that all have some rocks under water near the shore, for which you must keep your eyes peeled when you wish to anchor, and not anchor very near the shore, although the water is always very clear and you see the bottom. And among all these islands at a distance of two lombard[23] shots off-shore there is so much depth that you can't find bottom.

"These islands are very green and fertile and the air very balmy, and there may be many things that I don't know, for I do not wish to delay but to discover and go

---

[19] Alongside, or board to board.
[20] Long Island, the Bahamas; Columbus named the island Fernandina.
[21] Spanish copper coins.   [22] Tuesday, 16 October.
[23] A cannon used in the fifteenth and sixteenth centuries.

to many islands to find gold. And since these people make signs that it is worn on arms and legs, and it is gold all right because they point to some pieces that I have, I cannot fail (with Our Lord's help) to find out where it comes from.

"Standing in mid-channel between the two islands, i.e., this Santa Maria and that big one, to which I give the name Fernandina, I came upon a man alone in a dugout on his way from Santa Maria to Fernandina, and he carried a bit of his bread that would be about the size of your fist, and a calabash of water, and a lump of bright red earth powdered and then kneaded, and some dry leaves[24] which must be something much valued among them, since they offered me some at San Salvador as a gift. And he carried a basket of his own kind, in which he had a string of glass beads and two *blancas,* by which I knew that he had come from the island of San Salvador, had passed over to Santa Maria and was going on to Fernandina. And he came alongside the ship. I had him aboard (which he asked for) and had his dugout hoisted on deck, and had all he brought guarded, and ordered him to be given bread and honey and drink; and I shall give him passage to Fernandina and give him back all his stuff, that he may give a good account of us when (please Our Lord) Your Highnesses send hither and that those who come may be welcome and be given all they need."

1492–1493, 1825

from　LETTER OF VESPUCCI'S FIRST BRAZILIAN VOYAGE*

by　AMERIGO VESPUCCI (1454–1512)

[The "Reasoning Animals" of the New World]

Now we come to the reasoning animals. We found all the earth inhabited by people completely nude, men as well as women, without covering their shame. They have bodies well proportioned, white in color with black hair, and little or no beard. I tried very hard to understand their life and customs because for 27 days I ate and slept with them, and that which I learned of them follows:

They have no laws or faith, and live according to nature. They do not recognize the immortality of the soul, they have among them no private property, because everything is common; they have no boundaries of kingdoms and provinces, and no king! They obey nobody, each is lord unto himself; no justice, no gratitude, which to them is unnecessary because it is not part of their code. They live in common in houses made like very large cabins; and for people who have no iron or other metal, it is possible to say that their cabins are truly wonderful, for I have seen houses which are 200 *passi*[1] long and 30 wide and artfully made by craftsmen, and in one of these houses were 500 or perhaps 600 souls. They slept in nets[2] woven of cotton, exposed to the air without any other covering; they eat seated on the ground; their food is roots of herbs and many good fruits, an infinity

---

[24] Probably tobacco.

* Vespucci wrote this letter, known as the "Bartolozzi Letter," to his former employer, Lorenzo di Pier Francesco de' Medici, after Vespucci had returned to Lisbon, Portugal in September 1502 from his 1501 Brazilian voyage. The text was translated by Samuel E. Morison and Dr. Gino Corti.

[1] Portuguese measurements.　　[2] Hammocks.

of fish and great quantities of shellfish; crabs, oyster, lobster, crayfish, and many other things which the sea produces. The meat which they eat commonly is human flesh, as shall be told. When they can have other flesh of animals and birds they eat that too but they do not hunt for it much because they have no dogs and their land is very full of woods which are filled with fierce wild beasts, so they do not ordinarily enter the woods unless with a crowd of people.

1502, 1974

from RELATION OF NÚÑEZ CABEZA DE VACA*

by ALVAR NÚÑEZ CABEZA DE VACA (1490?–1557?)

Chapter 24: Customs of the Indians of That Country

From the Island of Malhado to this land,[1] all the Indians whom we saw have the custom from the time in which their wives find themselves pregnant, of not sleeping with them until two years after they have given birth. The children are suckled until the age of twelve years, when they are old enough to get support for themselves. We asked why they reared them in this manner; and they said because of the great poverty of the land, it happened many times, as we witnessed, that they were two or three days without eating, sometimes four, and consequently, in seasons of scarcity, the children were allowed to suckle, that they might not famish; otherwise those who lived would be delicate, having little strength.

If any one chance to fall sick in the desert, and cannot keep up with the rest, the Indians leave him to perish, unless it be a son or a brother; him they will assist, even to carrying on their back. It is common among them all to leave their wives when there is no conformity,[2] and directly they connect themselves with whom they please. This is the course of the men who are childless; those who have children remain with their wives and never abandon them. When they dispute and quarrel in their towns, they strike each other with the fists, fighting until exhausted, and then separate. Sometimes they are parted by the women going between them; the men never interfere. For no disaffection that arises do they resort to bows and arrows. After they have fought, or had out their dispute, they take their dwellings and go into the woods, living apart from each other until their heat has subsided. When no longer offended and their anger is gone, they return. From that time they are friends as if nothing had happened; nor is it necessary that any one should mend their friendships, as they in this way again unite them. If those that quarrel are single, they go to some neighboring people, and although these

---

* Cabeza de Vaca was part of a colonizing expedition led by Pánfilo de Narváez (1480?–1528), to Florida and eastern Mexico from Spain in 1527. The men were cast ashore on the island of Malhado, in the Gulf of Mexico, in 1528; the three hundred Europeans that had begun the expedition were soon drastically reduced in numbers by disease, exposure, starvation, and conflicts with hostile natives. Cabeza de Vaca remained on Malhado intermittently for five years while he eked out a meager existence as a trader among the natives and as a healer of the sick, a vocation at which he had considerable success. With three other survivors Cabeza de Vaca wandered along the Gulf Coast in search of rescue for a total of eight years; they finally reached Mexico City in 1536. The narrative, written after Cabeza de Vaca had reached Mexico, was first published in Spain in 1542.

[1] Eastern Texas.   [2] Customs or conventions.

should be enemies, they receive them well and welcome them warmly, giving them so largely of what they have, that when their animosity cools, and they return to their town, they go rich.

They are all warlike, and have as much strategy for protecting themselves against enemies as they could have were they reared in Italy in continual feuds. When they are in a part of the country where their enemies may attack them, they place their houses on the skirt of a wood, the thickest and most tangled they can find, and near it make a ditch in which they sleep. The warriors are covered by small pieces of stick through which are loop-holes; these hide them and present so false an appearance, that if come upon they are not discovered. They open a very narrow way, entering into the midst of the wood, where a spot is prepared on which the women and children sleep. When night comes they kindle fires in their lodges, that should spies be about, they may think to find them there; and before daybreak they again light those fires. If the enemy comes to assault the houses, they who are in the ditch make a sally; and from their trenches do much injury without those who are outside seeing or being able to find them. When there is no wood in which they can take shelter in this way, and make their ambuscades,[3] they settle on open ground at a place they select, which they invest with trenches covered with broken sticks, having apertures whence to discharge arrows. These arrangements are made for night.

While I was among the Aguenes,[4] their enemies[5] coming suddenly at midnight, fell upon them, killed three and wounded many, so that they ran from their houses to the fields before them. As soon as these ascertained that their assailants had withdrawn, they returned to pick up all the arrows the others had shot, and following after them in the most stealthy manner possible, came that night to their dwellings without their presence being suspected. At four o'clock in the morning the Aguenes attacked them, killed five, and wounded numerous others, and made them flee from their houses, leaving their bows with all they possessed. In a little while came the wives of the Quevenes to them and formed a treaty whereby the parties became friends. The women, however, are sometimes the cause of war. All these nations, when they have personal enmities, and are not of one family, assassinate at night, waylay, and inflict gross barbarities on each other.

Chapter 25: Vigilance of the Indians in War

They are the most watchful in danger of any people I ever knew. If they fear an enemy they are awake the night long, each with a bow at his side and a dozen arrows. He that would sleep tries his bow, and if it is not strung, he gives the turn necessary to the cord. They often come out from their houses, bending to the ground in such manner that they cannot be seen, looking and watching on all sides to catch every object. If they perceive anything about, they are at once in the bushes with their bows and arrows, and there remain until day, running from place to place where it is needful to be, or where they think their enemies are. When the light has come, they unbend their bows until they go out to hunt. The strings are the sinews of deer.

The method they have of fighting, is bending low to the earth, and whilst shot at they move about, speaking and leaping from one point to another, thus avoiding

---

[3] Ambushes.
[4] One of the native peoples that had held Cabeza de Vaca captive; also known as the Doguenes.
[5] The Quevenes.

the shafts of their enemies. So effectual is their manœuvring that they can receive very little injury from crossbow or arquebus;[6] they rather scoff at them; for these arms are of little value employed in open field, where the Indians move nimbly about. They are proper for defiles[7] and in water; everywhere else the horse will best subdue, being what the natives universally dread.[8] Whosoever would fight them must be cautious to show no fear, or desire to have anything that is theirs; while war exists they must be treated with the utmost rigor; for if they discover any timidity or covetousness, they are a race that well discern the opportunities for vengeance, and gather strength from any weakness of their adversaries. When they use arrows in battle and exhaust their store, each returns his own way, without the one party following the other, although the one be many and the other few, such being their custom. Oftentimes the body of an Indian is traversed by the arrow; yet unless the entrails of the heart be struck, he does not die but recovers from the wound.

I believe these people see and hear better, and have keener senses than any other in the world. They are great in hunger, thirst, and cold, as if they were made for the endurance of these more than other men, by habit and nature.

Thus much I have wished to say, beyond the gratification of that desire men have to learn the customs and manners of each other, that those who hereafter at some time find themselves amongst these people, may have knowledge of their usages and artifices, the value of which they will not find inconsiderable in such event.

1536, 1542

from THE NARRATIVE OF THE EXPEDITION OF CORONADO*

by PEDRO DE CASTEÑEDA (1510?–1570?)

Chapter 3: Of How They Killed the Negro Estevan[1] at Cibola, and Friar Marcos Returned in Flight

After Estevan had left the friars, he thought he could get all the reputation and honor himself, and that if he should discover those settlements with such famous high houses, alone, he would be considered bold and courageous. So he pro-

---

[6] A harquebus, an early type of portable gun.

[7] Narrow passages through which "troops" can march only in single file.

[8] A recollection of Narváez's experiences in Florida in 1528.

* Casteñeda was a member of the expeditions of Francisco Vasquez de Coronado (1510–1554), the governor of New Galicia, into what is now Arizona, New Mexico, Texas, Oklahoma, and Kansas. Friar Marcos de Niza (?–1558), or Marcos of Nice, returned from exploring land North of Mexico in 1539 with reports of vast riches in "Seven Golden Cities of Cibola," actually the Zuni Pueblos of present-day New Mexico. Coronado's expedition found such natural riches as the Grand Canyon but no gold. The narrative was started at least twenty years after the journey ended and was first translated into English in 1896 by George Parker Winship.

[1] A Moor who had followed his master, Andrés Dorante, to the New World from Spain on the unsuccessful expedition of Pánfilo de Narváez in 1528; Estevan was one of the four survivors, along with Alvar Núñez Cabeza de Vaca. Estevan led the scouting party of Friar Marcos.

ceeded with the people who had followed him, and attempted to cross the wilderness which lies between the country he had passed through and Cibola. He was so far ahead of the friars that, when these reached Chichilticalli,[2] which is on the edge of the wilderness, he was already at Cibola, which is eighty leagues beyond. It is 220 leagues from Culican[3] to the edge of the wilderness, and eighty across the desert, which makes 300, or perhaps ten more or less. As I said, Estevan reached Cibola loaded with the large quantity of turquoises they had given him and some beautiful women whom the Indians who followed him and carried his things were taking with them and had given him. These had followed him from all the settlements he had passed, believing that under his protection they could traverse the whole world without any danger. But as the people in this country were more intelligent than those who followed Estevan, they lodged him in a little hut they had outside their village, and the older men and the governors heard his story and took steps to find out the reason he had come to that country. For three days they made inquiries about him and held a council. The account which the negro gave them of two white men who were following him, sent by a great lord, who knew about the things in the sky, and how these were coming to instruct them in divine matters, made them think that he must be a spy or a guide from some nations who wished to come and conquer them, because it seemed to them unreasonable to say that the people were white in the country from which he came and that he was sent by them, he being black. Besides these other reasons, they thought it was hard of him to ask them for turquoises and women, and so they decided to kill him. They did this, but they did not kill any of those who went with him, although they kept some young fellows and let the others, about sixty persons, return freely to their own country. As these, who were badly scared, were returning in flight, they happened to come upon the friars in the desert sixty leagues from Cibola, and told them the sad news, which frightened them so much that they would not even trust these folks who had been with the negro, but opened the packs they were carrying and gave away everything they had except the holy vestments for saying mass. They returned from here by double marches, prepared for anything, without seeing any more of the country except what the Indians told them.

Chapter 4: Of How the Noble Don Antonio de Mendoza Made an Expedition to Discover Cibola

After Francisco Vazquez Coronado had sent Friar Marcos of Nice and his party on the search already related, he was engaged in Culiacan about some business that related to his government, when he heard an account of a province called Topira,[4] which was to the north of the country of Culiacan. He started to explore this region with several of the conquerors and some friendly Indians, but he did not get very far, because the mountain chains which they had to cross were very difficult. He returned without finding the least signs of a good country, and when he got back, he found the friars who had just arrived, and who told such great things about what the negro Estevan had discovered and what they had heard from the Indians, and other things they had heard about the South Sea[5] and islands and

---

[2] "Red House," as the Aztecs called this city, probably on or near the Río Gila in what is now southern Arizona.
[3] San Miguel Culiacan, in Sinaloa, northwestern Mexico.
[4] In Durango, Mexico; it is known for its rich mines.   [5] The Pacific Ocean.

other riches, that, without stopping for anything, the governor set off at once for the City of Mexico, taking Friar Marcos with him, to tell the viceroy about it. He made the things seem more important by not talking about them to anyone except his particular friends, under promise of the greatest secrecy, until after he had reached Mexico and seen Don Antonio de Mendoza.[6] Then it began to be noised abroad that the Seven Cities for which Nuño de Guzman[7] had searched had already been discovered, and a beginning was made in collecting an armed force and in bringing together people to go and conquer them. The noble viceroy arranged with the friars of the order of Saint Francis so that Friar Marcos was made father provincial, as a result of which the pulpits of that order were filled with such accounts of marvels and wonders that more than 300 Spaniards and about 800 natives of New Spain collected in a few days. There were so many men of such high quality among the Spaniards, that such a noble body was never collected in the Indies, nor so many men of quality in such a small body, there being 300 men. Francisco Vazquez Coronado, governor of New Galicia, was captain-general, because he had been the author of it all. The good viceroy Don Antonio did this because at this time Francisco Vazquez was his closest and most intimate friend, and because he considered him to be wise, skillful, and intelligent, besides being a gentleman. Had he paid more attention and regard to the position in which he was placed and the charge over which he was placed, and less to the estates he left behind in New Spain, or, at least, more to the honor he had and might secure from having such gentlemen under his command, things would not have turned out as they did. When this narrative is ended, it will be seen that he did not know how to keep his position nor the government that he held.[8]

1565?–1596, 1896

---

from VOYAGES OF SAMUEL DE CHAMPLAIN[*]

by SAMUEL DE CHAMPLAIN (1567–1635)

Chapter 9: Description of a Large Lake; An Encounter With the Enemy at This Lake

We set out on the next day,[1] continuing our course in the river as far as the entrance of the lake.[2] There are many pretty islands here, low, and containing very fine woods and meadows, with abundance of fowl and such animals of the chase as stags, fallow-deer, fawns, roe-bucks, bears, and others, which go from the

---

[6] Mendoza (1485?–1552) was the first viceroy of New Spain, or Mexico, from 1535 to 1549.

[7] Nuño Beltán de Guzmán (1485?–1544), a Spanish lawyer and soldier.

[8] Following his return Coronado was indicted twice for his conduct in having returned with no new-found riches.

[*] Champlain, best known for exploring Canada, agreed to aid his "savage" allies, the Algonquin, Huron, and Montagnais Indians of what is now southern Quebec and upper New York state, in a raid against their enemies, the Iroquois Indians, in 1609. In this confrontation, near present-day Fort Ticonderoga, New York, the Iroquois got their first look at the European musket, and a long period of hostility between the French and the Native Americans over control of the region began.

[1] July 13, 1609.   [2] Now Lake Champlain.

main land to these islands. We captured a large number of these animals. There are also many beavers, not only in this river, but also in numerous other little ones that flow into it. These regions, although they are pleasant, are not inhabited by any savages, on account of their wars; but they withdraw as far as possible from the rivers into the interior, in order not to be suddenly surprised.

The next day we entered the lake, which is of great extent, say eighty or a hundred leagues long, where I saw four fine islands, ten, twelve, and fifteen leagues long, which were formerly inhabited by the savages, like the River of the Iroquois; but they have been abandoned since the wars of the savages with one another prevail. There are also many rivers falling into the lake, bordered by many fine trees of the same kinds as those we have in France, with many vines finer than any I have seen in any other place; also many chestnut-trees on the border of this lake, which I had not seen before. There is also a great abundance of fish, of many varieties; among others, one called by the savages of the country *Chaousarou*,[3] which varies in length, the largest being, as the people told me, eight or ten feet long. I saw some five feet long, which were as large as my thigh; the head being as big as my two fists, with a snout two feet and a half long, and a double row of very sharp and dangerous teeth. Its body is, in shape, much like that of a pike; but it is armed with scales so strong that a poniard[4] could not pierce them. Its color is silver-gray. The extremity of its snout is like that of swine. This fish makes war upon all others in the lakes and rivers. It also possesses remarkable dexterity, as these people informed me, which is exhibited in the following manner. When it wants to capture birds, it swims in among the rushes, or reeds, which are found on the banks of the lake in several places, where it puts its snout out of water and keeps perfectly still: so that, when the birds come and light on its snout, supposing it to be only the stump of a tree, it adroitly closes it, which it had kept ajar, and pulls the birds by the feet down under water. The savages gave me the head of one of them, of which they make great account, saying that, when they have the headache, they bleed themselves with the teeth of this fish on the spot where they suffer pain, when it suddenly passes away.

Continuing our course over this lake on the western side, I noticed, while observing the country, some very high mountains[5] on the eastern side, on the top of which there was snow. I made inquiry of the savages whether these localities were inhabited, when they told me that the Iroquois dwelt there, and that there were beautiful valleys in these places, with plains productive in grain, such as I had eaten in this country, together with many kinds of fruit without limit. They said also that the lake extended near mountains, some twenty-five leagues distant from us, as I judge. I saw, on the south, other mountains,[6] no less high than the first, but without any snow. The savages told me that these mountains were thickly settled, and that it was there we were to find their enemies; but that it was necessary to pass a fall[7] in order to go there (which I afterwards saw), when we should enter another lake,[8] nine or ten leagues long. After reaching the end of the lake, we should have to go, they said, two leagues by land, and pass through a river[9] flowing into the sea on the Norumbegue coast, near that of Florida, whither it took them only two days to go by canoe, as I have since ascertained from some prisoners we captured, who gave me minute information in regard to all they had personal knowledge of, through some Algonquin interpreters, who understood the Iroquois language.

---

[3] The garpike.   [4] A dagger.   [5] Vermont's Green Mountains.   [6] New York's Adirondacks.
[7] Ticonderoga.   [8] Lake George.   [9] The Hudson River.

Now, as we began to approach within two or three days' journey of the abode of their enemies, we advanced only at night, resting during the day. But they did not fail to practise constantly their accustomed superstitions, in order to ascertain what was to be the result of their undertaking; and they often asked me if I had had a dream, and seen their enemies, to which I replied in the negative. Yet I did not cease to encourage them, and inspire in them hope. When night came, we set out on the journey until the next day, when we withdrew into the interior of the forest, and spent the rest of the day there. About ten or eleven o'clock, after taking a little walk about our encampment, I retired. While sleeping, I dreamed that I saw our enemies, the Iroquois, drowning in the lake near a mountain, within sight. When I expressed a wish to help them, our allies, the savages, told me we must let them all die, and that they were of no importance. When I awoke, they did not fail to ask me, as usual, if I had had a dream. I told them that I had, in fact, had a dream. This, upon being related, gave them so much confidence that they did not doubt any longer that good was to happen to them.

When it was evening, we embarked in our canoes to continue our course; and, as we advanced very quietly and without making any noise, we met on the 29th of the month the Iroquois, about ten o'clock at evening, at the extremity of a cape[10] which extends into the lake on the western bank. They had come to fight. We both began to utter loud cries, all getting their arms in readiness. We withdrew out on the water, and the Iroquois went on shore, where they drew up all their canoes close to each other and began to fell trees with poor axes, which they acquire in war sometimes, using also others of stone. Thus they barricaded themselves very well.

Our forces also passed the entire night, their canoes being drawn up close to each other, and fastened to poles, so that they might not get separated, and that they might be all in readiness to fight, if occasion required. We were out upon the water, within arrow range of their barricades. When they were armed and in array, they despatched two canoes by themselves to the enemy to inquire if they wished to fight, to which the latter replied that they wanted nothing else: but they said that, at present, there was not much light, and that it would be necessary to wait for daylight, so as to be able to recognize each other; and that, as soon as the sun rose, they would offer us battle. This was agreed to by our side. Meanwhile, the entire night was spent in dancing and singing, on both sides, with endless insults and other talk; as, how little courage we had, how feeble a resistance we should make against their arms, and that, when day came, we should realize it to our ruin. Ours also were not slow in retorting, telling them they would see such execution of arms as never before, together with an abundance of such talk as is not unusual in the siege of a town. After this singing, dancing, and bandying words on both sides to the fill, when day came, my companions and myself continued under cover, for fear that the enemy would see us. We arranged our arms in the best manner possible, being, however, separated, each in one of the canoes of the savage Montagnais. After arming ourselves with light armor, we each took an arquebuse,[11] and went on shore. I saw the enemy go out of their barricade, nearly two hundred in number, stout and rugged in appearance. They came at a slow pace towards us, with a dignity and assurance which greatly amused me, having three chiefs at their head. Our men also advanced in the same order, telling me that those who had three large plumes were the chiefs, and that they had only

---

[10] Crown Point.   [11] A harquebus, an early type of portable gun.

these three, and that they could be distinguished by these plumes, which were much larger than those of their companions, and that I should do what I could to kill them. I promised to do all in my power, and said that I was very sorry they could not understand me, so that I might give order and shape to their mode of attacking their enemies, and then we should, without doubt, defeat them all; but that this could not now be obviated, and that I should be very glad to show them my courage and good-will when we should engage in the fight.

As soon as we had landed, they began to run for some two hundred paces towards their enemies, who stood firmly, not having as yet noticed my companions, who went into the woods with some savages. Our men began to call me with loud cries; and, in order to give me a passage-way, they opened in two parts, and put me at their head, where I marched some twenty paces in advance of the rest, until I was within about thirty paces of the enemy, who at once noticed me, and, halting, gazed at me, as I did also at them. When I saw them making a move to fire at us, I rested my musket against my cheek, and aimed directly at one of the three chiefs. With the same shot, two fell to the ground; and one of their men was so wounded that he died some time after. I had loaded my musket with four balls. When our side saw this shot so favorable for them, they began to raise such loud cries that one could not have heard it thunder. Meanwhile, the arrows flew on both sides. The Iroquois were greatly astonished that two men had been so quickly killed, although they were quipped with armor woven from cotton thread, and with wood which was proof against their arrows. This caused great alarm among them. As I was loading again, one of my companions fired a shot from the woods, which astonished them anew to such a degree that, seeing their chiefs dead, they lost courage, and took to flight, abandoning their camp and fort, and fleeing into the woods, whither I pursued them, killing still more of them. Our savages also killed several of them, and took ten or twelve prisoners. The remainder escaped with the wounded. Fifteen or sixteen were wounded on our side with arrow-shots; but they were soon healed.

After gaining the victory, our men amused themselves by taking a great quantity of Indian corn and some meal from their enemies, also their armor, which they had left behind that they might run better. After feasting sumptuously, dancing and singing, we returned three hours after, with the prisoners. The spot where this attack took place is in latitude 43° and some minutes, and the lake was called Lake Champlain.

1619, 1907

Giovanni da Verrazzano
(1485?–1528)

Giovannni da Verrazzano, an explorer of North America, was the first to describe the coastline from Florida to Newfoundland. He called himself a Florentine but lived in Lyons, France. Probably from a distinguished family, Verrazzano was a "renaissance man" of many abilities, versed in the works of Aristotle as well as navigation and cartography. He is believed to have spent many years in the Mediterranean as a merchant, seaman, and explorer. In March 1524 he signed an agreement with King Francis I of France and with merchants from Florence and bankers from Lyons to undertake a voyage to the New World. The goal of the voyage was the discovery of a passage to China—the same goal that had inspired the voyages of Christopher Columbus and of John Cabot.

In spring 1524 the ship *La Dauphine,* with a crew of about fifty men, headed due West from a point off the Madeira Islands, near Morocco. Fifty days later the ship made landfall somewhere West of Cape Fear, off North Carolina. From there Verrazzano, in search of an opening (the "Northwest Passage") that would lead to Cathay (China), sailed some twenty-eight hundred miles along the Atlantic coast. The ship landed a number of times on its northeastern journey, probably at the eastern shore of Virginia, at the Delaware capes, in New York harbor (where there is now a bridge named after him), and at Newport, Rhode Island. The exploration ended in Newfoundland.

Verrazzano wrote of his journey in a letter to King Francis I. Amazed at the land that was "unknown to the ancients," Verrazzano carefully described its appearance and the character and customs of the Native Americans who inhabited it. Because Verrazzano looked at the New World from the perspective of someone who had studied the classics, he commonly viewed it in terms of classical antiquity. According to his letter to the king, Native Americans had features "like those of classical sculpture" and manners "very like the manners of the ancients." The behavior of these gentle people, who saved a sailor nearly drowned in the surf, contrast with that of Verrazzano and his men, who kidnapped a young boy and left a young woman behind only "because of the loud cries she uttered."

Verrazzano recognized the magnitude of what he had found, a land that appeared to be "larger than our Europe, than Africa, and almost larger than Asia." In describing this territory, he made one major error: he wrote of a two-hundred-mile-long isthmus (perhaps the outer banks of North Carolina) beyond which he thought he saw the Pacific Ocean. Nevertheless, his achievement is a major one. Verrazzano had undeniably identified an extensive new territory that, he wrote to the king, was "suitable for every kind of cultivation."

Apparently, Verrazzano's death occurred during a voyage in 1528. According to the chronicler Ramusio in his *Delle Navigazioni e Viaggi* (1550–1559), Verrazzano and some companions landed on the Caribbean island of Guadaloupe and were attacked and killed by its inhabitants. States Ramusio, "In the presence of those who had remained aboard the ship, they were roasted and eaten, such an unhappy *end* had this valorous gentleman," Verrazzano.

Richard Hakluyt, the famous sixteenth-century English compiler of voyages, recognized the importance of Verrazzano's letter. Hakluyt translated it from Italian into English for his *Diverse Voyages Touching on the Discovery of America* (1582?). Since then Verrazzano's letter has been read in many languages as one of the central documents in the story of the discovery of North America.

Suggested Readings: *The Voyages of Giovanni da Verrazzano, 1524–1528,* ed. L. C. Wroth, trans. S. Tarrow, 1970. S. E. Morison, *The European Discovery of America: The Northern Voyages,* A.D. *500–1600,* 1971.

Text Used: "Verrazzano's Voyage: 1524," *Old South Leaflets,* Gen. Series, No. 17, n.d.

VERRAZZANO'S VOYAGE*

1524

Captain John de Verrazzano to His Most Serene Majesty, the King of France, Writes:

Since the tempests which we encountered on the northern coasts, I have not written to your most Serene and Christian Majesty concerning the four ships sent out by your orders on the ocean to discover new lands, because I thought you must have been before apprized of all that had happened to us—that we had been compelled by the impetuous violence of the winds to put into Britany in distress with only the two ships Normandy and Dolphin; and that after having repaired these ships, we made a cruise in them, well armed, along the coast of Spain, as your Majesty must have heard, and also of our new plan of continuing our begun voyage with the Dolphin alone; from this voyage being now returned, I proceed to give your Majesty an account of our discoveries.

On the 17th of last January[1] we set sail from a desolate rock near the island of Madeira, belonging to his most Serene Majesty, the King of Portugal, with fifty men, having provisions sufficient for eight months, arms and other warlike munition and naval stores. Sailing westward with a light and pleasant easterly breeze, in twenty-five days we ran eight hundred leagues. On the 24th of February we encountered as violent a hurricane as any ship ever weathered, from which we escaped unhurt by the divine assistance and goodness, to the praise of the glorious and fortunate name of our good ship, that had been able to support the violent tossing of the waves. Pursuing our voyage towards the West, a little northwardly, in twenty-four days more, having run four hundred leagues, we reached a new country, which had never before been seen by any one, either in ancient or modern times. At first it appeared to be very low, but on approaching it to within a quarter of a league from the shore we perceived, by the great fires near the coast, that it was inhabited. We perceived that it stretched to the south, and coasted along in that direction in search of some port, in which we might come to anchor, and examine into the nature of the country, but for fifty leagues we could find none in which we could lie securely. Seeing the coast still stretch to the south, we resolved to change our course and stand to the northward, and as we still had the same difficulty, we drew in with the land and sent a boat on shore.[2] Many people who were seen coming to the sea-side fled at our approach, but occasionally stopping, they looked back upon us with astonishment, and some were at length induced, by various friendly signs, to come to us. These showed the greatest delight on beholding us, wondering at our dress, countenances and complexion. They then showed us by signs where we could more conveniently secure our boat, and offered us some of their provisions. That your Majesty may know all that we learned, while on shore, of their manners and customs of life, I will relate what

---

* This version of Verrazzano's letter to King Francis I of France is based on the Cèllere-Morgan Codex, first published in 1910.
[1] 1524.   [2] Near Cape Fear, North Carolina.

we saw as briefly as possible. They go entirely naked, except that about the loins they wear skins of small animals like martens fastened by a girdle of plaited grass, to which they tie, all round the body, the tails of other animals hanging down to the knees; all other parts of the body and the head are naked. Some wear garments similar to birds' feathers.

The complexion of these people is black, not much different from that of the Ethiopians; their hair is black and thick, and not very long, it is worn tied back upon the head in the form of a little tail. In person they are of good proportions, of middle stature, a little above our own, broad across the breast, strong in the arms, and well formed in the legs and other parts of the body; the only exception to their good looks is that they have broad faces, but not all, however, as we saw many that had sharp ones, with large black eyes and a fixed expression. They are not very strong in body, but acute in mind, active and swift of foot, as far as we could judge by observation. In these last two particulars they resemble the people of the east, especially those the most remote. We could not learn a great many particulars of their usages on account of our short stay among them, and the distance of our ship from the shore.

We found not far from this people another whose mode of life we judged to be similar. The whole shore is covered with fine sand, about fifteen feet thick, rising in the form of little hills about fifty paces broad. Ascending farther, we found several arms of the sea which make in through inlets, washing the shores on both sides as the coast runs. An outstretched country appears at a little distance rising somewhat above the sandy shore in beautiful fields and broad plains, covered with immense forests of trees, more or less dense, too various in colours, and too delightful and charming in appearance to be described. I do not believe that they are like the Hercynian forest[3] or the rough wilds of Scythia,[4] and the northern regions full of vines and common trees, but adorned with palms, laurels, cypresses, and other varieties unknown in Europe, that send forth the sweetest fragrance to a great distance, but which we could not examine more closely for the reasons before given, and not on account of any difficulty in traversing the woods, which, on the contrary, are easily penetrated.

As the "East" stretches around this country, I think it cannot be devoid of the same medicinal and aromatic drugs, and various riches of gold and the like, as is denoted by the colour of the ground. It abounds also in animals, as deer, stags, hares, and many other similar, and with a great variety of birds for every kind of pleasant and delightful sport. It is plentifully supplied with lakes and ponds of running water, and being in the latitude of 34, the air is salubrious, pure and temperate, and free from the extremes of both heat and cold. There are no violent winds in these regions, the most prevalent are the north-west and west. In summer, the season in which we were there, the sky is clear, with but little rain: if fogs and mists are at any time driven in by the south wind, they are instantaneously dissipated, and at once it becomes serene and bright again. The sea is calm, not boisterous, and its waves are gentle. Although the whole coast is low and without harbours, it is not dangerous for navigation, being free from rocks and bold, so that within four or five fathoms from the shore there is twenty-four feet of water at all times of tide, and this depth constantly increases in a uniform proportion. The holding ground is so good that no ship can part her cable, however

---

[3] An area in central Germany.   [4] An area in central Europe and Asia.

violent the wind, as we proved by experience; for while riding at anchor on the coast, we were overtaken by a gale in the beginning of March, when the winds are high, as is usual in all countries, we found our anchor broken before it started from its hold or moved at all.

We set sail from this place, continuing to coast along the shore, which we found stretching out to the west (east?); the inhabitants being numerous, we saw everywhere a multitude of fires. While at anchor on this coast, there being no harbour to enter, we sent the boat on shore with twenty-five men to obtain water, but it was not possible to land without endangering the boat, on account of the immense high surf thrown up by the sea, as it was an open roadstead. Many of the natives came to the beach, indicating by various friendly signs that we might trust ourselves on shore. One of their noble deeds of friendship deserves to be made known to your Majesty. A young sailor was attempting to swim ashore through the surf to carry them some knick-knacks, as little bells, looking-glasses, and other like trifles; when he came near three or four of them he tossed the things to them, and turned about to get back to the boat, but he was thrown over by the waves, and so dashed by them that he lay as it were dead upon the beach. When these people saw him in this situation, they ran and took him up by the head, legs and arms, and carried him to a distance from the surf; the young man, finding himself borne off in this way, uttered very loud shrieks in fear and dismay, while they answered as they could in their language, showing him that he had no cause for fear. Afterwards they laid him down at the foot of a little hill, when they took off his shirt and trowsers, and examined him, expressing the greatest astonishment at the whiteness of his skin. Our sailors in the boat seeing a great fire made up, and their companion placed very near it, full of fear, as is usual in all cases of novelty, imagined that the natives were about to roast him for food. But as soon as he had recovered his strength after a short stay with them, showing by signs that he wished to return aboard, they hugged him with great affection, and accompanied him to the shore, then leaving him, that he might feel more secure, they withdrew to a little hill, from which they watched him until he was safe in the boat. This young man remarked that these people were black like the others, that they had shining skins, middle stature, and sharper faces, and very delicate bodies and limbs, and that they were inferior in strength, but quick in their minds; this is all that he observed of them.

Departing hence,[5] and always following the shore, which stretched to the north, we came, in the space of fifty leagues, to another land,[6] which appeared very beautiful and full of the largest forests. We approached it, and going ashore with twenty men, we went back from the coast about two leagues, and found that the people had fled and hid themselves in the woods for fear. By searching around we discovered in the grass a very old woman and a young girl of about eighteen or twenty, who had concealed themselves for the same reason; the old woman carried two infants on her shoulders, and behind her neck a little boy eight years of age; when we came up to them they began to shriek and make signs to the men who had fled to the woods. We gave them a part of our provisions, which they accepted with delight, but the girl would not touch any; every thing we offered to her being thrown down in great anger. We took the little boy from the old woman

---

[5] Probably from the Outer Banks of Carolina.   [6] Probably from Kitty Hawk, North Carolina.

to carry with us to France, and would have taken the girl also, who was very beautiful and very tall, but it was impossible because of the loud shrieks she uttered as we attempted to lead her away; having to pass some woods, and being far from the ship, we determined to leave her and take the boy only. We found them fairer than the others, and wearing a covering made of certain plants, which hung down from the branches of the trees, tying them together with threads of wild hemp; their heads are without covering and of the same shape as the others. Their food is a kind of pulse[7] which there abounds, different in colour and size from ours, and of a very delicious flavour. Besides they take birds and fish for food, using snares and bows made of hard wood, with reeds for arrows, in the ends of which they put the bones of fish and other animals. The animals in these regions are wilder than in Europe from being continually molested by the hunters. We saw many of their boats made of one tree twenty feet long and four feet broad, without the aid of stone or iron or other kind of metal. In the whole country for the space of two hundred leagues, which we visited, we saw no stone of any sort. To hollow out their boats they burn out as much of a log as is requisite, and also from the prow and stern to make them float well on the sea. The land, in situation, fertility and beauty, is like the other, abounding also in forests filled with various kinds of trees, but not of such fragrance, as it is more northern and colder.

We saw in this country many vines growing naturally, which entwine about the trees, and run up upon them as they do in the plains of Lombardy.[8] These vines would doubtless produce excellent wine if they were properly cultivated and attended to, as we have often seen the grapes which they produce very sweet and pleasant, and not unlike our own. They must be held in estimation by them, as they carefully remove the shrubbery from around them, wherever they grow, to allow the fruit to ripen better. We found also wild roses, violets, lilies, and many sorts of plants and fragrant flowers different from our own. We cannot describe their habitations, as they are in the interior of the country, but from various indications we conclude they must be formed of trees and shrubs. We saw also many grounds for conjecturing that they often sleep in the open air, without any covering but the sky. Of their other usages we know nothing; we believe, however, that all the people we were among live in the same way.

After having remained here three days, riding at anchor on the coast, as we could find no harbour we determined to depart, and coast along the shore to the north-east, keeping sail on the vessel only by day, and coming to anchor by night. After proceeding one hundred leagues, we found a very pleasant situation among some steep hills, through which a very large river, deep at its mouth, forced its way to the sea; from the sea to the estuary of the river, any ship heavily laden might pass, with the help of the tide, which rises eight feet. But as we were riding at anchor in a good berth, we would not venture up in our vessel, without a knowledge of the mouth; therefore we took the boat, and entering the river, we found the country on its banks well peopled, the inhabitants not differing much from the others, being dressed out with the feathers of birds of various colours. They came towards us with evident delight, raising loud shouts of admiration, and showing us where we could most securely land with our boat. We passed up this river, about half a league, when we found it formed a most beautiful lake three

---

[7] A type of bean.   [8] A region of northern Italy.

leagues in circuit, upon which they were rowing thirty or more of their small boats, from one shore to the other, filled with multitudes who came to see us. All of a sudden, as is wont to happen to navigators, a violent contrary wind blew in from the sea, and forced us to return to our ship, greatly regretting to leave this region which seemed so commodious and delightful, and which we supposed must also contain great riches, as the hills showed many indications of minerals. Weighing anchor, we sailed fifty leagues toward the east, as the coast stretched in that direction, and always in sight of it; at length we discovered an island[9] of a triangular form, about ten leagues from the mainland, in size about equal to the island of Rhodes, having many hills covered with trees, and well peopled, judging from the great number of fires which we saw all around its shores; we gave it the name of your Majesty's illustrious mother.

We did not land there, as the weather was unfavourable, but proceeded to another place,[10] fifteen leagues distant from the island, where we found a very excellent harbour. Before entering it, we saw about twenty small boats full of people, who came about our ship, uttering many cries of astonishment, but they would not approach nearer than within fifty paces; stopping, they looked at the structure of our ship, our persons and dress, afterwards they all raised a loud shout together, signifying that they were pleased. By imitating their signs, we inspired them in some measure with confidence, so that they came near enough for us to toss to them some little bells and glasses, and many toys, which they took and looked at, laughing, and then came on board without fear. Among them were two kings more beautiful in form and stature than can possibly be described; one was about forty years old, the other about twenty-four, and they were dressed in the following manner: The oldest had a deer's skin around his body, artificially wrought in damask figures, his head was without covering, his hair was tied back in various knots; around his neck he wore a large chain ornamented with many stones of different colours. The young man was similar in his general appearance. This is the finest looking tribe, and the handsomest in their costumes, that we have found in our voyage. They exceed us in size, and they are of a very fair complexion (?); some of them incline more to a white (bronze?), and others to a tawny colour; their faces are sharp, their hair long and black, upon the adorning of which they bestow great pains; their eyes are black and sharp, their expression mild and pleasant, greatly resembling the antique. I say nothing to your Majesty of the other parts of the body, which are all in good proportion, and such as belong to well-formed men. Their women are of the same form and beautiful, very graceful, of fine countenances and pleasing appearance in manners and modesty; they wear no clothing except a deer skin, ornamented like those worn by the men; some wear very rich lynx skins upon their arms, and various ornaments upon their heads, composed of braids of hair, which also hang down upon their breasts on each side. Others wear different ornaments, such as the women of Egypt and Syria use. The older and the married people, both men and women, wear many ornaments in their ears, hanging down in the oriental manner. We saw upon them several pieces of wrought copper, which is more esteemed by them than gold, as this is not valued on account of its colour, but is considered by them as the most ordinary of

---

[9] Block Island, off Rhode Island.
[10] Newport, Rhode Island, inhabited by the Wampanoag Indians.

the metals—yellow being the colour especially disliked by them; azure and red are those in highest estimation with them. Of those things which we gave them, they prized most highly the bells, azure crystals, and other toys to hang in their ears and about their necks; they do not value or care to have silk or gold stuffs, or other kinds of cloth, nor implements of steel or iron. When we showed them our arms, they expressed no admiration, and only asked how they were made; the same was the case of the looking-glasses, which they returned to us, smiling, as soon as they had looked at them. They are very generous, giving away whatever they have. We formed a great friendship with them, and one day we entered into the port with our ship, having before rode at the distance of a league from the shore, as the weather was adverse. They came off to the ship with a number of their little boats, with their faces painted in divers colours, showing us real signs of joy, bringing us of their provisions, and signifying to us where we could best ride in safety with our ship, and keeping with us until we had cast anchor. We remained among them fifteen days, to provide ourselves with many things of which we were in want, during which time they came every day to see our ship, bringing with them their wives, of whom they were very careful; for, although they came on board themselves, and remained a long while, they made their wives stay in the boats, nor could we ever get them on board by any entreaties or any presents we could make them. One of the two kings often came with his queen and many attendants, to see us for his amusement; but he always stopped at the distance of about two hundred paces, and sent a boat to inform us of his intended visit, saying they would come and see our ship—this was done for safety, and as soon as they had an answer from us they came off, and remained awhile to look around; but on hearing the annoying cries of the sailors, the king sent the queen, with her attendants, in a very light boat, to wait, near an island a quarter of a league distant from us, while he remained a long time on board, talking with us by signs, and expressing his fanciful notions about every thing in the ship, and asking the use of all. After imitating our modes of salutation, and tasting our food, he courteously took leave of us. Sometimes, when our men stayed two or three days on a small island, near the ship, for their various necessities, as sailors are wont to do, he came with seven or eight of his attendants, to inquire about our movements, often asking us if we intended to remain there long, and offering us everything at his command, and then he would shoot with his bow, and run up and down with his people, making great sport for us. We often went five or six leagues into the interior,[11] and found the country as pleasant as is possible to conceive, adapted to cultivation of every kind, whether of corn, wine or oil; there are open plains twenty-five or thirty leagues in extent, entirely free from trees or other hindrances, and of so great fertility, that whatever is sown there will yield an excellent crop. On entering the woods, we observed that they might all be traversed by an army ever so numerous; the trees of which they were composed, were oaks, cypresses, and others, unknown in Europe. We found, also, apples, plumbs, filberts, and many other fruits, but all of a different kind from ours. The animals, which are in great numbers, as stags, deer, lynxes, and many other species, are taken by snares, and by bows, the latter being their chief implement; their arrows are wrought with great beauty, and for the heads of them, they use emery, jasper, hard marble, and other

[11] Pawtucket, Rhode Island.

sharp stones, in the place of iron. They also use the same kind of sharp stones in cutting down trees, and with them they construct their boats of single logs, hollowed out with admirable skill, and sufficiently commodious to contain ten or twelve persons; their oars are short, and broad at the end, and are managed in rowing by force of the arms alone, with perfect security, and as nimbly as they choose. We saw their dwellings, which are of a circular form, of about ten or twelve paces in circumference, made of logs split in halves, without any regularity of architecture, and covered with roofs of straw, nicely put on, which protect them from wind and rain. There is no doubt that they would build stately edifices if they had workmen as skilful as ours, for the whole seacoast abounds in shining stones, crystals, and alabaster, and for the same reason it has ports and retreats for animals. They change their habitations from place to place as circumstances of situation and season may require; this is easily done, as they have only to take with them their mats, and they have other houses prepared at once. The father and the whole family dwell together in one house in great numbers; in some we saw twenty-five or thirty persons. Their food is pulse, as with the other tribes, which is here better than elsewhere, and more carefully cultivated; in the time of sowing they are governed by the moon, the sprouting of grain, and many other ancient usages. They live by hunting and fishing, and they are long-lived. If they fall sick, they cure themselves without medicine, by the heat of the fire, and their death at last comes from extreme old age. We judge them to be very affectionate and charitable towards their relatives—making loud lamentations in their adversity, and in their misery calling to mind all their good fortune. At their departure out of life, their relations mutually join in weeping, mingled with singing, for a long while. This is all that we could learn of them. This region is situated in the parallel of Rome, being 41° 40' of north latitude, but much colder from accidental circumstances, and not by nature, as I shall hereafter explain to your Majesty, and confine myself at present to the description of its local situation. It looks towards the south, on which side the harbour is half a league broad; afterwards, upon entering it, the extent between the coast and north is twelve leagues, and then enlarging itself it forms a very large bay, twenty leagues in circumference, in which are five small islands, of great fertility and beauty, covered with large and lofty trees. Among these islands any fleet, however large, might ride safely, without fear of tempests or other dangers. Turning towards the south, at the entrance of the harbour, on both sides, there are very pleasant hills, and many streams of clear water, which flow down to the sea. In the midst of the entrance, there is a rock of freestone, formed by nature, and suitable for the construction of any kind of machine or bulwark for the defence of the harbour.[12]

Having supplied ourselves with every thing necessary, on the fifth of May we departed from the port, and sailed one hundred and fifty leagues, keeping so close to the coast as never to lose it from our sight; the nature of the country appeared much the same as before, but the mountains were a little higher, and all in appearance rich in minerals. We did not stop to land as the weather was very favorable for pursuing our voyage, and the country presented no variety. The shore stretched to the east, and fifty leagues beyond more to the north, where we found a more elevated country,[13] full of very thick woods of fir trees, cypresses and the

---

[12] Newport's harbor in the Narragansett Bay.   [13] Maine's coast.

like, indicative of a cold climate. The people[14] were entirely different from the others we had seen, whom we had found kind and gentle, but these were so rude and barbarous that we were unable by any signs we could make, to hold communication with them. They clothe themselves in the skins of bears, lynxes, seals and other animals. Their food, as far as we could judge by several visits to their dwellings, is obtained by hunting and fishing, and certain fruits, which are a sort of root of spontaneous growth. They have no pulse, and we saw no signs of cultivation; the land appears sterile and unfit for growing of fruit or grain of any kind. If we wished at any time to traffick with them, they came to the sea shore and stood upon the rocks, from which they lowered down by a cord to our boats beneath whatever they had to barter, continually crying out to us, not to come nearer, and instantly demanding from us that which was to be given in exchange; they took from us only knives, fish hooks and sharpened steel. No regard was paid to our courtesies; when we had nothing left to exchange with them, the men at our departure made the most brutal signs of disdain and contempt possible. Against their will we penetrated two or three leagues into the interior with twenty-five men; when we came to the shore, they shot at us with their arrows, raising the most horrible cries and afterwards fleeing to the woods. In this region we found nothing extraordinary except vast forests and some metalliferous hills, as we infer from seeing that many of the people wore copper ear-rings. Departing from thence, we kept along the coast, steering north-east, and found the country more pleasant and open, free from woods, and distant in the interior we saw lofty mountains but none which extended to the shore. Within fifty leagues we discovered thirty-two islands, all near the main land, small and of pleasant appearance, but high and so disposed as to afford excellent harbours and channels, as we see in the Adriatic gulph, near Illyria and Dalmatia.[15] We had no intercourse with the people, but we judge that they were similar in nature and usages to those we were last among. After sailing between east and north the distance of one hundred and fifty leagues more, and finding our provisions and naval stores nearly exhausted, we took in wood and water and determined to return to France, having discovered 502, that is 700 (sic) leagues of unknown lands.

As to the religious faith of all these tribes, not understanding their language, we could not discover either by sign or gestures any thing certain. It seemed to us that they had no religion nor laws, nor any knowledge of a First Cause or Mover, that they worshipped neither the heavens, stars, sun, moon nor other planets; nor could we learn if they were given to any kind of idolatry, or offered any sacrifices or supplications, or if they have temples or houses of prayer in their villages;—our conclusion was, that they have no religious belief whatever, but live in this respect entirely free. All which proceeds from ignorance, as they are very easy to be persuaded, and imitated us with earnestness and fervour in all which they saw us do as Christians in our acts of worship.

* * *

My intention in this voyage was to reach Cathay, on the extreme coast of Asia, expecting, however, to find in the newly discovered land some such an obstacle, as they have proved to be, yet I did not doubt that I should penetrate by some

---

[14] The Abnaki Indians.   [15] Western Yugoslavia.

passage to the eastern ocean. It was the opinion of the ancients, that our oriental Indian ocean is one and without any interposing land; Aristotle supports it by arguments founded on various probabilities; but is is contrary to that of the moderns and shown to be erroneous by experience; the country which has been discovered, and which was unknown to the ancients, is another world compared with that before known, being manifestly larger than our Europe, together with Africa and perhaps Asia, if we rightly estimate its extent, as shall now be briefly explained to your Majesty. The Spaniards have sailed south beyond the equator on a meridian 20 degrees west of the Fortunate Islands to the latitude of 54, and there still found land; turning about they steered northward on the same meridian and along the coast to the eighth degree of latitude near the equator, and thence along the coast more to the west and north-west, to the latitude of 21°, without finding a termination to the continent; they estimated the distance run as 89 degrees, which, added to the 20 first run west of the Canaries, make 109 degrees and so far west; they sailed from the meridian of these islands, but this may vary somewhat from truth; we did not make this voyage and therefore cannot speak from experience; we calculated it geometrically from the observations furnished by many navigators, who have made the voyage and affirm the distance to be 1,600 leagues, due allowance being made for the deviations of the ship from a straight course, by reason of contrary winds. I hope that we shall now obtain certain information on these points, by new voyages to be made on the same coasts. But to return to ourselves; in the voyage which we have made by order of your Majesty, in addition to the 92 degrees we run towards the west from our point of departure, before we reached land in the latitude of 34, we have to count 300 leagues which we ran north-east-wardly, and 400 nearly east along the coast before we reached the 50th parallel of north latitude, the point where we turned our course from the shore towards home. Beyond this point the Portuguese had already sailed as far north as the Arctic circle, without coming to the termination of the land. Thus adding the degrees of south latitude explored, which are 54, to those of the north, which are 66, the sum is 120, and therefore more than are embraced in the latitude of Africa and Europe, for the north point of Norway, which is the extremity of Europe, is in 71 north, and the Cape of Good Hope, which is the southern extremity of Africa, is in 35 south, and their sum is only 106, and if the breadth of this newly discovered country corresponds to its extent of sea coast, it doubtless exceeds Asia in size. In this way we find that the land forms a much larger portion of our globe than the ancients supposed, who maintained, contrary to mathematical reasoning, that it was less than the water, whereas actual experience proves the reverse, so that we judge in respect to extent of surface the land covers as much space as the water; and I hope more clearly and more satisfactorily to point out and explain to your Majesty the great extent of that new land, or new world, of which I have been speaking. The continent of Asia and Africa, we know for certain, is joined to Europe at the north in Norway and Russia, which disproves the idea of the ancients that all this part had been navigated from the Cimbric Chersonesus,[16] eastward as far as the Caspian Sea. They also maintained that the whole continent was surrounded by two seas situate to the east and west of it, which seas in fact do not surround either of the two continents, for as we have seen above, the land of the southern hemisphere at the latitude of 54 extends eastwardly an unknown dis-

---

[16] The Jutland Peninsula of northern Europe, home of the Cimbri, a Germanic people.

tance, and that of the northern passing the 66th parallel turns to the east, and has no termination as high as the 70th. In a short time, I hope, we shall have more certain knowledge of these things, by the aid of your Majesty, whom I pray Almighty God to prosper in lasting glory, that we may see the most important results of this our cosmography in the fulfilment of the holy words of the Gospel.[17]

On board the ship Dolphin, in the port of Dieppe in Normandy, the 8th of July, 1524.

Your humble servitor,

JOHN DE VERRAZZANO.
1524, 1556

Powhatan
(1550?–1618)

When Jamestown, Virginia, was founded in 1607, Wahunsonacock—or Powhatan, as the English called him, after his principal village, Powhatans—was the leader of the Algonquian confederacy of tidewater tribes dwelling near the English settlement. Powhatan, believed to have been born around 1550, appears to have lived in style: Captain John Smith first saw the "Emperour" bedecked with pearl necklaces, covered with raccoon skins and surrounded by attendants. Smith's account of that meeting, in *A True Relation of . . . Virginia* (1608), notes that Powhatan's will was law to his people, who revered their leader as "halfe a God."

With numbers far superior to those of the English and with a capacity for violence, Powhatan could have had the Jamestown Colony destroyed. He refrained from doing so, probably because he was confident that the feeble enterprise would soon extinguish itself and because he hoped to use the English as temporary allies against competing tribes. Meanwhile, the colonists desperately needed the food the Algonquians could provide. Thus, an uneasy accord developed. Powhatan and Smith tolerated each other partly because Pocahontas, Powhatan's favorite daughter, reportedly felt affection for Smith but mainly because they were concerned for their own interests. In 1608 Powhatan was given an elaborate coronation to ensure his subjection to the English, but the phony ceremony did not go smoothly. Powhatan refused to come to the English fort to be crowned, and when the ceremony was performed at one of his villages, he could not be persuaded to kneel. "At last," Smith reports, "he a little stooped, and . . . the Crowne [was placed] on his head."

Peace between Powhatan and the English temporarily ended in 1609, when Smith left Virginia. In 1612 the English kidnapped Pocahontas in an effort to control Powhatan. The Algonquian leader's refusal to negotiate might have ended in disaster for his daughter had she not charmed the Englishman John Rolfe, who married her in 1614. The ensuing peace lasted until the deaths of Pocahontas and Powhatan in 1617 and 1618, respectively. In 1622 Powhatan's successor, Opechancanough, attacked the James River settlements in

---

[17] "Their sound has gone out into every land," from Romans 9:18.

force, killing over three hundred colonists. Henceforth, the English had no cause to continue the policy of restraint pursued by Smith, and the deliberate extermination of Native Americans began.

Powhatan's significance lies in his role as the first Native-American leader to deal extensively with English colonists. His interactions with them—marked by disdain and distrust on the Native-American side and fear and condescension on the colonial side—predicted the interactions to follow. Smith viewed Powhatan as a "subtile Salvage," whose greed and cruelty (as well as strength and intelligence) were unquestionable. Later observers more sympathetic to the Native-American position have portrayed Powhatan as a victim of white treachery. Some truth lies in both views. Powhatan seems to have been a powerful ruler whose primary motive in 1607 was to put the English presence in Virginia to personal use. Yet, the unequal nature (and eventual outcome) of the struggle between Native Americans and whites lends sympathy to the leader finally doomed—as later tribe leaders would be—to see his lands confiscated, his authority removed, and his culture obliterated. Powhatan's speech to Smith during a meeting in 1609 can be interpreted (as Smith interpreted it) as a ploy to persuade the colonists to disarm themselves. Regardless of Powhatan's motives, his illusory vision of a harmonious relationship between Native Americans and whites and his prophetic vision of Native-American life style characterized by anxiety and deprivation provide a poignant picture of what might have been, and a tragic depiction of what was to be, in America.

Suggested Readings: G. Nash, *Red, White, and Black: The Peoples of Early America,* 1974. F. Jennings, *The Invasion of America,* 1974. K. Kupperman, *Settling With the Indians,* 1980. B. Sheehan, *Savagism and Civility,* 1980. J. Smith, *Complete Works of Captain John Smith,* 3 vols., ed. P. L. Barbour, 1986.

Text Used: S. G. Drake, *Biography and History of the Indians of North America,* 1841.

SPEECH TO CAPTAIN JOHN SMITH

I am now grown old, and must soon die; and the succession must descend, in order, to my brothers, *Opitchapan, Opekankanough,* and *Catataugh,* and then to my two sisters, and their two daughters. I wish their experience was equal to mine; and that your love to us might not be less than ours to you. Why should you take by force that from us which you can have by love? Why should you destroy us, who have provided you with food? What can you get by war? We can hide our provisions, and fly into the woods; and then you must consequently famish by wronging you friends. What is the cause of your jealousy? You see us unarmed, and willing to supply your wants, if you will come in a friendly manner, and not with swords and guns, as to invade an enemy. I am not so simple, as not to know it is better to eat good meat, lie well, and sleep quietly with my women and children; to laugh and be merry with the English; and, being their friend, to have copper, hatchets, and whatever else I want, than to fly from all, to lie cold in the woods, feed upon acorns, roots, and such trash, and to be so hunted, that I cannot rest, eat, or sleep. In such circumstances, my men must watch, and if a twig should but break, all would cry out, *"Here comes Capt. Smith"*; and so, in this miserable manner, to end my miserable life; and, Capt. Smith, this *might* be soon your fate too, through your rashness and unadvisedness. I, therefore, exhort you to peaceable councils; and, above all, I insist that the guns and swords, the cause of all our jealousy and uneasiness, be removed and sent away.

1609, 1841

John Smith
(1580–1631)

By age twenty-five John Smith had lived the romantic life of an English mercenary and adventurer throughout Europe, or so he claimed in *The True Travels, Adventures, and Observations of Captaine John Smith* (1630). Smith always played the hero of his own narratives, but evidence suggests that his stories generally are based on fact. Born in 1580 in Lincolnshire, England, to a freeman farmer, George Smith, and his wife Ann, John Smith received his first taste of adventure at seventeen when he fought in the Netherlands against Spain. Soon came more adventure: sea battles and abandonment by shipmates, combat against the Turks in the Balkans (off the Mediterranean Sea), capture and enslavement by the Turks, and even rescue by beautiful maidens. By the time he returned to England in 1605, he was Captain John Smith, still eager for travel. He then looked to America for adventure.

In 1606 England's King James chartered the London Trading Company to explore and settle the American mainland, hoping to compete with successful Spanish explorations. Smith left for Virginia as one of the settlement's seven leaders in December 1606. The unpleasant four-month-long voyage was especially dangerous for Smith; he was arrested for mutiny and kept from the governing board until 1607. Thus began a continuing conflict between Smith and other colonists, brought on, he claimed, by their jealousy. Hoping to find rich deposits of gold and other precious metals, the colonists were unprepared for the harsh conditions of Virginia. The group arrived at Jamestown in April 1607, but by September half the group members were lost to disease or fights with the natives. By the next spring only 38 out of the original 105 colonists had survived.

Smith's experience in survival soon proved valuable to the starving colonists, and he led the colony from September 1608 to August 1609. During an early exploration, he was captured by Native Americans and condemned to death. His first account of his capture, *A True Relation of . . . Virginia* (1608), made no mention of the Algonquian girl Pocahantas. His version sixteen years later, *The General History of Virginia, New England, and the Summer Isles* (1624), introduces the now-familiar story of his rescue by the Algonquian leader Powhatan's daughter. As is true of Smith's other writings, how much of the story is factual is unclear. However, it accurately depicts the uncertain, often violent relations with the natives. Smith was able to bargain with, even cajole, them for corn in order to keep the colonists from starving. Still, his severe rule did not win willing supporters. Seriously wounded in October 1609 by an accidental explosion of his gunpowder bag, Smith left for England to recover.

A map of Virginia engraved by William Hole and used by John Smith.

Although he never returned to Jamestown, Smith traveled in 1614 to the place he named "New England," what is now Maine and Massachusetts. After spending the winter, he returned to England, hoping to encourage others to settle in New England. He offered to lead the Pilgrims from the Netherlands, but they rejected his offer and later settled at Plymouth. Smith was never to travel to America again. Instead, he compiled travel narratives and wrote of his adventures. In *A Description of New England* (1616), *New England Trials* (1620), and especially *The General History of Virginia,* he provided a wealth of information and adventure stories for future colonists of America. He died in London in 1631.

Suggested Readings: E. Emerson, *Captain John Smith*, 1971. A. T. Vaughan, *American Genesis: Captain John Smith and the Founding of Virginia,* 1975.

Text Used: *The Travels and Works of Captaine John Smith,* 2 vols., ed. E. Arber, 1910 (some spelling and punctuation modernized).

from   THE DESCRIPTION OF NEW ENGLAND

[Growing Wealthy in New England]

I have not been so ill bred, but I have tasted of plenty and pleasure, as well as want and misery; nor does necessity yet, or occasion of discontent, force me to these endeavors; nor am I ignorant what small thanks I shall have for my pains, or that many would have the world imagine them to be of great judgement, that can but blemish these my designs,[1] by their witty objections and detractions. Yet (I hope) my reasons with my deeds will so prevail with some that I shall not want employment in these affairs, to make the most blind see his own senselessness and incredulity, hoping that gain will make them affect that which religion, charity, and the common good cannot. It were but a poor device in me to deceive myself, much more the King, State, my friends and country, with these inducements: which seeing His Majesty hath given permission, I wish all sorts of worthy, honest, industrious spirits would understand, and if they desire any further satisfaction, I will do my best to give it, not to persuade them to go only, but go with them; not leave them there, but live with them there.

I will not say, but by ill providing and undue managing, such courses may be taken [that] may make us miserable enough. But if I may have the execution of what I have projected; if they want to eat, let them eat or never digest[2] me. If I perform what I say, I desire but that reward out of the gains [which] may suit my pains, quality, and condition. And if I abuse you with my tongue, take my head for satisfaction. If any dislike at the year's end, defraying their charge, by my consent they should freely return. I fear not want of company sufficient, were it but known what I know of those countries; and by the proof of that wealth I hope yearly to return, if God please to bless me from such accidents as are beyond my power in reason to prevent. For I am not so simple to think that ever any other motive than wealth will ever erect there a commonwealth or draw company from their ease and humors[3] at home to stay in New England to effect my purposes.

And lest any should think the toil might be insupportable, though these things may be had by labor and diligence, I assure myself there are those who delight extremely in vain pleasure, that take much more pains in England to enjoy it than I should do here [New England] to gain wealth sufficient. And yet I think they should not have half such sweet content, for our pleasure here is still gains; in England charges and loss. Here nature and liberty afford us that freely which in England we want, or it costs us dearly. What pleasure can be more than (being tired with any occasion ashore, in planting vines, fruits, or herbs, in contriving their own grounds, to the pleasure of their own minds, their fields, gardens, orchards, buildings, ships, and other works, etc.) to recreate themselves[4] before their own doors, in their own boats upon the sea, where man, woman, and child, with a small hook and line, by angling may take diverse sorts of excellent fish at their pleasures? And is it not pretty sport to pull up two pence, six pence, and

---

[1] His plans to form a colony in New England.   [2] Tolerate.   [3] Fancies.   [4] To rest.

twelve pence as fast as you can haul and veer[5] a line? He is a very bad fisher [that] cannot kill in one day with his hook and line one, two, or three hundred cods, which dressed and dried, if they be sold there for ten shillings the hundred [pounds], though in England they will give more than twenty, may not both the servant, the master, and merchant be well content with this gain? If a man works but three days in seven he may get more than he can spend, unless he will be excessive. Now that carpenter, mason, gardener, tailor, smith, sailor, forgers, or what other, may they not make this a pretty recreation, though they fish but an hour in the day, to take more than they eat in a week? Or if they will not eat it, because there is so much better choice, yet sell it or change it with the fishermen or merchants for anything they want. And what sport does yield a more pleasing content and less hurt or charge than angling with a hook and crossing the sweet air from isle to isle, over the silent streams of a calm sea? Wherein the most curious may find pleasure, profit, and content.

Thus, though all men be not fishers, yet all men, whatsoever, may in other matters do as well. For necessity does in these cases so rule a commonwealth, and each in their several functions, as their labors in their qualities, may be as profitable because there is a necessary mutual use of all.

For gentlemen, what exercise should more delight them than ranging daily those unknown parts, using fowling and fishing, for hunting and hawking? And yet you shall see the wild hawks give you some pleasure, in seeing them stoop[6] (six or seven after one another) an hour or two together at the schools of fish in the fair harbors, as those ashore [do] at a fowl, and never trouble nor torment yourselves with watching, mewing,[7] feeding, and attending them, nor kill a horse and man with running and crying "See you not a hawk?" For hunting also, the woods, lakes, and rivers afford not only chase sufficient for any that delight in that kind of toil or pleasure, but such beast to hunt that besides the delicacy of their bodies for food, their skins are so rich as may well recompense thy daily labor with a Captain's pay.

For laborers, if those [in England] that sow hemp, rape,[8] turnips, parsnips, carrots, cabbage, and such like, give twenty, thirty, forty, fifty shillings yearly for an acre of ground, and meat, drink, and wages to use it and yet grow rich, when better or at least as good ground may be had [in New England] and cost nothing but labor, it seems strange to me any such should there grow poor.

My purpose is not to persuade children from their parents, men from their wives, nor servants from their masters; only such as with free consent may be spared. But that each parish or village, in city or country, that will but apparel[9] their fatherless children of thirteen or fourteen years of age, or young married people that have small wealth to live on, here by their labor may live exceedingly well: provided always that first there be a sufficient power to command them, houses to receive them, means to defend them, and meet[10] provisions for them, for any place may be overlain,[11] and it is most necessary to have a fortress (ere this grow to practice) and sufficient masters (as carpenters, masons, fishers, fowlers, gardeners, husbandmen,[12] sawyers,[13] smiths, spinners, tailors, weavers, and

---

[5] Let out.   [6] Swoop.   [7] Caging.
[8] A plant whose leaves are used as fodder for sheep and hogs.
[9] Make ready.   [10] Appropriate.   [11] Overtaken.
[12] Farmers.   [13] A person who saws wood.

such like) to take ten, twelve, or twenty, or as there is occasion, for apprentices. The masters by this may quickly grow rich; these [apprentices] may learn their trades themselves to do the like, to a general and an incredible benefit for king and country, master and servant.

1614, 1616

from   *THE GENERAL HISTORY OF VIRGINIA, NEW ENGLAND, AND THE SUMMER ISLES**

from   THE THIRD BOOK: THE PROCEEDINGS AND ACCIDENTS OF THE ENGLISH COLONY IN VIRGINIA

from Chapter I

It might well be thought a country so fair (as Virginia is) and a people so tractable would long ere this have been quietly possessed, to the satisfaction of the adventurers[1] and the eternizing of the memory of those that effected it. But because all the world does see a defailment,[2] this following treatise shall give satisfaction to all [in 1612], indifferent[3] readers how the business has been carried, where no doubt they will easily understand an answer to their question, how it came to pass there was no better speed and success in those proceedings.

Captain Bartholomew Gosnold, one of the first movers[4] of this plantation, having many years solicited many of his friends but found small assistance, at last prevailed with some gentlemen, as Captain John Smith, Master Edward-Maria Wingfield, Master Robert Hunt, and diverse others, who depended[5] a year upon his projects, but nothing could be effected till by their great charge[6] and industry it came to be apprehended by certain of the nobility, gentry, and merchants, so that his Majesty by his letters patent[7] [10 April 1606] gave commission for establishing councils to direct here,[8] and to govern and to execute there. To effect this, was spent another year, and by that, three ships were provided, one of 100 tons, another of 40, and a pinnace[9] of 20. The transportation of the company was committed to Captain Christopher Newport, a mariner well practiced for the western parts of America. But their orders for government were put in a box not to be opened nor the governors known until they arrived in Virginia.

On the 19th of December, 1606, we set sail from Blackwall[10] but by unprosperous winds were kept six weeks in the sight of England, all which time Master

---

* The Bermuda Islands.   [1] The English financial supporters of Jamestown.
[2] Smith's readers were well aware of the struggle for survival at Jamestown.   [3] Unbiased.
[4] Organizers.   [5] Waited.   [6] Expense.   [7] A royal charter.   [8] England.
[9] A ship with two masts.   [10] Near London, on the Thames River.

Hunt, our Preacher, was so weak and sick that few expected his recovery. Yet although he were but twenty miles from his habitation (the time we were in the Downs[11]) and notwithstanding the stormy weather nor the scandalous imputations (of some few, little better than atheists, of the greatest rank amongst us) suggested against him, all this could never force from his so much as a seeming desire to leave the business, but [he] preferred the service of God, in so good a voyage, before any affection to contest with his godless foes whose disastrous designs (could they have prevailed) had even then overthrown the business, so many discontents did then arise, had he not with the water of patience and his godly exhortations (but chiefly by his true devoted examples) quenched those flames of envy and dissension.

We watered at the Canaries; we traded with the savages at Dominica; three weeks we spent in refreshing ourselves amongst these West India isles; in Guadeloupe we found a bath so hot as in it we boiled pork as well as over the fire. And at a little isle called Monito, we took from the bushes with our hands near two hogsheads[12] full of birds in three or four hours. In Nevis, Mona, and the Virgin Isles we spent some time where, with a loathsome beast like a crocodile, called an iguana, tortoises, pelicans, parrots, and fishes, we daily feasted.

Gone from thence in search of Virginia, the company was not a little discomforted seeing the mariners had three days passed their reckoning and found no land, so that Captain Ratcliffe (Captain of the pinnace) rather desired to bear up the helm to return for England than make further search. But God the guider of all good actions, forcing them by an extreme storm to hull[13] all night, did drive them by His providence to their desired port, beyond all their expections, for never any of them had seen that coast.

The first land they made they called Cape Henry, where thirty of them recreating themselves[14] on shore were assaulted by five savages, who hurt two of the English very dangerously.

That night was the box opened and the orders read, in which Bartholomew Gosnold, John Smith, Edward Wingfield, Christopher Newport, John Ratcliffe, John Martin, and George Kendall were named to be the Council and [instructed] to choose a President amongst them for a year who with the Council should govern. Matters of moment were to be examined by a jury but determined by the major part of the Council, in which the President had two voices.[15]

Until the 13th of May [1607] they sought a place to plant[16] in; then the Council was sworn, Master Wingfield was chosen President, and an oration made why Captain Smith was not admitted of the Council as the rest.[17]

Now falleth every man to work, the Council contrive the fort, the rest cut down trees to make place to pitch their tents, some provide clapboard to reload the ships, some make gardens, some nets, etc. The savages often visited us kindly.[18] The President's overweening jealousy[19] would admit no exercise at arms or fortification but the boughs of trees cast together in the form of a half moon by the extraordinary pains and diligence of Captain Kendall.

Newport, Smith, and twenty others were sent to discover the head of the river; by diverse small habitations they passed; in six days they arrived at a town called

---

[11] An area near Kent, England, where ships were sheltered before crossing the Atlantic.
[12] Barrels.
[13] To travel with sails rolled and secured to the mast.   [14] Resting.   [15] Votes.   [16] Settle.
[17] Smith was excluded from the Council, having been charged with mutiny on the voyage.
[18] Fittingly.   [19] Conscientiousness.

Powhatan, consisting of some twelve houses pleasantly seated on a hill, before it three fertile isles, about it many of their cornfields; the place is very pleasant and strong by nature; of this place the Prince is called Powhatan and his people Powhatans. To this place the river is navigable, but higher within a mile, by reason of the rocks and isles, there is not passage for a small boat; this they call the Falls. The people in all parts kindly entreated them, till being returned within twenty miles of Jamestown, they gave just cause of jealousy,[20] but had God not blessed the discoverers otherwise than those at the fort, there had there been an end of that plantation, for at the fort, where they arrived the next day, they found seventeen men hurt and a boy slain by the savages, and had it not chanced a cross-bar[21] shot from the ships struck down a bough from a tree amongst them that caused them to retire, our men had all been slain, being securely all at work and their arms in dry vats.[22]

Hereupon the President was contented the fort should be palisaded, the Ordnance[23] mounted, his men armed and exercised, for many were the assaults and ambuscades of the savages, and our men by their disorderly straggling were often hurt, when the savages by the nimbleness of their heels well escaped.

What toil we had, with so small a power to guard our workmen by day, watch all night, resist our enemies, and effect our business, to reload the ships, cut down trees, and prepare the ground to plant our corn, etc., I refer to the reader's consideration.

Six weeks being spent in this manner, Captain Newport (who was hired only for our transportation) was to return with the ships.

Now Captain Smith, who all this time from their departure from the Canaries was restrained as a prisoner upon the scandalous suggestions of some of the chief (envying his repute) who feigned[24] he intended to usurp the government, murder the Council, and make himself king, that his confederates were dispersed in all the three ships, and that divers of his confederates that revealed it would affirm it; for this he was committed as a prisoner.

Thirteen weeks [24 Mar.–10 June 1607] he remained thus suspected, and by that time the ships should return, they pretended out of their commiserations to refer him to the Council in England to receive a check,[25] rather than by particulating[26] his designs [to] make him so odious to the world as to touch his life or utterly overthrow his reputation. But he so much scorned their charity and publicly defied the uttermost of their cruelty [that] he wisely prevented[27] their policies, though he could not suppress their envies; yet so well he demeaned[28] himself in this business as all the company did see his innocence and his adversaries' malice, and those suborned[29] to accuse him, accused his accusers of subornation; many untruths were alleged against him, but being so apparently disproved, [they] begat a general hatred in the hearts of the company against such unjust commanders [so] that the President [Wingfield] was adjudged to give him £200,[30] so that all he[31] had was seized upon in part of satisfaction, which Smith presently returned to the store[32] for the general use of the Colony.

Many were the mischiefs that daily sprung from their ignorant (yet ambitious) spirits, but the good Doctrine and exhortation of our Preacher, Master Hunt, rec-

---

[20] Here, watchfulness.   [21] A cannonball with projections.
[22] Storage trunks.   [23] Cannon.   [24] Stated untruthfully.
[25] To be reproached.   [26] Specifying.   [27] Circumvented.   [28] Conducted.
[29] Induced by illegal methods.   [30] Damages for false accusation.   [31] President Wingfield.
[32] A community warehouse.

onciled them and caused Captain Smith to be admitted of the Council [20 June, or rather on 10 June].

The next day all received the Communion; the day following [June 22], the savages voluntarily desired peace, and Captain Newport returned for England with news, leaving in Virginia 100, the 15th [or rather 22d] of June, 1607.

1606–1607, 1624

William Bradford
(1590–1657)

William Bradford, governor and principal historian of the Plymouth Colony, had probably intended to take over his father's small estate in Austerfield, Yorkshire, England, until Bradford heard the sermons of Richard Clyfton, a Nonconformist minister. That sermon moved Bradford, then age twelve, to join a Nonconformist congregation in nearby Scrooby. Born in Austerfield in 1590, Bradford had lost both his father and mother by 1597, leaving him to be raised locally by his grandparents and uncles. The Scrooby congregation became a spiritual home for young Bradford, against the wishes of his family. There Bradford acquired the dedicated spiritual piety that was to lead him from England to Holland and eventually to the New World.

By 1606 England's Reformation had reached such a pitch of self-purification that the Scrooby congregation, believing that even the Church of England was too corrupt to reform, decided to separate. Their decision to create a Separatist church was made in part out of fear that the recently crowned James I was sympathetic to the Catholic church. Believing Scripture to be a more trustworthy guide and authority than church hierarchy, the Scrooby congregation modeled the covenant made among its members on God's covenants with Adam and Abraham. Separation, however, was considered treason by the Crown, so in 1608 the group, including Bradford, traveled to Amsterdam and in 1609 to Leyden, the Netherlands, reportedly a haven for religious freedom. There Bradford bought a house and loom, went into business, and married Dorothy May in 1613—intending, like the others, to stay.

Making a living in the textile trade was difficult, and as time passed, the religious leaders discovered the younger members departing from the group. In *Of Plymouth Plantation* (not published until 1856), Bradford describes the decision in 1620 to travel to "those vast and unpeopled countries of America, which are fruitful and fit for habitation." The group, which Bradford called Pilgrims, successfully petitioned the Virginia Company of London for land in the Virginia Territory, which extended as far North as New York City today. But when the *Mayflower* was forced by storms to land at what is now Plymouth, Massachusetts, the winter weather and the immigrants' exhaustion convinced them to stay rather than continue southward.

Only about forty percent of the *Mayflower*'s passengers were part of the religious community; the others (including Myles Standish) were "strangers," many of whom were sent by London merchants to represent the financial backers' economic interests. Out of fear that this diversity would invite dissension, Bradford and other Pilgrims drew up the Mayflower Compact. That document legitimized a government to support the Pilgrims' desire for a religious society in Plymouth and provided the first quasidemocratic government in the New World. Upon the death of the Plymouth Colony's first governor, John Carver, Bradford was elected governor, a position he held thirty times between 1621 and 1656.

Having lost his first wife at the end of the voyage, Bradford married Alice Carpenter Southworth in 1623. In 1630 he began writing *Of Plymouth Plantation,* perhaps in response to the arrival of John Winthrop and the neighboring colonists of Massachusetts Bay. In fact, the arrival of the Puritans, part of the "Great Migration" of twenty thousand people between 1628 and 1642, opened a new market for the Plymouth Colony's food and goods. Reflecting the unique circumstances of the Pilgrims, Bradford's history is a very different document than Winthrop's *Journal* (begun in 1630 but published in 1790). *Of Plymouth Plantation* is more consciously crafted, shaped by Bradford's awareness that the Pilgrims' original goals and ideals were often diverted by human weaknesses or the machinations of Satan's henchmen. The portion written in 1630 begins with a prologue chronicling the "wars and oppositions" that "Satan hath raised, maintained and continued against the Saints," thus making the Pilgrims part of a universal battle between good and evil.

Essential to Bradford's history is its conscious parallel between the Pilgrims' migration and Old Testament accounts of the Israelites journeying out of captivity toward the Promised Land. God's providence provides for the Scrooby community in its journey from England to Holland and then to America, just as God had supported the Israelites' exodus. The first part of Bradford's history ends optimistically with the Pilgrims erecting their first house in the New World.

In 1646, when Bradford began writing the second book of his history, social changes dampened his enthusiasm. An economic depression and internal problems created a new plot for his history. Although the Plymouth community's holy covenant with God remains of utmost importance, the history depicts the main villains to be corrupt humans rather than Satan. The community's problems are less universal and more tied to historical circumstances. The conflicts themselves are in some cases morally ambiguous even to Bradford. For example, although tradition has depicted a harmonious relation between Pilgrims and Native Americans, Bradford's history reveals a dark side to the relationship. At first helped by a friendly alliance with the Wampanoag chief, Massasoit, the Pilgrims found themselves caught up in battles between the Narragansetts and the Mohegans. During the Pequot War in 1637, the combined New England colonies and the Narragansetts attacked the Pequot fort at Mystic, Connecticut, killing four hundred Pequots who had been sleeping inside. In *Of Plymouth Plantation* Bradford, not present during the attack, simply praises "God, who had wrought so wonderfully for" the Pilgrims.

The spiritual certainty and communal unity with which the Pilgrims arrived dissipates in *Of Plymouth Plantation* as more treachery and evil occurs in the community. As noted in *Of Plymouth Plantation,* in preparation for their trip to America the Pilgrims had anticipated John Winthrop's famous "Model of Christian Charity" sermon (given in 1630 but published in 1838) by declaring "We are knit together as a body in a most strict and sacred bond and covenant of the Lord." But at a much later date, in an aged hand Bradford added a footnote to this passage: "But (alas) that subtle serpent hath slyly wound in himself under fair pretences of necessity and the like, to untwist these sacred bonds and ties, and as it were insensibly by degrees to dissolve, or in a great measure to weaken, the same." Despite his doubts Bradford remained an able governor and honest historian until his death in 1657. In 1692 the Plymouth Colony merged with the more successful Massachusetts Bay Colony, and together they became an increasingly diverse and secular society.

Suggested Readings: B. Smith, *Bradford of Plymouth*, 1951. S. E. Morison, *Builders of the Bay Colony*, 1958. P. Gay, *A Loss of Mastery: Puritan Historians in Colonial America*, 1966.

Text Used: *Of Plymouth Plantation*, ed. S. E. Morison, 1952.

from   OF PLYMOUTH PLANTATION

from   Book I

Chapter IV: Showing the Reasons and Causes of Their Removal

After they had lived in this city[1] about some eleven or twelve years (which is the more observable being the whole time of that famous truce between that state and the Spaniards)[2] and sundry of them were taken away by death and many others began to be well stricken in years (the grave mistress of Experience having taught them many things), those prudent governors with sundry of the sagest members began both deeply to apprehend their present dangers and wisely to foresee the future and think of timely remedy. In the agitation of their thoughts, and much discourse of things hereabout, at length they began to incline to this conclusion: of removal to some other place. Not out of any newfangledness or other such like giddy humor by which men are oftentimes transported to their great hurt and danger, but for sundry weighty and solid reasons, some of the chief of which I will here briefly touch.

And first, they saw and found by experience the hardness of the place and country to be such as few in comparison would come to them, and fewer that would bide it out and continue with them. For many that came to them, and many more that desired to be with them, could not endure that great labour and hard fare, with other inconveniences which they underwent and were contented with. But though they loved their persons, approved their cause and honoured their sufferings, yet they left them as it were weeping, as Orpah did her mother-in-law Naomi,[3] or as those Romans did Cato[4] in Utica who desired to be excused and borne with, though they could not all be Catos. For many, though they desired to enjoy the ordinances of God in their purity and the liberty of the gospel with them, yet (alas) they admitted of bondage with danger of conscience, rather than to endure these hardships. Yea, some preferred and chose the prisons in England rather than this liberty in Holland with these afflictions.[5] But it was thought that if a better and easier place of living could be had, it would draw many and take away these discouragements. Yea, their pastor would often say that many of those who both wrote and preached now against them, if they were in a place where they might have liberty and live comfortably, they would then practice as they did.

---

[1] Leyden, the Netherlands.

[2] The twelve years' truce (of the Dutch war for independence from Spain), signed in 1609, was due to end in 1621.

[3] In Ruth 1:14, Orpah weeps when she must leave her mother-in-law, Naomi.

[4] Marcus Porcius (95–46 B.C.), a Roman statesman and philosopher, known as Cato the Younger, who committed suicide rather than surrender to Julius Caesar.

[5] The Netherlands were overpopulated during Bradford's time, and the standard of living was low.

Secondly. They saw that though the people generally bore all these difficulties very cheerfully and with a resolute courage, being in the best and strength of their years; yet old age began to steal on many of them; and their great and continual labours, with other crosses and sorrows, hastened it before the time. So as it was not only probably thought, but apparently seen, that within a few years more they would be in danger to scatter, by necessities pressing them, or sink under their burdens, or both. And therefore according to the divine proverb, that a wise man seeth the plague when it cometh, and hideth himself, Proverbs xxii.3, so they like skillful and beaten[6] soldiers were fearful either to be entrapped or surrounded by their enemies so as they should neither be able to fight nor fly. And therefore thought it better to dislodge betimes to some place of better advantage and less danger, if any such could be found.

Thirdly. As necessity was a taskmaster over them so they were forced to be such, not only to their servants but in a sort to their dearest children, the which as it did not a little wound the tender hearts of many a loving father and mother, so it produced likewise sundry sad and sorrowful effects. For many of their children that were of best dispositions and gracious inclinations, having learned to bear the yoke in their youth[7] and willing to bear part of their parents' burden, were oftentimes so oppressed with their heavy labours that though their minds were free and willing, yet their bodies bowed under the weight of the same, and became decrepit in their early youth, the vigour of nature being consumed in the very bud as it were. But that which was more lamentable, and of all sorrows most heavy to be borne, was that many of their children, by these occasions and the great licentiousness of youth in that country,[8] and the manifold temptations of the place, were drawn away by evil examples into extravagant and dangerous courses, getting the reins off their necks and departing from their parents. Some became soldiers, others took upon them far voyages by sea, and others some worse courses tending to dissoluteness and the danger of their souls, to the great grief of their parents and dishonour of God. So that they saw their posterity would be in danger to degenerate and be corrupted.[9]

Lastly (and which was not least), a great hope and inward zeal they had of laying some good foundation, or at least to make some way thereunto, for the propagating and advancing the gospel of the kingdom of Christ in those remote parts of the world; yea, though they should be but even as stepping-stones unto others for the performing of so great a work.

These and some other like reasons moved them to undertake this resolution of their removal; the which they afterward prosecuted with so great difficulties, as by the sequel will appear.

The place they had thoughts on was some of those vast and unpeopled countries of America, which are fruitful and fit for habitation, being devoid of all civil inhabitants, where there are only savage and brutish men which range up and down, little otherwise than the wild beasts of the same. This proposition being made public and coming to the scanning of all, it raised many variable opinions amongst men and caused many fears and doubts amongst themselves. Some, from their reasons and hopes conceived, laboured to stir up and encourage the rest to

---

[6] Experienced.   [7] "It is good for a man that he bear the yoke in his youth," from Lamentations 3:27.
[8] Unlike the English, the Dutch (especially children) feasted and enjoyed themselves after attending church on Sundays.
[9] The Pilgrims feared that their children would be assimilated into the Dutch "melting pot."

undertake and prosecute the same; others again, out of their fears, objected against it and sought to divert from it; alleging many things, and those neither unreasonable nor unprobable; as that it was a great design and subject to many unconceivable perils and dangers; as, besides the casualties of the sea (which none can be freed from), the length of the voyage was such as the weak bodies of women and other persons worn out with age and travail (as many of them were) could never be able to endure. And yet if they should, the miseries of the land which they should be exposed unto, would be too hard to be borne and likely, some or all of them together, to consume and utterly to ruinate them. For there they should be liable to famine and nakedness and the want, in a manner, of all things. The change of air, diet and drinking of water[10] would infect their bodies with sore sicknesses and grievous diseases. And also those which should escape or overcome these difficulties should yet be in continual danger of the savage people, who are cruel, barbarous and most treacherous, being most furious in their rage and merciless where they overcome; not being content only to kill and take away life, but delight to torment men in the most bloody manner that may be; flaying some alive with the shells of fishes, cutting off the members and joints of others by piecemeal and broiling on the coals, eat the collops[11] of their flesh in their sight whilst they live, with other cruelties horrible to be related.[12]

And surely it could not be thought but the very hearing of these things could not but move the very bowels of men to grate within them and make the weak to quake and tremble. It was further objected that it would require greater sums of money to furnish such a voyage and to fit them with necessaries, than their consumed estates would amount to; and yet they must as well look to be seconded with supplies as presently to be transported. Also many precedents of ill success and lamentable miseries befallen others in the like designs were easy to be found, and not forgotten to be alleded; besides their own experience, in their former troubles and hardships in their removal into Holland, and how hard a thing it was for them to live in that strange place, though it was a neighbour country and a civil and rich commonwealth.

It was answered, that all great and honourable actions are accompanied with great difficulties and must be both enterprised and overcome with answerable courages. It was granted the dangers were great, but not desperate. The difficulties were many, but not invincible. For though there were many of them likely, yet they were not certain. It might be sundry of the things feared might never befall; others by provident care and the use of good means might in a great measure be prevented; and all of them, through the help of God, by fortitude and patience, might either be borne or overcome. True it was that such attempts were not to be made and undertaken without good ground and reason, not rashly or lightly as many have done for curiosity or hope of gain, etc. But their condition was not ordinary, their ends were good and honourable, their calling lawful and urgent; and therefore they might expect the blessing of God in their proceeding. Yea, though they should lose their lives in this action, yet might they have comfort in the same and their endeavours would be honourable. They lived here but as men in exile and in a poor condition, and as great miseries might possibly befall them in this place; for the twelve years of truce were now out and there was nothing but

---

[10] During Bradford's time, well water was typically contaminated.   [11] Fatty folds.

[12] The travel narratives of the time made the Pilgrims respect the Native Americans and find the Spaniards in the New World distasteful.

beating of drums and preparing for war, the events whereof are always uncertain. The Spaniard might prove as cruel as the savages of America, and the famine and pestilence as sore here as there, and their liberty less to look out for remedy.

After many other particular things answered and alleged on both sides, it was fully concluded by the major part to put this design in execution and to prosecute it by the best means they could.

Chapter IX: Of Their Voyage, and How They Passed the Sea; and of Their Safe Arrival at Cape Cod

September 6.[1] These troubles being blown over, and now all being compact together in one ship,[2] they put to sea again with a prosperous wind, which continued divers days together, which was some encouragement unto them; yet, according to the usual manner, many were afflicted with seasickness. And I may not omit here a special work of God's providence. There was a proud and very profane young man, one of the seamen, of a lusty,[3] able body, which made him the more haughty; he would alway be contemning the poor people in their sickness and cursing them daily with grievous execrations; and did not let[4] to tell them that he hoped to help to cast half of them overboard before they came to their journey's end, and to make merry with what they had; and if he were by any gently reproved, he would curse and swear most bitterly. But it pleased God before they came half seas over, to smite this young man with a grievous disease, of which he died in a desperate manner, and so was himself the first that was thrown overboard. Thus his curses light on his own head, and it was an astonishment to all his fellows for they noted it to be the just hand of God upon him.

After they had enjoyed fair winds and weather for a season, they were encountered many times with cross winds and met with many fierce storms with which the ship was shroudly[5] shaken, and her upper works made very leaky; and one of the main beams in the midships was bowed and cracked, which put them in some fear that the ship could not be able to perform the voyage. So some of the chief of the company, perceiving the mariners to fear the sufficiency of the ship as appeared by their mutterings, they entered into serious consultation with the master and other officers of the ship, to consider in time of the danger, and rather to return than to cast themselves into a desperate and inevitable peril. And truly there was great distraction and difference of opinion amongst the mariners themselves; fain would they do what could be done for their wages' sake (being now near half the seas over) and on the other hand they were loath to hazard their lives too desperately. But in examining of all opinions, the master and others affirmed they knew the ship to be strong and firm under water; and for the buckling of the main beam, there was a great iron screw the passengers brought out of Holland, which would raise the beam into his place; the which being done, the carpenter and master affirmed that with a post put under it, set firm in the lower deck and otherways bound, he would make it sufficient. And as for the decks and upper works,

---

[1] Bradford used the Julian, not the Gregorian calendar, so his dates are 10 days earlier than they would be in our system.

[2] One of the two ships on which the Separatists set sail from England, the *Speedwell,* was not fit to make the voyage. Its passengers and cargo were transferred to the *Mayflower* back in England; the *Mayflower* then departed for America.

[3] Hardy, spirited.   [4] Hesitate.   [5] Shrewdly, originally meaning "wickedly."

they would caulk them as well as they could, and though with the working of the ship[6] they would not long keep staunch,[7] yet there would otherwise be no great danger, if they did not overpress her with sails. So they committed themselves to the will of God and resolved to proceed.

In sundry of these storms the winds were so fierce and the seas so high, as they could not bear a knot of sail, but were forced to hull[8] for diverse days together. And in one of them, as they thus lay at hull in a mighty storm, a lusty young man called John Howland, coming upon some occasion above the gratings[9] was, with a seele[10] of the ship, thrown into sea; but it pleased God that he caught hold of the topsail halyards which hung overboard and ran out at length. Yet he held his hold (though he was sundry fathoms under water) till he was hauled up by the same rope to the brim of the water, and then with a boat hook and other means got into the ship again and his life saved. And though he was something ill with it, yet he lived many years after and became a profitable member both in church and commonwealth. In all this voyage there died but one of the passengers, which was William Butten, a youth, servant to Samuel Fuller, when they drew near the coast.

But to omit other things (that I may be brief) after long beating at sea they fell with that land which is called Cape Cod;[11] the which being made and certainly known to be it, they were not a little joyful. After some deliberation had amongst themselves and with the master of the ship, they tacked about and resolved to stand for the southward (the wind and weather being fair) to find some place about Hudson's River for their habitation.[12] But after they had sailed that course about half the day, they fell amongst dangerous shoals and roaring breakers, and they were so far entangled therewith as they conceived themselves in great danger; and the wind shrinking upon them withal, they resolved to bear up again for the Cape and thought themselves happy to get out of those dangers before night overtook them, as by God's good providence they did. And the next day[13] they got into the Cape Harbor[14] where they rid in safety.

A word or two by the way of this cape. It was thus first named by Captain Gosnold and his company,[15] Anno 1602, and after by Captain Smith was called Cape James; but it retains the former name amongst seamen. Also, that point which first showed those dangerous shoals unto them they called Point Care, and Tucker's Terrour; but the French and Dutch to this day call it Malabar by reason of those perilous shoals and the losses they have suffered there.

Being thus arrived in a good harbor, and brought safe to land, they fell upon their knees and blessed the God of Heaven[16] who had brought them over the vast and furious ocean, and delivered them from all the perils and miseries thereof, again to set their feet on the firm and stable earth, their proper element. And no marvel if they were thus joyful, seeing wise Seneca[17] was so affected with sailing a few miles on the coast of his own Italy, as he affirmed, that he had rather remain

---

[6] Twisting of the ship's planks, creating leaks in the hull.

[7] Watertight.   [8] Under short sail, to drift with the wind.   [9] Wooden crossbars on the deck.

[10] Roll or toss.

[11] At daybreak on November 19 (9, with Bradford's timeframe), 1620, the Pilgrims first sighted the Cape Cod highlands.

[12] The English did not honor the Dutch's claims to the area and hoped to be the first to colonize it.

[13] November 21 (11), 1620; the journey from England took sixty-five days.

[14] Provincetown Harbor, today.

[15] Bradford's note: "Because they took much of that fish there."   [16] Daniel 2:19.

[17] A Roman philosopher and statesman (4 ? B.C.–A.D. 65).

twenty years on his way by land than pass by sea to any place in a short time, so tedious and dreadful was the same unto him.[18]

But here I cannot but stay and make a pause, and stand half amazed at this poor people's present condition; and so I think will the reader, too, when he well considers the same. Being thus passed the vast ocean, and a sea of troubles before in their preparation (as may be remembered by that which went before), they had now no friends to welcome them nor inns to entertain or refresh their weatherbeaten bodies; no houses or much less towns to repair to, to seek for succour. It is recorded in Scripture[19] as a mercy to the Apostle and his shipwrecked company, that the barbarians showed them no small kindness in refreshing them, but these savage barbarians, when they met with them (as after will appear) were readier to fill their sides full of arrows than otherwise. And for the season it was winter, and they that know the winters of that country know them to be sharp and violent, and subject to cruel and fierce storms, dangerous to travel to known places, much more to search an unknown coast. Besides, what could they see but a hideous and desolate wilderness, full of wild beasts and wild men—and what multitudes there might be of them they knew not. Neither could they, as it were, go up to the top of Pisgah[20] to view from this wilderness a more goodly country to feed their hopes; for which way soever they turned their eyes (save upward to the heavens) they could have little solace or content in respect of any outward objects. For summer being done, all things stand upon them with a weatherbeaten face, and the whole country, full of woods and thickets, represented a wild and savage hue. If they looked behind them, there was the mighty ocean which they had passed and was now as a main bar and gulf to separate them from all the civil parts of the world. If it be said they had a ship to succour them, it is true; but what heard they daily from the master and company? But that with speed they should look out a place (with their shallop[21]) where they would be, at some near distance; for the season was such as he would not stir from thence till a safe harbor was discovered by them, where they would be, and he might go without danger; and that victuals consumed apace but he must and would keep sufficient for themselves and their return. Yea, it was muttered by some that if they got not a place in time, they would turn them and their goods ashore and leave them. Let it also be considered what weak hopes of supply and succour they left behind them, that might bear up their minds in this sad condition and trials they were under; and they could not but be very small. It is true, indeed, the affections and love of their brethren at Leyden was cordial and entire towards them, but they had little power to help them or themselves; and how the case stood between them and the merchants[22] at their coming away hath already been declared.

What could now sustain them but the Spirit of God and His grace? May not and ought not the children of these fathers rightly say: "Our fathers were Englishmen which came over this great ocean, and were ready to perish in this wilderness; but they cried unto the Lord, and He heard their voice and looked on their adver-

---

[18] Bradford's note: "Epistle 53," referring to Seneca's *Epistles*.

[19] Bradford's note: "Acts xxviii," referring to Acts 28, verse 2, in which the shipwrecked Paul is helped by "barbarous people."

[20] The mountain on which Moses stood to view the Promised Land, in Deuteronomy 34:1–4.

[21] An open boat with at least one mast, used in shallow waters.

[22] Those who had financed the Pilgrims' voyage.

sity,"[23] etc. "Let them therefore praise the Lord, because He is good: and His mercies endure forever." "Yea, let them which have been redeemed of the Lord, shew how He hath delivered them from the hand of the oppressor. When they wandered in the desert wilderness out of the way, and found no city to dwell in, both hungry and thirsty, their soul was overwhelmed in them. Let them confess before the Lord His lovingkindness and His wonderful works before the sons of men."[24]

Chapter X: Showing How They Sought out a Place of Habitation; and What Befell Them Thereabout

Being thus arrived at Cape Cod the 11th of November, and necessity calling them to look out a place for habitation (as well as the master's and mariners' importunity); they having brought a large shallop[1] with them out of England, stowed in quarters in the ship, they now got her out and set their carpenters to work to trim her up; but being much bruised and shattered in the ship with foul weather, they saw she would be long in mending. Whereupon a few of them tendered themselves to go by land and discover those nearest places, whilst the shallop was in mending; and the rather because as they went into that harbor there seemed to be an opening some two or three leagues off, which the master judged to be a river. It was conceived there might be some danger in the attempt, yet seeing them resolute, they were permitted to go, being sixteen of them well armed under the conduct of Captain Standish,[2] having such instructions given them as was thought meet.

They set forth the 15th of November; and when they had marched about the space of a mile by the seaside, they espied five or six persons with a dog coming towards them, who were savages; but they fled from them and ran up into the woods, and the English followed them, partly to see if they could speak with them, and partly to discover if there might not be more of them lying in ambush. But the Indians seeing themselves thus followed, they again forsook the woods and ran away on the sands as hard as they could, so as they could not come near them but followed them by the track of their feet sundry miles and saw that they had come the same way. So, night coming on, they made their rendezvous and set out their sentinels, and rested in quiet that night; and the next morning followed their track till they had headed a great creek and so left the sands, and turned another way into the woods. But they still followed them by guess, hoping to find their dwellings; but they soon lost both them and themselves, falling into such thickets as were ready to tear their clothes and armor in pieces; but were most distressed for want of drink. But at length they found water and refreshed themselves, being the first New England water they drunk of, and was now in great thirst as pleasant unto them as wine or beer had been in foretimes.

Afterwards they directed their course to come to the other shore, for they knew it was a neck of land they were to cross over, and so at length got to the seaside

---

[23] Bradford's note: "Deuteronomy xxvi.5, 7," referring to the Israelites' deliverance from the bondage of Egypt.

[24] Bradford's note: "Psalms cvii, 1–5, 8."

[1] An open boat with at least one mast, used in shallow waters.

[2] Myles Standish (1584?–1656), a professional soldier, was not a Pilgrim. He was employed to aid the colonists in their military affairs and became a loyal supporter of them.

and marched to this supposed river, and by the way found a pond[3] of clear, fresh water, and shortly after a good quantity of clear ground where the Indians had formerly set corn, and some of their graves. And proceeding further they saw new stubble where corn had been set the same year; also they found where lately a house had been, where some planks and a great kettle was remaining, and heaps of sand newly paddled with their hands. Which, they digging up, found in them divers fair Indian baskets filled with corn, and some in ears, fair and good, of divers colours, which seemed to them a very goodly sight (having never seen any such before). This was near the place of that supposed river they came to seek, unto which they went and found it to open itself into two arms with a high cliff of sand in the entrance[4] but more like to be creeks of salt water than any fresh, for aught they saw; and that there was good harborage for their shallop, leaving it further to be discovered by their shallop, when she was ready. So, their time limited them being expired, they returned to the ship lest they should be in fear of their safety; and took with them part of the corn and buried up the rest. And so, like the men from Eshcol, carried with them of the fruits of the land and showed their brethren;[5] of which, and their return, they were marvelously glad and their hearts encouraged.

After this, the shallop being got ready, they set out again for the better discovery of this place, and the master of the ship desired to go himself. So there went some thirty men but found it[6] to be no harbour for ships but only for boats. There was also found two of their houses covered with mats, and sundry of their implements in them, but the people were run away and could not be seen. Also there was found more of their corn and of their beans of various colours; the corn and beans they brought away, purposing to give them full satisfaction when they should meet with any of them as, about some six months afterward they did, to their good content.

And here is to be noted a special providence of God, and a great mercy to this poor people, that here they got seed to plant them corn the next year, or else they might have starved, for they had none nor any likelihood to get any till the season had been past, as the sequel did manifest. Neither is it likely they had had this, if the first voyage had not been made, for the ground was now all covered with snow and hard frozen; but the Lord is never wanting unto His in their greatest needs; let His holy name have all the praise.

The month of November being spent in these affairs, and much foul weather falling in, the 6th of December they sent out their shallop again with ten of their principal men and some seamen, upon further discovery, intending to circulate that deep bay of Cape Cod. The weather was very cold and it froze so hard as the spray of the sea lighting on their coats, they were as if they had been glazed. Yet that night betimes they got down into the bottom of the bay, and as they drew near the shore they saw some ten or twelve Indians[7] very busy about something. They landed about a league or two from them, and had much ado to put ashore anywhere—it lay so full of flats. Being landed, it grew late and they made themselves a barricado with logs and boughs as well as they could in the time, and set out

[3] The pond for which Pond Village, Truro (in Massachusetts) was named.
[4] The Pamet River, a salt creek.
[5] In Numbers 13:23–26, grapes from the Valley of Eshcol were so heavy that two of Moses' scouts were needed to carry them.
[6] The mouth of the Pamet River, now Cold Harbor.
[7] Near Eastham, Massachusetts, home of the Nauset Indians.

their sentinel and betook them to rest, and saw the smoke of the fire the savages made that night. When morning was come they divided their company, some to coast along the shore in the boat, and the rest marched through the woods to see the land, if any fit place might be for their dwelling. They came also to the place where they saw the Indians the night before, and found they had been cutting up a great fish like a grampus,[8] being some two inches thick of fat like a hog, some pieces whereof they had left by the way. And the shallop found two more of these fishes dead on the sands, a thing usual after storms in that place, by reason of the great flats of sand that lie off.

So they ranged up and down all that day, but found no people, nor any place they liked. When the sun grew low, they hasted out of the woods to meet with their shallop, to whom they made signs to come to them into a creek hard by,[9] the which they did at high water; of which they were very glad, for they had not seen each other all that day since the morning. So they made them a barricado as usually they did every night, with logs, stakes and thick pine boughs, the height of a man, leaving it open to leeward, partly to shelter them from the cold and wind (making their fire in the middle and lying round about it) and partly to defend them from any sudden assaults of the savages, if they should surround them; so being very weary, they betook them to rest. But about midnight they heard a hideous and great cry, and their sentinel called "Arm! arm!" So they bestirred them and stood to their arms and shot off a couple of muskets, and then the noise ceased. They concluded it was a company of wolves or such like wild beasts, for one of the seamen told them he had often heard such a noise in Newfoundland.

So they rested till about five of the clock in the morning; for the tide, and their purpose to go from thence, made them be stirring betimes. So after prayer they prepared for breakfast, and it being day dawning it was thought best to be carrying things down to the boat. But some said it was not best to carry the arms down, others said they would be the readier, for they had lapped them up in their coats from the dew; but some three or four would not carry theirs till they went themselves. Yet as it fell out, the water being not high enough, they laid them down on the bank side and came up to breakfast.

But presently, all on the sudden, they heard a great and strange cry, which they knew to be the same voices they heard in the night, though they varied their notes; and one of their company being abroad came running in and cried, "Men, Indians! Indians!" And withal, their arrows came flying amongst them. Their men ran with all speed to recover their arms, as by the good providence of God they did. In the meantime, of those that were there ready, two muskets were discharged at them, and two more stood ready in the entrance of their rendezvous but were commanded not to shoot till they could take full aim at them. And the other two charged again with all speed, for there were only four had arms there, and defended the barricado, which was first assaulted. The cry of the Indians was dreadful, especially when they saw their men run out of the rendezvous toward the shallop to recover their arms, the Indians wheeling about upon them. But some running out with coats of mail on, and cutlasses in their hands, they soon got their arms and let fly amongst them and quickly stopped their violence. Yet there was a lusty man, and no less valiant, stood behind a tree within half a musket shot, and let his arrows fly at them; he was seen [to] shoot three arrows, which were all

---

[8] Most likely a blackfish.
[9] The mouth of Herring River in present-day Eastham.

avoided. He stood three shots of a musket, till one taking full aim at him and made the bark or splinters of the tree fly about his ears, after which he gave an extraordinary shriek and away they went, all of them. They[10] left some to keep the shallop and followed them about a quarter of a mile and shouted once or twice, and shot off two or three pieces, and so returned. This they did that they might conceive that they were not afraid of them or any way discouraged.

Thus it pleased God to vanquish their enemies and give them deliverance; and by His special providence so to dispose that not any one of them were either hurt or hit, though their arrows came close by them and on every side [of] them; and sundry of their coats, which hung up in the barricado, were shot through and through. Afterwards they gave God solemn thanks and praise for their deliverance, and gathered up a bundle of their arrows and sent them into England afterward by the master of the ship, and called that place the First Encounter.

From hence they departed and coasted all along but discerned no place likely for harbor; and therefore hasted to a place that their pilot (one Mr. Coppin who had been in the country before) did assure them was a good harbor, which he had been in, and they might fetch it before night; of which they were glad for it began to be foul weather.

After some hours' sailing it began to snow and rain, and about the middle of the afternoon the wind increased and the sea became very rough, and they broke their rudder, and it was as much as two men could do to steer her with a couple of oars. But their pilot bade them be of good cheer for he saw the harbor; but the storm increasing, and night drawing on, they bore what sail they could to get in, while they could see. But herewith they broke their mast in three pieces and their sail fell overboard in a very grown sea, so as they had like to have been cast away. Yet by God's mercy they recovered themselves, and having the flood[11] with them, struck into the harbor. But when it came to, the pilot was deceived in the place, and said the Lord be merciful unto them for his eyes never saw that place before; and he and the master's mate would have run her ashore in a cove full of breakers before the wind. But a lusty seaman which steered bade those which rowed, if they were men, about with her or else they were all cast away; the which they did with speed. So he bid them be of good cheer and row lustily, for there was a fair sound before them, and he doubted not but they should find one place or other where they might ride in safety. And though it was very dark and rained sore, yet in the end they got under the lee of a small island and remained there all that night in safety. But they knew not this to be an island till morning, but were divided in their minds; some would keep the boat for fear they might be amongst the Indians, other were so wet and cold they could not endure but got ashore, and with much ado got fire (all things being so wet); and the rest were glad to come to them, for after midnight the wind shifted to the northwest and it froze hard.

But though this had been a day and night of much trouble and danger unto them, yet God gave them a morning of comfort and refreshing (as usually He doth to His children) for the next day was a fair, sunshining day, and they found themselves to be on an island secure from the Indians, where they might dry their stuff, fix their pieces[12] and rest themselves; and gave God thanks for His mercies in their manifold deliverances. And this being the last day of the week, they prepared there to keep the Sabbath.

---

[10] The English.
[11] The flood tide, averaging 9 ft. there today.   [12] Armaments.

On Monday they sounded[13] the harbor and found it fit for shipping, and marched into the land and found divers cornfields and little running brooks, a place (as they supposed) fit for situation.[14] At least it was the best they could find, and the season and their present necessity made them glad to accept of it. So they returned to their ship again with this news to the rest of their people, which did much comfort their hearts.

On the 15th of December they weighed anchor to go to the place they had discovered, and came within two leagues of it, but were fain to bear up again; but the 16th day, the wind came fair, and they arrived safe in this harbor. And afterwards took better view of the place, and resolved where to pitch their dwelling; and the 25th day began to erect the first house for common use to receive them and their goods.

from   BOOK II

from   **Chapter XI: The Remainder of Anno 1620***
[The Mayflower Compact]

I shall a little return back, and begin with a combination[1] made by them before they came ashore; being the first foundation of their government in this place. Occasioned partly by the discontented and mutinous speeches that some of the strangers[2] amongst them had let fall from them in the ship: That when they came ashore they would use their own liberty, for none had power to command them, the patent they had being for Virginia and not for New England, which belonged to another government, with which the Virginia Company had nothing to do.[3] And partly that such an act by them done, this their condition considered, might be as firm as any patent,[4] and in some respects more sure.

The form was as followeth:[5]

IN THE NAME OF GOD, AMEN.

We whose names are underwritten, the loyal subjects of our dread Sovereign Lord King James, by the Grace of God of Great Britain, France, and Ireland King, Defender of the Faith, etc.

Having undertaken, for the Glory of God and advancement of the Christian Faith and Honour of our King and Country, a Voyage to plant the First Colony in the Northern Parts of Virginia,[6] do by these presents[7] solemnly and mutually in the presence of God and one of another, Covenant and Combine ourselves to-

---

[13] Measured the depth of.

[14] Morison's note: "Here is the only contemporary authority for the 'Landing of the Pilgrims on Plymouth Rock' on Monday 11 [21] Dec. 1620." The landing was made from the shallop while the *Mayflower* was in Provincetown Harbor; no women landed and no Native Americans greeted the landing party, which may not have landed on the boulder now called Plymouth Rock.

* Bradford numbered his manuscript only up to Chapter X; Morison uses these chapter numbers.

[1] An agreement.   [2] The Puritans' term for those outside their church.

[3] The Mayflower Compact, signed on November 21 (11), 1620, was drawn up to provide the Pilgrims with a document validating their colonization in New England, as their charter from the Virginia Company of London authorized colonization South of 41° N (as far North as New York City).

[4] A legal document signed by a sovereign to grant special privileges.

[5] Morison's note: "The original document has disappeared, so this may be regarded as the most authentic text of the Compact. It was first printed in *Mourt's Relation* (1622). . . . "

[6] New England.   [7] Provisions.

gether into a Civil Body Politic, for our[8] better ordering and preservation and furtherance of the ends aforesaid; and by virtue hereof to enact, constitute and frame such just and equal Laws, Ordinances, Acts, Constitutions and Offices, from time to time, as shall be thought most meet and convenient for the general good of the Colony, unto which we promise all due submission and obedience. In witness whereof we have hereunder subscribed our names at Cape Cod, the 11th of November, in the year of the reign of our Sovereign Lord King James, of England, France and Ireland the eighteenth, and of Scotland the fifty-fourth. Anno Domini 1620.

After this they chose, or rather confirmed, Mr. John Carver[9] (a man godly and well approved amongst them) their Governor for that year. And after they had provided a place for their goods, or common store (which were long in unlading[10] for want of boats, foulness of the winter weather and sickness of diverse)[11] and begun some small cottages for their habitation; as time would admit, they met and consulted of laws and orders, both for their civil and military government as the necessity of their condition did require, still adding thereunto as urgent occasion in several times, and as cases did require.

In these hard and difficult beginnings they found some discontents and murmurings arise amongst some, and mutinous speeches and carriages[12] in other; but they were soon quelled and overcome by the wisdom, patience, and just and equal carriage of things, by the Governor and better part, which clave[13] faithfully together in the main.

Chapter XXVIII: Anno Dom: 1637
[The Pequot War]

In the fore part of this year, the Pequots[1] fell openly upon the English at Connecticut, in the lower parts of the river,[2] and slew sundry of them as they were at work in the fields, both men and women, to the great terrour of the rest, and went away in great pride and triumph, with many high threats. They also assaulted a fort at the river's mouth, though strong and well defended; and though they did not there prevail, yet it struck them with much fear and astonishment to see their bold attempts in the face of danger. Which made them in all places to stand upon their guard and to prepare for resistance, and earnestly to solicit their friends and confederates in the Bay of Massachusetts to send them speedy aid, for they looked for more forcible assaults. Mr. Vane,[3] being then Governor, writ from their General Court to them here to join with them in this war. To which they were cordially willing, but took opportunity to write to them about some former things, as well as

---

[8] Bradford replaced "ye" with "our."

[9] John Carver (1575?–1621), a tradesman who had been appointed governor of the Pilgrim colony even before they set sail from England; his election after the compact was signed confirmed that appointment.

[10] Unloading.   [11] Various people.   [12] Conduct.   [13] Cleaved.

[1] An Algonquian Indian tribe of Connecticut; their disputes with the colonists ended in the Pequot War of 1637.

[2] The Connecticut River.

[3] Sir Henry Vane (1613–1662), then the Massachusetts Bay Colony's governor.

present, considerable hereabout. The which will best appear in the Governor's answer, which he returned to the same, which I shall here insert.

In the meantime, the Pequots, especially in the winter before, sought to make peace with the Narragansetts, and used very pernicious arguments to move them thereunto: as that the English were strangers and began to overspread their country, and would deprive them thereof in time, if they were suffered to grow and increase. And if the Narragansetts did assist the English to subdue them, they did but make way for their own overthrow, for if they were rooted out, the English would soon take occasion to subjugate them. And if they would hearken to them they should not need to fear the strength of the English, for they would not come to open battle with them but fire their houses, kill their cattle, and lie in ambush for them as they went abroad upon their occasions; and all this they might easily do without any or little danger to themselves. The which course being held, they well saw the English could not long subsist but they would either be starved with hunger or be forced to forsake the country. With many the like things; insomuch that the Narragansetts were once wavering and were half minded to have made peace with them, and joined against the English. But again, when they considered how much wrong they had received from the Pequots, and what an opportunity they now had by the help of the English to right themselves; revenge was so sweet unto them as it prevailed above all the rest, so as they resolved to join with the English against them, and did.

The Court here agreed forthwith to send fifty men at their own charge; and with as much speed as possibly they could, got them armed and had made them ready under sufficient leaders,[4] and provided a bark[5] to carry them provisions and tend upon them for all occasions. But when they were ready to march, with a supply from the Bay, they had word to stay; for the enemy was as good as vanquished and there would be no need.

I shall not take upon me exactly to describe their proceedings in these things, because I expect it will be fully done by themselves who best know the carriage and circumstances of things. I shall therefore but touch them in general. From Connecticut, who were most sensible of the hurt sustained and the present danger, they set out a party of men, and another party met them from the Bay, at Narragansetts', who were to join with them.[6] The Narragansetts were earnest to be gone before the English were well rested and refreshed, especially some of them which came last. It should seem their desire was to come upon the enemy suddenly and undiscovered. There was a bark of this place, newly put in there, which was come from Connecticut, who did encourage them to lay hold of the Indians' forwardness, and to show as great forwardness as they, for it would encourage them, and expedition might prove to their great advantage. So they went on and so ordered their march as the Indians brought them to a fort[7] of the enemy's (in which most of their chief men were) before day. They approached the same with great silence and surrounded it both with English and Indians, that they might not break out; and so assaulted them with great courage, shooting amongst them, and entered the fort with all speed. And those that first entered found sharp resistance from the

---

[4] Lieutenant William Holmes (?–1662); Thomas Prence (1600–1673), later a governor of the Plymouth Colony; and forty-two men.

[5] A sailing ship.

[6] The Connecticut party of ninety men was led by Captain John Mason (1588–1635), later a founder of the Dover Colony (New Hampshire); the Bay party of forty men was led by Captain John Underhill (1597?–1672), later a governor of the Dover Colony; one hundred more men were to follow.

[7] Mystic Fort, on the western bank of Connecticut's Mystic River.

enemy who both shot at and grappled with them; others ran into their houses and brought out fire and set them on fire, which soon took in their mat;[8] and standing close together, with the wind all was quickly on a flame, and thereby more were burnt to death than was otherwise slain; It burnt their bowstrings and made them unserviceable; those that scaped the fire were slain with the sword, some hewed to pieces, others run through with their rapiers, so as they were quickly dispatched and very few escaped. It was conceived they thus destroyed about 400 at this time. It was a fearful sight to see them thus frying in the fire and the streams of blood quenching the same, and horrible was the stink and scent thereof; but the victory seemed a sweet sacrifice,[9] and they gave the praise thereof to God, who had wrought so wonderfully for them, thus to enclose their enemies in their hands and give them so speedy a victory over so proud and insulting an enemy.

The Narragansett Indians all this while stood round about, but aloof from all danger and left the whole execution to the English, except it were the stopping of any that broke away. Insulting over their enemies in this their ruin and misery, when they saw them dancing in the flames, calling them by a word in their own language, signifying "O brave Pequots!" which they used familiarly among themselves in their own praise in songs of triumph after their victories. After this service was thus happily accomplished, they marched to the waterside where they met with some of their vessels, by which they had refreshing with victuals and other necessaries. But in their march the rest of the Pequots drew into a body and accosted them, thinking to have some advantage against them by reason of a neck of land. But when they saw the English prepare for them they kept aloof, so as they neither did hurt nor could receive any.

After their refreshing, and repair together for further counsel and directions, they resolved to pursue their victory and follow the war against the rest. But the Narragansett Indians, most of them, forsook them, and such of them as they had with them for guides or otherwise, they found them very cold and backward in the business, either out of envy, or that they saw the English would make more profit of the victory than they were willing they should; or else deprive them of such advantage as themselves desired, by having them become tributaries unto them, or the like.

For the rest of this business, I shall only relate the same as it is in a letter which came from Mr. Winthrop to the Governor here, as followeth.

That I may make an end of this matter, this Sassacus (the Pequots' chief sachem) being fled to the Mohawks, they cut off his head, with some other of the chief of them, whether to satisfy the English or rather the Narragansetts (who, as I have since heard, hired them to do it) or for their own advantage, I well know not; but thus this war took end. The rest of the Pequots were wholly driven from their place, and some of them submitted themselves to the Narragansetts and lived under them. Others of them betook themselves to the Mohegans under Uncas, their sachem, with the approbation of the English of Connecticut, under whose protection Uncas lived; and he and his men had been faithful to them in this war and done them very good service. But this did so vex the Narragansetts, that they had not the whole sway over them, as they have never ceased plotting and contriving how to bring them under; and because they cannot attain their ends, because of the English who have protected them, they have sought to raise a general conspiracy against the English, as will appear in another place.

---

[8] The wall and floor mats caught fire.
[9] In Leviticus 2:1–2, the priest's ceremonial burning was "a sweet savour unto the Lord."

from   *Chapter XXXVI: Anno Dom: 1646*

[*Winslow's Final Departure*]

This year Mr. Edward Winslow[1] went into England, upon this occasion: some discontented persons under the government of the Massachusetts sought to trouble their peace and disturb, if not innovate,[2] their government by laying many scandals upon them, and intended to prosecute against them in England by petitioning and complaining to the Parliament.[3] Also, Samuel Gorton and his company made complaints against them.[4] So as they made choice of Mr. Winslow to be their agent to make their defense, and gave him commission and instructions for that end. In which he so carried himself as did well answer their ends and cleared them from any blame or dishonour, to the shame of their adversaries. But by reason of the great alterations in the State,[5] he was detained longer than was expected, and afterwards fell into other employments there; so as he hath now been absent this four years, which hath been much to the weakening of this government, without whose consent he took these employments upon him.

Anno 1647.   And Anno 1648.[6]

1630–1651, 1856

John Winthrop
(1588–1649)

Born in Edwardstone, England, into the Old World culture of Elizabethan England in 1588, the year the Spanish Armada was launched against England, John Winthrop played a major role in shaping the New World fortunes of Puritan New England. Winthrop was the son of Anne Browne and Adam Winthrop, the successful lord of Groton Manor. At age fourteen Winthrop entered Trinity College, Cambridge. There, during an illness, he experienced the religious conversion that brought him to the Puritans, the conservative and reformist wing of the Church of England.

Winthrop's decision to immigrate to America resulted from the increasingly difficult economic and political conditions in England. A depression in the textile industry forced

---

[1] Edward Winslow (1595–1655), was the founder and a governor of the Plymouth Colony. An original *Mayflower* passenger, he returned to England in 1646 to defend the Massachusetts Bay Colony against depriving Church of England members of their civil and religious rights; once successful, Winslow remained in England.

[2] Disrupt.   [3] The Remonstrance and Petition to the General Court on May 6, 1646.

[4] Samuel Gorton (1592–1677), a notorious troublemaker in New England, was banished from four colonies and eventually founded Warwick, Rhode Island.

[5] The Puritan Revolution in England, in which King Charles was executed; Oliver Cromwell (1599–1658) was established as Lord Protector of the Commonwealth, now a Puritan republic.

[6] No entries follow this, completed in 1650. In 1651 Bradford added the names of the *Mayflower* passengers.

him into the practice of law in London, and in 1627 he was appointed attorney to the Court of Wards and Liveries. However, the new king, Charles I, was determined to keep the Puritans out of power. Winthrop eventually found himself out of a job. In 1629 Charles I dissolved Parliament, precipitating a crisis that eventually led to civil war. For Winthrop such events meant trouble. "I am veryly perswaded, God will bringe some heauye [heavy] Affliction vpon this lande," he wrote to his third wife (of four), Margaret Tyndal. But he added, "If the Lord seeth it wilbe good for vs, he will prouide a shelter and a hidinge place for vs and ours."

The shelter proved to be the Massachusetts Bay Company, a group of Puritans intent on colonizing America under royal charter. This charter, unlike most, did not require that the company hold meetings in England, so when Winthrop was elected governor of the company in 1629, the group found itself relatively independent. Even though the Puritans had not separated from the Church of England, as had the Pilgrims of Plymouth, they enjoyed a good deal of religious and political autonomy. When Winthrop left for New England on the *Arbella* in 1630, the ground was already prepared for the planting of seeds of a Puritan commonwealth based on strict religious principles.

In his famous 1630 sermon "A Model of Christian Charity" (not published until 1838), Winthrop articulated these underlying principles even as the *Arbella* sailed to New England. Foremost of these principles is "charity," or love, the force by which individual differences are overcome by a desire for connection to a larger body of people or to Christ himself. Using the metaphor of the body, Winthrop describes this company of Puritans as a single organic entity: "Christ and His church make one body . . . but when Christ comes and by His spirit and love knits all these parts to Himself and each to other, it is become the most perfect and best proportioned body in the world." Traveling from a deeply divided England under both a new charter and a new covenant with God, Winthrop hoped to protect the body politic from internal dissent and external danger. Whereas failure would mean that God might "withdraw his present help from us," the Puritans' success would

Nineteenth-century artists tended to paint romanticized visions of the early history of America and ignored the bitter hardships involved. This mural, Governor Winthrop Arrives at Salem on the *Arbella—1630, was painted by Charles Hoffbauer during the nineteenth century.*

insure that "The Lord will be our God, and delight to dwell among us as His own people."

Winthrop's sermon proved to be both a social blueprint and a warning of future problems for the young Massachusetts Bay Colony. Winthrop, serving as governor or deputy governor during most of the next two decades, faced several serious threats to the colony's unity and to his own authority. One of the first challenges was posed by Roger Williams, an iconoclastic religious radical who argued that Winthrop's colony should follow the Plymouth Colony's example and separate formally from the Church of England to achieve purity of religious doctrine. Winthrop rebutted him on this point, but Williams's later claim that the magistrate's power had come from the people and thus could not dictate religious matters, was too much for Winthrop, who believed his authority was derived from the colony's covenant with God. Williams fled to Rhode Island when he learned that Winthrop meant to send him back to England.

A more serious threat to the colony came from Anne Hutchinson and the "antinomian controversy" beginning in 1636. Hutchinson was "a woman of ready wit and bold spirit," according to Winthrop, but she attacked the colony's ministers for preaching the Old Covenant of works doctrine that "sanctification"—leading a righteous life and doing good works—is proof of salvation. Hutchinson believed that converts need look only for, and follow the indwelling of, the Holy Spirit in the New Covenant of faith, thus making ministers' sermons unnecessary for spiritual guidance. At her house (across the street from Winthrop's) Hutchinson began to hold meetings that grew to eighty women and men, including several influential merchants.

The crisis came to head in her trial of 1637. With Winthrop as her chief questioner, Hutchinson fended the accusations off by arguing that her beliefs were within the realm of Puritan orthodoxy, and it appeared that the case against her might collapse. But when she claimed to have gained knowledge by an immediate revelation from God in God's own words, the court convicted her of heresy and banished her to Rhode Island in November 1637. (When Hutchinson suffered a miscarriage, Winthrop called it 'proof' of God's displeasure with her.) Although this outcome insured the power of Winthrop and the clergy to control opinion and upheld the political model of government outlined in "A Model of Christian Charity," it also memorialized Hutchinson, on whose courage Nathaniel Hawthorne modeled Hester Prynne of *The Scarlet Letter* (1850), some two hundred years after Winthrop's death in 1649.

In his *Journal* (parts published in 1790; published in entirety as *The History of New England* [1825–1826]) Winthrop chronicled his conflicts with Anne Hutchinson as well as other matters—both serious and mundane—that occurred in the colony during its first nineteen years. Providing a day-to-day look at life in the New World, the *Journal* never loses its conviction that events and people are ultimately meaningful as expressions of God's will. In a ship's explosion, for example, Winthrop notes that "the judgment of God appeared, for the master and company were many of them profane scoffers at us, and at the ordinances of religion here." In describing the wars with the Pequot Indians, the disputes with Dutch settlers, and the punishments of internal troublemakers, Winthrop's *Journal* provides a revealing account of the Puritans' dedication and difficulties in establishing their "holy city on a hill."

Suggested Readings: P. Miller, *The New England Mind: The Seventeenth Century,* 1939. E. S. Morgan, *The Puritan Dilemma,* 1958. D. Rutman, *Winthrop's Boston,* 1965. T. Welde, "A Short Story of the Rise, Reign, and Ruin of the Antinomians, Familiasts & Libertines" in *The Antinomian Controversy 1636–1638,* ed. D. Hall, 1968.

Texts Used: "A Model of Christian Charity": *Winthrop Papers,* Vol. II, 1623–1630, ed. A. Forbes, 1931. The Anne Hutchinson Affair: *The History of New England,* Vols. I and II, ed. J. Savage, 1853, 1972. (Some spelling and punctuation modernized.)

from   A MODEL OF CHRISTIAN CHARITY*

Written on Boarde the Arbella, On the Atlantic Ocean. By the Honorable John Winthrop Esquire.

In His passage, (with the great Company of Religious people, of which Christian Tribes he was the Brave Leader and famous Governor;) from the Island of Great Britain, to New-England in the North America. Anno 1630.

CHRISTIAN CHARITY

A Model Hereof

God Almighty in his most holy and wise providence hath so disposed of the condition of mankind, as in all times some must be rich, some poor, some high and eminent in power and dignity; others mean and in subjection.

The Reason Hereof

1.REAS: First, to hold conformity with the rest of his works, being delighted to show forth the glory of his wisdom in the variety and difference of the creatures and the glory of his power, in ordering all these differences for the preservation and good of the whole; and the glory of his greatness, that as it is the glory of princes to have many officers, so this great King will have many stewards, counting himself more honored in dispensing his gifts to man by man than if he did it by his own immediate hand.

2.REAS: Secondly, that he might have the more occasion to manifest the work of his Spirit: first upon the wicked in moderating and restraining them, so that the rich and mighty should not eat up the poor, nor the poor and despised rise up against their superiors and shake off their yoke; secondly in the regenerate, in exercising his graces, in them, as in the great ones, their love, mercy, gentleness, temperance, etc.; in the poor and inferior sort, their faith patience, obedience, etc.

3.REAS: Thirdly, that every man might have need of other, and from hence they might be all knit more nearly together in the bond of brotherly affection. From hence it appears plainly that no man is made more honorable than another or more wealthy, etc., out of any particular and singular respect to himself, but for the glory of his Creator and the common good of the creature, man. Therefore God still reserves the property of these gifts to himself as [in] Ezekiel 16:17.[1] He there calls wealth his gold and his silver, etc. [In] Proverbs 3:9, he claims their service as his due, honor the Lord with thy riches, etc.[2] All men being thus (by divine providence) ranked into two sorts, rich and poor; under the first are comprehended

---

* This sermon was read by Winthrop on the *Arbella* during its journey to America in 1630. Although the original manuscript has been lost, copies were made and circulated in Winthrop's lifetime.

[1] "Thou hast also taken thy fair jewels of my gold and silver, which I had given thee, and madest to thyself images of men, and didst commit whoredom with them."

[2] "Honor the Lord with thy substance, and with the first fruits of all thine increase: so shall thy barns be filled with plenty, and thy presses burst out with new wine."

all such as are able to live comfortably by their own means duly improved; and all others are poor according to the former distribution. There are two rules whereby we are to walk one towards another: Justice and Mercy. These are always distinguished in their act and in their object, yet may they both concur in the same subject in each respect; as sometimes there may be an occasion of showing mercy to a rich man in some sudden danger of distress, and also doing of mere justice to a poor man in regard of some particular contract, etc. There is likewise a double law by which we are regulated in our conversation one towards another: in both the former respects, the law of nature and the law of grace, or the moral law or the law of the Gospel, to omit the rule of justice as not properly belonging to this purpose otherwise than it may fall into consideration in some particular cases. By the first of these laws man as he was enabled so withal [is] commanded to love his neighbor as himself.[3] Upon this ground stands all the precepts of the moral law, which concerns our dealings with men. To apply this to the works of mercy, this law requires two things: first, that every man afford his help to another in every want or distress; secondly, that he performed this out of the same affection which makes him careful of his own goods, according to that of our Savior. Math [7:12]:[4] "Whatsoever ye would that men should do to you." This was practiced by Abraham and Lot in entertaining the Angels and the old man of Gibeah.[5]

The law of grace or the Gospel hath some difference from the former, as in these respects: first, the law of nature was given to man in the estate of innocency; this of the Gospel in the estate of regeneracy.[6] Secondly, the former propounds one man to another, as the same flesh and image of God; this as a brother in Christ also, and in the communion of the same spirit, and so teacheth us to put a difference between Christians and others. Do good to all, especially to the household of faith:[7] Upon this ground the Israelites were to put a difference between the brethren of such as were strangers though not of the Canaanites.[8] Thirdly, the law of nature could give no rules for dealing with enemies, for all are to be considered as friends in the state of innocency, but the Gospel commands love to an enemy. Proof: "If thine Enemy hunger, feed him;"[9] "Love your Enemies, do good to them that hate you," Math 5:44.

This law of the Gospel propounds likewise a difference of seasons and occasions. There is a time when a Christian must sell all and give to the poor, as they did in the Apostles' times.[10] There is a time also when a Christian (though they give not all yet) must give beyond their ability, as they of Macedonia, Cor 2:8.[11] Likewise community of perils calls for extraordinary liberality, and so doth community in some special service for the Church. Lastly, when there is no other means whereby our Christian brother may be relieved in this distress, we must help him beyond our ability, rather than tempt God in putting him upon help by miraculous or extraordinary means.

* * *

[3] Matthew 5:43; 19:19.   [4] Matthew 7:12.

[5] In Genesis 18:1–2 Abraham entertains the angels; in Judges 19:16–21 an old man of Gibeah offers shelter to a traveling priest, a Levite, and defends him from enemies from a nearby city.

[6] "Man" is believed to have fallen to an unregenerate state after Adam and Eve sinned; Christ redeemed mankind through his suffering, and those who believe in him become saved or regenerate.

[7] Galatians 6:10.   [8] Those who live in Canaan, the Promised Land.

[9] Paraphrased from Proverbs 25:21.

[10] "Sell all that thou hast, and distribute unto the poor, and thou shalt have treasure in heaven," from Luke 18:22.

[11] 2 Corinthians 8[not 6]:1–4.

It rests now to make some application of this discourse by the present design, which gave the occasion of writing of it. Herein are 4 things to be propounded: first, the persons; secondly, the work; thirdly, the end; fourthly, the means.

First, for the persons. We are a company professing ourselves fellow members of Christ, in which respect only though we were absent from each other many miles, and had our employments as far distant, yet we ought to account ourselves knit together by this bond of love, and live in the exercise of it, if we would have comfort of our being in Christ. This was notorious in the practice of the Christians in former times; as is testified of the Waldenses,[12] from the mouth of one of the adversaries Æneas Sylvius,[13] "*mutuo solent amare penè antequam norint,*" they used to love any of their own religion even before they were acquainted with them.

Secondly, for the work we have in hand. It is by a mutual consent, through a special overruling providence, and a more than an ordinary approbation of the Churches of Christ, to seek out a place of cohabitation and consortship under a due form of government both civil and ecclesiastical. In such cases as this, the care of the public must oversway[14] all private respects, by which, not only conscience, but mere civil policy, doth bind us. For it is a true rule that particular estates cannot subsist in the ruin of the public.

Thirdly, the end is to improve our lives to do more service to the Lord; the comfort and increase of the body of Christ whereof we are members; that ourselves and posterity may be the better preserved from the common corruptions of this evil world, to serve the Lord and work out our salvation under the power and purity of his holy ordinances.

Fourthly, for the means whereby this must be effected. They are twofold, a conformity with the work and end we aim at. These we see are extraordinary, therefore we must not content ourselves with usual ordinary means. Whatsoever we did or ought to have done when we lived in England, the same must we do, and more also, where we go. That which the most in their churches maintain as a truth in profession only, we must bring into familiar and constant practice, as in this duty of love. We must love brotherly without dissimulation;[15] we must love one another with a pure heart fervently.[16] We must bear one another's burdens.[17] We must not look only on our own things, but also on the things of our brethren, neither must we think that the Lord will bear with such failings at our hands as he doth from those among whom we have lived; and that for 3 reasons.

First, in regard of the more near bond of marriage between him and us, wherein he hath taken us to be his after a most strict and peculiar manner, which will make him the more jealous of our love and obedience. So he tells the people of Israel, you only have I known of all the families of the earth, therefore will I punish you for your transgressions.[18] Secondly, because the Lord will be sanctified in them that come near him. We know that there were many that corrupted the service of the Lord, some setting up altars before his own, others offering both strange fire and strange sacrifices also; yet there came no fire from heaven, or other sudden judgment upon them, as did upon Nadab and Abihu,[19] who yet we may think did

[12] Followers of Pater Valdes (?–1217?), a French reformer who rejected the authority of the pope and believed the Bible to be the sole authority in religion.

[13] Pope Pius II, or Aeneas Sylvius Piccolomini (1405–1464), a scholar and historian who reigned as pope from 1458 to 1464.

[14] Outweigh.   [15] Paraphrased from Romans 12:9–10.   [16] Paraphrased from I Peter 1:22.

[17] Galatians 6:2.   [18] Amos 3:2.

[19] In Leviticus 10:1–2 two sons of Aaron who were destroyed for their sin in making an unauthorized offering to God.

not sin presumptuously. Thirdly, when God gives a special commission, he looks to have it strictly observed in every article. When he gave Saul a commission to destroy Amalek,[20] he indented with him upon certain articles, and because he failed in one of the least, and that upon a fair pretense, it lost him the kingdom, which should have been his reward if he had observed his commission. Thus stands the cause between God and us. We are entered into covenant[21] with him for this work. We have taken out a commission, the Lord hath given us leave to draw our own articles. We have professed to enterprise[22] these actions, upon these and those ends, we have hereupon besought him of favour and blessing. Now if the Lord shall please to hear us, and bring us in peace to the place we desire, then hath he ratified this covenant and sealed our commission, [and] will expect a strict performance of the articles contained in it; but if we shall neglect the observation of these articles which are the ends we have propounded, and, dissembling with our God, shall fall to embrace this present world and prosecute our carnal intentions, seeking great things for ourselves and our posterity, the Lord will surely break out in wrath against us, be revenged of such a perjured people and make us know the price of the breach of such a covenant.

Now the only way to avoid this shipwreck and to provide for our posterity is to follow the counsel of Micah,[23] to do justly, to love mercy, to walk humbly with our God. For this end, we must be knit together in this work as one man. We must entertain each other in brotherly affection. We must be willing to abridge ourselves of our superfluities, for the supply of other's necessities. We must uphold a familiar commerce together in all meekness, gentleness, patience and liberality. We must delight in each other, make other's conditions our own, rejoice together, mourn together, labour and suffer together, always having before our eyes our commission and community in the work, our community as members of the same body. So shall we keep the unity of the spirit in the bond of peace.[24] The Lord will be our God and delight to dwell among us, as his own people, and will command a blessing upon us in all our ways, so that we shall see much more of his wisdom, power, goodness and truth than formerly we have been acquainted with. We shall find that the God of Israel is among us, when ten of us shall be able to resist a thousand of our enemies; when he shall make us a praise and glory that men shall say of succeeding plantations, "the Lord make it like that of New England." For we must consider that we shall be as a city upon a hill.[25] The eyes of all people are upon us, so that if we shall deal falsely with our God in this work we have undertaken, and so cause him to withdraw his present help from us, we shall be made a story and a by-word through the world. We shall open the mouths of enemies to speak evil of the ways of God and all professors for God's sake. We shall shame the faces of many of God's worthy servants, and cause their prayers to be turned into curses upon us 'til we be consumed out of the good land whither we are going. And to shut up this discourse with that exhortation of Moses, that faithful

[20] In I Samuel 15:1–34 God ordered Saul to destroy the Amalekites and all they possessed, but Saul spared their sheep and oxen and so disobeyed God.

[21] A legal contract in which God offers protection to those who faithfully abide by His word.

[22] Undertake.

[23] A paraphrase of Micah 6:8, the words of the eighth-century B.C. prophet Micah: " . . . what doth the Lord require of thee, but to do justly, and to love mercy, and to walk humbly with thy God?"

[24] Ephesians 4:3.

[25] "Ye are the light of the world. A city that is set on a hill cannot be hid. Neither do men light a candle, and put it under a bushel, but on a candlestick; and it giveth light unto all that are in the house," from Matthew 5:14–15.

servant of the Lord, in his last farewell to Israel, Deut 30.[26] Beloved, there is now set before us life and good, death and evil, in that we are commanded this day to love the Lord our God, and to love one another, to walk in his ways and to keep his commandments and his ordinance, and his laws, and the articles of our covenant with him, that we may live and be multiplied, and that the Lord our God may bless us in the land whither we go to possess it. But if our hearts shall turn away so that we will not obey, but shall be seduced, and worship other gods, our pleasures and profits, and serve them; it is propounded unto us this day, we shall surely perish out of the good land whither we pass over this vast sea to possess it.

> Therefore let us choose life,[27]
> that we and our seed
> may live by obeying his
> voice and cleaving to him,
> for he is our life and
> our prosperity.

1630, 1838

from JOURNAL OF JOHN WINTHROP*

from VOLUME I

[*October 21, 1636*]

One Mrs. Hutchinson,[1] a member of the church of Boston, a woman of a ready wit and bold spirit, brought over with her two dangerous errors: 1. That the person of the Holy Ghost dwells in a justified[2] person. 2. That no sanctification can help to evidence to us our justification.—From these two grew many branches; as, 1, Our union with the Holy Ghost, so as a Christian remains dead to every spiritual action, and hath no gifts nor graces, other than such as are in hypocrites, nor any other sanctification but the Holy Ghost himself.

[26] "And it shall come to pass, when all these things are come upon come thee, the blessing and the curse, which I have set before thee, and thou shalt call them to mind among all the nations, whither the Lord thy God hath driven thee, and shalt return unto the Lord thy God, and shalt obey his voice according to all that I command thee this day, thou and thy children, with all thine heart, and with all thy soul; that then the Lord thy God will turn thy captivity, and have compassion upon thee, and will return and gather thee from all the nations, whither the Lord thy God hath scattered thee," from Deuteronomy 30:1–3.

[27] " . . . I have set before you life and death, blessing and cursing: therefore, choose life, that both thou and thy seed may live . . . ," from Deuteronomy 30:19.

* Parts of Winthrop's history were published as *Journal* in 1790; it was published in entirety as *The History of New England* from 1825 to 1826.

[1] Anne Hutchinson (1591–1643), whose antinomianism, a belief that the elect communicate personally with God and therefore do not need to interpret church doctrine, caused her to be convicted of heresy and eventually banished from the Massachusetts Bay Colony in 1637.

[2] A person chosen by God for salvation.

There joined with her in these opinions a brother of hers, one Mr. Wheelwright,[3] a silenced[4] minister sometimes in England.

[*October 25, 1636*]

The other ministers in the bay, hearing of these things, came to Boston at the time of a general court, and entered conference in private with them, to the end they might know the certainty of these things; that if need were, they might write to the church of Boston about them, to prevent (if it were possible) the dangers, which seemed hereby to hang over that and the rest of the churches. At this conference, Mr. Cotton[5] was present, and gave satisfaction to them, so as he agreed with them all in the point of sanctification, and so did Mr. Wheelwright; so as they all did hold, that sanctification did help to evidence justification. The same he had delivered plainly in public, diverse times; but, for the indwelling of the person of the Holy Ghost, he held that still, as some others of the ministers did, but not union with the person of the Holy Ghost, (as Mrs. Hutchinson and others did,) so as to amount to a personal union.

Mr. Cotton, being requested by the general court, with some other ministers, to assist some of the magistrates in compiling a body of fundamental laws, did this court, present a model of Moses his judicials, compiled in an exact method, which were taken into further consideration till the next general court.

[*October 30, 1636*]

Some of the church of Boston, being of the opinion of Mrs. Hutchinson, had labored to have Mr. Wheelwright to be called to be a teacher there. It was propounded the last Lord's day, and was moved again this day for resolution. One[6] of the church stood up and said, he could not consent, etc. His reason was, because the church being well furnished already with able ministers, whose spirits they knew, and whose labors God had blessed in much love and sweet peace, he thought it not fit (no necessity urging) to put the welfare of the church to the least hazard, as he feared they should do, by calling in one, whose spirit they knew not, and one who seemed to dissent in judgment, and instanced in two points, which he delivered in a late exercise there; 1. That a believer was more than a creature. 2. That the person of the Holy Ghost and a believer were united. Hereupon the governour spake, that he marvelled at this, seeing Mr. Cotton had lately approved his doctrine. To this Mr. Cotton answered, that he did not remember the first, and desired Mr. Wheelwright to explain his meaning. He denied not the points, but showed upon what occasion he delivered them. Whereupon, there being an endeavor to make a reconciliation, the first replied, that, although Mr. Wheelwright

---

[3] John Wheelwright (1592?–1662), a minister and Hutchinson's brother-in-law.
[4] Wheelwright is believed to have refused to swear loyalty to the Church of England.
[5] John Cotton (1584–1652), the Puritan clergyman whom Anne Hutchinson had followed.
[6] Most likely Winthrop himself.

and himself might likely agree about the point, and though he thought reverendly of his godliness and abilities, so as he could be content to live under such a ministry; yet, seeing he was apt to raise doubtful disputations, he could not consent to choose him to that place. Whereupon the church gave way, that he might be called to a new church, to be gathered at Mount Woollaston, now Braintree.[7]

* * *

[*November 1, 1637*]

The court also sent for Mrs. Hutchinson, and charged her with diverse matters, as her keeping two public lectures every week in her house, whereto sixty or eighty persons did usually resort, and for reproaching most of the ministers (viz., all except Mr. Cotton) for not preaching a covenant of free grace,[8] and that they had not the seal of the spirit, nor were able ministers of the New Testament; which were clearly proved against her, though she sought to shift it off.[9] And, after many speeches to and fro, at last she was so full as she could not contain, but vented her revelations;[10] amongst which this was one, that she had it revealed to her, that she should come into New England, and should here be persecuted, and that God would ruin us and our posterity, and the whole state, for the same. So the court proceeded and banished her; but, because it was winter, they committed her to a private house,[11] where she was well provided, and her own friends and the elders permitted to go to her, but none else.

The court called also Capt. Underhill,[12] and some five or six more of the principal, whose hands were to the said petition; and because they stood to justify it, they were disfranchised, and such as had public places were put from them.

The court also ordered, that the rest, who had subscribed the petition, (and would not acknowledge their fault, and which near twenty of them did,) and some others, who had been chief stirrers in these contentions, etc., should be disarmed. This troubled some of them very much, especially because they were to bring them in themselves; but at last, when they saw no remedy, they obeyed.[13]

All the proceedings of this court against these persons were set down at large, with the reasons and other observations, and were sent into England to be published there, to the end that all our godly friends might not be discouraged from coming to us, etc.[14]

---

[7] Savage's note: "A later hand, I suspect [Cotton] Mather's, wrote the last two words."

[8] Anne Hutchinson argued that, if grace is a gift of God, ministers teaching that God's grace can be earned by good behavior are incorrect.

[9] To qualify her statements.

[10] God, Hutchinson believed, spoke directly to her and sent her special revelations.

[11] In Roxbury, Massachusetts, now a suburb of Boston.

[12] Captain John Underhill (1597?–1672), later a governor of the Dover Colony (New Hampshire).

[13] They were forbidden, too, "to buy or borrow any guns, swords, pistols, powder, shot, or match, until this court shall take further order therein."

[14] Savage's note: "In the margin was written, in a hand I thought to be Cotton Mather's, 'This was printed by Mr. Wells about seven years after.' " "Mr. Wells" was Thomas Welde (1590?–1662), author of "A Short Story of the Rise, Reign, and Ruin of the Antinomians, Familiasts & Libertines" (1644).

[*Winter 1637–1638*]

Upon occasion of the censures of the court upon Mrs. Hutchinson and others, diverse other foul errors were discovered, which had been secretly carried by way of inquiry, but after were maintained by Mrs. Hutchinson and others; and so many of Boston were tainted with them, as Mr. Cotton, finding how he had been abused, and made (as himself said) their stalking horse, (for they pretended to hold nothing but what Mr. Cotton held, and himself did think the same,) did spend most of his time, both publicly and privately, to discover those errors, and to reduce such as were gone astray. And also the magistrates, calling together such of the elders as were near, did spend two days in consulting with them about the way to help the growing evils.

Some of the secret opinions were these:—

That there is no inherent righteousness in a child of God.

That neither absolute nor conditional promises belong to a Christian.

That we are not bound to the law, not as a rule, etc.

That the Sabbath is but as other days.

That the soul is mortal, till it be united to Christ, and then it is annihilated, and the body also, and a new given by Christ.

That there is no resurrection of the body.

[*February 1638*]

Diverse gentlemen and others, being joined in a military company, desired to be made a corporation, etc. But the council, considering (from the example of the Pretorian band among the Romans, and the Templars[15] in Europe) how dangerous it might be to erect a standing authority of military men, which might easily, in time, overthrow the civil power, thought fit to stop it betimes. Yet they were allowed to be a company, but subordinate to all authority.

About this time the Indians, which were in our families, were much frightened with Hobbamock (as they call the devil) appearing to them in diverse shapes, and persuading them to forsake the English, and not to come at the assemblies, nor to learn to read, etc.

[*February 26, 1638*]

Mr. Peirce,[16] in the Salem ship, the Desire, returned from the West Indies after seven months. He had been at Providence, and brought some cotton, and tobacco, and negroes, etc., from thence, and salt from Tertugos.[17] Dry fish and strong liquors are the only commodities for those parts. He met there two men-of-war, set forth by the lords, etc., of Providence with letters of mart, who had taken diverse prizes from the Spaniard, and many negroes.

---

[15] A medieval Christian military order, the Knights Templars.
[16] Captain William Peirce (1592?–1641), a ship's captain, who may have brought slaves for sale.
[17] Tortuga Island, in the West Indies.

[*March 1638*]

While Mrs. Hutchinson continued at Roxbury, diverse of the elders and others resorted to her, and finding her to persist in maintaining those gross errors before-mentioned, and many others, to the number of thirty or thereabout, some of them wrote to the church at Boston, offering to make proof of the same before the church, etc., 15; whereupon she was called, (the magistrates being desired to give her license to come,) and the lecture was appointed to begin at ten. (The general court being then at Newtown, the governour[18] and the treasurer, being members of Boston, were permitted to come down, but the rest of the court continued at Newtown.) When she appeared, the errors were read to her. The first was, that the souls of men are mortal by generation,[19] but, after, made immortal by Christ's purchase. This she maintained a long time; but at length she was so clearly convinced by reason and scripture, and the whole church agreeing that sufficient had been delivered for her conviction, that she yielded she had been in an error. Then they proceeded to three other errors: 1. That there was no resurrection of these bodies, and that these bodies were not united to Christ, but every person united hath a new body, etc. These were also clearly confuted, but yet she held her own; so as the church (all but two of her sons) agreed she should be admonished, and because her sons would not agree to it, they were admonished also.

Mr. Cotton pronounced the sentence of admonition with great solemnity, and with much zeal and detestation of her errors and pride of spirit. The assembly continued till eight at night, and all did acknowledge the special presence of God's spirit therein; and she was appointed to appear again the next lecture day.

* * *

[*March 22, 1638*]

Mrs. Hutchinson appeared again; (she had been licensed by the court, in regard she had given hope of her repentance, to be at Mr. Cotton's house, that both he and Mr. Davenport[20] might have the more opportunity to deal with her;) and the articles being again read to her, and her answer required, she delivered it in writing, wherein she made a retractation of near all, but with such explanations and circumstances as gave no satisfaction to the church; so as she was required to speak further to them. Then she declared, that it was just with God to leave her to herself, as he had done, for her slighting his ordinances, both magistracy and ministry;[21] and confessed that what she had spoken against the magistrates at the court (by way of revelation) was rash and ungrounded; and desired the church to pray for her. This gave the church good hope of her repentance; but when she was examined about some particulars, as that she had denied inherent righteousness,[22] etc., she affirmed that it was never her judgment; and though it was proved by many testimonies, that she had been of that judgment, and so had persisted, and maintained it by argument against diverse, yet she impudently persisted in her

---

[18] Winthrop.   [19] From the beginning.   [20] John Davenport (1597–1670), a Puritan minister.
[21] Her beliefs violated both civil and religious laws.
[22] She taught that righteousness is not inherent to humans but only to Christ.

affirmation, to the astonishment of all the assembly. So that, after much time and many arguments had been spent to bring her to see her sin, but all in vain, the church, with one consent, cast her out. Some moved to have her admonished once more; but, it being for manifest evil in matter of conversation, it was agreed otherwise; and for that reason also the sentence was denounced[23] by the pastor, matter of manners[24] belonging properly to his place.

After she was excommunicated,[25] her spirits, which seemed before to be somewhat dejected, revived again, and she gloried in her sufferings, saying, that it was the greatest happiness, next to Christ, that ever befel her. Indeed, it was a happy day to the churches of Christ here, and to many poor souls, who had been seduced by her, who, by what they heard and saw that day, were (through the grace of God) brought off quite from her errors, and settled again in the truth.

At this time the good providence of God so disposed, diverse of the congregation (being the chief men of the party, her husband being one) were gone to Naragansett[26] to seek out a new place for plantation, and taking liking of one in Plimouth patent, they went thither to have it granted them; but the magistrates there, knowing their spirit, gave them a denial, but consented they might buy of the Indians an island in the Naragansett Bay.[27]

After two or three days, the governour sent a warrant to Mrs. Hutchinson to depart this jurisdiction before the last of this month, according to the order of court, and for that end set her at liberty from her former constraint, so as she was not to go forth of her own house till her departure; and upon the 28th she went by water to her farm at the Mount, where she was to take water, with Mr. Wheelwright's wife and family, to go to Pascataquack; but she changed her mind, and went by land to Providence, and so to the island in the Naragansett Bay, which her husband and the rest of that sect had purchased of the Indians, and prepared with all speed to remove unto. For the court had ordered, that, except they were gone with their families by such a time, they should be summoned to the general court, etc.

[*September 1638*]

Mrs. Hutchinson, being removed to the Isle of Aquiday,[28] in the Naragansett Bay, after her time was fulfilled, that she expected deliverance of a child, was delivered of a monstrous birth, which, being diversely related in the country, (and, in the open assembly at Boston, upon a lecture day, declared by Mr. Cotton to be twenty-seven several lumps of man's seed, without any alteration, or mixture of any thing from the woman, and thereupon gathered, that it might signify her error in denying inherent righteousness, but that all was Christ in us, and nothing of ours in our faith, love, etc.) hereupon the governour wrote to Mr. Clarke,[29] a physician and a preacher to those of the island, to know the certainty thereof . . . .

---

[23] Proclaimed.
[24] She was sentenced by the pastor of the Boston church (John Wilson) rather than by a civil magistrate because she was found guilty of violating moral behavior, or manners, by speaking untruths.
[25] Banished; not excommunicated in the sense of the Roman Catholic Church.
[26] Part of Rhode Island.   [27] Now Rhode Island.   [28] Aquidneck, now part of Rhode Island.
[29] John Clarke (1609–1676), a Baptist clergyman and physician and a founder of Rhode Island.

from VOLUME II

[*June 21, 1641*]

Mrs. Hutchinson and those of Aquiday island broached new heresies every year. Diverse of them turned professed anabaptists,[30] and would not wear any arms, and denied all magistracy among christians, and maintained that there were no churches since those founded by the apostles and evangelists, nor could any be, nor any pastors ordained, nor seals[31] administered but by such, and that the church was to want[32] these all the time she[33] continued in the wilderness, as yet she was. Her son Francis and her son-in-law Mr. Collins (who was driven from Barbadoes where he had preached a time and done some good, but so soon as he came to her was infected with her heresies) came to Boston, and were there sent for to come before the governour and council. But they refused to come, except they were brought; so the officer led him, and being come (there were diverse of the elders present) he was charged with a letter he had written to some in our jurisdiction, wherein he charged all our churches and ministers to be antichristian, and many other reproachful speeches, terming our king, king of Babylon, and sought to possess the people's hearts with evil thoughts of our government and of our churches, etc. He acknowledged the letter, and maintained what he had written, yet sought to evade by confessing there was a true magistracy in the world, and that christians must be subject to it. He maintained also that there were no gentile churches (as he termed them) since the apostles' times, and that none now could ordain ministers, etc. Francis Hutchinson did agree with him in some of these, but not resolutely in all; but he had reviled the church of Boston (being then a member of it) calling her a strumpet. They were both committed to prison; and it fell out that one Stoddard,[34] being then one of the constables of Boston, was required to take Francis Hutchinson into his custody till the afternoon, and said withal to the governour, Sir, I came to observe what you did, that if you should proceed with a brother otherwise than you ought, I might deal with you in a church way. For this insolent behavior he was committed, but being dealt with by the elders and others, he came to see his error, which was that he did conceive that the magistrate ought not to deal with a member of the church before the church had proceeded with him. So the next Lord's day in the open assembly, he did freely and very affectionately confess his error and his contempt of authority, and being bound to appear at the next court, he did the like there to the satisfaction of all. Yet for example's sake he was fined 20*s.*,[35] which though some of the magistrates would have had it much less, or rather remitted, seeing his clear repentance and satisfaction in public left no poison or danger in his example, nor had the commonweath or any person sustained danger by it. At the same court Mr. Collins was fined £100[36] and Francis Hutchinson £50, and to remain in prison till they gave security for it. We assessed the fines the higher, partly that by occasion thereof they might be the

---

[30] A religious group who urged the separation of church and state, would not bear arms, and believed that religious matters are not under civil authority; their name stems from their objection to infant baptism.

[31] The Puritan sacraments of baptism and the Lord's Supper.   [32] Lack.   [33] The church.

[34] Anthony Stoddard (?–1684), father of the famous clergyman Solomon Stoddard.

[35] Twenty shillings.   [36] One hundred pounds.

longer kept in from doing harm, (for they were kept close prisoners,) and also because that family had put the country to so much charge in the synod and other occasions to the value of £500 at least: but after, because the winter drew on, and the prison was inconvenient, we abated them to £40 and £20. But they seemed not willing to pay any thing. They refused to come to the church assemblies except they were led, and so they came duly. At last we took their own bonds for their fine, and so dismissed them.

[*September 1643*]

The Indians near the Dutch, having killed 15 men, as is before related, proceeded on and began to set upon the English who dwelt under the Dutch. They came to Mrs. Hutchinson's[37] in way of friendly neighborhood, as they had been accustomed, and taking their opportunity, killed her and Mr. Collins, her son-in-law, (who had been kept prisoner in Boston, as is before related,) and all her family, and such of Mr. Throckmorton's and Mr. Cornhill's families as were at home; in all sixteen, and put their cattle into their houses and there burnt them. By a good providence of God, there was a boat came in there at the same instant, to which some women and children fled, and so were saved, but two of the boatmen going up to the houses were shot and killed.

These people had cast off ordinances and churches, and now at last their own people, and for larger accommodation had subjected themselves to the Dutch and dwelt scatteringly near a mile asunder: and some that escaped, who had removed only for want (as they said) of hay for their cattle which increased much, now coming back again to Aquiday, they wanted cattle for their grass. . . .

1630–1649; 1790, 1825–1826

Roger Williams
(1603?–1683)

Roger Williams was a thorn in the side of leaders from the Massachusetts Bay and Plymouth Colonies and of all Puritans who believed themselves endowed with a special covenant from God to settle New England. A determined and convincing dissenter, Williams defended liberty of conscience and the strict separation of church and state. When his beliefs got him in trouble, he founded the colony of Rhode Island. However, his arguments with John Winthrop, William Bradford, and many other Puritans should not be seen as anticipating the more liberal and humanistic discussions of the Revolution's founders

---

[37] Hutchinson had moved from Rhode Island to Long Island in 1642 after her husband's death. She was killed in a Native-American attack on what is now Pelham Bay.

during the eighteenth century. Rather, Williams's arguments stemmed from the strictness of his Puritanism and from his steadfast belief in the frailty and depravity of human actions on earth. Williams's scepticism about the Puritans' ambitions allowed him to become one of the first European immigrants to investigate and appreciate the original Native-American inhabitants of the region and to report on their language and culture.

Born most likely in 1603, Williams was the son of a tailor and textile merchant from Smithfield, on the outskirts of London. As a young man Williams caught the eye of the famous lawyer Sir Edward Coke, who supported Williams's education until he graduated from Cambridge University in 1627. No doubt influenced by Coke, Williams perfected his debating skills and throughout his life employed them often. In his employment, Williams also had a privileged view of the battles between England's largely Puritan Parliament and King Charles I over the king's authority to rule versus the right to religious freedom. In 1629 Williams, choosing religious freedom, talked of his late call to New England: he and his new wife, Mary Barnard, a housemaid, left aboard the *Lyon* in December 1630 for the Massachusetts Bay Colony, following John Winthrop's ship, the *Arbella,* which had left in March 1630.

Williams's commitment to religious freedom and especially to his belief in completely separating religious matters from earthly politics soon got him in trouble in the Massachusetts Bay Colony, which was still officially associated with the Church of England and thus tied to the king. At first Williams refused simply to accept the ministry in a non-Separatist Boston church, but as minister of the Salem church he was brought before the Massachusetts General Court in July 1635 and again in October, accused of "new and dangerous opinions against the authority of magistrates." Williams's opinions were indeed dangerous to the new colony. He argued that Native Americans were the true owners of the land, the king's charter being invalid, and that the jurisdiction of the civil magistrates extended only to the colonists' bodies, belongings, and outward state, not to their religious beliefs. His arguments undermined the basis of the theocentric government outlined in Winthrop's "A Model of Christian Charity" (1630; not published until 1838). Williams's intent was not to protect the current political system but to keep religion free from secular meddling. Learning that Winthrop and others intended to send him back to England, Williams fled to what is now Rhode Island, where he founded its first settlement, Providence, in 1636.

Under Williams's guidance Rhode Island became a haven for other religious dissenters. Anne Hutchinson, who held religious meetings at her house, was exiled there from Massachusetts in 1637, and later came Baptists, Seekers, Jews, and Quakers, all in search of religious freedom. Williams traveled to England in 1643 to obtain from the new Puritan government a charter for a Rhode Island colony, "Providence Plantations." Of great help to him in getting support for the colony was his friend Sir Henry Vane and the book Williams had published about the Narragansett Indians, *A Key Into the Language of America* (1643). Unlike the Pilgrims and Puritans, who were either generally hostile to Native Americans or wished to convert them to Christianity, Williams wanted his book to help the colonists converse with the Narragansetts and, according to its preface, "by such converse it may please the Father of Mercies to spread civilitie, (and in his owne most holy season) Christianitie." Although Williams's friendship with the Narragansetts had aided the colonies in their success against the warring Pequot Indians in 1637, he was able to achieve a remarkable degree of sympathy for, and understanding of, Native Americans. His belief that no nation has a special divine blessing from God, so that the Narragansetts were not inferior to, and no more or less depraved than, any other people (including the Puritans), was too controversial for his time.

A Key Into the Language of America is both a life history of the Narragansetts and a dictionary, translating common Native-American phrases into their English equivalents. These translations are followed by observations, based on Williams's personal experiences, about the Narragansetts' customs. A final, moral observation typically aimed at the settlers follows. For example, "It is a strange truth that a man shall generally finde more free entertainment and refreshing amongst these Barbarians, than amongst thousands that call themselves Christians." Williams's evident respect for the Narragansetts led him to mediate between the English settlers and Native Americans, especially during the Pequot War (1637) and King Philip's War (1675–1676).

From his home in Rhode Island Williams continued through most of his life to debate with the Massachusetts Bay Colony about the relationship between church and state. In the treatises *The Bloody Tenet of Persecution* (1644) and *The Bloody Tenet Yet More Bloody* (1652), largely attacks on the religious leader John Cotton, Williams argues that a magistrate's position, although "an Ordinance of God," has only those powers delegated by the people. Although it proved an unconvincing argument at the time, Williams's belief eventually became the central tenet of the U.S. Constitution and has made him the most famous dissenter of Puritan America. After returning from a trip to England in 1652, he served three terms as Rhode Island's governor. He was saddened in his last years by religious disputes and by having to side against the Narragansetts during King Philip's War. Williams died in 1683, having remained to the end a leader both of religious and of secular matters.

Suggested Readings: *The Complete Writings of Roger Williams*, 6 vols., ed. J. H. Trumball et al., 1866–1874; additional vol. ed. P. Miller, 1963. *The Correspondence of Roger Williams*, 2 vols., ed. G. LaFantasie, 1988. P. Miller, *Roger Williams*, 1953. E. S. Morgan, *Roger Williams: The Church and the State*, 1967. I. Polishook, ed., *Roger Williams, John Cotton, and Religious Freedom*, 1967.

Texts Used: *A Key Into the Language of America:* reprint of first edition, 1643, The Rhode Island and Providence Tercentenary Committee, 1936. *The Bloody Tenet of Persecution* and "A Letter to the Town of Providence": *The Complete Writings of Roger Williams*, Vol. III. (Some spelling and punctuation modernized.)

from A KEY INTO THE LANGUAGE OF AMERICA*

To My Dear and Well-Beloved Friends and Countrymen, in Old and New England

I present you with a Key; I have not heard of the like, yet framed, since it pleased God to bring that mighty continent of America to light. Others of my countrymen have often, and excellently, and lately written of the country (and none that I know beyond the goodness and worth of it).

This Key, respects the native language of it, and happily may unlock some rarities concerning the natives themselves, not yet discovered.

I drew the materials in a rude lump at sea, as a private help to my own memory, that I might not by my present absence lightly lose what I had so dearly bought in some few years hardship, and charges among the barbarians. Yet being reminded by some, what pity it were to bury those materials in my grave at land or sea; and

---

* Williams wrote this book primarily as a dictionary of the language of the Narragansett Indians; it also includes a series of verses praising the Narragansetts and admonishing the European settlers.

withal, remembering how oft I have been importuned by worthy friends, of all sorts, to afford them some helps this way.

I resolved (by the assistance of The Most High) to cast those materials into this Key, pleasant and profitable for all, but specially for my friends residing in those parts.

A little Key may open a box, where lies a bunch of keys.

With this I have entered into the secrets of those countries, wherever English dwell about two hundred miles, between the French and Dutch plantations; for want of this, I know what gross mistakes myself and others have run into.

There is a mixture of this language North and South, from the place of my abode, about six hundred miles; yet within the two hundred miles (aforementioned) their dialects do exceedingly differ; yet not so, but (within that compass) a man may, by this help, converse with thousands of natives all over the country: and by such converse it may please the Father of Mercies to spread civility, (and in his own most holy season) Christianity. For one candle will light ten thousand, and it may please God to bless a little leaven to season the mighty lump of those peoples and territories.

It is expected, that having had so much converse with these natives, I should write some little of them.

Concerning them (a little to gratify expectation) I shall touch upon four heads:

First, by what names they are distinguished.

Secondly, their original[1] and descent.

Thirdly, their religion, manners, customs, etc.

Fourthly, that great point of their conversion.

To the first, their names are of two sorts:

First, those of the English giving: as natives, savages, Indians, wildmen, (so the Dutch call them *wilden*) Abergeny[2] men, pagans, barbarians, heathen.

Secondly, their names which they give themselves.

I cannot observe that they ever had (before the coming of the English, French or Dutch amongst them) any names to difference themselves from strangers, for they knew none; but two sorts of names they had, and have amongst themselves:

First, general, belonging to all natives, as Nínnuock, Ninnimissinnûwock, Eniskeetompaûwog, which signifies Men, Folk, or People.

Secondly, particular names, peculiar to several nations, of them amongst themselves, as Nanhigganêuck, Massachusêuck, Cawasumsêuck, Cowwesêuck, Quintikóock, Qunnipiêuck, Pequttóog, etc.

They have often asked me, why we call them Indians, natives, etc. And understanding the reason, they will call themselves Indians, in opposition to English, etc.

For the second head proposed, their original and descent:

From Adam and Noah[3] that they spring, it is granted on all hands.

But for their later descent, and whence they came into those parts, it seems as hard to find, as to find the wellhead of some fresh stream, which running many miles out of the country to the salt ocean, hath met with many mixing streams by the way. They say themselves, that they have sprung and grown up in that very place, like the very trees of the wilderness.

[1] Place of origin.

[2] Aboriginal; not the Pequots, Narragansetts, Connecticuts, or Mohawks.

[3] Adam, the first man; and Noah, who, with his family, was all that remained of humankind after the biblical flood.

They say that their great god Cautantowwit created those parts, as I observed in the chapter of their religion. They have no clothes, books, nor letters, and conceive their fathers never had; and therefore they are easily persuaded that the God that made Englishmen is a greater God, because He hath so richly endowed the English above themselves. But when they hear that about sixteen hundred years ago, England and the inhabitants thereof were like unto themselves, and since have received from God clothes, books, etc., hope concerning themselves.

Wise and judicious men, with whom I have discoursed, maintain their original to be northward from Tarataria:[4] and at my now taking ship, at the Dutch plantation, it pleased the Dutch Governor, (in some discourse with me about the natives), to draw their line from Iceland, because the name Sackmakan (the name for an Indian prince, about the Dutch) is the name for a prince in Iceland.

Other opinions I could number up: under favor I shall present (not my opinion, but) my observations to the judgment of the wise.

First, others (and myself) have conceived some of their words to hold affinity with the Hebrew.

Secondly, they constantly anoint their heads as the Jews did.

Thirdly, they give dowries for their wives, as the Jews did.

Fourthly (and which I have not so observed amongst other nations as amongst the Jews, and these:) they constantly separate their women (during the time of their monthly sickness) in a little house alone by themselves four or five days, and hold it an irreligious thing for either father or husband or any male to come near them.

They have often asked me if it be so with women of other nations, and whether they are so separated: and for their practice they plead nature and tradition. Yet again I have found a greater affinity of their language with the Greek tongue.

2. As the Greeks and other nations, and ourselves call the seven stars (or Charles' Wain, the bear,[5]) so do the Mosk or Paukunnawaw, the Bear.

3. They have many strange relations of one Wétucks, a man that wrought great miracles amongst them, and walking upon the waters, etc. with some kind of broken resemblance to the Son of God.

Lastly, it is famous that the Sowwest (Sowaniu) is the great subject of their discourse. From thence their traditions. There they say (at the Southwest) is the court of their great god Cautantowwit: at the Southwest are their forefathers' souls: to the Southwest they go themselves when they die; from the Southwest came their corn, and beans out of their great god Cautantowwit's field: and indeed the further northward and westward from us their corn will not grow, but to the southward better and better. I dare not conjecture in these uncertainties. I believe they are lost, and yet hope (in the Lord's holy season) some of the wildest of them shall be found to share in the blood of the Son of God. To the third head, concerning their religion, customs, manners, etc. I shall here say nothing, because in those 32 chapters of the whole book,[6] I have briefly touched those of all sorts, from their birth to their burials, and have endeavored (as the nature of the work would give way) to bring some short observations and applications home to Europe from America.

---

[4] Mongolia.
[5] The consellation Ursa Major, also called the Great Bear or Charlemagne's Wagon.
[6] All thirty-two chapters of the *Key*.

Therefore fourthly, to that great point of their conversion, so much to be longed for, and by all New-English so much pretended, and I hope in truth.

For myself I have uprightly labored to suit my endeavors to my pretenses: and of later times (out of desire to attain their language) I have run through varieties of intercourses[7] with them day and night, summer and winter, by land and sea, particular passages tending to this, I have related diverse, in the chapter of their religion.

Many solemn discourses I have had with all sorts of nations of them, from one end of the country to another (so far as opportunity, and the little language I have could reach).

I know there is no small preparation in the hearts of multitudes of them. I know their many solemn confessions to myself, and one to another of their lost wandering conditions.

I know strong convictions upon the consciences of many of them, and their desires uttered that way.

I know not with how little knowledge and grace of Christ the Lord may save, and therefore, neither will despair, nor report much.

But since it hath pleased some of my worthy countrymen to mention (of late in print[8]) Wequash, the Pequot captain, I shall be bold so far to second their relations, as to relate mine own hopes of him (though I dare not be so confident as others).

Two days before his death, as I passed up to Qunníhticut[9] River, it pleased my worthy friend Mr. Fenwick, (whom I visited at his house in Saybrook Fort at the mouth of that river,) to tell me that my old friend Wequash lay very sick. I desired to see him, and himself was pleased to be my guide two miles where Wequash lay.

Amongst other discourse concerning his sickness and death (in which he freely bequeathed his son to Mr. Fenwick) I closed with him concerning his soul: he told me that some two or three years before he had lodged at my house, where I acquainted him with the condition of all mankind, & his own in particular; how God created man and all things; how man fell from God, and of his present enmity against God, and the wrath of God against him until repentance. Said he, "your words were never out of my heart to this present;" and said he, "me much pray to Jesus Christ." I told him so did many English, French, and Dutch, who had never turned to God, nor loved Him. He replied in broken English: "Me so big naughty heart, me heart all one stone!" Savory expressions using to breathe from compunct and broken hearts, and a sense of inward hardness and unbrokenness. I had many discourses with him in his life, but this was the sum of our last parting until our general meeting.[10]

Now because this is the great inquiry of all men: what Indians have been converted? What have the English done in those parts? What hopes of the Indians receiving the knowledge of Christ?

And because to this question, some put an edge from the boast of the Jesuits in Canada and Maryland, and especially from the wonderful conversions made by the Spaniards and Portugals in the West Indies, besides what I have here written, as also, beside what I have observed in the chapter of their religion, I shall further

[7] Conversations.
[8] In *New England's First Fruits* (1643), a publicity tract published in London.
[9] Connecticut.   [10] Judgment Day.

present you with a brief additional discourse concerning this great point, being comfortably persuaded that Father of Spirits, who was graciously pleased to persuade Japhet[11] (the Gentiles) to dwell in the tents of Shem[12] (the Jews), will, in his holy season (I hope approaching) persuade these gentiles of America to partake of the mercies of Europe, and then shall be fulfilled what is written, by the prophet Malachi,[13] from the rising of the sun (in Europe) to the going down of the same (in America), my name shall be great among the Gentiles. So I desire to hope and pray,

Your unworthy countryman,

Roger Williams.

1634?, 1643

from   **THE BLOODY TENET OF PERSECUTION, FOR CAUSE OF CONSCIENCE***

INTRODUCTION

To every courteous reader.

While I plead the cause of truth and innocency against the bloody doctrine of persecution for cause of conscience, I judge it not unfit to give alarm to myself, and all men to prepare to be persecuted or hunted for cause of conscience.

Whether thou standest charged with ten or but two talents,[1] if thou huntest any for cause of conscience, how canst thou say thou followest the Lamb of God[2] who so abhorred that practice?

If Paul, if Jesus Christ were present here at London, and the question were proposed what religion would they approve of: the Papists, Prelatists,[3] Presbyterians, Independents, etc. would each say, "Of mine, of mine."

But put the second question, if one of the several sorts should by major vote attain the sword of steel: what weapons doth Christ Jesus authorize them to fight with in His cause? Do not all men hate the persecutor, and every conscience true or false complain of cruelty, tyranny? etc.

Two mountains of crying guilt lie heavy upon the backs of all that name the name of Christ in the eyes of Jews, Turks and Pagans.

First, the blasphemies of their idolatrous inventions, superstitions, and most unchristian conversations.

Secondly, the bloody, irreligious and inhumane oppressions and destructions under the mask or veil of the name of Christ, etc.

---

[11] Japheth, the youngest of Noah's three sons, believed by some to be the forefather of all Indo-Europeans (see Genesis 9:18).

[12] Noah's eldest son, from whom the Jews (Semites) originated.

[13] A fifth-century B.C. Hebrew prophet: "For, from the rising of the sun, even unto the going down of the same, my name shall be great among the Gentiles . . . ," from Malachi 1:11.

* This tract, whose full title is *The Bloody Tenet of Persecution, for Cause of Conscience, in a Conference Between Truth and Peace*, was written as a response to John Cotton (1584–1652), a Massachusetts Bay Colony minister who was instrumental in Williams's banishment from the colony and opposed Williams's "cause of conscience."

[1] Individuals.   [2] Jesus.   [3] Episcopalians.

O how like is the jealous Jehovah, the consuming fire to end these present slaughters in a greater slaughter of the holy witnesses? Revelation 11.

Six years preaching of so much truth of Christ (as that time afforded in King Edward's[4] days) kindles the flames of Queen Mary's[5] bloody persecutions.

Who can now but expect that after so many scores of years preaching and professing of more truth, and amongst so many great contentions amongst the very best of Protestants, a fiery furnace should be heat, and who sees not now the fires kindling?

I confess I have little hopes till those flames are over, that this discourse against the doctrine of persecution for cause of conscience should pass current (I say not amongst the wolves and lions, but even amongst the sheep of Christ themselves) yet *liberavi animam meam*,[6] I have not hid within my breast my soul's belief: and although sleeping on the bed either of the pleasures or profits of sin thou thinkest thy conscience bound to smite at him that dares to waken thee? Yet in the midst of all these civil and spiritual wars[7] I hope we shall agree in these particulars.

First, however, the proud (upon the advantage of an higher earth or ground) overlook the poor and cry out schismatics, heretics, etc. shall blasphemers and seducers escape unpunished, etc. Yet there is a sorer punishment in the gospel for despising of Christ than Moses, even when the despiser of Moses was put to death without mercy, Hebrews 10:28–29. "He that believeth not shall be damned," Mark 16:16.

Secondly, whatever worship, ministry, ministration, the best and purest are practiced without faith and true persuasion that they are the true institutions of God, they are sin, sinful worships, ministries, etc. And however in civil things we may be servants unto men, yet in divine and spiritual things the poorest peasant must disdain the service of the highest prince: "Be ye not the servants of men," I Corinthians 14.

Thirdly, without search and trial no man attains this faith and right persuasion, I Thessalonians 5, "Try all things."

In vain have English Parliaments permitted English Bibles in the poorest English houses, and the simplest man or woman to search the Scriptures, if yet against their soul's persuasion from the Scripture, they should be forced (as if they lived in Spain or Rome itself without the sight of a Bible) to believe as the Church believes.

Fourthly, having tried, we must hold fast, I Thessalonians 5, upon the loss of a crown, Revelation 13, we must not let go for all the flea bitings of the present afflictions, etc. having bought truth dear, we must not sell it cheap, not the least grain of it for the whole world, no not for the saving of souls, though our own most precious; least of all for the bitter sweetening of a little vanishing pleasure.

For a little puff of credit and reputation from the changeable breath of uncertain sons of men.

For the broken bags of riches on eagles' wings: For a dream of these, any or all of these which on our deathbed vanish and leave tormenting stings behind them:

---

[4] Edward VI (1537–1553), king of England and Ireland from 1547 until his death, allowed the Reformation to advance rapidly.

[5] Mary I, or Mary Tudor (1516–1558), queen of England from the death of her half-brother Edward VI in 1553 until her death, halted the advance of the Reformation and allowed many Protestants to be burned at the stake for their beliefs.

[6] "I have freed my soul" (Latin).   [7] England experienced a civil war in 1642.

oh, how much better is it from the love of truth, from the love of the Father of lights, from whence it comes, from the love of the Son of God, who is the way and the truth, to say as He, John 18:37: "For this end was I born, and for this end came I into the world that I might bear witness to the truth."

1643–1644, 1644

TO THE TOWN OF PROVIDENCE*

[*January 1655*]

That ever I should speak or write a tittle,[1] that tends to such an infinite liberty of conscience, is a mistake, and which I have ever disclaimed and abhorred. To prevent such mistakes, I shall at present only propose this case: there goes many a ship to sea, with many hundred souls in one ship, whose weal and woe is common, and is a true picture of a commonwealth, or a human combination or society.[2] It hath fallen out sometimes, that both Papists and Protestants, Jews and Turks, may be embarked in one ship; upon which supposal I affirm, that all the liberty of conscience, that ever I pleaded for, turns upon these two hinges—that none of the Papists, Protestants, Jews, or Turks be forced to come to the ship's prayers or worship, nor compelled from their own particular prayers or worship, if they practice any. I further add, that I never denied, that notwithstanding this liberty, the commander of this ship ought to command the ship's course, yea, and also command that justice, peace and sobriety be kept and practiced, both among the seamen and all the passengers. If any of the seamen refuse to perform their services, or passengers to pay their freight; if any refuse to help, in person or purse, towards the common charges or defense; if any refuse to obey the common laws and orders of the ship, concerning their common peace or preservation; if any shall mutiny and rise up against their commanders and officers; if any should preach or write that there ought to be no commanders or officers, because all are equal in Christ, therefore no masters nor officers, no laws nor orders, nor corrections nor punishments; I say, I never denied, but in such cases, whatever is pretended, the commander or commanders may judge, resist, compel and punish such transgressors, according to their deserts and merits. This if seriously and honestly minded, may, if it so please the Father of lights, let in some light to such as willingly shut not their eyes.

I remain studious of your common peace and liberty.

Roger Williams
1654–1655?; 1655, 1874

* This letter is Williams's reply, written upon his return to Providence from England in 1654, to those who argued that freedom of conscience leads to anarchy; the debate over civil restraint versus religious freedom divided the Providence community.

[1] A tiny bit.

[2] Here Williams is addressing a misinterpretation of his *The Bloody Tenet of Persecution* (1644) that Williams had suggested that violators of civil laws could not be prosecuted if they claimed cause of conscience.

Thomas Morton
(1579?–1647?)

Adventurer, Royalist, profiteer, attorney, and vigorous anti-Puritan, Thomas Morton endures in history and legend as one of America's earliest folk heroes. Born in England probably in 1579, Morton married the widow Alice Miller in 1621. He left for the colonies in 1624 on the *Unity* and established the trading post "Ma-re Mount" (Merry Mount), now Quincy, Massachusetts. His life since then is readable as comedy, tragedy, or an exercise in capitalistic libertarianism in conflict with the Pilgrims' and Puritans' narrow political, theological, and social values. Repeatedly harassed by the authorities, jailed, and deported, Morton eventually died in exile in Maine.

Morton's problems with the New England authorities, particularly with the Plymouth Separatists under William Bradford's leadership, began with the establishment of Merry Mount. There he traded whiskey and guns to Native Americans, in exchange for furs. An early expression of Yankee free enterprise between white settlers and Native Americans, repeated for the next two centuries to the ultimate disadvantage of both, Morton's trade with the natives incensed the Pilgrims as much for its financial success as for its threat to the religious bases of their fledgling colony. According to Bradford's *Of Plymouth Plantation* (first published in 1857), Merry Mount was the ultimate "den of iniquity," a place loud with the shouts of drunken revelers, scofflaws of all types, and supposedly civilized Christians cavorting openly with savages. In 1627 Morton had a giant Maypole built as the centerpiece for spring revels that included drinking, dancing, and frolicking. That Maypole proved Morton's undoing.

Early in 1628 the Pilgrims, outraged at so visible a display of pagan ritual and phallic imagery, sent armed men led by Captain Myles Standish to arrest Morton. Charged with selling guns to Native Americans, Morton was deported to England for trial. Acquitted, he returned to the colonies and settled in Salem, Massachusetts. In 1630 he was again arrested, in effect charged with being a public nuisance. Before deporting him to England again, the authorities made an example of him by placing him in stocks, confiscating his property, and burning down his house.

Acquitted again, Morton wisely avoided New England during the next decade, but his time was not passed idly. In the mid-1630s he began to write a history of the New England colonies. Resolved to clear his reputation, to encourage others to seek their fortune in New England's vast untracked lands, and to satirize Puritan manners and narrowmindedness, Morton completed *New English Canaan* in 1635; it was printed in Holland in 1637, achieving most of those purposes. *New English Canaan* is noteworthy for being one of the few surviving non-Puritan accounts of life in newly settled New England and for displaying a unique variety of genres and styles. In richly descriptive prose Morton sets out the enticements of settlement in New England to promote migrations. Yet, in a mix of learned prose and satiric verse divided between two of the volume's three books, he serves his adversaries their just desserts via uncomplimentary contrasts between them and Native Americans, whom he depicts as humane, trustworthy, and, in their closeness to nature, more ideally Christian than savage.

Predictably, the book angered Morton's Puritan foes, yet he returned to New England one more time. Arriving in Massachusetts in 1643 he was promptly arrested and jailed in Boston on his reputation alone. Released in 1645 he set out for Maine, where he died about 1647. Although his death went largely unnoticed, Morton's colorful exploits and challenges to Puritan authority have been preserved through *New England Canaan* as well as through the literary imagination of writers such as Nathaniel Hawthorne, Henry Wadsworth Longfellow, Stephen Vincent Benét, and Robert Lowell.

Suggested Readings: C. Adams, Jr., "Editor's Introduction" in *The New English Canaan of Thomas Morton*, 1883. D. F. Connors, *Thomas Morton*, 1969.

Text Used: *New English Canaan: Or, New Canaan, Containing an Abstract of New England, Composed in Three Books*, 1632 (some spelling and punctuation modernized).

from   NEW ENGLISH CANAAN*

from   BOOK II

from   Chapter I: The General Survey of the Country

In the month of June, *Anno Salutis*[1] 1622, it was my chance to arrive in the parts of New England with 30 servants and provision of all sorts fit for a plantation; and while our houses were building, I did endeavor to take a survey of the country. The more I looked, the more I liked it. And when I had more seriously considered of the beauty of the place, with all her fair endowments, I did not think that in all the known world it could be paralleled for so many goodly groves of trees, dainty fine round rising hillocks, delicate fair large plains, sweet crystal fountains, and clear running streams that twine in fine meanders through the meads,[2] making so sweet a murmuring noise to hear as would even lull the senses with delight asleep, so pleasantly do they glide upon the pebble stones, jetting most jocundly where they do meet, and hand in hand run down to Neptune's[3] court, to pay the yearly tribute which they owe to him as sovereign lord of all the springs. Contained within the volume of the land, [are] fowls in abundance, [and] fish in multitude. And [I] discovered, besides, millions of turtledoves on the green boughs, which sat pecking of the full ripe pleasant grapes that were supported by the lusty trees, whose fruitful load did cause the arms to bend: [among] which here and there dispersed, you might see lilies and of [sic] the Daphnean-tree,[4] which made the land to me seem paradise. For mine eye t'was Nature's masterpiece, her chiefest magazine[5] of all where lives her store. If this land be not rich, then is the whole world poor.

---

* This work, whose full title is *New English Canaan: Or, New Canaan, Containing an Abstract of New England, Composed in Three Books*, contains one book describing the natives; one, the beauty and natural resources of the region; and one, the settlers. Canaan is the Promised Land to the Israelites.

[1] In the year of our prosperity.   [2] Meadows.   [3] According to Roman myth, the sea god.
[4] A laurel tree; according to Greek myth, the nymph Daphne was changed into that tree.
[5] A warehouse.

from BOOK III

Chapter XIV: Of the Revels of New Canaan
[*The Incident at Merry Mount*]

The inhabitants of Passonagessit[1] (having translated the name of their habitation from that ancient savage name to Ma-re Mount,[2] and being resolved to have the new name confirmed for a memorial to after ages) did devise amongst themselves to have it performed in a solemn manner, with revels and merriment after the old English custom; [they] prepared to set up a Maypole upon the festival day of Philip and Jacob,[3] and therefore brewed a barrel of excellent beer and provided a case of bottles to be spent, with other good cheer, for all comers of that day. And because they would have it in a complete form, they had prepared a song fitting to the time and present occasion. And upon May Day they brought the Maypole to the place appointed, with drums, guns, pistols, and other fitting instruments for that purpose, and there erected it with the help of savages that came thither of purpose to see the manner of our revels. A goodly pine tree 80 foot long was reared up, with a pair of buckhorns nailed on somewhat near unto the top of it, where it stood as a fair seamark for directions how to find out the way to mine host[4] of Ma-re Mount.

And because it should more fully appear to what end it was placed there, they had a poem in readiness made, which was fixed to the Maypole, to show the new name confirmed upon that plantation, which, although it were made according to the occurrence of the time, it being enigmatically composed, puzzled the Separatists[5] most pitifully to expound it, which (for the better information of the reader) I have here inserted.

THE POEM
Rise Oedipus,[6] and, if thou canst, unfold
What means Charybdis[7] underneath the mold,
When Scylla[8] solitary on the ground
(Sitting in form of Niobe[9] was found,
Till Amphitrite's darling[10] did acquaint
Grim Neptune with a tenor of her plaint

---

[1] To the Massachusetts Indians, "Little neck of land," now part of Braintree, Massachusetts.

[2] The settlement was first named Mount Wollaston and then Merry Mount; only Morton called it Ma-re Mount, or "place by the sea."

[3] May Day, May 1, is the feast day of Saints Philip and James (Jacob, in Latin).

[4] Morton, referring to himself in the third person.

[5] The Plymouth colonists, who, unlike the other Puritans, had separated from the Church of England.

[6] According to Greek myth, Oedipus solved the riddle of the Sphinx.

[7] According to Greek myth, a perilous whirlpool off Sicily.

[8] According to Greek myth, a monster who dwelled in a cave opposite Charybdis and consumed sailors.

[9] According to Greek myth, a queen who wept for her slain fourteen children and was turned into a weeping stone.

[10] According to myth, Venus (Roman), the goddess of love and daughter of Amphitrite (Greek) and Neptune (Roman sea god; Poseidon to the Greeks); she complained that Scylla needs a lover.

And caused him send forth Triton[11] with the sound
Of trumpet loud, at which the seas were found
So full of protean[12] forms that the bold shore
Presented Scylla a new paramour
So strong as Sampson[13] and so patient
As Job[14] himself, directed thus, by fate,
To comfort Scylla so unfortunate.
I do profess, by Cupid's beauteous mother,[15]
Here's Scogan's choice[16] for Scylla, and none other;
Though Scylla's sick with grief, because no sign
Can there be found of virtue masculine.
Asclepius[17] come; I know right well
His labor's lost when you may ring her knell.
The fatal sisters'[18] doom none can withstand,
Nor Cytherea's[19] power, who points to land
With proclamation that the first of May
At Ma-re Mount shall be kept holiday.

The setting up of this Maypole was a lamentable spectacle to the precise[20] Separatists that lived at New Plymouth. They termed it an idol; yea, they called it the Calf of Horeb[21] and stood at defiance with the place, naming it Mount Dagon, threatening to make it a woeful mount and not a merry mount.

The riddle, for want of Oedipus,[22] they could not expound, only they made some explication of part of it and said it was meant by Samson Job, the carpenter of the ship that brought over a woman to her husband that had been there long before and thrived so well that he sent for her and her children to come to him, where shortly after he died; having no reason but because of the sound of those two words, when as (the truth is) the man they applied it to was altogether unknown to the author.

There was likewise a merry song made, which (to make their revels more fashionable) was sung with a chorus, every man bearing his part, which they performed in a dance, hand in hand about the Maypole, while one of the company sang and filled out the good liquor, like Ganymede[23] and Jupiter.[24]

---

[11] According to Greek myth, Poseidon's son, typically portrayed blowing on a conch shell.

[12] Changing; according to Greek myth, Proteus was a minor sea god who could change form at will.

[13] An Israelite known for his great strength; as the Philistines honored their god Dagon, Sampson destroyed their temple.

[14] An Old Testament patriarch, who endured much suffering but retained his faith in God.

[15] According to Roman myth, Venus, the goddess of love and mother of Cupid, the god of love.

[16] John Scogan (1442–1483), court jester to England's King Edward IV, was condemned to hang; given his choice of gallows trees Scogan escaped execution because he found no tree to his liking.

[17] According to Greek myth, the god of healing.

[18] According to Greek myth, the Fates—three women who decide human destiny.

[19] According to Greek myth, Aphrodite, the goddess of love.   [20] Pious.

[21] In Exodus 32 and Deuteronomy 9:16, the golden idol falsely worshipped by Israelites as their deliverer from Egypt.

[22] For ignorance.   [23] According to Roman myth, the cupbearer to the gods.

[24] According to Roman myth, the god of the skies; the chief god.

THE SONG

[*Chorus*]
Drink and be merry, merry, merry boys;
Let all your delight be in the Hymen's[25] joys;
Io[26] to Hymen, now the day is come,
About the merry Maypole take a room.
    Make green garlands bring bottles out
    And fill sweet nectar freely about.
    Uncover thy head and fear no harm,
    For here's good liquor to keep it warm.
Then drink and be merry, etc.
Io to Hymen, etc.
    Nectar is a thing assigned
    By the Deity's own mind
    To cure the heart oppressed with grief,
    And of good liquors is the chief.
Then drink, etc.
Io to Hymen, etc.
    Give to the melancholy man
    A cup or two of't now and then;
    This physic will soon revive his blood,
    And make him be of a merrier mood.
Then drink, etc.
Io to Hymen, etc.
    Give to the nymph that's free from scorn
    No Irish stuff nor Scotch over worn.[27]
    Lasses in beaver coats[28] come away,
    Ye shall be welcome to us night and day.
To drink and be merry, etc.
Io to Hymen, etc.

This harmless mirth made by young men (that lived in hope to have wives brought over to them, that would save them a labor to make a voyage to fetch any over) was much distasted of the precise Separatists that keep much ado about the tithe of mint and cummin,[29] troubling their brains more than reason would require about things that are indifferent,[30] and from that time [they] sought occasion against my honest host of Ma-re Mount, to overthrow his undertakings and to destroy his plantation quite and clean. But because they presumed [that] with their imaginary gifts (which they have out of Phaon's box[31]) they could expound hidden mysteries (to convince them of blindness as well in this as in other matters of more conse-

---

[25] According to Greek myth, god of marriage.   [26] Hail.
[27] Worn-out Irish or Scottish woolen cloth.   [28] Indian women.
[29] "Woe unto you, scribes and Pharisees, hypocrites! for ye pay tithe of mint, and anise, and cummin, and have omitted the weightier matters of the law, judgement, mercy and faith. . .," Matthew 23:23.
[30] Not important.
[31] According to Greek myth, Phaon was an old boatman whom Aphrodite rewarded with a box containing elixir that made him young.

quence), I will illustrate the poem, according to the true intent of the authors of these revels, so much distasted by those moles.

Oedipus is generally received[32] for the absolute reader of riddles, who is invoked; Scylla and Charybdis are two dangerous places for seamen to encounter, near unto Venice, and have been by poets formerly resembled to man and wife. The like license the author challenged for a pair of his nomination, the one lamenting for the loss of the other, as Niobe for her children. Amphitrite is an arm of the sea, by which the news was carried up and down of a rich widow, now to be taken up or laid down. By Triton is the fame spread that caused the suitors to muster (as it had been to Penelope[33] of Greece), and, the coast lying circular, all our passage to and fro is made more convenient by sea than land. Many aimed at this mark, but he that played Proteus best and could comply with her humor must be the man that would carry her; and he had need have Sampson's strength to deal with a Delilah,[34] and as much patience as Job that should come there, for a thing that I did observe in the lifetime of the former.

But marriage and hanging (they say) come by destiny, and Scogan's choice is better [than] none at all. He that played Proteus (with the help of Priapus[35]) put their noses out of joint, as the proverb is.

And this the whole company of the revelers at Ma-re Mount knew to be the true sense and exposition of the riddle that was fixed to the Maypole, which the Separatists were at defiance with. Some of them affirmed that the first institution thereof was in memory of a whore,[36] not knowing that it was a trophy erected at first in honor of Maia,[37] The Lady of Learning which they despise, vilifying the two universities[38] with uncivil terms, accounting what is there obtained by study is but unnecessary learning, not considering that learning does enable men's minds to converse with elements of a higher nature than is to be found within the habitation of the mole.

Chapter XV: Of a Great Monster Supposed to Be at Ma-re Mount; and the Preparation Made to Destroy It

The Separatists, envying the prosperity and hope of the plantation at Ma-re Mount (which they perceived began to come forward and to be in a good way for gain in the beaver trade), conspired together against mine host especially (who was the owner of that plantation) and made up a party against him and mustered up what aid they could, accounting of him as of a great monster.

Many threatening speeches were given out both against his person and his habitation, which they divulged should be consumed with fire. And taking advantage of the time when his company (which seemed little to regard their threats) were gone up unto the inlands to trade with the savages for beaver, they set upon my

---

[32] Understood.

[33] According to Greek myth, Odysseus's wife, approached by many suitors when he was away.

[34] In Judges 16, Sampson's betrayer.

[35] According to Greek and Roman myth, the god of fertility.

[36] The Separatists attributed the May Day celebration to Roman feasts honoring Flora, the goddess of flowers, to them a symbol of idolatry.

[37] According to Greek and Roman myth, the goddess of the spring, to whom sacrifices were offered in May.

[38] England's Oxford and Cambridge Universities; the Separatists hated classical studies.

honest host at a place called Wessaguscus,[1] where, by accident, they found him. The inhabitants there were in good hope of the subversion of the plantation at Ma-re Mount (which they principally aimed at) and the rather because mine host was a man that endeavored to advance the dignity of the Church of England, which they (on the contrary part) would labor to vilify with uncivil terms, inveighing against the sacred Book of Common Prayer[2] and mine host that used it in a laudable manner amongst his family as a practice of piety.

There he would be a means to bring sacks to their mill (such is the thirst after beaver), and [it] helped the conspirators to surprise mine host (who was there all alone), and they charged him (because they would [want to] seem to have some reasonable cause against him, to set a gloss upon[3] their malice) with criminal things, which indeed had been done by such a person, but was of their conspiracy. Mine host demanded of the conspirators who it was that was author of that information that seemed to be their ground for what they now intended. And because they answered they would not tell him, he as peremptorily replied that he would not say whether he had or he had not done as they had been informed.

The answer made no matter (as it seemed) whether it had been negatively or affirmatively made, for they had resolved what he would suffer because (as they boasted) they were now become the greater number; they had shaken off their shackles of servitude and were become masters and masterless people.

It appears they were like bears' whelps[4] in former time when mine host's plantation was of as much strength as theirs, but now (theirs being stronger) they (like overgrown bears) seemed monstrous. In brief, mine host must endure to be their prisoner until they could contrive it so that they might send him for England (as they said), there to suffer according to the merit of the fact which they intended to father upon him, supposing (belike) it would prove a heinous crime.

Much rejoicing was made that they had gotten their capital enemy (as they concluded him) whom they purposed to hamper in such sort that he should not be able to uphold his plantation at Ma-re Mount.

The conspirators sported themselves at my honest host, that meant them no hurt, and were so jocund that they feasted their bodies and fell to tippling as if they had obtained a great prize, like the Trojans when they had the custody of Epeios' pinetree horse.[5]

Mine host feigned grief and could not be persuaded either to eat or drink, because he knew emptiness would be a means to make him as watchful as the geese kept in the roman Capital,[6] whereon, the contrary part, the conspirators would be so drowsy that he might have an opportunity to give them a slip instead of a tester.[7]

Six persons of the conspiracy were set to watch him at Wessaguscus. But he kept waking, and in the dead of the night (one lying on the bed for further surety), up gets mine host and got to the second door that he was to pass, which (notwith-

---

[1] A trading post near Morton's at Merry Mount; now Weymouth, Massachusetts, it is where Morton was first captured by the pilgrims.

[2] Set forth by the Church of England, this was opposed by the Separatists and Puritans for being inadequately Protestant.

[3] To explain.   [4] Cubs.

[5] The wooden horse, crafted by Epeios, that the Greeks used to conquer Troy.

[6] By hissing, the geese ruined the Gauls' surprise attack on the Romans in 390 B.C.

[7] A counterfeit coin in place of a sixpence.

standing the lock) he got open and shut it after him with such violence that it affrighted some of the conspirators.

The word which was given with an alarm was, "Oh, he's gone, he's gone, what shall we do, he's gone!" The rest (half asleep) start up in amaze[8] and like rams, ran their heads one at another full butt in the dark.

Their grand leader, Captain Shrimp,[9] took on most furiously and tore his clothes for anger, to see the empty nest and their bird gone.

The rest were eager to have torn their hair from their heads, but it was so short that it would give them no hold.[10] Now Captain Shrimp though in the loss of this prize (which he accounted his masterpiece), all his honor would be lost forever.

In the meantime mine host was got home to Ma-re Mount through the woods, eight miles round about the head of the river Monatoquit that parted the two plantations, finding his way by the help of the lightning (for it thundered as he went terribly), and there he prepared powder, three pounds dried, for his present employment, and four good guns for him and the two assistants left at his house, with bullets of several sizes, three hundred or thereabouts, to be used if the conspirators should pursue him thither; and these two persons promised their aids in the quarrel and confirmed that promise with health in good *rosa solis*.[11]

Now Captain Shrimp, the first captain in the land (as he supposed), must do some new act to repair this loss and to vindicate his reputation, who had sustained blemish by this oversight, begins now to study how to repair or survive his honor; in this manner, calling of council, they conclude.

He takes eight persons more to him, and (like the nine worthies[12] of New Canaan) they embark with preparation against Ma-re Mount, where this monster of a man (as their phrase was) had his den; the whole number (had the rest not been from home) being but seven, would have given Captain Shrimp (a *quondam* drummer[13]) such a welcome as would have made him wish for a drum as big as Diogenes' tub,[14] that he might have crept into it out of sight.

Now the nine worthies are approached, and mine host prepared, having intelligence by a savage that hastened in love from Wessaguscus to give him notice of their intent.

One of mine host's men proved a craven; the other had proved his wits to purchase a little valor, before mine host had observed his posture.

The nine worthies coming before the den of this supposed monster (this seven-headed hydra,[15] as they termed him) and began, like Don Quixote[16] against the windmill, to beat a parley[17] and to offer quarter[18] (if mine host would yield), for they resolved to send him to England and bade him lay by[19] his arms.

But he (who was the son of a soldier), having taken up arms in his just defense, replied that he would not lay by those arms because they were so needful at sea, if

[8] Amazement.
[9] Captain Myles Standish (1584?–1656), the Plymouth Colony's short, red-faced military leader.
[10] The Separatists disapproved of long hair, fashionable at the time.   [11] A red cordial.
[12] In the Middle Ages, nine heroes and kings considered to be the ideal of the human conduct: Hector of Troy, Alexander the Great, Julius Caesar, Joshua, David, Judas Maccabeus, King Arthur, and Geoffrey of Boulogne.
[13] A former drummer and, therefore, a man of low military rank.
[14] A Greek philosopher (412?–323? B.C.), said to have lived in a tub.
[15] According to Greek myth, a seven-headed monster slain by Hercules.
[16] The unrealistic hero of the novel *Don Quixote* (1605, 1615) by Miguel de Cervantes (1547–1616).
[17] To call a conference by beating a drum.   [18] Clemency.   [19] Put down.

he should be sent over. Yet, to save the effusion of so much worthy blood as would have issued out of the veins of these 9 worthies of New Canaan if mine host should have played upon them out at his portholes (for they came within danger like a flock of wild geese, as if they had been tailed[20] one to another, as colts to be sold at a fair), mine host was content to yield upon quarter and did capitulate with them in what manner it should be for more certainty, because he knew what Captain Shrimp was.

He expressed that no violence should be offered to his person, none to his goods, nor any of his household, but that he should have his arms and what else was requisite for the voyage (which their herald returns[21]); it was agreed upon and should be performed.

But mine host no sooner had set open the door and issued out, but instantly Captain Shrimp and the rest of the worthies stepped to him, laid hold of his arms, and had him down; and so eagerly was every man bent against him (not regarding any agreement made with such a carnal man), that they fell upon him as if they would have eaten him; some of them were so violent that they would have a slice with scabbard,[22] and all for haste, until an old soldier (of the Queen's, as the proverb is) that was there by accident, clapped his gun under the weapons and sharply rebuked these worthies for their unworthy practices. So the matter was taken into more deliberate consideration.

Captain Shrimp and the rest of the nine worthies made themselves (by this outrageous riot) masters of mine host of Ma-re Mount and disposed of what he had at his plantation.

This they knew (in the eye of the savages) would add to their glory and diminish the reputation of mine honest host, whom they practiced to be rid of upon any terms, as willingly as if he had been the very Hydra of the time.

Chapter XVI: How the Nine Worthies Put Mine Host of Ma-re Mount Into the Enchanted Castle at Plymouth and Terrified Him With the Monster Briareus*

The nine worthies of New Canaan having now the law in their own hands (there being no general governor in the land, nor none of the separation[1] that regarded the duty they owe their sovereign, whose natural-born subjects they were, though translated out of[2] Holland, from whence they had learned to work all to their own ends and made a great show of religion but no humanity), for they were now to sit in council on the cause.

And much it stood mine honest host upon to be very circumspect and to take Eacus[3] to task for that his voice was more allowed of than both the other; and had not mine host confounded all the arguments that Eacus could make in their defense and confuted him that swayed the rest, they would have made him unable to drink in such manner of merriment any more. So that following this private coun-

---

[20] Tied.   [21] Reports.   [22] They mistakenly took their scabbards to be swords, in their haste.

* According to Greek myth, a one-hundred-armed sea giant who battled the gods; Morton is referring to one of his captors.

[1] The Separatists.   [2] Taken from.

[3] According to Greek myth, one of the judges in Hades, the Underworld; Morton is referring to Samuel Fuller (?–1633), one of Morton's prosecutors (with William Bradford and Myles Standish).

=CONTEXTS=

The Bay Psalm Book

The Whole Booke of Psalmes Faithfully Translated Into English Metre (1640) was the first book both written and printed in America. *The Bay Psalm Book*, as it is commonly known, was the product of as many as thirteen New England clergy-men—including Richard Mather (1596–1669), a prominent preacher and grandfather of Cotton Mather—who sought to provide a plain translation of the Hebrew Psalms into English. The preface was written by the Puritan leader John Cotton (1584–1652). With the Bible and John Bunyan's *The Pilgrim's Progress* (1674), the *Bay Psalm Book* was for two centuries one of the most popular books in New England.

Psalm 1

O Blessed man, that in th' advice
    Of wicked doth not walk:
Nor stand in sinners' way, nor sit
    In chair of scornful folk.
But in the law of Jehovah
    Is his longing delight:
And in his law doth meditate,
    By day and eke by night.
And he shall be like to a tree
    Planted by water-rivers:
That in his season yields his fruit,
    And his leaf never withers.
And all he doth, shall prosper well,
    The wicked are not so:
But they are like unto the chaff,
    Which wind drives to and fro.
Therefore shall not ungodly men,
    Rise to stand in the doom,
Nor shall the sinners with the just,
    In their assembly come.
For of the righteous men, the Lord
    Acknowledgeth the way:
But the way of ungodly men,
    Shall utterly decay.

Various New England clergymen, 1640

---

sel, given him by one that knew who ruled the roost, the hurricane ceased that else would split his pinnace.[4]

A conclusion was made and sentence given that mine host should be sent to England a prisoner. But when he was brought to the ships for that purpose, no man dared be so foolhardy as to undertake to carry him. So these worthies set

[4] Sunk his ship.

mine host upon an island, without gun, powder, or shot, or dog, or so much as a knife to get anything to feed upon, or any other clothes to shelter him with at winter than a thin suit which he had on at that time. Home he could not get to Ma-re Mount. Upon this island he stayed a month at least and was relieved by savages that took notice that mine host was a sachem[5] of Passonagessit, and would bring bottles of strong liquor to him and unite themselves into a league of brotherhood with mine host, so full of humanity are these infidels before those Christians.

From this place for England sailed mine host in a Plymouth ship (that came into the land to fish upon the coast) that landed him safe in England at Plymouth; and he stayed in England until the ordinary time for shipping to set forth for these parts, and then returned,[6] no man being able to tax[7] him of anything.

But the worthies (in the meantime) hoped they had been rid of him.

1634–1635?, 1637

Anne Bradstreet
(1612?–1672)

Anne Bradstreet was colonial America's earliest published poet, its first woman poet, and one of its most admired. Born Anne Dudley in Northampton, England, around 1612, she was the second of the six children of Thomas Dudley and Dorothy Yorke. By age four Anne was living on the estate of the earl of Lincoln, where her father was the chief steward. Her religious training began early. In an undated letter "To my dear children," written shortly before her death, she recalled that when she was six or seven she was conscious of her capacity for sin and had begun a lifelong practice of taking "comfort from the Scriptures." She was nine years old when she met her husband-to-be, Simon Bradstreet, a twenty-one-year-old Cambridge University graduate, who joined the household in 1621 as an aide to Dudley. In 1624 the Dudleys moved to Boston, England. When she was sixteen she had smallpox, recovered, and married Simon Bradstreet. Although the marriage was probably arranged, it was by all accounts, especially Anne Bradstreet's, an extraordinarily happy one.

The Bradstreets and the Dudleys were among the Puritan dissenters in England who were the target of the anti-Puritan policies of King Charles I and Archbishop Laud. Possibly sensing their own danger after the earl of Lincoln was imprisoned for his refusal to pay a forced loan, the Bradstreets and Dudleys joined with other Puritans, notably John Winthrop and the preacher John Cotton, to form a "plantation" in the Massachusetts Bay. Carrying the charter for the settlement with them, these members of the Massachusetts Bay Company, of which Simon Bradstreet was secretary, set sail with eleven ships in April 1630. The Bradstreets and Dudleys were on the flagship, *Arbella,* which arrived in Salem harbor in late June. Conditions were much worse than they had expected. Remembering this experience, Anne Bradstreet wrote in the letter to her children, "I found a new world

---

[5] A ruling chief.   [6] In August 1629.
[7] Charge; the charges made against Morton in Plymouth were dismissed in London.

and new manners, at which my heart rose." Thomas Dudley was more explicit in a letter to the countess of Lincoln, writing that Salem was in unexpectedly poor condition with many who were "weak and sick" and the food hardly sufficient for "a fortnight." However, soon the two families had settled in Newtowne, now Cambridge, Massachusetts, and Anne Bradstreet yielded and joined the church at Boston.

From then until her death at age sixty in 1672, Bradstreet lived a harsh frontier existence and experienced a number of what she called "lingering sicknesses," one of which she explained in her first known poem, "Upon a Fit of Sickness, 1632." In this poem death seems like a relief from "care and strife." Her care included children; Bradstreet was no more than twenty-one when her first child, Simon, was born in 1633. Her last child, John, was born in 1642 when Bradstreet was forty. She writes in the poem "In Reference to Her Children" (1678), "I had eight birds hatched in one nest / Four Cocks there were, and Hens the rest."

For all its harshness and domestic care, Bradstreet's life was intellectually active, nurtured by her family and environment. Her father encouraged her to write poetry and sent her his own verses. When the Bradstreets moved to Ipswich, Massachusetts, in 1635, they were joined by some of the best-educated individuals in the Bay Colony, including John Winthrop, Jr., who possessed a fine library, and Nathaniel Ward, author of *The Simple Cobbler of Aggawam* (1646?). This accomplished group provided a ready audience for Bradstreet's work.

Moreover, unlike most women of the time, Bradstreet was educated and continued an active intellectual life in the New World. She read widely in history, science, and literature, especially the classics in translation. Her reading showed a particular interest in history, perhaps reflecting her realization that she was part of the Puritan "Great Migration" to a new Canaan, or Promised Land, in the wilderness. This migration, Puritans believe, was part of God's providential direction of history toward the millennium when evil would be banished from the earth and the righteous would remain. Her favorite reading of this time, Joshua Sylvester's translation of du Bartas's *Divine Weeks and Works* (1621), which contained du Bartas's long poem on the history of the Creation and Sir Walter Raleigh's *History of the World* (1614), provided her with material to support these views and with inspiration for her own writing.

Isolated though she was, Bradstreet followed the political developments in England but increasingly identified with the New World rather than the Old World. When in 1642 civil war broke out between the Puritans under the English revolutionary leader Oliver Cromwell and the Royalists under Charles I, Bradstreet viewed the situation as an episode in God's providential direction of history and responded with "A Dialogue Between Old England and New" (1642). In this poem the relationship between Old England and New England is that of mother and daughter: there is love but also separation. Old England must root out internal corruption and popery, or Catholicism, and prepare for the day of redemption. Until then, New England, sympathetic but distant, bids "farewell." For New England, and for Bradstreet, the wilderness was now home.

Most of all, Bradstreet was a writer of both poetry and prose, and with her writing she tested the tolerance of the Puritan community. Puritan men believed that a women should be silent and modest and ought to leave intellectual pursuits (such as writing) to men, whose wits were supposedly stronger. Writing about politics or controversial subjects was especially outside a woman's domain. Although some carping about her work evidently occurred, as Bradstreet suggests in her poem "The Prologue" (1650), she had little patience with it. Those who doubted female wits should look to Queen Elizabeth, who, Bradstreet asserted in her elegy "In Honour of Queen Elizabeth" (1643), was "argument enough to make you mute."

THE
TENTH MUSE
Lately ſprung up in AMERICA.
OR
Severall Poems, compiled
with great variety of VVit
and Learning, full of delight.
Wherein eſpecially is contained a com-
pleat diſcourſe and deſcription of
The Four { Elements,
Conſtitutions,
Ages of Man,
Seaſons of the Year.
Together with an Exact Epitomie of
the Four Monarchies, viz.
The { Aſſyrian,
Perſian,
Grecian,
Roman.
Alſo a Dialogue between Old England and
New, concerning the late troubles.
With divers other pleaſant and ſerious Poems.
By a Gentlewoman in thoſe parts.
Printed at London for Stephen Bowtell at the ſigne of the
Bible in Popes Head-Alley. 1650.

The title page of Anne Bradstreet's The Tenth Muse Lately Sprung Up in America.

Bradstreet's friends and relatives were proud of her work. Without her knowledge, John Woodbridge, her brother-in-law, carried to England a manuscript of thirteen of Bradstreet's poems and a number of commendatory verses written by her admirers. These were published by the printer Stephen Bowtell in 1650, under the title *The Tenth Muse Lately Sprung Up in America*. This volume contains a poem to her father; two long historical poems; elegies to the politician Sir Philip Sidney, the poet du Bartas, and Queen Elizabeth; the "Dialogue," a biblical paraphrase; and a poem on the "Vanity of All Worldy Creatures." The *Tenth Muse* was the first published book of English poetry written in America. Its publication was a surprise to the author, who was somewhat taken aback. In the poem "The Author to Her Book" (1678), Bradstreet recalls her concern at the appearance of her "ill-formed offspring," but, although apologetic for its faults, she immediately began to correct and polish her work.

Bradstreet continued to write poetry and prose, though nothing more was published in her lifetime. The then unpublished material is of a more private nature than the poems in *The Tenth Muse*. Whereas most of the poetry in *The Tenth Muse* concerns history, politics, and public figures and demonstrates the poet's learning, her private poems and prose give a picture of the poet's everyday concerns and of her relationship with her family. The private works also give a picture of her inner, spiritual life, the life that gave meaning to Bradstreet's, and to every Puritan's, existence in New England.

A number of these poems concern her husband, whose absences from home she frequently marked with a poem. Sometimes witty, anguished, or relieved, the poems reflect the depth of affection and confidence in this relationship and the physical as well as spiritual unity that characterized their marriage. Forthright, sincere, and assured in style and manner, these poems are much admired.

Some of these private poems and much of the prose deal with Bradstreet's family life, the subjects ranging from the fear of death in childbirth to the growth of her children into adulthood. A prose series, "Meditations Divine and Moral," which she began in 1664 for her son Simon reveals another dimension of her private life, demonstrating the moral wisdom and "spiritual advantage" she had gained in her maturity. Taken together with the domestic poems, the meditations complete a picture of Bradstreet's life—warm, spirited, and loving—certainly not the narrow, humorless life typically associated with Puritanism.

Most of all, the private poems and prose reveal Bradstreet's deeply spiritual nature and tell of her struggle to submit to God's will. The spiritual struggle is commonly discussed as a conflict between the attractions of this world and those of the next, a preoccupation suggesting to some readers that she had difficulty accepting the Puritan insistence that people may be in this world but not of it, and that she might have missed the rich life of the Old World when she accepted the hard life of the wilderness. In some poems, however, the poet appears to be at home in her New England environment and expresses an acceptance of human mortality. Such a poem is "Contemplations," probably written during the mid-1640s when the Bradstreet family had settled in the frontier town of Andover, Massachusetts. The first poem in the colonial New World to be inspired by the American landscape, "Contemplations" expresses an appreciation of nature as a manifestation of God's glory and an emblem of the eternal glory to come. The language, virtually free of classical allusions, is spare and direct, a good example of the Puritan plain style.

Most of the time Bradstreet's spiritual struggles were internal. As she wrote in the letter "To my dear children" (1867), she had "many times sinkings and droopings" in her spiritual pilgrimage. Yet, fits of sickness, concern for her absent children, or worry about her husband, who in 1662 was on a diplomatic mission in England, furnished the poet with occasions to consider "God's gracious dealings" with her. Moreover, she wrote in the letter, God never allowed her "long to sit loose" from Him and often chastised her with a sickness or a hardship that brought her to the recognition that her true life was "above." In her old age, Bradstreet's resignation to God's will underwent severe testing with the deaths of four of her eldest son's five children and his wife's death in childbirth. The elegies Bradstreet wrote for these children and their mother reveal a restrained and somber acceptance of God's power.

With Bradstreet's last known poem, "As Weary Pilgrim," written in 1669 and published in 1867, her struggle with the world appears to be over. Here, in the controlled voice of the mature poet, life offers the speaker "bryars and thornes," and she looks forward to throwing off her "corrupt carcass" for a "glorious body" in eternity. Such was the attitude that Bradstreet brought to her own last illness. According to an account by her son Simon, a minister, she suffered a "consumption," accompanied by an "issue" in her arm. Yet at this time in her life her submission to God's will was complete, and she accepted her suffering as a prerequisite to passage to salvation.

After Bradstreet's death the first American edition of her poems, entitled *Several Poems*, was published in 1678 by John Foster, who had set up the first printing press in Boston. In 1867 John Harvard Ellis published *The Works of Anne Bradstreet in Poetry and Prose*, which contains previously unpublished poems. Since that time, generations of readers have appreciated the work of Anne Bradstreet, which so eloquently expresses the spirit of Puritan life in New England.

Suggested Readings: *The Complete Works of Anne Bradstreet*, ed. J. R. McElrath, Jr., and A. P. Robb, 1981. J. K. Piercy, *Anne Bradstreet*, 1965. E. W. White, *Anne Bradstreet: The Tenth Muse*, 1971. A. Stratford, *Anne Bradstreet: The Worldy Puritan, an Introduction to Her Poetry*, 1974. W. Martin, *An American Triptych*, 1984.

Text Used: *The Works of Anne Bradstreet*, ed. J. Hensley, 1967.

THE PROLOGUE*

I

To sing of wars, of captains, and of kings,
Of cities founded, commonwealths begun,
For my mean[1] pen are too superior things:
Or how they all, or each their dates have run
Let poets and historians set these forth,
My obscure lines shall not so dim their worth.

2

But when my wond'ring eyes and envious heart
Great Bartas[2] sugared lines do but read o'er,
Fool I do grudge the Muses[3] did not part
'Twixt him and me that overfluent store;   10
A Bartas can do what a Bartas will
But simple I according to my skill.

3

From schoolboy's tongue no rhet'ric we expect,
Nor yet a sweet consort[4] from broken strings,
Nor perfect beauty where's a main defect:
My foolish, broken, blemished Muse so sings,
And this to mend, alas, no art is able,
'Cause nature made it so irreparable.

4

Nor can I, like that fluent sweet tongued Greek[5]
Who lisped at first, in future times speak plain.   20
By art he gladly found what he did seek,
A full requital of his striving pain.
Art can do much, but this maxim's most sure:
A weak or wounded brain admits no cure.

* "The Prologue," first published in *The Tenth Muse* (1650), prefaced Bradstreet's "Quaternions," a series of poems about the history of civilization.
[1] Humble.   [2] Guillaume du Bartas (1544–1590) a French poet much admired by the Puritans.
[3] According to Greek myth, the nine goddesses who preside over literature and the arts and sciences.
[4] Harmony.
[5] Demosthenes (384–322 B.C.), an Athenian statesman and orator who overcame a speech defect.

5

I am obnoxious to each carping tongue
Who says my hand a needle better fits,
A poet's pen all scorn I should thus wrong,
For such despite they cast on female wits:
If what I do prove well, it won't advance,
They'll say it's stol'n, or else it was by chance.   30

6

But sure the antique Greeks were far more mild
Else of our sex, why feigned they those nine
And poesy made Calliope's[6] own child;
So 'mongst the rest they placed the arts divine:
But this weak knot they will full soon untie,
The Greeks did nought, but play the fools and lie.

7

Let Greeks be Greeks, and women what they are
Men have precedency and still excel,
It is but vain unjustly to wage war;
Men can do best, and women know it well.   40
Preeminence in all and each is yours;
Yet grant some small acknowledgement of ours.

8

And oh ye high flown quills[7] that soar the skies,
And ever with your prey still catch your praise,
If e'er you deign these lowly lines your eyes,
Give thyme or parsley wreath, I ask no bays;[8]
This mean and unrefined ore of mine
Will make your glist'ring gold but more to shine.

1643?, 1650

AN EPITAPH ON MY DEAR AND EVER-HONOURED MOTHER MRS. DOROTHY DUDLEY, WHO DECEASED DECEMBER 27, 1643, AND OF HER AGE, 61

Here lies,
A worthy matron of unspotted life,
A loving mother and obedient wife,
A friendly neighbor, pitiful to poor,
Whom oft she fed and clothed with her store;
To servants wisely awful, but yet kind,
And as they did, so they reward did find.

[6] According to Greek myth, the Muse of epic poetry.
[7] Quill pens.   [8] Laurels used as a crown to adorn a poet's head.

A true instructor of her family,
The which she ordered with dexterity.
The public meetings ever did frequent,
And in her closet constant hours she spent;
Religious in all her words and ways,
Preparing still for death, till end of days:
Of all her children, children lived to see,
Then dying, left a blessed memory.

1643, 1678

CONTEMPLATIONS

[1]

Some time now past in the autumnal tide,
When Phoebus[1] wanted but one hour to bed,
The trees all richly clad, yet void of pride,
Where gilded o'er by his rich golden head.
Their leaves and fruits seemed painted, but was true,
Of green, of red, of yellow, mixed hue;
Rapt were my senses at this delectable view.

2

I wist[2] not what to wish, yet sure thought I,
If so much excellence abide below,
How excellent is He that dwells on high,   10
Whose power and beauty by his works we know?
Sure he is goodness, wisdom, glory, light,
That hath this under world so richly dight;[3]
More heaven than earth was here, no winter and no night.

3

Then on a stately oak I cast mine eye,
Whose ruffling top the clouds seemed to aspire;
How long since thou wast in thine infancy?
Thy strength, and stature, more thy years admire,
Hath hundred winters past since thou wast born?
Or thousand since thou brakest thy shell of horn?[4]   20
If so, all these as nought, eternity doth scorn.

4

Then higher on the glistering Sun I gazed,
Whose beams was shaded by the leavie tree;
The more I looked, the more I grew amazed,
And softly said, "What glory's like to thee?"
Soul of this world, this universe's eye,

---

[1] According to Greek myth, the personification of the sun god, Apollo.   [2] Knew.   [3] Decorated.
[4] An acorn.

No wonder some made thee a deity;
Had I not better known, alas, the same had I.

5

Thou as a bridegroom from thy chamber rushes,
And as a strong man, joys to run a race;[5]   30
The morn doth usher thee with smiles and blushes;
The Earth reflects her glances in thy face.
Birds, insects, animals with vegative,[6]
Thy heat from death and dullness doth revive,
And in the darksome womb of fruitful nature dive.

6

Thy swift annual and diurnal course,
Thy daily straight and yearly oblique path,
Thy pleasing fervor and thy scorching force,
All mortals here the feeling knowledge hath.
Thy presence makes it day, thy absence night,   40
Quaternal[7] seasons caused by thy might:
Hail creature, full of sweetness, beauty, and delight.

7

Art thou so full of glory that no eye
Hath strength thy shining rays once to behold?
And is thy splendid throne erect so high,
As to approach it, can no earthly mould?
How full of glory then must thy Creator be,
Who gave this bright light luster unto thee?
Admired, adored for ever, be that Majesty.

8

Silent alone, where none or saw, or heard,   50
In pathless paths I lead my wand'ring feet,
My humble eyes to lofty skies I reared
To sing some song, my mazed[8] Muse thought meet.[9]
My great Creator I would magnify,
That nature had thus decked liberally;
But Ah, and Ah, again, my imbecility.

9

I heard the merry grasshopper then sing.
The black-clad cricket bear a second part;
They kept one tune and played on the same string,
Seeming to glory in their little art.   60
Shall creatures abject thus their voices raise

---

[5] ". . .the sun, which is as a bridegroom coming out of his chamber, and rejoiceth as a strong man to run a race," from Psalms 19:5.
[6] Plants.   [7] Four.
[8] Amazed.   [9] Proper.

And in their kind resound their Maker's praise,
Whilst I, as mute, can warble forth no higher lays?[10]

10

When present times look back to ages past,
And men in being fancy those are dead,
It makes things gone perpetually to last,
And calls back months and years that long since fled.
It makes a man more aged in conceit[11]
Than was Methuselah,[12] or's grandsire great,
While of their persons and their acts his mind doth treat.   70

11

Sometimes in Eden fair he seems to be,
Sees glorious Adam there made lord of all,
Fancies the apple, dangle on the tree,
That turned his sovereign to a naked thrall.[13]
Who like a miscreant's driven from that place,
To get his bread with pain and sweat of face,
A penalty imposed on his backsliding race.

12

Here sits our grandame[14] in retired place,
And in her lap her bloody Cain new-born;
The weeping imp oft looks her in the face,   80
Bewails his unknown hap[15] and fate forlorn;
His mother sighs to think of Paradise,
And how she lost her bliss to be more wise,
Believing him that was, and is, father of lies.[16]

13

Here Cain and Abel come to sacrifice,
Fruits of the earth and fatlings[17] each do bring,
On Abel's gift the fire descends from skies,
But no such sign on false Cain's offering;
With sullen hateful looks he goes his ways,
Hath thousand thoughts to end his brother's days,   90
Upon whose blood his future good he hopes to raise.

14

There Abel keeps his sheep, no ill he thinks;
His brother comes, then acts his fratricide;
The virgin Earth of blood her first draught drinks,
But since that time she often hath been cloyed.
The wretch with ghastly face and dreadful mind

---

[10] Songs.   [11] Thought.   [12] In Genesis 5:27, Methuselah lived 969 years.   [13] A slave.
[14] Eve, the mother of Cain and Abel (see Genesis).   [15] Circumstances.
[16] In Genesis 3, Eve lost paradise by believing in Satan, the "father of lies."
[17] Young animals fattened for slaughter.

Thinks each he sees will serve him in his kind,
Though none on earth but kindred near then could he find.

15

Who fancies not his looks now at the bar,[18]
His face like death, his heart with horror fraught,   100
Nor malefactor ever felt like war,
When deep despair with wish of life hath fought,
Branded with guilt and crushed with treble woes,
A vagabond to Land of Nod[19] he goes.
A city builds, that walls might him secure from foes.

16

Who things not oft upon the father's ages,
Their long descent, how nephews' sons they saw,
The starry observations of those sages,
And how their precepts to their sons were law,
How Adam sighed to see his progeny,   110
Clothed all in his black sinful livery
Who neither guilt nor yet the punishment could fly.

17

Our life compare we with their length of days
Who to the tenth of theirs doth now arrive?
And though thus short, we shorten many ways,
Living so little while we are alive;
In eating, drinking, sleeping, vain delight
So unawares comes on perpetual night,
And puts all pleasures vain unto eternal flight.

18

When I behold the heavens as in their prime,   120
And then the earth (though old) still clad in green,
The stones and trees, insensible of time,
Nor age nor wrinkle on their front are seen;
If winter come and greenness then do fade,
A spring returns, and they more youthful made;
But man grows old, lied down, remains where once he's laid.

19

By birth more noble than those creatures all,
Yet seems by nature and by custom cursed,
No sooner born, but grief and care makes fall
That state obliterate he had at first;   130
Nor youth, nor strength, nor wisdom spring again,
Nor habitations long their names retain,
But in oblivion to the final day remain.

[18] A place of judgment.
[19] In Genesis 4:16, a land east of Eden, where Cain resided after slaying Abel.

20

Shall I then praise the heavens, the trees, the earth
Because their beauty and their strength last longer?
Shall I wish there, or never to had birth,
Because they're bigger, and their bodies stronger?
Nay, they shall darken, perish, fade and die,
And when unmade, so ever shall they lie,
But man was made for endless immortality.   140

21

Under the cooling shadow of a stately elm
Close sat I by a goodly river's side,
Where gliding streams the rocks did overwhelm,
A lonely place, with pleasures dignified.
I once that loved the shady woods so well,
Now thought the rivers did the trees excel,
And if the sun would ever shine, there would I dwell.

22

While on the stealing stream I fixt mine eye,
Which to the longed-for ocean held its course,
I marked, nor crooks, nor rubs[20] that there did lie   150
Could hinder ought,[21] but still augment its force.
"Oh happy flood," quoth I, "that holds thy race
Till thou arrive at thy beloved place,
Nor is it rocks or shoals that can obstruct thy pace,

23

Nor is't enough, that thou alone mayst slide,
But hundred brooks in thy clear waves do meet,
So hand in hand along with thee they glide
To Thetis' house,[22] where all embrace and greet.
Thou emblem true of what I count the best,
O could I lead my rivulets to rest,   160
So may we press to that vast mansion, ever blest."

24

Ye fish, which in this liquid region 'bide,
That for each season have your habitation,
Now salt, now fresh where you think best to glide
To unknown coasts to give a visitation,
In lakes and ponds you leave your numerous fry;[23]
So nature taught, and yet you know not why,
You wat'ry folk that know not your felicity.

25

Look how the wantons frisk to taste the air,
Then to the colder bottom straight they dive;   170

[20] Neither bends nor obstacles.   [21] Anything.
[22] The sea; according to Greek Myth, Thetis was a sea nymph.   [23] Young fish.

Eftsoon[24] to Neptune's glassy hall[25] repair
To see what trade they great ones there do drive,
Who forage o'er the spacious sea-green field,
And take the trembling prey before it yield,
Whose armour is their scales, their spreading fins their shield.

26

While musing thus with contemplation fed,
And thousand fancies buzzing in my brain,
The sweet-tongued Philomel[26] perched o'er my head
And chanted forth a most melodious strain
Which rapt me so with wonder and delight,   180
I judged my hearing better than my sight,
And wished me wings with her a while to take my flight.

27

"O merry Bird," said I, "that fears no snares,
That neither toils nor hoards up in thy barn,
Feels no sad thoughts nor cruciating[27] cares
To gain more good or shun what might thee harm.
Thy clothes ne'er wear, thy meat is everywhere,
Thy bed a bough, thy drink the water clear,
Reminds not what is past, nor what's to come dost fear."

28

"The dawning morn with songs thou dost prevent,[28]   190
Sets hundred notes unto thy feathered crew,
So each one tunes his pretty instrument,
And warbling out the old, begin anew,
And thus they pass their youth in summer season,
Then follow thee into a better region,
Where winter's never felt by that sweet airy legion."

29

Man at the best a creature frail and vain,
In knowledge ignorant, in strength but weak,
Subject to sorrows, losses, sickness, pain,
Each storm his state, his mind, his body break,   200
From some of these he never finds cessation,
But day or night, within, without, vexation,
Troubles from foes, from friends, from dearest, near'st relation.

30

And yet this sinful creature, frail and vain,
This lump of wretchedness, of sin and sorrow,

---

[24] Soon thereafter.   [25] The sea; according to Roman myth, Neptune was the sea god.
[26] The nightingale. According to Greek myth, Philomela, a princess of Athens, was turned into a nightingale after her brother-in-law raped her and tore out her tongue.
[27] Excruciating.   [28] Foresee.

This weatherbeaten vessel wracked with pain,
Joys not in hope of an eternal morrow;
Nor all his losses, crosses, and vexation,
In weight, in frequency and long duration
Can make him deeply groan for that divine translation.[29]　　210

31

The mariner that on smooth waves doth glide
Sings merrily and steers his bark with ease,
As if he had command of wind and tide,
And now become great master of the seas:
But suddenly a storm spoils all the sport,
And makes him long for a more quiet port,
Which 'gainst all adverse winds may serve for fort.

32

So he that saileth in this world of pleasure,
Feeding on sweets, that never bit of th' sour,
That's full of friends, of honour, and of treasure,　　220
Fond fool, he takes this earth ev'n for heav'n's bower.
But sad affliction comes and makes him see
Here's neither honour, wealth, nor safety;
Only above is found all with security.

33

O Time the fatal wrack[30] of mortal things,
That draws oblivion's curtains over kings;
Their sumptuous monuments, men know them not,
Their names without a record are forgot,
Their parts, their ports, their pomp's[31] all laid in th' dust
Nor wit nor gold, nor buildings scape times rust;　　230
But he whose name is graved in the white stone[32]
Shall last and shine when all of these are gone.

1666?, 1678

THE FLESH AND THE SPIRIT

In secret place where once I stood
Close by the banks of Lacrim flood,[1]
I heard two sisters reason on
Things that are past and things to come;
One flesh was called, who had her eye
On worldly wealth and vanity;

---

[29] Transformation.　[30] Destroyer.
[31] Their features, their shelters, their vanity.
[32] "To him that overcometh will I give. . . .a white stone, and in the stone a new name written, which no man knoweth saving him that receiveth it," from Revelation 2:17.
[1] The river of tears; *lacrima* is Latin for "tear.

The other Spirit, who did rear
Her thoughts unto a higher sphere:
Sister, quoth Flesh, what liv'st thou on,
Nothing but meditation?   10
Doth contemplation feed thee so
Regardlessly to let earth go?
Can speculation satisfy
Notion without reality?
Dost dream of things beyond the moon,
And dost thou hope to dwell there soon?
Hast treasures there laid up in store
That all in th' world thou count'st but poor?
Art fancy sick, or turned a sot[2]
To catch at shadows which are not?   20
Come, come, I'll show unto thy sense,
Industry hath its recompense.
What canst desire, but thou may'st see
True substance in variety?
Dost honour like? Acquire the same,
As some to their immortal fame,
And trophies to thy name erect
Which wearing time shall ne'er deject.
For riches doth thou long full sore?
Behold enough of precious store.   30
Earth hath more silver, pearls, and gold,
Than eyes can see or hands can hold.
Affect's[3] thou pleasure? Take thy fill,
Earth hath enough of what you will.
Then let not go, what thou may'st find
For things unknown, only in mind
Spirit: be still thou unregenerate[4] part,
Disturb no more my settled heart,
For I have vowed (and so will do)
Thee as a foe still to pursue.   40
And combat with thee will and must,
Until I see thee laid in th' dust.
Sisters we are, yea, twins we be,
Yet deadly feud 'twixt thee and me;
For from one father are we not,
Thou by old Adam wast begot,
But my arise is from above,
Whence my dear Father I do love.
Thou speak'st me fair, but hat'st me sore,
Thy flatt'ring shows I'll trust no more.   50
How oft thy slave, hast thou me made,
When I believed what thou hast said,
And never had more cause of woe
Than when I did what thou bad'st do.

[2] Turned a fool, or hallucinating.   [3] Seek.   [4] Unrepentant.

I'll stop mine ears at these thy charms.
And count them for my deadly harms.
Thy sinful pleasures I do hate,
Thy riches are to me no bait,
Thine honours do, nor will I love;
For my ambition lies above.　　　　　　60
My greatest honour it shall be
When I am victor over thee,
And triumph shall with laurel head,[5]
When thou my captive shalt be led,
How I do live, thou need'st not scoff,
For I have meat thou know'st not of;[6]
The hidden manna[7] I do eat,
The word of life it is my meat.
My thoughts do yield me more content
Than can thy hours in pleasure spent.　　70
Nor are they shadows which I catch,
Nor fancies vain at which I snatch,
But reach at things that are so high,
Beyond thy dull capacity;
Eternal substance I do see,
With which enriched I would be.
Mine eye doth pierce the heavens and see
What is invisible to thee.
My garments are not silk nor gold,
Nor such like trash which earth doth hold,　　80
But royal robes I shall have on,
More glorious than the glist'ring sun;
My crown not diamonds, pearls, and gold,
But such as angels' heads enfold.
The city[8] where I hope to dwell,
There's none on earth can parallel;
The stately walls both high and strong,
Are made of precious jasper stone;
The gates of pearl, both rich and clear,
And angels are for porters there;　　90
The streets thereof transparent gold,
Such as no eye did e'er behold;
A crystal river there doth run,
Which doth proceed from the Lamb's throne.
Of life, there are the waters sure,
Which shall remain forever pure,
Nor sun, nor moon, they have no need,
For glory doth from God proceed.
No candle there, nor yet torchlight,

---

[5] A crown of laurel, a symbol of victory.

[6] Paraphrasing Jesus' words to his disciples, "But he said unto them, I have meat to eat that ye know not of," from John 4:32.

[7] In Exodus 16:15, the spiritual food God sent to the Israelites in the wilderness.

[8] The description of this city follows that the New Jerusalem in Revelation 21 and 22.

For there shall be no darksome night.   100
From sickness and infirmity
For evermore they shall be free;
Nor withering age shall e'er come there,
But beauty shall be bright and clear;
This city pure is not for thee,
For things unclean there shall not be.
If I of heaven may have my fill,
Take thou the world and all that will.

                                                          1666?, 1678

THE AUTHOR TO HER BOOK*

Thou ill-formed offspring of my feeble brain,
Who after birth didst by my side remain,
Till snatched from thence by friends, less wise than true,
Who thee abroad, exposed to public view,
Made thee in rags, halting to th' press to trudge,
Where errors were not lessened (all may judge).
At thy return my blushing was not small,
My rambling brat (in print) should mother call,
I cast thee by as one unfit for light,
Thy visage was so irksome in my sight;   10
Yet being mine own, at length affection would
Thy blemishes amend, if so I could:
I washed thy face, but more defects I saw,
And rubbing off a spot still made a flaw.
I stretched thy joints to make thee even feet,[1]
Yet still thou run'st more hobbling than is meet;[2]
In better dress to trim thee was my mind,
But nought save homespun cloth i' th' house I find.
In this array 'mongst vulgars[3] may'st thou roam.
In critic's hands beware thou dost not come,   20
And take thy way where yet thou art not known;
If for thy father asked, say thou hadst none;
And for thy mother, she alas is poor,
Which caused her thus to send thee out of door.

                                                     1650?–1670, 1678

BEFORE THE BIRTH OF ONE OF HER CHILDREN

All things within this fading world hath end,
Adversity doth still our joys attend;

---

*The "book" is *The Tenth Muse* (1650), published without her knowledge; this poem appeared in its second edition.
[1] Metrical feet.   [2] Proper.   [3] Common people.

No ties so strong, no friends so dear and sweet,
But with death's parting blow is sure to meet.
The sentence past is most irrevocable,
A common thing, yet oh, inevitable.
How soon, my Dear, death may my steps attend,
How soon't may be thy lot to lose thy friend,
We both are ignorant, yet love bids me
These farewell lines to recommend to thee,   10
That when that knot's untied that made us one,
I may seem thine, who in effect am none.
And if I see not half my days that's due,
What nature would, God grant to yours and you;
The many faults that well you know I have
Let be interred in my oblivious grave;
If any worth or virtue were in me,
Let that live freshly in thy memory
And when thou feel'st no grief, as I no harms,
Yet love thy dead, who long lay in thine arms.   20
And when thy loss shall be repaid with gains
Look to my little babes, my dear remains.
And if thou love thyself, or loved'st me,
These O protect from step-dame's[1] injury.
And if chance to thine eyes shall bring this verse,
With some sad sighs honour my absent hearse;[2]
And kiss this paper for thy love's dear sake,
Who with salt tears this last farewell did take.

1640–1652?, 1678

TO MY DEAR AND LOVING HUSBAND

If ever two were one, then surely we.
If ever man were loved by wife, then thee;
If ever wife was happy in a man,
Compare with me, ye women, if you can.
I prize thy love more than whole mines of gold
Or all the riches that the East doth hold.
My love is such that rivers cannot quench,
Nor ought[1] but love from thee, give recompense.
Thy love is such I can no way repay,
The heavens reward thee manifold, I pray.   10
Then while we live, in love let's so persevere[2]
That when we live no more, we may live ever.

1641–1643?, 1678

---

[1] Stepmother's.   [2] Corpse.
[1] Anything.   [2] Then pronounced "pur-séver," i.e., rhymed with "ever."

A LETTER TO HER HUSBAND, ABSENT UPON PUBLIC EMPLOYMENT

My head, my heart, mine eyes, my life, nay, more,
My joy, my magazine[1] of earthly store,
If two be one, as surely thou and I,
How stayest thou there, whilst I at Ipswich[2] lie?
So many steps, head from the heart to sever,
If but a neck, soon should we be together.
I, like the Earth this season, mourn in black,
My Sun is gone so far in's zodiac,
Whom whilst I 'joyed, nor storms, nor frost I felt,
His warmth such frigid colds did cause to melt.   10
My chilled limbs now numbed lie forlorn;
Return, return, sweet Sol,[3] from Capricorn,[4]
In this dead time, alas, what can I more
Than view those fruits which through thy heat I bore?
Which sweet contentment yield me for a space,
True living pictures of their father's face.
O strange effect! now thou art southward gone,
I weary grow the tedious day so long;
But when thou northward to me shalt return,
I wish my Sun may never set, but burn   20
Within the Cancer[5] of my glowing breast,
The welcome house of him my dearest guest.
Where ever, ever stay, and go not thence,
Till nature's sad decree shall call thee hence;
Flesh of thy flesh, bone of thy bone,[6]
I here, thou there, yet both but one.

1641–1643?, 1678

ANOTHER

As loving hind[1] that (hartless)[2] wants her deer,
Scuds[3] through the woods and fern with hark'ning ear,
Perplext, in every bush and nook doth pry,
Her dearest deer, might answer ear or eye;
So doth my anxious soul, which now doth miss
A dearer dear (far dearer heart) than this.
Still wait with doubts, and hopes, and failing eye,

---

[1] A warehouse.
[2] Ipswich, Massachusetts (North of Boston) where the Bradstreets lived from about 1635 to 1645.
[3] The sun.   [4] The zodiac's tenth sign, indicating winter.
[5] The zodiac's fourth sign, indicating summer.
[6] Adam, from whose rib Eve was made, states "This is now bone of my bones, and flesh of my flesh: she shall be called Woman because she was taken out of Man," from Genesis 2:23.
[1] A female deer.   [2] A male deer: a pun on "heart" and "hart."   [3] Runs.

His voice to hear or person to descry.
Or as the pensive dove doth all alone
(On withered bough) most uncouthly bemoan   10
The absence of her love and loving mate,
Whose loss hath made her so unfortunate,
Ev'n thus do I, with many a deep sad groan,
Bewail my turtle[4] true, who now is gone,
His presence and his safe return still woos,
With thousand doleful sighs and mournful coos.
Or as the loving mullet, that true fish,
Her fellow lost, nor joy nor life do wish,
But launches on that shore, there for to die,
Where she her captive husband doth espy.   20
Mine being gone, I lead a joyless life,
I have a loving peer,[5] yet seem no wife;
But worst of all, to him can't steer my course,
I here, he there, alas, both kept by force.
Return my dear, my joy, my only love,
Unto thy hind, thy mullet, and thy dove,
Who neither joys in pasture, house, nor streams,
The substance gone, O me, these are but dreams.
Together at one tree, oh let us browse,
And like two turtles roost within one house,   30
And like the mullets in one river glide,
Let's still remain but one, till death divide.
      Thy loving love and dearest dear,
      At home, abroad, and everywhere.

1678

IN REFERENCE TO HER CHILDREN, 23 JUNE, 1659

I had eight birds hatched in one nest,
Four cocks there were, and hens the rest.
I nursed them up with pain and care,
Nor cost, nor labour did I spare,
Till at the last they felt their wing,
Mounted the trees, and learned to sing;
Chief of the brood then took his flight[1]
To regions far and left me quite.
My mournful chirps I after send,
Till he return, or I do end: 10
Leave not thy nest, thy dam and sire,
Fly back and sing amidst this choir.
My second bird did take her flight,[2]

---

[4] A turtledove.   [5] A mate.
[1] Her firstborn, Samuel, studied medicine in England from 1657 to 1661.
[2] Her daughter Dorothy married Rev. Seaborn Cotton in 1654 and moved first to Wethersfield, Connecticut, and then to Hampton, New Hampshire.

And with her mate flew out of sight;
Southward they both their course did bend,
And seasons twain they there did spend,
Till after blown by southern gales,
They norward steered with filled sails.
A prettier bird was no where seen,
Along the beach among the treen.[3]   20
I have a third[4] of colour white,
On whom I placed no small delight;
Coupled with mate loving and true,
Hath also bid her dam adieu;
And where Aurora[5] first appears,
She now hath perched to spend her years.
One to the academy flew[6]
To chat among that learned crew;
Ambition moves still in his breast
That he might chant above the rest,   30
Striving for more than to do well,
That nightingales he might excel.
My fifth, whose down is yet scarce gone,[7]
Is 'mongst the shrubs and bushes flown,
And as his wings increase in strength,
On higher boughs he'll perch at length.
My other three still with me nest,[8]
Until they're grown, then as the rest,
Or here or there they'll take their flight,
As is ordained, so shall they light.   40
If birds could weep, then would my tears
Let others know what are my fears
Lest this my brood some harm should catch,
And be surprised for want of watch,
Whilst pecking corn and void of care,
They fall un'wares in fowler's[9] snare,
Or whilst on trees they sit and sing,
Some untoward boy at them do fling,
Or whilst allured with bell and glass,
The net be spread, and caught, alas.   50
Or lest by lime-twigs they be foiled,[10]
Or by some greedy hawks be spoiled.
O would my young, ye saw my breast,
And knew what thoughts there sadly rest,
Great was my pain when I you bred,
Great was my care when I you fed,
Long did I keep you soft and warm,
And with my wings kept off all harm,

[3] Trees.
[4] Her daughter Sarah, who married Richard Hubbard and moved to Ipswich, Massachusetts.
[5] According to Roman myth, the goddess of the dawn.   [6] Her son Simon went to Harvard College.
[7] Most likely a reference to her seventh child, Dudley (skipping daughters Hannah and Mercy).
[8] Her children Hannah, Mercy, and John were still living at home.   [9] A birdcatcher.
[10] Birdlime, a sticky substance, was smeared on branches to catch birds.

My cares are more and fears than ever,
My throbs such now as 'fore were never.   60
Alas, my birds, you wisdom want,
Of perils you are ignorant;
Oft times in grass, on trees, in flight,
Sore accidents on you may light.
O to your safety have an eye,
So happy may you live and die.
Meanwhile my days in tunes I'll spend,
Till my weak lays[11] with me shall end.
In shady woods I'll sit and sing,
And things that past to mind I'll bring.   70
Once young and pleasant, as are you,
But former toys (no joys) adieu.
My age I will not once lament,
But sing, my time so near is spent.
And from the top bough take my flight
Into a country beyond sight,
Where old ones instantly grow young,
And there with seraphims[12] set song;
No seasons cold, nor storms they see;
But spring lasts to eternity.   80
When each of you shall in your nest
Among your young ones take your rest,
In chirping language, oft them tell,
You had a dam that loved you well,
That did what could be done for young,
And nursed you up till you were strong,
And 'fore she once would let you fly,
She showed you joy and misery;
Taught what was good, and what was ill,
What would save life, and what would kill.   90
Thus gone, amongst you I may live,
And dead, yet speak, and counsel give:
Farewell, my birds, farewell adieu,
I happy am, if well with you.

1659, 1678

IN MEMORY OF MY DEAR GRANDCHILD ELIZABETH BRADSTREET, WHO DECEASED AUGUST, 1665, BEING A YEAR AND HALF OLD

[1]
Farewell dear babe, my heart's too much content,
Farewell sweet babe, the pleasure of mine eye,
Farewell fair flower that for a space was lent,

---

[11] Songs.   [12] Angels.

Then ta'en away unto eternity.
Blest babe, why should I once bewail thy fate,
Or sigh thy days so soon were terminate,
Sith[1] thou art settled in an everlasting state.

2

By nature trees do rot when thy are grown,
And plums and apples thoroughly ripe do fall,
And corn and grass are in their season mown,   10
And time brings down what is both strong and tall.
And plants new set to be eradicate,
And buds new blown to have so short a date,
Is by His hand alone that guides nature and fate.

1665, 1678

HERE FOLLOWS SOME VERSES UPON THE BURNING OF OUR HOUSE JULY 10TH, 1666

COPIED OUT OF A LOOSE PAPER*

In silent night when rest I took
For sorrow near I did not look
I wakened was with thund'ring noise
And piteous shrieks of dreadful voice.
That fearful sound of "Fire!" and "Fire!"
Let no man know is my desire.
I, starting up, the light did spy,
And to my God my heart did cry
To strengthen me in my distress
And not to leave me succorless.   10
Then, coming out, beheld a space
The flame consume my dwelling place.
And when I could no longer look,
I blest His name that gave and took,[1]
That laid my goods now in the dust.
Yea, so it was, and so 'twas just.
It was His own, it was not mine,
Far be it that I should repine;
He might of all justly bereft
But yet sufficient for us left.   20
When by the ruins oft I past
My sorrowing eyes aside did cast,
And here and there the places spy

---

[1] Since.
* First published in *The Works of Anne Bradstreet* (ed. J. Ellis) in 1867, this poem was copied by Bradstreet's son Simon.
[1] "The Lord gave, and the Lord hath taken away; blessed be the name of the Lord," from Job 1:21.

Where oft I sat and long did lie:
Here stood that trunk, and there that chest,
There lay that store I counted best.
My pleasant things in ashes lie,
And them behold no more shall I.
Under thy roof no guest shall sit,
Nor at thy table eat a bit.   30
No pleasant tale shall e'er be told,
Nor things recounted done of old.
No candle e'er shall shine in thee,
Nor bridegroom's voice e'er heard shall be.
In silence ever shall thou lie,
Adieu, Adieu, all's vanity.[2]
Then straight I 'gin my heart to chide,
And did thy wealth on earth abide?
Didst fix thy hope on mold'ring dust?
The arm of flesh didst make thy trust?   40
Raise up thy thoughts above the sky
That dunghill mists away may fly.
Thou hast an house on high erect,
Framed by that mighty Architect,
With glory richly furnished,
Stands permanent though this be fled.
It's purchased and paid for too
By Him who hath enough to do.
A price so vast as is unknown
Yet by His gift is made thine own;   50
There's wealth enough, I need no more,
Farewell, my pelf,[3] farewell my store.
The world no longer let me love,
My hope and treasure lies above.

1666, 1867

AS WEARY PILGRIM

As weary pilgrim, now at rest,
  Hugs with delight his silent nest,
His wasted limbs now lie full soft
  That mirey steps have trodden oft,
Blesses himself to think upon
  His dangers past, and travails done.
The burning sun no more shall heat,
  Nor stormy rains on him shall beat.
The briars and thorns no more shall scratch,
  Nor hungry wolves at him shall catch.   10
He erring paths no more shall tread,

---

[2] "Vanity of vanities, saith the Preacher, vanity of vanities; all is vanity," from Ecclesiastes 1:2.
[3] Wealth or riches.

Nor wild fruits eat instead of bread.
For waters cold he doth not long
   For thirst no more shall parch his tongue.
No rugged stones his feet shall gall,[1]
   Nor stumps nor rocks cause him to fall.
All cares and fears he bids farewell
   And means in safety now to dwell.
A pilgrim I, on earth perplexed
   With sins, with cares and sorrows vext,   20
By age and pains brought to decay,
   And my clay house[2] mold'ring away.
Oh, how I long to be at rest
   And soar on thigh among the blest.
This body shall in silence sleep,
   Mine eyes no more shall ever weep,
No fainting fits shall me assail,
   Nor grinding pains my body frail,
With cares and fears ne'er cumb'red be
   Nor losses know, nor sorrows see.   30
What though my flesh shall there consume,
   It is the bed Christ did perfume,
And when a few years shall be gone,
   This mortal shall be clothed upon.
A corrupt carcass down it lays,
   A glorious body it shall rise.
In weakness and dishonour sown,
   In power 'tis raised by Christ alone.
Then soul and body shall unite
   And of their maker have the sight.   40
Such lasting joys shall there behold
   As ear ne'er heard nor tongue e'er told.
Lord make me ready for that day.
   Then come, dear Bridegroom,[3] come away.

                1669, 1867

Michael Wigglesworth
(1631–1705)

Whereas the modern social and literary sensibility exhibited in the poems of Anne Bradstreet and Edward Taylor are admired, neither Bradstreet nor Taylor had a contemporary following even remotely equal to Michael Wigglesworth's. Wigglesworth's verse is thor-

[1] Make sore.   [2] Body.
[3] "And Jesus said unto them, can the children of the bridechamber fast, while the bridegroom is with them? as long as they have the bridegroom with them, they cannot fast," from Mark 2:29; Christ is considered the bridegroom of the soul.

oughly moralistic and sermonic in tone, full of orthodox doctrinal expressions that appealed to Puritans and non-Puritans alike, and suitable to both recitative and meditative readings. Between 1662, when Wigglesworth's *The Day of Doom* was first printed, and the time of the American Revolution, only the *Bible* could compete with Wigglesworth's hold on America's readership.

Born in Yorkshire, England, in 1631, Wigglesworth arrived in New England with his nonconformist parents in 1638. They eventually settled in New Haven, Connecticut, and he was placed in the care of New England's most famous schoolmaster, Ezekiel Cheever. By age nine young Wigglesworth could write compositions in Latin. Attending Harvard College, he studied medicine and theology and earned an A.B. in 1651 and an A.M. in 1653. After staying on as a tutor at Harvard for two years, Wigglesworth began preaching in communities around Boston in 1655 (the year he married Mary Reyner), finally settling in Malden, Massachusetts, as minister in 1656.

Although Wigglesworth lived in Malden until his death in 1705, much of his life there was filled with melodrama over personal affairs and occasional conflicts with his congregation. Following Mary's death in 1659, Wigglesworth lapsed into a depression lasting until 1679, when he eloped with his housekeeper, Martha Mudge, twenty-five years his junior. The New England ecclesiastic hierarchy and the people of Malden were outraged; however, the match proved to be Wigglesworth's salvation. With one child by his first wife, he fathered six children with Martha and after her death another with Sybil Avery, whom he had married in 1691. Meanwhile, he had assumed full charge of the Malden ministry, had kept a modest medical practice, was asked to be Harvard's president in 1684 (but declined), and counseled New England's ministers and civil leaders.

In colonial times Wigglesworth was most highly regarded for his poetry. Most of his more than seventy poems were written in the 1660s and 1670s, during his depression. Although he had no formal training in poetry, Wigglesworth chose that form to serve his flock when depression kept him from preaching. Rich in biblical allusion and direct reference and written as a poetic ballad, *The Day of Doom* is a Puritan sermon in verse. The poem depicts Judgment Day and charges readers to look after their spiritual condition while persuading them of the justness of such doctrines as predestination. The poem's incredible array of sinners marched to judgment stands in severe contrast to the limited number of saints. Though Wigglesworth tries to reserve the poem's lesson until the concluding stanzas, that sinners cannot evade God's all-penetrating eye or hope to escape judgment and that all sinners must repent and be prepared to answer God's summons are apparent throughout.

Though sulfuric, self-righteous, and morally heavy-handed, *The Day of Doom* found interested audiences well into the nineteenth century. Wigglesworth also wrote *God's Controversy With New England* (1662), a long poetic tale of woe in which "backsliding" New Englanders are warned in Jehovah's voice to return to the religious ideals of New England's Pilgrim and Puritan founders, and *Meat Out of the Eater* (1670), a collection of largely introspective, meditational poems that argue for "the Necessity, End, and Usefulness of Afflictions." Thoroughly Puritan in purpose and sometimes personal in content, these poems owe much to Wigglesworth's sense of personal trial and hope for triumph over adversity. Like *The Day of Doom* they served to console as well as to edify both poet and readers.

Suggested Readings: *Meat Out of the Eater: Or, Meditations Concerning the Necessity, End, and Usefulness of Afflictions unto God's Children. . .*, 1670. *The Diary of Michael Wigglesworth, 1653–1657*, ed. E. S. Morgan, 1965. R. Crowder, *No Featherbed to Heaven: A Biography of Michael Wigglesworth*, 1962. R. M. Gummere, *Seven Wise Men of Colonial America*, 1967. R. Daly, *God's Altar: The World and the Flesh in Puritan Poetry*, 1978. R. A. Bosco, "Editor's Introduction" in *The Poems of Michael Wigglesworth*, 1989.

Text Used: *The Day of Doom: Or, a Poetical Description of the Great and Last Judgment*, ed. K. B. Murdock, 1929 (some spelling and punctuation modernized).

from THE DAY OF DOOM

I

The security of the   Still was the night, serene and bright,
world before   when all men sleeping lay;
Christ's coming to   Calm was the season, and carnal reason
judgment.   thought so 'twould last for ay.[1]
Luke 12:19   Soul, take thine ease, let sorrow cease,
                                       much good thou hast in store:
                                   This was their song, their cups among,
                                       the evening before.

2

                                   Wallowing in all kind of sin,
                                       vile wretches lay secure: 10
                                   The best of men had scarcely then
Mat. 25:5   their lamps kept in good ure.[2]
                                   Virgins unwise, who through disguise
                                       amongst the best were number'd,
                                   Had clos'd their eyes; yea, and the wise
                                       through sloth and frailty slumber'd.

3

                                   Like as of old, when men grow bold
Mat. 24:37, 38   God's threat'nings to contemn,[3]
                                   Who stopt their ear, and would not hear,
                                       when mercy warned them: 20
                                   But took their course, without remorse,
                                       till God began to power[4]
                                   Destruction the world upon
                                       in a tempestuous shower.

4

                                   They put away the evil day,
                                       And drown'd their care and fears,
                                   Till drown'd were they, and swept away
                                       by vengeance unawares:
1 Thes. 5:3   So at the last, whilst men sleep fast
                                       in their security,   30
                                   Supris'd they are in such a snare
                                       as cometh suddenly.

5

The suddenness,   For at midnight broke forth a light,
majesty, &   which turn'd the night to day,

---

[1] Aye, or forever.   [2] Use.   [3] To loathe.   [4] To pour, a variant spelling.

terror of Christ's
appearing.
Mat. 25:6
2 Pet. 3:10

And speedily an hideous cry
    did all the world dismay.
Sinners awake, their hearts do ache,
    trembling their loins surpriseth;
Amaz'd with fear, by what they hear,
    each one of them ariseth.   40

6

They rush from beds with giddy heads,
    and to their windows run,
Viewing this light, which shines more bright

Mat. 24:29, 30   then doth the noon-day Sun.
Straightway appears (they see't with tears)
    the Son of God most dread;
Who with his train[5] comes on amain[6]
    To judge both quick[7] and dead.

7

Before his face the heavn's gave place,

2 Pet. 3:10   and skies are rent asunder,   50
With mighty voice, and hideous noise,
    more terrible than thunder.
His brightness damps Heav'n's glorious lamps
    and makes them hide their heads,
As if afraid and quite dismay'd,
    they quit their wonted steads.[8]

8

Ye sons of men that durst contemn
    the threat'nings of God's word,
How cheer you now? your hearts, I trow,[9]
    are thrill'd[10] as with a sword.   60
Now atheist blind, whose brutish mind
    a God could never see,
Dost thou perceive, dost now believe,
    that Christ thy Judge shall be?

9

Stout courages,[11] (whose hardiness
    could death and Hell out-face)
Are you as bold now you behold
    your Judge draw near apace?
They cry, no, no: Alas! and woe!
    our courage all is gone: 70
Our hardiness (fool hardiness)
    hath us undone, undone.

10

No heart so bold, but now grows cold
    and almost dead with fear:

[5] Attendants.   [6] In full force.   [7] The living.   [8] Usual places.   [9] Trust.   [10] Pierced.
[11] Bold souls.

Rev. 6:16   No eye so dry, but now can cry,
            and pour out many a tear.
        Earth's potentates and pow'rful states,
            Captains and men of might
        Are quite abasht, their courage dasht
            at this most dreadful sight.   80

11

        Mean[12] men lament, great men do rent
            their robes, and tear their hair:
Mat. 24:30   They do not spare their flesh to tear
            through horrible despair.
        All kindreds wail: all hearts do fail:
            horror the world doth fill
        With weeping eyes, and loud out-cries,
            yet knows not how to kill.

12

Rev. 6:15, 16   Some hide themselves in caves and delves,[13]
            in places under ground:
        Some rashly leap into the deep,   90
            to scape[14] by being drown'd:
        Some to the rocks (O senseless blocks!)
            and woody mountains run,
        That there they might this fearful sight,
            and dreaded presence shun.

13

        In vain do they to mountains say,
            "Fall on us, and us hide
        From Judge's ire, more hot than fire,
            for who may it abide?"   100
        No hiding place can from his face,
            sinners at all conceal,
        Whose flaming eyes hid things doth 'spy,
            and darkest things reveal.

14

        The Judge draws nigh, exalted high
Mat. 25:31   upon a lofty throne,
        Amidst the throng of angels strong,
            lo, Israel's Holy One!
        The excellence of whose presence
            and awful majesty,
        Amazeth Nature, and every creature,   110
            doth more than terrify.

15

Rev. 6:14   The mountains smoke, the hills are shook,
            the earth is rent and torn,

[12] Ordinary.   [13] Dug-out pits.   [14] Escape.

As if she should be clean dissolv'd
　　or from the center born.
The sea doth roar, forsakes the shore,
　　and shrinks away for fear;
The wild beasts flee into the sea,
　　so soon as he draws near.   120

16
Whose glory bright, whose wondrous might,
　　whose power imperial,
So far surpass whatever was
　　in realms terrestrial;
That tongues of men (nor angel's pen)
　　cannot the same express,
And therefore I must pass it by,
　　lest speaking should transgress.

17
1 Thes. 4:16
Resurrection
of the dead.
John 5:28, 29

Before his throne a trump[15] is blown,
　　Proclaiming th' Day of Doom: 130
Forthwith he cries, "*Ye Dead arise,*
　　and unto Judgment come."
No sooner said, but 'tis obey'd;
　　Sepulchers open'd are:
Dead bodies all rise at his call,
　　and's mighty power declare.

18
Both sea and land, at his command,
　　their dead at once surrender:
The fire and air constrained are
　　also their dead to tender.   140
The mighty word of this great Lord
　　links body and soul together
Both of the just, and the unjust,
　　to part no more for ever.

19
The living
changed.

The same translates, from Mortal states
　　to immortality,
All that survive, and be alive,
　　i' th' twinkling of an eye:

Luk. 20:36
1 Cor. 15:52

That so they may abide for ay
　　to endless weal or woe;   150
Both the renate[16] and reprobate
　　are made to dy no more.

20
All brought
to Judgment.

His winged hosts flie through all coasts,
　　together gathering

[15] Trumpet.   [16] The reborn.

Mat. 24:31

Both good and bad, both quick and dead,
    and all to Judgment bring.
Out of their holes those creeping moles,
    that hid themselves for fear,
By force they take, and quickly make
    before the Judge appear.   160

21

2 Cor. 5:10
*The sheep
separated from
the goats.*
Mat. 25

Thus every one before the throne
    of Christ the Judge is brought,
Both righteous and impious
    that good or ill had wrought.
A separation, and diff'ring station[17]
    by Christ appointed is
(To sinners sad) 'twixt good and bad,
    'twixt heirs of woe and bliss.

22

*Who are
Christ's sheep.*
Mat. 5:10, 11

At Christ's right hand the sheep do stand,
    his holy martyrs, who   170
For his dear name suffering shame,
    calamity and woe,
Like champions stood, and with their blood
    their testimony sealed;
Whose innocence without offense,
    to Christ their Judge appealed.

23

Heb. 12:5, 6, 7

Next unto whom there find a room
    all Christ's afflicted ones,
Who being chastised, neither despised
    nor sank amidst their groans: 180
Who by the rod were turn'd to God,
    and loved him the more,
Not murmuring nor quarrelling
    when they were chast'ned sore.

24

Luke 7:41, 47

Moreover, such as loved much,
    that had not such a trial,
As might constrain to so great pain,
    and such deep self-denial:
Yet ready were the cross to bear,
    when Christ them call'd thereto,   190
And did rejoice to hear his voice,
    they're counted sheep also.

25

Joh. 21:15
Mat. 19:14

Christ's flock of lambs there also stands,
    whose faith was weak, yet true;

[17] Standing place.

Joh. 3:3

All sound believers (Gospel receivers)
    whose grace was small, but grew:
And them among an infant throng
    of babes, for whom Christ dy'd;
Whom for his own, by ways unknown
    to men, he sanctify'd.   200

26

All stand before their Saviour

Rev. 6:11
Phil. 3:21

    in long white roes yclad,[18]
Their countenance full of pleasance,
    appearing wondrous glad.
O glorious sight! Behold how bright
    dust heaps are made to shine,
Conformed so their Lord unto,
    whose glory is divine.

27

*The goats
described or the
several sorts of
reprobates on
the left hand.
Mat. 24:51*

At Christ's left hand the goats do stand,
    all whining hypocrites,   210
Who for self-ends did seem Christ's friends,
    but foster'd guileful sprites;[19]
Who sheep resembled, but they dissembled
    (their hearts were not sincere);
Who once did throng Christ's lambs among,
    but now must not come near.

28

Apostates[20] and run-aways,

Luk. 11:24, 26
Heb. 6:4, 5, 6
Heb. 10:29

    such as have Christ forsaken,
Of whom the Devil, with seven more evil,[21]
    hath fresh possession taken: 220
Sinners in grain[22] reserv'd to pain
    and torments most severe:
Because 'gainst light they sinn'd with spite,
    are also placed there.

29

There also stand a num'rous band,

Luk. :12, 47
Prov. 1:24, 26
Joh. 3:19

    that no profession made
Of godliness, nor to redress
    their ways at all essay'd:[23]
Who better knew, but (sinful crew)
    Gospel and law despised;   230
Who all Christ's knocks[24] withstood like blocks
    and would not be advised.

---

[18] Clothed.   [19] Spirits.   [20] Those who traitorously switch allegiance.
[21] Seven accomplices more evil than the Devil.   [22] Habitual.   [23] Tried out.
[24] Tries to gain admittance to their souls: "Behold, I stand at the door and knock," from Revelation
3:20.

30

Moreover, there with them appear
    a number, numberless

Gal. 3:10
1 Cor. 6:9
Rev. 21:8

Of great and small, vile wretches all,
    that did God's law transgress:
Idolators, false worshippers,
    Prophaners of God's name,
Who not at all thereon did call,
    or took in vain the same.   240

31

Blasphemers lewd, and swearers shrewd,
    Scoffers at purity,

Exed. 20:7, 8

They hated God, contemn'd his rod,
    and lov'd security;
Sabbath-polluters, saints persecuters,
    Presumptuous men and proud,

2 Thes. 1:6, 8, 9

Who never lov'd those that reprov'd;
    all stand amongst this crowd.

32

Heb. 13:4
1 Cor. 6:10

Adulterers and whoremongers
    were there, with all unchaste: 250
There covetous, and ravenous,
    that riches got too fast:
Who us'd vile ways themselves to raise
    t'estates and worldly wealth,
Oppression by, or knavery,
    by force, or fraud, or stealth.

33

Moreover, there together were
    Children flagitious,[25]

Zach. 5:3, 4
Gal. 5:19, 20, 21

And parents who did them undo
    by nurture vicious.   260
False-witness-bearers, and self-forswearers,
    Murd'rers, and men of blood,
Witches, inchanters, and ale-house-haunters,
    beyond account there stood.

* * *

219

*The saints rejoice
to see Judgment
executed upon the
wicked world.*
Ps. 58:10
Rev. 19:1, 2, 3

The saints behold with courage bold,
    and thankful wonderment,
To see all those that were their foes
    thus sent to punishment:
Then do they sing unto their King
    a song of endless praise: 270

---

[25] Shamefully wicked.

They praise his name, and do proclaim
    that just are all his ways.

220

They ascend with
Christ into Heaven
triumphing.
Mat. 25:46
1 Joh. 3:2
1 Cor. 13:12

Thus with great joy and melody
    to Heav'n they all ascend,
Him there to praise with sweetest lays,[26]
    and hymns that never end,
Where with long rest they shall be blest,
    and nought shall them annoy:
Where they shall see as seen they be,
    and whom they love enjoy.

221

Their eternal
happiness and
incomparable
glory there.

O glorious place! where face to face   280
    Jehovah may be seen,
By such as were sinners whilere[27]
    and no dark veil between.
Where the sun shine, and light divine,
    of God's bright countenance,
Doth rest upon them every one,
    with sweetest influence.

222

O blessed state of the renate!
    O wondrous happiness,
To which they're brought, beyond what thought   290
    can reach, or words express!

Rev. 21:4

Griefs water-course,[28] and sorrows source,
    are turn'd to joyful streams.
Their old distress and heaviness
    are vanished like dreams.

223

For God above in arms of love
    doth dearly them embrace.

Psal. 16:11

And fills their sprites with such delights;
    and pleasures in his grace;
As shall not fail, nor yet grow stale   300
    through frequency of use:
Nor do they fear God's favor there,
    to forfeit by abuse.

224

Heb. 12:23

For there the saints are perfect saints,
    and holy ones indeed,
From all the sin that dwelt within
    their mortal bodies freed:

[26] Songs.   [27] Once.   [28] Stream bed.

<table>
<tr><td>Rev. 1:6, 22:5</td><td>Made kings and priests to God through Christ's
dear loves transcendency,
There to remain, and there to reign
with him eternally.</td><td>310</td></tr>
</table>

1661, 1662

Edward Taylor
(1642?–1729)

The scholar Thomas H. Johnson's late 1930s discovery and initial publication of Edward Taylor's poetry in 1939 is one of the twentieth century's monumental contributions to the history of early New England life and letters. Taylor was virtually unknown—except as a preacher and physician in the frontier town of Westfield, Massachusetts—before Johnson found his manuscript poems in the Yale University Library. Whereas historians and literary critics of the nineteenth century typically measured the Puritan aesthetic by the poems of Anne Bradstreet and of Michael Wigglesworth and invariably found that aesthetic wanting, Taylor's work has offered more recent scholars a new and unexpected measure of Puritan influence on the quality of art in colonial America. Taylor, though every bit as much a Calvinist as his companion poets, eclipsed them as an artist. His religious convictions, personal humility, and love of God served as a moving inner source of poetic expression, not as an impediment to poetic expression, as some have argued is true for Bradstreet and Wigglesworth.

Because Taylor spent most of his life in frontier obscurity and because two centuries separate his death and the discovery of his poems, it is not surprising that details of Taylor's life are vague and largely conjectural. Born in Sketchley, England, around 1642, probably to dissenters, Taylor enjoyed a youth generally free of religious persecution. Although biographers have speculated that he began college studies at Cambridge University, no evidence has been found of his presence there before the Restoration—yet, after the Restoration his refusal to submit to the required loyalty oaths would have precluded his admission to study. By Taylor's own account, he taught school in the English countryside in the mid-1660s.

Eventually deciding to emigrate to the colonies, Taylor sailed for Massachusetts Bay in 1668 and, as did many Puritans before him, left home and family behind in search of religious freedom in the New World. Once in Massachusetts, he presented letters of introduction to Increase Mather, Master of the Mint John Hull, and others and began to study for the ministry at Harvard College. After graduating with a B.A. in 1671, he rode the one hundred miles to Westfield, where he had accepted a call as the town's only minister. He remained there for the next fifty-eight years, until his death in 1729. During those many years in Westfield, Taylor married twice (Elizabeth Fitch in 1674 and Ruth Wyllys in 1692) and fathered fourteen children, most of whom he survived. Though he was the correspondent and friend of persons such as Increase Mather and Samuel Sewall and a vigorous defender of the conservative wing of Puritanism, Taylor rarely came into the larger public view.

Edward Taylor's gravestone in Westfield, Massachusetts.

Given these few details and what we know of Taylor's theology, he would have been a likely candidate for the uncomplimentary treatment accorded Puritan poets by influential nineteenth-century literary critics such as Moses Coit Tyler. In *A History of American Literature, 1607–1765* (1878), Tyler summarizes the popular view of the relationship between Puritan faith and Puritan art in terms that targeted poets such as Bradstreet and Wigglesworth (and would have targeted Taylor, had his poetry been discovered): "the typical Puritan . . . believed that there was an inappeasable feud between religion and art; and hence, the duty of suppressing art was bound up in his soul with the master purpose of promoting religion. He cultivated the grim and the ugly . . . ." Our access to Taylor's poetry today allows us to reexamine the assumptions out of which such critics wrote and to examine the feeling, depth, and artistic sophistication in Puritan poetry.

Of all poets who wrote in America during the seventeenth and eighteenth centuries, Taylor is foremost for showing that Puritanism was not antithetical to art and that quite apart from "the grim and the ugly" the Puritan poets were said to have cultivated, they could cultivate opportunities for favoring images of the beautiful and the divine in their writings. In the work of Taylor (and by his example perhaps that of other Puritan poets as well) are found an appreciation of poetic precedent and a finely developed symbolic imagination. Among the precedents most often noticed, particularly in extravagant language and emotionalism of Taylor's meditational poems, is the influence of the English metaphysical and meditational verse traditions represented by Francis Quarles, John Donne, George Herbert, Richard Crashaw, and Andrew Marvell. Detectable in Taylor's poems, especially in his longer pieces, is an affinity for the dramatic representation of larger-than-life religious conflict, associated with poetic works such as John Milton's *Paradise Lost (1667)* and Wigglesworth's *The Day of Doom (1662)* and prose works such as John Bunyan's *The Holy War (1682)*.

At the same time, staples unique to the American Puritan poetic tradition abound in Taylor's poetry. Vestiges of the early Puritans' "plaine style" are noticeable, especially in the range of homelike and natural images Taylor introduces into his poems. Also apparent is the Puritans' fondness for typology, or symbolism. Favored by Puritan preachers and historians as well as poets, typology was understood in two contexts, and both are developed in Taylor's poems. Through typological treatment of the Bible individuals, places, or events in the Old Testament (the type) were interpreted as foreshadowings of individuals, places, or events in the New Testament (the antitype). Thus, Old Testament Passover rites were thought to foreshadow the rituals associated with the "Lord's Supper" in the New Testament; similarly, Old Testament images of captivity and bondage were thought to foreshadow the bondage in sin of New Testament figures who failed to yield to the redemptive power of grace. Typology also offered Puritans a way of seeing the world as a physical or material representation of the divine will toward humans. In Taylor's poetry, development of commonplace realities—a spider catching a fly, for instance, or the ravages of a "Sweeping Flood"—signals the poet's desire to plumb the material world for examples of the divine mind expressing its truths to humankind.

Following the topical and chronological arrangement in Taylor's manuscripts, his poetry is usually separated into three groups. Poems of the first group are collected under Taylor's own heading: *Gods Determinations touching his Elect*. Written during the late 1670s and early 1680s, the thirty-five poems that comprise *God's Determinations* attempt to trace the religious course of human history from Creation, through the Fall, to the point of man's opportunity for redemption through the suffering of Christ. Collectively, the poems present the prospect of a merciful God witnessing the battle between Christ and Satan for control of the elect (those chosen by God for salvation).

Emphasizing a God of mercy as opposed to the fire and brimstone God who dispenses justice in Wigglesworth's *The Day of Doom, God's Determinations* humanizes the Calvinists' typical portrait of the divine in a sometimes playful, but ultimately serious and affecting, manner. In "The Preface," for instance, Creator and Creation take on distinctly unorthodox characteristics: the Creator as sportsman in "this Bowling Alley" of a universe bowls the sun into place and as divine designer hangs the "Tapistry" of the world's landscape and decorates the sky with "twinckling Lanthorns" (lanterns). But throughout *God's Determinations,* lest the seriousness of his point be lost, Taylor repeatedly reminds the reader of the smallness of humans and of the need for divine support in the war between the forces of good and evil, a war in which humans would seem to be nothing more than unwitting pawns. But humans must fight, as well, against Satan's wiles and hoodwinks and against the doubts that compromise every Christian soldier's spirit when, as Taylor writes in "Some of Satan's Sophistry," the possibility of salvation through grace seems but a dim hope and sin looms so large as to seem unabsolvable. Yet, the reward for the enduring soldier—a ride heavenward in Christ's victory coach—justifies the struggle and is available for all who share Taylor's belief in God's final mercy toward the saints. That ride is assured in the refrain of "The Joy of Church Fellowship Rightly Attended": "in Christ's Coach they sweetly sing /As they to Glory ride therein."

The second group of Taylor's poems is the smallest of the three. Because the poems collected there use allegories based on natural events to demonstrate the poet coming to terms with necessity or to treat religious doctrine, they are intriguing and rewarding glimpses into the Puritan imagination. These occasional poems (poems for special occasions) were probably written in the 1680s. One, "Upon Wedlock, & Death of Children," is a particularly moving piece in which marital love, tried and strengthened by the loss of children, serves as a model for the poet's conversion of a trial of faith into a strengthening of his love for God and an expression of his willingness to accept the divine will. Marriage he calls a "Curious Knot," and by playing on the modern meaning of knot (the "True-Love Knot" that binds couples together) along with its archaic meaning (a garden), he reaffirms his love for his wife even as he surrenders the flowers of their love's labor to an untimely fate. The ultimate affirmation Taylor makes in the poem is to the will of God, and the poet pledges to "piecemeale pass" whatever additional flowers are required for God's glory.

Although none of Taylor's other occasional poems is quite so personal, most develop the symbolic content of events in a way that includes even the good Puritan preacher in their message. In "Upon the Sweeping Flood," for instance, Taylor interprets the ravages of rain and flood as heavenly "Excrements" sent to "drown [the] Carnal love" (that is, the worldliness) of a people incapable of crying over the effects of their sin. In "Upon a Spider Catching a Fly," the dance of death between spider, fly, and wasp symbolizes the spiritual dance of death between "Hell's Spider" (Satan), the unregenerate who court sin much as a "Silly Fly" might court death in a spider's web, and those born again in grace who, like a powerful wasp, have the ability to thwart all satanic "Stratigems."

Had they been all that survived, *God's Determinations* and the collection of occasional poems would have assured Taylor's reputation as a poet of rare merit. However, his enduring contribution to early-American letters will likely be *Preparatory Meditations,* his third group of poems. Composed between 1682 and 1725 and collected under the title *Preparatory Meditations Before My Approach to the Lord's Supper* by Taylor, the nearly two hundred meditations are the most unusual poetic expressions known to have been written in colonial America. In part, the meditations are thoroughly Puritan: many are typological studies, and some appear to portray the human condition with all the darkness and depravity suggested by the unmodified Calvinist writings of Wigglesworth or of Jonathan Edwards. Yet, the meditations are distinctly non-Puritan, and it is for their exception to practically every rule of Puritan poetry that they are most highly prized.

Taylor composed the meditations to put himself in the proper frame of mind prior to administering communion to his congregation. Neither the formal title nor the occasion suggests the depth of personal feeling and the sheer weight of personality revealed in the poems. For Taylor these meditations constituted a spiritual autobiography or an extended record of the spiritual content of his journey through this world. No Puritan poems equal in intensity Taylor's poetic confessions of love for God or of belief—almost to the point of presumption—in God's love for humans, and no Puritan poet has expressed the ecstasy that Taylor cannot conceal when he meditates on the efficacy of grace. Because words often seem insufficient to him to express the boundless love, indeed, the passion, flowing between God and poet, Taylor resorts to elaborate conceits and bold exaggerations. At these times, God's love becomes "matchless . . . [,] filling Heaven to the brim!" Taylor is always poised to admit his unworthiness, to confess himself the sinner desperate for, but not deserving of, redemption.

The majority of Taylor's contemporaries never read Taylor's writings. The responses of any who actually knew his poems remain shrouded in the obscurity in which the poems themselves languished for two centuries. That Taylor found poetry a congenial and inspiring medium for expressing his love of God and writing out his own interpretation of church doctrine is clear from the number of poems he wrote and from the fact that he wrote throughout his adult life. Ironically, in Edward Taylor New England Puritanism speaks with its most powerful, vital, and unique poetic voice, a voice that it never had the pleasure of hearing.

Suggested Readings: *Edward Taylor's Christographia,* ed. N. S. Grabo, 1962. *The Diary of Edward Taylor,* ed. F. Murphy, 1964. *A Transcript of Edward Taylor's Metrical History of Christianity,* ed. D. E. Stanford, 1977. *The Unpublished Writings of Edward Taylor,* 3 vols., ed. T. M. Davis and V. L. Davis, 1981. N. S. Grabo, *Edward Taylor,* 1961. *Early American Literature,* special Taylor issue, 4 (Winter 1969–1970). W. J. Scheick, *The Will and the Word: The Poetry of Edward Taylor,* 1974. K. Keller, *The Example of Edward Taylor,* 1975. K. E. Rowe, *Saint and Singer: Edward Taylor's Typology and the Poetics of Meditation,* 1986. J. Gatta, *Gracious Laughter: The Meditative Wit of Edward Taylor,* 1989.

Text Used: *The Poems of Edward Taylor,* ed. D. E. Stanford, 1960 (some spelling and punctuation modernized).

from GOD'S DETERMINATIONS*

THE PREFACE

Infinity, when all things it beheld
In nothing, and of nothing all did build,
Upon what base was fixed the lathe, wherein
He turn'd this globe, and riggaled[1] it so trim?
Who blew the bellows of his furnace vast?
Or held the mold wherein the world was cast?
Who laid its corner stone?[2] Or whose command?
Where stand the pillars upon which it stands?
Who laced and filleted[3] the earth so fine,
With rivers like green ribbons smaragdine?[4]   10
Who made the sea's its selvage,[5] and its locks
Like a quilt ball[6] within a silver box?
Who spread its canopy? Or curtains spun?
Who in this bowling alley bowled the sun?
Who made it always when it rises set
To go at once both down, and up to get?
Who th'curtain rods made for this tapestry?
Who hung the twinkling lanthorns[7] in the sky?
Who? who did this? or who is he? Why, know
Its only might almighty this did do.   20
His hand hath made this noble worke which stands
His glorious handywork not made by hands.

* Taylor wrote *God's Determinations Touching His Elect: And the Elect's Combat in Their Conversion, and Coming up to God in Christ, Together With the Comfortable Effects Thereof,* a series of lyrics and sermons in verse, to celebrate God's power and to trace the progress made by human souls since Creation.
[1] Grooved.
[2] "Where wast thou when I laid the foundations of the earth? . . . or who laid the cornerstone thereof: When the morning stars sang together, and all the sons of God shouted for joy?" from Job 38:4–8.
[3] Encircled with decoration.   [4] Emerald green.   [5] A border, as on a piece of cloth.
[6] A ball of yarn, which would unravel if not stored in a box.   [7] Lanterns.

Who spake all things from nothing; and with ease
Can speak all things to nothing, if he please.
Whose little finger at his pleasure can
Out mete[8] ten thousand worlds with half a span:
Whose might almighty can by half a looks
Root up the rocks and rock the hills by th'roots.
Can take this mighty world up in his hand,
And shake it like a squitchen[9] or a wand.   30
Whose single frown will make the heavens shake
Like as an aspen leaf the wind makes quake.
Oh! what a might is this whose single frown
Doth shake the world as it would shake it down?
Which all from nothing fet,[10] from nothing, all:
Hath all on nothing set, lets nothing fall.
Gave all to nothing man indeed, whereby
Through nothing man all might him glorify.
In nothing then imbossed the brightest gem
More precious than all preciousness in them.   40
But nothing man did throw down all by sin:
And darkened that lightsome gem in him.
    That now his brightest diamond is grown
    Darker by far than any coalpit stone.

                                       1680?, 1939

THE JOY OF CHURCH FELLOWSHIP RIGHTLY ATTENDED*

In Heaven soaring up, I dropped an ear
    On earth: and oh! sweet melody:
And listening, found it was the saints[1] who were
    Encoached for Heaven that sang for joy.
    For in Christ's coach[2] they sweetly sing;
    As they to glory ride therein.

Oh! joyous hearts! Enfired with holy flame!
    Is speech thus tassled[3] with praise?
Will not your inward fire of joy contain;
    That it in open flames doth blaze?   10
    For in Christ's coach saints sweetly sing,
    As they to glory ride therein.

And if a string[4] do slip, by chance, they soon
    Do screw it up again: whereby

---

[8] Outmeasure.   [9] A stick used for whipping.   [10] Made.
* The final poem in the *God's Determination* series.
[1] Those who, when alive, were church members—"visible saints."
[2] The church, the means by which the elect could rise to Heaven.
[3] Ornamented.   [4] A musical instrument's string; when it has slipped, it must be tightened.

They set it in a more melodious tune
   And a diviner harmony.
   For in Christ's coach they sweetly sing.
   As they to glory ride therein.

In all their acts, public, and private, nay
   And secret too, they praise impart.   20
But in their acts divine and worship, they
   With hymns do offer up their heart.
   Thus in Christ's coach they sweetly sing
   As they to glory ride therein.

Some few not in;[5] and some whose time, and place
   Block up this coach's way[6] do go
As travellers afoot, and so do trace
   The road that gives them right thereto
   While in this coach these sweetly sing
   As they to glory ride therein.   30

                                  1680?, 1939

from   *PREPARATORY MEDITATIONS**

THE REFLEXION

Lord, art thou at the table head above
   Meat, med'cine, sweetness, sparkling beauties to
Enamor souls with flaming flakes of love,
   And not my trencher,[1] nor my cup o'erflow?
   Be n't I a bidden guest? Oh! sweat mine eye.
   O'erflow with tears: Oh! draw thy fountains dry.

Shall I not smell thy sweet, oh! Sharon's rose?[2]
   Shall not mine eye salute thy beauty? Why?
Shall thy sweet leaves their beautious sweets upclose?
   As half ashamed my sight should on them lie?   10
   Woe's me! for this my sighs shall be in grain[3]
   Offer'd on sorrow's altar for the same.

---

[5] Those few who are saved but choose to remain outside the church.
[6] Those who are saved but live in non-Christian regions or preceded Christ.
* Published as *Preparatory Meditations Before My Approach to the Lord's Supper: Chiefly Upon the Doctrine Preached Upon the Day of Administration* [of Holy Communion].
[1] A wooden plate.
[2] "I am a rose of Sharon, a lily of the valleys," from Song of Solomon 2:1. The Plain of Sharon in Palestine was well known as a fertile coastal plain.
[3] Entirely.

Had not my soul's thy conduit, pipes stopped been
  With mud, what ravishment would'st thou convey?
Let grace's golden spade dig till the spring
  Of tears arise, and clear this filth away.
  Lord, let thy spirit raise my sighings till
  These pipes my soul do with thy sweetness fill.

Earth once was paradise of Heaven below
  Till inkfac'd sin had it with poison stocked   20
And chased this paradise away into
  Heav'n's upmost loft, and it in glory locked.
  But thou, sweet Lord, hast with thy golden key
  Unlocked the door, and made, a golden day.

Once at thy feast,[4] I saw thee pearl-like stand
  'Tween Heaven, and earth where heaven's bright glory all
In streams fell on thee, as a floodgate and,
  Like sunbeams through thee on the world to fall.
  Oh! sugar sweet then! my dear sweet Lord, I see
  Saints' Heavens-lost happiness restor'd by thee.   30

Shall Heaven, and earth's bright glory all up lie
  Like sunbeams bundled in the sun, in thee?
Dost thou sit rose at table head, where I
  Do sit, and carv'st no morsel sweet for me?
  So much before, so little now! Sprindge,[5] Lord,
  Thy rosy leaves, and me their glee afford.

Shall not thy rose my garden fresh perfume?
  Shall not thy beauty my dull heart assail?
Shall not thy golden gleams run through this gloom?
  Shall my black velvet mask thy fair face veil?   40
  Pass o'er my faults: shine forth, bright sun: arise
  Enthrone thy rosy-self within mine eyes.

1683, 1939

MEDITATION 8 (FIRST SERIES)

John 6:51. *I am the living bread.*[1]

I kenning[2] through astronomy divine
  The world's bright battlement,[3] wherein I spy

---

[4] The Eucharist, or Holy Communion, in which believers share in the blood and body of Christ.
[5] Spread.
[1] "I am the living bread which came down from heaven: if any man eat of this bread, he shall live for ever: and the bread that I will give is my flesh, which I will give for the life of the world," from John 6:51.
  [2] Discerning.   [3] The towers of Heaven.

A golden path my pencil cannot line,
  From that bright throne unto my threshold lie.
And while my puzzled thoughts about it pour,
  I find the bread of life in't at my door.

When that this bird of paradise[4] put in
  This wicker cage (my corpse) to tweedle[5] praise
Had pecked the fruit forbade: and so did fling
  Away its food; and lost its golden days;   10
  It fell into celestial famine sore:
  And never could attain a morsel more.

Alas! alas! Poor bird, what wilt thou do?
  The creature's field[6] no food for souls e'er gave.
And if thou knock at angels doors they show
  An empty barrel: they no soul bread have.
  Alas! Poor bird, the world's white loaf is done.
  And cannot yield thee here the smallest crumb.

In this sad state, God's tender bowels[7] run
  Out streams of grace: and he to end all strife   20
The purest wheat in Heaven, his dear-dear Son
  Grinds, and kneads up into this bread of life.
  Which bread of life from Heaven down came and stands
  Dished on thy table up by angel's hands.

Did God mold up this bread in Heaven, and bake,
  Which from his table came, and to thine goeth?
Doth he bespeak thee thus, this soul bread take.
  Come eat thy fill of this thy God's white loaf?
  It's food too fine for angels, yet come, take
  And eat thy fill. It's Heaven's sugar cake.   30

What grace is this knead in this loaf? This thing
  Souls are but petty things it to admire.
Yee angels, help: This fill would to the brim
  Heav'n's whelm'd-down[8] crystal meal bowl, yea and higher.
  This bread of life dropped in thy mouth, doth cry.
  Eat, eat me, soul, and thou shalt never die.

                                                    1684, 1939

MEDITATION 39 (FIRST SERIES)

1 John 2:1 *If any man sin, we have an advocate.*[1]

My sin! my sin, My God, these cursed dregs,
  Green, yellow, blue streaked poison hellish, rank,

---

[4] The human soul.   [5] To sing.   [6] The world of humans.
[7] The inner body, thought to be the source of compassion.   [8] Inverted.
[1] "And if any man sin, we have an advocate with the Father, Jesus Christ the righteous: And he is the propitiation for . . . the sins of the whole world," from 1 John 2:1–2.

Bubs[2] hatched in nature's nest on serpents' eggs,
   Yelp, chirp and cry; they set my soul acramp.
   I frown, chide, strike and fight them, mourn and cry
   To conquer them, but cannot them destroy.

I cannot kill nor coop them up: my curb
   'S less than a snaffle[3] in their mouth: my reins
They as a twine thread, snap: by hell they're spurred:
   And load my soul with swagging loads of pains.   10
   Black imps, young devils, snap, bite, drag to bring
   And pick me headlong hell's dread whirlpool in.

Lord, hold thy hand: for handle me thou may'st
   In wrath: but, oh, a twinkling ray of hope
Methinks I spy thou graciously display'st.
   There is an advocate: a door is ope.
   Sin's poison swell my heart would till it burst,
   Did not a hope hence creep in't thus, and nurse't.

Joy, joy, God's Son's the sinner's advocate
   Doth plead the sinner guiltless, and a saint.   20
But yet attorney's pleas spring from the state
   The case is in: if bad its bad in plaint.[4]
   My papers do contain no pleas that do
   Secure me from, but knock me down to, woe.

I have no plea mine advocate to give:
   What now? He'll anvil arguments great store
Out of his flesh and blood to make thee live.
   O dear bought arguments: Good pleas therefore.
   Nails made of heavenly steel, more choice than gold
   Drove home, well clenched, eternally will hold.   30

Oh! Dear bought plea, dear Lord, what buy't so dear?
   What with thy blood purchase thy plea for me?
Take argument out of thy grave t'appear
   And plead my case with, me from guilt to free.
   These maul both sins, and devils, and amaze
   Both saints, and angels; wreath their mouths with praise.

What shall I do, my Lord? what do, that I
   May have thee plead my case? I fee[5] thee will
With faith, repentance, and obediently
   Thy service gainst satanic sins fulfill.   40
   I'll fight thy fields while live I do, although
   I should be hacked in pieces by thy foe.

Make me thy friend, Lord, be my surety: I
   Will be thy client, be my advocate:

---

[2] Pustules.   [3] A bit on a horse's bridle.   [4] A written grievance.   [5] Pay.

My sins make thine, thy pleas make mine hereby.
Thou wilt me save, I will thee celebrate.
Thou'lt kill my sins that cut my heart within:
And my rough feet[6] shall thy smooth praises sing.

1684?, 1954

MEDITATION 7 (SECOND SERIES)

Psalms 105:17. *He sent a man before them, even Joseph, who was sold, etc.*[1]

All dull, my Lord, my spirits flat, and dead
    All water-soaked and sapless[2] to the skin.
Oh! Screw me up and make my spirit's bed
    Thy quickening virtue for my ink is dim,
    My pencil blunt. Doth Joseph type out thee?[3]
    Heralds of angels sing out, bow the knee.

Is Joseph's glorious shine a type of thee?
    How bright art thou? He envied was as well.
And so was thou. He's stripped, and picked, poor he,
    Into the pit. And so was thou. They shell   10
    Thee of thy kernel. He by Judas[4] sold
    For twenty bits, thirty for thee he'd told.

Joseph was tempted by his mistress vile.
    Thou by the Devil, but both shame the foe.
Joseph was cast into the jail awhile.
    And so was thou. Sweet apples mellow so.
    Joseph did from his jail to glory run.
    Thou from death's pallet rose like morning sun.

Joseph lays in[5] against the famine, and
    Thou dost prepare the bread of life for thine.   20
He bought with corn for pharaoh th'men and land.
    Thou with thy bread mak'st such themselves consign
    Over to thee, that eat it. Joseph makes
    His brethren bow before him. Thine too quake.

Joseph constrains his brethren till their sins
    Do gall their souls. Repentance babbles fresh.
Thou treatest sinners till repentance springs

---

[6] Metrical units of verse.

[1] "He sent a man before them, even Joseph, who was sold for a servant," from Psalms 105:17; Joseph, a son of Rachel and Jacob, was sold into slavery in Egypt by his jealous brothers but became a high-ranking official.

[2] Frail.

[3] Because of similarities between the events of Joseph's life and those of Jesus, Joseph has generally been considered to be a prefigurement, or type, of Jesus (see Genesis 37–50).

[4] In Matthew 26:14, 48, Judas Iscariot, the disciple who betrayed Jesus.   [5] Stores away goods.

Then with him sendst a Benjamin-like mess.[6]
Joseph doth cheer his humble brethren. Thou
Dost stud[7] with joy the mourning saints that bow.   30

Joseph's bright shine th'Eleven Tribes must preach.
    And thine Apostles now eleven, thine.
They bear his presents to his friends: thine reach
    Thine unto thine, thus now behold a shine.
    How hast thou pencilled out, my Lord, most bright
    Thy glorious image here, on Joseph's light.

This I bewail in me under this shine
    To see so dull a color in my skin.
Lord, lay thy brightsome colors on me thine.
    Scour thou my pipes then play thy tunes therein.   40
    I will not hang my harp in willows by,[8]
    While thy sweet praise, my tunes doth glorify.

                                                        1694, 1939

MEDITATION 150 (SECOND SERIES)

Canticles 7:3. *Thy two breasts are like two young roes that are twins.*[1]

My Blessed Lord, how doth thy beautious spouse[2]
    In stately stature rise in comeliness?
With her two breasts like two little roes that browse
    Among the lilies in their shining dress
    Like stately milk pails ever full and flow
    With spiritual milk to make her babes to grow.

Celestial nectar wealthier far than wine
    Wrought in the spirit's brew house and up tunned[3]
Within these vessels which are trussed up fine
    Likened to two pretty, neat twin roes that run'd   10
    Most pleasantly by their dam's sides like cades[4]
    And suckle with their milk Christ's spiritual babes.

Lord put these nibbles then my mouth into
    And suckle me therewith I humbly pray,

---

[6] A special meal; in Genesis 35:18 Benjamin was the favorite son of Jacob and Rachel.
[7] To ornament.
[8] "By the rivers of Babylon, there we [the Israelites] sat down, yea, we wept, when we rememberd Zion. On the willows there we hung our lyres. . . . How shall we sing the Lord's song in a strange land?" from Psalms 137:1–4.
[1] The poems of the Song of Solomon, or Canticles, celebrate love and the union of marriage; roes are small deer.
[2] The bride is considered to be God's spouse.
[3] Stored in barrels.   [4] Pets.

Then with this milk thy spiritual babe I'dst grow,
  And these two milk pails shall themselves display
  Like to these pretty twins in pairs round neat
  And shall sing forth thy praise over this meat.[5]

1719, 1960

UPON A SPIDER CATCHING A FLY

Thou sorrow, venom elf.
  Is this thy play,
To spin a web out of thyself
  To catch a fly?
    For why?

I saw a pettish[1] wasp
  Fall foul therein.
Whom yet thy whorl pins[2] did not clasp
  Lest he should fling
    His sting.   10

But as afraid, remote
  Didst stand hereat
And with thy little fingers stroke
  And gently tap
    His back.

Thus gently him didst treat
  Lest he should pet,[3]
And in a froppish,[4] waspish heat
  Should greatly fret
    Thy net.   20

Whereas the silly fly,
  Caught by its leg
Thou by the throat tookst hastily
  And 'hind the head
    Bite dead.

This goes to pot, that not
  Nature doth call.[5]
Strive not above what strength hath got
  Lest in the brawl
    Thou fall.   30

---

[5] The host, or food, that symbolizes Christ's flesh.
[1] Angry.   [2] The pins that catch the thread on a spinning wheel.   [3] Grow angry.   [4] Irritable.
[5] Those who do not call upon nature—natural reason, or, to the Puritans, the ability to know God's truth—are destroyed.

This fray seems thus to us.
    Hell's spider gets
His intrails spun to whip cords[6] thus
    And wove to nets
        And sets.[7]

To tangle Adam's race
    In's stratigems
To their destructions, spoil'd, made base
    By venom things
        Damn'd sins.   40

But mighty, gracious Lord
    Communicate
Thy grace to break the cord, afford
    Us glory's gate
        And state.

We'll nightingale sing like
    When pearched on high
In glory's cage, thy glory, bright,
    And thankfully,
        For joy.   50

1680–1682?, 1939

UPON A WASP CHILLED WITH COLD*

The bear[1] that breaths the northern blast
Did numb, torpedo-like,[2] a wasp
Whose stiffened limbs encramped, lay bathing
In Sol's[3] warm breath and shine as saving,
Which with her hands she chafes and stands
Rubbing her legs, shanks, thighs, and hands.
Her petty toes, and fingers' ends
Nipped with this breath, she out extends
Unto the sun, in great desire
To warm her digits at that fire.   10
Doth hold her temples in this state
Where pulse doth beat, and head doth ache.
Doth turn, and stretch her body small,
Doth comb her velvet capital.[4]
As if her little brain pan were

---

[6] Strong cords.   [7] Snares.
* Taylor's actual title was "Upon a Wasp Child With Cold."
[1] The Great Bear, the constellation Ursa Major; or the North wind.
[2] Like the torpedo fish, which stuns its victims by electric shock.   [3] The sun's.
[4] Head.

A volume of choice precepts clear.
As if her satin jacket hot
Contained apothecary's shop
Of nature's receipts,[5] that prevails
To remedy all her sad ails,   20
As if her velvet helmet high
Did turret[6] rationality.
She fans her wing up to the wind
As if her petticoat were lined,
With reason's fleece, and hoists sails
And humming flies in thankful gales
Unto her dun curled[7] palace hall
Her warm thanks offering for all.

    Lord clear my misted sight that I
May hence view thy divinity.   30
Some sparks whereof thou up dost hasp[8]
Within this little downy wasp
In whose small corporation[9] we
A school and a schoolmaster see
Where we may learn, and easily find
A nimble spirit bravely mind
Her work in ev'ry limb: and lace
It up neat with a vital grace,
Acting each part though ne'er so small
Here of this fustian[10] animal.   40
Till I enravished climb into
The Godhead on this ladder do.
Where all my pipes inspired upraise
An heavenly music furred[11] with praise.

                                            1674–1689?, 1943

HUSWIFERY*

Make me, O Lord, thy spinning wheel complete.
    Thy Holy Word my distaff[1] make for me.
Make mine affections thy swift flyers[2] neat
    And make my soul thy holy spool to be.
    My conversation make to be thy reel[3]
    And reel the yarn thereon spun of thy wheel.

Make me thy loom then, knit therein this twine:
    And make thy Holy Spirit, Lord, wind quills:[4]

---

[5] Recipes.   [6] Enclose, contain.   [7] Dark curved.   [8] Shut.   [9] Body.
[10] Coarse-clothed; fustian is a cloth similar to corduroy.   [11] Fur-trimmed.
* Housekeeping; here, specifically weaving.
[1] The part of a spinning wheel that holds the raw wool fibers.
[2] The revolving part of a spinning wheel that twists the fibers into yarn or thread.
[3] The spool of a spinning wheel on which yarn or thread is wound.   [4] Bobbins or spools.

Then weave the web thyself. The yarn is fine.
    Thine ordinances make my fulling mills.[5]   10
Then dye the same in heavenly colors choice,
    All pinked[6] with varnished[7] flowers of paradise.

Then clothe therewith mine understanding, will,
    Affections, judgment, conscience, memory
My words, and actions, that their shine may fill
    My ways with glory and thee glorify.
Then mine apparel shall display before ye
    That I am clothed in holy robes for glory.

1682–1683?, 1939

UPON WEDLOCK, AND DEATH OF CHILDREN

A curious knot[1] God made in paradise,
    And drew it out enameled neatly fresh.
It was the true-love knot, more sweet than spice
    And set with all the flowers of grace's dress.
    It's wedding's knot, that ne'er can be untied.
    No Alexander's sword can it divide.[2]

The slips[3] here planted, gay and glorious grow:
    Unless an hellish breath do singe their plumes.
Here primrose, cowslips, roses, lilies blow[4]
    With violets and pinks that void[5] perfumes.   10
    Whose beautious leaves o'erlaid with honey dew.
    And chanting birds chirp out sweet music true.

When in this knot I planted was, my stock[6]
    Soon knotted, and a manly flower[7] outbroke.
And after it my branch again did knot.
    Brought out another flower[8] its sweet breathed mate.
    One knot gave one t'other the t'other's place.
    Whence chuckling smiles fought in each other's face.

But oh! a glorious hand from glory came
    Guarded with angels, soon did crop this flower   20
Which almost tore the root up of the same
    At that unlooked for, dolesome, darksome hour.

---

[5] Mills where cloth is cleaned with soap, or fuller's earth.   [6] Adorned.   [7] Sparkling.
[1] A flower bed as well as the marital bond.
[2] According to legend, Alexander the Great (356–323 B.C.) cut the knot tied by King Gordius of Phrygia, a knot to be undone only by the future master of Asia; "to cut the Gordian knot" means to find a quick solution for a problem.
[3] Plant cuttings.   [4] Blossom.   [5] Give off.   [6] A plant's main stem or trunk.
[7] Taylor refers to four of his children, two of whom had died before the poem was written, as flowers. Here he means his son Samuel (1675–?).
[8] Taylor's daughter Elizabeth (1676–1677).

In prayer to Christ perfumed it did ascend,
And angels bright did it to Heaven tend.

But pausing on't, this sweet perfum'd my thought,
  Christ would in glory have a flower, choice, prime,
And having choice, chose this my branch forth brought.
  Lord take't. I thank thee, thou takst ought of mine,
  It is my pledge in glory,[9] part of me
  Is now in it, Lord, glorified with thee.   30

But praying o'er my branch, my branch did sprout
  And bore another manly flower,[10] and gay
And after that another,[11] sweet broke out.
  The which the former hand soon got away.
  But oh! the tortures, vomit, screechings, groans,
  And six weeks' fever would pierce hearts like stones.

Grief o'er doth flow: and nature fault would find
  Were not thy Will, my spell, charm, joy, and gem:
That as I said, I say, take, Lord, they're thine.
  I piecemeal pass to glory bright in them.   40
  I joy, may I sweet flowers for glory breed,
  Whether thou getst them green, or lets them seed.

                              1682–1683?, 1939

THE EBB AND FLOW

When first thou on me Lord wrought'st thy sweet print,
  My heart was made thy tinderbox.[1]
  My 'ffections were thy tinder in't.
    Where fell thy sparks by drops.
Those holy sparks of heavenly fire that came
Did ever catch and often out would flame.

But now my heart is made thy censear[2] trim,
  Full of thy golden altar's fire,
  To offer up sweet incense in
    Unto thyself entire: 10
I find my tinder scarce thy sparks can feel
That drop out from thy holy flint and steel.

---

[9] The assurance of a resting place in heaven.
[10] Taylor's son James (1678–?).   [11] Taylor's daughter Abigail (1681–1682).
[1] A box for holding tinder, flint, and steel for starting a fire.
[2] A receptacle used for burning incense.

Hence doubts out bud for fear thy fire in me
   'S a mocking ignis fatuus[3]
   Or lest thine altar's fire out be,
     Its hid in ashes thus.
Yet when the bellows of thy spirit blow
Away mine ashes, then thy fire doth glow.

1674–1689?, 1939

UPON THE SWEEPING FLOOD, AUG. 13–14, 1683

Oh! that I'd had a tear to've quenched that flame
   Which did dissolve the heavens above
   Into those liquid drops that came
     To drown our carnal[1] love.
Our cheeks were dry and eyes refused to weep.
Tears bursting out ran down the sky's dark cheek.

Were th'heavens sick? must we their doctors be
   And physic[2] them with pills, our sin?
   To make them purge and vomit, see,
     And excrements out fling?   10
We've griev'd them by such physic that they shed
Their excrements upon our lofty heads.

1683, 1943

A FIG FOR THEE OH! DEATH*

Thou king of terrors with thy gastly eyes
With butter[1] teeth, bare bones, grim looks likewise.
And grizzly hide, and clawing talons, fell,[2]
Op'ning to sinners vile, trap door of Hell,
That on in sin impenitently trip
The downfall[3] art of the infernal pit,
Thou struckst thy teeth deep in my Lord's bless'd side:
Who dashed it out, and all its venom 'stroyed
That now thy poundrill[4] shall only dash
My flesh and bones to bits, and cask[5] shall clash.   10
Thou'rt not so frightful now to me, thy knocks
Do crack my shell. Its heavenly kernel's box

---

[3] Foolish fire (Latin), a term used for natural phosphorescent lights over a swamp, which caused travelers to lose their way; a "will-o-the-wisp," or misleading influence.
[1] Earthly.   [2] To dose with medicine.
* "Fig" here means a trifling amount, something of no value.
[1] Yellowed.   [2] Deadly.   [3] Precipice.   [4] Pestle, or pounder.   [5] Body.

Abides most safe. Thy blows do break its shell,
Thy teeth its nut. Cracks are that on it fell.
Thence out its kernel fair and nut, by worms
Once vitiated out, new formed forth turns
And on the wings of some bright angel flies
Out to bright glory of God's blissful joys.
Hence thou to me with all thy gastly face
Art not so dreadful unto me through grace.   20
I am resolved to fight thee, and ne'er yield,
Blood up to th'ears; and in the battlefield
Chasing thee hence: But not for this my flesh,
My body, my vile harlot, its thy mess,[6]
Laboring to drown me into sin, disguise
By eating and by drinking such evil joys
Though grace preserv'd me that I ne'er have
Surprised been nor tumbled in such grave.[7]
Hence for my strumpet I'll ne'er draw my sword
Nor thee restrain at all by iron curb[8]   30
Nor for her safety will I 'gainst thee strive
But let thy frozen grips take her captive
And her imprison in thy dungeon cave
And grind to powder in thy mill the grave,
Which powder in thy van[9] thou'st safely keep
Till she hath slept out quite her fatal sleep.
When the last cock shall crow the last day[10] in
And the archangel's trumpet's sound shall ring
Then th'eye omniscient seek shall all there round
Each dust death's mill had very finely ground,   40
Which in death's smoky furnace well refined
And each to'ts fellow hath exactly joined,
Is raised up anew and made all bright
And crystallized; all top full of delight.
And entertains its soul again in bliss
And holy angels waiting all on this,
The soul and body now, as two true lovers
E'ry night how do they hug and kiss each other.
And going hand in hand thus through the skies
Up to eternal glory glorious rise.   50
Is this the worst thy terrors then canst, why
Then should this grimace at me terrify?
Why cam'st thou then so slowly? Mend[11] thy pace.
Thy slowness me detains from Christ's bright face.
Although thy terrors rise to th'high'st degree,
I still am where I was, a fig for thee.

[6] Meal.
[7] Lines 24–28 are clearer in an earlier version of this poem: "My harlot body, make thou it thy mess,/That oft ensnared me with its strumpet's guise/Of meat's and drink's dainty sensualities,/Yet grace ne'er suffer[ed] me to turn aside/As sinners oft fall in and do abide."
[8] A restrainer such as a horse's bit.   [9] A winnowing basket; possibly, a tomb.
[10] Judgment Day.   [11] Improve.

=CONTEXTS=

The New England Primer

For the Puritans, religion and learning were always linked. The Puritans believed that every Christian must be literate in order to read the Bible and other religious writing. This essential tie between learning and spiritual life was established for children through *The New England Primer*, first published in the Massachusetts Bay Colony before 1690. This book contains prayers, hymns, verse, and an illustrated alphabet accompanied by moral principles, so that the very act of learning to read became a religion lesson. Nearly every Puritan and Presbyterian household from the seventeenth through the mid-nineteenth century had a copy of the *Primer*, which was estimated to have sold over 5 million copies before 1850.

The Child's Guide.

A — In *Adam's* Fall
We finned all.

B — This *Book* attend,
Thy Life to mend.

C — The *Cat* does play,
And after flay.

D — The *Dog* doth bite
A Thief at Night.

E — An *Eagle's* flight
Is out of fight.

The Child's Guide.

F — The Idle *Fool*
Is whipt at School.

G — As runs the *Glafs*,
Man's Life doth
pafs.

H — My *Book* and *Heart*
Shall never part

I — *Jefus* did dye
For thee and I

K — King *Charles* the
Good,
No Man of Blood.

Two pages from *The New England Primer* (Anonymous, 1683?)

Mary Rowlandson
(1637?–1711?)

We have few facts about the life of Mary Rowlandson, the author of *The Narrative of the Captivity and Restoration of Mrs. Mary Rowlandson* (1682), one of the most widely read literary works to come out of the colonial period. She was probably born Mary White in 1637 in England but grew up in Salem, Massachusetts. In the early 1650s her father, John

White, a wealthy landowner, helped to establish the town of Lancaster, Massachusetts, about thirty miles West of Boston. There Mary settled with her husband, Joseph Rowlandson, the town's first minister. They had four children, one of whom died in infancy.

Mary Rowlandson lived on the frontier for a short but fierce period during the settlement of New England, called King Philip's War (1675?–1678). The war resulted from tensions between the Puritans and Native Americans—tensions building since the death of Massasoit, chief of the Wampanoag Indians of southeastern Massachusetts and ally of the Puritans, in 1661. The new chief was Metacomet, son of Massasoit. Called "King Philip," by the English, Metacomet remembered his father's status as a great chief before the Puritan arrival and sought to preserve the Wampanoag's dignity as a sovereign entity. With settlements crowding the Native Americans and their survival threatened, conflict was predictable. It broke out after Plymouth authorities executed three Wampanoags in January 1675 for the alleged murder of an Englishman. For the next eighteen months Wampanoags and Puritans fought, and the battleground typically was a frontier town.

In February 1676 a four-hundred-man war party consisting of Wampanoag, Quabaug, Nashaway, Narraganset, and Nipmuck Indians attacked Lancaster. The town had feared the raid, and Joseph Rowlandson was in Boston at the time, arranging for military aid. The Native Americans wounded Mary Rowlandson and her six-year-old daughter and took Rowlandson and her three children captives. Rowlandson was separated from her two oldest children, and her wounded daughter died nine days later. Until her release, nearly twelve weeks after her capture, Rowlandson was placed in the service of Quanopin, a sagamore (secondary chief) and brother-in-law of Metacomet, and Quanopin's wife, Wetamoo, who treated her decently.

From this experience Rowlandson composed *The Narrative*. It begins with a vigorous and unsentimental description of the nightmarish attack on Lancaster, including the savage treatment of so many of Rowlandson's relatives and neighbors. Twenty "removes," or relocations, to various campsites followed for the next eleven weeks and five days as Rowlandson endured freezing cold, sickness, loneliness, and fear—in what was ultimately a test of endurance. Against the day to day events are moments of unexpected confrontations with terror and death, which serve as dramatic punctuation in this tale of perseverance.

The Narrative is very much a Puritan's story. Framed as a tale of woe, it warns that God will punish Rowlandson and her community until they correct their ways and realize their complete dependence on God's will. The Native Americans are depicted as instruments of the Devil and as God's scourges sent to "afflict" the settlers until they reform. However, God's providence is reassuring, and Rowlandson's faith armed this New England Puritan against the terrors of the "howling wilderness." As Rowlandson explains in *The Narrative,* she could endure the hardships of the captivity because "God was carrying me along and bearing up my spirit." She searched for analogies between her experiences and passages in the Bible, referring to the Bible more than sixty-five times. Her release, she was convinced, was evidence of God's providential direction of her life and of the life of the colony.

Although *The Narrative* is didactic, finding a moral in every event, it is also realistic, giving a rare picture of Native-American life in this period of conflict. Along with their captives, the natives must live on nuts and berries, sleep out in the freezing New England winter, and meet death through war and privation. Even so, many Wampanoags find the means to "refresh" the starving Rowlandson from their limited resources, and she is thankful.

Many of the Wampanoags emerge from *The Narrative* with distinctive personalities, no one more than Metacomet, whom Rowlandson met at various times. To the reader, if not to Rowlandson, as he tries to profit from his captive, the chief appears somewhat more human than the ferocious enemy of the Puritans he was reputed to be. He instructs Rowlandson to stand before what he perhaps humorously calls "the General Court" and recommends the price of her ransom. Shortly thereafter, she is ransomed, apparently for the price of two coats, twenty pounds, half a bushel of seed corn, and some tobacco.

Rowlandson's release occurred near the end of King Philip's War, in which the Wampanoags were completely defeated. Whereas the colonists lost six hundred lives, the natives lost three thousand. Metacomet was killed, and his wife, children, and many other Native Americans were sold into slavery in the West Indies.

Once she and her children were freed, Rowlandson moved to Wethersfield, Connecticut, where her husband had accepted a ministry. When Rowlandson's husband died in 1678, the town gave her a pension for the remainder of her life. She is believed to have died in 1711.

Published in Boston in 1682, Rowlandson's *Narrative* was an immediate success, though her only known writing, and at least thirty editions of it have followed. It served as a model for other captivity narratives, commonly more sensational and sentimental than Rowlandson's. The captivity narrative entered American fiction in such stories about the Native American wars as James Fenimore Cooper's *The Last of the Mohicans* (1826). *The Narrative* remains important in its own right as a vigorous tale of frontier experience and for its heartfelt expression of a Puritan's deep religious experience. It is as well a powerful account of one of the Native American's many doomed attempts to halt colonial expansion.

Suggested Readings: *Narratives of the Indian Wars, 1675–1699*, ed. Charles H. Lincoln, 1913. *Held Captive by the Indians: Selected Narratives, 1642–1836*, ed. R. D. Van Der Beets, 1973. A. Keiser, *The Indian in American Literature*, 1933. R. H. Pearce, "The Significance of the Captivity Narrative" in *American Literature* XIX, 1947. R. Van Der Beets, *The Indian Captivity Narrative: An American Genre*, 1983. D. L. Greene, "New Light on Mary Rowlandson" in *Early American Literature* 20, 1985.

Text Used: *The Narrative of the Captivity and Restoration of Mrs. Mary Rowlandson*, 1930.

from THE NARRATIVE OF THE CAPTIVITY AND RESTORATION OF MRS. MARY ROWLANDSON*

On the tenth of February, 1675, [1] came the Indians in great numbers upon Lancaster.[2] Their first coming was about sun-rising. Hearing the noise of some guns, we looked out: several houses were burning, and the smoke ascending to heaven. There were five persons[3] taken in one house; the father, the mother, and a suckling child they knocked on the head; the other two they took and carried away

---

* Rowlandson's full title is *The Sovereignty and Goodness of GOD, Together With the Faithfulness of His Promises Displayed; Being a Narrative of the Captivity and Restoration of Mrs. Mary Rowlandson, Commended by Her, to All That Desires to Know the Lord's Doings to, and Dealings With Her. Especially to Her Dear Children and Relations. The Second Addition Corrected and Amended. Written by Her Own Hand for Her Private Use, and Now Made Public at the Earnest Desire of Some Friends, and for the Benefit of the Afflicted.*

[1] Rowlandson used the Julian, not the Gregorian, calendar, so her dates are ten days earlier than they would be in our system, and February was considered the last month of the year: her February 10, 1675/76 corresponds to our Thursday February 20, 1676.

[2] Lancaster, Massachusetts, Rowlandson's hometown and the site of her capture.

[3] The family of John Ball (?–1676), a tailor.

alive. There were two others, who being out of their garrison[4] upon some occasion, were set upon; one was knocked on the head, the other escaped. Another there was, who, running along, was shot and wounded, and fell down; he begged of them his life, promising them money, (as they told me,) but they would not hearken to him, but knocked him in head, and stripped him naked, and split open his bowels. Another, seeing many of the Indians about his barn, ventured and went out, but was quickly shot down. There were three others belonging to the same garrison[5] who were killed; the Indians getting up upon the roof of the barn, had advantage to shoot down upon them over their fortification. Thus these murderous wretches went on burning and destroying [all] before them.

At length they came and beset our own house, and quickly it was the dolefulest day that ever mine eyes saw. The house stood upon the edge of a hill; some of the Indians got behind the hill, others into the barn, and others behind any thing that would shelter them; from all which places they shot against the house, so that the bullets seemed to fly like hail; and quickly they wounded one man among us, then another, and then a third. About two hours (according to my observation in that amazing time) they had been about the house before they prevailed to fire it (which they did with flax and hemp which they brought out of the barn, there being no defense about the house,[6] only two flankers[7] at two opposite corners, and one of them not finished). They fired it once, and one ventured out and quenched it, but they quickly fired it again, and that took. Now is the dreadful hour come, that I have often heard (in time of war, as was the case with others) but now mine eyes see it. Some in our house were fighting for their lives, others wallowing in their blood, the house on fire over our heads, and the bloody heathen ready to knock us on the head if we stirred out. Now might we hear mothers and children crying out for themselves, and one another, "Lord, what shall we do?" Then I took my children (and one of my sisters her's) to go forth and leave the house: but as soon as we came to the door, and appeared, the Indians shot so thick, that the bullets rattled against the house, as if one had taken an handful of stones and threw them, so that we were fain to give back. We had six stout dogs belonging to our garrison, but none of them would stir, though [at] another time, if an Indian had come to the door, they were ready to fly upon him and tear him down. The Lord hereby would make us the more to acknowledge his hand, and to see that our help is always in him. But out we must go, the fire increasing, and coming along behind us, roaring, and the Indians gaping before us with their guns, spears, and hatchets, to devour us. No sooner were we out of the house, but my brother-in-law[8] (being before wounded, in defending the house, in or near the throat) fell down dead, whereat the Indians scornfully shouted, and hallooed, and were presently upon him, stripping off his clothes. The bullets flying thick, one went through my side, and the same (as [it] would seem) through the bowels and hand of my dear child in my arms.[9] One of my elder sister's children, named William,[10] had then his leg broken, which the Indians perceiving, they knocked him on the head. Thus were we butchered by those merciless heathens, standing amazed,

[4] A fortified house where people assembled for defense.
[5] The garrison of Richard Wheeler (?–1676).
[6] The Rowlandson house was not fortified and fell to the attackers.
[7] A projection for fortification.
[8] Ensign John Divoll (?–1676), commander of the garrison that day, was married to Rowlandson's youngest sister, Hannah.
[9] Rowlandson's daughter Sarah (1670–1676).
[10] William Kerley (1659–1676), son of Elizabeth and Lieut. Henry Kerley.

with the blood running down to our heels. My elder sister being yet in the house, and seeing those woeful sights, the infidels hauling mothers one way, and children another, and some wallowing in their blood, as her eldest son[11] telling her that her son William was dead, and myself was wounded, she said, And "Lord let me die with them": which was no sooner said, but she was struck with a bullet, and fell down dead over the threshold. I hope she is reaping the fruit of her good labors, being faithful to the service of God in her place. In her younger years she lay under much trouble upon spiritual accounts, till it pleased God to make that precious scripture take hold of her heart, 2 Corinthians xii:9. "And he said unto me, my grace is sufficient for thee." More than twenty years after, I have heard her tell how sweet and comfortable that place was to her. But to return: the Indians laid hold of us, pulling me one way, and the children another, and said, "Come, go along with us." I told them they would kill me. They answered, if I were willing to go along with them, they would not hurt me.

Oh! the doleful sight that now was to behold at this house! Come, behold the works of the Lord, what desolations he has made in the earth.[12] Of thirty-seven persons[13] who were in this one house, none escaped either present death, or a bitter captivity, save only one,[14] who might say as in Job i:15: And I only am escaped to tell the news. There were twelve killed, some shot, some stabbed with their spears, some knocked down with their hatchets. When we are in prosperity, oh, the little that we think of such dreadful sights, and to see our dear friends and relations lie bleeding out their heart's blood upon the ground. There was one who was chopped into the head with a hatchet, and stripped naked, and yet was crawling up and down. It is a solemn sight to see so many Christians lying in their blood, some here, and some there, like a company of sheep torn by wolves. All of them stripped naked by a company of hell-hounds, roaring, singing, ranting, and insulting, as if they would have torn our very hearts out; yet the Lord by his almighty power preserved a number of us from death, for there were twenty-four of us taken alive and carried captive.

I had often before this said, that if the Indians should come, I should choose rather to be killed by them, than taken alive; but when it came to the trial, my mind changed; their glittering weapons so daunted my spirit, that I chose rather to go along with those (as I may say) ravenous bears, than that moment to end my days. And that I may the better declare what happened to me during that grievous captivity, I shall particularly speak of the several removes[15] we had up and down the wilderness.

The First Remove

Now away we must go with those barbarous creatures, with our bodies wounded and bleeding, and our hearts no less than our bodies. About a mile we went that night, up upon a hill[16] within sight of the town, where they intended to lodge. There was hard by a vacant house (deserted by the English before, for fear of the

[11] Henry Kerley, Jr. (1657–?).   [12] Psalm 46:8.

[13] Current historians give numbers ranging from thirty-seven to more than fifty-five.

[14] Ephraim Roper. Unbeknownst to Rowlandson, three children of Elizabeth and John Kettle escaped, too.

[15] Moves to different areas; after each, the group spent a few days in camp. The first remove was made on February 10, 1675/76 [20, 1676].

[16] George hill, the highest elevation in Lancaster.

Indians). I asked them whether I might not lodge in the house that night, to which they made answer, what, will you love Englishmen still? This was the dolefulest night that ever my eyes saw. Oh the roaring and singing and dancing and yelling of those black creatures in the night, which made the place a lively resemblance of hell; and as miserable was the waste that was there made, of horses, cattle, sheep, swine, calves, lambs, roasting pigs, and fowl, (which they had plundered in the town,) some roasting, some lying and burning, and some boiling, to feed our merciless enemies, who were joyful enough, though we were disconsolate. To add to the dolefulness of the former day, and the dismalness of the present night, my thoughts ran upon my losses and sad bereaved condition. All was gone, my husband gone, (at least separated from me, he being in the Bay;[17] and to add to my grief, the Indians told me they would kill him as he came homeward; my children gone, my relations and friends gone, our house and home and all our comforts within door and without, all was gone, except my life, and I knew not but the next moment that might go too. There remained nothing to me but one poor wounded babe, and it seemed at present worse than death, that it was in such a pitiful condition, bespeaking compassion, and I had no refreshing for it, nor suitable things to revive it. Little do many think what is the savageness and brutishness of this barbarous enemy, even those that seem to profess more than others among them, when the English have fallen into their hands.

Those seven that were killed at Lancaster the summer before upon a Sabbath day,[18] and the one that was afterwards killed upon a week day, were slain and mangled in a barbarous manner, by One-eyed John, and Marlborough "Praying Indians," which Captain Moseley brought to Boston, as the Indians told me.

THE SECOND REMOVE[19]

But now, the next morning, I must turn my back upon the town, and travel with them into the vast and desolate wilderness, I knew not whither. It is not my tongue nor pen can express the sorrows of my heart, and bitterness of my spirit, that I had at this departure: but God was with me in a wonderful manner, carrying me along, and bearing up my spirit, that it did not quite fail. One of the Indians carried my poor wounded babe upon a horse; it went moaning all along, I shall die, I shall die. I went on foot after it, with sorrow that cannot be expressed. At length I took it off the horse and carried it in my arms till my strength failed, and I fell down with it. Then they set me upon a horse with my wounded child in my lap, and there being no furniture upon the horses back, as we went down a steep hill, we both fell over the horse's head at which they like inhuman creatures laughed, and rejoiced to see it, though I thought we should there have ended our days, overcome with many difficulties. But the Lord renewed my strength still, and carried me along that I might see more of his power; yea, so much that I could never have thought of, had I not experienced it.

After this it quickly began to snow and when night came on they stopped. And

---

[17] Rev. Rowlandson had gone to Boston (on Massachusetts Bay) to get help in case of a Native-American attack on Lancaster but was too late.

[18] August 22, 1675, when Lancaster was attacked by the Nashaway Indians, led by Monoco (?–1676), or One-eyed John, and Christianized Native Americans, or "Praying Indians," of Marlborough, Massachusetts (brought there by force by Captain Samuel Moseley).

[19] The group moved on Friday, February 11 [21], and camped at Princeton, Massachusetts.

now I must sit down in the snow before a little fire, and few boughs behind me, with my sick child in my lap, and calling much for water, being now (through the wound) fallen into a violent fever. My own wound also growing so stiff that I could scarce sit down or rise up; yet so it must be that I must sit all this cold winter night upon the cold snowy ground, with my sick child in my arms, looking that every hour would be the last of its life, and having no Christian friend near me, either to comfort or help me. Oh, I may see the wonderful power of God, that my spirit did not utterly sink under my afflictions; still the Lord upheld me with his gracious and merciful spirit, and we were both alive to see the light of the next morning.

THE THIRD REMOVE[20]

The morning being come, they prepared to go on their way. One of the Indians got up on a horse and they set me up behind him with my poor sick babe in my lap. A very wearisome and tedious day I had of it; what with my own wound, and my child being so exceedingly sick, and in a lamentable condition with her wound. It may be easily judged what a poor feeble condition we were in, there being not the least crumb of refreshment that came within either of our mouths from Wednesday night to Saturday night, except only a little cold water. This day in the afternoon, about an hour by sun, we came to the place where they intended, viz., an Indian town called Wenimesset, northward of Quabaug.[21] When we were come, oh the number of pagans (our merciless enemies) that there came about me! I might say as David, Psalm xxvii: 13. "I had fainted, unless I had believed," etc.[22] The next day was the Sabbath. I then remembered how careless I had been of God's holy time; how many Sabbaths I had lost and misspent, and how evilly I had walked in God's sight; which lay so closely upon my spirit, that it was easy for me to see how righteous it was with God to cut off the thread of my life, and cast me out of his presence forever. Yet the Lord still showed mercy to me, and upheld me; and as he wounded me with one hand, so he healed me with the other. This day there came to me one Robert Pepper (a man belonging to Roxbury) who was taken in Captain Beers' fight,[23] and had now been a considerable time with the Indians, and up with them almost as far as Albany to see King Philip, as he told me, and was now very lately come into these parts.[24] Hearing, I say, that I was in the Indian town, he obtained leave to come and see me. He told me he himself was wounded in the leg at Captain Beer's fight and was not able [for] some time to go, but as they carried him, and as he took oak leaves and laid to his wound, and through the blessing of God he was able to travel again. Then I took

[20] The group moved from Saturday, February 12 [22], to Sunday, February 27 [March 9], and camped at the Native-American village of Wenimesset, or Meminimisset (now New Braintree, Massachusetts), a stronghold of the Quabaug Indians.

[21] Now Brookfield, Massachusetts.

[22] "Unless I had believed to see the goodness of the Lord in the land of the living," from Psalm 27:13.

[23] Captain Richard Beers (?–1675) of Watertown, Massachusetts, and thirty-six men were waylaid by over one hundred native warriors on September 3, 1675, while attempting to save the nearby Northfield garrison. Beers and nineteen others were killed, Pepper was captured, and the rest escaped.

[24] Contrary to most historical accounts, this captive's statement indicates that King Philip, or Metacomet (1639?–1676), was not on hand to lead a Wampanoag attack on Lancaster; instead, the assault was led by the Quabaug chieftain Muttaump, along with Monoco and Sagamore Sam of the Nashaways, Quanopin of the Narragansets, and Matoonas of the Nipmucks.

oak leaves and laid to my side, and with the blessing of God it cured me also; yet before the cure was wrought, I may say, as it is in Psalm xxxviii: 5, 6. "My wounds stink and are corrupt, I am troubled, I am bowed down greatly, I go mourning all the day long." I sat much alone with my poor wounded child in my lap, which moaned night and day, having nothing to revive the body, or cheer the spirits of her; but instead of that, sometimes one Indian would come and tell me one hour, that "your master will knock your child in the head," and then a second, and then a third, "your master will quickly knock your child in the head."

This was all the comfort I had from them, miserable comforters are ye all, as he said.[25] Thus nine days I sat upon my knees with my babe upon my lap, till my flesh was raw again. My child being even ready to depart this sorrowful world, they bade me carry it out to another wigwam, (I suppose they would not be troubled with such spectacles,) whither I went with a very heavy heart, and down I sat with the picture of death in my lap. About two hours in the night my sweet babe, like a lamb, departed this life, on February 18, 1675,[26] it being about six years and five months old. It was about nine days from the first wounding in this miserable condition, without any refreshing of one nature or another, except a little cold water. I cannot but take notice, how at another time I could not bear to be in the room where any dead person was, but now the case is changed; I must, and can lie down by my dead babe, side by side, all the night after. I have thought since of the wonderful goodness of God to me, in preserving me in the use of my reason and sense in that distressed time, that I did not use wicked and violent means to end my own miserable life. In the morning when they understood that my child was dead, they sent for me home to my master's wigwam, (by my master in this writing must be understood Quanopin,[27] who was a Sagamore, and married King Philip's wife's sister; not that he first took me, but I was sold to him by another Narraganset Indian, who took me when first I came out of the garrison.) I went to take up my dead child in my arms to carry it with me, but they bid me let it alone: there was no resisting, but go I must and leave it. When I had been [awhile] at my master's wigwam, I took the first opportunity I could get to go look after my dead child. When I came I asked them what they had done with it. Then they told me it was upon the hill,—then they went and showed me where it was, where I saw the ground was newly digged, and there they told me they had buried it. There I left that child in the wilderness, and must commit it, and myself also, in this wilderness condition to him who is above all. God having taken away this dear child, I went to see my daughter Mary, who was at this same Indian town at a wigwam not very far off, though we had little liberty or opportunity to see one another. She was about ten years old, and taken from the door first by a Praying Indian and afterward sold for a gun. When I came in sight she would fall a-weeping, at which they were provoked, and would not let me come near her, but bade me be gone, which was a heart-cutting word to me. I had one child dead, another in the wilderness I knew not where, the third they would not let me come near to. "Me [as he said] have ye bereaved of my children, Joseph is not, and Simon is not, and ye will take Benjamin also: all these things are against me."[28] I could not sit still in

---

[25] "Then Job answered and said, I have heard many such things; miserable comforters are ye all," from Job 16:1–2.

[26] February 28, 1676, in the present system.

[27] Quanopin, or Quinnapin, husband of King Philip's sister Weetamoo (or the Queen of Pocasset), was a Narraganset sagamore, or subordinate chief. Rowlandson became Weetamoo's servant.

[28] In Genesis 42:36, Jacob's lament.

this condition, but kept walking from one place to another. And as I was going along, my heart was even overwhelmed with the thoughts of my condition, and that I should have children, and a nation which I knew not ruled over them. Whereupon I earnestly entreated the Lord that he would consider my low estate and show me a token for good, and if it were his blessed will, some sign and hope for some relief.

And indeed quickly the Lord answered, in some measure, my poor prayers; for as I was going up and down mourning and lamenting my condition, my son came to me and asked me how I did. I had not seen him before since the destruction of the town, and I knew not where he was, till I was informed by himself, that he was amongst a smaller parcel of Indians, whose place was about six miles off. With tears in his eyes he asked me whether his sister Sarah was dead, and told me he had seen his sister Mary, and prayed me that I would not be troubled in reference to himself. The occasion of his coming to see me at this time was this: There was, as I said, about six miles from us, a small plantation of Indians, where it seems he had been during his captivity, and at this time there were some forces of the Indians gathered out of our company, and some also from them, (amongst whom was my son's master) to go to the assault and burn Medfield.[29] In this time of the absence of his master, his dame brought him to see me. I took this to be some gracious answer to my earnest and unfeigned desire.

The next day, viz. to this, the Indians returned from Medfield; (all the company, for those that belonged to the other small company came through the town that now we were at.) But before they came to us, oh the outrageous roaring and whooping that there was! They began their din about a mile before they came to us. By their noise and whooping, they signified how many they had destroyed,[30] (which was at that time twenty-three.) Those that were with us at home were gathered together as soon as they heard the whooping, and every time that the other went over their number, these at home gave a shout, that the very earth rang again. And thus they continued till those that had been upon the expedition were come up to the Sagamore's wigwam; and then, oh the hideous insulting and triumphing that there was over some Englishmen's scalps that they had taken (as their manner is) and brought with them. I cannot but take notice of the wonderful mercy of God to me in those afflictions, in sending me a Bible. One of the Indians that came from Medfield fight had brought some plunder, came to me, and asked me if I would have a Bible. He had got one in his basket. I was glad of it and asked him whether he thought the Indians would let me read [it]. He answered, yes. So I took the Bible and in that melancholy time it came into my mind to read first the 28th chapter of Deuteronomy,[31] which I did. And when I had read it my dark heart wrought on this manner: That there was no mercy for me, that the blessings were gone and the curses came in their room, and that I had lost my opportunity. But the Lord helped me still to go on reading till I came to chapter 30, the seven first verses, where I found there was mercy promised again if we would return to him by repentence;[32] and though we were scattered from one end of the earth to the other, yet the Lord would gather us together, and turn all those

---

[29] Medfield, Massachusetts, outside Boston, was attacked on February 21 [March 3]; fifty homes were burned, and eighteen people killed.

[30] The number of enemy deaths and captives was customarily indicated by whooping.

[31] A chapter of blessings for those obedient to God and curses for the disobedient.

[32] "That then the Lord thy God will turn thy captivity, and have compassion upon thee, and will return and gather thee from all the nations . . . ," from Deuteronomy 30:3.

curses upon our enemies. I do not desire to live to forget this scripture, and what comfort it was to me.

Now the Indians began to talk of removing from this place, some one way, and some another. There were now besides myself nine English captives in this place, (all of them children, except one woman.) I got an opportunity to go and take my leave of them, they being to go one way and I another. I asked them whether they were earnest with God for deliverance. They told me they did as they were able and it was some comfort to me that the Lord stirred up children to look to him. The woman, viz. Goodwife Joslin,[33] told me she should never see me again and that she could find in her heart to run away. I wished her not to run away by any means, for we were near thirty miles from any English town and she very big with child, and had but one week to reckon; and another child in her arms, two years old, and bad rivers there were to go over, and we were feeble with our poor and coarse entertainment. I had my Bible with me: I pulled it out and asked her whether she would read. We opened the Bible and lighted on Psalm xxvii., in which Psalm we especially took notice of that verse viz., "Wait on the Lord, be of good courage, and he shall strengthen thine heart; wait I say on the Lord."[34]

THE FOURTH REMOVE[35]

And now I must part with that little company I had. Here I parted from my daughter Mary, (whom I never saw again till I saw her in Dorchester, returned from captivity,) and from four little cousins and neighbors, some of whom I never saw afterward: the Lord only knows the end of them. Amongst them also was that poor woman before mentioned,[36] who came to a sad end as some of the company told me in my travel; she having much grief upon her spirit, about her miserable condition, being so near her time, she would be often asking the Indians to let her go home. They not being willing to do that, and yet vexed with her importunity, gathered a great company about her and stripped her naked and set her in the midst of them. And when they had sung and danced about her (in their hellish manner) as long as they pleased, they knocked her on the head and the child in her arms with her. When they had done that, they made a fire and put them both into it and told the other children that were there with them that if they attempted to go home, they would serve them in like manner. The children said she did not shed one tear but prayed all the while. But to return to my own journey: we travelled about half a day or little more, and came to a desolate place in the wilderness where there were no wigwams or inhabitants before. We came about the middle of the afternoon to this place, cold and wet, and snowy, and hungry, and weary, and no refreshing for man but the cold ground to sit on and our poor Indian cheer.

Heart-aching thoughts here I had about my poor children who were scattered up and down among the wild beasts of the forest. My head was light and dizzy (either through hunger or hard lodging, or trouble, or all together), my knees feeble, my body raw by sitting double night and day, that I cannot express to man the afflic-

---

[33] Ann Joslin (?–1676), wife of Abraham Joslin (1650–1676); Ann was later killed in captivity, and her husband had died during the initial attack.

[34] Psalm 27:14.

[35] The group moved from Monday, February 38 [March 10], to Friday, March 3 [10], and camped at what is now Petersham, Massachusetts, near the Native-American village of Nichewaug.

[36] Ann Joslin, who was in her last months of pregnancy when she was killed.

tion that lay upon my spirit, but the Lord helped me at that time to express it to himself. I opened my Bible to read, and the Lord brought that precious scripture to me, Jeremiah xxxi:16. "Thus saith the Lord, refrain thy voice from weeping, and thine eyes from tears, for thy work shall be rewarded, and they shall come again from the land of the enemy." This was a sweet cordial[37] to me, when I was ready to faint, many and many a time have I sat down, and wept sweetly over this Scripture. At this place we continued about four days.

* * *

THE TWENTIETH REMOVE[38]

It was their unusual manner to remove when they had done any mischief, lest they should be found out; and so they did at this time. We went about three or four miles and there built a great wigwam, big enough to hold an hundred Indians, which they did in preparation to a great day of dancing. They would say now amongst themselves that the Governor would be so angry for his loss at Sudbury that they would send no more about the captives, which made me grieve and tremble. My sister being not far from the place where we now were, and hearing that I was here, desired her master to let her come and see me, and he was willing to it and would go with her. But she being ready before him, told him she would go before and was come within a mile or two of the place. Then he overtook her and began to rant as if he had been mad; and made her go back again in the rain, so that I never saw her till I saw her in Charlestown. But the Lord requited many of their ill doings, for this Indian, her master, was hanged afterwards in Boston.[39] The Indians now began to come from all quarters against their merry dancing day. Among some of them came one Goodwife Kettle.[40] I told her my heart was so heavy that is was ready to break. "So is mine too," said she, but yet said, "I hope we shall hear some good news shortly." I could hear how earnestly my sister desired to see me and I as earnestly desired to see her; and yet neither of us could get an opportunity. My daughter was also now about a mile off and I had not seen her in nine or ten weeks as I had not seen my sister since our first taking. I earnestly desired them to let me go and see them; yea, I entreated, begged, and persuaded them but to let me see my daughter; and yet so hard-hearted were they, that they would not suffer it. They made use of their tyrannical power whilst they had it, but through the Lord's wonderful mercy, their time now was short.

On a Sabbath-day, the sun being about an hour high in the afternoon, came Mr. John Hoar,[41] (the Council permitting him, and his own forward spirit inclining him,) together with the two aforementioned Indians, Tom and Peter, with their third letter from the Council. When they came, I was abroad; they presently called

[37] A medicine, something that stimulates the heart.

[38] The group moved from Friday, April 28 [May 8], to Tuesday, May 2 [12], and camped at Princeton, Massachusetts, near the southern shore of Wachusett Lake.

[39] Hannah Divoll's captor, Sagamore Sam, was hanged in Boston on September 26 [October 6], 1676.

[40] Elizabeth Kettle.

[41] John Hoar of Concord, Massachusetts, who, being friendly with the Native Americans, was asked by Rev. Rowlandson to negotiate with the Native-American council at Redemption Rock, Princeton, for the ransom of Mary Rowlandson. The agreement was made on May 2 [12], 1676.

me in and bade me sit down and not stir. Then they catched up their guns and away they ran, as if an enemy had been at hand, and the guns went off apace. I manifested some great trouble and they asked me what was the matter. I told them I thought they had killed the Englishman, (for they had in the meantime informed me that an Englishman was come.) They said no; they shot over his horse, and under and before his horse; and they pushed him this way and that way, at their pleasure, showing what they could do. Then they let them come to their wig-wams. I begged them to let me see the Englishman, but they would not; but there was I, fain to sit their pleasure. When they had talked their fill to him, they suf-fered me to go to him. We asked each other of our welfare, and how my husband did, and all my friends. He told me they were all well and would be glad to see me. Amongst other things which my husband sent me, there came a pound of tobacco, which I sold for nine shillings in money; for, many of the Indians for want of tobacco smoked hemlock and ground-ivy. It was a great mistake in any who thought I sent for tobacco, for through the favor of God that desire was overcome. I now asked them whether I should go home with Mr. Hoar. They answered no, one and another of them, and it being night we laid down with that answer. In the morning Mr. Hoar invited the sagamores to dinner, but when we went to get it ready, we found that they had stolen the greatest part of the provi-sions Mr. Hoar had brought, out of his bags, in the night. And we may see the wonderful power of God in that one passage, in that when there was such a great number of Indians together and so greedy of a little food, and no English there but Mr. Hoar and myself, that there they did not knock us in the head and take what we had, there being not only some provisions but trading-cloth,[42] a part of the twenty pounds agreed upon. But instead of doing us any mischief they seemed to be ashamed of the fact and said it were some Machit Indians[43] that did it. Oh, that we could believe that there is nothing too hard for God! God showed his power over the heathen in this, as he did over the hungry lions when Daniel was cast into the den.[44] Mr. Hoar called them betimes to dinner, but they ate very little, they being so busy in dressing themselves, and getting ready for their dance, which was carried on by eight of them, four men and four squaws, my master and his mistress being two. He was dressed in his Holland[45] shirt with great laces sewed at the tail of it. He had his silver buttons, his white stockings, his garters were hung round with shillings and he had girdles of wampum[46] upon his head and shoul-ders. She had a jersey[47] coat, and covered with girdles of wampum from the loins upward; her arms from her elbows to her hands were covered with bracelets; there were handfuls of necklaces about her neck and several sorts of jewels in her ears. She had fine red stockings and white shoes, her hair powdered and her face painted red, that was always before, black. And all the dancers were after the same manner. There were two others singing and knocking on a kettle for their music. They kept hopping up and down, one after another, with a kettle of water in the midst, standing warm upon some embers, to drink of when they were dry. They held on till it was almost night throwing out wampum to the standers-by. At night I asked them again if I should go home. They all as one said no, except[48] my husband come for me. When we were lain down my master went out of the wig-

---

[42] Cloth used in bartering.   [43] Bad Indians.
[44] In Daniel 6:1–29 the prophet Daniel was not harmed when cast into the lions' den.   [45] Linen.
[46] Encirclements made of shell beads, used as currency.   [47] A coarse woolen cloth.   [48] Unless.

wam, and by and by sent in an Indian called James the Printer,[49] who told Mr. Hoar, that my master would let me go tomorrow if he would let him have one pint of liquors. Then Mr. Hoar called his own Indians, Tom and Peter, and bid them go and see whether he would promise it before them three, and if he would he should have it; which he did, and he had it. Then Philip[50] smelling the business called me to him and asked me what I would give him to tell me some good news and speak a good word for me. I told him I could not tell what to give him; I would [give him] anything I had, and asked him what he would have. He said two coats and twenty shillings in money and half a bushel of feed corn and some tobacco. I thanked him for his love, but I knew the good news as well as the crafty fox. My master, after he had had his drink, quickly came ranting into the wigwam again, and called for Mr. Hoar, drinking to him and saying he was a good man, and then again he would say, hang him, rogue. Being almost drunk he would drink to him and yet presently say he should be hanged. Then he called for me. I trembled to hear him, yet I was fain to go to him, and he drank to me showing no incivility. He was the first Indian I saw drunk all the while that I was amongst them. At last his squaw ran out and he after her round the wigwam with his money jingling at his knees. But she escaped him, but having an old squaw he ran to her, and lo, through the Lord's mercy, we were no more troubled that night. Yet I had not a comfortable night's rest, for I think I can say, I did not sleep for three nights together. The night before the letter came from the Council I could not rest I was so full of fears and troubles, God many times leaving us most in the dark when deliverance is nearest; yea, at this time I could not rest night nor day. The next night I was overjoyed, Mr. Hoar being come, and that with such good tidings. The third night I was even swallowed up with the thoughts of things, viz., that ever I should go home again; and that I must go leaving my children behind me in the wilderness; so that sleep was now almost departed from mine eyes.

On Tuesday morning they called their General Court (as they call it) to consult and determine whether I should go home or no. And they all as one man did seemingly consent to it, that I should go home, except Philip, who would not come among them.

But before I go any further, I would take leave to mention a few remarkable passages of providence, which I took special notice of in my affliction.

1. Of the fair opportunity lost in the long march a little after the Fort Fight when our English army was so numerous, and in pursuit of the enemy, and so near as to take several and destroy them; and the enemy in such distress for food that our men might track them by their rooting in the earth for ground-nuts whilst they were flying for their lives. I say that then our Army should want provision, and be forced to leave their pursuit and return homeward; and the very next week the enemy came upon our town like bears bereft of their whelps or so many ravenous wolves, rending us and our lambs to death. But what shall I say? God seemed to leave his people to themselves and order all things for his own holy ends. "Shall there be evil in the city and the Lord hath not done it?"[51] "They are not grieved for the affliction of Joseph, therefore shall they go captive, with the first that go captive."[52] It is the Lord's doing and it should be marvelous in our eyes.

---

[49] A Praying Indian who had assisted Rev. John Eliot (1604–1690), a missionary, in printing a Bible for Native Americans.
[50] A Native American who had helped Rowlandson during her captivity.
[51] Amos 3:6.   [52] Amos 6:6–7.

2. I cannot but remember how the Indians derided the slowness and dullness of the English army in its setting out. For after the desolations of Lancaster and Medfield as I went along with them they asked me when I thought the English army would come after them. I told them I could not tell. "It may be they will come in May," said they. Thus did they scoff at us, as if the English would be a quarter of a year getting ready.

3. Which also I have hinted before, when the English army with new supplies were sent forth to pursue after the enemy, and they understanding it, fled before them till they came to Baquag River, where they forthwith went over safely: that that river should be impassable to the English. I can but admire to see the wonderful providence of God in preserving the heathen for farther affliction to our poor country. They could go in great numbers over, but the English must stop! God had an overruling hand in all those things.

4. It was thought, if the corn were cut down, they would starve and die with hunger; and all their corn that could be found was destroyed and they driven from the little they had in store into the woods in the midst of winter; and yet how to admiration did the Lord preserve them for his holy ends, and the destruction of many still amongst the English! Strangely did the Lord provide for them, that I did not see (all the time I was among them) one man, woman or child, die with hunger.

Though many times they would eat that, that a hog or dog would hardly touch, yet by that, God strengthened them to be a scourge to his people.

The chief and commonest food was ground-nuts. They eat also nuts and acorns, artichokes, lily-roots, ground-beans, and several other weeds and roots that I know not.

They would pick up old bones and cut them to pieces at the joints, and if they were full of worms and maggots they would scald them over the fire to make the vermin come out, and then boil them and drink up the liquor, and then beat the great ends of them in a mortar, and so eat them. They would eat horses' guts and ears and all sorts of wild birds which they would catch: also bear, venison, beaver, tortoise, frogs, squirrels, dogs, skunks, rattle-snakes, yea, the very bark of trees, besides all sorts of creatures and provisions which they plundered from the English. I can but stand in admiration to see the wonderful power of God in providing for such a vast number of enemies in the wilderness where there was nothing to be seen, but from hand to mouth. Many times in a morning the generality of them would eat up all they had and yet have some farther supply against they wanted. It is said, Psalm lxxxi: 13, 14, "Oh that my people had hearkened to me and Israel had walked in my ways, I should soon have subdued their enemies, and turned my hand against their adversaries." But now our perverse and evil carriages in the sight of the Lord have so offended him that instead of turning his hand against them, the Lord feeds and nourishes them up to be a scourge to the whole land.

5. Another thing that I would observe is, the strange providence of God in turning things about when the Indians were at the highest, and the English at the lowest. I was with the enemy eleven weeks and five days, and not one week passed without the fury of the enemy, and some desolation by fire and sword upon some place or another. They mourned (with their blackened faces) for their own losses yet triumphed and rejoiced in their inhumane and many times devilish cruelty to the English. They would boast much of their victories, saying that in two hours time they had destroyed such a captain and his company at such a place, and

such a captain and his company in such a place, and such a captain in such a place; and boast how many towns they had destroyed, and then scoff and say they had done them a good turn to send them to Heaven so soon. Again they would say this summer that they would knock all the rogues in the head or drive them into the sea or make them flee the country, thinking surely, Agag-like, "the bitterness of death is past."[53] Now the heathen begin to think all is their own; and the poor Christian hopes to fail (as to man) and now their eyes are more on God and their hearts sigh heavenward, and so say in good earnest, "Help, Lord or we perish." When the Lord had brought his people to this, that they saw no help in anything but himself, then he takes the quarrel into his own hand, and though they [i.e., the Indians] had made a pit (in their own imaginations) as deep as hell for the Christians that summer, yet the Lord hurled themselves into it. And the Lord had not so many ways before to preserve them but now he hath as many to destroy them.

But to return again to my going home, where we may see a remarkable change of providence. At first they were all against it except my husband would come for me, but afterwards they assented to it and seemed much to rejoice in it. Some asked me to send them some bread, others some tobacco, others shaking me by the hand offering me a hood and scarfe to ride in; not one moving hand or tongue against it. Thus hath the Lord answered my poor desire and the many earnest requests of others put up unto God for me. In my travels an Indian came to me and told me if I were willing he and his squaw would run away and go home along with me. I told him no; I was not willing to run away but desired to wait God's time that I might go home quietly and without fear. And now God hath granted me my desire. O the wonderful power of God that I have seen and the experience that I have had. I have been in the midst of those roaring lions and savage bears that feared neither God nor man nor the devil, by night and day, alone and in company, sleeping all sorts together, and yet not one of them ever offered me the least abuse of unchastity to me in word or action. Though some are ready to say, I speak it for my own credit; but I speak it in the presence of God, and to his glory. God's power is as great now, and as sufficient to save, as when he preserved Daniel in the Lion's den, or the three children in the fiery furnace.[54] I may well say as his Psalm cvii:12, "Oh give thanks unto the Lord for he is good for his mercy endureth for ever." Let the redeemed of the Lord say so, whom he hath redeemed from the hand of the enemy, especially that I should have come away in the midst of so many hundreds of enemies, quietly and peacefully, and not a dog moving his tongue. So I took my leave of them and in coming along my heart melted into tears more than all the while I was with them and I was almost swallowed up with the thoughts that ever I should go home again. About the sun going down, Mr. Hoar and myself and the two Indians came to Lancaster and a solemn sight it was to me. There had I lived many comfortable years amongst my relations and neighbors, and now not one Christian to be seen nor one house left standing. We went on to a farm-house[55] that was yet standing, where we lay all night; and a comfortable lodging we had, though nothing but straw to lie on. The Lord preserved us in safety that night and raised us up again in the morning and

---

[53] Agag, King of Amalek, was defeated by Saul (Israel's first king) but, thinking himself saved, was killed by Samuel (see 1 Samuel 15:32–33).

[54] In Daniel 3:12–27 the three captives Shadrach, Meshach, and Abednego were thrown into a furnace for worshipping false gods but were spared by an angel.

[55] Probably on the way to Marlborough, as no houses in Lancaster were left standing.

carried us along; thus before noon we came to Concord. Now was I full of joy and yet not without sorrow; joy to see such a lovely sight, so many Christians together and some of my neighbors. There I met with my brother and my brother-in-law[56] who asked me if I knew where his wife was. Poor heart, he had helped to bury her and knew it not, she being shot down by the house, was partly burned, so that those who were at Boston at the desolation of the town and came back afterwards and buried the dead, did not know her. Yet I was not without sorrow to think how many were looking and longing, and my own children among the rest, to enjoy that deliverance that I had now received, and I did not know whether ever I should see them again. Being recruited[57] with food and raiment we went to Boston that day where I met with my dear husband, but the thoughts of our dear children, one being dead, and the other we could not tell where, abated our comfort each to other. I was not before so much hemmed in with the merciless and cruel heathen, but now as much with pitiful tender-hearted and compassionate Christians. In that poor and distressed and beggerly condition I was received in, I was kindly entertained in several houses: so much love I received from several (some of whom I knew, and others I knew not) that I am not capable to declare it. But the Lord knows them all by name; the Lord reward them seven-fold into their bosoms of his spirituals for their temporals.[58]

The twenty pounds, the price of my redemption, was raised by some Boston gentlemen, and Mr. Usher,[59] whose bounty and religious charity, I would not forget to make mention of. Then Mr. Thomas Shepard of Charlestown received us into his house where we continued eleven weeks; and a father and mother they were to us. And many more tender-hearted friends we met with in that place. We were now in the midst of love, yet not without much and frequent heaviness of heart for our poor children and other relations who were still in affliction. The week following, after my coming in, the Governor and the Council sent forth to the Indians again, and that not without success, for they brought in my sister and Good-wife Kettle. Their not knowing where our children were, was a sore trial to us still, and yet we were not without secret hopes that we should see them again. That which was dead lay heavier upon my spirit than those which were living and amongst the heathen, thinking how it suffered with its wounds and I was no way able to relieve it, and how it was buried by the heathens in the wilderness from among all Christians. We were hurried up and down in our thoughts, sometimes we should hear a report that they had gone this way, and sometimes that. We kept inquiring and listening to hear concerning them, but no certain news as yet. About this time the Council had ordered a day of public thanksgiving,[60] though I thought I still had cause for mourning, and being unsettled in our minds, we thought we would ride toward the eastward to see if we could hear anything concerning our children. And as we were riding along (God is the wise disposer of all things) between Ipswich and Rowley we met with Mr. William Hubbard who told us that our son Joseph was come in to Major Waldron's[61] and another with him, which was my sister's son. I asked him how he knew it. He said the Major himself told him so. So along we went till we came to Newbury, and the minister there being absent, they desired my husband to preach the Thanksgiving for them. But he was not willing to stay there that night, but would go over to Salisbury, to hear further,

---

[56] Josiah White and Lt. Henry Kerley.   [57] Supplied.   [58] Worldy (nonspiritual) goods.
[59] Hezekiah Usher, a prominent Boston merchant.   [60] June 29 [July 9], 1676.
[61] Richard Waldron, Dover, New Hampshire's most distinguished citizen.

and come again in the morning; which he did, and preached there that day. At night, when he had done, one came and told him that his daughter was come in at Providence. Here was mercy on both hands. Now hath God fulfilled that precious scripture which was such a comfort to me in my distressed condition. When my heart was ready to sink into the earth (my children being gone I could not tell whither) and my knees trembled under me, and I was walking "through the valley of the shadow of death,"[62] then the Lord brought, and now has fulfilled, that reviving word unto me: Thus saith the Lord, "Refrain thy voice from weeping and thine eyes from tears for thy work shall be rewarded, saith the lord, and they shall come again from the land of the enemy."[63] Now were we between them, the one on the east, and the other on the west. Our son being nearest, we went to him first, to Portsmouth, where we met with him, and with the Major also, who told us he had done what he could, but could not redeem him under seven pounds, which the good people thereabouts were pleased to pay. The Lord reward the Major and all the rest, though unknown to me, for their labor of love. My sister's son was redeemed for four pounds, which the Council gave order for the payment of. Having now received one of our children, we hastened towards the other; going back through Newbury, my husband preached there on the Sabbath-day; for which they rewarded him many fold.

On Monday we came to Charlestown where we learned that the Governor of Rhode Island had sent over for our daughter, to take care of her, being now within his jurisdiction; which should not pass without our acknowledgments. But being nearer Rehoboth than Rhode Island, Mr. Newman[64] went over, and took care of her, and brought her to his own house. And the goodness of God was admirable to us in our low estate, in that he raised up passionate[65] friends on every side to us, when we had nothing to recompence any for their love.

The Indians were now gone that way [so] that it appeared dangerous to go to her. But the carts which carried provisions to the English army, being guarded, brought her with them to Dorchester where we received her safe: blessed be the Lord for it, for great is his power and he can do whatsoever seemeth him good. Her coming in was after this manner: she was travelling one day with the Indians, with her basket at her back; the company of Indians were got before her and gone out of sight, all except one squaw. She followed the squaw till night and then both of them lay down, having nothing over them but the heavens and under them but the earth. Thus she travelled three days together, not knowing whither she was going, having nothing to eat or drink but water and green whortleberries.[66] At last they came into Providence where she was kindly entertained by several of that town. The Indians often said that I should never have her under twenty pounds, but now the Lord hath brought her in upon free cost and given her to me the second time. The Lord make us a blessing indeed, each to others. Now have I seen that scripture also fulfilled, Deuteronomy xxx: 4, 7, "If any of thine be driven out to the outmost parts of heaven, from thence will the Lord thy God gather thee, and from thence will he fetch thee. And the Lord thy God will put all these curses upon thine enemies, and on them which hate thee, which persecuted thee." Thus hath the Lord brought me and mine out of that horrible pit and hath set us in the midst of tender-hearted and compassionate Christians. It is the desire of

---

[62] Psalm 23:4.   [63] Jeremiah 31:16.
[64] Rev. Noah Newman of Rehoboth, Massachusetts.   [65] Compassionate.
[66] Probably huckleberries.

my soul that we may walk worthy of the mercies received, and which we are receiving.

Our family being now gathered together (those of us that were living) the South Church in Boston hired an house for us. Then we removed from Mr. Shepard's (those cordial friends) and went to Boston where we continued about three quarters of a year. Still the Lord went along with us and provided graciously for us. I thought it somewhat strange to set up housekeeping with bare walls, but, as Solomon says, "Money answers all things."[67] And that we had through the benevolence of Christian friends, some in this town, and some in that, and others, and some from England, that in a little time we might look and see the house furnished with love. The Lord hath been exceeding good to us in our low estate, in that when we had neither house nor home nor other necessaries, the Lord so moved the hearts of these and those towards us that we wanted neither food nor raiment for ourselves and ours, Proverbs xviii:24, "There is a friend that sticketh closer than a brother." And how many such friends have we found, and now living amongst! And truly such a friend have we found him to be unto us, in whose house we lived, viz., Mr. James Whitcomb,[68] a friend unto us near hand, and afar off.

I can remember the time when I used to sleep quietly without working in my thoughts, whole nights together, but now it is otherwise with me. When all are fast about me and no eye open but his who ever waketh, my thoughts are upon things past, upon the awful dispensation of the Lord towards us, upon his wonderful power and might in carrying us through so many difficulties, in returning us to safety and suffering none to hurt us. I remember in the night season, how the other day I was in the midst of thousands of enemies and nothing but death before me. It was then hard work to persuade myself that ever I should be satisfied with bread again. But now we are fed with the finest of the wheat, and (as I may say) with "honey out of the rock."[69] Instead of the husk, we have the fatted calf.[70] The thoughts of these things in the particulars of them, and of the love and goodness of God towards us, make it true of me, what David[71] said to himself, Psalm vi: 5,[72] "I watered my couch with my tears." O the wonderful power of God that mine eyes have seen, affording matter enough for my thoughts to run in, that when others are sleeping mine eyes are weeping.

I have seen the extreme vanity of this world. One hour I have been in health, and wealth, wanting nothing, but the next hour in sickness, and wounds, and death, having nothing but sorrow and affliction.

Before I knew what affliction meant, I was ready sometimes to wish for it. When I lived in prosperity, having the comforts of the world about me, my relations by me, my heart cheerful, and taking little care for anything, and yet seeing many (whom I preferred before myself) under many trials and afflictions, in sickness, weakness, poverty, losses, crosses, and cares of the world, I should be sometimes jealous lest I should have my portion in this life, and that scripture would come to my mind, Hebrews xii: 6, "For whom the Lord loveth he chasteneth, and scourgeth every son whom he receiveth." But now I see the Lord had his time to scourge and chasten me. The portion of some is to have their affliction by drops, now one drop and then another, but the dregs of the cup, the wine of

---

[67] Ecclesiastes 10:19.   [68] A wealthy Boston citizen.

[69] "He should have fed them also with the finest of the wheat: and with honey out of the rock I should have satisfied thee," from Psalm 81:16.

[70] "And bring hither the fatted calf, and kill it; and let us eat, and be merry," from Luke 15:23.

[71] The second king of Israel, reportedly the author of many Psalms.   [72] Actually, Psalm 6:6.

astonishment (like a sweeping rain that leaveth no food) did the Lord prepare to be my portion. Affliction I wanted, and affliction I had, full measure (I thought) pressed down and running over. Yet I see when God calls a person to anything, and through never so many difficulties, yet he is fully able to carry them through, and make them see and say they have been gainers thereby. And I hope I can say in some measure, as David did, "It is good for me that I have been afflicted."[73] The Lord hath shown me the vanity of these outward things; that they are the "Vanity of vanities, and vexation of spirit;"[74] that they are but a shadow, a blast, a bubble, and things of no continuance; that we must rely on God himself, and our whole dependence must be upon him. If trouble with smaller things begin to arise in me, I have something at hand to check myself with, and say, why am I troubled? It was but the other day that if I had had the world, I would have given it for my freedom, or to have been a servant to a Christian. I have learned to look beyond present and smaller troubles, and to be quieted under them, as Moses said, Exodus xiv: 13, "Stand still and see the salvation of the Lord."

Finis

1682

Cotton Mather
(1663–1728)

Few early Americans equaled Cotton Mather in his dramatic involvement in the spiritual and political affairs of late seventeenth-century and early eighteenth-century New England. In colonial Boston, a community that relished foreshadowings of providence's blessing upon its endeavors, Mather's birth in 1663 must have appeared to be a particularly auspicious event. The grandson of the eminent first-generation Puritan ministers Richard Mather and John Cotton and the son of Maria Cotton and Increase Mather, then a rapidly rising figure in New England ecclesiastic circles, Cotton Mather was born into a position of privilege and promise. His accomplishments as a child and young man all seemed to validate the community's high expectations. He spent his formative years mastering Latin, Greek, and other ancient languages and practicing homiletic form (the form of sermons), graduated at age fifteen from Harvard College, and finished an M.A. there at age eighteen. Ordained his father's colleague at Boston's prestigious North Church in 1685, Mather published his first book, *The Call of the Gospel,* the following year.

Over the next forty years Mather lived through a succession of professional and personal ecstasies and agonies that possibly only a colonial Puritan could appreciate. He quickly joined his father in the vanguard of New England's political and ecclesiastic elite. Although both Mathers realized that old-style Puritanism was being eroded by an increasingly cosmopolitan, secular, and scientific temperament, neither fully understood that their collective activities actually encouraged the proliferation of that temperament. Cotton

[73] Psalm 119:71.

[74] "Vanity of vanities, all is vanity," from Ecclesiastes 1:2; "I have seen all the works that are done under the sun; and behold, all is vanity and vexation of spirit," from Ecclesiastes 1:14.

Mather was caught between familial and communal pressures to preserve the idealistic vision of New England's founders and a personal disposition to engage in scientific speculation, to believe in spiritual evidence in the physical world, and to endorse religious libertarianism even as he preached out of a virtually unmodified Calvinism. Mather endures as the most prolific and eloquent defender of the religious convictions under which New England was settled and as the most gifted, persistent voice providing the terms with which to challenge those convictions.

In more than four hundred books and sermons published during his lifetime and in a score of unpublished historical and theological manuscripts, Mather writes out all the paradoxes of his professional life. In the *Magnalia Christi Americana* (1702), his most famous work, he interprets the history of New England's first seventy years of settlement as a religious experience of epic proportions. He tries to move his contemporaries to follow in the footsteps of their ancestors, seemingly not realizing that American Puritanism had already passed its moment of glory or that, as Ralph Waldo Emerson explained many years later, each generation has to establish its own particular relation to God and the universe.

If Mather's historical writings, such as the *Magnalia,* fail to mesh his brand of religion, the expectations of the age, and his own intellectual curiosity, his writings that combine his typically contradictory scientific, speculative, theological, and humanitarian interests hardly fare much better. In these nonhistorical writings Mather vacillates between genius and blind superstition, arrogance, and simplicity. His belief in the existence of witches as a divine judgment against a sinful people and his fervid defense of the Salem witchcraft trials oddly juxtapose with his explicit distrust of "spectral evidence," as expressed in *The Wonders of the Invisible World* (1693). Throughout his ministerial career Mather harangued his congregation with awesome visions of divine retribution and believed he heard God's voice in the fury of storms as well as in angelic apparitions. Yet, he was an un-

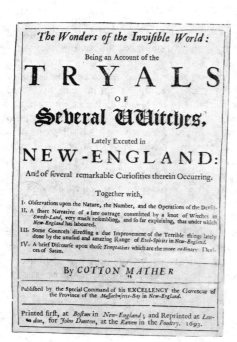

The title page of Cotton Mather's Wonders of the Invisible World.

commonly brilliant man whose extensive correspondence with foreign intellectuals merited his induction into the Royal Society of London in 1713. His writings on the necessity of doing good for one's fellows (especially the essay *Bonifacius* [1710]) exerted a profound and lasting influence on figures such as Benjamin Franklin. In 1721 Mather championed smallpox inoculation and then catalogued common maladies and their remedies in *The Angel of Bethesda* (1722), significantly advancing colonial medicine.

The extent to which Mather felt the difficulty of reconciling aspects of his old-style orthodoxy with his forward-looking intellectual curiosity is unknown. But as the product of an age that believed in the symbolic importance of events and as a leading proponent of that belief, Mather likely appreciated the awkwardness of his own situation. In his seven-volume *Diary* and autobiography *Paterna* (not published until 1911–1912 and 1976, respectively), he tended to write out of a sense of frustration over the course of his professional life and represents that frustration as an extension of his sometimes tragic personal life as well as of the inability of contemporaries to appreciate the quality of his mind. In Mather's private writing, between large meditational passages typical of Puritan spiritual writing are the trials of his professional career reconstituted in terrible private suffering, so that the professional and the personal become indistinguishable. This holds true for his diary's and autobiography's implications of disappointment over Mather's failing to succeed his father as Harvard's president and of his anguish over what he perceived as his failure to perpetuate the "Mather dynasty" (his favored son, named Increase after Mather's father, turned out to be a rogue more prone to carousing through the night than to preparing for the ministry). Mather's life seemed to offer few compensations for such disappointment and anguish. Although he fathered fifteen children, only two survived him, neither possessing an intellect or an imagination equal to those of their father or of their grandfather. Even marriage proved a trial: after two happy marriages (to Abigail Phillips in 1686 and to Elizabeth Clark Hubbard in 1703) cut short by death, Mather's third wife (as of 1715), Lydia Lee George, wrecked him financially and eventually went insane. It is little wonder that under such circumstances Mather, a few months before his death in 1728, concluded *Paterna*, composed over many years for the edification of his children, by imagining his death as a literal repetition of Christ's own crucifixion.

Mather's biographers have struggled with the complexities of his character and its relation to his time and place. Even fiction writers such as Washington Irving and Nathaniel Hawthorne have incorporated images of Mather into their narratives in an effort to explain to later generations the intricacies and eccentricities of life in Puritan America. Most biographers and writers agree that Mather stands as a stark representative of all that was powerful in New England's Puritan spirit and of all that ultimately proved its undoing. Few have been more succinct than the narrator of Hawthorne's *Grandfather's Chair* (1841) in expressing the paradoxical nature of Mather's character and the implicit relationship between Mather and his time: "It is difficult . . . to make you understand such a character as Cotton Mather's, in whom there was so much good, and yet so many failings and frailties."

Suggested Readings: *Diary of Cotton Mather*, 2 vols., ed. C. W. Ford, 1957. The Christian *Philosopher*, ed. J. K. Piercy, 1968. *Selected Letters of Cotton Mather*, ed. K. Silverman, 1971. O. T. Beall, Jr., and R. Shryock, *Cotton Mather: First Significant Figure in American Medicine*, 1954. B. Wendell, *Cotton Mather: The Puritan Priest*, ed. A. Heimert, 1963. R. Middlekauf, *The Mathers: Three Generations of Puritan Intellectuals, 1596–1728*, 1971. S. Bercovitch, "Cotton Mather" in *Major Writers of Early American Literature*, ed. E. Emerson, 1972. R. A. Bosco, "Editor's Introduction" in *Paterna: The Autobiography of Cotton Mather*, 1976. D. Levin, *Cotton Mather*, 1978. B. Levy, *Cotton Mather*, 1979. M. R. Breitwieser, *Cotton Mather and Benjamin Franklin: The Price of Representative Personality*, 1984. K. Silverman, *The Life and Times of Cotton Mather*, 1984. D. D. Knight, "Editor's Introduction" in *Cotton Mather's Verse in English*, 1989.

Texts Used: A People of God Settled in the Devil's Territories and "The Trial of Martha Carrier": *The Wonders of the Invisible World: Being an Account of the Trials of Several Witches Lately Executed in New-England*, 1862. "The Life of William Bradford, Esq., Governor of Plymouth Colony": *Magnalia Christi Americana: Or, the Ecclesiastical History of New-England*, Second Book, 1853. "Relative to Home and Neighborhood": *Bonifacius: An Essay Upon the Good*, ed. D. Levin, 1966. (Some spelling and punctuation modernized.)

from THE WONDERS OF THE INVISIBLE WORLD*

[*A People of God Settled in the Devil's Territories*]

The New-Englanders are a people of God settled in those, which were once the Devil's territories; and it may easily be supposed that the Devil was exceedingly disturbed, when he perceived such a people here accomplishing the promise of old made unto our blessed Jesus, *That He should have the utmost parts of the earth for his possession.*[1] There was not a greater uproar among the Ephesians,[2] when the Gospel was first brought among them, than there was among the powers of the air (after whom those Ephesians walked) when first the silver trumpets of the Gospel here made the joyful sound. The Devil thus irritated immediately tried all sorts of methods to overturn this poor plantation: and so much of the church, as was fled into this wilderness, immediately found the serpent cast out of his mouth a flood for the carrying of it away.[3] I believe that never were more satanical devices used for the unsettling of any people under the sun, than what have been employed for the extirpation of the vine which God has here planted, casting out the heathen, and preparing a room before it, and causing it to take deep root, and fill the land, so that it sent its boughs unto the Atlantic Sea eastward, and its branches unto the Connecticut River westward, and the hills were covered with the shadow thereof.[4] But, all those attempts of Hell, have hitherto been abortive, many an Ebenezer[5] has been erected unto the praise of God, by his poor people here; and having obtained help from God, we continue to this day. Wherefore the Devil is now making one attempt more upon us; an attempt more difficult, more surprising, more snarl'd with unintelligible circumstances than any that we have hitherto encountred; an attempt so critical, that if we get well through, we shall soon enjoy halcyon days[6] with all the vultures of Hell trodden under our feet. He has wanted his incarnate legions to persecute us, as the people of God have in the other hemi-

---

* Mather wrote *The Wonders of the Invisible World: Being an Account of the Trials of Several Witches Lately Executed in New-England* at the request of the judges of the 1692 Salem, Massachusetts, witchcraft trials.

[1] Psalm 2:8.

[2] The people of Ephesus, a city in ancient Ionia, now part of Turkey. Missionaries tried to convert the Ephesians but riots broke out following the missionaries' sermons (see Acts 19:21–40).

[3] "And the serpent cast out of his mouth water as a flood after the woman, that he might cause her to be carried away of the flood," from Revelation 12:15.

[4] "Thou hast brought a vine out of Egypt: thou hast cast out the heathen, and planted it. Thou preparedst room before it, and didst cause it to take deep root, and it filled the land. The hills were covered with the shadow of it, and the boughs thereof were like the goodly cedars. She sent out her boughs unto the sea and her branches unto the river," from Psalm 80:8–11.

[5] A stone monument commemorating the Israelites' victory over the Philistines (I Samuel 7:12).

[6] Idyllic times gone by.

sphere[7] been persecuted: he has therefore drawn forth his more spiritual ones to make an attack upon us. We have been advised by some credible Christians yet alive that a malefactor, accused of witchcraft as well as murder, and executed in this place more than forty years ago, did then give notice of an horrible plot against the country by witchcraft, and a foundation of witchcraft then laid, which if it were not seasonably discovered, would probably blow up, and pull down all the churches in the country. And we have now with horror seen the discovery of such a witchcraft! An army of Devils is horribly broke in upon the place which is the center, and after a sort, the first-born of our English settlements:[8] and the houses of the good people there are fill'd with the doleful shrieks of their children and servants, tormented by invisible hands, with tortures altogether preternatural. After the mischiefs there endeavored, and since in part conquered, the terrible plague of evil angels hath made its progress into some other places, where other persons have been in like manner diabolically handled. These our poor afflicted neighbors, quickly after they become infected and infested with these Dæmons, arrive to a capacity of discerning those which they conceive the shapes of their troublers; and notwithstanding the great and just suspicion, that the dæmons might impose the shapes of innocent persons in their spectral exhibitions upon the suffer-ers (which may perhaps prove no small part of the witch-plot in the issue), yet many of the persons thus represented, being examined, several of them have been convicted of a very damnable witchcraft: yea, more than one twenty have con-fessed, that they have signed unto a book, which the Devil show'd them, and engaged in his hellish design of bewitching and ruining our land. We know not, at least I know not, how far the delusions of Satan may be interwoven into some circumstances of the confessions; but one would think all the rules of understand-ing humane affairs are at an end, if after so many most voluntary harmonious confessions, made by intelligent persons of all ages, in sundry towns, at several times, we must not believe the main strokes wherein those confessions all agree: especially when we have a thousand preternatural things every day before our eyes, wherein the confessors do acknowledge their concernment, and give demon-stration of their being so concerned. If the devils now can strike the minds of men with any poisons of so fine a composition and operation, that scores of innocent people shall unite in confessions of a Crime, which we see actually committed, it is a thing prodigious beyond the wonders of the former ages, and it threatens no less than a sort of a dissolution upon the world. Now, by these confessions 'tis agreed that the Devil has made a dreadful knot[9] of witches in the country, and by the help of witches has dreadfully increased that knot: that these witches have driven a trade of commissioning their confederate spirits to do all sorts of mis-chiefs to the neighbors, whereupon there have ensued such mischievous conse-quences upon the bodies and estates of the neighborhood as could not otherwise be accounted for: yea that at prodigious witch-meetings the wretches have proceeded so far as to concert and consult the methods of rooting out the Christian religion from this country, and setting up instead of it perhaps a more gross diabolism than ever the world saw before. And yet it will be a thing little short of miracle, if in so spread a business as this, the Devil should not get in some of his juggles[10] to confound the discovery of all the rest.

---

[7] The Old World.
[8] Salem, the first settlement of the Massachusetts Bay Colony.   [9] Cluster or entanglement.
[10] Tricks.

V: The Trial of Martha Carrier

At the Court of Oyer and Terminer,[11] Held by Adjournment at Salem,
August 2, 1692

I. Martha Carrier was indicted for the bewitching certain persons, according to the form usual in such cases, pleading not guilty, to her indictment; there were first brought in a considerable number of the bewitched persons; who not only made the court sensible[12] of an horrid witchcraft committed upon them, but also deposed that it was Martha Carrier, or her shape, that grievously tormented them by biting, pricking, pinching and choking of them. It was further deposed that while this Carrier was on her examination before the magistrates, the poor people were so tortured that every one expected their death upon the very spot, but that upon the binding of Carrier they were eased. Moreover the look of Carrier then laid the afflicted people for dead; and her touch, if her eye at the same time were off them, raised them again: which things were also now seen upon her trial. And it was testified that upon the mention of some having their necks twisted almost round, by the shape of this Carrier, she replied, "It's no matter though their necks had been twisted quite off."

II. Before the trial of this prisoner, several of her own children had frankly and fully confessed not only that they were witches themselves, but that this their mother had made them so. This confession they made with great shows of repentance, and with much demonstration of truth. They related place, time, occasion; they gave an account of journeys, meetings and mischiefs by them performed, and were very credible in what they said. Nevertheless, this evidence was not produced against the prisoner at the bar,[13] inasmuch as there was other evidence enough to proceed upon.

III. Benjamin Abbot gave his testimony that last March was a twelvemonth, this Carrier was very angry with him, upon laying out some land near her husband's: her expressions in this anger were that she would stick as close to Abbot as the bark stuck to the tree; and that he should repent of it afore seven years came to an end, so as Doctor Prescot should never cure him. These words were heard by others besides Abbot himself, who also heard her say she would hold his nose as close to the grindstone as ever it was held since his name was Abbot. Presently after this, he was taken with a swelling in his foot, and then with a pain in his side, and exceedingly tormented. It bred into a sore, which was lanced by Doctor Prescot, and several gallons of corruption[14] ran out of it. For six weeks it continued very bad, and then another sore bred in the groin, which was also launced by Doctor Prescot. Another sore then bred in his groin, which was likewise cut, and put him to very great misery: He was brought unto death's door, and so remained until Carrier was taken, and carried away by the constable, from which very day he began to mend, and so grew better every day, and is well ever since.

Sarah Abbot also, his wife, testified that her husband was not only all this while afflicted in his body, but also that strange extraordinary and unaccountable

---

[11] "To hear and to determine" (Middle English), a commission authorizing judges to hear and determine criminal cases.
[12] Aware.   [13] In court.   [14] Pus.

calamities befel his cattle; their death being such as they could guess at no natural reason for.

IV. Allin Toothaker testified that Richard, the son of Martha Carrier, having some difference with him, pull'd him down by the hair of the head. When he rose again, he was going to strike at Richard Carrier but fell down flat on his back to the ground, and had not power to stir hand or foot, until he told Carrier he yielded; and then he saw the shape of Martha Carrier go off his breast.

This Toothaker had received a wound in the wars; and he now testified that Martha Carrier told him he should never be cured. Just afore the apprehending of Carrier, he could thrust a knitting needle into his wound, four inches deep; but presently after her being seized, he was thoroughly healed.

He further testified that when Carrier and he some times were at variance, she would clap her hands at him, and say he should get nothing by it; whereupon he several times lost his cattle by strange deaths, whereof no natural causes could be given.

V. John Rogger also testified that upon the threatening words of this malicious Carrier, his cattle would be strangely bewitched; as was more particularly then described.

VI. Samuel Preston testified that about two years ago, having some difference with Martha Carrier, he lost a cow in a strange preternatural unusual manner; and about a month after this, the said Carrier, having again some difference with him, she told him he had lately lost a cow, and it should not be long before he lost another; which accordingly came to pass; for he had a thriving and well-kept cow, which without any known cause quickly fell down and died.

VII. Phebe Chandler testified that about a fortnight before the apprehension of Martha Carrier, on a Lord's-day,[15] while the Psalm was singing in the church, this Carrier then took her by the shoulder and, shaking her, asked her where she lived: she made her no answer, although as Carrier, who lived next door to her father's house, could not in reason but know who she was. Quickly after this, as she was at several times crossing the fields, she heard a voice that she took to be Martha Carrier's, and it seemed as if it was over her head. The voice told her she should within two or three days be poisoned. Accordingly, within such a little time, one half of her right hand became greatly swollen, and very painful; as also part of her face: whereof she can give no account how it came. It continued very bad for some days; and several times since, she has had a great pain in her breast; and been so seized on her legs that she has hardly been able to go. She added that lately, going well to the house of God, Richard, the son of Martha Carrier, looked very earnestly upon her, and immediately her hand, which had formerly been poisoned, as is abovesaid, began to pain her greatly, and she had a strange burning at her stomach; but was then struck deaf, so that she could not hear any of the prayer, or singing, till the two or three last words of the Psalm.

VIII. One Foster, who confessed her own share in the witchcraft for which the prisoner stood indicted, affirmed that she had seen the prisoner at some of their witch-meetings, and that it was this Carrier who persuaded her to be a witch. She confessed that the Devil carried them on a pole to a witch-meeting; but the pole broke, and she hanging about Carrier's neck, they both fell down, and she then received an hurt by the fall, whereof she was not at this very time recovered.

IX. One Lacy, who likewise confessed her share in this witchcraft, now testi-

---

[15] Sunday.

fied that she and the prisoner were once bodily present at a witch-meeting in Salem Village; and that she knew the prisoner to be a witch, and to have been at a diabolical sacrament, and that the prisoner was the undoing of her, and her children, by enticing them into the snare of the Devil.

X. Another Lacy, who also confessed her share in this witchcraft, now testified that the prisoner was at the witch-meeting in Salem Village, where they had bread and wine administred unto them.

XI. In the time of this prisoner's trial, one Susanna Sheldon in open court had her hands unaccountably tied together with a wheel-band,[16] so fast that without cutting, it could not be loosed: it was done by a specter; and the sufferer affirmed it was the prisoner's.

Memorandum. This rampant hag, Martha Carrier, was the person of whom the confessions of the witches, and of her own children among the rest, agreed that the Devil had promised her she should be Queen of Heb.[17]

1692, 1693

from *MAGNALIA CHRISTI AMERICANA**

CHAPTER I: GALEACÍUS SECUNDUS[1]

The Life of William Bradford, Esq., Governor of Plymouth Colony

Omnium Somnos illius vigilantia defendit; omnium otium, illius Labor; omnium Delitias, illius Industria; omnium vacationem, illius occupatio.[2]

1. It has been a matter of some observation that although Yorkshire be one of the largest shires in England; yet, for all the fires of martyrdom which were kindled in the days of Queen Mary,[3] it afforded no more fuel than one poor leaf; namely, John Leaf, an apprentice, who suffered for the doctrine of the Reformation at the same time and stake with the famous John Bradford.[4] But when the reign of Queen Elizabeth[5] would not admit the Reformation of worship to proceed unto those degrees, which were proposed and pursued by no small number of the

---

[16] A strap that wraps around a wheel.   [17] Queen of Hebrews.

* *The Great Works of Christ in America* (Latin), subtitled *The Ecclesiastical History of New-England, From Its First Planting, in the Year 1620, Unto the Year of Our Lord 1698, in Seven Books,* was first published in London in 1702.

[1] "The second shield-bearer" (Latin); Bradford was the second governor of Plymouth. Galeazzo Caraccioli: (1517–1586) was a religious reformer and Protestant leader, as was Bradford.

[2] "His watchfulness guards others' slumbers; his toil secures others' rest; his diligence protects others' enjoyments; his constant application, others' leisure" (Latin).

[3] Mary I, or Mary Tudor (1516–1558); during her reign as queen of England (1553–1558), she had protestants executed to reestablish Roman Catholicism as the national church.

[4] John Bradford (1510?–1555), English theologian, was burned at the stake with John Leaf for their Protestant beliefs.

[5] Elizabeth I (1533–1603); during her reign as queen of England (1558–1603), she was faulted by Protestants for not fully forcing Roman Catholicism out of England.

faithful in those days, Yorkshire was not the least of the shires in England that afforded suffering witnesses thereunto. The churches there gathered were quickly molested with such a raging persecution, that if the spirit of separation in them did carry them unto a further extream than it should have done, one blameable cause thereof will be found in the extremity of that persecution. Their troubles made that cold country too hot for them, so that they were under a necessity to seek a retreat in the Low Countries;[6] and yet the watchful malice and fury of their adversaries rendred it almost impossible for them to find what they sought. For them to leave their native soil, their lands and their friends, and go into a strange place, where they must hear foreign language, and live meanly and hardly,[7] and in other employments than that of husbandry, wherein they had been educated, these must needs have been such discouragements as could have been conquered by none, save those who "sought first the kingdom of God, and the righteousness thereof." But that which would have made these discouragements the more unconquerable unto an ordinary faith was the terrible zeal of their enemies to guard all ports, and search all ships, that none of them should be carried off. I will not relate the sad things of this kind then seen and felt by this people of God; but only exemplify those trials with one short story. Diverse of this people having hired a Dutchman, then lying at Hull, to carry them over to Holland, he promised faithfully to take them in between Grimsly and Hull;[8] but they coming to the place a day or two too soon, the appearance of such a multitude alarmed the officers of the town adjoining, who came with a great body of soldiers to seize upon them. Now it happened that one boat full of men had been carried aboard, while the women were yet in a bark that lay aground in a creek at low water. The Dutchman perceiving the storm that was thus beginning ashore, swore by the sacrament that he would stay no longer for any of them; and so taking the advantage of a fair wind then blowing, he put out to sea for Zealand.[9] The women thus left near Grimsly-common, bereaved of their husbands, who had been hurried from them, and forsaken of their neighbors, of whom none durst in this fright stay with them, were a very rueful spectacle; some crying for fear, some shaking for cold, all dragged by troops of armed and angry men from one justice to another, till not knowing what to do with them, they even dismissed them to shift as well as they could for themselves. But by their singular afflictions, and by their Christian behaviors, the cause for which they exposed themselves did gain considerably. In the meantime, the men at sea found reason to be glad that their families were not with them, for they were surprised with an horrible tempest, which held them for fourteen days together, in seven whereof they saw not sun, moon or star, but were driven upon the coast of Norway. The mariners often despaired of life, and once with doleful shrieks gave over all, as thinking the vessel was foundered: but the vessel rose again, and when the mariners with sunk hearts often cried out, "We sink! we sink!" the passengers, without such distraction of mind, even while the water was running into their mouths and ears, would cheerfully shout, "Yet, Lord, thou canst save! Yet, Lord, thou canst save!" And the Lord accordingly brought them at last safe unto their desired haven: and not long after helped their distressed relations thither after them, where indeed they found upon almost all accounts a new world, but a world in which they found that they must live like strangers and pilgrims.

2. Among those devout people was our William Bradford, who was born Anno

---

[6] Holland, where some English Puritans traveled to constitute their own churches.
[7] Poorly and harshly.   [8] Two seaports in Humberside, England.   [9] The Netherlands.

1588,[10] in an obscure village called Ansterfield, where the people were as unacquainted with the Bible as the Jews do seem to have been with part of it in the days of Josiah;[11] a most ignorant and licentious people, and like unto their priest. Here, and in some other places, he had a comfortable inheritance left him of his honest parents, who died while he was yet a child, and cast him on the education, first of his grand parents, and then of his uncles, who devoted him, like his ancestors, unto the affairs of husbandry. Soon a long sickness kept him, as he would afterwards thankfully say, from the vanities of youth, and made him the fitter for what he was afterwards to undergo. When he was about a dozen years old, the reading of the Scriptures began to cause great impressions upon him; and those impressions were much assisted and improved, when he came to enjoy Mr. Richard Clifton's[12] illuminating ministry, not far from his abode; he was then also further befriended, by being brought into the company and fellowship of such as were then called professors;[13] though the young man that brought him into it did after become a prophane and wicked apostate.[14] Nor could the wrath of his uncles, nor the scoff of his neighbors, now turned upon him, as one of the Puritans, divert him from his pious inclinations.

3. At last, beholding how fearfully the evangelical and apostolical church-form, whereinto the churches of the primitive times were cast by the good spirit of God, had been deformed by the apostasy of the succeeding times; and what little progress the Reformation had yet made in many parts of Christendom towards its recovery, he set himself by reading, by discourse, by prayer, to learn whether it was not his duty to withdraw from the communion of the parish-assemblies, and engage with some society of the faithful, that should keep close unto the written word of God, as the rule of their worship. And after many distresses of mind concerning it, he took up a very deliberate and understanding resolution, of doing so; which resolution he chearfully prosecuted, although the provoked rage of his friends tried all the ways imaginable to reclaim him from it, unto all whom his answer was:

> "Were I like to endanger my life, or consume my estate by any ungodly courses, your counsels to me were very seasonable; but you know that I have been diligent and provident in my calling, and not only desirous to augment what I have, but also to enjoy it in your company; to part from which will be as great a cross as can befall me. Nevertheless, to keep a good conscience, and walk in such a way as God has prescribed in his Word, is a thing which I must prefer before you all, and above life it self. Wherefore, since 'tis for a good cause that I am like to suffer the disasters which you lay before me, you have no cause to be either angry with me, or sorry for me; yea, I am not only willing to part with every thing that is dear to me in this world for this cause, but I am also thankful that God has given me an heart to do, and will accept me so to suffer for him."

Some lamented him, some derided him, all dissuaded him: nevertheless, the more they did it, the more fixed he was in his purpose to seek the ordinances of

---

[10] Actually, 1590.

[11] Josiah (638?–608? B.C.), a king of Judah, worshipped false gods, as he did not know of the book of God's laws for Israel (see II Kings 22, 23).

[12] Clifton (?–1616), a Puritan minister of Scrooby, England, settled in Amsterdam with the Separatists.

[13] Those who profess their faith.   [14] One who disavows previous declarations of faith.

the gospel, where they should be dispensed with most of the commanded purity; and the sudden deaths of the chief relations which thus lay at[15] him, quickly after convinced him what a folly it had been to have quitted his profession, in expectation of any satisfaction from them. So to Holland he attempted a removal.

4. Having with a great company of Christians hired a ship to transport them for Holland, the master perfidiously betrayed them into the hands of those persecutors, who rifled and ransacked their goods, and clapped their persons into prison at Boston,[16] where they lay for a month together. But Mr. Bradford being a young man of about eighteen, was dismissed sooner than the rest, so that within a while he had opportunity with some others to get over to Zealand, through perils, both by land and sea not inconsiderable; where he was not long ashore ere a viper seized on his hand[17]—that is, an officer—who carried him unto the magistrates, unto whom an envious passenger had accused him as having fled out of England. When the magistrates understood the true cause of his coming thither, they were well satisfied with him; and so he repaired joyfully unto his brethren at Amsterdam, where the difficulties to which he afterwards stooped in learning and serving of a Frenchman at the working of silks, were abundantly compensated by the delight wherewith he sat under the shadow of our Lord, in his purely dispensed ordinances. At the end of two years, he did, being of age to do it, convert his estate in England into money; but setting up for himself, he found some of his designs by the providence of God frowned upon, which he judged a correction bestowed by God upon him for certain decays of internal piety, whereinto he had fallen; the consumption of his estate he thought came to prevent a consumption in his virtue. But after he had resided in Holland about half a score years, he was one of those who bore a part in that hazardous and generous[18] enterprise of removing into New-England, with part of the English church at Leyden, where, at their first landing, his dearest consort[19] accidentally falling overboard, was drowned in the harbor; and the rest of his days were spent in the services, and the temptations, of that American wilderness.

5. Here was Mr. Bradford, in the year 1621, unanimously chosen the governor of the plantation: the difficulties whereof were such, that if he had not been a person of more than ordinary piety, wisdom and courage, he must have sunk under them. He had, with a laudable industry, been laying up a treasure of experiences, and he had now occasion to use it: indeed, nothing but an experienced man could have been suitable to the necessities of the people. The potent nations of the Indians, into whose country they were come, would have cut them off, if the blessing of God upon his conduct had not quelled them; and if his prudence, justice and moderation had not over-ruled them, they had been ruined by their own distempers. One specimen of his demeanour is to this day particularly spoken of. A company of young fellows that were newly arrived, were very unwilling to comply with the governor's order for working abroad on the public account; and therefore on Christmas-day, when he had called upon them, they excused themselves, with a pretense that it was against their conscience to work such a day.[20] The governor gave them no answer, only that he would spare them till they were better informed; but by and by he found them all at play in the street, sporting themselves with various diversions; whereupon commanding the instruments of their games to be taken from them, he effectually gave them to understand, "That

---

[15] Harrassed.   [16] Boston, England.   [17] In Acts 28:3 a viper fastens on the Apostle Paul's hand.
[18] Noble-minded.   [19] Wife.   [20] The Puritans did not regard Christmas as a holiday.

it was against his conscience that they should play whilst others were at work: and that if they had any devotion to the day, they should show it at home in the exercises of religion, and not in the streets with pastime and frolics;" and this gentle reproof put a final stop to all such disorders for the future.

6. For two years together after the beginning of the colony, whereof he was now governor, the poor people had a great experiment of "man's not living by bread alone;"[21] for when they were left all together without one morsel of bread for many months one after another, still the good providence of God relieved them, and supplied them, and this for the most part out of the sea. In this low condition of affairs, there was no little exercise for the prudence and patience of the governor, who cheerfully bore his part in all: and, that industry might not flag, he quickly set himself to settle propriety[22] among the new-planters; foreseeing that while the whole country labored upon a common stock,[23] the husbandry and business of the plantation could not flourish, as Plato[24] and others long since dreamed that it would, if a community were established. Certainly, if the spirit which dwelt in the old puritans, had not inspired these new-planters, they had sunk under the burden of these difficulties; but our Bradford had a double portion of that spirit.

7. The plantation was quickly thrown into a storm that almost overwhelmed it, by the unhappy actions of a minister sent over from England by the adventurers[25] concerned for the plantation; but by the blessing of Heaven on the conduct of the governor, they weathered out that storm. Only the adventurers hereupon breaking to pieces, threw up all their concernments with the infant-colony; whereof they gave this as one reason, "That the planters dissembled with his Majesty and their friends in their petition, wherein they declared for a church-discipline, agreeing with the French and others of the reforming churches in Europe.[26] Whereas 'twas now urged, that they had admitted into their communion a person who at his admission utterly renounced the Churches of England, (which person, by the way, was that very man who had made the complaints against them,) and therefore, though they denied the name of Brownists,[27] yet they were the thing. In answer hereunto, the very words written by the governor were these:

> "Whereas you tax us with dissembling about the French discipline, you do us wrong, for we both hold and practice the discipline of the French and other Reformed Churches (as they have published the same in the Harmony of Confessions) according to our means, in effect and substance. But whereas you would tie us up to the French discipline in every circumstance, you derogate from the liberty we have in Christ Jesus. The Apostle Paul would have none to follow him in any thing, but wherein he follows Christ; must less ought any Christian or church in the world to do it. The French may err, we may err, and other churches may err, and doubtless do in many circumstances. That honor therefore belongs only to the infallible Word of God, and pure Testament of Christ, to be propounded and followed as the only rule and pattern for direction herein to all churches and Christians. And it is too

---

[21] "Man shall not live by bread along, buy by every word of God," from Luke 4:4.   [22] Property.
[23] Common property.
[24] Plato (427?–347? B.C.), a Greek philosopher, favored the establishment of a republic based on communally owned property.
[25] English investors who financed the Pilgrims' trip to America.
[26] European states were proclaimed as either Protestant or Catholic; in France the Edict of Nantes (1598) allowed religious independence for all without disavowing the authority of the Crown.
[27] Follower of Robert Browne (1550?–1633?), a Separatist clergyman who founded Congregationalism, a system in which each church is independent of any national church.

great arrogancy for any man or church to think that he or they have so sounded the Word of God unto the bottom, as precisely to set down the church's discipline without error in substance or circumstance, that no other without blame may digress or differ in any thing from the same. And it is not difficult to show that the Reformed Churches differ in many circumstances among themselves."

By which words it appears how far he was free from that rigid spirit of separation, which broke to pieces the Separatists themselves in the Low Countries, unto the great scandal of the reforming churches.[28] He was indeed a person of a well-tempered spirit, or else it had been scarce possible for him to have kept the affairs of Plymouth in so good a temper for thirty-seven years[29] together; in every one of which he was chosen their governor, except the three years wherein Mr. Winslow,[30] and the two years wherein Mr. Prince,[31] at the choice of the people, took a turn with him.

8. The leader of a people in a wilderness had need be a Moses;[32] and if a Moses had not led the people of Plymouth Colony, when this worthy person was their governor, the people had never with so much unanimity and importunity still called him to lead them. Among many instances thereof, let this one piece of self-denial be told for a memorial of him, wheresoever this history shall be considered: the patent of the colony was taken in his name, running in these terms: "To William Bradford, his heirs, associates, and assigns." But when the number of the freemen[33] was much increased, and many new townships erected, the General Court there desired of Mr. Bradford, that he would make a surrender of the same into their hands, which he willingly and presently assented unto, and confirmed it according to their desire by his hand and seal, reserving no more for himself than was his proportion, with others, by agreement. But as he found the providence of Heaven many ways recompensing his many acts of self-denial, so he gave this testimony to the faithfulness of the divine promises: "That he had forsaken friends, houses and lands for the sake of the gospel, and the Lord gave them him again." Here he prospered in his estate; and besides a worthy son which he had by a former wife, he had also two sons and a daughter by another, whom he married in this land.

9. He was a person for study as well as action; and hence, notwithstanding the difficulties through which he passed in his youth, he attained unto a notable skill in languages: the Dutch tongue was become almost as vernacular to him as the English; the French tongue he could also manage; the Latin and the Greek he had mastered; but the Hebrew he most of all studied, "Because," he said, "he would see with his own eyes the ancient oracles of God in their native beauty." He was also well skilled in history, in antiquity, and in philosophy; and for theology he became so versed in it, that he was an irrefragable[34] disputant against the errors, especially those of Anabaptism,[35] which with trouble he saw rising in his colony; wherefore he wrote some significant things for the confutation of those errors. But

---

[28] The Separatist movement ended in dissension; the scandal was the self-baptism of two English Puritans who claimed that there was no pure church to baptize them.

[29] Actually, Bradford served for thirty years as governor and for five years as assistant governor.

[30] Edward Winslow (1595–1655), who served three times as governor.

[31] Thomas Prince (1600–1673), who served three times as governor.

[32] The Hebrew lawgiver who led the Israelites out of slavery to the Promised Land.

[33] Those not indentured as servants, with full citizenship rights.   [34] Indisputable.

[35] A Protestant reformer movement against the baptism of children and supporting separation of church and state.

the crown of all was his holy, prayerful, watchful, and fruitful walk with God, wherein he was very exemplary.

10. At length he fell into an indisposition of body, which rendered him unhealthy for a whole winter; and as the spring advanced, his health yet more declined; yet he felt himself not what he counted sick, till one day; in the night after which, the God of heaven so filled his mind with ineffable consolations, that he seemed little short of Paul, rapt up unto the unutterable entertainments of Paradise.[36] The next morning he told his friends "that the good Spirit of God had given him a pledge of his happiness in another world, and the first-fruits of his eternal glory" and on the day following he died, May 9, 1657, in the 69th year[37] of his age—lamented by all the colonies of New-England, as a common blessing and father to them all.

O mihi si Similis Contingat Clausula Vitæ![38]

Plato's brief description of a governor is all that I will now leave as his character, in an

Epitaph
Νομευδ Τροφοδ ᾰγελ η δ ανθρωπινη δ.[39]
Men are but flocks: Bradford beheld their need,
And long did them at once both rule and feed.

1693–1702, 1702

from   BONIFACIUS: AN ESSAY UPON THE GOOD*

from   [Chapter Three: Relative to Home and Neighborhood]

§11. The useful man may now with a very good grace, extend and enlarge the sphere of his consideration. My next proposal now shall be: Let every man consider the relation, wherein the Sovereign God has placed him, and let him devise what good he may do, that may render his relatives, the better for him. One great way to prove ourselves really good, is to be relatively good. By this, more than by anything in the world, it is, that we adorn the doctrine of God our Saviour. It would be an excellent wisdom in a man, to make the interest he has in the good opinion and affection of anyone, an advantage to do good service for God upon them: He that has a friend will show himself indeed friendly, if he thinks, "Such an one loves me, and will hearken to me; what good shall I take advantage hence to persuade him to?"

---

[36] The Apostle Paul was converted to Christianity when a light from Heaven transfixed him (see Acts 9:3–5).
[37] Actually, his sixty-seventh year.
[38] "Oh, that I might reach a similar end of life" (Latin).
[39] "Shepherd and guardian of his human flock" (Greek).
* Mather's subtitle is *An Essay Upon the Good, That Is to Be Devised and Designed, by Those Who Desire to Answer the Great End of Life, and to Do Good While They Live.*

This will take place more particularly, where the endearing ties of natural relation do give us an interest. Let us call over our several relations, and let us have devices of something that may be called heroical goodness, in our discharging of them. Why should we not, at least once or twice in a week, make this relational goodness, the subject of our inquiries, and our purposes? Particularly, let us begin with our domestic relations, and provide for those of our own house, lest we deny some glorious rules and hopes of our Christian faith, in our negligence.

First, in the conjugal relation, how agreeably may the consorts[1] think on those words: "What knowest thou, O wife, whether thou shalt save thy husband?" Or, "How knowest thou, O man, whether thou shalt save thy wife?"

The husband will do well to think: "What shall I do, that my wife may have cause forever to bless God, for bringing her unto me?" And, "What shall I do that in my carriage[2] towards my wife, the kindness of the blessed Jesus towards His Church, may be followed and resembled?" That this question may be the more perfectly answered, Sir, sometimes ask her to help you in the answer; ask her to tell you, what she would have you to do.

But then, the wife also will do well to think: "Wherein may I be to my husband, a wife of that character: she will do him good, and not evil, all the days of his life?"

With my married people, I will particularly leave a good note, which I find in the memorials of Gervase Disney, Esq.[3] "Family passions, cloud faith, disturb duty, darken comfort." You'll do the more good unto one another, the more this note is thought upon. When the husband and wife are always contriving to be blessings unto one another, I will say with Tertullian, *Unde sufficiam ad enarrandam faelicitatem ejus matrimonii!*[4] O happy marriage!

Parents, Oh! how much ought you to be continually devising, and even travailing, for the good of your children. Often devise: how to make them wise children; how to carry on a desirable education for them; an education that shall render them desirable; how to render them lovely, and polite creatures, and serviceable in their generation. Often devise, how to enrich their minds with valuable knowledge; how to instill generous, and gracious, and heavenly principles into their minds; how to restrain and rescue them from the paths of the Destroyer, and fortify them against their special temptations. There is a world of good, that you have to do for them. You are without bowels,[5] Oh! be not such monsters! if you are not in a continual agony to do for them all the good that ever you can. It was no mistake of Pacatus Drepanius in his panegyric to Theodosius: *Instituente natura plus fere filios quam nosmetipsos diligimus.*[6]

I will prosecute this matter, by transcribing a copy of parental resolutions, which I have somewhere met withal.[7]

I. "At the birth of my children, I would use all explicit solemnity in the baptis-

---

[1] Marital partners.   [2] Behavior.

[3] A wealthy English landowner whose spiritual autobiography was published in 1692.

[4] "How can I find words to express the happiness of their marriage!" (Latin); Tertullian (A.D. 160?–230?) was a theologian from Carthage.

[5] Tender emotions.

[6] "Nature teaches us to love our children as ourselves" (Latin); Latinius Pacatus Drepanius was a Roman orator who lauded the Roman emperor Theodosius I (A.D. 346?–395).

[7] These resolutions were set down, or met, in Mather's autobiography, *Paterna*, published in entirety in 1976.

mal dedication and consecration of them unto the Lord. I would present them to the baptism of the Lord, not as a mere formality; but wondering at the grace of the infinite God, who will accept my children as His, I would resolve to do all I can that they may be His. I would now actually give them up unto God; entreating, that the child may be a child of God the Father, a subject of God the Son, a temple of God the Spirit, and be rescued from the condition of a child of wrath, and be possessed and employed by the Lord as an everlasting instrument of His glory.

II. "My children are no sooner grown capable of minding the admonitions, but I would often, often admonish them to be sensible of the baptismal engagements to be the Lord's. Often tell them, of their baptism, and of what it binds 'em to: oftener far, and more times than there are drops of water, that were cast on the infant, upon that occasion!

"Often say to them, 'Child, you have been baptized; you were washed in the name of the great God; now you must not sin against Him; to sin is to do a dirty, a filthy thing.' Say, 'Child, you must every day cry to God that He would be your Father, and your Savior, and your Leader; in your baptism He promised that He would be so, if you sought unto Him.' Say, 'Child, you must renounce the service of Satan, you must not follow the vanities of this world, you must lead a life of serious religion; in your baptism you were bound unto the service of your only Savior.' Tell the child: 'What is your name; you must sooner forget this name, that was given you in your baptism, than forget that you are a servant of a glorious Christ whose name was put upon you in your baptism.'

III. "Let my prayers for my children be daily, with constancy, with fervency, with agony; yea, by name let me mention each one of them, every day before the Lord. I would importunately beg for all suitable blessings to be bestowed upon them: that God would give them grace, and give them glory, and withhold no good thing from them; that God would smile on their education, and give His good angels the charge over them, and keep them from evil, that it may not grieve them; that when their father and mother shall forsake them, the Lord may take them up. With importunity I would plead that promise on their behalf: the Heavenly Father will give the Holy Spirit unto them that ask Him. Oh! happy children, if by asking I may obtain the Holy Spirit for them!

IV. "I would betimes entertain the children, with delightful stories out of the Bible. In the talk of the table, I would go through the Bible, when the olive-plants about my table[8] are capable of being so watered. But I would always conclude the stories with some lessons of piety, to be inferred from them.

V. "I would single out some Scriptural sentences of the greatest importance; and some also that have special antidotes in them against the common errors and vices of children. They shall quickly get those golden sayings by heart, and be rewarded with silver or gold, or some good thing, when they do it. Such as,

Psalm 111:10
The fear of the Lord, is the beginning of wisdom.
Matthew 16:26
What is a man profited, if he gain the whole world,
and lose his own soul.
I Timothy 1:15

---

[8] Mather's children.

Jesus Christ came into the world to save
sinners, of whom I am chief.
Matthew 6:6
Enter into thy closet, and when thou hast shut thy door,
pray to thy Father which is in secret.
Ecclesiastes 12:14
God shall bring every work into judgment, with every
secret thing.
Ephesians 5:25
Put away lying, speak everyone the truth.
Psalm 138:6
The Lord hath respect unto the lowly, but the proud
He knows afar off.
Romans 12:17, 19
Recompense to no one evil for evil. Dearly beloved,
avenge not yourselves.
Nehemiah 13:18
They bring wrath upon Israel, by profaning the
Sabbath.

A Jewish treatise quoted by Wagenseil[9] tells us, that among the Jews, when a child began to speak, the father was bound to teach him that verse: Deuteronomy 33:4, 'Moses commanded us a Law, even the inheritance of the Congregation of Jacob.' Oh! let me betimes make my children acquainted with the Law which our blessed Jesus has commanded us! 'Tis the best inheritance I can derive unto them.

VI. "I would betimes cause my children to learn the Catechism.[10] In catechizing of them, I would break the answer into many lesser and proper questions; and by their answer to them, observe and quicken their understandings. I would bring every truth, into some duty and practice, and expect them to confess it, and consent unto it, and resolve upon it. As we go on in our catechizing, they shall, when they are able, turn to the proofs, and read them, and say to me, what they prove, and how. Then, I will take my times, to put nicer[11] and harder questions to them; and improve the times of conversation with my family (which every man ordinarily has or may have) for conferences on matters of religion.

VII. "Restless would I be, till I may be able to say of my children, 'Behold, they pray!' I would therefore teach them to pray. But after they have learned a form of prayer, I will press them, to proceed unto points which are not in their form. I will show them the state of their own souls; and on every stroke inquire of them, what they think ought now to be their prayer. I will direct them, that every morning they shall take one text or two out of the Sacred Scripture, and shape it into a desire, which they shall add unto their usual prayer. When they have heard a sermon, I will mention to them over again the main subject of it, and ask them thereupon what they have now to pray for. I will charge them, with all possible cogency, to pray in secret; and often call upon them, 'Child, I hope, you don't forget my charge to you, about secret prayer: your crime is very great, if you do!'

---

[9] Johann Christoph Wagenseil (1633–1705), a Christian who studied the Jews' system of ethics and customs.
[10] A formal set of questions and answers for teaching religious principles.
[11] Finely discriminating.

VIII. "I would betimes do what I can, to beget a temper of benignity in my children, both towards one another, and towards all other people. I will instruct them how ready they should be to communicate unto others, a part of what they have; and they shall see my encouragements when they discover a loving, a courteous, an helpful disposition. I will give them now and then a piece of money, for them with their own little hands to dispense unto the poor. Yea, if any one has hurt them, or vexed them, I will not only forbid them all revenge, but also oblige them to do a kindness as soon as may be to the vexatious person. All coarseness of language or carriage in them, I will discountenance it.

IX. "I would be solicitous to have my children expert not only at reading handsomely, but also at writing a fair hand. I will then assign them such books to read, as I may judge most agreeable and profitable: obliging them to give me some account of what they read; but keep a strict eye upon them, that they don't stumble on the Devil's library, and poison themselves with foolish romances, or novels, or plays, or songs, or jests that are not convenient.[12] I will set them also, to write out such things, as may be of the greatest benefit unto them; and they shall have their blank books, neatly kept on purpose, to enter such passages as I advise them to. I will particularly require them now and then, to write a prayer of their own composing, and bring it unto me; that so I may discern, what sense they have of their own everlasting interests.

X. "I wish that my children may as soon as may be, feel the principles of reason and honor working in them, and that I may carry on their education, very much upon those principles. Therefore, first, I will wholly avoid that harsh, fierce, crabbed[13] usage of the children that would make them tremble, and abhor to come into my presence. I will so use them that they shall fear to offend me, and yet mightily love to see me, and be glad of my coming home, if I have been abroad at any time. I would have it looked upon as a severe and awful punishment for a crime in the family, to be forbidden for awhile to come into my presence. I would raise in them an high opinion of their father's love to them, and of his being better able to judge what is good for them, than they are for themselves. I would bring them to believe, 'tis best for them to be and do as I would have them. Hereupon I would continually magnify the matter to them, what a brave thing 'tis to know the things that are excellent; and more brave to do the things that are virtuous. I would have them to propose it as a reward of their well-doing at any time, I will now go to my father, and he will teach me something that I was never taught before. I would have them afraid of doing any base thing, from an horror of the baseness in it. My first animadversion[14] on a lesser fault in them, shall be a surprise, a wonder, vehemently expressed before them, that ever they should be guilty of doing so foolishly; a vehement belief, that they will never do the like again; a weeping resolution in them, that they will not. I will never dispense a blow, except it be for an atrocious crime, or for a lesser fault obstinately persisted in; either for an enormity, or for an obstinacy. I would ever proportion chastisements unto miscarriages;[15] not smite bitterly for a very small piece of childishness, and only frown a little for some real wickedness. Nor shall my chastisements ever be dispensed in a passion and a fury; but with them, I will first show them the command of God, by transgressing whereof they have displeased me. The slavish, raving, fighting way of education too commonly used, I look upon it, as a considerable article in the wrath and curse of God, upon a miserable world.

---

[12] Appropriate.   [13] Ill-tempered.   [14] An act of criticizing adversely.   [15] Failures.

XI. "As soon as we can, we'll get up to yet higher principles. I will often tell the children, what cause they have to love a glorious Christ, who has died for them. And, how much He will be well-pleased with their well-doing. And, what a noble thing, 'tis to follow His example; which example I will describe unto them. I will often tell them that the eye of God is upon them; the great God knows all they do, and hears all they speak. I will often tell them that there will be a time, when they must appear before the Judgment-Seat of the holy Lord; and they must now do nothing that may then be a grief and shame unto them. I will set before them the delights of that Heaven that is prepared for pious children; and the torments of that Hell that is prepared of old, for naughty ones. I will inform them, of the good offices[16] which the good angels do for little ones that have the fear of God, and are afraid of sin. And, how the devils tempt them to do ill things; how they hearken to the devils, and are like them, when they do such things; and what mischiefs the devils may get leave to do them in this world, and what a sad thing 'twill be, to be among the devils in the Place of Dragons.[17] I will cry to God, that He will make them feel the power of these principles.

XII. "When the children are of a fit age for it, I will sometimes closet[18] them; have them with me alone; talk with them about the state of their souls; their experiences, their proficiencies, their temptations; obtain their declared consent unto every stroke in the Covenant of Grace;[19] and then pray with them, and weep unto the Lord for His grace, to be bestowed upon them, and make them witnesses of the agony with which I am travailing to see the image of Christ formed in them. Certainly, they'll never forget such actions!

XIII. "I would be very watchful and cautious about the companions of my children. I will be very inquisitive what company they keep; if they are in hazard of being ensnared by any vicious company, I will earnestly pull them out of it, as brands out of the burning. I will find out, and procure, laudable companions for them.

XIV. "As in catechizing the children, so in the repetition of the public sermons, I would use this method. I will put every truth into a question to be answered still, with Yes, or No. By this method, I hope to awaken their attention as well as enlighten their understanding. And thus I shall have an opportunity to ask, 'Do you desire such or such a grace of God?' and the like. Yea, I may have opportunity to demand, and perhaps to obtain their early, and frequent, and why not sincere?, consent unto the glorious articles of the New Covenant. The spirit of grace may fall upon them in this action; and they may be seized by Him, and held as His temples, through eternal ages.

XV. "When a Day of Humiliation[20] arrives, I will make them know the meaning of the day. And after time given them to consider of it, I will order them to tell me: what special afflictions they have met withal? And, what good they hope to get by those afflictions? On a Day of Thanksgiving, they shall also be made to know the intent of the day. And after consideration, they shall tell me, what mercies of God unto them they take special notice of: And, what duties to God, they confess and resolve, under such obligations? Indeed, for something of this impor-

---

[16] Services.

[17] Hell; Satan is known as the Old Serpent, an archaic form of "dragon."

[18] To shut up in a private room for discussion.

[19] The Puritans' New Covenant, or the agreement God made with Adam after he ate the forbidden fruit and fell from grace.

[20] A day on which a child becomes aware of having offended God.

tance, to be pursued in my conversation with the children, I would not confine myself unto the solemn days, which may occur too seldom for it. Very particularly, when the birthdays of the children anniversarily arrive to any of them, I would then take them aside, and mind them of the age, which having obtained help from God they are come unto; how thankful they should be for the mercies of God, which they have hitherto lived upon; how fruitful they should be in all goodness, that so they may still enjoy their mercies. And I would inquire of them, whether they have ever yet begun to mind the work which God sent them into the world upon; how far they understand the work; and what good strokes they have struck at it; and, how they design to spend the rest of their time, if God still continue them in the world.

XVI. "When the children are in any trouble, as, if they be sick, or pained, I will take advantage therefrom to set before them the evil of sin, which brings all our trouble; and how fearful a thing it will be to be cast among the damned, who are in easeless and endless trouble. I will set before them the benefit of an interest in a Christ, by which their trouble will be sanctified unto them, and they will be prepared for death, and for fullness of joy in an happy eternity after death.

XVII. "I incline that among all the points of a polite education which I would endeavor for my children, they may each of them, the daughters as well as the sons, have so much insight into some skill, which lies in the way of gain (the limners',[21] or the scriveners',[22] or the apothecaries',[23] or some other mystery,[24] to which their own inclination may most carry them) that they may be able to subsist themselves, and get something of a livelihood, in case the providence of God should bring them into necessities. Why not they as well as Paul the Tent-Maker![25] The children of the best fashion, may have occasion to bless the parents, that make such a provision for them! The Jews have a saying; 'tis worth my remembering it: Quicunque filium suum non docet opificium, perinde est ac si eum doceret latrocinium.[26]

XVIII. "As soon as ever I can, I would make my children apprehensive of the main end for which they are to live; that so they may as soon as may be, begin to live; and their youth not be nothing but vanity. I would show them, that their main end must be to acknowledge the great God, and His glorious Christ; and bring others to acknowledge Him: and that they are never wise nor well, but when they are doing so. I would show them, what the acknowledgments are, and how they are to be made. I would make them able to answer the grand question, why they live; and what is the end of the actions that fill their lives? Teach them, how their Creator and Redeemer is to be obeyed in everything; and, how everything is to be done in obedience to Him; teach them, how even their diversions, and their ornaments,[27] and the tasks of their education, must all be to fit them for the further service of Him, to whom I have devoted them; and how in these also, His commandments must be the rule of all they do. I would sometimes therefore surprise them with an inquiry, 'Child, what is this for? Give me a good account, why you

---

[21] Those who illustrate manuscripts.   [22] Scribes.   [23] Pharmacists.
[24] A special skill known only to a small group.
[25] In Acts 18:3 the Apostle Paul is a tent maker by trade.
[26] "He who does not teach his son a craft, teaches him theft" (Latin).   [27] Adornments, attire.

do it?' How comfortably shall I see them walking in the light, if I may bring them wisely to answer this inquiry; and what children of the light?[28]

XIX. "I would oblige the children to retire sometimes, and ponder on that question: 'What shall I wish to have done, if I were now a-dying?' And report unto me, their own answer to the question; of which I would then take advantage, to inculcate the lessons of godliness upon them. I would also direct them and oblige them, at a proper time for it, seriously to realize their own appearance before the awful Judgment-Seat of the Lord Jesus Christ, and consider what they have to plead, that they may not be sent away into everlasting punishment; what they have to plead, that they may be admitted into the Holy City. I would instruct them, what plea to prepare; first, show them, how to get a part in the righteousness of Him that is to be their Judge; by receiving it with a thankful faith, as the gift of infinite grace unto the distressed and unworthy sinner: then, show them how to prove that their faith is not a counterfeit, by their continual endeavor to please Him in all things, who is to be their Judge, and to serve His Kingdom and interest in the world. And I would charge them, to make this preparation.

XX. "If I live to see the children marriageable, I would, before I consult with Heaven and earth for their best accommodation in the married state, endeavor the espousal of their souls unto their only Savior. I would as plainly, and as fully as I can, propose unto them the terms on which the glorious Redeemer would espouse them to Himself, in righteousness and judgment, and favor, and mercies forever; and solicit their consent unto His proposals and overtures. Then would I go on, to do what may be expected from a tender parent for them, in their temporal circumstances."

From these parental resolutions, how naturally, how reasonably may we pass on to say:

"Children, the Fifth Commandment[29] confirms all your other numberless and powerful obligations, often to devise, 'Wherein may I be a blessing to my parents?' Ingenuity would make this the very top of your ambition; to be a credit, and a comfort of your parents; to sweeten, and if it may be, to lengthen the lives of those, from whom, under God, you have received your lives. And God the Rewarder usually gives it, even in this life, a most observable recompense. But it is possible, you may be the happy instruments of more than a little good unto the souls of your parents (will you think, how!); yea, though they should be pious parents, you may by some exquisite methods, be the instruments of the growth in piety, and in preparation for the Heavenly world. O thrice and four times happy children! Among the Arabians, a father sometimes takes his name from an eminent Son, as well as a son from his reputed father. A man is called with an Abu, as well as an Ebn. Verily, a son may be such a blessing to his father that the best surname for the glad father would be, the father of such an one."

Masters, yea, and mistresses too, must have their devices, how to do good unto their servants; how to make them the servants of Christ, and the children of God. God whom you must remember to be your Master in Heaven, has brought them,

---

[28] ". . . for the children of this world are in their generation wiser than the children of light," from Luke 16:8.

[29] "Honor thy father and thy mother: that thy days may be long upon the land which the Lord thy God giveth thee," from Exodus 20:12.

and put them into your hands. Who can tell what good He has brought them for? How if they should be the elect of God, fetched from Africa, or the Indies, and brought into your families, on purpose, that by the means of their being there, they may be brought home unto the Shepherd of Souls? Oh! that the souls of our slaves, were of more account with us! that we gave a better demonstration that we despise not our own souls, by doing what we can for the souls of our slaves, and not using them as if they had no souls! that the poor slaves and blacks, which live with us, may by our means be made the candidates of the heavenly life! How can we pretend unto Christianity, when we do no more to Christianize our slaves! Verily, you must give an account unto God, concerning them. If they be lost, through your negligence, what answer can you make unto God the Judge of all! Methinks, common principles of gratitude should incline you to study the happiness of those by whose obsequious labors your lives are so much accommodated. Certainly, they would be the better servants to you, the more faithful, the more honest, the more industrious, and submissive servants to you, for your bringing them into the service of your common Lord.

But if any servant of God, may be so honored by Him, as to be made the successful instrument, of obtaining from a British Parliament, an act for the Christianizing of the slaves in the plantations; then it may be hoped, something more may be done, than has yet been done, that the blood of souls may not be found in the skirts of our nation: a controversy of Heaven with our colonies may be removed, and prosperity may be restored; or, however [whoever?] the honorable instrument, will have unspeakable peace and joy in the remembrance of his endeavors. In the meantime, the slave-trade is a spectacle that shocks humanity.

> The harmless natives basely they trepan,[30]
> And barter baubles for the souls of men.
> The wretches they to Christian climes bring o'er
> To serve worse heathens than they did before.

I have somewhere met with a paper under this title, "The Resolution of a Master," which may here afford an agreeable paragraph and parenthesis.

I. "I would always remember that my servants are in some sort my children. In a care that they may want nothing that may be good for them, I would make them as my children. And, as far as the methods of instilling piety, which I use with my children, may be properly and prudently used with these, they shall be partakers in them. Nor will I leave them ignorant of anything, wherein I may instruct them to be useful in their generation.

II. "I will see that my servants be furnished with Bibles, and able and careful to read the lively oracles.[31] I will put both Bibles and other good and fit books into their hands; and allow them time to read, but assure myself that they don't misspend this time. If I can discover any wicked books in their hands, I will take away from them, those pestilential instruments of wickedness. They shall also write as well as read, if I can bring them to it. And I will set them now and then such things to write, as may be for their greatest advantage.

III. "I will have my servants present at the religious exercises of my family; and let fall either in the speeches, or in the prayers, of the daily sacrifice in the family, such passages, as may have a tendency to quicken a sense of religion in them.

[30] Trap or trick.   [31] Divine announcements.

IV. "The catechizing stroke as far as the age or state of the servants will permit, that it may be done with decency, shall extend unto them also. And they shall be concerned in the conferences, wherein the repetition of the public sermons, may engage me with my family. If any of them, when they come to me, have not learned the Catechism, I will see to it that they shall do it, and give them a reward when they have done it.

V. "I will be very inquisitive and solicitous about the company chosen by my servants; and with all possible cogency rescue them from the snares of evil company: forbid their being the companions of fools.

VI. "Such of my servants as may be employed for that purpose, I will employ to teach lessons of piety unto my children, and recompense them for doing so. But I would with a particular artifice contrive them to be such lessons, as may be for their own edification too.

VII. "I will sometimes call my servants alone; talk with them about the state of their souls; tell them how to close with their only Savior; charge them to do well, and lay hold on eternal life; and show them very particularly, how they may render all the service they do for me, a service to the glorious Lord; how they may do all from a principle of obedience to the Lord, and become entitled unto the reward of the heavenly inheritance."[32]

I make this appendix to these resolutions. I have read such a passage as this:

"Age is well nigh sufficient with some masters to obliterate every letter and action, in the history of a meritorious life; and old services are generally buried under the ruins of an old carcass." And this passage, "It's a barbarous inhumanity in men towards their servants, to make their small failings to be a crime, without allowing their past services to have been a virtue. Good God, keep thy servant from such ingratitude! Worse than villainous ingratitude!"

But then, O servants, if you would arrive to the reward of the inheritance, you should set yourselves to devise: "How shall I approve myself such a servant, that the Lord may bless the house of my master, the more for my being in it?" Certainly, there are many ways, wherein servants may be blessings. Let your studies with your continual prayers for the welfare of the families to which you belong, and the example of your sober carriage, render you such. If you will remember but four words, and endeavor all that is comprised in them, obedience, honesty, industry, and piety, you will be the blessings and the Josephs[33] of the families to which you belong. Let those four heads be distinctly and frequently thought upon. And go cheerfully through all you have to do, upon this consideration: that it is an obedience to Heaven, and from thence will have a recompense. It was the observation even of a pagan that a master may receive a benefit from a servant. And, *Quod fit affectu amici, desinit esse ministerium.*[34] It is a friendship rather than a service, young man, if it be with the affection of a friend, that you do what you do for your master. Yea, even the maid-servants in the house may do an unknown service to it, by instructing the infants, and instilling the lessons of goodness into them. So, by Bilhah, and Zilpah,[35] may children be born again; the mistresses may by the travail of the maid-servants, have children, brought into the Kingdom of God.

---

[32] Salvation.

[33] Joseph, though sold into slavery by his brothers, was a credit to his parents, Jacob and Rachel, as he became a high-ranking official in Egypt (see Genesis 32:22–24).

[34] "What is done with the affection of a friend is no longer the act of a mere servant" (Latin).

[35] In Genesis 29:29 Bilhah is the handmaid of Jacob's wife Rachel; in Genesis 29:24 Zilpah is the handmaid of Jacob's wife Leah.

I will go on. Humanity teaches us to take notice of all that are our kindred. Nature bespeaks that which we call a natural affection to all that are akin to us. To be without it, is a very bad character; 'tis a brand on the worst of men; on such as forfeit the name of men. But now, Christianity is to improve it. Our natural affection is to be improved into a religious intention. Sir, take a catalogue of all your more distant relatives. Consider them one after another; and make every one of them the subjects of your good devices. Think: "Wherein may I pursue the good of such a relative?" And, "By what means may I render such a relative the better for me?" It is possible, you may do something, that may give them cause to bless God, that ever you have been related unto them. Have they no calamity, under which you may give them some relief? Is there no temptation against which you may give them some caution? Is there no article of their prosperity, to which you may be subservient? At least; with your affectionate prayers, you may go over your catalogue; you may successively pray for every one of them all by name; and, if you can, why should you not also put agreeable books of piety into their hands, to be lasting remembrancers of their duties to God, and of your desires for them?

§ 12. Methinks, this excellent zeal should be carried into our neighborhood. Neighbors, you stand related unto one another; and you should be full of devices, that all the neighbors may have cause to be glad of your being in the neighborhood. We read, "The righteous is more excellent than his neighbor." But we shall scarce own him so, except he be more excellent as a neighbor. He must excel in the duties of good neighborhood. Let that man be better than his neighbor, who labors to be a better neighbor; to do most good unto his neighbor.

And here, first, the poor people that lie wounded, must have wine and oil poured into their wounds. It was a charming stroke in the character with [which?] a modern prince had given to him, to be in distress, is to deserve his favor. O good neighbor, put on that princely, that more than royal quality. See who in the neighborhood may deserve the favor. We are told, this is pure religion and undefiled (a jewel, that neither is a counterfeit, nor has any flaws in it): to visit the fatherless and widows in their affliction. The orphans and the widows, and so all the children of affliction in the neighborhood, must be visited, and relieved with all agreeable kindnesses.

Neighbors, be concerned, that the orphans and widows in your neighborhood, may be well provided for. They meet with grievous difficulties; with unknown temptations. While their next relatives were yet living, they were, perhaps, but meanly[36] provided for. What must they now be in their more solitary condition? Their condition should be considered: and the result of the consideration should be that: I delivered the orphan, that had no helper, and I caused the heart of the widow to sing for joy.[37]

By consequence, all the afflicted in the neighborhood are to be thought upon. Sirs, would it be too much for you, at least once in a week, to think, "What neighbor is reduced into a pinching and painful poverty? Or in any degree impoverished with heavy losses?" Think, "What neighbor is languishing with sickness; especially if sick with sore maladies, and of some continuance?" Think, "What neighbor is heartbroken with sad bereavements; bereaved of desirable relatives?" And think: "What neighbor has a soul buffeted, and buried with violent assaults of the Wicked one?"[38] But then think, "What shall be done for such neighbors?"

---

[36] Poorly.   [37] Paraphrased from Job 29:12–13.   [38] Satan.

First, you will pity them. The evangelical precept is, have compassion one of another, be pitiful. It was of old, and ever will be, the just expectation, to him that is afflicted, pity should be shown. And let our pity to them, flame out in our prayer for them. It were a very lovely practice for you, in the daily prayer of your closet every evening, to think, "What miserable object have I seen today, that I may do well now to mention for the mercies of the Lord?"

But this is not all. 'Tis possible, 'tis probable, you may do well to visit them; and when you visit them, comfort them. Carry them some good word, which may raise a gladness, in an heart stooping with heaviness.

And lastly, Give them all the assistances that may answer their occasions: assist them with advice to them; assist them with address to others for them. And if it be needful, bestow your alms upon them; deal thy bread to the hungry; bring to thy house the poor that are cast out; when thou seest the naked, cover him.[39] At least, Nazianzen's[40] charity, I pray: Si nihil habes, da lacrymulam;[41] if you have nothing else to bestow upon the miserable, bestow a tear or two upon their miseries. This little, is better than nothing!

Would it be amiss for you, to have always lying by you, a list of the poor in your neighborhood, or of those whose calamities may call for the assistances of the neighborhood? Such a list would often furnish you with matter for an useful conversation, when you are talking with your friends, whom you may provoke to love and good works.

I will go on to say: Be glad of opportunities to do good in your neighborhood: yea, look out for them, lay hold on them, with a rapturous assiduity. Be sorry for all the bad circumstances of any neighbor, that bespeak your doing of good unto him. Yet, be glad, if any one tell you of them. Thank him who tells you, as having therein done you a very great civility. Let him know, that he could not by anything have more gratified you. Any civility that you can show, by lending, by watching, by—all the methods of courtesy; show it; and be glad you can show it. Show it, and give a pleasant countenance (cum munere vultum) in the showing of it. Let your wisdom cause your face always to shine; look, not with a cloudy but a serene and shining face, upon your neighbors; and shed the rays of your courtesy upon them, with such affability, that they may see they are welcome to all you can do for them. Yea, stay not until you are told of opportunities to do good. Inquire after them; let the inquiry be solicitous, be unwearied. The incomparable pleasure is worth an inquiry.

There was a generous pagan who counted a day lost if he had obliged nobody in the day. *Amici, diem perdidi!*[42] O Christian, let us try whether we can't attain to do something, for some neighbor or other, every day that comes over our head. Some do so; and with a better spirit than ever Titus Vespasian[43] was acted withal. Thrice in the Scriptures, we find the good angels rejoicing: 'tis always at the good of others. To rejoice in the good of others, and most of all in doing of good unto them, 'tis angelical goodness.

In moving for the devices of good neighborhood, a principal motion which I have to make is that you consult the spiritual interests of your neighborhood, as

---

[39] Paraphrased from Matthew 25:37–38.

[40] Of Gregory Nazianzen (A.D. 325?–390?), or Saint Gregory of Nazianzus.

[41] "If you have nothing, give a tear" (Latin).   [42] "Friends, I have lost the day!" (Latin).

[43] Vespasian (A.D. 9–79) was a much loved emperor of Rome (69–79) and founder of the Flavian dynasty.

well as the temporal. Be concerned, lest the deceitfulness of sin undo any of the neighbors. If there by any idle persons among them, I beseech you, cure them of their idleness; don't nourish 'em and harden 'em in that; but find employment for them. Find 'em work; set 'em to work; keep 'em to work. Then, as much of your other bounty to them, as you please.

If any children in the neighborhood are under no education, don't allow 'em to continue so. Let care be taken, that they may be better educated; and be taught to read; and be taught their Catechism; and the truths and ways of their only Savior.

Once more. If any in the neighborhood, are taking to bad courses, lovingly and faithfully admonish them. If any in the neighborhood are enemies to their own welfare, or their families, prudently dispense your admonitions unto them. If there are any prayerless families, never leave off entreating and exhorting of them, till you have persuaded them, to set up the worship of God. If there be any service of God, or of His people, to which any one may need to be excited, give him a tender excitation. Whatever snare you see any one in, be so kind as to tell him of his danger to be ensnared, and save him from it. By putting of good books into the hands of your neighbors, and gaining of them a promise to read the books, who can tell what good you may do unto them! It is possible you may in this way, with ingenuity, and with efficacy, administer those reproofs, which you may owe unto such neighbors, as are to be reproved for their miscarriages. The books will balk nothing that is to be said on the subjects that you would have the neighbors advised upon.

Finally. If there be any base houses, which threaten to debauch, and poison, and confound the neighborhood, let your charity to your neighbors, make you do all you can, for the suppression of them.

That my proposal to do good in the neighborhood, and as a neighbor, may be more fully formed and followed; I will conclude it, with minding you, that a world of self-denial is to be exercised in the execution of it. You must be armed against selfishness, all selfish and squinting intentions, in your generous resolutions. You shall see how my demands will grow upon you.

1710

Robert Calef
(1648–1719)

Robert Calef, born in 1648 (presumably in England) was a cloth-merchant who arrived in Boston in 1688 and served his community in such official capacities as constable, tax collector, and assessor. Between 1707 and 1710 he retired to Roxbury, Massachusetts, where he was a municipal-board member until his death in 1719. Calef's most famous public service is his authorship of *More Wonders of the Invisible World*, completed in 1697 and published in 1700. A response to clergyman Cotton Mather's *Wonders of the Invisible World* (1693), which defends the justice and necessity of the Salem witchcraft trials of 1692, Calef's work attacks the trials—and Mather's defense of them—from a number of directions. First, Calef reprints letters that Mather neglected to include: from witnesses recanting their testimony, from jurors and judges apologizing for their decisions, and from accused innocents and their frantic relatives—documents all suggesting that the witchcraft episode was, as modern historians have concluded, a tragic delusion rather than a terrible "visitation." Calef also printed an account of Mather's visit to Martha Rule, whom Mather believed to be persecuted by demons. The account showed Mather encouraging Rule to accuse others and laying his hands on her bare torso in an effort to relieve her torments.

Mather was outraged by Calef's book, calling it a "firebrand thrown by a madman" in the response *Some Few Remarks Upon a Scandalous Book* (1701). Mather's father, clergyman Increase Mather, was another target of Calef's charges and had the book publicly burned in Harvard Yard. Yet, Calef's primary target was not the Mathers but one idea underlying the trials: the notion that the Devil entered into covenants with certain individuals, who could then enlist demons (resembling their human employers) to torment others through supernatural means. The testimony of Salemites that they had been harassed by specters (ghosts) of their neighbors had, in fact, been the primary evidence used to indict these neighbors—and to justify their executions. Doubting the reliability of "specter evidence," Calef questioned the justice of courts into which such evidence was admitted. He noted that Cotton Mather's notion of contracts between witches and demons was not substantiated by Scripture and that if witches, in their demonic persecution of others, could flout natural laws, God would not be wholly in charge of nature. Recalling Satan's title of "father of lies," Calef asked with devastating irony, was it not possible that the Devil had asserted his power in New England, not by sponsoring supernatural wickedness but by encouraging deceitful testimony, false accusations, and unjust executions?

Calef has been praised for bringing the witchcraft episode to a close, but by the time his book appeared the trials had been over for eight years, Judge Samuel Sewall (who presided over the trials) and others had apologized, and hardly anyone was paying attention to the events of 1692. Only the Mathers seem to have taken Calef's book seriously—and their reasons were personal. Though lacking in seventeenth-century importance, *More Wonders* has considerable twentieth-century interest. Calef emphasized the doctrinal causes of the witchcraft episode rather than the psychological or sociological causes noted by recent historians. However, his book remains valuable for its ability to offer a refreshingly different Puritan voice, one marked by reason as well as piety, by fairness as well as conviction. A hodgepodge of letters and replies, charges and countercharges, Scriptural quotations, testimonies, and potent personal attacks, *More Wonders* is a noble contribution to American literature.

Suggested Readings: *Narratives of the Witchcraft Cases, 1648–1706,* ed. G. L. Burr, 1914. P. Miller, *The New England Mind: From Colony to Province,* 1953. K. Silverman, *The Life and Times of Cotton Mather,* 1985.

Text Used: *The Witchcraft Delusion in New England: Its Rise, Progress, and Termination, as Exhibited by Dr. Cotton Mather in "The Wonders of the Invisible World" and by Mr. Robert Calef in His "More Wonders of the Invisible World,"* Vol. III, ed. S. G. Drake, 1866; repr. in Woodward's Historical Series, No. VII, 1970 (some spelling and punctuation modernized).

from   MORE WONDERS OF THE INVISIBLE WORLD*

from   Postscript

[Witchcraft and Theocracy]

In the times of Sir Edmund Andros's government,[1] Goody Glover, a despised, crazy, ill-conditioned old woman, an Irish Roman Catholic, was tried for afflicting Goodwin's children;[2] by the account of which trial, taken in shorthand for the use of the jury, it may appear that the generality of her answers were nonsense, and her behavior like that of one distracted. Yet the doctors, finding her as she had been for many years, brought her in *compos mentis*;[3] and setting aside her crazy answers to some ensnaring questions, the proof against her was wholly deficient. The jury brought her in guilty.

Mr. Cotton Mather was the most active and forward of any minister in the country in those matters, taking home one of the children, and managing such intrigues with that child, and printing such an account of the whole in his *Memorable Providences,* as conduced much to the kindling of those flames, that in Sir William's time[4] threatened the destruction of this country.[5]

King Saul[6] in destroying the witches out of Israel is thought by many to have exceeded, and in his zeal to have slain the Gibeonites[7] wrongfully under that notion; yet went after this to a witch to know his fortune. For his wrongfully destroying the Gibeonites (besides the judgments of God upon the land) his sons were hanged; and for his going to the witch, himself was cut off. Our Sir William Phips did not do this; but, as appears by this book, had first his fortune told him, (by such as the author counts no better) and though he put it off (to his pastor, who he knew approved not thereof) as if it were brought to him in writing, without his seeking, etc., yet by his bringing it so far, and safe keeping it so many years, it appears he made some account for it; for which he gave the writer, after he had found the wreck, as a reward, more than two hundred pounds. His telling his wife that he should be a commander, should have a brick house in Greenlane,[8] etc., might be in confidence of some such prediction; and that he could foretell to him that he should be governor of New England, was probably such an one, the scriptures not having revealed it. Such predictions would have been counted, at Salem, pregnant proofs[9] of witchcraft, and much better than what were against several

---

* Calef's *More Wonders of the Invisible World* is an attack against the leaders of the witchcraft hysteria in Salem, Massachusetts, and Cotton Mather's *Wonders of the Invisible World* (1693), which defends the 1692 witchcraft trials; Calef points out the lack of real evidence in the trials, during which hundreds were accused of witchcraft and nineteen people sentenced to death.

[1] Andros (1637–1714) was an English governor of the colonies of New England, New York, and New Jersey (1685–1689) until Bostonians forced him out of office for levying taxes and enforcing the Navigation Acts, which excluded foreign ships from colonial trade.

[2] Those of John Goodwin.   [3] Of sound mind, sane.

[4] Sir William Phips (1651–1695), royal governor of Massachusetts from 1692 to 1694.

[5] Mather responded by denying that he was a leader in the "storm" raised at Salem; people assumed he was, Mather answered, because he spoke of the "honorable judges with as much honor as I could."

[6] The first king of Israel (see 1 Samuel 9).

[7] Inhabitants of Gibeon, condemned by Joshua (the successor of Moses) as "hewers of wood and drawers of water for the congregation and for the altar of the Lord . . . ," from Joshua 9:27.

[8] Salem Street, where Governor Phips resided.   [9] Significant evidence.

that suffered there. But Sir William, when the witchcrafts at Salem began (in his esteem) to look formidable, that he might act safely in this affair, asked the advice of the ministers in and near Boston. The whole of their advice and answer is printed in *Cases of Conscience,* the last pages. But lest the world should be ignorant who it was that drew the said advice, in this book of the life of Sir William Phips, are these words, "The ministers made to his excellency and the council a return, drawn up at their desire, by Mr. Mather the younger, as I have been informed." Mr. C. M. therein intending to beguile the world, and make them think that another, and not himself, had taken that notice of his (supposed) good service done therein, which otherwise would have been ascribed to those ministers in general; though indeed the advice then given looks most like a thing of his composing, as carrying both fire to increase, and water to quench, the conflagration; particularly after the Devil's testimony, by the supposed afflicted, had so prevailed as to take away the life of one, and the liberty of an hundred, and the whole country set into a most dreadful consternation, then this advice is given, ushered in with thanks for what was already done, and in conclusion, putting the government upon a speedy and vigorous prosecution, according to the laws of God, and the wholesome statutes of the English nation; so adding oil, rather than water, to the flame: for who so little acquainted with the proceedings of England, as not to know that they have taken some methods, with those here used, to discover who were witches? The rest of the advice, consisting of cautions and directions, is inserted in this book of the life of Sir William: so that if Sir William, looking upon the thanks for what was past, and exhortation to proceed, went on to take away the lives of nineteen more, this is according to the advice said to be given him by the ministers; and if the Devil, after those executions, be affronted by disbelieving his testimony, and by clearing and pardoning all the rest of the accused, yet this also is, according to that advice, but to cast the scale. The same that drew this advice saith, in *Wonders of the Invisible World, Enchantments Encountered,* that to have a hand in anything that may stifle or obstruct a regular detection of that witchcraft is what we may well with a holy fear avoid: their majesties' good subjects must not every day be torn to pieces by horrid witchcraft, and those bloody felons be wholly left unprosecuted; the witchcraft is a business that will not be shammed. The pastor of that church, of which Sir William was a member, being of this principle, and thus declaring it after the former advice, no wonder though it cast the scale against those cautions. It is rather a wonder that no more blood was shed; for if that advice of his pastor could still have prevailed with the governor, witchcraft had not been so shammed off[10] as it was. Yet now, in this book of the life of Sir William, the pardoning the prisoners when condemned, and clearing the jails, is called a vanquishing the Devil; adding this conquest to the rest of the noble achievements of Sir William, though performed not only without, but directly against, his pastor's advice. But this is not all; though this book pretends to raise a statue in honor of Sir William, yet it appears it was the least part of the design of the author to honor him, but it was rather to honor himself, and the ministers; it being so unjust to Sir William as to give a full account of the cautions given him, but designedly hiding from the reader the encouragements and exhortations to proceed that were laid before him (under the name of the ministers' advice); in effect telling the world that those executions at Salem were without and against the advice of the ministers, expressed in those cautions, purposely hiding their giving

---

[10] Fraudulent.

thanks for what was already done, and exhorting to proceed; thereby rendering Sir William of so sanguinary a complexion that the ministers had such cause to fear his going on with the tragedy, though against their advice, that they desired the president to write his *Cases of Conscience*, etc. To plead misinformation will not salve[11] here, however it may seem to palliate[12] other things, but is a manifest, designed travesty, or misrepresentation, of the minister's advice to Sir William, a hiding the truth, and a wronging the dead, whom the author so much pretends to honor; for which the acknowledgments ought to be as universal as the offense. But though the ministers' advice, or rather Mr. Cotton Mather's, was perfectly ambidexter,[13] giving as great or greater encouragement to proceed in those dark methods, than cautions against them; yet many eminent persons being accused, there was a necessity of a stop to be put to it. If it be true, what was said at the council board in answer to the commendations of Sir William for his stopping the proceedings about witchcraft, viz. that it was high time for him to stop it, his own lady being accused; if that assertion were a truth, then New England may seem to be more beholden to the accusers for accusing her, and thereby necessitating a stop, than to Sir William, or to the advice that was given him by his pastor.

Mr. Cotton Mather, having been very forward to write books of witchcraft, has not been so forward either to explain or to defend the doctrinal part thereof; and his belief (which he had a year's time to compose) he durst not venture, so as to be copied.[14] Yet in this book of the life of Sir William he sufficiently testifies his retaining that heterodox belief,[15] seeking by frightful stories of the sufferings of some, and the refined sight of others, etc., to obtrude upon the world, and confirm it in such a belief as hitherto he either cannot or will not defend, as if the blood already shed thereby were not sufficient.

Mr. I. Mather,[16] in his *Cases of Conscience*, tells of a bewitched eye, and that such can see more than others. They were certainly bewitched eyes, that could see as well shut as open, and that could see what never was; that could see the prisoners upon the afflicted, harming them, when those whose eyes were not bewitched could have sworn that they did not stir from the bar.[17] The accusers are said to have suffered much by biting, and the prints of just such a set of teeth, as those they accused had, would be seen on their flesh; but such as had not such bewitched eyes have seen the accusers bite themselves, and then complain of the accused. It has been seen, when the accused, instead of having just such a set of teeth, has not had one in his head. They were such bewitched eyes, that could see the poisonous powder (brought by specters) and that could see in the ashes the print of the brand, there invisibly heating to torment the pretended sufferers with, etc.[18]

These, with the rest of such legends, have this direct tendency, viz. to tell the world that the Devil is more ready to serve his votaries, by his doing for them

---

[11] Soothe.   [12] To alleviate.   [13] Two-sided.

[14] Certain answers in writing fell into Calef's hands, but with an injunction against his printing them.

[15] An opinion that disagrees with what is generally recognized as "right."

[16] The clergyman Increase Mather (1639–1723), the father of Cotton Mather.   [17] The court.

[18] According to Mather's "Life of Phips" in *Magnalia Christi Americana* (1702), ". . . the flesh of the afflicted was often bitten at such a rate that not only the print of teeth would be left on their flesh, but the very slaver [drool] of spittle too: as there would appear just such a set of teeth as was in the accused. . . . The miserable exclaimed extremely of branding irons heating at the fire on the hearth to mark them; now, though, the standers by could see no irons, yet they could see distinctly the print of them in the ashes, and smell them too as they were carried by the not-seen furies, unto the poor creatures for whom they were intended. . . ."

things above or against the course of nature, showing himself to them and making explicit contracts with them, etc., than the Divine Being is to his faithful servants; and that as he is willing, so also able, to perform their desires. The way whereby these people are believed to arrive at a power to afflict their neighbors is by a compact with the Devil, and that they have a power to commission him to those evils. However irrational, or unscriptural, such assertions are, yet they seem a necessary part of the faith of such as maintain the belief of such a sort of witches.

As the Scriptures know nothing of a covenanting or commissioning witch, so reason cannot conceive how mortals should by their wickedness arrive at a power to commission angels, fallen angels, against their innocent neighbors. But the Scriptures are full in it, and the instances numerous, that the Almighty Divine Being has this prerogative, to make use of what instruments he pleaseth, in afflicting any, and consequently to commission devils: and though this word, commissioning, in the author's former books, might be thought to be by inadvertency, yet now, after he hath been cautioned of it, still to persist in it seems highly criminal; and therefore, in the name of God, I here charge such belief as guilty of sacrilege in the highest nature, and so much worse than stealing church plate, etc., as it is a higher offense to steal any of the glorious attributes of the Almighty, to bestow them upon mortals, than it is to steal the utensils appropriated to his service. And whether to ascribe such power of commissioning devils to the worst of men, be not direct blasphemy, I leave to others better able to determine. Where the Pharisees[19] were so wicked as to ascribe to Beelzebub[20] the mighty works of Christ (whereby he did manifestly show forth his power and godhead) then it was that our Savior declared the sin against the Holy Ghost to be unpardonable.

1697, 1700

Samuel Sewall
(1652–1730)

Jurist, entrepreneur, early advocate for the civil rights of slaves, philanthropist, and devout Puritan, Samuel Sewall uniquely represents the social, political, and religious forces vying for supremacy in late seventeenth-century and early eighteenth-century New England, assimilated in the character and conduct of one individual. Born into a prosperous merchant family in Bishop Stoke, England, in 1652, Sewall was brought to American in 1661 by his parents. Escaping religious persecution during the Restoration, they settled first in Newbury, Massachusetts, and then in Boston, which would remain Sewall's home for much of his life.

Having studied for the ministry at Harvard College, from which he received an A.B. in

---

[19] Members of an ancient Jewish sect that observed written law as well as oral, or traditional, law.
[20] Satan.

1671 and A.M. in 1674, Sewall rejected the ministry and decided to seek his fortune in business and politics. His marriage in 1675 to Hannah Hull, the only child of John Hull, Massachusetts Bay Colony's wealthy Master of the Mint, seemed propitious to all parties. Between John Hull's access to persons and places of power and Sewall's initiative, the union quickly became a formidable colonial economic force. By the early 1690s Sewall had established himself as a banker, publisher, international trader, negotiator for colonial rights abroad, member of the colony's General Court, and judge—and was remarkably successsful and respected in most of those positions. In fact, Sewall's multiple success has led scholars to characterize him as an early version of the American "self-made man" later popularized by Benjamin Franklin and others.

The portrait of Sewall most noteworthy today is the literary portrait that emerges from his own *Diary* (published in three volumes, 1878–1882). Kept during an age in which religious practice—particularly among Puritans—required constant and vigilant self-examination, Sewall's *Diary* describes in minute detail the diarist's continual study of his spiritual condition. The *Diary* is also important for its evidence of colonial manners and political intrigues that demonstrate New England's evolution from a string of rude Puritan colonies to secular, cosmopolitan provinces.

Reminiscent of the diary written by the English Secretary of the Admiralty Samuel Pepys, Sewall's *Diary,* spanning from 1673 to 1729, contains all the ingredients of an engaging personal and cultural history. It is severely introspective when Sewall records details of his spiritual journey through this world. It is pseudo-speculative when he reports on scientific discoveries and natural phenomena, attempting to interpret Providence's attitude toward mankind as demonstrated through events. In other portions it is simply chatty and filled with remarks about people and events—from shrewd character analyses, to unwitting revelations about his own character, to trivial gossip. Whereas the introspective and speculative passages indicate that Sewall was very much a product of his time and place and are interesting to compare with passages in, for example, Cotton Mather's *Diary* (not published until 1911–1912) or Jonathan Edwards's *Personal Narrative* (not published until 1765), the chatty, more human passages disclose a wholly different Sewall. The Sewall found in these latter passages, particularly those in which he describes his business affairs or conducts the rites of courtship in a highly businesslike way, is the prototypical Yankee: worldly, pragmatic, and operating out of a value system predicated largely upon self-interest.

The *Diary* commonly merges introspection with speculation. This habit, typical of Puritan diarists and autobiographers, is one of the more prevalent features of Sewall's work and reveals his tendency to use commonplace events as the means to discover divine messages directed at him and his fellows. Feeding his chickens on January 13, 1677, for instance, he is humbled at the prospect of his own need of "spiritual food" and promises to be more diligent in his daily prayers. When a ferocious thunderstorm with hail the size of "Musquet Bullets" wrecks his home on April 29, 1695, a scared Sewall prays at the spectacle of this "awful Providence" and uses it as a reminder to be prepared for the time "when our [own] Clay-Tabernacles should be broken." For him and his contemporaries such activities represented intellectual and imaginative exercises by which to measure the progress of their journey through this world and into the next.

Similarly, Sewall drew a lesson from the adversity and misfortune that befell him between 1692, the year he sat as a judge at the trials of the Salem witches, and 1697. Moved by illness and death in his family and by business reversals, all of which he believed were providential messages, Sewall lent his voice to the increasing public outcry against the witchcraft trials and openly recanted his role in them. On January 14, 1697, a day set aside in Massachusetts for humiliation, fasting, and prayer, a humble Judge Sewall stood as his pastor read aloud Sewall's confession: "Samuel Sewall, . . . being sensible that as to the guilt contracted upon the opening of the late commission . . . at Salem[,] . . . desires to take the blame and shame of it, asking pardon of men, and especially desiring prayers that God . . . would pardon that sin . . . ."

Sewall's recantation of his role in the Salem trials demonstrates his perhaps unexpected depth of character: he was the only Puritan judge to question the wisdom or justice of the trials. That depth of character is again apparent in his *The Selling of Joseph* (1700), one of the earliest antislavery statements published in the New World. Although Sewall's *Diary* will likely remain the most interesting and accessible measure of the man, works such as *The Selling of Joseph, Phaenomena Quaedam Apocalyptica* (1697)—a Puritanical interpretation of America as the new "Heaven" or Jerusalem—and the several poems and funeral elegies he published or circulated privately are apt accompaniments to the *Diary* and underscore the authenticity of feelings and convictions recorded there.

Hannah Hull Sewall died in 1716, after enjoying forty-one years of marriage and bearing fourteen children. Sewall remarried in 1719, but his second wife, Abigail Tilley, died within six months. His subsequent courting of the widow Katherine Winthrop was a well-known episode recounted in his *Diary,* but he ultimately married Mary Gibbs in 1722. His death in 1730 marked the end of not only an unusually full and long life but also of an era. From Harvard student studying for the ministry in his early years to Chief Justice of Massachusetts in his later years, Sewall successfully traversed the boundaries of most career paths available in colonial America. Sewall emerges from his *Diary* as a flesh-and-blood representative of an important crossroad in American cultural history. In his political convictions he tended to be ahead of his time: he felt deeply about, and wrote on, subjects that Americans did not take seriously for another century or more. His social attitudes were a charming blend of old and new, of innocence and savoir-faire. His religious beliefs were very reflective of his time: thoroughly Puritan, but one of the last of that breed. Indeed, Samuel Sewall lived his life fully and well; no one has been able to tell it better than he.

Suggested Readings: O. Winslow, *Samuel Sewall of Boston,* 1964. H. Wish, "Introduction" in *The Diary of Samuel Sewall,* ed. H. Wish, 1967. S. E. Kagle, *American Diary Literature, 1620–1799,* 1979.

Texts Used: *The Diary of Samuel Sewall: The Diary of Samuel Sewall, 1674–1729,* 2 vols., ed. M. H. Thomas, 1973. Description of Plum Island: *Phaenomena Quaedam Apocalyptica,* 1697, 1975. *The Selling of Joseph: The Selling of Joseph: A Memorial,* ed. S. Kaplan, 1969. (Some spelling and punctuation modernized.)

from THE DIARY OF SAMUEL SEWALL*

from Volume I: 1674–1708

Jan. 13 [1677]. Giving my chickens meat,[1] it came to my mind that I gave them nothing save Indian corn and water, and yet they eat it and thrived very well, and that that food was necessary for them, how mean soever, which much affected me and convinced what need I stood in of spiritual food, and that I should not nauseat[2] daily duties of prayer, etc.

---

* Sewall's *Diary* begins on December 3, 1673, and ends on December 25, 1728. Sewall used the Julian, not the Gregorian, calendar, so February was considered the last month of the year.
[1] Food, chicken feed.   [2] Be repulsed by.

March 16 [1677]. Dr. Alcock[3] dies about midnight. Note, Mrs. Williams told us presently after Duties[4] how dangerously ill he was, and to get John to go for his grandmother. I was glad of that information, and resolved to go and pray earnestly for him; but going into the kitchen, fell into discourse with Tim[5] about metals, and so took up the time. The Lord forgive me and help me not to be so slack for time to come, and so easy to disregard and let die so good a resolution. Dr. Alcock was 39 years old.

July 8 [1677]. New Meeting House [the third, or South] *Mane:*[6] In sermon time there came in a female Quaker, in a canvas frock, her hair disheveled and loose like a periwigg,[7] her face as black as ink, led by two other Quakers, and two other followed. It occasioned the greatest and most amazing uproar that I ever saw. Isaiah I:12, 14.[8]

Thursday, Nov. 12 [1685]. Mr. Moodey[9] preaches from Isaiah 57:1. Mr. Cobbet's[10] funeral sermon; said also of Mr. Chauncy that he was a man of singular worth. Said but 2 of the first generation left.

After, the ministers of this town come to the court and complain against a dancing master who seeks to set up here and hath mixed dances, and his time of meeting is Lecture-Day;[11] and 'tis reported he should say that by one play[12] he could teach more divinity than Mr. Willard[13] or the Old Testament. Mr. Moodey said 'twas not a time for [New England] to dance. Mr. Mather[14] struck at the root, speaking against mixed dances.

Sabbath, Jan. 12 [1690]. Richard Dummer, a flourishing youth of 9 years old, dies of the smallpox. I tell Sam[15] of it and what need he had to prepare for death, and therefore to endeavor really to pray when he said over the Lord's Prayer: he seem'd not much to mind, eating an apple; but when he came to say, Our father, he burst out into a bitter cry, and when I asked what was the matter and he could speak, he burst out into a bitter cry and said he was afraid he should die. I pray'd with him, and read Scriptures comforting against death, as, O death where is thy sting, etc. All things yours. Life and immortality brought to light by Christ, etc. 'Twas at noon.

[3] Dr. Samuel Alcock (?–1677).   [4] Attending church.
[5] Timothy Dwight (1654–1692), apprentice to Sewall's father-in-law, the silversmith John Hull.
[6] Morning (Latin).
[7] A wig, generally powdered, worn by men in the seventeenth and eighteenth centuries.
[8] "When ye come to appear before me, who hath required this at your hand, to tread my courts," from Isaiah 1:12; "Your new moons and your appointed feasts my soul hateth: they are a trouble unto me, I am weary to bear them," from Isaiah 1:14. Some Quakers interrupted Puritan services to express their disrespect for the Puritan church.
[9] Joshua Moodey, minister of Boston's First Church.   [10] Thomas Cobbet (?–1685), a minister.
[11] Generally Thursday, a day for discussion of the Bible.
[12] Boston allowed no dramatic performances.
[13] Samuel Willard (1640–1707), minister of Boston's Old South Church, to which Sewall belonged.
[14] Increase Mather (1639–1723), a renowned Puritan minister, then president of Harvard College.
[15] Samuel Sewall, Jr. (1677–?), who later became a bookseller and farmer.

March 19 [1690]. Mr. C. Mather[16] preaches the lecture from Matthew 24 [:51] "and appoint his portion with the hypocrites": in his proem[17] said, *Totus mundus agit histrionem.*[18] Said one sign of a hypocrite was for a man to strain at a gnat and swallow a camel. Sign in 's throat discovered him; to be zealous against an innocent fashion, taken up and used by the best of men; and yet make no conscience of being guilty of great immoralities. Tis supposed means wearing of periwigs: said would deny themselves in any thing but parting with an opportunity to do God service; that so might not offend good Christians. Meaning, I suppose, was fain to wear a periwig for his health. I expected not to hear a vindication of periwigs in Boston pulpit by Mr. Mather; however, not from that text. The Lord give me a good heart and help to know, and not only to know but also to do his will; that my heart and head may be his.

About 10 o'clock Jan. 13 [1696]. Cousin Dummer came to invite me to go along with him to Cambridge to visit Mr. Danforth. About noon we set out, and at Mr. Danforth's gate, met with Mr. N. Hobart and Trowbridge; Mr. Danforth made us dine there; then after awhile, Mr. Hobart was called in to pray, which he did excellently, Mr Morton being by, who came with us from the college.[19] Note. When were there at first, Mr. Danforth bade me look on the cupboard's head for a book; I told him I saw there a law book, Wingate on the Common Law. He said he would lend it [to] me, I should speak to Amsden to call for it; and if he died, he would give it me. Again when [we] took leave after prayer, he said he lent me that book not to wrap up but to read, and if misliked it, [I] should tell him of it. By that time cousin and I could get to the ferry; 'twas quite dark. Capt. Hunting told us the river was full of ice and no getting over. But I went to Sheaf and he hallowed over John Russell again. Boat came to Ballard's Wharf below the lodged ice, from whence [I] had a very comfortable passage over with Madam Foxcroft.

When I came in, past 7 at night, my wife[20] met me in the entry and told me Betty[21] had surprised them. I was surprised with the abruptness of the relation. It seems Betty Sewall had given some signs of dejection and sorrow; but a little after dinner she burst out into an amazing cry, which caused all the family to cry too: her mother asked the reason; she gave none; at last said she was afraid she should go to Hell, her sins were not pardoned. She was first wounded by my reading a sermon of Mr. Norton's,[22] about the 5th of Jan. Text John 7:34, "Ye shall seek me and shall not find me." And those words in the sermon, John 8:21, "Ye shall seek me and shall die in your sins," ran in her mind, and terrified her greatly. And staying at home Jan. 12 she read out of Mr. Cotton Mather—"Why hath Satan filled thy heart," which increased her fear. Her mother asked her whether she prayed. She answered, "Yes," but feared her prayers were not heard because her sins not pardoned. Mr. Willard, though sent for timelier,[23] yet not being told of the message, till bruised Dindsdals [?] was given him; he came not till after I came home. He discoursed with Betty, who could not give a distinct account, but was confused as his phrase was, and as had experienced in himself. Mr. Willard prayed excellently. The Lord bring light and comfort out of this dark and dreadful cloud, and grant that Christ's being formed in my dear child, may be the issue of these painful pangs.

[16] Cotton Mather (1663–1728), a renowned Puritan minister and son of Increase Mather.
[17] Introduction or preface.   [18] "All the world plays a role" (Latin).   [19] Harvard College.
[20] Hannah Hull Sewall (1658–1717).   [21] Elisabeth Sewall (1680–?), one of Sewall's daughters.
[22] Rev. John Norton of Hingham, Massachusetts, a Harvard classmate of Sewall.   [23] Earlier.

Dec. 21 [1696]. A very great snow is on the ground. I go in the morn to Mr. Willard, to entreat him to choose his own time to come and pray with little Sarah:[24] he comes a little before night, and prays very fully and well. Mr. Mather, the president, had prayed with her in the time of the court's sitting. *Dec. 22.* being Catechizing day, I give Mr. Willard a note to pray for my daughter publicly, which he did. Note, this morn Madam Elisa. Bellingham came to our house and upbraided me with setting my hand to pass Mr. Wharton's account to the court, where he obtained a judgment for Eustace's farm. I was wheedled and hectored[25] into that business, and have all along been uneasy in the remembrance of it: and now there is one come who will not spare to lay load. The Lord take away my filthy garments, and give me change of raiment. This day I remove poor little Sarah into my bed-chamber, where about break of day Dec. 23. she gives up the ghost[26] in Nurse Cowell's arms. Born, Nov. 21, 1694. Neither I nor my wife were by: nurse not expecting so sudden a change, and having promised to call us. I thought of Christ's Words, could you not watch with me one hour! and would fain[27] have sat up with her: but fear of my wife's illness, who is very valetudinarious,[28] made me to lodge with her in the new hall, where [I] was called by Jane's cry,[29] to take notice of my dead daughter. Nurse did long and pathetically ask our pardon that she had not called us, and said she was surprised. Thus this very fair day is rendered foul to us by reason of the general sorrow and tears in the family. Master Chiever was here the evening before, I desired him to pray for my daughter. The chapter read in course on Dec. 23, morn, was Deuteronomy 22, which made me sadly reflect that I had not been so thoroughly tender of my daughter; nor so effectually careful of her defense and preservation as I should have been. The good Lord pity and pardon and help for the future as to those God has still left me.

Dec. 24 [1696]. Sam recites to me in Latin, Matthew 12, from the 6th to the end of the 12th verse. The 7th verse did awfully bring to mind the Salem tragedy.[30]

6th day, Dec. 25 [1696]. We bury our little daughter. In the chamber, Joseph[31] in course reads Ecclesiastes 3[d]: "A time to be born and a time to die"—Elisabeth, Revelation 22, Hannah, the 38th Psalm. I speak to each, as God helped, to our mutual comfort I hope. I ordered Sam. to read the 102 Psalm. Elisha Cooke, Edw. Hutchinson, John Baily, and Josia Willard bear my little daughter to the tomb.

Note. Twas wholly dry, and I went at noon to see in what order things were set; and there I was entertained with a view of, and converse with, the coffins of my dear father Hull, Mother Hull, Cousin Quinsey, and my six children:[32] for the little posthumous[33] was now took up and set in upon that that stands on John's: so

---

[24] Sarah Sewall (1694–1696), one of Sewall's daughters.   [25] Browbeaten.   [26] Dies.

[27] Gladly.   [28] Sickly.   [29] Jane Sewall, one of Sewall's daughters.

[30] "If ye had known what this meaneth, I will have mercy and not sacrifice, ye would not have condemned the guiltless," from Matthew 12:7, which reminded Sewall of the Salem witchcraft trials of 1692.

[31] Joseph Sewall (1688–1769), one of Sewall's sons, who later became a minister at Boston's Old South Church.

[32] Buried in the Hull/Sewall tomb (just a brick-lined excavation) were Sewall's father-in-law, John Hull, and his wife; Sewall's cousin Daniel Quinsey; and six of Sewall's children: John, Hannah, Hull, Henry, Stephen, and an unnamed stillborn son.

[33] Sarah, the dead child.

are three, one upon another twice, on the bench at the end. My mother lies on a lower bench, at the end, with head to her husband's head: and I ordered little Sarah to be set on her grandmother's feet. 'Twas an awfull yet pleasing treat; having said "the Lord knows who shall be brought hither next," I came away.

Mr. Willard prayed with us the night before; I gave him a ring worth about 20 shillings. Sent the president[34] one, who is sick of the gout. He prayed with my little daughter. Mr. Oakes, the physician, Major Townsend, Speaker, of whose wife I was a bearer,[35] and was joined with me in going to Albany and has been civil and treated me several times. Left a ring at Madam Cooper's for the governor. Gave not one pair of gloves save to the bearers. Many went to the church this day, I met them coming home, as [I] went to the tomb.

7ᵗʰ day, Dec. 26 [1696]. Roger Judd tells me of a ship arrived at Rhode Island from England, and after, that Mr. Ive has written that most judged the king of France was dead, or dying. Ship comes from New Castle, several weeks after the Falkland.

Jan. 15 [1697]. Copy of the bill[36] I put up on the fast day;[37] giving it to Mr. Willard as he passed by, and standing up at the reading of it, and bowing when finished; in the afternoon:

"Samuel Sewall, sensible of the reiterated strokes of God upon himself and family; and being sensible, that as to the guilt contracted, upon the opening of the late commission of Oyer and Terminer[38] at Salem (to which the order for this day relates) he is, upon many accounts, more concerned than any that he knows of, desires to take the blame and shame of it, asking pardon of men,[39] and especially desiring prayers that God, who has an unlimited authority, would pardon that sin and all other his sins; personal and relative: and according to his infinite benignity, and sovereignty, not visit the sin of him, or of any other, upon himself or any of his, nor upon the land: but that He would powerfully defend him against all temptations to sin, for the future; and vouchsafe him the efficacious, saving conduct of his Word and spirit."

Jan. 14ᵗʰ [1701]. Having been certified last night about 10 o'clock of the death of my dear mother at Newbury, Sam. and I set out with John Sewall, the messenger, for that place. Hired horses at Charlestown; set out about 10 o'clock in a great fog. Dined at Lewis's with Mr. Cushing of Salisbury. Sam. and I kept on in Ipswich Road, John went to accompany [my] brother from Salem. About Mr. Hubbard's in Ipswich farms, they overtook us. Sam. and I lodged at Crompton's in Ipswich. Brother and John stood on for Newbury by moon-shine.

Jan. 15ᵗʰ [1701]. Sam. and I set forward. Brother Northend meets us. Visit Aunt Northend, Mr. Payson. With brother and sister we set forward for Newbury:

---

[34] Increase Mather.   [35] Pallbearer.   [36] A legal petition.   [37] January 14.

[38] "To hear and to determine" (Middle English); a commission allowing the court to hear and determine criminal cases.

[39] Sewall is asking forgiveness for his part in the Salem witchcraft trials, as one of the seven judges overseeing the proceedings; he was the only one to publicly admit that the court's findings of guilt were incorrect.

where we find that day appointed for the funeral: 'twas a very pleasant comfortable day.

Bearers, John Kent of the Island, Lt. Cutting Noyes, Deacon William Noyes, Mr. Peter Tappan, Capt. Henry Somersby, Mr. Joseph Woodbridge. I followed the bier single. Then brother Sewall and sister Jane, brother Short and his wife, brother Moodey and his wife, brother Northend and his wife, brother Tappan and sister Sewall, Sam. and cous. Hannah Tappan. Mr. Payson of Rowley, Mr. Clark, minister of Excester, were there. Col. Pierce, Major Noyes, etc., cousins John, Richard and Betty Dummer. Went about 4 P.M. Nathan Bricket taking in hand to fill the grave, I said, forbear a little, and suffer me to say that amidst our bereaving sorrows we have the comfort of beholding this saint put into the rightful possession of that happiness of living desired and dying lamented. She lived commendably four and fifty years with her dear husband, and my dear father: and she could not well brook the being divided from him at her death; which is the cause of our taking leave of her in this place. She was a true and constant lover of God's Word, worship, and saints: and she always, with a patient cheerfulness, submitted to the divine decree of providing bread for her self and others in the sweat of her brows. And now her infinitely gracious and bountiful master has promoted her to the honor of higher employments, fully and absolutely discharged from all manner of toil, and sweat. My honored and beloved friends and neighbors! My dear mother never thought much of doing the most frequent and homely offices of love for me; and lavished away many thousands of words upon me, before I could return one word in answer: and therefore I ask and hope that none will be offended that I have now ventured to speak one word in her behalf; when she her self is become speechless. Made a motion with my hand for the filling of the grave. Note, I could hardly speak for passion and tears. Mr. Tappan prayed with us in the evening. I lodged at sister Gerrish's with Joseph. Brother and Sam. at brother Tappan's.

from   Volume II: 1709–1729

May, 29 [1720]. God having in his holy sovereignty put my wife out of the fore-seat,[40] I apprehended I had cause to be ashamed of my sin, and to loath my self for it; and retired into my pew. Mr. Williams of Deerfield preached in the morning from Romans 5; "Christ died for sinners." Mr. Sewall[41] administered the Lord's Supper. I put up a note to this purpose; Samuel Sewall, deprived of his dear wife by a very sudden and awful stroke, desires prayers that God would sanctify the same to himself, and children, and family. Writ and sent three; to the South, Old, and Mr. Colman's. Mr. Prince preaches P.M. Matthew 25. At midnight behold a cry was made.

7th 30 [Sept. 30, 1720]. Mr. Colman's lecture: daughter Sewall acquaints Madam Winthrop[42] that if she pleased to be within at 3 P.M. I would wait on her. She answered she would be at home.

[40] Hannah Hull Sewall had died on October 19, 1717; on October 29, 1719, Sewall had married the widow Abigail Tilley, who died suddenly.

[41] Joseph Sewall.

[42] Katherine Brattle Winthrop (1664–1725), widow of John Eyre, Sr., and Major-General Wait Still Winthrop; she was courted by Sewall after the death of his second wife; Winthrop and Sewall never married each other.

8th *1. Saturday* [Oct. 1, 1720]. I dine at Mr. Stoddard's:[43] from thence I went to Madam Winthrop's just at 3. Spake to her, saying, my loving wife [Abigail] died so soon and suddenly, 'twas hardly convenient for me to think of marrying again; however I came to this resolution, that I would not make my court to any person without first consulting with her. Had a pleasant discourse about 7 single persons sitting in the fore-seat 7th 29th,[44] viz. Madam Rebekah Dudley, Catharine Winthrop, Bridget Usher, Deliverance Legg, Rebekah Loyd, Lydia Colman, Elizabeth Bellingham. She propounded one and another for me; but none would do, said Mrs. Loyd was about her age.

October 3 [1720]. Waited on Madam Winthrop again; 'twas a little while before she came in. Her daughter Noyes[45] being there alone with me, I said, I hoped my waiting on her mother would not be disagreeable to her. She answered she should not be against that that might be for her comfort. I saluted[46] her, and told her I perceived I must shortly wish her a good time (her mother had told me she was with child, and within a month or two of her time). By and by in came Mr. Ayers, chaplain of the Castle,[47] and hanged up his hat, which I was a little startled at, it seeming as if he was to lodge there. At last Madam Winthrop came in. After a considerable time, I went up to her and said, if it might not be inconvenient I desired to speak with her. She assented, and spake of going into another room; but Mr. Ayers and Mrs. Noyes presently rose up, and went out, leaving us there alone. Then I ushered in discourse from the names in the fore-seat; at last I prayed that Katherine [Mrs. Winthrop] might be the person assigned for me. She instantly took it up in way of denial, as if she had catched at an opportunity to do it, saying she could not do it before she was asked. Said that was her mind unless she should change it, which she believed she should not; could not leave her children. I expressed my sorrow that she should do it so speedily, prayed her consideration, and asked her when I should wait on her again. She setting no time, I mentioned that day sennight.[48] Gave her Mr. Willard's *fountain*[49] opened with the little print and verses; saying, I hoped if we did well read that book, we should meet together hereafter, if we did not now. She took the book, and put it in her pocket. Took leave.

8th 6th [Oct. 6, 1720]. Lecture-Day, Mr. Cutler,[50] president of the Connecticut College, preached in Dr. C. Mather's turn. He made an excellent discourse from Hebrews 11:14, "For they that say such things, declare plainly that they seek a country." Brother Odlin,[51] son Sewall of Brookline,[52] and Mary Hirst[53] dine with me. I asked Mary of Madam Lord, Mr. Oliver and wife, and bid her present my service[54] to them.

---

[43] William Stoddard.

[44] The front pew was generally saved for widows; Sewall refers to September 29.

[45] Katherine Winthrop Noyes (1694–?), daughter of Katherine Winthrop and John Eyre, and wife of Dr. Oliver Noyes.

[46] Kissed.   [47] Obadiah Ayers, chaplain of Castle William, a fortified island in Boston Harbor.

[48] Seven-night, a week later.

[49] Samuel Willard's *The Fountain Opened: Or, the Great Gospel Privilege of Having Christ Exhibited to Sinful Men* (1700).

[50] Timothy Cutler, president of Yale College.   [51] Elisha Odlin.

[52] Samuel Sewall, Jr., of Brookline, Massachusetts.

[53] Sewall's granddaughter, who became Lady Pepperell by marriage.   [54] Offer my assistance.

8th 6th [Oct. 6, 1720]. A little after 6 P.M. I went to Madam Winthrop's. She was not within. I gave Sarah Chickering, the maid 2 shillings; Juno,[55] who brought in wood, 1 shilling. Afterward the nurse came in, I gave her 18 pence having no other small bill. After a while Dr. Noyes came in with his mother; and quickly after his wife came in: they sat talking, I think, till eight o'clock. I said I feared I might be some interruption to their business: Dr. Noyes replied pleasantly: he feared they might be an interruption to me, and went away. Madam seemed to harp upon the same string. Must take care of her children; could not leave that house and neighborhood where she had dwelt so long. I told her she might do her children as much or more good by bestowing what she laid out in house-keeping, upon them. Said her son would be of age the 7th of August. I said it might be inconvenient for her to dwell with her daughter-in-law, who must be mistress of the house. I gave her a piece of Mr. Belcher's cake and gingerbread[56] wrapped up in a clean sheet of paper; told her of her father's kindness to me when [he was] treasurer, and I constable. My daughter Judith was gone from me and I was more lonesome—might help to forward one another in our journey to Canaan.[57]—Mr. Eyre[58] came within the door; I saluted him, asked how Mr. Clark did, and he went away. I took leave about 9 o'clock. I told [Madam Winthrop] I came now to refresh her memory as to Monday night; said she had not forgot it. In discourse with her, I asked leave to speak with her sister;[59] I meant to gain Madam Mico's favor to persuade her sister. She seemed surprised and displeased, and said she was in the same condition!

8th 10th [Oct. 10, 1720]. Examine Mr. Briggs his account; said they could not find Mr. Whittemore. Mr. Willard offered to answer for him. But I showed the necessity of his being here; and appointed Wednesday 10 o'clock; and ordered notice to be given to the auditors to pray their assistance.

In the evening I visited Madam Winthrop, who treated me with a great deal of courtesy; wine, marmalade. I gave her the *News-Letter*[60] about the Thanksgiving proposals, for sake of the verses for David Jeffries.[61] She tells me Dr. Increase Mather visited her this day, in Mr. Hutchinson's coach.

It seems Dr. Cotton Mather's chimney fell a-fire yesterday, so as to interrupt the Assembly A.M. Mr. Cutler ceased preaching 1/4 of an hour.

8th 11th [Oct. 11, 1720]. I wrote a few Lines to Madam Winthrop to this purpose: "Madam, these wait on you with Mr. Mayhew's[62] sermon, and account of the state of the Indians on Martha's Vineyard. I thank you for your unmerited favors of yesterday; and hope to have the happiness of waiting on you tomorrow before eight o'clock after noon. I pray God to keep you, and give you a joyful entrance upon the two hundred and twenty-ninth year of Christopher Columbus his discovery; and take leave, who am, Madam, your humble servant.

S. S.

---

[55] A servant.

[56] Jonathan Belcher (1682–1757), who later became the governor of Massachusetts, had given Sewall leftovers from a party.

[57] Paradise.   [58] John Eyre, Jr. (1700–?).

[59] Mary Mico, Winthrop's sister and the widow of John Mico.

[60] The *Boston News-Letter*, the colonies' first newspaper; specifically, an article about the governor's Proclamation for Thanksgiving Day, 1720, already celebrated annually in Massachusetts.

[61] Winthrop's grandson, the son of Katherine Jeffries (later Noyes) and David Jeffries, Sr.

[62] Experience Mayhew (1673–1758) of Martha's Vineyard, a Puritan evangelist and missionary.

Sent this by Deacon Green, who delivered it to Sarah Chickering, her mistress not being at home.

8ᵗʰ 12 [Oct. 12, 1720]. Give Mr. Whittemore and Willard their oath to Dr. Mather's inventory. Visit Mr. Cooper. Go to the meeting at the widow Emons's: Mr. Manly prayed, I read half Mr. Henry's 12ᵗʰ Chapter of the Lord's Supper. Sung 1, 2, 3, 4, 5, 10, and 12ᵗʰ verses of the 30ᵗʰ Psalm. Brother Franklin concluded with prayer. At Madam Winthrop's steps I took leave of Capt. Hill, etc.

Mrs. Anne Cotton came to door (twas before 8), said Madam Winthrop was within, directed me into the little room, where she was full of work[63] behind a stand; Mrs. Cotton came in and stood. Madam Winthrop pointed to her to set me a chair. Madam Winthrop's countenance was much changed from what 'twas on Monday, looked dark and lowering. At last, the work, (black stuff or silk) was taken away, I got my chair in place, had some converse, but very cold and indifferent to what 'twas before. Asked her to acquit me of rudeness if I drew off her glove. Enquiring the reason, I told her 'twas great odds between handling a dead goat, and a living lady. Got it off. I told her I had one petition to ask of her, that was, that she would take off the negative she laid on me the third of October; She readily answered she could not, and enlarged upon it; she told me of it so soon as she could; could not leave her house, children, neighbors, business. I told her she might do some good to help and support me. Mentioning Mrs. Gookin, Nath, the widow Weld was spoken of; said I had visited Mrs. Denison. I told her "Yes!" Afterward I said, if after a first and second vagary she would accept of me returning, her victorious kindness and good will would be very obliging. She thanked me for my book, (Mr. Mayhew's sermon), but said not a word of the letter. When she insisted on the negative, I prayed there might be no more thunder and lightning, I should not sleep all night. I gave her Dr. Preston, *The Church's Marriage and the Church's Carriage,*[64] which cost me 6 shillings at the sale. The door standing open, Mr. Ayers came in, hung up his hat, and sat down. After a while, Madam Winthrop moving, he went out. John Eyre looked in, I said, "How do ye," or, "your servant, Mr. Eyre": but heard no word from him. Sarah filled a glass of wine, she drank to me, I to her, she sent Juno home with me with a good lantern, I gave her 6 pence and bid her thank her mistress. In some of our discourse, I told her I had rather go to the stone-house[65] adjoining to her than to come to her against her mind. Told her the reason why I came every other night was lest I should drink too deep draughts of pleasure. She had talked of canary,[66] her kisses were to me better than the best canary. Explained the expression concerning Columbus.

8ᵗʰ 15 [Oct. 15, 1720]. I dine on fish and oil at Mr. Stoddard's. Capt Hill wished me joy of my proceedings, i.e. with M[adam] Winthrop; sister Cooper applauded it, spake of visiting her: I said her complaisance of her visit would be obliging to me.

8ᵗʰ 16 [Oct. 16, 1720]. Lord's Day,[67] I upbraided my self that could be so solicitous about earthly things; and so cold and indifferent as to the love of Christ,

---

[63] Needlework.

[64] John Preston (1587–1628), theologian and author of *The Golden Scepter Held Forth to the Humble: With the Church's Dignity by Her Marriage, and the Church's Duty in Her Carriage* (1638).

[65] Prison.   [66] Wine made in the Canary Islands.   [67] Sunday.

who is altogether lovely. Mr. Prince administered. Dined at my son's with Mr. Cutler, and Mr. Shurtleff.[68] Mr. Cutler preaches in the afternoon from Ezekiel 16:30, "How weak is thy heart." Son reads the order for the Thanksgiving.

8th 17. Monday [Oct. 17, 1720]. Give Mr. Dan Willard, and Mr. Pelatiah Whittemore their oaths to their accounts; and Mr. John Briggs to his, as they are attorneys to Dr. Cotton Mather, administrator to the estate of Nathan Howell deceased. In the evening I visited Madam Winthrop, who treated me courteously, but not in clean linen as sometimes. She said she did not know whether I would come again, or no. I asked her how she could so impute inconstancy to me. (I had not visited her since Wednesday night, being unable to get over the indisposition received by the treatment received that night, and *I must* in it seemed to sound like a made piece of formality.) Gave her this day's gazette. Heard David Jeffries say the Lord's Prayer, and some other portions of the Scriptures. He came to the door, and asked me to go into chamber, where his grandmother was tending little Katie,[69] to whom she had given physic;[70] but I chose to sit below. Dr. Noyes and his wife came in, and sat a considerable time; had been visiting son and daughter Cooper.[71] Juno came home with me.

8th 18 [Oct. 18, 1720]. Visited Madam Mico, who came to me in a splendid dress. I said, "It may be you have heard of my visiting Madam Winthrop," her Sister. She answered her sister had told her of it. I asked her good will in the affair. She answered, if her sister were for it, she should not hinder it. I gave her Mr. Homes's sermon. She gave me a glass of canary, entertained me with good discourse, and a respectful remembrance of my first wife. I took leave.

8th 19 [Oct. 19, 1720]. Midweek, visited Madam Winthrop; Sarah told me she was at Mr. Walley's, would not come home till late. I gave her Hannah's 3 oranges with her duty, not knowing whether I should find her or no. Was ready to go home: but said if I knew she was there, I would go thither. Sarah seemed to speak with pretty good courage, she would be there. I went and found her there, with Mr. Walley and his wife in the little room below. At 7 o'clock I mentioned going home; at 8 I put on my coat, and quickly waited on her home. She found occasion to speak loud to the servant, as if she had a mind to be known. Was courteous to me; but took occasion to speak pretty earnestly about my keeping a coach: I said 'twould cost 100 pounds per annum; she said 'twould cost but 40 pounds. Spake much against John Winthrop, his false-heartedness. Mr. Eyre came in and sat awhile; I offered him Dr. Incr. Mather's sermons, whereof Mr. Appleton's ordination-sermon was one; said he had them already. I said I would give him another. Exit. Came away somewhat late.

8th 20 [Oct. 20, 1720]. Mr. Colman preaches from Luke 15:10, "Joy among the angels": made an excellent discourse.

At council, Col. Townsend spake to me of my hood: should get a wig.[72] I said

---

[68] William Shurtleff, minister of Newcastle, New Hampshire.
[69] Katherine Walley, daughter of Bethiah Eyre and John Walley.   [70] Medicine.
[71] Rev. William Cooper and his wife, Judith, Sewall's daughter.
[72] Winthrop thought Sewall should wear a judicial wig rather than a periwig, in addition to his judicial hood, to cover his baldness; instead he wore a velvet cap.

twas my chief ornament: I wore it for sake of the day. Brother Odlin, and Sam, Mary, and Jane Hirst dine with us. Promised to wait on the governor about 7. Madam Winthrop not being at lecture, I went thither first; found her very serene with her daughter Noyes, Mrs. Dering,[73] and the widow Shipreeve[74] sitting at a little table, she in her armed chair. She drank to me, and I to Mrs. Noyes. After a while prayed the favor to speak with her. She took one of the candles, and went into the best room, closed the shutters, sat down upon the couch. She told me Madam Usher had been there, and said the coach must be set on wheels, and not by rusting. She spake somthing of my needing a wig. Asked me what her sister said to me. I told her, she said, if her sister were for it, she would not hinder it. But I told her, she did not say she would be glad to have me for her brother. Said, "I shall keep you in the cold," and ask her if she would be within tomorrow night, for we had had but a running feast. She said she could not tell whether she should, or no. I took leave. As were drinking at the governor's, he said: "In England the ladies minded little more than that they might have money, and coaches to ride in." I said, "And New-England brooks its name.[75] At which Mr. Dudley smiled. Governor said they were not quite so bad here.

8th 21 [Oct. 21, 1720]. *Friday,* my son, the minister,[76] came to me P.M. by appointment and we pray one for another in the old chamber; more especially respecting my courtship. About 6 o'clock I go to Madam Winthrop's; Sarah told me her mistress was gone out, but did not tell me whither she went. She presently ordered me a fire; so I went in, having Dr. Sibb's *Bowels*[77] with me to read. I read the two first sermons, still nobody came in: at last about 9 o'clock Mr. John Eyre came in; I took the opportunity to say to him as I had done to Mrs. Noyes before, that I hoped my visiting his mother would not be disagreeable to him; he answered me with much respect. When 'twas after 9 o'clock he of himself said he would go and call her, she was but at one of his brothers: a while after I heard Madam Winthrop's voice, enquiring something about John. After a good while and clapping the garden door twice or thrice, she came in. I mentioned somthing of the lateness; she bantered me, and said I was later. She received me courteously. I asked when our proceedings should be made public: she said they were like to be no more public than they were already. Offered me no wine that I remember. I rose up at 11 o'clock to come away, saying I would put on my coat, she offered not to help me. I prayed her that Juno might light me home, she opened the shutter, and said 'twas pretty light abroad; Juno was weary and gone to bed. So I came home by starlight as well as I could. At my first coming in, I gave Sarah five shillings. I wrote Mr. Eyre his name in his book with the date October 21, 1720. It cost me 8 shillings. Jehovah jireh![78] Madam told me she had visited M. Mico, Wendell, and William Clark of the South [Church].

October 22 [1720]. Daughter Cooper visited me before my going out of town, stayed till about sunset. I brought her going near as far as the Orange Tree.[79]

---

[73] Elizabeth Packer Dering, wife of Henry Dering, Jr.

[74] Elizabeth Jeffries Shipreeve, widow of Charles Shipreeve and aunt of Katherine Noyes's first husband, David Jeffries, Sr.

[75] In New England it is the same.   [76] Joseph Sewall.

[77] Dr. Richard Sibbes (1577–1635), a Puritan theologian and author of *Bowels Opened: Or, a Discovery of the Near and Dear Love, Union and Communion Betwixt* Christ, and the Church (1641); bowels here means "heart," thought to be the source of compassion.

[78] "The Lord will provide," from Genesis 22:14.   [79] A roadside inn.

Coming back, near Leg's Corner, little David Jeffries saw me, and looking upon me very lovingly, asked me if I was going to see his grandmother? I said, Not tonight. Gave him a penny, and bid him present my service to his grandmother.

October 24 [1720]. I went in the hackney coach through the Common,[80] stopped at Madam Winthrop's (had told her I would take my departure from thence). Sarah came to the door with Katie in her arms: but I did not think to take notice of the child. Called her mistress. I told her, being encouraged by David Jeffries' loving eyes, and sweet words, I was come to enquire whether she could find in her heart to leave that house and neighborhood, and go and dwell with me at the South End;[81] I think she said softly, "Not yet." I told her it did not lie in my hands to keep a coach. If I should, I should be in danger to be brought to keep company with her neighbor Brooker (he was a little before sent to prison for debt). Told her I had an antipathy against those who would pretend to give themselves; but nothing of their estate. I would [give] a proportion of my estate with my self. And I supposed she would do so. As to a periwig, my best and greatest friend, I could not possibly have a greater, began to find me with hair before I was born, and had continued to do so ever since; and I could not find in my heart to go to another. She commended the book I gave her, Dr. Preston, *The Church's Marriage;* quoted him saying 'twas inconvenient keeping out of a fashion commonly used. I said the time and tide did circumscribe my visit. She gave me a dram of black-cherry brandy, and gave me a lump of the sugar that was in it. She wished me a good journey. I prayed God to keep her, and came away. Had a very pleasant journey to Salem.

October 31 [1720]. . . . At night I visited Madam Winthrop about 6 P.M. They told me she was gone to Madam Mico's. I went thither and found she was gone; so [I] returned to her house, read the Epistles to the Galatians, Ephesians in Mr. Eyre's Latin Bible. After the clock struck 8 I began to read the 103[d] Psalm. Mr. Wendell[82] came in from his warehouse. Asked me if I were alone? Spake very kindly to me, offered me to call Madam Winthrop. I told him, she would be angry, had been at M. Mico's; he helped me on with my coat and I came home: left the gazette in the Bible, which [I] told Sarah of, bid her present my service to M. Winthrop, and tell her I had been to wait on her if she had been at home.

Nov. 1 [1720]. I was so taken up that I could not go if I would.

Nov. 2 [1720]. Midweek, went again, and found Mrs. Alden[83] there, who quickly went out. Gave [Madam Winthrop] about 1/2 pound of sugar almonds, cost 3 shillings per pound. Carried them on Monday. She seemed pleased with them, asked what they cost. Spake of giving her a hundred pounds per annum if I died before her. Asked her what sum she would give me, if she should die first? Said I would give her time to consider of it. She said she heard as if I had given all to my children by deeds of gift. I told her 'twas a mistake, Point Judith[84] was mine, etc. That in England, I owned,[85] my father's desire was that it should go to

---

[80] A hired coach through Boston Common, a public park.   [81] Boston's South end area.
[82] Jacob Wendell, a Boston merchant and ancestor of Oliver Wendell Holmes.
[83] Probably Mary Drury Alden, wife of William Alden and daughter-in-law of Capt. John Alden.
[84] Now part of Rhode Island.   [85] Admitted.

my eldest son; 'twas 20 pounds per annum; she thought 'twas forty. I think when I seemed to excuse pressing this, she seemed to think 'twas best to speak of it; a long winter was coming on. Gave me a glass or two of canary.

Nov. 4ᵗʰ Friday [1720]. Went again about 7 o'clock; found there Mr. John Walley and his wife: sat discoursing pleasantly. I showed them Isaac Moses's [a Native American] writing. Madam W. served comfeits[86] to us. After a while a table was spread, and supper was set. I urged Mr. Walley to crave a blessing; but he put it upon me. About 9 they went away. I asked Madam what fashioned necklace I should present her with, she said, "none at all." I asked her whereabout we left off last time; [she] mentioned what I had offered to give her; [I] asked her what she would give me; she said she could not change her condition: she had said so from the beginning; could not be so far from her children, the lecture. Quoted the apostle Paul affirming that a single life was better than a married.[87] I answered that was for the present distress. Said she had not pleasure in things of that nature as formerly: I said, you are the fitter to make me a wife. If she held in that mind, I must go home and bewail my rashness in making more haste than good speed. However, considering the supper, I desired her to be within next Monday night, if we lived so long. Assented. She charged me with saying that she must put away Juno, if she came to me: I utterly denied it, it never came in my heart; yet she insisted upon it; saying it came in upon discourse about the Indian woman that obtained her freedom this court. About 10 I said I would not disturb the good orders of her house, and came away. She not seeming pleased with my coming away. Spake to her about David Jeffries, had not seen him.

Monday, Nov. 7ᵗʰ [1720]. My son prayed in the old chamber. Our time had been taken up by son and daughter Cooper's visit; so that I only read the 130ᵗʰ and 143ᵈ Psalm. 'Twas on the account of my courtship. I went to Mad. Winthrop; found her rocking her little Katie in the cradle. I excused my coming so late (near eight). She set me an armed chair and cushion; and so the cradle was between her armed chair and mine. Gave her the remnant of my almonds; she did not eat of them as before; but laid them away; I said I came to inquire whether she had altered her mind since Friday, or remained of the same mind still. She said, "thereabouts." I told her I loved her, and was so fond[88] as to think that she loved me: she said had a great respect for me. I told her, I had made her an offer, without asking any advice; she had so many to advise with, that 'twas a hindrance. The fire was come to one short brand besides the block, which brand was set up in end; at last it fell to pieces, and no recruit was made:[89] She gave me a glass of wine. I think I repeated again that I would go home and bewail my rashness in making more haste than good speed. I would endeavor to contain myself, and not go on to solicit her to do that which she could not consent to. Took leave of her. As came down the steps she bid me have a care. Treated me courteously. Told her she had entered the 4ᵗʰ year of her widowhood. I had given her the *News-Letter* before: I did not bid her draw off her glove, as sometime I had done. Her dress was not so clean as sometime it had been. Jehovah jireh!

---

[86] Fruit and nut preserves.

[87] "I say therefore to the unmarried and widows, It is good for them if they abide ever as I," from 1 Corinthians 7:8.

[88] Foolish.   [89] No logs were added, so Sewall assumed he was expected to leave.

Midweek, 9ᵗʰ 9ᵗʰ [Nov. 9, 1720]. Dine at brother Stoddard's:[90] were so kind as to inquire of me if they should invite Madam Winthrop; I answered no. Thanked my sister Stoddard for her courtesy; sat down at the table Simeon Stoddard, Esqr., Mad. Stoddard, Samuel Sewall, Mr. Colman, Madam Colman, Mr. Cooper, Mrs. Cooper, Mrs. Hannah Cooper, Mr. Samuel Sewall of Brookline, Mrs. Sewall, Mr. Joseph Sewall, Mrs. Lydia Walley, Mr. William Stoddard. Had a noble treat. At night our meeting was at the widow Belknap's. Gave each one of the meeting one of Mr. Homes's sermons, 12 in all; she sent her servant home with me with a lantern. Madam Winthrop's shutters were open as I passed by.

[Nov. 21, 1720]. About the middle of Dec. Madam Winthrop made a treat for her children; Mr. Sewall, Prince, Willoughby: I knew nothing of it; but the same day abode[91] in the council chamber for fear of the rain, and dined alone upon Kilby's pies and good beer.

1674–1729, 1878–1882

from *PHAENOMENA QUAEDAM APOCALYPTICA**

[*Description of Plum Island*]

As long as Plum Island shall faithfully keep the commanded post, notwithstanding all the hectoring[1] words and hard blows of the proud and boisterous ocean; as long as any salmon or sturgeon shall swim in the streams of Merrimack[2] or any perch or pickerel in Crane Pond; as long as the sea-fowl shall know the time of their coming, and not neglect seasonably to visit the places of their acquaintance; as long as any cattle shall be fed with the grass growing in the meadows, which do humbly bow down themselves before Turkey-Hill; as long as any sheep shall walk upon Old-Town Hills, and shall from thence pleasantly look down upon the River Parker, and the fruitful marshes lying beneath; as long as any free and harmless doves shall find a white oak or other tree within the township, to perch, or feed, or build a careless nest upon, and shall voluntarily present themselves to perform the office of gleaners[3] after barley harvest; as long as Nature shall not grow old and dote, but shall constantly remember to give the rows of

---

[90] Simeon Stoddard, Sewall's fellow council member and stepfather of Rev. William Cooper, Sewall's son-in-law.

[91] I remained.

* Sewall's *Phaenomena Quaedam Apocalyptica ad Aspectum Novi Orbis Configurata* was translated from Latin into English as *The New Heaven and the New Earth* (1697); it prophesizes that New England will become an earthly heaven if its citizens remain faithful, as in the Old Testament Book of Apocalypse, or Revelations. Plum Island lies along the northern coast of Massachusetts.

[1] Bullying.

[2] The Merrimack River, which feeds into Plum Island from New Hampshire; other sites mentioned are also geographic features on or near Plum Island.

[3] Grain collectors.

Indian corn their education by pairs; so long shall Christians be born there, and being first made meet, shall from thence be translated to be made partakers of the inheritance of the saints in light.

1697

from   THE SELLING OF JOSEPH*

Forasmuch as Liberty is in real value next unto Life: None ought to part with it themselves, or deprive others of it, but upon most mature Consideration.[1]

The numerousness of slaves at this day in the province, and the uneasiness of them under their slavery, hath put many upon thinking whether the foundation of it be firmly and well laid; so as to sustain the vast weight that is built upon it. It is most certain that all men, as they are sons of Adam, are co-heirs; and have equal right unto liberty, and all other outward comforts of life. "God hath given the earth [with all its commodities] unto the sons of Adam," Psalm 115:16. "And hath made of one blood, all nations of men, for to dwell on all the face of the earth, and hath determined the times before appointed, and the bounds of their habitation: That they should seek the Lord. Forasmuch then as we are the offspring of God," etc. Acts 17:26, 27, 29. Now although the title given by the last Adam doth infinitely better men's estates, respecting God and themselves; and grants them a most beneficial and inviolable lease under the broad seal of Heaven, who were before only tenants at will: yet through the indulgence of God to our first parents after the Fall,[2] the outward estate of all and every of their children remains the same, as to one another. So that originally, and naturally, there is no such thing as slavery. Joseph[3] was rightfully no more a slave to his brethren than they were to him: and they had no more authority to sell him than they had to slay him. And if they had nothing to do to sell him, the Ishmaelites[4] bargaining with them, and paying down twenty pieces of silver, could not make a title.[5] Neither could Potiphar[6] have any better interest in him than the Ishmaelites had, Genesis 37:20, 27, 28. For he that shall in this case plead alteration of property seems to have forfeited a great part of his own claim to humanity. There is no proportion between twenty pieces of silver and liberty. The commodity itself is the claimer. If Arabian

---

* Sewall's pamphlet was one of the first antislavery works published by a Puritan.

[1] Sewall's translation of a passage from *De Conscientia, et Eius Iure, Vel Casibus* (1623) by Dr. William Ames (1576–1633), a noted English theologian known as "the chief architect of Puritan ecclesiastical theory."

[2] Adam's sin of yielding to temptation by eating the forbidden fruit, and his subsequent fall from grace (see Genesis 3).

[3] The son of Rachel and Jacob, sold into slavery by his brothers; he became a high-ranking official in Egypt.

[4] Descendants of Ishmael, progenitor of the Arabs.

[5] "Come now therefore, and let us slay him, and cast him into some pit. . . . Come, let us sell him to the Ishmaelites, and let not our hand be upon him; for he is our brother and our flesh. . . . Then . . . they drew and lifted up Joseph out of the pit, and sold Joseph to the Ishmaelites for twenty pieces of silver: and they brought Joseph into Egypt," from Genesis 37:20–28.

[6] In Genesis 39, the Egyptian official to whom Joseph was sold.

gold be imported in any quantities, most are afraid to meddle with it, though they might have it at easy rates; lest if it should have been wrongfully taken from the owners, it should kindle a fire to the consumption of their whole estate. 'Tis pity there should be more caution used in buying a horse, or a little lifeless dust, than there is in purchasing men and women: whenas they are the offspring of God, and their liberty is *auro pretiosior omni.*[7]

And seeing God hath said, "He that stealeth a man and selleth him, or if he be found in his hand, he shall surely be put to death," Exodus 21:16. This law being of everlasting equity, wherein man stealing is ranked amongst the most atrocious of capital crimes: what louder cry can there be made of that celebrated warning, *caveat emptor!*[8]

And all things considered, it would conduce more to the welfare of the province, to have white servants for a term of years than to have slaves for life. Few can endure to hear of a Negro's being made free; and indeed they can seldom use their freedom well; yet their continual aspiring after their forbidden liberty renders them unwilling servants. And there is such a disparity in their conditions, color and hair that they can never embody with us, and grow up into orderly families, to the peopling of the land: but still remain in our body politic as a kind of extravasate blood.[9] As many Negro men as there are among us, so many empty places there are in our trainbands,[10] and the places taken up of men that might make husbands for our daughters. And the sons and daughters of New England would become more like Jacob, and Rachel, if this slavery were thrust quite out of doors. Moreover, it is too well known what temptations masters are under, to connive at the fornication of their slaves; lest they should be obliged to find them wives, or pay their fines. It seems to be practically pleaded that they might be lawless; 'tis thought much of, that the law should have satisfaction for their thefts, and other immoralities; by which means, holiness to the Lord is more rarely engraven upon this sort of servitude. It is likewise most lamentable to think, how in taking Negroes out of Africa, and selling of them here, that which God has joined together men do boldly rend asunder; men from their country, husbands from their wives, parents from their children. How horrible is the uncleanness, mortality, if not murder, that the ships are guilty of that bring great crowds of these miserable men, and women. Methinks, when we are bemoaning the barbarous usage of our friends and kinfolk in Africa: it might not be unseasonable to inquire whether we are not culpable in forcing the Africans to become slaves amongst ourselves. And it may be a question whether all the benefit received by Negro slaves will balance the account of cash laid out upon them; and for the redemption of our own enslaved friends out of Africa; besides all the persons and estates that have perished there.

Objection 1. These blackamoors are of the posterity of Cham,[11] and therefore are under the curse of slavery. Genesis 9:25, 26, 27.[12]

---

[7] "More precious than gold" (Latin), perhaps referring to the King James version of Isaiah 13:12, " I will make a man more precious than fine gold."

[8] "Let the buyer beware!" (Latin).

[9] Blood forced out of the proper vessels; Sewall believed that blacks are intrinsically different from whites.

[10] Bands of citizens trained as local militia.

[11] The dark-skinned Africans are descendants of eastern tribes.

[12] "And he said, Cursed be Canaan; a servant of servants shall be unto his brethren. And he said, Blessed be the Lord God of Shem; and Canaan shall be his servant. God shall enlarge Japheth, and he shall dwell in the tents of Shem; and Canaan shall be his servant."

Answer. Of all offices, one would not beg this; viz., uncalled for, to be an executioner of the vindictive wrath of God; the extent and duration of which is to us uncertain. If this ever was a commission, how do we know but that it is long since out of date? Many have found it to their cost, that a prophetical denunciation of judgment against a person or people would not warrant them to inflict that evil. If it would, Hazael[13] might justify himself in all he did against his master, and the Israelites, from II Kings 8:10, 12.[14]

But it is possible that by cursory reading, this text may have been mistaken. For Canaan is the person cursed three times over, without the mentioning of Cham. Good expositors suppose the curse entailed on him, and that this prophecy was accomplished in the extirpation of the Canaanites, and in the servitude of the Gibeonites.[15] *Vide Pareum.*[16] Whereas the blackamoors are not descended of Canaan, but of Cush.[17] Psalm 68:31, "Princes shall come out of Egypt [Mizraim]; Ethiopia [Cush] shall soon stretch out her hands unto God." Under which names, all Africa may be comprehended; and their promised conversion ought to be prayed for. Jeremiah 13:23, "Can the Ethiopian change his skin?" This shows that black men are the posterity of Cush, who time out of mind have been distinguished by their color. . . .

Objection 2. The Negroes are brought out of a pagan country into places where the Gospel is preached.

Answer. Evil must not be done, that good may come of it. The extraordinary and comprehensive benefit accruing to the church of God, and to Joseph personally, did not rectify his brethren's sale of him.

Objection 3. The Africans have wars one with another; our ships bring lawful captives taken in those wars.

Answer. For aught is known, their wars are much such as were between Jacob's sons and their brother Joseph. If they be between town and town, provincial, or national, every war is upon one side unjust. An unlawful war can't make lawful captives. And by receiving, we are in danger to promote, and partake in their barbarous cruelties. I am sure, if some gentlemen should go down to the Brewsters to take the air, and fish: and a stronger party from Hull[18] should surprise them, and sell them for slaves to a ship outward bound, they would think themselves unjustly dealt with; both by sellers and buyers. And yet 'tis to be feared, we have no other kind of title to our Negroes. "Therefore all things whatsoever ye would that men should do to you, do ye even so to them: for this is the law and the prophets," Matthew 7:12.

Objection 4. Abraham[19] had servants bought with his money, and born in his house.

---

[13] A king of Damascus; he killed Benhadad II and succeeded him to the throne.

[14] "And Elisha said unto him, Go, say unto him, Thou mayest certainly recover: howbeit the Lord hath showed me that he shall surely die. . . . And Hazael said, Why weepeth my lord? And he answered, Because I know the evil that thou wilt do unto the children of Israel: their strongholds wilt thou set on fire, and their young men wilt thou slay with the sword, and wilt dash their children, and rip up their women with child."

[15] Inhabitants of Gibeon, condemned by Joshua (the successor of Moses) as "hewers of wood and drawers of water for the congregation and for the altar of the Lord," from Joshua 9:27.

[16] "See Pareus" (Latin); David Pareus (1548–1635), a Protestant theologian of Heidelberg.

[17] In Genesis 10:8 Ethiopia, on the western shore of the Red Sea, inhabited by the descendants of Cush, a son of Ham.

[18] The Brewsters and Hull are locations in England.

[19] The biblical patriarch and ancestor of the Hebrews (see Genesis 12).

Answer. Until the circumstances of Abraham's purchase be recorded, no argument can be drawn from it. In the meantime, charity obliges us to conclude that he knew it was lawful and good.

It is observable that the Israelites were strictly forbidden the buying, or selling one another for slaves. Leviticus 25:39, 46.[20] Jeremiah 34:8–22.[21] And God gaged His blessing in lieu of any loss they might conceit they suffered thereby. Deuteronomy 15:18.[22] And since the partition wall is broken down, inordinate self love should likewise be demolished. God expects that Christians should be of a more ingenuous and benign frame of spirit. Christians should carry it to all the world, as the Israelites were to carry it one towards another. And for men obstinately to persist in holding their neighbors and brethren under the rigor of perpetual bondage seems to be no proper way of gaining assurance that God has given them spiritual freedom. Our blessed Savior has altered the measures of the ancient love-song, and set it to a most excellent new tune, which all ought to be ambitious of learning. Matthew 5:43, 44.[23] John 13:34.[24] These Ethiopians, as black as they are, seeing they are the sons and daughters of the first Adam, the brethren and sisters of the last Adam, and the offspring of God; they ought to be treated with a respect agreeable.

1700

Sarah Kemble Knight
(1666–1727)

A third-generation American, Sarah Kemble was born in Boston in 1666 to Elizabeth Trerice and the merchant Thomas Kemble. Before 1689 Sarah Kemble married Captain Richard Knight, a shipowner much older than herself. They had a daughter, Elizabeth, and

[20] "And if thy brother that dwelleth by thee be waxen poor, and be sold unto thee; thou shalt not compel him to serve as a bondservant . . . ; And ye shall take them as an inheritance . . . ; they shall be your bondmen forever, but over your brethren the children of Israel, ye shall not rule one over another with rigor."

[21] "This is the word that came unto Jeremiah from the Lord . . . ; That every man should let his manservant, and every man his maidservant, being an Hebrew or an Hebrewess, go free; that none should serve . . . of a Jew his brother. . . . All the princes, and all the people . . . obeyed, and let them go. But afterward they turned, and caused the servants and the handmaids, whom they had let go free, to return, and brought them into subjection. . . . Thus saith the Lord; Ye have not hearkened unto me, in proclaiming liberty, every one to his brother, and every man to his neighbor: behold, I proclaim a liberty for you, saith the Lord, to the sword, to the pestilence, and to the famine; and I will make you to be removed into all the kingdoms of the earth. . . . I will make the cities of Judah a desolation without an inhabitant."

[22] "It shall not seem hard unto thee, when thou sendest him away from thee; for he hath been worth a double hired servant to thee, in serving thee six years: and the Lord thy God shall bless thee in all that thou doest."

[23] "Ye have heard that it hath been said, Thou shalt love thy neighbor, and hate thine enemy. But I say unto you, Love your enemies, bless them that curse you, do good to them that hate you, and pray for them which despitefully use you, and persecute you."

[24] "A new commandment I give unto you, that ye love one another; as I have loved you, that ye also love one another."

Captain Knight died some time before 1706. Sarah Kemble Knight was a contemporary of another Bostonian, the indefatigable Puritan historiographer Cotton Mather. In the writing school she operated in Boston from 1706 to 1713, Madam Knight (as she was called in recognition of her writing and legal skills), is believed to have taught Mather's son Samuel and young Benjamin Franklin.

Knight's writing indicates that she was widely read in the standard literature of the time. Other than legal documents, the only surviving writing by the vigorous and quick-witted Knight is the journal of her journey by horse from Boston to New York City and back, between October 1704 and March 1705. First published in 1825, the slim volume *The Journal of Madam Knight* captures realities of colonial American life often lacking in Puritan literature: the rewards and hardships of travel, the variety of manners and characters, the collision of wilderness and culture, along with a genuine sense of the author's personality as an intrepid traveler in a rugged frontier.

Knight's journey probably resulted from her activity in the field of law. In 1704, one of her boarders, a young widow, married Knight's cousin, Caleb Trowbridge of New Haven, Connecticut. Within two months, the affluent Trowbridge died. Three weeks later Knight left Elizabeth in her grandmother's care in Boston and headed for New Haven to help Trowbridge's widow. Knight's familiarity with legal documents is probably what enabled her to act as lawyer for her cousin's widow.

Knight arrived in New Haven (126 miles away on today's roads) after five grueling days of travel recorded in vivid detail in her journal, with a series of guides, through a wilderness with few roads, bridges, and lodgings. She remained there for two months, attending to business and informing herself about the local manners and customs. When kinsman Thomas Trowbridge (probably Caleb's father) planned to go to New York City, Knight decided to accompany him. Leaving New Haven in early December, they arrived in New York City three days later. Within two weeks they had concluded their business,

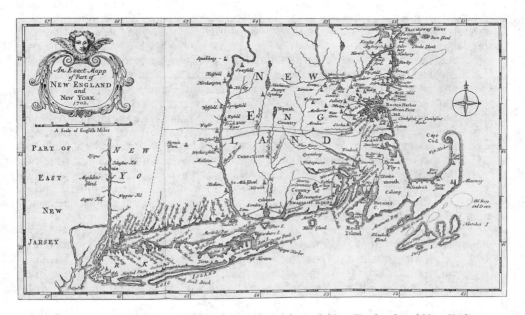

The 1702 map of Sarah Kemble Knight's journey through New England and New York.

while Knight again documented the local manners and customs. The trip from New York City back to New Haven took three days. The legal process continued slowly; Knight suspected the delays were intended to try her patience. Nevertheless, she persisted until she had achieved a happy settlement. Leaving New Haven in late February, Knight was back in Boston within a week and summed up this return trip quickly, without making separate entries for each day.

To be near her daughter, Knight moved to Connecticut in 1713. There Knight continued to prosper, buying farms and an inn. She died at age sixty-one in New London, Connecticut, leaving an estate valued at eighteen hundred pounds, more than one hundred times the wealth of the average person in 1727.

Suggested Readings: *The Journal of Madam Knight*, intro. G. P. Winship, pref. K. Silverman, 1970. A. Margolies, "The Editing and Publication of *The Journal of Madam Knight*" in *Papers of the Bibliographical Society of America* 1964, 58: 25–32. P. Thorpe, "Sarah Kemble Knight and the Picaresque Tradition" in *College Language Association Journal* 1966, 10: 114–121. R. D. Arner, "Sarah Kemble Knight" in *American Literature Before the 1800s*, ed. J. A. Levernier and D. R. Wilmes, 1983.

Text Used: *The Private Journal of a Journey From Boston to New York, in the Year 1704*, 1865 (spelling and punctuation modernized).

from THE PRIVATE JOURNAL OF A JOURNEY FROM BOSTON TO NEW YORK

Friday, Oct. Sixth [1704]. I got up very early, in order to hire somebody to go with me to New Haven, being in great perplexity at the thoughts of proceeding alone; which my most hospitable entertainer observing, himself went, and soon returned with a young gentleman of the town, who he could confide in to go with me; and about eight this morning, with Mr. Joshua Wheeler[1] my new guide, taking leave of this worthy gentleman, we advanced on toward Seabrook. The roads all along this way are very bad, encumbered with rocks and mountainous passages, which were very disagreeable to my tired carcass; but we went on with a moderate pace which made the journey more pleasant. But after about eight miles riding, in going over a bridge under which the river run very swift,[2] my horse stumbled, and very narrowly escaped falling over into the water; which extremely frightened me. But through God's goodness I met with no harm, and mounting again, in about half a mile's riding, come to an ordinary,[3] were well entertained by a woman of about seventy and vantage,[4] but of as sound intellectuals as one of seventeen. She entertained Mr. Wheeler with some passages of a wedding awhile ago at a place hard by, the bride's-groom being about her age or something above, saying his children was dreadfully against their father's marrying, which she condemned them extremely for.

From hence we went pretty briskly forward, and arrived at Saybrook ferry about two of the clock afternoon; and crossing it, we called at an inn to bait[5] (foreseeing we should not have such another opportunity 'til we come to Killingsworth). Landlady come in, with her hair about her ears, and hands at full pay[6] scratching. She told us she had some mutton which she would broil, which I

---

[1] Wheeler (1681–?) the son of John Wheeler, a shipping merchant of New London, Connecticut.
[2] Most likely the Niantic River.   [3] An inn.   [4] About age seventy or more.   [5] To rest.
[6] Busily.

was glad to hear; but I suppose forgot to wash her scratches; in a little time she brought it in; but it being pickled, and my guide said it smelled strong of head sauce,[7] we left it, and paid sixpence a piece for our dinners, which was only smell.

So we put forward with all speed, and about seven at night come to Kilingsworth, and were tolerably well with travelers' fare, and lodged there that night.

Saturday, Oct. 7th [1704], we set out early in the morning, and being something unaquainted with the way, having asked it of some we met, they told us we must ride a mile or two and turn down a lane on the right hand; and by their direction we rode on, but not yet coming to the turning, we met a young fellow and asked him how far it was to the lane which turned down towards Guilford. He said we must ride a little further, and turn down by the corner of Uncle Sam's lot. My guide vented his spleen at the lubber;[8] and we soon after came into the road, and keeping still on, without any thing further remarkable, about two o'clock [in the] afternoon we arrived at New Haven, where I was received with all possible respects and civility. Here I discharged Mr. Wheeler with a reward to his satisfaction, and took some time to rest after so long and toilsome a journey; and informed myself of the manners and customs of the place, and at the same time employed myself in the affair I went there upon.

They are governed by the same laws as we in Boston (or little differing), throughout this whole colony of Connecticut, and much the same say of church government, and many of them good, sociable people, and I hope religious too. . . .

Dec. 6th [1704].

* * *

The city of New York is a pleasant, well-compacted place, situated on a commodious river which is a fine harbor for shipping. The buildings brick generally, very stately and high, though not altogether like ours in Boston. The bricks in some of the houses are of diverse colors and laid in checkers, being glazed look very agreeable. The inside of them are neat to admiration, the wooden work, for only the walls are plastered, and the summers and gist[9] are plained and kept very white scowered as so is all the partitions if made of boards. The fireplaces have no jambs (as ours have) but the backs run flush with the walls, and the hearth is of tiles and is as far out into the room at the ends as before the fire, which is generally five foot in the lower rooms, and the piece over where the mantle tree should be is made as ours with joiners' work,[10] and as I suppose is fastened to iron rods inside. The house where the vendue[11] was had chimney corners like ours, and they and the hearths were laid with the finest tile that I ever see, and the staircases laid all with white tile which is ever clean,[12] and so are the walls of the kitchen which had a brick floor. They were making great preparations to receive their governor, Lord Cornbury[13] from the Jerseys, and for that end raised the militia to guard him on shore to the fort.

---

[7] Cheese sauce.   [8] Expressed his anger at the lout.
[9] The main beams and parallel horizontal supporting beams, or joists.
[10] Similar to carpenter's work but more finely finished.   [11] Auction.
[12] Set into the wall, forming a continuous border one tile in width.
[13] Edward Hyde (1661–1723), the governor of New Jersey and New York from 1702 to 1708.

They are generally of the Church of England and have a New England gentle-man[14] for their minister, and a very fine church set out with all customary requisites. There are also a Dutch and diverse conventicles[15] as they call them, *viz.* Baptist, Quakers, etc. They are not strict in keeping the sabbath as in Boston and other places where I had been, but seem to deal with great exactness as far as I see or deal with. They are sociable to one another and courteous and civil to strangers and fare well in their houses. The English go very fashionable in their dress. But the Dutch, especially the middling sort, differ from our women, in their habit go loose, wear French muchets which are like a cap and a headband in one, leaving their ears bare, which are set out with jewels of a large size and many in number. And their fingers hooped with rings, some with large stones in them of many colors as were their pendants in their ears, which you should see very old women wear as well as young.

They have vendues very frequently and make their earnings very well by them, for they treat with good liquor liberally, and the customers drink as liberally and generally for't as well, by paying for that which they bid up briskly for, after the sack[16] has gone plentifully about, though sometimes good penny worths are got there. Their diversions in the winter is riding sleighs about three or four miles out of town, where they have houses of entertainment at a place called the Bowery, and some go to friends' houses who handsomely treat them. Mr. Burroughs carried his spouse and daughter and myself out to one Madame Dowes, a gentlewoman that lived at a farm house, who gave us a handsome entertainment of five or six dishes and choice beer and metheglin,[17] cider, etc., all which she said was the produce of her farm. I believe we met 50 or 60 sleighs that day—they fly with great swiftness and some are so furious that they'll turn out of the path for none except a loaden cart. Nor do they spare for any diversion the place affords, and sociable to a degree, their tables being as free to their neighbors as to themselves.

Having here transacted the affair I went upon and some other that fell in the way, after about a fortnight's stay there I left New York with no little regret. . . .

1704–1705, 1825

Robert Beverley
(1673?–1722)

Robert Beverley was one of colonial America's first native-born gentlemen. Though educated in England, as were most males of early Virginia's aristocracy, Beverley always felt proud of his American birthplace. The work upon which his literary fame rests, *The His-*

[14] William Vesey (1674–1746), the rector of New York's Trinity Church.
[15] Religious assemblies held illegally by Protestant sects that disputed the Church of England's authority.
[16] Dry white wine, generally imported from Spain or the Canary Islands.
[17] A spiced alcoholic drink.

tory and Present State of Virginia (1705), was published anonymously and signed "By a *Native* and *Inhabitant* of the *PLACE*." Beverley saw himself so much a part of the New World that he writes as a Native American in *The History's* preface, "I am only an *Indian*, and don't pretend to be exact in my Language. . . ." By connecting the English planter and the Native American, Beverley is able to show the good and bad in both groups without treating either preferentially.

Similarly, Beverley's political sentiments were American rather than English. His cavalier father, Robert Beverley, Sr., became involved in local Virginia politics and ultimately led other Virginia planters in protest against the British governor Thomas Culpeper, whom the planters believed served only as a functionary for absentee British landlords. The elder Beverley died shortly after being forced to humiliate himself by begging the governor's pardon for having taken part in the protests. Beverley, Jr., was in London finishing his education at the time of his father's death in 1687. He returned to Virginia to inherit both his father's land holdings and his pro-American political leanings; he always stood for home rule when British colonial policies conflicted with the desires of American planters.

In 1697 Beverly wed Ursula Byrd, the sister of William Byrd II, but found himself a widower and a father less than a year later. He never remarried; instead, Beverley threw himself into business and politics. One of Virginia's richest landholders, he served as a Jamestown representative to the Virginia House of Burgesses and held various clerkships in the colony. On a trip to England in 1703 to litigate a property settlement, Beverley was asked by a bookseller to read the manuscript of John Oldmixon's *The British Empire in America* (1708). Finding Oldmixon's work to be exaggerated, patchy, and in some cases outright false, Beverley wrote his own history in response.

As a chronicler, Beverley took a new perspective on Virginia's short though dramatic history. He wrote about the colonies from an American point of view, removing many of the European prejudices that had built up about the New World. He refused to romanticize either the Edenic qualities of the American wilderness or America's improvements from interaction with European culture. Beverley portrays the land as a place that can be made fruitful by hard work. Through his nonromanticized perspective on the colonies and its inhabitants, Beverley balances the evils of Nathaniel Bacon's violent 1676 rebellion for social reform, Native-American attacks, and poor planting practices against descriptions of the land's lusciousness, intended to lure Europeans to settle in the New World. By combining both views of Virginia into one, Beverley's *History* is an accurate account as well as a promotional tract.

Beverley published little other than the 1705 edition of his *History*. He revised that work for a second edition in 1722, the year he completed his only other published work, *An Abridgment of the Public Laws of Virginia*. He died shortly thereafter that year and was buried in the family plot at Beverley Park in Virginia.

Suggested Readings: L. P. Simpson, *The Dispossessed Garden: Pastoral and History in Southern Literature*, 1975. R. D. Arner, "The Quest for Freedom: Style and Meaning in Robert Beverley's *History and Present State of Virginia*," *Southern Literary Journal*, 1976, 8.2: 79–98. W. R. Jacobs, "Robert Beverley: Colonial Ecologist and Indian Lover," *Essays in Early American Literature Honoring Richard Beale Davis*, ed. J. A. L. Lemay, 1977. J. J. Small, "Robert Beverley and the New World Garden," *American Literature*, 1983, 55: 525–540.

Text Used: *The History and Present State of Virginia*, Book I, ed. L. B. Wright, 1947 (some spelling and punctuation modernized).

from THE HISTORY AND PRESENT STATE OF VIRGINIA

from BOOK I*

Chap. I. Showing What Happened in the First Attempts to Settle Virginia, Before the Discovery of Chesapeake Bay

1. The learned and valiant Sir Walter Raleigh[1] having entertained some deeper and more serious considerations upon the state of the earth than most other men of his time, as may sufficiently appear by his incomparable book, *The History of the World:* and having laid together the many stories then in Europe concerning America; the native beauty, riches, and value of this part of the world; and the immense profits the Spaniards drew from a small settlement or two thereon made; resolved upon an adventure for further discoveries.

According to this purpose in the Year of our Lord, 1583, he got several men of great value and estate to join with him in an expedition of this nature: and for their encouragement obtained letters patents[2] from Queen Elizabeth,[3] bearing date the 25th of March, 1584, for turning their discoveries to their own advantage.

2. In April following they set out two small vessels under the command of Capt. Philip Amidas, and Capt. Arthur Barlow;[4] who, after a prosperous voyage, anchored at the inlet by Roanoke, at present under the government of North Carolina. They made good profit of the Indian truck,[5] which they bought for things of much inferior value, and returned. Being over-pleased with their profits, and finding all things there entirely new, and surprising, they gave a very advantageous account of matters; by representing the country so delightful, and desirable; so pleasant, and plentiful; the climate, and air, so temperate, sweet, and wholesome; the woods, and soil so charming, and fruitful; and all other things so agreeable, that Paradise itself seemed to be there, in its first native lustre.

They gave particular accounts of the variety of good fruits, and some whereof they had never seen the like before; but above all, that there were grapes in such abundance, as was never known in the world: stately and tall large oaks, and other timber; red cedar, cypress, pines, and other evergreens, and sweetwoods; for tallness and largeness exceeding all they had ever heard of: wild fowl, fish, deer, and other game in such plenty, and variety; that no epicure could desire more than this new world did seem naturally to afford.

And, to make it yet more desirable, they reported the native Indians (which were then the only inhabitants) so affable, kind, and good-natured; so uncultivated in learning, trades, and fashions; so innocent, and ignorant of all manner of politicks, tricks, and cunning; and so desirous of the company of the English: that they seemed rather to be like soft wax, ready to take any impression, than any

---

* The title of Book I is "The History of the First Settlement of Virginia and the Government Thereof, to the Present Time."

[1] Raleigh (1552?–1618) was a naval commander, explorer, poet, and author of *The History of the World* (1614).

[2] Public letters generally signed by a sovereign.

[3] Elizabeth I (1533–1603), queen of England from 1558 to 1603.

[4] Amadas (1550–1618); Barlow (1550?–1620?); Barlow's narrative of their journey was printed in Richard Hakluyt's *Principal Navigations* (1589).

[5] Commercial goods.

ways likely to oppose the settling of the English near them: they represented it as a scene laid open for the good and gracious Q. Elizabeth, to propagate the Gospel in, and extend her dominions over: as if purposely reserved for her Majesty, by a peculiar direction of providence, that had brought all former adventures in this affair to nothing: and to give a further taste of their discovery, they took with them in their return for England, two men of the native Indians, named Wanchese and Manteo.

3. Her Majesty accordingly took the hint, and espoused the project, as far as her present engagements in war with Spain[6] would let her; being so well pleased with the account given, that as the greatest mark of honor she could do the discovery, she called the country by the name of Virginia; as well, for that it was first discovered in her reign, a virgin queen, as that it did still seem to retain the virgin purity and plenty of the first Creation, and the people their primitive innocence; for they seemed not debauched nor corrupted with those pomps and vanities, which had depraved and enslaved the rest of mankind; neither were their hands hardened by labor, nor their minds corrupted by the desire of hoarding up treasure: they were without boundaries to their land; and without property in cattle; and seemed to have escaped, or rather not to have been concerned in the first curse, "*Of getting their bread by the sweat of their brows*":[7] for, by their pleasure alone, they supplied all their necessities, namely, by fishing, fowling, and hunting, skins being their only clothing; and these too, five sixth of the year thrown by: living without labor, and only gathering the fruits of the earth when ripe, or fit for use: neither fearing present want, nor solicitous for the future, but daily finding sufficient afresh for their subsistance.

4. This report was backed, nay much advanced, by the vast riches and treasure mentioned in several merchants' letters from Mexico and Peru to their correspondents in Spain; which letters were taken with their ships and treasure, by some of ours in her Majesty's service, in prosecution of the Spanish wars: this was encouragment enough for a new adventure, and set people's invention at work, till they had satisfied themselves, and made sufficient essays[8] for the further discovery of the country. Pursuant whereunto Sir Richard Greenville,[9] the chief of Sir Walter Raleigh's associates, having obtained seven sail of ships, well-laden with provision, arms, ammunition, and spare men to make a settlement, set out in person with them early in the spring of the succeeding year, to make further discoveries, taking back the two Indians with him; and according to his wish, in the latter end of May, arrived at the same place where the English had been the year before; there he made a settlement, sowed beans and peas, which he saw come up and grow to admiration while he stayed, which was about two months; and having made some little discoveries more in the Sound to the southward, and got some treasure in skins, furs, pearl, and other rarities of the country, for things of inconsiderable value, he returned for England, leaving one hundred and eight men upon Roanoke Island, under the command of Mr. Ralph Lane,[10] to keep possession.

---

[6] During 1583 a Spanish plot against Elizabeth was uncovered; war was declared against Spain in 1587.

[7] A paraphrase of God's curse of Adam in Genesis 3:19: "In the sweat of thy face shalt thou eat bread, till thou return unto the ground. . . ."

[8] Attempts.

[9] Actually Grenville (1541?–1591), a British naval officer who commanded the fleet for colonization of Virginia in 1585 for his cousin Sir Walter Raleigh.

[10] Sir Ralph Lane (1530?–1603), whose account of the Virginia settlement was published in Hakluyt's *Voyages* (1589).

5. As soon as Sir Richard Greenville was gone, they, according to order and their own inclination, set themselves earnestly about discovering the country, and ranged about a little too indiscreetly up the rivers, and into the land backward from the rivers, which gave the Indians a jealousy[11] of their meaning: for they cut off several stragglers of them, and had laid designs to destroy the rest, but were happily prevented. This put the English upon the precaution of keeping more within bounds, and not venturing themselves too defenseless abroad, who till then had depended too much upon the native's simplicity and innocence.

After the Indians had done this mischief, they never observed any real faith towards those English: for being naturally suspicious and revengeful themselves, they never thought the English could forgive them; and so by this jealousy, caused by cowardice of their nature, they were continually doing mischief.

The English, notwithstanding all this, continued their discoveries, but more carefully than they had done before, and kept the Indians in some awe by threatening them with the return of their companions again with a greater supply of men and goods: and, before the cold of winter became uneasy, they had extended their discoveries near a hundred miles along the sea-coast to the northward; but not reaching the southern cape of Chesapeake Bay in Virginia, they had as yet found no good harbor.

6. In this condition they maintained their settlement all the winter, and till August following; but were much distressed for want of provisions, not having learned to gather food, as the Indians did, not having conveniences like them of taking fish and fowl: besides, being now fallen out with the Indians, they feared to expose themselves to their contempt and cruelty; because they had not received the supply they talked of, and which had been expected in the spring.

All they could do under these distresses, and the despair of the recruits promised them this year, was only to keep a good looking out to seaward, if, perchance, they might find any means of escape, or recruit. And, to their great joy and satisfaction, in August aforesaid, they happened to espy, and make themselves be seen to Sir Francis Drake's[12] fleet, consisting of twenty-three sail, who being sent by her Majesty upon the coast of America, in search of the Spanish treasures, had orders from her Majesty to take a view of this plantation, and see what assistance or encouragement it wanted: their first petition to him was to grant them a fresh supply of men and provisions, with a small vessel, and boats to attend them; that so if they should be put to distress for want of relief, they might embark for England. This was as readily granted by Sir Francis Drake as asked by them; and a ship was appointed them, which ship they began immediately to fit up, and supply plentifully with all manner of stores for a long stay; but while they were a doing this, a great storm arose, and drove that very ship (with some others) from her anchor to sea, and so she was lost for that occasion.

Sir Francis would have given them another ship, but this accident coming on the back of so many hardships which they had undergone, daunted them, and put them upon imagining that providence was averse to their designs: and now having given over, for that year, the expectation of their promised supply from England, they consulted together, and agreed to desire Sir Francis Drake to take them along with him, which he did.

Thus their first intention of settlement fell, after discovering many things of the

---

[11] A suspicion.
[12] Drake (1540?–1596), an English navigator who plundered Spanish towns and ships, returned the Virginia colonists to England in 1586.

natural growth of the country, useful for the life of man, and beneficial to trade, they having observed a vast variety of fish, fowl and beasts; fruits, seeds, plants, roots, timber-trees, sweet-woods and gums: they had likewise attained some little knowledge in the language of the Indians, their religion, manners, and ways of correspondence one with another; and been made sensible of their cunning and treachery towards themselves.

7. While these things were thus acting in America, the adventurers in England were providing, though too tediously, to send them recruits. And though it was late before they could dispatch them (for they met with several disappointments, and had many squabbles among themselves). However, at last they provided four good ships, with all manner of recruits suitable for the colony, and Sir Walter Raleigh designed[13] to go in person with them.

Sir Walter got this ship ready first, and fearing the ill consequence of a delay, and the discouragement it might be to those that were left to make a settlement, he set sail by himself. And a fortnight after him Sir Richard Greenville sailed with the three other ships.

Sir Walter fell in with the land at Cape Hatteras,[14] a little to the southward of the place, where the 108 men had been settled, and after search not finding them, he returned: however, Sir Richard, with his ships, found the place where he had left the men, but entirely deserted, which was at first a great disheartening to him, thinking them all destroyed, because he knew not that Sir Francis Drake had been there, and taken them off; but he was a little better satisfied by Manteo's report that they were not cut off by the Indians, though he could give no good account what was become of them. However, notwithstanding this seeming discouragement, he again left fifty men in the same island of Roanoke, built them houses necessary, gave them two years' provision, and returned.

8. The next summer, being Anno 1587, three ships more were sent, under the command of Mr. John White,[15] who himself was to settle there as governor with more men, and some women, carrying also plentiful recruits of provisions.

In the latter end of July they arrived at Roanoke aforesaid, where they again encountered the uncomfortable news of the loss of these men also; who (as they were informed by Manteo) were secretly set upon by the Indians, some cut off, and the others fled, and not to be heard of, and their place of habitation now all grown up with weeds. However, they repaired the houses on Roanoke, and sat down there again.

The 13th of August they christened Manteo, and styled him Lord of Dassamonpeak, an Indian nation so called, in reward of the fidelity he had shown to the English from the beginning; who being the first Indian that was made a Christian in that part of the world, I thought it not amiss to remember him.

On the same occasion also may be mentioned the first child there born of Christian parentage, *viz.* a daughter of Mr. Ananias Dare. She was born the 18th of the same August upon Roanoke, and, after the name of the country, was christened Virginia.[16]

This seemed to be a settlement prosperously made, being carried on with much zeal and unanimity among themselves. The form of government consisted of a governor and twelve councellors, incorporated by the name of the governor and assistants of the city of Raleigh in Virginia.

---

[13] Intended.   [14] A cape on Hatteras Island, off what is now North Carolina.
[15] White (?–1593?) was an English cartographer.
[16] Virginia Dare (1587–?) was the granddaughter of Gov. John White.

Many nations of the Indians renewed their peace, and made firm leagues with the corporations: the chief men of the English also were so far from being disheartened at the former disappointments, that they disputed for the liberty of remaining on the spot; and by mere constraint compelled Mr. White, their governor, to return for England, to negotiate the business of their recruits and supply, as a man the most capable to manage that affair, leaving at his departure one hundred and fifteen in the corporation.

9. It was above two years before Mr. White could obtain any grant of supplies; and then, in the latter end of the year 1589, he set out from Plymouth with three ships, and sailed round by the Western and Carribbee Islands, they having hitherto not found any nearer way: for though they were skilled in navigation, and understood the use of the gloves, yet did example so much prevail upon them, that they chose to sail a thousand leagues about, rather than attempt a more direct passage.

Towards the middle of August, 1590, they arrived upon the coast, at Cape Hatteras, and went to search upon Roanoke for the people; but found, by letters on the trees, that they were removed to Croatan, one of the islands forming the Sound, and southward of Roanoke about twenty leagues, but no sign of distress. Thither they designed to sail to them in their ships; but a storm arising in the meanwhile lay so hard upon them that their cables broke; they lost three of their anchors, were forced to sea; and so returned home, without ever going near those poor people again for sixteen years following: and it is supposed that the Indians, seeing them forsaken by their country, and unfurnished of their expected supplies, cut them off: for to this day they were never more heard of.

Thus, after all this vast expense and trouble, and the hazard and loss of so many lives, Sir Walter Raleigh, the great projector and furtherer of these discoveries and settlements, being under trouble,[17] all thoughts of further prosecuting these designs lay dead for about twelve years following.

10. And then, in the year 1602 Capt. Gosnell,[18] who had made one in the former adventures, furnished out a small bark[19] from Dartmouth, and set sail in her himself, with thirty-odd men; designing a more direct course, and not to stand so far to the southward, nor pass by the Carribbee Islands, as all former adventurers had done. He attained his ends in that; but touched upon the coast of America much to the northward of any of the places where the former adventurers had landed. For he fell first among the islands, forming the northern side of Massachusetts Bay in New-England; but not finding the conveniencies that harbor affords, set sail again southward, and, as he thought, clear of land into the sea; but fell upon the bight[20] of Cape Cod.

Upon this coast, and a little to the southward, he spent some time in trade with the Indians; and gave names to the islands of Martha's Vineyard, and Elizabeth's Isle, which retain the same to this day. Upon Elizabeth's Isle he made an experiment of English grain, and found it spring up and grown to admiration, as it had done at Roanoke: here also his men built huts to shelter them in the nights, and bad weather; and made good profit by their Indian traffic of furs, skins, etc. And, as their pleasure invited them, would visit the main;[21] set receivers,[22] and save the gums, and juices distilling from sweet-woods; and try and examine the lesser vegetables.

---

[17] When Queen Elizabeth died in 1603, Raleigh was imprisoned in the Tower of London for conspiring against the new king, James I.

[18] Actually Batholomew Gosnold (?–1607), an English navigator who was second in command in the settling of Jamestown (1606–1607).

[19] A ship.   [20] Curved coastline.   [21] The mainland.   [22] Receiving tanks.

After a month's stay here, they returned for England, as well pleased with the natural beauty and richness of the place they had viewed as they were with the treasure they had gathered in it: neither had they a head, nor a finger that ached among them all the time.

11. The noise of this short, and most profitable of all the former voyages, set the Bristol merchants to work also; who early in the year 1603 sent two vessels in search of the same place and trade; which vessels fell luckily in with the same land. They followed the same methods Capt. Gosnell had done, and having got a rich lading,[23] they returned.

12. In the year 1605, a voyage was made from London in a single ship, with which they designed to fall in with the land about the latitude 39°; but the winds put her a little further northward, and she fell upon the eastern parts of Long-Island (as it is now called, but all went then under the name of Virginia). Here they trafficked with the Indians, as the others had done before them; made short trials of the soil by English grain, and found the Indians, as in all other places, very fair and courteous at first, till they got more knowledge of the English, and perhaps thought themselves over-reached, because one bought better penny-worths[24] than another; upon which afterwards they never failed to take revenge as they found their opportunity or advantage. So this company also returned with the ship, having ranged forty miles up Connecticut River, and called the harbor where they rid Pentecost Harbor because of their arrival there on Whitsunday.[25]

In all these latter voyages, they never so much as endeavored to come near the place where the first settlement was attempted at Cape Hatteras; neither had they any pity on those poor hundred and fifteen souls settled there in 1587 of whom there had never since been any account, no relief sent to them, nor so much as any inquiry made after them, whether they were dead or alive, till about three years after this, when Chesapeake Bay in Virginia was settled, which hitherto had never been seen by any English man. So strong was the desire of riches, and so eager the pursuit of a rich trade, that all concern for the lives of their fellow Christians, kindred, neighbors and country-men, weighed nothing in the comparison; though an inquiry might have been easily made, when they were so near them.

1705

William Byrd II
(1674–1744)

A premier example of southern colonial aristocracy, William Byrd II was born the first child of William Byrd and Mary Horsmanden in 1674 in what is now Richmond, Virginia. Designated his father's successor in business and politics, he was sent to school in Essex, England, in 1681; about 1690 he began to learn the world of business and trade, in Holland and then in London. He commenced the study of law at the Middle Temple, a London legal society, in 1692 and was subsequently admitted to the bar.

[23] Load.   [24] Bargains.
[25] Pentecost, the seventh Sunday after Easter; white garments were worn by Baptism candidates.

A polished gentleman trained to carry on his father's lucrative Native-American, colonial, and trans-Atlantic trade, Byrd joined Cotton Mather in 1696 as the only American members of London's Royal Society, the preeminent scientific body of its day. That year Byrd returned briefly to Virginia, was elected to the House of Burgesses there, and became the colony's representative before England's influential Board of Trade. In 1702 he lost that post by presenting directly to the king his constituents' protest against raising troops and taxes to defend New York's frontiers.

When Byrd journeyed to Westover, Virginia, to claim his inheritance in 1705, a year after his father's death, England was the home Byrd knew. He spent the next twenty-one years struggling to become a Virginian. His eighteenth-century English rearing, which emphasized classical education, balance, moderation, tolerance, and good taste, was fortunately compatible with his life as part of Virginia's ruling class. Byrd built a library of over thirty-six hundred volumes, second in size only to Cotton Mather's and second to none in its scope. But Westover was not London. Byrd's plantation was a retreat from city life and an anticipation of Jefferson's Monticello, just as Byrd, in the breadth of his humanistic and scientific concerns, anticipated Jefferson.

In 1706, as the newly appointed receiver general of Virginia, Byrd married Lucy Parke, whose father Daniel Parke was the only colonial to become a royal governor. Byrd's appointment in 1709 to the Council of Virginia marked a rise in political fortunes, but his underestimation and hasty assumption of his late father-in-law's debts in 1712, in return for Parke's estate, drained Bryd's resources almost until his death in 1744. Byrd became a Council leader, but spent years in London dealing with Parke's debts and, after Lucy's death in 1716, seeking a wealthy wife. After a year or two in Virginia, the council urged him back to England to try to preserve its powers. He married Maria Taylor in 1724, returned to Westover in 1726, and eventually expanded his father's 26,000 acres to 179,440 acres.

Byrd's role on the council enabled him to view himself first as a Virginian and second as an Englishman, a reconciliation echoed in his letters, in his "secret" diaries (written in a variation of shorthand), and in his major achievement, *The History of the Dividing Line* (first published in 1841). Based on Byrd's 1728 expeditions that set the boundary between Virginia and North Carolina, the work deemphasized the satire, sarcasm, and sexual humor of the previously written *Secret History* (first published in 1929) to reveal the expeditions as a myth-making process. That process captured the spirit of American frontier exploration and established the *History* as a prototype of discovery literature.

Suggested Readings: *The Secret History of the Line, in William Byrd's Histories of the Dividing Line Betwixt Virginia and North Carolina*, ed. W. K. Boyd, 1929. *The Secret Diary of William Byrd of Westover, 1709–1712*, ed. L. B. Wright and M. Tinling, 1941. A. Hatch, *The Byrds of Virginia*, 1969. R. C. Beatty, *William Byrd of Westover*, 1970. P. Marambaud, *William Byrd of Westover, 1674–1744*, 1971. K. A. Lockridge, *The Diary, and Life, of William Byrd II of Virginia, 1674–1744*, 1987. R. Turbet, *William Byrd: A Guide to Research*, 1987.

Text Used: *The Prose Works of William Byrd of Westover*, ed. L. B. Wright, 1966.

from   THE HISTORY OF THE DIVIDING LINE*

Before I enter upon the journal of the line between Virginia and North Carolina, it will be necessary to clear the way to it by showing how the other British colonies on the main have, one after another, been carved out of Virginia by grants from

---

* Byrd's *The History of the Dividing Line Betwixt Virginia and North Carolina* accounts the official survey to establish the boundary between the two states, begun on March 5, 1728.

His Majesty's royal predecessors. All that part of the northern American continent now under the dominion of the King of Great Britain and stretching quite as far as the Cape of Florida went at first under the general name of Virginia.

The only distinction in those early days was that all the coast to the southward of Chesapeake Bay was called South Virginia and all to the northward of it North Virginia.

The first settlement of this fine country was owing to that great ornament of the British nation, Sir Walter Raleigh,[1] who obtained a grant thereof from Queen Elizabeth,[2] of ever-glorious memory, by letters patent[3] dated March 25, 1584.

But whether that gentleman ever made a voyage thither himself is uncertain, because those who have favored the public with an account of his life mention nothing of it. However, thus much may be depended on, that Sir Walter invited sundry persons of distinction to share in his charter and join their purses with his in the laudable project of fitting out a colony to Virginia.

Accordingly, two ships were sent away that very year, under the command of his good friends Amadas and Barlow,[4] to take possession of the country in the name of his royal mistress, the Queen of England.

These worthy commanders, for the advantage of the trade winds, shaped their course first to the Caribbee Islands, thence, stretching away by the Gulf of Florida, dropped anchor not far from Roanoke Inlet.[5] They ventured ashore near that place upon an island now called Colleton Island,[6] where they set up the arms of England and claimed the adjacent country in right of their sovereign lady, the Queen; and this ceremony being duly performed, they kindly invited the neighboring Indians to traffic[7] with them.

These poor people at first approached the English with great caution, having heard much of the treachery of the Spaniards and not knowing but these strangers might be as treacherous as they. But at length, discovering a kind of good nature in their looks, they ventured to draw near and barter their skins and furs for the baubles and trinkets of the English.

These first adventurers made a very profitable voyage, raising at least a thousand per cent upon their cargo. Amongst other Indian commodities, they brought over some of that bewitching vegetable, tobacco. And this being the first that ever came to England, Sir Walter thought he could do no less than make a present of some of the brightest of it to his royal mistress for her own smoking. The Queen graciously accepted of it, but finding her stomach sicken after two or three whiffs, 'twas presently whispered by the Earl of Leicester's[8] faction that Sir Walter had certainly poisoned her. But Her Majesty, soon recovering her disorder, obliged the Countess of Nottingham and all her maids to smoke a whole pipe out amongst them.

As it happened some ages before to be the fashion to saunter to the Holy Land[9]

[1] Raleigh (1551?–1618) was a naval commander, explorer, poet, and author of *The History of the World* (1614).

[2] Elizabeth I (1533–1603), queen of England from 1558 to 1603.

[3] A public letter generally signed by a sovereign.

[4] Philip Amadas (1550–1618) and Arthur Barlow (1550?–1620?); Barlow's narrative of their journey was printed in Richard Hakluyt's *Principal Navigations* (1589).

[5] The colonists on Raleigh's 1585 expedition to Roanoke Island, off what is now North Carolina, returned to England; Raleigh led a second expedition to the same spot in 1587; three years later the island was found to be deserted and the colony "lost."

[6] Named for Sir John Colleton, an English official; now Colington Island.   [7] Trade, barter.

[8] Robert Dudley (1532?–1588), a man of eminent political power and Elizabeth's favorite at court.

[9] The Crusades; military expeditions Christians undertook to recover the Holy Land from the Muslims (11th–13th centuries).

and go upon other Quixote adventures,[10] so it was now grown the humor to take a trip to America. The Spaniards had lately discovered rich mines in their part of the West Indies, which made their maritime neighbors eager to do so too. This modish frenzy, being still more inflamed by the charming account given of Virginia by the first adventurers, made many fond of removing to such a Paradise.

Happy was he, and still happier she, that could get themselves transported, fondly expecting their coarsest utensils in that happy place would be of massy silver.

This made it easy for the Company[11] to procure as many volunteers as they wanted for their new colony, but, like most other undertakers who have no assistance from the public, they starved the design by too much frugality; for, unwilling to launch out at first into too much expense, they shipped off but few people at a time, and those but scantily provided. The adventurers were, besides, idle and extravagant and expected they might live without work in so plentiful a country.

These wretches were set ashore not far from Roanoke Inlet, but by some fatal disagreement or laziness were either starved or cut to pieces by the Indians.

Several repeated misadventures of this kind did for some time allay the itch of sailing to this new world, but the distemper broke out again about the year 1606. Then it happened that the Earl of Southampton[12] and several other persons eminent for their quality and estates were invited into the Company, who applied themselves once more to people the then almost abandoned colony. For this purpose they embarked about an hundred men, most of them reprobates of good families and related to some of the Company who were men of quality and fortune.

The ships that carried them made a shift to find a more direct way to Virginia and ventured through the capes into the Bay of Chesapeake. The same night they came to an anchor at the mouth of Powhatan,[13] the same as James River, where they built a small fort at a place called Point Comfort.

This settlement stood its ground from that time forward, in spite of all the blunders and disagreement of the first adventurers and the many calamities that befell the colony afterwards. The six gentlemen who were first named of the Company by the Crown and who were empowered to choose an annual president from among themselves were always engaged in factions and quarrels, while the rest detested work more than famine. At this rate the colony must have come to nothing had it not been for the vigilance and bravery of Captain Smith,[14] who struck a terror into all the Indians round about. This gentleman took some pains to persuade the men to plant Indian corn, but they looked upon all labor as a curse. They chose rather to depend upon the musty provisions that were sent from England; and when they failed they were forced to take more pains to seek for wild fruits in the woods than they would have taken in tilling the ground. Besides, this exposed them to be knocked in the head by the Indians and gave them fluxes[15] into the bargain, which thinned the plantation very much. To supply this mortality, they were reinforced the year following with a greater number of people, amongst which were fewer gentlemen and more laborers, who, however, took care not to kill themselves with work. These found the first adventurers in a very starving condition but relieved their wants with the fresh supply they brought with them. From Kecoughtan[16] they extended themselves as far as Jamestown, where, like

---

[10] Quixotic, or foolish, escapades, after *Don Quixote* (1605–1615), by Miguel de Cervantes.
[11] The Virginia Company of London.
[12] Henry Wriothesley (1573–1624), the third earl of Southampton.
[13] A site on the James River, under the rule of the Algonquian chief Powhatan (1550?–1618).
[14] John Smith (1580–1631), the founder of Virginia.   [15] Dysentery.   [16] Now Hampton, Virginia.

true Englishmen, they built a church that cost no more than fifty pounds and a tavern that cost five hundred.

They had now made peace with the Indians, but there was one thing wanting to make that peace lasting. The natives could by no means persuade themselves that the English were heartily their friends so long as they disdained to intermarry with them. And, in earnest, had the English consulted their own security and the good of the colony, had they intended either to civilize or convert these gentiles,[17] they would have brought their stomachs to embrace this prudent alliance.

The Indians are generally tall and well proportioned, which may make full amends for the darkness of their complexions. Add to this that they are healthy and strong, with constitutions untainted by lewdness and not enfeebled by luxury. Besides, morals and all considered, I cannot think the Indians were much greater heathens than the first adventurers, who, had they been good Christians, would have had the charity to take this only method of converting the natives to Christianity. For, after all that can be said, a sprightly lover is the most prevailing missionary that can be sent amongst these or any other infidels.

Besides, the poor Indians would have had less reason to complain that the English took away their land if they had received it by way of a portion with their daughters. Had such affinities been contracted in the beginning, how much bloodshed had been prevented and how populous would the country have been, and, consequently, how considerable! Nor would the shade of the skin have been any reproach at this day, for if a Moor may be washed white in three generations, surely an Indian might have been blanched in two.

The French, for their parts, have not been so squeamish in Canada, who upon trial find abundance of attraction in the Indians. Their late grand monarch thought it not below even the dignity of a Frenchman to become one flesh with this people and therefore ordered 100 livres[18] for any of his subjects, man or woman, that would intermarry with a native.

By this piece of policy we find the French interest very much strengthened amongst the savages and their religion, such as it is, propagated just as far as their love. And I heartily wish this well-concerted scheme don't hereafter give the French an advantage over His Majesty's good subjects on the northern continent of America.

About the same time New England was pared off from Virginia by letters patent bearing date April 10, 1608. Several gentlemen of the town and neighborhood of Plymouth obtained this grant, with the Lord Chief Justice Popham[19] at their head.

Their bounds were specified to extend from 38 to 45 degrees of northern latitude, with a breadth of one hundred miles from the seashore. The first fourteen years this company encountered many difficulties and lost many men, though, far from being discouraged, they sent over numerous recruits of Presbyterians every year, who for all that had much ado to stand their ground, with all their fighting and praying.

But about the year 1620 a large swarm of dissenters[20] fled thither from the severities of their stepmother, the church. These saints,[21] conceiving the same aversion to the copper complexion of the natives with that of the first adventurers

---

[17] Heathens.   [18] A French monetary denomination discontinued in the eighteenth century.
[19] Sir John Popham (1531?–1608?), an English magistrate.
[20] English Christians who renounced the rule of the Church of England.
[21] Those who followed the Puritan belief.

to Virginia, would on no terms contract alliances with them, afraid, perhaps, like the Jews of old, lest they might be drawn into idolatry by those strange women.

Whatever disgusted them I can't say, but this false delicacy, creating in the Indians a jealousy that the English were ill affected toward them, was the cause that many of them were cut off and the rest exposed to various distresses.

This reinforcement was landed not far from Cape Cod, where for their greater security they built a fort and near it a small town, which, in honor of the proprietors, was called New Plymouth. But they still had many discouragements to struggle with, though by being well supported from home they by degrees triumphed over them all.

Their brethren, after this, flocked over so fast that in a few years they extended the settlement one hundred miles along the coast, including Rhode Island and Martha's Vineyard.

Thus the colony throve apace and was thronged with large detachments of Independents and Presbyterians who thought themselves persecuted at home.

Though these people may be ridiculed for some pharisaical[22] particularities in their worship and behavior, yet they were very useful subjects, as being frugal and industrious, giving no scandal or bad example, at least by any open and public vices. By which excellent qualities they had much the advantage of the southern colony, who though their being members of the established church sufficient to sanctify very loose and profligate morals. For this reason New England improved much faster than Virginia, and in seven or eight years New Plymouth, like Switzerland, seemed too narrow a territory for its inhabitants.

* * *

[*March 10, 1728*]

10. The Sabbath happened very opportunely, to give some ease to our jaded people, who rested religiously from every work but that of cooking the kettle. We observed very few cornfields in our walks and those very small, which seemed the stranger to us because we could see no other tokens of husbandry or improvement. But upon further inquiry we were given to understand people only made corn for themselves and not for their stocks, which know very well how to get their own living. Both cattle and hogs ramble into the neighboring marshes and swamps, where they maintain themselves the whole winter long and are not fetched home till the spring. Thus these indolent wretches during one half of the year lose the advantage of the milk of their cattle, as well as their dung, and many of the poor creatures perish in the mire, into the bargain, by this ill management. Some who pique themselves more upon industry than their neighbors will now and then, in compliment to their cattle, cut down a tree whose limbs are loaded with the moss afore-mentioned. The trouble would be too great to climb the tree in order to gather this provender, but the shortest way (which in this country is always counted the best) is to fell it, just like the lazy Indians, who do the same by such trees as bear fruit and so make one harvest for all. By this bad husbandry milk is so scarce in the winter season that were a big-bellied woman to long for it she would tax her longing. And, in truth I believe this is often the case and at the same

---

[22] Hypocritical; after the Pharisees, an ancient Jewish sect that observed the written law but also accepted the oral, or traditional, law.

time a very good reason why so many people in this province are marked with a custard complexion.

The only business here is raising of hogs, which is managed with the least trouble and affords the diet they are most fond of. The truth of it is, the inhabitants of North Carolina devour so much swine's flesh that it fills them full of gross humors. For want, too, of a constant supply of salt, they are commonly obliged to eat it fresh, and that begets the highest taint of scurvy. Thus, whenever a severe cold happens to constitutions thus vitiated, 'tis apt to improve into the yaws,[23] called there very justly the country distemper. This has all the symptoms of the pox, with this aggravation, that no preparation of mercury will touch it. First it seizes the throat, next the palate, and lastly shows its spite to the poor nose, of which 'tis apt in a small time treacherously to undermine the foundation. This calamity is so common and familiar here that it ceases to be a scandal, and in the disputes that happen about beauty the noses have in some companies much ado to carry it. Nay, 'tis said that once, after three good pork years, a motion had like to have been made in the House of Burgesses that a man with a nose should be incapable of holding any place of profit in the province; which extraordinary motion could never have been intended without some hopes of a majority.

Thus, considering the foul and pernicious effects of eating swine's flesh in a hot country, it was wisely forbid and made an abomination to the Jews, who lived much in the same latitude with Carolina.

* * *

[March 25, 1728]

25. The air was chilled this morning with a smart Northwest wind, which favored the Dismalites[24] in their dirty march. They returned by the path they had made in coming out and with great industry arrived in the evening at the spot where the line had been discontinued. After so long and laborious a journey, they were glad to repose themselves on their couches of cypress bark, where their sleep was as sweet as it would have been on a bed of Finland down.

In the meantime, we who stayed behind had nothing to do but to make the best observations we could upon that part of the country. The soil of our landlord's plantation, though none of the best, seemed more fertile than any thereabouts, where the ground is near as sandy as the deserts of Africa and consequently barren. The road leading from thence to Edenton, being in distance about twenty-seven miles, lies upon a ridge called Sandy Ridge, which is so wretchedly poor that it will not bring potatoes. The pines in this part of the country are of a different species from those that grow in Virginia: their bearded leaves are much longer and their cones much larger. Each cell contains a seed of the size and figure of a black-eyed pea, which, shedding in November, is very good mast[25] for hogs and fattens them in a short time. The smallest of these pines are full of cones which are eight or nine inches long, and each affords commonly sixty or seventy seeds. This kind of mast has the advantage of all other by being more constant and less liable to be nipped by the frost or eaten by the caterpillars.

The trees also abound more with turpentine and consequently yield more tar than either the yellow or the white pine and for the same reason make more dura-

---

[23] A skin disease.   [24] Residents of the Dismal Swamp.   [25] Nuts used as feed for hogs.

ble timber for building. The inhabitants hereabouts pick up knots of lightwood in abundance, which they burn into tar and then carry it to Norfolk or Nansemond[26] for a market. The tar made in this method is less valuable because it is said to burn the cordage, though it is full as good for all other uses as that made in Sweden and Muscovy.[27]

Surely there is no place in the world where the inhabitants live with less labor than in North Carolina. It approaches nearer to the description of Lubberland[28] than any other, by the great felicity of the climate, the easiness of raising provisions, and the slothfulness of the people. Indian corn is of so great increase that a little pains will subsist a very large family with bread, and then they may have meat without any pains at all, by the help of the low grounds and the great variety of mast that grows on the high land. The men, for their parts, just like the Indians, impose all the work upon the poor women. They make their wives rise out of their beds early in the morning, at the same time that they lie and snore till the sun has risen one-third of his course and dispersed all the unwholesome damps.[29] Then, after stretching and yawning for half an hour, they light their pipes, and, under the protection of a cloud of smoke, venture out into the open air; though it if happen to be never so little cold they quickly return shivering into the chimney corner. When the weather is mild, they stand leaning with both their arms upon the cornfield fence and gravely consider whether they had best go and take a small heat at the hoe but generally find reasons to put it off till another time. Thus they loiter away their lives, like Solomon's sluggard,[30] with their arms across, and at the winding up of the year scarcely have bread to eat. To speak the truth, 'tis a thorough aversion to labor that makes people file off to North Carolina, where plenty and a warm sun confirm them in their disposition to laziness for their whole lives.

[*March 26, 1728*]

26. Since we were like to be confined to this place till the people returned out of the Dismal, 'twas agreed that our chaplain might safely take a turn to Edenton[31] to preach the Gospel to the infidels there and christen their children. He was accompanied thither by Mr. Little, one of the Carolina commissioners, who, to show his regard for the church, offered to treat him on the road with a fricassee of rum. They fried half a dozen rashers of very fat bacon in a pint of rum, both which being dished up together served the company at once both for meat and drink.

Most of the rum they get in this country comes from New England and is so bad and unwholesome that it is not improperly called "kill-devil." It is distilled there from foreign molasses, which, if skillfully managed, yields near gallon for gallon. Their molasses comes from the same country and has the name of "long sugar" in Carolina, I suppose from the ropiness of it, and serves all the purposes of sugar, both in their eating and drinking. When they entertain their friends bountifully, they fail not to set before them a capacious bowl of bombo, so called from the admiral of that name. This is a compound of rum and water in equal parts, made palatable with the said long sugar. As good humor begins to flow and

---

[26] A region in southeastern Virginia.   [27] Russia.
[28] From thirteenth-century fable, a land of riches and leisure.   [29] Dampness.
[30] In Proverbs 6:6–11 the wise King Solomon warns against laziness, using the ant as an example of industriousness.
[31] A commercial center and, unofficially, North Carolina's capital.

the bowl to ebb they take care to replenish it with sheer rum, of which there always is a reserve under the table.

But such generous doings happen only when that balsam of life is plenty; for they have often such melancholy times that neither landgraves nor caciques[32] can procure one drop for their wives when they lie in or are troubled with the colic or vapors. Very few in this country have the industry to plant orchards, which, in a dearth of rum, might supply them with much better liquor. The truth is, there is one inconvenience that easily discourages lazy people from making this improvement: very often, in autumn, when the apples begin to ripen, they are visited with numerous flights of parakeets,[33] that bite all the fruit to pieces in a moment for the sake of the kernels. The havoc they make is sometimes so great that whole orchards are laid waste, in spite of all the noises that can be made or mawkins[34] that can be dressed up to fright 'em away. These ravenous birds visit North Carolina only during the warm season and so soon as the cold begins to come on retire back toward the sun. They rarely venture so far north as Virginia, except in a very hot summer, when they visit the most southern parts of it. They are very beautiful but, like some other pretty creatures, are apt to be loud and mischievous.

[*March 27, 1728*]

27. Betwixt this [plantation] and Edenton there are many huckleberry slashes,[35] which afford a convenient harbor for wolves and foxes. The first of these wild beasts is not so large and fierce as they are in other countries more northerly. He will not attack a man in the keenest of his hunger but run away from him, as from an animal more mischievous than himself. The foxes are much bolder and will sometimes not only make a stand but likewise assault anyone that would balk them of their prey. The inhabitants hereabouts take the trouble to dig abundance of wolf pits, so deep and perpendicular that when a wolf is once tempted into them he can no more scramble out again than a husband who has taken the leap can scramble out of matrimony.

Most of the houses in this part of the country are log houses, covered with pine or cypress shingles, three feet long and one broad. They are hung upon lathes with pegs, and their doors, too, turn upon wooden hinges and have wooden locks to secure them, so that the building is finished without nails or other ironwork. They also set up their pales[36] without any nails at all, and, indeed, more securely than those that are nailed. There are three rails mortised[37] into the posts, the lowest of which serves as a sill, with a groove in the middle big enough to receive the end of the pales; the middle part of the pale rests against the inside of the next rail, and the top of it is brought forward to the outside of the uppermost. Such wreathing of the pales in and out makes them stand firm and much harder to unfix than when nailed in the ordinary way.

Within three or four miles of Edenton the soil appears to be a little more fertile, though it is much cut with slashes, which seem all to have a tendency toward the Dismal. This town is situated on the north side of Albemarle Sound, which is there about five miles over. A dirty slash runs all along the back of it, which in the summer is a foul annoyance and furnishes abundance of that Carolina plague,

---

[32] Princes nor Native-American chiefs.   [33] The Carolina parakeet, now extinct.   [34] Scarecrows.
[35] Swamps.   [36] Fenceposts.   [37] Fastened securely.

mosquitoes. There may be forty or fifty houses, most of them small and built without expense. A citizen here is counted extravagant if he has ambition enough to aspire to a brick chimney. Justice herself is but indifferently lodged, the court-house having much of the air of a common tobacco house. I believe this is the only metropolis in the Christian or Mahometan[38] world where there is neither church, chapel, mosque, synagogue, or any other place of public worship of any sect or religion whatsoever. What little devotion there may happen to be is much more private than their vices. The people seem easy without a minister as long as they are exempted from paying him. Sometimes the Society for Propagating the Gospel has had the charity to send over missionaries to this country; but, unfortunately, the priest has been too lewd for the people, or, which oftener happens, they too lewd for the priest. For these reasons these reverend gentlemen have always left their flocks as arrant heathen as they found them. Thus much, however, may be said for the inhabitants of Edenton, that not a soul has the least taint of hypocrisy or superstition, acting very frankly and aboveboard in all their exercises.

Provisions here are extremely cheap and extremely good, so that people may live plentifully at a trifling expense. Nothing is dear but law, physic,[39] and strong drink, which are all bad in their kind, and the last they get with so much difficulty that they are never guilty of the sin of suffering it to sour upon their hands. Their vanity generally lies not so much in having a handsome dining room as a hand-some house of office:[40] in this kind of structure they are really extravagant. They are rarely guilty of flattering or making any court to their governors but treat them with all the excesses of freedom and familarity. They are of opinion their rulers would be apt to grow insolent if they grew rich, and for that reason take care to keep them poorer and more dependent, if possible, than the saints in New England used to do their governors. They have very little coin, so they are forced to carry on their home traffic with paper money. This is the only cash that will tarry in the country, and for that reason the discount goes on increasing between that and real money and will do so to the end of the chapter.

* * *

[April 7, 1728]

7. The next day being Sunday, we ordered notice to be sent to all the neighbor-hood that there would be a sermon at this place an an opportunity of christening their children. But the likelihood of rain got the better of their devotion and, what perhaps might still be a stronger motive, of their curiosity. In the morning we dispatched a runner to the Nottoway[41] town to let the Indians know we intended them a visit that evening, and our honest landlord was so kind as to be our pilot thither, being about four miles from his house. Accordingly, in that afternoon we marched in good order to the town, where the female scouts, stationed on an eminence for that purpose, had no sooner spied us but they gave notice of our approach to their fellow citizens by continual whoops and cries, which could not possibly have been more dismal at the sight of their most implacable enemies. This signal assembled all their great men, who received us in a body and con-ducted us into the fort.

---

[38] Mohammedan.   [39] Medicine.   [40] A structure separate from the main house.
[41] A now-extinct Iroquoian people of southeastern Virginia (also "Nottaway").

This fort was a square piece of ground, enclosed with substantial puncheons or strong palisades[42] about ten feet high and leaning a little outwards to make a scalade[43] more difficult. Each side of the square might be about a hundred yards long, with loopholes at proper distances through which they may fire upon the enemy. Within this enclosure we found bark cabins sufficient to lodge all their people in case they should be obliged to retire thither. These cabins are no other but close arbors made of saplings, arched at the top and covered so well with bark as to be proof against all weather. The fire is made in the middle, according to the Hibernian[44] fashion, the smoke whereof finds no other vent but at the door and so keeps the whole family warm, at the expense both of their eyes and complexion. The Indians have no standing furniture in their cabins but hurdles[45] to repose their persons upon which they cover with mats or deerskins. We were conducted to the best apartments in the fort, which just before had been made ready for our reception and adorned with new mats that were very sweet and clean.

The young men had painted themselves in a hideous manner, not so much for ornament as terror. In that frightful equipage they entertained us with sundry war dances, wherein they endeavored to look as formidable as possible. The instrument they danced to was an Indian drum, that is, a large gourd with a skin braced taut over the mouth of it. The dancers all sang to this music keeping exact time with their feet while their head and arms were screwed into a thousand menacing postures.

Upon this occasion the ladies had arrayed themselves in all their finery. They were wrapped in their red and blue matchcoats,[46] thrown so negligently about them that their mahogany skins appeared in several parts, like the Lacedaemonian[47] damsels of old. Their hair was braided with white and blue peak and hung gracefully in a large roll upon their shoulders.

This peak consists of small cylinders cut out of a conch shell, drilled through and strung like beads. It serves them both for money and jewels, the blue being of much greater value than the white for the same reason that Ethiopian mistresses in France are dearer than French, because they are more scarce. The women wear necklaces and bracelets of these precious materials when they have a mind to appear lovely. Though their complexions be a little sad-colored, yet their shapes are very straight and well proportioned. Their faces are seldom handsome, yet they have an air of innocence and bashfulness that with a little less dirt would not fail to make them desirable. Such charms might have had their full effect upon men who had been so long deprived of female conversation but that the whole winter's soil was so crusted on the skins of those dark angels that it required a very strong appetite to approach them. The bear's oil with which they anoint their persons all over makes their skins soft and at the same time protects them from every species of vermin that use to be troublesome to other uncleanly people.

We were unluckily so many that they could not well make us the compliment of bedfellows according to the Indian rules of hospitality, though a grave matron whispered one of the commissioners very civilly in the ear that if her daughter had been but one year older she should have been at his devotion. It is by no means a loss of reputation among the Indians for damsels that are single to have intrigues with the men; on the contrary, they account it an argument of superior merit to be liked by a great number of gallants. However, like the ladies that game,[48] they are

---

[42] Wooden posts or stakes.   [43] Scaling of the walls.   [44] Irish or Celtic.
[45] Frames made of interlaced twigs.   [46] Loose wraps.   [47] Of ancient Sparta.
[48] Engage in prostitution.

a little mercenary in their amours and seldom bestow their favors out of stark love and kindness. But after these women have once appropriated their charms by marriage, they are from thenceforth faithful to their vows and will hardly ever be tempted by an agreeable gallant or be provoked by a brutal or even by a fumbling husband to go astray.

The little work that is done among the Indians is done by the poor women, while the men are quite idle or at most employed only in the gentlemanly diversions of hunting and fishing. In this, as well as in their wars, they now use nothing but firearms, which they purchase of the English for skins. Bows and arrows are grown into disuse, except only amongst their boys. Nor is it ill policy, but on the contrary very prudent, thus to furnish the Indians with firearms, because it makes them depend entirely upon the English, not only for their trade but even for their subsistence. Besides, they were really able to do more mischief while they made use of arrows, of which they would let silently fly several in a minute with wonderful dexterity, whereas now they hardly ever discharge their firelocks[49] more than once, which they insidiously do from behind a tree and then retire as nimbly as the Dutch horse used to do now and then formerly in Flanders.

We put the Indians to no expense but only of a little corn for our horses, for which in gratitude we cheered their hearts with what rum we had left, which they love better than they do their wives and children. Though these Indians dwell among the English and see in what plenty a little industry enables them to live, yet they choose to continue in their stupid idleness and to suffer all the inconveniences of dirt, cold, and want rather than disturb their heads with care or defile their hands with labor.

The whole number of people belonging to the Nottoway town, if you include women and children, amount to about two hundred. These are the only Indians of any consequence now remaining within the limits of Virginia. The rest are either removed or dwindled to a very inconsiderable number, either by destroying one another or else by the smallpox and other diseases. Though nothing has been so fatal to them as their ungovernable passion for rum, with which, I am sorry to say it, they have been but too liberally supplied by the English that live near them.

And here I must lament the bad success Mr. Boyle's[50] charity has hitherto had toward converting any of these poor heathens to Christianity. Many children of our neighboring Indians have been brought up in the College of William and Mary. They have been taught to read and write and been carefully instructed in the principles of the Christian religion till they came to be men. Yet after they returned home, instead of civilizing and converting the rest, they have immediately relapsed into infidelity and barbarism themselves.

And some of them, too, have made the worst use of the knowledge they acquired among the English by employing it against their benefactors. Besides, as they unhappily forget all the good they learn and remember the ill, they are apt to be more vicious and disorderly than the rest of their countrymen.

I ought not to quit this subject without doing justice to the great prudence of Colonel Spotswood[51] in this affair. That gentleman was Lieutenant Governor of

---

[49] An early type of musket.

[50] Robert Boyle (1627–1691), an English philosopher-scientist who bequeathed money to be used to spread Christianity among the "heathen"; some of the money went to the College of William and Mary for the education of Native Americans.

[51] Alexander Spotswood (1676–1740), Virginia's lieutenant governor from 1710 to 1722, who encouraged better relations with the Native Americans.

Virginia when Carolina was engaged in a bloody war with the Indians. At that critical time it was thought expedient to keep a watchful eye upon our tributary savages, who we knew had nothing to keep them to their duty but their fears. Then it was that he demanded of each nation a competent number of their great men's children to be sent to the College, where they served as so many hostages for the good behavior of the rest and at the same time were themselves principled in the Christian religion. He also placed a schoolmaster among the Saponi Indians, at the salary of 50 pounds per annum, to instruct their children. The person that undertook that charitable work was Mr. Charles Griffin, a man of a good family, who by the innocence of his life and the sweetness of his temper was perfectly well qualified for that pious undertaking. Besides, he had so much the secret of mixing pleasure with instruction that he had not a scholar who did not love him affectionately. Such talents must needs have been blessed with a proportionable success, had he not been unluckily removed to the College, by which he left the good work he had begun unfinished. In short, all the pains he had taken among the infidels had no other effect but to make them something cleanlier than other Indians are.

The care Colonel Spotswood took to tincture[52] the Indian children with Christianity produced the following epigram, which was not published during his administration for fear it might then have looked like flattery.

> Long has the furious priest assayed in vain,
> With sword and faggot, infidels to gain,
> But now the milder soldier wisely tries
> By gentler methods to unveil their eyes.
> Wonders apart, he knew 'twere vain t'engage
> The fixed preventions of misguided age.
> With fairer hopes he forms the Indian youth
> To early manners, probity, and truth.
> The lion's whelp thus, on the Libyan shore,
> Is tamed and gentled by the artful Moor,
> Not the grim sire, inured to blood before.

I am sorry I can't give a better account of the state of the poor Indians with respect to Christianity, although a great deal of pains has been and still continues to be taken with them. For my part, I must be of opinion, as I hinted before, that there is but one way of converting these poor infidels and reclaiming them from barbarity, and that is charitably to intermarry with them, according to the modern policy of the Most Christian King in Canada and Louisiana. Had the English done this at the first settlement of the colony, the infidelity of the Indians had been worn out at this day with their dark complexions, and the country had swarmed with people more than it does with insects. It was certainly an unreasonable nicety that prevented their entering into so good-natured an alliance. All nations of men have the same natural dignity, and we all know that very bright talents may be lodged under a very dark skin. The principal difference between one people and another proceeds only from the different opportunities of improvement. The Indians by no means want understanding and are in their figure tall and well proportioned. Even their copper-colored complexion would admit of blanching, if not in the first, at

---

[52] To permeate.

the farthest in the second, generation. I may safely venture to say, the Indian women would have made altogether as honest wives for the first planters as the damsels they used to purchase from aboard the ships. 'Tis strange, therefore, that any good Christian should have refused a wholesome, straight bedfellow, when he might have had so fair a portion with her as the merit of saving her soul.

* * *

[*October 1, 1728*]

1. There was a white frost this morning on the ground, occasioned by a northwest wind, which stood our friend in dispersing all aguish[53] damps and making the air wholesome at the same time that it made it cold. Encouraged, therefore, by the weather, our surveyors got to work early and, by the benefit of clear woods and level ground, drove the line twelve miles and twelve poles.[54]

At a small distance from our camp we crossed Great Creek and about seven miles farther Nutbush Creek, so called from the many hazel trees growing upon it. By good luck, many branches of these creeks were full of reeds, to the great comfort of our horses. Near five miles from thence we encamped on a branch that runs into Nutbush Creek, where those reeds flourished more than ordinary. The land we marched over was for the most part broken and stony and in some places covered over with thickets almost impenetrable.

At night the surveyors, taking advantage of a very clear sky, made a third trial of the variation and found it still something less than three degrees; so that it did not diminish by advancing toward the west or by approaching the mountains, nor yet by increasing our distance from the sea, but remained much the same we had found it at Currituck Inlet.

One of our Indians killed a large fawn, which was very welcome, though, like Hudibras' horse,[55] it had hardly flesh enough to cover its bones.

In the low grounds the Carolina gentlemen showed us another plant, which they said was used in their country to cure the bite of the rattlesnake. It put forth several leaves in figure like a heart and was clouded so like the common Asarabacca that I conceived it to be of that family.

[*October 2, 1728*]

2. So soon as the horses could be found, we hurried away the surveyors, who advanced the line 9 miles and 254 poles. About three miles from the camp they crossed a large creek, which the Indians called Massamony, signifying in their language "Paint Creek," because of the great quantity of red ocher found in its banks. This in every fresh tinges the water, just as the same mineral did formerly, and to this day continues to tinge, the famous river Adonis in Phoenicia,[56] by which there hangs a celebrated fable.

Three miles beyond that we passed another water with difficulty called

---

[53] Feverish.   [54] A measure equivalent to 5.5 yards.
[55] In Samuel Butler's parody *Hudibras* (1663–1678) a minister travels upon a starving horse.
[56] According to Greek myth, each spring this river becomes red with the blood of Adonis (the mortal love of the goddess Aphrodite), killed by a wild boar.

Yapatsco or Beaver Creek. Those industrious animals had dammed up the water so high that we had much ado to get over. 'Tis hardly credible how much work of this kind they will do in the space of one night. They bite young saplings into proper lengths with their foreteeth, which are exceeding strong and sharp, and afterwards drag them to the place where they intend to stop the water. Then they know how to join timber and earth together with so much skill that their work is able to resist the most violent flood that can happen. In this they are qualified to instruct their betters, it being certain their dams will stand firm when the strongest that are made by men will be carried down the stream. We observed very broad, low grounds upon this creek, with a growth of large trees and all the other signs of fertility, but seemed subject to be everywhere overflowed in a fresh.[57] The certain way to catch these sagacious animals is this: squeeze all the juice out of the large pride[58] of the beaver and six drops out of the small pride. Powder the inward bark of sassafras and mix it with this juice; then bait therewith a steel trap and they will eagerly come to it and be taken.

About three miles and a half farther we came to the banks of another creek, called in the Saponi language Ohimpamony, signifying "Jumping Creek," from the frequent jumping of fish during the spring season.

Here we encamped, and by the time the horses were hobbled our hunters brought us no less than a brace[59] and a half of deer, which made great plenty and consequently great content in our quarters. Some of our people had shot a great wildcat, which was that fatal moment making a comfortable meal upon a fox squirrel, and an ambitious sportsman of our company claimed the merit of killing this monster after it was dead. The wildcat is as big again as any household cat and much the fiercest inhabitant of the woods. Whenever it is disabled, it will tear its own flesh for madness. Although a panther will run away from a man, a wild-cat will only make a surly retreat, now and then facing about if he be too closely pursued, and will even pursue in his turn if he observe the least sign of fear or even of caution in those that pretend to follow him. The flesh of this beast, as well as of the panther, is as white as veal and altogether as sweet and delicious.

[*October 3, 1728*]

3. We got to work early this morning and carried the line 8 miles and 160 poles. We forded several runs of excellent water and afterwards traversed a large level of high land, full of lofty walnut, poplar, and white oak trees, which are certain proofs of a fruitful soil. This level was near two miles in length and of an unknown breadth, quite out of danger of being overflowed, which is a misfortune most of the low grounds are liable to in those parts. As we marched along, we saw many buffalo tracks and abundance of their dung very fresh but could not have the pleasure of seeing them. They either smelt us out, having that sense very quick,[60] or else were alarmed at the noise that so many people must necessarily make in marching along. At the sight of a man they will snort and grunt, cock up their ridiculous short tails, and tear up the ground with a sort of timorous fury. These wild cattle hardly ever range alone but herd together like those that are tame. They are seldom seen so far north as forty degrees of latitude, delighting much in canes and reeds which grow generally more southerly.

---

[57] A stream of fresh water.   [58] Testis.   [59] A pair.   [60] Keenly.

We quartered on the banks of a creek that the inhabitants call Tewahominy or Tuskarooda Creek,[61] because one of that nation had been killed thereabouts and his body thrown into the creek.

Our people had the fortune to kill a brace of does, one of which we presented to the Carolina gentlemen, who were glad to partake of the bounty of Providence at the same time that they sneered at us for depending upon it.

[*October 4, 1728*]

4. We hurried away the surveyors about nine this morning, who extended the line 7 miles and 160 poles, notwithstanding the ground was exceedingly uneven. At the distance of five miles we forded a stream to which we gave the name of Bluewing Creek because of the great number of those fowls[62] that then frequented it. About two and a half miles beyond that, we came upon Sugartree Creek, so called from the many trees of that kind[63] that grow upon it. By tapping this tree in the first warm weather in February, one may get from twenty to forty gallons of liquor, very sweet to the taste and agreeable to the stomach. This may be boiled into molasses first and afterward into very good sugar, allowing about ten gallons of liquor to make a pound. There is no doubt, too, that a very fine spirit may be distilled from the molasses, at least as good as rum. The sugar tree delights only in rich ground, where it grows very tall, and by the softness and sponginess of the wood should be a quick grower. Near this creek we discovered likewise several spice trees, the leaves of which are fragrant and the berries they bear are black when dry and of a hot taste, not much unlike pepper. The low grounds upon the creek are very wide, sometimes on one side, sometimes on the other, though most commonly upon the opposite shore the high land advances close to the bank, only on the north side of the line it spreads itself into a great breadth of rich low ground on both sides the creek for four miles together, as far as this stream runs into Hyco River, whereof I shall presently make mention. One of our men spied three buffaloes, but his piece being loaded only with goose shot, he was able to make no effectual impression on their thick hides; however, this disappointment was made up by a brace of bucks and as many wild turkeys killed by the rest of the company. Thus Providence was very bountiful to our endeavors, never disappointing those that faithfully rely upon it and pray heartily for their daily bread.

[*October 5, 1728*]

5. This day we met with such uneven grounds and thick underwoods that with all our industry we were able to advance the line but 4 miles and 312 poles. In this small distance it intersected a large stream four times, which our Indian at first mistook for the south branch of Roanoke River; but, discovering his error soon after, he assured us 'twas a river called Hycootomony, or Turkey Buzzard River, from the great number of those unsavory birds that roost on the tall trees growing near its banks.

Early in the afternoon, to our very great surprise, the commissioners of Carolina acquainted us with their resolution to return home. This declaration of theirs seemed the more abrupt because they had not been so kind as to prepare us by the

---

[61] Now Tuscarora Creek.   [62] The bluewinged teal.   [63] Sugar maples.

least hint of their intention to desert us. We therefore let them understand they appeared to us to abandon the business they came about with too much precipitation, this being but the fifteenth day since we came out the last time. But although we were to be so unhappy as to lose the assistance of their great abilities, yet we, who were concerned for Virginia, determined, by the grace of God, not to do our work by halves but, all deserted as we were like to be, should think it our duty to push the line quite to the mountains; and if their government should refuse to be bound by so much of the line as was run without their commissioners, yet at least it would bind Virginia and stand as a direction how far His Majesty's lands extend to the southward. In short, these gentlemen were positive, and the most we could agree upon was to subscribe plats[64] of our work as far as we had acted together; though at the same time we insisted these plats should be got ready by Monday noon at farthest, when we on the part of Virginia intended, if we were alive, to move forward without farther loss of time, the season being then too far advanced to admit of any unnecessary or complaisant delays.

[October 6, 1728]

6. We lay still this day, being Sunday, on the bank of Hyco River and had only prayers, our chaplain not having spirits enough to preach. The gentlemen of Carolina assisted not at our public devotions, because they were taken up all the morning in making a formidable protest against our proceeding on the line without them. When the divine service was over, the surveyors set about making the plats of so much of the line as we had run this last campaign. Our pious friends of Carolina assisted in this work with some seeming scruple, pretending it was a violation of the Sabbath, which we were the more surprised at because it happened to be the first qualm of conscience they had ever been troubled with during the whole journey. They had made no bones of staying from prayers to hammer out an unnecessary protest, though divine service was no sooner over but an unusual fit of godliness made them fancy that finishing the plats, which was now matter of necessity, was a profanation of the day. However, the expediency of losing no time, for us who thought it our duty to finish what we had undertaken, made such a labor pardonable.

In the afternoon, Mr. Fitzwilliam, one of the commissioners for Virginia, acquainted his colleagues it was his opinion that by His Majesty's order they could not proceed farther on the line but in conjunction with the commissioners of Carolina; for which reason he intended to retire the next morning with those gentlemen. This looked a little odd in our brother commissioner; though, in justice to him as well as to our Carolina friends, they stuck by us as long as our good liquor lasted and were so kind to us as to drink our good journey to the mountains in the last bottle we had left.

[October 7, 1728]

7. The duplicates of the plats could not be drawn fair this day before noon, where they were countersigned by the commissioners of each government. Then those of Carolina delivered their protest, which was by this time licked into form

---

[64] Maps.

and signed by them all. And we have been so just to them as to set it down at full length in the Appendix, that their reasons for leaving us may appear in their full strength. After having thus adjusted all our affairs with the Carolina commissioners and kindly supplied them with bread to carry them back, which they hardly deserved at our hands, we took leave both of them and our colleague, Mr. Fitzwilliam. This gentleman had still a stronger reason for hurrying him back to Williamsburg, which was that neither the General Court might lose an able judge nor himself a double salary, not despairing in the least but he should have the whole pay of commissioner into the bargain, though he did not half the work. This, to be sure, was relying more on the interest of his friends than on the justice of his cause; in which, however, he had the misfortune to miscarry when it came to be fairly considered.

It was two o'clock in the afternoon before these arduous affairs could be dispatched, and then, all forsaken as we were, we held on our course toward the west. But it was our misfortune to meet with so many thickets in this afternoon's work that we could advance no further than 2 miles and 260 poles. In this small distance we crossed the Hyco the fifth time and quartered near Buffalo Creek, so named from the frequent tokens we discovered of that American behemoth. Here the bushes were so intolerably thick that we were obliged to cover the bread bags with our deerskins, otherwise the joke of one of the Indians must have happened to us in good earnest: that in a few days we must cut up our house to make bags for the bread and so be forced to expose our backs in compliment to our bellies. We computed we had then biscuit enough left to last us, with good management, seven weeks longer; and this being our chief dependence, it imported us to be very careful both in the carriage and the distribution of it.

We had now no other drink but what Adam drank in Paradise, though to our comfort we found the water excellent, by the help of which we perceived our appetites to mend, our slumbers to sweeten, the stream of life to run cool and peaceably in our veins, and if ever we dreamt of women, they were kind.

Our men killed a very fat buck and several turkeys. These two kinds of meat boiled together, with the addition of a little rice or French barley, made excellent soup, and, what happens rarely in other good things, it never cloyed, no more than an engaging wife would do, by being a constant dish. Our Indian was very superstitious in this matter and told us, with a face full of concern, that if we continued to boil venison and turkey together we should for the future kill nothing, because the spirit that presided over the woods would drive all the game out of our sight. But we had the happiness to find this an idle superstition, and though his argument could not convince us, yet our repeated experience at last, with much ado, convinced him.

We observed abundance of coltsfoot and maidenhair in many places and nowhere a larger quantity than here. They are both excellent pectoral plants[65] and seem to have greater virtues much in this part of the world than in more northern climates; and I believe it may pass for a rule in botanics that where any vegetable is planted by the hand of Nature it had more virtue than in places whereto it is transplanted by the curiosity of man.

* * *

[65] Plants useful in curing diseases of the chest.

[*October 12, 1728*]

12. We were so cruelly entangled with bushes and grapevines all day that we could advance the line no farther than five miles and twenty-eight poles. The vines grew very thick in these woods, twining lovingly round the trees almost everywhere, especially to the saplings. This makes it evident how natural both the soil and climate of this country are to vines, though I believe most to our own vines. The grapes we commonly met with were black, though there be two or three kinds of white grapes that grow wild. The black are very sweet but small, because the strength of the vine spends itself in wood, though without question a proper culture would make the same grapes both larger and sweeter. But, with all these disadvantages, I have drunk tolerable good wine pressed from them, though made without skill. There is then good reason to believe it might admit of great improvement if rightly managed.[66]

Our Indian killed a bear, two years old, that was feasting on these grapes. He was very fat, as they generally are in that season of the year. In the fall the flesh of this animal has a high relish different from that of other creatures, though inclining nearest to that of pork, or rather of wild boar. A true woodsman prefers this sort of meat to that of the fattest venison, not only for the *haut goût*,[67] but also because the fat of it is well tasted and never rises in the stomach. Another proof of the goodness of this meat is that it is less apt to corrupt than any other we are acquainted with.

As agreeable as such rich diet was to the men, yet we who were not accustomed to it tasted it at first with some sort of squeamishness, that animal being of the dog kind, though a little use soon reconciled us to this American venison. And that its being of the dog kind might give us the less disgust, we had the example of that ancient and polite people, the Chinese, who reckon dog's flesh too good for any under the quality of a mandarin.[68] This beast is in truth a very clean feeder, living, while the season lasts, upon acorns, chestnuts, and chinquapins,[69] wild honey and wild grapes. They are naturally not carnivorous, unless hunger constrain them to it after the mast is all gone and the product of the woods quite exhausted. They are not provident enough to lay up any hoard like squirrels, nor can they, after all, live very long upon licking their paws, as Sir John Mandeville[70] and some travelers tell us, but are forced in the winter months to quit the mountains and visit the inhabitants. Their errand is then to surprise a poor hog at a pinch to keep them from starving. And to show that they are not flesh eaters by trade, they devour their prey very awkwardly. They don't kill it right out and feast upon its blood and entrails, like other ravenous beasts, but, having, after a fair pursuit, seized it with their paws, they begin first upon the rump and so devour one collop[71] after another till they come to the vitals, the poor animal crying all the while for several minutes together. However, in so doing, Bruin[72] acts a little imprudently, because the dismal outcry of the hog alarms the neighborhood, and 'tis odds but he pays the forfeit with his life before he can secure his retreat.

But bears soon grow weary of this unnatural diet, and about January, when

---

[66] Many colonists, including Byrd, attempted to establish vineyards in America.
[67] Gamy taste (French).   [68] A high-ranking Chinese official.
[69] The edible nut of members of the beech family.
[70] Mandeville (?–1372) was the compiler of French travel book's published between 1357 and 1371.
[71] A fold of fatty flesh.   [72] The bear in the medieval epic *Reynard the Fox*.

there is nothing to be gotten in the woods, they retire into some cave or hollow tree, where they sleep away two or three months very comfortably. But then they quit their holes in March, when the fish begin to run up the rivers, on which they are forced to keep Lent[73] till some fruit or berry comes in season. But bears are fondest of chestnuts, which grow plentifully toward the mountains, upon very large trees, where the soil happens to be rich. We were curious to know how it happened that many of the outward branches of those trees came to be broke off in that solitary place and were informed that the bears are so discreet as not to trust their unwieldy bodies on the smaller limbs of the tree that would not bear their weight, but after venturing as far as is safe, which they can judge to an inch, they bite off the end of the branch, which falling down, they are content to finish their repast upon the ground. In the same cautious manner they secure the acorns that grow on the weaker limbs of the oak. And it must be allowed that in these instances a bear carries instinct a great way and acts more reasonably than many of his betters, who indiscreetly venture upon frail projects that won't bear them.

[*October 13, 1728*]

13. This being Sunday we rested from our fatigue and had leisure to reflect on the signal mercies of Providence.

The great plenty of meat wherewith Bearskin[74] furnished us in these lonely woods made us once more shorten the men's allowance of bread from five to four pounds of biscuit a week. This was the more necessary because we knew not yet how long our business might require us to be out.

In the afternoon our hunters went forth and returned triumphantly with three brace of wild turkeys. They told us they could see the mountains distinctly from every eminence, though the atmosphere was so thick with smoke that they appeared at a greater distance than they really were.

In the evening we examined our friend Bearskin concerning the religion of his country, and he explained it to us without any of that reserve to which his nation is subject. He told us he believed there was one supreme god, who had several subaltern deities under him. And that this master god made the world a long time ago. That he told the sun, the moon, and stars their business in the beginning, which they, with good looking-after, have faithfully performed ever since. That the same power that made all things at first has taken care to keep them in the same method and motion ever since. He believed that God had formed many worlds before he formed this, but that those worlds either grew old and ruinous or were destroyed for the dishonesty of the inhabitants. That God is very just and very good, ever well pleased with those men who possess those godlike qualities. That he takes good people into his safe protection, makes them very rich, fills their bellies plentifully, preserves them from sickness and from being surprised or overcome by their enemies. But all such as tell lies and cheat those they have dealings with he

---

[73] To Christians, a time of penitence, in which meat is not eaten (making fish a larger part of the diet).

[74] An Indian guide who was helping them hunt.

never fails to punish with sickness, poverty, and hunger and, after all that, suffers them to be knocked on the head and scalped by those that fight against them.

He believed that after death both good and bad people are conducted by a strong guard into a great road, in which departed souls travel together for some time till at a certain distance this road forks into two paths, the one extremely level and the other stony and mountainous. Here the good are parted from the bad by a flash of lightning, the first being hurried away to the right, the other to the left. The right-hand road leads to a charming, warm country, where the spring is everlasting and every month is May; and as the year is always in its youth, so are the people, and particularly the women are bright as stars and never scold. That in this happy climate there are deer, turkeys, elks, and buffaloes innumerable, perpetually fat and gentle, while the trees are loaded with delicious fruit quite throughout the four seasons. That the soil brings forth corn spontaneously, without the curse of labor, and so very wholesome that none who have the happiness to eat of it are ever sick, grow old, or die. Near the entrance into this blessed land sits a venerable old man on a mat richly woven, who examines strictly all that are brought before him, and if they have behaved well, the guards are ordered to open the crystal gate and let them enter into the land of delight. The left-hand path is very rugged and uneven, leading to a dark and barren country where it is always winter. The ground is the whole year round covered with snow, and nothing is to be seen upon the trees but icicles. All the people are hungry yet have not a morsel of anything to eat except a bitter kind of potato, that gives them the dry gripes[75] and fills their whole body with loathsome ulcers that stink and are insupportably painful. Here all the women are old and ugly, having claws like a panther with which they fly upon the men that slight their passion. For it seems these haggard old furies are intolerably fond and expect a vast deal of cherishing. They talk much and exceedingly shrill, giving exquisite pain to the drum of the ear, which in that place of the torment is so tender that every sharp note wounds it to the quick. At the end of this path sits a dreadful old woman on a monstrous toadstool, whose head is covered with rattlesnakes instead of tresses, with glaring white eyes that strike a terror unspeakable into all that behold her. This hag pronounces sentence of woe upon all the miserable wretches that hold up their hands at her tribunal. After this they are delivered over to huge turkey buzzards, like harpies, that fly away with them to the place above-mentioned. Here, after they have been tormented a certain number of years according to their several degrees of guilt, they are again driven back into this world to try if they will mend their manners and merit a place the next time in the regions of bliss.

This was the substance of Bearskin's religion and was as much to the purpose as could be expected from a mere state of nature, without one glimpse of revelation or philosophy. It contained, however, the three great articles of natural religion: the belief of a god, the moral distinction betwixt good and evil, and the expectation of rewards and punishments in another world. Indeed, the Indian notion of a future happiness is a little gross and sensual, like Mahomet's Paradise. But how can it be otherwise in a people that are contented with Nature as they find her and have no other lights but what they receive from purblind tradition?

1728, 1841

---

[75] Vomiting.

Ebenezer Cook
(1667?–1733?)

Not everyone who described early America did so with relish. In his most famous work, *The Sot-Weed Factor* (1708), Ebenezer Cook (also spelled Cooke) satirically portrays the difficulties of life in colonial Maryland. However, Cook is not specifically a detractor of early-American society but uses the inability of an English emigrant to adapt to the colonial frontier in order to satirize the European image of America.

Little information about Cook's life exists except for a few scattered legal records. He was born in London around 1667 to Anne Bowyer and Andrew Cooke. Cook's signature on a 1694 petition against changing the capital of Maryland from St. Marys City to Annapolis indicates that he spent time in the colony long before the 1708 London publication of *The Sot-Weed Factor*, his first poem. Cook's father was an absentee landlord who owned a plantation in Maryland, and Cook was in America most likely to keep an eye on his father's estate. Inheriting the land in 1711, Cook probably traveled back and forth between England and America throughout his life. His last literary work, an elegy commemorating Benedict Leonard Calvert, was written in 1732; Cook is believed to have died a short time afterward.

Many critics read *The Sot-Weed Factor* as an autobiographical poem recounting Cook's own trials in Maryland. However, Cook's literary achievement in *The Sot-Weed Factor* was to create a narrative persona that is both realistic and burlesque to satirize the English narrator and the America he encounters. The story is told by a "sot-weed factor," that is, an agent (a factor), sent to trade in tobacco (sot-weed, the weed that causes intoxication). The factor has come to America to earn quickly as much money as possible because, like many colonists, he has left Europe impoverished. After a series of misadventure—encounters with a wild and corrupt frontier society—he returns to England less well off than when he left. Cook's Hudibrastic (burlesque) verse, modeled on Samuel Butler's mock-heroic poem *Hudibras* (1663–1678), uses the burlesque not only to exaggerate the difficulty of frontier life but to satirize through hyperbole the beliefs Europeans had of the Edenic New World portrayed in promotional tracts.

Cook, the "Poet Laureate of Maryland," wrote no other work as successful as *The Sot-Weed Factor*. Aside from a Hudibrastic poem, "The History of Colonel Nathaniel Bacon's Rebellion in Virginia" (1731), about the 1676 violent social-reform movement, and a few miscellaneous verses, Cook's only other published work is *Sotweed Redivivus* (1730), a sequel to his first poem. The later portrait of the Maryland colony depicts the land after settlement as poor and mismanaged. More serious and didactic than the original, *Sotweed Redivivus* deals with the overproduction of tobacco; it has not been widely read. Nevertheless, Cook has been immortalized in twentieth-century American literature as the central character in the novelist John Barth's satire *The Sot-weed Factor* (1960). A fictional biography of Cook, Barth's novel captures the compelling nature of the tension between the desire for economic gain and the detestation of wilderness culture portrayed in Cook's poem.

Suggested Readings: *Sotweed Redivivus: Or, the Planters Looking-Glass,* 1730. J. A. L. Lemay, *Men of Letters in Colonial Maryland,* 1972. E. H. Cohen, *Ebenezer Cooke: The Sot-Weed Canon,* 1975. R. D. Arner, "The Blackness of Darkness: Satire, Romance, and Ebenezer Cooke's *The Sot-Weed Factor,*" in *Tennessee Studies in Literature,* 1976, 21:1–10. R. Micklus, "The Case Against Ebenezer Cooke's *Sot-Weed Factor,*" in *American Literature,* 56:251–261, 1984.

Text Used: *The Sot-Weed Factor: Or, a Voyage to Maryland*, 1708, in *Shea's Early Southern Tracts*, No. II, 1865 (some spelling and punctuation modernized).

from   THE SOT-WEED FACTOR*

Condemned by fate, to wayward curse,
Of friends unkind, and empty purse,
Plagues worse than filled Pandora's box,[1]
I took my leave of Albion's rocks,[2]
With heavy heart, concerned that I
Was forced my native soil to fly,
And the old world must bid good-bye:
But Heaven ordained it should be so,
And to repine is vain, we know.
Freighted with fools, from Plymouth sound,   10
To Maryland our ship was bound;
Where we arrived, in dreadful pain,
Shocked by the terrors of the main;[3]
For full three months our wavering boat
Did through the surly ocean float,
And furious storms and threatening blasts,
Both tore our sails, and sprung our masts:
Wearied, yet pleased we did escape
Such ills, we anchored at the Cape;[4]
But weighing[5] soon, we plowed the Bay,   20
To cove it in Piscataway.[6]
Intending there to open store,
I put myself and goods ashore,
Where soon repaired a numerous crew
In shirts and drawers of Scotch-cloth blue[7]
With neither stockings, hat, nor shoe.
These sot-weed planters crowd the shore,
In hue as tawny as a Moor:
Figures so strange, no God designed
To be a part of humankind,   30
But wanton nature, void of rest,
Molded the brittle clay in jest.
At last, a fancy very odd
Took me, this was the Land of Nod,[8]

---

* The tobacco merchant.

[1] According to Greek myth, Pandora, the first woman, opened a box containing evils, which were let out and have plagued the human race.

[2] England.   [3] The high seas.

[4] Cook's note: "By the Cape is meant the Capes of Virginea, the first land on the coast of Virginia and Mary-Land."

[5] Cook's note: "To cove is to lie at anchor safe in harbor."

[6] Cook's note: "The Bay of Piscato-way, the usual place where our ships come to anchor in Mary-Land."

[7] Cook's note: "The planters generally wear blue linen."

[8] In Genesis 4:16 the country to which Cain fled after slaying his brother, Abel.

Planted at first when vagrant Cain
His brother had unjustly slain;
Then, conscious of the crime he'd done,
From vengeance dire, he hither run,
And in a hut supinely dwelt,
The first in furs and sot-weed dealt.   40
And ever since his time, the place
Has harbored a detested race,
Who, when they could not thrive at home,
For refuge to these worlds did roam,
In hopes by flight they might prevent
The Devil, and his fell intent;
Obtain from triple tree[9] reprieve,
And Heaven and Hell alike deceive:
But e're their manners I display,⎫
I think it fit I open lay   ⎬   50
My entertainment by the way: ⎭
That strangers well may be aware on
What homely diet they must fare on,
To touch that shore where no good sense is found,
But conversation's lost, and manners drowned.
I crossed unto the other side   ⎫
A river, whose impetuous tide   ⎬
The savage borders does divide; ⎭
In such a shining odd invention,
I scarce can give its due dimension.   60
The Indians call this watery wagon,
Canoe,[10] a vessel none can brag on;
Cut from a poplar tree, or pine,
And fashioned like a trough for swine:
In this most noble fishing-boat,
I boldly put myself afloat,
Standing erect, with legs stretched wide,
We paddled to the other side:
Where being landed safe by hap,
As Sol fell into Thetis' Lap.[11]   70
A ravenous gang, bent on the stroll,
Of wolves[12] for prey, began to howl;
This put me in a panic fright,
Lest I should be devoured quite:
But as I there a-musing stood
And quite benighted in a wood,
A female voice pierced through my ears,
Crying, "You rogue, drive home the steers."
I listened to th'attractive sound,   ⎫
And straight a herd of cattle found,   ⎬   80
Drove by a youth, and homeward bound;   ⎭
Cheered with the sight, I straight thought fit

[9] The gallows.
[10] Cook's note: "A canoo is an Indian boat, cut out of the body of a popular-tree."
[11] Sunset; according to myth, the Roman sun god Sol fell into the lap of the Greek sea nymph, Thetis, every evening.
[12] Cook's note: "Wolves are very numerous in Mary-Land."

To ask where I a bed might get.
The surly peasant bid me stay,
And asked from whom I'd run away.[13]
Surprised at such a saucy word,
I instantly lugged out my sword,
Swearing I was no fugitive,
But from Great Britain did arrive,
In hopes I better there might thrive.   90
To which he mildly made reply,
"I beg your pardon, Sir, that I
Should talk to you unmannerly;
But if you please to go with me
To yonder house, you'll welcome be."
Encountering soon the smoky seat,
The planter old did thus me greet:
"Whether you come from jail or college,
You're welcome, to my certain knowledge,
And if you please all night to stay,   100
My son shall put you in the way."
Which offer I most kindly took,
And for a seat did round me look;
When presently among the rest,
He placed his unknown English guest,
Who found them drinking, for a whet,[14]
A cask of cider[15] on the fret,[16]
'Til supper came upon the table,
On which I fed whilst I was able.
So after hearty entertainment,   110
Of drink and victuals, without payment;
For planters' tables, you must know,
Are free for all that come and go.
While pone[17] and milk, with mush[18] well stored,
In wooden dishes graced the board;
With hominy[19] and cider-pap,
(Which scarce a hungry dog would lap)
Well stuffed with fat from bacon fried,
Or with molasses dulcified.[20]
Then out our landlord pulls his pouch,   120
As greasy as the leather couch
On which he sat, and straight begun
To load with weed his Indian gun,[21]
In length, scarce longer than one's finger.
His pipe smoked out, with awful grace,
With aspect grave and solemn pace;

---

[13] Cook's note: " 'Tis supposed by the planters that all unknown persons run away from some master."

[14] An appetizer.

[15] Cook's note: "Syder-pap is a sort of food made of syder and small homine, like our oatmeal."

[16] Fermented.   [17] "Pon is bread made of Indian-Corn."

[18] Cook's note: "Mush is a sort of hasty-pudding made with water and Indian flower."

[19] Cook's note: "Homine is a dish that is made of boiled Indian wheat, eaten with molossus, or bacon-fat."

[20] Sweetened.   [21] Pipe.

The reverend Sire walks to a chest,
Of all his furniture the best,
Closely confined within a room,
Which seldom felt the weight of broom;   130
From thence he lugs a keg of rum,
And nodding to me, thus begun:
"I find," says he, "you don't much care
For this our Indian country fare;
But let me tell you, friend of mine,
You may be glad of it in time,
Though now your stomach is so fine;
And if within this land you stay,
You'll find it true what I do say."
This said, the rundlet[22] up he threw,   140
And bending backwards strongly drew;
I plucked as stoutly, for my part,
Although it made me sick at heart,
And got so soon into my head,
I scarce could find my way to bed;
Where I was instantly conveyed,
By one who passed for chambermaid,
Though by her loose and sluttish dress,
She rather seemed a Bedlam Bess.[23]
Curious to know from whence she came,   150
I pressed her to declare her name.
She blushing, seemed to hide her eyes,
And thus in civil terms replies:
"In better times, ere to this land
I was unhappily trepanned,[24]
Perchance as well I did appear,
As any lord or lady here,
Not then a slave for twice two year.[25]
My clothes were fashionably new,
Nor were my shifts of linen blue;   160
But things are changed: now at the hoe
I daily work, and barefoot go;
In weeding corn or feeding swine
I spend my melancholy time.
Kidnapped and fooled, I hither fled,
To shun a hated nuptial bed,[26]
And to my cost already find
Worse plagues than those I left behind."
Whate'er the wanderer did profess,
Good faith, I could not choose but guess   170
The cause which brought her to this place[27]
Was supping e'er the priest said Grace.

[22] A small keg.

[23] A servant in Bedlam, an infamous London insane asylum.   [24] Ensnared.

[25] Cook's note: "'Tis the custom for servants to be obliged for four years to very servile work; after which time they have their freedom."

[26] Cook's note: "These are the general excuses made by English women, which are sold, or sell themselves to Mary-Land."

[27] Which made her pregnant.

Quick as my thoughts, the slave was fled,
(Her candle left to show my bed)
Which, made of feathers soft and good,
Close in the chimney-corner stood;[28]
I threw me down, expecting rest,
To be in golden slumbers blessed,
But soon a noise disturbed my quiet,
And plagued me with nocturnal riot;   180
A puss,[29] which in the ashes lay,
With grunting pig began a fray;
And prudent dog, that feuds might cease,
Most strongly barked to keep the peace.
This quarrel scarcely was decided
By stick that ready lay provided;
But Reynard,[30] arch and cunning loon,
Broke into my apartment soon,
In hot pursuit of ducks and geese,
With fell intent the same to seize.   190
Their cackling 'plaints with strange surprise
Chased sleep's thick vapors from my eyes;
Raging, I jumped upon the floor,
And like a drunken sailor swore;
With sword I fiercely laid about,
And soon dispersed the feathered rout.
The poultry out of window flew,
And Reynard cautiously withdrew;
The dogs who this encounter heard,
Fiercely themselves to aid me reared,   200
And to the place of combat run,
Exactly as the field was won.
Fretting and hot as roasting capon,
And greasy as a flitch[31] of bacon,
I to the orchard did repair,
To breathe the cool and open air;
Expecting there the rising day,
Extended on a bank I lay;
But fortune here, that saucy whore,
Disturbed me worse, and plagued me more }   210
Than she had done the night before:
Hoarse croaking frogs[32] did 'bout me ring, }
Such peals the dead to life would bring,
A noise might move their wooden king.[33]
I stuffed my ears with cotton white,
For fear of being deaf outright,
And cursed the melancholy night;
But soon my vows I did recant,
And hearing as a blessing grant,

[28] Cook's note: "Beds stand in the chimney-corner in this country."   [29] A cat.
[30] The fox in the medieval epic *Reynara the Fox*.   [31] A side.
[32] Cook's note: "Frogs are called Virginea Bells and make (both in that country and Mary-Land) during the night, a very hoarse ungrateful noise."
[33] In Isaiah 45:20, a wooden idol.

When a confounded rattlesnake   220
With hissing made my heart to ache.
Not knowing how to fly the foe,
Or whither in the dark to go,
By strange good luck, I took a tree,
Prepared by fate to set me free;
Where, riding on a limb astride,
Night and the branches did me hide,
And I the Devil and snake defied.
Not yet from plagues exempted quite,
The cursed mosquitoes did me bite;   230
'Til rising morn and blushing day
Drove both my fears and ills away;
And from night's [t]errors set me free.
Discharged from hospitable tree,
I did to planter's booth repair,[34]
And there at breakfast nobly fare,
On rasher[35] broiled, of infant bear:
I thought the cub delicious meat,
Which ne'er did ought but chestnuts eat;
Nor was young Orson's[36] flesh the worse   240
Because he sucked a pagan nurse.
Our breakfast done, my landlord stout
Handed a glass of rum about;
Pleased with the treatment I did find,
I took my leave of host so kind,
Who, to oblige me, did provide
His eldest son to be my guide,
And lent me horses of his own,
A skittish colt, and aged roan,
The four-legged prop of his wife Joan: 250
Steering our barks in trot or pace,
We sailed directly for a place,
In Maryland, of high renown,
Known by the Name of Battletown:
To view the crowds did there resort,
Which justice made, and law, their sport,
In their sagacious county court:
Scarce had we entered on the way,
Which through the woods and marshes lay,
But Indian strange did soon appear,   260
In hot pursuit of wounded deer;
No mortal creature can express
His wild fantastic air and dress;
His painted skin, in colors dyed,
His sable hair, in satchel tied,
Showed savages not free from pride;
His tawny thighs, and bosom bare,
Disdained a useless coat to wear,
Scorned summer's heat and winter's air;

[34] A small room.   [35] A portion.
[36] In the French tale *Valentine and Orson*, Orson, an abandoned child, is nursed by a bear.

His manly shoulders, such as please   270
Widows and wives, were bathed in grease
Of cub and bear, whose supple oil,
Prepared his limbs in heat or toil. . . .

1708

=CONTEXTS=

The First Great Awakening

Beginning in the 1730s a series of religious revivals swept the American colonies. In New England the movement was led by Jonathan Edwards, who was both delighted and deeply troubled by the explosion of religious feeling. Because the revivals came at a time when religious devotion had been on the wane, the "Great Awakening," as they were called, seemed a blessing; but because Puritan doctrine had always stressed reason over emotionalism and sudden conversions, Edwards and other ministers were skeptical as well. The revival spread to the middle colonies and the South when the English Methodist preacher George Whitefield (1714–1770) toured America from 1739 to 1741. Doctrinal disputes in the Protestant churches over the role of emotion and immediate conversion led to a split of the clergy into two camps: "New Light" ministers, who favored the revival movement, and "Old Light" clergy, who rejected it. The College of New Jersey (now Princeton) was founded as a theological seminary for New Light ministers, and Jonathan Edwards was one of its first presidents.

Jonathan Edwards
(1703–1758)

Jonathan Edwards was born in East Windsor, Connecticut, in 1703 to the minister Timothy Edwards and Esther Stoddard. Her father, Solomon Stoddard, was one of the most powerful clergymen in New England; he became known as "Pope Stoddard" by those who feared and admired him. In 1727 Edwards married Sarah Pierpont of New Haven, Connecticut, a young woman of tremendous emotional fervor. The story of Jonathan Edwards is one of triumph and tragedy. Unlike some of his contemporaries, Edwards enjoyed an extremely happy marriage to a woman he loved deeply and whose support he enjoyed. At the same time, his ministry in Northampton, Massachusetts, was a failure. In 1750, twenty-one years after he had assumed the pulpit from Solomon Stoddard, the congregation overwhelmingly voted to dismiss Edwards as their minister. This defeat represented a rejection of a leading "New Light" minister, a spearheader of the Great Awakening of the 1730s and 1740s in New England.

Edwards was essentially exiled to Stockbridge, Massachusetts, where, with even less success than he had had in Northampton, he ministered to Native Americans. His world turned inward from the public meetings and mass gatherings of the preaching tour of New

The Jonathan Edwards Memorial by Herbert Adams, in the First Church of Northampton, Massachusetts.

England he had made with Rev. George Whitefield at the beginning of the Awakening. From the early 1740s and the decline of Edwards's ministry in Northampton to the time of his appointment as the third president of the College of New Jersey (now Princeton University) in 1758, he wrote many of the theological treatises for which he is now remembered. Thus, his long exile was quite productive for the development of American philosophy. Jonathan Edwards and Benjamin Franklin remain the two most prominent thinkers and influential figures in eighteenth-century American culture.

Young Edwards was tutored at home, a custom for Puritan children in New England. At age thirteen Edwards entered Yale College, where he remained after graduating in 1720 to read theology. In 1722 he became a minister at a Presbyterian church in New York City but withdrew after only nine months. From 1724 to 1725 he tutored at Yale, until his teaching career was interrupted by illness. In 1726 Edwards became assistant minister to Solomon Stoddard. He was elected to succeed Solomon Stoddard as minister to the Northampton congregation in 1729. Edwards's success with the evangelical awakening of the next twenty years was paralleled by a decline of influence with his own congregation. He had extremely poor relations with his flock, which resulted in petty squabbles. In 1744 he publicly listed persons from Northampton who were involved in "immoral practices," such as using "foul language" and reading a book about midwifery. He proceeded to read from the pulpit a long list that included many of the town's more prominent children, without bothering to distinguish between those who were accused of immoral practices and the accusers themselves.

As in all congregational matters, Edwards's timing was dreadful. He attempted to state his case from the pulpit, but his parishioners refused to listen. Finally, he was reduced to publishing his views in *An Humble Inquiry Into the Rules of the Word of God* (1749). Few parishioners bothered even to cut the pages open, as many extant copies of this dull volume clearly show. Edwards was finished as a minister long before he penned this defense. However, from a historical perspective, that he fully expressed his views is important. His reputation as a leading theologian rose dramatically because of his published works. Following his exile in Stockbridge, Edwards assumed the presidency of the College of New Jersey at Princeton. But soon he was inoculated with a primitive vaccine against small-pox; the inferior vaccine caused his death in 1758. Ironically, this inoculation, introduced into the colonies by Cotton Mather, was designed to preserve human life but ended the life of a man whose fifty-five years were spent showing others how to achieve eternal life.

In retrospect Edwards is now regarded as the most powerful thinker of colonial America, and Benjamin Franklin the most influential shaper of America's literary and philosophical discourse. Edwards and Franklin, both heirs to the Puritan ethic, perceived the world as spiritual and material and believed that man's first duty is to discover ways of comprehending the physical universe. For Franklin scientific investigation became the means to higher understanding; for Edwards nothing discovered in nature could contravene those truths revealed through the "word of God," Scripture. Since his youth Edwards had expressed a keen interest in the natural universe, writing descriptive pieces on spiders, lightning, and mathematics. The Connecticut Valley was very much frontier in the early eighteenth century. In 1715, at age twelve, Edwards composed his well-known dissertation on the spider, entitled "Of Insects." Edwards's interest in the natural world, unlike that of Franklin, was meant to reinforce the Bible's vision of Creation.

While at Yale Edwards read such works as Isaac Newton's *Principia Mathematica* (1687) and John Locke's *An Essay Concerning Human Understanding* (1690). These proponents of the "new science" profoundly influenced Edward's thinking and style of writing. Edwards emerged as a leading eighteenth-century philosopher and prominent American literary figure because of his concern to express his understanding of God's ideas in language that could be accommodated to reason and emotion. Following the attempts of his contemporaries to express things in ordered, rational forms, Edwards adopted a plain, direct style that employed images from the natural universe to communicate a vision of God that was frightening to the unregenerate and often comforting to the regenerate, or saved. The vehicle for his expression was the prose sermon and the essay or treatise. Edward's most influential sermon was *Sinners in the Hands of an Angry God* (1741); his most important philosophical essay was *A Treatise Concerning Religious Affections* (1746). The epistemology of the Great Awakening and the psychology of individual conversion are summarized in *Treatise*. Both documents reveal Edwards at his literary best, and each makes a peculiar contribution to the development of American literature.

Edwards was not unique in preaching a "born-again" theology, as Puritans had always stressed the value of transformation from a hardened heart of stone to the full measure of God's divine grace. But for Edwards this transforming experience was expressed in the language of sensory experience, as his *Personal Narrative* (written about 1740 but published in 1765) shows. His writings and preaching during the Great Awakening exhibit the power of God revealed in the beauty and perfection of the natural universe. His prose style is stimulating and powerful. Edwards's sermons reveal a conscious commitment to imagery, communicating God through the senses as well as through the language of Scripture. Edwards is best remembered for *Sinners in the Hands of an Angry God*. The sermon, first preached in 1741, is representative of Edwards as a literary stylist, but not because it shows him to be a "fire and brimstone" evangelist. Rather, this document shows careful craftsmanship, meticulous care in the arrangement of themes and images, and a close attention to the psychology of divine revelation. For Edwards the ultimate objective of the sermon's power was to bring about a wrenching conversion in his listener, a passage from terror and despair to the hope of salvation.

Edwards recorded many of his experiences in the *Personal Narrative,* less a chronology of his life's activities than a record of his inner life, that "habit of mind" by which the reader may eventually know Edwards as a thinker. In *Personal Narrative* he says that his own conversion led to a new way of perceiving the universe around him. Conversion and renewal bring about a heightened sense of the natural world, which in turn leads to further understanding of spiritual matters. Edwards makes it perfectly clear that this "new sense of things" is available only to the regenerate mind, that those not slated for election and regeneration would be like dumb animals in their efforts to comprehend God's natural manifestations. The new beginning or fresh start commonly associated with migration to America from Europe in the nineteenth century originated in the Puritan notion that conversion leads to a total transformation of an individual: each regenerated person would essentially have the opportunity to start over again, leaving the "old self" behind, just as the Old World had been abandoned in favor of the New World.

A History of the Work of Redemption, a series of sermons preached in 1739, was left in manuscript form at the time of Edwards's death and was not published until 1774. It gives the most complete summary of Edwards's orthodox and conservative approach to the eternal work of the Holy Spirit and contains a particularly illuminating section on the imagery of Scripture. His *A Faithful Narrative of the Surprising Work of God* (1737), *The Distinguishing Marks of a Work of the Spirit of God* (1741), and *Some Thoughts Concerning the Present Revival of Religion in New England* (1742) treat the revivalism of the Great Awakening and defend the work of the Holy Spirit in contemporary New England. Another important epistemological document is *Images or Shadows of Divine Things* (first published in 1948), a commonplace book in which Edwards recorded impressions and ideas in a journal format.

Edwards's perception of the natural world provided Christian theology with a new dimension. Edwards had entered nature organically, as American transcendentalists (such as Ralph Waldo Emerson and Henry David Thoreau) were to do a century later, his mind open to receive the impressions garnered through his experience, and the impressions themselves assisted his regenerate spirit in comprehending the mysteries of God's ways toward man. The effective communication of this comprehension through language and imagery constitutes Edwards's most significant contribution to American literature and culture.

Suggested Readings: *The Printed Writings of Jonathan Edwards, 1703–1758: A Bibliography,* ed. T. H. Johnson, 1940. *The Works of Jonathan Edwards,* 7 vols., ed. J. E. Smith, 1959. *Jonathan Edwards: A Reference Guide,* ed. M. X. Lesser, 1981. P. Miller, *Jonathan Edwards: The Life of the Mind,* 1949. E. H. Davidson, *Jonathan Edwards: The Narrative of a Puritan Mind,* 1966. R. Delattre, *Beauty and Sensibility in the Thought of Jonathan Edwards,* 1968. D. Shea, "Jonathan Edwards, Historian of Consciousness," in *Major Writers of Early American Literature,* ed. E. Emerson, 1972. J. Wilson, "Jonathan Edwards as Historian," in *Church History,* March 1977. M. Lowance, *The Language of Canaan: Metaphor and Symbol in New England From the Puritans to the Transcendentalists,* 1980. N. Fiering, *Jonathan Edwards's Moral Thought and Its British Context,* 1981. P. Tracy, *Jonathan Edwards: Pastor,* 1981.

Texts Used: Sarah Pierpont and *Personal Narrative*: *The Life of President Edwards,* ed. S. E. Dwight, 1830. *A Divine and Supernatural Light: The Works of President Edwards,* Vol. VI, ed. S. E. Dwight, 1829. *Sinners in the Hands of an Angry God: The Works of President Edwards,* Vol. VII. Letter to Rev. Dr. Benjamin Colman: *The Great Awakening,* ed. C. C. Goen, 1972. (Some spelling and punctuation modernized.)

SARAH PIERPONT*

They say there is a young lady in [New Haven] who is beloved of that Great Being, who made and rules the world, and that there are certain seasons in which this Great Being, in some way or other invisible, comes to her and fills her mind with exceeding sweet delight, and that she hardly cares for any thing, except to meditate on him—that she expects after a while to be received up where he is, to be raised up out of the world and caught up into heaven; being assured that he loves her too well to let her remain at a distance from him always. There she is to dwell with him, and to be ravished with his love and delight forever. Therefore, if you present all the world before her, with the richest of its treasures, she disregards it and cares not for it, and is unmindful of any pain or affliction. She has a strange sweetness in her mind, and singular purity in her affections; is most just and conscientious in all her conduct; and you could not persuade her to do any thing wrong or sinful, if you would give her all the world, lest she should offend this Great Being. She is of a wonderful sweetness, calmness and universal benevolence of mind; especially after this Great God has manifested himself to her mind. She will sometimes go about from place to place, singing sweetly; and seems to be always full of joy and pleasure; and no one knows for what. She loves to be alone, walking in the field and groves, and seems to have some one invisible always conversing with her.

1723, 1829

A DIVINE AND SUPERNATURAL LIGHT†

IMMEDIATELY IMPARTED TO THE SOUL BY THE SPIRIT OF GOD, SHOWN TO BE BOTH A SCRIPTURAL AND RATIONAL DOCTRINE

MATTHEW XVI: 17

And Jesus answered and said unto him, Blessed art thou, Simon Bar-jona:[1] for flesh and blood hath not revealed it unto thee, but my Father which is in heaven.

CHRIST addresses these words to Peter upon occasion of his professing his faith in him as the Son of God. Our Lord was inquiring of his disciples, whom men said that he was; not that he needed to be informed, but only to introduce and give occasion to what follows. They answer, that some said he was John the Baptist,

---

* Edwards wrote this tribute when he was twenty and Sarah Pierpont (1710–1758) was thirteen. They married in 1727.

† This sermon was delivered in 1733 in Northampton, Massachusetts, and, as requested by his congregration, was published the following year.

[1] Simon, son of Jonah: the Apostle Peter, or Saint Peter.

and some Elias, and others Jeremias, or one of the prophets.[2] When they had thus given an account whom others said that he was, Christ asks them, whom they said that he was? Simon Peter, whom we find always zealous and forward, was the first to answer: he readily replied to the question, Thou art Christ the Son of the living God.

Upon this occasion, Christ says as he does to him and of him in the text: in which we may observe,

1. That Peter is pronounced blessed on this account.—Blessed art thou— "Thou art an happy man, that thou art not ignorant of this, that I am Christ, the Son of the living God. Thou art distinguishingly happy. Others are blinded, and have dark and deluded apprehensions, as you have now given an account, some thinking that I am Elias, and some that I am Jeremias, and some one thing, and some another: but none of them thinking right all of them are misled. Happy art thou, that art so distinguished as to know the truth in this matter."

2. The evidence of this his happiness declared, viz. That God, and he only, had revealed it to him. This is an evidence of his being blessed.

First. As it shows how peculiarly favored he was of God above others; *q. d.*[3] "How highly favored art thou, that others, wise and great men, the scribes,[4] Pharisees,[5] and rulers, and the nation in general, are left in darkness, to follow their own misguided apprehensions; and that thou shouldst be singled out, as it were, by name, that my heavenly Father should thus set his love on thee, Simon Barjona.—This argues thee blessed, that thou shouldst thus be the object of God's distinguishing love."

Secondly. It evidences his blessedness also, as it intimates that this knowledge is above any that flesh and blood can reveal. "This is such knowledge as only my Father which is in heaven can give. It is too high and excellent to be communicated by such means as other knowledge is. Thou art blessed, that thou knowest what God alone can teach thee."

The original of this knowledge is here declared, both negatively and positively. Positively, as God is here declared the author of it. Negatively, as it is declared, that flesh and blood had not revealed it. God is the author of all knowledge and understanding whatsoever. He is the author of all moral prudence, and of the skill that men have in their secular business. Thus it is said of all in Israel that were wise-hearted, and skilled in embroidering, that God had filled them with the spirit of wisdom. Exodus xxviii: 3.[6]

God is the author of such knowledge; yet so that flesh and blood reveals it. Mortal men are capable of imparting the knowledge of human arts and sciences, and skill in temporal affairs. God is the author of such knowledge by those means: flesh and blood is employed as the mediate or second cause of it; he conveys it by the power and influence of natural means. But this spiritual knowledge, spoken of in the text, is what God is the author of, and none else: he reveals it, and flesh and blood reveals it not. He imparts this knowledge immediately, not making use of any intermediate natural causes, as he does in other knowledge.

What had passed in the preceding discourse naturally occasioned Christ to ob-

---

[2] The baptizer of Jesus; the prophet Elijah (New Testament); and the prophet Jeremiah (see Matthew 16:4).

[3] Quasi dicat, "as if he should say" (Latin).   [4] Interpreters of ancient Jewish law.

[5] An ancient sect, known for their arrogance, who accepted oral, or traditional, law and were antagonistic to Jesus (see Matthew 9).

[6] God commanded the Israelites to clothe Aaron (Israel's first high priest) for the priesthood.

serve this; because the disciples had been telling how others did not know him, but were generally mistaken about him, divided and confounded in their opinions of him: but Peter had declared his assured faith, that he was the Son of God. Now it was natural to observe, how it was not flesh and blood that had revealed it to him, but God; for if this knowledge were dependent on natural causes or means, how came it to pass that they, a company of poor fishermen, illiterate men, and persons of low education, attained to the knowledge of the truth; while the scribes and Pharisees, men of vastly higher advantages, and greater knowledge and sagacity, in other matters, remained in ignorance? This could be owing only to the gracious distinguishing influence and revelation of the Spirit of God. Hence, what I would make the subject of my present discourse, from these words, is this

Doctrine.

That there is such a thing as a spiritual and divine light, immediately imparted to the soul by God, of a different nature from any that is obtained by natural means. And on this subject I would,

I. Show what this divine light is.
II. How it is given immediately by God, and not obtained by natural means.
III. Show the truth of the doctrine.
And then conclude with a brief improvement.

I. I would show what this spiritual and divine light is. And in order to it would show,
First, In a few things, what it is not. And here,
1. Those convictions that natural men may have of their sin and misery, is not this spiritual and divine light. Men, in a natural condition, may have convictions of the guilt that lies upon them, and of the anger of God, and their danger of divine vengeance. Such convictions are from the light of truth. That some sinners have a greater conviction of their guilt and misery than others, is because some have more light, or more of an apprehension of truth than others. And this light and conviction may be from the Spirit of God; the Spirit convinces men of sin; but yet nature is much more concerned in it than in the communication of that spiritual and divine light that is spoken of in the doctrine; it is from the Spirit of God only as assisting natural principles, and not as infusing any new principles. Common grace differs from special, in that it influences only by assisting of nature; and not by imparting grace, or bestowing any thing above nature. The light that is obtained, is wholly natural, or of no superior kind to what mere nature attains to, though more of that kind be obtained than would be obtained, if men were left wholly to themselves; or, in other words, common grace only assists the faculties of the soul to do that more fully which they do by nature, as natural conscience or reason will by mere nature make a man sensible of guilt, and will accuse and condemn him when he has done amiss. Conscience is a principle natural to men; and the work that it doth naturally, or of itself, is to give an apprehension of right and wrong, and to suggest to the mind the relation that there is between right and wrong and a retribution. The Spirit of God, in those convictions which unregenerate men sometimes have, assists conscience to do this work in a further degree than it would do if they were left to themselves. He helps it against those things

that tend to stupify it, and obstruct its exercise. But in the renewing and sanctifying work of the Holy Ghost, those things are wrought in the soul that are above nature, and of which there is nothing of the like kind in the soul by nature; and they are caused to exist in the soul habitually, and according to such a stated constitution or law, that lays such a foundation for exercises in a continued course, as is called a principle of nature. Not only are remaining principles assisted to do their work more freely and fully, but those principles are restored that were utterly destroyed by the Fall;[7] and the mind thenceforward habitually exerts those acts that the dominion of sin had made it as wholly destitute of as a dead body is of vital acts.

The Spirit of God acts in a very different manner in the one case, from what he doth in the other. He may, indeed, act upon the mind of a natural man, but he acts in the mind of a saint[8] as an indwelling vital principle. He acts upon the mind of an unregenerate[9] person as an extrinsic occasional agent; for, in acting upon them, he doth not unite himself to them: for, notwithstanding all his influences that they may possess, they are still sensual, having not the Spirit. Jude 19.[10] But he unites himself with the mind of a saint, takes him for his temple, actuates and influences him as a new supernatural principle of life and action. There is this difference, that the Spirit of God, in acting in the soul of a godly man, exerts and communicates himself there in his own proper nature. Holiness is the proper nature of the Spirit of God. The Holy Spirit operates in the minds of the godly, by uniting himself to them, and living in them, and exerting his own nature in the exercise of their faculties. The Spirit of God may act upon a creature, and yet not in acting communicate himself. The Spirit of God may act upon inanimate creatures; as, the Spirit moved upon the face of the waters,[11] in the beginning of the Creation; so the Spirit of God may act upon the minds of men many ways, and communicate himself no more than when he acts upon an inanimate creature. For instance, he may excite thoughts in them, may assist their natural reason and understanding, or may assist other natural principles, and this without any union with the soul, but may act, as it were, upon an external object. But as he acts in his holy influences and spiritual operations, he acts in a way of peculiar communication of himself; so that the subject is thence denominated spiritual.

2. This spiritual and divine light does not consist in any impression made upon the imagination. It is no impression upon the mind, as though one saw any thing with the bodily eyes. It is no imagination or idea of an outward light or glory, or any beauty of form or countenance, or a visible lustre or brightness of any object. The imagination may be strongly impressed with such things; but this is not spiritual light. Indeed when the mind has a lively discovery of spiritual things, and is greatly affected with the power of divine light, it may, and probably very commonly doth, much affect the imagination; so that impressions of an outward beauty or brightness may accompany those spiritual discoveries. But spiritual light is not that impression upon the imagination, but an exceedingly different thing. Natural men may have lively impressions on their imaginations; and we cannot determine but that the devil, who transforms himself into an angel of light, may cause imaginations of an outward beauty, or visible glory, and of sounds and speeches, and other such things; but these are things of a vastly inferior nature to spiritual light.

[7] Adam's sin of yielding to temptation by eating the forbidden fruit, and his subsequent loss of grace.
[8] Here, a Christian who is committed to God's love and Christ's doctrines.
[9] A person who has not yet been saved.
[10] "These be they who separate themselves, sensual, having not the Spirit."   [11] Genesis 1:2.

3. This spiritual light is not the suggesting of any new truths or propositions not contained in the word of God. This suggesting of new truths or doctrines to the mind, independent of any antecedent revelations of those propositions, either in word or writing, is inspiration; such as the prophets and apostles had, and such as some enthusiasts[12] pretend to. But this spiritual light that I am speaking of, is quite a different thing from inspiration. It reveals no new doctrine, it suggests no new proposition to the mind, it teaches no new thing of God, or Christ, or another world, not taught in the Bible, but only gives a due apprehension of those things that are taught in the word of God.

4. It is not every affecting view that men have of religious things that is this spiritual and divine light. Men by mere principles of nature are capable of being affected with things that have a special relation to religion as well as other things. A person by mere nature, for instance, may be liable to be affected with the story of Jesus Christ, and the sufferings he underwent, as well as by any other tragical story. He may be the more affected with it from the interest he conceives mankind to have in it. Yea, he may be affected with it without believing it; as well as a man may be affected with what he reads in a romance, or sees acted in a stage-play. He may be affected with a lively and eloquent description of many pleasant things that attend the state of the blessed in heaven, as well as his imagination be entertained by a romantic description of the pleasantness of fairy land, or the like. And a common belief of the truth of such things, from education or otherwise, may help forward their affection. We read in Scripture of many that were greatly affected with things of a religious nature, who yet are there represented as wholly graceless, and many of them very ill[13] men. A person therefore may have affecting views of the things of religion, and yet be very destitute of spiritual light. Flesh and blood may be the author of this; one man may give another an affecting view of divine things with but common assistance; but God alone can give a spiritual discovery of them.—But I proceed to show,

Secondly, Positively what this spiritual and divine light is.

And it may be thus described: a true sense of the divine excellency of the things revealed in the word of God, and a conviction of the truth and reality of them thence arising. This spiritual light primarily consists in the former of these, viz. A real sense and apprehension of the divine excellency of things revealed in the word of God. A spiritual and saving conviction of the truth and reality of these things, arises from such a sight of their divine excellency and glory; so that this conviction of their truth is an effect and natural consequence of this sight of their divine glory. There is therefore in this spiritual light,

1. A true sense of the divine and superlative excellency of the things of religion; a real sense of the excellency of God and Jesus Christ, and of the work of redemption, and the ways and works of God revealed in the gospel. There is a divine and superlative glory in these things; an excellency that is of a vastly higher kind, and more sublime nature than in other things; a glory greatly distinguishing them from all that is earthly and temporal. He that is spiritually enlightened truly apprehends and sees it, or has a sense of it. He does not merely rationally believe that God is glorious, but he has a sense of the gloriousness of God in his heart. There is not only a rational belief that God is holy, and that holiness is a good thing, but there is a sense of the loveliness of God's holiness. There is not only a speculatively judging that God is gracious, but a sense how amiable God is on account of the beauty of this divine attribute.

---

[12] Those who spuriously claim to be inspired by God.   [13] Evil.

There is a twofold knowledge of good of which God has made the mind of man capable. The first, that which is merely notional; as when a person only speculatively judges that any thing is, which, by the agreement of mankind, is called good or excellent, viz. that which is most to general advantage, and between which and a reward there is a suitableness,—and the like. And the other is, that which consists in the sense of the heart; as when the heart is sensible of pleasure and delight in the presence of the idea of it. In the former is exercised merely the speculative faculty, or the understanding, in distinction from the will or disposition of the soul. In the latter, the will, or inclination, or heart, are mainly concerned.

Thus there is a difference between having an opinion, that God is holy and gracious, and having a sense of the loveliness and beauty of that holiness and grace. There is a difference between having a rational judgment that honey is sweet, and having a sense of its sweetness. A man may have the former, that knows not how honey tastes; but a man cannot have the latter unless he has an idea of the taste of honey in his mind. So there is a difference between believing that a person is beautiful, and having a sense of his beauty. The former may be obtained by hearsay, but the latter only by seeing the countenance. When the heart is sensible of the beauty and amiableness of a thing, it necessarily feels pleasure in the apprehension. It is implied in a person's being heartily sensible of the loveliness of a thing, that the idea of it is pleasant to his soul; which is a far different thing from having a rational opinion that it is excellent.

2. There arises from this sense of the divine excellency of things contained in the word of God, a conviction of the truth and reality of them; and that, either indirectly or directly.

First, Indirectly, and that two ways:

1. As the prejudices of the heart, against the truth of divine things, are hereby removed; so that the mind becomes susceptive of the due force of rational arguments for their truth. The mind of man is naturally full of prejudices against divine truth. It is full of enmity against the doctrines of the gospel; which is a disadvantage to those arguments that prove their truth, and causes them to lose their force upon the mind. But when a person has discovered to him the divine excellency of Christian doctrines, this destroys the enmity, removes those prejudices, sanctifies the reason, and causes it to lie open to the force of arguments for their truth.

Hence was the different effect that Christ's miracles had to convince the disciples, from what they had to convince the scribes and Pharisees. Not that they had a stronger reason, or had their reason more improved; but their reason was sanctified, and those blinding prejudices, that the scribes and Pharisees were under, were removed by the sense they had of the excellency of Christ, and his doctrine.

It not only removes the hinderances of reason, but positively helps reason. It makes even the speculative notions more lively. It engages the attention of the mind, with more fixedness and intenseness to that kind of objects; which causes it to have a clearer view of them, and enables it more clearly to see their mutual relations, and occasions it to take more notice of them. The ideas themselves that otherwise are dim and obscure, are by this means impressed with the greater strength, and have a light cast upon them; so that the mind can better judge of them. As he that beholds objects on the face of the earth, when the light of the sun is east upon them, is under greater advantage to discern them in their true forms and natural relations, than he that sees them in a dim twilight.

The mind, being sensible of the excellency of divine objects, dwells upon them with delight; and the powers of the soul are more awakened and enlivened to employ themselves in the contemplation of them, and exert themselves more fully and much more to the purpose. The beauty of the objects draws on the faculties, and draws forth their exercises; so that reason itself is under far greater advantages for its proper and free exercises, and to attain its proper end, free of darkness and delusion.—But,

Secondly, A true sense of the divine excellency of the things of God's word doth more directly and immediately convince us of their truth; and that because the excellency of these things is so superlative. There is a beauty in them so divine and godlike, that it greatly and evidently distinguishes them from things merely human, or that of which men are the inventors and authors; a glory so high and great, that when clearly seen, commands assent to their divine reality. When there is an actual and lively discovery of this beauty and excellency, it will not allow of any such thought as that it is the fruit of men's invention. This is a kind of intuitive and immediate evidence. They believe the doctrines of God's word to be divine, because they see a divine, and transcendent, and most evidently distinguishing glory in them; such a glory as, if clearly seen, does not leave room to doubt of their being of God, and not of men.

Such a conviction of the truth of religion as this, arising from a sense of their divine excellency, is included in saving faith. And this original of it, is that by which it is most essentially distinguished from that common assent, of which unregenerate men are capable.

II. I proceed now to the second thing proposed, viz. To show how this light is immediately given by God, and not obtained by natural means. And here,

1. It is not intended that the natural faculties are not used in it. They are the subject of this light: and in such a manner, that they are not merely passive, but active in it. God, in letting in this light into the soul, deals with man according to his nature, and makes use of his rational faculties. But yet this light is not the less immediately from God for that; the faculties are made use of as the subject, and not as the cause. As the use we make of our eyes in beholding various objects, when the sun arises, is not the cause of the light that discovers those objects to us.

2. It is not intended that outward means have no concern in this affair. It is not in this affair, as in inspiration, where new truths are suggested; for, by this light is given only a due apprehension of the same truths that are revealed in the word of God: and therefore it is not given without the word. The gospel is employed in this affair. This light is the "light of the glorious gospel of Christ." 2 Corinthians iv: 4.[14] The gospel is as a glass, by which this light is conveyed to us. 1 Corinthians xiii: 12.[15] "Now we see through a glass."—But,

3. When it is said that this light is given immediately by God, and not obtained by natural means, hereby is intended, that it is given by God without making use of any means that operate by their own power or natural force. God makes use of means; but it is not as mediate causes to produce this effect. There are not truly any second causes of it; but it is produced by God immediately. The word of God is no proper cause of this effect; but is made use of only to convey to the mind the subject-matter of this saving instruction: and this indeed it doth convey to us by

---

[14] "But if our gospel be hid, it is hid to them that are lost: In whom the god of this world hath blinded the minds of them which believe not, lest the light of the glorious gospel of Christ . . . should shine unto them."

[15] "For now we see through a glass, darkly; but then face to face."

natural force or influence. It conveys to our minds these doctrines; it is the cause of a notion of them in our heads, but not of the sense of their divine excellency in our hearts. Indeed a person cannot have spiritual light without the word. But that does not argue, that the word properly causes that light. The mind cannot see the excellency of any doctrine, unless that doctrine be first in the mind; but seeing the excellency of the doctrine may be immediately from the Spirit of God; though the conveying of the doctrine, or proposition, itself, may be by the word. So that the notions which are the subject-matter of this light, are conveyed to the mind by the word of God; but that due sense of the heart, wherein this light formally consists, is immediately by the Spirit of God. As, for instance, the notion that there is a Christ, and that Christ is holy and gracious, is conveyed to the mind by the word of God: But the sense of the excellency of Christ, by reason of that holiness and grace, is, nevertheless, immediately the work of the Holy Spirit.—I come now,

III. To show the truth of the doctrine; that is, to show that there is such a thing as that spiritual light that has been described, thus immediately let into the mind by God. And here I would show, briefly, that this doctrine is both scriptural and rational.

First, It is scriptural. My text is not only full to the purpose, but it is a doctrine with which the Scripture abounds. We are there abundantly taught, that the saints differ from the ungodly in this; that they have the knowledge of God, and a sight of God, and of Jesus Christ. I shall mention but few texts out of many: 1 John iii: 6. "Whosoever sinneth, hath not seen him, nor known him." 3 John 11. "He that doeth good, is of God: but he that doeth evil, hath not seen God." John xiv: 19. "The world seeth me no more; but ye see me." John xvii: 3. "And this is eternal life, that they might know thee, the only true God, and Jesus Christ whom thou hast sent." This knowledge, or sight of God and Christ, cannot be a mere speculative knowledge; because it is spoken of as that wherein they differ from the ungodly. And by these scriptures, it must not only be a different knowledge in degree and circumstances, and different in its effects, but it must be entirely different in nature and kind.

And this light and knowledge is always spoken of an immediately given of God; Matthew xi: 25—27. "At that time, Jesus answered and said, I thank thee, O Father, Lord of heaven and earth, because thou hast hid these things from the wise and prudent, and hast revealed them unto babes. Even so, Father, for so it seemed good in thy sight. All things are delivered unto me of my Father: and no man knoweth the Father, save the Son, and he to whomsoever the Son will reveal him." Here this effect is ascribed exclusively to the arbitrary operation and gift of God bestowing this knowledge on whom he will, and distinguishing those with it who have the least natural advantage or means for knowledge, even babes, when it is denied to the wise and prudent. And imparting this knowledge, is here appropriated to the Son of God, as his sole prerogative. And again, 2 Corinthians iv: 6. "For God, who commanded the light to shine out of darkness, hath shined in our hearts, to give the light of the knowledge of the glory of God, in the face of Jesus Christ." This plainly shows, that there is a discovery of the divine superlative glory and excellency of God and Christ, peculiar to the saints: and, also, that it is as immediately from God, as light from the sun: and that it is the immediate effect of his power and will. For it is compared to God's creating the light by his powerful word in the beginning of the Creation; and is said to be by the Spirit of the Lord, in the 18th verse of the preceding chapter. God is spoken of as giving the knowledge of Christ in conversion, as of what before was hidden and unseen;

Galatians i: 15, 16. "But when it pleased God, who separated me from my mother's womb, and called me by his grace, to reveal his son in me." The scripture also speaks plainly of such a knowledge of the word of God, as has been described as the immediate gift of God; Psalm cxix: 18. "Open thou mine eyes, that I may behold wondrous things out of thy law." What could the Psalmist mean, when he begged of God to open his eyes? Was he ever blind? Might he not have resort to the law, and see every word and sentence in it when he pleased? And what could he mean by those wondrous things? Were they the wonderful stories of the creation, and deluge, and Israel's passing through the Red Sea,[16] and the like? Were not his eyes open to read these strange things when he would? Doubtless, by wondrous things in God's law, he had respect to those distinguishing and wonderful excellencies, and marvelous manifestations of the divine perfections and glory contained in the commands and doctrines of the word, and those works and counsels of God that were there revealed. So the scripture speaks of a knowledge of God's dispensation, and covenant of mercy[17] and way of grace towards his people, as peculiar to the saints, and given only by God; Psalm xxv: 14. "The secret of the Lord is with them that fear him; and he will show them his covenant."

And that a true and saving belief of the truth of religion is that which arises from such a discovery, is, also, what the scripture teaches. As John vi: 40. "And this is the will of him that sent me, that every one who seeth the Son, and believeth on him, may have everlasting life;" where it is plain that a true faith is what arises from a spiritual sight of Christ. And John xvii: 6, 7, 8. "I have manifested thy name unto the men which thou gavest me out of the world. Now, they have known, that all things whatsoever thou hast given me, are of thee. For I have given unto them the words which thou gavest me, and they have received them, and have known surely, that I came out from thee, and they have believed that thou didst send me;" where Christ's manifesting God's name to the disciples, or giving them the knowledge of God, was that whereby they knew that Christ's doctrine was of God, and that Christ himself proceeded from him, and was sent by him. Again, John xii: 44, 45, 46. "Jesus cried and said, He that believeth on me, believeth not on me but on him that sent me. And he that seeth me, seeth him that sent me. I am come a light into the world, that whosoever believeth on me, should not abide in darkness." Their believing in Christ, and spiritually seeing him, are parallel.

Christ condemns the Jews, that they did not know that he was the Messiah, and that his doctrine was true, from an inward distinguishing taste and relish of what was divine, in Luke xii: 56, 57. He having there blamed the Jews, that, though they could discern the face of the sky and of the earth, and signs of the weather, that yet they could not discern those times—or, as it is expressed in Matthew, the signs of those times—adds, "yea, and why even of your ownselves, judge ye not what is right?" i.e. without extrinsic signs. Why have ye not that sense of true excellency, whereby ye may distinguish that which is holy and divine? Why have ye not that savor of the things of God, by which you may see the distinguishing glory, and evident divinity of me and my doctrine?

The apostle Peter mentions it as what gave him and his companions good and well-grounded assurance of the truth of the gospel, that they had seen the divine

---

[16] In Exodus 14:2 the Israelites were able to flee Egypt because the Red Sea parted for them.
[17] The agreement between Christ and his believers that they would be saved.

glory of Christ. 2 Peter i: 16. "For we have not followed cunningly-devised fables, when we made known unto you the power and coming of our Lord Jesus Christ, but were eye-witnesses of his majesty." The apostle has respect to that visible glory of Christ which they saw in his transfiguration. That glory was so divine, having such an ineffable appearance and semblance of divine holiness, majesty, and grace, that it evidently denoted him to be a divine person. But if a sight of Christ's outward glory might give a rational assurance of his divinity, why may not an apprehension of his spiritual glory do so too? Doubtless Christ's spiritual glory is in itself as distinguishing, and as plainly shows his divinity, as his outward glory—nay, a great deal more, for his spiritual glory is that wherein his divinity consists; and the outward glory of his transfiguration showed him to be divine, only as it was a remarkable image or representation of that spiritual glory. Doubtless, therefore, he that has had a clear sight of the spiritual glory of Christ, may say, I have not followed cunningly devised fables, but have been an eye-witness of his majesty, upon as good grounds as the apostle, when he had respect to the outward glory of Christ that he had seen. But this brings me to what was proposed next, viz. to show that,

Secondly, This doctrine is rational.[18]

1. It is rational to suppose, that there is really such an excellency in divine things—so transcendent and exceedingly different from what is in other things—that if it were seen, would most evidently distinguish them. We cannot rationally doubt but that things divine, which appertain to the supreme Being, are vastly different from things that are human; that there is a high, glorious, and god-like excellency in them, that does most remarkably difference them from the things that are of men; insomuch that if the difference were but seen, it would have a convincing, satisfying influence upon any one, that they are divine. What reason can be offered against it? unless we would argue, that God is not remarkably distinguished in glory from men.

If Christ should now appear to any one as he did on the mount at his transfiguration,[19] or if he should appear to the world in his heavenly glory, as he will do at the day of judgment;[20] without doubt, his glory and majesty would be such as would satisfy every one, that he was a divine person, and that his religion was true: and it would be a most reasonable, and well grounded conviction too. And why may there not be that stamp of divinity, or divine glory on the word of God, on the scheme and doctrine of the gospel, that may be in like manner distinguishing and as rationally convincing, provided it be but seen? It is rational to suppose, that when God speaks to the world, there should be something in his word vastly different from men's word. Supposing that God never had spoken to the world, but we had notice that he was about to reveal himself from heaven, and speak to us immediately himself, or that he should give us a book of his own inditing;[21] after what manner should we expect that he would speak? Would it not be rational to suppose, that his speech would be exceeding different from men's speech, that there should be such an excellency and sublimity in his word, such a stamp of wisdom, holiness, majesty, and other divine perfections, that the word of men,

[18] Understandable.

[19] "And after six days Jesus taketh Peter, James, and John his brother, and bringeth them up into an high mountain apart, And he was transfigured before them: and his face did shine like the sun, and his raiment was white as the light," from Matthew 17:1–2.

[20] See Revelation 4.   [21] Writing.

yea of the wisest of men, should appear mean and base in comparison of it? Doubtless it would be thought rational to expect this, and unreasonable to think otherwise. When a wise man speaks in the exercise of his wisdom, there is something in every thing he says, that is very distinguishable from the talk of a little child. So, without doubt, and much more is the speech of God, to be distinguished from that of the wisest of men; agreeable to Jeremiah xxiii: 28, 29. God having there been reproving the false prophets that prophesied in his name, and pretended that what they spake was his word, when indeed it was their own word, says "The prophet that hath a dream, let him tell a dream; and he that hath my word, let him speak my word faithfully: what is the chaff to the wheat? saith the Lord. Is not my word like as a fire? saith the Lord: and like a hammer that breaketh the rock in pieces?"

2. If there be such a distinguishing excellency in divine things; it is rational to suppose that there may be such a thing as seeing it. What should hinder but that it may be seen? It is no argument, that there is no such distinguishing excellency, or that it cannot be seen, because some do not see it, though they may be discerning men in temporal matters. It is not rational to suppose, if there be any such excellency in divine things, that wicked men should see it. Is it rational to suppose, that those whose minds are full of spiritual pollution, and under the power of filthy lusts, should have any relish or sense of divine beauty or excellency; or that their minds should be susceptive of that light that is in its own nature so pure and heavenly? It need not seem at all strange, that sin should so blind the mind, seeing that men's particular natural tempers and dispositions will so much blind them in secular matters; as when men's natural temper is melancholy, jealous, fearful, proud, or the like.

3. It is rational to suppose, that this knowledge should be given immediately by God, and not be obtained by natural means. Upon what account should it seem unreasonable, that there should be any immediate communication between God and the creature? It is strange, that men should make any matter of difficulty of it. Why should not he that made all things, still have something immediately to do with the things that he has made? Where lies the great difficulty, if we own the being of a God, and that he created all things out of nothing, of allowing some immediate influence of God on the creation still? And if it be reasonable to suppose it with respect to any part of the Creation, it is especially so with respect to reasonable, intelligent creatures; who are next to God in the gradation of the different orders of beings, and whose business is most immediately with God; and reason teaches, that man was made to serve and glorify his Creator. And if it be rational to suppose, that God immediately communicates himself to man in any affair, it is in this. It is rational to suppose, that God would reserve that knowledge and wisdom, which is of such a divine and excellent nature, to be bestowed immediately by himself; and that it should not be left in the power of second causes. Spiritual wisdom and grace is the highest and most excellent gift that ever God bestows on any creature; in this, the highest excellency and perfection of a rational creature consists. It is also immensely the most important of all divine gifts: it is that wherein man's happiness consists, and on which his everlasting welfare depends. How rational is it to suppose that God, however he has left lower gifts to second causes, and in some sort in their power, yet should reserve this most excellent, divine, and important of all divine communications, in his own hands, to be bestowed immediately by himself, as a thing too great for second causes to be concerned in. It is rational to suppose, that this blessing should be immediately

from God, for there is no gift or benefit that is in itself so nearly related to the divine nature. Nothing which the creature receives, is so much a participation of the Deity; it is a kind of emanation of God's beauty, and is related to God as the light is to the sun. It is, therefore, congruous and fit, that when it is given of God, it should be immediately from himself, and by himself, according to his own sovereign will.

It is rational to suppose, that it should be beyond man's power to obtain this light, by the mere strength of natural reason; for it is not a thing that belongs to reason, to see the beauty and loveliness of spiritual things; it is not a speculative thing, but depends on the sense of the heart. Reason, indeed, is necessary, in order to it, as it is by reason only that we are become the subjects of the means of it; which means, I have already shown to be necessary in order to it, though they have no proper causal influence in the affair. It is by reason that we become possessed of a notion of those doctrines that are the subject matter of this divine light, or knowledge; and reason may many ways be indirectly and remotely an advantage to it. Reason has also to do in the acts that are immediately consequent on this discovery: for, seeing the truth of religion from hence, is by reason; though it be but by one step, and the inference be immediate. So reason has to do in that accepting of, and trusting in Christ, that is consequent on it. But if we take reason strictly—not for the faculty of mental perception in general, but for ratiocination, or a power of inferring by arguments—the perceiving of spiritual beauty and excellency no more belongs to reason than it belongs to the sense of feeling to perceive colors, or to the power of seeing to perceive the sweetness of food. It is out of reason's province to perceive the beauty or loveliness of any thing: such a perception does not belong to that faculty. Reason's work is to perceive truth and not excellency. It is not ratiocination that gives men the perception of the beauty and amiableness of a countenance, though it may be many ways indirectly an advantage to it; yet it is no more reason that immediately perceives it, than it is reason that perceives the sweetness of honey: it depends on the sense of the heart. Reason may determine that a countenance is beautiful to others, it may determine that honey is sweet to others; but it will never give me a perception of its sweetness.

I will conclude with a very brief improvement of what has been said.

First, This doctrine may lead us to reflect on the goodness of God, that has so ordered it, that a saving evidence of the truth of the gospel is such, as is attainable by persons of mean capacities and advantages, as well as those that are of the greatest parts and learning. If the evidence of the gospel depended only on history, and such reasonings as learned men only are capable of, it would be above the reach of far the greatest part of mankind. But persons with an ordinary degree of knowledge, are capable, without a long and subtile train of reasoning, to see the divine excellency of the things of religion: they are capable of being taught by the Spirit of God, as well as learned men. The evidence that is this way obtained, is vastly better and more satisfying, than all that can be obtained by the arguings of those that are most learned, and greatest masters of reason. And babes are as capable of knowing these things, as the wise and prudent; and they are often hid from these, when they are revealed to those. 1 Corinthians i: 26, 27. For ye see your calling, brethren, how that not many wise men, after the flesh, not many mighty, not many noble, are called. But God hath chosen the foolish things of the world."

Secondly. This doctrine may well put us upon examining ourselves, whether we have ever had this divine light let into our souls. If there be such a thing, doubtless it is of great importance whether we have thus been taught by the Spirit of God; whether the light of the glorious gospel of Christ, who is the image of God, hath shined unto us, giving us the light of the knowledge of the glory of God in the face of Jesus Christ; whether we have seen the Son, and believed on him, or have that faith of gospel doctrines which arises from a spiritual sight of Christ.

Thirdly. All may hence be exhorted, earnestly to seek this spiritual light. To influence and move to it, the following things may be considered.

1. This is the most excellent and divine wisdom that any creature is capable of. It is more excellent than any human learning; it is far more excellent than all the knowledge of the greatest philosophers or statesmen. Yea, the least glimpse of the glory of God in the face of Christ doth more exalt and ennoble the soul, than all the knowledge of those that have the greatest speculative understanding in divinity without grace. This knowledge has the most noble object that can be, viz. the divine glory and excellency of God and Christ. The knowledge of these objects is that wherein consists the most excellent knowledge of the angels, yea, of God himself.

2. This knowledge is that which is above all others sweet and joyful. Men have a great deal of pleasure in human knowledge, in studies of natural things; but this is nothing to that joy which arises from this divine light shining into the soul. This light gives a view of those things that are immensely the most exquisitely beautiful, and capable of delighting the eye of the understanding. This spiritual light is the dawning of the light of glory in the heart. There is nothing so powerful as this to support persons in affliction, and to give the mind peace and brightness in this stormy and dark world.

3. This light is such as effectually influences the inclination, and changes the nature of the soul. It assimilates our nature to the divine nature, and changes the soul into an image of the same glory that is beheld. 2 Corinthians iii: 18. "But we all with open face, beholding as in a glass the glory of the Lord, are changed into the same image, from glory to glory, even as by the Spirit of the Lord." This knowledge will wean[22] from the world, and raise the inclination to heavenly things. It will turn the heart to God as the fountain of good, and to choose him for the only portion. This light, and this only, will bring the soul to a saving close with Christ. It conforms the heart to the gospel, mortifies its enmity and opposition against the scheme of salvation therein revealed; it causes the heart to embrace the joyful tidings, and entirely to adhere to, and acquiesce in, the revelation of Christ as our Savior; it causes the whole soul to accord and symphonize with it, admitting it with entire credit and respect, cleaving to it with full inclination and affection; and it effectually disposes the soul to give up itself entirely to Christ.

4. This light, and this only, has its fruit in an universal holiness of life. No merely notional or speculative understanding of the doctrines of religion will ever bring to this. But this light, as it reaches the bottom of the heart, and changes the nature, so it will effectually dispose to an universal obedience. It shows God as worthy to be obeyed and served. It draws forth the heart in a sincere love to God, which is the only principle of a true, gracious, and universal obedience: and it convinces of the reality of those glorious rewards that God has promised to them that obey him.

1733, 1734

---

[22] Withdraw.

PERSONAL NARRATIVE*

I had a variety of concerns and exercises[1] about my soul from my childhood, but had two more remarkable seasons of awakening[2] before I met with that change by which I was brought to those new dispositions and that new sense of things that I have since had. The first time was when I was a boy, some years before I went to college, at a time of remarkable awakening in my father's congregation. I was then very much affected for many months and concerned about the things of religion and my soul's salvation and was abundant in duties. I used to pray five times a day in secret, and to spend much time in religious talk with other boys and used to meet with them to pray together. I experienced I know not what kind of delight in religion. My mind was much engaged in it, and had much self-righteous pleasure; and it was my delight to abound in religious duties. I, with some of my schoolmates, joined together and built a booth in a swamp, in a very secret and retired place, for a place of prayer. And besides, I had particular secret places of my own in the woods, where I used to retire by myself, and used to be from time to time much affected. My affections seemed to be lively and easily moved, and I seemed to be in my element, when engaged in religious duties. And I am ready to think, many are deceived with such affections and such a kind of delight, as I then had in religion, and mistake it for grace.

But in process of time, my convictions and affections wore off; and I entirely lost all those affections and delights, and left off secret prayer, at least as to any constant performance of it, and returned like a dog to his vomit, and went on in ways of sin.[3]

Indeed, I was at some times very uneasy, especially towards the latter part of the time of my being at college. 'Til it pleased God, in my last year at college, at a time when I was in the midst of many uneasy thoughts about the state of my soul, to seize me with a pleurisy;[4] in which he brought me nigh to the grave, and shook me over the pit of hell.

But yet, it was not long after my recovery before I fell again into my old ways of sin. But God would not suffer me to go on with any quietness; but I had great and violent inward struggles: 'til after many conflicts with wicked inclinations and repeated resolutions and bonds that I laid myself under by a kind of vows to God, I was brought wholly to break off all former wicked ways and all ways of known outward sin, and to apply myself to seek my salvation and practice the duties of religion, but without that kind of affection and delight that I had formerly experienced. My concern now wrought more by inward struggles and conflicts and self-reflections. I made seeking my salvation the main business of my life. But yet it seems to me I sought after a miserable manner, which has made me sometimes since to question whether ever it issued in that which was saving,[5] being ready to doubt, whether such miserable seeking was ever succeeded. But yet I was brought to seek salvation in a manner that I never was before. I felt a spirit to part with all things in the world for an interest in Christ. My concern continued and prevailed, with many exercising thoughts and inward struggles; but yet it never seemed to be proper to express my concern that I had, by the name of terror.

---

* Edwards's autobiography was published in 1765 in *The Life and Character of the Late Rev. Mr. Jonathan Edwards* by his friend Samuel Hopkins; it was titled "An Account of His Conversions, Experiences, and Religious Exercises, Given by Himself."

[1] Religious activities.   [2] Religious arousing.

[3] "As a dog returneth to his vomit, so a fool returneth to his folly," from Proverb 26:11.

[4] A respiratory inflammation.   [5] Spiritually redeeming.

From my childhood up, my mind had been wont to be full of objections against the doctrine of God's sovereignty, in choosing whom he would to eternal life and rejecting whom he pleased, leaving them eternally to perish and be everlastingly tormented in hell. It used to appear like a horrible doctrine to me. But I remember the time very well when I seemed to be convinced, and fully satisfied, as to this sovereignty of God and his justice in thus eternally disposing of men according to his sovereign pleasure. But never could give an account how or by what means I was thus convinced; not in the least imagining, in the time of it nor a long time after, that there was any extraordinary influence of God's spirit in it; but only that now I saw further, and my reason apprehended the justice and reasonableness of it. However, my mind rested in it; and it put an end to all those cavils and objections, that had 'til then abode with me, all the proceeding part of my life. And there has been a wonderful alteration in my mind, with respect to the doctrine of God's sovereignty, from that day to this; so that I scarce ever have found so much as the rising of an objection against God's sovereignty, in the most absolute sense, in showing mercy to whom he will show mercy and hardening and eternally damning whom he will.[6] God's absolute sovereignty and justice, with respect to salvation and damnation, is what my mind seems to rest assured of, as much as of anything that I see with my eyes; at least it is so at times. But I have oftentimes since that first conviction had quite another kind of sense of God's sovereignty than I had then. I have often since not only had a conviction, but a delightful conviction. The doctrine of God's sovereignty has very often appeared an exceeding pleasant, bright and sweet doctrine to me; and absolute sovereignty is what I love to ascribe to God. By my first conviction was not with this.

The first that I remember that ever I found anything of that sort of inward, sweet delight in God and divine things, that I have lived much in since, was on reading those words, 1 Timothy 1:17, "Now unto the king eternal, immortal, invisible, the only wise God, be honor and glory for ever and ever, Amen." As I read the words, there came into my soul, and was as it were diffused through it, a sense of the glory of the Divine Being, a new sense, quite different from anything I ever experienced before. Never any words of scripture seemed to me as these words did. I thought with myself, how excellent a being that was, and how happy I should be if I might enjoy that God and be rapt[7] up to God in Heaven, and be as it were swallowed up in him. I kept saying, and as it were singing over these words of scripture to myself; and went to prayer to pray to God that I might enjoy him; and prayed in a manner quite different from what I used to do, with a new sort of affection. But it never came into my thought that there was anything spiritual or of a saving nature in this.

From about that time I began to have a new kind of apprehensions and ideas of Christ, and the work of redemption, and the glorious way of salvation by him. I had an inward, sweet sense of these things, that at times came into my heart; and my soul was led away in pleasant views and contemplations of them. And my mind was greatly engaged to spend my time in reading and meditating on Christ, and the beauty and excellency of his person, and the lovely way of salvation, by free grace in him. I found no books so delightful to me as those that treated of these subjects. Those words Canticles[8] 2:1, used to be abundantly with me: "I am the Rose of Sharon, the lily of the valleys." The words seemed to me, sweetly to

---

[6] "Therefore hath he mercy on whom he will have mercy, and whom he will be hardeneth," from Romans 9:18.
[7] Lifted.   [8] Another name for the biblical Song of Solomon.

represent the loveliness and beauty of Jesus Christ. And the whole book of Canticles used to be pleasant to me; and I used to be much in reading it, about that time. And found, from time to time, an inward sweetness that used, as it were, to carry me away in my contemplations, in what I know not how to express otherwise, than by a calm, sweet abstraction of soul from all the concerns of this world, and a kind of vision, or fixed ideas and imaginations, of being alone in the mountains or some solitary wilderness, far from all mankind, sweetly conversing with Christ, and rapt and swallowed up in God. The sense I had of divine things would often of a sudden as it were, kindle up a sweet burning in my heart, an ardor of my soul, that I know not how to express.

Not long after I first began to experience these things, I gave an account to my father of some things that had passed in my mind. I was pretty much affected by the discourse we had together. And when the discourse was ended, I walked abroad alone, in a solitary place in my father's pasture, for contemplation. And as I was walking there, and looked up on the sky and clouds; there came into my mind a sweet sense of the glorious majesty and grace of God that I know not how to express. I seemed to see them both in a sweet conjunction, majesty and meekness joined together. It was a sweet and gentle, and holy majesty; and also a majestic meekness; an awful sweetness; a high, and great, and holy gentleness.

After this my sense of divine things gradually increased, and became more and more lively, and had more of that inward sweetness. The appearance of everything was altered: there seemed to be, as it were, a calm, sweet cast, or appearance of divine glory, in almost everything. God's excellency, his wisdom, his purity and love, seemed to appear in everything: in the sun, moon and stars; in the clouds, and blue sky; in the grass, flowers, trees; in the water, and all nature; which used greatly to fix my mind. I often used to sit and view the moon for a long time, and so in the daytime spent much time in viewing the clouds and sky to behold the sweet glory of God in these things, in the meantime, singing forth with a low voice my contemplations of the Creator and Redeemer. And scarce anything, among all the works of nature, was so sweet to me as thunder and lightning. Formerly, nothing had been so terrible to me. I used to be a person uncommonly terrified with thunder, and it used to strike me with terror when I saw a thunderstorm rising. But now, on the contrary, it rejoiced me. I felt God at the first appearance of a thunderstorm. And used to take the opportunity at such times to fix myself to view the clouds, and see the lightnings play, and hear the majestic and awful voice of God's thunder, which often times was exceeding entertaining, leading me to sweet contemplations of my great and glorious God. And while I viewed, used to spend my time, as it always seemed natural to me, to sing or chant forth my meditations, to speak my thoughts in soliloquies, and speak with a singing voice.

I felt then a great satisfaction as to my good estate.[9] But that did not content me. I had vehement longings of soul after God and Christ, and after more holiness, wherewith my heart seemed to be full and ready to break: which often brought to mind the words of the psalmist, Psalm 119:28: "My soul breaketh for the longing it hath." I often felt a mourning and lamenting in my heart that I had not turned to God sooner, that I might have had more time to grow in grace. My mind was greatly fixed on divine things; I was almost perpetually in the contemplation of them. Spent most of my time in thinking of divine things, year after

---

[9] Spiritual condition.

year. And used to spend abundance of my time in walking alone in the woods and solitary places for meditation, soliloquy and prayer, and converse with God. And it was always my manner, at such times, to sing forth my contemplations. And was almost constantly in ejaculatory prayer, wherever I was. Prayer seemed to be natural to me, as the breath by which the inward burnings of my heart had vent.

The delights which I now felt in things of religion were of an exceeding different kind from those forementioned, that I had when I was a boy. They were totally of another kind; and what I then had no more notion or idea of, than one born blind has of pleasant and beautiful colors. They were of a more inward, pure, soul-animating and refreshing nature. Those former delights never reached the heart, and did not arise from any sight of the divine excellency of the things of God or any taste of the soul-satisfying and life-giving good there is in them.

My sense of divine things seemed gradually to increase, 'til I went to preach at New York,[10] which was about a year and a half after they began. While I was there, I felt them, very sensibly,[11] in a much higher degree, than I had done before. My longings after God and holiness, were much increased. Pure and humble, holy and heavenly Christianity appeared exceeding amiable to me. I felt in me a burning desire to be in everything a complete Christian, and conformed to the blessed image of Christ, and that I might live in all things, according to the pure, sweet and blessed rules of the gospel. I had an eager thirsting after progress in these things. My longings after it put me upon pursuing and pressing after them. It was my continual strife day and night, and constant inquiry, how I should be more holy, and live more holily, and more becoming a child of God, and disciple of Christ. I sought an increase of grace and holiness, and that I might live an holy life with vastly more earnestness than ever I sought grace, before I had it. I used to be continually examining myself, and studying and contriving for likely ways and means how I should live holily with far greater diligence and earnestness than ever I pursued anything in my life; but with too great a dependence on my own strength, which afterwards proved a great damage to me. My experience had not then taught me, as it has done since, my extreme feebleness and impotence, every manner of way, and the innumerable and bottomless depths of secret corruption and deceit that there was in my heart. However, I went on with my eager pursuit after more holiness, and sweet conformity to Christ.

The Heaven I desired was a heaven of holiness, to be with God, and to spend my eternity in divine love, and holy communion with Christ. My mind was very much taken up with contemplations on heaven, and the enjoyments of those there, and living there in perfect holiness, humility and love. And it used at that time to appear a great part of the happiness of heaven that there the saints could express their love to Christ. It appeared to me a great clog and hindrance and burden to me that what I felt within I could not express to God and give vent to as I desired. The inward ardor of my soul seemed to be hindered and pent up, and could not freely flame out as it would. I used often to think how in heaven this sweet principle should freely and fully vent and express itself. Heaven appeared to me exceeding delightful as a world of love. It appeared to me that all happiness consisted in living in pure, humble, heavenly, divine love.

I remember the thoughts I used then to have of holiness. I remember I then said

[10] From August 1722 to April 1723, Edwards assisted as pastor in a Presbyterian church in New York City.
[11] Perceptibly.

sometimes to myself, "I do certainly know that I love holiness such as the gospel prescribes." It appeared to me there was nothing in it but what was ravishingly lovely. It appeared to me to be the highest beauty and amiableness, above all other beauties, that it was a divine beauty, far purer than anything here upon earth; and that everything else, was like mire, filth and defilement in comparison of it.

Holiness, as I then wrote down some of my contemplations on it, appeared to me to be of a sweet, pleasant, charming, serene, calm nature. It seemed to me it brought an inexpressible purity, brightness, peacefulness and ravishment to the soul, and that it made the soul like a field or garden of God, with all manner of pleasant flowers; that is, all pleasant, delightful and undisturbed, enjoying a sweet calm, and the gently vivifying beams of the sun. The soul of a true Christian, as I then wrote my meditations, appeared like such a little white flower as we see in the spring of the year, low and humble on the ground, opening its bosom, to receive the pleasant beams of the sun's glory, rejoicing as it were, in a calm rapture, diffusing around a sweet fragrancy, standing peacefully and lovingly in the midst of other flowers round about, all in like manner opening their bosoms, to drink in the light of the sun.

There was no part of creature holiness that I then, and at other times, had so great a sense of the loveliness of, as humility, brokenness of heart and poverty of spirit, and there was nothing that I had such a spirit to long for. My heart, as it were, panted after this to lie low before God, and in the dust; that I might be nothing, and that God might be all; that I might become as a little child.[12]

While I was there at New York, I sometimes was much affected with reflections on my past life, considering how late it was, before I began to be truly religious and how wickedly I had lived 'til then; and once so as to weep abundantly, and for a considerable time together.

On January 12, [1723] I made a solemn dedication of myself to God, and wrote it down; giving up myself, and all that I had to God; to be for the future in no respect my own; to act as one that had no right to himself, in any respect. And solemnly vowed to take God for my whole portion and felicity, looking on nothing else as any part of my happiness, nor acting as if it were: and his law for the constant rule of my obedience, engaging to fight with all my might against the world, the flesh and the devil,[13] to the end of my life. But have reason to be infinitely humbled, when I consider, how much I have failed of answering my obligation.

I had then abundance of sweet religious conversation in the family where I lived, with Mr. John Smith, and his pious mother. My heart was knit in affection to those in whom were appearances of true piety, and I could bear the thoughts of no other companions but such as were holy, and the disciples of the blessed Jesus.

I had great longings for the advancement of Christ's kingdom in the world. My secret prayer used to be in great part taken up in praying for it. If I heard the least hint of anything that happened in any part of the world that appeared to me in some respect or other, to have a favorable aspect on the interest of Christ's kingdom, my soul eagerly catched at it; and it would much animate and refresh me. I

[12] ". . .Whosoever shall not receive the kingdom of God as a little child, he shall not enter therein," from Mark 10:15.

[13] "Good Lord, deliver us, From all inordinate and sinful affections; and from all the deceits of the world, the flesh, and the devil," from "Litany," the Anglican Book of Common Prayer.

used to be earnest to read public newsletters, mainly for that end, to see if I could not find some news favorable to the interest of religion in the world.

I very frequently used to retire into a solitary place, on the banks of Hudson's river, at some distance from the city, for contemplation on divine things and secret converse with God, and had many sweet hours there. Sometimes Mr. Smith and I walked there together to converse of the things of God, and our conversation used much to turn on the advancement of Christ's kingdom in the world, and the glorious things that God would accomplish for his church in the latter days.

I had then, and at other times, the greatest delight in the holy Scriptures, of any book whatsoever. Oftentimes in reading it, every word seemed to touch my heart. I felt an harmony between something in my heart, and those sweet and powerful words. I seemed often to see so much light exhibited by every sentence, and such a refreshing ravishing food communicated, that I could not get along in reading. Used oftentimes to dwell long on one sentence, to see the wonders contained in it; and yet almost every sentence seemed to be full of wonders.

I came away from New York in the month of April, 1723, and had a most bitter parting with Madam Smith and her son. My heart seemed to sink within me, at leaving the family and city, where I had enjoyed so many sweet and pleasant days. I went from New York to Weathersfield[14] by water. As I sailed away, I kept sight of the city as long as I could; and when I was out of sight of it, it would affect me much to look that way, with a kind of melancholy mixed with sweetness. However, that night after this sorrowful parting, I was greatly comforted in God at Westchester,[15] where we went ashore to lodge, and had a pleasant time of it all the voyage to Saybrook.[16] It was sweet to me to think of meeting dear Christians in heaven, where we should never part more. At Saybrook we went ashore to lodge on Saturday, and there kept sabbath where I had a sweet and refreshing season, walking alone in the fields.

After I came home to Windsor,[17] remained much in a like frame of my mind as I had been in at New York, but only sometimes felt my heart ready to sink with the thoughts of my friends at New York. And my refuge and support was in contemplations on the heavenly state, as I find in my diary of May 1, 1723. It was my comfort to think of that state where there is fulness of joy; where reigns heavenly, sweet, calm and delightful love, without alloy; where there are continually the dearest expressions of this love; where is the enjoyment of the persons loved without ever parting; where these persons that appear so lovely in this world will really be inexpressibly more lovely, and full of love to us. And how sweetly will the mutual lovers join together to sing the praises of God and the Lamb![18] How full will it fill us with joy to think that this enjoyment, these sweet exercises will never cease or come to an end, but will last to all eternity!

Continued much in the same frame in the general that I had been in at New York, 'til I went to New Haven to live there as tutor of the college,[19] having some special seasons of uncommon sweetness; particularly once at Bolton[20] in a journey from Boston, walking out alone in the fields. After I went to New Haven, I sunk in religion, my mind being diverted from my eager and violent pursuits after holiness by some affairs that greatly perplexed and distracted my mind.

[14] Wethersfield, Connecticut.   [15] Westchester, New York.   [16] Saybrook, Connecticut.
[17] Windsor, Connecticut.   [18] Christ.   [19] Yale College, in 1724.
[20] Bolton, Connecticut.

In September, 1725, was taken ill at New Haven, and endeavoring to go home to Windsor, was so ill at the North Village that I could go no further where I lay sick for about a quarter of a year. And in this sickness, God was pleased to visit me again with the sweet influences of his spirit. My mind was greatly engaged there on divine, pleasant contemplations and longings of soul. I observed that those who watched with me would often be looking out for the morning, and seemed to wish for it. Which brought to my mind those words of the psalmist, which my soul with sweetness made its own language: "My soul waitest for the Lord, more than they that watch for the morning, I say, more than they that watch for the morning."[21] And when the light of the morning came, and the beams of the sun came in at the windows, it refreshed my soul from one morning to another. It seemed to me to be some image of the sweet light of God's glory.

I remember, about that time, I used greatly to long for the conversion of some that I was concerned with. It seemed to me I could gladly honor them, and with delight be a servant to them, and lie at their feet, if they were but truly holy.

But sometime after this, I was again greatly diverted in my mind with some temporal concerns that exceedingly took up my thoughts, greatly to the wounding of my soul, and went on through various exercises, that it would be tedious to relate, that gave me much more experience of my own heart than ever I had before.

Since I came to this town,[22] I have often had sweet complacency in God, in views of his glorious perfections and the excellency of Jesus Christ. God has appeared to me a glorious and lovely Being, chiefly on the account of his holiness. The holiness of God has always appeared to me the most lovely of all his attributes. The doctrines of God's absolute sovereignty and free grace in showing mercy to whom he would show mercy, and man's absolute dependence on the operations of God's Holy Spirit, have very often appeared to me as sweet and glorious doctrines. These doctrines have been much my delight. God's sovereignty has ever appeared to me as great part of his glory. It has often been sweet to me to go to God and adore him as a sovereign God, and ask sovereign mercy of him.

I have loved the doctrines of the gospel; they have been to my soul like green pastures. The gospel has seemed to me to be the richest treasure, the treasure that I have most desired and longed that it might dwell richly in me. The way of salvation by Christ has appeared in a general way glorious and excellent, and most pleasant and beautiful. It has often seemed to me that it would in a great measure spoil heaven to receive it in any other way. That text has often been affecting and delightful to me, Isaiah 32:2: "A man shall be an hiding place from the wind, and a covert from the tempest," etc.

It has often appeared sweet to me to be united to Christ; to have him for my head, and to be a member of his body; and also to have Christ for my teacher and prophet. I very often think with sweetness and longings and pantings of soul, of being a little child, taking hold of Christ, to be led by him through the wilderness of this world. That text, Matthew 18:3 at the beginning, has often been sweet to me, "Except ye be converted, and become as little children, etc." I love to think of coming to Christ, to receive salvation of him, poor in spirit, and quite empty of

---

[21] Psalm 130:6.
[22] Northampton, Massachusetts, in 1726; he was appointed minister there in 1727.

self; humbly exalting him alone; cut entirely off from my own root, and to grow into and out of Christ; to have God in Christ to be all in all; and to live by faith on the Son of God, a life of humble, unfeigned confidence in him. That Scripture has often been sweet to me, Psalm 115:1: "Not unto us, O Lord, not unto us, but unto Thy name give glory, for Thy mercy, and for Thy truth's sake." And those words of Christ, Luke 10:21: "In that hour Jesus rejoiced in spirit, and said, I thank thee, O Father, Lord of heaven and earth, that Thou hast hid these things from the wise and prudent, and hast revealed them unto babes: Even so Father, for so it seemed good in Thy sight." That sovereignty of God that Christ rejoiced in seemed to me to be worthy to be rejoiced in, and that rejoicing of Christ seemed to me to show the excellency of Christ, and the spirit that he was of.

Sometimes only mentioning a single word causes my heart to burn within me, or only seeing the name of Christ or the name of some attribute of God. And God has appeared glorious to me on account of the Trinity. It has made me have exalting thoughts of God, that he subsists in three persons: Father, Son, and Holy Ghost.

The sweetest joys and delights I have experienced have not been those that have arisen from a hope of my own good estate, but in a direct view of the glorious things of the gospel. When I enjoy this sweetness it seems to carry me above the thoughts of my own safe estate. It seems at such times a loss that I cannot bear, to take off my eye from the glorious, pleasant object I behold without me, to turn my eye in upon myself, and my own good estate.

My heart has been much on the advancement of Christ's kingdom in the world. The histories of the past advancement of Christ's kingdom have been sweet to me. When I have read histories of past ages, the pleasantest thing in all my reading has been to read of the kingdom of Christ being promoted. And when I have expected in my reading to come to any such thing, I have lotted[23] upon it all the way as I read. And my mind has been much entertained and delighted with the Scripture promises and prophecies of the future glorious advancement of Christ's kingdom on earth.

I have sometimes had a sense of the excellent fullness of Christ, and his meetness and suitableness as a Savior; whereby he has appeared to me, far above all, the chief of ten thousands.[24] And His blood and atonement has appeared sweet, and His righteousness sweet; which is always accompanied with an ardency of spirit, and inward strugglings and breathings and groanings, that cannot be uttered, to be emptied of myself and swallowed up in Christ.

Once, as I rid out into the woods for my health, Anno 1737, and having lit from my horse in a retired place, as my manner commonly has been, to walk for divine contemplation and prayer, I had a view, that for me was extraordinary, of the glory of the Son of God, as mediator between God and man, and his wonderful, great, full, pure and sweet grace and love, and meek and gentle condescension. This grace, that appeared to me so calm and sweet, appeared great above the heavens. The person of Christ appeared ineffably excellent, with an excellency great enough to swallow up all thought and conception, which continued, as near as I can judge, about an hour, which kept me, the bigger part of the time, in a flood of tears, and weeping aloud. I felt withal an ardency of soul to be, what I

---

[23] Delighted.
[24] "My beloved is . . . the chiefest among ten thousand," from Song of Solomon 5:10.

know not otherwise how to express, than to be emptied and annihilated; to lie in the dust, and to be full of Christ alone; to love him with a holy and pure love; to trust in him; to live upon him; to serve and follow him, and to be totally wrapt up in the fullness of Christ; and to be perfectly sanctified and made pure with a divine and heavenly purity. I have several other times had views very much of the same nature and that have had the same effects.

I have many times had a sense of the glory of the third person in the Trinity in his office of sanctifier; in his holy operations communicating divine light and life to the soul. God in the communications of his Holy Spirit has appeared as an infinite fountain of divine glory and sweetness, being full and sufficient to fill and satisfy the soul, pouring forth itself in sweet communications, like the sun in its glory, sweetly and pleasantly diffusing light and life.

I have sometimes had an affecting sense of the excellency of the Word of God, as a word of life; as the light of life; a sweet, excellent, life-giving word, accompanied with a thirsting after that word, that it might dwell richly in my heart.

I have often, since I lived in this town, had very affecting views of my own sinfulness and vileness; very frequently so as to hold me in a kind of loud weeping, sometimes for a considerable time together, so that I have often been forced to shut myself up.[25] I have had a vastly greater sense of my wickedness, and the badness of my heart, since my conversion, than ever I had before. It has often appeared to me, that if God should mark iniquity against me, I should appear the very worst of all mankind, of all that have been since the beginning of the world of this time, and that I should have by far the lowest place in hell. When others that have come to talk with me about their soul concerns have expressed the sense they have had of their own wickedness by saying that it seemed to them that they were as bad as the devil himself, I thought their expressions seemed exceeding faint and feeble to represent my wickedness. I thought I should wonder that they should content themselves with such expressions as these, if I had any reason to imagine that their sin bore any proportion to mine. It seemed to me I should wonder at myself if I should express my wickedness in such feeble terms as they did.

My wickedness, as I am in myself, has long appeared to me perfectly ineffable and infinitely swallowing up all thought and imagination, like an infinite deluge or infinite mountains over my head. I know not how to express better what my sins appear to me to be than by heaping infinite upon infinite, and multiplying infinite by infinite. I go about very often, for this many years, with these expressions in my mind and in my mouth, "Infinite upon infinite. Infinite upon infinite!" When I look into my heart and take a view of my wickedness, it looks like an abyss infinitely deeper than hell. And it appears to me that were it not for free grace, exalted and raised up to the infinite height of all the fullness and glory of the great Jehovah,[26] and the arm of his power and grace stretched forth, in all the majesty of his power and in all the glory of his sovereignty, I should appear sunk down in my sins infinitely below hell itself, far beyond sight of everything but the piercing eye of God's grace, that can pierce even down to such a depth and to the bottom of such an abyss.

And yet I be not in the least inclined to think that I have a greater conviction of sin than ordinary. It seems to me my conviction of sin is exceeding small and faint. It appears to me enough to amaze me that I have no more sense of my sin. I

---

[25] To meditate alone in his study.   [26] In the Old Testament, the Hebrew God.

know certainly that I have very little sense of my sinfulness. That my sins appear to me so great don't seem to me to be because I have so much more conviction of sin than other Christians, but because I am so much worse and have so much more wickedness to be convinced of. When I have had these turns of weeping and crying for my sins, I thought I knew in the time of it that my repentance was nothing to my sin.

I have greatly longed of late for a broken heart and to lie low before God. And when I ask for humility of God, I can't bear the thoughts of being no more humble than other Christians. It seems to me that though their degrees of humility may be suitable for them, yet it would be a vile self-exaltation in me not to be the lowest in humility of all mankind. Others speak of their longing to be humbled to the dust. Though that may be a proper expression for them I always think for myself that I ought to be humbled down below hell. 'Tis an expression that it has long been natural for me to use in prayer to God. I ought to lie infinitely low before God.

It is affecting to me to think how ignorant I was, when I was a young Christian, of the bottomless, infinite depths of wickedness, pride, hypocrisy and deceit left in my heart.

I have vastly a greater sense of my universal, exceeding dependence on God's grace and strength and mere good pleasure, of late, than I used formerly to have, and have experienced more of an abhorrence of my own righteousness. The thought of any comfort or job, arising in me, on any consideration or reflection on my own amiableness, or any of my performances or experiences, or any goodness of heart or life is nauseous and detestable to me. And yet I am greatly afflicted with a proud and self-righteous spirit, much more sensibly than I used to be formerly. I see that serpent rising and putting forth its head, continually, everywhere, all around me.

Though it seems to me that in some respects I was a far better Christian for two or three years after my first conversion than I am now, and lived in a more constant delight and pleasure, yet of late years I have had a more full and constant sense of the absolute sovereignty of God and a delight in that sovereignty, and have had more of a sense of the glory of Christ as a mediator as revealed in the gospel. On one Saturday night in particular, had a particular discovery of the excellency of the gospel of Christ, above all other doctrines, so that I could not but say to myself, "This is my chosen light, my chosen doctrine," and of Christ, "This is my chosen prophet." It appeared to me to be sweet beyond all expression to follow Christ and to be taught and enlightened and instructed by him, to learn of him, and live to him.

Another Saturday night, January, [1739], had such a sense how sweet and blessed a thing it was to walk in the way of duty, to do that which was right and meet to be done and agreeable to the holy mind of God, that it caused me to break forth into a kind of a loud weeping, which held me some time, so that I was forced to shut myself up, and fasten the doors. I could not but as it were cry out, "How happy are they which do that which is right in the sight of God! They are blessed indeed, they are the happy ones!" I had at the same time, a very affecting sense how meet and suitable it was that God should govern the world, and order all things according to his own pleasure, and I rejoiced in it, and God reigned, and that his will was done.

1740, 1765

SINNERS IN THE HANDS OF AN ANGRY GOD*

DEUTERONOMY XXXII: 35

Their foot shall slide in due time.[1]

In this verse is threatened the vengeance of God on the wicked unbelieving Israelites, who were God's visible people, and who lived under the means of grace;[2] but who, nonwithstanding all God's wonderful works towards them, remained (as verse 28)[3] void of counsel, having no understanding in them. Under all the cultivations of heaven, they brought forth bitter and poisonous fruit; as in the two verses next preceding the text.[4]—The expression I have chosen for my text, Their foot shall slide in due time, seems to imply the following things, relating to the punishment and destruction to which these wicked Israelites were exposed.

1. That they were always exposed to destruction; as one that stands or walks in slippery places is always exposed to fall. This is implied in the manner of their destruction coming upon them, being represented by their foot sliding. The same is expressed, Psalm lxxiii: 18. "Surely thou didst set them in slippery places; thou castedst them down into destruction."

2. It implies, that they were always exposed to sudden unexpected destruction. As he that walks in slippery places is every moment liable to fall, he cannot foresee one moment whether he shall stand or fall the next; and when he does fall, he falls at once without warning: which is also expressed in Psalm lxxiii: 18, 19. "Surely thou didst set them in slippery places; thou castedst them down into destruction: How are they brought into desolation as in a moment!"

3. Another thing implied is, that they are liable to fall of themselves, without being thrown down by the hand of another; as he that stands or walks on slippery ground needs nothing but his own weight to throw him down.

4. That the reason why they are not fallen already, and do not fall now, is only that God's appointed time is not come. For it is said, that when that due time, or appointed time comes, their foot shall slide. Then they shall be left to fall, as they are inclined by their own weight. God will not hold them up in these slippery places any longer, but will let them go; and then, at that very instant, they shall fall into destruction; as he that stands on such slippery declining ground, on the edge of a pit, he cannot stand alone, when he is let go he immediately falls and is lost.

The observation from the words that I would now insist upon is this. "There is nothing that keeps wicked men at any one moment out of hell, but the mere plea-

---

* Edwards preached this sermon on July 8, 1741, in Enfield, Connecticut.

[1] "To me belongeth vengeance, and recompense; their foot shall slide in due time: for the day of their calamity is at hand . . . ."

[2] By the laws of the Ten Commandments; in comparison, the Puritans' "means of grace" meant preaching God's word, and administering the sacraments of the Lord's supper and baptism.

[3] "They are a nation void of counsel, neither is there any understanding in them," from Deuteronomy 32:28.

[4] "For their vine is of the vine of Sodom, and fields of Gomorrah: their grapes are grapes of gall, their clusters are bitter: their wine is the poison of dragons, and the cruel venom of asps," from Deuteronomy 32:32–33; in Genesis 19:28 Sodom and Gomorrah were cities destroyed for their wickedness.

sure of God." By the mere pleasure of God, I mean his sovereign pleasure, his arbitrary will, restrained by no obligation, hindered by no manner of difficulty, any more than if nothing else but God's mere will had in the least degree, or in any respect whatsoever, any hand in the preservation of wicked men one moment. The truth of this observation may appear by the following considerations.

1. There is no want of power in God to cast wicked men into hell at any moment. Men's hands cannot be strong when God rises up. The strongest have no power to resist him, nor can any deliver out of his hands. He is not only able to cast wicked men into hell, but he can most easily do it. Sometimes an earthly prince meets with a great deal of difficulty to subdue a rebel, who has found means to fortify himself, and has made himself strong by the numbers of his followers. But it is not so with God. There is no fortress that is any defense from the power of God. Though hand join in hand, and vast multitudes of God's enemies combine and associate themselves, they are easily broken in pieces. They are as great heaps of light chaff before the whirlwind; or large quantities of dry stubble before devouring flames. We find it easy to tread on and crush a worm that we see crawling on the earth; so it is easy for us to cut or singe a slender thread that any thing hangs by: thus easy is it for God, when he pleases, to cast his enemies down to hell. What are we, that we should think to stand before him, at whose rebuke the earth trembles, and before whom the rocks are thrown down?

2. They deserve to be cast into hell; so that divine justice never stands in the way, it makes no objection against God's using his power at any moment to destroy them. Yea, on the contrary, justice calls aloud for an infinite punishment of their sins. Divine justice says of the tree that brings forth such grapes of Sodom, "Cut it down, why cumbereth it the ground?" Luke xiii: 7. The sword of divine justice is every moment brandished over their heads, and it is nothing but the hand of arbitrary mercy, and God's mere will, that holds it back.

3. They are already under a sentence of condemnation to hell. They do not only justly deserve to be cast down thither, but the sentence of the law of God, that eternal and immutable rule of righteousness that God has fixed between him and mankind, is gone out against them, and stands against them; so that they are bound over already to hell. John iii: 18, "He that believeth not is condemned already." So that every unconverted man properly belongs to hell; that is his place; from thence he is, John viii: 23. "Ye are from beneath:" and thither he is bound; it is the place that justice, and God's word, and the sentence of his unchangeable law assign to him.

4. They are now the objects of that very same anger and wrath of God, that is expressed in the torments of hell. And the reason why they do not go down to hell at each moment, is not because God, in whose power they are, is not then very angry with them; as he is with many miserable creatures now tormented in hell, who there feel and bear the fierceness of his wrath. Yea, God is a great deal more angry with great numbers that are now on earth: yea, doubtless, with many that are now in this congregation, who it may be are at ease, than he is with many of those who are now in the flames of hell.

So that it is not because God is unmindful of their wickedness, and does not resent it, that he does not let loose his hand and cut them off. God is not altogether such an one as themselves, though they may imagine him to be so. The wrath of God burns against them, their damnation does not slumber; the pit is prepared, the fire is made ready, the furnace is now hot, ready to receive them; the flames do now rage and glow. The glittering sword is whet,[5] and held over them, and the pit hath opened its mouth under them.

5. The devil stands ready to fall upon them, and seize them as his own, at what moment God shall permit him. They belong to him; he has their souls in his possession, and under his dominion. The scripture represents them as his goods, Luke xi: 12.[6] The devils watch them; they are ever by them at their right hand; they stand waiting for them, like greedy hungry lions that see their prey, and expect to have it, but are for the present kept back. If God should withdraw his hand, by which they are restrained, they would in one moment fly upon their poor souls. The old serpent is gaping for them; hell opens its mouth wide to receive them; and if God should permit it, they would be hastily swallowed up and lost.

6. There are in the souls of wicked men those hellish principles reigning, that would presently kindle and flame out into hell fire, if it were not for God's restraints. There is laid in the very nature of carnal men, a foundation for the torments of hell. There are those corrupt principles, in reigning power in them, and in full possession of them, that are seeds of hell fire. These principles are active and powerful, exceeding violent in their nature, and if it were not for the restraining hand of God upon them, they would soon break out, they would flame out after the same manner as the same corruptions, the same enmity does in the hearts of damned souls, and would beget the same torments as they do in them. The souls of the wicked are in scripture compared to the troubled seas, Isaiah lvii: 20.[7] For the present, God restrains their wickedness by his mighty power, as he does the raging waves of the troubled sea, saying, "Hitherto shalt thou come, but no further;"[8] but if God should withdraw that restraining power, it would soon carry all before it. Sin is the ruin and misery of the soul; it is destructive in its nature; and if God should leave it without restraint, there would need nothing else to make the soul perfectly miserable. The corruption of the heart of man is immoderate and boundless in its fury; and while wicked men live here, it is like fire pent up by God's restraints, whereas if it were let loose, it would set on fire the course of nature; and as the heart is now a sink of sin, so if sin was not restrained, it would immediately turn the soul into a fiery oven, or a furnace of fire and brimstone.

7. It is no security to wicked men for one moment, that there are no visible means of death at hand. It is no security to a natural man, that he is now in health, and that he does not see which way he should now immediately go out of the world by any accident, and that there is no visible danger in any respect in his circumstances. The manifold and continual experience of the world in all ages, shows this is no evidence, that a man is not on the very brink of eternity, and that the next step will not be into another world. The unseen, unthought-of ways and means of persons going suddenly out of the world are innumerable and inconceivable. Unconverted men walk over the pit of hell on a rotten covering, and there are innumerable places in this covering so weak that they will not bear their weight, and these places are not seen. The arrows of death fly unseen at noonday;[9] the sharpest sight cannot discern them. God has so many different unsearchable ways of taking wicked men out of the world and sending them to hell, that

---

[5] Sharpened.   [6] "Or if he shall ask an egg, will he offer him a scorpion?"

[7] "But the wicked are like the troubled sea, when it cannot rest, whose waters cast up mire and dirt."

[8] Job 38:11.

[9] "Thou shalt not be afraid for the terror by night; nor for the arrow that flieth by day," from Psalm 91:5.

there is nothing to make it appear, that God had need to be at the expence of a miracle, or go out of the ordinary course of his providence, to destroy any wicked man, at any moment. All the means that there are of sinners going out of the world, are so in God's hands, and so universally and absolutely subject to his power and determination, that it does not depend at all the less on the mere will of God, whether sinners shall at any moment go to hell, than if means were never made use of, or at all concerned in the case.

8. Natural men's prudence and care to preserve their own lives, or the care of others to preserve them, do not secure them a moment. To this, divine providence and universal experience do also bear testimony. There is this clear evidence that men's own wisdom is no security to them from death; that if it were otherwise we should see some difference between the wise and politic men of the world, and others, with regard to their liableness to early and unexpected death: but how is it in fact? Ecclesiastes ii: 16. "How dieth the wise man? even as the fool."

9. All wicked men's pains and contrivance which they use to escape hell, while they continue to reject Christ, and so remain wicked men, do not secure them from hell one moment. Almost every natural[10] man that hears of hell, flatters himself that he shall escape it; he depends upon himself for his own security; he flatters himself in what he has done, in what he is now doing, or what he intends to do. Every one lays out matters in his own mind how he shall avoid damnation, and flatters himself that he contrives well for himself, and that his schemes will not fail. They hear indeed that there are but few saved, and that the greater part of men that have died heretofore are gone to hell; but each one imagines that he lays out matters better for his own escape than others have done. He does not intend to come to that place of torment; he says within himself, that he intends to take effectual care, and to order matters so for himself as not to fail.

But the foolish children of men miserably delude themselves in their own schemes, and in confidence in their own strength and wisdom; they trust to nothing but a shadow. The greater part of those who heretofore have lived under the same means of grace, and are now dead, are undoubtedly gone to hell; and it was not because they were not as wise as those who are now alive: it was not because they did not lay out matters as well for themselves to secure their own escape. If we could speak with them, and inquire of them, one by one, whether they expected, when alive, and when they used to hear about hell, ever to be the subjects of that misery: we doutless, should hear one and another reply, "No, I never intended to come here: I have laid out matters otherwise in my mind; I thought I should contrive well for myself: I thought my scheme good. I intended to take effectual care; but it came upon me unexpected; I did not look for it at that time, and in that manner; it came as a thief: Death outwitted me: God's wrath was too quick for me. Oh, my cursed foolishness! I was flattering myself, and pleasing myself with vain dreams of what I would do hereafter; and when I was saying, Peace and safety, then suddenly destruction came upon me."

10. God has laid himself under no obligation, by any promise to keep any natural man out of hell one moment. God certainly has made no promises either of eternal life, or of any deliverance or preservation from eternal death, but what are contained in the covenant of grace,[11] the promises that are given in Christ, in

---

[10] Unsaved.

[11] The covenant by which God restored the possibility of salvation (due to Jesus' atonement), previously unattainable because of the Covenant of Works, made by God after the fall of Adam.

whom all the promises are yea and amen. But surely they have no interest in the promises of the covenant of grace who are not the children of the covenant, who do not believe in any of the promises, and have no interest in the Mediator of the covenant.[12]

So that, whatever some have imagined and pretended about promises made to natural men's earnest seeking and knocking,[13] it is plain and manifest, that whatever pains a natural man takes in religion, whatever prayers he makes, till he believes in Christ, God is under no manner of obligation to keep him a moment from eternal destruction.

So that, thus it is that natural men are held in the hand of God, over the pit of hell; they have deserved the fiery pit, and are already sentenced to it; and God is dreadfully provoked, his anger is as great towards them as to those that are actually suffering the executions of the fierceness of his wrath in hell, and they have done nothing in the least to appease or abate that anger, neither is God in the least bound by any promise to hold them up one moment; the devil is waiting for them, hell is gaping for them, the flames gather and flash about them, and would fain lay hold on them, and swallow them up; the fire bent up in their own hearts is struggling to break out: and they have no interest in any Mediator, there are no means within reach that can be any security to them. In short, they have no refuge, nothing to take hold of; all that preserves them every moment is the mere arbitrary will, and uncovenanted, unobliged forbearance of an incensed God.

Application

The use of this awful[14] subject may be for awakening unconverted persons in this congregation. This that you have heard is the case of every one of you that are out of Christ. That world of misery, that lake of burning brimstone, is extended abroad under you. There is the dreadful pit of the glowing flames and of the wrath of God; there is hell's wide gaping mouth open; and you have nothing to stand upon, nor any thing to take hold of: there is nothing between you and hell but the air; it is only the power and mere pleasure of God that holds you up.

You probably are not sensible[15] of this; you find you are kept out of hell, but do not see the hand of God in it; but look at other things, as the good state of your bodily constitution, your care of your own life, and the means you use for your own preservation. But indeed these things are nothing; if God should withdraw his hand, they would avail no more to keep you from falling, than the thin air to hold up a person that is suspended in it.

Your wickedness makes you as it were heavy as lead, and to tend downwards with great weight and pressure towards hell; and if God should let you go, you would immediately sink and swiftly descend and plunge into the bottomless gulf, and your healthy constitution, and your own care and prudence, and best contrivance, and all your righteousness, would have no mere influence to uphold you and keep you out of hell, than a spider's web would have to stop a fallen rock. Were it not for the sovereign pleasure of God, the earth would not bear you one moment; for you are a burden to it; the creation groans with you; the creature[16] is made subject to the bondage of your corruption, not willingly; the sun does not willingly shine upon you to give you light to serve sin and Satan; the earth does not will-

---

[12] Jesus.   [13] To gain salvation.   [14] Awesome.   [15] Aware.   [16] Body.

ingly yield her increase to satisfy your lusts; nor is it willingly a stage for your wickedness to be acted upon; the air does not willingly serve you for breath to maintain the flame of life in your vitals, while you spend your life in the service of God's enemies. God's creatures are good, and were made for men to serve God with, and do not willingly subserve to any other purpose, and groan when they are abused to purposes so directly contrary to their nature and end. And the world would spew you out, were it not for the sovereign hand of him who hath subjected it in hope. There are black clouds of God's wrath now hanging directly over your heads, full of the dreadful storm, and big with thunder; and were it not for the restraining hand of God, it would immediately burst forth upon you. The sovereign pleasure of God, for the present, stays his rough wind; otherwise it would come with fury, and your destruction would come like a whirlwind, and you would be like the chaff of the summer threshing floor.

The wrath of God is like great waters that are dammed for the present; they increase more and more, and rise higher and higher, till an outlet is given; and the longer the stream is stopped, the more rapid and mighty is its course, when once it is let loose. It is true, that judgment against your evil works has not been executed hitherto; the floods of God's vengeance have been withheld; but your guilt in the mean time is constantly increasing, and you are every day treasuring up more wrath; the waters are constantly rising, and waxing more and more mighty; and there is nothing but the mere pleasure of God, that holds the waters back, that are unwilling to be stopped, and press hard to go forward. If God should only withdraw his hand from the flood-gate, it would immediately fly open, and the fiery floods of the fierceness and wrath of God, would rush forth with inconceivable fury, and would come upon you with omnipotent power; and if your strength were ten thousand times greater than it is, yea, ten thousand times greater than the strength of the stoutest, sturdiest devil in hell, it would be nothing to withstand or endure it.

The bow of God's wrath is bent, and the arrow made ready on the string, and justice bends the arrow at your heart, and strains the bow, and it is nothing but the mere pleasure of God, and that of an angry God, without any promise or obligation at all, that keeps the arrow one moment from being made drunk with your blood. Thus all you that never passed under a great change of heart, by the mighty power of the Spirit of God upon your souls; all you that were never born again, and made new creatures, and raised from being dead in sin, to a state of new, and before altogether unexperienced light and life, are in the hands of an angry God. However you may have reformed your life in many things, and may have had religious affections, and may keep up a form of religion in your families and closets,[17] and in the house of God, it is nothing but his mere pleasure that keeps you from being this moment swallowed up in everlasting destruction. However unconvinced you may now be of the truth of what you hear, by and by you will be fully convinced of it. Those that are gone from being in the like circumstances with you, see that it was so with them; for destruction came suddenly upon most of them; when they expected nothing of it, and while they were saying, peace and safety: now they see, that those things on which they depended for peace and safety, were nothing but thin air and empty shadows.

The God that holds you over the pit of hell, much as one holds a spider, or some loathsome insect over the fire, abhors you, and is dreadfully provoked: his

---

[17] Study rooms for meditation.

wrath towards you burns like fire; he looks upon you as worthy of nothing else, but to be cast into the fire; he is of purer eyes than to bear to have you in his sight; you are ten thousand times more abominable in his eyes, than the most hateful venomous serpent is in ours. You have offended him infinitely more than ever a stubborn rebel did his prince; and yet it is nothing but his hand that holds you from falling into the fire every moment. It is to be ascribed to nothing else, that you did not go to hell the last night; that you was suffered to awake again in this world, after you closed your eyes to sleep. And there is no other reason to be given, why you have not dropped into hell since you arose in the morning, but that God's hand has held you up. There is no other reason to be given why you have not gone to hell, since you have sat here in the house of God, provoking his pure eyes by your sinful wicked manner of attending his solemn worship. Yea, there is nothing else that is to be given as a reason why you do not this very moment drop down into hell.

O sinner! Consider the fearful danger you are in: it is a great furnace of wrath, a wide and bottomless pit, full of the fire of wrath, that you are held over in the hand of that God, whose wrath is provoked and incensed as much against you, as against many of the damned in hell. You hang by a slender thread, with the flames of divine wrath flashing about it, and ready every moment to singe it, and burn it asunder: and you have no interest in any Mediator, and nothing to lay hold of to save yourself, nothing to keep off the flames of wrath, nothing of your own, nothing that you ever have done, nothing that you can do, to induce God to spare you one moment.—And consider here more particularly,

1. Whose wrath it is: it is the wrath of the infinite God. If it were only the wrath of man, though it were of the most potent prince, it would be comparatively little to be regarded. The wrath of kings is very much dreaded, especially of absolute monarchs, who have the possessions and lives of their subjects wholly in their power, to be disposed of at their mere will. Proverbs xx: 2, "The fear of a king is as the roaring of a lion: Whoso provoketh him to anger, sinneth against his own soul." The subject that very much enrages an arbitrary prince, is liable to suffer the most extreme torments that human art can invent, or human power can inflict. But the greatest earthly potentates in their greatest majesty and strength, and when clothed in their greatest terrors, are but feeble, despicable worms of the dust, in comparison of the great and almighty Creator and King of heaven and earth. It is but little that they can do, when most enraged, and when they have exerted the utmost of their fury. All the kings of the earth, before God, are as grasshoppers; they are nothing, and less than nothing: both their love and their hatred is to be despised. The wrath of the great King of kings, is as much more terrible than theirs, as his majesty is greater. Luke xii: 4, 5, "And I say unto you, my friends, Be not afraid of them that kill the body, and after that, have no more that they can do. But I will forewarn you whom you shall fear: fear him, which after he hath killed, hath power to cast into hell; yea, I say unto you, Fear him."

2. It is the fierceness of his wrath that you are exposed to. We often read of the fury of God; as in Isaiah lix: 18. "According to their deeds, accordingly he will repay fury to his adversaries." So Isaiah lxvi: 15, "For behold, the Lord will come with fire, and with his chariots like a whirlwind, to render his anger with fury, and his rebuke with flames of fire." And in many other places. So, Revelation xix: 15, we read of "the wine press of the fierceness and wrath of Almighty God." The words are exceeding terrible. If it had only been said, "the wrath of God," the words would have implied that which is infinitely dreadful: but it is "the fierceness

and wrath of God." The fury of God! the fierceness of Jehovah![18] Oh, how dreadful must that be! Who can utter or conceive what such expressions carry in them! But it is also "the fierceness and wrath of Almighty God." As though there would be a very great manifestation of his almighty power in what the fierceness of his wrath should inflict, as though omnipotence should be as it were enraged, and exerted, as men are wont to exert their strength in the fierceness of their wrath. Oh! then, what will be the consequence! What will become of the poor worms that shall suffer it! Whose hands can be strong? And whose heart can endure? To what a dreadful, inexpressible, inconceivable depth of misery must the poor creature be sunk who shall be the subject of this!

Consider this, you that are here present, that yet remain in an unregenerate state. That God will execute the fierceness of his anger, implies, that he will inflict wrath without any pity. When God beholds the ineffable extremity of your case, and sees your torment to be so vastly disproportioned to your strength, and sees how your poor soul is crushed, and sinks down, as it were, into an infinite gloom; he will have no compassion upon you, he will not forbear the executions of his wrath, or in the least lighten his hand; there shall be no moderation or mercy, nor will God then at all stay his rough wind; he will have no regard to your welfare, nor be at all careful lest you should suffer too much in any other sense, than only that you not suffer beyond what strict justice requires. Nothing shall be withheld, because it is so hard for you to bear. Ezekekiel viii: 18, "Therefore will I also deal in fury: mine eye shall not spare, neither will I have pity; and though they cry in mine ears with a loud voice, yet I will not hear them." Now God stands ready to pity you; this is a day of mercy; you may cry now with some encouragement of obtaining mercy. But when once the day of mercy is past, your most lamentable and dolorous cries and shrieks will be in vain; you will be wholly lost and thrown away of God, as to any regard to your welfare. God will have no other use to put you to, but to suffer misery; you shall be continued in being to no other end; for you will be a vessel of wrath fitted to destruction; and there will be no other use of this vessel, but to be filled full of wrath. God will be so far from pitying you when you cry to him, that it is said he will only "laugh and mock," Proverbs i: 25, 26,[19] etc.

How awful are those words, Isaiah lxiii: 3, which are the words of the great God. "I will tread them in mine anger, and will trample them in my fury, and their blood shall be sprinkled upon my garments, and I will stain all my raiment. It is perhaps impossible to conceive of words that carry in them greater manifestations of these three things, viz. contempt, and hatred, and fierceness of indignation. If you cry to God to pity you, he will be so far from pitying you in your doleful case, or showing you the least regard or favor, that instead of that, he will only tread you under foot. And though he will know that you cannot bear the weight of omnipotence treading upon you, yet he will not regard that, but he will crush you under his feet without mercy; he will crush out your blood, and make it fly, and it shall be sprinkled on his garments, so as to stain all his raiment. He will not only hate you, but he will have you, in the utmost contempt: no place shall be thought fit for you, but under his feet to be trodden down as the mire of the streets.

3. The misery you are exposed to is that which God will inflict to that end, that

[18] In the Old Testament, The Hebrew God.

[19] "But ye have set at nought all my counsel, and would none of my reproof: I will also laugh at your calamity; I will mock you when your fear cometh."

he might show what that wrath of Jehovah is. God hath had it on his heart to show to angels and men, both how excellent his love is, and also how terrible his wrath is. Sometimes earthly kings have a mind to show how terrible their wrath is, by the extreme punishments they would execute on those that would provoke them. Nebuchadnezzar, that mighty and haughty monarch of the Chaldean[20] empire, was willing to show his wrath when enraged with Shadrack, Meshech, and Abed-nego;[21] and accordingly gave orders that the burning fiery furnace should be heated seven times hotter than it was before; doubtless, it was raised to the utmost degree of fierceness that human art could raise it.[22] But the great God is also willing to show his wrath, and magnify his awful majesty and mighty power in the extreme sufferings of his enemies. Romans ix: 22, "What if God, willing to show his wrath, and to make his power known, endure with much long-suffering the vessels of wrath fitted to destruction?" And seeing this is his design, and what he has determined, even to show how terrible the unrestrained wrath, the fury and fierceness of Jehovah is, he will do it to effect. There will be something accomplished and brought to pass that will be dreadful with a witness. When the great and angry God hath risen up and executed his awful vengeance on the poor sinner, and the wretch is actually suffering the infinite weight and power of his indignation, then will God call upon the whole universe to behold that awful majesty and mighty power that is to be seen in it. Isaiah xxxiii:12–14, "And the people shall be as the burnings of lime, as thorns cut up shall they be burnt in the fire. Hear ye that are far off, what I have done; and ye that are near, acknowledge my might. The sinners in Zion are afraid; fearfulness hath surprised the hypocrites," etc.

Thus it will be with you that are in an unconverted state, if you continue in it; the infinite might, and majesty, and terribleness of the omnipotent God shall be magnified upon you, in the ineffable strength of your torments. You shall be tormented in the presence of the holy angels, and in the presence of the Lamb;[23] and when you shall be in this state of suffering, the glorious inhabitants of heaven shall go forth and look on the awful spectacle, that they may see what the wrath and fierceness of the Almighty is; and when they have seen it, they will fall down and adore that great power and majesty. Isaiah lxvi: 23, 24, "And it shall come to pass, that from one new moon to another, and from one sabbath to another, shall all flesh come to worship before me, saith the Lord. And they shall go forth and look upon the carcasses of the men that have transgressed against me; for their worm[24] shall not die, neither shall their fire be quenched, and they shall be an abhorring unto all flesh."

4. It is everlasting wrath. It would be dreadful to suffer this fierceness and wrath of Almighty God one moment; but you must suffer it to all eternity. There will be no end to this exquisite horrible misery. When you look forward, you shall see a long for ever, a boundless duration before you, which will swallow up your thoughts, and amaze your soul; and you will absolutely despair of ever having any deliverance, any end, any mitigation, any rest at all. You will know certainly that you must wear out long ages, millions of millions of ages, in wrestling and conflicting with this almighty merciless vengeance; and then when you have so done, when so many ages have actually been spent by you in this manner, you will know

---

[20] A semitic people related to the Babylonians.
[21] In Daniel 3:12–27 three captives who emerged unharmed from a fiery furnace.
[22] Daniel 3:1–30.   [23] Jesus.   [24] The worm that gnaws at their carcasses.

that all is but a point to what remains. So that your punishment will indeed be infinite. Oh, who can express what the state of a soul in such circumstances is! All that we can possibly say about it, gives but a very feeble, faint representation of it; it is inexpressible and inconceivable: For "who knows the power of God's anger?"[25]

How dreadful is the state of those that are daily and hourly in the danger of this great wrath and infinite misery! But this is the dismal case of every soul in this congregation that has not been born again, however moral and strict, sober and religious, they may otherwise be. Oh that you would consider it, whether you be young or old! There is reason to think, that there are many in this congregation now hearing this discourse, that will actually be the subjects of this very misery to all eternity. We know not who they are, or in what seats they sit, or what thoughts they now have. It may be they are now at ease, and hear all these things without much disturbance, and are now flattering themselves that they are not the persons, promising themselves that they shall escape. If we knew that there was one person, and but one, in the whole congregation, that was to be the subject of this misery, what an awful thing would it be to think of! If we knew who it was, what an awful sight would it be to see such a person! How might all the rest of the congregation lift up a lamentable and bitter cry over him! But, alas! instead of one, how many is it likely will remember this discourse in hell? And it would be a wonder, if some that are now present should not be in hell in a very short time, even before this year is out. And it would be no wonder if some persons, that now sit here, in some seats of this meeting-house, in health, quiet and secure, should be there before to-morrow morning. Those of you that finally continue in a natural condition, that shall keep out of hell longest will be there in a little time! your damnation does not slumber; it will come swiftly, and, in all probability, very suddenly upon many of you. You have reason to wonder that you are not already in hell. It is doubtless the case of some whom you have seen and known, that never deserved hell more than you, and that heretofore appeared as likely to have been now alive as you. Their case is past all hope; they are crying in extreme misery and perfect despair; but here you are in the land of the living and in the house of God, and have an opportunity to obtain salvation. What would not those poor damned hopeless souls give for one day's opportunity such as you now enjoy!

And now you have an extraordinary opportunity, a day wherein Christ has thrown the door of mercy wide open, and stands in calling and crying with a loud voice to poor sinners; a day wherein many are flocking to him, and pressing into the kingdom of God. Many are daily coming from the east, west, north and south; many that were very lately in the same miserable condition that you are in, are now in a happy state, with their hearts filled with love to him who has loved them, and washed them from their sins in his own blood, and rejoicing in hope of the glory of God. How awful is it to be left behind at such a day! To see so many others feasting, while you are pining and perishing! To see so many rejoicing and singing for joy of heart, while you have cause to mourn for sorrow of heart, and howl for vexation of spirit! How can you rest one moment in such a condition?

[25] "Who knoweth the power of thine anger? even according to thy fear, so is thy wrath," from Psalm 90:11.

Are not your souls as precious as the souls of the people at Suffield,[26] where they are flocking from day to day to Christ?

Are there not many here who have lived long in the world, and are not to this day born again? and so are aliens from the commonwealth of Israel,[27] and have done nothing ever since they have lived, but treasure up wrath against the day of wrath? Oh, sirs, your case, in an especial manner, is extremely dangerous. Your guilt and hardness of heart is extremely great. Do you not see how generally persons of your years are passed over and left, in the present remarkable and wonderful dispensation of God's mercy? You had need to consider yourselves, and awake thoroughly out of sleep. You cannot bear the fierceness and wrath of the infinite God. And you, young men, and young women, will you neglect this precious season which you now enjoy, when so many others of your age are renouncing all youthful vanities, and flocking to Christ? You especially have now an extraordinary opportunity; but if you neglect it, it will soon be with you as with those persons who spent all the precious days of youth in sin, and are now come to such a dreadful pass in blindness and hardness. And you, children, who are unconverted, do not you know that you are going down to hell, to bear the dreadful wrath of that God, who is now angry with you every day and every night? Will you be content to be the children of the devil, when so many other children in the land are converted, and are become the holy and happy children of the King of kings?

And let every one that is yet of Christ, and hanging over the pit of hell, whether they be old men and women, or middle aged, or young people, or little children, now hearken to the loud calls of God's word and providence. This acceptable year of the Lord, a day of such great favors to some, will doubtless be a day of as remarkable vengeance to others. Men's hearts harden, and their guilt increases apace at such a day as this, if they neglect their souls; and never was there so great danger of such persons being given up to hardness of heart and blindness of mind. God seems now to be hastily gathering in his elect in all parts of the land; and probably the greater part of adult persons that ever shall be saved, will be brought in now in a little time, and that it will be as it was on the great out-pouring of the Spirit upon the Jews in the apostles' days;[28] the election will obtain, and the rest will be blinded. If this should be the case with you, you will eternally curse this day, and will curse the day that ever you was born, to see such a season of the pouring out of God's Spirit, and will wish that you had died and gone to hell before you had seen it. Now undoubtedly it is, as it was in the days of John the Baptist, the axe is in an extraordinary manner laid at the root of the trees, that every tree which brings not forth good fruit, may be hewn down and cast into the fire.[29]

Therefore, let every one that is out of Christ, now awake and fly from the wrath to come. The wrath of Almighty God is now undoubtedly hanging over a great part of this congregation: Let every one fly out of Sodom: "Haste and escape for your lives, look not behind you, escape to the mountain, lest you be consumed."[30]

1741

---

[26] Dwight's note: "A town in the neighborhood," in Connecticut.
[27] Are not among the Chosen, the elect.
[28] In Acts 2, Peter cautions a group to repent and to be converted.
[29] A paraphrase of Matthew 3:10.   [30] Genesis 19:17.

LETTER TO REV. DR. BENJAMIN COLMAN*

[*The Great Awakening*]

Northampton, May 30, 1735

Dear Sir:

In answer to your desire, I here send you a particular account of the present extraordinary circumstances of this town, and the neighboring towns with respect to religion. I have observed that the town for this several years have gradually been reforming; there has appeared less and less of a party spirit, and a contentious disposition, which before had prevailed for many years between two parties in the town.[1] The young people also have been reforming more and more; they by degrees left off their frolicking, and have been observably more decent in their attendance on the public worship. The winter before last there appeared a strange flexibleness in the young people of the town, and an unusual disposition to hearken to counsel, on this occasion. It had been their manner of a long time, and for aught I know, always, to make Sabbath-day nights and lecture days[2] to be especially times of diversion and company-keeping. I then preached a sermon on the Sabbath before the lecture, to show them the unsuitableness and inconvenience of the practice, and to persuade them to reform it; and urged it on heads of families that it should be a thing agreed among them to govern their families, and keep them in at those times. And there happened to be at my house the evening after, men that belonged to the several parts of the town, to whom I moved that they should desire the heads of families, in my name, to meet together in their several neighborhoods, that they might know each others' minds, and agree every one to restrain his family; which was done, and my motion complied with throughout the town. But the parents found little or no occasion for the exercise of government in the case; for the young people declared themselves convinced by what they had heard, and willing of themselves to comply with the counsel given them; and I suppose it was almost universally complied with thenceforward.

After this there began to be a remarkable religious concern among some farm houses at a place called Pascommuck[3] and five or six that I hoped were savingly wrought upon there. And in April [1734] there was a very sudden and awful death of a young man in town, in the very bloom of his youth, who was violently seized with a pleurisy[4] and taken immediately out of his head, and died in two days; which much affected many young people in the town. This was followed with

---

* Edwards's letter to Rev. Dr. Benjamin Colman (1673–1747), pastor of Boston's Brattle Street Church from 1699 to 1747, is the first report of the religious revivals, known as the Great Awakening, that began in 1734 in Northampton, Massachusetts, and had ended by the 1750s.

[1] Edwards refers to these two unnamed parties in more detail in a letter to Rev. Thomas Gillespie (1708–1774) of Scotland on July 1, 1751. In it Edwards states: "in one ecclesiastical controversy in Mr. Stoddard's days, wherein the church was divided into two parties, the heat of spirit was raised to such a height, that it came to hard blows; a member of one party met the head of the opposite party, and assaulted him and beat him unmercifully." "Mr. Stoddard" is Solomon Stoddard (1643–1729), Edwards's grandfather and predecessor as Northampton's pastor.

[2] Weekdays, when sermons were less formal than on the Sabbath.

[3] A community three miles from Northampton that was part of Edwards's congregation.

[4] A respiratory inflammation.

another death of a young married woman, who was in great distress in the beginning of her illness, but was hopefully converted before her death; so that she died
full of comfort, and in a most earnest and moving manner, warning and counsel-
ing others, which I believe much contributed to the solemnizing of the spirits of
the young people in the town; and there began evidently to appear more of a
religious concern upon people's minds. In the fall of the year I moved to the
young people that they should set up religious meetings, on evenings after lectures, which they complied with; this was followed with the death of an elderly
person in the town, which was attended with very unusual circumstances, which
much affected many people. About that time began the great noise that there was
in this part of the country about Arminianism,[5] which seemed strangely to be
overruled for the promoting of religion. People seemed to be put by it upon inquiring, with concern and engagedness of mind, what was the way of salvation, and
what were the terms of our acceptance with God; and what was said publicly on
that occasion, however found fault with by many elsewhere, and ridiculed by
some, was most evidently attended with a very remarkable blessing of heaven, to
the souls of the people in this town, to the giving of them an universal satisfaction
and engaging their minds with respect to the thing in question, the more earnestly
to see salvation in the way that had been made evident to them.

And then a concern about the great things of religion began, about the latter end
of December and the beginning of January [1735], to prevail abundantly in the
town, till in a very little time it became universal throughout the town, among old
and young, and from the highest to the lowest. All seemed to be seized with a
deep concern about their eternal salvation; all the talk in all companies, and upon
occasions was upon the things of religion, and no other talk was anywhere relished; and scarcely a single person in the whole town was left unconcerned about
the great things of the eternal world. Those that were wont to be the vainest, and
loosest persons in town seemed in general to be seized with strong convictions.
Those that were most disposed to contemn vital and experimental religion, and
those that had the greatest conceit of their own reason, the highest families in the
town, and the oldest persons in the town, and many little children were affected
remarkably; no one family that I know of, and scarcely a person, has been exempt. And the Spirit of God went on in his saving influences, to the appearance of
all human reason and charity, in a truly wonderful and astonishing manner. The
news of it filled the neighboring towns with talk, and there were many in them
that scoffed and made a ridicule of the religion that appeared in Northampton. But
it was observable that it was very frequent and common that those of other towns
that came into this town, and observed how it was here, were greatly affected, and
went home with wounded spirits, and were never more able to shake off the impression that it made upon them, till at length there began to appear a general
concern in several of the towns in the county.

In the month of March the people in New Hadley[6] seemed to be seized with a
deep concern about their salvation, all as it were at once, which has continued in a
very great degree ever since. About the same time there began to appear the like
concern in the west part of Suffield,[7] which has since spread into all parts of the

---

[5] A belief that man can save himself, unlike the Puritan belief that God alone determines man's
salvation.
[6] Later South Hadley, Massachusetts, about seven miles east of Northampton.
[7] Suffield, Connecticut.

town. It next began to appear at Sunderland,[8] and soon became universal, and to a very great degree. About the same time it began to appear in part of Deerfield,[9] called Green River, and since has filled the town. It began to appear also at a part of Hatfield,[10] and after than the whole town in the second week in April seemed to be seized at once, and there is a great and general concern there. And there gradually got in a considerable degree of the same concern into Hadley Old Society, and Mr. Hopkins'[11] parish in [West] Springfield, but it is nothing near so great as in many other places. The next place that we heard of was Northfield,[12] where the concern is very great and general. We have heard that there is a considerable degree of it at Longmeadow,[13] and there is something of it in Old Springfield in some parts of the society. About three weeks ago the town of Enfield[14] were struck down as it were at once, the worst persons in the town seemed to be suddenly seized with a great degree of concern about their souls, as I have been informed. And about the same time, Mr. Bull[15] of Westfield [said] that there began to be a great alteration there, and that there had been more done in one week before that time that I spoke with him than had been done in seven years before. The people of Westfield have till now above all other places, made a scoff and derision of this concern at Northampton. There has been a great concern of a like nature at Windsor,[16] on the west side of the [Connecticut] River, which began about the same time that it began to be general here at Northampton; and my father[17] has told me that there is an hopeful beginning on the east side in his society. Mr Noyes[18] writes me word that there is a considerable revival of religion at New Haven; and I have been credibly informed that there is something of it at Guilford and Lyme, as there also is at Coventry, Bolton, and a society in Lebanon[19] called The Crank. I yesterday saw Mr. White[20] of Bolton, and also last night saw a young man that belongs to [the church at] Coventry, who gave a very remarkable account of that town, of the manner in which the rude debauched young people there were suddenly seized with a concern about their souls.

As to the nature of persons' experiences, and the influences of that spirit that there is amongst us, persons when seized with concern are brought to forsake their vices, and ill practices; the looser sort are brought to forsake and to dread their former extravagances. Persons are soon brought to have done with their old quarrels; contention and intermeddling with other men's matters seems to be dead amongst us. I believe there never was so much done at confessing of faults to each other, and making up differences, as there has lately been. Where this concern comes it immediately puts an end to differences between ministers and people: there was a considerable uneasiness at New Hadley between some of the people and their minister, but when this concern came amongst them it immediately put an end to it, and the people are now universally united to their minister. There was an exceeding alienation at Sunderland, between the minister and many of the people; but when this concern came amongst them it all vanished at once, and the

---

[8] Sunderland, Massachusetts.   [9] Deerfield, Massachusetts.   [10] Hatfield, Massachusetts.
[11] Samuel Hopkins (1693–1755), pastor in West Springfield, Massachusetts.
[12] Northfield, Massachusetts.   [13] Longmeadow, Massachusetts.
[14] Enfield, Connecticut, where Edwards delivered *Sinners in the Hands of an Angry God* in 1741.
[15] Nehemiah Bull (1701–1740), pastor in Westfield, Massachusetts.
[16] Windsor, Connecticut.
[17] Timothy Edwards (1669–1758), pastor in East Windsor, Connecticut.
[18] Joseph Noyes (1688–1761), pastor at the First Church in New Haven.
[19] All are towns in Connecticut.   [20] Thomas White (1701–1763), pastor in Bolton.

people are universally united in hearty affection to their minister. There were some men at Deerfield, of turbulent spirits, that kept up an uneasiness there with Mr. Ashley,[21] but one of the chief of them has lately been influenced fully and freely to confess his fault to him, and is become his hearty friend.

People are brought off from inordinate engagedness after the world, and have been ready to run into the other extreme of too much neglecting their worldly business and to mind nothing but religion. Those that are under convictions are put upon it earnestly to inquire what they shall do to be saved, and diligently to use appointed means of grace, and apply themselves to all known duty. And those that obtain hope themselves, and the charity of others concerning their good estate, generally seem to be brought to a great sense of their own exceeding misery in a natural condition, and their utter helplessness, and insufficiency for themselves, and their exceeding wickedness and guiltiness in the sight of God; it seldom fails but that each one seems to think himself worse than anybody else, and they are brought to see that they deserve no mercy of God, that all their prayers and pains are exceeding worthless and polluted, and that God, notwithstanding all that they have done, or can do, may justly execute his eternal wrath upon them, and they seem to be brought to a lively sense of the excellency of Jesus Christ and his sufficiency and willingness to save sinners, and to be much weaned in their affections from the world, and to have their hearts filled with love to God and Christ, and a disposition to lie in the dust before him. They seem to have given [to] them a lively conviction of the truth of the Gospel, and the divine authority of the Holy Scriptures; though they can't have the exercise of this at all times alike, nor indeed of any other grace. They seem to be brought to abhor themselves for the sins of their past life, and to long to be holy, and to live holily, and to God's glory; but at the same time complain that they can do nothing, [for] they are poor impotent creatures, utterly insufficient to glorify their Creator and Redeemer. They commonly seem to be much more sensible of their own wickedness after their conversion than before, so that they are often humbled by it; it seems to them that they are really become more wicked, when at the same time they are evidently full of a gracious spirit. Their remaining sin seems to be their very great burden, and many of them seem to long after heaven, that there they may be rid of sin. They generally seem to be united in dear love and affection one to another, and to have a love to all mankind. I never saw the Christian spirit in love to enemies so exemplified in all my life as I have seen it within this half year. They commonly express a great concern for others' salvation; some say that they think they are far more concerned for others' conversion, after they themselves have been converted, than ever they were for their own; several have thought (though perhaps they might be deceived in it) that they could freely die for the salvation of any soul, of the meanest of mankind, of any Indian in the woods.

This town never was so full of love, nor so full of joy, nor so full of distress as it has lately been. Some persons have had those longing desires after Jesus Christ, that have been to that degree as to take away their strength, and very much to weaken them, and make them faint. Many have been even overcome with a sense of the dying love of Christ, so that the home of the body has been ready to fail under it; there was once three pious young persons in this town talking together of the dying love of Christ, till they all fainted away; though 'tis probable the fainting of the two latter was much promoted by the fainting of the first. Many express a sense of the glory of the divine perfections, and of the excellency and fullness of

[21] Jonathan Ashley (1712–1780), pastor in Deerfield and opponent of Edwards's religious revival.

Jesus Christ, and of their own littleness and unworthiness, in a manner truly wonderful and almost unparalleled; and so likewise of the excellency and wonderfulness of the way of salvation by Jesus Christ. Their esteem of the Holy Scriptures is exceedingly increased. Many of them say the Bible seems to be a new book to them, as though they never read it before. There have been some instances of persons that by only an accidental sight of the Bible, have been as much moved, it seemed to me, as a lover by the sight of his sweetheart. The preaching of the Word is greatly prized by them; they say they never heard preaching before: and so are God's Sabbaths, and ordinances,[22] and opportunities of public worship. The Sabbath is longed for before if comes; some by only hearing the bell ring on some occasion in the week time, have been greatly moved, because it has put them in mind of its ringing to call the people together to worship God. But no part of public worship has commonly [had] such an effect on them as singing God's praises. They have a greater respect to ministers than they used to have; there is scarcely a minister preaches here but gets their esteem and affection.

The experiences of some persons lately amongst [us] have been beyond almost all that ever I heard or read of. There is a pious woman in this town that is a very modest bashful person, that was moved by what she heard of the experiences of others earnestly to seek to God to give her more clear manifestations of himself, and evidences of her own good estate, and God answered her request, and gradually gave her more and more of a sense of his glory and love, which she had with intermissions for several days, till one morning the week before last she had it to a more than ordinary degree, and it prevailed more and more till towards the middle of the day, till her nature began to sink under it, as she was alone in the house; but there came somebody into the house, and found her in an unusual, extraordinary frame. She expressed what she saw and felt to him; it came to that at last that they raised the neighbors, [for] they were afraid she would die; I went up to see her and found her perfectly sober and in the exercise of her reason, but having her nature seemingly overborne and sinking, and when she could speak expressing in a manner that can't be described the sense she had of the glory of God, and particularly of such and such perfections, and her own unworthiness, her longing to lie in the dust, sometimes her longing to go to be with Christ, and crying out of the excellency of Christ, and the wonderfulness of his dying love; and so she continued for hours together, though not always in the same degree. At some times she was able to discourse to those about her; but it seemed to me [that] if God had manifested a little more of himself to her she would immediately have sunk and her frame dissolved under it. She has since been at my house, and continues as full as she can hold, but looks on herself not as an eminent saint,[23] but as the worst of all, and unworthy to go to speak with a minister; but yet now beyond any great doubt of her good estate.

There are two persons that belong to other towns that have had such a sense of God's exceeding greatness and majesty, that they were as it were swallowed up; they both of them told me to that purpose that if in the time of it they had had the least fear that they were not at peace with that great God, they should immediately have died. But there is a very vast variety of degrees of spiritual discoveries, that are made to those that we hope are godly, as there is also in the steps, and method of the Spirit's operation in convincing and converting sinners, and the length of time that persons are under conviction before they have comfort.

There is an alteration made in the town in a few months that strangers can

[22] Church laws.   [23] A "visible saint," one self-assured of salvation.

scarcely conceive of; our church I believe was the largest in New England be-fore,[24] but persons lately have thronged in, so that there are very few adult persons left out. There have been a great multitude hopefully converted; to many, I find, for me to declare abroad with credit to my judgment. The town seems to be full of the presence of God; our young people when they get together instead of frolick-ing as they used to do are altogether on pious subjects; 'til so at weddings and on all occasions. The children in this and the neighboring towns have been greatly affected and influenced by the Spirit of God, and many of them hopefully changed; the youngest in this town is between nine and ten years of age. Some of them seem to be full of love to Christ and have expressed great longings after him and willingness to die, and leave father and mother and all things in the world to go to him, together with a great sense of their unworthiness and admiration at the free grace of God towards them. And there have been many old people, many above fifty and several near seventy, that seem to be wonderfully changed and hopefully newborn. The good people that have been formerly converted in the town have many of them been wonderfully enlivened and increased.

This work seems to be upon every account an extraordinary dispensation of providence. 'Tis extraordinary upon the account of [the] universality of it in af-fecting all sorts, high and low, rich and poor, wise and unwise, old and young, vicious and moral; 'tis very extraordinary as to the numbers that are hopefully savingly wrought upon, and particularly the number of aged persons and children and loose livers; and also on the account of the quickness of the work of the Spirit on them, for many seem to have been suddenly taken from a loose way of living, and to be so changed as to become truly holy, spiritual, heavenly persons; 'tis extraordinary as to the degrees of gracious communications, and the abundant measures in which the Spirit of God has been poured out on many persons; 'tis extraordinary as to the extent of it, God's Spirit being so remarkably poured out on so many towns at once, and its making such swift progress from place to place. The extraordinariness of the thing has been, I believe, one principal cause that people abroad have suspected it.

There have been, as I have heard, many odd and strange stories that have been carried about the country of this affair, which it is a wonder some wise men should be so ready to believe. Some indeed under great terrors of conscience have had impressions on their imaginations; and also under the power of spiritual dis-coveries, they have had livelily impressed ideas of Christ shedding blood for sin-ners, his blood running from his veins, and of Christ in his glory in heaven and such like things, but they are always taught, and have been several times taught in public not to lay the weight of their hopes on such things and many have nothing of any such imaginations. There have been several persons that have had their natures overborne under strong convictions, have trembled, and han't been able to stand, they have had such a sense of divine wrath; but there are no new doctrines embraced, but people have been abundantly established in those that we account orthodox; there is no new way of worship affected. There is no oddity of behavior prevails; people are no more superstitious about their clothes, or anything else than they used to be. Indeed, there is a great deal of talk when they are together of one another's experiences, and indeed no other is to be expected in a town where the concern of the soul is so universally the concern, and that to so great a degree. And doubtless some persons under the strength of impressions that are made on

---

[24] Edwards claimed 620 adult members in November 1736, compared to 71 in 1669 under Solomon Stoddard.

their minds and under the power of strong affections,[25] are guilty of imprudences; their zeal may need to be regulated by more prudence, and they may need a guide to their assistance; as of old when the church of Corinth[26] had the extraordinary gifts of the Spirit, they needed to be told by the Apostle that the spirit of the prophets were subject to the prophets, and that their gifts were to be exercised with prudence, because God was not the author of confusion but of peace [I Corinthians 14:32–33].[27] There is no unlovely oddity in people's temper prevailing with this work, but on the contrary the face of things is much changed as to the appearance of a meek, humble, amiable behavior. Indeed, the Devil has not been idle, but his hand has evidently appeared in several instances endeavoring to mimic the work of the Spirit of God and to cast a slur upon it, and no wonder. And there has hereby appeared the need of the watchful eye of skillful guides, and of wisdom from above to direct them.

There lately came up hither a couple of ministers from Connecticut, viz. Mr. Lord[28] of [North] Preston, and Mr. Owen[29] of Groton, who had heard of the extraordinary circumstances of this and neighboring towns, who had heard the affair well represented by some, and also had heard many reports greatly to its disadvantage, who came on purpose to see and satisfy themselves; and that they might thoroughly acquaint themselves, went about and spent [the] good part of a day in hearing the accounts of many of our new converts, and examining of them, which was greatly to their satisfaction; and they took particular notice, among other things, of the modesty with which persons gave account of themselves, and said that the one-half was not told them, and could not be told them; and that if they renounced these persons' experiences they must renounce Christianity itself. And Mr. Owen said particularly as to their impressions on their imaginations, they were quite different from what had been represented, and that they were no more than might naturally be expected in such cases.

Thus, Sir, I have given you a particular account of this affair which Satan has so much misrepresented in the country.[30] This is a true account of the matter as far as I have opportunity to know, and I suppose I am under greater advantages to know than any person living. Having been thus long in the account, I forbear to make reflections, or to guess what God is about to do; I leave this to you, and shall only say, as I desire always to say from my heart, "To God be all the glory, whose work alone it is." And let him have an interest in your prayers, who so much needs divine help at this day, and is your affectionate brother and humble servant.

JONATHAN EDWARDS

Northampton, June 3, 1735

Since I wrote the foregoing letter, there has happened a thing of a very awful nature in the town. My Uncle Hawley,[31] the last Sabbath-day morning [June 1],

---

[25] Emotions.   [26] An ancient Greek city.

[27] "And the spirits of the prophets are subjects to the prophets. For God is not the author of confusion, but of peace. . . ."

[28] Hezekiah Lord (1698–1761), pastor in North Preston, Connecticut, and an active supporter of the Awakening.

[29] John Owen (1699–1753), pastor in Groton, Connecticut, and a promoter of the Awakening.

[30] It had been rumored that the revival produced frenzied emotions rather than genuinely converted Christians.

[31] Joseph Hawley (1682–1735), a leading Northampton merchant whose sister-in-law was Edwards's mother.

laid violent hands on himself, and put an end to his life, by cutting his own throat. He had been for a considerable time greatly concerned about the condition of his soul; till, by the ordering of a sovereign providence he was suffered to fall into deep melancholy, a distemper that the family are very prone to; he was much overpowered by it; the devil took the advantage and drove him into despairing thoughts. He was kept very much awake anights, so that he had but very little sleep for two months, till he seemed not to have his faculties in his own power. He was in a great measure past a capacity of receiving advice, or being reasoned with. The coroner's inquest judged him delirious. Satan seems to be in a great rage, at this extraordinary breaking forth of the work of God. I hope it is because he knows that he has but a short time. Doubtless he had a great reach,[32] in this violent attack of his against the whole affair. We have appointed a day of fasting in the town this week, by reason of this and other appearances of Satan's rage amongst us against poor souls. I yesterday saw a woman that belongs to [the church in] Durham [Connecticut], who says there is a considerable revival of religion there.

I am yours, etc.—
J.E.
1735, 1935

Benjamin Franklin
(1706–1790)

One of fifteen children, Benjamin Franklin was born in 1706 in Boston. His father, Josiah Franklin, a candle and soap maker, had come to America from England in 1682. Franklin's mother, Abiah Folger, was the daughter of a teacher, and the Franklins valued education highly, sending young Benjamin to the Boston Grammar School. Eventually unable to afford this luxury, Franklin was forced to return to work in the family business, which he disliked intensely. To provide him with a more stimulating occupation, Josiah Franklin apprenticed Benjamin at age twelve, to his older brother James, a printer. Under the pseudonym Silence Dogood, Benjamin Franklin, an eager student, published in his half-brother's newspaper; when James was imprisoned in 1722 for offending Massachusetts authorities, the paper was left in Ben's care, although he was only sixteen. The experience inspired Franklin's desire for independence, and one year later he abandoned his apprenticeship—a punishable offense—and left Boston for Philadelphia. There he flourished as a printer, and by age twenty-four was the publisher of the *Pennsylvania Gazette* and had commenced publication of *Poor Richard's Almanac* (1733–1758), issued under the pseudonym Richard Saunders. These immensely popular almanacs contain astronomical and astrological information and aphoristic wisdom with an emphasis on frugality, such as "a

---

[32] Influence.

penny saved is a penny earned." The printing shop, the newspaper, and the almanacs made Franklin very wealthy and able to retire at age forty-two from full-time business.

Franklin, whose image and life were popularized by the wide circulation of his *Autobiography* (1771–1790, published in entirety in 1867), came to represent the American Dream realized and actualized. His father had not provided him rank and privilege, and Franklin was able to rise from "rags to riches" in the New World during his lifetime. Not only was he wealthy at a relatively early age, but he became one of the most significant figures in the era of the American Revolution: a signer of the Declaration of Independence, a framer of the Constitution, and a negotiator of the Treaty of Paris (by which the Revolutionary War was ended in 1783). Franklin was a skilled writer as well. The *Autobiography* is his most significant contribution to the development of American literature and is one of the most widely circulated American works ever printed. The *Autobiography* reader must distinguish between real events of Franklin's life and the image of Franklin that appears in that text. The real events of the *Autobiography* carry the reader only to Franklin at age fifty-nine, though he lived to be eighty-four. Yet, the image of Franklin as perpetuated by the *Autobiography* is immortal. In a scant sixty years the *Autobiography's* subject moves from youthful apprenticeship to great wealth and prominence in public life. The image developed in the *Autobiography* creates a formula for success in America, a diagram by which a person may realize the secular American dream and enjoy its benefits while contributing to the community.

This image is as important as Franklin's life itself, for the *Autobiography* was translated into many languages during the nineteenth century. The account gave the world some idea of the type of new nation that was evolving under the highly experimental government, which was called "Democracy in America" (1835–1840) by Alexis de Tocqueville, a Frenchman who visited the United States in its infancy. As Ambassador to France for the new nation, Franklin established himself as a representative American and was known as being shrewd, politically tough, and extremely clever. That the *Autobiography* was initially published in French indicates just how completely immersed in European culture Franklin's image had become by the 1790s, following his death. This account was further popularized in America through translation and by the virtual resetting of the text by Parson Mason Weems, whose *Life of Benjamin Franklin* (1815) was one of a series of biographies Weems wrote and published to give the new nation an instant galaxy of heroes. These biographies were credible in their authority to report the events of the early political leaders' lives. However, much of what the accounts contain is image-making and the stuff of mythology. In Weems's *The Life and Memorable Actions of George Washington* (1800?), for example, we find for the only time in American literature the story of Washington cutting the cherry tree.

Franklin's own life story and satirical style are ideal material for Weems's mythologizing of the American hero. Together, both accounts of Franklin give the world a vision that wonderfully represents his own approach to the writing of literature: speaking through a mask, an invented persona, to an audience that is receptive to this process of image-making more than it is concerned about fidelity to truth and accuracy of portraiture. For example, in Franklin's essay "The Way to Wealth" (1758), the narrator, Richard Saunders, comes upon a group gathered in a public marketplace where an elderly man, Father Abraham, is "preaching" in a sermon that develops a strategy for monetary success. The quoted maxims become the text for the sermon, and most are taken from *Poor Richard's Almanac*.

The *Autobiography* consists of four parts; Part I commences with "Dear Son," an address to posterity, as though Franklin were writing to a young man who, in moving from adolescence to adulthood, would benefit from the wisdom of his parent. These words were addressed to William Franklin, Franklin's illegitimate son, then forty-two years old and the governor of New Jersey. Part I moves forward in a conventional autobiographical style, one that idealizes the subject and was borrowed from the Puritans, from whom Franklin was descended. Part I discusses generations past, with fathers instructing sons concerning their ancestors and with each succeeding generation improving the life of the preceding one. In Part II Franklin shifts away from the persona of a parent instructing a child and expands his audience to include all his followers who wish to learn how to become virtuous, industrious, and successful. He lists thirteen "virtues" and includes a chart by which he measured his personal habits, a programmed approach to personal living that has been adapted by self-improvement advisors. This section of the narrative is the best known and the most often quoted.

Parts III and IV indicate how the author's moral behavior led not only to worldly success but also to an expanded role as a public figure. Franklin's significant achievements of the late eighteenth century, such as his role in the Continental Congress and his ambassadorship in Paris, are not recorded in the *Autobiography*. However, that Franklin turned his own personal success into a contribution to the public good is clear. The persona of Benjamin Franklin that emerges as an adult is less judgmental and self-righteous than the youthful figure who during his lunch breaks drinks water and reads by himself while his peers indulge themselves with stronger drink and lengthy conversation. Even Franklin's marriage in 1730 to Deborah Read, the daughter of his first landlady, is recorded as a useful match, ultimately part of a programmed scheme for self-improvement and personal development. At the time, Read was married to John Rogers, a debtor who had left her without a divorce; thus, Franklin's relationship to her was a common-law marriage. The common-law arrangement was apparently very satisfactory to both parties and lasted forty-four years, until Read died in 1774.

Throughout his life Franklin was obsessed with scientific experimentation, and he especially indulged this passion after retiring from the printing business in 1746. He is credited with having invented the Franklin stove (a cast-iron heating stove) and bifocal glasses, and he founded the college that became the University of Pennsylvania. Like Thomas Jefferson, whose brilliant and comprehensive mind ranged from ancient philosophy to architecture and astronomy, Franklin believed the empirical or scientific method for establishing truth to be essential to learning and human development and throughout his career fought against superstition and religious dogmatism. In his "Letter to Ezra Stiles," printed in the *Autobiography*, Franklin asserts his simple faith, deism, which acknowledges that a supreme being created the universe but does not intervene in its functioning. In the letter Franklin expresses his doubts about the divinity of Jesus Christ, " . . . though it is a question I do not dogmatize upon, having never studied it." This cautious approach and undogmatic rejection of commitment in the face of little evidence characterizes Franklin's reasoning process and shows how steady a scientist he would have made. However, political and civic duties attracted him equally, and he was responsible for organizing the first lending library (1731) and the first fire department in Philadelphia and founded the American Philosophical Society. His close association with the evolving sentiment for revolution against England, and the military and political events that consumed the colonies between 1760 and 1787, left Franklin little time for scientific investigation other than his lightning and kite experiments, published in *Experiments and Observations on Electricity* (1751–1753).

Franklin spent his later years as a diplomat, living for long periods in London and Paris as well as Philadelphia. The unsophisticated runaway was by now a thoroughly urbane and successful diplomat who had taught himself French, Spanish, Italian, and Latin, all important to his negotiations at court and to his social popularity throughout Europe. He always

Benjamin Franklin's snake device, published in the Pennsylvania Gazette *in 1754, came to symbolize the colonies' growing resistance to England.*

dressed plainly and kept a personal profile that contrasted with that of the European court-
iers with whom he regularly associated. The diplomat Franklin was witty and charming,
learned and well versed. He also fathered several illegitimate children. His public life was
devoted to his emerging nation. More than any other American figure, including George
Washington, Franklin stood for the character, integrity, freedom, and opportunity that the
United States came to symbolize to the world. Important to Franklin's public life were
diplomatic missions abroad, to England (1757–1762 and 1764–1785) and to France
(1776–1785), during his "retirement." He also traveled in Germany and, with his son William, visited Holland and Belgium. In America Franklin had homes in Boston and Philadelphia, then the two most significant cultural centers in the New World.

Franklin's writings support the view that he was sophisticated and worldly, urbane and
scholarly. His penchant for satire, one of the most difficult literary genres to craft successfully, is realized in such works as "The Speech of Polly Baker" (1747), a narrative about a
pregnant defendant who is being tried for her social misconduct but cannot "conceive"
what she has done wrong, and Franklin's favorite satire, "Rules by Which a Great Empire
May Be Reduced to a Small One" (1773). In his "Father Abraham's Speech" (1758, 1774)
the author's persona narrator stands in the audience while his own dogmas are thrust upon
an admiring crowd of his peers by an elder statesman who resembles Franklin himself.
This document contains some of Franklin's finest satire and rhetorical strategies.

Many of Franklin's themes were inherited from the Puritans who preceded and surrounded him. His *Autobiography* was written in a form very well developed by Puritan
authors of spiritual autobiographies. Franklin adapted the form to a secular purpose and
used as his spiritual "text" the wisdom of the ancients and the practical wisdom of *Poor
Richard's Almanac*. The work ethic Franklin developed so fully in his *Autobiography* was
an extension of the Protestant/Puritan ethic of European and English origins, whereby the
most visible sign of sanctification and of being chosen by God is worldly success. (A sad
corollary of this ethic placed the impoverished in league with the Devil.) Even his
"Dogood Papers" (1722) were echoes of Cotton Mather's *Bonifacius: An Essay Upon the
Good* (1710). If Franklin's rhetorical style commonly resembles that of the English essayists Joseph Addison and Richard Steele and the satirist Jonathan Swift, his content is typically the legacy of American Puritanism.

The *Autobiography's* youthful runaway apprentice, who arrives in Philadelphia with a
loaf of bread under his arm, may prefigure Huckleberry Finn as an archetypal American
hero. However, this youth's development into an emergent American national figure,
larger than life, signals a new purpose in the Franklin image-building process: the continuous extension of, rather than the denial of, the purposes of New England Puritanism.
Franklin should be read in the context of America's gradual transition from the Puritan
seventeenth century to the Age of Enlightenment, a philosophical movement marked by
rationalism and the impetus toward empirical learning, in the eighteenth-century world of
Thomas Paine and Thomas Jefferson. Franklin's secular humanism, which embraced the
ethical morality of Puritanism and modernized it in the process, made it possible for gener-

ations of American readers to inherit the ethical legacy of Puritanism without having to embrace its spiritual tenets.

Franklin the man died in Philadelphia in 1790 shortly after signing a petition for Congress to abolish slavery. Over twenty thousand people attended his funeral, a massive public celebration of this genuine American hero. His image has endured, and his writings create and extend Franklin's influence well into modern times.

Suggested Readings: C. Van Doren, *Benjamin Franklin*, 1938. A. O. Aldridge, *Benjamin Franklin: Philosopher and Man*, 1965. M. Twain, "The Late Benjamin Franklin," in *Galaxy*, July 1870, 10:138–140. R. Amacher, *Benjamin Franklin*, 1962. D. Levin, "The *Autobiography* of Benjamin Franklin: The Puritan Experimenter in Life and Art," in *Yale Review*, December 1963, 43:258–275. B. I. Granger, *Benjamin Franklin: An American Man of Letters*, 1964. P. Miller, "Jonathan Edwards and Benjamin Franklin," in *Major Writers of America*, 1964. R. F. Sayre, *The Examined Self: Benjamin Franklin, Henry Adams, Henry James*, 1964. R. W. Ketcham, *Benjamin Franklin*, 1965. N. Fiering, "Benjamin Franklin and the Way to Virtue," in *American Quarterly*, Summer 1978. J. A. L. LeMay, "Benjamin Franklin: Universal Genius," in *The Renaissance Man in the Eighteenth Century*, 1978.

Texts Used: "The Way to Wealth": *The Papers of Benjamin Franklin*, Vol. 7, ed. L. W. Labaree, 1963. *The Autobiography of Benjamin Franklin*, ed. L. W. Labaree, R. L. Ketcham, H.C. Boatfield, and H. H. Fineman, 1964. All else: The Writings of Benjamin Franklin, Vols. VI–XI, ed. A. H. Smyth, 1906. (Some spelling and punctuation modernized.)

from   POOR RICHARD*

THE WAY TO WEALTH

Courteous Reader,

I have heard that nothing gives an author so great pleasure, as to find his works respectfully quoted by other learned authors. This pleasure I have seldom enjoyed; for tho' I have been, if I may say it without vanity, an eminent author of almanacs annually now a full quarter of a century, my brother authors in the same way, for what reason I know not, have ever been very sparing in their applauses; and no other author has taken the least notice of me, so that did not my writings produce me some solid pudding, the great deficiency of praise would have quite discouraged me.

I concluded at length, that the people were the best judges of my merit; for they buy my works; and besides, in my rambles, where I am not personally known, I have frequently heard one or other of my adages repeated, with, as Poor Richard says, at the end on't; this gave me some satisfaction, as it showed not only that my instructions were regarded, but discovered[1] likewise some respect for my author-

---

* This essay was published as the preface to *Poor Richard Improved*, an expanded version of *Poor Richard's Almanac*, for the twenty-fifth anniversary edition. The essay was also known as "Father Abraham's Speech." Franklin fictionalized an old man addressing an auction and using many of the maxims in earlier editions of *Poor Richard*.

[1] Showed.

ity; and I own, that to encourage the practice of remembering and repeating those wise sentences, I have sometimes quoted myself with great gravity.

Judge then how much I must have been gratified by an incident I am going to relate to you. I stopped my horse lately where a great number of people were collected at a vendue[2] of merchant goods. The hour of sale not being come, they were conversing on the badness of the times, and one of the company called to a plain clean old man, with white locks, "Pray, Father Abraham, what think you of the times? Won't these heavy taxes quite ruin the country? How shall we be ever able to pay them? What would you advise us to?" Father Abraham stood up, and replied, "If you'd have my advice, I'll give it you in short, for a *word to the wise is enough*, and *many words won't fill a bushel*, as *Poor Richard says*." They joined in desiring him to speak his mind, and gathering round him, he proceeded as follows:

"Friends, says he, and neighbors, the taxes are indeed very heavy, and if those laid on by the government were the only ones we had to pay, we might more easily discharge them; but we have many others, and much more grievous to some of us. We are taxed twice as much by our idleness, three times as much by our pride, and four times as much by our folly, and from these taxes the commissioners cannot ease or deliver us by allowing an abatement. However let us hearken to good advice, and something may be done for us; *God helps them that help themselves*, as Poor Richard says, in his almanac of 1733.[3]

"It would be thought a hard government that should tax its people one tenth part of their time, to be employed in its service. But idleness taxes many of us much more, if we reckon all that is spent in absolute sloth, or doing of nothing, with that which is spent in idle employments or amusements, that amount to nothing. Sloth, by bringing on diseases, absolutely shortens life. *Sloth, like rust, consumes faster than labor wears, while the used key is always bright*, as Poor Richard says. But *dost thou love life, then do not squander time, for that's the stuff life is made of*, as Poor Richard says. How much more than is necessary do we spend in sleep! forgetting that *the sleeping fox catches no poultry*, and that *there will be sleeping enough in the grave*, as Poor Richard says. If time be of all things the most precious, *wasting time* must be, as Poor Richard says, *the greatest prodigality*, since, as he elsewhere tells us, *lost time is never found again*, and what we call *time-enough, always proves little enough:* let us then be up and be doing, and doing to the purpose; so by diligence shall we do more with less perplexity. *Sloth makes all things difficult, but industry all easy*, as Poor Richard says; and *he that riseth late, must trot all day, and shall scarce overtake his business at night*. While *laziness travels so slowly, that poverty soon overtakes him*, as we read in Poor Richard, who adds, *drive thy business, let not that drive thee;* and *early to bed, and early to rise, makes a man healthy, wealthy and wise*.

"So what signifies wishing and hoping for better times. We may make these times better if we bestir ourselves. *Industry need not wish*, as Poor Richard says, and *he that lives upon hope will die fasting. There are no gains, without pains*, then *help hands, for I have no lands*, or if I have, they are smartly taxed. And, as Poor Richard likewise observes, *he that hath a trade hath an estate*, and *he that hath a calling hath an office of profit and honor;* but then the trade must be worked at, and the calling well followed, or neither the estate, nor the office, will enable us to pay our taxes. If we are industrious we shall never starve; for, as Poor

---

[2] An Auction.　　[3] Actually, 1736.

Richard says, *at the working man's house hunger looks in, but dares not enter.* Nor will the bailiff nor the constable enter, for *industry pays debts, while despair encreaseth them,* says Poor Richard. What though you have found no treasure, nor has any rich relation left you a legacy, *diligence is the mother of good luck,* as Poor Richard says, and *God gives all things to industry.* Then *plough deep, while sluggards sleep, and you shall have corn to sell and to keep,* says Poor Dick. Work while it is called today, for you know not how much you may be hindered tomorrow, which makes Poor Richard say, *one today is worth two tomorrows;* and farther, *have you somewhat to do tomorrow, do it today.* If you were a servant, would you not be ashamed that a good master should catch you idle? Are you then your own master, *be ashamed to catch yourself idle,* as Poor Dick says. When there is so much to be done for yourself, your family, your country, and your gracious king, be up by peep of day; *let not the sun look down and say, inglorious here he lies.* Handle your tools without mittens; remember that *the cat in gloves catches no mice,* as Poor Richard says. 'Tis true there is much to be done, and perphaps you are weak handed, but stick to it steadily, and you will see great effects, for *constant dropping wears away stones,* and by *diligence and patience the mouse ate in two the cable;* and *little strokes fell great oaks,* as Poor Richard says in his almanac, the year I cannot just now remember.

"Methinks I hear some of you say, must a man afford himself no leisure? I will tell thee, my friend, what Poor Richard says, *employ thy time well if thou meanest to gain leisure;* and, *since thou art not sure of a minute, throw not away an hour.* Leisure is time for doing something useful; this leisure the diligent man will obtain, but the lazy man never; so that, as Poor Richard says, a *life of leisure and a life of laziness are two things.* Do you imagine that sloth will afford you more comfort than labor? No, for as Poor Richard says, *trouble springs from idleness, and grievous toil from needless ease. Many without labor would live by their wits only, but they break for want of stock.*[4] Whereas industry gives comfort, and plenty, and respect: *fly*[5] *pleasures, and they'll follow you. The diligent spinner has a large shift,*[6] and *now I have a sheep and a cow, everybody bids me good morrow,* all which is well said by Poor Richard.

"But with our industry, we must likewise be steady, settled and careful, and oversee our own affairs with our own eyes, and not trust too much to others; for, as Poor Richard says,

> *I never saw an oft removed*[7] *tree,*
> *Nor yet an oft removed family,*
> *That throve so well as those that settled be.*

"And again, *three removes is as bad as a fire,* and again, *keep the shop, and thy shop will keep thee;* and again, *if you would have your business done, go; if not, send.* And again,

> *He that by the plough would thrive,*
> *Himself must either hold or drive.*

"And again, *the eye of a master will do more work than both his hands;* and again, *want of care does us more damage than want of knowledge;* and again, *not*

[4] For lack of a supply of wits. [5] Avoid. [6] Wardrobe. [7] Moved.

to oversee workmen is to leave them your purse open. Trusting too much to others' care is the ruin of many; for, as the almanac says, *in the affairs of this world men are saved not by faith, but by the want of it;* but a man's own care is profitable; for, saith Poor Dick, *learning is to the studious,* and *riches to the careful,* as well as *power to the bold,* and *Heaven to the virtuous.* And farther, *if you would have a faithful servant, and one that you like, serve yourself.* And again, he adviseth to circumspection and care, even in the smallest matters, because sometimes *a little neglect may breed great mischief;* adding, *for want of a nail the shoe was lost; for want of a shoe the horse was lost, and for want of a horse the rider was lost,* being overtaken and slain by the enemy, all for want of care about a horse-shoe nail.

"So much for industry, my friends, and attention to one's own business; but to these we must add frugality, if we would make our industry more certainly successful. A man may, if he knows not how to save as he gets, *keep his nose all his life to the grindstone,* and die not worth a *groat*[8] at last. *A fat kitchen makes a lean will,* as Poor Richard says; and,

> *Many estates are spent in the getting,*
> *Since women for tea forsook spinning and knitting,*
> *And men for punch forsook hewing and splitting.*

If you would be wealthy, says he, in another almanac, *think of saving as well as of getting: the Indies have not made Spain rich, because her outgoes are greater than her incomes.* Away then with your expensive follies, and you will not have so much cause to complain of hard times, heavy taxes, and chargeable families; for, as Poor Dick says,

> *Women and wine, game and deceit,*
> *Make the wealth small, and the wants great.*

And farther, *what maintains one vice, would bring up two children.* You may think perhaps that a little tea, or a little punch now and then, diet a little more costly, clothes a little finer, and a little entertainment now and then, can be no great Matter; but remember what Poor Richard says, *many* a little *makes a mickle,*[9] and farther, *beware of little expenses; a small leak will sink a great ship,* and again, *who dainties love, shall beggars prove,* and moreover, *fools make Feasts, and wise men eat them.*

"Here you are all got together at this vendue of fineries and knicknacks. You call them goods, but if you do not take care, they will prove evils to some of you. You expect they will be sold cheap, and perhaps they may for less than they cost; but if you have no occasion for them, they must be dear to you. Remember what Poor Richard says, *buy what thou hast no need of, and ere long thou shalt sell thy necessaries.* And again, *at a great pennyworth*[10] *pause a while:* he means, that perhaps the cheapness is apparent only, and not real; or the bargain, by straitning thee in thy business, may do thee more harm than good. For in another place he says, *many have been ruined by buying good pennyworths.* Again, Poor Richard says, *'tis foolish to lay our money in a purchase of repentance;* and yet this folly is

---

[8] A silver coin, roughly four pence.   [9] A lot.   [10] Bargain.

practised every day at vendues, for want of minding the almanac. *Wise men*, as Poor Dick says, *learn by others' harms, fools scarcely by their own*, but, *felix quem faciunt aliena pericula cautum*.[11] Many a one, for the sake of finery on the back, have gone with a hungry belly, and half starved their families; *silks and satins, scarlet and velvets*, as Poor Richard says, *put out the kitchen fire*. These are not the necessaries of life; they can scarcely be called the conveniencies, and yet only because they look pretty, how many want to have them. The artificial wants of mankind thus become more numerous than the natural; and, as Poor Dick says, *for one* poor *person, there are an hundred* indigent. By these, and other extravagancies, the genteel are reduced to poverty, and forced to borrow of those whom they formerly despised, but who through industry and frugality have maintained their standing; in which case it appears plainly, that a *ploughman on his legs is higher than a gentleman on his knees,* as Poor Richard says. Perhaps they have had a small estate left them, which they knew not the getting of; they think *'tis day, and will never be night;* that a little to be spent out of so much, is not worth minding; (*a child and a fool,* as Poor Richard says, *imagine twenty shillings and twenty years can never be spent*) but, *always taking out of the meal-tub, and never putting in, soon comes to the bottom;* then, as Poor Dick says, *when the well's dry, they know the worth of water*. But this they might have known before, if they had taken his advice; *if you would know the value of money, go and try to borrow some,* for, *he that goes a borrowing goes a sorrowing,* and indeed so does he that lends to such people, when he goes to get it in again. Poor Dick farther advises, and says,

> *Fond pride of dress, is sure a very curse;*
> *E'er fancy you consult, consult your purse.*

And again, *pride is as loud a beggar as want, and a great deal more saucy*. When you have bought one fine thing you must buy ten more, that your appearance may be all of a piece; but Poor Dick says, *'tis easier to suppress the first desire than to satisfy all that follow it*. And 'tis as truly folly for the poor to ape the rich, as for the frog to swell, in order to equal the ox.

> *Great estates may venture more,*
> *But little boats should keep near shore.*

'Tis however a folly soon punished; for *pride that dines on vanity sups on contempt,* as Poor Richards says. And in another place, *pride breakfasted with plenty, dined with poverty, and supped with infamy*. And after all, of what use is this *pride of appearance,* for which so much is risked, so much is suffered? It cannot promote health; or ease pain; it makes no increase of merit in the person, it creates envy, it hastens misfortune.

> *What is a butterfly? At best*
> *He's but a caterpillar dressed.*
> *The gaudy fop's his picture just,*

as Poor Richard says.

---

[11] "They are fortunate who have been made wary by the misfortunes of others" (Latin).

"But what madness must it be to run in debt for these superfluities! We are offered, by the terms of this vendue, six months' credit; and that perhaps has induced some of us to attend it, because we cannot spare the ready money, and hope now to be fine without it. But, ah, think what you do when you run in debt; *you give to another power over your liberty*. If you cannot pay at the time, you will be ashamed to see your creditor; you will be in fear when you speak to him, you will make poor pitiful sneaking excuses, and by degrees come to lose you veracity, and sink into base downright lying; for, as Poor Richard says, *the second vice is lying, the first is running in debt*. And again to the same purpose, *lying rides upon debt's back*. Whereas a freeborn Englishman ought not to be ashamed or afraid to see or speak to any man living. But poverty often deprives a man of all spirit and virtue: *'tis hard for an empty bag to stand upright*, as Poor Richard truly says. What would you think of that Prince, or that government, who should issue an edict forbidding you to dress like a gentleman or a gentlewoman, on pain of imprisonment or servitude? Would you not say, that you are free, have a right to dress as you please, and that such an edict would be a breach of your privileges, and such a government tyrannical? And yet you are about to put yourself under that tyranny when you run in debt for such dress! Your creditor has authority at his pleasure to deprive you of your liberty, by confining you in gaol[12] for life, or to sell you for a servant, if you should not be able to pay him! When you have got your bargain, you may, perhaps, think little of payment; but *creditors*, Poor Richard tells us, *have better memories than debtors*, and in another place says, *creditors are a superstitious sect, great observers of set days and times*. The day comes round before you are aware, and the demand is made before you are prepared to satisfy it. Or if you bear your debt in mind, the term which at first seemed so long, will, as it lessens, appear extreamly short. Time will seem to have added wings to his heels as well as shoulders. *Those have a short Lent*, saith Poor Richard, *who owe money to be paid at Easter*. Then since, as he says, *the borrower is a slave to the lender, and the debtor to the creditor*, disdain the chain, preserve your freedom; and maintain your independency: be industrious and free; be frugal and free. At present, perhaps, you may think yourself in thriving circumstances, and that you can bear a little extravagance without injury; but,

> For age and want, save while you may;
> No morning sun lasts a whole day,

as Poor Richard says. Gain may be temporary and uncertain, but ever while you live, expense is constant and certain; and *'tis easier to build two chimneys than to keep one in fuel*, as Poor Richard says. So *rather go to bed supperless than rise in debt*.

> Get what you can, and what you get hold;
> 'Tis the stone that will turn all your lead into gold,

as Poor Richard says. And when you have got the philosopher's stone,[13] sure you will no longer complain of bad times, or the difficulty of paying taxes.

"This doctrine, my friends, is reason and wisdom; but after all, do not depend too much upon your own industry, and frugality, and prudence, though excellent

---

[12] Jail.   [13] In alchemy, a substance thought to convert base metals into gold.

things, for they may all be blasted without the blessing of heaven; and therefore ask that blessing humbly, and be not uncharitable to those that at present seem to want it, but comfort and help them. Remember Job[14] suffered, and was afterwards prosperous.

"And now to conclude, *experience keeps a dear*[15] *school, but fools will learn in no other, and scarce in that,* for it is true, *we may give advice, but we cannot give conduct,* as Poor Richard says: however, remember this, *they that won't be counseled, can't be helped,* as Poor Richard says: and farther, that *if you will not hear reason, she'll surely rap your knuckles.*"

Thus the old gentleman ended his harangue. The people heard it, and approved the doctrine, and immediately practiced the contrary, just as if it had been a common sermon; for the vendue opened, and they began to buy extravagantly, notwithstanding all his cautions, and their own fear of taxes. I found the good man had thoroughly studied my almanacs, and digested all I had dropped on those topics during the course of five-and-twenty years. The frequent mention he made of me must have tired any one else, but my vanity was wonderfully delighted with it, though I was conscious that not a tenth part of the wisdom was my own which he ascribed to me, but rather the gleanings I had made of the sense of all ages and nations. However, I resolved to be the better for the echo of it; and though I had at first determined to buy stuff for a new coat, I went away resolved to wear my old one a little longer. Reader, if thou wilt do the same, thy profit will be as great as mine. I am, as ever, thine to serve thee,

Richard Saunders.[16]

July 7, 1757.

1757, 1758

AN EDICT BY THE KING OF PRUSSIA*

Dantzic,[1] Sept. 5

We have long wondered here at the supineness of the English nation, under the Prussian impositions upon its trade entering our port. We did not, till lately, know the claims, ancient and modern, that hang over that nation; and therefore could not suspect that it might submit to those impositions from a sense of duty or from principles of equity. The following edict, just made public, may, if serious, throw some light upon this matter.

"Frederic,[2] by the grace of God, king of Prussia, etc. etc., etc., to all present and to come, *(à tous présens et à venir)* health. The peace now enjoyed throughout our dominions, having afforded us leisure to apply ourselves to the regulation of commerce, the improvement of our finances, and at the same time the easing our domestic subjects in their taxes: for these causes, and other good considera-

---

[14] In the Old Testament a man who endured much suffering without losing faith.
[15] Expensive.   [16] The pseudonym Franklin used for *Poor Richard*.
* In this essay, published in the *Gentleman's Magazine* in October 1773, Franklin satirizes England's taxation of the American colonies, suggesting that the immigration of Germanic tribes into Britain during the fifth century gives modern Germany the right to tax the English. Prussia was formally dissolved in 1947 and is now part of northern Germany and Poland.
[1] Danzig, now Gdansk, Poland.
[2] Frederick II (1712–1786), or Frederick the Great, king of Prussia from 1740 to 1786.

tions us thereunto moving, we hereby make known, that, after having deliberated these affairs in our council, present our dear brothers, and other great officers of the state, members of the same, we, of our certain knowledge, full power, and authority royal, have made and issued this present edict, viz.

"Whereas it is well known to all the world that the first German settlements made in the Island of Britain were by colonies of people, subject to our renowned ducal ancestors, and drawn from their dominions, under the conduct of Hengist, Horsa, Hella, Uff, Cerdicus, Ida, and others;[3] and that the said colonies have flourished under the protection of our august house for ages past; have never been emancipated therefrom; and yet have hitherto yielded little profit to the same: and whereas we ourself have in the last war fought for and defended the said colonies, against the power of France, and thereby enabled them to make conquests from the said power in America, for which we have not yet received adequate compensation: and whereas it is just and expedient that a revenue should be raised from the said colonies in Britain, towards our indemnification; and that those who are descendants of our ancient subjects, and thence still owe us due obedience, should contribute to the replenishing of our royal coffers as they must have done, had their ancestors remained in the territories now to us appertaining: we do therefore hereby ordain and command, that, from and after the date of these presents, there shall be levied and paid to our officers of the customs, on all goods, wares, and merchandises, and on all grain and other produce of the earth, exported from the said Island of Britain, and on all goods of whatever kind imported into the same, a duty of four and a half per cent *ad valorem*,[4] for the use of us and our successors. And that the said duty may more effectually be collected, we do hereby ordain, that all ships or vessels bound from Great Britain to any other part of the world, or from any other part of the world to Great Britain, shall in their respective voyages touch at our port of Koningsberg,[5] there to be unladen, searched, and charged with the said duties.[6]

"And whereas there hath been from time to time discovered in the said island of Great Britain, by our colonists there, many mines or beds of iron-stone;[7] and sundry subjects of our ancient dominion, skillful in converting the said stone into metal, have in time past transported themselves thither, carrying with them and communicating that art; and the inhabitants of the said island, presuming that they had a natural right to make the best use they could of the natural productions of their country for their own benefit, have not only built furnaces for smelting the said stone into iron, but have erected plating-forges, slitting-mills, and steel-furnaces, for the more convenient manufacturing of the same; thereby endangering a diminution of the said manufacture in our ancient dominion; we do therefore hereby farther ordain, that, from and after the date hereof, no mill or other engine for slitting or rolling of iron, or any plating-forge to work with a tilt-hammer, or any furnace for making steel, shall be erected or continued in the said island of Great Britain: and the lord lieutenant of every county in the said island is hereby commanded, on information of any such erection within his county, to order and by force to cause the same to be abated and destroyed; as he shall answer the neglect thereof to us at his peril. But we are nevertheless graciously pleased to

---

[3] Ancient invaders of Britain.   [4] "Of their worth" (Latin).

[5] Konigsberg, now Kaliningrad, U.S.S.R.

[6] These demands mimicked the British Navigation Acts that helped to cause the Revolutionary War.

[7] Franklin mentions the British necessities of iron and, in the following paragraphs, wool and hat-making to represent the British exploitation of American products, such as tobacco.

permit the inhabitants of the said island to transport their iron into Prussia, there to be manufactured, and to them returned; they paying our Prussian subjects for the workmanship, with all the costs of commission, freight, and risk, coming and returning; any thing herein contained to the contrary notwithstanding.

"We do not, however, think fit to extend this our indulgence to the article of wool; but, meaning to encourage, not only the manufacturing of woollen cloth, but also the raising of wool, in our ancient dominions, and to prevent both, as much as may be, in our said island, we do hereby absolutely forbid the transportation of wool from thence, even to the mother country, Prussia; and that those islanders may be farther and more effectually restrained in making any advantage of their own wool in the way of manufacture, we command that none shall be carried out of one county into another; nor shall any worsted, bay, or woollen yarn, cloth, says, bays, kerseys, serges, frizes, druggets, cloth-serges, shalloons, or any other drapery stuffs, or woollen manufactures whatsoever, made up or mixed with wool in any of the said counties, be carried into any other county, or be waterborne even across the smallest river or creek, on penalty of forfeiture of the same, together with the boats, carriages, horses, etc., that shall be employed in removing them. Nevertheless, our loving subjects there are hereby permitted (if they think proper) to use all their wool as manure for the improvement of their lands.

"And whereas the art and mystery of making hats hath arrived at great perfection in Prussia, and the making of hats by our remoter subjects ought to be as much as possible restrained: and forasmuch as the islanders before mentioned, being in possession of wool, beaver and other furs, have presumptuously conceived they had a right to make some advantage thereof, by manufacturing the same into hats, to the prejudice of our domestic manufacture: we do therefore hereby strictly command and ordain, that no hats or felts whatsoever, dyed or undyed, finished or unfinished, shall be loaded or put into or upon any vessel, cart, carriage, or horse, to be transported or conveyed out of one county in the said island into another county, or to any other place whatsoever, by any person or persons whatsoever; on pain of forfeiting the same, with a penalty of five hundred pounds sterling for every offence. Nor shall any hat-maker, in any of the said counties, employ more than two apprentices, on penalty of five pounds sterling per month; we intending hereby, that such hatmakers, being so restrained, both in the production and sale of their commodity, may find no advantage in continuing their business. But, lest the said islanders should suffer inconveniency by the want of hats, we are farther graciously pleased to permit them to send their beaver furs to Prussia; and we also permit hats made thereof to be exported from Prussia to Britain; the people thus favoured to pay all costs and charges of manufacturing, interest, commission to our merchants, insurance and freight going and returning, as in the case of iron.

"And, lastly, being willing farther to favor our said colonies in Britain, we do hereby also ordain and command, that all the thieves, highway and street robbers, housebreakers, forgerers, murderers, s—d—tes,[8] and villains of every denomination, who have forfeited their lives to the law in Prussia; but whom we, in our great clemency, do not think fit here to hang, shall be emptied out of our gaols into the said island of Great Britain, for the better peopling of that country.

---

[8] Sodomites, literally inhabitants of the city of Sodom, which was destroyed for its sinfulness (see Genesis 18, 19). The British sent some criminals to the American colonies rather than keep them in British prisons, to the colonists' dismay.

"We flatter ourselves, that these our royal regulations and commands will be thought just and reasonable by our much-favored colonists in England; the said regulations being copied from their statutes of 10 and 11 William III. c. 10, 5 Geo. II. c. 22, 23, Geo. II. c. 29, 4 Geo. I. c. 11,[9] and from other equitable laws made by their parliaments; or from instructions given by their princes; or from resolutions of both houses, entered into for the good government of their own colonies in Ireland and America.

"And all persons in the said island are hereby cautioned not to oppose in any wise the execution of this our edict, or any part thereof, such opposition being high treason; of which all who are suspected shall be transported in fetters from Britain to Prussia, there to be tried and executed according to the Prussian law.

"Such is our pleasure.

"Given at Potsdam,[10] this twenty-fifth day of the month of August, one thousand seven hundred and seventy-three, and in the thirty-third year of our reign.
"By the king, in his council.

"Rechtmaessig, Sec."[11]

Some take this edict to be merely one of the king's *Jeux d'Esprit:*[12] others suppose it serious, and that he means a quarrel with England; but all here think the assertion it concludes with, "that these regulations are copied from acts of the English parliament respecting their colonies," a very injurious one; it being impossible to believe, that a people distinguished for their love of liberty, a nation so wise, so liberal in its sentiments, so just and equitable towards its neighbours, should, from mean and injudicious views of petty immediate profit, treat its own children in a manner so arbitrary and tyrannical!

1773

THE SALE OF THE HESSIANS*

FROM THE COUNT DE SCHAUMBERG TO THE BARON HOHENDORF, COMMANDING THE HESSIAN TROOPS IN AMERICA.

Rome, February 18, 1777.

Monsieur Le Baron: On my return from Naples, I received at Rome your letter of the 27th December of last year. I have learned with unspeakable pleasure the courage our troops exhibited at Trenton,[1] and you cannot imagine my joy on being

---

[9] William III (1650–1702), king of England from 1689 to 1702; George II (1683–1760), king of Great Britain and Ireland from 1727 to 1760; George I (1660–1727), king of Great Britain and Ireland from 1714 to 1727.

[10] Now in Germany. [11] "Legally authorized, Secretary" (German).

[12] "Witty remarks" (French).

* The British purchased the services of Hessians, German mercenaries from Hesse, to fight the American colonists during the Revolution. Franklin's letter, a satire of that purchase, between two imaginary German noblemen appeared in England in 1778 but was probably published earlier elsewhere (Franklin was serving as U.S. minister in Paris at the time).

[1] On Christmas Eve, 1776, George Washington defeated a force of Hessians, killing about twenty and taking nearly one thousand prisoners, in the Battle of Trenton (New Jersey). Franklin exaggerated the numbers.

told that of the 1,950 Hessians engaged in the fight, but 345 escaped. There were just 1,605 men killed, and I cannot sufficiently commend your prudence in sending an exact list of the dead to my minister in London. This precaution was the more necessary, as the report sent to the English ministry does not give but 1,455 dead. This would make 483,450 florins[2] instead of 643,500 which I am entitled to demand under our convention.[3] You will comprehend the prejudice which such an error would work in my finances, and I do not doubt you will take the necessary pains to prove that Lord North's[4] list is false and yours correct.

The court of London objects that there were a hundred wounded who ought not to be included in the list, nor paid for as dead; but I trust you will not overlook my instructions to you on quitting Cassel,[5] and that you will not have tried by human succor to recall the life of the unfortunates whose days could not be lengthened but by the loss of a leg or an arm. That would be making them a pernicious present, and I am sure they would rather die than live in a condition no longer fit for my service. I do not mean by this that you should assassinate them; we should be humane, my dear Baron, but you may insinuate to the surgeons with entire propriety that a crippled man is a reproach to their profession, and that there is no wiser course than to let every one of them die when he ceases to be fit to fight.

I am about to send to you some new recruits. Don't economize them. Remember glory before all things. Glory is true wealth. There is nothing degrades the soldier like the love of money. He must care only for honor and reputation, but this reputation must be acquired in the midst of dangers. A battle gained without costing the conqueror any blood is an inglorious success, while the conquered cover themselves with glory by perishing with their arms in their hands. Do you remember that of the 300 Lacedæmonians[6] who defended the defile of Thermopylæ,[7] not one returned? How happy should I be could I say the same of my brave Hessians!

It is true that their king, Leonidas, perished with them: but things have changed, and it is no longer the custom for princes of the empire to go and fight in America for a cause with which they have no concern. And besides, to whom should they pay the thirty guineas per man if I did not stay in Europe to receive them? Then, it is necessary also that I be ready to send recruits to replace the men you lose. For this purpose I must return to Hesse. It is true, grown men are becoming scarce there, but I will send you boys. Besides, the scarcer the commodity the higher the price. I am assured that the women and little girls have begun to till our lands, and they get on not badly. You did right to send back to Europe that Dr. Crumerus who was so successful in curing dysentery. Don't bother with a man who is subject to looseness of the bowels. That disease makes bad soldiers. One coward will do more mischief in an engagement than ten brave men will do good. Better that they burst in their barracks than fly in a battle, and tarnish the glory of our arms. Besides, you know that they pay me as killed for all who die from disease, and I don't get a farthing for runaways. My trip to Italy, which has cost me enormously, makes it desirable that there should be a great mortality among them. You will therefore promise promotion to all who expose themselves; you

---

[2] British coins, two shillings.   [3] Agreement.
[4] Frederick North (1732-1792), second earl of Guilford and British prime minister from 1770 to 1782.
[5] Capital of the eighteenth-century Germanic electorate Hesse-Cassel.   [6] Ancient Spartans.
[7] A mountain path in ancient Greece so narrow that troops had to march through in single file, where in 480 B.C. the Persians, led by Xerxes, destroyed a Spartan army, led by Leonidas.

will exhort them to seek glory in the midst of dangers; you will say to Major Maundorff that I am not at all content with his saving the 345 men who escaped the massacre of Trenton. Through the whole campaign he has not had ten men killed in consequence of his orders. Finally, let it be your principal object to prolong the war and avoid a decisive engagement on either side, for I have made arrangements for a grand Italian opera, and I do not wish to be obliged to give it up. Meantime I pray God, my dear Baron de Hohendorf, to have you in his holy and gracious keeping.

1777, 1778?

from INFORMATION TO THOSE WHO WOULD REMOVE TO AMERICA*

Many persons in Europe, having directly or by letters, expressed to the writer of this, who is well acquainted with North America, their desire of transporting and establishing themselves in that country; but who appear to have formed, through ignorance, mistaken ideas and expectations of what is to be obtained there; he thinks it may be useful, and prevent inconvenient, expensive, and fruitless removals and voyages of improper persons, if he gives some clearer and truer notions of that part of the world, than appear to have hitherto prevailed.

He finds it is imagined by numbers, that the inhabitants of North America are rich, capable of rewarding, and disposed to reward, all sorts of ingenuity; that they are at the same time ignorant of all the sciences, and, consequently, that strangers, possessing talents in the belles-lettres, fine arts, etc., must be highly esteemed, and so well paid, as to become easily rich themselves; that there are also abundance of profitable offices to be disposed of, which the natives are not qualified to fill; and that, having few persons of family among them, strangers of birth must be greatly respected, and of course easily obtain the best of those offices, which will make all their fortunes; that the governments too, to encourage emigrations from Europe, not only pay the expense of personal transportation, but give lands gratis to strangers, with Negroes to work for them, utensils of husbandry, and stocks of cattle. These are all wild imaginations; and those who go to America with expectations founded upon them will surely find themselves disappointed.

The truth is that though there are in that country few people so miserable as the poor of Europe, there are also very few that in Europe would be called rich; it is rather a general happy mediocrity that prevails. There are few great proprietors of the soil, and few tenants; most people cultivate their own lands, or follow some handicraft or merchandise; very few rich enough to live idly upon their rents or incomes, or to pay the high prices given in Europe for paintings, statues, architecture, and the other works of art, that are more curious than useful. Hence the natural geniuses that have arisen in America with such talents, have uniformly quitted that country for Europe, where they can be more suitably rewarded. It is true that letters and mathematical knowledge are in esteem there, but they are at

---

* This title was used on an edition published in 1784 without Franklin's permission; he used the title *Advice to Such As Would Remove to America* on his own edition of the pamphlet later that year in Paris, where he was serving as U.S. minister to France.

the same time more common than is apprehended; there being already existing nine colleges or universities, viz. four in New England, and one in each of the provinces of New York, New Jersey, Pennsylvania, Maryland, and Virginia, all furnished with learned professors; besides a number of smaller academies; these educate many of the youth in the languages, and those sciences that qualify men for the professions of divinity, law, or physic.[1] Strangers indeed are by no means excluded from exercising those professions; and the quick increase of inhabitants everywhere gives them a chance of employ, which they have in common with the natives. Of civil offices, or employments, there are few; no superflous ones, as in Europe; and it is a rule established in some of the states that no office should be so profitable as to make it desirable. The 36th Article of the Constitution of Pennsylvania runs expressly in these words: "As every freeman, to preserve his independence (if he has not a sufficient estate) ought to have some profession, calling, trade, or farm, whereby he may honestly subsist, there can be no necessity for, nor use in, establishing offices of profit; the usual effects of which are dependance and servility, unbecoming freemen, in the possessors and expectants; faction, contention, corruption, and disorder among the people. Wherefore, whenever an office, through increase of fees or otherwise, becomes so profitable, as to occasion many to apply for it, the profits ought to be lessened by the legislature."

These ideas prevailing more or less in all the United States, it cannot be worth any man's while, who has a means of living at home, to expatriate himself, in hopes of obtaining a profitable civil office in America; and, as to military offices, they are at an end with the war,[2] the armies being disbanded. Much less is it adviseable for a person to go thither, who has no other quality to recommend him but his birth. In Europe it has indeed its value; but it is a commodity that cannot be carried to a worse market than that of America, where people do not inquire concerning a stranger, "What is he?" but, "What can he do?" If he has any useful art, he is welcome; and if he exercises it, and behaves well, he will be respected by all that know him; but a mere man of quality, who, on that account, wants to live upon the public, buy some office or salary, will be despised and disregarded. The husbandman[3] is in honor there, and even the mechanic,[4] because their employments are useful. The people have a saying, that God Almighty is himself a mechanic, the greatest in the universe; and he is respected and admired more for the variety, ingenuity, and utility of his handyworks than for the antiquity of his family. They are pleased with the observation of a Negro, and frequently mention it, that *Boccarorra* (meaning the white men) *make de black man workee, make de horse workee, make de ox workee, make ebery ting workee; only de hog. He, de hog, no workee; he eat, he drink, he walk about, he go to sleep when he please, he libb like a gentleman.* According to these opinions of the Americans, one of them would think himself more obliged to a genealogist, who could prove for him that his ancestors and relations for ten generations had been ploughmen, smiths, carpenters, turners, weavers, tanners, or even shoemakers, and consequently that they were useful members of society; than if he could only prove that they were gentlemen, doing nothing of value, but living idly on the labor of others, mere *fruges consumere nati,*[5] and otherwise good for nothing, till by their death their estates, like the carcass of the Negro's gentleman-hog, come to be cut up.

[1] Medicine.   [2] The Revolutionary War.   [3] Farmer.   [4] Manual laborer.
[5] Franklin's note: " '. . . born Merely to eat up the corn'—Watts."

With regard to encouragements for strangers from government, they are really only what are derived from good laws and liberty. Strangers are welcome, because there is room enough for them all, and therefore the old inhabitants are not jealous of them; the laws protect them sufficiently, so that they have no need of the patronage of great men; and every one will enjoy securely the profits of his industry. But, if he does not bring a fortune with him, he must work and be industrious to live. One or two years' residence gives him all the rights of a citizen; but the government does not at present, whatever it may have done in former times, hire people to become settlers, by paying their passages, giving land, Negroes, utensil, stock, or any other kind of emolument whatsoever. In short, America is the land of labor, and by no means what the English call *Lubberland*,[6] and the French *Pays de Cocagne*,[7] where the streets are said to be paved with half-peck loaves, the houses tiled with pancakes, and where the fowls fly about ready roasted, crying, "Come eat me!"

1782, 1784

REMARKS CONCERNING THE SAVAGES OF NORTH AMERICA

Savages we call them because their manners differ from ours, which we think the perfection of civility; they think the same of theirs.

Perhaps, if we could examine the manners of different nations with impartiality; we should find no people so rude, as to be without any rules of politeness; nor any so polite, as not to have some remains of rudeness.

The Indian men, when young, are hunters and warriors; when old, counselors; for all their government is by counsel of the sages; there is no force, there are no prisons, no officers to compel obedience, or inflict punishment. Hence they generally study oratory, the best speaker having the most influence. The Indian women till the ground, dress the food, nurse and bring up the children, and preserve and hand down to posterity the memory of public transactions. These employments of men and women are accounted natural and honorable. Having few artificial wants, they have abundance of leisure for improvement by conversation. Our laborious manner of life, compared with theirs, they esteem slavish and base; and the learning, on which we value ourselves, they regard as frivolous and useless. An instance of this occurred at the Treaty of Lancaster, in Pennsylvania, Anno 1744, between the government of Virginia and the Six Nations.[1] After the principal business was settled, the commissioners from Virginia acquainted the Indians by a speech, that there was at Williamsburg a college, with a fund for educating Indian youth;[2] and that, if the Six Nations would send down half a dozen of their young lads to that college, the government would take care that they should be well provided for, and instructed in all the learning of the white people. It is one of the

---

[6] A land of slow, lazy people.   [7] Dreamland.

[1] A coalition of the Iroquois tribes Oneida, Onondaga, Mohawk, Seneca, Cayuga, and Tuscarora.

[2] Some of the money bequeathed by Robert Boyle (1627–1691), an English philosopher-scientist, to spread Christianity among the "heathen" went to the College of William and Mary for the education of Native Americans.

Indian rules of politeness not to answer a public proposition the same day that it is made; they think it would be treating it as a light matter, and that they show it respect by taking time to consider it, as of a matter important. They therefore deferred their answer till the day following; when their speaker began, by expressing their deep sense of the kindness of the Virginia government, in making them that offer; "for we know," says he, "that you highly esteem the kind of learning taught in those colleges, and that the maintenance of our young men, while with you, would be very expensive to you. We are convinced, therefore, that you mean to do us good by your proposal; and we thank you heartily. But you, who are wise, must know that different nations have different conceptions of things; and you will therefore not take it amiss, if our ideas of this kind of education happen not to be the same with yours. We have had some experience of it; several of our young people were formerly brought up at the colleges of the northern provinces; they were instructed in all your sciences; but, when they came back to us, they were bad runners, ignorant of every means of living in the woods, unable to bear either cold or hunger, knew neither how to build a cabin, take a deer, or kill an enemy, spoke our language imperfectly, were therefore neither fit for hunters, warriors, nor counselors; they were totally good for nothing. We are however not the less obliged by your kind offer, tho' we decline accepting it; and, to show our grateful sense of it, if the gentlemen of Virginia will send us a dozen of their sons, we will take great care of their education, instruct them in all we know, and make men of them."

Having frequent occasions to hold public councils, they have acquired great order and decency in conducting them. The old men sit in the foremost ranks, the warriors in the next, and the women and children in the hindmost. The business of the women is to take exact notice of what passes, imprint it in their memories (for they have no writing), and communicate it to their children. They are the records of the council, and they preserve traditions of the stipulations in treaties 100 years back; which, when we compare with our writings, we always find exact. He that would speak, rises. The rest observe a profound silence. When he has finished and sits down, they leave him 5 or 6 minutes to recollect, that, if he has omitted any thing he intended to say, or has any thing to add, he may rise again and deliver it. To interrupt another, even in common conversation, is reckoned highly indecent. How different this is from the conduct of a polite British House of Commons, where scarce a day passes without some confusion, that makes the speaker hoarse in calling "to order;" and how different from the mode of conversation in many polite companies of Europe, where, if you do not deliver your sentence with great rapidity, you are cut off in the middle of it by the impatient loquacity of those you converse with, and never suffered to finish it!

The politeness of these savages in conversation is indeed carried to excess, since it does not permit them to contradict or deny the truth of what is asserted in their presence. By this means they indeed avoid disputes; but then it becomes difficult to know their minds, or what impression you make upon them. The missionaries who have attempted to convert them to Christianity all complain of this as one of the great difficulties of their mission. The Indians hear with patience the truths of the Gospel explained to them, and give their usual tokens of assent and approbation; you would think they were convinced. No such matter. It is mere civility.

A Swedish minister, having assembled the chiefs of the Susquehannah Indians,[3] made a sermon to them, acquainting them with the principal historical facts on which our religion is founded; such as the fall of our first parents by eating an apple,[4] the coming of Christ to repair the mischief, his miracles and suffering, etc. When he had finished, an Indian orator stood up to thank him. "What you have told us," says he, "is all very good. It is indeed bad to eat apples. It is better to make them all into cider. We are much obliged by your kindness in coming so far, to tell us these things which you have heard from your mothers. In return, I will tell you some of those we have heard from ours. In the beginning, our fathers had only the flesh of animals to subsist on; and if their hunting was unsuccessful, they were starving. Two of our young hunters, having killed a deer, made a fire in the woods to broil some part of it. When they were about to satisfy their hunger, they beheld a beautiful young woman descend from the clouds, and seat herself on that hill, which you see yonder among the blue mountains. They said to each other, it is a spirit that has smelt our broiling venison, and wishes to eat of it; let us offer some to her. They presented her with the tongue; she was pleased with the taste of it, and said, 'Your kindness shall be rewarded; come to this place after thirteen moons, and you shall find something that will be of great benefit in nourishing you and your children to the latest generations.' They did so, and, to their surprise, found plants they had never seen before; but which, from that ancient time, have been constantly cultivated among us, to our great advantage. Where her right hand had touched the ground, they found maize; where her left hand had touched it, they found kidney beans; and where her backside had sat on it, they found tobacco." The good missionary, disgusted with this idle tale, said, "What I delivered to you were sacred truths; but what you tell me is mere fable, fiction, and falsehood." The Indian, offended, replied, "My brother, it seems your friends have not done you justice in your education; they have not well instructed you in the rules of common civility. You saw that we, who understand and practise those rules, believed all your stories; why do you refuse to believe ours?"

When any of them come into our towns, our people are apt to crowd round them, gaze upon them, and incommode them, where they desire to be private; this they esteem great rudeness, and the effect of the want of instruction in the rules of civility and good manners. "We have," say they, "as much curiosity as you, and when you come into our towns, we wish for opportunities of looking at you; but for this purpose we hide ourselves behind bushes, where you are to pass, and never intrude ourselves into your company."

Their manner of entering one another's village has likewise its rules. It is reckoned uncivil in traveling strangers to enter a village abruptly, without giving notice of their approach. Therefore, as soon as they arrive within hearing, they stop and hollow,[5] remaining there till invited to enter. Two old men usually come out to them, and lead them in. There is in every village a vacant dwelling, called the stranger's house. Here they are placed, while the old men go round from hut to hut, acquainting the inhabitants, that strangers are arrived, who are probably hun-

---

[3] An Iroquois tribe in Pennsylvania.

[4] In the old Testament the Fall, or Original Sin, in which Adam yielded to temptation by eating the forbidden fruit and subsequently fell from grace; "our first parents" are Adam and Eve.

[5] Cry out.

gry and weary; and every one sends them what he can spare of victuals, and skins to repose on. When the strangers are refreshed, pipes and tobacco are brought; and then, but not before, conversation begins, with enquiries who they are, whither bound, what news, etc; and it usually ends with offers of service, if the strangers have occasion of guides, or any necessaries for continuing their journey; and nothing is exacted for the entertainment.

The same hospitality, esteemed among them as a principal virtue, is practiced by private persons; of which Conrad Weiser, our interpreter, gave me the following instance. He had been naturalized among the Six Nations, and spoke well the Mohawk language. In going through the Indian country, to carry a message from our governor to the council at Onondaga, he called at the habitation of Canassatego, an old acquaintance, who embraced him, spread furs for him to sit on, placed before him some boiled beans and venison, and mixed some rum and water for his drink. When he was well refreshed, and had lit his pipe, Canassatego began to converse with him; asked how he had fared the many years since they had seen each other; whence he then came; what occasioned the journey, etc. Conrad answered all his questions; and when the discourse began to flag, the Indian, to continue it, said, "Conrad, you have lived long among the white people, and know something of their customs; I have been sometimes at Albany, and have observed, that once in seven days they shut up their shops, and assemble all in the great house; tell me what it is for? What do they do there?" "They meet there," says Conrad, "to hear and learn 'good things.'" "I do not doubt," says the Indian, "that they tell you so; they have told me the same; but I doubt the truth of what they say, and I will tell you my reasons. I went lately to Albany to sell my skins and buy blankets, knives, powder, rum, etc. You know I used generally to deal with Hans Hanson; but I was a little inclined this time to try some other merchant. However, I called first upon Hans, and asked him what he would give for beaver. He said he could not give any more than four shillings a pound; 'but' says he, 'I cannot talk on business now; this is the day when we meet together to learn "good things," and I am going to the meeting.' So I thought to myself, 'Since we cannot do any business today, I may as well go to the meeting too,' and I went with him. There stood up a man in black, and began to talk to the people very angrily. I did not understand what he said; but, perceiving that he looked much at me and at Hanson, I imagined he was angry at seeing me there; so I went out, sat down near the house, struck fire, and lit my pipe, waiting till the meeting should break up. I thought too, that the man had mentioned something of beaver, and I suspected it might be the subject of their meeting. So, when they came out, I accosted my merchant. 'Well, Hans' says I, 'I hope you have agreed to give more than four shillings a pound.' 'No,' says he, 'I cannot give so much; I cannot give more than three shillings and sixpence.' I then spoke to several other dealers, but they all sung the same song—three and sixpence, three and sixpence. This made it clear to me that my suspicion was right; and, that whatever they pretended of meeting to learn "good things," the real purpose was to consult how to cheat Indians in the price of beaver. Consider but a little, Conrad, and you must be of my opinion. If they met so often to learn "good things," they would certainly have learned some before this time. But they are still ignorant. You know our practice. If a white man, in travelling through our country, enters one of our cabins, we all treat him as I treat you; we dry him if he is wet, we warm him if he is cold, we give him meat and drink, that he may allay his thirst and hunger; and we spread soft furs for him to rest and sleep on; we demand nothing in return. But, if I go into a white man's house at Albany, and ask for victuals and drink, they say, 'Get out, you Indian dog.' You see they have not yet learned those little "good things," that we need no meetings to be instructed in, because our mothers taught them to us when we were children; and therefore it is impossible their meetings should be, as they say, for any such purpose, or have any such effect; they are only to contrive the cheating of Indians in the price of beaver."[6]

1784

AN ADDRESS TO THE PUBLIC

FROM THE PENNSYLVANIA SOCIETY FOR PROMOTING THE ABOLITION OF SLAVERY, AND THE RELIEF OF FREE NEGROES UNLAWFULLY HELD IN BONDAGE

It is with peculiar satisfaction we assure the friends of humanity, that, in prosecuting the design of our association, our endeavors have proved successful, far beyond our most sanguine expectations.

Encouraged by this success, and by the daily progress of that luminous and benign spirit of liberty, which is diffusing itself throughout the world, and humbly hoping for the continuance of the divine blessing on our labors, we have ventured to make an important addition to our original plan, and do therefore earnestly solicit the support and assistance of all who can feel the tender emotions of sympathy and compassion, or relish the exalted pleasure of beneficence.

Slavery is such an atrocious debasement of human nature, that its very extirpation, if not performed with solicitous care, may sometimes open a source of serious evils.

The unhappy man, who has long been treated as a brute animal, too frequently sinks beneath the common standard of the human species. The galling chains that bind his body, do also fetter his intellectual faculties, and impair the social affections of his heart. Accustomed to move like a mere machine, by the will of a master, reflection is suspended; he has not the power of choice; and reason and conscience have but little influence over his conduct, because he is chiefly governed by the passion of fear. He is poor and friendless; perhaps worn out by extreme labor, age, and disease.

Under such circumstances, freedom may often prove a misfortune to himself, and prejudicial to society.

Attention to emancipated black people, it is therefore to be hoped, will become a branch of our national policy; but, as far as we contribute to promote this eman-

---

[6] Franklin's note: "It is remarkable that in all ages and countries hospitality has been allowed as the virtue of those whom the civilized were pleased to call barbarians. The Greeks celebrated the Scythians for it. The Saracens possessed it eminently, and it is to this day the reigning virture of the wild Arabs. St. Paul, too, in the relation of his voyage and shipwreck on the Island of Melita says the barbarous people showed us no little kindness; for they kindled a fire, and received us every one, because of the present rain, and because of the cold."

cipation, so far that attention is evidently a serious duty incumbent on us, and which we mean to discharge to the best of our judgment and abilities.

To instruct, to advise, to qualify those, who have been restored to freedom, for the exercise and enjoyment of civil liberty, to promote in them habits of industry, to furnish them with employments suited to their age, sex, talents, and other circumstances, and to procure their children an education calculated for their future situation in life; these are the great outlines of the annexed plan, which we have adopted, and which we conceive will essentially promote the public good, and the happiness of these our hitherto too much neglected fellow creatures.

A plan so extensive cannot be carried into execution without considerable pecuniary resources, beyond the present ordinary funds of the Society. We hope much from the generosity of enlightened and benevolent freemen, and will gratefully receive any donations or subscriptions for this pupose, which may be made to our treasurer, James Starr, or to James Pemberton, chairman of our committee of correspondence.

Signed, by order of the Society,

B. Franklin, President.

Philadelphia, 9th of
    November, 1789.

1789

from   THE AUTOBIOGRAPHY*

PART ONE

Twyford,[1] at the Bishop of St. Asaph's 1771.

Dear Son,

I have ever had a Pleasure in obtaining any little Anecdotes of my Ancestors. You may remember the Enquiries I made among the Remains of my Relations when you were with me in England; and the Journey I took for that purpose.[2] Now imagining it may be equally agreeable to you to know the Circumstances of *my* Life, many of which you are yet unacquainted with; and expecting a Weeks uninterrupted Leisure in my present Country Retirement, I sit down to write them for you. To which I have besides some other Inducements. Having emerg'd from the Poverty and Obscurity in which I was born and bred, to a State of Affluence and some Degree of Reputation in the World, and having gone so far thro' Life with a considerable Share of Felicity, the conducing Means I made use of, which, with the Blessing of God, so well succeeded, my Posterity may like to know, as they

---

* In 1771 at age sixty-five Franklin began writing his *Autobiography,* which he called "Memoirs," for his son William (1731–1813), then governor of New Jersey. Franklin wrote three more sections during the next nineteen years, until just before his death in 1790, although the account stops at 1758, before he had begun his work in international diplomacy and in public service. Franklin never published his *Autobiography;* the text here retains the original spelling and punctuation.

[1] The country home of Jonathan Shipley, bishop of St. Asaph and Franklin's friend; near Winchester, England. Franklin was vacationing there.

[2] Franklin and his son William visited Ecton and Banbury, both in Northamptonshire, England, in 1758 to visit the homes of their ancestors and their remaining family.

may find some of them suitable to their own Situations, and therefore fit to be imitated. That Felicity, when I reflected on it, has induc'd me sometimes to say, that were it offer'd to my Choice, I should have no Objection to a Repetition of the same Life from its Beginning, only asking the Advantage Authors have in a second Edition to correct some Faults of the first. So would I if I might, besides corr[ectin]g the Faults, change some sinister Accidents and Events of it for others more favourable, but tho' this were deny'd, I should still accept the Offer. However, since such a Repetition is not to be expected, the next Thing most like living one's Life over again, seems to be a *Recollection* of that Life; and to make that Recollection as durable as possible, the putting it down in Writing. Hereby, too, I shall indulge the Inclination so natural in old Men, to be talking of themselves and their own past Actions, and I shall indulge it, without being troublesome to others who thro' respect to Age might think themselves oblig'd to give me a Hearing, since this may be read or not as any one pleases. And lastly, (I may as well confess it, since my Denial of it will be believ'd by no body) perhaps I shall a good deal gratify my own *Vanity*. Indeed I scarce ever heard or saw the introductory Words, *Without Vanity I may say,* etc., but some vain thing immediately follow'd. Most People dislike Vanity in others whatever Share they have of it themselves, but I give it fair Quarter[3] wherever I meet with it, being persuaded that it is often productive of Good to the Possessor and to others that are within his Sphere of Action: And therefore in many Cases it would not be quite absurd if a Man were to thank God for his Vanity among the other Comforts of Life.

And now I speak of thanking God, I desire with all Humility to acknowledge, that I owe the mention'd Happiness of my past Life to his kind Providence, which led me to the Means I us'd and gave them Success. My Belief of this, induces me to *hope,* tho' I must not *presume,* that the same Goodness will still be exercis'd towards me in continuing that Happiness, or in enabling me to bear a fatal Reverse, which I may experience as others have done, the Complexion of my future Fortune being known to him only: and in whose Power it is to bless to us even our Afflictions.

The Notes one of my Uncles[4] (who had the same kind of Curiosity in collecting Family Anecdotes) once put into my Hands, furnish'd me with several Particulars relating to our Ancestors. From these Notes I learnt that the Family had liv'd in the same Village, Ecton in Northamptonshire, for 300 Years, and how much longer he knew not (perhaps from the Time when the Name *Franklin* that before was the Name of an Order of People,[5] was assum'd by them for a Surname, when others took Surnames all over the Kingdom). (Here a Note)[6] on a Freehold[7] of about 30 Acres, aided by the Smith's Business which had continued in the Family till his Time, the eldest Son being always bred to that Business. A Custom which he and my Father both followed as to their eldest Sons. When I search'd the Register at Ecton, I found an Account of their Births, Marriages and Burials, from the Year 1555 only, there being no Register kept in that Parish at any time preceding. By that Register I perceiv'd that I was the youngest Son of the youngest Son for 5 Generations back.

My Grandfather Thomas, who was born in 1598, lived at Ecton till he grew too old to follow Business longer, when he went to live with his Son John, a Dyer at

---

[3] Consideration.   [4] Benjamin Franklin the Elder, or Uncle Benjamin.
[5] "Franklin" meant "freeholder" in medieval England—a landowner not of noble birth.
[6] Franklin never inserted the intended note.
[7] In feudal times, land free of other claims of ownership.

Banbury in Oxfordshire, with whom my Father serv'd an Apprenticeship. There my Grandfather died and lies buried. We saw his Gravestone in 1758. His eldest Son Thomas liv'd in the House at Ecton, and left it with the Land to his only Child, a Daughter, who with her Husband, one Fisher of Wellingborough sold it to Mr. Isted, now Lord of the Manor there. My Grandfather had 4 Sons that grew up, viz. Thomas, John, Benjamin and Josiah. I will give you what Account I can of them at this distance from my Papers, and if they are not lost in my Absence, you will among them find many more Particulars. Thomas was bred a Smith under his Father, but being ingenious, and encourag'd in Learning (as all his Brothers like wise were) by an Esquire Palmer[8] then the principal Gentleman in that Parish, he qualify'd for the Business of Scrivener,[9] became a considerable Man in the County Affairs, was a chief Mover of all publick Spirited Undertakings, for the County, or Town of Northampton and his own Village, of which many Instances were told us at Ecton and he was much taken Notice of and patroniz'd by the then Lord Halifax. He died in 1702, Jan. 6, old Stile,[10] just 4 Years to a Day before I was born. The Account we receiv'd of his Life and Character from some old People at Ecton, I remember struck you, as something extraordinary from its Similarity to what you knew of mine. Had he died on the same Day, you said one might have suppos'd a Transmigration.[11]

John was bred a Dyer, I believe of Woollens. Benjamin, was bred a Silk Dyer, serving an Apprenticeship at London. He was an ingenious Man, I remember him well, for when I was a Boy he came over to my Father in Boston, and lived in the House with us some Years. He lived to a great Age. His Grandson Samuel Franklin now lives in Boston. He left behind him two Quarto[12] Volumes, M.S. of his own Poetry, consisting of little occasional Pieces address'd to his Friends and Relations, of which the following sent to me, is a Specimen. (Here insert it.)[13] He had form'd a Shorthand of his own, which he taught me, but never practising it I have now forgot it. I was nam'd after this Uncle, there being a particular Affection between him and my Father. He was very pious, a great Attender of Sermons of the best Preachers, which he took down in his Shorthand and had with him many Volumes of them. He was also much of a Politician, too much perhaps for his Station. There fell lately into my Hands in London a Collection he had made of all the principal Pamphlets relating to Publick Affairs from 1641 to 1717. Many of the Volumes are wanting, as appears by the Numbering, but there still remains 8 Vols. Folio, and 24 in 4to and 8vo.[14] A Dealer in old Books met with them, and knowing me by my sometimes buying of him, he brought them to me. It seems my Uncle must have left them here when he went to America, which was above 50 Years since. There are many of his Notes in the Margins.

This obsure Family of ours was early in the Reformation, and continu'd Protestants thro' the Reign of Queen Mary,[15] when they were sometimes in Danger of

---

[8] John Palmer.   [9] A professional writer of legal documents.

[10] England changed over to the Gregorian, or "New Style," calendar in 1752 from the Julian, or "Old Style," calendar. Franklin's birthday in the New Style calendar was January 17.

[11] The soul's passage at death into another body.

[12] A book made from sheets with four pages printed on each side.

[13] Franklin made no insertion into the original manuscript.

[14] Book sizes ranging from large to small. A folio is made from sheets with two pages printed on each side; quarto ("4to"); and octavo ("8vo"), eight pages.

[15] Mary I (1516–1558), or Mary Tudor, queen of England from 1553–1558. She earned the name "Bloody Mary" for persecuting Protestants, in an attempt to restore Roman Catholicism as the state church.

Trouble on Account of their Zeal against Popery. They had got an English Bible, and to conceal and secure it,[16] it was fastned open with Tapes under and within the Frame of a Joint Stool.[17] When my Great Great Grandfather read in it to his Family, he turn'd up the Joint Stool upon his Knees, turning over the Leaves then under the Tapes. One of the Children stood at the Door to give Notice if he saw the Apparitor coming, who was an Officer of the Spiritual Court.[18] In that Case the Stool was turn'd down again upon its feet, when the Bible remain'd conceal'd under it as before. This Anecdote I had from my Uncle Benjamin. The Family continu'd all of the Church of England till about the End of Charles the 2ds[19] Reign, when some of the Ministers that had been outed for Nonconformity, holding Conventicles[20] in Northamptonshire, Benjamin and Josiah adher'd to them, and so continu'd all their Lives. The rest of the Family remain'd with the Episcopal Church.

Josiah, my Father, married young, and carried his Wife with three Children unto New England, about 1682.[21] The Conventicles having been forbidden by Law, and frequently disturbed, induced some considerable Men of his Acquaintance to remove to that Country, and he was prevail'd with to accompany them thither, where they expected to enjoy their Mode of Religion with Freedom. By the same Wife he had 4 Children more born there, and by a second Wife ten more, in all 17, of which I remember 13 sitting at one time at his Table, who all grew up to be Men and Women, and married. I was the youngest Son and the youngest Child but two, and was born in boston, N. England.

My Mother the 2d Wife was Abiah Folger, a Daughter of Peter Folger, one of the first Settlers of New England, of whom honourable mention is made by Cotton Mather, in his Church History of that Country, (entitled Magnalia Christi Americana)[22] as a *godly learned Englishman,* if I remember the words rightly. I have heard that he wrote sundry small occasional Pieces, but only one of them was printed[23] which I saw now many Years since. It was written in 1675, in the homespun Verse of that Time and People, and address'd to those then concern'd in the Government there. It was in favour of Liberty of Conscience, and in behalf of the Baptists, Quakers, and other Sectaries,[24] that had been under Persecution; ascribing the Indian Wars and other Distresses, that had befallen the Country to that Persecution, as so many Judgments of God, to punish so heinous an Offence; and exhorting a Repeal of those uncharitable Laws. The whole appear'd to me as written with a good deal of Decent Plainness and manly Freedom. The six last concluding Lines I remember, tho' I have forgotten the two first of the Stanza, but the Purport of them was that his Censures proceeded from *Goodwill,* and therefore he would be known as the Author,

> because to be a Libeller, (says he)
> I hate it with my Heart.

---

[16] Many Bibles were destroyed during Queen Mary's reign to eliminate Protestantism.

[17] A stool that is joined but not nailed together.

[18] An ecclesiastical court for the elimination of heresy.

[19] Charles II (1630–1685), king of England, Scotland, and Ireland from 1660 to 1685.

[20] Secret, illegal meetings of Nonconformists, who refused to follow the Church of England.

[21] Actually 1683; Josiah Franklin's first wife was Ann Child.   [22] Published in 1702.

[23] *A Looking Glass for the Times: Or, the Former Spirit of New England Revived in This Generation* (1676); Folger (1617–1690) was a pioneer of Nantucket.

[24] Members of a sect.

> From Sherburne Town[25] where now I dwell,
>   My Name I do put here,
> Without Offence, your real Friend,
>   It is Peter Folgier.

My elder Brothers were all put Apprentices to different Trades. I was put to the Grammar School at Eight Years of Age, my Father intending to devote me as the Tithe[26] of his Sons to the Service of the Church. My early Readiness in learning to read (which must have been very early, as I do not remember when I could not read) and the Opinion of all his Friends that I should certainly make a good Scholar, encourage'd him in this Purpose of his. My Uncle Benjamin too approv'd of it, and propos'd to give me all his Shorthand Volumes of Sermons I suppose as a Stock to set up with, if I would learn his Character.[27] I continu'd however at the Grammar School not quite one Year, tho' in that time I had risen gradually from the Middle of the Class of that Year to be the Head of it, and farther was remov'd into the next Class above it, in order to go with that into the third at the End of the Year. But my Father in the mean time, from a View of the Expence of a College Education which, having so large a Family, he could not well afford, and the mean Living many so educated were afterwards able to obtain, Reasons that he gave to his Friends in my Hearing, altered his first Intention, took me from the Grammar School, and sent me to a school for Writing and Arithmetic kept by a then famous Man, Mr. Geo. Brownell, very successful in his Profession generally, and that by mild encouraging Methods. Under him I acquired fair Writing pretty soon, but I fail'd in the Arithmetic, and made no Progress in it.

At Ten Years old, I was taken home to assist my Father in his Business, which was that of a Tallow Chandler and Sope-Boiler.[28] A Business he was not bred to, but had assumed on his Arrival in New England and on finding his Dying Trade would not maintain his Family, being in little Request. Accordingly I was employed in cutting Wick for the Candles, filling the Dipping Mold, and the Molds for cast Candles, attending the Shop, going of Errands, etc. I dislik'd the trade and had a strong Inclination for the Sea; but my Father declar'd against it; however, living near the Water, I was much in and about it, learnt early to swim well, and to manage Boats, and when in a Boat or Canoe with other Boys I was commonly allow'd to govern,[29] especially in any case of Difficulty; and upon other Occasions I was generally a Leader among the Boys, and sometimes led them into Scrapes, of which I will mention one Instance, as it shows an early projecting public Spirit, tho' not then justly conducted. There was a Salt Marsh that bounded part of the Mill Pond, on the Edge of which at Highwater, we us'd to stand to fish for Minews.[30] By much Trampling, we had made it a mere Quagmire. My Proposal was to build a Wharf there fit for us to stand upon, and I show'd my Comrades a large Heap of Stones which were intended for a new House near the Marsh, and which would very well suit our Purpose. Accordingly in the Evening when the Workmen were gone, I assembled a Number of my Playfellows, and working with them diligently like so many Emmets,[31] sometimes two or three to a Stone, we brought them all away and built our little Wharff. The next Morning the

[25] Franklin's note: "In the Island of Nantucket."
[26] One-tenth; literally a portion of income given to the church.   [27] Shorthand system.
[28] A maker of candles and soap.   [29] To steer.   [30] Minnows.   [31] Ants.

Workmen were surpriz'd at Missing the Stones; which were found in our Wharff; Enquiry was made after the Removers; we were discovered and complain'd of; several of us were corrected by our Fathers; and tho' I pleaded the Usefulness of the Work, mine convinc'd me that nothing was useful which was not honest.

I think you may like to know Something of his Person and Character. He had an excellent Constitution of Body, was of middle Stature, but well set and very strong. He was ingenious, could draw prettily, was skill'd a little in Music and had a clear pleasing Voice, so that when he play'd Psalm Tunes on his Violin and sung withal as he sometimes did in an Evening after the Business of the Day was over, it was extreamly agreable to hear. He had a mechanical Genius too, and on occasion was very handy in the Use of other Tradesmen's Tools. But his great Excellence lay in a sound Understanding, and solid Judgment in prudential Matters, both in private and publick Affairs. In the latter indeed he was never employed, the numerous Family he had to educate and the straitness of his Circumstances, keeping him close to his Trade, but I remember well his being frequently visited by leading People, who consulted him for his Opinion in Affairs of the Town or of the Church he belong'd to and show'd a good deal of Respect for his Judgment and Advice. He was also much consulted by private Persons about their Affairs when any Difficulty occur'd, and frequently chosen an Arbitrator between contending Parties. At his Table he lik'd to have as often as he could, some sensible Friend or Neighbour, to converse with, and always took care to start some ingenious or useful Topic for Discourse, which might tend to improve the Minds of his Children. By this means he turn'd our Attention to what was good, just, and prudent in the Conduct of Life; and little or no Notice was ever taken of what related to the Victuals on the Table, whether it was well or ill drest, in or out of season, of good or bad flavour, preferable or inferior to this or that other thing of the kind; so that I was bro't up in such a perfect Inattention to those Matters as to be quite Indifferent what kind of Food was set before me; and so unobservant of it, that to this Day, if I am ask'd I can scarce tell, a few Hours after Dinner, what I din'd upon. This has been a Convenience to me in travelling, where my Companions have been sometimes very unhappy for want of a suitable Gratification of their more delicate because better instructed Tastes and Appetites.

My Mother had likewise an excellent Constitution. She suckled all her 10 Children. I never knew either my Father or Mother to have any Sickness but that of which they dy'd he at 89 and she at 85 Years of age. They lie buried together at Boston, where I some Years since plac'd a Marble stone over their Grave with this Inscription

> Josiah Franklin
> And Abiah his Wife
> Lie here interred.
> They lived lovingly together in Wedlock
> Fifty-five Years.
> Without an Estate or any gainful Employment,[32]
> By constant labour and Industry,
> With God's Blessing,
> They maintained a large Family
> Comfortably;

[32] Without "privileged" employment, or an inheritance.

And brought up thirteen Children,
And seven Grand Children
Reputably.
From this Instance, Reader,
Be encouraged to Diligence in thy Calling,
And distrust not Providence.
He was a pious & prudent Man,
She a discreet and virtuous Woman.
Their youngest Son,
In filial Regard to their Memory,
Places this Stone.
J.F. born 1655—Died 1744. Ætat[33] 89
A.F. born 1667—died 1752———85

By my rambling Digressions I perceive my self to be grown old. I us'd to write more methodically. But one does not dress for private Company as for a publick Ball. 'Tis perhaps only Negligence.

To return. I continu'd thus employ'd in my Father's Business for two Years, that is till I was 12 Years old; and my Brother John,[34] who was bred to that Business having left my Father, married and set up for himself at Rhodeisland, there was all Appearance that I was destin'd to supply his Place and be a Tallow Chandler. But my Dislike to the Trade continuing, my Father was under Apprehensions that if he did not find one for me more agreable, I should break away and get to Sea, as his Son Josiah had done to his great Vexation. He therefore sometimes took me to walk with him, and see Joiners,[35] Bricklayers, Turners, Braziers,[36] etc. at their Work, that he might observe my Inclination, and endeavour to fix it on some Trade or other on Land. It has ever since been a Pleasure to me to see good Workmen handle their Tools; and it has been useful to me, having learnt so much by it, as to be able to do little Jobs my self in my House, when a Workman could not readily be got; and to construct little Machines for my Experiments while the Intention of making the Experiment was fresh and warm in my Mind. My Father at last fix'd upon the Cutler's Trade, and my Uncle Benjamin's Son Samuel who was bred to that Business in London being about that time establish'd in Boston, I was sent to be with him some time on liking. But his Expectations of a Fee with me displeasing my Father, I was taken home again.

From a Child I was fond of Reading, and all the little Money that came into my Hands was ever laid out in Books. Pleas'd with the Pilgrim's Progress, [37] my first Collection was of John Bunyan's Works, in separate little Volumes. I afterwards sold them to enable me to buy R. Burton's Historical Collections;[38] they were small Chapmen's [39] Books and cheap, 40 or 50 in all. My Father's little Library consisted chiefly of Books in polemic Divinity, most of which I read, and have since often regretted, that at a time when I had such a Thirst for Knowledge, more proper Books had not fallen in my Way, since it was now resolv'd I should not be

---

[33] "Aged" (Latin).

[34] John Franklin (1690–1756), Franklin's favorite brother; later, postmaster of Boston.

[35] Woodworkers.   [36] Latheworkers and brassworkers.

[37] *The Pilgrim's Progress* (1678), by the Puritan preacher John Bunyan (1628–1688).

[38] Nathaniel Crouch (1632?–1725?), popularizer of British history, wrote as Robert or Richard Burton.

[39] Peddlar's.

a Clergyman. Plutarch's Lives[40] there was, in which I read abundantly, and I still think that time spent to great Advantage. There was also a Book of Defoe's, called an Essay on Projects,[41] and another of Dr. Mather's, call'd Essays to do Good[42] which perhaps gave me a Turn of Thinking that had an Influence on some of the principal future Events of my Life.

This Bookish Inclination at length determin'd my Father to make me a Printer, tho' he had already one Son, (James)[43] of that Profession. In 1717 my Brother James return'd from England with a Press and Letters [44] to set up his Business in Boston. I lik'd it much better than that of my Father, but still had a Hankering for the Sea. To prevent the apprehended Effect of such an Inclination, my Father was impatient to have me bound[45] to my Brother. I stood out some time, but at last was persuaded and signed the Indentures, when I was yet but 12 Years old. I was to serve as an Apprentice till I was 21 Years of Age, only I was to be allow'd Journeyman's[46] Wages during the last Year. In a little time I made great Proficiency in the Business, and became a useful Hand to my Brother. I now had Access to better Books. An Acquaintance with the Apprentices of Booksellers, enabled me sometimes to borrow a small one, which I was careful to return soon and clean. Often I sat up in my Room reading the greatest Part of the Night, when the Book was borrow'd in the Evening and to be return'd early in the Morning lest it should be miss'd or wanted. And after some time an ingenious Tradesman Mr. Matthew Adams who had a pretty[47] Collection of Books, and who frequented our Printing House, took Notice of me, invited me to his Library, and very kindly lent me such Books as I chose to read. I now took a Fancy to Poetry, and made some little Pieces. My Brother, thinking it might turn to account encourag'd me, and put me on composing two occasional Ballads. One was called the *Light House Tragedy,* and contain'd an Account of the drowning of Capt. Worthilake with his Two Daughters; the other was a Sailor Song on the Taking of *Teach* or Blackbeard the Pirate.[48] They were wretched Stuff, in the Grubstreet Ballad Stile,[49] and when they were printed he sent me about the Town to sell them. The first sold wonderfully, the Event being recent, having made a great Noise. This flatter'd my Vanity. But my Father discourag'd me, by ridiculing my Performances, and telling me Verse-makers were generally Beggars; so I escap'd being a Poet, most probably a very bad one. But as Prose Writing has been of great Use to me in the Course of my Life, and was a principal Means of my Advancement, I shall tell you how in such a Situation I acquir'd what little Ability I have in that Way.

There was another Bookish Lad in the Town, John Collins by Name, with whom I was intimately acquainted. We sometimes disputed, and very fond we were of Argument, and very desirous of confuting one another. Which disputacious Turn, by the way, is apt to become a very bad Habit, making People often

---

[40] *Parallel Lives,* by the Greek writer Plutarch (A.D. 46–120), is a series of forty-six biographies of Greek and Roman notables.

[41] *Essay Upon Projects* (1697), by Daniel Defoe (1659?–1731), proposes schemes for civic and economic improvements.

[42] *Bonifacius: An Essay Upon the Good* (1710), by Cotton Mather, influenced Franklin's *Dogood Papers* (1722).

[43] James Franklin (1697–1735).   [44] Type.   [45] Apprenticed.   [46] Daily.   [47] Fine.

[48] The texts of the ballads are not known in entirety. George Worthylake, keeper of the Beacon Island light (in Boston Harbor), his wife, and a daughter drowned November 3, 1718; the pirate Edward Teach was attacked in North Carolina waters by forces from Virginia and killed November 22, 1718.

[49] London's Grub Street housed literary "hacks."

extreamly disagreable in Company, by the Contradiction that is necessary to bring it into Practice, and thence, besides souring and spoiling the Conversation, is productive of Disgusts and perhaps Enmities where you may have occasion for Friendship. I had caught it by reading my Father's Books of Dispute about Religion. Persons of good Sense, I have since observ'd, seldom fall into it, except Lawyers, University Men, and Men of all Sorts that have been bred at Edinborough. A Question was once some how or other started between Collins and me, of the Propriety of educating the Female Sex in Learning, and their Abilities for Study. He was of Opinion that it was improper; and that they were naturally unequal to it. I took the contrary Side, perhaps a little for Dispute sake. He was naturally more eloquent, had a ready Plenty of Words, and sometimes as I thought bore me down more by his Fluency than by the Strength of his Reasons. As we parted without settling the Point, and were not to see one another again for some time, I sat down to put my Arguments in writing, which I copied fair and sent to him. He answer'd and I reply'd. Three or four Letters of a Side had pass'd, when my Father happen'd to find my Papers, and read them. Without entring into the Discussion, he took occasion to talk to me about the Manner of my Writing, observ'd that tho' I had the Advantage of my Antagonist in correct Spelling and pointing[50] (which I ow'd to the Printing House) I fell far short in elegance of Expression, in Method and in Perspicuity of which he convinc'd me by several Instances. I saw the Justice of his Remarks, and thence grew more attentive to the *Manner* in Writing, and determin'd to endeavour at Improvement.

About this time I met with an odd Volume of the Spectator.[51] It was the third. I had never before seen any of them. I bought it, read it over and over, and was much delighted with it. I thought the Writing excellent, and wish'd if possible to imitate it. With that View, I took some of the Papers, and making short Hints of the Sentiment in each Sentence, laid them by a few Days, and then without looking at the Book, try'd to compleat the Papers again, by expressing each hinted Sentiment at length and as fully as it had been express'd before, in any suitable Words, that should come to hand.

Then I compar'd my Spectator with the Original, discover'd some of my Faults and corrected them. But I found I wanted a Stock of Words or a Readiness in recollecting and using them, which I thought I should have acquir'd before that time, if I had gone on making Verses, since the continual Occasion for Words of the same Import but of different Length, to suit the Measure,[52] or of different Sound for the Rhyme, would have laid me under a constant Necessity of searching for Variety, and also have tended to fix that Variety in my Mind, and make me Master of it. Therefore I took some of the Tales and turn'd them into Verse: And after a time, when I had pretty well forgotten the Prose, turn'd them back again. I also sometimes jumbled my Collections of Hints into Confusion, and after some Weeks, endeavour'd to reduce them into the best Order, before I began to form the full Sentences, and compleat the Paper. This was to teach me Method in the Arrangement of Thoughts. By comparing my work afterwards with the original, I discover'd many faults and amended them; but I sometimes had the Pleasure of Fancying that in certain Particulars of small Import, I had been lucky enough to

---

[50] Punctuation, which, along with spelling, was not standardized at the time.

[51] A popular English daily paper, published from March 1, 1711, to December 6, 1712, covered literary topics and contained essays by Joseph Addison (1672–1719) and Richard Steel (1672–1729).

[52] Meter.

improve the Method or the Language and this encourag'd me to think I might possibly in time come to be a tolerable English Writer, of which I was extreamly ambitious.

My time for these Exercises and for Reading, was at Night, after Work or before Work began in the Morning; or on Sundays, when I contrived to be in the Printing House alone, evading as much as I could the common Attendance on publick Worship, which my Father used to exact of me when I was under his Care: And which indeed I still thought a Duty; tho' I could not, as it seemed to me, afford the Time to practise it.

When about 16 Years of Age, I happen'd to meet with a Book, written by one Tryon,[53] recommending a Vegetable Diet. I determined to go into it. My Brother being yet unmarried, did not keep House, but boarded himself and his Apprentices in another Family. My refusing to eat Flesh occasioned an Inconveniency, and I was frequently chid for my singularity. I made my self acquainted with Tryon's Manner of preparing some of his Dishes, such as Boiling Potatoes or Rice, making Hasty Pudding,[54] and a few others, and then propos'd to my Brother, that if he would give me Weekly half the Money he paid for my Board I would board my self. He instantly agreed to it, and I presently found that I could save half what he paid me. This was an additional Fund for buying Books: But I had another Advantage in it. My Brother and the rest going from the Printing House to their Meals, I remain'd there alone, and dispatching presently my light Repast, (which often was no more than a Bisket or a Slice of Bread, a Handful of Raisins or a Tart from the Pastry Cook's, and a Glass of Water) had the rest of the Time till their Return, for Study, in which I made the greater Progress from that greater Clearness of Head and quicker Apprehension which usually attend Temperance in Eating and Drinking. And now it was that being on some Occasion made asham'd of my Ignorance in Figures, which I had twice failed in learning when at School, I took Cocker's Book of Arithmetick,[55] and went thro' the whole by my self with great Ease. I also read Seller's and Sturmy's Books of Navigation, and became acquainted with the little Geometry they contain, but never proceeded far in that Science. And I read about this Time Locke on Human Understanding, and the Art of Thinking by Messrs. du Port Royal.[56]

While I was intent on improving my Language, I met with an English Grammar (I think it was Greenwood's)[57] at the End of which there were two little Sketches of the Arts of Rhetoric and Logic, the latter finishing with a Specimen of a Dispute in the Socratic Method. And soon after I procur'd Xenophon's Memorable Things of Socrates,[58] wherein there are many Instances of the same Method. I was charm'd with it, adopted it, dropt my abrupt Contradiction, and positive Argu-

---

[53] *The Way to Wealth, Long Life and Happiness: Or, a Discourse of Temperance* (1683), by Thomas Tryon.

[54] Boiled oatmeal or cornmeal mush.

[55] One of several books on arithmetic by Edward Cocker (1631–1675).

[56] *An Epitome of the Art of Navigation* (1681), by John Seller; *The Mariner's Magazine: Or, Sturmy's Mathematical and Practical Arts* (1669), by Samuel Sturmy; *Essays Concerning Human Understanding* (1690), by John Locke (1632–1704); and *Logic: Or, the Art of Thinking* (1687), by Antoine Arnauld (1560–1619) and Pierre Nicole (1625?–1695).

[57] James Greenwood's *An Essay Towards a Practical English Grammar* (1711).

[58] *The Memorable Things of Socrates*, translated in 1712 by Edward Bysshe; the Athenian philosopher Socrates (470?–399 B.C.) used a method of teaching that involved a series of questions and answers.

mentation, and put on the humble Enquirer and Doubter. And being then, from reading Shaftsbury and Collins,[59] become a real Doubter in many Points of our Religious Doctrine, I found this Method safest for my self and very embarassing to those against whom I used it, therefore I took a Delight in it, practis'd it continually and grew very artful and expert in drawing People even of superior Knowledge into Concessions the Consequences of which they did not foresee, entangling them in Difficulties out of which they could not extricate themselves, and so obtaining Victories that neither my self nor my Cause always deserved.

I continu'd this Method some few Years, but gradually left it, retaining only the Habit of expressing my self in Terms of modest Diffidence, never using when I advance any thing that may possibly be disputed, the Words, *Certainly, undoubtedly*, or any others that give the Air of Positiveness to an Opinion; but rather say, I conceive, or I apprehend a Thing to be so or so, It appears to me, or I should think it so or so for such and such Reasons, or I imagine it to be so, or it is so if I am not mistaken. This Habit I believe has been of great Advantage to me, when I have had occasion to inculcate my Opinions and persuade Men into Measures that I have been from time to time engag'd in promoting. And as the chief Ends of Conversation are to *inform*, or to be *informed*, to *please* or to *persuade*, I wish wellmeaning sensible Men would not lessen their Power of doing Good by a Positive assuming Manner that seldom fails to disgust, tends to create Opposition, and to defeat every one of those Purposes for which Speech was given us, to wit, giving or receiving Information, or Pleasure: For if you would *inform*, a positive dogmatical Manner in advancing your Sentiments, may provoke Contradiction and prevent a candid Attention. If you wish Information and Improvement from the Knowledge of others and yet at the same time express your self as firmly fix'd in your present Opinions, modest sensible Men, who do not love Disputation, will probably leave you undisturb'd in the Possession of your Error; and by such a Manner you can seldom hope to recommend your self in *pleasing* your Hearers, or to persuade those whose Concurrence you desire. Pope says, judiciously,

> *Men should be taught as if you taught them not,*
> *And things unknown propos'd as things forgot,*

farther recommending it to us,

> *To speak tho' sure, with seeming Diffidence.*[60]

And he might have coupled with this Line that which he has coupled with another, I think less properly,

> *For Want of Modesty is Want of Sense.*[61]

---

[59] *Characteristics of Men, Manners, Opinions, Times* (1711), by Anthony Ashley Cooper (1671–1713), third earl of Shaftesbury; and *A Discourse of Free Thinking* (1713), by Anthony Collins (1676–1729).

[60] From *Essay on Criticism* (1711), by Alexander Pope (1688–1744); actually the first line here (line 574) reads "Men *must* be taught. . .," and the third line (line 577), "*And* speak tho' sure. . . . "

[61] From *Essay on Translated Verse* (1684), by Wentworth Dillon (1633?–1685), earl of Roscommon; actually this line (line 114) reads "For want of *decency*. . . . "

If you ask why, *less properly,* I must repeat the Lines;

> Immodest Words admit of *no* Defence;
> *For* Want of Modesty is Want of Sense.

Now is not *Want of Sense* (where a Man is so unfortunate as to want it) some Apology for his *Want of Modesty?* and would not the Lines stand more justly thus?

> Immodest words admit *but this* Defence,
> That Want of Modesty is Want of Sense.

My Brother had in 1720 or 21, begun to print a Newspaper. It was the second that appear'd in America, and was called *The New England Courant.*[62] The only one before it, was *the Boston News Letter.* I remember his being dissuaded by some of his Friends from the Undertaking, as not likely to succeed, one Newspaper being in their Judgment enough for America. At this time 1771 there are not less than five and twenty. He went on however with the Undertaking, and after having work'd in composing the Types and printing off the Sheets I was employ'd to carry the Papers thro' the Streets to the Customers. He had some ingenious Men among his Friends who amus'd themselves by writing little Pieces for this Paper, which gain'd it Credit, and made it more in Demand; and these Gentlemen often visited us. Hearing their Conversations, and their Accounts of the Approbation their Papers were receiv'd with, I was excited to try my Hand among them. But being still a Boy, and suspecting that my Brother would object to printing any Thing of mine in his Paper if he knew it to be mine, I contriv'd to disguise my Hand, and writing an anonymous Paper[63] I put it in at Night under the Door of the Printing House. It was found in the Morning and communicated to his Writing Friends when they call'd in as usual. They read it, commented on it in my Hearing, and I had the exquisite Pleasure, of finding it met with their Approbation, and that in their different Guesses at the Author none were named but Men of some Character among us for Learning and Ingenuity.

I suppose now that I was rather lucky in my Judges: And that perhaps they were not really so very good ones as I then esteem'd them. Encourag'd however by this, I wrote and convey'd in the same Way to the Press several more Papers, which were equally approv'd, and I kept my Secret till my small Fund of Sense for such Performances was pretty well exhausted, and then I discovered[64] it; when I began to be considered a little more by my Brother's Acquaintance, and in a manner that did not quite please him, as he thought, probably with reason, that it tended to make me too vain. And perhaps this might be one Occasion of the Differences that we frequently had about this Time. Tho' a Brother, he considered himself as my Master, and me as his Apprentice; and accordingly expected the

---

[62] Actually James Franklin's *New England Courant*, begun on August 7, 1721, followed *Public Occurrences* (only one issue was published, on September 25, 1690), the *Boston News Letter*, the *Boston Gazette*, and the *American Weekly Mercury*.

[63] The first of fourteen *Silence Dogood Letters*, published in the *Courant* between April 12 and October 8, 1722; Franklin's earliest surviving writings and the first essay series published in America.

[64] Revealed.

same Services from me as he would from another; while I thought he demean'd me too much in some he requir'd of me, who from a Brother expected more Indulgence. Our Disputes were often brought before our Father, and I fancy I was either generally in the right, or else a better Pleader, because the Judgment was generally in my favour: But my Brother was passionate and had often beaten me, which I took extreamly amiss; and thinking my Apprenticeship very tedious, I was continually wishing for some Opportunity of shortening it, which at length offered in a manner unexpected.[65]

One of the Pieces in our News-Paper, on some political Point which I have now forgotten, gave Offence to the Assembly.[66] He was taken up, censur'd and imprison'd for a Month by the Speaker's Warrant, I suppose because he would not discover his Author. I too was taken up and examin'd before the Council; but tho' I did not give them any Satisfaction, they contented themselves with admonishing me, and dismiss'd me; considering me perhaps as an Apprentice who was bound to keep his Master's Secrets. During my Brother's Confinement, which I resented a good deal, notwithstanding our private Differences, I had the Management of the Paper, and I made bold to give our Rulers some Rubs[67] in it, which my Brother took very kindly, while others began to consider me in an unfavourable Light, as a young Genius that had a Turn for Libelling and Satyr.[68] My Brother's Discharge was accompany'd with an Order of the House, (a very odd one) *that James Franklin should no longer print the Paper called the New England Courant.* There was a Consultation held in our Printing House among his Friends what he should do in this Case. Some propos'd to evade the Order by changing the Name of the Paper; but my Brother seeing Inconveniences in that, it was finally concluded on as a better Way, to let it be printed for the future under the Name of *Benjamin Franklin.* And to avoid the Censure of the Assembly that might fall on him, as still printing it by his Apprentice, the Contrivance was, that my old Indenture should be return'd to me with a full Discharge on the Back of it, to be shown on Occasion; but to secure to him the Benefit of my Service I was to sign new Indentures for the Remainder of the Term, which were to be kept private. A very flimsy Scheme it was, but however it was immediately executed, and the Paper went on accordingly under my Name for several Months.[69] At length a fresh Difference arising between my Brother and me, I took upon me to assert my Freedom, presuming that he would not venture to produce the new Indentures. It was not fair in me to take this Advantage, and this I therefore reckon one of the first Errata[70] of my Life: But the Unfairness of it weigh'd little with me, when under the Impressions of Resentment, for the Blows his Passion too often urg'd him to bestow upon me. Tho' he was otherwise not an ill-natur'd Man: Perhaps I was too saucy and provoking.

When he found I would leave him, he took care to prevent my getting Employ-

[65] Franklin's note: "I fancy his harsh and tyrannical Treatment of me, might be a means of impressing me with that Aversion to arbitrary Power that has stuck to me thro' my whole Life."

[66] The June 11, 1722, issue of the *Courant* insinuated that local authorities were in collusion with pirates raiding Boston Harbor; the Assembly, one house of the Massachusetts legislature, had James Franklin jailed for a month.

[67] Insults.   [68] Satire.

[69] Actually the *Courant* continued to appear in Benjamin Franklin's name until at least June 25, 1726, nearly three years after he had left Boston.

[70] "Errors" (Latin).

ment in any other Printing-House of the Town, by going round and speaking to every Master, who accordingly refus'd to give me Work. I then thought of going to New York as the nearest Place where there was a Printer: and I was the rather inclin'd to leave Boston, when I reflected that I had already made myself a little obnoxious to the governing Party; and from the arbitrary Proceedings of the Assembly in my Brother's Case it was likely I might if I stay'd soon bring myself into Scrapes; and farther that my indiscrete Disputations about Religion began to make me pointed at with Horror by good People, as an Infidel or Atheist. I determin'd on the Point: but my Father now siding with my Brother, I was sensible that if I attempted to go openly, Means would be used to prevent me. My Friend Collins therefore undertook to manage a little for me. He agreed with the Captain of a New York Sloop for my Passage, under the Notion of my being a young Acquaintance of his that had got a naughty Girl with Child, whose Friends would compel me to marry her, and therefore I could not appear or come away publickly. So I sold some of my Books to raise a little Money, Was taken on board privately, and as we had a fair Wind in three Days I found my self in New York near 300 Miles from home, a Boy of but 17, without the least Recommendation to or Knowledge of any Person in the Place, and with very little Money in my Pocket.

My Inclinations for the Sea, were by this time worne out, or I might now have gratify'd them. But having a Trade, and supposing my self a pretty good Workman, I offer'd my Service to the Printer of the Place, old Mr. Wm. Bradford,[71] (who had been the first Printer in Pensilvania, but remov'd from thence upon the Quarrel of Geo. Keith).[72] He could give me no Employment, having little to do, and Help enough already: But, says he, my Son[73] at Philadelphia has lately lost his principal Hand, Aquila Rose,[74] by Death. If you go thither I believe he may employ you. Philadelphia was 100 Miles farther. I set out, however, in a Boat for Amboy,[75] leaving my Chest and Things to follow me round by Sea. In crossing the Bay we met with a Squall that tore our rotten Sails to pieces, prevented our getting into the Kill,[76] and drove us upon Long Island. In our Way a drunken Dutchman, who was a Passenger too, fell over board; when he was sinking I reach'd thro' the Water to his shock Pate[77] and drew him up so that we got him in again. His Ducking sober'd him a little, and he went to sleep, taking first out of his Pocket a Book which he desir'd I would dry for him. It prov'd to be my old favourite Author Bunyan's Pilgrim's Progress in Dutch, finely printed on good Paper with copper Cuts, a Dress better than I had ever seen it wear in its own Language. I have since found that it has been translated into most of the Languages of Europe, and suppose it has been more generally read than any other Book except perhaps the Bible. Honest John was the first that I know of who mix'd Narration and Dialogue, a Method of Writing very engaging to the Reader, who in the most interesting Parts finds himself as it were brought into the Com-

---

[71] William Bradford (1663–1752), a pioneer American printer.

[72] George Keith (1638?–1716), a controversial Quaker missionary.

[73] Andrew Bradford (1686–1742), founder of the *American Weekly Mercury* in 1719 and Franklin's principal competitor in printing.

[74] Rose (1695?–1723) was a poet and printer working for Andrew Bradford.

[75] Perth Amboy, New Jersey.

[76] The Kill van Kull or the Arthur Kill, narrow channels separating Staten Island from New Jersey.

[77] Bushy hair.

pany, and present at the Discourse. Defoe in his Cruso, his Moll Flanders, Religious Courtship, Family Instructor, and other Pieces, has imitated it with Success. And Richardson has done the same in his Pamela, etc.[78]

When we drew near the Island we found it was at a Place where there could be no Landing, there being a great Surff on the stony Beach. So we dropt Anchor and swung round towards the Shore. Some People came down to the Water Edge and hallow'd to us, as we did to them. But the Wind was so high and the Surff so loud, that we could not hear so as to understand each other. There were Canoes on the Shore, and we made Signs and hallow'd that they should fetch us, but they either did not understand us, or thought it impracticable. So they went away, and Night coming on, we had no Remedy but to wait till the Wind should abate, and in the mean time the Boatman and I concluded to sleep if we could, and so crouded into the Scuttle[79] with the Dutchman who was still wet, and the Spray beating over the Head of our Boat, leak'd thro' to us, so that we were soon almost as wet as he. In this Manner we lay all Night with very little Rest. But the Wind abating the next Day, we made a Shift to reach Amboy before Night, having been 30 Hours on the Water without Victuals, or any Drink but a Bottle of filthy Rum: The Water we sail'd on being salt.

In the Evening I found my self very feverish, and went in to Bed. But having read somewhere that cold Water drank plentifully was good for a Fever, I follow'd the Prescription, sweat plentifully most of the Night, my Fever left me, and in the Morning crossing the Ferry, I proceeded on my Journey, on foot, having 50 Miles to Burlington[80] where I was told I should find Boats that would carry me the rest of the Way to Philadelphia.

It rain'd very hard all the Day, I was thoroughly soak'd and by Noon a good deal tir'd, so I stopt at a poor Inn, where I staid all Night, beginning now to wish I had never left home. I cut so miserable a Figure too, that I found by the Questions ask'd me I was suspected to be some runaway Servant, and in danger of being taken up on that Suspicion. However I proceeded the next Day, and got in the Evening to an Inn within 8 or 10 Miles of Burlington, kept by one Dr. Brown.[81]

He entred into Conversation with me while I took some Refreshment, and finnding I had read a little, became very sociable and friendly. Our Aquaintance continu'd as long as he liv'd. He had been, I imagine, an itinerant Doctor, for there was no Town in England, or Country in Europe, of which he could not give a very particular Account. He had some Letters,[82] and was ingenious, but much of an Unbeliever, and wickedly undertook some Years after to travesty the Bible in doggrel Verse as Cotton[83] had done Virgil. By this means he set many of the Facts in a very ridiculous Light, and might have hurt weak minds if his Work had been publish'd: but it never was. At his House I lay that Night, and the next Morning

---

[78] *Robinson Crusoe* (1719), *Moll Flanders* (1722), *Religious Courtship* (1722), and *The Family Instructor* (1715–1718), by Daniel Defoe; and *Pamela: Or, Virtue Rewarded* (1740), by Samuel Richardson (1689–1761). Franklin's 1744 reprinting of *Pamela* was the first novel published in America.

[79] An opening in a ship's deck or hull, with a lid.

[80] Then the capital of West Jersey, about eighteen miles North of Philadelphia.

[81] John Browne (1667?–1737), a Burlington innkeeper, physician, and religious skeptic.

[82] Education.

[83] Charles Cotton (1630–1687), English poet who satirized the Roman poet Virgil (70–19 B.C.) in *Scarronides: Or, the First Book of Virgil Travestied* (1664).

reach'd Burlington. But had the Mortification to find that the regular Boats were gone, a little before my coming, and no other expected to go till Tuesday, this being Saturday. Wherefore I return'd to an old Woman in the Town of whom I had bought Gingerbread to eat on the Water, and ask'd her Advice; she invited me to lodge at her house till a Passage by Water should offer: and being tired with my foot Travelling, I accepted the Invitation. She understanding I was a Printer, would have had me stay at that Town and follow my Business, being ignorant of the Stock necessary to begin with. She was very hospitable, gave me a Dinner of Ox Cheek with great Goodwill, accepting only a Pot of Ale in return. And I tho't my self fix'd till Tuesday should come. However walking in the Evening by the Side of the River a Boat came by, which I found was going towards Philadelphia, with several People in her. They took me in, and as there was no Wind, we row'd all the Way; and about Midnight not having yet seen the City, some of the Company were confident we must have pass'd it, and would row no farther, the others knew not where we were, so we put towards the Shore, got into a Creek, landed near an old Fence with the Rails of which we made a Fire, the Night being cold, in October, and there we remain'd till Daylight. Then one of the Company knew the Place to be Cooper's Creek a little above Philadelphia, which we saw as soon as we got out of the Creek, and arriv'd there about 8 or 9 a Clock, on the Sunday morning,[84] and landed at the Market street Wharff.

I have been the more particular in this Description of my Journey, and shall be so of my first Entry into that City, that you may in your mind compare such unlikely Beginnings with the Figure I have since made there. I was in my Working Dress, my best Cloaths being to come round by Sea. I was dirty from my Journey; my Pockets were stuff'd out with Shirts and Stockings; I knew no Soul, nor where to look for Lodging. I was fatigu'd with Travelling, Rowing and Want of Rest. I was very hungry, and my whole Stock of Cash consisted of a Dutch Dollar and about a Shilling in Copper. The latter I gave the People of the Boat for my Passage, who at first refus'd it on Account of my Rowing; but I insisted on their taking it, a Man being sometimes more generous when he has but a little Money than when he has plenty, perhaps thro' Fear of being thought to have but little.

Then I walk'd up the Street, gazing about, till near the Market House I met a Boy with Bread. I had made many a Meal on Bread, and inquiring where he got it, I went immediately to the Baker's he directed me to in second Street; and ask'd for Bisket, intending such as we had in Boston, but they it seems were not made in Philadelphia, then I ask'd for a threepenny Loaf, and was told they had none such: so not considering or knowing the Difference of Money and the greater Cheapness nor the Names of his Bread, I bad him give me three penny worth of any sort. He gave me accordingly three great Puffy Rolls. I was surpriz'd at the Quantity, but took it, and having no room in my Pockets, walk'd off, with a Roll under each Arm, and eating the other. Thus I went up Market Street as far as fourth Street, passing by the Door of Mr. Read, my future Wife's[85] Father, when she standing at the Door saw me, and thought I made as I certainly did a most awkward ridiculous Appearance. Then I turn'd and went down Chestnut Street and part of Walnut Street, eating my Roll all the Way, and coming round found my self again at Market Street Wharff, near the Boat I came in, to which I went for a Draught of the River Water, and being fill'd with one of my Rolls, gave the other two to a

---

[84] A Sunday in October 1723.   [85] Deborah Read (?–1774), whom Franklin married in 1730.

Woman and her Child that came down the River in a Boat with us and were waiting to go farther. Thus refresh'd I walk'd again up the Street, which by this time had many clean dress'd People in it who were all walking the same Way; I join'd them, and thereby was led into the great Meeting house of the Quakers near the Market. I sat down among them, and after looking round a while and hearing nothing said, being very drowzy thro' Labour and want of Rest the preceding Night, I fell fast asleep, and continu'd so till the Meeting broke up, when one was kind enough to rouse me. This was therefore the first House I was in or slept in, in Philadelphia.

Walking again down towards the River, and looking in the Faces of People, I met a young Quaker Man whose Countenance I lik'd, and accosting him requested he would tell me where a Stranger could get Lodging. We were then near the Sign of the Three Mariners. Here, says he, is one Place that entertains Strangers, but it is not a reputable House; if thee wilt walk with me, I'll show thee a better. He brought me to the Crooked Billet[86] in Water-Street. Here I got a Dinner. And while I was eating it, several sly Questions were ask'd me, as it seem'd to be suspected from my youth and Appearance, that I might be some Runaway. After Dinner my Sleepiness return'd: and being shown to a Bed, I lay down without undressing, and slept till Six in the Evening; was call'd to Supper; went to Bed again very early and slept soundly till the next Morning. Then I made my self as tidy as I could, and went to Andrew Bradford the Printer's. I found in the Shop the old Man his Father, whom I had seen at New York, and who travelling on horse back had got to Philadelphia before me. He introduc'd me to his Son, who receiv'd me civilly, gave me a Breakfast, but told me he did not at present want a Hand, being lately supply'd with one. But there was another Printer in town lately set up, one Keimer,[87] who perhaps might employ me; if not, I should be welcome to lodge at his House, and he would give me a little Work to do now and then till fuller Business should offer.

The old Gentleman said, he would go with me to the new Printer: And when we found him, Neighbour, says Bradford, I have brought to see you a young Man of your Business, perhaps you may want such a One. He ask'd me a few Questions, put a Composing Stick[88] in my Hand to see how I work'd, and then said he would employ me soon, tho' he had just then nothing for me to do. And taking old Bradford whom he had never seen before, to be one of the Towns People that had a Good Will for him, enter'd into a Conversation on his present Undertaking and Prospects; while Bradford not discovering that he was the other Printer's Father, on Keimer's saying he expected soon to get the greatest Part of the Business into his own Hands, drew him on by artful Questions and starting little Doubts, to explain all his Views, what Interest he rely'd on, and in what manner he intended to proceed. I who stood by and heard all, saw immediately that one of them was a crafty old Sophister,[89] and the other a mere Novice. Bradford left me with Keimer, who was greatly surpriz'd when I told him who the old Man was.

Keimer's Printing House I found, consisted of an old shatter'd Press, and one small worn-out Fount of English,[90] which he was then using himself, composing in it an Elegy on Aquila Rose beforementioned, an ingenious young Man of excellent Character much respected in the Town, Clerk of the Assembly, and a pretty

---

[86] A tavern.
[87] Samuel Keimer (1688?–1742), an English printer who had come Philadelphia the previous year; unsuccessful there, he left in 1730.
[88] An instrument for setting type.   [89] A trickster.   [90] An oversized font, or type.

Poet. Keimer made Verses, too, but very indifferently. He could not be said to write them, for his Manner was to compose them in the Types directly out of his Head; so there being no Copy, but one Pair of Cases,[91] and the Elegy likely to require all the Letter, no one could help him. I endeavour'd to put his Press (which he had not yet us'd, and of which he understood nothing) into Order fit to be work'd with; and promising to come and print off his Elegy as soon as he should have got it ready, I return'd to Bradford's who gave me a little Job to do for the present, and there I lodged and dieted.[92] A few Days after Keimer sent for me to print off the Elegy.[93] And now he had got another Pair of Cases, and a Pamphlet to reprint, on which he set me to work.

These two Printers I found poorly qualified for their Business. Bradford had not been bred to it, and was very illiterate; and Keimer tho' something of a Scholar, was a mere Compositor, knowing nothing of Presswork. He had been one of the French Prophets[94] and could act their enthusiastic Agitations. At this time he did not profess any particular Religion, but something of all on occasion; was very ignorant of the World, and had, as I afterwards found, a good deal of the Knave in his Composition. He did not like my Lodging at Bradford's while I work'd with him. He had a House indeed, but without Furniture, so he could not lodge me: But he got me a Lodging at Mr. Read's before-mentioned, who was the Owner of his House. And my Chest and Clothes being come by this time, I made rather a more respectable Appearance in the Eyes of Miss Read, than I had done when she first happen'd to see me eating my Roll in the Street.

I began now to have some Acquaintance among the young People of the Town, that were Lovers of Reading with whom I spent my Evenings very pleasantly and gaining Money by my Industry and Frugality, I lived very agreeably, forgetting Boston as much as I could, and not desiring that any there should know where I resided, except my Friend Collins who was in my Secret, and kept it when I wrote to him. At length an Incident happened that sent me back again much sooner than I had intended.

I had a Brother-in-law, Robert Holmes,[95] Master of a Sloop, that traded between Boston and Delaware. He being at New Castle 40 Miles below Philadelphia, heard there of me, and wrote me a Letter, mentioning the Concern of my Friends in Boston at my abrupt Departure, assuring me of their Goodwill to me, and that every thing would be accommodated to my Mind if I would return, to which he exhorted me very earnestly. I wrote an Answer to his Letter, thank'd him for his Advice, but stated my Reasons for quitting Boston fully, and in such a Light as to convince him I was not so wrong as he had apprehended.

Sir William Keith[96] Governor of the Province, was then at New Castle, and Capt. Holmes happening to be in Company with him when my Letter came to hand, spoke to him of me, and show'd him the Letter. The Governor read it, and seem'd surpriz'd when he was told my Age. He said I appear'd a young Man of promising Parts, and therefore should be encouraged: The Printers at Philadelphia were wretched ones, and if I would set up there, he made no doubt I should succeed; for his Part, he would procure me the publick Business, and do me every

---

[91] Trays containing uppercase and lowercase types.   [92] Boarded.

[93] *An Elegy on the Much Lamented Death of the Ingenious and Well-Beloved Aquila Rose, Clerk to the Honourable Assembly at Philadelphia, Who Died the 24th of the 4th Month,* 1723. *Aged* 28.

[94] French Protestant refugees in England in 1706, given to trances.

[95] Holmes, husband of Franklin's sister Mary, was a sea captain who died before 1743.

[96] Keith (1680–1749), governor of Pennsylvania from 1717 to 1726.

other Service in his Power. This my Brother-in-Law afterwards told me in Boston. But I knew as yet nothing of it; when one Day Keimer and I being at Work together near the Window, we saw the Governor and another Gentleman (which prov'd to be Col. French,[97] of New Castle) finely dress'd, come directly across the Street to our House, and heard them at the Door. Keimer ran down immediately, thinking it a Visit to him. But the Governor enquir'd for me, came up, and with a Condescension and Politeness I had been quite unus'd to, made me many Compliments, desired to be acquainted with me, blam'd me kindly for not having made my self known to him when I first came to the Place, and would have me away with him to the Tavern where he was going with Col. French to taste as he said some excellent Madeira. I was not a little supriz'd, and Keimer star'd like a Pig poison'd. I went however with the Governor and Col. French, to a Tavern the Corner of Third Street, and over the Madeira he propos'd my Setting up my Business, laid before me the Probabilities of Success, and both he and Col. French assur'd me I should have their Interest and Influence in procuring the Publick Business of both Governments. On my doubting whether my Father would assist me in it, Sir William said he would give me a Letter to him, in which he would state the Advantages, and he did not doubt of prevailing with him. So it was concluded I should return to Boston in the first Vessel with the Governor's Letter recommending me to my Father. In the mean time the Intention was to be kept secret, and I went on working with Keimer as usual, the Governor sending for me now and then to dine with him, a very great Honour I thought it, and conversing with me in the most affable, familiar, and friendly manner imaginable.

About the End of April 1724. a little Vessel offer'd for Boston. I took Leave of Keimer as going to see my Friends. The Governor gave me an ample Letter, saying many flattering things of me to my Father, and strongly recommending the Project of my setting up at Philadelphia, as a Thing that must make my Fortune. We struck on a Shoal in going down the Bay and sprung a Leak, we had a blustring time at Sea, and were oblig'd to pump almost continually, at which I took my Turn. We arriv'd safe however at Boston in about a Fortnight. I had been absent Seven Months and my friends had heard nothing of me; for my Br. Holmes was not yet return'd; and had not written about me. My unexpected Appearance surpriz'd the Family; all were however very glad to see me and made me Welcome, except my Brother. I went to see him at his Printing-House: I was better dress'd than ever while in his Service, having a genteel new Suit from Head to foot, a Watch, and my Pockets lin'd with near Five Pounds Sterling in Silver. He receiv'd me not very frankly, look'd me all over, and turn'd to his Work again. The Journey-Men were inquisitive where I had been, what sort of a Country it was, and how I lik'd it? I prais'd it much, and the happy Life I led in it; expressing strongly my Intention of returning to it; and one of them asking what kind of Money we had there, I produc'd a handful of Silver and spread it before them, which was a kind of Raree-Show[98] they had not been us'd to, Paper being the Money of Boston. Then I took an Opportunity of letting them see my Watch: and lastly, (my Brother still grum and sullen) I gave them a Piece of Eight to drink[99] and took my Leave. This Visit of mine offended him extreamly. For when my Mother some time after spoke to him of a Reconciliation, and of her Wishes to see us on good Terms together, and that we might live for the future as Brothers, he

---

[97] John French of New Castle, Delaware.   [98] A small street show.
[99] A Spanish dollar with which to buy drinks.

said, I had insulted him in such a Manner before his People that he could never forget or forgive it. In this however he was mistaken.

My Father receiv'd the Governor's Letter with some apparent Surprize; but said little of it to me for some Days; when Capt. Holmes returning, he show'd it to him, ask'd if he knew Keith, and what kind of a Man he was: Adding his Opinion that he must be of small Discretion, to think of setting a Boy up in Business who wanted yet 3 Years of being at Man's Estate. Homes said what he could in favour of the Project; but my Father was clear in the Impropriety of it; and at last gave a flat Denial to it. Then he wrote a civil Letter to Sir William thanking him for the Patronage he had so kindly offered me, but declining to assist me as yet in Setting up, I being in his Opinion too young to be trusted with the Management of a Business so important, and for which the Preparation must be so expensive.

My Friend and Companion Collins, who was a Clerk at the Post-Office, pleas'd with the Account I gave him of my new Country, determin'd to go thither also: And while I waited for my Fathers Determination, he set out before me by Land to Rhodeisland, leaving his Books which were a pretty Collection of Mathematicks and Natural Philosophy,[100] to come with mine and me to New York where he propos'd to wait for me. My Father, tho' he did not approve Sir William's Proposition was yet pleas'd that I had been able to obtain so advantageous a Character from a Person of such Note where I had resided, and that I had been so industrious and careful as to equip my self so handsomely in so short a time: therefore seeing no Prospect of an Accommodation between my Brother and me, he gave his Consent to my Returning again to Philadelphia, advis'd me to behave respectfully to the People there, endeavour to obtain the general Esteem, and avoid lampooning and libelling to which he thought I had too much Inclination; telling me, that by steady Industry and a prudent Parsimony, I might save enough by the time I was One and Twenty to set me up, and that if I came near the Matter he would help me out with the rest. This was all I could obtain, except some small Gifts as Tokens of his and my Mother's Love, when I embark'd again for New-York, now with their Approbation and their Blessing.

The Sloop putting in at Newport, Rhodeisland, I visited my Brother John, who had been married and settled there some Years. He received me very affectionately, for he always lov'd me. A Friend of his, one Vernon, having some Money due to him in Pensilvania, about 35 Pounds Currency, desired I would receive it for him, and keep it till I had his Directions what to remit it in. Accordingly he gave me an Order. This afterwards occasion'd me a good deal of Uneasiness. At Newport we took in a Number of Passengers for New York: Among which were two young Women, Companions, and a grave, sensible Matron-like Quaker-Woman with her Attendants. I had shown an obliging readiness to do her some little Services which impress'd her I suppose with a degree of Good-will towards me. Therefore when she saw a daily growing Familiarity between me and the two Young Women, which they appear'd to encourage, she took me aside and said, Young Man, I am concern'd for thee, as thou has no Friend with thee, and seems not to know much of the World, or of the Snares Youth is expos'd to; depend upon it those are very bad Women, I can see it in all their Actions, and if thee art not upon thy Guard, they will draw thee into some Danger: they are Strangers to thee, and I advise thee in a friendly Concern for thy Welfare, to have no Acquaintance with them. As I seem'd at first not to think so ill of them as she did, she

[100] Science.

mention'd some Things she had observ'd and heard that had escap'd my Notice; but now convinc'd me she was right. I thank'd her for her kind Advice, and promis'd to follow it. When we arriv'd at New York, they told me where they liv'd, and invited me to come and see them: but I avoided it. And it was well I did: For the next Day, the Captain miss'd a Silver Spoon and some other Things that had been taken out of his Cabbin, and knowing that these were a Couple of Strumpets, he got a Warrant to search their Lodgings, found the stolen Goods, and had the Thieves punish'd. So tho' we had escap'd a sunken Rock which we scrap'd upon in the Passage, I thought this Escape of rather more Importance to me.

At New York I found my friend Collins, who had arriv'd there some Time before me. We had been intimate from Children,[101] and had read the same Books together. But he had the Advantage of more time for reading, and Studying and a wonderful Genius for Mathematical Learning in which he far outstript me. While I liv'd in Boston most of my Hours of Leisure for Conversation were spent with him, and he continu'd a sober as well as an industrious Lad; was much respected for his Learning by several of the Clergy and other Gentlemen, and seem'd to promise making a good Figure in Life: but during my absence he had acquir'd a Habit of Sotting[102] with Brandy; and I found by his own Account and what I heard from others, that he had been drunk every day since his Arrival at New York, and behav'd very oddly. He had gam'd too and lost his Money, so that I was oblig'd to discharge[103] his Lodgings, and defray his Expences to and at Philadelphia: Which prov'd extreamly inconvenient to me. The then Governor of N York, Burnet,[104] Son of Bishop Burnet hearing from the Captain that a young Man, one of his Passengers, had a great many Books, desired he would bring me to see him. I waited upon him accordingly, and should have taken Collins with me but that he was not sober. The Governor treated me with great Civility, show'd me his Library, which was a very large one, and we had a good deal of Conversation about Books and authors. This was the second Governor who had done me the Honour to take Notice of me, which to a poor Boy like me was very pleasing.

We proceeded to Philadelphia. I received on the Way Vernon's Money, without which we could hardly have finish'd our Journey. Collins wish'd to be employ'd in some Counting House; but whether they discover'd his Dramming[105] by his Breath, or by his Behaviour, tho' he had some Recommendations, he met with no Success in any Application, and continu'd Lodging and Boarding at the same House with me and at my Expence. Knowing I had that Money of Vernon's he was continually borrowing of me, still promising Repayment as soon as he should be in Business. At length he had got so much of it, that I was distress'd to think what I should do, in case of being call'd on to remit it. His Drinking continu'd about which we sometimes quarrel'd, for when a little intoxicated he was very fractious. Once in a Boat on the Delaware with some other young Men, he refused to row in his Turn: I will be row'd home, says he. We will not row you, says I. You must or stay all Night on the Water, says he, just as you please. The others said, Let us row; what signifies it? But my Mind being soured with his other conduct, I continu'd to refuse. So he swore he would make me row, or throw me overboard; and coming along stepping on the Thwarts[106] towards me, when he

---

[101] Since childhood.

[102] Getting drunk.   [103] To pay for.

[104] William Burnet (1688–1729), governor of New York and New Jersey from 1720 to 1728, governor of Massachusetts from 1728 to 1729, and son of the Bishop of Salisbury.

[105] Drinking.   [106] Rowers' seats on a boat.

came up and struck at me I clapt my Hand under his Crutch,[107] and rising pitch'd him head-foremost into the River. I knew he was a good Swimmer, and so was under little Concern about him; but before he could get round to lay hold of the Boat, we had with a few Strokes pull'd her out of his Reach. And ever when he drew near the Boat, we ask'd if he would row, striking a few Strokes to slide her away from him. He was ready to die with Vexation, and obstinately would not promise to row; however seeing him at last beginning to tire, we lifted him in; and brought him home dripping wet in the Evening. We hardly exchang'd a civil Word afterwards; and a West India Captain who had a Commission to procure a Tutor for the Sons of a Gentleman at Barbadoes, happening to meet with him, agreed to carry him thither. He left me then, promising to remit me the first Money he should receive in order to discharge the Debt. But I never heard of him after.

The breaking into this Money of Vernon's was one of the first great Errata of my Life. And this Affair show'd that my father was not much out in his Judgment when he suppos'd me too young to manage Business of Importance. But Sir William, on reading his Letter, said he was too prudent. There was great Difference in Persons, and Discretion did not always accompany Years, nor was Youth always without it. And since he will not set you up, says he, I will do it my self. Give me an Inventory of the Things necessary to be had from England, and I will send for them. You shall repay me when you are able; I am resolv'd to have a good Printer here, and I am sure you must succeed. This was spoken with such an Appearance of Cordiality, that I had not the least doubt of his meaning what he said. I had hitherto kept the Proposition of my Setting up a Secret in Philadelphia, and I still kept it. Had it been known that I depended on the Governor, probably some Friend that knew him better would have advis'd me not to rely on him, as I afterwards heard it as his known Character to be liberal of Promises which he never meant to keep. Yet unsolicited as he was by me, how could I think his generous Offers insincere? I believ'd him one of the best Men in the World.

I presented him an Inventory of a little Printing House, amounting by my Computation to about £100 Sterling.[108] He lik'd it, but ask'd me if my being on the Spot in England to chuse the Types and see that every thing was good of the kind, might not be of some Advantage. Then, says he, when there, you may make Acquaintances and establish Correspondencies in the Bookselling and Stationary Way. I agreed that this might be advantageous. Then says he, get yourself ready to go with Annis;[109] which was the annual Ship, and the only one at that Time usually passing between London and Philadelphia. But it would be some Months before Annis sail'd, so I continu'd working with Keimer, fretting about the Money Collins had got from me, and in daily apprehensions of being call'd upon by Vernon, which however did not happen for some Years after.

I believe I have omitted mentioning that in my first Voyage from Boston, being becalm'd off Block Island,[110] our People set about catching Cod and hawl'd up a great many. Hitherto I had stuck to my Resolution of not eating animal food; and on this Occasion, I consider'd with my Master Tryon, the taking every Fish as a kind of unprovok'd Murder, since none of them had or never could do us any

---

[107] Crotch.

[108] One hundred pounds sterling; then, a pound weight of English silver pennies.

[109] Thomas Annis, captain of the *London Hope,* the "annual Ship" on which Franklin sailed to London in 1724.

[110] Off the Rhode Island coast.

Injury that might justify the Slaughter. All this seem'd very reasonable. But I had formerly been a great Lover of Fish, and when this came hot out of the Frying Pan, it smelt admirably well. I balanc'd some time between Principle and Inclination: till I recollected that when the Fish were opened, I saw smaller Fish taken out of their Stomachs: Then thought I, if you eat one another, I don't see why we mayn't eat you. So I din'd upon Cod very heartily and continu'd to eat with other People, returning only now and than occasionally to a vegetable Diet. So convenient a thing it is to be a *reasonable Creature,* since it enables one to find or make a Reason for every thing one has a mind to do.

Keimer and I liv'd on a pretty good familiar Footing and agreed tolerably well: for he suspected nothing of my Setting up. He retain'd a great deal of his old Enthusiasms, and lov'd Argumentation. We therefore had many Disputations. I us'd to work him so with my Socratic Method, and had trapann'd[111] him so often by Questions apparently so distant from any Point we had in hand, and yet by degrees led to the Point, and brought him into Difficulties and Contradictions that at last he grew ridiculously cautious, and would hardly answer me the most common Question, without asking first, *What do you intend to infer from that?* However it gave him so high an Opinion of my Abilities in the Confuting Way, that he seriously propos'd my being his Colleague in a Project he had of setting up a new Sect. He was to preach the Doctrines, and I was to confound all Opponents. When he came to explain with me upon the Doctrines, I found several Conundrums[112] which I objected to unless I might have my Way a little too, and introduce some of mine. Keimer wore his Beard at full Length, because somewhere in the Mosaic Law it is said, *thou shalt not mar the Corners of thy Beard.*[113] He likewise kept the seventh day Sabbath; and these two Points were Essentials with him. I dislik'd both, but agreed to admit them upon Condition of his adopting the Doctrine of using no animal Food. I doubt, says he, my Constitution will not bear that. I assur'd him it would, and that he would be the better for it. He was usually a great Glutton, and I promis'd my self some Diversion in half-starving him. He agreed to try the Practice if I would keep him Company. I did so and we held it for three Months. We had our Victuals dress'd and brought to us regularly by a Woman in the Neighbourhood, who had from me a List of 40 Dishes to be prepar'd for us at different times, in all which there was neither Fish Flesh nor Fowl, and the whim suited me the better at this time from the Cheapness of it, not costing us above 18*d.*[114] Sterling each, per Week. I have since kept several Lents most strictly, Leaving the common Diet for that, and that for the common, abruptly, without the least Inconvenience: So that I think there is little in the Advice of making those Changes by easy Gradations. I went on pleasantly, but poor Keimer suffer'd grievously, tir'd of the Project, long'd for the Flesh Pots of Egypt,[115] and order'd a roast Pig. He invited me and two Women friends to dine with him, but it being brought too soon upon table, he could not resist the Temptation, and ate it all up before we came.

I had made some Courtship during this time to Miss Read. I had a great Respect

---

[111] Ensnared.   [112] Puzzling questions.

[113] "Ye shall not round the corners of your heads, neither shalt thou mar the corners of thy beard," from Leviticus 19:27.

[114] Eighteen pence.

[115] "And the whole congregation of the children of Israel murmured against Moses and Aaron in the wilderness:. . .Would to God we had died by the hand of the Lord in the land of Egypt, when we sat by the flesh pots, and we did eat bread to the full," from Exodus 16:2–3.

and Affection for her, and had some Reason to believe she had the same for me: but as I was about to take a long Voyage, and we were both very young, only a little above 18. it was thought most prudent by her Mother to prevent our going too far at present, as a Marriage if it was to take place would be more convenient after my Return, when I should be as I expected set up in my Business. Perhaps too she thought my Expectations not so wellfounded as I imagined them to be.

My chief Acquaintances at this time were, Charles Osborne, Joseph Watson, and James Ralph;[116] All Lovers of Reading. The two first were Clerks to an eminent Scrivener or Conveyancer in the Town, Charles Brogden;[117] the other was Clerk to a Merchant. Watson was a pious sensible young Man, of great Integrity. The others rather more lax in their Principles of Religion, particularly Ralph, who as well as Collins had been unsettled by me, for which they both made me suffer. Osborne was sensible, candid, frank, sincere, and affectionate to his Friends; but in litterary Matters too fond of Criticising. Ralph, was ingenious, genteel in his Manners, and extreamly eloquent; I think I never knew a prettier Talker. Both of them great Admirers of Poetry, and began to try their Hands in little Pieces. Many pleasant Walks we four had together on Sundays into the Woods near Skuylkill,[118] where we read to one another and conferr'd on what we read.

Ralph was inclin'd to pursue the Study of Poetry, not doubting but he might become eminent in it and make his Fortune by it, alledging that the best Poets must when they first began to write, make as many Faults as he did. Osborne dissuaded him, assur'd him he had no Genius for Poetry, and advis'd him to think of nothing beyond the Business he was bred to; that in the mercantile way tho' he had no Stock, he might by his Diligence and Punctuality recommend himself to Employment as a Factor,[119] and in time acquire wherewith to trade on his own Account. I approv'd the amusing one's self with Poetry now and then, so far as to improve one's Language, but no farther. On this it was propos'd that we should each of us at our next Meeting produce a Piece of our own Composing, in order to improve by our mutual Observations, Criticisms and Corrections. As Language and Expression was what we had in View, we excluded all Considerations of Invention,[120] by agreeing that the Task should be a Version of the 18th Psalm, which describes the Descent of a Deity.[121] When the Time of our Meeting drew nigh, Ralph call'd on me first, and let me know his Piece was ready. I told him I had been busy, and having little Inclination had done nothing. He then show'd me his Piece for my Opinion; and I much approv'd it, as it appear'd to me to have great Merit. Now, says he, Osborne never will allow the least Merit in any thing of mine, but makes 1000 Criticisms out of mere Envy. He is not so jealous of you. I wish therefore you would take this Piece, and produce it as yours. I will pretend not to have had time, and so produce nothing: We shall then see what he will say to it. It was agreed, and I immediatley transcrib'd it that it might appear in my own hand. We met. Watson's Performance was read: there were some Beauties in it: but many Defects. Osborne's was read: It was much better. Ralph did it Justice, remark'd some Faults, but applauded the Beauties. He himself had nothing to produce. I was backward, seem'd desirous of being excus'd, had not had suffi-

---

[116] Watson (?–1728?); Ralph (1695?–1762), an unsuccessful poet but successful political writer in England, who helped Franklin propagandize for the colonies when Franklin returned to London in 1757.

[117] Charles Brockden (1683–1769), Philadelphia's conveyancer, or drafter of deeds and leases.

[118] Philadelphia's Schuylkill River.   [119] A merchant or agent.   [120] Originality.

[121] "He bowed the heavens also, and came down: and darkness was under his feet," from Psalm 18:9.

cient Time to correct; etc. but no Excuse could be admitted, produce I must. It was read and repeated; Watson and Osborne gave up the Contest; and join'd in applauding it immoderately. Ralph only made some Criticisms and propos'd some Amendments, but I defended my Text. Osborne was against Ralph, and told him he was no better a Critic than Poet; so he dropt the Argument. As they two went home together, Osborne express'd himself still more strongly in favour of what he thought my Production, having restrain'd himself before as he said, lest I should think it Flattery. But who would have imagin'd, says he, that Franklin had been capable of such a Performance; such Painting, such Force! such Fire! he has even improv'd the Original! In his common Conversation, he seems to have no Choice of Words; he hesitates and blunders; and yet, good God, how he writes! When we next met, Ralph discover'd the Trick, we had plaid him, and Osborne was a little laught at. This Transaction fix'd Ralph in his Resolution of becoming a Poet. I did all I could to dissuade him from it, but He continued scribbling Verses, till Pope cur'd him.[122] He became however a pretty good Prose Writer. More of him hereafter.

But as I may not have occasion again to mention the other two, I shall just remark here, that Watson died in my Arms a few Years after, much lamented, being the best of our Set. Osborne went to the West Indies, where he became an eminent Lawyer and made Money, but died young. He and I had made a serious Agreement, that the one who happen'd first to die, should if possible make a friendly Visit to the other, and acquaint him how he found things in that Separate State. But he never fulfill'd his Promise.

The Governor, seeming to like my Company, had me frequently to his House; and his Setting me up was always mention'd as a fix'd thing. I was to take with me Letters recommendatory to a Number of his friends, besides the Letter of Credit to furnish me with the necessary Money for purchasing the Press and Types, Paper, etc. For these Letters I was appointed to call at different times, when they were to be ready, but a future time was still[123] named. Thus we went on till the Ship whose Departure too had been several times postponed was on the Point of sailing. Then when I call'd to take my Leave and Receive the Letters, his Secretary, Dr. Bard,[124] came out to me and said the Governor was extreamly busy, in writing, but would be down at Newcastle[125] before the Ship, and there the Letters would be delivered to me.

Ralph, tho' married and having one Child, had determined to accompany me in this Voyage. It was thought he intended to establish a Correspondence, and obtain Goods to sell on Commission. But I found afterwards, that thro' some Discontent with his Wifes Relations, he purposed to leave her on their Hands, and never return again. Having taken leave of my Friends, and interchang'd some Promises with Miss Read, I left Philadelphia in the Ship, which anchor'd at Newcastle. The Governor was there. But when I went to his Lodging, the Secretary came to me from him with the civillest Message in the World, that he could not then see me being engag'd in Business of the utmost Importance; but should send the Letters to me on board, wish'd me heartily a good Voyage and a speedy Return, etc. I return'd on board, a little puzzled, but still not doubting.

[122] Alexander Pope, in response to Ralph's defense of some writers Pope attacks in his 1728 edition of the *Dunciad*, added this couplet in a later edition: "Silence, ye Wolves! while Ralph to Cynthia howls, / And makes Night hideous—Answer him ye Owls" (III. 159–160).
[123] Always.   [124] Patrick Baird, "Port Physician" of Philadelphia after 1720.
[125] New Castle, Delaware.

Mr. Andrew Hamilton,[126] a famous Lawyer of Philadelphia, had taken Passage in the same Ship for himself and Son: and with Mr. Denham[127] a Quaker Merchant, and Messrs. Onion and Russel Masters of an Iron Work in Maryland, had engag'd the Great Cabin; so that Ralph and I were forc'd to take up with a Birth in the Steerage:[128] And none on board knowing us, were considered as ordinary Persons. But Mr. Hamilton and his Son (it was James, since Governor) return'd from New Castle to Philadelphia, the Father being recall'd by a great Fee to plead for a seized Ship. And just before we sail'd Col. French coming on board, and showing me great Respect, I was more taken Notice of, and with my Friend Ralph invited by the other Gentlemen to come into the Cabin, there being now Room. Accordingly we remov'd thither.

Understanding that Col. French had brought on board the Governor's Dispatches, I ask'd the Captain for those Letters that were to be under my Care. He said all were put into the Bag together; and he could not then come at them; but before we landed in England, I should have an Opportunity of picking them out. So I was satisfy'd for the present, and we proceeded on our Voyage. We had a sociable Company in the Cabin, and lived uncommonly well, having the Addition of all Mr. Hamilton's Stores, who had laid in plentifully. In this Passage Mr. Denham contracted a Friendship for me that continued during his Life. The Voyage was otherwise not a pleasant one, as we had a great deal of bad Weather.

When we came into the Channel, the Captain kept his Word with me, and gave me an Opportunity of examining the Bag for the Governor's Letters. I found none upon which my Name was put, as under my Care; I pick'd out 6 or 7 that by the Hand writing I thought might be the promis'd Letters, especially as one of them was directed to Basket[129] the King's Printer, and another to some Stationer. We arriv'd in London the 24th of December, 1724. I waited upon the Stationer who came first in my Way, delivering the Letter as from Gov. Keith. I don't know such a Person, says he: but opening the Letter, O, this is from Riddlesden;[130] I have lately found him to be a compleat Rascal, and I will have nothing to do with him, nor receive any Letters from him. So putting the Letter into my Hand, he turn'd on his Heel and left me to serve some Customer. I was surprized to find these were not the Governor's Letters. And after recollecting and comparing Circumstances, I began to doubt his Sincerity. I found my Friend Denham, and opened the whole Affair to him. He let me into Keith's Character, told me there was not the least Probability that he had written any Letters for me, that no one who knew him had the smallest Dependance on him, and he laught at the Notion of the Governor's giving me a Letter of Credit, having as he said no Credit to give. On my expressing some Concern about what I should do: He advis'd me to endeavour getting some Employment in the Way of my Business. Among the Printers here, says he, you will improve yourself; and when you return to America, you will set up to greater Advantage.

We both of us happen'd to know, as well as the Stationer, that Riddlesden the Attorney, was a very Knave. He had half ruin'd Miss Read's Father by drawing

---

[126] Hamilton (1678?–1741) helped establish freedom of the press; his son James Hamilton (1710?–1783) served as Pennsylvania's governor four times between 1748 and 1773.

[127] Thomas Denham (?–1728), merchant and benefactor to Franklin.

[128] To share a berth in the least expensive portion of the ship, near the rudder.

[129] John Basket (?–1742).

[130] William Riddlesden, a renowned Maryland swindler, who died before 1733.

him in to be bound for him.[131] By his Letter it appear'd, there was a secret Scheme on foot to the Prejudice of Hamilton, (Suppos'd to be then coming over with us,) and that Keith was concern'd in it with Riddlesden. Denham, who was a Friend of Hamilton's, thought he ought to be acquainted with it. So when he arriv'd in England, which was soon after, partly from Resentment and Ill-Will to Keith and Riddlesden, and partly from Good Will to him: I waited on him, and gave him the Letter. He thank'd me cordially, the Information being of Importance to him. And from that time he became my Friend, greatly to my Advantage afterwards on many Occasions.

But what shall we think of a Governor's playing such pitiful Tricks, and imposing so grossly on a poor ignorant Boy! It was a Habit he had acquired. He wish'd to please every body; and having little to give, he gave Expectations. He was otherwise an ingenious sensible Man, a pretty good Writer, and a good Governor for the People, tho' not for his Constituents the Proprietaries,[132] whose Instructions he sometimes disregarded. Several of our best Laws were of his Planning, and pass'd during his Administration.

Ralph and I were inseparable Companions. We took Lodgings together in Little Britain[133] at 3s. 6d.[134] per Week, as much as we could then afford. He found some Relations, but they were poor and unable to assist him. He now let me know his Intentions of remaining in London, and that he never meant to return to Philadelphia. He had brought no Money with him, the whole he could muster having been expended in paying his Passage. I had 15 Pistoles:[135] So he borrowed occasionally of me, to subsist while he was looking out for Business. He first endeavoured to get into the Playhouse, believing himself qualify'd for an Actor; but Wilkes,[136] to whom he apply'd, advis'd him candidly not to think of that, Employment, as it was impossible he should succeed in it. Then he propos'd to Roberts, a Publisher in Paternoster Row,[137] to write for him a Weekly Paper like the Spectator, on certain Conditions, which Roberts did not approve. Then he endeavour'd to get Employment as a Hackney Writer[138] to copy for the Stationers and Lawyers about the Temple:[139] but could find no Vacancy.

I immediately got into Work at Palmer's then a famous Printing House in Bartholomew Close;[140] and here I continu'd near a Year. I was pretty diligent; but spent with Ralph a good deal of my Earnings in going to Plays and other Places of Amusement. We had together consum'd all my Pistoles, and now just rubb'd on from hand to mouth. He seem'd quite to forget his Wife and Child, and I by degrees my Engagements with Miss Read, to whom I never wrote more than one Letter, and that was to let her know I was not likely soon to return. This was another of the great Errata of my Life, which I should wish to correct if I were to live it over again. In fact, by our Expences, I was constantly kept unable to pay my Passage.

---

[131] By making Mr. Read responsible for Riddlesden's debts.

[132] The Proprietors of Pennsylvania, the Penn family, who owned the state's land until the Revolution.

[133] A short London street.

[134] Three shillings, six pence.   [135] Spanish gold coins, about eighteen shillings each.

[136] Robert Wilks (1665?–1732), an actor who managed two London theaters after 1709.

[137] The center of London's printing business.

[138] A hired writer working out of a hackney, or horse-drawn cab.

[139] One of four Inns of Court, buildings at the center of London's legal profession.

[140] Palmer's Printing House was run by Samuel Palmer (?–1732); Bartholomew Close was a square, just off Little Britain, that was a center for printing.

At Palmer's I was employ'd in composing for the second Edition of Woollaston's Religion of Nature.[141] Some of his Reasonings not appearing to me well-founded, I wrote a little metaphysical Piece, in which I made Remarks on them. It was entitled, *A Dissertation on Liberty and Necessity, Pleasure and pain*.[142] I inscrib'd it to my Friend Ralph. I printed a small Number. It occasion'd my being more consider'd by Mr. Palmer, as a young Man of some Ingenuity, tho' he seriously expostulated with me upon the Principles of my Pamphlet which to him appear'd abominable. My printing this Pamphlet was another Erratum.

While I lodg'd in Little Britain I made an Acquaintance with one Wilcox a Bookseller, whose Shop was at the next Door. He had an immense Collection of second-hand Books. Circulating Libraries were not then in Use;[143] but we agreed that on certain reasonable Terms which I have now forgotten, I might take, read and return any of his Books. This I esteem'd a great Advantage, and I made as much use of it as I could.

My Pamphlet by some means falling into the Hands of one Lyons,[144] a Surgeon, Author of a Book intituled *The Infallibility of Human Judgment*, it occasioned an Acquaintance between us; he took great Notice of me, call'd on me often, to converse on those Subjects, carried me to the Horns a pale Ale-House in [blank] Lane, Cheapside, and introduc'd me to Dr. Mandevile, Author of the Fable of the Bees.[145] who had a Club there, of which he was the Soul, being a most facetious entertaining Companion. Lyons too introduc'd me, to Dr. Pemberton,[146] at Batson's Coffee House,[147] who promis'd to give me an Opportunity some time or other of seeing Sir Isaac Newton, of which I was extreamly desirous; but this never happened.

I had brought over a few Curiosities among which the principal was a Purse made of the Asbestos, which purifies by Fire. Sir Hans Sloane[148] heard of it, came to see me, and invited me to his House in Bloomsbury Square, where he show'd me all his Curiosities, and persuaded me to let him add that to the Number, for which he paid me handsomely.

In our House there lodg'd a young Woman; a Millener, who I think had a Shop in the Cloisters.[149] She had been genteelly bred, was sensible and lively, and of most pleasing Conversation. Ralph read Plays to her in the Evenings, they grew intimate, she took another Lodging, and he follow'd her. They liv'd together some time, but he being still out of Business, and her Income not sufficient to maintain them with her Child, he took a Resolution of going from London, to try for a Country School, which he thought himself well qualify'd to undertake, as he

[141] Actually the third edition of *The Religion of Nature Delineated* (1722), by William Wollaston, (1660–1724), an Anglican clergyman and schoolmaster.

[142] Franklin's pamphlet, published in 1725, earned him charges of atheism, as the work denies the existence of vice and virtue.

[143] Franklin himself founded the first circulating library in 1731.

[144] William Lyons, a surgeon who wrote *The Infallibility, Dignity, and Excellence of Human Judgment* (1719).

[145] *The Fable of the Bees; Or, Private Vices Public Benefits* (1714), first published as *The Grumbling Hive; Or, Knaves Turned Honest* (1705), by Bernard Mandeville (1670?–1733).

[146] Henry Pemberton (1694–1771), a member of London's Royal Society and friend of Sir Isaac Newton (1642–1727), who produced theories of gravity, light, and color and was president of the Royal Society from 1703 to 1727.

[147] A favorite meeting-place of physicians that was disdained by literary men.

[148] Sloane (1660–1753) was a physician and eminent botanist who succeeded Newton as president of the Royal Society; Sloane's library and museum were used to form the British Museum.

[149] Possibly near St. Bartholomew's Church.

wrote an excellent Hand, and was a Master of Arithmetic and Accounts. This however he deem'd a Business below him, and confident of future better Fortune when he should be unwilling to have it known that he once was so meanly employ'd, he chang'd his Name, and did me the Honour to assume mine. For I soon after had a Letter from him, acquainting me, that he was settled in a small Village in Berkshire, I think it was, where he taught reading and writing to 10 or a dozen Boys at 6 pence each per Week, recommending Mrs. T. to my Care, and desiring me to write to him directing for Mr. Franklin Schoolmaster at such a Place. He continu'd to write frequently, sending me large Specimens of an Epic Poem, which he was then composing, and desiring my Remarks and Corrections. These I gave him from time to time, but endeavour'd rather to discourage his Proceeding. One of Young's Satires[150] was then just publish'd. I copy'd and sent him a great Part of it, which set in a strong Light the Folly of pursuing the Muses with any Hope of Advancement by them. All was in vain. Sheets of the Poem continu'd to come by every Post. In the mean time Mrs. T. having on his account lost her Friends and Business, was often in Distresses, and us'd to send for me, and borrow what I could spare to help her out of them. I grew fond of her Company, and being at this time under no Religious Restraints, and presuming on my Importance to her, I attempted Familiarities, (another Erratum) which she repuls'd with a proper Resentment, and acquainted him with my Behaviour. This made a Breach between us, and when he return'd again to London, he let me know he thought I had cancel'd all the Obligations he had been under to me. So I found I was never to expect his Repaying me what I lent to him or advanc'd for him. This was however not then of much Consequence, as he was totally unable. And in the Loss of his Friendship I found my self reliev'd from a Burthen. I now began to think of getting a little Money beforehand; and expecting better Work, I left Palmer's to work at Watt's[151] near Lincoln's Inn Fields, a still greater Printing House. Here I continu'd all the rest of my Stay in London.

At my first Admission into this Printing House, I took to working at Press, imagining I felt a Want of the Bodily Exercise I had been us'd to in America, where Presswork is mix'd with Composing. I drank only Water; the other Workmen, near 50 in Number, were great Guzzlers of Beer. On occasion I carried up and down Stairs a large Form of Types[152] in each hand, when others carried but one in both Hands. They wonder'd to see from this and several Instances that the Water-American as they call'd me was *stronger* than themselves who drank *strong* Beer. We had an Alehouse Boy who attended always in the House to supply the Workmen. My Companion at the Press, drank every day a Pint before Breakfast, a Pint at Breakfast with his Bread and Cheese; a Pint between Breakfast and Dinner; a Pint at Dinner; a Pint in the Afternoon about Six o'Clock, and another when he had done his Day's-Work. I thought it a detestable Custom. But it was necessary, he suppos'd, to drink *strong* Beer that he might be *strong* to labour. I endeavour'd to convince him that the Bodily Strength afforded by Beer could only be in proportion to the Grain or Flour of the Barley dissolved in the Water of which it was made; that there was more Flour in a Penny-worth of Bread, and therefore if he would eat that with a Pint of Water, it would give him more

---

[150] Probably the fourth satire in *Love of Fame, the Universal Passion* (1725–1728), by Edward Young (1683–1765).

[151] John Watts (1678?–1763).   [152] A body of type set in a metal frame.

Strength than a Quart of Beer. He drank on however, and had 4 or 5 Shillings to pay out of his Wages every Saturday Night for that muddling Liquor; an Expence I was free from. And thus these poor Devils keep themselves always under.[153]

Watts after some Weeks desiring to have me in the Composing Room, I left the Pressmen. A new *Bienvenu*[154] or Sum for Drink, being 5 *s.*, was demanded of me by the Compositors.[155] I thought it an Imposition, as I had paid below. The master thought so too, and forbad my Paying it. I stood out two or three Weeks, was accordingly considered as an Excommunicate, and had so many little Pieces of private Mischief done me, by mixing my Sorts,[156] transposing my Pages, breaking my Matter,[157] etc., etc., if I were ever so little out of the Room, and all ascrib'd to the Chapel[158] Ghost, which they said ever haunted those not regularly admitted, that notwithstanding the Master's Protection, I found myself oblig'd to comply and pay the Money; convinc'd of the Folly of being on ill Terms with those one is to live with continually. I was now on a fair Footing with them, and soon acquir'd considerable Influence. I propos'd some reasonable Alterations in their Chapel Laws, and carried them against all Opposition. From my Example a great Part of them, left their muddling Breakfast of Beer and Bread and Cheese, finding they could with me be supply'd from a neighbouring House with a large Porringer of hot Water-gruel, sprinkled with Pepper, crumb'd with Bread, and a Bit of Butter in it, for the Price of a Pint of Beer, viz, three halfpence. This was a more comfortable as well as cheaper Breakfast, and kept their Heads clearer. Those who continu'd sotting with Beer all day, were often, by not paying, out of Credit at the Alehouse, and us'd to make Interest with me to get Beer, *their Light,* as they phras'd it, *being out.* I watch'd the Pay table on Saturday Night, and collected what I stood engag'd for them, having to pay some times near Thirty Shillings a Week on their Accounts. This, and my being esteem'd a pretty good Riggitte,[159] that is a jocular verbal Satyrist, supported my Consequence in the Society. My constant Attendance, (I never making a St. Monday),[160] recommended me to the Master; and my uncommon Quickness at Composing, occasion'd my being put upon all Work of Dispatch which was generally better paid. So I went on now very agreably.

My Lodging in Little Britain being too remote, I found another in Duke-street opposite to the Romish Chapel.[161] It was two pair of Stairs backwards at an Italian Warehouse. A Widow Lady kept the House; she had a Daughter and a Maid Servant, and a Journeyman who attended the Warehouse, but lodg'd abroad. After sending to enquire my Character at the House where I last lodg'd, she agreed to take me in at the same Rate, 3*s.* 6*d.* per Week, cheaper as she said from the Protection she expected in having a Man lodge in the House. She was a Widow, an elderly Woman, had been bred a Protestant, being a Clergyman's Daughter, but was converted to the Catholic Religion by her Husband, whose Memory she much revered, had lived much among People of Distinction, and knew a 1000 Anecdotes of them as far back as the Times of Charles the Second. She was lame

[153] Poor.   [154] "Welcome" (French).   [155] Typesetters.   [156] Type, or letters.
[157] Type set for printing.
[158] Franklin's note: "A Printing House is always called a Chappel by the Workmen." Each group of journeymen printers had its own by-laws.
[159] A person who makes fun of others.
[160] Never absent on Monday because of weekend activities or a religious holiday.
[161] The Roman Catholic Chapel of Saints Anselm and Cecilia.

in her Knees with the Gout, and therefore seldom stirr'd out of her Room, so sometimes wanted Company; and hers was so highly amusing to me; that I was sure to spend an Evening with her whenever she desired it. Our Supper was only half an Anchovy each, on a very little Strip of Bread and Butter, and half a Pint of Ale between us. But the Entertainment was in her Conversation. My always keeping good Hours, and giving little Trouble in the Family, made her unwilling to part with me; so that when I talk'd of a Lodging I had heard of, nearer my Business, for 2s. a Week, which, intent as I now was on saving Money, made some Difference; she bid me not think of it, for she would abate me two Shillings a Week for the future, so I remain'd with her at 1s. 6d. as long as I staid in London.

In a Garret of her House there lived a Maiden Lady of 70 in the most retired Manner, of whom my Landlady gave me this Account, that she was a Roman Catholic, had been sent abroad when young and lodg'd in a Nunnery with an Intent of becoming a Nun: but the Country not agreeing with her, she return'd to England, where there being no Nunnery, she had vow'd to lead the Life of a Nun as near as might be done in those Circumstances: Accordingly she had given all her Estate to charitable Uses, reserving only Twelve Pounds a Year to live on, and out of this Sum she still gave a great deal in Charity, living her self on Watergruel only, and using no Fire but to boil it. She had lived many Years in that Garret, being permitted to remain there gratis by successive Catholic Tenants of the House below, as they deem'd it a Blessing to have her there. A Priest visited her, to confess her every Day. I have ask'd her, says my Landlady, how she, as she liv'd, could possibly find so much Employment for a Confessor? O, says she, it is impossible to avoid *vain Thoughts*. I was permitted once to visit her: She was chearful and polite, and convers'd pleasantly. The Room was clean, but had no other Furniture than a Matras, a Table with a Crucifix and Book, a Stool, which she gave me to sit on, and a Picture over the Chimney of St. Veronica, displaying her Handkerchief with the miraculous Figure of Christ's bleeding Face on it,[162] which she explain'd to me with great Seriousness. She look'd pale, but was never sick, and I give it as another Instance on how small an Income Life and Health may be supported.

At Watt's Printinghouse I contracted an Acquaintance with an ingenious young Man, one Wygate, who having wealthy Relations, had been better educated than most Printers, was a tolerable Latinist, spoke French, and lov'd Reading. I taught him, and a Friend of his, to swim, at twice going into the River, and they soon became good Swimmers. They introduc'd me to some Gentlemen from the Country who went to Chelsea by Water to see the College and Don Saltero's Curiosities.[163] In our Return, at the Request of the Company, whose Curiosity Wygate had excited, I stript and leapt into the River, and swam from near Chelsea to Blackfryars,[164] performing on the Way many Feats of Activity both upon and under Water, that surpriz'd and pleas'd those to whom they were Novelties. I had from a Child been ever delighted with this Exercise, had studied and practis'd all Thevenot's Motions and Positions,[165] added some of my own, aiming at the

---

[162] St. Veronica is said to have wiped the face of Christ as he bore the cross, and his image was supposedly retained on the cloth.

[163] Chelsea Hospital was errected in 1682 on the site of Chelsea College, founded in 1610; the coffee house and museum Don Saltero's Curiosities was opened in Chelsea in 1695 by James Salter, former servant of Hans Sloane.

[164] About three and a half miles away.

[165] *The Art of Swimming* (1699), by Melchisédeck de Thévenot.

graceful and easy, as well as the Useful. All these I took this Occasion of exhibiting to the Company, and was much flatter'd by their Admiration. And Wygate, who was desirous of becoming a Master, grew more and more attach'd to me, on that account, as well as from the Similarity of our Studies. He at length propos'd to me travelling all over Europe together, supporting ourselves everywhere by working at our Business. I was once inclin'd to it. But mentioning it to my good Friend Mr. Denham, with whom I often spent an Hour, when I had Leisure. He dissuaded me from it, advising me to think only of returning to Pensilvania, which he was now about to do.

I must record one Trait of this good Man's Character. He had formerly been in Business at Bristol, but fail'd in Debt to a Number of People, compounded[166] and went to America. There, by a close Application to Business as a Merchant, he acquir'd a plentiful Fortune in a few Years. Returning to England in the Ship with me, He invited his old Creditors to an Entertainment, at which he thank'd them for the easy Composition[167] they had favour'd him with, and when they expected nothing but the Treat, every Man at the first Remove,[168] found under his Plate an Order on a Banker for the full Amount of the unpaid Remainder with Interest.

He now told me he was about to return to Philadelphia, and should carry over a great Quantity of Goods in order to open a Store there: He propos'd to take me over as his Clerk, to keep his Books (in which he would instruct me) copy his Letters, and attend the Store. He added, that as soon as I should be acquainted with mercantile Business he would promote me by sending me with a Cargo of Flour and Bread etc., to the West Indies, and procure me Commissions from others; which would be profitable, and if I manag'd well, would establish me handsomely. The Thing pleas'd me, for I was grown tired of London, remember'd with Pleasure the happy Months I had spent in Pennsylvania, and wish'd again to see it. Therefore I immediately agreed, on the Terms of Fifty Pounds a Year, Pensilvania Money; less indeed than my present Gettings as a Compos[i]tor, but affording a better Prospect.

I now took Leave of Printing, as I thought for ever, and was daily employ'd in my new Business; going about with Mr. Denham among the Tradesmen, to purchase various Articles, and seeing them pack'd up, doing Errands, calling upon Workmen to dispatch, etc., and when all was on board, I had a few Days Leisure. On one of these Days I was to my Surprize sent for by a great Man I knew only by Name, a Sir William Wyndham[169] and I waited upon him. He had heard by some means or other of my Swimming from Chelsey to Blackfryars, and of my teaching Wygate and another young Man to swim in a few Hours. He had two Sons about to set out on their Travels; he wish'd to have them first taught Swimming; and propos'd to gratify me handsomely if I would teach them. They were not yet come to Town and my Stay was uncertain, so I could not undertake it. But from this Incident I thought it likely, that if I were to remain in England and open a Swimming School, I might get a good deal of Money. And it struck me so strongly, that had the Overture been sooner made me, probably I should not so soon have returned to America. After many Years, you and I had something of more Importance to do with one of these Sons of Sir William Wyndham, become Earl of Egremont, which I shall mention in its Place.[170]

---

[166] Partly settled his debts.   [167] Settlement.   [168] The removal of the first course's plates.
[169] Wyndham (1687–1740) was chancellor of the exchequer and a Tory leader.
[170] Franklin never mentions the son, Charles Wyndham (1710–1763), again.

Thus I spent about 18 Months in London. Most Part of the Time, I work'd hard at my Business, and spent but little upon my self except in seeing Plays and in Books. My Friend Ralph had kept me poor. He owed me about 27 Pounds; which I was now never likely to receive; a great Sum out of my small Earnings. I lov'd him notwithstanding, for he had many amiable Qualities. Tho' I had by no means improv'd my Fortune. But I had pick'd up some very ingenious Acquaintance whose Conversation was of great Advantage to me, and I had read considerably.

We sail'd from Gravesend[171] on the 23d of July 1726. For the Incidents of the Voyage, I refer you to my Journal, where you will find them all minutely related. Perhaps the most important Part of that Journal is the *Plan* to be found in it[172] which I formed at Sea, for regulating my future Conduct in Life. It is the more remarkable, as being form'd when I was so young, and yet being pretty faithfully adhered to quite thro' to Old Age. We landed In Philadelphia the 11th of October, where I found sundry Alterations. Keith was no longer Governor, being superceded by Major Gordon:[173] I met him walking the Streets as a common Citizen. He seem'd a little asham'd at seeing me, but pass'd without saying any thing. I should have been as much asham'd at seeing Miss Read, had not her Friends, despairing with Reason of my Return, after the Receipt of my Letter, persuaded her to marry another, one Rogers, a Potter, which was done in my Absence. With him however she was never happy, and soon parted from him, refusing to cohabit with him, or bear his Name It being now said that he had another Wife. He was a worthless Fellow tho' an excellent Workman which was the Temptation to her Friends. He got into Debt, and ran away in 1727 or 28. Went to the West Indies, and died there. Keimer had got a better House, a Shop well supply'd with Stationary, plenty of new Types, a number of Hands tho' none good, and seem'd to have a great deal of Business.

Mr. Denham took a Store in Water Street, where we open'd our Goods. I attended the Business diligently, studied Accounts, and grew in a little Time expert at selling. We lodg'd and boarded together, he counsell'd me as a Father, having a sincere Regard for me: I respected and lov'd him: and we might have gone on together very happily: But in the Beginning of Feby. 1726/7 when I had just pass'd my 21st Year, we both were taken ill. My Distemper was a Pleurisy,[174] which very nearly carried me off: I suffered a good deal, gave up the Point[175] in my own mind, and was rather disappointed when I found my Self recovering; regretting in some degree that I must now some time or other have all that disagreable Work to do over again. I forget what his Distemper was. It held him a long time, and at length carried him off. He left me a small Legacy in a nuncupative[176] Will, as a Token of his Kindness for me, and he left me once more to the wide World. For the Store was taken into the Care of his Executors, and my Employment under him ended: My Brother-in-law Homes, being now at Philadelphia, advis'd my Return to my Business. And Keimer tempted me with an Offer of large Wages by the Year to come and take the Management of his Printing-House, that he might better attend his Stationer's Shop. I had heard a bad Character of him in London, from his Wife and her Friends, and was not fond of having any more to do with him. I try'd for farther Employment as a Merchant's Clerk; but not readily meeting with any, I clos'd[177] again with Keimer.

---

[171] A port near London.   [172] The preamble and outline are all that remain of the *Plan*.
[173] Patrick Gordon (1644–1736), governor of Pennsylvania from 1726 to 1736.
[174] A respiratory inflammation.   [175] The will to live.   [176] Oral.   [177] Agreed on a contract.

I found in *his* House these Hands; Hugh Meredith[178] a Welsh-Pensilvanian, 30 Years of Age, bred to Country Work: honest, sensible, had a great deal of solid Observation, was something of a Reader, but given to drink: Stephen Potts,[179] a young Country Man of full Age, bred to the Same: of uncommon natural Parts,[180] and great Wit and Humour, but a little idle. These he had agreed with an extream low Wages, per Week, to be rais'd a Shilling every 3 Months, as they would deserve by improving in their Business, and the Expectation of these high Wages to come on hereafter was what he had drawn them in with. Meredith was to work at Press, Potts at Bookbinding, which he by Agreement, was to teach them, tho' he knew neither one nor t'other. John—a wild Irishman brought up to no Business, whose Service for 4 Years Keimer had purchas'd[181] from the Captain of a Ship. He too was to be made a Pressman. George Webb,[182] an Oxford Scholar, whose Time for 4 Years he had likewise bought, intending him for a Compositor: of whom more presently. And David Harry,[183] a Country Boy, whom he had taken Apprentice. I soon perceiv'd that the Intention of engaging me at Wages so much higher than he had been us'd to give, was to have these raw cheap Hands form'd thro' me, and as soon as I had instructed them, then, they being all articled to him,[184] he should be able to do without me. I went on however, very chearfully; put his Printing House in Order, which had been in great Confusion, and brought his Hands by degrees to mind their Business and to do it better.

It was an odd Thing to find an Oxford Scholar in the Situation of a bought Servant. He was not more than 18 Years of Age, and gave me this Account of himself; that he was born in Gloucester, educated at a Grammar School there, had been distinguish'd among the Scholars for some apparent Superiority in performing his Part when they exhibited Plays; belong'd to the Witty Club there, and had written some Pieces in Prose and Verse which were printed in the Gloucester Newspapers. Thence he was sent to Oxford; there he continu'd about a Year, but not well-satisfy'd, wishing of all things to see London and become a Player. At length receiving his Quarterly Allowance of 15 Guineas, instead of discharging his Debts, he walk'd out of Town, hid his Gown in a Furz Bush,[185] and footed it to London, where having no Friend to advise him, he fell into bad Company, soon spent his Guineas, found no means of being introduc'd among the Players, grew necessitous, pawn'd his Cloaths and wanted Bread. Walking the Street very hungry, and not knowing what to do with himself, a Crimp's Bill[186] was put into his Hand, offering immediate Entertainment and Encouragement to such as would bind themselves to serve in America. He went directly, sign'd the Indentures, was put into the Ship and came over; never writing a Line to acquaint his Friends what was become of him. He was lively, witty, good-natur'd, and a pleasant Companion, but idle, thoughtless and imprudent to the last Degree.

John the Irishman soon ran away. With the rest I began to live very agreably; for they all respected me, the more as they found Keimer incapable of instructing them, and that from me they learnt something daily. We never work'd on a Saturday, that being Keimer's Sabbath. So I had two Days for Reading. My Acquain-

---

[178] Meredith (1696?–1749) later became Franklin's business partner.
[179] Potts (?–1758) later became a bookseller and an innkeeper.   [180] Abilities.
[181] In exchange for service.   [182] Webb (1708–1736?) later became a printer.
[183] Harry (1708–1760) later became the first printer in Barbados.
[184] Contractually bound to work only for Keimer.   [185] Hid his academic robe in an evergreen bush.
[186] An ad to lure men into military or sea service or indentured servitude in return for passage to the colonies.

tance with Ingenious People in the Town, increased. Keimer himself treated me with great Civility, and apparent Regard; and nothing now made me uneasy but my Debt to Vernon, which I was yet unable to pay being hitherto but a poor Oeconomist. He however kindly made no Demand of it.

Our Printing-House often wanted Sorts,[187] and there was no Letter Founder in America. I had seen Types cast at James's in London,[188] but without much Attention to the Manner: However I now contriv'd a Mould, made use of the Letters we had, as Puncheons, struck the Matrices[189] in Lead, and thus supply'd in a pretty tolerable way all Deficiencies. I also engrav'd several Things on occasion. I made the Ink, I was Warehouse-man and every thing, in short quite a Factotum.[190]

But however serviceable I might be, I found that my Services became every Day of less Importance, as the other Hands improv'd in the Business. And when Keimer paid my second Quarter's Wages, he let me know that he felt them too heavy, and thought I should make an Abatement. He grew by degrees less civil, put on more of the Master, frequently found Fault, was captious and seem'd ready for an Out-breaking. I went on nevertheless with a good deal of Patience, thinking that his incumber'd Circumstances were partly the Cause. At length a Trifle snapt our Connexion. For a great Noise happening near the Courthouse, I put my Head out of the Window to see what was the Matter. Keimer being in the Street look'd up and saw me, call'd out to me in a loud Voice and angry Tone to mind my Business, adding some reproachful Words, that nettled me the more for their Publicity, all the Neighbours who were looking out on the same Occasion being Witnesses how I was treated. He came up immediately into the Printing-House, continu'd the Quarrel, high Words pass'd on both Sides, he gave me the Quarter's Warning we had stipulated, expressing a Wish that he had not been oblig'd to so long a Warning: I told him his Wish was unnecessary for I would leave him that Instant; and so taking my Hat walk'd out of Doors; desiring Meredith whom I saw below to take care of some Things I left, and bring them to my Lodging.

Meredith came accordingly in the Evening, when we talk'd my Affair over. He had conceiv'd a great Regard for me, and was very unwilling that I should leave the House while he remain'd in it. He dissuaded me from returning to my native Country[191] which I began to think of. He reminded me that Keimer was in debt for all he possess'd, that his Creditors began to be uneasy, that he kept his Shop miserably, sold often without Profit for ready Money, and often trusted without keeping Accounts. That he must therefore fail; which would make a Vacancy I might profit of. I objected my Want of Money. He then let me know, that his Father[192] had a high Opinion of me, and from some Discourse that had pass'd between them, he was sure would advance Money to set us up, if I would enter into Partnership with him. My Time, says he, will be out with Keimer in the Spring. By that time we may have our Press and Types in from London: I am sensible I am no Workman. If you like it, Your Skill in the Business shall be set against the Stock I furnish; and we will share the Profits equally. The Proposal was agreable, and I consented. His Father was in Town, and approv'd of it, the more as he saw I had great Influence with his Son, had prevail'd on him to abstain long from Dramdrinking,[193] and he hop'd might break him of that wretched Habit

---

[187] Lacked type fonts; a printer who was "out of sorts" was in trouble.
[188] Thomas James's type foundry, London's largest.
[189] Made use of the letters we had, as stamping tools, struck the casting molds in type.
[190] A jack-of-all-trades.   [191] Boston.   [192] Simon Meredith (?–1745?).
[193] Drinking small quantities of alcoholic beverages.

entirely, when we came to be so closely connected. I gave an Inventory to the Father, who carry'd it to a Merchant; the Things were sent for; the Secret was to be kept till they should arrive, and in the mean time I was to get work if I could at the other Printing House. But I found no Vacancy there, and so remain'd idle a few Days, when Keimer, on a Prospect of being employ'd to print some Paper-money, in New Jersey, which would require Cuts and various Types that I only could supply, and apprehending Bradford might engage me and get the Jobb from him, sent me a very civil Message, that old Friends should not part for a few Words, the Effect of sudden Passion, and wishing me to return. Meredith persuaded me to comply, as it would give more Opportunity for his Improvement under my daily Instructions. So I return'd, and we went on more smoothly than for some time before. The New Jersey Jobb was obtain'd. I contriv'd a Copper-Plate Press for it, the first that had been seen in the Country. I cut several Ornaments and Checks for the Bills. We went together to Burlington, where I executed the Whole to Satisfaction, and he received so large a Sum for the Work, as to be enabled thereby to keep his Head much longer above Water.

At Burlington I made an Acquaintance with many principal People of the Province. Several of them had been appointed by the Assembly a Committee to attend the Press, and take Care that no more Bills were printed than the Law directed. They were therefore by Turns constantly with us, and generally he who attended brought with him a Friend or two for Company. My Mind having been much more improv'd by Reading than Keimer's, I suppose it was for that Reason my Conversation seem'd to be more valu'd. They had me to their Houses, introduc'd me to their Friends and show'd me much Civility, while he, tho' the Master, was a little neglected. In truth he was an odd Fish, ignorant of common Life, fond of rudely opposing receiv'd Opinions, slovenly to extream dirtiness, enthusiastic in some Points of Religion, and a little Knavish withal. We continu'd there near 3 Months, and by that time I could reckon among my acquired Friends, Judge Allen, Samuel Bustill, the Secretary of the Province, Isaac Pearson, Joseph Cooper and several of the Smiths, Members of Assembly, and Isaac Decow the Surveyor General. The latter was a shrewd sagacious old Man, who told me that he began for himself when young by wheeling Clay for the Brickmakers, learnt to write after he was of Age, carry'd the Chain for Surveyors, who taught him Surveying, and he had now by his Industry acquir'd a good Estate; and says he, I foresee, that you will soon work this Man out of his Business and make a Fortune in it at Philadelphia. He had not then the least Intimation of my Intention to set up there or any where. These Friends were afterwards of great Use to me, as I occasionally was to some of them. They all continued their Regard for me as long as they lived.

Before I enter upon my public Appearance in Business it may be well to let you know the then State of my Mind, with regard to my Principles and Morals, that you may see how far those influenc'd the future Events of my Life. My Parents had early given me religious Impressions, and brought me through my Childhood piously in the Dissenting Way.[194] But I was scarce 15 when, after doubting by turns of several Points as I found them disputed in the different Books I read, I began to doubt of Revelation it self. Some Books against Deism fell into my Hands; they were said to be the Substance of Sermons preached at Boyle's Lectures.[195] It happened that they wrought an Effect on me quite contrary to what was

---

[194] As a Congregationalist or Presbyterian, as opposed to a follower of the Church of England.

[195] Lectures established in 1692 by the chemist Robert Boyle (1627–1691) to defend Christianity against nonbelievers.

intended by them: For the Arguments of the Deists which were quoted to be refuted, appeared to me much stronger than the Refutations. In short I soon became a thorough Deist. My Arguments perverted some others, particularly Collins and Ralph: but each of them having afterwards wrong'd me greatly without the least Compunction and recollecting Keith's Conduct towards me, (who was another Freethinker) and my own towards Vernon and Miss Read which at Times gave me great Trouble, I began to suspect that this Doctrine tho' it might be true, was not very useful. My London Pamphlet, which had for its Motto those Lines of Dryden

> —*Whatever is, is right.*—
> *Tho' purblind Man*
> *Sees but a Part of the Chain, the nearest Link,*
> *His Eyes not carrying to the equal Beam,*
> *That poizes all, above.*[196]

And from the Attributes of God, his infinite Wisdom, Goodness and Power concluded that nothing could possibly be wrong in the World, and that Vice and Virtue were empty Distinctions, no such Things existing: appear'd now not so clever a Performance as I once thought it; and I doubted whether some Error had not insinuated itself unperceiv'd into my Argument, so as to infect all that follow'd, as is common in metaphysical Reasonings. I grew convinc'd that *Truth, Sincerity and Integrity* in Dealings between Man and Man, were of the utmost Importance to the Felicity of Life, and I form'd written Resolutions, (which still remain in my Journal Book) to practice them ever while I lived. Revelation had indeed no weight with me as such; but I entertain'd an Opinion, that tho' certain Actions might not be bad *because* they were forbidden by it, or good *because* it commanded them; yet probably those Actions might be forbidden *because* they were bad for us, or commanded *because* they were beneficial to us, in their own Natures, all the Circumstances of things considered. And this Persuasion, with the kind hand of Providence, or some guardian Angel, or accidental favourable Circumstances and Situations, or all together, preserved me (thro' this dangerous Time of Youth and the hazardous Situations I was sometimes in among Strangers, remote from the Eye and Advice of my Father) without any *wilful* gross Immorality or Injustice that might have been expected from my Want of Religion. I say *wilful*, because the Instances I have mentioned, had something of *Necessity* in them, from my Youth, Inexperience, and the Knavery of others. I had therefore a tolerable Character to begin the World with, I valued it properly, and determin'd to preserve it.

We had not been long return'd to Philadelphia, before the New Types arriv'd from London. We settled with Keimer, and left him by his Consent before he heard of it. We found a House to hire near the Market, and took it. To lessen the Rent, (which was then but £24 a Year tho' I have since known it let for 70) We took in Tho' Godfrey a Glazier[197] and his Family, who were to pay a considerable Part of it to us, and we to board with them. We had scarce opened our Letters and

---

[196] The first line here is not from John Dryden (1631–1700) but from Alexander Pope, *Essays on Man* (1733), Epistle I, line 284; Franklin's London pamphlet *Of Liberty and Necessity, Pleasure and Pain* correctly quotes Dryden's *Oedipus* (1679), III.i.244–248: "Whatever is, is in its Causes just/ Since all Things are by Fate, but purblind Man. . . . "

[197] One who cuts and sets glass panes; Thomas Godfrey (1704–1749).

put our Press in Order, before George House, an Acquaintance of Mine, brought a Country-man to us; whom he had met in the Street enquiring for a Printer. All our Cash was now expended in the Variety of Particulars we had been obliged to procure and this Countryman's Five Shillings being our first Fruits, and coming so seasonably, gave me more Pleasure than any Crown[198] I have since earn'd; and from the Gratitude I felt towards House, has made me often more ready than perhaps I should otherwise have been to assist young Beginners.

There are Croakers in every Country always boding its Ruin. Such a one then lived in Philadelphia, a Person of Note, an elderly Man, with a wise Look, and very grave Manner of speaking. His Name was Samuel Mickle. This Gentleman, a Stranger to me, stopt one Day at my Door, and asked me if I was the young Man who had lately opened a new Printing House: Being answer'd in the Affirmative; he said he was sorry for me, because it was an expensive Undertaking and the Expence would be lost; for Philadelphia was a sinking Place,[199] the People already half Bankrupts or near being so; all Appearances of the contrary, such as new Buildings and the Rise of Rents being to his certain Knowledge fallacious, for they were in fact among the Things that would soon ruin us. And he gave me such a Detail of Misfortunes, now existing or that were soon to exist, that he left me half-melancholy. Had I known him before I engag'd in this Business, probably I never should have done it. This Man continu'd to live in this decaying Place; and to declaim in the same Strain, refusing for many Years to buy a House there, because all was going to Destruction, and at last I had the Pleasure of seeing him give five times as much for one as he might have bought it for when he first began his Croaking.

I should have mention'd before, that in the Autumn of the preceding Year I had form'd most of my ingenious Acquaintance into a Club for mutual Improvement, which we call'd the Junto.[200] We met on Friday Evenings. The Rules I drew up requir'd that every Member in his Turn should produce one or more Queries on any Point of Morals, Politics or Natural Philosophy, to be discuss'd by the Company, and once in three Months produce and read an Essay of his own Writing on any Subject he pleased. Our Debates were to be under the Direction of a President, and to be conducted in the sincere Spirit of Enquiry after Truth, without Fondness for Dispute, or Desire of Victory; and to prevent Warmth all Expressions of Positiveness in Opinion, or of direct Contradiction, were after some time made contraband and prohibited under small pecuniary Penalties. The first Members were Joseph Brientnal,[201] a Copyer of Deeds for the Scriveners; a good-natur'd friendly middle-ag'd Man, a great Lover of Poetry, reading all he could meet with, and writing some that was tolerable; very ingenious in many little Nicknackeries, and of sensible Conversation. Thomas Godfrey, a self-taught Mathematician, great in his Way, and afterwards Inventor of what is now call'd Hadley's Quadrant.[202] But he knew little out of his way, and was not a pleasing Companion, as like most Great Mathematicians I have met with, he expected unusual Precision in every thing said, or was forever denying or distinguishing upon Trifles, to the Disturbance of all Conversation. He soon left us. Nicholas Scull, a Surveyor, afterwards Surveyor-General, Who lov'd Books, and sometimes made

---

[198] A coin worth five shillings.   [199] Failing financially.
[200] Spanish for "joined," a small, secret group; many of its members went on to prominence.
[201] Brientnal (?–1746), who, like Franklin, was intrigued by science.
[202] A navigational instrument like a sextant.

a few Verses. William Parsons, bred a Shoemaker, but loving Reading, had ac-
quir'd a considerable Share of Mathematics, which he first studied with a View to
Astrology that he afterwards laught at. He also became Surveyor General. Wil-
liam Maugridge, a Joiner, a most exquisite Mechanic and a solid sensible Man.
Hugh Meredith, Stephen Potts, and George Webb, I have Characteris'd before.
Robert Grace, a young Gentleman of some Fortune, generous, lively and witty, a
Lover of Punning and of his Friends. And William Coleman,[203] then a Merchant's
Clerk, about my Age, who had the coolest clearest Head, the best Heart, and the
exactest Morals, of almost any Man I ever met with. He became afterwards a
Merchant of great Note, and one of our Provincial Judges: Our Friendship contin-
ued without Interruption to his Death upwards of 40 Years.

And the club continu'd almost as long and was the best School of Philosophy,
Morals and Politics that then existed in the Province; for our Queries which were
read the Week preceding their Discussion, put us on Reading with Attention upon
the several Subjects, that we might speak more to the purpose: and here too we
acquired better Habits of Conversation, every thing being studied in our Rules
which might prevent our disgusting each other. From hence the long Continuance
of the Club, which I shall have frequent Occasion to speak farther of hereafter;
But my giving this Account of it here, is to show something of the Interest I had,
every one of these exerting themselves in recommending Business to us. Brientnal
particularly procur'd us from the Quakers, the Printing 40 Sheets of their History,[204] the rest being to be done by Keimer: and upon this we work'd exceeding
hard, for the Price was low. It was a Folio, Pro Patria Size, in Pica with Long
Primer Notes.[205] I compos'd of it a Sheet a Day, and Meredith work'd it off at
Press. It was often 11 at Night and sometimes later, before I had finish'd my
Distribution[206] for the next days Work: For the little Jobbs sent in by our other
Friends now and then put us back. But so determin'd I was to continue doing a
Sheet a Day of the Folio, that one Night when having impos'd my Forms,[207] I
thought my Days Work over, one of them by accident was broken and two Pages
reduc'd to Pie,[208] I immediately distributed and compos'd it over again before I
went to bed. And this Industry visible to our Neighbours began to give us Character and Credit; particularly I was told, that mention being made of the new Printing Office at the Merchants every-night-Club, the general Opinion was that it must
fail, there being already two Printers in the Place, Keimer and Bradford; but Doctor Baird (whom you and I saw many Years after at his native Place, St. Andrews
in Scotland) gave a contrary Opinion; for the Industry of that Franklin, says he, is
superior to any thing I ever saw of the kind: I see him still at work when I go home
from Club; and he is at Work again before his Neighbours are out of bed. This
struck the rest, and we soon after had Offers from one of them to Supply us with
Stationary. But as yet we did not chuse to engage in Shop Business.

I mention this Industry the more particularly and the more freely, tho' it seems
to be talking in my own Praise, that those of my Posterity who shall read it, may

---

[203] Scull (1687–1761); Parsons (1701–1757), who later became surveyor-general and librarian of
Franklin's Library Company; Maugridge (?–1766), a ship's carpenter; Grace (1709–1766), whose
iron foundry later produced the Franklin stove; Colman (1704–1769).
[204] *The History of the Rise, Increase, and Progress of the Christian People Called Quakers* (1728),
by William Sewel.
[205] A large book set in 12-point type, with notes in 10-point type.
[206] Had returned the letters to their cases to be reused.
[207] Locked the type in preparation for printing.   [208] A confusing mess.

know the Use of that Virtue, when they see its Effects in my Favour throughout this Relation.

George Webb, who had found a Female Friend that lent him wherewith to purchase his Time of Keimer, now came to offer himself as a Journeyman to us. We could not then imploy him, but I foolishly let him know, as a Secret, that I soon intended to begin a Newspaper, and might then have Work for him. My Hopes of Success as I told him were founded on this, that the then only Newspaper,[209] printed by Bradford was a paltry thing, wretchedly manag'd, and no way entertaining; and yet was profitable to him. I therefore thought a good Paper could scarcely fail of good Encouragement. I requested Webb not to mention it, but he told it to Keimer, who immediately, to be beforehand with me, published Proposals for Printing one himself, on which Webb was to be employ'd. I resented this, and to counteract them, as I could not yet begin our Paper, I wrote several Pieces of Entertainment[210] for Bradford's Paper, under the Title of the Busy Body which Brientnal continu'd some Months. By this means the Attention of the Publick was fix'd on that Paper, and Keimers Proposals which we burlesqu'd and ridicul'd, were disregarded. He began his Paper however, and after carrying it on three Quarters of a Year, with at most only 90 Subscribers, he offer'd it to me for a Trifle, and I having been ready some time to go on with it, took it in hand directly, and it prov'd in a few Years extreamly profitable to me.[211]

I perceive that I am apt to speak in the singular Number, though our Partnership still continu'd. The Reason may be, that in fact the whole Management of the Business lay upon me. Meredith was no Compositor, a poor Pressman, and seldom sober. My Friends lamented my Connection with him, but I was to make the best of it.

Our first Papers made a quite different Appearance from any before in the Province, a better Type and better printed: but some spirited Remarks of my Writing on the Dispute then going on between Govr. Burnet and the Massachusetts Assembly, struck the principal People, occasion'd the Paper and the Manager of it to be much talk'd of, and in a few Weeks brought them all to be our Subscribers. Their Example was follow'd by many, and our Number went on growing continually. This was one of the first good Effects of my having learnt a little to scribble. Another was, that the leading Men, seeing a News Paper now in the hands of one who could also handle a Pen, thought it convenient to oblige and encourage me. Bradford still printed the Votes and Laws and other Publick Business. He had printed an Address of the House[212] to the Governor in a coarse blundering manner; We reprinted it elegantly and correctly, and sent one to every Member. They were sensible of the Difference, it strengthen'd the Hands of our Friends in the House, and they voted us their Printers for the Year ensuing.

Among my Friends in the House I must not forget Mr. Hamilton[213] before mentioned, who was now returned from England and had a Seat in it. He interested himself[214] for me strongly in that Instance, as he did in many others after-

---

[209] The *American Weekly Mercury*.

[210] Franklin wrote the first four numbers and parts of two others, appearing in the *American Weekly Mercury* in February and March 1729.

[211] Franklin and Meredith took over Keimer's *The Universal Instructor in all Arts and Sciences: And Pennsylvania Gazette* on October 2, 1729, and shortened the title to the *Pennsylvania Gazette;* the enormously successful paper was published until 1815 (Franklin was connected with it until 1766).

[212] The Pennsylvania Assembly.   [213] Andrew Hamilton was then speaker of the Assembly.

[214] Franklin's note: "I got his Son once £500;" Franklin convinced the legislature to pay Gov. James Hamilton's salary amid disagreements.

wards, continuing his Patronage till his Death. Mr. Vernon about this time put me in mind of the Debt I ow'd him: but did not press me. I wrote him an ingenuous Letter of Acknowledgments, crav'd his Forbearance a little longer which he allow'd me, and as soon as I was able I paid the Principal with Interest and many Thanks. So that *Erratum* was in some degree corrected.

But now another Difficulty came upon me, which I had never the least Reason to expect. Mr. Meredith's Father, who was to have paid for our Printing House according to the Expectations given me, was able to advance only one Hundred Pounds, Currency, which had been paid, and a Hundred more was due to the Merchant; who grew impatient and su'd us all. We gave Bail, but saw that if the Money could not be rais'd in time, the Suit must come to a Judgment and Execution,[215] and our hopeful Prospects must with us be ruined, as the Press and Letters must be sold for Payment, perhaps at half Price. In this Distress two true Friends whose Kindness I have never forgotten nor ever shall forget while I can remember any thing, came to me separately unknown to each other, and without any Application from me, offering each of them to advance me all the Money that should be necessary to enable me to take the whole Business upon my self if that should be practicable, but they did not like my continuing the Partnership with Meredith, who as they said was often seen drunk in the Streets, and playing at low Games in Alehouses, much to our Discredit. These two Friends were William Coleman and Robert Grace. I told them I could not propose a Separation while any Prospect remain'd of the Merediths fulfilling their Part of our Agreement. Because I thought myself under great Obligations to them for what they had done and would do if they could. But if they finally fail'd in their Performance, and our Partnership must be dissolv'd, I should then think myself at Liberty to accept the Assistance of my Friends.

Thus the matter rested for some time. When I said to my Partner, perhaps your Father is dissatisfied at the Part you have undertaken in this Affair of ours, and is unwilling to advance for you and me what he would for you alone: If that is the Case, tell me, and I will resign the whole to you and go about my Business. No says he, my Father has really been disappointed and is really unable; and I am unwilling to distress him farther. I see this is a Business I am not fit for. I was bred a Farmer, and it was a Folly in me to come to Town and put my Self at 30 Years of Age an Apprentice to learn a new Trade. Many of our Welsh People are going to settle in North Carolina where Land is cheap: I am inclin'd to go with them, and follow my old Employment. You may find Friends to assist you. If you will take the Debts of the Company upon you, return to my Father the hundred Pound he has advanc'd, pay my little personal Debts, and give me Thirty Pounds and a new Saddle, I will relinquish the Partnership and leave the whole in your Hands. I agreed to this Proposal. It was drawn up in Writing, sign'd and seal'd immediately. I gave him what he demanded and he went soon after to Carolina; from whence he sent me next Year two long Letters, containing the best Account that had been given of that Country, the Climate, Soil, Husbandry, etc. for in those Matters he was very judicious. I printed them in the Papers,[216] and they gave grate Satisfaction to the Publick.

As soon as he was gone, I recurr'd to my two Friends; and because I would not give an unkind Preference to either, I took half what each had offered and I wanted, of one, and half of the other; paid off the Company Debts, and went on

---

[215] A court-ordered seizure and sale of property.   [216] The *Pennsylvania Gazette*, May 6, 13, 1731.

with the Business in my own Name, advertising that the Partnership was dissolved. I think this was in or about the Year 1729.[217]

About this Time there was a Cry among the People for more Paper-Money, only £15,000 being extant in the Province and that soon to be sunk.[218] The wealthy Inhabitants oppos'd any Addition, being against all Paper Currency, from an Apprehension that it would depreciate as it had done in New England to the Prejudice of all Creditors. We had discuss'd this Point in our Junto, where I was on the Side of an Addition, being persuaded that the first small Sum struck in 1723 had done much good, by increasing the Trade Employment, and Number of Inhabitants in the Province, since I now saw all the old Houses inhabited, and many new ones building, where as I remember'd well, that when I first walk'd about the Streets of Philadelphia, eating my Roll, I saw most of the Houses in Walnut street between Second and Front streets with Bills[219] on their Doors, to be let; and many likewise in Chestnut Street, and other Streets; which made me then think the Inhabitants of the City were one after another deserting it. Our Debates possess'd me so fully of the Subject, that I wrote and printed an anonymous Pamphlet on it, entituled, *The Nature and Necessity of a Paper Currency*.[220] It was well receiv'd by the common People in general; but the Rich Men dislik'd it; for it increas'd and strengthen'd the Clamour for more Money; and they happening to have no Writers among them that were able to answer it, their Opposition slacken'd, and the Point was carried by a Majority in the House. My Friends there, who conceiv'd I had been of some Service, thought fit to reward me, by employing me in printing the Money, a very profitable Jobb, and a great Help to me.[221] This was another Advantage gain'd by my being able to write. The Utility of this Currency became by Time and Experience so evident, as never afterwards to be much disputed, so that it grew soon to £55000, and in 1739 to £80,000 since which it arose during War to upwards of £350,000. Trade, Building and Inhabitants all the while increasing. Tho' I now think there are Limits beyond which the Quantity may be hurtful.

I soon after obtain'd, thro' my Friend Hamilton, the Printing of the New Castle Paper Money,[222] another profitable Jobb, as I then thought it; small Things appearing great to those in small Circumstances. And these to me were really great Advantages, as they were great Encouragements. He procured me also the Printing of the Laws and Votes of that Government which continu'd in my Hands as long as I follow'd the Business.

I now open'd a little Stationer's Shop.[223] I had in it Blanks of all Sorts the correctest that ever appear'd among us, being assisted in that by my Friend Brientnal; I had also Paper, Parchment, Chapmen's Books, etc. One Whitemash[224] a Compositor I had known in London, an excellent Workman now came to me and work'd with me constantly and diligently, and I took an Apprentice the Son of Aquila Rose. I began now gradually to pay off the Debt I was under for the Printing-House. In order to secure my Credit and Character as a Tradesman, I took

---

[217] Actually, July 14, 1730; Meredith's name remained on the paper until May 11, 1732.
[218] Removed from circulation as it was worth so little.   [219] Posters.
[220] *A Modest Inquiry Into the Nature and Necessity of a Paper-Currency* (1729).
[221] Actually, Andrew Bradford printed £20,000 in 1729; Franklin was contracted to print £40,000 in 1731, for which he received £100 plus expenses.
[222] Delaware had the same proprietary governor as Pennsylvania then but a separate legislature; Andrew Hamilton presided over both Assemblies.
[223] About July 1730.   [224] Thomas Whitemarsh (?–1733), who left the next year for South Carolina.

care not only to be in *Reality* Industrious and frugal, but to avoid all *Appearances* of the Contrary. I drest plainly; I was seen at no Places of idle Diversion; I never went out a-fishing or shooting; a Book, indeed, sometimes debauch'd me from my Work; but that was seldom, snug, and gave no Scandal: and to show that I was not above my Business, I sometimes brought home the Paper I purchas'd at the Stores, thro' the Streets on a Wheelbarrow. Thus being esteem'd an industrious thriving young Man, and paying duly for what I bought, the Merchants who imported Stationary solicited my Custom, others propos'd supplying me with Books, and I went on swimmingly. In the mean time Keimer's Credit and Business declining daily, he was at last forc'd to sell his Printing-house to satisfy his Creditors. He went to Barbadoes, and there lived some Years, in very poor Circumstances.

His Apprentice David Harry, whom I had instructed while I work'd with him, set up in his Place at Philadelphia, having bought his Materials. I was at first apprehensive of a powerful Rival in Harry, as his Friends were very able, and had a good deal of Interest. I therefore propos'd a Partnership to him; which he, fortunately for me, rejected with Scorn. He was very proud, dress'd like a Gentleman, liv'd expensively, took much Diversion and Pleasure abroad, ran in debt, and neglected his Business, upon which all Business left him; and finding nothing to do, he follow'd Keimer to Barbadoes; taking the Printinghouse with him. There this Apprentice employ'd his former Master as a Journeyman. They quarrel'd often. Harry went continually behindhand, and at length was forc'd to sell his Types, and return to his Country Work in Pensilvania. The Person that bought them, employ'd Keimer to use them, but in a few years he died. There remain'd now no Competitor with me at Philadelphia, but the old one, Bradford, who was rich and easy, did a little Printing now and then by straggling Hands, but was not very anxious about the Business. However, as he kept the Post Office, it was imagined he had better Opportunities of obtaining News, his Paper was thought a better Distributer of Advertisements than mine, and therefore had many more, which was a profitable thing to him and a Disadvantage to me. For tho' I did indeed receive and send Papers by Post, yet the publick Opinion was otherwise; for what I did send was by Bribing the Riders[225] who took them privately: Bradford being unkind enough to forbid it: which occasion'd some Resentment on my Part; and I thought so meanly of him for it, that when I afterwards came into his Situation,[226] I took care never to imitate it.

I had hitherto continu'd to board with Godfrey who lived in Part of my House with his Wife and Children, and had one Side of the Shop for his Glazier's Business, tho' he work'd little, being always absorb'd in his Mathematics. Mrs. Godfrey projected a Match for me with a Relation's Daughter, took Opportunities of bringing us often together, till a serious Courtship on my Part ensu'd, the Girl being in herself very deserving. The old Folks encourag'd me by continual Invitations to Supper, and by leaving us together, till at length it was time to explain. Mrs. Godfrey manag'd our little Treaty. I let her know that I expected as much Money with their Daughter as would pay off my Remaining Debt for the Printinghouse,[227] which I believe was not then above a Hundred Pounds. She brought me

---

[225] Bribing the postal carriers to deliver the paper the same day as Bradford's.
[226] Franklin succeeded Bradford as Philadelphia's postmaster in 1737 and was named deputy postmaster-general of the colonies in 1753.
[227] Marriages were customarily arranged for financial reasons.

Word they had no such Sum to spare. I said they might mortgage their House in the Loan Office. The Answer to this after some Days was, that they did not approve the Match; that on Enquiry of Bradford they had been inform'd the Printing Business was not a profitable one, the Types would soon be worn out and more wanted, that S. Keimer and D. Harry had fail'd one after the other, and I should probably soon follow them; and therefore I was forbidden the House, and the Daughter shut up. Whether this was a real Change of Sentiment, or only Artifice, on a Supposition of our being too far engag'd in Affection to retract, and therefore that we should steal a Marriage, which would leave them at Liberty to give or withold what they pleas'd, I know not: But I suspected the latter, resented it, and went no more. Mrs. Godfrey brought me afterwards some more favourable Accounts of their Disposition, and would have drawn me on again: but I declared absolutely my Resolution to have nothing more to do with that Family. This was resented by the Godfreys, we differ'd, and they removed, leaving me the whole House, and I resolved to take no more Inmates.

But this Affair having turn'd my Thoughts to Marriage, I look'd round me, and made Overtures of Acquaintance in other Places; but soon found that the Business of a Printer being generally thought a poor one, I was not to expect Money with a Wife unless with such a one, as I should not otherwise think agreable. In the mean time, that hard-to-be-govern'd Passion of Youth, had hurried me frequently into Intrigues with low Women that fell in my Way, which were attended with some Expence and great Inconvenience, besides a continual Risque to my Health by a Distemper[228] which of all Things I dreaded, tho' by great good Luck I escaped it.

A friendly Correspondence as Neighbours and old Acquaintances, had continued between me and Mrs. Read's Family, who all had a Regard for me from the time of my first Lodging in their House. I was often invited there and consulted in their Affairs, wherein I sometimes was of service. I pity'd poor Miss Read's unfortunate Situation, who was generally dejected, seldom chearful, and avoided Company. I consider'd my Giddiness and Inconstancy when in London as in a great degree the Cause of her Unhappiness; tho' the Mother was good enough to think the Fault more her own than mine, as she had prevented our Marrying before I went thither, and persuaded the other Match in my Absence. Our mutual Affection was revived, but there were now great Objections to our Union. That Match was indeed look'd upon as invalid, a preceding Wife being said to be living in England; but this could not easily be prov'd, because of the Distance. And tho' there was a Report of his Death, it was not certain. Then tho' it should be true, he had left many Debts which his Successor might be call'd on to pay. We ventured however, over all these Difficulties, and I [took] her to Wife Sept. 1. 1730.[229] None of the Inconveniencies happened that we had apprehended, she prov'd a good and faithful Helpmate, assisted me much by attending the Shop, we throve together, and have ever mutually endeavour'd to make each other happy. Thus I corrected that great *Erratum* as well as I could.

About this Time our Club meeting, not at a Tavern, but in a little Room of Mr. Grace's set apart for that Purpose; a Proposition was made by me that since our Books were often referr'd to in our Disquisitions upon the Queries, it might be

---

[228] Syphilis.

[229] Read could not get her marriage to John Rogers annulled as she lacked full proof of his previous marriage in England, and Pennsylvania had no divorce law; had she and Franklin been "officially" married, they both could have been convicted of bigamy and imprisoned for life, but their common-law marriage was widely accepted.

convenient to us to have them all together where we met, that upon Occasion they might be consulted; and by thus clubbing our Books to a common Library, we should, while we lik'd to keep them together, have each of us the Advantage of using the Books of all the other Members, which would be nearly as beneficial as if each owned the whole. It was lik'd and agreed to, and we fill'd one End of the Room with such Books as we could best spare. The Number was not so great as we expected; and tho' they had been of great Use, yet some Inconveniencies occurring for want of due Care of them, the collection after about a Year was separated, and each took his Books home again.

And now I set on foot my first Project of a public Nature, that for a Subscription Library. I drew up the Proposals, got them put into Form by our great Scrivener Brockden, and by the help of my Friends in the Junto, procur'd Fifty Subscribers of 40s. each to begin with and 10s. a Year for 50 Years, the Term our Company was to continue. We afterwards obtain'd a Charter, the Company[230] being increas'd to 100. This was the Mother of all the N American Subscription Libraries now so numerous. It is become a great thing itself, and continually increasing. These Libraries have improv'd the general Conversation of the Americans, made the common Tradesmen and Farmers as intelligent as most Gentlemen from other Countries, and perhaps have contributed in some degree to the Stand so generally made throughout the Colonies in Defence of their Privileges.

Two Letters

Memo.

Thus far was written with the Intention express'd in the Beginning and therefore contains several little family Anecdotes of no Importance to others. What follows was written many Years after in compliance with the Advice contain'd in these Letters, and accordingly intended for the Publick. The Affairs of the Revolution occasion'd the Interruption.

Letter from Mr. Abel James[231] with Notes of my Life, to be here inserted. Also Letter from Mr. Vaughan[232] to the same purpose

My dear and honored Friend.

I have often been desirous of writing to thee, but could not be reconciled to the Thoughts that the Letter might fall into the Hands of the British, lest some Printer or busy Body should publish some Part of the Contents and give our Friends Pain and myself Censure.

Some Time since there fell into my Hands to my great Joy about 23 Sheets in thy own hand-writing containing an Account of the Parentage and Life of thyself, directed to thy Son ending in the Year 1730 with which there were Notes likewise in thy writing, a Copy of which I inclose in Hopes it may be a means if thou

---

[230] The Library Company of Philadelphia, the first circulating library in North America, founded by Franklin in 1731.

[231] James (1726?–1790) was a Quaker merchant in Philadelphia; he wrote the following letter to Franklin in 1782 while the colonies were at war with the British. Franklin's "Notes" were his outline of the autobiography.

[232] Benjamin Vaughan (1751–1835), English diplomat who edited the first collection of Franklin's work (1779) and was Franklin's personal emissary during and after the negotiation of the Treaty of Paris (1782–1785).

continuedst it up to a later period, that the first and latter part may be put together, and if it is not yet continued, I hope thou wilt not delay it, Life is uncertain as the Preacher tells us, and what will the World say if kind, humane and benevolent Ben Franklin should leave his Friends and the World deprived of so pleasing and profitable a Work, a Work which would be useful and entertaining not only to a few, but to millions.

The Influence Writings under that Class have on the Minds of Youth is very great, and has no where appeared so plain as in our public Friend's Journal. It almost insensibly leads the Youth into the Resolution of endeavouring to become as good and as eminent as the Journalist. Should thine for Instance when published, and I think it could not fail of it, lead the Youth to equal the Industry and Temperance of thy early Youth, what a Blessing with that Class would such a Work be. I know of no Character living nor many of them put together, who has so much in his Power as Thyself to promote a greater Spirit of Industry and early Attention to Business, Frugality and Temperance with the American Youth. Not that I think the Work would have no other Merit and Use in the World, far from it, but the first is of such vast Importance, that I know nothing that can equal it. . . . [233]   ABEL JAMES

The foregoing letter and the minutes accompanying it being shewn to a friend, I received from him the following:

Paris, January 31, 1783.

My dearest sir,

When I had read over your sheets of minutes of the principal incidents of your life, recovered for you by your Quaker acquaintance; I told you I would send you a letter expressing my reasons why I thought it would be useful to complete and publish it as he desired. Various concerns have for some time past prevented this letter being written, and I do not know whether it was worth any expectation: happening to be at leisure however at present, I shall by writing at least interest and instruct myself; but as the terms I am inclined to use may tend to offend a person of your manners, I shall only tell you how I would address any other person, who was as good and as great as yourself, but less diffident. I would say to him, Sir, I *solicit* the history of your life from the following motives.

Your history is so remarkable, that if you do not give it, somebody else will certainly give it; and perhaps so as nearly to do as much harm, as your own management of the thing might do good.

It will moreover present a table of the internal circumstances of your country, which will very much tend to invite to it settlers of virtuous and manly minds. And considering the eagerness with which such information is sought by them, and the extent of your reputation, I do not know of a more efficacious advertisement than your Biography would give.

All that has happened to you is also connected with the detail of the manners and situation of a *rising* people; and in this respect I do not think that the writings of Caesar and Tacitus[234] can be more interesting to a true judge of human nature and society.

---

[233] Ellipses are part of the Labaree et al. edition.

[234] Gaius Julius Caesar (100–44 B.C.) and Publius Cornelius Tacitus (A.D. 55?–118?), Roman statesmen also known for the histories they wrote.

But these, Sir, are small reasons in my opinion, compared with the chance which your life will give for the forming of future great men; and in conjunction with your Art of Virtue,[235] (which you design to publish) of improving the features of private character, and consequently of aiding all happiness both public and domestic.

The two works I allude to, Sir, will in particular give a noble rule and example of *self-education*. School and other education constantly proceed upon false principles, and shew a clumsy apparatus pointed at a false mark; but your apparatus is simple, and the mark a true one; and while parents and young persons are left destitute of other just means of estimating and becoming prepared for a reasonable course in life, your discovery that the thing is in many a man's private power, will be invaluable!

Influence upon the private character late in life, is not only an influence late in life, but a weak influence. It is in *youth* that we plant our chief habits and prejudices; it is in youth that we take our party[236] as to profession, pursuits, and matrimony. In youth therefore the turn is given; in youth the education even of the next generation is given; in youth the private and public character is determined; and the term of life extending but from youth to age, life ought to begin well from youth; and more especially *before* we take our party as to our principal objects.

But your Biography will not merely teach self-education, but the education of a *wise man;* and the wisest man will receive lights and improve his progress, by seeing detailed the conduct of another wise man. And why are weaker men to be deprived of such helps, when we see our race has been blundering on in the dark, almost without a guide in this particular, from the farthest trace of time? Shew then, Sir, how much is to be done, *both to sons and fathers;* and invite all wise men to become like yourself; and other men to become wise.

When we see how cruel statesmen and warriors can be to the humble race, and how absurd distinguished men can be to their acquaintance, it will be instructive to observe the instances multiply of pacific acquiescing manners; and to find how compatible it is to be great and *domestic;* enviable and yet *good-humored*.

The little private incidents which you will also have to relate, will have considerable use, as we want above all things, *rules of prudence in ordinary affairs;* and it will be curious to see how you have acted in these. It will be so far a sort of key to life, and explain many things that all men ought to have once explained to them, to give them a chance of becoming wise by foresight.

The nearest thing to having experience of one's own, is to have other people's affairs brought before us in a shape that is interesting; this is sure to happen from your pen. Your affairs and management will have an air of simplicity or importance that will not fail to strike; and I am convinced you have conducted them with as much originality as if you had been conducting discussions in politics or philosophy; and what more worthy of experiments and system, (its importance and its errors considered) than human life!

Some men have been virtuous blindly, others have speculated fantastically, and others have been shrewd to bad purposes; but you, Sir, I am sure, will give under your hand, nothing but what is at the same moment, wise, practical, and good.

---

[235] Franklin intended to write "The Art of Virtue" for the benefit of youth; Part Two of his autobiography is partly Franklin's attempt at that.
[236] Make our decisions.

Your account of yourself (for I suppose the parallel I am drawing for Dr. Franklin, will hold not only in point of character but of private history), will shew that you are ashamed of no origin; a thing the more important, as you prove how little necessary all origin is to happiness, virtue, or greatness.

As no end likewise happens without a means, so we shall find, Sir, that even you yourself framed a plan by which you became considerable; but at the same time we may see that though the event is flattering, the means are as simple as wisdom could make them; that is, depending upon nature, virtue, thought, and habit.

Another thing demonstrated will be the propriety of every man's waiting for his time for appearing upon the stage of the world. Our sensations being very much fixed to the moment, we are apt to forget that more moments are to follow the first, and consequently that man should arrange his conduct so as to suit the *whole* of a life. Your attribution appears to have been applied to your *life,* and the passing moments of it have been enlivened with content and enjoyment, instead of being tormented with foolish impatience or regrets. Such a conduct is easy for those who make virtue and themselves their standard, and who try to keep themselves in countenance by examples of other truly great men, of whom patience is so often the characteristic.

Your Quaker correspondent, Sir, (for here again I will suppose the subject of my letter resembling Dr. Franklin,) praised your frugality, diligence, and temperance, which he considered as a pattern for all youth: but it is singular that he should have forgotten your modesty, and your disinterestedness, without which you never could have waited for your advancement, or found your situation in the mean time comfortable; which is a strong lesson to shew the poverty of glory, and the importance of regulating our minds.

If this correspondent had know the nature of your reputation as well as I do, he would have said; your former writings and measures would secure attention to your Biography and Art of Virtue; and your Biography and Art of Virtue, in return, would secure attention to them. This is an advantage attendant upon a various character, and which brings all that belongs to it into greater play; and it is the more useful, as perhaps more persons are at a loss for the *means* of improving their minds and characters, than they are for the time or the inclination to do it.

But there is one concluding reflection, Sir, that will shew the use of your life as a mere piece of biography. This style of writing seems a little gone out of vogue, and yet it is a very useful one; and your specimen of it may be particularly serviceable, as it will make a subject of comparison with the lives of various public cutthroats and intriguers, and with absurd monastic self-tormentors, or vain literary triflers. If it encourages more writings of the same kind with your own, and induces more men to spend lives fit to be written; it will be worth all Plutarch's Lives put together.

But being tired of figuring to myself a character of which every feature suits only one man in the world, without giving him the praise of it; I shall end my letter, my dear Dr. Franklin, with a personal application to your proper self.

I am earnestly desirous then, my dear Sir, that you should let the world into the traits of your genuine character, as civil broils may otherwise tend to disguise or traduce it. Considering your great age, the caution of your character, and your peculiar style of thinking, it is not likely that any one besides yourself can be sufficiently master of the facts of your life, or the intentions of your mind.

Besides all this, the immense revolution of the present period, will necessarily turn our attention towards the author of it; and when virtuous principles have been pretended in it, it will be highly important to shew that such have really influenced; and, as your own character will be the principal one to receive a scrutiny, it is proper (even for its effects upon your vast and rising country, as well as upon England and upon Europe), that it should stand respectable and eternal. For the furtherance of human happiness, I have always maintained that it is necessary to prove that man is not even at present a vicious and detestable animal; and still more to prove that good management may greatly amend him; and it is for much the same reason, that I am anxious to see the opinion established, that there are fair characters existing among the individuals of the race; for the moment that all men, without exception, shall be conceived abandoned, good people will cease efforts deemed to be hopeless, and perhaps think of taking their share in the scramble of life, or at least of making it comfortable principally for themselves.

Take then, my dear Sir, this work most speedily into hand: shew yourself good as you are good, temperate as you are temperate; and above all things, prove yourself as one who from your infancy have loved justice, liberty, and concord, in a way that has made it natural and consistent for you to have acted, as we have seen you act in the last seventeen years of your life. Let Englishmen be made not only to respect, but even to love you. When they think well of individuals in your native country, they will go nearer to thinking well of your country; and when your countrymen see themselves well thought of by Englishmen, they will go nearer to thinking well of England. Extend your views even further; do not stop at those who speak the English tongue, but after having settled so many points in nature and politics, think of bettering the whole race of men.

As I have not read any part of the life in question, but know only the character that lived it, I write somewhat at hazard. I am sure however, that the life, and the treatise I allude to (on the Art of Virtue), will necessarily fulfil the chief of my expectations; and still more so if you take up the measure of suiting these performances to the several views above stated. Should they even prove unsuccessful in all that a sanguine admirer of yours hopes from them, you will at least have framed pieces to interest the human mind; and whoever gives a feeling of pleasure that is innocent to man, has added so much to the fair side of a life otherwise too much darkened by anxiety, and too much injured by pain.

In the hope therefore that you will listen to the prayer addressed to you in this letter, I beg to subscribe myself, my dearest Sir, etc., etc.

Benj. Vaughan.

Part Two

Continuation of the Account of my Life

Begun at Passy[1] 1784

It is some time since I receiv'd the above Letters, but I have been too busy till now to think of complying with the Request they contain. It might too be much better done if I were at home among my Papers, which would aid my Memory and help

---

[1] A Paris suburb; Franklin stayed at the Hotel de Valentois in Passy while he was negotiating the Treaty of Paris. Although the treaty was signed September 3, 1783, ending the Revolutionary War, Franklin remained in Paris as minister until July 1785.

to ascertain Dates. But my Return being uncertain, and having just now a little Leisure, I will endeavour to recollect and write what I can; if I live to get home, it may there be corrected and improv'd.

Not having any Copy here of what is already written, I know not whether an Account is given of the means I used to establish the Philadelphia publick Library, which from a small Beginning is now become so considerable, though I remember to have come down to near the Time of that Transaction, 1730. I will therefore begin here, with an Account of it, which may be struck out if found to have been already given.

At the time I establish'd my self in Pensylvania, there was not a good Bookseller's Shop in any of the Colonies to the Southward of Boston. In New-York and Philadelphia the Printers were indeed Stationers, they sold only Paper, etc., Almanacks, Ballads, and a few common School Books. Those who lov'd Reading were oblig'd to send for their Books from England. The Members of the Junto had each a few. We had left the Alehouse where we first met, and hired a Room to hold our Club in. I propos'd that we should all of us bring our Books to that Room, where they would not only be ready to consult in our Conferences, but become a common Benefit, each of us being at Liberty to borrow such as he wish'd to read at home. This was accordingly done, and for some time contented us. Finding the Advantage of this little Collection, I propos'd to render the Benefit from Books more common by commencing a Public Subscription Library. I drew a Sketch of the Plan and Rules that would be necessary, and got a skilful Conveyancer, Mr. Charles Brockden to put the whole in Form of Articles of Agreement to be subscribed; by which each Subscriber engag'd to pay a certain Sum down for the first Purchase of Books and an annual Contribution for encreasing them. So few were the Readers at that time in Philadelphia, and the Majority of us so poor, that I was not able with great Industry to find more than Fifty Persons, mostly young Tradesmen, willing to pay down for this purpose Forty shillings each, and Ten Shillings per Annum. On this little Fund we began. The Books were imported. The Library was open one Day in the Week for lending them to the Subscribers, on their Promisory Notes to pay Double the Value if not duly returned. The Institution soon manifested its Utility, was imitated by other Towns and in other Provinces, the Librarys were augmented by Donations, Reading became fashionable, and our People having no publick Amusements to divert their Attention from Study became better acquainted with Books, and in a few Years were observ'd by Strangers to be better instructed and more intelligent than People of the same Rank generally are in other Countries.

When we were about to sign the above-mentioned Articles, which were to be binding on us, our Heirs, etc., for fifty Years, Mr Brockden, the Scrivener, said to us, "You are young Men, but it is scarce probable that any of you will live to see the Expiration of the Term fix'd in this Instrument." A Number of us, however, are yet living: But the Instrument was after a few Years rendered null by a Charter that incorporated and gave Perpetuity to the Company.

The Objections, and Reluctances I met with in Soliciting the Subscriptions, made me soon feel the Impropriety of presenting one's self as the Proposer of any useful Project that might be suppos'd to raise one's Reputation in the smallest degree above that of one's Neighbours, when one has need of their Assistance to accomplish that Project. I therefore put my self as much as I could out of sight, and stated it as a Scheme of a *Number of Friends,* who had requested me to go about and propose it to such as they thought Lovers of Reading. In this way my Affair went on more smoothly, and I ever after practis'd it on such Occasions; and from my frequent Successes, can heartily recommend it. The present little Sacrifice of your Vanity will afterwards be amply repaid. If it remains a while uncertain to whom the Merit belongs, some one more vain than yourself will be encourag'd to claim it, and then even Envy will be dispos'd to do you Justice, by plucking those assum'd Feathers, and restoring them to their right Owner.

This Library afforded me the means of Improvement by constant Study, for which I set apart an Hour or two each Day; and thus repair'd in some Degree the Loss of the Learned Education my Father once intended for me. Reading was the only Amusement I allow'd my self. I spent no time in Taverns, Games, or Frolicks of any kind. And my Industry in my Business continu'd as indefatigable as it was necessary. I was in debt for my Printing-house, I had a young Family[2] coming on to be educated, and I had to contend with for Business two Printers who were establish'd in the Place before me. My Circumstances however grew daily easier: my original Habits of Frugality continuing. And my Father having among his Instructions to me when a Boy, frequently repeated a Proverb of Solomon, *"Seest thou a Man diligent in his Calling, he shall stand before Kings, he shall not stand before mean Men."*[3] I from thence consider'd Industry as a Means of obtaining Wealth and Distinction, which encourag'd me, tho' I did not think that I should ever literally stand before Kings, which however has since happened.—for I have stood before five,[4] and even had the honour of sitting down with one, the King of Denmark, to Dinner.

We have an English Proverb that says,

> He that would thrive
> Must ask his Wife;

it was lucky for me that I had one as much dispos'd to Industry and Frugality as my self. She assisted me chearfully in by Business, folding and stitching Pamphlets, tending Shop, purchasing old Linen Rags for the Paper-makers, etc., etc. We kept no idle Servants, our Table was plain and simple, our Furniture of the cheapest. For instance my Breakfast was a long time Bread and Milk, (no Tea) and I ate it out of a twopenny earthen Porringer[5] with a Pewter Spoon. But mark how Luxury will enter Families, and make a Progress, in Spite of Principle. Being call'd one Morning to Breakfast, I found it in a China Bowl with a Spoon of Silver. They had been bought for me without my Knowledge by my Wife, and had cost her the enormous Sum of three and twenty Shillings, for which she had no other Excuse or Apology to make, but that she thought *her* Husband deserv'd a Silver Spoon and China Bowl as well as any of his Neighbours. This was the first Appearance of Plate[6] and China in our House, which afterwards in a Course of Years as our Wealth encreas'd augmented gradually to several Hundred Pounds in Value.

I had been religiously educated as a Presbyterian, and tho' some of the Dogmas of the Persuasion, such as the Eternal Decrees of God, Election,[7] Reprobation, etc., appear'd to me unintelligible, others doubtful, and I early absented myself

---

[2] William, known as Billy; Frances Folger (1732–1736), known as Frankie; and Sarah (1743–?), known as Sally.

[3] Proverbs 22:29.

[4] King Christian VI of Denmark, Kings Louis XV and XVI of France, and Kings George II and III of Great Britain.

[5] A porridge bowl.   [6] Silver-plated ware.   [7] Selection for salvation by God.

from the Public Assemblies of the Sect, Sunday being my Studying-Day, I never was without some religious Principles; I never doubted, for instance, the Existance of the Deity, that he made the World, and govern'd it by his Providence; that the most acceptable Service of God was the doing Good to Man; that our Souls are immortal; and that all Crime will be punished and Virtue rewarded either here or hereafter; these I esteem'd the Essentials of every Religion, and being to be found in all the Religions we had in our Country I respected them all, tho' with different degrees of Respect as I found them more or less mix'd with other Articles which without any Tendency to inspire, promote or confirm Morality, serv'd principally to divide us and make us unfriendly to one another. This Respect to all, with an Opinion that the worst had some good Effects, induc'd me to avoid all Discourse that might tend to lessen the good Opinion another might have of his own Religion; and as our Province increas'd in People and new Places of worship were continually wanted, and generally erected by voluntary Contribution, my Mite[8] for such purpose, whatever might be the Sect, was never refused.

Tho' I seldom attended any Public Worship, I had still an Opinion of its Propriety, and of its Utility when rightly conducted, and I regularly paid my annual Subscription for the Support of the only Presbyterian Minister or Meeting we had in Philadelphia.[9] He us'd to visit me sometimes as a Friend, and admonish me to attend his Administrations, and I was now and then prevail'd on to do so, once for five Sundays successively. Had he been, *in my Opinion,* a good Preacher perhaps I might have continued, notwithstanding the occasion I had for the Sunday's Leisure in my Course of Study: But his Discourses were chiefly either polemic Arguments, or Explications of the peculiar Doctrines of our Sect, and were all to me very dry, uninteresting and unedifying, since not a single moral Principle was inculcated or enforc'd, their Aim seeming to be rather to make us Presbyterians than good Citizens. At length he took for his Text that Verse of the 4th Chapter of Philippians, *Finally, Brethren, Whatsoever Things are true, honest, just, pure, lovely, or of good report, if there be any virtue, or any praise, think on these Things;*[10] and I imagin'd in a Sermon on such a Text, we could not miss of having some Morality: But he confin'd himself to five Points only as meant by the Apostle, viz. 1. Keeping holy the Sabbath Day. 2. Being diligent in Reading the Holy Scriptures. 3. Attending duly the Publick Worship. 4. Partaking of the Sacrament. 5. Paying a due Respect to God's Ministers. These might be all good Things, but as they were not the kind of good Things that I expected from that Text, I despaired of ever meeting with them from any other, was disgusted, and attended his Preaching no more. I had some Years before compos'd a little Liturgy or Form of Prayer for my own private Use, viz, in 1728. entitled, *Articles of Belief and Acts of Religion.* I return'd to the Use of this, and went no more to the public Assemblies. My Conduct might be blameable, but I leave it without attempting farther to excuse it, my present purpose being to relate Facts, and not to make Apologies for them.

It was about this time that I conceiv'd the bold and arduous Project of arriving at moral Perfection. I wish'd to live without committing any Fault at any time; I would conquer all that either Natural Inclination, Custom, or Company might lead me into. As I knew, or thought I knew, what was right and wrong, I did not see why I might not *always* do the one and avoid the other. But I soon found I had undertaken a Task of more Difficulty than I had imagined. While my *Attention*

---

[8] Small contribution.   [9] Rev. Jedediah Andrews.   [10] A paraphrase of Philippians 4:8.

was taken up in guarding against one Fault, I was often surpriz'd by another. Habit took the Advantage of Inattention. Inclination was sometimes too strong for Reason. I concluded at length, that the mere speculative Conviction that it was our Interest to be compleatly virtuous, was not sufficient to prevent our Slipping, and that the contrary Habits must be broken and good ones acquired and established, before we can have any Dependance on a steady uniform Rectitude of Conduct. For this purpose I therefore contriv'd the following Method.

In the various Enumerations of the moral Virtues I had met with in my Reading, I found the Catalogue more or less numerous, as different Writers included more or fewer Ideas under the same Name. Temperance, for Example, was by some confin'd to Eating and Drinking, while by others it was extended to mean the moderating every other Pleasure, Appetite, Inclination or Passion, bodily or mental, even to our Avarice and Ambition. I propos'd to myself, for the sake of Clearness, to use rather more Names with fewer Ideas annex'd to each, than a few Names with more Ideas; and I included under Thirteen Names of Virtues all that at that time occurr'd to me as necessary or desirable, and annex'd to each a short Precept, which fully express'd the Extent I gave to its Meaning.

These Names of Virtues with their Precepts were

1. TEMPERANCE.

Eat not to Dulness.
Drink not to Elevation.

2. SILENCE.

Speak not but what may benefit others or yourself. Avoid trifling Conversation.

3. ORDER.

Let all your Things have their Places. Let each Part of your Business have its Time.

4. RESOLUTION.

Resolve to perform what you ought. Perform without fail what you resolve.

5. FRUGALITY.

Make no Expence but to do good to others or yourself: i.e. Waste nothing.

6. INDUSTRY.

Lose no Time. Be always employ'd in something useful. Cut off all unnecessary Actions.

7. SINCERITY.

Use no hurtful Deceit.
Think innocently and justly; and, if you speak, speak accordingly.

8. Justice.

Wrong none, by doing Injuries or omitting the Benefits that are your Duty.

9. Moderation.

Avoid Extreams. Forbear resenting Injuries so much as you think they deserve.

10. Cleanliness.

Tolerate no Uncleanness in Body, Cloaths or Habitation.

11. Tranquility.

Be not disturbed at Trifles, or at Accidents common or unavoidable.

12. Chastity.

Rarely use Venery but for Health or Offspring; Never to Dulness, Weakness, or the Injury of your own or another's Peace or Reputation.

13. Humility.

Imitate Jesus and Socrates.

My Intention being to acquire the *Habitude* of all these Virtues, I judg'd it would be well not to distract my Attention by attempting the whole at once, but to fix it on one of them at a time, and when I should be Master of that, then to proceed to another, and so on till I should have gone thro' the thirteen. And as the previous Acquisition of some might facilitate the Acquisition of certain others, I arrang'd them with that View as they stand above. *Temperance* first, as it tends to procure that Coolness and Clearness of Head, which is so necessary where constant Vigilance was to be kept up, and Guard maintained, against the unremitting Attraction of ancient Habits, and the Force of perpetual Temptations. this being acquir'd and establish'd, *Silence* would be more easy, and my Desire being to gain Knowledge at the same time that I improv'd in Virtue, and considering that in Conversation it was obtain'd rather by the use of the Ears than of the Tongue, and therefore wishing to break a Habit I was getting into of Prattling, Punning and Joking, which only made me acceptable to trifling Company, I gave *Silence* the second Place. This, and the next, *Order,* I expected would allow me more Time for attending to my Project and my Studies; Resolution, once become habitual, would keep me firm in my Endeavours to obtain all the subsequent Virtues; *Frugality* and *Industry,* by freeing me from my remaining Debt, and producing Affluence and Independance, would make more easy the Practice of *Sincerity* and *Justice,* etc., etc. Conceiving then that agreable to the Advice of Pythagoras[11] in his

---

[11] Pythagoras (6th century B.C.) was a Greek mathematician and philosopher; his "Golden Verses" were translated in Franklin's note: "Let sleep not close your eyes till you have thrice examined the transactions of the day: where have I strayed, what have I done, what good have I omitted?"

Golden Verses daily Examination would be necessary, I contriv'd the following Method for conducting that Examination.

I made a little Book in which I allotted a Page for each of the Virtues. I rul'd each Page with red Ink, so as to have seven Columns, one for each Day of the Week, marking each Column with a Letter for the Day. I cross'd these Columns with thirteen red Lines, marking the Beginning of each Line with the first Letter of one of the Virtues, on which Line and in its proper Column I might mark by a little black Spot every Fault I found upon Examination to have been committed respecting that Virtue upon that Day.

I determined to give a Week's strict Attention to each of the Virtues successively. Thus in the first Week my great Guard was to avoid every the least Offence against Temperance, leaving the other Virtues to their ordinary Chance, only marking every Evening the Faults of the Day. Thus if in the first Week I could keep my first Line marked T clear of Spots, I suppos'd the Habit of that Virtue so much strengthen'd and its opposite weaken'd, that I might venture extending my Attention to include the next, and for the following Week keep both Lines clear of Spots. Proceeding thus to the last, I could go thro' a Course compleat in Thirteen Weeks, and four Courses a Year. And like him who having a Garden to weed, does not attempt to eradicate all the bad Herbs at once, which would exceed his Reach and his Strength, but works on one of the Beds at a time, and having accomplish'd the first proceeds to a Second; so I should have, (I hoped) the encouraging Pleasure of seeing on my Pages the Progress I made in Virtue, by clearing successively my Lines of their Spots, till in the End by a Number of Courses, I should be happy in viewing a clean Book after thirteen Weeks daily Examination.

Form of the Pages

Temperance.						
Eat not to Dulness. *Drink not to Elevation.*						
	S	M	T	W	T	F	S
---	---	---	---	---	---	---	---
T							
S	••	•		•		•	
O	•	•	•		•	•	•
R			•			•	
F		•			•		
I			•	•			
S							
J							
M							
Cl.							
T							
Ch.							
H							

This my little Book had for its Motto these Lines from Addison's *Cato*;[12]

Here will I hold: If there is a Pow'r above us,
(And that there is, all Nature cries aloud

---

[12] Joseph Addison's *Cato, A Tragedy* (1713), v.i.15–18.

Thro' all her Works) he must delight in Virtue,
And that which he delights in must be happy.

Another from Cicero.[13]

O Vitœ Philosophia Dux! O Virtutum indagatrix, expultrixque vitiorum! Unus
dies bene, et ex preceptis tuis actus, peccanti immortalitati est anteponendus.

Another from the Proverbs of Solomon speaking of Wisdom or Virtue;

Length of Days is in her right hand, and in her Left Hand Riches and Honours;
Her Ways are Ways of Pleasantness, and all her Paths are Peace.

III, 16, 17.

And conceiving God to be the Fountain of Wisdom, I thought it right and necessary to solicit his Assistance for obtaining it; to this End I form'd the following
little Prayer, which was prefix'd to my Tables of Examination; for daily Use.

O Powerful Goodness! bountiful Father! merciful Guide! Increase in me that Wisdom which discovers my truest Interests; Strengthen my Resolutions to perform
what that Wisdom dictates. Accept my kind Offices to thy other Children, as the
only Return in my Power for thy continual Favours to me.

I us'd also sometimes a little Prayer which I took from Thomson's Poems.[14] viz

Father of Light and Life, thou Good supreme,
O teach me what is good, teach me thy self!
Save me from Folly, Vanity and Vice,
From every low Pursuit, and fill my Soul
With Knowledge, conscious Peace, and Virtue pure,
Sacred, substantial, neverfading Bliss!

The Precept of *Order* requiring that *every Part of my Business should have its
allotted Time,* one Page in my little Book contain'd the following Scheme of Employment for the Twenty-four Hours of a natural Day,　　[see p.396]
I enter'd upon the Execution of this plan for Self Examination, and continu'd it
with occasional Intermissions for some time. I was surpriz'd to find myself so
much fuller of Faults than I had imagined, but I had the Satisfaction of seeing
them diminish. To avoid the Trouble of renewing now and then my little Book,
which by scraping out the Marks on the Paper of old Faults to make room for new
Ones in a new Course, became full of Holes: I transferr'd my Tables and Precepts
to the Ivory Leaves of a Memorandum Book, on which the Lines were drawn with
red Ink that made a durable Stain, and on those Lines I mark'd my Faults with a
black Lead Pencil, which Marks I could easily wipe out with a wet Sponge. After

---

[13] Marcus Tullius Cicero (106–43 B.C.), a Roman philosopher, statesman, and orator. Several lines
of his *Tusculan Disputations* (V.ii.5), are missing after *vitiorum:* "Oh philosophy, guide of life! Oh
searcher out of virtues and expeller of vices! . . . One day lived well and according to thy precepts is
to be preferred to an eternity of sin."

[14] From *The Seasons* (1726), by James Thomson (1700–1748), "Winter," lines 218–223.

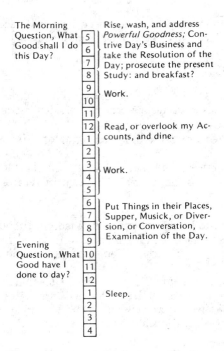

The Morning Question, What Good shall I do this Day?	5 6 7 8	Rise, wash, and address *Powerful Goodness;* Contrive Day's Business and take the Resolution of the Day; prosecute the present Study: and breakfast?
	9 10 11	Work.
	12 1	Read, or overlook my Accounts, and dine.
	2 3 4 5	Work.
	6 7 8 9	Put Things in their Places, Supper, Musick, or Diversion, or Conversation, Examination of the Day.
Evening Question, What Good have I done to day?	10 11 12	
	1 2 3 4	Sleep.

a while I went thro' one Course only in a Year, and afterwards only one in several Years, till at length I omitted them entirely, being employ'd in Voyages and Business abroad with a Multiplicity of Affairs, that interfered, but I always carried my little Book with me.

My Scheme of ORDER, gave me the most Trouble, and I found, that tho' it might be practicable where a Man's Business was such as to leave him the Disposition of his Time, that of a Journey-man Printer for instance, it was not possible to be exactly observ'd by a Master, who must mix with the World, and often receive People of Business at their own Hours. *Order* too, with regard to Places for Things, Papers, etc. I found extreamly difficult to acquire. I had not been early accustomed to *Method,* and having an exceeding good Memory, I was not so sensible of the Inconvenience attending Want of Method. This Article therefore cost me so much painful Attention and my Faults in it vex'd me so much, and I made so little Progress in Amendment, and had such frequent Relapses, that I was almost ready to give up the Attempt, and content my self with a faulty Character in that respect. Like the Man who in buying an Ax of a Smith my neighbour, desired to have the whole of its Surface as bright as the Edge; the Smith consented to grind it bright for him if he would turn the Wheel. He turn'd while the Smith press'd the broad Face of the Ax hard and heavily on the Stone, which made the Turning of it very fatiguing. The Man came every now and then from the Wheel to see how the Work went on; and at length would take his Ax as it was without farther Grinding. No, says the Smith, Turn on, turn on; we shall have it bright by and by; as yet 'tis only speckled. Yes, says the Man; but—*I think I like speckled Ax best.* And I believe this may have been the Case with many who having for want of some such Means as I employ'd found the Difficulty of obtaining good, and breaking bad Habits, in other Points of Vice and Virtue, have given up the Struggle, and concluded that *a speckled Ax was best.* For something that pretended to be Reason was every now and then suggesting to me, that such extream Nicety as I exacted of my self might be a kind of Foppery in Morals, which if it were known would make me ridiculous; that a perfect Character might be attended with the Inconvenience of being envied and hated; and that a benevolent Man should allow a few Faults in himself, to keep his Friends in Countenance.

In Truth I found myself incorrigible with respect to *Order;* and now I am grown old, and my Memory bad, I feel very sensibly the want of it. But on the whole, tho' I never arrived at the Perfection I had been so ambitious of obtaining, but fell far short of it, yet I was by the Endeavour a better and a happier Man than I otherwise should have been, if I had not attempted it; As those who aim at perfect Writing by imitating the engraved Copies, tho' they never reach the wish'd for Excellence of those Copies, their Hand is mended by the Endeavour, and is tolerable while it continues fair and legible.

And it may be well my Posterity should be informed, that to this little Artifice, with the Blessing of God, their Ancestor ow'd the constant Felicity of his Life down to his 79th Year in which this is written. What Reverses may attend the Remainder is in the Hand of Providence: But if they arrive the Reflection on past Happiness enjoy'd ought to help his Bearing them with more Resignation. To *Temperance* he ascribes his long-continu'd Health, and what is still left to him of a good Constitution. To *Industry* and *Frugality* the early Easiness of his Circumstances, and Acquisition of his Fortune, with all that Knowledge which enabled him to be an useful Citizen, and obtain'd for him some Degree of Reputation among the Learned. To *Sincerity* and *Justice* the Confidence of his Country, and the honourable Employs it conferr'd upon him. And to the joint Influence of the whole Mass of the Virtues, even in the imperfect State he was able to acquire them, all that Evenness of Temper, and that Chearfulness in Conversation which makes his Company still sought for, and agreable even to his younger Acquaintance. I hope therefore that some of my Descendants may follow the Example and reap the Benefit.

It will be remark'd that, tho' my Scheme was not wholly without Religion there was in it no Mark of any of the distinguishing Tenets of any particular Sect. I had purposely avoided them; for being fully persuaded of the Utility and Excellency of my Method, and that it might be serviceable to People in all Religions, and intending some time or other to publish it, I would not have any thing in it that should prejudice any one of any Sect against it. I purposed writing a little Comment on each Virtue, in which I would have shown the Advantages of possessing it, and the Mischiefs attending its opposite Vice; and I should have called my Book the ART *of Virtue,* because it would have shown the *Means* and *Manner* of obtaining Virtue, which would have distinguish'd it from the mere Exhortation to be good, that does not instruct and indicate the Means; but is like the Apostle's Man of verbal Charity, who only, without showing to the Naked and the Hungry *how* or where they might get Cloaths or Victuals, exhorted them to be fed and clothed. *James* II, 15, 16.[15]

---

[15] "If a brother or sister be naked, and destitute of daily food, And one of you say unto them, Depart in peace, be ye warmed and filled; notwithstanding ye give them not those things which are needful to the body; what doth it profit?"

But it so happened that my Intention of writing and publishing this Comment was never fulfilled. I did indeed, from time to time put down short Hints of the Sentiments, Reasonings, etc., to be made use of in it; some of which I have still by me: But the necessary close Attention to private Business in the earlier part of Life, and public Business since, have occasioned my postponing it. For it being connected in my Mind with a *great and extensive Project* that required the whole Man to execute, and which an unforeseen Succession of Employs prevented my attending to, it has hitherto remain'd unfinish'd.

In this Piece it was my Design to explain and enforce this Doctrine, that vicious Actions are not hurtful because they are forbidden, but forbidden because they are hurtful, the Nature of Man alone consider'd: That it was therefore every one's Interest to be virtuous, who wish'd to be happy even in this World. And I should from this Circumstance, there being always in the World a Number of rich Merchants, Nobility, States and Princes, who have need of honest Instruments for the Management of their Affairs, and such being so rare have endeavoured to convince young Persons, that no Qualities were so likely to make a poor Man's Fortune as those of Probity and Integrity.

My List of Virtues contain'd at first but twelve: But a Quaker Friend having kindly inform'd me that I was generally thought proud; that my Pride show'd itself frequently in Conversation; that I was not content with being in the right when discussing any Point, but was overbearing and rather insolent; of which he convinc'd me by mentioning several Instances; I determined endeavouring to cure myself if I could of this Vice or Folly among the rest, and I add *Humility* to my List, giving an extensive Meaning to the Word. I cannot boast of much Success in acquiring the *Reality* of this Virtue; but I had a good deal with regard to the *Appearance* of it. I made it a Rule to forbear all direct Contradiction to the Sentiments of others, and all positive Assertion of my own. I even forbid myself agreable to the old Laws of our Junto, the Use of every Word or Expression in the Language that imported[16] a fix'd Opinion; such as *certainly, undoubtedly,* etc., and I adopted instead of them, *I conceive, I apprehend,* or *I imagine* a thing to be so or so, or it so appears to me at present. When another asserted something, that I thought an Error, I deny'd my self the Pleasure of contradicting him abruptly, and of showing immediately some Absurdity in his Proposition; and in answering I began by observing that in certain Cases or Circumstances his Opinion would be right, but that in the present case there *appear'd* or *seem'd* to me some Difference, etc. I soon found the Advantage of this Change in my Manners. The Conversations I engag'd in went on more pleasantly. The modest way in which I propos'd my Opinions, procur'd them a readier Reception and less Contradiction; I had less Mortification when I was found to be in the wrong, and I more easily prevail'd with others to give up their Mistakes and join with me when I happen'd to be in the right. And this Mode, which I at first put on, with some violence to natural Inclination, became at length so easy and so habitual to me, that perhaps for these Fifty Years past no one has ever heard a dogmatical Expression escape me. And to this Habit (after my Character of Integrity) I think it principally owing, that I had early so much Weight with my Fellow Citizens, when I proposed new Institutions, or Alterations in the old; and so much Influence in public Councils when I became a Member. For I was but a bad Speaker, never eloquent, subject to much Hesita-

---

[16] Suggested.

tion in my choice of Words, hardly correct in Language, and yet I generally carried my Points.

In reality there is perhaps no one of our natural Passions so hard to subdue as *Pride*. Disguise it, struggle with it, beat it down, stifle it, mortify it as much as one pleases, it is still alive, and will every now and then peep out and show itself. You will see it perhaps often in this History. For even if I could conceive that I had compleatly overcome it, I should probably [be] proud of my Humility.

Thus far written at Passy 1784

1771–1790, 1791

=CONTEXTS=

Neoclassicism

The eighteenth century in Europe and America is commonly referred to as the Age of Reason or the Age of Enlightenment because of its renewed interest in science, empiricism, and philosophy. In literature and the arts the period was also characterized by a revival and imitation of the artistic principles of the ancient Greeks and Romans. Much of the poetry, painting, drama, and architecture of the eighteenth century exhibit the classical values of order, symmetry, elegance, and clarity. In American colleges, students adopted classical pseudonyms, such as Cicero and Augustus, as they imitated classical models in their poetry and essays. Another name for the period is the "Augustan Age." Public buildings and even farmhouses followed the Greco-Roman designs with classical colonnades and domes, a style that can still be viewed today in Washington, D.C., and throughout the South.

John Woolman
(1720–1772)

John Woolman, born in 1720, was the child of Quaker farmers who lived near Mount Holly, New Jersey. The Quaker sect, or the Religious Society of Friends, was founded in England during the 1650s to further purify the Puritan religion. The Quakers did away with paid clergy as well as liturgy, music, and the traditional adornments and hierarchy of organized religion. Believing in an "Inward Light" that was equally available to all people, Quakers gathered in simple, undecorated meeting houses for worship. Any person who felt inspired could stand and speak to the group. Those who demonstrated a special gift for the "vocal ministry" over a period of time were recorded as ministers. In America, the Quakers settled in Pennsylvania and the colony of West Jersey to avoid persecution from the Puritans. Woolman grew up in the self-contained Quaker Society in New Jersey and by age twenty-two was listed as a recorded minister by his local meeting.

By the time Woolman's talent for ministry was recognized, he had left his parents' farm and settled in Mount Holly, where he worked as a shopkeeper and tailor, supporting himself (and, as of 1749, his wife, Sarah Ellis) in a deliberately frugal manner. When his retail business became too successful, he dropped it and worked solely as a tailor and orchard keeper. All the while he continued to serve as a minister. It was the custom for Quaker ministers to travel among the far-flung colonial meetings, and in 1743 Woolman made the first of some thirty excursions, which ranged from New England to the Carolinas. During his travels Woolman had ample opportunity to witness slavery first hand. His observations led him to campaign to eliminate slave-holding within the Society of Friends. Woolman's campaign took great courage, as no organized antislavery movement existed at the time. Many respected Quaker elders held slaves, and as late as 1730 the Society of Friends had expelled an antislavery agitator from membership. However, Woolman persevered, and within a few years after his death in 1772, Quakers had abolished slavery within their ranks and had become leaders in the fledgling national abolition movement.

Woolman's antislavery work was carried on through personal contacts with slaveholders and through his writing. He wrote a number of essays on the topics of slavery and economic justice, essays that link political and economic issues to spiritual concerns. They reflect Woolman's belief that the key to social reform is devotion to the simple life, and they illustrate compassion that extends to all those at the bottom of the social hierarchy: slaves, Native Americans, the poor, and even overworked farm animals.

The same compassion and devotion to simplicity dominate Woolman's greatest work, his *Journal,* which was published posthumously in 1774. Though Woolman worked on the

The Quakers designed their churches to encourage members to speak out to one another when inspired, as in this anonymous painting The Quaker Meeting.

Journal until he contracted and died of smallpox while he was traveling in England, it is not a diary. Colonial Puritan diaries were kept as a private means of self-examination, a way of scrutinizing the soul for evidence of the gift of grace that meant the diarist was among the elect. In contrast, Quaker journals were spiritual autobiographies intended for publication, a public record of the workings of the Inward Light.

The clarity and simplicity of his style have contributed to a myth of Woolman as an "unlearned workingman," a myth promulgated by poet John Greenleaf Whittier in his introduction to a popular nineteenth-century edition of the *Journal*. Woolman was actually a careful stylist. He composed and revised the *Journal* over a period of many years; three successive drafts of the manuscript exist. (The published editions of Woolman's *Journal* are thought to include portions written by unidentified Quaker collaborators.) His simplicity of style reflects a Quaker aesthetic of plainness that extended to dress and architecture as well as to prose.

During his lifetime Woolman was little known outside the self-contained Quaker society. Yet, his *Journal*, intended for a relatively limited audience of fellow Quakers, has become an American classic. The *Journal* has continuously remained in print since its publication over two hundred years ago and has influenced writers as disparate as Ralph Waldo Emerson and Theodore Dreiser. It has received praise from American transcendentalists—the poet and biographer William Ellery Channing considered it the most sweet and pure of all autobiographies written in English—and from English romantics—the essayist and critic Charles Lamb said it was the only American book he had read twice, whereas the poet Samuel Coleridge said he should almost despair of the person who could read the story of Woolman's life and not be touched by it. Some more recent critics rank it alongside Franklin's *Autobiography* (published in entirety in 1867). Whereas Franklin's book has typically served as a manual for achieving the American dream of material success, Woolman's *Journal* joins Henry David Thoreau's *Walden* (1854) as a key text in a competing tradition—what the historian David Shi called the search for "the simple life." Like *Walden*, Woolman's *Journal* offers a model of how to combine, in the poet William Wordsworth's phrase, "plain living and high thinking." The *Journal* reveals the deep spiritual commitment of a man who has been called a Quaker saint. At the same time, it squarely confronts the major social issues of colonial America: slavery, the Native Americans, poverty, and war.

Suggested Readings: *Considerations on the Keeping of Negroes*, 1754. *A Plea for the Poor*, 1793. J. Whitney, *John Woolman: American Quaker*, 1942. S. V. James, *A People Among Peoples: Quaker Benevolence in Eighteenth-Century America*, 1963. E. Cady, *John Woolman*, 1965. P. Rosenblatt, *John Woolman*, 1969.

Text Used: *The Journal and Major Essays of John Woolman*, ed. P. P. Moulton, 1971 (some spelling and punctuation modernized).

from   JOURNAL OF JOHN WOOLMAN

[*Early Years and Vocation*]

I have often felt a motion of love to leave some hints in writing of my experience of the goodness of God, and now, in the thirty-sixth year of my age, I begin this work. I was born in Northampton, in Burlington County in West Jersey,[1] A.D. 1720, and before I was seven years old I began to be acquainted with the operations of divine love. Through the care of my parents, I was taught to read near as soon as I was capable of it, and as I went from school one Seventh Day,[2] I remember, while my companions went to play by the way, I went forward out of sight; and sitting down, I read the twenty-second chapter of the Revelations: "He showed me a river of water, clear as crystal, proceeding out of the throne of God and the Lamb, etc." And in reading it my mind was drawn to seek after that pure habitation which I then believed God had prepared for his servants. The place where I sat and the sweetness that attended my mind remains fresh in my memory.

This and the like gracious visitations[3] had that effect upon me, that when boys used ill language it troubled me, and through the continued mercies of God I was preserved from it. The pious instructions of my parents were often fresh in my mind when I happened amongst wicked children, and was of use to me. My parents, having a large family of children,[4] used frequently on First Days after meeting[5] to put us to read in the Holy Scriptures or some religious books, one after another, the rest sitting by without much conversation, which I have since often thought was a good practice. From what I had read and heard, I believed there had been in past ages people who walked in uprightness before God in a degree exceeding any that I knew, or heard of, now living; and the apprehension of there being less steadiness and firmness amongst people in this age than in past ages often troubled me while I was a child.

I had a dream about the ninth year of my age as follows: I saw the moon rise near the west and run a regular course eastward, so swift that in about a quarter of an hour she reached our meridian, when there descended from her a small cloud on a direct line to the earth, which lighted on a pleasant green about twenty yards from the door of my father's house (in which I thought I stood) and was immediately turned into a beautiful green tree. The moon appeared to run on with equal swiftness and soon set in the east, at which time the sun arose at the place where it commonly does in the summer, and shining with full radiance in a serene air, it appeared as pleasant a morning as ever I saw.

All this time I stood still in the door in an awful[6] frame of mind, and I observed that as heat increased by the rising sun, it wrought so powerfully on the little green tree that the leaves gradually withered; and before noon it appeared dry and dead. There then appeared a being, small of size, full of strength and resolution, moving swift from the north, southward, called a sun worm.[7]

Another thing remarkable in my childhood was that once, going to a neighbour's house, I saw on the way a robin sitting on her nest; and as I came near she went off, but having young ones, flew about and with many cries expressed her concern for them. I stood and threw stones at her, till one striking her, she fell

[1] Although the separate provinces East Jersey and West Jersey had been merged as New Jersey in 1702, residents perpetuated the distinction.

[2] Saturday, to the Quakers, who numbered days of the week to avoid honoring pagan gods (Saturday was named for Saturn, Roman god of agriculture).

[3] Instances when he felt God's presence.

[4] Samuel Woolman (1690–1750) and Elizabeth Burr had seven boys and six girls; John was the eldest.

[5] Quaker religious gatherings; their church is known as a "meetinghouse."   [6] Full of awe.

[7] An imaginary creature, perhaps representing a refraction of sunlight.

down dead. At first I was pleased with the exploit, but after a few minutes was seized with horror, as having in a sportive way killed an innocent creature while she was careful for her young. I beheld her lying dead and thought those young ones for which she was so careful must now perish for want of their dam to nourish them; and after some painful considerations on the subject, I climbed up the tree, took all the young birds and killed them, supposing that better than to leave them to pine away and die miserably, and believed in this case that Scripture proverb was fulfilled, "The tender mercies of the wicked are cruel."[8] I then went on my errand, but for some hours could think of little else but the cruelties I had committed, and was much troubled.

Thus he whose tender mercies are over all his works hath placed a principle in the human mind which incites to exercise goodness toward every living creature; and this being singly attended to, people become tender-hearted and sympathizing, but being frequently and totally rejected, the mind shuts itself up in a contrary disposition.

About the twelfth year of my age, my father being abroad,[9] my mother reproved me for some misconduct, to which I made an undutiful reply; and the next First Day as I was with my father returning from meeting, he told me he understood I had behaved amiss to my mother and advised me to be more careful in future. I knew myself blameable, and in shame and confusion remained silent. Being thus awakened to a sense of my wickedness, I felt remorse in my mind, and getting home I retired and prayed to the Lord to forgive me, and do not remember that I ever after that spoke unhandsomely to either of my parents, however foolish in other things.

Having attained the age of sixteen years, I began to love wanton company, and though I was preserved from profane language or scandalous conduct, still I perceived a plant in me which produced much wild grapes. Yet my merciful Father forsook me not utterly, but at times through his grace I was brought seriously to consider my ways, and the sight of my backsliding affected me with sorrow. But for want of rightly attending to the reproofs of instruction, vanity was added to vanity, and repentance to repentance; upon the whole my mind was more and more alienated from the Truth,[10] and I hastened toward destruction. While I meditate on the gulf toward which I travelled and reflect on my youthful disobedience, for these things I weep; mine eye runneth down with water.

Advancing in age the number of my acquaintance increased, and thereby my way grew more difficult. Though I had heretofore found comfort in reading the Holy Scriptures and thinking on heavenly things, I was now estranged therefrom. I knew I was going from the flock of Christ and had no resolution to return; hence serious reflections were uneasy to me and youthful vanities and diversions my greatest pleasure. Running in this road I found many like myself, and we associated in that which is reverse to true friendship.[11]

But in this swift race it pleased God to visit me with sickness, so that I doubted of recovering. And then did darkness, horror, and amazement with full force seize me, even when my pain and distress of body was very great. I thought it would have been better for me never to have had a being than to see the day which I now saw. I was filled with confusion, and in great affliction both of mind and body I

---

[8] From Proverbs 12:10.   [9] Away from home.   [10] Spiritual truth.
[11] To the practices of the Quakers, or the Religious Society of Friends.

lay and bewailed myself. I had not confidence to lift up my cries to God, whom I had thus offended, but in a deep sense of my great folly I was humbled before him, and at length that Word which is as a fire and a hammer[12] broke and dissolved my rebellious heart. And then my cries were put up in contrition, and in the multitude of his mercies I found inward relief, and felt a close engagement that if he was pleased to restore my health, I might walk humbly before him.

After my recovery this exercise[13] remained with me a considerable time; but by degrees giving way to youthful vanities, they gained strength, and getting with wanton[14] young people I lost ground. The Lord had been very gracious and spoke peace to me in the time of my distress, and I now most ungratefully turned again to folly, on which account at times I felt sharp reproof but did not get low enough to cry for help. I was not so hardy as to commit things scandalous, but to exceed in vanity and promote mirth was my chief study. Still I retained a love and esteem for pious people, and their company brought an awe upon me.

My dear parents several times admonished me in the fear of the Lord, and their admonition entered into my heart and had a good effect for a season, but not getting deep enough to pray rightly, the tempter when he came found entrance. I remember once, having spent a part of the day in wantonness, as I went to bed at night there lay in a window near my bed a Bible, which I opened, and first cast my eye on the text, "We lie down in our shame, and our confusion covers us."[15] This I knew to be my case, and meeting with so unexpected a reproof, I was somewhat affected with it and went to bed under remorse of conscience, which I soon cast off again.

Thus time passed on; my heart was replenished with mirth and wantonness, while pleasing scenes of vanity were presented to my imagination till I attained the age of eighteen years, near which time I felt the judgments of God in my soul like a consuming fire, and looking over my past life the prospect was moving. I was often sad and longed to be delivered from those vanities; then again my heart was strongly inclined to them, and there was in me a sore conflict. At times I turned to folly, and then again sorrow and confusion took hold of me. In a while I resolved totally to leave off some of my vanities, but there was a secret reserve in my heart of the more refined part of them, and I was not low enough to find true peace. Thus for some months I had great trouble, there remaining in me an unsubjected will which rendered my labors fruitless, till at length through the merciful continuance of heavenly visitations I was made to bow down in spirit before the Lord.

I remember one evening I had spent some time in reading a pious author, and walking out alone I humbly prayed to the Lord for his help, that I might be delivered from all those vanities which so ensnared me. Thus being brought low, he helped me; and as I learned to bear the cross I felt refreshment to come from his presence; but not keeping in that strength which gave victory, I lost ground again, the sense of which greatly affected me; and I sought deserts and lonely places and there with tears did confess my sins to God and humbly craved help of him. And I may say with reverence he was near to me in my troubles, and in those times of humiliation opened my ear to discipline.

---

[12] "Is not my word like as a fire? saith the Lord: and like a hammer that breaketh the rock in pieces?" from Jeremiah 23:29.
[13] Religious experience.   [14] Frivolous.   [15] From Jeremiah 3:25.

I was now led to look seriously at the means by which I was drawn from the pure Truth, and learned this: that if I would live in the life which the faithful servants of God lived in, I must not go into company as heretofore in my own will, but all the cravings of sense must be governed by a divine principle. In times of sorrow and abasement these instructions were sealed upon me, and I felt the power of Christ prevail over selfish desires, so that I was preserved in a good degree of steadiness. And being young and believing at that time that a single life was best for me, I was strengthened to keep from such company as had often been a snare to me.

I kept steady to meetings, spent First Days after noon chiefly in reading the Scriptures and other good books, and was early convinced in my mind that true religion consisted in an inward life, wherein the heart doth love and reverence God the Creator and learn to exercise true justice and goodness, not only toward all men but also toward the brute creatures; that as the mind was moved on an inward principle to love God as an invisible, incomprehensible being, on the same principle it was moved to love him in all his manifestations in the visible world; that as by his breath the flame of life was kindled in all animal and sensitive creatures, to say we love God as unseen and at the same time exercise cruelty toward the least creature moving by his life, or by life derived from him, was a contradiction in itself.

I found no narrowness respecting sects and opinions, but believed that sincere, upright-hearted people in every Society who truly loved God were accepted of him.

As I lived under the cross and simply followed the openings of Truth,[16] my mind from day to day was more enlightened; my former acquaintance was left to judge of me as they would, for I found it safest for me to live in private and keep these things sealed up in my own breast.

While I silently ponder on that change wrought in me, I find no language equal to it nor any means to convey to another a clear idea of it. I looked upon the works of God in this visible creation and an awfulness covered me; my heart was tender and often contrite, and a universal love to my fellow creatures increased in me. This will be understood by such who have trodden in the same path. Some glances of real beauty may be seen in their faces who dwell in true meekness. There is a harmony in the sound of that voice to which divine love gives utterance, and some appearance of right order in their temper and conduct whose passions are fully regulated. Yet all these do not fully show forth that inward life to such who have not felt it, but this white stone and new name is known rightly to such only who have it.[17]

Now though I had been thus strengthened to bear the cross, I still found myself in great danger, having many weaknesses attending me and strong temptations to wrestle with, in the feeling whereof I frequently withdrew into private places and often with tears besought the Lord to help me, whose gracious ear was open to my cry.

---

[16] As I was mindful of Christ's sacrifices and simply followed the direct messages from God (messages sent to those who constantly await them, according to the Quakers).

[17] "To him that overcometh I will give . . . him a white stone, and in the stone a new name written, which no men knoweth saving he that receiveth it," from Revelation 2:17.

All this time I lived with my parents and wrought on the plantation,[18] and having had schooling pretty well for a planter, I used to improve in winter evenings and other leisure times. And being now in the twenty-first year of my age, a man in much business shopkeeping and baking asked me if I would hire with him to tend shop and keep books. I acquainted my father with the proposal, and after some deliberation it was agreed for me to go.

At home I had lived retired, and now having a prospect of being much in the way of company, I felt frequent and fervent cries in my heart to God, the Father of Mercies, that he would preserve me from all taint and corruption, that in this more public employ I might serve him, my gracious Redeemer, in that humility and self-denial with which I had been in a small degree exercised in a very private life.

The man who employed me furnished a shop in Mount Holly,[19] about five miles from my father's house and six from his own, and there I lived alone and tended his shop. Shortly after my settlement here I was visited by several young people, my former acquaintance, who knew not but vanities would be as agreeable to me now as ever; and at these times I cried to the Lord in secret for wisdom and strength, for I felt myself encompassed with difficulties and had fresh occasion to bewail the follies of time past in contracting a familiarity with a libertine people. And as I had now left my father's house outwardly, I found my Heavenly Father to be merciful to me beyond what I can express.

By day I was much amongst people and had many trials to go through, but in evenings I was mostly alone and may with thankfulness acknowledge that in those times the spirit of supplication was often poured upon me, under which I was frequently exercised and felt my strength renewed.

In a few months after I came here, my master bought[20] several Scotch menservants from on board a vessel and brought them to Mount Holly to sell, one of which was taken sick and died. The latter part of his sickness he, being delirious, used to curse and swear most sorrowfully, and after he was buried I was left to sleep alone the next night in the same chamber where he died. I perceived in me a timorousness. I knew, however, I had not injured the man but assisted in taking care of him according to my capacity, and was not free to ask anyone on that occasion to sleep with me. Nature was feeble, but every trial was a fresh incitement to give myself up wholly to the service of God, for I found no helper like him in times of trouble.

After a while my former acquaintance gave over expecting me as one of their company, and I began to be known to some whose conversation was helpful to me. And now, as I had experienced the love of God through Jesus Christ to redeem me from many pollutions and to be a succour to me through a sea of conflicts, with which no person was fully acquainted, and as my heart was often enlarged in this heavenly principle, I felt a tender compassion for the youth who remained entangled in snares like those which had entangled me. From one month to another this love and tenderness increased, and my mind was more strongly engaged for the good of my fellow creatures.

I went to meetings in an awful frame of mind and endeavoured to be inwardly

---

[18] Worked on the family farm.   [19] Mount Holly, New Jersey.

[20] Bought the indentures of; men typically agreed to several years of indentured servitude in return for passage to the colonies, where their contracts could be renegotiated.

acquainted with the language of the True Shepherd. And one day being under a strong exercise of spirit, I stood up and said some words in a meeting, but not keeping close to the divine opening,[21] I said more than was required of me; and being soon sensible[22] of my error, I was afflicted in mind some weeks without any light or comfort, even to that degree that I could take satisfaction in nothing. I remembered God and was troubled, and in the depth of my distress he had pity upon me and sent the Comforter. I then felt forgiveness for my offense, and my mind became calm and quiet, being truly thankful to my gracious Redeemer for his mercies. And after this, feeling the spring of divine love opened and a concern[23] to speak, I said a few words in a meeting, in which I found peace. This I believe was about six weeks from the first time, and as I was thus humbled and disciplined under the cross, my understanding became more strengthened to distinguish the language of the pure Spirit which inwardly moves upon the heart[24] and taught [me] to wait in silence sometimes many weeks together, until I felt that rise which prepares the creature to stand like a trumpet through which the Lord speaks to his flock.

From an inward purifying, and steadfast abiding under it, springs a lively operative desire for the good of others. All faithful people are not called to the public ministry, but whoever are, are called to minister of that which they have tasted and handled spiritually. The outward modes of worship are various, but wherever men are true ministers of Jesus Christ it is from the operation of his spirit upon their hearts, first purifying them and thus giving them a feeling sense of the conditions of others. This truth was early fixed in my mind, and I was taught to watch the pure opening and to take heed lest while I was standing to speak, my own will should get uppermost and cause me to utter words from worldly wisdom and depart from the channel of the true gospel ministry.

In the management of my outward affairs I may say with thankfulness I found Truth to be my support, and I was respected in my master's family, who came to live in Mount Holly within two year after my going there.

About the twenty-third year of my age, I had many fresh and heavenly openings in respect to the care and providence of the Almighty over his creatures in general, and over man as the most noble amongst those which are visible. And being clearly convinced in my judgment that to place my whole trust in God was best for me, I felt renewed engagements that in all things I might act on an inward principle of virtue and pursue worldly business no further than as Truth opened my way therein.

About the time called Christmas[25] I observed many people from the country and dwellers in town who, resorting to the public houses, spent their time in drinking and vain sports, tending to corrupt one another, on which account I was much troubled. At one house in particular there was much disorder, and I believed it was a duty laid on me to go and speak to the master of that house. I considered I was young and that several elderly Friends in town had opportunity to see these things,

---

[21] Revelation; he wrongly spoke of worldly matters, not just spiritual matters.   [22] Aware.

[23] To the Quakers, something that one is compelled to do.

[24] To the Quakers, true "Inward Light," which comes from "disciplined understanding," is distinguishable from worldly, selfish desire.

[25] The Quakers consider all days to be holy; thus, Christmas was not a special holiday.

and though I would gladly have been excused, yet I could not feel my mind clear.

The exercise was heavy, and as I was reading what the Almighty said to Ezekiel[26] respecting his duty as a watchman, the matter was set home more clearly; and then with prayer and tears I besought the Lord for his assistance, who in loving-kindness gave me a resigned heart. Then at a suitable opportunity I went to the public house, and seeing the man amongst a company, I went to him and told him I wanted to speak with him; so we went aside, and there in the fear and dread of the Almighty I expressed to him what rested on my mind, which he took kindly, and afterward showed more regard to me than before. In a few years after, he died middle-aged, and I often thought that had I neglected my duty in that case it would have given me great trouble, and I was humbly thankful to my gracious Father, who had supported me herein.

My employer, having a Negro woman, sold her and directed me to write a bill of sale, the man being waiting who bought her. The thing was sudden, and though the thoughts of writing an instrument[27] of slavery for one of my fellow creatures felt uneasy,[28] yet I remembered I was hired by the year, that it was my master who directed me to do it, and that it was an elderly man, a member of our Society, who bought her; so through weakness I gave way and wrote it, but at the executing it, I was so afflicted in my mind that I said before my master and the Friend that I believed slavekeeping to be a practice inconsistent with the Christian religion. This in some degree abated my uneasiness, yet as often as I reflected seriously upon it I thought I should have been clearer if I had desired to be excused from it as a thing against my conscience, for such it was. And some time after this a young man of our Society spake to me to write an instrument of slavery, he having lately taken a Negro into his house. I told him I was not easy to write it, for though many kept slaves in our Society, as in others, I still believed the practice was not right, and desired to be excused from writing [it]. I spoke to him in good will, and he told me that keeping slaves was not altogether agreeable to his mind, but that the slave being a gift made to his wife, he had accepted of her.

[Writing About the Keeping of Slaves]

About this time believing it good for me to settle, and thinking seriously about a companion, my heart was turned to the Lord with desires that he would give me wisdom to proceed therein agreeable to his will; and he was pleased to give me a well-inclined damsel, Sarah Ellis,[29] to whom I was married the 18th day, 8th month, 1749.

In the fall of the year 1750 died my father Samuel Woolman with a fever, aged about sixty years. In his lifetime he manifested much care for us his children, that in our youth we might learn to fear the Lord, often endeavoring to imprint in our minds the true principles of virtue, and particularly to cherish in us a spirit of tenderness, not only toward poor people, but also towards all creatures of which we had the command.

---

[26] "Son of man, I have made thee a watchman unto the house of Israel; therefore hear the word at my mouth, and give them warning from me," from Ezekiel 3:17.

[27] A legal document.   [28] Woolman felt morally ill at ease.

[29] Ellis (1721-1787), who grew up near Mount Holly, was a childhood friend of Woolman.

After my return from Carolina I made some observations on keeping slaves, which I had some time before showed him, and he perused the manuscript,[30] proposed a few alterations, and appeared well satisfied that I found a concern on that account. And in his last sickness as I was watching with him one night, he being so far spent that there was no expectation of his recovery, but had the perfect use of his understanding, he asked me concerning the manuscript, whether I expected soon to offer it to the Overseers of the Press, and after some conversation thereon said, "I have all along been deeply affected with the oppression of the poor Negroes, and now at last my concern for them is as great as ever."

By his direction I had wrote his will in a time of health, and that night he desired me to read it to him, which I did, and he said it was agreeable to his mind. He then made mention of his end, which he believed was now near, and signified that though he was sensible of many imperfections in the course of his life, yet his experience of the power of Truth and of the love and goodness of God from time to time, even till now, was such that he had no doubt but that in leaving this life he should enter into one more happy.

The next day his sister Elizabeth came to see him and told him of the decease of their sister Anne, who died a few days before. He then said, "I reckon sister Anne was free to leave this world." Elizabeth said she was. He then said, "I also am free to leave it," and being in great weakness of body said, "I hope I shall shortly go to rest." He continued in a weighty[31] frame of mind and was sensible till near the last.

2nd day, 9th month, 1751. Feeling drawings in my mind to visit Friends at the Great Meadows, in the upper part of West Jersey, with the unity of our Monthly Meeting I went there and had some searching laborious exercise amongst Friends in those parts, and found inward peace therein.

In the 9th month, 1753, in company with my well-esteemed friend John Sykes,[32] and with the unity of Friends, we travelled about two weeks visiting Friends in Bucks County.[33] We labored in the love of the gospel according to the measure received, and through the mercies of him who is strength to the poor who trust in him, we found satisfaction in our visit. And in the next winter, way opening to visit Friends' families within the compass of our Monthly Meeting, partly by the labors of two friends from Pennsylvania, I joined some in it, having had a desire some time that it might go forward amongst us.

About this time a person at some distance lying sick, his brother came to me to write his will. I knew he had slaves, and asking his brother, was told he intended to leave them slaves to his children. As writing is a profitable employ, as offending sober people is disagreeable to my inclination, I was straitened[34] in my mind; but as I looked to the Lord, he inclined my heart to his testimony, and I told the man that I believed the practice of continuing slavery to this people was not right and had a scruple in mind against doing writings of that kind: that though many in our Society kept them as slaves, still I was not easy to be concerned in it and desired to be excused from going to write the will. I spake to him in the fear of the Lord, and he made no reply to what I said, but went away; he also had some concerns in the practice, and I thought he was displeased with me.

[30] Woolman's essay *Some Considerations on the Keeping of Negroes* (1754).   [31] Serious.
[32] Sykes (1682-1771) was a Quaker minister who frequently traveled with Woolman.
[33] In Pennsylvania.   [34] Troubled.

In this case I had a fresh confirmation that acting contrary to present outward interest from a motive of divine love and in regard to truth and righteousness, and thereby incurring the resentments of people, opens the way to a treasure better than silver and to a friendship exceeding the friendship of men.

On the 7th day, 2nd month, 1754, at night, I dreamed that I was walking in an orchard, it appeared to be about the middle of the afternoon; when on a sudden I saw two lights in the east resembling two suns, but of a dull and gloomy aspect. The one appeared about the height of the sun at three hours high, and the other more northward and one-third lower. In a few minutes the air in the east appeared to be mingled with fire, and like a terrible storm coming westward the streams of fire reached the orchard where I stood, but I felt no harm. I then found one of my acquaintances standing near me, who was greatly distressed in mind at this unusual appearance. My mind felt calm, and I said to my friend, "We must all once die, and if it please the Lord that our death be in this way, it is good for us to be resigned." Then I walked to a house hard by, and going upstairs, saw people with sad and troubled aspects, amongst whom I passed into another room where the floor was only some loose boards. There I sat down alone by a window, and looking out I saw in the south three great red streams standing at equal distance from each other, the bottom of which appeared to stand on the earth and the top to reach above the region of the clouds. Across those three streams went less ones, and from each end of such small stream others extended in regular lines to the earth, all red and appeared to extend through the whole southern firmament. There then appeared on a green plain a great multitude of men in a military posture, some of whom I knew. They came near the house, and passing on westward some of them, looking up at me, expressed themselves in a scoffing, taunting way, to which I made no reply; soon after, an old captain of the militia came to me, and I was told these men were assembled to improve in the discipline of war.

The manuscript before-mentioned having lain by me several years, the publication of it rested weightily upon me, and this year I offered it to the Overseers of the Press, who, having examined and made some small alterations in it, ordered a number of copies thereof to be published by the Yearly Meeting stock and dispersed amongst Friends.

* * *

[Taxes and Slavekeeping]

One evening a Friend came to our lodgings who was a justice of the peace and in a friendly way introduced the subject of refusing to pay taxes to support wars, and perceiving that I was one who scrupled the payment, said he had wanted an opportunity with some in that circumstance; whereupon we had some conversation in a brotherly way on some texts of Scripture relating thereto, in the conclusion of which he said that according to our way of proceeding it would follow that whenever administration of government was ill, we must suffer distraint[35] of goods rather than pay actively toward supporting it. To which I replied, "Men put in

[35] Seizure.

public stations are intended for good purposes, some to make good laws, others to take care that those laws are not broken. Now if those men thus set apart do not answer the design of their institution, our freely contributing to support them in that capacity when we certainly know that they are wrong is to strengthen them in a wrong way and tends to make them forget that it is so. But when from a clear understanding of the case we are really uneasy with the application of money, and in the spirit of meekness suffer distress to be made on our goods rather than to pay actively, this joined with an upright uniform life may tend to put men athinking about their own public conduct."

He said he would propose a medium: that is, where men in authority do not act agreeable to the mind of those who constituted them, he thought the people should rather remonstrate than refuse a voluntary payment of moneys so demanded, and added "Civil government is an agreement of free men by which they oblige themselves to abide by certain laws as a standard, and to refuse to obey in that case is of like nature as to refuse to do any particular act which we had convenanted to do."

I replied that in making covenants it was agreeable to honesty and uprightness to take care that we do not foreclose ourselves from adhering strictly to true virtue in all occurrences relating thereto. But if I should unwarily promise to obey the orders of a certain man, or number of men, without any proviso, and he or they command me to assist in doing some great wickedness, I may then see my error in making such promise, and an active obedience in that case would be adding one evil to another; that though by such promise I should be liable to punishment for disobedience, yet to suffer rather than act to me appears most virtuous.

The whole of our conversation was in calmness and good will. And here it may be noted that in Pennsylvania, where there are many Friends under that scruple, a petition was presented to the Assembly by a large number of Friends, asking that no law might be passed to enjoin the payment of money for such uses which they as a peaceable people could not pay for conscience' sake.

The Monthly Meeting of Philadelphia having been under a concern on account of some Friends who this summer, 1758, had bought Negro slaves, the said meeting moved it in their Quarterly Meeting to have the minute reconsidered in the Yearly Meeting which was made last on that subject. And the said Quarterly Meeting appointed a committee to consider it and report to their next, which committee having met once and adjourned, and I, going to Philadelphia to meet a committee of the Yearly Meeting, was in town the evening on which the Quarterly Meeting's committee met the second time, and finding an inclination to sit with them, was admitted; and Friends had a weighty conference on the subject. And soon after their next Quarterly Meeting I heard that the case was coming to our Yearly Meeting, which brought a weighty exercise upon me, and under a sense of my own infirmities and the great danger I felt of turning aside from perfect purity, my mind was often drawn to retire alone and put up my prayers to the Lord that he would be graciously pleased to strengthen me, that setting aside all views of self-interest and the friendship of this world, I might stand fully resigned to his holy will.

In this Yearly Meeting several weighty matters were considered, and toward the last, that in relation to dealing with persons who purchase slaves. During the several sittings of the said meeting, my mind was frequently covered with inward prayer, and I could say with David that tears were my meat day and night.[36] The case of slavekeeping lay heavy upon me, nor did I find any engagement to speak directly to any other matter before the meeting. Now when this case was opened, several faithful Friends spake weightily thereto, with which I was comforted, and feeling a concern to cast in my mite, I said in substance as follows:

> In the difficulties attending us in this life, nothing is more precious than the mind of Truth inwardly manifested, and it is my earnest desire that in this weighty matter we may be so truly humbled as to be favored with a clear understanding of the mind of Truth and follow it; this would be of more advantage to the Society than any mediums which are not in the clearness of divine wisdom. The case is difficult to some who have them, but if such set aside all self-interest and come to be weaned from the desire of getting estates, or even from holding them together when Truth requires the contrary, I believe way will open that they will know how to steer through those difficulties.

Many Friends appeared to be deeply bowed under the weight of the work and manifested much firmness in their love to the cause of truth and universal right-eousness in the earth. And though none did openly justify the practice of slavekeeping in general, yet some appeared concerned lest the meeting should go into such measures as might give uneasiness to many brethren, alleging that if Friends patiently continued under the exercise, the Lord in time to come might open a way for the deliverance of these people. And I, finding an engagement to speak, said:

> My mind is often led to consider the purity of the Divine Being and the justice of his judgments, and herein my soul is covered with awfulness. I cannot omit to hint of some cases where people have not been treated with the purity of justice, and the event hath been melancholy.
>
> Many slaves on this continent are oppressed, and their cries have reached the ears of the Most High! Such is the purity and certainty of his judgments that he cannot be partial in our favor. In infinite love and goodness he hath opened our understandings from one time to another concerning our duty toward this people, and it is not a time for delay.
>
> Should we now be sensible of what he requires of us, and through a respect to the private interest of some persons or through a regard to some friendships which do not stand on an immutable foundation, neglect to do our duty in firmness and con-stancy, still waiting for some extraordinary means to bring about their deliverance, it may be that by terrible things in righteousness God may answer us in this matter.

Many faithful brethren laboured with great firmness, and the love of Truth in a good degree prevailed. Several Friends who had Negroes expressed their desire that a rule might be made to deal with such Friends as offenders who bought slaves in future. To this it was answered that the root of this evil would never be effectually struck at until a thorough search was made into the circumstances of

---

[36] "My tears have been my meat day and night, while they continually say unto me, Where is thy God?" from Psalm 42:3; David, the second king of Israel, reputedly wrote many of the Psalms.

such Friends who kept Negroes, in regard to the righteousness of their motives in keeping them, that impartial justice might be administered throughout.

Several Friends expressed their desire that a visit might be made to such Friends who kept slaves, and many Friends declared that they believed liberty was the Negro's right, to which at length no opposition was made publicly, so that a minute was made more full on that subject than any heretofore and the names of several Friends entered who were free to join in a visit to such who kept slaves.

1756–1772, 1774

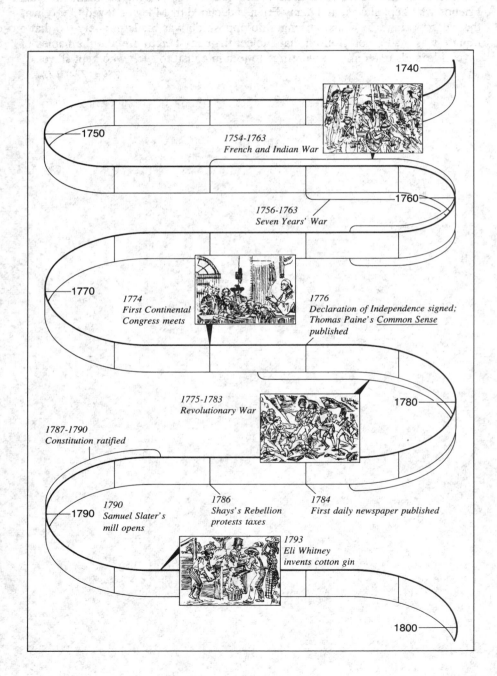

1740

1750

1754-1763
French and Indian War

1756-1763
Seven Years' War

1760

1770

1774
First Continental
Congress meets

1776
Declaration of Independence signed;
Thomas Paine's Common Sense
published

1775-1783
Revolutionary War

1780

1787-1790
Constitution ratified

1790
Samuel Slater's
mill opens

1786
Shays's Rebellion
protests taxes

1784
First daily newspaper published

1790

1793
Eli Whitney
invents cotton gin

1800

The Age of the Democratic Revolution

The Late 18th Century

In the latter half of the eighteenth century, Olaudah Equiano, an enslaved African, traveled through much of the British empire and keenly observed a wide range of societies from the British West Indies to South Carolina and Virginia to London. It was not obvious to him that mainland colonies were fated to be independent. However, during his lifetime the people of the mainland colonies came to feel distinctly different from other societies held by Britain and destined to separate from the British empire.

Over the course of a period historians have called "the long eighteenth century," 1689 to 1815, England and France were at war six times. These were transatlantic confrontations in which control of Atlantic commerce was at stake and in which the colonies of each nation were major suppliers of war material. English colonists and, during the American and French Revolutions, independent Americans fought in the armies and navies. The indigenous American peoples played complex roles as they sought to decrease European influence in America and also to use European presence to their own advantage.

The stakes steadily increased as did the European immigrant population in America, from 250,000 in 1700, to 1.15 million in 1750, to over 2 million by 1760. These immigrants were recruited from a wide range of countries—not only England, but various German principalities and Ireland (largely transplanted Scottish Protestants). As Parliament came to appreciate the formidable potential of the American colonies, it expanded its efforts to regulate their trade, particularly by taxing the highly profitable colonial trade with the French sugar islands. But taxes that seemed sensible to London legislators engaged in war with France seemed outrageous to colonists, who felt very distant from the European rivalries. An entire generation of colonial merchants and traders grew experienced at evading royal authority. Whereas the first three wars of the eighteenth century were fought largely at sea, the Seven Years' War (1756–1763) involved substantial confrontation on North American soil—deep in the West, as the French sought to exclude the English from the fur trade of the Ohio Valley, and in the Northeast, where major battles including colonial soldiers were fought for control of the fortresses guarding access to New France, in Nova Scotia. When peace was accomplished in 1763, the English had expelled France from North America.

Gratitude is not something to count on in international relations. Although the mainland colonies benefited from the removal of the French threat, colonists believed they had made major sacrifices in the venture. Nearly every working-class man in Boston had fought in the war, and many of them died; their impoverished widows and orphaned children were a painful legacy of the war. The proportion of poor people grew sharply in other cities as well. As the number of poor increased, the number of people with mixed feelings about the advantages of the British empire also swelled, and Americans' sense of dependence on their English mentors decreased. Legislators who had successfully struggled with colonial governors emerged with a new sense of competence.

However, the British Parliament understood the colonies to have been well served by the removal of the French threat. That removal had been expensive: the English national debt had doubled during the war. Americans were the least taxed people in the empire, indeed in the Atlantic world. There was now French-speaking Canada to support, peace to be maintained between Native Americans and settlers, and commerce to be managed, all requiring an enlarged British presence in the colonies and higher taxes to pay for that presence.

During the next ten years Parliament established a series of regulations intended to tighten and rationalize the administration of the colonies and a series of taxes generally calculated to be reasonable and mild. The strength and seriousness of colonial resistance to these measures and eventual defiance of British authority surprised not only Parliament but also colonial elites. Between 1764 and 1774 relations between the colonies and England were destabilized. In a series of now-famous crises many men and women took to the streets, sometimes violently, to express their resistance to English control. As they did so, internal political relationships within each colony were also destabilized. Group after group—lawyers objecting to stamp taxes on documents, merchants objecting to tight restrictions on shipping, consumers objecting to export and import taxes, artisans objecting to impressment into service in the British navy—rejected England's claims of benevolent rule, redefined themselves as deeply skeptical of the empire, and gradually claimed that their inheritance as free-born subjects entitled them to a final break with king and empire. These protests expressed an egalitarian ideology and a rejection of deference that infused American politics long after independence was accomplished.

The American Revolution

In each colony extralegal bodies bypassed official colonial governors and assemblies, trained militias, enforced boycotts of British goods, and obstructed British officials. Fighting broke out when the English General Thomas Gage sought to seize illegal stores of arms and ammunition in towns outside Boston. His detachment of men was met on the Lexington town common by seventy "minutemen." Eight Americans were killed, and the skirmish initiated both an undeclared war

The Declaration of Independence *(1786) by John Trumbull. (Yale University Art Gallery)*

with England and a civil war between patriots and Loyalists. Americans could not really explain what they were doing; successful rebellion of colonies against a powerful empire had not occurred since the Renaissance and not on so large a scale. Colonists were fighting for their traditional liberties as English subjects. It took fifteen months of public and private debate and the escalation of violence, during which Thomas Paine's extraordinary manifesto *Common Sense* (1776) was published, before the claim of independence could be articulated.

The war itself, as the historian John Shy wrote in *A People Numerous and Armed* (1976), was "a social process of political education." An estimated 250,000 men, eighty percent of adult males, served in the military at some point, and a higher percentage of the total population died than in any other American conflict except the Civil War. Men were held in the colonial army less by desperation and fear than by patriotism and commitment; to some extent this was also true of the British, with whom about 50,000 American Loyalists enlisted. The Revolution was one of the last wars in which women followed the armies of both sides, serving as an informal quartermaster corps—cooking food and laundering clothing for the soldiers.

The Revolutionary War stretched on for more than seven years; in American history, only the Vietnam War was longer. The British evacuated Boston shortly after the battle of Bunker Hill in 1776. The fighting then centered on the Middle Atlantic states, shifting to the South in 1778. General George Washington tried to avoid formal battles in which his vulnerable army was at risk, preferring harassment and skirmishing to wear down the British. In 1778 the Continental Congress negotiated a treaty of alliance with France, drawing French naval forces into the war on the American side—thus continuing the century-long Anglo-French hostility and eventually providing the margin of power that enabled the defeat of British forces in the battle of Yorktown in 1781. Even after the British surrender, skirmishing between American Loyalists and patriots continued, especially in the South, until the ratification of the Treaty of Paris ended the war in 1783. That treaty, brilliantly negotiated by John Adams, John Jay, and to a lesser extent Benjamin Franklin, defused French temptations to establish a peace between England and France that would have ignored American interests. The treaty recognized full independence, territorial claims to the Mississippi River, and American fishing rights off Nova Scotia's highly profitable Grand Banks.

The American Constitution

While the battles of the war for independence were being fought, Americans faced the challenge of institutionalizing the republic they had claimed. It was one thing to declare that they were no longer subjects of the king and that the people ought to rule themselves; it was quite another to invent the mechanism by which that could be done. Thomas Jefferson gave the claim to independence classic expression in 1776 in the Declaration of Independence. But several years passed before Americans identified themselves not as "inhabitants" of America or as "members" of their states but as "citizens." The concept of citizenship implies conscious choice: that people could become citizens of nations other than those into which they were born; that a citizen's primary obligation to the republic is loyalty. But citizenship was expressed in different modes for people of different sexes. By the example of the Roman republic of antiquity and the Italian republics of the Renaissance, only for men did citizenship include the obligation to bear arms in defense of the state and the right of property holders to vote for legislators. Furthermore, citizenship, as developed in America, was completely denied to slaves.

Each colony, using its long experience in colonial assemblies, declared itself to be a state, joined in a confederation of equals. Each created for itself a written constitution modeled on (but rarely duplicating) the old colonial charters given by the king to trading companies or proprietors. Into these new constitutions were embedded bills of rights, based on the British example but protecting citizen against state more broadly than the British model of protection of Parliament against king.

Post-Revolutionary America

After the Revolution American society was caught in major social transformations that shattered old rhythms of life. Could the new nation respond to political and social challenges in such a way as to confirm its republican assertions and to maintain its political integrity? The nation was populated with former soldiers, slaves who had learned the language of freedom and were making claims for their own, Native Americans who did not recognize England's peace treaty, and former Loyalists whose emotional connection to the new nation was tenuous. Could a people who had learned how to overthrow government be governed? In 1786 armed Massachusetts farmers led by war-veteran Daniel Shays demonstrated (in Shays's Rebellion) how intensely people might defy regressive taxes, deflationary monetary policies, and elite claims of political hegemony. Members of elites feared that Americans, having learned to sustain popular militancy, would make it the norm in the new republic. This fear reinforced other reasons for restlessness with the Articles of Confederation—America's first constitution, adopted in 1781—notably a confederation's weakness in dealing with matters of foreign policy and taxation, and strengthened those who called for a convention to revise the Articles of Confederation.

=CONTEXTS=

From the early 1770s through 1790s African-American slaves petitioned the state of Massachusetts to recognize their legal right to freedom. The ideas and language of these petitions first anticipated and later echoed the Declaration of Independence. The following excerpt is from a petition to the Massachusetts Bay Colony's House of Representatives (original spelling retained).

[The Early Abolition Movement]

The petition of A Great Number of Blackes detained in a State of slavery in the Bowels of a free & Christian Country Humbly shuwith that your Petitioners apprehend that they have in Common with all other men a Natural and Unaliable Right to that freedom which the Grat Parent of the Unavers hath Bestowed equalley on all menkind and which they have Never forfuted by any Compact or agreement whatever—but thay wher Unjustly Dragged by the hand of cruel Power from their Derest friends and sum of them Even torn from the Embraces of their tender Parents—from A popolous Pleasant and plentiful contry and in violation of Laws of Nature and off Nations and in defiance of all the tender feelings of humanity Brough hear Either to Be sold Like Beast of Burthen & Like them Condemnd to Slavery for Life—Among A People Profesing the mild Religion of Jesus A people Not Insensible of the Secrets of Rationable Being Nor without spirit to Resent the unjust endeavours of others to Reduce them to a state of Bondage and Subjection your honouer Need not to be informed that A Life of Slavery Like that of your petioners Deprived of Every social privilege of Every thing Requiset to Render Life Tolable is far worse then Nonexistance.

Your petioners . . . therfor humble Beseech your honours to give this petion its due weight & consideration and cause an act of the Legislatur to be past Wherby they may Be Restored to the Enjoyments of that which is the Naturel Right of all men—and their Children who wher Born in this Land of Liberty may not be heald as Slaves after they arive at the age of Twenty one years so may the Inhabitance of thes Stats No longer chargeable with the inconsistancey of acting themselves the part which they condem and oppose in others Be prospered in their present Glorious struggle for Liberty and have those Blessing to them, &c.

Anonymous black slaves, 1777

Fifty-five delegates from twelve states (all except Rhode Island) devised a strikingly new frame of government, sharply different from the Articles of Confederation they had set out to revise. The new government would have a national judiciary, a national Congress with the power to tax and to regulate foreign and interstate commerce, and a president. Members of the Senate were to be selected by state legislatures, the president by an electoral college. The new government was to have broad grants of power, such as authority to provide for the "general welfare of the United States."

Slavery was the most potentially explosive issue at the Constitutional Convention. Northern delegates who hoped for the natural erosion of the slave system settled for the avoidance of the term "slave" in the text and for the right to end the slave trade after 1808. Persons "held to service" were required to be "delivered up" to those who claimed them if they had fled across state lines. Most important, the Constitution provided that three-fifths of the slave population would be counted for purposes of representation (though not for the purposes of taxation, as originally proposed in the "Three-Fifth's Compromise"). Thus, slavery and sectional differences were inextricably bound in the new political order.

By including provision for amendment, the framers of the Constitution embedded in it the capacity for change. This resiliency was its salvation. Several states ratified it only on the understanding that it would quickly be amended to make explicit that Congress might not abridge freedom of speech, press, or religion; that it would protect individual rights to trial by "an impartial jury"; that citizens would not be "deprived of life, liberty, or property, without due process of law"; and that citizens would be "secure in their persons, houses, papers, and effects, against unreasonable searches and seizures." The ratification process, in which delegates especially elected for that purpose voted on the Constitution in special conventions in each state (1787–1790), was a dazzling political innovation that had already been developed for state constitutions during the war. The process clearly separated the statutory law of legislatures from the fundamental law of the Constitution; it was the mechanism by which "the people's" claims to sovereignty could be put into practice.

The combatants in the great political debates of the early republic—supporting or opposing a federal Constitution, subsequently opponents in the first party system of Federalists and Republicans—were locked in an uneasy dialectic made intense by the understanding that decisions once made were likely to set permanent precedents. The victors in a revolution typically define themselves as heirs of its principles and define their political opponents as counter-revolutionary. That happened in France in the 1790s, in many postcolonial African nations, and in the Soviet Union, Eastern Europe, and China in the twentieth century. During the party battles of the 1790s Jeffersonians defined their opponents as "monarchists"; Federalists called their opponents "seditious." But the postwar consensus that established the federal Constitution did not unravel into a repeated cycle of revolutions. Instead of dividing into pro- and anti-Revolutionary factions, American political parties groped toward a theory of legitimate opposition and modern political parties well before it was expressed elsewhere. In 1800 Thomas Jefferson became the first postrevolutionary leader ever to be elected head of state by the votes of an opposition party. Among the revolutionary generation's most important contributions to political theory is the concept of the "loyal opposition."

The New Republic's Emerging Culture

The Revolution did not produce an egalitarian economic order. A commercial revolution and the early stages of industrial revolution undermined traditions of artisan production. Recent studies of major cities reveal stunning disparities of wealth both before and after the Revolution. In *Render Them Submissive* (1980) the historian John Alexander reports that less than one percent of Philadelphia's taxpayers owned more taxable property than did the bottom seventy-five percent in 1800. The earliest factories for mass production of textiles—beginning with Samuel Slater's mill in Pawtucket, Rhode Island, in 1790—employed a work force largely composed of women and children and signaled a major shift in employer/employee relations. Whites continued to be made indentured servants; one out of five Americans remained enslaved.

The era of the early republic was a paradoxical moment in the history of slavery. On the one hand, the defense of slavery was shaken in theory by the Revolution's egalitarian principle. "See your Declaration, Americans!!! Do you understand your own language?" demanded the freeborn African-American David Walker in his powerful pamphlet *Appeal to the Colored Citizens of the World* (1829). The institution of slavery was shaken in practice when African-Americans served in patriot armies or fled with the British and took advantage of the disruptions of war to shape their own communities. During the 1780s slavery lost its legal foundations in much of the North. The phrase "all men are born free and equal" was interpreted by the Massachusetts courts to outlaw slavery implicitly. Pennsylvania, Rhode Island, New York, and Connecticut adopted gradual-emancipation laws. The Northwest Ordinance, one of the last statutes of the Continental Congress, forbade slavery in the region that is now Ohio, Indiana, Illinois, and Michigan. On the other hand, Eli Whitney's invention of the cotton gin in 1793, the subsequent invigoration of the cotton economy, and the opening of the Old Southwest to settlement and of the Old South to the slave trade until 1808 resulted in an extraordinary expansion of slavery in the postwar period. The historian Allan Kulikoff in his essay "Uprooted Peoples" (in *Slavery and Freedom in the Age of the American Revolution* [1983, Ira Berlin and Ronald Hoffman, eds.]) estimates that at least 250,000 slaves were forcibly moved from the Old South to the frontier and at least another 100,000 new slaves were imported during the quarter-century after the Treaty of Paris was signed. The phrase "all men are born free and equal" was interpreted by Virginia courts *not* to outlaw slavery, and emancipation was severely constrained by law in most southern states. These developments heightened the social differences between northern society, where slavery was declining, and southern society, where technology and geographic expansion supported the region's "peculiar institution."

══CONTEXTS══

After the Revolution, occupation of Native-American lands had government sanction through treaties. Because the native tribes were separated by great distances, their members did not consult among themselves about their property rights. The famous Shawnee leader Tecumseh (1768–1813) traveled across the Midwest and South, urging the many tribes to unite into one resisting political force. Although his plan failed he became legendary for his effort, initiative, and oratory. This speech was addressed to the Osage tribe of the Ohio River Valley.

[Tecumseh Speaks]

Brothers—We all belong to one family; we are all children of the Great Spirit; we walk in the same path; slake our thirst at the same spring; and now affairs of the greatest concern lead us to smoke the pipe around the same council fire!

Brothers—We are friends; we must assist each other to bear our burdens. The blood of many of our fathers and brothers has run like water on the ground, to satisfy the avarice of the white men. We, ourselves, are threatened with a great evil; nothing will pacify them but the destruction of all the red men.

Brothers—When the white men first set foot on our grounds, they were hungry; they had no place on which to spread their blankets, or to kindle their fires. They were feeble; they could do nothing for themselves. Our fathers commiserated their distress, and shared freely with them whatever the Great Spirit had given his red children. They gave them food when hungry, medicine when sick, spread skins for them to sleep on, and gave them grounds, that they might hunt and raise corn.

Brothers—The white people are like poisonous serpents: when chilled, they are feeble, and harmless, but invigorate them with warmth, and they sting their benefactors to death.

* * *

Brothers—Our Great Father [King George III] over the great waters is angry with the white people, our enemies. He will send his brave warriors against them; he will send us rifles, and whatever else we want—he is our friend, and we are his children.

Brothers—Who are the white people that we should fear them? They cannot run fast, and are good marks to shoot at: they are only men; our fathers have killed many of them; we are not squaws, and we will stain the earth red with their blood.

Brothers—The Great Spirit is angry with our enemies; he speaks in thunder, and the earth swallows up villages, and drinks up the Mississippi. The great waters will cover their lowlands; their corn cannot grow; and the Great Spirit will sweep those who escape to the hills from the earth with his terrible breath.

Brothers—We must be united; we must smoke the same pipe; we must fight each other's battles; and more than all, we must love the Great Spirit; he is for us; he will destroy our enemies, and make his red children happy.

                                                      Tecumseh, 1810

Despite an antimilitarist tradition and a rhetoric that proclaimed "no standing armies" and called for reliance on militia, the national government built a professional army. Within twenty-five years after the Revolution, the military establishment included 14 frontier forts, 13 frigates, and 6 arsenals. Struggle over how the national defense was to be managed became one of the distinguishing features of the debate between Federalists and Jeffersonians. In the end even the Jeffersonians conceded that to rely on the militia—egalitarian and democratic though it might be—risked anarchy and vulnerability. When Jefferson came to power, one of his first acts was to establish a military academy.

The army of the early republic was used mainly against Native Americans. Alliance with Britain and subsequent defeat had a profound impact on tribal cultures. New national policy offered native peoples the choice of forcible removal or complete disruption of their culture. Federal policy was shaped by ambivalence about the future place of indigenous peoples and by resentment of the ability of Native Americans to maintain control over substantial regions of the new nation, especially the Ohio Valley. Historians, once apt to assume that Native-American cultures were doomed to extinction before the inexorable pressures of "civilization," now tend to emphasize the dynamism of native cultures, the vigor of efforts of leaders such as Tecumseh to sustain the vitality of Native-American alliances, and the military force that was required to silence Native-American resistance.

Portrait of Tecumseh, by an unknown artist.

The Revolutionary era was one of major cultural shifts. One of the most deeply radical choices made by the Revolutionary generation was the separation of church and state. So long as the Anglican church, headed by the king of England, was established by the government, political revolution against the king could not help but be a religious revolution also. Many individuals, by refusing to take communion in the established church, may well have become aware that there might be secular concerns, as well, over which the state had no right to dictate. The separation of church and state was expressed in Thomas Jefferson's "Bill for Establishing Religious Freedom" (1786): "Our civil rights have no dependence on our religious opinions . . . truth is great and will prevail if left to herself . . . ."

Literacy in Post-Revolutionary America

The early years of the republic were marked by a growth of literacy and by the transition to a print culture. Because the increasingly commercial economy relied on written accounts and contracts, more people needed to learn to write and to use arithmetic. Historians of literacy now argue that the availability of print materials was the most important factor in the spread of literacy in America and in Europe. It engendered a "need" to read, write, and compute in order to carry out work, interact with merchants and traders, and connect with society outside one's own family and community. The first newspaper to be produced daily, the *Pennsylvania Packet* in 1784, made fresh reading material available every day in Philadelphia. The establishment of schools followed rather than initiated the spread of literacy. The growing understanding of reading, writing, and arithmetic now seems to have been due primarily to a commercial revolution that rewarded holders of these skills.

In addition, individuals possessing these skills had the psychological advantage of being less dependent on social superiors as sources of information and control. Although women's literacy lagged behind that of men of their own race and class, a gradual growth in the ability of women to read and write decreased their intellectual dependence on local sources of information such as ministers, parents, perhaps husbands; a woman could read broadsides and newspapers for herself and subscribe to books and magazines published elsewhere. The literacy gap between white men and women, substantial in the 1790s, virtually closed by the national census of 1840, which showed nearly universal literacy among northern whites and no gender disparity. At least fifty percent of free black people could read, a stunning accomplishment considering that slaves were generally denied access to print and that the free blacks of 1850 were likely to belong to the first generation in their families to be literate. To the extent that later marriages, a decline of household production, and the increasing availability of consumer goods permit control of one's life, these factors appear to have fostered the demographic transition denoted by a substantial decline in average family size among whites in the new republic.

Increased access to information accompanied a new understanding of citizenship; the "private" roles of wife and mother came to have an important political dimension. When Abigail Adams demanded that the new code of laws "remember the ladies," she proceeded to the issue of domestic violence: "Put it out of the power of husbands to use us with impunity; remember all men would be tyrants if they could," she wrote to John Adams in 1776. She understood that public and private arrangements were inextricably linked. The republic relied on mothers, it was understood, because mothers would socialize the next generation of virtuous citizens. But the new republic made no space for women as formal participants in political decision-making.

Many of the first novels written in America, the literary critic Cathy Davidson observes in *Revolution and the Word* (1986), "emphasized the class, gender and racial inequities in the new land." Lacking the optimism of the essayist Michel-Guillaume Jean de Crèvecoeur and the poets Philip Freneau and Joel Barlow, female novelists such as Susannah Haswell Rowson and Hannah Webster Foster stressed the dangers awaiting women in the new society: women's vulnerability to seduction and disaster when acting on their inclinations for independence and self-fulfillment, which the ideology of the early republic prescribed for men. When Thomas Jefferson scorned fiction and denied it to his daughter, he was barring her from virtually the only category of literature in which women were portrayed as active agents in shaping their own lives.

"Early national America" was a postrevolutionary society with problems of instability not unlike those that face other societies emerging from profoundly disruptive struggles. It was a society caught in the later stages of a commercial revolution and in the early stages of industrialization: a society in the early stages of becoming what we now call modern. It was a society committed to maintaining slavery and deferential patterns of race relations. But it was also a society developing a radically new political system and at the same time adjusting to new modes of communication, new styles of consumption, new patterns of family relations, and newly negotiated gender relations.

LATE 18TH-CENTURY NONFICTION PROSE

Nonfiction prose in seventeenth-century America was predominantly religious in tone and European in audience. In the eighteenth century the growing economic and political interdependence within the colonies altered both these emphases. Changing patterns of literary production and distribution transformed the cultural geography of the nation. Early in the eighteenth century the publishing center for American texts began to shift from London to America, a shift not completed until the nineteenth century. Books had been published as early as 1639 in Massachusetts; by 1763 all thirteen colonies had successful printers. The growth of an indigenous publishing industry was affected by the availability of transportation routes to facilitate distribution. With its underdeveloped roads and rural economy, the South lagged behind New England and the Middle Atlantic states. Even in New England, which produced a large number of texts, circulation was relatively restricted. The difficulty of travel prevented Boston and other New England towns from having easy access to outlying regions, possible in the more centrally located cities farther south.

The center of publishing relocated from Boston to New York and especially to Philadelphia. This relocation was accompanied by a broadening of the audience. Given the high cost of books—roughly three to four times modern prices—readers increasingly turned to lending libraries. In addition to circulating libraries, where individual books were rented for a small charge, and to institutional libraries attached to colleges, social or subscription libraries had appeared in most towns by the end of the eighteenth century. Members of such libraries paid an annual fee for the privilege of unlimited borrowing.

Those readers who found books too expensive or time-consuming turned to newspapers. Starting in 1690 with the short-lived Boston *Publick Occurrences*

Both Forreign and Domestick, by the publisher Benjamin Harris, most colonies had at least one weekly publication by mid-century. To supplement this periodical source of literature and politics, and as a partial outgrowth of it, printers issued pamphlets, almanacs, ballads, broadsides (large sheets of paper on which a political message or advertisement is printed), and other flimsily-bound publications sold individually at a low price. In the post-Revolutionary War period these mass-market issues were joined by somewhat more elitist magazines: the *Columbian Magazine,* the *American Museum,* the *Massachusetts Magazine,* and the *New York Magazine.*

The variety of these eighteenth-century publications and of their means of production challenges traditional assumptions about aesthetic value and even about "the book" as the primary object of literary study. These publications shared a common concern with the consolidation of the colonies into a political and cultural unit. Whereas seventeenth-century writers looked primarily to God for salvation and to England for population and approval, eighteenth-century writers characteristically looked homeward in an attempt to construct an independent cultural identity for America.

The shift in emphasis is clearest in descriptions of the land. Early accounts of America were highly rhetorical, overstating and at times mythicizing the country's charms to attract immigrants and income. By the end of the seventeenth century, writers had begun to study the landscape for its own sake. Samuel Sewall's 1697 Puritan celebration of the beauty of Plum Island foreshadows the rising concern with natural history and scientific observation. Subsequent thinkers such as Cotton Mather, Jonathan Edwards, and Benjamin Franklin were admired as much for their scientific endeavors as for their theology and politics. Travel narratives including the journal of Sarah Kemble Knight (first published in 1825) and nature descriptions, including botanist John Bartram's *Observations* (1751), marked the public's taste for realistic depictions of the countryside. This popular fascination with the picturesque quality of American geography culminated with Thomas Jefferson's masterful *Notes on the State of Virginia* (1785) and with *Travels* (1791) by William Bartram.

A similar realism infused the historical accounts of the period. The Puritan notion of history as providential, a progress report on God's ongoing plans for (and sometimes controversies with) His chosen people, continued in Cotton Mather's magisterial *Magnalia Christi Americana* (1702). But allegorical readings of the spiritual history of New England were overshadowed by more factual accounts of the colonies: Robert Beverley's *The History and Present State of Virginia* (1705); John Lawson *A New Voyage to Carolina* (1709); Thomas Prince's *Chronological History of New England in the Form of Animals* (1736); Cadwallader Colden's *History of the Five Indian Nations* (1727); and especially William Byrd's *The History of the Dividing Line* (first published in 1841). In his official account of the surveying trip that drew the line between Virginia and North Carolina, the Virginian Byrd epitomized the cultured man of the world who was quickly replacing the Boston theologian as the prototypical American.

Like the histories of the colonies, the personal histories of individuals became more worldly. The Puritan tradition of the spiritual autobiography continued in the biographical sections of Mather's *Magnalia* and in Edwards's unpublished "Personal Narrative" (written in 1740?). But like regionalism, sectarianism was giving way to a more inclusive view of the variety of religious experience. This ecumenical approach was evident in the interest in conversions of other sects, especially in Quaker narratives such as the *Journals* of Thomas Chalkley (1747) and of John Woolman (1774) and the *Accounts* of Elizabeth Ashbridge (1774) and of John Churchman (1779).

Although the famous secular diaries of Byrd and Knight were not published during the eighteenth century, their viewpoint was central to that period's most celebrated personal narrative—Franklin's *Autobiography* begun in 1771 but not published in entirety until 1867. Bostonian and Philadelphian, printer and writer, scientist and politician, entrepreneur and philanthropist, Franklin symbolized the transitional character of the late eighteenth century. By describing the purely secular pursuit of success with the spiritual intensity of the Puritans, Franklin

Many buildings from the eighteenth century, known as the neoclassical period, imitate ancient Greece and Rome architecturally. Thomas Jefferson's designs for his home, Monticello, helped promote a classical revival.

=CONTEXTS=

After the Revolution the nature of American versus "the King's" English was a subject of great controversy. In his essays, dictionaries, and schoolbooks, Noah Webster (1758–1843) led efforts to define a distinctive American language. The following excerpt is from his preface to *An American Dictionary of the English Language* (1828).

[American English]

It is not only important, but, in a degree necessary, that the people of this country, should have an *American Dictionary* of the English Language; for, although the body of the language is the same as in England, and it is desirable to perpetuate that sameness, yet some differences must exist. Language is the expression of idea; and if the people of one country cannot preserve an identity of ideas, they cannot retain an identity of language. Now an identity of ideas depends materially upon a sameness of things or objects with which the people of the two countries are conversant. But in no two portions of the earth, remote from each other, can such identity be found. Even physical objects must be different.

* * *

It has been my aim in this work, now offered to my fellow citizens, to ascertain the true principles of the language, in its orthography and structure; to purify it from some palpable errors, and reduce the number of its anomalies, thus giving it more regularity and consistency in its forms, both of words and sentences; and in this manner, to furnish a standard of our vernacular tongue, which we shall not be ashamed to bequeath to *three hundred millions of people*, who are destined to occupy, and I hope, to adorn the vast territory within our jurisdiction.

Noah Webster, 1828

---

completed the shift from piety to moralism already begun by Cotton Mather's brief moral handbook *Bonifacius* (1710). Adopting a falsely naïve narrative voice, Franklin defined a new American hero, one whose devotion to America was as religious as was the Puritans' devotion to the church.

Franklin's *Autobiography* was one of the stylistic jewels of its time and served as the model for an ongoing tradition of rags-to-riches success stories that includes the work of Horatio Alger, Mark Twain, Frederick Douglass, Louisa May Alcott, F. Scott Fitzgerald, Edna Ferber, and J. D. Salinger. Yet, the contradictions inherent in Franklin's celebration of individual ingenuity were faced more directly in the other new form of autobiography of the time—the slave narrative. Earlier narratives had depicted captivity by Native Americans as an emblem of the soul's enslavement to, and ultimate escape from, sin. The slave narrative found a parallel in the captivity not of individuals but of a whole race. Beginning in 1760 with Briton Hammon's *A Narrative of the Uncommon Sufferings, and Surprising*

Deliverance of Briton Hammon, a Negro Man, free blacks or fugitives such as John Marrant, James Albert Ukawsaw Gronniosaw, Venture Smith, and Abraham Johnstone recounted their persecution to argue for the redemptive power of religion and for the need to abolish the slave trade. The early masterpiece in this genre, *The Interesting Narrative of the Life of Olaudah Equiano, or Gustavus Vassa, the African* (1789), embodied the contradictions of the tradition and of the white culture that fostered it. Equiano's international identity and his black sense of self called into question the very notions of "America" and "liberty" then being institutionalized at the Constitutional Convention in Philadelphia. Equiano's mixture of morality and economics suggested even more fully than did Franklin's complacency the antisocial bias of the individualism that sponsored upward mobility.

The tension between individual advancement and group loyalty implicit throughout the secular biographies was explicit in the controversial publications of political pamphleteers. Like their English counterparts, Americans had always debated issues of general concern through pamphlet wars. The spiritual revivals of the 1730s, 1740s, and 1750s initiated an endless series of denunciations and vindications of the doctrine of original sin and of the role of religion in salvation. In the 1760s, however, the rising hostility to British colonialism combined with advances in printing technology to produce an unparalleled outpouring: nine thousand publications between 1763 and 1783, of which some two thousand were political pamphlets. Their rhetoric drew on established sermon techniques and on traditional English models of Joseph Addison, Richard Steele, Jonathan Swift, and Daniel Defoe. The theory in these pamphlets was equally eclectic—a mixture of Puritan theology, the views of John Locke and other Enlightenment philosophers, and the oppositional politics of the English Commonwealth and later English Whig-party republicans. These intellectual and rhetorical sources were turned against themselves thematically to cut the colonies' religious and political ties to Europe.

The value of many pamphlets—produced swiftly and anonymously, commonly as reprints from newspapers—lies more in their historical importance than in their literary sophistication. Yet, some writers wrote often enough to perfect their literary skills as well. James Otis's *The Rights of the British Colonies* (1764) and *A Vindication of the British Colonies* (1765) and especially John Dickinson's *Letters from a Farmer in Pennsylvania* (1768) address problems more universal than the local British injustices that occasioned the writings. The master of pamphlet rhetoric was Thomas Paine. The precise reasons for Paine's preeminence are unclear. His late entry into the debate may have heightened the originality of his voice; his English training may have given him a stylistic edge; that he was not a native American may have saved him from the regional envy that restricted the audience of the talented but very Yankee John Adams. Paine may simply have published *Common Sense* (1776), the first American call for immediate independence from England, at exactly the right moment. Whatever the reasons, that pamphlet quickly became an international bestseller, matched in popularity only by Paine's later defense of the French Revolution and attack on English aristocracy, *The Rights of Man* (1791–1792).

The paradoxical combination of universal truth and individualized voice generally characteristic of the pamphleteers informed the most important political documents of the period, The Declaration of Independence (1776) and the essays of *The Federalist* (1787–1788), which sought to ratify the Constitution. *The Federalist* interests modern readers less for its explanation (correct or not) of the theory of representative government than for its depiction of the confusion and uncertainties surrounding the Constitution's ratification. Via the split personality of "Publius," the pseudonym used by *The Federalist* authors, New Yorker Alexander Hamilton and Virginian James Madison acted out the compromises—between federalism and nationalism, elitism and populism, North and South—that characterized the uneasy unification of thirteen disparate colonies and cultures.

The diversity of the new republic's literature was perhaps best represented by the masterpiece that began the national tradition in American literature, Michel-Guillaume Jean de Crèvecoeur's *Letters From an American Farmer* (1782). The work and author were in every sense anomalies. Crèvecoeur was a French aristocrat who relocated to French Canada and subsequently became a naturalized British subject in upstate New York. Persecuted by both sides during the early years of the American Revolution, he fled to France in 1780 with his manuscript and subsequently published an account of these experiences. Crèvecoeur imitated the pamphleteer tradition through a discontinuous series of fictional "letters." The sentimental appreciation of the landscape, the close observation of nature, the value of travel, and the cultural differences throughout the Americas were all treated in turn. The account darkened with the approaching threat of war and with the twin problems of slavery and Indian hostility. Crèvecoeur's famous question "What is an American?" marked a turning point. For the first time American literature explicitly and directly confronted its own unique character. Yet, the answer was at best preliminary; Crèvecoeur's sense of America was limited by his perspective as a privileged white male.

Crèvecoeur's limitations and ambivalences summarize the contradictory thrust of his time. Despite Abigail Adams's famous warning to her husband, John, not to forget "the ladies," the Constitutional Convention neglected to include women as participants in the new government. The construction of an independent identity for America required the redefinition and exclusion of a wide range of cultural differences—in politics and theology as well as in race and gender. Just as the importance of the American Revolution has at times made it seem the sole event of the eighteenth century, so the political writings of the revolutionaries have obscured a wealth of other literature. Subsequent analyses of that burgeoning cultural identity have only further simplified the transition from colony to republic by isolating Jefferson's democratic philosophy from the slave society in which he practiced it, for example, or Crèvecoeur's hopeful predictions for America from the irony and despair in which his book and life ended. Only when we attend to the extraordinary range of voices within eighteenth-century American literature and to the full complexity of each individual voice can we truly understand the richness and depth of this eclectic period.

Thomas Jefferson
(1743–1826)

"I have sworn upon the altar of God, eternal hostility against every form of tyranny over the mind of man." When Thomas Jefferson wrote these words in a letter to the physician/ educator Benjamin Rush in 1800, Jefferson was at the midpoint of an already illustrious public career and would soon become president. A product of the Enlightenment, Jefferson believed that the United States offered the best hope for establishing a society based upon mankind's natural, inalienable rights. His writings, such as The Declaration of Independence (1776; of which he wrote the first draft), were typically the finest expression of the ideals that came to define the American national character.

Much of Jefferson's practical republicanism was the direct outgrowth of his early training. He was born in 1743 in Albemarle County, Virginia, to Jane Randolph and Peter Jefferson and into a lineage that combined the blue blood of the Virginia aristocracy with that of the self-made man. Throughout his life he fought against inherited privilege and preferment and argued in favor of a natural aristocracy, one open to all men but predicated upon virtue, merit, and achievement rather than on birthright. At age nine Jefferson studied Latin, Greek, and French; at fourteen he entered the school of Rev. James Maury. There Jefferson learned other languages and acquired a love of classical literature and gained a lifelong admiration for Greek and Roman ethical thought and self-discipline. At the College of William and Mary he was influenced by Dr. William Small, a professor of mathematics and philosophy, who developed Jefferson's knowledge of science and inductive reasoning. However, Jefferson made sharp distinctions between the learning he thought appropriate for women and that for men. As his letter to Nathaniel Burwell shows, he emphasized the practical, thought women should not study the classical languages, and was skeptical of fiction.

After graduating in 1762 Jefferson began a five-year intensive study of the law, particularly its guarantees of liberty, under the famed attorney George Wythe. Soon after Jefferson opened his law practice, he was elected to represent Albemarle County in the House of Burgesses in 1769. That year he began to build his home, Monticello. He married Martha Wayles Skelton in 1772, the year after his reelection; she died only ten years later after giving birth to their sixth child.

With the onset of the Revolution Jefferson became extraordinarily active in American politics. He represented Virginia in the Second Continental Congress in 1775, revised that state's legal code, drafted a public education bill, and, returning to the House of Burgesses (1776–1779), wrote the Statute of Virginia for Religious Freedom (not accepted until 1786). He then served as governor of Virginia (1779–1781) and as a congressman (1783–1784) and assisted Benjamin Franklin and John Adams with treaty negotiations in Paris in 1784 before succeeding Franklin as minister to France (1785–1789). From 1789 to 1793 Jefferson served as the first secretary of state and often opposed the extreme Federalist policies of Alexander Hamilton, favoring strong rights at the state and local levels.

Narrowly defeated for the presidency in 1776 by John Adams, Jefferson became vice-president, as was then the custom. As president from 1801 to 1809, he continued to champion individuals' and states' rights; made the Louisiana Purchase, which more than doubled America's size in 1803 and provided the land for individual ownership (which Jefferson considered necessary for human happiness); sponsored the Lewis and Clark expedition (1804–1806); and in 1806 signed a bill prohibiting the importation of slaves. After his political career ended, Jefferson sold his library of more than ten thousand volumes to the new nation in 1814 to form the core collection of the Library of Congress and founded the University of Virginia in 1817.

No summary of offices and achievements can present a full portrait of a man as complex as Jefferson. Politician, statesman, scientist, philosopher, architect, environmental planner, agriculturalist, inventor, writer, and patron of education and learning, he epitomized the eighteenth-century gentleman who did all things well and with easy grace. Yet, he was a man of paradoxes. An aristocrat, he established the small landowner as the ideal citizen; he loved Paris but promulgated the benefits of agrarian life; an indifferent orator, he was a master of prose; and although he kept a large number of slaves, he saw slavery as a moral evil.

More than any of his peers in the American Revolution, Jefferson captured the country's spirit in his writing. His stirring words were so apt that they became the foundation of the nation's civil religion. His statements in the Declaration of Independence were the natural outgrowths of his earlier highly influential work, *A Summary of the Rights of British America* (1774), and led to his bill establishing religious freedom in Virginia. But the literary Jefferson is best known from his only book, *Notes on the State of Virginia* (1785), and his correspondence. The *Notes* were Jefferson's responses to a series of questions put to him by François Marbois, the secretary to the French minister in Philadelphia. Jefferson's analyses and sweeping descriptions compensate for what the notes lack in formal unity. In answering Marbois's queries about America and particularly Virginia, Jefferson chose to present his view of the "state" of the new nation, its condition and governance. Jefferson used the *Notes* to justify the Declaration of Independence, to show that the United States would succeed, and to disprove the French naturalist Georges Buffon's theory that all species, including man, tended to degenerate in the New World.

After his second term as president Jefferson returned to Monticello and entered a very active retirement marked by an enormous increase in his correspondence. In many ways the letter was his ideal literary form; it showcased his wit, zest, and wisdom as he expounded his ideas on religion, ethics, language, education, politics, and American society. Jefferson honed his artfulness through practice; more than twenty-five thousand of his letters survive, and a definitive collected edition of his works would likely exceed sixty volumes. One highlight of his letter-writing skills was the series of letters he exchanged with John Adams from 1811 until just before their deaths on the same day, July 4, 1826, the fiftieth anniversary of the signing of the Declaration of Independence. Following the direct style that paced his letters, Jefferson ordered the following epitaph engraved on his tombstone to sum up his life: ". . .Author of the Declaration of American Independence, of the Statute of Virginia for Religious Freedom, and Father of the University of Virginia."

Suggested Readings: A. Koch, *The Philosophy of Thomas Jefferson*, 1943. D. Malone, *Jefferson and His Times*, 6 vols., 1948–1981. F. Brodie, *Thomas Jefferson: An Intimate History*, 1974. H. S. Commager, *Jefferson, Nationalism and the Enlightenment*, 1975. G. Wills, *Inventing America: Jefferson's Declaration of Independence*, 1978. C. A. Miller, *Jefferson and Nature: An Interpretation*, 1988.

Texts Used: The Declaration of Independence: *Old South Leaflets*, Gen. Series, No. 3, Vol. I, (n.d.). "Queries": *Notes on the State of Virginia*, ed. W. Peden, 1955. "To John Adams," Oct. 28, 1813 and July 5, 1814: *The Writings of Thomas Jefferson, 1807–1815*, Vol. IX, ed. P. L. Ford, 1898. "To John Adams," Aug. 16, 1816, and "To Nathaniel Burwell," March 14, 1818: *The Writings of Thomas Jefferson, 1816–1826*, Vol. X, ed. P. L. Ford, 1899.

A draft of the Declaration of Independence in Thomas Jefferson's handwriting.

THE DECLARATION OF INDEPENDENCE

THE UNANIMOUS DECLARATION OF THE THIRTEEN UNITED STATES OF AMERICA

In Congress, July 4, 1776.

When in the Course of human events, it becomes necessary for one people to dissolve the political bands which have connected them with another, and to assume among the Powers of the earth, the separate and equal station which the Laws of Nature and of Nature's God entitle them, a decent respect to the opinions of mankind requires that they should declare the causes which impel them to the separation.

We hold these truths to be self-evident, that all men are created equal, that they are endowed by their Creator with certain unalienable Rights, that among these are Life, Liberty and the pursuit of Happiness. That to secure these rights, Governments are instituted among Men, deriving their just powers from the consent of the governed, That whenever any Form of Government becomes destructive of these ends, it is the Right of the People to alter or to abolish it, and to institute new Government, laying its foundation on such principles and organizing its powers in such form, as to them shall seem most likely to effect their Safety and Happiness. Prudence, indeed, will dictate that Governments long established should not be changed for light and transient causes; and accordingly all experience hath shown, that mankind are more disposed to suffer, while evils are sufferable, than to right themselves by abolishing the forms to which they are accustomed. But when a long train of abuses and usurpations, pursuing invariably the same Object evinces a design to reduce them under absolute Despotism, it is their right, it is their duty, to throw off such Government, and to provide new Guards for their future security.—Such has been the patient sufferance of these Colonies; and such is now the necessity which constrains them to alter their former Systems of Government. The history of the present King of Great Britain is a history of repeated injuries and usurpations, all having in direct object the establishment of an absolute Tyranny over these States. To prove this, let Facts be submitted to a candid world.

He has refused his Assent to Laws, the most wholesome and necessary for the public good.

He has forbidden his Governors to pass Laws of immediate and pressing importance, unless suspended in their operation till his Assent should be obtained; and when so suspended, he has utterly neglected to attend to them.

He has refused to pass other Laws for the accommodation of large districts of people, unless those people would relinquish the right of Representation in the Legislature, a right inestimable to them and formidable to tyrants only.

He has called together legislative bodies at places unusual, uncomfortable, and distant from the depository of their Public Records, for the sole purpose of fatiguing them into compliance with his measures.

He has dissolved Representative Houses repeatedly, for opposing with manly firmness his invasions on the rights of the people.

He has refused for a long time, after such dissolutions, to cause others to be elected; whereby the Legislative Powers, incapable of Annihilation, have returned to the People at large for their exercise; the State remaining in the mean time exposed to all the dangers of invasion from without, and convulsions within.

He has endeavoured to prevent the population of these States; for that purpose obstructing the Laws for Naturalization of Foreigners; refusing to pass others to encourage their migration hither, and raising the conditions of new Appropriations of Lands.

He has obstructed the Administration of Justice, by refusing his Assent to Laws for establishing Judiciary Powers.

He has made Judges dependent on his Will alone, for the tenure of their offices, and the amount and payment of their salaries.

He has erected a multitude of New Offices, and sent hither swarms of Officers to harrass our People, and eat out their substance.

He has kept among us, in times of peace, Standing Armies without the Consent of our legislature.

He has affected to render the Military independent of and superior to the Civil Power.

He has combined with others to subject us to a jurisdiction foreign to our constitution, and unacknowledged by our laws; giving his Assent to their Acts of pretended Legislation:

For quartering large bodies of armed troops among us:

For protecting them, by a mock Trial, from Punishment for any Murders which they should commit on the Inhabitants of these States:

For cutting off our Trade with all parts of the world:

For imposing taxes on us without our Consent:

For depriving us in many cases, of the benefits of Trial by Jury:

For transporting us beyond Seas to be tried for pretended offences:

For abolishing the free System of English Laws in a neighbouring Province, establishing therein an Arbitrary government, and enlarging its Boundaries so as to render it at once an example and fit instrument for introducing the same absolute rule into these Colonies:

For taking away our Charters, abolishing our most valuable Laws, and altering fundamentally the Forms of our Governments:

For suspending our own Legislatures, and declaring themselves invested with Power to legislate for us in all cases whatsoever.

He has abdicated Government here, by declaring us out of his Protection and waging War against us.

He has plundered our seas, ravaged our Coasts, burnt our towns, and destroyed the lives of our people.

He is at this time transporting large armies of foreign mercenaries to compleat the works of death, desolation and tyranny, already begun with circumstances of Cruelty & perfidy scarcely paralleled in the most barbarous ages, and totally unworthy the Head of a civilized nation.

He has constrained our fellow Citizens taken Captive on the high Seas to bear Arms against their Country, to become the executioners of their friends and Brethren, or to fall themselves by their Hands.

He has excited domestic insurrections amongst us, and has endeavoured to bring on the inhabitants of our frontiers, the merciless Indian Savages, whose known rule of warfare, is an undistinguished destruction of all ages, sexes and conditions.

In every stage of these Oppressions We have Petitioned for Redress in the most humble terms: Our repeated Petitions have been answered only by repeated injury. A Prince, whose character is thus marked by every act which may define a Tyrant, is unfit to be the ruler of a free People.

Nor have We been wanting in attention to our Brittish brethren. We have warned them from time to time of attempts by their legislature to extend an unwarrantable jurisdiction over us. We have reminded them of the circumstances of our emigration and settlement here. We have appealed to their native justice and magnanimity, and we have conjured them by the ties of our common kindred to disavow these usurpations, which would inevitably interrupt our connections and correspondence. They too have been deaf to the voice of justice and of consanguinity. We must, therefore, acquiesce in the necessity, which denounces our Separation, and hold them, as we hold the rest of mankind, Enemies in War, in Peace Friends.

We, therefore, the Representatives of the united States of America, in General Congress, Assembled, appealing to the Supreme Judge of the world for the rectitude of our intentions, do, in the Name, and by Authority of the good People of these Colonies, solemnly publish and declare, That these United Colonies are, and of Right ought to be Free and Independent States; that they are Absolved from all Allegiance to the British Crown, and that all political connection between them and the State of Great Britain, is and ought to be totally dissolved; and that as Free and Independent States, they have full Power to levy War, conclude Peace, contract Alliances, establish Commerce, and to do all other Acts and Things which Independent States may of right do. And for the support of this Declaration, with a firm reliance on the Protection of Divine Providence, we mutually pledge to each other our Lives, our Fortunes and our sacred Honor.

1776

from NOTES ON THE STATE OF VIRGINIA*

from QUERY V: CASCADES

* * *

[Natural Bridge]

The *Natural Bridge*,[1] the most sublime of Nature's works, though not comprehended under the present head,[2] must not be pretermitted.[3] It is on the ascent of a hill, which seems to have been cloven through its length by some great convulsion. The fissure, just at the bridge, is, by some admeasurements, 270 feet deep, by others only 205. It is about 45 feet wide at the bottom, and 90 feet at the top; this of course determines the length of the bridge, and its height from the water. Its breadth in the middle, is about 60 feet, but more at the ends, and the thickness of the mass at the summit of the arch, about 40 feet. A part of this thickness is constituted by a coat of earth, which gives growth to many large trees. The residue, with the hill on both sides, is one solid rock of limestone. The arch ap-

---

* Jefferson wrote *Notes on the State of Virginia* in response to twenty-three queries by the French government, concerning Virginia's people, history, geography, and ecology.

[1] Near Lexington, Virginia, on land Jefferson owned.
[2] Not covered under the heading "Cascades."   [3] Omitted.

proaches the semi-elliptical form; but the larger axis of the ellipsis, which would be the cord of the arch, is many times longer than the semi-axis which gives its height. Though the sides of this bridge are provided in some parts with a parapet of fixed rocks, yet few men have resolution to walk to them and look over into the abyss. You involuntarily fall on your hands and feet, creep to the parapet and peep over it. Looking down from this height about a minute, gave me a violent head ache. This painful sensation is relieved by a short, but pleasing view of the Blue ridge along the fissure downwards, and upwards by that of the Short hills, which, with the Purgatory mountain is a divergence from the North ridge; and, descending then to the valley below, the sensation becomes delightful in the extreme. It is impossible for the emotions, arising from the sublime, to be felt beyond what they are here: so beautiful an arch, so elevated, so light, and springing, as it were, up to heaven, the rapture of the spectator is really indescribable! The fissure continues deep and narrow and, following the margin of the stream upwards about three eights of a mile you arrive at a limestone cavern, less remarkable, however, for height and extent than those before described. Its entrance into the hill is but a few feet above the bed of the stream. This bridge is in the county of Rockbridge, to which it has given name, and affords a public and commodious passage over a valley, which cannot be crossed elsewhere for a considerable distance. The stream passing under it is called Cedar creek. It is a water[4] of James river, and sufficient in the driest seasons to turn a grist-mill, though its fountain[5] is not more than two miles above.

from — QUERY VI: PRODUCTIONS MINERAL, VEGETABLE AND ANIMAL

* * *

The opinion advanced by the Count de Buffon,[1] is 1. That the animals common both to the old and new world, are smaller in the latter. 2. That those peculiar to the new, are on a smaller scale. 3. That those which have been domesticated in both, have degenerated in America: and 4. That on the whole it exhibits fewer species. And the reason he thinks is, that the heats of America are less; that more waters are spread over its surface by nature, and fewer of these drained off by the hand of man. In other words, that *heat* is friendly, and *moisture* adverse to the production and developement of large quadrupeds. I will not meet this hypothesis on its first doubtful ground, whether the climate of America be comparatively more humid? Because we are not furnished with observations sufficient to decide this question. And though, till it be decided, we are as free to deny, as others are to affirm the fact, yet for a moment let it be supposed. The hypothesis, after this supposition, proceeds to another; that *moisture* is unfriendly to animal growth. The truth of this is inscrutable to us by reasonings a priori. Nature has hidden from us her modus agendi. Our only appeal on such questions is to experience; and I think that experience is against the supposition. It is by the assistance of *heat* and *moisture* that vegetables are elaborated from the elements of earth, air, water, and fire. We accordingly see the more humid climates produce the greater quantity of vegetables. Vegetables are mediately or immediately the food of every animal:

----

[4] A tributary.   [5] Source.

[1] Georges Louis Leclerc de Buffon (1707–1788), a naturalist who proposed in *Natural History* (1749–1788) that North American species are degenerate.

and in proportion to the quantity of food, we see animals not only multiplied in their numbers, but improved in their bulk, as far as the laws of their nature will admit. Of this opinion is the Count de Buffon himself in another part of his work: "in general it seems that somewhat cold countries are better suited to our oxen than hot countries, and they are the heavier and bigger in proportion as the climate is damper and more abounding in pasture lands. The oxen of Denmark, of Podolie,[2] of the Ukraine, and of Tartary which is inhabited by the Calmouques,[3] are the largest of all." Here then a race of animals, and one of the largest too, has been increased in its dimensions by *cold* and *moisture,* in direct opposition to the hypothesis, which supposes that these two circumstances diminish animal bulk, and that it is their contraries *heat* and *dryness* which enlarge it. But when we appeal to experience, we are not to rest satisfied with a single fact. Let us therefore try our question on more general ground. Let us take two portions of the earth, Europe and America for instance, sufficiently extensive to give operation to general causes; let us consider the circumstances peculiar to each, and observe their effect on animal nature. America, running through the torrid as well as temperate zone, has more *heat,* collectively taken, than Europe. But Europe, according to our hypothesis, is the *dryest.* They are equally adapted then to animal productions; each being endowed with one of those causes which befriend animal growth, and with one which opposes it. If it be thought unequal to compare Europe with America, which is so much larger, I answer, not more so than to compare America with the whole world. Besides, the purpose of the comparison is to try an hypothesis, which makes the size of animals depend on the *heat* and *moisture* of climate. If therefore we take a region, so extensive as to comprehend a sensible distinction of climate, and so extensive too as that local accidents, or the intercourse of animals on its borders, may not materially affect the size of those in its interior parts, we shall comply with those conditions which the hypothesis may reasonably demand. The objection would be the weaker in the present case, because any intercourse of animals which may take place on the confines of Europe and Asia, is to the advantage of the former, Asia producing certainly larger animals than Europe. Let us then take a comparative view of the Quadrupeds of Europe and America, presenting them to the eye in three different tables, in one of which shall be enumerated those found in both countries; in a second those found in one only; in a third those which have been domesticated in both. To facilitate the comparison, let those of each table be arranged in gradation according to their sizes, from the greatest to the smallest, so far as their sizes can be conjectured. The weights of the large animals shall be expressed in the English avoirdupoise pound and its decimals: those of the smaller in the ounce and its decimals. Those which are marked thus *, are actual weights of particular subjects, deemed among the largest of their species. Those marked thus †, are furnished by judicious persons, well acquainted with the species, and saying, from conjecture only, what the largest individual they had seen would probably have weighed. The other weights are taken from Messrs. Buffon and D'Aubenton, and are of such subjects as came casually to their hands for dissection. This circumstance must be remembered where their weights and mine stand opposed: the latter being stated, not to produce a conclusion in favour of the American species, but to justify a suspension of opinion until we are better informed, and a suspicion in the mean time that there is no uniform difference in favour of either; which is all I pretend.

* * *

[2] A village in India.   [3] A Mongol tribe of nomads.

QUERY XVII: RELIGION

The first settlers in this country were emigrants from England, of the English church, just at a point of time when it was flushed with complete victory over the religious of all other persuasions. Possessed, as they became, of the powers of making, administering, and executing the laws, they shewed equal intolerance in this country with their Presbyterian brethren, who had emigrated to the northern government. The poor Quakers were flying from persecution in England. They cast their eyes on these new countries as asylums of civil and religious freedom; but they found them free only for the reigning sect. Several acts of the Virginia assembly of 1659, 1662, and 1693, had made it penal in parents to refuse to have their children baptized; had prohibited the unlawful assembling of Quakers; had made it penal for any master of a vessel to bring a Quaker into the state; had ordered those already here, and such as should come thereafter, to be imprisoned till they should abjure the country; provided a milder punishment for their first and second return, but death for their third; had inhibited all persons from suffering their meetings in or near their houses, entertaining them individually, or disposing of books which supported their tenets. If no capital execution took place here, as did in New-England, it was not owing to the moderation of the church, or spirit of the legislature, as may be inferred from the law itself; but to historical circumstances which have not been handed down to us. The Anglicans retained full possession of the country about a century. Other opinions began then to creep in, and the great care of the government to support their own church, having begotten an equal degree of indolence in its clergy, two-thirds of the people had become dissenters at the commencement of the present revolution. The laws indeed were still oppressive on them, but the spirit of the one party had subsided into moderation, and of the other had risen to a degree of determination which commanded respect.

The present state of our laws on the subject of religion is this. The convention of May 1776, in their declaration of rights, declared it to be a truth, and a natural right, that the exercise of religion should be free; but when they proceeded to form on that declaration the ordinance of government, instead of taking up every principle declared in the bill of rights, and guarding it by legislative sanction, they passed over that which asserted our religious rights, leaving them as they found them. The same convention, however, when they met as a member of the general assembly in October 1776, repealed all *acts of parliament* which had rendered criminal the maintaining any opinions in matters of religion, the forbearing to repair to church, and the exercising any mode of worship; and suspended the laws giving salaries to the clergy, which suspension was made perpetual in October 1779. Statutory oppressions in religion being thus wiped away, we remain at present under those only imposed by the common law, or by our own acts of assembly. At the common law, *heresy* was a capital offence, punishable by burning. Its definition was left to the ecclesiastical judges, before whom the conviction was, till the statute of the 1 El. c. 1.[1] circumscribed it, by declaring, that nothing should be deemed heresy, but what had been so determined by authority of the canonical scriptures, or by one of the four first general councils, or by some other council having for the grounds of their declaration the express and plain words of the scriptures. Heresy, thus circumscribed, being an offence at the common law, our act of assembly of October 1777, c. 17. gives cognizance of it to the general court, by declaring, that the jurisdiction of that court shall be general in all matters

[1] The first year of Queen Elizabeth's reign, 1558–1559.

at the common law. The execution is by the writ *De hæretico comburendo*.[2] By our own act of assembly of 1705, c. 30, if a person brought up in the Christian religion denies the being of a God, or the Trinity, or asserts there are more Gods than one, or denies the Christian religion to be true, or the scriptures to be of divine authority, he is punishable on the first offence by incapacity to hold any office or employment ecclesiastical, civil, or military; on the second by disability to sue, to take any gift or legacy, to be guardian, executor, or administrator, and by three years imprisonment, without bail. A father's right to the custody of his own children being founded in law on his right of guardianship, this being taken away, they may of course be severed from him, and put, by the authority of a court, into more orthodox hands. This is a summary view of that religious slavery, under which a people have been willing to remain, who have lavished their lives and fortunes for the establishment of their civil freedom.

The error seems not sufficiently eradicated, that the operations of the mind, as well as the acts of the body, are subject to the coercion of the laws.[3] But our rulers can have authority over such natural rights only as we have submitted to them. The rights of conscience we never submitted, we could not submit. We are answerable for them to our God. The legitimate powers of government extend to such acts only as are injurious to others. But it does me no injury for my neighbour to say there are twenty gods, or no god. It neither picks my pocket nor breaks my leg. If it be said, his testimony in a court of justice cannot be relied on, reject it then, and be the stigma on him. Constraint may make him worse by making him a hypocrite, but it will never make him a truer man. It may fix him obstinately in his errors, but will not cure them. Reason and free enquiry are the only effectual agents against error. Give a loose to them, they will support the true religion, by bringing every false one to their tribunal, to the test of their investigation. They are the natural enemies of error, and of error only. Had not the Roman government permitted free enquiry, Christianity could never have been introduced. Had not free enquiry been indulged, at the æra of the reformation, the corruptions of Christianity could not have been purged away. If it be restrained now, the present corruptions will be protected, and new ones encouraged. Was the government to prescribe to us our medicine and diet, our bodies would be in such keeping as our souls are now. Thus in France the emetic was once forbidden as a medicine, and the potatoe as an article of food. Government is just as infallible too when it fixes systems in physics. Galileo was sent to the inquisition for affirming that the earth was a sphere: the government had declared it to be as flat as a trencher, and Galileo was obliged to abjure his error. This error however at length prevailed, the earth became a globe, and Descartes[4] declared it was whirled round its axis by a vortex. The government in which he lived was wise enough to see that this was no question of civil jurisdiction, or we should all have been involved by authority in vortices. In fact, the vortices have been exploded, and the Newtonian principle of gravitation is now more firmly established, on the basis of reason, than it would be were the government to step in, and to make it an article of necessary faith. Reason and experiment have been indulged, and error has fled before them. It is error alone which needs the support of government. Truth can stand by itself. Subject opinion to coercion: whom will you make your inquisitors? Fallible men;

---

[2] "On the burning of a heretic" (Latin).

[3] Jefferson's note: "Furneaux passim." Philip Furneaux (1726–1783) was an English minister and author.

[4] René Descartes (1596–1650), a French philosopher and scientist.

men governed by bad passions, by private as well as public reasons. And why subject it to coercion? To produce uniformity. But is uniformity of opinion desireable? No more than of face and stature. Introduce the bed of Procrustes[5] then, and as there is danger that the large men may beat the small, make us all of a size, by lopping the former and stretching the latter. Difference of opinion is advantageous in religion. The several sects perform the office of a Censor morum[6] over each other. Is uniformity attainable? Millions of innocent men, women, and children, since the introduction of Christianity, have been burnt, tortured, fined, imprisoned; yet we have not advanced one inch towards uniformity. What has been the effect of coercion? To make one half the world fools, and the other half hypocrites. To support roguery and error all over the earth. Let us reflect that it is inhabited by a thousand millions of people. That these profess probably a thousand different systems of religion. That ours is but one of that thousand. That if there be but one right, and ours that one, we should wish to see the 999 wandering sects gathered into the fold of truth. But against such a majority we cannot effect this by force. Reason and persuasion are the only practicable instruments. To make way for these, free enquiry must be indulged; and how can we wish others to indulge it while we refuse it ourselves. But every state, says an inquisitor, has established some religion. No two, say I, have established the same. Is this a proof of the infallibility of establishments? Our sister states of Pennsylvania and New York, however, have long subsisted without any establishment at all. The experiment was new and doubtful when they made it. It has answered beyond conception. They flourish infinitely. Religion is well supported; of various kinds, indeed, but all good enough; all sufficient to preserve peace and order: or if a sect arises, whose tenets would subvert morals, good sense has fair play, and reasons and laughs it out of doors, without suffering the state to be troubled with it. They do not hang more malefactors than we do. They are not more disturbed with religious dissensions. On the contrary, their harmony is unparalleled, and can be ascribed to nothing but their unbounded tolerance, because there is no other circumstance in which they differ from every nation on earth. They have made the happy discovery, that the way to silence religious disputes, is to take no notice of them. Let us too give this experiment fair play, and get rid, while we may, of those tyrannical laws. It is true, we are as yet secured against them by the spirit of the times. I doubt whether the people of this country would suffer an execution for heresy, or a three years imprisonment for not comprehending the mysteries of the Trinity. But is the spirit of the people an infallible, a permanent reliance? Is it government? Is this the kind of protection we receive in return for the rights we give up? Besides, the spirit of the times may alter, will alter. Our rulers will become corrupt, our people careless. A single zealot may commence persecutor, and better men be his victims. It can never be too often repeated, that the time for fixing every essential right on a legal basis is while our rulers are honest, and ourselves united. From the conclusion of this war we shall be going down hill. It will not then be necessary to resort every moment to the people for support. They will be forgotten, therefore, and their rights disregarded. They will forget themselves, but in the sole faculty of making money, and will never think of uniting to effect a due respect for their rights. The shackles, therefore, which shall not be

---

[5] In classical mythology Procrustes was a highwayman who, to fit his iron bed, cut off or stretched his captives' legs.
[6] A critic of morals (Latin).

knocked off at the conclusion of this war, will remain on us long, will be made heavier and heavier, till our rights shall revive or expire in a convulsion.

QUERY XVIII: MANNERS

It is difficult to determine on the standard by which the manners of a nation may be tried, whether *catholic,*[1] or *particular*. It is more difficult for a native to bring to that standard the manners of his own nation, familiarized to him by habit. There must doubtless be an unhappy influence on the manners of our people produced by the existence of slavery among us. The whole commerce between master and slave is a perpetual exercise of the most boisterous passions, the most unremitting despotism on the one part, and degrading submissions on the other. Our children see this, and learn to imitate it; for man is an imitative animal. This quality is the germ of all education in him. From his cradle to his grave he is learning to do what he sees others do. If a parent could find no motive either in his philanthropy or his self-love, for restraining the intemperance of passion towards his slave, it should always be a sufficient one that his child is present. But generally it is not sufficient. The parent storms, the child looks on, catches the lineaments of wrath, puts on the same airs in the circle of smaller slaves, gives a loose to his worst of passions, and thus nursed, educated, and daily exercised in tyranny, cannot but be stamped by it with odious peculiarities. The man must be a prodigy who can retain his manners and morals undepraved by such circumstances. And with what execration should the statesman be loaded, who permitting one half the citizens thus to trample on the rights of the other, transforms those into despots, and these into enemies, destroys the morals of the one part, and the amor patriæ[2] of the other. For if a slave can have a country in this world, it must be any other in preference to that in which he is born to live and labour for another: in which he must lock up the faculties of his nature, contribute as far as depends on his individual endeavours to the evanishment of the human race, or entail[3] his own miserable condition on the endless generations proceeding from him. With the morals of the people, their industry also is destroyed. For in a warm climate, no man will labour for himself who can make another labour for him. This is so true, that of the proprietors of slaves a very small proportion indeed are ever seen to labour. And can the liberties of a nation be thought secure when we have removed their only firm basis, a conviction in the minds of the people that these liberties are of the gift of God? That they are not to be violated but with his wrath? Indeed I tremble for my country when I reflect that God is just: that his justice cannot sleep for ever: that considering numbers, nature and natural means only, a revolution of the wheel of fortune, an exchange of situation, is among possible events: that it may become probable by supernatural interference! The Almighty has no attribute which can take side with us in such a contest.—But it is impossible to be temperate and to pursue this subject through the various considerations of policy, of morals, of history natural and civil. We must be contented to hope they will force their way into every one's mind. I think a change already perceptible, since the origin of the present revolution. The spirit of the master is abating, that of the slave rising from the dust, his condition mollifying, the way I hope preparing,

[1] Universal.   [2] "Patriotism" (Latin).   [3] Impose.

under the auspices of heaven, for a total emancipation, and that this is disposed, in the order of events, to be with the consent of the masters, rather than by their extirpation.

Query XIX: Manufactures

We never had an interior trade of any importance. Our exterior commerce has suffered very much from the beginning of the present contest. During this time we have manufactured within our families the most necessary articles of cloathing. Those of cotton will bear some comparison with the same kinds of manufacture in Europe; but those of wool, flax and hemp are very coarse, unsightly, and unpleasant: and such is our attachment to agriculture, and such our preference for foreign manufactures, that be it wise or unwise, our people will certainly return as soon as they can, to the raising raw materials, and exchanging them for finer manufactures than they are able to execute themselves.

The political œconomists of Europe have established it as a principle that every state should endeavour to manufacture for itself: and this principle, like many others, we transfer to America, without calculating the difference of circumstance which should often produce a difference of result. In Europe the lands are either cultivated, or locked up against the cultivator. Manufacture must therefore be resorted to of necessity not of choice, to support the surplus of their people. But we have an immensity of land courting the industry of the husbandman.[1] Is it best then that all our citizens should be employed in its improvement, or that one half should be called off from that to exercise manufactures and handicraft arts for the other? Those who labour in the earth are the chosen people of God, if ever he had a chosen people, whose breasts he has made his peculiar deposit for substantial and genuine virtue. It is the focus in which he keeps alive that sacred fire, which otherwise might escape from the face of the earth. Corruption of morals in the mass of cultivators is a phænomenon of which no age nor nation has furnished an example. It is the mark set on those, who not looking up to heaven, to their own soil and industry, as does the husbandman, for their subsistence, depend for it on the casualties and caprice of customers. Dependance begets subservience and venality, suffocates the germ of virtue, and prepares fit tools for the designs of ambition. This, the natural progress and consequence of the arts, has sometimes perhaps been retarded by accidental circumstances: but, generally speaking, the proportion which the aggregate of the other classes of citizens bears in any state to that of its husbandmen, is the proportion of its unsound to its healthy parts, and is a good-enough barometer whereby to measure its degree of corruption. While we have land to labour then, let us never wish to see our citizens occupied at a work-bench, or twirling a distaff.[2] Carpenters, masons, smiths, are wanting in husbandry: but, for the general operations of manufacture, let our work-shops remain in Europe. It is better to carry provisions and materials to workmen there, than bring them to the provisions and materials, and with them their manners and principles. The loss by the transportation of commodities across the Atlantic will be made up in happiness and permanence of government. The mobs of great cities

---

[1] A farmer.   [2] The part of a spinning wheel on which wool is wound.

add just so much to the support of pure government, as sores do to the strength of the human body. It is the manners and spirit of a people which preserve a republic in vigour. A degeneracy in these is a canker which soon eats to the heart of its laws and constitution.

1781–1782, 1785

LETTERS TO JOHN ADAMS

[*Natural Aristocracy*]

Monticello October 28, 1813.

DEAR SIR,—

* * *

For I agree with you that there is a natural aristocracy among men. The grounds of this are virtue and talents. Formerly, bodily powers gave place among the aristoi.[1] But since the invention of gunpowder has armed the weak as well as the strong with missile death, bodily strength, like beauty, good humor, politeness and other accomplishments, has become but an auxiliary ground for distinction. There is also an artificial aristocracy, founded on wealth and birth, without either virtue or talents; for with these it would belong to the first class. The natural aristocracy I consider as the most precious gift of nature, for the instruction, the trusts, and government of society. And indeed, it would have been inconsistent in creation to have formed man for the social state, and not to have provided virtue and wisdom enough to manage the concerns of the society. May we not even say, that that form of government is the best, which provides the most effectually for a pure selection of these natural aristoi into the offices of government? The artificial aristocracy is a mischievous ingredient in government, and provision should be made to prevent its ascendency. On the question, what is the best provision, you and I differ; but we differ as rational friends, using the free exercise of our own reason, and mutually indulging its errors. You think it is best to put the pseudo-aristoi into a separate chamber of legislation, where they may be hindered from doing mischief by their co-ordinate branches, and where, also, they may be a protection to wealth against the Agrarian and plundering enterprises of the majority of the people. I think that to give them power in order to prevent them from doing mischief, is arming them for it, and increasing instead of remedying the evil. For if the co-ordinate branches can arrest their action, so may they that of the co-ordinates. Mischief may be done negatively as well as positively. Of this, a cabal in the Senate of the United States has furnished many proofs. Nor do I believe them necessary to protect the wealthy; because enough of these will find their way into every branch of the legislation, to protect themselves. From fifteen to twenty legislatures of our own, in action for thirty years past, have proved that no fears of an equalization of property are to be apprehended from them. I think the best remedy is exactly that provided by all our constitutions, to leave to the citizens the free election and separation of the aristoi from the pseudo-aristoi, of the wheat from

---

[1] "Aristocrats" (Greek).

the chaff. In general they will elect the really good and wise. In some instances, wealth may corrupt, and birth blind them; but not in sufficient degree to endanger the society.

It is probable that our difference of opinion may, in some measure, be produced by a difference of character in those among whom we live. From what I have seen of Massachusetts and Connecticut myself, and still more from what I have heard, and the character given of the former by yourself,[2] who know them so much better, there seems to be in those two States a traditionary reverence for certain families, which has rendered the offices of the government nearly hereditary in those families. I presume that from an early period of your history, members of those families happening to possess virtue and talents, have honestly exercised them for the good of the people, and by their services have endeared their names to them. In coupling Connecticut with you, I mean it politically only, not morally. For having made the Bible the common law of their land, they seemed to have modeled their morality on the story of Jacob and Laban.[3] But although this hereditary succession to office with you, may, in some degree, be founded in real family merit, yet in a much higher degree, it has proceeded from your strict alliance of Church and State. These families are canonized in the eyes of the people on common principles, "you tickle me, and I will tickle you." In Virginia we have nothing of this. Our clergy, before the revolution, having been secured against rivalship by fixed salaries, did not give themselves the trouble of acquiring influence over the people. Of wealth, there were great accumulations in particular families handed down from generation to generation, under the English law of entails.[4] But the only object of ambition for the wealthy was a seat in the King's Council.[5] All their court then was paid to the crown and its creatures; and they Philipised[6] in all collisions between the King and the people. Hence they were unpopular; and that unpopularity continues attached to their names. A Randolph, a Carter, or a Burwell[7] must have great personal superiority over a common competitor to be elected by the people even at this day. At the first session of our legislature after the Declaration of Independence, we passed a law abolishing entails. And this was followed by one abolishing the privilege of primogeniture,[8] and dividing the lands of intestates[9] equally among all their children, or other representatives. These laws, drawn by myself, laid the ax to the foot of pseudo-aristocracy. And had another which I prepared been adopted by the legislature, our work would have been complete. It was a bill for the more general diffusion of learning. This proposed to divide every county into wards of five or six miles square, like your townships; to establish in each ward a free school for reading, writing, and common arithmetic; to provide for the annual selection of the best subjects from these schools, who might receive, at the public expense, a higher degree of education at a district school; and from these district schools to select a certain number of the most promising subjects, to be completed at an University,

---

[2] Jefferson's note: "Vol.1, page 111." Jefferson is referring to Adams's *Defense of the Constitutions of Government of the United States* (1787).

[3] A dynastic family (see Genesis 24–31).

[4] Law by which an estate must pass via an established list of successors rather than via a written will.

[5] The Privy Council, an advisory council selected by the king.

[6] Fought against independence for the people.

[7] Virginian aristocrats John Randolph, Landon Carter, Lewis Burwell.

[8] An eldest son's right to his father's estates.

[9] Those who die without leaving a will.

where all the useful sciences should be taught. Worth and genius would thus have been sought out from every condition of life, and completely prepared by education for defeating the competition of wealth and birth for public trusts. My proposition had, for a further object, to impart to these wards those portions of self-government for which they are best qualified, by confiding to them the care of their poor, their roads, police, elections, the nomination of jurors, administration of justice in small cases, elementary exercises of militia; in short, to have made them little republics, with a warden at the head of each, for all those concerns which, being under their eye, they would better manage than the larger republics of the county or State. A general call of ward meetings by their wardens on the same day through the State, would at any time produce the genuine sense of the people on any required point, and would enable the State to act in mass, as your people have so often done, and with so much effect by their town meetings. The law for religious freedom, which made a part of this system, having put down the aristocracy of the clergy, and restored to the citizen the freedom of the mind, and those of entails and descents nurturing an equality of condition among them, this on education would have raised the mass of the people to the high ground of moral respectability necessary to their own safety, and to orderly government; and would have completed the great object of qualifying them to select the veritable aristoi, for the trusts of government, to the exclusion of the pseudalists; and the same Theognis[10] who has furnished the epigraphs of your two letters, assures us that "Ουδεμιαν πω, Κυρν,' αγαθοι πολιν ωλεσαν ανδρες."[11] Although this law has not yet been acted on but in a small and inefficient degree, it is still considered as before the legislature, with other bills of the revised code, not yet taken up, and I have great hope that some patriotic spirit will, at a favorable moment, call it up, and make it the key-stone of the arch of our government.

With respect to aristocracy, we should further consider, that before the establishment of the American States, nothing was known to history but the man of the old world, crowded within limits either small or overcharged, and steeped in the vices which that situation generates. A government adapted to such men would be one thing; but a very different one, that for the man of these States. Here every one may have land to labor for himself, if he chooses; or, preferring the exercise of any other industry, may exact for it such compensation as not only to afford a comfortable subsistence, but wherewith to provide for a cessation from labor in old age. Every one, by his property, or by his satisfactory situation, is interested in the support of law and order. And such men may safely and advantageously reserve to themselves a wholesome control over their public affairs, and a degree of freedom, which, in the hands of the *canaille*[12] of the cities of Europe, would be instantly perverted to the demolition and destruction of everything public and private. The history of the last twenty-five years of France,[13] and of the last forty years in America, nay of its last two hundred years, proves the truth of both parts of this observation.

But even in Europe a change has sensibly taken place in the mind of man. Science had liberated the ideas of those who read and reflect, and the American example had kindled feelings of right in the people. An insurrection has consequently begun, of science, talents, and courage, against rank and birth, which have fallen into contempt. It has failed in its first effort, because the mobs of the

---

[10] A Greek poet of the sixth century B.C.
[11] "Curnis, good men have never harmed any city" (Greek).
[12] "Mob" (French).   [13] Since the French Revolution, 1789.

cities, the instrument used for its accomplishment, debased by ignorance, poverty and vice, could not be restrained to rational action. But the world will recover from the panic of this first catastrophe. Science is progressive, and talents and enterprise on the alert. Resort may be had to the people of the country, a more governable power from their principles and subordination; and rank, and birth, and tinsel-aristocracy will finally shrink into insignificance, even there. This, however, we have no right to meddle with. It suffices for us, if the moral and physical condition of our own citizens qualifies them to select the able and good for the direction of their government, with a recurrence of elections at such short periods as will enable them to displace an unfaithful servant, before the mischief he meditates may be irremediable.

I have thus stated my opinion on a point on which we differ, not with a view to controversy, for we are both too old to change opinions which are the result of a long life of inquiry and reflection; but on the suggestions of a former letter of yours, that we ought not to die before we have explained ourselves to each other. We acted in perfect harmony, through a long and perilous contest for our liberty and independence. A constitution has been acquired, which, though neither of us thinks perfect, yet both consider as competent to render our fellow citizens the happiest and the securest on whom the sun has ever shone. If we do not think exactly alike as to its imperfections, it matters little to our country, which, after devoting to it long lives of disinterested labor, we have delivered over to our successors in life, who will be able to take care of it and of themselves.

Of the pamphlet on aristocracy which has been sent to you, or who may be its author, I have heard nothing but through your letter. If the person you suspect, it may be known from the quaint, mystical, and hyperbolical ideas, involved in affected, new-fangled and pedantic terms which stamp his writings. Whatever it be, I hope your quiet is not to be affected at this day by the rudeness or intemperance of scribblers; but that you may continue in tranquillity to live and to rejoice in the prosperity of our country until it shall be your own wish to take your seat among the aristoi who have gone before you. Ever and affectionately yours.

1813, 1829

[*Tyranny, Philosophy, and Education*]

Monticello, July 5, 1814.

DEAR SIR,—

Since mine of January the 24th, yours of March the 14th has been received. It was not acknowledged in the short one of May the 18th, by Mr. Rives, the only object of that having been to enable one of our most promising young men to have the advantage of making his bow to you. I learned with great regret the serious illness mentioned in your letter; and I hope Mr. Rives will be able to tell me you are entirely restored. But our machines have now been running seventy or eighty years, and we must expect that, worn as they are, here a pivot, there a wheel, now a pinion, next a spring, will be giving way; and however we may tinker them up for a while, all will at length surcease motion. Our watches, with works of brass and steel, wear out within that period. Shall you and I last to see the course the seven-fold wonders of the times will take? The Attila[1] of the age dethroned, the ruthless destroyer of ten millions of the human race, whose thirst for blood ap-

---

[1] Napoleon Bonaparte (1761–1821), emperor of France from 1804 to 1815.

peared unquenchable, the great oppressor of the rights and liberties of the world, shut up within the circle of a little island of the Mediterranean,[2] and dwindled to the condition of an humble and degraded pensioner on the bounty of those he had most injured. How miserably, how meanly, has he closed his inflated career! What a sample of the bathos will his history present! He should have perished on the swords of his enemies, under the walls of Paris.

> "Leon piagato a morte
> Sente mancar la vita,
> Guarda la sua ferita,
> Ne s'avilisce ancor.
>
> Cosi fra l'ire estrema
> Rugge, minaccia, e freme,
> Che fa tremar morendo
> Tal volta il cacciator."[3]
> —Metast. Adriano.

But Bonaparte was a lion in the field only. In civil life, a cold-blooded, calculating, unprincipled usurper, without a virtue: no statesman, knowing nothing of commerce, political economy, or civil government, and supplying ignorance by bold presumption. I had supposed him a great man until his entrance into the Assembly *des cinq cens*,[4] eighteen Brumaire (an. 8.). From that date, however, I set him down as a great scoundrel only. To the wonders of his rise and fall, we may add that of a Czar of Muscovy, dictating, *in Paris*, laws and limits to all the successors of the Cæsars, and holding even the balance in which the fortunes of this new world are suspended. I own, that while I rejoice, for the good of mankind, in the deliverance of Europe from the havoc which would never have ceased while Bonaparte should have lived in power, I see with anxiety the tyrant of the ocean remaining in vigor, and even participating in the merit of crushing his brother tyrant. While the world is thus turned up side down, on which of its sides are we? All the strong reasons, indeed, place us on the side of peace; the interests of the continent, their friendly dispositions, and even the interests of England. Her passions alone are opposed to it. Peace would seem now to be an easy work, the causes of the war being removed. Her orders of council will no doubt be taken care of by the allied powers, and, war ceasing, her impressment of our seamen ceases of course. But I fear there is foundation for the design intimated in the public papers, of demanding a cession of our right in the fisheries. What will Massachusetts say to this? I mean her majority, which must be considered as speaking through the organs it has appointed itself, as the index of its will. She chose to sacrifice the liberties of our seafaring citizens, in which we were all interested, and with them her obligations to the co-States, rather than war with England. Will she now sacrifice the fisheries to the same partialities? This question is interesting to her alone; for to the middle, the southern and western States, they are of no direct concern; of no more than the culture of tobacco, rice and cotton, to Massachusetts. I am really at a loss to conjecture what our refractory sister will say on this occasion. I know what, as a citizen of the Union, I would say to her. "Take this question *ad referendum*. It concerns you alone. If you would rather give up the fisheries than war with England, we give them up. If you

---

[2] In 1814 Napoleon was exiled to the island of Elba; he escaped in 1815 to lead the French armies until his defeat at Waterloo.

[3] "The lion stricken to death feels life draining away. It looks at its wounds from which it grows weaker and weaker. Then in its final wrath it roars, threatens, and rages, and thus in dying sometimes makes the hunter tremble" (Italian).

[4] "Of the five hundred" (French).

had rather fight for them, we will defend your interests to the last drop of our blood, choosing rather to set a good example than follow a bad one." And I hope she will determine to fight for them. With this, however, you and I shall have nothing to do; ours being truly the case wherein "*non tali auxilio, nec defensoribus istis tempus eget.*"[5] Quitting this subject, therefore, I will turn over a new leaf.

I am just returned from one of my long absences, having been at my other home for five weeks past. Having more leisure there than here for reading, I amused myself with reading seriously Plato's Republic.[6] I am wrong, however, in calling it amusement, for it was the heaviest task-work I ever went through. I had occasionally before taken up some of his other works, but scarcely ever had patience to go through a whole dialogue. While wading through the whimsies, the puerilities,[7] and unintelligible jargon of this work, I laid it down often to ask myself how it could have been, that the world should have so long consented to give reputation to such nonsense as this? How the *soi-disant*[8] Christian world, indeed, should have done it, is a piece of historical curiosity. But how could the Roman good sense do it? And particularly, how could Cicero[9] bestow such eulogies on Plato! Although Cicero did not wield the dense logic of Demosthenes,[10] yet he was able, learned, laborious, practised in the business of the world, and honest. He could not be the dupe of mere style, of which he was himself the first master in the world. With the moderns, I think, it is rather a matter of fashion and authority. Education is chiefly in the hands of persons who, from their profession, have an interest in the reputation and the dreams of Plato. They give the tone while at school, and few in their after years have occasion to revise their college opinions. But fashion and authority apart, and bringing Plato to the test of reason, take from him his sophisms, futilities and incomprehensibilities, and what remains? In truth, he is one of the race of genuine sophists,[11] who has escaped the oblivion of his brethren, first, by the elegance of his diction, but chiefly, by the adoption and incorporation of his whimsies into the body of artificial Christianity. His foggy mind is forever presenting the semblances of objects which, half seen through a mist, can be defined neither in form nor dimensions. Yet this, which should have consigned him to early oblivion, really procured him immortality of fame and reverence. The Christian priesthood, finding the doctrines of Christ levelled to every understanding, and too plain to need explanation, saw in the mysticism of Plato materials with which they might build up an artificial system, which might, from its indistinctness, admit everlasting controversy, give employment for their order, and introduce it to profit, power and pre-eminence. The doctrines which flowed from the lips of Jesus himself are within the comprehension of a child; but thousands of volumes have not yet explained the Platonisms engrafted on them; and for this obvious reason, that nonsense can never be explained. Their purposes, however, are answered. Plato is canonized; and it is now deemed as impious to question his merits as those of an Apostle of Jesus. He is peculiarly appealed to as an advocate of the immortality of the soul; and yet I will venture to

---

[5] "This time is in need of neither such aid nor such defense" (Latin).

[6] In his *Republic* Plato (427–347 B.C.) argues that the idea of a thing is the true, immutable reality behind the ever-changing appearance of the thing. This reality is inaccessible except through pure reason unaffected by sensation.

[7] Childlike qualities.   [8] "So-called" (French).

[9] Marcus Tullius Cicero (106–43 B.C.), a Roman orator and statesman.

[10] An Athenian orator and statesman (383–322 B.C.).   [11] Teachers of philosophy.

say, that were there no better arguments than his in proof of it, not a man in the world would believe it. It is fortunate for us, that Platonic republicanism has not obtained the same favor as Platonic Christianity; or we should now have been all living, men, women and children, pell mell together, like beasts of the field or forest. Yet "Plato is a great philosopher," said La Fontaine.[12] But, says Fontenelle, "Do you find his ideas very clear?" "Oh no! he is of an obscurity impenetrable." "Do you not find him full of contradictions?" "Certainly," replied La Fontaine, "he is but a sophist." Yet immediately after he exclaims again, "Oh, Plato was a great philosopher." Socrates had reason, indeed, to complain of the misrepresentations of Plato; for in truth, his dialogues are libels on Socrates.

But why am I dosing you with these antediluvian[13] topics? Because I am glad to have some one to whom they are familiar, and who will not receive them as if dropped from the moon. Our post-revolutionary youth are born under happier stars then you and I were. They acquire all learning in their mother's womb, and bring it into the world ready made. The information of books is no longer necessary; and all knowledge which is not innate, is in contempt, or neglect at least. Every folly must run its round; and so, I suppose, must that of self-learning and self-sufficiency; of rejecting the knowledge acquired in past ages, and starting on the new ground of intuition. When sobered by experience, I hope our successors will turn their attention to the advantages of education. I mean of education on the broad scale, and not that of the petty *academies*, as they call themselves, which are starting up in every neighborhood, and where one or two men, possessing Latin and sometimes Greek, a knowledge of the globes, and the first six books of Euclid, imagine and communicate this as the sum of science. They commit their pupils to the theater of the world, with just taste enough of learning to be alienated from industrious pursuits, and not enough to do service in the ranks of science. We have some exceptions, indeed. I presented one to you lately, and we have some others. But the terms I use are general truths. I hope the necessity will, at length, be seen of establishing institutions here, as in Europe, where every branch of science, useful at this day, may be taught in its highest degree. Have you ever turned your thoughts to the plan of such an institution? I mean to a specification of the particular sciences of real use in human affairs, and how they might be so grouped as to require so many professors only as might bring them within the views of a just but enlightened economy? I should be happy in a communication of your ideas on this problem, either loose or digested. But to avoid my being run away with by another subject, and adding to the length and ennui of the present letter, I will here present to Mrs. Adams and yourself, the assurance of my constant and sincere friendship and respect.

1814, 1829

[On Living One's Life Over]

Monticello, August 1, 1816

Dear Sir,—

Your two philosophical letters of May 4th and 6th have been too long in my carton of "letters to be answered." To the question, indeed, on the utility of grief, no

---

[12] Jean de La Fontaine (1621–1695), a French fabulist and poet.
[13] Ancient; literally, "before the flood."

answer remains to be given. You have exhausted the subject. I see that, with the other evils of life, it is destined to temper the cup we are to drink.

> Two urns by Jove's high throne have ever stood,
> The source of evil one, and one of good;
> From thence the cup of mortal man he fills,
> Blessings to these, to those distributes ills;
> To most he mingles both.[1]

Putting to myself your question, would I agree to live my seventy-three years over again forever? I hesitate to say. With Chew's[2] limitations from twenty-five to sixty, I would say yes; and I might go further back, but not come lower down. For, at the latter period, with most of us, the powers of life are sensibly on the wane, sight becomes dim, hearing dull, memory constantly enlarging its frightful blank and parting with all we have ever seen or known, spirits evaporate, bodily debility creeps on palsying every limb, and so faculty after faculty quits us, and where then is life? If, in its full vigor, of good as well as evil, your friend Vassall[3] could doubt its value, it must be purely a negative quantity when its evils alone remain. Yet I do not go into his opinion entirely. I do not agree that an age of pleasure is no compensation for a moment of pain. I think, with you, that life is a fair matter of account, and the balance often, nay generally, in its favor. It is not indeed easy, by calculation of intensity and time, to apply a common measure, or to fix the par between pleasure and pain; yet it exists and is measurable. On the question, for example, whether to be cut for the stone? The young, with a longer prospect of years, think these overbalance the pain of the operation. Dr. Franklin, at the age of eighty, thought his residuum of life not worth that price. I should have thought with him, even taking the stone out of the scale. There is a ripeness of time for death, regarding others as well as ourselves, when it is reasonable we should drop off, and make room for another growth. When we have lived our generation out, we should not wish to encroach on another. I enjoy good health; I am happy in what is around me, yet I assure you I am ripe for leaving all, this year, this day, this hour. If it could be doubted whether we would go back to twenty-five, how can it be whether we would go forward from seventy-three? Bodily decay is gloomy in prospect, but of all human contemplations the most abhorrent is body without mind. Perhaps, however, I might accept of time to read Grimm[4] before I go. Fifteen volumes of anecdotes and incidents, within the compass of my own time and cognizance, written by a man of genius, of taste, of point, an acquaintance, the measure and traverses of whose mind I know, could not fail to turn the scale in favor of life during their perusal. I must write to Ticknor[5] to add it to my catalogue, and hold on till it comes. There is a Mr. Van der

---

[1] From Alexander Pope's (1688–1744) translation of the *Iliad* (mid-eighth century B.C.), Bk. 24, by Homer.

[2] Benjamin Chew (1722–1810), a Philadelphia jurist, who remarked to John Adams that he wanted to "go back to twenty-five, to all Eternity" (as cited in Adams's letter of May 3, 1816, to Jefferson).

[3] William Vassall, a Massachusetts lawyer.

[4] Baron Friedrich Melchior von Grimm (1723–1807), who wrote *Letters, Literary, Philosophical and Critical* (1812) in seventeen volumes.

[5] George Ticknor (1791–1871), who founded the Boston Public Library and had visited Jefferson at Monticello.

Kemp[6] of New York, a correspondent, I believe, of yours, with whom I have exchanged some letters without knowing who he is. Will you tell me? I know nothing of the history of the Jesuits you mention in four volumes. Is it a good one? I dislike, with you, their restoration because it marks a retrograde step from light towards darkness. We shall have our follies without doubt. Some one or more of them will always be afloat. But ours will be the follies of enthusiasm, not of bigotry, not of Jesuitism. Bigotry is the disease of ignorance, of morbid minds; enthusiasm of the free and buoyant. Education and free discussion are the antidotes of both. We are destined to be a barrier against the returns of ignorance and barbarism. Old Europe will have to lean on our shoulders, and to hobble along by our side, under the monkish trammels of priests and kings, as she can. What a colossus shall we be when the southern continent comes up to our mark! What a stand will it secure as a ralliance for the reason and freedom of the globe! I like the dreams of the future better than the history of the past,—so good night! I will dream on, always fancying that Mrs. Adams and yourself are by my side marking the progress and the obliquities of ages and countries.

1816, 1829

LETTER TO NATHANIEL BURWELL

[*On Female Education*]

Monticello, March 14, 1818

DEAR SIR,—

Your letter of February 17th found me suffering under an attack of rheumatism, which has but now left me at sufficient ease to attend to the letters I have received. A plan of female education has never been a subject of systematic contemplation with me. It has occupied my attention so far only as the education of my own daughters occasionally required. Considering that they would be placed in a country situation, where little aid could be obtained from abroad, I thought it essential to give them a solid education, which might enable them, when become mothers, to educate their own daughters, and even to direct the course for sons, should their fathers be lost, or incapable, or inattentive. My surviving daughter accordingly, the mother of many daughters as well as sons, has made their education the object of her life, and being a better judge of the practical part than myself, it is with her aid and that of one of her élèves[1] that I shall subjoin a catalogue of the books for such a course of reading as we have practiced.

A great obstacle to good education is the inordinate passion prevalent for novels, and the time lost in that reading which should be instructively employed. When this poison infects the mind, it destroys its tone and revolts it against wholesome reading. Reason and fact, plain and unadorned, are rejected. Nothing can

---

[6] Rev. Francis Adrian Vander Kemp, who emigrated to New York from Holland.
[1] "Students" (French).

engage attention unless dressed in all the figments of fancy, and nothing so be-decked comes amiss. The result is a bloated imagination, sickly judgment, and disgust towards all the real businesses of life. This mass of trash, however, is not without some distinction; some few modelling their narratives, although fictitious, on the incidents of real life, have been able to make them interesting and useful vehicles of a sound morality. Such, I think, are Marmontel's[2] new moral tales, but not his old ones, which are really immoral. Such are the writings of Miss Edge-worth,[3] and some of those of Madame Genlis.[4] For a like reason, too, much po-etry should not be indulged. Some is useful for forming style and taste. Pope, Dryden, Thompson, Shakespeare, and of the French, Molière, Racine, the Cor-neilles,[5] may be read with pleasure and improvement.

The French language, become that of the general intercourse of nations, and from their extraordinary advances, now the depository of all science, is an indis-pensable part of education for both sexes. In the subjoined catalogue, therefore, I have placed the books of both languages indifferently, according as the one or the other offers what is best.

The ornaments too, and the amusements of life, are entitled to their portion of attention. These, for a female, are dancing, drawing, and music. The first is a healthy exercise, elegant and very attractive for young people. Every affectionate parent would be pleased to see his daughter qualified to participate with her com-panions, and without awkwardness at least, in the circles of festivity, of which she occasionally becomes a part. It is a necessary accomplishment, therefore, al-though of short use, for the French rule is wise, that no lady dances after mar-riage. This is founded in solid physical reasons, gestation and nursing leaving little time to a married lady when this exercise can be either safe or innocent. Drawing is thought less of in this country than in Europe. It is an innocent and engaging amusement, often useful, and a qualification not to be neglected in one who is to become a mother and an instructor. Music is invaluable where a person has an ear. Where they have not, it should not be attempted. It furnishes a delight-ful recreation for the hours of respite from the cares of the day, and lasts us through life. The taste of this country, too, calls for this accomplishment more strongly than for either of the others.

I need say nothing of household economy, in which the mothers of our country are generally skilled, and generally careful to instruct their daughters. We all know its value, and that diligence and dexterity in all its processes are inestimable treasures. The order and economy of a house are as honorable to the mistress as those of a farm to the master, and if either be neglected, ruin follows, and children destitute of the means of living.

This, Sir, is offered as a summary sketch on a subject on which I have not thought much. It probably contains nothing but what has already occurred to your-self, and claims your acceptance on no other ground than as a testimony of my respect for your wishes, and of my great esteem and respect.

1818

[2] Jean François Marmontel (1723–1799), a French dramatist and novelist who wrote *Moral Tales* (1781).

[3] Maria Edgeworth (1767–1849), an English novelist known for *Castle Rackrent* (1800).

[4] Stéphanie Félicité du Crest de Saint-Aubin, Comtesse de Genlis (1746–1830), a French novelist known for *Madame de Cleremont* (1802).

[5] Writers Alexander Pope (1688–1744), John Dryden (1631–1700), James Thompson (1700–1748), William Shakespeare (1564–1616), Molière (Jean Baptiste Poquelin, 1622–1673), Jean Baptiste Racine (1639–1699), and Pierre Corneille (1606–1684) and his brother Thomas (1625–1709).

John Adams
(1735–1826)

Although John Adams's formal writings are primarily political, his letters—especially those to his wife, Abigail, and to Thomas Jefferson— are engaging and diverse. A descendant of early Puritan settlers, Adams was born in 1735 in Braintree, Massachusetts. After graduating from Harvard College in 1755, he studied law. In 1764 Adams married Abigail Smith, a woman every bit his intellectual match, whose own correspondence is among the best in American literary history. They had five children, including John Quincy Adams, the sixth president of the United States.

John Adams became politically active during the early protests against the British Stamp Act of 1765. Yet, his sense of justice prevailed over popular opinion when he defended British soldiers accused of murder in the Boston Massacre of 1770. He won acquittal for all but two of them and proudly recalled his part in the case to be a true service to his country. In 1774 he was elected to the First Continental Congress. There he met Jefferson, and they were among those asked to draft an independence declaration.

During the ensuing Revolutionary War, Adams served as an ambassador to France, where he helped negotiate the war-ending Treaty of Paris. After the Revolution he was the first U.S. ambassador to the British royal court. During this ambassadorship he began writing *A Defence of the Constitutions* (1787–1788), a dense, three-volume work supporting ratification of the Constitution then under debate. Adams was elected first vice-president of the new United States, serving from 1789 to 1797. In 1796 he won the presidential election by a slim margin in the electoral college. His single term was marred by controversy and strong resistance from the Republican party, led by Vice-President Jefferson. When Jefferson defeated Adams's bid for a second term, Adams retired embittered and estranged from his former friend.

The estrangement lasted until New Year's Day 1812, when a mutual friend prompted Adams to write the first of a series of letters to Jefferson. Jefferson responded that Adams's letter "carries me back to the times when . . . we were fellow laborers in the same cause, struggling for what is most valuable to man, his right of self-government." Adams wrote back, "We ought not to die before we have explained ourselves to each other." Adams and Jefferson then carried on a remarkable correspondence, clarifying events of the Revolution; commenting on European politics, religion, science, and philosophy; and reporting poignantly about their own physical frailty.

Adams has been called a "skeptical realist," and Jefferson a "practical idealist." Adams's letters are warmer, more volatile, and also more playful at times than Jefferson's letters. Yet, the letters deepened their friendship. When Adams died on the Fourth of July in *1826*, his last words were "Thomas Jefferson survives." Adams did not know that Jefferson had died only hours earlier. The nation saw their deaths as a sign of the Revolution's true conclusion.

Suggested Readings: *The Works of John Adams*, ed. C. F. Adams, 1850–1856. *The Diary and Autobiography of John Adams*, ed. L. H. Butterfield, 1961. P. Shaw, *The Character of John Adams*, 1976.

Text Used: *The Adams-Jefferson Letters* Vol. 2, ed. L. J. Cappon, 1959.

LETTERS TO THOMAS JEFFERSON

[*Future Prospects*]

Quincy February 3, 1812

DEAR SIR

Sitting at My Fireside with my Daughter Smith, on the first of February My Servant brought me a Bundle of Letters and Newspapers from the Post Office in this Town: one of the first Letters that struck my Eye had the Post Mark of Milton 23. Jany. 1812. Milton is the next Town to Quincy and the Post Office in it is but three Miles from my House. How could the Letter be so long in coming three miles? Reading the Superscription, I instantly handed the Letter to Mrs. Smith. Is that not Mr. Jeffersons hand? Looking attentively at is, she answered it is very like it. How is it possible a letter from Mr. Jefferson, could get into the Milton Post office. Opening the Letter I found it, indeed from Monticello in the hand and with the Signature of Mr. Jefferson: but this did not much diminish my Surprize. How is it possible a Letter can come from Mr. Jefferson to me in seven or Eight days? I had no Expectation of an Answer, thinking the Distance so great and the Roads so embarrassed under two or three Months. This History would not be worth recording but for the Discovery it made of a Fact, very pleasing to me, vizt. that the Communication between Us is much easier, surer and may be more frequent than I had ever believed or suspected to be possible.

The Material of the Samples of American Manufacture which I sent you was not Wool nor Cotton, nor Silk nor Flax nor Hemp nor Iron nor Wood. They were spun from the Brain of John Quincy Adams and consist in two Volumes of his Lectures on Rhetorick and oratory, delivered when he was a Professor of that Science in our University of Cambridge. A Relation of mine, a first Cousin of my ever honoured, beloved and revered Mother, Nicholas Boylston, a rich Merchant of Boston, bequeathed by his Will a Donation for establishing a professorship, and John Quincy Adams, having in his Veins so much of the Blood of the Founder, was most earnestly solicited to become the first Professor. The Volumes I sent you are the Fruit of his Labour during the short time he held that office. But it ought to be remembered that he attended his Duty as a Senator of the United States during the same Period. It is with some Anxiety submitted to your Judgment.

Your Account of the flourishing State of Manufactures in Families in your Part of the Country is highly delightful to me. I wish the Spirit may spread and prevail through the Union. Within my Memory We were much in the same Way in New England: but in later Times We have run a gadding abroad too much to seek for Eatables, Drinkables and Wearables.

Your Life and mine for almost half a Century have been nearly all of a Piece, resembling in the whole, mine in The Gulph Stream, chaced by three British Frigates, in a Hurricane from the North East and a hideous Tempest of Thunder and Lightning, which cracked our Mainmast, struck three and twenty Men on Deck, wounded four and killed one. I do not remember that my Feelings, during those three days were very different from what they have been for fifty Years.

What an Exchange have you made? Of Newspapers for Newton! Rising from the lower deep of the lowest deep of Dulness and Bathos to the Contemplation of the Heavens and the heavens of Heavens. Oh that I had devoted to Newton and his Fellows that time which I fear has been wasted on Plato and Aristotle, Bacon (Nat) Acherly, Bolin[g]broke, De Lolme, Harrington, Sidney, Hobbes, Plato Redivivus, Marchmont, Nedham, with twenty others upon Subjects which Mankind is determined never to Understand, and those who do Understand them are resolved never to practice, or countenance.

Your Memoranda of the past, your Sense of the present and the Prospect for the Future seem to be well founded, as far as I see. But the Latter i.e. the Prospect of the Future, will depend on the Union: and how is that Union to be preserved? Concordia Res parvae crescunt, Discordia Maximae dilabuntur.[1] Our Union is an immense Structure. In Russia, I doubt not, a Temple or Pallace might be erected of Wood, Brick or Marble, which should be cemented only with Ice. A sublime and beautiful Building it might be; surpassing St. Sophia, St. Peters, St. Pauls, Notre Dame or St. Genevieve. But the first Week, if not the first day of the *Debacle* would melt all the Cement and Tumble The Glass and Marble, the Gold and Silver, the Timber and the Iron into one promiscuous chaotic or anarchic heap.

I will not at present point out the precise Years Days and Months when; nor the Names of the Men by whom this Union has been put in jeopardy. Your Recollection can be at no more loss than mine.

Cobbets, Callenders, Peter Markoes, Burrs and Hamiltons may and have passed away. But Conquerors do not so easily disappear. Battles and Victories are irresis[t]able by human Nature. When a Man is once acknowledged by the People in the Army and the Country to be the Author of a Victory, there is no longer any Question. He is undoubtedly a great and good Man. Had Hamilton, [or] Burr obtained a recent Victory, neither You, nor Jay nor I should have stood any Chance against them or either of them more than a Swallow or a Sparrow.

The Union is still to me an Object of as much Anxiety as ever Independence was. To this I have sacrificed my Popularity in New England and yet what Treatment do I still receive from the Randolphs and Sheffeys of Virginia. By the Way are not these Eastern Shore Men? My Senectutal Loquacity has more than retaliated your "Senile Garrulity."

I have read Thucidides and Tacitus, so often, and at such distant Periods of my Life, that elegant, profound and enchanting as is their Style, I am weary of them. When I read them I seem to be only reading the History of my own Times and my own Life. I am heartily weary of both; i.e. of recollecting the History of both; for I am not weary of Living. Whatever a peevish Patriarch might say, I have never yet seen the day in which I could say I have had no Pleasure; or that I have had more Pain than Pleasure.

Gerry, Paine, and J. Adams, R. R. Livingston, B. Rush and George Clymer and yourself, are all that I can recollect, of the Subscribers to Independence who remain. Gerry is acting a decided and a splendid Part. So daring and so hazardous a Part; but at the same time so able and upright, that I say: "God save the Governor." and "prosper long our noble Governor."

I walk every fair day, sometimes 3 or 4 miles. Ride now and then but very rarely more than ten or fifteen Miles. But I have a Complaint that Nothing but the Ground can cure, that is the Palsy; a king of a Paralytic Affection of the Nerves, which makes my hands tremble, and renders it difficult to write at all and impossible to write well.

I have the Start of you in Age by at least ten Years: but you are advanced to the Rank of a Great Grandfather before me. Of 13 Grand Children I have two, Wil-

---

[1] "Small communities grow great through harmony, great ones fall to pieces through discord" (Latin), Sallust (83–35? B.C.), a Roman historian.

liam and John Smith, and three Girls, Caroline Smith, Susanna and Abigail Adams, who might have made me Great Grand Children enough. But they are not likely to employ their Talents very soon. They are all good Boys and Girls however, and are the solace of my Age. I cordially reciprocate your Professions of Esteem and Respect. Madam joins and sends her kind Regards to your Daughter and your Grand Children as well as to yourself.

JOHN ADAMS

P. S. I forgot to remark your Preference to Savage over civilized life. I have Something to say upon that Subject. If I am in an Error, you can set me Right, but by all I know of one or the other I would rather be the poorest Man in France or England, with sound health of Body and Mind, than the proudest King, Sachem or Warriour of any Tribe of Savages in America.

1812, 1850–1856

[*Purposes of Grief*]

Quincy May 6 1816

DEAR SIR

Neither Eyes Fingers or Paper held out, to dispatch all the Trifles I wished to write in my last Letter.

In your favour of April 8th, You "wonder for what good End the Sensations of Grief could be intended"? You ["]wish the Pathologists would tell Us, what the Use of Grief, in Our Œconmy, and of what good it is the Cause proximate or remote." When I approach such questions as this, I consider myself, like one of those little Eels in Vinaigre, or one of those Animalcules in black or red Peper or in the Horse radish Root, that bite our Tongues so cruelly, reasoning upon the το παν ["totality"]. Of what Use is this Sting upon the Tongue? Why might We not have the Benefit of these Stimulants, without the Sting? Why might We not have the fragrance and Beauty of the Rose without the Thorn?

In the first place, however, We know not the Connections between pleasure and Pain. They seem to be mechanical and inseperable. How can We conceive a strong Passion, a Sanguine Hope suddenly disappointed without producing Pain? or Grief? Swift at 70, recollected the Fish he had angled out of Water when a Boy, which broke loose from his hoock, and said I feel the disappointment at this Moment. A Merchant plans all his fortune and all his Credit, in a single India or China Ship. She Arrives at the Viniard with a Cargo worth a Million, in Order. Sailing round the Cape for Boston a sudden Storm wrecks her, Ship Cargo and Crew all lost. Is it possible that the Merchant ruined, bankrupt sent to Prison by his Creditors, his Wife and Children starving, should not grieve? Suppose a young Couple, with every Advant[a]ge of Persons, fortunes and Connection on the Point of an indissoluble Union. A flash of Lightening or any one of those millions of Accidents which are alloted to Humanity prove fatal to one of the Lovers. Is it possible that the other, and all the Friends of both should not grieve? It should seem that Grief, as a mere Passion must necesarily be in Proportion to Sensibility.

Did you ever see a Portrait or a Statue of a great Man, without perceiving strong Traits of Paine and Anxiety? These Furrows were all ploughed in the Countenance, by Grief. Our juvenile Oracle, Sir Edward Coke, thought that none were fit for Legislators and Magistrates, but "*Sad Men.*" And Who were these sad Men?

They were aged Men, who had been tossed and buffeted in the Vicissitudes of Life, forced upon profound Reflection by Grief and disappointments and taught to command their Passions and Prejudices.

But, All this, You will say, is nothing to the purpose. It is only repeating and exemplifying a Fact, which my question supposed to be well known, viz the Existence of Grief; and is no Answer to my Question, "What Are the Uses of Grief." This is very true, and you are very right: but may not the Uses of Grief be inferred, or at least suggested by such Exemplifications of known facts? Grief Compels the India Merchant to think; to reflect upon the plan of his Voyage. "Have I not been rash, to trust my Fortune, my Family, my Liberty, to the Caprices of Winds and Waves in a single Ship? I will never again give a loose to my Imagination and Avarice." ["]It had been wiser and more honest to have traded on a smaller scale upon my own Capital." The dessolated Lover and disappointed Connections, are compelled by their Grief to reflect on the Vanity of human Wishes and Expectations; to learn the essential Lesson of Resignation; to review their own Conduct towards the deceased; to correct any Errors or faults in their future Conduct towards their remaining friends and towards all Men; to recollect the Virtues of the lost Friend and resolve to imitate them; his Follies and Vices if he had any and resolve to avoid them. Grief drives Men into habits of serious Reflection sharpens the Understanding and softens the heart; it compells them to arrouse their Reason, to assert its Empire over their Passions Propensities and Prejudices; to elevate them to a Superiority over all human Events; to give them the Felicis Annimi immotan tranquilitatem ["the imperturbable tranquillity of a happy heart"]; in short to make them Stoicks and Christians.

After all, as Grief is a Pain, it stands in the Predicament of all other Evil and the great question Occurs what is the Origin and what the final cause of Evil. This perhaps is known only to Omnicience. We poor Mortals have nothing to do with it, but to fabricate all the good We can out of all inevitable Evils, and to avoid all that are avoidable, and many such there are, among which are our own unnecessary Apprehensions and imaginary Fears. Though Stoical Apathy is impossible, Yet Patience and Resignation and tranquility may be acquired by Consideration in a great degree, very much for the hapiness of Life.

I have read Grim, in fifteen Volumes of more than five hundred pages each. I will not say, like Uncle Tobey "You shall not die till you have read him." But you ought to read him, if possible. It is the most entertaining Work I ever read. He appears exactly as you represent him. What is most of all remarkable, is his Impartiality. He spares no Characters, but Necker and Diderot. Voltaire, Buffon, D'Alembert, Helvetius Rousseau, Marmontel, Condorcet, La Harpe, Beaumarchais and all others are lashed without Ceremony. Their Portraits as faithfully drawn as possible. It is a compleat Review of French Litterature and fine Arts from 1753 to 1790. No Politicks. Criticisms very just. Anecdotes with out number, and very merry. One ineffably ridiculous I wish I could send you, but it is immeasurably long. D'Argens, a little out of health and shivering with the cold in Berlin asked leave of the King to take a ride to Gascony his Native Province. He was absent so long that Frederick concluded the Air of the South of France was like to detain his Friend and as he wanted his Society and Services he contrived a Trick to bring him back. He fabricated a Mandement in the Name of the Archbishop of Aix, commanding all the Faithful to seize The Marquis D'Argens, Author of Ocellus, Timæus and Julian, Works Atheistical, Deistical, Heretical and impious in the highest degree. This Mandement composed in a Style of Ecclesiastical Eloquence that never was exceeded by Pope, Jesuite, Inquisitor, or Sorbonite he sent in Print by a Courier to D'Argens, who frightened out of his Witts fled by cross roads out of France and back to Berlin, to the greater Joy of the Philosophical Court for the laugh of Europe which they had raised at the Expence of the learned Marquis.

I do not like the late Resurrection of the Jesuits.[1] They have a General, now in Russia, in correspondence with the Jesuits in the U. S. who are more numerous than every body knows. Shall We not have Swarms of them here? In as many shapes and disguises as ever a King of the Gypsies, Bamfie[l]d More Carew himself, assumed? In the shape of Printers, Editors, Writers School masters etc. I have lately read Pascalls Letters over again and four Volumes of the History of the Jesuits. If ever any Congregation of Men could merit, eternal Perdition on Earth and in Hell, According to these Historians though like Pascal true Catholicks, it is this Company of Loiola. Our System however of Religious Liberty must afford them an Assylum. But if they do not put the Purity of our Elections to a severe Tryal, it will be a Wonder.

J. ADAMS
1816, 1850–1856

[*Aging Founders*]

Montezillo June 11th. 1822.

DEAR SIR,

Half an hour ago I received, and this moment have heard read for the third or fourth time, the best letter that ever was written by an Octogenearian, dated June the 1st. It is so excellent that I am almost under an invincible temptation to commit a breach of trust by lending it to a printer. My Son, Thomas Boylston, says it would be worth five hundred dollars to any newspaper in Boston, but I dare not betray your confidence.

I have not sprained my wrist, but both my Arms and hands are so over strained that I cannot write a line. Poor Starke remembered nothing, and talked of nothing, but the Battle of Bennington. Poor Thomson is not quite so reduced. I cannot mount my Horse, but I can walk three miles over a rugged rockey Mountain, and have done it within a Month. Yet I feel when setting in my chair, as if I could not rise out of it, and when risen, as if I could not walk across the room; my sight is very dim; hearing pritty good; memory poor enough.

I answer your question, Is Death an Evil? It is not an Evil. It is a blessing to the individual, and to the world. Yet we ought not to wish for it till life becomes insupportable; we must wait the pleasure and convenience of this great teacher. Winter is as terrible to me, as to you. I am almost reduced in it, to the life of a Bear or a torpid swallow. I cannot read, but my delight is to hear others read, and I tease all my friends most unmercifully and tyrannically, against their consent. The Ass has kicked in vain, all men say the dull animal has missed the mark.

This globe is a Theatre of War, its inhabitants are all heroes. I believe the little Eels in Vinegar and the animacule in pepper water, I believe are quarrelsome. The Bees are as warlike as Romans, Russians, Britains, or Frenchmen. Ants or Cater-

---

[1] The Jesuit sect, banished from most Catholic countries during the 1760s, was dissolved by the pope in 1773, but was reconstituted in 1814.

pilars and Canker worms are the only tribes amongst whom I have not seen battles. And Heaven itself, if we believe Hindoos, Jews, and Christians, has not always been at peace. We need not trouble ourselves about these things nor fret ourselves because of Evil doers but safely trust the ruler with his skies. Nor need we dread the approach of dotage, let it come if it must. Thomson, it seems, still delights in his four stories. And Starke remembers to the last his Bennington, and exulted in his Glory. The worst of the Evil is that our friends will suffer more by our imbecility than we ourselves.

Diplomatic flickerings, it seemes, have not yet ceased. It seems as if a Council of Ambassadors could never agree.

In wishing for your health and happiness I am very selfish, for I hope for more letters; this is worth more than five hundred dollars to me, for it has already given me, and will continue to give me more pleasure than a thousand. Mr. Jay who is about your age I am told experiences more decay than you do. I am your old friend

JOHN ADAMS

1822, 1850–1856

Abigail Adams
(1744–1818)

Abigail Adams was one of America's most distinguished letter writers as well as its second first lady. Born Abigail Smith in 1744 in Weymouth, Massachusetts, she was the second daughter of the Congregational minister William Smith and of Elizabeth Quincy. Abigail Smith was a descendant of the Puritan founders. When she married John Adams, the son of a Braintree, Masachusetts, farmer in October 1764, her family may have felt she was stepping down in the world. However, this Harvard-educated lawyer proved a devoted husband and an adventurous political leader—a signer of the Declaration of Independence, a minister to France and England, and America's first vice-president and its second president.

The Adamses were separated through many of the early years of their marriage and through most of the American Revolution. Abigail managed the family's farm and finances and the education of their one daughter and three sons. (Her eldest son, John Quincy Adams, became the sixth president of the United States.) In 1784 she joined her husband in Paris and thereafter accompanied him on his assignments. Throughout her travels she kept her New England sensibilities. She retired to the farm in Quincy and died at the age of seventy-four in 1818, not an afternoon's horseback ride from where she was born.

Adams's correspondence with her husband extends throughout the years of their courtship and marriage and amounts to over three hundred letters. Her lifelong correspondence includes her children and extended family, numerous friends (such as James and Mercy Otis Warren), and political leaders (such as Thomas Jefferson, James Madison, and George Washington). Observant, intelligent, honest, and imaginative, she loved political controversy. Her letters about the American Revolution are among the most informative and incisive of the period, exhibiting "a kind of picture of the manners, opinions, and principles of these times of perplexity, danger and distress," as John Adams observed in a 1774 letter to her. Her correspondence from Europe is no less revealing as she judged European society and found it wanting: "I do not feel at all captivated either with the manners or politics of Europe" (from a 1786 letter to Mercy Otis Warren).

A woman of independent judgment, and a partner and a friend to her husband, Adams expressed her views frankly in her letters, especially her conviction that the status of women needed to be improved. Sensitive to the implications of the American Revolution and its promise of an end to tyranny, she urged that the legal statutes that would follow the revolution should "remember the ladies" and put an end to the almost absolute power over wives that husbands were allowed by law. Regretful of her own lack of a formal education, she argued for the education of women, on the premise that no free country could survive without learned women. In addition, she and her husband abhorred slavery. In 1774 she wrote him of her wish that "there was not a slave in the Province."

Although she admired the famous letter writers from Cicero to the earl of Chesterfield, Adams insisted on her own manner: "It is not the studied sentence, nor the elaborate period, which pleases, but the general sentiments of the heart expressed with simplicity" (written to Lucy Cranch, her niece, in 1785). Her grandson Charles Francis Adams, recognizing the genius of her letters, published a collection of them in 1840. Ever since, her letters have been widely read for their disarmingly candid view of eighteenth-century colonial society through the eyes of one of its most extraordinary women.

Suggested Readings: *Letters of Mrs. Adams the Wife of John Adams*, ed. C. F. Adams, 1848. *Familiar Letters of John Adams and His Wife Abigail Adams, During the Revolution*, ed. C. F. Adams, 1876. *Adams Family Correspondence*, ed. L. H. Butterfield, 1963–1973. C. W. Akers, *Abigail Adams*, 1980. L. Whithey, *Dearest Friend, A Life of Abigail Adams*, 1981. P. C. Nagel, *The Adams Women: Abigail and Louisa Adams, Their Sisters and Daughters*, 1987.

Text Used: *The Book of Abigail and John*, ed. L. H. Butterfield, M. Freidlaender, and M. Kline, 1975.

LETTERS TO JOHN ADAMS

[*The Passion for Liberty*]

Braintree March 31 1776

I wish you would ever write me a Letter half as long as I write you; and tell me if you may where your Fleet are gone? What sort of Defence Virginia can make against our common Enemy? Whether it is so situated as to make an able Defence? Are not the Gentery Lords and the common people vassals, are they not like the uncivilized Natives Brittain represents us to be? I hope their Riffel Men who have shewen themselves very savage and even Blood thirsty; are not a specimen of the Generality of the people.

I am willing to allow the Colony great merit for having produced a Washington but they have been shamefully duped by a Dunmore.[1]

I have sometimes been ready to think that the passion for Liberty cannot be Eaquelly Strong in the Breasts of those who have been accustomed to deprive their fellow Creatures of theirs. Of this I am certain that it is not founded upon that generous and christian principal of doing to others as we would that others should do unto us.

---

[1] John, earl of Dunmore and governor of Virginia, a proponent of the Loyalist view.

Do not you want to see Boston; I am fearfull of the small pox, or I should have been in before this time. I got Mr. Crane[2] to go to our House and see what state it was in. I find it has been occupied by one of the Doctors of a Regiment, very dirty, but no other damage has been done to it. The few things which were left in it are all gone. Cranch[3] has the key which he never deliverd up. I have wrote to him for it and am determined to get it cleand as soon as possible and shut it up. I look upon it a new acquisition of property, a property which one month ago I did not value at a single Shilling, and could with pleasure have seen it in flames.

The Town in General is left in a better state than we expected, more oweing to a percipitate flight than any Regard to the inhabitants, tho some individuals discoverd a sense of honour and justice and have left the rent of the Houses in which they were, for the owners and the furniture unhurt, or if damaged suffcient to make it good.

Others have committed abominable Ravages. The Mansion House of your President is safe and the furniture unhurt whilst both the House and Furniture of the Solisiter General have fallen a prey to their own merciless party. Surely the very Fiends feel a Reverential awe for Virtue and patriotism, whilst they Detest the paricide and traitor.

I feel very differently at the approach of spring to what I did a month ago. We knew not then whether we could plant or sow with safety, whether when we had toild we could reap the fruits of our own industery, whether we could rest in our own Cottages, or whether we should not be driven from the sea coasts to seek shelter in the wilderness, but now we feel as if we might sit under our own vine and eat the good of the land.

I feel a gaieti de Coar[4] to which before I was a stranger. I think the Sun looks brighter, the Birds sing more melodiously, and Nature puts on a more chearfull countanance. We feel a temporary peace, and the poor fugitives are returning to their deserted habitations.

Tho we felicitate ourselves, we sympathize with those who are trembling least the Lot of Boston should be theirs. But they cannot be in similar circumstances unless pusilanimity and cowardise should take possession of them. They have time and warning given them to see the Evil and shun it.—I long to hear that you have declared an independancy—and by the way in the new Code of Laws[5] which I suppose it will be necessary for you to make I desire you would Remember the Ladies, and be more generous and favourable to them than your ancestors. Do not put such unlimited power into the hands of the Husbands. Remember all Men would be tyrants if they could. If perticuliar care and attention is not paid to the Laidies we are determined to foment a Rebelion, and will not hold ourselves bound by any Laws in which we have no voice, or Representation.

That your Sex are Naturally Tyrannical is a Truth so thoroughly established as to admit of no dispute, but such of you as wish to be happy willingly give up the harsh title of Master for the more tender and endearing one of Friend. Why then, not put it out of the power of the vicious and the Lawless to use us with cruelty and indignity with impunity. Men of Sense in all Ages abhor those customs which treat us only as the vassals of your Sex. Regard us then as Beings placed by

---

[2] Abigail's agent in Boston.   [3] Should probably read "Crane."
[4] *gaité de coeur* (French): lightheartedness.
[5] What later became the Declaration of Independence.

providence under your protection and in immitation of the Supreem Being make use of that power only for our happiness.

1776, 1876

[*Independent States*]

Boston July 13 1776

I must begin with apoligising to you for not writing since the 17 of June. I have really had so many cares upon my Hands and Mind, with a bad inflamation in my Eyes that I have not been able to write. I now date from Boston where I yesterday arrived and was with all 4 of our Little ones innoculated for the small pox. My unkle and Aunt were so kind as to send me an invitation with my family. Mr. Cranch[1] and wife and family, My Sister Betsy and her Little Neice, Cotton Tufts[2] and Mr. Thaxter,[3] a maid who has had the Distemper and my old Nurse compose our family. A Boy too I should have added. 17 in all. My unkles maid with his Little daughter and a Negro Man are here. We had our Bedding &c. to bring. A Cow we have driven down from B[raintre]e and some Hay I have put into the Stable, wood &c. and we have really commenced housekeepers here. The House was furnished with almost every article (except Beds) which we have free use of, and think ourselves much obliged by the fine accommodations and kind offer of our Friends. All our necessary Stores we purchase jointly. Our Little ones stood the opperation Manfully. Dr. Bulfinch is our Physician. Such a Spirit of innoculation never before took place; the Town and every House in it, are as full as they can hold. I believe there are not less than 30 persons from Braintree. Mrs. Quincy, Mrs. Lincoln, Miss Betsy and Nancy are our near Neighbours. God Grant that we may all go comfortably thro the Distemper, the phisick part is bad enough I know. I knew your mind so perfectly upon the subject that I thought nothing, but our recovery would give you eaquel pleasure, and as to safety there was none. The Soldiers innoculated privately, so did many of the inhabitants and the paper curency spread it everywhere. I immediately determined to set myself about it, and get ready with my children. I wish it was so you could have been with us, but I submit.

I received some Letters from you last Saturday Night 26 of June. You mention a Letter of the 16 which I have never received, and I suppose must relate something to private affairs which I wrote about in May and sent by Harry.

As to News we have taken several fine prizes since I wrote you as you will see by the news papers. The present Report is of Lord Hows[4] comeing with unlimited powers. However suppose it is so, I believe he little thinks of treating with us as independant States. How can any person yet dreem of a settlement, accommodations &c. They have neither the spirit nor feeling of Men, yet I see some who never were call'd Tories, gratified with the Idea of Lord Hows being upon his passage with such powers.

1776, 1876

---

[1] Richard Cranch (1726–1811), Abigail's brother-in-law.

[2] Cotton Tufts, Jr. (1757–1833), Abigail's first cousin.

[3] John Thaxter, Jr. (1755–1791), John Adams's clerk and private secretary.

[4] Admiral Richard Howe (1726–1799), sent by Britain to mollify the committee from the Continental Congress.

[*The Deficiency of Education*]

August 14 1776

I wrote you to day by Mr. Smith[1] but as I suppose this will reach you sooner, I omitted mentioning anything of my family in it.

Nabby[2] has enough of the small Pox for all the family beside. She is pretty well coverd, not a spot but what is so soar that she can neither walk sit stand or lay with any comfort. She is as patient as one can expect, but they are a very soar sort. If it was a disorder to which we could be subject more than once I would go as far as it was possible to avoid it. She is sweld a good deal. You will receive a perticuliar account before this reaches you of the uncommon manner in which the small Pox acts, it bafels the skill of the most Experience'd here. Billy Cranch[3] is now out with about 40, and so well as not to be detained at Home an hour for it. Charlly[4] remains in the same state he did.

Your Letter of August 3 came by this days Post. I find it very conveniant to be so handy. I can receive a Letter at Night, sit down and reply to it, and send it of in the morning.

You remark upon the deficiency of Education in your Countrymen. It never I believe was in a worse state, at least for many years. The Colledge is not in the state one could wish, the Schollars complain that their professer in Philosophy is taken of by publick Buisness to their great detriment. In this Town I never saw so great a neglect of Education. The poorer sort of children are wholly neglected, and left to range the Streets without Schools, without Buisness, given up to all Evil. The Town is not as formerly divided into Wards. There is either too much Business left upon the hands of a few, or too little care to do it. We daily see the Necessity of a regular Government.—You speak of our Worthy brother.[5] I often lament it that a Man so peculiarly formed for the Education of youth, and so well qualified as he is in many Branches of Litrature, excelling in Philosiphy and the Mathematicks, should not be imployd in some publick Station. I know not the person who would make half so good a Successor to Dr. Winthrope.[6] He has a peculiar easy manner of communicating his Ideas to Youth, and the Goodness of his Heart, and the purity of his morrals without an affected austerity must have a happy Effect upon the minds of Pupils.

If you complain of neglect of Education in sons, What shall I say with regard to daughters, who every day experience the want of it. With regard to the Education of my own children, I find myself soon out of my debth, and destitute and deficient in every part of Education.

I most sincerely wish that some more liberal plan might be laid and executed for the Benefit of the rising Generation, and that our new constitution may be distinguished for Learning and Virtue. If we mean to have Heroes, Statesmen and Philosophers, we should have learned women. The world perhaps would laugh at me, and accuse me of vanity, But you I know have a mind too enlarged and liberal to disregard the Sentiment. If much depends as is allowed upon the early Education of youth and the first principals which are instilld take the deepest root, great benifit must arise from litirary accomplishments in women.

[1] A visitor from South Carolina.   [2] The Adamses' daughter, Abigail.
[3] Abigail's nephew.   [4] The Adamses' son Charles.
[5] Most likely Richard Cranch, later a judge of Court of the Common Pleas in Massachusetts.
[6] Dr. John Winthrope (?–1779), a professor of mathematics and natural philosophy at Harvard College.

Excuse me my pen has run away with me. I have no thoughts of comeing to P[hiladelphi]a. The length of time I have [and] shall be detaind here would have prevented me, even if you had no thoughts of returning till December, but I live in daily Expectation of seeing you here. Your Health I think requires your immediate return. I expected Mr. Gerry[7] would have set off before now, but he finds it perhaps very hard to leave his Mistress[8]—I wont say harder than some do to leave their wives. Mr. Gerry stood very high in my Esteem—what is meat for one is not for an other—no accounting for fancy. She is a queer dame and leads people wild dances.

But hush—Post, dont betray your trust and loose my Letter.

Nabby is poorly this morning. The pock are near the turn, 6 or 7 hundred boils are no agreable feeling. You and I know not what a feeling it is. Miss Katy can tell. I had but 3 they were very clever and fill'd nicely. The Town instead of being clear of this distemper are now in the height of it, hundreds having it in the natural way through the deceitfulness of innoculation.

Adieu ever yours. Breakfast waits.

PORTIA[9]
1776, 1876

[*Service to Your Country*]

My Dearest Friend   April 10th. 1782

How great was my joy to see the well known Signature of my Friend after a Melancholy Solicitude of many months in which my hopes and fears alternately preponderated.

It was January when Charles arrived. By him I expected Letters, but found not a line; instead of which the heavy tidings of your illness reachd me. I then found my Friends had been no strangers of what they carefully conceald from me. Your Letter to Charles dated in November was the only consolation I had; by that I found that the most dangerous period of your illness was pass'd, and that you considerd yourself as recovering tho feeble. My anxiety and apprehensions from that day untill your Letters arrived, which was near 3 months, conspired to render me unhappy. Capt. Trowbridge in the Fire Brand arrived with your favours of October and December and in some measure dispeld the gloom which hung heavy at my heart. How did it leap for joy to find I was not the miserable Being I sometimes feared I was. I felt that Gratitude to Heaven which great deliverances both demand and inspire. I will not distrust the providential Care of the supreem disposer of events, from whose Hand I have so frequently received distinguished favours. Such I call the preservation of my dear Friend and children from the uncertain Element upon which they have frequently embarked; their preservation from the hands of their enimies I have reason to consider in the same view, especially when I reflect upon the cruel and inhumane treatment experienced by a Gentleman of Mr. Laurences[1] age and respectable character.

---

[7] Elbridge Gerry (1744–1814), a signer of the Declaration of Independence, a delegate to the Second Continental Congress, and U.S. vice-president from 1813 to 1814.

[8] Catherine Hunt, whom Gerry would not marry because she could not read or write and thus correspond with him.

[9] After marriage, Abigail used this signature, from Shakespeare's *The Merchant of Venice* (1596–1597); Portia's clever mediations help her lover's best friend.

[1] John Laurence (1750–1810), a judge who served in the U. S. Senate from 1797 to 1800.

The restoration of my dearest Friend from so dangerous a Sickness, demands all my gratitude, whilst I fail not to supplicate Heaven for the continuance of a Life upon which my temporal happiness rests, and deprived of which my own existance would become a burden. Often has the Question which you say staggerd your philosophy occured to me, nor have I felt so misirable upon account of my own personal Situation, when I considerd that according to the common course of Nature, more than half my days were allready passt, as for those in whom our days are renewed. Their hopes and prospects would vanish, their best prospects, those of Education, would be greatly diminished—but I will not anticipate those miseries which I would shun. Hope is my best Friend and kindest comforter; she assures me that the pure unabated affection, which neither time or absence can allay or abate, shall e'er long be crowned with the completion of its fondest wishes, in the safe return of the beloved object; the age of romance has long ago past, but the affection of almost Infant years has matured and strengthened untill it has become a vital principle, nor has the world any thing to bestow which could in the smallest degree compensate for the loss. Desire and Sorrow were denounced upon our Sex; as a punishment for the transgression of Eve. I have sometimes thought that we are formed to experience more exquisite Sensations than is the Lot of your Sex. More tender and susceptable by Nature of those impression[s] which create happiness or misiry, we Suffer and enjoy in a higher degree. I never wonderd at the philosopher who thanked the Gods that he was created a Man rather than a Woman.

I cannot say, but that I was dissapointed when I found that your return to your native land was a still distant Idea. I think your Situation cannot be so dissagreable as I feared it was, yet that dreadful climate is my terror.—You mortify me indeed when you talk of sending Charles to Colledge, who it is not probable will be fit under three or four years. Surely my dear Friend fleeting as time is I cannot reconcile myself to the Idea of living in this cruel State of Seperation for [4?] or even three years to come. Eight years have already past, since you could call yourself an Inhabitant of this State. I shall assume the Signature of Penelope, for my dear Ulysses[2] has already been a wanderer from me near half the term of years that, that Hero was encountering Neptune, Calipso, the Circes, and Syrens.[3] In the poetical Language of Penelope I shall address you

> "Oh! haste to me! A Little longer Stay
> Will ev'ry grace, each fancy'd charm decay:
> Increasing cares, and times resistless rage
> Will waste my bloom, and wither it to age."

You will ask me I suppose what is become of my patriotick virtue? It is that which most ardently calls for your return. I greatly fear that the climate in which you now reside will prove fatal to your Life, whilst your Life and usefullness might be many years of Service to your Country in a more Healthy climate. If the Essentials of her political system are safe, as I would fain hope they are, yet the

---

[2] In Homer's *Odyssey* (eighth century B.C.), king and queen of Ithaca. Ulysses, a leader in the Trojan War, did not return home until ten years after the war had ended; Penelope faithfully awaited her beloved husband's return.

[3] In mythology, Neptune, Roman god of the sea; Calypso, the divine nymph with whom Ulysses lived after he washed ashore on her island; Circe, a sorceress who transformed Ulysses's men into swine; Syrens, female creatures who lured sailors to their island by singing.

impositions and injuries, to which she is hourly liable, and daily suffering, call for the exertions of her wisest and ablest citizens. You know by many years experience what it is to struggle with difficulties—with wickedness in high places—from thence you are led to covet a private Station as the post of Honour, but should such an Idea generally prevail, who would be left to stem the torrent?

Should we at this day possess those invaluable Blessings transmitted us by our venerable Ancestors, if they had not inforced by their example, what they taught by their precepts?

> "While pride, oppression and injustice reign
> the World will still demand her Catos[4] presence."

Why should I indulge an Idea, that whilst the active powers of my Friend remain, they will not be devoted to the Service of his country?

Can I believe that the Man who fears neither poverty or dangers, who sees not charms sufficient either in Riches, power or places to tempt him in the least to swerve from the purest Sentiments of Honour and Delicacy; will retire, unnoticed, Fameless to a Rustick cottage there by dint of Labour to earn his Bread. I need not much examination of my heart to say I would not willing[ly] consent to it.

Have not Cincinnatus and Regulus[5] been handed down to posterity, with immortal honour?

Without fortune it is more than probable we shall end our days, but let the well earned Fame of having Sacrificed those prospects, from a principal of universal Benevolence and good will to Man, descend as an inheritance to our offspring. The Luxery of Foreign Nations may possibly infect them but they have not before them an example of it, so far as respects their domestick life. They are not Bred up with the Idea of possessing Hereditary Riches or Grandeur. Retired from the Capital, they see little of the extravagance or dissipation, which prevails there, and at the close of the day, in lieu of the Card table, some usefull Book employs their leisure hours. These habits early fixed, and daily inculcated, will I hope render them usefull and ornamental Members of Society.—But we cannot see into futurity.—With Regard to politicks, it is rather a dull season for them, we are recruiting for the Army.

The Enemy make sad Havock with our Navigation. Mr. Lovell[6] is appointed continental Receiver of taxes and is on his way to this state.

It is difficult to get Gentlemen of abilities and Integrity to serve in congress, few very few are willing to Sacrifice their Interest as others have done before them.

Your favour of december 18th came by way of Philadelphia, but all those Letters sent by Capt. Reeler[7] were lost, thrown over Board. Our Friends are well and desire to be rememberd to you. Charles will write if he is able to, before the vessel

---

[4] Either Cato the Elder (234–149 B.C.), a Roman statesman, or Cato the Younger (95–46 B.C.), a Roman philosopher.

[5] Lucius Quinctius Cincinnatus (fifth century B.C.), a Roman dictator sent to rescue Minucius from the seige of Aequu. Cincinnatus then stepped down and returned to his farm; Marcus Atilius Regulus (?–250? B.C.), in command of Roman troops in Africa, was defeated and captured in Carthage. He was sent to Rome to arrange a prisoner exchange in 250 B.C. He is said to have been tortured to death after voluntarily returning to Carthage.

[6] James Lovell (1737–1814), a delegate to the General Congress from Massachusetts.

[7] Commander of a merchant ship and friend of the Adamses.

sails, but he is sick at present, threatned I fear with a fever. I received one Letter from my young Russian to whom I shall write—and 2 from Mr. Thaxter.[8] If the vessel gives me time I shall write. We wait impatiently for the result of your demand. These slow slugish wheels move not in unison with our feelings.

Adieu my dear Friend. How gladly would I visit you and partake of your Labours and cares, sooth you to rest, and alleviate your anxieties were it given me to visit you even by moon Light, as the faries are fabled to do.

I cheer my Heart with the distant prospect. All that I can hope for at present, is to hear of your welfare which of all things lies nearest the Heart of Your ever affectionate

PORTIA
1782, 1876

Thomas Paine
(1737–1809)

"Independence is my happiness, and I view things as they are, without regard to place or purpose; my country is the world, and my religion is to do good." Although these words from Thomas Paine's *The Rights of Man* (1791–1792) did not produce the same passionate response as did his "These are the times that try men's souls" from *The American Crisis* (1776), they tell more of his central core of vision than do his many well-known quotations. The work of this inspired agitator had international ramifications and belonged to the Enlightenment in its broadest terms. Whether Paine sought wage and labor reform or the direct overthrow of a monarchy, his quest was for human dignity and independence, for the creation of democratic republics, and ultimately for world peace. Paine saw the United States as the key to completing what he called the "circle of civilization." If each state could come together for the common good, then so could nations.

This early promoter of a utopian global village was born to Joseph Paine and Frances Cocke in Thetford, England, in 1737. At age thirteen Paine apprenticed with his father as a corset maker but ran away three years later to become a sailor. He then commenced a series of unsuccessful careers as a corset maker, excise (tax) officer, teacher, tobacconist, and grocer. Between 1757 and 1774 he married twice. In 1768, Paine wrote his first known pamphlet, *The Case of the Officers of Excise* (1772), to organize the excise collectors to raise their salary, and solicited the aid of British writer Oliver Goldsmith to influence Parliament. Obstinate and argumentative, Paine identified with those whose lives were limited by social class, poverty, or a repressive government and fought to improve their lot. In 1774 he was discharged as an excise officer for neglecting his duties.

Thirty-seven years old, penniless, and with poor prospects for employment, Paine set sail for America, bringing little more with him than a modest statement of his abilities in a letter of introduction from his recent acquaintance Benjamin Franklin. Arriving in November 1774 Paine found himself in a unique moment in history. Within a year he became the editor of the *Pennsylvania Magazine* and tripled its circulation via his powerful essays, one

---

[8] John Thaxter, Abigail's cousin and tutor to her son John Quincy.

of which, "A Serious Thought," anticipated much of the Declaration of Independence. Paine had studied the anti-British pamphlets written since 1760 and the proceedings of the First Continental Congress and kept abreast of the worsening relationship with the English government.

Common Sense, Paine's first master stroke in the American cause, was published anonymously in January 1776. The one hundred thousand copies circulated in the following months rallied immense support for the Revolution and proved Paine's genius as a propagandist. Late that year, when George Washington retreated across the Delaware at perhaps one of the darkest times of the war, Paine again rallied American resistance. His essay *The American Crisis* united the colonies into a force composed of far more than the "summer soldier and the sunshine patriot" and directly influenced the American victory at Trenton.

Employed by Congress and then the Pennsylvania Assembly, Paine wrote fifteen more Crisis papers over the next seven years. They formed a compelling record of the ebb and flow of American fortunes in the war. His poor finances at the end of the Revolution mirrored those of his country. Out of gratitude his countrymen provided him with $3,000 and a confiscated Tory estate in New Rochelle, New York, but no employment. The resourceful Paine turned to invention, creating a smokeless candle and a single-span iron bridge. He sailed for France in 1787 to follow the spirit of revolution as much as to patent and promote his bridge.

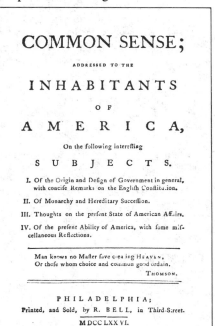

The title page of Thomas Paine's Common Sense.

Well received in France and England, Paine was soon at work. His *The Rights of Man*, an attack on Edmund Burke's *Reflections on the Revolution in France*, espoused mankind's natural rights and the overthrow of hereditary monarchy. Paine was indicted for treason in 1792 but escaped to France, where he was greeted enthusiastically, was elected a representative to the National Assembly, and became an honorary citizen. Too revolutionary for the British, Paine proved too moderate for the radical French. His opposition to France's Reign of Terror and to the execution of the king and queen resulted in his arrest in

1793 and confinement in Luxembourg prison for ten months. Escaping the guillotine by mere luck, he was finally freed through the efforts of James Monroe, then ambassador to France.

Just before his imprisonment Paine gave the first part of *The Age of Reason* (1794) to his friend Joel Barlow for publication. In it and in the second part (1795), Paine brings his arsenal of effective rhetoric, satire, ridicule, and emotional appeal to bear on the abuses of organized religion and on the Bible as a source of divine revelation. Although his belief in God is clearly stated in this work, Paine was condemned as an atheist. His former popularity was further undercut by his *Letter to George Washington* (1796), a series of scathing attacks that accused the president of betraying their friendship by allowing Paine to remain in prison.

Impoverished and in ill health, Paine was invited to return to the United States in 1802 by his old friend, President Thomas Jefferson. Paine's last years were far from happy. Forgotton by all but the orthodox Christians who reviled him, the Revolution's premier pamphleteer experienced an assassination attempt, was denied the right to vote, and was refused Quaker burial. Only a handful of people attended Paine's funeral on his farm in 1809.

Paine was not to rest easy even in death. William Cobbett, an enthusiastic admirer, illegally exhumed the casket in 1819 and shipped it to England to make it part of a monument he planned to erect in Paine's memory. The scheme failed and the remains were up for auction as part of Cobbett's estate in 1835. Morbidly, legend has kept track of the scattered parts of Paine's skeleton. The courageous revolutionary, the articulate exponent of liberal political thought and republican virtue, the humanitarian who tried to be the social conscience of an age, was never laid to rest; neither were the ideas to which he gave such eloquent voice.

Suggested Readings: P. Davidson, *Propaganda and the American Revolution, 1763–1783*, 1941. B. Bailyn, *The Ideological Origins of the American Revolution*, 1969. E. Foner, *Tom Paine and Revolutionary America*, 1976. A. O. Aldridge, *Thomas Paine's American Ideology*, 1984. I. Dyck, *Citizen of the World: Essays on Thomas Paine*, 1987. A. J. Ayer, *Thomas Paine*, 1988.

Texts Used: "An Occasional Letter on the Female Sex," "Introduction" and "Thoughts on the Present State of American Affairs" from *Common Sense*, and "The Crisis No. 1" from *The American Crisis: The Writings of Thomas Paine, 1774–1779*, Vol. I, ed. M. D. Conway, 1894. All others from *The Age of Reason*, Pt. I: *The Writings of Thomas Paine*, Vol IV, ed. M. D. Conway, 1967.

AN OCCASIONAL LETTER ON THE FEMALE SEX

> *O Woman! lovely Woman!*
> *Nature made thee to temper man,*
> *We had been Brutes without you.*
> OTWAY

If we take a survey of ages and of countries, we shall find the women, almost—without exception—at all times and in all places, adored and oppressed. Man, who has never neglected an opportunity of exerting his power, in paying homage to their beauty, has always availed himself of their weakness. He has been at once their tyrant and their slave.

Nature herself, in forming beings so susceptible and tender, appears to have been more attentive to their charms than to their happiness. Continually surrounded with griefs and fears, the women more than share all our miseries, and are besides subjected to ills which are peculiarly their own. They cannot be the means of life without exposing themselves to the loss of it; every revolution which they undergo, alters their health, and threatens their existence. Cruel distempers attack their beauty—and the hour, which confirms their release from those, is perhaps the most melancholy of their lives. It robs them of the most essential characteristic of their sex. They can then only hope for protection from the humiliating claims of pity, or the feeble voice of gratitude.

Society, instead of alleviating their condition, is to them the source of new miseries. More than one half of the globe is covered with savages; and among all these people women are completely wretched. Man, in a state of barbarity, equally cruel and indolent, active by necessity, but naturally inclined to repose, is acquainted with little more than the physical effects of love; and, having none of those moral ideas which only can soften the empire of force, he is led to consider it as his supreme law, subjecting to his despotism those whom reason had made his equal, but whose imbecility betrayed them to his strength. "Nothing"(says Professor Miller, speaking of the women of barbarous nations) "can exceed the dependence and subjection in which they are kept, or the toil and drudgery which they are obliged to undergo. The husband, when he is not engaged in some warlike exercise, indulges himself in idleness, and devolves upon his wife the whole burden of his domestic affairs. He disdains to assist her in any of those servile employments. She sleeps in a different bed, and is seldom permitted to have any conversation or correspondence with him."

The women among the Indians of America are what the Helots[1] were among the Spartans, a vanquished people, obliged to toil for their conquerors. Hence on the banks of the Oroonoko,[2] we have seen mothers slaying their daughters out of compassion, and smothering them in the hour of their birth. They consider this barbarous pity as a virtue.

> "The men (says Commodore Byron, in his account of the inhabitants of South-America) exercise a most despotic authority over their wives, whom they consider in the same view they do any other part of their property, and dispose of them accordingly: Even their common treatment of them is cruel; for though the toil and hazard of procuring food lies entirely on the women, yet they are not suffered to touch any part of it till the husband is satisfied; and then he assigns them their portion, which is generally very scanty, and such as he has not a stomach for himself."

Among the nations of the East we find another kind of despotism and dominion prevail—the Seraglio,[3] and the domestic servitude of woman, authorised by the manners and established by the laws. In Turkey, in Persia, in India, in Japan, and over the vast empire of China, one half of the human species is oppressed by the other.

The excess of oppression in those countries springs from the excess of love.

All Asia is covered with prisons, where beauty in bondage waits the caprices of

---

[1] The lowest class of serfs in Sparta.   [2] The Orinoco River in Venezuela.   [3] A harem.

a master. The multitude of women there assembled have no will, no inclinations but his: Their triumphs are only for a moment; and their rivalry, their hate, and their animosities, continue till death. There the lovely sex are obliged to repay even their servitude with the most tender affections; or, what is still more mortifying, with the counterfeit of an affection, which they do not feel: There the most gloomy tyranny has subjected them to creatures, who, being of neither sex, are a dishonour to both: There, in short, their education tends only to debase them; their virtues are forced; their very pleasures are involuntary and joyless; and after an existence of a few years—till the bloom of youth is over—their period of neglect commences, which is long and dreadful. In the temperate latitude where the climates, giving less ardour to passion, leave more confidence in virtue, the women have not been deprived of their liberty, but a severe legislation has, at all times, kept them in a state of dependence. One while, they were confined to their own apartments, and debarred at once from business and amusement; at other times, a tedious guardianship defrauded their hearts, and insulted their understandings. Affronted in one country by polygamy, which gives them their rivals for their inseparable companions; inslaved in another by indissoluble ties, which often join the gentle to the rude, and sensibility to brutality: Even in countries where they may be esteemed most happy, constrained in their desires in the disposal of their goods, robbed of freedom of will by the laws, the slaves of opinion, which rules them with absolute sway, and construes the slightest appearances into guilt; surrounded on all sides by judges, who are at once tyrants and their seducers, and who, after having prepared their faults, punish every lapse with dishonour—nay, usurp the right of degrading them on suspicion! Who does not feel for the tender sex? Yet such, I am sorry to say, is the lot of woman over the whole earth. Man with regard to them, in all climates, and in all ages, has been either an insensible husband or an oppressor; but they have sometimes experienced the cold and deliberate oppression of pride, and sometimes the violent and terrible tyranny of jealousy. When they are not beloved they are nothing; and, when they are, they are tormented. They have almost equal cause to be afraid of indifference and of love. Over three quarters of the globe nature has placed them between contempt and misery.

"The melting desires, or the fiery passions," says Professor Ferguson,[4] "which in one climate take place between the sexes, are, in another, changed into a sober consideration, or a patience of mutual disgust. This change is remarked in crossing the Mediterranean, in following the course of the Mississippi, in ascending the mountains of Caucasus, and in passing from the Alps and the Pyrenees to the shores of the Baltic.

"The burning ardours and torturing jealousies of the Seraglio and Harem, which have reigned so long in Asia and Africa, and which, in the southern parts of Europe, have scarcely given way to the differences of religion and civil establishments, are found, however, with an abatement of heat in the climate, to be more easily changed, in one latitude, into a temporary passion, which engrosses the mind without infeebling it, and which excites to romantic atchievments. By a farther progress

---

[4] Adam Ferguson (1723–1816), a professor of moral philosophy at the University of Edinburgh, who wrote *Essay on the History of Civil Society* (1767) and *Institutes of Moral Philosophy* (1769).

to the north it is changed into a spirit of gallantry, which employs the wit and fancy more than the heart, which prefers intrigue to enjoyment, and substitutes affection and vanity where sentiment and desire have failed. As it departs from the sun, the same passion is farther composed into a habit of domestic connection, or frozen into a state of insensibility, under which the sexes at freedom scarcely choose to unite their society."

Even among people where beauty received the highest homage, we find men who would deprive the sex of every kind of reputation: "The most virtuous woman," says a celebrated Greek, "is she who is least talked of." That morose man, while he imposes duties upon women, would deprive them of the sweets of public esteem, and in exacting virtues from them, would make it a crime to aspire at honour.

If a woman were to defend the cause of her sex, she might address him in the following manner:

"How great is your injustice? If we have an equal right with you to virtue, why should we not have an equal right to praise? The public esteem ought to wait upon merit. Our duties are different from yours, but they are not therefore less difficult to fulfil, or of less consequence to society: They are the fountains of your felicity, and the sweetness of life. We are wives and mothers. 'T is we who form the union and the cordiality of families: 'T is we who soften that savage rudeness which considers everything as due to force, and which would involve man with man in eternal war. We cultivate in you that humanity which makes you feel for the misfortunes of others, and our tears forewarn you of your own danger. Nay, you cannot be ignorant that we have need of courage not less than you: More feeble in ourselves, we have perhaps more trials to encounter. Nature assails us with sorrow, law and custom press us with constraint, and sensibility and virtue alarm us with their continual conflict. Sometimes also the name of citizen demands from us the tribute of fortitude. When you offer your blood to the State think that it is ours. In giving it our sons and our husbands we give more than ourselves. You can only die on the field of battle, but we have the misfortune to survive those whom we love most. Alas! while your ambitious vanity is unceasingly labouring to cover the earth with statues, with monuments, and with inscriptions to eternize, if possible, your names, and give yourselves an existence, when this body is no more, why must we be condemned to live and to die unknown? Would that the grave and eternal forgetfulness should be our lot. Be not our tyrants in all: Permit our names to be sometimes pronounced beyond the narrow circle in which we live: Permit friendship, or at least love, to inscribe its emblems on the tomb where our ashes repose; and deny us not that public esteem which, after the esteem of one's self, is the sweetest reward of well doing."

All men, however, it must be owned, have not been equally unjust to their fair companions. In some countries public honours have been paid to women. Art has erected them monuments. Eloquence has celebrated their virtues, and History has collected whatever could adorn their character.

1775

from COMMON SENSE*

INTRODUCTION

Perhaps the sentiments contained in the following pages, are not *yet* sufficiently fashionable to procure them general Favor; a long Habit of not thinking a Thing *wrong,* gives it a superficial appearance of being *right,* and raises at first a formidable outcry in defence of Custom. But the Tumult soon subsides. Time makes more Converts than Reason.

As a long and violent abuse of power is generally the means of calling the right of it in question, (and in matters too which might never have been thought of, had not the sufferers been aggravated into the inquiry,) and as the King of England hath undertaken in his *own right,* to support the Parliament in what he calls *Theirs,* and as the good People of this Country are grievously oppressed by the Combination, they have an undoubted privilege to enquire into the Pretensions of both, and equally to reject the Usurpation of *either*.

In the following Sheets, the Author hath studiously avoided every thing which is personal among ourselves. Compliments as well as censure to individuals make no part thereof. The wise and the worthy need not the triumph of a Pamphlet; and those whose sentiments are injudicious or unfriendly will cease of themselves, unless too much pains is bestowed upon their conversions.

The cause of America is in a great measure the cause of all mankind. Many circumstances have, and will arise, which are not local, but universal, and through which the principles of all lovers of mankind are affected, and in the event of which their affections are interested. The laying a country desolate with fire and sword, declaring war against the natural rights of all mankind, and extirpating the defenders thereof from the face of the earth, is the concern of every man to whom nature hath given the power of feeling; of which class, regardless of party censure, is

The Author.

Postscript to Preface in the third edition

P.S. The Publication of this new Edition hath been delayed, with a view of taking notice (had it been necessary) of any attempt to refute the Doctrine of Independence: As no answer hath yet appeared, it is now presumed that none will, the time needful for getting such a Performance ready for the Public being considerably past.

Who the Author of this Production is, is wholly unnecessary to the Public, as the Object for Attention is the *Doctrine itself,* not the *Man.* Yet it may not be unnecessary to say, That he is unconnected with any party, and under no sort of Influence, public or private, but the influence of reason and principle.

Philadelphia, February 14, 1776.

* This pamphlet was published with the title COMMON SENSE: Addressed to the Inhabitants of America, on the following Interesting Subjects, viz.: I. Of the Origin and Design of Government in General; with Concise Remarks on the English Constitution.   II. Of Monarchy and Hereditary Succession.   III. Thoughts on the Present State of American Affairs.   IV. Of the Present Ability of America; with some Miscellaneous Reflections.

THOUGHTS ON THE PRESENT STATE OF AMERICAN AFFAIRS

In the following pages I offer nothing more than simple facts, plain arguments, and common sense: and have no other preliminaries to settle with the reader, than that he will divest himself of prejudice and prepossession, and suffer his reason and his feelings to determine for themselves: that he will put on, or rather that he will not put off, the true character of a man, and generously enlarge his views beyond the present day.

Volumes have been written on the subject of the struggle between England and America. Men of all ranks have embarked in the controversy, from different motives, and with various designs; but all have been ineffectual, and the period of debate is closed. Arms as the last resource decide the contest; the appeal was the choice of the King, and the Continent has accepted the challenge.

It hath been reported of the late Mr. Pelham[1] (who tho' an able minister was not without his faults) that on his being attacked in the House of Commons on the score that his measures were only of a temporary kind, replied, *"they will last my time."* Should a thought so fatal and unmanly possess the Colonies in the present contest, the name of ancestors will be remembered by future generations with detestation.

The Sun never shined on a cause of greater worth. 'Tis not the affair of a City, a County, a Province, or a Kingdom; but of a Continent—of at least one eighth part of the habitable Globe. 'Tis not the concern of a day, a year, or an age; posterity are virtually involved in the contest, and will be more or less affected even to the end of time, by the proceedings now. Now is the seed-time of Continental union, faith and honour. The least fracture now will be like a name engraved with the point of a pin on the tender rind of a young oak; the wound would enlarge with the tree, and posterity read it in full grown characters.

By referring the matter from argument to arms, a new æra for politics is struck—a new method of thinking hath arisen. All plans, proposals, &c. prior to the nineteenth of April, *i.e.* to the commencement of hostilities,[2] are like the almanacks of the last year; which tho' proper then, are superceded and useless now. Whatever was advanced by the advocates on either side of the question then, terminated in one and the same point, viz. a union with Great Britain; the only difference between the parties was the method of effecting it; the one proposing force, the other friendship; but it hath so far happened that the first hath failed, and the second hath withdrawn her influence.

As much hath been said of the advantages of reconciliation, which, like an agreeable dream, hath passed away and left us as we were, it is but right that we should examine the contrary side of the argument, and enquire into some of the many material injuries which these Colonies sustain, and always will sustain, by being connected with and dependant on Great-Britain. To examine that connection and dependance, on the principles of nature and common sense, to see what we have to trust to, if separated, and what we are to expect, if dependant.

I have heard it asserted by some, that as America has flourished under her former connection with Great-Britain, the same connection is necessary towards

---

[1] Henry Pelham, British prime minister from 1743 to 1754.

[2] The start of the American Revolution at Lexington, Massachusetts, where the "minutemen" defended their ammunitions against the English on April 19, 1775.

her future happiness, and will always have the same effect. Nothing can be more fallacious than this kind of argument. We may as well assert that because a child has thrived upon milk, that it is never to have meat, or that the first twenty years of our lives is to become a precedent for the next twenty. But even this is admitting more than is true; for I answer roundly, that America would have flourished as much, and probably much more, had no European power taken any notice of her. The commerce by which she hath enriched herself are the necessaries of life, and will always have a market while eating is the custom of Europe.

But she has protected us, say some. That she hath engrossed us is true, and defended the Continent at our expense as well as her own, is admitted; and she would have defended Turkey from the same motive, *viz.* for the sake of trade and dominion.

Alas! we have been long led away by ancient prejudices and made large sacrifices to superstition. We have boasted the protection of Great Britain, without considering, that her motive was *interest* not *attachment;* and that she did not protect us from *our enemies* on *our account;* but from *her enemies* on *her own account,* from those who had no quarrel with us on any *other account,* and who will always be our enemies on the *same account.* Let Britain waive her pretensions to the Continent, or the Continent throw off the dependance, and we should be at peace with France and Spain, were they at war with Britain. The miseries of Hanover last war[3] ought to warn us against connections.

It hath lately been asserted in parliament, that the Colonies have no relation to each other but through the Parent Country, *i.e.* that Pennsylvania and the Jerseys,[4] and so on for the rest, are sister Colonies by the way of England; this is certainly a very roundabout way of proving relationship, but it is the nearest and only true way of proving enmity (or enemyship, if I may so call it.) France and Spain never were, nor perhaps ever will be, our enemies as *Americans,* but as our being the *subjects of Great Britain.*

But Britain is the parent country, say some. Then the more shame upon her conduct. Even brutes do not devour their young, nor savages make war upon their families; Wherefore, the assertion, if true, turns to her reproach; but it happens not to be true, or only partly so, and the phrase *parent* or *mother country* hath been jesuitically adopted by the King and his parasites, with a low papistical design of gaining an unfair bias on the credulous weakness of our minds. Europe, and not England, is the parent country of America. This new World hath been the asylum for the persecuted lovers of civil and religious liberty from *every part* of Europe. Hither have they fled, not from the tender embraces of the mother, but from the cruelty of the monster, and it is so far true of England, that the same tyranny which drove the first emigrants from home, pursues their descendants still.

In this extensive quarter of the globe, we forget the narrow limits of three hundred and sixty miles (the extent of England) and carry our friendship on a larger scale; we claim brotherhood with every European Christian, and triumph in the generosity of the sentiment.

It is pleasant to observe by what regular gradations we surmount the force of local prejudices, as we enlarge our acquaintance with the World. A man born in any town in England divided into parishes, will naturally associate most with his

---

[3] The Seven Years' War of 1756 to 1763. Britain's King George III descended from the Prussian House of Hanover.

[4] East and West Jersey, separated at that time.

fellow parishioners (because their interests in many cases will be common) and distinguish him by the name of *neighbour,* if he meet him but a few miles from home, he drops the narrow idea of a street, and salutes him by the name of *townsman;* if he travel out of the county and meet him in any other, he forgets the minor divisions of street and town, and calls him *countryman, i.e. countyman;* but if in their foreign excursions they should associate in France, or any other part of Europe, their local remembrance would be enlarged into that of *Englishmen.* And by a just parity of reasoning, all Europeans meeting in America, or any other quarter of the globe, are *countrymen;* for England, Holland, Germany, or Sweden, when compared with the whole, stand in the same places on the larger scale, which the divisions of street, town, and county do on the smaller ones; Distinctions too limited for Continental minds. Not one third of the inhabitants, even of this province, [Pennsylvania], are of English descent. Wherefore, I reprobate the phrase of Parent or Mother Country applied to England only, as being false, selfish, narrow and ungenerous.

But, admitting that we were all of English descent, what does it amount to? Nothing. Britain, being now an open enemy, extinguishes every other name and title: and to say that reconciliation is our duty, is truly farcical. The first king of England, of the present line (William the Conqueror) was a Frenchman, and half the peers of England are descendants from the same country; wherefore, by the same method of reasoning, England ought to be governed by France.

Much hath been said of the united strength of Britain and the Colonies, that in conjunction they might bid defiance to the world: But this is mere presumption; the fate of war is uncertain, neither do the expressions mean any thing; for this continent would never suffer itself to be drained of inhabitants, to support the British arms in either Asia, Africa, or Europe.

Besides, what have we to do with setting the world at defiance? Our plan is commerce, and that, well attended to, will secure us the peace and friendship of all Europe; because it is the interest of all Europe to have America a free port. Her trade will always be a protection, and her barrenness of gold and silver secure her from invaders.

I challenge the warmest advocate for reconciliation to show a single advantage that this continent can reap by being connected with Great Britain. I repeat the challenge; not a single advantage is derived. Our corn will fetch its price in any market in Europe, and our imported goods must be paid for buy them where we will.

But the injuries and disadvantages which we sustain by that connection, are without number; and our duty to mankind at large, as well as to ourselves, instruct us to renounce the alliance: because, any submission to, or dependance on, Great Britain, tends directly to involve this Continent in European wars and quarrels, and set us at variance with nations who would otherwise seek our friendship, and against whom we have neither anger nor complaint. As Europe is our market for trade, we ought to form no partial connection with any part of it. It is the true interest of America to steer clear of European contentions, which she never can do, while, by her dependance on Britain, she is made the make-weight in the scale of British politics.

Europe is too thickly planted with Kingdoms to be long at peace, and whenever a war breaks out between England and any foreign power, the trade of America goes to ruin, *because of her connection with Britain*. The next war may not turn out like the last,[5] and should it not, the advocates for reconciliation now will be wishing for separation then, because neutrality in the case would be a safer convoy than a man of war. Everything that is right or reasonable pleads for separation. The blood of the slain, the weeping voice of nature cries, 'TIS TIME TO PART. Even the distance at which the Almighty hath placed England and America is a strong and natural proof that the authority of the one over the other, was never the design of Heaven. The time likewise at which the Continent was discovered, adds weight to the argument, and the manner in which it was peopled, encreases the force of it. The Reformation was preceded by the discovery of America: As if the Almighty graciously meant to open a sanctuary to the persecuted in future years, when home should afford neither friendship nor safety.

The authority of Great Britain over this continent, is a form of government, which sooner or later must have an end: And a serious mind can draw no true pleasure by looking forward, under the painful and positive conviction that what he calls "the present constitution" is merely temporary. As parents, we can have no joy, knowing that this government is not sufficiently lasting to ensure any thing which we may bequeath to posterity: And by a plain method of argument, as we are running the next generation into debt, we ought to do the work of it, otherwise we use them meanly and pitifully. In order to discover the line of our duty rightly, we should take our children in our hand, and fix our station a few years farther into life; that eminence will present a prospect which a few present fears and prejudices conceal from our sight.

Though I would carefully avoid giving unnecessary offence, yet I am inclined to believe, that all those who espouse the doctrine of reconciliation, may be included within the following descriptions.

Interested men, who are not to be trusted, weak men who *cannot* see, prejudiced men who will not see, and a certain set of moderate men who think better of the European world than it deserves; and this last class, by an ill-judged deliberation, will be the cause of more calamities to this Continent than all the other three.

It is the good fortune of many to live distant from the scene of present sorrow; the evil is not sufficiently brought to their doors to make them feel the precariousness with which all American property is possessed. But let our imaginations transport us a few moments to Boston; that seat of wretchedness will teach us wisdom, and instruct us for ever to renounce a power in whom we can have no trust.[6] The inhabitants of that unfortunate city who but a few months ago were in ease and affluence, have now no other alternative than to stay and starve, or turn out to beg. Endangered by the fire of their friends if they continue within the city, and plundered by the soldiery if they leave it, in their present situation they are prisoners without the hope of redemption, and in a general attack for their relief they would be exposed to the fury of both armies.

Men of passive tempers look somewhat lightly over the offences of Great Britain, and, still hoping for the best, are apt to call out, *Come, come, we shall be friends again for all this*. But examine the passions and feelings of mankind: bring the doctrine of reconciliation to the touchstone of nature and then tell me whether you can hereafter love, honour, and faithfully serve the power that hath carried fire and sword into your land? If you cannot do all these, then are you only deceiving yourselves, and by your delay bringing ruin upon posterity. Your future con-

---

[5] When the Seven Years' War had ended, all French territory in North America was handed over to Britain by the Treaty of Paris in 1763.

[6] For six months Boston was barricaded under British military control.

nection with Britain, whom you can neither love nor honour, will be forced and unnatural, and being formed only on the plan of present convenience, will in a little time fall into a relapse more wretched than the first. But if you say, you can still pass the violations over, then I ask, hath your house been burnt? Hath your property been destroyed before your face? Are your wife and children destitute of a bed to lie on, or bread to live on? Have you lost a parent or a child by their hands, and yourself the ruined and wretched survivor? If you have not, then are you not a judge of those who have. But if you have, and can still shake hands with the murderers, then are you unworthy the name of husband, father, friend, or lover, and whatever may be your rank or title in life, you have the heart of a coward, and the spirit of a sycophant.

This is not inflaming or exaggerating matters, but trying them by those feelings and affections which nature justifies, and without which we should be incapable of discharging the social duties of life, or enjoying the felicities of it. I mean not to exhibit horror for the purpose of provoking revenge, but to awaken us from fatal and unmanly slumbers, that we may pursue determinately some fixed object. 'Tis not in the power of Britain or of Europe to conquer America, if she doth not conquer herself by delay and timidity. The present winter is worth an age if rightly employed, but if lost or neglected the whole Continent will partake of the misfortune; and there is no punishment which that man doth not deserve, be he who, or what, or where he will, that may be the means of sacrificing a season so precious and useful.

'Tis repugnant to reason, to the universal order of things, to all examples from former ages, to suppose that this Continent can long remain subject to any external power. The most sanguine in Britain doth not think so. The utmost stretch of human wisdom cannot, at this time, compass a plan, short of separation, which can promise the continent even a year's security. Reconciliation is *now* a fallacious dream. Nature hath deserted the connection, and art cannot supply her place. For, as Milton wisely expresses, "never can true reconcilement grow where wounds of deadly hate have pierced so deep."[7]

Every quiet method for peace hath been ineffectual. Our prayers have been rejected with disdain; and hath tended to convince us that nothing flatters vanity or confirms obstinacy in Kings more than repeated petitioning—and nothing hath contributed more than that very measure to make the Kings of Europe absolute. Witness Denmark and Sweden.[8] Wherefore, since nothing but blows will do, for God's sake let us come to a final separation, and not leave the next generation to be cutting throats under the violated unmeaning names of parent and child.

To say they will never attempt it again is idle and visionary; we thought so at the repeal of the stamp act, yet a year or two undeceived us; as well may we suppose that nations which have been once defeated will never renew the quarrel.

As to government matters, 'tis not in the power of Britain to do this continent justice: the business of it will soon be too weighty and intricate to be managed with any tolerable degree of convenience, by a power so distant from us, and so very ignorant of us; for if they cannot conquer us, they cannot govern us. To be always running three or four thousand miles with a tale or a petition, waiting four of five months for an answer, which, when obtained, requires five or six more to explain it in, will in a few years be looked upon as folly and childishness. There was a time when it was proper, and there is a proper time for it to cease.

---

[7] From John Milton's *Paradise Lost* (1674, IV. 98–99).
[8] Both recently threatened by absolute monarchies.

Small islands not capable of protecting themselves are the proper objects for government to take under their care; but there is something absurd, in supposing a Continent to be perpetually governed by an island. In no instance hath nature made the satellite larger than its primary planet; and as England and America, with respect to each other, reverse the common order of nature, it is evident that they belong to different systems. England to Europe: America to itself.

I am not induced by motives of pride, party, or resentment to espouse the doctrine of separation and independence; I am clearly, positively, and conscientiously persuaded that it is the true interest of this Continent to be so; that everything short of *that* is mere patchwork, that it can afford no lasting felicity,—that it is leaving the sword to our children, and shrinking back at a time when a little more, a little further, would have rendered this Continent the glory of the earth.

As Britain hath not manifested the least inclination towards a compromise, we may be assured that no terms can be obtained worthy the acceptance of the Continent, or any ways equal to the expence of blood and treasure we have been already put to.

The object contended for, ought always to bear some just proportion to the expense. The removal of North,[9] or the whole detestable junto, is a matter unworthy the millions we have expended. A temporary stoppage of trade was an inconvenience , which would have sufficiently ballanced the repeal of all the acts complained of, had such repeals been obtained; but if the whole Continent must take up arms, if every man must be a soldier, 'tis scarcely worth our while to fight against a contemptible ministry only. Dearly, dearly do we pay for the repeal of the acts, if that is all we fight for; for, in a just estimation 'tis as great a folly to pay a Bunker-hill price[10] for law as for land. As I have always considered the independancy of this continent, as an event which sooner or later must arrive, so from the late rapid progress of the Continent to maturity, the event cannot be far off. Wherefore, on the breaking out of hostilities, it was not worth the while to have disputed a matter which time would have finally redressed, unless we meant to be in earnest: otherwise it is like wasting an estate on a suit at law, to regulate the trespasses of a tenant whose lease is just expiring. No man was a warmer wisher for a reconciliation than myself, before the fatal nineteenth of April, 1775,[11] but the moment the event of that day was made known, I rejected the hardened, sullen-tempered Pharaoh of England[12] for ever; and disdain the wretch, that with the pretended title of FATHER OF HIS PEOPLE can unfeelingly hear of their slaughter, and composedly sleep with their blood upon his soul.

But admitting that matters were now made up, what would be the event? I answer, the ruin of the Continent. And that for several reasons.

First. The powers of governing still remaining in the hands of the king, he will have a negative over the whole legislation of this Continent. And as he hath shown himself such an inveterate enemy to liberty, and discovered such a thirst for arbitrary power, is he, or is he not, a proper person to say to these colonies, *You shall make no laws but what I please!?* And is there any inhabitant of America so ignorant as not to know, that according to what is called the *present constitution,* this

---

[9] Frederick North, earl of Guilford and British prime minister from 1770 to 1782, who was blamed for exploiting the colonies via taxation.
[10] The high price of extensive casualties at the Battle of Bunker Hill, June 17, 1775.
[11] Date of the battles of Lexington and Concord.   [12] King George III.

Continent can make no laws but what the king gives leave to; and is there any man so unwise as not to see, that (considering what has happened) he will suffer no law to be made here but such as suits *his* purpose? We may be as effectually enslaved by the want of laws in America, as by submitting to laws made for us in England. After matters are made up (as it is called) can there be any doubt, but the whole power of the crown will be exerted to keep this continent as low and humble as possible? Instead of going forward we shall go backward, or be perpetually quarrelling, or ridiculously petitioning. We are already greater than the King wishes us to be, and will he not hereafter endeavor to make us less? To bring the matter to one point, Is the Power who is jealous of our prosperity, a proper power to govern us? Whoever says *No*, to this question, is an Independant for independency means no more than this, whether we shall make our own laws or, whether the King, the greatest enemy this continent hath, or can have, shall tell us *there shall be no laws but such as I like*.

But the King, you will say, has a negative in England; the people there can make no laws without his consent. In point of right and good order, it is something very ridiculous that a youth of twenty-one (which hath often happened) shall say to several millions of people older and wiser than himself, "I forbid this or that act of yours to be law." But in this place I decline this sort of reply, though I will never cease to expose the absurdity of it, and only answer that England being the King's residence, and America not so, makes quite another case. The King's negative here is ten times more dangerous and fatal than it can be in England; for there he will scarcely refuse his consent to a bill for putting England into as strong a state of defense as possible, and in America he would never suffer such a bill to be passed.

America is only a secondary object in the system of British politics. England consults the good of this country no further than it answers her own purpose. Wherefore, her own interest leads her to suppress the growth of ours in every case which doth not promote her advantage, or in the least interferes with it. A pretty state we should soon be in under such a second hand government, considering what has happened! Men do not change from enemies to friends by the alteration of a name: And in order to show that reconciliation now is a dangerous doctrine, I affirm, *that it would be policy in the King at this time to repeal the acts, for the sake of reinstating himself in the government of the provinces;* In order that HE MAY ACCOMPLISH BY CRAFT AND SUBTLETY, IN THE LONG RUN, WHAT HE CANNOT DO BY FORCE AND VIOLENCE IN THE SHORT ONE. Reconciliation and ruin are nearly related.

Secondly. That as even the best terms which we can expect to obtain can amount to no more than a temporary expedient, or a kind of government by guardianship, which can last no longer than till the Colonies come of age, so the general face and state of things in the interim will be unsettled and unpromising. Emigrants of property will not choose to come to a country whose form of government hangs but by a thread, and who is every day tottering on the brink of commotion and disturbance; and numbers of the present inhabitants would lay hold of the interval to dispose of their effects, and quit the Continent.

But the most powerful of all arguments is, that nothing but independance, *i.e.* a Continental form of government, can keep the peace of the Continent and preserve it inviolate from civil wars. I dread the event of a reconciliation with Britain now, as it is more than probable that it will be followed by a revolt some where or other, the consequences of which may be far more fatal than all the malice of Britain.

Thousands are already ruined by British barbarity; (thousands more will probably suffer the same fate.) Those men have other feelings than us who have nothing suffered. All they now possess is liberty; what they before enjoyed is sacrificed to its service, and having nothing more to lose they disdain submission. Besides, the general temper of the Colonies, towards a British government will be like that of a youth who is nearly out of his time; they will care very little about her: And a government which cannot preserve the peace is no government at all, and in that case we pay our money for nothing; and pray what is it that Britain can do, whose power will be wholly on paper, should a civil tumult break out the very day after reconciliation? I have heard some men say, many of whom I believe spoke without thinking, that they dreaded an independance, fearing that it would produce civil wars: It is but seldom that our first thoughts are truly correct, and that is the case here; for there is ten times more to dread from a patched up connection than from independance. I make the sufferer's case my own, and I protest, that were I driven from house and home, my property destroyed, and my circumstances ruined, that as a man, sensible of injuries, I could never relish the doctrine of reconciliation, or consider myself bound thereby.

The Colonies have manifested such a spirit of good order and obedience to Continental government, as is sufficient to make every reasonable person easy and happy on that head. No man can assign the least pretence for his fears, on any other grounds, than such as are truly childish and ridiculous, viz., that one colony will be striving for superiority over another.

Where there are no distinctions there can be no superiority; perfect equality affords no temptation. The Republics of Europe are all (and we may say always) in peace. Holland and Switzerland are without wars, foreign or domestic: Monarchical governments, it is true, are never long at rest: the crown itself is a temptation to enterprising ruffians at home; and that degree of pride and insolence ever attendant on regal authority, swells into a rupture with foreign powers in instances where a republican government, by being formed on more natural principles, would negociate the mistake.

If there is any true cause of fear respecting independance, it is because no plan is yet laid down. Men do not see their way out. Wherefore, as an opening into that business I offer the following hints; at the same time modestly affirming, that I have no other opinion of them myself, than that they may be the means of giving rise to something better. Could the straggling thoughts of individuals be collected, they would frequently form materials for wise and able men to improve into useful matter.

Let the assemblies be annual, with a president only. The representation more equal, their business wholly domestic, and subject to the authority of a Continental Congress.

Let each Colony be divided into six, eight, or ten, convenient districts, each district to send a proper number of Delegates to Congress, so that each Colony send at least thirty. The whole number in Congress will be at least 390. Each congress to sit and to choose a President by the following method. When the Delegates are met, let a Colony be taken from the whole thirteen Colonies by lot, after which let the Congress choose (by ballot) a president from out of the Delegates of that Province. In the next Congress, let a Colony be taken by lot from twelve only, omitting that Colony from which the president was taken in the former Congress, and so proceeding on till the whole thirteen shall have had their proper rotation. And in order that nothing may pass into a law but what is satisfactorily just, not less than three fifths of the Congress to be called a majority. He that will promote discord, under a government so equally formed as this, would have joined Lucifer in his revolt.

But as there is a peculiar delicacy from whom, or in what manner, this business must first arise, and as it seems most agreeable and consistent that it should come from some intermediate body between the governed and the governors, that is, between the Congress and the People, let a Continental Conference be held in the following manner, and for the following purpose,

A Committee of twenty six members of congress, *viz*. Two for each Colony. Two Members from each House of Assembly, or Provincial Convention; and five Representatives of the people at large, to be chosen in the capital city or town of each Province, for, and in behalf of the whole Province, by as many qualified voters as shall think proper to attend from all parts of the Province for that purpose; or, if more convenient, the Representatives may be chosen in two or three of the most populous parts thereof. In this conference, thus assembled, will be united the two grand principles of business, *knowledge* and *power*. The Members of Congress, Assemblies, or Conventions, by having had experience in national concerns, will be able and useful counsellors, and the whole, being impowered by the people, will have a truly legal authority.

The conferring members being met, let their business be to frame a Continental Charter, or Charter of the United Colonies; (answering to what is called the Magna Charta of England) fixing the number and manner of choosing Members of Congress, Members of Assembly, with their date of sitting; and drawing the line of business and jurisdiction between them: Always remembering, that our strength is Continental, not Provincial. Securing freedom and property to all men, and above all things, the free exercise of religion, according to the dictates of conscience; with such other matter as it is necessary for a charter to contain. Immediately after which, the said conference to dissolve, and the bodies which shall be chosen conformable to the said charter, to be the Legislators and Governors of this Continent for the time being: Whose pease and happiness, may GOD preserve. AMEN.

Should any body of men be hereafter delegated for this or some similar purpose, I offer them the following extracts from that wise observer on Governments, Dragonetti. "The science," says he, "of the Politician consists in fixing the true point of happiness and freedom. Those men would deserve the gratitude of ages, who should discover a mode of government that contained the greatest sum of individual happiness, with the least national expense." (Dragonetti on "Virtues and Reward.")[13]

But where, say some, is the King of America? I'll tell you, friend, he reigns above, and doth not make havoc of mankind like the Royal Brute of Great Britain. Yet that we may not appear to be defective even in earthly honours, let a day be solemnly set apart for proclaiming the Charter; let it be brought forth placed on the Divine Law, the Word of God; let a crown be placed thereon, by which the world may know, that so far as we approve of monarchy, that in America the law is king. For as in absolute governments the King is law, so in free countries the law ought to be king; and there ought to be no other. But lest any ill use should after-

---

[13] *Le Virtù ed i Premi* (1767) by Giacinto Dragonetti.

wards arise, let the Crown at the conclusion of the ceremony be demolished, and scattered among the people whose right it is.

A government of our own is our natural right: and when a man seriously reflects on the precariousness of human affairs, he will become convinced that it is infinitely wiser and safer, to form a constitution of our own in a cool deliberate manner, while we have it in our power, than to trust such an interesting event to time and chance. If we omit it now, some Massanello[14] may hereafter arise, who, laying hold of popular disquietudes, may collect together the desperate and the discontented, and by assuming to themselves the powers of government, finally sweep away the liberties of the Continent like a deluge. Should the government of America return again into the hands of Britain, the tottering situation of things will be a temptation for some desperate adventurer to try his fortune; and in such a case, what relief can Britain give? Ere she could hear the news, the fatal business might be done; and ourselves suffering like the wretched Britons under the oppression of the Conqueror. Ye that oppose independance now, ye know not what ye do: ye are opening a door to eternal tyranny, by keeping vacant the seat of government. There are thousands and tens of thousands, who would think it glorious to expel from the Continent, that barbarous and hellish power, which hath stirred up the Indians and the Negroes to destroy us; the cruelty hath a double guilt, it is dealing brutally by us, and treacherously by them.

To talk of friendship with those in whom our reason forbids us to have faith, and our affections wounded thro' a thousand pores instruct us to detest, is madness and folly. Every day wears out the little remains of kindred between us and them; and can there be any reason to hope, that as the relationship expires, the affection will encrease, or that we shall agree better when we have ten times more and greater concerns to quarrel over than ever?

Ye that tell us of harmony and reconciliation, can ye restore to us the time that is past? Can ye give to prostitution its former innocence? neither can ye reconcile Britain and America. The last cord now is broken, the people of England are presenting addresses against us. There are injuries which nature cannot forgive; she would cease to be nature if she did. As well can the lover forgive the ravisher of his mistress, as the Continent forgive the murders of Britain. The Almighty hath implanted in us these unextinguishable feelings for good and wise purposes. They are the Guardians of his Image in our hearts. They distinguish us from the herd of common animals. The social compact would dissolve, and justice be extirpated from the earth, or have only a casual existence were we callous to the touches of affection. The robber and the murderer would often escape unpunished, did not the injuries which our tempers sustain, provoke us into justice.

O! ye that love mankind! Ye that dare oppose not only the tyranny but the tyrant, stand forth! Every spot of the old world is overrun with oppression. Freedom hath been hunted round the Globe. Asia and Africa have long expelled her. Europe regards her like a stranger, and England hath given her warning to depart. O! receive the fugitive, and prepare in time an asylum for mankind.

1776

[14] Paine's note: "Thomas Anello, otherwise Massanello, a fisherman of Naples, who after spiriting up his countrymen in the public marketplace, against the oppression of the Spaniards, to whom the place was then subject, prompted them to revolt, and in the space of a day became King."

from THE AMERICAN CRISIS

THE CRISIS No. I

These are the times that try men's souls. The summer soldier and the sunshine patriot will, in this crisis, shrink from the service of their country; but he that stands it *now*, deserves the love and thanks of man and woman. Tyranny, like hell, is not easily conquered; yet we have this consolation with us, that the harder the conflict, the more glorious the triumph. What we obtain too cheap, we esteem too lightly: it is dearness only that gives every thing its value. Heaven knows how to put a proper price upon its goods; and it would be strange indeed if so celestial an article as FREEDOM should not be highly rated. Britain, with an army to enforce her tyranny, has declared that she has a right (*not only to* TAX) but "to BIND *us in* ALL CASES WHATSOEVER,"[1] and if being *bound in that manner,* is not slavery, then is there not such a thing as slavery upon earth. Even the expression is impious; for so unlimited a power can belong only to God.

Whether the independence of the continent was declared too soon, or delayed too long, I will not now enter into as an argument; my own simple opinion is, that had it been eight months earlier, it would have been much better. We did not make a proper use of last winter, neither could we, while we were in a dependant state. However, the fault, if it were one, was all our own;[2] we have none to blame but ourselves. But no great deal is lost yet. All that Howe[3] has been doing for this month past, as rather a ravage than a conquest, which the spirit of the Jerseys,[4] a year ago, would have quickly repulsed, and which time and a little resolution will soon recover.

I have as little superstition in me as any man living, but my secret opinion has ever been, and still is, that God Almighty will not give up a people to military destruction, or leave them unsupportedly to perish, who have so earnestly and so repeatedly sought to avoid the calamities of war, by every decent method which wisdom could invent. Neither have I so much of the infidel in me, as to suppose that He has relinquished the government of the world, and given us up to the care of devils; and as I do not, I cannot see on what grounds the king of Britain can look up to heaven for help against us: a common murderer, a highwayman, or a house-breaker, has as good a pretence as he.

'Tis surprising to see how rapidly a panic will sometimes run through a country. All nations and ages have been subject to them: Britain has trembled like an ague[5] at the report of a French fleet of flat bottomed boats; and in the fourteenth [fifteenth] century the whole English army, after ravaging the kingdom of France, was driven back like men petrified with fear; and this brave exploit was performed by a few broken forces collected and headed by a woman, Joan of Arc. Would

---

[1] From the Declaratory Act of Parliament, February 1776, regarding British authority over the colonies.

[2] Paine's note, cited from *Common Sense:* "The present winter is worth an age, if rightly employed; but, if lost or neglected, the whole continent will partake of the evil; and there is no punishment that man does not deserve, be he who, or what, or where he will, that may be the means of sacrificing a season so precious and useful."

[3] Lord William Howe (1729–1814), a British general.

[4] East Jersey and West Jersey, separated at that time.   [5] One who is cold.

that heaven might inspire some Jersey maid to spirit up her countrymen, and save her fair fellow sufferers from ravage and ravishment! Yet panics, in some cases, have their uses; they produce as much good as hurt. Their duration is always short; the mind soon grows through them, and acquires a firmer habit than before. But their peculiar advantage is, that they are the touchstones of sincerity and hypocrisy, and bring things and men to light, which might otherwise have lain forever undiscovered. In fact, they have the same effect on secret traitors, which an imaginary apparition would have upon a private murderer. They sift out the hidden thoughts of man, and hold them up in public to the world. Many a disguised tory[6] has lately shown his head, that shall penitentially solemnize with curses the day on which Howe arrived upon the Delaware.

As I was with the troops at Fort Lee, and marched with them to the edge of Pennsylvania, I am well acquainted with many circumstances, which those who live at a distance know but little or nothing of. Our situation there was exceedingly cramped, the place being a narrow neck of land between the North River[7] and the Hackensack. Our force was inconsiderable, being not one fourth so great as Howe could bring against us. We had no army at hand to have relieved the garrison, had we shut ourselves up and stood on our defence. Our ammunition, light artillery, and the best part of our stores, had been removed, on the apprehension that Howe would endeavor to penetrate the Jerseys, in which case fort Lee could be of no use to us; for it must occur to every thinking man, whether in the army or not, that these kind of field forts are only for temporary purposes, and last in use no longer than the enemy directs his force against the particular object, which such forts are raised to defend. Such was our situation and condition at fort Lee on the morning of the 20th of November, when an officer arrived with information that the enemy with 200 boats had landed about seven miles above: Major General [Nathaniel] Green, who commanded the garrison, immediately ordered them under arms, and sent express to General Washington at the town of Hackensack, distant by the way of the ferry = six miles. Our first object was to secure the bridge over the Hackensack, which laid up the river between the enemy and us, about six miles from us, and three from them. General Washington arrived in about three quarters of an hour, and marched at the head of the troops towards the bridge, which place I expected we should have a brush for; however, they did not choose to dispute it with us, and the greatest part of our troops went over the bridge, the rest over the ferry, except some which passed at a mill on a small creek, between the bridge and the ferry, and made their way through some marshy grounds up to the town of Hackensack, and there passed the river. We brought off as much baggage as the wagons could contain, the rest was lost. The simple object was to bring off the garrison, and march them on till they could be strengthened by the Jersey or Pennsylvania militia, so as to be enabled to make a stand. We staid four days at Newark, collected our out-posts with some of the Jersey militia, and marched out twice to meet the enemy, on being informed that they were advancing, though our numbers were greatly inferior to theirs. Howe, in my little opinion, committed a great error in generalship in not throwing a body of forces off from Staten Island through Amboy, by which means he might have seized all our stores at Brunswick, and intercepted our march into Pennsylvania; but if we believe the power of hell to be limited, we must likewise believe that their agents are under some providential controul.

[6] The Tories supported the king.   [7] The Hudson River.

I shall not now attempt to give all the particulars of our retreat to the Delaware; suffice it for the present to say, that both officers and men, though greatly harassed and fatigued, frequently without rest, covering, or provision, the inevitable consequences of a long retreat, bore it with a manly and martial spirit. All their wishes centred in one, which was, that the country would turn out and help them to drive the enemy back. Voltaire has remarked that king William[8] never appeared to full advantage but in difficulties and in action; the same remark may be made on General Washington, for the character fits him. There is a natural firmness in some minds which cannot be unlocked by trifles, but which, when unlocked, discovers a cabinet of fortitude; and I reckon it among those kind of public blessings, which we do not immediately see, that God hath blessed him with uninterrupted health, and given him a mind that can even flourish upon care.

I shall conclude this paper with some miscellaneous remarks on the state of our affairs; and shall begin with asking the following question, Why is it that the enemy have left the New-England provinces, and made these middle ones the seat of war? The answer is easy: New-England is not infested with tories, and we are. I have been tender in raising the cry against these men, and used numberless arguments to show them their danger, but it will not do to sacrifice a world either to their folly or their baseness. The period is now arrived, in which either they or we must change our sentiments, or one or both must fall. And what is a tory? Good God! what is he? I should not be afraid to go with a hundred whigs[9] against a thousand tories, were they to attempt to get into arms. Every tory is a coward; for servile, slavish, self-interested fear is the foundation of toryism; and a man under such influence, though he may be cruel, never can be brave.

But, before the line of irrecoverable separation be drawn between us, let us reason the matter together: Your conduct is an invitation to the enemy, yet not one in a thousand of you has heart enough to join him. Howe is as much deceived by you as the American cause is injured by you. He expects you will all take up arms, and flock to his standard, with muskets on your shoulders. Your opinions are of no use to him, unless you support him personally, for 'tis soldiers, and not tories, that he wants.

I once felt all that kind of anger, which a man ought to feel, against the mean principles that are held by the tories: a noted one, who kept a tavaern at Amboy,[10] was standing at his door, with as pretty a child in his hand, about eight or nine years old, as I ever saw, and after speaking his mind as freely as he thought was prudent, finished with this unfatherly expression, "*Well! give me peace in my day.*" Not a man lives on the continent but fully believes that a separation must some time or other finally take place, and a generous parent should have said, "*If there must be trouble, let it be in my day, that my child may have peace;*" and this single reflection, well applied, is sufficient to awaken every man to duty. Not a place upon earth might be so happy as America. Her situation is remote from all the wrangling world, and she has nothing to do but to trade with them. A man can distinguish himself between temper and principle, and I am as confident, as I am that God governs the world, that America will never be happy till she gets clear of foreign dominion. Wars, without ceasing, will break out till that period arrives,

[8] William III (1650–1702), king of England from 1689 until his death.
[9] The Whigs supported the Revolution.
[10] Amboy, New Jersey, where Paine was stationed in the Continental Army.

and the continent must in the end be conqueror; for though the flame of liberty may sometimes cease to shine, the coal can never expire.

America did not, nor does not want force; but she wanted a proper application of that force. Wisdom is not the purchase of a day, and it is no wonder that we should err at the first setting off. From an excess of tenderness, we were unwilling to raise an army, and trusted our cause to the temporary defence of a well-meaning militia. A summer's experience has now taught us better; yet with those troops, while they were collected, we were able to set bounds to the progress of the enemy, and thank God! they are again assembling. I always considered militia as the best troops in the world for sudden exertion, but they will not do for a long campaign. Howe, it is probable, will make an attempt on this city;[11] should he fail on this side the Delaware, he is ruined: if he succeeds, our cause is not ruined. He stakes all on his side against a part on ours; admitting he succeeds, the consequence will be, that armies from both ends of the continent will march to assist their suffering friends in the middle states; for he cannot go everywhere, it is impossible. I consider Howe as the greatest enemy the tories have; he is bringing a war into their country, which, had it not been for him and partly for themselves, they had been clear of. Should he now be expelled, I wish with all the devotion of a Christian, that the names of whig and tory may never more be mentioned; but should the tories give him encouragement to come, or assistance if he come, I as sincerely wish that our next year's arms may expel them from the continent, and the congress appropriate their possessions to the relief of those who have suffered in well-doing. A single successful battle next year will settle the whole. America could carry on a two years war by the confiscation of the property of disaffected persons, and be made happy by their expulsion. Say not that this is revenge, call it rather the soft resentment of a suffering people, who, having no object in view but the *good* of *all,* have staked their *own all* upon a seemingly doubtful event. Yet it is folly to argue against determined hardness; eloquence may strike the ear, and the language of sorrow draw forth the tear of compassion, but nothing can reach the heart that is steeled with prejudice.

Quitting this class of men, I turn with the warm ardor of a friend to those who have nobly stood, and are yet determined to stand the matter out: I call not upon a few, but upon all: not on *this* state or *that* state, but on *every* state: up and help us; lay your shoulders to the wheel; better have too much force than too little, when so great an object is at stake. Let it be told to the future world, that in the depth of winter, when nothing but hope and virtue could survive, that the city and country, alarmed at one common danger, came forth to meet and to repulse it. Say not that thousands are gone, turn out your tens of thousands;[12] throw not the burden of the day upon Providence, but *"show your faith by your works,"*[13] that God may bless you. It matters not where you live, or what rank of life you hold, the evil or the blessing will reach you all. The far and the near, the home counties and the back, the rich and the poor, will suffer or rejoice alike. The heart that feels not now, is dead: the blood of his children will curse his cowardice, who shrinks back at a time when a little might have saved the whole, and made *them* happy. I love the man that can smile in trouble, that can gather strength from distress, and grow

---

[11] Philadelphia.

[12] "Saul hath slain his thousands, and David his ten thousands," from I Samuel 18:7.

[13] "Show me thy faith without thy works, and I will show thee my faith by my works," from James 2:18.

brave by reflection. 'Tis the business of little minds to shrink; but he whose heart is firm, and whose conscience approves his conduct, will pursue his principles unto death. My own line of reasoning is to myself as straight and clear as a ray of light. Not all the treasures of the world, so far as I believe, could have induced me to support an offensive war, for I think it murder; but if a thief breaks into my house, burns and destroys my property, and kills or threatens to kill me, or those that are in it, and to *"bind me in all cases whatsoever"*[14] to his absolute will, am I to suffer it? What signifies it to me, whether he who does it is a king or a common man; my countryman or not my countryman; whether it be done by an individual villain, or an army of them? If we reason to the root of things we shall find no difference; neither can any just cause be assigned why we should punish in the one case and pardon in the other. Let them call me rebel, and welcome, I feel no concern from it; but I should suffer the misery of devils, were I to make a whore of my soul by swearing allegiance to one whose character is that of a sottish, stupid, stubborn, worthless, brutish man. I conceive likewise a horrid idea in receiving mercy from a being, who at the last day shall be shrieking to the rocks and mountains to cover him, and fleeing with terror from the orphan, the widow, and the slain of America.

There are cases which cannot be overdone by language, and this is one. There are persons, too, who see not the full extent of the evil which threatens them; they solace themselves with hopes that the enemy, if he succeed, will be merciful. It is the madness of folly, to expect mercy from those who have refused to do justice; and even mercy, where conquest is the object, is only a trick of war; the cunning of the fox is as murderous as the violence of the wolf, and we ought to guard equally against both. Howe's first object is, partly by threats and partly by promises, to terrify or seduce the people to deliver up their arms and receive mercy. The ministry recommended the same plan to Gage,[15] and this is what the tories call making their peace, *"a peace which passeth all understanding" indeed!*[16] A peace which would be the immediate forerunner of a worse ruin than any we have yet thought of. Ye men of Pennsylvania, do reason upon these things! Were the back counties to give up their arms, they would fall an easy prey to the Indians, who are all armed: this perhaps is what some tories would not be sorry for. Were the home counties to deliver up their arms, they would be exposed to the resentment of the back counties, who would then have it in their power to chastise their defection at pleasure. And were any one state to give up its arms, *that* state must be garrisoned by all Howe's army of Britons and Hessians[17] to preserve it from the anger of the rest. Mutual fear is the principal link in the chain of mutual love, and woe be to the state that breaks the compact. Howe is mercifully inviting you to barbarous destruction, and men must be either rogues or fools that will not see it. I dwell not upon the vapours of imagination: I bring reason to your ears, and, in language as plain as A, B, C hold up truth to your eyes.

I thank God, that I fear not. I see no real cause for fear. I know our situation well, and can see the way out of it. While our army was collected, Howe dared not risk a battle; and it is no credit to him that he decamped from the White Plains, and waited a mean opportunity to ravage the defenceless Jerseys; but it is great

---

[14] From the Declaratory Act of Parliment.

[15] General Thomas Gage (1721–1787), commander of the British armies from 1763 to 1775.

[16] "And the peace of God, which passeth all understanding, shall keep your hearts and minds through Christ Jesus," from Philippians 4:7.

[17] German mercenaries.

credit to us, that, with a handful of men, we sustained an orderly retreat for near an hundred miles, brought off our ammunition, all our field pieces, the greatest part of our stores, and had four rivers to pass. None can say that our retreat was precipitate, for we were near three weeks in performing it, that the country[18] might have time to come in. Twice we marched back to meet the enemy, and remained out till dark. The sign of fear was not seen in our camp, and had not some of the cowardly and disaffected inhabitants spread false alarms through the country, the Jerseys had never been ravaged. Once more we are again collected and collecting; our new army at both ends of the continent is recruiting fast, and we shall be able to open the next campaign with sixty thousand men, well armed and clothed. This is our situation, and who will may know it. By perseverance and fortitude we have the prospect of a glorious issue; by cowardice and submisssion, the sad choice of a variety of evils—a ravaged country—a depopulated city—habitations without safety, and slavery without hope—our homes turned into barracks and bawdy houses for Hessians, and a future race to provide for, whose fathers we shall doubt of. Look on this picture and weep over it! and if there yet remains one thoughtless wretch who believes it not, let him suffer it unlamented.

Common Sense.

1776

from *THE AGE OF REASON*

Chapter I. The Author's Profession of Faith

It has been my intention, for several years past, to publish my thoughts upon religion; I am well aware of the difficulties that attend the subject, and from that consideration, had reserved it to a more advanced period of life. I intended it to be the last offering I should make to my fellow-citizens of all nations, and that at a time when the purity of the motive that induced me to it could not admit of a question, even by those who might disapprove the work.

The circumstance that has now taken place in France,[1] of the total abolition of the whole national order of priesthood, and of everything appertaining to compulsive systems of religion, and compulsive articles of faith, has not only precipitated my intention, but rendered a work of this kind exceedingly necessary, lest, in the general wreck of superstition, of false systems of government, and false theology, we lose sight of morality, of humanity, and of the theology that is true.

As several of my colleagues, and others of my fellow-citizens of France, have given me the example of making their voluntary and individual profession of faith, I also will make mine; and I do this with all that sincerity and frankness with which the mind of man communicates with itself.

I believe in one God, and no more; and I hope for happiness beyond this life.

I believe the equality of man, and I believe that religious duties consist in doing justice, loving mercy, and endeavouring to make our fellow-creatures happy.

---

[18] Local volunteers.

[1] By 1792 the Catholic church in France had been dissolved by the French Revolution's leaders, and churches had closed.

But, lest it should be supposed that I believe many other things in addition to these, I shall, in the progress of this work, declare the things I do not believe, and my reasons for not believing them.

I do not believe in the creed professed by the Jewish church, by the Roman church, by the Greek church, by the Turkish church, by the Protestant church, nor by any church that I know of. My own mind is my own church.

All national institutions of churches, whether Jewish, Christian, or Turkish, appear to me no other than human inventions set up to terrify and enslave mankind, and monopolize power and profit.

I do not mean by this declaration to condemn those who believe otherwise; they have the same right to their belief as I have to mine. But it is necessary to the happiness of man, that he be mentally faithful to himself. Infidelity does not consist in believing, or in disbelieving; it consists in professing to believe what he does not believe.

It is impossible to calculate the moral mischief, if I may so express it, that mental lying has produced in society. When a man has so far corrupted and prostituted the chastity of his mind, as to subscribe his professional belief to things he does not believe, he has prepared himself for the commission of every other crime. He takes up the trade of a priest for the sake of gain, and, in order to qualify himself for that trade, he begins with a perjury. Can we conceive anything more destructive to morality than this?

Soon after I had published the pamphlet COMMON SENSE, in America, I saw the exceeding probability that a revolution in the system of government would be followed by a revolution in the system of religion. The adulterous connection of church and state, wherever it had taken place, whether Jewish, Christian, or Turkish, had so effectually prohibited, by pains and penalties, every discussion upon established creeds, and upon first principles of religion, that until the system of government should be changed, those subjects could not be brought fairly and openly before the world; but that whenever this should be done, a revolution in the system of religion would follow. Human inventions and priest-craft would be detected; and man would return to the pure, unmixed, and unadulterated belief of one God, and no more.

CHAPTER IV. OF THE BASES OF CHRISTIANITY

It is upon this plain narrative of facts, together with another case I am going to mention, that the Christian mythologists, calling themselves the Christian Church, have erected their fable, which for absurdity and extravagance is not exceeded by anything that is to be found in the mythology of the ancients.

The ancient mythologists tell us that the race of Giants made war against Jupiter, and that one of them threw a hundred rocks against him at one throw; that Jupiter defeated him with thunder, and confined him afterwards under Mount Etna,[1] and that every time the Giant turns himself, Mount Etna belches fire. It is here easy to see that the circumstance of the mountain, that of its being a volcano, suggested the idea of the fable; and that the fable is made to fit and wind itself up with that circumstance.

The Christian mythologists tell that their Satan made war against the Almighty,

[1] A volcano in Sicily.

who defeated him, and confined him afterwards, not under a mountain, but in a pit. It is here easy to see that the first fable suggested the idea of the second; for the fable of Jupiter and the Giants was told many hundred years before that of Satan.

Thus far the ancient and the Christian mythologists differ very little from each other. But the latter have contrived to carry the matter much farther. They have contrived to connect the fabulous part of the story of Jesus Christ with the fable originating from Mount Etna; and, in order to make all the parts of the story tye together, they have taken to their aid the traditions of the Jews; for the Christian mythology is made up partly from the ancient mythology, and partly from the Jewish traditions.

The Christian mythologists, after having confined Satan in a pit, were obliged to let him out again to bring on the sequel of the fable. He is then introduced into the garden of Eden in the shape of a snake, or a serpent, and in that shape he enters into familiar conversation with Eve, who is no ways surprised to hear a snake talk; and the issue of this tête-à-tête is, that he persuades her to eat an apple, and the eating of that apple damns all mankind.

After giving Satan this triumph over the whole creation, one would have supposed that the church mythologists would have been kind enough to send him back again to the pit, or, if they had not done this, that they would have put a mountain upon him, (for they say that their faith can remove a mountain) or have put him under a mountain, as the former mythologists had done, to prevent his getting again among the women, and doing more mischief. But instead of this, they leave him at large, without even obliging him to give his parole. The secret of which is, that they could not do without him; and after being at the trouble of making him, they bribed him to stay. They promised him ALL the Jews, ALL the Turks by anticipation, nine-tenths of the world beside, and Mahomet into the bargain. After this, who can doubt the bountifulness of the Christian Mythology?

Having thus made an insurrection and a battle in heaven, in which none of the combatants could be either killed or wounded—put Satan into the pit—let him out again—given him a triumph over the whole creation—damned all mankind by the eating of an apple, these Christian mythologists bring the two ends of their fable together. They represent this virtuous and amiable man, Jesus Christ, to be at once both God and man, and also the Son of God, celestially begotten, on purpose to be sacrificed, because they say that Eve in her longing had eaten an apple.

Chapter X. Concerning God, and the Lights Cast on His Existence and Attributes by the Bible

The only idea man can affix to the name of God, is that of a *first cause,* the cause of all things. And, incomprehensibly difficult as it is for a man to conceive what a first cause is, he arrives at the belief of it, from the tenfold greater difficulty of disbelieving it. It is difficult beyond description to conceive that space can have no end; but it is more difficult to conceive an end. It is difficult beyond the power of man to conceive an eternal duration of what we call time; but it is more impossible to conceive a time when there shall be no time.

In like manner of reasoning, everything we behold carries in itself the internal evidence that it did not make itself. Every man is an evidence to himself, that he did not make himself; neither could his father make himself, nor his grandfather, nor any of his race; neither could any tree, plant, or animal make itself; and it is the conviction arising from this evidence, that carries us on, as it were, by necessity, to the belief of a first cause eternally existing, of a nature totally different to any material existence we know of, and by the power of which all things exist; and this first cause, man calls God.

It is only by the exercise of reason, that man can discover God. Take away that reason, and he would be incapable of understanding anything; and in this case it would be just as consistent to read even the book called the Bible to a horse as to a man. How then is it that those people pretend to reject reason?

Almost the only parts in the book called the Bible, that convey to us any idea of God, are some chapters in Job, and the 19th Psalm; I recollect no other. Those parts are true *deistical* compositions; for they treat of the *Deity* through his works. They take the book of Creation as the word of God; they refer to no other book: and all the inferences they make are drawn from that volume.

I insert in this place the 19th Psalm, as paraphrased into English verse by Addison.[1] I recollect not the prose, and where I write this[2] I have not the opportunity of seeing it.

> The spacious firmament on high,
> With all the blue etherial sky,
> And spangled heavens, a shining frame,
> Their great original proclaim.
> The unwearied sun, from day to day,
> Does his Creator's power display,
> And publishes to every land
> The work of an Almighty hand.
> Soon as the evening shades prevail,
> The moon takes up the wondrous tale,
> And nightly to the list'ning earth
> Repeats the story of her birth;
> Whilst all the stars that round her burn,
> And all the planets, in their turn,
> Confirm the tidings as they roll,
> And spread the truth from pole to pole.
> What though in solemn silence all
> Move round this dark terrestrial ball;
> What though no real voice, nor sound,
> Amidst their radiant orbs be found,
> In reason's ear they all rejoice,
> And utter forth a glorious voice,
> Forever singing as they shine,
> THE HAND THAT MADE US IS DIVINE.

What more does man want to know, than that the hand or power that made these things is divine, is omnipotent? Let him believe this, with the force it is impossible to repel if he permits his reason to act, and his rule of moral life will follow of course.

[1] Joseph Addison (1672–1719), an English poet and essayist.   [2] Paine was in a French prison.

The allusions in Job have all of them the same tendency with this Psalm; that of deducing or proving a truth that would be otherwise unknown, from truths already known.

I recollect not enough of the passages in Job to insert them correctly; but there is one that occurs to me that is applicable to the subject I am speaking upon. "Canst thou by searching find out God; canst thou find out the Almighty to perfection?"[3]

I know not how the printers have pointed[4] this passage, for I keep no Bible; but it contains two distinct questions that admit of distinct answers.

First, Canst thou by *searching* find out God? Yes. Because, in the first place, I know I did not make myself, and yet I have existence; and by *searching* into the nature of other things, I find that no other thing could make itself; and yet millions of other things exist; therefore it is, that I know, by positive conclusion resulting from this search, that there is a power superior to all those things, and that power is God.

Secondly, Canst thou find out the Almighty to *perfection?* No. Not only because the power and wisdom He has manifested in the structure of the Creation that I behold is to me incomprehensible; but because even this manifestation, great as it is, is probably but a small display of that immensity of power and wisdom, by which millions of other worlds, to me invisible by their distance, were created and continue to exist.

It is evident that both of these questions were put to the reason of the person to whom they are supposed to have been addressed; and it is only by admitting the first question to be answered affirmatively, that the second could follow. It would have been unnecessary, and even absurd, to have put a second question, more difficult than the first if the first question had been answered negatively. The two questions have different objects; the first refers to the existence of God, the second to his attributes. Reason can discover the one, but it falls infinitely short in discovering the whole of the other.

I recollect not a single passage in all the writings ascribed to the men called apostles, that conveys any idea of what God is. Those writings are chiefly controversial; and the gloominess of the subject they dwell upon, that of a man dying in agony on a cross, is better suited to the gloomy genius of a monk in a cell, by whom it is not impossible they were written, than to any man breathing the open air of the Creation. The only passage that occurs to me, that has any reference to the works of God, by which only his power and wisdom can be known, is related to have been spoken by Jesus Christ, as a remedy against distrustful care. "Behold the lilies of the field, they toil not, neither do they spin."[5] This, however, is far inferior to the allusions in Job and in the 19th Psalm; but it is similar in idea, and the modesty of the imagery is correspondent to the modesty of the man.

RECAPITULATION

Having now extended the subject to a greater length than I first intended, I shall bring it to a close by abstracting a summary from the whole.

First, That the idea or belief of a word of God existing in print, or in writing, or in speech, is inconsistent in itself for the reasons already assigned. These reasons,

---

[3] From Job 11:7.   [4] Punctuated.   [5] From Matthew 6:28.

among many others, are the want of an universal language; the mutability of language; the errors to which translations are subject; the possibility of totally suppressing such a word; the probability of altering it, or of fabricating the whole, and imposing it upon the world.

Secondly, That the Creation we behold is the real and ever existing word of God, in which we cannot be deceived. It proclaimeth his power, it demonstrates his wisdom, it manifests his goodness and beneficence.

Thirdly, That the moral duty of man consists in imitating the moral goodness and beneficence of God manifested in the creation towards all his creatures. That seeing as we daily do the goodness of God to all men, it is an example calling upon all men to practise the same towards each other; and, consequently, that every thing of persecution and revenge between man and man, and every thing of cruelty to animals, is a violation of moral duty.

I trouble not myself about the manner of future existence. I content myself with believing, even to positive conviction, that the power that gave me existence is able to continue it, in any form and manner he pleases, either with or without this body; and it appears more probable to me that I shall continue to exist hereafter than that I should have had existence, as I now have, before that existence began.

It is certain that, in one point, all nations of the earth and all religions agree. All believe in a God, The things in which they disagree are the redundancies annexed to that belief; and therefore, if ever an universal religion should prevail, it will not be believing any thing new, but in getting rid of redundancies, and believing as man believed at first.[1] Adam, if ever there was such a man, was created a Deist; but in the mean time, let every man follow, as he has a right to do, the religion and worship he prefers.

1793, 1794

Michel-Guillaume Jean de Crèvecoeur
(1735–1813)

When the novelist and poet D.H. Lawrence included Michel-Guillaume Jean de Crèvecoeur's *Letters From an American Farmer* (1782) in his *Studies in Classic American Literature* (1923), Lawrence noted that Benjamin "Franklin is the real *practical* prototype of the American" and "Crèvecoeur is the emotional." In both analyses Lawrence mistook life for art: the historical Franklin for the literary character Franklin created in his *Autobiography* (1867) and likewise Crèvecoeur for his fictional American farmer, James. Lawrence, nevertheless, correctly identified the antithesis that helped to define the American national consciousness, a tension and polarity perhaps best expressed in Crèvecoeur's work.

Crèvecoeur's early life prepared him for the diversity of the American experience. Born in 1735, in Caen, France, Crèvecoeur was trained by Jesuits and then educated in England. At age nineteen he left for Canada and eventually served as a surveyor and cartogra-

---

[1] "In the childhood of the world," according to the first (French) version.

pher under General Montcalm during part of the French and Indian War. Becoming an officer in 1758, Crèvecoeur was wounded the following year in the Battle of Quebec, subsequently sold his commission, and went to New York. (There he changed his name to J. Hector St. John.) For the next ten years he traveled extensively in the wilderness of New York and Vermont and toured the Atlantic seaboard, the Ohio Valley, and the Great Lakes region. In 1769 he married an American, Mehitable Tippet, bought a farm in Orange County, New York, and began to write about America.

What seemed an ideal bucolic existence was shattered by the Revolutionary War. New York was soon occupied by the British, and Orange County became a target for Native-American and Tory raiders. Crèvecoeur's stance of neutrality made him suspect by both sides. In 1778 he petitioned to return to France with his son, leaving his wife and two younger children at home. Arrested by the British as a suspected spy in 1779, Crèvecoeur was not allowed to sail to Dublin until the next year and apparently suffered a nervous breakdown. In London in 1781 he sold the manuscripts that were later published as *Letters* and made his way to France. As French consul Crèvecoeur returned to New York in autumn 1783 and discovered that his house had been burned, his wife had died, and his children had been adopted and taken to Boston.

Reunited with his children the following year, Crèvecoeur undertook his consular duties with some success. He kept the relationship between France and America cordial, aided in developing trans-Atlantic trade, and pursued his love of horticulture and literature. His *Lettres d'un Cultivateur Américain,* more than a mere translation of *Letters,* was published in Paris in 1784. This revision and expansion included some previously unpublished essays; more material was eventually uncovered and published in 1925 as *Sketches of Eighteenth-Century America.* After he returned to France in 1790 because of ill health, Crèvecoeur never saw the United States again. A lesser aristocrat, he avoided execution in the French Revolution's Reign of Terror and spent the last twenty-three years of his life in relative seclusion with his children in Germany and France. He died in Normandy in 1813.

Before Crèvecoeur, the European image of America was drawn more from Central and South America and the Caribbean than from the English colonies. His works, particularly the *Letters,* were instrumental in shifting the European focus to the emergence of the United States. In *Letters,* the narrator, James, describes the physical conditions in America; then discusses the ideas that are basic to happiness; and ends on the disruptive note that evil, in the form of war and slavery, are an inseparable part of humankind. Thus, Crèvecoeur forced James to drop his naïveté and to confront the serpent in his paradise. However, Crèvecoeur's final book, *Le Voyage dans la Haute Pensylvanie et dans l'État de New-York* (1801), reaffirms his original views of America as the best hope of the world, although in a complex, convoluted style barely reminiscent of the *Letters.*

Crèvecoeur's *Letters* was extraordinarily popular for half a century in Europe but only for a decade in the United States. For many citizens the realities of a fledgling nation struggling to survive were likely incompatible with Crèvecoeur's glowing descriptions. His pacifism and Tory inclinations were also possible factors that led to the financial failure of Mathew Carey's American edition of *Letters* published in 1793. Such was not the case in Europe. A precise fit with the romanticist's imagination, *Letters* was translated into French, Dutch, and German, and published in Dublin, Belfast, Leyden, Maastricht, Leipzig, Berlin, London, and Paris. Crèvecoeur literally provided two generations of Europeans with their views of America.

Nineteenth-century appreciation for Crèvecoeur's achievement was negligible after about 1830, except for the perceptive comments of the critic William Hazlitt in the *Edinburgh Review.* Hazlitt applauded Crèvecoeur's "power to sympathize with nature, without thinking of ourselves or others." Hazlitt also saw in *Letters* how "American scenery and manners may be treated with a lively, poetic interest" and how "not only the objects, but the feelings of a new country" could be admirably captured in literature. Hazlitt, like D.H. Lawrence, seemed to sense Crèvecoeur's importance in helping to develop an American self-identity.

For the most part an optimist, Crèvecoeur accepted the contradictory impulses in his *new American,* a citizen who combined civilization and the wilderness, the Old World and the New, aristocracy and democracy. Crèvecoeur's hope for the future blanketed many incongruities and he shared the Enlightenment ideals of many of his American counterparts. Like Benjamin Franklin, he knew that in America industry and thrift could lead to wealth. Like Thomas Paine, he had an intense distrust of organized religion and its tendency to limit personal freedom. Like Thomas Jefferson, he believed man to be at his best immersed in the activities and values of agrarian life. With them all he also believed in, and through James in *Letters* gave admirable voice to, the hopeful dreams of a new society that could yoke innocence together with progress, without seeing a paradox. Crèvecoeur saw America as a melting pot and its people as the agents who would create a new golden age.

Suggested Readings: P. G. Adams, *Introduction to 'Crèvecoeur's Eighteenth-Century Travels in Pennsylvania & New York'*, 1961. T. Philbrick, *St. John de Crèvecoeur*, 1970. E. Emerson, "Hector St. John de Crèvecoeur and the Promise of America" in *Forms and Functions of History in American Literature*, ed. W. Flunk, J. Peper, and W. P. Adams, 1981. G. W. Allen and R. Asselineau, *St. Jean de Crèvecoeur: The Life of an American Farmer*, 1987.

Text Used: *Letters From an American Farmer and Sketches of Eighteenth-Century America*, ed. A. E. Stone, 1981.

from LETTERS FROM AN AMERICAN FARMER

LETTER III: WHAT IS AN AMERICAN?

I wish I could be acquainted with the feelings and thoughts which must agitate the heart and present themselves to the mind of an enlightened Englishman when he first lands on this continent. He must greatly rejoice that he lived at a time to see this fair country discovered and settled; he must necessarily feel a share of national pride when he views the chain of settlements which embellish these extended shores. When he says to himself, "This is the work of my countrymen, who, when convulsed by factions,[1] afflicted by a variety of miseries and wants, restless and impatient, took refuge here. They brought along with them their national genius, to which they principally owe what liberty they enjoy and what substance they possess." Here he sees the industry of his native country displayed in a new manner and traces in their works the embryos of all the arts, sciences, and ingenuity which flourish in Europe. Here he beholds fair cities, substantial villages, extensive fields, an immense country filled with decent houses, good roads, orchards, meadows, and bridges where an hundred years ago all was wild, woody, and uncultivated! What a train of pleasing ideas this fair spectacle must suggest; it is a prospect which must inspire a good citizen with the most heart-felt pleasure. The difficulty consists in the manner of viewing so extensive a scene. He is arrived on a new continent; a modern society offers itself to his contemplation, different from

[1] Conflicts.

what he had hitherto seen. It is not composed, as in Europe, of great lords who possess everything and of a herd of people who have nothing. Here are no aristocratical families, no courts, no kings, no bishops, no ecclesiastical dominion, no invisible power giving to a few a very visible one, no great manufactures employing thousands, no great refinements of luxury. The rich and the poor are not so far removed from each other as they are in Europe. Some few towns excepted, we are all tillers of the earth, from Nova Scotia to West Florida. We are a people of cultivators scattered over an immense territory, communicating with each other by means of good roads and navigable rivers, united by the silken bands of mild government, all respecting the laws without dreading their power, because they are equitable. We are all animated with the spirit of an industry which is unfettered and unrestrained, because each person works for himself. If he travels through our rural districts, he views not the hostile castle and the haughty mansion, contrasted with the clay-built hut and miserable cabin, where cattle and men help to keep each other warm and dwell in meanness, smoke, and indigence. A pleasing uniformity of decent competence appears throughout our habitations. The meanest of our log-houses is a dry and comfortable habitation. Lawyer or merchant are the fairest titles our towns afford; that of a farmer is the only appellation of the rural inhabitants of our country. It must take some time ere he can reconcile himself to our dictionary, which is but short in words of dignity and names of honour. There, on a Sunday, he sees a congregation of respectable farmers and their wives, all clad in neat homespun, well mounted, or riding in their own humble waggons. There is not among them an esquire, saving the unlettered magistrate. There he sees a parson as simple as his flock, a farmer who does not riot on the labour of others. We have no princes for whom we toil, starve, and bleed; we are the most perfect society now existing in the world. Here man is free as he ought to be, nor is this pleasing equality so transitory as many others are. Many ages will not see the shores of our great lakes replenished with inland nations, nor the unknown bounds of North America entirely peopled. Who can tell how far it extends? Who can tell the millions of men whom it will feed and contain? For no European foot has as yet travelled half the extent of this mighty continent!

The next wish of this traveller will be to know whence came all these people. They are a mixture of English, Scotch, Irish, French, Dutch, Germans, and Swedes. From this promiscuous breed, that race now called Americans have arisen. The eastern provinces[2] must indeed be excepted as being the unmixed descendants of Englishmen. I have heard many wish that they had been more intermixed also; for my part, I am no wisher and think it much better as it has happened. They exhibit a most conspicuous figure in this great and variegated picture; they too enter for a great share in the pleasing perspective displayed in these thirteen provinces. I know it is fashionable to reflect on them, but I respect them for what they have done; for the accuracy and wisdom with which they have settled their territory; for the decency of their manners; for their early love of letters; their ancient college,[3] the first in this hemisphere; for their industry, which to me who am but a farmer is the criterion of everything. There never was a people, situated as they are, who with so ungrateful a soil have done more in so short a time. Do you think that the monarchical ingredients which are more prevalent in other governments have purged them from all foul stains? Their histories assert the contrary.

---

[2] New England.   [3] Harvard College, founded in 1636.

In this great American asylum, the poor of Europe have by some means met together, and in consequence of various causes; to what purpose should they ask one another what countrymen they are? Alas, two thirds of them had no country. Can a wretch who wanders about, who works and starves, whose life is a continual scene of sore affliction or pinching penury—can that man call England or any other kingdom his country? A country that had no bread for him, whose fields procured him no harvest, who met with nothing but the frowns of the rich, the severity of the laws, with jails and punishments, who owned not a single foot of the extensive surface of this planet? No! Urged by a variety of motives, here they came. Everything has tended to regenerate them: new laws, a new mode of living, a new social system; here they are become men: in Europe they were as so many useless plants, wanting vegetative mould and refreshing showers; they withered, and were mowed down by want, hunger, and war; but now, by the power of transplantation, like all other plants they have taken root and flourished! Formerly they were not numbered in any civil lists[4] of their country, except in those of the poor; here they rank as citizens. By what invisible power hath this surprising metamorphosis been performed? By that of the laws and that of their industry. The laws, the indulgent laws, protect them as they arrive, stamping on them the symbol of adoption; they receive ample rewards for their labours; these accumulated rewards procure them lands; those lands confer on them the title of freemen, and to that title every benefit is affixed which men can possibly require. This is the great operation daily performed by our laws. Whence proceed these laws? From our government. Whence that government? It is derived from the original genius and strong desire of the people ratified and confirmed by the crown. This is the great chain which links us all, this is the picture which every province exhibits. Nova Scotia excepted. There the crown has done all;[5] either there were no people who had genius or it was not much attended to; the consequence is that the province is very thinly inhabited indeed; the power of the crown in conjunction with the musketos has prevented men from settling there. Yet some parts of it flourished once, and it contained a mild, harmless set of people. But for the fault of a few leaders, the whole was banished. The greatest political error the crown ever committed in America was to cut off men from a country which wanted nothing but men!

What attachment can a poor European emigrant have for a country where he had nothing? The knowledge of the language, the love of a few kindred as poor as himself, were the only cords that tied him; his country is now that which gives him his land, bread, protection, and consequence; *Ubi panis ibi patria*[6] is the motto of all emigrants. What, then, is the American, this new man? He is neither an European nor the descendant of an European; hence that strange mixture of blood, which you will find in no other country. I could point out to you a family whose grandfather was an Englishman, whose wife was Dutch, whose son married a French woman, and whose present four sons have now four wives of different nations. *He* is an American, who, leaving behind him all his ancient prejudices and manners, receives new ones from the new mode of life he has embraced, the new government he obeys, and the new rank he holds. He becomes an American by being received in the broad lap of our great Alma Mater. Here individuals of all nations are melted into a new race of men, whose labours and posterity will one

[4] Those employed in the civil government, such as judges and ambassadors.
[5] The French settlers were exiled from Nova Scotia by the English in 1755.
[6] "Where there is bread, there is one's country" (Latin).

day cause great changes in the world. Americans are the western pilgrims who are carrying along with them that great mass of arts, sciences, vigour, and industry which began long since in the East; they will finish the great circle. The Americans were once scattered all over Europe; here they are incorporated into one of the finest systems of population which has ever appeared, and which will hereafter become distinct by the power of the different climates they inhabit. The American ought therefore to love this country much better than that wherein either he or his forefathers were born. Here the rewards of his industry follow with equal steps the progress of his labour; his labour is founded on the basis of nature, self-interest; can it want a stronger allurement? Wives and children, who before in vain demanded of him a morsel of bread, now, fat and frolicsome, gladly help their father to clear those fields whence exuberant crops are to arise to feed and to clothe them all, without any part being claimed, either by a despotic prince, a rich abbot, or a mighty lord. Here religion demands but little of him: a small voluntary salary to the minister and gratitude to God; can he refuse these? The American is a new man, who acts upon new principles; he must therefore entertain new ideas and form new opinions. From involuntary idleness, servile dependence, penury, and useless labour, he has passed to toils of a very different nature, rewarded by ample subsistence. This is an American.

British America is divided into many provinces, forming a large association scattered along a coast of 1,500 miles extent and about 200 wide. This society I would fain examine, at least such as it appears in the middle provinces; if it does not afford that variety of tinges and gradations which may be observed in Europe, we have colours peculiar to ourselves. For instance, it is natural to conceive that those who live near the sea must be very different from those who live in the woods; the intermediate space will afford a separate and distinct class.

Men are like plants; the goodness and flavour or the fruit proceeds from the peculiar soil and exposition in which they grow. We are nothing but what we derive from the air we breathe, the climate we inhabit, the government we obey, the system of religion we profess, and the nature of our employment. Here you will find but few crimes; these have acquired as yet no root among us. I wish I were able to trace all my ideas; if my ignorance prevents me from describing them properly, I hope I shall be able to delineate a few of the outlines, which is all I propose.

Those who live near the sea feed more on fish than on flesh and often encounter that boisterous element. This renders them more bold and enterprising; this leads them to neglect the confined occupations of the land. They see and converse with a variety of people; their intercourse with mankind becomes extensive. The sea inspires them with a love of traffic, a desire of transporting produce from one place to another, and leads them to a variety of resources which supply the place of labour. Those who inhabit the middle settlements, by far the most numerous, must be very different; the simple cultivation of the earth purifies them, but the indulgences of the government, the soft remonstrances of religion, the rank of independent freeholders, must necessarily inspire them with sentiments, very little known in Europe among a people of the same class. What do I say? Europe has no such class of men; the early knowledge they acquire, the early bargains they make, give them a great degree of sagacity. As freemen, they will be litigious; pride and obstinacy are often the cause of lawsuits; the nature of our laws and governments may be another. As citizens, it is easy to imagine that they will carefully read the newspapers, enter into every political disquisition, freely blame or censure governors and others. As farmers, they will be careful and anxious to get as much as they can, because what they get is their own. As northern men, they will love the cheerful cup. As Christians, religion curbs them not in their opinions; the general indulgence leaves every one to think for themselves in spiritual matters; the law inspects our actions; our thoughts are left to God. Industry, good living, selfishness, litigiousness, country politics, the pride of freemen, religious indifference, are their characteristics. If you recede still farther from the sea, you will come into more modern settlements; they exhibit the same strong lineaments, in a ruder appearance. Religion seems to have still less influence, and their manners are less improved.

Now we arrive near the great woods, near the last inhabited districts;[7] there men seem to be placed still farther beyond the reach of government, which in some measure leaves them to themselves. How can it pervade every corner, as they were driven there by misfortunes, necessity of beginnings, desire of acquiring large tracks of land, idleness, frequent want of economy, ancient debts; the reunion of such people does not afford a very pleasing spectacle. When discord, want of unity and friendship, when either drunkenness or idleness prevail in such remote districts, contention, inactivity, and wretchedness must ensue. There are not the same remedies to these evils as in a long-established community. The few magistrates they have are in general little better than the rest; they are often in a perfect state of war; that of man against man, sometimes decided by blows, sometimes by means of the law; that of man against every wild inhabitant of these venerable woods, of which they are come to dispossess them. There men appear to be no better than carnivorous animals of a superior rank, living on the flesh of wild animals when they can catch them, and when they are not able, they subsist on grain. He who would wish to see America in its proper light and have a true idea of its feeble beginnings and barbarous rudiments must visit our extended line of frontiers, where the last settlers dwell and where he may see the first labours of settlement, the mode of clearing the earth, in all their different appearances, where men are wholly left dependent on their native tempers and on the spur of uncertain industry, which often fails when not sanctified by the efficacy of a few moral rules. There, remote from the power of example and check of shame, many families exhibit the most hideous parts of our society. They are a kind of forlorn hope, preceding by ten or twelve years the most respectable army of veterans which come after them. In that space, prosperity will polish some, vice and the law will drive off the rest, who, uniting again with others like themselves, will recede still farther, making room for more industrious people, who will finish their improvements, convert the log-house into a convenient habitation, and rejoicing that the first heavy labours are finished, will change in a few years that hitherto barbarous country into a fine, fertile, well-regulated district. Such is our progress; such is the march of the Europeans toward the interior parts of this continent. In all societies there are off-casts; this impure part serves as our precursors or pioneers; my father himself was one of that class, but he came upon honest principles and was therefore one of the few who held fast; by good conduct and temperance, he transmitted to me his fair inheritance, when not above one in fourteen of his contemporaries had the same good fortune.[8]

Forty years ago, this smiling country was thus inhabited; it is now purged, a general decency of manners prevails throughout, and such has been the fate of our best countries.

---

[7] The frontier.   [8] Crèvecoeur's father never came to America.

Exclusive of those general characteristics, each province has its own, founded on the government, climate, mode of husbandry, customs, and peculiarity of circumstances. Europeans submit insensibly to these great powers and become, in the course of a few generations, not only Americans in general, but either Pennsylvanians, Virginians, or provincials under some other name. Whoever traverses the continent must easily observe those strong differences, which will grow more evident in time. The inhabitants of Canada, Massachusetts, the middle provinces, the southern ones, will be as different as their climates; their only points of unity will be those of religion and language.

As I have endeavoured to show you how Europeans become Americans, it may not be disagreeable to show you likewise how the various Christian sects introduced wear out and how religious indifference becomes prevalent. When any considerable number of a particular sect happen to dwell contiguous to each other, they immediately erect a temple and there worship the Divinity agreeably to their own peculiar ideas. Nobody disturbs them. If any new sect springs up in Europe, it may happen that many of its professors will come and settle in America. As they bring their zeal with them, they are at liberty to make proselytes if they can and to build a meeting and to follow the dictates of their consciences; for neither the government nor any other power interferes. If they are peaceable subjects and are industrious, what is it to their neighbours how and in what manner they think fit to address their prayers to the Supreme Being? But if the sectaries are not settled close together, if they are mixed with other denominations, their zeal will cool for want of fuel, and will be extinguished in a little time. Then, the Americans become as to religion what they are as to country, allied to all. In them the name of Englishman, Frenchman, and European is lost, and in like manner, the strict modes of Christianity as practised in Europe are lost also. This effect will extend itself still farther hereafter, and though this may appear to you as a strange idea, yet it is a very true one. I shall be able, perhaps, hereafter to explain myself better; in the meanwhile, let the following example serve as my first justification.

Let us suppose you and I to be travelling; we observe that in this house, to the right, lives a Catholic, who prays to God as he has been taught and believes in transsubstantiation;[9] he works and raises wheat, he has a large family of children, all hale and robust; his belief, his prayers, offend nobody. About one mile farther on the same road, his next neighbour may be a good, honest, plodding German Lutheran, who addresses himself to the same God, the God of all, agreeable to the modes he has been educated in, and believes in consubstantiation;[10] by so doing, he scandalizes nobody; he also works in his field, embellishes the earth, clears swamps, etc. What has the world to do with his Lutheran principles? He persecutes nobody, and nobody persecutes him; he visits his neighbours, and his neighbours visit him. Next to him lives a seceder,[11] the most enthusiastic of all sectaries;[12] his zeal is hot and fiery, but separated as he is from others of the same complexion, he has no congregation of his own to resort to where he might cabal[13] and mingle religious pride with worldly obstinacy. He likewise raises good crops, his house is handsomely painted, his orchard is one of the fairest in the neighbourhood. How does it concern the welfare of the country, or of the province at

---

[9] The Roman Catholic belief that the Eucharistic bread and wine change into the true presence of Christ.

[10] The belief that the Eucharist is only a symbol of Christ's presence through faith.

[11] One who has withdrawn from a religious congregation.

[12] One who opposes the established Church.   [13] Plot.

large, what this man's religious sentiments are, or really whether he has any at all? He is a good farmer, he is a sober, peaceable, good citizen; William Penn himself would not wish for more. This is the visible character; the invisible one is only guessed at, and is nobody's business. Next, again, lives a Low Dutchman,[14] who implicitly believes the rules laid down by the synod of Dort.[15] He conceives no other idea of a clergyman than that of an hired man; if he does his work well, he will pay him the stipulated sum; if not, he will dismiss him, and do without his sermons, and let his church be shut up for years. But notwithstanding this coarse idea, you will find his house and farm to be the neatest in all the country; and you will judge by his waggon and fat horses that he thinks more of the affairs of this world than of those of the next. He is sober and laborious; therefore, he is all he ought to be as to the affairs of this life. As for those of the next, he must trust to the great Creator. Each of these people instruct their children as well as they can, but these instructions are feeble compared to those which are given to the youth of the poorest class in Europe. Their children will therefore grow up less zealous and more indifferent in matters of religion than their parents. The foolish vanity or, rather, the fury of making proselytes is unknown here; they have no time, the seasons call for all their attention, and thus in a few years this mixed neighbourhood will exhibit a strange religious medley that will be neither pure Catholicism nor pure Calvinism. A very perceptible indifference, even in the first generation, will become apparent; and it may happen that the daughter of the Catholic will marry the son of the seceder and settle by themselves at a distance from their parents. What religious education will they give their children? A very imperfect one. If there happens to be in the neighbourhood any place of worship, we will suppose a Quaker's meeting; rather than not show their fine clothes, they will go to it, and some of them may perhaps attach themselves to that society. Others will remain in a perfect state of indifference; the children of these zealous parents will not be able to tell what their religious principles are, and their grandchildren still less. The neighbourhood of a place of worship generally leads them to it, and the action of going thither is the strongest evidence they can give of their attachment to any sect. The Quakers are the only people who retain a fondness for their own mode of worship; for be they ever so far separated from each other, they hold a sort of communion with the society and seldom depart from its rules, at least in this country. Thus all sects are mixed, as well as all nations; thus religious indifference is imperceptibly disseminated from one end of the continent to the other, which is at present one of the strongest characteristics of the Americans. Where this will reach no one can tell; perhaps it may leave a vacuum fit to receive other systems. Persecution, religious pride, the love of contradiction, are the food of what the world commonly calls religion. These motives have ceased here; zeal in Europe is confined; here it evaporates in the great distance it has to travel; there it is a grain of powder inclosed; here it burns away in the open air and consumes without effect.

But to return to our back settlers. I must tell you that there is something in the proximity of the woods which is very singular. It is with men as it is with the plants and animals that grow and live in the forests; they are entirely different from those that live in the plains. I will candidly tell you all my thoughts, but you are not to expect that I shall advance any reasons. By living in or near the woods,

---

[14] A person from Holland, not Belgium.

[15] In 1618, the synod (church council) of Dort endeavored to settle debates between Protestant Reformed Churches.

their actions are regulated by the wildness of the neighbourhood. The deer often come to eat their grain, the wolves to destroy their sheep, the bears to kill their hogs, the foxes to catch their poultry. This surrounding hostility immediately puts the gun into their hands; they watch these animals, they kill some; and thus by defending their property, they soon become professed hunters; this is the progress; once hunters, farewell to the plough. The chase renders them ferocious, gloomy, and unsocial; a hunter wants no neighbour, he rather hates them because he dreads the competition. In a little time, their success in the woods makes them neglect their tillage. They trust to the natural fecundity of the earth and therefore do little; carelessness in fencing often exposes what little they sow to destruction; they are not at home to watch; in order, therefore, to make up the deficiency, they go oftener to the woods. That new mode of life brings along with it a new set of manners, which I cannot easily describe. These new manners being grafted on the old stock produce a strange sort of lawless profligacy, the impressions of which are indelible. The manners of the Indian natives are respectable compared with this European medley. Their wives and children live in sloth and inactivity; and having no proper pursuits, you may judge what education the latter receive. Their tender minds have nothing else to contemplate but the example of their parents; like them, they grow up a mongrel breed, half civilized, half savage, except nature stamps on them some constitutional propensities. That rich, that voluptuous sentiment is gone that struck them so forcibly; the possession of their freeholds[16] no longer conveys to their minds the same pleasure and pride. To all these reasons you must add their lonely situation, and you cannot imagine what an effect on manners the great distances they live from each other has! Consider one of the last settlements in its first view: of what is it composed? Europeans who have not that sufficient share of knowledge they ought to have in order to prosper; people who have suddenly passed from oppression, dread of government, and fear of laws into the unlimited freedom of the woods. This sudden change must have a very great effect on most men, and on that class particularly. Eating of wild meat, whatever you may think, tends to alter their temper, though all the proof I can adduce is that I have seen it, and having no place of worship to resort to, what little society this might afford is denied them. The Sunday meetings, exclusive of religious benefits, were the only social bonds that might have inspired them with some degree of emulation in neatness. Is it, then, suprising to see men thus situated, immersed in great and heavy labours, degenerate a little? It is rather a wonder the effect is not more diffusive. The Moravians[17] and the Quakers are the only instances in exception to what I have advanced. The first never settle singly; it is a colony of the society which emigrates; they carry with them their forms, worship, rules, and decency. The others never begin so hard; they are always able to buy improvements,[18] in which there is a great advantage, for by that time the country is recovered from its first barbarity. Thus our bad people are those who are half cultivators and half hunters; and the worst of them are those who have degenerated altogether into the hunting state. As old ploughmen and new men of the woods, as Europeans and new-made Indians, they contract the vices of both; they adopt the moroseness and ferocity of a native, without his mildness or even his industry at home. If

[16] Owned estates (property and land).
[17] A religious sect whose followers gave up personal property and were renowned for their industry and frugality.
[18] Developed land.

manners are not refined, at least they are rendered simple and inoffensive by till-ing the earth. All our wants are supplied by it; our time is divided between labour and rest, and leaves none for the commission of great misdeeds. As hunters, it is divided between the toil of the chase, the idleness of repose, or the indulgence of inebriation. Hunting is but a licentious idle life, and if it does not always pervert good dispositions, yet, when it is united with bad luck, it leads to want: want stimulates that propensity to rapacity and injustice, too natural to needy men, which is the fatal gradation. After this explanation of the effects which follow by living in the woods, shall we yet vainly flatter ourselves with the hope of convert-ing the Indians? We should rather begin with converting our back-settlers; and now if I dare mention the name of religion, its sweet accents would be lost in the immensity of these woods. Men thus placed are not fit either to receive or remem-ber its mild instructions; they want temples and ministers, but as soon as men cease to remain at home and begin to lead an erratic life, let them be either tawny or white, they cease to be its disciples.

Thus have I faintly and imperfectly endeavoured to trace our society from the sea to our woods! Yet you must not imagine that every person who moves back acts upon the same principles or falls into the same degeneracy. Many families carry with them all their decency of conduct, purity of morals, and respect of religion, but these are scarce; the power of example is sometimes irresistible. Even among these back-settlers, their depravity is greater or less according to what nation or province they belong. Were I to adduce proofs of this, I might be accused of partiality. If there happens to be some rich intervals, some fertile bot-toms, in those remote districts, the people will there prefer tilling the land to hunt-ing and will attach themselves to it; but even on these fertile spots you may plainly perceive the inhabitants to acquire a great degree of rusticity and selfishness.

It is in consequence of this straggling situation and the astonishing power it has on manners that the back-settlers of both the Carolinas, Virginia, and many other parts have been long a set of lawless people; it has been even dangerous to travel among them. Government can do nothing in so extensive a country; better it should wink at these irregularities than that it should use means inconsistent with its usual mildness. Time will efface those stains: in proportion as the great body of population approaches them they will reform and become polished and subordi-nate. Whatever has been said of the four New England provinces, no such degen-eracy of manners has ever tarnished their annals; their back-settlers have been kept within the bounds of decency, and government, by means of wise laws, and by the influence of religion. What a detestable idea such must have given to the na-tives of the Europeans! They trade with them; the worst of people are permitted to do that which none but persons of the best characters should be employed in. They get drunk with them and often defraud the Indians. Their avarice, removed from the eyes of their superior, knows no bounds; and aided by a little superiority of knowledge, these traders deceive them and even sometimes shed blood. Hence those shocking violations, those sudden devastations which have so often stained our frontiers, when hundreds of innocent people have been sacrificed for the crimes of a few. It was in consequence of such behaviour that the Indians took the hatchet against the Virginians in 1774. Thus are our first steps trodden, thus are our first trees felled, in general, by the most vicious of our people; and thus the path is opened for the arrival of a second and better class, the true American freeholders, the most respectable set of people in this part of the world: respect-able for their industry, their happy independence, the great share of freedom they possess, the good regulation of their families, and for extending the trade and the dominion of our mother country.

Europe contains hardly any other distinctions but lords and tenants; this fair country alone is settled by freeholders, the possessors of the soil they cultivate, members of the government they obey, and the framers of their own laws, by means of their representatives. This is a thought which you have taught me to cherish; our distance from Europe, far from diminishing, rather adds to our usefulness and consequence as men and subjects. Had our forefathers remained there, they would only have crowded it and perhaps prolonged those convulsions which had shaken it so long. Every industrious European who transports himself here may be compared to a sprout growing at the foot of a great tree; it enjoys and draws but a little portion of sap; wrench it from the parent roots, transplant it, and it will become a tree bearing fruit also. Colonists are therefore entitled to the consideration due to the most useful subjects; a hundred families barely existing in some parts of Scotland will here in six years cause an annual exportation of 10,000 bushels of wheat, 100 bushels being but a common quantity for an industrious family to sell if they cultivate good land. It is here, then, that the idle may be employed, the useless become useful, and the poor become rich; but by riches I do not mean gold and silver—we have but little of those metals; I mean a better sort of wealth—cleared lands, cattle, good houses, good clothes, and an increase of people to enjoy them.

There is no wonder that this country has so many charms and presents to Europeans so many temptations to remain in it. A traveller in Europe becomes a stranger as soon as he quits his own kingdom; but it is otherwise here. We know, properly speaking, no strangers; his is every person's country; the variety of our soils, situations, climates, governments, and produce hath something which must please everybody. No sooner does an European arrive, no matter of what condition, than his eyes are opened upon the fair prospect: he hears his language spoke; he retraces many of his own country manners; he perpetually hears the names of families and towns with which he is acquainted; he sees happiness and prosperity in all places disseminated; he meets with hospitality, kindness, and plenty everywhere; he beholds hardly any poor; he seldom hears of punishments and executions; and he wonders at the elegance of our towns, those miracles of industry and freedom. He cannot admire enough our rural districts, our convenient roads, good taverns, and our many accommodations; he involuntarily loves a country where everything is so lovely. When in England, he was a mere Englishman; here he stands on a larger portion of the globe, not less than its fourth part, and may see the productions of the north, in iron and naval stores; the provisions of Ireland; the grain of Egypt; the indigo, the rice of China. He does not find, as in Europe, a crowded society where every place is overstocked; he does not feel that perpetual collision of parties, that difficulty of beginning, that contention which oversets so many. There is room for everybody in America; has he any particular talent or industry? He exerts it in order to procure a livelihood, and it succeeds. Is he a merchant? The avenues of trade are infinite. Is he eminent in any respect? He will be employed and respected. Does he love a country life? Pleasant farms present themselves; he may purchase what he wants and thereby become an American farmer. Is he a labourer, sober and industrious? He need not go many miles nor receive many informations before he will be hired, well fed at the table of his employer, and paid four or five times more than he can get in Europe. Does he want uncultivated lands? Thousands of acres present themselves, which he may purchase cheap. Whatever be his talents or inclinations, if they are moderate, he may satisfy them. I do not mean that every one who comes will grow rich in a little time; no, but he may procure an easy, decent maintenance by his industry. Instead of starving, he will be fed; instead of being idle, he will have employment: and these are riches enough for such men as come over here. The rich stay in Europe; it is only the middling and poor that emigrate. Would you wish to travel in independent idleness, from north to south, you will find easy access, and the most cheerful reception at every house; society without ostentation; good cheer without pride; and every decent diversion which the country affords, with little expense. It is no wonder that the European who has lived here a few years is desirous to remain; Europe with all its pomp is not to be compared to this continent for men of middle stations or labourers.

An European, when he first arrives, seems limited in his intentions, as well as in his views; but he very suddenly alters his scale; two hundred miles formerly appeared a very great distance, it is now but a trifle; he no sooner breathes our air than he forms schemes and embarks in designs he never would have thought of in his own country. There the plenitude of society confines many useful ideas and often extinguishes the most laudable schemes, which here ripen into maturity. Thus Europeans become Americans.

But how is this accomplished in that crowd of low, indigent people who flock here every year from all parts of Europe? I will tell you; they no sooner arrive than they immediately feel the good effects of that plenty of provisions we possess: they fare on our best food, and are kindly entertained; their talents, character, and peculiar industry are immediately inquired into; they find countrymen everywhere disseminated, let them come from whatever part of Europe. Let me select one as an epitome of the rest: he is hired, he goes to work, and works moderately; instead of being employed by a haughty person, he finds himself with his equal, placed at the substantial table of the farmer, or else at an inferior one as good; his wages are high, his bed is not like that bed of sorrow on which he used to lie; if he behaves with propriety, and is faithful, he is caressed, and becomes as it were a member of the family. He begins to feel the effects of a sort of resurrection; hitherto he had not lived, but simply vegetated; he now feels himself a man because he is treated as such; the laws of his own country had overlooked him in his insignificancy; the laws of this cover him with their mantle. Judge what an alteration there must arise in the mind and the thoughts of this man. He begins to forget his former servitude and dependence; his heart involuntarily swells and glows; this first swell inspires him with those new thoughts which constitute an American. What love can he entertain for a country where his existence was a burthen to him; if he is a generous, good man, the love of this new adoptive parent will sink deep into his heart. He looks around and sees many a prosperous person who but a few years before was as poor as himself. This encourages him much; he begins to form some little scheme, the first, alas, he ever formed in his life. If he is wise, he thus spends two or three years, in which time he acquires knowledge, the use of tools, the modes of working the lands, felling trees, etc. This prepares the foundation of a good name, the most useful acquisition he can make. He is encouraged, he has gained friends; he is advised and directed; he feels bold, he purchases some land; he gives all the money he has brought over, as well as what he has earned, and trusts to the God of harvests for the discharge of the rest. His good name procures him credit.

He is now possessed of the deed, conveying to him and his posterity the fee sim-ple[19] and absolute property of two hundred acres of land, situated on such a river. What an epocha in this man's life! He is become a freeholder, from perhaps a German boor. He is now an American, a Pennsylvanian, an English subject. He is naturalized; his name is enrolled with those of the other citizens of the province. Instead of being a vagrant, he has a place of residence; he is called the inhabitant of such a county, or of such a district, and for the first time in his life counts for something, for hitherto he had been a cypher. I only repeat what I have heard many say, and no wonder their hearts should glow and be agitated with a multi-tude of feelings, not easy to describe. From nothing to start into being; from a servant to the rank of a master; from being the slave of some despotic prince, to become a free man, invested with lands to which every municipal blessing is an-nexed! What a change indeed! It is in consequence of that change that he becomes an American. This great metamorphosis has a double effect: it extinguishes all his European prejudices, he forgets that mechanism of subordination, that servility of disposition which poverty had taught him; and sometimes he is apt to forget it too much, often passing from one extreme to the other. If he is a good man, he forms schemes of future prosperity, he proposes to educate his children better than he has been educated himself; he thinks of future modes of conduct, feels an ardour to labour he never felt before. Pride steps in and leads him to everything that the laws do not forbid; he respects them; with a heart-felt gratitude he looks toward the east, toward that insular government from whose wisdom all his new felicity is derived and under whose wings and protection he now lives. These reflections constitute him the good man and the good subject. Ye poor Europeans—ye who sweat and work for the great; ye who are obliged to give so many sheaves to the church, so many to your lords, so many to your government, and have hardly any left for yourselves; ye who are held in less estimation than favourite hunters[20] or useless lap-dogs; ye who only breathe the air of nature because it cannot be with-holden from you—it is here that ye can conceive the possibility of those feelings I have been describing; it is here the laws of naturalization invite every one to par-take of our great labours and felicity, to till unrented, untaxed lands! Many, cor-rupted beyond the power of amendment, have brought with them all their vices, and disregarding the advantages held to them, have gone on in their former career of iniquity until they have been overtaken and punished by our laws. It is not every emigrant who succeeds; no, it is only the sober, the honest, and industrious. Happy those to whom this transition has served as a powerful spur to labour, to prosperity, and to the good establishment of children, born in the days of their poverty and who had no other portion to expect but the rags of their parents had it not been for their happy emigration. Others, again, have been led astray by this enchanting scene; their new pride, instead of leading them to the fields, has kept them in idleness; the idea of possessing lands is all that satisfied them—though surrounded with fertility, they have mouldered away their time in inactivity, mis-informed husbandry, and ineffectual endeavours. How much wiser, in general, the honest Germans than almost all other Europeans; they hire themselves to some of their wealthy landsmen, and in that apprenticeship learn everything that is necessary. They attentively consider the prosperous industry of others, which imprints in their minds a strong desire of possessing the same advantages. This forcible idea never quits them; they launch forth, and by dint of sobriety, rigid

[19] A legal possession.   [20] Horses used in hunting.

parsimony, and the most persevering industry, they commonly succeed. Their astonishment at their first arrival from Germany is very great—it is to them a dream; the contrast must be very powerful indeed; they observe their countrymen flourishing in every place; they travel through whole counties where not a word of English is spoken; and in the names and the language of the people, they retrace Germany. They have been an useful acquisition to this continent, and to Pennsylvania in particular; to them it owes some share of its prosperity: to their mechanical knowledge and patience it owes the finest mills in all America, the best teams of horses, and many other advantages. The recollection of their former poverty and slavery never quits them as long as they live.

The Scotch and the Irish might have lived in their own country perhaps as poor, but enjoying more civil advantages; the effects of their new situation do not strike them so forcibly, nor has it so lasting an effect. Whence the difference arises I know not, but out of twelve families of emigrants of each country, generally seven Scotch will succeed, nine German, and four Irish. The Scotch are frugal and laborious, but their wives cannot work so hard as German women, who on the contrary vie with their husbands, and often share with them the most severe toils of the field, which they understand better. They have therefore nothing to struggle against but the common casualties of nature. The Irish do not prosper so well; they love to drink and to quarrel; they are litigious and soon take to the gun, which is the ruin of everything; they seem beside to labour under a greater degree of ignorance in husbandry than the others; perhaps it is that their industry had less scope and was less exercised at home. I have heard many relate how the land was parcelled out in that kingdom; their ancient conquest has been a great detriment to them, by oversetting their landed property. The lands possessed by a few are leased down ad infinitum, and the occupiers often pay five guineas an acre. The poor are worse lodged there than anywhere else in Europe; their potatoes, which are easily raised, are perhaps an inducement to laziness: their wages are too low and their whisky too cheap.

There is no tracing observations of this kind without making at the same time very great allowances, as there are everywhere to be found a great many exceptions. The Irish themselves, from different parts of that kingdom, are very different. It is difficult to account for this surprising locality; one would think on so small an island an Irishman must be an Irishman. Yet it is not so; they are different in their aptitude to and in their love of labour.

The Scotch, on the contrary, are all industrious and saving; they want nothing more than a field to exert themselves in, and they are commonly sure of succeeding. The only difficulty they labour under is that technical American knowledge which requires some time to obtain; it is not easy for those who seldom saw a tree to conceive how it is to be felled, cut up, and split into rails and posts.

As I am fond of seeing and talking of properous families, I intend to finish this letter by relating to you the history of an honest Scotch Hebridean who came here in 1774, which will show you in epitome what the Scotch can do wherever they have room for the exertion of their industry. Whenever I hear of any new settlement, I pay it a visit once or twice a year, on purpose to observe the different steps each settler takes; the gradual improvements; the different tempers of each family, on which their prosperity in a great measure depends; their different modifications of industry; their ingenuity and contrivance; for being all poor, their life requires sagacity and prudence. In an evening, I love to hear them tell their stories; they furnish me with new ideas; I sit still and listen to their ancient misfortunes, observing in many of them a strong degree of gratitude to God and the government. Many a well-meant sermon have I preached to some of them. When I found laziness and inattention prevail, who could refrain from wishing well to these new countrymen, after having undergone so many fatigues. Who could withhold good advice? What a happy change it must be to descend from the high, sterile, bleak lands of Scotland, where everything is barren and cold, and to rest on some fertile farms in these middle provinces! Such a transition must have afforded the most pleasing satisfaction.

The following dialogue passed at an out-settlement, where I lately paid a visit:

"Well, friend, how do you do now; I am come fifty odd miles on purpose to see you; how do you go on with your new cutting and slashing?" "Very well, good sir; we learn the use of the axe bravely, we shall make it out; we have a belly full of victuals every day; our cows run about and come home full of milk; our hogs get fat of themselves in the woods. Oh, this is a good country! God bless the king and William Penn; we shall do very well by and by, if we keep our healths." "Your log-house looks neat and light; where did you get these shingles?" "One of our neighbours is a New England man, and he showed us how to split them out of chestnut-trees. Now for a barn, but all in good time; here are fine trees to build it with." "Who is to frame it; sure you do not understand that work yet?" "A countryman of ours who has been in America these ten years offers to wait for his money until the second crop is lodged in it." "What did you give for your land?" "Thirty-five shillings per acre, payable in seven years." "How many acres have you got?" "A hundred and fifty." "That is enough to begin with; is not your land pretty hard to clear?" "Yes, sir, hard enough, but it would be harder still if it was already cleared, for then we should have no timber, and I love the woods much; the land is nothing without them." "Have not you found out any bees yet?" "No, sir; and if we had, we should not know what to do with them." "I will tell you by and by." "You are very kind." "Farewell, honest man; God prosper you; whenever you travel toward——, inquire for J.S. He will entertain you kindly, provided you bring him good tidings from your family and farm."

In this manner I often visit them and carefully examine their houses, their modes of ingenuity, their different ways; and make them relate all they know and describe all they feel. These are scenes which I believe you would willingly share with me. I well remember your philanthropic turn of mind. Is it not better to contemplate under these humble roofs the rudiments of future wealth and population than to behold the accumulated bundles of litigious papers in the office of a lawyer? To examine how the world is gradually settled, how the howling swamp is converted into a pleasing meadow, the rough ridge into a fine field; and to hear the cheerful whistling, the rural song, where there was no sound heard before, save the yell of the savage, the screech of the owl or the hissing of the snake? Here an European, fatigued with luxury, riches, and pleasures, may find a sweet relaxation in a series of interesting scenes, as affecting as they are new. England, which now contains so many domes, so many castles, was once like this: a place woody and marshy; its inhabitants, now the favourite nation for arts and commerce, were once painted like our neighbours. This country will flourish in its turn, and the same observations will be made which I have just delineated. Posterity will look back with avidity and pleasure to trace, if possible, the era of this or that particular settlement.

Pray, what is the reason that the Scots are in general more religious, more faithful, more honest, and industrious than the Irish? I do not mean to insinuate national reflections, God forbid! It ill becomes any man, and much less an American; but as I know men are nothing of themselves, and that they owe all their different modifications either to government or other local circumstances, there must be some powerful causes which constitute this great national difference.

Agreeable to the account which several Scotchmen have given me of the north of Britain, of the Orkneys, and the Hebride Islands, they seem, on many accounts, to be unfit for the habitation of men; they appear to be calculated only for great sheep pastures. Who, then, can blame the inhabitants of these countries for transporting themselves hither? This great continent must in time absorb the poorest part of Europe; and this will happen in proportion as it becomes better known and as war, taxation, oppression, and misery increase there. The Hebrides appear to be fit only for the residence of malefactors, and it would be much better to send felons there than either to Virginia or Maryland. What a strange compliment has our mother country paid to two of the finest provinces in America! England has entertained in that respect very mistaken ideas; what was intended as a punishment is become the good fortune of several; many of those who have been transported as felons are now rich, and strangers to the stings of those wants that urged them to violations of the laws: they are become industrious, exemplary, and useful citizens. The English government should purchase the most northern and barren of those islands; it should send over to us the honest, primitive Hebrideans, settle them here on good lands as a reward for their virtue and ancient poverty, and replace them with a colony of her wicked sons. The severity of the climate, the inclemency of the seasons, the sterility of the soil, the tempestuousness of the sea, would afflict and punish enough. Could there be found a spot better adapted to retaliate the injury it had received by their crimes? Some of those islands might be considered as the hell of Great Britain, where all evil spirits should be sent. Two essential ends would be answered by this simple operation; the good people, by emigration, would be rendered happier; the bad ones would be placed where they ought to be. In a few years the dread of being sent to that wintry region would have a much stronger effect than that of transportation. This is no place of punishment; were I a poor, hopeless, breadless Englishman, and not restrained by the power of shame, I should be very thankful for the passage. It is of very little importance how and in what manner an indigent man arrives; for if he is but sober, honest, and industrious, he has nothing more to ask of heaven. Let him go to work, he will have opportunities enough to earn a comfortable support, and even the means of procuring some land, which ought to be the utmost wish of every person who has health and hands to work. I knew a man who came to this country, in the literal sense of the expression, stark naked; I think he was a Frenchman and a sailor on board an English man-of-war. Being discontented, he had stripped himself and swam on-shore, where, finding clothes and friends, he settled afterwards at Maraneck, in the county of Chester, in the province of New York. He married and left a good farm to each of his sons. I knew another person who was but twelve years old when he was taken on the frontiers of Canada by the Indians; at his arrival at Albany, he was purchased by a gentleman who generously bound him apprentice to a tailor. He lived to the age of ninety and left behind him a fine estate and a numerous family, all well settled; many of them I am acquainted with. Where is, then, the industrious European who ought to despair?

After a foreigner from any part of Europe is arrived and become a citizen, let him devoutly listen to the voice of our great parent, which says to him, "Welcome to my shores, distressed European; bless the hour in which thou didst see my verdant fields, my fair navigable rivers, and my green mountains! If thou wilt work, I have bread for thee; if thou wilt be honest, sober, and industrious, I have greater rewards to confer on thee—ease and independence. I will give thee fields to feed and clothe thee, a comfortable fireside to sit by and tell thy children by what means thou hast prospered, and a decent bed to repose on. I shall endow thee beside with the immunities of a freeman. If thou wilt carefully educate thy children, teach them gratitude to God and reverence to that government, that philanthropic government, which has collected here so many men and made them happy, I will also provide for thy progeny; and to every good man this ought to be the most holy, the most powerful, the most earnest wish he can possibly form, as well as the most consolatory prospect when he dies. Go thou and work and till; thou shalt prosper, provided thou be just, grateful, and industrious."

LETTER IX: DESCRIPTION OF CHARLES TOWN; THOUGHTS ON SLAVERY; ON PHYSICAL EVIL; A MELANCHOLY SCENE

Charles Town is, in the north, what Lima[1] is in the south; both are capitals of the richest provinces of their respective hemispheres; you may therefore conjecture that both cities must exhibit the appearances necessarily resulting from riches. Peru abounding in gold, Lima is filled with inhabitants who enjoy all those gradations of pleasure, refinement, and luxury which proceed from wealth. Carolina produces commodities more valuable perhaps than gold because they are gained by greater industry; it exhibits also on our northern stage a display of riches and luxury, inferior indeed to the former, but far superior to what are to be seen in our northern towns. Its situation is admirable, being built at the confluence of two large rivers, which receive in their course a great number of inferior streams, all navigable in the spring for flat boats. Here the produce of this extensive territory concentres; here therefore is the seat of the most valuable exportation; their wharfs, their docks, their magazines,[2] are extremely convenient to facilitate this great commercial business. The inhabitants are the gayest in America; it is called the centre of our *beau monde*[3] and is always filled with the richest planters in the province, who resort hither in quest of health and pleasure. Here is always to be seen a great number of valetudinarians[4] from the West Indies, seeking for the renovation of health, exhausted by the debilitating nature of their sun, air, and modes of living. Many of these West Indians have I seen, at thirty, loaded with the infirmities of old age; for nothing is more common in those countries of wealth than for persons to lose the abilities of enjoying the comforts of life at a time when we northern men just begin to taste the fruits of our labour and prudence. The round of pleasure and the expenses of those citizens' tables are much superior to what you would imagine; indeed, the growth of this town and province has been astonishingly rapid. It is pity that the narrowness of the neck on which it stands prevents it from increasing; and which is the reason why houses are so dear. The heat of the climate, which is sometimes very great in the interior parts of the country, is always temperate in Charles Town, though sometimes when they have no sea breezes, the sun is too powerful. The climate renders excesses of all kinds very dangerous, particularly those of the table; and yet, insensible or fearless of

---

[1] Charleston, South Carolina; Lima, Peru.   [2] Warehouses.   [3] "High society" (French).
[4] Invalids.

danger, they live on and enjoy a short and a merry life. The rays of their sun seem to urge them irresistibly to dissipation and pleasure: on the contrary, the women, from being abstemious, reach to a longer period of life and seldom die without having had several husbands. An European at his first arrival must be greatly surprised when he sees the elegance of their houses, their sumptuous furniture, as well as the magnificence of their tables. Can he imagine himself in a country the establishment of which is so recent?

The three principal classes of inhabitants are lawyers, planters, and merchants; this is the province which has afforded to the first the richest spoils, for nothing can exceed their wealth, their power, and their influence. They have reached the *ne plus ultra*[5] of worldly felicity; no plantation is secured, no title is good, no will is valid, but what they dictate, regulate, and approve. The whole mass of provincial property is become tributary to this society, which, far above priests and bishops, disdain to be satisfied with the poor Mosaical portion of the tenth.[6] I appeal to the many inhabitants who, while contending perhaps for their right to a few hundred acres, have lost by the mazes of the law their whole patrimony. These men are more properly lawgivers than interpreters of the law and have united here, as well as in most other provinces, the skill and dexterity of the scribe with the power and ambition of the prince; who can tell where this may lead in a future day? The nature of our laws and the spirit of freedom, which often tends to make us litigious, must necessarily throw the greatest part of the property of the colonies into the hands of these gentlemen. In another century, the law will possess in the north what now the church possesses in Peru and Mexico.

While all is joy, festivity, and happiness in Charles Town, would you imagine that scenes of misery overspread in the country? Their ears by habit are become deaf, their hearts are hardened; they neither see, hear, nor feel for the woes of their poor slaves, from whose painful labours all their wealth proceeds. Here the horrors of slavery, the hardship of incessant toils, are unseen; and no one thinks with compassion of those showers of sweat and of tears which from the bodies of Africans daily drop and moisten the ground they till. The cracks of the whip urging these miserable beings to excessive labour are far too distant from the gay capital to be heard. The chosen race eat, drink, and live happy, while the unfortunate one grubs up the ground, raises indigo, or husks the rice, exposed to a sun full as scorching as their native one, without the support of good food, without the cordials of any cheering liquor. This great contrast has often afforded me subjects of the most afflicting meditations. On the one side, behold a people enjoying all that life affords most bewitching and pleasurable, without labour, without fatigue, hardly subjected to the trouble of wishing. With gold, dug from Peruvian mountains, they order vessels to the coasts of Guinea; by virtue of that gold, wars, murders, and devastations are committed in some harmless, peaceable African neighbourhood where dwelt innocent people who even knew not but that all men were black. The daughter torn from her weeping mother, the child from the wretched parents, the wife from the loving husband; whole families swept away and brought through storms and tempests to this rich metropolis! There, arranged like horses at a fair, they are branded like cattle and then driven to toil, to starve, and to languish for a few years on the different plantations of these citizens. And for whom must they work? For persons they know not, and who have no other

---

[5] "The highest point" (Latin).

[6] In the Old Testament, the law stating that one tenth of one's worldly possessions should be offered to God.

power over them than that of violence, no other right than what this accursed metal has given them! Strange order of things! Oh, Nature, where art thou? Are not these blacks thy children as well as we? On the other side, nothing is to be seen but the most diffusive misery and wretchedness, unrelieved even in thought or wish! Day after day they drudge on without any prospect of ever reaping for themselves; they are obliged to devote their lives, their limbs, their will, and every vital exertion to swell the wealth of masters who look not upon them with half the kindness and affection with which they consider their dogs and horses. Kindness and affection are not the portion of those who till the earth, who carry burthens, who convert the logs into useful boards. This reward, simple and natural as one would conceive it, would border on humanity; and planters must have none of it!

If Negroes are permitted to become fathers, this fatal indulgence only tends to increase their misery; the poor companions of their scanty pleasures are likewise the companions of their labours; and when at some critical seasons they could wish to see them relieved, with tears in their eyes they behold them perhaps doubly oppressed, obliged to bear the burden of Nature—a fatal present—as well as that of unabated tasks. How many have I seen cursing the irresistible propensity and regretting that by having tasted of those harmless joys they had become the authors of double misery to their wives. Like their masters, they are not permitted to partake of those ineffable sensations with which Nature inspires the hearts of fathers and mothers; they must repel them all and become callous and passive. This unnatural state often occasions the most acute, the most pungent of their afflictions; they have no time, like us, tenderly to rear their helpless offspring, to nurse them on their knees, to enjoy the delight of being parents. Their paternal fondness is embittered by considering that if their children live, they must live to be slaves like themselves; no time is allowed them to exercise their pious office; the mothers must fasten them on their backs and, with this double load, follow their husbands in the fields, where they too often hear no other sound than that of the voice or whip of the taskmaster and the cries of their infants, broiling in the sun. These unfortunate creatures cry and weep like their parents, without a possibility of relief; the very instinct of the brute, so laudable, so irresistible, runs counter here to their master's interest; and to that god, all the laws of Nature must give way. Thus planters get rich; so raw, so inexperienced am I in this mode of life that were I to be possessed of a plantation, and my slaves treated as in general they are here, never could I rest in peace; my sleep would be perpetually disturbed by a retrospect of the frauds committed in Africa in order to entrap them, frauds surpassing in enormity everything which a common mind can possibly conceive. I should be thinking of the barbarous treatment they meet with on shipboard, of their anguish, of the despair necessarily inspired by their situation, when torn from their friends and relations, when delivered into the hands of a people differently coloured, whom they cannot understand, carried in a strange machine over an ever agitated element, which they had never seen before, and finally delivered over to the severities of the whippers and the excessive labours of the field. Can it be possible that the force of custom should ever make me deaf to all these reflections and as insensible to the injustice of that trade and to their miseries as the rich inhabitants of this town seem to be? What, then, is man, this being who boasts so much of the excellence and dignity of his nature among that variety of unscrutable mysteries, of unsolvable problems, with which he is surrounded? The reason why man has been thus created is not the least astonishing! It is said, I know, that they are much happier here than in the West Indies because, land being cheaper upon this continent than in those islands, the fields allowed them to raise their subsistence from are in general more extensive. The only possible chance of any alleviation depends on the humour of the planters, who, bred in the midst of slaves, learn from the example of their parents to despise them and seldom conceive either from religion or philosophy any ideas that tend to make their fate less calamitous, except some strong native tenderness of heart, some rays of philanthropy, overcome the obduracy contracted by habit.

I have not resided here long enough to become insensible of pain for the objects which I every day behold. In the choice of my friends and acquaintance, I always endeavour to find out those whose dispositions are somewhat congenial with my own. We have slaves likewise in our northern provinces; I hope the time draws near when they will be all emancipated, but how different their lot, how different their situation, in every possible respect! They enjoy as much liberty as their masters; they are as well clad and as well fed; in health and sickness, they are tenderly taken care of; they live under the same roof and are, truly speaking, a part of our families. Many of them are taught to read and write, and are well instructed in the principles of religion; they are the companions of our labours, and treated as such; they enjoy many perquisites, many established holidays, and are not obliged to work more than white people. They marry where inclination leads them, visit their wives every week; are as decently clad as the common people; they are indulged in educating, cherishing, and chastising their children, who are taught subordination to them as to their lawful parents: in short, they participate in many of the benefits of our society without being obliged to bear any of its burthens. They are fat, healthy, and hearty; and far from repining at their fate, they think themselves happier than many of the lower class of whites; they share with their masters the wheat and meat provision they help to raise; many of those whom the good Quakers have emancipated have received that great benefit with tears of regret and have never quitted, though free, their former masters and benefactors.

But is it really true, as I have heard it asserted here, that those blacks are incapable of feeling the spurs of emulation and the cheerful sound of encouragement? By no means; there are a thousand proofs existing of their gratitude and fidelity: those hearts in which such noble dispositions can grow are then like ours; they are susceptible of every generous sentiment, of every useful motive of action; they are capable of receiving lights,[7] of imbibing ideas that would greatly alleviate the weight of their miseries. But what methods have in general been made use of to obtain so desirable an end? None; the day in which they arrive and are sold is the first of their labours, labours which from that hour admit of no respite; for though indulged by law with relaxation on Sundays, they are obliged to employ that time which is intended for rest to till their little plantations. What can be expected from wretches in such circumstances? Forced from their native country, cruelly treated when on board, and not less so on the plantations to which they are driven, is there anything in this treatment but what must kindle all the passions, sow the seeds of inveterate resentment, and nourish a wish of perpetual revenge? They are left to the irresistible effects of those strong and natural propensities; the blows they receive, are they conducive to extinguish them or to win their affections? They are neither soothed by the hopes that their slavery will ever terminate but with their lives or yet encouraged by the goodness of their food or the mildness of their treatment. The very hopes held out to mankind by religion, that consolatory sys-

---

[7] A spiritual glow.

tem, so useful to the miserable, are never presented to them; neither moral nor physical means are made use of to soften their chains; they are left in their original and untutored state, that very state wherein the natural propensities of revenge and warm passions are so soon kindled. Cheered by no one single motive that can impel the will or excite their efforts, nothing but terrors and punishments are presented to them; death is denounced[8] if they run away; horrid delaceration if they speak with their native freedom; perpetually awed by the terrible cracks of whips or by the fear of capital punishments, while even those punishments often fail of their purpose.

A clergyman settled a few years ago at George Town, and feeling as I do now, warmly recommended to the planters, from the pulpit, a relaxation of severity; he introduced the benignity of Christianity and pathetically made use of the admirable precepts of that system to melt the hearts of his congregation into a greater degree of compassion toward their slaves than had been hitherto customary. "Sir," said one of his hearers, "we pay you a genteel salary to read to us the prayers of the liturgy and to explain to us such parts of the Gospel as the rule of the church directs, but we do not want you to teach us what we are to do with our blacks." The clergyman found it prudent to withhold any further admonition. Whence this astonishing right, or rather this barbarous custom, for most certainly we have no kind of right beyond that of force? We are told, it is true, that slavery cannot be so repugnant to human nature as we at first imagine because it has been practised in all ages and in all nations; the Lacedaemonians[9] themselves, those great asserters of liberty, conquered the Helotes with the design of making them their slaves; the Romans, whom we consider as our masters in civil and military policy, lived in the exercise of the most horrid oppression; they conquered to plunder and to enslave. What a hideous aspect the face of the earth must then have exhibited! Provinces, towns, districts, often depopulated! Their inhabitants driven to Rome, the greatest market in the world, and there sold by thousands! The Roman dominions were tilled by the hands of unfortunate people who had once been, like their victors, free, rich, and possessed of every benefit society can confer, until they became subject to the cruel right of war and to lawless force. Is there, then, no superintending power who conducts the moral operations of the world, as well as the physical? The same sublime hand which guides the planets round the sun with so much exactness, which preserves the arrangement of the whole with such exalted wisdom and paternal care, and prevents the vast system from falling into confusion—doth it abandon mankind to all the errors, the follies, and the miseries, which their most frantic rage and their most dangerous vices and passions can produce?

The history of the earth! Doth it present anything but crimes of the most heinous nature, committed from one end of the world to the other? We observe avarice, rapine, and murder, equally prevailing in all parts. History perpetually tells us of millions of people abandoned to the caprice of the maddest princes, and of whole nations devoted to the blind fury of tyrants. Countries destroyed, nations alternately buried in ruins by other nations, some parts of the world beautifully cultivated, returned again into their pristine state, the fruits of ages of industry, the toil of thousands in a short time destroyed by few! If one corner breathes in peace for a few years, it is, in turn subjected, torn, and levelled; one would almost believe the principles of action in man, considered as the first agent of this planet,

---

[8] The death sentence is pronounced.   [9] Ancient Spartans.

to be poisoned in their most essential parts. We certainly are not that class of beings which we vainly think ourselves to be; man, an animal of prey, seems to have rapine and the love of bloodshed implanted in his heart, nay, to hold it the most honourable occupation in society; we never speak of a hero of mathematics, a hero of knowledge or humanity, no, this illustrious appellation is reserved for the most successful butchers of the world. If Nature has given us a fruitful soil to inhabit, she has refused us such inclinations and propensities as would afford us the full enjoyment of it. Extensive as the surface of this planet is, not one half of it is yet cultivated, not half replenished; she created man and placed him either in the woods or plains and provided him with passions which must forever oppose his happiness; everything is submitted to the power of the strongest; men, like the elements, are always at war; the weakest yield to the most potent; force, subtlety, and malice always triumph over unguarded honesty and simplicity. Benignity, moderation, and justice are virtues adapted only to the humble paths of life; we love to talk of virtue and to admire its beauty while in the shade of solitude and retirement, but when we step forth into active life, if it happen to be in competition with any passion or desire, do we observe it to prevail? Hence so many religious impostors have triumphed over the credulity of mankind and have rendered their frauds the creeds of succeeding generations during the course of many ages until, worn away by time, they have been replaced by new ones. Hence the most unjust war, if supported by the greatest force, always succeeds; hence the most just ones, when supported only by their justice, as often fail. Such is the ascendancy of power, the supreme arbiter of all the revolutions which we observe in this planet; so irresistible is power that it often thwarts the tendency of the most forcible causes and prevents their subsequent salutary effects, though ordained for the good of man by the Governor of the universe. Such is the perverseness of human nature; who can describe it in all its latitude?

In the moments of our philanthropy, we often talk of an indulgent nature, a kind parent, who for the benefit of mankind has taken singular pains to vary the genera of plants, fruits, grain, and the different productions of the earth and has spread peculiar blessings in each climate. This is undoubtedly an object of contemplation which calls forth our warmest gratitude; for so singularly benevolent have those paternal intentions been, that where barrenness of soil or severity of climate prevail, there she has implanted in the heart of man sentiments which overbalance every misery and supply the place of every want. She has given to the inhabitants of these regions an attachment to their savage rocks and wild shores, unknown to those who inhabit the fertile fields of the temperate zone. Yet if we attentively view this globe, will it not appear rather a place of punishment than of delight? And what misfortune that those punishments should fall on the innocent, and its few delights be enjoyed by the most unworthy! Famine, diseases, elementary convulsions, human feuds, dissensions, etc., are the produce of every climate; each climate produces, besides, vices and miseries peculiar to its latitude. View the frigid sterility of the north, whose famished inhabitants, hardly acquainted with the sun, live and fare worse than the bears they hunt and to which they are superior only in the faculty of speaking. View the arctic and antarctic regions, those huge voids where nothing lives, regions of eternal snow where winter in all his horrors has established his throne and arrested every creative power of nature. Will you call the miserable stragglers in these countries by the name of men? Now contrast this frigid power of the north and south with that of the sun; examine the parched lands of the torrid zone, replete with sulphureous exhalations; view those countries of Asia subject to pestilential infections which lay Nature waste; view this globe, often convulsed both from within and without, pouring forth from several mouths rivers of boiling matter which are imperceptibly leaving immense subterranean graves wherein millions will one day perish! Look at the poisonous soil of the equator, at those putrid slimy tracks, teeming with horrid monsters, the enemies of the human race; look next at the sandy continent, scorched perhaps by the fatal approach of some ancient comet, now the abode of desolation. Examine the rains, the convulsive storms of those climates, where masses of sulphur, bitumen, and electrical fire, combining their dreadful powers, are incessantly hovering and bursting over a globe threatened with dissolution. On this little shell, how very few are the spots where man can live and flourish? Even under those mild climates which seem to breathe peace and happiness, the poison of slavery, the fury of despotism, and the rage of superstition are all combined against man! There only the few live and rule whilst the many starve and utter ineffectual complaints; there human nature appears more debased, perhaps, than in the less favoured climates. The fertile plains of Asia, the rich lowlands of Egypt and of Diarbeck,[10] the fruitful fields bordering on the Tigris and the Euphrates, the extensive country of the East Indies in all its separate districts—all these must to the geographical eye seem as if intended for terrestrial paradises; but though surrounded with the spontaneous riches of nature, though her kindest favours seem to be shed on those beautiful regions with the most profuse hand, yet there in general we find the most wretched people in the world. Almost everywhere, liberty so natural to mankind is refused, or rather enjoyed but by their tyrants; the word slave is the appellation of every rank who adore as a divinity a being worse than themselves, subject to every caprice and to every lawless rage which unrestrained power can give. Tears are shed, perpetual groans are heard, where only the accents of peace, alacrity, and gratitude should resound. There the very delirium of tyranny tramples on the best gifts of nature and sports with the fate, the happiness, the lives of millions; there the extreme fertility of the ground always indicates the extreme misery of the inhabitants!

Everywhere one part of the human species is taught the art of shedding the blood of the other, of setting fire to their dwellings, of levelling the works of their industry: half of the existence of nations regularly employed in destroying other nations. What little political felicity is to be met with here and there has cost oceans of blood to purchase, as if good was never to be the portion of unhappy man. Republics, kingdoms, monarchies, founded either on fraud or successful violence, increase by pursuing the steps of the same policy until they are destroyed in their turn, either by the influence of their own crimes or by more successful but equally criminal enemies.

If from this general review of human nature we descend to the examination of what is called civilized society, there the combination of every natural and artificial want makes us pay very dear for what little share of political felicity we enjoy. It is a strange heterogeneous assemblage of vices and virtues and of a variety of other principles, forever at war, forever jarring, forever producing some dangerous, some distressing extreme. Where do you conceive, then, that nature intended we should be happy? Would you prefer the state of men in the woods to that of men in a more improved situation? Evil preponderates in both; in the first they often eat each other for want of food, and in the other they often starve each other

---

[10] Southeast Turkey.

for want of room. For my part, I think the vices and miseries to be found in the latter exceed those of the former, in which real evil is more scarce, more supportable, and less enormous. Yet we wish to see the earth peopled, to accomplish the happiness of kingdoms, which is said to consist in numbers. Gracious God! To what end is the introduction of so many beings into a mode of existence in which they must grope amidst as many errors, commit as many crimes, and meet with as many diseases, wants, and sufferings!

The following scene will, I hope, account for these melancholy reflections and apologize for the gloomy thoughts with which I have filled this letter: my mind is, and always has been, oppressed since I became a witness to it. I was not long since invited to dine with a planter who lived three miles from ———, where he then resided. In order to avoid the heat of the sun, I resolved to go on foot, sheltered in a small path leading through a pleasant wood. I was leisurely travelling along, attentively examining some peculiar plants which I had collected, when all at once I felt the air strongly agitated, though the day was perfectly calm and sultry. I immediately cast my eyes toward the cleared ground, from which I was but a small distance, in order to see whether it was not occasioned by a sudden shower, when at that instant a sound resembling a deep rough voice, uttered, as I thought, a few inarticulate monosyllables. Alarmed and surprised, I precipitately looked all round, when I perceived at about six rods distance something resembling a cage, suspended to the limbs of a tree, all the branches of which appeared covered with large birds of prey, fluttering about and anxiously endeavouring to perch on the cage. Actuated by an involuntary motion of my hands more than by any design of my mind, I fired at them; they all flew to a short distance, with a most hideous noise, when, horrid to think and painful to repeat, I perceived a Negro, suspended in the cage and left there to expire! I shudder when I recollect that the birds had already picked out his eyes; his cheek-bones were bare; his arms had been attacked in several places; and his body seemed covered with a multitude of wounds. From the edges of the hollow sockets and from the lacerations with which he was disfigured, the blood slowly dropped and tinged the ground beneath. No sooner were the birds flown than swarms of insects covered the whole body of this unfortunate wretch, eager to feed on his mangled flesh and to drink his blood. I found myself suddenly arrested by the power of affright and terror; my nerves were convulsed; I trembled; I stood motionless, involuntarily contemplating the fate of this Negro in all its dismal latitude. The living spectre, though deprived of his eyes, could still distinctly hear, and in his uncouth dialect begged me to give him some water to allay his thirst. Humanity herself would have recoiled back with horror; she would have balanced whether to lessen such reliefless distress or mercifully with one blow to end this dreadful scene of agonizing torture! Had I had a ball in my gun, I certainly should have dispatched him, but finding myself unable to perform so kind an office, I sought, though trembling, to relieve him as well as I could. A shell ready fixed to a pole, which had been used by some Negroes, presented itself to me; filled it with water, and with trembling hands I guided it to the quivering lips of the wretched sufferer. Urged by the irresistible power of thirst, he endeavoured to meet it, as he instinctively guessed its approach by the noise it made in passing through the bars of the cage. "Tanky you, white man; tanky you; puta some poison and give me." "How long have you been hanging there?" I asked him. "Two days, and me no die; the birds, the birds; aaah me!" Oppressed with the reflections which this shocking spectacle afforded me, I mustered strength enough to walk away and soon reached the house at which I intended to dine. There I heard that the reason for this slave's being thus punished was on account of his having killed the overseer of the plantation. They told me that the laws of self-preservation rendered such executions necessary, and supported the doctrine of slavery with the arguments generally made use of to justify the practice, with the repetition of which I shall not trouble you at present. Adieu.

1769–1781, 1782

William Bartram
(1739–1823)

William Bartram's *Travels,* published in Philadelphia in 1791, began as a diary or journal made by Bartram during a four-year-long journey that started with the preparations for an extensive foray into the southern colonies in autumn 1772. From this diary, itself an extensive document, Bartram wrote his *Travels* for publication some twenty years later, in much the same way that Henry David Thoreau recapitulated in *Walden* (1850) his experience of two years spent at Walden Pond. Like Thoreau, Bartram was a keen observer of nature whose scientific investigations of the New World gave readers in England a clear sense of the natural beauty and power of America. A writer of considerable merit, Bartram shaped a document that was successful not only as an exploration of natural phenomena but as a work of literature.

Born in Philadelphia in 1739, Bartram was the son of Quaker John Bartram, now regarded to be the first American-born botanist. Both in England and America the eighteenth century was a period of intense interest in the natural universe. The Bartram family maintained a botanical garden at Kingseesing, on the Schuylkill River near Philadelphia, where father and son experimented with plant development. By 1772 William Bartram was exceptionally well prepared for the extensive journey and for the composition of the journal that became the foundation for his *Travels* narrative. He had already traveled with his father, who authored *Observations . . . From Pensilvania to Lake Ontario* (1751) and *A Description of Florida* (1769). Like these accounts, William Bartram's *Travels* includes long passages in which nature is observed in technical detail at close range, so that the reader is given an accurate, even scientific, picture of the writer's observations. Credibility and veracity were important to both Bartrams, even if their observations may, by modern scientific standards of data gathering and observation, appear to be amateurish.

Bartram's *Travels* goes beyond his father's work by attempting, like Thomas Jefferson's *Notes on the State of Virginia* (1785), to present a cultural and anthropological portrait of the inhabitants of North America, together with some observations about their customs and manners. The anthropological commentary and the philosophical excursions based on natural observations give *Travels* its unique quality and render it a fit transition piece between the purely descriptive accounts of the New World, which date back to the earliest explorations—with travel narratives written largely to justify the exploration to a partron or sponsor—and the type of personal, literary account Thoreau provided in *Walden*. Unlike *Walden*, which was revised by the author several times, *Travels* remains a large-scale canvas, one in which all elements of the experience are communicated to the reader as separate parts with less of the cohesive, pervasively metaphorical structure of Thoreau's work.

William Bartram enjoyed the sponsorship of Dr. John Fothergill, a British botanist who advised Bartram to keep a journal of the local soil types, flora, and fauna. But Bartram's finished product goes far beyond this challenge. It is an anthropological return to the Garden of Eden and a literary work that gives mythic proportion to the vast wilderness of America. That Bartram's *Travels* influenced writers such as Samuel Coleridge, William Wordsworth, and Thomas Jefferson is commonly acknowledged, and scholars attribute the inclusion of engravings in Benjamin Barton's *Elements of Botany* (1808) to the drawings of William Bartram. *Travels* was translated into several languages soon after its publication—a clear sign of its influence and success. For modern readers the formal language and long sentences may appear to be complex; however, by considering the historical context, *Travels* provides an understanding and perception unavailable before Bartram made his arduous journey through the southern colonies.

Suggested Readings: *The Travels of William Bartram,* ed. M. Van Doren, 1940. *Travels in Georgia and Florida, 1773-1774: A Report to Dr. John Fothergill,* ed. F. Harper, 1944. N. B. Fagin, *William Bartram: Interpreter of the American Landscape,* 1933. *John and William Bartram's America: Selections From the Writings,* ed. H. G. Cruikshank, 1957.

Text Used: *The Travels of William Bartram,* ed. F. Harper, 1958.

William Bartram's 1788 drawing of Franklinia alatamaha, *the flowering tree he and his father saved from extinction by planting its seeds in their garden; it was last seen growing wild in 1803.*

from   TRAVELS*

from   CHAPTER VII

A Journey From Spalding's Lower Trading House to Talahasochte
or White King's Town, on the River Little St. Juan, Thirty Miles Above
Fort St. Marks in the Bay of Apalatche

On my return to the trading house, from my journey to the great savanna, I found the trading company for Little St. Juan's,[1] were preparing for that post.

My mind yet elate with the various scenes of rural nature, which as a lively animated picture, had been presented to my view; the deeply engraven impression, a pleasing flattering contemplation, gave strength and agility to my steps, anxiously to press forward to the delightful fields and groves of Apalatche.

The trading company for Talahasochte being now in readiness to proceed for that quarter, under the direction of our chief trader, in the cool of the morning we set off, each of us having a good horse to ride, besides having in our caravan several pack horses laden with provisions, camp equipage and other necessaries; a young man from St. Augustine, in the service of the governor of East Florida accompanied us, commissioned to purchase of the Indians and traders, some Siminole horses. They are the most beautiful and sprightly species of that noble creature, perhaps any where to be seen; but are of a small breed, and as delicately formed as the American roe buck. A horse in the Creek or Muscogulge tongue is echoclucco, that is the great deer, (echo is a deer and clucco is big:) the Siminole horses are said to descend originally from the Andalusian breed, brought here by the Spaniards when they first established the colony of East Florida. From the forehead to their nose is a little arched or aquiline, and so are the fine Chactaw horses among the Upper Creeks, which are said to have been brought thither from New-Mexico across Mississippi, by those nations of Indians who emigrated from the West, beyond the river. These horses are every way like the Siminole breed, only being larger, and perhaps not so lively and capricious. It is a matter of conjecture and enquiry, whether or not the different soil and situation of the country, may have contributed in some measure, in forming and establishing the difference in size and other qualities betwixt them. I have observed the horses and other animals in the high hilly country of Carolina, Georgia, Virginia and all along our shores, are of a much larger and stronger make, than those which are bred in the flat country next the sea coast; a buck-skin of the Upper Creeks and Cherokees will weigh twice as heavy as those of the Siminoles or Lower Creeks, and those bred in the low flat country of Carolina.

Our first days journey was along the Alachua roads, twenty-five miles to the Half-way Pond, where we encamped, the musquitoes were excessively troublesome the whole night.

Decamped early next morning, still pursuing the road to Alachua, until within a

---

* The full title is *Travels Through North and South Carolina, Georgia, East and West Florida, the Cherokee Country, the Extensive Territories of the Muscogulges, or Creek Confederacy, and the Country of the Chactaws, Containing an Account of the Soil and Natural Productions of Those Regions, Together With Observations on the Manners of the Indians,* from Pt. II.

[1] The Saint John's River, which runs northward through Florida.

few miles of Cuscowilla, when the road dividing, one for the town and the other for the great savanna; here our company separated, one party chose to pass through the town, having some concerns there; I kept with the party that went through the savanna, it being the best road, leading over a part of the savanna, when entering the groves on its borders, we travelled several miles over these fertile eminences and delightful, shady, fragrant forests, then again entered upon the savanna, and crossed a charming extensive green cove or bay of it, covered with a vivid green grassy turf, when we again ascended the woodland hills, through fruitful Orange groves and under shadowy Palms and Magnolias. Now the Pine forests opened to view, we left the magnificent savanna and its delightful groves, passing through a level, open, airy Pine forest, the stately trees scatteringly planted by nature, arising strait and erect from the green carpet, embellished with various grasses and flowering plants, and gradually ascending the sand hills soon came into the trading path to Talahasochte; which is generally, excepting a few deviations, the old Spanish highway to St. Mark's. At about five miles distance beyond the great savanna, we came to camp late in the evening, under a little grove of Live Oaks just by a group of shelly rocks, on the banks of a beautiful little lake, partly environed by meadows. The rocks as usual in these regions partly encircled a spacious sink or grotto, which communicates with the waters of the lake; the waters of the grotto are perfectly transparent, cool and pleasant, and well replenished with fish. Soon after our arrival here, our companions who passed through Cuscowilla joined us. A brisk cool wind during the night kept the persecuting musquitoes at a distance.

The morning pleasant, we decamped early, proceeding on, rising gently for several miles, over sandy, gravelly ridges, we find ourselves in an elevated, high, open, airy region, somewhat rocky, on the backs of the ridges, and presents to view on every side, the most dreary, solitary, desart waste I had ever beheld; groups of bare rocks emerging out of the naked gravel and drifts of white sand; the grass thinly scattered and but few trees; the Pines, Oaks, Olives and Sideroxilons,[2] poor, misshapen and tattered; scarce an animal to be seen or noise heard, save the symphony of the Western breeze, through the bristly Pine leaves, or solitary sand crickets screech, or at best the more social converse of the frogs, in solemn chorus with the swift breezes, brought from distant fens and forests. Next we joyfully enter the borders of the level Pine forest and savannas, which continued for many miles, never out of sight of little lakes or ponds, environed with illumined meadows, the clear waters sparkling through the tall Pines.

Having a good spirited horse under me, I generally kept a-head of my companions, which I often chose to do, as circumstances offered or invited, for the sake of retirement and observation.

The high road being here open and spacious, at a good distance before me, I observed a large hawk on the ground, in the middle of the road; he seemed to be in distress, endeavouring to rise; when, coming up near him, I found him closely bound up by a very long coach-whip snake, that had wreathed himself several times round the hawk's body, who had but one of his wings at liberty; beholding their struggles a while, I alighted off my horse with an intention of parting them; when, on coming up, they mutually agreed to separate themselves, each one seeking his own safety, probably considering me as their common enemy. The bird rose aloft and fled away as soon as he recovered his liberty, and the snake as

[2] Buckthorn.

eagerly made off, I soon overtook him but could not perceive that he was wounded.

I suppose the hawk had been the aggressor, and fell upon the snake with an intention of making a prey of him, and that the snake dexterously and luckily threw himself in coils round his body, and girded him so close as to save himself from destruction.

The coach-whip snake is a beautiful creature; when full grown they are six and seven feet in length, and the largest part of their body not so thick as a cane or common walking stick; their head not larger than the end of a man's finger; their neck is very slender, and from the abdomen tapers away in the manner of a small switch or coach-whip; the top of the head and neck, for three or four inches, is as black and shining as a raven; the throat and belly as white as snow; and the upper side of their body of a chocolate colour, excepting the tail part, almost from the abdomen to the extremity, which is black: it may be proper to observe, however, that they vary in respect to the colour of the body; some I have seen almost white or cream colour, others of a pale chocolate or clay colour, but in all the head and neck is black, and the tail dark brown or black. They are extremely swift, seeming almost to fly over the surface of the ground, and that which is very singular, they can run swiftly on only their tail part, carrying their head and body upright: one very fine one accompanied me along the road side, at a little distance, raising himself erect, now and then looking me in the face, although I proceeded on a good round trot on purpose to observe how fast they could proceed in that position. His object seemed mere curiosity or observation; with respect to venom they are as innocent as a worm, and seem to be familiar with man. They seem a particular inhabitant of East Florida, though I have seen some of them in the maritime parts of Carolina and Georgia, but in these regions they are neither so large or beautiful.

We rise again, passing over sand ridges of gentle elevation, savannas and open Pine forests. Masses or groups of rocks present to view on every side, as before mentioned, and with difficulty we escaped the circular infundibuliform[3] cavities or sinks in the surface of the earth; generally a group of rocks, shaded by Palms, Live Oaks and Magnolias, is situated on their limb: some are partly filled up with earth, whilst others and the greater number of them are partly filled with transparent cool water, which discover the well or perforation through the rocks in the center. This day being remarkably sultry, we came to camp early, having chosen our situation under some stately Pines, near the verge of a spacious savanna.

After some refreshment, our hunters went out into the forest, and returned towards evening; amongst other game, they brought with them a savanna crane which they shot in the adjoining meadows. This stately bird is above six feet in length from the toes to the extremity of the beak when extended, and the wings expand eight or nine feet; they are above five feet high when standing erect; the tail is remarkably short, but the flag or pendant feathers which fall down off the rump on each side, are very long and sharp pointed, of a delicate texture, and silky softness; the beak is very long, strait and sharp pointed; the crown of the head bare of feathers, of a reddish rose colour, thinly barbed with short, stiff, black hair; the legs and thighs are very long, and bare of feathers a great space above the knees; the plumage of this bird is generally of a pale ash colour, with shades or clouds of pale brown and sky blue, the brown prevails on the shoulders

---

[3] Funnel-shaped.

and back; the barrels of the prime quill-feathers are long and of a large diameter, leaving a large cavity when extracted from the wing: all the bones of this bird have a thin shell, and consequently a large cavity or medullary receptacle. When these birds move their wings in flight, their strokes are slow, moderate and regular, and even when at a considerable distance or high above us, we plainly hear the quill-feathers, their shafts and webs upon one another, creak as the joints or working of a vessel in a tempestuous sea.

We had this fowl dressed for supper and it made excellent soup; nevertheless as long as I can get any other necessary food I shall prefer his seraphic music in the etherial skies, and my eyes and understanding gratified in observing their economy and social communities, in the expansive green savannas of Florida.

Next morning we arose early, and proceeding, gradually descended again, and continued many miles along a flat, level country, over delightful green savannas, decorated with hommocks[4] or islets of dark groves, consisting of Magnolia grandiflora, Morus, tilia, Zanthoxilon, Laurus Borbonia, Sideroxilon, Quercus sempervirens, Halesia diptera, Callicarpa, Corypha palma, &c. there are always groups of whitish testaceous[5] rocks and sinks where these hommocks are. We next crossed a wet savanna, which is the beginning of a region still lower than we had traversed; here we crossed a rapid rivulet of exceeding cool, pleasant water, where we halted to refresh ourselves. But it must be remarked here, that this rivulet, though lively and rapid at this time, is not a permanent stream, but was formed by a heavy rain that fell the day before, as was apparent from its bed, besides it is at best but a jet or mere phantom of a brook, as the land around is rocky and hollow, abounding with wells and cavities. Soon after leaving the brook we passed off to the left hand, along the verge of an extensive savanna, and meadows many miles in circumference, edged on one border with detached groves and pompous Palms, and embellished with a beautiful sparkling lake; its verges decorated with tall, waving grass and floriferous plants; the pellucid[6] waters gently rolling on to a dark shaded grotto, just under a semicircular, swelling, turfy ascent or bank, skirted by groves of Magnolias, Oaks, Laurels and Palms. In these expansive and delightful meadows, were feeding and roving troops of the fleet Siminole horse. We halted a while at this grotto, and after refreshing ourselves we mounted horse and proceeded across a charming lawn, part of the savanna, entering on it through a dark grove. In this extensive lawn were several troops of horse, and our company had the satisfaction of observing several belonging to themselves. One occurrence, remarkable here, was a troop of horse under the control and care of a single black dog, which seemed to differ in no respect from the wolf of Florida, except his being able to bark as the common dog. He was very careful and industrious in keeping them together, and if any one strolled from the rest at too great a distance, the dog would spring up, head the horse and bring him back to the company. The proprietor of these horses is an Indian in Talahasochte, about ten miles distance from this place, who, out of humour and experiment, trained his dog up from a puppy to this business; he follows his master's horses only, keeping them in a separate company where they range, and when he is hungry or wants to see his master, in the evening he returns to town, but never stays at home a night.

The region we had journeyed through, since we decamped this morning, is of a far better soil and quality than we had yet seen since we left Alachua; generally a dark greyish, and sometimes brown and black loam, on a foundation of whitish

---

[4] Hummocks, or low, rounded hills.   [5] Shell-like.   [6] Transparent.

marl, chalk and testaceous limestone rocks, and ridges of a loose, coarse, reddish sand, producing stately Pines in the plains, and Live Oak, Mulberry, Magnolia, Palm, Zanthoxilon, etc. in the hommocks, and also in great plenty the perennial Indigo; it grows here five, six and seven feet high, and as thick together as if it had been planted and cultivated. The higher ridges of hills afford great quantities of a species of iron ore, of that kind found in New-Jersey and Pennsylvania, and there called bog ore; it appears on the surface of the ground in large detached masses and smaller fragments; it is ponderous and seemed rich of that most useful metal; but one property remarkable in these terrigenous stones is, they appeared to be blistered, somewhat resembling cinders, or as if they had suffered a violent action of fire.

Leaving the charming savanna and fields of Capola, we passed several miles through delightful plains and meadows, little differing from the environs of Capola, diversified with rocky islets or hommocks of dark woodland.

We next entered a vast forest of the most stately Pine trees that can be imagined, planted by nature at a moderate distance, on a level, grassy plain, enamelled with a variety of flowering shrubs, viz. Viola, Ruellia infundibuliformea, Amaryllis atamasco, Mimosa sensitiva, Mimosa intsia and many others new to me. This sublime forest continued five or six miles, when we came to dark groves of Oaks, Magnolias, Red bays, Mulberrys, &c. through which proceeding near a mile, we entered open fields and arrived at the town of Talahasochte, on the banks of Little St. Juan.

The river Little St. Juan may, with singular propriety, be termed the pellucid river. The waters are the clearest and purest of any river I ever saw, transmitting distinctly the natural form and appearance of the objects moving in the transparent floods, or reposing on the silvery bed, with the finny inhabitants sporting in its gently flowing stream.

The river at the town is about two hundred yards over, and fifteen or twenty feet in depth. The great swamp and lake Oaquaphenogaw[7] is said to be its source, which is about one hundred miles by land North of this place, which would give the river a course of near two hundred miles from its source to the sea, to follow its meanders; as in general our rivers, that run any considerable distance through the country to the sea, by their windings and roving about to find a passage through the ridges and heights, at least double their distance.

The Indians and traders say that this river has no branches or collateral brooks or rivers tributary to it, but that it is fed or augmented by great springs which break out through the banks. From the accounts given by them, and my own observations on the country round about, it seems a probable assertion, for there was not a creek or rivulet, to be seen, running on the surface of the ground, from the great Alachua Savanna to this river, a distance of about seventy miles; yet, perhaps, no part of the earth affords a greater plenty of pure, salubrious waters. The unparalleled transparency of these waters furnishes an argument for such a conjecture, that amounts at least to a probability, were it not confirmed by ocular demonstration; for in all the flat countries of Carolina and Florida, except this isthmus, the waters of the rivers are, in some degree, turgid, and have a dark hue, owing to the annual firing of the forests and plains, and afterwards the heavy rains washing the light surface of the burnt earth into rivulets, and these rivulets running rapidly over the surface of the earth, flow into the rivers, and tinge the waters the

[7] The Okenfenokee Swamp in southeast Georgia.

colour of lye or beer, almost down to the tide near the sea coast. But here behold how different the appearance, and how manifest the cause; for although the surface of the ground produces the same vegetable substances, the soil the same, and suffers in like manner a general conflagration, and the rains, in impetuous showers, as liberally descend upon the parched surface of the ground; but the earth being so hollow and porous, these superabundant waters cannot constitute a rivulet or brook to continue any distance on its surface, before they are arrested in their course and swallowed up, thence descending, are filtered through the sands and other strata of earth, to the horizontal beds of porous rocks, which being composed of thin separable laminae,[8] lying generally in obliquely horizontal directions over each other, admit these waters to pass on by gradual but constant percolation; which collecting and associating, augment and form little rills, brooks and even subterraneous rivers, which wander in darkness beneath the surface of the earth, by innnumerable doublings, windings and secret labyrinths; no doubt in some places forming vast reservoirs and subterranean lakes, inhabited by multitudes of fish and aquatic animals: and possibly, when collected into large rapid brooks, meeting irresistible obstructions in their course, they suddenly break through these perforated fluted rocks, in high, perpendicular jets, nearly to their former level, flooding large districts of land: thus by means of those subterranean courses, the waters are purified and finally carried to the banks of great rivers, where they emerge and present themselves to open day-light, with their troops of finny inhabitants, in those surprising vast fountains near the banks of this river; and likewise on and near the shores of Great St. Juan, on the East coast of the isthmus, some of which I have already given an account of.

On our arrival at Talahasochte, in the evening we repaired to the trading house formerly belonging to our chief, where were a family of Indians, who immediately and complaisantly moved out to accommodate us. The White King with most of the male inhabitants were out hunting or tending their Corn plantations.

The town is delightfully situated on the elevated East banks of the river, the ground level to near the river, when it descends suddenly to the water; I suppose the perpendicular elevation of the ground may be twenty or thirty feet. There are near thirty habitations constructed after the mode of Cuscowilla; but here is a more spacious and neat council-house.

These Indians have large handsome canoes, which they form out of the trunks of Cypress trees (Cupressus disticha) some of them commodious enough to accomodate twenty or thirty warriors. In these large canoes they descend the river on trading and hunting expeditions on the sea coast, neighbouring islands and keys, quite to the point of Florida, and sometimes cross the gulph, extending their navigations to the Bahama islands and even to Cuba: a crew of these adventurers had just arrived, having returned from Cuba but a few days before our arrival, with a cargo of spirituous liquors, Coffee, Sugar and Tobacco. One of them politely presented me with a choice piece of Tobacco, which he told me he had received from the governor of Cuba.

They deal in the way of barter, carrying with them deer skins, furs, dry fish, bees-wax, honey, bear's oil and some other articles. They say the Spaniards receive them very friendly, and treat them with the best spirituous liquors.

* * *

---

[8] Layers.

We came up to this vast plain where the ancient Spanish high way crosses it to Pensacola; there yet remain plain vestiges of the grand causeway, which is open like a magnificent avenue, and the Indians have a bad road or pathway on it. The ground or soil of the plain is a perfectly black, rich soapy earth, like a stiff clay or marle, wet and boggy near shore, but, further in, firm and hard enough in the summer season, but wet and in some places under water during the winter.

This vast plain together with the forests contiguous to it, if permitted (by the Siminoles who are sovereigns of these realms) to be in possession and under the culture of industrious planters and mechanicks, would in a little time exhibit other scenes than it does at present, delightful as it is; for by the arts of agriculture and commerce, almost every desirable thing in life might be produced and made plentiful here, and thereby establish a rich, populous and delightful region; as this soil and climate appear to be of a nature favourable for the production of almost all the fruits of the earth, as Corn, Rice, Indigo, Sugar-cane, Flax, Cotton, Silk, Cochineal and all the varieties of esculent [9] vegetables; and I suppose no part of the earth affords such endless range and exuberant pasture for cattle, deer, sheep, &c. the waters every where, even in the holes in the earth abound with varieties of excellent fish; and the forests and native meadows with wild game, as bear, deer, turkeys, quail, and in the winter season geese, ducks and other fowl; and lying contiguous to one of the most beautiful navigable rivers in the world; and not more than thirty miles from St. Marks on the great bay of Mexico; is most conveniently situated for the West-India trade and the commerce of all the world.

After indulging my imagination in the contemplation of these grand diversified scenes, we turned to the right hand, riding over the charming green terrace dividing the forests from the plains, and then entering the groves again, continued eight or nine miles up the river, four or five miles distance from its banks; having continually in view on one side or other, expansive green fields, groves and high forests; the meadows glittering with distant lakes and ponds, alive with cattle, deer and turkeys, and frequently present to view remains of ancient Spanish plantations. At length, towards evening, we turned about and came within sight of the river, where falling on the Indian trading path, we continued along it to the landing-place opposite the town, when hallooing and discharging our pieces, an Indian with a canoe came presently over and conducted us to the town before dark.

On our arrival at the trading house, our chief was visited by the head men of the town, when instantly the White King's arrival in town was announced; a messenger had before been sent in to prepare a feast, the king and his retinue having killed several bears. A fire is now kindled in the area of the public square; the royal standard is displayed, and the drum beats to give notice to the town of the royal feast.

The ribs and the choice pieces of the three great fat bears already well barbecued or broiled, are brought to the banqueting house in the square, with hot bread; and honeyed water for drink.

When the feast was over in the square, (where only the chiefs and warriors were admitted, with the white people) the chief priest, attended by slaves, came with baskets and carried off the remainder of the victuals etc. which was distributed amongst the families of the town; the king then withdrew, repairing to the

[9] Edible.

council house in the square, whither the chiefs and warriors, old and young, and such of the whites as chose, repaired also; the king, war-chief and several ancient chiefs and warriors were seated on the royal cabins, the rest of the head men and warriors, old and young, sat on the cabins on the right hand of the king's, and the cabins of seats on the left, and on the same elevation are always assigned for the white people, Indians of other towns, and such of their own people as chose.

Our chief, with the rest of the white people in town, took their seats according to order; Tobacco and pipes are brought, the calumet[10] is lighted and smoked, circulating according to the usual forms and ceremony, and afterwards black drink concluded the feast. The king conversed, drank Cassine[11] and associated familiarly with his people and with us.

After the public entertainment was over, the young people began their music and dancing in the square, whither the young of both sexes repaired, as well as the old and middle aged; this frolick continued all night.

The White King of Talahasochte is a middle aged man, of moderate stature, and though of a lofty and majestic countenance and deportment, yet I am convinced this dignity which really seems graceful, is not the effect of vain supercilious pride, for his smiling countenance and his cheerful familiarity bespeak magnanimity and benignity.

Next a council and treaty was held, they requested to have a trading house again established in the town, assuring us that every possible means should constantly be pursued to prevent any disturbance in future on their part; they informed us that the murderers of M'Gee[12] and his associates, were to be put to death, that two of them were already shot, and they were in pursuit of the other.

Our chief trader in answer, informed them that the re-establishment of friendship and trade was the chief object of his visit, and that he was happy to find his old friends of Talahasochte in the same good disposition, as they ever were towards him and the white people, that it was his wish to trade with them, and that he was now come to collect his pack-horses to bring them goods. The king and the chiefs having been already acquainted with my business and pursuits amongst them, received me very kindly; the king in particular complimented me, saying that I was as one of his own children or people, and should be protected accordingly, while I remained with them, adding, "Our whole country is before you, where you may range about at pleasure, gather physic plants and flowers, and every other production;" thus the treaty terminated friendly and peaceably.

Next day early in the morning we left the town and the river, in order to fix our encampment in the forests about twelve miles from the river, our companions with the pack-horses went a head to the place of rendezvous, and our chief conducted me another way to shew me a very curious place, called the Alligator-Hole, which was lately formed by an extraordinary eruption or jet of water; it is one of those vast circular sinks, which we behold almost every where about us as we traversed these forests, after we left the Alachua savanna: this remarkable one is on the verge of a spacious meadow, the surface of the ground round about uneven by means of gentle rising knolls; some detached groups of rocks and large spreading Live-Oaks shade it on every side; it is about sixty yards over, and the surface of the water six or seven feet below the rim of the funnel or bason; the water is transparent, cool and pleasant to drink, and well stored with fish; a very large

---

[10] A ceremonial pipe, a "peace pipe."   [11] A drink made from the holly tree's leaves.
[12] The leader of a Georgia family whose camp was attacked by predatory Indians.

alligator at present is lord or chief; many have been killed here, but the throne is never long vacant, the vast neighbouring ponds so abound with them.

The account that this gentleman, who was an eye-witness of the last eruption, gave me of its first appearance; being very wonderful, I proceed to relate what he told me whilst we were in town, which was confirmed by the Indians, and one or more of our companions, who also saw its progress, as well as my own observations after I came to the ground.

This trader being near the place (before it had any visible existence in its present appearance) about three years ago (as he was looking for some horses which he expected to find in these parts) when, on a sudden, he was astonished by an inexpressible rushing noise, like a mighty hurricane or thunder storm, and looking around, he saw the earth overflowed by torrents of water, which came, wave after wave, rushing down a vale or plain very near him, which it filled with water, and soon began to overwhelm the higher grounds, attended with a terrific noise and tremor of the earth; recovering from his first surprise, he immediately resolved to proceed for the place from whence the noise seemed to come, and soon came in sight of the incomparable fountain, and saw, with amazement, the floods rushing upwards many feet high, and the expanding waters, which prevailed every way, spreading themselves far and near: he at length concluded (he said) that the fountains of the deep were again broken up, and that an universal deluge had commenced, and instantly turned about and fled to alarm the town, about nine miles distance, but before he could reach it he met several of the inhabitants, who, already alarmed by the unusual noise, were hurrying on towards the place, upon which he returned with the Indians, taking their stand on an eminence to watch its progress and the event: it continued to jet and flow in this manner for several days, forming a large, rapid creek or river, descending and following the various courses and windings of the valley, for the distance of seven or eight miles, emptying itself into a vast savanna, where was a lake and sink which received and gave vent to its waters.

The fountain, however, gradually ceased to overflow, and finally withdrew itself beneath the common surface of the earth, leaving this capacious bason of waters, which, though continually near full, hath never since overflowed. There yet remains, and will, I suppose, remain for ages, the dry bed of the river or canal, generally four, five and six feet below the natural surface of the land; the perpendicular, ragged banks of which, on each side, shew the different strata of the earth, and at places, where ridges or a swelling bank crossed and opposed its course and fury, are vast heaps of fragments of rocks, white chalk, stones and pebbles, which were collected and thrown into the lateral valleys, until the main stream prevailed over and forced them aside, overflowing the levels and meadows, for some miles distance from the principal stream, on either side. We continued down the great vale, along its banks, quite to the savanna and lake where it vented itself, while its ancient subterranean channel was gradually opening, which, I imagine, from some hidden event or cause had been choaked up, and which, we may suppose, was the immediate cause of the eruption.

In the evening having gained our encampment, on a grassy knoll or eminence, under the cover of spreading Oaks, just by the grotto or sink of the lake, which lay as a sparkling gem on the flowery bosom of the ample savanna; our roving associates soon came in from ranging the forests; we continued our encampment at this place for several days, ranging around the delightful country to a great distance, every days excursion presenting new scenes of wonder and delight.

Early in the morning our chief invited me with him on a visit to the town, to take a final leave of the White King. We were graciously received, and treated with the utmost civility and hospitality; there was a noble entertaintment and repast provided against our arrival, consisting of bears ribs, venison, varieties of fish, roasted turkeys (which they call the white man's dish) hot corn cakes, and a very agreeable, cooling sort of jelly, which they call conte; this is prepared from the root of the China brier.

* * *

About midnight, having fallen asleep, I was awakened and greatly surprised at finding most of my companions up in arms, and furiously engaged with a large alligator but a few yards from me. One of our company, it seems, awoke in the night, and perceived the monster within a few paces of the camp, who giving the alarm to the rest, they readily came to his assistance, for it was a rare piece of sport; some took fire-brands and cast them at his head, whilst others formed javelins of saplins, pointed and hardened with fire; these they thrust down his throat into his bowels, which caused the monster to roar and bellow hideously, but his strength and fury was so great that he easily wrenched or twisted them out of their hands, which he wielded and brandished about and kept his enemies at distance for a time; some were for putting an end to his life and sufferings with a rifle ball, but the majority thought this would too soon deprive them of the diversion and pleasure of exercising their various inventions of torture; they at length however grew tired, and agreed in one opinion, that he had suffered sufficiently, and put an end to his existence. This crocodile was about twelve feet in length: we supposed that he had been allured by the fishy scent of our birds, and encouraged to undertake and pursue this hazardous adventure which cost him his life; this, with other instances already recited, may be sufficient to prove the intrepidity and subtilty of those voracious, formidable animals.

We set off early next morning, and soon after falling into the trading path, accomplished about twenty miles of our journey, and in the evening encamped as usual, near the banks of savannas and ponds, for the benefit of water and accommodations of pasture for our creatures. Next day we passed over part of the great and beautiful Alachua Savanna, whose exuberant green meadows, with the fertile hills which immediately encircle it, would if peopled and cultivated after the manner of the civilized countries of Europe, without crouding or incommoding families, at a moderate estimation, accommodate in the happiest manner, above one hundred thousand human inhabitants, besides millions of domestic animals; and I make no doubt this place will at some future day be one of the most populous and delightful seats on earth.

We came to camp in the evening, on the banks of a creek but a few miles distance from Cuscowilla, and two days more moderate travelling brought us safe back again to the lower trading-house, on St. Juan, having been blessed with health and a prosperous journey.

On my arrival at the stores, I was happy to find all well as we had left them, and our bringing with us friendly talks from the Siminole towns, and the Nation likewise, compleated the hopes and wishes of the trading company, with respect to their commercial concerns with the Indians, which, as the chearing light of the sun-beams after a dark, tempestuous night, diffused joy and conviviality throughout the little community, where were a number of men with their families, who had been put out of employment and subsistence, anxiously waiting the happy event.

1772-1776, 1791

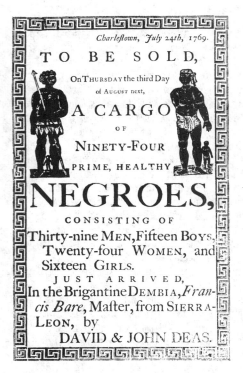

A broadside advertising a sale of slaves in South Carolina.

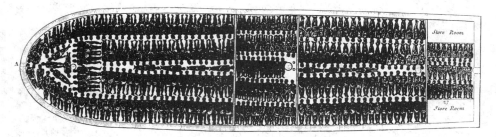

The slave ship Brookes *out of Liverpool was able to hold a "cargo" of 454 slaves, according to an act of 1788; the hold was only 22 inches high.*

Olaudah Equiano (Gustavus Vassa)
(1745?–1801?)

Born in 1745 in what is now Nigeria, Olaudah Equiano was kidnapped at age eleven by African slave traders. Carried to Africa's western coast, he was sold to white traders and transported to Barbados. During the Atlantic crossing and after being bought and shipped to a Virginia plantation, he experienced the horrors of slavery. Yet, his circumstances improved somewhat when he was purchased by Michael Henry Pascal, a British naval lieutenant, who brought Equiano to England, treated him well, and renamed him Gustavus Vassa, after a Swedish king.

During the Seven Years' War between England and France (1756 to 1763), Equiano, assuming that he would be freed after the war, bravely served his master in several important naval engagements. Instead, he was transported to the Caribbean isle of Montserrat and purchased by a Quaker merchant, Philadelphian Robert King. King also treated Equiano well, allowing the slave to become a sailor on merchant vessels in the Caribbean and encouraging him to earn a tiny income through small trading ventures. However, Equiano continued to experience slavery's emotional abuses and to long for freedom.

His loyalty to his master and his efficient and responsible service were rewarded when Equiano was freed in 1766. In 1767 he returned to London and became a valet for a physician, Charles Irving. In summer 1773, he and Irving joined an Arctic expedition, becoming trapped in the Greenland ice and narrowly escaping. On voyages to Turkey, Portugal, and Italy and return trips to the West Indies, Equiano discovered that free blacks were everywhere vulnerable to abuse, prejudice, and reenslavement.

In 1774 Equiano underwent a powerful conversion experience and joined the Methodist church. That move led him to travel with Irving the next year to what is now Nicaragua, where Equiano hoped not only to further Irving's mercantile interests but also to convert the local natives. After barely avoiding being resold into slavery, he returned to England in 1777. During the 1780s, when abolitionist sentiment ran high in England, Equiano brought cases of slave abuse before the public, lectured on slavery, worked to organize an African resettlement effort, and published *The Interesting Narrative of the Life of Olaudah Equiano, or Gustavus Vassa, the African, Written by Himself* (1789). Exceedingly popular, this book went through many editions in England and America. In 1792 Equiano married Susanna Cullen. Their only child died less than three months after her father, probably in 1801.

Equiano's *Narrative* is the most important predecessor of nineteenth-century slave narratives, which provided materials for white abolitionist authors, such as Harriet Beecher Stowe, and helped create a literary genre that influenced many African-American authors, including Booker T. Washington, Richard Wright, Ralph Ellison, and Toni Morrison. Widening the range of American literature, the slave narrative and its recent fictional offspring have promoted black self-expression, demonstrated black creativity, and built black self-respect. Yet, with its memorable accounts of African, Caribbean, American, and European cultures, of Equiano's adventures, and of slave suffering and religious decision, the *Narrative* is important in its own right. With its emphasis on moral improvement and financial progress à la Benjamin Franklin, its emphasis on religious conversion à la

Jonathan Edwards, and its emphasis on the evils of oppression à la Thomas Jefferson, Equiano's *Narrative* is an unforgettable portrait of an interestingly American mind.

Suggested Readings: *The Interesting Narrative*, ed. P. Edwards, 1969. *Great Slave Narratives*, ed. A. Bontemps, 1969. M. Starkey, *Striving to Make It My Home*, 1964. F. D. Adams and B. Sanders, *Three Black Writers in Eighteenth-Century England*, 1971. V. Smith, *Self-Discovery and Authority in Afro-American Narrative*, 1987.

Text Used: *The Interesting Narrative of the Life of Olaudah Equiano, or Gustavus Vassa, the African*, 1814, in *The Classic Slave Narratives*, ed. H. L. Gates, Jr., 1987.

from   THE INTERESTING NARRATIVE OF THE LIFE OF OLAUDAH EQUIANO

Chapter II

I. I hope the reader will not think I have trespassed on his patience, in introducing myself to him with some account of the manners and customs of my country. They had been implanted in me with great care, and made an impression on my mind, which time could not erase, and which all adversity and variety of fortune I have since experienced, served only to rivet and record; for, whether the love of one's country be real or imaginary, a lesson of reason or an instinct of nature, I still look back with pleasure on the first scenes of my life, though that pleasure has been for the most part mingled with sorrow.

I have already acquainted the reader with the time and place of my birth. My father, besides many slaves, had a numerous family, of which seven lived to grow up, including myself and a sister, who was the only daughter. As I was the youngest of the sons, I became, of course, the greatest favourite with my mother, and was always with her, and she used to take particular pains to form my mind. I was trained up from my earliest years in the art of war: my daily exercise was shooting and throwing javelins; and my mother adorned me with emblems, after the manner of our greatest warriors. In this way I grew up till I was turned the age of eleven, when an end was put to my happiness in the following manner:—When the grown people in the neighbourhood were gone far in the fields to labour, the children generally assembled together in some of the neighbours' premises to play; and some of us often used to get up into a tree to look out for any assailant, or kidnapper, that might come upon us. For they sometimes took those opportunities of our parents' absence, to attack and carry off as many as they could seize. One day, as I was watching at the top of a tree in our yard, I saw one of those people come into the yard of our next neighbour but one, to kidnap, there being many stout young people in it. Immediately on this I gave the alarm of the rogue, and he was surrounded by the stoutest of them, who entangled him with cords, so that he could not escape till some of the grown people came and secured him.

II. But alas! ere long it was my fate to be thus attacked, and to be carried off, when none of the grown people were nigh. One day, when all our people were gone out to their work as usual, and only I and my sister were left to mind the house, two men and a woman got over our walls, and in a moment seized us both; and without giving us time to cry out, or to make any resistance, they stopped our mouths and ran off with us into the nearest wood. Here they tied our hands, and continued to carry us as far as they could, till night came on, when we reached a small house, where the robbers halted for refreshment and spent the night. We were then unbound, but were unable to take any food; and being quite overpowered by fatigue and grief, our only relief was some sleep, which allayed our misfortune for a short time. The next morning we left the house, and continued travelling all the day. For a long time we had kept the woods, but at last we came into a road which I believed I knew. I had now some hopes of being delivered; for we had advanced but a little way before I discovered some people at a distance, on which I began to cry out for their assistance; but my cries had no other effect than to make them tie me faster and stop my mouth; they then put me into a large sack. They also stopped my sister's mouth, and tied her hands; and in this manner we proceeded till we were out of sight of these people.

When we went to rest the following night, they offered us some victuals; but we refused it; and the only comfort we had was in being in one another's arms all that night, and bathing each other with tears. But alas! we were soon deprived of even the small comfort of weeping together. The next day proved one of greater sorrow than I had yet experienced; for my sister and I were then separated, while we lay clasped in each other's arms. It was in vain that we besought them not to part us; she was torn from me, and immediately carried away, while I was left in a state of distraction not to be described. I cried and grieved continually; and for several days did not eat any thing but what they forced into my mouth. At length, after many days' travelling, during which I had often changed masters, I got into the hands of a chieftain, in a pleasant country. This man had two wives and some children; and they all used me extremely well, and did all they could to comfort me; particularly the first wife, who was something like my mother. Although I was a great many days' journey from my father's house, yet these people spoke exactly the same language with us. This first master of mine, as I may call him, was a smith,[1] and my principal employment was working his bellows, which were the same kind as I had seen in my vicinity. They were in some respects not unlike the stoves here in gentlemen's kitchens; and were covered over with leather, and in the middle of that leather a stick was fixed, and a person stood up and worked it, in the same manner as is done to pump water out of a cask with a hand pump. I believe it was gold he worked, for it was of a lovely bright yellow colour, and was worn by the women on their wrists and ankles.

I was there, I suppose, about a month, and they at length used to trust me some little distance from the house. I employed this liberty in embracing every opportunity to inquire the way to my own home: and I also sometimes, for the same purpose, went with the maidens, in the cool of the evenings, to bring pitchers of water from the springs for the use of the house. I had also remarked where the sun rose in the morning, and set in the evening, as I had travelled along: and had observed that my father's house was towards the rising of the sun. I therefore determined to seize the first opportunity of making my escape, and to shape my course for that quarter; for I was quite oppressed and weighed down by grief after my mother and friends; and my love of liberty, ever great, was strengthened by the mortifying circumstance of not daring to eat with the free-born children, although I was mostly their companion.

III. While I was projecting my escape, one day an unlucky event happened, which quite disconcerted my plan, and put an end to my hopes. I used to be sometimes employed in assisting an elderly woman slave to cook and take care of the poultry: and one morning, while I was feeding some chickens, I happened to

---

[1] A goldsmith.

toss a small pebble at one of them, which hit in on the middle, and directly killed it. The old slave having soon after missed the chicken, inquired after it; and on my relating the accident (for I told her the truth, because my mother would never suffer me to tell a lie) she flew into a violent passion, threatened that I should suffer for it; and, my master being out, she immediately went and told her mistress what I had done. This alarmed me very much, and I expected an instant flogging, which to me was uncommonly dreadful; for I had seldom been beaten at home. I therefore resolved to fly; and accordingly I ran into a thicket that was hard by, and hid myself in the bushes. Soon afterwards my mistress and the slave returned, and, not seeing me, they searched all the house, but not finding me, and I not making answer when they called me, they thought I had run away, and the whole neighbourhood was raised in the pursuit of me.

In that part of the country, as well as in ours, the houses and villages were skirted with woods, or shrubberies, and the bushes were so thick that a man could readily conceal himself in them, so as to elude the strictest search. The neighbours continued the whole day looking for me, and several times many of them came within a few yards of the place where I lay hid. I expected every moment, when I heard a rustling among the trees, to be found out, and punished by my master. But they never discovered me, though they often were so near that I even heard their conjectures, as they were looking about for me; and I now learned from them, that any attempt to return home would be hopeless. Most of them supposed I had fled towards home; but the distance was so great, and the way so intricate, that they thought I could never reach it, and that I should be lost in the woods. When I heard this I was seized with a violent panic, and abandoned myself to despair. Night too began to approach, and aggravated all my fears. I had before entertained hopes of getting home and had determined when it should be dark to make the attempt; but I was now convinced it was fruitless, and began to consider that, if possibly I could escape all other animals, I could not those of the human kind; and that, not knowing the way, I must perish in the woods. Thus was I like the hunted deer:

> Ev'ry leaf, and ev'ry whisp'ring breath
> Convey'd a foe, and ev'ry foe a death.

I heard frequent rustlings among the leaves, and being pretty sure they were snakes, I expected every instant to be stung by them. This increased my anguish, and the horror of my situation became now quite insupportable. I at length quitted the thicket, very faint and hungry, for I had not eaten nor drunk any thing all the day. I crept to my master's kitchen, from whence I set out at first, which was an open shed, and laid myself down in the ashes with an anxious wish for death to relieve me from all my pains. I was scarcely awake in the morning, when the old woman slave, who was the first up, came to light the fire, and saw me in the fire place. She was very much surprised to see me, and could scarcely believe her own eyes. She now promised to intercede for me, and went for her master, who soon after came, and, having slightly reprimanded me, ordered me to be taken care of, and not ill treated.

IV. Soon after this my master's only daughter and child by his first wife, sickened and died, which affected him so much that for some time he was almost frantic, and really would have killed himself, had he not been watched and prevented. However, in a small time afterwards he recovered, and I was again sold. I was now carried to the left of the sun's rising, through many dreary wastes and dismal woods, amidst the hideous roaring of wild beasts. The people I was sold to used to carry me very often, when I was tired, either on their shoulders or on their backs. I saw many convenient well-built sheds along the road, at proper distances, to accommodate the merchants and travellers. They lie in those buildings along with their wives, who often accompany them: and they always go well armed.

From the time I left my own nation I always found somebody that understood me till I came to the sea coast. The languages of different nations did not totally differ, nor were they so copious as those of the Europeans, particularly the English. They were therefore easily learned; and, while I was journeying thus through Africa, I acquired two or three different tongues. In this manner I had been travelling for a considerable time, when one evening, to my great surprise, whom should I see brought to the house where I was, but my dear sister? As soon as she saw me she gave a loud shriek, and ran into my arms. I was quite overpowered: neither of us could speak; but for a considerable time, clung to each other in mutual embraces, unable to do any thing but weep. Our meeting affected all who saw us; and indeed I must acknowledge, in honour of those sable destroyers of human rights, that I never met with any ill treatment, or saw any offered to their slaves, except tying them, when necessary, to keep them running away.

When these people knew we were brother and sister, they indulged us to be together; and the man, to whom I supposed we belonged, lay with us, he in the middle, while she and I held one another by the hands across his breast all night; and thus for a while we forgot our misfortunes in the joy of being together. But even this small comfort was soon to have an end, for scarcely had the fatal morning appeared, when she was again torn from me for ever! I was now more miserable, if possible, than before. The small relief which her presence gave me from pain was gone, and the wretchedness of my situation was redoubled by my anxiety after her fate, and my apprehensions lest her sufferings should be greater than mine, when I could not be with her to alleviate them.

Yes, dear partner of all my childish sports! Sharer of my joys and sorrows; happy should I have ever esteemed myself to encounter every misery for you, and to procure your freedom by the sacrifice of my own! Though you were early forced from my arms, your image has been always rivetted in my heart, from which neither time nor fortune has been able to remove it: so that, while the thoughts of your sufferings have damped my prosperity, they have mingled with adversity and increased its bitterness. To that Heaven, which protects the weak from the strong, I commit the care of your innocence and virtues, if they have not already received their full reward, and if your youth and delicacy have not long since fallen victims to the violence of the African trader, the pestilential stench of a Guinea ship, the seasoning in the European colonies, or the lash and lust of a brutal and unrelenting overseer.

I did not long remain after my sister. I was again sold, and carried through a number of places, till, after travelling a considerable time, I came to a town called Tinmah, in the most beautiful country I had yet seen in Africa: It was extremely rich, and there were many rivulets which flowed through it, and supplied a large pond in the centre of the town, where the people washed. Here I first saw and tasted cocoa nuts, which I thought superior to any nuts I had ever tasted before; and the trees which were loaded, were also interspersed among the houses, which had commodious shades adjoining, and were in the same manner as ours, the insides being neatly plastered and whitewashed. Here I also saw and tasted, for the first time, sugar-cane. Their money consisted of little white shells, the size of the fingernail. I was sold for one hundred and seventy-two of these, by a merchant who lived at this place. I had been about two or three days at his house, when a wealthy widow, a neighbour of his came there one evening, and brought with her an only son, a young gentleman about my own age and size. Here they saw me; and, having taken a fancy to me, I was bought of the merchant, and went home with them. Her house and premises were situated close to one of those rivulets I have mentioned, and were the finest I ever saw in Africa: they were very extensive, and she had a number of slaves to attend her. The next day I was washed and perfumed, and when meal-time came, I was led into the presence of my mistress, and ate and drank before her with her son. This filled me with astonishment; and I could scarcely avoid expressing my surprise that the young gentleman should suffer me, who was bound, to eat with him who was free; and not only so, but that he would not at any time either eat or drink till I had taken first, because I was the eldest, which was agreeable to our custom. Indeed every thing here, and their treatment of me, made me forget that I was a slave. The language of these people resembled ours so nearly, that we understood each other perfectly. They had also the very same customs as we. There were likewise slaves daily to attend us, while my young master and I, with other boys, sported with our darts, and bows and arrows, as I had been used to do at home. In this resemblance to my former happy state, I passed about two months; and now I began to think I was to be adopted into the family, and was beginning to be reconciled to my situation, and to forget by degrees my misfortunes, when all at once the delusion vanished; for, without the least previous knowledge, one morning, early, while my dear master and companion was still asleep, I was awakened out of my reverie to fresh sorrow, and hurried away even amongst the uncircumcised.[2]

Thus, at the very moment I dreamed of the greatest happiness, I found myself most miserable; and it seemed as if fortune wished to give me this taste of joy only to render the reverse more poignant. The change I now experienced was as painful as it was sudden and unexpected. It was a change indeed from a state of bliss to a scene which is inexpressible by me, as it discovered to me an element I had never before beheld, and of which till then had no idea; and wherein such instances of hardship and cruelty continually occurred, as I can never reflect on but with horror.

V. All the nations and people I had hitherto passed through resembled our own in their manners, customs, and language: but I came at length to a country, the inhabitants of which differed from us in all these particulars. I was very much struck with this difference, especially when I came among a people who did not circumcise, and who ate without washing their hands. They cooked their provisions also in iron pots, and had European cutlasses and cross bows, which were unknown to us; and fought with their fists among themselves. Their women were not so modest as ours, for they ate, drank, and slept with their men. But, above all, I was amazed to see no sacrifices or offerings among them. In some of those places the people ornamented themselves with scars, and likewise filed their teeth very sharp. They sometimes wanted to ornament me in the same manner, but I would not suffer them; hoping that I might sometime be among a people who did not thus disfigure themselves, as I thought they did. At last I came to the banks of a large river, covered with canoes, in which the people appeared to live, with their

---

[2] Treated like a heathen.

household utensils, and provisions of all kinds. I was beyond measure astonished at this, as I had never before seen any water larger than a pond or a rivulet: and my surprise was mingled with no small fear when I was put into one of these canoes, and we began to paddle and move along the river. We continued going on thus till night; and when we came to land, and made fires on the banks, each family by themselves, some dragged their canoes on shore, others cooked in theirs, and laid in them all night. Those on the land had mats, of which they made tents, some in the shape of little houses: in these we slept: and after the morning meal, we embarked again, and proceeded as before. I was often very much astonished to see some of the women as well as the men, jump into the water, dive to the bottom, come up again, and swim about. Thus I continued to travel, both by land and by water, through different countries and various nations, till at the end of six or seven months after I had been kidnapped, I arrived at the sea coast.

It would be tedious and uninteresting to relate all the incidents which befell me during this journey, and which I have not yet forgotten, or to mention the various lands I passed through, and the manners and customs of the different people among whom I lived: I shall therefore only observe, that in all the places where I was, the soil was exceedingly rich; the pomkins, aedas,[3] plantains, yams, &c. &c. were in great abundance, and of incredible size. There were also large quantities of different gums, though not used for any purpose; and every where a great deal of tobacco. The cotton even grew quite wild; and there was plenty of red wood. I saw no mechanics whatever in all the way, except such as I have mentioned. The chief employment in all these countries was agriculture, and both the males and females, as with us, were brought up to it, and trained in the arts of war.

The first object that saluted my eyes when I arrived on the coast was the sea, and a slave ship, which was then riding at anchor, and waiting for its cargo. These filled me with astonishment, that was soon converted into terror, which I am yet at a loss to describe, and much more the then feelings of my mind when I was carried on board. I was immediately handled and tossed up to see if I was sound, by some of the crew; and I was now persuaded that I had got into a world of bad spirits, and that they were going to kill me. Their complexions too, differing so much from ours, their long hair, and the language they spoke, which was very different from any I had ever heard, united to confirm me in this belief. Indeed such were the horrors of my views and fears at the moment, that if ten thousand worlds had been my own, I would have freely parted with them all to have exchanged my condition with the meanest slave in my own country. When I looked round the ship too, and saw a large furnace or copper boiling and a multitude of black people, of every description, chained together, every one of their countenances expressing dejection and sorrow, I no longer doubted of my fate; and, quite overpowered with horror and anguish, I fell motionless on the deck, and fainted. When I recovered a little, I found some black people about me, who I believed were some of those who brought me on board, and had been receiving their pay: they talked to me in order to cheer me, but all in vain. I asked them if we were not to be eaten by those white men with horrible looks, red faces, and long hair. They told me I was not: and one of the crew brought me a small portion of spirituous liquor in a wine glass; but, being afraid of him, I would not take it out of his hand. One of the blacks therefore took it from him and gave it to me, and I took a little down my palate, which, instead of reviving me, as they thought

---

[3] Pumpkins; eddoes (edible tropical roots).

it would, threw me into the greatest consternation at the strange feeling it produced, having never tasted any such liquor before.

Soon after this the blacks who brought me on board went off, and left me abandoned to despair. I now saw myself deprived of all chance of returning to my native country, or even the least glimpse of gaining the shore, which I now considered as friendly; and I even wished for my former slavery, in preference to my present situation, which was filled with horrors of every kind, still heightened by my ignorance of what I was to undergo. I was not long suffered to indulge my grief. I was soon put down under the decks, and there I received such a salutation in my nostrils as I had never experienced in my life: so that, with the loathsomeness of the stench, and with my crying together, I became so sick and low that I was not able to eat, nor had I the least desire to taste any thing. I now wished for the last friend, death, to relieve me; but soon, to my grief, two of the white men offered me eatables; and, on my refusing to eat, one of them held me fast by the hands, and laid me across, I think, the windlass, and tied my feet, while the other flogged me severely. I had never experienced any thing of this kind before, and although, not being used to the water, I naturally feared that element the first time I saw it, yet nevertheless, could I have got over the nettings, I would have jumped over the side, but I could not; and besides the crew used to watch us very closely, who were not chained down to the decks, lest we should leap into the water. I have seen some of these poor African prisoners most severely cut for attempting to do so, and hourly whipped for not eating. This indeed was often the case with myself. In a little time after, amongst the poor chained men, I found some of my own nation, which in a small degree gave ease to my mind. I inquired of these what was to be done with us. They gave me to understand we were to be carried to these white people's country to work for them. I was then a little revived, and thought if it were no worse than working, my situation was not so desperate. But still I feared I should be put to death, the white people looked and acted, as I thought, in so savage a manner; for I had never seen among any people such instances of brutal cruelty: and this is not only shewn towards us blacks, but also to some of the whites themselves. One white man in particular I saw, when we were permitted to be on deck, flogged so unmercifully with a large rope near the foremast, that he died in consequence of it; and they tossed him over the side as they would have done a brute. This made me fear these people the more; and I expected nothing less than to be treated in the same manner. I could not help expressing my fearful apprehensions to some of my countrymen; I asked them if these people had no country, but lived in this hollow place, the ship. They told me they did not, but came from a distant one. 'Then,' said I, 'how comes it, that in all our country we never heard of them?' They told me, because they lived so very far off. I then asked, where their women were: had they any like themselves. I was told they had. 'And why,' said I, 'do we not see them?' They answered, because they were left behind. I asked how the vessel could go. They told me they could not tell; but that there was cloth put upon the masts by the help of the ropes I saw, and then the vessel went on; and the white men had some spell or magic they put in the water, when they liked, in order to stop the vessel. I was exceedingly amazed at this account, and really thought they were spirits. I therefore wished much to be from amongst them, for I expected they would sacrifice me; but my wishes were in vain, for we were so quartered that it was impossible for any of us to make our escape.

VI. While we stayed on the coast I was mostly on deck; and one day, to my great astonishment, I saw one of these vessels coming in with the sails up. As soon as the whites saw it, they gave a great shout, at which we were amazed; and the more so as the vessel appeared larger by approaching nearer. At last she came to an anchor in my sight, and when the anchor was let go, I and my countrymen who saw it, were lost in astonishment to observe the vessel stop, and were now convinced it was done by magic. Soon after this the other ship got her boats out, and they came on board of us, and the people of both ships seemed very glad to see each other. Several of the strangers also shook hands with us black people, and made motions with their hands, signifying, I suppose, we were to go to their country; but we did not understand them. At last, when the ship, in which we were, had got in all her cargo, they made ready with many fearful noises, and we were all put under deck, so that we could not see how they managed the vessel.

But this disappointment was the least of my grief. The stench of the hold, while we were on the coast, was so intolerably loathsome, that it was dangerous to remain there for any time, and some of us had been permitted to stay on the deck for the fresh air; but now that the whole ship's cargo were confined together, it became absolutely pestilential. The closeness of the place, and the heat of the climate, added to the number in the ship, being so crowded that each had scarcely room to turn himself, almost suffocated us. This produced copious perspirations, so that the air soon became unfit for respiration, from a variety of loathsome smells, and brought on a sickness among the slaves, of which many died, thus falling victims to the improvident avarice, as I may call it, of their purchasers. This deplorable situation was again aggravated by the galling of the chains, now become insupportable; and the filth of necessary tubs, into which the children often fell, and were almost suffocated. The shrieks of the women, and the groans of the dying, rendered it a scene of horror almost inconceivable. Happily, perhaps, for myself, I was soon reduced so low here that it was thought necessary to keep me almost continually on deck; and from my extreme youth, I was not put in fetters. In this situation I expected every hour to share the fate of my companions, some of whom were almost daily brought upon deck at the point of death, and I began to hope that death would soon put an end to my miseries. Often did I think many of the inhabitants of the deep much more happy than myself; I envied them the freedom they enjoyed, and as often wished I could change my condition for theirs. Every circumstance I met with served only to render my state more painful, and heighten my apprehensions and my opinion of the cruelty of the whites. One day they had taken a number of fishes; and when they had killed and satisfied themselves with as many as they thought fit, to our astonishment who were on deck, rather than give any of them to us to eat, as we expected, they tossed the remaining fish into the sea again, although we begged and prayed for some as well as we could, but in vain; and some of my countrymen, being pressed by hunger, took an opportunity, when they thought no one saw them, of trying to get a little privately; but were discovered, and the attempt procured for them some very severe floggings.

One day, when we had a smooth sea and moderate wind, two of my wearied countrymen, who were chained together, (I was near them at the time) preferring death to such a life of misery, somehow made through the nettings and jumped into the sea: immediately another quite dejected fellow, who on account of his illness was suffered to be out of irons also followed their example; and I believe many more would very soon have done the same, if they had not been prevented by the ship's crew, who were instantly alarmed. Those of us who were the most active were in a moment put down under the deck; and there was such a noise and confusion amongst the people of the ship as I never heard before, to stop her and get the boat out to go after the slaves. However, two of the wretches were drowned; but they got the other, and afterward flogged him unmercifully, for thus attempting to prefer death to slavery. In this manner we continued to undergo more hardships than I can now relate, hardships which are inseparable from this accursed trade. Many a time we were near suffocation from the want of fresh air, being deprived thereof for days together. This, and the stench of the necessary tubs, carried off many.

VII. During our passage I first saw flying fishes, which surprised me very much: they used frequently to fly across the ship, and many of them fell on the deck. I also now first saw the use of the quadrant. I had often with astonishment seen the mariners make observations with it, and I could not think what it meant. They at last took notice of my surprise: and one of them, willing to increase it, as well as to gratify my curiosity, made me one day look through it. The clouds appeared to me to be land, which disappeared as they passed along. This heightened my wonder; and I was now more persuaded than ever that I was in another world, and that every thing about me was magic. At last we came in sight of the island of Barbadoes, at which the whites on board gave a great shout, and made many signs of joy to us. We did not know what to think of this, but as the vessel drew nearer we plainly saw the harbour, and other ships of different kinds and sizes; and we soon anchored amongst them off Bridge Town. Many merchants and planters now came on board, though it was in the evening. They put us in separate parcels, and examined us attentively. They also made us jump, and pointed to the land, signifying we were to go there. We thought by this we should be beaten by these ugly men, as they appeared to us; and, when soon after we were all put down under the deck again, there was much dread and trembling among us, and nothing but bitter cries to be heard all the night from these apprehensions, insomuch that at last the white people got some old slaves from the land to pacify us. They told us we were not to be eaten, but to work, and were soon to go on land, where we should see many of our country people. This report eased us much; and, sure enough, soon after we landed, there came to us Africans of all languages.

We were conducted immediately to the merchant's yard, where we were all pent up together like so many sheep in a fold, without regard to sex or age. As every object was new to me, every thing I saw filled me with surprise. What struck me first was that the houses were built with bricks in stories,[4] and were in every other respect different from those I had seen in Africa; but I was still more astonished at seeing people on horseback. I did not know what this could mean; and indeed I thought these people full of nothing but magical arts. While I was in this astonishment one of my fellow prisoners spoke to a countryman of his about the horses, who said they were the same kind they had in their country. I understood them, though they were from a distant part of Africa, and I thought it odd I had not seen any horses there; but afterwards, when I came to converse with different Africans, I found they had many horses amongst them, and much larger than those I then saw.

We were not many days in the merchants' custody before we were sold after the usual manner, which is this:—On a signal given, such as the beat of a drum,

---

[4] The houses had two stories.

the buyers rush at once into the yard where the slaves are confined, and make choice of that parcel they like best. The noise and clamour with which this is attended, and the eagerness visible in the countenances of the buyers, serve not a little to increase the apprehensions of the terrified Africans, who may well be supposed to consider them the ministers of that destruction to which they think themselves devoted. In this manner, without scruple, are relations and friends separated, most of them never to see each other again. I remember in the vessel in which I was brought over in, in the man's apartment, there were several brothers, who, in the sale, were sold in different lots; and it was very moving on this occasion to see their distress and hear their cries at parting. O, ye nominal[5] Christians! might not an African ask you, "learned you this from your God, who says unto you, Do unto all men as you would men should do unto you? Is it not enough that we are torn from our country and friends, to toil for your luxury and lust of gain? Must every tender feeling be likewise sacrificed to your avarice? Are the dearest friends and relations now rendered more dear by their separation from the rest of their kindred, still to be parted from each other, and thus prevented from cheering the gloom of slavery, with the small comfort of being together, and mingling their sufferings and sorrows? Why are parents to lose their children, brothers their sisters, or husbands their wives? Surely this is a new refinement in cruelty, which, while it has no advantage to atone for it, thus aggravates distress, and adds fresh horrors even to the wretchedness of slavery."

1789

The Federalist
(1787–1788)

The drafters of the Articles of Confederation (America's first constitution), approved in 1776 by thirteen colonies determined to wage a successful war for independence against Britain, were hardly eager to create a strong central government for America, one that could substitute a republican tyranny for a monarchical one. Thus, they created only one institution—the Continental Congress—and denied this body the ability to control commerce or levy taxes, a prohibition that seriously undermined the war effort. After peace came in 1783, further problems arose as states placed tariffs on imports from other states, seized the ships of their neighbors, argued over boundaries, printed their own money, and otherwise behaved as tiny uncooperative nations. Conversely, the Continental Congress successfully concluded the war, negotiated a favorable peace treaty, and permitted the states a wide range of options in enacting a republican government.

In early 1787, after four years of discord, the Continental Congress endorsed the idea of a convention for the purpose of revising the Articles. Yet, the delegates who met in Philadelphia the following summer did more than revise. They drafted a constitution that entirely replaced the Articles, calling for a two-chambered national legislature with the

[5] In name only.

power to levy taxes, regulate commerce, and raise and support an army; a chief magistrate who could veto Congressional laws, make treaties, and command the army; and federal judges, appointed for life by the president. On September 20 the Continental Congress voted to send the Constitution to the states for ratification. Although the approval of only nine states was required, the refusal of any state to ratify would have greatly weakened the new nation.

Because New York City was then the nation's capital and a major commercial center, the vote in New York state was particularly important. One New York delegate to the Constitutional Convention and strong supporter of the Constitution, Alexander Hamilton, decided to influence its outcome. Born in the West Indies in 1757, Hamilton had come to America at age sixteen, studied at King's College (now Columbia University), and risen from the ranks to become Washington's aide-de-camp during the Revolution. In 1782, Hamilton was elected to Congress. A strong defender of vigorous, powerful, and even "splendid" government, Hamilton wanted to model America's political system after Britain's (with a president and senators serving for life, an executive with absolute veto, and the near elimination of state governments) but was willing to support the new Constitution as an improvement over the status quo.

An effective writer, Hamilton decided to promote the Constitution in New York City newspapers, enlisting the help of James Madison and John Jay. Born into an influential Virginia family in 1751, graduated from Princeton University, and elected to Congress in 1780, Madison was the most influential delegate at the Constitutional Convention. Less impressed with the idea of a glorious America than was Hamilton, Madison saw a strong national government as merely necessary to protect rights and ensure justice but agreed with Hamilton on the need for a new Constitution. Jay, a New Yorker born in 1745 and a King's College graduate, served as president of Congress in 1778 and helped to negotiate the peace treaty with Britain. Planning to participate fully in Hamilton's propaganda offensive, Jay was forced to withdraw from the project almost entirely because of illness.

Hamilton's first essay, "The Federalist No. 1," appeared in the *Independent Journal* in October 1787. Eighty-four more essays followed over the next ten months, printed two or three a week in up to four newspapers. All eighty-five were published as *The Federalist* in 1788. Hamilton wrote 51; Madison, 29; and Jay, 5. All three authors signed their essays 'Publius' to hide their identities, to present a united front, and to link their government-building enterprise with that of Publius Valerius, a consul who established a stable republic in Rome after the last Roman king was overthrown.

The "anti-Federalists," or opponents of the Constitution, believed in participatory democracy, preferred small nations of like-minded citizens, and opposed large governments with complex systems of representation. Conversely, the Federalists were committed to a "republican" system in which representatives rather than the people themselves governed. Federalists preferred leaders who were superior to their constituents in education and in status. They admired large nations in which governments arbitrated the diverse interests of heterogeneous populations. The Federalists made certain unflattering assumptions about human nature. In *The Federalist* No. 1 Hamilton insists that people are prone to "angry and malignant passions," particularly in times of political crisis. In Nos. 10 and 54, Madison views self-interested behavior—in individuals, political groups, and states—as equally inevitable. According to both writers, government's primary aim is to keep these negative human traits from threatening the public welfare.

The Federalist papers were hailed by Thomas Jefferson, and some later commentators have similarly placed them among the classics of political theory. Critics have found them vague, self-contradictory, and unenlightened in their acceptance of the notion of slaves as

```
         T  H  E

FEDERALIST:

      A   COLLECTION

          O  F

E      S      S      A      Y      S,

       WRITTEN IN FAVOUR OF THE

NEW   CONSTITUTION,

   AS AGREED UPON BY THE FEDERAL CONVENTION,
           SEPTEMBER 17, 1787.


        IN  TWO  VOLUMES.


            VOL.  I.


            NEW-YORK:

    PRINTED AND SOLD BY J. AND A. M'LEAN,
         No. 41, HANOVER-SQUARE,
            M,DCC,LXXXVIII.
```

The title page of
The Federalist.

subhuman. Clearly, the essays are historically important as the plainest and fullest expression of the founding fathers' interpretation of America's most basic political document. The essays also have obvious literary value. Through the learnedness, reasonableness, and civility of their discourse, *The Federalist* authors invented a new literary genre, raising the standards for journalistic political debate, lifting it above the name-calling and vituperation of earlier political writing. Through the vividness of their account of a balanced government, smoothly functioning within a complex society of happily competitive persons, *The Federalist* authors also prove that political writing can be as imaginative as other forms of literature.

Thanks in part to the power and persuasiveness of *The Federalist,* the eventual vote in the New York convention was 30 to 27 in favor of ratification. Hamilton, Madison, and Jay later became secretary of the treasury, president, and chief justice, respectively, of the nation they helped to create. Partly because of the *Federalist* authors' willingness to build into their political system a capacity for change, that nation has continued to function—much as they imagined—for more than two hundred years.

Suggested Readings: *The Federalist,* ed. I. Kramnick, 1987. G. Wood, *The Creation of the American Republic, 1776-1787,* 1972. H. J. Storing, *What the Anti-Federalists Were For,* 1981. A. Furtwangler, *The Authority of Publius,* 1984.

Text Used: *The Federalist,* ed. B. F. Wright, 1961.

from   THE FEDERALIST

Number 1: Introduction

[*by Alexander Hamilton*]

To the People of the State of New York:

After an unequivocal experience of the inefficiency of the subsisting[1] federal government, you are called upon to deliberate on a new Constitution for the United States of America. The subject speaks its own importance; comprehending in its consequences nothing less than the existence of the UNION, the safety and welfare of the parts of which it is composed, the fate of an empire in many respects the most interesting in the world. It has been frequently remarked that it seems to have been reserved to the people of this country, by their conduct and example, to decide the important question, whether societies of men are really capable or not of establishing good government from reflection and choice, or whether they are forever destined to depend for their political constitutions on accident and force. If there be any truth in the remark, the crisis at which we are arrived may with propriety be regarded as the era in which that decision is to be made; and a wrong election of the part we shall act may, in this view, deserve to be considered as the general misfortune of mankind.

This idea will add the inducements of philanthropy to those of patriotism, to heighten the solicitude which all considerate and good men must feel for the event. Happy will it be if our choice should be directed by a judicious estimate of our true interests, unperplexed and unbiased by considerations not connected with the public good. But this is a thing more ardently to be wished than seriously to be expected. The plan offered to our deliberations affects too many particular interests, innovates upon too many local institutions, not to involve in its discussion a variety of objects foreign to its merits, and of views, passions and prejudices little favorable to the discovery of truth.

Among the most formidable of the obstacles which the new Constitution will have to encounter may readily be distinguished the obvious interest of a certain class of men in every State to resist all changes which may hazard a diminution of the power, emolument, and consequence of the offices they hold under the State establishments; and the perverted ambition of another class of men, who will either hope to aggrandize themselves by the confusions of their country, or will flatter themselves with fairer prospects of elevation from the subdivision of the empire into several partial confederacies than from its union under one government.

It is not, however, my design to dwell upon observations of this nature. I am well aware that it would be disingenuous to resolve indiscriminately the opposition of any set of men (merely because their situations might subject them to suspicion) into interested or ambitious views. Candor will oblige us to admit that even such men may be actuated by upright intentions; and it cannot be doubted that much of the opposition which has made its appearance, or may hereafter make its appearance, will spring from sources, blameless at least, if not respect-

[1] Present.

able—the honest errors of minds led astray by preconceived jealousies and fears. So numerous indeed and so powerful are the causes which serve to give a false bias to the judgment, that we, upon many occasions, see wise and good men on the wrong as well as on the right side of questions of the first magnitude to society. This circumstance, if duly attended to, would furnish a lesson of moderation to those who are ever so much persuaded of their being in the right in any controversy. And a further reason for caution, in this respect, might be drawn from the reflection that we are not always sure that those who advocate the truth are influenced by purer principles than their antagonists. Ambition, avarice, personal animosity, party opposition, and many other motives not more laudable than these, are apt to operate as well upon those who support as those who oppose the right side of a question. Were there not even inducements to moderation, nothing could be more ill-judged than that intolerant spirit which has, at all times, characterized political parties. For in politics, as in religion, it is equally absurd to aim a making proselytes by fire and sword. Heresies in either can rarely be cured by persecution.

And yet, however just these sentiments will be allowed to be, we have already sufficient indications that it will happen in this as in all former cases of great national discussion. A torrent of angry and malignant passions will be let loose. To judge from the conduct of the opposite parties, we shall be led to conclude that they will mutually hope to evince the justness of their opinions, and to increase the number of their converts by the loudness of their declamations and the bitterness of their invectives. An enlightened zeal for the energy and efficiency of government will be stigmatized as the offspring of a temper fond of despotic power and hostile to the principles of liberty. An overscrupulous jealousy of danger to the rights of the people, which is more commonly the fault of the head than of the heart, will be represented as mere pretence and artifice, the stale bait for popularity at the expense of the public good. It will be forgotten, on the one hand, that jealousy is the usual concomitant of love, and that the noble enthusiasm of liberty is apt to be infected with a spirit of narrow and illiberal distrust. On the other hand, it will be equally forgotten that the vigor of government is essential to the security of liberty; that, in the contemplation of a sound and well-informed judgment, their interest can never be separated; and that a dangerous ambition more often lurks behind the specious mask of zeal for the rights of the people than under the forbidding appearance of zeal for the firmness and efficiency of government. History will teach us that the former has been found a much more certain road to the introduction of despotism than the latter, and that of those men who have overturned the liberties of republics, the greatest number have begun their career by paying an obsequious court to the people; commencing demagogues, and ending tyrants.

In the course of the preceding observations, I have had an eye, my fellow-citizens, to putting you upon your guard against all attempts, from whatever quarter, to influence your decision in a matter of the utmost moment to your welfare, by any impressions other than those which may result from the evidence of truth. You will, no doubt, at the same time, have collected from the general scope of them, that they proceed from a source not unfriendly to the new Constitution. Yes, my countrymen, I own to you that, after having given it an attentive consideration, I am clearly of opinion it is your interest to adopt it. I am convinced that this is the safest course for your liberty, your dignity, and your happiness. I affect not reserves which I do not feel. I will not amuse you with an appearance of deliberation when I have decided. I frankly acknowledge to you my convictions, and I will freely lay before you the reasons on which they are founded. The consciousness of good intentions disdains ambiguity. I shall not, however, multiply professions on this head. My motives must remain in the depository of my own breast. My arguments will be open to all, and may be judged of by all. They shall at least be offered in a spirit which will not disgrace the cause of truth.

I propose, in a series of papers, to discuss the following interesting particulars: — *The utility of the UNION to your political prosperity — The insufficiency of the present Confederation to preserve that Union — The necessity of a government at least equally energetic with the one proposed, to the attainment of this object —The conformity of the proposed Constitution to the true principles of republican government — Its analogy to your own State constitution — and lastly, The additional security which its adoption will afford to the preservation of that species of government, to liberty, and to property.*

In the progress of this discussion I shall endeavor to give a satisfactory answer to all the objections which shall have made their appearance, that may seem to have any claim to your attention.

It may perhaps be thought superfluous to offer arguments to prove the utility of the UNION, a point, no doubt, deeply engraved on the hearts of the great body of the people in every State, and one, which it may be imagined, has no adversaries. But the fact is, that we already hear it whispered in the private circles of those who oppose the new Constitution, that the thirteen States are of too great extent for any general system, and that we must of necessity resort to separate confederacies of distinct portions of the whole.[2] This doctrine will, in all probability, be gradually propagated, till it has votaries enough to countenance an open avowal of it. For nothing can be more evident, to those who are able to take an enlarged view of the subject, than the alternative of an adoption of the new Constitution or a dismemberment of the Union. It will therefore be of use to begin by examining the advantages of that Union, the certain evils, and the probable dangers, to which every State will be exposed from its dissolution. This shall accordingly constitute the subject of my next address.

PUBLIUS[3]

NUMBER 10: THE SIZE AND VARIETY OF THE UNION AS A CHECK ON FACTION

[by James Madison]

To the People of the State of New York:

Among the numerous advantages promised by a well-constructed Union, none deserves to be more accurately developed than its tendency to break and control the violence of faction. The friend of popular governments never finds himself so much alarmed for their character and fate, as when he contemplates their propensity to this dangerous vice. He will not fail, therefore, to set a due value on any plan which, without violating the principles to which he is attached, provides a

---

[2] Publius's note: "The same idea, tracing the arguments to their consequences is held out in several of the late publications against the new Constitution."

[3] The pseudonym adopted by the *The Federalist* authors Hamilton, Madison, and Jay, whose identity was known to most eighteenth-century readers.

proper cure for it. The instability, injustice, and confusion introduced into the public councils, have, in truth, been the mortal diseases under which popular governments have everywhere perished; as they continue to be the favorite and fruitful topics from which the adversaries to liberty derive their most specious declamations. The valuable improvements made by the American constitutions on the popular models, both ancient and modern, cannot certainly be too much admired; but it would be an unwarrantable partiality, to contend that they have as effectually obviated the danger on this side, as was wished and expected. Complaints are everywhere heard from our most considerate and virtuous citizens, equally the friends of public and private faith, and of public and personal liberty, that our governments are too unstable, that the public good is disregarded in the conflicts of rival parties, and that measures are too often decided, not according to the rules of justice and the rights of the minor party, but by the superior force of an interested and overbearing majority. However anxiously we may wish that these complaints had no foundation, the evidence of known facts will not permit us to deny that they are in some degree true. It will be found, indeed, on a candid review of our situation, that some of the distresses under which we labor have been erroneously charged on the operation of our governments; but it will be found, at the same time, that other causes will not alone account for many of our heaviest misfortunes; and, particularly, for that prevailing and increasing distrust of public engagements, and alarm for private rights, which are echoed from one end of the continent to the other. These must be chiefly, if not wholly, effects of the unsteadiness and injustice with which a factious spirit has tainted our public administrations.

By a faction, I understand a number of citizens, whether amounting to a majority or minority of the whole, who are united and actuated by some common impulse of passion, or of interest, adverse to the rights of other citizens, or to the permanent and aggregate interests of the community.

There are two methods of curing the mischiefs of faction: the one, by removing its causes; the other, by controlling its effects.

There are again two methods of removing the causes of faction: the one, by destroying the liberty which is essential to its existence; the other, by giving to every citizen the same opinions, the same passions, and the same interests.

It could never be more truly said than of the first remedy, that it was worse than the disease. Liberty is to faction what air is to fire, an aliment[1] without which it instantly expires. But it could not be less folly to abolish liberty, which is essential to political life, because it nourishes faction, than it would be to wish the annihilation of air, which is essential to animal life, because it imparts to fire its destructive agency.

The second expedient is as impracticable as the first would be unwise. As long as the reason of man continues fallible, and he is at liberty to exercise it, different opinions will be formed. As long as the connection subsists between his reason and his self-love, his opinions and his passions will have a reciprocal influence on each other: and the former will be objects to which the latter will attach themselves. The diversity in the faculties of men, from which the rights of property originate, is not less an insuperable obstacle to a uniformity of interests. The protection of these faculties is the first object of government. From the protection of

---

[1] Nutriment.

different and unequal faculties of acquiring property, the possession of different degrees and kinds of property immediately results; and from the influence of these on the sentiments and views of the respective proprietors, ensues a division of the society into different interests and parties.

The latent causes of faction are thus sown in the nature of man; and we see them everywhere brought into different degrees of activity, according to the different circumstances of civil society. A zeal for different opinions concerning religion, concerning government, and many other points, as well of speculation as of practice; an attachment to different leaders ambitiously contending for preeminence and power; or to persons of other descriptions whose fortunes have been interesting to the human passions, have, in turn, divided mankind into parties, inflamed them with mutual animosity, and rendered them much more disposed to vex and oppress each other than to co-operate for their common good. So strong is this propensity of mankind to fall into mutual animosities, that where no substantial occasion presents itself, the most frivolous and fanciful distinctions have been sufficient to kindle their unfriendly passions and excite their most violent conflicts. But the most common and durable source of factions has been the various and unequal distribution of property. Those who hold and those who are without property have ever formed distinct interests in society. Those who are creditors, and those who are debtors, fall under a like discrimination. A landed interest, a manufacturing interest, a mercantile interest, a moneyed interest, with many lesser interests, grow up of necessity in civilized nations, and divide them into different classes, actuated by different sentiments and views. The regulation of these various and interfering interests forms the principal task of modern legislation, and involves the spirit of party and faction in the necessary and ordinary operations of the government.

No man is allowed to be a judge in his own cause, because his interest would certainly bias his judgment, and, not improbably, corrupt his integrity. With equal, nay with greater reason, a body of men are unfit to be both judges and parties at the same time; yet what are many of the most important acts of legislation, but so many judicial determinations, not indeed concerning the rights of single persons, but concerning the rights of large bodies of citizens? And what are the different classes of legislators but advocates and parties to the causes which they determine? Is a law proposed concerning private debts? It is a question to which the creditors are parties on one side and the debtors on the other. Justice ought to hold the balance between them. Yet the parties are, and must be, themselves the judges; and the most numerous party, or, in other words, the most powerful faction must be expected to prevail. Shall domestic manufactures be encouraged, and in what degree, by restrictions on foreign manufactures? are questions which would be differently decided by the landed and the manufacturing classes, and probably by neither with a sole regard to justice and the public good. The apportionment of taxes on the various descriptions of property is an act which seems to require the most exact impartiality; yet there is, perhaps, no legislative act in which greater opportunity and temptation are given to a predominant party to trample on the rules of justice. Every shilling with which they overburden the inferior number, is a shilling saved to their own pockets.

It is in vain to say that enlightened statesmen will be able to adjust these clashing interests, and render them all subservient to the public good. Enlightened statesmen will not always be at the helm. Nor, in many cases, can such an adjustment be made at all without taking into view indirect and remote considerations, which will rarely prevail over the immediate interest which one party may find in disregarding the rights of another or the good of the whole.

The inference to which we are brought is, that the *causes* of faction cannot be removed, and that relief is only to be sought in the means of controlling its *effects*.

If a faction consists of less than a majority, relief is supplied by the republican principle, which enables the majority to defeat its sinister views by regular vote. It may clog the administration, it may convulse the society; but it will be unable to execute and mask its violence under the forms of the Constitution. When a majority is included in a faction, the form of popular government, on the other hand, enables it to sacrifice to its ruling passion or interest both the public good and the rights of other citizens. To secure the public good and private rights against the danger of such a faction, and at the same time to preserve the spirit and the form of popular government, is then the great object to which our inquiries are directed. Let me add that it is the great desideratum[2] by which this form of government can be rescued from the opprobrium under which it has so long labored, and be recommended to the esteem and adoption of mankind.

By what means is this object attainable? Evidently by one of two only. Either the existence of the same passion or interest in a majority at the same time must be prevented, or the majority, having such coexistent passion or interest, must be rendered, by their number and local situation, unable to concert and carry into effect schemes of oppression. If the impulse and the opportunity be suffered to coincide, we well know that neither moral nor religious motives can be relied on as an adequate control. They are not found to be such on the injustice and violence of individuals, and lose their efficacy in proportion to the number combined together, that is, in proportion as their efficacy becomes needful.

From this view of the subject it may be concluded that a pure democracy, by which I mean a society consisting of a small number of citizens, who assemble and administer the government in person, can admit of no cure for the mischiefs of faction. A common passion or interest will, in almost every case, be felt by a majority of the whole; a communication and concert result from the form of government itself; and there is nothing to check the inducements to sacrifice the weaker party or an obnoxious individual. Hence it is that such democracies have ever been spectacles of turbulence and contention; have ever been found incompatible with personal security or the rights of property; and have in general been as short in their lives as they have been violent in their deaths. Theoretic politicians, who have patronized this species of government, have erroneously supposed that by reducing mankind to a perfect equality in their political rights, they would, at the same time, be perfectly equalized and assimilated in their possessions, their opinions, and their passions.

A republic, by which I mean a government in which the scheme of representation takes place, opens a different prospect, and promises the cure for which we are seeking. Let us examine the points in which it varies from pure democracy, and we shall comprehend both the nature of the cure and the efficacy which it must derive from the Union.

The two great points of difference between a democracy and a republic are: first, the delegation of the government, in the latter, to a small number of citizens elected by the rest; secondly, the greater number of citizens, and greater sphere of country, over which the latter may be extended.

---

[2] That which is desired or thought to be necessary.

The effect of the first difference is, on the one hand, to refine and enlarge the public views, by passing them through the medium of a chosen body of citizens, whose wisdom may best discern the true interest of their country, and whose patriotism and love of justice will be least likely to sacrifice it to temporary or partial considerations. Under such a regulation, it may well happen that the public voice, pronounced by the representatives of the people, will be more consonant to the public good than if pronounced by the people themselves, convened for the purpose. On the other hand, the effect may be inverted. Men of factious tempers, of local prejudices, or of sinister designs, may, by intrigue, by corruption, or by other means, first obtain the suffrages,[3] and then betray the interests, of the people. The question resulting is, whether small or extensive republics are more favorable to the election of proper guardians of the public weal;[4] and it is clearly decided in favor of the latter by two obvious considerations:

In the first place, it is to be remarked that, however small the republic may be, the representatives must be raised to a certain number, in order to guard against the cabals[5] of a few; and that, however large it may be, they must be limited to a certain number, in order to guard against the confusion of a multitude. Hence, the number of representatives in the two cases not being in proportion to that of the two constituents, and being proportionally greater in the small republic, it follows that, if the proportion of fit characters be not less in the large than in the small republic, the former will present a greater option, and consequently a greater probability of a fit choice.

In the next place, as each representative will be chosen by a greater number of citizens in the large than in the small republic, it will be more difficult for unworthy candidates to practise with success the vicious arts by which elections are too often carried; and the suffrages of the people being more free, will be more likely to centre in men who possess the most attractive merit and the most diffusive and established characters.

It must be confessed that in this, as in most other cases, there is a mean, on both sides of which inconveniences will be found to lie. By enlarging too much the number of electors, you render the representative too little acquainted with all their local circumstances and lesser interests; as by reducing it too much, you render him unduly attached to these, and too little fit to comprehend and pursue great and national objects. The federal Constitution forms a happy combination in this respect; the great and aggregate interests being referred to the national, the local and particular to the State legislatures.

The other point of difference is, the greater number of citizens and extent of territory which may be brought within the compass of republican than of democratic government; and it is this circumstance principally which renders factious combinations less to be dreaded in the former than in the latter. The smaller the society, the fewer probably will be the distinct parties and interests composing it; the fewer the distinct parties and interests, the more frequently will a majority be found of the same party; and the smaller the number of individuals composing a majority, and the smaller the compass within which they are placed, the most easily will they concert and execute their plans of oppression. Extend the sphere, and you take in a greater variety of parties and interests; you make it less probable that a majority of the whole will have a common motive to invade the rights of other citizens; or if such a common motive exists, it will be more difficult for all

---

[3] Votes.   [4] Well-being.   [5] Plots.

who feel it to discover their won strength, and to act in unison with each other. Besides other impediments, it may be remarked that, where there is a consciousness of unjust or dishonorable purposes, communication is always checked by distrust in proportion to the number whose concurrence is necessary.

Hence, it clearly appears, that the same advantage which a republic has over a democracy, in controlling the effects of faction, is enjoyed by a large over a small republic, — is enjoyed by the Union over the States composing it. Does the advantage consist in the substitution of representatives whose enlightened views and virtuous sentiments render them superior to local prejudices and to schemes of injustice? It will not be denied that the representation of the Union will be most likely to possess these requisite endowments. Does it consist in the greater security afforded by a greater variety of parties, against the event of any one party being able to outnumber and oppress the rest? In an equal degree does the increased variety of parties comprised within the Union, increase this security? Does it, in fine,[6] consist in the greater obstacles opposed to the concert and accomplishment of the secret wishes of an unjust and interested majority? Here, again, the extent of the Union gives it the most palpable advantage.

The influence of factious leaders may kindle a flame within their particular States, but will be unable to spread a general conflagration through the other states. A religious sect may degenerate into a political faction in a part of the Confederacy; but the variety of sects dispersed over the entire face of it must secure the national councils against any danger from that source. A rage for paper money, for an abolition of debts, for an equal division of property, or for any other improper or wicked project, will be less apt to pervade the whole body of the Union than a particular member of it; in the same proportion as such a malady is more likely to taint a particular county or district, than an entire State.

In the extent and proper structure of the Union, therefore, we behold a republican remedy for the diseases most incident to republican government. And according to the degree of pleasure and pride we feel in being republicans, ought to be our zeal in cherishing the spirit and supporting the character of Federalists.

PUBLIUS

NUMBER 54: THE APPORTIONMENT OF REPRESENTATIVES AND OF TAXES

[by James Madison]

To the People of the State of New York:

The next view which I shall take of the House of Representatives relates to the apportionment of its members to the several States, which is to be determined by the same rule with that of direct taxes.

It is not contended that the number of people in each State ought not to be the standard for regulating the proportion of those who are to represent the people of each State. The establishment of the same rule for the apportionment of taxes will probably be as little contested; though the rule itself, in this case, is by no means founded on the same principle. In the former case, the rule is understood to refer to the personal rights of the people, with which it has a natural and universal

---

[6] In the end.

connection. In the latter, it has reference to the proportion of wealth, of which it is in no case a precise measure, and in ordinary cases a very unfit one. But notwithstanding the imperfection of the rule as applied to the relative wealth and contributions of the States, it is evidently the least objectionable among the practicable rules, and had too recently obtained the general sanction of America, not to have found a ready preference with the convention.

All this is admitted, it will perhaps be said; but does it follow, from an admission of numbers for the measure of representation, or of slaves combined with free citizens as a ratio of taxation, that slaves ought to be included in the numerical rule of representation? Slaves are considered as property, not as persons. They ought therefore to be comprehended in estimates of taxation which are founded on property, and to be excluded from representation which is regulated by a census of persons. This is the objection, as I understand it, stated in its full force. I shall be equally candid in stating the reasoning which may be offered on the opposite side.

"We subscribe to the doctrine," might one of our Southern brethren observe, "that representation relates more immediately to persons, and taxation more immediately to property, and we join in the application of this distinction to the case of our slaves. But we must deny the fact, that slaves are considered merely as property, and in no respect whatever as persons. The true state of the case is, that they partake of both these qualities: being considered by our laws, in some respects, as persons, and in other respects as property. In being compelled to labor, not for himself, but for a master; in being vendible by one master to another master; and in being subject at all times to be restrained in his liberty and chastised in his body, by the capricious will of another,—the slave may appear to be degraded from the human rank, and classed with those irrational animals which fall under the legal denomination of property. In being protected, on the other hand, in his life and in his limbs, against the violence of all others, even the master of his labor and his liberty; and in being punishable himself for all violence committed against others,—the slave is no less evidently regarded by the law as a member of the society, not as a part of the irrational creation; as a moral person, not as a mere article of property. The federal Constitution, therefore, decides with great propriety on the case of our slaves, when it views them in the mixed character of persons and of property. This is in fact their true character. It is the character bestowed on them by the laws under which they live; and it will not be denied, that these are the proper criterion; because it is only under the pretext that the laws have transformed the negroes into subjects of property, that a place is disputed them in the computation of numbers; and it is admitted, that if the laws were to restore the rights which have been taken away, the negroes could no longer be refused an equal share of representation with the other inhabitants.

"This question may be placed in another light. It is agreed on all sides, that numbers are the best scale of wealth and taxation, as they are the only proper scale of representation. Would the convention have been impartial or consistent, if they had rejected the slaves from the list of inhabitants, when the shares of representation were to be calculated, and inserted them on the lists when the tariff of contributions was to be adjusted? Could it be reasonably expected, that the Southern States would concur in a system, which considered their slaves in some degree as men, when burdens were to be imposed, but refused to consider them in the same light, when advantages were to be conferred? Might not some surprise also be expressed, that those who reproach the Southern States with the barbarous policy of considering as property a part of their human brethren, should themselves contend, that the government to which all the States are to be parties, ought to consider this unfortunate race more completely in the unnatural light of the property, than the very laws of which they complain?

"It may be replied, perhaps, that slaves are not included in the estimate of representatives in any of the States possessing them. They neither vote themselves nor increase the votes of their masters. Upon what principle, then, ought they to be taken into the federal estimate of representation? In rejecting them altogether, the Constitution would, in this respect, have followed the very laws which have been appealed to as the proper guide.

"This objection is repelled by a single observation. It is a fundamental principle of the proposed Constitution, that as the aggregate number of representatives allotted to the several States is to be determined by a federal rule, founded on the aggregate numbers of inhabitants, so the right of choosing this allotted number in each State is to be exercised by such part of the inhabitants as the State itself may designate. The qualifications on which the right of suffrage depend are not, perhaps, the same in any two States. In some of the States the difference is very material. In every State, a certain proportion of inhabitants are deprived of this right by the constitution of the State, who will be included in the census by which the federal Constitution apportions the representatives. In this point of view the Southern States might retort the complaint, by insisting that the principle laid down by the convention required that no regard should be had to the policy of particular States towards their own inhabitants; and consequently that the slaves, as inhabitants, should have been admitted into the census according to their full number, in like manner with other inhabitants, who, by the policy of other States, are not admitted to all the rights of citizens. A rigorous adherence, however, to this principle, is waived by those who would be gainers by it. All that they ask is that equal moderation be shown on the other side. Let the case of the slaves be considered, as it is in truth, a peculiar one. Let the compromising expedient of the Constitution be mutually adopted, which regards them as inhabitants, but as debased by servitude below the equal level of free inhabitants; which regards the *slave* as divested of two fifths of the *man*.

"After all, may not another ground be taken on which this article of the Constitution will admit of a still more ready defence? We have hitherto proceeded on the idea that representation related to persons only, and not at all to property. But is it a just idea? Government is instituted no less for protection of the property, than of the persons, of individuals. The one as well as the other therefore, may be considered as represented by those who are charged with the government. Upon this principle it is, that in several of the States, and particularly in the State of New York, one branch of the government is intended more especially to be the guardian of property, and is accordingly elected by that part of the society which is most interested in this object of government. In the federal Constitution, this policy does not prevail. The rights of property are committed into the same hands with the personal rights. Some attention ought, therefore, to be paid to property in the choice of those hands.

"For another reason, the votes allowed in the federal legislature to the people of each State, ought to bear some proportion to the comparative wealth of the States. States have not, like individuals, an influence over each other, arising from superior advantages of fortune. If the law allows an opulent citizen but a single vote in the choice of his representative, the respect and consequence which he derives from his fortunate situation very frequently guide the votes of others to the objects of his choice; and through this imperceptible channel the rights of property are conveyed into the public representation. A State possesses no such influence over other States. It is not probable that the richest State in the Confederacy will ever influence the choice of a single representative in any other State. Nor will the representatives of the larger and richer States possess any other advantage in the federal legislature, over the representatives of other States, than what may result from their superior number alone. As far, therefore, as their superior wealth and weight may justly entitle them to any advantage, it ought to be secured to them by a superior share of representation. The new Constitution is, in this respect, materially different from the existing Confederation, as well as from that of the United Netherlands, and other similar confederacies. In each of the latter, the efficacy of the federal resolutions depends on the subsequent and voluntary resolutions of the states composing the union. Hence the states, though possessing an equal vote in the public councils, have an unequal influence, corresponding with the unequal importance of these subsequent and voluntary resolutions. Under the proposed Constitution, the federal acts will take effect without the necessary intervention of the individual States. They will depend merely on the majority of votes in the federal legislature, and consequently each vote, whether proceeding from a large or smaller State, or a State more or less wealthy or powerful, will have an equal weight and efficacy: in the same manner as the votes individually given in a State legislature, by the representatives of unequal counties or other districts, have each a precise equality of value and effect; or if there be any difference in the case, it proceeds from the difference in the personal character of the individual representative, rather than from any regard to the extent of the district from which he comes."

Such is the reasoning which an advocate for the Southern interests might employ on this subject; and although it may appear to be a little strained in some points, yet, on the whole, I must confess that it fully reconciles me to the scale of representation which the convention have established.

In one respect, the establishment of a common measure for representation and taxation will have a very salutary effect. As the accuracy of the census to be obtained by the Congress will necessarily depend, in a considerable degree, on the disposition, if not on the coöperation, of the States, it is of great importance that the States should feel as little bias as possible, to swell or to reduce the amount of their numbers. Were their share of representation alone to be governed by this rule, they would have an interest in exaggerating their inhabitants. Were the rule to decide their share of taxation alone, a contrary temptation would prevail. By extending the rule to both objects, the States will have opposite interests, which will control and balance each other, and produce the requisite impartiality.

PUBLIUS

1787, 1787–1788

LATE 18TH-CENTURY POETRY

In Royall Tyler's play *The Contrast* (1787), the unlearned bumpkin Jonathan admits to his would-be love that he cannot woo her with high-flown verses; the only poems he knows are the Psalms and "Yankee Doodle." We tend to assume that

Jonathan's ignorance represents a widespread disinterest in poetry in eighteenth-century America. Yet, poetry was then a highly respected form of literature. Not only was poetry an accepted genre in which to argue philosophical, theological, and political points, versification was an essential skill of the educated, required of all college students. However crude Jonathan's poetic recitations were, *The Contrast* began, in the accepted mode of eighteenth-century drama, with an elegant prologue in heroic couplets (rhymed pairs of lines), delivered by the actor who played the unversed Jonathan.

The importance of poetry in the Revolutionary period is disguised in part by our modern desire to differentiate poetry from prose. In the eighteenth century such distinctions were less important, and many works now labeled prose include poetic passages. Theater dialogue regularly incorporated verse. Comedies typically alternated scenes of poetry and of prose, whereas heroic dramas such as those of Mercy Otis Warren and William Dunlap, modeled on the great Elizabethan tragedies, were written entirely in blank verse. Similarly, most of the novels of Revolutionary time contained poetry, either as chapter epigraphs or within the narrative itself. And though much of the novels' verse was drawn from English sources, some was American. For example, the title page of Susanna Rowson's *Charlotte Temple* (1794) quotes one of Rowson's earlier ballads. William Hill Brown's *The Power of Sympathy* (1789) includes not only numerous passages of original poetry but an extended defense of the way in which poetry "enlarges and strengthens the mind, refines the taste and improves the judgment," especially of "ladies."

Nonfiction prose incorporated poetry as regularly as did fiction. Even so prosaic a soul as Benjamin Franklin felt the need to versify. When Franklin was only sixteen, his character Silence Dogood attacked the Puritan tradition of writing elegies by producing her own satirical versions of their funeral poetry. Dogood's satire was directed against the content, not the form, of Puritan poetry. Franklin's later persona, Poor Richard, employed the balanced cadences of poetry. Most of his sayings—such as the celebrated "Early to bed and early to rise . . ."—were constructed explicitly as poetic couplets or triplets.

There was no lack of verse in the eighteenth century. The conceptual difficulty began when poetry began to be separated from prose as an independent genre. The very popularity of poetry made it a less profitable form of writing than prose; with so much verse available, poets, unlike prose writers, were rarely paid for newspaper publication of their work. Moreover, a poet's market tended to be very localized and class-specific. Such writers as Joel Barlow and Robert Treat Paine, Jr., who were able to realize some profits on their poetry, did so largely through pre-selling the work on subscription to a small circle of highly supportive friends. Unintentionally, such narrow marketing fostered an elitism at odds with the generally democratic thrust of the poets' messages.

The necessary limitations surrounding distribution were compounded by the more subtle limitations of the literary form itself. The reigning poetic genres in this so-called neoclassical period were the epic, the satire, the pastoral (a poem about rural life), and the prospect poem (combining naturalistic description and nationalistic prophecy). The preferred meter was the "closed" heroic couplet, two lines of rhyming iambic pentameter (five bisyllabic metrical units per line) generally expressing a single idea. The preeminent masters of these forms were the English writers Alexander Pope and Samuel Johnson. However, the rhetorical symmetry and metrical regularity most admired in their aristocratic, neoclassical poetry was not always appropriate for the anti-establishment sentiments of the American Revolution. Pope's preference for rules over inspiration did not answer well the poetic needs of a youthful nation searching for identity.

Some American poetry of the Revolutionary period resolved this tension between aristocratic form and democratic content conservatively by ridiculing the limitations of American culture. These satires from a loosely interconnected group of poets known as the Connecticut Wits culminated in the collaborative *The Anarchiad* (1786–1787), a multifaceted critique of the postwar period, patterned on Pope's angry *The Dunciad* (1728). But the conservative thrust of the Wits was most clearly (and successfully) represented in the burlesques of John Trumbull. Trumbull's *The Progress of Dulness* (1772–1773) exposed the inadequacies of American education. His later *M'Fingal* (1782) presented itself as a political account of the conflict with England. Yet, apart from mildly ridiculing Tory rhetoric, Trumbull's tone was far from the incendiarism of Thomas Paine's *Common Sense* (1776) and genial enough to please both sides in the Revolution.

The conservative irony of American satires masked more progressive elements in their social vision. If in his burlesques Trumbull minimized the achievements of the new nation, fellow Wits Timothy Dwight and Joel Barlow expressed both support for the age's political programs and faith in literature's ability to accelerate social change. Dwight's Calvinism, a legacy from his grandfather Jonathan Edwards, occasionally seemed old-fashioned, even gloomy. In Dwight's *The Triumph of Infidelity* (1788) Satan reviews in placid heroic couplets the westward progress not of civilization but of ignorance and irreligion. Dwight's religious rhetoric generally serves more positively as a bridge between America's Puritan past and its republican future. In *The Conquest of Canaan* (1785) Dwight retells the Biblical story of Joshua's military victory as an allegory of the American Revolution, suggesting both the promise of America and its potential for backsliding and failure. In *Greenfield Hill* (1794) Dwight, finding in America a natural fecundity absent in the "deserted" English villages, prophesies an economic and spiritual utopia, revising his skeptical predictions from the Satanic "Triumph."

The epic visions of Joel Barlow similarly combine optimistic prophecy and social critique without resolving the tensions between the two. Barlow's major poetic work, *The Vision of Columbus* (1787), revised as *The Columbiad* (1807), is an account of contemporary American culture. *Vision* relates an angel's prophecy to an imprisoned Columbus. The poem's contradictory mixture of Puritan imagery and social activism marks Barlow's youthful attraction to religion and politics. His return to these issues after his conversion from piety to the secular philosophies of the Enlightenment eliminates the narrative contradictions without improving the poetry. Although structurally more complex than *Vision,* the expanded *Columbiad* courted a cosmopolitan readership only by sacrificing the symbolic richness of the provincial version. The aesthetic failure of this revision suggests the difficulty with which Barlow imagined his audience. He knew his American readers to be in

John Singleton Copley's Watson and the Shark *(1778) displays the grandiose manner and balanced neoclassical composition that characterize the efforts of poets such as Joel Barlow to create American epics. (Museum of Fine Arts, Boston)*

some senses "vulgar" and understood his own share in that vulgarity as both a source of power and something to be overcome. Barlow never resolved these dilemmas of audience or narrative voice; only in his brief mock-epic *The Hasty Pudding* (1796) was he able to combine successfully the sophisticated diction of Enlightenment rhetoric and a truly American celebration.

In their elevation of science and lawfulness, Enlightenment thinkers typically dismissed poetic imagination as mere "fancy" and saw the mind as a passive processor of sensations. Even the Scottish common sense philosophers, who saw imagination as more than delusion, described the operation of imagination via a mechanistic rhetoric. Such a mechanistic theory of knowledge handicapped even the most imaginative American poet of the generation, Philip Freneau. More technically adept and politically engaged than the Wits, Freneau experimented with a wide variety of poetic forms and topics. His gentle lyrics in such poems as "The Wild Honey Suckle" (1786) anticipate romantic nature poetry. Equally powerful are his topical works such as the antislavery address "To Sir Toby" (1792) or the sea allegory *The Hurricane* (1786), in which a realistic description of a storm images widespread social problems. Even his explicitly propagandistic works of the late 1790s and 1800s display poetic invention and typically caustic wit, as in "To a New England Poet" (1832), a cutting attack on Washington Irving's Anglophilia. Though able to reconcile the poet's private and public roles more skillfully than the Wits, Freneau was, like them, unable to believe in the creative power of literature. In "To an Author" (1788) Freneau complains of the bleakness of American culture, in which reason overpowers "lovely Fancy." Yet, his own failure to attribute to poetry any more forceful characteristic than "loveliness" insured that imagination as "fancy" would remain subordinate to reason.

The sole Revolutionary poet to suspect that poetry's persuasive power rests as fully in its form as in its argument was ironically the one who profited least from the Revolution's liberating power—the black female poet Phillis Wheatley. African-American poetry did not begin with Wheatley. She was preceded in the eighteenth century by the public poets Lucy Terry and Jupiter Hammons; and the anonymous poetry of folk tales and spirituals was fairly extensive when Wheatley began writing in the 1760s. Her importance rests instead in her subtle intertwining of the themes of political liberation, racial and sexual subordination, and aesthetic creativity. Required to adapt her beliefs for an audience sensitive to the needs of neither women nor blacks, Wheatley's protests were carefully muted. Yet, in such poems as "America" (1768, unpublished) or "To the Right Honorable William, Earl of Dartmouth" (1773), Wheatley's comparison of political liberty to her own youth in Africa implies that England's mistreatment of the colonies was not the only tyranny.

In striking anticipation of romanticism, Wheatley's poem "On Imagination" (1773), unlike Freneau's "The Power of Fancy" (1770), acknowledges the creative potential of the mind. For Wheatley imagination was itself divine. Like all Revolutionary poets, she was limited by her environment—by discriminatory presuppositions about race and gender and more generally about the social role of poets. In her ability to stretch these bounds, Wheatley epitomized the weaknesses and strengths of eighteenth-century poetry in America. The poets of the American Revolution sought to express through traditional forms an antitraditional message: to offer in aristocratic diction a call to liberation, and in symbolic discourse a practical social influence. Even the most successful of these poets realized their goals only partly and sporadically. In their failure as fully as in their triumphs, these founders of our national poetic tradition capture the transitional character of this initial stage of American writing.

Phillis Wheatley
(1753–1784)

In her short life, Phillis Wheatley, the first published African-American poet, received both national and international recognition. As a frail child of about seven, Phillis arrived in Boston from Africa in 1761, wrapped, so the story goes, in dirty carpet, missing her front teeth, and speaking not a word of English. According to one account she was purchased "for a trifle" by Susannah Wheatley, the wife of the prosperous tailor John Wheatley. The Wheatleys were part of a trans-Atlantic Methodist reform movement that was deeply skeptical of slavery. Some sixteen months after her arrival, Phillis (the name given to her by the Wheatleys) had learned to read and write English, was reading the Bible and English literature, and had begun to study Latin—all at a time when most white women were unable to read or write.

Provided with a fire and a candle in her room so that she could compose her thoughts even at night, Phillis concentrated on writing poetry. Fostering her talent, the Wheatleys gave her light domestic duties and encouraged her to read her work to their circle of acquaintances. Boston society soon recognized her as a phenomenon, a child prodigy, a slave with extraordinary creativity and intellectual gifts.

In 1770, at age seventeen, Wheatley published the elegy "On the Death of Mr. George Whitefield," about the noted Methodist minister who had earned international fame for his fiery preaching. The poem appeared in numerous editions both in the colonies and in London. It attracted the attention of the countess of Huntingdon, leader of the Methodists in London and patron of Rev. Whitefield. It was through her influence that Olaudah Equiano was able to purchase his freedom. By invitation of the countess, Wheatley traveled to London in June 1773. There she came to be known as the "Sable Muse" and was among such notables as Benjamin Franklin and the lord mayor of London, who gave her a volume of John Milton's *Paradise Lost* (1667). At age twenty Wheatley published *Poems on Various Subjects, Religious and Moral* (1773) in London. This collection of her poems was prefaced by an attestation from eighteen leaders of Massachusetts, including Governor Thomas Hutchinson and John Hancock, that this was indeed the work of a female slave who but a few years earlier had been "an uncultivated barbarian from Africa."

Wheatley returned to the colonies in July 1773 to find Susannah Wheatley dying and the people of Boston preparing for revolution. At the request of the poet's "friends" in England, John Wheatley freed her. Soon Boston was under siege, and the patriot army, led by General George Washington, had camped at Cambridge. Firmly on the patriot side, Phillis Wheatley sent Washington the laudatory poem "To His Excellency General Washington" in late 1775. After a few months, the twenty-three-year-old poet was invited to his headquarters, where she received the "polite attention" of the general and of other officers.

Her career as a prodigy soon came to an end. The country, turning its attention to war, had little interest in poetry. With the death of John Wheatley in 1778 and of his daughter shortly thereafter, the poet was left very much on her own. Her life changed abruptly and for the worse. In April of 1778, Phillis married John Peters, a freed man about whom little is known for certain, except that he and Phillis lived in poverty. In 1779 Phillis Wheatley Peters tried to publish a second volume of verse but did not succeed. Meanwhile, she bore two children who died in infancy and tried to run a small school. When that failed, she had to earn her own living (Peters had been imprisoned for nonpayment of debts) in a boarding house for African Americans. With her third child, a mortally ill infant, at her side, Wheatley died at age thirty-one in 1784. An unknown observer recorded that she "was carried to her last earthly resting-place, without one of the friends of her prosperity to follow her, and without a stone to mark her grave." Her prized volume of *Paradise Lost* was sold to pay John Peters's debts and is now in the possession of Harvard University.

Within her lifetime Phillis Wheatley had published one book of verse, over fifty other pieces of poetry, and some prose in broadsides, pamphlets, and newspapers in America and abroad. Most of her poems are elegies to well-known contemporaries or personal acquaintances, philosophical poems, translations and biblical paraphrases, and poems on subjects taken from the Bible. They are neoclassical in form and express the poet's deep piety. Unavailable immediately after her death, her work was reprinted by abolitionists in

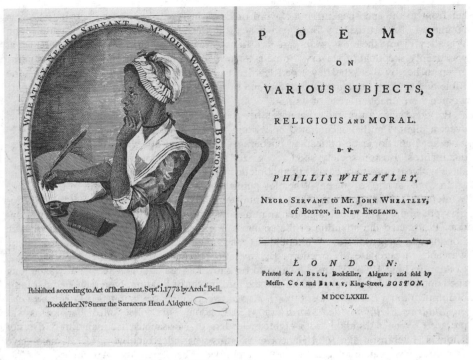

P O E M S

O N

VARIOUS SUBJECTS,

RELIGIOUS AND MORAL.

B Y

PHILLIS WHEATLEY,

NEGRO SERVANT to Mr. JOHN WHEATLEY,
of BOSTON, in NEW ENGLAND.

L O N D O N:
Printed for A. BELL, Bookseller, Aldgate; and sold by
Messrs. COX and BERRY, King-Street, BOSTON.

M DCC LXXIII.

Published according to Act of Parliament, Sept. 1. 1773 by Arch.d Bell.
Bookseller No. 8 near the Saracens Head Aldgate.

The frontispiece and title page of Phillis Wheatley's Poems.

the 1830s. Since then, her *Poems* has been reprinted more than two dozen times, and her poetry is regularly anthologized.

While acknowledging her achievement as remarkable, many critics have observed that much of Wheatley's poetry is conventional and derived from other sources, reflecting the middle-class values of the Wheatleys. For many, her work is evidence of unfulfilled potential; this female African-American slave in Revolutionary Boston, writing for a predominantly white audience, may not have had a chance to reach the full measure of her abilities.

Yet, Wheatley's work has much to offer. It commonly questions the assumptions of her society, especially in regard to slavery. In this respect she belongs with other colonial writers, such as Philip Freneau, who questioned the established order even as they used conventional neoclassical forms. Although she wrote that her own experience with slavery, having introduced her to Christianity, was fortunate, Wheatley consistently opposed the institution of slavery and the attitudes that made it possible. She was a nineteen-year-old slave when she addressed a poem published in 1773 to the earl of Dartmouth, urging freedom for America on the basis of a slave's own knowledge of "tyrannic sway." Her poem "On the Death of General Wooster" wondered aloud why God should help the Americans win freedom while they "hold in bondage Afric's blameless race." Once free, Wheatley continued to publish her views on the evil of slavery, most notably in a strong antislavery letter published in a number of New England newspapers in 1774. In the letter, she points out the "universal Love of Freedom . . . , impatient of oppression," of which she says "I humbly think it does not require the penetration of a philosopher to determine."

As writing by African-American women is increasingly becoming available, the recognition of Phillis Wheatley as a pioneer and a significant poet during the American Revolution grows. Readers find a consistent poetic voice, from her earliest work to her latest. That voice is pious and humble yet firm in its conviction of self worth and its concern with freedom.

Suggested Readings: *The Collected Works of Phillis Wheatley,* ed. J. C. Shields, 1988. M. A. Richmond, *Bid the Vassal Soar: Interpretive Essays on the Life and Poetry of Phillis Wheatley and George Moses Horton,* 1974. W. H. Robinson, *Phillis Wheatley and Her Writings,* 1984. D. Grimsted, "Anglo-American Racism and Phillis Wheatley's 'Sable Veil,' 'Knitted Heart,'" in R. Hoffmann, ed., *Women in the Age of the American Revolution,* 1989.

Text Used: *The Poems of Phillis Wheatley,* ed. J. Mason, Jr., 1966.

ON BEING BROUGHT FROM AFRICA TO AMERICA

'Twas mercy brought me from my *Pagan* land,
Taught my benighted soul to understand
That there's a God, that there's a *Saviour* too:
Once I redemption neither sought nor knew.
Some view our sable race with scornful eye,
"Their colour is a diabolic die."
Remember, *Christians, Negros,* black as *Cain,*
May be refin'd, and join th' angelic train.

1773

TO THE UNIVERSITY OF CAMBRIDGE,[1]
IN NEW-ENGLAND

While an intrinsic ardor prompts to write,
The muses promise to assist my pen;
'Twas not long since I left my native shore
The land of errors,[2] and *Egyptian* gloom:
Father of mercy, 'twas thy gracious hand
Brought me in safety from those dark abodes.

Students, to you 'tis giv'n to scan the heights
Above, to traverse the ethereal space,
And mark the systems of revolving worlds.
Still more, ye sons of science[3] ye receive   10
The blissful news by messengers from heav'n,
How *Jesus'* blood for your redemption flows.
See him with hands out-stretcht upon the cross;
Immense compassion in his bosom glows;

---

[1] Harvard University.
[2] Africa, land of "theological errors" because its people had not been converted to Christianity.
[3] Knowledge.

He hears revilers, nor resents their scorn:
What matchless mercy in the Son of God!
When the whole human race by sin had fall'n,
He deign'd to die that they might rise again,
And share with him in the sublimest skies,
Life without death, and glory without end.   20

Improve your privileges while they stay,
Ye pupils, and each hour redeem, that bears
Or good or bad report of you to heav'n.
Let sin, that baneful evil to the soul,
By you be shunn'd, nor once remit your guard;
Suppress the deadly serpent in its egg.
Ye blooming plants of human race devine,
An *Ethiop*[4] tells you 'tis your greatest foe;
Its transient sweetness turns to endless pain,
And in immense perdition sinks the soul.   30

1767, 1773

ON THE DEATH OF THE REV. MR. GEORGE WHITEFIELD[1] 1770

Hail, happy saint, on thine immortal throne,
Possest of glory, life and bliss unknown;
We hear no more the music of thy tongue,
Thy wonted[2] auditories cease to throng.
Thy sermons in unequall'd accents flow'd,
And ev'ry bosom with devotion glow'd;
Thou didst in strains of eloquence refin'd
Inflame the heart, and captivate the mind.
Unhappy we the setting sun deplore,
So glorious once, but ah! it shines no more.   10

Behold the prophet in his tow'ring flight!
He leaves the earth for heav'n's unmeasur'd height,
And worlds unknown receive him from our sight.
There *Whitefield* wings with rapid course his way,
And sails to *Zion*[3] through vast seas of day.
Thy pray'rs, great saint, and thine incessant cries
Have pierc'd the bosom of thy native skies.
Thou moon hast seen, and all the stars of light,
How he has wrestled with his God by night.

[4] Ethiopian.
[1] George Whitefield (1714–1770), an English follower of John Wesley (founder of Methodism) and a well-known revivalist, who died in Newburyport, Massachusetts.
[2] Accustomed.
[3] The city of God.

He pray'd that grace in ev'ry heart might dwell,   20
He long'd to see *America* excel;
He charg'd its youth that ev'ry grace divine
Should with full lustre in their conduct shine;
That Saviour, which his soul did first receive,
The greatest gift that ev'n a God can give,
He freely offer'd to the num'rous throng,
That on his lips with list'ning pleasure hung.

   "Take him, ye wretched, for your only good,
"Take him ye starving sinners, for your food;
"Ye thirsty, come to this life-giving stream,   30
"Ye preachers, take him for your joyful theme;
"Take him my dear *Americans*, he said,
"Be your complaints on this kind bosom laid:
"Take him, ye *Africans,* he longs for you,
"*Impartial Saviour* is his title due:
"Wash'd in the fountain of redeeming blood,
"You shall be sons, and kings, and priests to God."

   Great *Countess,*[4] we *Americans* revere
Thy name, and mingle in thy grief sincere;
New England deeply feels, the *Orphans* mourn,   40
Their more than father will no more return.

   But, though arrested by the hand of death,
Whitefield no more exerts his lab'ring breath,
Yet let us view him in th' eternal skies,
Let ev'ry heart to this bright vision rise;
While the tomb safe retains its sacred trust,
Till life divine re-animates his dust.

1770

ON IMAGINATION

Thy various works, imperial queen, we see,
How bright their forms! how deck'd with pomp by thee!
Thy wond'rous acts in beauteous order stand,
And all attest how potent is thine hand.

   From *Helicon's*[1] refulgent heights attend,
Ye sacred choir, and my attempts befriend:
To tell her glories with a faithful tongue,
Ye blooming graces, triumph in my song.

---

[4] The countess of Huntingdon, Selina Shirley Hastings (1707–1791), a supporter of her chaplain, Whitefield.
[1] According to Greek Myth, Mount Helicon is home to the Muses, the nine goddesses presiding over literature, art, and music.

Now here, now there, the roving *Fancy* flies,   10
Till some lov'd objects strikes her wand'ring eyes,
Whose silken fetters all the senses bind,
And soft captivity involves the mind.

Imagination! who can sing thy force?
Or who describe the swiftness of thy course?
Soaring through air to find the bright abode,
Th' empyreal palace of the thund'ring God,
We on thy pinions[2] can surpass the wind,
And leave the rolling universe behind:
From star to star the mental optics rove,
Measure the skies, and range the realms above.   20
There in one view we grasp the mighty whole,
Or with new worlds amaze th' unbounded soul.

Though *Winter* frowns to *Fancy's* raptur'd eyes
The fields may flourish, and gay scenes arise;
The frozen deeps may break their iron bands,
And bid their waters murmur o'er the sands.
Fair *Flora*[3] may resume her fragrant reign,
And with her flow'ry riches deck the plain;
Sylvanus[4] may diffuse his honours round,
And all the forest may with leaves be crown'd: 30
Show'rs may descend, and dews their gems disclose,
And nectar sparkle on the blooming rose.

Such is thy pow'r, nor are thine orders vain,
O thou the leader of the mental train:
In full perfection all thy works are wrought,
And thine the sceptre o'er the realms of thought.
Before thy throne the subject-passions bow,
Of subject-passions sov'reign ruler Thou,
At thy command joy rushes on the heart,
And through the glowing veins the spirits dart.   40

Fancy might now her silken pinions try
To rise from earth, and sweep th' expanse on high;
From *Tithon's* bed now might *Aurora*[5] rise, ⎫
Her cheeks all glowing with celestial dies,   ⎬
While a pure stream of light o'erflows the skies. ⎭
The monarch of the day I might behold,
And all the mountains tipt with radiant gold,
But I reluctant leave the pleasing views,
Which *Fancy* dresses to delight the *Muse;*
Winter austere forbids me to aspire,   50

---

[2] Wings.   [3] The Roman goddess of flowers.   [4] The Roman god of the forest.
[5] The Roman goddess of the dawn, equivalent to the Greek Eos, who loved Tithonus.

And northern tempests damp the rising fire;
They chill the tides of *Fancy's* flowing sea,
Cease then, my song, cease the unequal lay.[6]

1767?–1773, 1773

THOUGHTS ON THE WORKS OF PROVIDENCE

Arise, my soul, on wings enraptur'd, rise
To praise the monarch of the earth and skies,
Whose goodness and beneficence appear
As round its centre moves the rolling year,
Or when the morning glows with rosy charms,
Or the sun slumbers in the ocean's arms:
Of light divine be a rich portion lent
To guide my soul, and favour my intent.
Celestial muse, my arduous flight sustain,
And raise my mind to a seraphic[1] strain!   10

Ador'd for ever be the God unseen,
Which round the sun revolves this vast machine,
Though to his eye its mass a point appears:
Ador'd the God that whirls surrounding spheres,
Which first ordain'd that mighty *Sol*[2] should reign
The peerless monarch of th' ethereal train:
Of miles twice forty millions is his height,
And yet his radiance dazzles mortal sight
So far beneath—from him th' extended earth
Vigour derives, and ev'ry flow'ry birth: 20
Vast through her orb she moves with easy grace
Around her *Phœbus*[3] in unbounded space;
True to her course th' impetuous storm derides,
Triumphant o'er the winds, and surging tides.

Almighty, in these wond'rous works of thine,
What *Pow'r,* what *Wisdom,* and what *Goodness* shine?
And are thy wonders, Lord, by men explor'd,
And yet creating glory unador'd!

Creation smiles in various beauty gay,
While day to night, and night succeeds to day: 30
That *Wisdom,* which attends *Jehovah's* ways,
Shines most conspicuous in the solar rays:
Without them, destitute of heat and light,
This world would be the reign of endless night:
In their excess how would our race complain,

[6] Ballad.
[1] Angelic.   [2] The sun.   [3] The Greek sun god, Apollo.

Abhorring life! how hate its length'ned chain!
From air adust what num'rous ills would rise?
What dire contagion taint the burning skies?
What pestilential vapours, fraught with death,
Would rise, and overspread the lands beneath?   40

Hail, smiling morn, that from the orient main[4]
Ascending dost adorn the heav'nly plain!
So rich, so various are thy beauteous dies,
That spread through all the circuit of the skies,
That, full of thee, my soul in rapture soars,
And thy great God, the cause of all adores.

O'er beings infinite his love extends,
His *Wisdom* rules them, and his *Pow'r* defends.
When tasks diurnal[5] tire the human frame,
The spirits faint, and dim the vital flame,   50
Then too that ever active bounty shines,
Which not infinity of space confines.
The sable veil, and *Night* in silence draws,
Conceals effects, but shes th' *Almighty Cause;*
Night seals in sleep the wide creation fair,
And all is peaceful but the brow of care.
Again, gay *Phœbus,* as the day before,
Wakes ev'ry eye, but what shall wake no more;
Again the face of nature is renew'd,
Which still appears harmonious, fair, and good.   60
May grateful strains salute the smiling morn,
Before its beams the eastern hills adorn!

Shall day to day, and night to night conspire
To show the goodness of the Almighty Sire?
This mental voice shall man regardless hear,
And never, never raise the filial pray'r?
To-day, O hearken, nor your folly mourn
For time mispent, that never will return.
But see the sons of vegetation rise,
And spread their leafy banners to the skies.   70
All-wise Almighty providence we trace
In trees, and plants, and all the flow'ry race;
As clear as in the nobler frame of man,
All lovely copies of the Maker's plan.
The pow'r the same that forms a ray of light,
That call'd creation from eternal night.
"Let there be light,"[6] he said: from his profound
Old *Chaos* heard, and trembled at the sound:
Swift as the word, inspir'd by pow'r divine,

[4] Eastern ocean.   [5] Daily.   [6] From Genesis 1.3.

Behold the light around its maker shine,   80
The first fair product of th' omnific God,
And now through all his works diffus'd abroad.

As reason's pow'rs by day our God disclose,
So we may trace him in the night's repose:
Say what is sleep? and dreams how passing strange!
When action ceases, and ideas range
Licentious and unbounded o'er the plains,
Where *Fancy's*[7] queen in giddy triumph reigns.
Here in soft strains the dreaming lover sigh
To a kind fair, or rave in jealousy;   90
On pleasure now, and now on vengeance bent,
The lab'ring passions struggle for a vent.
What pow'r, Oh man! thy *reason* then restores,
So long suspended in nocturnal hours?
What secret hand returns the mental train,
And gives improv'd thine active pow'rs again?
From thee, O man, what gratitude should rise!
And, when from balmy sleep thou op'st thine eyes,
Let first thoughts be praises to the skies.
How merciful our God who thus imparts   100
O'erflowing tides of joy to human hearts,
When wants and woes might be our righteous lot,
Our God forgetting, by our God forgot!

Among the mental pow'rs a question rose,
"What must the image of th' Eternal shows?"
When thus to *Reason* (so let *Fancy* rove)
Her great companion spoke immortal *Love*.

"Say, mighty pow'r, how long shall strife prevail,
"And with its murmurs load the whisp'ring gale?
"Refer the cause to *Recollection's* shrine,   110
"Who loud proclaims my origin divine,
"The cause whence heav'n and earth began to be,
"And is not man immortaliz'd by me?
"*Reason* let this most causeless strife subside."
Thus *Love* pronounc'd, and *Reason* thus reply'd.

"Thy birth, celestial queen! 'tis mine to own,
"In thee resplendent is the Godhead shown;
"Thy words persuade, my soul enraptur'd feels
"Resistless beauty which thy smile reveals."
Ardent she spoke, and, kindling at her charms,   120
She clasp'd the blooming goddess in her arms.

[7] Imagination's.

Infinite *Love* wher'er we turn our eyes
Appears: this ev'ry creature's wants supplies;
This most is heard in *Nature's* constant voice,
This makes the morn, and this the eve rejoice;
This bids the fost'ring rains and dews descend
To nourish all, to serve one gen'ral end,
The good of man; yet man ungrateful pays
But little homage, and but little praise.
To him, whose works array'd with mercy shine,   130
What songs should rise, how constant, how divine!

                                                    1767?–1773, 1773

TO S. M.,[1] A YOUNG AFRICAN PAINTER, ON SEEING HIS WORKS

To show the lab'ring bosom's deep intent,
And thought in living characters to paint,
When first thy pencil did those beauties give,
And breathing figures learnt from thee to live,
How did those prospects give my soul delight,
A new creation rushing on my sight?
Still, wond'rous youth! each noble path pursue,
On deathless glories fix thine ardent view:
Still may the painter's and the poet's fire
To aid thy pencil, and thy verse conspire!   10
And may the charms of each seraphic[2] theme
Conduct thy footsteps to immortal fame!
High to the blissful wonders of the skies
Elate thy soul, and raise thy wishful eyes.
Thrice happy, when exalted to survey
That splendid city, crown'd with endless day,
Whose twice six gates[3] on radiant hinges ring:
Celestial *Salem*[4] blooms in endless spring.

Calm and serene thy moments glide along,
And may the muse inspire each future song!   20
Sill, with the sweets of contemplation bless'd,
May peace with balmy winds your soul invest!
But when these shades of time are chas'd away,
And darkness ends in everlasting day,
On what seraphic pinions[5] shall we move,
And view the landscapes in the realms above?
There shall thy tongue in heav'nly murmurs flow,

---

[1] Identified by Benjamin Brawley in *The Negro in Literature and Art* (1934) as Scipio Moorhead, "a young man who exhibited some talent for drawing and who was a servant of the Rev. John Moorhead of Boston."
[2] Angelic.   [3] The twelve gates of Heaven.   [4] "Jerusalem" or Heaven.   [5] Angelic wings.

And there my muse with heav'nly transport glow:
No more to tell of *Damon's*[6] tender sighs,
Or rising radiance of *Aurora's*[7] eyes,   30
For nobler themes demand a nobler strain,
And purer language on th' ethereal plain.
Cease, gentle muse! the solemn gloom of night
Now seals the fair creation from my sight.

1767?–1773, 1773

TO HIS EXCELLENCY GENERAL WASHINGTON*

SIR,

I have taken the freedom to address your Excellency in the enclosed poem, and
entreat your acceptance, though I am not insensible of its inaccuracies. Your being
appointed by the Grand Continental Congress to be Generalissimo of the armies of
North America, together with the fame of your virtues, excite sensations not easy
to suppress. Your generosity, therefore, I presume, will pardon the attempt. Wishing your Excellency all possible success in the great cause you are so generously
engaged in. I am,

Your Excellency's most obedient humble servant,
PHILLIS WHEATLEY.

Providence, Oct. 26, 1775.
His Excellency Gen. Washington.

Celestial choir! enthron'd in realms of light,
Columbia's[1] scenes of glorious toils I write.
While freedom's cause her anxious breast alarms,
She flashes dreadful in refulgent arms.
See mother earth her offspring's fate bemoan,
And nations gaze at scenes before unknown!
See the bright beams of heaven's revolving light
Involved in sorrows and the veil of night!
    The goddess comes, she moves divinely fair,
Olive and laurel[2] binds her golden hair: 10
Wherever shines this native of the skies,
Unnumber'd charms and recent graces rise.
    Muse! bow propitious while my pen relates
How pour her armies through a thousand gates:
As when Eolus[3] heaven's fair face deforms,
Enwrapp'd in tempest and a night of storms;
Astonish'd ocean feels the wild uproar,

---

[6] According to classical myth, Damon pledged his life for his friend Pythias.
[7] The Roman goddess of the dawn.
* First printed in *The Pennsylvania Magazine* 2:93 (April 1776), while Thomas Paine was editor.
[1] America's.   [2] Signs of victory.   [3] Roman god of the winds.

The refluent surges beat the sounding shore;
Or thick as leaves in Autumn's golden reign,
Such and so many, moves the warrior's train.   20
In bright array they seek the work of war,
Where high unfurl'd the ensign waves in air.
Shall I to Washington their praise recite?
Enough thou know'st them in the fields of fight.
Thee, first in peace and honours,—we demand
The grace and glory of thy martial band.
Fam'd for thy valour, for thy virtues more,
Hear every tongue thy guardian aid implore!
    One century scarce perform'd its destined round,
When Gallic[4] powers Columbia's fury found;   30
And so may you, whoever dares disgrace
The land of freedom's heaven-defended race!
Fix'd are the eyes of nations on the scales,
For in their hopes Columbia's arm prevails.
Anon Britannia droops the pensive head,
While round increase the rising hills of dead.
Ah! cruel blindness to Columbia's state!
Lament thy thirst of boundless power too late.
    Proceed, great chief, with virtue on thy side,
Thy ev'ry action let the goddess guide.   40
A crown, a mansion, and a throne that shine,
With gold unfading, WASHINGTON! be thine.

                                                1775, 1776

Philip Freneau
(1752–1832)

Born in New York City in 1752, Philip Freneau was the son of a prosperous wine merchant of French descent and a well-to-do New Jersey farmer's daughter. The Freneaus reared their children according to the doctrines of orthodox Calvinism. Following his father's death in 1767, Freneau entered the College of New Jersey (now Princeton University), expecting to become a minister. There, however, along with his classmates James Madison and Hugh Henry Brackenridge, he became involved in the patriotic ferment that preceded the Revolutionary War. Discovering in himself a literary bent, Freneau began to produce poems. The most important of these, "The Rising Glory of America," was cowritten with Brackenridge, who read the poem at their class commencement ceremony in 1771. The poem celebrates the promising future of an America seen in its dedication to liberty rather than to gold, as morally superior to the colonies of Spain.

---

[4] The French and Indian Wars (1689–1763), thought to have begun with King William's War (1689–1697), included four wars between France and England.

In 1775 Freneau traveled to New York and again jumped into the political fray, contributing anti-British and pro-American odes, satires, and other verses to local magazines and newspapers. By 1780 he had earned the title "Poet of the Revolution." Exhausted by political strife, he abandoned New York in 1776 and sailed to Santa Cruz in the Caribbean. There he enjoyed the beauties of the isles, noted the horrors of slavery, and likely had an affair with an island belle. In 1778, however, he returned to America, enlisted in the New Jersey militia, and saw action on blockade runners. Two years later, Freneau's ship, the *Aurora,* was captured by a British vessel. Freneau spent six grueling weeks on a British prison ship and, after becoming ill, six worse weeks on a British hospital ship moored in New York City's East River. Sick and exhausted, he was freed in July 1780, having enhanced his hatred of the British.

After recuperating at his mother's home in Mt. Pleasant, New Jersey (to which he regularly returned throughout his life), Freneau went to Philadelphia. There, in the *Freeman's Journal* he continued to vilify the British and their American sympathizers. After the Revolutionary War ended in 1783, he briefly returned to the Caribbean. On the way, he encountered the worst hurricane to hit the region in decades; he describes the experience in his popular poem "The Hurricane" (1785). From 1785 to 1789 he served as captain on merchant vessels shuttling between New Jersey and South Carolina. Perhaps depressed by the war ending, by his hurricane experience, or (most likely) by a woman's rejection, Freneau began to write more personal poems, such as "The Wild Honey Suckle" (1786) and "The Indian Burying Ground" (1788), marked by an emphasis on life's transience. In 1788 he published *The Miscellaneous Works of Philip Freneau,* which contains not only poetry from his dark period but lighter prose essays previously contributed to magazines, under various pseudonyms.

Freneau married the wealthy and beautiful Eleanor Forman in 1790, whereupon his poetry immediately lost much of its gloom. He soon returned to public affairs, contributing republican, anti-Federalist rhetoric to the *National Gazette,* which he edited. Freneau's staunch republicanism led Thomas Jefferson to insist that Freneau had kept the country from "galloping into monarchy" during the 1790s. Yet, Freneau's continual characterization of George Washington as the "monarchical" successor to England's King George III led Washington to dub him a "rascal." Though publication of the *National Gazette* ended in 1793, Freneau was henceforth remembered as a partisan debater, an image that overshadowed his reputation as a poet.

From 1795 to 1798 Freneau edited a country newspaper (in which he published essays under the pseudonym Tomo-Cheeki, an imaginary Creek Indian chief supposedly living in Philadelphia) and a literary magazine. Between 1798 and 1815 he managed the family farm in New Jersey and served again as a merchant captain. He also published more essays under the pseudonym Robert Slender, a cobbler who pretended humility and naïveté while attacking federalism and Britain and defending republicanism and France. Collections of Freneau's poetry appeared in 1795, 1809, and 1815. During his later years, Freneau's verse expressed a deistic confidence in a benevolent nature wholly absent from his poetry of the 1780s. Yet, as an old man Freneau experienced poverty and professional neglect, seeing his lands sold at auction and his poems pass out of print. He died near his home in 1832 after losing his way in a snowstorm.

Freneau's writings—like his life—manifest considerable variety, ranging from political propaganda to philosophical speculation, from urbane essay to lyric effusion, from pious optimism to atheistical despair. Moreover, Freneau seems to alternate between eighteenth-century neoclassicism, with its regard for reason and its imitative theory of literature, and nineteenth-century romanticism, with its emphasis on emotion and its redefinition of literature as the expression of the writer's feelings. Despite his fluctuations, Freneau is consistent in his preromantic preference for traditional verse forms, his belief in the natural goodness of human beings, his determination to see corrupting social and political institutions abolished, and his loyalty to the themes of liberty and the ability to change. Whether describing the cruelties of slavery or the tyrannies of George III, the beaches of Santa Cruz or the freedoms available in a "glorious" America, Freneau was convinced that liberty is essential to the happiness of every human being. And whether describing the destructive power of a hurricane, or the brief lifetime of a honeysuckle, or the poignant doom of the last apple on a tree, he likewise was aware that, even if life goes on, individual lives must end.

Freneau's work has continuing importance. Having composed two dozen memorable poems and a number of valuable essays, Freneau is something other than a study in failure, as has been suggested, and something more than a precursor of Edgar Allan Poe and Ralph Waldo Emerson, as has been argued also. Freneau's vision of America may now seem naïve, his patriotic tone shrill, and his fear of federalism slightly paranoid, but his public writings will continue to inspire so long as freedom remains important. And though Freneau's emphasis on death and decay may now seem quaint or morbid, his best private writings will likewise be widely read so long as people continue to love life enough to mourn its loss.

Suggested Readings: *The Prose of Philip Freneau,* ed. P. M. Marsh, 1955. L. Leary, *That Rascal Freneau,* 1941. R. C. Vitzhum, *Land and Sea,* 1978.

Texts Used: "On the Emigration to America" and "To Sir Toby": *Poems of Philip Freneau,* Vol. II, ed. F. L. Pattee, 1902–1907. "On Observing a Large Red-Streak Apple": *The Last Poems of Philip Freneau,* ed. L. Leary, 1945. All others: *The Poems of Philip Freneau,* No. 19, ed. H. H. Clark, 1929.

ON THE EMIGRATION TO AMERICA

And Peopling the Western Country

To western woods, and lonely plains,
Palemon[1] from the crowd departs,
Where Nature's wildest genius reigns,
To tame the soil, and plant the arts—
What wonders there shall freedom show,
What mighty states successive grow!

From Europe's proud, despotic shores
Hither the stranger takes his way,
And in our new found world explores
A happier soil, a milder sway,   10
Where no proud despot holds him down,
No slaves insult him with a crown.

What charming scenes attract the eye,
On wild Ohio's savage stream!
There Nature reigns, whose works outvie

---

[1] An adventurer, from a character in Geoffrey Chaucer's *The Canterbury Tales* (1395?).

The boldest pattern art can frame;
There ages past have rolled away,
And forests bloomed but to decay.

From these fair plains, these rural seats,
So long concealed, so lately known,   20
The unsocial Indian far retreats,
To make some other clime his own,
When other streams, less pleasing, flow,
And darker forests round him grow.

Great Sire[2] of floods! whose varied wave
Through climes and countries takes its way,
To whom creating Nature gave
Ten thousand steams to swell thy sway!
No longer shall they useless prove,
Nor idly through the forests rove;   30

Nor longer shall your princely flood
From distant lakes be swelled in vain,
Nor longer through a darksome wood
Advance, unnoticed, to the main,
Far other ends, the heavens decree—
And commerce plans new freights for thee.

While virtue warms the generous breast,
There heaven-born freedom shall reside,
Nor shall the voice of war molest,
Nor Europe's all-aspiring pride—   40
There Reason shall new laws devise,
And order from confusion rise.

Forsaking kings and regal state,
With all their pomp and fancied bliss,
The traveller owns, convinced though late,
No realm so free, so blest as this—
The east is half to slaves consigned,
Where kings and priests enchain the mind.

O come the time, and haste the day,
When man shall man no longer crush,   50
When Reason shall enforce her sway,
Nor these fair regions raise our blush,
Where still the African complains,
And mourns his yet unbroken chains.

Far brighter scenes a future age,
The muse predicts, these States will hail,

---

[2] Freneau's note: "Mississippi."

Whose genius may the world engage,
Whose deeds may over death prevail,
And happier systems bring to view,
Than all the eastern sages knew.   60

1784, 1785

TO SIR TOBY*

A SUGAR PLANTER IN THE INTERIOR PARTS OF JAMAICA, NEAR THE CITY OF
SAN JAGO DE LA VEGA (SPANISH TOWN), 1784

"The motions of his spirit are black as night,
And his affections dark as Erebus." [1]
—SHAKESPEARE. [2]

If there exists a hell—the case is clear—
Sir Toby's slaves enjoy that portion here:
Here are no blazing brimstone lakes—'tis true;
But kindled Rum too often burns as blue;
In which some fiend, whom nature must detest,
Steeps Toby's brand, and marks poor Cudjoe's breast. [3]
    Here whips on whips excite perpetual fears,
And mingled howlings vibrate on my ears:
Here nature's plagues abound, to fret and teaze,
Snakes, scorpions, despots, lizards, centipees—   10
No art, no care escapes the busy lash;
All have their dues—and all are paid in cash—
The eternal driver keeps a steady eye
On a black herd, who would his vengeance fly,
But chained, imprisoned, on a burning soil,
For the mean avarice of a tyrant, toil!
The lengthy cart-whip guards this monster's reign—
And cracks, like pistols, from the fields of cane.
    Ye powers! who formed these wretched tribes, relate,
What had they done, to merit such a fate!   20
Why were they brought from Eboe's [4] sultry waste,
To see that plenty which they must not taste—
Food, which they cannot buy, and dare not steal;
Yams and potatoes—many a scanty meal!—
    One, with a gibbet [5] wakes his negro's fears,

---

* From the edition of 1809 (lines 13-16 added then); first published in the *National Gazette*, July 21,
1792, as "The Island Field Hand."
    [1] According to Greek myth, the region through which the dead pass from the earth to Hades.
    [2] From *The Merchant of Venice*, 5.1.79. Freneau substituted "black as night" for "dull as night."
    [3] Freneau's note: "This passage has a reference to the West India custom (sanctioned by law) of
branding a newly imported slave on the breast, with a red hot iron, as an evidence of the purchaser's
property."
    [4] Freneau's note: "A small negro kingdom near the river Senegal."
    [5] Gallows.

One to the windmill nails him by the ears;
One keeps his slave in darkened dens, unfed,
One puts the wretch in pickle ere he's dead:
This, from a tree suspends him by the thumbs,
That, from his table grudges even the crumbs!   30
    O'er yond' rough hills a tribe of females go,
Each with her gourd, her infant, and her hoe;
Scorched by a sun that has no mercy here,
Driven by a devil, whom men call overseer—
In chains, twelve wretches to their labours haste;
Twice twelve I saw, with iron collars graced!—
    Are such the fruits that spring from vast domains?
Is wealth, thus got, Sir Toby, worth your pains!—
Who would your wealth on terms, like these, possess,
Where all we see is pregnant with distress—   40
Angola's[6] natives scourged by ruffian hands,
And toil's hard product shipp'd to foreign lands.
    Talk not of blossoms, and your endless spring;
What joy, what smile, can scenes of misery bring?—
Though Nature, here, has every blessing spread,
Poor is the labourer—and how meanly fed!—
    Here Stygian[7] paintings light and shade renew,
Pictures of hell, that Virgil's[8] pencil drew:
Here, surly Charons[9] make their annual trip,
And ghosts arrive in every Guinea ship,[10]   50
To find what beasts these western isles afford,
Plutonian[11] scourges, and despotic lords:—
    Here, they, of stuff determined to be free,
Must climb the rude cliffs of the Liguanee;[12]
Beyond the clouds, in sculking haste repair,
And hardly safe from brother traitors[13] there.—

1784, 1792

THE WILD HONEY SUCKLE

Fair flower, that dost so comely grow,
Hid in this silent, dull retreat,
Untouched thy honied blossoms blow,[1]

---

[6] A Portuguese colony in West Africa.   [7] Hell-like.

[8] Freneau's note: "See Eneid, Book 6th.—and Fenelon's Telemachus, Book 18." Virgil (70–19 B.C.), a Latin poet, wrote the *Aeniad* (30–19 B.C.), in which Aeneas reaches the underworld; Francois de Salignac de la Mothe-Fénelon (1651–1715), a theologian, wrote *Télemaque* (1699), about Ulysses and his son.

[9] According to Greek myth, the ferryman who carried the dead over the river Styx to Hades.

[10] Ship carrying slaves from West Africa.   [11] Reference to the Greek underworld god, Pluto.

[12] Freneau's note: "The mountains northward of Kingston."

[13] Freneau's note: "Alluding to the *Independent* negroes in the blue mountains, who for a stipulated reward, deliver up every fugitive that falls into their hands, to the English Government."

[1] Bloom.

Unseen thy little branches greet:
  No roving foot shall crush thee here,
  No busy hand provoke a tear.

By Nature's self in white arrayed,
She bade thee shun the vulgar[2] eye,
And planted here the guardian shade,
And sent soft waters murmuring by;   10
  Thus quietly thy summer goes,
  Thy days declining to repose.

Smit with those charms, that must decay,
I grieve to see your future doom;
They died—nor were those flowers more gay,
The flowers that did in Eden bloom;
  Unpitying frosts, and Autumn's power
  Shall leave no vestige of this flower.

From morning suns and evening dews
At first thy little being came: 20
If nothing once, you nothing lose,
For when you die you are the same;
  The space between, is but an hour,
  The frail duration of a flower.

                                                          1786

THE INDIAN BURYING GROUND

In spite of all the learned have said,
I still my old opinion keep;
'The *posture,* that *we* give the dead,
Points out the soul's eternal sleep.

Not so the ancients of these lands—
The Indian, when from life released,
Again is seated with his friends,
And shares again the joyous feast.[1]

His imaged birds, and painted bowl,
And venison, for a journey dressed.   10
Bespeak the nature of the soul,
  ACTIVITY, that knows no rest.

----

[2] Common.

[1] Freneau's note: "The North American Indians bury their dead in a sitting posture; decorating the corpse with wampum, the images of birds, quadrupeds, etc: And (if that of a warrior) with bows, arrows, tomhawks and other military weapons."

His bow, for action ready bent,
And arrows, with a head of stone,
Can only mean that life is spent,
And not the old ideas gone.

Thou, stranger, that shalt come this way,
No fraud upon the dead commit—
Observe the swelling turf, and say
They do not *lie*, but here they *sit*.   20

Here still a lofty rock remains,
On which the curious eye may trace
(Now wasted, half, by wearing rains)
The fancies of a ruder race.

Here still an aged elm aspires,
Beneath whose far-projecting shade
(And which the shepherd still admires)
The children of the forest played!

There oft a restless Indian queen
(Pale *Shebah*,[2] with her braided hair)   30
And many a barbarous form is seen
To chide the man that lingers there.

By midnight moons, o'er moistening dews,
In habit for the chase arrayed,
The hunter still the deer pursues,
The hunter and the deer, a shade![3]

And long shall timorous fancy see
The painted chief, and pointed spear,
And Reason's self shall bow the knee
To shadows and delusions here.   40

1787

ON MR. PAINE'S RIGHTS OF MAN*

Thus briefly sketched the sacred RIGHTS OF MAN,
How inconsistent with the ROYAL PLAN!
Which for itself exclusive honour craves,
Where some are masters born, and millions slaves.
With what contempt must every eye look down

---

[2] The Queen of Shebah, known for her wisdom and beauty (1 Kings 10.1–10.13).   [3] A ghost.
* Originally titled "To a Republican with Mr. Paine's *Rights of Man*," a response to Edmund Burke's
Reflections on the French Revolution (1790) and Thomas Paine's *Rights of Man* (1791–1792).

On that base, childish bauble called a *crown,*
The gilded bait, that lures the crowd, to come,
Bow down their necks, and meet a slavish doom;
The source of half the miseries men endure,
The quack that kills them, while it seems to cure.   10
 Roused by the REASON of his manly page,
Once more shall PAINE a listening world engage:
From Reason's source, a bold reform he brings,
In raising up *mankind,* he pulls down *kings,*
Who, source of discord, patrons of all wrong,
On blood and murder have been fed too long:
Hid from the world, and tutored to be base,
The curse, the scourge, the ruin of our race,
Their's was the task, a dull designing few,
To shackle beings that they scarcely knew,   20
Who made this globe the residence of slaves,
And built their thrones on systems formed by knaves
—Advance, bright years, to work their final fall,
And haste the period that shall crush them all.
Who, that has read and scann'd the historic page
But glows, at every line, with kindling rage,
To see by them the rights of men aspersed,
Freedom restrain'd, and Nature's law reversed,
Men, ranked with beasts, by monarchs *will'd* away,
And bound young fools, or madmen to obey: 30
Now driven to wars, and now oppressed at home,
Compelled in crowds o'er distant seas to roam,
From India's climes the plundered prize to bring
To glad the strumpet, or to glut the king.
 COLUMBIA,[1] hail! immortal be thy reign:
Without a king, we till the smiling plain;
Without a king, we trace the unbounded sea,
And traffic round the globe, through each degree;
Each foreign clime our honour'd flag reveres,
Which asks no monarch, to support the STARS: 40
Without a *king,* the laws maintain their sway,
While honour bids each generous heart obey.
Be ours the task the ambitious to restrain,
And this great lesson teach—that kings are vain;
That warring realms to certain ruin haste,
That kings subsist by war, and wars are waste:
So shall our nation, form'd on Virtue's plan.
Remain the guardian of the Rights of Man,
A vast Republic, famed through every clime,
Without a king, to see the end of time.   50

          1792, 1795

---

[1] America.

TO AN AUTHOR

Your leaves bound up compact and fair,
In neat array at length prepare,
To pass their hour on learning's stage,
To meet the surly critic's rage;
The statesman's slight, the smatterer's sneer—
Were these, indeed, your only fear,
You might be tranquil and resigned:
What most should touch your fluttering mind;
Is that, few critics will be found
To sift your works, and deal the wound.   10

Thus, when one fleeting year is past
On some bye-shelf *your* book is cast—
Another comes, with *something new,*
And drives you fairly out of view:
With some to praise, *but more to blame,*
The mind returns to—whence it came;
And some alive, who *scarce could read*
Will publish satires on the dead.

Thrice happy Dryden,[1] who could meet
Some rival bard in every street!   20
When all were bent on writing well
It was some credit to excel:—

Thrice happy Dryden, who could find
A *Milbourne*[2] for his sport designed—
And *Pope,*[3] who saw the harmless rage
Of *Dennis*[4] bursting o'er his page
Might justly spurn the *critic's aim,*
Who only helped to swell his fame.

On these bleak climes by Fortune thrown,
Where rigid *Reason* reigns alone,   30
Where lovely *Fancy* has no sway,
Nor magic forms about us play—
Nor nature takes her summer hue
Tell me, what has the muse to do?—

An age employed in edging steel
Can no poetic raptures feel;

[1] Freneau's note: "See Johnson's lives of the English Poets." In *Lives of the Poets* (1779–1781) Samuel Johnson (1709–1784) discusses John Dryden (1631–1700), an English poet.
[2] English poet (1649–1720) whom Dryden considered "the worst poet of the age."
[3] Alexander Pope (1688–1744), an English poet.
[4] John Dennis (1657–1734), a writer satirized by Pope as being pompous.

No solitude's attracting power,
No leisure of the noon day hour,
No shaded stream, no quiet grove
Can this fantastic century move;   40

The muse of love in no request—
Go—try your fortune with the rest,
One of the nine you should engage,
To meet the follies of the age:—
On *one,* we fear, your choice must fall—
The least engaging of them all—
Her visage stern—an angry style—
A clouded brow—malicious smile—
A mind on *murdered victims* placed—
She, only she, can please the taste!   50

1787?, 1788

ON THE RELIGION OF NATURE

The power, that gives with liberal hand
    The blessings man enjoys, while here,
And scatters through a smiling land
    Abundant products of the year;
        That power of nature, ever bless'd,
        Bestow'd religion with the rest.

Born with ourselves, her early sway
    Inclines the tender mind to take
The path of right, fair virtue's way
    Its own felicity to make.   10
        This universally extends
        And leads to no mysterious ends.

Religion, such as nature taught,
    With all divine perfection suits;
Had all mankind this system sought
    Sophists[1] would cease their vain disputes,
        And from this source would nations know
        All that can make their heaven below.

This deals not curses on mankind,
    Or dooms them to perpetual grief,   20
If from its aid no joys they find,
    It damns them not for unbelief;

---

[1] Teachers of philosophy.

Upon a more exalted plan
Creatress nature dealt with man—

Joy to the day, when all agree
  On such grand systems to proceed,
From fraud, design, and error free,
  And which to truth and goodness lead:
    The persecution will retreat
    And man's religion be complete.   30

1815

ON OBSERVING A LARGE RED-STREAK APPLE

In spite of ice, in spite of snow,
In spite of all the winds that blow,
In spite of hail and biting frost,
Suspended here I see you tossed
You still retain your wonted[1] hold
Though days are short and nights are cold.

Amidst this system of decay
How could you have one wish to stay?
If fate or fancy kept you there
They meant you for a *Solitaire*.[2]   10
Were it not better to descend,
Or in the cider mill to end
Than thus to shiver in the storm
And not a leaf to keep you warm—
A moment then, had buried all,
Nor you have doomed so late a fall.

But should the stem to which you cling
Uphold you to another spring,
Another race would round you rise
And view the *stranger* with surprize,   20
And, peeping from the blossoms say
Away old dotard,[3] get away!

Alas! small pleasure can there be
To dwell, a hermit, on the tree—
Your old companions, all, are gone,
Have dropt and perished, every one;
You only stay to face the blast,
A sad memento of the past.

[1] Usual.   [2] An isolated case.   [3] A foolish old person.

Would fate or nature hear my prayer,
I would your bloom of youth repair   30
I would the wrongs of time restrain
And bring your blossom state again:
But fate and nature both say no;
And you, though late must perish too.

What can we say, what can we hope?
Ere from the branch I see you drop,
All I can do, all in my power
Will be to watch your parting hour:
When from the branch I see you fall,
A grave we dig a-south the wall.   40
There you shall sleep 'till from your core,
Of youngsters rises three or four;
These shall salute the coming spring
And Red streaks to perfection bring
When years have brought them to their prime
And they shall have their summer's time:
This, this is all you can attain,
And thus, I bid you, live again!

1822

Joel Barlow
(1754–1812)

Born in 1754, Joel Barlow spent the first nineteen years of his life on his family's farm in Redding, Connecticut. There he tended crops and livestock and became familiar with rural tasks and customs. In 1774 he entered Yale College, but his education was disrupted by the Revolutionary War. When the governor of Connecticut called for volunteers to defend New York City in 1776, Barlow joined the Revolutionary Army for a summer, returning to Yale only after the Battle of Long Island had been lost. At his graduation in 1778 Barlow, named class poet, read "The Prospect of Peace," the first of his several poetical envisionings of an ideal postrevolutionary America.

After graduation, Barlow moved to Hartford, Connecticut, where he married Ruth Baldwin and, over the next ten years, held the jobs of newspaper editor, bookseller, teacher, and lawyer. From 1780 to 1782 he served as chaplain of a Revolutionary War brigade quartered in New Jersey. Having heard Barlow's patriotic sermons praised, George Washington invited the youthful chaplain to dinner.

In the mid-1780s Barlow joined other Hartford writers to produce a series of satiric newspaper articles describing *The Anarchiad* (1786–1787), a fictitious serial poem celebrating the triumph of political chaos. Calling themselves the Connecticut Wits, Barlow and his friends used their commentary on *The Anarchiad* to decry the leveling tendencies then observable in American politics and to encourage the conservative political reaction that culminated in the Constitutional Convention of 1787. In that year Barlow completed and published *The Vision of Columbus*. Written in heroic couplets (rhymed pairs of lines), this long poem describes the settling of America, the Revolutionary War, an American future marked by scientific progress, the end of language differences and political hostilities in the Western Hemisphere, and the unification of all Western peoples under the American banner of democracy. Popular with an audience eager to hear America praised, *The Vision of Columbus* became a bestseller after the Revolutionary War.

In 1788 Barlow left for Europe, having accepted a position to sell parcels of American farmland to potential immigrants. By 1790, however, he had become deeply involved in European politics, associating with Thomas Paine, Mary Wollstonecraft, and other major critics of monarchical government, and abandoning the political conservatism of his own Hartford years. When Edmund Burke's *Reflections on the Revolution in France* appeared in 1790, Barlow expedited the publication of Paine's *The Rights of Man* (1791–1792), the most influential reply to Burke, and published his own reply, *Advice to the Privileged Orders* (1792). In *Advice* Barlow lodges careful complaints against such institutions as kings, established churches, and standing armies; praises the libertarian reforms of France's new French government; and cites the positive steps taken in America during and after its own revolution.

Barlow argues in *Advice* that Burke's defense of authoritarian social and political structures was based on the faulty assumption that human beings are unable to recognize or promote their own best interests—and thus need to be led by political and religious "superiors." Barlow suggests that although people have been manipulated into believing that such is the case, a state of equality is the only natural state for human beings. This will inevitably occur, Barlow predicts, when people lose their "superstitious" regard for oppressive institutions. The reasonableness of Barlow's tone was not sufficient to disguise the radicalness of his argument: following the publication of his book, he was forced to leave London.

More popular in Paris, Barlow was made an honorary French citizen in 1793 and sought election (in vain) to the French National Assembly that year. While campaigning in Savoy, France, he received from his friends a dish of hasty pudding, the cornmeal mush he had enjoyed as a boy. In the guise of a mock-epic tribute to this familiar food, Barlow produced *The Hasty Pudding* (1796), a defense of American folk rituals and critique of European traditions. Despite France's Reign of Terror, in which many citizens were executed, Barlow retained his confidence in the ultimate success of the French Revolution. In 1793 he launched a business shipping goods to France, eventually amassing a considerable fortune. In the late 1790s Barlow expressed in a letter his fear that the Federalists in Washington would provoke a confrontation between the United States and France. Published without authorization, the letter caused some Americans to view Barlow as disloyal to his country. However, upon the ascension of his friend Thomas Jefferson to the presidency in 1800, Barlow's reputation was restored. In 1805, after an absence of seventeen years, he and his wife returned to America and bought an expensive home in Washington, D.C.

Barlow's last major work was *The Columbiad* (1807), a reworking of *The Vision of Columbus*. As before, an angelic spirit visits a dejected Columbus in prison and reveals to him the glorious future of the lands he discovered. New to the poem is a critique of American slavery, portrayed as incongruous in a libertarian America. In 1811 Barlow was appointed minister to France by President James Madison and sent to negotiate a treaty with Napoleon. Barlow journeyed to the Russian front, where feelings of revulsion inspired him to compose "Advice to a Raven in Russian" (published in 1843). In the midst of Napoleon's retreat from Russia in 1812, Barlow died of pneumonia in Poland.

Barlow's literary significance lies partly in his conviction that America is a prime subject for epic poetry and that the serious American poet is obliged to tackle this subject. Barlow was the first in a line of poets, including Walt Whitman, Hart Crane, William Carlos Williams, and Allen Ginsberg, to view themselves as America's bards. Barlow is important, too, for his vision of America as a place where persons of all races could for the first time in human history achieve a society characterized by social equality, political freedom, and perpetual peace. Although America has never achieved perfect equality, peace, and freedom, Barlow's vision remains valuable. Through his poems and equally powerful prose, Barlow suggests that just as the most troubling social and political problems—racism, tyranny, war—stem from the fears and misconceptions of the human mind, so do solutions to these problems become possible when people are able to change their attitudes and to throw off their mental shackles. With his heroic couplets, hasty pudding, and old-fashioned revolutionary optimism, Barlow implies that cynicism is itself a manacle of the mind, a limiting habit of thought.

Suggested Readings: *Advice to the Privileged Orders.* 1956. *Writings of Joel Barlow*, 2 vols., ed. W. K. Bottorff and A. L. Ford, 1970. L. Howard, *The Connecticut Wits,*1943. L. Lemay, "The Contexts and Themes of 'The Hasty-Pudding,' " in *Early American Literature* 17 (1982)."

Texts Used: *The Hasting Pudding:* J. Woodress, *A Yankee's Odyssey: The Life of Joel Barlow*, 1958. "Advice to a Raven in Russia": L. Howard, "Joel Barlow and Napoleon," in *The Huntington Library Quarterly* 2:1 (October 1938), (some spelling and punctuation modernized).

THE HASTY PUDDING

A Poem, in Three Cantos

WRITTEN AT CHAMBERY, IN SAVOY,[1] JANUARY, 1793

Omne tulit punctum qui miscuit utile dulci.[2]
He makes a good breakfast who mixes pudding with molasses.

Preface

A simplicity in diet, whether it be considered with reference to the happiness of individuals or the prosperity of a nation, is of more consequence than we are apt to imagine. In recommending so important an object to the rational part of mankind, I wish it were in my power to do it in such a manner as would be likely to gain their attention. I am sensible that it is one of those subjects in which example has infinitely more power than the most convincing arguments or the highest charms of poetry. Goldsmith's *Deserted Village*,[3] though possessing these two advantages

---

[1] A region of France.
[2] "He who combines the useful and the pleasing wins the approval of all" (Latin), from Horace (65–8 B.C.) *Ars Poetica* (8? B.C.).
[3] The poem *The Deserted Village* (1770) by Oliver Goldsmith, which idealizes rural life in England.

in a greater degree than any other work of the kind, had not prevented villages in England from being deserted. The apparent interest of the rich individuals, who form the taste as well as the laws in that country, has been against him; and with that interest it has been vain to contend.

The vicious habits which in this little piece I endeavor to combat, seem to me not so difficult to cure. No class of people has any interest in supporting them; unless it be the interest which certain families may feel in vying with each other in sumptuous entertainments. There may indeed be some instances of depraved appetites, which no arguments will conquer; but these must be rare. There are very few persons but what would always prefer a plain dish for themselves, and would prefer it likewise for their guests, if there were no risk of reputation in the case. This difficulty can only be removed by example; and the example should proceed from those whose situation enables them to take the lead in forming the manners of a nation. Persons of this description in America, I should hope, are neither above nor below the influence of truth and reason, when conveyed in language suited to the subject.

Whether the manner I have chosen to address my arguments to them be such as to promise any success is what I cannot decide. But I certainly had hopes of doing some good, or I should not have taken the pains of putting so many rhymes together. The example of domestic virtues has doubtless a great effect. I only wish to rank simplicity of diet among the virtues. In that case I should hope it will be cherished and more esteemed by others than it is at present.

The Author

Canto I

Ye Alps audacious, through the heavens that rise,
To cramp the day and hide me from the skies;
Ye Gallic flags[4] that o'er their heights unfurled,
Bear death of kings and freedom to the world,
I sing not you. A softer theme I choose,
A virgin theme, unconscious of the muse,
But fruitful, rich, well suited to inspire
The purest frenzy of poetic fire.

Despise it not, ye bards to terror steeled,
Who hurl your thunders round the epic field;   10
Nor ye who strain your midnight throats to sing
Joys that the vineyard and the stillhouse[5] bring;
Or on some distant fair[6] your notes employ,
And speak of raptures that you ne'er enjoy.
I sing the sweets I know, the charms I feel,
My morning incense, and my evening meal—
The sweets of Hasty Pudding. Come, dear bowl,
Glide o'er my palate, and inspire my soul.
The milk beside thee, smoking from the kine,[7]

---

[4] French flags. Savoy, once part of Sardinia, was annexed by France in 1792; Barlow supported this.
[5] A distillery.   [6] Fair lady.   [7] Cattle.

Its substance mingled, married in with thine,   20
Shall cool and temper thy superior heat,
And save the pains of blowing while I eat.

Oh! could the smooth, the emblematic song
Flow like the genial juices o'er my tongue,
Could those mild morsels in my numbers[8] chime,
And, as they roll in substance, roll in rime,
No more thy awkward, unpoetic name
Should shun the muse or prejudice thy fame;
But rising grateful to the accustomed ear,
All bards should catch it, and all realms revere!   30

Assist me first with pious toil to trace
Through wrecks of time, thy lineage and thy race;
Declare what lovely squaw, in days of yore,
(Ere great Columbus sought thy native shore)
First gave thee to the world; her works of fame
Have lived indeed, but lived without a name.
Some tawny Ceres,[9] goddess of her days,
First learned with stones to crack the well-dried maize,
Through the rough sieve to shake the golden shower,
In boiling water stir the yellow flour: 40
The yellow flour, bestrewed and stirred with haste,
Swells in the flood and thickens to a paste,
Then puffs and wallops,[10] rises to the brim,
Drinks the dry knobs that on the surface swim;
The knobs at last the busy ladle breaks,
And the whole mass its true consistence takes.

Could but her sacred name, unknown so long,
Rise, like her labors, to the son of song,
To her, to them I'd consecrate my lays,
And blow her pudding with the breath of praise.   50
If 'twas Oella[11] whom I sang before,
I here ascribe her one great virtue more.
Not through the rich, Peruvian realms alone
The fame of Sol's[12] sweet daughter should be known,
But o'er the world's wide climes should live secure,
Far as his rays extend, as long as they endure.

Dear Hasting Pudding, what unpromised joy
Expands my heart, to meet thee in Savoy!
Doomed o'er the world through devious paths to roam,
Each clime my country, and each house my home,   60

[8] Metrical verse.
[9] The Roman goddess of agriculture and grain.   [10] Boils and bubbles.
[11] Legendary princess of the Incas, daughter of the sun and inventor of spinning; Barlow cited her in his *Vision of Columbus* (1787).
[12] The sun's.

My soul is soothed, my cares have found an end;
I greet my long-lost, unforgotten friend.

For thee through Paris, that corrupted town,
How long in vain I wandered up and down,
Where shameless Bacchus,[13] with his drenching hoard,
Cold from his cave usurps the morning board.
London is lost in smoke and steeped in tea;
No Yankee there can lisp the name of thee;
The uncouth word, a libel on the town,
Would call a proclamation from the crown.[14]   70
For climes oblique, that fear the sun's full rays,
Chilled in their fogs, exclude the generous maize;
A grain whose rich, luxuriant growth requires
Short, gentle showers, and bright, ethereal fires.

But here, though distant from our native shore,
With mutual glee, we meet and laugh once more.
The same! I know thee by that yellow face,
That strong complexion of true Indian race,
Which time can never change, nor soil impair,
Nor Alpine snows, nor Turkey's morbid air;   80
For endless years, through every mild domain,
Where grows the maize, there thou art sure to reign.

But man, more fickle, the bold licence claims,
In different realms to give thee different names.
Thee the soft nations round the warm Levant[15]
Polanta[16] call; the French of course, *Polante.*
E'en in thy native regions, how I blush
To hear the Pennsylvanians call thee *Mush!*
On Hudson's banks, while men of Belgic-spawn[17]
Insult and eat thee by the name *Suppawn.*[18]   90
All spurious appellations, void of truth;
I've better known thee from my earliest youth:
Thy name is *Hasty Pudding!* thus my sire
Was wont to greet thee fuming from his fire;
And while he argued in thy just defense
With logic clear he thus explained the sense:
"In haste the boiling caldron, o'er the blaze,
Receives and cooks the ready powdered maize;
In haste 'tis served, and then in equal haste,
With cooling milk, we make the sweet repast.   100
No carving to be done, no knife to grate

---

[13] Greek and Roman god of wine.
   [14] Barlow's note: "A certain king, at the time when this was written, was publishing proclamations to prevent American principles from being propagated in his country." Refers to George III.
   [15] Coastlands off the eastern Mediteranean Sea.   [16] Cooked cereal usually (polenta).
[17] Of Dutch ancestry.   [18] Cornmeal mush.

The tender ear and wound the stony plate;
But the smooth spoon, just fitted to the lip,
And taught with art the yielding mass to dip,
By frequent journeys to the bowl well stored,
Performs the hasty honors of the board."
Such is thy name, significant and clear,
A name, a sound to every Yankee dear,
But most to me, whose heart and palate chaste
Preserve my pure, hereditary taste.   110

There are who strive to stamp with disrepute
The luscious food, because it feeds the brute;
In tropes[19] of high-strained wit, while gaudy prigs
Compare thy nursling, man, to pampered pigs;
With sovereign scorn I treat the vulgar jest,
Nor fear to share thy bounties with the beast.
What thought the generous cow gives me to quaff
The milk nutritious: am I then a calf?
Or can the genius of the noisy swine,
Though nursed on pudding, thence lay claim to mine?   120
Sure the sweet song I fashion to thy praise,
Runs more melodious than the notes they raise.

My song, resounding in its grateful glee,
No merit claims: I praise myself in thee.
My father loved thee through his length of days!
For thee his fields were shaded o'er with maize;
From thee what health, what vigor he possessed,
Ten sturdy freemen from his loins attest;
Thy constellation ruled my natal morn,
And all my bones were made of Indian corn.   130
Delicious grain, whatever form it take,
To roast or boil, to smother or to bake,
In every dish 'tis welcome still to me,
But most, my Hasty Pudding, most in thee.

Let the green succotash with thee contend;
Let beans and corn their sweetest juices blend;
Let butter drench them in its yellow tide,
And a long slice of bacon grace their side;
Not all the plate, how famed soe'er it be,
Can please my palate like a bowl of thee.   140
Some talk of hoe-cake, fair Virginia's pride!
Rich johnny-cake this mouth has often tried;
Both please me well, their virtues much the same,
Alike their fabric, as allied their fame,
Except in dear New England, where the last
Receives a dash of pumpkin in the paste,

[19] Metaphors.

To give it sweetness and improve the taste.
But place them all before me, smoking hot,
The big, round dumpling, rolling from the pot;
The pudding of the bag, whose quivering breast,   150
With suet lined, leads on the Yankee feast;
The charlotte brown, within whose crusty sides
A belly soft the pulpy apple hides;
The yellow bread whose face like amber glows,
And all of Indian that the bakepan knows—
You tempt me not; my favorite greets my eyes,
To that loved bowl my spoon by instinct flies.

Canto II

To mix the food by vicious rules of art,
To kill the stomach and to sink the heart,
To make mankind to social virtue sour,   160
Cram o'er each dish, and be what they devour;
For this the kitchen muse first framed her book,
Commanding sweats to stream from every cook;
Children no more their antic gambols tried,
And friends to physic[20] wondered why they died.

Not so the Yankee: his abundant feast,
With simples[21] furnished and with plainness dressed,
A numerous offspring gathers round the board,
And cheers alike the servant and the lord;
Whose well-bought hunger prompts the joyous taste,   170
And health attends them from the short repast.

While the full pail rewards the milkmaid's toil,
The mother sees the morning caldron boil;
To stir the pudding next demands their care;
To spread the table and the bowls prepare;
To feed the household as their portions cool
And send them all to labor or to school.

Yet may the simplest dish some rules impart,
For nature scorns not all the aids of art.
E'en Hasty Pudding, purest of all food,   180
May still be bad, indifferent, or good,
As sage experience the short process guides,
Or want of skill, or want of care presides.
Who'er would form it on the surest plan,
To rear the child and long sustain the man;
To shield the morals while it mends the size,
And all the powers of every food supplies—

---

[20] The art of healing.   [21] Herbs.

Attend the lesson that the muse shall bring,
Suspend your spoons, and listen while I sing.

But since, O man! thy life and health demand   190
Not food alone, but labor from thy hand,
First, in the field, beneath the sun's strong rays,
Ask of thy mother earth the needful maize;
She loves the race that courts her yielding soil,
And gives her bounties to the sons of toil.

When now the ox, obedient to thy call,
Repays the loan that filled the winter stall,
Pursue his traces o'er the furrowed plain,
And plant in measured hills the golden grain.
But when the tender germ begins to shoot,   200
And the green spire declares the sprouting root,
Then guard your nursling from each greedy foe,
The insidious worm, the all-devouring crow.
A little ashes sprinkled round the spire,
Soon steeped in rain, will bid the worm retire;
The feathered robber with his hungry maw
Swift flies the field before your man of straw,
A frightful image, such as schoolboys bring
When met to burn the Pope[22] or hang the King.

Thrice in the season, through each verdant row,   210
Wield the strong plowshare and the faithful hoe;
The faithful hoe, a double task that takes,
To till the summer corn and roast the winter cakes.

Slow springs the blade while checked by chilling rains,
Ere yet the sun the seat of Cancer[23] gains;
But when his fiercest fires emblaze the land,
Then start the juices, then the roots expand;
Then, like a column of Corinthian mold,[24]
The stalk struts upward and the leaves unfold;
The bushy branches all the ridges fill,   220
Entwine their arms, and kiss from hill to hill.
Here cease to vex them; all your cares are done:
Leave the last labors to the parent sun;
Beneath his genial smiles, the well-dressed field,
When autumn calls, a plenteous crop shall yield.

Now the strong foliage bears the standards high,
And shoots the tall top-gallants[25] to the sky;

[22] Probably a reference to Guy Fawkes Day, November 5, when effigies of the Pope were burned in England.
[23] Zodiac sign that begins on the summer solstice, June 21.
[24] A Greek architectural column embellished with leaves on the capital.
[25] The upper masts and sails on a ship.

The suckling ears their silky fringes bend,
And pregnant grown, their swelling coats distend;
The loaded stalk, while still the burden grows,   230
O'erhangs the space that runs between the rows;
High as a hop-field waves the silent grove,
A safe retreat for little thefts of love,
When the pledged roasting-ears invite the maid
To meet her swain beneath the new-formed shade;
Her generous hand unloads the cumbrous hill,
And the green spoils her ready basket fill;
Small compensation for the twofold bliss,
The promised wedding, and the present kiss.

    Slight depredations these; but now the moon   240
Calls from his hollow tree the sly raccoon;
And while by night he bears his prize away,
The bolder squirrel labors through the day.
Both thieves alike, but provident of time,
A virtue rare, that almost hides their crime.
Then let them steal the little stores they can,
And fill their granaries from the toils of man;
We've one advantage where they take no part—
With all their wiles, they ne'er have found the art
To boil the Hasty Pudding; here we shine   250
Superior far to tenants of the pine;
This envied boon to man shall still belong,
Unshared by them in substance or in song.

    At last the closing season browns the plain,
And ripe October gathers in the grain;
Deep-loaded carts the spacious corn-house fill;
The sack distended marches to the mill;
The laboring mill beneath the burden groans,
And showers the future pudding from the stones;[26]
Till the glad housewife greets the powdered gold,   260
And the new crop exterminates the old.
Ah who can sing what every wight must feel,
The joy that enters with the bag of meal,
A general jubilee pervades the house,
Wakes every child and gladdens every mouse.[27]

Canto III

    The days grow short; but though the falling sun
To the glad swain proclaims his day's work done,
Night's pleasing shades his various tasks prolong,
And yield new subjects to my various song.

---

[26] Grindstones.   [27] Lines 262–265 were added in 1796.

For now, the corn-house filled, the harvest home,
The invited neighbors to the husking[28] come:
A frolic scene, where work, and mirth, and play,
Unite their charms to chase the hours away.
Where the huge heap lies centered in the hall,   270
The lamp suspended from the cheerful wall,
Brown, corn-fed nymphs, and strong, hard-handed beaux,
Alternate ranged, extend the circling rows,
Assume their seats, the solid mass attack;
The dry husks rustle, and the corncobs crack;
The song, the laugh, alternate notes resound,
And the sweet cider trips in silence round.

    The laws of husking every wight[29] can tell;
And sure no laws he ever keeps so well:
For each red ear a general kiss he gains,   280
With each smut ear[30] she smuts the luckless swains;
But when to some sweet maid a prize is cast,
Red as her lips and taper as her waist,
She walks the round and culls one favored beau,
Who leaps the luscious tribute to bestow.
Various the sport, as are the wits and brains
Of well-pleased lasses and contending swains;
Till the vast mound of corn is swept away,
And he that gets the last ear wins the day.
Meanwhile, the housewife urges all her care,   290
The well-earned feast to hasten and prepare.
The sifted meal already waits her hand,
The milk is strained, the bowls in order stand,
The fire flames high; and as a pool—that takes
The headlong stream that o'er the milldam breaks—
Foams, roars, and rages with incessant toils,
So the vexed caldron rages, roars, and boils.

    First with clean salt she seasons well the food,
Then strews the flour, and thickens all the flood.
Long o'er the simmering fire she lets it stand;   300
To stir it well demands a stronger hand;
The husband takes his turn; and round and round
The ladle flies; at last the toil is crowned;
When to the board the thronging huskers pour,
And take their seats as at the corn before.

    I leave them to their feast. There still belong
More useful matters to my faithful song.
For rules there are, though ne'er unfolded yet,
Nice rules and wise, how pudding should be ate.
Some with molasses line the luscious treat,   310
And mix, like bards, the useful with the sweet.

---

[28] A party for corn husking.   [29] Person.   [30] Damaged by fungal growth.

A wholesome dish, and well deserving praise,
A great resource in those bleak wintry days,
When the chilled earth lies buried deep in snow,
And raging Boreas[31] dries the shivering cow.

Blest cow! thy praise shall still my notes employ,
Great source of health, the only source of joy;
Mother of Egypt's god[32] but sure, for me,
Were I to leave my god, I'd worship thee.
How oft thy teats these pious hands have pressed!
How oft thy bounties proved my only feast!
How oft I've fed thee with my favorite grain!   320
And roared, like thee, to see thy children slain!

Ye swains who know her various worth to prize,
Ah! house her well from winter's angry skies.
Potatoes, pumpkins, should her sadness cheer,
Corn from your crib, and mashes from your beer;
When spring returns, she'll well acquit the loan,
And nurse at once your infants and her own.
Milk then with pudding I should always choose;
To this in future I confine my muse,
Till she in haste some further hints unfold,   330
Well for the young, nor useless to the old.
First in your bowl the milk abundant take,
Then drop with care along the silver lake
Your flakes of pudding; these at first will *hide*
Their little bulk beneath the swelling tide;
But when their growing mass no more can sink,
When the soft island looms above the brink,
Then check your hand; you've got the portion due;
So taught our sires, and what they taught is true.

There is a choice in spoons. Though small appear   340
The nice distinction, yet to me 'tis clear.
The deep-bowled Gallic spoon, contrived to scoop
In ample draughts the thin, diluted soup,
Performs not well in those substantial things,
Whose mass adhesive to the metal clings;
Where the strong labial muscles must embrace
The gentle curve, and sweep the hollow space
With ease to enter and discharge the freight,
A bowl less concave, but still more dilate,
Becomes the pudding best. The shape, the size,   350
A secret rests, unknown to vulgar eyes.
Experienced feeders can alone impart
A rule so much above the lore of art.
These tuneful lips that thousand spoons have tried,
With just precision could the point decide,

---

[31] The north wind.   [32] The goddess Nut, Osiris's mother, typically portrayed as a cow.

Though not in song; the muse but poorly shines
In cones, and cubes, and geometric lines;
Yet the true form, as near as she can tell,
Is that small section of a goose-egg shell,
Which in two equal portions shall divide   360
The distance from the center to the side.

    Fear not to slaver; 'tis no sin.
Like the free Frenchman, from your joyous chin
Suspend the ready napkin; or, like me,
Poise with one hand your bowl upon your knee;
Just in the zenith your wise head project,
Your full spoon, rising in a line direct,
Bold as a bucket, heeds no drops that fall;
The wide-mouthed bowl will surely catch them all!

                          1793, 1796

ADVICE TO A RAVEN IN RUSSIA

DECEMBER, 1812

    Black fool, why winter here? These frozen skies,
Worn by your wings and deafen'd by your cries,
Should warn you hence, where milder suns invite,
And day alternates with his mother night.
    You fear perhaps your food will fail you there,
Your human carnage, that delicious fare
That lured you hither, following still your friend
The great Napoleon to the world's bleak end.
You fear, because the southern climes pour'd forth
Their clustering nations to infest the north,   10
Barvarians, Austrians, those who Drink the Po[1]
And those who skirt the Tuscan seas below,
With all Germania, Neustria, Belgia, Gaul,[2]
Doom'd here to wade thro slaughter to their fall,
You fear he left behind no wars, to feed
His feather'd canibals and nurse the breed.
    Fear not, my screamer, call your greedy train,
Sweep over Europe, hurry back to Spain,
You'll find his legions there; the valliant crew
Please best their master when they toil for you.   20
Abundant there they spread the country o'er
And taint the breeze with every nation's gore,
Iberian, Lusian,[3] British widely strown,
But still more wide and copious flows their own.

---

[1] A river in Italy that runs from the Alps to the Adriatic Sea.
[2] Germany, northern France, the Netherlands, France.
[3] Lusitania, roughly equivalent to Portugal today.

Go where you will; Calabria,[4] Malta, Greece,
Egypt and Syria still his fame increase,
Domingo's[5] fatten'd isle and India's plains
Glow deep with purple drawn from Gallic veins.
No Raven's wing can stretch the flight so far
As the torn bandrols[6] of Napoleon's war.   30
Choose then your climate, fix your best abode,
He'll make you deserts and he'll bring you blood.
   How could you fear a dearth? have not mankind,
Tho slain by millions, millions left behind?
Has not CONSCRIPTION still the power to weild
Her annual faulchion[7] o'er the human field?
A faithful harvester! or if a man
Escape that gleaner, shall he scape the ban?[8]
The triple BAN, that like the hound of hell[9]
Gripes with three joles,[10] to hold his victim well.   40
   Fear nothing then, hatch fast your ravenous brood,
Teach them to cry to Bonaparte for food;
They'll be like you, of all his suppliant train,
The only class that never cries in vain.
For see what mutual benefits you lend!
(The surest way to fix the mutual friend)
While on his slaughter'd troops your tribes are fed,
You cleanse his camp and carry off his dead.
Imperial Scavenger! but now you know
Your work is vain amid these hills of snow.   50
His tentless troops are marbled thro with frost
And change to crystal when the breath is lost.
Mere trunks of ice, tho limb'd like human frames
And lately warm'd with life's endearing flames,
They cannot taint the air, the world impest,[11]
Nor can you tear one fiber from their breast.
No! from their visual sockets, as they lie,
With beak and claws you cannot pluck an eye.
The frozen orb, preserving still its form,
Defies your talons as it braves the storm,   60
But stands and stares to God, as if to know
In what curst hands he leaves his world below.
   Fly then, or starve; tho all the dreadful road
From Minsk to Moskow with their bodies strow'd
May count some Myriads, yet they can't suffice
To feed you more beneath these dreary skies.
Go back, and winter in the wilds of Spain;
Feast there awhile, and in the next campaign
Rejoin your master; for you'll find him then,
With his new million of the race of men,   70
Clothed in his thunders, all his flags unfurl'd,

---

[4] In southern Italy.   [5] Of the West Indies.   [6] Flags carried in war.   [7] Sword.   [8] Curse.
[9] According to Greek myth, Cerberus, the three-headed dog who guards the gates of Hades.
[10] Jaws.   [11] Infect.

Raging and storming o'er the prostrate world.
    War after war his hungry soul requires,
State after State shall sink beneath his fires,
Yet other Spains in victim smoke shall rise
And other Moskows suffocate the skies,
Each land lie reeking with its people's slain
And not a stream run bloodless to the main.
Till men resume their souls, and dare to shed
Earth's total vengeance on the monster's head,   80
Hurl from his blood-built throne this king of woes,
Dash him to dust, and let the world repose.

1812, 1843

LATE 18TH-CENTURY DRAMA

In eighteenth-century American art and letters, the issues of political independence and cultural self-definition emerge as supremely important, dominating all others—the former culminating in the American Revolution, the latter in a peculiarly nationalistic, or "American," view of art. This twin theme of national emergence pervades and in fact inspired the bourgeoning drama of the period, whether

The Federal Street Theater, designed by Charles Bulfinch and built in 1794, was New England's first theater.

written as entertainment or propaganda. A sense of striking historical immediacy gives that drama, sparse and uneven as it is, charm and interest as well as significance today. Both the form and the sociopolitical overtones of American drama may be attributed to its simultaneous emergence with the national consiciousness and the spirit of revolution. As discontent with England began to rise, American drama began to sustain momentum.

The early eighteenth century was a time when a stern tradition of Puritan and Quaker opposition to all things theatrical pervaded the New England colonies. That view was intensified by the influence of the Great Awakening at mid-century, when a new sense of religious urgency spread throughout America. In the Cavalier areas of the South, where the Church of England held sway, theater was tolerated; in some areas, such as Charleston, it even flourished. North of Virginia, though, theater was discouraged; not until 1794 did New England have its first site for the production of plays, Boston's Federal Street Theater. Discouragement commonly took the form of law. Typical perhaps is the fate of *Ye Bare and Ye Cubb* (1665), the first play written for performance in America. Whether it ever reached the stage is not clear because the author, William Darby, was arrested merely for having proposed its performance. For having agreed to act in it, two performers were jailed for immorality.

=CONTEXTS=

The early Puritan rejection of drama as sinful continued to influence attitudes in post-Revolutionary America. While plays were produced, moralists such as John Witherspoon (1723–1794), president of Princeton University and a Declaration of Independence signer, condemned the stage. The following excerpt is from Witherspoon's sermon "A Serious Inquiry Into the Nature and Effects of the Stage."

[Debate Over Drama]

It is very plain, that were men but seriously disposed, and without prejudice desiring the knowledge of their duty, it would not be necessary, in order to show the unlawfulness of the stage, as it now is, to combat it in its imaginary reformed state. Such a reformation, were not men by the prevalence of vicious and corrupt affections, in love with it, even in its present condition, would have been long ago given up as a hopeless and visionary project, and the whole trade or employment detested, on account of the abuses that had always adhered to it. But since all advocates for the stage have and do still defend it in this manner, by forming an idea of it separate from its evil qualities; since they defend it so far with success, that many who would otherwise abstain, do, upon this very account, allow themselves in attending the theatre sometimes, to their own hurt and that of others; and, as I am convinced on the most mature deliberation, that the reason why there never was a well regulated stage, in fact, is because it cannot be, the nature of the thing not admitting of it. I will endeavor to shew, that PUBLIC THEATRICAL REPRESENTATIONS, either tragedy or comedy, are, in their general nature or in their best possible state, unlawful, contrary to the purity of our religion: and that writing, acting, or attending them, is inconsistent with the character of a Christian.

John Witherspoon, 1757

Theater remained under a cloud of suspicion for two more centuries in religious America. Even the troops under George Washington, himself an avid theater-goer, were forbidden by the Continental Congress from frequenting professional theaters, such as Philadelphia's Southwark. Yet, while official disapproval of theater continued in the eighteenth century, American drama began to emerge. With the English Restoration of 1660 came a brilliant revival of theater, previously banished from Puritan England, and increased toleration of theater in the American colonies. Furthermore, at the same time in America, power began to shift from the Puritan patriarchs to the royal governors, who were appointed by the Crown. Wherever the Crown stationed British troops before and during the Revolution—in Boston, Philadelphia, Albany, New York City—drama was in special demand. To some extent, the great influence of the British aristocracy neutralized religious opposition to the theater, allowing that art form to grow. Ironically, the very first plays by American writers, made possible by the tone set by the British aristocracy, were attacks on the British Crown and its colonial appointees. For their own amusement British officers, trapped in an alien wilderness far from home, satirized the locals; local Patriots, emulating the British, satirized the Crown.

Thus, even though American theater is said to have begun in the revolutionary years, not all that is classified as "American" drama in that period is either stage-able or American, except in the loosest possible sense of having been written in America. One Tory playwright living in America was Jonathan Sewall, whose *The Americans Roused, in a Cure for the Spleen* was first performed for British troops in 1774. Another was the legendary British general John Burgoyne, who added his own efforts to the tradition of a time in which soldiers amused themselves by writing, staging, and acting in plays typically about themselves.

Most of the patriotic dramas of the day were essentially dialogues without conventional plot structure and with scant potential for stage success. Into this category fall the works of Hugh Henry Brackenridge and of America's foremost patriotic, dramatic propagandist, Mercy Otis Warren. Written before independence was declared, two of Warren's plays satirized Boston politics. *The Adulateur* (1773) ridicules Massachusetts governor Thomas Hutchinson; *The Group* (1775) attacks powerful politicians who remained loyal to George III even after the Crown repeatedly broke agreements. Other timely political dramas, including *The Blockheads* (1776) and *The Motley Assembly* (1779), have been attributed to Warren, and she continued to write after the war ended. Critics of drama, however, have found more literary merit in Hugh Henry Brackenridge's two long dramatic poems of patriotism, which were never intended for performance: *The Battle of Bunker Hill* (1776) and *The Death of General Montgomery, at the Siege of Quebec* (1777).

To find eighteenth-century political dramas indisputably intended for stage production, historians must turn to playwrights other than Warren and Brackenridge. One such playwright was New York's Governor Robert Hunter whose *Androboros* appeared in 1714; another reputedly was John Leacock, whose chronicle play *The Fall of British Tyranny* appeared in 1776. *Androboros,* thought to be the first play published in America, anticipates the slapstick and ribaldry of the nineteenth-century minstrel show. Aimed at New York politicians named in the list of characters, the play is enlivened by raucous and effective tricks of broad comedy, including dialects, malapropisms, nonsense legislative parlance, and scatology. The title character, General Francis Nicholson, is pushed into a collapsing chair, soaked with a bucket of sludge, sprayed with a mouthful of ale, belched on, and has snuff thrown in his eyes. The interplay of dramatic action and contemporary historical action takes an interesting turn in this play when Hunter includes himself as a character.

The revolutionary period was an extraordinary time in the history of drama because of this intersection of history and drama. Commonly, only a few hours lapsed between the events being played out in real life and the same events being presented on stage, actually blurring the lines between historical and dramatic events. Throughout the century this immediacy was underscored by the close relationship between the military and the theater. Plays about military engagements were written and performed by soldiers, usually for audiences of soldiers. One of the most dramatic examples is *The Blockade of Boston* (1776) by General John Burgoyne: While satirizing Americans, a cast of British soldiers on stage in Faneuil Hall received word that the Americans were attacking British forces a few miles away at Bunker Hill—a bulletin that caused the soldier–actors to run hastily for cover. This episode then became the subject of Mercy Otis Warren's satire *The Blockheads*. Warren's *The Group* was supposedly published in 1775 on the day before the battles of Lexington and Concord were fought.

Some other dramas written in the eighteenth century about eighteenth-century events are less political and more retrospective. *Ponteach* (1766), by Major Robert Rogers, reputedly is the first serious dramatic treatment of Native Americans. William Dunlap's *André,* (1798), about an event in the Revolutionary War, was written by America's first professional playwright and first theater historian. These highly playable works best exemplify the eighteenth-century and nineteenth-century popularity of the drama of American history, and both illustrate character types popular for over a century: the noble Native American and George Washington. Even in these two retrospective plays, however, the element of immediacy is striking. For example, after an illustrious career fighting Native Americans, Rogers turned his hand to a drama about a conflict that he knew intimately. Unpredictably, the hero of *Ponteach* is a Native American rather than a white man, and the murderous seducers of innocence come from the Christian civilization for which the playwright had spent his career fighting.

Events touching Dunlap's *André* illustrate the same extraordinary intersections of eighteenth-century American history and theater. Both Major André, a famous Revolutionary War figure, and playwright Dunlap were at different times soldiers, actors, and painters in America and performed or wrote about their lives. According to legend, Dunlap in his youth had seen the soldier André on stage, and in Dunlap's theatrical prime, while backstage in Philadelphia years after the first production of *André,* he had stumbled upon a theatrical scene painted by the protagonist of his successful play.

Dunlap's play illustrates how far the revolutionary drama had come by the end of the century. Removed from the heat of the subject, the play, unlike its episodic precursors, observes the three unities: unity of time, setting, and plot. It has a modest cast of characters, including George Washington, who was then and continued to be a popular character type. *André,* a sophisticated study of a complex situation into which the human element has been introduced, is essentially without villainous characters. André, the condemned spy, and his adversary, George Washington, are heroic figures in their own way. André's personal courage and humanity emerge in contradiction to the nature of his military mission; Washington reveals ambivalent complexity despite his heroism, condemning to death two basically good men who acted from conscience. In fact, Washington, though always regarded as the play's hero, comes very close to petty and bureaucratic inflexibility. With *André,* the play about the American Revolution came of age.

Other plays, still American in sentiment but distinctly British in form and style, were written in the eighteenth century by Americans. Two of the few extant dramas in this vein, one a tragedy and one a comedy, are *The Prince of Parthia* (published in 1765 and produced in 1767) by Thomas Godfrey and *The Contrast* (1787) by Royall Tyler. The attitude of *The Prince of Parthia* is fundamentally American despite the play's heavy debt to five or six Shakespearean tragedies and histories and its first-century B.C. setting. Like Rogers's *Ponteach,* Godfrey's play celebrates a noble-blooded hero who belongs to a disintegrating golden age. The heroes of both plays are warriors who must battle with enemies outside the tribe and within the family, the characters in effect reenacting the enmity between Cain and Abel on the outskirts of Paradise. Although *The Prince of Parthia,* thought to be the first professionally produced play written by an American, is classified in the tradition of the drama of America's noble savage, the play anticipates George Henry Boker's *Francesca Da Rimini* (1855), the major romantic tragedy of the nineteenth-century American stage.

Tyler's *The Contrast,* sometimes cited as the first indigenous American comedy, reflects the English comedy of manners. Its theme is the contrast between slaves to a shallow European fashion and an independent-minded American hero who is unpretentious, down-to-earth, and solid. In short, the play is a cultural contrast between appearance and substance. That Tyler used Richard Sheridan's *School for Scandal* (1777) as a model for his American theme is telegraphed to the audience by the rustic Jonathan, the prototype of many rural stage Yankees to follow. Jonathan, having seen Sheridan's play on stage and mistaking it for an actual occurrence, gives his own comic interpretation of that play. Tyler's smooth, quick-paced comedy reads and plays extremely well, as though it emerged from the pen of a seasoned theatrical professional instead of an attorney with very little stage or drama experience.

Considered as a group, the plays of the eighteenth-century are distinctly American. More than any other artistic genre of the period, they reinforce values that we associate with the "Party of Nature," as Emerson called it, laying some of the groundwork for the romanticism that flowered in all literary genres of the nineteenth-century American Renaissance. The values that emerge from these plays—simplicity, natural nobility, action, courage, truthfulness, rusticity—are clearly opposed to those of eighteenth-century and Restoration drama in England, which stressed style, elegance, and cultivation and studied wit and grace. Long before

Emerson, Poe, and other nineteenth-century figures philosophically expressed the problem of America's artistic subservience to Britain and Europe, the battle for cultural independence was being waged in dramatic fashion on the stages of America.

Mercy Otis Warren
(1728–1814)

Mercy Otis Warren, poet, dramatist, and historian of the American Revolution, was born Mercy Otis in 1728 into one of the leading Mayflower families of southeastern Massachusetts, deeply involved in Massachusetts politics. By studying with James Otis, her brother, as he prepared for Harvard College, she was educated beyond the standards of most women of the period. When she married James Warren, also a Mayflower descendant, she married a man who shared her interest in politics and who encouraged her ambition to be a writer.

Sensitive to the conventions that required respectable women to stay out of politics, Warren at first focused her attention on raising five sons. Also, she conducted behind-the-scenes political activity through meetings with such leaders as John and Abigail Adams at her home in Plymouth. She began a lifelong friendship with Abigail Adams, who shared Warren's interest in women's rights.

A turning point in Warren's life came when James Otis, nicknamed "the Patriot" for his eloquent opposition to British use of writs of assistance (or general search warrants), suffered a mental breakdown under the stress of his political activity. Warren responded with three anonymous dramatic sketches printed in the Massachusetts press, attacking the British leadership and especially the American-born governor, Thomas Hutchinson. These plays—*The Adulateur: A Tragedy, as It Is Now Acted in Upper Servia* (1772), *The Defeat* (1773), and *The Group* (1775)—were part of the propaganda war that helped to bring hostilities with the British to the boiling point. Reflecting Warren's Puritan values, the plays define the issues of the coming revolution along moral lines, showing that the British presence was destroying the social fabric of shared values that made good government in Massachusetts possible. In her plays Warren says the Crown promoted the corrupt and dismissed the virtuous. That is what she believed had happened in March 1774 when General Thomas Gage appointed a group of mandamus councillors (representatives) to the Massachusetts Council in place of the elected representatives. These councillors appear in *The Group,* Warren's most widely distributed play. A "group" of American "sycophants," they are thoroughly corrupted by the British and despite some pangs of conscience are ready to betray family or country. This corruption has no solution but war, which the play predicts the Patriots will win because "they fight for virtue."

When the American Revolution began, Warren used her pen to promote independence. After the war she remained committed to the Revolution's democratic values and was deeply skeptical of the conservative drift of many former revolutionaries. Her pamphlet on *Observations on the New Constitution* (1788) vigorously criticized Federalists for having forgotten the goals of the Revolution. Though all that she wrote will never be known, by her death at age eighty-six in 1814 Warren had published under her own name a collection of poems, two "anonymous" dramas, and a three-volume *History of the Rise, Progress, and Termination of the American Revolution* (1805). She also left a large correspondence with the Revolution's leaders, most notably with John and Abigail Adams.

Unfortunately, Warren's typically formal style has been a barrier for readers, and her writing has never had a large audience. However, with the recent revival of interest in women's literature and in the literature of the American Revolution, readers have been more ready to attempt to appreciate her work. What they find is one of the best representations available of the American Revolution from the perspective of a New England descendant of the Puritans and an undiluted supporter of the republic.

Suggested Readings: A. Brown, *Mercy Warren*, 1968. J. Fritz, *Cast for a Revolution*, 1972. E. Hayes, "The Private Poems of Mercy Otis Warren" in *New England Quarterly*, 53:2, 1981.

Text Used: *The Plays and Poems of Mercy Otis Warren*, ed. B. Franklin V, 1980.

from THE GROUP

DRAMATIS PERSONAE

LORD CHIEF JUSTICE HAZLEROD

JUDGE MEAGRE

BRIGADIER HATEALL

HUM HUMBUG, ESQ.

SIR SPARROW SPENDALL

HECTOR MUSHROOM,—COL.

BEAU TRUMPS

DICK, THE PUBLICAN

SIMPLE SAPLING, ESQ.

MONSIEUR DE FRANCOIS

CRUSTY CROWBAR, ESQ.

DUPE,—SECRETARY OF STATE

SCRIBBLERIUS FRIBBLE

COMMODORE BATTEAU

COLLATERALIS,—A NEW MADE JUDGE

Attended by a swarm of court sycophants, hungry harpies,[1] and unprincipled danglers, collected from the neighboring villages, hovering over the stage in the shape of locusts, led by Massachusettensis[2] in the form of a basilisk,[3] the rear brought up by Proteus,[4] bearing a torch in one hand, and a powder-flask in the other: The whole supported by a mighty army and navy, from blunderland, for the laudible purpose of enslaving its best friends.

[1] Greedy or grasping persons.
[2] A name of Native-American origin, after the Massachuset Indians.
[3] A cannon.   [4] In Greek mythology, a sea god who could change form at will.

ACT I, SCENE I

Scene, a little dark parlour, guards standing at the door.

HAZLEROD, CRUSTY CROWBAR, SIMPLE-SAPLING, HATEALL,
AND HECTOR MUSHROOM.

SIMPLE.   I know not what to think of these sad times,
   The people arm'd— and all resolv'd to die
   E're they'll submit.————————
CRUSTY CROWBAR.   I too am almost sick of the parade
   Of honours purchas'd at the price of peace.
SIMPLE.   Fond as I am of greatness and her charms
   Elate with prospects of my rising name,
   Push'd into place,—a place I ne'er expected,
   My bounding heart leapt in my feeble breast
   And ecstasies entranc'd my slender brain.   10
   But yet, ere this I hop'd more solid gains,
   As my low purse demands a quick supply.————
   Poor Sylvia weeps,—and urges my return
   To rural peace and humble happiness,
   As my ambition beggars all her babes.
CRUSTY.   When first I listed in the desp'rate cause,
   And blindly swore obedience to his will,
   So wise, so just, so good I thought Rapatio,[5]
   That if salvation rested on his word
   I'd pin my faith and risk my hopes thereon.   20
HAZLEROD.   And why not now?—What staggers thy belief?
CRUSTY.   Himself————his perfidy[6] appears————
   It is too plain he has betray'd his country.
   And we're the wretched tools by him mark'd out
   To seal its ruins—tear up the ancient forms,
   And every vestige treacherously destroy,
   Nor leave a trait of freedom in the land.
   Nor did I think hard fate would call me up
   From drudging o'er my acres,————————
   Treading the glade, and sweating at the plough,   30
   To dangle at the tables of the great;
   At bowls and cards, to spend my frozen years;
   To sell my friends, my country, and my conscience;
   Profane the sacred sabbaths of my God;
   Scorn'd by the very men who want my aid
   To spread distress o'er this devoted people.
HAZLEROD.   Pho—what misgivings—why these idle qualms
   This shrinking backwards at the bugbear[7] conscience?

---

[5] Warren's name for Thomas Hutchinson (1711–1780), governor of Massachusetts from 1771 to 1774.
   [6] Treachery.   [7] An object of extreme fear or concern.

In early life I heard the phantom nam'd,
And the grave sages prate[8] of moral sense   40
Presiding in the bosom of the just;
Or panting thongs about the guilty heart.
Bound by these shackles, long my lab'ring mind
Obscurely trod the lower walks of life,
In hopes by honesty my bread to gain;
But neither commerce, or my conjuring rods,
Nor yet mechanics, or newfangled drills,
Or all the Iron-mongers curious arts,
Gave me a competence of shining ore,
Or gratify'd my itching palm for more;   50
Till I dismiss'd the bold intruding guest,
And banish'd conscience from my wounded breast.

CRUSTY.   Happy expedient!—Could I gain the art,
Then balmy sleep might sooth my waking lids.
And rest once more refresh my weary soul.—

HAZLEROD.   Resolv'd more rapidly to gain my point,
I mounted high in justice's sacred seat,
With flowing robes, and head equip'd without,
A heart unfeeling and a stubborn soul,
As qualify'd as e'er a Jefferies was;   60
Save in the knotty rudiments of law,
The smallest requisite for modern times,
When wisdom, law, and justice, are supply'd
By swords, dragoons, and ministerial nods,
Sanctions most sacred in the pander's[9] creed,
I sold my country for a splendid bribe.
Now let her sink——and all the dire alarms
Of war, confusion, pestilence and blood,
And tenfold mis'ry be her future doom—
Let civil discord lift her sword on high,   70
Nay sheathe its hilt even in my brother's blood;
It ne'er shall move the purpose of my soul;
Though once I trembled at a thought so bold;
By Philalethes's[10] arguments, convinc'd
We may live Demons, as we die like brutes,
I give my tears, and conscience to the winds.

HATEALL.   Curse on their coward fears, and dastard souls,
Their soft compunctions and relenting qualms,
Compassion ne'er shall seize my steadfast breast
Though blood and carnage spread through all the land;   80
Till streaming purple tinge the verdant[11] turf,
Till ev'ry street shall float with human gore,
I Nero[12] like, the capital in flames,

---

[8] Chatter.   [9] Procurer's.
[10] The penname of John, King of Saxony.   [11] Green with vegetation; inexperienced.
[12] A Roman emperor (A.D. 54–68), Nero perhaps gave the order for the disastrous fire that ravaged half of Rome in A.D. 64.

Could laugh to see her glutted sons expire,
Though much too rough my soul to touch the lyre.
SIMPLE.   I fear the brave, the injur'd multitude,
   Repeated wrongs, arouse them to resent,
   And every patriot like old Brutus[13] stands,
   The shining steel half drawn——its glitt'ring point
   Scarce hid beneath the scabbard's friendly cell   90
   Resolv'd to die, or see their country free.
HATEALL.   Then let them die—The dogs we will keep down—
   While N——'s my friend, and G—— approves the deed,
   Though hell and all its hell-hounds should unite,
   I'll not recede to save from swift perdition
   My wife, my country, family or friends.
   G——'s mandamus[14] I more highly prize
   Than all the mandates of the etherial king.
HECTOR MUSHROOM.   Will our abettors in the distant towns
   Support us long against the common cause,   100
   When they shall see from Hampshire's northern bound
   Through the wide western plains to southern shores
   The whole united continent in arms?—
HATEALL.   They shall—as sure as oaths or bonds can bind;
   I've boldly sent my new-born brat abroad,
   The association of my morbid brain,
   To which each minion must affix his name.
   As all our hope depends on brutal force
   On quick destruction, misery and death;
   Soon may we see dark ruin stalk around,   110
   With murder, rapine,[15] and inflicted pains,
   Estates confiscate, slav'ry and despair,
   Wrecks, halters, axes, gibbeting[16] and chains,
   All the dread ills that wait on civil war;—
   How I could glut my vengeful eyes to see
   The weeping maid thrown helpless on the world,
   Her fire cut off.—Her orphan brothers stand
   While the big tear rolls down the manly cheek.
   Robb'd of maternal care by grief's keen shaft,
   The sorrowing mother mourns her starving babes.   120
   Her murder'd lord torn guiltless from her side,
   And flees for shelter to the pitying grave
   To screen at once from slavery and pain.
HAZLEROD.   But more complete I view this scene of woe,
   By the incursions of a savage foe,
   Of which I warn'd them, if they dare refuse
   The badge of slaves, and bold resistance use.
   Now let them suffer—I'll no pity feel.

---

[13] Marcus Junius Brutus (85–42 B.C.), the prime assassin of Julius Caesar.
[14] A written order issued by a superior court mandating a public official or a lower court to perform a specific duty.
[15] Plunder.   [16] Execution by hanging.

HATEALL.   Nor I—But had I power, as I have the Will
    I'd send them murm'ring to the shades of hell.   130

* * *

ACT II, SCENE II

COLLATERALIS————DICK THE PUBLICAN

PUBLICAN.   This dull inaction will no longer do;
    Month after Month the idle troops have lain,
    Nor struck one stroke that leads us to our wish.
            The trifling bickering's at the city gates,
    Or bold outrages of their midnight routs,
    Bring us no nearer to the point in view.
    Though much the daily suff'rings of the people,
    Commerce destroy'd, and government unhing'd,
    No talk to tame submission yet I hear.

COLLATERALIS.   No————not the least————
    ————————they're more resolved than ever.   140
    They're firm, united, bold, undaunted, brave,
    And every villa boasts their marshall'd ranks,
    The warlike Clarion sounds through ev'ry street;
    Both vig'rous youth, and the grey headed fire
    Bear the Fusee,[17] in regimental garbs,
    Repairing to defend invaded right,
    And if push'd hard, by manly force repel;
    And though Britannia sends her legions over,
    To plant her daggers in her children's breast,
    It will rebound————New whetted, the keen point,   150
    Will find a sheath in every tyrant's heart.

* * *

SCENE III

*The fragments of the broken Council appear with trembling servile Gestures,
showing several applications to the General from the Under-Tools[18] in the distant
Counties, begging each a guard of myrmidons[19] to protect them from the armed
multitudes (which the guilty horrors of their wounded consciences hourly presented to their frighted imaginations) approaching to take speedy vengeance on
the Court Parasites, who had fled for refuge to the Camp, by immediate destruction to their Pimps. Panders and Sycophants left behind.*

————SYLLA *walking in great Perplexity.*

---

[17] A large-headed match able to burn in strong winds.   [18] Underlings.
[19] Followers who carry out orders without question. According to Greek myth, the Myrmidons of
ancient Thessaly were followers of Achilles in the Trojan War.

SYLLA.   Pray, how will it comport with my pretence
 For building walls, and shutting up the Town,
 Erecting fortresses, and strong redoubts,
 To keep my troops from any bold inroads
 A brave insulted people might attempt,
 If I send out my little scatter'd parties,
 And the long suff'ring, gen'rous patriot's Care
 Prevents a Skirmish.
        Though they're the sport of wanton cruel power,   160
 And Hydra[20] headed ill, start up around,
 Till the last hope of redress cut off
 Their humane feeling, Urge them to forbear,
 And wait some milder means to bring relief.
HATEALL.   'Tis now the time to try their daring tempers.
 Send out a few——and if they are cut off,
 What are a thousand souls, sent swiftly down
 To Pluto's[21] gloomy shades,—to tell in anguish
 Half their compeers shall fit pandimonic,[22]
 E're we will suffer Liberty to reign,   170
 Or see her sons triumphant win the day.
        I feign would push them to the last extreme,
 To draw their swords against their legal King,
 Then short's the process to complete destruction.
SECRETARY DUPE.   Be not so sanguine—the day is not our own,
 And much I fear it never will be won.
 Their discipline is equal to our own,
 Their valor has been try'd,–and in a field
 They're not less brave than are a Fred'rick's[23] troops,
 Those members formidable pour along,   180
 While virtue's banners shroud each warrior's head
 Stern Justice binds the helmet on his brow,
 And liberty fits perch'd on ev'ry shield.
 But who's apply'd, and ask'd the General's aid,
 Or wish'd his peaceful Villa such a curse,
 As posting Troops beside the peasant's cot?
JUDGE MEAGRE.   None but the very dregs of all mankind.
 The Stains of Nature—The blots of human race,
 Yet that's no matter, still they are our friends,
 'Twill help our projects if we give them aid.   190

* * *

MEAGRE.   Let not thy soft timidity of heart
 Urge thee to terms, till the last stake is thrown.
        Tis not my temper ever to forgive,
 When once resentment's kindled in my breast.

---

[20] According to Greek myth, a poisonous snake with numerous heads; when one head was cut off another grew in its place.
[21] Roman god of the dead.   [22] Their companions will be wildly disrupted or confused.
[23] Friedrich Augustus, King of Saxony.

I hated Brutus for his noble stand
Against the oppressors of his injur'd country.
    I hate the leaders of these restless factions,
For all their gen'rous efforts to be free.
    I curse the senate which defeats our bribes,
Who Hazlerod impeach'd for the same crime.   200
    I hate the people, who, no longer gull'd,
See through the schemes of our aspiring clan.
And from the rancor of my venom'd mind,
I look askance on all the human race,
And if they're not to be appall'd by fear,
I wish the earth might drink that vital stream
That warms the heart, and feeds the manly glow,
The love inherent, planted in the breast,
To equal liberty, confer'd on man,
By him who form'd the peasant and the King!   210
    Could we erase these notions from their minds,
Then (paramount to these ideal whims,
Utopian dreams, of patriotic virtue,
Which long has danc'd in their distemper'd brains)
    We'd smoothly glide on midst a race of slaves,
Nor heave one sigh though all the human race
Were plung'd in darkness, slavery and vice.
If we could keep our foot-hold in the stirrup,
And, like the noble Claudia[24] of old,
Ride o'er the people, if they don't give way;   220
Or wish their fates were all involv'd in one;
For I've a *Brother,* as the roman dame,
Who would strike off the rebel neck at once.
SECRETARY.   No[t] all is o'er unless the sword decides,
    Which cuts down Kings, and kingdoms oft divides.
    By that appeal I think we can't prevail,
    Their valor's great, and justice holds the scale.
    They fight for freedom, while we stab the breast
    Of every man, who is her friend professed.
    They fight in virtue's ever sacred cause,   230
    While we tread on divine and human laws.
    Glory and victory, and lasting fame,
    Will crown their arms and bless each Hero's name!
MEAGRE.   Away with all thy foolish, trifling cares;
    And to the winds give all thy empty fears;
    Let us repair and urge brave Sylla on,
    I long to see the sweet revenge begun.
    As fortune is a fickle, sportive dame,
    She may for us the victory proclaim,
    And with success our busy ploddings crown,   240
    Though injured justice stern and solemn frown.

---

[24] According to Roman myth, Claudia Quinta proved her chastity, said soothsayers, by succeeding in moving a ship that had gotten stuck in the mouth of the Tiber River.

Then they shall smart for ev'ry bold offense,
Estates confiscated will pay th' expense;
On their lost fortunes we a while will plume
And strive to think there is no after doom.

Exit all—
As they pass off the stage the curtain draws up, and discovers to the audience a
Lady nearly connected with one of the principal actors in the group, reclined in an
adjoining alcove, who in mournful accents accosts them—thus——

What painful scenes are hov'ring o'er the morn,
When spring again invigorates the lawn!
Instead of the gay landscape's beauteous dies,
Must the stain'd field salute our weeping eyes,
Must the green turf, and all the mournful glades,   250
Drench'd in the stream, absorb their dewy heads,
Whilst the tall oak, and quiv'ring willow bends
To make a covert for their country's friends,
Deny'd a grave!—amid the hurrying scene
Of routed armies scouring o'er the plain.
Till British troops shall to Columbia[25] yield,
And freedom's sons are Masters of the field;
The o'er the purpl'd plain the victors tread
Among the slain to seek each patriot dead,
(While Freedom weeps that merit could not save   260
But conq'ring Hero's must enrich the Grave)
An adamantine[26] monument they rear
With this inscription—Virtue's Sons lie here!

FINIS

1774–1775, 1775

Royall Tyler
(1757–1826)

Royall Tyler is best known as the author of the first successful American comedy produced
on stage in the United States. *The Contrast: A Comedy in Five Acts,* a sophisticated comedy of manners, was first staged in New York City on April 16, 1787. This play introduced into American legend the characters of the homespun Jonathan, the typical Yankee;
the practical, noble Colonel Manly, veteran of the Revolution; and the bourgeois father,
with an eye on the "main chance." Despite its reliance on English models, *The Contrast* is

---

[25] America, personified as a woman.   [26] Unbreakable.

a very American story that reveals the social, political, and legal limitations on freedom in the new nation, especially as they applied to women. Tyler claimed he wrote the play in three weeks, immediately before its first staging. After several performances in various cities, the play was printed in 1790. By the middle of the nineteenth century, however, it had disappeared. In 1876 a Vermont book collector spotted *The Contrast* in a list of George Washington's books to be auctioned in Philadelphia and bought the signed copy for a few dollars. (In 1919 it sold for $2800.) Since that time the play has been reprinted and performed frequently.

America's first successful playwright spent most of his professional life as a Vermont lawyer and judge. Born into a prominent Anglican family in Boston in 1757, he was baptized William Clark Tyler. When his father, a wealthy merchant, died, the fourteen-year-old boy legally changed his first name to Royall. The elder Royall Tyler had been a Boston representative and king's councillor and a member of the Sons of Liberty, supporting the colonists in their opposition to the British. The younger Tyler received a strong classical education at Boston Latin School and Harvard College, where he graduated in 1776 with a reputation for his wit. Remaining in Cambridge, Massachusetts, to study law, Tyler served briefly in 1778 in the American Army during an unsuccessful attack on the British at Newport, Rhode Island. He returned to Harvard and received an M.A. in 1779.

With a sizable inheritance from his father, Tyler during his Harvard years led a dissipated social life of an affluent young man: drinking, carousing, and discussing literature, painting, and politics. He left Massachusetts to practice law in Maine in 1780 but moved in 1782 to Braintree (now Quincy), Massachusetts, where he fell in love with and proposed to seventeen-year-old Abigail (Nabby) Adams, daughter of future president John Adams. Her father, however, ordered Nabby to join him in Europe in 1784, not wanting a dissipated poet for a son-in-law.

Tyler slowly recovered from this rejection and set up a law practice in Boston in 1785. Boarding with the Palmer family, he met Mary Palmer, still a young girl. Ten years later, in May 1794, they secretly married. Eleven children were born to the couple, who appear to have had a very strong marriage. Mary's journal and reminiscences provide information about their life and attest to her singular devotion throughout her husband's periods of depression, political and literary triumphs, and last years of pain and sickness.

In the decade before his marriage, Tyler had matured as lawyer, diplomat, and writer, with a strong Federalist bent. In January 1787 he helped to quell Shays' Rebellion at Springfield, Massachusetts. Leading a state militia troop, Tyler helped convince the farmers, angered by the unstable postwar economy, to end their rebellion. His next mission was to convince the governor of Vermont not to grant political asylum to David Shays, who had escaped capture and fled to Vermont. Tyler was sent to New York City to negotiate for militia support against the rebels. At this time *The Contrast*, was presented on stage in New York. The play can be considered Tyler's personal response to those deeply dissatisfied with what the American Revolution had wrought. On May 19, one month after the opening of *The Contrast*, New Yorkers were treated to a second Tyler play, the musical *May Day in Town*.

In 1791 Tyler reestablished his law practice in the remote village of Guilford, Vermont. From 1794 to 1801 he served as a state's attorney and wrote a newspaper column with Joseph Dennie, an editor and early champion of American literature. In the first piece, the pair advertised themselves as "Mess. COLON & SPONDEE [types of metrical units in poetry], WHOLESALE DEALERS IN VERSE, PROSE, & MUSIC." Over the years they published hundreds of columns in numerous newspapers, combining light satirical essays (by Dennie as "Colon") and verse (by Tyler as "Spondee") on politics, manners, religion, and literature. When Tyler was elected to the Vermont Supreme Court in 1801, he stopped

"DO YOU WANT TO KILL THE COLONEL?"[1]

The frontispiece of Royall Tyler's The Contrast,
*engraved by P. R. Maverick from a drawing
by William Dunlap.*

contributing to the columns. In 1802 he was named a trustee of the University of Vermont,
where he became professor of jurisprudence in 1811. From 1807 to 1813 he served as
chief justice of the Vermont Supreme Court. His bid for election to the U.S. Senate in
1812 was unsuccessful, and in 1813 he lost his place on the court.

Throughout these years Tyler continued to write, although sometimes hastily or superficially. In 1795 he reported he was working on another comedy, an opera, and a book of
poetry. At this time he was also beginning his longest published work, *The Algerine Captive* (1797), a hybrid novel following the adventures of the narrator, Dr. Updike Underhill,
whose education in the classics ill prepared him for life in the new republic. Underhill,
born into an impoverished New Hampshire family, reaches the age of twenty-one in 1783,
the year the colonies achieved independence. He thus represents the United States in its
coming of age. *The Algerine Captive* begins as a picaresque adventure tracing the narrator's education and early career, revealing the limitations of American democracy. The
book's second volume becomes a captivity narrative in which Underhill's experience as a
slave in Algiers reflects on the question of slavery in a nation where all men are defined as
equally endowed with "certain inalienable rights."

The end of Tyler's life was marked by the pain of cancer and the poverty that followed his failure to be recalled to the Supreme Court. During these years he completed four plays and a long poem and attempted to turn *The Algerine Captive* into an autobiographical novel, *The Bay Boy*. Tyler died in 1826, exactly a half-century following the beginning of the Revolution that had transformed America. His death, like the deaths of John Adams and Thomas Jefferson, signaled an end to the early republic Tyler had chronicled.

Suggested Readings: *The Algerine Captive: Or, the Life and Adventures of Doctor Updike Under-hill, Six Years a Prisoner Among the Algerines*, ed. J.B. Moore, 1967. *The Verse of Royall Tyler*, ed. M.B. Péladeau, 1968. *The Prose of Royall Tyler*, ed. M. B. Péladeau, 1972. G. T. Tanselle, *Royall Tyler*, 1967.

Text Used: *The Contrast: A Comedy in Five Acts*, ed. J. B. Wilbur, 1970.

THE CONTRAST

A Comedy in Five Acts

Characters

COL. MANLY	CHARLOTTE
DIMPLE	MARIA
VAN ROUGH	LETITIA
JESSAMY	JENNY
JONATHAN	SERVANTS

Scene, *NEW–YORK*

Prologue

WRITTEN BY A YOUNG GENTLEMAN OF NEW-YORK,
AND SPOKEN BY MR. WIGNELL[1]

EXULT, each patriot heart!—this night is shewn
A piece, which we may fairly call our own;
Where the proud titles of "My Lord! Your Grace!"
To humble *Mr.* and plain *Sir* give place.
Our Author pictures not from foreign climes
The fashions or the follies of the times;
But has confin'd the subject of his work
To the gay scenes—the circles of New-York.
On native themes his Muse displays her pow'rs;
If ours the faults, the virtues too are ours.
Why should our thoughts to distant countries roam,
When each refinement may be found at home?

[1] Thomas Wignell (1753–1803), a comic actor who first played the character Jonathan in *The Contrast*.

Who travels now to ape the rich or great,
To deck an equipage and roll in state;
To court the graces, or to dance with ease,
Or by hypocrisy to strive to please?
Our free-born ancestors such arts despis'd;
Genuine sincerity alone they priz'd;
Their minds, with honest emulation fir'd;
To solid good—not ornament—aspir'd;
Or, if ambition rous'd a bolder flame,
Stern virtue throve, where indolence was shame.

But modern youths, with imitative sense,
Deem taste in dress the proof of excellence;
And spurn the meanness of your homespun arts,
Since homespun habits would obscure their parts;
Whilst all, which aims at splendour and parade,
Must come from Europe, *and be ready made*.
Strange! we should thus our native worth disclaim,
And check the progress of our rising fame.
Yet *one*, whilst imitation bears the sway,
Aspires to nobler heights, and points the way.
Be rous'd, my friends! his bold example view;
Let your own Bards be proud to copy *you!*
Should rigid critics reprobate our play,
At least the patriotic heart will say,
"Glorious our fall, since in a noble cause.
"The bold *attempt alone* demands applause."
Still may the wisdom of the Comic Muse
Exalt your merits, or your faults accuse.
But think not, 't is her aim to be severe;—
We all are mortals, and as mortals err.
If candour pleases, we are truly blest;
Vice trembles, when compell'd to stand confess'd.
Let not light Censure on your faults offend,
Which aims not to expose them, but amend.
Thus does our Author to your candour trust;
Conscious, the *free* are generous, as just.

Act I

Scene, an Apartment at CHARLOTTE'S
CHARLOTTE *and* LETITIA *discovered*

LETITIA.   And so, Charlotte, you really think the pocket-hoop[2] unbecoming.
CHARLOTTE.   No, I don't say so. It may be very becoming to saunter round the house of a rainy day; to visit my grand-mamma, or to go to Quakers' meeting: But to swim in a minuet, with the eyes of fifty well dressed beaux upon me, to trip it

---

[2] A type of hoop skirt, smaller than the "bell hoop" mentioned later.

in the mall,[3] or walk on the battery,[4] give me the luxurious, jaunty, flowing, bell-hoop. It would have delighted you to have seen me the last evening, my charming girl! I was dangling o'er the battery with Billy Dimple; a knot of young fellows were upon the platform; as I passed them I faultered with one of the most bewitching false steps you ever saw, and then recovered myself with such a pretty confusion, flirting my hoop to discover a jet black shoe and brilliant buckle. Gad! how my little heart thrilled to hear the confused raptures of—*"Demme,[5] Jack, what a delicate foot!" "Ha! General, what a well-turned—"*

LETITIA. Fie! fie! Charlotte [*stopping her mouth*], I protest you are quite a libertine.

CHARLOTTE. Why my dear little prude, are we not all such libertines? Do you think, when I sat tortured two hours under the hands of my friseur,[6] and an hour more at my toilet, that I had any thoughts of my aunt Susan, or my cousin Betsey? though they are both allowed to be critical judges of dress.

LETITIA. Why, who should we dress to please, but those who are judges of its merit?

CHARLOTTE. Why a creature who does not know *Buffon* from *Souflée—* Man!—my Letitia— Man! for whom we dress, walk, dance, talk, lisp, languish, and smile. Does not the grave Spectator[7] assure us that even our much bepraised diffidence, modesty, and blushes are all directed to make ourselves good wives and mothers as fast as we can? Why, I'll undertake with one flirt of this hoop to bring more beaux to my feet in one week than the grave Maria, and her sentimental circle, can do, by sighing sentiment till their hairs are grey.

LETITIA. Well, I won't argue with you; you always out-talk me; let us change the subject. I hear that Mr. Dimple and Maria are soon to be married.

CHARLOTTE. You hear true. I was consulted in the choice of the wedding clothes. She is to be married in a delicate white sattin, and has a monstrous pretty brocaded lutestring[8] for the second day. It would have done you good to have seen with what an affected indifference the dear sentimentalist turned over a thousand pretty things, just as if her heart did not palpitate with her approaching happiness, and at last made her choice and arranged her dress with such apathy as if she did not know that plain white sattin and a simple blond lace would shew her clear skin and dark hair to the greatest advantage.

LETITIA. But they say her indifference to dress, and even to the gentleman himself, is not entirely affected.

CHARLOTTE. How?

LETITIA. It is whispered that if Maria gives her hand to Mr. Dimple, it will be without her heart.

CHARLOTTE. Though the giving the heart is one of the last of all laughable considerations in the marriage of a girl of spirit, yet I should like to hear what antiquated notions the dear little piece of old-fashioned prudery has got in her head.

LETITIA. Why, you know that old Mr. John-Richard-Robert-Jacob-Isaac-Abraham-Cornelius Van Dumpling, Billy Dimple's father (for he has thought fit to soften his name, as well as manners, during his English tour), was the most

---

[3] In Manhattan, a vogue place to stroll.   [4] Battery Park, at the southern end of Manhattan.
[5] Damn me.   [6] Hairdresser.
[7] *The Spectator*, an eighteenth-century English publication in which papers on the morals and literature of the time were introduced under the name "Mr. Spectator."
[8] A shiny silk fabric.

intimate friend of Maria's father. The old folks, about a year before Mr. Van Dumpling's death, proposed this match: The young folks were accordingly introduced, and told they must love one another. Billy was then a good-natured, decent-dressing young fellow, with a little dash of the coxcomb,[9] such as our young fellows of fortune usually have. At this time, I really believe she thought she loved him; and had they then been married, I doubt not they might have jogged on, to the end of the chapter, a good kind of a sing-song lack-a-daysaical life, as other honest married folks do.

CHARLOTTE.   Why did they not then marry?

LETITIA.   Upon the death of his father, Billy went to England to see the world and rub off a little of the patroon rust.[10] During his absence, Maria, like a good girl, to keep herself constant to her *nown true-love,* avoided company, and betook herself, for her amusement, to her books, and her dear Billy's letters. But, alas! how many ways has the mischievous demon of inconstancy of stealing into a woman's heart! Her love was destroyed by the very means she took to support it.

CHARLOTTE.   How?—Oh! I have it—some likely young beau found the way to her study.

LETITIA.   Be patient, Charlotte; your head so runs upon beaux. Why, she read Sir Charles Grandison, Clarissa Harlow, Shenstone, and the Sentimental Journey;[11] and between whiles, as I said, Billy's letters. But, as her taste improved, her love declined. The contrast was so striking betwixt the good sense of her books and the flimsiness of her love-letters, that she discovered she had unthinkingly engaged her hand without her heart; and then the whole transaction, managed by the old folks, now appeared so unsentimental, and looked so like bargaining for a bale of goods, that she found she ought to have rejected, according to every rule of romance, even the man of her choice, if imposed upon her in that manner. Clary Harlow would have scorned such a match.

CHARLOTTE.   Well, how was it on Mr. Dimple's return? Did he meet a more favourable reception than his letters?

LETITIA.   Much the same. She spoke of him with respect abroad, and with contempt in her closet.[12] She watched his conduct and conversation, and found that he had by travelling acquired the wickedness of Lovelace[13] without his wit, and the politeness of Sir Charles Grandison without his generosity. The ruddy youth, who washed his face at the cistern every morning, and swore and looked eternal love and constancy, was now metamorphosed into a flippant, palid, polite beau, who devotes the morning to his toilet, reads a few pages of Chesterfield's letters,[14] and then minces out, to put the infamous principles in practice upon every woman he meets.

CHARLOTTE.   But, if she is so apt at conjuring up these sentimental bugbears, why does she not discard him at once?

LETITIA.   Why, she thinks her word too sacred to be trifled with. Besides, her

---

[9] An arrogant man.   [10] Country manners.

[11] *Sir Charles Grandison* (1753–1754) and *Clarissa Harlow[e]* (1747–1758), novels by Samuel Richardson (1689–1761); William Shenstone (1714–1763), a poet who wrote "Pastoral Ballad" and *A Sentimental Journey* (1768), a novel by Laurence Sterne (1713–1768). All are works in which sentimentality is a primary element.

[12] Study.   [13] The villain in *Clarissa Harlowe*.

[14] The earl of Chesterfield, Philip Stanhope (1694–1773), wrote letters to teach his son good manners; however, when they were published in 1774, they were quickly criticized for being hypocritical and frivolous.

father, who has a great respect for the memory of his deceased friend, is ever telling her how he shall renew his years in their union, and repeating the dying injunctions of old Van Dumpling.

CHARLOTTE.   A mighty pretty story! And so you would make me believe that the sensible Maria would give up Dumpling manor, and the all-accomplished Dimple as a husband, for the absurd, ridiculous reason, forsooth, because she despises and abhors him. Just as if a lady could not be privileged to spend a man's fortune, ride in his carriage, be called after his name, and call him her *nown dear lovee* when she wants money, without loving and respecting the great he-creature. Oh! my dear girl, you are a monstrous prude.

LETITIA.   I don't say what I would do; I only intimate how I suppose she wishes to act.

CHARLOTTE.   No, no, no! A fig for sentiment. If she breaks, or wishes to break, with Mr. Dimple, depend upon it, she has some other man in her eye. A woman rarely discards one lover until she is sure of another. Letitia little thinks what a clue I have to Dimple's conduct. The generous man submits to render himself disgusting to Maria, in order that she may leave him at liberty to address me. I must change the subject.   [*Aside, and rings a bell.*

Enter SERVANT

Frank, order the horses to.——Talking of marriage, did you hear that Sally Bloomsbury is going to be married next week to Mr. Indigo, the rich Carolinian?

LETITIA.   Sally Bloomsbury married!—why, she is not yet in her teens.

CHARLOTTE.   I do not know how that is, but you may depend upon it, 'tis a done affair. I have it from the best authority. There is my aunt Wyerly's Hannah. You know Hannah; though a black, she is a wench that was never caught in a lie in her life. Now, Hannah has a brother who courts Sarah, Mrs. Catgut the milliner's girl, and she told Hannah's brother, and Hannah, who, as I said before, is a girl of undoubted veracity, told it directly to me, that Mrs. Catgut was making a new cap for Miss Bloomsbury, which, as it was very dressy, it is very probable is designed for a wedding cap. Now, as she is to be married, who can it be but to Mr. Indigo? Why, there is no other gentleman that visits at her papa's.

LETITIA.   Say not a word more, Charlotte. Your intelligence[15] is so direct and well grounded, it is almost a pity that it is not a piece of scandal.

CHARLOTTE.   Oh! I am the pink of prudence. Though I cannot charge myself with ever having discredited a tea-party by my silence, yet I take care never to report anything of my acquaintance, especially if it is to their credit, —*discredit,* I mean,—until I have searched to the bottom of it. It is true, there is infinite pleasure in this charitable pursuit. Oh! how delicious to go and condole with the friends of some backsliding sister, or to retire with some old dowager or maiden aunt of the family, who love scandal so well that they cannot forbear gratifying their appetite at the expense of the reputation of their nearest relations! And then to return full fraught with a rich collection of circumstances, to retail to the next circle of our acquaintance under the strongest injunctions of secrecy,—ha, ha, ha!—interlarding the melancholy tale with so many doleful shakes of the head, and more doleful "Ah! who would have thought it! so amiable, so prudent a young

---

[15] News.

lady, as we all thought her, what a monstrous pity! well, I have nothing to charge myself with; I acted the part of a friend, I warned her of the principles of that rake,[16] I told her what would be the consequence; I told her so, I told her so."— Ha, ha, ha!

LETITIA.   Ha, ha, ha! Well, but, Charlotte, you don't tell me what you think of Miss Bloomsbury's match.

CHARLOTTE.   Think! why I think it is probable she cried for a plaything, and they have given her a husband. Well, well, well, the puling chit[17] shall not be deprived of her plaything: 'tis only exchanging London dolls for American babies.—Apropos, of babies, have you heard what Mrs. Affable's high-flying notions of delicacy have come to?

LETITIA.   Who, she that was Miss Lovely?

CHARLOTTE.   The same; she married Bob Affable of Schenectady. Don't you remember?

Enter SERVANT

SERVANT.   Madam, the carriage is ready.

LETITIA.   Shall we go to the stores first, or visiting?

CHARLOTTE.   I should think it rather too early to visit, especially Mrs. Prim; you know she is so particular.

LETITIA.   Well, but what of Mrs. Affable?

CHARLOTTE.   Oh, I'll tell you as we go; come, come, let us hasten. I hear Mrs. Catgut has some of the prettiest caps arrived you ever saw. I shall die if I have not the first sight of them.   [*Exeunt*.

SCENE II

A Room in VAN ROUGH'S *House*

MARIA *sitting disconsolate at a Table, with Books, Etc.*

SONG[18]

I

The sun sets in night, and the stars shun the day;
But glory remains when their lights fade away!
Begin, ye tormentors! your threats are in vain,
For the son of Alknomook shall never complain.

II

Remember the arrows he shot from his bow;
Remember your chiefs by his hatchet laid low:
Why so slow?—do you wait till I shrink from the pain?
No—the son of Alknomook will never complain.

[16] Rakehell, a degenerate man.   [17] A childish, sniveling woman.
[18] The author of this poem is unknown; however, it has been credited to a number of poets, including Royall Tyler and Philip Freneau.

III

Remember the wood where in ambush we lay,
And the scalps which we bore from your nation away:
Now the flame rises fast, you exult in my pain;
But the son of Alknomook can never complain.

IV

I go to the land where my father is gone;
His ghost shall rejoice in the fame of his son:
Death comes like a friend, he relieves me from pain;
And thy son, Oh Alknomook! has scorn'd to complain.

There is something in this song which ever calls forth my affections. The manly virtue of courage, that fortitude which steels the heart against the keenest misfortunes, which interweaves the laurel of glory amidst the instruments of torture and death, displays something so noble, so exalted, that in despite of the prejudices of education I cannot but admire it, even in a savage. The prepossession which our sex is supposed to entertain for the character of a soldier is, I know, a standing piece of raillery[19] among the wits. A cockade,[20] a lapell'd coat, and a feather, they will tell you, are irresistible by a female heart. Let it be so. Who is it that considers the helpless situation of our sex, that does not see that we each moment stand in need of a protector, and that a brave one too? Formed of the more delicate materials of nature, endowed only with the softer passions, incapable, from our ignorance of the world, to guard against the wiles of mankind, our security for happiness often depends upon their generosity and courage. Alas! how little of the former do we find! How inconsistent! that man should be leagued to destroy that honour upon which solely rests his respect and esteem. Ten thousand temptations allure us, ten thousand passions betray us; yet the smallest deviation from the path of rectitude is followed by the contempt and insult of man, and the more remorseless pity of woman; years of penitence and tears cannot wash away the stain, nor a life of virtue obliterate its remembrance. Reputation is the life of woman; yet courage to protect it is masculine and disgusting; and the only safe asylum a woman of delicacy can find is in the arms of a man of honour. How naturally, then should we love the brave and the generous; how gratefully should we bless the arm raised for our protection, when nerv'd by virtue and directed by honour! Heaven grant that the man with whom I may be connected—may be connected! Whither has my imagination transported me—whither does it now lead me? Am I not indissolubly engaged, "by every obligation of honour which my own consent and my father's approbation can give," to a man who can never share my affections, and whom a few days hence it will be criminal for me to disapprove—to disapprove! would to heaven that were all—to despise. For, can the most frivolous manners, actuated by the most depraved heart, meet, or merit, anything but contempt from every woman of delicacy and sentiment?

[VAN ROUGH *without*. Mary!]

Ha! my father's voice—Sir!——

---

[19] Satire.   [20] A medallion worn on the hat, part of a military uniform.

Enter VAN ROUGH

VAN ROUGH.   What, Mary, always singing doleful ditties, and moping over these plaguy[21] books.

MARIA.   I hope, Sir, that it is not criminal to improve my mind with books, or to divert my melancholy with singing, at my leisure hours.

VAN ROUGH.   Why, I don't know that, child; I don't know that. They us'd to say, when I was a young man, that if a woman knew how to make a pudding, and to keep herself out of fire and water, she knew enough for a wife. Now, what good have these books done you? have they not made you melancholy? as you call it. Pray, what right has a girl of your age to be in the dumps? haven't you everything your heart can wish; an't you going to be married to a young man of great fortune; an't you going to have the quit-rent[22] of twenty miles square?

MARIA.   One-hundredth part of the land, and a lease for life of the heart of a man I could love, would satisfy me.

VAN ROUGH.   Pho, pho, pho! child; nonsense, downright nonsense, child. This comes of your reading your story-books; your Charles Grandisons, your Sentimental Journals, and your Robinson Crusoes, and such other trumpery. No, no, no! child; it is money makes the mare go; keep your eye upon the main chance, Mary.

MARIA.   Marriage, Sir, is, indeed, a very serious affair.

VAN ROUGH.   You are right, child; you are right. I am sure I found it so, to my cost.

MARIA.   I mean, Sir, that as marriage is a portion for life, and so intimately involves our happiness, we cannot be too considerate in the choice of our companion.

VAN ROUGH.   Right, child; very right. A young woman should be very sober when she is making her choice, but when she has once made it, as you have done, I don't see why she should not be as merry as a grig;[23] I am sure she has reason enough to be so. Solomon says that "there is a time to laugh, and a time to weep."[24] Now, a time for a young woman to laugh is when she has made sure of a good rich husband. Now, a time to cry, according to you, Mary, is when she is making choice of him; but I should think that a young woman's time to cry was when she despaired of *getting* one. Why, there was your mother, now: to be sure, when I popp'd the question to her she did look a little silly; but when she had once looked down on her apron-strings, as all modest young women us'd to do, and drawled out ye—s, she was as brisk and as merry as a bee.

MARIA.   My honoured mother, Sir, had no motive to melancholy; she married the man of her choice.

VAN ROUGH.   The man of her choice! And pray, Mary, an't you going to marry the man of your choice—what trumpery notion is this? It is these vile books [*throwing them away*]. I'd have you to know, Mary, if you won't make young Van Dumpling the man of *your* choice, you shall marry him as the man of *my* choice.

MARIA.   You terrify me, Sir. Indeed, Sir, I am all submission. My will is yours.

---

[21] Plaguing, annoying.   [22] A fixed fee, such as rent.   [23] A cricket.
[24] From Ecclesiastes 3:4.

VAN ROUGH.   Why, that is the way your mother us'd to talk. "My will is yours, my dear Mr. Van Rough, my will is yours"; but she took special care to have her own way, though, for all that.

MARIA.   Do not reflect upon my mother's memory, Sir——

VAN ROUGH.   Why not, Mary, why not? She kept me from speaking my mind all her *life,* and do you think she shall henpeck me now she is *dead* too? Come, come; don't go to sniveling; be a good girl, and mind the main chance. I'll see you well settled in the world.

MARIA.   I do not doubt your love, Sir, and it is my duty to obey you. I will endeavour to make my duty and inclination go hand in hand.

VAN ROUGH.   Well, well, Mary; do you be a good girl, mind the main chance, and never mind inclination. Why, do you know that I have been down in the cellar this very morning to examine a pipe[25] of Madeira which I purchased the week you were born, and mean to tap on your wedding day?—That pipe cost me fifty pounds sterling. It was well worth sixty pounds; but I overreach'd[26] Ben Bulkhead, the supercargo.[27] I'll tell you the whole story. You must know that——

Enter SERVANT

SERVANT.   Sir, Mr. Transfer, the broker, is below.   [*Exit.*

VAN ROUGH.   Well, Mary, I must go. Remember, and be a good girl, and mind the main chance.   [*Exit.*

MARIA [*alone*].   How deplorable is my situation! How distressing for a daughter to find her heart militating with her filial duty! I know my father loves me tenderly; why then do I reluctantly obey him? Heaven knows! with what reluctance I should oppose the will of a parent, or set an example of filial disobedience; at a parent's command, I could wed awkwardness and deformity. Were the heart of my husband good, I would so magnify his good qualities with the eye of conjugal affection, that the defects of his person and manners should be lost in the emanation of his virtues. At a father's command, I could embrace poverty. Were the poor man my husband, I would learn resignation to my lot; I would enliven our frugal meal with good humour, and chase away misfortune from our cottage with a smile. At a father's command, I could almost submit to what every female heart knows to be the most mortifying, to marry a weak man, and blush at my husband's folly in every company I visited. But to marry a depraved wretch, whose only virtue is a polished exterior; who is actuated by the unmanly ambition of conquering the defenceless; whose heart, insensible to the emotions of patriotism, dilates at the plaudits of every unthinking girl; whose laurels are the sighs and tears of the miserable victims of his specious behaviour,—can he, who has no regard for the peace and happiness of other families, ever have a due regard for the peace and happiness of his own? Would to heaven that my father were not so hasty in his temper? Surely, if I were to state my reasons for declining this match, he would not compel me to marry a man, whom, though my lips may solemnly promise to honour, I find my heart must ever despise.   [*Exit.*

END OF THE FIRST ACT

[25] A cask to hold wine.   [26] Outsmarted.
[27] A ship's officer who takes care of the commercial matters of a voyage.

ACT II. SCENE I

Enter CHARLOTTE *and* LETITIA

CHARLOTTE [*at entering*]. Betty, take those things out of the carriage and carry them to my chamber; see that you don't tumble them. My dear, I protest, I think it was the homeliest of the whole. I declare I was almost tempted to return and change it.

LETITIA.   Why would you take it?

CHARLOTTE.   Didn't Mrs. Catgut say it was the most fashionable?

LETITIA.   But, my dear, it will never fit becomingly on you.

CHARLOTTE.   I know that; but did not you hear Mrs. Catgut say it was fashionable?

LETITIA.   Did you see that sweet airy cap with the white sprig?

CHARLOTTE.   Yes, and I longed to take it; but, my dear, what could I do? Did not Mrs. Catgut say it was the most fashionable; and if I had not taken it, was not that awkward gawky, Sally Slender, ready to purchase it immediately?

LETITIA.   Did you observe how she tumbled over the things at the next shop, and then went off without purchasing anything, nor even thanking the poor man for his trouble? But, of all the awkward creatures, did you see Miss Blouze endeavouring to thrust her unmerciful arm into those small kid gloves?

CHARLOTTE.   Ha, ha, ha, ha!

LETITIA.   Then did you take notice with what an affected warmth of friendship she and Miss Wasp met? when all their acquaintance know how much pleasure they take in abusing each other in every company.

CHARLOTTE.   Lud![1] Letitia, is that so extraordinary? Why, my dear, I hope you are not going to turn sentimentalist. Scandal, you know, is but amusing ourselves with the faults, foibles, follies, and reputations of our friends; indeed, I don't know why we should have friends, if we are not at liberty to make use of them. But no person is so ignorant of the world as to suppose, because I amuse myself with a lady's faults, that I am obliged to quarrel with her person every time we meet: believe me, my dear, we should have very few acquaintance at that rate.

SERVANT *enters and delivers a letter to* CHARLOTTE, *and*——   [*Exit.*

CHARLOTTE.   You'll excuse me, my dear.   [*Opens and reads to herself.*

LETITIA.   Oh, quite excusable.

CHARLOTTE.   As I hope to be married, my brother Henry is in the city.

LETITIA.   What, your brother, Colonel Manly?

CHARLOTTE.   Yes, my dear; the only brother I have in the world.

LETITIA.   Was he never in this city?

CHARLOTTE.   Never nearer than Harlem Heights,[2] where he lay with his regiment.

LETITIA.   What sort of a being is this brother of yours? If he is as chatty, as pretty, as sprightly as you, half the belles in the city will be pulling caps for him.

CHARLOTTE.   My brother is the very counterpart and reverse of me: I am gay,

---

[1] Variant of "Lord!"

[2] Now an area in New York City, a site of a battle in the American Revolution.

he is grave; I am airy, he is solid; I am ever selecting the most pleasing objects for my laughter, he has a tear for every pitiful one. And thus, whilst he is plucking the briars and thorns from the path of the unfortunate, I am strewing my own path with roses.

LETITIA.   My sweet friend, not quite so poetical, and a little more particular.

CHARLOTTE.   Hands off, Letitia. I feel the rage of simile upon me; I can't talk to you in any other way. My brother has a heart replete with the noblest sentiments, but then, it is like—it is like—Oh! you provoking girl, you have deranged all my ideas—it is like—Oh! I have it—his heart is like an old maiden lady's bandbox; it contains many costly things, arranged with the most scrupulous nicety, yet the misfortune is that they are too delicate, costly, and antiquated for common use.

LETITIA.   By what I can pick out of your flowery description, your brother is no beau.

CHARLOTTE.   No, indeed; he makes no pretension to the character. He'd ride, or rather fly, an hundred miles to relieve a distressed object, or to do a gallant act in the service of his country; but should you drop your fan or bouquet in his presence, it is ten to one that some beau at the farther end of the room would have the honour of presenting it to you before he had observed that it fell. I'll tell you one of his antiquated, anti-gallant notions. He said once in my presence, in a room full of company,—would you believe it?—in a large circle of ladies, that the best evidence a gentleman could give a young lady of his respect and affection was to endeavour in a friendly manner to rectify her foibles. I protest I was crimson to the eyes, upon reflecting that I was known as his sister.

LETITIA.   Insupportable creature! tell a lady of her faults! if he is so grave, I fear I have no chance of captivating him.

CHARLOTTE.   His conversation is like a rich, old-fashioned brocade,—it will stand alone; every sentence is a sentiment. Now you may judge what a time I had with him, in my twelve months' visit to my father. He read me such lectures, out of pure brotherly affection, against the extremes of fashion, dress, flirting, and coquetry, and all the other dear things which he knows I doat upon, that I protest his conversation made me as melancholy as if I had been at church; and heaven knows, though I never prayed to go there but on one occasion, yet I would have exchanged his conversation for a psalm and a sermon. Church is rather melancholy, to be sure; but then I can ogle the beaux, and be regaled with "here endeth the first lesson," but his brotherly *here,* you would think had no end. You captivate him! Why, my dear, he would as soon fall in love with a box of Italian flowers. There is Maria, now, if she were not engaged, she might do something. Oh! how I should like to see that pair of pensorosos[3] together, looking as grave as two sailors' wives of a stormy night, with a flow of sentiment meandering through their conversation like purling streams in modern poetry.

LETITIA.   Oh! my dear fanciful——

CHARLOTTE.   Hush! I hear some person coming through the entry.

Enter SERVANT

SERVANT.   Madam, there's a gentleman below who calls himself Colonel Manly; do you chuse to be at home?

---

[3] Superfluously thoughtful persons.

CHARLOTTE.   Shew him in. [*Exit Servant.*] Now for a sober face.

Enter COLONEL MANLY

MANLY.   My dear Charlotte, I am happy that I once more enfold you within the arms of fraternal affection. I know you are going to ask (amiable impatience!) how our parents do,—the venerable pair transmit you their blessing by me. They totter on the verge of a well-spent life, and wish only to see their children settled in the world, to depart in peace.

CHARLOTTE.   I am very happy to hear that they are well. [*Coolly.*] Brother, will you give me leave to introduce you to our uncle's ward, one of my most intimate friends?

MANLY.   [*Saluting Letitia*]. I ought to regard your friends as my own.

CHARLOTTE.   Come, Letitia, do give us a little dash of your vivacity; my brother is so sentimental and so grave, that I protest he'll give us the vapours.[4]

MANLY.   Though sentiment and gravity, I know, are banished the polite world, yet I hoped they might find some countenance in the meeting of such near connections as brother and sister.

CHARLOTTE.   Positively, brother, if you go one step further in this strain, you will set me crying, and that, you know, would spoil my eyes; and then I should never get the husband which our good papa and mamma have so kindly wished me—never be established in the world.

MANLY.   Forgive me, my sister,—I am no enemy to mirth; I love your sprightliness; and I hope it will one day enliven the hours of some worthy man; but when I mention the respectable authors of my existence,—the cherishers and protectors of my helpless infancy, whose hearts glow with such fondness and attachment that they would willingly lay down their lives for my welfare,—you will excuse me if I am so unfashionable as to speak of them with some degree of respect and reverence.

CHARLOTTE.   Well, well, brother; if you won't be gay, we'll not differ; I will be as grave as you wish. [*Affects gravity.*] And so, brother, you have come to the city to exchange some of your commutation notes[5] for a little pleasure?

MANLY.   Indeed you are mistaken; my errand is not of amusement, but business; and as I neither drink nor game, my expenses will be so trivial, I shall have no occasion to sell my notes.

CHARLOTTE.   Then you won't have occasion to do a very good thing. Why, here was the Vermont General—he came down some time since, sold all his musty notes at one stroke, and then laid the cash out in trinkets for his dear Fanny. I want a dozen pretty things myself; have you got the notes with you?

MANLY.   I shall be ever willing to contribute, as far as it is in my power, to adorn or in any way to please my sister; yet I hope I shall never be obliged for this to sell my notes. I may be romantic, but I preserve them as a sacred deposit. Their full amount is justly due to me, but as embarrassments, the natural consequences of a long war, disable my country from supporting its credit, I shall wait with patience until it is rich enough to discharge them. If that is not in my day, they shall be transmitted as an honourable certificate to posterity, that I have humbly

---

[4] Make us melancholy.

[5] At the end of the American Revolution, officers of the then dissolved Continental Army were given notes with a promise of payment equal to five year's full pay. Many officers cashed in the notes before they were due, and typically at a large discount.

imitated our illustrious WASHINGTON, in having exposed my health and life in the service of my country, without reaping any other reward than the glory of conquering in so arduous a contest.

CHARLOTTE.   Well said heroics. Why, my dear Henry, you have such a lofty way of saying things, that I protest I almost tremble at the thought of introducing you to the polite circles in the city. The belles would think you were a player[6] run mad, with your head filled with old scraps of tragedy; and as to the beaux, they might admire, because they would not understand you. But, however, I must, I believe, introduce you to two or three ladies of my acquaintance.

LETITIA.   And that will make him acquainted with thirty or forty beaux.

CHARLOTTE.   Oh! brother, you don't know what a fund of happiness you have in store.

MANLY.   I fear, sister, I have not refinement sufficient to enjoy it.

CHARLOTTE.   Oh! you cannot fail being pleased.

LETITIA.   Our ladies are so delicate and dressy.

CHARLOTTE.   And our beaux so dressy and delicate.

LETITIA.   Our ladies chat and flirt so agreeably.

CHARLOTTE.   And our beaux simper and bow so gracefully.

LETITIA.   With their hair so trim and neat.

CHARLOTTE.   And their faces so soft and sleek.

LETITIA.   Their buckles so tonish[7] and bright.

CHARLOTTE.   And their hands so slender and white.

LETITIA.   I vow, Charlotte, we are quite poetical.

CHARLOTTE.   And then, brother, the faces of the beaux are of such a lily-white hue! None of that horrid robustness of constitution, that vulgar cornfed glow of health, which can only serve to alarm an unmarried lady with apprehension, and prove a melancholy memento to a married one, that she can never hope for the happiness of being a widow. I will say this to the credit of our city beaux, that such is the delicacy of their complexion, dress, and address, that, even had I no reliance upon the honour of the dear Adonises, I would trust myself in any possible situation with them, without the least apprehensions of rudeness.

MANLY.   Sister Charlotte!

CHARLOTTE.   Now, now, now, brother [*interrupting him*], now don't go to spoil my mirth with a dash of your gravity; I am so glad to see you, I am in tiptop spirits. Oh! that you could be with us at a little snug party. There is Billy Simper, Jack Chaffé, and Colonel Van Titter, Miss Promonade, and the two Miss Tambours, sometimes make a party, with some other ladies, in a side-box at the play. Everything is conducted with such decorum. First we bow round to the company in general, then to each one in particular, then we have so many inquiries after each other's health, and we are so happy to meet each other, and it is so many ages since we last had that pleasure, and if a married lady is in company, we have such a sweet dissertation upon her son Bobby's chin-cough;[8] then the curtain rises, then our sensibility is all awake, and then, by the mere force of apprehension, we torture some harmless expression into a double meaning, which the poor author never dreamt of, and then we have recourse to our fans, and then we blush, and then the gentlemen jog one another, peep under the fan, and make the prettiest remarks; and then we giggle and they simper, and they giggle and we simper, and then the curtain drops, and then for nuts and oranges, and then we bow, and it's

---

[6] Actor.   [7] Fashionable.   [8] Whooping cough.

pray, Ma'am, take it, and pray, Sir, keep it, and oh! not for the world, Sir; and then the curtain rises again, and then we blush and giggle and simper and bow all over again. Oh! the sentimental charms of a side-box conversation!   [*All laugh.*

MANLY.   Well, sister, I join heartily with you in the laugh; for, in my opinion, it is as justifiable to laugh at folly as it is reprehensible to ridicule misfortune.

CHARLOTTE.   Well, but, brother, positively I can't introduce you in these clothes: why, your coat looks as if it were calculated for the vulgar purpose of keeping yourself comfortable.

MANLY.   This coat was my regimental coat in the late war. The public tumults of our state have induced me to buckle on the sword in support of that government which I once fought to establish. I can only say, sister, that there was a time when this coat was respectable, and some people even thought that those men who had endured so many winter campaigns in the service of their country, without bread, clothing, or pay, at least deserved that the poverty of their appearance should not be ridiculed.

CHARLOTTE.   We agree in opinion entirely, brother, though it would not have done for me to have said it: it is the coat makes the man respectable. In the time of the war, when we were almost frightened to death, why, your coat was respectable, that is fashionable; now another kind of coat is fashionable, that is, respectable. And pray direct the taylor to make yours the height of the fashion.

MANLY.   Though it is of little consequence to me of what shape my coat is, yet, as to the height of the fashion, there you will please to excuse me, sister. You know my sentiments on that subject. I have often lamented the advantage which the French have over us in that particular. In Paris, the fashions have their dawnings, their routine, and declensions, and depend as much upon the caprice of the day as in other countries; but there every lady assumes a right to deviate from the general *ton*[9] as far as will be of advantage to her own appearance. In America, the cry is, what is the fashion? and we follow it indiscriminately, because it is so.

CHARLOTTE.   Therefore it is, that when large hoops are in fashion, we often see many a plump girl lost in the immensity of a hoop-petticoat, whose want of height and *en-bon-point*[10] would never have been remarked in any other dress. When the high head-dress is the mode, how then do we see a lofty cushion, with a profusion of gauze, feathers, and ribband, supported by a face no bigger than an apple! whilst a broad full-faced lady, who really would have appeared tolerably handsome in a large head-dress, looks with her smart chapeau as masculine as a soldier.

MANLY.   But remember, my dear sister, and I wish all my fair country-women would recollect, that the only excuse a young lady can have for going extravagantly into a fashion is because it makes her look extravagantly handsome.—Ladies, I must wish you a good morning.

CHARLOTTE.   But, brother, you are going to make home with us.

MANLY.   Indeed I cannot. I have seen my uncle and explained that matter.

CHARLOTTE.   Come and dine with us, then. We have a family dinner about half-past four o'clock.

MANLY.   I am engaged to dine with the Spanish ambassador. I was introduced to him by an old brother officer; and instead of freezing me with a cold card of compliment to dine with him ten days hence, he, with the true old Castilian frankness, in a friendly manner, asked me to dine with him to-day—an honour I could

---

[9] Fashion.   [10] Plumpness.

not refuse. Sister, adieu—Madam, your most obedient——   [*Exit.*

CHARLOTTE.   I will wait upon you to the door, brother; I have something particular to say to you.   [*Exit.*

LETITIA [*alone*].   What a pair!—She the pink of flirtation, he the essence of everything that is *outré*[11] and gloomy.—I think I have completely deceived Charlotte by my manner of speaking of Mr. Dimple; she's too much the friend of Maria to be confided in. He is certainly rendering himself disagreeable to Maria, in order to break with her and proffer his hand to me. This is what the delicate fellow hinted in our last conversation.   [*Exit.*

SCENE II

The Mall

Enter JESSAMY

JESSAMY.   Positively this Mall is a very pretty place. I hope the cits[12] won't ruin it by repairs. To be sure, it won't do to speak of in the same day with Ranelegh or Vauxhall;[13] however, it's a fine place for a young fellow to display his person to advantage. Indeed, nothing is lost here; the girls have taste, and I am very happy to find they have adopted the elegant London fashion of looking back, after a genteel fellow like me has passed them.—Ah! who comes here? This, by his awkwardness, must be the Yankee colonel's servant. I'll accost him.

Enter JONATHAN

Votre très-humble serviteur, Monsieur.[14] I understand Colonel Manly, the Yankee officer, has the honour of your services.

JONATHAN.   Sir!——

JESSAMY.   I say, Sir, I understand that Colonel Manly has the honour of having you for a servant.

JONATHAN.   Servant! Sir, do you take me for a neger,—I am Colonel Manly's waiter.

JESSAMY.   A true Yankee distinction, egad, without a difference. Why, Sir, do you not perform all the offices of a servant? do you not even blacken his boots?

JONATHAN.   Yes; I do grease them a bit sometimes; but I am a true blue son of liberty, for all that. Father said I should come as Colonel Manly's waiter, to see the world, and all that; but no man shall master me. My father has as good a farm as the colonel.

JESSAMY.   Well, Sir, we will not quarrel about terms upon the eve of an acquaintance from which I promise myself so much satisfaction;—therefore, sans ceremonie——

JONATHAN.   What?——

JESSAMY.   I say I am extremely happy to see Colonel Manly's waiter.

JONATHAN.   Well, and I vow, too, I am pretty considerably glad to see you; but

---

[11] Fantastic, odd.   [12] Disparaging word for "citizens."
[13] Public parks around London.
[14] "Your most humble servant, Sir" (French).

what the dogs need of all this outlandish lingo? Who may you be, Sir, if I may be so bold?

JESSAMY.   I have the honour to be Mr. Dimple's servant, or, if you please, waiter. We lodge under the same roof, and should be glad of the honour of your acquaintance.

JONATHAN.   You a waiter! by the living jingo, you look so topping, I took you for one of the agents to Congress.

JESSAMY.   The brute has discernment, notwithstanding his appearance.—Give me leave to say I wonder then at your familiarity.

JONATHAN.   Why, as to the matter of that, Mr.——; pray, what's your name?

JESSAMY.   Jessamy, at your service.

JONATHAN.   Why, I swear we don't make any great matter of distinction in our state between quality and other folks.

JESSAMY.   This is, indeed, a levelling principle.—I hope, Mr. Jonathan, you have not taken part with the insurgents.

JONATHAN.   Why, since General Shays has sneaked off and given us the bag to hold, I don't care to give my opinion; but you'll promise not to tell—put your ear this way—you won't tell?—I vow I did think the sturgeons were right.

JESSAMY.   I thought, Mr. Jonathan, you Massachusetts men always argued with a gun in your hand. Why didn't you join them?

JONATHAN.   Why, the colonel is one of those folks called the Shin—Shin[15]— dang it all, I can't speak them lignum vitae[16] words—you know who I mean— there is a company of them—they wear a china goose at their button-hole—a kind of gilt thing.—Now the colonel told father and brother,—you must know there are, let me see—there is Elnathan, Silas, and Barnabas, Tabitha—no, no, she's a she—tarnation, now I have it—there's Elnathan, Silas, Barnabas, Jonathan, that's I—seven of us, six went into the wars, and I staid at home to take care of mother. Colonel said that it was a burning shame for the true blue Bunker Hill sons of liberty, who had fought Governor Hutchinson, Lord North, and the Devil, to have any hand in kicking up a cursed dust against a government which we had, every mother's son of us, a hand in making.

JESSAMY.   Bravo!—Well, have you been abroad in the city since your arrival? What have you seen that is curious and entertaining?

JONATHAN.   Oh! I have seen a power of fine sights. I went to see two marble-stone men and a leaden horse that stands out in doors in all weathers; and when I came where they was, one had got no head, and t'other wern't there. They said as how the leaden man was a damn'd tory, and that he took wit in his anger and rode off in the time of the troubles.

JESSAMY.   But this was not the end of your excursion?

JONATHAN.   Oh, no; I went to a place they call Holy Ground.[17] Now I counted this was a place where folks go to meeting; so I put my hymn-book in my pocket, and walked softly and grave as a minister; and when I came there, the dogs a bit of a meetinghouse could I see. At last I spied a young gentlewoman standing by one of the seats which they have here at the doors. I took her to be the deacon's daughter, and she looked so kind, and so obliging, that I thought I would go and ask her the way to lecture, and—would you think it?—she called me dear, and

---

[15] The Society of the Cincinnati, an organization founded in 1783 by officers of the American Revolution.

[16] "Wood of life" (Latin).

[17] Land owned by Trinity Church, where the brothel district of New York City was located.

sweeting, and honey, just as if we were married: by the living jingo, I had a month's mind to buss[18] her.

JESSAMY.   Well, but how did it end?

JONATHAN.   Why, as I was standing talking with her, a parcel of sailor men and boys got round me, the snarl-headed curs fell a-kicking and cursing of me at such a tarnal[19] rate, that I vow I was glad to take to my heels and split home, right off, tail on end, like a stream of chalk.

JESSAMY.   Why, my dear friend, you are not acquainted with the city; that girl you saw was a——   *[Whispers.*

JONATHAN.   Mercy on my soul! was that young woman a harlot!—Well! if this is New-York Holy Ground, what must the Holy-day Ground be!

JESSAMY.   Well, you should not judge of the city too rashly. We have a number of elegant, fine girls here that make a man's leisure hours pass very agreeably. I would esteem it an honour to announce you to some of them.—Gad! that announce is a select word; I wonder where I picked it up.

JONATHAN.   I don't want to know them.

JESSAMY.   Come, come, my dear friend, I see that I must assume the honour of being the director of your amusements. Nature has given us passions and youth and opportunity stimulate to gratify them. It is no shame, my dear Blueskin,[20] for a man to amuse himself with a little gallantry.

JONATHAN.   Girl huntry! I don't altogether understand. I never played at that game. I know how to play hunt the squirrel, but I can't play anything with the girls; I am as good as married.

JESSAMY.   Vulgar, horrid brute! Married, and above a hundred miles from his wife, and thinks that an objection to his making love to every woman he meets! He never can have read, no, he never can have been in a room with a volume of the divine Chesterfield.—So you are married?

JONATHAN.   No, I don't say so; I said I was as good as married, a kind of promise.

JESSAMY.   As good as married!——

JONATHAN.   Why, yes; there's Tabitha Wymen, the deacon's daughter, at home; she and I have been courting a great while, and folks say as how we are to be married; and so I broke a piece of money[21] with her when we parted, and she promised not to spark it with Solomon Dyer while I am gone. You wou'dn't have me false to my true-love, would you?

JESSAMY.   May be you have another reason for constancy; possibly the young lady has a fortune? Ha! Mr. Jonathan, the solid charms: the chains of love are never so binding as when the links are made of gold.

JONATHAN.   Why, as to fortune, I must needs say her father is pretty dumb rich; he went representative for our town last year. He will give her—let me see—four times seven is—seven times four—nought and carry one,—he will give her twenty acres of land—somewhat rocky though—a Bible, and a cow.

JESSAMY.   Twenty acres of rock, a Bible, and a cow! Why, my dear Mr. Jonathan, we have servant-maids, or, as you would more elegantly express it, wait-resses, in this city, who collect more in one year from their mistresses' cast clothes.

JONATHAN.   You don't say so!——

---

[18] Kiss.   [19] Damned.

[20] Slang for a supporter of the American Revolution, originating from the blue uniforms worn by the soldiers.

[21] Old custom in which a pledge is sealed by the two parties breaking a coin and each keeping a half.

JESSAMY.   Yes, and I'll introduce you to one of them. There is a little lump of flesh and delicacy that lives at next door, waitress to Miss Maria; we often see her on the stoop.

JONATHAN.   But are you sure she would be courted by me?

JESSAMY.   Never doubt it; remember a faint heart never—blisters on my tongue—I was going to be guilty of a vile proverb; flat against the authority of Chesterfield. I say there can be no doubt that the brilliancy of your merit will secure you a favourable reception.

JONATHAN.   Well, but what must I say to her?

JESSAMY.   Say to her! why, my dear friend, though I admire your profound knowledge on every other subject, yet, you will pardon my saying that your want of opportunity has made the female heart escape the poignancy of your penetration. Say to her! Why, when a man goes a-courting, and hopes for success, he must begin with doing, and not saying.

JONATHAN.   Well, what must I do?

JESSAMY.   Why, when you are introduced you must make five or six elegant bows.

JONATHAN.   Six elegant bows! I understand that; six, you say? Well——

JESSAMY.   Then you must press and kiss her hand; then press and kiss, and so on to her lips and cheeks; then talk as much as you can about hearts, darts, flames, nectar and ambrosia—the more incoherent the better.

JONATHAN.   Well, but suppose she should be angry with I?

JESSAMY.   Why, if she should pretend—please to observe, Mr. Jonathan—if she should pretend to be offended, you must—But I'll tell you how my master acted in such a case: He was seated by a young lady of eighteen upon a sofa, plucking with a wanton hand the blooming sweets of youth and beauty. When the lady thought it necessary to check his ardour, she called up a frown upon her lovely face, so irresistibly alluring, that it would have warmed the frozen bosom of age; remember, said she, putting her delicate arms upon his, remember your character and my honour. My master instantly dropped upon his knees, with eyes swimming with love, cheeks glowing with desire, and in the gentlest modulation of voice he said: My dear Caroline, in a few months our hands will be indissolubly united at the altar; our hearts I feel are already so; the favours you now grant as evidence of your affection are favours indeed; yet, when the ceremony is once past, what will now be received with rapture will then be attributed to duty.

JONATHAN.   Well, and what was the consequence?

JESSAMY.   The consequence!—Ah! forgive me, my dear friend, but you New England gentlemen have such a laudable curiosity of seeing the bottom of everything;—why, to be honest, I confess I saw the blooming cherub of a consequence smiling in its angelic mother's arms, about ten months afterwards.

JONATHAN.   Well, if I follow all your plans, make them six bows, and all that, shall I have such little cherubim consequences?

JESSAMY.   Undoubtedly.—What are you musing upon?

JONATHAN.   You say you'll certainly make me acquainted?—Why, I was thinking then how I should contrive to pass this broken piece of silver—won't it buy a sugar-dram?[22]

JESSAMY.   What is that, the love-token from the deacon's daughter?—You come on bravely. But I must hasten to my master. Adieu, my dear friend.

JONATHAN.   Stay, Mr. Jessamy—must I buss her when I am introduced to her?

---

[22] Drink of punch.

JESSAMY.   I told you, you must kiss her.

JONATHAN.   Well, but must I buss her?

JESSAMY.   Why kiss and buss, and buss and kiss, is all one.

JONATHAN.   Oh! my dear friend, though you have a profound knowledge of all, a pugnency of tribulation, you don't know everything.   [*Exit.*

JESSAMY [*alone*]. Well, certainly I improve; my master could not have insinuated himself with more address into the heart of a man he despised. Now will this blundering dog sicken Jenny with his nauseous pawings, until she flies into my arms for very ease. How sweet will the contrast be between the blundering Jonathan and the courtly and accomplished Jessamy!

END OF THE SECOND ACT

ACT III. SCENE I

DIMPLE'S *Room*

DIMPLE *discovered at a Toilet*

DIMPLE [*reading*]: "Women have in general but one object, which is their beauty." Very true, my lord; positively very true. "Nature has hardly formed a woman ugly enough to be insensible to flattery upon her person." Extremely just, my lord; every day's delightful experience confirms this. "If her face is so shocking that she must, in some degree, be conscious of it, her figure and air, she thinks, make ample amends for it." The sallow Miss Wan is a proof of this. Upon my telling the distasteful wretch, the other day, that her countenance spoke the pensive language of sentiment, and that Lady Wortley Montagu[1] declared that if the ladies were arrayed in the garb of innocence, the face would be the last part which would be admired, as Monsieur Milton expresses it, she grinn'd horribly a ghastly smile. "If her figure is deformed, she thinks her face counterbalances it."[2]

Enter JESSAMY *with letters*

Where got you these, Jessamy?

JESSAMY.   Sir, the English packet[3] is arrived.

DIMPLE [*opens and reads a letter enclosing notes*]:

"Sir,

"I have drawn bills on you in favour of Messrs. Van Cash and Co. as per margin. I have taken up your note to Col. Piquet, and discharged your debts to my Lord Lurcher and Sir Harry Rook. I herewith enclose you copies of the bills, which I have no doubt will be immediately honoured. On failure, I shall empower some lawyer in your country to recover the amounts.

"I am, Sir,

"Your most humble servant,

"JOHN HAZARD."

Now, did not my lord expressly say that it was unbecoming a well-bred man to be in a passion, I confess I should be ruffled. [*Reads.*] "There is no accident so

[1] English poet (1689–1762).   [2] A quote from Lord Chesterfield's *Letters* (to his son).
[3] A ship that carries mail and passengers on a set schedule.

unfortunate, which a wise man may not turn to his advantage; nor any accident so fortunate, which a fool will not turn to his disadvantage."[4] True, my lord; but how advantage can be derived from this I can't see. Chesterfield himself, who made, however, the worst practice of the most excellent precepts, was never in so embarrassing a situation. I love the person of Charlotte, and it is necessary I should command the fortune of Letitia. As to Maria!—I doubt not by my *sang-froid*[5] behaviour I shall compel her to decline the match; but the blame must not fall upon me. A prudent man, as my lord says, should take all the credit of a good action to himself, and throw the discredit of a bad one upon others. I must break with Maria, marry Letitia, and as for Charlotte—why, Charlotte must be a companion to my wife.—Here, Jessamy!

Enter JESSAMY

DIMPLE *folds and seals two letters*

DIMPLE.   Here, Jessamy, take this letter to my love.   [*Gives one*.
JESSAMY.   To which of your honour's loves?—Oh! [*reading*] to Miss Letitia, your honour's rich love.
DIMPLE.   And this [*delivers another*] to Miss Charlotte Manly. See that you deliver them privately.
JESSAMY.   Yes, your honour.   [*Going*.
DIMPLE.   Jessamy, who are these strange lodgers that came to the house last night?
JESSAMY.   Why, the master is a Yankee colonel; I have not seen much of him; but the man is the most unpolished animal your honour ever disgraced your eyes by looking upon. I have had one of the most *outré* conversations with him!—He really has a most prodigious effect upon my risibility.
DIMPLE.   I ought, according to every rule of Chesterfield, to wait on him and insinuate myself into his good graces.——Jessamy, wait on the colonel with my compliments, and if he is disengaged I will do myself the honour of paying him my respects.—Some ignorant, unpolished boor——

JESSAMY *goes off and returns*

JESSAMY.   Sir, the colonel is gone out, and Jonathan his servant says that he is gone to stretch his legs upon the Mall.—Stretch his legs! what an indelicacy of diction!
DIMPLE.   Very well. Reach me my hat and sword. I'll accost him there, in my way to Letitia's, as by accident; pretend to be struck by his person and address, and endeavour to steal into his confidence. Jessamy, I have no business for you at present.   [*Exit*.
JESSAMY [*taking up the book*]. My master and I obtain our knowledge from the same source;—though, gad! I think myself much the prettier fellow of the two. [*Surveying himself in the glass*.] That was a brilliant thought, to insinuate that I folded my master's letters for him; the folding is so neat, that it does honour to the operator. I once intended to have insinuated that I wrote his letters too; but that was before I saw them; it won't do now; no honour there, positively.—"Nothing looks more vulgar, [*reading affectedly*] ordinary, and illiberal than ugly, uneven,

---

[4] From Chesterfield's *Letters*.   [5] Composed.

and ragged nails; the ends of which should be kept even and clean, not tipped with black, and cut in small segments of circles."[6] —Segments of circles! surely my lord did not consider that he wrote for the beaux. Segments of circles; what a crabbed term! Now I dare answer that my master, with all his learning, does not know that this means, according to the present mode, let the nails grow long, and then cut them off even at top. [*Laughing without.*] Ha! that's Jenny's titter. I protest I despair of ever teaching that girl to laugh; she has something so execrably natural in her laugh, that I declare it absolutely discomposes my nerves. How came she into our House! [*Calls.*] Jenny!

Enter JENNY

Prythee, Jenny, don't spoil your fine face with laughing.

JENNY.   Why, mustn't I laugh, Mr. Jessamy?

JESSAMY.   You may smile, but, as my lord says, nothing can authorise a laugh.

JENNY.   Well, but I can't help laughing.—Have you seen him, Mr. Jessamy? ha, ha, ha!

JESSAMY.   Seen whom?

JENNY.   Why, Jonathan, the New England colonel's servant. Do you know he was at the play last night, and the stupid creature don't know where he has been. He would not go to a play for the world; he thinks it was a show, as he calls it.

JESSAMY.   As ignorant and unpolished as he is, do you know, Miss Jenny, that I propose to introduce him to the honour of your acquaintance?

JENNY.   Introduce him to me! for what?

JESSAMY.   Why, my lovely girl, that you may take him under your protection, as Madame Rambouillet did young Stanhope; that you may, by your plastic hand, mould this uncouth cub into a gentleman. He is to make love to you.

JENNY.   Make love to me!——

JESSAMY.   Yes, Mistress Jenny, make love to you; and, I doubt not, when he shall become *domesticated* in your kitchen, that this boor, under your auspices, will soon become *un amiable* [aimable] *petit Jonathan.*[7]

JENNY.   I must say, Mr. Jessamy, if he copies after me, he will be vastly, monstrously polite.

JESSAMY.   Stay here one moment, and I will call him.—Jonathan!—Mr. Jonathan!—   [*Calls.*

JONATHAN [*within*]. Holla! there.—[*Enters.*] You promise to stand by me—six bows you say.   [*Bows.*

JESSAMY.   Mrs. Jenny, I have the honour of presenting Mr. Jonathan, Colonel Manly's waiter, to you. I am extremely happy that I have it in my power to make two worthy people acquainted with each other's merits.

JENNY.   So, Mr. Jonathan, I hear you were at the play last night.

JONATHAN.   At the play! why, did you think I went to the devil's drawing-room?

JENNY.   The devil's drawing-room!

JONATHAN.   Yes; why an't cards and dice the devil's device, and the play-house the shop where the devil hangs out the vanities of the world upon the tenter-hooks of temptation? I believe you have not heard how they were acting the old

---

[6] From Chesterfield's *Letters.*   [7] "A well-behaved little Jonathan" (French).

boy one night, and the wicked one came among them sure enough, and went right off in a storm, and carried one quarter of the play-house with him. Oh! no, no, no! you won't catch me at a play-house, I warrant you.

JENNY.   Well, Mr. Jonathan, though I don't scruple your veracity, I have some reasons for believing you were there: pray, where were you about six o'clock?

JONATHAN.   Why, I went to see one Mr. Morrison, the *hocus pocus* man; they said as how he could eat a case knife.

JENNY.   Well, and how did you find the place?

JONATHAN.   As I was going about here and there, to and again, to find it, I saw a great crowd of folks going into a long entry that had lanterns over the door; so I asked a man whether that was not the place where they played *hocus pocus?* He was a very civil, kind man, though he did speak like the Hessians;[8] he lifted up his eyes and said, "They play *hocus pocus* tricks enough there, Got knows, mine friend."

JENNY.   Well—

JONATHAN.   So I went right in, and they shewed me away, clean up to the garret, just like meetinghouse gallery. And so I saw a power of topping folks, all sitting round in little cabbins,[9] "just like father's corn-cribs"; and then there was such a squeaking with the fiddles, and such a tarnal blaze with the lights, my head was near turned. At last the people that sat near me set up such a hissing—hiss— like so many mad cats; and then they went thump, thump, thump, just like our Peleg threshing wheat, and stampt away, just like the nation;[10] and called out for one Mr. Langolee,—I suppose he helps act the tricks.

JENNY.   Well, and what did you do all this time?

JONATHAN.   Gor, I—I liked the fun, and so I thumpt away, and hiss'd as lustily as the best of 'em. One sailor-looking man that sat by me, seeing me stamp, and knowing I was a cute felllow, because I could make a roaring noise, clapt me on the shoulder and said, "You are a d——d hearty cock, smite my timbers!" I told him so I was, but I thought he need not swear so, and make use of such naughty words.

JESSAMY.   The savage!—Well, and did you see the man with his tricks?

JONATHAN.   Why, I vow, as I was looking out for him, they lifted up a great green cloth and let us look right into the next neighbour's house. Have you a good many houses in New-York made so in that 'ere way?

JENNY.   Not many; but did you see the family?

JONATHAN.   Yes, swamp it; I see'd the family.

JENNY.   Well, and how did you like them?

JONATHAN.   Why, I vow they were pretty much like other families;—there was a poor, good-natured, curse of a husband, and a sad rantipole[11] of a wife.

JENNY.   But did you see no other folks?

JONATHAN.   Yes. There was one youngster; they called him Mr. Joseph; he talked as sober and as pious as a minister; but, like some ministers that I know, he was a sly tike in his heart for all that. He was going to ask a young woman to spark it with him, and—the Lord have mercy on my soul!—she was another man's wife.

JESSAMY.   The Wabash![12]

---

[8] German peasants from Hesse whom the British hired as mercenary soldiers in the American Revolution.
[9] Theater boxes.   [10] Damnation.   [11] Wild person.   [12] A cheat.

JENNY.   And did you see any more folks?

JONATHAN.   Why, they came on as thick as mustard. For my part, I thought the house was haunted. There was a soldier fellow, who talked about his row de dow, dow, and courted a young woman; but, of all the cute folk I saw, I liked one little fellow——

JENNY.   Aye! who was he?

JONATHAN.   Why, he had red hair, and a little round plump face like mine, only not altogether so handsome. His name was—Darby;—that was his baptizing name; his other name I forgot. Oh! it was Wig—Wag—Wag-all, Darby Wag-all,[13]—pray, do you know him?—I should like to take a sling[14] with him, or a drap of cyder with a pepper-pod in it, to make it warm and comfortable.

JENNY.   I can't say I have that pleasure.

JONATHAN.   I wish you did; he is a cute fellow. But there was one thing I didn't like in that Mr. Darby; and that was, he was afraid of some of them 'ere shooting irons, such as your troopers wear on training days. How, I'm a true born Yankee American son of liberty, and I never was afraid of a gun yet in all my life.

JENNY.   Well, Mr. Jonathan, you were certainly at the play-house.

JONATHAN.   I at the play-house!—Why didn't I see the play then?

JENNY.   Why, the people you saw were players.

JONATHAN.   Mercy on my soul! did I see the wicked players?—Mayhap that 'ere Darby that I liked so was the old serpent himself, and had his cloven foot in his pocket. Why, I vow, now I come to think on't, the candles seemed to burn blue, and I am sure where I sat it smelt tarnally of brimstone.

JESSAMY.   Well, Mr. Jonathan, from your account, which I confess is very accurate, you must have been at the play-house.

JONATHAN.   Why, I vow, I began to smell a rat. When I came away, I went to the man for my money again; you want your money? says he; yes, says I; for what? says he; why, says I, no man shall jocky me out of my money; I paid my money to see the sights, and the dogs a bit of a sight have I seen, unless you call listening to people's private business a sight. Why, says he, it is the School for Scandalization.[15]—The School for Scandalization!—Oh! ho! no wonder you New-York folks are so cute at it, when you go to school to learn it; and so I jogged off.

JESSAMY.   My dear Jenny, my master's business drags me from you; would to heaven I knew no other servitude than to your charms.

JONATHAN.   Well, but don't go; you won't leave me so——

JESSAMY.   Excuse me.—Remember the cash.   [*Aside to him, and —Exit.*

JENNY.   Mr. Jonathan, won't you please to sit down? Mr. Jessamy tells me you wanted to have some conversation with me.

                                                    [*Having brought forward two chairs, they sit.*

JONATHAN.   Ma'am!——

JENNY.   Sir!——

JONATHAN.   Ma'am!——

JENNY.   Pray, how do you like the city, Sir?

JONATHAN.   Ma'am!——

JENNY.   I say, Sir, how do you like New-York?

---

[13] Thomas Wignell (see Prologue, note 1).   [14] A drink of water and sugar mixed with liquor.

[15] *The School for Scandal,* a play by Richard Sheridan (*1751–1816*), was produced in New York shortly before *The Contrast* opened.

JONATHAN.   Ma'am!——

JENNY.   The stupid creature! but I must pass some little time with him, if it is only to endeavour to learn whether it was his master that made such an abrupt entrance into our house, and my young mistress's heart, this morning. [*Aside.*] As you don't seem to like to talk, Mr. Jonathan—do you sing?

JONATHAN.   Gor, I—I am glad she asked that, for I forgot what Mr. Jessamy bid me say, and I dare as well be hanged as act what he bid me do, I'm so ashamed. [*Aside.*] Yes, Ma'am, I can sing—I can sing Mear, Old Hundred, and Bangor.[16]

JENNY.   Oh! I don't mean psalm tunes. Have you no little song to please the ladies such as Roslin Castle, or the Maid of the Mill?[17]

JONATHAN.   Why, all my tunes go to meeting tunes, save one, and I count you won't altogether like that 'ere.

JENNY.   What is it called?

JONATHAN.   I am sure you have heard folks talk about it; it is called Yankee Doodle.

JENNY.   Oh! it is the tune I am fond of; and if I know anything of my mistress, she would be glad to dance to it. Pray, sing!

JONATHAN [*sings*].

> Father and I went up to camp,
> Along with Captain Goodwin;
> And there we saw the men and boys,
> As thick as hasty-pudding.
>
> > Yankee doodle do, etc.
>
> And there we saw a swamping gun,
> Big as log of maple,
> On a little deuced cart,
> A load for father's cattle.
>
> > Yankee doodle do, etc.
>
> And every time they fired it off
> It took a horn of powder,
> It made a noise—like father's gun,
> Only a nation louder.
>
> > Yankee doodle do, etc.
>
> There was a man in our town,
> His name was——

No, no, that won't do. Now, if I was with Tabitha Wymen and Jemima Cawley down at father Chase's, I shouldn't mind singing this all out before them—you would be affronted if I was to sing that, though that's a lucky thought; if you should be affronted, I have something dang'd cute, which Jessamy told me to say to you.

JENNY.   Is that all! I assure you I like it of all things.

JONATHAN.   No, no; I can sing more; some other time, when you and I are better acquainted, I'll sing the whole of it—no, no—that's a fib—I can't sing but a hundred and ninety verses; our Tabitha at home can sing it all.—   [*Sings.*

[16] Familiar tunes to which hymns were sung.   [17] Popular eighteenth-century songs.

> Marblehead's a rocky place,
> And Cape-Cod is sandy;
> Charlestown is burnt down,
> Boston is the dandy.
>
> Yankee doodle, doodle do, etc.

I vow, my own town song has put me into such topping spirits that I believe I'll begin to do a little, as Jessamy says we must when we go a-courting—[*Runs and kisses her.*] Burning rivers! cooling flames! red-hot roses! pig-nuts! hasty-pudding and ambrosia!

JENNY.   What means this freedom? you insulting wretch.   [*Strikes him.*

JONATHAN.   Are you affronted?

JENNY.   Affronted! with what looks shall I express my anger?

JONATHAN.   Looks! why as to the matter of looks, you look as cross as a witch.

JENNY.   Have you no feeling for the delicacy of my sex?

JONATHAN.   Feeling! Gor, I—I feel the delicacy of your sex pretty smartly [*rubbing his cheek*], though, I vow, I thought when you city ladies courted and married, and all that, you put feeling out of the question. But I want to know whether you are really affronted, or only pretend to be so? 'Cause, if you are certainly right down affronted, I am at the end of my tether; Jessamy didn't tell me what to say to you.

JENNY.   Pretend to be affronted!

JONATHAN.   Aye aye, if you only pretend, you shall hear how I'll go to work to make cherubim consequences.   [*Runs up to her.*

JENNY.   Begone, you brute!

JONATHAN.   That looks like mad; but I won't lose my speech. My dearest Jenny—your name is Jenny, I think?—My dearest Jenny, though I have the highest esteem for the sweet favours you have just now granted me—Gor, that's a fib, though; but Jessamy says it is not wicked to tell lies to the women. [*Aside.*] I say, though I have the highest esteem for the favours you have just now granted me, yet you will consider that, as soon as the dissolvable knot is tied, they will no longer be favours, but only matters of duty and matters of course.

JENNY.   Marry you! you audacious monster! get out of my sight, or, rather, let me fly from you.   [*Exit hastily.*

JONATHAN.   Gor! she's gone off in a swinging passion, before I had time to think of consequences. If this is the way with your city ladies, give me the twenty acres of rock, the Bible, the cow, and Tabitha, and a little peaceable bundling.[18]

SCENE II.

The Mall
Enter MANLY

MANLY.   It must be so, Montague! and it is not all the tribe of Mandevilles[19] that shall convince me that a nation, to become great, must first become dissipated. Luxury is surely the bane of a nation: Luxury! which enervates both soul

---

[18] A wintertime courtship ritual of a couple occupying the same bed, fully dressed.

[19] Edward Montagu (1713–1776) and Bernard de Mandeville (1670–1733), who wrote of the follies of mankind.

and body, by opening a thousand new sources of enjoyment, opens, also, a thousand new sources of contention and want: Luxury! which renders a people weak at home, and accessible to bribery, corruption, and force from abroad. When the Grecian states knew no other tools than the axe and the saw, the Grecians were a great, a free, and a happy people. The kings of Greece devoted their lives to the service of their country, and her senators knew no other superiority over their fellow-citizens than a glorious pre-eminence in danger and virtue. They exhibited to the world a noble spectacle,—a number of independent states united by a similarity of language, sentiment, manners, common interest, and common consent in one grand mutual league of protection. And, thus united, long might they have continued the cherishers of arts and sciences, the protectors of the oppressed, the scourge of tyrants, and the safe asylum of liberty. But when foreign gold, and still more pernicious foreign luxury, had crept among them, they sapped the vitals of their virtue. The virtues of their ancestors were only found in their writings. Envy and suspicion, the vices of little minds, possessed them. The various states engendered jealousies of each other; and, more unfortunately, growing jealous of their great federal council, the Amphictyons,[20] they forgot that their common safety had existed, and would exist, in giving them an honourable extensive prerogative. The common good was lost in the pursuit of private interest; and that people who, by uniting, might have stood against the world in arms, by dividing, crumbled into ruin;—their name is now only known in the page of the historian, and what they once were is all we have left to admire. Oh! that America! Oh! that my country, would, in this her day, learn the things which belong to her peace!

Enter DIMPLE

DIMPLE. You are Colonel Manly, I presume?

MANLY. At your service, Sir.

DIMPLE. My name is Dimple, Sir. I have the honour to be a lodger in the same house with you, and, hearing you were in the Mall, came hither to take the liberty of joining you.

MANLY. You are very obliging, Sir.

DIMPLE. As I understand you are a stranger here, Sir, I have taken the liberty to introduce myself to your acquaintance, as possibly I may have it in my power to point out some things in this city worthy your notice.

MANLY. An attention to strangers is worthy a liberal mind, and must ever be gratefully received. But to a soldier, who has no fixed abode, such attentions are particularly pleasing.

DIMPLE. Sir, there is no character so respectable as that of a soldier. And, indeed, when we reflect how much we owe to those brave men who have suffered so much in the service of their country, and secured to us those inestimable blessings that we now enjoy, our liberty and independence, they demand every attention which gratitude can pay. For my own part, I never meet an officer, but I embrace him as my friend, nor a private in distress, but I insensibly extend my charity to him.——I have hit the Bumkin off very tolerably.   [*Aside*.

MANLY. Give me your hand, Sir! I do not proffer this hand to everybody; but you steal into my heart. I hope I am as insensible to flattery as most men; but I

---

[20] Religious assemblies of Greek states.

declare (it may be my weak side) that I never hear the name of soldier mentioned with respect, but I experience a thrill of pleasure which I never feel on any other occasion.

DIMPLE.   Will you give me leave, my dear Colonel, to confer an obligation on myself, by shewing you some civilities during your stay here, and giving a similar opportunity to some of my friends?

MANLY.   Sir, I thank you; but I believe my stay in this city will be very short.

DIMPLE.   I can introduce you to some men of excellent sense, in whose company you will esteem yourself happy; and, by way of amusement, to some fine girls, who will listen to your soft things with pleasure.

MANLY.   Sir, I should be proud of the honour of being acquainted with those gentlemen;—but, as for the ladies, I don't understand you.

DIMPLE.   Why, Sir, I need not tell you, that when a young gentleman is alone with a young lady he must say some soft things to her fair cheek—indeed, the lady will expect it. To be sure, there is not much pleasure when a man of the world and a finished coquette meet, who perfectly know each other; but how delicious is it to excite the emotions of joy, hope, expectation, and delight in the bosom of a lovely girl who believes every tittle of what you say to be serious!

MANLY.   Serious, Sir! In my opinion, the man who, under pretensions of marriage, can plant thorns in the bosom of an innocent, unsuspecting girl is more detestable than a common robber, in the same proportion as private violence is more despicable than open force, and money of less value than happiness.

DIMPLE.   How he awes me by the superiority of his sentiments. [*Aside*.] As you say, Sir, a gentleman should be cautious how he mentions marriage.

MANLY.   Cautious, Sir! No person more approves of an intercourse between the sexes than I do. Female conversation softens our manners, whilst our discourse, from the superiority of our literary advantages, improves their minds. But, in our young country, where there is no such thing as gallantry, when a gentleman speaks of love to a lady, whether he mentions marriage or not, she ought to conclude either that he meant to insult her or that his intentions are the most serious and honourable. How mean, how cruel, is it, by a thousand tender assiduities, to win the affections of an amiable girl, and, though you leave her virtue unspotted, to betray her into the appearance of so many tender partialities, that every man of delicacy would suppress his inclination towards her, by supposing her heart engaged! Can any man, for the trivial gratification of his leisure hours, affect the happiness of a whole life! His not having spoken of marriage may add to his perfidy, but can be no excuse for his conduct.

DIMPLE.   Sir, I admire your sentiments;—they are mine. The light observations that fell from me were only a principle of the tongue; they came not from the heart; my practice has ever disapproved these principles.

MANLY.   I believe you, sir. I should with reluctance suppose that those pernicious sentiments could find admittance into the heart of a gentleman.

DIMPLE.   I am now, Sir, going to visit a family, where, if you please, I will have the honour of introducing you. Mr. Manly's ward, Miss Letitia, is a young lady of immense fortune; and his niece, Miss Charlotte Manly, is a young lady of great sprightliness and beauty.

MANLY.   That gentleman, Sir, is my uncle, and Miss Manly my sister.

DIMPLE.   The devil she is! [*Aside*.] Miss Manly your sister, Sir? I rejoice to hear it, and feel a double pleasure in being known to you.——Plague on him! I wish he was at Boston again, with all my soul.   [*Aside*.

MANLY.   Come, Sir, will you go?

DIMPLE.   I will follow you in a moment, Sir. [*Exit* MANLY.] Plague on it! this is unlucky. A fighting brother is a cursed appendage to a fine girl. Egad! I just stopped in time; had he not discovered himself, in two minutes more I should have told him how well I was with his sister. Indeed, I cannot see the satisfaction of an intrigue, if one can't have the pleasure of communicating it to our friends.   [*Exit.*

END OF THE THIRD ACT

ACT IV. SCENE I

CHARLOTTE'S Apartment
CHARLOTTE leading in MARIA

CHARLOTTE.   This is so kind, my sweet friend, to come to see me at this moment. I declare, if I were going to be married in a few days, as you are, I should scarce have found time to visit my friends.

MARIA.   Do you think, then, that there is an impropriety in it?—How should you dispose of your time?

CHARLOTTE.   Why, I should be shut up in my chamber; and my head would so run upon—upon—upon the solemn ceremony that I was to pass through!—I declare, it would take me above two hours merely to learn that little monosyllable— *Yes*. Ah! my dear, your sentimental imagination does not conceive what that little tiny word implies.

MARIA.   Spare me your raillery, my sweet friend; I should love your agreeable vivacity at any other time.

CHARLOTTE.   Why, this is the very time to amuse you. You grieve me to see you look so unhappy.

MARIA.   Have I not reason to look so?

CHARLOTTE.   What new grief distresses you?

MARIA.   Oh! how sweet it is, when the heart is borne down with misfortune, to recline and repose on the bosom of friendship! Heaven knows that, although it is improper for a young lady to praise a gentleman, yet I have ever concealed Mr. Dimple's foibles, and spoke of him as of one whose reputation I expected would be linked with mine; but his late conduct towards me has turned my coolness into contempt. He behaves as if he meant to insult and disgust me; whilst my father, in the last conversation on the subject of our marriage, spoke of it as a matter which lay near his heart, and in which he would not bear contradiction.

CHARLOTTE.   This works well; oh! the generous Dimple. I'll endeavour to excite her to discharge him. [*Aside.*] But, my dear friend, your happiness depends on yourself. Why don't you discard him? Though the match has been of long standing, I would not be forced to make myself miserable: no parent in the world should oblige me to marry the man I did not like.

MARIA.   Oh! my dear, you never lived with your parents, and do not know what influence a father's frowns have upon a daughter's heart. Besides, what have I to alledge against Mr. Dimple, to justify myself to the world? He carries himself so smoothly, that every one would impute the blame to me, and call me capricious.

CHARLOTTE.   And call her capricious! Did ever such an objection start into the heart of woman? For my part, I wish I had fifty lovers to discard, for no other reason than because I did not fancy them. My dear Maria, you will forgive me; I know your candour and confidence in me; but I have at times, I confess, been led to suppose that some other gentleman was the cause of your aversion to Mr. Dimple.

MARIA.   No, my sweet friend, you may be assured, that though I have seen many gentlemen I could prefer to Mr. Dimple, yet I never saw one that I thought I could give my hand to, until this morning.

CHARLOTTE.   This morning!

MARIA.   Yes; one of the strangest accidents in the world. The odious Dimple, after disgusting me with his conversation, had just left me, when a gentleman, who, it seems, boards in the same house with him, saw him coming out of our door, and, the houses looking very much alike, he came into our house instead of his lodgings; nor did he discover his mistake until he got into the parlour, where I was; he then bowed so gracefully, made such a genteel apology, and looked so manly and noble!——

CHARLOTTE.   I see some folks, though it is so great an impropriety, can praise a gentleman, when he happens to be the man of their fancy.   [*Aside.*

MARIA.   I don't know how it was,—I hope he did not think me indelicate,—but I asked him, I believe, to sit down, or pointed to a chair. He sat down, and, instead of having recourse to observations upon the weather, or hackneyed criticisms upon the theatre, he entered readily into a conversation worthy a man of sense to speak, and a lady of delicacy and sentiment to hear. He was not strictly handsome, but he spoke the language of sentiment, and his eyes looked tenderness and honour.

CHARLOTTE.   Oh! [*eagerly*] you sentimental, grave girls, when your hearts are once touched, beat us rattles a bar's length. And so you are quite in love with this he-angel?

MARIA.   In love with him! How can you rattle so, Charlotte? am I not going to be miserable? [*Sighs.*] In love with a gentleman I never saw but one hour in my life, and don't know his name! No; I only wished that the man I shall marry may look, and talk, and act, just like him. Besides, my dear, he is a married man.

CHARLOTTE.   Why, that was good-natured—he told you so, I suppose, in mere charity, to prevent you falling in love with him?

MARIA.   He didn't tell me so; [*peevishly*] he looked as if he was married.

CHARLOTTE.   How, my dear; did he look sheepish?

MARIA.   I am sure he has a susceptible heart, and the ladies of his acquaintance must be very stupid not to——

CHARLOTTE.   Hush! I hear some person coming.

Enter LETITIA

LETITIA.   My dear Maria, I am happy to see you. Lud! what a pity it is that you have purchased your wedding clothes.

MARIA.   I think so.   [*Sighing.*

LETITIA.   Why, my dear, there is the sweetest parcel of silks come over you ever saw! Nancy Brilliant has a full suit come; she sent over her measure, and it fits her to a hair; it is immensely dressy, and made for a court-hoop. I thought they said the large hoops were going out of fashion.

CHARLOTTE.   Did you see the hat? Is it a fact that the deep laces round the border is still the fashion?

DIMPLE [*within*].   Upon my honour, Sir.

MARIA.   Ha! Dimple's voice! My dear, I must take leave of you. There are some things necessary to be done at our house. Can't I go through the other room?

Enter DIMPLE *and* MANLY

DIMPLE.   Ladies, your most obedient.

CHARLOTTE.   Miss Van Rough, shall I present my brother Henry to you? Colonel Manly, Maria,—Miss Van Rough, brother.

MARIA.   Her brother! [*Turns and sees* MANLY.] Oh! my heart! the very gentleman I have been praising.

MANLY.   The same amiable girl I saw this morning!

CHARLOTTE.   Why, you look as if you were acquainted.

MANLY.   I unintentionally intruded into this lady's presence this morning, for which she was so good as to promise me her forgiveness.

CHARLOTTE.   Oh ho! is that the case! Have these two penserosos been together? Were they Henry's eyes that looked so tenderly? [*Aside.*] And so you promised to pardon him? and could you be so good-natured? have you really forgiven him? I beg you would do it for my sake [*whispering loud to* MARIA]. But, my dear, as you are in such haste, it would be cruel to detain you; I can show you the way through the other room.

MARIA.   Spare me, my sprightly friend.

MANLY.   The lady does not, I hope, intend to deprive us of the pleasure of her company so soon.

CHARLOTTE.   She has only a mantua-maker[1] who waits for her at home. But, as I am to give my opinion of the dress, I think she cannot go yet. We were talking of the fashions when you came in, but I suppose the subject must be changed to something of more importance now. Mr. Dimple, will you favour us with an account of the public entertainments?

DIMPLE.   Why, really, Miss Manly, you could not have asked me a question more *mal-apropos*.[2] For my part, I must confess that, to a man who has travelled, there is nothing that is worthy the name of amusement to be found in this city.

CHARLOTTE.   Except visiting the ladies.

DIMPLE.   Pardon me, Madam; that is the avocation of a man of taste. But for amusement, I positively know of nothing that can be called so, unless you dignify with that title the hopping once a fortnight to the sound of two or three squeaking fiddles, and the clattering of the old tavern windows, or sitting to see the miserable mummers, whom you call actors, murder comedy and make a farce of tragedy.

MANLY.   Do you never attend the theatre, Sir?

DIMPLE.   I was tortured there once.

CHARLOTTE.   Pray, Mr. Dimple, was it a tragedy or a comedy?

DIMPLE.   Faith, Madam, I cannot tell; for I sat with my back to the stage all the time, admiring a much better actress than any there—a lady who played the fine woman to perfection; though, by the laugh of the horrid creatures round me, I suppose it was comedy. Yet, on second thoughts, it might be some hero in a tragedy, dying so comically as to set the whole house in an uproar. Colonel, I presume you have been in Europe?

---

[1] A dressmaker.   [2] Inappropriate.

MANLY.   Indeed, Sir, I was never ten leagues from the continent.

DIMPLE.   Believe me, Colonel, you have an immense pleasure to come; and when you shall have seen the brilliant exhibitions of Europe, you will learn to despise the amusements of this country as much as I do.

MANLY.   Therefore I do not wish to see them; for I can never esteem that knowledge valuable which tends to give me a distaste for my native country.

DIMPLE.   Well, Colonel, though you have not travelled, you have read.

MANLY.   I have, a little; and by it have discovered that there is a laudable partiality which ignorant, untravelled men entertain for everything that belongs to their native country. I call it laudable; it injures no one; adds to their own happiness; and, when extended, becomes the noble principle of patriotism. Travelled gentlemen rise superior, in their own opinion, to this; but if the contempt which they contract for their country is the most valuable acquisition of their travels, I am far from thinking that their time and money are well spent.

MARIA.   What noble sentiments!

CHARLOTTE.   Let my brother set out where he will in the fields of conversation, he is sure to end his tour in the temple of gravity.

MANLY.   Forgive me, my sister. I love my country; it has its foibles undoubtedly;—some foreigners will with pleasure remark them—but such remarks fall very ungracefully from the lips of her citizens.

DIMPLE.   You are perfectly in the right, Colonel—America has her faults.

MANLY.   Yes, Sir; and we, her children, should blush for them in private, and endeavour, as individuals, to reform them. But, if our country has its errors in common with other countries, I am proud to say America—I mean the United States—has displayed virtues and achievements which modern nations may admire, but of which they have seldom set us the example.

CHARLOTTE.   But, brother, we must introduce you to some of our gay folks, and let you see the city, such as it is. Mr. Dimple is known to almost every family in town; he will doubtless take a pleasure in introducing you?

DIMPLE.   I shall esteem every service I can render your brother an honour.

MANLY.   I fear the business I am upon will take up all my time, and my family will be anxious to hear from me.

MARIA.   His family! but what is it to me that he is married! [*Aside.*] Pray, how did you leave your lady, Sir?

CHARLOTTE.   My brother is not married [*observing her anxiety*]; it is only an odd way he has of expressing himself. Pray, brother, is this business, which you make your continual excuse, a secret?

MANLY.   No, sister; I came hither to solicit the honourable Congress, that a number of my brave old soldiers may be put upon the pension-list, who were, at first, not judged to be so materially wounded as to need the public assistance. My sister says true [*to* MARIA]: I call my late soldiers my family. Those who were not in the field in the late glorious contest, and those who were, have their respective merits; but, I confess, my old brother-soldiers are dearer to me than the former description. Friendships made in adversity are lasting; our countrymen may forget us, but that is no reason why we should forget one another. But I must leave you; my time of engagement approaches.

CHARLOTTE.   Well, but, brother, if you will go, will you please to conduct my fair friend home? You live in the same street——I was to have gone with her myself—[*Aside.*] A lucky thought.

MARIA.   I am obliged to your sister, Sir, and was just intending to go. [*Going*.
MANLY.   I shall attend her with pleasure.

[*Exit with* MARIA, *followed by* DIMPLE *and* CHARLOTTE.

MARIA.   Now, pray, don't betray me to your brother.
CHARLOTTE.   [*Just as she sees him make a motion to take his leave*.] One word
with you, brother, if you please.   [*Follows them out*.
                                                    [*Manent*,³ DIMPLE *and* LETITIA.

DIMPLE.   You received the billet⁴ I sent you, I presume?
LETITIA.   Hush!—Yes.
DIMPLE.   When shall I pay my respects to you?
LETITIA.   At eight I shall be unengaged.

Reënter CHARLOTTE

DIMPLE.   Did my lovely angel receive my billet? [*To* CHARLOTTE.]
CHARLOTTE.   Yes.
DIMPLE.   What hour shall I expect with impatience?
CHARLOTTE.   At eight I shall be at home unengaged.
DIMPLE.   Unfortunate! I have a horrid engagement of business at that hour.
Can't you finish your visit earlier and let six be the happy hour?
CHARLOTTE.   You know your influence over me.   [*Exeunt severally*.

SCENE II

VAN ROUGH'S *House*

VAN ROUGH [*alone*]. It cannot possibly be true! The son of my old friend can't
have acted so unadvisedly. Seventeen thousand pounds! in bills! Mr. Transfer
must have been mistaken. He always appeared so prudent, and talked so well
upon money matters, and even assured me that he intended to change his dress for
a suit of clothes which would not cost so much, and look more substantial, as soon
as he married. No, no, no! it can't be; it cannot be. But, however, I must look out
sharp. I did not care what his principles or his actions were, so long as he minded
the main chance. Seventeen thousand pounds! If he had lost it in trade, why the
best men may have ill-luck; but to game it away, as Transfer says—why, at this
rate, his whole estate may go in one night, and what is ten times worse, mine into
the bargain. No, no; Mary is right. Leave women to look as if they didn't know a
journal from a ledger, when their interest is concerned they know what's what;
they mind the main chance as well as the best of us. I wonder Mary did not tell me
she knew of his spending his money so foolishly. Seventeen thousand pounds!
Why, if my daughter was standing up to be married, I would forbid the banns,⁵ if
I found it was to a man who did not mind the main chance.—Hush! I hear somebody coming. 'Tis Mary's voice; a man with her too! I shouldn't be surprised

---

³ There remain.   ⁴ Note.   ⁵ Announcement of marriage.

if this should be the other string to her bow. Aye, aye, let them alone; women understand the main chance.—Though, i' faith, I'll listen a little.

[*Retires into a closet.*

MANLY *leading in* MARIA

MANLY.   I hope you will excuse my speaking upon so important a subject so abruptly; but, the moment I entered your room, you struck me as the lady whom I had long loved in imagination, and never hoped to see.

MARIA.   Indeed, Sir, I have been led to hear more upon this subject than I ought.

MANLY.   Do you, then, disapprove my suit, Madam, or the abruptness of my introducing it? If the latter, my peculiar situation, being obliged to leave the city in a few days, will, I hope, be my excuse; if the former, I will retire, for I am sure I would not give a moment's inquietude to her whom I could devote my life to please. I am not so indelicate as to seek your immediate approbation; permit me only to be near you, and by a thousand tender assiduities to endeavour to excite a grateful return.

MARIA.   I have a father, whom I would die to make happy; he will dis-approve——

MANLY.   Do you think me so ungenerous as to seek a place in your esteem without his consent? You must—you ever ought to consider that man as unworthy of you who seeks an interest in your heart contrary to a father's approbation. A young lady should reflect that the loss of a lover may be supplied, but nothing can compensate for the loss of a parent's affection. Yet, why do you suppose your father would disapprove? In our country, the affections are not sacrificed to riches or family aggrandizement: should you approve, my family is decent, and my rank honourable.

MARIA.   You distress me, Sir.

MANLY.   Then I will sincerely beg your excuse for obtruding so disagreeable a subject, and retire.   [*Going.*

MARIA.   Stay, Sir! your generosity and good opinion of me deserve a return; but why must I declare what, for these few hours, I have scarce suffered myself to think?—I am——

MANLY.   What?

MARIA.   Engaged, Sir; and, in a few days to be married to the gentleman you saw at your sister's.

MANLY.   Engaged to be married! And I have been basely invading the rights of another? Why have you permitted this? Is this the return for the partiality I de-clared for you?

MARIA.   You distress me, Sir. What would you have me say? you are too gen-erous to wish the truth. Ought I to say that I dared not suffer myself to think of my engagement, and that I am going to give my hand without my heart? Would you have me confess a partiality for you? If so, your triumph is compleat, and can be only more so when days of misery with the man I cannot love will make me think of him whom I could prefer.

MANLY.   [*after a pause*].   We are both unhappy; but it is your duty to obey your parent—mine to obey my honour. Let us, therefore, both follow the path of rectitude; and of this we may be assured, that if we are not happy, we shall, at least, deserve to be so. Adieu! I dare not trust myself longer with you.

[*Exeunt severally.*

END OF THE FOURTH ACT

ACT V. SCENE I

DIMPLE'S *Lodgings*
JESSAMY *meeting* JONATHAN

JESSAMY.   Well, Mr. Jonathan, what success with the fair?

JONATHAN.   Why, such a tarnal cross tike you never saw! You would have counted she had lived upon crab-apples and vinegar for a fortnight. But what the rattle makes you look so tarnation glum?

JESSAMY.   I was thinking, Mr. Jonathan, what could be the reason of her carrying herself so coolly to you.

JONATHAN.   Coolly, do you call it? Why, I vow, she was fire-hot angry: may be it was because I buss'd her.

JESSAMY.   No, no, Mr. Jonathan; there must be some other cause; I never yet knew a lady angry at being kissed.

JONATHAN.   Well, if it is not the young woman's bashfulness, I vow I can't conceive why she shouldn't like me.

JESSAMY.   May be it is because you have not the Graces, Mr. Jonathan.

JONATHAN.   Grace! Why, does the young woman expect I must be converted before I court her?

JESSAMY.   I mean graces of person: for instance, my lord tells us that we must cut off our nails even at top, in small segments of circles—though you won't understand that; in the next place, you must regulate your laugh.

JONATHAN.   Maple-log seize it! don't I laugh natural?

JESSAMY.   That's the very fault, Mr. Jonathan. Besides, you absolutely misplace it. I was told by a friend of mine that you laughed outright at the play the other night, when you ought only to have tittered.

JONATHAN.   Gor! I—what does one go to see fun for if they can't laugh.

JESSAMY.   You may laugh; but you must laugh by rule.

JONATHAN.   Swamp it—laugh by rule! Well, I should like that tarnally.

JESSAMY.   Why, you know, Mr. Jonathan, that to dance, a lady to play with her fan, or a gentleman with his cane, and all other natural motions, are regulated by art. My master has composed an immensely pretty gamut,[1] by which any lady or gentleman, with a few years' close application, may learn to laugh as gracefully as if they were born and bred to it.

JONATHAN.   Mercy on my soul! A gamut for laughing—just like fa, la, sol?

JESSAMY.   Yes. It comprises every possible display of jocularity, from an *affettuoso* smile to a *piano* titter, or full chorus *fortissimo*[2] ha, ha, ha! My master employs his leisure hours in marking out the plays, like a cathedral chanting-

---

[1] The full range of musical notes.   [2] "Affectionate," "soft," and "very loud" (Italian).

book, that the ignorant may know where to laugh; and that pit, box, and gallery[3] may keep time together, and not have a snigger in one part of the house, a broad grin in the other, and a d——d grum[4] look in the third. How delightful to see the audience all smile together, then look on their books, then twist their mouths into an agreeable simper, then altogether shake the house with a general ha, ha, ha! loud as a full chorus of Handel's at an Abbey commemoration.[5]

JONATHAN.   Ha, ha, ha! that's dang'd cute, I swear.

JESSAMY.   The gentlemen, you see, will laugh the tenor; the ladies will play the counter-tenor; the beaux will squeak the treble; and our jolly friends in the gallery a thorough base, ho, ho, ho!

JONATHAN.   Well, can't you let me see that gamut?

JESSAMY.   Oh! yes, Mr. Jonathan; here it is [*Takes out a book.*] Oh! no, this is only a titter with its variations. Ah, here it is. [*Takes out another.*] Now, you must know, Mr. Jonathan, this is a piece written by Ben Johnson,[6] which I have set to my master's gamut. The places where you must smile, look grave, or laugh out-right, are marked below the line. Now look over me. "There was a certain man"—now you must smile.

JONATHAN.   Well, read it again; I warrant I'll mind my eye.

JESSAMY.   "There was a certain man, who had a sad scolding wife,"—now you must laugh.

JONATHAN.   Tarnation! That's no laughing matter though.

JESSAMY.   "And she lay sick a-dying";—now you must titter.

JONATHAN.   What, snigger when the good woman's a-dying! Gor, I——

JESSAMY.   Yes, the notes say you must—"and she asked her husband leave to make a will,"—now you must begin to look grave; "and her husband said"——

JONATHAN.   Ay, what did her husband say? Something dang'd cute, I reckon.

JESSAMY.   "And her husband said, you have had your will all your life-time, and would you have it after you are dead, too?"

JONATHAN.   Ho, ho, ho! There the old man was even with her; he was up to the notch—ha, ha, ha!

JESSAMY.   But, Mr. Jonathan, you must not laugh so. Why you ought to have tittered *piano,* and you have laughed *fortissimo.* Look here; you see these marks, A, B, C, and so on; these are the references to the other part of the book. Let us turn to it, and you will see the directions how to manage the muscles. This [*turns over*] was note D you blundered at.—You must purse the mouth into a smile, then titter, discovering the lower part of the three front upper teeth.

JONATHAN.   How? read it again.

JESSAMY.   "There was a certain man"—very well!—"who had a sad scolding wife,"—why don't you laugh?

JONATHAN.   Now, that scolding wife sticks in my gizzard so pluckily that I can't laugh for the blood and nowns of me.[7] Let me look grave here, and I'll laugh your belly full, where the old creature's a-dying.

JESSAMY.   "And she asked her husband"—[*Bell rings.*] My master's bell! he's returned, I fear.—Here, Mr. Jonathan, take this gamut; and I make no doubt but with a few years' close application, you may be able to smile gracefully.

[*Exeunt severally.*

[3] Region nearest the stage, theater box, and balcony.   [4] Grim.
[5] A performance by George Frederick Handel (1685–1759), a British composer, given at London's Westminster Abbey.
[6] An English dramatist (1572–1637).   [7] Taken from the oath "God's blood and wounds."

SCENE II

CHARLOTTE'S *Apartment*
Enter MANLY

MANLY.   What, no one at home? How unfortunate to meet the only lady my heart was ever moved by, to find her engaged to another, and confessing her partiality for me! Yet engaged to a man who, by her intimation, and his libertine conversation with me, I fear, does not merit her. Aye! there's the sting; for, were I assured that Maria was happy, my heart is not so selfish but that it would dilate in knowing it, even though it were with another. But to know she is unhappy!—I must drive these thoughts from me. Charlotte has some books; and this is what I believe she calls her little library.   [*Enters a closet.*

Enter DIMPLE *leading* LETITIA

LETITIA.   And will you pretend to say now, Mr. Dimple, that you propose to break with Maria? Are not the banns published?[8] Are not the clothes purchased? Are not the friends invited? In short, is it not a done affair?

DIMPLE.   Believe me, my dear Letitia, I would not marry her.

LETITIA.   Why have you not broke with her before this, as you all along deluded me by saying you would?

DIMPLE.   Because I was in hopes she would, ere this, have broke with me.

LETITIA.   You could not expect it.

DIMPLE.   Nay, but be calm a moment; 'twas from my regard to you that I did not discard her.

LETITIA.   Regard to me!

DIMPLE.   Yes; I have done everything in my power to break with her, but the foolish girl is so fond of me that nothing can accomplish it. Besides, how can I offer her my hand when my heart is indissolubly engaged to you?

LETITIA.   There may be reason in this; but why so attentive to Miss Manly?

DIMPLE.   Attentive to Miss Manly! For heaven's sake, if you have no better opinion of my constancy, pay not so ill a compliment to my taste.

LETITIA.   Did I not see you whisper her to-day?

DIMPLE.   Possibly I might—but something of so very trifling a nature that I have already forgot what it was.

LETITIA.   I believe she has not forgot it.

DIMPLE.   My dear creature, how can you for a moment suppose I should have any serious thoughts of that trifling, gay, flighty coquette, that disagreeable——

Enter CHARLOTTE

My dear Miss Manly, I rejoice to see you; there is a charm in your conversation that always marks your entrance into company as fortunate.

LETITIA.   Where have you been, my dear?

CHARLOTTE.   Why, I have been about to twenty shops, turning over pretty things, and so have left twenty visits unpaid. I wish you would step into the car-

---

[8] Hasn't the wedding been publicly announced?

riage and whisk round, make my apology, and leave my cards where our friends are not at home; that, you know, will serve as a visit. Come, do go.

LETITIA.   So anxious to get me out! but I'll watch you. [*Aside.*] Oh! yes, I'll go; I want a little exercise. Positively [DIMPLE *offering to accompany her*], Mr. Dimple, you shall not go; why, half my visits are cake and candle visits; it won't do, you know, for you to go.

[*Exit, but returns to the door in the back scene and listens.*

DIMPLE.   This attachment of your brother to Maria is fortunate.

CHARLOTTE.   How did you come to the knowledge of it?

DIMPLE.   I read it in their eyes.

CHARLOTTE.   And I had it from her mouth. It would have amused you to have seen her! She, that thought it so great an impropriety to praise a gentleman that she could not bring out one word in your favour, found a redundancy to praise him.

DIMPLE.   I have done everything in my power to assist his passion there: your delicacy, my dearest girl, would be shocked at half the instances of neglect and misbehaviour.

CHARLOTTE.   I don't know how I should bear neglect; but Mr. Dimple must misbehave himself indeed, to forfeit my good opinion.

DIMPLE.   Your good opinion, my angel, is the pride and pleasure of my heart; and if the most respectful tenderness for you, and an utter indifference for all your sex besides, can make me worthy of your esteem, I shall richly merit it.

CHARLOTTE.   All my sex besides, Mr. Dimple!—you forgot your tête-à-tête with Letitia.

DIMPLE.   How can you, my lovely angel, cast a thought on that insipid, wry-mouthed, ugly creature!

CHARLOTTE.   But her fortune may have charms.

DIMPLE.   Not to a heart like mine. The man, who has been blessed with the good opinion of my Charlotte, must despise the allurements of fortune.

CHARLOTTE.   I am satisfied.

DIMPLE.   Let us think no more on the odious subject, but devote the present hour to happiness.

CHARLOTTE.   Can I be happy, when I see the man I prefer going to be married to another?

DIMPLE.   Have I not already satisfied my charming angel, that I can never think of marrying the puling Maria? But, even if it were so, could that be any bar to our happiness? for, as the poet sings,

> "Love, free as air, at sight of human ties,
> Spreads his light wings, and in a moment flies."[9]

Come, then, my charming angel! why delay our bliss? The present moment is ours; the next is in the hand of fate.   [*Kissing her.*

CHARLOTTE.   Begone, Sir! By your delusions you had almost lulled my honour asleep.

DIMPLE.   Let me lull the demon to sleep again with kisses.

[*He struggles with her; she screams.*

---

[9] From "Eloisa to Abelard" (1717), a poem by Alexander Pope (1688–1744).

Enter MANLY

MANLY.   Turn, villain! and defend yourself.——

[*Draws.*

VAN ROUGH *enters and beats down their swords*

VAN ROUGH.   Is the devil in you? are you going to murder one another?

[*Holding* DIMPLE.

DIMPLE.   Hold him, hold him,—I can command my passion.

Enter JONATHAN

JONATHAN.   What the rattle ails you? Is the old one[10] in you? Let the colonel alone, can't you? I feel chock-full of fight,—do you want to kill the colonel?——

MANLY.   Be still, Jonathan; the gentleman does not want to hurt me.

JONATHAN.   Gor! I—I wish he did; I'd shew him Yankee boys play, pretty quick.—Don't you see you have frightened the young woman into the *hystrikes?*[11]

VAN ROUGH.   Pray, some of you explain this; what has been the occasion of all this racket?

MANLY.   That gentleman can explain it to you; it will be a very diverting story for an intended father-in-law to hear.

VAN ROUGH.   How was this matter, Mr. Van Dumpling?

DIMPLE.   Sir,—upon my honour,—all I know is, that I was talking to this young lady, and this gentleman broke in on us in a very extraordinary manner.

VAN ROUGH.   Why, all this is nothing to the purpose; can you explain it, Miss?

[*To* CHARLOTTE.

Enter LETITIA *through the back scene*

LETITIA.   I can explain it to that gentleman's confusion. Though long betrothed to your daughter [*to* VAN ROUGH], yet, allured by my fortune, it seems (with shame do I speak it) he has privately paid his addresses to me. I was drawn in to listen to him by his assuring me that the match was made by his father without his consent, and that he proposed to break with Maria, whether he married me or not. But, whatever were his intentions respecting your daughter, Sir, even to me he was false; for he has repeated the same story, with some cruel reflections upon my person, to Miss Manly.

JONATHAN.   What a tarnal curse!

LETITIA.   Nor is this all, Miss Manly. When he was with me this very morning, he made the same ungenerous reflections upon the weakness of your mind as he has so recently done upon the defects of my person.

JONATHAN.   What a tarnal curse and damn, too.

DIMPLE.   Ha! since I have lost Letitia, I believe I had as good make it up with Maria. Mr. Van Rough, at present I cannot enter into particulars; but, I believe, I can explain everything to your satisfaction in private.

VAN ROUGH.   There is another matter, Mr. Van Dumpling, which I would have

---

[10] The devil.   [11] Hysterics.

you explain. Pray, Sir, have Messrs. Van Cash & Co. presented you those bills for acceptance?

DIMPLE.   The deuce! Has he heard of those bills! Nay, then, all's up with Maria, too; but an affair of this sort can never prejudice me among the ladies; they will rather long to know what the dear creature possesses to make him so agreeable. [*Aside*.] Sir, you'll hear from me.   [*To* MANLY.

MANLY.   And you from me, Sir——

DIMPLE.   Sir, you wear a sword——

MANLY.   Yes, Sir. This sword was presented to me by that brave Gallic hero, the Marquis De la Fayette.[12] I have drawn it in the service of my country, and in private life, on the only occasion where a man is justified in drawing his sword, in defence of a lady's honour. I have fought too many battles in the service of my country to dread the imputation of cowardice. Death from a man of honour would be a glory you do not merit; you shall live to bear the insult of man and the contempt of that sex whose general smiles afforded you all your happiness.

DIMPLE.   You won't meet me, Sir? Then I'll post you for a coward.

MANLY.   I'll venture that, Sir. The reputation of my life does not depend upon the breath of a Mr. Dimple. I would have you to know, however, Sir, that I have a cane to chastise the insolence of a scoundrel, and a sword and the good laws of my country to protect me from the attempts of an assassin——

DIMPLE.   Mighty well! Very fine, indeed! Ladies and gentlemen, I take my leave; and you will please to observe in the case of my deportment the contrast between a gentleman who has read Chesterfield and received the polish of Europe and an unpolished, untravelled American.   [*Exit*.

Enter MARIA

MARIA.   Is he indeed gone?——

LETITIA.   I hope, never to return.

VAN ROUGH.   I am glad I heard of those bills; though it's plaguy unlucky; I hoped to see Mary married before I died.

MANLY.   Will you permit a gentleman, Sir, to offer himself as a suitor to your daughter? Though a stranger to you, he is not altogether so to her, or unknown in this city. You may find a son-in-law of more fortune, but you can never meet with one who is richer in love for her, or respect for you.

VAN ROUGH.   Why, Mary, you have not let this gentleman make love to you without my leave?

MANLY.   I did not say, Sir——

MARIA.   Say, Sir!——I—the gentleman, to be sure, met me accidentally.

VAN ROUGH.   Ha, ha, ha! Mark me, Mary; young folks think old folks to be fools; but old folks know young folks to be fools. Why, I knew all about this affair. This was only a cunning way I had to bring it about. Hark ye! I was in the closet when you and he were at our house. [*Turns to the company*.] I heard that little baggage say she loved her old father, and would die to make him happy! Oh! how I loved the little baggage! And you talked very prudently, young man. I have inquired into your character, and find you to be a man of punctuality and mind the main chance. And so, as you love Mary and Mary loves you, you shall have my

---

[12] A French general (1757–1834) who served in the Continental Army during the American Revolution.

consent immediately to be married. I'll settle my fortune on you, and go and live with you the remainder of my life.

MANLY.   Sir, I hope——

VAN ROUGH.   Come, come, no fine speeches; mind the main chance, young man, and you and I shall always agree.

LETITIA.   I sincerely wish you joy [*advancing to* MARIA]; and hope your pardon for my conduct.

MARIA.   I thank you for your congratulations, and hope we shall at once forget the wretch who has given us so much disquiet, and the trouble that he has occasioned.

CHARLOTTE.   And I, my dear Maria,—how shall I look up to you for forgiveness? I, who, in the practice of the meanest arts, have violated the most sacred rights of friendship? I never can forgive myself, or hope charity from the world; but, I confess, I have much to hope from such a brother; and I am happy that I may soon say, such a sister.

MARIA.   My dear, you distress me; you have all my love.

MANLY.   And mine.

CHARLOTTE.   If repentence can entitle me to forgiveness, I have already much merit; for I despise the littleness of my past conduct. I now find that the heart of any worthy man cannot be gained by invidious attacks upon the rights and characters of others;—by countenancing the addresses of a thousand;—or that the finest assemblage of features, the greatest taste in dress, the genteelest address, or the most brilliant wit, cannot eventually secure a coquette from contempt and ridicule.

MANLY.   And I have learned that probity, virtue, honour, though they should not have received the polish of Europe, will secure to an honest American the good graces of his fair countrywomen, and I hope, the applause of THE PUBLIC.

THE END

1787, 1790

LATE 18TH-CENTURY FICTION

Is it not a little hard . . . that not one gentleman's daughter in a thousand should be brought to read or understand her own natural tongue, or be the judge of the easiest books that are written in it? . . . I hope you will recommend the study of Mr. [Noah] *Webster's* Grammatical Institute, as the best work in our language to facilitate the knowledge of Grammar. I cannot but think Mr. *Webster* intended his valuable book for the benefit of his countrywomen; for while he delivers his *rules* in a pure, precise, and elegant style, he *explains* his meaning by *examples* which are calculated to inspire the female mind with a thirst for emulation, and a desire for virtue.

Although this epigraph may seem to be part of an early-American sermon or advice book, it actually appears in *The Power of Sympathy* (1789) by William Hill Brown, then a twenty-three-year-old clockmaker's son. Both the factuality and the highly sensationalized plot (involving adultery and incest) of *The Power of Sympathy*, now widely accepted as the first American novel, set the tone for many

subsequent novels. Even the novel's frontispiece exploits one of postrevolu-
tionary-Boston's most notorious scandals, the story of Fanny Apthorp. Fanny
committed suicide after her illicit liaison with her sister's husband, a Harvard University graduate and Patriot, Perez Morton, was publicly disclosed. Fanny's
neighbor, Brown sympathizes with her in *The Power of Sympathy* and even names
her "Ophelia," after Shakespeare's tragic heroine. Morton, however, was a genuine seducer/villain. He becomes "Martin" in the novel, a manuever clearly designed to expose the guilty.

That Brown would interrupt his plot for a digression on the best way to improve
women's illiteracy may strike the contemporary reader as particularly strange,
given the novel's lurid aspects. Yet, somewhere in their plots, virtually all early-
American novels advocated greater literacy, education, and practical wisdom for
the young female reader. The preface to *The Power of Sympathy* explicitly promises that the "dangerous Consequences of SEDUCTION are exposed, and the Advantages of FEMALE EDUCATION set forth and recommended." The implicit
equation here and in many other novels of the period is that education can better
prepare a woman for life: that, more explicitly, a woman's intellectual and sexual
well being are directly related. For example, allegories of education and seduction
appear in the two bestselling novels of the era, Susanna Haswell Rowson's *Charlotte Temple* (1791) and Hannah Webster Foster's *The Coquette* (1797). Charlotte
Temple is misled by a handsome young soldier, her own naïveté, and a conniving
French schoolmistress. The heroine of *The Coquette,* Eliza Wharton, is both older
and better educated than Charlotte but nonetheless has received the kind of genteel
female education typical of the period, an education that in no way prepares Eliza
to support herself or to be sensible about the unequal gender politics of matrimony. For different reasons, and with differing degrees of self-awareness, both
Charlotte and Eliza fall prey to seducing men, and each meets a grim death during
childbirth.

Conversely, Judith Sargent Murray's indomitable Margaretta Melworth of *The
Story of Margaretta* (1798) receives a superior education in traditionally male subjects, ranging from accounting to geography, as well as in the traditionally feminine curriculum of painting, needlepoint, piano playing, and French. Because she
had a sound education, Margaretta is not fooled by the ominously named Sinis-
terus Courtland and instead rationally assesses and then chooses the admirable
Edward Hamilton. The plots by Brown, Rowson, Foster, and Murray illustrated
for American readers the ways in which a woman's intellect had to be improved in
order for her to cope with a social situation in which her income, social identity,
and even physical well-being were determined by her husband.

Much fiction of the new republic is explicitly or implicitly directed to the female reader, who by eighteenth-century American law and custom had few rights
of her own. She could not vote (except, in New Jersey, briefly) or serve on a jury
and even had few rights to her own body. Inheriting property was difficult, if
not illegal, for her; in general, her personal wealth or income simply became her
husband's. Given these restrictions, the question of matrimony loomed large in
the advice books of the time and equally large in the early novel. Behind much
fiction of the new republic is the insistent message that precisely because women

continued to be relatively powerless within the postrevolutionary economy, they had to be especially shrewd in their marital choices. They literally could not afford to make a mistake.

Although not all early-American novels were addressed to the female reader, the novel tradition was so commonly associated with women that Hugh Henry Brackenridge overtly and explicitly explains in the preface to *Modern Chivalry* (1792–1815), that he is addressing a male readership. Education is an issue, even in *Modern Chivalry* because, as Brackenridge shows, a democracy cannot survive an uneducated voting population. Brackenridge confronts issues of class, race, nationality, religion and, in a few instances, gender. This is perhaps the most important point: whether addressed explicitly to a female readership or a male readership, the late eighteenth-century American novel took social responsibilities seriously. Different novelists responded to social issues in dramatically different ways (and not always in ways that twentieth-century readers would find admirable), but virtually all early-American novelists realized they were reshaping a European form to the specific political, economic, and social problems of a new nation.

Yet, for all its social consciousness, the novel did not receive universal approval, partly because some novels championed causes that many social authorities found to be disruptive to the broad fabric of America. Three U.S. presidents, myriad lesser elected officials, critics, college teachers, and ministers debated the nature and merits of the genre. Whether approved or despised (or, as Thomas Jefferson thought, fine for gentlemen but potentially dangerous for young women and lower-class workers), the novel was considered significant enough for its social effects as well as its literary merits to be debated. Newspapers and magazines of the day were filled with commentaries, including such hyperbolically negative essays as "Novel Reading, a Cause of Female Depravity"(1802, anonymous) about the novel as a genre. No matter what the critics had to say, they all acknowledged that by the 1790s the "whole land" was filled with "modern travels and novels almost as incredible," as Royall Tyler notes in the preface to his novel *The Algerine Captive* (1797).

Many reasons for the popularity of novels in late eighteenth-century America can be postulated, but the most important economic factor contributing to the prevalence of the form was the concurrent establishment of lending libraries. Buying a novel was prohibitively expensive for most Americans. A typical early-American novel cost between seventy-five cents and a dollar at the time when that was a full day's wages for a laborer in Massachusetts or a week's salary for a serving girl. Especially in poor, rural areas, a female schoolteacher might have earned as little as seventy-five cents or a dollar a week (plus free room and board with a local family). For the price of an average novel, an upper-middle-class gentleman could have spent a night at the theater, or his wife could have purchased a season's supply of fashionable Parisian ribbons. A less wealthy woman could have purchased enough homespun to make dresses for herself and two or three of her daughters, or a family lower on the social ladder could have bought a substantial portion of their monthly diet—a bushel of potatoes and a half-bushel of corn.

╔═CONTEXTS═══╗

The teaching of literature in American colleges during the late eighteenth century was strongly influenced by thinkers of the Scottish Common-sense School of philosophy. A subject of much critical debate was the potential moral harm or benefit of novels (sometimes called "fictional histories"). Whereas many condemned fiction outright, the moderate views of Rev. Hugh Blair (1718–1800), a professor at Edinburgh University, were quite influential. The following excerpt is from his *Lectures on Rhetoric and Belles Lettres* (1783), a standard college text.

[Debate Over Fiction]

There remains to be treated of, another species of Composition in prose, which comprehends a very numerous, though, in general, a very insignificant class of Writings, known by the name of Romances and Novels. These may, at first view, seem too insignificant, to deserve that any particular notice should be taken of them. But I cannot be of this opinion. . . . For any kind of Writing, how trifling soever in appearance, that obtains a general currency, and especially that early preoccupies the imagination of the youth of both sexes, must demand particular attention. Its influence is likely to be considerable, both on the morals, and taste of a nation.

    In fact, fictitious histories might be employed for very useful purposes. They furnish one of the best channels for conveying instruction, for painting human life and manners, for showing the errors into which we are betrayed by our passions, for rendering virtue amiable and vice odious. The effect of well contrived stories, towards accomplishing these purposes, is stronger than any effect that can be produced by simple and naked instruction. . . .

                                                  Rev. Hugh Blair, 1783

╚══╝

Clearly, buying a novel was a luxury. Yet, lending libraries made novels available to all but the very lowest, most impoverished class of Americans. For as little as three to six dollars a year, payable in installments, a reader could borrow up to three novels a day from libraries such as Hocquet Caritat's Circulating Library in New York City, which stocked nearly fifteen hundred novels. According to diaries of the time, readers typically shared their borrowed novels with friends. In group tasks such as quilting, one person was commonly designated as "the reader" and would read aloud while others worked. A laborer in Philadelphia; a serving girl in Pelham, Massachusetts; a mechanic in New Haven; a farmhand in the small village of Harwinton, Connecticut; and even a pioneer in the frontier outpost of Belpre, Ohio, all had access to lending libraries. There, unaffordable novels were borrowed and anyone could read about a wide range of characters, including itinerants, factory girls, beggar maids, orphans, the illegitimate, and others deemed social outcasts by genteel society.

    Despite the widespread popularity of fiction, no American novelist before James Fenimore Cooper was able to support herself or himself solely by writing fiction. Susanna Rowson comes closest to having been America's first professional novelist, but she wrote plays, songs, advice books, and textbooks as well as

SECOND STREET *North from Market S.ᵗ ʷ.* CHRIST CHURCH.
PHILADELPHIA.

*During the eighteenth century, Philadelphia was a major publishing center (and also
the U.S. capital from 1790 to 1800). W. Birch & Son's engraving shows Second Street
in 1799.*

novels (and later turned her attention to running a progressive school for young
women in order to support herself and her family). As expensive as buying a
novel was, printing and publishing one during the early years of the republic was
even more expensive. Books had to be set by hand; paper was handmade from
expensive (and typically scarce) rags; and bindings, even of cheap books, were
hand sewn. No writer got rich from an early-American novel, and no printer did,
either. In fact, printing was generally a cottage industry, in which every family
member (female as well as male, child as well as adult) participated, and rarely
yielded an affluent life style. Significantly, out of the hundreds of colonial and
postcolonial American publishers, only one establishment (that of Mathew Carey)
managed to survive into the middle of the nineteenth century.

Beside the cost of producing books before mechanization was the matter of authors' royalties. The absence of national and international copyright laws wors-
ened the economics of authorship. Little in early-American law favored books
written by Americans and published in the new United States. On the contrary, the
Tariff Act of 1789, in which Congress placed sliding taxes on imported goods in
order to aid American manufacturers, neglected to mention books or the book
trade.

Because London had a large, concentrated population, publishing books was significantly cheaper in England than in the United States. American publishers simply waited to see what English novels did well on the English market and then had buyers purchase large quantities of these books, typically at a discounted price, and ship them to America. Otherwise, American importers bought remaindered books (books that did not sell) at bargain-basement prices in England and essentially dumped the books in America, where fewer literary choices were available. These cheap imports flooded the American market and threatened to destroy the early-American novel just as it was getting started.

Similarly, the absence of copyright laws enabled a publisher to reproduce with impunity a popular book on his (or rarely, her) own press. After 1790 and the passage of the first national copyright regulations, the reprinting of English novels was still possible. Thus, Rowson's *Charlotte Temple,* which was first published in England but became a bestseller only in America, apparently earned Rowson no royalties. In letters to Rowson, Mathew Carey praises her on the excellent sales of her book but never mentions profits that she could receive from her novel's various reprintings. Not until 1830, when the first international copyright laws were passed, did the pirating of foreign imprints (without due payment to the original author or publisher) become illegal.

Economics fostered a taste for British fiction and to a lesser extent French fiction, also. Americans certainly suffered the insecurities of cultural imperialism experienced in many postcolonial societies, then as now. In fashion, anything French was esteemed over clothing tailored at home; in literature, books from England had more status than did the local product. Although a war with England had been fought and won, many Americans insisted that England was still the intellectual and cultural fountainhead of America. As if to legitimate their own creative attempts, a number of new republic novelists defensively allude to English writers—Henry Fielding, Samuel Richardson, and Lawrence Sterne. However, rather than these highly praised (and now canonical) writers, the English writers most often sought by late eighteenth-century booksellers, lending libraries, and readers were Robert Bage, "Monk" Lewis, and Ann Radcliffe. Henry Brooke's *The Fool of Quality* (1766–1770), a popular English title now as obscure as most early American ones, was the novel most likely to be found in American bookshops or libraries.

For the most part, American writers did not ape their British counterparts. Hannah Webster Foster mentioned English novelists to disparage their morals as much as to praise their skill. Whereas American writers read British authors, British writers read American authors, too. Charles Brockden Brown read virtually everything by feminist philosopher Mary Wollstonecraft and her husband, William Godwin. In the preface to *Mandeville* (1817), Godwin returned the compliment by acknowledging his debt to Brown. A generation later, novelist Mary Godwin Shelley, the daughter of Wollstonecraft and Godwin, and Mary's husband, poet Percy Bysshe Shelley, were inspired by Brown. A persisting postcolonial inferiority complex may have deemphasized such a linkage, so that Mary Shelley's *Frankenstein* (1818) is rarely considered in the same breath as Brown's earlier tales of misguided intellect wreaking havoc on the unsuspecting.

Only recently has American fiction before Washington Irving and James Fenimore Cooper been given the attention it deserves. Against almost impossible odds, a curious band of women and men tried to reshape an evolving European narrative tradition into a genre that addressed the social and political conditions of the new republic. These authors produced a remarkably diverse body of work. The early-American novel took many forms and, in a very real way, fictionalized the aspirations of the new republic and voiced a profound critique of American society in its formative moments.

Hugh Henry Brackenridge
(1748–1816)

A lawyer, politician, judge, journalist, and civic leader, Hugh Henry Brackenridge wrote poems and plays; fictional, satirical, and historical works; propaganda; and sermons. His literary reputation rests chiefly on the picaresque satire *Modern Chivalry,* published in installments (1792–1815). *Modern Chivalry* follows Captain John Farrago and his illiterate Irish servant, Teague O'Regan, as they travel "to see how things were going on here and there and to observe human nature." The two are on a quest, looking for the real meaning of this new country called America. The aristocratic Farrago (which means hodgepodge) is a quixotic knight-errant, educated more by books than by the world. O'Regan's worldly knowledge far exceeds his learning. His escapades give the captain endless opportunities to moralize on the folly of ignorance and ambition, major threats to the democratic experiment as it evolved in the first quarter-century after the Revolution.

Born in 1748 in Scotland, Brackenridge was five years old when his family emigrated to Pennsylvania. Poor farmers, the family settled in York County, where young Brackenridge learned the rigors of frontier farming and the dangers of Native-American attacks. Education was especially important to his mother, and the boy often walked thirty miles to borrow books and newspapers.

At fifteen, Brackenridge began teaching school. In 1768 he entered Princeton University, then the College of New Jersey, where he studied the classics, history, mathematics, philosophy, and science. There, with his friends Philip Freneau and James Madison, Brackenridge became active in the Whig Society, writing "Satires Against the Tories" (1767–1771). In 1770 Brackenridge and Freneau wrote *Father Bombo's Pilgrimage to Mecca,* a novel of which only fragments survive. The high point of Brackenridge's Princeton career came when the epic poem "The Rising Glory of America," co-written with Freneau, was read at graduation in 1771 and published the next year. In the poem, Brackenridge celebrates commerce, learning, and science in an American landscape from South America and the Great Plains to Boston (comparable to Athens or Rome), where "fair freedom shall forever reign."

During the next decade, Brackenridge explored what an educated young man in America could do. He tutored at Princeton while studying for the ministry (but was never ordained), receiving an M.A. in 1774. Returning to schoolteaching, Brackenridge wrote two patriotic plays performed by his students. In 1776 he became a chaplain in George Washington's army and preached political sermons against the British, published as *Six Political Discourses Founded on the Scriptures* (1778).

Leaving the army in 1778, Brackenridge went to Philadelphia to start the *United States Magazine* to educate his countrymen in a "United States [where] the path to office and preferment lies open to every individual." The magazine was to be both "library" and "literary coffee-house of public conversation." Despite publishing numerous contributions from Freneau and Brackenridge's "The Cave of Vanhest," the magazine lasted only a year. Having invested his life savings in the failed magazine, Brackenridge turned to the study of law at Annapolis and finished in 1780.

In 1781 Brackenridge began practicing law in the small frontier town of Pittsburgh. He married in about 1785 and had a son, but within three years his wife died. In 1790 he remarried Sabina Wolfe, the daughter of a German farmer, after proposing on their first meeting. They had two sons and a daughter.

Although Brackenridge had been elected to the state legislature in 1786, he was not chosen to represent his district at the Constitutional Convention in Philadelphia the following year. His Eastern outlook clashed with the western frontiersman's distrust of government, and the people elected Irishman William Findley instead. Brackenridge satirized his opponent as Traddle, an illiterate Irish weaver ill-equipped for public office. As the community of Pittsburgh grew, Brackenridge helped establish the *Pittsburgh Gazette,* the Academy (now the University of Pittsburgh), and the first bookstore. Turning political defeat into literary gold, Brackenridge published in the *Gazette* in 1787 a version of his satiric poem about the character of Traddle. In this version, Traddle became O'Regan and over the next quarter-century evolved into the first genuinely American underclass hero, a sterotypical red-haired Irishman with a brogue, short on education but long on ambition.

Brackenridge's writing ranges from a grisly narrative of a Native-American attack on American troops (*Narratives of a Late Expedition Against the Indians* [1783]), to a masque (a combination of drama, music, and dance) honoring General Washington (1784), to court cases. *Incidents of the Insurrection* (1795) records his involvement in the Whiskey Rebellion of 1793–1794, when federal excise officers attempted to collect taxes from ruggedly independent western liquor distillers. Brackenridge attempted to negotiate with the rebels to prevent civil war. Appointed to the Pennsylvania Supreme Court in 1799, he moved east to Carlisle, Pennsylvania, in 1801 and continued to study and write law until his death in 1816.

All of Brackenridge's experiences found their way into *Modern Chivalry.* Two volumes were published in 1792; four more in 1793, 1797, 1804, and 1805; and an enlarged six-volume edition in 1815. Its enduring popularity indicates Brackenridge had learned to use as a gentle rod, not as a knife, his wit, intellect, classical training, and skill at observation and analytical thinking. Brackenridge has been called a trained classicist who yearned for the coffeehouses of London, a vigorous orator who beseeched his "rough countrymen to accept the new Federal Constitution that would limit their liberties," and a frontier eccentric, notes the biographer Daniel Marder (1970). Brackenridge was tall, stoopshouldered, and reserved, with a facetious sense of humor. Careless about his appearance, Brackenridge often heard cases while in his shirtsleeves, unshaven, and barefoot, his feet "propped on the bar of justice." Once seen riding naked in the rain, he explained he was protecting his one suit of clothes.

These several selves of Hugh Henry Brackenridge meet to create a dialogue in *Modern Chivalry.* No single authorial persona controls the narrative. Instead, as the presumed narrator yields to the voices of Farrago, Traddle, and many others, the result is a panoramic view of the American scene that indicates the proper course is neoclassical moderation.

Through *Modern Chivalry* Brackenridge taught his compatriots lessons in democracy, insisting that humans without reason are little more than beasts.

Suggested Readings: *A Hugh Henry Brackenridge Reader, 1770–1815*, ed. D. Marder, 1970. "The Rising Glory of America" (with Philip Freneau), in *American Writers of the Early Republic, Dictionary of Literary Biography* 37:317–322. C.M. Newlin, *The Life and Writings of Hugh Henry Brackenridge*, 1932.

Text Used: *Modern Chivalry*, ed. C.M. Newlin, 1937.

from   MODERN CHIVALRY

from   BOOK I, CHAPTER I

John Farrago, was a man of about fifty-three years of age, of good natural sense, and considerable reading; but in some things whimsical, owing perhaps to his greater knowledge of books than of the world; but, in some degree, also, to his having never married, being what they call an old batchelor, a characteristic of which is, usually, singularity and whim. He had the advantage of having had in early life, an academic education; but having never applied himself to any of the learned professions, he had lived the greater part of his life on a small farm, which he cultivated with servants or hired hands, as he could conveniently supply himself with either. The servant that he had at this time, was an Irishman, whose name was Teague Oregan. I shall say nothing of the character of this man, because the very name imports what he was.

A strange idea came into the head of Captain Farrago about this time; for, by the bye, I had forgot to mention that having been chosen captain of a company of militia in the neighbourhood, he had gone by the name of Captain ever since; for the rule is, once a captain, and always a captain; but, as I was observing, the idea had come in to his head, to saddle an old horse that he had, and ride about the world a little, with his man Teague at his heels, to see how things were going on here and there, and to observe human nature. For it is a mistake to suppose, that a man cannot learn man by reading him in a corner, as well as on the widest space of transaction. At any rate, it may yield amusement.

BOOK I, CHAPTER III

The Captain rising early next morning, and setting out on his way, had now arrived at a place where a number of people were convened, for the purpose of electing persons to represent them in the legislature of the state. There was a weaver who was a candidate for this appointment, and seemed to have a good deal of interest among the people. But another, who was a man of education, was his competitor. Relying on some talent of speaking which he thought he possessed, he addressed the multitude.

Said he, Fellow citizens, I pretend not to any great abilities; but am conscious to myself that I have the best good will to serve you. But it is very astonishing to me, that this weaver should conceive himself qualified for the trust. For though my acquirements are not great, yet his are still less. The mechanical business which he pursues, must necessarily take up so much of his time, that he cannot apply himself to political studies. I should therefore think it would be more answerable to your dignity, and conducive to your interest, to be represented by a man at least of some letters, than by an illiterate handicraftsman like this. It will be more honourable for himself, to remain at his loom and knot threads, than to come forward in a legislative capacity: because, in the one case, he is in the sphere where God and nature has placed him; in the other, he is like a fish out of water, and must struggle for breath in a new element.

Is it possible he can understand the affairs of government, whose mind has been concentered to the small object of weaving webs; to the price by the yard, the grist of the thread, and such like matters as concern a manufacturer of cloths? The feet of him who weaves, are more occupied than the head, or at least as much; and therefore the whole man must be, at least, but in half accustomed to exercise his mental powers. For these reasons, all other things set aside, the chance is in my favour, with respect to information. However, you will decide, and give your suffrages to him or to me, as you shall judge expedient.

The Captain hearing these observations, and looking at the weaver, could not help advancing, and undertaking to subjoin something in support of what had been just said. Said he, I have no prejudice against a weaver more than another man. Nor do I know any harm in the trade; save that from the sedentary life in a damp place, there is usually a paleness of the countenance: but this is a physical, not a moral evil. Such usually occupy subterranean apartments; not for the purpose, like Demosthenes,[1] of shaving their heads, and writing over eight times the history of Thucydides,[2] and perfecting a stile of oratory; but rather to keep the thread moist; or because this is considered but as an inglorious sort of trade, and is frequently thrust away into cellars, and damp outhouses, which are not occupied for a better use.

But to rise from the cellar to the senate house, would be an unnatural hoist. To come from counting threads, and adjusting them to the splits of a reed, to regulate the finances of a government, would be preposterous; there being no congruity in the case. There is no analogy between knotting threads and framing laws. It would be a reversion of the order of things. Not that a manufacturer of linen or woolen, or other stuff, is an inferior character, but a different one, from that which ought to be employed in affairs of state. It is unnecessary to enlarge on this subject; for you must all be convinced of the truth and propriety of what I say. But if you will give me leave to take the manufacturer aside a little, I think I can explain to him my ideas on the subject; and very probably prevail with him to withdraw his pretensions. The people seeming to acquiesce, and beckoning to the weaver, they drew aside, and the Captain addressed him in the following words: Mr. Traddle, said he, for that was the name of the manufacturer, I have not the smallest idea of wounding your sensibility; but it would seem to me, it would be more your interest to pursue your occupation, than to launch out into that of which you have no knowledge. When you go to the senate house, the application to you will not be to warp a web; but to make laws for the commonwealth. Now, suppose that the

[1] Orator of ancient Athens (384?–322 B.C.).
[2] Historian of ancient Athens (460–400 B.C.), whose account of the Peloponnesian war set the criteria for future chronicles.

making these laws, requires a knowledge of commerce, or of the interests of agriculture, or those principles upon which the different manufactures depend, what service could you render. It is possible you might think justly enough; but could you speak? You are not furnished with those common place ideas, with which even very ignorant men can pass for knowing something. There is nothing makes a man so ridiculous as to attempt what is above his sphere. You are no tumbler for instance; yet should you give out that you could vault upon a man's back; or turn head over heels, like the wheels of a cart; the stiffness of your joints would encumber you; and you would fall upon your backside to the ground. Such a squash as that would do you damage. The getting up to ride on the state is an unsafe thing to those who are not accustomed to such horsemanship. It is a disagreeable thing for a man to be laughed at, and there is no way of keeping ones self from it but by avoiding all affectation.

While they were thus discoursing, a bustle had taken place among the croud. Teague hearing so much about elections, and serving the government, took it into his head, that he could be a legislator himself. The thing was not displeasing to the people, who seemed to favour his pretensions; owing, in some degree, to there being several of his countrymen among the croud; but more especially to the fluctuation of the popular mind, and a disposition to what is new and ignoble. For though the weaver was not the most elevated object of choice, yet he was still preferable to this tatter-demalion,[3] who was but a menial servant, and had so much of what is called the brogue on his tongue, as to fall far short of an elegant speaker.

The Captain coming up, and finding what was on the carpet, was greatly chagrined at not having been able to give the multitude a better idea of the importance of a legislative trust; alarmed also, from an apprehension of the loss of his servant. Under these impressions he resumed his address to the multitude. Said he, This is making the matter still worse, gentlemen: this servant of mine is but a bog-trotter,[4] who can scarcely speak the dialect in which your laws ought to be written; but certainly has never read a single treatise on any political subject; for the truth is, he cannot read at all. The young people of the lower class, in Ireland, have seldom the advantage of a good education; especially the descendants of the ancient Irish, who have most of them a great assurance of countenance, but little information, or literature. This young man, whose family name is Oregan, has been my servant for several years. And, except a too great fondness for women, which now and then brings him into scrapes, he has demeaned himself in a manner tolerable enough. But he is totally ignorant of the great principles of legislation; and more especially, the particular interests of government. A free government is a noble possession to a people: and this freedom consists in an equal right to make laws, and to have the benefit of the laws when made. Though doubtless, in such a government, the lowest citizen may become chief magistrate; yet it is sufficient to possess the right; not absolutely necessary to exercise it. Or even if you should think proper, now and then, to shew your privilege, and exert, in a signal manner, the democratic prerogative, yet is it not descending too low to filch away from me a hireling, which I cannot well spare, to serve your purpose. You are surely carrying the matter too far, in thinking to make a senator of this hostler;[5] to take him away from an employment to which he has been bred, and put him to another, to which he has served no apprenticeship: to set those hands which have been lately

---

[3] A tattered person.   [4] Disparaging expression for an Irish immigrant.   [5] A stable boy.

employed in currying my horse, to the draughting bills, and preparing business for the house.

The people were tenacious of their choice, and insisted on giving Teague their suffrages; and by the frown upon their brows, seemed to indicate resentment at what has been said; as indirectly charging them with want of judgment; or calling in question their privilege to do what they thought proper. It is a very strange thing, said one of them, who was a speaker for the rest, that after having conquered Burgoyne[6] and Cornwallis,[7] and got a government of our own, we cannot put in it whom we please. This young man may be your servant, or another man's servant; but if we chuse to make him a delegate, what is that to you. He may not be yet skilled in the matter, but there is a good day a-coming. We will impower him; and it is better to trust a plain man like him, than one of your high flyers, that will make laws to suit their own purposes.

Said the Captain, I had much rather you would send the weaver, though I thought that improper, than to invade my household, and thus detract from me the very person that I have about me to brush my boots, and clean my spurs. The prolocutor of the people gave him to understand that his surmises were useless, for the people had determined on the choice, and Teague they would have, for a representative.

Finding it answered no end to expostulate with the multitude, he requested to speak a word with Teague by himself. Stepping aside, he said to him, composing his voice, and addressing him in a soft manner; Teague, you are quite wrong in this matter they have put into your head. Do you know what it is to be a member of a deliberate body? What qualifications are necessary? Do you understand any thing of geography? If a question should be, to make a law to dig a canal in some part of the state, can you describe the bearing of the mountains, and the course of the rivers? Or if commerce is to be pushed to some new quarter, by the force of regulations, are you competent to decide in such a case? There will be questions of law, and astronomy on the carpet. How you must gape and state like a fool, when you come to be asked your opinion on these subjects? Are you acquainted with the abstract principles of finance; with the funding public securities; the ways and means of raising the revenue; providing for the discharge of the public debts, and all other things which respect the economy of the government? Even if you had knowledge, have you a facility of speaking? I would suppose you would have too much pride to go to the house just to say, Ay, or No. This is not the fault of your nature, but of your education; having been accustomed to dig turf in your early years, rather than instructing yourself in the classics, or common school books.

When a man becomes a member of a public body, he is like a racoon, or other beast that climbs up the fork of a tree; the boys pushing at him with pitch-forks, or throwing stones, or shooting at him with an arrow, the dogs barking in the mean time. One will find fault with your not speaking; another with your speaking, if you speak at all. They will have you in the newspapers, and ridicule you as a perfect beast. There is what they call the carcatura; that is, representing you with a dog's head, or a cat's claw. As you have a red head, they will very probably make a fox of you, or a sorrel horse, or a brindled cow. It is the devil in hell to be

---

[6] John Burgoyne (1722–1792), the British General defeated in the Battle of Saratoga during the American Revolution; also known as Gentleman Johnny.

[7] Charles Cornwallis (1735–1805), named marquis for his accomplishments as a British general, was forced to surrender to General Washington after the Battle of Yorktown, which signaled the end of the Revolution in 1781.

exposed to the squibs and crackers[8] of the gazette wits and publications. You know no more about these matters than a goose; and yet you would undertake rashly, without advice, to enter on the office; nay, contrary to advice. For I would not for a thousand guineas, though I have not the half of it to spare, that the breed of the Oregans should come to this; bringing on them a worse stain than stealing sheep; to which they are addicted. You have nothing but your character, Teague, in a new country to depend upon. Let it never be said, that you quitted an honest livelihood, the taking care of my horse, to follow the new fangled whims of the times, and to be a statesman.

Teague was moved chiefly with the last part of the address, and consented to give up the object.

The Captain, glad of this, took him back to the people, and announced his disposition to decline the honour which they had intended him.

Teague acknowledged that he had changed his mind, and was willing to remain in a private station.

The people did not seem well pleased with the Captain; but as nothing more could be said about the matter, they turned their attention to the weaver, and gave him their suffrages.

BOOK II, CHAPTER I

There was, in a certain great city, a society[1] who called themselves Philosophers. They had published books, they called Transactions. These contained dissertations on the nature and causes of things; from the stars of the heaven to the fire-flies of the earth; and from the sea-crab to the woodland buffaloe. Such disquisitions, are doubtless useful and entertaining to an inquisitive mind.

There is no question, but there were in this body some very great men; whose investigations of the arcana[2] of nature, deserve attention. But so it was, there had been introduced, by some means, many individuals, who were no philosophers at all. This is no unusual thing with institutions of this nature; though, by the bye, it is a very great fault. For it lessens the incentives of honour, to have the access made so easy, that every one may obtain admission. It has been a reproach to some colleges, that a diploma could be purchased for half a crown. This society were still more moderate; for the bare scratching the backside of a member has been known to procure a fellowship. At least, there have been those admitted who appeared capable of nothing else.

Nevertheless, it was necessary, even in these cases, for the candidates to procure some token of a philosophical turn of mind; such as the skin of a dead cat, or some odd kind of a mouse-trap, or the like; or have some phrases in their mouths, about minerals and petrifactions; so as just to support some idea of natural knowledge, and pass muster. There was one who had got in by finding, accidentally, the tail of a rabbit, which had been taken off in a boy's trap. Another by means of a squirrel's scalp, which he had taken care to stretch and dry on a bit of osier,[3] bended in the form of a hoop. The beard of an old fox, taken off and dried in the sun, was the means of introducing one whom I knew very well: Or rather, as I have already hinted, it was beforehand intended he should be introduced; and

---

[8] Sarcasm and insults.
[1] The American Philosophical Society of Philadelphia.   [2] Secrets.   [3] Willow.

these exuviae, or spoils of the animal kingdom, were but the tokens and apologies for admission.

It happened, as the Captain was riding this day, and Teague trotting after him, he saw a large owl, that had been shot by some body, and was placed in the crotch of a tree about the height of a man's head from the ground, for those that passed by to look at. The Captain being struck with it, as somewhat larger than such birds usually are, desired Teague to reach it to him; and tying it to the hinder part of his saddle, rode alone.

Passing by the house of one who belonged to the society, the bird was noticed at the saddle-skirts, and the philosopher coming out, made enquiry with regard to the genus and nature of the fowl. Said the Captain, I know nothing more about it, than that it is nearly as large as a turkey buzzard. It is doubtless, said the other, the great Canada owl, that comes from the Lakes; and if your honour will give me leave, I will take it and submit it to the society, and have yourself made a member. As to the first, the Captain consented; but as to the last, the being a member, he chose rather to decline it; conceiving himself unqualified for a place in such a body. The other assured him that he was under a very great mistake; for there were persons there who scarcely knew a B from a bull's foot. That may be, said the Captain; but if others chuse to degrade themselves, by suffering their names to be used in so preposterous a way as that, it was no reason he should.

The other gave him to understand, that the society would certainly wish to express their sense of his merit, and shew themselves not inattentive to a virtuoso; that as he declined the honour himself, he probably might not be averse to let his servant take a seat among them.

Said the Captain, he is but a simple Irishman, and of a low education; his language being that spoken by the aborigines of his country. And if he speaks a little English, it is with the brogue on his tongue; which would be unbecoming in a member of your body. It would seem to me, that a philosopher ought to know how to write, or at least to read. But Teague can neither write nor read. He can sing a song, or whistle an Irish tune; but is totally illiterate in all things else. I question much if he could tell you how many new moons there are in a year; or any the most common thing you could ask him. He is a long-legged fellow, it is true; and might be of service in clambering over rocks, or going to the shores of rivers, to gather curiosities. But could you not get persons to do this, without making them members? I have more respect for science, than to suffer this bog-trotter to be so advanced at its expence.

In these American states, there is a wide field for philosophic search; and these researches may be of great use in agriculture, mechanics, and astronomy. There is but little immediate profit attending these pursuits; but if there can be inducements of honour, these may supply the place. What more alluring to a young man, than the prospect of being, one day, received into the society of men truly learned; the admission being a test and a proof of distinguished knowledge. But the fountain of honour, thus contaminated by a sediment foreign from its nature, who would wish to drink of it?

Said the philosopher, At the first institution of the society by Dr. Franklin and others, it was put upon a narrow basis, and only men of science were considered proper to compose it; and this might be a necessary policy at that time, when the institution was in its infancy, and could not bear much draw-back of ignorance. But it has not been judged so necessary of late years. The matter stands now on a broad and catholic bottom; and, like the gospel itself, it is our orders to go out into the highways and hedges, and compel them to come in. There are hundreds, whose names you may see on our list, who are not more instructed than this lad of yours.

They must be a sad set indeed then, said the Captain. Sad or no sad, said the other, it is the case; and if you will let Teague go, I will engage him a member-ship.

I take it very ill of you, Mr. Philosopher, said the Captain, to put this nonsense in his head. If you knew what trouble I have lately had with a parcel of people that were for sending him to Congress, you would be unwilling to draw him from me for the purpose of making him a philosopher. It is not an easy matter to get hire-lings now-a-days; and when you do get one, it is a mere chance, whether he is faithful, and will suit your purpose. It would be a very great loss to me, to have him taken off at this time, when I have equipped myself for a journey.

Teague was a good deal incensed at this refusal of his master, and insisted that he would be a philospher. You are an ignoramus, said the Captain. It is not the being among philosophers will make you one.

Teague insisted that he had a right to make the best of his fortune: and as there was a door open to his advancement he did not see why he might not make use of it.

The Captain finding that it answered no end to dispute the matter with him, but words of sense and reason, took a contrary way to manage him.

Teague, said he, I have a regard for you, and would wish to see you do well. But before you take this step, I would wish to speak a word or two in private. If you will go, I may perhaps suggest some things that may be of service to you, for your future conduct in that body.

Teague consenting, they stepped aside; and the Captain addressed him in the following manner:

Teague, said he, do you know what you are about? It is a fine thing at first sight, to be a philosopher, and get into this body. And indeed, if you are a real philosopher, it might be some honor, and also safe, to take that leap. But do you think it is to make a philosopher of you that they want you? Far from it. It is their great study to find curiosities; and because this man saw you coming after me, with a red head, trotting like an Esquimaux Indian, it has struck his mind to pick you up, and pass you for one. Nay, it is possible, they may intend worse; and when they have examined you awhile, take the skin off you, and pass you for an overgrown otter, or a musk-rat; or some outlandish animal, for which they will themselves, invent a name. If you were at the museum of one of these societies, to observe the quantity of skins and skeletons they have, you might be well assured they did not come by them honestly. I know so much of these people, that I am well persuaded they would think no more of throwing you into a kettle of boiling water, than they would a tarapin;[4] and having scraped you out to a shell, present you as the relics of an animal they had procured, at an immense price, from some Guinea[5] merchant. Or if they should not at once turn you to this use, how, in the mean time, will they dispose of you? They will have you away through the bogs and marshes, catching flies and mire-snipes; or send you to the woods for a pole-cat; or oblige you to descend into draw-wells for fog, and phlogistic[6] air, and the Lord knows what. You must go into wolves dens, and catch bears by the tail; run over mountains like an opossum, and dig the earth like a ground hog. You will

---

[4] A turtle.   [5] West African.   [6] Flaming.

have to climb upon trees, and get yourself bit by flying squirrels. There will be no end to the musquetoes you will have to dissect. What is all this to diving into mill-dams and rivers, to catch craw-fish? Or if you go to the ocean there are alligators to devour you like a cat-fish. Who knows but it may come your turn, in a windy night, to go aloft to the heavens, to rub down the stars, and give the goats and rams that are there, fodder. The keeping the stars clean, is a laborious work, a great deal worse than scouring andirons, or brass kettles. There is a bull there would think no more of tossing you on his horns than he would a puppy dog. If the crab should get you into his claws he would squeeze you like a lobster. But what is all that to your having no place to stand on? How would you like to be up at the moon, and to fall down when you had missed your hold, like a boy from the top-mast of a ship, and have your brains beat out upon the top of some great mountain; where the devil might take your skeleton and give it to the turkey-buzzards?

Or if they should, in the mean time, excuse you from such out of door services, they will rack and torture you with hard questions. You must tell them how long the rays of light are coming from the sun; how many drops of rain fall in a thunder gust; what makes the grasshopper chirp when the sun is hot; how muscle shells get up to the top of the mountains; how the Indians got over to America. You will have to prove absolutely that the negroes were once white; and that their flat noses came by some cause in the compass of human means to produce. These are puzzling questions; and yet you must solve them all. Take my advice, and stay where you are. Many men have ruined themselves by their ambition, and made bad worse. There is another kind of philosophy, which lies more within your sphere; that is moral philosophy. Every hostler or hireling can study this, and you have the most excellent opportunity of acquiring this knowledge in our traverses through the country; or communications at the different taverns or villages, where we may happen to sojourn.

Teague had long ago given up all thoughts of the society; and would not for the world have any more to do with it; therefore, without bidding the philosopher adieu, they pursued their route as usual.

Book III, Chapter I

It was somewhat late when the Captain arrived at an inn this evening. There was there before him, a young clergyman, who had been preaching that day to a neighbouring congregation; but had not as usual, gone home with an elder; but had come thus far on his way towards another place, where he was to preach the next day.

The Captain entering into conversation with the clergyman, sat up pretty late. The subject was what might be expected; *viz.* the affairs of religion and the church. The clergyman was a good young man; but with a leaning to fanaticism, and being righteous over much: The Captain on the other hand, somewhat sceptical in his notions of religion: Hence, a considerable opposition of sentiment between the two. But at length, drowziness seizing both, candles were called for, and they went to bed.

It was about an hour or two after, when an uproar was heard in a small chamber to the left of the stair-case which led to the floor on which they slept. It was Teague, who had got to bed to the girl of the house. For as they would neither let him go to Congress, nor be a philosopher, he must be doing something. The girl not being apprized, or not chusing his embraces, made a great outcry and lamentation. The clergyman, who slept in an adjoining chamber, and hearing this, out of the zeal of his benevolence and humanity, leaped out of bed in his shirt, and ran in to see what was the cause of the disturbance. The Captain also jumping up, followed soon after, and was scarcely in the chamber before the landlord coming up with a candle, found them all together.

The maid gave this account of the matter, *viz.* That between sleeping and waking she felt a man's hand lifting up the bed-clothes; upon which she called out murder. But whether it was any body there present, or some one else, she could not tell.

Teague, whose natural parts[1] were not bad, and presence of mind considerable, instantly took the resolution to throw the matter on the clergyman. By shaint Patrick, said he, I was aslape in my own bed, as sound as the shates that were about me, when I heard the sound of this young crature's voice crying out like a shape in a pasture; and when after I had heard, aslape as I was, and come here, I found this praste, who was so wholy, and praching all night, upon the top of the bed, with his arms round this young crature's neck; and if I had not given him a twitch by the nose, and bid him ly over, dear honey, he would have ravished her virginity, and murdered her, save her soul, and the paple of the house not the wiser for it.

The clergyman stared with his mouth open; for the palpable nature of the falsehood, had shocked him beyond the power of speech.

But the landlady, who in the mean time was come up, and had heard what Teague had said, was enraged, and could supply speech for them both. Hey, said she, this comes of your preaching and praying, Mr. Minister. I have lodged many a gentleman; but never had such doings here before. It is a pretty story that a minister of the gospel should be the first to bring a scandal upon the house.

The Captain interrupted her, and told her there was no harm done. The maid was not actually ravished; and if there was no noise made about it, all matters might be set right.

The clergyman had by this time recovered himself so much as to have the use of his tongue; and began by protesting his innocence, and that it was no more him that made the attack upon the main, than the angel Gabriel.

The Captain, interrupting him, and wishing to save his feelings, began by excusing or extenuating the offence. It is no great affair, said he, after all that is said or done. The love of women is a natural sin, and the holiest men in all ages have been propense to this indulgence. There was Abraham that got to bed to his maid Hagar, and had a bastard by her, whom he named Ishmael.[2] Joshua, who took Jericho by the sound of ram's horns, saved a likely slut of the name of Rahab, under a pretence that she had been civil to the spies he had sent out, but in reality because he himself took a fancy for her.[3] I need say nothing about David, who wrote the Psalms, and set them to music; and yet in his old days had a girl to sleep with him.[4] Human nature is human nature still; and it is not all the preaching and praying on earth can extinguish it.

The clergyman averred his innocence, and that it was that red-headed gentleman himself, meaning Teague, who was in the room first, and had been guilty of the outrage. Teague was beginning to make the sign of the cross, and to put him-

---

[1] Abilities.   [2] From Genesis 16 and 21.   [3] From Joshua 2.
[4] From I Samuel 17 through I Kings 2.

self into an attitude of swearing, when the Captain thinking it of no consequence who was the person, put an end to the matter, by ordering Teague to bed, and himself bidding the company good night.

The clergyman finding no better could be made of it, took the advice of the landlord, and retired also. The landlady seemed disposed to hush the matter up, and the maid went to sleep as usual.

1790–1815, 1792–1815

Susanna Haswell Rowson
(1762–1824)

Feisty, independent, determined, a woman of wit, talent, and sensitivity, Susanna Haswell Rowson achieved fame and professional success as an actress, dramatist, poet, novelist, and teacher. She was America's first bestselling novelist. Rowson demonstrated resourcefulness and independence in a period of history that encouraged female docility.

Susanna Haswell was born in Portsmouth, England, in 1762. Her mother died soon afterwards, and her father, a British naval officer, traveled to New England as a revenue collector, leaving his young daughter in the care of relatives. When she was five years old, she sailed from England to rejoin her father, by then remarried and settled at Nantasket, near Boston. The stormy crossing ended in shipwreck: she later used this experience in several of her novels. The Haswells settled into a comfortably genteel life at Nantasket, and by the time she was twelve Susanna gained a reputation for learning.

As English Loyalists, the Haswells suffered during the American Revolution: Their property was confiscated, Haswell was declared a prisoner of war, and for over two years, the family moved frequently, living in poverty and humiliation. In 1778 Haswell and his family were returned to London as part of a prisoner exchange. Susanna Haswell began working as a governess for the family of the duchess of Devonshire (and later dedicated her first novel, *Victoria* [1786] to the duchess). As a member of this aristocratic household, she met the prince of Wales, obtained a pension for her father, and toured Europe, gaining insights into the lives of the wealthy and powerful.

In 1786 Susanna married William Rowson. Charming but irresponsible, unreliable, and excessively fond of drink, he was equally unsuccessful as a hardware merchant, musician, and actor. The couple remained in London until William's hardware business failed in 1792. During that period Susanna Rowson published two volumes of poetry, including *A Trip to Parnassus*, (1788), a long dramatic poem; four more novels, including *Charlotte Temple* (1794), her most well-known work; and a collection of moralistic letters and stories, *Mentoria; Or, the Young Lady's Friend* (1791), which includes an essay on women's education.

Charlotte Temple, the first American bestseller, has been called a literary classic, a book that barely rises above literacy's lower limits, the epitome of the seduction novel, an allegory of early America's changing sociopolitical conditions, and a powerful work that provides sisterly, affectionate "counsel" to girls who feel alone because they have no identity of their own legally or politically. It tells the story of the seduction of a fifteen-year-old English schoolgirl and her abandonment in New York by a British officer, Montraville, during the American Revolution. Other characters include the conniving Mademoiselle La Rue and the villainous Belcour. Both sexes conspire, Rowson shows, to ensnare a helpless young girl like Charlotte.

Published in England in 1791 as *Charlotte: A Tale of Truth,* the first American edition came out in 1794, and during Rowson's lifetime forty more editions appeared. By the end of the nineteenth century more than two hundred editions had been printed, and Charlotte had become an important figure in American legend. For many readers, this was indeed a tale of truth. Over the years thousands wept at a tombstone marked "Charlotte Temple" at Trinity Church in New York City, where she supposedly was buried. The tradition that the story is based on the actual elopement of Rowson's cousin John Montresor and Charlotte Stanley is generally considered apocryphal today.

William Rowson's business went bankrupt, and the couple took theater jobs at Edinburgh, where the actor Thomas Wignell (who had played the lead in Royall Tyler's *The Contrast* in New York in 1787) persuaded them to join a new theater company in Philadelphia in 1793. Thus, Susanna Rowson lived the second half of her life in the United States, where she continued her theater career, singing, dancing, playing instruments, and composing songs, librettos, and plays, as well as acting in Annapolis and Philadelphia. She joined Boston's Federal Street Theater in 1796. The most successful of Rowson's seven plays is *Slaves in Algiers* (1794), which combines an attack on slavery with a feminist message.

SLAVES in ALGIERS;

OR, A

STRUGGLE for FREEDOM:

A PLAY,

INTERSPERSED WITH SONGS,

IN THREE ACTS.

By Mrs. ROWSON.

AS PERFORMED

AT THE

NEW THEATRES,

IN

PHILADELPHIA and BALTIMORE.

PHILADELPHIA:

PRINTED FOR THE AUTHOR, BY WRIGLEY AND BERRIMAN, N° 149, CHESNUT-STREET.

M,DCC,XCIV

The title page of the first American edition of Susannah Haswell Rowson's Slaves in Algiers.

In 1797 Rowson left the theater and opened a highly regarded academy for young ladies in Boston, remaining there until her retirement in 1822. She was innovative in providing a far more rigorous and varied education than was commonly available for girls, adding mathematics, science, geography, and history to the usual diet of needlework, music, and dancing. She was also a popular public lecturer and for many years headed Boston's charitable society for widows and orphans. She died at age sixty-three in 1824.

Rowson's professional life demonstrates the energy that characterized the early republic from 1793 to 1824. She saw young women as her primary audience and, through her writings and her example, tried to teach them resourcefulness and independence. Despite her declining health, she continued to write: plays, three more novels, poetry, biographies of famous women, a spelling dictionary, magazine pieces, songs, and textbooks in geography, Bible and church history, and history. Moreover, she was the main provider in a family that included not only the shiftless William but an adopted daughter, William's sister and her children, and William's illegitimate son. At the end of her life Rowson was working on a sequel called *Charlotte's Daughter: Or, The Three Orphans* (later retitled *Lucy Temple*), published four years after her death.

Suggested Readings: *Trials of the Human Heart*, 1795. *Sarah: Or, The Exemplary Wife*, 1813. D. Weil, *In Defense of Women: Susanna Rowson (1762–1824)*, 1976. P. L. Parker, *Susanna Rowson*, 1986.

Texts Used: *Charlotte Temple*, Vol. I, ed. C. N. Davidson, 1986.

from   CHARLOTTE TEMPLE

PREFACE

For the perusal of the young and thoughtless of the fair sex, this Tale of Truth is designed; and I could wish my fair readers to consider it as not merely the effusion of Fancy, but as a reality. The circumstances on which I have founded this novel were related to me some little time since by an old lady who had personally known Charlotte, though she concealed the real names of the characters, and likewise the place where the unfortunate scenes were acted: yet as it was impossible to offer a relation to the public in such an imperfect state, I have thrown over the whole a slight veil of fiction, and substituted names and places according to my own fancy. The principal characters in this little tale are now consigned to the silent tomb: it can therefore hurt the feelings of no one; and may, I flatter myself, be of service to some who are so unfortunate as to have neither friends to advise, or understanding to direct them, through the various and unexpected evils that attend a young and unprotected woman in her first entrance into life.

While the tear of compassion still trembled in my eye for the fate of the unhappy Charlotte, I may have children of my own, said I, to whom this recital may be of use, and if to your own children, said Benevolence, why not to the many daughters of Misfortune who, deprived of natural friends, or spoilt by a mistaken education, are thrown on an unfeeling world without the least power to defend themselves from the snares not only of the other sex, but from the more dangerous arts of the profligate of their own.

Sensible as I am that a novel writer, at a time when such a variety of works are ushered into the world under that name, stands but a poor chance for fame in the annals of literature, but conscious that I wrote with a mind anxious for the happiness of that sex whose morals and conduct have so powerful an influence on mankind in general; and convinced that I have not wrote a line that conveys a wrong idea to the head or a corrupt wish to the heart, I shall rest satisfied in the purity of my own intentions, and if I merit not applause, I feel that I dread not censure.

If the following tale should save one hapless fair one from the errors which ruined poor Charlotte, or rescue from impending misery the heart of one anxious parent, I shall feel a much higher gratification in reflecting on this trifling performance, than could possibly result from the applause which might attend the most elegant finished piece of literature whose tendency might deprave the heart or mislead the understanding.

from   CHAPTER VII: NATURAL SENSE OF PROPRIETY INHERENT IN THE FEMALE BOSOM

"I cannot think we have done exactly right in going out this evening, Mademoiselle," said Charlotte, seating herself when she entered her apartment: "nay, I am sure it was not right; for I expected to be very happy, but was sadly disappointed."

"It was your own fault, then," replied Mademoiselle: "for I am sure my cousin omitted nothing that could serve to render the evening agreeable."

"True," said Charlotte: "but I thought the gentlemen were very free in their manner: I wonder you would suffer them to behave as they did."

"Prithee, don't be such a foolish little prude," said the artful woman, affecting anger: "I invited you to go in hopes it would divert you, and be an agreeable change of scene; however, if your delicacy was hurt by the behaviour of the gentlemen, you need not go again; so there let it rest."

"I do not intend to go again," said Charlotte, gravely taking off her bonnet, and beginning to prepare for bed: "I am sure, if Madame Du Pont knew we had been out to-night, she would be very angry; and it is ten to one but she hears of it by some means or other."

"Nay, Miss," said La Rue, "perhaps your mighty sense of propriety may lead you to tell her yourself: and in order to avoid the censure you would incur, should she hear of it by accident, throw the blame on me: but I confess I deserve it: it will be a very kind return for that partiality which led me to prefer you before any of the rest of the ladies; but perhaps it will give you pleasure," continued she, letting fall some hypocritical tears, "to see me deprived of bread, and for an action which by the most rigid could only be esteemed an inadvertency, lose my place and character, and be driven again into the world, where I have already suffered all the evils attendant on poverty."

This was touching Charlotte in the most vulnerable part: she rose from her seat, and taking Mademoiselle's hand—"You know, my dear La Rue," said she, "I love you too well, to do anything that would injure you in my governess's opinion: I am only sorry we went out this evening."

"I don't believe it, Charlotte," said she, assuming a little vivacity; "for if you had not gone out, you would not have seen the gentleman who met us crossing the field; and I rather think you were pleased with his conversation."

"I had seen him once before," replied Charlotte, "and thought him an agreeable man; and you know one is always pleased to see a person with whom one has passed several chearful hours. "But," said she pausing, and drawing the letter from her pocket, while a gentle suffusion of vermillion tinged her neck and face, "he gave me this letter; what shall I do with it?"

"Read it, to be sure," returned Mademoiselle.

"I am afraid I ought not," said Charlotte: "my mother has often told me, I should never read a letter given me by a young man, without first giving it to her."

"Lord bless you, my dear girl," cried the teacher smiling, "have you a mind to be in leading strings all your life time. Prithee open the letter, read it, and judge for yourself; if you show it your mother, the consequence will be, you will be taken from school, and a strict guard kept over you; so you will stand no chance of ever seeing the smart young officer again."

"I should not like to leave school yet," replied Charlotte, "till I have attained a greater proficiency in my Italian and music. But you can, if you please, Mademoiselle, take the letter back to Montraville, and tell him I wish him well, but cannot, with any propriety, enter into a clandestine correspondence with him." She laid the letter on the table, and began to undress herself.

"Well," said La Rue, "I vow you are an unaccountable girl: have you no curiosity to see the inside now? for my part I could no more let a letter addressed to me lie unopened so long, than I could work miracles: he writes a good hand," continued she, turning the letter, to look at the superscription.

"'Tis well enough," said Charlotte, drawing it towards her.

"He is a genteel young fellow," said La Rue carelessly, folding up her apron at the same time; "but I think he is marked with the small pox."

"Oh you are greatly mistaken," said Charlotte eagerly; "he has a remarkable clear skin and fine complexion."

"His eyes, if I could judge by what I saw," said La Rue, "are grey and want expression."

"By no means," replied Charlotte; "they are the most expressive eyes I ever saw."

"Well, child, whether they are grey or black is of no consequence: you have determined not to read his letter; so it is likely you will never either see or hear from him again."

Charlotte took up the letter, and Mademoiselle continued—"He is most probably going to America; and if ever you should hear any account of him, it may possibly be that he is killed; and though he loved you ever so fervently, though his last breath should be spent in a prayer for your happiness, it can be nothing to you: you can feel nothing for the fate of the man, whose letters you will not open, and whose suffering you will not alleviate, by permitting him to think you would remember him when absent, and pray for his safety."

Charlotte still held the letter in her hand: her heart swelled at the conclusion of Mademoiselle's speech, and a tear dropped upon the wafer that closed it.

"The wafer is not dry yet," said she, "and sure there can be no great harm—" She hesitated. La Rue was silent. "I may read it, Mademoiselle, and return it afterwards."

"Certainly," replied Mademoiselle.

Hannah Webster Foster
(1758–1840)

The Coquette (1797), the first of only two books published by Hannah Webster Foster, has been called the best early American novel. It is a sentimental novel made up of 74 letters written by seven different characters. These letters tell the story of a spirited, attractive, but not wealthy young woman who wants to sow her wild oats before settling down to a constricting societal role. The story relates the tragic consequences of her decision.

The full title of Foster's first novel is *The Coquette: or the History of Eliza Wharton; A Novel; Founded on Fact*. It was an immediate success, earning distinction as one of two American bestsellers published before 1800 (the other was Susanna Haswell Rowson's *Charlotte Temple* [1794]). *The Coquette* remained popular into the early nineteenth century and was reprinted more than twenty times. At least part of its popularity derived from its sources in the tragedy of a real woman, Elizabeth Whitman of Hartford, Connecticut. Like Foster's character Eliza Wharton, Whitman found herself free after the death of the preacher to whom she had been engaged by her mother and then torn between a second preacher and a seducer, father of the child whose birth speeded her death. The story of Whitman's sad end at the Bell Tavern in Danvers, Massachusetts, in July 1788 was well known by the time Foster created her fictionalized account.

The Coquette rises above the stereotypical seduction novel by reformulating the heroine's problem. For Eliza, neither of her choices in the marriage market is really a choice. She finds the Rev. John Boyer, who wants to marry her, boring; the man who excites her, Major Peter Sanford, is a debauched rake who cynically realizes that he must marry a wealthy woman to maintain his affluent life style. Foster avoids a narrowly moralistic labeling of Eliza as a fallen woman who reaps the wages of sin; instead the author creates a dynamic portrait, filtered through the many lenses of her letter writers, that manages to engage the reader on the horns of the dilemma Eliza experienced.

Little is known of Foster's life beyond its mere outlines. She was born Hannah Webster in Salisbury, Massachusetts, a small coastal town near the Maine border, in 1758. Her father was a merchant who traded in Boston, and her mother died before Hannah was four years old. At this time Hannah was probably sent to a boarding school. Her experiences there provided the basis for her thoughts on women's education, included in her second book, *The Boarding School* (1798). By 1771 she was living in Boston. In 1785, at age twenty-six, she married Rev. John Foster, four years younger than herself and educated at Dartmouth University. He served as pastor of the First Church in Brighton, Massachusetts, for forty-five years. Of their six children, two daughters, Eliza Lanesford Cushing and Harriet Vaughan Cheney, became novelists. Both settled in Montreal, where Foster moved after her husband's death in 1830; she died there at age eighty-one.

Suggested Readings: *The Boarding School: Or, Lessons of a Preceptress to Her Pupils*, 1798. C. Bolton, *The Elizabeth Whitman Mystery*, 1912. H. Brown, *The Sentimental Novel in America, 1798–1869*, 1940. C. Davidson, *Revolution and the Word, The Rise of the Novel in America*, 1986.

Text Used: *The Coquette*, ed. C. N. Davidson, 1987.

from THE COQUETTE

LETTER IX: TO MISS LUCY FREEMAN

New-Haven.

I am not so happy to day in the recollection of last evening's entertainment, as I was in the enjoyment.

The explanation which I promised you from Mrs. Richman yesterday, I could not obtain. When I went down to dinner, some friends of General Richman's had accidentally dropped in, which precluded all particular conversation. I retired soon to dress, and saw Mrs. Richman no more, till I was informed that Major Sanford waited for me. But I was surprised on going into the parlour to find Mr. Boyer there. I blushed and stammered; but I know not why; for certain I am, that I neither love nor fear the good man yet, whatever I may do some future day. I would not be understood that I do not respect and esteem him; for I do both. But these are calm passions, which sooth rather than agitate the mind. It was not the consciousness of any impropriety of conduct; for I was far from feeling any. The entertainment for which I was prepared was such as virtue would not dissapprove, and my gallant was a man of fortune, fashion, and for ought I knew, of unblemished character.

But Mr. Boyer was much more disconcerted than myself. Indeed he did not recover his philosophy while I staid. I believe, by some hints I have received since, that he had some particular views, in which he was disappointed.

Our ball had every charm which could render a ball delightful. My partner was all ease, politeness, and attention; and your friend was as much flattered and caressed as variety itself could wish. We returned to General Richman's about two. Major Sanford asked leave to call and inquire after my health, this morning, and I am now expecting him. I rose to breakfast. The late hour of retiring to rest had not depressed, but rather exhilerated my spirits. My friends were waiting for me in the parlor. They received me sociably, inquired after my health, my last evening's entertainment, the company, &c. When, after a little pause, Mrs. Richman said, and how do you like Major Sanford, Eliza? Very well indeed, madam: I think him a finished gentleman. Will you, who are a connoisieur, allow him that title? No, my dear: in my opinion, he falls far below it; since he is deficient in one of the great essentials of the character, and that is, *virtue*. I am surprised, said I: but how has he incurred so severe a censure? By being a professed libertine; by having but too successfully practised the arts of seduction; by triumphing in the destruction of innocence and the peace of families!

O, why was I not informed of this before? But, perhaps, these are old affairs; the effects of juvenile folly; crimes of which he may have repented, and which charity ought to obliterate. No, my dear, they are recent facts; facts which he dares not deny; facts for which he ought to be banished from all virtuous society. I should have intimated this to you before, but your precipitate acceptance of his invitation deprived me of an opportunity, until it was too late to prevent your going with him; and we thought it best to protract your enjoyment as long as possible, not doubting but your virtue and delicacy would, in future, guard you against the like deception.

Must I then become an avowed prude at once; and refuse him admission, if he call, in compliance with the customary forms? By no means. I am sensible, that even the false maxims of the world must be complied with in a degree. But a man of Major Sanford's art can easily distinguish between a forbidding, and an encouraging reception. The former may, in this case, be given without any breach of the rules of politeness. Astonished, and mortified, I knew not what further to say. I had been so pleased with the man, that I wished to plead in his favor; but virtue and prudence forbade. I therefore rose and retired. He is this moment, I am told, below stairs. So that I must bid you adieu, until the next post.

ELIZA WHARTON.

LETTER X: To THE SAME

New-Haven.

Upon closing my last, I walked down, and found Major Sanford alone. He met me at the door of the parlor; and taking my hand with an air of affectionate tenderness, led me to a seat, and took one beside me. I believe the gloom of suspicion had not entirely forsaken my brow. He appeared, however, not to notice it; but after the compliments of the day had passed, entered into an easy and agreeable conversation on the pleasures of society: a conversation perfectly adapted to my taste, and calculated to dissipate my chagrin, and pass the time imperceptibly. He inquired the place of my native abode; and having informed him, he said he had thoughts of purchasing the seat of Capt. Pribble, in that neighborhood, for his residence; and could he be assured of my society and friendship, his resolution would be fixed. I answered his compliment only by a slight bow. He took leave, and I retired to dress for the day, being engaged to accompany my cousin to dine at Mr. Laurence's, a gentleman of fortune and fashion, in this vicinity. Mr. Laurence has but one daughter, heiress to a large estate, with an agreeable form, but a countenance, which to me, indicates not much soul. I was surprised in the afternoon to see Major Sanford alight at the gate. He entered with the familiarity of an old acquaintance; and, after accosting each of the company, told me, with a low bow, that he did not expect the happiness of seeing me again so soon. I received his compliment with a conscious awkwardness. Mrs. Richman's morning lecture still rung in my head; and her watchful eye now traced every turn of mine, and every action of the major's. Indeed, his assiduity was painful to me; yet I found it impossible to disengage myself a moment from him, till the close of the day brought our carriage to the door; when he handed me in, and pressing my hand to his lips, retired.

What shall I say about this extraordinary man? Shall I own to you, my friend, that he is pleasing to me? His person, his manners, his situation, all combine to charm my fancy; and to my lively imagination, strew the path of life with flowers. What a pity, my dear Lucy, that the graces and virtues are not oftner united! They must, however, meet in the man of my choice; and till I find such a one, I shall continue to subscribe my name

ELIZA WHARTON.

LETTER XI: TO MR. CHARLES DEIGHTON

New-Haven.

Well, Charles, I have been manœuvring to day, a little revengefully. That, you will say, is out of character. So baleful a passion does not easily find admission among those softer ones, which you well know I cherish. However, I am a mere Proteus, and can assume any shape that will best answer my purpose.

I called this forenoon, as I told you I intended, at Gen. Richman's. I waited some time in the parlor alone, before Eliza appeared; and when she did appear, the distant reserve of her manners and the pensiveness of her countenance convinced me that she had been vexed, and I doubted not but Peter Sanford was the occasion. Her wise cousin, I could have sworn, had been giving her a detail of the vices of her gallant; and warning her against the danger of associating with him in future. Notwithstanding, I took no notice of any alteration in her behavior; but entered with the utmost facetiousness into a conversation which I thought most to her taste. By degrees, she assumed her usual vivacity; cheerfulness and good humor again animated her countenance. I tarried as long as decency would admit. She having intimated that they were to dine at my friend Lawrence's, I caught at this information; and determined to follow them, and teaze the jealous Mrs. Richman, by playing off all the gallantry I was master of in her presence.

I went, and succeeded to the utmost of my wishes, as I read in the vexation, visible in the one; and the ease and attention displayed by the other. I believe too, that I have charmed the eye at least, of the amiable Eliza. Indeed, Charles, she is a fine girl. I think it would hurt my conscience to wound her mind or reputation. Were I disposed to marry, I am persuaded she would make an excellent wife; but that you know is no part of my plan, so long as I can keep out of the noose. Whenever I do submit to be shackled, it must be from a necessity of mending my fortune. This girl would be far from doing that. However, I am pleased with her acquaintance, and mean not to abuse her credulity and good nature, if I can help it.

PETER SANFORD.
1796, 1797

Judith Sargent Murray
(1751–1820)

The eldest of four surviving children of Judith Saunders and Captain Winthrop Sargent, a prosperous merchant and shipowner, Judith Sargent was born in Gloucester, Massachusetts, in 1751. She was fortunate to share the education of her brother, Winthrop, two years younger than she, until he entered Harvard College. She was fully competitive in her mastery of the classics and neoclassical rhetoric, style, and form, as her essays demonstrate. Her classical training seriously affected her style, which is filled with abstractions, personifications, classical allusions, Latinate diction, and archaic verb forms, all embedded in convoluted sentences. Her education taught her that girls are every bit as strong and capable as are boys. Her feminist line is spelled out in "On the Equality of the Sexes"

(1790), an essay published in the *Massachusetts Magazine,* and throughout her writing.

Judith Sargent remained in Gloucester after her marriage to the merchant-captain John Stevens when she was eighteen; they had no children. Her only known publication during this marriage was "The Utility of Encouraging a Degree of Self-Complacency in Female Bosoms" (1784), although she was already writing verse. She became interested in universalism (a doctrine preaching that all people would be saved) and supported the early ministry of universalism's founder in America, John Murray, an Englishman who settled in Gloucester. In 1786 huge debts caused John Stevens to flee to the West Indies, where he soon died. Shortly afterward in 1788 Judith Sargent Stevens married John Murray and returned to writing. One child, a daughter born in 1791, lived.

Between 1789 and 1805 Judith Murray published many poems and essays. She wrote a series of essays in a monthly column in the *Massachusetts Magazine* between 1792 and 1794. These essays, which read like a sentimental novel, were reprinted as Volume I of *The Gleaner* (1798), her major achievement. A work in three volumes, *The Gleaner* was built around the story of "Mr. Gleaner" and his family, especially Gleaner's adopted daughter, Margaretta. Two plays, *The Traveller Returned* and *Virtue Triumphant,* were printed in *The Gleaner.* In the former, Murray reaffirms the value of reason over passion and the need for a mean between extremes. She skillfully combines mystery, love, comedy, and (averted) tragedy, carefully plotted with a large cast of stock characters.

In 1793 the Murrays moved to Boston, where the two plays in *The Gleaner* were produced in 1795 and 1796. Murray financed the publication of *The Gleaner* by collecting subscriptions and dedicated the work to President John Adams, hoping his name would help the book's sales. She also published editions of John Murray's letters and sermons (1812–1813) and autobiography (1816). After 1808 she devoted herself to caring for her husband, who had been paralyzed by a stroke. He died in 1815, and Murray moved to Natchez, Mississippi, to live with their daughter. Murray died there five years later.

Murray's central theme is equality, the equality of American genius and the classical past, of American genius and European models, of all writers, of women and men. (In *The Gleaner* she used a male pseudonym, Mr. Virgillius, who writes as Mr. Gleaner, to assure herself an equal hearing with men.) She demonstrated she could compete with men by publishing periodical essays on lofty topics such as heroism, virtue, and the formation of an "American" character, as well as publishing drama and formal verse.

Suggested Readings: "On the Equality of the Sexes," in *The Feminist Papers,* ed. A. S. Rossi, 1988. V. B. Field, *Constantia: A Study of the Life and Works of Judith Sargent Murray, 1751–1820,* 1931.

Text Used: *The Gleaner,* Vol. I, 1798 (some spelling and punctuation modernized).

from   THE GLEANER*

PREFACE TO THE READER

My Readers will not call my veracity in question, when I assure them that I am ardently anxious for their approbation.[1] A lover of humanity, I do not remember the period when I was not solicitous to render myself acceptable to all those who

---

* A person who gathers grain left behind by reapers; someone who collects things bit by bit.

[1] Approval; sanction.

were naturally or adventitiously my associates. Had I possessed ability, I should have advanced every individual of my species to the highest state of felicity, of which the present scene is susceptible; but circumscribed within very narrow bounds, I have, I had almost said momently; been reduced to the necessity of lamenting the inefficacy of my wishes. Yet this my *ruling passion,*[2] a fondness to stand well in the opinion of the world, having given a prevalent hue to every important action of my life, hath operated powerfully upon my ambition, stimulated my efforts, and implanted in my bosom an invincible desire to present myself before a public which I reverence, irresistibly impelling me to become a candidate for that complacency we naturally feel toward those persons, or that performance, which hath contributed to our emolument,[3] or even amusement.

My desires are, I am free to own, aspiring—perhaps presumptuously so. I would be distinguished and respected by my contemporaries; I would be continued in grateful remembrance when I make my exit; and I would descend with celebrity to posterity.

Had I been mistress of talents for an achievement so meritorious, my first object in writing would have been the information and improvement of my readers; nor will I deny that a pleasing hope plays about my heart, suggesting a possibility of my becoming in some small degree beneficial to those young people, who, just entering the career of life, may turn, with all the endearing ardour of youthful enthusiasm, to a *New Book,* to an *American Author;*[4] and while with partial avidity they pursue the *well intended* pages, they may select a hint, or treasure up a remark, which may become useful in the destined journey of life.

But vanity, in the most extravagant moments of her triumph, having never flattered me with the capability of conveying instruction to those, whose understandings have passed the age of adolescence, my view has only been to *amuse;* and if I can do this without offending, I shall be honoured with a place in some gentle bosom where I should else have been unknown; I shall obtain a portion of esteem, and my *ruling passion* will be thus far gratified.

To have presented a finished or perfect production, (such is my fondness for literary fame) I would gladly have relinquished my *present mode of existence;* nay, more—I would have laboured for the completion of such a composition through a long succession of lengthening years, although my life had been a scene of *penury*[5] and *hardship*.

With such sentiments I shall not be suspected of writing hastily or carelessly. The truth is, I have penned every essay as cautiously as if I had been assured my reputation rested solely upon that single effort: yet defects of almost every description may too probably occur; the Grammarian, the Rhetorician, the Poet, these may all trace such palpable deviations from the given standard, as may render me, in their opinion, an unpardonable offender against the rules of language, and the elegance and graces of style. Possibly too, thus laid open to all the severity of criticism, I may be arraigned, tried and condemned; and in this case it is certainly true, that I am preparing for myself the severest pangs. But, be this as it may, I rest assured, that the feelings of the Moralist being in no instance wounded, he will accept with complacency my efforts in the common cause, and humanely shield me from those shafts which might otherwise transfix my peace.

---

[2] To be a writer.   [3] Compensation.   [4] Young people would read her book.
[5] Extreme poverty.

HAVING, in the concluding Essays, given my reasons for assuming the masculine character, I have only further to observe, that those who admit the utility of conveying instruction and amusement by allegory or metaphor, and who allow the propriety of giving a tongue to the inanimate world, and speech to the inferior orders of the creation, will not object to the liberty I have taken. It is superfluous to add, that allegory and fable are not only authorized by the best moral writers, but are also sanctioned by holy writ.

I CANNOT urge in defence of my *temerity,*[6] that the importunity of friends hath drawn me forth—certainly not. But, worthy reader, I repeat that I have been animated, in this my arduous pursuit, *by a desire to be introduced to thee, by a wish to make one in the number of thy friends. I am solicitous to obtain an establishment in the bosom of virtue*—I would advance my claim to the sweetly soothing trains of just applause; and I would secure for myself, and for my infant daughter, (should our future exigencies require it) thy amity and thy patronage.

IF thou proceedest through the volumes before thee, we shall pass on together through many a page; the sentiments of my heart will be unreservedly pourtrayed; and I fondly persuade myself that thou wilt, without reluctance, embrace in the arms of thy complacency, thy most obedient, and sincerely devoted friend, and very humble servant,

CONSTANTIA.

Boston, March 16, 1797.

from   NUMBER I

Yes, I confess I love the paths of fame,
And ardent wish to glean a brightening name.

Observing in the general preface, published in the *December* Magazine,[1] a hint which I have construed into a desire to increase the number of your miscellaneous correspondents; and stimulated by the delicate reproof upon literary indolence, and that elegant exordium contains, I feel myself, while fitting quite at my leisure, on this evening of January 27th, 1792, strongly incited by my *good* or *bad genius—the event* must determine the character of the spright which is goading me on, to take into my serious consideration, the solicitation which in said preface is so modestly urged, and which squares so wonderfully well with my ideas of the reason and fitness of things.

Not that I shall aim at palming myself upon the public, for a son of literature, a votary of the nine,[2] or a dabbler in wit. I have no pretension to any of these characters. I am *rather* a plain man, who, after spending the day in

---

[6] Foolishness.

[1] Murray's Note: "The reader is requested to remember, that the Essays which compose this First Volume were written purposely for the Monthly Museum, in which they originally appeared; and that they now stand precisely in the order, and nearly in the manner, in which they were first presented." *December Magazine* was a short-lived literary journal that has been lost from periodical records.

[2] Worshipper of the nine Muses who, in Greek mythology, were regarded as the inspirers of learning and the arts.

making provision for my little family, sit myself comfortably down by a clean hearth, and a good fire, enjoying, through these long evenings, with an exquisite zest, the pleasures of the hour, whether they happen to be furnished by an amusing tale, a well written book, or a social friend. Possibly I might have jogged on to the end of my journey, in this sober, tranquil manner: but alas, for some time past, I think, as near as I can remember, ever since the commencement of your Magazine, I have been seized with a violent desire to become a writer. To combat this unaccountable itch for scribbling, it is in vain that I have endeavoured; it follows me through all the busy scenes which the day presents; it is my constant accompaniment in every nocturnal haunt; and it often keeps me waking, when, I verily believe, but for this restless desire, I might enjoy, in the fullest latitude, every blessing which hath ever yet been ascribed to sleep.

The many comprehensive titles, and alluring signatures, which have from time to time embellished your Magazine, have well near captivated my reason; and among many *et ceteras,* which might be enumerated, the following appellations have had for me peculiar charms: An ample field seemed opening in the title page of the *General Observer;* the name *Philo* appeared replete with studious lore; the *Politician* was indefatigable for the good of the nation; the *Philanthropist* bled sympathy; and with the *Rivulet* I was enraptured. At the bar of fancy, many a title for my intended essays hath been tried, and hath been successively condemned. A variety of signatures have been deliberately adopted, and as deliberately displaced, until my pericranium[3] hath been nearly turned with thinking. Unfortunately, with my wish to commence author, originated also, a most inordinate ambition, and an insatiable thirst for applause. In whatever line I made my appearance, I was solicitous to stand unequalled—I would be Cesar, or I would be nothing. The smoothness of Addison's page, the purity, strength and correctness of Swift, the magic numbers of Pope—these must all veil to me. The Homers and Virgils of antiquity, I would rival; and, audacious as I am, from the Philenia's[4] of the present age, I would arrogantly snatch the bays. Strange as is this account, it is nevertheless true. And, moreover, all these wild extravagancies have been engendered in a brain, which it may be, doth not possess abilities adequate to the furnishing a paragraph in a common newspaper! My case, I assure you, Gentlemen, hath been truly pitiable, while, for three years past, I have been struggling with an inflatus, which hath been almost irresistible. Reason, however, aided, as I said, by a conviction of inferiority, hath hitherto restrained me; but your last preface hath done the business—it hath interested my feelings, and induced *even reason* to enlist under the banners of temerity—the fire thus long pent up, cannot now be smothered, but acquiring, from its confinement, additional fervour, it at length produces me a candidate for that applause, by a prospect of which, you are solicitous to engage your readers in the arduous pursuit of fame.

Thus resolved, the die is cast, and this ungovernable mania admits of one only remedy. But having once made up my mind to write, an appellation is the next

---

[3] The skin of the skull.

[4] Refers to Sarah Wentworth Morton (1759–1846), an American poet using the pseudonym "Philenia," probably a female variant on "Philenon," who according to Greek myth triumphed over Meander in literary contests despite Meander's superior talent.

thing to be considered; for as to subjects, my sanguine hopes assure me they will follow of course. A writer of facetious memory, hath represented his dear Jenny, when she could not obtain the tissued robe, as meekly assuming the humblest garb which frugality could furnish. I am fond of respectable examples, and I have humility enough to be influenced by them.

My title having much exercised my mind, and being convinced that any considerable achievements are beyond my grasp, upon mature deliberation I have thought best to adopt, and I do hereby adopt, the name, character, and avocation of a Gleaner; and this appellation, I do freely confess, gives a full and complete idea of my present amazingly curtailed views.

Here pride suggests a question, What is any modern scribbler better than a Gleaner? But I very *sagaciously*[5] reply, Let my brethren and sisters of the quill characterize themselves; I shall not thus, upon the very threshold of the vocation of my election, enter the lists.

The truth is, I am very fond of my title: I conceive that I shall find it in many respects abundantly convenient; more especially, should an accusation of plagiarism be lodged against me, my very *title* will plead my apology; for it would be indeed pitiful if the opulent reaper, whose granaries are confessedly large, and variously supplied, should grudge the poor Gleaner what little he industriously collects, and what, from the richness and plenty of his ample harvest, he can never want.

With diligence then, I shall ransack the fields, the meadows, and the groves; each secret haunt, however sequestered, with avidity I shall explore; deeming myself privileged to crop with impunity a hint from one, an idea from another, and to aim at improvement upon a sentence from a third. I shall give to my materials whatever texture my fancy directs; and, as I said, feeling myself entitled to toleration as a Gleaner, in this expressive name I shall take shelter, standing entirely regardless of every charge relative to property, originality, and every thing of this nature, which may be preferred against me.

. . . I shall haste to present the precious gift, a fit offering at the shrine of the Massachusetts Magazine.[6] Thus having, as far as it lays with me, adjusted preliminaries, I propose myself, Gentlemen, as a candidate for a place in your Magazine. If my pretensions are judged inadmissible, presiding in your respectable divan, you have but to wave your oblivious wand, and I am *forever* silenced. I confess, however, that I have no violent inclination to see the Gleaner among your list of acknowledgments to correspondents, set up as a mark for the shafts of wit, however burnished they may be.

You, Gentlemen, possess the specific at which I have already hinted, and by which I may be radically cured; and if this attempt is really as absurd as I am even now, at times, inclined to think it, your noninsertion of, and silence thereto, will operate as effectually as the severest reprehension, and will be regarded by the Gleaner as a judgment from which there is no appeal.

1792–1797, 1798

---

[5] Shrewdly.

[6] Also known as *Monthly Museum of Knowledge and Rational Entertainment;* Murray published two serials there from 1792 to 1794.

Charles Brockden Brown
(1771–1810)

Charles Brockden Brown, America's first professional novelist, was born in Philadelphia in 1771. His Quaker parents instilled in their son both a distaste for the tenets of Calvinism and a preoccupation with individual morality, which greatly influenced his later writings. After attending a Quaker school from 1781 to 1787, Brown was apprenticed to a lawyer but abandoned legal study in 1793 because of his moral reservations about the legal profession and his growing literary interests: in 1789 his first essays had been published in a local magazine. Upon leaving the law Brown moved to New York City and joined the Friendly Society. This group of freethinkers was enchanted with the radical ideas of novelists Mary Wollstonecraft, who in *Vindication of the Rights of Woman* (1792) calls for equal education for women, and her husband William Godwin, who in *Political Justice* (1793) argues for human perfectibility and against society's corrupting influences.

In 1798 the period of Brown's greatest literary productivity began. Living in New York that year with bachelor friends—the closest being the poet and physician Elihu Smith—Brown published the fictional *Alcuin: A Dialogue,* lamenting the situation of women within the constraints of marriage, and *Wieland,* his first and perhaps greatest novel. In 1799 yellow fever struck New York and killed Smith, who had charitably shared his apartment with a fellow physician afflicted with the disease; Brown was himself temporarily afflicted. Yet, during 1799 Brown produced three more novels (*Ormond,* Part I of *Arthur Mervyn,* and *Edgar Huntly*), apparently by working on more than one at a time. From 1799 to 1800, he also edited the *Monthly Magazine and Literary Review,* in which he regularly called for the creation of an indigenous American literature. After publishing Part II of *Arthur Mervyn* in 1800, Brown returned to Philadelphia and entered the family importing business, having failed to earn a secure income as an author despite his hard work.

Distant from the literary circles of New York and involved in business affairs, Brown nevertheless continued to pursue literary interests. He produced two more novels, *Clara Howard* and *Jane Talbot* in 1801, edited two magazines between 1803 and 1809, and added to his "History of the Carrils," a fictional family chronicle never published in its entirety. During these years Brown also pursued interests in politics and geography, publishing pamphlets in 1803 and 1809 urging the forcible annexation of the Louisiana Territories to the United States and calling for an end to Thomas Jefferson's embargo on American trade with England and France. Brown struggled as well to complete a lengthy "Topographical, Statistical, and Descriptive Survey of the Earth." Over the objections of his Quaker parents, Brown married Elizabeth Linn, the daughter of a Presbyterian minister, in 1804. Together they lived happily until he died of tuberculosis in 1810.

Despite his attempts to enhance the literary reputation of his nation, Brown's works received little American notice during his lifetime: only one of his novels, *Edgar Huntly,* sold well enough to deserve reprinting. Ironically, however, his novels were praised by English reviewers, by his English mentor, William Godwin, and by the English poets John

Keats and Percy Bysshe Shelley. Some years after Brown's death, his novels were also praised by Edgar Allan Poe and Nathaniel Hawthorne—and by the critic and writer Margaret Fuller, who appreciated Brown's support for women's issues. The appearance of an American edition of Brown's *Collected Novels* in 1827 attests to the American reading public's increasing interest in his work.

Today, a quartet of Brown's novels—*Wieland, Ormond, Edgar Huntly,* and *Arthur Mervyn*—form the primary basis of his literary reputation. To some extent, these novels all rely on Gothic melodrama and horror: on depraved and powerful villains, on virginal damsels in distress, on darkness, mystery, and motifs of enclosure and burial. Yet, as Brown notes in his preface to *Edgar Huntly,* they eschew much of the paraphernalia of European Gothicism, replacing barons and castles with middle-class American characters and ordinary American locales. Tending to substitute the psychological for the supernatural, all four novels also reveal Brown's paramount concern with the human mind, particularly under extreme physical, sexual, moral, or financial stress. Despite Brown's later interest in national affairs, his novels pay little attention to the world beyond the mind, rarely alluding to the social and political issues that confronted America in the late 1790s and early 1800s. Their similarities and their contemporaneity notwithstanding, Brown's four major novels are, however, valuably different: throughout his literary career Brown continued to try new techniques and explore new subjects. Based on a real episode in New York history, *Wieland* is the story of a young man who comes to believe God has ordered him to kill his wife and children. In addition to the dangers of religious obsession, the novel underscores the perils of mistaken perception. *Wieland*'s title character is wrongly convinced that he has heard God's voice, and the novel's narrator, Wieland's sister Clara, is likewise continually misled by her senses—and thus continually mistaken in both her assessments of physical reality and her judgments of people. The novel's villain, a dark stranger named Carwin, derives power from his ability (as a ventriloquist) to mislead people such as Clara. Nevertheless, *Wieland* is optimistic in its suggestion that human reason and moral firmness can protect at least some individuals from being destroyed by perceptual error: Clara's rationality and morality finally save her from the tragedy that befalls her brother. Brown's inclusion of this temporarily baffled but ultimately triumphant character demonstrates both his feminist respect for the intellectual and moral capacities of women and his Godwinian confidence in the fundamental resources of human nature.

Though it contains another strong female character, Constantia Dudley, Brown's *Ormond* raises very different issues. As the novel begins, Constantia's wealthy, artistic, and self-indulgent father suffers financial reverses, leaving her to cope more or less single-handedly with poverty, illness, and social isolation. Whenever her father's spirits flag (and they often do), Constantia is true to her name, remaining optimistic and courageous. She must display other virtues once she encounters the novel's title character. Ormond is a man who speaks his mind no matter how impolite the truth might be and who has arrogantly decided that his own reason is superior to everyone else's. He makes another young woman his mistress (rather than his wife) because he finds her mental attributes less appealing than her physical ones. He is attracted to Constantia (because she possesses a good mind and the virtues he lacks), and he attempts to rape her. By way of the highly intelligent but utterly selfish character Ormond, the novel calls into question the eighteenth-century conflation of morality and reason. Thus, differing from *Wieland* in theme, *Ormond* differs as well in technique: unlike Clara Wieland, *Ormond*'s narrator, Constantia's friend Sophia Westwyn is only tangentially involved in the action and provides a generally knowledgeable and even omniscient point of view. More panoramic than *Wieland, Ormond* is also less horrific.

Very different from *Ormond* and *Wieland*, *Edgar Huntly* is set in a wild region full of mountains, caves, panthers, and Native Americans, far from civilization. Curious about a guilty-looking young man named Clithero, who wanders nightly in the recesses of rural Pennsylvania, the novel's narrator/title character, is drawn into strange wanderings of his own. Waking up in a pitch-black cave and having no idea how he got there, Huntly must battle hunger, thirst, physical exhaustion, cruel savages, and especially his own tendency to lose hope, all in order to make his way back to civilization. His discovery that his adventures have resulted from sleepwalking (as had the nocturnal excursions of Clithero), helps to explain the significance of these adventures. Afflicted by mental tensions resembling Clithero's, Huntly has relieved these tensions through his wanderings. Signaling Brown's movement in new directions, *Edgar Huntly* points not only toward James Fenimore Cooper's work with its wilderness setting and Native-American episodes but also toward the work of Poe and Hawthorne with its use of psychological landscape and brilliant analysis of neurotic behavior.

In some ways *Arthur Mervyn: Or, Memoirs of the Year 1793* is a combination of *Ormond* and *Wieland*. Part I describes the triumph of the apparently virtuous title character over many of the adversities that beset Constantia Dudley; Part II casts serious doubt on the principles of Mervyn, again raising the issue of appearance and reality. Yet, *Arthur Mervyn* moves beyond *Ormond* and *Wieland* by focusing on the moral development of a single character. In Part I the youthful Mervyn, having recently arrived in the city, comes under the influence of an evil schemer named Welbeck, who quickly involves Mervyn in criminal activities and from whom Mervyn must eventually detach himself. As Part I ends, Mervyn seems determined only to clear his name and to rescue other victims of Welbeck's frauds and manipulations. Part II greatly alters the reader's attitude toward Mervyn. Rumors arise suggesting that the life story Mervyn told to the novel's kindly narrator in Part I was a veil of half-truths, disguising unpleasant aspects of Mervyn's character. Moreover, having won the love of the charming Eliza Hadwin, whose father befriended him during the crises of Part I, Mervyn first concludes that he cannot marry her, then, when she appears to have become an heiress, decides he can. However, he marries someone else when Eliza's fortune proves illusory. Possessing characteristics of Welbeck, the mature Mervyn may represent Brown's ironic commentary on the notions of success as promoted by writers such as Benjamin Franklin and those prevalent in America in the 1790s.

Brown's greatest liability as a writer is his penchant for unrealistic manipulation of events. Unlikely coincidences abound in his novels, and his endings are rather contrived. Some coincidences in Brown's novels (such as the character doublings in *Edgar Huntly*) may be strategic rather than accidental, designed to underscore Brown's subtle psychological themes; and his narrative idiosyncrasies (including his contrived endings) may be attributable not to his incompetence as a writer but to his desire to characterize his narrators through the unsatisfactoriness of their narratives. Nevertheless, all the problems with Brown's plots are not likely to be transformable into virtues. Brown was simply a writer with great talents—and a few rather obvious limitations.

Brown has been called "the first man of letters in America," but with his career a brief and unprosperous one, with Philip Freneau writing before him, and with no "first woman of letters" having been named, both the title and Brown's nomination seem suspect. Brown cannot be accurately called "the father of American fiction." Although some of his themes anticipate those of later American authors, evidence that Brown had a major direct influence on these authors is lacking. Moreover, if Brown's themes have proved popular with later authors, other themes have proved equally popular: Brown can be given credit for introducing only a few significant strands into the fabric of American fiction. Brown continues, however, to seem more creative and original than other early American novelists, including Susanna Haswell Rowson and Hugh Henry Brackenridge, who treat traditional subjects in traditional ways. The works of these authors are less diverse than Brown's, less engrossing as narratives, and less thematically complex. Thus, whereas Brown's other designations have rightly been stripped from him, the title of "America's premier early novelist" is likely to remain his—derived from four innovative and powerful novels, which after nearly two hundred years are still easy to admire and difficult to forget.

Suggested Readings: *Charles Brockden Brown's Novels*, 1963. N. Grabo, *The Coincidental Art of Charles Brockden Brown*, 1981. *Critical Essays on Charles Brockden Brown*, ed. B. Rosenthal, 1981. A. Axelrod, *Charles Brockden Brown: An American Tale*, 1983.

Texts Used: *Arthur Mervyn: Or, Memoirs of the Year 1793: The Novels and Related Works of Charles Brockden Brown*, Pt. I, ed. S. J. Krause, S. W. Reid, N. S. Grabo, and M. L. Williams, Jr., 1980. *Wieland: Or, The Transformation: The Novels and Related Works of Charles Brockden Brown*, ed. S. J. Krausse, S. W. Reid, and A. Cowie, 1977.

from ARTHUR MERVYN

from CHAPTER XV[1]

These meditations did not enfeeble my resolution, or slacken my pace. In proportion as I drew near the city, the tokens of its calamitous condition became more apparent. Every farm-house was filled with supernumerary tenants; fugitives from home, and haunting the skirts of the road, eager to detain every passsenger with inquiries after news. The passengers were numerous; for the tide of emigration was by no means exhausted. Some were on foot, bearing in their countenances the tokens of their recent terror, and filled with mournful reflections on the forlornness of their state. Few had secured to themselves an asylum; some were without the means of paying for victuals or lodging for the coming night; others, who were not thus destitute, yet knew not whither to apply for entertainment, every house being already over-stocked with inhabitants, or barring its inhospitable doors at their approach.

Families of weeping mothers, and dismayed children, attended with a few pieces of indispensable furniture, were carried in vehicles of every form. The parent or husband had perished; and the price of some moveable, or the pittance handed forth by public charity, had been expended to purchase the means of retiring from this theatre of disasters; though uncertain and hopeless of accommodation in the neighbouring districts.

Between these and the fugitives whom curiosity had led to the road, dialogues frequently took place, to which I was suffered to listen. From every mouth the tale

---

[1] During the summer of 1793 Philadelphia suffered a yellow fever epidemic that left thousands dead. In this scene Arthur Mervyn enters the city as families who have lost loved ones and left everything behind are fleeing for their lives.

of sorrow was repeated with new aggravations. Pictures of their own distress, or of that of their neighbours, were exhibited in all the hues which imagination can annex to pestilence and poverty.

My preconceptions of the evil now appeared to have fallen short of the truth. The dangers into which I was rushing, seemed more numerous and imminent than I had previously imagined. I wavered not in my purpose. A panick crept to my heart, which more vehement exertions were necessary to subdue or control; but I harboured not a momentary doubt that the course which I had taken was pre-scribed by duty. There was no difficulty or reluctance in proceeding. All for which my efforts were demanded, was to walk in this path without tumult or alarm.

Various circumstances had hindered me from setting out upon this journey as early as was proper. My frequent pauses to listen to the narratives of travellers, contributed likewise to procrastination. The sun had nearly set before I reached the precincts of the city. I pursued the track which I had formerly taken, and entered High-street after nightfall. Instead of equipages[2] and a throng of passengers, the voice of levity and glee, which I had formerly observed, and which the mildness of the season would, at other times, have produced, I found nothing but a dreary solitude.

The market-place, and each side of this magnificent avenue were illuminated, as before, by lamps; but between the verge of Schuylkill[3] and the heart of the city, I met not more than a dozen figures; and these were ghost-like, wrapt in cloaks, from behind which they cast upon me glances of wonder and suspicion; and, as I approached, changed their course, to avoid touching me. Their clothes were sprin-kled with vinegar; and their nostrils defended from contagion by some powerful perfume.

I cast a look upon the houses, which I recollected to have formerly been, at this hour, brilliant with lights, resounding with lively voices, and thronged with busy faces. Now they were closed, above and below; dark, and without tokens of being inhabited. From the upper windows of some, a gleam sometimes fell upon the pavement I was traversing, and shewed that their tenants had not fled, but were secluded or disabled.

These tokens were new, and awakened all my panicks. Death seemed to hover over this scene, and I dreaded that the floating pestilence had already lighted on my frame. I had scarcely overcome these tremors, when I approached an house, the door of which was open, and before which stood a vehicle, which I presently recognized to be an *hearse*.

The driver was seated on it. I stood still to mark his visage, and to observe the course which he proposed to take. Presently a coffin, bourne by two men, issued from the house. The driver was a negro, but his companions were white. Their features were marked by ferocious indifference to danger or pity. One of them as he asssisted in thrusting the coffin into the cavity provided for it, said, I'll be damned if I think the poor dog was quite dead. It wasn't the *fever* that ailed him, but the sight of the girl and her mother on the floor. I wonder how they all got into that room. What carried them there?

---

[2] Carriages.   [3] The Schuylkill River.

The other surlily muttered, Their legs to be sure.

But what should they hug together in one room for?

To save us trouble to be sure.

And I thank them with all my heart; but damn it, it wasn't right to put him in his coffin before the breath was fairly gone. I thought the last look he gave me, told me to stay a few minutes.

Pshaw! He could not live. The sooner dead the better for him; as well as for us. Did you mark how he eyed us, when we carried away his wife and daughter? I never cried in my life, since I was knee-high, but curse me if I ever felt in better tune for the business than just then. Hey! continued he, looking up, and observing me standing a few paces distant, and listening to their discourse, What's wanted? Any body dead?

* * *

1798–1799, 1799

from   WIELAND

CHAPTER XVII[1]

I had no inclination nor power to move from this spot. For more than an hour, my faculties and limbs seemed to be deprived of all activity. The door below creaked on its hinges, and steps ascended the stairs. My wandering and confused thoughts were instantly recalled by these sounds, and dropping the curtain of the bed, I moved to a part of the room where any one who entered should be visible; such are the vibrations of sentiment, that notwithstanding the seeming fulfilment of my fears, and increase of my danger, I was conscious, on this occasion, to no turbulence but that of curiosity.

At length he entered the apartment, and I recognized my brother. It was the same Wieland whom I had ever seen. Yet his features were pervaded by a new expression. I supposed him unacquainted with the fate of his wife, and his appearance confirmed this persuasion. A brow expanding into exultation I had hitherto never seen in him, yet such a brow did he now wear. Not only was he unapprized of the disaster that had happened, but some joyous occurrence had betided. What a reverse was preparing to annihilate his transitory bliss! No husband ever doated more fondly, for no wife ever claimed so boundless a devotion. I was not uncertain as to the effects to flow from the discovery of her fate. I confided not at all in the efforts of his reason or his piety. There were few evils which his modes of thinking would not disarm or their sting; but here, all opiates to grief, and all

---

[1] As the scene opens Clara, the speaker and Wieland's sister, has just discovered the body of her sister-in-law, murdered in Clara's bed. Not yet suspecting her brother to be the killer, she greets her "transformed" brother.

compellers of patience were vain. This spectacle would be unavoidably followed by the outrages of desperation, and a rushing to death.

For the present, I neglected to ask myself what motive brought him hither. I was only fearful of the effects to flow from the sight of the dead. Yet could it be long concealed from him? Some time and speedily he would obtain this knowledge. No stratagems could considerably or usefully prolong his ignorance. All that could be sought was to take away the abruptness of the change, and shut out the confusion of despair, and the inroads of madness: but I knew my brother, and knew that all exertions to console him would be fruitless.

What could I say? I was mute, and poured forth those tears on his account, which my own unhappiness had been unable to extort. In the midst of my tears, I was not unobservant of his motions. These were of a nature to rouse some other sentiment than grief, or, at least, to mix with it a portion of astonishment.

His countenance suddenly became troubled. His hands were clasped with a force that left the print of his nails in his flesh. His eyes were fixed on my feet. His brain seemed to swell beyond its continent. He did not cease to breathe, but his breath was stifled into groans. I had never witnessed the hurricane of human passions. My element had, till lately, been all sunshine and calm. I was unconversant with the altitudes and energies of sentiment, and was transfixed with inexplicable horror by the symptoms which I now beheld.

After a silence and a conflict which I could not interpret, he lifted his eyes to heaven, and in broken accents exclaimed,"This is too much! Any victim but this, and thy will be done. Have I not sufficiently attested my faith and my obedience? She that is gone, they that have perished, were linked with my soul by ties which only thy command would have broken; but here is sanctity and excellence surpassing human. This workmanship is thine, and it cannot be thy will to heap it into ruins."

Here suddenly unclasping his hands, he struck one of them against his forehead, and continued—"Wretch! who made thee quicksighted in the councils of thy Maker? Deliverance from mortal fetters is awarded to this being, and thou art the minister of this decree."

So saying, Wieland advanced towards me. His words and his motions were without meaning, except on one supposition. The death of Catharine was already known to him, and that knowledge, as might have been suspected, had destroyed his reason. I had feared nothing less; but now that I beheld the extinction of a mind the most luminous and penetrating that ever dignified the human form, my sensations were fraught with new and insupportable anguish.

I had not time to reflect in what way my own safety would be affected by this revolution, or what I had to dread from the wild conceptions of a mad-man. He advanced towards me. Some hollow noises were wafted by the breeze. Confused clamours were succeeded by many feet traversing the grass, and then crowding into the piazza.

These sounds suspended my brother's purpose, and he stood to listen. The signals multiplied and grew louder; perceiving this, he turned from me, and hurried out of my sight. All about me was pregnant with motives to astonishment. My sister's corpse, Wieland's frantic demeanour, and, at length, this crowd of visitants so little accorded with my foresight, that my mental progress was stopped. The impulse had ceased which was accustomed to give motion and order to my thoughts.

Footsteps thronged upon the stairs, and presently many faces shewed[2] themselves within the door of my apartment. These looks were full of alarm and watchfulness. They pryed into corners as if in search of some fugitive; next their gaze was fixed upon me, and betokened all the vehemence of terror and pity. For a time I questioned whether these were not shapes and faces like that which I had seen at the bottom of the stairs, creatures of my fancy or airy existences.

My eye wandered from one to another, till at length it fell on a countenance which I well knew. It was that of Mr. Hallet. This man was a distant kinsman of my mother, venerable for his age, his uprightness, and sagacity. He had long discharged the functions of a magistrate and good citizen. If any terrors remained, his presence was sufficient to dispel them.

He approached, took my hand with a compassionate air, and said in a low voice, "Where, my dear Clara, are your brother and sister?" I made no answer, but pointed to the bed. His attendants drew aside the curtain, and while their eyes glared with horror at the spectacle which they beheld, those of Mr. Hallet overflowed with tears.

After considerable pause, he once more turned to me. "My dear girl, this sight is not for you. Can you confide in my care, and that of Mrs. Baynton's? We will see performed all that circumstances require."

I made strenuous opposition to this request. I insisted on remaining near her till she were interred. His remonstrances, however, and my own feelings, shewed me the propriety of a temporary dereliction. Louisa stood in need of a comforter, and my brother's children of a nurse. My unhappy brother was himself an object of solicitude and care. At length, I consented to relinquish the corpse, and go to my brother's, whose house, I said, would need a mistress, and his children a parent.

During this discourse, my venerable friend struggled with his tears, but my last intimation called them forth with fresh violence. Meanwhile, his attendants stood round in mournful silence, gazing on me and at each other. I repeated my resolution, and rose to execute it; but he took my hand to detain me. His countenance betrayed irresolution and reluctance. I requested him to state the reason of his opposition to this measure. I entreated him to be explicit. I told him that my brother had just been there, and that I knew his condition. This misfortune had driven him to madness, and his offspring must not want a protector. If he chose, I would resign Wieland to his care; but his innocent and helpless babes stood in instant need of nurse and mother, and these offices I would by no means allow another to perform while I had life.

Every word that I uttered seemed to augment his perplexity and distress. At last he said, "I think, Clara, I have entitled myself to some regard from you. You have professed your willingness to oblige me. Now I call upon you to confer upon me the highest obligation in your power. Permit Mrs. Baynton to have the management of your brother's house for two or three days; then it shall be yours to act in it as you please. No matter what are my motives in making this request; perhaps I think your age, your sex, or the distress which this disaster must occasion, incapacitates you for the office. Surely you have no doubt of Mrs. Baynton's tenderness or discretion."

New ideas now rushed into my mind. I fixed my eyes stedfastly on Mr. Hallet.

[2] Showed.

"Are they well?"said I. "Is Louisa well? Are Benjamin, and William, and Constantine, and Little Clara, are they safe? Tell me truly, I beseech you!"

"They are well." he replied; "they are perfectly safe."

"Fear no effeminate weakness in me: I can bear to hear the truth. Tell me truly, are they well?"

He again assured me that they were well.

"What then," resumed I, "do you fear? Is it possible for any calamity to disqualify me for performing my duty to these helpless innocents? I am willing to divide the care of them with Mrs. Baynton; I shall be grateful for her sympathy and aid; but what should I be to desert them at an hour like this!"

I will cut short this distressful dialogue. I still persisted in my purpose, and he still persisted in his opposition. This excited my suspicions anew; but these were removed by solemn declarations of their safety. I could not explain this conduct in my friend; but at length consented to go to the city, provided I should see them for a few minutes at present, and should return on the morrow.

Even this arrangement was objected to. At length he told me they were removed to the city. Why were they removed, I asked, and whither? My importunities would not now be eluded. My suspicions were roused, and no evasion or artifice was sufficient to allay them. Many of the audience began to give vent to their emotions in tears. Mr. Hallet himself seemed as if the conflict were too hard to be longer sustained. Something whispered to my heart that havoc had been wider than I now witnessed. I suspected this concealment to arise from apprehensions of the effects which a knowledge of the truth would produce in me. I once more entreated him to inform me truly of their state. To enforce my entreaties, I put on an air of insensibility. "I can guess," said I, "what has happened—They are indeed beyond the reach of injury, for they are dead! Is it not so?" My voice faltered in spite of my courageous efforts.

"Yes," said he, "they are dead! Dead by the same fate, and by the same hand, with their mother!"

"Dead!" replied I; "what, all?"

"All!" replied he: "he spared *not one!*"

Allow me, my friends, to close my eyes upon the afterscene. Why should I protract a tale which I already begin to feel is too long? Over this scene at least let me pass lightly. Here, indeed, my narrative would be imperfect. All was tempestuous commotion in my heart and in my brain. I have no memory for ought but unconscious transitions and rueful sights. I was ingenious and indefatigable in the invention of torments. I would not dispense with any spectacle adapted to exasperate my grief. Each pale and mangled form I crushed to my bosom. Louisa, whom I loved with so ineffable a passion, was denied to me at first, but my obstinacy conquered their reluctance.

They led the way into a darkened hall. A lamp pendant from the ceiling was uncovered, and they pointed to a table. The assassin had defrauded me of my last and miserable consolation. I sought not in her visage, for the tinge of the morning, and lustre of heaven. These had vanished with life; but I hoped for liberty to print a last kiss upon her lips. This was denied me; for such had been the merciless blow that destroyed her, that *not a lineament*[3] *remained!*

I was carried hence to the city. Mrs. Hallet was my companion and my nurse.

---

[3] A facial feature.

Why should I dwell upon the rage of fever, and the effusions of delirium? Carwin was the phantom that pursued my dreams, the giant oppressor under whose arm I was for ever on the point of being crushed. Strenuous muscles were required to hinder my flight, and hearts of steel to withstand the eloquence of my fears. In vain I called upon them to look upward, to mark his sparkling rage and scowling contempt. All I sought was to fly from the stroke that was lifted. Then I heaped upon my guards the most vehement reproaches, or betook myself to wailing on the haplessness of my condition.

This malady, at length, declined, and my weeping friends began to look for my restoration. Slowly, and with intermitted beams, memory revisited me. The scenes that I had witnessed were revived, became the theme of deliberation and deduction, and called forth the effusions of more rational sorrow.

1798

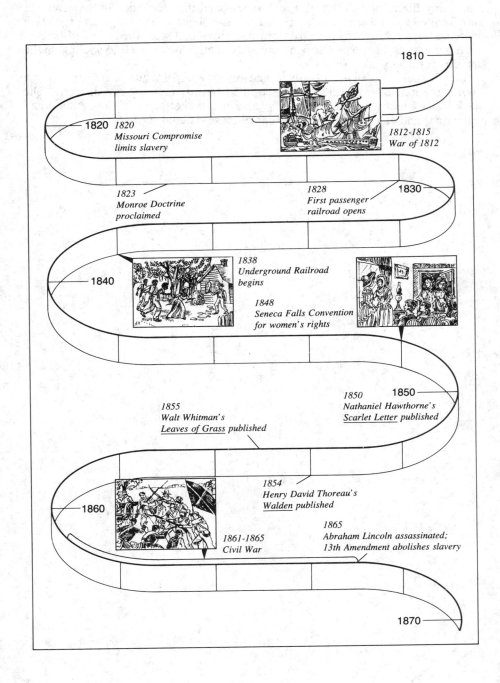

1810

1820
1820
Missouri Compromise
limits slavery

1812-1815
War of 1812

1823
Monroe Doctrine
proclaimed

1828
First passenger
railroad opens

1830

1840

1838
Underground Railroad
begins

1848
Seneca Falls Convention
for women's rights

1850
1850
Nathaniel Hawthorne's
Scarlet Letter published

1855
Walt Whitman's
Leaves of Grass published

1854
Henry David Thoreau's
Walden published

1860

1861-1865
Civil War

1865
Abraham Lincoln assassinated;
13th Amendment abolishes slavery

1870

PART THREE

Progress and Crisis

The Early to Middle 19th Century

The years from the founding of the republic to the outbreak of civil war were short enough to encompass a single life span. Washington Irving, for example, was born in 1783, the year the Treaty of Paris ended the Revolutionary War. He died in 1859; Abraham Lincoln was elected to the presidency the following year. James Fenimore Cooper was born in 1789, the year of George Washington's first inauguration. Lydia Maria Child was born two years into the nineteenth century; she died in 1880, after Reconstruction had come to an end. Ralph Waldo Emerson was a year younger than Child and outlived her by two years.

Their generation experienced an astonishing political and economic transformation. America once again faced England in war—the War of 1812, which arose over the British impressment of American seamen into naval service. (Before the British retreated at the Battle of New Orleans two and a half years after the war began, Washington, D.C., was in partial ruins.) Many problems we still face—in race relations, in the management of technological innovation, in the roles of men and women in an industrializing society—developed in the first half of the nineteenth century, and the ways in which they were understood still infuse our language. While this generation was alive, the physical size of the nation tripled: in 1783 the western boundary had been the Mississippi River; by 1860 it stretched to the Pacific. The Northwest Ordinance of 1787 provided the pattern by which new territory could be integrated into the political community, avoiding colonial status; the Missouri Compromise of 1820 determined which regions, new or extant, could maintain slaves. By mid-century the original thirteen states had increased to twenty-nine. The population size doubled nearly every twenty years, from 4 million people in 1790 to 30 million in 1860, although the average family size decreased sharply. A white woman in 1860 on average bore five children, compared to seven in 1800. The population growth came largely from foreign immigration in the 1840s and 1850s, a factor that changed the composition of the population; before 1840 an overwhelming majority of the population had been born in the United States.

Industrialization and Expansion

Postrevolutionary America was largely an agricultural nation. From North or South, slave or free, most Americans lived in the countryside and grew crops for market. As late as 1870, seventy percent of the population was defined as rural. In fact, the census bureau did not make a distinction between rural and urban populations until 1870, when a town with only eight thousand people was considered a city.

Nevertheless, the postrevolutionary generation experienced an extraordinary industrial transformation, which affected rural as well as urban life. Masters became capitalists; artisans became employees. The use of steam power to drive gears—resulting in steampowered boats, railroads, and textile machinery—restructured economic life. Despite a rhetoric of *laissez faire* and free trade, state support for the development of America's industrial capacity was widespread. States issued bonds in the 1820s and 1830s for building canals and in the 1840s and thereafter for building railroads, culminating in major federal land grants of the 1860s. Mill towns—Lowell, Massachusetts, was perhaps the most famous—embodied a new relationship between owners, employees, and technology. At its formation in the 1820s, Lowell attracted young, unmarried women who saw structured toil in factories as an improvement over unremitting toil on marginal New England family farms. Some found independence in the cash they received, but they came to resent a system in which they worked twelve hours a day, six days a week. Discrimination by gender and class was locked into the American factory system from the beginning; women could never earn wages comparable to men, who held all supervisory roles. The Lowell mill "girls" staged one of the nation's earliest industrial strikes in 1834. In the 1840s they were innovative in making demands not only of employers but of the state government: they demanded a ten-hour work day and the first state legislative hearing on industrial working conditions.

The major cities—Boston, New York, Philadelphia, and Charleston—were also transformed in the early nineteenth century. They became centers for national finance and communications, commerce, publishing, and small scale manufactures. The opening of the first passenger railroad in 1828 enabled business to be carried on over a wider region than was easily possible previously. Commercial development heightened inequities of wealth and power: in 1848 the poorest eighty percent of Boston's population owned only four percent of the city's wealth, while the richest one percent controlled thirty-seven percent of the city's wealth (E. Pessen, *Wealth Class, and Power Before the Civil War,* 1973).

The world of the farmer was rapidly transformed by technological innovation. Westward expansion provided cheap land; by 1840 5 million people, one-third of the U.S. population, lived west of the Appalachians. Inventions such as John Deere's steel plow and Cyrus McCormick's harvester made it possible to harvest larger crops, and steam-powered transportation on rivers and railroads made it possible to get the food to market faster so it could be sold more cheaply. The availability of inexpensive agricultural products in the cities resulted in cheap food for industrial workers and improved the ability of Americans to compete effectively in international markets.

The growth America experienced in the first half of the nineteenth century depended on the clearing of land for homesteads, as in this woodcut by J. A. Ayres.

In Europe industrialization forced massive disruption to rural populations, but in the United States it led to vibrant rural expansion. This expansion was not simply a matter of "manifest destiny"; it was the result of clear political choice and an insistence that there be no political limitations on westward movement—including no interference from Europe, as proclaimed by President James Monroe in 1823, in what became known as the Monroe Doctrine. By setting cheap prices for federal land, Congress encouraged farmers to move West. Congress supported white settlers' pressure for the repeated removal of native populations from desirable lands, even when, as in the case of the Cherokees in Georgia, the Native Americans had a sophisticated political system, a substantial number of English-speaking members, and a profitable economy. In 1837 federal troops forced the southeastern Cherokees across the Mississippi to what is now Oklahoma and Missouri; one out of four Cherokees died along the way. Other federal troops were used in guerrilla warfare against Seminoles in Florida and Sauks and Foxes in Illinois and Wisconsin.

The claim of manifest destiny was used also to rationalize American annexation of part of northern Mexico. During the 1830s slaveholding American settlers entered Mexico, which did not recognize slavery. In 1835 the slaveholders organized a revolt that the Mexican government resisted but lacked the force to squelch. When the independent republic of Texas appealed to Congress for annexation, Congress accepted, even though it meant war with Mexico; the Mexican War began in 1846. The resulting victory in 1848 brought under American control 500,000 square miles, including what is now California, Nevada, Utah, and most of New Mexico and Arizona. With this land came millions of Native-American and Hispanic inhabitants.

Slavery and the Economy. Slavery, which had developed in part as a response to a need for cheap labor, was now enlarged and strengthened. Although the slave plantation appeared to be a rural, agricultural enterprise, it, too, was embedded in a system of capitalist industrial production. The invention of the cotton gin and the development of large-scale textile mills in the Northeast and in Great Britain contributed to a virtually insatiable demand for cotton produced on new lands in the Southwest, including Texas. Cotton production soared from less than 500,000 bales in 1817 to 3 million bales in 1850. The British bought whatever northern mills did not; textile manufacturing was the single most important industry in America.

The profitability of textile production energized slavery, giving more white Americans, both northerners and southerners, a stake in its continuation and expansion. Although the foreign slave trade was ended in 1808, the internal slave trade remained a multimillion dollar "industry." At least 300,000 Virginia slaves were transported South between 1830 and 1850, and the number of slaves in America increased from 1.5 million in 1820 to 4 million by the eve of the Civil War. Slavery was profitable: just prior to the Civil War, a plantation slave produced on average about $80 in cotton earnings per year for the master, who spent less than half that much to provide the slave with marginal nutrition, clothing, and housing. Prices for slaves, which tripled between 1840 and 1860, reflected this profitability.

The profitability of slavery locked the South into economic underdevelopment in other ways as well. There was little industry and a far less developed railroad system than in the North. Less than one-third of white families owned slaves, and most of those owned very few. The majority of the rural white population consisted of marginal yeoman farmers whose opportunities for prosperity were far more limited than those of their northern counterparts.

African-American resentment of slavery occasionally exploded in violence. In 1831 Nat Turner, whose father had escaped slavery and whose African-born mother had brought him up to resist it, led an uprising in Southampton County, Virginia. Driven by rage, Turner and his associates killed some sixty white men, women, and children; in the aftermath about two hundred blacks were murdered by white vigilantes or executed in accordance with the law. After the rebellion slavery was placed under stricter legal controls throughout the South, and slave resistance took forms compatible with survival—notably running away and sabotage. Masters' fear of slave rebellion contributed to a political rigidity that not only inhibited manumission but pervaded much of southern political life and sharpened the distinctions between North and South.

Cultural Effects of Industrialization. The industrial revolution in America had important psychological dimensions. Faster, cheaper printing led to a virtual flood of printed materials—newspapers, pamphlets, books—after 1830. The availability of printed materials fostered literacy. The census of 1840 was the first to ask whether respondents could read and write. It established that the literacy gap between white men and white women in the North had virtually closed; in the south the ratio of literate white men to literate white women was five to four. Railroads allowed for faster, more reliable, and cheaper mail; coupled with inexpensive printing, a wider-ranging intellectual community was formed. Special-interest newspapers and pamphlets—such as William Lloyd Garrison's abolitionist newspaper, *The Liberator,* and Lydia Maria Child's abolitionist pamphlets—could be sent quickly and cheaply throughout the country. Subscribers, perhaps the lone abolitionist or temperance advocate in their own small towns, knew that they were not alone. Because it was easier and safer for women to travel by train than by stagecoach, railroads made a major change in what might be called the political culture of travel. Elizabeth Cady Stanton and other women's rights advocates have testified to the psychological freedom that rail travel brought women, and abolitionist organizations sent women as well as men on speaking tours. But perhaps the most stunning psychological impact of the industrial revolution was the invisible revolution generated by clocks. As clocks became less costly and more pervasive in the 1830s and 1840s, they transformed the rhythms by which people allocated time and organized their lives. The agricultural workday proceeded from sunrise to sunset, so that the workday was shorter in the winter than in the summer, but the factory workday was marked by the clock, which rang out twelve hours in both winter and summer and marked short lunch and dinner breaks as well. Railroads ran on rigid schedules. By mid-century, efficiency in the use of time was an essential ingredient of a "modern" way of life.

Political Growth and Polarization

During the first half of the nineteenth century, mass political parties developed in America. Property requirements for white male voters moved steadily downward and by mid-century had generally been eliminated. Voter participation was widely encouraged in rallies, parades, and conventions. While restrictions based on class were eliminated, and in some states (notably in New England) suffrage restrictions based on race also eroded, restrictions based on gender intensified. However, white women were part of the political community, and they organized themselves in groups that addressed a wide range of reform issues, particularly temperance and abolition. The difficulty of addressing such issues without the right to vote—and the persistence of the old rules of coverture, laws that denied married women control over their own property—led to a demand for the vote and for the right of married women to control property and to exercise the primary rights of citizenship.

Political parties raised money, selected and promoted candidates, and encouraged voter turnout. National parties linked vastly different regions and bridged the gap between the two political cultures of free workers and slaveowners. But the link between the two political economies had been brittle since the negotiation of the Three-fifths Compromise at the Constitutional Convention, and after the Mexican War it was subjected to strains it could not withstand. The territory acquired in the war was rich agricultural land. Northern farmers who wanted to move West did not want to compete with slave labor. Many among them were against slavery and wanted it excluded from the new territory. Southerners saw no reason why slaveowners should not take advantage of opportunity for profit. Political decisions had to be made about this new territory. In the course of the argument, issues of free speech (should northern abolitionists have the right to proselytize freely in the South?), of free press (could abolitionist newspapers circulate freely?), of the right to petition (might Congress table abolitionist petitions and refuse even to read them?) of women's rights (should abolitionist organizations exclude women so as not to alienate men who would otherwise support the anti-slavery cause?), and of the Fugitive Slave Act of 1850 (did free people have a moral obligation to return fugitive slaves?) polarized people who did not care much about slavery but did care about civil liberties. The politics of the 1850s were poisoned by the debate over slavery in the new territories, resulting in civil disobedience, guerilla warfare in Kansas and Nebraska, and the breakdown of national churches into regional ones and national political parties into regionally based parties. The two sides were polarized between those insisting that the principles of local autonomy and majority rule gave local majorities the right to install slavery in at least part of the new territories, and those insisting on the moral primacy of freedom and maintaining that there are things that even majorities may not do. When Abraham Lincoln was elected president in 1860, it was with a pledge not to interfere with slavery as it existed in the South. Although he won overwhelmingly in the North, he received no support from southern states, which announced that the Constitution they had signed in 1787 was violated. As states, they reclaimed their right to withdraw from the Union they had made.

The Civil War

The Civil War remains the greatest national trauma of American life. One-third of all American men served in one of the armies. Nearly one-fifth of those who served died: 360,000 northern men and 260,000 southern men were killed, and more than 500,000 men were maimed permanently. The losses of the Civil War were greater than the combined losses of all other American wars, including Vietnam. The South was devastated: it is estimated that more than forty percent of its wealth (excluding that invested in slaves) was destroyed, and major cities, including Atlanta and Richmond, were burned to the ground. The cheerful assumptions with which most men on both sides had marched to battle in 1861—that courage, self-confidence, and heroism would overcome all obstacles—gave way to irony and depression. A war that began with violence limited to the battlefield (picnickers from Washington, D.C., went out to observe the first Battle of Bull Run in July 1861) ended with Union General William Tecumseh Sherman's March to the Sea, a conscious effort to demoralize civilians and a model of the total war, which would be characteristic of World War I, World War II, and Vietnam. By the end of 1864 the desertion rate in the Army of the Confederacy was fifty percent.

At the outset the advantage appeared to lie with the South, which was self-sufficient in food production and fighting on familiar ground, and which had a

═CONTEXTS═

The Fugitive Slave Act

In summer 1850 the controversies over the admission of California into the Union and the extension of slavery into the territories led to talk of secession among certain groups of southerners. The only concession Congress made to the South in the ensuing Compromise of 1850 was to pass a stricter fugitive slave law, requiring that northerners aid the capture of runaway slaves. The constitutionality of the Fugitive Slave Act, intended to hamper the operation of the Underground Railroad, was soon being debated by some of the most prominent lawyers in the country. James Russell Lowell, John Greenleaf Whittier, and Henry David Thoreau were among the prominent literary figures who raised their pens against the passage of this act. At the same time, American's mainstream clergy, businessmen, and industrialists in the cities and politicians in Congress were working hard to convince the public that opposition to the law's enforcement would lead to disruption of the Union.

William Still (1821–1902), corresponding secretary of the Underground Railroad's Vigilance Committee, kept records that describe the divisive effect the Fugitive Slave Act had on America. By writing and preserving these records during the 1850s, Still risked heavy fines and long imprisonment under the penalties of the Fugitive Slave Act. Still published his account in *The Underground Railroad* in 1871.

The Slave-Hunting Tragedy in Lancaster County, in September, 1851

. . . . The deepest feelings of loathing, contempt and opposition were manifested by the opponents of Slavery on every hand. Anti-slavery papers, lecturers, preachers, etc., arrayed themselves boldly against [the Fugitive Slave Act] on the ground of its inhumanity and violation of the laws of God.

On the other hand, the slave-holders South, and their pro-slavery adherents in the North demanded the most abject obedience from all parties, regardless of conscience or obligation to God. In order to compel such obedience, as well as to prove the practicability of the law, unbounded zeal daily marked the attempt on the part of the slave-holders and slave-catchers to refasten the fetters on the limbs of fugitives in different parts of the North, whither they had escaped.

In this dark hour, when colored men's rights were so insecure, as a matter of self-defence, they felt called upon to arm themselves and resist all kidnapping intruders, although clothed with the authority of wicked law. . . .

William Still, 1871

strong military tradition. All the South had to do was to maintain a separate army and make the war too expensive for the North to fight. But as time went on the balance shifted, partly because Lincoln defined his powers as a wartime president aggressively and partly because the advantages of the North's industrial base, eight times greater than that of the South, became more important with time. The North mobilized human and economic resources on a scale America had never experienced before—by selling treasury bonds and imposing substantial new taxes (including the first federal income tax) and high tariffs. In the process, the North improved its capacity to wage war: it increased its industrial capacity, adding an additional five thousand miles of railroad track, and tied the interests of business classes to the success of the Union. The South did not have a comparable war capacity, partly because it lacked the resources and partly because, having left the Union to ensure the right of states to dissent, the Confederate government was not in a position to assert claims to centralized power. Also, the South, always an industrially underdeveloped region, lost most of what limited industrial capacity it had.

Most significantly, the war destabilized and then ended slavery. Lincoln's early pledge not to interfere with slavery where it existed made it possible to keep border states—Maryland, Kentucky, Delaware, and Missouri—in the Union. But Lincoln was slowly and inexorably driven to define the war as one to end slavery. In 1861 Union General Benjamin Franklin Butler refused to return any slave who escaped behind Union lines. They were "contraband of war," he said, thus avoiding argument over whether they were or were not property, and he gave them sanctuary. As the war progressed, sentiment for abolition in the North strengthened, and in 1863 Lincoln issued the Emancipation Proclamation, which freed those slaves who were not in the border states nor at that moment under the control of federal armies. The Emancipation Proclamation transformed the Civil War into a revolutionary struggle. It encouraged the enlistment of African Americans in the Union Army, and thousands responded to the challenge. "By the war's end," writes Eric Foner, "180,000 blacks had served in the Union Army—over one-fifth of the nation's adult male black population under age forty-five" (*Reconstruction*, 1989). They served as soldiers, laborers, and sailors. Uncounted numbers of African-American women served in military camps as cooks and laundresses. In effect what occurred was a great slave rebellion, although it was not perceived as such because whites believed that a slave rebellion consisted of race riots and massacres. When the war was over, 3 million slaves were free, and a constitutional amendment, the thirteenth, guaranteed that freedom.

The assassination of Abraham Lincoln only five days after General Robert E. Lee's surrender in Appomattox Court House, Virginia, in 1865 was an eerie precursor of the violence and profound disruption that continued to characterize American life even after the Civil War had officially ended. The meaning of the Civil War remained contested. To many northerners the war had increasingly come to have a moral component, and victory seemed to validate the increased power of the central government, which had directed the war, and also to commit the nation to a revolution in race relations. For many white southerners, defeat in war signified simply an end to claims of southern independence and to the system of slavery. Many thought they could return to life as it had been before the guns fired on Fort Sumter in Charleston: that is, to a system of race relations in which whites were dominant and blacks were submissive, and to a political system in which the white men who had controlled politics would resume their seats in Congress and in state legislatures as though nothing had happened.

EARLY TO MIDDLE 19TH-CENTURY FICTION

American fiction of the first half of the nineteenth century is an original and diverse body of work that ranges from the comic fables of Washington Irving to the Gothic tales of Edgar Allan Poe, from the frontier adventures of James Fenimore Cooper to the grotesque yarns of Southwest Humorists, from the psychological romances of Nathaniel Hawthorne to the social realism of Rebecca Harding Davis, from the narrative quests of Herman Melville to the moral protests of Harriet Beecher Stowe. The lack of an international copyright law prior to 1830 posed a burden to all these writers. Publishers pirated the work of well-known British authors rather than pay royalties to aspiring Americans. But strategies of publishing simultaneously in England and the United States (with copyright protection in each country), together with a growing audience for writing that focused on American subjects, helped to foster the development of a uniquely American body of fiction by the middle of the nineteenth century. The wide popularity of Irving's *Sketch-Book* (1819–1820), containing such stories as "Rip Van Winkle" and "The Legend of Sleepy Hollow," and of Cooper's early novels, among them *The Spy* (1821) and *The Pioneers* (1823), demonstrated that there was an international market for American fiction that could find its way to publication.

The legacies of Cooper and Irving are demonstrably vital to the development of American literature. Cooper's sagas of the frontier spawned hundreds of imitations throughout the nineteenth century and resulted in the genre we call the "western." Irving's work contributed to the creation of a new literary genre, the short story, which Americans would continue to adapt to their own purposes. In three stories recounting the activities of the criminologist C. Auguste Dupin (a Sherlock Holmes-type sleuth who appeared more than fifty years before Holmes), Edgar Allan Poe invented the modern detective story. During this time Nathaniel Hawthorne explored new directions for the short story in such narratives as "My Kinsman, Major Molineux" (1832) and "The Birth-Mark" (1843). And in later years writers as different as O. Henry (William Sydney Porter), Flannery O'Connor, and Ann Beattie have continued to find the short story congenial to their own form of literary art.

During the decades in which American writers conceived and perfected the short story, another type of short fiction, earthy and vibrant, came into existence. Beginning with the various tellings of the adventures of the real Tennessee frontiersman-turned-politician, Davy Crockett, a group of writers from the Old Southwest (Georgia, Alabama, Louisiana, and Arkansas) transformed the traditions of the tall tale and the resources of regional dialect into fiction. Whereas the short story is distinguished by unity and compression and by an emphasis on character and moral nuance, the tall tale is marked by exaggeration, orality, and the conflict between gentility and unrefined comedy.

With their unromantic views of human relations, their coarse depictions of backwoods life, and their relentless use of vernacular speech, Southwest Humorists such as George Washington Harris and Thomas Bangs Thorpe made a unique contribution to the development of prose fiction in America. To examine Thorpe's

=CONTEXTS=

The Second Great Awakening

The reform movements from about 1800 to 1840—concerning everything from slavery to temperance to impovements in education—were a hallmark of American romanticism. At roughly the same time, a renewed interest in religion, known as the Second Great Awakening, swept the United States. Historians credit James Mc-Gready (1758?–1817), a preacher from North Carolina, with starting the custom of camp meetings, the first of which was held in Logan County, Kentucky, about 1800. At these meetings people were encouraged to pray and sing as much and as loud as they pleased. The traditional "welcome" extended to everyone, no matter what age, sex, race, or denomination—children and blacks as well as Native-American converts to Protestantism preached and reproved sin in equal voice with white women and men. The emphasis on the individual in the services agreed with the character of frontier society (although conservatives considered immoral the revivalist practice of men and women praying together in public). A typical camp meeting is described in the following excerpt from the eyewitness account of Dr. Richard Furman of Charleston:

[Camp Meetings]

. . . The numbers which assembled from various parts of the country, formed a very large congregation, the amount of which has been variously estimated; to me there appeared to be 3000 or perhaps 4000 persons; but some supposed there were 7000 or 8000. . . . The encampment was laid out in an oblong form, extending from the top of a hill down the south side of it, toward a stream of water. . . . Lines of tents were erected on every side of this space; and between them, and behind, were the waggons and riding carriages placed; the space itself being reserved for the assembling of the congregation. . . . Two stands were fixed on for this purpose: at the one a stage was erected under some lofty trees, which afforded an ample shade; at the other, which was not so well provided with shade, a waggon was placed for the rostrum. . . . Several persons suffered at this meeting those bodily affections, which have been experienced at Kentucky, North Carolina, and at other places, where the extraordinary revivals in religion within this year or two have taken place. Some of them fell instantaneously, as though struck with lightning, and continued insensible for a length of time; other were more mildly affected, and soon recovered their bodily strength, with a proper command of their mental powers. . . . These general meetings have a great tendency to excite the attention, and engage it to religion. . . .

Dr. Richard Furman, 1802

"Big Bear of Arkansas" (1841) is to see that the interaction of social classes, the speech patterns, and the sheer exuberance of the fiction prefigures the later and more accomplished work of Mark Twain and of William Faulkner. Moreover, the humor and hyperbole of Thorpe's tale, and of the tall tale as a subgenre, would prove influential beyond the boundaries of prose fiction. Abraham Lincoln's political style, which evolved throughout the 1840s in small midwestern and southern towns, owed much to the defining characteristics of the tall tale.

The distinction between the tall tale and the short story rests fundamentally on a difference in treatment or representation, a difference between caricature and a more realistic depiction of event and character. And in much of the long fiction of this period, a similar distinction can be observed. Both Nathaniel Hawthorne and the southern writer William Gilmore Simms distinguished between the novel and the romance, Hawthorne in his preface to *The House of the Seven Gables* (1851), Simms in a preface to the 1850 edition of *The Yemassee* (1835). The novel, according to Hawthorne, "is presumed to aim at a very minute fidelity" to the "probable and ordinary course" of human experience, whereas the romance has "a certain latitude" of choice and presentation. The novel, according to Simms, derives from the newspaper story and recent events, whereas the romance traces its lineage to the fairy tale. Clearly, both writers think of the novel as more realistic than the romance, more social in subject and manner. The appeal of the romance is that it can fashion a world of its own and feature exaggerations of action and of character.

Late in the eighteenth century Charles Brockden Brown adapted the British-born Gothic romance—devised by Horace Walpole in *The Castle of Otranto* (1765) and popularly exemplified by Mary Shelley's *Frankenstein* (1818)—to American settings in such works as *Wieland* (1798) and *Arthur Mervyn* (1799). And in the mid-nineteenth century such writers as Poe, Hawthorne, and Melville infused their work with the mystery and extravagance of Gothic fiction. No longer did they employ the trappings of Gothicism—dark castles, haunted passageways, ghosts in armor; instead, they internalized the spirit of Gothicism, made it a feature of minds obsessed with a desire for wealth or revenge or truth. In temperament and imagination these three writers were drawn to the Gothic strain in fiction and not to the realism that developed out of the sentimental novels of Samuel Richardson in England and reached an apotheosis at the turn of the nineteenth century in the domestic novels of Jane Austen. Their concern with evil and abnormality—whether in Poe's *Narrative of Arthur Gordon Pym* (1838), Hawthorne's *Scarlet Letter* (1850), or Melville's *Moby-Dick* (1851)—stems from a central focus on the self rather than on society and on the elaborate web of social entanglements that characterize the more realistic form of the novel.

The romance and the novel, however, have never been mutually exclusive forms. Elements of social realism are present in such works as *The Scarlet Letter* and *The House of the Seven Gables* and even in *Moby-Dick* (when Captains Bildad and Peleg sign on the crew of the *Pequod* and, more importantly, when Chief Mate Starbuck says he came on the voyage to hunt whales, not his commander's vengeance). And Gothic interludes can be found even in such straightforward novels as Henry James's *The American* (1877). Moreover, even in the first half of the nineteenth century many people used the term "novel" to describe all long forms of fictional narrative, as we do now. But a definable Gothicism remains a vital force in American fiction, in the novels of William Faulkner and Robert Penn Warren, for example, and in the work of contemporary writers such as Joyce Carol Oates and Stephen King.

Until recently, literary historians have considered such late nineteenth-century novelists as William Dean Howells, Mark Twain, and Henry James as America's original realists. Their theories of the novel developed, as Howells argued in his critical essays, from French and Russian models. We have come to understand of late, however, that the achievement of these realists was preceded by the earlier accomplishments of a number of American women novelists, some of whom found a model in the work of Jane Austen. These writers understood the tastes of their audience, wrote novels that sold far better than did the works of their male counterparts, and were able to support themselves with their pens.

The audience for fiction in the early and middle nineteenth century was for the most part made up of women, and their taste was less for metaphysical quests and characters isolated by obsession than for domestic fiction—novels about the trials, strength, and perseverance of women characters and the place of women in a male-dominated society. In critical circles the work of female novelists was accorded little status: to critics, they took refuge in formulas and consequently produced bestsellers. In an 1855 letter to his publisher Hawthorne himself commented (doubtless with more than a tinge of jealousy) on the "d——d mob of scribbling women" whose novels consistently outsold his. We now recognize that the best of the fiction written by these women has a dramatic eloquence that transcends formula and brings us to understand the issues of power and compliance at stake in the domestic world. Such novels as Susan Warner's *The Wide, Wide World* (1850), the first literary work by an American to sell over a million copies; Fanny Fern's *Ruth Hall* (1855), praised even by Hawthorne; E. D. E. N. Southworth's *The Hidden Hand* (1859), whose protagonist, Capitola the Madcap, is in some ways a female precursor of Huckleberry Finn; Rebecca Harding Davis's "Life in the Iron-Mills" (1861), a pioneer work of American realism; and Harriet

The Lowell Offering, *begun in 1842 by Harriet Farley, was a literary magazine containing the writings of female mill workers in Lowell, Massachusetts.*

Beecher Stowe's classic *Uncle Tom's Cabin* (1852) have taken their place in the canon of work that defines the achievement of American literature. They also provide a context in which to gain a fresh understanding of the darker symbolic romances of Hawthorne and of Melville.

As is true of any body of work that shares similarities and is eventually grouped together, the novels written by women in the middle nineteenth century were not nearly so monolithic as easy categorizing suggests. Although some of these books dealt with little beyond their domestic contexts, others were driven by social concerns. Davis's story "Life in the Iron-Mills" explores in achingly realistic detail the terrible working and living conditions of industrial workers in America's rapidly growing cities. *Uncle Tom's Cabin* depicts with startling moral fervor the evils of slavery. For Stowe this blatantly abolitionist novel was pointedly and consciously intended to appeal to the emotions of readers as it doggedly emphasized the cruelty and hypocrisy of southern slaveholders who thought of themselves as good Christians.

Social criticism was certainly not new to American writing nor to nineteenth-century fiction. Irving and Cooper were often pronounced in their criticisms of human conformity and the sometimes stultifying nature of civilization in America. Hawthorne and Melville could be severe in their criticisms of Ralph Waldo Emerson and the transcendentalists. Indeed, close examination suggests that fiction in the first half of the nineteenth century was contending with nonfiction as the principal vehicle in America for social commentary. And with its diversity, originality, and vitality, fiction was also replacing nonfiction prose as our dominant literary genre—a position that fiction, primarily in the form of the novel, continues to occupy. It is the power and diversity of fiction that accounts more than anything else for its influence in America, and that power and diversity is found in abundance in American fiction of the early to middle nineteenth century.

Washington Irving
(1783–1859)

Although Washington Irving no longer presides as the "Father of American Letters," the particular "firsts" of his literary career assure his place in American social and cultural history. He was the first American to succeed as a writer of "high" literature for commercial sale and the first American to win a reputation both at home and abroad for such writing. During his lifetime international acclaim for his work appeased nationalistic yearnings for an American literary culture; after his death his reputation as a founder promoted the status of American literature as a legitimate field of study. But early and perhaps excessive praise inevitably diminished. Much twentieth-century Irving scholarship pursues the problem formulated by Edgar Allan Poe in an 1838 letter to Nathan C. Brooks, that of distinguishing "between what is due to the pioneer solely, and what to the writer." Praise of the pioneer has generally outpaced praise of the writer; yet, a handful of Irving's works continue to command attention on their own merit.

Irving was born in New York City in 1783. He was the youngest of eleven children of an English mother and a Scottish father, a prosperous merchant. He attended private schools and went on to study law but, though an apt learner when interested, was generally a desultory student. Some of the things that did interest Irving are evident in his first work, "The Letters of Jonathan Oldstyle, Gent." (1802–1803), which satirizes New York theater and society life and was published in the *Morning Chronicle,* edited by his brother Peter. Following a tour of Europe from 1804 to 1806, Irving returned to New York and the law. He soon turned to writing again, collaborating with his brothers William and Peter and William's brother-in-law James Kirke Paulding on a series of satirical sketches called *Salmagundi: Or, the Whim-Whams and Opinions of Launcelot Langstaff, Esq., and Others* (1807–1808), which brought local celebrity to its authors. Conservative in attitude and sportive in manner, these sketches established the tone and stance Irving would cultivate throughout his career. His next work featured the creation of Diedrich Knickerbocker as the antiquarian narrator of *A History of New-York From the Beginning of the World to the End of the Dutch Dynasty, by Diedrich Knickerbocker* (1809). At once a burlesque of the "heroic" mode of history-writing, a lampoon of the city and its founders, and a satire of Jeffersonian republicanism, *A History of New-York* brought Irving immediate fame and two thousand dollars.

This triumph was followed by ten years of near silence. During the completion of *A History of New-York* in 1809, Irving was devastated by the death of his fiancée, Matilda Hoffman, from consumption; the loss affected both his life and his work, and he never married. During these years he lobbied in Washington, D.C., on trade issues, published Thomas Campbell's poetry, and edited the *Analectic Magazine,* among other occupations. In 1815, "weary of everything," he sailed for Europe with a plan to study and write, only to become further dispirited by the protracted failure of the family business and the death of his mother.

Irving extricated himself from grief and financial necessity with the personal, commercial, and literary success of *The Sketch Book of Geoffrey Crayon, Gent.* (1819–1820), which includes "Rip Van Winkle" and "The Legend of Sleepy Hollow." The writing itself marked the onset of *vocation* in Irving's work, and his tales and sketches, bound together by the persona of Geoffrey Crayon, were well received upon their serial publication in New York. To protect his work against pirating, Irving arranged with the help of the Scottish poet and novelist Sir Walter Scott to publish a London edition, which was also very successful. Irving's next work, *Bracebridge Hall* (1822), a loosely plotted collection of sketches centered on an old English country estate, interestingly casts light on the success of *The Sketch Book.* With *Bracebridge Hall* Irving refined his commercial technique, securing his copyright with near-simultaneous publication in England and America. He also reflected in *Bracebridge Hall* that one source of his earlier success had been that an American could write "tolerable English." Finally, the centrality of *The Sketch Book* to Irving's image as a writer can be inferred by the fact that *Bracebridge Hall* came to be called the "English *Sketch Book.*"

Bracebridge Hall sold well but did not receive resounding critical praise. And Irving's next collection, *Tales of a Traveller* (1824), drew bad reviews outright. At this point Irving's career, which had already shifted from youthful satires to genial sketches, took a successful turn into history and biography, genres that had been lampooned in Knickerbocker's *History of New-York.* Joining the American legation in Madrid, Irving seized the opportunity to reshape historical documents and Spanish works into the *Life and Voyages of Christopher Columbus* (1828). This he followed with *Chronicle of the Conquest of Granada* (1829), *Voyages and Discoveries of the Companions of Columbus* (1831), and

The Return of Rip Van Winkle *(1849?)*, *by John Quidor, inspired by the Washington Irving story, demonstrates the continuing link between literature and art.*

another popular collection of sketches, *The Alhambra* (1832), later called the "Spanish *Sketch Book.*" These Spanish works secured Irving's reputation, although he had already left Spain to join the American legation in London. In 1831 he received an honorary degree from Oxford University, and in 1832, after seventeen years' absence, he returned to his native land.

Perhaps sensitive to critical doubts about his Americanness, Irving immediately avowed his love for his country and set about demonstrating it in works about the American West. He traveled to the Oklahoma frontier and drew on that experience for *A Tour on the Prairies* (1835). Two other western books came by way of the library: *Astoria* (1836) and *Adventures of Captain Bonneville* (1837) are second-hand celebrations of American expansion. Settling at Sunnyside, his home near Tarrytown, New York (by Sleepy Hollow Valley), Irving composed no major works between 1837 and 1842. He then resumed government service, first as U.S. minister to Spain and later, in London, as an American publicist on the Oregon Question (a disagreement over who had the rights to the Oregon Territory— America or England). Two major projects dominated his later years. The fifteen-volume Author's Revised Edition (1848–1851) of his histories and fiction offered him an occasion to smooth some of the remaining edges in his earlier works. But the greatest achievement of the final years—and, to Irving's mind, of his career—was the five-volume *Life of Washington* (1855–1859), a biography of his namesake, George Washington. Conceived in 1825, begun in the 1840s, and completed only months before his death in 1859, *Life of Washington* crowned Irving's work by reforging the link between "the Father of His Country" and the author who was popularly understood to be his literary counterpart.

Suggested Readings: *The Complete Works of Washington Irving,* 19 of 27 vols. completed, ed. R. D. Rust, 1960– . S. T. Williams, *The Life of Washington Irving,* 2 vols., 1935. W. L. Hedges, *Washington Irving: An America Study,* 1965. H. Springer, *Washington Irving: A Reference Guide,* 1976. M. Roth, *Comedy and America: The Lost World of Washington Irving,* 1976. A. B. Myers, ed., *A Century of Commentary on the Works of Washington Irving,* 1976. M. W. Bowden, *Washington Irving,* 1981. S. Browdin, ed., *The Old and New World Romanticism of Washington Irving,* 1986. J. Rubin-Dorsky, *Adrift in the Old World: The Psychological Pilgrimage of Washington Irving,* 1988.

Text Used: *The Sketch Book of Geoffrey Crayon, Gent.*, ed. H. Springer, from *The Complete Works of Washington Irving,* Vol. VIII, 1978.

from   THE SKETCH BOOK OF GEOFFREY CRAYON, GENT.*

THE AUTHOR'S ACCOUNT OF HIMSELF

I am of this mind with Homer, that as the snaile that crept out of her shel was turned eftsoones into a Toad, and thereby was forced to make a stoole to sit on; so the traveller that stragleth from his owne country is in a short time transformed into so monstrous a shape that he is faine to alter his mansion with his manners and to live where he can, not where he would.

LYLY'S EUPHUES[1]

I was always fond of visiting new scenes and observing strange characters and manners. Even when a mere child I began my travels and made many tours of discovery into foreign parts and unknown regions of my native city; to the frequent alarm of my parents and the emolument of the town cryer.[2] As I grew into boyhood I extended the range of my observations. My holyday afternoons were spent in rambles about the surrounding country. I made myself familiar with all its places famous in history or fable. I knew every spot where a murder or robbery had been committed or a ghost seen. I visited the neighbouring villages and added greatly to my stock of knowledge, by noting their habits and customs, and conversing with their sages and great men. I even journeyed one long summer's day to the summit of the most distant hill, from whence I stretched my eye over many a mile of terra incognita,[3] and was astonished to find how vast a globe I inhabited.

This rambling propensity strengthened with my years. Books of voyages and travels became my passion, and in devouring their contents I neglected the regular exercises of the school. How wistfully would I wander about the pier heads in fine weather, and watch the parting ships, bound to distant climes. With what longing

---

* Written under the pseudonym of Geoffrey Crayon, Gent., *The Sketch Book* was published serially in the United States in 1819 and 1820 and in England in 1820. This first version includes "The Author's Account of Himself" and "Rip Van Winkle." Irving later expanded *The Sketch Book* to a total of thirty-two tales and sketches.

[1] From *Euphues and His England* (1580), by John Lyly (1554?–1606). The epigraph serves as a mock warning about travel to the confirmed traveler, Geoffrey Crayon.

[2] Here the "town cryer" was paid to announce that a child was lost.

[3] "Unknown land" (Latin); frequently used on early maps.

eyes would I gaze after their lessening sails, and waft myself in imagination to the ends of the earth.

Further reading and thinking, though they brought this vague inclination into more reasonable bounds, only served to make it more decided. I visited various parts of my own country, and had I been merely a lover of fine scenery, I should have felt little desire to seek elsewhere its gratification, for on no country have the charms of nature been more prodigally lavished. Her mighty lakes, like oceans of liquid silver; her mountains with their bright aerial tints; her valleys teeming with wild fertility; her tremendous cataracts thundering in their solitudes; her boundless plains waving with spontaneous verdure; her broad deep rivers, rolling in solemn silence to the ocean; her trackless forests, where vegetation puts forth all its magnificence; her skies kindling with the magic of summer clouds and glorious sunshine—no, never need an American look beyond his own country for the sublime and beautiful of natural scenery.

But Europe held forth the charms of storied and poetical association. There were to be seen the masterpieces of art, the refinements of highly cultivated society, the quaint peculiarities of ancient and local custom. My native country was full of youthful promise; Europe was rich in the accumulated treasures of age. Her very ruins told the history of times gone by, and every mouldering stone was a chronicle. I longed to wander over the scenes of renowned achievement—to tread as it were in the footsteps of antiquity—to loiter about the ruined castle—to meditate on the falling tower—to escape in short, from the commonplace realities of the present, and lose myself among the shadowy grandeurs of the past.

I had, beside all this, an earnest desire to see the great men of the earth. We have, it is true, our great men in America—not a city but has an ample share of them. I have mingled among them in my time, and been almost withered by the shade into which they cast me; for there is nothing so baleful to a small man as the shade of a great one, particularly the great man of a city. But I was anxious to see the great men of Europe; for I had read in the works of various philosophers, that all animals degenerated in America, and man among the number.[4] A great man of Europe, thought I, must therefore be as superior to a great man of America, as a peak of the Alps to a highland of the Hudson; and in this idea I was confirmed by observing the comparative importance and swelling magnitude of many English travellers among us; who, I was assured, were very little people in their own country.—I will visit this land of wonders, thought I, and see the gigantic race from which I am degenerated.

It has been either my good or evil lot to have my roving passion gratified. I have wandered through different countries and witnessed many of the shifting scenes of life. I cannot say that I have studied them with the eye of a philosopher, but rather with the sauntering gaze with which humble lovers of the picturesque stroll from the window of one print shop to another; caught sometimes by the delineations of beauty, sometimes by the distortions of caricature and sometimes by the loveliness of landscape. As it is the fashion for modern tourists to travel pencil in hand, and bring home their portfolios filled with sketches, I am disposed to get up a few for the entertainment of my friends. When I look over, however,

---

[4] In his influential *Natural History* (44 vols., 1749–1788), the French scientist George Louis Leclerc de Buffon (1707–1788) maintained that the environment in America would cause animals and humans to degenerate. After Thomas Jefferson sent him a panther skin, the skeleton of a moose, and a copy of Jefferson's *Notes on the State of Virginia* (1785), Buffon changed his view.

the hints and memorandums I have taken down for the purpose, my heart almost fails me at finding how my idle humour has led me aside from the great objects studied by every regular traveller who would make a book. I fear I shall give equal disappointment with an unlucky landscape painter, who had travelled on the continent, but following the bent of his vagrant inclination, had sketched in nooks and corners and bye places. His sketch book was accordingly crowded with cottages, and landscapes, and obscure ruins; but he had neglected to paint St. Peter's or the Coliseum; the cascade of Terni[5] or the Bay of Naples; and had not a single Glacier or Volcano in his whole collection.

1819

RIP VAN WINKLE

The following Tale was found among the papers of the late Diedrich Knickerbocker, an old gentleman of New York, who was very curious in the Dutch history of the province, and the manners of the descendants from its primitive settlers. His historical researches, however, did not lie so much among books, as among men; for the former are lamentably scanty on his favourite topics; whereas he found the old burghers,[1] and still more, their wives, rich in that legendary lore so invaluable to true history. Whenever, therefore, he happened upon a genuine Dutch family, snugly shut up in its low roofed farm house, under a spreading sycamore, he looked upon it as a little clasped volume of black letter,[2] and studied it with the zeal of a bookworm.

The result of all these researches was a history of the province, during the reign of the Dutch governors, which he published some years since. There have been various opinions as to the literary character of his work and, to tell the truth, it is not a whit better than it should be. Its chief merit is its scrupulous accuracy, which indeed was a little questioned on its first appearance, but has since been completely established; and it is now admitted into all historical collections as a book of unquestionable authority.[3]

The old gentleman died shortly after the publication of his work, and now that he is dead and gone, it cannot do much harm to his memory to say that his time might have been much better employed in weightier labours. He, however, was apt to ride his hobby his own way; and though it did now and then kick up the dust a little in the eyes of his neighbours, and grieve the spirit of some friends for whom he felt the truest deference and affection; yet his errors and follies are remembered "more in sorrow than in anger,"[4] and it begins to be suspected that he never intended to injure or offend. But however his memory may be appreciated by criticks, it is still held dear by many folk whose good opinion is well worth

---

[5] St Peter's Cathedral in Rome is the largest church in the world; the Coliseum, an amphitheater in Rome, is a famous ruin dating from the first century A.D.; the cascade of Terni is a waterfall in northern Italy.

[1] Inhabitants of boroughs or towns.

[2] A typeface used in early printed books, now called Gothic or Old English. Some of these books had clasps so they could be snapped shut.

[3] Irving refers to his comic *History of New-York* (1809), "written" by his earlier persona, Diedrich Knickerbocker, whose extravagant pedantry is comic but hardly accurate.

[4] From Shakespeare's *Hamlet,* (I.1.232).

having; particularly by certain biscuit bakers, who have gone so far as to imprint his likeness on their new year cakes, and have thus given him a chance for immortality, almost equal to being stamped on a Waterloo medal, or a Queen Anne's farthing.[5]

Rip Van Winkle[6]

A POSTHUMOUS WRITING OF DIEDRICH KNICKERBOCKER

> *By Woden,[7] God of Saxons,*
> *From whence comes Wensday, that is Wodensday,*
> *Truth is a thing that ever I will keep*
> *Unto thylke[8] day in which I creep into*
> *My sepulchre—*
>   CARTWRIGHT [9]

Whoever has made a voyage up the Hudson must remember the Kaatskill mountains.[10] They are a dismembered branch of the great Appalachian family, and are seen away to the west of the river swelling up to noble height and lording it over the surrounding country. Every change of season, every change of weather, indeed every hour of the day, produces some change in the magical hues and shapes of these mountains, and they are regarded by all the good wives far and near as perfect barometers. When the weather is fair and settled they are clothed in blue and purple, and print their bold outlines on the clear evening sky; but sometimes, when the rest of the landscape is cloudless, they will gather a hood of grey vapours about their summits, which, in the last rays of the setting sun, will glow and light up like a crown of glory.

At the foot of these fairy mountains the voyager may have descried the light smoke curling up from a village, whose shingle roofs gleam among the trees, just where the blue tints of the upland melt away into the fresh green of the nearer landscape. It is a little village of great antiquity, having been founded by some of the Dutch colonists in the early times of the province, just about the beginning of the government of the good Peter Stuyvesant,[11] (may he rest in peace!) and there were some of the houses of the original settlers standing within a few years; built of small yellow bricks brought from Holland, having latticed windows and gable fronts, surmounted with weathercocks.

---

[5] Waterloo medals, commemorating the British victory over Napoleon in 1815, were issued to everyone who took part in the historic battle; Queen Anne's farthings were small, supposedly rare coins minted during the reign of Queen Anne (1702–1714).

[6] In both "Rip Van Winkle" and "The Legend of Sleepy Hollow," Irving adapted German folk legends to American settings. His immediate source for "Rip" is J. C. C. N. Otmar's "Peter Klaus" (1800), in which the protagonist sleeps for twenty years. Irving brings the tale to America and has Rip Van Winkle sleep through the American Revolution.

[7] According to Norse myth, the supreme god and creator.   [8] "The" or "that".

[9] From the play *The Ordinary* (1651) (III.1. 1050–1054), by William Cartwright (1611–1643), an English clergyman, poet, and dramatist.

[10] The Catskill Mountains in southeastern New York.

[11] Stuyvesant (1592–1672) served as the last governor of New Netherlands from 1647 to 1664. In 1655 he led the Dutch forces to victory over Swedish colonists at Fort Christina, near what is now Wilmington, Delaware, as described in mock-epic terms in Knickerbocker's *History of New-York*.

In that same village, and in one of these very houses (which to tell the precise truth was sadly time worn and weather beaten) there lived many years since, while the country was yet a province of Great Britain, a simple good natured fellow of the name of Rip Van Winkle. He was a descendant of the Van Winkles who figured so gallantly in the chivalrous days of Peter Stuyvesant, and accompanied him to the siege of Fort Christina. He inherited, however, but little of the martial character of his ancestors. I have observed that he was a simple good natured man; he was moreover a kind neighbour, and an obedient, henpecked husband. Indeed to the latter circumstance might be owing that meekness of spirit which gained him such universal popularity; for those men are most apt to be obsequious and conciliating abroad, who are under the discipline of shrews at home. Their tempers doubtless are rendered pliant and malleable in the fiery furnace of domestic tribulation, and a curtain lecture[12] is worth all the sermons in the world for teaching the virtues of patience and long suffering. A termagant wife may therefore in some respects be considered a tolerable blessing—and if so, Rip Van Winkle was thrice blessed.

Certain it is that he was a great favourite among all the good wives of the village, who as usual with the amiable sex, took his part in all family squabbles, and never failed, whenever they talked those matters over in their evening gossippings, to lay all the blame on Dame Van Winkle. The children of the village too would shout with joy whenever he approached. He assisted at their sports, made their play things, taught them to fly kites and shoot marbles, and told them long stories of ghosts, witches and Indians. Whenever he went dodging about the village he was surrounded by a troop of them hanging on his skirts, clambering on his back and playing a thousand tricks on him with impunity; and not a dog would bark at him throughout the neighbourhood.

The great error in Rip's composition was an insuperable aversion to all kinds of profitable labour. It could not be from the want of assiduity or perseverance; for he would sit on a wet rock, with a rod as long and heavy as a Tartar's lance, and fish all day without a murmur, even though he should not be encouraged by a single nibble. He would carry a fowling piece on his shoulder for hours together, trudging through woods, and swamps and up hill and down dale, to shoot a few squirrels or wild pigeons; he would never refuse to assist a neighbour even in the roughest toil, and was a foremost man at all country frolicks for husking Indian corn, or building stone fences; the women of the village too used to employ him to run their errands and to do such little odd jobs as their less obliging husbands would not do for them—in a word Rip was ready to attend to any body's business but his own; but as to doing family duty, and keeping his farm in order, he found it impossible.

In fact he declared it was of no use to work on his farm; it was the most pestilent little piece of ground in the whole country; everything about it went wrong and would go wrong in spite of him. His fences were continually falling to pieces; his cow would either go astray or get among the cabbages, weeds were sure to grow quicker in his fields than any where else; the rain always made a point of setting in just as he had some outdoor work to do. So that though his patrimonial estate had dwindled away under his management, acre by acre until there was little more left than a mere patch of Indian corn and potatoes, yet it was the worst conditioned farm in the neighbourhood.

---

[12] A scolding of a husband by his wife after the bed curtains have been drawn.

His children too were as ragged and wild as if they belonged to nobody. His son Rip, an urchin begotten in his own likeness, promised to inherit the habits with the old clothes of his father. He was generally seen trooping like a colt at his mother's heels, equipped in a pair of his father's cast off galligaskins,[13] which he had much ado to hold up with one hand, as a fine lady does her train in bad weather.

Rip Van Winkle, however, was one of those happy mortals of foolish, well oiled dispositions, who take the world easy, eat white bread or brown, whichever can be got with least thought or trouble, and would rather starve on a penny than work for a pound. If left to himself, he would have whistled life away in perfect contentment, but his wife kept continually dinning in his ears about his idleness, his carelessness and the ruin he was bringing on his family. Morning noon and night her tongue was incessantly going, and every thing he said or did was sure to produce a torrent of household eloquence. Rip had but one way of replying to all lectures of the kind, and that by frequent use had grown into a habit. He shrugged his shoulders, shook his head, cast up his eyes, but said nothing. This, however, always provoked a fresh volley from his wife, so that he was fain to draw off his forces and take to the outside of the house—the only side which in truth belongs to a henpecked husband.

Rip's sole domestic adherent was his dog Wolf who was as much henpecked as his master, for Dame Van Winkle regarded them as companions in idleness, and even looked upon Wolf with an evil eye as the cause of his master's going so often astray. True it is, in all points of spirit befitting an honourable dog, he was as courageous an animal as ever scoured the woods—but what courage can withstand the ever during and all besetting terrors of a woman's tongue? The moment Wolf entered the house his crest fell, his tail drooped to the ground or curled between his legs, he sneaked about with a gallows air, casting many a sidelong glance at Dame Van Winkle, and at the least flourish of a broomstick or ladle he would fly to the door with yelping precipitation.

Times grew worse and worse with Rip Van Winkle as years of matrimony rolled on; a tart temper never mellows with age, and a sharp tongue is the only edged tool that grows keener with constant use. For a long while he used to console himself when driven from home, by frequenting a kind of perpetual club of the sages, philosophers and other idle personages of the village which held its sessions on a bench before a small inn, designated by a rubicund portrait of his majesty George the Third. Here they used to sit in the shade, through a long lazy summer's day, talking listlessly over village gossip, or telling endless sleepy stories about nothing. But it would have been worth any statesman's money to have heard the profound discussions that sometimes took place, when by chance an old newspaper fell into their hands from some passing traveller. How solemnly they would listen to the contents as drawled out by Derrick Van Bummel the schoolmaster, a dapper, learned little man, who was not to be daunted by the most gigantic word in the dictionary; and how sagely they would deliberate upon public events some months after they had taken place.

The opinions of this junto[14] were completely controlled by Nicholaus Vedder, a patriarch of the village, and landlord of the inn, at the door of which he took his seat from morning till night, just moving sufficiently to avoid the sun and keep in

---

[13] Loose breeches or pants.
[14] A committee; "a club of the sages," as Irving describes these men with mild irony.

the shade of a large tree; so that the neighbours could tell the hour by his movements as accurately as by a sun dial. It is true he was rarely heard to speak, but smoked his pipe incessantly. His adherents, however (for every great man has his adherents), perfectly understood him and knew how to gather his opinions. When any thing that was read or related displeased him, he was observed to smoke his pipe vehemently and to send forth short, frequent and angry puffs; but when pleased he would inhale the smoke slowly and tranquilly and emit it in light and placid clouds, and sometimes taking the pipe from his mouth and letting the fragrant vapour curl about his nose, would gravely nod his head in token of perfect approbation.

From even this strong hold the unlucky Rip was at length routed by his termagant wife who would suddenly break in upon the tranquility of the assemblage and call the members all to naught; nor was that august personage Nicholaus Vedder himself sacred from the daring tongue of this terrible virago, who charged him outright with encouraging her husband in habits of idleness.

Poor Rip was at last reduced almost to despair; and his only alternative to escape from the labour of the farm and the clamour of his wife, was to take gun in hand and stroll away into the woods. Here he would sometimes seat himself at the foot of a tree and share the contents of his wallet[15] with Wolf, with whom he sympathised as a fellow sufferer in persecution. "Poor Wolf," he would say, "thy mistress leads thee a dog's life of it, but never mind my lad, whilst I live thou shalt never want a friend to stand by thee!" Wolf would wag his tail, look wistfully in his master's face, and if dogs can feel pity I verily believe he reciprocated the sentiment with all his heart.

In a long ramble of the kind on a fine autumnal day, Rip had unconsciously scrambled to one of the highest parts of the Kaatskill mountains. He was after his favourite sport of squirrel shooting and the still solitudes had echoed and re-echoed with the reports of his gun. Panting and fatigued he threw himself, late in the afternoon, on a green knoll, covered with mountain herbage, that crowned the brow of a precipice. From an opening between the trees he could overlook all the lower country for many a mile of rich woodland. He saw at a distance the lordly Hudson, far, far below him, moving on its silent but majestic course, with the reflection of a purple cloud, or the sail of a lagging bark here and there sleeping on its glassy bosom, and at last losing itself in the blue highlands.

On the other side he looked down into a deep mountain glen, wild, lonely and shagged, the bottom filled with fragments from the impending cliffs and scarcely lighted by the reflected rays of the setting sun. For some time Rip lay musing on this scene, evening was gradually advancing, the mountains began to throw their long blue shadows over the valleys, he saw that it would be dark, long before he could reach the village, and he heaved a heavy sigh when he thought of encountering the terrors of Dame Van Winkle.

As he was about to descend he heard a voice from a distance hallooing "Rip Van Winkle! Rip Van Winkle!" He looked around, but could see nothing but a crow winging its solitary flight across the mountain. He thought his fancy must have deceived him and turned again to descend, which he heard the same cry ring through the still evening air: "Rip Van Winkle! Rip Van Winkle!"—at the same time Wolf bristled up his back and giving a low growl, skulked to his master's side, looking fearfully down into the glen. Rip now felt a vague apprehension

---

[15] A pouch or knapsack.

stealing over him; he looked anxiously in the same direction and perceived a strange figure slowly toiling up the rocks and bending under the weight of something he carried on his back. He was surprised to see any human being in this lonely and unfrequented place, but supposing it to be some one of the neighbourhood in need of his assistance he hastened down to yield it.

On nearer approach he was still more surprised at the singularity of the stranger's appearance. He was a short, square built old fellow, with thick bushy hair and a grizzled beard. His dress was of the antique Dutch fashion, a cloth jerkin[16] strapped round the waist, several pair of breeches, the outer one of ample volume decorated with rows of buttons down the sides and bunches at the knees. He bore on his shoulder a stout keg that seemed full of liquor, and made signs for Rip to approach and assist him with the load. Though rather shy and distrustful of this new acquaintance Rip complied with his usual alacrity, and mutually relieving each other they clambered up a narrow gully apparently the dry bed of a mountain torrent. As they ascended Rip every now and then heard long rolling peals like distant thunder, that seemed to issue out of a deep ravine or rather cleft between lofty rocks, toward which their rugged path conducted. He paused for an instant, but supposing it to be the muttering of one of those transient thunder showers which often take place in mountain heights, he proceeded. Passing through the ravine they came to a hollow like a small amphitheatre, surrounded by perpendicular precipices, over the brinks of which impending trees shot their branches, so that you only caught glimpses of the azure sky and the bright evening cloud. During the whole time Rip and his companion had laboured on in silence, for though the former marvelled greatly what could be the object of carrying a keg of liquor up this wild mountain, yet there was something strange and incomprehensible about the unknown, that inspired awe and checked familiarity.

On entering the amphitheatre new objects of wonder presented themselves. On a level spot in the centre was a company of odd looking personages playing at ninepins. They were dressed in a quaint outlandish fashion—some wore short doublets,[17] others jerkins with long knives in their belts and most of them had enormous breeches of similar style with that of the guide's. Their visages too were peculiar. One had a large head, broad face and small piggish eyes. The face of another seemed to consist entirely of nose, and was surmounted by a white sugar-loaf hat, set off with a little red cock's tail. They all had beards of various shapes and colours. There was one who seemed to be the Commander. He was a stout old gentleman, with a weatherbeaten countenance. He wore a laced doublet, broad belt and hanger,[18] high crowned hat and feather, red stockings and high heel'd shoes with roses in them. The whole group reminded Rip of the figures in an old Flemish painting, in the parlour of Dominie[19] Van Schaick the village parson, and which had been brought over from Holland at the time of the settlement.

What seemed particularly odd to Rip was, that though these folks were evidently amusing themselves, yet they maintained the gravest faces, the most mysterious silence, and were, withal, the most melancholy party of pleasure he had ever witnessed. Nothing interrupted the stillness of the scene, but the noise of the balls, which, whenever they were rolled, echoed along the mountains like rumbling peals of thunder.

---

[16] A jacket or short coat, generally armless.   [17] A close-fitting, commonly elaborate jacket.
[18] A short sword, originally hung from the belt.   [19] Pastor.

As Rip and his companion approached them they suddenly desisted from their play and stared at him with such fixed statue like gaze, and such strange uncouth, lack lustre countenances, that his heart turned within him, and his knees smote together. His companion now emptied the contents of the keg into large flagons and made signs to him to wait upon the company. He obeyed with fear and trembling; they quaffed the liquor in profound silence and then returned to their game.

By degrees Rip's awe and apprehension subsided. He even ventured, when no eye was fixed upon him, to taste the beverage, which he found had much of the flavour of excellent hollands.[20] He was naturally a thirsty soul and was soon tempted to repeat the draught. One taste provoked another, and he reiterated his visits to the flagon so often that at length his senses were overpowered, his eyes swam in his head—his head gradually declined and he fell into a deep sleep.

On awaking he found himself on the green knoll from whence he had first seen the old man of the glen. He rubbed his eyes—it was a bright, sunny morning. The birds were hopping and twittering among the bushes, and the eagle was wheeling aloft and breasting the pure mountain breeze. "Surely," thought Rip, "I have not slept here all night." He recalled the occurrences before he fell asleep. The strange man with a keg of liquor—the mountain ravine—the wild retreat among the rocks—the woe begone party at ninepins—the flagon—"ah! that flagon! that wicked flagon!" thought Rip—"what excuse shall I make to Dame Van Winkle?"

He looked round for his gun, but in place of the clean well oiled fowling piece he found an old firelock lying by him, the barrel encrusted with rust; the lock falling off and the stock worm eaten. He now suspected that the grave roysters of the mountain had put a trick upon him, and having dosed him with liquor, had robbed him of his gun. Wolf too had disappeared, but he might have strayed away after a squirrel or partridge. He whistled after him and shouted his name—but all in vain; the echoes repeated his whistle and shout, but no dog was to be seen.

He determined to revisit the scene of the last evening's gambol, and if he met with any of the party, to demand his dog and gun. As he arose to walk he found himself stiff in the joints and wanting in his usual activity. "These mountain beds do not agree with me," thought Rip, "and if this frolick should lay me up with a fit of the rheumatism, I shall have a blessed time with Dame Van Winkle." With some difficulty he got down into the glen; he found the gully up which he and his companion had ascended the preceding evening, but to his astonishment a mountain stream was now foaming down it; leaping from rock to rock, and filling the glen with babbling murmurs. He, however, made shift to scramble up its sides working his toilsome way through thickets of birch, sassafras and witch hazel, and sometimes tripped up or entangled by the wild grape vines that twisted their coils and tendrils from tree to tree, and spread a kind of net work in his path.

At length he reached to where the ravine had opened through the cliffs, to the amphitheatre—but no traces of such opening remained. The rocks presented a high impenetrable wall over which the torrent came tumbling in a sheet of feathery foam, and fell into a broad deep basin black from the shadows of the surrounding forest. Here then poor Rip was brought to a stand. He again called and whistled after his dog—he was only answered by the cawing of a flock of idle crows, sporting high in air about a dry tree that overhung a sunny precipice; and who,

---

[20] Dutch gin.

secure in their elevation seemed to look down and scoff at the poor man's perplexities.

What was to be done? The morning was passing away and Rip felt famished for want of his breakfast. He grieved to give up his dog and gun; he dreaded to meet his wife; but it would not do to starve among the mountains. He shook his head, shouldered the rusty fire lock and with a heart full of trouble and anxiety, turned his steps homeward.

As he approached the village he met a number of people, but none whom he knew, which somewhat surprised him, for he had thought himself acquainted with every one in the country round. Their dress too was of a different fashion from that to which he was accustomed. They all stared at him with equal marks of surprise, and whenever they cast their eyes upon him, invariably stroked their chins. The constant recurrence of this gesture induced Rip involuntarily to do the same, when to his astonishment he found his beard had grown a foot long!

He had now entered the skirts of the village. A troop of strange children ran at his heels, hooting after him and pointing at his grey beard. The dogs too, not one of which he recognized for an old acquaintance, barked at him as he passed. The very village was altered—it was larger and more populous. There were rows of houses which he had never seen before, and those which had been his familiar haunts had disappeared. Strange names were over the doors—strange faces at the windows—every thing was strange. His mind now misgave him; he began to doubt whether both he and the world around him were not bewitched. Surely this was his native village which he had left but the day before. There stood the Kaatskill mountains—there ran the silver Hudson at a distance—there was every hill and dale precisely as it had always been—Rip was sorely perplexed—"That flagon last night," thought he, —"has addled my poor head sadly!"

It was with some difficulty that he found the way to his own house, which he approached with silent awe, expecting every moment to hear the shrill voice of Dame Van Winkle. He found the house gone to decay—the roof fallen in, the windows shattered and the doors off the hinges. A half starved dog that looked like Wolf was skulking about it. Rip called him by name but the cur snarled, shewed his teeth and passed on. This was an unkind cut indeed—"My very dog," sighed poor Rip, "has forgotten me!"

He entered the house, which, to tell the truth, Dame Van Winkle had always kept in neat order. It was empty, forlorn and apparently abandoned. This desolateness overcame all his connubial fears—he called loudly for his wife and children—the lonely chambers rung for a moment with his voice, and then all again was silence.

He now hurried forth and hastened to his old resort, the village inn—but it too was gone. A large, ricketty wooden building stood in its place, with great gaping windows, some of them broken, and mended with old hats and petticoats, and over the door was printed "The Union Hotel, by Jonathan Doolittle." Instead of the great tree, that used to shelter the quiet little Dutch inn of yore, there now was reared a tall naked pole with something on top that looked like a red night cap,[21] and from it was fluttering a flag on which was a singular assemblage of stars and stripes—all this was strange and incomprehensible. He recognized on the sign,

---

[21] A liberty pole and liberty cap, or Phrygian cap worn by slaves freed by the Romans, symbols of the American and French Revolutions.

however, the ruby face of King George under which he had smoked so many a peaceful pipe, but even this was singularly metamorphosed. The red coat was changed for one of blue and buff;[22] a sword was held in the hand instead of a sceptre; the head was decorated with a cocked hat, and underneath was printed in large characters GENERAL WASHINGTON.

There was as usual a crowd of folk about the door; but none that Rip recollected. The very character of the people seemed changed. There was a busy, bustling disputatious tone about it, instead of the accustomed phlegm and drowsy tranquility. He looked in vain for the sage Nicholaus Vedder with his broad face, double chin and fair long pipe, uttering clouds of tobacco smoke instead of idle speeches. Or Van Bummel the schoolmaster doling forth the contents of an ancient newspaper. In place of these a lean bilious looking fellow with his pockets full of hand bills, was haranguing vehemently about rights of citizens—elections—members of Congress—liberty—Bunker's hill—heroes of seventy six—and other words which were a perfect babylonish jargon[23] to the bewildered Van Winkle.

The appearance of Rip with his long grizzled beard, his rusty fowling piece,[24] his uncouth dress and an army of women and children at his heels soon attracted the attention of the tavern politicians. They crowded around him eying him from head to foot, with great curiosity. The orator bustled up to him, and drawing him partly aside, enquired "on which side he voted?"—Rip stared in vacant stupidity. Another short but busy little fellow, pulled him by the arm and rising on tiptoe, enquired in his ear "whether he was Federal or Democrat?"[25]—Rip was equally at a loss to comprehend the question—when a knowing, self important old gentleman, in a sharp cocked hat, made his way through the crowd, putting them to the right and left with his elbows as he passed, and planting himself before Van Winkle, with one arm akimbo, the other resting on his cane, his keen eyes and sharp hat penetrating as it were into his very soul, demanded in an austere tone—"what brought him to the election with a gun on his shoulder and a mob at his heels, and whether he meant to breed a riot in the village?"—"Alas gentlemen," cried Rip, somewhat dismayed, "I am a poor quiet man, a native of the place, and a loyal subject of the King—God bless him!"

Here a general shout burst from the byestanders—"A tory! a tory! a spy! a Refugee! hustle him! away with him!"—It was with great difficulty that the self important man in the cocked hat restored order; and having assumed a ten fold austerity of brow demanded again of the unknown culprit, what he came there for and whom he was seeking. The poor man humbly assured him that he meant no harm; but merely came there in search of some of his neighbours, who used to keep about the tavern.

"—Well—who are they?—name them."

Rip bethought himself a moment and enquired, "Where's Nicholaus Vedder?"

There was a silence for a little while, when an old man replied, in a thin, piping voice, "Nicholaus Vedder? why he is dead and gone these eighteen years! There

[22] Colors of Revolutionary Army uniforms.
[23] A puzzle; in Genesis 11:1–9 the "Confusion of Tongues" occurs at the Tower of Babel (Babel is apparently confused with Babylon).
[24] A shotgun for killing fowl.
[25] Political parties that grew during George Washington's administration: the first conservative, the second liberal.

was a wooden tombstone in the church yard that used to tell all about him, but that's rotted and gone too."

"Where's Brom Dutcher?"

"Oh he went off to the army in the beginning of the war; some say he was killed at the storming of Stoney Point—others say he was drowned in a squall at the foot of Antony's Nose[26]—I don't know—he never came back again."

"Where's Van Bummel the schoolmaster?"

"He went off to the wars too—was a great militia general, and is now in Congress."

Rip's heart died away at hearing of these sad changes in his home and friends, and finding himself thus alone in the world—every answer puzzled him too by treating of such enormous lapses of time and of matters which he could not understand—war—Congress, Stoney Point—he had no courage to ask after any more friends, but cried out in despair, "Does nobody here know Rip Van Winkle?"

"Oh. Rip Van Winkle?" exclaimed two or three—oh to be sure!—that's Rip Van Winkle—yonder—leaning against the tree."

Rip looked and beheld a precise counterpart of himself, as he went up the mountain: apparently as lazy and certainly as ragged! The poor fellow was now completely confounded. He doubted his own identity, and whether he was himself or another man. In the midst of his bewilderment the man in the cocked hat demanded who he was,—what was his name?

"God knows," exclaimed he, at his wit's end. "I'm not myself.—I'm somebody else—that's me yonder—no—that's somebody else got into my shoes—I was myself last night; but I fell asleep on the mountain—and they've changed my gun—and every thing's changed—and I'm changed—and I can't tell what's my name, or who I am!"

The byestanders began now to look at each other, nod, wink significantly and tap their fingers against their foreheads. There was a whisper also about securing the gun, and keeping the old fellow from doing mischief—at the very suggestion of which, the self important man in the cocked hat retired with some precipitation. At this critical moment a fresh likely looking woman pressed through the throng to get a peep at the greybearded man. She had a chubby child in her arms, which frightened at his looks began to cry. "Hush Rip," cried she, "hush you little fool, the old man won't hurt you." The name of the child, the air of the mother, the tone of her voice all awakened a train of recollections in his mind. "What is your name my good woman?" asked he.

"Judith Gardenier."

"And your father's name?"

"Ah, poor man, Rip Van Winkle was his name, but it's twenty years since he went away from home with his gun and never has been heard of since—his dog came home without him—but whether he shot himself, or was carried away by the Indians no body can tell. I was then but a little girl."

Rip had but one question more to ask, but he put it with a faltering voice—

"Where's your mother?"

Oh she too had died but a short time since—she broke a blood vessel in a fit of passion at a New England pedlar.—

---

[26] In July 1779 General Anthony Wayne (1745–1796) captured the British fort at Stony Point, on the Hudson River; Antony's Nose is a promontory on the Hudson, near West Point.

There was a drop of comfort at least in this intelligence. The honest man could contain himself no longer—he caught his daughter and her child in his arms.—"I am your father!" cried he—"Young Rip Van Winkle once—old Rip Van Winkle now!—does nobody know poor Rip Van Winkle!"

All stood amazed, until an old woman tottering out from among the crowd put her hand to her brow and peering under it in his face for a moment exclaimed— "Sure enough!—it is Rip Van Winkle—it is himself—welcome home again old neighbour—why, where have you been these twenty long years?"

Rip's story was soon told, for the whole twenty years had been to him but as one night. The neighbours stared when they heard it; some were seen to wink at each other and put their tongues in their cheeks, and the self important man in the cocked hat, who when the alarm was over had returned to the field, screwed down the corners of his mouth and shook his head—upon which there was a general shaking of the head throughout the assemblage.

It was determined, however, to take the opinion of old Peter Vanderdonk, who was seen slowly advancing up the road. He was a descendant of the historian of that name,[27] who wrote one of the earliest accounts of the province. Peter was the most ancient inhabitant of the village and well versed in all the wonderful events and traditions of the neighbourhood. He recollected Rip at once, and corroborated his story in the most satisfactory manner. He assured the company that it was a fact handed down from his ancestor the historian, that the Kaatskill mountains had always been haunted by strange beings. That it was affirmed that the great Hendrick Hudson,[28] the first discoverer of the river and country, kept a kind of vigil there every twenty years, with his crew of the Half Moon—being permitted in this way to revisit the scenes of his enterprize and keep a guardian eye upon the river and the great city called by his name. That his father had once seen them in their old Dutch dresses playing at nine pins in a hollow of the mountain; and that he himself had heard one summer afternoon the sound of their balls, like distant peals of thunder.

To make a long story short—the company broke up, and returned to the more important concerns of the election. Rip's daughter took him home to live with her; she had a snug well furnished house, and a stout cheery farmer for a husband whom Rip recollected for one of the urchins that used to climb upon his back. As to Rip's son and heir, who was the ditto of himself seen leaning against the tree; he was employed to work on the farm; but evinced an hereditary disposition to attend to any thing else but his business.

Rip now resumed his old walks and habits; he soon found many of his former cronies, though all rather the worse for the wear and tear of time; and preferred making friends among the rising generation, with whom he soon grew into great favour. Having nothing to do at home, and being arrived at that happy age when a man can be idle, with impunity, he took his place once more on the bench at the inn door and was reverenced as one of the patriarchs of the village and a chronicle of the old times "before the war." It was some time before he could get into the regular track of gossip, or could be made to comprehend the strange events that had taken place during his torpor. How that there had been a revolutionary war—

[27] Adriaen Van der Donck (1620?–1655), a Dutchman who wrote a history of New Netherland, published in Amsterdam in 1655 and (in an English translation) in New Netherland in 1656.

[28] Henry Hudson (?–1611), an English navigator employed by the Dutch to explore what is now call the Hudson River; Irving uses a Dutch form of the name Henry. The "great city called by his name" is Hudson, New York, on the East bank of the river.

that the country had thrown off the yoke of Old England and that instead of being a subject of his majesty George the Third, he was now a free citizen of the United States. Rip in fact was no politician; the changes of states and empires made but little impression on him; but there was one species of despotism under which he had long groaned and that was petticoat government. Happily that was at an end— he had got his neck out of the yoke of matrimony, and could go in and out whenever he pleased without dreading the tyranny of Dame Van Winkle. Whenever her name was mentioned, however, he shook his head, shrugged his shoulders and cast up his eyes; which might pass either for an expression of resignation to his fate or joy at his deliverance.

He used to tell his story to every stranger that arrived at Mr. Doolittle's Hotel. He was observed at first to vary on some points, every time he told it, which was doubtless owing to his having so recently awaked. It at last settled down precisely to the tale I have related and not a man woman or child in the neighbourhood but knew it by heart. Some always pretended to doubt the reality of it, and insisted that Rip had been out of his head, and that this was one point on which he always remained flighty. The old Dutch inhabitants, however, almost universally gave it full credit—Even to this day they never hear a thunder storm of a summer afternoon about the Kaatskill, but they say Hendrick Hudson and his crew are at their game of nine pins; and it is a common wish of all henpecked husbands in the neighbourhood, when life hangs heavy on their hands, that they might have a quieting draught out of Rip Van Winkle's flagon.

NOTE

The foregoing tale one would suspect had been suggested to Mr. Knickerbocker by a little German superstition about the emperor Frederick *der Rothbart* and the Kypphauser Mountain;[29] the subjoined note, however, which he had appended to the tale, shews that it is an absolute fact, narrated with his usual fidelity.—

"The story of Rip Van Winkle may seem incredible to many, but nevertheless I give it my full belief, for I know the vicinity of our old Dutch settlements to have been very subject to marvellous events and appearances. Indeed I have heard many stranger stories than this, in the villages along the Hudson; all of which were too well authenticated to admit of a doubt. I have even talked with Rip Van Winkle myself, who when last I saw him was a very venerable old man and so perfectly rational and consistent on every other point, that I think no conscientious person could refuse to take this into the bargain—nay I have seen a certificate on the subject taken before a country justice and signed with a cross in the justice's own hand writing. The story therefore is beyond the possibility of doubt. D.K."

POSTSCRIPT

The following are travelling notes from a memorandum book of Mr. Knickerbocker.[30]

[29] The "superstition" of Frederick Barbarossa, the Holy Roman Emperor Frederick I (1123?–1190), asleep at a table in the Kyffhaüser Mountain of Germany: when his red beard (the translation of *Barbarossa* [Latin] and *Rothbart* [German]) circles the table three times, he will awaken and lead Germany to world preeminence.

[30] This postscript takes Irving's fiction back from post-Revolutionary days and the clutter of Dutch colonial times to a region of peace ruled by Native-American legends. It traces a path to a mythic source that flows into history and the present day, thus linking fable and fact.

The Kaatsberg or Catskill mountains have always been a region full of fable. The Indians considered them the abode of spirits who influenced the weather, spreading sunshine or clouds over the landscape and sending good or bad hunting seasons. They were ruled by an old squaw spirit, said to be their mother. She dwelt on the highest peak of the Catskills and had charge of the doors of day and night to open and shut them at the proper hour. She hung up the new moons in the skies and cut up the old ones into stars. In times of drought, if properly propitiated, she would spin light summer clouds out of cobwebs and morning dew, and send them off, from the crest of the mountain, flake after flake, like flakes of carded cotton to float in the air: until, dissolved by the heat of the sun, they would fall in gentle showers, causing the grass to spring, the fruits to ripen and the corn to grow an inch an hour. If displeased, however, she would brew up clouds black as ink, sitting in the midst of them like a bottle bellied spider in the midst of its web; and when these clouds broke—woe betide the valleys!

In old times say the Indian traditions, there was a kind of Manitou or Spirit, who kept about the wildest recesses of the Catskill mountains, and took a mischievous pleasure in wreaking all kinds of evils and vexations upon the red men. Sometimes he would assume the form of a bear a panther or a deer, lead the bewildered hunter a weary chace through tangled forests and among rugged rocks; and then spring off with a loud ho! ho! leaving him aghast on the brink of a beetling precipice or raging torrent.

The favorite abode of this Manitou is still shewn. It is a great rock or cliff in the loneliest part of the mountains, and, from the flowering vines which clamber about it, and the wild flowers which abound in its neighborhood, is known by the name of the Garden Rock. Near the foot of it is a small lake the haunt of the solitary bittern, with water snakes basking in the sun on the leaves of the pond lillies which lie on the surface. This place was held in great awe by the Indians, insomuch that the boldest hunter would not pursue his game within its precincts. Once upon a time, however, a hunter who had lost his way, penetrated to the garden rock where he beheld a number of gourds placed in the crotches of trees. One of these he seized and made off with it, but in the hurry of his retreat he let it fall among the rocks, when a great stream gushed forth which washed him away and swept him down precipices where he was dashed to pieces, and the stream made its way to the Hudson and continues to flow to the present day: being the identical stream known by the name of the Kaaters-kill.

1819

THE LEGEND OF SLEEPY HOLLOW

(Found among the Papers of the late Diedrich Knickerbocker)

A pleasing land of drowsy head it was,
Of dreams that wave before the half-shut eye;
And of gay castles in the clouds that pass,
Forever flushing round a summer sky.
                    CASTLE OF INDOLENCE[1]

---

[1] By the Scottish poet James Thomson (1700–1748), I. 46–49.

In the bosom of one of those spacious coves which indent the eastern shore of the Hudson, at that broad expansion of the river denominated by the ancient Dutch navigators the Tappaan Zee,[2] and where they always prudently shortened sail, and implored the protection of St. Nicholas when they crossed, there lies a small market town or rural port, which by some is called Greensburgh, but which is more generally and properly known by the name of Tarry Town. This name was given, we are told, in former days, by the good housewives of the adjacent country, from the inveterate propensity of their husbands to linger about the village tavern on market days. Be that as it may, I do not vouch for the fact, but merely advert to it, for the sake of being precise and authentic. Not far from this village, perhaps about two miles, there is a little valley, or rather lap of land among high hills, which is one of the quietest places in the whole world. A small brook glides through it, with just murmur enough to lull one to repose, and the occasional whistle of a quail, or tapping of a woodpecker, is almost the only sound that ever breaks in upon the uniform tranquillity.

I recollect that when a stripling, my first exploit in squirrel shooting was in a grove of tall walnut trees that shades one side of the valley. I had wandered into it at noon time, when all nature is peculiarly quiet, and was startled by the roar of my own gun, as it broke the sabbath stillness around, and was prolonged and reverberated by the angry echoes. If ever I should wish for a retreat, whither I might steal from the world and its distractions, and dream quietly away the remnant of a troubled life, I know of none more promising than this little valley.

From the listless repose of the place, and the peculiar character of its inhabitants, who are descendants from the original Dutch settlers, this sequestered glen has long been known by the name of SLEEPY HOLLOW, and its rustic lads are called the Sleepy Hollow Boys throughout all the neighbouring country. A drowsy, dreamy influence seems to hang over the land, and to pervade the very atmosphere. Some say that the place was bewitched by a high German[3] doctor during the early days of the settlement; others, that an old Indian chief, the prophet or wizard of his tribe, held his powwows there before the country was discovered by Master Hendrick Hudson.[4] Certain it is, the place still continues under the sway of some witching power, that holds a spell over the minds of the good people, causing them to walk in a continual reverie. They are given to all kinds of marvellous beliefs; are subject to trances and visions, and frequently see strange sights, and hear music and voices in the air. The whole neighbourhood abounds with local tales, haunted spots, and twilight superstitions; stars shoot and meteors glare oftener across the valley than in any other part of the country, and the night mare, with her whole nine fold,[5] seems to make it the favourite scene of her gambols.

The dominant spirit, however, that haunts this enchanted region, and seems to be commander in chief of all the powers of the air, is the apparition of a figure on horseback without a head. It is said by some to be the ghost of a Hessian[6] trooper, whose head had been carried away by a cannon ball, in some nameless battle

---

[2] A widening in the Hudson River near Tarrytown, New York, wide enough to be called a sea or "Zee." St. Nicholas was known as the protector of sailors—hence the Dutch navigators "implored" his protection.

[3] From southern Germany.

[4] Henry Hudson (?–1611), an English navigator employed by the Dutch to explore what is now called the Hudson River; Irving uses a Dutch form of the name Henry.

[5] In folklore, the nightmare had nine foals or imps (see Shakespeare's *King Lear*, III. iv. 128).

[6] A mercenary soldier from Hesse, Germany, hired by the British to fight in the Revolutionary War.

during the revolutionary war, and who is ever and anon seen by the country folk, hurrying along in the gloom of night, as if on the wings of the wind. His haunts are not confined to the valley, but extend at times to the adjacent roads, and especially to the vicinity of a church at no great distance. Indeed, certain of the most authentic historians of those parts, who have been careful in collecting and collating the floating facts concerning this spectre, allege, that the body of the trooper having been buried in the church yard, the ghost rides forth to the scene of battle in nightly quest of his head, and that the rushing speed with which he sometimes passes along the hollow, like a midnight blast, is owing to his being belated, and in a hurry to get back to the church yard before day break.[7]

Such is the general purport of this legendary superstition, which has furnished materials for many a wild story in that region of shadows; and the spectre is known, at all the country firesides, by the name of The Headless Horseman of Sleepy Hollow.

It is remarkable, that the visionary propensity I have mentioned is not confined to the native inhabitants of the valley, but is unconsciously imbibed by every one who resides there for a time. However wide awake they may have been before they entered that sleepy region, they are sure, in a little time, to inhale the witching influence of the air, and begin to grow imaginative—to dream dreams, and see apparitions.

I mention this peaceful spot with all possible laud; for it is in such little retired Dutch valleys, found here and there embosomed in the great state of New York, that population, manners, and customs, remain fixed, while the great torrent of migration and improvement, which is making such incessant changes in other parts of this restless country, sweeps by them unobserved. They are like those little nooks of still water, which border a rapid stream, where we may see the straw and bubble riding quietly at anchor, or slowly revolving in their mimic harbour, undisturbed by the rush of the passing current. Though many years have elapsed since I trod the drowsy shades of Sleepy Hollow, yet I question whether I should not still find the same trees and the same families vegetating in its sheltered bosom.

In this by place of nature there abode, in a remote period of American history, that is to say, some thirty years since, a worthy wight[8] of the name of Ichabod Crane, who sojourned, or, as he expressed it, "tarried," in Sleepy Hollow, for the purpose of instructing the children of the vicinity. He was a native of Connecticut, a state which supplies the Union with pioneers for the mind as well as for the forest, and sends forth yearly its legions of frontier woodmen and country schoolmasters, The cognomen of Crane was not inapplicable to his person. He was tall, but exceedingly lank, with narrow shoulders, long arms and legs, hands that dangled a mile out of his sleeves, feet that might have served for shovels, and his whole frame most loosely hung together. His head was small, and flat at top, with huge ears, large green glassy eyes, and a long snipe nose, so that it looked like a weathercock perched upon his spindle neck, to tell which way the wind blew. To see him striding along the profile of a hill on a windy day, with his clothes bag-

---

[7] According to superstition, ghosts must return to their graves before dawn.

[8] Irving has just defined a "remote period" of American history as approximately thirty years; now he uses the nine-hundred year old word *wight* (creature) in referring to Ichabod Crane. Irving pretends a legendary time his country did not have as the condition of his fiction.

ging and fluttering about him, one might have mistaken him for the genius[9] of famine decending upon the earth, or some scarecrow eloped from a cornfield.

His school house was a low building of one large room, rudely constructed of logs; the windows partly glazed, and partly patched with leaves of old copy books. It was most ingeniously secured at vacant hours, by a withe[10] twisted in the handle of the door, and stakes set against the window shutters; so that though a thief might get in with perfect ease, he would find some embarrassment in getting out; an idea most probably borrowed by the architect, Yost Van Houten, from the mystery of an eelpot.[11] The school house stood in a rather lonely but pleasant situation, just at the foot of a woody hill, with a brook running close by, and a formidable birch tree growing at one end of it. From hence the low murmur of his pupils' voices conning over their lessons, might be heard of a drowsy summer's day, like the hum of a bee hive; interrupted now and then by the authoritative voice of the master, in the tone of menace or command, or peradverture, by the appalling sound of the birch, as he urged some tardy loiterer along the flowery path of knowledge. Truth to say, he was a conscientious man, and ever bore in mind the golden maxim, "spare the rod and spoil the child."[12]—Ichabod Crane's scholars certainly were not spoiled.

I would not have it imagined, however, that he was one of those cruel potentates of the school, who joy in the smart[13] of their subjects; on the contrary, he administered justice with discrimination rather than severity; taking the burthen off the backs of the weak, and laying it on those of the strong. Your mere puny stripling, that winced at the least flourish of the rod, was passed by with indulgence; but the claims of justice were satisfied, by inflicting a double portion on some little, tough, wrong headed, broad skirted Dutch urchin, who sulked and swelled and grew dogged and sullen beneath the birch. All this he called "doing his duty by their parents;" and he never inflicted a chastisement without following it by the assurance, so consolatory to the smarting urchin, that "he would remember it and thank him for it the longest day he had to live."

When school hours were over, he was even the companion and playmate of the larger boys; and on holyday afternoons would convoy some of the smaller ones home, who happened to have pretty sisters, or good housewives for mothers, noted for the comforts of the cupboard. Indeed, it behooved him to keep on good terms with his pupils. The revenue arising from his school was small, and would have been scarcely sufficient to furnish him with daily bread, for he was a huge feeder, and though lank, had the dilating powers of an Anaconda;[14] but to help out his maintenance, he was, according to country custom in those parts, boarded and lodged at the houses of the farmers, whose children he instructed. With these he lived successively a week at a time, thus going the rounds of the neighbourhood, with all his worldly effects tied up in a cotton handkerchief.

That all this might not be too onerous on the purses of his rustic patrons, who are apt to consider the costs of schooling a grievous burthen, and schoolmasters as mere drones, he had various ways of rendering himself both useful and agreeable.

---

[9] A spirit presiding over the destiny of a place.

[10] A slender branch used in place of a rope.   [11] An eel trap.

[12] From *Hudibras* (1664), by the English poet Samuel Butler (1612–1680), 2. II. 844; the maxim goes back to the Book of Proverbs, 13:24, "He that spareth his rod, hateth his son."

[13] Here, pain (from whipping).

[14] A large snake that can stretch its gullet to swallow large animals whole.

He assisted the farmers occasionally in the lighter labours of their farms, helped to make hay, mended the fences, took the horses to water, drove the cows from pasture, and cut wood for the winter fire. He laid aside, too, all the dominant dignity and absolute sway, with which he lorded it in his little empire, the school, and became wonderfully gentle and ingratiating. He found favour in the eyes of the mothers, by petting the children, particularly the youngest, and like the lion bold, which whilome[15] so magnanimously the lamb did hold,[16] he would sit with a child on one knee, and rock a cradle with his foot, for whole hours together.

In addition to his other vocations, he was the singing master of the neighbourhood, and picked up many bright shillings by instructing the young folks in psalmody.[17] It was a matter of no little vanity to him on Sundays, to take his station in front of the church gallery, with a band of chosen singers; where, in his own mind, he completely carried away the palm from the parson. Certain it is, his voice resounded far above all the rest of the congregation, and there are peculiar quavers still to be heard in that church, and which may even be heard half a mile off, quite to the opposite side of the mill pond, of a still Sunday morning, which are said to be legitimately descended from the nose of Ichabod Crane. Thus, by diverse little make shifts, in that ingenious way which is commonly denominated "by hook and by crook,"[18] the worthy pedagogue got on tolerably enough, and was thought, by all who understood nothing of the labour of headwork, to have a wonderfully easy life of it.

The schoolmaster is generally a man of some importance in the female circle of a rural neighbourhood, being considered a kind of idle gentleman like personage, of vastly superior taste and accomplishments to the rough country swains, and, indeed, inferior in learning only to the parson. His appearance, therefore, is apt to occasion some little stir at the tea table of a farm house, and the addition of a supernumerary dish of cakes or sweetmeats, or, peradventure, the parade of a silver tea pot. Our man of letters, therefore, was peculiarly happy in the smiles of all the country damsels. How he would figure among them in the church yard, between services on Sundays; gathering grapes for them from the wild vines that overrun the surrounding trees; reciting for their amusement all the epitaphs on the tombstones, or sauntering, with a whole bevy of them, along the banks of the adjacent mill pond; while the more bashful country bumpkins hung sheepishly back, envying his superior elegance and address.

From his half itinerant life, also, he was a kind of travelling gazette, carrying the whole budget of local gossip from house to house; so that his appearance was always greeted with satisfaction. He was, moreover, esteemed by the women as a man of great erudition, for he had read several books quite through, and was a perfect master of Cotton Mather's History of New England Witchcraft,[19] in which, by the way, he most firmly and potently believed.

He was, in fact, an odd mixture of small shrewdness and simple credulity. His appetite for the marvellous, and his powers of digesting it, were equally extraordinary; and both had been increased by his residence in this spell bound region. No

---

[15] Formerly.

[16] In *The New England Primer* (1683?) the couplet for the letter "L" reads "The lion bold / The lamb doth hold," accompanied by a biblical illustration portraying Isaiah 11:6–9.

[17] The singing of psalms.

[18] From "Colyn Cloute" (1519?), by the English poet John Skelton (1460?–1529).

[19] Actually, Cotton Mather (1663–1728) wrote *Memorable Providences Relating to Witchcraft* (1689) and *The Wonders of the Invisible World* (1693), both dealing with witchcraft in New England.

tale was too gross or monstrous for his capacious swallow.[20] It was often his delight, after his school was dismissed of an afternoon, to stretch himself on the rich bed of clover, bordering the little brook that whimpered by his school house, and there con[21] over old Mather's direful tales, until the gathering dusk of evening made the printed page a mere mist before his eyes. Then, as he wended his way, by swamp and stream and awful[22] woodland, to the farm house where he happened to be quartered, every sound of nature, at that witching hour, fluttered his excited imagination; the moan of the whip-poor-will[23] from the hill side; the boding cry of the tree toad, that harbinger of storm; the dreary hooting of the screech owl; or the sudden rustling in the thicket, of birds frightened from their roost. The fire flies, too, which sparkled most vividly in the darkest places, now and then startled him, as one of uncommon brightness would stream across his path; and if, by chance, a huge blockhead of a beetle came winging his blundering flight against him, the poor varlet was ready to give up the ghost, with the idea that he was struck with a witch's token. His only resource on such occasions, either to drown thought, or drive away evil spirits, was to sing psalm tunes;—and the good people of Sleepy Hollow, as they sat by their doors of an evening, were often filled with awe, at hearing his nasal melody, "in linked sweetness long drawn out,"[24] floating from the distant hill, or along the dusky road.

Another of his sources of fearful pleasure was, to pass long winter evenings with the old Dutch wives, as they sat spinning by the fire, with a row of apples roasting and sputtering along the hearth, and listen to their marvellous tales of ghosts and goblins, and haunted fields and haunted brooks, and haunted bridges and haunted houses, and particularly of the headless horseman, or galloping Hessian of the Hollow, as they sometimes called him. He would delight them equally by his anecdotes of witchcraft, and of the direful omens and portentous sights and sounds in the air, which prevailed in the earlier times of Connecticut; and would frighten them woefully with speculations upon comets and shooting stars, and with the alarming fact that the world did absolutely turn round, and that they were half the time topsy-turvy!

But if there was a pleasure in all this, while snugly cuddling in the chimney corner of a chamber that was all of a ruddy glow from the crackling wood fire, and where, of course, no spectre dared to show its face, it was dearly purchased by the terrors of his subsequent walk homewards. What fearful shapes and shadows beset his path, amidst the dim and ghastly glare of a snowy night!—With what wistful look did he eye every trembling ray of light streaming across the waste fields from some distant window!—How often was he appalled by some shrub covered with snow, which like a sheeted spectre beset his very path!—How often did he shrink with curdling awe at the sound of his own steps on the frosty crust beneath his feet; and dread to look over his shoulder, lest he should behold some uncouth being tramping close behind him!—and how often was he thrown into complete dismay by some rushing blast, howling among the trees, in the idea that it was the gallopping Hessian on one of his nightly scourings.

All these, however, were mere terrors of the night, phantoms of the mind, that walk in darkness; and though he had seen many spectres in his time, and been

---

[20] Like a child, Ichabod will swallow anything.   [21] Study.   [22] Frightening.
[23] Irving's note: "The whip-poor-will is a bird which is only heard at night. It receives its name from its note which is thought to resemble those words."
[24] From "L'Allegro" (1632), line 140, by the English poet John Milton (1608–1674).

more than once beset by Satan in diverse shapes, in his lonely perambulations, yet daylight put an end to all these evils; and he would have passed a pleasant life of it, in despite of the Devil and all his works, if his path had not been crossed by a being that causes more perplexity to mortal man, than ghosts, goblins, and the whole race of witches put together, and that was—a woman.

Among the musical disciples who assembled, one evening in each week, to receive his instructions in psalmody, was Katrina Van Tassel, the daughter and only child of a substantial Dutch farmer. She was a blooming lass of fresh eighteen; plump as a partridge; ripe and melting and rosy cheeked as one of her father's peaches, and universally famed, not merely for her beauty, but her vast expectations. She was withal a little of a coquette, as might be perceived even in her dress, which was a mixture of ancient and modern fashions, as most suited to set off her charms. She wore the ornaments of pure yellow gold, which her great great grandmother had brought over from Saardam;[25] the tempting stomacher[26] of the olden time, and withal a provokingly short petticoat, to display the prettiest foot and ankle in the country round.

Ichabod Crane had a soft and foolish heart toward the sex;[27] and it is not to be wondered at, that so tempting a morsel soon found favour in his eyes, more especially after he had visited her in her paternal mansion. Old Baltus Van Tassel was a perfect picture of a thriving, contented, liberal hearted farmer. He seldom, it is true, sent either his eyes or his thoughts beyond the boundaries of his own farm; but within those every thing was snug, happy, and well conditioned. He was satisfied with his wealth, but not proud of it, and piqued himself upon the hearty abundance, rather than the style in which he lived. His strong hold was situated on the banks of the Hudson, in one of those green, sheltered, fertile nooks, in which the Dutch farmers are so fond of nestling. A great elm tree spread its broad branches over it, at the foot of which bubbled up a spring of the softest and sweetest water, in a little well, formed of a barrel, and then stole sparkling away through the grass, to a neighbouring brook, that babbled along among elders and dwarf willows. Hard by the farm house was a vast barn, that might have served for a church; every window and crevice of which seemed bursting forth with the treasures of the farm; the flail[28] was busily resounding within it from morning to night; swallows and martins skimmed twittering about the eaves, and rows of pigeons, some with one eye turned up, as if watching the weather, some with their heads under their wings, or buried in their bosoms, and others, swelling, and cooing, and bowing about their dames, were enjoying the sunshine on the roof. Sleek unwieldy porkers were grunting in the repose and abundance of their pens, from whence sallied forth, now and then, troops of sucking pigs, as if to snuff the air. A stately squadron of snowy geese were riding in an adjoining pond, convoying whole fleets of ducks; regiments of turkeys were gobbling through the farm yard, and guinea fowls fretting about it like ill tempered housewives, with their peevish discontented cry. Before the barn door strutted the gallant cock, that pattern of a husband, a warrior, and a fine gentleman, clapping his burnished wings, and crowing in the pride and gladness of his heart—sometimes tearing up the earth with his feet, and then generously calling his ever hungry family of wives and children to enjoy the rich morsel which he had discovered.

---

[25] Now Zaandam, about five miles northwest of Amsterdam.
[26] A decorated waistband worn over a dress.   [27] Women.
[28] An instrument for threshing grain by hand.

The pedagogue's mouth watered, as he looked upon this sumptuous promise of luxurious winter fare. In his devouring mind's eye, he pictured to himself every roasting pig running about with a pudding in his belly, and an apple in his mouth; the pigeons were snugly put to bed in a comfortable pie, and tucked in with a coverlet of crust; the geese were swimming in their own gravy; and the ducks pairing cosily in dishes, like snug married couples, with a decent competency of onion sauce; in the porkers he saw carved out the future sleek side of bacon, and juicy relishing ham; not a turkey, but he beheld daintily trussed up, with its gizzard under its wing, and, peradventure, a necklace of savoury sausages; and even bright chanticleer[29] himself lay sprawling on his back, in a side dish, with uplifted claws, as if craving that quarter,[30] which his chivalrous spirit disdained to ask while living.

As the enraptured Ichabod fancied all this, and as he rolled his great green eyes over the fat meadow lands, the rich fields of wheat, of rye, of buckwheat, and Indian corn, and the orchards burthened with ruddy fruit, which surrounded the warm tenement[31] of Van Tassel, his heart yearned after the damsel who was to inherit these domains, and his imagination expanded with the idea, how they might be readily turned into cash, and the money invested in immense tracts of wild land, and shingle palaces in the wilderness. Nay, his busy fancy already realized his hopes, and presented to him the blooming Katrina, with a whole family of children, mounted on the top of a waggon loaded with household trumpery, with pots and kettles dangling beneath; and he beheld himself bestriding a pacing mare, with a colt at her heels, setting out for Kentucky, Tennessee, or the Lord knows where!

When he entered the house, the conquest of his heart was complete. It was one of those spacious farm houses, with high ridged, but lowly sloping roofs, built in the style handed down from the first Dutch settlers. The low, projecting eaves formed a piazza along the front, capable of being closed up in bad weather. Under this were hung flails, harness, various utensils of husbandry, and nets for fishing in the neighbouring river. Benches were built along the sides for summer use; and a great spinning wheel at one end, and a churn at the other, showed the various uses to which this important porch might be devoted. From this piazza the wondering Ichabod entered the hall, which formed the centre of the mansion, and the place of usual residence. Here, rows of resplendent pewter, ranged on a long dresser, dazzled his eyes. In one corner stood a huge bag of wool ready to be spun; in another a quantity of linsey-woolsey just from the loom; ears of Indian corn, and strings of dried apples and peaches, hung in gay festoons along the walls, mingled with the gaud[32] of red peppers; and a door left ajar, gave him a peep into the best parlour, where the claw footed chairs, and dark mahogany tables, shone like mirrors; andirons, with their accompanying shovel and tongs, glistened from their covert of asparagus tops; mock oranges[33] and conch shells decorated the mantlepiece; strings of various coloured birds' eggs were suspended above it; a great ostrich egg was hung from the centre of the room, and a corner cupboard, knowingly left open, displayed immense treasures of old silver and well mended china.

[29] A rooster.   [30] Mercy or clemency.
[31] A dwelling place, residence; the Van Tassel house is later called a "mansion."
[32] A bright or gaudy display.
[33] The andirons in the fireplace glisten from their hiding place in the midst of asparagus tops, used as decoration; "mock oranges" are probably orange-colored gourds.

From the moment Ichabod laid his eyes upon these regions of delight, the peace of his mind was at an end, and his only study was how to gain the affections of the peerless daughter of Van Tassel. In this enterprize, however, he had more real difficulties than generally fell to the lot of a knight errant[34] of yore, who seldom had any thing but giants, enchanters, fiery dragons, and such like easily conquered adversaries, to contend with; and had to make his way merely through gates of iron and brass, and walls of adamant, to the castle keep,[35] where the lady of his heart was confined; all which he achieved as easily as a man would carve his way to the centre of a Christmas pie, and then the lady gave him her hand as a matter of course. Ichabod, on the contrary, had to win his way to the heart of a country coquette, beset with a labyrinth of whims and caprices, which were for ever presenting new difficulties and impediments, and he had to encounter a host of fearful adversaries of real flesh and blood, the numerous rustic admirers, who beset every portal to her heart, keeping a watchful and angry eye upon each other, but ready to fly out in the common cause against any new competitor.

Among these, the most formidable, was a burly, roaring, roystering blade, of the name of Abraham, or, according to the Dutch abbreviation, Brom Van Brunt, the hero of the country round, which rung with his feats of strength and hardihood. He was broad shouldered and double jointed, with short curly black hair, and a bluff, but not unpleasant countenance, having a mingled air of fun and arrogance. From his Herculean frame and great powers of limb, he had received the nick name of Brom Bones, by which he was universally known. He was famed for great knowledge and skill in horsemanship, being as dexterous on horseback as a Tartar.[36] He was foremost at all races and cock fights, and with the ascendancy which bodily strength acquires in rustic life, was the umpire in all disputes, setting his hat on one side, and giving his decisions with an air and tone admitting of no gainsay or appeal. He was always ready for either a fight or a frolick; but had more mischief than ill will in his composition; and with all his overbearing roughness, there was a strong dash of waggish good humour at bottom. He had three or four boon companions, who regarded him as their model, and at the head of whom he scoured the country, attending every scene of feud or merriment for miles round. In cold weather he was distinguished by a fur cap, surmounted with a flaunting fox's tail, and when the folks at a country gathering descried this well known crest at a distance, whisking about among a squad of hard riders, they always stood by for a squall. Sometimes his crew would be heard dashing along past the farm houses at midnight, with whoop and halloo, like a troop of Don Cossacks,[37] and the old dames, startled out of their sleep, would listen for a moment till the hurry scurry had clattered by, and then exclaim, "aye, there goes Brom Bones and his gang!" The neighbours looked upon him with a mixture of awe, admiration, and good will; and when any mad cap prank, or rustic brawl, occurred in the vicinity, always shook their heads, and warranted Brom Bones was at the bottom of it.

This rantipole[38] hero had for some time singled out the blooming Katrina for the object of his uncouth gallantries, and though his amorous toyings were something like the gentle caresses and endearments of a bear, yet it was whispered that she did not altogether discourage his hopes. Certain it is, his advances were sig-

---

[34] A knight who searches for adventure, commonly to save a maiden in distress.
[35] Walls of extremely hard stone, to the dungeon.   [36] A fierce Asian warrior.
[37] The cavalry of the Don River area in Russia.   [38] Wild, boisterous.

nals for rival candidates to retire, who felt no inclination to cross a lion in his amours; insomuch, that when his horse was seen tied to Van Tassel's paling,[39] of a Sunday night, (a sure sign that his master was courting, or, as it is termed, "sparking," within,) all other suitors passed by in despair, and carried the war into other quarters.

Such was the formidable rival with whom Ichabod Crane had to contend, and, considering all things, a stouter man than he would have shrunk from the competition, and a wiser man would have despaired. He had, however, a happy mixture of pliability and perserverance in his nature; he was in form and spirit like a supple jack[40]—yielding, but tough; though he bent, he never broke; and though he bowed beneath the slightest pressure, yet, the moment it was away—jerk!—he was as erect, and carried his head as high as ever.

To have taken the field openly against his rival, would have been madness; for he was not a man to be thwarted in his amours, any more than that stormy lover, Achilles.[41] Ichabod, therefore, made his advances in a quiet and gently insinuating manner. Under cover of his character of singing master, he made frequent visits at the farm house; not that he had any thing to apprehend from the meddlesome interference of parents, which is so often a stumbling block in the path of lovers. Balt Van Tassel was an easy indulgent soul; he loved his daughter better even than his pipe, and like a reasonable man, and an excellent father, let her have her way in every thing. His notable little wife too, had enough to do to attend to her housekeeping and manage her poultry, for, as she sagely observed, ducks and geese are foolish things, and must be looked after, but girls can take care of themselves. Thus while the busy dame bustled about the house, or plied her spinning wheel at one end of the piazza, honest Balt would sit smoking his evening pipe at the other, watching the achievements of a little wooden warrior, who, armed with a sword in each hand, was most valiantly fighting the wind on the pinnacle of the barn.[42] In the mean time, Ichabod would carry on his suit with the daughter by the side of the spring under the great elm, or sauntering along in the twilight, that hour so favourable to the lover's eloquence.

I profess not to know how women's hearts are wooed and won. To me they have always been matters of riddle and admiration. Some seem to have but one vulnerable point, or door of access; while others have a thousand avenues, and may be captured in a thousand different ways. It is a great triumph of skill to gain the former, but a still greater proof of generalship to maintain possession of the latter, for a man must battle for his fortress at every door and window. He who wins a thousand common hearts, is therefore entitled to some renown; but he who keeps undisputed sway over the heart of a coquette, is indeed a hero. Certain it is, this was not the case with the redoutable Brom Bones; and from the moment Ichabod Crane made his advances, the interests of the former evidently declined; his horse was no longer seen tied at the palings on Sunday nights, and a deadly feud gradually arose between him and the preceptor of Sleepy Hollow.

Brom, who had a degree of rough chivalry in his nature, would fain have carried matters to open warfare, and have settled their pretensions to the lady, ac-

---

[39] Fence.   [40] A climbing vine with tough, pliant stems.

[41] In Homer's *Iliad* Achilles becomes angry when the captive maiden Briseis is taken from him by King Agamemnon. In mock-heroic manner Irving associates the gullible Ichabod Crane with a renowned Greek warrior, just as he likens Brom Bones and his pranksters to fabled Russian cavalry.

[42] A wind gauge in the form of a soldier.

cording to the mode of those most concise and simple reasoners, the knights errant of yore—by single combat; but Ichabod was too conscious of the superior might of his adversary to enter the lists against him; he had overheard a boast of Bones, that he would "double the schoolmaster up, and lay him on a shelf of his own school house;" and he was too wary to give him an opportunity. There was something extremely provoking in this obstinately pacific system; it left Brom no alternative but to draw upon the funds of rustic waggery in his disposition, and to play off boorish practical jokes upon his rival. Ichabod became the object of whimsical persecution to Bones, and his gang of rough riders. They harried his hitherto peaceful domains; smoked out his singing school, by stopping up the chimney; broke into the school house at night, in spite of its formidable fastenings of withe and window stakes, and turned every thing topsy-turvy, so that the poor schoolmaster began to think all the witches in the country held their meetings there. But what was still more annoying, Brom took all opportunities of turning him into ridicule in presence of his mistress, and had a scoundrel dog, whom he taught to whine in the most ludicrous manner, and introduced as a rival of Ichabod's, to instruct her in psalmody.

In this way, matters went on for some time, without producing any material effect on the relative situations of the contending powers. On a fine autumnal afternoon, Ichabod, in pensive mood, sat enthroned on the lofty stool from whence he usually watched all the concerns of his little literary realm. In his hand he swayed a ferule, that sceptre of despotic power; the birch of justice reposed on three nails, behind the throne, a constant terror to evil doers; while on the desk before him might be seen sundry contraband articles and prohibited weapons, detected upon the persons of idle urchins, such as half munched apples, popguns, whirligigs, fly cages, and whole legions of rampant little paper game cocks.[43] Apparently there had been some appalling act of justice recently inflicted, for his scholars were all busily intent upon their books, or slyly whispering behind them with one eye kept upon the master; and a kind of buzzing stillness reigned throughout the school room. It was suddenly interrupted by the appearance of a negro in tow cloth jacket and trowsers, a round crowned fragment of a hat, like the cap of Mercury,[44] and mounted on the back of a ragged, wild, half broken colt, which he managed with a rope by way of halter. He came clattering up to the school door with an invitation to Ichabod to attend a merry making, or "quilting frolick," to be held that evening at Mynheer Van Tassel's, and having delivered his message with that air of importance, and effort at fine language, which a negro is apt to display on petty embassies[45] of the kind, he dashed over the brook, and was seen scampering away up the hollow, full of the importance and hurry of his mission.

All was now bustle and hubbub in the late quiet school room. The scholars were hurried through their lessons, without stopping at trifles; those who were nimble, skipped over half with impunity, and those who were tardy, had a smart application now and then in the rear, to quicken their speed, or help them over a tall word. Books were flung aside, without being put away on the shelves; ink-

---

[43] Whirligigs: toys that spin like a top; fly cages: small containers for imprisoning flies; rampant paper game cocks: figures of male game fowl in threatening posture.
[44] According to Roman myth, the cap of Mercury, the gods' messenger, symbolized speed.
[45] Errands.

stands were overturned, benches thrown down, and the whole school was turned loose an hour before the usual time; bursting forth like a legion of young imps, yelping and racketing about the green, in joy at their early emancipation.

The gallant Ichabod now spent at least an extra half hour at his toilet, brushing and furbishing up his best, and indeed only suit of rusty black, and arranging his looks by a bit of broken looking glass, that hung up in the school house. That he might make his appearance before his mistress in the true style of a cavalier, he borrowed a horse from the farmer with whom he was domiciliated, a choleric old Dutchman, of the name of Hans Van Ripper, and thus gallantly mounted, issued forth like a knight errant in quest of adventures. But it is meet[46] I should, in the true spirit of romantic story, give some account of the looks and equipments of my hero and his steed. The animal he bestrode was a broken down plough horse, that had outlived almost every thing but his viciousness. He was gaunt and shagged, with a ewe neck[47] and a head like a hammer; his rusty mane and tail were tangled and knotted with burrs; one eye had lost its pupil, and was glaring and spectral, but the other had the gleam of a genuine devil in it. Still he must have had fire and mettle in his day, if we may judge from the name he bore of Gunpowder. He had, in fact, been a favourite steed of his master's, the cholerick Van Ripper, who was a furious rider, and had infused, very probably, some of his own spirit into the animal, for, old and broken down as he looked, there was more of the lurking devil in him than in any young filly in the country.

Ichabod was a suitable figure for such a steed. He rode with short stirrups, which brought his knees nearly up to the pommel of the saddle; his sharp elbows stuck out like grasshoppers'; he carried his whip perpendicularly in his hand, like a sceptre, and as his horse jogged on, the motion of his arms was not unlike the flapping of a pair of wings. A small wool hat rested on the top of his nose, for so his scanty strip of forehead might be called, and the skirts of his black coat fluttered out almost to the horse's tail. Such was the appearance of Ichabod and his steed, as they shambled out of the gate of Hans Van Ripper, and it was altogether such an apparition as is seldom to be met with in broad day light.

It was, as I have said, a fine autumnal day, the sky was clear and serene, and nature wore that rich and golden livery which we always associate with the idea of abundance. The forests had put on their sober brown and yellow, while some trees of the tenderer kind had been nipped by the frosts into brilliant dyes of orange, purple, and scarlet. Streaming files of wild ducks began to make their appearance high in the air; the bark of the squirrel might be heard from the groves of beech and hickory nuts, and the pensive whistle of the quail at intervals from the neighbouring stubble field.

The small birds were taking their farewell banquets. In the fullness of their revelry, they fluttered, chirping and frolicking, from bush to bush, and tree to tree, capricious from the very profusion and variety around them. There was the honest cock robin, the favourite game of stripling sportsmen, with its loud querulous note; and the twittering blackbirds flying in sable clouds; and the golden winged woodpecker, with his crimson crest, his broad black gorget,[48] and splendid plumage; and the cedar bird, with its red tipt wings and yellow tipt tail, and its little monteiro cap of feathers;[49] and the blue jay, that noisy coxcomb, in his gay

---

[46] Fitting, appropriate.   [47] A thin, sheeplike neck.   [48] Throat.
[49] The bird's plume is like a huntsman's round cap with a flap.

light blue coat and white under clothes, screaming and chattering, nodding, and bobbing, and bowing, and pretending to be on good terms with every songster of the grove.

As Ichabod jogged slowly on his way, his eye, ever open to every symptom of culinary abundance, ranged with delight over the treasures of jolly autumn. On all sides he beheld vast store of apples, some hanging in oppressive opulence on the trees, some gathered into baskets and barrels for the market, others heaped up in rich piles for the cider press. Further on he beheld great fields of Indian corn, with its golden ears peeping from their leafy coverts, and holding out the promise of cakes and hasty pudding; and the yellow pumpkins lying beneath them, turning up their fair round bellies to the sun, and giving ample prospects of the most luxurious of pies; and anon he passed the fragrant buckwheat fields, breathing the odour of the bee hive, and as he beheld them, soft anticipations stole over his mind of dainty slap jacks, well buttered, and garnished with honey or treacle,[50] by the delicate little dimpled hand of Katrina Van Tassel.

Thus feeding his mind with many sweet thoughts and "sugared suppositions," he journeyed along the sides of a range of hills which look out upon some of the goodliest scenes of the mighty Hudson. The sun gradually wheeled his broad disk down into the west. The wide bosom of the Tappaan Zee lay motionless and glassy, excepting that here and there a gentle undulation waved and prolonged the blue shadow of the distant mountain: a few amber clouds floated in the sky, without a breath of air to move them. The horizon was of a fine golden tint, changing gradually into a pure apple green, and from that into the deep blue of the mid-heaven. A slanting ray lingered on the woody crests of the precipices that overhung some parts of the river, giving greater depth to the dark grey and purple of their rocky sides. A sloop was loitering in the distance, dropping slowly down with the tide, her sail hanging uselessly against the mast, and as the reflection of the sky gleamed along the still water, it seemed as if the vessel was suspended in the air.

It was toward evening that Ichabod arrived at the castle of the Heer Van Tassel, which he found thronged with the pride and flower of the adjacent country. Old farmers, a spare, leathern faced race, in homespun coats and breeches, blue stockings, huge shoes and magnificent pewter buckles. Their brisk withered little dames in close crimped caps, long waisted short gowns, homespun petticoats, with scissors and pincushions, and gay calico pockets, hanging on the outside. Buxom lasses, almost as antiquated as their mothers, excepting where a straw hat, a fine ribband, or perhaps a white frock, gave symptoms of city innovation. The sons, in short square skirted coats with rows of stupendous brass buttons, and their hair generally queued in the fashion of the times, especially if they could procure an eel skin for the purpose, it being esteemed throughout the country as a potent nourisher and strengthener of the hair.

Brom Bones, however, was the hero of the scene, having come to the gathering on his favourite steed Daredevil, a creature, like himself, full of mettle and mischief, and which no one but himself could manage. He was in fact noted for preferring vicious animals, given to all kinds of tricks, which kept the rider in constant risk of his neck, for he held a tractable well broken horse as unworthy of a lad of spirit.

[50] Molasses.

Fain would I pause to dwell upon the world of charms that burst upon the enraptured gaze of my hero,[51] as he entered the state parlour of Van Tassel's mansion. Not those of the bevy of buxom lasses, with their luxurious display of red and white: but the ample charms of a genuine Dutch country tea table, in the sumptuous time of autumn. Such heaped up platters of cakes of various and almost indescribable kinds, known only to experienced Dutch housewives. There was the doughty dough nut, the tenderer oly koek,[52] and the crisp and crumbling cruller; sweet cakes and short cakes, ginger cakes and honey cakes, and the whole family of cakes. And then there were apple pies and peach pies and pumpkin pies; besides slices of ham and smoked beef; and moreover delectable dishes of preserved plums, and peaches, and pears, and quinces; not to mention broiled shad and roasted chickens; together with bowls of milk and cream, all mingled higgledy-piggledy, pretty much as I have enumerated them, with the motherly tea pot sending up its clouds of vapour from the midst—Heaven bless the mark! I want[53] breath and time to discuss this banquet as it deserves, and am too eager to get on with my story. Happily, Ichabod Crane was not in so great a hurry as his historian, but did ample justice to every dainty.

He was a kind and thankful creature, whose heart dilated in proportion as his skin was filled with good cheer, and whose spirits rose with eating, as some men's do with drink. He could not help, too, rolling his large eyes round him as he ate, and chuckling with the possibility that he might one day be lord of all this scene of almost unimaginable luxury and splendour. Then, he thought, how soon he'd turn his back upon the old school house; snap his fingers in the face of Hans Van Ripper, and every other niggardly patron, and kick any itinerant pedagogue out of doors that should dare to call him comrade!

Old Baltus Van Tassel moved about among his guests with a face dilated with content and good humour, round and jolly as the harvest moon. His hospitable attentions were brief, but expressive, being confined to a shake of the hand, a slap on the shoulder, a loud laugh, and a pressing invitation to "fall to, and help themselves."

And now the sound of the music from the common room or hall, summoned to the dance. The musician was an old grey headed negro, who had been the itinerant orchestra of the neighbourhood for more than half a century. His instrument was as old and battered as himself. The greater part of the time he scraped away on two or three strings, accompanying every movement of the bow with a motion of the head; bowing almost to the ground, and stamping with his foot whenever a fresh couple were to start.

Ichabod prided himself upon his dancing as much as upon his vocal powers. Not a limb, not a fibre about him was idle, and to have seen his loosely hung frame in full motion, and clattering about the room, you would have thought Saint Vitus[54] himself, that blessed patron of the dance, was figuring before you in person. He was the admiration of all the negroes, who, having gathered, of all ages and sizes, from the farm and the neighbourhood, stood forming a pyramid of

---

[51] In the previous paragraph Brom Bones is the "hero" of this social occasion, whereas here Ichabod Crane is "my hero." Bones is a hero prized by society, Crane by the writer.

[52] Oil cake: sweetened dough fried in lard.   [53] Lack.

[54] An early Christian martyr, patron of those suffering from chorea, a nervous disorder characterized by spasmodic jerking known as St. Vitus' dance.

shining black faces at every door and window, gazing with delight at the scene, rolling their white eye balls, and showing grinning rows of ivory from ear to ear. How could the flogger of urchins be otherwise than animated and joyous; the lady of his heart was his partner in the dance; and smiling graciously in reply to all his amorous oglings, while Brom Bones, sorely smitten with love and jealousy, sat brooding by himself in one corner.

When the dance was at an end, Ichabod was attracted to a knot of the sager folks, who, with old Van Tassel, sat smoking at one end of the piazza, gossiping over former times, and drawling out long stories about the war.

This neighbourhood, at the time of which I am speaking, was one of those highly favoured places which abound with chronicle and great men. The British and American line had run near it during the war; it had, therefore, been the scene of marauding, and been infested with refugees, cow boys,[55] and all kinds of border chivalry. Just sufficient time had elapsed to enable each story teller to dress up his tale with a little becoming fiction, and in the indistinctness of his recollection, to make himself the hero of every exploit.

There was the story of Doffue Martling, a large, blue bearded Dutchman, who had nearly taken a British frigate with an old iron nine pounder from a mud breastwork,[56] only that his gun burst at the sixth discharge. And there was an old gentleman who shall be nameless, being too rich a mynheer[57] to be lightly mentioned, who in the battle of Whiteplains,[58] being an excellent master of defence, parried a musket ball with a small sword, insomuch that he absolutely felt it whiz round the blade, and glance off at the hilt: in proof of which, he was ready at any time to show the sword, with the hilt a little bent. There were several more who had been equally great in the field, not one of whom but was persuaded that he had a considerable hand in bringing the war to a happy termination.

But all these were nothing to the tales of ghosts and apparitions that succeeded. The neighbourhood is rich in legendary treasures of the kind. Local tales and superstitions thrive best in these sheltered, long settled retreats; but are trampled under foot, by the shifting throng that forms the population of most of our country places. Besides, there is no encouragement for ghosts in most of our villages, for they have scarce had time to finish their first nap, and turn themselves in their graves, before their surviving friends have travelled away from the neighbourhood, so that when they turn out of a night to walk the rounds, they have no acquaintance left to call upon. This is perhaps the reason why we so seldom hear of ghosts except in our long established Dutch communities.

The immediate cause, however, of the prevalence of supernatural stories in these parts, was doubtless owing to the vicinity of Sleepy Hollow. There was a contagion in the very air that blew from that haunted region; it breathed forth an atmosphere of dreams and fancies infecting all the land. Several of the Sleepy Hollow people were present at Van Tassel's, and, as usual, were doling out their wild and wonderful legends. Many dismal tales were told about funeral trains, and mournful cries and wailings heard and seen about the great tree where the unfortu-

---

[55] Tory guerillas, active in the Tarrytown area, who aided the British during the American Revolution.

[56] A cannon firing nine-pound cannonballs from a chest-high fortification, built in haste.

[57] "Gentleman" (Dutch).

[58] The British defeated George Washington at the battle of White Plains, near New York City, in 1776.

nate Major André[59] was taken, and which stood in the neighbourhood. Some mention was made also of the woman in white, that haunted the dark glen at Raven Rock, and was often heard to shriek on winter nights before a storm, having perished there in the snow. The chief part of the stories, however, turned upon the favourite spectre of Sleepy Hollow, the headless horseman, who had been heard several times of late, patroling the country; and it was said, tethered his horse nightly among the graves in the church yard.

The sequestered situation of this church seems always to have made it a favourite haunt of troubled spirits. It stands on a knoll, surrounded by locust trees and lofty elms, from among which its decent, whitewashed walls shine modestly forth, like Christian purity, beaming through the shades of retirement. A gentle slope descends from it to a silver sheet of water, bordered by high trees, between which, peeps may be caught at the blue hills of the Hudson. To look upon its grass grown yard, where the sunbeams seem to sleep so quietly, one would think that there at least the dead might rest in peace. On one side of the church extends a wide woody dell, along which raves a large brook among broken rocks and trunks of fallen trees. Over a deep black part of the stream, not far from the church, was formerly thrown a wooden bridge; the road that led to it, and the bridge itself, were thickly shaded by overhanging trees, which cast a gloom about it, even in the day time; but occasioned a fearful darkness at night. Such was one of the favourite haunts of the headless horseman, and the place where he was most frequently encountered. The tale was told of old Brouwer, a most heretical disbeliever in ghosts, how he met the horseman returning from his foray into Sleepy Hollow, and was obliged to get up behind him; how they gallopped over bush and brake, over hill and swamp, until they reached the bridge, when the horseman suddenly turned into a skeleton, threw old Brouwer into the brook, and sprang away over the tree tops with a clap of thunder.

This story was immediately matched by a thrice marvellous adventure of Brom Bones, who made light of the gallopping Hessian as an arrant jockey.[60] He affirmed, that on returning one night from the neighbouring village of Sing-Sing,[61] he had been overtaken by this midnight trooper; that he had offered to race with him for a bowl of punch, and should have won it too, for Daredevil beat the goblin horse all hollow, but just as they came to the church bridge, the Hessian bolted, and vanished in a flash of fire.

All these tales, told in that drowsy under tone with which men talk in the dark, the countenances of the listeners only now and then receiving a casual gleam from the glare of a pipe, sunk deep in the mind of Ichabod. He repaid them in kind with large extracts from his invaluable author, Cotton Mather, and added many very marvellous events that had taken place in his native state of Connecticut, and fearful sights which he had seen in his nightly walks about Sleepy Hollow.

The revel now gradually broke up. The old farmers gathered together their families in their wagons, and were heard for some time rattling along the hollow roads, and over the distant hills. Some of the damsels, mounted on pillions[62] be-

---

[59] Major John André (1751–1780), a British officer involved in Benedict Arnold's attempt to betray West Point. André was tried at George Washington's headquarters as a spy and hanged at Tappan, across the Hudson River from Tarrytown.

[60] A fraud or fake.   [61] Now Ossining, New York.

[62] Small pads behind the saddle for an extra rider.

hind their favourite swains, and their light hearted laughter mingling with the clatter of hoofs, echoed along the silent woodlands, sounding fainter and fainter until they gradually died away—and the late scene of noise and frolick was all silent and deserted. Ichabod only lingered behind, according to the custom of country lovers, to have a tête-a-tête[63] with the heiress; fully convinced that he was now on the high road to success. What passed at this interview I will not pretend to say, for in fact I do not know. Something, however, I fear me, must have gone wrong, for he certainly sallied forth, after no very great interval, with an air quite desolate and chopfallen—Oh these women! these women! Could that girl have been playing off any of her coquettish tricks?—Was her encouragement of the poor pedagogue all a mere sham to secure her conquest of his rival?—Heaven only knows, not I!—Let it suffice to say, Ichabod stole forth with the air of one who had been sacking a hen roost, rather than a fair lady's heart. Without looking to the right or left to notice the scene of rural wealth, on which he had so often gloated, he went straight to the stable, and with several hearty cuffs and kicks, roused his steed most uncourteously from the comfortable quarters in which he was soundly sleeping, dreaming of mountains of corn and oats, and whole valleys of timothy and clover.

It was the very witching time of night[64] that Ichabod, heavy hearted and crest fallen, pursued his travel homewards, along the sides of the lofty hills which rise above Tarry Town, and which he had traversed so cheerily in the afternoon. The hour was as dismal as himself. Far below him the Tappaan Zee spread its dusky and indistinct waste of waters, with here and there the tall mast of a sloop, riding quietly at anchor under the land. In the dead hush of midnight, he could even hear the barking of the watch dog from the opposite shore of the Hudson; but it was so vague and faint as only to give an idea of his distance from this faithful companion of man. Now and then, too, the long drawn crowing of a cock, accidentally awakened, would sound far, far off, from some farm house away among the hills—but it was like a dreaming sound in his ear. No signs of life occurred near him, but occasionally the melancholy chirp of a cricket, or perhaps the guttural twang of a bull frog, from a neighbouring marsh, as if sleeping uncomfortably, and turning suddenly in his bed.

All the stories of ghosts and goblins that he had heard in the afternoon, now came crowding upon his recollection. The night grew darker and darker; the stars seemed to sink deeper in the sky, and driving clouds occasionally hid them from his sight. He had never felt so lonely and dismal. He was, moreover, approaching the very place where many of the scenes of the ghost stories had been laid. In the centre of the road stood an enormous tulip tree, which towered like a giant above all the other trees of the neighbourhood, and formed a kind of land mark. Its limbs were gnarled, and fantastic, large enough to form trunks for ordinary trees, twisting down almost to the earth, and rising again into the air. It was connected with the tragical story of the unfortunate André, who had been taken prisoner hard by; and was universally known by the name of Major André's tree. The common people regarded it with a mixture of respect and superstition, partly out of sympathy for the fate of its ill starred namesake, and partly from the tales of strange sights, and doleful lamentations, told concerning it.

As Ichabod approached this fearful tree, he began to whistle; he thought his

---

[63] "Head-to-head" (French), a private conversation.
[64] An allusion to Shakespeare's *Hamlet* (III. ii. 406): "Tis now the very witching time of night."

whistle was answered: it was but a blast sweeping sharply through the dry branches. As he approached a little nearer, he thought he saw something white, hanging in the midst of the tree: he paused and ceased whistling; but on looking more narrowly, perceived that it was a place where the tree had been scathed by lightning, and the white wood laid bare. Suddenly he heard a groan—his teeth chattered, and his knees smote against the saddle: it was but the rubbing of one huge bough upon another, as they were swayed about by the breeze. He passed the tree in safety, but new perils lay before him.

About two hundred yards from the tree, a small brook crossed the road, and ran into a marshy and thickly wooded glen, known by the name of Wiley's Swamp. A few rough logs, laid side by side, served for a bridge over this stream. On that side of the road where the brook entered the wood, a group of oaks and chestnuts, matted thick with wild grape vines, threw a cavernous gloom over it. To pass this bridge, was the severest trial. It was at this identical spot that the unfortunate André was captured, and under the covert of those chestnuts and vines were the sturdy yeomen concealed who surprised him. This has ever since been considered a haunted stream, and fearful are the feelings of the schoolboy who has to pass it alone after dark.

As he approached the stream, his heart began to thump; he, however, summoned up all his resolution, gave his horse half a score of kicks in the ribs, and attempted to dash briskly across the bridge; but instead of starting forward, the perverse old animal made a lateral movement, and ran broadside against the fence. Ichabod, whose fears increased with the delay, jerked the reins on the other side, and kicked lustily with the contrary foot: it was all in vain; his steed started, it is true, but it was only to plunge to the opposite side of the road into a thicket of brambles and alder bushes. The schoolmaster now bestowed both whip and heel upon the starvelling ribs of old Gunpowder, who dashed forward, snuffling and snorting, but came to a stand just by the bridge with a suddenness that had nearly sent his rider sprawling over his head. Just at this moment a plashy tramp by the side of the bridge caught the sensitive ear of Ichabod. In the dark shadow of the grove, on the margin of the brook, he beheld something huge, misshapen, black and towering. It stirred not, but seemed gathered up in the gloom, like some gigantic monster ready to spring upon the traveller.

The hair of the affrighted pedagogue rose upon his head with terror. What was to be done? To turn and fly was now too late; and besides, what chance was there of escaping ghost or goblin, if such it was, which could ride upon the wings of the wind? Summoning up, therefore, a show of courage, he demanded in stammering accents—"who are you?" He received no reply. He repeated his demand in a still more agitated voice.—Still there was no answer. Once more he cudgelled the sides of the inflexible Gunpowder, and shutting his eyes, broke forth with involuntary fervour into a psalm tune. Just then the shadowy object of alarm put itself in motion, and with a scramble and a bound, stood at once in the middle of the road. Though the night was dark and dismal, yet the form of the unknown might now in some degree be ascertained. He appeared to be a horseman of large dimensions, and mounted on a black horse of powerful frame. He made no offer of molestation or sociability, but kept aloof on one side of the road, jogging along on the blind side of old Gunpowder, who had now got over his fright and waywardness.

Ichabod, who had no relish for this strange midnight companion, and bethought himself of the adventure of Brom Bones with the galloping Hessian, now quickened his steed, in hopes of leaving him behind. The stranger, however, quickened his horse to an equal pace; Ichabod pulled up, and fell into a walk, thinking to lag behind—the other did the same. His heart began to sink within him; he endeavoured to resume his psalm tune, but his parched tongue clove to the roof of his mouth, and he could not utter a stave.[65] There was something in the moody and dogged silence of this pertinacious companion, that was mysterious and appalling. It was soon fearfully accounted for. On mounting arising ground, which brought the figure of his fellow traveller in relief against the sky, gigantic in height, and muffled in a cloak, Ichabod was horror struck, on perceiving that he was headless! but his horror was still more increased, on observing, that the head, which should have rested on his shoulders, was carried before him on the pommel of the saddle! His terror rose to desperation; he rained a shower of kicks and blows upon Gunpowder, hoping, by a sudden movement, to give his companion the slip—but the spectre started full jump with him. Away, then, they dashed, through thick and thin; stones flying, and sparks flashing, at every bound. Ichabod's flimsy garments fluttered in the air, as he stretched his long lank body away over his horse's head, in the eagerness of his flight.

They had now reached the road which turns off to Sleepy Hollow; but Gunpowder, who seemed possessed with a demon, instead of keeping up it, made an opposite turn, and plunged headlong down hill to the left. This road leads through a sandy hollow shaded by trees for about a quarter of a mile, where it crosses the bridge famous in goblin story, and just beyond swells the green knoll on which stands the whitewashed church.

As yet the panic of the steed had given his unskilful rider an apparent advantage in the chace, but just as he had got half way through the hollow, the girths of the saddle gave way, and he felt it slipping from under him; he seized it by the pommel, and endeavoured to hold it firm, but in vain; and had just time to save himself by clasping old Gunpowder round the neck, when the saddle fell to the earth, and he heard it trampled under foot by his pursuer. For a moment the terror of Hans Van Ripper's wrath passed across his mind—for it was his Sunday saddle; but this was no time for petty fears: the goblin was hard on his haunches; and (unskilful rider that he was!) he had much ado to maintain his seat; sometimes slipping on one side, sometimes on another, and sometimes jolted on the high ridge of his horse's back bone, with a violence that he verily feared would cleave him asunder.

An opening in the trees now cheered him with the hopes that the Church Bridge was at hand. The wavering reflection of a silver star in the bosom of the brook told him that he was not mistaken. He saw the walls of the church dimly glaring under the trees beyond. He recollected the place where Brom Bones' ghostly competitor had disappeared. "If I can but reach that bridge," thought Ichabod, "I am safe."[66] Just then he heard the black steed panting and blowing close behind him; he even fancied that he felt his hot breath. Another convulsive kick in the ribs, and old Gunpowder sprung upon the bridge; he thundered over the resounding planks; he gained the opposite side, and now Ichabod cast a look behind to see if his pursuer should vanish, according to rule, in a flash of fire and brimstone. Just then he saw the goblin rising in his stirrups, and in the very act of hurling his head at him.[67]

---

[65] A verse.   [66] According to superstition, ghosts or evil spirits can not cross water.

[67] A chase climaxed by the throwing of a head occurs in the Rübezahl legends of Germany, Irving's source for this scene.

Ichabod endeavoured to dodge the horrible missile, but too late. It encounted his cranium with a tremendous crash—he was tumbled headlong into the dust, and Gunpowder, the black steed, and the goblin rider, passed by like a whirl-wind.———

The next morning the old horse was found without his saddle, and with the bridle under his feet, soberly cropping the grass at his master's gate. Ichabod did not make his appearance at breakfast—dinner hour came, but no Ichabod. The boys assembled at the schoolhouse, and strolled idly about the banks of the brook; but no schoolmaster. Hans Van Ripper now began to feel some uneasiness about the fate of poor Ichabod, and his saddle. An inquiry was set on foot, and after diligent investigation they came upon his traces. In one part of the road leading to the church, was found the saddle trampled in the dirt; the tracks of horses' hoofs deeply dented in the road, and evidently at furious speed, were traced to the bridge, beyond which, on the bank of a broad part of the brook, where the water ran deep and black, was found the hat of the unfortunate Ichabod, and close be-side it a shattered pumpkin.

The brook was searched, but the body of the schoolmaster was not to be dis-covered. Hans Van Ripper, as executor of his estate, examined the bundle which contained all his worldly effects. They consisted of two shirts and a half; two stocks[68] for the neck; a pair or two of worsted stockings; an old pair of corduroy small clothes; a rusty razor; a book of psalm tunes, full of dog's ears;[69] and a broken pitch pipe. As to the books and furniture of the schoolhouse, they be-longed to the community, excepting Cotton Mather's History of Witchcraft, a New England Almanack, and a book of dreams and fortune telling, in which last was a sheet of foolscap much scribbled and blotted, in several fruitless attempts to make a copy of verses in honour of the heiress of Van Tassel. These magic books and the poetic scrawl were forthwith consigned to the flames by Hans Van Ripper, who from that time forward determined to send his children no more to school, observing, that he never knew any good come of this same reading and writing. Whatever money the schoolmaster possessed, and he had received his quarter's pay but a day or two before, he must have had about his person at the time of his disappearance.

The mysterious event caused much speculation at the Church on the following Sunday. Knots of gazers and gossips were collected in the church yard, at the bridge, and at the spot where the hat and pumpkin had been found. The stories of Brouwer, of Bones, and a whole budget of others, were called to mind; and when they had diligently considered them all, and compared them with the symptoms of the present case, they shook their heads, and came to the conclusion, that Ichabod had been carried off by the gallopping Hessian. As he was a bachelor, and in nobody's debt, nobody troubled his head any more about him, the school was removed to a different quarter of the hollow, and another pedagogue reigned in his stead.

It is true, an old farmer, who had been down to New York on a visit several years after, and from whom this account of the ghostly adventure was received, brought home the intelligence that Ichabod Crane was still alive; that he had left the neighbourhood partly through fear of the goblin and Hans Van Ripper, and partly in mortification of having been suddenly dismissed by the heiress; that he had changed his quarters to a distant part of the country; had kept school and

---

[68] Scarves, early versions of the necktie.   [69] With many dog-eared pages, with corners bent.

studied law at the same time; had been admitted to the bar, turned politician, electioneered, written for the newspapers, and finally had been made a Justice of the Ten Pound Court.[70] Brom Bones too, who, shortly after his rival's disappearance, conducted the blooming Katrina in triumph to the altar, was observed to look exceedingly knowing whenever the story of Ichabod was related, and always burst into a hearty laugh at the mention of the pumpkin; which led some to suspect that he knew more about the matter than he chose to tell.

The old country wives, however, who are the best judges of these matters, maintain to this day, that Ichabod was spirited away by supernatural means; and it is a favourite story often told about the neighbourhood round the winter evening fire. The bridge became more than ever an object of superstitious awe, and that may be the reason why the road has been altered of late years, so as to approach the church by the border of the millpond. The schoolhouse being deserted, soon fell to decay, and was reported to be haunted by the ghost of the unfortunate pedagogue; and the plough boy, loitering homeward of a still summer evening, has often fancied his voice at a distance, chanting a melancholy psalm tune among the tranquil solitudes of Sleepy Hollow.

POSTSCRIPT

(Found in the Handwriting of Mr. Knickerbocker)

The preceding Tale is given, almost in the precise words in which I heard it related at a corporation meeting of the ancient city of Manhattoes,[71] at which were present many of its sagest and most illustrious burghers. The narrator was a pleasant, shabby, gentlemanly old fellow, in pepper and salt clothes, with a sadly humourous face, and one whom I strongly suspected of being poor, he made such efforts to be entertaining. When his story was concluded, there was much laughter and approbation, particularly from two or three deputy aldermen, who had been asleep the greater part of the time. There was, however, one tall, dry looking old gentleman, with beetling eye brows, who maintained a grave and rather severe face throughout; now and then folding his arms, inclining his head, and looking down upon the floor, as if turning a doubt over in his mind. He was one of your wary men, who never laugh but upon good grounds—when they have reason and the law on their side. When the mirth of the rest of the company had subsided, and silence was restored, he leaned one arm on the elbow of his chair, and sticking the other akimbo, demanded, with a slight, but exceedingly sage motion of the head, and contraction of the brow, what was the moral of the story, and what it went to prove.

The story teller, who was just putting a glass of wine to his lips, as a refreshment after his toils, paused for a moment, looked at his inquirer with an air of infinite deference, and lowering the glass slowly to the table, observed, that the story was intended most logically to prove,

"That there is no situation in life but has it advantages and pleasures, provided we will but take a joke as we find it:

"That, therefore, he that runs races with goblin troopers, is likely to have rough riding of it:

"Ergo, for a country schoolmaster to be refused the hand of a Dutch heiress, is a certain step to high preferment in the state."

The cautious old gentleman knit his brows tenfold closer after this explanation,

---

[70] A small claims court, trying cases of no more than £10.   [71] New York City.

being sorely puzzled by the ratiocination of the syllogism; while methought the one in pepper and salt eyed him with something of a triumphant leer. At length he observed, that all this was very well, but still he thought the story a little on the extravagant—there were one or two points on which he had his doubts.

"Faith, sir," replied the story teller, "as to that matter, I don't believe one half of it myself."

D.K.

1820

James Fenimore Cooper
(1789–1851)

A year after James Cooper's birth in Burlington, New Jersey, in 1789, his parents Elizabeth Fenimore and Judge William Cooper moved their family to what would become the family estate in a town that was later named for them, Cooperstown, New York. The novelist's imposing father had acquired vast tracts of land in the area of Lake Otsego after the American Revolution. After a period of private tutoring, at age fourteen Cooper entered Yale University but was expelled in 1806 for committing a series of pranks and for unruly behavior. His father then sent him to sea, where Cooper served first on a merchant ship and later as a midshipman in the U.S. Navy from 1808 to 1811. Following his departure from the navy, Cooper married Susan De Lancy, daughter of a wealthy New York family. Soon afterward the death of his father left him an inheritance of more than $50,000, which allowed him to live as a country gentleman in Cooperstown and Scarsdale, New York. He lived well; by 1819 his inheritance had not only dwindled, but he had incurred heavy debts and he already had five children to care for (two more were yet to come).

According to his daughter Susan in her journal *Rural Hours* (1850), Cooper began writing by chance when his wife laughed at his claim that he could improve on the "newly imported novel" he was reading aloud to her. Thus, the man "who disliked writing even a letter" undertook *Precaution* (1820), an imitative drawing-room novel set in England, and began a prodigious career that encompassed thirty-two novels; four volumes of comments on Europe, *Gleanings in Europe* (1837–1838); a history of the American Navy (1839); and several books of social criticism. Dissatisfied with his efforts in *Precaution*, Cooper turned to the subject of the Revolutionary War for *The Spy* (1821), a novel praised both in the United States and in Europe. Next came *The Pilot* (1823), the first of Cooper's eleven sea novels, written to show that his knowledge of the sea surpassed that of Sir Walter Scott in *The Pirate* (1822). In the same year Cooper finished *The Pioneers* (1823), in which he relied on his memories of Lake Otsego and Cooperstown. It was the first of the five "Leather-Stocking Tales," the novels for which Cooper is best known, and it introduced (as an aging hunter) the figure of Natty Bumppo, or Leather-Stocking, who moves West to get away from society because he is "made for the wilderness." In the popular *Last of the Mohicans* (1826), Cooper made Natty younger, taking him back to the colonial wars of the 1750s as an intrepid scout who witnesses the death of the heroic Uncas—and thus the symbolic extinction of a Native-American tribe. In *The Prairie*, published in 1827, an aged Leather-Stocking dies, succumbing not simply to his infirmities but to the destructive

Leatherstocking Meets the Law *(1832), by John Quidor.*

thrust of civilization. At this point (as his letters show), Cooper saw *The Prairie* as the final novel in the Leather-Stocking series.

Once again financially secure, James Fenimore Cooper (he added his mother's maiden name at this time) took his family abroad in 1826 and toured several countries in Europe, but he spent most of his seven-year sojourn in Lyons, France. As a reply to English critics of American society, he published the fictional letters *Notions of the Americans* in 1828. Cooper continued writing fiction, notably the provocative *Wept of Wish-ton-Wish* in 1829 but also a trilogy—consisting of *The Bravo* (1831), *The Heidenmauer* (1832), and *The Headsman* (1833)—that undercuts the glamor of a feudal past and suggests the moral superiority of democracy.

When Cooper returned to the United States in 1833, he did not find the country he had remembered—or had imagined as its spokesman. What he did find from his evolving conservative perspective was a society leveled by mediocrity and democratic excess, manifestations of Jacksonian America that troubled his patrician spirit. Cooper's writing in these years expressed the depth of his disappointment and alienated a public that had once applauded his work: the homiletic tone of *A Letter to His Countrymen* (1834), the crude satire of *The Monikins* (1835), and the lofty assurance of *The American Democrat* (1838) spell out his differences with American society. The novels *Homeward Bound* (1838) and *Home As Found* (1838) cast the same strictures into narrative form. When a character in *Home As Found* laments "that the days of the Leather-Stocking are over," we sense Cooper's frustration with the present as well as his nostalgia for a time and a vision that had brought him confidence and success.

Cooper resurrected Leather-Stocking, first in *The Pathfinder* (1840), then in the final novel of the series, *The Deerslayer* (1841), which presents Natty Bumppo at his youngest and most innocent. The setting of *The Deerslayer* is once again Lake Otsego (here called Lake Glimmerglass)—but years before the burgeoning village of Templeton in *The Pioneers* comes to occupy and transform the same locale. An undefiled wilderness provides the mood of the novel. Cooper is dreaming back to origins in *The Deerslayer*, putting Natty in a time prior to the civilization he can no longer escape by going West.

In the 1840s Cooper was once again at odds with critics and with society: arguing, bickering, engaged in an astonishing number of lawsuits. Yet, he continued to produce novels during this decade, among them the disturbing *Wyandotte* (1843), which deals with the outbreak of the Revolutionary War in upstate New York, and the trilogy that follows three generations of the Littlepage family to the "Anti-Rent War" of the 1840s—*Satanstoe* (1845), *The Chainbearer* (1845), and *The Redskins* (1846). He died in Cooperstown in 1851 and was eulogized by William Cullen Bryant.

His letters suggest that Cooper was both ambitious as a writer and at times strangely unaware of the significance of his work. The man who thought of naming the final novel of the Leather-Stocking series "Judith and Hetty: Or, the Girls of the Glimmerglass" rather than *The Deerslayer* could hardly have seen the meaning of that narrative in the way we have come to see it. Still, with a ponderousness that made him an easy target for Mark Twain in "Fenimore Cooper's Literary Offences" (1895), Cooper wrote novels that engaged American history, sea narratives that commanded the respect of such writers as Herman Melville and Joseph Conrad, and, above all, the Leather-Stocking Tales, at once prophetic and nostalgic, which tell us of the world we had before we made it into the world we have.

Suggested Readings: *The Letters and Journals of James Fenimore Cooper*, 6 vols., ed. J. F. Beard, 1969–1968. *The Writings of James Fenimore Cooper*, ed. J. F. Beard et al., 1980– . H. N. Smith, *Virgin Land: The American West as Symbol and Myth*, 1950. J. P. McWilliams, Jr., *Political Justice in a Republic*, 1972. B. Nevius, *Cooper's Landscapes: An Essay on the Picturesque Vision*, 1976. H. D. Peck, *A World by Itself*, 1977. S. Railton, *Fenimore Cooper: A Study of His Life and Imagination*, 1981. W. Franklin, *The New World of James Fenimore Cooper*, 1982. W. P. Kelly, *Plotting America's Past: Fenimore Cooper and the Leather-Stocking Tales*, 1983. J. D. Wallace, *Early Cooper and His Audience*, 1986.

Texts Used: *Notions of the Americans: Picked Up by a Travelling Bachelor*, Vol. II, 1828. *The Deerslayer: Or, the First War-Path* (Darley edition), 1870.

from NOTIONS OF THE AMERICANS*

[*Literature in the United States: Obstacles and Prospects*]

TO THE ABBATE GIROMACHI, ETC., ETC., FLORENCE

Washington,———

You ask me to write freely on the subject of the literature and the arts of the United States. The subjects are so meagre as to render it a task that would require no small portion of the talents necessary to figure in either, in order to render them

---

* *Notions of the Americans: Picked Up by A Travelling Bachelor* is a fictitious travel book consisting of letters supposedly written from the United States by a young English count to members of a club of bachelors, among them the Italian abbot Giromachi in Florence. The book was intended to counteract the biased descriptions of American society written by European travelers in the early nine-

of interest. Still, as the request has come in so urgent a form, I shall endeavour to oblige you.

The Americans have been placed, as respects moral and intellectual advancement, different from all other infant nations. They have never been without the wants of civilization, nor have they ever been entirely without the means of a supply. Thus pictures, and books, and statuary, and every thing else which appertains to elegant life, have always been known to them in an abundance, and of a quality exactly proportioned to their cost. Books, being the cheapest, and the nation having great leisure and prodigious zest for information, are not only the most common, as you will readily suppose, but they are probably more common than among any other people. I scarcely remember ever to have entered an American dwelling, however humble, without finding fewer or more books. As they form the most essential division of the subject, not only on account of their greater frequency, but on account of their far greater importance, I shall give them the first notice in this letter.

Unlike the progress of the two professions in the countries of our hemisphere, in America the printer came into existence before the author. Reprints of English works gave the first employment to the press. Then came almanacks, psalmbooks, religious tracts, sermons, journals, political essays, and even rude attempts at poetry. All these preceded the revolution. The first journal was established in Boston at the commencement of the last century.[1] There are several original polemical works of great originality and power that belong to the same period. I do not know that more learning and talents existed at that early day in the states of New England than in Virginia, Maryland and the Carolinas, but there was certainly a stronger desire to exhibit them.

* * *

It is quite obvious, that, so far as taste and forms alone are concerned, the literature of England and that of America must be fashioned after the same models. The authors, previously to the revolution, are common property, and it is quite idle to say that the American has not just as good a right to claim Milton, and Shakspeare, and all the old masters of the language, for his countrymen, as an Englishman. The Americans having continued to cultivate, and to cultivate extensively, an acquaintance with the writers of the mother country, since the separation, it is evident they must have kept pace with the trifling changes of the day. The only peculiarity that can, or ought to be expected in their literature, is that which is connected with the promulgation of their distinctive political opinions. They have not been remiss in this duty, as any one may see, who chooses to examine their books. But we will devote a few minutes to a more minute account of the actual condition of American literature.

* * *

The literature of the United States has, indeed, [two] powerful obstacles to conquer before (to use a mercantile expression) it can ever enter the markets of its

---

teenth century (by 1825 almost forty such books had appeared). The count writes of such matters as elections, Congress, New York City, slavery, and General Marquis de Lafayette's visit to the United States in 1824 (which Cooper had applauded warmly).

[1] Actually, in 1690, but the Boston *Publick Occurrences* disappeared in less than a week.

own country on terms of perfect equality with that of England. Solitary and individual works of genius may, indeed, be occasionally brought to light, under the impulses of the high feeling which has conceived them; but, I fear, a good, wholesome, profitable, and continued pecuniary support is the applause that talent most craves. The fact, that an American publisher can get an English work without money, must, for a few years longer (unless legislative protection shall be extended to their own authors), have a tendency to repress a national literature. No man will pay a writer for an epic, a tragedy, a sonnet, a history, or a romance, when he can get a work of equal merit for nothing.[2] I have conversed with those who are conversant on the subject, and I confess, I have been astonished at the information they imparted.

A capital American publisher has assured me that there are not a dozen writers in this country, whose works he should feel confidence in publishing at all, while he reprints hundreds of English books without the least hesitation. This preference is by no means so much owing to any difference in merit, as to the fact that, when the price of the original author is to be added to the uniform hazard which accompanies all literary speculations, the risk becomes too great. . . .

* * *

The second obstacle against which American literature has to contend is in the poverty of materials. There is scarcely an ore which contributes to the wealth of the author, that is found, here, in veins as rich as in Europe. There are no annals for the historian; no follies (beyond the most vulgar and common place) for the satirist; no manners for the dramatist; no obscure fictions for the writer of romance; no gross and hardy offences against decorum for the moralist; nor any of the rich artificial auxiliaries of poetry. The weakest hand can extract a spark from the flint, but it would baffle the strength of a giant to attempt kindling a flame with a pudding stone.[3] I very well know there are theorists who assume that the society and institutions of this country are, or ought to be, particularly favourable to novelties and variety. But the experience of one month, in these States, is sufficient to show any observant man the falsity of their position. The effect of a promiscuous assemblage any where, is to create a standard of deportment; and great liberty permits every one to aim at its attainment. I have never seen a nation so much alike in my life, as the people of the United States, and what is more, they are not only like each other, but they are remarkably like that which common sense tells them they ought to resemble. No doubt, traits of character that are a little peculiar, without, however, being either very poetical, or very rich, are to be found in remote districts; but they are rare, and not always happy exceptions. In short, it is not possible to conceive a state of society in which more of the attributes of plain good sense, or fewer of the artificial absurdities of life, are to be found, than here. There is no costume for the peasant, (there is scarcely a peasant at all,) no wig for the judge, no baton for the general, no diadem for the chief magistrate. The darkest ages of their history are illuminated by the light of truth; the utmost efforts of their chivalry are limited by the laws of God; and even the deeds of their sages and heroes are to be sung in a language that would differ but little from a version of

---

[2] Because of the lack of an international copyright law before 1891, American publishers could reprint English books with no payment to the authors, whereas they had to pay royalties to American writers.

[3] Rock too sandy to be used as flintstone.

the ten commandments. However useful and respectable all this may be in actual life, it indicates but one direction to the man of genius.

It is very true there are a few young poets now living in this country, who have known how to extract sweets from even these wholesome, but scentless native plants. They have, however, been compelled to seek their inspiration in the universal laws of nature, and they have succeeded, precisely in proportion as they have been most general in their application. Among these gifted young men, there is one (Halleck[4]) who is remarkable for an exquisite vein of ironical wit, mingled with a fine, poetical, and, frequently, a lofty expression. This gentleman commenced his career as a satirist in one of the journals of New York. Heaven knows, his materials were none of the richest; and yet the melody of his verse, the quaintness and force of his comparisons, and the exceeding humour of his strong points, brought him instantly into notice. He then attempted a general satire, by giving the history of the early days of a *belle*.[5] He was again successful, though every body, at least every body of any talent, felt that he wrote in leading-strings.[6] But he happened, shortly after the appearance of the little volume just named (Fanny), to visit England. Here his spirit was properly excited, and, probably on a rainy day, he was induced to try his hand at a *jeu d'esprit*,[7] in the mother country. The result was one of the finest semi-heroic ironical descriptions to be found in the English language.[8] This simple fact, in itself, proves the truth of a great deal of what I have just been writing, since it shews the effect a superiority of material can produce on the efforts of a man of true genius.

Notwithstanding the difficulties of the subject, talent has even done more than in the instance of Mr. Halleck. I could mention several other young poets of this country of rare merit. By mentioning Bryant, Percival, and Sprague,[9] I shall direct your attention to the names of those whose works would be most likely to give you pleasure. Unfortunately they are not yet known in Italian, but I think even you would not turn in distaste from the task of translation which the best of their effusions will invite.

The next, though certainly an inferior branch of imaginative writing, is fictitious composition. From the facts just named, you cannot expect that the novelists, or romance writers of the United States, should be very successful. The same reason will be likely, for a long time to come, to repress the ardour of dramatic genius. Still, tales and plays are no novelties in the literature of this country. Of the former, there are many as old as soon after the revolution; and a vast number have been published within the last five years. One of their authors of romance, who curbed his talents by as few allusions as possible to actual society, is distin-

---

[4] Fitz-Greene Halleck (1790–1867), a New York poet and secretary to the wealthy John Jacob Astor (1763–1848).

[5] "A pretty woman" (French); the "satire" Cooper mentions is *Fanny* (1819), a burlesque poem that satirizes New York society.

[6] He was led or helped along by another poet: *Fanny* was judged to be imitative of Lord Byron's *Don Juan*, which also appeared in 1819.

[7] "A play of the wit" (French): a witty piece of writing.

[8] Cooper's note: "This little *morceau* [piece] of pleasant irony is called Alnwick Castle." Cooper is generous in his estimate of *Alnwick Castle* (1827), which owes much to the example of Sir Walter Scott (1771–1832).

[9] William Cullen Bryant (1794–1878); James Gates Percival (1795–1856), who translated poems from Hungarian, Serbian, and Russian and wrote the play *Zamor* (1815) and the long poem "Prometheus" (1821); and Charles Sprague (1791–1875), a banker and occasional poet who delivered his *Shakespeare Ode* at the Boston Theater in 1823.

guished for power and comprehensiveness of thought. I remember to have read one of his books (Wieland) when a boy, and I take it to be a never-failing evidence of genius, that, amid a thousand similar pictures which have succeeded, the images it has left still stand distinct and prominent in my recollection. This author (Mr. Brockden Brown[10]) enjoys a high reputation among his countrymen, whose opinions are sufficiently impartial, since he flattered no particular prejudice of the nation in any of his works.

The reputation of Irving[11] is well known to you. He is an author distinguished for a quality (humour) that has been denied his countrymen; and his merit is the more rare, that it has been shewn in a state of society so cold and so restrained. Besides these writers, there are many others of a similar character, who enjoy a greater or less degree of favour in their own country. The works of two or three have even been translated (into French) in Europe, and a great many are reprinted in England. Though every writer of fiction in America has to contend against the difficulties I have named, there is a certain interest in the novelty of the subject, which is not without its charm. I think, however, it will be found that they have all been successful, or the reverse, just as they have drawn warily, or freely, on the distinctive habits of their own country. I now speak of their success purely as writers of romance. It certainly would be possible for an American to give a description of the manners of his own country, in a book that he might choose to call a romance, which should be read, because the world is curious on the subject, but which would certainly never be read for that nearly indefinable poetical interest which attaches itself to a description of manners less bald and uniform. All the attempts to blend history with romance in America, have been comparative failures, (and perhaps fortunately,) since the subjects are too familiar to be treated with the freedom that the imagination absolutely requires. Some of the descriptions of the progress of society on the borders, have had a rather better success, since there is a positive, though no very poetical, novelty in the subject; but, on the whole, the books which have been best received, are those in which the authors have trusted most to their own conceptions of character, and to qualities that are common to the rest of the world and to human nature. This fact, if its truth be admitted, will serve to prove that the American writer must seek his renown in the exhibition of qualities that are general, while he is confessedly compelled to limit his observations to a state of society that has a wonderful tendency not only to repress passion, but to equalize humours.

The Americans have always been prolific writers on polemics and politics. Their sermons and fourth of July orations are numberless. Their historians, without being very classical or very profound, are remarkable for truth and good sense. There is not, perhaps, in the language a closer reasoner in metaphysics than Edwards;[12] and their theological writers find great favour among the sectarians of their respective schools.

The stage of the United States is decidedly English. Both plays and players, with few exceptions, are imported. Theatres are numerous, and they are to be found in places where a traveller would little expect to meet them. Of course, they are of all sizes and of every degree of decoration and architectural beauty known

[10] Charles Brockden Brown (1771–1810), author of *Wieland: Or, the Transformation* (1798).

[11] Washington Irving (1783–1859), well known as a writer by the time Cooper's *Notions* appeared. Cooper's assessment is brief, possibly because of his conviction that Irving had become Europeanized during his years abroad.

[12] Jonathan Edwards (1703–1758), an American theologian and philosopher.

in Europe, below the very highest. The facade of the principal theatre in Philadelphia is a chaste specimen in marble, of the Ionic,[13] if my memory is correct. In New York, there are two theatres about as large as the Théatre Français[14] (in the interior), and not much inferior in embellishments. Besides these, there is a very pretty little theatre, where lighter pieces are performed, and another with a vast stage for melo-dramas. There are also one or two other places of dramatic representation in this city, in which horses and men contend for the bays.

The Americans pay well for dramatic talent. Cooke,[15] the greatest English tragedian of our age, died on this side of the Atlantic; and there are few players of eminence in the mother country who are not tempted, at some time or other, to cross the ocean. Shakspeare, is of course, the great author of America, as he is of England, and I think he is quite as well relished here as there. In point of taste, if all the rest of the world be any thing against England, that of America is the best, since it unquestionably approaches nearest to that of the continent of Europe. Nearly one half of the theatrical taste of the English is condemned by their own judgments, since the stage is not much supported by those who have had an opportunity of seeing any other. You will be apt to ask me how it happens, then, that the American taste is better? Because the people, being less exaggerated in their habits, are less disposed to tolerate caricatures, and because the theatres are not yet sufficiently numerous (though that hour is near) to admit of a representation that shall not be subject to the control of a certain degree of intelligence. I have heard an English player complain that he never saw such a dull audience as the one before which he had just been exhibiting; and I heard the same audience complain that they never listened to such dull jokes. Now, there was talent enough in both parties; but the one had formed his taste in a coarse school, and the others had formed theirs under the dominion of common sense. Independently of this peculiarity, there is a vast deal of acquired, travelled taste in this country. English tragedy, and high English comedy, both of which, you know, are excellent, never fail here, if well played; that is, they never fail under the usual limits of all amusement. One will cloy of sweets. But the fact of the taste and judgment of these people, in theatrical exhibitions, is proved by the number of their good theatres, compared to their population.

Of dramatic writers there are none, or next to none. The remarks I have made in respect to novels apply with double force to this species of composition. A witty and successful American comedy could only proceed from extraordinary talent. There would be less difficulty, certainly, with a tragedy; but still, there is rather too much foreign competition, and too much domestic employment in other pursuits, to invite genius to so doubtful an enterprise. The very baldness of ordinary American life is in deadly hostility to scenic representation. The character must be supported solely by its intrinsic power. The judge, the footman, the clown, the lawyer, the belle, or the beau, can receive no great assistance from dress. Melo-dramas, except the scene should be laid in the woods, are out of the question. It would be necessary to seek the great clock, which is to strike the portentous twelve blows, in the nearest church; a vaulted passage would degenerate into a cellar; and, as for ghosts, the country was discovered, since their visita-

---

[13] The Ionic style of architecture, which featured spiral-like ornamentation at the top of columns.
[14] The national theater in Paris.
[15] George Frederick Cooke (1756–1811), an English Shakespearean actor.

tions have ceased.[16] The smallest departure from the incidents of ordinary life would do violence to every man's experience; and, as already mentioned, the passions which belong to human nature must be delineated, in America, subject to the influence of that despot—common sense.

Notwithstanding the overwhelming influence of British publications, and all the difficulties I have named, original books are getting to be numerous in the United States. The impulses of talent and intelligence are bearing down a thousand obstacles. I think the new works will increase rapidly, and that they are destined to produce a powerful influence on the world. We will pursue this subject another time.—Adieu.

1828

PREFACE TO THE LEATHER-STOCKING TALES*

This series of Stories, which has obtained the name of "The Leather-Stocking Tales," has been written in a very desultory and inartificial manner. The order in which the several books appeared was essentially different from that in which they would have been presented to the world, had the regular course of their incidents been consulted. In the Pioneers, the first of the series written, the Leather-Stocking is represented as already old, and driven from his early haunts in the forest, by the sound of the axe, and the smoke of the settler. "The Last of the Mohicans," the next book in the order of publication, carried the readers back to a much earlier period in the history of our hero, representing him as middle-aged, and in the fullest vigor of manhood. In the Prairie, his career terminates, and he is laid in his grave. There, it was originally the intention to leave him, in the expectation that, as in the case of the human mass, he would soon be forgotten. But a latent regard for this character induced the author to resuscitate him in "The Pathfinder," a book that was not long after succeeded by "The Deerslayer," thus completing the series as it now exists.

While the five books that have been written were originally published in the order just mentioned, that of the incidents, insomuch as they are connected with the career of their principal character, is, as has been stated, very different. Taking the life of the Leather-Stocking as a guide, "The Deerslayer" should have been the opening book, for in that work he is seen just emerging into manhood; to be succeeded by "The Last of the Mohicans," "The Pathfinder," "The Pioneers," and "The Prairie." This arrangement embraces the order of events, though far from being that in which the books at first appeared. "The Pioneers" was published in 1822;[1] "The Deerslayer" in 1841; making the interval between them nineteen years. Whether these progressive years have had a tendency to lessen the value of the last-named book, by lessening the native fire of its author, or of adding some-

---

[16] After their visitations had ceased.

* This preface was written in 1850 for an edition of the five "Leather-Stocking Tales," which were published between 1823 and 1841, about the life of Leather-Stocking (or Natty Bumppo or Deerslayer).

[1] Actually, February 1823.

what in the way of improved taste and a more matured judgment, is for others to decide.

If anything from the pen of the writer of these romances is at all to outlive himself, it is, unquestionably, the series of "The Leather-Stocking Tales." To say this, is not to predict a very lasting reputation for the series itself, but simply to express the belief it will outlast any, or all, of the works from the same hand.

It is undeniable that the desultory manner in which "The Leather-Stocking Tales" were written, has, in a measure, impaired their harmony, and otherwise lessened their interest. This is proved by the fate of the two books last published, though probably the two most worthy an enlightened and cultivated reader's notice. If the facts could be ascertained, it is probable the result would show that of all those (in America, in particular) who have read the three first books of the series, not one in ten has a knowledge of the existence even of the two last. Several causes have tended to produce this result. The long interval of time between the appearance of "The Prairie" and that of "The Pathfinder," was itself a reason why the later books of the series should be overlooked. There was no longer novelty to attract attention, and the interest was materially impaired by the manner in which events were necessarily anticipated, in laying the last of the series first before the world. With the generation that is now coming on the stage this fault will be partially removed by the edition contained in the present work, in which the several tales will be arranged solely in reference to their connexion with each other.

The author has often been asked if he had any original in his mind, for the character of Leather-Stocking. In a physical sense, different individuals known to the writer in early life, certainly presented themselves as models, through his recollections; but in a moral sense this man of the forest is purely a creation. The idea of delineating a character that possessed little of civilization but its highest principles as they are exhibited in the uneducated, and all of savage life that is not incompatible with these great rules of conduct, is perhaps natural to the situation in which Natty was placed. He is too proud of his origin to sink into the condition of the wild Indian, and too much a man of the woods not to imbibe as much as was at all desirable, from his friends and companions. In a moral point of view it was the intention to illustrate the effect of seed scattered by the way side. To use his own language, his "gifts" were "white gifts," and he was not disposed to bring on them discredit. On the other hand, removed from nearly all the temptations of civilized life, placed in the best associations of that which is deemed savage, and favorably disposed by nature to improve such advantages, it appeared to the writer that his hero was a fit subject to represent the better qualities of both conditions, without pushing either to extremes.

There was no violent stretch of the imagination, perhaps, in supposing one of civilized associations in childhood, retaining many of his earliest lessons amid the scenes of the forest. Had these early impressions, however, not been sustained by continued, though casual connexion with men of his own color, if not of his own caste, all our information goes to show he would soon have lost every trace of his origin. It is believed that sufficient attention was paid to the particular circumstances in which this individual was placed, to justify the picture of his qualities that has been drawn. The Delawares early attracted the attention of the missionaries, and were a tribe unusually influenced by their precepts and example. In many instances they became Christians, and cases occurred in which their subsequent lives gave proof of the efficacy of the great moral changes that had taken place within them.

A leading character in a work of fiction has a fair right to the aid which can be obtained from a poetical view of the subject. It is in this view, rather than in one more strictly circumstantial, that Leather-Stocking has been drawn. The imagination has no great task in portraying to itself a being removed from the every-day inducements to err, which abound in civilized life, while he retains the best and simplest of his early impressions; who sees God in the forest; hears him in the winds; bows to him in the firmament that o'ercanopies all; submits to his sway in a humble belief of his justice and mercy; in a word, a being who finds the impress of the Deity in all the works of nature, without any of the blots produced by the expedients, and passion, and mistakes of man. This is the most that has been attempted in the character of Leather-Stocking. Had this been done without any of the drawbacks of humanity, the picture would have been, in all probability, more pleasing than just. In order to preserve the *vrai-semblable*,[2] therefore, traits derived from the prejudices, tastes, and even the weaknesses of his youth, have been mixed up with these higher qualities and longings, in a way, it is hoped, to represent a reasonable picture of human nature, without offering to the spectator a "monster of goodness."

It has been objected to these books that they give a more favorable picture of the red man than he deserves. The writer apprehends that much of this objection arises from the habits of those who have made it. One of his critics, on the appearance of the first work in which Indian character was portrayed, objected that its "characters were Indians of the school of Heckewelder,[3] rather than of the school of nature." These words quite probably contain the substance of the true answer to the objection. Heckewelder was an ardent, benevolent missionary, bent on the good of the red man, and seeing in him one who had the soul, reason, and characteristics of a fellow-being. The critic is understood to have been a distinguished agent of the government, one very familiar with Indians, as they are seen at the councils to treat for the sale of their lands, where little or none of their domestic qualities come in play, and where, indeed, their evil passions are known to have the fullest scope. As just would it be to draw conclusions of the general state of American society from the scenes of the capital, as to suppose that the negotiating of one of these treaties is a fair picture of Indian life.

It is the privilege of all writers of fiction, more particularly when their works aspire to the elevation of romances, to present the *beau-idéal*[4] of their characters to the reader. This it is which constitutes poetry, and to suppose that the red man is to be represented only in the squalid misery or in the degraded moral state that certainly more or less belongs to his condition, is, we apprehend, taking a very narrow view of an author's privileges. Such criticism would have deprived the world of even Homer.

1850

---

[2] "True semblance" (French): verisimilitude or realism.

[3] John Gottlieb Heckewelder (1743–1823), an early Moravian missionary among the Native Americans of Ohio; Cooper's information about Native-American customs came primarily from Heckewelder's *Account of the History, Manners, and Customs of the Indian Nations Who Once Inhabited Pennsylvania and the Neighboring States* (1819). Cooper quotes Lewis Cass (1782–1866), a governor of the Michigan territory; Cass's assessment of Cooper appeared in the *North American Review*, January 1826.

[4] "Ideal of beauty" (French).

from   THE DEERSLAYER*

from   CHAPTER VII

[Deerslayer Is Named Hawkeye by His Dying Foe]

When about a hundred yards from the shore,[1] Deerslayer rose in the canoe, gave three or four vigorous strokes with the paddle, sufficient of themselves to impel the bark to land, and then quickly laying aside the instrument of labor, he seized that of war. He was in the very act of raising the rifle, when a sharp report was followed by the buzz of a bullet that passed so near his body, as to cause him involuntarily to start. The next instant Deerslayer staggered, and fell his whole length in the bottom of the canoe. A yell—it came from a single voice—followed, and an Indian leaped from the bushes upon the open area of the point, bounding towards the canoe. This was the moment the young man desired. He rose on the instant, and levelled his own rifle at his uncovered foe; but his finger hesitated about pulling the trigger on one whom he held at such a disadvantage. This little delay, probably, saved the life of the Indian, who bounded back into the cover as swiftly as he had broken out of it. In the meantime Deerslayer had been swiftly approaching the land, and his own canoe reached the point just as his enemy disappeared. As its movements had not been directed, it touched the shore a few yards from the other boat;[2] and though the rifle of his foe had to be loaded, there was not time to secure his prize, and to carry it beyond danger, before he would be exposed to another shot. Under the circumstances, therefore, he did not pause an instant, but dashed into the woods and sought a cover.

On the immediate point there was a small open area, partly in native grass, and partly beach, but a dense fringe of bushes lined its upper side. This narrow belt of dwarf vegetation passed, one issued immediately into the high and gloomy vaults of the forest. The land was tolerably level for a few hundred feet, and then it rose precipitously in a mountain-side. The trees were tall, large, and so free from under-brush, that they resembled vast columns, irregularly scattered, upholding a dome of leaves. Although they stood tolerably close together, for their ages and size, the eye could penetrate to considerable distances; and bodies of men, even, might have engaged beneath their cover, with concert and intelligence.

Deerslayer knew that his adversary must be employed in re-loading, unless he had fled. The former proved to be the case, for the young man had no sooner placed himself behind a tree, than he caught a glimpse of the arm of the Indian,

---

* The title of *The Deerslayer* (1841) refers to Cooper's frontiersman and skilled hunter Nathaniel or Natty Bumppo, often called Leather-Stocking because of his characteristic apparel in the forest. Here the youthful Deerslayer is fired upon by a Native-American enemy during a colonial war between England and France, engages in one-to-one combat, and is named "Hawkeye" by the foe he conquers—the first human being he has killed. Cooper's frontiersman is called Hawkeye throughout the *The Last of the Mohicans,* published fifteen years earlier. In *The Deerslayer* Cooper goes back in time, presenting a very young Natty Bumppo.

[1] Deerslayer is guiding his canoe across Lake Glimmerglass (Lake Otsego, near what is now Cooperstown, New York). Although the novel is set in the mid-1750s, Cooper manages to suggest a pristine locale, "a world by itself."

[2] This "other boat" belongs to Deerslayer's acquaintances.

his body being concealed by an oak, in the very act of forcing the leathered bullet home. Nothing would have been easier than to spring forward, and decide the affair by a close assault on his unprepared foe; but every feeling of Deerslayer revolted at such a step, although his own life had just been attempted from a cover. He was yet unpractised in the ruthless expedients of savage warfare, of which he knew nothing except by tradition and theory, and it struck him as an unfair advantage to assail an unarmed foe. His color had heightened, his eye frowned, his lips were compressed, and all his energies were collected and ready; but, instead of advancing to fire, he dropped his rifle to the usual position of a sportsman in readiness to catch his aim, and muttered to himself, unconscious that he was speaking—

"No, no—that may be red-skin warfare, but it's not a Christian's gifts.[3] Let the miscreant charge, and then we'll take it out like men; for the canoe he *must* not, and *shall* not have. No, no; let him have time to load, and God will take care of the right!"

All this time the Indian had been so intent on his own movements, that he was even ignorant that his enemy was in the wood. His only apprehension was, that the canoe would be recovered and carried away before he might be in readiness to prevent it. He had sought the cover from habit, but was within a few feet of the fringe of bushes, and could be at the margin of the forest in readiness to fire in a moment. The distance between him and his enemy was about fifty yards, and the trees were so arranged by nature that the line of sight was not interrupted, except by the particular trees behind which each party stood.

His rifle was no sooner loaded, than the savage glanced around him, and advanced incautiously as regarded the real, but stealthily as respected the fancied position of his enemy, until he was fairly exposed. Then Deerslayer stepped from behind his own cover, and hailed him.

"This-a-way, red-skin; this-a-way, if you're looking for me," he called out. "I'm young in war, but not so young as to stand on an open beach to be shot down like an owl, by daylight. It rests on yourself whether it's peace or war atween us; for my gifts are white gifts, and I'm not one of them that thinks it valiant to slay human mortals, singly, in the woods."

The savage was a good deal startled by this sudden discovery of the danger he ran. He had a little knowledge of English, however, and caught the drift of the other's meaning. He was also too well schooled to betray alarm, but, dropping the butt of his rifle to the earth, with an air of confidence, he made a gesture of lofty courtesy. All this was done with the ease and self-possession of one accustomed to consider no man his superior. In the midst of this consummate acting, however, the volcano that raged within caused his eyes to glare, and his nostrils to dilate, like those of some wild beast that is suddenly prevented from taking the fatal leap.

"Two canoe," he said, in the deep guttural tones of his race, holding up the number of fingers he mentioned, by way of preventing mistakes; "one for you— one for me."

"No, no, Mingo,[4] that will never do. You own neither; and neither shall you have, as long as I can prevent it. I know it's war atween your people and mine,

---

[3] Throughout the five Leather-Stocking novels Natty Bumppo distinguishes between red and white "gifts" or codes of ethics and of warfare. (White codes are assumed to be Christian.) Thus, a Native American may scalp a conquered foe but a white man may not.

[4] An Iroquois or Sioux brave.

but that's no reason why human mortals should slay each other, like savage creatur's that meet in the woods; go your way, then, and leave me to go mine. The world is large enough for us both; and when we meet fairly in battle, why, the Lord will order the fate of each of us."

"Good!" exclaimed the Indian; "my brother missionary—great talk; all about Manitou."[5]

"Not so—not so, warrior. I'm not good enough for the Moravians,[6] and am too good for most of the other vagabonds that preach about in the woods. No, no, I'm only a hunter, as yet, though afore the peace is made, 'tis like enough there'll be occasion to strike a blow at some of your people. Still, I wish it to be done in fair fight, and not in a quarrel about the ownership of a miserable canoe."

"Good! My brother very young—but he very wise. Little warrior—great talker. Chief, sometimes, in council."

"I don't know this, nor do I say it, Injin," returned Deerslayer, coloring a little at the ill-concealed sarcasm of the other's manner; "I look forward to a life in the woods, and I only hope it may be a peaceable one. All young men must go on the war-path, when there's occasion, but war isn't needfully massacre. I've seen enough of the last, this very night, to know that Providence frowns on it; and I now invite you to go your own way, while I go mine; and hope that we may part fri'nds."

"Good! My brother has two scalp—grey hair under t'other. Old wisdom—young tongue."

Here the savage advanced with confidence, his hand extended, his face smiling, and his whole bearing denoting amity and respect. Deerslayer met his offered friendship in a proper spirit, and they shook hands cordially, each endeavoring to assure the other of his sincerity and desire to be at peace.

"All have his own," said the Indian; "my canoe, mine; your canoe, your'n. Go look; if your'n, you keep; if mine, I keep."

"That's just, red-skin; though you must be wrong in thinking the canoe your property. Howsever, seein' is believin', and we'll go down to the shore, where you may look with your own eyes; for it's likely you'll object to trustin' altogether to mine."

The Indian uttered his favorite exclamation of "good!" and then they walked side by side, towards the shore. There was no apparent distrust in the manner of either, the Indian moving in advance, as if he wished to show his companion that he did not fear turning his back to him. As they reached the open ground, the former pointed towards Deerslayer's boat, and said emphatically—

"No mine—pale-face canoe. *This* red-man's. No want other man's canoe—want his own."

"You're wrong, red-skin, you're altogether wrong. This canoe was left in old Hutter's keeping, and is his'n according to all law, red or white, till its owner comes to claim it. Here's the seats and the stitching of the bark to speak for themselves. No man ever know'd an Injin to turn off such work."

"Good! My brother little ole—big wisdom. Injin no made him. White man's work."

---

[5] Among various native tribes, an august power or deity that controls the forces of nature, synonomous with "God."

[6] A Protestant sect of missionaries who preached to Native Americans; Natty Bumppo learned Christian principles from them.

"I'm glad you think so, for holding out to the contrary might have made ill blood atween us; every one having a right to take possession of his own. I'll just shove the canoe out of reach of dispute at once, as the quickest way of settling difficulties."

While Deerslayer was speaking, he put a foot against the end of the light boat, and giving a vigorous shove, he sent it out into the lake a hundred feet or more, where, taking the true current, it would necessarily float past the point, and be in no further danger of coming ashore. The savage started at this ready and decided expedient, and his companion saw that he cast a hurried and fierce glance at his own canoe, or that which contained the paddles. The change of manner, however, was but momentary, and then the Iroquois resumed his air of friendliness, and a smile of satisfaction.

"Good!" he repeated, with stronger emphasis than ever. "Young head, old mind. Know how to settle quarrel. Farewell, brother. He go to house in water—muskrat house[7]—Injin go to camp; tell chiefs no find canoe."

Deerslayer was not sorry to hear this proposal, for he felt anxious to join the females, and he took the offered hand of the Indian very willingly. The parting words were friendly, and, while the red-man walked calmly towards the wood, with the rifle in the hollow of his arm, without once looking back in uneasiness or distrust, the white man moved towards the remaining canoe, carrying his piece in the same pacific manner, it is true, but keeping his eyes fastened on the movements of the other. This distrust, however, seemed to be altogether uncalled for, and, as if ashamed to have entertained it, the young man averted his look, and stepped carelessly up to his boat. Here he began to push the canoe from the shore, and to make his other preparations for departing. He might have been thus employed a minute, when, happening to turn his face towards the land, his quick and certain eye told him, at a glance, the imminent jeopardy in which his life was placed. The black, ferocious eyes of the savage were glancing on him, like those of the crouching tiger, through a small opening in the bushes, and the muzzle of his rifle seemed already to be opening in a line with his own body.

Then, indeed, the long practice of Deerslayer, as a hunter, did him good service. Accustomed to fire with the deer on the bound, and often when the precise position of the animal's body had in a manner to be guessed at, he used the same expedients here. To cock and poise his rifle were the acts of a single moment and a single motion; then, aiming almost without sighting, he fired into the bushes where he knew a body ought to be, in order to sustain the appalling countenance which alone was visible. There was not time to raise the piece any higher, or to take a more deliberate aim. So rapid were his movements, that both parties discharged their pieces at the same instant, the concussions mingling in one report. The mountains, indeed, gave back but a single echo. Deerslayer dropped his piece, and stood, with head erect, steady as one of the pines in the calm of a June morning, watching the result; while the savage gave the yell that has become historical for its appalling influence, leaped through the bushes and came bounding across the open ground, flourishing a tomahawk. Still Deerslayer moved not, but stood with his unloaded rifle fallen against his shoulders, while, with a hunter's habits, his hands were mechanically feeling for the powder-horn and charger. When about forty feet from his enemy, the savage hurled his keen weapon; but it

---

[7] The houseboat of Floating Tom Hutter, a muskrat trapper who lives with his daughters, Hetty and Judith, in the middle of the lake.

was with an eye so vacant, and a hand so unsteady and feeble, that the young man caught it by the handle as it was flying past him. At that instant the Indian staggered and fell his whole length on the ground.

"I know'd it—I know'd it!" exclaimed Deerslayer, who was already preparing to force a fresh bullet into his rifle; "I know'd it must come to this, as soon as I had got the range from the creatur's eyes. A man sights suddenly, and fires quick when his own life's in danger; yes, I know'd it would come to this. I was about the hundredth part of a second too quick for him, or it might have been bad for me! The riptyle's bullet has just grazed my side—but, say what you will for or ag'in em, a red-skin is by no means as sartain with powder and ball as a white man. Their gifts don't seem to lie that-a-way. Even Chingachgook,[8] great as he is in other matters, isn't downright deadly with the rifle."

By this time the piece was reloaded, and Deerslayer, after tossing the tomahawk into the canoe, advanced to his victim, and stood over him, leaning on his rifle, in melancholy attention. It was the first instance in which he had seen a man fall in battle—it was the first fellow-creature against whom he had ever seriously raised his own hand. The sensations were novel; and regret, with the freshness of our better feelings, mingled with his triumph. The Indian was not dead, though shot directly through the body. He lay on his back motionless, but his eyes, now full of consciousness, watched each action of his victor—as the fallen bird regards the fowler—jealous of every movement. The man probably expected the fatal blow which was to precede the loss of his scalp; or perhaps he anticipated that this latter act of cruelty would precede his death. Deerslayer read his thoughts; and he found a melancholy satisfaction in relieving the apprehensions of the helpless savage.

"No, no, red-skin," he said; "you've nothing more to fear from me. I am of a Christian stock, and scalping is not of my gifts. I'll just make sartain of your rifle, and then come back and do you what sarvice I can. Though here I can't stay much longer, as the crack of three rifles will be apt to bring some of your devils down upon me."

The close of this was said in a sort of a soliloquy, as the young man went in quest of the fallen rifle. The piece was found where its owner had dropped it, and was immediately put into the canoe. Laying his own rifle at its side, Deerslayer then returned and stood over the Indian again.

"All inmity atween you and me's at an ind, red-skin," he said; "and you may set your heart at rest on the score of the scalp, or any further injury. My gifts are white, as I've told you; and I hope my conduct will be white also!"

Could looks have conveyed all they meant, it is probable Deerslayer's innocent vanity on the subject of color would have been rebuked a little; but he comprehended the gratitude that was expressed in the eyes of the dying savage, without in the least detecting the bitter sarcasm that struggled with the better feeling.

"Water!" ejaculated the thirsty and unfortunate creature; "give poor Injin water."

"Aye, water you shall have, if you drink the lake dry. I'll just carry you down to it, that you may take your fill. This is the way, they tell me, with all wounded people—water is their greatest comfort and delight."

So saying, Deerslayer raised the Indian in his arms, and carried him to the lake.

---

[8] Natty Bumppo's lifelong companion, a Mohican chief; he dies at an advancaed age in *The Pioneers* (1823).

Here he first helped him to take an attitude in which he could appease his burning thirst; after which he seated himself on a stone, and took the head of his wounded adversary in his own lap, and endeavored to soothe his anguish in the best manner he could.

* * *

. . . With the high innate courtesy that so often distinguishes the Indian warrior before he becomes corrupted by too much intercourse with the worst class of the white men, he endeavored to express his thankfulness for the other's good intentions, and to let him understand that they were appreciated.

"Good!" he repeated, for this was an English word much used by the savages—"good—young head; young *heart,* too, *Old* heart tough; no shed tear. Hear Indian when he die, and no want to lie—what he call him?"

"Deerslayer is the name I bear now, though the Delawares[9] have said that when I get back from this war-path, I shall have a more manly title, provided I can 'arn one."

"That good name for boy—poor name for warrior. He get better quick. No fear *there*"—the savage had strength sufficient, under the strong excitement he felt, to raise a hand and tap the young man on his breast—"eye sartain—finger lightning—aim, death—great warrior soon. No Deerslayer—Hawkeye—Hawkeye—Hawkeye. Shake hand."

Deerslayer—or Hawkeye, as the youth was then first named, for in after years he bore the appellation throughout all that region—Deerslayer took the hand of the savage, whose last breath was drawn in that attitude, gazing in admiration at the countenance of a stranger, who had shown so much readiness, skill, and firmness, in a scene that was equally trying and novel. . . .

1841

Edgar Allan Poe
(1809–1849)

Edgar Allan Poe's inventive brilliance, commitment to craft, and genius at transforming gothic formulas into surreal structures of the imagination are well-known aspects of his achievement as a writer. Yet, any such catalogue of praise yields only a partial portrait of this embattled virtuoso, whose chronic instability and self-destructive behavior consistently threatened to overshadow his literary achievement. Poe was and remains a complex figure, best understood by the very contradictions that made his life and career so difficult.

Edgar Poe was born in Boston to traveling actors in 1809, and his earliest years prefigured the lack of moorings in his later life: not long after Poe's birth his father, David Poe, Jr., deserted the family, and in 1811 his mother, Elizabeth Arnold Hopkins, died while on

---

[9] The Delaware Indians fought with the British in the colonial wars, the Iroquois with the French. The Mohicans were part of the large Delaware nation.

tour in Richmond, Virginia. Poe was taken in by the family of Frances and John Allan, a prosperous Richmond merchant, and eventually baptized Edgar Allan Poe by the man he then regarded as his benefactor. When Poe was seventeen he entered the University of Virginia and did well in his study of French and Latin. His fellow students knew him as an aspiring poet and a heavy drinker. He also had a reputation for gambling—not well, apparently, for he ran up gambling debts to the total of $2000. When John Allan refused to pay these debts, Poe left Virginia in anger, went to Boston, and enlisted in the army as Edgar A. Perry. In 1827, during his army service, he arranged for the publication of his first slender volume of verse, *Tamerlane and Other Poems*. Two years later, following his release from the army, he published a second volume, *Al Aaraaf, Tamerlane, and Minor Poems*.

Poe's complaints that Allan would not help him in times of distress have led many to see Allan as an insensitive and mean-spirited man of wealth who would not lend support to a foster child and aspiring artist. To read Poe's letters, however, is to see how the writer might have alienated Allan (or anyone) with his whining, self-dramatic, and condemnatory appeals for money. Repeatedly, Poe promises that he will never again ask for money; repeatedly he does ask, spends with astonishing speed what money may have been sent him, and says that Allan will be responsible for his destruction and death if further funds are not forthcoming. There is no doubt that throughout much of his life Poe was in need of money and that Allan refused to give it. But Allan's role in Poe's life must have been exasperating. It is no doubt easier to appreciate Poe from the distance of a century and a half.

The 1830s introduced Poe to a dizzying array of jobs and events. After a temporary reconciliation in 1830, Allan helped him secure an appointment to West Point. But during Poe's eight months at the academy it became clear that the man and the institution were not made for each other. A series of minor infractions brought about his dismissal from the academy in 1831. Undaunted by his severance, Poe turned to the writing of fiction and in 1832 published five stories in the Philadelphia *Saturday Courier*. The following year his story "MS. Found in a Bottle" won the $100 first prize in a short-story contest run by a Baltimore magazine. Also in 1833 he was named editor of the *Southern Literary Messenger* in Richmond, a magazine in which he published poems, stories, and over eighty reviews. Three years later, when he was twenty-seven, he married his thirteen-year-old cousin Virginia Clemm. Shortly after they married Poe left the *Southern Literary Messenger*, having had one of his many bitter arguments with magazine publishers over his drinking, his authoritarian editorial style, and the hatchetlike quality of his reviews.

During the 1830s and early 1840s Poe also published much fiction, including *The Narrative of Arthur Gordon Pym* (1838), "Ligeia" (1838), "The Fall of the House of Usher" (1839), and a collection of stories, *Tales of the Grotesque and Arabesque* (1840). Yet, Poe earned little money from these works we have come to prize (his collection of stories sold fewer than 750 copies). Despite a developing pattern of difficult behavior, he was able to obtain positions of responsibility on magazines: he became co-editor of *Burton's Gentleman's Magazine* in 1839, only to be discharged after several months because of arguments with the publisher over his reviews and his drinking. Soon afterward he became the editor of *Graham's Magazine* and wrote such tales as "A Descent Into the Maelstrom" (1841) and "The Masque of the Red Death" (1842) while he held that position.

Although Poe continued to write throughout the 1840s, he remained deeply in the grasp of poverty. Not even the popularity of "The Raven" (1844) and an increasing reputation as a writer could bring him financial security. In 1845 he became the editor of the *Broadway Journal* and wrote a series of articles suggesting that Henry Wadsworth Longfellow (already revered in New England) was a plagiarist—perhaps to enhance the circulation of the

Journal, perhaps also because of an evolving paranoia that led Poe to wonder (quite incorrectly) if Nathaniel Hawthorne had not plagiarized from Poe's work. But the *Broadway Journal* failed in 1846, Poe's young wife died of tuberculosis in 1847, and Poe found it difficult to maintain professional or personal equilibrium after that time—although his provocative effort in cosmology, *Eureka: A Prose Poem* (1848), displays a strange combination of elation, erudition, and comedy. Toward the end of his life Poe returned to Richmond and became engaged to Elmira Royster Shelton, a widow who had been a neighbor of the Allans and the sweetheart of Poe's early years. During two tranquil months in Richmond he wrote "Annabel Lee" (posthumously published in 1849), gave readings of his poetry, and joined the Sons of Temperance in a final effort to change his habits. On his way to Philadelphia to receive payment for some freelance editing he had done, however, he stopped in Baltimore, disappeared mysteriously for several days, and was found unconscious on the street. Four days later, on October 7, 1849, he died.

There is no doubt that Poe's life presents a melodramatic and vexed scenario. He seemed to court literary feuds and to resent the prominence and assurance of the New England literary establishment. In a review he sneered, for example, at the "so-called poetry of the so-called Transcendentalists" and attacked numerous writers as literary hacks. In return, he was called "the jingle man" by Emerson because of the sing-song quality of his poetry and was described memorably by James Russell Lowell in "A Fable for Critics" (1848) as "three-fifths . . . genius and two-fifths sheer fudge."

The range and quality of Poe's achievement is undeniable. Not only did he perfect the modern form of the short story, but also he established many of the conventions of the modern detective story with his character C. Auguste Dupin—shrewd, logical, eccentric—who appears in "The Murders in the Rue Morgue" (1841), "The Mystery of Marie Roget" (1842–1843), and "The Purloined Letter" (1845). Additionally, in the midst of an emerging American romanticism to which he contributed both manner and substance, Poe advocated the idea of the poet as craftsman, one who constructs and shapes a poem and for

A portrait of Elmira Royster Shelton, Edgar Allan Poe's childhood sweetheart, reportedly sketched by Poe.

whom the form is integral to the meaning. That idea recommended Poe to the French symbolists and anticipated the disciplined poetics of some modernist poets in the twentieth century. More idiosyncratic was Poe's assertion that to preserve a necessary unity of effect a poem should be capable of being read at one sitting. The logical consequence, as Poe took pains to say, is that there is no such thing as a long poem. No matter the traditional praise heaped upon epic poems: Homer's *Iliad*, Poe boldly contended, proceeds from an imperfect sense of poetry; John Milton's *Paradise Lost* (1667) is a series of short poems with what is essentially prose sandwiched between them.

Poe's fiction thrives on wordplay, puzzles, and anagrams. The secret of "The Gold-Bug" (a prize-winning story first published in 1843 in a Philadelphia magazine) depends on a cryptograph and reflects an interest in deciphering codes, which brought Poe to write the essay "Cryptography," published in *Graham's Magazine* in 1841. "The Balloon Hoax," written as a news story in the New York *Sun* in 1844, details the supposed journey of a "Steering Balloon" from England to South Carolina. Even "The Philosophy of Composition" (1846), which purports to explain how Poe wrote "The Raven," may well be an after-the-fact parade of gamesmanship. A more bizarre type of playing can be seen in Poe's tales that defy consequences: the narrator of "Loss of Breath" (1835), for example, suffers a fractured skull and a hanging, yet relates his misadventures in the tone of one who is having a bad day. In "A Predicament" (1838) the case is even more extreme—the narrator has her head cut off by the minute hand of a clock and goes on talking with studied nonchalance. What Poe gives us in these tales is not the unreliable narrator we have come to know and mistrust but the indestructible narrator, a creature alien to our expectations yet confidential and even presumptuous in disclosure.

In a society that prized the domestic and valued the didactic for its moral utility, Poe became militantly antididactic, mischievously antidomestic. The narrator of "The Black Cat" (1843) presents the garish violence of his tale as "a series of mere household events." Fortunato in "The Cask of Amontillado" (1846) exults in the memory of revenge taken fifty years before—although some readers, uneasy at the amoral calisthenics of this tale, see the narrative as confessional and not celebratory. The point is that Poe was part of the society in which he wrote: he knew its values and pieties and inverted them for the complex purposes of his fiction.

Perhaps most importantly, in some of his best-known work Poe explores the intricate and baffling nature of the perverse. Characteristically, he uses first-person narrators who bid us watch as they destroy the "I"—the "self" that is glorified in the work of Ralph Waldo Emerson, of Henry David Thoreau, and of Walt Whitman, the *self* that is driven in Poe's fiction by the "unfathomable longing of the soul *to vex itself*—to offer violence to its own nature" (as we read in "The Black Cat"). The narrator of "The Tell-Tale Heart" (1843) is obsessed by the "eye" of the victim in that tale; without passion or object, he decides "to take the life of the old man, and thus rid myself of the eye forever." Given Poe's fondness for puns, it is an easy move to substitute an "eye" for an "I" in this context. Given Poe's addiction to anagrams it is tempting to see that the letters of "perverse" can also spell "preserve" and thereby understand the profound interrelationship between perversity and preservation in the world of Poe's fiction.

Poe's choice of Rufus Wilmot Griswold, a prominent journalist and editor, as his literary executor is a curious one. Griswold wrote the first biography of Poe, a malicious and distorted portrait that left the study of Poe's life in disarray for more than a century. As twentieth-century scholars have discovered, Griswold also changed the text of some Poe letters that had been left in his charge. Clearly, Griswold felt a deep antipathy of which Poe seems to have been unaware. Yet, the consequence suggests a reprise on the relationship between perversity and preservation: if it was (unconsciously) perverse for Poe to name Griswold as his literary executor, the act has helped to preserve his reputation at the expense of Griswold's. If Griswold is known at all, he is known as the biographer who falsified the facts and the documents of Poe's life. The dimensions of Poe's achievement, however, have become secure. Unstable and histrionic as he may have been as an editor, erratic as he may have become as a writer, Poe nonetheless produced haunted narratives that are triumphs of psychological exploration, mood poems that yearn beyond the boundaries of the finite world, and critical ideas that proclaim the enduring importance of form in the creation of art.

Suggested Readings: *The Complete Works of Edgar Allan Poe*, 17 vols., ed. J. A. Harrison, 1902. *The Letters of Edgar Allan Poe*, 2 vols., ed. J. W. Ostrom, 1966. *Collected Works*, 3 vols., ed. T. O. Mabbott et al., 1969–1978. *The Short Fiction of Edgar Allan Poe: An Annotated Edition*, ed. S. Levine and S. Levine, 1976. C. Baudelaire, *Baudelaire on Poe*, 1852. A. H. Quinn, *Edgar Allan Poe: A Critical Biography*, 1966. M. L. Allen, *Poe and the British Magazine Tradition*, 1969. D. Hoffman, *Poe, Poe, Poe, Poe, Poe, Poe, Poe*, 1973. G. R. Thompson, *Poe's Fiction: Romantic Irony in the Gothic Tales*, 1973. J. Dayan, *Fables of Mind: An Inquiry into Poe's Fiction*, 1987. J. G. Kennedy, *Poe, Death, and the Life of Writing*, 1987. D. Thomas and D. K. Jackson, eds., *The Poe Log: A Documentary Life of Edgar Allan Poe, 1809–1849*, 1987. J. P. Muller and W. J. Richardson, eds., *The Purloined Poe: Lacan, Derrida, and Psychoanalytic Reading*, 1988. M. J. S. Williams, *A World of Words: Language and Displacement in the Fiction of Edgar Allan Poe*, 1988.

Texts Used: "Ligeia": *The Complete Works*, Vol. I. "The Fall of the House of Usher": *The Complete Works*, Vol. III. "The Tell-Tale Heart" and "The Black Cat": *The Complete Works*, Vol. V. "The Cask of Amontillado": *The Complete Works*, Vol. VI. All poems: *The Complete Works*, Vol. VII. Review of *Twice-Told Tales*: *The Complete Works*, Vol. XI. "The Philosophy of Composition": *The Complete Works*, Vol. XIV.

LIGEIA*

And the will therein lieth, which dieth not. Who knoweth the mysteries of the will, with its vigor? For God is but a great will pervading all things by nature of its intentness. Man doth not yield himself to the angels, nor unto death utterly, save only through the weakness of his feeble will.

Joseph Glanvill[1]

I cannot, for my soul, remember how, when, or even precisely where, I first became acquainted with the lady Ligeia. Long years have since elapsed, and my memory is feeble through much suffering. Or, perhaps, I cannot *now* bring these points to mind, because, in truth, the character of my beloved, her rare learning, her singular yet placid cast of beauty, and the thrilling and enthralling eloquence of her low musical language, made their way into my heart by paces so steadily and stealthily progressive that they have been unnoticed and unknown. Yet I believe that I met her first and most frequently in some large, old, decaying city near the Rhine. Of her family—I have surely heard her speak. That it is of a remotely ancient date cannot be doubted. Ligeia! Ligeia! Buried in studies of a nature more

---

* First published in *The American Museum* in 1838. Poe may have found the name "Ligeia" in Book IV of Virgil's *Georgics* (37?–30? B.C.), which is concerned with beekeeping, or in John Milton's *Comus* (1634), a masque, or theatrical entertainment.

[1] No such statement can be found in the work of Joseph Glanvill (1638–1680), a Cambridge Platonist, or seventeenth-century English religious philosopher. Poe probably made up the quotation for the purposes of his story.

than all else adapted to deaden impressions of the outward world, it is by that
sweet word alone—by Ligeia—that I bring before mine eyes in fancy the image
of her who is no more. And now, while I write, a recollection flashes upon me
that I have *never known* the paternal name of her who was my friend and my
betrothed, and who became the partner of my studies, and finally the wife of my
bosom. Was it a playful charge on the part of my Ligeia? or was it a test of my
strength of affection, that I should institute no inquiries upon this point ? or was it
rather a caprice of my own—a wildly romantic offering on the shrine of the most
passionate devotion? I but indistinctly recall the fact itself—what wonder that I
have utterly forgotten the circumstances which originated or attended it? And,
indeed, if ever that spirit which is entitled *Romance*—if ever she, the wan and the
misty-winged *Ashtophet*[2] of idolatrous Egypt, presided, as they tell, over marriages ill-omened, then most surely she presided over mine.

There is one dear topic, however, on which my memory fails me not. It is the
person of Ligeia. In stature she was tall, somewhat slender, and, in her latter
days, even emaciated. I would in vain attempt to portray the majesty, the quiet
ease, of her demeanor, or the incomprehensible lightness and elasticity of her
footfall. She came and departed as a shadow. I was never made aware of her
entrance into my closed study save by the dear music of her low sweet voice, as
she placed her marble hand upon my shoulder. In beauty of face no maiden ever
equalled her. It was the radiance of an opium-dream—an airy and spirit-lifting
vision more wildly divine than the phantasies which hovered about the slumbering
souls of the daughters of Delos.[3] Yet her features were not of that regular mould
which we have been falsely taught to worship in the classical labors of the heathen. "There is no exquisite beauty," says Bacon, Lord Verulam, speaking truly
of all the forms and *genera* of beauty, "without some *strangeness* in the proportion."[4] Yet, although I saw that the features of Ligeia were not of a classic regularity—although I perceived that her loveliness was indeed "exquisite," and felt that
there was much of "strangeness" pervading it, yet I have tried in vain to detect the
irregularity and to trace home my own perception of "the strange." I examined the
contour of the lofty and pale forehead—it was faultless—how cold indeed that
word when applied to a majesty so divine!—the skin rivalling the purest ivory, the
commanding extent and repose, the gentle prominence of the regions above the
temples; and then the raven-black, the glossy, the luxuriant and naturally-curling
tresses, setting forth the full force of the Homeric epithet, "hyacinthine!"[5] I looked
at the delicate outlines of the nose—and nowhere but in the graceful medallions of
the Hebrews had I beheld a similar perfection. There were the same luxurious
smoothness of surface, the same scarcely perceptible tendency to the aquiline,[6] the
same harmoniously curved nostrils speaking the free spirit. I regarded the sweet
mouth. Here was indeed the triumph of all things heavenly—the magnificent turn
of the short upper lip—the soft, voluptuous slumber of the under—the dimples
which sported, and the color which spoke—the teeth glancing back, with a brilliancy almost startling, every ray of the holy light which fell upon them in her
serene and placid, yet most exultingly radiant of all smiles. I scrutinized the for-

---

[2] Ashtoreth, a Phoenecian goddess of fertility.

[3] A small island in the Aegean Sea; according to Greek myth, the birthplace of Apollo, the god of
music and the arts, and of Artemis, goddess of the hunt; and the site of great festivals in their honor.

[4] From the essay "Of Beauty" (1625) by Francis Bacon (1561–1626), Baron Verulam; Poe uses "exquisite" in place of Bacon's "excellent."

[5] In Homer's *Odyssey*, Book VI, the curly hair of Odysseus is likened to a hyacinth.   [6] Curved.

mation of the chin—and here, too, I found the gentleness of breadth, the softness and the majesty, the fullness and the spirituality, of the Greek—the contour which the god Apollo revealed but in a dream, to Cleomenes,[7] the son of the Athenian. And then I peered into the large eyes of Ligeia.

For eyes we have no models in the remotely antique. It might have been, too, that in these eyes of my beloved lay the secret to which Lord Verulam alludes. They were, I must believe, far larger than the ordinary eyes of our own race. They were even fuller than the fullest of the gazelle eyes of the tribe of the valley of Nourjahad.[8] Yet it was only at intervals—in moments of intense excitement—that this peculiarity became more than slightly noticeable in Ligeia. And at such moments was her beauty—in my heated fancy thus it appeared perhaps—the beauty of beings either above or apart from the earth—the beauty of the fabulous Houri of the Turk.[9] The hue of the orbs was the most brilliant of black, and, far over them, hung jetty lashes of great length. The brows, slightly irregular in outline, had the same tint. The "strangeness," however, which I found in the eyes, was of a nature distinct from the formation, or the color, or the brilliancy of the features, and must, after all, be referred to the *expression*. Ah, word of no meaning! behind whose vast latitude of mere sound we intrench our ignorance of so much of the spiritual. The expression of the eyes of Ligeia! How for long hours have I pondered upon it! How have I, through the whole of a midsummer night, struggled to fathom it! What was it—that something more profound than the well of Democritus[10]—which lay far within the pupils of my beloved? What *was* it? I was possessed with a passion to discover. Those eyes! those large, those shining, those divine orbs! they became to me twin stars of Leda,[11] and I to them devoutest of astrologers.

There is no point, among the many incomprehensible anomalies of the science of mind, more thrillingly exciting than the fact—never, I believe, noticed in the schools—that, in our endeavors to recall to memory something long forgotten, we often find ourselves *upon the very verge* of remembrance, without being able, in the end, to remember. And thus how frequently, in my intense scrutiny of Ligeia's eyes, have I felt approaching the full knowledge of their expression—felt it approaching—yet not quite be mine—and so at length entirely depart! And (strange, oh strangest mystery of all!) I found, in the commonest objects of the universe, a circle of analogies to that expression. I mean to say that, subsequently to the period when Ligeia's beauty passed into my spirit, there dwelling as in a shrine, I derived, from many existences in the material world, a sentiment such as I felt always aroused within me by her large and luminous orbs. Yet not the more could I define that sentiment, or analyze, or even steadily view it. I recognized it, let me repeat, sometimes in the survey of a rapidly-growing vine—in the contemplation of a moth, a butterfly, a chrysalis, a stream of running water. I have felt it in the

---

[7] An Athenian artist who reputedly sculpted the original statue of the Venus de Medici in the third century B.C.

[8] From *The History of Nourjahad* (1767), an Oriental romance by the English writer Frances Sheridan (1724–1766).

[9] Beautiful maidens who wait in Paradise for deserving Mohammedans, from *The History of Nourjahad*.

[10] A fifth century B.C. Greek philosopher who characteristically laughed at the follies of mankind (according to the Roman satirist Juvenal), and said that "Truth lies at the bottom of a well."

[11] According to Greek myth, the rape of Leda by Zeus resulted in twin sons, Castor and Pollux, who were eventually reincarnated as stars in the constellation Gemini.

ocean; in the falling of a meteor. I have felt it in the glances of unusually aged people. And there are one or two stars in heaven—(one especially, a star of the sixth magnitude, double and changeable, to be found near the large star in Lyra[12]) in a telescopic scrutiny of which I have been made aware of the feeling. I have been filled with it by certain sounds from stringed instruments, and not unfrequently by passages from books. Among innumerable other instances, I well remember something in a volume of Joseph Glanvill, which (perhaps merely from its quaintness—who shall say?) never failed to inspire me with the sentiment;— "And the will therein lieth, which dieth not. Who knoweth the mysteries of the will, with its vigor? For God is but a great will pervading all things by nature of its intentness. Man doth not yield him to the angels, nor unto death utterly, save only through the weakness of his feeble will."

Length of years, and subsequent reflection, have enabled me to trace, indeed, some remote connection between this passage in the English moralist and a portion of the character of Ligeia. An *intensity* in thought, action, or speech, was possibly, in her, a result, or at least an index, of that gigantic volition which, during our long intercourse, failed to give other and more immediate evidence of its existence. Of all the women whom I have ever known, she, the outwardly calm, the ever-placid Ligeia, was the most violently a prey to the tumultuous vultures of stern passion. And of such passion I could form no estimate, save by the miraculous expansion of those eyes which at once so delighted and appalled me—by the almost magical melody, modulation, distinctness and placidity of her very low voice—and by the fierce energy (rendered doubly effective by contrast with her manner of utterance) of the wild words which she habitually uttered.

I have spoken of the learning of Ligeia: it was immense—such as I have never known in woman. In the classical tongues was she deeply proficient, and as far as my own acquaintance extended in regard to the modern dialects of Europe, I have never known her at fault. Indeed upon any theme of the most admired, because simply the most abstruse of the boasted erudition of the academy, have I *ever* found Ligeia at fault? How singularly—how thrillingly, this one point in the nature of my wife has forced itself, at this late period only, upon my attention! I said her knowledge was such as I have never known in woman—but where breathes the man who has traversed, and successfully, *all* the wide areas of moral, physical, and mathematical science? I saw not then what I now clearly perceive, that the acquisitions of Ligeia were gigantic, were astounding; yet I was sufficiently aware of her infinite supremacy to resign myself, with a child-like confidence, to her guidance through the chaotic world of metaphysical investigation at which I was most busily occupied during the earlier years of our marriage. With how vast a triumph—with how vivid a delight—with how much of all that is ethereal in hope—did I *feel*, as she bent over me in studies but little sought—but less known—that delicious vista by slow degrees expanding before me, down whose long, gorgeous, and all untrodden path, I might at length pass onward to the goal of a wisdom too divinely precious not to be forbidden!

How poignant, then, must have been the grief with which, after some years, I beheld my well-grounded expectations take wings to themselves and fly away! Without Ligeia I was but as a child groping benighted. Her presence, her readings alone, rendered vividly luminous the many mysteries of the transcendentalism in

---

[12] The "large star" in the constellation Lyra is Vega, or Alpha Lyrae.

which we were immersed. Wanting the radiant lustre of her eyes, letters, lambent and golden, grew duller than Saturnian lead.[13] And now those eyes shone less and less frequently upon the pages over which I pored. Ligeia grew ill. The wild eyes blazed with a too—too glorious effulgence; the pale fingers became of the transparent waxen hue of the grave, and the blue veins upon the lofty forehead swelled and sank impetuously with the tides of the most gentle emotion. I saw that she must die—and I struggled desperately in spirit with the grim Azrael.[14] And the struggles of the passionate wife were, to my astonishment, even more energetic than my own. There had been much in her stern nature to impress me with the belief that, to her, death would have come without its terrors;—but not so. Words are impotent to convey any just idea of the fierceness of resistance with which she wrestled with the Shadow.[15] I groaned in anguish at the pitiable spectacle. I would have soothed—I would have reasoned; but, in the intensity of her wild desire for life,—for life—*but* for life—solace and reason were alike the uttermost of folly. Yet not until the last instance, amid the most convulsive writhings of her fierce spirit, was shaken the external placidity of her demeanor. Her voice grew more gentle—grew more low—yet I would not wish to dwell upon the wild meaning of the quietly uttered words. My brain reeled as I hearkened, entranced, to a melody more than mortal—to assumptions and aspirations which mortality had never before known.

That she loved me I should not have doubted; and I might have been easily aware that, in a bosom such as hers, love would have reigned no ordinary passion. But in death only, was I fully impressed with the strength of her affection. For long hours, detaining my hand, would she pour out before me the overflowing of a heart whose more than passionate devotion amounted to idolatry. How had I deserved to be so blessed by such confessions?—how had I deserved to be so cursed with the removal of my beloved in the hour of her making them? But upon this subject I cannot bear to dilate. Let me say only, that in Ligeia's more than womanly abandonment to a love, alas! all unmerited, all unworthily bestowed, I at length recognized the principle of her longing with so wildly earnest a desire for the life which was now fleeing so rapidly away. It is this wild longing—it is this eager vehemence of desire for life—*but* for life—that I have no power to portray—no utterance capable of expressing.

At high noon of the night in which she departed, beckoning me, peremptorily, to her side, she bade me repeat certain verses composed by herself not many days before. I obeyed her.—They were these:

> Lo! 't is a gala night
>   Within the lonesome latter years!
> An angel throng, bewinged, bedight[16]
>   In veils, and drowned in tears,
> Sit in a theatre, to see
>   A play of hopes and fears,
> While the orchestra breathes fitfully
>   The music of the spheres.[17]

[13] In alchemy Saturn is the term for lead; to astrologers, the planet Saturn causes gloominess and sluggishness.
[14] The Angel of Death in both Jewish and Moslem legend.   [15] Death.   [16] Adorned, arrayed.
[17] Melodies produced by the revolution of stars and planets, according to ancient astronomers.

Mimes, in the form of God on high,
   Mutter and mumble low,
And hither and thither fly—
   Mere puppets they, who come and go
At bidding of vast formless things
   That shift the scenery to and fro,
Flapping from out their Condor wings
   Invisible Wo!

That motley drama!—oh, be sure
   It shall not be forgot!
With its Phantom chased forever more,
   By a crowd that seize it not,
Through a circle that ever returneth in
   To the self-same spot,
And much of Madness and more of Sin,
   And Horror the soul of the plot.

But see, amid the mimic rout,
   A crawling shape intrude!
A blood-red thing that writes from out
   The scenic solitude!
It writhes!—it writhes!—with mortal pangs
   The mimes become its food,
And the seraphs sob at vermin fangs
   In human gore imbued.

Out—out are the lights—out all!
   And over each quivering form,
The curtain, a funeral pall,
   Comes down with the rush of a storm,
And the angels, all pallid and wan,
   Uprising, unveiling, affirm
That the play is the tragedy, "Man,"
   And its hero the Conqueror Worm.[18]

"O God!" half shrieked Ligeia, leaping to her feet and extending her arms aloft with a spasmodic movement, as I made an end of these lines—"O God! O Divine Father!—shall these things be undeviatingly so?—shall this Conqueror be not once conquered? Are we not part and parcel in Thee? Who—who knoweth the mysteries of the will with its vigor? Man doth not yield him to the angels, *nor unto death utterly,* save only through the weakness of his feeble will."

And now, as if exhausted with emotion, she suffered her white arms to fall, and returned solemnly to her bed of death. And as she breathed her last sighs, there came mingled with them a low murmur from her lips. I bent to them my ear and distinguished, again, the concluding words of the passage in Glanvill—"*Man doth*

---

[18] This poem was first published as "The Conqueror Worm" in *Graham's Magazine* in January 1843 and was incorporated into "Ligeia" in 1845.

not yield him to the angels, nor unto death utterly, save only through the weakness of his feeble will."

She died;—and I, crushed into the very dust with sorrow, could no longer endure the lonely desolation of my dwelling in the dim and decaying city by the Rhine. I had no lack of what the world calls wealth. Ligeia had brought me far more, very far more than ordinarily falls to the lot of mortals. After a few months, therefore, of weary and aimless wandering, I purchased, and put in some repair, an abbey, which I shall not name, in one of the wildest and least frequented portions of fair England. The gloomy and dreary grandeur of the building, the almost savage aspect of the domain, the many melancholy and time-honored memories connected with both, had much in unison with the feelings of utter abandonment which had driven me into that remote and unsocial region of the country. Yet although the external abbey, with its verdant decay hanging about it, suffered but little alteration, I gave way, with a child-like perversity, and perchance with a faint hope of alleviating my sorrows, to a display of more than regal magnificence within.—For such follies, even in childhood, I had imbibed a taste and now they came back to me as if in the dotage of grief. Alas, I feel how much even of incipient madness might have been discovered in the gorgeous and fantastic draperies, in the solemn carvings of Egypt, in the wild cornices and furniture, in the Bedlam[19] patterns of the carpets of tufted gold! I had become a bounden slave in the trammels[20] of opium, and my labors and my orders had taken a coloring from my dreams. But these absurdities I must not pause to detail. Let me speak only of that one chamber, ever accursed, whither in a moment of mental alienation, I led from the altar as my bride—as the successor of the unforgotten Ligeia—the fair-haired and blue-eyed Lady Rowena Trevanion, of Tremaine.

There is no individual portion of the architecture and decoration of that bridal chamber which is not now visibly before me. Where were the souls of the haughty family of the bride, when, through thirst of gold, they permitted to pass the threshold of an apartment *so* bedecked, a maiden and a daughter so beloved? I have said that I minutely remember the details of the chamber—yet I am sadly forgetful on topics of deep moment—and here there was no system, no keeping, in the fantastic display, to take hold upon the memory. The room lay in a high turret of the castellated abbey, was pentagonal in shape, and of capacious size. Occupying the whole southern face of the pentagon was the sole window—an immense sheet of unbroken glass from Venice—a single pane, and tinted of a leaden hue, so that the rays of either the sun or moon, passing through it, fell with a ghastly lustre on the objects within. Over the upper portion of this huge window, extended the trellice-work of an aged vine, which clambered up the massy walls of the turret. The ceiling, of gloomy-looking oak, was excessively lofty, vaulted, and elaborately fretted[21] with the wildest and most grotesque specimens of a semi-Gothic, semi-Druidical[22] device. From out the most central recess of this melancholy vaulting, depended, by a single chain of gold with long links, a huge censer of the same metal, Saracenic in pattern,[23] and with many perforations so contrived

---

[19] Insane, crazy. "Bedlam" is short for "Bethlehem Hospital," a London asylum for the mentally deranged.
[20] Restraints.   [21] Ornamented with intersecting patterns.
[22] The Druids were a mysterious priestly class in ancient Britain and Ireland.
[23] A container (of gold) for burning incense, with an Arabian design.

that there writhed in and out of them, as if endued with a serpent vitality, a continual succession of parti-colored fires.

Some few ottomans and golden candelabra, of Eastern figure, were in various stations about—and there was the couch, too—the bridal couch—of an Indian model, and low, and sculptured of solid ebony, with a pall-like canopy above. In each of the angles of the chamber stood on end a gigantic sarcophagus[24] of black granite, from the tombs of the kings over against Luxor,[25] with their aged lids full of immemorial sculpture. But in the draping of the apartment lay, alas! the chief phantasy of all. The lofty walls, gigantic in height—even unproportionably so—were hung from summit to foot, in vast folds, with a heavy and massive-looking tapestry—tapestry of a material which was found alike as a carpet on the floor, as a covering for the ottomans and the ebony bed, as a canopy for the bed, and as the gorgeous volutes[26] of the curtains which partially shaded the window. The material was the richest cloth of gold. It was spotted all over, at irregular intervals, with arabesque[27] figures, about a foot in diameter, and wrought upon the cloth in patterns of the most jetty black. But these figures partook of the true character of the arabesque only when regarded from a single point of view. By a contrivance now common, and indeed traceable to a very remote period of antiquity, they were made changeable in aspect. To one entering the room, they bore the appearance of simple monstrosities; but upon a farther advance, this appearance gradually departed; and step by step, as the visiter moved his station in the chamber, he saw himself surrounded by an endless succession of the ghastly forms which belong to the superstition of the Norman,[28] or arise in the guilty slumbers of the monk. The phantasmagoric effect was vastly heightened by the artificial introduction of a strong continual current of wind behind the draperies—giving a hideous and uneasy animation to the whole.

In halls such as these—in a bridal chamber such as this—I passed, with the Lady of Tremaine, the unhallowed hours of the first month of our marriage—passed them with but little disquietude. That my wife dreaded the fierce moodiness of my temper—that she shunned me and loved me but little—I could not help perceiving; but it gave me rather pleasure than otherwise. I loathed her with a hatred belonging more to demon than to man. My memory flew back, (oh, with what intensity of regret!) to Ligeia, the beloved, the august, the beautiful, the entombed. I revelled in recollections of her purity, of her wisdom, of her lofty, her ethereal nature, of her passionate, her idolatrous love. Now, then, did my spirit fully and freely burn with more than all the fires of her own. In the excitement of my opium dreams (for I was habitually fettered in the shackles of the drug) I would call aloud upon her name, during the silence of the night, or among the sheltered recesses of the glens by day, as if, through the wild eagerness, the solemn passion, the consuming ardor of my longing for the departed, I could restore her to the pathway she had abandoned—ah, *could* it be forever?—upon the earth.

About the commencement of the second month of the marriage, the Lady

---

[24] A coffin.   [25] A city in ancient Egypt and site of famous ruins.

[26] Spiral or scroll-like designs.

[27] Intricate designs of flowers and fruit interlaced with figures of humans and animals. Poe called his first collection of tales, including "Ligeia", *Tales of the Grotesque and Arabesque* (1840).

[28] The Normans (or "Northmen," the term Poe used in *The American Museum* in 1838) were the Vikings who conquered the section of France known as Normandy; their art is known for its intricate designs.

Rowena was attacked with sudden illness, from which her recovery was slow. The fever which consumed her rendered her nights uneasy; and in her perturbed state of half-slumber, she spoke of sounds, and of motions, in and about the chamber of the turret, which I concluded had no origin save in the distemper of her fancy, or perhaps in the phantasmagoric influences of the chamber itself. She became at length convalescent—finally well. Yet but a brief period elapsed, ere a second more violent disorder again threw her upon a bed of suffering; and from this attack her frame, at all times feeble, never altogether recovered. Her illnesses were, after this epoch, of alarming character, and of more alarming recurrence, defying alike the knowledge and the great exertions of her physicians. With the increase of the chronic disease which had thus, apparently, taken too sure hold upon her constitution to be eradicated by human means, I could not fail to observe a similar increase in the nervous irritation of her temperament, and in her excitability by trivial causes of fear. She spoke again, and now more frequently and pertinaciously, of the sounds—of the slight sounds—and of the unusual motions among the tapestries, to which she had formerly alluded.

One night, near the closing in of September, she pressed this distressing subject with more than usual emphasis upon my attention. She had just awakened from an unquiet slumber, and I had been watching, with feelings half of anxiety, half of vague terror, the workings of her emaciated countenance. I sat by the side of her ebony bed, upon one of the ottomans of India. She partly arose, and spoke, in an earnest low whisper, of sounds which she *then* heard, but which I could not hear—of motions which she *then* saw, but which I could not perceive. The wind was rushing hurriedly behind the tapestries, and I wished to show her (what, let me confess it, I could not *all* believe) that those almost inarticulate breathings, and those very gentle variations of the figures upon the wall, were but the natural effects of that customary rushing of the wind. But a deadly pallor, overspreading her face, had proved to me that my exertions to reassure her would be fruitless. She appeared to be fainting, and no attendants were within call. I remembered where was deposited a decanter of light wine which had been ordered by her physicians, and hastened across the chamber to procure it. But, as I stepped beneath the light of the censer, two circumstances of a startling nature attracted my attention. I had felt that some palpable although invisible object had passed lightly by my person; and I saw that there lay upon the golden carpet, in the very middle of the rich lustre thrown from the censer, a shadow—a faint, indefinite shadow of angelic aspect—such as might be fancied for the shadow of a shade. But I was wild with the excitement of an immoderate dose of opium, and heeded these things but little, nor spoke of them to Rowena. Having found the wine, I recrossed the chamber, and poured out a goblet-ful, which I held to the lips of the fainting lady. She had now partially recovered, however, and took the vessel herself, while I sank upon an ottoman near me, with my eyes fastened upon her person. It was then that I became distinctly aware of a gentle foot-fall upon the carpet, and near the couch; and in a second thereafter, as Rowena was in the act of raising the wine to her lips, I saw, or may have dreamed that I saw, fall within the goblet, as if from some invisible spring in the atmosphere of the room, three or four large drops of a brilliant and ruby colored fluid. If this I saw—not so Rowena. She swallowed the wine unhesitatingly, and I forbore to speak to her of a circumstance which must, after all, I considered, have been but the suggestion of a vivid imagination, rendered morbidly active by the terror of the lady, by the opium, and by the hour.

Yet I cannot conceal it from my own perception that, immediately subsequent to the fall of the ruby-drops, a rapid change for the worse took place in the disorder of my wife; so that, on the third subsequent night, the hands of her menials prepared her for the tomb, and on the fourth, I sat alone, with her shrouded body, in that fantastic chamber which had received her as my bride.—Wild visions, opium-engendered, flitted, shadow-like, before me. I gazed with unquiet eye upon the sarcophagi in the angles of the room, upon the varying figures of the drapery, and upon the writhing of the parti-colored fires in the censer overhead. My eyes then fell, as I called to mind the circumstances of a former night, to the spot beneath the glare of the censer where I had seen the faint traces of the shadow. It was there, however, no longer; and breathing with greater freedom, I turned my glances to the pallid and rigid figure upon the bed. Then rushed upon me a thousand memories of Ligeia—and then came back upon my heart, with the turbulent violence of a flood, the whole of that unutterable wo with which I had regarded *her* thus enshrouded. The night waned; and still, with a bosom full of bitter thoughts of the one only and supremely beloved, I remained gazing upon the body of Rowena.

It might have been midnight, or perhaps earlier, or later, for I had taken no note of time, when a sob, low, gentle, but very distinct, startled me from my revery.— I *felt* that it came from the bed of ebony—the bed of death. I listened in an agony of superstitious terror—but there was no repetition of the sound. I strained my vision to detect any motion in the corpse—but there was not the slightest perceptible. Yet I could not have been deceived. I *had* heard the noise, however faint, and my soul was awakened within me. I resolutely and perseveringly kept my attention riveted upon the body. Many minutes elapsed before any circumstance occurred tending to throw light upon the mystery. At length it became evident that a slight, a very feeble, and barely noticeable tinge of color had flushed up within the cheeks, and along the sunken small veins of the eyelids. Through a species of unutterable horror and awe, for which the language of mortality has no sufficiently energetic expression, I felt my heart cease to beat, my limbs grow rigid where I sat. Yet a sense of duty finally operated to restore my self-possession. I could no longer doubt that we had been precipitate in our preparations—that Rowena still lived. It was necessary that some immediate exertion be made; yet the turret was altogether apart from the portion of the abbey tenanted by the servants—there were none within call—I had no means of summoning them to my aid without leaving the room for many minutes—and this I could not venture to do. I therefore struggled alone in my endeavors to call back the spirit still hovering. In a short period it was certain, however, that a relapse had taken place; the color disappeared from both eyelid and cheek, leaving a wanness even more than that of marble; the lips became doubly shrivelled and pinched up in the ghastly expression of death; a repulsive clamminess and coldness overspread rapidly the surface of the body; and all the usual rigorous stiffness immediately supervened. I fell back with a shudder upon the couch from which I had been so startlingly aroused, and again gave myself up to passionate waking visions of Ligeia.

An hour thus elapsed when (could it be possible?) I was a second time aware of some vague sound issuing from the region of the bed. I listened—in extremity of horror. The sound came again—it was a sigh. Rushing to the corpse, I saw— distinctly saw—a tremor upon the lips. In a minute afterward they relaxed, disclosing a bright line of the pearly teeth. Amazement now struggled in my bosom with the profound awe which had hitherto reigned there alone. I felt that my vision grew dim, that my reason wandered; and it was only by a violent effort that I at length succeeded in nerving myself to the task which duty thus once more had pointed out. There was now a partial glow upon the forehead and upon the cheek and throat; a perceptible warmth pervaded the whole frame; there was even a slight pulsation at the heart. The lady *lived*; and with redoubled ardor I betook myself to the task of restoration. I chafed and bathed the temples and the hands, and used every exertion which experience, and no little medical reading, could suggest. But in vain. Suddenly, the color fled, the pulsation ceased, the lips resumed the expression of the dead, and, in an instant afterward, the whole body took upon itself the icy chilliness, the livid hue, the intense rigidity, the sunken outline, and all the loathsome peculiarities of that which has been, for many days, a tenant of the tomb.

And again I sunk into visions of Ligeia—and again, (what marvel that I shudder while I write?) *again* there reached my ears a low sob from the region of the ebony bed. But why shall I minutely detail the unspeakable horrors of that night? Why shall I pause to relate how, time after time, until near the period of the gray dawn, this hideous drama of revivification was repeated; how each terrific relapse was only into a sterner and apparently more irredeemable death; how each agony wore the aspect of a struggle with some invisible foe; and how each struggle was succeeded by I know not what of wild change in the personal appearance of the corpse? Let me hurry to a conclusion.

The greater part of the fearful night had worn away, and she who had been dead, once again stirred—and now more vigorously than hitherto, although arousing from a dissolution more appalling in its utter hopelessness than any. I had long ceased to struggle or to move, and remained sitting rigidly upon the ottoman, a helpless prey to a whirl of violent emotions, of which extreme awe was perhaps the least terrible, the least consuming. The corpse, I repeat, stirred, and now more vigorously than before. The hues of life flushed up with unwonted energy into the countenance—the limbs relaxed—and, save that the eyelids were yet pressed heavily together, and that the bandages and draperies of the grave still imparted their charnel[29] character to the figure, I might have dreamed that Rowena had indeed shaken off, utterly, the fetters of Death. But if this idea was not, even then, altogether adopted, I could at least doubt no longer, when, arising from the bed, tottering, with feeble steps, with closed eyes, and with the manner of one bewildered in a dream, the thing that was enshrouded advanced boldly and palpably into the middle of the apartment.

I trembled not—I stirred not—for a crowd of unutterable fancies connected with the air, the stature, the demeanor of the figure, rushing hurriedly through my brain, had paralyzed—had chilled me into stone. I stirred not—but gazed upon the apparition. There was a mad disorder in my thoughts—a tumult unappeasable. Could it, indeed, be the *living* Rowena who confronted me? Could it indeed be Rowena *at all*—the fair-haired, the blue-eyed Lady Rowena Trevanion of Tremaine? Why, *why* should I doubt it? The bandage lay heavily about the mouth— but then might it not be the mouth of the breathing Lady of Tremaine? And the cheeks—there were the roses as in her noon of life—yes, these might indeed be the fair cheeks of the living Lady of Tremaine. And the chin, with its dimples, as in health, might it not be hers?—but *had she then grown taller since her malady?* What inexpressible madness seized me with that thought? One bound, and I had

[29] Gravelike.

reached her feet! Shrinking from my touch, she let fall from her head, unloosened, the ghastly cerements[30] which had confined it, and there streamed forth, into the rushing atmosphere of the chamber, huge masses of long and dishevelled hair; *it was blacker than the raven wings of the midnight!* And now slowly opened *the eyes* of the figure which stood before me. "Here then, at least," I shrieked aloud, "can I never—can I never be mistaken—these are the full, and the black, and the wild eyes—of my lost love—of the lady—of the LADY LIGEIA."

1838

THE FALL OF THE HOUSE OF USHER*

> *Son cœur est un luth suspendu;*
> *Sitôt qu'on le touche il résonne.*
> DE BÉRANGER[1]

During the whole of a dull, dark, and soundless day in the autumn of the year, when the clouds hung oppressively low in the heavens, I had been passing alone, on horseback, through a singularly dreary tract of country; and at length found myself, as the shades of the evening drew on, within view of the melancholy House of Usher. I know not how it was—but, with the first glimpse of the building, a sense of insufferable gloom pervaded my spirit. I say insufferable; for the feeling was unrelieved by any of that half-pleasurable, because poetic, sentiment, with which the mind usually receives even the sternest natural images of the desolate or terrible. I looked upon the scene before me—upon the mere house, and the simple landscape features of the domain—upon the bleak walls—upon the vacant eye-like windows—upon a few rank sedges—and upon a few white trunks of decayed trees—with an utter depression of soul which I can compare to no earthly sensation more properly than to the after-dream of the reveller upon opium—the bitter lapse into everyday life—the hideous dropping off of the veil. There was an iciness, a sinking, a sickening of the heart—an unredeemed dreariness of thought which no goading of the imagination could torture into aught of the sublime. What was it—I paused to think—what was it that so unnerved me in the contemplation of the House of Usher? It was a mystery all insoluble; nor could I grapple with the shadowy fancies that crowded upon me as I pondered. I was forced to fall back upon the unsatisfactory conclusion, that while, beyond doubt, there *are* combinations of very simple natural objects which have the power of thus affecting us, still the analysis of this power lies among considerations beyond our depth. It was possible, I reflected, that a mere different arrangement of the particulars of the scene, of the details of the picture, would be sufficient to modify, or perhaps to annihilate its capacity for sorrowful impression; and, acting upon this idea, I reined my horse to the precipitous brink of a black and lurid tarn[2] that lay in

---

[30] Shrouds.

* First published in *Burton's Gentleman's Magazine* in 1839 and collected in *Tales of the Grotesque and Arabesque* (1840).

[1] "His heart is a lute strung tight; / As soon as one touches it, it resounds," from the poem "Le Refus" (1831) by Pierre-Jean de Béranger (1780–1857); Poe changed "My heart" to "His heart."

[2] A small mountain lake.

unruffled lustre by the dwelling, and gazed down—but with a shudder even more thrilling than before—upon the remodelled and inverted images of the gray sedge, and the ghastly tree-stems, and the vacant and eye-like windows.

Nevertheless, in this mansion of gloom I now proposed to myself a sojourn of some weeks. Its proprietor, Roderick Usher, had been one of my boon companions in boyhood; but many years had elapsed since our last meeting. A letter, however, had lately reached me in a distant part of the country—a letter from him—which, in its wildly importunate nature, had admitted of no other than a personal reply. The MS. gave evidence of nervous agitation. The writer spoke of acute bodily illness—of a mental disorder which oppressed him—and of an earnest desire to see me, as his best, and indeed his only personal friend, with a view of attempting, by the cheerfulness of my society, some alleviation of his malady. It was the manner in which all this, and much more, was said—it was the apparent *heart* that went with his request—which allowed me no room for hesitation; and I accordingly obeyed forthwith what I still considered a very singular summons.

Although, as boys, we had been even intimate associates, yet I really knew little of my friend. His reserve had been always excessive and habitual. I was aware, however, that his very ancient family had been noted, time out of mind, for a peculiar sensibility of temperament, displaying itself, through long ages, in many works of exalted art, and manifested, of late, in repeated deeds of munificent yet unobtrusive charity, as well as in a passionate devotion to the intricacies, perhaps even more than to the orthodox and easily recognisable beauties, of musical science. I had learned, too, the very remarkable fact, that the stem of the Usher race, all time-honoured as it was, had put forth, at no period, any enduring branch; in other words, that the entire family lay in the direct line of descent, and had always, with very trifling and very temporary variation, so lain. It was this deficiency, I considered, while running over in thought the perfect keeping of the character of the premises with the accredited character of the people, and while speculating upon the possible influence which the one, in the long lapse of centuries, might have exercised upon the other—it was this deficiency, perhaps, of collateral issue, and the consequent undeviating transmission, from sire to son, of the patrimony with the name, which had, at length, so identified the two as to merge the original title of the estate in the quaint and equivocal appellation of the "House of Usher"—an appellation which seemed to include, in the minds of the peasantry who used it, both the family and the family mansion.

I have said that the sole effect of my somewhat childish experiment—that of looking down within the tarn—had been to deepen the first singular impression. There can be no doubt that the consciousness of the rapid increase of my superstition—for why should I not so term it?—served mainly to accelerate the increase itself. Such, I have long known, is the paradoxical law of all sentiments having terror as a basis. And it might have been for this reason only, that, when I again uplifted my eyes to the house itself, from its image in the pool, there grew in my mind a strange fancy—a fancy so ridiculous, indeed, that I but mention it to show the vivid force of the sensations which oppressed me. I had so worked upon my imagination as really to believe that about the whole mansion and domain there hung an atmosphere peculiar to themselves and their immediate vicinity—an atmosphere which had no affinity with the air of heaven, but which had reeked up from the decayed trees, and the gray wall, and the silent tarn—a pestilent and mystic vapour, dull, sluggish, faintly discernible, and leaden-hued.

Shaking off from my spirit what *must* have been a dream, I scanned more narrowly the real aspect of the building. Its principal feature seemed to be that of an excessive antiquity. The discoloration of ages had been great. Minute fungi overspread the whole exterior, hanging in a fine tangled web-work from the eaves. Yet all this was apart from any extraordinary dilapidation. No portion of the masonry had fallen; and there appeared to be a wild inconsistency between its still perfect adaptation of parts, and the crumbling condition of the individual stones. In this there was much that reminded me of the specious totality of old wood-work which has rotted for long years in some neglected vault, with no disturbance from the breath of the external air. Beyond this indication of extensive decay, however, the fabric gave little token of instability. Perhaps the eye of a scrutinising observer might have discovered a barely perceptible fissure, which, extending from the roof of the building in front, made its way down the wall in a zigzag direction, until it became lost in the sullen waters of the tarn.

Noticing these things, I rode over a short causeway to the house. A servant in waiting took my horse, and I entered the Gothic archway of the hall. A valet, of stealthy step, thence conducted me, in silence, through many dark and intricate passages in my progress to the *studio* of his master. Much that I encountered on the way contributed, I know not how, to heighten the vague sentiments of which I have already spoken. While the objects around me—while the carvings of the ceilings, the sombre tapestries of the walls, the ebon blackness of the floors, and the phantasmagoric armorial trophies which rattled as I strode, were but matters to which, or to such as which, I had been accustomed from my infancy—while I hesitated not to acknowledge how familiar was all this—I still wondered to find how unfamiliar were the fancies which ordinary images were stirring up. On one of the staircases, I met the physician of the family. His countenance, I thought, wore a mingled expression of low cunning and perplexity. He accosted me with trepidation and passed on. The valet now threw open a door and ushered me into the presence of his master.

The room in which I found myself was very large and lofty. The windows were long, narrow, and pointed, and at so vast a distance from the black oaken floor as to be altogether inaccessible from within. Feeble gleams of encrimsoned light made their way through the trellised panes, and served to render sufficiently distinct the more prominent objects around; the eye, however, struggled in vain to reach the remoter angles of the chamber, or the recesses of the vaulted and fretted ceiling. Dark draperies hung upon the walls. The general furniture was profuse, comfortless, antique, and tattered. Many books and musical instruments lay scattered about, but failed to give any vitality to the scene. I felt that I breathed an atmosphere of sorrow. An air of stern, deep, and irredeemable gloom hung over and pervaded all.[3]

Upon my entrance, Usher arose from a sofa on which he had been lying at full length, and greeted me with a vivacious warmth which had much in it, I at first thought, of an overdone cordiality—of the constrained effort of the *ennuyé*[4] man of the world. A glance, however, at his countenance, convinced me of his perfect sincerity. We sat down; and for some moments, while he spoke not, I gazed upon him with a feeling half of pity, half of awe. Surely, man had never before so

---

[3] The poet Richard Wilbur has observed that the interior of the house is an analogue of Usher's "visionary Mind" (*The Recognition of Poe*, ed. E. Carlson, 1966).

[4] "Bored" (French).

terribly altered, in so brief a period, as had Roderick Usher! It was with difficulty that I could bring myself to admit the identity of the wan being before me with the companion of my early boyhood. Yet the character of his face had been at all times remarkable. A cadaverousness of complexion; an eye large, liquid, and luminous beyond comparison; lips somewhat thin and very pallid, but of a surpassingly beautiful curve; a nose of a delicate Hebrew model, but with a breadth of nostril unusual in similar formations; a finely moulded chin, speaking, in its want of prominence, of a want of moral energy; hair of a more than web-like softness and tenuity; these features, with an inordinate expansion above the regions of the temple, made up altogether a countenance not easily to be forgotten. And now in the mere exaggeration of the prevailing character of these features, and of the expression they were wont to convey, lay so much of change that I doubted to whom I spoke. The now ghastly pallor of the skin, and the now miraculous lustre of the eye, above all things startled and even awed me. The silken hair, too, had been suffered to grow all unheeded, and as, in its wild gossamer texture, it floated rather than fell about the face, I could not, even with effort, connect its Arabesque[5] expression with any idea of simple humanity.

In the manner of my friend I was at once struck with an incoherence—an inconsistency; and I soon found this to arise from a series of feeble and futile struggles to overcome an habitual trepidancy—an excessive nervous agitation. For something of this nature I had indeed been prepared, no less by his letter, than by reminiscences of certain boyish traits, and by conclusions deduced from his peculiar physical conformation and temperament. His action was alternately vivacious and sullen. His voice varied rapidly from a tremulous indecision (when the animal spirits seemed utterly in abeyance) to that species of energetic concision—that abrupt, weighty, unhurried, and hollow-sounding enunciation—that leaden, self-balanced and perfectly modulated guttural utterance, which may be observed in the lost drunkard, or the irreclaimable eater of opium, during the periods of his most intense excitement.

It was thus that he spoke of the object of my visit, of his earnest desire to see me, and of the solace he expected me to afford him. He entered, at some length, into what he conceived to be the nature of his malady. It was, he said, a constitutional and a family evil, and one for which he despaired to find a remedy—a mere nervous affection, he immediately added, which would undoubtedly soon pass off. It displayed itself in a host of unnatural sensations. Some of these, as he detailed them, interested and bewildered me; although, perhaps, the terms, and the general manner of the narration had their weight. He suffered much from a morbid acuteness of the senses; the most insipid food was alone endurable; he could wear only garments of certain texture; the odours of all flowers were oppressive; his eyes were tortured by even a faint light; and there were but peculiar sounds, and these from stringed instruments, which did not inspire him with horror.

To an anomalous species of terror I found him a bounden slave. "I shall perish," said he, "I *must* perish in this deplorable folly. Thus, thus, and not otherwise, shall I be lost. I dread the events of the future, not in themselves, but in their results. I shudder at the thought of any, even the most trivial, incident, which may operate upon this intolerable agitation of soul. I have, indeed, no abhorrence of

[5] Here, complex or unfamiliar.

danger, except in its absolute effect—in terror. In this unnerved—in this pitiable condition—I feel that the period will sooner or later arrive when I must abandon life and reason together, in some struggle with the grim phantasm, FEAR."

I learned, moreover, at intervals, and through broken and equivocal hints, another singular feature of his mental condition. He was enchained by certain superstitious impressions in regard to the dwelling which he tenanted, and whence, for many years, he had never ventured forth—in regard to an influence whose supposititious force was conveyed in terms too shadowy here to be re-stated—an influence which some peculiarities in the mere form and substance of his family mansion, had, by dint of long sufferance, he said, obtained over his spirit—an effect which the *physique* of the gray walls and turrets, and of the dim tarn into which they all looked down, had, at length, brought about upon the *morale* of his existence.

He admitted, however, although with hesitation, that much of the peculiar gloom which thus afflicted him could be traced to a more natural and far more palpable origin—to the severe and long-continued illness—indeed to the evidently approaching dissolution—of a tenderly beloved sister—his sole companion for long years—his last and only relative on earth. "Her decease," he said, with a bitterness which I can never forget, "would leave him (him the hopeless and the frail) the last of the ancient race of the Ushers." While he spoke, the lady Madeline (for so was she called) passed slowly through a remote portion of the apartment, and, without having noticed my presence, disappeared. I regarded her with an utter astonishment not unmingled with dread—and yet I found it impossible to account for such feelings. A sensation of stupor oppressed me, as my eyes followed her retreating steps. When a door, at length, closed upon her, my glance sought instinctively and eagerly the countenance of the brother—but he had buried his face in his hands, and I could only perceive that a far more than ordinary wanness had overspread the emaciated fingers through which trickled many passionate tears.

The disease of the lady Madeline had long baffled the skill of her physicians. A settled apathy, a gradual wasting away of the person, and frequent although transient affections of a partially cataleptical[6] character, were the unusual diagnosis. Hitherto she had steadily borne up against the pressure of her malady, and had not betaken herself finally to bed; but, on the closing in of the evening of my arrival at the house, she succumbed (as her brother told me at night with inexpressible agitation) to the prostrating power of the destroyer; and I learned that the glimpse I had obtained of her person would thus probably be the last I should obtain—that the lady, at least while living, would be seen by me no more.

For several days ensuing, her name was unmentioned by either Usher or myself: and during this period I was busied in earnest endeavours to alleviate the melancholoy of my friend. We painted and read together; or I listened, as if in a dream, to the wild improvisations of his speaking guitar. And thus, as a closer and still closer intimacy admitted me more unreservedly into the recesses of his spirit, the more bitterly did I perceive the futility of all attempt at cheering a mind from which darkness, as if an inherent positive quality, poured forth upon all objects of the moral and physical universe, in one unceasing radiation of gloom.

I shall ever bear about me a memory of the many solemn hours I thus spent

---

[6] Without complete consciousness.

alone with the master of the House of Usher. Yet I should fail in any attempt to convey an idea of the exact character of the studies, or of the occupations, in which he involved me, or led me the way. An excited and highly distempered ideality threw a sulphureous lustre over all. His long improvised dirges will ring forever in my ears. Among other things, I hold painfully in mind a certain singular perversion and amplification of the wild air of the last waltz of Von Weber.[7] From the paintings over which his elaborate fancy brooded, and which grew, touch by touch, into vaguenesses at which I shuddered the more thrillingly, because I shuddered knowing not why;—from these paintings (vivid as their images now are before me) I would in vain endeavour to educe more than a small portion which should lie within the compass of merely written words. By the utter simplicity, by the nakedness of his designs, he arrested and overawed attention. If ever mortal painted an idea, that mortal was Roderick Usher. For me at least—in the circumstances then surrounding me—there arose out of the pure abstractions which the hypochondriac contrived to throw upon his canvas, an intensity of intolerable awe, no shadow of which felt I ever yet in the contemplation of the certainly glowing yet too concrete reveries of Fuseli.[8]

One of the phantasmagoric conceptions of my friend, partaking not so rigidly of the spirit of abstraction, may be shadowed forth, although feebly, in words. A small picture presented the interior of an immensely long and rectangular vault or tunnel, with low walls, smooth, white, and without interruption or device. Certain accessory points of the design served well to convey the idea that this excavation lay at an exceeding depth below the surface of the earth. No outlet was observed in any portion of its vast extent, and no torch, or other artificial source of light was discernible; yet a flood of intense rays rolled throughout, and bathed the whole in a ghastly and inappropriate splendour.

I have just spoken of that morbid condition of the auditory nerve which rendered all music intolerable to the sufferer, with the exception of certain effects of stringed instruments. It was, perhaps, the narrow limits to which he thus confined himself upon the guitar, which gave birth, in great measure, to the fantastic character of his performances. But the fervid *facility* of his *impromptus* could not be so accounted for. They must have been, and were, in the notes, as well as in the words of his wild fantasias (for he not unfrequently accompanied himself with rhymed verbal improvisations), the result of that intense mental collectedness and concentration to which I have previously alluded as observable only in particular moments of the highest artificial excitement. The words of one of these rhapsodies I have easily remembered. I was, perhaps, the more forcibly impressed with it, as he gave it, because, in the under or mystic current of its meaning, I fancied that I perceived, and for the first time, a full consciousness on the part of Usher, of the tottering of his lofty reason upon her throne. The verses, which were entitled "The Haunted Palace,"[9] ran very nearly, if not accurately, thus:

---

[7] "The Last Waltz of Von Weber," by Karl Gottlieb Reissiger (1798–1859), is a tribute to Karl Maria Von Weber (1786–1826), renowned creator of German romantic opera. In his edition of Poe's tales, Thomas O. Mabbott suggests that Usher is playing a dirge for himself at this point.

[8] Henry Fuseli (1741–1825), a Swiss-born painter whose career flourished in London, largely due to his interest in the supernatural and the terrifying.

[9] This poem was published separately in the *American Museum of Science, Literature, and the Arts,* in April 1839, five months before the publication of "The Fall of the House of Usher."

I

In the greenest of our valleys,
  By good angels tenanted,
Once a fair and stately palace—
  Radiant palace—reared its head.
In the monarch Thought's dominion—
  It stood there!
Never seraph spread a pinion
  Over fabric half so fair.

II

Banners yellow, glorious, golden,
  On its roof did float and flow;
(This—all this—was in the olden
  Time long ago)
And every gentle air that dallied,
  In that sweet day,
Along the ramparts plumed and pallid,
  A winged odour went away.

III

Wanderers in that happy valley
  Through two luminous windows saw
Spirits moving musically
  To a lute's well-tunèd law,
Round about a throne, where sitting
  (Porphyrogene![10])
In state his glory well befitting,
  The ruler of the realm was seen.

IV

And all with pearl and ruby glowing
  Was the fair palace door,
Through which came flowing, flowing, flowing,
  And sparkling evermore,
A troop of Echoes whose sweet duty
  Was but to sing,
In voices of surpassing beauty,
  The wit and wisdom of their king.

V

But evil things, in robes of sorrow,
  Assailed the monarch's high estate;
(Ah, let us mourn, for never morrow
  Shall dawn upon him, desolate!)

---

[10] Born to the purple, of royal birth; Poe assembled this word from Greek roots.

And, round about his home, the glory
    That blushed and bloomed
Is but a dim-remembered story
    Of the old time entombed.

VI
And travellers now within that valley,
    Through the red-litten[11] windows, see
Vast forms that move fantastically
    To a discordant melody;
While, like a rapid ghastly river,
    Through the pale door,
A hideous throng rush out forever,
    And laugh—but smile no more.

I well remember that suggestions arising from this ballad led us into a train of thought wherein there became manifest an opinion of Usher's which I mention not so much on account of its novelty, (for other men[12] have thought thus,) as on account of the pertinacity with which he maintained it. This opinion, in its general form, was that of the sentience of all vegetable things. But, in his disordered fancy, the idea had assumed a more daring character, and trespassed, under certain conditions, upon the kingdom of inorganization. I lack words to express the full extent, or the earnest *abandon* of his persuasion. The belief, however, was connected (as I have previously hinted) with the gray stones of the home of his forefathers. The conditions of the sentience had been here, he imagined, fulfilled in the method of collocation of these stones—in the order of their arrangement, as well as in that of the many *fungi* which overspread them, and of the decayed trees which stood around—above all, in the long undisturbed endurance of this arrangement, and in its reduplication in the still waters of the tarn. Its evidence—the evidence of the sentience—was to be seen, he said, (and I here started as he spoke,) in the gradual yet certain condensation of an atmosphere of their own about the waters and the walls. The result was discoverable, he added, in that silent, yet importunate and terrible influence which for centuries had moulded the destinies of his family, and which made *him* what I now saw him—what he was. Such opinions need no comment, and I will make none.

Our books—the books which, for years, had formed no small portion of the mental existence of the invalid—were, as might be supposed, in strict keeping with this character of phantasm. We pored together over such works as the Ververt et Chartreuse of Gresset;[13] the Belphegor of Machiavelli; the Heaven and

---

[11] Red-lighted.

[12] Poe's note: "Watson, Dr. Percival, Spallanzani, and especially the Bishop of Landaff.—See 'Chemical Essays,' vol. v." Richard Watson (1737–1816), Bishop of Llandaff, wrote *Chemical Essays*, 5 vols. (1781 and 1787); Thomas Percival (1740–1804), an English scientist, published an article on the sensory perceptions of vegetables in 1785; and the Abbe Lazzaro Spallanzani (1739–1799), an Italian researcher, wrote *Dissertations Relative to the Natural History of Animals and Vegetables* (trans. 1784). Usher's ultimate suggestion is that all matter is sentient, or able to sense.

[13] The books are real, and most deal with the supernatural, demonism, and persecution: Jean Baptiste Louis Gresset (1709–1777), a French anticleric; Niccolo Macchiavelli (1469–1527), author of *Bel-*

Hell of Swedenborg; the Subterranean Voyage of Nicholas Klimm by Holberg; the Chiromancy of Robert Flud, of Jean D'Indaginé, and of De la Chambre; the Journey into the Blue Distance of Tieck; and the City of the Sun of Campanella. One favourite volume was a small octavo edition of the *Directorium Inquisitorum,* by the Dominican Eymeric de Gironne; and there were passages in Pomponius Mela, about the old African Satyrs and Ægipans,[14] over which Usher would sit dreaming for hours. His chief delight, however, was found in the perusal of an exceedingly rare and curious book in quarto Gothic—the manual of a forgotten church—the *Vigiliæ Mortuorum secundum Chorum Ecclesiæ Maguntinæ.*[15]

I could not help thinking of the wild ritual of this work, and of its probable influence upon the hypochondriac, when, one evening, having informed me abruptly that the lady Madeline was no more, he stated his intention of preserving her corpse for a fortnight, (previously to its final interment,) in one of the numerous vaults within the main walls of the building. The worldly reason, however, assigned for this singular proceeding, was one which I did not feel at liberty to dispute. The brother had been led to his resolution (so he told me) by considerations of the unusual character of the malady of the deceased, of certain obtrusive and eager inquiries on the part of her medical men, and of the remote and exposed situation of the burial-ground of the family. I will not deny that when I called to mind the sinister countenance of the person whom I met upon the staircase, on the day of my arrival at the house, I had no desire to oppose what I regarded as at best but a harmless, and by no means an unnatural, precaution.[16]

At the request of Usher, I personally aided him in the arrangements for the temporary entombment. The body having been encoffined, we two alone bore it to its rest. The vault in which we placed it (and which had been so long unopened that our torches, half smothered in its oppressive atmosphere, gave us little opportunity for investigation) was small, damp, and entirely without means of admission for light; lying, at great depth, immediately beneath that portion of the building in which was my own sleeping apartment. It had been used, apparently, in remote feudal times, for the worst purposes of a donjon-keep,[17] and, in later days, as a place of deposit for powder, or some other highly combustible substance, as a portion of its floor, and the whole interior of a long archway through which we reached it, were carefully sheathed with copper. The door, of massive iron, had

---

phegor (1553), in which a devil arrives on earth to prove that women lure men to Hell; Emanuel Swedenborg (1688–1772), a Swedish mystic and author of *Heaven and Hell* (1758); Ludwig Holberg (1684–1754), the apocalyptic Danish author of *Niels Klim's Underground Journey* (1741); Robert Fludd (1574–1637), Jean D'Indaginé (early 16th century), and Martin Cureau de la Chambre (1594–1669), investigators of chiromancy, or palm reading; Ludwig Tieck (1773–1853), author of *Blue Distance,* a narrative of a journey to another world; Tommaso Campanella (1568–1639), author of the utopian *City of the Sun* (1623); Nicholas Eymerico (1320–1399), Spain's grand inquisitor from 1356 to 1399 and author of *Directorium Inquisitorium* (1503), which chronicles the torture of heretics during the Inquisition; Pomponius Mela (A.D. 1st century), a Roman geographer who describes strange beasts in his *De Situ Orbis* (A.D. 43?).

[14] According to Greek myth, creatures that are half-goat, half-man.

[15] *"Vigils for the Dead According to the Church-Choir of Mayence"* (Latin), an anonymous book of requiem rituals printed in Switzerland around 1500.

[16] A precaution against Madeline's body being stolen from the grave and sold to medical students and doctors needing cadavers for dissection.

[17] A dungeon.

been, also, similarly protected. Its immense weight caused an unusually sharp grating sound, as it moved upon its hinges.

Having deposited our mournful burden upon tressels within this region of horror, we partially turned aside the yet unscrewed lid of the coffin, and looked upon the face of the tenant. A striking similitude between the brother and sister now first arrested my attention; and Usher, divining, perhaps, my thoughts, murmured out some few words from which I learned that the deceased and himself had been twins, and that sympathies of a scarcely intelligible nature had always existed between them. Our glances, however, rested not long upon the dead—for we could not regard her unawed. The disease which had thus entombed the lady in the maturity of youth, had left, as usual in all maladies of a strictly cataleptical character, the mockery of a faint blush upon the bosom and the face, and that suspiciously lingering smile upon the lip which is so terrible in death. We replaced and screwed down the lid, and, having secured the door of iron, made our way, with toil, into the scarcely less gloomy apartments of the upper portion of the house.

And now, some days of bitter grief having elapsed, an observable change came over the features of the mental disorder of my friend. His ordinary manner had vanished. His ordinary occupations were neglected or forgotten. He roamed from chamber to chamber with hurried, unequal, and objectless step. The pallor of his countenance had assumed, if possible, a more ghastly hue—but the luminousness of his eye had utterly gone out. The once occasional huskiness of his tone was heard no more; and a tremulous quaver, as if of extreme terror, habitually characterized his utterance. There were times, indeed, when I thought his unceasingly agitated mind was labouring with some oppressive secret, to divulge which he struggled for the necessary courage. At times, again, I was obliged to resolve all into the mere inexplicable vagaries of madness, for I beheld him gazing upon vacancy for long hours, in an attitude of the profoundest attention, as if listening to some imaginary sound. It was no wonder that his condition terrified—that it infected me. I felt creeping upon me, by slow yet certain degrees, the wild influences of his own fantastic yet impressive superstitions.

It was, especially, upon retiring to bed late in the night of the seventh or eighth day after the placing of the lady Madeline within the donjon, that I experienced the full power of such feelings. Sleep came not near my couch—while the hours waned and waned away. I struggled to reason off the nervousness which had dominion over me. I endeavoured to believe that much, if not all of what I felt, was due to the bewildering influence of the gloomy furniture of the room—of the dark and tattered draperies, which, tortured into motion by the breath of a rising tempest, swayed fitfully to and fro upon the walls, and rustled uneasily about the decorations of the bed. But my efforts were fruitless. An irrepressible tremour gradually pervaded my frame; and, at length, there sat upon my very heart an incubus[18] of utterly causeless alarm. Shaking this off with a gasp and a struggle, I uplifted myself upon the pillows, and, peering earnestly within the intense darkness of the chamber, hearkened—I know not why, except that an instinctive spirit prompted me—to certain low and indefinite sounds which came, through the pauses of the storm, at long intervals, I knew not whence. Overpowered by an intense sentiment of horror, unaccountable yet unendurable, I threw on my clothes with haste (for I felt that I should sleep no more during the night), and en-

---

[18] An evil spirit; here, an oppressive burden.

deavoured to arouse myself from the pitiable condition into which I had fallen, by pacing rapidly to and fro through the apartment.

I had taken but few turns in this manner, when a light step on an adjoining staircase arrested my attention. I presently recognised it as that of Usher. In an instant afterward he rapped, with a gentle touch, at my door, and entered, bearing a lamp. His countenance was, as usual, cadaverously wan—but, moreover, there was a species of mad hilarity in his eyes—an evidently restrained *hysteria* in his whole demeanour. His air appalled me—but anything was preferable to the solitude which I had so long endured, and I even welcomed his presence as a relief.

"And you have not seen it?" he said abruptly, after having stared about him for some moments in silence—"you have not then seen it?—but, stay! you shall." Thus speaking, and having carefully shaded his lamp, he hurried to one of the casements, and threw it freely open to the storm.

The impetuous fury of the entering gust nearly lifted us from our feet. It was, indeed, a tempestuous yet sternly beautiful night, and one wildly singular in its terror and its beauty. A whirlwind had apparently collected its force in our vicinity; for there were frequent and violent alterations in the direction of the wind; and the exceeding density of the clouds (which hung so low as to press upon the turrets of the house) did not prevent our perceiving the life-like velocity with which they flew careering from all points against each other, without passing away into the distance. I say that even their exceeding density did not prevent our perceiving this—yet we had no glimpse of the moon or stars—nor was there any flashing forth of the lightning. But the under surfaces of the huge masses of agitated vapour, as well as all terrestrial objects immediately around us, were glowing in the unnatural light of a faintly luminous and distinctly visible gaseous exhalation which hung about and enshrouded the mansion.

"You must not—you shall not behold this!" said I, shudderingly, to Usher, as I led him, with a gentle violence, from the window to a seat. "These appearances, which bewilder you, are merely electrical phenomena not uncommon—or it may be that they have their ghastly origin in the rank miasma of the tarn. Let us close this casement;—the air is chilling and dangerous to your frame. Here is one of your favourite romances. I will read, and you shall listen;—and so we will pass away this terrible night together."

The antique volume which I had taken up was the "Mad Trist" of Sir Launcelot Canning;[19] but I had called it a favourite of Usher's more in sad jest than in earnest; for, in truth, there is little in its uncouth and unimaginative prolixity which could have had interest for the lofty and spiritual ideality of my friend. It was, however, the only book immediately at hand; and I indulged a vague hope that the excitement which now agitated the hypochondriac, might find relief (for the history of mental disorder is full of similar anomalies) even in the extremeness of the folly which I should read. Could I have judged, indeed, by the wild overstrained air of vivacity with which he hearkened, or apparently hearkened, to the words of the tale, I might well have congratulated myself upon the success of my design.

I had arrived at the well-known portion of the story where Ethelred, the hero of the Trist, having sought in vain for peaceable admission into the dwelling of the hermit, proceeds to make good an entrance by force. Here, it will be remembered, the words of the narrative run thus:

[19] A volume and author invented by Poe. "Trist" signifies a fated meeting or encounter.

"And Ethelred, who was by nature of a doughty heart, and who was now mighty withal, on account of the powerfulness of the wine which he had drunken, waited no longer to hold parley with the hermit, who, in sooth, was of an obstinate and maliceful turn, but, feeling the rain upon his shoulders, and fearing the rising of the tempest, uplifted his mace outright, and, with blows, made quickly room in the plankings of the door for his gauntleted hand; and now pulling therewith sturdily, he so cracked, and ripped, and tore all asunder, that the noise of the dry and hollow-sounding wood alarmed and reverberated throughout the forest."

At the termination of this sentence I started, and for a moment, paused; for it appeared to me (although I at once concluded that my excited fancy had deceived me)—it appeared to me that, from some very remote portion of the mansion, there came, indistinctly, to my ears, what might have been, in its exact similarity of character, the echo (but a stifled and dull one certainly) of the very cracking and ripping sound which Sir Launcelot had so particularly described. It was, beyond doubt, the coincidence alone which had arrested my attention; for, amid the rattling of the sashes of the casements, and the ordinary commingled noises of the still increasing storm, the sound, in itself, had nothing, surely, which should have interested or disturbed me. I continued the story:

"But the good champion Ethelred, now entering within the door, was sore enraged and amazed to perceive no signal of the maliceful hermit; but, in the stead thereof, a dragon of a scaly and prodigious demeanour, and of a fiery tongue, which sate in guard before a palace of gold, with a floor of silver; and upon the wall there hung a shield of shining brass with this legend enwritten—

Who entereth herein, a conqueror hath bin;
Who slayeth the dragon, the shield he shall win;

And Ethelred uplifted his mace, and struck upon the head of the dragon, which fell before him, and gave up his pesty breath, with a shriek so horrid and harsh, and withal so piercing, that Ethelred had fain to close his ears with his hands against the dreadful noise of it, the like whereof was never before heard."

Here again I paused abruptly, and now with a feeling of wild amazement—for there could be no doubt whatever that, in this instance, I did actually hear (although from what direction it proceeded I found it impossible to say) a low and apparently distant, but harsh, protracted, and most unusual screaming or grating sound—the exact counterpart of what my fancy had already conjured up for the dragon's unnatural shriek as described by the romancer.

Oppressed, as I certainly was, upon the occurrence of the second and most extraordinary coincidence, by a thousand conflicting sensations, in which wonder and extreme terror were predominant, I still retained sufficient presence of mind to avoid exciting, by any observation, the sensitive nervousness of my companion. I was by no means certain that he had noticed the sounds in question; although, assuredly, a strange alteration had, during the last few minutes, taken place in his demeanour. From a position fronting my own, he had gradually brought round his chair, so as to sit with his face to the door of the chamber; and thus I could but partially perceive his features, although I saw that his lips trembled as if he were murmuring inaudibly. His head had dropped upon his breast—yet I knew that he was not asleep, from the wide and rigid opening of the eye as I caught a glance of it in profile. The motion of his body, too, was at variance with this idea—for he rocked from side to side with a gentle yet constant and uniform sway. Having rapidly taken notice of all this, I resumed the narrative of Sir Launcelot, which thus proceeded:

"And now, the champion, having escaped from the terrible fury of the dragon, bethinking himself of the brazen shield, and of the breaking up of the enchantment which was upon it, removed the carcass from out of the way before him, and approached valorously over the silver pavement of the castle to where the shield was upon the wall; which in sooth tarried not for his full coming, but fell down at his feet upon the silver floor, with a mighty great and terrible ringing sound."

No sooner had these syllables passed my lips, than—as if a shield of brass had indeed, at the moment, fallen heavily upon a floor of silver—I became aware of a distinct, hollow, metallic, and clangorous, yet apparently muffled reverberation. Completely unnerved, I leaped to my feet; but the measured rocking movement of Usher was undisturbed. I rushed to the chair in which he sat. His eyes were bent fixedly before him, and throughout his whole countenance there reigned a stony rigidity. But, as I placed my hand upon his shoulder, there came a strong shudder over his whole person; a sickly smile quivered about his lips; and I saw that he spoke in a low, hurried, and gibbering murmur, as if unconscious of my presence. Bending closely over him, I at length drank in the hideous import of his words.

"Not hear it?—yes, I hear it, and *have* heard it. Long—long—long—many minutes, many hours, many days, have I heard it—yet I dared not—oh, pity me, miserable wretch that I am!—I dared not—I *dared* not speak! *We have put her living in the tomb!* Said I not that my senses were acute? I *now* tell you that I heard her first feeble movements in the hollow coffin. I heard them—many, many days ago—yet I dared not—*I dared not speak!* And now—to-night—Ethelred—ha! ha!—the breaking of the hermit's door, and the death-cry of the dragon, and the clangour of the shield!—say, rather, the rending of her coffin, and the grating of the iron hinges of her prison, and her struggles within the coppered archway of the vault! Oh whither shall I fly? Will she not be here anon? Is she not hurrying to upbraid me for my haste? Have I not heard her footstep on the stair? Do I not distinguish that heavy and horrible beating of her heart? MADMAN!" here he sprang furiously to his feet, and shrieked out his syllables, as if in the effort he were giving up his soul—"MADMAN! I TELL YOU THAT SHE NOW STANDS WITHOUT THE DOOR!"

As if in the superhuman energy of his utterance there had been found the potency of a spell—the huge antique panels to which the speaker pointed, threw slowly back, upon the instant, their ponderous and ebony jaws. It was the work of the rushing gust—but then without those doors there DID stand the lofty and enshrouded figure of the lady Madeline of Usher. There was blood upon her white robes, and the evidence of some bitter struggle upon every portion of her emaciated frame. For a moment she remained trembling and reeling to and fro upon the threshold, then, with a low moaning cry, fell heavily inward upon the person of her brother, and in her violent and now final death-agonies, bore him to the floor a corpse, and a victim to the terrors he had anticipated.

From that chamber, and from that mansion, I fled aghast. The storm was still abroad in all its wrath as I found myself crossing the old causeway. Suddenly there shot along the path a wild light, and I turned to see whence a gleam so unusual could have issued; for the vast house and its shadows were alone behind me. The radiance was that of the full, setting, and blood-red moon which now shone vividly through that once barely-discernible fissure of which I have before spoken as extending from the roof of the building, in a zigzag direction, to the base. While I gazed, this fissure rapidly widened—there came a fierce breath of the whirlwind—the entire orb of the satellite burst at once upon my sight—my brain reeled as I saw the mighty walls rushing asunder—there was a long tumultuous shouting sound like the voice of a thousand waters—and the deep and dank tarn at my feet closed sullenly and silently over the fragments of the "HOUSE OF USHER."

1839

THE TELL-TALE HEART*

True!—nervous—very, very dreadfully nervous I had been and am; but why *will* you say that I am mad? The disease had sharpened my senses—not destroyed—not dulled them. Above all was the sense of hearing acute. I heard all things in the heaven and in the earth. I heard many things in hell. How, then, am I mad? Hearken! and observe how healthily—how calmly I can tell you the whole story.

It is impossible to say how first the idea entered my brain; but once conceived, it haunted me day and night. Object there was none. Passion there was none. I loved the old man. He had never wronged me. He had never given me insult. For his gold I had no desire. I think it was his eye! yes, it was this! He had the eye of a vulture—a pale blue eye, with a film over it. Whenever it fell upon me, my blood ran cold; and so by degrees—very gradually—I made up my mind to take the life of the old man, and thus rid myself of the eye forever.[1]

Now this is the point. You fancy me mad. Madmen know nothing. But you should have seen *me*. You should have seen how wisely I proceeded—with what caution—with what foresight—with what dissimulation I went to work! I was never kinder to the old man than during the whole week before I killed him. And every night, about midnight, I turned the latch of his door and opened it—oh so gently! And then, when I had made an opening sufficient for my head, I put in a dark lantern,[2] all closed, closed, so that no light shone out, and then I thrust in my head. Oh, you would have laughed to see how cunningly I thrust it in! I moved it slowly—very, very slowly, so that I might not disturb the old man's sleep. It took me an hour to place my whole head within the opening so far that I could see him as he lay upon his bed. Ha!—would a madman have been so wise as this? And then, when my head was well in the room, I undid the lantern cautiously—oh, so cautiously—cautiously (for the hinges creaked)—I undid it just so much that a single thin ray fell upon the vulture eye. And this I did for seven long nights—every night just at midnight—but I found the eye always closed; and so it was impossible to do the work; for it was not the old man who vexed me, but his Evil Eye. And every morning, when the day broke, I went boldly into the chamber, and spoke courageously to him, calling him by name in a hearty tone, and inquiring how he had passed the night. So you see he would have been a very profound

---

* First published in *The Pioneer* in 1843.

[1] Poe, who relished word games, seems to imply that the murderer identifies with his victim and in some way he is attacking himself: the narrator, the "I," determined to rid himself of the "eye" forever.

[2] A lantern with shutters to block the light.

old man, indeed, to suspect that every night, just at twelve, I looked in upon him while he slept.

Upon the eighth night I was more than usually cautious in opening the door. A watch's minute hand moves more quickly than did mine. Never before that night, had I *felt* the extent of my own powers—of my sagacity. I could scarcely contain my feelings of triumph. To think that there I was, opening the door, little by little, and he not even to dream of my secret deeds or thoughts. I fairly chuckled at the idea; and perhaps he heard me; for he moved on the bed suddenly, as if startled. Now you may think that I drew back—but no. His room was as black as pitch with the thick darkness, (for the shutters were close fastened, through fear of robbers,) and so I knew that he could not see the opening of the door, and I kept pushing it on steadily, steadily.

I had my head in, and was about to open the lantern, when my thumb slipped upon the tin fastening, and the old man sprang up in bed, crying out—"Who's there?"

I kept quite still and said nothing. For a whole hour I did not move a muscle, and in the meantime I did not hear him lie down. He was still sitting up in the bed listening;—just as I have done, night after night, hearkening to the death watches[3] in the wall.

Presently I heard a slight groan, and I knew it was the groan of mortal terror. It was not a groan of pain or of grief—oh, no!—it was the low stifled sound that arises from the bottom of the soul when overcharged with awe. I knew the sound well. Many a night, just at midnight, when all the world slept, it has welled up from my own bosom, deepening, with its dreadful echo, the terrors that distracted me. I say I knew it well. I knew what the old man felt, and pitied him, although I chuckled at heart. I knew that he had been lying awake ever since the first slight noise, when he had turned in the bed. His fears had been ever since growing upon him. He had been trying to fancy them causeless, but could not. He had been saying to himself—"It is nothing but the wind in the chimney—it is only a mouse crossing the floor," or "it is merely a cricket which has made a single chirp." Yes, he had been trying to comfort himself with these suppositions: but he had found all in vain. *All in vain;* because Death, in approaching him had stalked with his black shadow before him, and enveloped the victim. And it was the mournful influence of the unperceived shadow that caused him to feel—although he neither saw nor heard—to *feel* the presence of my head within the room.

When I had waited a long time, very patiently, without hearing him lie down, I resolved to open a little—a very, very little crevice in the lantern. So I opened it—you cannot imagine how stealthily, stealthily—until, at length a simple dim ray, like the thread of the spider, shot from out the crevice and fell full upon the vulture eye.

It was open—wide, wide open—and I grew furious as I gazed upon it. I saw it with perfect distinctness—all a dull blue, with a hideous veil over it that chilled the very marrow in my bones; but I could see nothing else of the old man's face or person: for I had directed the ray as if by instinct, precisely upon the damned spot.

And have I not told you that what you mistake for madness is but over acuteness of the senses?—now, I say, there came to my ears a low, dull, quick sound, such as a watch makes when enveloped in cotton. I knew *that* sound well, too. It

---

[3] Small insects (such as beetles) that make a ticking sound superstitiously thought to predict death. Note the analogy made between the old man and the narrator.

was the beating of the old man's heart. It increased my fury, as the beating of a drum stimulates the soldier into courage.

But even yet I refrained and kept still. I scarcely breathed. I held the lantern motionless. I tried how steadily I could maintain the ray upon the eye. Meantime the hellish tattoo of the heart increased. It grew quicker and quicker, and louder and louder every instant. The old man's terror *must* have been extreme! It grew louder, I say, louder every moment!—do you mark me well? I have told you that I am nervous: so I am. And now at the dead hour of the night, amid the dreadful silence of that old house, so strange a noise as this excited me to uncontrollable terror. Yet, for some minutes longer I refrained and stood still. But the beating grew louder, louder! I thought the heart must burst. And now a new anxiety seized me—the sound would be heard by a neighbour! The old man's hour had come! With a loud yell, I threw open the lantern and leaped into the room. He shrieked once—once only. In an instant I dragged him to the floor, and pulled the heavy bed[4] over him. I then smiled gaily, to find the deed so far done. But, for many minutes, the heart beat on with a muffled sound. This, however, did not vex me; it would not be heard through the wall. At length it ceased. The old man was dead. I removed the bed and examined the corpse. Yes, he was stone, stone dead. I placed my hand upon the heart and held it there many minutes. There was no pulsation. He was stone dead. His eye would trouble me no more.

If still you think me mad, you will think so no longer when I describe the wise precautions I took for the concealment of the body. The night waned, and I worked hastily, but in silence. First of all I dismembered the corpse. I cut off the head and the arms and the legs.

I then took up three planks from the flooring of the chamber, and deposited all between the scantlings.[5] I then replaced the boards so cleverly, so cunningly, that no human eye—not even *his*—could have detected any thing wrong. There was nothing to wash out—no stain of any kind—no blood-spot whatever. I had been too wary for that. A tub had caught all—ha! ha!

When I had made an end of these labors, it was four o'clock—still dark as midnight. As the bell sounded the hour, there came a knocking at the street door. I went down to open it with a light heart,—for what had I *now* to fear? There entered three men, who introduced themselves, with perfect suavity, as officers of the police. A shriek had been heard by a neighbour during the night; suspicion of foul play had been aroused; information had been lodged at the police office, and they (the officers) had been deputed to search the premises.

I smiled,—for *what* had I to fear? I bade the gentlemen welcome. The shriek, I said, was my own in a dream. The old man, I mentioned, was absent in the country. I took my visitors all over the house. I bade them search—search *well*. I led them, at length, to *his* chamber. I showed them his treasures, secure, undisturbed. In the enthusiasm of my confidence, I brought chairs into the room, and desired them *here* to rest from their fatigues, while I myself, in the wild audacity of my perfect triumph, placed my own seat upon the very spot beneath which reposed the corpse of the victim.

The officers were satisfied. My *manner* had convinced them. I was singularly at ease. They sat, and while I answered cheerily, they chatted of familiar things. But, ere long, I felt myself getting pale and wished them gone. My head ached, and I fancied a ringing in my ears: but still they sat and still they chatted. The ringing

---

[4] Bedclothes or heavy comforter.   [5] Beams that support floor boards.

became more distinct:—it continued and became more distinct: I talked more freely to get rid of the feeling: but it continued and gained definiteness—until, at length, I found that the noise was *not* within my ears.

No doubt I now grew *very* pale;—but I talked more fluently, and with a heightened voice. Yet the sound increased—and what could I do? It was *a low, dull, quick sound—much such a sound as a watch makes when enveloped in cotton.*[6] I gasped for breath—and yet the officers heard it not. I talked more quickly—more vehemently; but the noise steadily increased. I arose and argued about trifles, in a high key and with violent gesticulations; but the noise steadily increased. Why *would* they not be gone? I paced the floor to and fro with heavy strides, as if excited to fury by the observations of the men—but the noise steadily increased. Oh God! what *could* I do? I foamed—I raved—I swore! I swung the chair upon which I had been sitting, and grated it upon the boards, but the noise arose over all and continually increased. It grew louder—louder—*louder!* And still the men chatted pleasantly, and smiled. Was it possible they heard not? Almighty God!— no, no! They heard!—they suspected!—they *knew!*—they were making a mockery of my horror!—this I thought, and this I think. But anything was better than this agony! Anything was more tolerable than this derision! I could bear those hypocritical smiles no longer! I felt that I must scream or die! and now—again!— hark! louder! louder! louder! *louder!*

"Villains!" I shrieked, "dissemble no more! I admit the deed!—tear up the planks! here, here!—it is the beating of his hideous heart!"

1843

THE BLACK CAT*

For the most wild, yet most homely narrative which I am about to pen, I neither expect nor solicit belief. Mad indeed would I be to expect it, in a case where my very senses reject their own evidence. Yet, mad am I not—and very surely do I not dream. But tomorrow I die, and to-day I would unburthen my soul. My immediate purpose is to place before the world, plainly, succinctly, and without comment, a series of mere household events.[1] In their consequences, these events have terrified—have tortured—have destroyed me. Yet I will not attempt to expound them. To me, they have presented little but Horror—to many they will seem less terrible than *baroques*.[2] Hereafter, perhaps, some intellect may be found which will reduce my phantasm to the common-place—some intellect more calm, more logical, and far less excitable than my own, which will perceive, in the circumstances I detail with awe, nothing more than an ordinary succession of very natural causes and effects.

From my infancy I was noted for the docility and humanity of my disposition. My tenderness of heart was even so conspicuous as to make me the jest of my companions. I was especially fond of animals, and was indulged by my parents

---

[6] The sound is a ticking, an echo of the death-watch ticking the narrator has heard before.

* First published in the *United States Saturday Post,* a Philadelphia weekly paper, in 1843.

[1] Among nineteenth-century American writers, only Poe would present the lurid events of this tale as "a series of mere household events." "The Black Cat" is a prime example of mock-domestic fiction.

[2] Bizarre, weird.

with a great variety of pets. With these I spent most of my time, and never was so happy as when feeding and caressing them. This peculiarity of character grew with my growth, and, in my manhood, I derived from it one of my principal sources of pleasure. To those who have cherished an affection for a faithful and sagacious dog, I need hardly be at the trouble of explaining the nature or the intensity of the gratification thus derivable. There is something in the unselfish and self-sacrificing love of a brute, which goes directly to the heart of him who has had frequent occasion to test the paltry friendship and gossamer fidelity of mere *Man*.

I married early, and was happy to find in my wife a disposition not uncongenial with my own. Observing my partiality for domestic pets, she lost no opportunity of procuring those of the most agreeable kind. We had birds, gold fish, a fine dog, rabbits, a small monkey, and *a cat*.

This latter was a remarkably large and beautiful animal, entirely black, and sagacious to an astonishing degree. In speaking of his intelligence, my wife, who at heart was not a little tinctured with superstition, made frequent allusion to the ancient popular notion, which regarded all black cats as witches in disguise. Not that she was ever *serious* upon this point—and I mention the matter at all for no better reason than that it happens, just now, to be remembered.

Pluto[3]—this was the cat's name—was my favorite pet and playmate. I alone fed him, and he attended me wherever I went about the house. It was even with difficulty that I could prevent him from following me through the streets.

Our friendship lasted, in this manner, for several years, during which my general temperament and character—through the instrumentality of the Fiend Intemperance—had (I blush to confess it) experienced a radical alteration for the worse. I grew, day by day, more moody, more irritable, more regardless of the feelings of others. I suffered myself to use intemperate language to my wife. At length, I even offered her personal violence. My pets, of course, were made to feel the change in my disposition. I not only neglected, but ill-used them. For Pluto, however, I still retained sufficient regard to restrain me from maltreating him, as I made no scruple of maltreating the rabbits, the monkey, or even the dog, when by accident, or through affection, they came in my way. But my disease grew upon me—for what disease is like Alcohol!—and at length even Pluto, who was now becoming old, and consequently somewhat peevish—even Pluto began to experience the effects of my ill temper.

One night, returning home, much intoxicated, from one of my haunts about town, I fancied that the cat avoided my presence. I seized him; when, in his fright at my violence, he inflicted a slight wound upon my hand with his teeth. The fury of a demon instantly possessed me. I knew myself no longer. My original soul seemed, at once, to take its flight from my body; and a more than fiendish malevolence, gin-nurtured, thrilled every fibre of my frame. I took from my waistcoat-pocket a pen-knife, opened it, grasped the poor beast by the throat, and deliberately cut one of its eyes from the socket! I blush, I burn, I shudder, while I pen the damnable atrocity.

When reason returned with the morning—when I had slept off the fumes of the night's debauch—I experienced a sentiment half of horror, half of remorse, for the crime of which I had been guilty; but it was, at best, a feeble and equivocal feeling, and the soul remained untouched. I again plunged into excess, and soon drowned in wine all memory of the deed.

---

[3] According to Roman myth, the god of the dead and ruler of the underworld.

In the meantime the cat slowly recovered. The socket of the lost eye presented, it is true, a frightful appearance, but he no longer appeared to suffer any pain. He went about the house as usual, but, as might be expected, fled in extreme terror at my approach. I had so much of my old heart left, as to be at first grieved by this evident dislike on the part of a creature which had once so loved me. But this feeling soon gave place to irritation. And then came, as if to my final and irrevocable overthrow, the spirit of PERVERSENESS. Of this spirit philosophy takes no account. Yet I am not more sure that my soul lives, than I am that perverseness is one of the primitive impulses of the human heart—one of the indivisible primary faculties, or sentiments, which give direction to the character of Man. Who has not, a hundred times, found himself committing a vile or a silly action, for no other reason than because he knows he should *not?* Have we not a perpetual inclination, in the teeth of our best judgment, to violate that which is *Law,* merely because we understand it to be such? This spirit of perverseness, I say, came to my final overthrow. It was this unfathomable longing of the soul *to vex itself*—to offer violence to its own nature—to do wrong for the wrong's sake only[4]—that urged me to continue and finally to consummate the injury I had inflicted upon the unoffending brute. One morning, in cool blood, I slipped a noose about its neck and hung it to the limb of a tree;—hung it with the tears streaming from my eyes, and with the bitterest remorse at my heart;—hung it *because* I knew that it had loved me, and *because* I felt it had given me no reason of offence;—hung it *because* I knew that in so doing I was committing a sin—a deadly sin that would so jeopardize my immortal soul as to place it—if such a thing were possible—even beyond the reach of the infinite mercy of the Most Merciful and Most Terrible God.

On the night of the day on which this cruel deed was done, I was aroused from sleep by the cry of fire. The curtains of my bed were in flames. The whole house was blazing. It was with great difficulty that my wife, a servant, and myself, made our escape from the conflagration. The destruction was complete. My entire worldly wealth was swallowed up, and I resigned myself thenceforward to despair.

I am above the weakness of seeking to establish a sequence of cause and effect, between the disaster and the atrocity. But I am detailing a chain of facts—and wish not to leave even a possible link imperfect. On the day succeeding the fire, I visited the ruins. The walls, with one exception, had fallen in. This exception was found in a compartment wall, not very thick, which stood about the middle of the house, and against which had rested the head of my bed. The plastering had here, in great measure, resisted the action of the fire—a fact which I attributed to its having been recently spread. About this wall a dense crowd were collected, and many persons seemed to be examining a particular portion of it with very minute and eager attention. The words "strange!" "singular!" and other similar expressions, excited my curiosity. I approached and saw, as if graven in *bas relief*[5] upon the white surface, the figure of a gigantic *cat.* The impression was given with an accuracy truly marvellous. There was a rope about the animal's neck.

When I first beheld this apparition—for I could scarcely regard it as less—my wonder and my terror were extreme. But at length reflection came to my aid. The cat, I remembered, had been hung in a garden adjacent to the house. Upon the

---

[4] This definition of "perverseness" is the most concise to be found in Poe's fiction, even more dramatic in its clarity than the explanation given in "The Imp of the Perverse" (1845).

[5] Low relief; in sculpture, the slight (or low) projection of a figure from a flat background.

alarm of fire, this garden had been immediately filled by the crowd—by some one of whom the animal must have been cut from the tree and thrown, through an open window, into my chamber. This had probably been done with the view of arousing me from sleep. The falling of other walls had compressed the victim of my cruelty into the substance of the freshly-spread plaster; the line of which, with the flames, and the *ammonia* from the carcass, had then accomplished the portraiture as I saw it.

Although I thus readily accounted to my reason, if not altogether to my conscience, for the startling fact just detailed, it did not the less fail to make a deep impression upon my fancy. For months I could not rid myself of the phantasm of the cat; and, during this period, there came back into my spirit a half-sentiment that seemed, but was not, remorse. I went so far as to regret the loss of the animal, and to look about me, among the vile haunts which I now habitually frequented, for another pet of the same species, and of somewhat similar appearance, with which to supply its place.

One night as I sat, half stupified, in a den of more than infamy, my attention was suddenly drawn to some black object, reposing upon the head of one of the immense hogsheads[6] of Gin, or of Rum, which constituted the chief furniture of the apartment. I had been looking steadily at the top of this hogshead for some minutes, and what now caused me surprise was the fact that I had not sooner perceived the object thereupon. I approached it, and touched it with my hand. It was a black cat—a very large one—fully as large as Pluto, and closely resembling him in every respect but one. Pluto had not a white hair upon any portion of his body; but this cat had a large, although indefinite splotch of white, covering nearly the whole region of the breast.

Upon my touching him, he immediately arose, purred loudly, rubbed against my hand, and appeared delighted with my notice. This, then, was the very creature of which I was in search. I at once offered to purchase it of the landlord; but this person made no claim to it—knew nothing of it—had never seen it before.

I continued my caresses, and, when I prepared to go home, the animal evinced a disposition to accompany me. I permitted it to do so; occasionally stooping and patting it as I proceeded. When it reached the house it domesticated itself at once, and became immediately a great favorite with my wife.

For my own part, I soon found a dislike to it arising within me. This was just the reverse of what I had anticipated; but I know not how or why it was—its evident fondness for myself rather disgusted and annoyed. By slow degrees, these feelings of disgust and annoyance rose into the bitterness of hatred. I avoided the creature; a certain sense of shame, and the remembrance of my former deed of cruelty, preventing me from physically abusing it. I did not, for some weeks, strike, or otherwise violently ill use it; but gradually—very gradually—I came to look upon it with unutterable loathing, and to flee silently from its odious presence, as from the breath of a pestilence.

What added, no doubt, to my hatred of the beast, was the discovery, on the morning after I brought it home, that, like Pluto, it also had been deprived of one of its eyes. This circumstance, however, only endeared it to my wife, who, as I have already said, possessed, in a high degree, that humanity of feeling which had once been my distinguishing trait, and the source of many of my simplest and purest pleasures.

With my aversion to this cat, however, its partiality for myself seemed to in-

6 Large casks containing up to 140 gallons.

crease. It followed my footsteps with a pertinacity which it would be difficult to make the reader comprehend. Whenever I sat, it would crouch beneath my chair, or spring upon my knees, covering me with its loathsome caresses. If I arose to walk it would get between my feet and thus nearly throw me down, or, fastening its long and sharp claws in my dress, clamber, in this manner, to my breast. At such times, although I longed to destroy it with a blow, I was yet withheld from so doing, partly by a memory of my former crime, but chiefly—let me confess it at once—by absolute *dread* of the beast.

This dread was not exactly a dread of physical evil—and yet I should be at a loss how otherwise to define it. I am almost ashamed to own—yes, even in this felon's cell, I am almost ashamed to own—that the terror and horror with which the animal inspired me, had been heightened by one of the merest chimæras[7] it would be possible to conceive. My wife had called my attention, more than once, to the character of the mark of white hair, of which I have spoken, and which constituted the sole visible difference between the strange beast and the one I had destroyed. The reader will remember that this mark, although large, had been originally very indefinite; but, by slow degrees—degrees nearly imperceptible, and which for a long time my Reason struggled to reject as fanciful—it had, at length, assumed a rigorous distinctness of outline. It was now the representation of an object that I shudder to name—and for this, above all, I loathed, and dreaded, and would have rid myself of the monster *had I dared*—it was now, I say, the image of a hideous—of a ghastly thing—of the GALLOWS!—oh, mournful and terrible engine of Horror and of Crime—of Agony and of Death!

And now was I indeed wretched beyond the wretchedness of mere Humanity. And *a brute beast*—whose fellow I had contemptuously destroyed—*a brute beast* to work out for *me*—for me a man, fashioned in the image of the High God—so much of insufferable wo! Alas! neither by day nor by night knew I the blessing of Rest any more! During the former the creature left me no moment alone; and, in the latter, I started, hourly, from dreams of unutterable fear, to find the hot breath of *the thing* upon my face, and its vast weight—an incarnate Night-Mare that I had no power to shake off—incumbent eternally upon my *heart!*

Beneath the pressure of torments such as these, the feeble remnant of the good within me succumbed. Evil thoughts became my sole intimates—the darkest and most evil of thoughts. The moodiness of my usual temper increased to hatred of all things and of all mankind; while, from the sudden, frequent, and ungovernable outbursts of a fury to which I now blindly abandoned myself, my uncomplaining wife, alas! was the most usual and the most patient of sufferers.

One day she accompanied me, upon some household errand, into the cellar of the old building which our poverty compelled us to inhabit. The cat followed me down the steep stairs, and, nearly throwing me headlong, exasperated me to madness. Uplifting an axe, and forgetting, in my wrath, the childish dread which had hitherto stayed my hand, I aimed a blow at the animal which, of course, would have proved instantly fatal had it descended as I wished. But this blow was arrested by the hand of my wife. Goaded, by the interference, into a rage more than demoniacal, I withdrew my arm from her grasp and buried the axe in her brain. She fell dead upon the spot, without a groan.

This hideous murder accomplished, I set myself forthwith, and with entire deliberation, to the task of concealing the body. I knew that I could not remove it

---

[7] Frightening and incredible fancies.

from the house, either by day or by night, without the risk of being observed by the neighbors. Many projects entered my mind. At one period I thought of cutting the corpse into minute fragments, and destroying them by fire. At another, I resolved to dig a grave for it in the floor of the cellar. Again, I deliberated about casting it in the well in the yard—about packing it in a box, as if merchandize, with the usual arrangements, and so getting a porter to take it from the house. Finally I hit upon what I considered a far better expedient than either of these. I determined to wall it up in the cellar—as the monks of the middle ages are recorded to have walled up their victims.

For a purpose such as this the cellar was well adapted. Its walls were loosely constructed, and had lately been plastered throughout with a rough plaster, which the dampness of the atmosphere had prevented from hardening. Moreover, in one of the walls was a projection, caused by a false chimney, or fireplace, that had been filled up, and made to resemble the rest of the cellar. I made no doubt that I could readily displace the bricks at this point, insert the corpse, and wall the whole up as before, so that no eye could detect anything suspicious.

And in this calculation I was not deceived. By means of a crow-bar I easily dislodged the bricks, and, having carefully deposited the body against the inner wall, I propped it in that position, while, with little trouble, I re-laid the whole structure as it originally stood. Having procured mortar, sand, and hair, with every possible precaution, I prepared a plaster which could not be distinguished from the old, and with this I very carefully went over the new brick-work. When I had finished, I felt satisfied that all was right. The wall did not present the slightest appearance of having been disturbed. The rubbish on the floor was picked up with the minutest care. I looked around triumphantly, and said to myself—"Here at least, then, my labor has not been in vain."

My next step was to look for the beast which had been the cause of so much wretchedness; for I had, at length, firmly resolved to put it to death. Had I been able to meet with it, at the moment, there could have been no doubt of its fate; but it appeared that the crafty animal had been alarmed at the violence of my previous anger, and forebore to present itself in my present mood. It is impossible to describe, or to imagine, the deep, the blissful sense of relief which the absence of the detested creature occasioned in my bosom. It did not make its appearance during the night—and thus for one night at least, since its introduction into the house, I soundly and tranquilly slept; aye, *slept* even with the burden of murder upon my soul!

The second and the third day passed, and still my tormentor came not. Once again I breathed as a free-man. The monster, in terror, had fled the premises forever! I should behold it no more! My happiness was supreme! The guilt of my dark deed disturbed me but little. Some few inquiries had been made, but these had been readily answered. Even a search had been instituted—but of course nothing was to be discovered. I looked upon my future felicity as secured.

Upon the fourth day of the assassination, a party of the police came, very unexpectedly, into the house, and proceeded again to make rigorous investigation of the premises. Secure, however, in the inscrutability of my place of concealment, I felt no embarrassment whatever. The officers bade me accompany them in their search. They left no nook or corner unexplored. At length, for the third of fourth time, they descended into the cellar. I quivered not in a muscle. My heart beat calmly as that of one who slumbers in innocence. I walked the cellar from end to end. I folded my arms upon my bosom, and roamed easily to and fro. The police were thoroughly satisfied and prepared to depart. The glee at my heart was too strong to be restrained. I burned to say if but one word, by way of triumph, and to render doubly sure their assurance of my guiltlessness.

"Gentlemen," I said at last, as the party ascended the steps, "I delight to have allayed your suspicions. I wish you all health, and a little more courtesy. By the bye, gentlemen, this—this is a very well constructed house." [In the rabid desire to say something easily, I scarcely knew what I uttered at all.]—"I may say an *excellently* well constructed house. These walls—are you going, gentlemen?— these walls are solidly put together;" and here, through the mere phrenzy of bravado, I rapped heavily, with a cane which I held in my hand, upon that very portion of the brick-work behind which stood the corpse of the wife of my bosom.

But may God shield and deliver me from the fangs of the Arch-Fiend! No sooner had the reverberation of my blows sunk into silence, than I was answered by a voice from within the tomb!—by a cry, at first muffled and broken, like the sobbing of a child, and then quickly swelling into one long, loud, and continuous scream, utterly anomalous and inhuman—a howl—a wailing shriek, half of horror and half of triumph, such as might have arisen only out of hell, conjointly from the throats of the damned in their agony and of the demons that exult in the damnation.

Of my own thoughts it is folly to speak. Swooning, I staggered to the opposite wall. For one instant the party upon the stairs remained motionless, through extremity of terror and of awe. In the next, a dozen stout arms were toiling at the wall. It fell bodily. The corpse, already greatly decayed and clotted with gore, stood erect before the eyes of the spectators. Upon its head, with red extended mouth and solitary eye of fire, sat the hideous beast whose craft had seduced me into murder, and whose informing voice had consigned me to the hangman. I had walled the monster up within the tomb!

1843

THE CASK OF AMONTILLADO*

The thousand injuries of Fortunato I had borne as I best could, but when he ventured upon insult I vowed revenge. You, who so well know the nature of my soul, will not suppose, however, that I gave utterance to a threat. *At length* I would be avenged; this was a point definitely settled—but the very definitiveness with which it was resolved precluded the idea of risk. I must not only punish but punish with impunity. A wrong is unredressed when retribution overtakes its redresser. It is equally unredressed when the avenger fails to make himself felt as such to him who has done the wrong.[1]

It must be understood that neither by word nor deed had I given Fortunato cause to doubt my good will. I continued, as was my wont, to smile in his face, and he did not perceive that my smile *now* was at the thought of his immolation.

He had a weak point—this Fortunato—although in other regards he was a man to be respected and even feared. He prided himself on his connoisseurship in

* First published in *Godey's Lady's Book* in 1846. Amontillado is a pale, dry Spanish sherry.
[1] The narrator's conditions for revenge are: you must not get caught, and you must perform the act of vengeance yourself.

wine. Few Italians have the true virtuoso spirit. For the most part their enthusiasm is adopted to suit the time and opportunity, to practise imposture upon the British and Austrian *millionaires*. In painting and gemmary,[2] Fortunato, like his country-men, was a quack, but in the matter of old wines he was sincere. In this respect I did not differ from him materially;—I was skilful in the Italian vintages myself,[3] and bought largely whenever I could.

It was about dusk, one evening during the supreme madness of the carnival season, that I encountered my friend. He accosted me with excessive warmth, for he had been drinking much. The man wore motley.[4] He had on a tight-fitting parti-striped dress, and his head was surmounted by the conical cap and bells. I was so pleased to see him that I thought I should never have done wringing his hand.

I said to him—"My dear Fortunato, you are luckily met. How remarkably well you are looking to-day. But I have received a pipe[5] of what passes for Amontil-lado, and I have my doubts."

"How?" said he. "Amontillado? A pipe? Impossible! And in the middle of the carnival!"

"I have my doubts," I replied; "and I was silly enough to pay the full Amontil-lado price without consulting you in the matter. You were not to be found, and I was fearful of losing a bargain."

"Amontillado!"

"I have my doubts."

"Amontillado!"

"And I must satisfy them."

"Amontillado!"

"As you are engaged, I am on my way to Luchresi. If any one has a critical turn it is he. He will tell me—"

"Luchresi cannot tell Amontillado from Sherry."[6]

"And yet some fools will have it that his taste is a match for his own."

"Come, let us go."

"Whither?"

"To your vaults."

"My friend, no; I will not impose upon your good nature. I perceive you have an engagement. Luchresi—"

"I have no engagement;—come."

"My friend, no. It is not the engagement, but the severe cold with which I perceive you are afflicted. The vaults are insufferably damp. They are encrusted with nitre."[7]

"Let us go, nevertheless. The cold is merely nothing. Amontillado! You have been imposed upon. And as for Luchresi, he cannot distinguish Sherry from Amontillado."

Thus speaking, Fortunato possessed himself of my arm; and putting on a mask of black silk and drawing a *roquelaire*[8] closely about my person, I suffered him to hurry me to my palazzo.[9]

---

[2] Knowledge of gems and jewels.
[3] A curious remark, as no Italian wines are mentioned in the story.
[4] A multicolored costume worn by clowns and jesters. "Fortunato" means "lucky."
[5] An immense cask holding from 150 to 250 gallons.
[6] He cannot tell fine sherry from ordinary sherry.
[7] Potassium nitrate, a whitish mineral deposited in water.   [8] A cloak.
[9] "Palace" (Italian), or large home.

There were no attendants at home; they had absconded to make merry in honour of the time. I had told them that I should not return until the morning, and had given them explicit orders not to stir from the house. These orders were sufficient, I well knew, to insure their immediate disappearance, one and all, as soon as my back was turned.

I took from their sconces two flambeaux,[10] and giving one to Fortunato, bowed him through several suites of rooms to the archway that led into the vaults. I passed down a long and winding staircase, requesting him to be cautious as he followed. We came at length to the foot of the descent, and stood together upon the damp ground of the catacombs of the Montresors.

The gait of my friend was unsteady, and the bells upon his cap jingled as he strode.

"The pipe," he said.

"It is farther on," said I; "but observe the white web-work which gleams from these cavern walls."

He turned towards me, and looked into my eyes with two filmy orbs that distilled the rheum of intoxication.

"Nitre?" he asked, at length.

"Nitre," I replied, "How long have you had that cough?"

"Ugh! ugh! ugh!—ugh! ugh! ugh!—ugh! ugh! ugh!—ugh! ugh! ugh!—ugh! ugh! ugh!"

My poor friend found it impossible to reply for many minutes.

"It is nothing," he said, at last.

"Come," I said, with decision, "we will go back; your health is precious. You are rich, respected, admired, beloved; you are happy, as once I was. You are a man to be missed. For me it is no matter. We will go back; you will be ill, and I cannot be responsible. Besides, there is Luchresi—"

"Enough," he said; "the cough is a mere nothing; it will not kill me. I shall not die of a cough."

"True—true," I replied; "and, indeed, I had no intention of alarming you unnecessarily—but you should use all proper caution. A draught of this Medoc[11] will defend us from the damps."

Here I knocked off the neck of a bottle which I drew from a long row of its fellows that lay upon the mould.

"Drink," I said, presenting him the wine.

He raised it to his lips with a leer. He paused and nodded to me familiarly, while his bells jingled.

"I drink," he said, "to the buried that repose around us."

"And I to your long life."

He again took my arm, and we proceeded.

"These vaults," he said, "are extensive."

"The Montresors," I replied, "were a great and numerous family."

"I forget your arms."[12]

"A huge human foot d'or, in a field azure;[13] the foot crushes a serpent rampant whose fangs are imbedded in the heel."

---

[10] Flaming torches, taken from holders (sconces) fixed to the wall.

[11] A red wine from the Bordeaux region of France.

[12] The family's coat of arms; that Fortunato cannot recall the coat of arms of the narrator's "great and numerous" family is an insult to the name of Montresor.

[13] Foot of gold in a field of blue.

"And the motto?"

"*Nemo me impune lacessit.*"[14]

"Good!" he said.

The wine sparkled in his eyes and the bells jingled. My own fancy grew warm with the Medoc. We had passed through long walls of piled skeletons, with casks and puncheons[15] intermingling, into the inmost recesses of the catacombs. I paused again, and this time I made bold to seize Fortunato by an arm above the elbow.

"The nitre!" I said; "see, it increases. It hangs like moss upon the vaults. We are below the river's bed. The drops of moisture trickle among the bones. Come, we will go back ere it is too late. Your cough—"

"It is nothing," he said; "let us go on. But first, another draught of the Medoc."

I broke and reached him a flagon of De Grâve.[16] He emptied it at a breath. His eyes flashed with a fierce light. He laughed and threw the bottle upwards with a gesticulation I did not understand.

I looked at him in surprise. He repeated the movement—a grotesque one.

"You do not comprehend?" he said.

"Not I," I replied.

"Then you are not of the brotherhood."

"How?"

"You are not of the masons."[17]

"Yes, yes," I said; "yes, yes."

"You? Impossible! A mason?"

"A mason," I replied.

"A sign," he said, "a sign."

"It is this," I answered, producing from beneath the folds of my *roquelaire* a trowel.

"You jest," he exclaimed, recoiling a few paces. "But let us proceed to the Amontillado."

"Be it so," I said, replacing the tool beneath the cloak and again offering him my arm. He leaned upon it heavily. We continued our route in search of the Amontillado. We passed through a range of low arches, descended, passed on, and descending again, arrived at a deep crypt, in which the foulness of the air caused our flambeaux rather to glow than flame.

At the most remote end of the crypt there appeared another less spacious. Its walls had been lined with human remains, piled to the vault overhead, in the fashion of the great catacombs of Paris. Three sides of this interior crypt were still ornamented in this manner. From the fourth side the bones had been thrown down, and lay promiscuously upon the earth, forming at one point a mound of some size. Within the wall thus exposed by the displacing of the bones, we perceived a still interior crypt or recess, in depth about four feet, in width three, in height six or seven. It seemed to have been constructed for no especial use within itself, but formed merely the interval between two of the colossal supports of the

[14] "No one insults me with impunity" (Latin); or "No one insults me and gets away with it."

[15] Large casks.

[16] A large bottle of white wine from the Bordeaux region of France, the name used perhaps as a foreboding.

[17] The Freemasons, an international organization with secret signs and symbols. Fortunato again slights the narrator by saying it is "impossible" that he could be a mason; when asked for a sign to prove his membership, the narrator produces a trowel.

roof of the catacombs, and was backed by one of their circumscribing walls of solid granite.

It was in vain that Fortunato, uplifting his dull torch, endeavoured to pry into the depth of the recess. Its termination the feeble light did not enable us to see.

"Proceed," I said; "herein is the Amontillado. As for Luchresi—"

"He is an ignoramus," interrupted my friend, as he stepped unsteadily forward, while I followed immediately at his heels. In an instant he had reached the extremity of the niche, and finding his progress arrested by the rock, stood stupidly bewildered. A moment more and I had fettered him to the granite. In its surface were two iron staples, distant from each other about two feet, horizontally. From one of these depended a short chain, from the other a padlock. Throwing the links about his waist, it was but the work of a few seconds to secure it. He was too much astounded to resist. Withdrawing the key I stepped back from the recess.

"Pass your hand," I said, "over the wall; you cannot help feeling the nitre. Indeed, it is *very* damp. Once more let me *implore* you to return. No? Then I must positively leave you. But I must first render you all the little attentions in my power."

"The Amontillado!" ejaculated my friend, not yet recovered from his astonishment.

"True," I replied; "the Amontillado."

As I said these words I busied myself among the pile of bones of which I have before spoken. Throwing them aside, I soon uncovered a quantity of building stone and mortar. With these materials and with the aid of my trowel, I began vigorously to wall up the entrance of the niche.

I had scarcely laid the first tier of the masonry when I discovered that the intoxication of Fortunato had in a great measure worn off. The earliest indication I had of this was a low moaning cry from the depth of the recess. It was *not* the cry of a drunken man. There was then a long and obstinate silence. I laid the second tier, and the third, and the fourth; and then I heard the furious vibrations of the chain. The noise lasted for several minutes, during which, that I might hearken to it with the more satisfaction, I ceased my labours and sat down upon the bones. When at last the clanking subsided, I resumed the trowel, and finished without interruption the fifth, the sixth, and the seventh tier. The wall was now nearly upon a level with my breast. I again paused, and holding the flambeaux over the mason-work, threw a few feeble rays upon the figure within.

A succession of loud and shrill screams, bursting suddenly from the throat of the chained form, seemed to thrust me violently back. For a brief moment I hesitated, I trembled. Unsheathing my rapier, I began to grope with it about the recess; but the thought of an instant reassured me. I placed my hand upon the solid fabric of the catacombs, and felt satisfied. I reapproached the wall; I replied to the yells of him who clamoured. I re-echoed, I aided, I surpassed them in volume and in strength. I did this, and the clamourer grew still.

It was now midnight, and my task was drawing to a close. I had completed the eighth, the ninth and the tenth tier. I had finished a portion of the last and the eleventh; there remained but a single stone to be fitted and plastered in. I struggled with its weight; I placed it partially in its destined position. But now there came from out the niche a low laugh that erected the hairs on my head. It was succeeded by a sad voice, which I had difficulty in recognizing as that of the noble Fortunato. The voice said—

"Ha! ha! ha!—he! he! he!—a very good joke, indeed—an excellent jest. We will have many a rich laugh about it at the palazzo—he! he! he!—over our wine—he! he! he!"

"The Amontillado!" I said.

"He! he! he!—he! he! he!—yes, the Amontillado. But is it not getting late? Will not they be awaiting us at the palazzo, the Lady Fortunato and the rest? Let us be gone."

"Yes," I said, "let us be gone."

"*For the love of God, Montresor!*"

"Yes," I said, "for the love of God!"

But to these words I hearkened in vain for a reply. I grew impatient. I called aloud—

"Fortunato!"

No answer. I called again—

"Fortunato!"

No answer still. I thrust a torch through the remaining aperture and let it fall within. There came forth in return only a jingling of the bells. My heart grew sick; it was the dampness of the catacombs that made it so. I hastened to make an end of my labour. I forced the last stone into its position; I plastered it up. Against the new masonry I re-erected the old rampart of bones. For the half of a century no mortal has disturbed them. *In pace requiescat!*[18]

1846

SONNET—TO SCIENCE*

Science! true daughter of Old Time thou art!
   Who alterest all things with thy peering eyes.
Why preyest thou thus upon the poet's heart,
   Vulture, whose wings are dull realities?
How should he love thee? or how deem thee wise,
   Who wouldst not leave him in his wandering
To seek for treasure in the jewelled skies,
   Albeit he soared with an undaunted wing?
Hast thou not dragged Diana[1] from her car?
   And driven the Hamadryad[2] from the wood   10
To seek a shelter in some happier star?
   Hast thou not torn the Naiad[3] from her flood,
The Elfin from the green grass, and from me
The summer dream beneath the tamarind tree?[4]

1829

[18] "Rest in peace!" (Latin).

* First printed in *Al Aaraaf, Tamerlane, and Minor Poems*, in 1829. In this sonnet, science is the adversary of the imagination and of poetry.

[1] According to Roman myth, the moon-goddess who drives through the sky in her chariot or "car."

[2] According to Greek myth, a nymph who lives as a spirit within a tree and perishes when her tree dies.

[3] A female spirit who lives in fountains and streams.   [4] A brightly colored tropical tree.

TO HELEN*

Helen, thy beauty is to me
    Like those Nicéan barks[1] of yore,
That gently, o'er a perfumed sea,
    The weary, way-worn wanderer bore
    To his own native shore.

On desperate seas long wont to roam,
    Thy hyacinth[2] hair, thy classic face,
Thy Naiad[3] airs have brought me home
    To the glory that was Greece,
    And the grandeur that was Rome.   10

Lo! in yon brilliant window-niche
    How statue-like I see thee stand,
The agate[4] lamp within thy hand!
    Ah, Psyche,[5] from the regions which
    Are Holy-Land!

                                    1831

ISRAFEL*

In Heaven a spirit doth dwell
    "Whose heart-strings are a lute;"
None sing so wildly well
As the angel Israfel,[1]
And the giddy stars (so legends tell)

* First published in *Poems* in 1831, then revised and reworked at various times in the next twelve years; this version was included in *The Raven and Other Poems* (1845). In its public dimension the poem honors Helen of Troy, according to Greek myth the beautiful daughter of the chief god Zeus; she was the fabled cause of the Trojan war. As Poe admitted privately in an 1848 letter to Sarah Helen Whitman, the poem was inspired by the "first, purely ideal love of my soul," Mrs. Jane Stith Stanard, mother of Poe's schoolmate Robert Stanard, in Richmond, Virginia.
[1] Victorious (from the Greek *nike*) "victory" ships. Critics agree that the sound of "Nicéan," suggestive of a gentle homecoming in a classical world, contributes to the total effect of the poem.
[2] Luxuriant and curling.
[3] Nymphlike; according to Greek myth, Naiads are female spirits who inhabit fountains and streams.
[4] This word first appeared in the final revision of the poem in 1843. According to Thomas O. Mabbott the agate "is named for 'fidus Acates,'" the *faithful* friend of Aeneas" in Virgil's *Aenead*. Agate is a translucent variety of quartz, with a waxlike luster.
[5] "Soul" (Greek); according to Roman myth, Psyche was a damsel so beautiful that the goddess of love, Venus, was jealous of her. Thus, the poet's sign for this spiritualized beauty who comes from the "Holy-Land" of idealized love.
* First published in *Poems* in 1831, revised and reprinted in various journals in the 1830s and 1840s, and included in *The Raven and Other Poems* (1845). Poe added this note to the title: "And the angel Israfel, whose heart-strings are a lute, and who has the sweetest voice of all God's creatures.— KORAN," from the "Preliminary Discourse" to George Sale's translation of the Koran (1734).
[1] The source of Poe's idea for the "angel Israfel" is *Lalla Rookh* (1817), a series of Oriental tales by the Irish poet Thomas Moore (1779–1852), in which Israfel has an enchanting and wondrous voice.

Ceasing their hymns, attend the spell
  Of his voice, all mute.

Tottering above
  In her highest noon,
  The enamoured moon   10
Blushes with love,
  While, to listen, the red levin[2]
  (With the rapid Pleiads,[3] even,
  Which were seven,)
  Pauses in Heaven.

And they say (the starry choir
  And the other listening things)
That Israfeli's fire
Is owing to that lyre
  By which he sits and sings—   20
The trembling living wire
Of those unusual strings.

But the skies that angel trod,
  Where deep thoughts are a duty—
Where Love's a grown-up God[4]—
  Where the Houri[5] glances are
Imbued with all the beauty
  Which we worship in a star.

Therefore, thou art not wrong,
  Israfeli, who despisest   30
An unimpassioned song;
To thee the laurels belong,
  Best bard, because the wisest!
Merrily live, and long!

The ecstasies above
  With thy burning measures suit—
Thy grief, thy joy, thy hate, thy love,
  With the fervour of thy lute—
  Well may the stars be mute!

Yes, Heaven is thine; but this   40
  Is a world of sweets and sours;
  Our flowers are merely—flowers,
And the shadow of thy perfect bliss
  Is the sunshine of ours.

[2] Lightning.
[3] According to Greek myth, the Pleiades were seven sisters pursued by the giant hunter Orion; both he and they were turned into heavenly constellations.
[4] According to Greek myth, the god of love, Eros, is a man.
[5] Dark-eyed nymphs of the Mohammedan paradise.

If I could dwell
Where Israfel
   Hath dwelt, and he where I,
He might not sing so wildly well
   A mortal melody,
While a bolder note than this might swell   50
   From my lyre within the sky.

1831

THE SLEEPER*

At midnight, in the month of June,
I stand beneath the mystic moon.
An opiate vapour, dewy, dim,
Exhales from out her golden rim,
And, softly dripping, drop by drop,
Upon the quiet mountain top,
Steals drowsily and musically
Into the universal valley.
The rosemary nods upon the grave;
The lily lolls upon the wave;   10
Wrapping the fog about its breast,
The ruin moulders into rest;
Looking like Lethe,[1] see! the lake
A conscious slumber seems to take,
And would not, for the world, awake.
All Beauty sleeps!—and lo! where lies
Irene,[2] with her Destinies!

Oh, lady bright! can it be right—
This window open to the night?
The wanton airs, from the tree-top,   20
Laughingly through the lattice drop—
The bodiless airs, a wizard rout,
Flit through thy chamber in and out,
And wave the curtain canopy
So fitfully—so fearfully—
Above the closed and fringéd lid
'Neath which thy slumb'ring soul lies hid,

That, o'er the floor and down the wall,
Like ghosts the shadows rise and fall!

---

* First published as "Irene" in *Poems* in 1831, revised and printed in journals principally in the early 1840s, and included in *The Raven and Other Poems* (1845).

[1] According to Greek myth, the river of forgetfulness in Hades, the underworld, where the spirits of the dead reside.

[2] According to Greek myth, the goddess of peace.

Oh, lady dear, hast thou no fear?   30
Why and what art thou dreaming here?
Sure thou art come o'er far-off seas,
A wonder to these garden trees!
Strange is thy pallor! strange thy dress!
Strange, above all, thy length of tress,[3]
And this all solemn silentness!

The lady sleeps! Oh, may her sleep,
Which is enduring, so be deep!
Heaven have her in its sacred keep!
This chamber changed for one more holy,   40
This bed for one more melancholy,
I pray to God that she may lie
Forever with unopened eye,
While the pale sheeted ghosts go by!

My love, she sleeps! Oh, may her sleep,
As it is lasting, so be deep!
Soft may the worms about her creep![4]
Far in the forest, dim and old,
For her may some tall vault unfold—
Some vault that oft hath flung its black   50
And wingéd panels fluttering back,
Triumphant, o'er the crested palls,
Of her grand family funerals—
Some sepulchre, remote, alone,
Against whose portal she hath thrown,
In childhood, many an idle stone—
Some tomb from out whose sounding door
She ne'er shall force an echo more,
Thrilling to think, poor child of sin![5]
It was the dead who groaned within.   60

1831

THE CITY IN THE SEA*

Lo! Death has reared himself a throne
In a strange city lying alone
Far down within the dim West,

---

[3] Popular belief held that hair continues to grow after death.

[4] In the original version of the poem, "Irene," this line read, "No icy worms about her creep." The invocation was common usage in Poe's day, though morbid today.

[5] The Original Sin of Adam and Eve, which makes everyone a "child of sin."

* First published as "The Doomed City" in *Poems* in 1831, revised and reprinted in journals in the 1830s and 1840s, and included in *The Raven and Other Poems* (1845). Although there are many legends of sunken cities, Poe seems to have had in mind the biblical cities of Sodom or Gomorrah, which were destroyed for their wickedness and sunk into the Dead Sea.

Where the good and the bad and the worst and the best
Have gone to their eternal rest.
There shrines and palaces and towers
(Time-eaten towers that tremble not!)
Resemble nothing that is ours.[1]
Around, by lifting winds forgot,
Resignedly beneath the sky   10
The melancholoy waters lie.

No rays from the holy heaven come down
On the long night-time of that town;
But light from out the lurid sea
Streams up the turrets silently—
Gleams up the pinnacles far and free—
Up domes—up spires—up kingly halls—
Up fanes—up Babylon-like walls[2]—
Up shadowy long-forgotten bowers
Of sculptured ivy and stone flowers—   20
Up many and many a marvellous shrine
Whose wreathéd friezes intertwine
The viol, the violet, and the vine.
Resignedly beneath the sky
The melancholy waters lie.
So blend the turrets and shadows there
That all seem pendulous in air,
While from a proud tower in the town
Death looks gigantically down.

There open fanes and gaping graves   30
Yawn level with the luminous waves;
But not the riches there that lie
In each idol's diamond eye—
Not the gaily-jewelled dead
Tempt the waters from their bed;
For no ripples curl, alas!
Along that wilderness of glass—
No swellings tell that winds may be
Upon some far-off happier sea—
No heavings hint that winds have been   40
On seas less hideously serene.[3]

But lo, a stir is in the air!
The wave—there is a movement there!
As if the towers had thrust aside,

---

[1] Characteristically, Poe cancels out the familiar and the finite to achieve his dreamlike effects.
[2] Up temples, up walls that, along with the city of Babylon, are doomed to destruction, according to the Old Testament.
[3] This oxymoron removes the image of the sea from normal contexts into the realm of Poe's imagination.

In slightly sinking, the dull tide—
As if their tops had feebly given
A void within the filmy Heaven.
The waves have now a redder glow—
The hours are breathing faint and low—
And when, amid no earthly moans,   50
Down, down that town shall settle hence,
Hell, rising from a thousand thrones,[4]
Shall do it reverence.

1831

SONNET—SILENCE*

There are some qualities—some incorporate[1] things,
　　That have a double life, which thus is made
A type of that twin entity which springs
　　From matter and light, evinced in solid and shade.
There is a two-fold *Silence*—sea and shore—
　　Body and soul. One dwells in lonely places,
　　Newly with grass o'ergrown; some solemn graces,
Some human memories and tearful lore,
Render him terrorless: his name's "No More."
He is the corporate Silence: dread him not!   10
　　No power hath he of evil in himself;
But should some urgent fate (untimely lot!)
　　Bring thee to meet his shadow (nameless elf,
That haunteth the lone regions where hath trod
No foot of man,) commend thyself to God![2]

1840

DREAM-LAND*

By a route obscure and lonely,
Haunted by ill angels only,
Where an Eidolon,[1] named NIGHT,

---

　[4] "Hell . . . stirreth up the dead for thee. . .; it hath raised up from their thrones all the kings of the nations," from Isaiah 14:9.
　* First published in the Philadelphia *Saturday Courier* in 1840, reprinted in journals in the 1840s, and included in *The Raven and Other Poems* (1845). This fifteen-line poem is a variation on the traditional fourteen-line sonnet.
　[1] Incorporeal, spiritual.
　[2] The silence of the body, which has a name ("No More") and is a product of memory, need not be feared; but the silence of the soul, nameless and alien, makes one ask for God's mercy.
　* First published in *Graham's Magazine* in 1844, reprinted in the *Broadway Journal* in 1845, and included in *The Raven and Other Poems* (1845).
　[1] A phantom.

On a black throne reigns upright,
I have reached these lands but newly
From an ultimate dim Thule[2]—
From a wild weird clime that lieth, sublime,
    Out of SPACE—out of TIME.[3]

Bottomless vales and boundless floods,
And chasms, and caves and Titan[4] woods,   10
With forms that no man can discover
For the tears that drip all over;
Mountains toppling evermore
Into seas without a shore;
Seas that restlessly aspire,
Surging, unto skies of fire;
Lakes that endlessly outspread
Their lone waters—lone and dead,—
Their still waters—still and chilly
With the snows of the lolling lily.   20

By the lakes that thus outspread
Their lone waters, lone and dead,—
Their sad waters, sad and chilly
With the snows of the lolling lily,—
By the mountains—near the river
Murmuring lowly, murmuring ever,—
By the grey woods,—by the swamp
Where the toad and the newt encamp,—
By the dismal tarns[5] and pools
    Where dwell the Ghouls,—   30
By each spot the most unholy—
In each nook most melancholy,—
There the traveller meets, aghast,
Sheeted Memories of the Past—
Shrouded forms that start and sigh
As they pass the wanderer by—
White-robed forms of friends long given,
In agony, to the Earth—and Heaven.

For the heart whose woes are legion
'T is a peaceful, soothing region—   40
For the spirit that walks in shadow
'T is—oh 't is an Eldorado![6]

---

[2] Among ancient geographers, an island North of Britain, thought to be the northernmost part of the habitable world (used in the phrase "ultima Thule," the most remote place).

[3] Poe moves his setting beyond space and time, cancels out limits known by human experience (valleys have no bottoms, seas no shores), and thus arrives in a region of the imagination where the dreamer is supreme.

[4] Enormous, titanic; according to Greek myth, the Titans were giant gods deposed by the gods of Olympus.

[5] Small mountain lakes.

[6] A legendary land of gold and riches sought by Spanish conquerors of South America.

But the traveller, travelling through it,
May not—dare not openly view it;
Never its mysteries are exposed
To the weak human eye unclosed;
So wills its King, who hath forbid
The uplifting of the fringéd lid;
And thus the sad Soul that here passes
Beholds it but through darkened glasses.   50

By a route obscure and lonely,
Haunted by ill angels only,
Where an Eidolon, named Night,
On a black throne reigns upright,
I have wandered home but newly
From this ultimate dim Thule.

1844

THE RAVEN*

Once upon a midnight dreary, while I pondered, weak and weary,
Over many a quaint and curious volume of forgotten lore—
While I nodded, nearly napping, suddenly there came a tapping,
As of some one gently rapping, rapping at my chamber door.
"'T is some visiter," I muttered, "tapping at my chamber door—
          Only this and nothing more."

Ah, distinctly I remember it was in the bleak December;
And each separate dying ember wrought its ghost upon the floor.
Eagerly I wished the morrow;—vainly I had sought to borrow
From my books surcease of sorrow—sorrow for the lost Lenore—   10
For the rare and radiant maiden whom the angels name Lenore—
          Nameless *here* for evermore.[1]

And the silken, sad, uncertain rustling of each purple curtain
Thrilled me—filled me with fantastic terrors never felt before;
So that now, to still the beating of my heart, I stood repeating
"'T is some visiter entreating entrance at my chamber door—
Some late visiter entreating entrance at my chamber door;—
          This it is and nothing more."

Presently my soul grew stronger; hesitating then no longer,
"Sir," said I, "or Madam, truly your forgiveness I implore;   20
But the fact is I was napping, and so gently you came rapping,

---

* First typeset for the February 1845 issue of the *American Review,* but before that issue appeared it was printed in the New York *Evening Mirror* on January 29, 1845. The poem was reprinted in other periodicals in that year and was included in *The Raven and Other Poems* (1845). Instantly popular, it has remained Poe's best-known poem.
[1] Because Lenore has died, she will no longer be part of this world.

And so faintly you came tapping, tapping at my chamber door,
That I scarce was sure I heard you"—here I opened wide the door;———
          Darkness there and nothing more.

Deep into that darkness peering, long I stood there wondering, fearing,
Doubting, dreaming dreams no mortal ever dared to dream before;
But the silence was unbroken, and the stillness gave no token,
And the only word there spoken was the whispered word, "Lenore!"
This I whispered, and an echo murmured back the word "Lenore!"
          Merely this and nothing more.   30

Back into the chamber turning, all my soul within me burning,
Soon again I heard a tapping somewhat louder than before.
"Surely," said I, "surely that is something at my window lattice;
Let me see, then, what thereat is, and this mystery explore—
Let my heart be still a moment and this mystery explore;—
          'T is the wind and nothing more!"

Open here I flung the shutter, when, with many a flirt[2] and flutter
In there stepped a stately Raven of the saintly days of yore.
Not the least obeisance made he; not a minute stopped or stayed he;
But, with mien of lord or lady, perched above my chamber door—   40
Perched upon a bust of Pallas[3] just above my chamber door—
          Perched, and sat, and nothing more.

Then this ebony bird beguiling my sad fancy into smiling,
By the grave and stern decorum of the countenance it wore,
"Though thy crest be shorn and shaven, thou," I said, "art sure no craven,[4]
Ghastly grim and ancient Raven wandering from the Nightly shore—
Tell me what thy lordly name is on the Night's Plutonian[5] shore!"
          Quoth the Raven, "Nevermore."

Much I marvelled this ungainly fowl to hear discourse so plainly,
Though its answer little meaning—little relevancy bore;   50
For we cannot help agreeing that no living human being
Ever yet was blessed with seeing bird above his chamber door—
Bird or beast upon the sculptured bust above his chamber door,
          With such name as "Nevermore."

But the Raven, sitting lonely on the placid bust, spoke only
That one word, as if his soul in that one word he did outpour.
Nothing farther then he uttered—not a feather then he fluttered—

---

[2] A jerky movement.   [3] Pallas Athena: according to Greek myth, the goddess of wisdom.
[4] As Thomas O. Mabbott observes, a cowardly or craven knight sometimes had his head (crest) shaved. Mabbott also points out Poe's pun ("Nightly shore") in the following line.
[5] Black; according to Roman myth, Pluto is the ruler of the underworld of the dead.

Till I scarcely more than muttered "Other friends have flown before—
On the morrow *he* will leave me, as my hopes have flown before."
             Then the bird said "Nevermore."   60

Startled at the stillness broken by reply so aptly spoken,
"Doubtless," said I, "what it utters is its only stock and store
Caught from some unhappy master whom unmerciful Disaster
Followed fast and followed faster till his songs one burden bore—
Till the dirges of his Hope that melancholy burden bore
             Of 'Never—nevermore.'"

But the Raven still beguiling all my fancy into smiling,
Straight I wheeled a cushioned seat in front of bird, and bust and door;
Then, upon the velvet sinking, I betook myself to linking
Fancy unto fancy, thinking what this ominous bird of yore—   70
What this grim, ungainly, ghastly, gaunt, and ominous bird of yore
             Meant in croaking "Nevermore."

This I sat engaged in guessing, but no syllable expressing
To the fowl whose fiery eyes now burned into my bosom's core;
This and more I sat divining, with my head at ease reclining
On the cushion's velvet lining that the lamp-light gloated[6] o'er,
But whose velvet violet lining with the lamp-light gloating o'er,
             She shall press, ah, nevermore!

Then, methought, the air grew denser, perfumed from an unseen censer
Swung by Seraphim[7] whose foot-falls tinkled on the tufted floor.   80
 "Wretch," I cried, "thy God hath lent thee—by these angels he hath sent thee
Respite—respite and nepenthe[8] from thy memories of Lenore;
Quaff, oh quaff this kind nepenthe and forget this lost Lenore!"
             Quoth the Raven "Nevermore."

"Prophet!" said I, "thing of evil! prophet still, if bird or devil!—
Whether Tempter sent, or whether tempest tossed thee here ashore,
Desolate yet all undaunted, on this desert land enchanted—
On this home by Horror haunted—tell me truly, I implore—
Is there—*is* there balm in Gilead?[9]—tell me—tell me, I implore!"
             Quoth the Raven "Nevermore."   90

"Prophet!" said I, "thing of evil!—prophet still, if bird or devil!
By that Heaven that bends above us—by that God we both adore—

---

[6] Glowed as well as shone down maliciously.
[7] Angels (with bells, or tinkling foot-falls, at their ankles).
[8] A legendary drug that soothes and relieves anguish.
[9] "Is there no balm in Gilead?" from Jeremiah 8:22. Evergreens growing in Gilead, near the Sea of Galilee in Jordan, supplied a medicinal balm.

Tell this soul with sorrow laden if, within the distant Aidenn,[10]
It shall clasp a sainted maiden whom the angels name Lenore.—
Clasp a rare and radiant maiden whom the angels name Lenore."
    Quoth the Raven "Nevermore."

"Be that word our sign of parting, bird or fiend!" I shrieked, upstarting—
"Get thee back into the tempest and the Night's Plutonian shore!
Leave no black plume as a token of that lie thy soul hath spoken!
Leave my loneliness unbroken!—quit the bust above my door!   100
Take thy beak from out my heart, and take thy form from off my door!"
    Quoth the Raven "Nevermore."

And the Raven, never flitting, still is sitting, *still* is sitting
On the pallid bust of Pallas just above my chamber door;
And his eyes have all the seeming of a demon's that is dreaming,
And the lamp-light o'er him streaming throws his shadow on the floor;
And my soul from out that shadow that lies floating on the floor
    Shall be lifted—nevermore!

            1845

ULALUME*

 The skies they were ashen and sober;
  The leaves they were crispèd and sere—
  The leaves they were withering and sere;
 It was night in the lonesome October
  Of my most immemorial[1] year;
 It was hard by the dim lake of Auber,[2]
  In the misty mid region of Weir[3]—
 It was down by the dank tarn[4] of Auber,
  In the ghoul-haunted woodland of Weir.

 Here once, through an alley Titanic,[5]   10
  Of cypress, I roamed with my Soul—
  Of cypress, with Psyche, my Soul.
 These were days when my heart was volcanic
  As the scoriac rivers[6] that roll—

---

[10] Eden or Heaven, from the Arabic *Adn*.
 * First published in the *American Review* in 1847 and reprinted in journals in 1848 and 1849. Poe may have taken his title from the Latin *ululare*, to wail. Along with rhyme and reiteration, the sound of place names adds much to the atmosphere of the poem.
 [1] Memorable.   [2] After Daniel Auber (1782–1871), a French composer.
 [3] After Robert Walter Weir (1803–1889), an American landscape painter.
 [4] A small mountain lake.
 [5] Enormous; according to Greek myth, the Titans were giant gods deposed by the gods of Olympus.
 [6] Rivers of slaggy, loose lava.

As the lavas that restlessly roll
Their sulphurous currents down Yaanek[7]
In the ultimate climes of the pole—
That groan as they roll down Mount Yaanek
In the realms of the boreal pole.[8]

Our talk had been serious and sober,   20
But our thoughts they were palsied and sere—
Our memories were treacherous and sere—
For we knew not the month was October,
And we marked not the night of the year—
(Ah, night of all nights in the year![9])
We noted not the dim lake of Auber—
(Though once we had journeyed down here)—
Remembered not the dank tarn of Auber,
Nor the ghoul-haunted woodland of Weir.

And now, as the night was senescent[10]   30
And star-dials pointed to morn—
As the star-dials hinted of morn—
At the end of our path a liquescent
And nebulous lustre was born,
Out of which a miraculous crescent
Arose with a duplicate horn—
Astarte's[11] bediamonded crescent
Distinct with its duplicate horn.

And I said—"She is warmer than Dian:[12]
She rolls through an ether of sighs—   40
She revels in a region of sighs:
She has seen that the tears are not dry on
These cheeks, where the worm never dies[13]
And has come past the stars of the Lion[14]
To point us the path to the skies—
To the Lethean[15] peace of the skies—
Come up, in despite of the Lion,
To shine on us with her bright eyes—

---

[7] Poe probably invented this mountain and gave it an evocative name that would rhyme with "volcanic."

[8] "Boreal" means northern (from Boreas, the North wind); but some Poe scholars, including Thomas O. Mabbott, feel that because of the volcanic activity mentioned in the poem, "boreal" here means "southern": an active volcano had been discovered on Antarctica in 1840.

[9] All Hallows' Eve, or Halloween.   [10] Growing old.

[11] A Phoenician goddess of fertility and sexual love, also regarded as a moon goddess; in Poe's lines, the moon is crescent-shaped.

[12] Diana, the Roman moongoddess, also identified with hunting and chastity; the "warmer" Astarte is contrasted with the chaste Diana.

[13] In Isaiah 66:24 and Mark 9:48, "the worm [that devours the dead] shall not die" for sinners.

[14] The constellation Leo.

[15] Forgetful; according to Greek and Roman myth, "oblivion." Souls about to be reincarnated drink from the waters of the river Lethe in Hades to forget their previous existence.

Come up through the lair of the Lion,
 With love in her luminous eyes."   50

But Psyche,[16] uplifting her finger,
 Said—"Sadly this star I mistrust—
 Her pallor I strangely mistrust:—
Oh, hasten!—oh, let us not linger!
 Oh, fly!—let us fly!—for we must."
In terror she spoke, letting sink her
 Wings until they trailed in the dust—
In agony sobbed, letting sink her
 Plumes till they trailed in the dust—
 Till they sorrowfully trailed in the dust.   60

I replied—"This is nothing but dreaming:
 Let us on by this tremulous light!
 Let us bathe in this crystalline light!
Its Sibyllic[17] splendor is beaming
 With Hope and in Beauty to-night:—
 See!—it flickers up the sky through the night!
Ah, we safely may trust to its gleaming,
 And be sure it will lead us aright—
We safely may trust to a gleaming
 That cannot but guide us aright,   70
 Since it flickers up to Heaven through the night."

Thus I pacified Psyche and kissed her,
 And tempted her out of her gloom—
 And conquered her scruples and gloom;
And we passed to the end of the vista,
 But were stopped by the door of a tomb—
 By the door of a legended[18] tomb;
And I said—"What is written, sweet sister,
 On the door of this legended tomb?"
She replied—"Ulalume—Ulalume—   80
 'T is the vault of thy lost Ulalume!"

Then my heart it grew ashen and sober
 As the leaves that were crispèd and sere—
 As the leaves that were withering and sere,
And I cried—"It was surely October
 On *this* very night of last year
 That I journeyed—I journeyed down here—
 That I brought a dread burden down here—
 On this night of all nights in the year,
 Ah, what demon has tempted me here?   90
Well I know, now, this dim lake of Auber—
 This misty mid region of Weir—

[16] The soul, personified as a butterfly.
[17] Prophetic; according to Greek and Roman myth, the Sibyls could foretell the future.
[18] Inscribed.

Well I know, now, this dank tarn of Auber,
    This ghoul-haunted woodland of Weir."

Said we,[19] then—the two, then—"Ah, can it
    Have been that the woodlandish ghouls—
    The pitiful, the merciful ghouls,
To bar up our way and to ban it
    From the secret that lies in these wolds[20]   100
    From the thing that lies in these wolds—
Have drawn up the spectre of a planet
    From the limbo[21] of lunary souls—
This sinfully scintillant[22] planet
    From the Hell of the planetary souls?"

1847

ANNABEL LEE*

It was many and many a year ago,
    In a kingdom by the sea,
That a maiden there lived whom you may know
    By the name of ANNABEL LEE;
And this maiden she lived with no other thought
    Than to love and be loved by me.

I was a child and *she* was a child,
    In this kingdom by the sea,
But we loved with a love that was more than love—
    I and my ANNABEL LEE—   10
With a love that the wingèd seraphs of heaven
    Coveted her and me.

And this was the reason that, long ago,
    In this kingdom by the sea,
A wind blew out of a cloud, chilling
    My beautiful ANNABEL LEE;
So that her highborn kinsmen came
    And bore her away from me,
To shut her up in a sepulchre
    In this kingdom by the sea.   20

[19] The speaker of the poem and Psyche. At the suggestion of Sarah Helen Whitman, a poet to whom Poe was engaged, he omitted this final stanza from some printings of "Ulalume."

[20] Elevated plains.

[21] The resting place of souls who can enter neither Heaven nor Hell (such as infants and the unbaptized).

[22] Shining, scintillating.

* First published in the *New-York Tribune* on October 9, 1849, two days after Poe's death. In July 1849 Poe had sold the poem for publication to *Sartain's Union Magazine*, then given copies to several people who had helped him financially; some of them had the poem printed before *Sartain's* published it in January 1850.

The angels, not half so happy in heaven,
 Went envying her and me—
Yes!—that was the reason (as all men know,
 In this kingdom by the sea)
That the wind came out of the cloud by night,
 Chilling and killing my ANNABEL LEE.

But our love it was stronger by far than the love
 Of those who were older than we—
 Of many far wiser than we—
And neither the angels in heaven above,   30
 Nor the demons down under the sea,
Can ever dissever my soul from the soul
 Of the beautiful ANNABEL LEE:

For the moon never beams, without bringing me dreams
 Of the beautiful ANNABEL LEE;
And the stars never rise, but I feel the bright eyes
 Of the beautiful ANNABEL LEE:
And so, all the night-tide, I lie down by the side
Of my darling—my darling—my life and my bride,
 In the sepulchre there by the sea—   40
 In her tomb by the sounding sea.[1]

1849

ELDORADO*

 Gaily bedight,[1]
 A gallant knight,
In sunshine and in shadow,
 Had journeyed long,
 Singing a song,
In search of Eldorado.

 But he grew old—
 This knight so bold—
And o'er his heart a shadow
 Fell as he found   10
 No spot of ground
That looked like Eldorado.

---

[1] Early manuscript versions of the poem contain this final line, but in a late revision Poe altered it to read, "In her tomb by the side of the sea." Most critics prefer the earlier version.

* First published in *The Flag of Our Union* in 1849. The occasion for the poem was the California gold rush, but the ballad meter and archaic diction of the poem remove it from any specific context and make it a fable of the human search for an "Eldorado," a land of gold and riches like that sought by Spanish conquistadores.

[1] Adorned, dressed.

And as his strength
Failed him at length,
He met a pilgrim[2] shadow—
"Shadow," said he,
"Where can it be—
This land of Eldorado?"

"Over the Mountains
Of the Moon,   20
Down the Valley of the Shadow,
Ride, boldly ride,"
The shade replied,—
"If you seek for Eldorado."

1849

from REVIEW OF NATHANIEL HAWTHORNE'S
*TWICE-TOLD TALES**

We said a few hurried words about Mr. Hawthorne in our last number, with the
design of speaking more fully in the present.[1] We are still, however, pressed for
room, and must necessarily discuss his volumes more briefly and more at random
than their high merits deserve.

The book professes to be a collection of *tales,* yet is, in two respects, mis-
named. These pieces are now in their third republication, and, of course, are
thrice-told.[2] Moreover, they are by no means *all* tales, either in the ordinary or in
the legitimate understanding of the term. Many of them are pure essays; for example, "Sights from a Steeple," "Sunday at Home," "Little Annie's Ramble," "A
Rill from the Town Pump," "The Toll-Gatherer's Day," "The Haunted Mind,"
"The Sister Years," "Snow-Flakes," "Night Sketches," and "Foot-Prints on the
Sea-Shore." We mention these matters chiefly on account of their discrepancy
with that marked precision and finish by which the body of the work is distinguished.

Of the essays just named, we must be content to speak in brief. They are each
and all beautiful, without being characterised by the polish and adaptation so visible in the tales proper. A painter would at once note their leading or predominant
feature, and style it *repose.* There is no attempt at effect. All is quiet, thoughtful,
subdued. Yet this repose may exist simultaneously with high originality of
thought; and Mr. Hawthorne has demonstrated the fact. At every turn we meet
with novel combinations; yet these combinations never surpass the limits of the
quiet. We are soothed as we read; and withal is a calm astonishment that ideas so

---

[2] Wandering.

* This review was first published in *Graham's Magazine* in May 1842.

[1] For the April issue of *Graham's,* Poe had written a brief assessment of Hawthorne's collection of
tales.

[2] The present tales and sketches had first appeared in magazines and periodicals, then in book form in
1837 as *Twice-Told Tales.* Poe is reviewing an 1842 edition of *Twice-Told Tales,* so the contents of
the volumes are "thrice-told."

apparently obvious have never occurred or been presented to us before. Herein our author differs materially from Lamb or Hunt or Hazlitt[3]— who, with vivid originality of manner and expression, have less of the true novelty of thought than is generally supposed, and whose originality, at best, has an uneasy and meretricious quaintness, replete with startling effects unfounded in nature, and inducing trains of reflection which lead to no satisfactory result. The Essays of Hawthorne have much of the character of Irving,[4] with more of originality, and less of finish; while, compared with the Spectator, they have a vast superiority at all points. The Spectator,[5] Mr. Irving, and Mr. Hawthorne have in common that tranquil and subdued manner which we have chosen to denominate *repose;* but, in the case of the two former, this repose is attained rather by the absence of novel combination, or of originality, than otherwise, and consists chiefly in the calm, quiet, unostentatious expression of commonplace thoughts, in an unambitious, unadulterated Saxon. In them, by strong effort, we are made to conceive the absence of all. In the essays before us the absence of effort is too obvious to be mistaken, and a strong under-current of *suggestion* runs continuously beneath the upper stream of the tranquil thesis. In short, these effusions of Mr. Hawthorne are the product of a truly imaginative intellect, restrained, and in some measure repressed, by fastidiousness of taste, by constitutional melancholy and by indolence.

But it is of his tales that we desire principally to speak. The tale proper, in our opinion, affords unquestionably the fairest field for the exercise of the loftiest talent, which can be afforded by the wide domains of mere prose. Were we bidden to say how the highest genius could be most advantageously employed for the best display of its own powers, we should answer, without hesitation—in the composition of a rhymed poem, not to exceed in length what might be perused in an hour. Within this limit alone can the highest order of true poetry exist. We need only here say, upon this topic, that, in almost all classes of composition, the unity of effect or impression is a point of the greatest importance. It is clear, moreover, that this unity cannot be thoroughly preserved in productions whose perusal cannot be completed at one sitting. We may continue the reading of a prose composition, from the very nature of prose itself, much longer than we can persevere, to any good purpose, in the perusal of a poem. This later, if truly fulfilling the demands of the poetic sentiment, induces an exaltation of the soul which cannot be long sustained. All high excitements are necessarily transient. Thus a long poem is a paradox. And, without unity of impression, the deepest effects cannot be brought about. Epics were the offspring of an imperfect sense of Art, and their reign is no more. A poem *too* brief may produce a vivid, but never an intense or enduring impression. Without a certain continuity of effort—without a certain duration or repetition of purpose—the soul is never deeply moved. There must be the dropping of the water upon the rock. De Béranger[6] has wrought brilliant things—pungent and spirit-stirring—but, like all immassive[7] bodies, they lack *momentum,* and thus fail to satisfy the Poetic Sentiment. They sparkle and excite, but, from want of continuity, fail deeply to impress. Extreme brevity will degener-

---

[3] The English essayists Charles Lamb (1775–1834), Leigh Hunt (1784–1859), and William Hazlitt (1778–1830).

[4] Washington Irving (1783–1859), a leading American writer of sketches and tales; Poe's April review had compared Hawthorne's "Essays" to Irving's *Tales of a Traveller* (1824).

[5] An English periodical that published highly respected essays by such writers as the *Spectator's* editors, Joseph Addison (1672–1719) and Richard Steele (1672–1729).

[6] Pierre-Jean de Béranger (1780–1857), a French poet.   [7] Massless.

ate into epigrammatism; but the sin of extreme length is even more unpardonable. *In medio tutissimus ibis.*[8]

Were we called upon, however, to designate that class of composition which, next to such a poem as we have suggested, should best fulfil the demands of high genius—should offer it the most advantageous field of exertion—we should un-hesitatingly speak of the prose tale, as Mr. Hawthorne has here exemplified it. We allude to the short prose narrative, requiring from a half-hour to one or two hours in its perusal. The ordinary novel is objectionable, from its length, for reasons already stated in substance. As it cannot be read at one sitting, it deprives itself, of course, of the immense force derivable from *totality*. Worldly interests interven-ing during the pauses of perusal, modify, annul, or counteract, in a greater or less degree, the impressions of the book. But simple cessation in reading, would, of itself, be sufficient to destroy the true unity. In the brief tale, however, the author is enabled to carry out the fulness of his intention, be it what it may. During the hour of perusal the soul of the reader is at the writer's control. There are no exter-nal or extrinsic influences—resulting from weariness or interruption.

A skilful literary artist has constructed a tale. If wise, he has not fashioned his thoughts to accommodate his incidents; but having conceived, with deliberate care, a certain unique or single *effect* to be wrought out, he then invents such incidents—he then combines such events as may best aid him in establishing this preconceived effect. If his very initial sentence tend not to the outbringing of this effect, then he has failed in his first step. In the whole composition there should be no word written, of which the tendency, direct or indirect, is not to the one pre-established design. And by such means, with such care and skill, a picture is at length painted which leaves in the mind of him who contemplates it with a kindred art, a sense of the fullest satisfaction. The idea of the tale has been presented unblemished, because undisturbed; and this is an end unattainable by the novel. Undue brevity is just as exceptionable here as in the poem; but undue length is yet more to be avoided.

We have said that the tale has a point of superiority even over the poem. In fact, while the *rhythm* of this latter is an essential aid in the development of the poet's highest idea—the idea of the Beautiful—the artificialities of this rhythm are an inseparable bar to the development of all points of thought or expression which have their basis in *Truth*. But Truth is often, and in very great degree, the aim of the tale. Some of the finest tales are tales of ratiocination.[9] Thus the field of this species of composition, if not in so elevated a region on the mountain of Mind, is a table-land of far vaster extent than the domain of the mere poem. Its products are never so rich, but infinitely more numerous, and more appreciable by the mass of mankind. The writer of the prose tale, in short, may bring to his theme a vast variety of modes or inflections of thought and expression—(the ratiocinative, for example, the sarcastic, or the humorous) which are not only antagonistical to the nature of the poem, but absolutely forbidden by one of its most peculiar and indis-pensable adjuncts; we allude, of course, to rhythm. It may be added here, *par parenthèse,*[10] that the author who aims at the purely beautiful in a prose tale is laboring at great disadvantage. For Beauty can be better treated in the poem. Not so with terror, or passion, or horror, or a multitude of such other points. And here it will be seen how full of prejudice are the usual animadversions[11] against those

---

[8] "You will go most safely in a middle course" (Latin).   [9] Logic, reasoning.
[10] "Parenthetically" (French).   [11] Criticisms.

tales of effect, many fine examples of which were found in the earlier numbers of Blackwood.[12] The impressions produced were wrought in a legitimate sphere of action, and constituted a legitimate although sometimes an exaggerated interest. They were relished by every man of genius: although there were found many men of genius who condemned them without just ground. The true critic will but demand that the design intended be accomplished, to the fullest extent, by the means most advantageously applicable.

We have very few American tales of real merit—we may say, indeed, none, with the exception of "The Tales of a Traveller" of Washington Irving, and these "Twice-Told Tales" of Mr. Hawthorne. Some of the pieces of Mr. John Neal[13] abound in vigor and originality; but in general, his compositions of this class are excessively diffuse, extravagant, and indicative of an imperfect sentiment of Art. Articles at random are, now and then, met with in our periodicals which might be advantageously compared with the best effusions of the British Magazines; but, upon the whole, we are far behind our progenitors in this department of literature.

Of Mr. Hawthorne's Tales we would say, emphatically, that they belong to the highest region of Art—an Art subservient to genius of a very lofty order. We had supposed, with good reason for so supposing, that he had been thrust into his present position by one of the impudent *cliques* which beset our literature, and whose pretensions it is our full purpose to expose at the earliest opportunity; but we have been most agreeably mistaken. We know of few compositions which the critic can more honestly commend than these "Twice-Told Tales." As Americans, we feel proud of the book.

Mr. Hawthorne's distinctive trait is invention, creation, imagination, originality—a trait which, in the literature of fiction, is positively worth all the rest. But the nature of originality, so far as regards its manifestation in letters, is but imperfectly understood. The inventive or original mind as frequently displays itself in novelty of *tone* as in novelty of matter. Mr. Hawthorne is original at *all* points.

It would be a matter of some difficulty to designate the best of these tales; we repeat that, without exception, they are beautiful. "Wakefield" is remarkable for the skill with which an old idea—a well-known incident—is worked up or discussed. A man of whims conceives the purpose of quitting his wife and residing *incognito,* for twenty years, in her immediate neighborhood. Something of this kind actually happened in London. The force of Mr. Hawthorne's tale lies in the analysis of the motives which must or might have impelled the husband to such folly, in the first instance, with the possible causes of his perseverance. Upon this thesis a sketch of singular power has been constructed.

"The Wedding Knell" is full of the boldest imagination—an imagination fully controlled by taste. The most captious critic could find no flaw in this production.

"The Minister's Black Veil" is a masterly composition of which the sole defect is that to the rabble its exquisite skill will be *caviare.* The *obvious* meaning of this article will be found to smother its insinuated one. The *moral* put into the mouth of the dying minister will be supposed to convey the *true* import of the narrative; and that a crime of dark dye, (having reference to the "young lady") has been committed, is a point which only minds congenial with that of the author will perceive.

* * *

[12] *Blackwood's Edinburgh Magazine,* a British monthly that Poe knew well, published many Gothic tales of terror.

[13] Neal (1793–1876) was an energetic American writer who published articles (on American writers and other subjects) in *Blackwood's Edinburgh Magazine* in the 1820s and also wrote tales and novels.

In the way of objection we have scarcely a word to say of these tales. There is, perhaps, a somewhat too general or prevalent *tone*—a tone of melancholy and mysticism. The subjects are insufficiently varied. There is not so much of *versatility* evinced as we might well be warranted in expecting from the high powers of Mr. Hawthorne. But beyond these trivial exceptions we have really none to make. The style is purity itself. Force abounds. High imagination gleams from every page. Mr. Hawthorne is a man of the truest genius. We only regret that the limits of our Magazine will not permit us to pay him that full tribute of commendation, which, under other circumstances, we should be so eager to pay.

1842

THE PHILOSOPHY OF COMPOSITION*

Charles Dickens, in a note now lying before me, alluding to an examination I once made of the mechanism of "Barnaby Rudge,"[1] says—"By the way, are you aware that Godwin wrote his 'Caleb Williams' backwards?[2] He first involved his hero in a web of difficulties, forming the second volume, and then, for the first, cast about him for some mode of accounting for what had been done."

I cannot think this the *precise* mode of procedure on the part of Godwin—and indeed what he himself acknowledges, is not altogether in accordance with Mr. Dickens' idea—but the author of "Caleb Williams" was too good an artist not to perceive the advantage derivable from at least a somewhat similar process. Nothing is more clear than that every plot, worth the name, must be elaborated to its *dénouement*[3] before anything be attempted with the pen. It is only with the *dénouement* constantly in view that we can give a plot its indispensable air of consequence, or causation, by making the incidents, and especially the tone at all points, tend to the development of the intention.

There is a radical error, I think, in the usual mode of constructing a story. Either history affords a thesis—or one is suggested by an incident of the day—*or,* at best, the author sets himself to work in the combination of striking events to form merely the basis of his narrative—designing, generally, to fill in with description, dialogue, or authorial comment, whatever crevices of fact, or action, may, from page to page, render themselves apparent.

I prefer commencing with the consideration of an *effect*. Keeping originality *always* in view—for he is false to himself who ventures to dispense with so obvious and so easily attainable a source of interest—I say to myself, in the first place, "Of the innumerable effects, or impressions, of which the heart, the intellect, or (more generally) the soul is susceptible, what one shall I, on the present occasion, select?" Having chosen a novel, first, and secondly a vivid effect, I consider whether it can be best wrought by incident or tone—whether by ordinary incidents and peculiar tone, or the converse, or by peculiarity both of incident and tone—

---

* First published in *Graham's Magazine* in 1846; in this famous essay Poe purports to explain step-by-step how he wrote "The Raven." Whether or not his explanation is serious, the idea of the artist as a deliberate craftsman is central to Poe's theory of art.

[1] While Dickens's novel *Barnaby Rudge* was being serialized in 1842, Poe wrote an analytical review predicting the conclusion and correctly identifying the murderer.

[2] In an 1832 preface to the novel *Caleb Williams* (1794), William Godwin (1756–1836) claims that he planned his novel from the ending to the beginning.

[3] The unraveling of the plot.

afterward looking about me (or rather within) for such combinations of event, or tone, as shall best aid me in the construction of the effect.

I have often thought how interesting a magazine paper[4] might be written by any author who would—that is to say who could—detail, step by step, the processes by which any one of his compositions attained its ultimate point of completion. Why such a paper has never been given to the world, I am much at a loss to say—but, perhaps, the autorial vanity has had more to do with the omission than any one other cause. Most writers—poets in especial—prefer having it understood that they compose by a species of fine frenzy—an ecstatic intuition—and would positively shudder at letting the public take a peep behind the scenes, at the elaborate and vacillating crudities of thought—at the true purposes seized only at the last moment—at the innumerable glimpses of idea that arrived not at the maturity of full view—at the fully matured fancies discarded in despair as unmanageable—at the cautious selections and rejections—at the painful erasures and interpolations—in a word, at the wheels and pinions—the tackle for scene-shifting—the step-ladders and demon-traps—the cock's feathers, the red paint and the black patches, which, in ninety-nine cases out of the hundred, constitute the properties of the literary *histrio*.[5]

I am aware, on the other hand, that the case is by no means common, in which an author is at all in condition to retrace the steps by which his conclusions have been attained. In general, suggestions, having arisen pell-mell, are pursued and forgotten in a similar manner.

For my own part, I have neither sympathy with the repugnance alluded to, nor, at any time the least difficulty in recalling to mind the progressive steps of any of my compositions; and, since the interest of an analysis, or reconstruction, such as I have considered a *desideratum*,[6] is quite independent of any real or fancied interest in the thing analyzed, it will not be regarded as a breach of decorum on my part to show the *modus operandi*[7] by which some one of my own works was put together. I select "The Raven," as most generally known. It is my design to render it manifest that no one point in its composition is referrible either to accident or intuition—that the work proceeded, step by step, to its completion with the precision and rigid consequence of a mathematical problem.

Let us dismiss, as irrelevant to the poem, *per se,* the circumstance—or say the necessity—which, in the first place, gave rise to the intention of composing *a* poem that should suit at once the popular and the critical taste.

We commence, then, with this intention.

The initial consideration was that of extent. If any literary work is too long to be read at one sitting, we must be content to dispense with the immensely important effect derivable from unity of impression—for, if two sittings be required, the affairs of the world interfere, and every thing like totality is at once destroyed. But since, *ceteris paribus,*[8] no poet can afford to dispense with *any thing* that may advance his design, it but remains to be seen whether there is, in extent, any advantage to counterbalance the loss of unity which attends it. Here I say no, at once. What we term a long poem is, in fact, merely a succession of brief ones— that is to say, of brief poetical effects. It is needless to demonstrate that a poem is such, only inasmuch as it intensely excites, by elevating, the soul; and all intense excitements are, through a psychal[9] necessity, brief. For this reason, at least one

---

[4] Article.   [5] "Artist" or "performer" (Latin).   [6] "A thing to be desired" (Latin).
[7] "Mode of operation" (Latin).
[8] "Other things being equal" (Latin).   [9] Psychological.

half of the "Paradise Lost"[10] is essentially prose—a succession of poetical excitements interspersed, *inevitably,* with corresponding depressions—the whole being deprived, through the extremeness of its length, of the vastly important artistic element, totality, or unity, of effect.

It appears evident, then, that there is a distinct limit, as regards length, to all works of literary art—the limit of a single sitting—and that, although in certain classes of prose composition, such as "Robinson Crusoe,"[11] (demanding no unity,) this limit may be advantageously overpassed, it can never properly be overpassed in a poem. Within this limit, the extent of a poem may be made to bear mathematical relation to its merit—in other words, to the excitement or elevation—again in other words, to the degree of the true poetical effect which it is capable of inducing; for it is clear that the brevity must be in direct ratio of the intensity of the intended effect:—this, with one proviso—that a certain degree of duration is absolutely requisite for the production of any effect at all.

Holding in view these considerations, as well as that degree of excitement which I deemed not above the popular, while not below the critical, taste, I reached at once what I conceived the proper *length* for my intended poem—a length of about one hundred lines. It is, in fact, a hundred and eight.

My next thought concerned the choice of an impression, or effect, to be conveyed: and here I may as well observe that, throughout the construction, I kept steadily in view the design of rendering the work *universally* appreciable. I should be carried too far out of my immediate topic were I to demonstrate a point upon which I have repeatedly insisted, and which, with the poetical, stands not in the slightest need of demonstration—the point, I mean, that Beauty is the sole legitimate province of the poem. A few words, however, in elucidation of my real meaning, which some of my friends have evinced a disposition to misrepresent. That pleasure which is at once the most intense, the most elevating, and the most pure, is, I believe, found in the contemplation of the beautiful. When, indeed, men speak of Beauty, they mean, precisely, not a quality, as is supposed, but an effect—they refer, in short, just to that intense and pure elevation of *soul—not* of intellect, or of heart—upon which I have commented, and which is experienced in consequence of contemplating "the beautiful." Now I designate Beauty as the province of the poem, merely because it is an obvious rule of Art that effects should be made to spring from direct causes—that objects should be attained through means best adapted for their attainment—no one as yet having been weak enough to deny that the peculiar elevation alluded to is *most readily* attained in the poem. Now the object, Truth, or the satisfaction of the intellect, and the object Passion, or the excitement of the heart, are, although attainable, to a certain extent, in poetry, far more readily attainable in prose. Truth, in fact, demands a precision, and Passion a *homeliness* (the truly passionate will comprehend me) which are absolutely antagonistic to that Beauty which, I maintain, is the excitement, or pleasurable elevation, of the soul. It by no means follows from any thing here said, that passion, or even truth, may not be introduced, and even profitably introduced, into a poem—for they may serve in elucidation, or aid the general effect, as do discords in music, by contrast—but the true artist will always contrive, first, to tone them into proper subservience to the predominant aim, and,

---

[10] *Paradise Lost* (1667), an epic poem in twelve books by John Milton (1608–1674). In length, this ambitious poem about human disobedience and the loss of Paradise comes to more than 10,500 lines.

[11] *The Life and Strange Surprising Adventures of Robinson Crusoe* (1719), an episodic novel of shipwreck in the Caribbean Sea and the adventures following Crusoe's rescue, by Daniel Defoe (1660–1731).

secondly, to enveil them, as far as possible, in that Beauty which is the atmosphere and the essence of the poem.

Regarding, then, Beauty as my province, my next question referred to the *tone* of its highest manifestation—and all experience has shown that this tone is one of *sadness*. Beauty of whatever kind, in its supreme development, invariably excites the sensitive soul to tears. Melancholy is thus the most legitimate of all the poetical tones.

The length, the province, and the tone, being thus determined, I betook myself to ordinary induction, with the view of obtaining some artistic piquancy which might serve me as a key-note in the construction of the poem—some pivot upon which the whole structure might turn. In carefully thinking over all the usual artistic effects—or more properly *points*, in the theatrical sense—I did not fail to perceive immediately that no one had been so universally employed as that of the *refrain*. The universality of its employment sufficed to assure me of its intrinsic value, and spared me the necessity of submitting it to analysis. I considered it, however, with regard to its susceptibility of improvement, and soon saw it to be in a primitive condition. As commonly used, the *refrain*, or burden, not only is limited to lyric verse, but depends for its impression upon the force of monotone— both in sound and thought. The pleasure is deduced solely from the sense of identity—of repetition. I resolved to diversify, and so heighten, the effect, by adhering, in general, to the monotone of sound, while I continually varied that of thought: that is to say, I determined to produce continuously novel effects, by the variation *of the application* of the *refrain*—the *refrain* itself remaining, for the most part, unvaried.

These points being settled, I next bethought me of the *nature* of my *refrain*. Since its application was to be repeatedly varied, it was clear that the *refrain* itself must be brief, for there would have been an insurmountable difficulty in frequent variations of application in any sentence of length. In proportion to the brevity of the sentence, would, of course, be the facility of the variation. This led me at once to a single word as the best *refrain*.

The question now arose as to the *character* of the word. Having made up my mind to a *refrain*, the division of the poem into stanzas was, of course, a corollary: the *refrain* forming the close of each stanza. That such a close, to have force, must be sonorous and susceptible of protracted emphasis, admitted no doubt: and these considerations inevitably led me to the long *o* as the most sonorous vowel, in connection with *r* as the most producible consonant.

The sound of the *refrain* being thus determined, it became necessary to select a word embodying this sound, and at the same time in the fullest possible keeping with that melancholy which I had predetermined as the tone of the poem. In such a search it would have been absolutely impossible to overlook the word "Nevermore." In fact, it was the very first which presented itself.

The next *desideratum* was a pretext for the continuous use of the one word "nevermore." In observing the difficulty which I at once found in inventing a sufficiently plausible reason for its continuous repetition, I did not fail to perceive that this difficulty arose solely from the pre-assumption that the word was to be so continuously or monotonously spoken by *a human* being—I did not fail to perceive, in short, that the difficulty lay in the reconciliation of this monotony with the exercise of reason on the part of the creature repeating the word. Here, then, immediately arose the idea of a *non*-reasoning creature capable of speech; and, very naturally, a parrot, in the first instance, suggested itself, but was superseded forthwith by a Raven, as equally capable of speech, and infinitely more in keeping with the intended *tone*.

I had now gone so far as the conception of a Raven—the bird of ill omen—monotonously repeating the one word, "Nevermore," at the conclusion of each stanza, in a poem of melancholy tone, and in length about one hundred lines. Now, never losing sight of the object *supremeness,* or perfection, at all points, I asked myself—"Of all melancholy topics, what, according to the *universal* understanding of mankind, is the *most* melancholy?" Death—was the obvious reply. "And when," I said, "is this most melancholy of topics most poetical?" From what I have already explained at some length, the answer, here also, is obvious—"When it most closely allies itself to *Beauty:* the death, then, of a beautiful woman is, unquestionably, the most poetical topic in the world—and equally is it beyond doubt that the lips best suited for such topic are those of a bereaved lover."

I had now to combine the two ideas, of a lover lamenting his deceased mistress and a Raven continuously repeating the word "Nevermore."—I had to combine these, bearing in mind my design of varying, at every turn, the *application* of the word repeated; but the only intelligible mode of such combination is that of imagining the Raven employing the word in answer to the queries of the lover. And here it was that I saw at once the opportunity afforded for the effect on which I had been depending—that is to say, the effect of the *variation of application*. I saw that I could make the first query propounded by the lover—the first query to which the Raven should reply "Nevermore"—that I could make this first query a commonplace one—the second less so—the third still less, and so on—until at length the lover, startled from his original *nonchalance* by the melancholy character of the word itself—by its frequent repetition—and by a consideration of the ominous reputation of the fowl that uttered it—is at length excited to superstition, and wildly propounds queries of a far different character—queries whose solution he has passionately at heart—propounds them half in superstition and half in that species of despair which delights in self-torture—propounds them not altogether because he believes in the prophetic or demoniac character of the bird (which, reason assures him, is merely repeating a lesson learned by rote) but because he experiences a phrenzied pleasure in so modeling his questions as to receive from the *expected* "Nevermore" the most delicious because the most intolerable of sorrow. Perceiving the opportunity thus afforded me—or, more strictly, thus forced upon me in the progress of the construction—I first established in mind the climax, or concluding query—that query to which "Nevermore" should be in the last place an answer—that in reply to which this word "Nevermore" should involve the utmost conceivable amount of sorrow and despair.

Here then the poem may be said to have its beginning—at the end, where all works of art should begin—for it was here, at this point of my preconsiderations, that I first put pen to paper in the composition of the stanza:

> "Prophet," said I, "thing of evil! prophet still if bird or devil!
> By that heaven that bends above us—by that God we both adore,
> Tell this soul with sorrow laden, if within the distant Aidenn,
> It shall clasp a sainted maiden whom the angels name Lenore—
> Clasp a rare and radiant maiden whom the angels name Lenore."
>   Quoth the raven "Nevermore."

I composed this stanza, at this point, first that, by establishing the climax, I might the better vary and graduate, as regards seriousness and importance, the preceding queries of the lover—and, secondly, that I might definitely settle the rhythm, the metre, and the length and general arrangement of the stanza—as well as graduate the stanzas which were to precede, so that none of them might surpass this in rhythmical effect. Had I been able, in the subsequent composition, to construct more vigorous stanzas, I should, without scruple, have purposely enfeebled them, so as not to interfere with the climacteric[12] effect.

And here I may as well say a few words of the versification. My first object (as usual) was originality. The extent to which this has been neglected, in versification, is one of the most unaccountable things in the world. Admitting that there is little possibility of variety in mere *rhythm,* it is still clear that the possible varieties of metre and stanza are absolutely infinite—and yet, *for centuries, no man, in verse, has ever done, or ever seemed to think of doing, an original thing.* The fact is, that originality (unless in minds of very unusual force) is by no means a matter, as some suppose, of impulse or intuition. In general, to be found, it must be elaborately sought, and although a positive merit of the highest class, demands in its attainment less of invention than negation.

Of course, I pretend to no originality in either the rhythm or metre of the "Raven." The former is trochaic—the latter is octameter acatalectic, alternating with heptameter catalectic[13] repeated in the *refrain* of the fifth verse, and terminating with tetrameter catalectic. Less pedantically—the feet employed throughout (trochees) consist of a long syllable followed by a short: the first line of the stanza consists of eight of these feet—the second of seven and a half (in effect two-thirds)—the third of eight—the fourth of seven and a half—the fifth the same—the sixth three and a half. Now each of these lines, taken individually, has been employed before, and what originality the "Raven" has, is in their *combination into stanza;* nothing even remotely approaching this combination has ever been attempted. The effect of this originality of combination is aided by other unusual, and some altogether novel effects, arising from an extension of the application of the principles of rhyme and alliteration.

The next point to be considered was the mode of bringing together the lover and the Raven—and the first branch of this consideration was the *locale.* For this the most natural suggestion might seem to be a forest, or the fields—but it has always appeared to me that a close *circumscription of space* is absolutely necessary to the effect of insulated incident:—it has the force of a frame to a picture. It has an indisputable moral power in keeping concentrated the attention, and, of course, must not be confounded with mere unity of place.

I determined, then, to place the lover in his chamber—in a chamber rendered sacred to him by memories of her who had frequented it. The room is represented as richly furnished—this in mere pursuance of the ideas I have already explained on the subject of Beauty, as the sole true poetical thesis.

The *locale* being thus determined, I had now to introduce the bird—and the thought of introducing him through the window, was inevitable. The idea of making the lover suppose, in the first instance, that the flapping of the wings of the bird against the shutter, is a "tapping" at the door, originated in a wish to increase, by prolonging, the reader's curiosity, and in a desire to admit the incidental effect

---

[12] Climactic.

[13] The former composed of trochees, or metrical feet with one accented and one unaccented syllable; the latter is an eight-measure line of poetry with a complete syllable at the end, alternating with a five-measure line lacking a syllable at the end.

arising from the lover's throwing open the door, finding all dark, and thence adopting the half-fancy that it was the spirit of his mistress that knocked.

I made the night tempestuous, first, to account for the Raven's seeking admission, and secondly, for the effect of contrast with the (physical) serenity within the chamber.

I made the bird alight on the bust of Pallas,[14] also for the effect of contrast between the marble and the plumage—it being understood that the bust was absolutely *suggested* by the bird—the bust of *Pallas* being chosen, first, as most in keeping with the scholarship of the lover, and, secondly, for the sonorousness of the word, Pallas, itself.

About the middle of the poem, also, I have availed myself of the force of contrast, with a view of deepening the ultimate impression. For example, an air of the fantastic—approaching as nearly to the ludicrous as was admissible—is given to the Raven's entrance. He comes in "with many a flirt and flutter."

> Not the *least obeisance made he*—not a moment stopped or stayed he,
> *But with mien of lord or lady,* perched above my chamber door.

In the two stanzas which follow, the design is more obviously carried out:—

> Then this ebony bird beguiling my sad fancy into smiling
> By the *grave and stern decorum of the countenance it wore,*
> "Though thy *crest be shorn and shaven* thou," I said, "art sure no craven,
> Ghastly grim and ancient Raven wandering from the nightly shore—
> Tell me what thy lordly name is on the Night's Plutonian shore?"
>   Quoth the Raven "Nevermore."

> Much I marvelled *this ungainly fowl* to hear discourse so plainly
> Though its answer little meaning—little relevancy bore;
> For we cannot help agreeing that no living human being
> *Ever yet was blessed with seeing bird above his chamber door—*
> *Bird or beast upon the sculptured bust above his chamber door,*
>   With such name as "Nevermore."

The effect of the *dénouement* being thus provided for, I immediately drop the fantastic for a tone of the most profound seriousness:—this tone commencing in the stanza directly following the one last quoted, with the line,

> But the Raven, sitting lonely on that placid bust, spoke only, etc.

From this epoch the lover no longer jests—no longer sees any thing even of the fantastic in the Raven's demeanor. He speaks of him as a "grim, ungainly, ghastly, gaunt, and ominous bird of yore," and feels the "fiery eyes" burning into his "bosom's core." This revolution of thought, or fancy, on the lover's part, is intended to induce a similar one on the part of the reader—to bring the mind into a proper frame for the *dénouement*—which is now brought about as rapidly and as *directly* as possible.

---

[14] Pallas Athena: according to Greek myth, the goddess of wisdom and art.

With the *dénouement* proper—with the Raven's reply, "Nevermore," to the lover's final demand if he shall meet his mistress in another world—the poem, in its obvious phase, that of a simple narrative, may be said to have its completion. So far, every thing is within the limits of the accountable—of the real. A raven, having escaped from the custody of its owner, is driven at midnight, through the violence of a storm, to seek admission at a window from which a light still gleams—the chamber-window of a student, occupied half in poring over a volume, half in dreaming of a beloved mistress deceased. The casement being thrown open at the fluttering of the bird's wings, the bird itself perches on the most convenient seat out of the immediate reach of the student, who, amused by the incident and the oddity of the visitor's demeanor, demands of it, in jest and without looking for a reply, its name. The raven addressed, answers with its customary word, "Nevermore"—a word which finds immediate echo in the melancholy heart of the student, who, giving utterance aloud to certain thoughts suggested by the occasion, is again startled by the fowl's repetition of "Nevermore." The student now guesses the state of the case, but is impelled, as I have before explained, by the human thirst for self-torture, and in part by superstition, to propound such queries to the bird as will bring him, the lover, the most of the luxury of sorrow, through the anticipated answer "Nevermore." With the indulgence, to the extreme, of this self-torture, the narration, in what I have termed its first or obvious phase, has a natural termination, and so far there has been no overstepping of the limits of the real.

But in subjects so handled, however skilfully, or with however vivid an array of incident, there is always a certain hardness or nakedness, which repels the artistical eye. Two things are invariably required—first, some amount of complexity, or more properly, adaptation; and, secondly, some amount of suggestiveness—some under-current, however indefinite, of meaning. It is this latter, in especial, which imparts to a work of art so much of that *richness* (to borrow from colloquy a forcible term) which we are too fond of confounding with *the ideal*. It is the *excess* of the suggested meaning—it is the rendering this the upper instead of the under current of the theme—which turns into prose (and that of the very flattest kind) the so called poetry of the so called transcendentalists.

Holding these opinions, I added the two concluding stanzas of the poem—their suggestiveness being thus made to pervade all the narrative which has preceded them. The under-current of meaning is rendered first apparent in the lines—

> "Take thy beak from out *my heart,* and take thy form from off my door!"
>   Quoth the Raven "Nevermore!"

It will be observed that the words, "from out my heart," involve the first metaphorical expression in the poem. They, with the answer, "Nevermore," dispose the mind to seek a moral in all that has been previously narrated. The reader begins now to regard the Raven as emblematical[15]—but it is not until the very last line of the very last stanza, that the intention of making him emblematical of *Mournful and Never-ending Remembrance* is permitted distinctly to be seen:

---

[15] Symbolic.

And the Raven, never flitting, still is sitting, still is sitting,
On the pallid bust of Pallas, just above my chamber door;
And his eyes have all the seeming of a demon's that is dreaming,
And the lamplight o'er him streaming throws his shadow on the floor;
And my soul *from out that shadow* that lies floating on the floor
          Shall be lifted—nevermore.

1846

Augustus Baldwin Longstreet
(1790–187c)

In describing *Georgia Scenes* (1835), his masterpiece of regional humor, Augustus Baldwin Longstreet declared that his intention was to set forth "the manners, customs, amusements, wit, [regional] dialect, as they appear in all grades of society to an ear and eye witness of them." Longstreet accomplished more than this aim, however; his collection of tales marked the beginning of the tradition of Southwest Humor. Many writers would follow his lead in depicting, in the Addisonian, or polished, prose of a refined traveler, the antics of the Old Southwest's backwoodsmen.

Like the gentlemen narrators of his sketches, Longstreet was a southern aristocrat. Born in 1790 in Augusta, Georgia, he followed the example of many wealthy Georgians and left his native state to be educated in New England. After graduating from Yale University in 1813, he began a series of careers as minister, politician, judge, and president of no less than four colleges and universities—first Emory University in Atlanta, then Centenary College in Shreveport, Louisiana, and later the Universities of Mississippi and South Carolina. His social position and political ability enabled him to become an influential spokesman for the rights of the southern states against the federal government. As the Civil War approached, Longstreet fought hard for southern secession. The war itself proved a devastating blow to his personal life and finances. He and his family managed to flee Oxford, Mississippi, just before federal troops seized the town, but during the occupation the Longstreet house was burned to the ground—the fire apparently set with the writer's collection of private papers. After the Civil War he returned to the ruins of Oxford and lived to see the town, the future home of William Faulkner, rebuilt. With the war over and the southern cause lost, however, Longstreet found both his cherished antebellum society and the frontier nearly vanished. He died in Oxford in 1870, two years after his wife's death.

Longstreet considered his writing a gentlemanly pursuit rather than a professional activity. He published other stories and one novel, *Master William Mitten* (1858), but modern audiences remember him for the realistic tales of *Georgia Scenes* (1835). Those stories feature an urbane narrator whose comments frame the action of a rustic population, poking fun at their crudeness, reacting with horror to their violence. Despite this narrative distance, the nineteen tales in the collection throb with the energy of a region just opened to settlement. "The Horse Swap," for example, depicts a double cheat, a favorite subject of the Southwest Humorists; sketches such as "The Fight" portray the barbarism that lay beneath the surface of the South's code of honor. Anticipating criticism of the language and detail of his tales, Longstreet published his book anonymously as "A Native Georgian." But the mask did not hide the identity of the man, and the anomaly of a college president writing a book such as *Georgia Scenes* later caused him some embarrassment. Partial as he was to the South, Longstreet did not gild the harsher aspects of the region's way of life. Other Southwest Humorists, and American realists as well, are indebted to his pioneering work.

Suggested Readings: *Georgia Scenes, Characters, Incidents, Etc., in the First Half-Century of the Republic*, 1835, rpt. 1957. O. P. Fitzgerald, *Judge Longstreet*, 1891. M. T. Inge, ed., *The Frontier Humorists: Critical Views*, 1975. K. King, *Augustus Baldwin Longstreet*, 1984.

Text Used: *Humor of the Old Southwest*, ed. H. Cohen and W. B. Dillingham, 1964.

THE HORSE SWAP*

During the session of the Superior Court, in the village of ———, about three weeks ago, when a number of people were collected in the principal street of the village, I observed a young man riding up and down the street, as I supposed, in a violent passion. He galloped this way, then that, and then the other. Spurred his horse to one group of citizens, then to another. Then dashed off at half speed, as if fleeing from danger; and suddenly checking his horse, returned—first in a pace, then in a trot, and then in a canter. While he was performing these various evolutions, he cursed, swore, whooped, screamed, and tossed himself in every attitude which man could assume on horse back. In short, he *cavorted* most magnanimously, (a term which, in our tongue, expresses all that I have described, and a little more) and seemed to be setting all creation at defiance. As I like to see all that is passing, I determined to take a position a little nearer to him, and to ascertain if possible, what it was that affected him so sensibly.[1] Accordingly, I approached a crowd before which he had stopt for a moment, and examined it with the strictest scrutiny. —But I could see nothing in it, that seemed to have anything to do with the cavorter. Every man appeared to be in a good humor, and all minding their own business. Not one so much as noticed the principal figure. Still he went on. After a semicolon pause,[2] which my appearance seemed to produce, (for he eyed me closely as I approached) he fetched a whoop, and swore that "he could out-swap any live man, woman or child, that ever walked these hills, or that ever straddled horse flesh since the days of old daddy Adam." "Stranger," said he to me, "did you ever see the *Yellow* Blossom from Jasper?"

"No," said I, "but I have often heard of him."

"I'm the boy," continued he; "perhaps a *leetle*—jist a *leetle* of the best man, at a horse swap, that ever trod shoe-leather."

---

* First published in the Milledgeville, Georgia, *Southern Recorder*, a newspaper, in 1833, then included in *Georgia Scenes, Characters, Incidents, Etc., in the First Half Century of the Republic* (1835). "The Horse Swap" presents a situation that William Faulkner adapted for his own comic purposes in *The Hamlet* (1940).

[1] Appreciably.

[2] Blossom's pause is longer than a comma would indicate, but not a full stop like that signaled by a colon: hence, a semicolon pause.

I began to feel my situation a little awkward, when I was relieved by a man somewhat advanced in years, who stept up and began to survey the "*Yellow Blossom's*" horse with much apparent interest. This drew the rider's attention, and he turned the conversation from me to the stranger.

"Well, my old coon,"[3] said he, "do you want to swap *hosses?*"

"Why, I don't know," replied the stranger; "I believe I've got a beast I'd trade with you for that one, if you like him."

"Well, fetch up your nag, my old cock;[4] you're jist the lark I wanted to get hold of. I am perhaps a *leetle*, jist a *leetle*, of the best man at a horse swap, that ever stole *cracklins* out of his mammy's fat gourd.[5] Where's your *hoss?*"

"I'll bring him presently; but I want to examine your horse a little."

"Oh! look at him," said the Blossom, alighting and hitting him a cut—"look at him. He's the best piece of *hoss* flesh in the thirteen united universal worlds.[6] There's no sort o' mistake in little Bullet. He can pick up miles on his feet and fling 'em behind him as fast as the next man's *hoss,* I don't care where he comes from.—And he can keep at it as long as the Sun can shine without resting."

During this harangue, little Bullet looked as if he understood it all, believed it, and was ready at any moment to verify it. He was a horse of goodly countenance, rather expressive of vigilance than fire; though an unnatural appearance of fierceness was thrown into it, by the loss of his ears, which had been cropt pretty close to his head. Nature had done but little for Bullet's head and neck; but he managed, in a great measure, to hide their defects, by bowing perpetually. He had obviously suffered severely for corn;[7] but if his ribs and hip bones had not disclosed the fact, *he* never would have done it; for he was in all respects, as cheerful and happy, as if he commanded all the corn-cribs and fodder stacks in Georgia. His height was about twelve hands;[8] but as his shape partook somewhat of that of the Giraffe, his haunches stood much lower. They were short, strait,[9] peaked and concave. Bullet's tail, however, made amends for all his defects. All that the artist could do to beautify it, had been done; and all that horse could do to compliment the artist, Bullet did. His tail was nicked[10] in superior style, and exhibited the line of beauty in so many directions, that it could not fail to hit the most fastidious taste in some of them. From the root it dropt into a graceful festoon; then rose in a handsome curve; then resumed its first direction; and then mounted suddenly upwards like a cypress knee[11] to a perpendicular of about two and a half inches. The whole had a careless and bewitching inclination to the right. Bullet obviously knew where his beauty lay, and took all occasions to display it to the best advantage. If a stick cracked, or if any one moved suddenly about him, or coughed, or hawked,[12] or spoke a little louder than common, up went Bullet's tail like lightning; and if the *going up* did not please, the *coming down* must of necessity, for it was as different from the other movement, as was its direction. The first, was a bold and rapid flight upward; usually to an angle of forty-five degrees. In this position he kept his interesting appendage, until he satisfied himself that nothing in particular was to

---

[3] Racoon.   [4] Rooster; Blossom then calls the old gentleman a "lark," or prankster.

[5] Crisp rinds of roasted pork stolen from a large container in which his mother saved fat.

[6] The thirteen original states.   [7] Bullet has had very little corn to eat.

[8] One hand is now considered to be 4 inches.   [9] Tight.

[10] Cut on the underside so that the horse carries it higher.

[11] Wood growth at the base of a cypress tree.

[12] Made an unpleasant sound by coughing up phlegm.

be done; when he commenced dropping it by half inches, in second beats—then in triple time—then faster and shorter, and faster and shorter still; until it finally died away imperceptibly into its natural position. If I might compare sights to sounds, I should say, its *settling*, was more like the note of a locust than anything else in nature.

Either from native sprightliness of disposition, from uncontrolable activity, or from an unconquerable habit of removing flies by the stamping of the feet, Bullet never stood still; but always kept up a gentle fly-scaring movement of his limbs, which was peculiarly interesting.

"I tell you, man," proceeded the Yellow Blossom, "he's the best live hoss that ever trod the grit of Georgia. Bob Smart knows the hoss. Come here, Bob, and mount this hoss and show Bullet's motions." Here, Bullet bristled up, and looked as if he had been hunting for Bob all day long, and had just found him. Bob sprang on his back. "Boo-oo-oo,!" said Bob, with a fluttering noise of the lips; and away went Bullet, as if in a quarter race,[13] with all his beauties spread in handsome style.

"Now fetch him back," said Blossom. Bullet turned and came in pretty much as he went out.

"Now trot him by." Bullet reduced his tail to "*customary*"—sidled to the right and left airily, and exhibited at least three varieties of trot, in the short space of fifty yards.

"Make him pace!" Bob commenced twitching the bridle and kicking at the same time. These inconsistent movements obviously (and most naturally) disconcerted Bullet: for it was impossible for him to learn, from them, whether he was to proceed or stand still. He started to trot—and was told that wouldn't do. He attempted a canter—and was checked again. He stopt—and was urged to go on. Bullet now rushed into the wide field of experiment, and struck out a gait of his own, that completely turned the tables upon his rider, and certainly deserved a patent. It seemed to have derived its elements from the jig, the minuet and the cotillion.[14] If it was not a pace, it certainly had *pace* in it; and no man would venture to call it anything else; so it passed off to the satisfaction of the owner.

"Walk him!" Bullet was now at home again; and he walked as if money was staked on him.

The stranger, whose name I afterwards learned was Peter Ketch, having examined bullet to his heart's content, ordered his son Neddy to go and bring up Kit. Neddy soon appeared upon Kit; a well formed sorrel[15] of the middle size, and in good order. His *tout ensemble*[16] threw Bullet entirely in the shade; though a glance was sufficient to satisfy anyone, that Bullet had the decided advantage of him in point of intellect.

"Why man," said Blossom, "do you bring such a hoss as that to trade for Bullet? Oh, I see you're no notion of trading."

"Ride him off, Neddy!" said Peter. Kit put off at a handsome lope.

"Trot him back!" Kit came in at a long, sweeping trot, and stopt suddenly at the crowd.

---

[13] A quarter-mile-long race.

[14] A fast, lively dance; a slow, stately ballroom dance; a brisk, lively ballroom dance.

[15] A light reddish-brown horse.   [16] "Whole attire" (French).

"Well," said Blossom, "let me look at him; may be he'll do to plough."

"Examine him!" said Peter, taking hold of the bridle close to the mouth; "He's nothing but a tacky.[17] He an't as *pretty* a horse as Bullet, I know; but he'll do. Start 'em together for a hundred and fifty *mile;* and if Kit an't twenty mile ahead of him at the coming out, any man may take Kit for nothing. But he's a monstrous mean horse, gentlemen; any man may see that. He's the scariest horse, too, you ever saw. He won't do to hunt on, no how. Stranger, will you let Neddy have your rifle to shoot off him? Lay the rifle between his ears, Neddy, and shoot at the blaze[18] in that stump. Tell me when his head is high enough."

Ned fired, and hit the blaze; and Kit did not move a hair's breadth.

"Neddy, take a couple of sticks and beat on that hogshead[19] at Kit's tail."

Ned made a tremendous rattling; at which *Bullet* took fright, broke his bridle and dashed off in grand style; and would have stopt all farther negotiations, by going home in disgust, had not a traveller arrested him and brought him back; but Kit did not move.

"I tell you, gentlemen," continued Peter, "he's the scariest horse you ever saw. He an't as gentle as Bullet; but we won't do any harm if you watch him. Shall I put him in a cart, gig,[20] or wagon for you, stranger? He'll cut the same capers there he does here. He's a monstrous mean horse."

During all this time, Blossom was examining him with the nicest scrutiny. Having examined his frame and limbs, he now looked at his eyes.

"He's got a curious look out of his eyes," said Blossom.

"Oh yes, sir," said Peter, "just as blind as a bat. Blind horses always have clear eyes. Make a motion at his eyes, if you please, sir."

Blossom did so, and Kit threw up his head rather as if something pricked him under the chin, than as if fearing a blow. Blossom repeated the experiment, and Kit jirked back in considerable astonishment.

"Stone blind, you see, gentlemen," proceeded Peter; "but he's just as good to travel of a dark night as if he had eyes."

"Blame my buttons," said Blossom, "if I like them eyes."

"No," said Peter, "nor I neither. I'd rather have 'em made of diamonds; but they'll do, if they don't show as much white as Bullet's."

"Well," said Blossom, "Make a pass at me."[21]

"No," said Peter, "you made the banter; now make your pass."

"Well I'm never afraid to price my hosses. You must give me twenty-five dollars boot."[22]

"Oh certainly; say fifty, and my saddle and bridle in. Here, Neddy, my son, take away daddy's horse."

"Well," said Blossom, "I've made my pass; now you make yours."

"I'm for short talk in a horse swap; and therefore always tell a gentleman, at once, what I mean to do. You must give me ten dollars."

Blossom swore absolutely, roundly and profanely, that he never would give boot.

"Well," said Peter, "I didn't care about trading; but you cut such high shines,

---

[17] Dowdy in appearance.   [18] The trail marker.   [19] A large cask containing up to 140 gallons.
[20] An open carriage drawn by one horse.   [21] Make me an offer.
[22] You give me your horse and twenty-five dollars extra (to boot).

that I thought I'd like to back you out; and I've done it. Gentlemen, you see I've brought him to a hack."[23]

"Come, old man," said Blossom, "I've been joking with you, I begin to think you do want to trade; therefore, give me five dollars and take Bullet. I'd rather lose ten dollars, any time, than not make a trade; though I hate to fling away a good hoss."

"Well," said Peter, "I'll be as clever[24] as you are. Just put the five dollars on Bullet's back and hand him over, it's a trade."

Blossom swore again, as roundly as before, that he would not give boot; and, said he, "Bullet wouldn't hold five dollars on his back, no how. But as I bantered you, if you say an even swap, here's at you."

"I told you," said Peter, "I'd be as clever as you; therefore, here goes two dollars more, just for trade sake. Give me three dollars, and it's a bargain."

Blossom repeated his former assertion; and here the parties stood for a long time, and the by-standers (for many were now collected,) began to taunt both parties. After some time, however, it was pretty unanimously decided that the old man had backed Blossom out.

At length Blossom swore he "never would be backed out, for three dollars, after bantering a man;" and accordingly they closed the trade.

"Now," said Blossom, as he handed Peter the three dollars, "I'm a man, that when he makes a bad trade, makes the most of it until he can make a better. I'm for no rues and after-claps."[25]

"That's just my way," said Peter; "I never goes to law to mend my bargains."

"Ah, you're the kind of boy I love to trade with. Here's your hoss, old man. Take the saddle and bridle off him, and I'll strip yours; but lift up the blanket easy from Bullet's back, for he's a mighty tender-backed hoss."

The old man removed the saddle, but the blanket stuck fast. He attempted to raise it, and Bullet bowed himself, switched his tail, danced a little, and gave signs of biting.

"Don't hurt him, old man," said Blossom archly; —take it off easy. I am, perhaps, a leetle of the best man at a horse-swap that ever catched a coon."

Peter continued to pull at the blanket more and more roughly; and Bullet became more and more *cavortish;* in so much, that when the blanket came off, he had reached the *kicking* point in good earnest.

The removal of the blanket, disclosed a sore on Bullet's back-bone, that seemed to have defied all medical skill. It measured six full inches in length, and four in breadth; and had as many features as Bullet had motions. My heart sickened at the sight; and I felt that the brute who had been riding him in that situation, deserved the halter.[26]

The prevailing feeling, however, was that of mirth. The laugh became loud and general, at the old man's expense; and rustic witticisms were liberally bestowed upon him and his late purchase. These, Blossom continued to provoke by various remarks. He asked the old man, "if he thought Bullet would let five dollars lie on his back." He declared most seriously, that he had owned that horse three months,

---

[23] An insult for horse traders: Peter has reduced Blossom to the condition of a hack, a bedraggled horse for hire.
[24] Amiable.   [25] Regrets or unexpected aftereffects.   [26] The hangman's noose.

and had never discovered before, that he had a sore back, "or he never should have thought of trading him," etc., etc.

The old man bore it all with the most philosophic composure. He evinced no astonishment at his late discovery, and made no replies. But his son, Neddy, had not disciplined his feelings quite so well. His eyes opened, wider and wider, from the first to the last pull of the blanket; and when the whole sore burst upon his view, astonishment and fright seemed to contend for the mastery of his countenance. As the blanket disappeared, he stuck his hands in his breeches pockets, heaved a deep sigh, and lapsed into a profound reverie; from which he was only roused by the cuts at his father. He bore them as long as he could; and when he could contain himself no longer, he began, with a certain wildness of expression, which gave a peculiar interest to what he uttered: "His back's mighty bad off; but dod drot my soul, if he's put it to daddy as bad as he thinks he has, for old Kit's both blind and *deef*, I'll be dod drot if he eint."

"The devil he is," said Blossom. "Yes, dod drot my soul if he *eint*. You walk him and see if he *eint*. His eyes don't look like it; but he *jist as live go agin* the house with you, or in a ditch, as any how.[27] Now you go try him." The laugh was now turned on Blossom; and many rushed to test the fidelity of the little boy's report. A few experiments established its truth, beyond controversy.

"Neddy," said the old man, "you oughtn't to try and make people discontented with their things." "Stranger, don't mind what the little boy says. If you can only get Kit rid of them little failing, you'll find him all sorts of a horse. You are a *leetle* the best man, at a horse swap, that ever I got hold of; but don't fool away Kit. Come, Neddy, my son, let's be moving; the stranger seems to be getting snappish."

1835

Thomas Bangs Thorpe
(1815–1878)

Born in 1815 in Westfield, Massachusetts, Thomas Bangs Thorpe spent his teen years in New York City, where he studied painting with John Quidor (known for his illustrations of Washington Irving). Despite Thorpe's talent, his artistic ambitions were frustrated by lack of funds. Unable to raise the money to study art in Europe, he enrolled at Wesleyan University in Connecticut in 1834. By 1836, however, he left Wesleyan, suffering from poor health and poor grades. Hoping for a more healthful climate and a chance to make money painting portraits, he moved to Baton Rouge, Louisiana. The move was the turning point

[27] The horse is just as likely to carry a rider into the side of a house or into a ditch as anywhere else. It is the little boy who makes this speech, beginning with "Yes, dod drot my soul. . . ."

of his career: rather than finding subjects for his portraits, Thorpe found ample subject matter for colorful tales about life on the southwestern frontier.

Thorpe's first tale, "Tom Owen, the Bee Hunter," was published in 1839 in William T. Porter's the *Spirit of the Times,* a journal that Thorpe later edited. Thorpe went on to publish many successful tales in the *Spirit,* among them his classic "Big Bear of Arkansas" in 1841 and others, which he collected in *The Mysteries of the Backwoods* (1846). From 1840 until his death in 1878 he wrote scores of articles, dealing with the fine arts, fishing, hunting, and the American landscape, which he published in magazines as diverse as *Harper's* and *Forest and Stream.* Today, however, Thorpe is remembered for his tall tales of southwestern life. Although his second collection of these stories, *The Hive of The Bee Hunter* (1854), established him as a major southern humorist, he never became completely southern in his sympathies. After serving as a colonel in the Mexican War, he returned to New York in 1853 and shortly afterward published *The Master's House: A Tale of Southern Life* (1854), a novel that attacks slavery. During the Civil War Thorpe served as a colonel with the Union forces that occupied New Orleans. In 1864 he again returned to New York, where he received a Customs House appointment, which he held until his death in 1878.

During his years in the Old Southwest, Thorpe observed the vanishing of the wilderness as a result of the progress of white settlers. He recorded the importation of outside refinements, such as a town's first piano in the story "A Piano in 'Arkansaw'." As his exuberant descriptions of the Arkansas backwoods demonstrate, he always retained his painter's sensitivity for landscape. "The Big Bear of Arkansas," for example, celebrates the incredible fertility of "the creation state" and records the passing of the frontier that makes such tall tales possible. Widely reprinted, Thorpe's story of an "unhuntable" bear is representative of the entire genre of Southwest Humor. As scholars agree, it stands as the beginning of the "Big Bear" tradition in American writing, which not only includes other bear stories in Southwest Humor but later fiction such as William Faulkner's "The Bear" (1942). "The Big Bear" contains a "ringtail roarer," a loud boaster, who speaks the dialect of the region, a fantastic "bar" hunt, and a vision of a fertile American wilderness that, like the big bear itself, seems ever beyond the pursuer's grasp.

Suggested Readings: *The Big Bear of Arkansas, and Other Sketches Illustrative of Characters and Incidents in the South and South-West,* ed. W. T. Porter, 1845. *The Mysteries of the Backwoods: Or, Sketches of the Southwest,* 1846. *The Master's House: A Tale of Southern Life,* 1854. N. W. Yates, *William T. Porter and "The Spirit of the Times": A Study of the "Big Bear" School of Humor,* 1957. M. Rickels, *Thomas Bangs Thorpe: Humorist of the Old Southwest,* 1962. E. Miles, *Southwest Humorists,* 1969.

Text Used: *Humor of the Old Southwest,* ed. H. Cohen and W. B. Dillingham, 1964.

THE BIG BEAR OF ARKANSAS[*]

A steamboat on the Mississippi, frequently, in making her regular trips, carries between places varying from one to two thousand miles apart; and, as these boats advertise to land passengers and freight at "all intermediate landings," the hetero-

---

[*] First published in *The Spirit of the Times* in 1841; later included in the collection *The Hive of The Bee-Hunter* (1854).

geneous character of the passengers of one of these up-country boats can scarcely be imagined by one who has never seen it with his own eyes.

Starting from New Orleans in one of these boats, you will find yourself associated with men from every State in the Union, and from every portion of the globe; and a man of observation need not lack for amusement or instruction in such a crowd, if he will take the trouble to read the great book of character so favorably opened before him.

Here may be seen, jostling together, the wealthy Southern planter and the pedler of tin-ware from New England—the Northern merchant and the Southern jockey—a venerable bishop, and a desperate gambler—the land speculator, and the honest farmer—professional men of all creeds and characters—Wolvereens, Suckers, Hoosiers, Buckeyes, and Corncrackers,[1] beside a "plentiful sprinkling" of the half-horse and half-alligator species of men,[2] who are peculiar to "old Mississippi," and who appear to gain a livelihood by simply going up and down the river. In the pursuit of pleasure or business, I have frequently found myself in such a crowd.

On one occasion, when in New Orleans, I had occasion to take a trip of a few miles up the Mississippi, and I hurried on board the well-known "high-pressure-and-beat-every-thing" steamboat "Invincible," just as the last note of the last bell was sounding; and when the confusion and bustle that is natural to a boat's getting under way had subsided, I discovered that I was associated in as heterogeneous a crowd as was ever got together. As my trip was to be of a few hours' duration only, I made no endeavors to become acquainted with my fellow-passengers, most of whom would be together many days. Instead of this, I took out of my pocket the "latest paper," and more critically than usual examined its contents; my fellow-passengers, at the same time, disposed of themselves in little groups.

While I was thus busily employed in reading, and my companions were more busily still employed, in discussing such subjects as suited their humors best, we were most unexpectedly startled by a loud Indian whoop, uttered in the "social hall," that part of the cabin fitted off for a bar; then was to be heard a loud crowing, which would not have continued to interest us—such sounds being quite common in that *place of spirits*—had not the hero of these windy accomplishments stuck his head into the cabin, and hallooed out, "Hurra for the Big Bear of Arkansaw!"

Then might be heard a confused hum of voices, unintelligible, save in such broken sentences as "horse," "screamer," "lightning is slow," etc.

As might have been expected, this continued interruption, attracted the attention of every one in the cabin; all conversation ceased, and in the midst of this surprise, the "Big Bear" walked into the cabin, took a chair, put his feet on the stove, and looking back over his shoulder, passed the general and familiar salute—"Strangers, how are you?"

He then expressed himself as much at home as if he had been at "the Forks of Cypress," and "prehaps a little more so."

Some of the company at this familiarity looked a little angry, and some astonished; but in a moment every face was wreathed in a smile. There was something

---

[1] Nicknames for inhabitants of Michigan, Illinois, Indiana, Ohio, and Kentucky, respectively.

[2] Boastful, rowdy backwoodsmen from Kentucky and Tennessee and raftsmen on the Mississippi River.

about the intruder that won the heart on sight. He appeared to be a man enjoying perfect health and contentment; his eyes were as sparkling as diamonds, and good-natured to simplicity. Then his perfect confidence in himself was irresistibly droll.

"Prehaps," said he, "gentlemen," running on without a person interrupting, "prehaps you have been to New Orleans often; I never made *the first visit before,* and I don't intend to make another in a crow's life. I am thrown away in that ar place, and useless, that ar a fact. Some of the gentlemen thar called me *green*— well, prehaps I am, said I, *but I arn't so at home;* and if I ain't off my trail much, the heads of them perlite chaps themselves wern't much the hardest; for according to my notion, they were *real know-nothings,* green as a pumpkin-vine—couldn't, in farming, I'll bet, raise a crop of turnips; and as for shooting, they'd miss a barn if the door was swinging, and that, too, with the best rifle in the country. And then they talked to me 'bout hunting, and laughed at my calling the principal game in Arkansaw poker, and high-low-jack.

"'Prehaps,' said I, 'you prefer checkers and roulette;' at this they laughed harder than ever, and asked me if I lived in the woods, and didn't know what *game* was?

"At this, I rather think *I* laughed.

"'Yes,' I roared, and says, I, 'Strangers, if you'd ask me *how we got our meat* in Arkansaw, I'd a told you at once, and given you a list of varmints that would make a caravan, beginning with the bar, and ending off with the cat; that's *meat* though, not game.

"Game, indeed,—that's what city folks call it; and with them it means chippen-birds and shite-pokes;[3] may be such trash live in my diggins, but I arn't noticed them yet: a bird anyway is too trifling. I never did shoot at but one, and I'd never forgiven myself for that, had it weighed less than forty pounds. I wouldn't draw a rifle on anything less heavy than that; and when I meet with another wild turkey of the same size, I will drap him."

"A wild turkey weighing forty pounds!" exclaimed twenty voices in the cabin at once.

"Yes, strangers, and wasn't it a whopper? You see, the thing was so fat that it couldn't fly far; and when he fell out of the tree, after I shot him, on striking the ground he bust open behind, and the way the pound gobs of tallow rolled out of the opening was perfectly beautiful."

"Where did all that happen?" asked a cynical-looking Hoosier.

"Happen! happened in Arkansaw: where else could it have happened, but in the creation State, the finishing-up country—a State where the *sile* runs down to the centre of the 'arth, and government gives you a title to every inch of it? Then its airs—just breathe them, and they will make you snort like a horse. It's a State without a fault, it is."

"Excepting mosquitoes," cried the Hoosier.

"Well, stranger, except them; for it ar a fact that they are rather *enormous,* and do push themselves in somewhat troublesome. But, stranger, they never stick twice in the same place; and give them a fair chance for a few months, and you will get as much above noticing them as an alligator. They can't hurt my feelings, for they lay under the skin; and I never knew but one case of injury resulting from them, and that was to a Yankee: and they take worse to foreigners, any how, than

---

[3] Chirping sparrows and green herons.

they do to natives. But the way they used that fellow up! first they punched him until he swelled up and busted; then he sup-per-a-ted, as the doctor called it, until he was as raw as beef; then, owing to the warm weather, he tuck the ager,[4] and finally he tuck a steamboat and left the country. He was the only man that ever tuck mosquitoes at heart that I knowd of.

"But mosquitoes is natur, and I never find fault with her. If they ar large, Arkansaw is large, her varmints ar large, her trees ar large, her rivers ar large, and a small mosquito would be of no more use in Arkansaw than preaching in a cane-brake."

This knock-down argument in favor of big mosquitoes used the Hoosier up, and the logician started on a new track, to explain how numerous bear were in his "diggins," where he represented them to be "about as plenty as blackberries, and a little plentifuller."

Upon the utterance of this assertion, a timid little man near me inquired, if the bear in Arkansaw ever attacked the settlers in numbers.

"No," said our hero, warming with the subject, "no, stranger, for you see it ain't the natur of bear to go in droves; but the way they squander about in pairs and single ones is edifying.

"An then the way I hunt them—the old black rascals know the crack of my gun as well as they know a pig's squealing. They grow thin in our parts, it frightens them so, and they do take the noise dreadfully, poor things. That gun of mine is a perfect *epidemic among bear:* if not watched closely, it will go off as quick on a warm scent as my dog Bowieknife[5] will: and then that dog—whew! why the fellow thinks that the world is full of bear, he finds them so easy. It's lucky he don't talk as well as think; for with his natural modesty, if he should suddenly learn how much he is acknowledged to be ahead of all other dogs in the universe, he would be astonished to death in two minutes.

"Strangers, that dog knows a bear's way as well as a horse-jockey knows a woman's: he always barks at the right time, bites at the exact place, and whips without getting a scratch.

"I never could tell whether he was made expressly to hunt bear, or whether bear was made expressly for him to hunt; any way, I believe they were ordained to go together as naturally as Squire Jones says a man and woman is, when he moralizes in marrying a couple. In fact, Jones once said, said he, 'Marriage according to law is a civil contract of divine origin; it's common to all countries as well as Arkansaw, and people take to it as naturally as Jim Doggett's Bowieknife takes to bear.'"

"What season of the year do your hunts take place?" inquired a gentlemanly foreigner, who, from some peculiarities of his baggage, I suspected to be an Englishman, on some hunting expedition, probably at the foot of the Rocky Mountains.

"The season for bear hunting, stranger," said the man of Arkansaw, "is generally all the year round, and the hunts take place about as regular. I read in history that varmints have their fat season, and their lean season. That is not the case in Arkansaw, feeding as they do upon the *spontenacious* productions of the sile, they

---

[4] Ague (chills and fever).
[5] The dog is named for the knife, which in turn is named for the frontiersman and soldier James Bowie (1799–1836), who died at the Alamo.

have one continued fat season the year round; though in winter things in this way is rather more greasy than in summer, I must admit. For that reason bear with us run in warm weather, but in winter they only waddle.

"Fat, fat! its an enemy to speed; it tames every thing that has plenty of it. I have seen wild turkeys, from its influence, as gentle as chickens. Run a bear in this fat condition, and the way it improves the critter for eating is amazing; it sort of mixes the ile[6] up with the meat, until you can't tell t'other from which. I've done this often.

"I recollect one perty morning in particular, of putting an old he fellow on the stretch, and considering the weight he carried, he run well. But the dogs soon tired him down, and when I came up with him wasn't he in a beautiful sweat—I might say fever; and then to see his tongue sticking out of his mouth a feet,[7] and his sides sinking and opening like a bellows, and his cheeks so fat that he couldn't look cross. In this fix I blazed[8] at him, and pitch me naked into a briar patch, if the steam didn't come out of the bullet-hole ten foot in a straight line. The fellow, I reckon, was made on the high-pressure system, and the lead sort of bust his biler."[9]

"That column of steam was rather curious, or else the bear must have been very *warm*," observed the foreigner, with a laugh.

"Stranger, as you observe, that bear was WARM, and the blowing off of the steam show'd it, and also how hard the varmint had been run. I have no doubt if he had kept on two miles farther his insides would have been stewed; and I expect to meet with a varmint yet of extra bottom, that will run himself into a skinfull of bear's grease: it is possible; much onlikelier things have happened."

"Whereabouts are these bears so abundant?" inquired the foreigner, with increasing interest.

"Why, stranger, they inhabit the neighborhood of my settlement, one of the prettiest places on old Mississipp—a perfeet location, and no mistake; a place that had some defects until the river made the 'cut-off'[10] at 'Shirt-tail bend,' and that remedied the evil, as it brought my cabin on the edge of the river—a great advantage in wet weather, I assure you, as you can now roll a barrel of whiskey into my yard in high water from a boat, as easy as falling off a log. It's a great improvement, as toting it by land in a jug, as I used to do, *evaporated* it too fast, and it became expensive.

"Just stop with me, stranger, a month or two, or a year, if you like, and you will appreciate my place. I can give you plenty to eat; for beside hog and hominy, you can have bear-ham, and bear-sausages, and a mattrass of bear-skins to sleep on, and a wildcat-skin, pulled off hull,[11] stuffed with corn-shucks, for a pillow. That bed would put you to sleep if you had the rheumatics in every joint in your body. I call that ar bed, a *quietus*.[12]

"Then look at my 'pre-emption'—the government ain't got another like it to dispose of. Such timber, and such bottom land,—why you can't preserve anything natural you plant in it unless you pick it young, things thar will grow out of shape so quick.

"I once planted in those diggins a few potatoes and beets; they took a fine start,

---

[6] Oil.   [7] Probably "foot."   [8] Fired shots rapidly.   [9] Boiler.
[10] A new channel made when a river cuts across a narrow bend, sometimes leaving towns miles from water; here, bringing a settlement to the river's edge.
[11] Whole.   [12] An end, such as death or sleep.

and after that, an ox team couldn't have kept them from growing. About that time I went off to old Kaintuck on business, and did not hear from them things in three months, when I accidentally stumbled on a fellow who had drapped in at my place, with an idea of buying me out.

" 'How did you like things?' said I.

" 'Pretty well,' said he; 'the cabin is convenient, and the timber land is good; but that bottom land ain't worth the first red cent.'"

" 'Why?' said I.

" ''Cause,' said he.

" ''Cause what?' said I.

" ''Cause it's full of cedar stumps and Indian mounds, and *can't be cleared.'*

" 'Lord,' said I, 'them ar "cedar stumps" is beets, and them ar "Indian mounds" tater hills.'

"As I had expected, the crop was overgrown and useless: the sile is too rich, *and planting in Arkansaw is dangerous.*

"I had a good-sized sow killed in that same bottom land. The old thief stole an ear of corn, and took it down to eat where she slept at night. Well, she left a grain or two on the ground, and lay down on them: before morning the corn shot up, and the percussion killed her dead. I don't plant any more: natur intended Arkansaw for a hunting ground, and I go according to natur."

The questioner, who had thus elicited the description of our hero's settlement, seemed to be perfectly satisfied, and said no more; but the "Big Bear of Arkansaw" rambled on from one thing to another with a volubility perfectly astonishing, occasionally disputing with those around him, particularly with a "live Sucker" from Illinois, who had the daring to say that our Arkansaw friend's stories "smelt rather tall."

The evening was nearly spent by the incidents we have detailed; and conscious that my own association with so singular a personage would probably end before morning, I asked him if he would not give me a description of some particular bear hunt; adding, that I took great interest in such things, though I was no sportsman. The desire seemed to please him, and he squared himself round towards me, saying, that he could give me an idea of a bear hunt that was never beat in this world, or in any other. His manner was so singular, that half of his story consisted in his excellent way of telling it, the great peculiarity of which was, the happy manner he had of emphasizing the prominent parts of his conversation. As near as I can recollect, I have italicized the words, and given the story in his own way.

"Stranger," said he, "in bear hunts *I am numerous,* and which particular one, as you say, I shall tell, puzzles me.

"There was the old she devil I shot at the Hurricane last fall—then there was the old hog thief I popped over at the Bloody Crossing, and then—Yes, I have it! I will give you an idea of a hunt, in which the greatest bear was killed that ever lived, *none excepted;* about an old fellow that I hunted, more or less, for two or three years; and if that ain't a *particular bear hunt,* I ain't got one to tell.

"But in the first place, stranger, let me say, I am pleased with you, because you ain't ashamed to gain information by asking and listening; and that's what I say to Countess's pups every day when I'm home; and I have got great hopes of them ar pups, because they are continually *nosing* about; and though they stick it sometimes in the wrong place, they gain experience any how, and may learn something useful to boot.

"Well, as I was saying about his big bear, you see when I and some more first settled in our region, we were drivin to hunting naturally; we soon liked it, and after that we found it an easy matter to make the thing our business. One old chap who had pioneered 'afore us, gave us to understand that we had settled in the right place. He dwelt upon its merits until it was affecting, and showed us, to prove his assertions, more scratches on the bark of the sassafras trees, than I ever saw chalk marks on a tavern door 'lection time.[13]

" 'Who keeps that ar reckoning?' said I.

" 'The bear,' said he.

" 'What for?' said I.

" 'Can't tell,' said he; 'but so it is: the bear bite the bark and wood too, at the highest point from the ground they can reach, and you can tell, by the marks,' said he, 'the length of the bear to an inch.'

" 'Enough,' said I; 'I've learned something here a'ready, and I'll put it in practice.'

"Well, stranger, just one month from that time I killed a bear, and told its exact length before I measured it, by those very marks; and when I did that, I swelled up considerably—I've been a prouder man ever since.

"So I went on, larning something every day, until I was reckoned a buster,[14] and allowed to be decidedly the best bear hunter in my district; and that is a reputation as much harder to earn than to be reckoned first man in Congress, as an iron ramrod is harder than a toadstool.

"Do the varmints grow over-cunning by being fooled with by greenhorn hunters, and by this means get troublesome, they send for me, as a matter of course; and thus I do my own hunting, and most of my neighbors'. I walk into the varmints though, and it has become about as much the same to me as drinking. It is told in two sentences—

"A bear is started, and he is killed.

"The thing is somewhat monotonous now—I know just how much they will run, where they will tire, how much they will growl, and what a thundering time I will have in getting their meat home. I could give you the history of the chase with all the particulars at the commencement, I know the signs so well—*Stranger, I'm certain*. Once I met with a match, though, and I will tell you about it; for a common hunt would not be worth relating.

"On a fine fall day, long time ago, I was trailing about for bear, and what should I see but fresh marks on the sassafras trees, about eight inches above any in the forests that I knew of. Says I, 'Them marks is a hoax, or it indicates the d—t bear that was ever grown.' In fact, stranger, I couldn't believe it was real, and I went on. Again I saw the same marks, at the same height, and *I knew the thing lived*. That conviction came home to my soul like an earthquake.

"Says I, 'Here is something a-purpose for me: that bear is mine, or I give up the hunting business.' The very next morning, what should I see but a number of buzzards hovering over my corn-field. 'The rascal has been there,' said I, 'for that sign is certain'; and, sure enough, on examining, I found the bones of what had been as beautiful a hog the day before, as was ever raised by a Buckeye. Then I tracked the critter out of the field to the woods, and all the marks he left behind, showed me that he was *the bear*.

---

[13] At election time, candidates often bought drinks for voters, and tavern keepers marked the reckoning on the doors.

[14] A record-buster.

"Well, stranger, the first fair chase I ever had with that big critter, I saw him no less than three distinct times at a distance; the dogs run him over eighteen miles and broke down, my horse gave out, and I was as nearly used up as a man can be, made on *my* principle, *which is patent.*[15]

"Before this adventure, such things were unknown to me as possible; but, strange as it was, that bear got me used to it before I was done with him; for he got so at last, that he would leave me on a long chase *quite easy.* How he did it, I never could understand.

"That a bear runs at all, is puzzling; but how this one could tire down and bust up a pack of hounds and a horse, that were used to overhauling everything they started after in no time, was past my understanding. Well, stranger, that bear finally got so sassy, that he used to help himself to a hog off my premises whenever he wanted one; the buzzards followed after what he left, and so, between *bear and buzzard,* I rather think I got *out of pork.*

"Well, missing that bear so often took hold of my vitals, and I wasted away. The thing had been carried too far, and it reduced me in flesh faster than an ager. I would see that bear in every thing I did: *he hunted me,* and that, too, like a devil, which I began to think he was.

"While in this shaky fix, I made preparations to give him a last brush, and be done with it. Having completed everything to my satisfaction, I started at sunrise, and to my great joy, I discovered from the way the dogs run, that they were near him. Finding his trail was nothing, for that had become as plain to the pack as a turnpike road.[16]

"On we went, and coming an an open country, what should I see but the bear very leisurely ascending a hill, and the dogs close at his heels, either a match for him this time in speed, or else he did not care to get out of their way—I don't know which. But wasn't he a beauty, though! I loved him like a brother.

"On he went, until he came to a tree, the limbs of which formed a crotch about six feet from the ground. Into this crotch he got and seated himself, the dogs yelling all around it; and there he sat eyeing them as quiet as a pond in low water.

"A greenhorn friend of mine, in company, reached shooting distance before me, and blazed away, hitting the critter in the centre of his forehead. The bear shook his head as the ball struck it, and then walked down from that tree, as gently as a lady would from a carriage.

"'Twas a beautiful sight to see him do that—he was in such a rage, that he seemed to be as little afraid of the dogs as if they had been sucking pigs; and the dogs warn't slow in making a ring around him at a respectful distance, I tell you; even Bowieknife himself, stood off. Then the way his eyes flashed!—why the fire of them would have singed a cat's hair; in fact, that bear was in a *wrath all over.* Only one pup came near him, and he was brushed out so totally with bear's left paw, that he entirely disappeared; and that made the old dogs more cautious still. In the mean time, I came up, and taking deliberate aim, as a man should do, at his side, just back of his foreleg, *if my gun did not snap,*[17] call me a coward, and I won't take it personal.

"Yes, stranger, *it snapped,* and I could not find a cap[18] about my person. While in this predicament, I turned round to my fool friend—'Bill,' says I, 'you're an ass—you're a fool—you might as well have tried to kill that bear by barking the

---

[15] Clear, evident.   [16] A toll road.   [17] Misfire.
[18] A percussion cap, containing explosive powder.

tree[19] under his belly, as to have done it by hitting him in the head. Your shot has made a tiger of him; and blast me, if a dog gets killed or wounded when they come to blows, I will stick my knife into your liver, I will————.' My wrath was up. I had lost my caps, my gun had snapped, the fellow with me had fired at the bear's head, and I expected every moment to see him close in with the dogs and kill a dozen of them at least. In this thing I was mistaken; for the bear leaped over the ring formed by the dogs, and giving a fierce growl, was off—the pack, of course, in full cry after him. The run this time was short, for coming to the edge of a lake, the varmint jumped in, and swam to a little island in the lake, which it reached, just a moment before the dogs.

" 'I'll have him now,' said I, for I had found my caps in the *lining of my coat*—so, rolling a log into the lake, I paddled myself across to the island, just as the dogs had cornered the bear in a thicket. I rushed up and fired—at the same time the critter leaped over the dogs and came within three feet of me, running like mad; he jumped into the lake, and tried to mount the log I had just deserted, but every time he got half his body on it, it would roll over and send him under; the dogs, too, got around him, and pulled him about, and finally Bowieknife clenched with him, and they sunk into the lake together.

"Stranger, about this time I was excited, and I stripped off my coat, drew my knife, and intended to have taken a part with Bowieknife myself, when the bear rose to the surface. But the varmint staid under—Bowieknife came up alone, more dead than alive, and with the pack came ashore.

" 'Thank God!' said I, 'the old villain has got his deserts at last.'

"Determined to have the body, I cut a grape-vine for a rope, and dove down where I could see the bear in the water, fastened my rope to his leg, and fished him, with great difficulty, ashore. Stranger, may I be chawed to death by young alligators, if the thing I looked at wasn't a *she bear, and not the old critter after all*.

"The way matters got mixed on that island was onaccountably curious, and thinking of it made me more than ever convinced that I was hunting the devil himself. I went home that night and took to my bed—the thing was killing me. The entire team of Arkansaw in bear-hunting acknowledged himself used up, and the fact sunk into my feelings as a snagged boat will in the Mississippi. I grew as cross as a bear with two cubs and a sore tail. The thing got out 'mong my neighbors, and I was asked how come on that individ-u-al that never lost a bear when once started?[20] and if that same individ-u-al didn't wear telescopes when he turned a she-bear, of ordinary size, into an old he one, a little larger than a horse?

" 'Prehaps,' said I, 'friends'—getting wrathy—'prehaps you want to call somebody a liar?'

" 'Oh, no,' said they, 'we only heard of such things being *rather common* of late, but we don't believe one word of it; oh, no,'—and then they would ride off, and laugh like so many hyenas over a dead nigger.

"It was too much, and I determined to catch that bear, go to Texas, or die,—and I made my preparations accordin'.

"I had the pack shut up and rested. I took my rifle to pieces, and iled it.

"I put caps in every pocket about my person, *for fear of the lining*.

"I then told my neighbors, that on Monday morning—naming the day—I would start THAT BEAR, and bring him home with me, or they might divide my settlement among them, the owner having disappeared.

---

[19] Shooting into the tree, creating splinters.   [20] Flushed out of hiding.

"Well, stranger, on the morning previous to the great day of my hunting expedition, I went into the woods near my house, taking my gun and Bowieknife along, just *from habit,* and there sitting down, also from habit,[21] what should I see, getting over my fence, but *the bear!* Yes, the old varmint was within a hundred yards of me, and the way he walked *over that fence*—stranger; he loomed up like a *black mist,* he seemed so large, and he walked right towards me.

"I raised myself, took deliberate aim, and fired. Instantly the varmint wheeled, gave a yell, and *walked through the fence,* as easy as a falling tree would through a cobweb.

"I started after, but was tripped up by my inexpressibles,[22] which, either from habit or the excitement of the moment, were about my heels, and before I had really gathered myself up, I heard the old varmint groaning, like a thousand sinners, in a thicket near by, and, by the time I reached him, he was a corpse.

"Stranger, it took five niggers and myself to put that carcass on a mule's back, and old long-ears waddled under his load, as if he was foundered[23] in every leg of his body; and with a common whopper of a bear, he would have trotted off, and enjoyed himself.

" 'Twould astonish you to know how big he was: I made a *bedspread of his skin,* and the way it used to cover my bear mattress, and leave several feet on each side to tuck up, would have delighted you. It was, in fact, a creation[24] bear, and if it had lived in Samson's[25] time, and had met him in a fair fight, he would have licked him in the twinkling of a dice-box.

"But, stranger, I never like the way I hunted him, *and missed him.* There is something curious about it, that I never could understand,—and I never was satisfied at his giving in *so easy at last.* Prehaps he had heard of my preparations to hunt him the next day, so he jist guv up, like Captain Scott's coon,[26] to save his wind to grunt with in dying; but that ain't likely. My private opinion is, that that bear was an *unhuntable bear, and died when his time come.*"[27]

When this story was ended, our hero sat some minutes with his auditors, in a grave silence; I saw there was a mystery to him connected with the bear whose death he had just related, that had evidently made a strong impression on his mind. It was also evident that there was some superstitious awe connected with the affair,—a feeling common with all "children of the wood," when they meet with any thing out of their every-day experience.

He was the first one, however, to break the silence, and, jumping up, he asked all present to "liquor" before going to bed,—a thing which he did, with a number of companions, evidently to his heart's content.

Long before day, I was put ashore at my place of destination, and I can only follow with the reader, in imagination, our Arkansas friend, in his adventures at the "Forks of Cypress," on the Mississippi.

1841

---

[21] Having his habitual morning bowel movement.   [22] Underwear.
[23] Had gone lame.   [24] An original bear, dating from creation.
[25] In Judges 13–16, an Israelite hero famous for great strength.
[26] From a tall tale about the excellent marksman Captain Martin Scott, in which a raccoon (aware of Scott's prowess with the rifle) surrenders to him.
[27] The bear hunt episode here has many similarities with the final hunt for the bear Old Ben in William Faulkner's *Go Down, Moses* (1942). The notion that the bear dies only when his time has come is central to both works.

Nineteenth-century writers and painters were awed by the beauty of the American West, such as that of California's giant redwoods, captured here by Albert Bierstadt.

Henry Clay Lewis
(1825–1850)

Among humorists of the Old Southwest, Henry Clay Lewis is in many ways an anomaly. He was born in Charleston, South Carolina, in 1825 to a Jewish family that moved to Cincinnati in 1829. After being sent to live with a brother in Yazoo City, Mississippi, Lewis ran away—at age ten—to work on steamboats. Put out of work by the financial crash of 1837, Lewis did menial labor until 1841, when his brother consented to arrange for Lewis to serve a medical apprenticeship in Yazoo City. At that time he joined a group of young men who staged theatrical productions and met to discuss literature. Lewis became an avid reader of the developing school of Southwest Humor as it was fostered in William T. Porter's New York newspaper the *Spirit of the Times* and quickly learned to mimic the styles of Augustus Baldwin Longstreet, Thomas Bangs Thorpe, Joseph Glover Baldwin, and other writers with whom Lewis's name is now associated.

In 1844 Lewis began medical training at the Louisville Medical Institute. He also began to write in the hyperbolic idiom that he cultivated, publishing his first exaggerated piece in the *Spirit of the Times* in 1845. After finishing his M.D. degree in 1846, Lewis answered an advertisement for a doctor in northern Louisiana and set up practice in Madison Parish on the Tensas River. In those frontier surroundings he found enough patients to support himself comfortably and enough time to write the volume of stories published in 1850 as *Odd Leaves From the Life of a Louisiana "Swamp Doctor."* He also found a name, Madison Tensas, to use in his fiction to disguise his personal experiences, albeit thinly.

Anomalous in its own right, *Odd Leaves* is presented as the fictional autobiography of Madison Tensas, M.D. Its various stories reflect Lewis's experiences, including his medical apprenticeship, his time in Louisville, and his life in the bayou country of unsettled Louisiana. Typically gruesome, they blend medical curiosity and physical humor even as they show an awareness of what other Southwest Humorists were writing. "The Indefatigable Bear Hunter" (1850), for example, demonstrates Lewis's thorough training in this subgenre: the name Mik-hoo-tah alludes both to Mike Hooter, a figure employed by other humorists as the stock figure of the wild frontiersman and (more specifically) to Thorpe's "Big Bear of Arkansas" (1841). When Mik claims "So I detarmined to strike out in a new track for glory and title myself to be called the 'bear hunter of Ameriky,'" Lewis is transparently measuring Thorpe's hunter.

Many of Lewis's tales are dark, somber, almost meditative in their use of landscape. The irony of his vision is epitomized in his final tale, "A Struggle for Life" (1850), in which Madison Tensas wonders what friends will say when "on a visit to the sick, I disappeared in the swamp and was never heard of more." In this case, fiction presaged fact: while on a medical errand in the Louisiana bayou in 1850, Lewis drowned in a flooded river. His death when he was only twenty-five silenced an American voice that was distinctive, outrageous, and always intriguing.

Suggested Readings: J. Q. Anderson, *Louisiana Swamp Doctor: The Life and Writing of Henry Clay Lewis*, 1962. N. Schmitz, *Of Huck and Alice: Humorous Writing in American Literature*, 1983.

Text Used: *Odd Leaves From the Life of a Louisiana "Swamp Doctor"*, 1849.

THE INDEFATIGABLE BEAR-HUNTER*

In my round of practice, I occasionally meet with men whose peculiarities stamp them as belonging to a class composed only of themselves. So different are they in appearance, habits, taste, from the majority of mankind, that it is impossible to

---

* First published in *Odd Leaves From the Life of a Louisiana 'Swamp Doctor'* in 1849 under the pseudonym Madison Tensas, M.D. Tensas, the narrator of this story, is a swamp doctor like his creator, Henry Clay Lewis.

classify them, and you have therefore to set them down as queer birds "of a feather," that none resemble sufficiently to associate with.

I had a patient once who was one of these queer ones; gigantic in stature, uneducated, fearless of real danger, yet timorous as a child of superstitious perils, born literally in the woods, never having been in a city in his life, and his idea of one being that it was a place where people met together to make whiskey, and form plans for swindling country folks. To view him at one time, you would think him only a whiskey-drinking, bear-fat-loving mortal; at other moments, he would give vent to ideas, proving that beneath his rough exterior there ran a fiery current of high enthusiastic ambition.

It is a favorite theory of mine, and one that I am fond of consoling myself with, for my own insignificance, that there is no man born who is not capable of attaining distinction, and no occupation that does not contain a path leading to fame. To bide our time is all that is necessary. I had expressed this view in the hearing of Mik-hoo-tah,[1] for so was the subject of this sketch called, and it seemed to chime in with his feelings exactly. Born in the woods, and losing his parents early, he had forgotten his real name, and the bent of his genius inclining him to the slaying of bears, he had been given, even when a youth, the name of Mik-hoo-tah, signifying "the grave of bears," by his Indian associates and admirers.

To glance in and around his cabin, you would have thought that the place had been selected for ages past by the bear tribe to yield up their spirits in, so numerous were the relics. Little chance, I ween,[2] had the cold air to whistle through that hut, so thickly was it tapestried with the soft, downy hides, the darkness of the surface relieved occasionally by the skin of a tender fawn, or the short-haired irascible panther. From the joists depended[3] bear-hams and tongues innumerable, and the ground outside was literally white with bones. Ay, he was a bear-hunter, in its most comprehensive sense—the chief of that vigorous band, whose occupation is nearly gone—crushed beneath the advancing strides of romance-destroying civilization. When his horn sounded—so tradition ran—the bears began to draw lots to see who should die that day, for painful experience had told them the uselessness of all endeavoring to escape. The "Big Bear of Arkansas" would not have given him an hour's extra work,[4] or raised a fresh wrinkle on his already care-corrugated brow. But, though almost daily imbruing his hands in the blood of Bruin,[5] Mik-hoo-tah had not become an impious or cruel-hearted man. Such was his piety, that he never killed a bear without getting down on his knees—to skin it—and praying to be d—ned if it warn't a buster;[6] and such his softness of heart, that he often wept, when he, by mistake, had killed a suckling bear—depriving her poor offspring of a mother's care—and found her too poor to be eaten. So indefatigable had he become in his pursuit, that the bears bid fair to disappear from the face of the swamp, and be known to posterity only through the one mentioned in Scripture,[7] that assisted Elisha to punish the impertinent children, when an accident occurred to the hunter, which raised their hopes of not being entirely exterminated.

One day, Mik happened to come unfortunately in contact with a stray grizzly fellow, who, doubtless in the indulgence of an adventurous spirit, had wandered

---

[1] Mike Hooter.   [2] Think.   [3] Hung down.

[4] Obvious one-upmanship with reference to Thomas Bangs Thorpe's "The Big Bear of Arkansas" (1841), emphasized further when Lewis's Mik-hoo-tah wants to be the "bar-hunter of Ameriky."

[5] A bear, from the medieval epic *Reynard the Fox*.   [6] A record-buster.

[7] In II Kings 2:23-24, two bears "tore" the boys who insulted the propet Elisha.

away from the Rocky Mountains, and formed a league for mutual protection with his black and more effeminate brethren of the swamp. Mik saluted him, as he approached, with an ounce ball in the forehead, to avenge half a dozen of his best dogs, who lay in fragments around; the bullet flattened upon his impenetrable skull, merely infuriating the monster; and before Mik could reload, it was upon him. Seizing him by the leg, it bore him to the ground, and ground the limb to atoms. But before it could attack a more vital part, the knife of the dauntless hunter had cloven its heart, and it dropped dead upon the bleeding form of its slayer, in which condition they were shortly found by Mik's comrades. Making a litter of branches, they placed Mik upon it, and proceeded with all haste to their camp, sending one of the company by a near cut for me, as I was the nearest physician. When I reached their temporary shelter I found Mik doing better than I could have expected, with the exception of his wounded leg, and that, from its crushed and mutilated condition, I saw would have to be amputated immediately, of which I informed Mik. As I expected, he opposed it vehemently; but I convinced him of the impossibility of saving it, assuring him if it were not amputated, he would certainly die, and appealed to his good sense to grant permission, which he did at last. The next difficulty was to procure amputating instruments, the rarity of surgical operations, and the generally slender purse of the "Swamp Doctor," not justifying him in purchasing expensive instruments. A couple of bowie-knives, one ingeniously hacked and filed into a saw—a tourniquet made of a belt and piece of stick—a gun-screw converted for the time into a tenaculum[8]—and some buckskin slips for ligatures, completed my case of instruments for amputation. The city physician may smile at this recital, but I assure him many a more difficult operation than the amputation of a leg, has been performed by his humble brother in the "swamp," with far more simple means than those I have mentioned. The preparations being completed, Mik refused to have his arms bound, and commenced singing a bear song; and throughout the whole operation, which was necessarily tedious, he never uttered a groan, or missed a single stave.[9] The next day, I had him conveyed by easy stages to his pre-emption;[10] and tending assiduously, in the course of a few weeks, he had recovered sufficiently for me to cease attentions. I made him a wooden leg, which answered a good purpose; and with a sigh of regret for the spoiling of such a good hunter, I struck him from my list of patients.

A few months passed over and I heard nothing more of him. Newer, but not brighter, stars were in the ascendant, filling with their deeds the clanging trump of bear-killing fame, and, but for the quantity of bear-blankets in the neighboring cabins, and the painful absence of his usual present of bear-hams, Mik-hoo-tah bid fair to suffer that fate most terrible to aspiring ambitionists—forgetfulness during life. The sun, in despair at the stern necessity which compelled him to yield up his tender offspring, day, to the gloomy grave of darkness, had stretched forth his long arms, and, with the tenacity of a drowning man clinging to a straw, had clutched the tender whispering straw-like topmost branches of the trees—in other words it was near sunset—when I arrived at home from a long wearisome semi-ride-and-swim through the swamp. Receiving a negative to my inquiry whether there were any new calls, I was felicitating myself upon a quiet night beside my tidy bachelor hearth, undisturbed by crying children, babbling women, or amo-

---

[8] A surgical instrument for handling blood vessels.　　[9] Note.
[10] A bit of land that Mik has preempted, probably on which he has squatted.

rous cats—the usual accompaniments of married life—when, like a poor henpecked Benedick[11] crying for peace when there is no peace, I was doomed to
disappointment. Hearing the splash of a paddle in the bayou running before the
door, I turned my head towards the bank, and soon beheld, first the tail of a
coon,[12] next his body, a human face, and, the top of the bank being gained, a
full-proportioned form clad in the garments which, better than any printed label,
wrote him down raftsman, trapper, bear-hunter. He was a messenger from the
indefatigable bear-hunter, Mik-hoo-tah. Asking him what was the matter, as soon
as he could get the knots untied which two-thirds drunkenness had made in his
tongue, he informed me, to my sincere regret, that Mik went out that morning on
a bear-hunt, and in a fight with one had got his leg broke all to flinders,[13] if
possible worse than the other, and that he wanted me to come quickly. Getting
into the canoe, which awaited me, I wrapped myself in my blanket, and yielding
to my fatigue, was soon fast asleep. I did not awaken until the canoe striking
against the bank, as it landed at Mik's pre-emption, nearly threw me in the bayou,
and entirely succeeded with regard to my half-drunken paddler, who—like the
sailor who circumnavigated the world and then was drowned in a puddle-hole in
his own garden—had escaped all the perils of the tortuous bayou to be pitched
overboard when there was nothing to do but step out and tie the dug-out. Assisting
him out of the water, we proceeded to the house, when, to my indignation, I learnt
that the drunken messenger had given me the long trip for nothing, Mik only
wanting me to make him a new wooden leg, the old one having been completely
demolished that morning.

Relieving myself by a satisfactory oath, I would have returned that night, but
the distance was too great for one fatigued as I was, so I had to content myself
with such accommodations as Mik's cabin afforded, which, to one blessed like
myself with the happy faculty of ready adaptation to circumstances, was not a
very difficult task.

I was surprised to perceive the change in Mik's appearance. From nearly a
giant, he had wasted to a mere huge bony frame-work; the skin of his face clung
tightly to the bones, and showed nothing of those laughter-moving features that
were wont to adorn his visage; only his eye remained unchanged, and it had lost
none of its brilliancy—the flint had lost none of its fire.

"What on earth is the matter with you, Mik? I have never seen any one fall off
so fast; you have wasted to a skeleton—surely you must have the consumption."

"Do you think so, Doc? I'll soon show you whether the old bellows has lost
any of its force!" and hopping to the door, which he threw wide open, he gave a
death-hug rally to his dogs, in such a loud and piercing tone, that I imagined a
steam whistle was being discharged in my ear, and for several moments could
hear nothing distinctly.

"That will do! stop!" I yelled, as I saw Mik drawing in his breath preparatory to
another effort of his vocal strength; "I am satisfied you have not got consumption;
but what has wasted you so, Mik? Surely, you ain't in love?"

"Love! h-ll! you don't suppose, Doc, even if I was 'tarmined to make a cussed
fool of myself, that there is any gal in the swamp that could stand that hug, do
you?" and catching up a huge bull-dog, who lay basking himself by the fire, he

---

[11] Here, a married man: from the character Benedick in Shakespeare's *Much Ado About Nothing*
(1600), a newly married man who has long been a bachelor.
[12] A racoon.   [13] Splinters, fragments.

gave him such a squeeze that the animal yelled with pain, and for a few moments appeared dead. "No, Doc, it's grief, pure sorrur, sorrur, Doc! when I looks at what I is now and what I used to be! Jes think, Doc, of the fust hunter in the swamp having his sport spilte, like bar-meat in summer without salt! Jes think of a man standin' up one day and blessing old Master for having put bar in creation, and the next cussing high heaven and low h-ll 'cause he couldn't 'sist in puttin' them out! Warn't it enough to bring tears to the eyes of an Injun tater,[14] much less take the fat off a bar-hunter? Doc, I fell off like 'simmons arter frost, and folks as doubted me, needn't had asked whether I war 'ceitful or not, for they could have seed plum threw[15] me! The bar and painter[16] got so saucy that they'd cum to the tother side of the bayou and see which could talk the impudentest! 'Don't you want some bar-meat or painter blanket?' they'd ask: 'bars is monstrous fat, and painter's hide is mighty warm!' Oh! Doc, I was a miserable man! The sky warn't blue for me, the sun war always cloudy, and the shade-trees gin no shade for me. Even the dogs forgot me, and the little children quit coming and asking, 'Please, Mr. Bar-Grave, cotch me a young bar or a painter kitten.' Doc, the tears would cum in my eyes and the hot blood would cum biling[17] up from my heart, when I'd hobble out of a sundown and hear the boys tell, as they went by, of the sport they'd had that day, and how the bar fit 'fore he was killed, and how fat he war arter he was slayed. Long arter they was gone, and the whip-poor-will had eat up their voices, I would sit out there on the old stump, and think of the things that used to hold the biggest place in my mind when I was a boy, and p'raps sense I've bin a man.

"I'd heard tell of distinction and fame, and people's names never dying, and how Washington and Franklin, and Clay and Jackson,[18] and a heap of political dicshunary-folks, would live when their big hearts had crumbled down to a rifle-charge of dust; and I begun, too, to think, Doc, what a pleasant thing it would be to know folks a million years off would talk of me like them, and it made me 'tarmine to 'stinguish myself, and have my name put in a book with a yaller kiver.[19] I warn't a genus, Doc, I nude[20] that, nor I warn't dicshunary; so I de-tarmined to strike out in a new track for glory, and 'title myself to be called the 'bear-hunter of Ameriky.' Doc, my heart jumpt up, and I belted my hunting-shirt tighter for fear it would lepe out when I fust spoke them words out loud.

"'The bar-hunter of Ameriky!' Doc, you know whether I war earnin' the name when I war ruined. There is not a child, white, black, Injun, or nigger, from the Arkansas line to Trinity,[21] but what has heard of me, and I were happy when"— here a tremor of his voice and a tear glistening in the glare of the fire told the old fellow's emotion—"when—but les take a drink—Doc, I found I was dying—I war gettin' weaker and weaker—I nude your truck warn't what I needed, or I'd sent for you. A bar-hunt war the medsin that my systum required, a fust class bar-hunt, the music of the dogs, the fellers a screaming, the cane poppin', the rifles crackin', the bar growlin', the fight hand to hand, slap goes his paw, and a dog's hide hangs on one cane and his body on another, the knife glistenin' and then goin' plump up to the handle in his heart!—Oh! Doc, this was what I needed,

---

[14] A sweet potato.   [15] Through.   [16] Panther.   [17] Boiling.
[18] George Washington and Benjamin Franklin; Henry Clay (1777–1852), perennial U.S. senator and representative from Kentucky, and Andrew Jackson (1767–1845), seventh U.S. president (1829–1837), from Tennessee.
[19] A yellow cover.   [20] Knewed (knew).   [21] Probably Trinity, Kentucky, on the Ohio River.

and I swore, since death were huggin' me, anyhow, I mite as well feel his last grip in a bar-hunt.

"I seed the boys goin' long one day, and haled them to wait awhile, as I believed I would go along too. I war frade if I kept out of a hunt much longer I wood get outen practis. They laughed at me, thinkin' I war jokin'; for wat cood a sick, old, one-legged man do in a bar-hunt? how cood he get threw the swamp, and vines, and canes, and backwater? and s'pose he mist the bar, how war he to get outen the way?

"But I war 'tarmined on goin'; my dander was up, and I swore I wood go, tellin' them if I coodent travel 'bout much, I could take a stand. Seein' it war no use tryin' to 'swade me, they saddled my poney, and off we started. I felt better right off. I knew I cuddent do much in the chase, so I told the fellers I would go to the cross-path stand, and wate for the bar, as he would be sarten to cum by thar. You have never seed the cross-path stand, Doc. It's the singularest place in the swamp. It's rite in the middle of a canebrake,[22] thicker than har on a bar-hide, down in a deep sink, that looks like the devil had cummenst diggin' a skylite for his pre-emption. I knew it war a dangersome place for a well man to go in, much less a one-leg cripple; but I war 'tarmined that time to give a deal on the dead wood, and play my hand out. The boys gin me time to get to the stand, and then cummenst the drive. The bar seemd 'tarmined on disappinting me, for the fust thing I heard of the dogs and bar, they was outen hearing. Everything got quiet, and I got so wrathy at not being able to foller up the chase, that I cust till the trees cummenst shedding their leaves and small branches, when I herd them lumbrin back, and I nude they war makin' to me. I primed old 'bar death' fresh, and rubbed the frizin, for it war no time for rifle to get to snappin'.[23] Thinks I, if I happen to miss, I'll try what virtue there is in a knife—when, Doc, my knife war gone. H-ll! bar, for God's sake have a soft head, and die easy, for I *can't* run!

"Doc, you've hearn a bar bustin' threw a cane-brake, and know how near to a harrycane it is. I almost cummenst dodgin' the trees, thinkin' it war the best in the shop one a comin', for it beat the loudest thunder ever I heard; that ole bar did, comin' to get his death from an ole, one-legged cripple, what had slayed more of his brethren than his nigger foot had ever made trax in the mud. Doc, he heerd a *monstrus long ways ahead of the dogs*. I warn't skeered, but I must own, as I had but one shot, an' no knife, I wud have prefurd they had been closer. But here he cum! he bar—big as a bull—boys off h-ll-wards—dogs nowhar—no knife—but one shot—*and only one leg that cood run!*

"The bar 'peered s'prised to see me standin' ready for him in the openin'; for it war currently reported 'mong his brethren that I war either dead, or no use for bar. I thought fust he war skeered; and, Doc, I b'leve he war, till he cotch a sight of my wooden leg, and that toch his pride, for he knew he would be hist outen every she bear's company, ef he run from a poor, sickly, one-legged cripple, so on he cum, a small river of slobber pourin from his mouth, and the blue smoke curlin outen his ears. I tuck good aim at his left, and let drive. The ball struck him on the eyebrow, and glanced off, only stunnin' him for a moment, jes givin' me time to club my rifle, an' on he kum, as fierce as old grizzly. As he got in reach, I gin him a lick 'cross the temples, brakin' the stock in fifty pieces, an' knockin' him senseless. I struv to foller up the lick, when, Doc, I war fast—my timber toe had run inter the ground, and I cuddent git out, though I jerked hard enuf almost to bring my thigh out of joint. I stuped to unscrew the infurnal thing, when the bar cum

---

[22] A dense growth of cane plants.   [23] Misfiring.

too, and cum at me agen. Vim! I tuck him over the head, and, cochunk, he keeled over. H-ll! but I cavorted and pitched. Thar war my wust enemy, watin' for me to giv him a finisher, an' *I cuddent* git at him. I'd cummense unscrewin' leg—here cum bar—vim—cochunk—he'd fall out of reach—and, Doc, *I cuddent git to him*. I kept workin' my body round, so as to unscrew the leg, and keep the bar off till I cood 'complish it, when jes as I tuck the last turn, and got loose from the d——d thing, here cum bar, more venimous than ever, and I nude thar war death to one out, and comin' shortly. I let him get close, an' then cum down with a perfect tornado on his head, as I thought; but the old villin had learnt the dodge— the barrel jes struck him on the side of the head, and glanst off, slinging itself out of my hands bout twenty feet 'mongst the thick cane, and thar I war in a fix sure. Bar but little hurt—no gun—no knife—no dogs—no frens—no chance to climb—*an' only one leg that cood run*. Doc, I jes cummenst makin' 'pologies to ole Master,[24] when an idee struck me. Doc, did you ever see a piney woods nigger pullin at a sassafras root? or a suckin' pig in a tater patch arter the big yams? You has! Well, you can 'magin how I jurkt at that wudden leg, for it war the last of pea-time with me, sure, if I didn't rise 'fore bar did. At last, they both cum up, bout the same time, and I braced myself for a death struggle.

"We fit all round that holler! Fust I'd foller bar, and then bar would chase me! I'd make a lick, he'd fend off, and showin' a set of teeth that no doctor, 'cept natur, had ever wurkt at, cum tearin' at me! We both 'gan to git tired, I heard the boys and dogs cummin', so did bar, and we were both anxshus to bring the thing to a close 'fore they cum up, though I wuddent thought they were intrudin' ef they had cum up some time afore.

"I'd worn the old leg pretty well off to the second jint, when, jest 'fore I made a lick, the noise of the boys and the dogs cummin' sorter confused bar, and he made a stumble, and bein' off his guard I got a fair lick! The way that bar's flesh giv in to the soft impresshuns of that leg war an honor to the mederkal perfeshun for having invented sich a weepun! I hollered—but you have heered me holler an' I won't describe it—I had whipped a bar in a fair hand to hand fight—me, an old sickly, one-legged bar-hunter! The boys cum up, and, when they seed the ground we had fit over, they swore they would hav thought, 'stead of a bar-fight, that I had been cuttin' cane and deadenin' timber for a corn-patch, the sile[25] war so worked up, they then handed me a knife to finish the work.

"Doc, les licker,[26] it's a dry talk—when will you make me another leg? for bar-meat is not over plenty in the cabin, and I feel like tryin' another!"

1849

George Washington Harris
(1814–1869)

Born in Allegheny City, Pennsylvania in 1814 and raised in Knoxville, Tennessee, George Washington Harris worked at a number of jobs in his early years: he was a metalsmith, a

---

[24] God: Mik had just begun to pray.   [25] Soil.   [26] "Let's have a drink."

farmer, a postmaster, a copper miner, a railroad worker, and one of the youngest steam-boat captains on the Tennessee River. He also wrote political articles for newspapers throughout the region and gained a reputation both for his flamboyant journalism and his flamboyant life style.

Harris's career as a humorist began in 1845 with "The Knob Dance—A Tennessee Frolic," published under the pseudonym Mr. Free in William T. Porter's *The Spirit of the Times*. There followed a series of sketches and "yarns" that describe in raucous detail and wondrous dialect the backwoods customs of eastern Tennessee. Harris combined such dialect and detail with a relish for mayhem in the character Sut Lovingood, who first appeared in "Sut Lovingood's Daddy, Acting Horse" in 1854. Apparently modeled on an illiterate and crude practical joker Harris had known among the hill people around Knoxville, Sut is coarse and amoral, dedicated to wreaking havoc among his neighbors. At the same time, the figure Sut exposes the hypocrisy Harris saw in such nineteenth-century institutions as religion, civil authority, conventional morality, and the all-too-wrongly educated class (exemplified by the encyclopedia writer in "Rare Ripe Garden-Seed" [1867]).

Sut's stories are as interesting for their technique as for their content. Sut tells the stories to "George," an obvious representation of the author, who according to convention should mediate between his outlandish creation and the reader. But "George" exercises much less control than do the mediating voices in the tales of Henry Clay Lewis, Augustus Baldwin Longstreet, and Thomas Bangs Thorpe. In "Sut Lovingood's Daddy" George describes Sut as "a queer looking, long legged, short bodied, small headed, white haired, hog eyed, funny sort of a genius." As a general rule, however, the lurid vitality of Sut's voice overrides authorial supervision, rejoicing in the comical chaos of his misadventures even while lamenting his fate as a "nat'ral born durn'd fool." It is Sut who, in "Sut's Sermon," lists among his "pow'ful strong pints ove karactar" the fact that in place of a soul he has only "a whisky proof gizzard, sorter like the wust half ove a ole par ove saddil bags." And it is Sut who, in "Blown Up With Soda," marvels at the charms of Sicily Burns by saying, "Sich a buzzim! Jis' think ove two snow balls wif a strawberry stuck but-ainded intu bof on em."

The unvarnished energy of Sut's idiom brought Edmund Wilson to describe Harris's collection *Sut Lovingood. Yarns Spun by a "Nat'ral Born Durn'd Fool,"* (1867) as "by far the most repellent book of any real literary merit in American literature" (in *Patriotic Gore,* 1962). From a different perspective, M. Thomas Inge sees Harris's innovative use of dialect as leading to the narrative achievements of Mark Twain and William Faulkner. Both critics are right: Sut's yarns are commonly offensive in style and substance yet demonstrably important to a colloquial tradition.

Harris's wife of thirty-two years, Mary Emeline Nance, died in 1867. He was preparing a second story collection, to be named *High Times and Hard Times*, when he fell ill on a train in 1869, weeks after marrying the young widow Jane Pride. He died suddenly, and his original manuscript was never recovered. Its title has since been used on previously uncollected Harris stories.

Suggested Readings: *High Times and Hard Times: Sketches and Tales by George Washington Harris,* ed. M. T. Inge, 1967. *Sut Lovingood: Yarns Spun by a "Nat'ral Born Durn'd Fool,"* Warped and Wove for Public Wear, ed. M. T. Inge (rep. of 1867 ed.), 1987. M. Rickels, *George Washington Harris,* 1965. W. B. Clark and W. C. Turner, eds., *Critical Essays on American Humor,* 1984. C. S. Brown, *The Tall Tale in American Folklore and Literature,* 1987.

Text Used: *Humor of the Old Southwest,* ed. H. Cohen and W. B. Dillingham, 1964.

RARE RIPE GARDEN-SEED*

"I tell yu now, I minds my fust big skeer[1] jis' es well as rich boys mind thar fust boots, ur seein the fust spotted hoss sirkis.[2] The red top ove them boots am still a rich red stripe in thar minds, an' the burnin red ove my fust skeer hes lef es deep a scar ontu my thinkin works. Mam hed me a standin atwixt her knees. I kin feel the knobs ove her jints[3] a-rattlin a-pas' my ribs yet. She didn't hev much petticoats tu speak ove, an' I hed but one, an' hit wer calliker[4] slit frum the nap ove my naik tu the tail, hilt tugether at the top wif a draw-string, an' at the bottom by the hem; hit wer the handiest close[5] I ever seed, an' wud be pow'ful cumfurtin in summer if hit warn't fur the flies. Ef they was good tu run in, I'd war one yet. They beats pasted shuts,[6] an' britches, es bad es a feather bed beats a bag ove warnut shells fur sleepin on.

"Say, George,[7] wudn't yu like tu see me intu one 'bout haf fadid, slit, an' a-walkin jis' so, up the middil street[8] ove yure city chuch, a-aimin fur yure pew pen, an' hit chock full ove yure fine city gal friends, jis' arter the peopil hed sot down frum the fust prayer, an' the orgin beginin tu groan; what wud yu du in sich a margincy? say hoss?"

"Why, I'd shoot you dead, Monday morning before eight o'clock," was my reply.

"Well, I speck yu wud; but yu'd take a rale ole maid faint fus,[9] rite amung them ar gals. Lordy! wudn't yu be shamed ove me! Yit why not ten[10] chuch in sich a suit, when yu hesn't got no store clothes?

"Well, es I wer sayin mam wer feedin us brats ontu mush an' milk, wifout the milk, an' es I were the baby then, she hilt me so es to see that I got my sheer.[11] Whar thar ain't enuf feed, big childer roots littil childer outen the troff, an' gobbils up thar part. Jis' so the yeath over:[12] bishops eats elders, elders eats common peopil; they eats sich cattil es me, I eats possums, possums eats chickins, chickins swallers wums, an' wums am content tu eat dus, an' the dus am the aind ove hit all. Hit am all es regilur es the souns frum the tribil[13] down tu the bull base ove a fiddil in good tchune, an' I speck hit am right, ur hit wudn't be 'lowed.[14]

" '*The sheriff!*' his'd[15] mam in a keen trimblin whisper; hit sounded tu me like the skreech ove a hen when she sez 'hawk,' tu her little roun-sturn'd, fuzzy, bead-eyed, stripid-backs.

"I actid jis' adzacly as they dus; I darted on all fours onder mam's petticoatails, an' thar I met, face tu face, the wooden bowl, an' the mush, an' the spoon what she slid onder frum tuther side. I'se mad at mysef yet, fur rite thar I show'd the fust flash ove the nat'ral born durn fool what I now is. I orter et hit[16] all up, in jestis tu my stumick an' my growin, while the sheriff wer levyin ontu the bed an'

---

* First published in *Sut Lovingood: Yarns Spun by a "Nat'ral Born Durn'd Fool," Warped and Wove for Public Wear* in 1867. As reproduced by Harris, Sut Lovingood's dialect is made up of earthy expressions, backwoods metaphors, and a semiphonetic spelling that gives the text a bizarre look. It is often helpful to read aloud.
[1] Scare.   [2] The first spotted-horse circus.   [3] Joints.   [4] Calico.   [5] Clothes.
[6] Starched shirts.
[7] Presumably George Washington Harris, who comes into these stories as a listener. Sut frequently talks to "George" at the beginning of stories and calls George (and other people he meets) "hoss."
[8] The middle aisle.   [9] You'd take a real old maid faint, first.   [10] Attend.   [11] Share.
[12] It's just so, the earth over.   [13] Sounds from the treble.   [14] Allowed.   [15] Hissed.
[16] I ought to eat it.

the cheers.[17] Tu this day, ef enybody sez 'sheriff,' I feels skeer, an' ef I hears constabil menshun'd, my laigs goes thru runnin moshuns, even ef I is asleep. Did yu ever watch a dorg dreamin ove rabbit huntin? Thems the moshuns, an' the feelin am the rabbit's.

"Sherifs am orful 'spectabil peopil; everybody looks up tu em. I never adzacly seed the 'spectabil part mysef. I'se too fear'd ove em, I reckon, tu 'zamin fur hit[18] much. One thing I knows, no country atwix yere an' Tophit[19] kin ever 'lect me tu sell out widders' plunder, ur poor men's co'n, an' the tho'ts ove hit gins me a good feelin; hit sorter flashes thru my heart when I thinks ove hit. I axed a passun onst,[20] whan hit cud be, an' he pernounced hit tu be *onregenerit*[21] *pride,* what I orter squelch in prayer, an' in tendin chuch on colleckshun days. I wer in hopes hit mout be 'ligion, ur sense, a-soakin intu me; hit feels good, enyhow, an' I don't keer ef every suckit rider[22] outen jail knows hit. Sheriffs' shuts allers hes nettil dus[23] ur fleas inside ove em when they lies down tu sleep, an' I'se glad ove hit, fur they'se allers discumfortin me, durn em. I scarcely ever git tu drink a ho'n,[24] ur eat a mess in peace. I'll hurt one sum day, see ef I don't. Show me a sheriff a-steppin softly roun, an' a-sorter sightin at me, an' I'll show yu a far sampil ove the speed ove a express ingine, fired up wif rich, dry, rosiny skeers. They don't ketch me *much,* usin only human laigs es wepuns.

"Ole John Doltin wer a 'spectabil sheriff, monsusly so, an' hed the bes' scent fur poor fugatif devils, an' wimen, I ever seed; he wer sure fire. Well, he toted a warrun[25] fur this yere skinful ove durn'd fool, 'bout that ar misfortnit nigger meetin bisness, ontil he wore hit intu six seperit squar bits,[26] an' hed wore out much shoe leather a-chasin ove me. I'd foun a doggery in full milk, an' hated pow'ful bad tu leave that settilment while hit suck'd free;[27] so I sot intu sorter try an' wean him off frum botherin me so much. I suckseedid so well that he not only quit racin ove me, an' wimen, but he wer tetotaly[28] spiled es as a sheriff, an' los' the 'spectabil seckshun ove his karacter. Tu make yu fool fellers onderstan how hit wer done, I mus' interjuice yure minds tu one Wat Mastin, a bullit-headed yung blacksmith.

"Well, las' year—no hit wer the year afore las'—in struttin an' gobblin time,[29] Wat felt his keepin right warm, so he sot intu bellerin[30] an' pawin up dus in the neighborhood roun the ole widder McKildrin's. The more dus he flung up, the wus he got, ontil at las' he jis cudn't stan the ticklin sensashuns anuther minnit; so he put fur the county clark's offis, wif his hans sock'd down deep intu his britchis pockets, like he wer fear'd ove pick-pockets, his back roach'd roun, an' a-chompin his teef ontil he splotch'd his whiskers wif foam. Oh! he wer yearnis' hot,[31] an' es restless es a cockroach in a hot skillit."

---

[17] The sheriff arrives to seize property, specifically the bed and the chairs.
[18] To examine for it: Sut has heard that sheriffs are respectable but is too afraid of them to examine the matter closely.
[19] Tophet, or Hell.   [20] I asked a parson once.   [21] Unregenerate, or obstinate.
[22] Circuit rider, a preacher who rode from town to town for religious services.
[23] Sheriff's shirts always have nettle dust, the gritty powder from prickly plants (nettles).
[24] A large drinking mug.
[25] Warrant. The sheriff is carrying a warrant for Sut's arrest because of mayhem he had caused in another episode; occasionally, Sut refers to events from other stories.
[26] The warrant was torn into six pieces.
[27] Sut had found a situation he could really milk, and he hated to leave it.
[28] Totally; a feeble pun on "teetotal" (the sheriff was turned into a nondrinking man).
[29] Springtime, when the juices flow and the young men strut.
[30] Wat was sexually aroused, so he started bellowing.   [31] Hot in earnest.

"What was the matter with this Mr. Mastin? I cannot understand you, Mr. Lovingood; had he hydrophobia?" remarked a man in a square-tail coat, and cloth gaiters, who was obtaining subscribers for some forthcoming Encyclopedia of Useful Knowledge, who had quartered at our camp, uninvited, and really unwanted.

"What du yu mean by high-dry-foby?" and Sut looked puzzled.

"A madness produced by being bit by some rabid animal," explained Square-tail, in a pompous manner.

"Yas, hoss, he hed high-dry-foby *orful*,[32] an' Mary McKildrin, the widder McKildrin's only darter, hed gin him the complaint; I don't know whether she bit 'im ur not; he mout a-cotch hit frum her bref,[33] an' he wer now in the roach back, chompin stage ove the sickness, so he wer arter the clark fur a tickit tu the hospital. Well, the clark sole 'im a piece ove paper, part printin an' part ritin, wif a picter ove two pigs' hearts, what sum boy hed shot a arrer thru, an' lef hit stickin, printed at the top. That paper wer a splicin pass[34]—sum calls hit a par ove licins— an' that very nite he tuck Mary, fur better, fur wus, tu hev an' tu hole tu him his heirs, an'—"

"Allow me to interrupt you," said our guest; "you do not quote the marriage ceremony correctly."

"Yu go tu *hell*, mistofer; yu bothers me."

This outrageous rebuff took the stranger all aback, and he sat down.

"Whar wer I? Oh, yas, he married Mary tight an' fas', an' nex day he wer abil tu be about. His coat tho', an' his trousis look'd jis' a skrimshun too big, loose like, an' heavy tu tote. I axed him ef he felt soun. He sed yas, but he'd welded a steamboat shaftez[35] the day afore, an' wer sorter tired like. Thar he tole a durn lie, fur he'd been a-ho'nin up dirt mos' ove the day, roun the widder's garden, an' bellerin in the orchard. Mary an' him sot squar[36] intu hous'-keepin, an' 'mung uther things he bot a lot ove *rar ripe garden-seed*, frum a Yankee peddler. Rar ripe co'n, rar ripe peas, rar ripe taters, rar ripe everything, an' the two yung durn'd fools wer dreadfully exercis'd[37] 'bout hit. Wat sed he ment tu git him a rar ripe hammer an' anvil, an' Mary vow'd tu grashus, that she'd hev a rar ripe wheel an' loom, ef money wud git em. Purty soon arter he hed made the garden, he tuck a noshun tu work a spell down tu Ataylanty,[38] in the railroad shop, es he sed he hed a sorter ailin in his back, an' he tho't weldin rail car-tire an' ingine axiltrees, wer lighter work nur[39] sharpinin plows, an' puttin lap-links in trace-chains. So down he went, an' foun hit agreed wif him, fur he didn't cum back ontil the middil ove August. The fust thing he seed when he landid intu his cabin-door, wer a shoebox wif rockers onder hit, an' the nex thing he seed, wer Mary hersef, propped up in bed, an' the nex thing he seed arter that, wer a par ove littil rat-eyes a-shinin abuv the aind ove the quilt, ontu Mary's arm, an' the next an' las thing he seed wer the two littil rat-eyes aforesed, a-turnin into two hundred thousand big green stars, an' a-swingin roun an' roun the room, faster an' faster, ontil they mix'd intu one orful green flash. He drap't intu a limber pile on the floor. The durn'd fool what hed weldid the steamboat shaftez hed fainted safe an' soun es a gal skeered at a mad bull. Mary fotch a weak cat-scream, an' kivered her hed, an' sot intu work ontu a whifflin dry cry,[40] while littil Rat-eyes gin hitssef up tu suckin. Cryin an' suckin bof at onst ain't far; mus' cum pow'ful strainin on the

---

[32] Awful.   [33] He might have caught it from her breath.   [34] A wedding license.

[35] A metal bar used to support rotating pieces for transmitting power.   [36] Set directly.

[37] Excited.   [38] Atlanta.   [39] Than.   [40] A tearless "cry" with little whiffs of breath.

wet seckshun ove an' 'oman's constitushun;[41] yet hit am ofen dun, an' more too. Ole Missis McKildrin, what wer a-nussin Mary, jis' got up frum knittin, an' flung a big gourd ove warter squar intu Wat's face, then she fotch a glass bottil ove swell-skull whisky[42] outen the three-cornered cupboard, an' stood furnint Wat, a-holdin hit in wun han, an' the tin-cup in tuther, waitin fur Wat tu cum to. She wer the piusses[43] lookin ole 'oman jis' then, yu ever seed outside ove a prayer-meetin. Arter a spell, Wat begun tu move, twitchin his fingers, an' battin his eyes, sorter 'stonished like. That pius lookin statue sed tu him:

"'My son, jis' take a drap ove sperrits, honey. Yu'se very sick, dumplin, don't take on darlin, ef yu kin help hit, ducky, fur poor Margarit Jane am mons'ous ailin, an' the leas' nise ur takin on[44] will kill the poor sufferin dear, an' yu'll loose yure tuckil[45] ducky duv ove a sweet wifey, arter all she's dun gone thru fur yu. My dear son Watty, yu mus' consider her feelins a littil.' Sez Wat, a-turnin up his eyes at that vartus[46] ole relick, sorter sick like—

"'I is a-considerin em a heap, rite now.'

"'Oh that's right, my good kine child.'

"Oh dam ef ole muther-in-lors can't plaster humbug over a feller, jis' es saft an' easy es they spreads a camrick hanketcher[47] over a three hour ole baby's face; yu don't feel hit at all, but hit am thar, a plum inch thick, an' stickin fas es court-plaster. She raised Wat's head, an' sot the aidge ove the tin cup agin his lower teef, an' turned up the bottim slow an' keerful, a-winkin at Mary, hu[48] wer a-peepin over the aidge ove the coverlid, tu see ef Wat *tuck the perskripshun,*[49] fur a heap ove famerly cumfort 'pended on that ar ho'n ove sperrits. *Wun* ho'n allers saftens[50] a man, the yeath over. Wat keep a-battin his eyes, wus nur[51] a owl in daylight; at las' he raised hissef ontu wun elbow, an' rested his head in that han, sorter weak like. Sez he, mons'ous trimblin an' slow: 'Aprile—May—June—July—an' mos'—haf—ove—August,' a-countin the munths ontu the fingers ove tuther han, wif the thumb, a-shakin ove his head, an' lookin at his spread fingers like they warn't his'n, ur they wer nastied wif sumfin. Then he counted em agin, slower, Aprile—May—June—July—an', mos' haf ove August, an' he run his thumb atwixt his fingers, es meaning mos' haf ove August, an' look'd at the pint ove hit, like hit mout be a snake's head.[52] He raised his eyes tu the widder's face, who wer standin jis' es steady es a hitchin pos', an' still a-warin that pius 'spression ontu her pussonal feturs, an' a flood ove saft luv fur Wat, a-shining strait frum her eyes intu his'n. Sez he, 'That jis' makes four munths, an' mos' a half, don't hit, Missis McKildrin?' She never sed one word. Wat reached fur the hath,[53] an' got a dead fire-coal; then he made a mark clean acrost a floor-plank. Sez he, 'Aprile,' a-holdin down the coal ontu the aind ove the mark, like he wer fear'd hit mout blow away afore he got hit christened Aprile. Sez he, 'May'—an' he marked across the board agin; then he counted the marks, one, two, a-dottin at em wif the coal. 'June,' an' he marked agin, one, two three; counted wif the pint[54]

---

[41] Sut thinks that crying and nursing at the same time must be a powerful strain on the "wet seckshun" of a woman's constitution.

[42] Whiskey that would swell your skull, rot gut.   [43] Most pious.

[44] The least noise or carrying on.   [45] Turtle.   [46] Virtuous.

[47] A cambric, or fine-clothed, handkerchief.   [48] Who.

[49] Bought the story, believed what his mother-in-law told him.

[50] *One* mug of whiskey always softens.   [51] Worse than.

[52] Wat puts his thumb between his fingers, a crude sexual gesture, to indicate half of August, then looks at it as if it were a snake's head.

[53] Hearth.   [54] Point.

ove the coal. He scratched his head wif the littil finger ove the han holdin the charcoal, an' he drawed hit slowly acrost the board agin, peepin onder his wrist tu see when hit reached the crack, an' sez he 'July,' es he lifted the coal; 'one, two three, four,' countin frum lef tu right, an' then frum right tu lef. 'That haint but four, no way I kin fix hit. Ole Pike hissef cudn't make hit five, ef he wer tu sifer[55] ontu hit until his laigs turned intu figger eights.' Then he made a mark, haf acrost a plank, spit on his finger, an' rubbed off a haf inch ove the aind, an' sez he, 'Mos' haf ove August.' He looked up at the widder, an' thar she wer, same es ever, still a-holdin the flask agin her bussum, an' sez he 'Four months, an' mos' a haf. *Haint enuf, is hit mammy?* hits jis' 'bout (lackin a littil) *haf enuf,* haint hit, mammy?'

"Missis McKildrin shuck her head sorter onsartin like, an' sez she, 'Take a drap more sperrits, Watty, my dear pet; dus yu mine[56] buyin that ar rar ripe seed, frum the peddler?' Wat nodded his head, an' looked 'what ove hit,' but didn't say hit.

" 'This is what cums ove hit, an' four months an' a half am rar ripe time fur babys, adzackly. Tu be sure, hit lacks a day ur two, but Margarit Jane wer allers a pow'ful interprizin gal, an' a yearly rizer.'[57] Sez Wat,

" 'How about the 'taters?'

" 'Oh, *we* et 'taters es big es goose aigs, afore ole Missis Collinze's blossomed.'

" 'How 'bout co'n?'

" 'Oh, we shaved down roasin years afore hern tassel'd[58]—'

" 'An' peas?'

" 'Yes son, we hed gobs an' lots in three weeks. Everything cums in adzackly half the time that hit takes the ole sort, an' yu *knows,* my darlin son, yu planted hit waseful.[59] I tho't then yu'd rar ripe everything on the place. Yu planted *often,* too, didn't yu luv? fur fear hit wudn't cum up.'[60]

" 'Ye-ye-s-s he—he did,' sed Mary a-cryin. Wat studied pow'ful deep a spell, an' the widder jis' waited. Widders allers wait, an' allers win. At las, sez he, 'Mammy.' She looked at Mary, an' winked these yere words at her, es plain es she cud a-talked em. 'Yu hearn him call me *mammy twiste.*[61] I'se *got him* now. His back-bone's a-limberin fas', he'll own the baby yet, see ef he don't. Jis' hole still my darter, an' let yer mammy knead this dough, then yu may bake hit es brown es yu please.'

" 'Mammy, when I married on the fust day of Aprile"—The widder look'd oneasy; she tho't he mout be a-cupplin that day,[62] his weddin, an' the idear, dam fool, tugether. But he warn't, fur he sed 'That day I gin ole man Collins my note ove han fur a hundred dullars, jew in one year arter date, the balluns on this lan.[63] Dus yu think that ar seed will change the *time* eny, ur will hit alter the *amount?*' An' Wat looked at her powerful ankshus. She raised the whisky bottil way abuv her head, wif her thumb on the mouf, an' fotch the bottim down ontu her han, spat. Sez she, 'Watty, my dear b'lovid son, pripar tu pay *two* hundred dullars 'bout the fust ove October, fur hit'll be jew jis' then, *es* sure es that littil black-eyed angel in the bed thar, am yer darter.'

---

[55] Cipher, figure.   [56] Do you remember?   [57] An early riser.
[58] We harvested roastings ears before she grew: the corn grew in half the time.   [59] Wastefully.
[60] Planting here takes on a sexual meaning.   [61] Twice.
[62] Putting together dates that would make him suspicious.
[63] A $100 promissory note, due one year later, for the balance on this land.

"Wat drap't his head, an' sed, '*Then hits a dam sure thing*.' Rite yere, the baby fotch a rattlin loud squall, (I speck Mary wer sorter figetty jis' then, an' hurt hit). 'Yas,' sez Wat, a-wallin a red eye[64] to'ards the bed; 'my littil she—what wer hit yu called her name, mammy?' 'I called her a sweet littil angel, an' she is wun, es sure es yu're her daddy, my b'loved son.' 'Well,' sez Wat, 'my littil sweet, patent rar ripe she angel, ef yu lives tu marryin time, yu'll 'stonish sum man body outen his shut, ef yu don't rar ripe lose hits vartu arter the fust plantin, that's all.' He rared up on aind, wif his mouf pouch'd out. He had a pow'ful forrid,[65] fur-reaching, bread funnel, enyhow—cud a-bit the aigs outen a catfish, in two-foot warter, wifout wettin his eyebrows. 'Dod durn rar ripe seed, an' rar ripe pedlers, an' rar ripe notes tu the hottes' corner ove—'

" 'Stop Watty, *darlin*, don't swar; 'member yu belongs tu meetin.'[66]

" 'My blacksmith's fire,' ainded Wat, an' he studied a long spell; sez he,

" 'Did you save eny ove that infunnel[67] doubil-trigger seed?' 'Yas,' sez the widder, 'thar in that bag by the cupboard.' Wat got up ofen the floor, tuck a countin sorter look[68] at the charcoal marks, an' reached down the bag; he went tu the door an' called 'Suke, muley! Suke, Suke, cow, chick, chick, chicky chick.' 'What's yu gwine tu du now, my dear son?' sed Missis McKildrin. 'I'se jis' gwine tu feed this actif *smart* truck[69] tu the cow, an' the hens, that's what I'se gwine tu du. Ole muley haint hed a calf in two years, an' I'll eat sum rar ripe aigs.' Mary now venter'd tu speak: 'Husban, I ain't sure hit'll work on hens; cum an' kiss me my luv.' 'I haint sure hit'll work on hens, either,' sed Wat. 'They's powerful onsartin in thar ways, well es wimen,' an' he flung out a hanful spiteful like. 'Takin the rar ripe invenshun all tugether, frum 'taters an' peas tu notes ove han, an' childer, I can't say I likes hit much,' an' he flung out anuther hanful. 'Yer mam hed thuteen the ole way, an' ef this truck stays 'bout the hous', yu'se good fur twenty-six,[70] maybe thuty, fur yu'se a pow'ful interprizin gal, yer mam sez', an' he flung out anuther hanful, over-handid, es hard es ef he wer flingin rocks at a stealin sow. 'Make yere mine[71] easy,' sed the widder; 'hit never works on married folks only the fust time.' 'Say them words agin,' sed Wat, 'I'se glad tu hear em. Is hit the same way wif notes ove han?' 'I speck hit am,' answer'd the widder, wif jis' a taste ove strong vinegar in the words, es she sot the flask in the cupboard wif a push.

"Jis' then ole Doltin, the sheriff, rid up, an' started 'stonished when he seed Wat, but he, quick es an 'oman[72] kin hide a strange hat, drawed the puckerin-string ove that legil face ove his'n, an' fotch hit up tu the 'know'd yu wer at home,' sorter look, an' wishin Wat much joy, sed he'd fotch the baby a present, a par ove red shoes, an' a calliker dress, fur the luv he bore hits granmam. Missis McKildrin tole him what the rar ripe hed dun, an' he swore hit allers worked jis' that way, an' wer 'stonished at Wat's not knowin hit; an' they talked so fas', an' so much, that the more Wat listened the less he know'd.

"Arter the sheriff lef, they onrolled the bundil, an' Wat straitched out the calliker in the yard. He step't hit off keerfully, ten yards, an a littil the rise. He puss'd up[73] his mouf, an' blow'd out a whistil seven foot long, lookin up an'

---

[64] Looking wall-eyed (sideways); his eye may be red from whiskey and a mounting anger.
[65] Forehead.   [66] You belong to a church.   [67] Infernal.   [68] He looks as though to count again.
[69] Active, smart vegetables: the rare ripe garden-seed.
[70] Although Wat counted slowly when he was making charcoal marks on the floor, he has no trouble doubling thirteen and getting twenty-six as the number of "childer," or children, Mary could have.
[71] Mind.   [72] Any woman.   [73] Pursed.

down the middil stripe ove the drygoods, frum aind tu aind. Sez he, 'Missis Mc-Kildrin, that'll make Rar Ripe a good *full* frock, won't hit?' 'Y-a-s,' sed she, wif her hans laid up along her jaw, like she wer studyin the thing keerfully. 'My son, I thinks hit will, an' I wer jis' a-thinkin ef hit wer cut tu 'vantage, thar *mout* be nuff lef, squeezed out tu make yu a Sunday shutin shut, making the ruffils an' ban[74] outen sumthin else.' 'Put hit in the bag what the rar ripe wer in, an' by mornin thar'll be nuff fur the ruffils an' bans, an' yu mout make the tail tu drag the yeath, wifout squeezin ur pecin',[75] sez Wat, an' he put a few small wrinkils in the pint ove his nose, what seemed tu bother the widder tu make out the meanin ove; they look'd mons'ous like the outward signs ove an onb'lever.[76] Jis' then his eyes sot fas' ontu sumthin a-lyin on the groun whar he'd onrolled the bundil; he walk'd up tu hit slow, sorter like a feller goes up tu a log, arter he thinks he seed a snake run onder. He walk'd clean roun hit twiste, never takin his eyes ofen hit. At las' he lifted hit on his instep, an' hilt out his laig strait at that widdered muther-in-lor ove his'n. Sez he, 'What mout yu call that? Red baby's shoes don't giner'lly hev teeth, dus they?' 'Don't yu *know* hits a tuckin comb,[77] Watty? The store-keeper's made a sorter blunder, I speck,' sed that vartus petticoatful ove widder-hood. 'Maybe he hes; I'se durn sure I *hes*,' sed Wat, an' he wrinkil'd his nose agin, mons'ous botherinly tu that watchful widder. He scratched his head a spell; sez he, 'Ten yards an' the rise fur a baby's frock, *an' hit rar ripe at that, gits me;* an' that ar tuckin comb gits me wus.' 'Oh, fiddlesticks an' flusterashun,' sez she. 'Save the comb; baby'll soon want hit.' 'That's so, mammy, I'm dam ef hit don't,' an' he slip't his foot frum onder hit, an' hit scarcely totch[78] the yeath afore he stomp't hit, an' the teeth flew all over the widder. He look'd like he'd been stompin a blowin adder,[79] an' went apas' the 'oman intu the cabin, in a rale Aprile tucky[80] gobbler strut. When he tore the rapper off the sheriff's present, I seed a littil bit ove white paper fall out. Onbenowenst tu enybody, I sot my foot ontu hit, an' when they went in I socked hit deep intu my pocket, an' went over tu the still-'ous.[81] I tuck Jim Dunkin out, an' arter swarin 'im wif a uplifted han', tu keep dark,[82] got him tu read hit tu me, ontil hit wer printed on the mindin[83] seck-shun ove my brain. Hit run jis' so:

> "My sweet Mary:
>
> I mayn't git the chance tu talk eny tu yu, so when Wat gits home, an' axes enything 'bout the *comb* an' *calliker,* yu tell him yer mam foun the bundil in the road. She'll back yu up in that ar statemint, ontil thar's enuf white fros' in hell tu kill snapbeans.
>
> *Notey Beney.*[84]—I hope Wat'll stay in Atlanty ontil the merlenium,[85] don't yu, my dear duv?
>
> Yures till deth,
>
> Doltin

An' tu that ar las' remark he'd sot a big D. I reckon he ment that fur dam Wat.

---

[74] A Sunday shouting shirt (for church meetings) with ruffles and bands.
[75] Piecing fabric together.
[76] Wat, having wrinkled his nose, looks monstrously as though he does not believe the story.
[77] A comb for "tucking" long hair, obviously a present for a woman, not a baby.
[78] Touched.   [79] Snake.   [80] Turkey.   [81] The building in which the still was kept.
[82] Quiet: Sut Lovingood is illiterate and must have someone read the note to him.   [83] Memory.
[84] *Nota bene:* "note well," or take careful note (Latin).
[85] Millennium; the thousand years mentioned in the Book of Revelation.

"Now, I jis' know'd es long es I hed that paper, I hilt four aces ontu the sheriff, an' I ment tu bet on the han, an' *go halves wif Wat,* fur I wer sorry fur him, he wer so infunely 'posed upon. I went tu school tu Sicily Burns, tu larn 'oman tricks, an' I tuck a dirplomer,[86] I did, an' now I'd jes' like tu see the pussonal feeters[87] ove the she 'oman what cud stock rar ripe kerds[88] on me, durn'd fool es I is. I hed a talk wif Wat, an' soon foun out that his mine hed simmer'd down intu a strong belief that the sheriff an' Mary wer doin thar weavin in the same loom.

"Then I show'd him my four aces, an' that chip made the pot bile[89] over, an' he jis' 'greed tu be led by me, spontanashusly.

"Jis' think on that fac' a minnit boys; a man what hed sense enuf tu turn a hoss shoe, an' then nail hit on toe aind foremos' bein led by me, looks sorter like a plum tree barin tumil bug-balls,[90] but hit wer jis' so, an' durn my pictur, ef I didn't lead him tu victory, strait along.

"Wat narrated hit,[91] that he b'leved strong in rar ripe, frum beans, thru notes ove han, plum tu babys, an' that his cabin shud never be wifout hit. The widder wer cheerful, Mary wer luvin, an' the sheriff wer told on the sly, by ole Mister McKildrin's remainin, an' mos' pius she half,[92] that Wat wer es plum blind es ef his eyes wer two tuckil aigs. So the wool grow'd over *his* eyes, ontil hit wer fit tu shear, an' *dam ef I warn't at the shearin.*

"Things, tharfore, went smoof, an' es quiet es a greased waggin, runnin in san. Hits allers so, jis' afore a tarin big storm.

"By the time littil Rar Ripe wer ten weeks ole, Doltin begun tu be pow'ful plenty in the neighborhood. Even the brats know'd his hoss's tracks, an' go whar he wud, the road led ni[93] ontu Wat's, ur the widder's, tu git thar. My time tu play my four aces hed 'bout cum."

"And so has orderly bed time. I wish to repose," remarked the man of Useful Knowledge, in the square-tail coat, and cloth gaiters.

Sut opened his eyes in wonder.

"Yu wish tu du what?"

"I wish to go to sleep."

"Then why the h—l didn't yu say so? Yu mus' talk Inglish tu me, ur not git yersef onderstood. I warn't edikated at no Injun ur nigger school. Say, bunty,[94] warn't yu standid deep in sum creek, when the taylure man put the string to yu, fur that ar cross atwix a rounabout[95] an' a flour barril, what yu'se got on in place of a coat?"

My self-made guest looked appealingly at me, as he untied his gaiters,[96] evidently deeply insulted. I shook my head at Sut, who was lying on his breast, with his arms crossed for a pillow, but with head elevated like a lizard's, watching the traveler's motions with great interest.

"Say, George, what dus repose mean? That wurd wer used at me jis' now."

"Repose means rest."

"Oh, the devil hit dus! I'se glad tu hear hit. I tho't hit wer pussonal. I kin

---

[86] A diploma; in other stories Sut has adventures with Sicily Burns, from whom he learns about women.

[87] Personal features.   [88] Seeds.   [89] Boil.   [90] Swollen growths caused by insects.

[91] Pretended to believe it.   [92] The widow.

[93] Nigh; wherever Doltin went, he seemed to go by way of Wat's house or the widow's (where Mary might be).

[94] Saggy ("bunt" is the saggy part of a fishing net); according to Sut, the encyclopedia salesman's clothes are saggy.

[95] A short, tight coat.   [96] Spats or leggings.

repose now, mysef. Say, ole Onsightly Peter, repose sum tu, ef yu kin in that flour barril. I ain't gwine tu hunt fur yure har ontil mor—" and Sut slept. When morning broke, the Encyclopedia, or Onsightly Peter as Sut pronounced it, had

"Folded his tent like the Arab,
And as silently stole away."[97]

1867

Nathaniel Hawthorne
(1804–1864)

Born on the Fourth of July, 1804, in Salem, Massachusetts, Nathaniel Hawthorne was the descendant of determined Puritans. One of his Puritan ancestors, William Hathorne, came to Salem in 1630 and gained notoriety for persecuting Quakers; another, John Hathorne, was a judge at the Salem witchcraft trials in 1692. A keen sense of these two ancestors brought Hawthorne (the author himself added the "w" to his surname) to envision them in "The Custom–House" (1850) as stern men resolute in their intolerance, who would disapprove of him as a writer of storybooks. Following the death of his father, a sea captain, in Dutch Guiana in 1808, Hawthorne moved with his family to the home of relatives, the Mannings, in Raymond, Maine. In that rural setting he passed the years of his youth, reading extensively in the English classics and nursing the hope of becoming a writer.

Hawthorne entered Bowdoin College in Brunswick, Maine, in autumn 1821. Henry Wadsworth Longfellow and Horatio Bridge (later, a naval officer and an author) were members of Hawthorne's class; Franklin Pierce, the future president, was in the class ahead. Hawthorne joined the convivial Pot-8-o Club, demonstrated ability in Latin and English composition, and graduated eighteenth in a class of thirty-eight in September 1825. Clearly, he did not make a full commitment to academic success. During his years at Bowdoin he was distracted from formal study by his attempts to write fiction. The best evidence suggests that at this time he was working on the novel *Fanshawe* (1828) and "Seven Tales of My Native Land," which was never published. Following his graduation he returned to his mother's house. The family had moved back to Salem from Raymond in summer 1822, and thus Hawthorne went to Salem to live and write.

The years 1825 to 1837 have often been termed the years of solitude in Hawthorne's life. Although he was in no way a recluse, Hawthorne did cultivate habits of seclusion during this period to practice his craft as a writer. His claim of having been "the obscurest man of letters in America," prefacing his 1851 edition of *Twice-Told Tales,* refers not to any patterns of retirement, however, but to the fate of his early tales and sketches: for, because of editorial policies, all of Hawthorne's work before the initial publication of *Twice-Told Tales* in 1837 appeared anonymously or pseudonymously. In 1829 he wrote to the publisher Samuel G. Goodrich about a collection of his work to be called "Provincial Tales." Goodrich read the tales, as he said "with great pleasure." Rather than bring out the

---

[97] Adapted from Henry Wadsworth Longfellow's *Evangeline* (1847).

collection as a book, Goodrich chose to publish the tales individually in the *Token*—an annual that he edited. After putting four tales in the 1832 issue he explained in a letter to Hawthorne that because "they are anonymous, no objection arises from having so many pages by one author, particularly as they are as good, if not better, than anything else I get."

Throughout the early 1830s two, three, or four of Hawthorne's tales appeared in each issue of the *Token;* the 1837 issue contained no less than nine. And in 1835 the *New England Magazine* published eight of his tales and sketches. Hawthorne was publishing regularly but earning little money. To augment his income he edited the *American Magazine of Useful and Entertaining Knowledge* from March to August 1836. And despite a growing dissatisfaction with Goodrich, Hawthorne assembled—with assistance from his sister Elizabeth—*Peter Parley's Universal History* for Goodrich in 1836. The popular history was a financial success for the publisher but earned only $100 for the author.

The circumstances of periodical publication thus helped to keep Hawthorne anonymous. In 1836, harried by scrambling editorial work and having seen another collection of tales dismantled for magazine publication, he was understandably depressed about his career. To his rescue came Horatio Bridge, who had repeatedly urged Hawthorne to appear before the public under his own name. Without Hawthorne's knowledge Bridge arranged for the publication of a volume of his friend's tales and supplied $250 to guarantee the publishers against loss. Thus, *Twice-Told Tales,* containing eighteen of the thirty-six tales and sketches previously published in periodicals, appeared in 1837. Response to the volume was favorable, if not widespread. But the book sold well enough to enable the publisher to refund Bridge's money. After twelve years of writing in what he called his "dismal chamber," Hawthorne had achieved a literary reputation that went beyond the confines of editorial offices.

Hawthorne met Sophia Peabody in autumn 1838 and quickly came to see her as someone who had rescued him from a treacherous half-life, as a savior who made him whole, humanized by love. His letters to Sophia are eloquent testimonials to the enduring depth of his feeling. In January 1839 he was appointed measurer of salt and coal in the Boston Customhouse at an annual salary of $1500. With Sophia now his intended wife, he needed the security offered by a regular salary. From 1839 to 1840 he stayed in the Boston Customhouse, working hard, writing to Sophia of his "coal-begrimed visage and salt-befrosted locks." Early in 1841 he made a bold personal experiment: he invested $1000 in Brook Farm, George Ripley's utopian community near West Roxbury, Massachusetts, and went to live there. Several weeks after Hawthorne's arrival he wrote happily to his sister Louisa that he was "transformed into a complete farmer." He had loaded manure carts, planted potatoes and peas, and milked cows. But Hawthorne had not gone to Brook Farm out of transcendentalist convictions: he thought Brook Farm might afford an economical home for Sophia and himself after they married. When he came to believe that it would not, toward the end of 1841, he left the community in disenchantment.

After their marriage in 1842 Hawthorne and Sophia lived at the Old Manse in Concord, Massachusetts, the house in which Ralph Waldo Emerson had written *Nature* in 1836. The three years at the Old Manse were perhaps the happiest of Hawthorne's life, but the difficulty of earning a living was a nagging problem. "I did not come to see you," he wrote to Bridge in March 1843, "because I was very short of cash." Such difficulties "make me sigh for the regular monthly payments of the customhouse." During these years Hawthorne published almost two dozen tales and sketches. Most of them were included in *Mosses From an Old Manse,* which appeared in 1846 and contributed to a reputation that had been growing since the publication of *Twice-Told Tales*. But some readers preferred Hawthorne's first book. Edgar Allan Poe, for example, who had praised Hawthorne's genius in

The Old Manse of Concord, Massachusets, built by Ralph Waldo Emerson's grandfather, was home to, and made famous by, Nathaniel Hawthorne.

Twice-Told Tales, objected to the allegorical nature of *Mosses.* And Herman Melville, reading *Twice-Told Tales* after having lavished praise on *Mosses,* felt that the quality of the "earlier vintage" surpassed that of the later. Hawthorne himself announced that unless he could "do better" he would publish no more collections of tales. *Mosses,* however, contains some of Hawthorne's most respected work—including "Rappaccini's Daughter," "The Birth-Mark," and, perhaps most notably, "Young Goodman Brown," which Hawthorne had passed over for both the first and second editions of *Twice-Told Tales.*

In April 1846 Hawthorne secured an appointment as surveyor of the Salem Customhouse at an annual salary of $1200. Once again, however, working at a monotonous job meant abandoning the role of author. Though his duties were undemanding, Hawthorne wrote little during his three years in the customhouse. Dismissed in January 1849, he was somewhat frustrated and bitter; the machinations of small-time politics, he felt, had victimized him. But under Sophia's influence he turned to his writing, and by early February 1850 he had completed *The Scarlet Letter,* which was published one month later.

The early 1850s was for Hawthorne a time of intense literary activity. *The Scarlet Letter* was followed by *The House of the Seven Gables* (1851) and by *The Blithedale Romance* (1852). And he found the energy for other work as well. *True Stories From History and Biography* (1851), *A Wonder-Book for Girls and Boys* (1852), *The Life of Franklin Pierce* (1852), and *Tanglewood Tales for Girls and Boys* (1853) evidence his ability to write for different markets. In 1852, with *Blithedale* completed, he announced his intention of beginning a new work "in a day or two." But the period of burgeoning literary activity was over. It was not until 1860 that Hawthorne published another romance—*The Marble Faun,* his last completed work of fiction.

From 1853 to 1857 Hawthorne served as U.S. consul at Liverpool, having been appointed by President Franklin Pierce. The financial advantage of the consular post (important now that he had three children to support), plus a desire to see England, encouraged Hawthorne to go abroad at this time. And see England he did, as his journal entries show. A record of his observations, he hoped, would prove useful for an English romance he planned to write. But that romance was never to be completed. A series of essays on England, first published in the *Atlantic Monthly* and then collected under the title *Our Old Home* in 1863, came instead from the penetrating sketches and observations in his journal—a charming but disappointing harvest from the rich soil of his recorded English experiences. In a studied and deeply personal act of gratitude Hawthorne dedicated *Our Old Home* to Franklin Pierce, the man who had made his years in England possible. Because Pierce had consistently advocated a moderate policy regarding slavery (in a vain hope of holding the Union together), many people regarded him as less a patriot than a temporizer. His popularity, never of magnitude in the North, had waned appreciably. By insisting that *Our Old Home* be dedicated to Pierce, Hawthorne thus made a point of his friendship with a man exceedingly out of fashion. Emerson was so irritated by Hawthorne's public thanks to Pierce that he ripped the dedicatory page from his copy of the book.

Hawthorne resigned his post in Liverpool in August 1857 and early in 1858 left for Italy. There during the final years of the decade he met artists and poets, visited cathedrals and museums, and assessed the mighty dimensions of the past. As his notebooks suggest, Italy challenged Hawthorne as no other experience in his life had done. All too often he could view the rich legacy of the Italian past only through the distracting lens of the Italian present. He could not ignore the dirt of Roman byways and even less the ever-present beggars, whose numbers exceeded the capacity of one man's charity. His daughter Una's illness in November 1858 cost him anxious weeks in an environment in which he felt himself to be essentially a stranger. Troubling and complex, Hawthorne's Italian experience was nonetheless rich in implication. For out of it came the idea for *The Marble Faun*, which he wrote in England after leaving Italy in 1859.

In 1860 Hawthorne returned to the United States and to his former home of Concord. During the final years of his life he began work on four romances—*Dr. Grimshawe's Secret, Septimius Felton, The Ancestral Footstep,* and *The Dolliver Romance*—none of which he could complete. In the context of the Civil War, his attempts to bring his kind of fiction into coherent form met with failure. He could not breathe vitality into the idea of a lost estate in England or of an elixir of life when the life of the nation was itself at stake. The effect of the Civil War does not fully explain Hawthorne's inability to complete these late romances: a loss of health also contributed to his difficulties. And perhaps he would have been unable to work successfully under the most favorable of circumstances. But his admission (in the preface to *Our Old Home*) that "the Present, the Immediate, the Actual, has proved too potent for me" suggests the way in which the war overpowered his imagination.

Shortly after Hawthorne's funeral in May 1864, Emerson wrote in his journal "I thought him a greater man than any of his works betray." The statement reveals Hawthorne's stature as a human being. But an artist is judged finally by the quality of his or her art. And in the best of his tales and romances Hawthorne created a literary art of enduring significance.

Suggested Readings: *The Centenary Edition of the Works of Nathaniel Hawthorne,* 20 vols., ed. W. Charvat et al., 1962–1988. *Hawthorne's Lost Notebooks, 1835-1841,* ed. B. Mouffe, 1978. H. James, *Hawthorne,* 1879. R. H. Pearce, ed., *Hawthorne Centenary Essays,* 1964. M. D. Bell, *Hawthorne and the Historical Romance of New England,* 1971. N. Baym, *The Shape of Hawthorne's Career,* 1976. E. Dryden, *Nathaniel Hawthorne: The Poetics of Enchantment,* 1977. A. Turner, *Nathaniel Hawthorne: A Biography,* 1980. J. R. Mellow, *Nathaniel Hawthorne in His Times,* 1980. T. Martin, *Nathaniel Hawthorne,* 1983. M. Colacurcio, *The Province of Piety: Moral History in Hawthorne's Early Tales,* 1984. L. S. Luedtke, *Hawthorne and the Romance of the Orient,* 1989.

Texts Used: "My Kinsman, Major Molineux," "Alice Doane's Appeal," and "Ethan Brand": *The Snow-Image and Uncollected Tales*, in *The Centenary Edition*, Vol. XI, 1974. "Young Goodman Brown," "Rappaccini's Daughter," and "The Birth-Mark": *Mosses From an Old Manse*, in *The Centenary Edition*, Vol. X, 1974. "The Minister's Black Veil" and "Wakefield": *Twice-Told Tales*, in *The Centenary Edition*, Vol. IX, 1974. Preface: *The House of the Seven Gables*, in *The Centenary Edition*, Vol. II, 1965. *The Scarlet Letter: The Centenary Edition*, Vol. I, 1962. All else: *The American Notebooks*, in *The Centenary Edition*, Vol. VIII, 1973.

MY KINSMAN, MAJOR MOLINEUX*

After the kings of Great Britain had assumed the right of appointing the colonial governors, the measures of the latter seldom met with the ready and general approbation, which had been paid to those of their predecessors, under the original charters.[1] The people looked with most jealous scrutiny to the exercise of power, which did not emanate from themselves, and they usually rewarded the rulers with slender gratitude, for the compliances, by which, in softening their instructions from beyond the sea, they had incurred the reprehension of those who gave them. The annals of Massachusetts Bay will inform us, that of six governors, in the space of about forty years from the surrender of the old charter, under James II., two were imprisoned by a popular insurrection; a third, as Hutchinson[2] inclines to believe, was driven from the province by the whizzing of a musket ball; a fourth, in the opinion of the same historian, was hastened to his grave by continual bickerings with the House of Representatives; and the remaining two, as well as their successors, till the Revolution, were favored with few and brief intervals of peaceful sway. The inferior members of the court party,[3] in times of high political excitement, led scarcely a more desirable life. These remarks may serve as preface to the following adventures, which chanced upon a summer night, not far from a hundred years ago. The reader, in order to avoid a long and dry detail of colonial affairs, is requested to dispense with an account of the train of circumstances, that had caused much temporary inflammation of the popular mind.

It was near nine o'clock of a moonlight evening, when a boat crossed the ferry with a single passenger, who had obtained his conveyance, at that unusual hour, by the promise of an extra fare. While he stood on the landing-place, searching in either pocket for the means of fulfilling his agreement, the ferryman lifted a lantern, by the aid of which, and the newly risen moon, he took a very accurate survey of the stranger's figure. He was a youth of barely eighteen years, evidently country-bred, and now, as it should seem, upon his first visit to town. He was clad in a coarse grey coat, well worn, but in excellent repair; his under garments[4] were durably constructed of leather, and sat tight to a pair of serviceable and well-shaped limbs; his stockings of blue yarn, were the incontrovertible handiwork of a mother or a sister; and on his head was a three-cornered hat, which in its better days had perhaps sheltered the graver brow of the lad's father. Under his left arm was a heavy cudgel, formed of an oak sapling, and retaining a part of the hardened

---

* First published in *The Token* in 1832 and collected in *The Snow-Image, and Other Twice-Told Tales* (1851).

[1] King James II (1633–1701) of England appointed the first royal governor in 1685, after King Charles II (1630–1685) had rescinded the Massachusetts Charter in 1684.

[2] Thomas Hutchinson (1711–1780), the last royal governor of Massachusetts (1771–1774), who wrote *The History of the Colony and Province of Massachusetts-Bay* (1764, 1767).

[3] The Royalist party.   [4] The clothes on the lower half of his body.

root; and his equipment was completed by a wallet,[5] not so abundantly stocked as to incommode the vigorous shoulders on which it hung. Brown, curly hair, well-shaped features, and bright cheerful eyes, were nature's gifts, and worth all that art could have done for his adornment.

The youth, one of whose names was Robin, finally drew from his pocket the half of a little province-bill[6] of five shillings, which, in the depreciation of that sort of currency, did but satisfy the ferryman's demand, with the surplus of a sexangular piece of parchment valued at three pence. He then walked forward into the town, with as light a step, as if his day's journey had not already exceeded thirty miles, and with as eager an eye, as if he were entering London city, instead of the little metropolis of a New England colony.[7] Before Robin had proceeded far, however, it occurred to him, that he knew not whither to direct his steps; so he paused, and looked up and down the narrow street, scrutinizing the small and mean wooden buildings, that were scattered on either side.

"This low hovel cannot be my kinsman's dwelling," thought he, "nor yonder old house, where the moonlight enters at the broken casement; and truly I see none hereabouts that might be worthy of him. It would have been wise to inquire my way of the ferryman, and doubtless he would have gone with me, and earned a shilling from the Major for his pains. But the next man I meet will do as well."

He resumed his walk, and was glad to perceive that the street now became wider, and the houses more respectable in their appearance. He soon discerned a figure moving on moderately in advance, and hastened his steps to overtake it. As Robin drew nigh, he saw that the passenger was a man in years, with a full peri-wig of grey hair, a wide-skirted coat of dark cloth, and silk stockings rolled about his knees. He carried a long and polished cane, which he struck down perpendicu-larly before him, at every step; and at regular intervals he uttered two successive hems, of a peculiarly solemn and sepulchral intonation. Having made these obser-vations, Robin laid hold of the skirt of the old man's coat, just when the light from the open door and windows of a barber's shop, fell upon both their figures.

"Good evening to you, honored Sir," said he, making a low bow, and still retaining his hold of the skirt. "I pray you to tell me whereabouts is the dwelling of my kinsman, Major Molineux?"

The youth's question was uttered very loudly; and one of the barbers, whose razor was descending on a well-soaped chin, and another who was dressing a Ramillies wig,[8] left their occupations, and came to the door. The citizen, in the meantime, turned a long favored countenance[9] upon Robin, and answered him in a tone of excessive anger and annoyance. His two sepulchral hems, however, broke into the very centre of his rebuke, with most singular effect, like a thought of the cold grave obtruding among wrathful passions.

"Let go my garment, fellow! I tell you, I know not the man you speak of. What! I have authority, I have—hem, hem—authority; and if this be the respect you show your betters, your feet shall be brought acquainted with the stocks,[10] by daylight, tomorrow morning!"

Robin released the old man's skirt, and hastened away, pursued by an ill-man-

---

[5] A knapsack.   [6] Paper money issued by a province or colony.   [7] Boston.

[8] An ornate powdered wig with a braided tail, named for a British victory in Ramillies, Belgium, in 1706.

[9] A long face.

[10] A device for public punishment: a wooden frame with holes for locking in the feet and sometimes the hands.

nered roar of laughter from the barber's shop. He was at first considerably surprised by the result of his question, but, being a shrewd youth, soon thought himself able to account for the mystery.

"This is some country representative," was his conclusion, "who has never
seen the inside of my kinsman's door, and lacks the breeding to answer a stranger
civilly. The man is old, or verily—I might be tempted to turn back and smite him
on the nose. Ah, Robin, Robin! even the barber's boys laugh at you, for choosing
such a guide! You will be wiser in time, friend Robin."

He now became entangled in a succession of crooked and narrow streets, which
crossed each other, and meandered at no great distance from the water-side. The
smell of tar was obvious to his nostrils, the masts of vessels pierced the moonlight
above the tops of the buildings, and the numerous signs, which Robin paused to
read, informed him that he was near the centre of business. But the streets were
empty, the shops were closed, and lights were visible only in the second stories of
a few dwelling-houses. At length, on the corner of a narrow lane, through which
he was passing, he beheld the broad countenance of a British hero swinging before
the door of an inn,[11] whence proceeded the voices of many guests. The casement
of one of the lower windows was thrown back, and a very thin curtain permitted
Robin to distinguish a party at supper, round a well-furnished table. The fragrance
of the good cheer steamed forth into the outer air, and the youth could not fail to
recollect, that the last remnant of his travelling stock of provision had yielded to
his morning appetite, and that noon had found, and left him, dinnerless.

"Oh, that a parchment three-penny might give me a right to sit down at yonder
table," said Robin, with a sigh. "But the Major will make me welcome to the best
of his victuals; so I will even step boldly in, and inquire my way to his dwelling."

He entered the tavern, and was guided by the murmur of voices, and fumes of
tobacco, to the public room. It was a long and low apartment, with oaken walls,
grown dark in the continual smoke, and a floor, which was thickly sanded, but of
no immaculate purity. A number of persons, the larger part of whom appeared to
be mariners, or in some way connected with the sea, occupied the wooden
benches, or leather-bottomed chairs, conversing on various matters, and occasionally lending their attention to some topic of general interest. Three or four little
groups were draining as many bowls of punch, which the great West India trade
had long since made a familiar drink[12] in the colony. Others, who had the aspect
of men who lived by regular and laborious handicraft, preferred the insulated bliss
of an unshared potation, and became more taciturn under its influence. Nearly all,
in short, evinced a predilection for the Good Creature[13] in some of its various
shapes, for this is a vice, to which, as the Fast-day[14] sermons of a hundred years
ago will testify, we have a long hereditary claim. The only guests to whom
Robin's sympathies inclined him, were two or three sheepish countrymen, who
were using the inn somewhat after the fashion of a Turkish Caravansary;[15] they
had gotten themselves into the darkest corner of the room, and, heedless of the
Nicotian[16] atmosphere, were supping on the bread of their own ovens, and the
bacon cured in their own chimney-smoke. But though Robin felt a sort of brotherhood with these strangers, his eyes were attracted from them, to a person who

---

[11] On a signboard.   [12] Punch made with rum.
[13] Alcoholic drinks; an allusion to I Timothy 4:4: "For every creature of God is good."
[14] Days designated for penance.   [15] An inn catering to those who travel in a caravan.
[16] Smoke-filled: "Nicotian" and "nicotine" come from Jean Nicot (1530?–1600), who brought tobacco to France in 1560 when he served as French ambassador to Portugal.

stood near the door, holding whispered conversation with a group of ill-dressed associates. His features were separately striking almost to grotesqueness, and the whole face left a deep impression in the memory. The forehead bulged out into a double prominence, with a vale between; the nose came boldly forth in an irregular curve, and its bridge was of more than a finger's breadth; the eyebrows were deep and shaggy, and the eyes glowed beneath them like fire in a cave.

While Robin deliberated of whom to inquire respecting his kinsman's dwelling, he was accosted by the innkeeper, a little man in a stained white apron, who had come to pay his professional welcome to the stranger. Being in the second generation from a French Protestant,[17] he seemed to have inherited the courtesy of his parent nation; but no variety of circumstance was ever known to change his voice from the one shrill note in which he now addressed Robin.

"From the country, I presume, Sir?" said he, with a profound bow. "Beg to congratulate you on your arrival, and trust you intend a long stay with us. Fine town here, Sir, beautiful buildings, and much that may interest a stranger. May I hope for the honor of your commands in respect to supper?"

"The man sees a family likeness! the rogue has guessed that I am related to the Major!" thought Robin, who had hitherto experienced little superfluous civility.

All eyes were now turned on the country lad, standing at the door, in his worn three-cornered hat, grey coat, leather breeches, and blue yarn stockings, leaning on an oaken cudgel, and bearing a wallet on his back.

Robin replied to the courteous innkeeper, with such an assumption of consequence, as befitted the Major's relative.

"My honest friend," he said, "I shall make it a point to patronize your house on some occasion, when—" here he could not help lowering his voice—"I may have more than a parchment three-pence in my pocket. My present business," continued he, speaking with lofty confidence, "is merely to inquire the way to the dwelling of my kinsman, Major Molineux."

There was a sudden and general movement in the room, which Robin interpreted as expressing the eagerness of each individual to become his guide. But the innkeeper turned his eyes to a written paper on the wall, which he read, or seemed to read, with occasional recurrences to the young man's figure.

"What have we here?" said he, breaking his speech into little dry fragments. " 'Left the house of the subscriber, bounden servant,[18] Hezekiah Mudge— had on, when he went away, grey coat, leather breeches, master's third best hat. One pound currency reward to whoever shall lodge him in any jail in the province.' Better trudge, boy, better trudge!"

Robin had begun to draw his hand towards the lighter end of the oak cudgel, but a strange hostility in every countenance, induced him to relinquish his purpose of breaking the courteous innkeeper's head. As he turned to leave the room, he encountered a sneering glance from the bold-featured personage whom he had before noticed; and no sooner was he beyond the door, than he heard a general laugh, in which the innkeeper's voice might be distinguished, like the dropping of small stones into a kettle.

"Now is it not strange," thought Robin, with his usual shrewdness, "is it not

---

[17] Numerous French Protestants, or Huguenots, came to Massachusetts after 1685 when King Louis XIV issued the Edict of Nantes, which denied them religious liberty.

[18] Someone indentured or "bound" as a paid servant, generally for a period of seven years, in exchange for transportation to the colonies. The innkeeper has checked a wanted sign to see if Robin is dressed like Hezekiah Mudge, who evidently left his employer, or "subscriber," before his term of indenture expired.

strange, that the confession of an empty pocket, should outweigh the name of my kinsman, Major Molineux? Oh, if I had one of these grinning rascals in the woods, where I and my oak sapling grew up together, I would teach him that my arm is heavy, though my purse be light!"

On turning the corner of the narrow lane, Robin found himself in a spacious street, with an unbroken line of lofty houses on each side, and a steepled building at the upper end, whence the ringing of a bell announced the hour of nine. The light of the moon, and the lamps from numerous shop windows, discovered people promenading on the pavement, and amongst them, Robin hoped to recognize his hitherto inscrutable relative. The result of his former inquiries made him unwilling to hazard another, in a scene of such publicity, and he determined to walk slowly and silently up the street, thrusting his face close to that of every elderly gentleman, in search of the Major's lineaments. In his progress, Robin encountered many gay and gallant figures. Embroidered garments, of showy colors, enormous periwigs, gold-laced hats, and silver hilted swords, glided past him and dazzled his optics. Travelled youths, imitators of the European fine gentlemen of the period, trod jauntily along, half-dancing to the fashionable tunes which they hummed, and making poor Robin ashamed of his quiet and natural gait. At length, after many pauses to examine the gorgeous display of goods in the shop windows, and after suffering some rebukes for the impertinence of his scrutiny into people's faces, the Major's kinsman found himself near the steepled building, still unsuccessful in his search. As yet, however, he had seen only one side of the thronged street; so Robin crossed, and continued the same sort of inquisition down the opposite pavement, with stronger hopes than the philosopher seeking an honest man,[19] but with no better fortune. He had arrived about midway towards the lower end, from which his course began, when he overheard the approach of some one, who struck down a cane on the flag-stones at every step, uttering, at regular intervals, two sepulchral hems.

"Mercy on us!" quoth Robin, recognizing the sound.

Turning a corner, which chanced to be close at his right hand, he hastened to pursue his researches, in some other part of the town. His patience was now wearing low, and he seemed to feel more fatigue from his rambles since he crossed the ferry, than from his journey of several days on the other side. Hunger also pleaded loudly within him, and Robin began to balance the propriety of demanding, violently and with lifted cudgel, the necessary guidance from the first solitary passenger, whom he should meet. While a resolution to this effect was gaining strength, he entered a street of mean appearance, on either side of which, a row of ill-built houses was straggling towards the harbor. The moonlight fell upon no passenger along the whole extent, but in the third domicile which Robin passed, there was a half-opened door, and his keen glance detected a woman's garment within.

"My luck may be better here," said he to himself.

Accordingly, he approached the door, and beheld it shut closer as he did so; yet an open space remained, sufficing for the fair occupant to observe the stranger, without a corresponding display on her part. All that Robin could discern was a strip of scarlet petticoat, and the occasional sparkle of an eye, as if the moonbeams were trembling on some bright thing.

"Pretty mistress,"—for I may call her so with a good conscience, thought the

---

[19] The Greek philosopher Diogenes (412?–323 B.C.) supposedly roamed the world in search of an honest man.

shrewd youth, since I know nothing to the contrary—"my sweet pretty mistress, will you be kind enough to tell me whereabouts I must seek the dwelling of my kinsman, Major Molineux?"

Robin's voice was plaintive and winning, and the female, seeing nothing to be shunned in the handsome country youth, thrust open the door, and came forth into the moonlight. She was a dainty little figure, with a white neck, round arms, and a slender waist, at the extremity of which her scarlet petticoat jutted out over a hoop, as if she were standing in a balloon. Moreover, her face was oval and pretty, her hair dark beneath the little cap, and her bright eyes possessed a sly freedom, which triumphed over those of Robin.

"Major Molineux dwells here," said this fair woman.

Now her voice was the sweetest Robin had heard that night, the airy counterpart of a stream of melted silver; yet he could not help doubting whether that sweet voice spoke Gospel truth. He looked up and down the mean street, and then surveyed the house before which they stood. It was a small, dark edifice of two stories, the second of which projected over the lower floor; and the front apartment had the aspect of a shop for petty commodities.

"Now truly I am in luck," replied Robin, cunningly, "and so indeed is my kinsman, the Major, in having so pretty a housekeeper. But I prithee trouble him to step to the door; I will deliver him a message from his friends in the country, and then go back to my lodgings at the inn."

"Nay, the Major has been a-bed this hour or more," said the lady of the scarlet petticoat; "and it would be to little purpose to disturb him to-night, seeing his evening draught[20] was of the strongest. But he is a kind-hearted man, and it would be as much as my life's worth, to let a kinsman of his turn away from the door. You are the good old gentleman's very picture,[21] and I could swear that was his rainy-weather hat. Also, he has garments very much resembling those leather— But come in, I pray, for I bid you hearty welcome in his name."

So saying, the fair and hospitable dame took our hero by the hand; and though the touch was light, and the force was gentleness, and though Robin read in her eyes what he did not hear in her words, yet the slender waisted woman, in the scarlet petticoat, proved stronger than the athletic county youth. She had drawn his half-willing footsteps nearly to the threshold, when the opening of a door in the neighborhood, startled the Major's housekeeper, and, leaving the Major's kinsman, she vanished speedily into her own domicile. A heavy yawn preceded the appearance of a man, who, like the Moonshine of Pyramus and Thisbe,[22] carried a lantern, needlessly aiding his sister luminary in the heavens. As he walked sleepily up the street, he turned his broad, dull face on Robin, and displayed a long staff, spiked at the end.

"Home, vagabond, home!" said the watchman, in accents that seemed to fall asleep as soon as they were uttered. "Home, or we'll set you in the stocks by peep of day!"

"This is the second hint of the kind," thought Robin. "I wish they would end my difficulties, by setting me there to-night."

Nevertheless, the youth felt an instinctive antipathy towards the guardian of midnight order, which at first prevented him from asking his usual question. But

---

[20] Drink.   [21] You look just like the major.

[22] Moonshine appears in a comic rendition of the love story of Pyramus and Thisbe in Shakespeare's *A Midsummer Night's Dream* (III.i).

just when the man was about to vanish behind the corner, Robin resolved not to lose the opportunity, and shouted lustily after him—

"I say, friend! will you guide me to the house of my kinsman, Major Molineux?"

The watchman made no reply, but turned the corner and was gone; yet Robin seemed to hear the sound of drowsy laughter stealing along the solitary street. At that moment, also, a pleasant titter saluted him from the open window above his head; he looked up, and caught the sparkle of a saucy eye; a round arm beckoned to him, and next he heard light footsteps descending the staircase within. But Robin, being of the household of a New England cleryman, was a good youth, as well as a shrewd one; so he resisted temptation, and fled away.

He now roamed desperately, and at random, through the town, almost ready to believe that a spell was on him, like that, by which a wizard of his country, had once kept three pursuers wandering, a whole winter night, within twenty paces of the cottage which they sought. The streets lay before him, strange and desolate, and the lights were extinguished in almost every house. Twice, however, little parties of men, among whom Robin distinguished individuals in outlandish attire, came hurrying along, but though on both occasions they paused to address him, such intercourse did not at all enlighten his perplexity. They did but utter a few words in some language of which Robin knew nothing, and perceiving his inability to answer, bestowed a curse upon him in plain English, and hastened away. Finally, the lad determined to knock at the door of every mansion that might appear worthy to be occupied by his kinsman, trusting that perseverance would overcome the fatality which had hitherto thwarted him. Firm in this resolve, he was passing beneath the walls of a church, which formed the corner of two streets, when, as he turned into the shade of its steeple, he encountered a bulky stranger, muffled in a cloak. The man was proceeding with the speed of earnest business, but Robin planted himself full before him, holding the oak cudgel with both hands across his body, as a bar to further passage.

"Halt, honest man, and answer me a question," said he, very resolutely. "Tell me, this instant, whereabouts is the dwelling of my kinsman, Major Molineux?"

"Keep your tongue between your teeth, fool, and let me pass," said a deep, gruff voice, which Robin partly remembered. "Let me pass, I say, or I'll strike you to the earth!"

"No, no, neighbor!" cried Robin, flourishing his cudgel, and then thrusting its larger end close to the man's muffled face. "No, no, I'm not the fool you take me for, nor do you pass, till I have an answer to my question. Whereabouts is the dwelling of my kinsman, Major Molineux?"

The stranger, instead of attempting to force his passage, stept back into the moonlight, unmuffled his own face and stared full into that of Robin.

"Watch here an hour, and Major Molineux will pass by," said he.

Robin gazed with dismay and astonishment, on the unprecedented physiognomy of the speaker. The forehead with its double prominence, the broad-hooked nose, the shaggy eyebrows, and fiery eyes, were those which he had noticed at the inn, but the man's complexion had undergone a singular, or, more properly, a two-fold change. One side of the face blazed of an intense red, while the other was black as midnight, the division line being in the broad bridge of the nose; and a mouth, which seemed to extend from ear to ear, was black or red, in contrast to the color of the cheek. The effect was as if two individual devils, a fiend of fire and a fiend of darkness, had united themselves to form this infernal visage. The stranger grinned in Robin's face, muffled his parti-colored features, and was out of sight in a moment.

"Strange things we travellers see!" ejaculated Robin.

He seated himself, however, upon the steps of the church-door, resolving to wait the appointed time for his kinsman's appearance. A few moments were consumed in philosophical speculations, upon the species of the *genus homo*, who had just left him, but having settled this point shrewdly, rationally, and satisfactorily, he was compelled to look elsewhere for amusement. And first he threw his eyes along the street; it was of more respectable appearance than most of those into which he had wandered, and the moon, "creating, like the imaginative power, a beautiful strangeness in familiar objects," gave something of romance to a scene, that might not have possessed it in the light of day. The irregular, and often quaint architecture of the houses, some of whose roofs were broken into numerous little peaks; while others ascended, steep and narrow, into a single point; and others again were square; the pure milk-white of some of their complexions, the aged darkness of others, and the thousand sparklings reflected from bright substances in the plastered walls of many; these matters engaged Robin's attention for awhile, and then began to grow wearisome. Next he endeavored to define the forms of distant objects, starting away with almost ghostly indistinctness, just as his eye appeared to grasp them; and finally he took a minute survey of an edifice, which stood on the opposite side of the street, directly in front of the church-door, where he was stationed. It was a large square mansion, distinguished from its neighbors by a balcony, which rested on tall pillars, and by an elaborate Gothic window, communicating therewith.

"Perhaps this is the very house I have been seeking," thought Robin.

Then he strove to speed away the time, by listening to a murmur, which swept continually along the street, yet was scarcely audible, except to an unaccustomed ear like his; it was a low, dull, dreamy sound, compounded of many noises, each of which was at too great a distance to be separately heard. Robin marvelled at this snore of a sleeping town, and marvelled more, whenever its continuity was broken, by now and then a distant shout, apparently loud where it originated. But altogether it was a sleep-inspiring sound, and to shake off its drowsy influence, Robin arose, and climbed a window-frame, that he might view the interior of the church. There the moonbeans came trembling in, and fell down upon the deserted pews, and extended along the quiet aisles. A fainter, yet more awful radiance, was hovering round the pulpit, and one solitary ray had dared to rest upon the opened page of the great Bible. Had Nature, in that deep hour, become a worshipper in the house, which man had builded? Or was that heavenly light the visible sanctity of the place, visible because no earthly and impure feet were within the walls? The scene made Robin's heart shiver with a sensation of loneliness, stronger than he had ever felt in the remotest depths of his native woods; so he turned away, and sat down again before the door. There were graves around the church, and now an uneasy thought obtruded into Robin's breast. What if the object of his search, which had been so often and so strangely thwarted, were all the time mouldering in his shroud? What if his kinsmen should glide through yonder gate, and nod and smile to him in passing dimly by?

"Oh, that any breathing thing were here with me!" said Robin.

Recalling his thoughts from this uncomfortable track, he sent them over forest, hill, and stream, and attempted to imagine how that evening of ambiguity and weariness, had been spent by his father's household. He pictured them assembled at the door, beneath the tree, the great old tree, which had been spared for its huge twisted trunk, and venerable shade, when a thousand leafy brethren fell. There, at the going down of the summer sun, it was his father's custom to perform domestic worship, that the neighbors might come and join with him like brothers of the family, and that the wayfaring man might pause to drink at that fountain, and keep his heart pure by freshening the memory of home. Robin distinguished the seat of every individual of the little audience; he saw the good man in the midst, holding the Scriptures in the golden light that shone from the western clouds; he beheld him close the book, and all rise up to pray. He heard the old thanksgivings for daily mercies, the old supplications for their continuance, to which he had so often listened in weariness, but which were now among his dear remembrances. He perceived the slight inequality of his father's voice when he came to speak of the Absent One; he noted how his mother turned her face to the broad and knotted trunk; how his elder brother scorned, because the beard was rough upon his upper lip, to permit his features to be moved; how his younger sister drew down a low hanging branch before her eyes; and how the little one of all, whose sports had hitherto broken the decorum of the scene, understood the prayer for her playmate, and burst into clamorous grief. Then he saw them go in at the door; and when Robin would have entered also, the latch tinkled into its place, and he was excluded from his home.

"Am I here, or there?" cried Robin, starting; for all at once, when his thoughts had become visible and audible in a dream, the long, wide, solitary street shone out before him.

He aroused himself, and endeavored to fix his attention steadily upon the large edifice which he had surveyed before. But still his mind kept vibrating between fancy and reality; by turns, the pillars of the balcony lengthened into the tall, bare stems of pines, dwindled down to human figures, settled again in their true shape and size, and then commenced a new succession of changes. For a single moment, when he deemed himself awake, he could have sworn that a visage, one which he seemed to remember, yet could not absolutely name as his kinsman's, was looking towards him from the Gothic window. A deeper sleep wrestled with, and nearly overcame him, but fled at the sound of footsteps along the opposite pavement. Robin rubbed his eyes, discerned a man passing at the foot of the balcony, and addressed him in a loud, peevish, and lamentable cry.

"Halloo, friend! must I wait here all night for my kinsman, Major Molineux?"

The sleeping echoes awoke, and answered the voice; and the passenger, barely able to discern a figure sitting in the oblique shade of the steeple, traversed the street to obtain a nearer view. He was himself a gentleman in his prime, of open, intelligent, cheerful, and altogether prepossessing countenance. Perceiving a country youth, apparently homeless and without friends, he accosted him in a tone of real kindness, which had become strange to Robin's ears.

"Well, my good lad, why are you sitting here?" inquired he. "Can I be of service to you in any way?"

"I am afraid not, Sir," replied Robin, despondingly; "yet I shall take it kindly, if you'll answer me a single question. I've been searching half the night for one Major Molineux; now, Sir, is there really such a person in these parts, or am I dreaming?"

"Major Molineux! The name is not altogether strange to me," said the gentleman, smiling. "Have you any objection to telling me the nature of your business with him?"

Then Robin briefly related that his father was a clergyman, settled on a small salary, at a long distance back in the country, and that he and Major Molineux were brothers' children. The Major, having inherited riches, and acquired civil and military rank, had visited his cousin in great pomp a year or two before; had manifested much interest in Robin and an elder brother, and, being childless himself, had thrown out hints respecting the future establishment of one of them in life. The elder brother was destined to succeed to the farm, which his father cultivated, in the interval of sacred duties; it was therefore determined that Robin should profit by his kinsman's generous intentions, especially as he had seemed to be rather the favorite, and was thought to possess other necessary endowments.

"For I have the name of being a shrewd youth," observed Robin, in this part of his story.

"I doubt not you deserve it," replied his new friend, good naturedly; "but pray proceed."

"Well, Sir, being nearly eighteen years old, and well grown, as you see," continued Robin, raising himself to his full height, "I thought it high time to begin the world. So my mother and sister put me in handsome trim, and my father gave me half the remnant of his last year's salary, and five days ago I started for this place, to pay the Major a visit. But would you believe it, Sir? I crossed the ferry a little after dusk, and have yet found nobody that would show me the way to his dwelling; only an hour or two since, I was told to wait here, and Major Molineux would pass by."

"Can you describe the man who told you this?" inquired the gentleman.

"Oh, he was a very ill-favored fellow, Sir," replied Robin, "with two great bumps on his forehead, a hook nose, fiery eyes, and, what struck me as the strangest, his face was of two different colors. Do you happen to know such a man, Sir?"

"Not intimately," answered the stranger, "but I chanced to meet him a little time previous to your stopping me. I believe you may trust his word, and that the Major will very shortly pass through this street. In the mean time, as I have a singular curiosity to witness your meeting, I will sit down here upon the steps, and bear you company."

He seated himself accordingly, and soon engaged his companion in animated discourse. It was but of brief continuance, however, for a noise of shouting, which had long been remotely audible, drew so much nearer, that Robin inquired its cause.

"What may be the meaning of this uproar?" asked he. "Truly, if your town be always as noisy, I shall find little sleep, while I am an inhabitant."

"Why, indeed, friend Robin, there do appear to be three or four riotous fellows abroad to-night," replied the gentleman. "You must not expect all the stillness of your native woods, here in our streets. But the watch will shortly be at the heels of these lads, and—"

"Aye, and set them in the stocks by peep of day," interrupted Robin, recollecting his own encounter with the drowsy lantern-bearer. "But, dear Sir, if I may trust my ears, an army of watchmen would never make head against such a multitude of rioters. There were at least a thousand voices went to make up that one shout."

"May not one man have several voices, Robin, as well as two complexions?" said his friend.

"Perhaps a man may; but Heaven forbid that a woman should!" responded the shrewd youth, thinking of the seductive tones of the Major's housekeeper.

The sounds of a trumpet in some neighboring street now became so evident and continual, that Robin's curiosity was strongly excited. In addition to the shouts, he heard frequent bursts from many instruments of discord, and a wild and confused laughter filled up the intervals. Robin rose from the steps, and looked wistfully towards a point, whither several people seemed to be hastening.

"Surely some prodigious merrymaking is going on," exclaimed he. "I have laughed very little since I left home, Sir, and should be sorry to lose an opportunity. Shall we just step round the corner by that darkish house, and take our share of the fun?"

"Sit down again, sit down, good Robin," replied the gentleman, laying his hand on the skirt of the grey coat. "You forget that we must wait here for your kinsman; and there is reason to believe that he will pass by, in the course of a very few moments."

The near approach of the uproar had now disturbed the neighborhood; windows flew open on all sides; and many heads, in the attire of the pillow, and confused by sleep suddenly broken, were protruded to the gaze of whoever had leisure to observe them. Eager voices hailed each other from house to house, all demanding the explanation, which not a soul could give. Half-dressed men hurried towards the unknown commotion, stumbling as they went over the stone steps, that thrust themselves into the narrow foot-walk. The shouts, the laughter, and the tuneless bray, the antipodes of music, came onward with increasing din, till scattered individuals, and then denser bodies, began to appear round a corner, at the distance of a hundred yards.

"Will you recognize your kinsman, Robin, if he passes in this crowd?" inquired the gentleman.

"Indeed, I can't warrant it, Sir; but I'll take my stand here, and keep a bright look out," answered Robin, descending to the outer edge of the pavement.

A mighty stream of people now emptied into the street, and came rolling slowly towards the church. A single horseman wheeled the corner in the midst of them, and close behind him came a band of fearful wind-instruments, sending forth a fresher discord, now that no intervening buildings kept it from the ear. Then a redder light disturbed the moonbeams, and a dense multitude of torches shone along the street, concealing by their glare whatever object they illuminated. The single horseman, clad in a military dress, and bearing a drawn sword, rode onward as the leader, and, by his fierce and variegated countenance, appeared like war personified; the red of one cheek was an emblem of fire and sword; the blackness of the other betokened the mourning which attends them. In his train, were wild figures in the Indian dress, and many fantastic shapes without a model, giving the whole march a visionary air, as if a dream had broken forth from some feverish brain, and were sweeping visibly through the midnight streets. A mass of people, inactive, except as applauding spectators, hemmed the procession in, and several women ran along the sidewalks, piercing the confusion of heavier sounds, with their shrill voices of mirth or terror.

"The double-faced fellow has his eye upon me," muttered Robin, with an indefinite but uncomfortable idea, that he was himself to bear a part in the pageantry.

The leader turned himself in the saddle, and fixed his glance full upon the country youth, as the steed went slowly by. When Robin had freed his eyes from those fiery ones, the musicians were passing before him, and the torches were close at hand; but the unsteady brightness of the latter formed a veil which he could not penetrate. The rattling of wheels over the stones sometimes found its way to his ear, and confused traces of a human form appeared at intervals, and then melted into the vivid light. A moment more, and the leader thundered a command to halt; the trumpets vomited a horrid breath, and held their peace; the shouts and laughter of the people died away, and there remained only a universal hum, nearly allied to silence. Right before Robin's eyes was an uncovered cart. There the torches blazed the brightest, there the moon shone out like day, and there, in tar-and-feathery dignity, sat his kinsman, Major Molineux!

He was an elderly man, of large and majestic person, and strong, square features, betokening a steady soul; but steady as it was, his enemies had found the means to shake it. His face was pale as death, and far more ghastly; the broad forehead was contracted in his agony, so that his eyebrows formed one grizzled line; his eyes were red and wild, and the foam hung white upon his quivering lip. His whole frame was agitated by a quick, and continual tremor, which his pride strove to quell, even in those circumstances of overwhelming humiliation. But perhaps the bitterest pang of all was when his eyes met those of Robin; for he evidently knew him on the instant, as the youth stood witnessing the foul disgrace of a head that had grown grey in honor. They stared at each other in silence, and Robin's knees shook, and his hair bristled, with a mixture of pity and terror. Soon, however, a bewildering excitement began to seize upon his mind; the preceding adventures of the night, the unexpected appearance of the crowd, the torches, the confused din, and the hush that followed, the spectre of his kinsman reviled by that great multitude, all this, and more than all, a perception of tremendous ridicule in the whole scene, affected him with a sort of mental inebriety. At that moment a voice of sluggish merriment saluted Robin's ears; he turned instinctively, and just behind the corner of the church stood the lantern-bearer, rubbing his eyes, and drowsily enjoying the lad's amazement. Then he heard a peal of laughter like the ringing of silvery bells; a woman twitched his arm, a saucy eye met his, and he saw the lady of the scarlet petticoat. A sharp, dry cachinnation[23] appealed to his memory, and standing on tiptoe in the crowd, with his white apron over his head, he beheld the courteous little innkeeper. And lastly, there sailed over the heads of the multitude a great, broad laugh, broken in the midst by two sepulchral hems; thus—

"Haw, haw, haw—hem, hem—haw, haw, haw, haw!"

The sound proceeded from the balcony of the opposite edifice, and thither Robin turned his eyes. In front of the Gothic window stood the old citizen, wrapped in a wide gown, his grey periwig exchanged for a nightcap, which was thrust back from his forehead, and his silk stockings hanging down about his legs. He supported himself on his polished cane in a fit of convulsive merriment, which manifested itself on his solemn old features, like a funny inscription on a tombstone. Then Robin seemed to hear the voices of the barbers; of the guests of the inn; and of all who had made sport of him that night. The contagion was spreading among the multitude, when, all at once, it seized upon Robin, and he sent forth a shout of laughter that echoed through the street; every man shook his sides, every man emptied his lungs, but Robin's shout was the loudest there. The cloud-spirits peeped from their silvery islands, as the congregated mirth went roaring up the sky! The Man in the Moon heard the far bellow; "Oho," quoth he, "the old Earth is frolicsome to-night!"

When there was a momentary calm in that tempestuous sea of sound, the leader

---

[23] Laugh.

gave the sign, the procession resumed its march. On they went, like fiends that throng in mockery round some dead potentate, mighty no more, but majestic still in his agony. On they went, in counterfeited pomp, in senseless uproar, in frenzied merriment, trampling all on an old man's heart. On swept the tumult, and left a silent street behind.

"Well, Robin, are you dreaming?" inquired the gentleman, laying his hand on the youth's shoulder.

Robin started, and withdrew his arm from the stone post, to which he had instinctively clung, while the living stream rolled by him. His cheek was somewhat pale, and his eye not quite so lively as in the earlier part of the evening.

"Will you be kind enough to show me the way to the ferry?" said he, after a moment's pause.

"You have then adopted a new subject of inquiry?" observed his companion, with a smile.

"Why, yes, Sir," replied Robin, rather dryly. "Thanks to you, and to my other friends, I have at last met my kinsman, and he will scarce desire to see my face again. I begin to grow weary of a town life, Sir. Will you show me the way to the ferry?"

"No, my good friend Robin, not to-night, at least," said the gentleman. "Some few days hence, if you continue to wish it, I will speed you on your journey. Or, if you prefer to remain with us, perhaps, as you are a shrewd youth, you may rise in the world, without the help of your kinsman, Major Molineux."

1832

ALICE DOANE'S APPEAL*

On a pleasant afternoon of June, it was my good fortune to be the companion of two young ladies in a walk. The direction of our course being left to me, I led them neither to Legge's Hill, nor to the Cold Spring, nor to the rude shores and old batteries of the Neck, nor yet to Paradise; though if the latter place were rightly named, my fair friends would have been at home there. We reached the outskirts of the town,[1] and turning aside from a street of tanners and curriers,[2] began to ascend a hill, which at a distance, by its dark slope and the even line of its summit, resembled a green rampart along the road. It was less steep than its aspect threatened. The eminence formed part of an extensive tract of pasture land, and was traversed by cow paths in various directions; but, strange to tell, though the whole slope and summit were of a peculiarly deep green; scarce a blade of grass was visible from the base upward. This deceitful verdure was occasioned by a plentiful crop of "wood-wax,"[3] which wears the same dark and glossy green throughout the summer, except at one short period, when it puts forth a profusion of yellow blossoms. At that season to a distant spectator, the hill appears abso-

---

* Evidence suggests that a version of "Alice Doane's Appeal" was written in the late 1820s for Hawthorne's projected collection "Seven Tales of My Native Land." The tale was originally published in *The Token* in 1835 and was never collected in a volume during Hawthorne's lifetime.

[1] Salem, Massachusetts; the names in the preceding sentence are places near Salem.

[2] One who tans hides and one who curries or dresses leather after it is tanned.

[3] A yellow-flowered Eurasian shrub that grows wild in North America.

lutely overlaid with gold, or covered with a glory of sunshine, even beneath a clouded sky. But the curious wanderer on the hill will perceive that all the grass, and every thing that should nourish man or beast, has been destroyed by this vile and ineradicable weed: its tufted roots make the soil their own, and permit nothing else to vegetate among them; so that a physical curse may be said to have blasted the spot, where guilt and phrenzy[4] consummated the most execrable scene, that our history blushes to record. For this was the field where superstition won her darkest triumph; the high place where our fathers set up their shame, to the mournful gaze of generations far remote. The dust of martyrs was beneath our feet. We stood on Gallows Hill.[5]

For my own part, I have often courted the historic influence of the spot. But it is singular, how few come on pilgrimage to this famous hill; how many spend their lives almost at its base, and never once obey the summons of the shadowy past, as it beckons them to the summit. Till a year or two since, this portion of our history had been very imperfectly written, and, as we are not a people of legend or tradition, it was not every citizen of our ancient town that could tell, within half a century, so much as the date of the witchcraft delusion. Recently, indeed, an historian has treated the subject in a manner that will keep his name alive, in the only desirable connection with the errors of our ancestry, by converting the hill of their disgrace into an honorable monument of his own antiquarian lore, and of that better wisdom, which draws the moral while it tells the tale. But we are a people of the present and have no heartfelt interest in the olden time. Every fifth of November, in commemoration of they know not what, or rather without an idea beyond the momentary blaze, the young men scare the town with bonfires on this haunted height, but never dream of paying funeral honors to those who died so wrongfully, and without a coffin or a prayer, were buried here.

Though with feminine susceptibility, my companions caught all the melancholy associations of the scene, yet these could but imperfectly overcome the gayety of girlish spirits. Their emotions came and went with quick vicissitude, and sometimes combined to form a peculiar and delicious excitement, the mirth brightening the gloom into a sunny shower of feeling, and a rainbow in the mind. My own more sombre mood was tinged by theirs. With now a merry word and next a sad one, we trod among the tangled weeds, and almost hoped that our feet would sink into the hollow of a witch's grave. Such vestiges were to be found within the memory of man, but have vanished now, and with them, I believe, all traces of the precise spot of the executions. On the long and broad ridge of the eminence, there is no very decided elevation of any one point, nor other prominent marks, except the decayed stumps of two trees, standing near each other, and here and there the rocky substance of the hill, peeping just above the wood-wax.

There are few such prospects of town and village, woodland and cultivated field, steeples and country seats, as we beheld from this unhappy spot. No blight had fallen on old Essex;[6] all was prosperity and riches, healthfully distributed. Before us lay our native town, extending from the foot of the hill to the harbor, level as a chess board, embraced by two arms of the sea, and filling the whole peninsula with a close assemblage of wooden roofs, overtopt by many a spire, and intermixed with frequent heaps of verdure,[7] where trees threw up their shade from

---

[4] Old spelling of "frenzy."
[5] Outside Salem, the site where those convicted of witchcraft were hanged in November 1692.
[6] Gallows Hill and Salem are in Essex County.   [7] Vegetation.

unseen trunks. Beyond, was the bay and its islands, almost the only objects, in a country unmarked by strong natural features, on which time and human toil had produced no change. Retaining these portions of the scene, and also the peaceful glory and tender gloom of the declining sun, we threw, in imagination, a veil of deep forest over the land, and pictured a few scattered villages, and this old town itself a village, as when the prince of hell[8] bore sway there. The idea thus gained, of its former aspect, its quaint edifices standing far apart, with peaked roofs and projecting stories, and its single meeting house pointing up a tall spire in the midst; the vision, in short, of the town in 1692, served to introduce a wondrous tale of those old times.

I had brought the manuscript in my pocket. It was one of a series written years ago, when my pen, now sluggish and perhaps feeble, because I have not much to hope or fear, was driven by stronger external motives, and a more passionate impulse within, than I am fated to feel again. Three or four of these tales had appeared in the Token,[9] after a long time and various adventures, but had incumbered me with no troublesome notoriety, even in my birth place.[10] One great heap had met a brighter destiny: they had fed the flames; thoughts meant to delight the world and endure for ages, had perished in a moment, and stirred not a single heart but mine. The story now to be introduced, and another, chanced to be in kinder custody at the time, and thus by no conspicuous merits of their own, escaped destruction.[11]

The ladies, in consideration that I had never before intruded my performances on them, by any but the legitimate medium, through the press, consented to hear me read. I made them sit down on a moss-grown rock, close by the spot where we chose to believe that the death-tree[12] had stood. After a little hesitation on my part, caused by a dread of renewing my acquaintance with fantasies that had lost their charm, in the ceaseless flux of mind, I began the tale, which opened darkly with the discovery of a murder.

A hundred years, and nearly half that time, have elapsed since the body of a murdered man was found, at about the distance of three miles, on the old road to Boston. He lay in a solitary spot, on the bank of a small lake, which the severe frost of December had covered with a sheet of ice. Beneath this, it seemed to have been the intention of the murderer to conceal his victim in a chill and watery grave, the ice being deeply hacked, perhaps with the weapon that had slain him, though its solidity was too stubborn for the patience of a man with blood upon his hand. The corpse therefore reclined on the earth, but was separated from the road by a thick growth of dwarf pines. There had been a slight fall of snow during the night, and as if Nature were shocked at the deed, and strove to hide it with her frozen tears, a little drifted heap had partly buried the body, and lay deepest over the pale dead face. An early traveller, whose dog had led him to the spot, ventured to uncover the features, but was affrighted by their expression. A look of evil and scornful triumph had hardened on them, and made death so life-like and so terri-

---

[8] The Devil.
[9] The annual gift-book in which a number of Hawthorne's stories had appeared and in which this story would appear.
[10] Salem.
[11] Hawthorne reportedly burned some of the "Seven Tales of My Native Land" when they were rejected for publication in book form. Two of the stories, including the Gothic tale of Alice Doane the narrator now reads, apparently survived because the manuscripts had been loaned to friends.
[12] The tree from which the convicted witches were hanged.

ble, that the beholder at once took flight, as swiftly as if the stiffened corpse would rise up and follow.

I read on, and identified the body as that of a young man, a stranger in the country, but resident during several preceding months in the town which lay at our feet. The story described, at some length, the excitement caused by the murder, the unavailing quest after the perpetrator, the funeral ceremonies, and other common place matters, in the course of which, I brought forward the personages who were to move among the succeeding events. They were but three. A young man and his sister; the former characterized by a diseased imagination and morbid feelings; the latter, beautiful and virtuous, and instilling something of her own excellence into the wild heart of her brother, but not enough to cure the deep taint of his nature. The third person was a wizard; a small, gray, withered man, with fiendish ingenuity in devising evil, and superhuman power to execute it, but senseless as an idiot and feebler than a child, to all better purposes. The central scene of the story was an interview between this wretch and Leonard Doane, in the wizard's hut, situated beneath a range of rocks at some distance from the town. They sat beside a smouldering fire, while a tempest of wintry rain was beating on the roof. The young man spoke of the closeness of the tie which united him and Alice, the concentrated fervor of their affection from childhood upwards, their sense of lonely sufficiency to each other, because they only of their race[13] had escaped death, in a night attack by the Indians. He related his discovery, or suspicion of a secret sympathy between his sister and Walter Brome, and told how a distempered jealousy had maddened him. In the following passage, I threw a glimmering light on the mystery of the tale.

"Searching," continued Leonard, "into the breast of Walter Brome, I at length found a cause why Alice must inevitably love him. For he was my very counterpart! I compared his mind by each individual portion, and as a whole, with mine. There was a resemblance from which I shrank with sickness, and loathing, and horror, as if my own features had come and stared upon me in a solitary place, or had met me in struggling through a crowd. Nay! the very same thoughts would often express themselves in the same words from our lips, proving a hateful sympathy in our secret souls. His education, indeed, in the cities of the old world, and mine in this rude wilderness, had wrought a superficial difference. The evil of his character, also, had been strengthened and rendered prominent by a reckless and ungoverned life, while mine had been softened and purified by the gentle and holy nature of Alice. But my soul had been conscious of the germ of all the fierce and deep passions, and of all the many varieties of wickedness, which accident had brought to their full maturity in him. Nor will I deny, that in the accursed one, I could see the withered blossom of every virtue, which by a happier culture, had been made to bring forth fruit in me. Now, here was a man, whom Alice might love with all the strength of sisterly affection, added to that impure passion which alone engrosses all the heart. The stranger would have more than the love which had been gathered to me from the many graves of our household—and I be desolate!"

Leonard Doane went on to describe the insane hatred that had kindled his heart into a volume of hellish flame. It appeared, indeed, that his jealousy had grounds, so far as that Walter Brome had actually sought the love of Alice, who also had betrayed an undefinable, but powerful interest in the unknown youth. The latter,

---

[13] Family.

in spite of his passion for Alice, seemed to return the loathful antipathy of her brother; the similarity of their dispositions made them like joint possessors of an individual nature, which could not become wholly the property of one, unless by the extinction of the other. At last, with the same devil in each bosom, they chanced to meet, they two on a lonely road. While Leonard spoke, the wizard had sat listening to what he already knew, yet with tokens of pleasurable interest, manifested by flashes of expression across his vacant features, by grisly smiles and by a word here and there, mysteriously filling up some void in the narrative. But when the young man told, how Walter Brome had taunted him with indubitable proofs of the shame of Alice, and before the triumphant sneer could vanish from his face, had died by her brother's hand, the wizard laughed aloud. Leonard started, but just then a gust of wind came down the chimney, forming itself into a close resemblance of the slow, unvaried laughter, by which he had been interrupted. "I was deceived," thought he; and thus pursued his fearful story.

"I trod out his accursed soul, and knew that he was dead; for my spirit bounded as if a chain had fallen from it and left me free. But the burst of exulting certainty soon fled, and was succeeded by a torpor over my brain and a dimness before my eyes, with the sensation of one who struggles through a dream. So I bent down over the body of Walter Brome, gazing into his face, and striving to make my soul glad with the thought, that he, in very truth, lay dead before me. I know not what space of time I had thus stood, nor how the vision came. But it seemed to me that the irrevocable years, since childhood had rolled back, and a scene, that had long been confused and broken in my memory, arrayed itself with all its first distinctness. Methought I stood a weeping infant by my father's hearth; by the cold and blood-stained hearth where he lay dead. I heard the childish wail of Alice, and my own cry arose with hers, as we beheld the features of our parent, fierce with the strife and distorted with the pain, in which his spirit had passed away. As I gazed, a cold wind whistled by, and waved my father's hair. Immediately, I stood again in the lonesome road, no more a sinless child, but a man of blood, whose tears were falling fast over the face of his dead enemy. But the delusion was not wholly gone; that face still wore a likeness of my father; and because my soul shrank from the fixed glare of the eyes, I bore the body to the lake, and would have buried it there. But before his icy sepulchre was hewn, I heard the voices of two travellers and fled."

Such was the dreadful confession of Leonard Doane. And now tortured by the idea of his sister's guilt, yet sometimes yielding to a conviction of her purity; stung with remorse for the death of Walter Brome, and shuddering with a deeper sense of some unutterable crime, perpetrated, as he imagined, in madness or a dream; moved also by dark impulses, as if a fiend were whispering him to meditate violence against the life of Alice; he had sought this interview with the wizard, who, on certain conditions, had no power to withhold his aid in unravelling the mystery. The tale drew near its close.

The moon was bright on high; the blue firmament appeared to glow with an inherent brightness; the greater stars were burning in their spheres; the northern lights threw their mysterious glare far over the horizon; the few small clouds aloft were burthened with radiance; but the sky with all its variety of light, was scarcely so brilliant as the earth. The rain of the preceding night had frozen as it fell, and, by that simple magic, had wrought wonders. The trees were hung with diamonds and many-colored gems; the houses were overlaid with silver, and the streets paved with slippery brightness; a frigid glory was flung over all familiar things, from the cottage chimney to the steeple of the meeting house, that gleamed upward to the sky. This living world, where we sit by our firesides, or go forth to meet beings like ourselves, seemed rather the creation of wizard power, with so much of resemblance to known objects, that a man might shudder at the ghostly shape of his old beloved dwelling, and the shadow of a ghostly tree before his door. One looked to behold inhabitants suited to such a town, glittering in icy garments, with motionless features, cold, sparkling eyes, and just sensation enough in their frozen hearts to shiver at each other's presence.

By this fantastic piece of description, and more in the same style, I intended to throw a ghostly glimmer round the reader, so that his imagination might view the town through a medium that should take off its every day aspect, and make it a proper theatre for so wild a scene as the final one. Amid this unearthly show, the wretched brother and sister were represented as setting forth, at midnight, through the gleaming streets, and directing their steps to a grave yard, where all the dead had been laid, from the first corpse in that ancient town, to the murdered man who was buried three days before. As they went, they seemed to see the wizard gliding by their sides, or walking dimly on the path before them. But here I paused, and gazed into the faces of my two fair auditors, to judge whether, even on the hill where so many had been brought to death by wilder tales than this,[14] I might venture to proceed. Their bright eyes were fixed on me; their lips apart. I took courage, and led the fated pair to a new made grave, where for a few moments, in the bright and silent midnight, they stood alone. But suddenly, there was a multitude of people among the graves.

Each family tomb had given up its inhabitants, who, one by one, through distant years, had been borne to its dark chamber, but now came forth and stood in a pale group together. There was the gray ancestor, the aged mother, and all their descendants, some withered and full of years, like themselves, and others in their prime; there, too, were the children who went prattling to the tomb, and there the maiden who yielded her early beauty to death's embrace, before passion had polluted it. Husbands and wives arose, who had lain many years side by side, and young mothers who had forgotten to kiss their first babes, though pillowed so long on their bosoms. Many had been buried in the habiliments of life, and still wore their ancient garb; some were old defenders of the infant colony,[15] and gleamed forth in their steel caps and bright breast-plates, as if starting up at an Indian war-cry; other venerable shapes had been pastors of the church, famous among the New England clergy, and now leaned with hands clasped over their grave stones, ready to call the congregation to prayer. There stood the early settlers, those old illustrious ones, the heroes of tradition and fireside legends, the men of history whose features had been so long beneath the sod, that few alive could have remembered them. There, too, were faces of former townspeople, dimly recollected from childhood, and others, whom Leonard and Alice had wept in later years, but who now were most terrible of all, by their ghastly smile of recognition. All, in short, were there; the dead of other generations, whose moss-grown names could scarce be read upon their tomb stones, and their successors, whose graves were not yet green; all whom black funerals had followed slowly thither, now re-ap-

[14] The testimony by which people were hanged on Gallows Hill was "wilder" than the fantastic story the narrator has been relating.
[15] Citizens of the Massachusetts Bay Colony when it was new.

peared where the mourners left them. Yet none but souls accursed were there, and fiends counterfeiting the likeness of departed saints.[16]

The countenances of those venerable men, whose very features had been hallowed by lives of piety, were contorted now by intolerable pain or hellish passion, and now by an unearthly and derisive merriment. Had the pastors prayed, all saintlike as they seemed, it had been blasphemy. The chaste matrons, too, and the maidens with untasted lips, who had slept in their virgin graves apart from all other dust, now wore a look from which the two trembling mortals shrank, as if the unimaginable sin of twenty worlds were collected there. The faces of fond lovers, even of such as had pined into the tomb, because there their treasure was, were bent on one another with glances of hatred and smiles of bitter scorn, passions that are to devils, what love is to the blest. At times, the features of those, who had passed from a holy life to heaven, would vary to and fro, between their assumed aspect and the fiendish lineaments whence they had been transformed. The whole miserable multitude, both sinful souls and false spectres of good men, groaned horribly and gnashed their teeth, as they looked upward to the calm loveliness of the midnight sky, and beheld those homes of bliss where they must never dwell. Such was the apparition, though too shadowy for language to portray; for here would be the moonbeams on the ice, glittering through a warrior's breastplate, and there the letters of a tomb stone, on the form that stood before it; and whenever a breeze went by, it swept the old men's hoary heads, the women's fearful beauty, and all the unreal throng, into one indistinguishable cloud together.

I dare not give the remainder of the scene, except in a very brief epitome. This company of devils and condemned souls had come on a holiday, to revel in the discovery of a complicated crime; as foul a one as ever was imagined in their dreadful abode. In the course of the tale, the reader had been permitted to discover, that all the incidents were results of the machinations of the wizard, who had cunningly devised that Walter Brome should tempt his unknown sister to guilt and shame, and himself perish by the hand of his twin-brother. I described the glee of the fiends, at this hideous conception, and their eagerness to know if it were consummated. The story concluded with the Appeal of Alice to the spectre of Walter Brome; his reply, absolving her from every stain; and the trembling awe with which ghost and devil fled, as from the sinless presence of an angel.

The sun had gone down. While I held my page of wonders in the fading light, and read how Alice and her brother were left alone among the graves, my voice mingled with the sigh of a summer wind, which passed over the hill top with the broad and hollow sound, as of the flight of unseen spirits. Not a word was spoken, till I added, that the wizard's grave was close beside us, and that the wood-wax had sprouted originally from his unhallowed bones. The ladies started; perhaps their cheeks might have grown pale, had not the crimson west been blushing on them; but after a moment they began to laugh, while the breeze took a livelier motion, as if responsive to their mirth. I kept an awful solemnity of visage, being indeed a little piqued, that a narrative which had good authority in our ancient superstitions, and would have brought even a church deacon to Gallows Hill, in old witch times, should now be considered too grotesque and extravagant, for timid maids to tremble at. Though it was past supper time, I detained them for a

---

[16] In the apocalyptic vision the narrator conjures up, everyone appears damned—some because of their evil lives, others ("departed saints") because fiends or devils are "counterfeiting" their likeness.

while longer on the hill, and made a trial whether truth were more powerful than fiction.

We looked again towards the town, no longer arrayed in that icy splendor of earth, tree and edifice, beneath the glow of a wintry midnight, which, shining afar through the gloom of a century, had made it appear the very home of visions in visionary streets. An indistinctness had begun to creep over the mass of buildings and blend them with the intermingled tree tops, except where the roof of a statelier mansion, and the steeples and brick towers of churches, caught the brightness of some cloud that yet floated in the sunshine. Twilight over the landscape was congenial to the obscurity of time. With such eloquence as my share of feeling and fancy could supply, I called back hoar[17] antiquity, and bade my companions imagine an ancient multitude of people, congregated on the hill side, spreading far below, clustering on the steep old roofs, and climbing the adjacent heights, wherever a glimpse of this spot might be obtained. I strove to realize and faintly communicate, the deep, unutterable loathing and horror, the indignation, the affrighted wonder, that wrinkled on every brow, and filled the universal heart. See! the whole crowd turns pale and shrinks within itself, as the virtuous emerge from yonder street. Keeping pace with that devoted company, I described them one by one; here tottered a woman in her dotage,[18] knowing neither the crime imputed her, nor its punishment; there another, distracted by the universal madness, till feverish dreams were remembered as realities, and she almost believed her guilt. One, a proud man once, was so broken down by the intolerable hatred heaped upon him, that he seemed to hasten his steps, eager to hide himself in the grave hastily dug, at the foot of the gallows. As they went slowly on, a mother looked behind, and beheld her peaceful dwelling; she cast her eyes elsewhere, and groaned inwardly, yet with bitterest anguish; for there was her little son among the accusers. I watched the face of an ordained pastor, who walked onward to the same death; his lips moved in prayer, no narrow petition for himself alone, but embracing all, his fellow sufferers and the frenzied multitude; he looked to heaven and trod lightly up the hill.

Behind their victims came the afflicted, a guilty and miserable band; villains who had thus avenged themselves on their enemies, and viler wretches, whose cowardice had destroyed their friends; lunatics, whose ravings had chimed in with the madness of the land; and children, who had played a game that the imps of darkness[19] might have envied them, since it disgraced an age, and dipped a people's hands in blood. In the rear of the procession rode a figure on horseback, so darkly conspicuous, so sternly triumphant, that my hearers mistook him for the visible presence of the fiend himself; but it was only his good friend, Cotton Mather,[20] proud of his well won dignity, as the representative of all the hateful features of his time; the one blood-thirsty man, in whom were concentrated those vices of spirit and errors of opinion, that sufficed to madden the whole surrounding multitude. And thus I marshalled them onward, the innocent who were to die, and the guilty who were to grow old in long remorse—tracing their every step, by rock, and shrub, and broken track, till their shadowy visages had circled round the

---

[17] Aged.   [18] Feeble-minded because of age.

[19] Demons; some of the accusations against so-called witches were made by children, who might, Hawthorne implies, have been playing a terrible game.

[20] Mather (1663–1728) was a scholar, pedant, and leading Puritan minister who recommended that those possessed by the Devil should be treated by fasting and penance rather than executed but concurred in the verdicts and made no move to stop the executions.

hill-top, where we stood. I plunged into my imagination for a blacker horror, and a deeper woe, and pictured the scaffold—

But here my companions seized an arm on each side; their nerves were trembling; and sweeter victory still, I had reached the seldom trodden places of their hearts, and found the well-spring of their tears. And now the past had done all it could. We slowly descended, watching the lights as they twinkled gradually through the town, and listening to the distant mirth of boys at play, and to the voice of a young girl, warbling somewhere in the dusk, a pleasant sound to wanderers from old witch times. Yet ere we left the hill, we could not but regret, that there is nothing on its barren summit, no relic of old, nor lettered stone of later days, to assist the imagination in appealing to the heart. We build the memorial column on the height which our fathers made sacred with their blood, poured out in a holy cause. And here in dark, funereal stone, should rise another monument, sadly commemorative of the errors of an earlier race, and not to be cast down, while the human heart has one infirmity that may result in crime.

1835

WAKEFIELD*

In some old magazine or newspaper, I recollect a story, told as truth, of a man— let us call him Wakefield—who absented himself for a long time, from his wife. The fact, thus abstractedly stated, is not very uncommon, nor—without a proper distinction of circumstances—to be condemned either as naughty or nonsensical. Howbeit, this, though far from the most aggravated, is perhaps the strangest instance, on record, of marital delinquency; and, moreover, as remarkable a freak as may be found in the whole list of human oddities. The wedded couple lived in London. The man, under pretence of going a journey, took lodgings in the next street to his own house, and there, unheard of by his wife or friends, and without the shadow of a reason for such self-banishment, dwelt upwards of twenty years. During that period, he beheld his home every day, and frequently the forlorn Mrs. Wakefield. And after so great a gap in his matrimonial felicity—when his death was reckoned certain, his estate settled, his name dismissed from memory, and his wife, long, long ago, resigned to her autumnal widowhood—he entered the door one evening, quietly, as from a day's absence, and became a loving spouse till death.

This outline is all that I remember. But the incident, though of the purest originality, unexampled, and probably never to be repeated, is one, I think, which appeals to the general sympathies of mankind. We know, each for himself, that none of us would perpetrate such a folly, yet feel as if some other might. To my own contemplations, at least, it has often recurred, always exciting wonder, but with a sense that the story must be true, and a conception of its hero's character. Whenever any subject so forcibly affects the mind, time is well spent in thinking of it. If the reader choose, let him do his own meditation; or if he prefer to ramble with me through the twenty years of Wakefield's vagary, I bid him welcome; trusting that there will be a pervading spirit and a moral, even should we fail to

* First published in *The New-England Magazine* in 1835 and included in *Twice-Told Tales* (1837).

find them, done up neatly, and condensed into the final sentence. Thought has always its efficacy, and every striking incident its moral.

What sort of a man was Wakefield? We are free to shape out our own idea, and call it by his name. He was now in the meridian[1] of life; his matrimonial affections, never violent, were sobered into a calm, habitual sentiment; of all husbands, he was likely to be the most constant, because a certain sluggishness would keep his heart at rest, wherever it might be placed. He was intellectual, but not actively so; his mind occupied itself in long and lazy musings, that tended to no purpose, or had not vigor to attain it; his thoughts were seldom so energetic as to seize hold of words. Imagination, in the proper meaning of the term, made no part of Wakefield's gifts. With a cold, but not depraved nor wandering heart, and a mind never feverish with riotous thoughts, nor perplexed with originality, who could have anticipated, that our friend would entitle himself to a foremost place among the doers of eccentric deeds? Had his acquaintances been asked, who was the man in London, the surest to perform nothing to-day which should be remembered on the morrow, they would have thought of Wakefield. Only the wife of his bosom might have hesitated. She, without having analyzed his character, was partly aware of a quiet selfishness, that had rusted into his inactive mind—of a peculiar sort of vanity, the most uneasy attribute about him—of a disposition to craft, which had seldom produced more positive effects than the keeping of petty secrets, hardly worth revealing—and, lastly, of what she called a little strangeness, sometimes, in the good man. This latter quality is indefinable, and perhaps nonexistent.

Let us now imagine Wakefield bidding adieu to his wife. It is the dusk of an October evening. His equipment is a drab great-coat, a hat covered with an oilcloth, top-boots, an umbrella in one hand and a small portmanteau[2] in the other. He has informed Mrs. Wakefield that he is to take the night-coach into the country. She would fain inquire the length of his journey, its object, and the probable time of his return; but, indulgent to his harmless love of mystery, interrogates him only by a look. He tells her not to expect him positively by the return coach, nor to be alarmed should he tarry three or four days; but, at all events, to look for him at supper on Friday evening. Wakefield himself, be it considered, has no suspicion of what is before him. He holds out his hand; she gives her own, and meets his parting kiss, in the matter-of-course way of a ten years' matrimony; and forth goes the middle-aged Mr. Wakefield, almost resolved to perplex his good lady by a whole week's absence. After the door has closed behind him, she perceives it thrust partly open, and a vision of her husband's face, through the aperture, smiling on her, and gone in a moment. For the time, this little incident is dismissed without a thought. But, long afterwards, when she has been more years a widow than a wife, that smile recurs, and flickers across all her reminiscences of Wakefield's visage. In her many musings, she surrounds the original smile with a multitude of fantasies, which make it strange and awful; as, for instance, if she imagines him in a coffin, that parting look is frozen on his pale features; or, if she dreams of him in Heaven, still his blessed spirit wears a quiet and crafty smile. Yet, for its sake, when all others have given him up for dead, she sometimes doubts whether she is a widow.

But, our business is with the husband. We must hurry after him, along the street, ere he loses his individuality, and melt into the great mass of London life. It would be vain searching for him there. Let us follow close at his heels, therefore,

[1] The mid-point.   [2] A large suitcase.

until, after several superfluous turns and doublings, we find him comfortably established by the fireside of a small apartment, previously bespoken. He is in the next street to his own, and at his journey's end. He can scarcely trust his good fortune, in having got thither unperceived—recollecting that, at one time, he was delayed by the throng, in the very focus of a lighted lantern; and, again, there were footsteps, that seemed to tread behind his own, distinct from the multitudinous tramp around him; and, anon, he heard a voice shouting afar, and fancied that it called his name. Doubtless, a dozen busy-bodies had been watching him, and told his wife the whole affair. Poor Wakefield! Little knowest thou thine own insignificance in this great world! No mortal eye but mine has traced thee. Go quietly to thy bed, foolish man; and, on the morrow, if thou wilt be wise, get thee home to good Mrs. Wakefield, and tell her the truth. Remove not thyself, even for a little week, from thy place in her chaste bosom. Were she, for a single moment, to deem thee dead, or lost, or lastingly divided from her, thou wouldst be woefully conscious of a change in thy true wife, forever after. It is perilous to make a chasm in human affections; not that they gape so long and wide—but so quickly close again!

Almost repenting of his frolic, or whatever it may be termed, Wakefield lies down betimes, and starting from his first nap, spreads forth his arms into the wide and solitary waste of the unaccustomed bed. "No"—thinks he, gathering the bedclothes about him—"I will not sleep alone another night."

In the morning, he rises earlier than usual, and sets himself to consider what he really means to do. Such are his loose and rambling modes of thought, that he has taken this very singular step, with the consciousness of a purpose, indeed, but without being able to define it sufficiently for his own contemplation. The vagueness of the project, and the convulsive effort with which he plunges into the execution of it, are equally characteristic of a feeble-minded man. Wakefield sifts his ideas, however, as minutely as he may, and finds himself curious to know the progress of matters at home—how his exemplary wife will endure her widowhood, of a week; and, briefly, how the little sphere of creatures and circumstances, in which he was a central object, will be affected by his removal. A morbid vanity, therefore, lies nearest the bottom of the affair. But, how is he to attain his ends? Not, certainly, by keeping close in this comfortable lodging, where, though he slept and awoke in the next street to his home, he is as effectually abroad, as if the stage-coach had been whirling him away all night. Yet, should he reappear, the whole project is knocked in the head. His poor brains being hopelessly puzzled with this dilemma, he at length ventures out, partly resolving to cross the head of the street, and send one hasty glance towards his forsaken domicile. Habit—for he is a man of habits—takes him by the hand, and guides him, wholly unaware, to his own door, where, just at the critical moment, he is aroused by the scraping of his foot upon the step. Wakefield! whither are you going?

At that instant, his fate was turning on the pivot. Little dreaming of the doom to which his first backward step devotes him, he hurries away, breathless with agitation hitherto unfelt, and hardly dares turn his head, at the distant corner. Can it be, that nobody caught sight of him? Will not the whole household—the decent Mrs. Wakefield, the smart maid-servant, and the dirty little foot-boy—raise a hue-and-cry, through London streets, in pursuit of their fugitive lord and master? Wonderful escape! He gathers courage to pause and look homeward, but is perplexed with a sense of change about the familiar edifice, such as affects us all, when, after a separation of months or years, we again see some hill or lake, or work of art, with which we were friends, of old. In ordinary cases, this indescribable impression is caused by the comparison and contrast between our imperfect reminiscences and the reality. In Wakefield, the magic of a single night has wrought a similar transformation, because, in that brief period, a great moral change has been effected. But this is a secret from himself. Before leaving the spot, he catches a far and momentary glimpse of his wife, passing athwart the front window, with her face turned towards the head of the street. The crafty nincompoop takes to his heels, scared with the idea, that, among a thousand such atoms of mortality, her eye must have detected him. Right glad is his heart, though his brain be somewhat dizzy, when he finds himself by the coal-fire of his lodgings.

So much for the commencement of this long whim-wham.[3] After the initial conception, and the stirring up of the man's sluggish temperament to put it in practice, the whole matter evolves itself in a natural train. We may suppose him, as the result of deep deliberation, buying a new wig, of reddish hair, and selecting sundry garments, in a fashion unlike his customary suit of brown, from a Jew's old-clothes bag. It is accomplished. Wakefield is another man. The new system being now established, a retrograde movement to the old would be almost as difficult as the step that placed him in his unparalleled position. Furthermore, he is rendered obstinate by a sulkiness, occasionally incident to his temper, and brought on, at present, by the inadequate sensation which he conceives to have been produced in the bosom of Mrs. Wakefield. He will not go back until she be frightened half to death. Well, twice or thrice has she passed before his sight, each time with a heavier step, a paler cheek, and more anxious brow; and, in the third week of his non-appearance, he detects a portent of evil entering the house, in the guise of an apothecary.[4] Next day, the knocker is muffled. Towards night-fall, comes the chariot of a physician, and deposits its big-wigged and solemn burthen at Wakefield's door, whence, after a quarter of an hour's visit, he emerges, perchance the herald of a funeral. Dear woman! Will she die? By this time, Wakefield is excited to something like energy of feeling, but still lingers away from his wife's bedside, pleading with his conscience, that she must not be disturbed at such a juncture. If aught else restrains him, he does not know it. In the course of a few weeks, she gradually recovers; the crisis is over; her heart is sad, perhaps, but quiet; and, let him return soon or late, it will never be feverish for him again. Such ideas glimmer through the mist of Wakefield's mind, and render him indistinctly conscious, that an almost impassable gulf divides his hired apartment from his former home. "It is but in the next street!" he sometimes says. Fool! it is in another world. Hitherto, he has put off his return from one particular day to another; henceforward, he leaves the precise time undetermined. Not to-morrow—probably next week—pretty soon. Poor man! The dead have nearly as much chance of re-visiting their earthly homes, as the self-banished Wakefield.

Would that I had a folio to write, instead of an article of a dozen pages! Then might I exemplify how an influence, beyond our control, lays its strong hand on every deed which we do, and weaves its consequences into an iron tissue of necessity. Wakefield is spell-bound. We must leave him, for ten years or so, to haunt around his house, without once crossing the threshold, and to be faithful to his wife, with all the affection of which his heart is capable, while he is slowly fading out of hers. Long since, it must be remarked, he has lost the perception of singularity in his conduct.

---

[3] A fanciful notion or action based on a whim.
[4] One who prepares and sells drugs for medical purposes.

Now for a scene! Amid the throng of a London street, we distinguish a man, now waxing elderly, with few characteristics to attract careless observers, yet bearing, in his whole aspect, the hand-writing of no common fate, for such as have the skill to read it. He is meager; his low and narrow forehead is deeply wrinkled; his eyes, small and lustreless, sometimes wander apprehensively about him, but oftener seem to look inward. He bends his head, but moves with an indescribable obliquity of gait,[5] as if unwilling to display his full front to the world. Watch him, long enough to see what we have described, and you will allow, that circumstances—which often produce remarkable men from nature's ordinary handiwork—have produced one such here. Next, leaving him to sidle along the foot-walk, cast your eyes in the opposite direction, where a portly female, considerably in the wane of life, with a prayer-book in her hand, is proceeding to yonder church. She has the placid mien[6] of settled widowhood. Her regrets have either died away, or have become so essential to her heart, that they would be poorly exchanged for joy. Just as the lean man and well conditioned woman are passing, a slight obstruction occurs, and brings these two figures directly in contact. Their hands touch; the pressure of the crowd forces her bosom against his shoulder; they stand, face to face, staring into each other's eyes. After a ten years' separation, thus Wakefield meets his wife!

The throng eddies away, and carries them asunder. The sober widow, resuming her former pace, proceeds to church, but pauses in the portal, and throws a perplexed glance along the street. She passes in, however, opening her prayer-book as she goes. And the man? With so wild a face, that busy and selfish London stands to gaze after him, he hurries to his lodgings, bolts the door, and throws himself upon the bed. The latent feelings of years break out; his feeble mind acquires a brief energy from their strength; all the miserable strangeness of his life is revealed to him at a glance; and he cries out, passionately—"Wakefield! Wakefield! You are mad!"

Perhaps he was so. The singularity of his situation must have so moulded him to itself, that, considered in regard to his fellow-creatures and the business of life, he could not be said to possess his right mind. He had contrived, or rather he had happened, to dissever himself from the world—to vanish—to give up his place and privileges with living men, without being admitted among the dead. The life of a hermit is nowise parallel to his. He was in the bustle of the city, as of old; but the crowd swept by, and saw him not; he was, we may figuratively say, always beside his wife, and at his hearth, yet must never feel the warmth of the one, nor the affection of the other. It was Wakefield's unprecedented fate, to retain his original share of human sympathies, and to be still involved in human interests, while he had lost his reciprocal influence on them. It would be a most curious speculation, to trace out the effect of such circumstances on his heart and intellect, separately, and in unison. Yet, changed as he was, he would seldom be conscious of it, but deem himself the same man as ever; glimpses of the truth, indeed, would come, but only for the moment; and still he would keep saying—"I shall soon go back!"—nor reflect, that he had been saying so for twenty years.

I conceive, also, that these twenty years would appear, in the retrospect, scarcely longer than the week to which Wakefield had at first limited his absence. He would look on the affair as no more than an interlude in the main business of his life. When, after a little while more, he should deem it time to re-enter his parlor, his wife would clap her hands for joy, on beholding the middle-aged Mr.

---

[5] Slightly sideways.   [6] Appearance.

Wakefield. Alas, what a mistake! Would Time but await the close of our favorite follies, we should be young men, all of us, and till Doom's Day.

One evening, in the twentieth year since he vanished, Wakefield is taking his customary walk towards the dwelling which he still calls his own. It is a gusty night of autumn, with frequent showers, that patter down upon the pavement, and are gone, before a man can put up his umbrella. Pausing near the house, Wakefield discerns, through the parlor-windows of the second floor, the red glow, and the glimmer and fitful flash, of a comfortable fire. On the ceiling, appear a grotesque shadow of good Mrs. Wakefield. The cap, the nose and chin, and the broad waist, form an admirable caricature, which dances, moreover, with the up-flickering and down-sinking blaze, almost too merrily for the shade of an elderly widow. At this instant, a shower chances to fall, and is driven, by the unmannerly gust, full into Wakefield's face and bosom. He is quite penetrated with its autumnal chill. Shall he stand, wet and shivering here, when his own hearth has a good fire to warm him, and his own wife will run to fetch the gray coat and small-clothes,[7] which, doubtless, she has kept carefully in the closet of their bed-chamber? No! Wakefield is no such fool. He ascends the steps—heavily!—for twenty years have stiffened his legs, since he came down—but he knows it not. Stay, Wakefield! Would you go to the sole home that is left you? Then step into your grave! The door opens. As he passes in, we have a parting glimpse of his visage, and recognize the crafty smile, which was the precursor of the little joke, that he has ever since been playing off at his wife's expense. How unmercifully has he quizzed[8] the poor woman! Well; a good night's rest to Wakefield!

This happy event—supposing it to be such—could only have occurred at an unpremeditated moment. We will not follow our friend across the threshold. He has left us much food for thought, a portion of which shall lend its wisdom to a moral; and be shaped into a figure. Amid the seeming confusion of our mysterious world, individuals are so nicely adjusted to a system, and systems to one another, and to a whole, that, by stepping aside for a moment, a man exposes himself to a fearful risk of losing his place forever. Like Wakefield, he may become, as it were, the Outcast of the Universe.

1835

YOUNG GOODMAN BROWN*

Young Goodman Brown came forth, at sunset, into the street of Salem[1] village, but put his head back, after crossing the threshold, to exchange a parting kiss with his young wife. And Faith, as the wife was aptly named, thrust her own pretty head into the street, letting the wind play with the pink ribbons of her cap, while she called to Goodman Brown.

"Dearest heart," whispered she, softly and rather sadly, when her lips were close to his ear, "pr'y thee, put off your journey until sunrise, and sleep in your

---

[7] Close-fitting knee britches.   [8] Played a practical joke on.

* First published in *The New-England Magazine* in 1835 and included in *Mosses From an Old Manse* (1846). "Goodman" is a polite form of address for a man of humble birth who headed a household. The common surname Brown suggests that Hawthorne's Goodman is an ordinary person.

[1] Salem, Massachusetts, the site of witchcraft trials and executions in 1692.

own bed to-night. A lone woman is troubled with such dreams and such thoughts, that she's afeard of herself, sometimes. Pray, tarry with me this night, dear husband, of all nights in the year!"

"My love and my Faith," replied young Goodman Brown, "of all nights in the year, this one night must I tarry away from thee. My journey, as thou callest it, forth and back again, must needs be done 'twixt now and sunrise. What, my sweet, pretty wife, dost thou doubt me already, and we but three months married!"

"Then, God bless you!" said Faith, with the pink ribbons, "and may you find all well, when you come back."

"Amen!" cried Goodman Brown, "Say thy prayers, dear Faith, and go to bed at dusk, and no harm will come to thee!"

So they parted; and the young man pursued his way, until, being about to turn the corner by the meeting-house, he looked back, and saw the head of Faith still peeping after him, with a melancholy air, in spite of her pink ribbons.

"Poor little Faith!" thought he, for his heart smote him. "What a wretch am I, to leave her on such an errand! She talks of dreams, too. Methought, as she spoke, there was trouble in her face, as if a dream had warned her what work is to be done to-night. But, no, no! 'twould kill her to think it. Well; she's a blessed angel on earth; and after this one night, I'll cling to her skirts and follow her to Heaven."

With this excellent resolve for the future, Goodman Brown felt himself justified in making more haste on his present evil purpose. He had taken a dreary road, darkened by all the gloomiest trees of the forest, which barely stood aside to let the narrow path creep through, and closed immediately behind. It was all as lonely as could be; and there is this peculiarity in such a solitude, that the traveller knows not who may be concealed by the innumerable trunks and the thick boughs overhead; so that, with lonely footsteps, he may yet be passing through an unseen multitude.

"There may be a devilish Indian behind every tree," said Goodman Brown, to himself; and he glanced fearfully behind him, as he added, "What if the devil himself should be at my very elbow!"

His head being turned back, he passed a crook of the road, and looking forward again, beheld a figure of a man, in grave and decent attire, seated at the foot of an old tree. He arose, at Goodman Brown's approach, and walked onward, side by side with him.

"You are late, Goodman Brown," said he. "The clock of the Old South[2] was striking as I came through Boston; and that is full fifteen minutes agone."

"Faith kept me back awhile," replied the young man, with a tremor in his voice, caused by the sudden appearance of his companion, though not wholly unexpected.

It was now deep dusk in the forest, and deepest in that part of it where these two were journeying. As nearly as could be discerned, the second traveller was about fifty years old, apparently in the same rank of life as Goodman Brown, and bearing a considerable resemblance to him, though perhaps more in expression than features. Still, they might have been taken for father and son. And yet, though the elder person was as simply clad as the younger, and as simple in manner too, he had an indescribable air of one who knew the world, and would not

---

[2] Boston's Old South Church, built in 1669. That this "figure" has come from Boston to Salem in just fifteen minutes signifies supernatural powers.

have felt abashed at the governor's dinner-table, or in King William's court,[3] were it possible that his affairs should call him thither. But the only thing about him, that could be fixed upon as remarkable, was his staff, which bore the likeness of a great black snake, so curiously wrought, that it might almost be seen to twist and wriggle itself, like a living serpent. This, of course, must have been an ocular deception, assisted by the uncertain light.

"Come, Goodman Brown!" cried his fellow-traveller, "this is a dull pace for the beginning of a journey. Take my staff, if you are so soon weary."

"Friend," said the other, exchanging his slow pace for a full stop, "having kept covenant by meeting thee here, it is my purpose now to return whence I came. I have scruples, touching the matter thou wot'st[4] of."

"Sayest thou so?" replied he of the serpent, smiling apart. "Let us walk on, nevertheless, reasoning as we go, and if I convince thee not, thou shalt turn back. We are but a little way in the forest, yet."

"Too far, too far!" exclaimed the goodman, unconsciously resuming his walk. "My father never went into the woods on such an errand, nor his father before him. We have been a race of honest men and good Christians, since the days of the martyrs.[5] And shall I be the first of the name of Brown, that ever took this path, and kept—"

"Such company, thou wouldst say," observed the elder person, interpreting his pause. "Well said, Goodman Brown! I have been as well acquainted with your family as with ever a one among the Puritans; and that's no trifle to say. I helped your grandfather, the constable, when he lashed the Quaker woman so smartly through the streets of Salem.[6] And it was I that brought your father a pitch-pine knot, kindled at my own hearth, to set fire to an Indian village, in King Philip's war.[7] They were my good friends, both; and many a pleasant walk have we had along this path, and returned merrily after midnight. I would fain be friends with you, for their sake."

"If it be as thou sayest," replied Goodman Brown, "I marvel they never spoke of these matters. Or, verily, I marvel not, seeing that the least rumor of the sort would have driven them from New-England. We are a people of prayer, and good works, to boot, and abide no such wickedness."

"Wickedness or not," said the travellers with the twisted staff, "I have a very general acquaintance here in New-England. The deacons of many a church have drunk the communion wine with me; the selectmen,[8] of divers towns, make me their chairman; and a majority of the Great and General Court[9] are firm supporters of my interest. The governor and I, too—but these are state-secrets."

"Can this be so!" cried Goodman Brown, with a stare of amazement at his undisturbed companion. "Howbeit, I have nothing to do with the governor and council; they have their own ways, and are no rule for a simple husbandman,[10]

---

[3] That of King William III (1650–1702), who ruled England from 1689 to 1702 with his wife, Queen Mary II (1662–1694), until her death.

[4] The matter you know.

[5] Protestants persecuted during the reign of Mary Tudor (1516–1558), queen of England from 1553 to 1558, called "Bloody Mary" because of her severity.

[6] A Puritan law passed in 1661 commanded that Quakers who broke the law be "whipped through the town."

[7] The war waged by the Wampanoag Indians against the colonists in 1675; King Philip is the name the English gave to Metacomet (?–1676), the Wampanoag chief.

[8] Village officials.   [9] The colony's legislature.

[10] Ordinarily, a farmer; here, a man of modest status. Hawthorne plays on the word husbandman as he does on goodman.

like me. But, were I to go on with thee, how should I meet the eye of that good old man, our minister, at Salem village? Oh, his voice would make me tremble, both Sabbath-day and lecture-day!"[11]

Thus far, the elder traveller had listened with due gravity, but now burst into a fit of irrepressible mirth, shaking himself so violently, that his snake-like staff actually seemed to wriggle in sympathy.

"Ha! ha! ha!" shouted he, again and again; then composing himself, "Well go on, Goodman Brown, go on; but pr'y thee, don't kill me with laughing!"

"Well, then, to end the matter at once," said Goodman Brown, considerably nettled, "there is my wife, Faith. It would break her dear little heart; and I'd rather break my own!"

"Nay, if that be the case," answered the other, "e'en go thy ways, Goodman Brown. I would not, for twenty old women like the one hobbling before us, that Faith should come to any harm."

As he spoke, he pointed his staff at a female figure on the path, in whom Goodman Brown recognized a very pious and exemplary dame, who had taught him his catechism, in youth, and was still his moral and spiritual adviser, jointly with the minister and Deacon Gookin.

"A marvel, truly, that Goody[12] Cloyse should be so far in the wilderness, at night-fall!" said he. "But, with your leave, friend, I shall take a cut through the woods, until we have left this Christian woman behind. Being a stranger to you, she might ask whom I was consorting with, and whither I was going."

"Be it so," said his fellow-traveller. "Betake you to the woods, and let me keep the path."

Accordingly, the young man turned aside, but took care to watch his companion, who advanced softly along the road, until he had come within a staff's length of the old dame. She, meanwhile, was making the best of her way, with singular speed for so aged a woman, and mumbling some indistinct words, a prayer, doubtless, as she went. The traveller put forth his staff, and touched her withered neck with what seemed the serpent's tail.

"The devil!" screamed the pious old lady.

"Then Goody Cloyse knows her old friend?" observed the traveller, confronting her, and leaning on his writhing stick.

"Ah, forsooth, and is it your worship, indeed?" cried the good dame. "Yea, truly is it, and in the very image of my old gossip, Goodman Brown, the grandfather of the silly fellow that now is. But—would your worship believe it?—my broomstick hath strangely disappeared, stolen, as I suspect, by the unhanged witch, Goody Cory, and that, too, when I was all anointed with the juice of smallage and cinque-foil and wolf's-bane—"[13]

"Mingled with fine wheat and the fat of a new-born babe," said the shape of old Goodman Brown.

"Ah, your worship knows the receipt," cried the old lady, cackling aloud. "So, as I was saying, being all ready for the meeting, and no horse to ride on, I made up my mind to foot it; for they tell me, there is a nice young man to be taken into communion to-night. But now your good worship will lend me your arm, and we shall be there in a twinkling."

---

[11] The midweek sermon day, generally Wednesday or Thursday.

[12] A contraction of "Goodwife," a polite term of address for a married woman of humble rank. Both Goody Cloyse and Goody Cory (later called an "unhanged witch") were sentenced to death at the Salem witchcraft trials.

[13] Plants associated with witchcraft.

"That can hardly be," answered her friend. "I may not spare you my arm, Goody Cloyse, but here is my staff, if you will."

So saying, he threw it down at her feet, where, perhaps, it assumed life, being one of the rods which its owner had formerly lent to the Egyptian Magi.[14] Of this fact, however, Goodman Brown could not take cognizance. He had cast up his eyes in astonishment, and looking down again, beheld neither Goody Cloyse nor the serpentine staff, but his fellow-traveller alone, who waited for him as calmly as if nothing had happened.

"That old woman taught me my catechism!" said the young man; and there was a world of meaning in this simple comment.

They continued to walk onward, while the elder traveller exhorted his companion to make good speed and persevere in the path, discoursing so aptly, that his arguments seemed rather to spring up in the bosom of his auditor, than to be suggested by himself. As they went, he plucked a branch of maple, to serve for a walking-stick, and began to strip it of the twigs and little boughs, which were wet with evening dew. The moment his fingers touched them, they became strangely withered and dried up, as with a week's sunshine. Thus the pair proceeded, at a good free pace, until suddenly, in a gloomy hollow of the road, Goodman Brown sat himself down on the stump of a tree, and refused to go any farther.

"Friend," said he, stubbornly, "my mind is made up. Not another step will I budge on this errand. What if a wretched old woman do choose to go to the devil, when I thought she was going to Heaven! Is that any reason why I should quit my dear Faith, and go after her?"

"You will think better of this, by-and-by," said his acquaintance, composedly. "Sit here and rest yourself awhile; and when you feel like moving again, there is my staff to help you along."

Without more words, he threw his companion the maple stick, and was as speedily out of sight, as if he had vanished into the deepening gloom. The young man sat a few moments, by the road-side, applauding himself greatly, and thinking with how a clear a conscience he should meet the minister, in his morning-walk, nor shrink from the eye of good old Deacon Gookin. And what calm sleep would be his, that very night, which was to have been spent so wickedly, but purely and sweetly now, in the arms of Faith! Amidst these pleasant and praiseworthy meditations, Goodman Brown heard the tramp of horses along the road, and deemed it advisable to conceal himself within the verge of the forest, conscious of the guilty purpose that had brought him thither, though now so happily turned from it.

On came the hoof-tramps and the voices of the riders, two grave old voices, conversing soberly as they drew near. These mingled sounds appeared to pass along the road, within a few yards of the young man's hiding-place; but owing, doubtless, to the depth of the gloom, at that particular spot, neither the travellers nor their steeds were visible. Though their figures brushed the small boughs by the way-side, it could not be seen that they intercepted, even for a moment, the faint gleam from the strip of bright sky, athwart which they must have passed. Goodman Brown alternately crouched and stood on tip-toe, pulling aside the branches, and thrusting forth his head as far as he durst, without discerning so much as a shadow. It vexed him the more, because he could have sworn, were such a thing possible, that he recognized the voices of the minister and Deacon

---

[14] Magicians; in Exodus 7:11 the magicians of Egypt turned their rods into serpents.

Gookin, jogging along quietly, as they were wont to do, when bound to some ordination or ecclesiastical council. While yet within hearing, one of the riders stopped to pluck a switch.

"Of the two, reverend Sir," said the voice like the deacon's, "I had rather miss an ordination-dinner[15] than to-night's meeting. They tell me that some of our community are to be here from Falmouth[16] and beyond, and others from Connecticut and Rhode-Island; besides several of the Indian powows,[17] who, after their fashion, know almost as much deviltry as the best of us. Moreover, there is a goodly young woman to be taken into communion."

"Mighty well, Deacon Gookin!" replied the solemn old tones of the minister. "Spur up, or we shall be late. Nothing can be done, you know, until I get on the ground."

The hoofs clattered again, and the voices, talking so strangely in the empty air, passed on through the forest, where no church had ever been gathered, nor solitary Christian prayed. Whither, then, could these holy men be journeying, so deep into the heathen wilderness? Young Goodman Brown caught hold of a tree, for support, being ready to sink down on the ground, faint and overburthened with the heavy sickness of his heart. He looked up to the sky, doubting whether there really was a Heaven above him. Yet, there was the blue arch, and the stars brightening in it.

"With Heaven above, and Faith below, I will yet stand firm against the devil!" cried Goodman Brown.

While he still gazed upward, into the deep arch of the firmament, and had lifted his hands to pray, a cloud, though no wind was stirring, hurried acros the zenith, and hid the brightening stars. The blue sky was still visible, except directly overhead, where this black mass of cloud was sweeping swiftly northward. Aloft in the air, as if from the depths of the cloud, came a confused and doubtful sound of voices. Once, the listener fancied that he could distinguish the accents of town's-people of his own, men and women, both pious and ungodly, many of whom he had met at the communion-table, and had seen others rioting at the tavern. The next moment, so indistinct were the sounds, he doubted whether he had heard aught but the murmur of the old forest, whispering without a wind. Then came a stronger swell of those familiar tones, heard daily in the sunshine, at Salem village, but never, until now, from a cloud of night. There was one voice, of a young woman, uttering lamentations, yet with an uncertain sorrow, and entreating for some favor, which, perhaps, it would grieve her to obtain. And all the unseen multitude, both saint and sinners, seemed to encourage her onward.

"Faith!" shouted Goodman Brown, in a voice of agony and desperation; and the echoes of the forest mocked him, crying—"Faith! Faith!" as if bewildered wretches were seeking her, all through the wilderness.

The cry of grief, rage, and terror, was yet piercing the night, when the unhappy husband held his breath for a response. There was a scream, drowned immediately in a louder murmur of voices, fading into far-off laughter, as the dark cloud swept away, leaving the clear and silent sky above Goodman Brown. But something fluttered lightly down through the air, and caught on the branch of a tree. The young man seized it, and beheld a pink ribbon.

"My Faith is gone!" cried he, after one stupefied moment. "There is no good on

---

[15] A dinner to celebrate the ordination of a Puritan minister.
[16] Falmouth, Massachusetts, on Cape Cod.   [17] Medicine men.

earth; and sin is but a name. Come, devil! for to thee is this world given."

And maddened with despair, so that he laughed loud and long, did Goodman Brown grasp his staff and set forth again, at such a rate, that he seemed to fly along the forest-path, rather than to walk or run. The road grew wilder and drearier, and more faintly traced, and vanished at length, leaving him in the heart of the dark wilderness, still rushing onward, with the instinct that guides mortal man to evil. The whole forest was peopled with frightful sounds; the creaking of the trees, the howling of wild beasts, and the yell of Indians; while, sometimes, the wind tolled like a distant church-bell, and sometimes gave a broad roar around the traveller, as if all Nature were laughing him to scorn. But he was himself the chief horror of the scene, and shrank not from its other horrors.

"Ha! ha! ha!" roared Goodman Brown, when the wind laughed at him. "Let us hear which will laugh loudest! Think not to frighten me with your deviltry! Come witch, come wizard, come Indian powow, come devil himself! and here comes Goodman Brown. You may as well fear him as he fear you!"

In truth, all through the haunted forest, there could be nothing more frightful than the figure of Goodman Brown. On he flew, among the black pines, brandishing his staff with frenzied gestures, now giving vent to an inspiration of horrid blasphemy, and now shouting forth such laughter, as set all the echoes of the forest laughing like demons around him. The fiend in his own shape is less hideous, than when he rages in the breast of man. Thus sped the demoniac on his course, until, quivering among the trees, he saw a red light before him, as when the felled trunks and branches of a clearing have been set on fire, and throw up their lurid blaze against the sky, at the hour of midnight. He paused, in a lull of the tempest that had driven him onward, and heard the swell of what seemed a hymn, rolling solemnly from a distance, with the weight of many voices. He knew the tune; it was a familiar one in the choir of the village meeting-house. The verse died heavily away, and was lengthened by a chorus, not of human voices, but of all the sounds of the benighted wilderness, pealing in awful harmony together. Goodman Brown cried out; and his cry was lost to his own ear, by its unison with the cry of the desert.

In the interval of silence, he stole forward, until the light glared full upon his eyes. At one extremity of an open space, hemmed in by the dark wall of the forest, arose a rock, bearing some rude, natural resemblance either to an altar or a pulpit, and surrounded by four blazing pines, their tops aflame, their stems untouched, like candles at an evening meeting. The mass of foliage, that had overgrown the summit of the rock, was all on fire, blazing high into the night, and fitfully illuminating the whole field. Each pendent twig and leafy festoon was in a blaze. As the red light arose and fell, a numerous congregation alternately shone forth, then disappeared in shadow, and again grew, as it were, out of the darkness, peopling the heart of the solitary woods at once.

"A grave and dark-clad company!" quoth Goodman Brown.

In truth, they were such. Among them, quivering to-and-fro, between gloom and splendor, appeared faces that would be seen, next day, at the council-board of the province, and others which, Sabbath after Sabbath, looked devoutly heavenward, and benignantly over the crowded pews, from the holiest pulpits in the land. Some affirm, that the lady of the governor[18] was there. At least, there were high dames well known to her, and wives of honored husbands, and widows, a great

---

[18] The wife of Sir William Phips (1651–1695), royal governor of Massachusetts from 1692 to 1694, was accused but never tried for witchcraft in 1692.

multitude, and ancient maidens, all of the excellent repute, and fair young girls, who trembled, lest their mothers should espy them. Either the sudden gleams of light, flashing over the obscure field, bedazzled Goodman Brown, or he recognized a score of the church-members of Salem village, famous for their especial sanctity. Good old Deacon Gookin had arrived, and waited at the skirts of that venerable saint, his revered pastor. But, irreverently consorting with these grave, reputable, and pious people, these elders of the church, these chaste dames and dewy virgins, there were men of dissolute lives and women of spotted fame, wretches given over to all mean and filthy vice, and suspected even of horrid crimes. It was strange to see, that the good shrank not from the wicked, nor were the sinners abashed by the saints. Scattered, also, among their pale-faced enemies, were the Indian priests, or powows, who had often scared their native forest with more hideous incantations than any known to English witchcraft.

"But, where is Faith?" thought Goodman Brown; and, as hope came into his heart, he trembled.

Another verse of the hymn arose, a slow and mournful strain, such as the pious love, but joined to words which expressed all that our nature can conceive of sin, and darkly hinted at far more. Unfathomable to mere mortals is the lore of fiends. Verse after verse was sung, and still the chorus of the desert swelled between, like the deepest tone of a mighty organ. And, with the final peal of that dreadful anthem, there came a sound, as if the roaring wind, the rushing streams, the howling beasts, and every other voice of the unconverted wilderness, were mingling and according with the voice of guilty man, in homage to the prince of all. The four blazing pines threw up a loftier flame, and obscurely discovered shapes and visages of horror on the smoke-wreaths, above the impious assembly. At the same moment, the fire on the rock shot redly forth, and formed a glowing arch above its base, where now appeared a figure. With reverence be it spoken, the figure bore no slight similitude, both in garb and manner, to some grave divine of the New-England churches.

"Bring forth the converts!" cried a voice, that echoed through the field and rolled into the forest.

At the word, Goodman Brown stept forth from the shadow of the trees, and approached the congregation, with whom he felt a loathful brotherhood, by the sympathy of all that was wicked in his heart. He could have well nigh sworn, that the shape of his own dead father beckoned him to advance, looking downward from a smoke-wreath, while a woman, with dim features of despair, threw out her hand to warn him back. Was it his mother? But he had no power to retreat one step, nor to resist, even in thought, when the minister and good old Deacon Gookin seized his arms, and led him to the blazing rock. Thither came also the slender form of a veiled female, led between Goody Cloyse, that pious teacher of the catechism, and Martha Carrier,[19] who had received the devil's promise to be queen of hell. A rampant hag was she! And there stood the proselytes,[20] beneath the canopy of fire.

"Welcome, my children," said the dark figure, "to the communion of your race! Ye have found, thus young, your nature and your destiny. My children, look behind you!"

---

[19] Carrier was hanged as a witch in Salem in 1692. During her trial she "confessed" that the Devil promised that she would be queen of Hell.

[20] New converts.

They turned; and flashing forth, as it were, in a sheet of flame, the fiend-worshippers were seen; the smile of welcome gleamed darkly on every visage.

"There," resumed the sable[21] form, "are all whom ye have reverenced from youth. Ye deemed them holier than yourselves, and shrank from your own sin, contrasting it with their lives of righteousness, and prayerful aspirations heavenward. Yet, here are they all, in my worshipping assembly! This night it shall be granted to you to know their secret deeds; how hoary-bearded elders of the church have whispered wanton words to the young maids of their households; how many a woman, eager for widow's weeds, has given her husband a drink at bed-time, and let him sleep his last sleep in her bosom; how beardless youths have made haste to inherit their fathers' wealth; and how fair damsels—blush not, sweet ones!—have dug little graves in the garden, and bidden me, the sole guest, to an infant's funeral. By the sympathy of your human hearts for sin, ye shall scent out all the places—whether in church, bed-chamber, street, field, or forest—where crime has been committed, and shall exult to behold the whole earth one stain of guilt, one mighty blood-spot. Far more than this! It shall be yours to penetrate, in every bosom, the deep mystery of sin, the fountain of all wicked arts, and which inexhaustibly supplies more evil impulses than human power—than my power, at its utmost!—can make manifest in deeds. And now, my children, look upon each other."

They did so; and, by the blaze of the hell-kindled torches, the wretched man beheld his Faith, and the wife her husband, trembling before that unhallowed altar.

"Lo! there ye stand, my children," said the figure, in a deep and solemn tone, almost sad, with its despairing awfulness, as if his once angelic nature could yet mourn for our miserable race. "Depending upon one another's hearts, ye had still hoped, that virtue were not all a dream. Now are ye undeceived! Evil is the nature of mankind. Evil must be your only happiness. Welcome, again, my children, to the communion of your race!"

"Welcome!" repeated the fiend-worshippers, in one cry of despair and triumph.

And there they stood, the only pair, as it seemed, who were yet hesitating on the verge of wickedness, in this dark world. A basin was hollowed, naturally, in the rock. Did it contain water, reddened by the lurid light? or was it blood? or, perchance, a liquid flame? Herein did the Shape of Evil dip his hand, and prepare to lay the mark of baptism upon their foreheads, that they might be partakers of the mystery of sin, more conscious of the secret guilt of others, both in deed and thought, than they could now be of their own. The husband cast one look at his pale wife, and Faith at him. What polluted wretches would the next glance shew them to each other, shuddering alike at what they disclosed and what they saw!

"Faith! Faith!" cried the husband. "Look up to Heaven, and resist the Wicked One!"

Whether Faith obeyed, he knew not. Hardly had he spoken, when he found himself amid calm night and solitude, listening to a roar of the wind, which died heavily away through the forest. He staggered against the rock and felt it chill and damp, while a hanging twig, that had been all on fire, besprinkled his cheek with the coldest dew.

The next morning, young Goodman Brown came slowly into the street of Salem village, staring around him like a bewildered man. The good old minister was taking a walk along the grave-yard, to get an appetite for breakfast and medi-

---

[21] Black.

tate his sermon, and bestowed a blessing, as he passed, on Goodman Brown. He shrank from the venerable saint, as if to avoid an anathema.[22] Old Deacon Gookin was at domestic worship, and the holy words of his prayer were heard through the open window. "What God doth the wizard pray to?" quoth Goodman Brown. Goody Cloyse, that excellent old Christian, stood in the early sunshine, at her own lattice, catechising a little girl, who had brought her a pint of morning's milk. Goodman Brown snatched away the child, as from the grasp of the fiend himself. Turning the corner by the meeting-house, he spied the head of Faith, with the pink ribbons, gazing anxiously forth, and bursting into such joy at sight of him, that she skipt along the street, and almost kissed her husband before the whole village. But, Goodman Brown looked sternly and sadly into her face, and passed on without a greeting.

Had Goodman Brown fallen asleep in the forest, and only dreamed a wild dream of a witch-meeting?

Be it so, if you will. But, alas! it was a dream of evil omen for young Goodman Brown. A stern, a sad, a darkly meditative, a distrustful, if not a desperate man, did he become, from the night of that fearful dream. On the Sabbath-day, when the congregation were singing a holy psalm, he could not listen, because an anthem of sin rushed loudly upon his ear, and drowned all the blessed strain. When the minister spoke from the pulpit, with power and fervid eloquence, and, with his hand on the open Bible, of the sacred truths of our religion, and of saint-like lives and triumphant deaths, and of future bliss or misery unutterable, then did Goodman Brown turn pale, dreading, lest the roof should thunder down upon the gray blasphemer and his hearers. Often, awakening suddenly at midnight, he shrank from the bosom of Faith, and at morning or eventide, when the family knelt down at prayer, he scowled, and muttered to himself, and gazed sternly at his wife, and turned away. And when he had lived long, and was borne to his grave, a hoary corpse, followed by Faith, an aged woman, and children and grandchildren, a goodly procession, besides neighbors, not a few, they carved no hopeful verse upon his tomb-stone; for his dying hour was gloom.

1835

THE MINISTER'S BLACK VEIL*

A PARABLE[1]

The sexton stood in the porch of Milford[2] meeting-house, pulling lustily at the bell-rope. The old people of the village came stooping along the street. Children, with bright faces, tript merrily beside their parents, or mimicked a graver gait, in the conscious dignity of their Sunday clothes. Spruce bachelors looked sidelong at the pretty maidens, and fancied that the Sabbath sunshine made them prettier than

[22] A solemn curse.

* First published in *The Token* in 1836 and included in *Twice-Told Tales* (1837).

[1] Hawthorne's note: "Another clergyman in New England, Mr. Joseph Moody, of York, Maine, who died about eighty years since, made himself remarkable by the same eccentricity that is here related of the Reverend Mr. Hooper. In his case, however, the symbol had a different import. In early life he had accidentally killed a beloved friend; and from that day till the hour of his own death, he hid his face from men."

[2] Milford, Massachusetts, southwest of Boston.

on week-days. When the throng had mostly streamed into the porch, the sexton began to toll the bell, keeping his eye on the Reverend Mr. Hooper's door. The first glimpse of the clergyman's figure was the signal for the bell to cease its summons.

"But what has good Parson Hooper got upon his face?" cried the sexton in astonishment.

All within hearing immediately turned about, and beheld the semblance of Mr. Hooper, pacing slowly his meditative way towards the meeting-house. With one accord they started, expressing more wonder than if some strange minister were coming to dust the cushions of Mr. Hooper's pulpit.

"Are you sure it is our parson?" inquired Goodman Gray of the sexton.

"Of a certainty it is good Mr. Hooper," replied the sexton. "He was to have exchanged pulpits with Parson Shute of Westbury; but Parson Shute sent to excuse himself yesterday, being to preach a funeral sermon."

The cause of so much amazement may appear sufficiently slight. Mr. Hooper, a gentlemanly person of about thirty, though still a bachelor, was dressed with due clerical neatness, as if a careful wife had starched his band,[3] and brushed the weekly dust from his Sunday's garb. There was but one thing remarkable in his appearance. Swathed about his forehead, and hanging down over his face, so low as to be shaken by his breath, Mr. Hooper had on a black veil. On a nearer view, it seemed to consist of two folds of crape, which entirely concealed his features, except the mouth and chin, but probably did not intercept his sight, farther than to give a darkened aspect to all living and inanimate things. With this gloomy shade before him, good Mr. Hooper walked onward, at a slow and quiet pace, stooping somewhat and looking on the ground, as is customary with abstracted men, yet nodding kindly to those of his parishioners who still waited on the meeting-house steps. But so wonder-struck were they, that his greeting hardly met with a return.

"I can't really feel as if good Mr. Hooper's face was behind that piece of crape," said the sexton.

"I don't like it," muttered an old woman, as she hobbled into the meeting-house. "He has changed himself into something awful, only by hiding his face."

"Our parson has gone mad!" cried Goodman Gray, following him across the threshold.

A rumor of some unaccountable phenomenon had preceded Mr. Hooper into the meeting-house, and set all the congregation astir. Few could refrain from twisting their heads towards the door; many stood upright, and turned directly about; while several little boys clambered upon the seats, and came down again with a terrible racket. There was a general bustle, a rustling of the women's gowns and shuffling of the men's feet, greatly at variance with that hushed repose which should attend the entrance of the minsiter. But Mr. Hooper appeared not to notice the perturbation of his people. He entered with an almost noiseless step, bent his head mildly to the pews on each side, and bowed as he passed his oldest parishioner, a white-haired great-grandsire, who occupied an arm-chair in the centre of the aisle. It was strange to observe, how slowly this venerable man became conscious of something singular in the appearance of his pastor. He seemed not fully to partake of the prevailing wonder, till Mr. Hooper had ascended the stairs, and showed himself in the pulpit, face to face with his congregation, except for the black veil. That mysterious emblem was never once withdrawn. It shook with his measured breath as he gave out the psalm; it threw its obscurity between him and

---

[3] The collar of a clerical gown.

the holy page, as he read the Scriptures; and while he prayed, the veil lay heavily on his uplifted countenance. Did he seek to hide it from the dread Being whom he was addressing?

Such was the effect of this simple piece of crape, that more than one woman of delicate nerves was forced to leave the meeting-house. Yet perhaps the pale-faced congregation was almost as fearful a sight to the minister, as his black veil to them.

Mr. Hooper had the reputation of a good preacher, but not an energetic one: he strove to win his people heaven-ward, by mild persuasive influences, rather than to drive them thither, by the thunders of the Word. The sermon which he now delivered, was marked by the same characteristics of style and manner, as the general series of his pulpit oratory. But there was something, either in the sentiment of the discourse itself, or in the imagination of the auditors, which made it greatly the most powerful effort that they had ever heard from their pastor's lips. It was tinged, rather more darkly than usual, with the gentle gloom of Mr. Hooper's temperament. The subject had reference to secret sin, and those sad mysteries which we hide from our nearest and dearest, and would fain conceal from our own consciousness, even forgetting that the Omniscient can detect them. A subtle power was breathed into his words. Each member of the congregation, the most innocent girl, and the man of hardened breast, felt as if the preacher had crept upon them, behind his awful veil, and discovered their hoarded iniquity of deed or thought. Many spread their clasped hands on their bosoms. There was nothing terrible in what Mr. Hooper said; at least, no violence; and yet, with every tremor of his melancholy voice, the hearers quaked. An unsought pathos came hand in hand with awe. So sensible were the audience of some unwonted attribute in their minister, that they longed for a breath of wind to blow aside the veil, almost believing that a stranger's visage would be discovered, though the form, gesture, and voice were those of Mr. Hooper.

At the close of the services, the people hurried out with indecorous confusion, eager to communicate their pent-up amazement, and conscious of lighter spirits, the moment they lost sight of the black veil. Some gathered in little circles, huddled closely together, with their mouths all whispering in the centre; some went homeward alone, wrapt in silent meditation; some talked loudly, and profaned the Sabbath-day with ostentatious laughter. A few shook their sagacious heads, intimating that they could penetrate the mystery; while one or two affirmed that there was no mystery at all, but only that Mr. Hooper's eyes were so weakened by the midnight lamp, as to require a shade. After a brief interval, forth came good Mr. Hooper also, in the rear of his flock. Turning his veiled face from one group to another, he paid due reverence to the hoary heads, saluted the middle-aged with kind dignity, as their friend and spiritual guide, greeted the young with mingled authority and love, and laid his hands on the little children's heads to bless them. Such was always his custom on the Sabbath-day. Strange and bewildered looks repaid him for his courtesy. None, as on former occasions, aspired to the honor of walking by their pastor's side. Old Squire Saunders, doubtless by an accidental lapse of memory, neglected to invite Mr. Hooper to his table, where the good clergyman had been wont to bless the food, almost every Sunday since his settlement. He returned, therefore, to the parsonage, and, at the moment of closing the door, was observed to look back upon the people, all of whom had their eyes fixed upon the minister. A sad smile gleamed faintly from beneath the black veil, and flickered about his mouth, glimmering as he disappeared.

"How strange," said a lady, "that a simple black veil, such as any woman might wear on her bonnet, should become such a terrible thing on Mr. Hooper's face!"

"Something must surely be amiss with Mr. Hooper's intellects," observed her husband, the physician of the village. "But the strangest part of the affair is the effect of this vagary, even on a sober-minded man like myself. The black veil, though it covers only our pastor's face, throws its influence over his whole person, and makes him ghost-like from head to foot. Do you not feel it so?"

"Truly do I," replied the lady; "and I would not be alone with him for the world. I wonder he is not afraid to be alone with himself!"

"Men sometimes are so," said her husband.

The afternoon service was attended with similar circumstances. At its conclusion, the bell tolled for the funeral of a young lady. The relatives and friends were assembled in the house, and the more distant acquaintances stood about the door, speaking of the good qualities of the deceased, when their talk was interrupted by the appearance of Mr. Hooper, still covered with his black veil. It was now an appropriate emblem. The clergyman stepped into the room where the corpse was laid, and bent over the coffin, to take a last farewell of his deceased parishioner. As he stooped, the veil hung straight down from his forehead, so that, if her eye-lids had not been closed for ever, the dead maiden might have seen his face. Could Mr. Hooper be fearful of her glance, that he so hastily caught back the black veil? A person, who watched the interview between the dead and living, scrupled not to affirm, that, at the instant when the clergyman's features were disclosed, the corpse had slightly shuddered, rustling the shroud and muslin cap, though the countenance retained the composure of death. A superstitious old woman was the only witness of this prodigy. From the coffin, Mr. Hooper passed into the chamber of the mourners, and thence to the head of the staircase, to make the funeral prayer. It was a tender and heart-dissolving prayer, full of sorrow, yet so imbued with celestial hopes, that the music of a heavenly harp, swept by the fingers of the dead, seemed faintly to be heard among the saddest accents of the minister. The people trembled, though they but darkly understood him, when he prayed that they, and himself, and all of mortal race, might be ready, as he trusted this young maiden had been, for the dreadful hour that should snatch the veil from their faces. The bearers went heavily forth, and the mourners followed, saddening all the street, with the dead before them, and Mr. Hooper in his black veil behind.

"Why do you look back?" said one in the procession to his partner.

"I had a fancy," replied she, "that the minister and the maiden's spirit were walking hand in hand."

"And so had I, at the same moment," said the other.

That night, the handsomest couple in Milford village were to be joined in wedlock. Though reckoned a melancholy man, Mr. Hooper had a placid cheerfulness for such occasions, which often excited a sympathetic smile, where livelier merriment would have been thrown away. There was no quality of his disposition which made him more beloved than this. The company at the wedding awaited his arrival with impatience, trusting that the strange awe, which had gathered over him throughout the day, would now be dispelled. But such was not the result. When Mr. Hooper came, the first thing that their eyes rested on was the same horrible black veil, which had added deeper gloom to the funeral, and could portend nothing but evil to the wedding. Such was its immediate effect on the guests, that a cloud seemed to have rolled duskily from beneath the black crape, and dimmed the light of the candles. The bridal pair stood up before the minister. But the bride's cold fingers quivered in the tremulous hand of the bridegroom, and her death-like paleness caused a whisper, that the maiden who had been buried a few hours before, was come from her grave to be married. If ever another wedding were so dismal, it was that famous one, where they tolled the wedding-knell.[4] After performing the ceremony, Mr. Hooper raised a glass of wine to his lips, wishing happiness to the new-married couple, in a strain of mild pleasantry that ought to have brightened the features of the guests, like a cheerful gleam from the hearth. At that instant, catching a glimpse of his figure in the looking-glass, the black veil involved his own spirit in the horror with which it overwhelmed all others. His frame shuddered—his lips grew white—he spilt the untasted wine upon the carpet—and rushed forth into the darkness. For the Earth, too, had on her Black Veil.

The next day, the whole village of Milford talked of little else than Parson Hooper's black veil. That, and the mystery concealed behind it, supplied a topic for discussion between acquaintances meeting in the street, and good women gossiping at their open windows. It was the first item of news that the tavern-keeper told to his guests. The children babbled of it on their way to school. One imitative little imp covered his face with an old black handkerchief, thereby so affrighting his playmates, that the panic seized himself, and he well nigh lost his wits by his own waggery.[5]

It was remarkable, that, of all the busy-bodies and impertinent people in the parish, not one ventured to put the plain question to Mr. Hooper, wherefore he did this thing. Hitherto, whenever there appeared the slightest call for such interference, he had never lacked advisers, nor shown himself averse to be guided by their judgment. If he erred at all, it was by so painful a degree of self-distrust, that even the mildest censure would lead him to consider an indifferent action as a crime. Yet, though so well acquainted with this amiable weakness, no individual among his parishioners chose to make the black veil a subject of friendly remonstrance. There was a feeling of dread, neither plainly confessed nor carefully concealed, which caused each to shift the responsibility upon another, till at length it was found expedient to send a deputation of the church, in order to deal with Mr. Hooper about the mystery, before it should grow into a scandal. Never did an embassy so ill discharge its duties. The minister received them with friendly courtesy, but became silent, after they were seated, leaving to his visiters the whole burthen[6] of introducing their important business. The topic, it might be supposed, was obvious enough. There was the black veil, swathed around Mr. Hooper's forehead, and concealing every feature above his placid mouth, on which, at times, they could perceive the glimmering of a melancholy smile. But that piece of crape, to their imagination, seemed to hang down before his heart, the symbol of a fearful secret between him and them. Were the veil but cast aside, they might speak freely of it, but not till then. Thus they sat a considerable time, speechless, confused, and shrinking uneasily from Mr. Hooper's eye, which they felt to be fixed upon them with an invisible glance. Finally, the deputies returned abashed to their constituents, pronouncing the matter too weighty to be handled, except by a council of the churches, if, indeed, it might not require a general synod.[7]

But there was one person in the village, unappalled by the awe with which the

---

[4] Hawthorne alludes to his own story "The Wedding Knell," published in *The Token* in 1836 and in *Twice-Told Tales*.

[5] A mischievous joke.   [6] Burden.   [7] A church council.

black veil had impressed all beside herself. When the deputies returned without an explanation, or even venturing to demand one, she, with the calm energy of her character, determined to chase away the strange cloud that appeared to be settling round Mr. Hooper, every moment more darkly than before. As his plighted wife, it should be her privilege to know what the black veil concealed. At the minister's first visit, therefore, she entered upon the subject, with a direct simplicity, which made the task easier both for him and her. After he had seated himself, she fixed her eyes steadfastly upon the veil, but could discern nothing of the dreadful gloom that had so overawed the multitude: it was but a double fold of crape, hanging down from his forehead to his mouth, and slightly stirring with his breath.

"No," said she aloud, and smiling, "there is nothing terrible in this piece of crape, except that it hides a face which I am always glad to look upon. Come, good sir, let the sun shine from behind the cloud. First lay aside your black veil: then tell me why you put it on."

Mr. Hooper's smile glimmered faintly.

"There is an hour to come," said he, "when all of us shall cast aside our veils. Take it not amiss, beloved friend, if I wear this piece of crape till then."

"Your words are a mystery too," returned the young lady. "Take away the veil from them, at least."

"Elizabeth, I will," said he, "so far as my vow may suffer me. Know, then, this veil is a type and a symbol, and I am bound to wear it ever, both in light and darkness, in solitude and before the gaze of multitudes, and as with strangers, so with my familiar friends. No mortal eye will see it withdrawn. This dismal shade must separate me from the world: even you, Elizabeth, can never come behind it!"

"What grievous affliction hath befallen you," she earnestly inquired, "that you should thus darken your eyes for ever?"

"If it be a sign of mourning," replied Mr. Hooper, "I, perhaps, like most other mortals, have sorrows dark enough to by typified by a black veil."

"But what if the world will not believe that it is the type of an innocent sorrow?" urged Elizabeth. "Beloved and respected as you are, there may be whispers, that you hide your face under the consciousness of secret sin. For the sake of your holy office, do away this scandal!"

The color rose into her cheeks, as she intimated the nature of the rumors that were already abroad in the village. But Mr. Hooper's mildness did not forsake him. He even smiled again—that same sad smile, which always appeared like a faint glimmering of light, proceeding from the obscurity beneath the veil.

"If I hide my face for sorrow, there is cause enough," he merely replied; "and if I cover it for secret sin, what mortal might not do the same?"

And with this gentle, but unconquerable obstinacy, did he resist all her entreaties. At length Elizabeth sat silent. For a few moments she appeared lost in thought, considering, probably, what new methods might be tried, to withdraw her lover from so dark a fantasy, which, if it had no other meaning, was perhaps a symptom of mental disease. Though of a firmer character than his own, the tears rolled down her cheeks. But, in an instant, as it were, a new feeling took the place of sorrow: her eyes were fixed insensibly on the black veil, when, like a sudden twilight in the air, its terrors fell around her. She arose, and stood trembling before him.

"And do you feel it then at last?" said he mournfully.

She made no reply, but covered her eyes with her hand, and turned to leave the room. He rushed forward and caught her arm.

"Have patience with me, Elizabeth!" cried he passionately. "Do not desert me, though this veil must be between us here on earth. Be mine, and hereafter there shall be no veil over my face, no darkness between our souls! It is but a mortal veil—it is not for eternity! Oh! you know not how lonely I am, and how frightened to be alone behind my black veil. Do not leave me in this miserable obscurity for ever!"

"Lift the veil but once, and look me in the face," said she.

"Never! It cannot be!" replied Mr. Hooper.

"Then, farewell!" said Elizabeth.

She withdrew her arm from his grasp, and slowly departed, pausing at the door, to give one long, shuddering gaze, that seemed almost to penetrate the mystery of the black veil. But, even amid his grief, Mr. Hooper smiled to think that only a material emblem had separated him from happiness, though the horrors which it shadowed forth, must be drawn darkly between the fondest of lovers.

From that time no attempts were made to remove Mr. Hooper's black veil, or, by a direct appeal, to discover the secret which it was supposed to hide. By persons who claimed a superiority to popular prejudice, it was reckoned merely an eccentric whim, such as often mingles with the sober actions of men otherwise rational, and tinges them all with its own semblance of insanity. But with the multitude, good Mr. Hooper was irreparably a bugbear.[8] He could not walk the streets with any peace of mind, so conscious was he that the gentle and timid would turn aside to avoid him, and that others would make it a point of hardihood to throw themselves in his way. The impertinence of the latter class compelled him to give up his customary walk, at sunset, to the burial ground; for when he leaned pensively over the gate, there would always be faces behind the gravestones, peeping at his black veil. A fable went the rounds, that the stare of the dead people drove him thence. It grieved him, to the very depth of his kind heart, to observe how the children fled from his approach, breaking up their merriest sports, while his melancholy figure was yet afar off. Their instinctive dread caused him to feel, more strongly than aught else, that a preternatural horror was interwoven with the threads of the black crape. In truth, his own antipathy to the veil was known to be so great, that he never willingly passed before a mirror, nor stooped to drink at a still fountain, lest, in its peaceful bosom, he should be affrighted by himself. This was what gave plausibility to the whispers, that Mr. Hooper's conscience tortured him for some great crime, too horrible to be entirely concealed, or otherwise than so obscurely intimated. Thus, from beneath the black veil, there rolled a cloud into the sunshine, an ambiguity of sin or sorrow, which enveloped the poor minister, so that love or sympathy could never reach him. It was said, that ghost and fiend consorted with him there. With self-shudderings and outward terrors, he walked continually in its shadow, groping darkly within his own soul, or gazing through a medium that saddened the whole world. Even the lawless wind, it was believed, respected his dreadful secret, and never blew aside the veil. But still good Mr. Hooper sadly smiled, at the pale visages of the worldly throng as he passed by.

Among all its bad influences, the black veil had the one desirable effect, of making its wearer a very efficient clergyman. By the aid of his mysterious emblem—for there was no other apparent cause—he became a man of awful power, over souls that were in agony for sin. His converts always regarded him with a

---

[8] An object of dread.

dread peculiar to themselves, affirming, though but figuratively, that, before he brought them to celestial light, they had been with him behind the black veil. Its gloom, indeed, enabled him to sympathize with all dark affections. Dying sinners cried aloud for Mr. Hooper, and would not yield their breath till he appeared; though ever, as he stooped to whisper consolation, they shuddered at the veiled face so near their own. Such were the terrors of the black veil, even when Death had bared his visage! Strangers came long distances to attend service at his church, with the mere idle purpose of gazing at his figure, because it was forbidden them to behold his face. But many were made to quake ere they departed! Once, during Governor Belcher's[9] administration, Mr. Hooper was appointed to preach the election sermon.[10] Covered with his black veil, he stood before the chief magistrate, the council, and the representatives, and wrought so deep an impression, that the legislative measures of that year, were characterized by all the gloom and piety of our earliest ancestral sway.

In this manner Mr. Hooper spent a long life, irreproachable in outward act, yet shrouded in dismal suspicions; kind and loving, though unloved, and dimly feared; a man apart from men, shunned in their health and joy, but ever summoned to their aid in mortal anguish. As years wore on, shedding their snows above his sable[11] veil, he acquired a name throughout the New-England churches, and they called him Father Hooper. Nearly all his parishioners, who were of mature age when he was settled, had been borne away by many a funeral: he had one congregation in the church, and a more crowded one in the church-yard; and having wrought so late into the evening, and done his work so well, it was now good Father Hooper's turn to rest.

Several persons were visible by the shaded candlelight, in the death-chamber of the old clergyman. Natural connections he had none. But there was the decorously grave, though unmoved physician, seeking only to mitigate the last pangs of the patient whom he could not save. There were the deacons, and other eminently pious members of his church. There, also, was the Reverend Mr. Clark, of Westbury, a young and zealous divine, who had ridden in haste to pray by the bed-side of the expiring minister. There was the nurse, no hired handmaiden of death, but one whose calm affection had endured thus long, in secresy, in solitude, amid the chill of age, and would not perish, even at the dying hour. Who, but Elizabeth! And there lay the hoary head of good Father Hooper upon the death-pillow, with the black veil still swathed about his brow and reaching down over his face, so that each more difficult gasp of his faint breath caused it to stir. All through life that piece of crape had hung between him and the world: it had separated him from cheerful brotherhood and woman's love, and kept him in that saddest of all prisons, his own heart; and still it lay upon his face, as if to deepen the gloom of his darksome chamber, and shade him from the sunshine of eternity.

For some time previous, his mind had been confused, wavering doubtfully between the past and the present, and hovering forward, as it were, at intervals, into the indistinctness of the world to come. There had been feverish turns, which

---

[9] Jonathan Belcher (1682–1757) served as governor of Massachusetts and New Hampshire from 1730 to 1741.

[10] A sermon delivered at the inauguration of a governor; it was an honor to be chosen to give this sermon.

[11] Black.

tossed him from side to side, and wore away what little strength he had. But in his most convulsive struggles, and in the wildest vagaries of his intellect, when no other thought retained its sober influence, he still showed an awful solicitude lest the black veil should slip aside. Even if his bewildered soul could have forgotten, there was a faithful woman at his pillow, who, with averted eyes, would have covered that aged face, which she had last beheld in the comeliness of manhood. At length the death-stricken old man lay quietly in the torpor of mental and bodily exhaustion, with an imperceptible pulse, and breath that grew fainter and fainter, except when a long, deep, and irregular inspiration seemed to prelude the flight of his spirit.

The minister of Westbury approached the bedside.

"Venerable Father Hooper," said he, "the moment of your release is at hand. Are you ready for the lifting of the veil, that shuts in time from eternity?"

Father Hooper at first replied merely by a feeble motion of his head; then, apprehensive, perhaps, that his meaning might be doubtful, he exerted himself to speak.

"Yea," said he, in faint accents, "my soul hath a patient weariness until that veil be lifted."

"And is it fitting," resumed the Reverend Mr. Clark, "that a man so given to prayer, of such a blameless example, holy in deed and thought, so far as mortal judgment may pronounce; is it fitting that a father in the church should leave a shadow on his memory, that may seem to blacken a life so pure? I pray you, my venerable brother, let not this thing be! Suffer us to be gladdened by your triumphant aspect, as you go to your reward. Before the veil of eternity be lifted, let me cast aside this black veil from your face!"

And thus speaking, the Reverend Mr. Clark bent forward to reveal the mystery of so many years. But, exerting a sudden energy, that made all the beholders stand aghast, Father Hooper snatched both his hands from beneath the bed-clothes, and pressed them strongly on the black veil, resolute to struggle, if the minister of Westbury would contend with a dying man.

"Never!" cried the veiled clergyman. "On earth, never!"

"Dark old man!" exclaimed the affrighted minister, "with what horrible crime upon your soul are you now passing to the judgment?"

Father Hooper's breath heaved; it rattled in his throat; but, with a mighty effort, grasping forward with his hands, he caught hold of life, and held it back till he should speak. He even raised himself in bed; and there he sat, shivering with the arms of death around him, while the black veil hung down, awful, at that last moment, in the gathered terrors of a life-time. And yet the faint, sad smile, so often there, now seemed to glimmer from its obscurity, and linger on Father Hooper's lips.

"Why do you tremble at me alone?" cried he, turning his veiled face round the circle of pale spectators. "Tremble also at each other! Have men avoided me, and women shown no pity, and children screamed and fled, only for my black veil? What, but the mystery which it obscurely typifies, has made this piece of crape so awful? When the friend shows his inmost heart to his friend; the lover to his best-beloved; when man does not vainly shrink from the eye of his Creator, loath-somely treasuring up the secret of his sin; then deem me a monster, for the symbol beneath which I have lived, and die! I look around me, and, lo! on every visage a Black Veil!"

While his auditors shrank from one another, in mutual affright, Father Hooper fell back upon his pillow, a veiled corpse, with a faint smile lingering on the lips. Still veiled, they laid him in his coffin, and a veiled corpse they bore him to the grave. The grass of many years has sprung up and withered on that grave, the burial-stone is moss-grown, and good Mr. Hooper's face is dust; but awful is still the thought, that it mouldered beneath the Black Veil!

1836

THE BIRTH-MARK*

In the latter part of the last century, there lived a man of science—an eminent proficient in every branch of natural philosophy—who, not long before our story opens, had made experience of a spiritual affinity, more attractive than any chemical one. He had left his laboratory to the care of an assistant, cleared his fine countenance from the furnace-smoke, washed the stain of acids from his fingers, and persuaded a beautiful woman to become his wife. In those days, when the comparatively recent discovery of electricity, and other kindred mysteries of nature, seemed to open paths into the region of miracle, it was not unusual for the love of science to rival the love of woman, in its depth and absorbing energy. The higher intellect, the imagination, the spirit, and even the heart, might all find their congenial aliment in pursuits which, as some of their ardent votaries believed, would ascend from one step of powerful intelligence to another, until the philosopher should lay his hand on the secret of creative force, and perhaps make new worlds for himself. We know not whether Aylmer possessed this degree of faith in man's ultimate control over nature. He had devoted himself, however, too unreservedly to scientific studies, ever to be weaned from them by any second passion. His love for his young wife might prove the stronger of the two; but it could only be by intertwining itself with his love of science, and uniting the strength of the latter to its own.

Such a union accordingly took place, and was attended with truly remarkable consequences, and a deeply impressive moral. One day, very soon after their marriage, Aylmer sat gazing at his wife, with a trouble in his countenance that grew stronger, until he spoke.

"Georgiana," said he, "has it never occurred to you that the mark upon your cheek might be removed?"

"No, indeed," said she, smiling; but perceiving the seriousness of his manner, she blushed deeply. "To tell you the truth, it has been so often called a charm, that I was simple enough to imagine it might be so."

"Ah, upon another face, perhaps it might," replied her husband. "But never on yours! No, dearest Georgiana, you came so nearly perfect from the hand of Nature, that this slightest possible defect—which we hesitate whether to term a defect or a beauty—shocks me, as being the visible mark of earthly imperfection."

"Shocks you, my husband!" cried Georgiana, deeply hurt; at first reddening with momentary anger, but then bursting into tears. "Then why did you take me from my mother's side? You cannot love what shocks you!"

* First published in the *Pioneer Magazine* in 1843 and included in *Mosses From an Old Manse* (1846).

To explain this conversation, it must be mentioned, that, in the centre of Georgiana's left cheek, there was a singular mark, deeply interwoven, as it were, with the texture and substance of her face. In the usual state of her complexion,—a healthy, though delicate bloom,—the mark wore a tint of deeper crimson, which imperfectly defined its shape amid the surrounding rosiness. When she blushed, it gradually became more indistinct, and finally vanished amid the triumphant rush of blood, that bathed the whole cheek with its brilliant glow. But, if any shifting emotion caused her to turn pale, there was the mark again, a crimson stain upon the snow, in what Aylmer sometimes deemed an almost fearful distinctness. Its shape bore not a little similarity to the human hand, though of the smallest pigmy size. Georgiana's lovers were wont to say, that some fairy, at her birth-hour, had laid her tiny hand upon the infant's cheek, and left this impress there, in token of the magic endowments that were to give her such sway over all hearts. Many a desperate swain would have risked life for the privilege of pressing his lips to the mysterious hand. It must not be concealed, however, that the impression wrought by this fairy sign-manual varied exceedingly, according to the difference of temperament in the beholders. Some fastidious persons—but they were exclusively of her own sex—affirmed that the Bloody Hand, as they chose to call it, quite destroyed the effect of Georgiana's beauty, and rendered her countenance even hideous. But it would be as reasonable to say, that one of those small blue stains, which sometimes occur in the purest statuary marble, would convert the Eve of Powers[1] to a monster. Masculine observers, if the birth-mark did not heighten their admiration, contented themselves with wishing it away, that the world might possess one living specimen of ideal loveliness, without the semblance of a flaw. After his marriage—for he thought little or nothing of the matter before—Aylmer discovered that this was the case with himself.

Had she been less beautiful—if Envy's self could have found aught else to sneer at—he might have felt his affection heightened by the prettiness of this mimic hand, now vaguely portrayed, now lost, now stealing forth again, and glimmering to-and-fro with every pulse of emotion that throbbed within her heart. But, seeing her otherwise so perfect, he found this one defect grow more and more intolerable, with every moment of their united lives. It was the fatal flaw of humanity, which Nature, in one shape or another, stamps ineffaceably on all her productions, either to imply that they are temporary and finite, or that their perfection must be wrought by toil and pain. The Crimson Hand expressed the ineludible gripe, in which mortality clutches the highest and purest of earthly mould, degrading them into kindred with the lowest, and even with the very brutes, like whom their visible frames return to dust. In this manner, selecting it as the symbol of his wife's liability to sin, sorrow, decay, and death, Alymer's sombre imagination was not long in rendering the birth-mark a frightful object, causing him more trouble and horror than ever Georgiana's beauty, whether of soul or sense, had given him delight.

At all the seasons which should have been their happiest, he invariably, and without intending it—nay, in spite of a purpose to the contrary—reverted to this one disastrous topic. Trifling as it at first appeared, it so connected itself with innumerable trains of thought, and modes of feeling, that it became the central point of all. With the morning twilight, Aylmer opened his eyes upon his wife's

---

[1] The marble statue *Eve Before the Fall* (1842?), produced by the American sculptor Hiram Powers (1805–1873) in Florence.

face, and recognized the symbol of imperfection; and when they sat together at the evening hearth, his eyes wandered stealthily to her cheek, and beheld, flickering with the blaze of the wood fire, the spectral Hand that wrote mortality, where he would fain have worshipped. Georgiana soon learned to shudder at his gaze. It needed but a glance, with the peculiar expression that his face often wore, to change the roses of her cheek into a deathlike paleness, amid which the Crimson Hand was brought strongly out, like a bas-relief[2] of ruby on the whitest marble.

Late, one night, when the lights were growing dim, so as hardly to betray the stain on the poor wife's cheek, she herself, for the first time, voluntarily took up the subject.

"Do you remember, my dear Aylmer," said she, with a feeble attempt at a smile—"have you any recollection of a dream, last night, about this odious Hand?"

"None!—none whatever!" replied Aylmer, starting; but then he added in a dry, cold tone, affected for the sake of concealing the real depth of his emotion:—"I might well dream of it; for before I fell asleep, it had taken a pretty firm hold of my fancy."

"And you did dream of it," continued Georgiana, hastily; for she dreaded lest a gush of tears should interrupt what she had to say—"A terrible dream! I wonder that you can forget it. Is it possible to forget this one expression?—Reflect, my husband; for by all means I would have you recall that dream."

The mind is in a sad note, when Sleep, the all-involving, cannot confine her spectres within the dim region of her sway, but suffers them to break forth, affrighting this actual life with secrets that perchance belong to a deeper one. Aylmer now remembered his dream. He had fancied himself, with his servant Aminadab, attempting an operation for the removal of the birth-mark. But the deeper went the knife, the deeper sank the Hand, until at length its tiny grasp appeared to have caught hold of Georgiana's heart; whence, however, her husband was inexorably resolved to cut or wrench it away.

When the dream had shaped itself perfectly in his memory, Aylmer sat in his wife's presence with a guilty feeling. Truth often finds its way to the mind close-muffled in robes of sleep, and then speaks with uncompromising directness of matters in regard to which we practise an unconscious self-deception, during our waking moments. Until now, he had not been aware of the tyrannizing influence acquired by one idea over his mind, and of the lengths which he might find in his heart to go, for the sake of giving himself peace.

"Aylmer," resumed Georgiana, solemnly, "I know not what may be the cost to both of us, to rid me of this fatal birth-mark. Perhaps its removal may cause cureless deformity. Or, it may be, the stain goes as deep as life itself. Again, do we know that there is a possibility, on any terms, of unclasping the firm grip of this little Hand, which was laid upon me before I came into the world?"

"Dearest Georgiana, I have spent much thought upon the subject," hastily interrupted Aylmer—"I am convinced of the perfect practicability of its removal."

"If there be the remotest possibility of it," continued Georgiana, "let the attempt be made, at whatever risk. Danger is nothing to me; for life—while this hateful mark makes me the object of your horror and disgust—life is a burthen which I would fling down with joy. Either remove this dreadful Hand, or take my wretched life! You have deep science! All the world bears witness of it. You have

[2] "Low relief" (French); slightly raised.

achieved great wonders! Cannot you remove this little, little mark, which I cover with the tips of two small fingers? Is this beyond your power, for the sake of your own peace, and to save your poor wife from madness?"

"Noblest—dearest—tenderest wife!" cried Aylmer, rapturously. "Doubt not my power. I have already given this matter the deepest thought—thought which might almost have enlightened me to create a being less perfect than yourself. Georgiana, you have led me deeper than ever into the heart of science. I feel myself fully competent to render this dear cheek as faultless as its fellow; and then, most beloved, what will be my triumph, when I shall have corrected what Nature left imperfect, in her fairest work! Even Pygmalion,[3] when his sculptured woman assumed life, felt not greater ecstasy than mine will be."

"It is resolved, then," said Georgiana, faintly smiling,—"And, Aylmer, spare me not, though you should find the birth-mark take refuge in my heart at last."

Her husband tenderly kissed her cheek—her right cheek—not that which bore the impress of the Crimson Hand.

The next day, Aylmer apprized his wife of a plan that he had formed, whereby he might have opportunity for the intense thought and constant watchfulness, which the proposed operation would require; while Georgiana, likewise, would enjoy the perfect repose essential to its success. They were to seclude themselves in the extensive apartments occupied by Aylmer as a laboratory, and where, during his toil-some youth, he had made discoveries in the elemental powers of nature, that had roused the admiration of all the learned societies in Europe. Seated calmly in this laboratory, the pale philosopher had investigated the secrets of the highest cloud-region, and of the profoundest mines; he had satisfied himself of the causes that kindled and kept alive the fires of the volcano; and had explained the mystery of fountains, and how it is that they gush forth, some so bright and pure, and others with such rich medicinal virtues, from the dark bosom of the earth. Here, too, at an earlier period, he had studied the wonders of the human frame, and attempted to fathom the very process by which Nature assimilates all her precious influences from earth and air, and from the spiritual world, to create and foster Man, her masterpiece. The latter pursuit, however, Aylmer had long laid aside, in unwilling recognition of the truth, against which all seekers sooner or later stumble, that our great creative Mother, while she amuses us with apparently working in the broadest sunshine, is yet severely careful to keep her own secrets, and, in spite of her pretended openness, shows us nothing but results. She permits us indeed, to mar, but seldom to mend, and, like a jealous patentee, on no account to make. Now, however, Aylmer resumed these half-forgotten investigations; not, of course, with such hopes or wishes as first suggested them; but because they involved much physiological truth, and lay in the path of his proposed scheme for the treatment of Georgiana.

As he led her over the threshold of the laboratory, Georgiana was cold and tremulous. Aylmer looked cheerfully into her face, with intent to reassure her, but was so startled with the intense glow of the birth-mark upon the whiteness of her cheek, that he could not restrain a strong convulsive shudder. His wife fainted.

"Aminadab! Aminadab!" shouted Aylmer, stamping violently on the floor.

Forthwith, there issued from an inner apartment a man of low stature, but bulky frame, with shaggy hair hanging about his visage, which was grimed with the

---

[3] According to Greek myth, a king of Cyprus who fell in love with a beautiful statue he had sculpted; Aphrodite, the goddess of love, brought the statue to life, and he married his creation.

vapors of the furnace. This personage had been Aylmer's under-worker during his whole scientific career, and was admirably fitted for that office by his great mechanical readiness, and the skill with which, while incapable of comprehending a single principle, he executed all the practical details of his master's experiments. With his vast strength, his shaggy hair, his smoky aspect, and the indescribable earthiness that incrusted him, he seemed to represent man's physical nature; while Aylmer's slender figure, and pale, intellectual face, were no less apt a type of the spiritual element.

"Throw open the door of the boudoir, Aminadab," said Aylmer, "and burn a pastille."[4]

"Yes, master," answered Aminadab, looking intently at the lifeless form of Georgiana; and then he muttered to himself:—"If she were my wife, I'd never part with that birth-mark."

When Georgiana recovered consciousness, she found herself breathing an atmosphere of penetrating fragrance, the gentle potency of which had recalled her from her deathlike faintness. The scene around her looked like enchantment. Aylmer had converted those smoky, dingy, sombre rooms, where he had spent his brightest years in recondite pursuits, into a series of beautiful apartments, not unfit to be the secluded abode of a lovely woman. The walls were hung with gorgeous curtains, which imparted the combination of grandeur and grace, that no other species of adornment can achieve; and as they fell from the ceiling to the floor, their rich and ponderous folds, concealing all angles and straight lines, appeared to shut in the scene from infinite space. For aught Georgiana knew, it might be a pavilion among the clouds. And Aylmer, excluding the sunshine, which would have interfered with his chemical processes, had supplied its place with perfumed lamps, emitting flames of various hue, but all uniting in a soft, empurpled radiance. He now knelt by his wife's side, watching her earnestly, but without alarm; for he was confident in his science, and felt that he could draw a magic circle round her, within which no evil might intrude.

"Where am I?—Ah, I remember!" said Georgiana, faintly; and she placed her hand over her cheek, to hide the terrible mark from her husband's eyes.

"Fear not, dearest!" exclaimed he. "Do not shrink from me! Believe me, Georgiana, I even rejoice in this single imperfection, since it will be such rapture to remove it."

"Oh, spare me!" sadly replied his wife—"Pray do not look at it again. I never can forget that convulsive shudder."

In order to soothe Georgiana, and, as it were, to release her mind from the burthen of actual things, Aylmer now put in practice some of the light and playful secrets, which science had taught him among its profounder lore. Airy figures, absolutely bodiless ideas, and forms of unsubstantial beauty, came and danced before her, imprinting their momentary footsteps on beams of light. Though she had some indistinct idea of the method of these optical phenomena, still the illusion was almost perfect enough to warrant the belief, that her husband possessed sway over the spiritual world. Then again, when she felt a wish to look forth from her seclusion, immediately, as if her thoughts were answered, the procession of external existence flitted across a screen. The scenery and the figures of actual life were perfectly represented, but with that bewitching, yet indescribable difference, which always makes a picture, an image, or a shadow, so much more attractive

---

[4] A pellet of aromatic paste-like incense.

than the original. When wearied of this, Aylmer bade her cast her eyes upon a vessel, containing a quantity of earth. She did so, with little interest at first, but was soon startled, to perceive the germ of a plant, shooting upward from the soil. Then came the slender stalk—the leaves gradually unfolded themselves—and amid them was a perfect and lovely flower.

"It is magical!" cried Georgiana, "I dare not touch it."

"Nay, pluck it," answered Aylmer, "pluck it, and inhale its brief perfume while you may. The flower will wither in a few moments, and leave nothing save its brown seed-vessels—but thence may be perpetuated a race as ephemeral as itself."

But Georgiana had no sooner touched the flower than the whole plant suffered a blight, its leaves turning coal-black, as if by the agency of fire.

"There was too powerful a stimulus," said Aylmer thoughtfully.

To make up for this abortive experiment, he proposed to take her portrait by a scientific process of his own invention. It was to be effected by rays of light striking upon a polished plate of metal.[5] Georgiana assented—but, on looking at the result, was affrighted to find the features of the portrait blurred and indefinable; while the minute figure of a hand appeared where the cheek should have been. Aylmer snatched the metallic plate, and threw it into a jar of corrosive acid.

Soon, however, he forgot these mortifying failures. In the intervals of study and chemical experiment, he came to her, flushed and exhausted, but seemed invigorated by her presence, and spoke in glowing language of the resources of his art. He gave a history of the long dynasty of the Alchemists, who spent so many ages in quest of the universal solvent, by which the Golden Principle might be elicted from all things vile and base. Aylmer appeared to believe, that, by the plainest scientific logic, it was altogether within the limits of possibility to discover this long-sought medium; but, he added, a philosopher who should go deep enough to acquire the power, would attain too lofty a wisdom to stoop to the exercise of it. Not less singular were his opinions in regard to the Elixir Vitæ.[6] He more than intimated, that it was his option to concoct a liquid that should prolong life for years—perhaps interminably—but that it would produce a discord in nature, which all the world, and chiefly the quaffer of the immortal nostrum, would find cause to curse.

"Aylmer, are you in earnest?" asked Georgiana, looking at him with amazement and fear; "it is terrible to possess such power, or even to dream of possessing it!"

"Oh, do not tremble, my love!" said her husband, "I would not wrong either you or myself by working such inharmonious effects upon our lives. But I would have you consider how trifling, in comparison, is the skill requisite to remove this little Hand."

At the mention of the birth-mark, Georgiana, as usual, shrank, as if a red-hot iron had touched her cheek.

Again Aylmer applied himself to his labors. She could hear his voice in the distant furnace-room, giving directions to Aminadab, whose harsh, uncouth, misshapen tones were audible in response, more like the grunt or growl of a brute

---

[5] To accentuate Aylmer's inventive genius, Hawthorne has him anticipate the process of making a daguerreotype, an early photographic method introduced in 1839.

[6] "Elixir of life" (Latin): alchemists tried to turn base metal into gold, to discover the universal cure for diseases, and to develop an elixir that would prolong human life indefinitely.

than human speech. After hours of absence, Aylmer reappeared, and proposed that she should now examine his cabinets of chemical products, and natural treasures of the earth. Among the former he showed her a small vial, in which, he remarked, was contained a gentle yet most powerful fragrance, capable of impregnating all the breezes that blow across a kingdom. They were of inestimable value, the contents of that little vial; and, as he said so, he threw some of the perfume into the air, and filled the room with piercing and invigorating delight.

"And what is this?" asked Georgiana, pointing to a small crystal globe, containing a gold-colored liquid. "It is so beautiful to the eye, that I could imagine it the Elixir of Life."

"In one sense it is," replied Aylmer, "or rather the Elixir of Immortality. It is the most precious poison that ever was concocted in this world. By its aid, I could apportion the lifetime of any mortal at whom you might point your finger. The strength of the dose would determine whether he were to linger out years, or drop dead in the midst of a breath. No king, on his guarded throne, could keep his life, if I, in my private station, should deem that the welfare of millions justified me in depriving him of it."

"Why do you keep such a terrific drug?" inquired Georgiana in horror.

"Do not mistrust me, dearest!" said her husband, smiling; "its virtuous potency is yet greater than its harmful one. But, see! here is a powerful cosmetic. With a few drops of this, in a vase of water, freckles may be washed away as easily as the hands are cleansed. A stronger infusion would take the blood out of the cheek, and leave the rosiest beauty a pale ghost."

"Is it with this lotion that you intend to bathe my cheek?" asked Georgiana anxiously.

"Oh, no!" hastily replied her husband—"this is merely superficial. Your case demands a remedy that shall go deeper."

In his interviews with Georgiana, Aylmer generally made minute inquiries as to her sensations, and whether the confinement of the rooms, and the temperature of the atmosphere, agreed with her. These questions had such a particular drift, that Georgiana began to conjecture that she was already subjected to certain physical influences, either breathed in with the fragrant air, or taken with her food. She fancied, likewise—but it might be altogether fancy—that there was a stirring up of her system,—a strange indefinite sensation creeping through her veins, and tingling, half painfully, half pleasurably, at her heart. Still, whenever she dared to look into the mirror, there she beheld herself, pale as a white rose, and with the crimson birth-mark stamped upon her cheek. Not even Aylmer now hated it so much as she.

To dispel the tedium of the hours which her husband found it necessary to devote to the processes of combination and analysis, Georgiana turned over the volumes of his scientific library. In many dark old tomes, she met with chapters full of romance and poetry. They were the works of the philosophers of the middle ages, such as Albertus Magnus, Cornelius Agrippa, Paracelsus, and the famous friar who created the prophetic Brazen Head.[7] All these antique naturalists stood in advance of their centuries, yet were imbued with some of their credulity, and therefore were believed, and perhaps imagined themselves, to have acquired from

---

[7] Medieval and early Renaissance philosophers and scientists interested in alchemy and magic: Saint Albertus Magnus (1200?–1280); Agrippa (1486?–1535); Philippus Aureolus Paracelsus (1493?–1541); and Roger Bacon (1214–1294?), who fashioned a head made of brass to forecast such things as changes of climate and personal health.

the investigation of nature a power above nature, and from physics a sway over the spiritual world. Hardly less curious and imaginative were the early volumes of the Transactions of the Royal Society,[8] in which the members, knowing little of the limits of natural possibility, were continually recording wonders, or proposing methods whereby wonders might be wrought.

But, to Georgiana, the most engrossing volume was a large folio from her husband's own hand, in which he had recorded every experiment of his scientific career, with its original aim, the methods adopted for its development, and its final success or failure, with the circumstances to which either event was attributable. The book, in truth, was both the history and emblem of his ardent, ambitious, imaginative, yet practical and laborious, life. He handled physical details, as if there were nothing beyond them; yet spiritualized them all, and redeemed himself from materialism, by his strong and eager aspiration towards the infinite. In his grasp, the veriest clod of earth assumed a soul. Georgiana, as she read, reverenced Aylmer, and loved him more profoundly than ever, but with a less entire dependence on his judgment than heretofore. Much as he had accomplished, she could not but observe that his most splendid successes were almost invariably failures, if compared with the ideal at which he aimed. His brightest diamonds were the merest pebbles, and felt to be so by himself, in comparison with the inestimable gems which lay hidden beyond his reach. The volume, rich with achievements that had won renown for its author, was yet as melancholy a record as ever mortal hand had penned. It was the sad confession, and continual exemplification, of the short-comings of the composite man—the spirit burthened with clay and working in matter—and of the despair that assails the higher nature, at finding itself so miserably thwarted by the earthly part. Perhaps every man of genius, in whatever sphere, might recognize the image of his own experience in Aylmer's journal.

So deeply did these reflections affect Georgiana, that she laid her face upon the open volume, and burst into tears. In this situation she was found by her husband.

"It is dangerous to read in a sorcerer's books," said he, with a smile, though his countenance was uneasy and displeased. "Georgiana, there are pages in that volume, which I can scarcely glance over and keep my senses. Take heed lest it prove as detrimental to you!"

"It has made me worship you more than ever," said she.

"Ah! wait for this one success," rejoined he, "then worship me if you will. I shall deem myself hardly unworthy of it. But, come! I have sought you for the luxury of your voice. Sing to me, dearest!"

So she poured out the liquid music of her voice to quench the thirst of his spirit. He then took his leave, with a boyish exuberance of gaiety, assuring her that her seclusion would endure but a little longer, and that the result was already certain. Scarcely had he departed, when Georgiana felt irresistibly impelled to follow him. She had forgotten to inform Aylmer of a symptom, which, for two or three hours past, had begun to excite her attention. It was a sensation in the fatal birth-mark, not painful, but which induced a restlessness throughout her system. Hastening after her husband, she intruded, for the first time, into the laboratory.

The first thing that struck her eye was the furnace, that hot and feverish worker, with the intense glow of its fire, which, by the quantities of soot clustered above it, seemed to have been burning for ages. There was a distilling apparatus in full

---

[8] The Royal Society of London, established in 1660 to promote scientific discussion.

operation. Around the room were retorts, tubes, cylinders, crucibles, and other apparatus of chemical research. An electrical machine stood ready for immediate use. The atmosphere felt oppressively close, and was tainted with gaseous odors, which had been tormented forth by the process of science. The severe and homely simplicity of the apartment, with its naked walls and brick pavement, looked strange, accustomed as Georgiana had become to the fantastic elegance of her boudoir. But what chiefly, indeed almost solely, drew her attention, was the aspect of Aylmer himself.

He was pale as death, anxious, and absorbed, and hung over the furnace as if it depended upon his utmost watchfulness whether the liquid, which it was distilling, should be the draught of immortal happiness or misery. How different from the sanguine and joyous mien that he had assumed for Georgiana's encouragement!

"Carefully now, Aminadab! Carefully, thou human machine! Carefully, thou man of clay!" muttered Aylmer, more to himself than his assistant. "Now, if there be a thought too much or too little, it is all over!"

"Hoh! hoh!" mumbled Aminadab—"look, master, look!"

Aylmer raised his eyes hastily, and at first reddened, then grew paler than ever, on beholding Georgiana. He rushed towards her, and seized her arm with a gripe that left the print of his fingers upon it.

"Why did you come hither? Have you no trust in your husband?" cried he impetuously. "Would you throw the blight of that fatal birth-mark over my labors? It is not well done. Go, prying woman, go!"

"Nay, Aylmer," said Georgiana, with the firmness of which she possessed no stinted endowment, "it is not you that have a right to complain. You mistrust your wife! You have concealed the anxiety with which you watch the development of this experiment. Think not so unworthily of me, my husband! Tell me all the risk we run; and fear not that I shall shrink, for my share in it is far less than your own!"

"No, no, Georgiana!" said Aylmer impatiently, "it must not be."

"I submit," replied she calmly. "And, Aylmer, I shall quaff whatever draught you bring me; but it will be on the same principle that would induce me to take a dose of poison, if offered by your hand."

"My noble wife," said Aylmer, deeply moved, "I knew not the height and depth of your nature, until now. Nothing shall be concealed. Know, then, that this Crimson Hand, superficial as it seems, has clutched its grasp into your being, with a strength of which I had no previous conception. I have already administered agents powerful enough to do aught except to change your entire physical system. Only one thing remains to be tried. If that fail us, we are ruined!"

"Why did you hesitate to tell me this?" asked she.

"Because, Georgiana," said Aylmer, in a low voice, "there is danger!"

"Danger? There is but one danger—that this horrible stigma shall be left upon my cheek!" cried Georgiana. "Remove it! remove it!—whatever be the cost—or we shall both go mad!"

"Heaven knows, your words are too true," said Aylmer, sadly. "And now, dearest, return to your boudoir. In a little while, all will be tested."

He conducted her back, and took leave of her with a solemn tenderness, which spoke far more than his words how much was now at stake. After his departure, Georgiana became wrapt in musings. She considered the character of Aylmer, and did it completer justice than at any previous moment. Her heart exulted, while it trembled, at his honorable love, so pure and lofty that it would accept nothing less than perfection, nor miserably make itself contented with an earthlier nature than he had dreamed of. She felt how much more precious was such a sentiment, than that meaner kind which would have borne with the imperfection for her sake, and have been guilty of treason to holy love, by degrading its perfect idea to the level of the actual. And, with her whole spirit, she prayed, that, for a single moment, she might satisfy his highest and deepest conception. Longer than one moment, she well knew, it could not be; for his spirit was ever on the march—ever ascending—and each instant required something that was beyond the scope of the instant before.

The sound of her husband's footsteps aroused her. He bore a crystal goblet, containing a liquor colorless as water, but bright enough to be the draught of immortality. Aylmer was pale; but it seemed rather the consequence of a highly wrought state of mind, and tension of spirit, than of fear or doubt.

"The concoction of the draught has been perfect," said he, in answer to Georgiana's look. "Unless all my science have deceived me, it cannot fail."

"Save on your account, my dearest Aylmer," observed his wife, "I might wish to put off this birth-mark of mortality by relinquishing mortality itself, in preference to any other mode. Life is but a sad possession of those who have attained precisely the degree of moral advancement at which I stand. Were I weaker and blinder, it might be happiness. Were I stronger, it might be endured hopefully. But, being what I find myself, methinks I am of all mortals the most fit to die."

"You are fit for heaven without tasting death!" replied her husband. "But why do we speak of dying? The draught cannot fail. Behold its effect upon this plant!"

On the window-seat there stood a geranium, diseased with yellow blotches, which had overspread all its leaves. Aylmer poured a small quantity of the liquid upon the soil in which it grew. In a little time, when the roots of the plant had taken up the moisture, the unsightly blotches began to be extinguished in a living verdure.

"There needed no proof," said Georgiana, quietly. "Give me the goblet. I joyfully stake all upon your word."

"Drink then, thou lofty creature!" exclaimed Aylmer, with fervid admiration. "There is no taint of imperfection on thy spirit. Thy sensible frame, too, shall soon be all perfect!"

She quaffed the liquid, and returned the goblet to his hand.

"It is grateful," said she, with a placid smile. "Methinks it is like water from a heavenly fountain; for it contains I know not what of unobtrusive fragrance and deliciousness. It allays a feverish thirst, that had parched me for many days. Now, dearest, let me sleep. My earthly senses are closing over my spirit, like the leaves round the heart of a rose, at sunset."

She spoke the last words with a gentle reluctance, as if it required almost more energy than she could command to pronounce the faint and lingering syllables. Scarcely had they loitered through her lips, ere she was lost in slumber. Aylmer sat by her side, watching her aspect with the emotions proper to a man, the whole value of whose existence was involved in the process now to be tested. Mingled with this mood, however, was the philosophic investigation, characteristic of the man of science. Not the minutest symptom escaped him. A heightened flush of the cheek—a slight irregularity of breath—a quiver of the eyelid—a hardly perceptible tremor through the frame—such were the details which, as the moments passed, he wrote down in his folio volume. Intense thought had set its stamp upon every previous page of that volume; but the thoughts of years were all concentrated upon the last.

While thus employed, he failed not to gaze often at the fatal Hand, and not without a shudder. Yet once, by a strange and unaccountable impulse, he pressed it with his lips. His spirit recoiled, however, in the very act, and Georgiana, out of the midst of her deep sleep, moved uneasily and murmured, as if in remonstrance. Again, Aylmer resumed his watch. Nor was it without avail. The Crimson Hand, which at first had been strongly visible upon the marble paleness of Georgiana's cheek now grew more faintly outlined. She remained not less pale than ever; but the birth-mark, with every breath that came and went, lost somewhat of its former distinctness. Its presence had been awful; its departure was more awful still. Watch the stain of the rainbow fading out of the sky; and you will know how that mysterious symbol passed away.

"By Heaven, it is well nigh gone!" said Aylmer to himself, in almost irrepressible ecstasy. "I can scarcely trace it now. Success! Success! And now it is like the faintest rose-color. The slightest flush of blood across her cheek would overcome it. But she is so pale!"

He drew aside the window-curtain, and suffered the light of natural day to fall into the room, and rest upon her cheek. At the same time, he heard a gross, hoarse chuckle, which he had long known as his servant Aminadab's expression of delight.

"Ah clod! Ah, earthly mass!" cried Aylmer, laughing in a sort of frenzy. "You have served me well! Matter and Spirit—Earth and Heaven—have both done their part in this! Laugh, thing of senses! You have earned the right to laugh."

These exclamations broke Georgiana's sleep. She slowly unclosed her eyes, and gazed into the mirror, which her husband had arranged for that purpose. A faint smile flitted over her lips, when she recognized how barely perceptible was now that Crimson Hand, which had once blazed forth with such disastrous brilliancy as to scare away all their happiness. But then her eyes sought Aylmer's face, with a trouble and anxiety that he could by no means account for.

"My poor Aylmer!" murmured she.

"Poor? Nay, richest! Happiest! Most favored!" exclaimed he. "My peerless bride, it is successful! You are perfect!"

"My poor Aylmer!" she repeated, with a more than human tenderness. "You have aimed loftily!—you have done nobly! Do not repent, that, with so high and pure a feeling, you have rejected the best that earth could offer. Aylmer—dearest Aylmer—I am dying!"

Alas, it was too true! The fatal Hand had grappled with the mystery of life, and was the bond by which an angelic spirit kept itself in union with a mortal frame. As the last crimson tint of the birth-mark—that sole token of human imperfection—faded from her cheek, the parting breath of the now perfect woman passed into the atmosphere, and her soul, lingering a moment near her husband, took its heavenward flight. Then a hoarse, chuckling laugh was heard again! Thus ever does the gross Fatality of Earth exult in its invariable triumph over the immortal essence, which, in this dim sphere of half-development, demands the completeness of a higher state. Yet, had Aylmer reached a profounder wisdom, he need not thus have flung away the happiness, which would have woven his mortal life of the self-same texture with the celestial. The momentary circumstance was too strong for him; he failed to look beyond the shadowy scope of Time, and living once for all in Eternity, to find the perfect Future in the present.

1843

RAPPACCINI'S DAUGHTER*

FROM THE WRITINGS OF AUBÉPINE[1]

We do not remember to have seen any translated specimens of the productions of M. de l'Aubépine; a fact the less to be wondered at, as his very name is unknown to many of his own countrymen, as well as to the student of foreign literature. As a writer, he seems to occupy an unfortunate position between the Transcendental-ists (who, under one name or another, have their share in all the current literature of the world), and the great body of pen-and-ink men who address the intellect and sympathies of the multitude. If not too refined, at all events too remote, too shadowy and unsubstantial in his modes of development, to suit the taste of the latter class, and yet too popular to satisfy the spiritual or metaphysical requisitions of the former, he must necessarily find himself without an audience; except here and there an individual, or possibly an isolated clique. His writings, to do them justice, are not altogether destitute of fancy and originality; they might have won him greater reputation but for an inveterate love of allegory, which is apt to invest his plots and characters with the aspect of scenery and people in the clouds, and to steal away the human warmth out of his conceptions. His fictions are sometimes historical, sometimes of the present day, and sometimes, so far as can be discov-ered, have little or no reference either to time or space. In any case, he generally contents himself with a very slight embroidery of outward manners,—the faintest possible counterfeit of real life,—and endeavors to create an interest by some less obvious peculiarity of the subject. Occasionally, a breath of nature, a rain-drop of pathos and tenderness, or a gleam of humor, will find its way into the midst of his fantastic imagery, and make us feel as if, after all, we were yet within the limits of our native earth. We will only add to this very cursory notice, that M. de l'Aubépine's productions, if the reader chance to take them in precisely the proper point of view, may amuse a leisure hour as well as those of a brighter man; if otherwise, they can hardly fail to look excessively like nonsense.

Our author is voluminous; he continues to write and publish with as much praiseworthy and indefatigable prolixity, as if his efforts were crowned with the brilliant success that so justly attends those of Eugene Sue.[2] His first appearance was by a collection of stories, in a long series of volumes, entitled "*Contes deux fois racontées.*"[3] The titles of some of his more recent works (we quote from memory) are as follows:—"*Le Voyage Céleste à Chemin de Fer,*" 3 tom. 1838. "*Le nouveau Père Adam et la nouvelle Mère Eve,*" 2 tom. 1839. "*Roderic; ou le Serpent à l'estomac,*" 2 tom. 1840. "*Le Culte du Feu,*" a folio volume of ponder-ous research into the religion and ritual of the old Persian Ghebers,[4] published in 1841. "*La Soirée du Chateau en Espagne,*" I tom. 8vo. 1842; and "*L'Artiste du*

---

* First published in *The Democratic Review* in 1844 and included in *Mosses From an Old Manse* (1846).

[1] "Hawthorne" (French).   [2] Sue (1804–1857) was a popular French novelist.

[3] "*Twice-Told Tales*" (French), published in 1837. Hawthorne's tongue-in-cheek account of his own career concludes with the titles of some of his tales translated into French: "The Celestial Railroad," "The New Adam and the New Eve," "Egotism; or the Bosom Serpent," "Fire-Worship," and "The Artist of the Beautiful; or the Mechanical Butterfly." With these titles he includes one nonexistent work, *La Soirée du Chateau en Espagne* (*The Evening in a Castle in Spain*). The mock-bibliographi-cal citations include the supposed volume, or tom. (tome) and size ("8vo" means octavo, a book of pages folded into eight leaves; and "4to," quarto, a book of pages folded into four leaves) of these works, but all were short stories.

[4] Zoroastrians.

Beau; ou le Papillon Mécanique," 5 tom. 4to. 1843. Our somewhat wearisome perusal of this startling catalogue of volumes has left behind it a certain personal affection and sympathy, though by no means admiration, for M. de l'Aubépine; and we would fain do the little in our power towards introducing him favorably to the American public. The ensuing tale is a translation of his *"Beatrice; ou la Belle Empoisonneuse,"* recently published in *"La Revue Anti-Aristocratique."*[5] This journal, edited by the Comte de Bearhaven,[6] has, for some years past, led the defence of liberal principles and popular rights, with a faithfulness and ability worthy of all praise.

A young man, named Giovanni Guasconti, came, very long ago, from the more southern region of Italy, to pursue his studies at the University of Padua.[7] Giovanni, who had but a scanty supply of gold ducats in his pocket, took lodgings in a high and gloomy chamber of an old edifice, which looked not unworthy to have been the palace of a Paduan noble, and which, in fact, exhibited over its entrance the armorial bearings of a family long since extinct. The young stranger, who was not unstudied in the great poem of his country, recollected that one of the ancestors of this family, and perhaps an occupant of this very mansion, had been pictured by Dante[8] as a partaker of the immortal agonies of his Inferno. These reminiscences and associations, together with the tendency to heart-break natural to a young man for the first time out of his native sphere, caused Giovanni to sigh heavily, as he looked around the desolate and ill-furnished apartment.

"Holy Virgin, Signor," cried old dame Lisabetta, who, won by the youth's remarkable beauty of a person, was kindly endeavoring to give the chamber a habitable air, "what a sigh was that to come out of a young man's heart! Do you find this old mansion gloomy? For the love of heaven, then, put your head out of the window, and you will see as bright sunshine as you have left in Naples."

Guasconti mechanically did as the old woman advised, but could not quite agree with her that the Paduan sunshine was as cheerful as that of southern Italy. Such as it was, however, it fell upon a garden beneath the window, and expended its fostering influences on a variety of plants, which seemed to have been cultivated with exceeding care.

"Does this garden belong to the house?" asked Giovanni.

"Heaven forbid, Signor!—unless it were fruitful of better pot-herbs than any that grow there now," answered old Lisabetta. "No; that garden is cultivated by the own hands of Signor Giacomo Rappaccini, the famous Doctor, who, I warrant him, has been heard of as far as Naples. It is said that he distils these plants into medicines that are as potent as a charm. Oftentimes you may see the Signor Doctor at work, and perchance the Signora his daughter, too, gathering the strange flowers that grow in the garden."

The old woman had now done what she could for the aspect of the chamber, and, commending the young man to the protection of the saints, took her departure.

Giovanni still found no better occupation than to look down into the garden beneath his window. From its appearance, he judged it to be one of those botanic

---

[5] "Beatrice; or the Poisonous Beauty," recently published in *"The Democratic Review"* (French).
[6] John O'Sullivan, Hawthorne's friend.   [7] Padua, Italy.
[8] Dante Alighieri (1265–1321), the poet known for *The Divine Comedy,* the first section of which is *The Inferno.*

gardens, which were of earlier date in Padua than elsewhere in Italy, or in the world. Or, not improbably, it might once have been the pleasure-place of an opulent family; for there was the ruin of a marble fountain in the centre, sculptured with rare art, but so wofully shattered that it was impossible to trace the original design from the chaos of remaining fragments. The water, however, continued to gush and sparkle into the sunbeams as cheerfully as ever. A little gurgling sound ascended to the young man's window, and made him feel as if the fountain were an immortal spirit, that sung its song unceasingly, and without heeding the vicissitudes around it; while one century embodied it in marble, and another scattered the perishable garniture on the soil. All about the pool into which the water subsided, grew various plants, that seemed to require a plentiful supply of moisture for the nourishment of gigantic leaves, and, in some instances, flowers gorgeously magnificent. There was one shrub in particular, set in marble vase in the midst of the pool, that bore a profusion of purple blossoms, each of which had the lustre and richness of a gem; and the whole together made a show so resplendent that it seemed enough to illuminate the garden, even had there been no sunshine. Every portion of the soil was peopled with plants and herbs, which, if less beautiful, still bore tokens of assiduous care; as if all had their individual virtues, known to the scientific mind that fostered them. Some were placed in urns, rich with old carving, and others in common garden-pots; some crept serpent-like along the ground, or climbed on high, using whatever means of ascent was offered them. One plant had wreathed itself round a statue or Vertumnus,[9] which was thus quite veiled and shrouded in a drapery of hanging foliage, so happily arranged that it might have served a sculptor for a study.

While Giovanni stood at the window, he heard a rustling behind a screen of leaves, and became aware that a person was at work in the garden. His figure soon emerged into view, and showed itself to be that of no common laborer, but a tall, emaciated, sallow, and sickly-looking man, dressed in a scholar's garb of black. He was beyond the middle term of life, with grey hair, a thin grey beard, and a face singularly marked with intellect and cultivation, but which could never, even in his more youthful days, have expressed much warmth of heart.

Nothing could exceed the intentness with which this scientific gardener examined every shrub which grew in his path; it seemed as if he was looking into their inmost nature, making observations in regard to their creative essence, and discovering why one leaf grew in this shape, and another in that, and wherefore such and such flowers differed among themselves in hue and perfume. Nevertheless, in spite of this deep intelligence on his part, there was no approach to intimacy between himself and these vegetable existences. On the contrary, he avoided their actual touch, or the direct inhaling of their odors, with a caution that impressed Giovanni most disagreeably; for the man's demeanor was that of one walking among malignant influences, such as savage beasts, or deadly snakes, or evil spirits, which, should he allow them one moment of license, would wreak upon him some terrible fatality. It was strangely frightful to the young man's imagination, to see this air of insecurity in a person cultivating a garden, that most simple and innocent of human toils, and which had been alike the joy and labor of the unfallen parents of the race. Was this garden, then, the Eden of the present world?— and this man, with such a perception of harm in what his own hands caused to grow, was he the Adam?

[9] According to Roman myth, the god of orchards and fruit, who presided over the seasons.

The distrustful gardener, while plucking away the dead leaves or pruning the too luxuriant growth of the shrubs, defended his hands with a pair of thick gloves. Nor were these his only armor. When, in his walk through the garden, he came to the magnificent plant that hung its purple gems beside the marble fountain, he placed a kind of mask over his mouth and nostrils, as if all this beauty did but conceal a deadlier malice. But finding his task still too dangerous, he drew back, removed the mask, and called loudly, but in the infirm voice of a person affected with inward disease:

"Beatrice!—Beatrice!"[10]

"Here am I, my father! What would you?" cried a rich and youthful voice from the window of the opposite house; a voice as rich as a tropical sunset, and which made Giovanni, though he knew not why, think of deep hues of purple or crimson, and of perfumes heavily delectable.—"Are you in the garden?"

"Yes, Beatrice," answered the gardener, "and I need your help."

Soon there emerged from under a sculptured portal the figure of a young girl, arrayed with as much richness of taste as the most splendid of the flowers, beautiful as the day, and with a bloom so deep and vivid that one shade more would have been too much. She looked redundant with life, health, and energy; all of which attributes were bound down and compressed, as it were, and girdled tensely, in their luxuriance, by her virgin zone.[11] Yet Giovanni's fancy must have grown morbid, while he looked down into the garden; for the impression which the fair stranger made upon him was as if here were another flower, the human sister of those vegetable ones, as beautiful as they—more beautiful than the richest of them—but still to be touched only with a glove, nor to be approached without a mask. As Beatrice came down the garden path, it was observable that she handled and inhaled the odor of several of the plants, which her father had most sedulously avoided.

"Here, Beatrice," said the latter,—"see how many needful offices require to be done to our chief treasure. Yet, shattered as I am, my life might pay the penalty of approaching it so closely as circumstances demand. Henceforth, I fear, this plant must be consigned to your sole charge."

"And gladly will I undertake it," cried again the rich tones of the young lady, as she bent towards the magnificent plant, and opened her arms as if to embrace it. "Yes, my sister, my splendor, it shall be Beatrice's task to nurse and serve thee; and thou shalt reward her with thy kisses and perfumed breath, which to her is as the breath of life!"

Then, with all the tenderness in her manner that was so strikingly expressed in her words, she busied herself with such attentions as the plant seemed to require; and Giovanni, at his lofty window, rubbed his eyes, and almost doubted whether it were a girl tending her favorite flower, or one sister performing the duties of affection to another. The scene soon terminated. Whether Doctor Rappaccini had finished his labors in the garden, or that his watchful eye had caught the stranger's face, he now took his daughter's arm and retired. Night was already closing in; oppressive exhalations seemed to proceed from the plants, and steal upward past the open window; and Giovanni, closing the lattice,[12] went to his couch, and

---

[10] Beatrice Portinari (1266–1290) was Dante's idealized love, celebrated in *The Divine Comedy* as the guide who leads Dante the pilgrim to a vision of Paradise.

[11] A wide belt customarily worn by a young unmarried woman.

[12] A shutter made of crossed wooden strips.

dreamed of a rich flower and beautiful girl. Flower and maiden were different and yet the same, and fraught with some strange peril in either shape.

But there is an influence in the light of morning that tends to rectify whatever errors of fancy, or even of judgment, we may have incurred during the sun's decline, or among the shadows of the night, or in the less wholesome glow of moonshine. Giovanni's first movement on starting from sleep, was to throw open the window, and gaze down into the garden which his dreams had made so fertile of mysteries. He was surprised, and a little ashamed, to find how real and matter-of-fact an affair it proved to be, in the first rays of the sun, which gilded the dew-drops that hung upon leaf and blossom, and, while giving a brighter beauty to each rare flower, brought everything within the limits of ordinary experience. The young man rejoiced, that, in the heart of the barren city, he had the privilege of overlooking this spot of lovely and luxuriant vegetation. It would serve, he said to himself, as a symbolic language, to keep him in communion with Nature. Neither the sickly and thought-worn Doctor Giacomo Rappaccini, it is true, nor his brilliant daughter, were now visible; so that Giovanni could not determine how much of the singularity which he attributed to both, was due to their own qualities, and how much to his wonder-working fancy. But he was inclined to take a most rational view of the whole matter.

In the course of the day, he paid his respects to Signor Pietro Baglioni, professor of medicine in the University, a physician of eminent repute, to whom Giovanni had brought a letter of introduction. The Professor was an elderly personage, apparently of genial nature, and habits that might almost be called jovial; he kept the young man to dinner, and made himself very agreeable by the freedom and liveliness of his conversation, especially when warmed by a flask or two of Tuscan[13] wine. Giovanni, conceiving that men of science, inhabitants of the same city, must needs be on familiar terms with one another, took an opportunity to mention the name of Doctor Rappaccini. But the Professor did not respond with so much cordiality as he had anticipated.

"Ill would it become a teacher of the divine art of medicine," said Professor Pietro Baglioni, in answer to a question of Giovanni, "to withhold due and well-considered praise of a physician so eminently skilled as Rappaccini. But, on the other hand, I should answer it but scantily to my conscience, were I to permit a worthy youth like yourself, Signor Giovanni, the son of an ancient friend, to imbibe erroneous ideas respecting a man who might hereafter chance to hold your life and death in his hands. The truth is, our worshipful Doctor Rappaccini has as much science as any member of the faculty—with perhaps one single exception—in Padua, or all Italy. But there are certain grave objections to his professional character."

"And what are they?" asked the young man.

"Has my friend Giovanni any disease of body or heart, that he is so inquisitive about physicians?" said the Professor, with a smile. "But as for Rappaccini, it is said of him—and I, who know the man well, can answer for its truth—that he cares infinitely more for science than for mankind. His patients are interesting to him only as subjects for some new experiment. He would sacrifice human life, his own among the rest, or whatever else was dearest him, for the sake of adding so much as a grain of mustard-seed to the great heap of his accumulated knowledge."

"Methinks he is an awful[14] man, indeed," remarked Guasconti, mentally recall-

---

[13] From Tuscany, a region in Italy.   [14] Awe-inspiring.

ing the cold and purely intellectual aspect of Rappaccini. "And yet, worshipful Professor, is it not a noble spirit? Are there many men capable of so spiritual a love of science?"

"God forbid," answered the Professor, somewhat testily—"at least, unless they take sounder views of the healing art than those adopted by Rappaccini. It is his theory, that all medicinal virtues are comprised within those substances which we term vegetable poisons. These he cultivates with his own hands, and is said even to have produced new varieties of poison, more horribly deleterious than Nature, without the assistance of this learned person, would ever have plagued the world withal. That the Signor Doctor does less mischief than might be expected, with such dangerous substances, is undeniable. Now and then, it must be owned, he has effected—or seemed to effect—a marvellous cure. But, to tell you my private mind, Signor Giovanni, he should receive little credit for such instances of success—they being probably the work of chance—but should be held strictly accountable for his failures, which may justly be considered his own work."

The youth might have taken Baglioni's opinions with many grains of allowance, had he know that there was a professional warfare of long continuance between him and Doctor Rappaccini, in which the latter was generally thought to have gained the advantage. If the reader be inclined to judge for himself, we refer him to certain black-letter tracts[15] on both sides, preserved in the medical department of the University of Padua.

"I know not, most learned Professor," returned Giovanni, after musing on what had been said of Rappaccini's exclusive zeal for science—"I know not how dearly this physician may love his art; but surely there is one object more dear to him. He has a daughter."

"Aha!" cried the Professor with a laugh. "So now our friend Giovanni's secret is out. You have heard of this daughter, whom all the young men in Padua are wild about, though not half a dozen have ever had the good hap to see her face. I know little of the Signora Beatrice, save that Rappaccini is said to have instructed her deeply in his science, and that, young and beautiful as fame reports her, she is already qualified to fill a professor's chair. Perchance her father destines her for mine! Other absurd rumors there be, not worth talking about, or listening to. So now, Signor Giovanni, drink off your glass of Lacryma."[16]

Guasconti returned to his lodgings somewhat heated with the wine he had quaffed, and which caused his brain to swim with strange fantasies in reference to Doctor Rappaccini and the beautiful Beatrice. On his way, happening to pass by a florist's, he bought a fresh bouquet of flowers.

Ascending to his chamber, he seated himself near the window, but within the shadow thrown by the depth of the wall, so that he could look down into the garden with little risk of being discovered. All beneath his eye was a solitude. The strange plants were basking in the sunshine, and now and then nodding gently to one another, as if in acknowledgment of sympathy and kindred. In the midst, by the shattered fountain, grew the magnificent shrub, with its purple gems clustering all over it; they glowed in the air, and gleamed back again out of the depths of the pool, which thus seemed to overflow with colored radiance from the rich reflection that was steeped in it. At first, as we have said, the garden was a solitude. Soon, however,—as Giovanni had half-hoped, half-feared, would be the case,—a

---

[15] A document printed with heavy-faced type.
[16] Lachryma Christi, or "Tears of Christ", (Latin), a well-known Italian white wine.

figure appeared beneath the antique sculptured portal, and came down between the rows of plants, inhaling their various perfumes, as if she were one of those beings of old classic fable, that lived upon sweet odors. On again beholding Beatrice, the young man was even startled to perceive how much her beauty exceeded his recollection of it; so brilliant, so vivid was its character, that she glowed amid the sunlight, and, as Giovanni whispered to himself, positively illuminated the more shadowy intervals of the garden path. Her face being now more revealed than on the former occasion, he was struck by its expression of simplicity and sweetness; qualities that had not entered into his idea of her character, and which made him ask anew, what manner of mortal she might be. Nor did he fail again to observe, or imagine, an analogy between the beautiful girl and the gorgeous shrub that hung its gem-like flowers over the fountain; a resemblance which Beatrice seemed to have indulged a fantastic humor in heightening, both by the arrangement of her dress and the selection of its hues.

Approaching the shrub, she threw open her arms, as with a passionate ardor, and drew its branches into an intimate embrace; so intimate, that her features were hidden in its leafy bosom, and her glistening ringlets all intermingled with the flowers.

"Give me thy breath, my sister," exclaimed Beatrice; "for I am faint with common air! And give me this flower of thine, which I separate with gentlest fingers from the stem, and place it close beside my heart."

With these words, the beautiful daughter of Rappaccini plucked one of the richest blossoms of the shrub, and was about to fasten it in her bosom. But now, unless Giovanni's draughts of wine had bewildered his senses, a singular incident occurred. A small orange-colored reptile, of the lizard or chameleon species, chanced to be creeping along the path, just at the feet of Beatrice. It appeared to Giovanni—but, at the distance from which he gazed, he could scarcely have seen anything so minute—it appeared to him, however, that a drop or two of moisture from the broken stem of the flower descended upon the lizard's head. For an instant, the reptile contorted itself violently, and then lay motionless in the sunshine. Beatrice observed this remarkable phenomenon, and crossed herself, sadly, but without surprise; nor did she therefore hesitate to arrange the fatal flower in her bosom. There it blushed, and almost glimmered with the dazzling effect of a precious stone, adding to her dress and aspect the one appropriate charm, which nothing else in the world could have supplied. But Giovanni, out of the shadow of his window, bent forward and shrank back, and murmured and trembled.

"Am I awake? Have I my senses?" said he to himself. "What is this being?—beautiful, shall I call her?—or inexpressibly terrible?"

Beatrice now strayed carelessly through the garden, approaching closer beneath Giovanni's window, so that he was compelled to thrust his head quite out of its concealment in order to gratify the intense and painful curiosity which she excited. At this moment, there came a beautiful insect over the garden wall; it had perhaps wandered through the city and found no flowers nor verdure among those antique haunts of men, until the heavy perfumes of Doctor Rappaccini's shrubs had lured it from afar. Without alighting on the flowers, this winged brightness seemed to be attracted by Beatrice, and lingered in the air and fluttered about her head. Now, here it could not be but that Giovanni Guasconti's eyes deceived him. Be that as it might, he fancied that while Beatrice was gazing at the insect with childish delight, it grew faint and fell at her feet;—its bright wings shivered; it was dead—from no cause that he could discern, unless it were the atmosphere of her breath.

Again Beatrice crossed herself and sighed heavily, as she bent over the dead insect.

An impulsive movement of Giovanni drew her eyes to the window. There she beheld the beautiful head of the young man—rather a Grecian than an Italian head, with fair, regular features, and a glistening of gold among his ringlets—gazing down upon her like a being that hovered in mid-air. Scarcely knowing what he did, Giovanni threw down the bouquet which he had hitherto held in his hand.

"Signora," said he, "there are pure and healthful flowers. Wear them for the sake of Giovanni Guasconti!"

"Thanks, Signor," replied Beatrice, with her rich voice, that came forth as it were like a gush of music; and with a mirthful expression half childish and half woman-like. "I accept your gift, and would fain recompense it with this precious purple flower; but if I toss it into the air, it will not reach you. So Signor Guasconti must even content himself with my thanks."

She lifted the bouquet from the ground, and then as if inwardly ashamed at having stepped aside from her maidenly reserve to respond to a stranger's greeting, passed swiftly homeward through the garden. But, few as the moments were, it seemed to Giovanni when she was on the point of vanishing beneath the sculptured portal, that his beautiful bouquet was already beginning to wither in her grasp. It was an idle thought; there could be no possibility of distinguishing a faded flower from a fresh one at so great a distance.

For many days after this incident, the young man avoided the window that looked into Doctor Rappaccini's garden, as if something ugly and monstrous would have blasted his eye-sight, had he been betrayed into a glance. He felt conscious of having put himself, to a certain extent, within the influence of an unintelligible power, by the communication which he had opened with Beatrice. The wisest course would have been, if his heart were in any real danger, to quit his lodgings and Padua itself, at once; the next wiser, to have accustomed himself, as far as possible, to the familiar and day-light view of Beatrice; thus bringing her rigidly and systematically within the limits of ordinary experience. Least of all, while avoiding her sight, ought Giovanni to have remained so near this extraordinary being, that the proximity and possibility even of intercouse, should give a kind of substance and reality to the wild vagaries which his imagination ran riot continually in producing. Guasconti had not a deep heart—or at all events, its depths were not sounded now—but he had a quick fancy, and an ardent southern temperament, which rose every instant to a higher fever-pitch. Whether or no Beatrice possessed those terrible attributes—that fatal breath—the affinity with those so beautiful and deadly flowers—which were indicated by what Giovanni had witnessed, she had at least instilled a fierce and subtle poison into his system. It was not love, although her rich beauty was a madness to him; nor horror, even while he fancied her spirit to be imbued with the same baneful essence that seemed to pervade her physical frame; but a wild offspring of both love and horror that had each parent in it, and burned like one and shivered like the other. Giovanni knew not what to dread; still less did he know what to hope; yet hope and dread kept a continual warfare in his breast, alternately vanquishing one another and starting up afresh to renew the contest. Blessed are all simple emotions, be they dark or bright! It is the lurid intermixture of the two that produces the illuminating blaze of the infernal regions.

Sometimes he endeavored to assuage the fever of his spirit by a rapid walk through the streets of Padua, or beyond its gates; his footsteps kept time with the throbbings of his brain, so that the walk was apt to accelerate itself to a race. One day, he found himself arrested; his arm was seized by a portly personage who had turned back on recognizing the young man, and expended much breath in overtaking him.

"Signor Giovanni!—stay, my young friend!" cried he. "Have you forgotten me? That might well be the case, if I were as much altered as yourself."

It was Baglioni, whom Giovanni had avoided, ever since their first meeting, from a doubt that the Professor's sagacity would look too deeply into his secrets. Endeavoring to recover himself, he stared forth wildly from his inner world into the outer one, and spoke like a man in a dream:

"Yes; I am Giovanni Guasconti. You are Professor Pietro Baglioni. Now let me pass!"

"Not yet—not yet, Signor Giovanni Guasconti," said the Professor, smiling, but at the same time scruntizing the youth with an earnest glance.—"What; did I grow up side by side with your father, and shall his son pass me like a stranger, in these old streets of Padua? Stand still, Signor Giovanni; for we must have a word or two, before we part."

"Speedily, then, most worshipful Professor, speedily!" said Giovanni, with feverish impatience. "Does not your worship see that I am in haste?"

Now, while he was speaking, there came a man in black along the street, stooping and moving feebly, like a person in inferior health. His face was all overspread with a most sickly and sallow hue, but yet so pervaded with an expression of piercing and active intellect, that an observer might easily have overlooked the merely physical attributes, and have seen only this wonderful energy. As he passed, this person exchanged a cold and distant salutation with Baglioni, but fixed his eyes upon Giovanni with an intentness that seemed to bring out whatever was within him worthy of notice. Nevertheless, there was a peculiar quietness in the look, as if taking merely a speculative, not a human, interest in the young man.

"It is Doctor Rappaccini!" whispered the Professor, when the stranger had passed.—"Has he ever seen your face before?"

"Not that I know," answered Giovanni, starting at the name.

"He *has* seen you!—he must have seen you!" said Baglioni, hastily. "For some purpose or other, this man of science is making a study of you. I know that look of his! It is the same that coldly illuminates his face, as he bends over a bird, a mouse, or a butterfly, which, in pursuance of some experiment, he has killed by the perfume of a flower;—a look as deep as Nature itself, but without Nature's warmth of love. Signor Giovanni, I will stake my life upon it, you are the subject of one of Rappaccini's experiments!"

"Will you make a fool of me?" cried Giovanni, passionately. "*That,* Signor Professor, were an untoward experiment."

"Patience, patience!" replied the imperturbable Professor.—"I tell thee, my poor Giovanni, that Rappaccini has a scientific interest in thee. Thou hast fallen into fearful hands! And the Signora Beatrice? What part does she act in this mystery?"

But Guasconti, finding Baglioni's pertinacity intolerable, here broke away, and was gone before the Professor could again seize his arm. He looked after the young man intently, and shook his head.

"This must not be," said Baglioni to himself. "The youth is the son of my old friend, and shall not come to any harm from which the arcana of medical science can preserve him. Besides, it is too insufferable an impertinence in Rappaccini, thus to snatch the lad out of my own hands, as I may say, and make use of him for his infernal experiments. This daughter of his! It shall be looked to. Perchance, most learned Rappaccini, I may foil you where you little dream of it!"

Meanwhile, Giovanni had pursued a circuitous route, and at length found himself at the door of his lodgings. As he crossed the threshold, he was met by old Lisabetta, who smirked and smiled, and was evidently desirous to attract his attention; vainly, however, as the ebullition of his feelings had momentarily subsided into a cold and dull vacuity. He turned his eyes full upon the withered face that was puckering itself into a smile, but seemed to behold it not. The old dame, therefore, laid her grasp upon his cloak.

"Signor!—Signor!" whispered she, still with a smile over the whole breadth of her visage, so that it looked not unlike a grotesque carving in wood, darkened by centuries—"Listen, Signor! There is a private entrance into the garden!"

"What do you say?" exclaimed Giovanni, turning quickly about, as if an inanimate thing should start into feverish life.—"A private entrance into Doctor Rappaccini's garden!"

"Hush! hush!—not so loud!" whispered Lisabetta, putting her hand over his mouth. "Yes; into the worshipful Doctor's garden, where you may see all his fine shrubbery. Many a young man in Padua would give gold to be admitted among those flowers."

Giovanni put a piece of gold into her hand.

"Show me the way," said he.

A surmise, probably excited by his conversation with Baglioni, crossed his mind, that this interposition of old Lisabetta might perchance be connected with the intrigue, whatever were its nature, in which the Professor seemed to suppose that Doctor Rappaccini was involving him. But such a suspicion, though it disturbed Giovanni, was inadequte to restrain him. The instant that he was aware of the possibility of approaching Beatrice, it seemed an absolute necessity of his existence to do so. It mattered not whether she were angel or demon; he was irrevocably within her sphere, and must obey the law that whirled him onward, in ever lessening circles, towards a result which he did not attempt to foreshadow. And yet, strange to say, there came across him a sudden doubt, whether this intense interest on his part were not delusory—whether it were really of so deep and positive a nature as to justify him in now thrusting himself into an incalculable position—whether it were not merely the fantasy of a young man's brain, only slightly, or not at all, connected with his heart!

He paused—hesitated—turned half about—but again went on. His withered guide led him along several obscure passages, and finally undid a door, through which, as it was opened, there came the sight and sound of rustling leaves, with the broken sunshine glimmering among them. Giovanni stepped forth, and forcing himself through the entanglement of a shrub that wreathed its tendrils over the hidden entrance, he stood beneath his own window, in the open area of Doctor Rappaccini's garden.

How often is it the case, that, when impossibilities have come to pass, and dreams have condensed their misty substance into tangible realities, we find ourselves calm, and even coldly self-possessed, amid circumstances which it would have been a delirium of joy or agony to anticipate! Fate delights to thwart us thus. Passion will choose his own time to rush upon the scene, and lingers sluggishly behind, when an appropriate adjustment of events would seem to summon his appearance. So was it now with Giovanni. Day after day, his pulses had throbbed with feverish blood, at the improbable idea of an interview with Beatrice, and of standing with her, face to face, in this very garden, basking in the Oriental sunshine of her beauty, and snatching from her full gaze the mystery which he deemed the riddle of his own existence. But now there was a singular and untimely equanimity within his breast. He threw a glance around the garden to discover if Beatrice or her father were present, and perceiving that he was alone, began a critical observation of the plants.

The aspect of one and all of them dissatisfied him; their gorgeousness seemed fierce, passionate, and even unnatural. There was hardly an individual shrub which a wanderer, straying by himself through a forest, would not have been startled to find growing wild, as if an unearthly face had glared at him out of the thicket. Several, also, would have shocked a delicate instinct by an appearance of artificialness, indicating that there had been such commixture, and, as it were, adultery of various vegetable species, that the production was no longer of God's making, but the monstrous offspring of man's depraved fancy, glowing with only an evil mockery of beauty. They were probably the result of experiment, which, in one or two cases, had succeeded in mingling plants individually lovely into a compound possessing the questionable and ominous character that distinguished the whole growth of the garden. In fine, Giovanni recognized but two or three plants in the collection, and those of a kind that he well knew to be poisonous. While busy with these contemplations, he heard the rustling of a silken garment, and turning, beheld Beatrice emerging from beneath the sculptured portal.

Giovanni had not considered with himself what should be his deportment; whether he should apologize for his intrusion into the garden, or assume that he was there with the privity, at least, if not by the desire, of Doctor Rappaccini or his daughter. But Beatrice's manner placed him at his ease, though leaving him still in doubt by what agency he had gained admittance. She came lightly along the path, and met him near the broken fountain. There was surprise in her face, but brightened by a simple and kind expression of pleasure.

"You are a connoisseur in flowers, Signor," said Beatrice with a smile, alluding to the bouquet which he had flung her from the window. "It is no marvel, therefore, if the sight of my father's rare collection has tempted you to take a nearer view. If he were here, he could tell you many strange and interesting facts as to the nature and habits of these shrubs, for he has spent a life-time in such studies, and this garden is his world."

"And yourself, lady"—observed Giovanni,—"if fame says true—you, likewise, are deeply skilled in the virtues indicated by these rich blossoms, and these spicy perfumes. Would you deign to be my instructress, I should prove an apter scholar than if taught by Signor Rappaccini himself."

"Are there such idle rumors?" asked Beatrice, with the music of a pleasant laugh. "Do people say that I am skilled in my father's science of plants? What a jest is there! No; though I have grown up among these flowers, I know no more of them than their hues and perfume; and sometimes, methinks I would fain rid myself of even that small knowledge. There are many flowers here, and those not the least brilliant, that shock and offend me, when they meet my eye. But, pray, Signor, do not believe these stories about my science. Believe nothing of me save what you see with your own eyes."

"And must I believe all that I have seen with my own eyes?" asked Giovanni pointedly, while the recollection of former scenes made him shrink. "No, Signora, you demand too little of me. Bid me believe nothing, save what comes from your own lips."

It would appear that Beatrice understood him. There came a deep flush to her cheek; but she looked full into Giovanni's eyes, and responded to his gaze of uneasy suspicion with a queen-like haughtiness.

"I do so bid you, Signor!" she replied. "Forget whatever you may have fancied in regard to me. If true to the outward senses, still it may be false in its essence. But the words of Beatrice Rappaccini's lips are true from the depths of the heart outward. Those you may believe!"

A fervor glowed in her whole aspect, and beamed upon Giovanni's consciousness like the light of truth itself. But while she spoke, there was a fragrance in the atmosphere around her, rich and delightful, though evanescent, yet which the young man, from an indefinable reluctance, scarcely dared to draw into his lungs. It might be the odor of the flowers. Could it be Beatrice's breath, which thus embalmed her words with a strange richness, as if by steeping them in her heart? A faintness passed like a shadow over Giovanni, and flitted away; he seemed to gaze through the beautiful girl's eyes into her transparent soul, and felt no more doubt or fear.

The tinge of passion that had colored Beatrice's manner vanished; she became gay, and appeared to derive a pure delight from her communion with the youth, not unlike what the maiden of a lonely island might have felt, conversing with a voyager from the civilized world. Evidently her experience of life had been confined within the limits of that garden. She talked now about matters as simple as the daylight or summer-clouds, and now asked questions in reference to the city, or Giovanni's distant home, his friends, his mother, and his sisters; questions indicating such seclusion, and such lack of familiarity with modes and forms, that Giovanni responded as if to an infant. Her spirit gushed out before him like a fresh rill, that was just catching its first glimpse of the sunlight, and wondering at the reflections of earth and sky which were flung into its bosom. There came thoughts, too, from a deep source, and fantasies of a gem-like brilliancy, as if diamonds and rubies sparkled upward among the bubbles of the fountain. Ever and anon, there gleamed across the young man's mind a sense of wonder, that so wrought upon his imagination—whom he had idealized in such hues of terror—in whom he had positively witnessed such manifestations of dreadful attributes—that he should be conversing with Beatrice like a brother, and should find her so human and so maiden-like. But such reflections were only momentary; the effect of her character was too real, not to make itself familiar at once.

In this free intercourse, they had strayed through the garden, and now, after many turns among its avenues, were come to the shattered fountain, beside which grew the magnificent shrub with its treasury of glowing blossoms. A fragrance was diffused from it, which Giovanni recognized as identical with that which he had attributed to Beatrice's breath, but incomparably more powerful. As her eyes fell upon it, Giovanni beheld her press her hand to her bosom, as if her heart were throbbing suddenly and painfully.

"For the first time in my life," murmured she, addressing the shrub, "I had forgotten thee!"

"I remember, Signora," said Giovanni, "that you once promised to reward me with one of these living gems for the bouquet, which I had the happy boldness to fling to your feet. Permit me not to pluck it as a memorial of this interview."

He made a step towards the shrub, with extended hand. But Beatrice darted forward, uttering a shriek that went through his heart like a dagger. She caught his hand, and drew it back with the whole force of her slender figure. Giovanni felt her touch thrilling through his fibres.

"Touch it not!" exclaimed she, in a voice of agony. "Not for thy life! It is fatal!"

Then, hiding her face, she fled from him, and vanished beneath the sculptured portal. As Giovanni followed her with his eyes, he beheld the emaciated figure and pale intelligence of Doctor Rappaccini, who had been watching the scene, he knew not how long, within the shadow of the entrance.

No sooner was Guasconti alone in his chamber, than the image of Beatrice came back to his passionate musings, invested with all the witchery that had been gathering around it ever since his first glimpse of her, and now likewise imbued with a tender warmth of girlish womanhood. She was human: her nature was endowed with all gentle and feminine qualities; she was worthiest to be worshipped; she was capable, surely, on her part, of the height and heroism of love. Those tokens, which he had hitherto considered as proofs of a frightful peculiarity in her physical and moral system, were now either forgotten, or, by the subtle sophistry of passion, transmuted into a golden crown of enchantment, rendering Beatrice the more admirable, by so much as she was the more unique. Whatever had looked ugly, was now beautiful; or, if incapable of such a change, it stole away and hid itself among those shapeless half-ideas, which throng the dim region beyond the daylight of our perfect consciousness. Thus did he spend the night, nor fell asleep, until the dawn had begun to awake the slumbering flowers in Doctor Rappaccini's garden, wither Giovanni's dreams doubtless led him. Up rose the sun in his due season, and flinging his beams upon the young man's eyelids, awoke him to a sense of pain. When thoroughly aroused, he became sensible of a burning and tingling agony in his hand—in his right hand—the very hand which Beatrice had grasped in her own, when he was on the point of plucking one of the gem-like flowers. On the back of that hand there was now a purple print, like that of four small fingers, and the likeness of a slender thumb upon his wrist.

Oh, how stubbornly does love—or even that cunning semblance of love which flourishes in the imagination, but strikes no depth of root into the heart—how stubbornly does it hold its faith, until the moment come, when it is doomed to vanish into thin mist! Giovanni wrapt a handkerchief about his hand, and wondered what evil thing had stung him, and soon forgot his pain in a reverie of Beatrice.

After the first interview, a second was in the inevitable course of what we call fate. A third; a fourth; and a meeting with Beatrice in the garden was no longer an incident in Giovanni's daily life, but the whole space in which he might be said to live; for the anticipation and memory of that ecstatic hour made up the remainder. Nor was it otherwise with the daughter of Rappaccini. She watched for the youth's appearance, and flew to his side with confidence as unreserved as if they had been playmates from early infancy—as if they were such playmates still. If, by any unwonted chance, he failed to come at the appointed moment, she stood beneath the window, and sent up the rich sweetness of her tones to float around him in his chamber, and echo and reverberate throughout his heart—"Giovanni! Giovanni! Why tarriest thou? Come down!"—And down he hastened into that Eden of poisonous flowers.

But, with all this intimate familiarity, there was still a reserve in Beatrice's demeanor, so rigidly and invariably sustained, that the idea of infringing it scarcely occurred to his imagination. By all appreciable signs, they loved; they had looked love, with eyes that conveyed the holy secret from the depths of one soul into the depths of the other, as if it were too sacred to be whispered by the way; they had even spoken love, in those gushes of passion when their spirits darted forth in articulated breath, like tongues of long-hidden flame; and yet there had been no seal of lips, no clasp of hands, nor any slightest caress, such as love claims and hallows. He had never touched one of the gleaming ringlets of her hair; her garment—so marked was the physical barrier between them—had never been waved against him by a breeze. On the few occasions when Giovanni had seemed tempted to overstep the limit, Beatrice grew so sad, so stern, and withal wore such a look of desolate separation, shuddering at itself, that not a spoken word was requisite to repel him. At such times, he was startled at the horrible suspicions that rose, monster-like, out of the caverns of his heart, and stared him in the face; his love grew thin and faint as the morning-mist; his doubts alone had substance. But when Beatrice's face brightened again, after the momentary shadow, she was transformed at once from the mysterious, questionable being, whom he had watched with so much awe and horror; she was now the beautiful and unsophisticated girl, whom he felt that his spirit knew with a certainty beyond all other knowledge.

A considerable time had now passed since Giovanni's last meeting with Baglioni. One morning, however, he was disagreeably surprised by a visit from the Professor, whom he had scarcely thought of for whole weeks, and would willingly have forgotten still longer. Given up, as he had long been, to a pervading excitement, he could tolerate no companions, except upon condition of their perfect sympathy with his present state of feeling. Such sympathy was not to be expected from Professor Baglioni.

The visitor chatted carelessly, for a few moments, about the gossip of the city and the University, and then took up another topic.

"I have been reading an old classic author lately," said he, "and met with a story that strangely interested me. Possibly you may remember it. It is of an Indian prince, who sent a beautiful woman as a present to Alexander the Great.[17] She was as lovely as the dawn, and gorgeous as the sunset; but what especially distinguished her was a certain rich perfume in her breath—richer than a garden of Persian roses. Alexander, as was natural to a youthful conqueror, fell in love at first sight with this magnificent stranger. But a certain sage physician, happening to be present, discovered a terrible secret in regard to her."[18]

"And what was that?" asked Giovanni, turning his eyes downward to avoid those of the Professor.

"That this lovely woman," continued Baglioni, with emphasis, "had been nourished with poisons from her birth upward, until her whole nature was so imbued with them, that she herself had become the deadliest poison in existence. Poison was her element of life. With that rich perfume of her breath, she blasted the very air. Her love would have been poison!—her embrace death! Is not this a marvelous tale?"

"A childish fable," answered Giovanni, nervously starting from his chair. "I

---

[17] Alexander, king of Macedon (356–323 B.C.), was the conqueror of Persia and northern India.
[18] Sir Thomas Brown (1605–1682) reports this story in *Vulgar Errors* (1646), Book VII.

marvel how your worship finds time to read such nonsense, among your graver studies."

"By the bye," said the Professor, looking uneasily about him, "what singular fragrance is this in your apartment? Is it the perfume of your gloves? It is faint, but delicious, and yet, after all, by no means agreeable. Were I to breathe it long, methinks it would make me ill. It is like the breath of a flower—but I see no flowers in the chamber."

"Nor are there any," replied Giovanni, who had turned pale as the Professor spoke; "nor, I think, is there any fragrance, except in your worship's imagination. Odors, being a sort of element combined of the sensual and the spiritual, are apt to deceive us in this manner. The recollection of a perfume—the bare idea of it—may easily be mistaken for a present reality."

"Aye; but my sober imagination does not often play such tricks," said Baglioni; "and were I to fancy any kind of odor, it would be that of some vile apothecary drug, wherewith my fingers are likely enough to be imbued. Our worshipful friend Rappaccini, as I have heard, tinctures his medicaments with odors richer than those of Araby. Doubtless, likewise, the fair and learned Signora Beatrice would minister to her patients with draughts as sweet as a maiden's breath. But wo to him that sips them!"

Giovanni's face evinced many contending emotions. The tone in which the Professor alluded to the pure and lovely daughter of Rappaccini was a torture to his soul; and yet, the intimation of a view of her character, opposite to his own, gave instantaneous distinctness to a thousand dim suspicions, which now grinned at him like so many demons. But he strove hard to quell them, and to respond to Baglioni with a true lover's perfect faith.

"Signor Professor," said he, "you were my father's friend—perchance, too, it is your purpose to act a friendly part towards his son. I would fain feel nothing towards you, save respect and deference. But I pray you to observe, Signor, that there is one subject on which we must not speak. You know not the Signora Beatrice. You cannot, therefore, estimate the wrong—the blasphemy, I may even say—that is offered to her character by a light or injurious word."

"Giovanni!—my poor Giovanni!" answered the Professor, with a calm expression of pity, "I know this wretched girl far better than yourself. You shall hear the truth in respect to the poisoner Rappaccini, and his poisonous daughter. Yes; poisonous as she is beautiful! Listen; for even should you do violence to my grey hairs, it shall not silence me. That old fable of the Indian woman has become a truth, by the deep and deadly science of Rappaccini, and in the person of the lovely Beatrice!"

Giovanni groaned and hid his face.

"Her father," continued Baglioni, "was not restrained by natural affection from offering up his child, in this horrible manner, as the victim of his insane zeal for science. For—let us do him justice—he is as true a man of science as ever distilled his own heart in an alembic.[19] What, then, will be your fate? Beyond a doubt, you are selected as the material of some new experiment. Perhaps the result is to be death—perhaps a fate more awful still! Rappaccini, with what he calls the interest of science before his eyes, will hesitate at nothing."

"It is a dream!" muttered Giovanni to himself, "surely it is a dream!"

---

[19] An apparatus for distilling liquids.

"But," resumed the Professor, "be of good cheer, son of my friend! It is not yet too late for the rescue. Possibly, we may even succeed in bringing back this miserable child within the limits of ordinary nature, from which her father's madness has estranged her. Behold this little silver vase! It was wrought by the hands of the renowned Benvenuto Cellini,[20] and is well worthy to be a love-gift to the fairest dame in Italy. But its contents are invaluable. One little sip of this antidote would have rendered the most virulent poisons of the Borgias[21] innocuous. Doubt not that it will be as efficacious against those of Rappaccini. Bestow the vase, and the precious liquid within it, on your Beatrice, and hopefully await the result."

Baglioni laid a small, exquisitely wrought silver phial on the table, and withdrew, leaving what he had said to produce its effect upon the young man's mind.

"We will thwart Rappaccini yet!" thought he, chuckling to himself, as he descended the stairs. "But, let us confess the truth of him, he is a wonderful man!— a wonderful man indeed! A vile empiric,[22] however, in his practice, and therefore not to be tolerated by those who respect the good old rules of the medical profession!"

Throughout Giovanni's whole acquaintance with Beatrice, he had occasionally, as we have said, been haunted by dark surmises as to her character. Yet, so thoroughly had she made herself felt by him as a simple, natural, most affectionate and guileless creature, that the image now held up by Professor Baglioni, looked as strange and incredible, as if it were not in accordance with his own original conception. True, there were ugly recollections connected with his first glimpses of the beautiful girl; he could not quite forget the bouquet that withered in her grasp, and the insect that perished amid the sunny air, by no ostensible agency, save the fragrance of her breath. These incidents, however, dissolving in the pure light of her character, had no longer the efficacy of facts, but were acknowledged as mistaken fantasies, by whatever testimony of the senses they might appear to be substantiated. There is something truer and more real, than what we can see with the eyes, and touch with the finger. On such better evidence, had Giovanni founded his confidence in Beatrice, though rather by the necessary force of her high attributes, than by any deep and generous faith, on his part. But, now, his spirit was incapable of sustaining itself at the height to which the early enthusiasm of passion had exalted it; he fell down, grovelling among earthly doubts, and defiled therewith the pure whiteness of Beatrice's image. Not that he gave her up; he did but distrust. He resolved to institute some decisive test that should satisfy him, once for all, whether there were those dreadful peculiarities in her physical nature, which could not be supposed to exist without some corresponding monstrosity of soul. His eyes, gazing down afar, might have deceived him as to the lizard, the insect, and the flowers. But if he could witness, at the distance of a few paces, the sudden blight of one fresh and healthful flower in Beatrice's hand, there would be room for no further question. With this idea, he hastened to the florist's, and purchased a bouquet that was still gemmed with the morning dew-drops.

It was now the customary hour of his daily interview with Beatrice. Before descending into the garden, Giovanni failed not to look at his figure in the mirror;

---

[20] Cellini (1500–1571), was an Italian sculptor, metalsmith, and author.

[21] An aristocratic Italian family influential in Renaissance politics and notorious for corruption and even for the murder of their enemies, especially by poisoning.

[22] A follower of the empirical method (relying on practice rather than theory), but also a quack and charlatan.

a vanity to be expected in a beautiful young man, yet, as displaying itself at that troubled and feverish moment, the token of a certain shallowness of feeling and insincerity of character. He did gaze, however, and said to himself, that his features had never before possessed so rich a grace, nor his eyes such vivacity, nor his cheeks so warm a hue of superabundant life.

"At least," thought he, "her poison has not yet insinuated itself into my system. I am no flower to perish in her grasp!"

With that thought, he turned his eyes on the bouquet, which he had never once laid aside from his hand. A thrill of indefinable horror shot through his frame, on perceiving that those dewy flowers were already beginning to droop; they wore the aspect of things that had been fresh and lovely, yesterday. Giovanni grew white as marble, and stood motionless before the mirror, staring at his own reflection there, as at the likeness of something frightful. He remembered Baglioni's remark about the fragrance that seemed to pervade the chamber. It must have been the poison in his breath! Then he shuddered—shuddered at himself! Recovering from his stupor, he began to watch, with curious eye, a spider that was busily at work, hanging its web from the antique cornice of the apartment, crossing and re-crossing the artful system of interwoven lines, as vigorous and active a spider as ever dangled from an old ceiling. Giovanni bent towards the insect, and emitted a deep, long breath. The spider suddenly ceased its toil; the web vibrated with a tremor originating in the body of the small artizan. Again Giovanni sent forth a breath, deeper, longer, and imbued with a venomous feeling out of his heart; he knew not whether he were wicked or only desperate. The spider made a convulsive gripe with his limbs, and hung dead across the window.

"Accursed! Accursed!" muttered Giovanni, addressing himself. "Hast thou grown so poisonous, that this deadly insect perishes by thy breath?"

At that moment, a rich, sweet voice came floating up from the garden:—

"Giovanni! Giovanni! It is past the hour! Why tarriest thou! Come down!"

"Yes," muttered Giovanni again. "She is the only being whom my breath may not slay! Would that it might!"

He rushed down, and in an instant, was standing before the bright and loving eyes of Beatrice. A moment ago, his wrath and despair had been so fierce that he could have desired nothing so much as to wither her by a glance. But, with her actual presence, there came influences which had too real an existence to be shaken off; recollections of the delicate and benign power of her feminine nature, which had so often enveloped him in a religious calm; recollections of many a holy and passionate outgush of her heart, when the pure fountain had been unsealed from its depths, and made visible in its transparency to his mental eye; recollections which, had Giovanni known how to estimate them, would have assured him that all this ugly mystery was but an earthly illusion, and that, whatever mist of evil might seem to have gathered over her, the real Beatrice was a heavenly angel. Incapable as he was of such high faith, still her presence had not utterly lost its magic. Giovanni's rage was quelled into an aspect of sullen insensibility. Beatrice, with a quick spiritual sense, immediately felt that there was a gulf of blackness between them, which neither he nor she could pass. They walked on together, sad and silent, and came thus to the marble fountain, and to its pool of water on the ground, in the midst of which grew the shrub that bore gem-like blossoms. Giovanni was affrighted at the eager enjoyment—the appetite, as it were—with which he found himself inhaling the fragrance of the flowers.

"Beatrice," asked he abruptly, "whence came this shrub?"

"My father created it!" answered she, with simplicity.

"Created it! created it!" repeated Giovanni. "What mean you, Beatrice?"

"He is a man fearfully acquainted with the secrets of nature," replied Beatrice; "and, at the hour when I first drew breath, this plant sprang from the soil, the offspring of his science, of his intellect, while I was but his earthly child. Approach it not!" continued she, observing with terror that Giovanni was drawing nearer to the shrub. "It has qualities that you little dream of. But I, dearest Giovanni,—I grew up and blossomed with the plant, and was nourished with its breath. It was my sister, and I loved it with a human affection: for—alas! hast thou not suspected it? there was an awful doom."

Here Giovanni frowned so darkly upon her that Beatrice paused and trembled. But her faith in his tenderness reassured her, and made her blush that she had doubted for an instant.

"There was an awful doom," she continued,—"the effect of my father's fatal love of science—which estranged me from all society of my kind. Until Heaven sent thee, dearest Giovanni, Oh! how lonely was thy poor Beatrice!"

"Was it a hard doom?" asked Giovanni, fixing his eyes upon her.

"Only of late have I known how hard it was," answered she tenderly. "Oh, yes; but my heart was torpid, and therefore quiet."

Giovanni's rage broke forth from his sullen gloom like a lightning-flash out of a dark cloud.

"Accursed one!" cried he, with venomous scorn and anger. "And finding thy solitude wearisome, thou hast severed me, likewise, from all the warmth of life, and enticed me into thy region of unspeakable horror!"

"Giovanni!" exclaimed Beatrice, turning her large bright eyes upon his face. The force of his words had not found its way into her mind; she was merely thunder-struck.

"Yes, poisonous thing!" repeated Giovanni, beside himself with passion. "Thou hast done it! Thou hast blasted me! Thou hast filled my veins with poison! Thou hast made me as hateful, as ugly, as loathsome and deadly a creature as thyself,—a world's wonder of hideous monstrosity! Now—if our breath be happily as fatal to ourselves as to all others—let us join our lips in one kiss of unutterable hatred, and so die!"

"What has befallen me?" murmured Beatrice, with a low moan out of her heart. "Holy Virgin pity me, a poor heartbroken child!"

"Thou! Dost thou pray?" cried Giovanni, still with the same fiendish scorn. "Thy very prayers, as they come from thy lips, taint the atmosphere with death. Yes, yes; let us pray! Let us to church, and dip our fingers in the holy water at the portal! They that come after us will perish as by a pestilence. Let us sign crosses in the air! It will be scattering curses abroad in the likeness of holy symbols!"

"Giovanni," said Beatrice calmly, for her grief was beyond passion, "why dost thou join thyself with me thus in those terrible words? I, it is true, am the horrible thing thou namest me. But thou!—what hast thou to do, save with one other shudder at my hideous misery to go forth out of the garden and mingle with thy race, and forget that there ever crawled on earth such a monster as poor Beatrice?"

"Dost thou pretend ignorance?" asked Giovanni, scowling upon her. "Behold! This power have I gained from the pure daughter of Rappaccini!"

There was a swarm of summer-insects flitting through the air, in search of the food promised by the flower-odors of the fatal garden. They circled round Giovanni's head, and were evidently attracted towards him by the same influence which had drawn them, for an instant, within the sphere of several of the shrubs. He sent forth a breath among them, and smiled bitterly at Beatrice, as at least a score of the insects fell dead upon the ground.

"I see it! I see it!" shrieked Beatrice. "It is my father's fatal science! No, no, Giovanni; it was not I! Never, never! I dreamed only to love thee, and be with thee a little time, and so let thee pass away, leaving but thine image in mine heart. For, Giovanni—believe it—though my body be nourished with poison, my spirit is God's creature, and craves love as its daily food. But my father!—he has united us in this fearful sympathy. Yes; spurn me!—tread upon me!—kill me! Oh, what is death, after such words as thine? But it was not I! Not for a world of bliss would I have done it!"

Giovanni's passion had exhausted itself in its outburst from his lips. There now came across him a sense, mournful, and not without tenderness, of the intimate and peculiar relationship between Beatrice and himself. They stood, as it were, in an utter solitude, which would be made none the less solitary by the densest throng of human life. Ought not, then, the desert of humanity around them to press this insulated pair closer together? If they should be cruel to one another, who was there to be kind to them? Besides, thought Giovanni, might there not still be a hope of his returning within the limits of ordinary nature, and leading Beatrice—the redeemed Beatrice—by the hand? Oh, weak, and selfish, and unworthy spirit, that could dream of an earthly union and earthly happiness as possible, after such deep love had been so bitterly wronged as was Beatrice's love by Giovanni's blighting words! No, no; there could be no such hope. She must pass heavily, with that broken heart, across the borders of Time—she must bathe her hurts in some fount of Paradise, and forget her grief in the light of immortality—and *there* be well!

But Giovanni did not know it.

"Dear Beatrice," said he, approaching her, while she shrank away, as always at his approach, but now with a different impulse—"dearest Beatrice, our fate is not yet so desperate. Behold! There is a medicine, potent, as a wise physician has assured me, and almost divine in its efficacy. It is composed of ingredients the most opposite to those by which thy awful father has brought this calamity upon thee and me. It is distilled of blessed herbs. Shall we not quaff it together, and thus be purified from evil?"

"Give it me!" said Beatrice, extending her hand to receive the little silver phial which Giovanni took from his bosom. She added, with a peculiar emphasis: "I will drink—but do thou await the result."

She put Baglioni's antidote to her lips; and, at the same moment, the figure of Rappaccini emerged from the portal, and came slowly towards the marble fountain. As he drew near, the pale man of science seemed to gaze with a triumphant expression at the beautiful youth and maiden, as might an artist who should spend his life in achieving a picture or a group of statuary, and finally be satisfied with his success. He paused—his bent form grew erect with conscious power, he spread out his hands over them, in the attitude of a father imploring a blessing upon his children. But those were the same hands that had thrown poison into the stream of their lives! Giovanni trembled. Beatrice shuddered nervously, and pressed her hand upon her heart.

"My daughter," said Rappaccini, "thou art no longer lonely in the world! Pluck one of those precious gems from thy sister shrub, and bid thy bridegroom wear it in his bosom. It will not harm him now! My science, and the sympathy between thee and him, have so wrought within his system, that he now stands apart from common men, as thou dost, daughter of my pride and triumph, from ordinary women. Pass on, then, through the world, most dear to one another, and dreadful to all besides!"

"My father," said Beatrice, feebly—and still, as she spoke, she kept her hand upon her heart—"wherefore didst thou inflict this miserable doom upon thy child?"

"Miserable!" exclaimed Rappaccini. "What mean you, foolish girl? Dost thou deem it misery to be endowed with marvellous gifts, against which no power nor strength could avail an enemy? Misery, to be able to quell the mightiest with a breath? Misery, to be as terrible as thou art beautiful? Wouldst thou, then, have preferred the condition of a weak woman, exposed to all evil, and capable of none?"

"I would fain have been loved, not feared," murmured Beatrice, sinking down upon the ground.—"But now it matters not; I am going, father, where the evil, which thou hast striven to mingle with my being, will pass away like a dream— like the fragrance of these poisonous flowers, which will no longer taint my breath among the flowers of Eden. Farewell, Giovanni! Thy words of hatred are like lead within my heart—but they, too, will fall away as I ascend. Oh, was there not, from the first, more poison in thy nature than in mine?"

To Beatrice—so radically had her earthly part been wrought upon by Rappaccini's skill—as poison had been life, so the powerful antidote was death. And thus the poor victim of man's ingenuity and of thwarted nature, and of the fatality that attends all such efforts of perverted wisdom, perished there, at the feet of her father and Giovanni. Just at that moment, Professor Pietro Baglioni looked forth from the window, and called loudly, in a tone of triumph mixed with horror, to the thunder-stricken man of science:

"Rappaccini! Rappaccini! And is *this* the upshot of your experiment?"

1844

ETHAN BRAND*

A CHAPTER FROM AN ABORTIVE ROMANCE

Bartram, the lime-burner,[1] a rough, heavy-looking man, begrimed with charcoal, sat watching his kiln, at nightfall, while his little son played at building houses with the scattered fragments of marble; when, on the hill-side below them, they heard a roar of laughter, not mirthful, but slow, and even solemn, like a wind shaking the boughs of the forest.

"Father, what is that?" asked the little boy, leaving his play, and pressing betwixt his father's knees.

"Oh, some drunken man, I suppose," answered the lime-burner;—"some merry fellow from the bar-room in the village, who dared not laugh loud enough

---

* First published in the *Boston Weekly Museum* in 1850 and included in *The Snow-Image and Other Twice-Told Tales* (1851). As the subtitle and internal evidence suggest, Hawthorne may have intended this story to be part of a longer narrative.
[1] One who burns limestone to extract pure lime, which is used for cement.

within doors, lest he should blow the roof of the house off. So here he is, shaking his jolly sides, at the foot of the Graylock."[2]

"But father," said the child, more sensitive than the obtuse, middle-aged clown, "he does not laugh like a man that is glad. So the noise frightens me!"

"Don't be a fool, child!" cried his father, gruffly. "You will never make a man, I do believe; there is too much of your mother in you. I have known the rustling of a leaf startle you. Hark! Here comes the merry fellow now. You shall see that there is no harm in him."

Bartram and his little son, while they were talking thus, sat watching the same lime-kiln[3] that had been the scene of Ethan Brand's solitary and meditative life, before he began his search for the Unpardonable Sin. Many years, as we have seen, had now elapsed, since that portentous night when the IDEA was first developed. The kiln, however, on the mountainside, stood unimpaired, and was in nothing changed, since he had thrown his dark thoughts into the intense glow of its furnace, and melted them, as it were, into the one thought that took possession of his life. It was a rude, round, towerlike structure, about twenty feet high, heavily built of rough stones, and with a hillock of earth heaped about the larger part of its circumference; so that blocks and fragments of marble might be drawn by cartloads, and thrown in at the top. There was an opening at the bottom of the tower, like an oven-mouth, but large enough to admit a man in a stooping posture, and provided with a massive iron door. With the smoke and jets of flame issuing from the chinks and crevices of this door, which seemed to give admittance into the hillside, it resembled nothing so much as the private entrance to the infernal regions, which the shepherds of the Delectable Mountains were accustomed to show to pilgrims.[4]

There are many such lime-kilns in that tract of country, for the purpose of burning the white marble which composes a large part of the substance of the hills. Some of them, built years ago, and long deserted, with weeds growing in the vacant round of the interior, which is open to the sky, and grass and wild flowers rooting themselves into the chinks of the stones, look already like relics of antiquity, and may yet be overspread with the lichens of centuries to come. Others, where the lime-burner still feeds his daily and night-long fire, afford points of interest to the wanderer among the hills, who seats himself on a log of wood or a fragment of marble, to hold chat with the solitary man. It is a lonesome, and when the character is inclined to thought, may be an intensely thoughtful occupation; as it proved in the case of Ethan Brand, who had mused to such strange purpose, in days gone by, while the fire in this very kiln was burning.

The man, who now watched the fire, was of a different order, and troubled himself with no thoughts save the very few that were requisite to his business. At frequent intervals he flung back the clashing weight of the iron door, and, turning his face from the insufferable glare, thrust in huge logs of oak, or stirred the immense brands with a long pole. Within the furnace, was seen the curling and riotous flames, and the burning marble, almost molten with the intensity of heat;

---

[2] The highest mountain in the Berkshires in western Massachusetts.

[3] The preferred pronunciation of the lime-burning furnace is "lime-kill," a foreboding detail in this story.

[4] In *Pilgrim's Progress* (1678, 1684), by John Bunyan (1628–1688), the pilgrims are taken to the top of the Delectable Mountains, from which point they can see the gates of the Celestial City (Heaven) and also the entrance to Hell.

while, without, the reflection of the fire quivered on the dark intricacy of the surrounding forest, and showed, in the foreground, a bright and ruddy little picture of the hut, the spring beside its door, the athletic and coal-begrimed figure of the lime-burner, and the half-frightened child, shrinking into the protection of his father's shadow. And when, again, the iron door was closed, then re-appeared the tender light of the half-full moon, which vainly strove to trace out the indistinct shapes of the neighboring mountains; and, in the upper sky, there was a flitting congregation of clouds, still faintly tinged with the rosy sunset, though, thus far down into the valley, the sunshine had vanished long and long ago.

The little boy now crept still closer to his father, as footsteps were heard ascending the hill-side, and a human form thrust aside the bushes that clustered beneath the trees.

"Halloo! who is it?" cried the lime-burner, vexed at his son's timidity, yet half-infected by it. "Come forward, and show yourself, like a man; or I'll fling this chunk of marble at your head!"

"You offer me a rough welcome," said a gloomy voice, as the unknown man drew nigh. "Yet I neither claim nor desire a kinder one, even at my own fireside."

To obtain a distincter view, Bartram threw open the iron door of the kiln, whence immediately issued a gush of fierce light, that smote full upon the stranger's face and figure. To a careless eye, there appeared nothing very remarkable in his aspect, which was that of a man in a coarse, brown, country-made suit of clothes, tall and thin, with the staff and heavy shoes of a wayfarer. As he advanced, he fixed his eyes, which were very bright, intently upon the brightness of the furnace, as if he beheld, or expected to behold, some object worthy of note within it.

"Good evening, stranger," said the lime-burner, "whence come you, so late in the day?"

"I come from my search," answered the wayfarer; "for, at last, it is finished."

"Drunk, or crazy!" muttered Bartram to himself. "I shall have trouble with the fellow. The sooner I drive him away, the better."

The little boy, all in a tremble, whispered to his father, and begged him to shut the door of the kiln, so that there might not be so much light; for that there was something in the man's face which he was afraid to look at, yet could not look away from. And, indeed, even the lime-burner's dull and torpid sense began to be impressed by an indescribable something in that thin, rugged, thoughtful visage, with the grizzled hair hanging wildly about it, and those deeply sunken eyes, which gleamed like fires within the entrance of a mysterious cavern. But, as he closed the door, the stranger turned towards him, and spoke in a quiet, familiar way, that made Bartram feel as if he were a sane and sensible man, after all.

"Your task draws to an end, I see," said he. "This marble has already been burning three days. A few hours more will convert the stone to lime."

"Why, who are you?" exclaimed the lime-burner. "You seem as well acquainted with my business as I myself."

"And well I may be," said the stranger, "for I followed the same craft, many a long year and here, too, on this very spot. But you are a new comer to these parts. Did you never hear of Ethan Brand?"

"The man that went in search of the Unpardonable Sin?" asked Bartram, with a laugh.

"The same," answered the stranger. "He has found what he sought, and therefore he comes back again."

"What! then you are Ethan Brand, himself?" cried the lime-burner in amazement. "I am a new comer here, as you say; and they call it eighteen years since you left the foot of Graylock. But, I can tell you, the good folks still talk about Ethan Brand, in the village yonder, and what a strange errand took him away from his lime-kiln. Well, and so you have found the Unpardonable Sin?"

"Even so!" said the stranger, calmly.

"If the question is a fair one," proceeded Bartram, "where might it be?"

Ethan Brand laid his finger on his own heart. "Here!" replied he.

And then, without mirth in his countenance, but as if moved by an involuntary recognition of the infinite absurdity of seeking throughout the world for what was the closest of all things to himself, and looking into every heart, save his own, for what was hidden in no other breast, he broke into a laugh of scorn. It was the same slow, heavy laugh, that had almost appalled the lime-burner, when it heralded the wayfarer's approach.

The solitary mountain-side was made dismal by it. Laughter, when out of place, mistimed, or bursting forth from a disordered state of feeling, may be the most terrible modulation of the human voice. The laughter of one asleep, even if it be a little child—the madman's laugh—the wild, screaming laugh of a born idiot, are sounds that we sometimes tremble to hear, and would always willingly forget. Poets have imagined no utterance of fiends or hobgoblins so fearfully appropriate as a laugh. And even the obtuse lime-burner felt his nerves shaken, as this strange man looked inward at his own heart, and burst into laughter that rolled away into the night, and was indistinctly reverberated among the hills.

"Joe," said he to his little son, "scamper down to the tavern in the village, and tell the jolly fellows there that Ethan Brand has come back, and that he has found the Unpardonable Sin!"

The boy darted away on his errand, to which Ethan Brand made no objection, nor seemed hardly to notice it. He sat on a log of wood, looking steadfastly at the iron door of the kiln. When the child was out of sight, and his swift and light footsteps ceased to be heard, treading first on the fallen leaves, and then on the rocky mountain-path, the lime-burner began to regret his departure. He felt that the little fellow's presence had been a barrier between his guest and himself, and that he must now deal, heart to heart, with a man who, on his own confession, had committed the only crime for which Heaven could afford no mercy. That crime, in its indistinct blackness, seemed to overshadow him. The lime-burner's own sins rose up within him, and made his memory riotous with a throng of evil shapes that asserted their kindred with the Master Sin, whatever it might be, which it was within the scope of man's corrupted nature to conceive and cherish. They were all of one family; they went to and fro between his breast and Ethan Brand's, and carried dark greetings from one to the other.

Then Bartram remembered the stories which had grown traditionary in reference to this strange man, who had come upon him like a shadow of the night, and was making himself at home in his old place, after so long absence that the dead people, dead and buried for years, would have had more right to be at home, in any familiar spot, than he. Ethan Brand, it was said, had conversed with Satan himself, in the lurid blaze of this very kiln. The legend had been matter of mirth heretofore, but looked grisly now. According to this tale, before Ethan Brand departed on his search, he had been accustomed to evoke a fiend from the hot furnace of the lime-kiln, night after night, in order to confer with him about the Unpardonable Sin; the Man and the Fiend each laboring to frame the image of some mode of guilt, which could neither be atoned for, nor forgiven. And, with the first gleam of light upon the mountain-top, the fiend crept in at the iron door, there to abide in the intensest element of fire, until again summoned forth to share in the dreadful task of extending man's possible guilt beyond the scope of Heaven's else infinite mercy.

While the lime-burner was struggling with the horror of these thoughts, Ethan Brand rose from the log and flung open the door of the kiln. The action was in such accordance with the idea in Bartram's mind, that he almost expected to see the Evil One issue forth, red-hot from the raging furnace.

"Hold, hold!" cried he, with a tremulous attempt to laugh; for he was ashamed of his fears, although they overmastered him. "Don't, for mercy's sake, bring out your devil now!"

"Man!" sternly replied Ethan Brand, "what need have I of the devil? I have left him behind me on my track. It is with such half-way sinners as you that he busies himself. Fear not, because I open the door. I do but act by old custom, and am going to trim your fire, like a lime-burner, as I was once."

He stirred the vast coals, thrust in more wood, and bent forward to gaze into the hollow prison-house of the fire, regardless of the fierce glow that reddened upon his face. The lime-burner sat watching him, and half suspected his strange guest of a purpose, if not to evoke a fiend, at least to plunge bodily into the flames, and thus vanish from the sight of man. Ethan Brand, however, drew quietly back, and closed the door of the kiln.

"I have looked," said he, "into many a human heart that was seven times hotter with sinful passions than yonder furnace is with fire. But I found not there what I sought. No; not the Unpardonable Sin!"

"What is the Unpardonable Sin?" asked the lime-burner; and then he shrank farther from his companion, trembling lest his question should be answered.

"It is a sin that grew within my own breast," replied Ethan Brand, standing erect, with the pride that distinguishes all enthusiasts of his stamp. "A sin that grew nowhere else! The sin of an intellect that triumphed over the sense of brotherhood with man, and reverence for God, and sacrificed everything to its own mighty claims! The only sin that deserves a recompense of immortal agony! Freely, were it to do again, would I incur the guilt. Unshrinkingly, I accept the retribution!"

"The man's head is turned," muttered the lime-burner to himself. "He may be a sinner, like the rest of us—nothing more likely—but I'll be sworn, he is a madman, too."

Nevertheless, he felt uncomfortable at his situation, alone with Ethan Brand on the wild mountain-side, and was right glad to hear the rough murmur of tongues, and the footsteps of what seemed a pretty numerous party, stumbling over the stones, and rustling through the underbrush. Soon appeared the whole lazy regiment that was wont to infest the village tavern, comprehending three or four individuals who had drunk flip[5] beside the bar-room fire, through all the winters, and smoked their pipes beneath the stoop, through all the summers since Ethan Brand's departure. Laughing boisterously, and mingling all their voices together in unceremonious talk, they now burst into the moonshine and narrow streaks of fire-light that illuminated the open space before the lime-kiln. Bartram set the door

---

[5] A spicy, sweetened ale or beer.

ajar again, flooding the spot with light, that the whole company might get a fair view of Ethan Brand, and he of them.

There, among other old acquaintances, was a once ubiquitous man, now almost extinct, but who we were formerly sure to encounter at the hotel of every thriving village throughout the country. It was the stage-agent. The present specimen of the genus was a wilted and smoke-dried man, wrinkled and red-nosed, in a smartly cut, brown, bob-tailed coat, with brass buttons, who, for a length of time unknown, had kept his desk and corner in the bar-room, and was still puffing what seemed to be the same cigar that he had lighted twenty years before. He had great fame as a dry joker, though, perhaps, less on account of any intrinsic humor, than from a certain flavor of brandy-toddy and tobacco-smoke, which impregnated all his ideas and expressions, as well as his person. Another well-remembered, though strangely-altered face was that of Lawyer Giles, as people still called him in courtesy; an elderly ragamuffin, in his soiled shirt-sleeves and tow-cloth[6] trowsers. This poor fellow had been an attorney, in what he called his better days, a sharp practitioner, and in great vogue among the village litigants; but flip, and sling, and toddy,[7] and cocktails, imbibed at all hours, morning, noon, and night, had caused him to slide from intellectual, to various kinds and degrees of bodily labor, till, at last, to adopt his own phrase, he slid into a soap-vat. In other words, Giles was now a soap-boiler, in a small way. He had come to be but the fragment of a human being, a part of one foot having been chopped off by an axe, and an entire hand torn away by the devilish gripe of a steam-engine. Yet, though the corporeal hand was gone, a spiritual member remained; for, stretching forth the stump, Giles steadfastly averred, that he felt an invisible thumb and fingers, with as vivid a sensation as before the real ones were amputated. A maimed and miserable wretch he was; but one, nevertheless, whom the world could not trample on, and had no right to scorn, either in this or any previous stage of his misfortunes, since he had still kept up the courage and spirit of a man, asked nothing in charity, and, with his one hand—and that the left one—fought a stern battle against want and hostile circumstances.

Among the throng, too, came another personage, who, with certain points of similarity to Lawyer Giles, had more of difference. It was the village Doctor, a man of some fifty years, whom, at an earlier period of his life, we should have introduced as paying a professional visit to Ethan Brand, during the latter's supposed insanity. He was now a purple-visaged, rude, and brutal, yet half-gentlemanly figure, with something wild, ruined, and desperate in his talk, and in all the details of his gesture and manners. Brandy possessed this man like an evil spirit, and made him as surly and savage as a wild beast, and as miserable as a lost soul; but there was supposed to be in him such wonderful skill, such native gifts of healing, beyond any which medical science could impart, that society caught hold of him, and would not let him sink out of its reach. So, swaying to and fro upon his horse, and grumbling thick accents at the bedside, he visited all the sick chambers for miles about among the mountain towns; and sometimes raised a dying man, as it were, by miracle, or, quite as often, no doubt, sent his patient to a grave that was dug many a year too soon. The Doctor had an everlasting pipe in his mouth, and, as somebody said, in allusion to his habit of swearing, it was always alight with hell-fire.

---

[6] Coarse cloth.   [7] Gin and water mixed with lemon and sugar; and rum and sweetened hot water.

These three worthies pressed forward, and greeted Ethan Brand, each after his own fashion, earnestly inviting him to partake of the contents of a certain black bottle; in which, as they averred, he would find something far better worth seeking for, than the Unpardonable Sin. No mind, which has wrought itself, by intense and solitary meditation, into a high state of enthusiasm, can endure the kind of contact with low and vulgar modes of thought and feeling, to which Ethan Brand was now subjected. It made him doubt—and, strange to say, it was a painful doubt—whether he had indeed found the Unpardonable Sin, and found it within himself. The whole question on which he had exhausted life, and more than life, looked like a delusion.

"Leave me," he said bitterly, "ye brute beasts, that have made yourselves so, shrivelling up you souls with fiery liquors! I have done with you. Years and years ago, I groped into your hearts and found nothing there for my purpose. Get ye gone!"

"Why you uncivil scoundrel," cried the Fierce Doctor, "is that the way you respond to the kindness of your best friends? Then let me tell you the truth. You have no more found the Unpardonable Sin than yonder boy Joe has. You are but a crazy fellow, and the fit companion of old Humphrey, here!"

He pointed to an old man, shabbily dressed, with long white hair, thin visage, and unsteady eyes. For some years past, this aged person had been wandering about among the hills, inquiring of all travellers whom he met, for his daughter. The girl, it seemed, had gone off with a company of circus-performers; and, occasionally, tidings of her came to the village, and fine stories were told of her glittering appearance, as she rode on horseback in the ring, or performed marvellous feats on the tight-rope.

The white-haired father now approached Ethan Brand, and gazed unsteadily into his face.

"They tell me you have been all over the earth," said he, wringing his hands with earnestness. "You must have seen my daughter; for she makes a grand figure in the world, and everybody goes to see her. Did she send any word to her old father, or say when she is coming back?"

Ethan Brand's eye quailed beneath the old man's. That daughter, from whom he so earnestly desired a word of greeting, was the Esther of our tale;[8] the very girl whom, with such cold and remorseless purpose, Ethan Brand had made the subject of a psychological experiment, and wasted, absorbed, and perhaps annihilated her soul, in the process.

"Yes," murmured he, turning away from the hoary wanderer; "it is no delusion. There is an Unpardonable Sin!"

While these things were passing, a merry scene was going forward in the area of cheerful light, besides the spring and before the door of the hut. A number of the youth of the village, young men and girls, had hurried up the hill-side, impelled by curiosity to see Ethan Brand, the hero of so many a legend familiar to their childhood. Finding nothing, however, very remarkable in his aspect—nothing but a sunburnt wayfarer, in plain garb and dusty shoes, who sat looking into the fire, as if he fancied pictures among the coals—these young people speedily grew tired of observing him. As it happened, there was other amusement at hand.

---

[8] Because there is no Esther in this tale, this must be a loose end suggestive of Hawthorne's intention to tell a fuller story of Ethan Brand.

An old German Jew, travelling with a diorama[9] on his back, was passing down the mountain-road towards the village, just as the party turned aside from it; and, in hopes of eking out the profits of the day, the showman had kept them company to the lime-kiln.

"Come, old Dutchman," cried one of the young men, "let us see your pictures, if you can swear they are worth looking at!"

"Oh, yes, Captain," answered the Jew—whether as a matter of courtesy or craft, he styled everybody Captain—"I shall show you, indeed, some very superb pictures!"

So, placing his box in a proper position, he invited the young men and girls to look through the glass orifices of the machine, and proceeded to exhibit a series of the most outrageous scratchings and daubings, as specimens of the fine arts, that ever an itinerant showman had the face to impose upon his circle of spectators. The pictures were worn out, moreover, tattered, full of cracks and wrinkles, dingy with tobacco-smoke, and otherwise in most pitiable condition. Some purported to be cities, public edifices, and ruined castles, in Europe; others represented Napoleon's battles, and Nelson's[10] sea-fights; and in the midst of these would be seen a gigantic, brown, hairy hand—which might have been mistaken for the Hand of Destiny, though, in truth, it was only the showman's—pointing its forefinger to various scenes of the conflict, while its owner gave historical illustrations. When, with much merriment at its abominable deficiency of merit, the exhibition was concluded, the German bade little Joe put his head into the box. Viewed through the magnifying glasses, the boy's round, rosy visage assumed the strangest imaginable aspect of an immense, Titanic[11] child, the mouth grinning broadly, and the eyes, and every other feature, overflowing with fun at the joke. Suddenly, however, that merry face turned pale, and its expression changed to horror; for this easily impressed and excitable child had become sensible that the eye of Ethan Brand was fixed upon him through the glass.

"You make the little man to be afraid, Captain," said the German Jew, turning up the dark and strong outline of his visage, from his stooping posture. "But, look again; and, by chance, I shall cause you to see somewhat that is very fine, upon my word!"

Ethan Brand gazed into the box for an instant, and then starting back, looked fixedly at the German. What had he seen? Nothing, apparently; for a curious youth, who had peeped in, almost at the same moment, beheld only a vacant space of canvass.

"I remember you now," muttered Ethan Brand to the showman.

"Ah, Captain," whispered the Jew of Nuremberg, with a dark smile, "I find it to be a heavy matter in my show-box—this Unpardonable Sin! By my faith, Captain, it has wearied my shoulders, this long day, to carry it over the mountain."

"Peace!" answered Ethan Brand, sternly, "or get thee into the furnace yonder!"

The Jew's exhibition had scarcely concluded, when a great, elderly dog—who seemed to be his own master, as no person in the company laid claim to him—saw fit to render himself the object of public notice. Hitherto, he had shown himself a

---

[9] A box with a lens for viewing inserted pictures and paintings.

[10] Horatio Nelson (1758–1805), a British admiral whose greatest victory was a defeat over the combined fleets of France and Spain at Trafalgar in 1805.

[11] According to Greek myth, the Titans were a race of giant gods.

very quiet, well-disposed old dog, going round from one to another, and, by way of being sociable, offering his rough head to be patted by any kindly hand that would take so much trouble. But, now, all of a sudden, this grave and venerable quadruped, of his own mere notion, and without the slightest suggestion from anybody else, began to run round after his tail, which, to heighten the absurdity of the proceeding, was a great deal shorter than it should have been. Never was seen such headlong eagerness in pursuit of an object that could not possibly be attained; never was heard such a tremendous outbreak of growling, snarling, barking, and snapping—as if one end of the ridiculous brute's body were at deadly and most unforgivable enmity with the other. Faster and faster, roundabout went the cur; and faster and still faster fled the unapproachable brevity of his tail; and louder and fiercer grew his yells of rage and animosity; until, utterly exhausted, and as far from the goal as ever, the foolish old dog ceased his performance as suddenly as he had begun it. The next moment, he was as mild, quiet, sensible, and respectable in his deportment, as when he first scraped acquaintance with the company.

As may be supposed, the exhibition was greeted with universal laughter, clapping of hands, and shouts of encore; to which the canine performer responded by wagging all that there was to wag of his tail, but appeared totally unable to repeat his very successful effort to amuse the spectators.

Meanwhile, Ethan Brand had resumed his seat upon the log; and moved, it might be, by a perception of some remote analogy between his own case and that of this self-pursuing cur, he broke into the awful laugh, which, more than any other token, expressed the condition of his inward being. From that moment, the merriment of the party was at an end; they stood aghast, dreading lest the inauspicious sound should be reverberated around the horizon, and that mountain would thunder it to mountain, and so the horror be prolonged upon their ears. Then, whispering one to another, that it was late—that the moon was almost down—that the August night was growing chill—they hurried homeward, leaving the lime-burner and little Joe to deal as they might with their unwelcome guest. Save for these three human beings, the open space on the hill-side was a solitude, set in a vast gloom of forest. Beyond that darksome verge, the fire-light glimmered on the stately trunks and almost black foliage of pines, intermixed with the lighter verdure of sapling oaks, maples, and poplars, while, here and there, lay the gigantic corpses of dead trees, decaying on the leaf-strewn soil. And it seemed to little Joe—a timorous and imaginative child—that the silent forest was holding its breath, until some fearful thing should happen.

Ethan Brand thrust more wood into the fire, and closed the door of the kiln; then looking over his shoulder at the lime-burner and his son, he bade, rather than advised, them to retire to rest.

"For myself I cannot sleep," said he, "I have matters that it concerns me to meditate upon. I will watch the fire, as I used to do in the old time."

"And call the devil out of the furnace to keep you company, I suppose," muttered Bartram, who had been making intimate acquaintance with the black bottle above-mentioned. "But watch, if you like, and call as many devils as you like! For my part, I shall be all the better for a snooze. Come, Joe!"

As the boy followed his father into the hut, he looked back to the wayfarer, and the tears came into his eyes; for his tender spirit had an intuition of the bleak and terrible loneliness in which this man had enveloped himself.

When they had gone, Ethan Brand sat listening to the crackling of the kindled wood, and looking at the little spirts of fire that issued through the chinks of the door. These trifles, however, once so familiar, had but the slightest hold of his attention; while deep within his mind, he was reviewing the gradual, but marvellous change, that had been wrought upon him by the search to which he had devoted himself. He remembered how the night-dew had fallen upon him—how the dark forest had whispered to him—how the stars had gleamed upon him—a simple and loving man, watching his fire in the years gone by, and ever musing as it burned. He remembered with what tenderness, with what love and sympathy for mankind, and what pity for human guilt and woe, he had first begun to contemplate those ideas which afterwards became the inspiration of his life; with what reverence he had then looked into the heart of man, viewing it as a temple originally divine, and however desecrated, still to be held sacred by a brother; with what awful fear he had deprecated the success of his pursuit, and prayed that the Unpardonable Sin might never be revealed to him. Then ensued that vast intellectual development, which, in its progress, disturbed the counterpoise between his mind and heart. The Idea that possessed his life had operated as a means of education; it had gone on cultivating his powers to the highest point of which they were susceptible; it had raised him from the level of an unlettered laborer, to stand on a star-light eminence, whither the philosophers of the earth, laden with the lore of universities, might vainly strive to clamber after him. So much for the intellect! But where was the heart? That, indeed, had withered—had contracted—had hardened—had perished! It had ceased to partake of the universal throb. He had lost his hold of the magnetic chain of humanity. He was no longer a brother-man, opening the chambers or the dungeons of our common nature by the key of holy sympathy, which gave him a right to share in all its secrets; he was now a cold observer, looking on mankind as the subject of his experiment, and, at length, converting man and woman to be his puppets, and pulling the wires that moved them to such degrees of crime as were demanded for his study.

Thus Ethan Brand became a fiend. He began to be so from the moment that his moral nature had ceased to keep the pace of improvement with his intellect. And now, as his highest effort and inevitable development—as the bright and gorgeous flower, and rich, delicious fruit of his life's labor—he had produced the Unpardonable Sin!

"What more have I to seek? What more to achieve?" said Ethan Brand to himself. "My task is done, and well done!"

Starting from the log with a certain alacrity in his gait, and ascending the hillock of earth that was raised against the stone circumference of the lime-kiln, he thus reached the top of the structure. It was a space of perhaps ten feet across, from edge to edge, presenting a view of the upper surface of the immense mass of broken marble with which the kiln was heaped. All these innumerable blocks and fragments of marble were red-hot, and vividly on fire, sending up great spouts of blue flame, which quivered aloft and danced madly, as within a magic circle, and sank and rose again, with continual and multitudinous activity. As the lonely man bent forward over this terrible body of fire, the blasting heat smote up against his person with a breath that, it might be supposed, would have scorched and shrivelled him up in a moment.

Ethan Brand stood erect and raised his arms on high. The blue flames played upon his face, and imparted the wild and ghastly light which alone could have suited its expression; it was that of a fiend on the verge of plunging into his gulf of intensest torment.

"Oh, Mother Earth," cried he, "who art no more my Mother, and into whose bosom this frame shall never be resolved! Oh, mankind, whose brotherhood I have cast off, and trampled thy great heart beneath my feet! Oh, stars of Heaven, that shone on me of old, as if to light me onward and upward!—farewell all, and forever! Come, deadly element of Fire—henceforth my familiar friend! Embrace me as I do thee!"

That night the sound of a fearful peal of laughter rolled heavily through the sleep of the lime-burner and his little son; dim shapes of horror and anguish haunted their dreams, and seemed still present in the rude hovel when they opened their eyes to the daylight.

"Up, boy, up!" cried the lime-burner, starting about him. "Thank Heaven, the night is gone at last; and rather than pass such another, I would watch my lime-kiln, wide awake, for a twelvemonth. This Ethan Brand, with his humbug of an Unpardonable Sin, has done me no such mighty favor in taking my place!"

He issued from the hut, followed by little Joe, who kept fast hold of his father's hand. The early sunshine was already pouring its gold upon the mountain-tops, and though the valleys were still in shadow, they smiled cheerfully in the promise of the bright day that was hastening onward. The village, completely shut in by hills, which swelled away gently about it, looked as if it had rested peacefully in the hollow the great hand of Providence. Every dwelling was distinctly visible; the little spires of the two churches pointed upward, and caught a fore-glimmering of brightness from the sun-gilt skies upon their gilded weathercocks. The tavern was astir, and the figure of the old, smoke-dried stage-agent, cigar in mouth, was seen beneath the stoop. Old Graylock was glorified with a golden cloud upon his head. Scattered, likewise, over the breasts of the surrounding mountains, there were heaps of hoary mist, in fantastic shapes, some of them far down into the valley, others high up towards the summits, and still others, of the same family of mist or cloud, hovering in the gold radiance of the upper atmosphere. Stepping from one to another of the clouds that rested on the hills, and thence to the loftier brotherhood that sailed in air, it seemed almost as if a mortal man might thus ascend into the heavenly regions. Earth was so mingled with sky that it was a day-dream to look at it.

To supply that charm of the familiar and homely, which Nature so readily adopts into a scene like this, the stagecoach was rattling down the mountain-road, and the driver sounded his horn; while echo[12] caught up the notes and intertwined them into a rich, and varied, and elaborate harmony, of which the original performer could lay claim to little share. The great hills played a concert among themselves, each contributing a strain of airy sweetness.

Little Joe's face brightened at once.

"Dear father," cried he, skipping cheerily to and fro, "that strange man is gone, and the sky and the mountains all seem glad of it!"

"Yes," growled the lime-burner with an oath, "but he has let the fire go down, and no thanks to him, if five hundred bushels of lime are not spoilt. If I catch the fellow hereabouts again I shall feel like tossing him into the furnace!"

With his long pole in his hand he ascended to the top of the kiln. After a moment's pause he called to his son.

---

[12] According to Greek myth, the nymph Echo was loved by Pan (the god of sheep and shepherds); when she fled from him she was changed into a voice that could only repeat the last words spoken to her.

"Come up here, Joe!" said he.

So little Joe ran up the hillock and stood by his father's side. The marble was all burnt into perfect, snow-white lime. But on its surface, in the midst of the circle—snow-white too, and thoroughly converted into lime—lay a human skeleton, in the attitude of a person who, after long toil, lies down to long repose. Within the ribs—strange to say—was the shape of a human heart.

"Was the fellow's heart made of marble?" cried Bartram, in some perplexity at this phenomenon. "At any rate, it is burnt into what looks like special good lime; and, taking all the bones together, my kiln is half a bushel the richer for him."

So saying, the rude lime-burner lifted his pole, and letting it fall upon the skeleton, the relics of Ethan Brand were crumbled into fragments.

1850

from THE HOUSE OF THE SEVEN GABLES

Preface*

When a writer calls his work a Romance, it need hardly be observed that he wishes to claim a certain latitude, both as to its fashion and material, which he would not have felt himself entitled to assume, had he professed to be writing a Novel. The latter form of composition is presumed to aim at a very minute fidelity, not merely to the possible, but to the probable and ordinary course of man's experience. The former—while, as a work of art, it must rigidly subject itself to laws, and while it sins unpardonably, so far as it may swerve aside from the truth of the human heart—has fairly a right to present that truth under circumstances, to a great extent, of the writer's own choosing or creation. If he think fit, also, he may so manage his atmospherical medium as to bring out or mellow the lights and deepen and enrich the shadows of the picture. He will be wise, no doubt, to make a very moderate use of the privileges here stated, and, especially, to mingle the Marvellous rather as a slight, delicate, and evanescent flavor, than as any portion of the actual substance of the dish offered to the Public. He can hardly be said, however, to commit a literary crime, even if he disregard this caution.

In the present work, the Author has proposed to himself (but with what success, fortunately, it is not for him to judge) to keep undeviatingly within his immunities. The point of view in which this Tale comes under the Romantic definition, lies in the attempt to connect a by-gone time with the very Present that is flitting away from us. It is a Legend, prolonging itself, from an epoch now gray in the distance, down into our own broad daylight, and bringing along with it some of its legendary mist, which the Reader, according to his pleasure, may either disregard, or allow it to float almost imperceptibly about the characters and events, for the sake of a picturesque effect. The narrative, it may be, is woven of

---

* In his preface to *The House of the Seven Gables* (1851), Hawthorne makes a distinction between the "novel" and the "romance," which was common at the time. It amounts to a rationale for his type of fiction.

so humble a texture as to require this advantage, and, at the same time, to render it the more difficult of attainment.

Many writers lay very great stress upon some definite moral purpose, at which they profess to aim their works. Not to be deficient, in this particular, the Author has provided himself with a moral;—the truth, namely, that the wrong-doing of one generation lives into the successive ones, and, divesting itself of every temporary advantage, becomes a pure and uncontrollable mischief;—and he would feel it a singular gratification, if this Romance might effectually convince mankind (or, indeed, any one man) of the folly of tumbling down an avalanche of ill-gotten gold, or real estate, on the heads of an unfortunate posterity, thereby to maim and crush them, until the accumulated mass shall be scattered abroad in its original atoms. In good faith, however, he is not sufficiently imaginative to flatter himself with the slightest hope of this kind. When romances do really teach anything, or produce any effective operation, it is usually through a far more subtle process than the ostensible one. The Author has considered it hardly worth his while, therefore, relentlessly to impale the story with its moral, as with an iron rod—or rather, as by sticking a pin through a butterfly—thus at once depriving it of life, and causing it to stiffen in an ungainly and unnatural attitude. A high truth, indeed, fairly, finely, and skilfully wrought out, brightening at every step, and crowning the final development of a work of fiction, may add an artistic glory, but is never any truer, and seldom any more evident, at the last page than at the first.

The Reader may perhaps choose to assign an actual locality to the imaginary events of this narrative. If permitted by the historical connection, (which, though slight, was essential to his plan,) the Author would very willingly have avoided anything of this nature. Not to speak of other objections, it exposes the Romance to an inflexible and exceedingly dangerous species of criticism, by bringing his fancy-pictures almost into positive contact with the realities of the moment. It has been no part of his object, however, to describe local manners, nor in any way to meddle with the characteristics of a community for whom he cherishes a proper respect and a natural regard. He trusts not to be considered as unpardonably offending, by laying out a street that infringes upon nobody's private rights, and appropriating a lot of land which had no visible owner, and building a house, of materials long in use for constructing castles in the air. The personages of the Tale—though they give themselves out to be of ancient stability and considerable prominence—are really of the Author's own making, or, at all events, of his own mixing; their virtues can shed no lustre, nor their defects redound, in the remotest degree, to the discredit of the venerable town[1] of which they profess to be inhabitants. He would be glad, therefore, if—especially in the quarter to which he alludes—the book may be read strictly as a Romance, having a great deal more to do with the clouds overhead, than with any portion of the actual soil of the County of Essex.

Lenox, January 27, 1851.

1851

---

[1] Salem, in Essex County, Massachusetts.

from   THE AMERICAN NOTEBOOKS

[*Thoughts on Perfection: Toward "The Birth-Mark"**]

from   OCTOBER 25th, 1836

Those who are very difficult in choosing wives seem as if they would take none of Nature's ready-made works, but want a woman manufactured particularly to their order.

from   OCTOBER 16th, 1837

A person to be in possession of something as perfect as mortal man has a right to demand; he tries to make it better, and ruins it entirely.

A person to spend all his life and splendid talents in trying to achieve something naturally impossible,—as to make a conquest over Nature.

from   JANUARY 4th, 1839

A person to be the death of his beloved in trying to raise her to more than mortal perfection; yet this should be a comfort to him for having aimed so highly and holily.

[*On Thoreau**]

from   APRIL 7th, 1843

. . . So I arose, and began this record in the Journal, almost at the commencement of which I was interrupted by a visit from Mr. Thoreau, who came to return a book, and to announce his purpose of going to reside at Staten Island, as private tutor in the family of Mr. Emerson's brother.[1] We had some conversation upon this subject, and upon the spiritual advantages of change of place, and upon the Dial,[2] and upon Mr. Alcott,[3] and other kindred or concatenated subjects. I am glad, on Mr. Thoreau's own account, that he is going away; as he is physically out of health, and, morally and intellectually, seems not to have found exactly the

---

* Many of Hawthorne's notebook entries consist of ideas for stories. These entries from the 1830s contain his earliest thoughts on the theme of "The Birth-Mark" (1843).

* Henry David Thoreau (1817–1862), Hawthorne's fellow-townsman in Concord, Massachusetts.

[1] In 1843 Thoreau took a position as tutor in the family of William Emerson (brother of Ralph Waldo Emerson) on Staten Island, New York.

[2] The quarterly magazine of the transcendentalist movement in New England, published from July 1840 until April 1844.

[3] Bronson Alcott (1799–1888), a philosopher and educator, an idealistic resident of Concord, and the father of Louisa May Alcott, author of *Little Women* (1868); he named *The Dial*.

guiding clue; and in all these respects, he may be benefitted by his removal;— also, it is one step towards a circumstantial position in the world. On my account, I should like to have him remain here; he being one of the few persons, I think, with whom to hold intercourse is like hearing the wind among the boughs of a forest-tree; and with all this wild freedom, there is high and classic cultivation in him too. He says that Ellery Channing[4] is coming back to Concord, and that he (Mr. Thoreau) has concluded a bargain, in his behalf, for the hire of a small house, with land attached, at $55 per year. I am rather glad than otherwise; but Ellery, so far as he has been developed to my observation, is but a poor substitute for Mr. Thoreau.

[*On Emerson's Praise of Margaret Fuller**]

from   APRIL 8th, 1843

Mr. Emerson came, with a sunbeam in his face; and we had as good a talk as I ever remember experiencing with him. My little wife,[1] I know, will demand to know every word that was spoken; but she knows me too well to anticipate anything of the kind. He seemed fullest of Margaret Fuller, who, he says, has risen perceptibly into a higher state, since their last meeting. He apotheosized her as the greatest woman, I believe, of ancient or modern times, and the one figure in the world worth considering. . . .

[*The Unpardonable Sin**]

from   JULY 27th, 1844

The search of an investigator for the Unpardonable Sin;—he at last finds it in his own heart and practice.

* * *

The Unpardonable Sin might consist in a want of love and reverence for the Human Soul; in consequence of which, the investigator pried into its dark depths, not with a hope or purpose of making it better, but from a cold philosophical curiosity,—content that it should be wicked in what ever kind or degree, and only desiring to study it out. Would not this, in other words, be the separation of the intellect from the heart?[1]

---

[4] William Ellery Channing (1818–1901), a close friend of Thoreau and a disciple of Emerson.

* Ralph Waldo Emerson (1803–1882), Hawthorne's famous fellow-townsman in Concord, Massachusetts; and Margaret Fuller (1810–1850), a brilliant advocate of transcendental ideas, women's rights, and thus human rights, who edited *The Dial* from 1840 to 1842.

[1] Sophia Peabody (1809–1871), whom Hawthorne had married the previous summer; at this time they lived in the Old Manse in Concord.

* This notebook entry shows Hawthorne considering the idea that became central to his story "Ethan Brand" (1850).

[1] Hawthorne's most villainous characters suffer from the "separation of the intellect from the heart."

[*The Idea of the "Neutral Ground"**]

OCTOBER 13th, 1848

During this moon, I have two or three evenings, sat sometime in our sitting-room, without light, except from the coal-fire and the moon. Moonlight produces a very beautiful effect in the room; falling so white upon the carpet, and showing its figures so distinctly; and making all the room so visible, and yet so different from a morning or noontide visibility. There are all the familiar things;—every chair, the tables, the couch, the bookcase, all the things that we are accustomed to in the daytime; but now it seems as if we were remembering them through a lapse of years rather than seeing them with the immediate eye. A child's shoe—the doll, sitting in her little wicker-carriage—all objects, that have been used or played with during the day, though still as familiar as ever, are invested with something like strangeness and remoteness. I cannot in any measure express it. Then the somewhat dim coal-fire throws its unobtrusive tinge through the room—a faint ruddiness upon the wall—which has a not unpleasant effect in taking from the colder spirituality of the moonbeams. Between both these lights, such a medium is created that the room seems just fit for the ghosts of persons very dear, who have lived in the room with us, to glide noiselessly in, and sit quietly down, without affrighting us. It would be like a matter of course, to look round, and find some familiar form in one of the chairs. If one of the white curtains happen to be down before the windows, the moonlight makes a delicate tracery with the branches of the trees, the leaves somewhat thinned by the progress of autumn, but still pretty abundant. It is strange how utterly I have failed to give anything of the effect of moonlight in a room.

The fire-light diffuses a mild, heart-warm influence through the room; but is scarcely visible, unless you particularly look for it—and then you become conscious of a faint tinge upon the cieling ![sic], of a reflected gleam from the mahogany furniture; and if your eyes fall on the glass, deep within it you perceive the glow of the burning anthracite.

I hate to leave such a scene; and when retiring to bed, after closing the sitting-room door, I re-open it, again and again, to peep back at the warm, cheerful, solemn repose, the white light, the faint ruddiness, the dimness,—all like a dream, and which makes me feel as if I were in a conscious dream.

[*A Visit From Herman Melville**]

from AUGUST 1st, 1851

Returning to the Post Office, I got Mr. Tappan's[1] mail and my own, and proceeded homeward, but clambered over the fence and sat down in Love Grove, to

---

* In its details and tone this notebook entry anticipates the meditation on moonlight and a fanciful atmosphere in "The Custom-House" preface to *The Scarlet Letter* (1850). There Hawthorne uses the metaphor of a "neutral ground" between reality and dream to define the conditions for bringing his type of fiction into existence.

* Melville (1819–1891) was Hawthorne's younger and enthusiastic friend in the early 1850s when both lived in the Berkshires in western Massachusetts.

[1] W. A. Tappan, Hawthorne's neighbor and landlord.

read the papers. While thus engaged, a cavalier on horseback came along the road, and saluted me in Spanish; to which I replied by touching my hat, and went on with the newspaper. But the cavalier renewing his salutation, I regarded him more attentively, and saw that it was Herman Melville! So, hereupon, Julian[2] and I hastened to the road, where ensued a greeting, and we all went homeward together, talking as we went. Soon, Mr. Melville alighted, and put Julian into the saddle; and the little man was highly pleased, and sat on the horse with the freedom and fearlessness of an old equestrian, and had a ride of at least a mile homeward.

I asked Mrs. Peters[3] to make some tea for Herman Melville; and so she did, and he drank a cup, but was afraid to drink much, because it would keep him awake. After supper, I put Julian to bed; and Melville and I had a talk about time and eternity, things of this world and of the next, and books, and publishers, and all possible and impossible matters, that lasted pretty deep into the night; and if truth must be told, we smoked cigars even within the sacred precincts of the sitting-room. At last, he arose, and saddled his horse (whom we had put into the barn) and rode off for his own domicile; and I hastened to make the most of what little sleeping-time remained for me.

1835–1853, 1868

THE SCARLET LETTER*

PREFACE TO THE SECOND EDITION

Much to the author's surprise, and (if he may say so without additional offence) considerably to his amusement, he finds that his sketch of official life, introductory to *The Scarlet Letter,* has created an unprecedented excitement in the respectable community immediately around him. It could hardly have been more violent, indeed, had he burned down the Custom-House, and quenched its last smoking ember in the blood of a certain venerable personage, against whom he is supposed to cherish a peculiar malevolence. As the public disapprobation would weigh very heavily on him, were he conscious of deserving it, the author begs leave to say, that he has carefully read over the introductory pages, with a purpose to alter or expunge whatever might be found amiss, and to make the best reparation in his power for the atrocities of which he has been adjudged guilty. But it appears to him, that the only remarkable features of the sketch are its frank and genuine good-humor, and the general accuracy with which he has conveyed his sincere

---

[2] Julian Hawthorne (1846–1934), Hawthorne's son, who was then five.

[3] The Hawthornes' housekeeper; ordinarily, Sophia Hawthorne (1809–1871) would have been present to welcome Melville, but she was visiting relatives in Boston at the time.

* Hawthorne began writing *The Scarlet Letter* when he was dismissed from his appointment as surveyor, or tax officer, at the customhouse (where customs, or duties, are paid on goods transported by ship) in Salem, Massachusetts, in June 1849. He completed it in February 1850; it was published in Boston a month later. He introduced the novel with the sketch "The Custom-House," which was in part intended to criticize the Whig politicians (those opposing the Democrats from 1834 to 1852, until the Republican party emerged) who had him dismissed.

impressions of the characters therein described. As to enmity, or ill-feeling of any kind, personal or political, he utterly disclaims such motives. The sketch might, perhaps, have been wholly omitted, without loss to the public, or detriment to the book; but, having undertaken to write it, he conceives that it could not have been done in a better or a kindlier spirit, nor, so far as his abilities availed, with a livelier effect of truth.

The author is constrained, therefore, to republish his introductory sketch without the change of a word.

SALEM, *March* 30, 1850.

THE CUSTOM-HOUSE

Introductory to "The Scarlet Letter"

It is a little remarkable, that—though disinclined to talk overmuch of myself and my affairs at the fireside, and to my personal friends—an autobiographical impulse should twice in my life have taken possession of me, in addressing the public. The first time was three or four years since, when I favored the reader—inexcusably, and for no earthly reason, that either the indulgent reader or the intrusive author could imagine—with a description of my way of life in the deep quietude of an Old Manse.[1] And now—because, beyond my deserts, I was happy enough to find a listener or two on the former occasion—I again seize the public by the button, and talk of my three years' experience in a Custom-House. The example of the famous "P. P., Clerk of this Parish,"[2] was never more faithfully followed. The truth seems to be, however, that, when he casts his leaves forth upon the wind, the author addresses, not the many who will fling aside his volume, or never take it up, but the few who will understand him, better than most of his schoolmates and lifemates. Some authors, indeed, do far more than this, and indulge themselves in such confidential depths of revelation as could fittingly be addressed, only and exclusively, to the one heart and mind of perfect sympathy; as if the printed book, thrown at large on the wide world, were certain to find out the divided segment of the writer's own nature, and complete his circle of existence by bringing him into communion with it. It is scarcely decorous, however, to speak all, even where we speak impersonally. But—as thoughts are frozen and utterance benumbed, unless the speaker stand in some true relation with his audience—it may be pardonable to imagine that a friend, a kind and apprehensive, though not the closest friend, is listening to our talk; and then, a native reserve being thawed by this genial consciousness, we may prate of the circumstances that lie around us, and even of ourself, but still keep the inmost Me behind its veil. To

---

[1] Hawthorne lived in the Old Manse in Concord, Massachusetts, from 1842 to 1845 and completed his collection of tales and sketches *Mosses From an Old Manse* (1846) at that time. He alludes to "The Author Makes the Reader Acquainted With His Abode," the introduction to *Mosses From an Old Manse (1846)*.

[2] The anonymous *Memoirs of P. P., Clerk of This Parish,* a parody of the pompous autobiography of Bishop Gilbert Burnet (1643–1715), *A History of My Own Times* (1723).

this extent and within these limits, an author, methinks, may be autobiographical, without violating either the reader's rights or his own.

It will be seen, likewise, that this Custom-House sketch has a certain propriety, of a kind always recognized in literature, as explaining how a large portion of the following pages came into my possession, and as offering proofs of the authenticity of a narrative therein contained. This, in fact,—a desire to put myself in my true position as editor, or very little more, of the most prolix among the tales that make up my volume,[3]—this, and no other, is my true reason for assuming a personal relation with the public. In accomplishing the main purpose, it has appeared allowable, by a few extra touches, to give a faint representation of a mode of life not heretofore described, together with some of the characters that move in it, among whom the author happened to make one.

In my native town of Salem, at the head of what, half a century ago, in the days of old King Derby,[4] was a bustling wharf,—but which is now burdened with decayed wooden warehouses, and exhibits few or no symptoms of commercial life; except, perhaps, a bark or brig, half-way down its melancholy length, discharging hides; or, nearer at hand, a Nova Scotia schooner, pitching out her cargo of firewood,—at the head, I say, of this dilapidated wharf, which the tide often overflows, and along which, at the base and in the rear of the row of buildings, the track of many languid years is seen in a border of unthrifty grass,—here, with a view from its front windows adown this not very enlivening prospect, and thence across the harbour, stands a spacious edifice of brick. From the loftiest point of its roof, during precisely three and a half hours of each forenoon, floats or droops, in breeze or calm, the banner of the republic; but with the thirteen stripes turned vertically, instead of horizontally, and thus indicating that a civil, and not a military post of Uncle Sam's government, is here established. Its front is ornamented with a portico of half a dozen wooden pillars, supporting a balcony, beneath which a flight of wide granite steps descends towards the street. Over the entrance hovers an enormous specimen of the American eagle, with outspread wings, a shield before her breast, and, if I recollect aright, a bunch of intermingled thunderbolts and barbed arrows in each claw. With the customary infirmity of temper that characterizes this unhappy fowl, she appears, by the fierceness of her beak and eye and the general truculency of her attitude, to threaten mischief to the inoffensive community; and especially to warn all citizens, careful of their safety, against intruding on the premises which she overshadows with her wings. Nevertheless, vixenly as she looks, many people are seeking, at this very moment, to shelter themselves under the wing of the federal eagle; imagining, I presume, that her bosom has all the softness and snugness of an eider-down pillow. But she has no great tenderness, even in her best of moods, and, sooner or later,—oftener soon than late,—is apt to fling off her nestlings with a scratch of her claw, a dab of her beak, or a rankling wound from her barbed arrows.

The pavement round about the above-described edifice—which we may as well name at once as the Custom-House of the port—has grass enough growing in its chinks to show that it has not, of late days, been worn by any multitudinous resort of business. In some months of the year, however, there often chances a forenoon

---

[3] Hawthorne had originally planned to publish *The Scarlet Letter* with several shorter works in a volume entitled "Old-Time Legends: Together With Sketches, Experimental and Ideal."

[4] Elias Hasket Derby (1739–1799), a wealthy shipowner in Salem.

when affairs move onward with livelier tread. Such occasions might remind the elderly citizen of that period, before the last war with England,[5] when Salem was a port by itself; not scorned, as she is now, by her own merchants and ship-owners, who permit her wharves to crumble to ruin, while their ventures go to swell, needlessly and imperceptibly, the mighty flood of commerce at New York or Boston. On some such morning, when three or four vessels happen to have arrived at once,—usually from Africa or South America,—or to be on the verge of their departure thitherward, there is a sound of frequent feet, passing briskly up and down the granite steps. Here, before his own wife has greeted him, you may greet the sea-flushed ship-master, just in port, with his vessel's papers under his arm in a tarnished tin box. Here, too, comes his owner, cheerful or sombre, gracious or in the sulks, accordingly as his scheme of the now accomplished voyage has been realized in merchandise that will readily be turned to gold, or has buried him under a bulk of incommodities, such as nobody will care to rid him of. Here likewise,—the germ of the wrinkle-browed, grizzly-bearded, careworn merchant,—we have the smart young clerk, who gets the taste of traffic as a wolf-cub does of blood, and already sends adventures in his master's ships, when he had better be sailing mimic boats upon a mill-pond. Another figure in the scene is the outward-bound sailor, in quest of a protection;[6] or the recently arrived one, pale and feeble, seeking a passport to the hospital. Nor must we forget the captains of the rusty little schooners that bring firewood from the British provinces; a rough-looking set of tarpaulins, without the alertness of the Yankee aspect, but contributing an item of no slight importance to our decaying trade.

Cluster all these individuals together, as they sometimes were, with other miscellaneous ones to diversify the group, and, for the time being, it made the Custom-House a stirring scene. More frequently, however, on ascending the steps, you would discern—in the entry, if it were summer time, or in their appropriate rooms, if wintry or inclement weather—a row of venerable figures, sitting in old-fashioned chairs, which were tipped on their hind legs back against the wall. Oftentimes they were asleep, but occasionally might be heard talking together, in voices between speech and a snore, and with that lack of energy that distinguishes the occupants of alms-houses, and all other human beings who depend for subsistence on charity, on monopolized labor, or any thing else but their own independent exertions. These old gentlemen—seated, like Matthew,[7] at the receipt of custom, but not very liable to be summoned thence, like him, for apostolic errands—were Custom-House officers.

Furthermore, on the left hand as you enter the front door, is a certain room or office, about fifteen feet square, and of a lofty height; with two of its arched windows commanding a view of the aforesaid dilapidated wharf, and the third looking across a narrow lane, and along a portion of Derby Street.[8] All three give glimpses of the shops of grocers, block-makers, slop-sellers, and ship-chandlers;[9] around the doors of which are generally to be seen, laughing and gossiping, clusters of old salts, and such other wharf-rats as haunt the Wapping[10] of a seaport. The room itself is cobwebbed, and dingy with old paint; its floor is strewn with

---

[5] The War of 1812.　　[6] A passport or document verifying citizenship.

[7] In Matthew 9:9 Matthew was "sitting at the receipt of custom" when he was summoned to be one of Christ's apostles.

[8] The street on which the customhouse was located.

[9] Pulley-makers, dealers in clothing and supplies for sailors, and grocers and outfitters.

[10] A run-down district of wharves in London.

gray sand, in a fashion that has elsewhere fallen into long disuse; and it is easy to conclude, from the general slovenliness of the place, that this is a sanctuary into which womankind, with her tools of magic, the broom and mop, has very infrequent access. In the way of furniture, there is a stove with a voluminous funnel; an old pine desk, with a three-legged stool beside it; two or three wooden-bottom chairs, exceedingly decrepit and infirm; and,—not to forget the library,—on some shelves, a score or two of volumes of the Acts of Congress, and a bulky Digest of the Revenue Laws. A tin pipe ascends through the ceiling, and forms a medium of vocal communication with other parts of the edifice. And here, some six months ago,—pacing from corner to corner, or lounging on the long-legged stool, with his elbow on the desk, and his eyes wandering up and down the columns of the morning newspaper,—you might have recognized, honored reader, the same individual who welcomed you into his cheery little study, where the sunshine glimmered so pleasantly through the willow branches, on the western side of the Old Manse. But now, should you go thither to seek him, you would inquire in vain for the Loco-foco[11] Surveyor. The besom[12] of reform has swept him out of office; and a worthier successor wears his dignity and pockets his emoluments.

This old town of Salem—my native place, though I have dwelt much away from it, both in boyhood and maturer years—possesses, or did possess, a hold on my affections, the force of which I have never realized during my seasons of actual residence here. Indeed, so far as its physical aspect is concerned, with its flat, unvaried surface, covered chiefly with wooden houses, few or none of which pretend to architectural beauty,—its irregularity, which is neither picturesque nor quaint, but only tame,—its long and lazy street, lounging wearisomely through the whole extent of the peninsula, with Gallows Hill and New Guinea at one end,[13] and a view of the alms-house at the other,—such being the features of my native town, it would be quite as reasonable to form a sentimental attachment to a disarranged checkerboard. And yet, though invariably happiest elsewhere, there is within me a feeling for old Salem, which, in lack of a better phrase, I must be content to call affection. The sentiment is probably assignable to the deep and aged roots which my family has struck into the soil. It is now nearly two centuries and a quarter since the original Briton, the earliest emigrant of my name,[14] made his appearance in the wild and forest-bordered settlement, which has since become a city. And here his descendants have been born and died, and have mingled their earthy substance with the soil; until no small portion of it must necessarily be akin to the mortal frame wherewith, for a little while, I walk the streets. In part, therefore, the attachment which I speak of is the mere sensuous sympathy of dust for dust. Few of my countrymen can know what it is; nor, as frequent transplantation is perhaps better for the stock, need they consider it desirable to know.

But the sentiment has likewise its moral quality. The figure of that first ances-

---

[11] Locofocos were matches; the Whigs applied the name to Democrats after an 1835 political meeting in which a radical group of Democrats, plunged into darkness by opponents in their party, relighted lamps with the new "lucifer" matches, or locofocos, and continued the debate.

[12] Broom.

[13] Salem is situated on a peninsula that includes the areas New Guinea and Gallow's Hill, reportedly where those found guilty of witchcraft were executed.

[14] William Hathorne (1607–1681) came to Massachusetts in 1630 with John Winthrop (1588–1649) and grew to be a powerful civil and military leader in Salem. Nathaniel Hawthorne added the "w" to his family name.

tor, invested by family tradition with a dim and dusky grandeur, was present to my boyish imagination, as far back as I can remember. It still haunts me, and induces a sort of home-feeling with the past, which I scarcely claim in reference to the present phase of the town. I seem to have a stronger claim to a residence here on account of this grave, bearded, sable-cloaked, and steeple-crowned progenitor,—who came so early, with his Bible and his sword, and trode the unworn street with such a stately port, and made so large a figure, as a man of war and peace,—a stronger claim than for myself, whose name is seldom heard and my face hardly known. He was a soldier, legislator, judge; he was a ruler in the Church; he had all the Puritanic traits, both good and evil. He was likewise a bitter persecutor; as witness the Quakers, who have remembered him in their histories, and relate an incident of his hard severity towards a woman of their sect, which will last longer, it is to be feared, than any record of his better deeds, although these were many.[15] His son,[16] too, inherited the persecuting spirit, and made himself so conspicuous in the martyrdom of the witches, that their blood may fairly be said to have left a stain upon him. So deep a stain, indeed, that his old dry bones, in the Charter Street burial-ground, must still retain it, if they have not crumbled utterly to dust! I know not whether these ancestors of mine bethought themselves to repent, and ask pardon of Heaven for their cruelties; or whether they are now groaning under the heavy consequences of them, in another state of being. At all events, I, the present writer, as their representative, hereby take shame upon myself for their sakes, and pray that any curse incurred by them—as I have heard, and as the dreary and unprosperous condition of the race, for many a long year back, would argue to exist—may be now and henceforth removed.

Doubtless, however, either of these stern and black-browed Puritans would have thought it quite a sufficient retribution for his sins, that, after so long a lapse of years, the old trunk of the family tree, with so much venerable moss upon it, should have borne, as its topmost bough, an idler like myself. No aim, that I have ever cherished, would they recognize as laudable; no success of mine—if my life, beyond its domestic scope, had ever been brightened by success—would they deem otherwise than worthless, if not positively disgraceful. "What is he?" murmurs one gray shadow of my forefathers to the other. "A writer of story-books! What kind of business in life,—what mode of glorifying God, or being serviceable to mankind in his day and generation,—may that be? Why, the degenerate fellow might as well have been a fiddler!" Such are the compliments bandied between my great-grandsires and myself, across the gulf of time! And yet, let them scorn me as they will, strong traits of their nature have intertwined themselves with mine.[17]

Planted deep, in the town's earliest infancy and childhood, by these two earnest and energetic men, the race has ever since subsisted here; always, too, in respectability; never, so far as I have known, disgraced by a single unworthy member; but seldom or never, on the other hand, after the first two generations, performing any memorable deed, or so much as putting forward a claim to public notice. Gradually, they have sunk almost out of sight; as old houses, here and there about the streets, get covered half-way to the eaves by the accumulation of new soil. From

---

[15] In "The Gentle Boy" (1832) Hawthorne wrote of the Puritan harshness toward the Quakers.

[16] John Hathorne (1641–1717), a judge at the Salem witchcraft trials in 1692.

[17] In "Main-Street," originally intended for publication with *The Scarlet Letter*, Hawthorne writes of the Puritans: "Let us thank God for having given us such ancestors; and let each successive generation thank Him, not less fervently, for being one step further from them in the march of ages."

father to son, for above a hundred years, they followed the sea; a gray-headed shipmaster, in each generation, retiring from the quarter-deck to the homestead, while a boy of fourteen took the hereditary place before the mast, confronting the salt spray and the gale, which had blustered against his sire and grandsire. The boy, also, in due time, passed from the forecastle to the cabin,[18] spent a tempestuous manhood, and returned from his world-wanderings, to grow old, and die, and mingle his dust with the natal earth. This long connection of a family with one spot, as its place of birth and burial, creates a kindred between the human being and the locality, quite independent of any charm in the scenery or moral circumstances that surround him. It is not love, but instinct. The new inhabitant—who came himself from a foreign land, or whose father or grandfather came—has little claim to be called a Salemite; he has no conception of the oyster-like tenacity with which an old settler, over whom his third century is creeping, clings to the spot where his successive generations have been imbedded. It is no matter that the place is joyless for him; that he is weary of the old wooden houses, the mud and dust, the dead level of site and sentiment, the chill east wind, and the chillest of social atmospheres;—all these, and whatever faults besides he may see or imagine, are nothing to the purpose. The spell survives, and just as powerfully as if the natal spot were an earthly paradise. So has it been in my case. I felt it almost as a destiny to make Salem my home; so that the mould of features and cast of character which had all along been familiar here—ever, as one representative of the race lay down in his grave, another assuming, as it were, his sentry-march along the Main Street—might still in my little day be seen and recognized in the old town. Nevertheless, this very sentiment is an evidence that the connection, which has become an unhealthy one, should at last be severed. Human nature will not flourish, any more than a potato, if it be planted and replanted, for too long a series of generations, in the same worn-out soil. My children have had other birthplaces, and, so far as their fortunes may be within my control, shall strike their roots into unaccustomed earth.

On emerging from the Old Manse, it was chiefly this strange, indolent, unjoyous attachment for my native town, that brought me to fill a place in Uncle Sam's brick edifice,[19] when I might as well, or better, have gone somewhere else. My doom was on me. It was not the first time, nor the second, that I had gone away,—as it seemed, permanently,—but yet returned, like the bad half-penny; or as if Salem were for me the inevitable centre of the universe. So, one fine morning, I ascended the flight of granite steps, with the President's commission in my pocket, and was introduced to the corps of gentlemen who were to aid me in my weighty responsibility, as chief executive officer of the Custom-House.

I doubt greatly—or rather, I do not doubt at all—whether any public functionary of the United States, either in the civil or military line, has ever had such a patriarchal body of veterans under his orders as myself. The whereabouts of the Oldest Inhabitant was at once settled, when I looked at them. For upwards of twenty years before this epoch, the independent position of the Collector had kept the Salem Custom-House out of the whirlpool of political vicissitude, which makes the tenure of office generally so fragile. A soldier,—New England's most

---

[18] Worked his way up from ordinary seaman to captain.

[19] The Salem Customhouse, where Hawthorne was the surveyor from 1846 to 1849, commissioned by President James K. Polk (1795–1849).

distinguished soldier,[20]—he stood firmly on the pedestal of his gallant services; and, himself secure in the wise liberality of the successive administrations through which he had held office, he had been the safety of his subordinates in many an hour of danger and heart-quake. General Miller was radically conservative; a man over whose kindly nature habit had no slight influence; attaching himself strongly to familiar faces, and with difficulty moved to change, even when change might have brought unquestionable improvement. Thus, on taking charge of my department, I found few but aged men. They were ancient sea-captains, for the most part, who, after being tost on every sea, and standing up sturdily against life's tempestuous blast, had finally drifted into this quiet nook; where, with little to disturb them, except the periodical terrors of a Presidential election, they one and all acquired a new lease of existence. Though by no means less liable than their fellow-men to age and infirmity, they had evidently some talisman or other that kept death at bay. Two or three of their number, as I was assured, being gouty and rheumatic, or perhaps bed-ridden, never dreamed of making their appearance at the Custom-House, during a large part of the year; but, after a torpid winter, would creep out into the warm sunshine of May or June, go lazily about what they termed duty, and, at their own leisure and convenience, betake themselves to bed again. I must plead guilty to the charge of abbreviating the official breath of more than one of these venerable servants of the republic. They were allowed, on my representation, to rest from their arduous labors, and soon afterwards—as if their sole principle of life had been zeal for their country's service; as I verily believe it was—withdrew to a better world. It is a pious consolation to me, that, through my interference, a sufficient space was allowed them for repentance of the evil and corrupt practices, into which, as a matter of course, every Custom-House officer must be supposed to fall. Neither the front nor the back entrance of the Custom-House opens on the road to Paradise.

The greater part of my officers were Whigs. It was well for their venerable brotherhood, that the new Surveyor was not a politician, and, though a faithful Democrat in principle, neither received nor held his office with any reference to political services. Had it been otherwise,—had an active politician been put into this influential post, to assume the easy task of making head against a Whig Collector, whose infirmities withheld him from the personal administration of his office,—hardly a man of the old corps would have drawn the breath of official life, within a month after the exterminating angel had come up the Custom-House steps. According to the received code in such matters, it would have been nothing short of duty, in a politician, to bring every one of those white heads under the axe of the guillotine. It was plain enough to discern, that the old fellows dreaded some such discourtesy at my hands. It pained, and at the same time amused me, to behold the terrors that attended my advent; to see a furrowed cheek, weather-beaten by half a century of storm, turn ashy pale at the glance of so harmless an individual as myself; to detect, as one or another addressed me, the tremor of a voice, which, in long-past days, had been wont to bellow through a speaking-trumpet, hoarsely enough to frighten Boreas[21] himself to silence. They knew,

---

[20] General James F. Miller (1776–1851), renowned for his bravery in the War of 1812, was the first territorial governor of Arkansas (1819–1825) and chief officer, or collector, of the Salem Custom-house from 1825 to 1849.

[21] According to Greek myth, the god of the North wind.

these excellent old persons, that, by all established rule,—and, as regarded some of them, weighed by their own lack of efficiency for business,—they ought to have given place to younger men, more orthodox in politics, and altogether fitter than themselves to serve our common Uncle. I knew it too, but could never quite find in my heart to act upon the knowledge. Much and deservedly to my own discredit, therefore, and considerably to the detriment of my official conscience, they continued, during my incumbency, to creep about the wharves, and loiter up and down the Custom-House steps. They spent a good deal of time, also, asleep in their accustomed corners, with their chairs tilted back against the wall; awaking, however, once or twice in a forenoon, to bore one another with the several thousandth repetition of old sea-stories, and mouldy jokes, that had grown to be passwords and countersigns among them.

The discovery was soon made, I imagine, that the new Surveyor had no great harm in him. So, with lightsome hearts, and the happy consciousness of being usefully employed,—in their own behalf, at least, if not for our beloved country,—these good old gentlemen went through the various formalities of office. Sagaciously, under their spectacles, did they peep into the holds of vessels! Mighty was their fuss about little matters, and marvellous, sometimes, the obtuseness that allowed greater ones to slip between their fingers! Whenever such a mischance occurred,—when a wagon-load of valuable merchandise had been smuggled ashore, at noonday, perhaps, and directly beneath their unsuspicious noses,—nothing could exceed the vigilance and alacrity with which they proceeded to lock, and double-lock, and secure with tape and sealing-wax, all the avenues of the delinquent vessel. Instead of a reprimand for their previous negligence, the case seemed rather to require an eulogium on their praiseworthy caution, after the mischief had happened; a grateful recognition of the promptitude of their zeal, the moment that there was no longer any remedy!

Unless people are more than commonly disagreeable, it is my foolish habit to contract a kindness for them. The better part of my companion's character, if it have a better part, is that which usually comes uppermost in my regard, and forms the type whereby I recognize the man. As most of these old Custom-House officers had good traits, and as my position in reference to them, being paternal and protective, was favorable to the growth of friendly sentiments, I soon grew to like them all. It was pleasant, in the summer forenoons,—when the fervent heat, that almost liquefied the rest of the human family, merely communicated a genial warmth to their half-torpid systems,—it was pleasant to hear them chatting in the back entry, a row of them all tipped against the wall, as usual; while the frozen witticisms of past generations were thawed out, and came bubbling with laughter from their lips. Externally, the jollity of aged men has much in common with the mirth of children; the intellect, any more than a deep sense of humor, has little to do with the matter; it is, with both, a gleam that plays upon the surface, and imparts a sunny and cheery aspect alike to the green branch, and gray, mouldering trunk. In one case, however, it is real sunshine; in the other, it more resembles the phosphorescent glow of decaying wood.

It would be sad injustice, the reader must understand, to represent all my excellent old friends as in the dotage. In the first place, my coadjutors were not invariably old; there were men among them in their strength and prime, of marked ability and energy, and altogether superior to the sluggish and dependent mode of life on which their evil stars had cast them. Then, moreover, the white locks of age were sometimes found to be the thatch of an intellectual tenement in good repair. But, as respects the majority of my corps of veterans, there will be no wrong done, if I characterize them generally as a set of wearisome old souls, who had gathered nothing worth preservation from their varied experience of life. They seemed to have flung away all the golden grain of practical wisdom, which they had enjoyed so many opportunities of harvesting, and most carefully to have stored their memories with the husks. They spoke with far more interest and unction of their morning's breakfast, or yesterday's, today's, or to-morrow's dinner, than of the shipwreck of forty or fifty years ago, and all the world's wonders which they had witnessed with their youthful eyes.

The father of the Custom-House—the patriarch, not only of this little squad of officials, but, I am bold to say, of the respectable body of tide-waiters[22] all over the United States—was a certain permanent Inspector. He might truly be termed a legitimate son of the revenue system, dyed in the wool, or rather, born in the purple; since his sire, a Revolutionary colonel, and formerly collector of the port, had created an office for him, and appointed him to fill it, at a period of the early ages which few living men can now remember. This Inspector, when I first knew him, was a man of fourscore years, or thereabouts, and certainly one of the most wonderful specimens of winter-green that you would be likely to discover in a lifetime's search. With his florid cheek, his compact figure, smartly arrayed in a bright-buttoned blue coat, his brisk and vigorous step, and his hale and hearty aspect, altogether, he seemed—not young, indeed—but a kind of new contrivance of Mother Nature in the shape of man, whom age and infirmity had no business to touch. His voice and laugh, which perpetually reëchoed through the Custom-House, had nothing of the tremulous quaver and cackle of an old man's utterance; they came strutting out of his lungs, like the crow of a cock, or the blast of a clarion. Looking at him merely as an animal,—and there was very little else to look at,—he was a most satisfactory object, from the thorough healthfulness and wholesomeness of his system, and his capacity, at that extreme age, to enjoy all, or nearly all, the delights which he had ever aimed at, or conceived of. The careless security of his life in the Custom-House, on a regular income, and with but slight and infrequent apprehensions of removal, had no doubt contributed to make time pass lightly over him. The original and more potent causes, however, lay in the rare perfection of his animal nature, the moderate proportion of intellect, and the very trifling admixture of moral and spiritual ingredients; these latter qualities, indeed, being in barely enough measure to keep the old gentleman from walking on all-fours. He possessed no power of thought, no depth of feeling, no troublesome sensibilities; nothing, in short, but a few commonplace instincts, which, aided by the cheerful temper that grew inevitably out of his physical well-being, did duty very respectably, and to general acceptance, in lieu of a heart. He had been the husband of three wives, all long since dead; the father of twenty children, most of whom, at every age of childhood or maturity, had likewise returned to dust. Here, one would suppose, might have been sorrow enough to imbue the sunniest disposition, through and through, with a sable tinge. Not so with our old Inspector! One brief sigh sufficed to carry off the entire burden of these dismal reminiscences. The next moment, he was as ready for sport as any unbreeched infant; far readier than the Collector's junior clerk, who, at nineteen years, was much the elder and graver man of the two.

I used to watch and study this patriarchal personage with, I think, livelier curi-

---

[22] Customs officers who board incoming ships to tally the cargo.

osity than any other form of humanity there presented to my notice. He was, in truth, a rare phenomenon; so perfect in one point of view; so shallow, so delusive, so impalpable, such an absolute nonentity, in every other. My conclusion was that he had no soul, no heart, no mind; nothing, as I have already said, but instincts; and yet, withal, so cunningly had the few materials of his character been put together, that there was no painful perception of deficiency, but, on my part, an entire contentment with what I found in him. It might be difficult—and it was so—to conceive how he should exist hereafter, so earthy and sensuous did he seem; but surely his existence here, admitting that it was to terminate with his last breath, had been not unkindly given; with no higher moral responsibilities than the beasts of the field, but with a larger scope of enjoyment than theirs, and with all their blessed immunity from the dreariness and duskiness of age.

One point, in which he had vastly the advantage over his four-footed brethren, was his ability to recollect the good dinners which it had made no small portion of the happiness of his life to eat. His gourmandism was a highly agreeable trait; and to hear him talk of roast-meat was as appetizing as a pickle or an oyster. As he possessed no higher attribute, and neither sacrificed nor vitiated any spiritual endowment by devoting all his energies and ingenuities to subserve the delight and profit of his maw, it always pleased and satisfied me to hear him expatiate on fish, poultry, and butcher's meat, and the most eligible methods of preparing them for the table. This reminiscences of good cheer, however ancient the date of the actual banquet, seemed to bring the savor of pig or turkey under one's very nostrils. There were flavors on his palate, that had lingered there not less than sixty or seventy years, and were still apparently as fresh as that of the mutton-chop which he had just devoured for his breakfast. I have heard him smack his lips over dinners, every guest at which, except himself, had long been food for worms. It was marvelous to observe how the ghosts of bygone meals were continually rising up before him; not in anger or retribution, but as if grateful for his former appreciation, and seeking to reduplicate an endless series of enjoyment, at once shadowy and sensual. A tenderloin of beef, a hind-quarter of veal, a spare-rib of pork, a particular chicken, or a remarkably praiseworthy turkey, which had perhaps adorned his board in the days of the elder Adams,[23] would be remembered; while all the subsequent experience of our race, and all the events that brightened or darkened his individual career, had gone over him with as little permanent effect as the passing breeze. The chief tragic event of the old man's life, so far as I could judge, was his mishap with a certain goose, which lived and died some twenty or forty years ago; a goose of most promising figure, but which, at table, proved so inveterately tough that the carving-knife would make no impression on its carcass; and it could only be divided with an axe and handsaw.

But it is time to quit this sketch; on which, however, I should be glad to dwell at considerably more length, because, of all men whom I have ever known, this individual was fittest to be a Custom-House officer. Most persons, owing to causes which I may not have space to hint at, suffer moral detriment from this peculiar mode of life. The old Inspector was incapable of it, and, were he to continue in office to the end of time, would be just as good as he was then, and sit down to dinner with just as good an appetite.

There is one likeness, without which my gallery of Custom-House portraits

---

[23] John Adams (1735–1826), second U.S. president (1797–1801) and father of John Quincy Adams (1767–1848), sixth U.S. president (1825–1829).

would be strangely incomplete; but which my comparatively few opportunities for observation enable me to sketch only in the merest outline. It is that of the Collector, our gallant old General, who, after his brilliant military service, subsequently to which he had ruled over a wild Western territory, had come hither, twenty years before, to spend the decline of his varied and honorable life. The brave soldier had already numbered, nearly or quite, his threescore years and ten, and was pursuing the remainder of his earthly march, burdened with infirmities which even the martial music of his own spirit-stirring recollections could do little towards lightening. The step was palsied now, that had been foremost in the charge. It was only with the assistance of a servant, and by leaning his hand heavily on the iron balustrade, that he could slowly and painfully ascend the Custom-House steps, and, with a toilsome progress across the floor, attain his customary chair beside the fireplace. There he used to sit, gazing with a somewhat dim serenity of aspect at the figures that came and went; amid the rustle of papers, the administering of oaths, the discussion of business, and the casual talk of the office; all which sounds and circumstances seemed but indistinctly to impress his senses, and hardly to make their way into his inner sphere of contemplation. His countenance, in this repose, was mild and kindly. If his notice was sought, an expression of courtesy and interest gleamed out upon his features; proving that there was light within him, and that it was only the outward medium of the intellectual lamp that obstructed the rays in their passage. The closer you penetrated to the substance of his mind, the sounder it appeared. When no longer called upon to speak, or listen, either of which operations cost him an evident effort, his face would briefly subside into its former not uncheerful quietude. It was not painful to behold this look; for, though dim, it had not the imbecility of decaying age. The framework of his nature, originally strong and massive, was not yet crumbled into ruin.

To observe and define his character, however, under such disadvantages, was as difficult a task as to trace out and build up anew, in imagination, an old fortress, like Ticonderoga,[24] from a view of its gray and broken ruins. Here and there, perchance, the walls may remain almost complete; but elsewhere may be only a shapeless mound, cumbrous[25] with its very strength, and overgrown, through long years of peace and neglect, with grass and alien weeds.

Nevertheless, looking at the old warrior with affection,—for, slight as was the communication between us, my feeling towards him, like that of all bipeds and quadrupeds who knew him, might not improperly be termed so,—I could discern the main points of his portrait. It was marked with the noble and heroic qualities which showed it to be not by a mere accident, but of good right, that he had won a distinguished name. His spirit could never, I conceive, have been characterized by an uneasy activity; it must, at any period of his life, have required an impulse to set him in motion; but, once stirred up, with obstacles to overcome, and an adequate object to be attained, it was not in the man to give out or fail. The heat that had formerly pervaded his nature, and which was not yet extinct, was never of the kind that flashes and flickers in a blaze, but, rather, a deep, red glow, as of iron in a furnace. Weight, solidity, firmness; this was the expression of his repose, even in such decay as had crept untimely over him, at the period of which I speak. But I could imagine, even then, that, under some excitement which should go deeply

---

[24] Fort Ticonderoga in upstate New York, captured from the British in 1775. In 1836 Hawthorne depicted this fort in "Old Ticonderoga: A Picture of the Past."
[25] Cumbersome.

into his consciousness,—roused by a trumpet-peal, loud enough to awaken all of his energies that were not dead, but only slumbering,—he was yet capable of flinging off his infirmities like a sick man's gown, dropping the staff of age to seize a battle-sword, and starting up once more a warrior. And, in so intense a moment, his demeanour would have still been calm. Such an exhibition, however, was but to be pictured in fancy; not to be anticipated, nor desired. What I saw in him—as evidently as the indestructible ramparts of Old Ticonderoga, already cited as the most appropriate simile—were the features of stubborn and ponderous endurance, which might well have amounted to obstinacy in his earlier days; of integrity, that, like most of his other endowments, lay in a somewhat heavy mass, and was just as unmalleable and unmanageable as a ton of iron ore; and of benevolence, which, fiercely as he led the bayonets on at Chippewa or Fort Erie,[26] I take to be of quite as genuine a stamp as what actuates any or all the polemical philanthropists of the age. He had slain men with his own hand, for aught I know;— certainly, they had fallen, like blades of grass at the sweep of the scythe, before the charge to which his spirit imparted its triumphant energy;—but, be that as it might, there was never in his heart so much cruelty as would have brushed the down off a butterfly's wing. I have not known the man, to whose innate kindliness I would more confidently make an appeal.

Many characteristics—and those, too, which contribute not the least forcibly to impart resemblance in a sketch—must have vanished, or been obscured, before I met the General. All merely graceful attributes are usually the most evanescent; nor does Nature adorn the human ruin with blossoms of new beauty, that have their roots and proper nutriment only in the chinks and crevices of decay, as she sows wall-flowers over the ruined fortress of Ticonderoga. Still, even in respect of grace and beauty, there were points well worth noting. A ray of humor, now and then, would make its way through the veil of dim obstruction, and glimmer pleasantly upon our faces. A trait of native elegance, seldom seen in the masculine character after childhood or early youth, was shown in the General's fondness for the sight and fragrance of flowers. An old soldier might be supposed to prize only the bloody laurel on his brow; but here was one, who seemed to have a young girl's appreciation of the floral tribe.

There, beside the fireplace, the brave old General used to sit; while the Surveyor—though seldom, when it could be avoided, taking upon himself the difficult task of engaging him in conversation—was fond of standing at a distance, and watching his quiet and almost slumberous countenance. He seemed away from us, although we saw him but a few yards off; remote, though we passed close beside his chair; unattainable, though we might have stretched forth our hands and touched his own. It might be, that he lived a more real life within his thoughts, than amid the unappropriate environment of the Collector's office. The evolutions of the parade; the tumult of the battle; the flourish of old, heroic music, heard thirty years before;—such scenes and sounds, perhaps, were all alive before his intellectual sense. Meanwhile, the merchants and ship-masters, the spruce clerks, and uncouth sailors, entered and departed; the bustle of this commercial and Custom-House life kept up its little murmur roundabout him; and neither with the men nor their affairs did the General appear to sustain the most distant relation. He was as much out of place as an old sword—now rusty, but which had flashed once in the battle's front, and showed still a bright gleam along its blade—would have

---

[26] Important battles on the Niagara frontier during the War of 1812.

been, among the inkstands, paper-folders, and mahogany rulers, on the Deputy Collector's desk.

There was one thing that much aided me in renewing and re-creating the stalwart soldier of the Niagara frontier,—the man of true and simple energy. It was the recollection of those memorable words of his,—"I'll try, Sir!"[27]—spoken on the very verge of a desperate and heroic enterprise, and breathing the soul and spirit of New England hardihood, comprehending all perils, and encountering all. If, in our country, valor were rewarded by heraldic honor, this phrase—which it seems so easy to speak, but which only he, with such a task of danger and glory before him, has ever spoken—would be the best and fittest of all mottoes for the General's shield of arms.

It contributes greatly towards a man's moral and intellectual health, to be brought into habits of companionship with individuals unlike himself, who care little for his pursuits, and whose sphere and abilities he must go out of himself to appreciate. The accidents of my life have often afforded me this advantage, but never with more fulness and variety than during my continuance in office. There was one man, especially, the observation of whose character gave me a new idea of talent. His gifts were emphatically those of a man of business; prompt, acute, clear-minded; with an eye that saw through all perplexities, and a faculty of arrangement that made them vanish, as by the waving of an enchanter's wand. Bred up from boyhood in the Custom-House, it was his proper field of activity; and the many intricacies of business, so harassing to the interloper, presented themselves before him with the regularity of a perfectly comprehended system. In my contemplation, he stood as the ideal of his class. He was, indeed, the Custom-House in himself; or, at all events, the main-spring that kept its variously revolving wheels in motion; for, in an institution like this, where its officers are appointed to subserve their own profit and convenience, and seldom with a leading reference to their fitness for the duty to be performed, they must perforce seek elsewhere the dexterity which is not in them. Thus, by an inevitable necessity, as a magnet attracts steel-filings, so did our man of business draw to himself the difficulties which everybody met with. With an easy condescension, and kind forbearance towards our stupidity,—which, to his order of mind, must have seemed little short of crime,—would he forthwith, by the merest touch of his finger, make the incomprehensible as clear as daylight. The merchants valued him not less than we, his esoteric friends. His integrity was perfect; it was a law of nature with him, rather than a choice or a principle; nor can it be otherwise than the main condition of an intellect so remarkably clear and accurate as his, to be honest and regular in the administration of affairs. A stain on his conscience, as to any thing that came within the range of his vocation, would trouble such a man very much in the same way, though to a far greater degree, than an error in the balance of an account, or an ink-blot on the fair page of a book of record. Here, in a word,—and it is a rare instance in my life,—I had met with a person thoroughly adapted to the situation which he held.

Such were some of the people with whom I now found myself connected. I took it in good part at the hands of Providence, that I was thrown into a position so little akin to my past habits; and set myself seriously to gather from it whatever profit was to be had. After my fellowship of toil and impracticable schemes, with

---

[27] Words attributed to General Miller when General Winfield Scott (1786–1866) commanded him to capture a British battery at Lundy's Lane, Ontario, near Niagara Falls.

the dreamy brethren of Brook Farm;[28] after living for three years within the subtile influence of an intellect like Emerson's;[29] after those wild, free days on the Assabeth, indulging fantastic speculations beside our fire of fallen boughs, with Ellery Channing; after talking with Thoreau about pine-trees and Indian relics, in his hermitage at Walden; after growing fastidious by sympathy with the classic refinement of Hillard's[30] culture; after becoming imbued with poetic sentiment at Longfellow's[31] hearth-stone;—it was time, at length, that I should exercise other faculties of my nature, and nourish myself with food for which I had hitherto had little appetite. Even the old Inspector was desirable, as a change of diet, to a man who had known Alcott.[32] I looked upon it as an evidence, in some measure, of a system naturally well balanced, and lacking no essential part of a thorough organization, that, with such associates to remember, I could mingle at once with men of altogether different qualities, and never murmur at the change.

Literature, its exertions and objects, were now of little moment in my regard. I cared not, at this period, for books; they were apart from me. Nature,—except it were human nature,—the nature that is developed in earth and sky, was, in one sense, hidden from me; and all the imaginative delight, wherewith it had been spiritualized, passed away out of my mind. A gift, a faculty, if it had not departed, was suspended and inanimate within me. There would have been something sad, unutterably dreary, in all this, had I not been conscious that it lay at my own option to recall whatever was valuable in the past. It might be true, indeed, that this was a life which could not, with impunity, be lived too long; else, it might make me permanently other than I had been, without transforming me into any shape which it would be worth my while to take. But I never considered it as other than a transitory life. There was always a prophetic instinct, a low whisper in my ear, that, within no long period, and whenever a new change of custom should be essential to my good, a change would come.

Meanwhile, there I was, a Surveyor of the Revenue, and, so far as I have been able to understand, as good a Surveyor as need be. A man of thought, fancy, and sensibility, (had he ten times the Surveyor's proportion of those qualities,) may, at any time, be a man of affairs, if he will only choose to give himself the trouble. My fellow-officers, and the merchants and sea-captains with whom my official duties brought me into any manner of connection, viewed me in no other light, and probably knew me in no other character. None of them, I presume, had ever read a page of my inditing, or would have cared a fig the more for me, if they had read them all; nor would it have mended the matter, in the least, had those same unprofitable pages been written with a pen like that of Burns or of Chaucer,[33] each

---

[28] The transcendentalist community founded in 1841 at West Roxbury, Massachusetts, officially the Brook Farm Institute of Agriculture and Education. Hawthorne lived there from April to November 1841 and based his third novel, *The Blithedale Romance* (1852), on the communal experiment.

[29] After leaving Brook Farm, Hawthorne married and moved to Concord, Massachusetts, near the Assabeth River in central Massachusetts (1842–1845). His neighbors included the noted transcendentalists Ralph Waldo Emerson (1803–1882), William Ellery Channing (1818–1901), and Henry David Thoreau (1817–1862).

[30] George S. Hillard (1808–1879), Boston lawyer, writer, and friend of literary figures.

[31] Henry Wadsworth Longfellow (1806–1882), a classmate of Hawthorne at Bowdoin College.

[32] Amos Bronson Alcott (1799–1888), whom Hawthorne knew at Brook Farm; he was the father of Louisa May Alcott (1832–1888).

[33] Robert Burns (1759–1796), a Scottish poet and collector of excise taxes in Dumfries, Scotland, from 1789 to 1791; Geoffrey Chaucer (1340?–1400), an English poet and controller of customs in London from 1374 to 1386.

of whom was a Custom-House officer in his day, as well as I. It is a good lesson—though it may often be a hard one—for a man who has dreamed of literary fame, and of making for himself a rank among the world's dignitaries by such means, to step aside out of the narrow circle in which his claims are recognized, and to find how utterly devoid of significance, beyond that circle, is all that he achieves, and all he aims at. I know not that I especially needed the lesson, either in the way of warning or rebuke; but, at any rate, I learned it thoroughly; nor, it gives me pleasure to reflect, did the truth, as it came home to my perception, ever cost me a pang, or require to be thrown off in a sigh. In the way of literary talk, it is true, the Naval Officer—an excellent fellow, who came into office with me, and went out only a little later—would often engage me in a discussion about one or the other of his favorite topics, Napoleon or Shakspeare. The Collector's junior clerk, too,—a young gentleman who, it was whispered, occasionally covered a sheet of Uncle Sam's letter-paper with what, (at the distance of a few yards,) looked very much like poetry,—used now and then to speak of me of books, as matters with which I might possibly be conversant. This was my all of lettered intercourse; and it was quite sufficient for my necessities.

No longer seeking nor caring that my name should be blazoned abroad on title-pages, I smiled to think that it had now another kind of vogue. The Custom-House marker imprinted it, with a stencil and black paint, on pepper-bags, and baskets of anatto,[34] and cigar-boxes, and bales of all kinds of dutiable merchandise, in testimony that these commodities had paid the impost,[35] and gone regularly through the office. Borne on such queer vehicle of fame, a knowledge of my existence, so far as a name conveys it, was carried where it had never been before, and, I hope, will never go again.

But the past was not dead. Once in a great while, the thoughts, that had seemed so vital and so active, yet had been put to rest so quietly, revived again. One of the most remarkable occasions, when the habit of bygone days awoke in me, was that which brings it within the law of literary propriety to offer the public the sketch which I am now writing.

In the second story of the Custom-House, there is a large room, in which the brick-work and naked rafters have never been covered with panelling and plaster. The edifice—originally projected on a scale adapted to the old commercial enterprise of the port, and with an idea of subsequent prosperity destined never to be realized—contains far more space than its occupants know what to do with. This airy hall, therefore, over the Collector's apartments, remains unfinished to this day, and, in spite of the aged cobwebs that festoon its dusky beams, appears still to await the labor of the carpenter and mason. At one end of the room, in a recess, were a number of barrels, piled one upon another, containing bundles of official documents. Large quantities of similar rubbish lay lumbering[36] the floor. It was sorrowful to think how many days, and weeks, and months, and years of toil, had been wasted on these musty papers, which were now only an encumbrance on earth, and were hidden away in this forgotten corner, never more to be glanced at by human eyes. But, then, what reams of other manuscripts—filled, not with the dulness of official formalities, but with the thought of inventive brains and the rich effusion of deep hearts—had gone equally to oblivion; and that, moreover, without serving a purpose in their day, as these heaped-up papers had, and—saddest

---

[34] Annatto, a yellowish-red dye made from the pulp of seeds from a tropical tree.
[35] The tax due on imported goods.   [36] Cluttering.

of all—without purchasing for their writers the comfortable livelihood which the clerks of the Custom-House had gained by these worthless scratchings of the pen! Yet not altogether worthless, perhaps, as materials of local history. Here, no doubt, statistics of the former commerce of Salem might be discovered, and memorials of her princely merchants,—old King Derby,—old Billy Gray,—old Simon Forrester,[37]—and many another magnate in his day; whose powdered head, however, was scarcely in the tomb, before his mountain-pile of wealth began to dwindle. The founders of the greater part of the families which now compose the aristocracy of Salem might here be traced, from the petty and obscure beginnings of their traffic, at periods generally much posterior to the Revolution, upward to what their children look upon as long-established rank.

Prior to the Revolution, there is a dearth of records; the earlier documents and archives of the Custom-House having, probably, been carried off to Halifax, when all the King's officials accompanied the British army in its flight from Boston.[38] It has often been a matter of regret with me; for, going back, perhaps, to the days of the Protectorate,[39] those papers must have contained many references to forgotten or remembered men, and to antique customs, which would have affected me with the same pleasure as when I used to pick up Indian arrow-heads in the field near the Old Manse.

But, one idle and rainy day, it was my fortune to make a discovery of some little interest. Poking and burrowing into the heaped-up rubbish in the corner; unfolding one and another document, and reading the names of vessels that had long ago foundered at sea or rotted at the wharves, and those of merchants, never heard of now on 'Change,[40] nor very readily decipherable on their mossy tombstones; glancing at such matters with the saddened, weary, half-reluctant interest which we bestow on the corpse of dead activity,—and exerting my fancy, sluggish with little use, to raise up from these dry bones an image of the old town's brighter aspect, when India was a new region, and only Salem knew the way thither,—I chanced to lay my hand on a small package, carefully done up in a piece of ancient yellow parchment. This envelope had the air of an official record of some period long past, when clerks engrossed their stiff and formal chirography on more substantial materials than at present. There was something about it that quickened an instinctive curiosity, and made me undo the faded red tape, that tied up the package, with the sense that a treasure would here be brought to light. Unbending the rigid folds of the parchment cover, I found it to be a commission, under the hand and seal of Governor Shirley,[41] in favor of one Jonathan Pue,[42] as Surveyor of his Majesty's Customs for the port of Salem, in the Province of Massachusetts Bay. I remembered to have read (probably in Felt's Annals) a notice of the decease of Mr. Surveyor Pue, about fourscore years ago; and likewise, in a

---

[37] William Gray (1750–1825) and Simon Forrester (1776–1851), like Derby, were wealthy Salem shipowners.

[38] When George Washington attacked the British forces in Boston in 1776, General William Howe (1729–1814) evacuated the British troops to Nova Scotia.

[39] The years 1653 to 1660, when first Oliver Cromwell (1599–1658) and then his son Richard (1626–1712) ruled as lords protector of England.

[40] Exchange, comparable to the modern stock exchange.

[41] William Shirley (1694–1771), governor of Massachusetts from 1741 to 1749 and from 1753 to 1756.

[42] A customs surveyor in Salem in 1752, whose death is recorded in Joseph B. Felt's *Annals of Salem From Its First Settlement* (1827) as having taken place on March 24, 1760. Hawthorne gleaned much information about colonial times from Felt's *Annals*.

newspaper of recent times, an account of the digging up of his remains in the little grave-yard of St. Peter's Church,[43] during the renewal of that edifice. Nothing, if I rightly call to mind, was left of my respected predecessor, save an imperfect skeleton, and some fragments of apparel, and a wig of majestic frizzle; which, unlike the head that it once adorned, was in very satisfactory preservation. But, on examining the papers which the parchment commission served to envelop, I found more traces of Mr. Pue's mental part, and the internal operations of his head, than the frizzled wig had contained of the venerable skull itself.

They were documents, in short, not official, but of a private nature, or, at least, written in his private capacity, and apparently with his own hand. I could account for their being included in the heap of Custom-House lumber only by the fact, that Mr. Pue's death had happened suddenly; and that these papers, which he probably kept in his official desk, had never come to the knowledge of his heirs, or were supposed to relate the business of the revenue. On the transfer of the archives to Halifax, this package, proving to be of no public concern, was left behind, and had remained ever since unopened.

The ancient Surveyor—being little molested, I suppose, at that early day, with business pertaining to his office—seems to have devoted some of his many leisure hours to researches as a local antiquarian, and other inquisitions of a similar nature. These supplied material for petty activity to a mind that would otherwise have been eaten up with rust. A portion of his facts, by the by, did me good service in the preparation of the article entitled "MAIN STREET,"[44] included in the present volume. The remainder may perhaps be applied to purposes equally valuable, hereafter; or not impossibly may be worked up, so far as they go, into a regular history of Salem, should my veneration for the natal soil ever impel me to so pious a task. Meanwhile, they shall be at the command of any gentleman, inclined, and competent, to take the unprofitable labor off my hands. As a final disposition, I contemplate depositing them with the Essex Historical Society.[45]

But the object that most drew my attention, in the mysterious package, was a certain affair of fine red cloth, much worn and faded. There were traces about it of gold embroidery, which, however, was greatly frayed and defaced; so that none, or very little, of the glitter was left. It had been wrought, as was easy to perceive, with wonderful skill of needlework; and the stitch (as I am assured by ladies conversant with such mysteries) gives evidence of a now forgotten art, not to be recovered even by the process of picking out the threads. This rag of scarlet cloth,—for time, and wear, and a sacrilegious moth, had reduced it to little other than a rag,—on careful examination, assumed the shape of a letter. It was the capital letter A. By an accurate measurement, each limb proved to be precisely three inches and a quarter in length. It had been intended, there could be no doubt, as an ornamental article of dress; but how it was to be worn, or what rank, honor, and dignity, in by-past times, were signified by it, was a riddle which (so evanescent are the fashions of the world in these particulars) I saw little hope of solving. And yet it strangely interested me. My eyes fastened themselves upon the old scarlet letter, and would not be turned aside. Certainly, there was some deep meaning in it, most worthy of interpretation, and which, as it were, streamed forth

[43] The first Anglican church in Salem, established in 1633.

[44] One of the sketches Hawthorne had planned to include in *The Scarlet Letter*.

[45] An institution that contains valuable historical material concerning colonial Massachusetts; the documents Hawthorne mentions are fictional.

from the mystic symbol, subtly communicating itself to my sensibilities, but evading the analysis of my mind.

While thus perplexed,—and cogitating, among other hypotheses, whether the letter might not have been one of those decorations which the white men used to contrive, in order to take the eyes of Indians,—I happened to place it on my breast. It seemed to me,—the reader may smile, but must not doubt my word,—it seemed to me, then, that I experienced a sensation not altogether physical, yet almost so, as of burning heat; and as if the letter were not of red cloth, but red-hot iron. I shuddered, and involuntarily let it fall upon the floor.

In the absorbing contemplation of the scarlet letter, I had hitherto neglected to examine a small roll of dingy paper, around which it had been twisted. This I now opened, and had the satisfaction to find, recorded by the old Surveyor's pen, a reasonably complete explanation of the whole affair. There were several foolscap sheets,[46] containing many particulars respecting the life and conversation of one Hester Prynne, who appeared to have been rather a noteworthy personage in the view of our ancestors. She had flourished during a period between the early days of Massachusetts and the close of the seventeenth century. Aged persons, alive in the time of Mr. Surveyor Pue, and from whose oral testimony he had made up his narrative, remembered her, in their youth, as a very old, but not decrepit woman, of a stately and solemn aspect. It had been her habit, from an almost immemorial date, to go about the country as a kind of voluntary nurse, and doing whatever miscellaneous good she might; taking upon herself, likewise, to give advice in all matters, especially those of the heart; by which means, as a person of such propensities inevitably must, she gained from many people the reverence due to an angel, but, I should imagine, was looked upon by others as an intruder and a nuisance. Prying farther into the manuscript, I found the record of other doings and sufferings of this singular woman, for most of which the reader is referred to the story entitled "THE SCARLET LETTER"; and it should be borne carefully in mind, that the main facts of that story are authorized and authenticated by the document of Mr. Surveyor Pue. The original papers, together with the scarlet letter itself,— a most curious relic,—are still in my possession, and shall be freely exhibited to whomsoever, induced by the great interest of the narrative, may desire a sight of them. I must not be understood as affirming, that, in the dressing up of the tale, and imagining the motives and modes of passion that influenced the characters who figure in it, I have invariably confined myself within the limits of the old Surveyor's half a dozen sheets of foolscap. On the contrary, I have allowed myself, as to such points, nearly or altogether as much license as if the facts had been entirely of my own invention. What I contend for is the authenticity of the outline.

This incident recalled my mind, in some degree, to its old track. There seemed to be here the groundwork of a tale. It impressed me as if the ancient Surveyor, in his garb of a hundred years gone by, and wearing his immortal wig,— which was buried with him, but did not perish in the grave,—had met me in the deserted chamber of the Custom-House. In his port[47] was the dignity of one who had borne his Majesty's commission, and who was therefore illuminated by a ray of the splendor that shone so dazzlingly about the throne. How unlike, alas! the hang-dog look of a republican official, who, as the servant of the people, feels himself less than the least, and below the lowest, of his masters. With his own ghostly

---

[46] Sheets of paper measuring 13 by 16 inches unfolded; often folded into four smaller pages.
[47] Deportment.

hand, the obscurely seen, but majestic, figure had imparted to me the scarlet symbol, and the little roll of explanatory manuscript. With his own ghostly voice, he had exhorted me, on the sacred consideration of my filial duty and reverence towards him,—who might reasonably regard himself as my official ancestor,—to bring his mouldy and moth-eaten lucubrations[48] before the public. "Do this," said the ghost of Mr. Surveyor Pue, emphatically nodding the head that looked so imposing within its memorable wig, "do this, and the profit shall be all your own! You will shortly need it; for it is not in your days as it was in mine, when a man's office was a life-lease, and often-times an heirloom. But, I charge you, in this matter of old Mistress Prynne, give to your predecessor's memory the credit which will be rightfully its due!" And I said to the ghost of Mr. Surveyor Pue,— "I will!"

On Hester Prynne's story, therefore, I bestowed much thought. It was the subject of my meditations for many an hour, while pacing to and fro across my room, or traversing, with a hundredfold repetition, the long extent from the front-door of the Custom-House to the side-entrance, and back again. Great were the weariness and annoyance of the old Inspector and the Weighers and Gaugers, whose slumbers were disturbed by the unmercifully lengthened tramp of my passing and returning footsteps. Remembering their own former habits, they used to say that the Surveyor was walking the quarter-deck. They probably fancied that my sole object—and, indeed, the sole object for which a sane man could ever put himself into voluntary motion—was, to get an appetite for dinner. And to say the truth, an appetite, sharpened by the east-wind that generally blew along the passage, was the only valuable result of so much indefatigable exercise. So little adapted is the atmosphere of a Custom-House to the delicate harvest of fancy and sensibility, that, had I remained there through ten Presidencies yet to come, I doubt whether the tale of "The Scarlet Letter" would ever have been brought before the public eye. My imagination was a tarnished mirror. It would not reflect, or only with miserable dimness, the figures with which I did my best to people it. The characters of the narrative would not be warmed and rendered malleable, by any heat that I could kindle at my intellectual forge. They would take neither the glow of passion nor the tenderness of sentiment, but retained all the rigidity of dead corpses, and stared me in the face with a fixed and ghastly grin of contemptuous defiance. "What have you to do with us?" that expression seemed to say. "The little power you might once have possessed over the tribe of unrealities is gone! You have bartered it for a pittance of the public gold. Go, then, and earn your wages!" In short, the almost torpid creatures of my own fancy twitted me with imbecility, and not without fair occasion.

It was not merely during the three hours and a half which Uncle Sam claimed as his share of my daily life, that this wretched numbness held possession of me. It went with me on my sea-shore walks and rambles into the country, whenever— which was seldom and reluctantly—I bestirred myself to seek that invigorating charm of Nature, which used to give me such freshness and activity of thought, the moment that I stepped across the threshold of the Old Manse. The same torpor, as regarded the capacity for intellectual effort, accompanied me home, and weighed upon me in the chamber which I most absurdly termed my study. Nor did it quit me, when, late at night, I sat in the deserted parlour, lighted only by the glimmering coal-fire and the moon, striving to picture forth imaginary scenes,

---

[48] Studious labors, laborious writing.

which, the next day, might flow out on the brightening page in many-hued description.

If the imaginative faculty refused to act at such an hour, it might well be deemed a hopeless case. Moonlight, in a familiar room, falling so white upon the carpet, and showing all its figures so distinctly,—making every object so minutely visible, yet so unlike a morning or noontide visibility,—is a medium the most suitable for a romance-writer to get acquainted with his illusive guests. There is the little domestic scenery of the well-known apartment; the chairs, with each its separate individuality; the centre-table, sustaining a work-basket, a volume or two, and an extinguished lamp; the sofa; the book-case; the picture on the wall;—all these details, so completely seen, are so spiritualized by the unusual light, that they seem to lose their actual substance, and become things of intellect. Nothing is too small or too trifling to undergo this change, and acquire dignity thereby. A child's shoe; the doll, seated in her little wicker carriage; the hobby-horse;—whatever, in a word, has been used or played with, during the day, is now invested with a quality of strangeness and remoteness, though still almost as vividly present as by daylight. Thus, therefore, the floor of our familiar room has become a neutral territory, somewhere between the real world and fairy-land, where the Actual and the Imaginary may meet, and each imbue itself with the nature of the other.[49] Ghosts might enter here, without affrighting us. It would be too much in keeping with the scene to excite surprise, were we to look about us and discover a form, beloved, but gone hence, now sitting quietly in a streak of this magic moonshine, with an aspect that would make us doubt whether it had returned from afar, or had never once stirred from our fireside.

The somewhat dim coal-fire has an essential influence in producing the effect which I would describe. It throws its unobtrusive tinge throughout the room, with a faint ruddiness upon the walls and ceiling, and a reflected gleam from the polish of the furniture. This warmer light mingles itself with the cold spirituality of the moonbeams, and communicates, as it were, a heart and sensibilities of human tenderness to the forms which fancy summons up. It converts them from snow-images into men and women. Glancing at the looking-glass, we behold—deep within its haunted verge—the smouldering glow of the half-extinguished anthracite, the white moonbeams on the floor, and a repetition of all the gleam and shadow of the picture, with one remove farther from the actual, and nearer to the imaginative. Then, at such an hour, and with this scene before him, if a man, sitting all alone, cannot dream strange things, and make them look like truth, he need never try to write romances.

But, for myself, during the whole of my Custom-House experience, moonlight and sunshine, and the glow of fire-light, were just alike in my regard; and neither of them was of one whit more avail than the twinkle of a tallow-candle. An entire class of susceptibilities, and a gift connected with them,—of no great richness or value, but the best I had,—was gone from me.

It is my belief, however, that, had I attempted a different order of composition, my faculties would not have been found so pointless and inefficacious. I might, for instance, have contented myself with writing out the narratives of a veteran shipmaster, one of the Inspectors, whom I should be most ungrateful not to men-

---

[49] The prefaces to Hawthorne's other romances—*The House of the Seven Gables* (1851), *The Blithedale Romance,* and *The Marble Faun* (1860)—show his concern for setting up some sort of "neutral territory" as the condition of his fiction.

tion; since scarcely a day passed that he did not stir me to laughter and admiration by his marvellous gifts as a story-teller. Could I have preserved the picturesque force of his style, and the humorous coloring which nature taught him how to throw over his descriptions, the result, I honestly believe, would have been something new in literature. Or I might readily have found a more serious task. It was a folly, with the materiality of this daily life pressing so intrusively upon me, to attempt to fling myself back into another age; or to insist on creating the semblance of a world out of airy matter, when, at every moment, the impalpable beauty of my soap-bubble was broken by the rude contact of some actual circumstance. The wiser effort would have been, to diffuse thought and imagination through the opaque substance of to-day, and thus to make it a bright transparency; to spiritualize the burden that began to weigh so heavily; to seek, resolutely, the true and indestructible value that lay hidden in the petty and wearisome incidents, and ordinary characters, with which I was now conversant. The fault was mine. The page of life that was spread out before me seemed dull and commonplace, only because I had not fathomed its deeper import. A better book than I shall ever write was there; leaf after leaf presenting itself to me, just as it was written out by the reality of the flitting hour, and vanishing as fast as written, only because my brain wanted the insight and my hand the cunning to transcribe it. At some future day, it may be, I shall remember a few scattered fragments and broken paragraphs, and write them down, and find the letters turn to gold upon the page.

These perceptions have come too late. At the instant, I was only conscious that what would have been a pleasure once was now a hopeless toil. There was no occasion to make much moan about this state of affairs. I had ceased to be a writer of tolerably poor tales and essays, and had become a tolerably good Surveyor of the Customs. That was all. But, nevertheless, it is any thing but agreeable to be haunted by a suspicion that one's intellect is dwindling away; or exhaling, without your consciousness, like ether out of a phial; so that, at every glance, you find a smaller and less volatile residuum. Of the fact, there could be no doubt; and examining myself and others, I was led to conclusions in reference to the effect of public office on the character, not very favorable to the mode of life in question. In some other form, perhaps, I may hereafter develop these effects. Suffice it here to say, that a Custom-House officer, of long continuance, can hardly be a very praiseworthy or respectable personage, for many reasons; one of them, the tenure by which he holds his situation, and another, the very nature of his business, which—though, I trust, an honest one—is of such a sort that he does not share in the united effort of mankind.

An effect—which I believe to be observable, more or less, in every individual who has occupied the position—is, that, while he leans on the mighty arm of the Republic, his own proper strength departs from him. He loses, in an extent proportioned to the weakness or force of his original nature, the capability of self-support. If he possess an unusual share of native energy, or the enervating magic of place do not operate too long upon him, his forfeited powers may be redeemable. The ejected officer—fortunate in the unkindly shove that sends him forth betimes, to struggle amid a struggling world—may return to himself, and become all that he has ever been. But this seldom happens. He usually keeps his ground just long enough for his own ruin, and is then thrust out, with sinews all unstrung, to totter along the difficult footpath of life as he best may. Conscious of his own infirmity,—that his tempered steel and elasticity are lost,—he for ever afterwards looks wistfully about him in quest of support external to himself. His pervading and continual hope—a hallucination, which, in the face of all discouragement, and making light of impossibilities, haunts him while he lives, and, I fancy, like the convulsive throes of the cholera, torments him for a brief space after death— is, that, finally, and in no long time, by some happy coincidence of circumstances, he shall be restored to office. This faith, more than any thing else, steals the pith and availability out of whatever enterprise he may dream of undertaking. Why should he toil and moil, and be at so much trouble to pick himself up out of the mud, when, in a little while hence, the strong arm of his Uncle will raise and support him? Why should he work for his living here, or go to dig gold in California,[50] when he is so soon to be made happy, at monthly intervals, with a little pile of glittering coin out of his Uncle's pocket? It is sadly curious to observe how slight a taste of office suffices to infect a poor fellow with this singular disease. Uncle Sam's gold—meaning no disrespect to the worthy old gentleman—has, in this respect, a quality of enchantment like that of the Devil's wages. Whoever touches it should look well to himself, or he may find the bargain to go hard against him, involving, if not his soul, yet many of its better attributes; its sturdy force, its courage and constancy, its truth, its self-reliance, and all that gives the emphasis to manly character.

Here was a fine prospect in the distance! Not that the Surveyor brought the lesson home to himself, or admitted that he could be so utterly undone, either by continuance in office, or ejectment. Yet my reflections were not the most comfortable. I began to grow melancholy and restless; continually prying into my mind, to discover which of its poor properties were gone, and what degree of detriment had already accrued to the remainder. I endeavoured to calculate how much longer I could stay in the Custom-House, and yet go forth a man. To confess the truth, it was my greatest apprehension,—as it would never be a measure of policy to turn out so quiet an individual as myself, and it being hardly in the nature of a public officer to resign,—it was my chief trouble, therefore, that I was likely to grow gray and decrepit in the Surveyorship, and become much such another animal as the old Inspector. Might it not, in the tedious lapse of official life that lay before me, finally be with me as it was with this venerable friend,—to make the dinner-hour the nucleus of the day, and to spend the rest of it, as an old dog spends it, asleep in the sunshine or the shade? A dreary look-forward this, for a man who felt it to be the best definition of happiness to live throughout the whole range of his faculties and sensibilities! But, all this while, I was giving myself very unnecessary alarm. Providence had meditated better things for me than I could possibly imagine for myself.

A remarkable event of the third year of my Surveyorship—to adopt the tone of "P.P."—was the election of General Taylor[51] to the Presidency. It is essential, in order to form a complete estimate of the advantages of official life, to view the incumbent at the in-coming of a hostile administration. His position is then one of the most singularly irksome, and, in every contingency, disagreeable, that a wretched mortal can possibly occupy; with seldom an alternative of good, on either hand, although what presents itself to him as the worst event may very probably be the best. But it is a strange experience, to a man of pride and sensibility, to know that his interests are within the control of individuals who neither love nor

---

[50] The California Gold Rush of 1849.

[51] Zachary Taylor (1784–1850), a Whig and twelfth U.S. president (1849–1850); his election in 1848 led to Hawthorne's dismissal from the customhouse.

understand him, and by whom, since one or the other must needs happen, he would rather be injured than obliged. Strange, too, for one who has kept his calmness throughout the contest, to observe the bloodthirstiness that is developed in the hour of triumph, and to be conscious that he is himself among its objects! There are few uglier traits of human nature than this tendency—which I now witnessed in men no worse than their neighbours—to grow cruel, merely because they possessed the power of inflicting harm. If the guillotine, as applied to officeholders, were a literal fact, instead of one of the most apt of metaphors, it is my sincere belief, that the active members of the victorious party were sufficiently excited to have chopped off all our heads, and have thanked Heaven for the opportunity! It appears to me—who have been a calm and curious observer, as well in victory as defeat—that this fierce and bitter spirit of malice and revenge has never distinguished the many triumphs of my own party as it now did that of the Whigs. The Democrats take the offices, as a general rule, because they need them, and because the practice of many years has made it the law of political warfare, which, unless a different system be proclaimed, it were weakness and cowardice to murmur at. But the long habit of victory has made them generous. They know how to spare, when they see occasion; and when they strike, the axe may be sharp, indeed, but its edge is seldom poisoned with ill-will; nor is it their custom ignominiously to kick the head which they have just struck off.

In short, unpleasant as was my predicament, at best, I saw much reason to congratulate myself that I was on the losing side, rather than the triumphant one. If, heretofore, I had been none of the warmest of partisans, I began now, at this season of peril and adversity, to be pretty acutely sensible with which party my predilections lay; nor was it without something like regret and shame, that, according to a reasonable calculation of chances, I saw my own prospect of retaining office to be better than those of my Democratic brethren.[52] But who can see an inch into futurity, beyond his nose? My own head was the first that fell!

The moment when a man's head drops off is seldom or never, I am inclined to think, precisely the most agreeable of his life. Nevertheless, like the greater part of our misfortunes, even so serious a contingency brings its remedy and consolation with it, if the sufferer will but make the best, rather than the worst, of the accident which has befallen him. In my particular case, the consolatory topics were close at hand, and, indeed, had suggested themselves to my meditations a considerable time before it was a requisite to use them. In view of my previous weariness of office, and vague thoughts of resignation, my fortune somewhat resembled that of a person who should entertain an idea of committing suicide, and, altogether beyond his hopes, meet with the good hap to be murdered. In the Custom-House, as before in the Old Manse, I had spent three years; a term long enough to rest a weary brain; long enough to break off old intellectual habits, and make room for new ones; long enough, and too long, to have lived in an unnatural state, doing what was really of no advantage nor delight to any human being, and withholding myself from toil that would, at least, have stilled an unquiet impulse in me. Then, moreover, as regarded his unceremonious ejectment, the late Surveyor was not altogether ill-pleased to be recognized by the Whigs as an enemy; since his inactivity in political affairs,—his tendency to roam, at will, in that broad and quiet field where all mankind may meet, rather than confine himself to

---

[52] Hawthorne, a Democrat appointed surveyor with the support of both Whigs and Democrats, wrongly believed his appointment was safe regardless of which party won the election.

those narrow paths where brethren of the same household must diverge from one another,—had sometimes made it questionable with his brother Democrats whether he was a friend. Now, after he had won the crown of martyrdom, (though with no longer a head to wear it on,) the point might be looked upon as settled. Finally, little heroic as he was, it seemed more decorous to be overthrown in the downfall of the party with which he had been content to stand, than to remain a forlorn survivor, when so many worthier men were falling; and, at last, after subsisting for four years on the mercy of a hostile administration, to be compelled then to define his position anew, and claim the yet more humiliating mercy of a friendly one.

Meanwhile, the press had taken up my affair, and kept me, for a week or two, careering[53] through the public prints, in my decapitated state, like Irving's Headless Horseman;[54] ghastly and grim, and longing to be buried, as a politically dead man ought. So much for my figurative self. The real human being, all this time, with his head safely on his shoulders, had brought himself to the comfortable conclusion, that every thing was for the best; and, making an investment in ink, paper, and steel-pens, had opened his long-disused writing-desk, and was again a literary man.

Now it was, that the lucubrations of my ancient predecessor, Mr. Surveyor Pue, came into play. Rusty through long idleness, some little space was requisite before my intellectual machinery could be brought to work upon the tale, with an effect in any degree satisfactory. Even yet, though my thoughts were ultimately much absorbed in the task, it wears, to my eye, a stern and sombre aspect; too much ungladdened by genial sunshine; too little relieved by the tender and familiar influences which soften almost every scene of nature and real life, and, undoubtedly, should soften every picture of them. This uncaptivating effect is perhaps due to the period of hardly accomplished revolution, and still seething turmoil, in which the story shaped itself. It is no indication, however, of a lack of cheerfulness in the writer's mind; for he was happier, while straying through the gloom of these sunless fantasies, than at any time since he had quitted the Old Manse. Some of the briefer articles, which contribute to make up the volume, have likewise been written since my involuntary withdrawal from the toils and honors of public life, and the remainder are gleaned from annuals and magazines, of such antique date that they have gone round the circle, and come back to novelty again.[55] Keeping up the metaphor of the political guillotine, the whole may be considered as the POSTHUMOUS PAPERS OF A DECAPITATED SURVEYOR; and the sketch which I am now bringing to a close, if too autobiographical for a modest person to publish in his lifetime, will readily be excused in a gentleman who writes from beyond the grave. Peace be with all the world! My blessing on my friends! My forgiveness to my enemies! For I am in the realm of quiet!

The life of the Custom-House lies like a dream behind me. The old Inspector,—who, by the by, I regret to say, was overthrown and killed by a horse, some time ago; else he would certainly have lived for ever,—he, and all those other venerable personages who sat with him at the receipt of custom, are but shadows in my view; white-headed and wrinkled images, which my fancy used to

---

[53] Running headlong.

[54] The headless horseman in "The Legend of Sleepy Hollow" (1820), by Washington Irving (1783–1859).

[55] Hawthorne's note: "At the time of writing this article, the author intended to publish, along with 'The Scarlet Letter,' several shorter tales and sketches. These it has been thought advisable to defer."

sport with, and has now flung aside for ever. The merchants,—Pingree, Phillips, Shepard, Upton, Kimball, Bertram, Hunt,—these, and many other names, which had such a classic familiarity for my ear six months ago,—these men of traffic, who seemed to occupy so important a position in the world,—how little time has it required to disconnect me from them all, not merely in act, but recollection! It is with an effort that I recall the figures and appellations of these few. Soon, likewise, my old native town will loom upon me through the haze of memory, a mist brooding over and around it; as if it were no portion of the real earth, but an overgrown village in cloud-land, with only imaginary inhabitants to people its wooden houses, and walk its homely lanes, and the unpicturesque prolixity of its main street. Henceforth, it ceases to be a reality of my life. I am a citizen of somewhere else. My good townspeople will not much regret me; for—though it has been as dear an object as any, in my literary efforts, to be of some importance in their eyes, and to win myself a pleasant memory in this abode and burial-place of so many of my forefathers—there has never been, for me, the genial atmosphere which a literary man requires, in order to ripen the best harvest of his mind. I shall do better amongst other faces; and these familiar ones, it need hardly be said, will do just as well without me.

It may be, however,—O, transporting and triumphant thought!—that the great-grandchildren of the present race may sometimes think kindly of the scribbler of bygone days, when the antiquary of days to come, among the sites memorable in the town's history, shall point out the locality of the THE TOWN-PUMP![56]

THE SCARLET LETTER

I: The Prison-Door

A throng of bearded men, in sad-colored garments and gray, steeple-crowned hats, intermixed with women, some wearing hoods, and others bareheaded, was assembled in front of a wooden edifice, the door of which was heavily timbered with oak, and studded with iron spikes.

The founders of a new colony, whatever Utopia of human virtue and happiness they might originally project, have invariably recognized it among their earliest practical necessities to allot a portion of the virgin soil as a cemetery, and another portion as the site of a prison. In accordance with this rule, it may safely be assumed that the forefathers of Boston had built the first prison-house, somewhere in the vicinity of Cornhill, almost as seasonably as they marked out the first burial-ground, on Isaac Johnson's lot,[1] and round about his grave, which subsequently became the nucleus of all the congregated sepulchres in the old church-yard of King's Chapel. Certain it is, that, some fifteen or twenty years after the settlement of the town,[2] the wooden jail was already marked with weather-stains

[56] In his sketch "A Rill From the Town Pump" (1835), Hawthorne describes the daily activities of Salem from the point of view of the town pump.

[1] Isaac Johnson (1601–1630) died shortly after emigrating to Massachusetts; his land became the site for a grave yard, a prison, and King's Chapel, Boston's first Anglican church (built in 1688).

[2] Boston was settled in 1630. The events of the novel begin in 1642 and end in 1649: the action of the second half of the romance occurs within a week after the death of Governor John Winthrop in 1649, mentioned in Ch. XII, and is noted to be seven years later than the opening scene.

and other indications of age, which gave a yet darker aspect to its beetle-browed and gloomy front. The rust on the ponderous iron-work of its oaken door looked more antique than any thing else in the new world. Like all that pertains to crime, it seemed never to have known a youthful era. Before this ugly edifice, and between it and the wheel-track of the street, was a grass-plot, much overgrown with burdock, pig-weed, apple-peru,[3] and such unsightly vegetation, which evidently found something congenial in the soil that had so early borne the black flower of civilized society, a prison. But, on one side of the portal, and rooted almost at the threshold, was a wild rose-bush, covered, in this month of June, with its delicate gems, which might be imagined to offer their fragrance and fragile beauty to the prisoner as he went in, and to the condemned criminal as he came forth to his doom, in token that the deep heart of Nature could pity and be kind to him.

This rose-bush, by a strange chance, has been kept alive in history; but whether it had merely survived out of the stern old wilderness, so long after the fall of the gigantic pines and oaks that originally overshadowed it,—or whether, as there is fair authority for believing, it had sprung up under the footsteps of the sainted Ann Hutchinson,[4] as she entered the prison-door,—we shall not take upon us to determine. Finding it so directly on the threshold of our narrative, which is now about to issue from that inauspicious portal, we could hardly do otherwise than pluck one of its flowers and present it to the reader. It may serve, let us hope, to symbolize some sweet moral blossom, that may be found along the track, or relieve the darkening close of a tale of human frailty and sorrow.

II: The Market-Place

The grass-plot before the jail, in Prison Lane, on a certain summer morning, not less than two centuries ago, was occupied by a pretty large number of the inhabitants of Boston; all with their eyes intently fastened on the iron-clamped oaken door. Amongst any other population, or at a later period in the history of New England, the grim rigidity that petrified the bearded physiognomies of these good people would have augured some awful business in hand. It could have betokened nothing short of the anticipated execution of some noted culprit, on whom the sentence of a legal tribunal had but confirmed the verdict of public sentiment. But, in that early severity of the Puritan character, an inference of this kind could not so indubitably be drawn. It might be that a sluggish bond-servant, or an undutiful child, whom his parents had given over to the civil authority, was to be corrected at the whipping-post. It might be, that an Antinomian, a Quaker, or other heterodox religionist, was to be scourged out of the town, or an idle and vagrant Indian, whom the white man's fire-water had made riotous about the streets, was to be driven with stripes[5] into the shadow of the forest. It might be, too, that a witch, like old Mistress Hibbins,[6] the bitter-tempered widow of the magistrate, was to die

---

[3] A coarse weed with burrs, a family of shrubs with small, green flowers, and a thorn apple (the apple of Peru).

[4] Hutchinson (1591–1643), a persuasive religious figure, came to Massachusetts in 1634. She taught antinomianism, which emphasized the individual's responsibility to the Spirit within and the idea that salvation depends on faith alone. The Puritans regarded her ideas as subversive and banished her in 1637.

[5] Driven out by whipping.

[6] Ann Hibbins was tried for witchcraft in 1655, evidently because of her disagreeable and contentious temper; she was executed on June 19, 1656.

upon the gallows. In either case, there was very much the same solemnity of demeanour on the part of the spectators; as befitted a people amongst whom religion and law were almost identical, and in whose character both were so thoroughly interfused, that the mildest and the severest acts of public discipline were alike made venerable and awful. Meagre, indeed, and cold, was the sympathy that a transgressor might look for, from such bystanders at the scaffold. On the other hand, a penalty which, in our days, would infer a degree of mocking infamy and ridicule, might then be invested with almost as stern a dignity as the punishment of death itself.

It was a circumstance to be noted, on the summer morning when our story begins its course, that the women, of whom there were several in the crowd, appeared to take a peculiar interest in whatever penal infliction might be expected to ensue. The age had not so much refinement, that any sense of impropriety restrained the wearers of petticoat and farthingale[7] from stepping forth into the public ways, and wedging their not unsubstantial persons, if occasion were, into the throng nearest to the scaffold at an execution. Morally, as well as materially, there was a coarser fibre in those wives and maidens of old English birth and breeding, than in their fair descendants, separated from them by a series of six or seven generations; for, throughout that chain of ancestry, every successive mother has transmitted to her child a fainter bloom, a more delicate and briefer beauty, and a slighter physical frame, if not a character of less force and solidity, than her own. The women, who were now standing about the prison-door, stood within less than half a century of the period when the man-like Elizabeth[8] had been the not altogether unsuitable representative of the sex. They were her countrywomen; and the beef and ale of their native land, with a moral diet not a whit more refined, entered largely into their composition. The bright morning sun, therefore, shone on broad shoulders and well-developed busts, and on round and ruddy cheeks, that had ripened in the far-off island, and had hardly yet grown paler or thinner in the atmosphere of New England. There was, moreover, a boldness and rotundity of speech among these matrons, as most of them seemed to be, that would startle us at the present day, whether in respect to its purport or its volume of tone.

"Goodwives," said a hard-featured dame of fifty, "I'll tell ye a piece of my mind. It would be greatly for the public behoof, if we women, being of mature age and church-members in good repute, should have the handling of such malefactresses as this Hester Prynne. What think ye, gossips?[9] If the hussy stood up for judgment before us five, that are now here in a knot together, would she come off with such a sentence as the worshipful magistrates have awarded? Marry, I trow[10] not!"

"People say," said another, "that the Reverend Master Dimmesdale, her godly pastor, takes it very grievously to heart that such a scandal should have come upon his congregation."

"The magistrates are God-fearing gentlemen, but merciful overmuch,—that is a truth," added a third autumnal matron. "At the very least, they should have put the brand of a hot iron on Hester Prynne's forehead. Madam Hester would have winced at that, I warrant me. But she,—the naughty baggage,—little will she care what they put upon the bodice of her gown! Why, look you, she may cover it with a brooch, or such like heathenish adornment, and so walk the streets as brave as ever!"

---

[7] A hoop skirt.   [8] Elizabeth I (1533–1603), queen of England from 1558 to 1603.
[9] Friends (originally "good sibs," or relatives).   [10] "Indeed, I believe not."

"Ah, but," interposed, more softly, a young wife, holding a child by the hand, "let her cover the mark as she will, the pang of it will be always in her heart."[11]

"What do we talk of marks and brands, whether on the bodice of her gown, or the flesh of her forehead?" cried another female, the ugliest as well as the most pitiless of these self-constituted judges. "This woman has brought shame upon us all, and ought to die. Is there not law for it? Truly there is, both in the Scripture and the statute-book.[12] Then let the magistrates, who have made it of no effect, thank themselves if their own wives and daughters go astray!"

"Mercy on us, goodwife," exclaimed a man in the crowd, "is there no virtue in woman, save what springs from a wholesome fear of the gallows? That is the hardest word yet! Hush, now, gossips; for the lock is turning in the prison-door, and here comes Mistress Prynne herself."

The door of the jail being flung open from within, there appeared, in the first place, like a black shadow emerging into the sunshine, the grim and grisly presence of the town-beadle,[13] with a sword by his side and his staff of office in his hand. This personage prefigured and represented in his aspect the whole dismal severity of the Puritanic code of law, which it was his business to administer in its final and closest application to the offender. Stretching forth the official staff in his left hand, he laid his right upon the shoulder of a young woman, whom he thus drew forward; until, on the threshold of the prison-door, she repelled him, by an action marked with natural dignity and force of character, and stepped into the open air, as if by her own free-will. She bore in her arms a child, a baby of some three months old, who winked and turned aside its little face from the too vivid light of day; because its existence, heretofore, had brought it acquainted only with the gray twilight of a dungeon, or other darksome apartment of the prison.

When the young woman—the mother of this child—stood fully revealed before the crowd, it seemed to be her first impulse to clasp the infant closely to her bosom; not so much by an impulse of motherly affection, as that she might thereby conceal a certain token, which was wrought or fastened into her dress. In a moment, however, wisely judging that one token of her shame would but poorly serve to hide another, she took the baby on her arm, and, with a burning blush, and yet a haughty smile, and a glance that would not be abashed, looked around at her townspeople and neighbours. On the breast of her gown, in fine red cloth, surrounded with an elaborate embroidery and fantastic flourishes of gold thread, appeared the letter A.[14] It was so artistically done, and with so much fertility and gorgeous luxuriance of fancy, that it had all the effect of a last and fitting decoration to the apparel which she wore; and which was of a splendor in accordance with the taste of the age, but greatly beyond what was allowed by the sumptuary regulations[15] of the colony.

The young woman was tall, with a figure of perfect elegance, on a large scale.

---

[11] This compassionate young wife is specifically mentioned in Chapter XXII as having died, whereas the rest of the group remains to stare again at Hester's letter.

[12] The Puritans justified such cruel punishments for adultery as public humiliation, branding, whipping, and (rarely) execution as instructions from the Bible: "Thou shalt not commit adultery," from Exodus 20:14, and "The adulterer and the adulteress shall surely be put to death," from Leviticus 20:10.

[13] A constable.

[14] The Plymouth Colony enacted a law in 1636 that adulterers should be whipped and made to wear "two Capitall letters viz. AD" on their garments. Felt's *Annals of Salem* records a 1694 Massachusetts law that required adulterers to be whipped and to wear "a capital A, two inches long," on the clothing.

[15] Laws limiting extravagance of conduct or dress, primarily on moral or religious grounds.

She had dark and abundant hair, so glossy that it threw off the sunshine with a gleam, and a face which, besides being beautiful from regularity of feature and richness of complexion, had the impressiveness belonging to a marked brow and deep black eyes. She was lady-like, too, after the manner of the feminine gentility of those days; characterized by a certain state and dignity, rather than by the delicate, evanescent, and indescribable grace, which is now recognized as its indication. And never had Hester Prynne appeared more lady-like, in the antique interpretation of the term, than as she issued from the prison. Those who had before known her, and had expected to behold her dimmed and obscured by a disastrous cloud, were astonished, and even startled, to perceive how her beauty shone out, and made a halo of the misfortune and ignominy in which she was enveloped. It may be true, that, to a sensitive observer, there was something exquisitely painful in it. Her attire, which, indeed, she had wrought for the occasion, in prison, and had modelled much after her own fancy, seemed to express the attitude of her spirit, the desperate recklessness of her mood, by its wild and picturesque peculiarity. But the point which drew all eyes, and, as it were, transfigured the wearer,—so that both men and women, who had been familiarly acquainted with Hester Prynne, were now impressed as if they beheld her for the first time,—was that SCARLET LETTER, so fantastically embroidered and illuminated upon her bosom. It had the effect of a spell, taking her out of the ordinary relations with humanity, and inclosing her in a sphere by herself.

"She hath good skill at her needle, that's certain," remarked one of the female spectators; "but did ever a woman, before this brazen hussy, contrive such a way of showing it! Why, gossips, what is it but to laugh in the faces of our godly magistrates, and make a pride out of what they, worthy gentlemen, meant for a punishment?"

"It were well," muttered the most iron-visaged of the old dames, "if we stripped Madam Hester's rich gown off her dainty shoulders; and as for the red letter, which she hath stitched so curiously, I'll bestow a rag of mine own rheumatic flannel, to make a fitter one!"

"O, peace, neighbours, peace!" whispered their youngest companion. "Do not let her hear you! Not a stitch in that embroidered letter, but she has felt it in her heart."

The grim beadle now made a gesture with his staff.

"Make way, good people, make way, in the King's name," cried he. "Open a passage; and, I promise ye, Mistress Prynne shall be set where man, woman, and child may have a fair sight of her brave apparel, from this time till an hour past meridian. A blessing on the righteous Colony of the Massachusetts, where iniquity is dragged out into the sunshine! Come along, Madam Hester, and show your scarlet letter in the market-place!"

A lane was forthwith opened through the crowd of spectators. Preceded by the beadle, and attended by an irregular procession of stern-browed men and unkindly-visaged women, Hester Prynne set forth towards the place appointed for her punishment. A crowd of eager and curious schoolboys, understanding little of the matter in hand, except that it gave them a half-holiday, ran before her progress, turning their heads continually to stare into her face, and at the winking baby in her arms, and at the ignominious letter on her breast. It was no great distance, in those days, from the prison-door to the market-place. Measured by the prisoner's experience, however, it might be reckoned a journey of some length; for, haughty as her demeanour was, she perchance underwent an agony from every footstep of those that thronged to see her, as if her heart had been flung into the street for them all to spurn and trample upon. In our nature, however, there is a provision, alike marvellous and merciful, that the sufferer should never know the intensity of what he endures by its present torture, but chiefly by the pang that rankles after it. With almost a serene deportment, therefore, Hester Prynne passed through this portion of her ordeal, and came to a sort of scaffold, at the western extremity of the market-place. It stood nearly beneath the eaves of Boston's earliest church, and appeared to be a fixture there.

In fact, this scaffold constituted a portion of a penal machine, which now, for two or three generations past, has been merely historical and traditionary among us, but was held, in the old time, to be as effectual an agent in the promotion of good citizenship, as ever was the guillotine among the terrorists of France.[16] It was, in short, the platform of the pillory; and above it rose the framework of that instrument of discipline, so fashioned as to confine the human head in its tight grasp, and thus hold it up to the public gaze. The very ideal of ignominy was embodied and made manifest in this contrivance of wood and iron. There can be no outrage, methinks, against our common nature,—whatever be the delinquencies of the individual,—no outrage more flagrant than to forbid the culprit to hide his face for shame; as it was the essence of this punishment to do. In Hester Prynne's instance, however, as not unfrequently in other cases, her sentence bore, that she should stand a certain time upon the platform, but without undergoing that gripe about the neck and confinement of the head, the proneness to which was the most devilish characteristic of this ugly engine. Knowing well her part, she ascended a flight of wooden steps, and was thus displayed to the surrounding multitude, at about the height of a man's shoulders above the street.

Had there been a Papist among the crowd of Puritans, he might have seen in this beautiful woman, so picturesque in her attire and mien, and with the infant at her bosom, an object to remind him of the image of Divine Maternity, which so many illustrious painters have vied with one another to represent; something which should remind him, indeed, but only by contrast, of that sacred image of sinless motherhood, whose infant was to redeem the world. Here, there was the taint of deepest sin in the most sacred quality of human life, working such effect, that the world was only the darker for this woman's beauty, and the more lost for the infant that she had borne.

The scene was not without a mixture of awe, such as must always invest the spectacle of guilt and shame in a fellow-creature, before society shall have grown corrupt enough to smile, instead of shuddering, at it. The witnesses of Hester Prynne's disgrace had not yet passed beyond their simplicity. They were stern enough to look upon her death, had that been the sentence, without a murmur at its severity, but had none of the heartlessness of another social state, which would find only a theme for jest in an exhibition like the present. Even had there been a disposition to turn the matter into ridicule, it must have been repressed and overpowered by the solemn presence of men no less dignified than the Governor, and several of his counsellors, a judge, a general, and the ministers of the town; all of whom sat or stood in a balcony of the meeting-house, looking down upon the platform. When such personages could constitute a part of the spectacle, without risking the majesty or reverence of rank and office, it was safely to be inferred that the infliction of a legal sentence would have an earnest and effectual meaning. Accordingly, the crowd was sombre and grave. The unhappy culprit sustained

---

[16] The murderous revolutionaries during France's Reign of Terror (1793–1794).

herself as best a woman might, under the heavy weight of a thousand unrelenting eyes, all fastened upon her, and concentred at her bosom. It was almost intolerable to be borne. Of an impulsive and passionate nature, she had fortified herself to encounter the stings and venomous stabs of public contumely, wreaking itself in every variety of insult; but there was a quality so much more terrible in the solemn mood of the popular mind, that she longed rather to behold all those rigid countenances contorted with scornful merriment, and herself the object. Had a roar of laughter burst from the multitude,—each man, each woman, each little shrill-voiced child, contributing their individual parts,—Hester Prynne might have repaid them all with a bitter and disdainful smile. But, under the leaden infliction which it was her doom to endure, she felt, at moments, as if she must needs shriek out with the full power of her lungs, and cast herself from the scaffold down upon the ground, or else go mad at once.

Yet there were intervals when the whole scene, in which she was the most conspicuous object, seemed to vanish from her eyes, or, at least, glimmered indistinctly before them, like a mass of imperfectly shaped and spectral images. Her mind, and especially her memory, was preternaturally active, and kept bringing up other scenes than this roughly hewn street of a little town, on the edge of the Western wilderness; other faces than were lowering upon her from beneath the brims of those steeple-crowned hats. Reminiscences, the most trifling and immaterial, passages of infancy and school-days, sports, childish quarrels, and the little domestic traits of her maiden years, came swarming back upon her, intermingled with recollections of whatever was gravest in her subsequent life; one picture precisely as vivid as another; as if all were of similar importance, or all alike a play. Possibly, it was an instinctive device of her spirit, to relieve itself, by the exhibition of these phantasmagoric forms, from the cruel weight and hardness of the reality.

Be that as it might, the scaffold of the pillory was a point of view that revealed to Hester Prynne the entire track along which she had been treading, since her happy infancy. Standing on that miserable eminence, she saw again her native village, in Old England, and her paternal home; a decayed house of gray stone, with a poverty-stricken aspect, but retaining a half-obliterated shield of arms over the portal, in token of antique gentility. She saw her father's face, with its bald brow, and reverend white beard, that flowed over the old-fashioned Elizabethan ruff; her mother's, too, with the look of heedful and anxious love which it always wore in her remembrance, and which, even since her death, had so often laid the impediment of a gentle remonstrance in her daughter's pathway. She saw her own face, glowing with girlish beauty, and illuminating all the interior of the dusky mirror in which she had been wont to gaze at it. There she beheld another countenance, of a man well stricken in years, a pale, thin, scholar-like visage, with eyes dim and bleared by the lamp-light that had served them to pore over many ponderous books. Yet those same bleared optics had a strange, penetrating power, when it was their owner's purpose to read the human soul. This figure of the study and the cloister, as Hester Prynne's womanly fancy failed not to recall, was slightly deformed, with the left shoulder a trifle higher than the right. Next rose before her, in memory's picture-gallery, the intricate and narrow thoroughfares, the tall, gray houses, the huge cathedrals, and the public edifices, ancient in date and quaint in architecture, of a Continental city;[17] where a new life had awaited her,

[17] Amsterdam, where many English Puritans fled before they came to North America.

still in connection with the misshapen scholar; a new life, but feeding itself on time-worn materials, like a tuft of green moss on a crumbling wall. Lastly, in lieu of these shifting scenes, came back the rude market-place of the Puritan settlement, with all the townspeople assembled and levelling their stern regards at Hester Prynne,—yes, at herself,—who stood on the scaffold of the pillory, an infant on her arm, and the letter A, in scarlet, fantastically embroidered with gold thread, upon her bosom!

Could it be true? She clutched the child so fiercely to her breast, that it sent forth a cry; she turned her eyes downward at the scarlet letter, and even touched it with her finger, to assure herself that the infant and the shame were real. Yes!— these were her realities,—all else had vanished!

III: The Recognition

From this intense consciousness of being the object of severe and universal observation, the wearer of the scarlet letter was at length relieved by discerning, on the outskirts of the crowd, a figure which irresistibly took possession of her thoughts. An Indian, in his native garb, was standing there; but the red men were not so infrequent visitors of the English settlements, that one of them would have attracted any notice from Hester Prynne, at such a time; much less would he have excluded all other objects and ideas from her mind. By the Indian's side, and evidently sustaining a companionship with him, stood a white man, clad in a strange disarray of civilized and savage costume.

He was small in stature, with a furrowed visage, which, as yet, could hardly be termed aged. There was a remarkable intelligence in his features, as of a person who had so cultivated his mental part that it could not fail to mould the physical to itself, and become manifest by unmistakable tokens. Although, by a seemingly careless arrangement of his heterogeneous garb, he had endeavoured to conceal or abate the peculiarity, it was sufficiently evident to Hester Prynne, that one of this man's shoulders rose higher than the other. Again, at the first instant of perceiving that thin visage, and the slight deformity of the figure, she pressed her infant to her bosom, with so convulsive a force that the poor babe uttered another cry of pain. But the mother did not seem to hear it.

At his arrival in the market-place, and some time before she saw him, the stranger had bent his eyes on Hester Prynne. It was carelessly, at first, like a man chiefly accustomed to look inward, and to whom external matters are of little value and import, unless they bear relation to something within his mind. Very soon, however, his look became keen and penetrative. A writhing horror twisted itself across his features, like a snake gliding swiftly over them, and making one little pause, with all its wreathed intervolutions in open sight. His face darkened with some powerful emotion, which, nevertheless, he so instantaneously controlled by an effort of his will, that, save at a single moment, its expression might have passed for calmness. After a brief space, the convulsion grew almost imperceptible, and finally subsided into the depths of his nature. When he found the eyes of Hester Prynne fastened on his own, and saw that she appeared to recognize him, he slowly and calmly raised his finger, made a gesture with it in the air, and laid it on his lips.

Then, touching the shoulder of a townsman who stood next to him, he addressed him in a formal and courteous manner.

"I pray you, good Sir," said he, "who is this woman?—and wherefore is she here set up to public shame?"

"You must needs be a stranger in this region, friend," answered the townsman, looking curiously at the questioner and his savage companion; "else you would surely have heard of Mistress Hester Prynne, and her evil doings. She hath raised a great scandal, I promise you, in godly Master Dimmesdale's church."

"You say truly," replied the other. "I am a stranger, and have been a wanderer, sorely against my will. I have met with grievous mishaps by sea and land, and have been long held in bonds among the heathen-folk, to the southward; and am now brought hither by this Indian, to be redeemed out of my captivity. Will it please you, therefore, to tell me of Hester Prynne's—have I her name rightly?— of this woman's offences, and what has brought her to yonder scaffold?"

"Truly, friend, and methinks it must gladden your heart, after your troubles and sojourn in the wilderness," said the townsman, "to find yourself, at length, in a land where iniquity is searched out, and punished in the sight of rulers and people; as here in our godly New England. Yonder woman, Sir, you must know, was the wife of a certain learned man, English by birth, but who had long dwelt in Amsterdam, whence, some good time agone, he was minded to cross over and cast in his lot with us of the Massachusetts. To this purpose, he sent his wife before him, remaining himself to look after some necessary affairs. Marry, good Sir, in some two years, or less, that the woman has been a dweller here in Boston, no tidings have come of this learned gentleman, Master Prynne; and his young wife, look you, being left to her own misguidance—"

"Ah!—aha!—I conceive you," said the stranger, with a bitter smile. "So learned a man as you speak of should have learned this too in his books. And who, by your favor, Sir, may be the father of yonder babe—it is some three or four months old, I should judge—which Mistress Prynne is holding in her arms?"

"Of a truth, friend, that matter remaineth a riddle; and the Daniel[18] who shall expound it is yet a-wanting," answered the townsman. "Madam Hester absolutely refuseth to speak, and the magistrates have laid their heads together in vain. Peradventure the guilty one stands looking on at this sad spectacle, unknown of man, and forgetting that God sees him."

"The learned man," observed the stranger, with another smile, "should come himself to look into the mystery."

"It behooves him well, if he be still in life," responded the townsman. "Now good Sir, our Massachusetts magistracy, bethinking themselves that this woman is youthful and fair, and doubtless was strongly tempted to her fall;—and that, moreover, as is most likely, her husband may be at the bottom of the sea;—they have not been bold to put in force the extremity of our righteous law against her. The penalty thereof is death. But, in their great mercy and tenderness of heart, they have doomed Mistress Prynne to stand only a space of three hours on the platform of the pillory, and then and thereafter, for the remainder of her natural life, to wear a mark of shame upon her bosom."

"A wise sentence!" remarked the stranger, gravely bowing his head. "Thus she will be a living sermon against sin, until the ignominious letter be engraved upon her tombstone. It irks me, nevertheless, that the partner of her iniquity should not, at least, stand on the scaffold by her side. But he will be known!—he will be known!—he will be known!"

---

[18] The Old Testament prophet with the ability to interpret cryptic signs, or "riddles," the "handwriting on the wall" (see Daniel 5).

He bowed courteously to the communicative townsman, and, whispering a few words to his Indian attendant, they both made their way through the crowd.

While this passed, Hester Prynne had been standing on her pedestal, still with a fixed gaze towards the stranger; so fixed a gaze, that, at moments of intense absorption, all other objects in the visible world seemed to vanish, leaving only him and her. Such an interview, perhaps, would have been more terrible than even to meet him as she now did, with the hot, midday sun burning down upon her face, and lighting up its shame; with the scarlet token of infamy on her breast; with the sin-born infant in her arms; with a whole people, drawn forth as to a festival, staring at the features that should have been seen only in the quiet gleam of the fireside, in the happy shadow of a home, or beneath a matronly veil, at church. Dreadful as it was, she was conscious of a shelter in the presence of these thousand witnesses. It was better to stand thus, with so many betwixt him and her, than to greet him, face to face, they two alone. She fled for refuge, as it were, to the public exposure, and dreaded the moment when its protection should be withdrawn from her. Involved in these thoughts, she scarcely heard a voice behind her, until it had repeated her name more than once, in a loud and solemn tone, audible to the whole multitude.

"Hearken unto me, Hester Prynne!" said the voice.

It has already been noticed, that directly over the platform on which Hester Prynne stood was a kind of balcony, or open gallery, appended to the meeting-house. It was the place whence proclamations were wont to be made, amidst an assemblage of the magistracy, with all the ceremonial that attended such public observances in those days. Here, to witness the scene which we are describing, sat Governor Bellingham[19] himself, with four sergeants[20] about his chair, bearing halberds, as a guard of honor. He wore a dark feather in his hat, a border of embroidery on his cloak, and a black velvet tunic beneath; a gentleman advanced in years, and with a hard experience written in his wrinkles. He was not ill fitted to be the head and representative of a community, which owed its origin and progress, and its present state of development, not to the impulses of youth, but to the stern and tempered energies of manhood, and the sombre sagacity of age; accomplishing so much, precisely because it imagined and hoped so little. The other eminent characters, by whom the chief ruler was surrounded, were distinguished by a dignity of mien, belonging to a period when the forms of authority were felt to possess the sacredness of divine institutions. They were, doubtless, good men, just, and sage. But, out of the whole human family, it would not have been easy to select the same number of wise and virtuous persons, who should be less capable of sitting in judgment on an erring woman's heart, and disentangling its mesh of good and evil, than the sages of rigid aspect towards whom Hester Prynne now turned her face. She seemed conscious, indeed, that whatever sympathy she might expect lay in the larger and warmer heart of the multitude; for, as she lifted her eyes towards the balcony, the unhappy woman grew pale and trembled.

The voice which had called her attention was that of the reverend and famous

---

[19] Richard Bellingham (1592–1672), governor of Massachusetts in 1641 and 1654 and from 1665 to 1672.

[20] Civil officers, who carry out the orders of government officials, bearing long-handled weapons that combine a spear and an ax-head (used for combat in the fifteenth and sixteenth centuries, for ceremonial purposes later).

John Wilson,[21] the eldest clergyman of Boston, a great scholar, like most of his contemporaries in the profession, and withal a man of kind and genial spirit. This last attribute, however, had been less carefully developed than his intellectual gifts, and was, in truth, rather a matter of shame than self-congratulation with him. There he stood, with a border of grizzled locks beneath his skull-cap; while his gray eyes, accustomed to the shaded light of his study, were winking, like those of Hester's infant, in the unadulterated sunshine. He looked like the darkly engraved portraits which we see prefixed to old volumes of sermons; and had no more right than one of those portraits would have, to step forth, as he now did, and meddle with a question of human guilt, passion, and anguish.

"Hester Prynne," said the clergyman, "I have striven with my young brother here, under whose preaching of the word you have been privileged to sit,"—here Mr. Wilson laid his hand on the shoulder of a pale young man beside him,—"I have sought, I say, to persuade this godly youth, that he should deal with you, here in the face of Heaven, and before these wise and upright rulers, and in hearing of all the people, as touching the vileness and blackness of your sin. Knowing your natural temper better than I, he could the better judge what arguments to use, whether of tenderness or terror, such as might prevail over your hardness and obstinacy; insomuch that you should no longer hide the name of him who tempted you to this grievous fall. But he opposes to me, (with a young man's oversoftness, albeit wise beyond his years,) that it were wronging the very nature of woman to force her to lay open her heart's secrets in such broad daylight, and in presence of so great a multitude. Truly, as I sought to convince him, the shame lay in the commission of the sin, and not in the showing of it forth. What say you to it, once again, brother Dimmesdale? Must it be thou or I that shall deal with this poor sinner's soul?"

There was a murmur among the dignified and reverend occupants of the balcony; and Governor Bellingham gave expression to its purport, speaking in an authoritative voice, although tempered with respect towards the youthful clergyman whom he addressed.

"Good Master Dimmesdale," said he, "the responsibility of this woman's soul lies greatly with you. It behooves you, therefore, to exhort her to repentance, and to confession, as a proof and consequence thereof."

The directness of this appeal drew the eyes of the whole crowd upon the Reverend Mr. Dimmesdale; a young clergyman, who had come from one of the great English universities, bringing all the learning of the age into our wild forest-land. His eloquence and religious fervor had already given the earnest of high eminence in his profession. He was a person of very striking aspect, with a white, lofty, and impending brow, large, brown, melancholy eyes, and a mouth which, unless when he forcibly compressed it, was apt to be tremulous, expressing both nervous sensibility and a vast power of self-restraint. Notwithstanding his high native gifts and scholar-like attainments, there was an air about this young minister,—an apprehensive, a startled, a half-frightened look,—as of a being who felt himself quite astray and at a loss in the pathway of human existence, and could only be at ease in some seclusion of his own. Therefore, so far as his duties would permit, he

---

[21] Wilson (1591?–1667) came to Massachusetts in 1630 with John Winthrop; for this romance Hawthorne made the character Rev. Wilson seem more aged and patriarchal than Wilson would have been at the time (thus he contrasts all the better with Arthur Dimmesdale).

trode in the shadowy by-paths, and thus kept himself simple and childlike; coming forth, when occasion was, with a freshness, and fragrance, and dewy purity of thought, which, as many people said, affected them like the speech of an angel.

Such was the young man whom the Reverend Mr. Wilson and the Governor had introduced so openly to the public notice, bidding him speak, in the hearing of all men, to that mystery of a woman's soul, so sacred even in its pollution. The trying nature of his position drove the blood from his cheek, and made his lips tremulous.

"Speak to the woman, my brother," said Mr. Wilson. "It is of moment to her soul, and therefore, as the worshipful Governor says, momentous to thine own, in whose charge hers is. Exhort her to confess the truth!"

The Reverend Mr. Dimmesdale bent his head, in silent prayer, as it seemed, and then came forward.

"Hester Prynne," said he, leaning over the balcony, and looking down stedfastly into her eyes, "thou hearest what this good man says, and seest the accountability under which I labor. If thou feelest it to be for thy soul's peace, and that thy earthly punishment will thereby be made more effectual to salvation, I charge thee to speak out the name of thy fellow-sinner and fellow-sufferer! Be not silent from any mistaken pity and tenderness for him; for, believe me, Hester, though he were to step down from a high place, and stand there beside thee, on thy pedestal of shame, yet better were it so, than to hide a guilty heart through life. What can thy silence do for him, except it tempt him—yea, compel him, as it were—to add hypocrisy to sin? Heaven hath granted thee an open ignominy, that thereby thou mayest work out an open triumph over the evil within thee, and the sorrow without. Take heed how thou deniest to him—who, perchance, hath not the courage to grasp it for himself—the bitter, but wholesome, cup that is now presented to thy lips!"

The young pastor's voice was tremulously sweet, rich, deep, and broken. The feeling that it so evidently manifested, rather than the direct purport of the words, caused it to vibrate within all hearts, and brought the listeners into one accord of sympathy. Even the poor baby, at Hester's bosom, was affected by the same influence; for it directed its hitherto vacant gaze towards Mr. Dimmesdale, and held up its little arms, with a half pleased, half plaintive murmur. So powerful seemed the minister's appeal, that the people could not believe but that Hester Prynne would speak out the guilty name; or else that the guilty one himself, in whatever high or lowly place he stood, would be drawn forth by an inward and inevitable necessity, and compelled to ascend the scaffold.

Hester shook her head.

"Woman, transgress not beyond the limits of Heaven's mercy!" cried the Reverend Mr. Wilson, more harshly than before. "That little babe hath been gifted with a voice, to second and confirm the counsel which thou hast heard. Speak out the name! That, and thy repentance, may avail to take the scarlet letter off thy breast."

"Never!" replied Hester Prynne, looking, not at Mr. Wilson, but into the deep and troubled eyes of the younger clergyman. "It is too deeply branded. Ye cannot take it off. And would that I might endure his agony, as well as mine!"

"Speak, woman!" said another voice, coldly and sternly, proceeding from the crowd about the scaffold. "Speak; and give your child a father!"

"I will not speak!" answered Hester, turning pale as death, but responding to this voice, which she too surely recognized. "And my child must seek a heavenly Father; she shall never know an earthly one!"

"She will not speak!" murmured Mr. Dimmesdale, who, leaning over the balcony, with his hand upon his heart, had awaited the result of his appeal. He now drew back, with a long respiration. "Wondrous strength and generosity of a woman's heart! She will not speak!"

Discerning the impracticable state of the poor culprit's mind, the elder clergyman, who had carefully prepared himself for the occasion, addressed to the multitude a discourse on sin, in all its branches, but with continual reference to the ignominious letter. So forcibly did he dwell upon this symbol, for the hour or more during which his periods were rolling over the people's heads, that it assumed new terrors in their imagination, and seemed to derive its scarlet hue from the flames of the infernal pit. Hester Prynne, meanwhile, kept her place upon the pedestal of shame, with glazed eyes, and an air of weary indifference. She had borne, that morning, all that nature could endure; and as her temperament was not of the order that escapes from too intense suffering by a swoon, her spirit could only shelter itself beneath a stony crust of insensibility, while the faculties of animal life remained entire. In this state, the voice of the preacher thundered remorselessly, but unavailingly, upon her ears. The infant, during the latter portion of her ordeal, pierced the air with its wailings and screams; she strove to hush it, mechanically, but seemed scarcely to sympathize with its trouble. With the same hard demeanour, she was led back to prison, and vanished from the public gaze within its iron-clamped portal. It was whispered, by those who peered after her, that the scarlet letter threw a lurid gleam along the dark passage-way of the interior.

IV: The Interview

After her return to the prison, Hester Prynne was found to be in a state of nervous excitement that demanded constant watchfulness, lest she should perpetrate violence on herself, or do some half-frenzied mischief to the poor babe. As night approached, it proving impossible to quell her insubordination by rebuke or threats of punishment, Master Brackett, the jailer, thought fit to introduce a physician. He described him as a man of skill in all Christian modes of physical science, and likewise familiar with whatever the savage people could teach, in respect to medicinal herbs and roots that grew in the forest. To say the truth, there was much need of professional assistance, not merely for Hester herself, but still more urgently for the child; who, drawing its sustenance from the maternal bosom, seemed to have drank in with it all the turmoil, the anguish, and despair, which pervaded the mother's system. It now writhed in convulsions of pain, and was a forcible type,[22] in its little frame, of the moral agony which Hester Prynne had borne throughout the day.

Closely following the jailer into the dismal apartment, appeared that individual, of singular aspect, whose presence in the crowd had been of such deep interest to the wearer of the scarlet letter. He was lodged in the prison, not as suspected of any offence, but as the most convenient and suitable mode of disposing of him,

[22] A symbol or emblem.

until the magistrates should have conferred with the Indian sagamores[23] respecting his ransom. His name was announced as Roger Chillingworth. The jailer, after ushering him into the room, remained a moment, marvelling at the comparative quiet that followed his entrance; for Hester Prynne had immediately become as still as death, although the child continued to moan.

"Prithee, friend, leave me alone with my patient," said the practitioner. "Trust me, good jailer, you shall briefly have peace in your house; and, I promise you, Mistress Prynne shall hereafter be more amenable to just authority than you may have found her heretofore."

"Nay, if your worship can accomplish that," answered Master Brackett, "I shall own you for a man of skill indeed! Verily, the woman hath been like a possessed one; and there lacks little, that I should take in hand to drive Satan out of her with stripes."

The stranger had entered the room with the characteristic quietude of the profession to which he announced himself as belonging. Nor did his demeanour change, when the withdrawal of the prison-keeper left him face to face with the woman, whose absorbed notice of him, in the crowd, had intimated so close a relation between himself and her. His first care was given to the child; whose cries, indeed, as she lay writhing on the trundle-bed, made it of peremptory necessity to postpone all other business to the task of soothing her. He examined the infant carefully, and then proceeded to unclasp a leathern case, which he took from beneath his dress. It appeared to contain certain medical preparations, one of which he mingled with a cup of water.

"My old studies in alchemy," observed he, "and my sojourn, for above a year past, among a people well versed in the kindly properties of simples,[24] have made a better physician of me than many that claim the medical degree. Here, woman! The child is yours,—she is none of mine,—neither will she recognize my voice or aspect as a father's. Administer this draught, therefore, with thine own hand."

Hester repelled the offered medicine, at the same time gazing with strongly marked apprehension into his face.

"Wouldst thou avenge thyself on the innocent babe?" whispered she.

"Foolish woman!" responded the physician, half coldly, half soothingly. "What should ail me to harm this misbegotten and miserable babe? The medicine is potent for good; and were it my child,—yea, mine own, as well as thine!—I could do no better for it."

As she still hesitated, being, in fact, in no reasonable state of mind, he took the infant in his arms, and himself administered the draught. It soon proved its efficacy, and redeemed the leech's[25] pledge. The moans of the little patient subsided; its convulsive tossings gradually ceased; and in a few moments, as is the custom of young children after relief from pain, it sank into a profound and dewy slumber. The physician, as he had a fair right to be termed, next bestowed his attention on the mother. With calm and intent scrutiny, he felt her pulse, looked into her eyes,—a gaze that made her heart shrink and shudder, because so familiar, and yet so strange and cold,—and, finally, satisfied with his investigation, proceeded to mingle another draught.

"I know not Lethe nor Nepenthe,"[26] remarked he; "but I have learned many

---

[23] Subordinate chiefs.   [24] Medications made from herbs and plants.

[25] Physician's (for the practice of trying to heal by bloodletting with leeches).

[26] According to Greek myth, the water of the river Lethe, in Hades, causes forgetfulness in those who drink it; the drug Nepenthe causes forgetfulness.

new secrets in the wilderness, and here is one of them,—a recipe that an Indian taught me, in requital of some lessons of my own, that were as old as Paracelsus.[27] Drink it! It may be less soothing than a sinless conscience. That I cannot give thee. But it will calm the swell and heaving of thy passion, like oil thrown on the waves of a tempestuous sea."

He presented the cup to Hester, who received it with a slow, earnest look into his face; not precisely a look of fear, yet full of doubt and questioning, as to what his purposes might be. She looked also at her slumbering child.

"I have thought of death," said she,—"have wished for it,—would even have prayed for it, were it fit that such as I should pray for any thing. Yet, if death be in this cup, I bid thee think again, ere thou beholdest me quaff it. See! It is even now at my lips."

"Drink, then," replied he, still with the same cold composure. "Dost thou know me so little, Hester Prynne? Are my purposes wont to be so shallow? Even if I imagine a scheme of vengeance, what could I do better for my object than to let thee live,—than to give thee medicines against all harm and peril of life,—so that this burning shame may still blaze upon thy bosom?"—As he spoke, he laid his long forefinger on the scarlet letter, which forthwith seemed to scorch into Hester's breast, as if it had been red-hot. He noticed her involuntary gesture, and smiled.—"Live, therefore, and bear about thy doom with thee, in the eyes of men and women,—in the eyes of him whom thou didst call thy husband,—in the eyes of yonder child! And, that thou mayest live, take off this draught."

Without further expostulation or delay, Hester Prynne drained the cup, and, at the motion of the man of skill, seated herself on the bed where the child was sleeping; while he drew the only chair which the room afforded, and took his own seat beside her. She could not be tremble at these preparations; for she felt that—having now done all that humanity, or principle, or, if so it were, a refined cruelty, impelled him to do, for the relief of physical suffering—he was next to treat with her as the man whom she had most deeply and irreparably injured.

"Hester," said he, "I ask not wherefore, nor how, thou has fallen into the pit, or say rather, thou hast ascended to the pedestal of infamy, on which I found thee. The reason is not far to seek. It was my folly, and thy weakness. I,—a man of thought,—the book-worm of great libraries,—a man already in decay, having given my best years to feed the hungry dream of knowledge,—what had I to do with youth and beauty like thine own! Misshapen from my birth-hour, how could I delude myself with the idea that intellectual gifts might veil physical deformity in a young girl's fantasy! Men call me wise. If sages were ever wise in their own behoof, I might have foreseen all this. I might have known that, as I came out of the vast and dismal forest, and entered this settlement of Christian men, the very first object to meet my eyes would be thyself, Hester Prynne, standing up, a statue of ignominy, before the people. Nay, from the moment when we came down the old church-steps together, a married pair, I might have beheld the bale-fire[28] of that scarlet letter blazing at the end of our path!"

"Thou knowest," said Hester,—for, depressed as she was, she could not endure this last quiet stab at the token of her shame,—"thou knowest that I was frank with thee. I felt no love, nor feigned any."

"True!" replied he. "It was my folly! I have said it. But, up to that epoch of my

---

[27] Philippus Aureolus Paracelsus (1493?–1541), a Swiss alchemist and physician.
[28] Warning fire or signal fire.

life, I had lived in vain. The world had been so cheerless! My heart was a habitation large enough for many guests, but lonely and chill, and without a household fire. I longed to kindle one! It seemed not so wild a dream,—old as I was, and sombre as I was, and misshapen as I was,—that the simple bliss, which is scattered far and wide, for all mankind to gather up, might yet be mine. And so, Hester, I drew thee into my heart, into its innermost chamber, and sought to warm thee by the warmth which thy presence made there!"

"I have greatly wronged thee," murmured Hester.

"We have wronged each other," answered he. "Mine was the first wrong, when I betrayed thy budding youth into a false and unnatural relation with my decay. Therefore, as a man who has not thought and philosophized in vain, I seek no vengeance, plot no evil against thee. Between thee and me, the scale hangs fairly balanced. But, Hester, the man lives who has wronged us both! Who is he?"

"Ask me not!" replied Hester Prynne, looking firmly into his face. "That thou shalt never know!"

"Never, sayest thou?" rejoined he, with a smile of dark and self-relying intelligence. "Never know him! Believe me, Hester, there are few things,—whether in the outward world, or, to a certain depth, in the invisible sphere of thought,—few things hidden from the man, who devotes himself earnestly and unreservedly to the solution of a mystery. Thou mayest cover up thy secret from the prying multitude. Thou mayest conceal it, too, from the ministers and magistrate, even as thou didst this day, when they sought to wrench the name out of thy heart, and give thee a partner on thy pedestal. But, as for me, I come to the inquest with other senses than they possess. I shall see this man, as I have sought truth in books; as I have sought gold in alchemy. There is a sympathy that will make me conscious of him. I shall see him tremble. I shall feel myself shudder, suddenly and unawares. Sooner or later, he must needs be mine!"

The eyes of the wrinkled scholar glowed so intensely upon her, that Hester Prynne clasped her hands over her heart, dreading lest he should read the secret there at once.

"Thou wilt not reveal his name? Not the less he is mine," resumed he, with a look of confidence, as if destiny were at one with him. "He bears no letter of infamy wrought into his garment, as thou dost; but I shall read it on his heart. Yet fear not for him! Think not that I shall interfere with Heaven's own method of retribution, or, to my own loss, betray him to the gripe[29] of human law. Neither do thou imagine that I shall contrive aught against his life; no, nor against his fame, if, as I judge, he be a man of fair repute. Let him live! Let him hide himself in outward honor, if he may! Not the less he shall be mine!"

"Thy acts are like mercy," said Hester, bewildered and appalled. "But thy words interpret thee as a terror!"

"One thing, thou that wast my wife, I would enjoin upon thee," continued the scholar. "Thou hast kept the secret of thy paramour. Keep, likewise, mine! There are none in this land that know me. Breathe not, to any human soul, that thou didst ever call me husband! Here, on this wild outskirt of the earth, I shall pitch my tent; for, elsewhere a wanderer, and isolated from human interests, I find here a woman, a man, a child, amongst whom and myself there exist the closest ligaments. No matter whether of love or hate; no matter whether of right or wrong!

---

[29] Archaic spelling of "grip."

Thou and thine, Hester Prynne, belong to me. My home is where thou art, and where he is. But betray me not!"

"Wherefore dost thou desire it?" inquired Hester, shrinking, she hardly knew why, from this secret bond. "Why not announce thyself openly, and cast me off at once?"

"It may be," he replied, "because I will not encounter the dishonor that besmirches the husband of a faithless woman. It may be for other reasons. Enough, it is my purpose to live and die unknown. Let, therefore, thy husband be to the world as one already dead, and of whom no tidings shall ever come. Recognize me not, by word, by sign, by look! Breathe not the secret, above all, to the man thou wottest[30] of. Shouldst thou fail me in this, beware! His fame, his position, his life, will be in my hands. Beware!"

"I will keep thy secret, as I have his," said Hester.

"Swear it!" rejoined he.

And she took the oath.

"And now, Mistress Prynne," said old Roger Chillingworth, as he was hereafter to be named, "I leave thee alone; alone with thy infant, and the scarlet letter! How is it, Hester? Doth thy sentence bind thee to wear the token in thy sleep? Art thou not afraid of nightmares and hideous dreams?"

"Why dost thou smile so at me?" inquired Hester, troubled at the expression of his eyes. "Art thou like the Black Man[31] that haunts the forest round about us? Hast thou enticed me into a bond that will prove the ruin of my soul?"

"Not thy soul," he answered, with another smile. "No, not thine!"

V: Hester at Her Needle

Hester Prynne's term of confinement was now at an end. Her prison-door was thrown open, and she came forth into the sunshine, which, falling on all alike, seemed, to her sick and morbid heart, as if meant for no other purpose than to reveal the scarlet letter on her breast. Perhaps there was a more real torture in her first unattended footsteps from the threshold of the prison, than even in the procession and spectacle that have been described, where she was made the common infamy, at which all mankind was summoned to point its finger. Then, she was supported by an unnatural tension of the nerves, and by all the combative energy of her character, which enabled her to convert the scene into a kind of lurid triumph. It was, moreover, a separate and insulated event, to occur but once in her lifetime, and to meet which, therefore, reckless of economy, she might call up the vital strength that would have sufficed for many quiet years. The very law that condemned her—a giant of stern features, but with vigor to support, as well as to annihilate, in his iron arm—had held her up, through the terrible ordeal of her ignominy. But now, with this unattended walk from her prison-door, began the daily custom, and she must either sustain and carry it forward by the ordinary resources of her nature, or sink beneath it. She could no longer borrow from the future, to help her through the present grief. To-morrow would bring its own trial with it; so would the next day, and so would the next, each its own trial, and yet the very same that was now so unutterably grievous to be borne. The days of the

---

[30] Knowest (from the archaic "wit," to know).   [31] The Devil, in folklore.

far-off future would toil onward, still with the same burden for her to take up, and bear along with her, but never to fling down; for the accumulating days, and added years, would pile up their misery upon the heap of shame. Throughout them all, giving up her individuality, she would become the general symbol at which the preacher and moralist might point, and in which they might vivify and embody their images of woman's frailty and sinful passion. Thus the young and pure would be taught to look at her, with the scarlet letter flaming on her breast,— at her, the child of honorable parents,—at her, the mother of a babe, that would hereafter be a woman,—at her, who had once been innocent,—as the figure, the body, the reality of sin. And over her grave, the infamy that she must carry thither would be her only monument.

It may seem marvellous, that, with the world before her,—kept by no restrictive clause of her condemnation within the limits of the Puritan settlement, so remote and so obscure,—free to return to her birthplace, or to any other European land, and there hide her character and identity under a new exterior, as completely as if emerging into another state of being,—and having also the passes of the dark, inscrutable forest open to her, where the wildness of her nature might assimilate itself with a people whose customs and life were alien from the law that had condemned her,—it may seem marvellous, that this woman should still call that place her home, where, and where only, she must needs be the type of shame. But there is a fatality, a feeling so irresistible and inevitable that it has the force of doom, which almost invariably compels human beings to linger around and haunt, ghost-like, the spot where some great and marked event has given the color to their lifetime; and still the more irresistibly, the darker the tinge that saddens it. Her sin, her ignominy, were the roots which she had struck into the soil. It was as if a new birth, with stronger assimilations than the first, had converted the forest-land, still so uncongenial to every other pilgrim and wanderer, into Hester Prynne's wild and dreary, but life-long home. All other scenes of earth—even that village of rural England, where happy infancy and stainless maidenhood seemed yet to be in her mother's keeping, like garments put off long ago—were foreign to her, in comparison. The chain that bound her here was of iron links, and galling to her inmost soul, but never could be broken.

It might be, too,—doubtless it was so, although she hid the secret from herself, and grew pale whenever it struggled out of her heart, like a serpent from its hole,—it might be that another feeling kept her within the scene and pathway that had been so fatal. There dwelt, there trode the feet of one with whom she deemed herself connected in a union, that, unrecognized on earth, would bring them together before the bar of final judgment, and make that their marriage-altar, for a joint futurity of endless retribution. Over and over again, the tempter of souls had thrust this idea upon Hester's contemplation, and laughed at the passionate and desperate joy with which she seized, and then strove to cast it from her. She barely looked the idea in the face, and hastened to bar it in its dungeon. What she compelled herself to believe,—what, finally, she reasoned upon, as her motive for continuing a resident of New England,—was half a truth, and half a self-delusion. Here, she said to herself, had been the scene of her guilt, and here should be the scene of her earthly punishment; and so, perchance, the torture of her daily shame would at length purge her soul, and work out another purity than that which she had lost; more saint-like, because the result of martyrdom.

Hester Prynne, therefore, did not flee. On the outskirts of the town, within the verge of the peninsula, but not in close vicinity to any other habitation, there was a small thatched cottage. It had been built by an earlier settler, and abandoned, because the soil about it was too sterile for cultivation, while its comparative remoteness put it out of the sphere of that social activity which already marked the habits of the emigrants. It stood on the shore, looking across a basin of the sea at the forest-covered hills, towards the west. A clump of scrubby trees, such as alone grew on the peninsula, did not so much conceal the cottage from view, as seem to denote that here was some object which would fain have been, or at least ought to be, concealed. In this little, lonesome dwelling, with some slender means that she possessed, and by the license of the magistrates, who still kept an inquisitorial watch over her, Hester established herself, with her infant child. A mystic shadow of suspicion immediately attached itself to the spot. Children, too young to comprehend wherefore this woman should be shut out from the sphere of human charities, would creep nigh enough to behold her plying her needle at the cottage-window, or standing in the door-way, or laboring in her little garden, or coming forth along the pathway that led townward; and, discerning the scarlet letter on her breast, would scamper off, with a strange, contagious fear.

Lonely as was Hester's situation, and without a friend on earth who dared to show himself, she, however, incurred no risk of want. She possessed an art that sufficed, even in a land that afforded comparatively little scope for its exercise, to supply food for her thriving infant and herself. It was the art—then, as now, almost the only one within a woman's grasp—of needle-work. She bore on her breast, in the curiously embroidered letter, a specimen of her delicate and imaginative skill, of which the dames of a court might gladly have availed themselves, to add the richer and more spiritual adornment of human ingenuity to their fabrics of silk and gold. Here, indeed, in the sable simplicity that generally characterized the Puritanic modes of dress, there might be an infrequent call for the finer productions of her handiwork. Yet the taste of the age, demanding whatever was elaborate in compositions of this kind, did not fail to extend its influence over our stern progenitors, who had cast behind them so many fashions which it might seem harder to dispense with. Public ceremonies, such as ordinations, the installation of magistrates, and all that could give majesty to the forms in which a new government manifested itself to the people, were, as a matter of policy, marked by a stately and well-conducted ceremonial, and a sombre, but yet a studied magnificence. Deep ruffs, painfully wrought bands, and gorgeously embroidered gloves, were all deemed necessary to the official state of men assuming the reins of power; and were readily allowed to individuals dignified by rank or wealth, even while sumptuary laws forbade these and similar extravagances to the plebeian order. In the array of funerals, too,—whether for the apparel of the dead body, or to typify, by manifold emblematic devices of sable cloth and snowy lawn,[32] the sorrow of the survivors,—there was a frequent and characteristic demand for such labor as Hester Prynne could supply. Baby-linen—for babies then wore robes of state—afforded still another possibility of toil and emolument.

By degrees, nor very slowly, her handiwork became what would now be termed the fashion. Whether from commiseration for a woman of so miserable a destiny; or from the morbid curiosity that gives a fictitious value even to common or worthless things; or by whatever other intangible circumstance was then, as now, sufficient to bestow, on some persons, what others might seek in vain; or because Hester really filled a gap which must otherwise have remained vacant; it

---

[32] Dark cloth and sheer white linen or cotton.

is certain that she had ready and fairly requited employment for as many hours as she saw fit to occupy with her needle. Vanity, it may be, chose to mortify itself, by putting on, for ceremonials of pomp and state, the garments that had been wrought by her sinful hands. Her needle-work was seen on the ruff of the Governor; military men wore it on their scarfs, and the minister on his band; it decked the baby's little cap; it was shut up, to be mildewed and moulder away, in the coffins of the dead. But it is not recorded that, in a single instance, her skill was called in aid to embroider the white veil which was to cover the pure blushes of a bride. The exception indicated the ever relentless vigor with which society frowned upon her sin.

Hester sought not to acquire any thing beyond a subsistence, of the plainest and most ascetic description, for herself, and a simple abundance for her child. Her own dress was of the coarsest materials and the most sombre hue; with only that one ornament,—the scarlet letter,—which it was her doom to wear. The child's attire, on the other hand, was distinguished by a fanciful, or, we might rather say, a fantastic ingenuity, which served, indeed, to heighten the airy charm that early began to develop itself in the little girl, but which appeared to have also a deeper meaning. We may speak further of it hereafter. Except for that small expenditure in the decoration of her infant, Hester bestowed all her superfluous means in charity, on wretches less miserable than herself, and who not unfrequently insulted the hand that fed them. Much of the time, which she might readily have applied to the better efforts of her art, she employed in making coarse garments for the poor. It is probable that there was an idea of penance in this mode of occupation, and that she offered up a real sacrifice of enjoyment, in devoting so many hours to such rude handiwork. She had in her nature a rich, voluptuous, Oriental characteristic,—a taste for the gorgeously beautiful, which, save in the exquisite productions of her needle, found nothing else, in all the possibilities of her life, to exercise itself upon. Women derive a pleasure, incomprehensible to the other sex, from the delicate toil of the needle. To Hester Prynne it might have been a mode of expressing, and therefore soothing, the passion of her life. Like all other joys, she rejected it as sin. This morbid meddling of conscience with an immaterial matter betokened, it is to be feared, no genuine and stedfast penitence, but something doubtful, something that might be deeply wrong, beneath.

In this manner, Hester Prynne came to have a part to perform in the world. With her native energy of character, and rare capacity, it could not entirely cast her off, although it had set a mark upon her, more intolerable to a woman's heart than that which branded the brow of Cain.[33] In all her intercourse with society, however, there was nothing that made her feel as if she belonged to it. Every gesture, every word, and even the silence of those with whom she came in contact, implied, and often expressed, that she was banished, and as much alone as if she inhabited another sphere, or communicated with the common nature by other organs and senses than the rest of human kind. She stood apart from mortal interests, yet close beside them, like a ghost that revisits the familiar fireside, and can no longer make itself seen or felt; no more smile with the household joy, nor mourn with the kindred sorrow; or, should it succeed in manifesting its forbidden sympathy, awakening only terror and horrible repugnance. These emotions, in fact, and its bitterest scorn besides, seemed to be the sole portion that she retained in the universal heart. It was not an age of delicacy; and her position, although she

[33] In Genesis 4:15 " . . . the Lord set a mark upon Cain," who murdered his brother, Abel.

understood it well, and was in little danger of forgetting it, was often brought before her vivid self-perception, like a new anguish, by the rudest touch upon the tenderest spot. The poor, as we have already said, whom she sought out to be the objects of her bounty, often reviled the hand that was stretched forth to succor them. Dames of elevated rank, likewise, whose doors she entered in the way of her occupation, were accustomed to distil drops of bitterness into her heart; sometimes through that alchemy of quiet malice, by which women can concoct a subtile poison from ordinary trifles; and sometimes, also, by a coarser expression, that fell upon the sufferer's defenceless breast like a rough blow upon an ulcerated wound. Hester had schooled herself long and well; she never responded to these attacks, save by a flush of crimson that rose irrepressibly over her pale cheek, and again subsided into the depths of her bosom. She was patient,—a martyr, indeed,—but she forbore to pray for her enemies; lest, in spite of her forgiving aspirations, the words of the blessing should stubbornly twist themselves into a curse.

Continually, and in a thousand other ways, did she feel the innumerable throbs of anguish that had been so cunningly contrived for her by the undying, the ever-active sentence of the Puritan tribunal. Clergymen paused in the street to address words of exhortation, that brought a crowd, with its mingled grin and frown, around the poor, sinful woman. If she entered a church, trusting to share the Sabbath smile of the Universal Father, it was often her mishap to find herself the text of the discourse. She grew to have a dread of children; for they had imbibed from their parents a vague idea of something horrible in this dreary woman, gliding silently through the town, with never any companion but one only child. Therefore, first allowing her to pass, they pursued her at a distance with shrill cries, and the utterance of a word that had no distinct purport to their own minds, but was none the less terrible to her, as proceeding from lips that babbled it unconsciously. It seemed to argue so wide a diffusion of her shame, that all nature knew of it; it could have caused her no deeper pang, had the leaves of the trees whispered the dark story among themselves,—had the summer breeze murmured about it,—had the wintry blast shrieked it aloud! Another peculiar torture was felt in the gaze of a new eye. When strangers looked curiously at the scarlet letter,—and none ever failed to do so,—they branded it afresh into Hester's soul; so that, oftentimes, she could scarcely refrain, yet always did refrain, from covering the symbol with her hand. But then, again, an accustomed eye had likewise its own anguish to inflict. Its cool stare of familiarity was intolerable. From first to last, in short, Hester Prynne had always this dreadful agony in feeling a human eye upon the token; the spot never grew callous; it seemed, on the contrary, to grow more sensitive with daily torture.

But sometimes, once in many days, or perchance in many months, she felt an eye—a human eye—upon the ignominious brand, that seemed to give a momentary relief, as if half of her agony were shared. The next instant, back it all rushed again, with still a deeper throb of pain; for, in that brief interval, she had sinned anew. Had Hester sinned alone?

Her imagination was somewhat affected, and, had she been of a softer moral and intellectual fibre, would have been still more so, by the strange and solitary anguish of her life. Walking to and fro, with those lonely footsteps, in the little world with which she was outwardly connected, it now and then appeared to Hester,—if altogether fancy, it was nevertheless too potent to be resisted,—she felt or fancied, then, that the scarlet letter had endowed her with a new sense. She shuddered to believe, yet could not help believing, that it gave her a sympathetic knowledge of the hidden sin in other hearts. She was terror-stricken by the revelations that were thus made. What were they? Could they be other than the insidious whispers of the bad angel,[34] who would fain have persuaded the struggling woman, as yet only half his victim, that the outward guise of purity was but a lie, and that, if truth were everywhere to be shown, a scarlet letter would blaze forth on many a bosom besides Hester Prynne's? Or, must she receive those intimations—so obscure, yet so distinct—as truth? In all her miserable experience, there was nothing else so awful and so loathsome as this sense. It perplexed, as well as shocked her, by the irreverent inopportuneness of the occasions that brought it into vivid action. Sometimes, the red infamy upon her breast would give a sympathetic throb, as she passed near a venerable minister or magistrate, the model of piety and justice, to whom that age of antique reverence looked up, as to a mortal man in fellowship with angels. "What evil thing is at hand?" would Hester say to herself. Lifting her reluctant eyes, there would be nothing human within the scope of view, save the form of this earthly saint! Again, a mystic sisterhood would contumaciously assert itself, as she met the sanctified frown of some matron, who, according to the rumor of all tongues, had kept cold snow within her bosom throughout life. That unsunned snow in the matron's bosom, and the burning shame on Hester Prynne's,—what had the two in common? Or, once more, the electric thrill would give her warning,—"Behold, Hester, here is a companion!"—and, looking up, she would detect the eyes of a young maiden glancing at the scarlet letter, shyly and aside, and quickly averted, with a faint, chill crimson in her cheeks; as if her purity were somewhat sullied by that momentary glance. O Fiend, whose talisman was that fatal symbol, wouldst thou leave nothing, whether in youth or age, for this poor sinner to revere?—Such loss of faith is ever one of the saddest results of sin. Be it accepted as a proof that all was not corrupt in this poor victim of her own frailty, and man's hard law, that Hester Prynne yet struggled to believe that no fellow-mortal was guilty like herself.

The vulgar, who, in those dreary old times, were always contributing a grotesque horror to what interested their imaginations, had a story about the scarlet letter which we might readily work up into a terrific legend. They averred, that the symbol was not mere scarlet cloth, tinged in an earthly dye-pot, but was red-hot with infernal fire, and could be seen glowing all alight, whenever Hester Prynne walked abroad in the night-time. And we must needs say, it seared Hester's bosom so deeply, that perhaps there was more truth in the rumor than our modern incredulity may be inclined to admit.

VI: Pearl

We have as yet hardly spoken of the infant; that little creature, whose innocent life had sprung, by the inscrutable decree of Providence, a lovely and immortal flower, out of the rank luxuriance of a guilty passion. How strange it seemed to the sad woman, as she watched the growth, and the beauty that became every day more brilliant, and the intelligence that threw its quivering sunshine over the tiny features of this child! Her Pearl!—For so had Hester called her; not as a name expressive of her aspect, which had nothing of the calm, white, unimpassioned

---

[34] Lucifer, or Satan.

lustre that would be indicated by the comparison. But she named the infant "Pearl," as being of great price,[35]—purchased with all she had,—her mother's only treasure! How strange, indeed! Man had marked this woman's sin by a scarlet letter, which had such potent and disastrous efficacy that no human sympathy could reach her, save it were sinful like herself. God, as a direct consequence of the sin which man thus punished, had given her a lovely child, whose place was on that same dishonored bosom, to connect her parent for ever with the race and descent of mortals, and to be finally a blessed soul in heaven! Yet these thoughts affected Hester Prynne less with hope than apprehension. She knew that her deed had been evil; she could have no faith, therefore, that its result would be for good. Day after day, she looked fearfully into the child's expanding nature; ever dreading to detect some dark and wild peculiarity, that should correspond with the guiltiness to which she owed her being.

Certainly, there was no physical defect. By its perfect shape, its vigor, and its natural dexterity in the use of all its untried limbs, the infant was worthy to have been brought forth in Eden; worthy to have been left there, to be the plaything of the angels, after the world's first parents were driven out. The child had a native grace which does not invariably coexist with faultless beauty; its attire, however simple, always impressed the beholder as if it were the very garb that precisely became it best. But little Pearl was not clad in rustic weeds. Her mother, with a morbid purpose that may be better understood hereafter, had bought the richest tissues that could be procured, and allowed her imaginative faculty its full play in the arrangement and decoration of the dresses which the child wore, before the public eye. So magnificent was the small figure, when thus arrayed, and such was the splendor of Pearl's own proper beauty, shining through the gorgeous robes which might have extinguished a paler loveliness, that there was an absolute circle of radiance around her, on the darksome cottage-floor. And yet a russet gown, torn and soiled with the child's rude play, made a picture of her just as perfect. Pearl's aspect was imbued with a spell of infinite variety; in this one child there were many children, comprehending the full scope between the wild-flower prettiness of a peasant-baby, and the pomp, in little, of an infant princess. Throughout all, however, there was a trait of passion, a certain depth of hue, which she never lost; and if, in any of her changes, she had grown fainter or paler, she would have ceased to be herself;—it would have been no longer Pearl!

This outward mutability indicated, and did not more than fairly express, the various properties of her inner life. Her nature appeared to possess depth, too, as well as variety; but—or else Hester's fears deceived her—it lacked reference and adaptation to the world into which she was born. The child could not be made amenable to rules. In giving her existence, a great law had been broken; and the result was a being, whose elements were perhaps beautiful and brilliant, but all in disorder; or with an order peculiar to themselves, amidst which the point of variety and arrangement was difficult or impossible to be discovered. Hester could only account for the child's character—and even then, most vaguely and imperfectly—by recalling what she herself had been, during that momentous period while Pearl was imbibing her soul from the spiritual world, and her bodily frame from its material of earth. The mother's impassioned state had been the medium through which were transmitted to the unborn infant the rays of its moral life;

[35] "The kingdom of heaven is like unto a merchant man, seeking goodly pearls: Who, when he had found one pearl of great price, went out and sold all he had, and bought it," from Matthew 13:45–46.

and, however white and clear originally, they had taken the deep stains of crimson and gold, the fiery lustre, the black shadow, and the untempered light, of the intervening substance. Above all, the warfare of Hester's spirit, at that epoch, was perpetuated in Pearl. She could recognize her wild, desperate, defiant mood, the flightiness of her temper, and even some of the very cloud-shapes of gloom and despondency that had brooded in her heart. They were now illuminated by the morning radiance of a young child's disposition, but, later in the day of earthly existence, might be prolific of the storm and whirlwind.

The discipline of the family, in those days, was of a far more rigid kind than now. The frown, the harsh rebuke, the frequent application of the rod, enjoined by Scriptural authority,[36] were used, not merely in the way of punishment for actual offences, but as a wholesome regimen for the growth and promotion of all childish virtues. Hester Prynne, nevertheless, the lonely mother of this one child, ran little risk of erring on the side of undue severity. Mindful, however, of her own errors and misfortunes, she early sought to impose a tender, but strict, control over the infant immortality that was committed to her charge. But the task was beyond her skill. After testing both smiles and frowns, and proving that neither mode of treatment possessed any calculable influence, Hester was ultimately compelled to stand aside, and permit the child to be swayed by her own impulses. Physical compulsion or restraint was effectual, of course, while it lasted. As to any other kind of discipline, whether addressed to her mind or heart, little Pearl might or might not be within its reach, in accordance with the caprice that ruled the moment. Her mother, while Pearl was yet an infant, grew acquainted with a certain peculiar look, that warned her when it would be labor thrown away to insist, persuade, or plead. It was a look so intelligent, yet inexplicable, so perverse, sometimes so malicious, but generally accompanied by a wild flow of spirits, that Hester could not help questioning, at such moments, whether Pearl was a human child. She seemed rather an airy sprite, which, after playing its fantastic sports for a little while upon the cottage-floor, would flit away with a mocking smile. Whenever that look appeared in her wild, bright, deeply black eyes, it invested her with a strange remoteness and intangibility; it was as if she were hovering in the air and might vanish, like a glimmering light that comes we know not whence, and goes we know not whither. Beholding it, Hester was constrained to rush towards the child,—to pursue the little elf in the flight which she invariably began,—to snatch her to her bosom, with a close pressure and earnest kisses,—not so much from overflowing love, as to assure herself that Pearl was flesh and blood, and not utterly delusive. But Pearl's laugh, when she was caught, though full of merriment and music, made her mother more doubtful than before.

Heart-smitten at this bewildering and baffling spell, that so often came between herself and her sole treasure, whom she had bought so dear, and who was all her world, Hester sometimes burst into passionate tears. Then, perhaps,—for there was no foreseeing how it might affect her,—Pearl would frown, and clench her little fist, and harden her small features into a stern, unsympathizing look of discontent. Not seldom, she would laugh anew, and louder than before, like a thing incapable and unintelligent of human sorrow. Or—but this more rarely happened—she would be convulsed with a rage of grief, and sob out her love for her mother, in broken words, and seem intent on proving that she had a heart, by

---

[36] "He that spareth his rod hateth his son: but he that loveth him chasteneth him betimes," from Proverbs 13:24 (more popularly, "spare the rod and spoil the child").

breaking it. Yet Hester was hardly safe in confiding herself to that gusty tenderness; it passed, as suddenly as it came. Brooding over all these matters, the mother felt like one who has evoked a spirit, but, by some irregularity in the process of conjuration, has failed to win the master-word that should control this new and incomprehensible intelligence. Her only real comfort was when the child lay in the placidity of sleep. Then she was sure of her, and tasted hours of quiet, sad, delicious happiness; until—perhaps with that perverse expression glimmering from beneath her opening lids—little Pearl awoke!

How soon—with what strange rapidity, indeed!—did Pearl arrive at an age that was capable of social intercourse, beyond the mother's ever-ready smile and nonsense-words! And then what a happiness would it have been, could Hester Prynne have heard her clear, bird-like voice mingling with the uproar of other childish voices, and have distinguished and unravelled her own darling's tones, amid all the entangled outcry of a group of sportive children! But this could never be. Pearl was a born outcast of the infantile world. An imp of evil, emblem and product of sin, she had no right among christened infants. Nothing was more remarkable than the instinct, as it seemed, with which the child comprehended her loneliness; the destiny that had drawn an inviolable circle round about her; the whole peculiarity, in short, of her position in respect to other children. Never, since her release from prison, had Hester met the public gaze without her. In all her walks about the town, Pearl, too, was there; first as the babe in arms, and afterwards as the little girl, small companion of her mother, holding a forefinger with her whole grasp, and tripping along at the rate of three or four footsteps to one of Hester's. She saw the children of the settlement, on the grassy margin of the street, or at the domestic thresholds, disporting themselves in such grim fashion as the Puritanic nurture would permit; playing at going to church, perchance; or at scourging Quakers; or taking scalps in a sham-fight with the Indians; or scaring one another with freaks of imitative witchcraft. Pearl saw, and gazed intently, but never sought to make acquaintance. If spoken to, she would not speak again. If the children gathered about her, as they sometimes did, Pearl would grow positively terrible in her puny wrath, snatching up stones to fling at them, with shrill, incoherent exclamations that made her mother tremble, because they had so much the sound of a witch's anathemas in some unknown tongue.

The truth was, that the little Puritans, being of the most intolerant brood that ever lived, had got a vague idea of something outlandish, unearthly, or at variance with ordinary fashions, in the mother and child; and therefore scorned them in their hearts, and not unfrequently reviled them with their tongues. Pearl felt the sentiment, and requited it with the bitterest hatred that can be supposed to rankle in a childish bosom. These outbreaks of a fierce temper had a kind of value, and even comfort, for her mother; because there was at least an intelligible earnestness in the mood, instead of the fitful caprice that so often thwarted her in the child's manifestations. It appalled her, nevertheless, to discern here, again, a shadowy reflection of the evil that had existed in herself. All this enmity and passion had Pearl inherited, by inalienable right, out of Hester's heart. Mother and daughter stood together in the same circle of seclusion from human society; and in the nature of the child seemed to be perpetuated those unquiet elements that had distracted Hester Prynne before Pearl's birth, but had since begun to be soothed away by the softening influences of maternity.

At home, within and around her mother's cottage, Pearl wanted not a wide and various circle of acquaintance. The spell of life went forth from her ever creative spirit, and communicated itself to a thousand objects, as a torch kindles a flame wherever it may be applied. The unlikeliest materials, a stick, a bunch of rags, a flower, were the puppets of Pearl's witchcraft, and, without undergoing any outward change, became spiritually adapted to whatever drama occupied the stage of her inner world. Her one baby-voice served a multitude of imaginary personages, old and young, to talk withal. The pine-trees, aged, black, and solemn, and flinging groans and other melancholy utterances on the breeze, needed little transformation to figure as Puritan elders; the ugliest weeds of the garden were their children, whom Pearl smote down and uprooted, most unmercifully. It was wonderful, the vast variety of forms into which she threw her intellect, with no continuity, indeed, but darting up and dancing, always in a state of preternatural activity,—soon sinking down, as if exhausted by so rapid and feverish a tide of life,—and succeeded by other shapes of a similar wild energy. It was like nothing so much as the phantasmagoric play of the northern lights. In the mere exercise of the fancy, however, and the sportiveness of a growing mind, there might be little more than was observable in other children of bright faculties; except as Pearl, in the dearth of human playmates, was thrown more upon the visionary throng which she created. The singularity lay in the hostile feelings with which the child regarded all these offspring of her own heart and mind. She never created a friend, but seemed always to be sowing broadcast the dragon's teeth, whence sprung a harvest of armed enemies,[37] against whom she rushed to battle. It was inexpressibly sad—then what depth of sorrow to a mother, who felt in her own heart the cause!—to observe, in one so young, this constant recognition of an adverse world, and so fierce a training of the energies that were to make good her cause, in the contest that must ensue.

Gazing at Pearl, Hester Prynne often dropped her work upon her knees, and cried out, with an agony which she would fain have hidden, but which made utterance for itself, betwixt speech and a groan,—"O Father in Heaven,—if Thou art still my Father,—what is this being which I have brought into the world!" And Pearl, overhearing the ejaculation, or aware, through some more subtle channel, of those throbs of anguish, would turn her vivid and beautiful little face upon her mother, smile with sprite-like intelligence, and resume her play.

One peculiarity of the child's deportment remains yet to be told. The very first thing which she had noticed, in her life, was—what?—not the mother's smile, responding to it, as other babies do, by that faint, embryo smile of the little mouth, remembered so doubtfully afterwards, and with such fond discussion whether it were indeed a smile. By no means! But that first object of which Pearl seemed to become aware was—shall we say it?—the scarlet letter on Hester's bosom! One day, as her mother stooped over the cradle, the infant's eyes had been caught by the glimmering of the gold embroidery about the letter; and, putting up her little hand, she grasped at it, smiling, not doubtfully, but with a decided gleam that gave her face the look of a much older child. Then, gasping for breath, did Hester Prynne clutch the fatal token, instinctively endeavouring to tear it away; so infinite was the torture inflicted by the intelligent touch of Pearl's baby-hand. Again, as if her mother's agonized gesture were meant only to make sport for her, did little Pearl look into her eyes, and smile! From that epoch, except when the child was asleep, Hester had never felt a moment's safety; not a moment's calm

---

[37] According to Greek myth, the hero Cadmus planted dragon's teeth that grew into armed warriors. Hawthorne's "The Dragon's Teeth" (1853) retells the story for children.

enjoyment of her. Weeks, it is true, would sometimes elapse, during which Pearl's gaze might never once be fixed upon the scarlet letter; but then, again, it would come at unawares, like the stroke of sudden death, and always with that peculiar smile, and odd expression of the eyes.

Once, this freakish, elfish cast came into the child's eyes, while Hester was looking at her own image in them, as mothers are fond of doing; and, suddenly,—for women in solitude, and with troubled hearts, are pestered with unaccountable delusions,—she fancied that she beheld, not her own miniature portrait, but another face in the small black mirror of Pearl's eye. It was a face, fiend-like, full of smiling malice, yet bearing the semblance of features that she had known full well, though seldom with a smile, and never with malice, in them. It was as if an evil spirit possessed the child, and had just then peeped forth in mockery. Many a time afterwards had Hester been tortured, though less vividly, by the same illusion.

In the afternoon of a certain summer's day, after Pearl grew big enough to run about, she amused herself with gathering handfuls of wild-flowers, and flinging them, one by one, at her mother's bosom; dancing up and down, like a little elf, whenever she hit the scarlet letter. Hester's first motion had been to cover her bosom with her clasped hands. But, whether from pride or resignation, or a feeling that her penance might best be wrought out by this unutterable pain, she resisted the impulse, and sat erect, pale as death, looking sadly into little Pearl's wild eyes. Still came the battery of flowers, almost invariably hitting the mark, and covering the mother's breast with hurts for which she could find no balm in this world, nor knew how to seek it in another. At last, her shot being all expended, the child stood still and gazed at Hester, with that little, laughing image of a fiend peeping out—or, whether it peeped or no, her mother so imagined it—from the unsearchable abyss of her black eyes.

"Child, what art thou?" cried the mother.

"O, I am your little Pearl!" answered the child.

But, while she said it, Pearl laughed and began to dance up and down, with the humorsome gesticulation of a little imp, whose next freak[38] might be to fly up the chimney.

"Art thou my child, in very truth?" asked Hester.

Nor did she put the question altogether idly, but, for the moment, with a portion of genuine earnestness; for, such was Pearl's wonderful intelligence, that her mother half doubted whether she were not acquainted with the secret spell of her existence, and might not now reveal herself.

"Yes; I am little Pearl!" repeated the child, continuing her antics.

"Thou art not my child! Thou art no Pearl of mine!" said the mother, half playfully; for it was often the case that a sportive impulse came over her, in the midst of her deepest suffering. "Tell me, then, what thou art, and who sent thee hither?"

"Tell me, mother!" said the child, seriously, coming up to Hester, and pressing herself close to her knees. "Do thou tell me!"

"Thy Heavenly Father sent thee!" answered Hester Prynne.

But she said it with a hesitation that did not escape the acuteness of the child. Whether moved only by her ordinary freakishness, or because an evil spirit prompted her, she put up her small forefinger, and touched the scarlet letter.

[38] Whim or fancy.

"He did not send me!" cried she, positively. "I have no Heavenly Father!"

"Hush, Pearl, hush! Thou must not talk so!" answered the mother, suppressing a groan. "He sent us all into this world. He sent even me, thy mother. Then, much more, thee! Or, if not, thou strange and elfish child, whence didst thou come?"

"Tell me! Tell me!" repeated Pearl, no longer seriously, but laughing, and capering about the floor. "It is thou that must tell me!"

But Hester could not resolve the query, being herself in a dismal labyrinth of doubt. She remembered—betwixt a smile and a shudder—the talk of the neighbouring townspeople; who, seeking vainly elsewhere for the child's paternity, and observing some of her odd attributes, had given out that poor little Pearl was a demon offspring;[39] such as, ever since old Catholic times, had occasionally been seen on earth, through the agency of their mothers' sin, and to promote some foul and wicked purpose. Luther, according to the scandal of his monkish enemies, was a brat of that hellish breed; nor was Pearl the only child to whom this inauspicious origin was assigned, among the New England Puritans.

VII: The Governor's Hall

Hester Prynne went, one day, to the mansion of Governor Bellingham, with a pair of gloves, which she had fringed and embroidered to his order, and which were to be worn on some great occasion of state; for, though the chances of a popular election had caused this former ruler to descend a step or two from the highest rank, he still held an honorable and influential place among the colonial magistracy.[40]

Another and far more important reason than the delivery of a pair of embroidered gloves impelled Hester, at this time, to seek an interview with a personage of so much power and activity in the affairs of the settlement. It had reached her ears, that there was a design on the part of some of the leading inhabitants, cherishing the more rigid order of principles in religion and government, to deprive her of her child. On the supposition that Pearl, as already hinted, was of demon origin, these good people not unreasonably argued that a Christian interest in the mother's soul required them to remove such a stumbling-block from her path. If the child, on the other hand, were really capable of moral and religious growth, and possessed the elements of ultimate salvation, then, surely, it would enjoy all the fairer prospect of these advantages by being transferred to wiser and better guardianship than Hester Prynne's. Among those who promoted the design, Governor Bellingham was said to be one of the most busy. It may appear singular, and, indeed, not a little ludicrous, that an affair of this kind, which, in later days, would have been referred to no higher jurisdiction than that of the selectmen of the town, should then have been a question publicly discussed, and on which statesmen of eminence took sides. At that epoch of pristine simplicity, however, matters of even slighter public interest, and of far less intrinsic weight than the welfare of Hester and her child, were strangely mixed up with the deliberations of legislators and acts of state. The period was hardly, if at all, earlier than that of our story, when a dispute concerning the right of property in a pig, not only

---

[39] Before the Protestant Reformation and establishment of the Church of England in the sixteenth century, led by Martin Luther (1483–1546).

[40] Bellingham became a magistrate, or deputy governor, in 1642, between terms as governor.

caused a fierce and bitter contest in the legislative body of the colony, but resulted in an important modification of the framework itself of the legislature.[41]

Full of concern, therefore,—but so conscious of her own right, that it seemed scarcely an unequal match between the public, on the one side, and a lonely woman, backed by the sympathies of nature, on the other,—Hester Prynne set forth from her solitary cottage. Little Pearl, of course, was her companion. She was now of an age to run lightly along by her mother's side, and, constantly in motion from morn till sunset, could have accomplished a much longer journey than that before her. Often, nevertheless, more from caprice than necessity, she demanded to be taken up in arms, but was soon as imperious to be set down again, and frisked onward before Hester on the grassy pathway, with many a harmless trip and tumble. We have spoken of Pearl's rich and luxuriant beauty; a beauty that shone with deep and vivid tints; a bright complexion, eyes possessing intensity both of depth and glow, and hair already of a deep, glossy brown, and which, in after years, would be nearly akin to black. There was fire in her and throughout her; she seemed the unpremeditated offshoot of a passionate moment. Her mother, in contriving the child's garb, had allowed the gorgeous tendencies of her imagination their full play; arraying her in a crimson velvet tunic, of a peculiar cut, abundantly embroidered with fantasies and flourishes of gold thread. So much strength of coloring, which must have given a wan and pallid aspect to cheeks of a fainter bloom, was admirably adapted to Pearl's beauty, and made her the very brightest little jet of flame that ever danced upon the earth.

But it was a remarkable attribute of this garb, and, indeed, of the child's whole appearance, that it irresistibly and inevitably reminded the beholder of the token which Hester Prynne was doomed to wear upon her bosom. It was the scarlet letter in another form; the scarlet letter endowed with life! The mother herself—as if the red ignominy were so deeply scorched into her brain, that all her conceptions assumed its form—had carefully wrought out the similitude; lavishing many hours of morbid ingenuity, to create an analogy between the object of her affection, and the emblem of her guilt and torture. But, in truth, Pearl was the one, as well as the other; and only in consequence of that identity had Hester contrived so perfectly to represent the scarlet letter in her appearance.

As the two wayfarers came within the precincts of the town, the children of the Puritans looked up from their play,—or what passed for play with those sombre little urchins,—and spake gravely one to another:—

"Behold, verily, there is the woman of the scarlet letter; and, of a truth, moreover, there is the likeness of the scarlet letter running along by her side! Come, therefore, and let us fling mud at them!"

But Pearl, who was a dauntless child, after frowning, stamping her foot, and shaking her little hand with a variety of threatening gestures, suddenly made a rush at the knot of her enemies, and put them all to flight. She resembled, in her fierce pursuit of them, an infant pestilence,—the scarlet fever, or some such half-fledged angel of judgment,—whose mission was to punish the sins of the rising generation. She screamed and shouted, too, with a terrific volume of sound, which doubtless caused the hearts of the fugitives to quake within them. The victory accomplished, Pearl returned quietly to her mother, and looked up smiling into her face.

---

[41] The so-called Sow Case, *Sherman* v. *Keayne* (1642–1643), led to the dividing of the Massachusetts General Court, or legislature, into two houses.

Without further adventure, they reached the dwelling of Governor Bellingham. This was a large wooden house, built in a fashion of which there are specimens still extant in the streets of our elder towns; now moss-grown, crumbling to decay, and melancholy at heart with the many sorrowful or joyful occurrences, remembered or forgotten, that have happened, and passed away, within their dusky chambers. Then, however, there was the freshness of the passing year on its exterior, and the cheerfulness, gleaming forth from the sunny windows, of a human habitation into which death had never entered. It had indeed a very cheery aspect; the walls being overspread with a kind of stucco, in which fragments of broken glass were plentifully intermixed; so that, when the sunshine fell aslant-wise over the front of the edifice, it glittered and sparkled as if diamonds had been flung against it by the double handful. The brilliancy might have befitted Aladdin's palace,[42] rather than the mansion of a grave old Puritan ruler. It was further decorated with strange and seemingly cabalistic[43] figures and diagrams, suitable to the quaint taste of the age, which had been drawn in the stucco when newly laid on, and had now grown hard and durable, for the admiration of after times.

Pearl, looking at this bright wonder of a house, began to caper and dance, and imperatively required that the whole breadth of sunshine should be stripped off its front, and given her to play with.

"No, my little Pearl!" said her mother. "Thou must gather thine own sunshine. I have none to give thee!"

They approached the door; which was of an arched form, and flanked on each side by a narrow tower or projection of the edifice, in both of which were lattice-windows, with wooden shutters to close over them at need. Lifting the iron hammer than hung at the portal, Hester Prynne gave a summons, which was answered by one of the Governor's bond-servants; a free-born Englishman, but now a seven years' slave. During that term he was to be the property of his master, and as much a commodity of bargain and sale as an ox, or a joint-stool. The serf wore the blue coat, which was the customary garb of serving-men at that period, and long before, in the old hereditary halls of England.

"Is the worshipful Governor Bellingham within?" inquired Hester.

"Yea, forsooth," replied the bond-servant, staring with wide-open eyes at the scarlet letter, which, being a new-comer in the country, he had never before seen. "Yea, his honorable worship is within. But he hath a godly minister or two with him, and likewise a leech. Ye may not see his worship now."

"Nevertheless, I will enter," answered Hester Prynne; and the bond-servant, perhaps judging from the decision of her air and the glittering symbol in her bosom, that she was a great lady in the land, offered no opposition.

So the mother and little Pearl were admitted into the hall of entrance. With many variations, suggested by the nature of his building-materials, diversity of climate, and a different mode of social life, Governor Bellingham had planned his new habitation after the residences of gentlemen of fair estate in his native land. Here, then, was a wide and reasonably lofty hall, extending through the whole depth of the house, and forming a medium of general communication, more or less directly, with all the other apartments. At one extremity, this spacious room was lighted by the windows of the two towers, which formed a small recess on

[42] In the *Arabian Nights,* the palace of the boy who finds a magic lamp and ring, which enable him to summon genii who grant his wishes.
[43] Occult, mysterious.

either side of the portal. At the other end, though partly muffled by a curtain, it was more powerfully illuminated by one of those embowed hall-windows which we read of in old books, and which was provided with a deep and cushioned seat. Here, on the cushion, lay a folio tome, probably of the Chronicles of England,[44] or other such substantial literature; even as, in our own days, we scatter gilded volumes on the centre-table, to be turned over by the casual guest. The furniture of the hall consisted of some ponderous chairs, the backs of which were elaborately carved with wreaths of oaken flowers; and likewise a table in the same taste; the whole being of the Elizabethan age, or perhaps earlier, and heirlooms, transferred hither from the Governor's paternal home. On the table—in token that the sentiment of old English hospitality had not been left behind—stood a large pewter tankard, at the bottom of which, had Hester or Pearl peeped into it, they might have seen the frothy remnant of a recent draught of ale.

On the wall hung a row of portraits, representing the forefathers of the Bellingham lineage, some with armour on their breasts, and others with stately ruffs and robes of peace. All were characterized by the sternness and severity which old portraits so invariably put on; as if they were the ghosts, rather than the pictures, of departed worthies, and were gazing with harsh and intolerant criticism at the pursuits and enjoyments of living men.

At about the centre of the oaken panels, that lined the hall, was suspended a suit of mail, not, like the pictures, an ancestral relic, but of the most modern date; for it had been manufactured by a skilful armorer in London, the same year in which Governor Bellingham came over to New England. There was a steel headpiece, a cuirass, a gorget, and greaves,[45] with a pair of gauntlets and a sword hanging beneath; all, and especially the helmet and breastplate, so highly burnished as to glow with white radiance, and scatter an illumination everywhere about upon the floor. This bright panoply was not meant for mere idle show, but had been worn by the Governor on many a solemn muster and training field, and had glittered, moreover, at the head of a regiment in the Pequod[46] war. For, though bred a lawyer, and accustomed to speak of Bacon, Coke, Noye, and Finch,[47] as his professional associates, the exigencies of this new country had transformed Governor Bellingham into a soldier, as well as a statesman and ruler.

Little Pearl—who was as greatly pleased with the gleaming armour as she had been with the glittering frontispiece of the house—spent some time looking into the polished mirror of the breastplate.

"Mother," cried she, "I see you here. Look! Look!"

Hester looked, by way of humoring the child; and she saw that, owing to the peculiar effect of this convex mirror, the scarlet letter was represented in exaggerated and gigantic proportions, so as to be greatly the most prominent feature of her appearance. In truth, she seemed absolutely hidden behind it. Pearl pointed upward, also, at a similar picture in the headpiece; smiling at her mother, with the elfish intelligence that was so familiar an expression on her small physiognomy.

---

[44] *Chronicles of England, Scotland, and Ireland* (1577), a well-known source of historical information, by Raphael Holinshed (?–1580?).

[45] Protective armor for the chest, for the neck, and for the shins.

[46] The Pequot Indians of Connecticut fought colonial forces from Massachusetts Bay, Plymouth, and Connecticut in 1637 and were slaughtered.

[47] Francis Bacon (1561–1626), a famous essayist and philosopher; Edward Coke (1552–1634), a prominent jurist who served as Lord Chief Justice; William Noye (1577–1634), Attorney General under Charles I; and John Finch (1584–1660), Chief Justice of the Commons Pleas Court.

That look of naughty merriment was likewise reflected in the mirror, with so much breadth and intensity of effect, that it made Hester Prynne feel as if it could not be the image of her own child, but of an imp who was seeking to mould itself into Pearl's shape.

"Come along, Pearl!" said she, drawing her away. "Come and look into this fair garden. It may be, we shall see flowers there; more beautiful ones than we find in the woods."

Pearl, accordingly, ran to the bow-window, at the farther end of the hall, and looked along the vista of a garden-walk, carpeted with closely shaven grass, and bordered with some rude and immature attempt at shrubbery. But the proprietor appeared already to have relinquished, as hopeless, the effort to perpetuate on this side of the Atlantic, in a hard soil and amid the close struggle for subsistence, the native English taste for ornamental gardening. Cabbages grew in plain sight; and a pumpkin vine, rooted at some distance, had run across the intervening space, and deposited one of its gigantic products directly beneath the hall-window; as if to warn the Governor that this great lump of vegetable gold was as rich an ornament as New England earth would offer him. There were a few rose-bushes, however, and a number of apple-trees, probably the descendants of those planted by the Reverend Mr. Blackstone,[48] the first settler of the peninsula; that half mythological personage who rides through our early annals, seated on the back of a bull.

Pearl, seeing the rose-bushes, began to cry for a red rose, and would not be pacified.

"Hush, child, hush!" said her mother earnestly. "Do not cry, dear little Pearl! I hear voices in the garden. The Governor is coming, and gentlemen along with him!"

In fact, adown the vista of the garden-avenue, a number of persons were seen approaching towards the house. Pearl, in utter scorn of her mother's attempt to quiet her, gave an eldritch[49] scream, and then became silent; not from any notion of obedience, but because the quick and mobile curiosity of her disposition was excited by the appearance of these new personages.

VIII: The Elf-Child and the Minister

Governor Bellingham, in a loose gown and easy cap,—such as elderly gentlemen loved to indue themselves with, in their domestic privacy,—walked foremost, and appeared to be showing off his estate, and expatiating on his projected improvements. The wide circumference of an elaborate ruff, beneath his gray beard, in the antiquated fashion of King James's reign,[50] caused his head to look not a little like that of John the Baptist in a charger.[51] The impression made by his aspect, so rigid and severe, and frost-bitten with more than autumnal age, was hardly in keeping with the appliances of worldly enjoyment wherewith he had evidently done his utmost to surround himself. But it is an error to suppose that our grave forefa-

---

[48] William Blackstone (1595–1675), an Anglican minister who came to New England in 1623 and joined Native-American settlements in Rhode Island because of disputes with the Puritans, who arrived in 1630. He is said to have been the first white settler in the Boston area.

[49] Unearthly or eerie.

[50] James I (1566–1625) ruled England from 1603 to 1625.

[51] In Matthew 14:6–11 John the Baptist was beheaded, and his head was served on a charger, or platter.

thers—though accustomed to speak and think of human existence as a state merely of trial and warfare, and though unfeignedly prepared to sacrifice goods and life at the behest of duty—made it a matter of conscience to reject such means of comfort, or even luxury, as lay fairly within their grasp. This creed was never taught, for instance, by the venerable pastor, John Wilson, whose beard, white as a snow-drift, was seen over Governor Bellingham's shoulder; while its wearer suggested that pears and peaches might yet be naturalized in the New England climate, and that purple grapes might possibly be compelled to flourish, against the sunny garden-wall. The old clergyman, nurtured at the rich bosom of the English Church, had a long established and legitimate taste for all good and comfortable things; and however stern he might show himself in the pulpit, or in his public reproof of such transgressions as that of Hester Prynne, still, the genial benevolence of his private life had won him warmer affection than was accorded to any of his professional contemporaries.

Behind the Governor and Mr. Wilson came two other guests; one, the Reverend Arthur Dimmesdale, whom the reader may remember, as having taken a brief and reluctant part in the scene of Hester Prynne's disgrace; and, in close companionship with him, old Roger Chillingworth, a person of great skill in physic,[52] who, for two or three years past, had been settled in the town. It was understood that this learned man was the physician as well as friend of the young minister, whose health had severely suffered, of late, by his too unreserved self-sacrifice to the labors and duties of the pastoral relation.

The Governor, in advance of his visitors, ascended one or two steps, and, throwing open the leaves of the great hall window, found himself close to little Pearl. The shadow of the curtain fell on Hester Prynne, and partially concealed her.

"What have we here?" said Governor Bellingham, looking with surprise at the scarlet little figure before him. "I profess, I have never seen the like, since my days of vanity, in old King James's time, when I was wont to esteem it a high favor to be admitted to a court mask! There used to be a swarm of these small apparitions, in holiday-time; and we called them children of the Lord of Misrule.[53] But how gat such a guest into my hall?"

"Ay, indeed!" cried good old Mr. Wilson. "What little bird of scarlet plumage may this be? Methinks I have seen just such figures, when the sun has been shining through a richly painted window, and tracing out the golden and crimson images across the floor. But that was in the old land.[54] Prithee, young one, who art thou, and what has ailed thy mother to bedizen thee in this strange fashion? Art thou a Christian child,—ha? Dost know thy catechism? Or art thou one of those naughty elfs or fairies, whom we thought to have left behind us, with other relics of Papistry, in merry old England?"

"I am mother's child," answered the scarlet vision, "and my name is Pearl!"

"Pearl?—Ruby, rather!—or Coral!—or Red Rose, at the very least, judging from thy hue!" responded the old minister, putting forth his hand in a vain attempt to pat little Pearl on the cheek. "But where is this mother of thine? Ah! I see," he added; and, turning to Governor Bellingham, whispered,—"This is the selfsame

---

[52] Medicine or healing.

[53] The title of the master of revels at Christmas games, prior to the advent of Puritan government in England; He was sometimes assisted by "swarms" of children.

[54] England.

child of whom we have held speech together; and behold here the unhappy woman, Hester Prynne, her mother!"

"Sayest thou so?" cried the Governor. "Nay, we might have judged that such a child's mother must needs be a scarlet woman, and a worthy type of her of Babylon![55] But she comes at a good time; and we will look into this matter forthwith."

Governor Bellingham stepped through the window into the hall, followed by his three guests.

"Hester Prynne," said he, fixing his naturally stern regard on the wearer of the scarlet letter, "there hath been much question concerning thee, of late. The point hath been weightily discussed, whether we, that are of authority and influence, do well discharge our consciences by trusting an immortal soul, such as there is in yonder child, to the guidance of one who hath stumbled and fallen, amid the pitfalls of this world. Speak thou, the child's own mother! Were it not, thinkest thou, for thy little one's temporal and eternal welfare, that she be taken out of thy charge, and clad soberly, and disciplined strictly, and instructed in the truths of heaven and earth? What canst thou do for the child, in this kind?"

"I can teach my little Pearl what I have learned from this!" answered Hester Prynne, laying her finger on the red token.

"Woman, it is thy badge of shame!" replied the stern magistrate. "It is because of the stain which that letter indicates, that we would transfer thy child to other hands."

"Nevertheless," said the mother calmly, though growing more pale, "this badge hath taught me,—it daily teaches me,—it is teaching me at this moment,—lessons whereof my child may be the wiser and better, albeit they can profit nothing to myself."

"We will judge warily," said Bellingham, "and look well what we are about to do. Good Master Wilson, I pray you, examine this Pearl,—since that is her name,—and see whether she hath had such Christian nurture as befits a child of her age."

The old minister seated himself in an arm-chair, and made an effort to draw Pearl betwixt his knees. But the child, unaccustomed to the touch or familiarity of any but her mother, escaped through the open window and stood on the upper step, looking like a wild, tropical bird, of rich plumage, ready to take flight into the upper air. Mr. Wilson, not a little astonished at this outbreak,—for he was a grandfatherly sort of personage, and usually a vast favorite with children,—essayed, however, to proceed with the examination.

"Pearl," said he, with great solemnity, "thou must take heed to instruction, that so, in due season, thou mayest wear in thy bosom the pearl of great price.[56] Canst thou tell me, my child, who made thee?"

Now Pearl knew well enough who made her; for Hester Prynne, the daughter of a pious home, very soon after her talk with the child about her Heavenly Father, had begun to inform her of those truths which the human spirit, at whatever stage of immaturity, imbibes with such eager interest. Pearl, therefore, so large were the attainments of her three years' lifetime, could have borne a fair examination in the New England Primer, or the first column of the Westminister Catechism,[57] al-

---

[55] In Revelations 17:1–5 the "scarlet woman," or city of Babylon, is denounced as an abomination; during the reformation the Catholic church was denounced as the "whore of Babylon."

[56] In Matthew 13:45–46 the "pearl of great price" is linked to godliness, the "kingdom of Heaven."

[57] *The New England Primer* (1683?), a Puritan schoolbook, illustrates the alphabet with woodcuts and religious rhymes; the *Westminster Catechism,* formulated by the Westminster Assembly (1645–

though unacquainted with the outward form of either of those celebrated works. But that perversity, which all children have more or less of, and of which little Pearl had a tenfold portion, now, at the most inopportune moment, took thorough possession of her, and closed her lips, or impelled her to speak words amiss. After putting her finger in her mouth, with many ungracious refusals to answer good Mr. Wilson's question, the child finally announced that she had not been made at all, but had been plucked by her mother off the bush of wild roses, that grew by the prison-door.

This fantasy was probably suggested by the near proximity of the Governor's red roses, as Pearl stood outside of the window; together with her recollection of the prison rose-bush, which she had passed in coming hither.

Old Roger Chillingworth, with a smile on his face, whispered something in the young clergyman's ear. Hester Prynne looked at the man of skill, and even then, with her fate hanging in the balance, was startled to perceive what a change had come over his features,—how much uglier they were,—how his dark complexion seemed to have grown duskier, and his figure more misshapen,—since the days when she had familiarly known him. She met his eyes for an instant, but was immediately constrained to give all her attention to the scene now going forward.

"This is awful!" cried the Governor, slowly recovering from the astonishment into which Pearl's response had thrown him. "Here is a child of three years old, and she cannot tell who made her! Without question, she is equally in the dark as to her soul, its present depravity, and future destiny! Methinks, gentlemen, we need inquire no further."

Hester caught hold of Pearl, and drew her forcibly into her arms, confronting the old Puritan magistrate with almost a fierce expression. Alone in the world, cast off by it, and with this sole treasure to keep her heart alive, she felt that she possessed indefeasible rights against the world, and was ready to defend them to the death.

"God gave me the child!" cried she. "He gave her, in requital of all things else, which ye had taken from me. She is my happiness!—she is my torture, none the less— Pearl keeps me here in life! Pearl punishes me too! See ye not, she is the scarlet letter, only capable of being loved, and so endowed with a million-fold the power of retribution for my sin? Ye shall not take her! I will die first!"

"My poor woman," said the not unkind old minister, "the child shall be well cared for!—far better than thou canst do it."

"God gave her into my keeping," repeated Hester Prynne, raising her voice almost to a shriek. "I will not give her up!"—And here, by a sudden impulse, she turned to the young clergyman, Mr. Dimmesdale, at whom, up to this moment, she had seemed hardly so much as once to direct her eyes.—"Speak thou for me!" cried she. "Thou wast my pastor, and hadst charge of my soul, and knowest me better than these men can. I will not lose the child! Speak for me! Thou knowest,—for thou hast sympathies which these men lack!—thou knowest what is in my heart, and what are a mother's rights, and how much the stronger they are, when that mother has but her child and the scarlet letter! Look thou to it! I will not lose the child! Look to it!"

At this wild and singular appeal, which indicated that Hester Prynne's situation had provoked her to little less than madness, the young minister at once came

---

1647) and adopted in 1648 by Presbyterians and Congregationalists, sets Calvinistic ideas in question-and-answer form for purposes of instruction.

forward, pale, and holding his hand over his heart, as was his custom whenever his peculiarly nervous temperament was thrown into agitation. He looked now more careworn and emaciated than as we described him at the scene of Hester's public ignominy; and whether it were his failing health, or whatever the cause might be, his large dark eyes had a world of pain in their troubled and melancholy depth.

"There is truth in what she says," began the minister, with a voice sweet, tremulous, but powerful, insomuch that the hall reëchoed, and the hollow armour rang with it,—"truth in what Hester says, and in the feeling which inspires her! God gave her the child, and gave her, too, an instinctive knowledge of its nature and requirements,—both seemingly so peculiar,—which no other mortal being can possess. And, moreover, is there not a quality of awful sacredness in the relation between this mother and this child?"

"Ay!—how is that, good Master Dimmesdale?" interrupted the Governor. "Make that plain, I pray you!"

"It must be even so," resumed the minister. "For if we deem it otherwise, do we not thereby say that the Heavenly Father, the Creator of all flesh, hath lightly recognized a deed of sin, and made of no account the distinction between unhallowed lust and holy love? This child of its father's guilt and its mother's shame hath come from the hand of God, to work in many ways upon her heart, who pleads so earnestly, and with such bitterness of spirit, the right to keep her. It was meant for a blessing; for the one blessing of her life! It was meant, doubtless, as the mother herself hath told us, for a retribution too; a torture, to be felt at many an unthought of moment; a pang, a sting, an ever-recurring agony, in the midst of a troubled joy! Hath she not expressed this thought in the garb of the poor child, so forcibly reminding us of that red symbol which sears her bosom?"

"Well said, again!" cried good Mr. Wilson. "I feared the woman had no better thought than to make a mountebank of her child!"

"O, not so!—not so!" continued Mr. Dimmesdale. "She recognizes, believe me, the solemn miracle which God hath wrought, in the existence of that child. And may she feel, too,—what, methinks, is the very truth,—that this boon was meant, above all things else, to keep the mother's soul alive, and to preserve her from blacker depths of sin into which Satan might else have sought to plunge her! Therefore it is good for this poor, sinful woman that she hath an infant immortality, a being capable of eternal joy or sorrow, confided to her care,—to be trained up by her to righteousness,—to remind her, at every moment, of her fall,—but yet to teach her, as it were by the Creator's sacred pledge, that, if she bring the child to heaven, the child also will bring its parent thither! Herein is the sinful mother happier than the sinful father. For Hester Prynne's sake, then, and no less for the poor child's sake, let us leave them as Providence hath seen fit to place them!"

"You speak, my friend, with a strange earnestness," said old Roger Chillingworth, smiling at him.

"And there is weighty import in what my young brother hath spoken," added the Reverend Mr. Wilson. "What say you, worshipful Master Bellingham? Hath he not pleaded well for the poor woman?"

"Indeed hath he," answered the magistrate, "and hath adduced such arguments, that we will even leave the matter as it now stands; so long, at least, as there shall be no further scandal in the woman. Care must be had, nevertheless, to put the child to due and stated examination in the catechism at thy hands or Master

Dimmesdale's. Moreover, at a proper season, the tithing-men[58] must take heed that she go both to school and to meeting."

The young minister, on ceasing to speak, had withdrawn a few steps from the group, and stood with his face partially concealed in the heavy folds of the window-curtain; while the shadow of his figure, which the sunlight cast upon the floor, was tremulous with the vehemence of his appeal. Pearl, that wild and flighty little elf, stole softly towards him, and, taking his hand in the grasp of both her own, laid her cheek against it; a caress so tender, and withal so unobtrusive, that her mother, who was looking on, asked herself,—"Is that my Pearl?" Yet she knew that there was love in the child's heart, although it mostly revealed itself in passion, and hardly twice in her lifetime had been softened by such gentleness as now. The minister,—for, save the long-sought regards of woman, nothing is sweeter than these marks of childish preference, accorded spontaneously by a spiritual instinct, and therefore seeming to imply in us something truly worthy to be loved,—the minister looked round, laid his hand on the child's head, hesitated an instant, and then kissed her brow. Little Pearl's unwonted mood of sentiment lasted no longer; she laughed, and went capering down the hall, so airily, that old Mr. Wilson raised a question whether even her tiptoes touched the floor.

"The little baggage hath witchcraft in her, I profess," said he to Mr. Dimmesdale. "She needs no old woman's broomstick to fly withal!"

"A strange child!" remarked old Roger Chillingworth. "It is easy to see the mother's part in her. Would it be beyond a philosopher's research, think ye, gentlemen, to analyze that child's nature, and, from its make and mould, to give a shrewd guess at the father?"

"Nay; it would be sinful, in such a question, to follow the clew of profane philosophy," said Mr. Wilson. "Better to fast and pray upon it; and still better, it may be, to leave the mystery as we find it, unless Providence reveal it of its own accord. Thereby, every good Christian man hath a title to show a father's kindness towards the poor, deserted babe."

The affair being so satisfactorily concluded, Hester Prynne, with Pearl, departed from the house. As they descended the steps, it is averred that the lattice of a chamber-window was thrown open, and forth into the sunny day was thrust the face of Mistress Hibbins, Governor Bellingham's bitter-tempered sister, and the same who, a few years later, was executed as a witch.

"Hist, hist!" said she, while her ill-omened physiognomy seemed to cast a shadow over the cheerful newness of the house. "Wilt thou go with us to-night! There will be a merry company in the forest; and I wellnigh promised the Black Man that comely Hester Prynne should make one."

"Make my excuse to him, so please you!" answered Hester, with a triumphant smile. "I must tarry at home, and keep watch over my little Pearl. Had they taken her from me, I would willingly have gone with thee into the forest, and signed my name in the Black Man's book too, and that with mine own blood!"

"We shall have thee there anon!" said the witch-lady, frowning, as she drew back her head.

But here—if we suppose this interview betwixt Mistress Hibbins and Hester Prynne to be authentic, and not a parable—was already an illustration of the young minister's argument against sundering the relation of a fallen mother to the

---

[58] Parish officials responsible for maintaining order (originally, collectors of tithes, one-tenth the parishioners' incomes, given to the church).

offspring of her frailty. Even thus early had the child saved her from Satan's snare.

IX: The Leech

Under the appellation of Roger Chillingworth, the reader will remember, was hidden another name, which its former wearer had resolved should never more be spoken. It has been related, how, in the crowd that witnessed Hester Prynne's ignominious exposure, stood a man, elderly, travel-worn, who, just emerging from the perilous wilderness, beheld the woman, in whom he hoped to find embodied the warmth and cheerfulness of home, set up as a type of sin before the people. Her matronly fame was trodden under all men's feet. Infamy was babbling around her in the public market-place. For her kindred, should the tidings ever reach them, and for the companions of her unspotted life, there remained nothing but the contagion of her dishonor; which would not fail to be distributed in strict accordance and proportion with the intimacy and sacredness of their previous relationship. Then why—since the choice was with himself—should the individual, whose connection with the fallen woman had been the most intimate and sacred of them all, come forward to vindicate his claim to an inheritance so little desirable? He resolved not to be pilloried beside her on her pedestal of shame. Unknown to all but Hester Pyrnne, and possessing the lock and key of her silence, he chose to withdraw his name from the roll of mankind, and, as regarded his former ties and interests, to vanish out of life as completely as if he indeed lay at the bottom of the ocean, whither rumor had long ago consigned him. This purpose once effected, new interests would immediately spring up, and likewise a new purpose; dark, it is true, if not guilty, but of force enough to engage the full strength of his faculties.

In pursuance of this resolve, he took up his residence in the Puritan town, as Roger Chillingworth, without other introduction than the learning and intelligence of which he possessed more than a common measure. As his studies, at a previous period of his life, had made him extensively acquainted with the medical science of the day, it was as a physician that he presented himself, and as such was cordially received. Skilful men, of the medical and chirurgical[59] profession, were of rare occurrence in the colony. They seldom, it would appear, partook of the religious zeal that brought other emigrants across the Atlantic. In their researches into the human frame, it may be that the higher and more subtile faculties of such men were materialized, and that they lost the spiritual view of existence amid the intricacies of that wondrous mechanism, which seemed to involve art enough to comprise all of life within itself. At all events, the health of the good town of Boston, so far as medicine had aught to do with it, had hitherto lain in the guardianship of an aged deacon and apothecary, whose piety and godly deportment were stronger testimonials in his favor, than any that he could have produced in the shape of a diploma. The only surgeon was one who combined the occasional exercise of that noble art with the daily and habitual flourish of a razor. To such a professional body Roger Chillingworth was a brilliant acquisition. He soon manifested his familiarity with the ponderous and imposing machinery of antique physic; in which

---

[59] Surgical.

every remedy contained a multitude of far-fetched and heterogeneous ingredients, as elaborately compounded as if the proposed result had been the Elixir of Life.[60] In his Indian captivity, moreover, he had gained much knowledge of the properties of native herbs and roots; nor did he conceal from his patients, that these simple medicines, Nature's boon to the untutored savage, had quite as large a share of his own confidence as the European pharmacopœia,[61] which so many learned doctors had spent centuries in elaborating.

This learned stranger was exemplary, as regarded at least the outward forms of a religious life, and, early after his arrival, had chosen for his spiritual guide the Reverend Mr. Dimmesdale. The young divine, whose scholar-like renown still lived in Oxford, was considered by his more fervent admirers as little less than a heaven-ordained apostle, destined, should he live and labor for the ordinary term of life, to do as great deeds for the now feeble New England Church, as the early Fathers had achieved for the infancy of the Christian faith. About this period, however, the health of Mr. Dimmesdale had evidently begun to fail. By those best acquainted with his habits, the paleness of the young minister's cheek was accounted for by his too earnest devotion to study, his scrupulous fulfilment of parochial duty, and, more than all, by the fasts and vigils of which he made a frequent practice, in order to keep the grossness of this earthly state from clogging and obscuring his spiritual lamp. Some declared, that, if Mr. Dimmesdale were really going to die, it was cause enough, that the world was not worthy to be any longer trodden by his feet. He himself, on the other hand, with characteristic humility, avowed his belief, that, if Providence should see fit to remove him, it would be because of his own unworthiness to perform its humblest mission here on earth. With all this difference of opinion as to the cause of his decline, there could be no question of the fact. His form grew emaciated; his voice, though still rich and sweet, had a certain melancholy prophecy of decay in it; he was often observed, on any slight alarm or other sudden accident, to put his hand over his heart, with first a flush and then a paleness, indicative of pain.

Such was the young clergyman's condition, and so imminent the prospect that his dawning light would be extinguished, all untimely, when Roger Chillingworth made his advent to the town. His first entry on the scene, few people could tell whence, dropping down, as it were, out of the sky, or starting from the nether earth, had an aspect of mystery, which was easily heightened to the miraculous. He was now known to be a man of skill; it was observed that he gathered herbs, and the blossoms of wild-flowers, and dug up roots and plucked off twigs from the forest-trees, like one acquainted with hidden virtues in what was valueless to common eyes. He was heard to speak of Sir Kenelm Digby,[62] and other famous men,—whose scientific attainments were esteemed hardly less than supernatural,—as having been his correspondents or associates. Why, with such rank in the learned world, had he come hither? What could he, whose sphere was in great cities, be seeking in the wilderness? In answer to this query, a rumor gained ground,—and, however absurd, was entertained by some very sensible people,— that Heaven had wrought an absolute miracle, by transporting an eminent Doctor of Physic, from a German university, bodily through the air, and setting him

---

[60] A secret mixture of drugs thought to prolong life indefinitely.

[61] A list of approved medicines.

[62] Digby (1603–1665) was an English scientist, naval commander, diplomat, and writer.

down at the door of Mr. Dimmesdale's study! Individuals of wiser faith, indeed, who knew that Heaven promotes its purposes without aiming at the stage-effect of what is called miraculous interposition, were inclined to see a providential hand in Roger Chillingworth's so opportune arrival.

This idea was countenanced by the strong interest which the physician ever manifested in the young clergyman; he attached himself to him as a parishioner, and sought to win a friendly regard and confidence from his naturally reserved sensibility. He expressed great alarm at his pastor's state of health, but was anxious to attempt the cure, and, if early undertaken, seemed not despondent of a favorable result. The elders, the deacons, the motherly dames, and the young and fair maidens, of Mr. Dimmesdale's flock, were alike importunate that he should make trial of the physician's frankly offered skill. Mr. Dimmesdale gently repelled their entreaties.

"I need no medicine," said he.

But how could the young minister say so, when, with every successive Sabbath, his cheek was paler and thinner, and his voice more tremulous than before,—when it had now become a constant habit, rather than a casual gesture, to press his hand over his heart? Was he weary of his labors? Did he wish to die? These questions were solemnly propounded to Mr. Dimmesdale by the elder ministers of Boston and the deacons of his church, who, to use their own phrase, "dealt with him" on the sin of rejecting the aid which Providence so manifestly held out. He listened in silence, and finally promised to confer with the physician.

"Were it God's will," said the Reverend Mr. Dimmesdale, when, in fulfilment of this pledge, he requested old Roger Chillingworth's professional advice, "I could be well content, that my labors, and my sorrows, and my sins, and my pains, should shortly end with me, and what is earthly of them be buried in my grave, and the spiritual go with me to my eternal state, rather than that you should put your skill to the proof in my behalf."

"Ah," replied Roger Chillingworth, with that quietness which, whether imposed or natural, marked all his deportment, "it is thus that a young clergyman is apt to speak. Youthful men, not having taken a deep root, give up their hold of life so easily! And saintly men, who walk with God on earth, would fain be away, to walk with him on the golden pavements of the New Jerusalem."[63]

"Nay," rejoined the young minister, putting his hand to his heart, with a flush of pain flitting over his brow, "were I worthier to walk there, I could be better content to toil here."

"Good men ever interpret themselves too meanly," said the physician.

In this manner, the mysterious old Roger Chillingworth became the medical adviser of the Reverend Mr. Dimmesdale. As not only the disease interested the physician, but he was strongly moved to look into the character and qualities of the patient, these two men, so different in age, came gradually to spend much time together. For the sake of the minister's health, and to enable the leech to gather plants with healing balm in them, they took long walks on the sea-shore, or in the forest; mingling various talk with the plash and murmur of the waves, and the solemn wind-anthem among the tree-tops. Often, likewise, one was the guest of the other, in his place of study and retirement. There was a fascination for the minister in the company of the man of science, in whom he recognized an intellectual cultivation of no moderate depth or scope; together with a range and freedom

---

[63] Heaven; the heavenly city in Revelation 21:2.

of ideas, that he would have vainly looked for among the members of his own profession. In truth, he was startled, if not shocked, to find this attribute in the physician. Mr. Dimmesdale was a true priest, a true religionist, with the reverential sentiment largely developed, and an order of mind that impelled itself powerfully along the track of a creed, and wore its passage continually deeper with the lapse of time. In no state of society would he have been what is called a man of liberal views; it would always be essential to his peace to feel the pressure of a faith about him, supporting, while it confined him within its iron framework. Not the less, however, though with a tremulous enjoyment, did he feel the occasional relief of looking at the universe through the medium of another kind of intellect than those with which he habitually held converse. It was as if a window were thrown open, admitting a freer atmosphere into the close and stifled study, where his life was wasting itself away, amid lamp-light, or obstructed day-beams, and the musty fragrance, be it sensual or moral, that exhales from books. But the air was too fresh and chill to be long breathed, with comfort. So the minister, and the physician with him, withdrew again within the limits of what their church defined as orthodox.

Thus Roger Chillingworth scrutinized his patient carefully, both as he saw him in his ordinary life, keeping an accustomed pathway in the range of thoughts familiar to him, and as he appeared when thrown amidst other moral scenery, the novelty of which might call out something new to the surface of his character. He deemed it essential, it would seem, to know the man, before attempting to do him good. Wherever there is a heart and an intellect, the diseases of the physical frame are tinged with the peculiarities of these. In Arthur Dimmesdale, thought and imagination were so active, and sensibility so intense, that the bodily infirmity would be likely to have its groundwork there. So Roger Chillingworth—the man of skill, the kind and friendly physician—strove to go deep into his patient's bosom, delving among his principles, prying into his recollections, and probing every thing with a cautious touch, like a treasure-seeker in a dark cavern. Few secrets can escape an investigator, who has opportunity and license to undertake such a quest, and skill to follow it up. A man burdened with a secret should especially avoid the intimacy of his physician. If the latter possess native sagacity, and a nameless something more,—let us call it intuition; if he show no intrusive egotism, nor disagreeably prominent characteristics of his own; if he have the power, which must be born with him, to bring his mind into such affinity with his patient's, that this last shall unawares have spoken what he imagines himself only to have thought; if such revelations be received without tumult, and acknowledged not so often by an uttered sympathy, as by silence, an inarticulate breath, and here and there a word, to indicate that all is understood; if, to these qualifications of a confidant be joined the advantages afforded by his recognized character as a physician;—then, at some inevitable moment, will the soul of the sufferer be dissolved, and flow forth in a dark, but transparent stream, bringing all its mysteries into the daylight.

Roger Chillingworth possessed all, or most, of the attributes above enumerated. Nevertheless, time went on; a kind of intimacy, as we have said, grew up between these two cultivated minds, which had as wide a field as the whole sphere of human thought and study, to meet upon; they discussed every topic of ethics and religion, of public affairs, and private character; they talked much, on both sides, of matters that seemed personal to themselves; and yet no secret, such as the physician fancied must exist there, ever stole out of the minister's consciousness into his companion's ear. The latter had his suspicions, indeed, that even the nature of Mr. Dimmesdale's bodily disease had never fairly been revealed to him. It was a strange reserve!

After a time, at a hint from Roger Chillingworth, the friends of Mr. Dimmesdale effected an arrangement by which the two were lodged in the same house; so that every ebb and flow of the minister's life-tide might pass under the eye of his anxious and attached physician. There was much joy throughout the town, when this greatly desirable object was attained. It was held to be the best possible measure for the young clergyman's welfare; unless, indeed, as often urged by such as felt authorized to do so, he had selected some one of the many blooming damsels, spiritually devoted to him, to become his devoted wife. This latter step, however, there was no present prospect that Arthur Dimmesdale would be prevailed upon to take; he rejected all suggestions of the kind, as if priestly celibacy were one of his articles of church-discipline. Doomed by his own choice, therefore, as Mr. Dimmesdale so evidently was, to eat his unsavory morsel always at another's board, and endure the life-long chill which must be his lot who seeks to warm himself only at another's fireside, it truly seemed that this sagacious, experienced, benevolent, old physician, with his concord of paternal and reverential love for the young pastor, was the very man, of all mankind, to be constantly within reach of his voice.

The new abode of the two friends was with a pious widow, of good social rank, who dwelt in a house covering pretty nearly the site on which the venerable structure of King's Chapel has since been built. It had the grave-yard, originally Isaac Johnson's home-field, on one side, and so was well adapted to call up serious reflections, suited to their respective employments, in both minister and man of physic. The motherly care of the good widow assigned to Mr. Dimmesdale a front apartment, with a sunny exposure, and heavy window-curtains to create a noontide shadow, when desirable. The walls were hung round with tapestry, said to be from the Gobelin looms, and, at all events, representing the Scriptural story of David and Bathsheba, and Nathan the Prophet,[64] in colors still unfaded, but which made the fair woman of the scene almost as grimly picturesque as the woe-denouncing seer. Here, the pale clergyman piled up his library, rich with parchment-bound folios of the Fathers,[65] and the lore of Rabbis, and monkish erudition, of which the Protestant divines, even while they vilified and decried that class of writers, were yet constrained often to avail themselves. On the other side of the house, old Roger Chillingworth arranged his study and laboratory; not such as a modern man of science would reckon even tolerably complete, but provided with a distilling apparatus, and the means of compounding drugs and chemicals, which the practised alchemist knew well how to turn to purpose. With such commodiousness of situation, these two learned persons sat themselves down, each in his own domain, yet familiarly passing from one apartment to the other, and bestowing a mutual and not incurious inspection into one another's business.

And the Reverend Arthur Dimmesdale's best discerning friends, as we have intimated, very reasonably imagined that the hand of Providence had done all this, for the purpose—besought in so many public, and domestic, and secret prayers—of restoring the young minister to health. But—it must now be said—another

---

[64] The Gobelin family of Paris produced valuable tapestries in the fifteenth century; in II Samuel 11–12 David, Israel's second king, was denounced by the prophet Nathan for sending Bathsheba's first husband to certain death in battle so that David could marry her.

[65] The traditions and doctrines of the early Christian church.

portion of the community had latterly begun to take its own view of the relation betwixt Mr. Dimmesdale and the mysterious old physician. When an uninstructed multitude attempts to see with its eyes, it is exceedingly apt to be deceived. When, however, it forms its judgment, as it usually does, on the intuitions of its great and warm heart, the conclusions thus attained are often so profound and so unerring, as to possess the character of truths supernaturally revealed. The people, in the case of which we speak, could justify its prejudice against Roger Chillingworth by no fact or argument worthy of serious refutation. There was an aged handicrafts-man, it is true, who had been a citizen of London at the period of Sir Thomas Overbury's murder,[66] now some thirty years agone; he testified to having seen the physician, under some other name, which the narrator of the story had now for-gotten, in company with Doctor Forman, the famous old conjurer, who was impli-cated in the affair of Overbury. Two or three individuals hinted, that the man of skill, during his Indian captivity, had enlarged his medical attainments by joining in the incantations of the savage priests; who were universally acknowledged to be powerful enchanters, often performing seemingly miraculous cures by their skill in the black art. A large number—and many of these were persons of such sober sense and practical observation, that their opinions would have been valuable, in other matters—affirmed that Roger Chillingworth's aspect had undergone a re-markable change while he had dwelt in town, and especially since his abode with Mr. Dimmesdale. At first, his expression had been calm, meditative, scholar-like. Now, there was something ugly and evil in his face, which they had not previ-ously noticed, and which grew still the more obvious to sight, the oftener they looked upon him. According to the vulgar idea, the fire in his laboratory had been brought from the lower regions, and was fed with infernal fuel; and so, as might be expected, his visage was getting sooty with the smoke.

To sum up the matter, it grew to be a widely diffused opinion, that the Rever-end Arthur Dimmesdale, like many other personages of especial sanctity, in all ages of the Christian world, was haunted either by Satan himself, or Satan's emis-sary, in the guise of old Roger Chillingworth. This diabolical agent had the Divine permission, for a season, to burrow into the clergyman's intimacy, and plot against his soul. No sensible man, it was confessed, could doubt on which side the victory would turn. The people looked, with an unshaken hope, to see the minister come forth out of the conflict, transfigured with the glory which he would unques-tionably win. Meanwhile, nevertheless, it was sad to think of the perchance mortal agony through which he must struggle towards his triumph.

Alas, to judge from the gloom and terror in the depths of the poor minister's eyes, the battle was a sore one, and the victory any thing but secure!

X: The Leech and His Patient

Old Roger Chillingworth, throughout life, had been calm in temperament, kindly, though not of warm affections, but ever, and in all his relations with the world, a pure and upright man. He had begun an investigation, as he imagined, with the severe and equal integrity of a judge, desirous only of truth, even as if the ques-

---

[66] Overbury (1581–1613), aware of the profligacy of the countess of Essex, tried to stop his em-ployer, the earl of Rochester, from marrying her. The countess had Overbury imprisoned in the Tower of London and had Ann Turner (a friend of Ann Hibbins) poison him. The countess conspired with the notorious Dr. Simon Forman (1552–1611), among other things an astrologer and concocter of love potions.

tion involved no more than the air-drawn lines and figures of a geometrical problem, instead of human passions, and wrongs inflicted on himself. But, as he proceeded, a terrible fascination, a kind of fierce, though still calm, necessity seized the old man within its gripe, and never set him free again, until he had done all its bidding. He now dug into the poor clergyman's heart, like a miner searching for gold; or, rather, like a sexton[67] delving into a grave, possibly in quest of a jewel that had been buried on the dead man's bosom, but likely to find nothing save mortality and corruption. Alas for his own soul, if these were what he sought!

Sometimes, a light glimmered out of the physician's eyes, burning blue and ominous, like the reflection of a furnace, or, let us say, like one of those gleams of ghastly fire that darted from Bunyan's awful door-way in the hill-side,[68] and quivered on the pilgrim's face. The soil where this dark miner was working had perchance shown indications that encouraged him.

"This man," said he, at one such moment, to himself, "pure as they deem him,—all spiritual as he seems,—hath inherited a strong animal nature from his father or his mother. Let us dig a little farther in the direction of this vein!"

Then, after long search into the minister's dim interior, and turning over many precious materials, in the shape of high aspirations for the welfare of his race, warm love of souls, pure sentiments, natural piety, strengthened by thought and study, and illuminated by revelation,—all of which invaluable gold was perhaps no better than rubbish to the seeker,—he would turn back, discouraged, and begin his quest towards another point. He groped along as stealthily, with as cautious a tread, and as wary an outlook, as a thief entering a chamber where a man lies only half asleep,—or, it may be, broad awake,—with purpose to steal the very treasure which this man guards as the apple of his eye. In spite of his premeditated carefulness, the floor would now and then creak; his garments would rustle; the shadow of his presence, in a forbidden proximity, would be thrown across his victim. In other words, Mr. Dimmesdale, whose sensibility of nerve often produced the effect of spiritual intuition, would become vaguely aware that something inimical to his peace had thrust itself into relation with him. But old Roger Chillingworth, too, had perceptions that were almost intuitive; and when the minister threw his startled eyes towards him, there the physician sat; his kind, watchful, sympathizing, but never intrusive friend.

Yet Mr. Dimmesdale would perhaps have seen this individual's character more perfectly, if a certain morbidness, to which sick hearts are liable, had not rendered him suspicious of all mankind. Trusting no man as his friend, he could not recognize his enemy when the latter actually appeared. He therefore still kept up a familiar intercourse with him, daily receiving the old physician in his study; or visiting the laboratory, and, for recreation's sake, watching the processes by which weeds were converted into drugs of potency.

One day, leaning his forehead on his hand, and his elbow on the sill of the open window, that looked towards the grave-yard, he talked with Roger Chillingworth, while the old man was examining a bundle of unsightly plants.

"Where," asked he, with a look askance at them,—for it was the clergyman's peculiarity that he seldom, now-a-days, looked straightforth at any object,

---

[67] A church custodian, gravedigger, and burial supervisor.

[68] In John Bunyan's *Pilgrim's Progress* (1678) there is a doorway to Hell on the hill that leads to Heaven, the Celestial City; Hawthorne's "The Celestial Railroad" (1843) is an updated version of Bunyan's allegory.

whether human or inanimate,—"where, my kind doctor, did you gather those herbs, with such a dark, flabby leaf?"

"Even in the grave-yard, here at hand," answered the physician, continuing his employment. "They are new to me. I found them growing on a grave, which bore no tombstone, nor other memorial of the dead man, save these ugly weeds that have taken upon themselves to keep him in remembrance. They grew out of his heart, and typify, it may be, some hideous secret that was buried with him, and which he had done better to confess during his lifetime."

"Perchance," said Mr. Dimmesdale, "he earnestly desired it, but could not."

"And wherefore?" rejoined the physician. "Wherefore not; since all the powers of nature call so earnestly for the confession of sin, that these black weeds have sprung up out of a buried heart, to make manifest an unspoken crime?"

"That, good Sir, is but a fantasy of yours," replied the minister. "There can be, if I forebode aright, no power, short of the Divine mercy, to disclose, whether by uttered words, or by type or emblem, the secrets that may be buried with a human heart. The heart, making itself guilty of such secrets, must perforce hold them, until the day when all hidden things shall be revealed. Nor have I so read or interpreted Holy Writ, as to understand that the disclosure of human thoughts and deeds, then to be made, is intended as a part of the retribution. That, surely, were a shallow view of it. No; these revelations, unless I greatly err, are meant merely to promote the intellectual satisfaction of all intelligent beings, who will stand waiting, on that day, to see the dark problem of this life made plain. A knowledge of men's hearts will be needful to the completest solution of that problem. And I conceive, moreover, that the hearts holding such miserable secrets as you speak of will yield them up, at the last day,[69] not with reluctance, but with a joy unutterable."

"Then why not reveal them here?" asked Roger Chillingworth, glancing quietly aside at the minister. "Why should not the guilty ones sooner avail themselves of this unutterable solace?"

"They mostly do," said the clergyman, griping hard at his breast, as if afflicted with an importunate throb of pain. "Many, many a poor soul hath given its confidence to me, not only on the death-bed, but while strong in life, and fair in reputation. And ever, after such an outpouring, O, what a relief have I witnessed in those sinful brethren! even as in one who at last draws free air, after long stifling with his own polluted breath. How can it be otherwise? Why should a wretched man, guilty, we will say, of murder, prefer to keep the dead corpse buried in his own heart, rather than fling it forth at once, and let the universe take care of it!"

"Yet some men bury their secrets thus," observed the calm physician.

"True, there are such men," answered Mr. Dimmesdale. "But, not to suggest more obvious reasons, it may be that they are kept silent by the very constitution of their nature. Or,—can we not suppose it?—guilty as they may be, retaining, nevertheless, a zeal for God's glory and man's welfare, they shrink from displaying themselves black and filthy in the view of men; because, thenceforward, no good can be achieved by them; no evil of the past be redeemed by better service. So, to their own unutterable torment, they go about among their fellow-creatures, looking pure as new-fallen snow; while their hearts are all speckled and spotted with iniquity of which they cannot rid themselves."

"These men deceive themselves," said Roger Chillingworth, with somewhat

---

[69] On Judgment Day.

more emphasis than usual, and making a slight gesture with his forefinger. "They fear to take up the shame that rightfully belongs to them. Their love for man, their zeal for God's service,—these holy impulses may or may not coexist in their hearts with the evil inmates to which their guilt has unbarred the door, and which must needs propagate a hellish breed within them, But, if they seek to glorify God, let them not lift heavenward their unclean hands! If they would serve their fellow-men, let them to do it by making manifest the power and reality of conscience, in constraining them to penitential self-abasement! Wouldst thou have me to believe, O wise and pious friend, that a false show can be better—can be more for God's glory, or man's welfare—than God's own truth? Trust me, such men deceive themselves!"

"It may be so," said the young clergyman indifferently, as waiving a discussion that he considered irrelevant or unseasonable. He had a ready faculty, indeed, of escaping from any topic that agitated his too sensitive and nervous temperament. —"But, now, I would ask of my well-skilled physician, whether, in good sooth, he deems me to have profited by his kindly care of this weak frame of mine?"

Before Roger Chillingworth could answer, they heard the clear, wild laughter of a young child's voice, proceeding from the adjacent burial-ground. Looking instinctively from the open window,—for it was summer-time,—the minister beheld Hester Prynne and little Pearl passing along the footpath that traversed the inclosure. Pearl looked as beautiful as the day, but was in one of those moods of perverse merriment which, whenever they occurred, seemed to remove her entirely out of the sphere of sympathy or human contact. She now skipped irreverently from one grave to another; until, coming to the broad, flat, armorial tombstone of a departed worthy,—perhaps of Isaac Johnson himself,—she began to dance upon it. In reply to her mother's command and entreaty that she would behave more decorously, little Pearl paused to gather the prickly burrs from a tall burdock, which grew beside the tomb. Taking a handful of these, she arranged them along the lines of the scarlet letter that decorated the maternal bosom, to which the burrs, as their nature was, tenaciously adhered. Hester did not pluck them off.

Roger Chillingworth had by this time approached the window, and smiled grimly down.

"There is no law, nor reverence for authority, no regard for human ordinances or opinions, right or wrong, mixed up with that child's composition," remarked he, as much to himself as to his companion. "I saw her, the other day, bespatter the Governor himself with water, at the cattle-trough in Spring Lane. What, in Heaven's name, is she? Is the imp altogether evil? Hath she affections? Hath she any discoverable principle of being?"

"None,—save the freedom of a broken law," answered Mr. Dimmesdale, in a quiet way, as if he had been discussing the point within himself. "Whether capable of good, I know not."

The child probably overheard their voices; for, looking up to the window, with a bright, but naughty smile of mirth and intelligence, she threw one of the prickly burrs at the Reverend Mr. Dimmesdale. The sensitive clergyman shrunk, with nervous dread, from the light missile. Detecting his emotion, Pearl clapped her little hands in the most extravagant ecstasy. Hester Prynne, likewise, had involuntarily looked up; and all these four persons, old and young, regarded one another in silence, till the child laughed aloud, and shouted,—"Come away, mother!

Come away, or yonder old Black Man will catch you! He hath got hold of the minister already. Come away, mother, or he will catch you! But he cannot catch little Pearl!"

So she drew her mother away, skipping, dancing, and frisking fantastically among the hillocks of the dead people, like a creature that had nothing in common with a bygone and buried generation, nor owned herself akin to it. It was as if she had been made afresh, out of new elements, and must perforce be permitted to live her own life, and be a law unto herself, without her eccentricities being reckoned to her for a crime.

"There goes a woman," resumed Roger Chillingworth, after a pause, "who, be her demerits what they may, hath none of that mystery of hidden sinfulness which you deem so grievous to be borne. Is Hester Prynne the less miserable, think you, for that scarlet letter on her breast?"

"I do verily believe it," answered the clergyman. "Nevertheless, I cannot answer for her. There was a look of pain in her face, which I would gladly have been spared the sight of. But still, methinks, it must needs be better for the sufferer to be free to show his pain, as this poor woman Hester is, than to cover it all up in his heart."

There was another pause; and the physician began anew to examine and arrange the plants which he had gathered.

"You inquired of me, a little time agone," said he, at length, "my judgment as touching your health."

"I did," answered the clergyman, "and would gladly learn it. Speak frankly, I pray you, be it for life or death."

"Freely, then, and plainly," said the physician, still busy with his plants, but keeping a wary eye on Mr. Dimmesdale, "the disorder is a strange one; not so much in itself, nor as outwardly manifested,—in so far, at least, as the symptoms have been laid open to my observation. Looking daily at you, my good Sir, and watching the tokens of your aspect, now for months gone by, I should deem you a man sore sick, it may be, yet not so sick but that an instructed and watchful physician might well hope to cure you. But—I know not what to say—the disease is what I seem to know, yet know it not."

"You speak in riddles, learned Sir," said the pale minister, glancing aside out of the window.

"Then, to speak more plainly," continued the physician, "and I crave pardon, Sir,—should it seem to require pardon,—for this needful plainness of my speech. Let me ask,—as your friend,—as one having charge, under Providence, of your life and physical well-being,—hath all the operation of this disorder been fairly laid open and recounted to me?"

"How can you question it?" asked the minister. "Surely, it were child's play to call in a physician, and then hide the sore!"

"You would tell me, then, that I know all?" said Roger Chillingworth, deliberately, and fixing an eye, bright with intense and concentrated intelligence, on the minister's face. "Be it so! But, again! He to whom only the outward and physical evil is laid open knoweth, oftentimes, but half the evil which he is called upon to cure. A bodily disease, which we look upon as whole and entire within itself, may, after all, be but a symptom of some ailment in the spiritual part. Your pardon, once again, good Sir, if my speech give the shadow of offence. You, Sir, of all men whom I have known, are he whose body is the closest conjoined, and imbued, and identified, so to speak, with the spirit whereof it is the instrument."

"Then I need ask no further," said the clergyman, somewhat hastily rising from his chair. "You deal not, I take it, in medicine for the soul!"

"Thus, a sickness," continued Roger Chillingworth, going on, in an unaltered tone, without heeding the interruption,—but standing up, and confronting the emaciated and white-cheeked minister with his low, dark, and misshapen figure,—"a sickness, a sore place, if we may so call it, in your spirit, hath immediately its appropriate manifestation in your bodily frame. Would you, therefore, that your physician heal the bodily evil? How may this be, unless you first lay open to him the wound or trouble in your soul?"

"No!—not to thee!—not to an earthly physician!" cried Mr. Dimmesdale, passionately, and turning his eyes, full and bright, and with a kind of fierceness, on old Roger Chillingworth. "Not to thee! But, if it be the soul's disease, then do I commit myself to the one Physician of the soul! He, if it stand with his good pleasure can cure; or he can kill! Let him do with me as, in his justice and wisdom, he shall see good. But who art thou, that meddlest in this matter?—that dares thrust himself between the sufferer and his God?"

With a frantic gesture, he rushed out of the room.

"It is as well to have made this step," said Roger Chillingworth to himself, looking after the minister with a grave smile. "There is nothing lost. We shall be friends again anon. But see, now, how passion takes hold upon this man, and hurrieth him out of himself! As with one passion, so with another! He hath done a wild thing ere now, this pious Master Dimmesdale, in the hot passion of his heart!"

It proved not difficult to reëstablish the intimacy of the two companions, on the same footing and in the same degree as heretofore. The young clergyman, after a few hours of privacy, was sensible that the disorder of his nerves had hurried him into an unseemly outbreak of temper, which there had been nothing in the physician's words to excuse or palliate. He marvelled, indeed, at the violence with which he had thrust back the kind old man, when merely proffering the advice which it was his duty to bestow, and which the minister himself had expressly sought. With these remorseful feelings, he lost no time in making the amplest apologies, and besought his friend still to continue the care, which, if not successful in restoring him to health, had, in all probability, been the means of prolonging his feeble existence to that hour. Roger Chillingworth readily assented, and went on with his medical supervision of the minister; doing his best for him, in all good faith, but always quitting the patient's apartment, at the close of a professional interview, with a mysterious and puzzled smile upon his lips. This expression was invisible in Mr. Dimmesdale's presence, but grew strongly evident as the physician crossed the threshold.

"A rare case!" he muttered. "I must needs look deeper into it. A strange sympathy betwixt soul and body! Were it only for the art's sake, I must search this matter to the bottom!"

It came to pass, not long after the scene above recorded, that the Reverend Mr. Dimmesdale, at noonday, and entirely unawares, fell into a deep, deep slumber, sitting in his chair, with a large black-letter volume[70] open before him on the table. It must have been a work of vast ability in the somniferous school of literature. The profound depth of the minister's repose was the more remarkable; inas-

---

[70] A heavy-faced Gothic type modeled on medieval script.

much as he was one of those persons whose sleep, ordinarily, is as light, as fitful, and as easily scared away, as a small bird hopping on a twig. To such an unwonted remoteness, however, had his spirit now withdrawn into itself, that he stirred not in his chair, when old Roger Chillingworth, without any extraordinary precaution, came into the room. The physician advanced directly in front of his patient, laid his hand upon his bosom, and thrust aside the vestment, that, hitherto, had always covered it even from the professional eye.

Then, indeed, Mr. Dimmesdale shuddered, and slightly stirred.

After a brief pause, the physician turned away.

But with what a wild look of wonder, joy, and horror! With what a ghastly rapture, as it were, too mighty to be expressed only by the eye and features, and therefore bursting forth through the whole ugliness of his figure, and making itself even riotously manifest by the extravagant gestures with which he threw up his arms towards the ceiling, and stamped his foot upon the floor! Had a man seen old Roger Chillingworth, at that moment of his ecstasy, he would have had no need to ask how Satan comports himself, when a precious human soul is lost to heaven, and won into his kingdom.

But what distinguished the physician's ecstasy from Satan's was the trait of wonder in it!

XI: *The Interior of a Heart*

After the incident last described, the intercourse between the clergyman and the physician, though externally the same, was really of another character than it had previously been. The intellect of Roger Chillingworth had now a sufficiently plain path before it. It was not, indeed, precisely that which he had laid out for himself to tread. Calm, gentle, passionless, as he appeared, there was yet, we fear, a quiet depth of malice, hitherto latent, but active now, in this unfortunate old man, which led him to imagine a more intimate revenge than any mortal had ever wreaked upon an enemy. To make himself the one trusted friend, to whom should be confided all the fear, the remorse, the agony, the ineffectual repentance, the backward rush of sinful thoughts, expelled in vain! All that guilty sorrow, hidden from the world, whose great heart would have pitied and forgiven, to be revealed to him, the Pitiless, to him, the Unforgiving! All that dark treasure to be lavished on the very man, to whom nothing else could so adequately pay the debt of vengeance!

The clergyman's shy and sensitive reserve had balked this scheme. Roger Chillingworth, however, was inclined to be hardly, if at all, less satisfied with the aspect of affairs, which Providence—using the avenger and his victim for its own purposes, and, perchance, pardoning, where it seemed most to punish—had substituted for his black devices. A revelation, he could almost say, had been granted to him. It mattered little, for his object, whether celestial, or from what other region. By its aid, in all the subsequent relations betwixt him and Mr. Dimmesdale, not merely the external presence, but the very inmost soul of the latter seemed to be brought out before his eyes, so that he could see and comprehend its every movement. He became, thenceforth, not a spectator only, but a chief actor, in the poor minister's interior world. He could play upon him as he chose. Would he arouse him with a throb of agony? The victim was for ever on the rack; it needed only to know the spring that controlled the engine;—and the physician knew it well! Would he startle him with sudden fear? As at the waving of a magician's wand, uprose a grisly phantom,—uprose a thousand phantoms,—in many shapes, of death, or more awful shame, all flocking round-about the clergyman, and pointing with their fingers at his breast!

All this was accomplished with a subtlety so perfect, that the minister, though he had constantly a dim perception of some evil influence watching over him, could never gain a knowledge of its actual nature. True, he looked doubtfully, fearfully,—even, at times, with horror and the bitterness of hatred,—at the deformed figure of the old physician. His gestures, his gait, his grizzled beard, his slightest and most indifferent acts, the very fashion of his garments, were odious in the clergyman's sight; a token, implicitly to be relied on, of a deeper antipathy in the breast of the latter than he was willing to acknowledge to himself. For, as it was impossible to assign a reason for such distrust and abhorrence, so Mr. Dimmesdale, conscious that the poison of one morbid spot was infecting his heart's entire substance, attributed all his presentiments to no other cause. He took himself to task for his bad sympathies in reference to Roger Chillingworth, disregarded the lesson that he should have drawn from them, and did his best to root them out. Unable to accomplish this, he nevertheless, as a matter of principle, continued his habits of social familiarity with the old man, and thus gave him constant opportunities for perfecting the purpose to which—poor, forlorn creature that he was, and more wretched than his victim—the avenger had devoted himself.

While thus suffering under bodily disease, and gnawed and tortured by some black trouble of the soul, and given over to the machinations of his deadliest enemy, the Reverend Mr. Dimmesdale had achieved a brilliant popularity in his sacred office. He won it, indeed, in great part, by his sorrows. His intellectual gifts, his moral perceptions, his power of experiencing and communicating emotion, were kept in a state of preternatural activity by the prick and anguish of his daily life. His fame, though still on its upward slope, already overshadowed the soberer reputations of his fellow-clergymen, eminent as several of them were. There were scholars among them, who had spent more years in acquiring abstruse lore, connected with the divine profession, than Mr. Dimmesdale had lived; and who might well, therefore, be more profoundly versed in such solid and valuable attainments than their youthful brother. There were men, too, of a sturdier texture of mind than his, and endowed with a far greater share of shrewd, hard, iron or granite understanding; which, duly mingled with a fair proportion of doctrinal ingredient, constitutes a highly respectable, efficacious, and unamiable variety of the clerical species. There were others, again, true saintly fathers, whose faculties had been elaborated by weary toil among their books, and by patient thought, and etherealized, moreover, by spiritual communications with the better world, into which their purity of life had almost introduced these holy personages, with their garments of mortality still clinging to them. All that they lacked was the gift that descended upon the chosen disciples, at Pentecost, in tongues of flame; symbolizing, it would seem, not the power of speech in foreign and unknown languages, but that of addressing the whole human brotherhood in the heart's native language. These fathers, otherwise so apostolic, lacked Heaven's last and rarest attestation of their office, the Tongue of Flame.[71] They would have vainly sought—

---

[71] In Acts 2:1–8 the Holy Spirit came to Jesus' apostles in the form of "cloven tongues like as of fire" on the day of Pentecost, enabling them to speak to all nations.

had they ever dreamed of seeking—to express the highest truths through the humblest medium of familiar words and images. Their voices came down, afar and indistinctly, from the upper heights where they habitually dwelt.

Not improbably, it was to this latter class of men that Mr. Dimmesdale, by many of his traits of character, naturally belonged. To their high mountain-peaks of faith and sanctity he would have climbed, had not the tendency been thwarted by the burden, whatever it might be, of crime or anguish, beneath which it was his doom to totter. It kept him down, on a level with the lowest; him, the man of ethereal attributes, whose voice the angels might else have listened to and answered! But this very burden it was, that gave him sympathies so intimate with the sinful brotherhood of mankind; so that his heart vibrated in unison with theirs, and received their pain into itself, and sent its own throb of pain through a thousand other hearts, in gushes of sad, persuasive eloquence. Oftenest persuasive, but sometimes terrible! The people knew not the power that moved them thus. They deemed the young clergyman a miracle of holiness. They fancied him the mouthpiece of Heaven's messages of wisdom, and rebuke, and love. In their eyes, the very ground on which he trod was sanctified. The virgins of his church grew pale around him, victims of a passion so imbued with religious sentiment that they imagined it to be all religion, and brought it openly, in their white bosoms, as their most acceptable sacrifice before the altar. The aged members of his flock, beholding Mr. Dimmesdale's frame so feeble, while they were themselves so rugged in their infirmity, believed that he would go heavenward before them, and enjoined it upon their children, that their old bones should be buried close to their young pastor's holy grave. And, all this time, perchance, when poor Mr. Dimmesdale was thinking of his grave, he questioned with himself whether the grass would ever grow on it, because an accursed thing must there be buried!

It is inconceivable, the agony with which this public veneration tortured him! It was his genuine impulse to adore the truth, and to reckon all things shadow-like, and utterly devoid of weight or value, that had not its divine essence as the life within their life. Then, what was he?—a substance?—or the dimmest of all shadows? He longed to speak out, from his own pulpit, at the full height of his voice, and tell the people what he was. "I, whom you behold in these black garments of the priesthood,—I, who ascend the sacred desk, and turn my pale face heavenward, taking upon myself to hold communion, in your behalf, with the Most High Omniscience,—I, in whose daily life you discern the sanctity of Enoch,[72]—I, whose footsteps, as you suppose, leave a gleam along my earthly track, whereby the pilgrims that shall come after me may be guided to the regions of the blest,— I, who have laid the hand of baptism upon your children,—I, who have breathed the parting prayer over your dying friends, to whom the Amen sounded faintly from a world which they had quitted,—I, your pastor, whom you so reverence and trust, am utterly a pollution and a lie!"

More than once, Mr. Dimmesdale had gone into the pulpit, with a purpose never to come down its steps, until he should have spoken words like the above. More than once, he had cleared his throat, and drawn in the long, deep, and tremulous breath, which, when sent forth again, would come burdened with the black secret of his soul. More than once—nay, more than a hundred times—he had actually spoken! Spoken! But how? He had told his hearers that he was alto-

---

[72] In Genesis 5:21–24 Enoch "walked with God," interpreted in Hebrews 11:5 by the Apostle Paul to mean that God had "translated" Enoch to Heaven without Enoch having died.

gether vile, a viler companion of the vilest, the worst of sinners, an abomination, a thing of unimaginable iniquity; and that the only wonder was, that they did not see his wretched body shrivelled up before their eyes, by the burning wrath of the Almighty! Could there be plainer speech than this? Would not the people start up in their seats, by a simultaneous impulse, and tear him down out of the pulpit which he defiled? Not so, indeed! They heard it all, and did but reverence him the more. They little guessed what deadly purport lurked in those self-condemning words. "The godly youth!" said they among themselves. "The saint on earth! Alas, if he discern such sinfulness in his own white soul, what horrid spectacle would he behold in thine or mine!" The minister well knew—subtle, but remorseful hypocrite that he was!—the light in which his vague confession would be viewed. He had striven to put a cheat upon himself[73] by making the avowal of a guilty conscience, but had gained only one other sin, and a self-acknowledged shame, without the momentary relief of being self-deceived. He had spoken the very truth, and transformed it into the veriest falsehood. And yet, by the constitution of his nature, he loved the truth, and loathed the lie, as few men ever did. Therefore, above all things else, he loathed his miserable self!

His inward trouble drove him to practices, more in accordance with the old, corrupted faith of Rome, than with the better light of the church in which he had been born and bred. In Mr. Dimmesdale's secret closet, under lock and key, there was a bloody scourge.[74] Oftentimes, this Protestant and Puritan divine had plied it on his own shoulders; laughing bitterly at himself the while, and smiting so much the more pitilessly, because of that bitter laugh. It was his custom, too, as it has been that of many other pious Puritans, to fast,—not, however, like them, in order to purify the body and render it the fitter medium of celestial illumination,—but rigorously, and until his knees trembled beneath him, as an act of penance. He kept vigils, likewise, night after night, sometimes in utter darkness; sometimes with a glimmering lamp; and sometimes, viewing his own face in a looking-glass, by the most powerful light which he could throw upon it. He thus typified the constant introspection wherewith he tortured, but could not purify, himself. In these lengthened vigils, his brain often reeled, and visions seemed to flit before him; perhaps seen doubtfully, and by a faint light of their own, in the remote dimness of the chamber, or more vividly, and close beside him, within the looking-glass. Now it was a herd of diabolic shapes, that grinned and mocked at the pale minister, and beckoned him away with them; now a group of shining angels, who flew upward heavily, as sorrow-laden, but grew more ethereal as they rose. Now came the dead friends of his youth, and his white-bearded father, with a saint-like frown, and his mother, turning her face away as she passed by. Ghost of a mother,—thinnest fantasy of a mother,—methinks she might yet have thrown a pitying glance towards her son! And now, through the chamber which these spectral thoughts had made so ghastly, glided Hester Prynne, leading along little Pearl, in her scarlet garb, and pointing her forefinger, first, at the scarlet letter on her bosom, and then at the clergyman's own breast.

None of these visions ever quite deluded him. At any moment, by an effort of his will, he could discern substances through their misty lack of substance, and convince himself that they were not solid in their nature, like yonder table of carved oak, or that big, square, leathern-bound and brazen-clasped volume of divinity. But, for all that, they were, in one sense, the truest and most substantial things which the poor minister now dealt with. It is the unspeakable misery of a

---

[73] To fool himself.   [74] A whip.

life so false as his, that it steals the pith and substance out of whatever realities there are around us, and which were meant by Heaven to be the spirit's joy and nutriment. To the untrue man, the whole universe is false,—it is impalpable,—it shrinks to nothing within his grasp. And he himself, in so far as he shows himself in a false light, becomes a shadow, or, indeed, ceases to exist. The only truth, that continued to give Mr. Dimmesdale a real existence on this earth, was the anguish in his inmost soul, and the undissembled expression of it in his aspect. Had he once found power to smile, and wear a face of gayety, there would have been no such man!

On one of those ugly nights, which we have faintly hinted at, but forborne to picture forth, the minister started from his chair. A new thought had struck him. There might be a moment's peace in it. Attiring himself with as much care as if it had been for public worship, and precisely in the same manner, he stole softly down the staircase, undid the door, and issued forth.

XII: The Minister's Vigil

Walking in the shadow of a dream, as it were, and perhaps actually under the influence of a species of somnambulism, Mr. Dimmesdale reached the spot, where, now so long since, Hester Prynne had lived through her first hour of public ignominy. The same platform or scaffold, black and weather-stained with the storm or sunshine of seven long years, and foot-worn, too, with the tread of many culprits who had since ascended it, remained standing beneath the balcony of the meeting-house. The minister went up the steps.

It was an obscure night of early May. An unvaried pall of cloud muffled the whole expanse of sky from zenith to horizon. If the same multitude which had stood as eyewitnesses while Hester Prynne sustained her punishment could now have been summoned forth, they would have discerned no face above the platform, nor hardly the outline of a human shape, in the dark gray of the midnight. But the town was all asleep. There was no peril of discovery. The minister might stand there, if it so pleased him, until morning should redden in the east, without other risk than that the dank and chill night-air would creep into his frame, and stiffen his joints with rheumatism, and clog his throat with catarrh and cough; thereby defrauding the expectant audience of to-morrow's prayer and sermon. No eye could see him, save that ever-wakeful one which had seen him in his closet, wielding the bloody scourge. Why, then, had he come hither? Was it but the mockery of penitence? A mockery, indeed, but in which his soul trifled with itself! A mockery at which angels blushed and wept, while fiends rejoiced, with jeering laughter! He had been driven hither by the impulse of that Remorse which dogged him everywhere, and whose own sister and closely linked companion was that Cowardice which invariably drew him back, with her tremulous gripe, just when the other impulse had hurried him to the verge of a disclosure. Poor, miserable man! what right had infirmity like his to burden itself with crime? Crime is for the iron-nerved, who have their choice either to endure it, or, if it press too hard, to exert their fierce and savage strength for a good purpose, and fling it off at once! This feeble and most sensitive of spirits could do neither, yet continually did one thing or another, which intertwined, in the same inextricable knot, the agony of heaven-defying guilt and vain repentance.

And thus, while standing on the scaffold, in this vain show of expiation, Mr. Dimmesdale was overcome with a great horror of mind, as if the universe were gazing at a scarlet token on his naked breast, right over his heart. On that spot, in very truth, there was, and there had long been, the gnawing and poisonous tooth of bodily pain. Without any effort of his will, or power to restrain himself, he shrieked aloud; an outcry that went pealing through the night, and was beaten back from one house to another, and reverberated from the hills in the background; as if a company of devils, detecting so much misery and terror in it, had made a plaything of the sound, and were bandying it to and fro.

"It is done!" muttered the minister, covering his face with his hands. "The whole town will awake, and hurry forth, and find me here!"

But it was not so. The shriek had perhaps sounded with a far greater power, to his own startled ears, than it actually possessed. The town did not awake; or, if it did, the drowsy slumberers mistook the cry either for something frightful in a dream, or for the noise of witches; whose voices, at that period, were often heard to pass over the settlements or lonely cottages, as they rode with Satan through the air. The clergyman, therefore, hearing no symptoms of disturbance, uncovered his eyes and looked about him. At one of the chamber-windows of Governor Bellingham's mansion, which stood at some distance, on the line of another street, he beheld the appearance of the old magistrate himself, with a lamp in his hand, a white night-cap on his head, and a long white gown enveloping his figure. He looked like a ghost, evoked unseasonably from the grave. The cry had evidently startled him. At another window of the same house, moreover, appeared old Mistress Hibbins, the Governor's sister, also with a lamp, which, even thus far off, revealed the expression of her sour and discontented face. She thrust forth her head from the lattice, and looked anxiously upward. Beyond the shadow of a doubt, this venerable witch-lady had heard Mr. Dimmesdale's outcry and interpreted it, with its multitudinous echoes and reverberations, as the clamor of the fiends and night-hags, with whom she was well known to make excursions into the forest.

Detecting the gleam of Governor Bellingham's lamp, the old lady quickly extinguished her own, and vanished. Possibly, she went up among the clouds. The minister saw nothing further of her motions. The magistrate, after a wary observation of the darkness—into which, nevertheless, he could see but little farther than he might into a mill-stone—retired from the window.

The minister grew comparatively calm. His eyes, however, were soon greeted by a little, glimmering light, which, at first a long way off, was approaching up the street. It threw a gleam of recognition on here a post, and there a garden-fence, and here a latticed window-pane, and there a pump, with its full trough of water, and here, again, an arched door of oak, with an iron knocker, and a rough log for the door-step. The Reverend Mr. Dimmesdale noted all these minute particulars, even while firmly convinced that the doom of his existence was stealing onward, in the footsteps which he now heard; and that the gleam of the lantern would fall upon him, in a few moments more, and reveal his long-hidden secret. As the light drew nearer, he beheld, within its illuminated circle, his brother clergyman,—or, to speak more accurately, his professional father, as well as highly valued friend,— the Reverend Mr. Wilson; who, as Mr. Dimmesdale now conjectured, had been praying at the bedside of some dying man. And so he had. The good old minister came freshly from the death-chamber of Governor Winthrop,[75]

[75] John Winthrop, who had arrived in Massachusetts in 1630, served as governor from 1630 to 1634, 1637 to 1640, 1642 to 1644, and 1646 to 1649. Although he died on March 26, 1649, Hawthorne sets the scaffold scene in "early May" of that year.

who had passed from earth to heaven within that very hour. And now, surrounded, like the saint-like personages of olden times, with a radiant halo, that glorified him amid this gloomy night of sin,—as if the departed Governor had left him an inheritance of his glory, or as if he had caught upon himself the distant shine of the celestial city, while looking thitherward to see the triumphant pilgrim pass within its gates,—now, in short, good Father Wilson was moving homeward, aiding his footsteps with a lighted lantern! The glimmer of this luminary suggested the above conceits to Mr. Dimmesdale, who smiled,—nay, almost laughed at them,—and then wondered if he were going mad.

As the Reverend Mr. Wilson passed beside the scaffold, closely muffling his Geneva cloak[76] about him with one arm, and holding the lantern before his breast with the other, the minister could hardly restrain himself from speaking.

"A good evening to you, venerable Father Wilson! Come up hither, I pray you, and pass a pleasant hour with me!"

Good heavens! Had Mr Dimmesdale actually spoken? For one instant, he believed that these words had passed his lips. But they were uttered only within his imagination. The venerable Father Wilson continued to step slowly onward, looking carefully at the muddy pathway before his feet, and never once turning his head towards the guilty platform. When the light of the glimmering lantern had faded quite away, the minister discovered, by the faintness which came over him, that the last few moments had been a crisis of terrible anxiety; although his mind had made an involuntary effort to relieve itself by a kind of lurid playfulness.

Shortly afterwards, the like grisly sense of humorous again stole in among the solemn phantoms of his thought. He felt his limbs growing stiff with the unaccustomed chilliness of the night, and doubted whether he should be able to descend the steps of the scaffold. Morning would break, and find him there. The neighbourhood would begin to rouse itself. The earliest riser, coming forth in the dim twilight, would perceive a vaguely defined figure aloft on the place of shame; and, half crazed betwixt alarm and curiosity, would go, knocking from door to door, summoning all the people to behold the ghost—as he needs must think it—of some defunct transgressor. A dusky tumult would flap its wings from one house to another. Then—the morning light still waxing stronger—old patriarchs would rise up in great haste, each in his flannel gown, and matronly dames, without pausing to put off their night-gear. The whole tribe of decorous personages, who had never heretofore been seen with a single hair of their heads awry, would start into public view, with the disorder of a nightmare in their aspects. Old Governor Bellingham would come grimly forth, with his King James's ruff fastened askew; and Mistress Hibbins, with some twigs of the forest clinging to her skirts, and looking sourer than ever, as having hardly got a wink of sleep after her night ride; and good Father Wilson, too, after spending half the night at a death-bed, and liking ill to be disturbed, thus early, out of his dreams about the glorified saints. Hither, likewise, would come the elders and deacons of Mr. Dimmesdale's church, and the young virgins who so idolized their minister, and had made a shrine for him in their white bosoms; which, now, by the by, in their hurry and confusion, they would scantly have given themselves time to cover with their kerchiefs. All people, in a word, would come stumbling over their thresholds, and turning up their amazed and horror-stricken visages around the scaffold. Whom would they discern there, with the red eastern light upon his brow? Whom, but the

---

[76] A traditional black clerical robe worn by Calvinist ministers in Geneva, Switzerland.

Reverend Arthur Dimmesdale, half frozen to death, overwhelmed with shame, and standing where Hester Prynne had stood!

Carried away by the grotesque horror of this picture, the minister, unawares, and to his own infinite alarm, burst into a great peal of laughter. It was immediately responded to by a light, airy, childish laugh, in which, with a thrill of the heart,—but he knew not whether of exquisite pain, or pleasure as acute,—he recognized the tones of little Pearl.

"Pearl! Little Pearl!" cried he, after a moment's pause; then, suppressing his voice,—"Hester! Hester Prynne! Are you there?"

"Yes; it is Hester Prynne!" she replied, in a tone of surprise; and the minister heard her footsteps approaching from the sidewalk, along which she had been passing.—"It is I, and my little Pearl."

"Whence come you, Hester?" asked the minister. "What sent you hither?"

"I have been watching at a death-bed," answered Hester Prynne;—"at Governor Winthrop's death-bed, and have taken his measure for a robe, and am now going homeward to my dwelling."

"Come up hither, Hester, thou and little Pearl," said the Reverend Mr. Dimmesdale. "Ye have both been here before, but I was not with you. Come up hither once again, and we will stand all three together!"

She silently ascended the steps, and stood on the platform, holding little Pearl by the hand. The minister felt for the child's other hand, and took it. The moment that he did so, there came what seemed a tumultuous rush of new life, other life than his own, pouring like a torrent into his heart, and hurrying through all his veins, as if the mother and the child were communicating their vital warmth to his half-torpid system. The three formed an electric chain.

"Minister!" whispered little Pearl.

"What wouldst thou say, child?" asked Mr. Dimmesdale.

"Wilt thou stand here with mother and me, to-morrow noontide?" inquired Pearl.

"Nay; not so, my little Pearl!" answered the minister; for, with the new energy of the moment, all the dread of public exposure, that had so long been the anguish of his life, had returned upon him; and he was already trembling at the conjunction in which—with a strange joy, nevertheless—he now found himself. "Not so, my child. I shall, indeed, stand with thy mother and thee one other day, but not to-morrow!"

Pearl laughed, and attempted to pull away her hand. But the minister held it fast.

"A moment longer, my child!" said he.

"But wilt thou promise," asked Pearl, "to take my hand, and mother's hand, to-morrow noontide?"

"Not then, Pearl," said the minister, "but another time!"

"And what other time?" persisted the child.

"At the great judgment day!" whispered the minister,—and, strangely enough, the sense that he was a professional teacher of the truth impelled him to answer the child so. "Then, and there, before the judgment-seat, thy mother, and thou, and I, must stand together! But the daylight of this world shall not see our meeting!"

Pearl laughed again.

But, before Mr. Dimmesdale had done speaking, a light gleamed far and wide over all the muffled sky. It was doubtless caused by one of those meteors, which the night-watcher may so often observe burning out to waste, in the vacant regions of the atmosphere. So powerful was its radiance, that it thoroughly illuminated the dense medium of cloud betwixt the sky and earth. The great vault brightened, like the dome of an immense lamp. It showed the familiar scene of the street, with the distinctness of mid-day, but also with the awfulness that is always imparted to familiar objects by an unaccustomed light. The wooden houses, with their jutting stories and quaint gable-peaks; the doorsteps and thresholds, with the early grass springing up about them; the garden-plots, black with freshly turned earth; the wheel-track, little worn, and, even in the market-place, margined with green on either side;—all were visible, but with a singularity of aspect that seemed to give another moral interpretation to the things of this world than they had ever borne before. And there stood the minister, with his hand over his heart; and Hester Prynne with the embroidered letter glimmering on her bosom; and little Pearl, herself a symbol, and the connecting link between those two. They stood in the noon of that strange and solemn splendor, as if it were the light that is to reveal all secrets, and the daybreak that shall unite all who belong to one another.

There was witchcraft in little Pearl's eyes; and her face, as she glanced upward at the minister, wore that naughty smile which made its expression frequently so elfish. She withdrew her hand from Mr. Dimmesdale's, and pointed across the street. But he clasped both his hands over his breast, and cast his eyes towards the zenith.

Nothing was more common, in those days, than to interpret all meteoric appearances, and other natural phenomena, that occurred with less regularity than the rise and set of sun and moon, as so many revelations from a supernatural source. Thus, a blazing spear, a sword of flame, a bow, or a sheaf of arrows, seen in the midnight sky, prefigured Indian warfare. Pestilence was known to have been foreboded by a shower of crimson light. We doubt whether any marked event, for good or evil, ever befell New England, from its settlement down to Revolutionary times, of which the inhabitants had not been previously warned by some spectacle of this nature. Not seldom, it had been seen by multitudes. Oftener, however, its credibility rested on the faith of some lonely eyewitness, who beheld the wonder through the colored, magnifying, and distorting medium of his imagination, and shaped it more distinctly in his after-thought. It was, indeed, a majestic idea, that the destiny of nations should be revealed, in these awful hieroglyphics, on the cope[77] of heaven. A scroll so wide might not be deemed too expansive for Providence to write a people's doom upon. The belief was a favorite one with our forefathers, as betokening that their infant commonwealth was under a celestial guardianship of peculiar intimacy and strictness. But what shall we say, when an individual discovers a revelation, addressed to himself alone, on the same vast sheet of record! In such a case, it could only be the symptom of a highly disordered mental state, when a man, rendered morbidly self-contemplative by long, intense, and secret pain, had extended his egotism over the whole expanse of nature, until the firmament itself should appear no more than a fitting page for his soul's history and fate.

We impute it, therefore, solely to the disease in his own eye and heart, that the minister, looking upward to the zenith, beheld there the appearance of an immense letter,—the letter A,—marked out in lines of dull red light. Not but the meteor may have shown itself at that point, burning duskily through a veil of cloud; but with no such shape as his guilty imagination gave it; or, at least, with so little definiteness, that another's guilt might have seen another symbol in it.

There was a singular circumstance that characterized Mr. Dimmesdale's psy-

[77] Canopy.

chological state, at this moment. All the time that he gazed upward to the zenith, he was, nevertheless, perfectly aware that little Pearl was pointing her finger towards old Roger Chillingworth, who stood at no great distance from the scaffold. The minister appeared to see him, with the same glance that discerned the miraculous letter. To his features, as to all other objects, the meteoric light imparted a new expression; or it might well be that the physician was not careful then, as at all other times, to hide the malevolence with which he looked upon his victim. Certainly, if the meteor kindled up the sky, and disclosed the earth, with an awfulness that admonished Hester Prynne and the clergyman of the day of judgment, then might Roger Chillingworth have passed with them for the arch-fiend, standing there, with a smile and scowl, to claim his own. So vivid was the expression, or so intense the minister's perception of it, that it seemed still to remain painted on the darkness, after the meteor had vanished, with an effect as if the street and all things else were at once annihilated.

"Who is that man, Hester?" gasped Mr. Dimmesdale, overcome with terror. "I shiver at him! Dost thou know the man? I hate him, Hester!"

She remembered her oath, and was silent.

"I tell thee, my soul shivers at him," muttered the minister again. "Who is he? Who is he? Canst thou do nothing for me? I have a nameless horror of the man."

"Minister," said little Pearl, "I can tell thee who he is!"

"Quickly, then, child!" said the minister, bending his ear close to her lips. "Quickly!—and as low as thou canst whisper."

Pearl mumbled something into his ear, that sounded, indeed, like human language, but was only such gibberish as children may be heard amusing themselves with, by the hour together. At all events, if it involved any secret information in regard to old Roger Chillingworth, it was in a tongue unknown to the erudite clergyman, and did but increase the bewilderment of his mind. The elfish child then laughed aloud.

"Does thou mock me now?" said the minister.

"Thou wast not bold!—thou wast not true!" answered the child. "Thou wouldst not promise to take my hand, and mother's hand, to-morrow noontide!"

"Worthy Sir," said the physician, who had now advanced to the foot of the platform. "Pious Master Dimmesdale! can this be you? Well, well, indeed! We men of study, whose heads are in our books, have need to be straitly looked after! We dream in our waking moments, and walk in our sleep. Come, good Sir, and my dear friend, I pray you, let me lead you home!"

"How knewest thou that I was here?" asked the minister, fearfully.

"Verily, and in good faith," answered Roger Chillingworth, "I knew nothing of the matter. I had spent the better part of the night at the bedside of the worshipful Governor Winthrop, doing what my poor skill might to give him ease. He going home to a better world, I, likewise, was on my way homeward, when this strange light shone out. Come with me, I beseech you, Reverend Sir; else you will be poorly able to do Sabbath duty to-morrow. Aha! see now, how they trouble the brain,—these books!—these books! You should study less, good Sir, and take a little pastime; or these night-whimseys will grow upon you!"

"I will go home with you," said Mr. Dimmesdale.

With a chill despondency, like one awaking, all nerveless, from an ugly dream, he yielded himself to the physician, and was led away.

The next day, however, being the Sabbath, he preached a discourse which was held to be the richest and most powerful, and the most replete with heavenly influences, that had ever proceeded from his lips. Souls, it is said, more souls than one, were brought to the truth by the efficacy of that sermon, and vowed within themselves to cherish a holy gratitude towards Mr. Dimmesdale throughout the long hereafter. But, as he came down the pulpit-steps, the gray-bearded sexton met him, holding up a black glove, which the minister recognized as his own.

"It was found," said the sexton, "this morning, on the scaffold, where evil-doers are set up to public shame. Satan dropped it there, I take it, intending a scurrilous jest against your reverence. But, indeed, he was blind and foolish, as he ever and always is. A pure hand needs no glove to cover it!"

"Thank you, my good friend," said the minister gravely, but startled at heart; for, so confused was his remembrance, that he had almost brought himself to look at the events of the past night as visionary. "Yes, it seems to be my glove indeed!"

"And, since Satan saw fit to steal it, your reverence must needs handle him without gloves, henceforward," remarked the old sexton, grimly smiling. "But did your reverence hear of the portent that was seen last night? A great red letter in the sky,—the letter A,—which we interpret to stand for Angel. For, as our good Governor Winthrop was made an angel this past night, it was doubtless held fit that there should be some notice thereof!"

"No," answered the minister. "I had not heard of it."

XIII: Another View of Hester

In her late singular interview with Mr. Dimmesdale, Hester Prynne was shocked at the condition to which she found the clergyman reduced. His nerve seemed absolutely destroyed. His moral force was abased into more than childish weakness. It grovelled helpless on the ground, even while his intellectual faculties retained their pristine strength, or had perhaps acquired a morbid energy, which disease only could have given them. With her knowledge of a train of circumstances hidden from all others, she could readily infer, that, besides the legitimate action of his own conscience, a terrible machinery had been brought to bear, and was still operating, on Mr. Dimmesdale's well-being and respose. Knowing what this poor, fallen man had once been, her whole soul was moved by the shuddering terror with which he had appealed to her,—the outcast woman,—for support against his instinctively discovered enemy. She decided, moreover, that he had a right to her utmost aid. Little accustomed, in her long seclusion from society, to measure her ideas of right and wrong by any standard external to herself, Hester saw—or seemed to see—that there lay a responsibility upon her, in reference to the clergyman, which she owed to no other, nor to the whole world besides. The links that united her to the rest of human kind—links of flowers, or silk, or gold, or whatever the material—had all been broken. Here was the iron link of mutual crime, which neither he nor she could break. Like all other ties, it brought along with it its obligations.

Hester Prynne did not now occupy precisely the same position in which we beheld her during the earlier periods of her ignominy. Years had come, and gone. Pearl was now seven years old. Her mother, with the scarlet letter on her breast, glittering in its fantastic embroidery, had long been a familiar object to the townspeople. As is apt to be the case when a person stands out in any prominence before the community, and, at the same time, interferes neither with public nor individual interests and convenience, a species of general regard had ultimately grown up in reference to Hester Prynne. It is to the credit of human nature, that, except where its selfishness is brought into play, it loves more readily than it hates. Hatred, by a gradual and quiet process, will even be transformed to love, unless the change be impeded by a continually new irritation of the original feeling of hostility. In this matter of Hester Prynne, there was neither irritation nor irksomeness. She never battled with the public, but submitted uncomplainingly to its worst usage; she made no claim upon it, in requital for what she suffered; she did not weigh upon its sympathies. Then, also, the blameless purity of her life, during all these years in which she had been set apart to infamy, was reckoned largely in her favor. With nothing now to lose, in the sight of mankind, and with no hope, and seemingly no wish, of gaining any thing, it could only be a genuine regard for virtue that had brought back the poor wanderer to its paths.

It was perceived, too, that, while Hester never put forward even the humblest title to share in the world's privileges,—farther than to breathe the common air, and earn daily bread for little Pearl and herself by the faithful labor of her hands,—she was quick to acknowledge her sisterhood with the race of man, whenever benefits were to be conferred. None so ready as she to give of her little substance to every demand of poverty; even though the bitter-hearted pauper threw back a gibe in requital of the food brought regularly to his door, or the garments wrought for him by the fingers that could have embroidered a monarch's robe. None so self-devoted as Hester, when pestilence stalked through the town. In all seasons of calamity, indeed, whether general or of individuals, the outcast of society at once found her place. She came, not as a guest, but as a rightful inmate, into the household that was darkened by trouble; as if its gloomy twilight were a medium in which she was entitled to hold intercourse with her fellow-creatures. There glimmered the embroidered letter, with comfort in its unearthly ray. Elsewhere the token of sin, it was the taper of the sick-chamber. It had even thrown its gleam, in the sufferer's hard extremity, across the verge of time. It had shown him where to set his foot, while the light of earth was fast becoming dim, and ere the light of futurity could reach him. In such emergencies, Hester's nature showed itself warm and rich; a well-spring of human tenderness, unfailing to every real demand, and inexhaustible by the largest. Her breast, with its badge of shame, was but the softer pillow for the head that needed one. She was self-ordained a Sister of Mercy; or, we may rather say, the world's heavy hand had so ordained her, when neither the world nor she looked forward to this result. The letter was the symbol of her calling. Such helpfulness was found in her,—so much power to do, and power to sympathize,—that many people refused to interpret the scarlet A by its original signification. They said that it meant Able; so strong was Hester Prynne, with a woman's strength.

It was only the darkened house that could contain her. When sunshine came again, she was not there. Her shadow had faded across the threshold. The helpful inmate had departed, without one backward glance to gather up the meed[78] of gratitude, if any were in the hearts of those whom she had served so zealously. Meeting them in the street, she never raised her head to receive their greeting. If they were resolute to accost her, she laid her finger on the scarlet letter, and passed on. This might be pride, but was so like humility, that it produced all the softening influence of the latter quality on the public mind. The public is despotic in its temper; it is capable of denying common justice, when too strenuously de-

[78] Reward.

manded as a right; but quite as frequently it awards more than justice, when the appeal is made, as despots love to have it made, entirely to its generosity. Interpreting Hester Prynne's deportment as an appeal of this nature, society was inclined to show its former victim a more benign countenance than she cared to be favored with, or, perchance, than she deserved.

The rulers, and the wise and learned men of the community, were longer in acknowledging the influence of Hester's good qualities than the people. The prejudices which they shared in common with the latter were fortified in themselves by an iron framework of reasoning, that made it a far tougher labor to expel them. Day by day, nevertheless, their sour and rigid wrinkles were relaxing into something which, in the due course of years, might grow to be an expression of almost benevolence. Thus it was with the men of rank, on whom their eminent position imposed the guardianship of the public morals. Individuals in private life, meanwhile, had quite forgiven Herster Prynne for her frailty; nay, more, they had begun to look upon the scarlet letter as the token, not of that one sin, for which she had borne so long and dreary a penance, but of her many good deeds since. "Do you see that woman with the embroidered badge?" they would say to strangers. "It is our Hester,—the town's own Hester,—who is so kind to the poor, so helpful to the sick, so comfortable to the afflicted!" Then, it is true, the propensity of human nature to tell the very worst of itself, when embodied in the person of another, would constrain them to whisper the black scandal of bygone years. It was none the less a fact, however, that, in the eyes of the very men who spoke thus, the scarlet letter had the effect of the cross on a nun's bosom. It imparted to the wearer a kind of sacredness, which enabled her to walk securely amid all peril. Had she fallen among thieves, it would have kept her safe. It was reported, and believed by many, that an Indian had drawn his arrow against the badge, and that the missile struck it, but fell harmless to the ground.

The effect of the symbol—or rather, of the position in respect to society that was indicated by it—on the mind of Hester Prynne herself, was powerful and peculiar. All the light and graceful foliage of her character had been withered up by this red-hot brand, and had long ago fallen away, leaving a bare and harsh outline, which might have been repulsive, had she possessed friends or companions to be repelled by it. Even the attractiveness of her person had undergone a similar change. It might be partly owing to the studied austerity of her dress, and partly to the lack of demonstration in her manners. It was a sad transformation, too, that her rich and luxuriant hair had either been cut off, or was so completely hidden by a cap, that not a shining lock of it ever once gushed into the sunshine. It was due in part to all these causes, but still more to something else, that there seemed to be no longer any thing in Hester's face for Love to dwell upon; nothing in Hester's form, though majestic and statue-like, that Passion would ever dream of clasping in its embrace; nothing in Hester's bosom, to make it ever again the pillow of Affection. Some attribute had departed from her, the permanence of which had been essential to keep her a woman. Such is frequently the fate, and such the stern development, of the feminine character and person, when the woman has encountered, and lived through, an experience of peculiar severity. If she be all tenderness, she will die. If she survive, the tenderness will either be crushed out of her, or—and the outward semblance is the same—crushed so deeply into her heart that it can never show itself more. The latter is perhaps the truest theory. She who has once been woman, and ceased to be so, might at any moment become a woman again, if there were only the magic touch to effect the transfiguration. We shall see whether Hester Prynne were ever afterwards so touched, and so transfigured.

Much of the marble coldness of Hester's impression was to be attributed to the circumstance that her life had turned, in a great measure, from passion and feeling, to thought. Standing alone in the world,—alone, as to any dependence on society, and with little Pearl to be guided and protected,—alone, and hopeless of retrieving her position, even had she not scorned to consider it desirable,—she cast away the fragments of a broken chain. The world's law was no law for her mind. It was an age in which the human intellect, newly emancipated, had taken a more active and a wider range than for many centuries before. Men of the sword had overthrown nobles and kings. Men bolder than these had overthrown and rearranged—not actually, but within the sphere of theory, which was their most real abode—the whole system of ancient prejudice, wherewith was linked much of ancient principle. Hester Prynne imbibed this spirit. She assumed a freedom of speculation, then common enough on the other side of the Atlantic, but which our forefathers, had they known of it, would have held to be a deadlier crime than that stigmatized by the scarlet letter. In her lonesome cottage, by the sea-shore, thoughts visited her, such as dared to enter no other dwelling in New England; shadowy guests, that would have been as perilous as demons to their entertainer, could they have been seen so much as knocking at her door.

It is remarkable, that persons who speculate the most boldly often conform with the most perfect quietude to the external regulations of society. The thought suffices them, without investing itself in the flesh and blood of action. So it seemed to be with Hester. Yet, had little Pearl never come to her from the spiritual world, it might have been far otherwise. Then, she might have come down to us in history, hand in hand with Ann Hutchinson, as the foundress of a religious sect. She might, in one of her phases, have been a prophetess. She might, and not improbably would, have suffered death from the stern tribunals of the period, for attempting to undermine the foundations of the Puritan establishment. But, in the education of her child, the mother's enthusiasm of thought had something to wreak itself upon. Providence, in the person of this little girl, had assigned to Hester's charge the germ and blossom of womanhood, to be cherished and developed amid a host of difficulties. Every thing was against her. The world was hostile. The child's own nature had something wrong in it, which continually betokened that she had been born amiss,—the effluence of her mother's lawless passion,—and often impelled Hester to ask, in bitterness of heart, whether it were for ill or good that the poor little creature had been born at all.

Indeed, the same dark question often rose into her mind, with reference to the whole race of womanhood. Was existence worth accepting, even to the happiest among them? As concerned her own individual existence, she had long ago decided in the negative, and dismissed the point as settled. A tendency to speculation, though it may keep woman quiet, as it does man, yet makes her sad. She discerns, it may be, such a hopeless task before her. As a first step, the whole system of society is to be torn down, and built up anew. Then, the very nature of the opposite sex, or its long hereditary habit, which has become like nature, is to be essentially modified, before woman can be allowed to assume what seems a fair and suitable position. Finally, all other difficulties being obviated, woman cannot take advantage of these preliminary reforms, until she herself shall have undergone a still mightier change; in which, perhaps, the ethereal essence, wherein she has her truest life, will be found to have evaporated. A woman never overcomes these problems by any exercise of thought. They are not to be solved, or only in one way. If her heart chance to come uppermost, they vanish. Thus, Hester Prynne, whose heart had lost its regular and healthy throb, wandered without a clew in the dark labyrinth of mind; now turned aside by an insurmountable precipice; now starting back from a deep chasm. There was wild and ghastly scenery all around her, and a home and comfort nowhere. At times, a fearful doubt strove to possess her soul, whether it were not better to send Pearl at once to heaven, and go herself to such futurity as Eternal Justice should provide.

The scarlet letter had not done its office.

Now, however, her interview with the Reverend Mr. Dimmesdale, on the night of his vigil, had given her a new theme of reflection, and held up to her an object that appeared worthy of any exertion and sacrifice for its attainment. She had witnessed the intense misery beneath which the minister struggled, or, to speak more accurately, had ceased to struggle. She saw that he stood on the verge of lunacy, if he had not already stepped across it. It was impossible to doubt, that, whatever painful efficacy there might be in the secret sting of remorse, a deadlier venom had been infused into it by the hand that proffered relief. A secret enemy had been continually by his side, under the semblance of a friend and helper, and had availed himself of the opportunities thus afforded for tampering with the delicate springs of Mr. Dimmesdale's nature. Hester could not but ask herself, whether there had not originally been a defect of truth, courage, and loyalty, on her own part, in allowing the minister to be thrown into a position where so much evil was to be foreboded, and nothing auspicious to be hoped. Her only justification lay in the fact, that she had been able to discern no method of rescuing him from a blacker ruin than had overwhelmed herself, except by acquiescing in Roger Chillingworth's scheme of disguise. Under that impulse, she had made her choice, and had chosen, as it now appeared, the more wretched alternative of the two. She determined to redeem her error, so far as it might yet be possible. Strengthened by years of hard and solemn trial, she felt herself no longer so inadequate to cope with Roger Chillingworth as on that night, abased by sin, and half maddened by the ignominy that was still new, when they had talked together in the prison-chamber. She had climbed her way, since then, to a higher point. The old man, on the other hand, had brought himself nearer to her level, or perhaps below it, by the revenge which he had stooped for.

In fine, Hester Prynne resolved to meet her former husband, and do what might be in her power for the rescue of the victim on whom he had so evidently set his gripe. The occasion was not long to seek. One afternoon, walking with Pearl in a retired part of the peninsula, she beheld the old physician, with a basket on one arm, and a staff in the other hand, stooping along the ground, in quest of roots and herbs to concoct his medicines withal.

XIV: *Hester and the Physician*

Hester bade little Pearl run down to the margin of the water, and play with the shells and tangled seaweed, until she should have talked awhile with yonder gatherer of herbs. So the child flew away like a bird, and, making bare her small white feet, went pattering along the moist margin of the sea. Here and there, she came to a full stop, and peeped curiously into a pool, left by the retiring tide as a mirror for Pearl to see her face in. Forth peeped at her, out of the pool, with dark, glistening curls around her head, and an elf-smile in her eyes, the image of a little maid, whom Pearl, having no other playmate, invited to take her hand and run a race with her. But the visionary little maid, on her part, beckoned likewise, as if to say,—"This is a better place! Come thou into the pool!" And Pearl, stepping in, mid-leg deep, beheld her own white feet at the bottom; while, out of a still lower depth, came the gleam of a kind of fragmentary smile, floating to and fro in the agitated water.

Meanwhile, her mother had accosted the physician.

"I would speak a word with you," said she,—"a word that concerns us much."

"Aha! And is it Mistress Hester that has a word for old Roger Chillingworth?" answered he, raising himself from his stooping posture. "With all my heart! Why, Mistress, I hear good tidings of you on all hands! No longer ago than yester-eve, a magistrate, a wise and godly man, was discoursing of your affairs, Mistress Hester, and whispered me that there had been question concerning you in the council. It was debated whether or no, with safety to the common weal, yonder scarlet letter might be taken off your bosom. On my life, Hester, I made my entreaty to the worshipful magistrate that it might be done forthwith!"

"It lies not in the pleasure of the magistrates to take off this badge," calmly replied Hester. "Were I worthy to be quit of it, it would fall away of its own nature, or be transformed into something that should speak a different purport."

"Nay, then, wear it, if it suit you better," rejoined he. "A woman must needs follow her own fancy, touching the adornment of her person. The letter is gayly embroidered, and shows right bravely on your bosom!"

All this while, Hester had been looking steadily at the old man, and was shocked, as well as wonder-smitten, to discern what a change had been wrought upon him within the past seven years. It was not so much that he had grown older; for though the traces of advancing life were visible, he bore his age well, and seemed to retain a wiry vigor and alertness. But the former aspect of an intellectual and studious man, calm and quiet, which was what she best remembered in him, had altogether vanished, and been succeeded by an eager, searching, almost fierce, yet carefully guarded look. It seemed to be his wish and purpose to mask this expression with a smile; but the latter played him false, and flickered over his visage so derisively, that the spectator could see his blackness all the better for it. Ever and anon, too, there came a glare of red light out of his eyes; as if the old man's soul were on fire, and kept on smouldering duskily within his breast, until, by some casual puff of passion, it was blown into a momentary flame. This he repressed as speedily as possible, and strove to look as if nothing of the kind had happened.

In a word, old Roger Chillingworth was a striking evidence of man's faculty of transforming himself into a devil, if he will only, for a reasonable space of time, undertake a devil's office. This unhappy person had effected such a transformation by devoting himself, for seven years, to the constant analysis of a heart full of torture, and deriving his enjoyment thence, and adding fuel to those fiery tortures which he analyzed and gloated over.

The scarlet letter burned on Hester Prynne's bosom. Here was another ruin, the responsibility of which came partly home to her.

"What see you in my face," asked the physician, "that you look at it so earnestly?"

"Something that would make me weep, if there were any tears bitter enough for it," answered she. "But let it pass! It is of yonder miserable man that I would speak."

"And what of him?" cried Roger Chillingworth eagerly, as if he loved the topic, and were glad of an opportunity to discuss it with the only person of whom he could make a confidant. "Not to hide the truth, Mistress Hester, my thoughts happen just now to be busy with the gentleman. So speak freely; and I will make answer."

"When we last spake together," said Hester, "now seven years ago, it was your pleasure to extort a promise of secrecy, as touching the former relation betwixt yourself and me. As the life and good fame of yonder man were in your hands, there seemed no choice to me, save to be silent, in accordance with your behest. Yet it was not without heavy misgivings that I thus bound myself; for, having cast off all duty towards other human beings, there remained a duty towards him; and something whispered me that I was betraying it, in pledging myself to keep your counsel. Since that day, no man is so near to him as you. You tread behind his every footstep. You are beside him, sleeping and waking. You search his thoughts. You burrow and rankle in his heart! Your clutch is on his life, and you cause him to die daily a living death; and still he knows you not. In permitting this, I have surely acted a false part by the only man to whom the power was left me to be true!"

"What choice had you?" asked Roger Chillingworth. "My finger, pointed at this man, would have hurled him from his pulpit into a dungeon,—thence, peradventure, to the gallows!"

"It had been better so!" said Hester Prynne.

"What evil have I done the man?" asked Roger Chillingworth again. "I tell thee, Hester Prynne, the richest fee that ever physician earned from monarch could not have bought such care as I have wasted on this miserable priest! But for my aid, his life would have burned away in torments, within the first two years after the perpetration of his crime and thine. For, Hester, his spirit lacked the strength that could have borne up, as thine has, beneath a burden like thy scarlet letter. O, I could reveal a goodly secret! But enough! What art can do, I have exhausted on him. That he now breathes, and creeps about on earth, is owing all to me!"

"Better he had died at once!" said Hester Prynne.

"Yea, woman, thou sayest truly!" cried old Roger Chillingworth, letting the lurid fire of his heart blaze out before her eyes. "Better had he died at once! Never did mortal suffer what this man has suffered. And all, all, in the sight of his worst enemy! He has been conscious of me. He has felt an influence dwelling always upon him like a curse. He knew, by some spiritual sense,—for the Creator never made another being so sensitive as this,—he knew that no friendly hand was pulling at his heart-strings, and that an eye was looking curiously into him, which sought only evil, and found it. But he knew not that the eye and hand were mine! With the superstition common to his brotherhood, he fancied himself given over to a fiend, to be tortured with frightful dreams, and desperate thoughts, the sting of remorse, and despair of pardon; as a foretaste of what awaits him beyond the grave. But it was the constant shadow of my presence!—the closest propinquity of the man whom he had most vilely wronged!—and who had grown to exist only by this perpetual poison of the direst revenge! Yea, indeed!—he did not err!—there was a fiend at his elbow! A mortal man, with once a human heart, has become a fiend for his especial torment!"

The unfortunate physician, while uttering these words, lifted his hands with a look of horror, as if he had beheld some frightful shape, which he could not recognize, usurping the place of his own image in a glass. It was one of those moments—which sometimes occur only at the interval of years—when a man's moral aspect is faithfully revealed to his mind's eye. Not improbably, he had never before viewed himself as he did now.

"Hast thou not tortured him enough?" said Hester, noticing the old man's look. "Has he not paid thee all?"

"No!—no!—He has but increased the debt!" answered the physician; and, as he proceeded, his manner lost its fiercer characteristics, and subsided, into gloom. "Dost thou remember me, Hester, as I was nine years agone? Even then, I was in the autumn of my days, nor was it the early autumn. But all my life had been made up of earnest, studious, thoughtful, quiet years, bestowed faithfully for the increase of mine own knowledge, and faithfully, too, though this latter object was but casual to the other,—faithfully for the advancement of human welfare. No life had been more peaceful and innocent than mine; few lives so rich with benefits conferred. Dost thou remember me? Was I not, though you might deem me cold, nevertheless a man thoughtful for others, craving little for himself,—kind, true, just, and of constant, if not warm affections? Was I not all this?"

"All this, and more," said Hester.

"And what am I now?" demanded he, looking into her face, and permitting the whole evil within him to be written on his features. "I have already told thee what I am! A fiend! Who made me so?"

"It was myself!" cried Hester, shuddering. "It was I, not less than he. Why hast thou not avenged thyself on me?"

"I have left thee to the scarlet letter," replied Roger Chillingworth. "If that have not avenged me, I can do no more!"

He laid his finger on it, with a smile.

"It has avenged thee!" answered Hester Prynne.

"I judged no less," said the physician. "And now what wouldst thou with me touching this man?"

"I must reveal the secret," answered Hester, firmly. "He must discern thee in thy true character. What may be the result, I know not. But this long debt of confidence, due from me to him, whose bane and ruin I have been, shall at length be paid. So far as concerns the overthrow or preservation of his fair fame and his earthly state, and perchance his life, he is in thy hands. Nor do I,—whom the scarlet letter has disciplined to truth, though it be the truth of red-hot iron, entering into the soul,—nor do I perceive such advantage in his living any longer a life of ghastly emptiness, that I shall stoop to implore thy mercy. Do with him as thou wilt! There is no good for him,—no good for me,—no good for thee! There is no good for little Pearl! There is no path to guide us out of this dismal maze!"

"Woman, I could wellnigh pity thee!" said Roger Chillingworth, unable to restrain a thrill of admiration too; for there was a quality almost majestic in the despair which she expressed. "Thou hadst great elements. Peradventure, hadst thou met earlier with a better love than mine, this evil had not been. I pity thee, for the good that has been wasted in thy nature!"

"And I thee," answered Hester Prynne, "for hatred that has transformed a wise and just man to a fiend! Wilt thou yet purge it out of thee, and be once more human? If not for his sake, then doubly for thine own! Forgive, and leave his further retribution to the Power that claims it! I said, but now, that there could be no good event for him, or thee, or me, who are here wandering together in this gloomy maze of evil, and stumbling, at every step, over the guilt wherewith we have strewn our path. It is not so! There might be good for thee, and thee alone, since thou hast been deeply wronged, and hast it at thy will to pardon. Wilt thou give up that only privilege? Wilt thou reject that priceless benefit?"

"Peace, Hester, peace!" replied the old man, with gloomy sternness. "It is not granted me to pardon. I have no such power as thou tellest me of. My old faith, long forgotten, comes back to me, and explains all that we do, and all we suffer. By thy first step awry, thou didst plant the germ of evil; but, since that moment, it has all been a dark necessity. Ye that have wronged me are not sinful, save in a kind of typical illusion; neither am I fiend-like, who have snatched a fiend's office from his hands. It is our fate. Let the black flower blossom as it may! Now go thy ways, and deal as thou wilt with yonder man."

He waved his hand, and betook himself again to his employment of gathering herbs.

XV: Hester and Pearl

So Roger Chillingworth—a deformed old figure, with a face that haunted men's memories longer than they liked—took leave of Hester Prynne, and went stooping away along the earth. He gathered here and there an herb, or grubbed up a root, and put it into the basket on his arm. His gray beard almost touched the ground, as he crept onward. Hester gazed after him a little while, looking with a half-fantastic curiosity to see whether the tender grass of early spring would not be blighted beneath him, and show the wavering track of his footsteps, sere and brown, across its cheerful verdure. She wondered what sort of herbs they were, which the old man was so sedulous to gather. Would not the earth, quickened to an evil purpose by the sympathy of his eye, greet him with poisonous shrubs, of species hitherto unknown, that would start up under his fingers? Or might it suffice him, that every wholesome growth should be converted into something deleterious and malignant at his touch? Did the sun, which shone so brightly everywhere else, really fall upon him? Or was there, as it rather seemed, a circle of ominous shadow moving along with his deformity, whichever way he turned himself? And whither was he now going? Would he not suddenly sink into the earth, leaving a barren and blasted spot, where, in due course of time, would be seen deadly nightshade, dogwood, henbane[79] and whatever else of vegetable wickedness the climate could produce, all flourishing with hideous luxuriance? Or would he spread bat's wings and flee away, looking so much the uglier, the higher he rose towards heaven?

"Be it sin or no," said Hester Prynne bitterly, as she still gazed after him, "I hate the man!"

She upbraided herself for the sentiment, but could not overcome or lessen it. Attempting to do so, she thought of those long-past days, in a distant land, when he used to emerge at eventide from the seclusion of his study, and sit down in the fire-light of their home, and in the light of her nuptial smile. He needed to bask himself in that smile, he said, in order that the chill of so many lonely hours among his books might be taken off the scholar's heart. Such scenes had once appeared not otherwise than happy, but now, as viewed through the dismal medium of her subsequent life, they classed themselves among her ugliest remembrances. She marvelled how such scenes could have been! She marvelled how she

---

[79] Deadly nightshade (or belladonna) and henbane are poisonous plants; all three plants are associated with witchcraft.

could ever have been wrought upon to marry him! She deemed it her crime most to be repented of, that she had ever endured, and reciprocated, the lukewarm grasp of his hand, and had suffered the smile of her lips and eyes to mingle and melt into his own. And it seemed a fouler offence committed by Roger Chillingworth, than any which had since been done him, that, in the time when her heart knew no better, he had persuaded her to fancy herself happy by his side.

"Yes, I hate him!" repeated Hester, more bitterly than before. "He betrayed me! He has done me worse wrong than I did him!"

Let men tremble to win the hand of woman, unless they win along with it the utmost passion of their heart! Else it may be their miserable fortune, as it was Roger Chillingworth's, when some mightier touch than their own may have awakened all her sensibilities, to be reproached even for the calm content, the marble image of happiness, which they will have imposed upon her as the warm reality. But Hester ought long ago to have done with this injustice. What did it betoken? Had seven long years, under the torture of the scarlet letter, inflicted so much of misery, and wrought out no repentance?

The emotions of that brief space, while she stood gazing after the crooked figure of old Roger Chillingworth, threw a dark light on Hester's state of mind, revealing much that she might not otherwise have acknowledged to herself.

He being gone, she summoned back her child.

"Pearl! Little Pearl! Where are you?"

Pearl, whose activity of spirit never flagged, had been at no loss for amusement while her mother talked with the old gatherer of herbs. At first, as already told, she had flirted fancifully with her own image in a pool of water, beckoning the phantom forth, and—as it declined to venture—seeking a passage for herself into its sphere of impalpable earth and unattainable sky. Soon finding, however, that either she or the image was unreal, she turned elsewhere for better pastime. She made little boats out of birch-bark, and freighted them with snail-shells, and sent out more ventures on the mighty deep than any merchant in New England; but the larger part of them foundered near the shore. She seized a live horseshoe[80] by the tail, and made prize of several five-fingers,[81] and laid out a jelly-fish to melt in the warm sun. Then she took up the white foam, that streaked the line of the advancing tide, and threw it upon the breeze, scampering after it with winged footsteps, to catch the great snow-flakes ere they fell. Perceiving a flock of beach-birds, that fed and fluttered along the shore, the naughty child picked up her apron full of pebbles, and, creeping from rock to rock after these small sea-fowl, displayed remarkable dexterity in pelting them. One little gray bird, with a white breast, Pearl was almost sure, had been hit by a pebble, and fluttered away with a broken wing. But then the elf-child sighed, and gave up her sport; because it grieved her to have done harm to a little being that was as wild as the sea-breeze, or as wild as Pearl herself.

Her final employment was to gather sea-weed, of various kinds, and make herself a scarf, or mantle, and a head-dress, and thus assume the aspect of a little mermaid. She inherited her mother's gift for devising drapery and costume. As the last touch to her mermaid's garb, Pearl took some eel-grass, and imitated, as best she could, on her own bosom, the decoration with which she was so familiar on her mother's. A letter,—the letter A,—but freshly green, instead of scarlet!

---

[80] A horseshoe crab.   [81] Starfish.

The child bent her chin upon her breast, and contemplated this device with strange interest; even as if the one only thing for which she had been sent into the world was to make out its hidden import.

"I wonder if mother will ask me what it means!" thought Pearl.

Just then, she heard her mother's voice, and, flitting along as lightly as one of the little sea-birds, appeared before Hester Prynne, dancing, laughing, and pointing her finger to the ornament upon her bosom.

"My little Pearl," said Hester, after a moment's silence, "the green letter, and on thy childish bosom, has no purport. But dost thou know, my child, what this letter means which thy mother is doomed to wear?"

"Yes, mother," said the child. "It is the great letter A. Thou hast taught it me in the horn-book."[82]

Hester looked steadily into her little face; but, though there was that singular expression which she had so often remarked in her black eyes, she could not satisfy herself whether Pearl really attached any meaning to the symbol. She felt a morbid desire to ascertain the point.

"Dost thou know, child, wherefore thy mother wears this letter?"

"Truly do I!" answered Pearl, looking brightly into her mother's face. "It is for the same reason that the minister keeps his hand over his heart!"

"And what reason is that?" asked Hester, half smiling at the absurd incongruity of the child's observation; but, on second thoughts, turning pale. "What has the letter to do with any heart, save mine?"

"Nay, mother, I have told all I know," said Pearl, more seriously than she was wont to speak. "Ask yonder old man whom thou hast been talking with! It may be he can tell. But in good earnest now, mother dear, what does this scarlet letter mean?—and why dost thou wear it on thy bosom?—and why does the minister keep his hand over his heart?"

She took her mother's hand in both her own, and gazed into her eyes with an earnestness that was seldom seen in her wild and capricious character. The thought occurred to Hester, that the child might really be seeking to approach her with childlike confidence, and doing what she could, and as intelligently as she knew how, to establish a meeting-point of sympathy. It showed Pearl in an unwonted aspect. Heretofore, the mother, while loving her child with the intensity of a sole affection, had schooled herself to hope for little other return than the waywardness of an April breeze; which spends its time in airy sport, and has its gusts of inexplicable passion, and is petulant in its best of moods, and chills oftener than caresses you, when you take it to your bosom; in requital of which misdemeanours, it will sometimes, of its own vague purpose, kiss your cheek with a kind of doubtful tenderness, and play gently with your hair, and then begone about its other idle business, leaving a dreamy pleasure at your heart. And this, moreover, was a mother's estimate of the child's disposition. Any other observer might have seen few but unamiable traits, and have given them a far darker coloring. But now the idea came strongly into Hester's mind, that Pearl, with her remarkable precocity and acuteness, might already have approached the age when she could be made a friend, and intrusted with as much of her mother's sorrows as could be imparted, without irreverence either to the parent or the child. In the little

---

[82] A primer, used to teach spelling and reading, that consisted of a single page protected by a transparent sheet of horn.

chaos of Pearl's character, there might be seen emerging—and could have been, from the very first—the steadfast principles of an unflinching courage,—an uncontrollable will,—a sturdy pride, which might be disciplined into self-respect,—and a bitter scorn of many things, which, when examined, might be found to have the taint of falsehood in them. She possessed affections, too, though hitherto acrid and disagreeable, as are the richest flavors of unripe fruit. With all these sterling attributes, thought Hester, the evil which she inherited from her mother must be great indeed, if a noble woman do not grow out of this elfish child.

Pearl's inevitable tendency to hover about the enigma of the scarlet letter seemed an innate quality of her being. From the earliest epoch of her conscious life, she had entered upon this as her appointed mission. Hester had often fancied that Providence had a design of justice and retribution, in endowing the child with this marked propensity; but never, until now, had she bethought herself to ask, whether, linked with that design, there might not likewise be a purpose of mercy and beneficence. If little Pearl were entertained with faith and trust, as a spirit-messenger no less than an earthly child, might it not be her errand to soothe away the sorrow that lay cold in her mother's heart, and converted it into a tomb?—and to help her to overcome the passion, once so wild, and even yet neither dead nor asleep, but only imprisoned within the same tomb-like heart?

Such were some of the thoughts that now stirred in Hester's mind, with as much vivacity of impression as if they had actually been whispered into her ear. And there was little Pearl, all this while, holding her mother's hand in both her own, and turning her face upward, while she put these searching questions, once, and again, and still a third time.

"What does the letter mean, mother?—and why dost thou wear it?—and why does the minister keep his hand over his heart?"

"What shall I say?" thought Hester to herself.—"No! If this be the price of the child's sympathy, I cannot pay it!"

Then she spoke aloud.

"Silly Pearl," said she, "what questions are these? There are many things in this world that a child must not ask about. What know I of the minister's heart? And as for the scarlet letter, I wear it for the sake of its gold thread!"

In all the seven bygone years, Hester Prynne had never before been false to the symbol on her bosom. It may be that it was the talisman of a stern and severe, but yet a guardian spirit, who now forsook her; as recognizing that, in spite of his strict watch over her heart, some new evil had crept into it, or some old one had never been expelled. As for little Pearl, the earnestness soon passed out of her face.

But the child did not see fit to let the matter drop. Two or three times, as her mother and she went homeward, and as often at supper-time, and while Hester was putting her to bed, and once after she seemed to be fairly asleep, Pearl looked up, with mischief gleaming in her black eyes.

"Mother," said she, "what does the scarlet letter mean?"

And the next morning, the first indication the child gave of being awake was by popping up her head from the pillow, and making that other inquiry, which she had so unaccountably connected with her investigations about the scarlet letter:—

"Mother!—Mother!—Why does the minister keep his hand over his heart?"

"Hold thy tongue, naughty child!" answered her mother, with an asperity that she had never permitted to herself before. "Do not tease me; else I shall shut thee into the dark closet!"

XVI: A Forest Walk

Hester Prynne remained constant in her resolve to make known to Mr. Dimmesdale, at whatever risk of present pain or ulterior consequences, the true character of the man who had crept into his intimacy. For several days, however, she vainly sought an opportunity of addressing him in some of the meditative walks which she knew him to be in the habit of taking, along the shores of the peninsula, or on the wooded hills of the neighbouring country. There would have been no scandal, indeed, nor peril to the holy whiteness of the clergyman's good fame, had she visited him in his own study; where many a penitent, ere now, had confessed sins of perhaps as deep a dye as the one betokened by the scarlet letter. But, partly that she dreaded the secret or undisguised interference of old Roger Chillingworth, and partly that her conscious heart imputed suspicion where none could have been felt, and partly that both the minister and she would need the whole wide world to breathe in, while they talked together,—for all these reasons, Hester never thought of meeting him in any narrower privacy than beneath the open sky.

At last, while attending in a sick-chamber, whither the Reverend Mr. Dimmesdale had been summoned to make a prayer, she learnt that he had gone, the day before, to visit the Apostle Eliot,[83] among his Indian converts. He would probably return, by a certain hour, in the afternoon of the morrow. Betimes, therefore, the next day, Hester took little Pearl,—who was necessarily the companion of all her mother's expeditions, however inconvenient her presence,—and set forth.

The road, after the two wayfarers had crossed from the peninsula to the mainland, was no other than a footpath. It straggled onward into the mystery of the primeval forest. This hemmed it in so narrowly, and stood so black and dense on either side, and disclosed such imperfect glimpses of the sky above, that, to Hester's mind, it imaged not amiss the moral wilderness in which she had so long been wandering. The day was chill and sombre. Overhead was a gray expanse of cloud, slightly stirred, however, by a breeze; so that a gleam of flickering sunshine might now and then be seen at its solitary play along the path. This flitting cheerfulness was always at the farther extremity of some long vista through the forest. The sportive sunlight—feebly sportive, at best, in the predominant pensiveness of the day and scene—withdrew itself as they came nigh, and left the spots where it had danced the drearier, because they had hoped to find them bright.

"Mother," said little Pearl, "the sunshine does not love you. It runs away and hides itself, because it is afraid of something on your bosom. Now, see! There it is, playing, a good way off. Stand you here, and let me run and catch it. I am but a child. It will not flee from me; for I wear nothing on my bosom yet!"

"Nor ever will, my child, I hope," said Hester.

"And why not, mother? asked Pearl, stopping short, just at the beginning of her race. "Will not it come of its own accord, when I am a woman grown?"

"Run away, child," answered her mother, "and catch the sunshine! It will soon be gone."

Pearl set forth, at a great pace, and, as Hester smiled to perceive, did actually catch the sunshine, and stood laughing in the midst of it, all brightened by its splendor, and scintillating with the vivacity excited by rapid motion. The light

---

[83] John Eliot (1604–1690) one of the few Puritans who took an interest in converting the local Native-American tribes; he became known as the "Apostle to the Indians."

lingered about the lonely child, as if glad of such a playmate, until her mother had drawn almost nigh enough to step into the magic circle too.

"It will go now!" said Pearl, shaking her head.

"See!" answered Hester, smiling, "Now I can stretch out my hand, and grasp some of it."

As she attempted to do so, the sunshine vanished; or, to judge from the bright expression that was dancing on Pearl's features, her mother could have fancied that the child had absorbed it into herself, and would give it forth again, with a gleam about her path, as they should plunge into some gloomier shade. There was no other attribute that so much impressed her with a sense of new and untransmitted vigor in Pearl's nature, as this never-failing vivacity of spirits; she had not the disease of sadness, which almost all children, in these latter days, inherit, with the scrofula,[84] from the troubles of their ancestors. Perhaps this too was a disease, and but the reflex of the wild energy with which Hester had fought against her sorrows, before Pearl's birth. It was certainly a doubtful charm, imparting a hard, metallic lustre to the child's character. She wanted—what some people want throughout life—a grief that should deeply touch her, and thus humanize and make her capable of sympathy. But there was time enough yet for little Pearl!

"Come, my child!" said Hester, looking about her, from the spot where Pearl had stood still in the sunshine. "We will sit down a little way within the wood, and rest ourselves."

"I am not aweary, mother," replied the little girl. "But you may sit down, if you will tell me a story meanwhile."

"A story, child!" said Hester. "And about what?"

"O, a story about the Black Man!" answered Pearl, taking hold of her mother's gown, and looking up, half earnestly, half mischievously, into her face. "How he haunts this forest, and carries a book with him,—a big, heavy book, with iron clasps; and how this ugly Black Man offers his book and an iron pen to every body that meets him here among the trees; and they are to write their names with their own blood. And then he sets his mark on their bosoms! Didst thou ever meet the Black Man, mother?"

"And who told you this story, Pearl?" asked her mother, recognizing a common superstition of the period.

"It was the old dame in the chimney-corner, at the house where you watched last night," said the child. "But she fancied me asleep while she was talking of it. She said that a thousand and a thousand people had met him here, and had written in his book, and have his mark on them. And that ugly-tempered lady, old Mistress Hibbins, was one. And, mother, the old dame said that this scarlet letter was the Black Man's mark on thee, and that it glows like a red flame when thou meetest him at midnight, here in the dark wood. Is it true, mother? And dost thou go to meet him in the night-time?"

"Didst thou ever awake, and find thy mother gone?" asked Hester.

"Not that I remember," said the child. "If thou fearest to leave me in our cottage, thou mightest take me along with thee. I would very gladly go! But, mother, tell me now! Is there such a Black Man? And didst thou ever meet him? And is this his mark?"

"Wilt thou let me be at peace, if I once tell thee?" asked her mother.

"Yes, if thou tellest me all," answered Pearl.

---

[84] Tuberculosis of the lymph glands, typically affecting children.

"Once in my life I met the Black Man!" said her mother. "This scarlet letter is his mark!"

Thus conversing, they entered sufficiently deep into the wood to secure themselves from the observation of any casual passenger along the forest-track. Here they sat down on a luxuriant heap of moss; which, at some epoch of the preceding century, had been a gigantic pine, with its roots and trunk in the darksome shade, and its head aloft in the upper atmosphere. It was a little dell where they had seated themselves, with a leaf-strewn bank rising gently on either side, and a brook flowing through the midst, over a bed of fallen and drowned leaves. The trees impending over it had flung down great branches, from time to time, which choked up the current, and compelled it to form eddies and black depths at some points; while, in its swifter and livelier passages, there appeared a channel-way of pebbles, and brown, sparkling sand. Letting the eyes follow along the course of the stream, they could catch the reflected light from its water, at some short distance within the forest, but soon lost all traces of it amid the bewilderment of tree-trunks and underbrush, and here and there a huge rock, covered over with gray lichens. All these giant trees and boulders of granite seemed intent on making a mystery of the course of this small brook; fearing, perhaps, that, with its never-ceasing loquacity, it should whisper tales out of the heart of the old forest whence it flowed, or mirror its revelations on the smooth surface of a pool. Continually, indeed, as it stole onward, the streamlet kept up a babble, kind, quiet, soothing, but melancholy, like the voice of a young child that was spending its infancy without playfulness, and knew not how to be merry among sad acquaintance and events of sombre hue.

"O brook! O foolish and tiresome little brook!" cried Pearl, after listening awhile to its talk. "Why art thou so sad? Pluck up a spirit, and do not be all the time sighing and murmuring!"

But the brook, in the course of its little lifetime among the forest-trees, had gone through so solemn an experience that it could not help talking about it, and seemed to have nothing else to say. Pearl resembled the brook, inasmuch as the current of her life gushed from a well-spring as mysterious, and had flowed through scenes shadowed as heavily with gloom. But, unlike the little stream, she danced and sparkled, and prattled airily along her course.

"What does this sad little brook say, mother?" inquired she.

"If thou hadst a sorrow of thine own, the brook might tell thee of it," answered her mother, "even as it is telling me of mine! But now, Pearl, I hear a footstep along the path, and the noise of one putting aside the branches. I would have thee betake thyself to play, and leave me to speak with him that comes yonder."

"Is it the Black Man?" asked Pearl.

"Wilt thou go and play, child?" repeated her mother. "But do not stray far into the wood. And take heed that thou come at my first call."

"Yes, mother," answered Pearl. "But, if it be the Black Man, wilt thou not let me stay a moment, and look at him, with his big book under his arm?"

"Go, silly child!" said her mother, impatiently. "It is no Black Man! Thou canst see him now through the trees. It is the minister!"

"And so it is!" said the child. "And, mother, he has his hand over his heart! Is it because, when the minister wrote his name in the book, the Black Man set his mark in that place? But why does he not wear it outside his bosom, as thou dost, mother?"

"Go now, child, and thou shalt tease me as thou wilt another time!" cried

Hester Prynne. "But do not stray far. Keep where thou canst hear the babble of the brook."

The child went singing away, following up the current of the brook, and striving to mingle a more lightsome cadence with its melancholy voice. But the little stream would not be comforted, and still kept telling its unintelligible secret of some very mournful mystery that had happened—or making a prophetic lamentation about something that was yet to happen—within the verge of the dismal forest. So Pearl, who had enough of shadow in her own little life, chose to break off all acquaintance with this repining brook. She set herself, therefore, to gathering violets and wood-anemones, and some scarlet columbines that she found growing in the crevices of a high rock.

When her elf-child had departed, Hester Prynne made a step or two towards the track that led through the forest, but still remained under the deep shadow of the trees. She beheld the minister advancing along the path, entirely alone, and leaning on a staff which he had cut by the way-side. He looked haggard and feeble, and betrayed a nerveless despondency in his air, which had never so remarkably characterized him in his walks about the settlement, nor in any other situation where he deemed himself liable to notice. Here it was wofully visible, in this intense seclusion of the forest, which of itself would have been a heavy trial to the spirits. There was a listlessness in his gait; as if he saw no reason for taking one step farther, nor felt any desire to do so, but would have been glad, could he be glad of any thing, to fling himself down at the root of the nearest tree, and lie there passive for evermore. The leaves might bestrew him, and the soil gradually accumulate and form a little hillock over his frame, no matter whether there were life in it or no. Death was too definite an object to be wished for, or avoided.

To Hester's eye, the Reverend Mr. Dimmesdale exhibited no symptom of positive and vivacious suffering, except that, as little Pearl had remarked, he kept his hand over his heart.

XVII: *The Pastor and His Parishioner*

Slowly as the minister walked, he had almost gone by, before Hester Prynne could gather voice enough to attract his observation. At length, she succeeded.

"Arthur Dimmesdale!" she said, faintly at first; then louder, but hoarsely. "Arthur Dimmesdale!"

"Who speaks?" answered the minister.

Gathering himself quickly up, he stood more erect, like a man taken by surprise in a mood to which he was reluctant to have witnesses. Throwing his eyes anxiously in the direction of the voice, he indistinctly beheld a form under the trees, clad in garments so sombre, and so little relieved from the gray twilight into which the clouded sky and the heavy foliage had darkened the noontide, that he knew not whether it were a woman or a shadow. It may be, that his pathway through life was haunted thus, by a spectre that had stolen out from among his thoughts.

He made a step nigher, and discovered the scarlet letter.

"Hester! Hester Prynne!" said he. "Is it thou? Art thou in life?"

"Even so!" she answered. "In such life as has been mine these seven years past! And thou, Arthur Dimmesdale, dost thou yet live?"

It was no wonder that they thus questioned one another's actual and bodily existence, and even doubted of their own. So strangely did they meet, in the dim wood, that it was like the first encounter, in the world beyond the grave, of two spirits who had been intimately connected in their former life, but now stood coldly shuddering, in mutual dread; as not yet familiar with their state, nor wonted to the companionship of disembodied beings. Each a ghost, and awe-stricken at the other ghost! They were awe-stricken likewise at themselves; because the crisis flung back to them their consciousness, and revealed to each heart its history and experience, as life never does, except at such breathless epochs. The soul beheld its features in the mirror of the passing moment. It was with fear, and tremulously, and, as it were, by a slow, reluctant necessity, that Arthur Dimmesdale put forth his hand, chill as death, and touched the chill hand of Hester Prynne. The grasp, cold as it was, took away what was dreariest in the interview. They now felt themselves, at least, inhabitants of the same sphere.

Without a word more spoken,—neither he nor she assuming the guidance, but with an unexpressed consent,—they glided back into the shadow of the woods, whence Hester had emerged, and sat down on the heap of moss where she and Pearl had before been sitting. When they found voice to speak, it was, at first, only to utter remarks and inquiries such as any two acquaintance might have made, about the gloomy sky, the threatening storm, and, next, the health of each. Thus they went onward, not boldly, but step by set, into the themes that were brooding deepest in their hearts. So long estranged by fate and circumstances, they needed something slight and casual to run before, and throw open the doors of intercourse, so that their real thoughts might be led across the threshold.

After a while, the minister fixed his eyes on Hester Prynne's.

"Hester," said he, "hast thou found peace?"

She smiled drearily, looking down upon her bosom.

"Hast thou?" she asked.

"None!—nothing but despair!" he answered. "What else could I look for, being what I am, and leading such a life as mine? Were I an atheist,—a man devoid of conscience,—a wretch with coarse and brutal instincts,—I might have found peace, long ere now. Nay, I never should have lost it! But, as matters stand with my soul, whatever of good capacity there originally was in me, all of God's gifts that were the choicest have become the ministers of spiritual torment. Hester, I am most miserable!"

"The people reverence thee," said Hester. "And surely thou workest good among them! Doth this bring thee no comfort?"

"More misery, Hester!—only the more misery!" answered the clergyman, with a bitter smile. "As concerns the good which I may appear to do, I have no faith in it. It must needs be a delusion. What can a ruined soul, like mine, effect towards the redemption of other souls?—or a polluted soul, towards their purification? And as for the people's reverence, would that it were turned to scorn and hatred! Canst thou deem it, Hester, a consolation, that I must stand up in my pulpit, and meet so many eyes turned upward to my face, as if the light of heaven were beaming from it!—must see my flock hungry for the truth, and listening to my words as if a tongue of Pentecost were speaking!—and then look inward, and discern the black reality of what they idolize? I have laughed, in bitterness and agony of heart, at the contrast between what I seem and what I am! And Satan laughs at it!"

"You wrong yourself in this," said Hester, gently. "You have deeply and sorely repented. Your sin is left behind you, in the days long past. Your present life is not less holy, in very truth, than it seems in people's eyes. Is there no reality in the penitence thus sealed and witnessed by good works? And wherefore should it not bring you peace?"

"No, Hester, no!" replied the clergyman. "There is no substance in it! It is cold and dead, and can do nothing for me! Of penance I have had enough! Of penitence there has been none! Else, I should long ago have thrown off these garments of mock holiness, and have shown myself to mankind as they will see me at the judgment-seat. Happy are you, Hester, that wear the scarlet letter openly upon your bosom! Mine burns in secret! Thou little knowest what a relief it is, after the torment of a seven years' cheat, to look into an eye that recognizes me for what I am! Had I one friend,—or were it my worst enemy!—to whom, when sickened with the praises of all other men, I could daily betake myself, and be known as the vilest of all sinners, methinks my soul might keep itself alive thereby. Even thus much of truth would save me! But, now, it is all falsehood!—all emptiness!—all death!"

Hester Prynne looked into his face, but hesitated to speak. Yet, uttering his long-restrained emotions so vehemently as he did, his words here offered her the very point of circumstances in which to interpose what she came to say. She conquered her fears, and spoke.

"Such a friend as thou hast even now wished for," said she, "with whom to weep over thy sin, thou hast in me, the partner of it!"—Again she hesitated, but brought out the words with an effort.—"Thou hast long had such an enemy, and dwellest with him under the same roof!"

The minister started to his feet, gasping for breath, and clutching at his heart as if he would have torn it out of his bosom.

"Ha! What sayest thou?" cried he. "An enemy! And under mine own roof! What mean you?"

Hester Prynne was now fully sensible of the deep injury for which she was responsible to this unhappy man, in permitting him to lie for so many years, or, indeed, for a single moment, at the mercy of one, whose purposes could not be other than malevolent. The very contiguity of his enemy, beneath whatever mask the latter might conceal himself, was enough to disturb the magnetic sphere of a being so sensitive as Arthur Dimmesdale. There had been a period when Hester was less alive to this consideration; or, perhaps, in the misanthropy of her own trouble, she left the minister to bear what she might picture to herself as a more tolerable doom. But of late, since the night of his vigil, all her sympathies towards him had been both softened and invigorated. She now read his heart more accurately. She doubted not, that the continual presence of Roger Chillingworth,—the secret poison of his malignity, infecting all the air about him,—and his authorized interference, as a physician, with the minister's physical and spiritual infirmities,—that these bad opportunities had been turned to a cruel purpose. By means of them, the sufferer's conscience had been kept in an irritated state, the tendency of which was, not to cure by wholesome pain, but to disorganize and corrupt his spiritual being. Its result, on earth, could hardly fail to be insanity, and hereafter, that eternal alienation from the Good and True, of which madness is perhaps the earthly type.

Such was the ruin to which she had brought the man, once,—nay, why should we not speak it?—still so passionately loved! Hester felt that the sacrifice of the clergyman's good name, and death itself, as she had already told Roger Chillingworth, would have been infinitely preferable to the alternative which she had taken upon herself to choose. And now, rather than have had this grievous wrong to confess, she would gladly have lain down on the forest-leaves, and died there, at Arthur Dimmesdale's feet.

"Oh Arthur," cried she, "forgive me! In all things else, I have striven to be true! Truth was the one virtue which I might have held fast, and did hold fast through all extremity; save when thy good,—thy life,—thy fame,—were put in question! Then I consented to a deception. But a lie is never good, even though death threaten on the other side! Dost thou not see what I would say? That old man!—the physician!—he whom they call Roger Chillingworth!—he was my husband!"

The minister looked at her, for an instant, with all that violence of passion, which—intermixed, in more shapes than one, with his higher, purer, softer qualities—was, in fact, the portion of him which the Devil claimed, and through which he sought to win the rest. Never was there a blacker or a fiercer frown, than Hester now encountered. For the brief space that it lasted, it was a dark transfiguration. But his character had been so much enfeebled by suffering, that even its lower energies were incapable of more than a temporary struggle. He sank down on the ground, and buried his face in his hands.

"I might have known it!" murmured he. "I did know it! Was not the secret told me in the natural recoil of my heart, at the first sight of him, and as often as I have seen him since? Why did I not understand? O Hester Prynne, thou little, little knowest all the horror of this thing! And the shame!—the indelicacy!—the horrible ugliness of this exposure of a sick and guilty heart to the very eye that would gloat over it! Woman, woman, thou art accountable for this! I cannot forgive thee!"

"Thou shalt forgive me!" cried Hester, flinging herself on the fallen leaves beside him. "Let God punish! Thou shalt forgive!"

With sudden and desperate tenderness, she threw her arms around him, and pressed his head against her bosom; little caring though his cheek rested on the scarlet letter. He would have released himself, but strove in vain to do so. Hester would not set him free, lest he should look her sternly in the face. All the world had frowned on her,—for seven long years had it frowned upon this lonely woman,—and still she bore it all, nor ever once turned away her firm, sad eyes. Heaven, likewise, had frowned upon her, and she had not died. But the frown of this pale, weak, sinful, and sorrow-stricken man was what Hester could not bear, and live!

"Wilt thou yet forgive me?" she repeated, over and over again. "Wilt thou not frown? Wilt thou forgive?"

"I do forgive you, Hester," replied the minister, at length, with a deep utterance out of an abyss of sadness, but no anger. "I freely forgive you now. May God forgive us both! We are not, Hester, the worst sinners in the world. There is one worse than even the polluted priest! That old man's revenge has been blacker than my sin. He has violated, in cold blood, the sanctity of a human heart. Thou and I, Hester, never did so!"

"Never, never!" whispered she. "What we did had a consecration of its own. We felt it so! We said so to each other! Hast thou forgotten it?"

"Hush, Hester!" said Arthur Dimmesdale, rising from the ground. "No; I have not forgotten!"

They sat down again, side by side, and hand clasped in hand, on the mossy trunk of the fallen tree. Life had never brought them a gloomier hour; it was the point whither their pathway had so long been tending, and darkening ever, as it stole along;—and yet it inclosed a charm that made them linger upon it, and claim another, and another, and, after all, another moment. The forest was obscure around them, and creaked with a blast that was passing through it. The boughs were tossing heavily above their heads; while one solemn old tree groaned dolefully to another, as it telling the sad story of the pair that sat beneath, or constrained to forbode evil to come.

And yet they lingered. How dreary looked the forest-track that led backward to the settlement, where Hester Prynne must take up again the burden of her ignominy, and the minister the hollow mockery of his good name! So they lingered an instant longer. No golden light had ever been so precious as the gloom of this dark forest. Here, seen only by his eyes, the scarlet letter need not burn into the bosom of the fallen woman! Here, seen only by her eyes, Arthur Dimmesdale, false to God and man, might be, for one moment, true!

He started at a thought that suddenly occurred to him.

"Hester," cried he, "here is a new horror! Roger Chillingworth knows your purpose to reveal his true character. Will he continue, then, to keep our secret? What will now be the course of his revenge?"

"There is a strange secrecy in his nature," replied Hester, thoughtfully; "and it has grown upon him by the hidden practices of his revenge. I deem it not likely that he will betray the secret. He will doubtless seek other means of satiating his dark passion."

"And I!—how am I to live longer, breathing the same air with this deadly enemy?" exclaimed Arthur Dimmesdale, shrinking within himself, and pressing his hand nervously against his heart,—a gesture that had grown involuntary with him. "Think for me, Hester! Thou art strong. Resolve for me!"

"Thou must dwell no longer with this man," said Hester, slowly and firmly. "Thy heart must be no longer under his evil eye!"

"It were far worse than death!" replied the minister. "But how to avoid it? What choice remains to me? Shall I lie down again on these withered leaves, where I cast myself when thou didst tell me what he was? Must I sink down there, and die at once?"

"Alas, what a ruin has befallen thee!" said Hester, with the tears gushing into her eyes. "Wilt thou die for very weakness? There is no other cause!"

"The judgment of God is on me," answered the conscience-stricken priest. "It is too mighty for me to struggle with!"

"Heaven would show mercy," rejoined Hester, "hadst thou but the strength to take advantage of it."

"Be thou strong for me!" answered he. "Advise me what to do."

"Is the world then so narrow?" exclaimed Hester Prynne, fixing her deep eyes on the minister's, and instinctively exercising a magnetic power over a spirit so shattered and subdued, that it could hardly hold itself erect. "Doth the universe lie within the compass of yonder town, which only a little time ago was but a leaf-strewn desert, as lonely as this around us? Whither leads yonder forest-track? Backward to the settlement, thou sayest! Yes; but onward, too! Deeper it goes, and deeper, into the wilderness, less plainly to be seen at every step; until, some few miles hence, the yellow leaves will show no vestige of the white man's tread. There thou art free! So brief a journey would bring thee from a world where thou hast been most wretched, to one where thou mayest still be happy! Is there not shade enough in all this boundless forest to hide thy heart from the gaze of Roger Chillingworth?"

"Yes, Hester; but only under the fallen leaves!" replied the minister, with a sad smile.

"Then there is the broad pathway of the sea!" continued Hester. "It brought thee hither. If thou so choose, it will bear thee back again. In our native land, whether in some remote rural village or in vast London,—or, surely, in Germany, in France, in pleasant Italy,—thou wouldst be beyond his power and knowledge! And what hast thou to do with all these iron men, and their opinions? They have kept thy better part in bondage too long already!"

"It cannot be!" answered the minister, listening as if he were called upon to realize a dream. "I am powerless to go. Wretched and sinful as I am, I have had no other thought than to drag on my earthly existence in the sphere where Providence hath placed me. Lost as my own soul is, I would still do what I may for other human souls! I dare not quit my post, though an unfaithful sentinel, whose sure reward is death and dishonor, when his dreary watch shall come to an end!"

"Thou art crushed under this seven years' weight of misery," replied Hester, fervently resolved to buoy him up with her own energy. "But thou shalt leave it all behind thee! It shall not cumber thy steps, as thou treadest along the forest path; neither shalt thou freight the ship with it, if thou prefer to cross the sea. Leave this wreck and ruin here where it hath happened! Meddle no more with it! Begin all anew! Hast thou exhausted possibility in the failure of this one trial? Not so! The future is yet full of trial and success. There is happiness to be enjoyed! There is good to be done! Exchange this false life of thine for a true one. Be, if thy spirit summon thee to such a mission, the teacher and apostle of the red men. Or,—as is more thy nature,—be a scholar and a sage among the wisest and the most renowned of the cultivated world. Preach! Write! Act! Do any thing, save to lie down and die! Give up this name of Arthur Dimmesdale, and make thyself another, and a high one, such as thou canst wear without fear or shame. Why shouldst thou tarry so much as one other day in the torments that have so gnawed into thy life!—that have made thee feeble to will and to do!—that will leave thee powerless even to repent! Up, and away!"

"O Hester!" cried Arthur Dimmesdale, in whose eyes a fitful light, kindled by her enthusiasm, flashed up and died away, "thou tellest of running a race to a man whose knees are tottering beneath him! I must die here. There is not the strength or courage left me to venture into the wide, strange, difficult world, alone!"

It was the last expression of the despondency of a broken spirit. He lacked energy to grasp the better fortune that seemed within his reach.

He repeated the word.

"Alone, Hester!"

"Thou shalt not go alone!" answered she, in a deep whisper.

Then, all was spoken!

XVIII: A Flood of Sunshine

Arthur Dimmesdale gazed into Hester's face with a look in which hope and joy shone out, indeed, but with fear betwixt them, and a kind of horror at her boldness, who had spoken what he vaguely hinted at, but dared not speak.

But Hester Prynne, with a mind of native courage and activity, and for so long a period not merely estranged, but outlawed, from society, had habituated herself to such latitude of speculation as was altogether foreign to the clergyman. She had wandered, without rule or guidance, in a moral wilderness; as vast, as intricate and shadowy, as the untamed forest, amid the gloom of which they were now holding a colloquy that was to decide their fate. Her intellect and heart had their home, as it were, in desert places, where she roamed as freely as the wild Indian in his woods. For years past she had looked from this estranged point of view at human institutions, and whatever priests or legislators had established; criticizing all with hardly more reverence than the Indian would feel for the clerical band, the judicial robe, the pillory, the gallows, the fireside, or the church. The tendency of her fate and fortunes had been to set her free. The scarlet letter was her passport into regions where other women dared not tread. Shame, Despair, Solitude! These had been her teachers,—stern and wild ones,—and they had make her strong, but taught her much amiss.

The minister, on the other hand, had never gone through an experience calculated to lead him beyond the scope of generally received laws; although, in a single instance, he had so fearfully transgressed one of the most sacred of them. But this had been a sin of passion, not of principle, nor even purpose. Since that wretched epoch, he had watched, with morbid zeal and minuteness, not his acts,—for those it was easy to arrange,—but each breath of emotion, and his every thought. At the head of the social system, as the clergymen of that day stood, he was only the more trammelled by its regulations, its principles, and even its prejudices. As a priest, the framework of his order inevitably hemmed him in. As a man who had once sinned, but who kept his conscience all alive and painfully sensitive by the fretting of an unhealed wound, he might have been supposed safer within the line of virtue, than if he had never sinned at all.

Thus, we seem to see that, as regarded Hester Prynne, the whole seven years of outlaw and ignominy had been little other than a preparation for this very hour. But Arthur Dimmesdale! Were such a man once more to fall, what plea could be urged in extenuation of his crime? None; unless it avail him somewhat, that he was broken down by long and exquisite suffering; that his mind was darkened and confused by the very remorse which harrowed it; that, between fleeing as an avowed criminal, and remaining as a hypocrite, conscience might find it hard to strike the balance; that it was human to avoid the peril of death and infamy, and the inscrutable machinations of an enemy; that, finally, to this poor pilgrim, on his dreary and desert path, faint, sick, miserable, there appeared a glimpse of human affection and sympathy, a new life, and a true one, in exchange for the heavy doom which he was now expiating. And be the stern and sad truth spoken, that the breach which guilt has once made into the human soul is never, in this mortal state, repaired. It may be watched and guarded; so that the enemy shall not force his way again into the citadel, and might even, in his subsequent assaults, select some other avenue, in preference to that where he had formerly succeeded. But there is still the ruined wall, and, near it, the stealthy tread of the foe that would win over again his unforgotten triumph.

The struggle, if there were one, need not be described. Let if suffice, that the clergyman resolved to flee, and not alone.

"If, in all these past seven years," thought he, "I could recall one instant of peace or hope, I would yet endure, for the sake of that earnest of Heaven's mercy. But now,—since I am irrevocably doomed,—wherefore should I not snatch the solace allowed to the condemned culprit before his execution? Or, if this be the path to a better life, as Hester would persuade me, I surely give up no fairer prospect by pursuing it! Neither can I any longer live without her companionship;

so powerful is she to sustain,—so tender to soothe! O Thou to whom I dare not lift mine eyes, wilt Thou yet pardon me!"

"Thou wilt go!" said Hester calmly, as he met her glance.

The decision once made, a glow of strange enjoyment threw its flickering brightness over the trouble of his breast. It was the exhilarating effect—upon a prisoner just escaped from the dungeon of his own heart—of breathing the wild, free atmosphere of an unredeemed, unchristianized, lawless region. His spirit rose, as it were, with a bound, and attained a nearer prospect of the sky, than throughout all the misery which had kept him grovelling on the earth. Of a deeply religious temperament, there was inevitably a tinge of the devotional in his mood.

"Do I feel joy again?" cried he, wondering at himself. "Methought the germ of it was dead in me! O Hester, thou art my better angel! I seem to have flung myself—sick, sin-stained, and sorrow-blackened—down upon these forest-leaves, and to have risen up all made anew, and with new powers to glorify Him that hath been merciful! This is already the better life! Why did we not find it sooner?"

"Let us not look back," answered Hester Prynne. "The past is gone! Wherefore should we linger upon it now? See! With this symbol, I undo it all, and make it as it had never been!"

So speaking, she undid the clasp that fastened the scarlet letter, and, taking it from her bosom, threw it to a distance among the withered leaves. The mystic token alighted on the hither verge of the stream. With a hand's breadth farther flight it would have fallen into the water, and have given the little brook another woe to carry onward, besides the unintelligible tale which it still kept murmuring about. But there lay the embroidered letter, glittering like a lost jewel, which some ill-fated wonderer might pick up, and thenceforth be haunted by strange phantoms of guilt, sinkings of the heart, and unaccountable misfortune.

The stigma gone, Hester heaved a long, deep sigh, in which the burden of shame and anguish departed from her spirit. O exquisite relief! She had not known the weight, until she felt the freedom! By another impulse, she took off the formal cap that confined her hair; and down it fell upon her shoulders, dark and rich, with at once a shadow and a light in its abundance, and imparting the charm of softness to her features. There played around her mouth, and beamed out of her eyes, a radiant and tender smile, that seemed gushing from the very heart of womanhood. A crimson flush was glowing on her cheek, that had been long so pale. Her sex, her youth, and the whole richness of her beauty, came back from what men call the irrevocable past, and clustered themselves, with her maiden hope, and a happiness before unknown, within the magic circle of this hour. And, as if the gloom of the earth and sky had been but the effluence of these two mortal hearts, it vanished with their sorrow. All at once, as with a sudden smile of heaven, forth burst the sunshine, pouring a very flood into the obscure forest, gladdening each green leaf, transmuting the yellow fallen ones to gold, and gleaming adown the gray trunks of the solemn trees. The objects that had made a shadow hitherto, embodied the brightness now. The course of the little brook might be traced by its merry gleam afar into the wood's heart of mystery, which had become a mystery of joy.

Such was the sympathy of Nature—that wild, heathen Nature of the forest, never subjugated by human law, nor illumined by higher truth—with the bliss of these two spirits! Love, whether newly born, or aroused from a deathlike slumber, must always create a sunshine, filling the heart so full of radiance, that it overflows upon the outward world. Had the forest still kept its gloom, it would have been bright in Hester's eyes, and bright in Arthur Dimmesdale's!

Hester looked at him with the thrill of another joy.

"Thou must know Pearl!" said she. "Our little Pearl! Thou hast seen her,—yes, I know it!—but thou wilt see her now with other eyes. She is a strange child! I hardly comprehend her! But thou wilt love her dearly, as I do, and wilt advise me how to deal with her."

"Dost thou think the child will be glad to know me?" asked the minister, somewhat uneasily. "I have long shrunk from children, because they often show a distrust,—a backwardness to be familiar with me. I have even been afraid of little Pearl!"

"Ah, that was sad!" answered the mother. "But she will love thee dearly, and thou her. She is not far off. I will call her! Pearl! Pearl!"

"I see the child," observed the minister. "Yonder she is, standing in a streak of sunshine, a good way off, on the other side of the brook. So thou thinkest the child will love me?"

Hester smiled, and again called to Pearl, who was visible, at some distance, as the minister had described her, like a bright-apparelled vision, in a sunbeam, which fell down upon her through an arch of boughs. The ray quivered to and fro, making her figure dim or distinct,—now like a real child, now like a child's spirit,—as the splendor went and came again. She heard her mother's voice, and approached slowly through the forest.

Pearl had not found the hour pass wearisomely, while her mother sat talking with the clergyman. The great black forest—stern as it showed itself to those who brought the guilt and troubles of the world into its bosom—became the playmate of the lonely infant, as well as it knew how. Sombre as it was, it put on the kindest of its moods to welcome her. It offered her the partridge-berries, the growth of the preceding autumn, but ripening only in the spring, and now red as drops of blood upon the withered leaves. These Pearl gathered, and was pleased with their wild flavor. The small denizens of the wilderness hardly took pains to move out of her path. A partridge, indeed, with a brood of ten behind her, ran forward threateningly, but soon repented of her fierceness, and clucked to her young ones not to be afraid. A pigeon, alone on a low branch, allowed Pearl to come beneath, and uttered a sound as much of greeting as alarm. A squirrel, from the lofty depths of his domestic tree, chattered either in anger or merriment,—for a squirrel is such a choleric and humorous little personage that it is hard to distinguish between his moods,—so he chattered at the child, and flung down a nut upon her head. It was a last year's nut, and already gnawed by his sharp tooth. A fox, startled from his sleep by her light footstep on the leaves, looked inquisitively at Pearl, as doubting whether it were better to steal off, or renew his nap on the same spot. A wolf, it is said,—but here the tale has surely lapsed into the improbable,—came up, and smelt of Pearl's robe, and offered his savage head to be patted by her hand. The truth seems to be, however, that the mother-forest, and these wild things which it nourished, all recognized a kindred wildness in the human child.

And she was gentler here than in the grassy-margined streets of the settlement, or in her mother's cottage. The flowers appeared to know it; and one and another whispered, as she passed, "Adorn thyself with me, thou beautiful child, adorn thyself with me!"—and, to please them, Pearl gathered the violets, and anemones, and columbines, and some twigs of the freshest green, which the old trees held down before her eyes. With these she decorated her hair, and her young waist, and became a nymph-child, or an infant dryad,[85] or whatever else was in closest

---

[85] According to Greek myth, a wood nymph.

sympathy with the antique wood. In such guise had Pearl adorned herself, when she heard her mother's voice, and came slowly back.

Slowly; for she saw the clergyman!

XIX: *The Child at the Brook-Side*

Thou wilt love her dearly," repeated Hester Prynne, as she and the minister sat watching little Pearl. "Dost thou not think her beautiful? And see with what natural skill she has made those simple flowers adorn her! Had she gathered pearls, and diamonds, and rubies, in the wood, they could not have become her better. She is a splendid child! But I know whose brow she has!"

"Dost thou know, Hester," said Arthur Dimmesdale, with an unquiet smile, "that this dear child, tripping about always at thy side, hath caused me many an alarm? Methought—O Hester, what a thought is that, and how terrible to dread it!—that my own features were partly repeated in her face, and so strikingly that the world might see them! But she is mostly thine!"

"No, no! Not mostly!" answered the mother with a tender smile. "A little longer, and thou needest not to be afraid to trace whose child she is. But how strangely beautiful she looks, with those wild flowers in her hair! It is as if one of the fairies, whom we left in our dear old England, had decked her out to meet us."

It was with a feeling which neither of them had ever before experienced, that they sat and watched Pearl's slow advance. In her was visible the tie that united them. She had been offered to the world, these seven years past, as the living hieroglyphic, in which was revealed the secret they so darkly sought to hide,—all written in this symbol,—all plainly manifest,—had there been a prophet or magician skilled to read the character of flame! And Pearl was the oneness of their being. Be the foregone evil what it might, how could they doubt that their earthly lives and future destinies were conjoined, when they beheld at once the material union, and the spiritual idea, in whom they met, and were to dwell immortally together? Thoughts like these—and perhaps other thoughts, which they did not acknowledge or define—threw an awe about the child, as she came onward.

"Let her see nothing strange—no passion nor eagerness—in thy way of accosting her," whispered Hester. "Our Pearl is a fitful and fantastic little elf, sometimes. Especially, she is seldom tolerant of emotion, when she does not fully comprehend the why and wherefore. But the child hath strong affections! She loves me, and will love thee!"

"Thou canst not think," said the minister, glancing aside at Hester Prynne, "how my heart dreads this interview, and yearns for it! But, in truth, as I already told thee, children are not readily won to be familiar with me. They will not climb my knee, nor prattle in my ear, nor answer to my smile; but stand apart, and eye me strangely. Even little babes, when I take them in my arms, weep bitterly. Yet Pearl, twice in her little lifetime, hath been kind to me! The first time,—thou knowest it well! The last was when thou ledst her with thee to the house of yonder stern old Governor."

"And thou didst plead so bravely in her behalf and mine!" answered the mother. "I remember it; and so shall little Pearl. Fear nothing! She may be strange and shy at first, but will soon learn to love thee!"

By this time Pearl had reached the margin of the brook, and stood on the farther side, gazing silently at Hester and the clergyman, who still sat together on the mossy tree-trunk, waiting to receive her. Just where she had paused the brook chanced to form a pool, so smooth and quiet that it reflected a perfect image of her little figure, with all the brilliant picturesqueness of her beauty, in its adornment of flowers and wreathed foliage, but more refined and spiritualized than the reality. This image, so nearly identical with the living Pearl, seemed to communicate somewhat of its own shadowy and intangible quality to the child herself. It was strange, the way in which Pearl stood, looking so stedfastly at them through the dim medium of the forest-gloom; herself, meanwhile, all glorified with a ray of sunshine, that was attracted thitherward as by a certain sympathy. In the brook beneath stood another child,—another and the same,—with likewise its ray of golden light. Hester felt herself, in some indistinct and tantalizing manner, es- tranged from Pearl; as if the child, in her lonely ramble through the forest, had strayed out of the sphere in which she and her mother dwelt together, and was now vainly seeking to return to it.

There was both truth and error in the impression; the child and mother were estranged, but through Hester's fault, not Pearl's. Since the latter rambled from her side, another inmate had been admitted within the circle of the mother's feel- ings, and so modified the aspect of them all, that Pearl, the returning wanderer, could not find her wonted place, and hardly knew where she was.

"I have a strange fancy," observed the sensitive minister, "that this brook is the boundary between two worlds, and that thou canst never meet thy Pearl again. Or is she an elfish spirit, who, as the legends of our childhood taught us, is forbidden to cross a running stream? Pray hasten her; for this delay has already imparted a tremor to my nerves."

"Come, dearest child!" said Hester encouragingly, and stretching out both her arms. "How slow thou art! When hast thou been so sluggish before now? Here is a friend of mine, who must be thy friend also. Thou wilt have twice as much love, henceforward, as thy mother alone could give thee! Leap across the brook and come to us. Thou canst leap like a young deer!"

Pearl, without responding in any manner to these honey-sweet expressions, re- mained on the other side of the brook. Now she fixed her bright, wild eyes on her mother, now on the minister, and now included them both in the same glance; as if to detect and explain to herself the relation which they bore to one another. For some unaccountable reason, as Arthur Dimmesdale felt the child's eyes upon him- self, his hand—with that gesture so habitual as to have become involuntary—stole over his heart. At length, assuming a singular air of authority, Pearl stretched out her hand, with the small forefinger extended, and pointing evidently towards her mother's breast. And beneath, in the mirror of the brook, there was the flower- girdled and sunny image of little Pearl, pointing her small forefinger too.

"Thou strange child, why dost thou not come to me?" exclaimed Hester.

Pearl still pointed with her forefinger; and a frown gathered on her brow; the more impressive from the childish, the almost baby-like aspect of the features that conveyed it. As her mother still kept beckoning to her, and arraying her face in a holiday suit of unaccustomed smiles, the child stamped her foot with a yet more imperious look and gesture. In the brook, again, was the fantastic beauty of the image, with its reflected frown, its pointed finger, and imperious gesture, giving emphasis to the aspect of little Pearl.

"Hasten, Pearl; or I shall be angry with thee!" cried Hester Prynne, who, how- ever inured to such behaviour on the elf-child's part at other seasons, was natu- rally anxious for a more seemly deportment now. "Leap across the brook, naughty child, and run hither! Else I must come to thee!"

But Pearl, not a whit startled at her mother's threats, any more than mollified by her entreaties, now suddenly burst into a fit of passion, gesticulating violently, and throwing her small figure into the most extravagant contortions. She accompanied this wild outbreak with piercing shrieks, which the woods reverberated on all sides; so that, alone as she was in her childish and unreasonable wrath, it seemed as if a hidden multitude were lending her their sympathy and encouragement. Seen in the brook, once more, was the shadowy wrath of Pearl's image, crowned and girdled with flowers, but stamping its foot, wildly gesticulating, and, in the midst of all, still pointing its small forefinger at Hester's bosom!

"I see what ails the child," whispered Hester to the clergyman, and turning pale in spite of a strong effort to conceal her trouble and annoyance. "Children will not abide any, the slightest, change in the accustomed aspect of things that are daily before their eyes. Pearl misses something which she has always seen me wear!"

"I pray you," answered the minister, "if thou hast any means of pacifying the child, do it forthwith! Save it were the cankered wrath of an old witch, like Mistress Hibbins," added he, attempting to smile, "I know nothing that I would not sooner encounter than this passion in a child. In Pearl's young beauty, as in the wrinkled witch, it has a preternatural effect. Pacify her, if thou lovest me!"

Hester turned again towards Pearl, with a crimson blush upon her cheek, a conscious glance aside at the clergyman, and then a heavy sigh; while, even before she had time to speak, the blush yielded to a deadly pallor.

"Pearl," said she, sadly, "look down at thy feet! There!—before thee!—on the hither side of the brook!"

The child turned her eyes to the point indicated; and there lay the scarlet letter, so close upon the margin of the stream, that the gold embroidery was reflected in it.

"Bring it hither!" said Hester.

"Come thou and take it up!" answered Pearl.

"Was there ever such a child!" observed Hester aside to the minister. "O, I have much to tell thee about her. But, in very truth, she is right as regards this hateful token. I must bear its torture yet a little longer,—only a few days longer,—until we shall have left this region, and look back hither as to a land which we have dreamed of. The forest cannot hide it! The mid-ocean shall take it from my hand, and swallow it up for ever!"

With these words, she advanced to the margin of the brook, took up the scarlet letter, and fastened it again into her bosom. Hopefully, but a moment ago, as Hester had spoken of drowning it in the deep sea, there was a sense of inevitable doom upon her, as she thus received back this deadly symbol from the hand of fate. She had flung it into infinite space!—she had drawn an hour's free breath!—and here again was the scarlet misery, glittering on the old spot! So it ever is, whether thus typified or no, that an evil deed invests itself with the character of doom. Hester next gathered up the heavy tresses of her hair, and confined them beneath her cap. As it there were a withering spell in the sad letter, her beauty, the warmth and richness of her womanhood, departed, like fading sunshine; and a gray shadow seemed to fall across her.

When the dreary change was wrought, she extended her hand to Pearl.

"Dost thou know thy mother now, child?" asked she, reproachfully, but with a subdued tone. "Wilt thou come across the brook, and own thy mother, now that she has her shame upon her,—now that she is sad?"

"Yes; now I will!" answered the child, bounding across the brook, and clasping Hester in her arms. "Now thou art my mother indeed! And I am thy little Pearl!"

In a mood of tenderness that was not usual with her, she drew down her mother's head, and kissed her brow with both her cheeks. But then—by a kind of necessity that always impelled this child to alloy whatever comfort she might chance to give with a throb of anguish—Pearl put up her mouth, and kissed the scarlet letter too!

"That was not kind!" said Hester. "When thou hast shown me a little love, thou mockest me!"

"Why doth the minister sit yonder?" asked Pearl.

"He waits to welcome thee," replied her mother. "Come thou, and entreat his blessing! He loves thee, my little Pearl, and loves thy mother too. Wilt thou not love him? Come! he longs to greet thee!"

"Doth he love us?" said Pearl, looking up with acute intelligence into her mother's face. "Will he go back with us, hand in hand, we three together, into the town?"

"Not now, dear child," answered Hester. "But in days to come he will walk hand in hand with us. We will have a home and a fireside of our own; and thou shalt sit upon his knee; and he will teach thee many things, and love thee dearly. Thou wilt love him; wilt thou not?"

"And will he always keep his hand over his heart?" inquired Pearl.

"Foolish child, what a question is that!" exclaimed her mother. "Come and ask his blessing!"

But, whether influenced by the jealousy that seems instinctive with every petted child towards a dangerous rival, or from whatever caprice of her freakish nature, Pearl would show no favor to the clergyman. It was only by an exertion of force that her mother brought her up to him, hanging back, and manifesting her reluctance by odd grimaces; of which, ever since her babyhood, she had possessed a singular variety, and could transform her mobile physiognomy into a series of different aspects, with a new mischief in them, each and all. The minister—painfully embarrassed, but hoping that a kiss might prove a talisman to admit him into the child's kindlier regards—bent forward, and impressed one on her brow. Hereupon, Pearl broke away from her mother, and, running to the brook, stooped over it, and bathed her forehead, until the unwelcome kiss was quite washed off, and diffused through a long lapse of the gliding water. She then remained apart, silently watching Hester and the clergyman; while they talked together, and made such arrangements as were suggested by their new position, and the purposes soon to be fulfilled.

And now this fateful interview had come to a close. The dell was to be left a solitude among its dark, old trees, which, with their multitudinous tongues, would whisper long of what had passed there, and no mortal be the wiser. And the melancholy brook would add this other tale to the mystery with which its little heart was already overburdened, and whereof it still kept up a murmuring babble, with not a whit more cheerfulness of tone than for ages heretofore.

XX: The Minister in a Maze

As the minister departed, in advance of Hester Prynne and little Pearl, he threw a backward glance; half expecting that he should discover only some faintly traced features or outline of the mother and the child, slowly fading into the twilight of the woods. So great a vicissitude in his life could not at once be received as real. But there was Hester, clad in her gray robe, still standing beside the tree-trunk, which some blast had overthrown a long antiquity ago, and which time had ever since been covering with moss, so that these two fated ones, with earth's heaviest burden on them, might there sit down together, and find a single hour's rest and solace. And there was Pearl, too, lightly dancing from the margin of the brook,—now that the intrusive third person was gone,— and taking her old place by her mother's side. So the minister had not fallen asleep, and dreamed!

In order to free his mind from this indistinctness and duplicity of impression, which vexed it with a strange disquietude, he recalled and more thoroughly defined the plans which Hester and himself had sketched for their departure. It had been determined between them, that the Old World, with its crowds and cities, offered them a more eligible shelter and concealment than the wilds of New England, or all America, with its alternatives of an Indian wigwam, or the few settlements of Europeans, scattered thinly along the seaboard. Not to speak of the clergyman's health, so inadequate to sustain the hardships of a forest life, his native gifts, his culture, and his entire development would secure him a home only in the midst of civilization and refinement; the higher the state, the more delicately adapted to it the man. In furtherance of this choice, it so happened that a ship lay in the harbour; one of those questionable cruisers, frequent at that day, which, without being absolutely outlaws of the deep, yet roamed over its surface with a remarkable irresponsibility of character. This vessel had recently arrived from the Spanish Main, and, within three days' time, would sail for Bristol.[86] Hester Prynne—whose vocation, as a self-enlisted Sister of Charity, had brought her acquainted with the captain and crew—could take upon herself to secure the passage of two individuals and a child, with all the secrecy which circumstances rendered more than desirable.

The minister had inquired of Hester, with no little interest, the precise time at which the vessel might be expected to depart. It would probably be on the fourth day from the present. "That is most fortunate!" he had then said to himself. Now, why the Reverend Mr. Dimmesdale considered it so very fortunate, we hesitate to reveal. Nevertheless,—to hold nothing back from the reader,—it was because, on the third day from the present, he was to preach the Election Sermon;[87] and, as such an occasion formed an honorable epoch in the life of a New England clergyman, he could not have chanced upon a more suitable mode and time of terminating his professional career. "At least, they shall say of me," thought this exemplary man, "that I leave no public duty unperformed, nor ill performed!" Sad, indeed, that an introspection so profound and acute as this poor minister's should be so miserably deceived! We have had, and may still have, worse things to tell of him; but none, we apprehend, so pitiably weak; no evidence, at once so slight and irrefragable, of a subtle disease, that had long since begun to eat into the real substance of his character. No man, for any considerable period, can wear one face to himself, and another to the multitude, without finally getting bewildered as to which may be the true.

The excitement of Mr. Dimmesdale's feelings, as he returned from his interview with Hester, lent him unaccustomed physical energy, and hurried him townward at a rapid pace. The pathway among the woods seemed wilder, more uncouth with its rude natural obstacles, and less trodden by the foot of man, than he

---

[86] A seaport in western England.

[87] A sermon preached on the day a new governor was elected; it was a high honor to be chosen to deliver this sermon.

remembered it on his outward journey. But he leaped across the plashy places, thrust himself through the clinging underbrush, climbed the ascent, plunged into the hollow, and overcame, in short, all the difficulties of the track, with an unweariable activity that astonished him. He could not but recall how feebly, and with what frequent pauses for breath, he had toiled over the same ground only two days before. As he drew near the town, he took an impression of change from the series of familiar objects that presented themselves. It seemed not yesterday, not one, nor two, but many days, or even years ago, since he had quitted them. There, indeed, was each former trace of the street, as he remembered it, and all the peculiarities of the houses, with the due multitude of gable-peaks, and a weathercock at every point where his memory suggested one. Not the less, however, came this importunately obtrusive sense of change. The same was true as regarded the acquaintances whom he met, and all the well-known shapes of human life, about the little town. They looked neither older nor younger, now; the beards of the aged were no whiter, nor could the creeping babe of yesterday walk on his feet to-day; it was impossible to describe in what respect they differed from the individuals on whom he had so recently bestowed a parting glance; and yet the minister's deepest sense seemed to inform him of their mutability. A similar impression struck him most remarkably, as he passed under the walls of his own church. The edifice had so very strange, and yet so familiar, an aspect, that Mr. Dimmesdale's mind vibrated between two ideas; either that he had seen it only in a dream hitherto, or that he was merely dreaming about it now.

This phenomenon, in the various shapes which it assumed, indicated no external change, but so sudden and important a change in the spectator of the familiar scene, that the intervening space of a single day had operated on his consciousness like the lapse of years. The minister's own will, and Hester's will, and the fate that grew between them, had wrought this transformation. It was the same town as heretofore; but the same minister returned not from the forest. He might have said to the friends who greeted him,—"I am not the man for whom you take me! I left him yonder in the forest, withdrawn into a secret dell, by a mossy tree-trunk, and near a melancholy brook! Go, seek your minister, and see if his emaciated figure, his thin cheek, his white, heavy, pain-wrinkled brow, be not flung down there like a cast-off garment!" His friends, no doubt, would still have insisted with him,— "Thou art thyself the man!"—but the error would have been their own, not his.

Before Mr. Dimmesdale reached home, his inner man gave him other evidences of a revolution in the sphere of thought and feeling. In truth, nothing short of a total change of dynasty and moral code, in that interior kingdom, was adequate to account for the impulses now communicated to the unfortunate and startled minister. At every step he was incited to do some strange, wild, wicked thing or other, with a sense that it would be at once involuntary and intentional; in spite of himself, yet growing out of a profounder self than that which opposed the impulse. For instance, he met one of his own deacons. The good old man addressed him with the paternal affection and patriarchal privilege, which his venerable age, his upright and holy character, and his station in the Church, entitled him to use; and, conjoined with this, the deep, almost worshipping respect, which the minister's professional and private claims alike demanded. Never was there a more beautiful example of how the majesty of age and wisdom may comport with the obeisance and respect enjoined upon it, as from a lower social rank and inferior order of endowment, towards a higher. Now, during a conversation of some two or three moments between the Reverend Mr. Dimmesdale and this excellent and hoary-bearded deacon, it was only by the most careful self-control that the former could refrain from uttering certain blasphemous suggestions that rose into his mind, respecting the communion-supper. He absolutely trembled and turned pale as ashes, lest his tongue should wag itself, in utterance of these horrible matters, and plead his own consent for so doing, without his having fairly given it. And, even with this terror in his heart, he could hardly avoid laughing to imagine how the sanctified old patriarchal deacon would have been petrified by his minister's impiety!

Again, another incident of the same nature. Hurrying along the street, the Reverend Mr. Dimmesdale encountered the eldest female member of his church; a most pious and exemplary old dame; poor, widowed, lonely, and with a heart as full of reminiscences about her dead husband and children, and her dead friends of long ago, as a burial-ground is full of storied grave-stones. Yet all this, which would else have been such heavy sorrow, was made almost a solemn joy to her devout old soul by religious consolations and the truths of Scripture, wherewith she had fed herself continually for more than thirty years. And, since Mr. Dimmesdale had taken her in charge, the good grandam's chief earthly comfort— which, unless it had been likewise a heavenly comfort, would have been none at all—was to meet her pastor, whether casually, or of set purpose, and be refreshed with a word of warm, fragrant, heaven-breathing Gospel truth from his beloved lips into her dulled, but rapturously attentive ear. But, on this occasion, up to the moment of putting his lips to the old woman's ear, Mr. Dimmesdale, as the great enemy of souls would have it, could recall no text of Scripture, nor aught else, except a brief, pithy, and, as it then appeared to him, unanswerable argument against the immortality of the human soul. The instilment thereof into her mind would probably have caused this aged sister to drop down dead, at once, as by the effect of an intensely poisonous infusion. What he really did whisper, the minister could never afterwards recollect. There was, perhaps, a fortunate disorder in his utterance, which failed to impart any distinct idea to the good widow's comprehension, or which Providence interpreted after a method of its own. Assuredly, as the minister looked back, he beheld an expression of divine gratitude and ecstasy that seemed like the shine of the celestial city on her face, so wrinkled and ashy pale.

Again, a third instance. After parting from the old church-member, he met the youngest sister of them all. It was a maiden newly won—and won by the Reverend Mr. Dimmesdale's own sermon, on the Sabbath after his vigil—to barter the transitory pleasures of the world for the heavenly hope, that was to assume brighter substance as life grew dark around her, and which would gild the utter gloom with final glory. She was fair and pure as a lily that had bloomed in Paradise. The minister knew well that he was himself enshrined within the stainless sanctity of her heart, which hung its snowy curtains about his image, imparting to religion the warmth of love, and to love a religious purity. Satan, that afternoon, had surely led the poor young girl away from her mother's side, and thrown her into the pathway of this sorely tempted, or—shall we not rather say?—this lost and desperate man. As she drew nigh, the arch-fiend whispered him to condense into small compass and drop into her tender bosom a germ of evil that would be sure to blossom darkly soon, and bear black fruit betimes. Such was his sense of power over this virgin soul, trusting him as she did, that the minister felt potent to blight all the field of innocence with but one wicked look, and develop all its opposite with but a word. So—with a mightier struggle than he had yet sustained—he held his Geneva cloak before his face, and hurried onward, making no sign of recognition, and leaving the young sister to digest his rudeness as she might. She ransacked her conscience,—which was full of harmless little matters, like her pocket or her work-bag,—and took herself to task, poor thing, for a thousand imaginary faults; and went about her household duties with swollen eyelids the next morning.

Before the minister had time to celebrate his victory over this last temptation, he was conscious of another impulse, more ludicrous, and almost as horrible. It was,—we blush to tell it,—it was to stop short in the road, and teach some very wicked words to a knot of little Puritan children who were playing there, and had but just begun to talk. Denying himself this freak, as unworthy of his cloth, he met a drunken seaman, one of the ship's crew from the Spanish Main. And, here, since he had so valiantly forborne all other wickedness, poor Mr. Dimmesdale longed, at least, to shake hands with the tarry blackguard, and recreate himself with a few improper jests, such as dissolute sailors so abound with, and a volley of good, round, solid, satisfactory, and heaven-defying oaths! It was not so much a better principle, as partly his natural good taste, and still more his buckramed[88] habit of clerical decorum, that carried him safely through the latter crisis.

"What is it that haunts and tempts me thus?" cried the minister to himself, at length, pausing in the street, and striking his hand against his forehead. "Am I mad? or am I given over utterly to the fiend? Did I make a contract with him in the forest, and sign it with my blood? And does he now summon me to its fulfilment, by suggesting the performance of every wickedness which his most foul imagination can conceive?"

At that moment when the Reverend Mr. Dimmesdale thus communed with himself, and struck his forehead with his hand, old Mistress Hibbins, the reputed witch-lady, is said to have been passing by. She made a very grand appearance; having on a high head-dress, a rich gown of velvet, and a ruff done up with the famous yellow starch, of which Ann Turner, her especial friend, had taught her the secret, before this last good lady had been hanged for Sir Thomas Overbury's murder. Whether the witch had read the minister's thoughts, or no, she came to a full stop, looked shrewdly into his face, smiled craftily, and—though little given to converse with clergymen—began a conversation.

"So, reverend Sir, you have made a visit into the forest," observed the witch-lady, nodding her high head-dress at him. "The next time, I pray you to allow me only a fair warning, and I shall be proud to bear you company. Without taking overmuch upon myself, my good word will go far towards gaining any strange gentleman a fair reception from yonder potentate you wot of!"

"I profess, madam," answered the clergyman, with a grave obeisance, such as the lady's rank demanded, and his own good-breeding made imperative,—"I profess, on my conscience and character, that I am utterly bewildered as touching the purport of your words! I went not into the forest to seek a potentate; neither do I, at any future time, design a visit thither, with a view to gaining the favor of such personage. My one sufficient object was to greet that pious friend of mine, the Apostle Eliot, and rejoice with him over the many precious souls he hath won from heathendom!"

"Ha, ha, ha!" cackled the old witch-lady, still nodding her high head-dress at the minister. "Well, well, we must needs talk thus in the daytime! You carry it off

[88] Stiff or rigid, like the cloth buckram; formal.

like an old hand! But at midnight, and in the forest, we shall have other talk together!"

She passed on with her aged stateliness, but often turning back her head and smiling at him, like one willing to recognize a secret intimacy of connection.

"Have I then sold myself," thought the minister, "to the fiend whom, if men say true, this yellow-starched and velveted old hag has chosen for her prince and master!"

The wretched minister! He had made a bargain very like it! Tempted by a dream of happiness, he had yielded himself with deliberate choice, as he had never done before, to what he knew was deadly sin. And the infectious poison of that sin had been thus rapidly diffused throughout his moral system. It had stupefied all blessed impulses, and awakened into vivid life the whole brotherhood of bad ones. Scorn, bitterness, unprovoked malignity, gratuitous desire of ill, ridicule of whatever was good and holy, all awoke, to tempt, even while they frightened him. And this encounter with old Mistress Hibbins, if it were a real incident, did but show his sympathy and fellowship with wicked mortals and the world of perverted spirits.

He had by this time reached his dwelling, on the edge of the burial-ground, and, hastening up the stairs, took refuge in his study. The minister was glad to have reached this shelter, without first betraying himself to the world by any of those strange and wicked eccentricities to which he had been continually impelled while passing through the streets. He entered the accustomed room, and looked around him on its books, its windows, its fireplace, and the tapestried comfort of the walls, with the same perception of strangeness that had haunted him throughout his walk from the forest-dell into the town, and thitherward. Here he had studied and written; here, gone through fast and vigil, and come forth half alive; here, striven to pray; here, borne a hundred thousand agonies! There was the Bible, in its rich old Hebrew, with Moses and the Prophets speaking to him, and God's voice through all! There, on the table, with the inky pen beside it, was an unfinished sermon, with a sentence broken in the midst, where his thoughts had ceased to gush out upon the page two days before. He knew that it was himself, the thin and white-cheeked minister, who had done and suffered these things, and written thus far into the Election Sermon! But he seemed to stand apart, and eye this former self with scornful, pitying, but half-envious curiosity. That self was gone! Another man had returned out of the forest; a wiser one; with a knowledge of hidden mysteries which the simplicity of the former never could have reached. A bitter kind of knowledge that!

While occupied with these reflections, a knock came at the door of the study, and the minister said, "Come in!"—not wholly devoid of an idea that he might behold an evil spirit. And so he did! It was old Roger Chillingworth that entered. The minister stood, white and speechless, with one hand on the Hebrew Scriptures, and the other spread upon his breast.

"Welcome home, reverend Sir!" said the physician. "And how found you that godly man, the Apostle Eliot? But methinks, dear Sir, you look pale; as if the travel through the wilderness had been too sore for you. Will not my aid be requisite to put you in heart and strength to preach your Election Sermon?"

"Nay, I think not so," rejoined the Reverend Mr. Dimmesdale. "My journey, and the sight of the holy Apostle yonder, and the free air which I have breathed, have done me good, after so long confinement in my study. I think to need no more of your drugs, my kind physician, good though they be, and administered by a friendly hand."

All this time, Roger Chillingworth was looking at the minister with the grave and intent regard of a physician towards his patient. But, in spite of this outward show, the latter was almost convinced of the old man's knowledge, or, at least, his confident suspicion, with respect to his own interview with Hester Prynne. The physician knew, then, that, in the minister's regard, he was no longer a trusted friend, but his bitterest enemy. So much being known, it would appear natural that a part of it should be expressed. It is singular, however, how long a time often passes before words embody things; and with what security two persons, who choose to avoid a certain subject, may approach its very verge, and retire without disturbing it. Thus, the minister felt no apprehension that Roger Chillingworth would touch, in express words, upon the real position which they sustained towards one another. Yet did the physician, in his dark way, creep frightfully near the secret.

"Were it not better," said he, "that you use my poor skill to-night? Verily, dear Sir, we must take pains to make you strong and vigorous for this occasion of the Election discourse. The people look for great things from you; apprehending that another year may come about, and find their pastor gone."

"Yea, to another world," replied the minister, with pious resignation. "Heaven grant it be a better one; for, in good sooth, I hardly think to tarry with my flock through the flitting seasons of another year! But, touching your medicine, kind Sir, in my present frame of body I need it not."

"I joy to hear it," answered the physician. "It may be that my remedies, so long administered in vain, begin now to take due effect. Happy man were I, and well deserving of New England's gratitude, could I achieve this cure!"

"I thank you from my heart, most watchful friend," said the Reverend Mr. Dimmesdale, with a solemn smile. "I thank you, and can but requite your good deeds with my prayers."

"A good man's prayers are golden recompense!" rejoined old Roger Chillingworth, as he took his leave. "Yea, they are the current gold coin of the New Jerusalem, with the King's own mint-mark on them!"

Left alone, the minister summoned a servant of the house, and requested food, which, being set before him, he ate with ravenous appetite. Then, flinging the already written pages of the Election Sermon into the fire, he forthwith began another, which he wrote with such an impulsive flow of thought and emotion, that he fancied himself inspired; and only wondered that Heaven should see fit to transmit the grand and solemn music of its oracles through so foul an organ-pipe as he. However, leaving that mystery to solve itself, or go unsolved for ever, he drove his task onward, with earnest haste and ecstasy. Thus the night fled away, as it were a winged steed, and he careering on it; morning came, and peeped blushing through the curtains; and at last sunrise threw a golden beam into the study, and laid it right across the minister's bedazzled eyes. There he was, with the pen still between his fingers, and a vast, immeasurable tract of written space behind him!

XXI: The New England Holiday

Betimes[89] in the morning of the day on which the new Governor was to receive his office at the hands of the people, Hester Prynne and little Pearl came into the

---

[89] Early.

market-place. It was already thronged with the craftsmen and other plebeian inhabitants of the town, in considerable numbers; among whom, likewise, were
many rough figures, whose attire of deer-skins marked them as belonging to some
of the forest settlements, which surrounded the little metropolis of the colony.

On this public holiday, as on all other occasions, for seven years past, Hester
was clad in a garment of coarse gray cloth. Not more by its hue than by some
indescribable peculiarity in its fashion, it had the effect of making her fade personally out of sight and outline; while, again, the scarlet letter brought her back from
this twilight indistinctness, and revealed her under the moral aspect of its own
illumination. Her face, so long familiar to the townspeople, showed the marble
quietude which they were accustomed to behold there. It was like a mask; or
rather, like the frozen calmness of a dead woman's features; owing this dreary
resemblance to the fact that Hester was actually dead, in respect to any claim
of sympathy, and had departed out of the world with which she still seemed to
mingle.

It might be, on this one day, that there was an expression unseen before, nor,
indeed, vivid enough to be detected now; unless some preternaturally gifted observer should have first read the heart, and have afterwards sought a corresponding development in the countenance and mien. Such a spiritual seer might have
conceived, that, after sustaining the gaze of the multitude through seven miserable
years as a necessity, a penance, and something which it was a stern religion to
endure, she now, for one last time more, encountered it freely and voluntarily, in
order to convert what had so long been agony into a kind of triumph. "Look your
last on the scarlet letter and its wearer!"—the people's victim and life-long bond-
slave, as they fancied her, might say to them. "Yet a little while, and she will be
beyond your reach! A few hours longer, and the deep, mysterious ocean will
quench and hide for ever the symbol which ye have caused to burn upon her
bosom!" Nor were it an inconsistency too improbable to be assigned to human
nature, should we suppose a feeling of regret in Hester's mind, at the moment
when she was about to win her freedom from the pain which had been thus deeply
incorporated with her being. Might there not be an irresistible desire to quaff a
last, long, breathless draught of the cup of wormwood and aloes, with which
nearly all her years of womanhood had been perpetually flavored? The wine of
life, henceforth to be presented to her lips, must be indeed rich, delicious, and
exhilarating, in its chased and golden beaker; or else leave an inevitable and weary
languor, after the lees of bitterness wherewith she had been drugged, as with a
cordial of intensest potency.

Pearl was decked out with airy gayety. It would have been impossible to guess
that this bright and sunny apparition owed its existence to the shape of gloomy
gray; or that a fancy, at once so gorgeous and so delicate as must have been
requisite to contrive the child's apparel, was the same that had achieved a task
perhaps more difficult, in imparting so distinct a peculiarity to Hester's simple
robe. The dress, so proper was it to little Pearl, seemed an effluence, or inevitable
development and outward manifestation of her character, no more to be separated
from her than the many-hued brilliancy from a butterfly's wing, or the painted
glory from the leaf of a bright flower. As with these, so with the child; her garb
was all of one idea with her nature. On this eventful day, moreover, there was a
certain singular inquietude and excitement in her mood, resembling nothing so
much as the shimmer of a diamond, that sparkles and flashes with the varied
throbbings of the breast on which it is displayed. Children have always a sympathy in the agitations of those connected with them; always, especially, a sense of

any trouble or impending revolution, of whatever kind, in domestic circumstances; and therefore Pearl, who was the gem on her mother's unquiet bosom, betrayed, by the very dance of her spirits, the emotions which none could detect in the marble passiveness of Hester's brow.

This effervescence made her flit with a bird-like movement, rather than walk by her mother's side. She broke continually into shouts of a wild, inarticulate, and sometimes piercing music. When they reached the market-place, she became still more restless, on perceiving the stir and bustle that enlivened the spot; for it was usually more like the broad and lonesome green before a village meeting-house, than the centre of a town's business.

"Why, what is this, mother?" cried she. "Wherefore have all the people left their work to-day? Is it a play-day for the whole world? See, there is the blacksmith! He has washed his sooty face, and put on his Sabbath-day clothes, and looks as if he would gladly be merry, if any kind body would only teach him how! And there is Master Brackett, the old jailer, nodding and smiling at me. Why does he do so, mother?"

"He remembers thee a little babe, my child," answered Hester.

"He should not nod and smile at me, for all that,—the black, grim, ugly-eyed old man!" said Pearl. "He may nod at thee if he will; for thou art clad in gray, and wearest the scarlet letter. But, see, mother, how many faces of strange people, and Indians among them, and sailors! What have they all come to do here in the market-place?"

"They wait to see the procession pass," said Hester. "For the Governor and the magistrates are to go by, and the ministers, and all the great people and good people, with the music, and the soldiers marching before them."

"And will the minister be there?" asked Pearl. "And will he hold out both his hands to me, as when thou ledst me to him from the brook-side?"

"He will be there, child," answered her mother. "But he will not greet thee to-day; nor must thou greet him."

"What a strange, sad man is he!" said the child, as if speaking partly to herself. "In the dark night-time, he calls us to him, and holds thy hand and mine, as when we stood with him on the scaffold yonder! And in the deep forest, where only the old trees can hear, and the strip of sky see it, he talks with thee, sitting on a heap of moss! And he kisses my forehead, too, so that the little brook would hardly wash it off! But here in the sunny day, and among all the people, he knows us not; nor must we know him! A strange, sad man is he, with his hand always over his heart!"

"Be quiet, Pearl! Thou understandest not these things," said her mother. "Think not now of the minister, but look about thee, and see how cheery is every body's face to-day. The children have come from their schools, and the grown people from their workshops and their fields, on purpose to be happy. For, to-day, a new man is beginning to rule over them; and so—as has been the custom of mankind ever since a nation was first gathered—they make merry and rejoice; as if a good and golden year were at length to pass over the poor old world!"

It was as Hester said, in regard to the unwonted jollity that brightened the faces of the people. Into this festal season of the year—as it already was, and continued to be during the greater part of two centuries—the Puritans compressed whatever mirth and public joy they deemed allowable to human infirmity; thereby so far dispelling the customary cloud, that, for the space of a single holiday, they appeared scarcely more grave than most other communities at a period of general affliction.

But we perhaps exaggerate the gray or sable tinge, which undoubtedly characterized the mood and manners of the age. The persons now in the market-place of Boston had not been born to an inheritance of Puritanic gloom. They were native Englishmen, whose fathers had lived in the sunny richness of the Elizabethan epoch; a time when the life of England, viewed as one great mass, would appear to have been as stately, magnificent, and joyous, as the world has ever witnessed. Had they followed their hereditary taste, the New England settlers would have illustrated all events of public importance by bonfires, banquets, pageantries, and processions. Nor would it have been impracticable, in the observance of majestic ceremonies, to combine mirthful recreation with solemnity, and give, as it were, a grotesque and brilliant embroidery to the great robe of state, which a nation, at such festivals, puts on. There was some shadow of an attempt of this kind in the mode of celebrating the day on which the political year of the colony commenced. The dim reflection of a remembered splendor, a colorless and manifold diluted repetition of what they had beheld in proud old London,—we will not say at a royal coronation, but at a Lord Mayor's show,[90]—might be traced in the customs which our forefathers instituted, with reference to the annual installation of magistrates. The fathers and founders of the commonwealth—the statesman, the priest, and the soldier—deemed it a duty then to assume the outward state and majesty, which, in accordance with antique style, was looked upon as the proper garb of public or social eminence. All came forth, to move in procession before the people's eye, and thus impart a needed dignity to the simple framework of a government so newly constructed.

Then, too, the people were countenanced, if not encouraged, in relaxing the severe and close application to their various modes of rugged industry, which, at all other times, seemed of the same piece and material with their religion. Here, it is true, were none of the appliances which popular merriment would so readily have found in the England of Elizabeth's time, or that of James,[91]—no rude shows of a theatrical kind; no minstrel with his harp and legendary ballad, nor gleeman, with an ape dancing to his music; no juggler, with his tricks of mimic witchcraft; no Merry Andrew,[92] to stir up the multitude with jests, perhaps hundreds of years old, but still effective, by their appeals to the very broadest sources of mirthful sympathy. All such professors of the several branches of jocularity would have been sternly repressed, not only by the rigid discipline of law, but by the general sentiment which gives law its vitality. Not the less, however, the great, honest face of the people smiled, grimly, perhaps, but widely too. Nor were sports wanting, such as the colonists had witnessed, and shared in, long ago, at the country fairs and on the village-greens of England; and which it was thought well to keep alive on this new soil, for the sake of the courage and manliness that were essential in them. Wrestling-matches, in the differing fashions of Cornwall and Devonshire, were seen here and there about the market-place; in one corner, there was a friendly bout at quarterstaff;[93] and —what attracted most interest of all—on the platform of the pillory, already so noted in our pages, two masters of defence were commencing an exhibition with the buckler[94] and broadsword. But, much to the disappointment of the crowd, this latter business was broken off by

---

[90] Inaugural ceremonies honoring the lord mayor of London.
[91] Elizabeth I and James I reigned before the Puritans came to power in the 1640s.
[92] A clown or jester.   [93] A fight with a long wooden staff.   [94] A shield.

the interposition of the town beadle, who had no idea of permitting the majesty of the law to be violated by such an abuse of one of its consecrated places.

It may not be too much to affirm, on the whole, (the people being then in the first stages of joyless deportment, and the offspring of sires who had known how to be merry, in their day,) that they would compare favorably, in point of holiday keeping, with their descendants, even at so long an interval as ourselves. Their immediate posterity, the generation next to the early emigrants, wore the blackest shade of Puritanism, and so darkened the national visage with it, that all the subsequent years have not sufficed to clear it up. We have yet to learn again the forgotten art of gayety.

The picture of human life in the market-place, though its general tint was the sad gray, brown, or black of the English emigrants, was yet enlivened by some diversity of hue. A party of Indians—in their savage finery of curiously embroidered deer-skin robes, wampum-belts, red and yellow ochre, and feathers, and armed with the bow and arrow and stone-headed spear—stood apart, with countenances of inflexible gravity, beyond what even the Puritan aspect could attain. Nor, wild as were these painted barbarians, were they the wildest feature of the scene. This distinction could more justly be claimed by some mariners,—a part of the crew of the vessel from the Spanish Main,—who had come ashore to see the humors of Election Day. They were rough-looking desperadoes, with sun-blackened faces, and an immensity of beard; their wide, short trousers were confined about the waist by belts, often clasped with a rough plate of gold, and sustaining always a long knife, and, in some instances, a sword. From beneath their broad-brimmed hats of palm-leaf, gleamed eyes which, even in good nature and merriment, had a kind of animal ferocity. They transgressed, without fear or scruple, the rules of behaviour that were binding on all others; smoking tobacco under the beadle's very nose, although each whiff would have cost a townsman a shilling; and quaffing, at their pleasure, draughts of wine or aqua-vitæ[95] from pocket-flasks, which they freely tendered to the gaping crowd around them. It remarkably characterized the incomplete morality of the age, rigid as we call it, that a license was allowed the seafaring class, not merely for their freaks on shore, but for far more desperate deeds on their proper element. The sailor of that day would go near to be arraigned as a pirate in our own. There could be little doubt, for instance, that this very ship's crew, though no unfavorable specimens of the nautical brotherhood, had been guilty, as we should phrase it, of depredations on the Spanish commerce, such as would have perilled all their necks in a modern court of justice.

But the sea, in those old times, heaved and swelled, and foamed very much at its own will, or subject only to the tempestuous wind, with hardly any attempts at regulation by human law. The buccaneer on the wave might relinquish his calling, and become at once, if he chose, a man of probity and piety on land; nor, even in the full career of his reckless life, was he regarded as a personage with whom it was disreputable to traffic, or casually associate. Thus, the Puritan elders, in their black cloaks, starched bands, and steeple-crowned hats, smiled not unbenignantly at the clamor and rude deportment of these jolly seafaring men; and it excited neither surprise nor animadversion when so reputable a citizen as old Roger Chillingworth, the physician, was seen to enter the market-place, in close and familiar talk with the commander of the questionable vessel.

The latter was by far the most showy and gallant figure, so far as apparel went,

---

[95] Brandy.

anywhere to be seen among the multitude. He wore a profusion of ribbons on his garment, and gold lace on his hat, which was also encircled by a gold chain, and surmounted with a feather. There was a sword at his side, and a sword-cut on his forehead, which, by the arrangement of his hair, he seemed anxious rather to display than hide. A landsman could hardly have worn this garb and shown this face, and worn and shown them both with such a galliard[96] air, without undergoing stern question before a magistrate, and probably incurring fine or imprisonment, or perhaps an exhibition in the stocks. As regarded the shipmaster, however, all was looked upon as pertaining to the character, as to a fish his glistening scales.

After parting from the physician, the commander of the Bristol ship strolled idly though the market-place; until, happening to approach the spot where Hester Prynne was standing, he appeared to recognize, and did not hesitate to address her. As was usually the case wherever Hester stood, a small, vacant area—a sort of magic circle—had formed itself about her, into which, though the people were elbowing one another at a little distance, none ventured, or felt disposed to intrude. It was a forcible type of the moral solitude in which the scarlet letter enveloped its fated wearer; partly by her own reserve, and partly by the instinctive, though no longer so unkindly, withdrawal of her fellow-creatures. Now, if never before, it answered a good purpose, by enabling Hester and the seaman to speak together without risk of being overheard; and so changed was Hester Prynne's repute before the public, that the matron in town most eminent for rigid morality could not have held such intercourse with less result of scandal than herself.

"So, mistress," said the mariner, "I must bid the steward make ready one more berth than you bargained for! No fear of scurvy or ship-fever, this voyage! What with the ship's surgeon and this other doctor, our only danger will be from drug or pill; more by token, as there is a lot of apothecary's stuff aboard, which I traded for with a Spanish vessel."

"What mean you?" inquired Hester, startled more than she permitted to appear. "Have you another passenger?"

"Why know you not," cried the shipmaster, "that this physician here—Chillingworth, he calls himself—is minded to try my cabin-fare with you? Ay, ay, you must have known it; for he tells me he is of your party, and a close friend to the gentleman you spoke of,—he that is in peril from these sour old Puritan rulers!"

"They know each other well, indeed," replied Hester, with a mien of calmness, though in the utmost consternation. "They have long dwelt together."

Nothing further passed between the mariner and Hester Prynne. But, at that instant, she beheld old Roger Chillingworth himself, standing in the remotest corner of the marketplace, and smiling on her; a smile which—across the wide and bustling square, and through all the talk and laughter, and various thoughts, moods, and interests of the crowd—conveyed secret and fearful meaning.

XXII: *The Procession*

Before Hester Prynne could call together her thoughts, and consider what was practicable to be done in this new and startling aspect of affairs, the sound of military music was heard approaching along a contiguous street. It denoted the

---

[96] Lively.

advance of the procession of magistrates and citizens, on its way towards the meeting-house; where, in compliance witth a custom thus early established, and ever since observed, the Reverend Mr. Dimmesdale was to deliver an Election Sermon.

Soon the head of the procession showed itself, with a slow and stately march, turning a corner, and making its way across the market-place. First came the music. It comprised a variety of instruments, perhaps imperfectly adapted to one another, and played with no great skill, but yet attaining the great object for which the harmony of drum and clarion addresses itself to the multitude,—that of imparting a higher and more heroic air to the scene of life that passes before the eye. Little Pearl at first clapped her hands, but then lost, for an instant, the restless agitation that had kept her in a continual effervescence throughout the morning; she gazed silently, and seemed to be borne upward, like a floating sea-bird, on the long heaves and swells of sound. But she was brought back to her former mood by the shimmer of the sunshine on the weapons and bright armour of the military company,[97] which followed after the music, and formed the honorary escort of the procession. This body of soldiery—which still sustains a corporate existence, and marches down from past ages with an ancient and honorable fame—was composed of no mercenary materials. Its ranks were filled with gentlemen, who felt the stirrings of martial impulse, and sought to establish a kind of College of Arms,[98] where, as in an association of Knights Templars,[99] they might learn the science, and, so far as peaceful exercise would teach them, the practices of war. The high estimation then placed upon the military character might be seen in the lofty port of each individual member of the company. Some of them, indeed, by their services in the Low Countries[100] and on other fields of European warfare, had fairly won their title to assume the name and pomp of soldiership. The entire array, moreover, clad in burnished steel, and with plumage nodding over their bright morions,[101] had a brilliancy of effect which no modern display can aspire to equal.

And yet the men of civil eminence, who came immediately behind the military escort, were better worth a thoughtful observer's eye. Even in outward demeanour they showed a stamp of majesty that made the warrior's haughty stride look vulgar, if not absurd. It was an age when what we call talent had far less consideration than now, but the massive materials which produce stability and dignity of character a great deal more. The people possessed, by hereditary right, the quality of reverence; which, in their descendants, if it survive at all, exists in smaller proportion, and with a vastly diminshed force in the selection and estimate of public men. The change may be for good or ill, and is partly, perhaps, for both. In that old day, the English settler on these rude shores,—having left king, nobles, and all degrees of awful rank behind, while still the faculty and necessity of reverence were strong in him,—bestowed it on the white hair and venerable brow of age; on long-tried integrity; on solid wisdom and sad-colored experience; on endowments of that grave and weighty order, which gives the idea of permanence,

---

[97] The Ancient and Honorable Artillery Company of Massachusetts, founded in 1638.

[98] The Herald's College of England, a royal corporation established in the fifteenth century to keep records of genealogies and coats of arms. The Puritans in Hawthorne's scene are trying to emulate the Herald's College.

[99] An order of military and religious crusaders in the twelfth century.

[100] The Netherlands, Belgium, and Luxembourg.

[101] A footsoldier's visorless high-crested helmet, curved up in front and back.

and comes under the general definition of respectability. These primitive states-men, therefore,—Bradstreet, Endicott, Dudley,[102] Bellingham, and their com-peers,—who were elevated to power by the early choice of the people, seem to have been not often brilliant, but distinguished by a ponderous sobriety, rather than activity of intellect. They had fortitude and self-reliance, and, in time of difficulty or peril, stood up for the welfare of the state like a line of cliffs against a tempestuous tide. The traits of character here indicated were well represented in the square cast of countenance and large physical development of the new colonial magistrates. So far as a demeanour of natural authority was concerned, the mother country need not have been ashamed to see these foremost men of an actual de-mocracy adopted into the House of Peers,[103] or made the Privy Council of the sovereign.

Next in order to the magistrates came the young and eminently distinguished divine, from whose lips the religious discourse of the anniversary was expected. His was the profession, at that era, in which intellectual ability displayed itself far more than in political life; for—leaving a higher motive out of the question—it offered inducements powerful enough, in the almost worshipping respect of the community, to win the most aspiring ambition into its service. Even political power—as in the case of Increase Mather[104]—was within the grasp of a successful priest.

It was the observation of those who beheld him now, that never, since Mr. Dimmesdale first set his foot on the New England shore, had he exhibited such energy as was seen in the gait and air with which he kept his pace in the proces-sion. There was no feebleness of step, as at other times; his frame was not bent; nor did his hand rest ominously upon his heart. Yet, if the clergyman were rightly viewed, his strength seemed not of the body. It might be spiritual, and imparted to him by angelic ministrations. It might be the exhilaration of that potent cordial, which is distilled only in the furnace-glow of earnest and long-continued thought. Or, perchance, his sensitive temperament was invigorated by the loud and pierc-ing music, that swelled heavenward, and uplifted him on its ascending wave. Nevertheless, so abstracted was his look, it might be questioned whether Mr. Dimmesdale even heard the music. There was his body, moving onward, and with an unaccustomed force. But where was his mind? Far and deep in its own region, busying itself, with preternatural activity, to marshal a procession of stately thoughts that were soon to issue thence; and so he saw nothing, heard nothing, knew nothing, of what was around him; but the spiritual element took up the feeble frame, and carried it along, unconscious of the burden, and converting it to spirit like itself. Men of uncommon intellect, who have grown morbid, possess this occasional power of mighty effort, into which they throw the life of many days, and then are lifeless for as many more.

Hester Prynne, gazing stedfastly at the clergyman, felt a dreary influence come over her, but wherefore or whence she knew not; unless that he seemed so remote from her own sphere, and utterly beyond her reach. One glance of recognition,

---

[102] Simon Bradstreet (1603–1697), husband of the poet Anne Bradstreet (1612–1672); John Endicott (1589?–1665); and Thomas Dudley (1576–1653): all were colonial governors of Massachusetts (as was Bellingham), between 1679 and 1692.

[103] The House of Lords in the British Parliament.

[104] Mather (1639–1723), father of Cotton Mather (1663–1728), a powerful Puritan minister, presi-dent of Harvard College from 1685 to 1701, and a persecutor of "witches" in Salem.

she had imagined, must needs pass between them. She thought of the dim forest, with its little dell of solitude, and love, and anguish, and the mossy tree-trunk, where, sitting hand in hand, they had mingled their sad and passionate talk with the melancholy murmur of the brook. How deeply had they known each other them! And was this the man? She hardly knew him now! He, moving proudly past, enveloped, as it were, in the rich music, with the procession of majestic and venerable fathers; he, so unattainable in his worldly position, and still more so in that far vista of his unsympathizing thoughts, through which she now beheld him! Her spirit sank with the idea that all must have been a delusion, and that, vividly as she had dreamed it, there could be no real bond betwixt the clergyman and herself. And thus much of woman was there in Hester, that she could scarcely forgive him,—least of all now, when the heavy footstep of their approaching Fate might be heard, nearer, nearer, nearer!—for being able so completely to withdraw himself from their mutual world; while she groped darkly, and stretched forth her cold hands, and found him not.

Pearl either saw and responded to her mother's feelings, or herself felt the remoteness and intangibility that had fallen around the minister. While the procession passed, the child was uneasy, fluttering up and down, like a bird on the point of taking flight. When the whole had gone by, she looked up into Hester's face.

"Mother," said she, "was that the same minister that kissed me by the brook?"

"Hold thy peace, dear little Pearl!" whispered her mother. "We must not always talk in the market-place of what happens to us in the forest."

"I could not be sure that it was he; so strange he looked," continued the child. "Else I would have run to him, and bid him kiss me now, before all the people; even as he did yonder among the dark old trees. What would the minister have said, mother? Would he have clapped his hand over his heart, and scowled on me, and bid me begone?"

"What should he say, Pearl," answered Hester, "save that it was no time to kiss, and that kisses are not to be given in the market-place? Well for thee, foolish child, that thou didst not speak to him!"

Another shade of the same sentiment, in reference to Mr. Dimmesdale, was expressed by a person whose eccentricities—or insanity, as we should term it—led her to do what few of the townspeople would have ventured on; to begin a conversation with the wearer of the scarlet letter, in public. It was Mistress Hibbins, who, arrayed in great magnificence, with a triple ruff, a broidered stomacher, a gown of rich velvet, and a gold-headed cane, had come forth to see the procession. As this ancient lady had the renown (which subsequently cost her no less a price than her life) of being a principal actor in all the works of necromancy that were continually going forward, the crowd gave way before her, and seemed to fear the touch of her garment, as if it carried the plague among its gorgeous folds. Seen in conjunction with Hester Prynne,—kindly as so many now felt towards the latter,—the dread inspired by Mistress Hibbins was doubled, and caused a general movement from that part of the market-place in which the two women stood.

"Now, what mortal imagination could conceive it!" whispered the old lady confidently to Hester. "Yonder divine man! That saint on earth, as the people uphold him to be, and as—I must needs say—he really looks! Who, now, that saw him pass in the procession, would think how little while it is since he went forth out of his study,—chewing a Hebrew text of Scripture in his mouth, I warrant,—to take an airing in the forest! Aha! we know what that means, Hester Prynne! But, truly, forsooth, I find it hard to believe him the same man. Many a church-member saw I, walking behind the music, that has danced in the same measure with me, when Somebody was fiddler, and, it might be, an Indian powwow[105] or a Lapland wizard changing hands with us! That is but a trifle, when a woman knows the world. But this minister! Couldst thou surely tell, Hester, whether he was the same man that encountered thee on the forest-path!"

"Madam, I know not of what you speak," answered Hester Prynne, feeling Mistress Hibbins to be of infirm mind; yet strangely startled and awe-stricken by the confidence with which she affirmed a personal connection between so many persons (herself among them) and the Evil One. "It is not for me to talk lightly of a learned and pious minister of the Word, like the Reverend Mr. Dimmesdale!"

"Fie, woman, fie!" cried the old lady, shaking her finger at Hester. "Dost thou think I have been to the forest so many times, and have yet no skill to judge who else has been there? Yea; though no leaf of the wild garlands, which they wore while they danced, be left in their hair! I know thee, Hester; for I behold the token. We may all see it in the sunshine; and it glows like a red flame in the dark. Thou wearest it openly; so there need be no question about that. But this minister! Let me tell thee in thine ear! When the Black Man sees one of his own servants, signed and sealed, so shy of owning to the bond as is the Reverend Mr. Dimmesdale, he hath a way of ordering matters so that the mark shall be disclosed in open daylight to the eyes of all the world! What is it that the minister seeks to hide, with his hand always over his heart? Ha, Hester Prynne!"

"What is it, good Mistress Hibbins?" eagerly asked little Pearl. "Hast thou seen it?"

"No matter, darling!" responded Mistress Hibbins, making Pearl a profound reverence. "Thou thyself wilt see it, one time or another. They say, child, thou art of the lineage of the Prince of the Air![106] Wilt thou ride with me, some fine night, to see thy father? Then thou shalt know wherefore the minister keeps his hand over his heart!"

Laughing so shrilly that all the market-place could hear her, the weird old gentlewoman took her departure.

By this time the preliminary prayer had been offered in the meeting-house, and the accents of the Reverend Mr. Dimmesdale were heard commencing his discourse. An irresistible feeling kept Hester near the spot. As the sacred edifice was too much thronged to admit another auditor, she took up her position close beside the scaffold of the pillory. It was in sufficient proximity to bring the whole sermon to her ears, in the shape of an indistinct, but varied, murmur and flow of the minister's very peculiar voice.

This vocal organ was in itself a rich endowment; insomuch that a listener, comprehending nothing of the language in which the preacher spoke, might still have been swayed to and fro by the mere tone and cadence. Like all other music, it breathed passion and pathos, and emotions high or tender, in a tongue native to the human heart, wherever educated. Muffled as the sound was by its passage through the church-walls, Hester Prynne listened with such intentness, and sympathized so intimately, that the sermon had throughout a meaning for her, entirely

---

[105] A medicine man.

[106] Satan. In Ephesians 2:2 Satan is described as "the prince of the power of the air. . . . "

apart from its indistinguishable words. These, perhaps, if more distinctly heard, might have been only a grosser medium, and have clogged the spiritual sense. Now she caught the low undertone, as of the wind sinking down to repose itself; then ascended with it, as it rose through progressive gradations of sweetness and power, until its volume seemed to envelop her with an atmosphere of awe and solemn grandeur. And yet, majestic as the voice sometimes became, there was for ever in it an essential character of plaintiveness. A loud or low expression of anguish,—the whisper, or the shriek, as it might be conceived, of suffering humanity, that touched a sensibility in every bosom! At times this deep strain of pathos was all that could be heard, and scarcely heard, sighing amid a desolate silence. But even when the minister's voice grew high and commanding,—when it gushed irrepressibly upward,—when it assumed its utmost breadth and power, so overfilling the church as to burst its way through the solid walls, and diffuse itself in the open air,—still, if the auditor listened intently, and for the purpose, he could detect the same cry of pain. What was it? The complaint of a human heart, sorrow-laden, perchance guilty, telling its secret, whether of guilt or sorrow, to the great heart of mankind; beseeching its sympathy or forgiveness,—at every moment,—in each accent,—and never in vain! It was this profound and continual undertone that gave the clergyman his most appropriate power.

During all this time Hester stood, statue-like, at the foot of the scaffold. If the minister's voice had not kept her there, there would nevertheless have been an inevitable magnetism in that spot, whence she dated the first hour of her life of ignominy. There was a sense within her,—too ill-defined to be made a thought, but weighing heavily on her mind,—that her whole orb of life, both before and after, was connected with this spot, as with the one point that gave it unity.

Little Pearl, meanwhile, had quitted her mother's side, and was playing at her own will about the market-place. She made the sombre crowd cheerful by her erratic and glistening ray; even as a bird of bright plumage illuminates a whole tree of dusky foliage by darting to and fro, half seen and half concealed, amid the twilight of the clustering leaves. She had an undulating, but, oftentimes, a sharp and irregular movement. It indicated the restless vivacity of her spirit, which to-day was doubly indefatigable in its tiptoe dance, because it was played upon and vibrated with her mother's disquietude. Whenever Pearl saw any thing to excite her ever active and wandering curiosity, she flew thitherward, and, as we might say, seized upon that man or thing as her own property, so far as she desired it; but without yielding the minutest degree of control over her motions in requital. The Puritans looked on, and, if they smiled, were none the less inclined to pronounce the child a demon offspring, from the indescribable charm of beauty and eccentricity that shone through her little figure, and sparkled with its activity. She ran and looked the wild Indian in the face; and he grew conscious of a nature wilder than his own. Thence, with native audacity, but still with a reserve as characteristic, she flew into the midst of a group of mariners, the swarthy-cheeked wild men of the ocean, as the Indians were of the land; and they gazed wonderingly and admiringly at Pearl, as if a flake of the sea-foam had taken the shape of a little maid, and were gifted with a soul of the sea-fire, that flashes beneath the prow in the night-time.

One of these seafaring men—the shipmaster, indeed, who had spoken to Hester Prynne—was so smitten with Pearl's aspect, that he attempted to lay hands upon her, with purpose to snatch a kiss. Finding it as impossible to touch her as to catch a humming-bird in the air, he took from his hat the gold chain that was twisted about it, and threw it to the child. Pearl immediately twined it around her neck and waist, with such happy skill, that, once seen there, it became a part of her, and it was difficult to imagine her without it.

"Thy mother is yonder woman with the scarlet letter," said the seaman. "Wilt thou carry her a message from me?"

"If the message pleases me I will," answered Pearl.

"Then tell her," rejoined he, "that I spake again with the black-a-visaged, hump-shouldered old doctor, and he engages to bring his friend, the gentleman she wots of, aboard with him. So let thy mother take no thought, save for herself and thee. Wilt thou tell her this, thou witch-baby?"

"Mistress Hibbins says my father is the Prince of the Air!" cried Pearl, with her naughty smile. "If thou callest me that ill name, I shall tell him of thee; and he will chase thy ship with a tempest!"

Pursuing a zigzag course across the market-place, the child returned to her mother, and communicated what the mariner had said. Hester's strong, calm, stedfastly enduring spirit almost sank, at last, on beholding this dark and grim countenance of an inevitable doom, which—at the moment when a passage seemed to open for the minister and herself out of their labyrinth of misery— showed itself, with an unrelenting smile, right in the midst of their path.

With her mind harassed by the terrible perplexity in which the shipmaster's intelligence involved her, she was also subjected to another trial. There were many people present, from the country roundabout, who had often heard of the scarlet letter, and to whom it had been made terrific by a hundred false or exaggerated rumors, but who had never beheld it with their own bodily eyes. These, after exhausting other modes of amusement, now thronged about Hester Prynne with rude and boorish intrusiveness. Unscrupulous as it was, however, it could not bring them nearer than a circuit of several yards. At that distance they accordingly stood, fixed there by the centrifugal force of the repugnance which the mystic symbol inspired. The whole gang of sailors, likewise, observing the press of spectators, and learning the purport of the scarlet letter, came and thrust their sunburnt and desperado-looking faces into the ring. Even the Indians were affected by a sort of cold shadow of the white man's curiosity, and, gliding through the crowd, fastened their snake-like black eyes on Hester's bosom; conceiving, perhaps, that the wearer of this brilliantly embroidered badge must needs be a personage of high dignity among her people. Lastly, the inhabitants of the town (their own interest in this worn-out subject languidly reviving itself, by sympathy with what they saw others feel) lounged idly to the same quarter, and tormented Hester Prynne, perhaps more than all the rest, with their cool, well-acquainted gaze at her familiar shame. Hester saw and recognized the self-same faces of that group of matrons, who had awaited her forthcoming from the prison-door, seven years ago; all save one, the youngest and only compassionate among them, whose burial-robe she had since made. At the final hour, when she was so soon to fling aside the burning letter, it had strangely become the centre of more remark and excitement, and was thus made to sear her breast more painfully, than at any time since the first day she put it on.

While Hester stood in that magic circle of ignominy, where the cunning cruelty of her sentence seemed to have fixed her for ever, the admirable preacher was looking down from the sacred pulpit upon an audience, whose very inmost spirits had yielded to his control. The sainted minister in the church! The woman of the scarlet letter in the market-place! What imagination would have been irreverent enough to surmise that the same scorching stigma was on them both?

XXIII: *The Revelation of the Scarlet Letter*

The eloquent voice, on which the souls of the listening audience had been borne aloft, as on the swelling waves of the sea, at length came to a pause. There was a momentary silence, profound as what should follow the utterance of oracles. Then ensued a murmur and half-hushed tumult; as if the auditors, released from the high spell that had transported them into the region of another's mind, were returning into themselves, with all their awe and wonder still heavy on them. In a moment more, the crowd began to gush forth from the doors of the church. Now that there was an end, they needed other breath, more fit to support the gross and earthly life into which they relapsed, than that atmosphere which the preacher had converted into words of flame, and had burdened with the rich fragrance of his thought.

In the open air their rapture broke into speech. The street and the market-place absolutely babbled, from side to side, with applauses of the minister. His hearers could not rest until they had told one another of what each knew better than he could tell or hear. According to their united testimony, never had man spoken in so wise, so high, and so holy a spirit, as he that spake this day; nor had inspiration ever breathed through mortal lips more evidently than it did through his. Its influence could be seen, as it were, descending upon him, and possessing him, and continually lifting him out of the written discourse that lay before him, and filling him with ideas that must have been as marvellous to himself as to his audience. His subject, it appeared, had been the relation between the Deity and the communities of mankind, with a special reference to the New England which they were here planting in the wilderness. And, as he drew towards the close, a spirit as of prophecy had come upon him, constraining him to its purpose as mightily as the old prophets of Israel were constrained; only with this difference, that, whereas the Jewish seers had denounced judgments and ruin on their country, it was his mission to foretell a high and glorious destiny for the newly gathered people of the Lord. But, throughout it all, and through the whole discourse, there had been a certain deep, sad undertone of pathos, which could not be interpreted otherwise than as the natural regret of one soon to pass away. Yes; their minister whom they so loved—and who so loved them all, that he could not depart heavenward without a sigh—had the foreboding of untimely death upon him, and would soon leave them in their tears! This idea of his transitory stay on earth gave the last emphasis to the effect which the preacher had produced; it was as if an angel, in his passage to the skies, had shaken his bright wings over the people for an instant,—at once a shadow and a splendor,—and had shed down a shower of golden truths upon them.

Thus, there had come to the Reverend Mr. Dimmesdale—as to most men, in their various spheres, though seldom recognized until they see it far behind them—an epoch of life more brilliant and full of triumph than any previous one, or than any which could hereafter be. He stood, at this moment, on the very proudest eminence of superiority, to which the gifts of intellect, rich lore, prevailing eloquence, and a reputation of whitest sanctity, could exalt a clergyman in New England's earliest days, when the professional character was of itself a lofty pedestal. Such was the position which the minister occupied, as he bowed his head forward on the cushions of the pulpit, at the close of his Election Sermon.[107] Meanwhile, Hester Prynne was standing beside the scaffold of the pillory, with the scarlet letter still burning on her breast!

Now was heard again the clangor of the music, and the measured tramp of the military escort, issuing from the church-door. The procession was to be marshalled thence to the town-hall, where a solemn banquet would complete the ceremonies of the day.

Once more, therefore, the train of venerable and majestic fathers was seen moving through a broad pathway of the people, who drew back reverently, on either side, as the Governor and magistrates, the old and wise men, the holy ministers, and all that were eminent and renowned, advanced into the midst of them. When they were fairly in the market-place, their presence was greeted by a shout. This—though doubtless it might acquire additional force and volume from the childlike loyalty which the age awarded to its rulers—was felt to be an irrepressible outburst of the enthusiasm kindled in the auditors by that high strain of eloquence which was yet reverberating in their ears. Each felt the impulse in himself, and, in the same breath, caught it from his neighbour. Within the church, it had hardly been kept down; beneath the sky, it pealed upward to the zenith. There were human beings enough, and enough of highly wrought and symphonious feeling, to produce that more impressive sound than the organ-tones of the blast, or the thunder, or the roar of the sea; even that mighty swell of many voices, blended into one great voice by the universal impulse which makes likewise one vast heart out of the many. Never, from the soil of New England, had gone up such a shout! Never, on New England soil, had stood the man so honored by his mortal brethren as the preacher!

How fared it with him them? Were there not the brilliant particles of a halo in the air about his head? So etherealized by spirit as he was, and so apotheosized by worshipping admirers, did his footsteps in the procession really tread upon the dust of earth?

As the ranks of military men and civil fathers moved onward, all eyes were turned towards the point where the minister was seen to approach among them. The shout died into a murmur, as one portion of the crowd after another obtained a glimpse of him. How feeble and pale he looked amid all his triumph! The energy—or say, rather, the inspiration which had held him up, until he should have delivered the sacred message that brought its own strength along with it from heaven—was withdrawn, now that it had so faithfully performed its office. The glow, which they had just before beheld burning on his cheek, was extinguished, like a flame that sinks down hopelessly among the late-decaying embers. It seemed hardly the face of a man alive, with such a deathlike hue; it was hardly a man with life in him, that tottered on his path so nervelessly, yet tottered, and did not fall!

One of his clerical brethren,—it was the venerable John Wilson,—observing the state in which Mr. Dimmesdale was left by the retiring wave of intellect and sensibility, stepped forward hastily to offer his support. The minister tremulously, but decidedly, repelled the old man's arm. He still walked onward, if that move-

---

[107] There is no evidence that Dimmesdale had decided to make his revelation on the scaffold prior to this point; his decision comes suddenly without mention of a specific motive. It is within the dramatic logic of the narrative to see his final and greatest sermon as a factor in motivating his confession.

ment could be so described, which rather resembled the wavering effort of an infant, with its mother's arms in view, outstretched to tempt him forward. And now, almost imperceptible as were the latter steps of his progress, he had come opposite the well-remembered and weather-darkened scaffold, where, long since, with all that dreary lapse of time between, Hester Prynne had encountered the world's ignominious stare. There stood Hester, holding little Pearl by the hand! And there was the scarlet letter on her breast! The minister here made a pause; although the music still played the stately and rejoicing march to which the procession moved. It summoned him onward,—onward to the festival!—but here he made a pause.

Bellingham, for the last few moments, had kept an anxious eye upon him. He now left his own place in the procession, and advanced to give assistance; judging from Mr. Dimmesdale's aspect that he must otherwise inevitably fall. But there was something in the latter's expression that warned back the magistrate, although a man not readily obeying the vague intimations that pass from one spirit to another. The crowd, meanwhile, looked on with awe and wonder. This earthly faintness was, in their view, only another phase of the minister's celestial strength; nor would it have seemed a miracle too high to be wrought for one so holy, had he ascended before their eyes, waxing dimmer and brighter, and fading at last into the light of heaven!

He turned towards the scaffold, and stretched forth his arms.

"Hester," said he, "come hither! Come, my Pearl!"

It was a ghastly look with which he regarded them; but there was something at once tender and strangely triumphant in it. The child, with the bird-like motion which was one of her characteristics, flew to him, and clasped her arms about his knees. Hester Prynne—slowly, as if impelled by inevitable fate, and against her strongest will—likewise drew near, but paused before she reached him. At this instant old Roger Chillingworth thrust himself through the crowd,—or, perhaps, so dark, disturbed, and evil was his look, he rose up out of some nether region,—to snatch back his victim from what he sought to do! Be that as it might, the old man rushed forward and caught the minister by the arm.

"Madman, hold! What is your purpose?" whispered he. "Wave back that woman! Cast off this child! All shall be well! Do not blacken your fame, and perish in dishonor! I can yet save you! Would you bring infamy on your sacred profession?"

"Ha, tempter! Methinks thou art too late!" answered the minister, encountering his eye, fearfully, but firmly. "Thy power is not what it was! With God's help, I shall escape thee now!"

He again extended his hand to the woman of the scarlet letter.

"Hester Prynne," cried he, with a piercing earnestness, "in the name of Him, so terrible and so merciful, who gives me grace, at this last moment, to do what—for my own heavy sin and miserable agony—I withheld myself from doing seven years ago, come hither now, and twine thy strength about me! Thy strength, Hester; but let it be guided by the will which God hath granted me! This wretched and wronged old man is opposing it with all his might!—with all his own might and the fiend's! Come, Hester, come! Support me up yonder scaffold!"

The crowd was in a tumult. The men of rank and dignity, who stood more immediately around the clergyman, were so taken by surprise, and so perplexed as to the purport of what they saw,—unable to receive the explanation which most readily presented itself, or to imagine any other,—that they remained silent and inactive spectators of the judgment which Providence seemed about to work. They beheld the minister, leaning on Hester's shoulder and supported by her arm around him, approach the scaffold, and ascend its steps; while still the little hand of the sin-born child was clasped in his. Old Roger Chillingworth followed, as one intimately connected with the drama of guilt and sorrow in which they had all been actors, and well entitled, therefore, to be present at its closing scene.

"Hadst thou sought the whole earth over," said he, looking darkly at the clergyman, "there was no one place so secret,—no high place nor lowly place, where thou couldst have escaped me,—save on this very scaffold!"

"Thanks be to Him who hath led me hither!" answered the minister.

Yet he trembled, and turned to Hester with an expression of doubt and anxiety in his eyes, not the less evidently betrayed, that there was feeble smile upon his lips.

"Is not this better," murmured he, "than what we dreamed of in the forest?"

"I know not! I know not!" she hurriedly replied. "Better? Yea; so we may both die, and little Pearl die with us!"

"For thee and Pearl, be it as God shall order," said the minister; "and God is merciful! Let me now do the will which he hath made plain before my sight. For, Hester, I am a dying man. So let me make haste to take my shame upon me."

Partly supported by Hester Prynne, and holding one hand of little Pearl's, the Reverend Mr. Dimmesdale turned to the dignified and venerable rulers; to the holy ministers, who were his brethren; to the people, whose great heart was thoroughly appalled, yet overflowing with tearful sympathy, as knowing that some deep life-matter—which, if full of sin, was full of anguish and repentance likewise—was now to be laid open to them. The sun, but little past its meridian, shone down upon the clergyman, and gave a distinctness to his figure, as he stood out from all the earth to put in his plea of guilty at the bar of Eternal Justice.

"People of New England!" cried he, with a voice that rose over them, high, solemn, and majestic,—yet had always a tremor through it, and sometimes a shriek, struggling up out of a fathomless depth of remorse and woe,—"ye, that have loved me!—ye, that have deemed me holy!—behold me here, the one sinner of the world. At last!—at last!—I stand upon the spot where, seven years since, I should have stood; here, with this woman, whose arm, more than the little strength wherewith I have crept hitherward, sustains me, at this dreadful moment, from grovelling down upon my face! Lo, the scarlet letter which Hester wears! Ye have all shuddered at it! Wherever her walk hath been,—wherever, so miserably burdened, she may have hoped to find repose,—it hath cast a lurid gleam of awe and horrible repugnance roundabout her. But there stood one in the midst of you, at whose brand of sin and infamy ye have not shuddered!"

It seemed, at this point, as if the minister must leave the remainder of his secret undisclosed. But he fought back the bodily weakness,—and, still more, the faintness of heart,—that was striving for the mastery with him. He threw off all assistance, and stepped passionately forward a pace before the woman and the child.

"It was on him!" he continued, with a kind of fierceness; so determined was he to speak out the whole. "God's eye beheld it! The angels were for ever pointing at it! The Devil knew it well, and fretted it continually with the touch of his burning finger! But he hid it cunningly from men, and walked among you with the mien of a spirit, mournful, because so pure in a sinful world!—and sad, because he missed his heavenly kindred! Now, at the death-hour, he stands up before you! He bids you look again at Hester's scarlet letter! He tells you, that, with all its mysterious horror, it is but the shadow of what he bears on his own breast, and that even this, his own red stigma, is no more than the type of what has seared his inmost heart! Stand any here that question God's judgment on a sinner? Behold! Behold a dreadful witness of it!"

With a convulsive motion he tore away the ministerial band from before his breast. It was revealed! But it were irreverent to describe that revelation. For an instant the gaze of the horror-stricken multitude was concentred on the ghastly miracle; while the minister stood with a flush of triumph in his face, as one who, in the crisis of acutest pain, had won a victory. Then, down he sank upon the scaffold! Hester partly raised him, and supported his head against her bosom. Old Roger Chillingworth knelt down beside him, with a blank, dull countenance, out of which the life seemed to have departed.

"Thou hast escaped me!" he repeated more than once. "Thou hast escaped me!"

"May God forgive thee!" said the minister. "Thou, too, hast deeply sinned!"

He withdrew his dying eyes from the old man, and fixed them on the woman and the child.

"My little Pearl," said he feebly,—and there was a sweet and gentle smile over his face, as of a spirit sinking into deep repose; nay, now that the burden was removed, it seemed almost as if he would be sportive with the child,—"dear little Pearl, wilt thou kiss me now? Thou wouldst not yonder, in the forest! But now thou wilt?"

Pearl kissed his lips. A spell was broken. The great scene of grief, in which the wild infant bore a part, had developed all her sympathies; and as her tears fell upon her father's cheek, they were the pledge that she would grow up amid human joy and sorrow, nor for ever do battle with the world, but be a woman in it. Towards her mother, too, Pearl's errand as a messenger of anguish was all fulfilled.

"Hester," said the clergyman, "farewell!"

"Shall we not meet again?" whispered she, bending her face down close to his. "Shall we not spend our immortal life together? Surely, surely, we have ransomed one another, with all this woe! Thou lookest far into eternity, with those bright dying eyes! Then tell me what thou seest?"

"Hush, Hester, hush!" said he, with tremulous solemnity. "The law we broke!—the sin here so awfully revealed!—let these alone be in thy thoughts! I fear! I fear! It may be, that, when we forgot our God,—when we violated our reverence each for the other's souls,—it was thenceforth vain to hope that we could meet hereafter, in an everlasting and pure reunion. God knows; and He is merciful! He hath proved his mercy, most of all, in my afflictions. By giving me this burning torture to bear upon my breast! By sending yonder dark and terrible old man, to keep the torture always at red-heat! By bringing me hither, to die this death of triumphant ignominy before the people! Had either of these agonies been wanting, I had been lost for ever! Praised be his name! His will be done! Farewell!"

That final word came forth with the minister's expiring breath. The multitude, silent till then, broke out in a strange, deep voice of awe and wonder, which could not as yet find utterance, save in this murmur that rolled so heavily after the departed spirit.

XXIV: Conclusion

After many days, when time sufficed for the people to arange their thoughts in reference to the foregoing scene, there was more than one account of what had been witnessed on the scaffold.

Most of the spectators testified to having seen, on the breast of the unhappy minister, a SCARLET LETTER—the very semblance of that worn by Hester Prynne—imprinted in the flesh. As regarded its origin, there were various explanations, all of which must necessarily have been conjectural. Some affirmed that the Reverend Mr. Dimmesdale, on the very day when Hester Prynne first wore her ignominious badge, had begun a course of penance, which he afterwards, in so many futile methods, followed out,—by inflicting a hideous torture on himself. Others contended that the stigma had not been produced until a long time subsequent, when old Roger Chillingworth, being a potent necromancer, had caused it to appear, through the agency of magic and poisonous drugs. Others, again,—and those best able to appreciate the minister's peculiar sensibility, and the wonderful operation of his spirit upon the body,—whispered their belief, that the awful symbol was the effect of the ever active tooth of remorse, gnawing from the inmost heart outwardly, and at last manifesting Heaven's dreadful judgment by the visible presence of the letter. The reader may choose among these theories. We have thrown all the light we could acquire upon the portent, and would gladly, now that it has done its office, erase its deep print out of our own brain; where long meditation has fixed it in very undesirable distinctness.

It is singular, nevertheless, that certain persons, who were spectators of the whole scene, and professed never once to have removed their eyes from the Reverend Mr. Dimmesdale, denied that there was any mark whatever on his breast, more than on a new-born infant's. Neither, by their report, had his dying words acknowledged, nor even remotely implied, any, the slightest connection, on his part, with the guilt for which Hester Prynne had so long worn the scarlet letter. According to these highly respectable witnesses, the minister, conscious that he was dying,—conscious, also, that the reverence of the multitude placed him already among saints and angels,—had desired, by yielding up his breath in the arms of that fallen woman, to express to the world how utterly nugatory is the choicest of man's own righteousness. After exhausting life in his efforts for mankind's spiritual good, he had made the manner of his death a parable, in order to impress on his admirers the mighty and mournful lesson, that, in the view of Infinite Purity, we are sinners all alike. It was to teach them, that the holiest among us has but attained so far above his fellows as to discern more clearly the Mercy which looks down, and repudiate more utterly the phantom of human merit, which would look aspiringly upward. Without disputing a truth so momentous, we must be allowed to consider this version of Mr. Dimmesdale's story as only an instance of that stubborn fidelity with which a man's friends—and especially a clergyman's—will sometimes uphold his character; when proofs, clear as the mid-day sunshine on the scarlet letter, establish him a false and sin-stained creature of the dust.

The authority which we have chiefly followed—a manuscript of old date, drawn up from the verbal testimony of individuals, some of whom had known Hester Prynne, while others had heard the tale from contemporary witnesses—fully confirms the view taken in the foregoing pages. Among many morals which press upon us from the poor minister's miserable experience, we put only this into a sentence:—"Be true! Be true! Be true! Show freely to the world, if not your worst, yet some trait whereby the worst may be inferred!"

Nothing was more remarkable than the change which took place, almost immediately after Mr. Dimmesdale's death, in the appearance and demeanour of the old man known as Roger Chillingworth. All his strength and energy—all his vital and intellectual force—seemed at once to desert him; insomuch that he positively withered up, shrivelled away, and almost vanished from mortal sight, like an uprooted weed that lies wilting in the sun. This unhappy man had made the very principle of his life to consist in the pursuit and systematic exercise of revenge; and when, by its completest triumph and consummation, that evil principle was left with no further material to support it,—when, in short, there was no more devil's work on earth for him to do, it only remained for the unhumanized mortal to betake himself whither his Master would find him tasks enough, and pay him his wages duly. But, to all these shadowy beings, so long our near acquaintances,—as well Roger Chillingworth as his companions,—we would fain be merciful. It is a curious subject of observation and inquiry, whether hatred and love be not the same thing at bottom. Each, in its utmost development, supposes a high degree of intimacy and heart-knowledge; each renders one individual dependent for the food of his affections and spiritual life upon another; each leaves the passionate lover, or the no less passionate hater, forlorn and desolate by the withdrawal of his object. Philosophically considered, therefore, the two passions seem essentially the same, except that one happens to be seen in a celestial radiance, and the other in a dusky and lurid glow. In the spiritual world, the old physician and the minister—mutual victims as they have been—may, unawares, have found their earthly stock of hatred and antipathy transmuted into golden love.

Leaving this discussion apart, we have a matter of business to communicate to the reader. At old Roger Chillingworth's decease (which took place within the year), and by his last will and testament, of which Governor Bellingham and the Reverend Mr. Wilson were executors, he bequeathed a very considerable amount of property, both here and in England, to little Pearl, the daughter of Hester Prynne.

So Pearl—the elf-child,—the demon offspring, as some people, up to that epoch, persisted in considering her—became the richest heiress of her day, in the New World. Not improbably, this circumstance wrought a very material change in the public estimation; and, had the mother and child remained here, little Pearl, at a marriageable period of life, might have mingled her wild blood with the lineage of the devoutest Puritan among them all. But, in no long time after the physician's death, the wearer of the scarlet letter disappeared, and Pearl along with her. For many years, though a vague report would now and then find its way across the sea,—like a shapeless piece of driftwood tost ashore, with the initials of a name upon it,—yet no tidings of them unquestionably authentic were received. The story of the scarlet letter grew into a legend. Its spell, however, was still potent, and kept the scaffold awful where the poor minister had died, and likewise the cottage by the sea-shore, where Hester Prynne had dwelt. Near this latter spot, one afternoon, some children were at play, when they beheld a tall woman, in a gray robe, approach the cottage-door. In all those years it had never once been opened; but either she unlocked it, or the decaying wood and iron yielded to her hand, or she glided shadow-like through these impediments,—and, at all events, went in.

On the threshold she paused,—turned partly round,—for, perchance, the idea of entering, all alone, and all so changed, the home of so intense a former life, was more dreary and desolate that even she could bear. But her hesitation was only for an instant, though long enough to display a scarlet letter on her breast.

And Hester Prynne had returned, and taken up her long forsaken shame. But where was little Pearl? If still alive, she must now have been in the flush and bloom of early womanhood. None knew—nor ever learned, with the fulness of perfect certainty—whether the elf-child had gone thus untimely to a maiden grave; or whether her wild, rich nature had been softened and subdued, and made capable of a woman's gentle happiness. But, through the remainder of Hester's life, there were indications that the recluse of the scarlet letter was the object of love and interest with some inhabitant of another land. Letters came, with armorial seals upon them, though of bearings unknown to English heraldry. In the cottage there were articles of comfort and luxury, such as Hester never cared to use, but which only wealth could have purchased, and affection have imagined for her. There were trifles, too, little ornaments, beautiful tokens of a continual remembrance, that must have been wrought by delicate fingers, at the impulse of a fond heart. And, once, Hester was seen embroidering a baby-garment, with such a lavish richness of golden fancy as would have raised a public tumult, had any infant, thus apparelled, been shown to our sombre-hued community.

In fine, the gossips of that day believed,—and Mr. Surveyor Pue, who made investigations a century later, believed,—and one of his recent successors in office, moreover, faithfully believes,—that Pearl was not only alive, but married, and happy, and mindful of her mother; and that she would most joyfully have entertained that sad and lonely mother at her fireside.

But there was a more real life for Hester Prynne, here, in New England, than in that unknown region where Pearl had found a home. Here had been her sin; here, her sorrow; and here was yet to be her penitence. She had returned, therefore, and resumed,—of her own free will, for not the sternest magistrate of that iron period would have imposed it,—resumed the symbol of which we have related so dark a tale. Never afterwards did it quit her bosom. But, in the lapse of the toilsome, thoughtful, and self-devoted years that made up Hester's life, the scarlet letter ceased to be a stigma which attracted the world's scorn and bitterness, and became a type of something to be sorrowed over, and looked upon with awe, yet with reverence too. And, as Hester Prynne had no selfish ends, nor lived in any measure for her own profit and enjoyment, people brought all their sorrows and perplexities, and besought her counsel, as one who had herself gone through a mighty trouble. Women, more especially,—in the continually recurring trials of wounded, wasted, wronged, misplaced, or erring and sinful passion,—or with the dreary burden of a heart unyielded, because unvalued and unsought,—came to Hester's cottage, demanding why they were so wretched, and what the remedy! Hester comforted and counselled them, as best she might. She assured them, too, of her firm belief, that, at some brighter period, when the world should have grown ripe for it, in Heaven's own time, a new truth would be revealed, in order to establish the whole relation between man and woman on a surer ground of mutual happiness. Earlier in life, Hester had vainly imagined that she herself might be the destined prophetess, but had long since recognized the impossibility that any mission of divine and mysterious truth should be confided to a woman stained with sin, bowed down with shame, or even burdened with a life-long sorrow. The angel and apostle of the coming revelation must be a woman, indeed, but lofty, pure, and beautiful; and wise, moreover, not through dusky grief, but the ethereal medium of joy; and showing how sacred love should make us happy, by the truest test of a life successful to such an end!

So said Hester Prynne, and glanced her sad eyes downward at the scarlet letter. And, after many, many years, a new grave was delved, near an old and sunken one, in that burial-ground beside which King's Chapel has since been built. It was near that old and sunken grave, yet with a space between, as if the dust of the two sleepers had no right to mingle. Yet one tombstone served for both. All around, there were monuments carved with armorial bearings; and on this simple slab of slate—as the curious investigator may still discern, and perplex himself with the purport—there appeared the semblance of an engraved escutcheon.[108] It bore a device, a herald's wording of which might serve for a motto and brief description of our now concluded legend; so sombre is it, and relieved only by one ever glowing point of light gloomier than the shadow:—

"ON A FIELD, SABLE, THE LETTER A, GULES."[109]

1849–1850, 1850

Herman Melville
(1819–1891)

"Until I was twenty-five," Herman Melville wrote to his friend Nathaniel Hawthorne in 1850, "I had no development at all. From my twenty-fifth year I date my life." Melville had good reason to date his life from 1844, the year he returned without prospects or much formal education from a long stint as a common seaman on several whaling ships and an American man-of-war. During the next sixteen years he published five novels and established his reputation as a promising author; when he wrote to Hawthorne in 1850 Melville was working on his masterpiece, *Moby-Dick* (1851). But the curve of Melville's public career had peaked: *Moby-Dick* was not a popular success, his novel *Pierre* (1852) frustrated critics and public alike, and his obscure satire *The Confidence-Man* (1857) almost went unread. At his death in 1891 Melville was unknown beyond a small group of admirers; not until the Melville revival of the 1920s was his work given the attention it deserves. The shape of Melville's public career—early success, obscurity, posthumous vindication—exercises a powerful fascination as a model of tragic authorship, but it is more than matched by the extraordinary drama of his inward development, which continued submerged but unabated through the years of public neglect.

Born in 1819 in New York City, Melville was the third of eight children of Maria Gansevoort and Allan Melvill (the "e" was added in the 1830s). Maria was the only daughter of General Peter Gansevoort, a Revolutionary War hero; Allan's father, Major Thomas Melvill, had taken part in the Boston Tea Party. This patrician ancestry helped shape Melville's life and work. As a child he was considered somewhat backward in development,

---

[108] A shield.   [109] Heraldic wording that means "on a black background, the letter A in red."

especially in comparison with his more precocious brother Gansevoort, but his early years seem to have been happy. Melville was eleven when his father, a prosperous importer, was forced into bankruptcy in 1830. The family then moved to Albany, where for a short time their fortunes improved; but the business failed again, and Allan Melvill died in 1832 after suffering a mental and physical breakdown.

The trauma of his father's early death is reflected throughout Melville's fiction in the persistent concern with absent fathers; more immediately, however, it forced Melville to find a career. During the next few years he tried various professions—clerk, farmhand, bookkeeper, schoolmaster—with little pleasure or success. In 1839 he took the decisive step of working as a cabin boy on a packet ship bound for Liverpool; this first taste of a sailor's often brutal life provided material for his fourth novel, *Redburn* (1849). Back in the United States later that year, Melville briefly taught school and made a trip to Illinois, during which he took a steamboat excursion up the Mississippi River (the setting of *The Confidence-Man*). Returning East with no definite prospects, he left New Bedford, Massachusetts, in January 1841 on the *Acushnet*, a whaler bound for the South Pacific. Conditions on the ship proved intolerable: the captain was despotic, whales were scarce, and when the *Acushnet* reached the Marquesas Islands in July 1842, Melville and a shipmate, Richard Tobias Greene, jumped ship, intending to seek refuge with a friendly tribe. By error they made their way to the reputedly cannibalistic Taipis (Typees), with whom Melville remained for a month before escaping on an Australian whaler. Conditions on that ship were no better than those aboard the *Acushnet*, however, and Melville reluctantly joined a rebellion that landed him in a Tahitian prison. Soon released, he spent several months beachcombing before shipping out on the homeward-bound frigate *United States*. He was discharged from the navy in October 1844 with a valuable store of tales and a permanently altered perspective on western culture.

Encouraged by family and friends, Melville began writing about his South Pacific adventures, supplementing personal experience with information from secondary sources—a method of composition he used throughout his career. Published in England in 1846, *Typee: Or, a Peep at Polynesian Life* was an immediate success, although many readers were offended by Melville's critique of the hypocrisy and ethnocentric cruelty of Christian missionaries in the South Pacific. Reaction was so strong that to Melville's disgust an expurgated edition was published in the United States the following year. The novel *Omoo: A Narrative of Adventures in the South Seas* (1847) capitalized on *Typee*'s success by portraying Melville's adventures in Tahiti. By the time he began *Mardi* in 1848, however, Melville was beginning to feel the constraints of the picaresque travel narrative; because some critics had doubted the factual basis of his two novels, he proposed to write "a romance of Polynesian adventure." *Mardi* (1849) opens as a straightforward adventure tale but soon enters uncharted seas as the protagonist, Taji, voyages through an imaginary archipelago in search of an illusive maiden. At once allegory, satire, and philosophical speculation, *Mardi* reflects Melville's readings in Edmund Spenser, Dante, François Rabelais, and Thomas Browne and his own increasing interest in what he called "the great art of Telling the Truth."

Mardi was neither the critical success that Melville had expected nor the commercial success his circumstances demanded. In 1847 he had married Elizabeth Shaw, daughter of Lemuel Shaw (an influential judge who had been a good friend of Melville's father), and the first of their four children was born in 1849. To support his family Melville pushed himself to write two novels in rapid succession: *Redburn*, a tale of initiation based on his voyage to Liverpool, and *White-Jacket* (1850), about life on a man-of-war. Both offered nautical adventures of the sort Melville's audience had come to expect, and although they were popular successes Melville considered them hack work, written "to buy some tobacco

A watercolor drawing of the whaling ship Acushnet, *on which Herman Melville sailed to the South Seas in 1841, by Henry Johnson (1847)*.

with." This judgment is certainly too severe; both novels combine psychological observation and social commentary in ways that anticipate Melville's best work.

After Melville returned from a trip to England to arrange advantageous copyright terms for *White-Jacket*, he began a new book about the whaling industry. *Moby-Dick* bears the special impress of his readings in Thomas Carlyle, Johann Wolfgang von Goethe, the Bible, and William Shakespeare; the most formative influence, however, was exercised by Nathaniel Hawthorne. In August 1850 Melville published a buoyant nationalistic review of Hawthorne's *Mosses From an Old Manse* (1846) for the New York *Literary World*, touting the American writer as Shakespeare's equal and claiming him as a fellow traveler toward "the blackness of darkness beyond." The same month the two writers found themselves neighbors, Melville at Arrowhead, the 160-acre farm he had recently purchased near Pittsfield, Massachusetts, and Hawthorne in his little red house just outside nearby Lenox. They soon became friends, although the more demonstrative Melville noted in an 1851 letter to the editor Evert Duyckinck the lack of "plump sphericity" in Hawthorne and suggested a corrective diet of "roast-beef, done rare." Nevertheless, with Hawthorne, Melville could discourse freely about what he called "ontological heroics," and he found the support and inspiration needed to push *Moby-Dick* beyond its initially more conventional design. In his masterpiece Melville balances Captain Ahab's monomaniacal search for vengeance on the white whale with the narrator Ishmael's open-ended voyage for understanding his place as a cosmic orphan—a voyage the attentive reader must also make. Ballasted with facts about whales and whaling, *Moby-Dick* mixes sermons, drama, and dramatic monologues in a work whose dominant characteristics are its driving imaginative energy and linguistic exuberance. The book is dedicated to Hawthorne, "in token of my admiration for his genius."

Hawthorne responded knowingly to *Moby-Dick*, but many reviewers were confused by what an October 1851 London *Athenaeum* called "an ill-compounded mixture of romance and matter-of-fact." Once again, as Melville wrote Hawthorne in 1851, "what I feel most moved to write, that is banned—it will not pay. Yet, altogether, write the *other* way I cannot." Melville nevertheless determined to write his next novel "the other way"; it was going to be "a rural bowl of milk," as he explained to Hawthorne's wife, Sophia. But Melville could not refrain from extending pious formulas to parodic, and destructive, lengths. *Pierre: Or, the Ambiguities* is a disturbing psychological tale that follows the protagonist from gushy innocence to aggressive defiance and finally to death. With its own perverse brilliance, it is perhaps Melville's most personal work. The overwrought, subversive style, however, left many readers confused, offended at the spectacle of sentimental romance transformed to nightmare.

Profoundly disappointed by the reception of *Moby-Dick* and *Pierre,* Melville nevertheless continued to write. When he failed to receive an appointment as U.S. Consul to the Sandwich Islands (Hawaii), he turned to short fiction and published fourteen stories (among them "Bartleby the Scrivener" [1853]) between 1853 and 1856, mostly in *Putnam's* and *Harper's* magazines. The stories did little to reestablish Melville's reputation, even when some were collected in *The Piazza Tales* in 1856. Additionally, Melville wrote the restrained short novel *Israel Potter* about the life of a Revolutionary War soldier; serialized by *Putnam's,* it appeared in book form in 1855. During this period he began work on the last novel to be published during his lifetime, *The Confidence-Man: His Masquerade.* Set on a Mississippi River steamboat that begins its journey on April Fools' Day, this work is a picaresque philosophical and theological excursion that targets the optimistic philosophies of mid-century America. The ambivalent prose and mysterious cast of characters did not satisfy an audience expecting a more intelligible satire on American manners.

The years between 1850 and 1856 had taken a heavy toll on Melville, both physically and psychologically. In October 1856, after selling half his farm and accepting a loan from Judge Shaw, he set out on a voyage to Europe and the Near East in hope of regaining his health. In Liverpool he strolled with Hawthorne (then U.S. consul) and talked, as Hawthorne noted in his journal, "of Providence and futurity, and of everything that lies beyond human ken"—including their disbelief in "a temperance heaven." In mid-November Melville boarded a steamer for the Holy Land, which would provide the background for his long narrative poem *Clarel* (1876), and quickly toured Europe before returning to Liverpool. Back in the United States in May 1857, he tried lecturing on such topics as "Statues in Rome" and "The South Seas" but without much success, and after a voyage to San Francisco in 1860 he moved his family to New York City, where a legacy from Judge Shaw (who died in 1861) soon allowed them to live comfortably. In 1866, at age forty-seven, Melville began working as a customs inspector for the port of New York—a position that he held for almost twenty years. Although inheritances from several relatives eased the Melvilles' financial situation, personal tragedies continued: their oldest son, Malcolm, committed suicide in 1867; the second son, Stanwix, died almost twenty years later in San Francisco after years of unfocused wandering; and one daughter, Frances, felt so bitter toward her father because of his erratic and sometimes violent behavior that she would not speak to him.

The silence of Melville's last twenty-five years, however, is a matter of public rather than of private record: after *The Confidence-Man* Melville turned from prose fiction to the more private genre of poetry. In 1866 *Battle-Pieces,* a collection of poems about the Civil War, was published. In powerful but metrically irregular verse that found no critical acclaim, Melville probed the pain of war and conflated the healing of national wounds with hope for his own renewal. *Clarel,* a dense, eighteen thousand-line philosophical poem on faith and doubt that Melville had published with money provided by his uncle Peter Gansevoort, went virtually unnoticed. Undaunted, Melville published volumes of poetry at his own expense in 1888 and 1891 and at the time of his death had nearly completed *Billy*

Budd, his only long prose fiction after *The Confidence-Man.* Although it was published in 1923, an authoritative text of *Billy Budd* was not available until 1962, and in some ways this tale of an innocent sailor's tragic confrontation with authority continues to resist definitive interpretation. Nevertheless, it shows Melville still questing for truth of character and action in a fallen world, still unwilling to rest in easy solutions. At the end of his career Melville remained an exemplary member of what he called the "corps of thought-divers, that have been diving & coming up again with bloodshot eyes since the world began," in an 1849 letter to Duyckinck.

Suggested Readings: *Clarel,* ed. W. Bezanson, 1959. *Writings of Herman Melville,* 16 vols. projected (Northwestern-Newberry Edition), ed. H. Hayford, H. Parker, and G. T. Tanselle, 1968– . *The Melville Log: A Documentary Life of Herman Melville,* 2 vols., ed. J. Leyda, 1969. *The Collected Poems,* ed. H. P. Vincent, 1981. C. Olson, *Call Me Ishmael,* 1958. H. Parker, ed., *The Recognition of Herman Melville: Selected Criticism Since 1846,* 1967. E. A. Dryden, *Melville's Thematics of Form: The Great Art of Telling the Truth,* 1969. J. Seelye, *Melville: The Ironic Diagram,* 1970. R. A. Sherrill, *The Prophetic Melville: Experience, Transcendence, and Tragedy,* 1979. T. W. Herbert, *Marquesan Encounters: Melville and the Meaning of Civilization,* 1980. C. L. Karcher, *Shadow Over the Promised Land: Slavery, Race, and Violence in Melville's America,* 1980. S. Cameron, *The Corporeal Self: Allegories of the Body in Melville and Hawthorne,* 1981. M. P. Rogin, *Subversive Geneology: The Politics and Art of Herman Melville,* 1985. W. B. Dillingham, *Melville's Later Novels,* 1986. M. Sealts, *Melville's Reading,* 1988. N. L. Tolchin, *Mourning, Gender, and Creativity in the Art of Herman Melville,* 1988. J. Samson, *White Lies: Melville's Narrative of Facts,* 1989.

Texts Used: "Bartleby the Scrivener" and "Benito Cereno": *The Piazza Tales,* 1856. "The Paradise of Bachelors and the Tartarus of Maids": *Harper's New Monthly Magazine,* April 1855: 670–678. *Billy Budd,* ed. H. Hayford and M. M. Sealts, 1962. Poetry: *Poems,* 1924. "Hawthorne and His Mosses": *Billy Budd and Other Prose Pieces,* ed. R. W. Weaver, 1924. Letters: *Correspondence,* ed. L. Howth, 1990.

BARTLEBY THE SCRIVENER*

A Story of Wall Street

I am a rather elderly man. The nature of my avocations, for the last thirty years, has brought me into more than ordinary contact with what would seem an interesting and somewhat singular set of men, of whom, as yet, nothing, that I know of, has ever been written—I mean, the law-copyists, or scriveners. I have known very many of them, professionally and privately, and, if I pleased, could relate divers histories, at which good-natured gentlemen might smile, and sentimental souls might weep. But I waive the biographies of all other scriveners, for a few passages in the life of Bartleby, who was a scrivener, the strangest I ever saw, or heard of. While, of other law-copyists, I might write the complete life, of Bartleby nothing of that sort can be done. I believe that no materials exist, for a full and satisfactory biography of this man. It is an irreparable loss to literature. Bartleby was one of those beings of whom nothing is ascertainable, except from the original sources, and, in his case, those are very small. What my own astonished eyes saw of Bartleby, *that* is all I know of him, except, indeed, one vague report, which will appear in the sequel.

---

* First published in *Putnam's Monthly Magazine* in November and December 1853 and included in *The Piazza Tales* (1856), under the title "Bartleby." A scrivener is a writer (originally, "scribe").

Ere introducing the scrivener, as he first appeared to me, it is fit I make some mention of myself, my *employés,* my business, my chambers, and general surroundings; because some such description is indispensable to an adequate understanding of the chief character about to be presented. Imprimis:[1] I am a man who, from his youth upwards, has been filled with a profound conviction that the easiest way of life is the best. Hence, though I belong to a profession proverbially energetic and nervous, even to turbulence, at times, yet nothing of that sort have I ever suffered to invade my peace. I am one of those unambitious lawyers who never addresses a jury, or in any way draws down public applause; but, in the cool tranquillity of a snug retreat, do a snug business among rich men's bonds, and mortgages, and title-deeds. All who know me, consider me an eminently *safe* man. The late John Jacob Astor,[2] a personage little given to poetic enthusiasm, had no hesitation in pronouncing my first grand point to be prudence; my next, method. I do not speak it in vanity, but simply record the fact, that I was not unemployed in my profession by the late John Jacob Astor; a name which, I admit, I love to repeat; for it hath a rounded and orbicular sound to it, and rings like unto bullion. I will freely add, that I was not insensible to the late John Jacob Astor's good opinion.

Some time prior to the period at which this little history begins, my avocations had been largely increased. The good old office, now extinct in the State of New York, of a Master in Chancery,[3] had been conferred upon me. It was not a very arduous office, but very pleasantly remunerative. I seldom lose my temper; much more seldom indulge in dangerous indignation at wrongs and outrages; but, I must be permitted to be rash here, and declare, that I consider the sudden and violent abrogation of the office of Master in Chancery, by the new Constitution, as a —premature act; inasmuch as I had counted upon a life-lease of the profits, whereas I only received those of a few short years. But this is by the way.

My chambers were up stairs, at No. — Wall street. At one end, they looked upon the white wall of the interior of a spacious sky-light shaft, penetrating the building from top to bottom.

This view might have been considered rather tame than otherwise, deficient in what landscape painters call "life." But, if so, the view from the other end of my chambers offered, at least, a contrast, if nothing more. In that direction, my windows commanded an unobstructed view of a lofty brick wall, black by age and everlasting shade; which wall required no spy-glass to bring out its lurking beauties, but, for the benefit of all near-sighted spectators, was pushed up to within ten feet of my window panes. Owing to the great height of the surrounding buildings, and my chambers being on the second floor, the interval between this wall and mine not a little resembled a huge square cistern.

At the period just preceding the advent of Bartleby, I had two persons as copyists in my employment, and a promising lad as an office-boy. First, Turkey; second, Nippers; third, Ginger Nut. These may seem names, the like of which are not usually found in the Directory.[4] In truth, they were nicknames, mutually conferred upon each other by my three clerks, and were deemed expressive of their respective persons or characters. Turkey was a short, pursy[5] Englishman, of about

---

[1] "In the first place" (Latin).

[2] Astor (1763–1848) was an American millionaire who made his fortune in the fur trade and in real-estate dealings.

[3] A new New York state constitution in 1846 had abolished the office of Master of Chancery as part of an outdated court system.

[4] The city directory of residents.   [5] Short-winded from being fat.

my own age—that is, somewhere not far from sixty. In the morning, one might say, his face was of a fine florid hue, but after twelve o'clock, meridian[6]—his dinner hour—it blazed like a grate full of Christmas coals; and continued blazing—but, as it were, with a gradual wane—till six o'clock, P.M., or thereabouts; after which, I saw no more of the proprietor of the face, which, gaining its meridian with the sun, seemed to set with it, to rise, culminate, and decline the following day, with the like regularity and undiminished glory. There are many singular coincidences I have known in the course of my life, not the least among which was the fact, that, exactly when Turkey displayed his fullest beams from his red and radiant countenance, just then, too, at that critical moment, began the daily period when I considered his business capacities as seriously disturbed for the remainder of the twenty-four hours. Not that he was absolutely idle, or averse to business, then; far from it. The difficulty was, he was apt to be altogether too energetic. There was a strange, inflamed, flurried, flighty recklessness of activity about him. He would be incautious in dipping his pen into his inkstand. All his blots upon my documents were dropped there after twelve o'clock, meridian. Indeed, not only would he be reckless, and sadly given to making blots in the afternoon, but, some days, he went further, and was rather noisy. At such times, too, his face flamed with augmented blazonry, as if cannel coal had been heaped on anthracite.[7] He made an unpleasant racket with his chair; spilled his sand-box;[8] in mending his pens, impatiently split them all to pieces, and threw them on the floor in a sudden passion; stood up, and leaned over his table, boxing his papers about in a most indecorous manner, very sad to behold in an elderly man like him. Nevertheless, as he was in many ways a most valuable person to me, and all the time before twelve o'clock, meridian, was the quickest, steadiest creature, too, accomplishing a great deal of work in a style not easily to be matched—for these reasons, I was willing to overlook his eccentricities, though, indeed, occasionally, I remonstrated with him. I did this very gently, however, because, though the civilest, nay, the blandest and most reverential of men in the morning, yet, in the afternoon, he was disposed, upon provocation, to be slightly rash with his tongue—in fact, insolent. Now, valuing his morning services as I did, and resolved not to lose them—yet, at the same time, made uncomfortable by his inflamed ways after twelve o'clock—and being a man of peace, unwilling by my admonitions to call forth unseemly retorts from him, I took upon me, one Saturday noon (he was always worse on Saturdays) to hint to him, very kindly, that, perhaps, now that he was growing old, it might be well to abridge his labors; in short, he need not come to my chambers after twelve o'clock, but, dinner over, had best go home to his lodgings, and rest himself till tea-time. But no; he insisted upon his afternoon devotions.[9] His countenance became intolerably fervid, as he oratorically assured me—gesticulating with a long ruler at the other end of the room—that if his services in the morning were useful, how indispensable, then, in the afternoon?

"With submission, sir," said Turkey, on this occasion, "I consider myself your right-hand man. In the morning I but marshal and deploy my columns; but in the afternoon I put myself at their head, and gallantly charge the foe, thus"—and he made a violent thrust with the ruler.

---

[6] Noon.

[7] Cannel coal (soft) burns quickly and brightly; anthracite (hard) burns more slowly and intensely.

[8] A box containing sand for blotting ink.

[9] He is devoted to his work. The religious overtones give this sentence a gentle irony.

"But the blots, Turkey," intimated I.

"True; but, with submission, sir, behold these hairs! I am getting old. Surely, sir, a blot or two of a warm afternoon is not to be severely urged against gray hairs. Old age—even if it blot the page—is honorable. With submission, sir, we *both* are getting old."

This appeal to my fellow-feeling was hardly to be resisted. At all events, I saw that go he would not. So, I made up my mind to let him stay, resolving, nevertheless, to see to it that, during the afternoon, he had to do with my less important papers.

Nippers, the second on my list, was a whiskered, sallow, and, upon the whole, rather piratical-looking young man, of about five and twenty. I always deemed him the victim of two evil powers—ambition and indigestion. The ambition was evinced by a certain impatience of the duties of a mere copyist, an unwarrantable usurpation of strictly professional affairs, such as the original drawing up of legal documents. The indigestion seemed betokened in an occasional nervous testiness and grinning irritability, causing the teeth to audibly grind together over mistakes committed in copying; unnecessary maledictions, hissed, rather than spoken, in the heat of business; and especially by a continual discontent with the height of the table where he worked. Though of a very ingenious mechanical turn, Nippers could never get this table to suit him. He put chips under it, blocks of various sorts, bits of pasteboard, and at last went so far as to attempt an exquisite adjustment, by final pieces of folded blotting-paper. But no invention would answer. If, for the sake of easing his back, he brought the table lid at a sharp angle well up towards his chin, and wrote there like a man using the steep roof of a Dutch house for his desk, then he declared that it stopped the circulation in his arms. If now he lowered the table to his waistbands, and stooped over it in writing, then there was a sore aching in his back. In short, the truth of the matter was, Nippers knew not what he wanted. Or, if he wanted anything, it was to be rid of a scrivener's table altogether. Among the manifestations of his diseased ambition was a fondness he had for receiving visits from certain ambiguous-looking fellows in seedy coats, whom he called his clients. Indeed, I was aware that not only was he, at times, considerable of a ward-politician, but he occasionally did a little business at the Justices' courts, and was not unknown on the steps of the Tombs.[10] I have good reason to believe, however, that one individual who called upon him at my chambers, and who, with a grand air, he insisted was his client, was no other than a dun,[11] and the alleged title-deed, a bill. But, with all his failings, and the annoyances he caused me, Nippers, like his compatriot Turkey, was a very useful man to me; wrote a neat, swift hand; and, when he chose, was not deficient in a gentlemanly sort of deportment. Added to this, he always dressed in a gentlemanly sort of way; and so, incidentally, reflected credit upon my chambers. Whereas, with respect to Turkey, I had much ado to keep him from being a reproach to me. His clothes were apt to look oily, and smell of eating-houses. He wore his pantaloons very loose and baggy in summer. His coats were execrable; his hat not to be handled. But while the hat was a thing of indifference to me, inasmuch as his natural civility and deference, as a dependent Englishman, always led him to doff

---

[10] A New York City prison built in 1839, officially the Halls of Justice and House of Detention, the Tombs was named after the Egyptian Revival style of architecture that imitated Egyptian temples and tombs. Because Nippers is an ambitious "ward-politician," his presence at courts of law and on the steps of the city prison suggests to the narrator some questionable activities on his employee's part.

[11] A bill collector.

it the moment he entered the room, yet his coat was another matter. Concerning his coats, I reasoned with him; but with no effect. The truth was, I suppose, that a man with so small an income could not afford to sport such a lustrous face and a lustrous coat at one and the same time. As Nippers once observed, Turkey's money went chiefly for red ink. One winter day, I presented Turkey with a highly respectable-looking coat of my own—a padded gray coat, of a most comfortable warmth, and which buttoned straight up from the knee to the neck. I thought Turkey would appreciate the favor, and abate his rashness and obstreperousness of afternoons. But no; I verily believe that buttoning himself up in so downy and blanket-like a coat had a pernicious effect upon him—upon the same principle that too much oats are bad for horses. In fact, precisely as a rash, restive horse is said to feel his oats, so Turkey felt his coat. It made him insolent. He was a man whom prosperity harmed.

Though, concerning the self-indulgent habits of Turkey, I had my own private surmises, yet, touching Nippers, I was well persuaded that, whatever might be his faults in other respects, he was, at least, a temperate young man. But, indeed, nature herself seemed to have been his vintner, and, at his birth, charged him so thoroughly with an irritable, brandy-like disposition, that all subsequent potations were needless. When I consider how, amid the stillness of my chambers, Nippers would sometimes impatiently rise from his seat, and stooping over his table, spread his arms wide apart, seize the whole desk, and move it, and jerk it, with a grim, grinding motion on the floor, as if the table were a perverse voluntary agent, intent on thwarting and vexing him, I plainly perceive that, for Nippers, brandy-and-water were altogether superfluous.

It was fortunate for me that, owing to its peculiar cause—indigestion—the irritability and consequent nervousness of Nippers were mainly observable in the morning, while in the afternoon he was comparatively mild. So that, Turkey's paroxysms only coming on about twelve o'clock, I never had to do with their eccentricities at one time. Their fits relieved each other, like guards. When Nippers's was on, Turkey's was off; and *vice versa*. This was a good natural arrangement, under the circumstances.

Ginger Nut, the third on my list, was a lad, some twelve years old. His father was a carman,[12] ambitious of seeing his son on the bench instead of a cart, before he died. So he sent him to my office, as student at law, errand-boy, cleaner and sweeper, at the rate of one dollar a week. He had a little desk to himself, but he did not use it much. Upon inspection, the drawer exhibited a great array of the shells of various sorts of nuts. Indeed, to this quick-witted youth, the whole noble science of the law was contained in a nut-shell. Not the least among the employments of Ginger Nut, as well as one which he discharged with the most alacrity, was his duty as cake and apple purveyor for Turkey and Nippers. Copying law-papers being proverbially a dry, husky sort of business, my two scriveners were fain to moisten their mouths very often with Spitzenbergs,[13] to be had at the numerous stalls nigh the Custom House and Post Office. Also, they sent Ginger Nut very frequently for that peculiar cake—small, flat, round, and very spicy—after which he had been named by them. Of a cold morning, when business was but dull, Turkey would gobble up scores of these cakes, as if they were mere wafers—indeed, they sell them at the rate of six or eight for a penny—the scrape of his pen blending with the crunching of the crisp particles in his mouth. Of all the

---

[12] A wagon driver.   [13] A type of apple.

fiery afternoon blunders and flurried rashnesses of Turkey, was his once moistening a ginger-cake between his lips, and clapping it on to a mortgage, for a seal. I came within an ace of dismissing him then. But he mollified me by making an oriental bow, and saying—

"With submission, sir, it was generous of me to find you in stationery on my own account."[14]

Now my original business—that of a conveyancer and title hunter, and drawer-up of recondite documents of all sorts[15]—was considerably increased by receiving the master's office. There was now great work for scriveners. Not only must I push the clerks already with me, but I must have additional help.

In answer to my advertisement, a motionless young man one morning stood upon my office threshold, the door being open, for it was summer. I can see that figure now—pallidly neat, pitiably respectable, incurably forlorn! It was Bartleby.

After a few words touching his qualifications, I engaged him, glad to have among my corps of copyists a man of so singularly sedate an aspect, which I thought might operate beneficially upon the flighty temper of Turkey, and the fiery one of Nippers.

I should have stated before that ground glass folding-doors divided my premises into two parts, one of which was occupied by my scriveners, the other by myself. According to my humor, I threw open these doors, or closed them. I resolved to assign Bartleby a corner by the folding-doors, but on my side of them, so as to have this quiet man within easy call, in case any trifling thing was to be done. I placed his desk close up to a small side-window in that part of the room, a window which originally had afforded a lateral view of certain grimy backyards and bricks, but which, owing to subsequent erections, commanded at present no view at all, though it gave some light. Within three feet of the panes was a wall, and the light came down from far above, between two lofty buildings, as from a very small opening in a dome. Still further to a satisfactory arrangement, I procured a high green folding screen, which might entirely isolate Bartleby from my sight, though not remove him from my voice. And thus, in a manner, privacy and society were conjoined.

At first, Bartleby did an extraordinary quantity of writing. As if long famishing for something to copy, he seemed to gorge himself on my documents. There was no pause for digestion. He ran a day and night line, copying by sun-light and by candle-light. I should have been quite delighted with his application, had he been cheerfully industrious. But he wrote on silently, palely, mechanically.

It is, of course, an indispensable part of a scrivener's business to verify the accuracy of his copy, word by word. Where there are two or more scriveners in an office, they assist each other in this examination, one reading from the copy, the other holding the original. It is a very dull, wearisome, and lethargic affair. I can readily imagine that, to some sanguine temperaments, it would be altogether intolerable. For example, I cannot credit that the mettlesome poet, Byron, would have contentedly sat down with Bartleby to examine a law document of, say five hundred pages, closely written in a crimpy hand.

Now and then, in the haste of business, it had been my habit to assist in com-

---

[14] To supply you with stationery at my own expense.

[15] The narrator works on legal transfers of property, checks titles of ownership to be sure they are free and clear, and draws up complicated documents.

paring some brief document myself, calling Turkey or Nippers for this purpose. One object I had, in placing Bartleby so handy to me behind the screen, was, to avail myself of his services on such trivial occasions. It was on the third day, I think, of his being with me, and before any necessity had arisen for having his own writing examined, that, being much hurried to complete a small affair I had in hand, I abruptly called to Bartleby. In my haste and natural expectancy of instant compliance, I sat with my head bent over the original on my desk, and my right hand sideways, and somewhat nervously extended with the copy, so that, immediately upon emerging from his retreat, Bartleby might snatch it and proceed to business without the least delay.

In this very attitude did I sit when I called to him, rapidly stating what it was I wanted him to do—namely, to examine a small paper with me. Imagine my surprise, nay, my consternation, when, without moving from his privacy, Bartleby, in a singularly mild, firm voice, replied, "I would prefer not to."

I sat awhile in perfect silence, rallying my stunned faculties. Immediately it occurred to me that my ears had deceived me, or Bartleby had entirely misunderstood my meaning. I repeated my request in the clearest tone I could assume; but in quite as clear a one came the previous reply, "I would prefer not to."

"Prefer not to," echoed I, rising in high excitement, and crossing the room with a stride. "What do you mean? Are you moon-struck? I want you to help me compare this sheet here—take it," and I thrust it towards him.

"I would prefer not to," said he.

I looked at him steadfastly. His face was leanly composed; his gray eye dimly calm. Not a wrinkle of agitation rippled him. Had there been the least uneasiness, anger, impatience or impertinence in his manner; in other words, had there been any thing ordinarily human about him, doubtless I should have violently dismissed him from the premises. But as it was, I should have as soon thought of turning my pale plaster-of-paris bust of Cicero[16] out of doors. I stood gazing at him awhile, as he went on with his own writing, and then reseated myself at my desk. This is very strange, thought I. What had one best do? But my business hurried me. I concluded to forget the matter for the present, reserving it for my future leisure. So calling Nippers from the other room, the paper was speedily examined.

A few days after this, Bartleby concluded four lengthy documents, being quadruplicates of a week's testimony taken before me in my High Court of Chancery. It became necessary to examine them. It was an important suit, and great accuracy was imperative. Having all things arranged, I called Turkey, Nippers and Ginger Nut, from the next room, meaning to place the four copies in the hand of my four clerks, while I should read from the original. Accordingly, Turkey, Nippers, and Ginger Nut had taken their seats in a row, each with his document in his hand, when I called to Bartleby to join this interesting group.

"Bartleby! quick, I am waiting."

I heard a slow scrape of his chair legs on the uncarpeted floor, and soon he appeared standing at the entrance of his hermitage.

"What is wanted?" said he, mildly.

"The copies, the copies," said I, hurriedly. "We are going to examine them. There"—and I held towards him the fourth quadruplicate.

"I would prefer not to," he said, and gently disappeared behind the screen.

---

[16] Marcus Tullius Cicero (106–43 B.C.), a Roman philosopher, statesman, and orator.

For a few moments I was turned into a pillar of salt,[17] standing at the head of my seated column of clerks. Recovering myself, I advanced towards the screen, and demanded the reason for such extraordinary conduct.

"*Why* do you refuse?"

"I would prefer not to."

With any other man I should have flown outright into a dreadful passion, scorned all further words, and thrust him ignominiously from my presence. But there was something about Bartleby that not only strangely disarmed me, but, in a wonderful manner, touched and disconcerted me. I began to reason with him.

"These are your own copies we are about to examine. It is labor saving to you, because one examination will answer for your four papers. It is common usage. Every copyist is bound to help examine his copy. Is it not so? Will you not speak? Answer!"

"I would prefer not to," he replied in a flutelike tone. It seemed to me that, while I had been addressing him, he carefully revolved every statement that I made; fully comprehended the meaning; could not gainsay the irresistible conclusion; but, at the same time, some paramount consideration prevailed with him to reply as he did.

"You are decided, then, not to comply with my request—a request made according to common usage and common sense?"

He briefly gave me to understand, that on that point my judgment was sound. Yes: his decision was irreversible.

It is not seldom the case that, when a man is browbeaten in some unprecedented and violently unreasonable way, he begins to stagger in his own plainest faith. He begins, as it were, vaguely to surmise that, wonderful as it may be, all the justice and all the reason is on the other side. Accordingly, if any disinterested persons are present, he turns to them for some reinforcement for his own faltering mind.

"Turkey," said I, "what do you think of this? Am I not right?"

"With submission, sir," said Turkey, in his blandest tone, "I think that you are."

"Nippers," said I, "what do *you* think of it?"

"I think I should kick him out of the office."

(The reader, of nice[18] perceptions, will here perceive that, it being morning, Turkey's answer is couched in polite and tranquil terms, but Nippers replies in ill-tempered ones. Or, to repeat a previous sentence, Nippers's ugly mood was on duty, and Turkey's off.)

"Ginger Nut," said I, willing to enlist the smallest suffrage[19] in my behalf, "what do *you* think of it?"

"I think, sir, he's a little *luny*," replied Ginger Nut, with a grin.

"You hear what they say," said I, turning towards the screen, "come forth and do your duty."

But he vouchsafed no reply. I pondered a moment in sore perplexity. But once more business hurried me. I determined again to postpone the consideration of this dilemma to my future leisure. With a little trouble we made out to examine the papers without Bartleby, though at every page or two Turkey deferentially

---

[17] In Genesis 19:26, for her disobedience, Lot's wife is turned into a pillar of salt; here, the unoffending narrator suffers this fate metaphorically.

[18] Discriminative.   [19] Vote of support.

dropped his opinion, that this proceeding was quite out of the common; while Nippers, twitching in his chair with a dyspeptic nervousness, ground out, between his set teeth, occasional hissing maledictions against the stubborn oaf behind the screen. And for his (Nippers's) part, this was the first and the last time he would do another man's business without pay.

Meanwhile Bartleby sat in his hermitage, oblivious to everything but his own peculiar business there.

Some days passed, the scrivener being employed upon another lengthy work. His late remarkable conduct led me to regard his ways narrowly. I observed that he never went to dinner; indeed, that he never went anywhere. As yet I had never, of my personal knowledge, known him to be outside of my office. He was a perpetual sentry in the corner. At about eleven o'clock though, in the morning, I noticed that Ginger Nut would advance toward the opening in Bartleby's screen, as if silently beckoned thither by a gesture invisible to me where I sat. The boy would then leave the office, jingling a few pence, and reappear with a handful of ginger-nuts, which he delivered in the hermitage, receiving two of the cakes for his trouble.

He lives, then, on ginger-nuts, thought I; never eats a dinner, properly speaking; he must be a vegetarian, then; but no; he never eats even vegetables, he eats nothing but ginger-nuts. My mind then ran on in reveries concerning the probable effects upon the human constitution of living entirely on ginger-nuts. Ginger-nuts are so called, because they contain ginger as one of their peculiar constituents, and the final flavoring one. Now, what was ginger? A hot, spicy thing. Was Bartleby hot and spicy? Not at all. Ginger, then, had no effect upon Bartleby. Probably he preferred it should have none.

Nothing so aggravates an earnest person as a passive resistance. If the individual so resisted be of a not inhumane temper, and the resisting one perfectly harmless in his passivity, then, in the better moods of the former, he will endeavor charitably to construe to his imagination what proves impossible to be solved by his judgment. Even so, for the most part, I regarded Bartleby and his ways. Poor fellow! thought I, he means no mischief; it is plain he intends no insolence; his aspect sufficiently evinces that his eccentricities are involuntary. He is useful to me. I can get along with him. If I turn him away, the chances are he will fall in with some less-indulgent employer, and then he will be rudely treated, and perhaps driven forth miserably to starve. Yes. Here I can cheaply purchase a delicious self-approval. To befriend Bartleby; to humor him in his strange willfulness, will cost me little or nothing, while I lay up in my soul what will eventually prove a sweet morsel for my conscience. But this mood was not invariable with me. The passiveness of Bartleby sometimes irritated me. I felt strangely goaded on to encounter him in new opposition—to elicit some angry spark from him answerable to my own. But, indeed, I might as well have essayed to strike fire with my knuckles against a bit of Windsor soap.[20] But one afternoon the evil impulse in me mastered me, and the following little scene ensued:

"Bartleby," said I, "when those papers are all copied, I will compare them with you."

"I would prefer not to."

"How? Surely you do not mean to persist in that mulish vagary?"

No answer.

---

[20] A brand of hand soap.

I threw open the folding-doors near by, and, turning upon Turkey and Nippers, exclaimed:

"Bartleby a second time says, he won't examine his papers. What do you think of it, Turkey?"

It was afternoon, be it remembered. Turkey sat glowing like a brass boiler; his bald head steaming; his hands reeling among his blotted papers.

"Think of it?" roared Turkey; "I think I'll just step behind his screen, and black his eyes for him!"

So saying, Turkey rose to his feet and threw his arms into a pugilistic position. He was hurrying away to make good his promise, when I detained him, alarmed at the effect of incautiously rousing Turkey's combativeness after dinner.

"Sit down, Turkey," said I, "and hear what Nippers has to say. What do you think of it, Nippers? Would I not be justified in immediately dismissing Bartleby?"

"Excuse me, that is for you to decide, sir. I think his conduct quite unusual, and, indeed, unjust as regards Turkey and myself. But it may only be a passing whim."

"Ah," exclaimed I, "you have strangely changed your mind, then—you speak very gently of him now."

"All beer," cried Turkey; "gentleness is effects of beer—Nippers and I dined together to-day. You see how gentle *I* am, sir. Shall I go and black his eyes?"

"You refer to Bartleby, I suppose. No, not to-day, Turkey," I replied; "pray, put up your fists."

I closed the doors, and again advanced towards Bartleby. I felt additional incentives tempting me to my fate. I burned to be rebelled against again. I remembered that Bartleby never left the office.

"Bartleby," said I, "Ginger Nut is away; just step around to the Post Office, won't you? (it was but a three minutes' walk), and see if there is anything for me."

"I would prefer not to."

"You *will* not?"

"I *prefer* not."

I staggered to my desk, and sat there in a deep study. My blind inveteracy returned. Was there any other thing in which I could procure myself to be ignominiously repulsed by this lean, penniless wight?—my hired clerk? What added thing is there, perfectly reasonable, that he will be sure to refuse to do?

"Bartleby!"

No answer.

"Bartleby," in a louder tone.

No answer.

"Bartleby," I roared.

Like a very ghost, agreeably to the laws of magical invocation, at the third summons, he appeared at the entrance of his hermitage.

"Go to the next room, and tell Nippers to come to me."

"I prefer not to," he respectfully and slowly said, and mildly disappeared.

"Very good, Bartleby," said I, in a quiet sort of serenely-severe self-possessed tone, intimating the unalterable purpose of some terrible retribution very close at hand. At the moment I half intended something of the kind. But upon the whole, as it was drawing towards my dinner-hour, I thought it best to put on my hat and walk home for the day, suffering much from perplexity and distress of mind.

Shall I acknowledge it? The conclusion of this whole business was, that it soon became a fixed fact of my chambers, that a pale young scrivener, by the name of Bartleby, had a desk there; that he copied for me at the usual rate of four cents a folio (one hundred words); but he was permanently exempt from examining the work done by him, that duty being transferred to Turkey and Nippers, out of compliment, doubtless, to their superior acuteness; moreover, said Bartleby was never, on any account, to be dispatched on the most trivial errand of any sort; and that even if entreated to take upon him such a matter, it was generally understood that he would "prefer not to"—in other words, that he would refuse point-blank.

As days passed on, I became considerably reconciled to Bartleby. His steadiness, his freedom from all dissipation, his incessant industry (except when he chose to throw himself into a standing revery behind his screen), his great stillness, his unalterableness of demeanor under all circumstances, made him a valuable acquisition. One prime thing was this—*he was always there*—first in the morning, continually through the day, and the last at night. I had a singular confidence in his honesty. I felt my most precious papers perfectly safe in his hands. Sometimes, to be sure, I could not, for the very soul of me, avoid falling into sudden spasmodic passions with him. For it was exceeding difficult to bear in mind all the time those strange peculiarities, privileges, and unheard of exemptions, forming the tacit stipulations on Bartleby's part under which he remained in my office. Now and then, in the eagerness of dispatching pressing business, I would inadvertently summon Bartleby, in a short, rapid tone, to put his finger, say, on the incipient tie of a bit of red tape with which I was about compressing some papers. Of course, from behind the screen the usual answer, "I prefer not to," was sure to come; and then, how could a human creature, with the common infirmities of our nature, refrain from bitterly exclaiming upon such perverseness—such unreasonableness. However, every added repulse of this sort which I received only tended to lessen the probability of my repeating the inadvertence.

Here it must be said, that according to the custom of most legal gentlemen occupying chambers in densely-populated law buildings, there were several keys to my door. One was kept by a woman residing in the attic, which person weekly scrubbed and daily swept and dusted my apartments. Another was kept by Turkey for convenience sake. The third I sometimes carried in my own pocket. The fourth I knew not who had.

Now, one Sunday morning I happened to go to Trinity Church,[21] to hear a celebrated preacher, and finding myself rather early on the ground I thought I would walk round to my chambers for a while. Luckily I had my key with me; but upon applying it to the lock, I found it resisted by something inserted from the inside. Quite surprised, I called out; when to my consternation a key was turned from within; and thrusting his lean visage at me, and holding the door ajar, the apparition of Bartleby appeared, in his shirt sleeves, and otherwise in a strangely tattered deshabille,[22] saying quietly that he was sorry, but he was deeply engaged just then, and—preferred not admitting me at present. In a brief word or two, he moreover added, that perhaps I had better walk round the block two or three times, and by that time he would probably have concluded his affairs.

Now, the utterly unsurmised appearance of Bartleby, tenanting my law-chambers of a Sunday morning, with his cadaverously gentlemanly *nonchalance*, yet withal firm and self-possessed, had such a strange effect upon me, that inconti-

---

[21] An Episcopal church in New York City's financial district (apparently near the narrator's office).
[22] Dishabille, or clothing in disarray.

nently I slunk away from my own door, and did as desired. But not without sundry twinges of impotent rebellion against the mild effrontery of this unaccountable scrivener. Indeed, it was his wonderful mildness chiefly, which not only disarmed me, but unmanned me as it were. For I consider that one, for the time, is a sort of unmanned when he tranquilly permits his hired clerk to dictate to him, and order him away from his own premises. Furthermore, I was full of uneasiness as to what Bartleby could possibly be doing in my office in his shirt sleeves, and in an otherwise dismantled condition of a Sunday morning. Was anything amiss going on? Nay, that was out of the question. It was not to be thought of for a moment that Bartleby was an immoral person. But what could he be doing there?—copying? Nay again, whatever might be his eccentricities, Bartleby was an eminently decorous person. He would be the last man to sit down to his desk in any state approaching to nudity. Besides, it was Sunday; and there was something about Bartleby that forbade the supposition that he would by any secular occupation violate the proprieties of the day.

Nevertheless, my mind was not pacified; and full of a restless curiosity, at last I returned to the door. Without hindrance I inserted my key, opened it, and entered. Bartleby was not to be seen. I looked round anxiously, peeped behind his screen; but it was very plain that he was gone. Upon more closely examining the place, I surmised that for an indefinite period Bartleby must have ate, dressed, and slept in my office, and that, too without plate, mirror, or bed. The cushioned seat of a ricketty old sofa in one corner bore the faint impress of a lean, reclining form. Rolled away under his desk, I found a blanket; under the empty grate, a blacking box and brush; on a chair, a tin basin, with soap and a ragged towel; in a newspaper a few crumbs of ginger-nuts and a morsel of cheese. Yes, thought I, it is evident enough that Bartleby has been making his home here, keeping bachelor's hall all by himself. Immediately then the thought came sweeping across me, what miserable friendlessness and loneliness are here revealed! His poverty is great; but his solitude, how horrible! Think of it. Of a Sunday, Wall-street is deserted as Petra;[23] and every night of every day it is an emptiness. This building, too, which of week-days hums with industry and life, at nightfall echoes with sheer vacancy, and all through Sunday is forlorn. And here Bartleby makes his home; sole spectator of a solitude which he has seen all populous—a sort of innocent and transformed Marius[24] brooding among the ruins of Carthage!

For the first time in my life a feeling of overpowering stinging melancholy seized me. Before, I had never experienced aught but a not unpleasing sadness. The bond of a common humanity now drew me irresistibly to gloom. A fraternal melancholy! For both I and Bartleby were sons of Adam. I remembered the bright silks and sparkling faces I had seen that day, in gala trim, swan-like sailing down the Mississippi of Broadway; and I contrasted them with the pallid copyist, and thought to myself, Ah, happiness courts the light, so we deem the world is gay; but misery hides aloof, so we deem that misery there is none. These sad fancyings—chimeras, doubtless, of a sick and silly brain—led on to other and more special thoughts, concerning the eccentricities of Bartleby. Presentiments of

[23] An ancient city in what is now Jordan; its ruins were discovered in 1812.

[24] Gaius Marius (157?–86 B.C.), a Roman general and statesman who was exiled from Rome. Captured by his enemies, he finally escaped to Africa and, in a message to the Roman governor, said that he was sitting "amid the ruins of Carthage"—the man and the city having met similar fates. Marius became popularized in nineteenth-century American art and literature.

strange discoveries hovered round me. The scrivener's pale form appeared to me laid out, among uncaring strangers, in its shivering winding sheet.

Suddenly I was attracted by Bartleby's closed desk, the key in open sight left in the lock.

I mean no mischief, seek the gratification of no heartless curiosity, thought I; besides, the desk is mine, and its contents, too, so I will make bold to look within. Everything was methodically arranged, the papers smoothly placed. The pigeon holes were deep, and removing the files of documents, I groped into their recesses. Presently I felt something there, and dragged it out. It was an old bandanna handkerchief, heavy and knotted. I opened it, and saw it was a savings's [sic] bank.

I now recalled all the quiet mysteries which I had noted in the man. I remembered that he never spoke but to answer; that, though at intervals he had considerable time to himself, yet I had never seen him reading—no, not even a newspaper; that for long periods he would stand looking out, at his pale window behind the screen, upon the dead brick wall; I was quite sure he never visited any refectory or eating house; while his pale face clearly indicated that he never drank beer like Turkey, or tea and coffee even, like other men; that he never went anywhere in particular that I could learn; never went out for a walk, unless, indeed, that was the case at present; that he had declined telling who he was, or whence he came, or whether he had any relatives in the world; that though so thin and pale, he never complained of ill health. And more than all, I remembered a certain unconscious air of pallid—how shall I call it?—of pallid haughtiness, say, or rather an austere reserve about him, which had positively awed me into my tame compliance with his eccentricities, when I had feared to ask him to do the slightest incidental thing for me, even though I might know, from his long-continued motionlessness, that behind his screen he must be standing in one of those dead-wall reveries of his.

Revolving all these things, and coupling them with the recently discovered fact, that he made my office his constant abiding place and home, and not forgetful of his morbid moodiness; revolving all these things, a prudential feeling began to steal over me. My first emotions had been those of pure melancholy and sincerest pity; but just in proportion as the forlornness of Bartleby grew and grew to my imagination, did that same melancholy merge into fear, that pity into repulsion. So true it is, and so terrible, too, that up to a certain point the thought or sight of misery enlists our best affections; but, in certain special cases, beyond that point it does not. They err who would assert that invariably this is owing to the inherent selfishness of the human heart. It rather proceeds from a certain hopelessness of remedying excessive and organic ill. To a sensitive being, pity is not seldom pain. And when at last it is perceived that such pity cannot lead to effectual succor, common sense bids the soul be rid of it. What I saw that morning persuaded me that the scrivener was the victim of innate and incurable disorder. I might give alms to his body; but his body did not pain him; it was his soul that suffered, and his soul I could not reach.

I did not accomplish the purpose of going to Trinity Church that morning. Somehow, the things I had seen disqualified me for the time from church-going. I walked homeward, thinking what I would do with Bartleby. Finally, I resolved upon this—I would put certain calm questions to him the next morning, touching his history, etc., and if he declined to answer them openly and unreservedly (and I supposed he would prefer not), then to give him a twenty dollar bill over and above whatever I might owe him, and tell him his services were no longer required; but that if in any other way I could assist him, I would be happy to do so, especially if he desired to return to his native place, wherever that might be, I would willingly help to defray the expenses. Moreover, if, after reaching home, he found himself at any time in want of aid, a letter from him would be sure of a reply.

The next morning came.

"Bartleby," said I, gently calling to him behind his screen.

No reply.

"Bartleby," said I, in a still gentler tone, "come here; I am not going to ask you to do anything you would prefer not to do—I simply wish to speak to you."

Upon this he noiselessly slid into view.

"Will you tell me, Bartleby, where you were born?"

"I would prefer not to."

"Will you tell me *anything* about yourself?"

"I would prefer not to."

"But what reasonable objection can you have to speak to me? I feel friendly towards you."

He did not look at me while I spoke, but kept his glance fixed upon my bust of Cicero, which, as I then sat, was directly behind me, some six inches above my head.

"What is your answer, Bartleby," said I, after waiting a considerable time for a reply, during which his countenance remained immovable, only there was the faintest conceivable tremor of the white attenuated mouth.

"At present I prefer to give no answer," he said, and retired into his hermitage.

It was rather weak in me I confess, but his manner, on this occasion, nettled me. Not only did there seem to lurk in it a certain calm disdain, but his perverseness seemed ungrateful, considering the undeniable good usage and indulgence he had received from me.

Again I sat ruminating what I should do. Mortified as I was at his behavior, and resolved as I had been to dismiss him when I entered my office, nevertheless I strangely felt something superstitious knocking at my heart, and forbidding me to carry out my purpose, and denouncing me for a villain if I dared to breathe one bitter word against this forlornest of mankind. At last, familiarly drawing my chair behind his screen, I sat down and said: "Bartleby, never mind, then, about revealing your history; but let me entreat you, as a friend, to comply as far as may be with the usages of this office. Say now, you will help to examine papers to-morrow or next day: in short, say now, that in a day or two you will begin to be a little reasonable:—say so, Bartleby."

"At present I would prefer not to be a little reasonable," was his mildly cadaverous reply.

Just then the folding-doors opened, and Nippers approached. He seemed suffering from an unusually bad night's rest, induced by severer indigestion than common. He overheard those final words of Bartleby.

"*Prefer not*, eh?" gritted Nippers—"I'd *prefer* him, if I were you, sir," addressing me—"I'd *prefer* him; I'd give him preferences, the stubborn mule! What is it, sir, pray, that he *prefers* not to do now?"

Bartleby moved not a limb.

"Mr. Nippers," said I, "I'd prefer that you would withdraw for the present."

Somehow, of late, I had got into the way of involuntarily using this word "prefer" upon all sorts of not exactly suitable occasions. And I trembled to think that my contact with the scrivener had already and seriously affected me in a mental way. And what further and deeper aberration might it not yet produce? This apprehension had not been without efficacy in determining me to summary measures.

As Nippers, looking very sour and sulky, was departing, Turkey blandly and deferentially approached.

"With submission, sir," said he, "yesterday I was thinking about Bartleby here, and I think that if he would but prefer to take a quart of good ale every day, it would do much towards mending him, and enabling him to assist in examining his papers."

"So you have got the word, too," said I, slightly excited.

"With submission, what word, sir," asked Turkey, respectfully crowding himself into the contracted space behind the screen, and by so doing, making me jostle the scrivener. "What word, sir?"

"I would prefer to be left alone here," said Bartleby, as if offended at being mobbed in his privacy.

"*That's* the word, Turkey," said I—"*that's* it."

"Oh, *prefer?* oh yes—queer word. I never use it myself. But, sir, as I was saying, if he would but prefer—"

"Turkey," interrupted I, "you will please withdraw."

"Oh certainly, sir, if you prefer that I should."

As he opened the folding-door to retire, Nippers at his desk caught a glimpse of me, and asked whether I would prefer to have a certain paper copied on blue paper or white. He did not in the least roguishly accent the word prefer. It was plain that it involuntarily rolled from his tongue. I thought to myself, surely I must get rid of a demented man, who already has in some degree turned the tongues, if not the heads of myself and clerks. But I thought it prudent not to break the dismission at once.

The next day I noticed that Bartleby did nothing but stand at his window in his dead-wall revery. Upon asking him why he did not write, he said that he had decided upon doing no more writing.

"Why, how now? what next?" exclaimed I, "do no more writing?"

"No more."

"And what is the reason?"

"Do you not see the reason for yourself," he indifferently replied.

I looked steadfastly at him, and perceived that his eyes looked dull and glazed. Instantly it occurred to me, that his unexampled diligence in copying by his dim window for the first few weeks of his stay with me might have temporarily impaired his vision.

I was touched. I said something in condolence with him. I hinted that of course he did wisely in abstaining from writing for a while; and urged him to embrace that opportunity of taking wholesome exercise in the open air. This, however, he did not do. A few days after this, my other clerks being absent, and being in a great hurry to dispatch certain letters by the mail, I thought that, having nothing else earthly to do, Bartleby would surely be less inflexible than usual, and carry these letters to the post-office. But he blankly declined. So, much to my inconvenience, I went myself.

Still added days went by. Whether Bartleby's eyes improved or not, I could not say. To all appearance, I thought they did. But when I asked him if they did, he vouchsafed no answer. At all events, he would do no copying. At last, in reply to my urgings, he informed me that he had permanently given up copying.

"What!" exclaimed I; "suppose your eyes should get entirely well—better than ever before—would you not copy then?"

"I have given up copying," he answered, and slid aside.

He remained as ever, a fixture in my chamber. Nay—if that were possible—he became still more of a fixture than before. What was to be done? He would do nothing in the office; why should he stay there? In plain fact, he had now become a millstone to me, not only useless as a necklace, but afflictive to bear. Yet I was sorry for him. I speak less than truth when I say that, on his own account, he occasioned me uneasiness. If he would but have named a single relative or friend, I would instantly have written, and urged their taking the poor fellow away to some convenient retreat. But he seemed alone, absolutely alone in the universe. A bit of wreck in the mid Atlantic. At length, necessities connected with my business tyrannized over all other considerations. Decently as I could, I told Bartleby that in six days time he must unconditionally leave the office. I warned him to take measures, in the interval, for procuring some other abode. I offered to assist him in this endeavor, if he himself would but take the first step towards a removal. "And when you finally quit me, Bartleby," added I, "I shall see that you go not away entirely unprovided. Six days from this hour, remember."

At the expiration of that period, I peeped behind the screen, and lo! Bartleby was there.

I buttoned up my coat, balanced myself; advanced slowly towards him, touched his shoulder, and said, "The time has come; you must quit this place; I am sorry for you; here is money; but you must go."

"I would prefer not," he replied, with his back still towards me.

"You *must*."

He remained silent.

Now I had an unbounded confidence in this man's common honesty. He had frequently restored to me sixpences and shillings carelessly dropped upon the floor, for I am apt to be very reckless in such shirt-button[25] affairs. The proceeding, then, which followed will not be deemed extraordinary.

"Bartleby," said I, "I owe you twelve dollars on account; here are thirty-two; the odd twenty are yours—Will you take it?" and I handed the bills towards him.

But he made no motion.

"I will leave them here, then," putting them under a weight on the table. Then taking my hat and cane and going to the door, I tranquilly turned and added— "After you have removed your things from these offices, Bartleby, you will of course lock the door—since everyone is now gone for the day but you—and if you please, slip your key underneath the mat, so that I may have it in the morning. I shall not see you again; so good-by to you. If, hereafter, in your new place of abode, I can be of any service to you, do not fail to advise me by letter. Good-by, Bartleby, and fare you well."

But he answered not a word; like the last column of some ruined temple, he remained standing mute and solitary in the middle of the otherwise deserted room.

As I walked home in a pensive mood, my vanity got the better of my pity. I could not but highly plume myself on my masterly management in getting rid of Bartleby. Masterly I call it, and such it must appear to any dispassionate thinker. The beauty of my procedure seemed to consist in its perfect quietness. There was no vulgar bullying, no bravado of any sort, no choleric hectoring, and striding to

---

[25] Small or insignificant.

and fro across the apartment, jerking out vehement commands for Bartleby to bundle himself off with his beggarly traps. Nothing of the kind. Without loudly bidding Bartleby depart—as an inferior genius might have done—I *assumed* the ground that depart he must; and upon that assumption built all I had to say. The more I thought over my procedure, the more I was charmed with it. Nevertheless, next morning, upon awakening, I had my doubts—I had somehow slept off the fumes of vanity. One of the coolest and wisest hours a man has, is just after he awakes in the morning. My procedure seemed as sagacious as ever—but only in theory. How it would prove in practice—there was the rub. It was truly a beautiful thought to have assumed Bartleby's departure; but, after all, that assumption was simply my own, and none of Bartleby's. The great point was, not whether I had assumed that he would quit me, but whether he would prefer so to do. He was more a man of preferences than assumptions.

After breakfast, I walked down town, arguing the probabilities *pro* and *con*. One moment I thought it would prove a miserable failure, and Bartleby would be found all alive at my office as usual; the next moment it seemed certain that I should find his chair empty. And so I kept veering about. At the corner of Broadway and Canal street, I saw quite an excited group of people standing in earnest conversation.

"I'll take odds he doesn't," said a voice as I passed.

"Doesn't go?—done!" said I, "put up your money."

I was instinctively putting my hand in my pocket to produce my own, when I remembered that this was an election day. The words I had overheard bore no reference to Bartleby, but to the success or non-success of some candidate for the mayoralty. In my intent frame of mind, I had, as it were, imagined that all Broadway shared in my excitement, and were debating the same question with me. I passed on, very thankful that the uproar of the street screened my momentary absent-mindedness.

As I had intended, I was earlier than usual at my office door. I stood listening for a moment. All was still. He must be gone. I tried the knob. The door was locked. Yes, my procedure had worked to a charm; he indeed must be vanished. Yet a certain melancholy mixed with this: I was almost sorry for my brilliant success. I was fumbling under the door mat for the key, which Bartleby was to have left there for me, when accidentally my knee knocked against a panel, producing a summoning sound, and in response a voice came to me from within—"Not yet; I am occupied."

It was Bartleby.

I was thunderstruck. For an instant I stood like the man who, pipe in mouth, was killed one cloudless afternoon long ago in Virginia, by summer lightning; at his own warm open window he was killed, and remained leaning out there upon the dreamy afternoon, till some one touched him, when he fell.

"Not gone!" I murmured at last. But again obeying that wondrous ascendancy which the inscrutable scrivener had over me, and from which ascendancy, for all my chafing, I could not completely escape, I slowly went downstairs and out into the street, and while walking round the block, considered what I should next do in this unheard-of perplexity. Turn the man out by an actual thrusting I could not; to drive him away by calling him hard names would not do; calling in the police was an unpleasant idea; and yet, permit him to enjoy his cadaverous triumph over me—this, too, I could not think of. What was to be done? or, if nothing could be done, was there anything further that I could *assume* in the matter? Yes, as before

I had prospectively assumed that Bartleby would depart, so now I might retrospectively assume that departed he was. In the legitimate carrying out of this assumption, I might enter my office in a great hurry, and pretending not to see Bartleby at all, walk straight against him as if he were air. Such a proceeding would in a singular degree have the appearance of a home-thrust.[26] It was hardly possible that Bartleby could withstand such an application of the doctrine of assumptions. But upon second thoughts the success of the plan seemed rather dubious. I resolved to argue the matter over with him again.

"Bartleby," said I, entering the office, with a quietly severe expression, "I am seriously displeased. I am pained, Bartleby. I had thought better of you. I had imagined you of such a gentlemanly organization, that in any delicate dilemma a slight hint would suffice—in sort, an assumption. But it appears I am deceived. Why," I added, unaffectedly starting, "you have not even touched that money yet," pointing to it, just where I had left it the evening previous.

He answered nothing.

"Will you, or will you not, quit me?" I now demanded in a sudden passion, advancing close to him.

"I would prefer *not* to quit you," he replied gently emphasizing the *not*.

"What earthly right have you to stay here? Do you pay any rent? Do you pay my taxes? Or is this property yours?"

He answered nothing.

"Are you ready to go on and write now? Are your eyes recovered? Could you copy a small paper for me this morning? or help examine a few lines? or step round to the post-office? In a word, will you do anything at all, to give a coloring to your refusal to depart the premises?"

He silently retired into his hermitage.

I was now in such a state of nervous resentment that I thought it but prudent to check myself at present from further demonstrations. Bartleby and I were alone. I remembered the tragedy of the unfortunate Adams[27] and the still more unfortunate Colt in the solitary office of the latter; and how poor Colt, being dreadfully incensed by Adams, and imprudently permitting himself to get wildly excited, was at unawares hurried into his fatal act—an act which certainly no man could possibly deplore more than the actor himself. Often it had occurred to me in my ponderings upon the subject, that had that altercation taken place in the public street, or at a private residence, it would not have terminated as it did. It was the circumstance of being alone in a solitary office, upstairs, of a building entirely unhallowed by humanizing domestic associations—an uncarpeted office, doubtless, of a dusty, haggard sort of appearance—this it must have been, which greatly helped to enhance the irritable desperation of the hapless Colt.

But when this old Adam[28] of resentment rose in me and tempted me concerning Bartleby, I grappled him and threw him. How? Why, simply by recalling the divine injunction: "A new commandment give I unto you, that ye love one another."[29] Yes, this it was that saved me. Aside from higher considerations, charity often operates as a vastly wise and prudent principle—a great safeguard to its

---

[26] A blow that hits home.

[27] The printer Samuel Adams, who was axe murdered by John C. Colt in 1841 when Adams tried to collect a debt. Prior to his arrest and conviction for murder, Colt apparently crated Adams's body for shipment to New Orleans. Shortly before his scheduled hanging, Colt married his mistress in his jail cell and was found stabbed to death soon afterward. Great material for a mini-series.

[28] The human tendency to sin.   [29] From John 13:34.

possessor. Men have committed murder for jealousy's sake, and anger's sake, and hatred's sake, and selfishness' sake, and spiritual pride's sake; but no man, that ever I heard of, ever committed a diabolical murder for sweet charity's sake. Mere self-interest, then, if no better motive can be enlisted, should, especially with high-tempered men, prompt all beings to charity and philanthropy. At any rate, upon the occasion in question, I strove to drown my exasperated feelings towards the scrivener by benevolently construing his conduct. Poor fellow, poor fellow! thought I, he don't mean anything; and besides, he has seen hard times, and ought to be indulged.

I endeavored, also, immediately to occupy myself, and at the same time to comfort my despondency. I tried to fancy, that in the course of the morning, at such time as might prove agreeable to him, Bartleby, of his own free accord, would emerge from his hermitage and take up some decided line of march in the direction of the door. But no. Half-past twelve o'clock came; Turkey began to glow in the face, overturn his inkstand, and become generally obstreperous; Nippers abated down into quietude and courtesy; Ginger Nut munched his noon apple; and Bartleby remained standing at his window in one of his profoundest dead-wall reveries. Will it be credited? Ought I to acknowledge it? That afternoon I left the office without saying one further word to him.

Some days now passed, during which, at leisure intervals I looked a little into "Edwards on the Will," and "Priestley on Necessity."[30] Under the circumstances, those books induced a salutary feeling. Gradually I slid into the persuasion that these troubles of mine, touching the scrivener, had been all predestinated from eternity, and Bartleby was billeted upon me for some mysterious purpose of an allwise Providence, which it was not for a mere mortal like me to fathom. Yes, Bartleby, stay there behind your screen, thought I; I shall persecute you no more; you are harmless and noiseless as any of these old chairs; in short, I never feel so private as when I know you are here. At last I see it, I feel it; I penetrate to the predestinated purpose of my life. I am content. Others may have loftier parts to enact; but my mission in this world, Bartleby, is to furnish you with office-room for such period as you may see fit to remain.

I believe that this wise and blessed frame of mind would have continued with me, had it not been for the unsolicited and uncharitable remarks obtruded upon me by my professional friends who visited the rooms. But thus it often is, that the constant friction of illiberal minds wears out at last the best resolves of the more generous. Though to be sure, when I reflected upon it, it was not strange that people entering my office should be struck by the peculiar aspect of the unaccountable Bartleby, and so be tempted to throw out some sinister observations concerning him. Sometimes an attorney, having business with me, and calling at my office, and finding no one but the scrivener there, would undertake to obtain some sort of precise information from him touching my whereabouts; but without heeding his idle talk, Bartleby would remain standing immovable in the middle of the room. So after contemplating him in that position for a time, the attorney would depart, no wiser than he came.

Also, when a reference[31] was going on, and the room full of lawyers and wit-

---

[30] *Freedom of the Will* (1754), by Jonathan Edwards (1703–1758), and *Doctrine of Philosophical Necessity Illustrated* (1777), by Joseph Priestley (1733–1804). The American clergyman Edwards and the English scientist Priestley both believed that the will is not free.

[31] A matter referred to a judge or referee.

nesses, and business driving fast, some deeply-occupied legal gentleman present, seeing Bartleby wholly unemployed, would request him to run round to his (the legal gentleman's) office and fetch some papers for him. Thereupon, Bartleby would tranquilly decline, and yet remain idle as before. Then the lawyer would give a great stare, and turn to me. And what could I say? At last I was made aware that all through the circle of my professional acquaintance, a whisper of wonder was running round, having reference to the strange creature I kept at my office. This worried me very much. And as the idea came upon me of his possibly turning out a long-lived man, and keep occupying my chambers, and denying my authority; and perplexing my visitors; and scandalizing my professional reputation; and casting a general gloom over the premises; keeping soul and body together to the last upon his savings (for doubtless he spent but half a dime a day), and in the end perhaps outlive me, and claim possession of my office by right of his perpetual occupancy: as all these dark anticipations crowded upon me more and more, and my friends continually intruded their relentless remarks upon the apparition in my room; a great change was wrought in me. I resolved to gather all my faculties together, and forever rid me of this intolerable incubus.

Ere revolving any complicated project, however, adapted to this end, I first simply suggested to Bartleby the propriety of his permanent departure. In a calm and serious tone, I commended the idea to his careful and mature consideration. But, having taken three days to meditate upon it, he apprised me, that his original determination remained the same; in short, that he still preferred to abide with me.

What shall I do? I now said to myself, buttoning up my coat to the last button. What shall I do? what ought I to do? what does conscience say I *should* do with this man, or, rather, ghost. Rid myself of him, I must; go, he shall. But how? You will not thrust him, the poor, pale, passive mortal—you will not thrust such a helpless creature out of your door? you will not dishonor yourself by such cruelty? No, I will not, I cannot do that. Rather would I let him live and die here, and then mason up his remains in the wall. What, then, will you do? For all your coaxing, he will not budge. Bribes he leaves under your own paper-weight on your table; in short, it is quite plain that he prefers to cling to you.

Then something severe, something unusual must be done. What! surely you will not have him collared by a constable, and commit his innocent pallor to the common jail? And upon what ground could you procure such a thing to be done?—a vagrant, is he? What! he a vagrant, a wanderer, who refuses to budge? It is because he will *not* be a vagrant, then, that you seek to count him *as* a vagrant. That is too absurd. No visible means of support: there I have him. Wrong again: for indubitably he *does* support himself, and that is the only unanswerable proof that any man can show of his possessing the means so to do. No more, then. Since he will not quit me, I must quit him. I will change my offices; I will move elsewhere, and give him fair notice, that if I find him on my new premises I will then proceed against him as a common trespasser.

Acting accordingly, next day I thus addressed him: "I find these chambers too far from the City Hall; the air is unwholesome. In a word, I propose to remove my offices next week, and shall no longer require your services. I tell you this now, in order that you may seek another place."

He made no reply, and nothing more was said:

On the appointed day I engaged carts and men, proceeded to my chambers, and, having but little furniture, everything was removed in a few hours. Throughout, the scrivener remained standing behind the screen, which I directed to be removed the last thing. It was withdrawn; and, being folded up like a huge folio, left him the motionless occupant of a naked room. I stood in the entry watching him a moment, while something from within me upbraided me.

I re-entered, with my hand in my pocket—and—and my heart in my mouth.

"Good-by, Bartleby; I am going—good-by, and God some way bless you; and take that," slipping something in his hand. But it dropped upon the floor, and then—strange to say—I tore myself from him whom I had so longed to be rid of.

Established in my new quarters, for a day or two I kept the door locked, and started at every footfall in the passages. When I returned to my rooms, after any little absence, I would pause at the threshold for an instant, and attentively listen, ere applying my key. But these fears were needless. Bartleby never came nigh me.

I thought all was going well, when a perturbed-looking stranger visited me, inquiring whether I was the person who had recently occupied rooms at No.— Wall street.

Full of forebodings, I replied that I was.

"Then, sir," said the stranger, who proved a lawyer, "you are responsible for the man you left there. He refuses to do any copying; he refuses to do anything; he says he prefers not to; and he refuses to quit the premises."

"I am very sorry, sir," said I, with assumed tranquillity, but an inward tremor, "but, really, the man you allude to is nothing to me[32]—he is no relation or apprentice of mine, that you should hold me responsible for him."

"In mercy's name, who is he?"

"I certainly cannot inform you. I know nothing about him. Formerly I employed him as a copyist; but he has done nothing for me now for some time past."

"I shall settle him, then—good morning, sir."

Several days passed, and I heard nothing more; and, though I often felt a charitable prompting to call at the place and see poor Bartleby, yet a certain squeamishness, of I know not what, withheld me.

All is over with him, by this time, thought I, at last, when, through another week, no further intelligence reached me. But, coming to my room the day after, I found several persons waiting at my door in a high state of nervous excitement.

"That's the man—here he comes," cried the foremost one, whom I recognized as the lawyer who had previously called upon me alone.

"You must take him away, sir, at once," cried a portly person among them, advancing upon me, and whom I knew to be the landlord of No.— Wall street. "These gentlemen, my tenants, cannot stand it any longer; Mr. B—," pointing to the lawyer, "has turned him out of his room, and he now persists in haunting the building generally, sitting upon the banisters of the stairs by day, and sleeping in the entry by night. Everybody is concerned; clients are leaving the offices; some fears are entertained of a mob; something you must do, and that without delay."

Aghast at this torrent, I fell back before it, and would fain have locked myself in my new quarters. In vain I persisted that Bartleby was nothing to me—no more than to any one else. In vain—I was the last person known to have anything to do with him, and they held me to the terrible account. Fearful, then, of being exposed in the papers (as one person present obscurely threatened), I considered the matter, and, at length, said, that if the lawyer would give me a confidential interview

---

[32] An echo of Saint Peter's denial of Christ (see Mark 14:68, 70–71).

with the scrivener, in his (the lawyer's) own room, I would, that afternoon, strive my best to rid them of the nuisance they complained of.

Going up stairs to my old haunt, there was Bartleby silently sitting upon the banister at the landing.

"What are you doing here, Bartleby?" said I.

"Sitting upon the banister," he mildly replied.

I motioned him into the lawyer's room, who then left us.

"Bartleby" said I, "are you aware that you are the cause of great tribulation to me, by persisting in occupying the entry after being dismissed from the office?"

No answer.

"Now one of two things must take place. Either you must do something, or something must be done to you. Now what sort of business would you like to engage in? Would you like to re-engage in copying for some one?"

"No; I would prefer not to make any change."

"Would you like a clerkship in a dry-goods store?"

"There is too much confinement about that. No, I would not like a clerkship; but I am not particular."

"Too much confinement," I cried, "why you keep yourself confined all the time!"

"I would prefer not to take a clerkship," he rejoined, as if to settle that little item at once.

"How would a bar-tender's business suit you? There is no trying of the eyesight in that."

"I would not like it at all; though, as I said before, I am not particular."

His unwonted wordiness inspirited me. I returned to the charge.

"Well, then, would you like to travel through the country collecting bills for the merchants? That would improve your health."

"No, I would prefer to be doing something else."

"How, then, would going as a companion to Europe, to entertain some young gentleman with your conversation—how would that suit you?"

"Not at all. It does not strike me that there is anything definite about that. I like to be stationary. But I am not particular."

"Stationary you shall be, then," I cried, now losing all patience, and, for the first time in all my exasperating connection with him, fairly flying into a passion. "If you do not go away from these premises before night, I shall feel bound—indeed, I *am* bound—to—to—to quit the premises myself!" I rather absurdly concluded, knowing not with what possible threat to try to frighten his immobility into compliance. Despairing of all further efforts, I was precipitately leaving him, when a final thought occurred to me—one which had not been wholly unindulged before.

"Bartleby," said I, in the kindest tone I could assume under such exciting circumstances, "will you go home with me now—not to my office, but my dwelling—and remain there till we can conclude upon some convenient arrangement for you at our leisure? Come, let us start now, right away."

"No: at present I would prefer not to make any change at all."

I answered nothing; but, effectually dodging every one by the suddenness and rapidity of my flight, rushed from the building, ran up Wall street towards Broadway, and, jumping into the first omnibus, was soon removed from pursuit. As soon as tranquillity returned, I distinctly perceived that I had now done all that I possibly could, both in respect to the demands of the landlord and his tenants, and with regard to my own desire and sense of duty, to benefit Bartleby, and shield him from rude persecution. I now strove to be entirely care-free and quiescent; and my conscience justified me in the attempt; though, indeed, it was not so successful as I could have wished. So fearful was I of being again hunted out by the incensed landlord and his exasperated tenants, that, surrendering my business to Nippers, for a few days, I drove about the upper part of the town and through the suburbs, in my rockaway;[33] crossed over to Jersey City and Hoboken, and paid fugitive visits to Manhattanville and Astoria.[34] In fact, I almost lived in my rockaway for the time.

When again I entered my office, lo, a note from the landlord lay upon the desk. I opened it with trembling hands. It informed me that the writer had sent to the police, and had Bartleby removed to the Tombs as a vagrant. Moreover, since I knew more about him than any one else, he wished me to appear at that place, and make a suitable statement of the facts. These tidings had a conflicting effect upon me. At first I was indignant; but, at last, almost approved. The landlord's energetic, summary disposition, had led him to adopt a procedure which I do not think I would have decided upon myself; and yet, as a last resort, under such peculiar circumstances, it seemed the only plan.

As I afterwards learned, the poor scrivener, when told that he must be conducted to the Tombs, offered not the slightest obstacle, but, in his pale, unmoving way, silently acquiesced.

Some of the compassionate and curious bystanders joined the party; and headed by one of the constables arm in arm with Bartleby, the silent procession filed its way through all the noise, and heat, and joy of the roaring thoroughfares at noon.

The same day I received the note, I went to the Tombs, or, to speak more properly, the Halls of Justice. Seeking the right officer, I stated the purpose of my call, and was informed that the individual I described was, indeed, within. I then assured the functionary that Bartleby was a perfectly honest man, and greatly to be compassionated, however unaccountably eccentric. I narrated all I knew, and closed by suggesting the idea of letting him remain in as indulgent confinement as possible, till something less harsh might be done—though, indeed, I hardly knew what. At all events, if nothing else could be decided upon, the alms-house must receive him. I then begged to have an interview.

Being under no disgraceful charge, and quite serene and harmless in all his ways, they had permitted him freely to wander about the prison, and, especially, in the inclosed grass-platted yards thereof. And so I found him there, standing all alone in the quietest of the yards, his face towards a high wall, while all around, from the narrow slits of the jail windows, I thought I saw peering out upon him the eyes of murderers and thieves.

"Bartleby!"

"I know you," he said, without looking round—"and I want nothing to say to you."

"It was not I that brought you here, Bartleby," said I, keenly pained at his implied suspicion. "And to you, this should not be so vile a place. Nothing reproachful attaches to you by being here. And see, it is not so sad a place as one might think. Look, there is the sky, and here is the grass."

---

[33] A carriage with open sides and a top.

[34] Jersey City and Hoboken are in New Jersey; Manhattanville is on Manhattan Island, and Astoria, on Long Island.

"I know where I am," he replied, but would say nothing more, and so I left him.

As I entered the corridor again, a broad meat-like man, in an apron, accosted me, and, jerking his thumb over his shoulder, said—"Is that your friend?"

"Yes."

"Does he want to starve? If he does, let him live on the prison fare, that's all."

"Who are you?" asked I, not knowing what to make of such an unofficially speaking person in such a place.

"I am the grub-man. Such gentlemen as have friends here, hire me to provide them with something good to eat."

"Is this so?" said I, turning to the turnkey.

He said it was.

"Well, then," said I, slipping some silver into the grub-man's hands (for so they called him), "I want you to give particular attention to my friend there; let him have the best dinner you can get. And you must be as polite to him as possible."

"Introduce me, will you?" said the grub-man, looking at me with an expression which seemed to say he was all impatience for an opportunity to give a specimen of his breeding.

Thinking it would prove of benefit to the scrivener, I acquiesced; and, asking the grub-man his name, went up with him to Bartleby.

"Bartleby, this is a friend; you will find him very useful to you."

"Your sarvant, sir, your sarvant," said the grub-man, making a low salutation behind his apron. "Hope you find it pleasant here, sir; nice grounds—cool apartments—hope you'll stay with us some time—try to make it agreeable. What will you have for dinner to-day?"

"I prefer not to dine to-day," said Bartleby, turning away. "It would disagree with me; I am unused to dinners." So saying, he slowly moved to the other side of the inclosure, and took up a position fronting the dead-wall.

"How's this?" said the grub-man, addressing me with a stare of astonishment. "He's odd, ain't he?"

"I think he is a little deranged," said I, sadly.

"Deranged? deranged is it? Well, now, upon my word, I thought that friend of yourn was a gentleman forger; they are always pale and genteel-like, them forgers. I can't help pity 'em—can't help it, sir. Did you know Monroe Edwards?"[35] he added, touchingly, and paused. Then, laying his hand piteously on my shoulder, sighed, "he died of consumption at Sing-Sing. So you weren't acquainted with Monroe?"

"No, I was never socially acquainted with any forgers. But I cannot stop longer. Look to my friend yonder. You will not lose by it. I will see you again."

Some few days after this, I again obtained admission to the Tombs, and went through the corridors in quest of Bartleby; but without finding him.

"I saw him coming from his cell not long ago," said a turnkey, "may be he's gone to loiter in the yards."

So I went in that direction.

"Are you looking for the silent man?" said another turnkey, passing me. "Yon-

---

[35] Edwards (1808–1847) was convicted in 1842 of defrauding two firms of $25,000 each, with forged letters of credit. First imprisoned in the Tombs, he was sent to Sing-Sing prison in Ossining, New York, where he died.

der he lies—sleeping in the yard there. 'Tis not twenty minutes since I saw him lie down."

The yard was entirely quiet. It was not accessible to the common prisoners. The surrounding walls, of amazing thickness, kept off all sounds behind them. The Egyptian character of the masonry weighed upon me with its gloom. But a soft imprisoned turf grew under foot. The heart of the eternal pyramids, it seemed, wherein, by some strange magic, through the clefts, grass-seed, dropped by birds, had sprung.

Strangely huddled at the base of the wall, his knees drawn up, and lying on his side, his head touching the cold stones, I saw the wasted Bartleby. But nothing stirred. I paused; then went close up to him; stooped over, and saw that his dim eyes were open; otherwise he seemed profoundly sleeping. Something prompted me to touch him. I felt his hand, when a tingling shiver ran up my arm and down my spine to my feet.

The round face of the grub-man peered upon me now. "His dinner is ready. Won't he dine to-day, either? Or does he live without dining?"

"Lives without dining," said I, and closed the eyes.

"Eh!—He's asleep, ain't he?"

"With kings and counselors," murmured I.[36]

There would seem little need for proceeding further in this history. Imagination will readily supply the meagre recital of poor Bartleby's interment. But, ere parting with the reader, let me say, that if this little narrative has sufficiently interested him, to awaken curiosity as to who Bartleby was, and what manner of life he led prior to the present narrator's making his acquaintance, I can only reply, that in such curiosity I fully share, but am wholly unable to gratify it. Yet here I hardly know whether I should divulge one little item of rumor, which came to my ear a few months after the scrivener's decease. Upon what basis it rested, I could never ascertain; and hence, how true it is I cannot now tell. But, inasmuch as this vague report has not been without a certain suggestive interest to me, however sad, it may prove the same with some others; and so I will briefly mention it. The report was this: that Bartleby had been a subordinate clerk in the Dead Letter Office at Washington, from which he had been suddenly removed by a change in the administration. When I think over this rumor, hardly can I express the emotions which seize me. Dead letters! does it not sound like dead men? Conceive a man by nature and misfortune prone to a pallid hopelessness, can any business seem more fitted to heighten it than that of continually handling these dead letters, and assorting them for the flames? For by the cart-load they are annually burned. Sometimes from out the folded paper the pale clerk takes a ring—the finger it was meant for, perhaps, moulders in the grave; a bank-note sent in swiftest charity—he whom it would relieve, nor eats nor hungers any more; pardon for those who died despairing; hope for those who died unhoping; good tidings for those who died stifled by unrelieved calamities. On errands of life, these letters speed to death.

Ah, Bartleby! Ah, humanity!

1853

---

[36] In his sufferings Job wishes he were " . . . at rest, With kings and counsellors of the earth which built desolate places for themselves," from Job 3:14.

BENITO CERENO*

In the year 1799, Captain Amasa Delano,[1] of Duxbury, in Massachusetts, commanding a large sealer[2] and general trader, lay at anchor with a valuable cargo, in the harbor of St. Maria—a small, desert, uninhabited island toward the southern extremity of the long coast of Chili. There he had touched for water.

On the second day, not long after dawn, while lying in his berth, his mate came below, informing him that a strange sail was coming into the bay. Ships were then not so plenty in those waters as now. He rose, dressed, and went on deck.

The morning was one peculiar to that coast. Everything was mute and calm; everything gray. The sea, though undulated into long roods[3] of swells, seemed fixed, and was sleeked at the surface like waved lead that has cooled and set in the smelter's mould. The sky seemed a gray surtout.[4] Flights of troubled gray fowl, kith and kin with flights of troubled gray vapors among which they were mixed, skimmed low and fitfully over the waters, as swallows over meadows before storms. Shadows present, foreshadowing deeper shadows to come.

To Captain Delano's surprise, the stranger, viewed through the glass,[5] showed no colors; though to do so upon entering a haven, however uninhabited in its shores, where but a single other ship might be lying, was the custom among peaceful seamen of all nations. Considering the lawlessness and loneliness of the spot, and the sort of stories, at that day, associated with those seas, Captain Delano's surprise might have deepened into some uneasiness had he not been a person of a singularly undistrustful goodnature, not liable, except on extraordinary and repeated incentives, and hardly then, to indulge in personal alarms, any way involving the imputation of malign evil in man. Whether, in view of what humanity is capable, such a trait implies, along with a benevolent heart, more than ordinary quickness and accuracy of intellectual perception, may be left to the wise to determine.

But whatever misgivings might have obtruded on first seeing the stranger, would almost, in any seaman's mind, have been dissipated by observing that, the ship, in navigating into the harbor, was drawing too near the land; a sunken reef making out[6] off her bow. This seemed to prove her a stranger, indeed, not only to the sealer, but the island; consequently, she could be no wonted freebooter[7] on that ocean. With no small interest, Captain Delano continued to watch her—a proceeding not much facilitated by the vapors partly mantling the hull, through which the far matin[8] light from her cabin streamed equivocally enough; much like the sun—by this time hemisphered on the rim of the horizon, and, apparently, in company with the strange ship entering the harbor—which, wimpled[9] by the same

* First published serially in *Putnam's Magazine* in October through December 1855 and was included in *Piazza Tales* (1856).

[1] Melville's plot is based on incidents related in Chapter 18 of Captain Amasa Delano's *Narrative of Voyages and Travels in the Northern and Southern Hemispheres* (1817). In adapting this *Narrative*, Melville moved the story from 1805 to 1799 and renamed the Spanish ship *Tryal* the *San Dominick* and the American ship *Perseverance* the *Bachelor's Delight*.

[2] A ship for seal hunting.   [3] Rods, units of linear measure.   [4] An overcoat.
[5] Spyglass, or telescope.   [6] Existing; the reef represents hidden danger.
[7] A pirate familiar with the waters.   [8] Early morning.   [9] Veiled.

low, creeping clouds, showed not unlike a Lima intriguante's one sinister eye peering across the Plaza from the Indian loop-hole of her dusk *saya-y-manta*.[10]

It might have been but a deception of the vapors, but, the longer the stranger was watched the more singular appeared her manœuvres. Ere long it seemed hard to decide whether she meant to come in or no—what she wanted, or what she was about. The wind, which had breezed up a little during the night, was now extremely light and baffling,[11] which the more increased the apparent uncertainty of her movements.

Surmising, at last, that it might be a ship in distress, Captain Delano ordered his whale-boat to be dropped, and, much to the wary opposition of his mate, prepared to board her, and, at the least, pilot her in. On the night previous, a fishing-party of the seamen had gone a long distance to some detached rocks out of sight from the sealer, and, an hour or two before daybreak, had returned, having met with no small success. Presuming that the stranger might have been long off soundings,[12] the good captain put several baskets of the fish, for presents, into his boat, and so pulled away. From her continuing too near the sunken reef, deeming her in danger, calling to his men, he made all haste to apprise those on board of their situation. But, some time ere the boat came up, the wind, light though it was, having shifted, had headed the vessel off, as well as partly broken the vapors from about her.

Upon gaining a less remote view, the ship, when made signally visible on the verge of the leaden-hued swells, with the shreds of fog here and there raggedly furring her, appeared like a white-washed monastery after a thunder-storm, seen perched upon some dun cliff among the Pyrenees.[13] But it was no purely fanciful resemblance which now, for a moment, almost led Captain Delano to think that nothing less than a ship-load of monks was before him. Peering over the bulwarks were what really seemed, in the hazy distance, throngs of dark cowls; while, fitfully revealed through the open port-holes, other dark moving figures were dimly descried, as of Black Friars[14] pacing the cloisters.

Upon a still nigher approach, this appearance was modified, and the true character of the vessel was plain—a Spanish merchantman of the first class, carrying negro slaves, amongst other valuable freight, from one colonial port to another. A very large, and, in its time, a very fine vessel, such as in those days were at intervals encountered along that main; sometimes superseded Acapulco treasure-ships, or retired frigates of the Spanish king's navy, which, like superannuated Italian palaces, still, under a decline of masters, preserved signs of former state.

As the whale-boat drew more and more nigh, the cause of the peculiar pipe-clayed[15] aspect of the stranger was seen in the slovenly neglect pervading her. The spars, ropes, and great part of the bulwarks, looked woolly, from long unacquaintance with the scraper, tar, and the brush. Her keel seemed laid, her ribs put together, and she launched, from Ezekiel's Valley of Dry Bones.[16]

---

[10] "Skirt and shawl" (Spanish); the shawl could cover the face so that only one eye of an intrigant, one involved in intrigue, would show.

[11] Uncertain.   [12] A long time away from shallow water.

[13] Mountains between France and Spain.

[14] Dominicans, an order of preaching friars who wore black hoods; Melville named the *San Dominick* after them.

[15] Whitened.

[16] "The Lord . . . set [Ezekiel] down in the midst of the valley which was full of bones," from Ezekiel 37:1.

In the present business in which she was engaged, the ship's general model and rig appeared to have undergone no material change from their original warlike and Froissart pattern.[17] However, no guns were seen.

The tops[18] were large, and were railed about with what had once been octagonal net-work, all now in sad disrepair. These tops hung overhead like three ruinous aviaries, in one of which was seen perched, on a ratlin, a white noddy,[19] a strange fowl, so called from its lethargic, somnambulistic character, being frequently caught by hand at sea. Battered and mouldy, the castellated forecastle[20] seemed some ancient turret, long ago taken by assault, and then left to decay. Toward the stern, two high-raised quarter galleries[21]—the balustrades here and there covered with dry, tindery sea-moss—opening out from the unoccupied state-cabin, whose dead-lights,[22] for all the mild weather, were hermetically closed and calked—these tenantless balconies hung over the sea as if it were the grand Venetian canal. But the principal relic of faded grandeur was the ample oval of the shield-like stern-piece, intricately carved with the arms of Castile and Leon,[23] medallioned about by groups of mythological or symbolical devices; uppermost and central of which was a dark satyr in a mask, holding his foot on the prostrate neck of a writhing figure, likewise masked.

Whether the ship had a figure-head, or only a plain beak, was not quite certain, owing to canvas wrapped about that part, either to protect it while undergoing a re-furbishing, or else decently to hide its decay. Rudely painted or chalked, as in a sailor freak,[24] along the forward side of a sort of pedestal below the canvas, was the sentence, "*Seguid vuestro jefe,*" (follow your leader); while upon the tarnished headboards, near by, appeared, in stately capitals, once gilt, the ship's name "SAN DOMINICK," each letter streakingly corroded with tricklings of copper-spike rust; while, like mourning weeds, dark festoons of sea-grass slimily swept to and fro over the name, with every hearse-like roll of the hull.

As, at last, the boat was hooked from the bow along toward the gangway amidship, its keel, while yet some inches separated from the hull, harshly grated as on a sunken coral reef. It proved a hugh bunch of conglobated[25] barnacles adhering below the water to the side like a wen[26]—a token of baffling airs and long calms passed somewhere in those seas.

Climbing the side, the visitor was at once surrounded by a clamorous throng of whites and blacks, but the latter outnumbering the former more than could have been expected, negro transportation-ship as the stranger in port was. But, in one language, and as with one voice, all poured out a common tale of suffering; in which the negresses, of whom there were not a few, exceeded the others in their dolorous vehemence. The scurvy, together with the fever, had swept off a great part of their number, more especially the Spaniards. Off Cape Horn they had narrowly escaped shipwreck; then, for days together, they had lain tranced with-

---

[17] A medieval or ancient pattern; Jean Froissart (1333?–1400?) was a medieval French historian who wrote about the wars between France and England.

[18] Small platforms in the masts, used by lookouts.

[19] On the step of a rope ladder, a stout-bodied tern.

[20] The forward part of a ship's upper deck.   [21] Platforms on the side of a ship.

[22] Shutters that close over the port holes.

[23] Old kingdoms of Spain, united in 1230; the "shield-like stern-piece" displays a castle (Castile) and a lion (Leon). The other ornaments are ominous in nature.

[24] A joke.   [25] Ball-shaped.   [26] A cyst.

out wind; their provisions were low; their water next to none; their lips that moment were baked.

While Captain Delano was thus made the mark of all eager tongues, his one eager glance took in all faces, with every other object about him.

Always upon first boarding a large and populous ship at sea, especially a foreign one, with a nondescript crew such as Lascars or Manilla men,[27] the impression varies in a peculiar way from that produced by first entering a strange house with strange inmates in a strange land. Both house and ship—the one by its walls and blinds, the other by its high bulwarks like ramparts––hoard from view their interiors till the last moment: but in the case of the ship there is this addition; that the living spectacle it contains, upon its sudden and complete disclosure, has, in contrast with the blank ocean which zones it, something of the effect of enchantment. The ship seems unreal; these strange costumes, gestures, and faces, but a shadowy tableau just emerged from the deep, which directly must receive back what it gave.

Perhaps it was some such influence, as above is attempted to be described, which, in Captain Delano's mind, heightened whatever, upon a staid scrutiny, might have seemed unusual; especially the conspicuous figures of four elderly grizzled negroes, their heads like black, doddered[28] willow tops, who, in venerable contrast to the tumult below them, were couched, sphynx-like, one on the starboard cat-head,[29] another on the larboard, and the remaining pair face to face on the opposite bulwarks above the main-chains. They each had bits of unstranded old junk in their hands, and, with a sort of stoical self-content, were picking the junk into oakum,[30] a small heap of which lay by their sides. They accompanied the task with a continuous, low, monotonous chant; droning and druling[31] away like so many gray-headed bag-pipers playing a funeral march.

The quarter-deck rose into an ample elevated poop, upon the forward verge of which, lifted, like the oakum-pickers, some eight feet above the general throng, sat along in a row, separated by regular spaces, the cross-legged figures of six other blacks; each with a rusty hatchet in his hand, which, with a bit of brick and a rag, he was engaged like a scullion[32] in scouring; while between each two was a small stack of hatchets, their rusted edges turned forward awaiting a like operation. Though occasionally the four oakum-pickers would briefly address some person or persons in the crowd below, yet the six hatchet-polishers neither spoke to others, nor breathed a whisper among themselves, but sat intent upon their task, except at intervals, when, with the peculiar love in negroes of uniting industry with pastime, two and two they sideways clashed their hatchets together, like cymbals, with a barbarous din. All six, unlike the generality, had the raw aspect of unsophisticated Africans.

But that first comprehensive glance which took in those ten figures, with scores less conspicuous, rested but an instant upon them, as, impatient of the hubbub of voices, the visitor turned in quest of whomsoever it might be that commanded the ship.

But as if not unwilling to let nature make known her own case among his suffering charge, or else in despair of restraining it for the time, the Spanish captain,

---

[27] Sailors from East India or the Philippines.   [28] Without branches, due to age or decay.
[29] Projecting timber, near the bow, to which the anchor is secured.
[30] The worn-out rope into loose hemp fibers, used for caulking.
[31] Moaning.   [32] A kitchen worker.

a gentlemanly, reserved-looking, and rather young man to a stranger's eye, dressed with singular richness, but bearing plain traces of recent sleepless cares and disquietudes, stood passively by, leaning against the main-mast, at one moment casting a dreary, spiritless look upon his excited people, at the next an unhappy glance toward his visitor. By his side stood a black of small stature, in whose rude face, as occasionally, like a shepherd's dog, he mutely turned it up into the Spaniard's, sorrow and affection were equally blended.

Struggling through the throng, the American advanced to the Spaniard, assuring him of his sympathies, and offering to render whatever assistance might be in his power. To which the Spaniard returned for the present but grave and ceremonious acknowledgments, his national formality dusked by the saturnine mood of ill-health.

But losing no time in mere compliments, Captain Delano, returning to the gangway, had his basket of fish brought up; and as the wind still continued light, so that some hours at least must elapse ere the ship could be brought to the anchorage, he bade his men return to the sealer, and fetch back as much water as the whale-boat could carry, with whatever soft bread the steward might have, all the remaining pumpkins on board, with a box of sugar, and a dozen of his private bottles of cider.

Not many minutes after the boat's pushing off, to the vexation of all, the wind entirely died away, and the tide turning, began drifting back the ship helplessly seaward. But trusting this would not long last, Captain Delano sought, with good hopes, to cheer up the strangers, feeling no small satisfaction that, with persons in their condition, he could—thanks to his frequent voyages along the Spanish main[33]—converse with some freedom in their native tongue.

While left alone with them, he was not long in observing some things tending to heighten his first impressions; but surprise was lost in pity, both for the Spaniards and blacks, alike evidently reduced from scarcity of water and provisions; while long-continued suffering seemed to have brought out the less good-natured qualities of the negroes, besides, at the same time, impairing the Spaniard's authority over them. But, under the circumstances, precisely this condition of things was to have been anticipated. In armies, navies, cities, or families, in nature herself, nothing more relaxes good order than misery. Still, Captain Delano was not without the idea, that had Benito Cereno been a man of greater energy, misrule would hardly have come to the present pass. But the debility, constitutional or induced by hardships, bodily and mental, of the Spanish captain, was too obvious to be overlooked. A prey to settled dejection, as if long mocked with hope he would not now indulge it, even when it had ceased to be a mock, the prospect of that day, or evening at furthest, lying at anchor, with plenty of water for his people, and a brother captain to counsel and befriend, seemed in no perceptible degree to encourage him. His mind appeared unstrung, if not still more seriously affected. Shut up in these oaken walls, chained to one dull round of command, whose unconditionality cloyed him, like some hypochondriac abbot he moved slowly about, at times suddenly pausing, starting, or staring, biting his lip, biting his finger-nail, flushing, paling, twitching his beard, with other symptoms of an absent or moody mind. This distempered spirit was lodged, as before hinted, in as distempered a frame. He was rather tall, but seemed never to have been robust, and now with nervous suffering was almost worn to a skeleton. A tendency to

---

[33] The mainland coast of Spanish-owned South America.

some pulmonary complaint appeared to have been lately confirmed. His voice was like that of one with lungs half gone—hoarsely suppressed, a husky whisper. No wonder that, as in this state he tottered about, his private servant apprehensively followed him. Sometimes the negro gave his master his arm, or took his handkerchief out of his pocket for him; performing these and similar offices with that affectionate zeal which transmutes into something filial or fraternal acts in themselves but menial; and which has gained for the negro the repute of making the most pleasing body-servant in the world; one, too, whom a master need be on no stiffly superior terms with, but may treat with familiar trust; less a servant than a devoted companion.

Marking the noisy indocility of the blacks in general, as well as what seemed the sullen inefficiency of the whites it was not without humane satisfaction that Captain Delano witnessed the steady good conduct of Babo.

But the good conduct of Babo, hardly more than the ill-behavior of others, seemed to withdraw the half-lunatic Don[34] Benito from his cloudy languor. Not that such precisely was the impression made by the Spaniard on the mind of his visitor. The Spaniard's individual unrest was, for the present, but noted as a conspicuous feature in the ship's general affliction. Still, Captain Delano was not a little concerned at what he could not help taking for the time to be Don Benito's unfriendly indifference towards himself. The Spaniard's manner, too, conveyed a sort of sour and gloomy disdain, which he seemed at no pains to disguise. But this the American in charity ascribed to the harassing effects of sickness, since, in former instances, he had noted that there are peculiar natures on whom prolonged physical suffering seems to cancel every social instinct of kindness; as if, forced to black bread themselves, they deemed it but equity that each person coming nigh them should, indirectly, by some slight or affront, be made to partake of their fare.

But ere long Captain Delano bethought him that, indulgent as he was at the first, in judging the Spaniard, he might not, after all, have exercised charity enough. At bottom it was Don Benito's reserve which displeased him; but the same reserve was shown towards all but his faithful personal attendant. Even the formal reports which, according to sea-usage, were, at stated times, made to him by some petty underling, either a white, mulatto or black, he hardly had patience enough to listen to, without betraying contemptuous aversion. His manner upon such occasions was, in its degree, not unlike that which might be supposed to have been his imperial countryman's, Charles V.,[35] just previous to the anchoritish retirement of that monarch from the throne.

This splenetic disrelish of his place was evinced in almost every function pertaining to it. Proud as he was moody, he condescended to no personal mandate. Whatever special orders were necessary, their delivery was delegated to his body-servant, who in turn transferred them to their ultimate destination, through runners, alert Spanish boys or slave boys, like pages or pilot-fish[36] within easy call continually hovering round Don Benito. So that to have beheld this undemonstrative invalid gliding about, apathetic and mute, no landsman could have dreamed

---

[34] A title (corresponding to "Sir") prefixed to the first name of a Spanish gentleman.

[35] Charles V (1500–1558), who became king of Spain in 1517 and Holy Roman Emperor in 1519. He began the passage of African slaves to the American colonies in 1517 and conducted wars with France, Germany, and Turkey. In 1556 he abdicated his titles and retired to a monastery.

[36] Small fish that swim near sharks and seem to escort them.

that in him was lodged a dictatorship beyond which, while at sea, there was no earthly appeal.

Thus, the Spaniard, regarded in his reserve, seemed the involuntary victim of mental disorder. But, in fact, his reserve might, in some degree, have proceeded from design. If so, then here was evinced the unhealthy climax of that icy though conscientious policy; more or less adopted by all commanders of large ships, which, except in signal emergencies, obliterates alike the manifestation of sway with every trace of sociality; transforming the man into a block, or rather into a loaded cannon, which, until there is call for thunder, has nothing to say.

Viewing him in this light, it seemed but a natural token of the perverse habit induced by a long course of such hard self-restraint, that, notwithstanding the present condition of his ship, the Spaniard should still persist in a demeanor, which, however harmless, or, it may be, appropriate, in a well-appointed vessel, such as the San Dominick might have been at the outset of the voyage, was anything but judicious now. But the Spaniard, perhaps, thought that it was with captains as with gods: reserve, under all events, must still be their cue. But probably this appearance of slumbering dominion might have been but an attempted disguise to conscious imbecility—not deep policy, but shallow device. But be all this as it might, whether Don Benito's manner was designed or not, the more Captain Delano noted its pervading reserve, the less he felt uneasiness at any particular manifestation of that reserve towards himself.

Neither were his thoughts taken up by the captain alone. Wonted to the quiet orderliness of the sealer's comfortable family of a crew, the noisy confusion of the San Dominick's suffering host repeatedly challenged his eye. Some prominent breaches, not only of discipline but of decency, were observed. These Captain Delano could not but ascribe, in the main, to the absence of those subordinate deck-officers to whom, along with higher duties, is intrusted what may be styled the police department of a populous ship. True, the old oakum-pickers appeared at times to act the part of monitorial constables to their countrymen, the blacks; but though occasionally succeeding in allaying trifling outbreaks now and then between man and man, they could do little or nothing toward establishing general quiet. The San Dominick was in the condition of a transatlantic emigrant ship, among whose multitude of living freight are some individuals, doubtless, as little troublesome as crates and bales; but the friendly remonstrances of such with their ruder companions are of not so much avail as the unfriendly arm of the mate. What the San Dominick wanted was, what the emigrant ship has, stern superior officers. But on these decks not so much as a fourth-mate was to be seen.

The visitor's curiosity was roused to learn the particulars of those mishaps which had brought about such absenteeism, with its consequences; because, though deriving some inkling of the voyage from the wails which at the first moment had greeted him, yet of the details no clear understanding had been had. The best account would, doubtless, be given by the captain. Yet at first the visitor was loth to ask it, unwilling to provoke some distant rebuff. But plucking up courage, he at last accosted Don Benito, renewing the expression of his benevolent interest, adding, that did he (Captain Delano) but know the particulars of the ship's misfortunes, he would, perhaps, be better able in the end to relieve them. Would Don Benito favor him with the whole story.

Don Benito faltered; then, like some somnambulist suddenly interfered with, vacantly stared at his visitor, and ended by looking down on the deck. He maintained this posture so long, that Captain Delano, almost equally disconcerted, and involuntarily almost as rude, turned suddenly from him, walking forward to accost one of the Spanish seamen for the desired information. But he had hardly gone five paces, when, with a sort of eagerness, Don Benito invited him back, regretting his momentary absence of mind, and professing readiness to gratify him.

While most part of the story was being given, the two captains stood on the after part of the main-deck, a privileged spot, no one being near but the servant.

"It is now a hundred and ninety days," began the Spaniard, in his husky whisper, "that this ship, well officered and well manned, with several cabin passengers—some fifty Spaniards in all—sailed from Buenos Ayres bound to Lima, with a general cargo, hardware, Paraguay tea and the like—and," pointing forward, "that parcel of negroes, now not more than a hundred and fifty, as you see, but then numbering over three hundred souls. Off Cape Horn we had heavy gales. In one moment, by night, three of my best officers, with fifteen sailors, were lost, with the main-yard; the spar snapping under them in the slings, as they sought, with heavers,[37] to beat down the icy sail. To lighten the hull, the heavier sacks of mata[38] were thrown into the sea, with most of the water-pipes[39] lashed on deck at the time. And this last necessity it was, combined with the prolonged detentions afterwards experienced, which eventually brought about our chief causes of suffering. When—"

Here there was a sudden fainting attack of his cough, brought on, no doubt, by his mental distress. His servant sustained him, and drawing a cordial[40] from his pocket placed it to his lips. He a little revived. But unwilling to leave him unsupported while yet imperfectly restored, the black with one arm still encircled his master, at the same time keeping his eye fixed on his face, as if to watch for the first sign of complete restoration, or relapse, as the event might prove.

The Spaniard proceeded, but brokenly and obscurely, as one in a dream.

—"Oh, my God! rather than pass through what I have, with joy I would have hailed the most terrible gales; but—"

His cough returned and with increased violence; this subsiding, with reddened lips and closed eyes he fell heavily against his supporter.

"His mind wanders. He was thinking of the plague that followed the gales," plaintively sighed the servant; "my poor, poor master!" wringing one hand, and with the other wiping the mouth. "But be patient, Señor," again turning to Captain Delano, "these fits do not last long; master will soon be himself."

Don Benito reviving, went on; but as this portion of the story was very brokenly delivered, the substance only will here be set down.

It appeared that after the ship had been many days tossed in storms off the Cape, the scurvy broke out, carrying off numbers of the whites and blacks. When at last they had worked round into the Pacific, their spars and sails were so damaged, and so inadequately handled by the surviving mariners, most of whom were become invalids, that, unable to lay her northerly course by the wind, which was powerful, the unmanageable ship, for successive days and nights, was blown northwestward, where the breeze suddenly deserted her, in unknown waters, to sultry calms. The absence of the water-pipes now proved as fatal to life as before their presence had menaced it. Induced, or at least aggravated, by the more than

---

[37] In the ropes that attach yardarms to masts, as they sought to control the flapping sail, with bars used as levers.

[38] Mate, or Paraguay tea.   [39] Water casks.   [40] A medicine or liqueur that stimulates the heart.

scanty allowance of water, a malignant fever followed the scurvy; with the excessive heat of the lengthened calm, making such short work of it as to sweep away, as by billows, whole families of the Africans, and a yet larger number, proportionably, of the Spaniards, including, by a luckless fatality, every remaining officer on board. Consequently, in the smart west winds eventually following the calm, the already rent sails, having to be simply dropped, not furled, at need, had been gradually reduced to the beggars' rags they were now. To procure substitutes for his lost sailors, as well as supplies of water and sails, the captain, at the earliest opportunity, had made for Baldivia, the southernmost civilized port of Chili and South America; but upon nearing the coast the thick weather had prevented him from so much as sighting that harbor. Since which period, almost without a crew, and almost without canvas and almost without water, and, at intervals, giving its added dead to the sea, the San Dominick had been battle-dored[41] about by contrary winds, inveigled by currents, or grown weedy in calms. Like a man lost in woods, more than once she had doubled upon her own track.

"But throughout these calamities," huskily continued Don Benito, painfully turning in the half embrace of his servant, "I have to thank those negroes you see, who, though to your inexperienced eyes appearing unruly, have, indeed, conducted themselves with less of restlessness than even their owner could have thought possible under such circumstances."

Here he again fell faintly back. Again his mind wandered; but he rallied, and less obscurely proceeded.

"Yes, their owner was quite right in assuring me that no fetters would be needed with his blacks; so that while, as is wont in this transportation, those negroes have always remained upon deck—not thrust below, as in the Guinea-men[42]—they have, also, from the beginning, been freely permitted to range within given bounds at their pleasure."

Once more the faintness returned—his mind roved—but, recovering, he resumed:

"But it is Babo here to whom, under God, I owe not only my own preservation, but likewise to him, chiefly, the merit is due, of pacifying his more ignorant brethren, when at intervals tempted to murmurings."

"Ah, master," sighed the black, bowing his face, "don't speak of me; Babo is nothing; what Babo has done was but duty."

"Faithful fellow!" cried Captain Delano. "Don Benito, I envy you such a friend; slave I cannot call him."

As master and man stood before him, the black upholding the white, Captain Delano could not but bethink him of the beauty of that relationship which could present such a spectacle of fidelity on the one hand and confidence on the other. The scene was heightened by the contrast in dress, denoting their relative positions. The Spaniard wore a loose Chili jacket of dark velvet; white small-clothes and stockings, with silver buckles at the knee and instep; a high-crowned sombrero, of fine grass; a slender sword, silver mounted, hung from a knot in his sash—the last being an almost invariable adjunct, more for utility than ornament, of a South American gentlemen's dress to this hour. Excepting when his occasional nervous contortions brought about disarray, there was a certain precision in his attire curiously at variance with the unsightly disorder around; especially in the belittered Ghetto, forward of the main-mast, wholly occupied by the blacks.

---

[41] Batted back and forth.   [42] Ships that carried slaves from Guinea, on the West coast of Africa.

The servant wore nothing but wide trowsers, apparently, from their coarseness and patches, made out of some old topsail; they were clean, and confined at the waist by a bit of unstranded rope, which, with his composed, deprecatory air at times, made him look something like a begging friar of St. Francis.

However unsuitable for the time and place, at least in the blunt-thinking American's eyes, and however strangely surviving in the midst of all his afflictions, the toilette of Don Benito might not, in fashion at least, have gone beyond the style of the day among South Americans of his class. Though on the present voyage sailing from Buenos Ayres, he had avowed himself a native and resident of Chili, whose inhabitants had not so generally adopted the plain coat and once plebeian pantaloons; but, with a becoming modification, adhered to their provincial costume, picturesque as any in the world. Still, relatively to the pale history of the voyage, and his own pale face, there seemed something so incongruous in the Spaniard's apparel, as almost to suggest the image of an invalid courtier tottering about London streets in the time of the plague.

The portion of the narrative which, perhaps, most excited interest, as well as some surprise, considering the latitudes in question, was the long calms spoken of, and more particularly the ship's so long drifting about. Without communicating the opinion, of course, the American could not but impute at least part of the detentions both to clumsy seamanship and faulty navigation. Eying Don Benito's small, yellow hands, he easily inferred that the young captain had not got into command at the hawse-hole,[43] but the cabin-window; and if so, why wonder at incompetence, in youth, sickness, and gentility united?

But drowning criticism in compassion, after a fresh repetition of his sympathies, Captain Delano, having heard out his story, not only engaged, as in the first place, to see Don Benito and his people supplied in their immediate bodily needs, but, also, now further promised to assist him in procuring a large permanent supply of water, as well as some sails and rigging; and, though it would involve no small embarrassment to himself, yet he would spare three of his best seamen for temporary deck officers; so that without delay the ship might proceed to Conception,[44] there fully to refit for Lima, her destined port.

Such generosity was not without its effect, even upon the invalid. His face lighted up; eager and hectic, he met the honest glance of his visitor. With gratitude he seemed overcome.

"This excitement is bad for master," whispered the servant, taking his arm, and with soothing words gently drawing him aside.

When Don Benito returned, the American was pained to observe that his hopefulness, like the sudden kindling in his cheek, was but febrile and transient.

Ere long, with a joyless mien, looking up towards the poop, the host invited his guest to accompany him there, for the benefit of what little breath of wind might be stirring.

As, during the telling of the story, Captain Delano had once or twice started at the occasional cymballing of the hatchet-polishers, wondering why such an interruption should be allowed, especially in that part of the ship, and in the ears of an invalid; and moreover, as the hatchets had anything but an attractive look, and the

---

[43] A hole in a ship's bow, through which cables pass, implying that Don Benito has not worked his way up from the bottom but has come directly into authority.

[44] Concepción, Chile.

handlers of them still less so, it was, therefore, to tell the truth, not without some lurking reluctance, or even shrinking, it may be, that Captain Delano, with apparent complaisance, acquiesced in his host's invitation. The more so, since, with an untimely caprice of punctilio, rendered distressing by his cadaverous aspect, Don Benito, with Castilian[45] bows, solemnly insisted upon his guest's preceding him up the ladder leading to the elevation; where, one on each side of the last step, sat for armorial supporters and sentries two of the ominous file. Gingerly enough stepped good Captain Delano between them, and in the instant of leaving them behind, like one running the gauntlet, he felt an apprehensive twitch in the calves of his legs.

But when, facing about, he saw the whole file, like so many organ-grinders, still stupidly intent on their work, unmindful of everything beside, he could not but smile at his late fidgety panic.

Presently, while standing with his host, looking forward upon the decks below, he was struck by one of those instances of insubordination previously alluded to. Three black boys, with two Spanish boys, were sitting together on the hatches, scraping a rude wooden platter, in which some scanty mess had recently been cooked. Suddenly, one of the black boys, enraged at a word dropped by one of his white companions, seized a knife, and, though called to forbear by one of the oakum-pickers, struck the lad over the head, inflicting a gash from which blood flowed.

In amazement, Captain Delano inquired what this meant. To which the pale Don Benito dully muttered, that it was merely the sport of the lad.

"Pretty serious sport, truly," rejoined Captain Delano. "Had such a thing happened on board the Bachelor's Delight, instant punishment would have followed."

At these words the Spaniard turned upon the American one of his sudden, staring, half-lunatic looks; then, relapsing into his torpor, answered, "Doubtless, doubtless, Señor."

Is it, thought Captain Delano, that this hapless man is one of those paper captains I've known, who by policy wink at what by power they cannot put down? I know no sadder sight than a commander who has little of command but the name.

"I should think, Don Benito," he now said, glancing towards the oakum-picker who had sought to interfere with the boys, "that you would find it advantageous to keep all your blacks employed, especially the younger ones, no matter at what useless task, and no matter what happens to the ship. Why, even with my little band, I find such a course indispensable. I once kept a crew on my quarter-deck thrumming[46] mats for my cabin, when, for three days, I had given up my ship— mats, men, and all—for a speedy loss, owing to the violence of a gale, in which we could do nothing but helplessly drive before it."

"Doubtless, doubtless," muttered Don Benito.

"But," continued Captain Delano, again glancing upon the oakum-pickers and then at the hatchet-polishers, near by, "I see you keep some, at least, of your host employed."

"Yes," was again the vacant response.

"Those old men there, shaking their pows[47] from their pulpits," continued Captain Delano, pointing to the oakum-pickers, "seem to act the part of old domin-

---

[45] Courtly.   [46] Weaving with pieces of rope yarn and canvas.   [47] Heads.

ies[48] to the rest, little heeded as their admonitions are at time. Is this voluntary on their part, Don Benito, or have you appointed them shepherds to your flock of black sheep?"

"What posts they fill, I appointed them," rejoined the Spaniard, in an acrid tone, as if resenting some supposed satiric reflection.

"And these others, these Ashantee[49] conjurors here," continued Captain Delano, rather uneasily eying the brandished steel of the hatchet-polishers, where, in spots, it had been brought to a shine, "this seems a curious business they are at, Don Benito?"

"In the gales we met," answered the Spaniard, "what of our general cargo was not thrown overboard was much damaged by the brine. Since coming into calm weather, I have had several cases of knives and hatchets daily brought up for overhauling and cleaning."

"A prudent idea, Don Benito. You are part owner of ship and cargo, I presume; but none of the slaves, perhaps?"

"I am owner of all you see," impatiently returned Don Benito, "except the main company of blacks, who belonged to my late friend, Alexandro Aranda."

As he mentioned this name, his air was heart-broken; his knees shook; his servant supported him.

Thinking he divined the cause of such unusual emotion, to confirm his surmise, Captain Delano, after a pause, said: "And may I ask, Don Benito, whether—since awhile ago you spoke of some cabin passengers—the friend, whose loss so afflicts you, at the outset of the voyage accompanied his blacks?"

"Yes."

"But died of the fever?"

"Died of the fever. Oh, could I but—"

Again quivering, the Spaniard paused.

"Pardon me," said Captain Delano, lowly, "but I think that, by a sympathetic experience, I conjecture, Don Benito, what it is that gives the keener edge to your grief. It was once my hard fortune to lose, at sea, a dear friend, my own brother, then supercargo.[50] Assured of the welfare of his spirit, its departure I could have borne like a man; but that honest eye, that honest hand—both of which had so often met mine—and that warm heart; all, all—like scraps to the dogs—to throw all to the sharks! It was then I vowed never to have for fellow-voyager a man I loved, unless, unbeknown to him, I had provided every requisite, in case of a fatality, for embalming his mortal part for interment on shore. Were your friend's remains now on board this ship, Don Benito, not thus strangely would the mention of his name affect you."

"On board this ship?" echoed the Spaniard. Then, with horrified gestures, as directed against some spectre, he unconsciously fell into the ready arms of his attendant, who, with a silent appeal toward Captain Delano, seemed beseeching him not again to broach a theme so unspeakably distressing to his master.

This poor fellow now, thought the pained American, is the victim of that sad superstition which associates goblins with the deserted body of man, as ghosts with an abandoned house. How unlike are we made! What to me, in like case, would have been a solemn satisfaction, the bare suggestion, even, terrifies the Spaniard into this trance. Poor Alexandro Aranda! what would you say could you

---

[48] Schoolmasters or clergymen.   [49] Ashanti, a West African tribe.
[50] An officer in charge of the commercial concerns of a voyage.

here see your friend—who, on former voyages, when you, for months, were left behind, has, I dare say, often longed, and longed, for one peep at you—now transported with terror at the least thought of having you anyway nigh him.

At this moment, with a dreary grave-yard toll, betokening a flaw, the ship's forecastle bell, smote by one of the grizzled oakum-pickers, proclaimed ten o'clock, through the leaden calm; when Captain Delano's attention was caught by the moving figure of a gigantic black, emerging from the general crowd below, and slowly advancing towards the elevated poop. An iron collar was about his neck, from which depended a chain, thrice wound round his body; the terminating links padlocked together at a broad band of iron, his girdle.

"How like a mute Atufal moves," murmured the servant.

The black mounted the steps of the poop, and, like a brave prisoner, brought up to receive sentence, stood in unquailing muteness before Don Benito, now recovered from his attack.

At the first glimpse of his approach, Don Benito had started, a resentful shadow swept over his face; and, as with the sudden memory of bootless[51] rage, his white lips glued together.

This is some mulish mutineer, thought Captain Delano, surveying, not without a mixture of admiration, the colossal form of the negro.

"See, he waits your question, master," said the servant.

Thus reminded, Don Benito, nervously averting his glance, as if shunning, by anticipation, some rebellious response, in a disconcerted voice, thus spoke:—

"Atufal, will you ask my pardon, now?"

The black was silent.

"Again, master," murmured the servant, with bitter upbraiding eyeing his countryman, "Again, master; he will bend to master yet."

"Answer," said Don Benito, still averting his glance, "say but the one word, *pardon*, and your chains shall be off."

Upon this, the black, slowly raising both arms, let them lifelessly fall, his links clanking, his head bowed; as much as to say, "no, I am content."

"Go," said Don Benito, with inkept and unknown emotion.

Deliberately as he had come, the black obeyed.

"Excuse me, Don Benito," said Captain Delano, "but this scene surprises me; what means it, pray?"

"It means that that negro alone, of all the band, has given me peculiar cause of offense. I have put him in chains; I—"

Here he paused; his hand to his head, as if there were a swimming there, or a sudden bewilderment of memory had come over him; but meeting his servant's kindly glance seemed reassured, and proceeded:—

"I could not scourge such a form. But I told him he must ask my pardon. As yet he has not. At my command, every two hours he stands before me."

"And how long has this been?"

"Some sixty days."

"And obedient in all else? And respectful?"

"Yes."

"Upon my conscience, then," exclaimed Captain Delano, impulsively, "he has a royal spirit in him, this fellow."

---

[51] Useless, unavailing.

"He may have some right to it," bitterly returned Don Benito, "he says he was king in his own land."

"Yes," said the servant, entering a word, "those slits in Atufal's ears once held wedges of gold; but poor Babo here, in his own land, was only a poor slave; a black man's slave was Babo, who now is the white's."

Somewhat annoyed by these conversational familiarities, Captain Delano turned curiously upon the attendant, then glanced inquiringly at his master; but, as if long wonted to these little informalities, neither master nor man seemed to understand him.

"What, pray, was Atufal's offense, Don Benito?" asked Captain Delano; "if it was not something very serious, take a fool's advice, and, in view of his general docility, as well as in some natural respect for his spirit, remit him his penalty."

"No, no, master never will do that," here murmured the servant to himself, "proud Atufal must first ask master's pardon. The slave there carries the padlock, but master here carries the key."

His attention thus directed, Captain Delano now noticed for the first, that, suspended by a slender silken cord, from Don Benito's neck, hung a key. At once, from the servant's muttered syllables, divining the key's purpose, he smiled and said:—"So, Don Benito—padlock and key—significant symbols, truly."

Biting his lip, Don Benito faltered.

Though the remark of Captain Delano, a man of such native simplicity as to be incapable of satire or irony, had been dropped in playful allusion to the Spaniard's singularly evidenced lordship over the black; yet the hypochondriac seemed some way to have taken it as a malicious reflection upon his confessed inability thus far to break down, at least, on a verbal summons, the entrenched will of the slave. Deploring this supposed misconception, yet despairing of correcting it, Captain Delano shifted the subject; but finding his companion more than ever withdrawn, as if still sourly digesting the lees[52] of the presumed affront above-mentioned, by-and-by Captain Delano likewise became less talkative, oppressed, against his own will, by what seemed the secret vindictiveness of the morbidly sensitive Spaniard. But the good sailor, himself of a quite contrary disposition, refrained, on his part, alike from the appearance as from the feeling of resentment, and if silent, was only so from contagion.

Presently the Spaniard, assisted by his servant somewhat discourteously crossed over from his guest; a procedure which, sensibly enough, might have been allowed to pass for idle caprice of ill-humor, had not master and man, lingering round the corner of the elevated skylight, began whispering together in low voices. This was unpleasing. And more; the moody air of the Spaniard, which at times had not been without a sort of valetudinarian[53] stateliness, now seemed anything but dignified; while the menial familiarity of the servant lost its original charm of simple-hearted attachment.

In his embarrassment, the visitor turned his face to the other side of the ship. By so doing, his glance accidentally fell on a young Spanish sailor, a coil of rope in his hand, just stepped from the deck to the first round of the mizzen-rigging.[54] Perhaps the man would not have been particularly noticed, were it not that, during his ascent to one of the yards, he, with a sort of covert intentness, kept his eye fixed on Captain Delano, from whom, presently, it passed, as if by a natural sequence, to the two whisperers.

---

[52] Dregs.   [53] Infirm, sickly.   [54] The rigging on the mast near the stern.

His own attention thus redirected to that quarter, Captain Delano gave a slight start. From something in Don Benito's manner just then, it seemed as if the visitor had, at least partly, been the subject of the withdrawn consultation going on—a conjecture as little agreeable to the guest as it was little flattering to the host.

The singular alternations of courtesy and ill-breeding in the Spanish captain were unaccountable, except on one of two suppositions—innocent lunacy, or wicked imposture.

But the first idea, though it might naturally have occurred to an indifferent observer, and, in some respect, had not hitherto been wholly a stranger to Captain Delano's mind, yet, now that, in an incipient way, he began to regard the stranger's conduct something in the light of an intentional affront, of course the idea of lunacy was virtually vacated. But if not a lunatic, what then? Under the circumstances, would a gentleman, nay, any honest boor, act the part now acted by his host? The man was an impostor. Some low-born adventurer, masquerading as an oceanic grandee;[55] yet so ignorant of the first requisites of mere gentleman-hood as to be betrayed into the present remarkable indecorum. That strange cere-moniousness, too, at other times evinced, seemed not uncharacteristic of one play-ing a part above his real level. Benito Cereno—Don Benito Cereno—a sounding[56] name. One, too, at that period, not unknown, in the surname, to supercargoes and sea captains trading along the Spanish Main, as belonging to one of the most enterprising and extensive mercantile families in all those provinces; several mem-bers of it having titles; a sort of Castilian Rothschild,[57] with a noble brother, or cousin, in every great trading town of South America. The alleged Don Benito was in early manhood, about twenty-nine or thirty. To assume a sort of roving cadetship[58] in the maritime affairs of such a house, what more likely scheme for a young knave of talent and spirit? But the Spaniard was a pale invalid. Never mind. For even to the degree of simulating mortal disease, the craft of some tricksters had been known to attain. To think that, under the aspect of infantile weakness, the most savage energies might be couched—those velvets of the Spaniard but the silky paw to his fangs.

From no train of thought did these fancies come; not from within, but from without; suddenly, too, and in one throng, like hoar frost; yet as soon to vanish as the mild sun of Captain Delano's good-nature regained its meridian.

Glancing over once more towards his host—whose side-face, revealed above the skylight, was not turned towards him—he was struck by the profile, whose clearness of cut was refined by the thinness, incident to ill-health, as well as enno-bled about the chin by the beard. Away with suspicion. He was a true off-shoot of a true hidalgo[59] Cereno.

Relieved by these and other better thoughts, the visitor, lightly humming a tune, now began indifferently pacing the poop, so as not to betray to Don Benito that he had at all mistrusted incivility, much less duplicity; for such mistrust would yet be proved illusory, and by the event; though, for the present, the circumstance which had provoked that distrust remained unexplained. But when that little mys-tery should have been cleared up, Captain Delano thought he might extremely regret it, did he allow Don Benito to become aware that he had indulged in ungen-

---

[55] The highest rank of Spanish noblemen.   [56] High-sounding, bombastic.
[57] A famous German banking family with widespread European interests.
[58] An apprenticeship.   [59] A Spanish nobleman, below the rank of grandee.

erous surmises. In short, to the Spaniard's black-letter text,[60] it was best, for awhile, to leave open margin.[61]

Presently, his pale face twitching and overcast, the Spaniard, still supported by his attendant, moved over towards his guest, when, with even more than his usual embarrassment, and a strange sort of intriguing intonation in his husky whisper, the following conversation began:—

"Señor, may I ask how long you have lain at this isle?"

"Oh, but a day or two, Don Benito."

"And from what port are you last?"

"Canton."[62]

"And there, Señor, you exchanged your sealskins for teas and silks, I think you said?"

"Yes. Silks, mostly."

"And the balance you took in specie,[63] perhaps?"

Captain Delano, fidgeting a little, answered—

"Yes; some silver; not a very great deal, though."

"Ah—well. May I ask how many men have you, Señor?"

Captain Delano slightly started, but answered—

"About five-and-twenty, all told."

"And at present, Señor, all on board, I suppose?"

"All on board, Don Benito," replied the Captain, now with satisfaction.

"And will be to-night, Señor?"

At this last question, following so many pertinacious ones, for the soul of him Captain Delano could not but look very earnestly at the questioner, who, instead of meeting the glance, with every token of craven discomposure dropped his eyes to the deck; presenting an unworthy contrast to his servant, who, just then, was kneeling at his feet, adjusting a loose shoe-buckle; his disengaged face meantime, with humble curiosity, turned openly up into his master's downcast one.

The Spaniard, still with a guilty shuffle, repeated his question:

"And—and will be to-night, Señor?"

"Yes, for aught I know," returned Captain Delano— "but nay," rallying himself into fearless truth, "some of them talked of going off on another fishing party about midnight."

"Your ships generally go—go more or less armed, I believe, Señor?"

"Oh, a six-pounder or two, in case of emergency," was the intrepidly indifferent reply, "with a small stock of muskets, sealing-spears, and cutlasses, you know."

As he thus responded, Captain Delano again glanced at Don Benito, but the latter's eyes were averted; while abruptly and awkwardly shifting the subject, he made some peevish allusion to the calm, and then, without apology, once more, with his attendant, withdrew to the opposite bulwarks, where the whispering was resumed.

At this moment, and ere Captain Delano could cast a cool thought upon what had just passed, the young Spanish sailor, before mentioned, was seen descending from the rigging. In act of stooping over to spring inboard to the deck, his voluminous, unconfined frock, or shirt, of coarse woolen, much spotted with tar, opened out far down the chest, revealing a soiled under garment of what seemed the finest

---

[60] A text printed in ornate script.   [61] To reserve judgment (with no marginal notes).
[62] A port in China.   [63] A coin of precious metal.

linen, edged, about the neck, with a narrow blue ribbon, sadly faded and worn. At this moment the young sailor's eye was again fixed on the whisperers, and Captain Delano thought he observed a lurking significance in it, as if silent signs, of some Freemason[64] sort, had that instant been interchanged.

This once more impelled his own glance in the direction of Don Benito, and, as before, he could not but infer that himself formed the subject of the conference. He paused. The sound of the hatchet-polishing fell on his ears. He cast another swift side-look at the two. They had the air of conspirators. In connection with the late questionings, and the incident of the young sailor, these things now begat such return of involuntary suspicion, that the singular guilelessness of the American could not endure it. Plucking up a gay and humorous expression, he crossed over to the two rapidly, saying:—"Ha, Don Benito, your black here seems high in your trust; a sort of privy-counselor, in fact."

Upon this, the servant looked up with a good-natured grin, but the master started as from a venomous bite. It was a moment or two before the Spaniard sufficiently recovered himself to reply; which he did, at last, with cold constraint:—"Yes, Señor, I have trust in Babo."

Here Babo, changing his previous grin of mere animal humor into an intelligent smile, not ungratefully eyed his master.

Finding that the Spaniard now stood silent and reserved, as if involuntarily, or purposely giving hint that his guest's proximity was inconvenient just then, Captain Delano, unwilling to appear uncivil even to incivility itself, made some trivial remark and moved off; again and again turning over in his mind the mysterious demeanor of Don Benito Cereno.

He had descended from the poop, and, wrapped in thought, was passing near a dark hatchway, leading down into the steerage, when, perceiving motion there, he looked to see what moved. The same instant there was a sparkle in the shadowy hatchway, and he saw one of the Spanish sailors, prowling there, hurriedly placing his hand in the bosom of his frock, as if hiding something. Before the man could have been certain who it was that was passing, he slunk below out of sight. But enough was seen of him to make it sure that he was the same young sailor before noticed in the rigging.

What was that which so sparkled? thought Captain Delano. It was no lamp—no match—no live coal. Could it have been a jewel? But how come sailors with jewels?—or with silk-trimmed under-shirts either? Has he been robbing the trunks of the dead cabin-passengers? But if so, he would hardly wear one of the stolen articles on board ship here. Ah, ah—if, now, that was, indeed, a secret sign I saw passing between this suspicious fellow and his captain awhile since; if I could only be certain that, in my uneasiness, my senses did not deceive me, then—

Here, passing from one suspicious thing to another, his mind revolved the strange questions put to him concerning his ship.

By a curious coincidence, as each point was recalled, the black wizards of Ashantee would strike up with their hatchets, as in ominous comment on the white stranger's thoughts. Pressed by such enigmas and portents, it would have been almost against nature, had not, even into the least distrustful heart, some ugly misgivings obtruded.

---

[64] A fraternal society of men, founded in the eighteenth century, that was secret and a political force in some countries. An active anti-Masonic movement influenced American politics in the 1820s and 1830s.

Observing the ship, now helplessly fallen into a current, with enchanted sails, drifting with increased rapidity seaward; and noting that, from a lately intercepted projection of the land, the sealer was hidden, the stout mariner began to quake at thoughts which he barely durst confess to himself. Above all, he began to feel a ghostly dread of Don Benito. And yet, when he roused himself, dilated his chest, felt himself strong on his legs, and coolly considered it—what did all these phantoms amount to?

Had the Spaniard any sinister scheme, it must have reference not so much to him (Captain Delano) as to his ship (the Bachelor's Delight). Hence the present drifting away of the one ship from the other, instead of favoring any such possible scheme, was, for the time, at least, opposed to it. Clearly any suspicion, combining such contradictions, must need be delusive. Beside, was it not absurd to think of a vessel in distress—a vessel by sickness almost dismanned of her crew—a vessel whose inmates were parched for water—was it not a thousand times absurd that such a craft should, at present, be of a piratical character; or her commander, either for himself or those under him, cherish any desire but for the speedy relief and refreshment? But then, might not general distress, and thirst in particular, be affected? And might not that same undiminished Spanish crew, alleged to have perished off to a remnant, be at that very moment lurking in the hold? On heart-broken pretense of entreating a cup of cold water, fiends in human form had got into lonely dwellings, nor retired until a dark deed had been done. And among the Malay pirates, it was no unusual thing to lure ships after them into their treacherous harbors, or entice boarders from a declared enemy at sea, by the spectacle of thinly manned or vacant decks, beneath which prowled a hundred spears with yellow arms ready to upthrust them through the mats. Not that Captain Delano had entirely credited such things. He had heard of them—and now, as stories, they recurred. The present destination of the ship was the anchorage. There she would be near his own vessel. Upon gaining that vicinity, might not the San Dominick, like a slumbering volcano, suddenly let loose energies now hid?

He recalled the Spaniard's manner while telling his story. There was a gloomy hesitancy and subterfuge about it. It was just the manner of one making up his tale for evil purposes, as he goes. But if that story was not true, what was the truth? That the ship had unlawfully come into the Spaniard's possession? But in many of its details, especially in reference to the more calamitous parts, such as the fatalities among the seamen, the consequent prolonged beating about, the past sufferings from obstinate calms, and still continued suffering from thirst; in all these points, as well as others, Don Benito's story had corroborated not only the wailing ejaculations of the indiscriminate multitude, white and black, but likewise—what seemed impossible to be counterfeit—by the very expression and play of every human feature, which Captain Delano saw. If Don Benito's story was, throughout, an invention, then every soul on board, down to the youngest negress, was his carefully drilled recruit in the plot: an incredible inference. And yet, if there was ground for mistrusting his veracity, that inference was a legitimate one.

But those questions of the Spaniard. There, indeed, one might pause. Did they not seem put with much the same object with which the burglar or assassin, by day-time, reconnoitres the walls of a house? But, with ill purposes, to solicit such information openly of the chief person endangered, and so, in effect, setting him on his guard; how unlikely a procedure was that? Absurd, then, to suppose that those questions had been prompted by evil designs. Thus, the same conduct, which, in this instance, had raised the alarm, served to dispel it. In short, scarce any suspicion or uneasiness, however apparently reasonable at the time, which was not now, with equal apparent reason, dismissed.

At last he began to laugh at his former forebodings; and laugh at the strange ship for, in its aspect, someway siding with them, as it were; and laugh, too, at the odd-looking blacks, particularly those old scissors-grinders, the Ashantees; and those bed-ridden old knitting women, the oakum-pickers; and almost at the dark Spaniard himself, the central hobgoblin of all.

For the rest, whatever in a serious way seemed enigmatical, was now good-naturedly explained away by the thought that, for the most part, the poor invalid scarcely knew what he was about; either sulking in black vapors, or putting idle questions without sense or object. Evidently, for the present, the man was not fit to be intrusted, with the ship. On some benevolent plea withdrawing the command from him, Captain Delano would yet have to send her to Conception, in charge of his second mate, a worthy person and good navigator—a plan not more conven-ient for the San Dominick than for Don Benito; for, relieved from all anxiety, keeping wholly to his cabin, the sick man, under the good nursing of his servant, would, probably, by the end of the passage, be in a measure restored to health, and with that he should also be restored to authority.

Such were the American's thoughts. They were tranquilizing. There was a dif-ference between the idea of Don Benito's darkly pre-ordaining Captain Delano's fate, and Captain Delano's lightly arranging Don Benito's. Nevertheless, it was not without something of relief that the good seaman presently perceived his whale-boat in the distance. Its absence had been prolonged by unexpected deten-tion at the sealer's side, as well as its returning trip lengthened by the continual recession of the goal.

The advancing speck was observed by the blacks. Their shouts attracted the attention of Don Benito, who, with a return of courtesy, approaching Captain Delano, expressed satisfaction at the coming of some supplies, slight and tempo-rary as they must necessarily prove.

Captain Delano responded; but while doing so, his attention was drawn to something passing on the deck below: among the crowd climbing the landward bulwarks, anxiously watching the coming boat, two blacks, to all appearances accidentally incommoded by one of the sailors, violently pushed him aside, which the sailor someway resenting, they dashed him to the deck, despite the earnest cries of the oakum-pickers.

"Don Benito," said Captain Delano quickly, "do you see what is going on there? Look!"

But, seized by his cough, the Spaniard staggered, with both hands to his face, on the point of falling. Captain Delano would have supported him, but the servant was more alert, who, with one hand sustaining his master, with the other applied the cordial. Don Benito restored, the black withdrew his support, slipping aside a little, but dutifully remaining within call of a whisper. Such discretion was here evinced as quite wiped away, in the visitor's eyes, any blemish of impropriety which might have attached to the attendant, from the indecorous conferences be-fore mentioned; showing, too, that if the servant were to blame, it might be more the master's fault than his own, since, when left to himself, he could conduct thus well.

His glance called away from the spectacle of disorder to the more pleasing one before him, Captain Delano could not avoid again congratulating his host upon possessing such a servant, who, though perhaps a little too forward now and then, must upon the whole be invaluable to one in the invalid's situation.

"Tell me, Don Benito," he added, with a smile—"I should like to have your man here, myself—what will you take for him? Would fifty doubloons[65] be any object?"

"Master wouldn't part with Babo for a thousand doubloons," murmured the black, overhearing the offer, and taking it in earnest, and, with the strange vanity of a faithful slave, appreciated by his master, scorning to hear so paltry a valuation put upon him by a stranger. But Don Benito, apparently hardly yet completely restored, and again interrupted by his cough, made but some broken reply.

Soon his physical distress became so great, affecting his mind, too, apparently, that, as if to screen the sad spectacle, the servant gently conducted his master below.

Left to himself, the American, to while away the time till his boat should arrive, would have pleasantly accosted some one of the few Spanish seamen he saw; but recalling something that Don Benito had said touching their ill conduct, he refrained; as a shipmaster indisposed to countenance cowardice or unfaithfulness in seamen.

While, with these thoughts, standing with eye directed forward towards that handful of sailors, suddenly he thought that one or two of them returned the glance and with a sort of meaning. He rubbed his eyes, and looked again; but again seemed to see the same thing. Under a new form, but more obscure than any previous one, the old suspicions recurred, but, in the absence of Don Benito, with less of panic than before. Despite the bad account given of the sailors, Captain Delano resolved forthwith to accost one of them. Descending the poop, he made his way through the blacks, his movement drawing a queer cry from the oakum-pickers, prompted by whom, the negroes, twitching each other aside, divided before him; but, as if curious to see what was the object of this deliberate visit to their Ghetto, closing in behind, in tolerable order, followed the white stranger up. His progress thus proclaimed as by mounted kings-at-arms,[66] and escorted as by a Caffre[67] guard of honor, Captain Delano, assuming a good-humored, off-handed air, continued to advance; now and then saying a blithe word to the negroes, and his eye curiously surveying the white faces, here and there sparsely mixed in with the blacks, like stray white pawns venturously involved in the ranks of the chessmen opposed.

While thinking which of them to select for his purpose, he chanced to observe a sailor seated on the deck engaged in tarring the strap of a large block, a circle of blacks squatted round him inquisitively eying the process.

The mean employment of the man was in contrast with something superior in his figure. His hand, black with continually thrusting it into the tar-pot held for him by a negro, seemed not naturally allied to his face, a face which would have been a very fine one but for its haggardness. Whether this haggardness had aught to do with criminality, could not be determined; since, as intense heat and cold, though unlike, produce like sensations, so innocence and guilt, when, through casual association with mental pain, stamping any visible impress, use one seal—a hacked one.

---

[65] Would you object to Spanish gold coins (equal to sixteen silver dollars each)?
[66] Heraldic officers.   [67] Kaffir, a Bantu tribe in South Africa, known for their height.

Not again that this reflection occurred to Captain Delano at the time, charitable man as he was. Rather another idea. Because observing so singular a haggardness combined with a dark eye, averted as in trouble and shame, and then again recalling Don Benito's confessed ill opinion of his crew, insensibly he was operated upon by certain general notions which, while disconnecting pain and abashment from virtue, invariably link them with vice.

If, indeed, there be any wickedness on board this ship, thought Captain Delano, be sure that man there has fouled his hand in it, even as now he fouls it in the pitch. I don't like to accost him. I will speak to this other, this old Jack here on the windlass.[68]

He advanced to an old Barcelona tar, in ragged red breeches and dirty nightcap, cheeks trenched and bronzed, whiskers dense as thorn hedges. Seated between two sleepy-looking Africans, this mariner, like his younger shipmate, was employed upon some rigging—splicing a cable—the sleepy-looking blacks performing the inferior function of holding the outer parts of the ropes for him.

Upon Captain Delano's approach, the man at once hung his head below its previous level; the one necessary for business. It appeared as if he desired to be thought absorbed, with more than common fidelity, in his task. Being addressed, he glanced up, but with what seemed a furtive, diffident air, which sat strangely enough on his weather-beaten visage, much as if a grizzly bear, instead of growling and biting, should simper and cast sheep's eyes. He was asked several questions concerning the voyage—questions purposely referring to several particulars in Don Benito's narrative, not previously corroborated by those impulsive cries greeting the visitor on first coming on board. The questions were briefly answered, confirming all that remained to be confirmed of the story. The negroes about the windlass joined in with the old sailor; but, as they became talkative, he by degrees became mute, and at length quite glum, seemed morosely unwilling to answer more questions, and yet, all the while, this ursine[69] air was somehow mixed with his sheepish one.

Despairing of getting into unembarrassed talk with such a centaur,[70] Captain Delano, after glancing round for a more promising countenance, but seeing none, spoke pleasantly to the blacks to make way for him; and so, amid various grins and grimaces, returned to the poop, feeling a little strange at first, he could hardly tell why, but upon the whole with regained confidence in Benito Cereno.

How plainly, thought he, did that old whiskerando[71] yonder betray a consciousness of ill desert. No doubt, when he saw me coming, he dreaded lest I, apprised by his Captain of the crew's general misbehavior, came with sharp words for him, and so down with his head. And yet—and yet, now that I think of it, that very old fellow, if I err not, was one of those who seemed so earnestly eying me here awhile since. Ah, these currents spin one's head round almost as much as they do the ship. Ha, there now's a pleasant sort of sunny sight; quite sociable, too.

His attention had been drawn to a slumbering negress, partly disclosed through the lacework of some rigging, lying, with youthful limbs carelessly disposed, under the lee of the bulwarks, like a doe in the shade of a woodland rock. Sprawling at her lapped breasts, was her wide-awake fawn, stark naked, its black little body half lifted from the deck, crosswise with its dam's; its hands, like two paws, clambering upon her; its mouth and nose ineffectually rooting to get at the mark;

---

[68] This sailor here on the winch, or hoist.   [69] Bearlike.
[70] According to Greek myth, a half-man, half-horse.   [71] A bearded sailor.

and meantime giving a vexatious half-grunt blending with the composed snore of the negress.

The uncommon vigor of the child at length roused the mother. She started up, at a distance facing Captain Delano. But as if not at all concerned at the attitude in which she had been caught, delightedly she caught the child up, with maternal transports, covering it with kisses.

There's naked nature, now; pure tenderness and love, thought Captain Delano, well pleased.

This incident prompted him to remark the other negresses more particuarly than before. He was gratified with their manners: like most uncivilized women, they seemed at once tender of heart and tough of constitution; equally ready to die for their infants or fight for them. Unsophisticated as leopardesses; loving as doves. Ah! thought Captain Delano, these, perhaps, are some of the very women whom Ledyard[72] saw in Africa, and gave such a noble account of.

These natural sights somehow insensibly deepened his confidence and ease. At last he looked to see how his boat was getting on; but it was still pretty remote. He turned to see if Don Benito had returned; but he had not.

To change the scene, as well as to please himself with a leisurely observation of the coming boat, stepping over into the mizzen-chains,[73] he clambered his way into the starboard quarter-gallery—one of those abandoned Venetian-looking water-balconies previously mentioned—retreats cut off from the deck. As his foot pressed the half-damp, half-dry sea-mosses matting the place, and a chance phantom catspaw[74]—an islet of breeze, unheralded, unfollowed—as this ghostly cats paw came fanning his cheek; as his glance fell upon the row of small, round dead-lights—all closed like coppered eyes of the coffined—and the state-cabin door, once connecting with the gallery, even as the dead-lights had once looked out upon it, but now calked fast like a sarcophagus lid; and to a purple-black tarred-over, panel, threshold, and post; and he bethought him of the time, when that state-cabin and this state-balcony had heard the voices of the Spanish king's officers, and the forms of the Lima viceroy's daughters had perhaps leaned where he stood—as these and other images flitted through his mind, as the cats-paw through the calm, gradually he felt rising a dreamy inquietude, like that of one who alone on the prairie feels unrest from the repose of the noon.

He leaned against the carved balustrade, again looking off toward his boat; but found his eye falling upon the ribbon grass, trailing along the ship's water-line, straight as a border of green box; and parterres[75] of sea-weed, broad ovals and crescents, floating nigh and far, with what seemed long formal alleys between, crossing the terraces of swells, and sweeping round as if leading to the grottoes below. And overhanging all was the balustrade by his arm, which, partly stained with pitch and partly embossed with moss, seemed the charred ruin of some summer-house in a grand garden long running to waste.

Trying to break one charm, he was but becharmed anew. Though upon the wide sea, he seemed in some far inland country; prisoner in some deserted châ-

---

[72] John Ledyard (1751–1789), an American traveler and writer, whose account of African woman, *Proceedings of the Association for Promoting the Discovery of the Interior Parts of Africa* (1790) was quoted by the famous Scottish explorer Mungo Park (1771–1806) in his *Travels in the Interior of Africa* (1799). Melville gave Park credit for the quotation in the *Putnam's Magazine* version of "Benito Cereno," then substituted Ledyard's name for Park's in *The Piazza Tales*.
[73] Supports for the mizzen rigging.   [74] A mild breeze (as light as a cat's paw).
[75] Ornamental gardens of flower beds.

teau, left to stare at empty grounds, and peer out at vague roads, where never wagon or wayfarer passed.

But these enchantments were a little disenchanted as his eye fell on the corroded mainchains.[76] Of an ancient style, massy and rusty in link, shackle and bolt, they seemed even more fit for the ship's present business than the one for which she had been built.

Presently he thought something moved nigh the chains. He rubbed his eyes, and looked hard. Groves of rigging were about the chains; and there, peering from behind a great stay,[77] like an Indian from behind a hemlock, a Spanish sailor, a marlingspike[78] in his hand, was seen, who made what seemed an imperfect gesture towards the balcony, but immediately, as if alarmed by some advancing step along the deck within, vanished into the recesses of the hempen forest, like a poacher.

What meant this? Something the man had sought to communicate, unbeknown to any one, even to his captain. Did the secret involve aught unfavorable to his captain? Were those previous misgivings of Captain Delano's about to be verified? Or, in his haunted mood at the moment, had some random, unintentional motion of the man, while busy with the stay, as if repairing it, been mistaken for a significant beckoning?

Not unbewildered, again he gazed off for his boat. But it was temporarily hidden by a rocky spur of the isle. As with some eagerness he bent forward, watching for the first shooting view of its beak, the balustrade gave way before him like charcoal. Had he not clutched an outreaching rope he would have fallen into the sea. The crash, though feeble, and the fall, though hollow, of the rotten fragments, must have been overheard. He glanced up. With sober curiosity peering down upon him was one of the old oakum-pickers, slipped from his perch to an outside boom;[79] while below the old negro, and, invisible to him, reconnoitering from a port-hole like a fox from the mouth of its den, crouched the Spanish sailor again. From something suddenly suggested by the man's air, the mad idea now darted into Captain Delano's mind, that Don Benito's plea of indisposition, in withdrawing below, was but a pretense: that he was engaged there maturing his plot, of which the sailor, by some means gaining an inkling, had a mind to warn the stranger against; incited, it may be, by gratitude for a kind word on first boarding the ship. Was it from foreseeing some possible interference like this, that Don Benito had, beforehand, given such a bad character[80] of his sailors, while praising the negroes; though, indeed, the former seemed as docile as the latter the contrary? The whites, too, by nature, were the shrewder race. A man with some evil design, would he not be likely to speak well of that stupidity which was blind to his depravity, and malign that intelligence from which it might not be hidden? Not unlikely, perhaps. But if the whites had dark secrets concerning Don Benito, could then Don Benito be any way in complicity with the blacks? But they were too stupid. Besides, who ever heard of a white so far a renegade as to apostatize[81] from his very species almost, by leaguing in against it with negroes? These difficulties recalled former ones. Lost in their mazes, Captain Delano, who had now regained the deck, was uneasily advancing along it, when he observed a new face; an aged sailor seated cross-legged near the main hatchway. His skin was shrunk

---

[76] Supports for the mainmast rigging.   [77] A strong rope used to support a mast.
[78] A pointed iron tool used in splicing.   [79] A spar extending from a mast to hold a sail.
[80] A reference.   [81] To abandon a faith.

up with wrinkles like a pelican's empty pouch; his hair frosted; his countenance grave and composed. His hands were full of ropes, which he was working into a large knot. Some blacks were about him obligingly dipping the strands for him, here and there, as the exigencies of the operation demanded.

Captain Delano crossed over to him, and stood in silence surveying the knot; his mind, by a not uncongenial transition, passing from its own entanglements to those of the hemp. For intricacy, such a knot he had never seen in an American ship, nor indeed any other. The old man looked like an Egyptian priest, making Gordian knots for the temple of Ammon.[82] The knot seemed a combination of double-bowline-knot, treble-crown-knot, back-handed-well-knot, knot-in-and-out-knot, and jamming-knot.

At last, puzzled to comprehend the meaning of such a knot, Captain Delano addressed the knotter:—

"What are you knotting there, my man?"

"The knot," was the brief reply, without looking up.

"So it seems; but what is it for?"

"For some one else to undo," muttered back the old man, plying his fingers harder than ever, the knot being now nearly completed.

While Captain Delano stood watching him, suddenly the old man threw the knot towards him, saying in broken English—the first heard in the ship—something to this effect: "Undo it, cut it, quick." It was said lowly, but with such condensation of rapidity, that the long, slow words in Spanish, which had preceded and followed, almost operated as covers to the brief English between.

For a moment, knot in hand, and knot in head, Captain Delano stood mute; while, without further heeding him, the old man was now intent upon other ropes. Presently there was a slight stir behind Captain Delano. Turning, he saw the chained negro, Atufal, standing quietly there. The next moment the old sailor rose, muttering, and, followed by his subordinate negroes, removed to the forward part of the ship, where in the crowd he disappeared.

An elderly negro, in a clout[83] like an infant's, and with a pepper and salt head, and a kind of attorney air, now approached Captain Delano. In tolerable Spanish, and with a good-natured, knowing wink, he informed him that the old knotter was simple-witted, but harmless; often playing his odd tricks. The negro concluded by begging the knot, for of course the stranger would not care to be troubled with it. Unconsciously, it was handed to him. With a sort of congé,[84] the negro received it, and, turning his back, ferreted into it like a detective custom-house officer after smuggled laces. Soon, with some African word, equivalent to pshaw, he tossed the knot overboard.

All this is very queer now, thought Captain Delano, with a qualmish sort of emotion; but, as one feeling incipient sea-sickness, he strove, by ignoring the symptoms, to get rid of the malady. Once more he looked off for his boat. To his delight, it was now again in view, leaving the rocky spur astern.

The sensation here experienced, after at first relieving his uneasiness, with unforeseen efficacy soon began to remove it. The less distant sight of that well-known boat—showing it, not as before, half blended with the haze, but with out-

---

[82] The oracle at the temple of Ammon in Egypt prophesied that whoever untied King Gordius's intricate knot would become master of Asia. Alexander the Great simply cut the knot with his sword (and later defeated the Persian army).

[83] A patch of cloth.　　[84] A low bow.

line defined, so that its individuality, like a man's, was manifest; that boat, Rover by name, which, though now in strange seas, had often pressed the beach of Captain Delano's home, and, brought to its threshold for repairs, had familiarly lain there, as a Newfoundland dog; the sight of that household boat evoked a thousand trustful associations, which, contrasted with previous suspicions, filled him not only with lightsome confidence, but somehow with half humorous self-reproaches at his former lack of it.

"What, I, Amasa Delano—Jack of the Beach, as they called me when a lad—I, Amasa; the same that, duck-satchel in hand, used to paddle along the water-side to the school-house made from the old hulk—I, little Jack of the Beach, that used to go berrying with cousin Nat and the rest; I to be murdered here at the ends of the earth, on board a haunted pirate-ship by a horrible Spaniard? Too nonsensical to think of! Who would murder Amasa Delano? His conscience is clean. There is some one above. Fie, fie, Jack of the Beach! you are a child indeed; a child of the second childhood, old boy; you are beginning to dote and drule, I'm afraid."

Light of heart and foot, he stepped aft, and there was met by Don Benito's servant, who, with a pleasing expression, responsive to his own present feelings, informed him that his master has recovered from the effects of his coughing fit, and had just ordered him to go present his compliments to his good guest, Don Amasa, and say that he (Don Benito) would soon have the happiness to rejoin him.

There now, do you mark that? again thought Captain Delano, walking the poop. What a donkey I was. This kind gentleman who here sends me his kind compliments, he, but ten minutes ago, dark-lantern in hand, was dodging round some old grind-stone in the hold, sharpening a hatchet for me, I thought. Well, well; these long calms have a morbid effect on the mind, I've often heard, though I never believed it before. Ha! glancing towards the boat; there's Rover; good dog; a white bone in her mouth.[85] A pretty big bone though, seems to me.—What? Yes, she has fallen afoul of the bubbling tide-rip there. It sets her the other way, too, for the time. Patience.

It was now about noon, though, from the grayness of everything, it seemed to be getting towards dusk.

The calm was confirmed. In the far distance, away from the influence of land, the leaden ocean seemed laid out and leaded up, its course finished, soul gone, defunct. But the current from landward, where the ship was, increased; silently sweeping her further and further towards the tranced waters beyond.

Still, from his knowledge of those latitudes, cherishing hopes of a breeze, and a fair and fresh one, at any moment, Captain Delano, despite present prospects, buoyantly counted upon bringing the San Dominick safely to anchor ere night. The distance swept over was nothing; since, with a good wind, ten minutes' sailing would retrace more than sixty minutes, drifting. Meantime, one moment turning to mark "Rover" fighting the tide-rip, and the next to see Don Benito approaching, he continued walking the poop.

Gradually he felt a vexation arising from the delay of his boat; this soon merged into uneasiness; and at last—his eye falling continually, as from a stage-box into the pit,[86] upon the strange crowd before and below him, and, by-and-by, recognizing there the face—now composed to indifference—of the Spanish sailor who

---

[85] A metaphor for a boat with sea foam under the bow.   [86] An orchestra pit.

had seemed to beckon from the main-chains—something of his old trepidations returned.

Ah, thought he—gravely enough—this is like the ague:[87] because it went off, it follows not that it won't come back.

Though ashamed of the relapse, he could not altogether subdue it; and so, exerting his good-nature to the utmost, insensibly he came to a compromise.

Yes, this is a strange craft; a strange history, too, and strange folks on board. But—nothing more.

By way of keeping his mind out of mischief till the boat should arrive, he tried to occupy it with turning over and over, in a purely speculative sort of way, some lesser peculiarities of the captain and crew. Among others, four curious points recurred:

First, the affair of the Spanish lad assailed with a knife by the slave boy; an act winked at by Don Benito. Second, the tyranny in Don Benito's treatment of Atufal, the black; as if a child should lead a bull of the Nile by the ring in his nose. Third, the trampling of the sailor by the two negroes; a piece of insolence passed over without so much as a reprimand. Fourth, the cringing submission to their master, of all the ship's underlings, mostly blacks; as if by the least inadvertence they feared to draw down his despotic displeasure.

Coupling these points, they seemed somewhat contradictory. But what then, thought Captain Delano, glancing towards his now nearing boat—what then? Why, Don Benito is a very capricious commander. But he is not the first of the sort I have seen; though it's true he rather exceeds any other. But as a nation—continued he in his reveries—these Spaniards are all an odd set; the very word Spaniard has a curious, conspirator, Guy-Fawkish[88] twang to it. And yet, I dare say, Spaniards in the main are as good folks as any in Duxbury, Massachusetts. Ah good! At last "Rover" has come.

As, with its welcome freight, the boat touched the side, the oakum-pickers, with venerable gestures, sought to restrain the blacks, who, at the sight of three gurried[89] water-casks in its bottom, and a pile of wilted pumpkins in its bow, hung over the bulwarks in disorderly raptures.

Don Benito, with his servant, now appeared; his coming, perhaps, hastened by hearing the noise. Of him Captain Delano sought permission to serve out the water, so that all might share alike, and none injure themselves by unfair excess. But sensible, and, on Don Benito's account, kind as this offer was, it was received with what seemed impatience; as if aware that he lacked energy as a commander, Don Benito, with the true jealousy of weakness, resented as an affront any interference. So, at least, Captain Delano inferred.

In another moment the casks were being hoisted in, when some of the eager negroes accidentally jostled Captain Delano, where he stood by the gangway; so that, unmindful of Don Benito, yielding to the impulse of the moment, with good-natured authority he bade the blacks stand back; to enforce his words making use of a half-mirthful, half-menacing gesture. Instantly the blacks paused, just where they were, each negro and negress suspended in his or her posture, exactly as the

---

[87] Fever and chills.

[88] Guy Fawkes (1570–1606), a Catholic conspirator, was involved in the Gunpowder Plot to blow up the English Parliament building in 1605. Fawkes was executed, and Guy Fawkes Day became an occasion for anti-Catholic sentiment and suspicion.

[89] Slimy from fish entrails.

word had found them—for a few seconds continuing so—while, as between the responsive posts of a telegraph, an unknown syllable ran from man to man among the perched oakum-pickers. While the visitors attention was fixed by this scene, suddenly the hatchet-polishers half rose, and a rapid cry came from Don Benito.

Thinking that at the signal of the Spaniard he was about to be massacred, Captain Delano would have sprung for his boat, but paused, as the oakum-pickers, dropping down into the crowd with earnest exclamations, forced every white and every negro back, at the same moment, with gestures friendly and familiar, almost jocose, bidding him, in substance, not be a fool. Simultaneously the hatchet-polishers resumed their seats, quietly as so many tailors, and at once, as if nothing had happened, the work of hoisting in the casks was resumed, whites and blacks singing at the tackle.

Captain Delano glanced towards Don Benito. As he saw his meagre form in the act of recovering itself from reclining in the servant's arms, into which the agitated invalid had fallen, he could not but marvel at the panic by which himself had been surprised, on the darting supposition that such a commander, who, upon a legitimate occasion, so trivial, too, as it now appeared, could lose all self-command, was, with energetic iniquity, going to bring about his murder.

The casks being on deck, Captain Delano was handed a number of jars and cups by one of the steward's aids, who, in the name of his captain, entreated him to do as he had proposed—dole out the water. He complied, with republican impartiality as to this republican element, which always seeks one level, serving the oldest white no better than the youngest black; excepting, indeed, poor Don Benito, whose condition, if not rank, demanded an extra allowance. To him, in the first place, Captain Delano presented a fair pitcher of the fluid; but, thirsting as he was for it, the Spaniard quaffed not a drop until after several grave bows and salutes. A reciprocation of courtesies which the sight-loving Africans hailed with clapping of hands.

Two of the less wilted pumpkins being reserved for the cabin table, the residue were minced up on the spot for the general regalement. But the soft bread, sugar, and bottled cider, Captain Delano would have given the whites alone, and in chief Don Benito; but the latter objected; which disinterestedness not a little pleased the American; and so mouthfuls all around were given alike to whites and blacks; excepting one bottle of cider, which Babo insisted upon setting aside for his master.

Here it may be observed that as, on the first visit of the boat, the American had not permitted his men to board the ship, neither did he now; being unwilling to add to the confusion of the decks.

Not uninfluenced by the peculiar good-humor at present prevailing, and for the time oblivious of any but benevolent thoughts, Captain Delano, who, from recent indications, counted upon a breeze within an hour or two at furthest, dispatched the boat back to the sealer, with orders for all the hands that could be spared immediately to set about rafting casks to the watering-place and filling them. Likewise he bade word be carried to his chief officer, that if, against present expectation, the ship was not brought to anchor by sunset, he need be under no concern; for as there was to be a full moon that night, he (Captain Delano) would remain on board ready to play the pilot, come the wind soon or late.

As the two Captains stood together, observing the departing boat—the servant, as it happened, having just spied a spot on his master's velvet sleeve, and silently engaged rubbing it out—the American expressed his regrets that the San Dominick had no boats; none, at least, but the unseaworthy old hulk of the long-boat, which, warped as a camel's skeleton in the desert, and almost as bleached, lay pot-wise inverted amid-ships, one side a little tipped, furnishing a subterranean sort of den for family groups of the blacks, mostly women and small children; who, squatting on old mats below, or perched above in the dark dome, on the elevated seats, were descried, some distance within, like a social circle of bats, sheltering in some friendly cave; at intervals, ebon flights of naked boys and girls, three or four years old, darting in and out of the den's mouth.

"Had you three or four boats now, Don Benito," said Captain Delano, "I think that, by tugging at the oars, your negroes here might help along matters some. Did you sail from port without boats, Don Benito?"

"They were stove in the gales, Señor."

"That was bad. Many men, too, you lost then. Boats and men. Those must have been hard gales, Don Benito."

"Past all speech," cringed the Spaniard.

"Tell me, Don Benito," continued his companion with increased interest, "tell me, were these gales immediately off the pitch[90] of Cape Horn?"

"Cape Horn?—who spoke of Cape Horn?"

"Yourself did, when giving me an account of your voyage," answered Captain Delano, with almost equal astonishment at this eating of his own words, even as he ever seemed eating his own heart, on the part of the Spaniard. "You yourself, Don Benito, spoke of Cape Horn," he emphatically repeated.

The Spaniard turned, in a sort of stooping posture, pausing an instant, as one about to make a plunging exchange of elements, as from air to water.

At this moment a messenger-boy, a white, hurried by, in the regular performance of his function carrying the last expired half hour[91] forward to the forecastle, from the cabin time-piece, to have it struck at the ship's large bell.

"Master," said the servant, discontinuing his work on the coat sleeve, and addressing the rapt Spaniard with a sort of timid apprehensiveness, as one charged with a duty, the discharge of which, it was foreseen, would prove irksome to the very person who had imposed it, and for whose benefit it was intended, "master told me never mind where he was, or how engaged, always to remind him, to a minute, when shaving-time comes. Miguel has gone to strike the half-hour afternoon. It is *now*, master. Will master go into the cuddy?"[92]

"Ah—yes," answered the Spaniard, starting, as from dreams into realities; then turning upon Captain Delano, he said that ere long he would resume the conversation.

"Then if master means to talk more to Don Amasa," said the servant, "why not let Don Amasa sit by master in the cuddy, and master can talk, and Don Amasa can listen, while Babo here lathers and strops."

"Yes," said Captain Delano, not unpleased with this sociable plan, "yes, Don Benito, unless you had rather not, I will go with you."

"Be it so, Señor."

As the three passed aft, the American could not but think it another strange instance of his host's capriciousness, this being shaved with such uncommon punctuality in the middle of the day. But he deemed it more than likely that the

[90] The point.
[91] The eighth half-hour in a ship's four-hour watch (one bell is struck for every half-hour in the watch). The messenger boy is going to strike eight bells, signaling the end of one four-hour watch and the beginning of another.
[92] A small cabin.

servant's anxious fidelity had something to do with the matter; inasmuch as the timely interruption served to rally his master from the mood which had evidently been coming upon him.

The place called the cuddy was a light deck-cabin formed by the poop, a sort of attic to the large cabin below. Part of it had formerly been the quarters of the officers; but since their death all the partitionings had been thrown down, and the whole interior converted into one spacious and airy marine hall; for absence of fine furniture and picturesque disarray of odd appurtenances, somewhat answering to the wide, cluttered hall of some eccentric bachelor-squire in the country, who hangs his shooting-jacket and tobacco-pouch on deer antlers, and keeps his fishing-rod, tongs, and walking-stick in the same corner.

The similitude was heightened, if not originally suggested, by glimpses of the surrounding sea; since, in one aspect, the country and the ocean seem cousins-german.[93]

The floor of the cuddy was matted. Overhead, four or five old muskets were stuck into horizontal holes along the beams. On one side was a claw-footed old table lashed to the deck; a thumbed missal[94] on it, and over it a small, meagre crucifix attached to the bulk-head. Under the table lay a dented cutlass or two, with a hacked harpoon, among some melancholy old rigging, like a heap of poor friars' girdles.[95] There were also two long, sharp-ribbed settees of Malacca cane, black with age, and uncomfortable to look at as inquisitors' racks, with a large, misshapen arm-chair, which, furnished with a rude barber's crotch[96] at the back, working with a screw, seemed some grotesque engine of torment. A flag locker was in one corner, open, exposing various colored bunting, some rolled up, others half unrolled, still others tumbled. Opposite was a cumbrous washstand, of black mahogany, all of one block, with a pedestal, like a font, and over it a railed shelf, containing combs, brushes, and other implements of the toilet. A torn hammock of stained grass swung near; the sheets tossed, and the pillow wrinkled up like a brow, as if who ever slept here slept but illy, with alternate visitations of sad thoughts and bad dreams.

The further extremity of the cuddy, overhanging the ship's stern, was pierced with three openings, windows or port-holes, according as men or cannon might peer, socially or unsocially, out of them. At present neither men nor cannon were seen, though huge ring-bolts and other rusty iron fixtures of the wood-work hinted of twenty-four-pounders.

Glancing towards the hammock as he entered, Captain Delano said, "You sleep here, Don Benito?"

"Yes, Señor, since we got into mild weather."

"This seems a sort of dormitory, sitting-room, sail-loft, chapel, armory, and private closet all together, Don Benito," added Captain Delano, looking round.

"Yes, Señor; events have not been favorable to much order in my arrangements."

Here the servant, napkin on arm, made a motion as if waiting his master's good pleasure. Don Benito signified his readiness, when seating him in the Malacca arm-chair, and for the guest's convenience drawing opposite one of the settees, the servant commenced operations by throwing back his master's collar and loosening his cravat.

There is something in the negro which, in a peculiar way, fits him for avoca-

---

[93] First cousins.   [94] A prayer book.
[95] Rope belts worn by Franciscans and other religious orders.   [96] Headrest.

tions about one's person. Most negroes are natural valets and hair-dressers; taking to the comb and brush congenially as to the castinets, and flourishing them apparently with almost equal satisfaction. There is, too, a smooth tact about them in this employment, with a marvelous, noiseless, gliding briskness, not ungraceful in its way, singularly pleasing to behold, and still more so to be the manipulated subject of. And above all is the great gift of good-humor. Not the mere grin or laugh is here meant. Those were unsuitable. But a certain easy cheerfulness, harmonious in every glance and gesture; as though God had set the whole negro to some pleasant tune.

When to this is added the docility arising from the unaspiring contentment of a limited mind, and that susceptibility of blind attachment sometimes inhering in indisputable inferiors, one readily perceives why those hypochondriacs, Johnson and Byron—it may be, something like the hypochondriac Benito Cereno—took to their hearts, almost to the exclusion of the entire white race, their serving men, the negroes, Barber and Fletcher.[97] But if there be that in the negro which exempts him from the inflicted sourness of the morbid or cynical mind, how, in his most prepossessing aspects, must he appear to a benevolent one? When at ease with respect to exterior things, Captain Delano's nature was not only benign, but familiarly and humorously so. At home, he had often taken rare satisfaction in sitting in his door, watching some free man of color at his work or play. If on a voyage he chanced to have a black sailor, invariably he was on chatty and half-gamesome terms with him. In fact, like most men of good, blithe heart, Captain Delano took to negroes, not philanthropically, but genially, just as other men to Newfoundland dogs.

Hitherto, the circumstances in which he found the San Dominick had repressed the tendency. But in the cuddy, relieved from his former uneasiness, and, for various reasons, more sociably inclined than at any previous period of the day, and seeing the colored servant, napkin on arm, so debonair about his master, in a business so familiar as that of shaving, too, all his old weakness for negroes returned.

Among other things, he was amused with an odd instance of the African love of bright colors and fine shows, in the black's informally taking from the flag-locker a great piece of bunting of all hues, and lavishly tucking it under his master's chin for an apron.

The mode of shaving among the Spaniards is a little different from what it is with other nations. They have a basin, specifically called a barber's basin, which on one side is scooped out, so as accurately to receive the chin, against which it is closely held in lathering; which is done, not with a brush, but with soap dipped in the water of the basin and rubbed on the face.

In the present instance salt-water was used for lack of better; and the parts lathered were only the upper lip, and low down under the throat, all the rest being cultivated beard.

The preliminaries being somewhat novel to Captain Delano, he sat curiously eying them, so that no conversation took place, nor, for the present, did Don Benito appear disposed to renew any.

Setting down his basin, the negro searched among the razors, as for the sharpest, and having found it, gave it an additional edge by expertly strapping it on the

---

[97] Francis Barber, the devoted black servant of Samuel Johnson (1709–1784) for thirty years, and William Fletcher, the white valet of Lord Byron (1788–1824). Melville apparently confused Fletcher with the black servant of Byron's friend Edward Trelawny.

firm, smooth, oily skin of his open palm; he then made a gesture as if to begin, but midway stood suspended for an instant, one hand elevating the razor, the other professionally dabbling among the bubbling suds on the Spaniard's lank neck. Not unaffected by the close sight of the gleaming steel, Don Benito nervously shuddered; his usual ghastliness was heightened by the lather, which lather, again, was intensified in its hue by the contrasting sootiness of the negro's body. Altogether the scene was somewhat peculiar, at least to Captain Delano, nor, as he saw the two thus postured, could he resist the vagary, that in the black he saw a headsman, and in the white a man at the block.[98] But this was one of those antic conceits, appearing and vanishing in a breath, from which, perhaps, the best regulated mind is not always free.

Meantime the agitation of the Spaniard had a little loosened the bunting from around him, so that one broad fold swept curtain-like over the chair-arm to the floor, revealing, amid a profusion of armorial bars and ground-colors—black, blue, and yellow—a closed castle in a blood-red field diagonal with a lion rampant in a white.

"The castle and the lion," exclaimed Captain Delano—"why, Don Benito, this is the flag of Spain you use here. It's well it's only I, and not the King, that sees this," he added, with a smile, "but"—turning towards the black—"it's all one, I suppose, so the colors be gay;" which playful remark did not fail somewhat to tickle the negro.

"Now, master," he said, readjusting the flag, and pressing the head gently further back into the crotch of the chair; "now, master," and the steel glanced nigh the throat.

Again Don Benito faintly shuddered.

"You must not shake so, master. See, Don Amasa, master always shakes when I shave him. And yet master knows I never yet have drawn blood, though it's true, if master will shake so, I may some of these times. Now master," he continued. "And now, Don Amasa, please go on with your talk about the gale, and all that; master can hear, and, between times, master can answer."

"Ah yes, these gales," said Captain Delano; "but the more I think of your voyage, Don Benito, the more I wonder, not at the gales, terrible as they must have been, but at the disastrous interval following them. For here, by your account, have you been these two months and more getting from Cape Horn to St. Maria, a distance which I myself, with a good wind, have sailed in a few days. True, you had calms, and long ones, but to be becalmed for two months, that is, at least, unusual. Why, Don Benito, had almost any other gentleman told me such a story, I should have been half disposed to a little incredulity."

Here an involuntary expression came over the Spaniard, similar to that just before on the deck, and whether it was the start he gave, or a sudden gawky roll of the hull in the calm, or a momentary unsteadiness of the servant's hand, however it was, just then the razor drew blood, spots of which stained the creamy lather under the throat: immediately the black barber drew back his steel, and, remaining in his professional attitude, back to Captain Delano, and face to Don Benito, held up the trickling razor, saying, with a sort of half humorous sorrow, "See, master—you shook so—here's Babo's first blood."

---

[98] An executioner, and in the white a man at the chopping block. Captain Delano repeatedly gets flashes of the true situation on the ship but reasons them away with his optimism and his tendency to stereotype blacks.

No sword drawn before James the First of England,[99] no assassination in that timid King's presence, could have produced a more terrified aspect than was now presented by Don Benito.

Poor fellow, thought Captain Delano, so nervous he can't even bear the sight of barber's blood; and this unstrung, sick man, is it credible that I should have imagined he meant to spill all my blood, who can't endure the sight of one little drop of his own? Surely, Amasa Delano, you have been beside yourself this day. Tell it not when you get home, sappy Amasa. Well, well, he looks like a murderer, doesn't he? More like as if himself were to be done for. Well, well, this day's experience shall be a good lesson.

Meantime, while these things were running through the honest seaman's mind, the servant had taken the napkin from his arm, and to Don Benito had said—"But answer Don Amasa, please, master, while I wipe this ugly stuff off the razor, and strop it again."

As he said the words, his face was turned half round, so as to be alike visible to the Spaniard and the American, and seemed, by its expression, to hint, that he was desirous, by getting his master to go on with the conversation, considerably to withdraw his attention from the recent annoying accident. As if glad to snatch the offered relief, Don Benito resumed, rehearsing to Captain Delano, that not only were the calms of unusual duration, but the ship had fallen in with obstinate currents; and other things he added, some of which were but repetitions of former statements, to explain how it came to pass that the passage from Cape Horn to St. Maria had been so exceedingly long; now and then mingling with his words, incidental praises, less qualified than before, to the blacks, for their general good conduct. These particulars were not given consecutively, the servant, at convenient times, using his razor, and so, between the intervals of shaving, the story and panegyric went on with more than usual huskiness.

To Captain Delano's imagination, now again not wholly at rest, there was something so hollow in the Spaniard's manner, with apparently some reciprocal hollowness in the servant's dusky comment of silence, that the idea flashed across him, that possibly master and man, for some unknown purpose, were acting out, both in word and deed, nay, to the very tremor of Don Benito's limbs, some juggling play before him. Neither did the suspicion of collusion lack apparent support, from the fact of those whispered conferences before mentioned. But then, what could be the object of enacting this play of the barber before him? At last, regarding the notion as a whimsy, insensibly suggested, perhaps, by the theatrical aspect of Don Benito in his harlequin ensign,[100] Captain Delano speedily banished it.

The shaving over, the servant bestirred himself with a small bottle of scented waters, pouring a few drops on the head, and then diligently rubbing; the vehemence of the exercise causing the muscles of his face to twitch rather strangely.

His next operation was with comb, scissors, and brush; going round and round, smoothing a curl here, clipping an unruly whisker-hair there, giving a graceful sweep to the temple-lock, with other impromptu touches evincing the hand of a master; while, like any resigned gentleman in barber's hands, Don Benito bore all, much less uneasily, at least, than he had done the razoring; indeed, he sat so

---

[99] James I (1566–1625), who reigned from 1604 to 1625, lived in fear of assassination by Catholics, especially after the Gunpowder Plot in 1605.

[100] The colorful Spanish flag.

pale and rigid now, that the negro seemed a Nubian[101] sculptor finishing off a white statue-head.

All being over at last, the standard of Spain removed, tumbled up, and tossed back into the flag-locker, the negro's warm breath blowing away any stray hair which might have lodged down his master's neck; collar and cravat readjusted; a speck of lint whisked off the velvet lapel; all this being done; backing off a little space, and pausing with an expression of subdued self-complacency, the servant for a moment surveyed his master, as, in toilet at least, the creature of his own tasteful hands.

Captain Delano playfully complimented him upon his achievement; at the same time congratulating Don Benito.

But neither sweet waters, nor shampooing, nor fidelity, nor sociality, delighted the Spaniard. Seeing him relapsing into forbidding gloom, and still remaining seated, Captain Delano, thinking that his presence was undesired just then, withdrew, on the pretense of seeing whether, as he had prophesied, any signs of a breeze were visible.

Walking forward to the main-mast, he stood awhile thinking over the scene, and not without some undefined misgivings, when he heard a noise near the cuddy and turning, saw the negro, his hand to his cheek. Advancing, Captain Delano perceived that the cheek was bleeding. He was about to ask the cause, when the negro's wailing soliloquy enlightened him.

"Ah, when will master get better from his sickness; only the sour heart that sour sickness breeds made him serve Babo so; cutting Babo with the razor, because, only by accident, Babo had given master one little scratch; and for the first time in so many a day, too. Ah, ah, ah," holding his hand to his face.

Is it possible, thought Captain Delano; was it to wreak in private his Spanish spite against this poor friend of his, that Don Benito, by his sullen manner, impelled me to withdraw? Ah, this slavery breeds ugly passions in man.—Poor fellow!

He was about to speak in sympathy to the negro, but with a timid reluctance he now reentered the cuddy.

Presently master and man came forth; Don Benito leaning on his servant as if nothing had happened.

But a sort of love-quarrel, after all, thought Captain Delano.

He accosted Don Benito, and they slowly walked together. They had gone but a few paces, when the steward—a tall, rajah-looking mulatto, orientally set off with a pagoda turban formed by three or four Madras handkerchiefs[102] wound about his head, tier on tier—approaching with a salaam,[103] announced lunch in the cabin.

On their way thither, the two captains were preceded by the mulatto, who, turning round as he advanced, with continual smiles and bows, ushered them on, a display of elegance which quite completed the insignificance of the small bareheaded Babo, who, as if not unconscious of inferiority, eyed askance the graceful steward. But in part, Captain Delano imputed his jealous watchfulness to that peculiar feeling which the full-blooded African entertains for the adulterated one. As for the steward, his manner, if not bespeaking much dignity of self-respect, yet

---

[101] A native of Nubia, now part of the Sudan.
[102] Colorful cotton handkerchiefs from Madras, India.
[103] "Health" (Arabic), a Moslem greeting.

evidenced his extreme desire to please; which is doubly meritorious, as at once Christian and Chesterfieldian.[104]

Captain Delano observed with interest that while the complexion of the mulatto was hybrid, his physiognomy was European—classically so.

"Don Benito," whispered he, "I am glad to see this usher-of-the-golden-rod[105] of yours; the sight refutes an ugly remark once made to me by a Barbadoes planter; that when a mulatto has a regular European face, look out for him; he is a devil. But see, your steward here has features more regular than King George's of England; and yet there he nods, and bows, and smiles; a king, indeed—the king of kind hearts and polite fellows. What a pleasant voice he has, too?"

"He has, Señor."

"But tell me, has he not, so far as you have known him, always proved a good, worthy fellow?" said Captain Delano, pausing, while with a final genuflexion the steward disppeared into the cabin; "come, for the reason just mentioned, I am curious to know."

"Francesco is a good man," a sort of sluggishly responded Don Benito, like a phlegmatic appreciator, who would neither find fault nor flatter.

"Ah, I thought so. For it were strange, indeed, and not very creditable to us whiteskins, if a little of our blood mixed with the African's, should, far from improving the latter's quality, have the sad effect of pouring vitriolic acid into black broth; improving the hue, perhaps, but not the wholesomeness."

"Doubtless, doubtless, Señor, but"—glancing at Babo—"not to speak of negroes, your planter's remark I have heard applied to the Spanish and Indian intermixtures in our provinces. But I know nothing about the matter," he listlessly added.

And here they entered the cabin.

The lunch was a frugal one. Some of Captain Delano's fresh fish and pumpkins, biscuit and salt beef, the reserved bottle of cider, and the San Dominick's last bottle of Canary.[106]

As they entered, Francesco, with two or three colored aids, was hovering over the table giving the last adjustments. Upon perceiving their master they withdrew, Francesco making a smiling congé and the Spaniard, without condescending to notice it, fastidiously remarking to his companion that he relished not superfluous attendance.

Without companions, host and guest sat down, like a childless married couple, at opposite ends of the table, Don Benito waving Captain Delano to his place, and, weak as he was, insisting upon that gentleman being seated before himself.

The negro placed a rug under Don Benito's feet, and a cushion behind his back, and then stood behind, not his master's chair, but Captain Delano's. At first, this a little surprised the latter. But it was soon evident that, in taking his position, the black was still true to his master; since by facing him he could the more readily anticipate his slightest want.

"This is an uncommonly intelligent fellow of yours, Don Benito," whispered Captain Delano across the table.

"You say true, Señor."

---

[104] Philip Dormer Stanhope (1694–1773), the fourth earl of Chesterfield, advocated a worldly code of conduct and ethics in letters to his illegitimate son, the opposite of that personified by Christ.

[105] Ushers walked formally before a person of rank; they were known by the color of the rod or staff they carried.

[106] Wine from the Canary Islands.

During the repast, the guest again reverted to parts of Don Benito's story, begging further particulars here and there. He inquired how it was that the scurvy and fever should have committed such wholesale havoc upon the whites, while destroying less than half of the blacks. As if this question reproduced the whole scene of plague before the Spaniard's eyes, miserably reminding him of his solitude in a cabin where before he had had so many friends and officers round him, his hand shook, his face became hueless, broken words escaped; but directly the sane memory of the past seemed replaced by insane terrors of the present. With starting eyes he stared before him at vacancy. For nothing was to be seen but the hand of his servant pushing the Canary over towards him. At length a few sips served partially to restore him. He made random reference to the different constitution of races, enabling one to offer more resistance to certain maladies than another. The thought was new to his companion.

Presently Captain Delano, intending to say something to his host concerning the pecuniary part of the business he had undertaken for him, especially—since he was strictly accountable to his owners—with reference to the new suit of sails, and other things of that sort; and naturally preferring to conduct such affairs in private, was desirous that the servant should withdraw; imagining that Don Benito for a few minutes could dispense with his attendance. He, however, waited awhile; thinking that, as the conversation proceeded, Don Benito, without being prompted, would perceive the propriety of the step.

But it was otherwise. At last catching his host's eye, Captain Delano, with a slight backward gesture of his thumb, whispered, "Don Benito, pardon me, but there is an interference with the full expression of what I have to say to you."

Upon this the Spaniard changed countenance; which was imputed to his resenting the hint, as in some way a reflection upon his servant. After a moment's pause, he assured his guest that the black's remaining with them could be of no disservice; because since losing his officers he had made Babo (whose original office, it now appeared, had been captain of the slaves) not only his constant attendant and companion, but in all things his confidant.

After this, nothing more could be said; though, indeed, Captain Delano could hardly avoid some little tinge of irritation upon being left ungratified in so inconsiderable a wish, by one, too, for whom he intended such solid services. But it is only his querulousness, thought he; and so filling his glass he proceeded to business.

The price of the sails and other matters was fixed upon. But while this was being done, the American observed that, though his original offer of assistance had been hailed with hectic animation, yet now when it was reduced to a business transaction, indifference and apathy were betrayed. Don Benito, in fact, appeared to submit to hearing the details more out of regard to common propriety, than from any impression that weighty benefit to himself and his voyage was involved.

Soon, his manner became still more reserved. The effort was vain to seek to draw him into social talk. Gnawed by his splenetic[107] mood, he sat twitching his beard, while to little purpose the hand of his servant, mute as that on the wall, slowly pushed over the Canary.

Lunch being over, they sat down on the cushioned transom;[108] the servant placing a pillow behind his master. The long continuance of the calm had now affected the atmosphere. Don Benito sighed heavily, as if for breath.

---

[107] Melancholy and peevish.   [108] A large crossbeam at a ship's stern.

"Why not adjourn to the cuddy," said Captain Delano; "there is more air there." But the host sat silent and motionless.

Meantime his servant knelt before him, with a large fan of feathers. And Francesco coming in on tiptoes, handed the negro a little cup of aromatic waters, with which at intervals he chafed his master's brow; smoothing the hair along the temples as a nurse does a child's. He spoke no word. He only rested his eye on his master's, as if, amid all Don Benito's distress, a little to refresh his spirit by the silent sight of fidelity.

Presently the ship's bell sounded two o'clock; and through the cabin windows a slight rippling of the sea was discerned; and from the desired direction.

"There," exclaimed Captain Delano, "I told you so, Don Benito, look!"

He had risen to his feet, speaking in a very animated tone, with a view the more to rouse his companion. But though the crimson curtain of the stern-window near him that moment fluttered against his pale cheek, Don Benito seemed to have even less welcome for the breeze than the calm.

Poor fellow, thought Captain Delano, bitter experience has taught him that one ripple does not make a wind, any more than one swallow a summer. But he is mistaken for once. I will get his ship in for him, and prove it.

Briefly alluding to his weak condition, he urged his host to remain quietly where he was, since he (Captain Delano) would with pleasure take upon himself the responsibility of making the best use of the wind.

Upon gaining the deck, Captain Delano started at the unexpected figure of Atufal, monumentally fixed at the threshold, like one of those sculptured porters of black marble guarding the porches of Egyptian tombs.

But this time the start was, perhaps, purely physical. Atufal's presence, singularly attesting docility even in sullenness, was contrasted with that of the hatchet-polishers, who in patience evinced their industry; while both spectacles showed, that lax as Don Benito's general authority might be, still, whenever he chose to exert it, no man so savage or colossal but must, more or less, bow.

Snatching a trumpet which hung from the bulwarks, with a free step Captain Delano advanced to the forward edge of the poop, issuing his orders in his best Spanish. The few sailors and many negroes, all equally pleased, obediently set about heading the ship towards the harbor.

While giving some directions about setting a lower stu'n'-sail,[109] suddenly Captain Delano heard a voice faithfully repeating his orders. Turning, he saw Babo, now for the time acting, under the pilot, his original part of captain of the slaves. This assistance proved valuable. Tattered sails and warped yards were soon brought into some trim. And no brace or halyard was pulled but to the blithe songs of the inspirited negroes.

Good fellows, thought Captain Delano, a little training would make fine sailors of them. Why see, the very women pull and sing too. These must be some of those Ashantee negresses that make such capital soldiers, I've heard. But who's at the helm. I must have a good hand there.

He went to see.

The San Dominick steered with a cumbrous tiller, with large horizontal pullies attached. At each pully-end stood a subordinate black, and between them, at the tiller-head, the responsible post, a Spanish seaman, whose countenance evinced his due share in the general hopefulness and confidence at the coming of the breeze.

---

[109] A studdingsail, an auxiliary sail set out in good weather.

He proved the same man who had behaved with so shame-faced an air on the windlass.

"Ah,—it is you, my man," exclaimed Captain Delano—"well, no more sheep's-eyes now;—look straight forward and keep the ship so. Good hand, I trust? And want to get into the harbor, don't you?"

The man assented with an inward chuckle, grasping the tiller-head firmly. Upon this, unperceived by the American, the two blacks eyed the sailor intently.

Finding all right at the helm, the pilot went forward to the forecastle, to see how matters stood there.

The ship now had way enough to breast the current. With the approach of evening, the breeze would be sure to freshen.

Having done all that was needed for the present, Captain Delano, giving his last orders to the sailors, turned aft to report affairs to Don Benito in the cabin; perhaps additionally incited to rejoin him by the hope of snatching a moment's private chat while the servant was engaged upon deck.

From opposite sides, there were, beneath the poop, two approaches to the cabin; one further forward than the other, and consequently communicating with a longer passage. Marking the servant still above, Captain Delano, taking the nighest entrance—the one last named, and at whose porch Atufal still stood—hurried on his way, till, arrived at the cabin threshold, he paused an instant, a little to recover from his eagerness. Then, with the words of his intended business upon his lips, he entered. As he advanced toward the seated Spaniard, he heard another footstep, keeping time with his. From the opposite door, a salver in hand, the servant was likewise advancing.

"Confound the faithful fellow," thought Captain Delano; "what a vexatious coincidence."

Possibly, the vexation might have been something different, were it not for the brisk confidence inspired by the breeze. But even as it was, he felt a slight twinge, from a sudden indefinite association in his mind of Babo with Atufal.

"Don Benito," said he, "I give you joy; the breeze will hold, and will increase. By the way, your tall man and time-piece, Atufal, stands without. By your order, of course?"

Don Benito recoiled, as if at some bland satirical touch, delivered with such adroit garnish of apparent good breeding as to present no handle for retort.

He is like one flayed alive, thought Captain Delano; where may one touch him without causing a shrink?

The servant moved before his master, adjusting a cushion; recalled to civility, the Spaniard stiffly replied: "you are right. The slave appears where you saw him, according to my command; which is, that if at the given hour I am below, he must take his stand and abide my coming."

"Ah now, pardon me, but that is treating the poor fellow like an ex-king indeed. Ah, Don Benito," smiling, "for all the license you permit in some things, I fear lest, at bottom, you are a bitter hard master."

Again Don Benito shrank; and this time, as the good sailor thought, from a genuine twinge of his conscience.

Again conversation became constrained. In vain Captain Delano called attention to the now perceptible motion of the keel gently cleaving the sea; with lacklustre eye, Don Benito returned words few and reserved.

By-and-by, the wind having steadily risen, and still blowing right into the harbor, bore the San Dominick swiftly on. Rounding a point of land, the sealer at distance came into open view.

Meantime Captain Delano had again repaired to the deck, remaining there some time. Having at last altered the ship's course, so as to give the reef a wide berth, he returned for a few moments below.

I will cheer up my poor friend, this time, thought he.

"Better and better, Don Benito," he cried as he blithely re-entered: "there will soon be an end to your cares, at least for awhile. For when, after a long, sad voyage, you know, the anchor drops into the haven, all its vast weight seems lifted from the captain's heart. We are getting on famously, Don Benito. My ship is in sight. Look through this side-light here; there she is; all a-taunt-o![110] The Bachelor's Delight, my good friend. Ah, how this wind braces one up. Come, you must take a cup of coffee with me this evening. My old steward will give you as fine a cup as ever any sultan tasted. What say you, Don Benito, will you?"

At first, the Spaniard glanced feverishly up, casting a longing look towards the sealer, while with mute concern his servant gazed into his face. Suddenly the old ague of coldness returned, and dropping back to his cushions he was silent.

"You do not answer. Come, all day you have been my host; would you have hospitality all on one side?"

"I cannot go," was the response.

"What? it will not fatigue you. The ships will lie together as near as they can, without swinging foul. It will be little more than stepping from deck to deck; which is but as from room to room. Come, come, you must not refuse me."

"I cannot go," decisively and repulsively repeated Don Benito.

Renouncing all but the last appearance of courtesy, with a sort of cadaverous sullenness, and biting his thin nails to the quick, he glanced, almost glared, at his guest, as if impatient that a stranger's presence should interfere with the full indulgence of his morbid hour. Meantime the sound of the parted waters came more and more gurglingly and merrily at the windows; as reproaching him for his dark spleen, as telling him that, sulk as he might, and go mad with it, nature cared not a jot; since, whose fault was it, pray?

But the foul mood was now at its depth, as the fair wind at its height.

There was something in the man so far beyond any mere unsociality or sourness previously evinced, that even the forbearing good-nature of his guest could no longer endure it. Wholly at a loss to account for such demeanor, and deeming sickness with eccentricity, however extreme, no adequate excuse, well satisfied, too, that nothing in his own conduct could justify it, Captain Delano's pride began to be roused. Himself became reserved. But all seemed one to the Spaniard. Quitting him, therefore, Captain Delano once more went to the deck.

The ship was now within less than two miles of the sealer. The whale-boat was seen darting over the interval.

To be brief, the two vessels, thanks to the pilot's skill, ere long in neighborly style lay anchored together.

Before returning to his own vessel, Captain Delano had intended communicating to Don Benito the smaller details of the proposed services to be rendered. But, as it was, unwilling anew to subject himself to rebuffs, he resolved, now that he had seen the San Dominick safely moored, immediately to quit her, without further allusion to hospitality or business. Indefinitely postponing his ulterior plans, he would regulate his future actions according to future circumstances. His boat

---

[110] Fully rigged, looking fit.

was ready to receive him; but his host still tarried below. Well, thought Captain Delano, if he had little breeding, the more need to show mine. He descended to the cabin to bid a ceremonious, and, it may be, tacitly rebukeful adieu. But to his great satisfaction, Don Benito, as if he began to feel the weight of that treatment with which his slighted guest had, not indecorously, retaliated upon him, now supported by his servant, rose to his feet, and grasping Captain Delano's hand, stood tremulous; too much agitated to speak. But the good augury hence drawn was suddenly dashed, by his resuming all his previous reserve, with augmented gloom, as, with half-averted eyes, he silently reseated himself on his cushions. With a corresponding return of his own chilled feelings, Captain Delano bowed and withdrew.

He was hardly midway in the narrow corridor, dim as a tunnel, leading from the cabin to the stairs, when a sound, as of the tolling for execution in some jail-yard, fell on his ears. It was the echo of the ship's flawed bell, striking the hour, drearily reverberated in this subterranean vault. Instantly, by a fatality not to be withstood, his mind, responsive to the portent, swarmed with superstitious suspicions. He paused. In images far swifter than these sentences, the minutest details of all his former distrusts swept through him.

Hitherto, credulous good-nature had been too ready to furnish excuses for reasonable fears. Why was the Spaniard, so superfluously punctilious at times, now heedless of common propriety in not accompanying to the side his departing guest? Did indisposition forbid? Indisposition had not forbidden more irksome exertion that day. His last equivocal demeanor recurred. He had risen to his feet, grasped his guest's hand, motioned toward his hat; then, in an instant, all was eclipsed in sinister muteness and gloom. Did this imply one brief, repentant relenting at the final moment, from some iniquitous plot, followed by remorseless return to it? His last glance seemed to express a calamitous, yet acquiescent farewell to Captain Delano forever. Why decline the invitation to visit the sealer that evening? Or was the Spaniard less hardened than the Jew,[111] who refrained not from supping at the board of him whom the same night he meant to betray? What imported all those day-long enigmas and contradictions, except they were intended to mystify, preliminary to some stealthy blow? Atufal, the pretended rebel, but punctual shadow, that moment lurked by the threshold without. He seemed a sentry, and more. Who, by his own confession, had stationed him there? Was the negro now lying in wait?

The Spaniard behind—his creature before: to rush from darkness to light was the involuntary choice.

The next moment, with clenched jaw and hand, he passed Atufal, and stood unharmed in the light. As he saw his trim ship lying peacefully at anchor, and almost within ordinary call; as he saw his household boat, with familiar faces in it, patiently rising and falling on the short waves by the San Dominick's side; and then, glancing about the decks where he stood, saw the oakum-pickers still gravely plying their fingers; and heard the low, buzzing whistle and industrious hum of the hatchet-polishers, still bestirring themselves over their endless occupation; and more than all, as he saw the benign aspect of nature, taking her innocent repose in the evening; the screened sun in the quiet camp of the west shining out like the mild light from Abraham's[112] tent; as charmed eye and ear took in all

---

[111] Judas Iscariot, who betrayed Christ after the Last Supper (see Matthew 26:20–25).
[112] An Old Testament patriarch (see Genesis 18:1).

these, with the chained figure of the black, clenched jaw and hand relaxed. Once again he smiled at the phantoms which had mocked him, and felt something like a tinge of remorse, that, by harboring them even for a moment, he should, by implication, have betrayed an atheist doubt of the ever-watchful Providence above.

There was a few minutes' delay, while, in obedience to his orders, the boat was being hooked along to the gangway. During this interval, a sort of saddened satisfaction stole over Captain Delano, at thinking of the kindly offices he had that day discharged for a stranger. Ah, thought he, after good actions one's conscience is never ungrateful, however much so the benefited party may be.

Presently, his foot, in the first act of descent into the boat, pressed the first round of the side-ladder, his face presented inward upon the deck. In the same moment, he heard his name courteously sounded; and, to his pleased surprise, saw Don Benito advancing—an unwonted energy in his air, as if, at the last moment, intent upon making amends for his recent discourtesy. With instinctive good feeling, Captain Delano, withdrawing his foot, turned and reciprocally advanced. As he did so, the Spaniard's nervous eagerness increased, but his vital energy failed; so that, the better to support him, the servant, placing his master's hand on his naked shoulder, and gently holding it there, formed himself into a sort of crutch.

When the two captains met, the Spaniard again fervently took the hand of the American, at the same time casting an earnest glance into his eyes, but, as before, too much overcome to speak.

I have done him wrong, self-reproachfully thought Captain Delano; his apparent coldness has deceived me; in no instance has he meant to offend.

Meantime, as if fearful that the continuance of the scene might too much unstring his master, the servant seemed anxious to terminate it. And so, still presenting himself as a crutch, and walking between the two captains, he advanced with them towards the gangway; while still, as if full of kindly contrition, Don Benito would not let go the hand of Captain Delano, but retained it in his, across the black's body.

Soon they were standing by the side, looking over into the boat, whose crew turned up their curious eyes. Waiting a moment for the Spaniard to relinquish his hold, the now embarrassed Captain Delano lifted his foot, to overstep the threshold of the open gangway; but still Don Benito would not let go his hand. And yet, with an agitated tone, he said, "I can go no further; here I must bid you adieu. Adieu, my dear, dear Don Amasa. Go—go!" suddenly tearing his hand loose, "go, and God guard you better than me, my best friend."

Not unaffected, Captain Delano would now have lingered; but catching the meekly admonitory eye of the servant, with a hasty farewell he descended into his boat, followed by the continual adieus of Don Benito, standing rooted in the gangway.

Seating himself in the stern, Captain Delano, making a last salute, ordered the boat shoved off. The crew had their oars on end. The bowsmen pushed the boat a sufficient distance for the oars to be lengthwise dropped. The instant that was done, Don Benito sprang over the bulwarks, falling at the feet of Captain Delano; at the same time calling towards his ship, but in tones so frenzied, that none in the boat could understand him. But, as if not equally obtuse, three sailors, from three different and distant parts of the ship, splashed into the sea, swimming after their captain, as if intent upon his rescue.

The dismayed officer of the boat eagerly asked what this meant. To which, Captain Delano, turning a disdainful smile upon the unaccountable Spaniard, answered that, for his part, he neither knew nor cared; but it seemed as if Don Benito had taken it into his head to produce the impression among his people that the boat wanted to kidnap him. "Or else—give way[113] for your lives," he wildly added, starting at a clattering hubbub in the ship, above which rang the tocsin[114] of the hatchet-polishers; and seizing Don Benito by the throat he added, "this plotting pirate means murder!" Here, in apparent verification of the words, the servant, a dagger in his hand, was seen on the rail overhead, poised, in the act of leaping, as if with desperate fidelity to befriend his master to the last; while, seemingly to aid the black, the three white sailors were trying to clamber into the hampered bow. Meantime, the whole host of negroes, as if inflamed at the sight of their jeopardized captain, impended in one sooty avalanche over the bulwarks.

All this, with what preceded, and what followed, occurred with such involutions of rapidity, that past, present, and future seemed one.

Seeing the negro coming, Captain Delano had flung the Spaniard aside, almost in the very act of clutching him, and, by the unconscious recoil, shifting his place, with arms thrown up, so promptly grappled the servant in his descent, that with dagger presented at Captain Delano's heart, the black seemed of purpose to have leaped there as to his mark. But the weapon was wrenched away, and the assailant dashed down into the bottom of the boat, which now, with disentangled oars, began to speed through the sea.

At this juncture, the left hand of Captain Delano, on one side, again clutched the half-reclined Don Benito, heedless that he was in a speechless faint, while his right foot, on the other side, ground the prostrate negro; and his right arm pressed for added speed on the after oar, his eye bent forward, encouraging his men to their utmost.

But here, the officer of the boat, who had at last succeeded in beating off the towing sailors, and was now, with face turned aft, assisting the bowsman at his oar, suddenly called to Captain Delano, to see what the black was about; while a Portuguese oarsman shouted to him to give heed to what the Spaniard was saying.

Glancing down at his feet, Captain Delano saw the freed hand of the servant aiming with a second dagger—a small one, before concealed in his wool[115]—with this he was snakishly writhing up from the boat's bottom, at the heart of his master, his countenance lividly vindictive, expressing the centred purpose of his soul; while the Spaniard, half-choked, was vainly shrinking away, with husky words, incoherent to all but the Portuguese.

That moment, across the long-benighted mind of Captain Delano, a flash of revelation swept, illuminating, in unanticipated clearness, his host's whole mysterious demeanor, with every enigmatic event of the day, as well as the entire past voyage of the San Dominick. He smote Babo's hand down, but his own heart smote him harder. With infinite pity he withdrew his hold from Don Benito. Not Captain Delano, but Don Benito, the black, in leaping into the boat, had intended to stab.

Both the black's hands were held, as, glancing up towards the San Dominick, Captain Delano, now with scales dropped from his eyes, saw the negroes, not in misrule, not in tumult; not as if frantically concerned for Don Benito, but with mask torn away, flourishing hatchets and knives, in ferocious piratical revolt. Like delirious black dervishes,[116] the six Ashantees danced on the poop. Pre-

---

[113] Row.   [114] An alarm bell.   [115] Hair.   [116] Muslims who whirl as part of religious services.

vented by their foes from springing into the water, the Spanish boys were hurrying up to the topmost spars, while such of the few Spanish sailors, not already in the sea, less alert, were descried, helplessly mixed in, on deck, with the blacks.

Meantime Captain Delano hailed his own vessel, ordering the ports up, and the guns run out. But by this time the cable of the San Dominick had been cut; and the fag-end, in lashing out, whipped away the canvas shroud about the beak, suddenly revealing, as the bleached hull swung round towards the open ocean, death for the figure-head, in a human skeleton; chalky comment on the chalked words below, *"Follow your leader."*

At the sight, Don Benito, covering his face, wailed out: "'Tis he, Aranda! my murdered, unburied friend!"

Upon reaching the sealer, calling for ropes, Captain Delano bound the negro, who made no resistance, and had him hoisted to the deck. He would then have assisted the now almost helpless Don Benito up the side; but Don Benito, wan as he was, refused to move, or be moved, until the negro should have been first put below out of view. When, presently assured that it was done, he no more shrank from the ascent.

The boat was immediately dispatched back to pick up the three swimming sailors. Meantime, the guns were in readiness, though, owing to the San Dominick having glided somewhat astern of the sealer, only the aftermost one could be brought to bear. With this, they fired six times; thinking to cripple the fugitive ship by bringing down her spars. But only a few inconsiderable ropes were shot away. Soon the ship was beyond the gun's range, steering broad out of the bay; the blacks thickly clustering round the bowsprit,[117] one moment with taunting cries towards the whites, the next with upthrown gestures hailing the now dusky moors of ocean—cawing crows escaped from the hand of the fowler.

The first impulse was to slip the cables and give chase. But, upon second thoughts, to pursue with whale-boat and yawl seemed more promising.

Upon inquiring of Don Benito what firearms they had on board the San Dominick, Captain Delano was answered that they had none that could be used; because, in the earlier stages of the mutiny, a cabin-passenger, since dead, had secretly put out of order the locks of what few muskets there were. But with all his remaining strength, Don Benito entreated the American not to give chase, either with ship or boat; for the negroes had already proved themselves such desperadoes, that, in case of a present assault, nothing but a total massacre of the whites could be looked for. But, regarding this warning as coming from one whose spirit had been crushed by misery the American did not give up his design.

The boats were got ready and armed. Captain Delano ordered his men into them. He was going himself when Don Benito grasped his arm.

"What! have you saved my life, Señor, and are you now going to throw away your own?"

The officers also, for reasons connected with their interests and those of the voyage, and a duty owing to the owners, strongly objected against their commander's going. Weighing their remonstrances a moment, Captain Delano felt bound to remain; appointing his chief mate—an athletic and resolute man, who had been a privateer's man[118]—to head the party. The more to encourage the

[117] A large spar extending from a ship's bow.

[118] A private ship commissioned by a government to serve as a naval vessel to seize enemy ships; in *Putnam's Magazine* Melville added "and, as his enemies whispered, a pirate."

sailors, they were told, that the Spanish captain considered his ship good as lost; that she and her cargo, including some gold and silver, were worth more than a thousand doubloons. Take her, and no small part should be theirs. The sailors replied with a shout.

The fugitives had now almost gained an offing.[119] It was nearly night; but the moon was rising. After hard, prolonged pulling, the boats came up on the ship's quarters, at a suitable distance laying upon their oars to discharge their muskets. Having no bullets to return; the negroes sent their yells. But, upon the second volley, Indian-like, they hurtled their hatchets. One took off a sailor's fingers. Another struck the whale-boat's bow, cutting off the rope there, and remaining stuck in the gunwale like a woodman's axe. Snatching it, quivering from it's lodgment, the mate hurled it back. The returned gauntlet now stuck in the ship's broken quarter-gallery, and so remained.

The negroes giving too hot a reception, the whites kept a more respectful distance. Hovering now just out of reach of the hurtling hatchets, they, with a view to the close encounter which must soon come, sought to decoy the blacks into entirely disarming themselves of their most murderous weapons in a hand-to-hand fight, by foolishly flinging them, as missiles, short of the mark, into the sea. But, ere long, perceiving the stratagem, the negroes desisted, though not before many of them had to replace their lost hatchets with handspikes; an exchange which, as counted upon, proved, in the end, favorable to the assailants.

Meantime, with a strong wind, the ship still clove the water; the boats alternately falling behind, and pulling up, to discharge fresh volleys.

The fire was mostly directed towards the stern, since there, chiefly, the negroes, at present, were clustering. But to kill or maim the negroes was not the object. To take them, with the ship, was the object. To do it, the ship must be boarded; which could not be done by boats while she was sailing so fast.

A thought now struck the mate. Observing the Spanish boys still aloft, high as they could get, he called to them to descend to the yards, and cut adrift the sails. It was done. About this time, owing to causes hereafter to be shown, two Spaniards, in the dress of sailors, and conspicuously showing themselves, were killed; not by volleys, but by deliberate marksman's shots; while, as it afterwards appeared, by one of the general discharges, Atufal, the black, and the Spaniard at the helm likewise were killed. What now, with the loss of the sails, and loss of leaders, the ship became unmanageable to the negroes.

With creaking masts, she came heavily round to the wind; the prow slowly swinging into view of the boats, its skeleton gleaming in the horizontal moonlight, and casting a gigantic ribbed shadow upon the water. One extended arm of the ghost seemed beckoning the whites to avenge it.

"Follow your leader!" cried the mate; and, one on each bow, the boats boarded. Sealing-spears and cutlasses crossed hatchets and handspikes. Huddled upon the long-boat amidships, the negresses raised a wailing chant, whose chorus was the clash of the steel.

For a time, the attack wavered; the negroes wedging themselves to beat it back; the half-repelled sailors, as yet unable to gain a footing, fighting as troopers in the saddle, one leg sideways flung over the bulwarks, and one without, plying their cutlasses like carters' whips. But in vain. They were almost overborne, when, rallying themselves into a squad as one man, with a huzza, they sprang inboard,

[119] Reached deep water.

where, entangled, they involuntarily separated again. For a few breaths' space, there was a vague, muffled, inner sound, as of submerged sword-fish rushing hither and thither through shoals of black-fish. Soon, in a reunited band, and joined by the Spanish seamen, the whites came to the surface, irresistibly driving the negroes toward the stern. But a barricade of casks and sacks, from side to side, had been thrown up by the mainmast. Here the negroes faced about, and though scorning peace or truce, yet fain would have had respite. But, without pause, overleaping the barrier, the unflagging sailors again closed. Exhausted, the blacks now fought in despair. Their red tongues lolled, wolf-like, from their black mouths. But the pale sailors' teeth were set; not a word was spoken; and, in five minutes more, the ship was won.

Nearly a score of the negroes were killed. Exclusive of those by the balls,[120] many were mangled; their wounds—mostly inflicted by the long-edged sealing-spears, resembling those shaven ones of the English at Preston Pans,[121] made by the poled scythes of the Highlanders. On the other side, none were killed, though several were wounded; some severely, including the mate. The surviving negroes were temporarily secured, and the ship, towed back into the harbor at midnight, once more lay anchored.

Omitting the incidents and arrangements ensuing, suffice it that, after two days spent in refitting, the ships sailed in company for Conception, in Chili, and thence for Lima, in Peru; where, before the vice-regal courts, the whole affair, from the beginning, underwent investigation.

Though, midway on the passage, the ill-fated Spaniard, relaxed from constraint, showed some signs of regaining health with free-will; yet, agreeably to his own foreboding, shortly before arriving at Lima, he relapsed, finally becoming so reduced as to be carried ashore in arms. Hearing of his story and plight, one of the many religious institutions of the City of Kings opened an hospitable refuge to him, where both physician and priest were his nurses, and a member of the order volunteered to be his one special guardian and consoler, by night and by day.

The following extracts, translated from one of the official Spanish documents, will, it is hoped, shed light on the preceding narrative, as well as, in the first place, reveal the true port of departure and true history of the San Dominick's voyage, down to the time of her touching at the island of St. Maria.

But, ere the extracts come, it may be well to preface them with a remark.

The document selected, from among many others, for partial translation, contains the deposition of Benito Cereno; the first taken in the case. Some disclosures therein were, at the time, held dubious for both learned and natural reasons. The tribunal inclined to the opinion that the deponent, not undisturbed in his mind by recent events, raved of some things which could never have happened. But subsequent depositions of the surviving sailors, bearing out the revelations of their captain in several of the strangest particulars, gave credence to the rest. So that the tribunal, in its final decision, rested its capital sentences upon statements which, had they lacked confirmation, it would have deemed it but duty to reject.

I, Don Jose de Abos and Padilla, His Majesty's Notary for the Royal Revenue, and Register of this Province, and Notary Public of the Holy Crusade of this Bishopric, etc.

---

[120] Those killed by musket balls.

[121] At the battle of Prestonpans, Scotland, in 1745, Scottish Highlanders armed with swords and with scythes fastened to poles defeated British forces.

Do certify and declare, as much as is requisite in law, that, in the criminal cause commenced the twenty-fourth of the month of September, in the year seventeen hundred and ninety-nine, against the negroes of the ship San Dominick, the following declaration before me was made:[122]

Declaration of the first witness, DON BENITO CERENO.

The same day, and month, and year, His Honor, Doctor Juan Martinez de Rozas, Councilor of the Royal Audience of this Kingdom, and learned in the law of this Intendency,[123] ordered the captain of the ship San Dominick, Don Benito Cereno, to appear; which he did in his litter,[124] attended by the monk Infelez; of whom he received the oath, which he took by God, our Lord, and a sign of the Cross; under which he promised to tell the truth of whatever he should know and should be asked;—and being interrogated agreeably to the tenor of the act commencing the process, he said, that on the twentieth of May last, he set sail with his ship from the port of Valparaiso, bound to that of Callao;[125] loaded with the produce of the country beside thirty cases of hardware and one hundred and sixty blacks, of both sexes, mostly belonging to Don Alexandro Aranda, gentleman, of the city of Mendoza;[126] that the crew of the ship consisted of thirty-six men, beside the persons who went as passengers; that the negroes were in part as follows:

[*Here, in the original, follows a list of some fifty names, descriptions, and ages, compiled from certain recovered documents of Aranda's, and also from recollections of the deponent, from which portions only are extracted.*]

—One, from about eighteen to nineteen years, named José, and this was the man that waited upon his master, Don Alexandro, and who speaks well the Spanish, having served him four or five years; * * * a mulatto, named Francesco, the cabin steward, of a good person and voice, having sung in the Valparaiso churches, native of the province of Buenos Ayres, aged about thirty-five years. * * * A smart negro, named Dago, who had been for many years a grave-digger among the Spaniards, aged forty-six years. * * * Four old negroes, born in Africa, from sixty to seventy, but sound, calkers by trade, whose names are as follows:—the first was named Muri, and he was killed (as was also his son named Diamelo); the second, Nacta; the third, Yola, likewise killed; the fourth, Ghofan; and six full-grown negroes, aged from thirty to forty-five, all raw, and born among the Ashantees—Matiluqui, Yan, Lecbe, Mapenda, Yambaio, Akim; four of whom were killed; * * * a powerful negro named Atufal, who being supposed to have been a chief in Africa, his owner set great store by him. * * * And a small negro of Senegal, but some years among the Spaniards, aged about thirty, which negro's name was Babo; * * * that he does not remember the names of the others, but that still expecting the residue of Don Alexandro's papers will be found, will then take due account of them all, and remit to the court; * * * and thirty-nine women and children of all ages.

---

[122] Melville edited and revised Delano's *Narrative*. He makes Babo more intelligent and subtle than he is in the official deposition of Benito Cereno; the Spanish captain's self-serving testimony is also more obvious. In the pages that follow, the brackets, italics, and ellipses are Melville's.

[123] A court district over which a provincial officer presides.

[124] A seat on which a person can be carried.

[125] Valparaiso, Chile; Callao, Peru.   [126] Mendoza, Argentina.

[*The catalogue over, the deposition goes on*]

* * * That all the negroes slept upon deck, as is customary in this navigation, and none wore fetters, because the owner, his friend Aranda, told him that they were all tractable; * * * that on the seventh day after leaving port, at three o'clock in the morning, all the Spaniards being asleep except the two officers on the watch, who were the boatswain,[127] Juan Robles, and the carpenter, Juan Bautista Gayete, and the helmsman and his boy, the negroes revolted suddenly, wounded dangerously the boatswain and the carpenter, and successively killed eighteen men of those who were sleeping upon deck, some with hand-spikes and hatchets, and others by throwing them alive overboard, after tying them; that of the Spaniards upon deck, they left about seven, as he thinks, alive and tied, to manœuvre the ship, and three or four more, who hid themselves, remained also alive. Although in the act of revolt the negroes made themselves masters of the hatchway, six or seven wounded went through it to the cockpit,[128] without any hindrance on their part; that during the act of revolt, the mate and another person, whose name he does not recollect, attempted to come up through the hatchway, but being quickly wounded, were obliged to return to the cabin; that the deponent resolved at break of day to come up the companion-way, where the negro Babo was, being the ringleader, and Atufal, who assisted him, and having spoken to them, exhorted them to cease committing such atrocities, asking them, at the same time, what they wanted and intended to do, offering, himself, to obey their commands; that notwithstanding this, they threw, in his presence, three men, alive and tied, overboard; that they told the deponent to come up, and that they would not kill him; which having done, the negro Babo asked him whether there were in those seas any negro countries where they might be carried, and he answered them, No; that the negro Babo afterwards told him to carry them to Senegal, or to the neighboring islands of St. Nicholas; and he answered, that this was impossible, on account of the great distance, the necessity involved of rounding Cape Horn, the bad condition of the vessel, the want of provisions, sails, and water; but that the negro Babo replied to him he must carry them in any way; that they would do and conform themselves to everything the deponent should require as to eating and drinking; that after a long conference, being absolutely compelled to please them, for they threatened to kill all the whites if they were not, at all events, carried to Senegal, he told them that what was most wanting for the voyage was water; that they would go near the coast to take it; and thence they would proceed on their course; that the negro Babo agreed to it; and the deponent steered towards the intermediate ports, hoping to meet some Spanish or foreign vessel that would save them; that within ten or eleven days they saw the land, and continued their course by it in the vicinity of Nasca;[129] that the deponent observed that the negroes were now restless and mutinous, because he did not effect the taking in of water, the negro Babo having required, with threats, that it should be done, without fail, the following day; he told him he saw plainly that the coast was steep, and the rivers designated in the maps were not to be found, with other reasons suitable to the circumstances; that the best way would be to go to the island of Santa Maria, where they might water easily, it being a solitary island, as the foreigners did; that the deponent did not go to Pisco,[130] that was near, nor make any other port of the coast, because the negro Babo had intimated to him several times, that he would

---

[127] A ship's officer in charge of the deck crew. [128] Sleeping quarters for junior officers.
[129] Nasca, Peru. [130] Pisco, Peru.

kill all the whites the very moment he should perceive any city, town, or settlement of any kind on the shores to which they should be carried: that having determined to go to the island of Santa Maria, as the deponent had planned, for the
purpose of trying whether, on the passage or near the island itself, they could find
any vessel that should favor them, or whether he could escape from it in a boat to
the neighboring coast of Arraco,[131] to adopt the necessary means he immediately
changed his course, steering for the island; that the negroes Babo and Atufal held
daily conferences, in which they discussed what was necessary for their design of
returning to Senegal, whether they were to kill all the Spaniards, and particularly
the deponent; that eight days after parting from the coast of Nasca, the deponent
being on the watch a little after day-break, and soon after the negroes had their
meeting, the negro Babo came to the place where the deponent was, and told him
that he had determined to kill his master, Don Alexandro Aranda, both because he
and his companions could not otherwise be sure of their liberty, and that to keep
the seamen in subjection, he wanted to prepare a warning of what road they
should be made to take did they or any of them oppose him; and that, by means of
the death of Don Alexandro, that warning would best be given; but, that what this
last meant, the deponent did not at the time comprehend, nor could not, further
than that the death of Don Alexandro was intended; and moreover the negro Babo
proposed to the deponent to call the mate Raneds, who was sleeping in the cabin,
before the thing was done, for fear, as the deponent understood it, that the mate,
who was a good navigator, should be killed with Don Alexandro and the rest; that
the deponent, who was the friend, from youth, of Don Alexandro, prayed and
conjured, but all was useless; for the negro Babo answered him that the thing
could not be prevented, and that all the Spaniards risked their death if they should
attempt to frustrate his will in this matter, or any other; that, in this conflict, the
deponent called the mate, Raneds, who was forced to go apart, and immediately
the negro Babo commanded the Ashantee Martinqui and the Ashantee Lecbe to go
and commit the murder; that those two went down with hatchets to the berth of
Don Alexandro; that, yet half alive and mangled, they dragged him on deck; that
they were going to throw him overboard in that state, but the negro Babo stopped
them, bidding the murder be completed on the deck before him, which was done,
when, by his orders, the body was carried below, forward; that nothing more was
seen of it by the deponent for three days; * * * that Don Alonzo Sidonia, an old
man, long resident at Valparaiso, and lately appointed to a civil office in Peru,
whither he had taken passage, was at the time sleeping in the berth opposite Don
Alexandro's; that awakening at his cries, surprised by them, and at the sight of the
negroes with their bloody hatchets in their hands, he threw himself into the sea
through a window which was near him, and was drowned, without it being in the
power of the deponent to assist or take him up; * * * that a short time after killing
Aranda, they brought upon deck his german-cousin, of middle-age, Don Francisco Masa, of Mendoza, and the young Don Joaquin, Marques de Aramboalaza,
then lately from Spain, with his Spanish servant Ponce, and the three young clerks
of Aranda, José Mozairi, Lorenzo Bargas, and Hermenegildo Gandix, all of
Cadiz; that Don Joaquin and Hermenegildo Gandix, the negro Babo, for purposes
hereafter to appear, preserved alive; but Don Francisco Masa, José Mozairi, and
Lorenzo Bargas, with Ponce the servant, beside the boatswain, Juan Robles, the
boatswain's mates, Manuel Viscaya and Roderigo Hurta, and four of the sailors,
the negro Babo ordered to be thrown alive into the sea, although they made no

---

[131] Arraco, or Arica, Chile.

resistance, nor begged for anything else but mercy; that the boatswain, Juan Robles, who knew how to swim, kept the longest above water, making acts of contrition, and, in the last words he uttered, charged this deponent to cause mass to be said for his soul to our Lady of Succor: * * * that, during the three days which followed, the deponent, uncertain what fate had befallen the remains of Don Alexandro, frequently asked the negro Babo where they were, and, if still on board, whether they were to be preserved for interment ashore, entreating him so to order it; that the negro Babo answered nothing till the fourth day, when at sunrise, the deponent coming on deck, the negro Babo showed him a skeleton, which had been substituted for the ship's proper figure-head—the image of Christopher Colon, the discoverer of the New World; that the negro Babo asked him whose skeleton that was, and whether, from its whiteness, he should not think it a white's; that, upon discovering his face, the negro Babo, coming close, said words to this effect: "Keep faith with the blacks from here to Senegal, or you shall in spirit, as now in body, follow your leader," pointing to the prow; * * * that the same morning the negro Babo took by succession each Spaniard forward, and asked him whose skeleton that was, and whether, from its whiteness, he should not think it a white's; that each Spaniard covered his face; that then to each the negro Babo repeated the words in the first place said to the deponent; * * * that they (the Spaniards) being then assembled aft, the negro Babo harangued them, saying that he had now done all; that the deponent (as navigator for the negroes) might pursue his course, warning him and all of them that they should, soul and body, go the way of Don Alexandro, if he saw them (the Spaniards) speak or plot anything against them (the negroes)—a threat which was repeated every day; that, before the events last mentioned, they had tied the cook to throw him overboard, for it is not known what thing they heard him speak, but finally the negro Babo spared his life, at the request of the deponent; that a few days after, the deponent, endeavoring not to omit any means to preserve the lives of the remaining whites, spoke to the negroes peace and tranquillity, and agreed to draw up a paper, signed by the deponent and the sailors who could write, as also by the negro Babo, for himself and all the blacks, in which the deponent obliged himself to carry them to Senegal, and they not to kill any more, and he formally to make over to them the ship, with the cargo, with which they were for that time satisfied and quieted.* * * But the next day, the more surely to guard against the sailors' escape, the negro Babo commanded all the boats to be destroyed but the long-boat, which was unseaworthy, and another, a cutter in good condition, which knowing it would yet be wanted for towing the water casks, he had it lowered down into the hold.

*   *   *   *   *   *   *   *

[*Various particulars of the prolonged and perplexed navigation ensuing here follow, with incidents of a calamitous calm, from which portion one passage is extracted, to wit:*]

—That on the fifth day of the calm, all on board suffering much from the heat, and want of water, and five having died in fits, and mad, the negroes became irritable, and for a chance gesture, which they deemed suspicious—though it was harmless—made by the mate, Raneds, to the deponent in the act of handing a quadrant,[132] they killed him; but that for this they afterwards were sorry, the mate being the only remaining navigator on board, except the deponent.

*   *   *   *   *   *   *   *   *

---

[132] An instrument of navigation, used to determine latitude.

—That omitting other events, which daily happened, and which can only serve uselessly to recall past misfortunes and conflicts, after seventy-three days' navigation, reckoned from the time they sailed from Nasca, during which they navigated under a scanty allowance of water, and were afflicted with the calms before mentioned, they at last arrived at the island of Santa Maria, on the seventeenth of the month of August, at about six o'clock in the afternoon, at which hour they cast anchor very near the American ship, Bachelor's Delight, which lay in the same bay, commanded by the generous Captain Amasa Delano; but at six o'clock in the morning, they had already descried the port, and the negroes became uneasy, as soon as at distance they saw the ship, not having expected to see one there; that the negro Babo pacified them, assuring them that no fear need be had; that straightway he ordered the figure on the bow to be covered with canvas, as for repairs, and had the decks a little set in order; that for a time the negro Babo and the negro Atufal conferred; that the negro Atufal was for sailing away, but the negro Babo would not, and, by himself, cast about what to do; that at last he came to the deponent, proposing to him to say and do all that the deponent declares to have said and done to the American captain;

*   *   *   *   *   *   *   *   *

that the negro Babo warned him that if he varied in the least, or uttered any word, or gave any look that should give the least intimation of the past events or present state, he would instantly kill him, with all his companions, showing a dagger, which he carried hid, saying something which, as he understood it, meant that that dagger would be alert as his eye; that the negro Babo then announced the plan to all his companions, which pleased them; that he then, the better to disguise the truth, devised many expedients, in some of them uniting deceit and defense; that of this sort was the device of the six Ashantees before named, who were his bravoes;[133] that them he stationed on the break of the poop, as if to clean certain hatchets (in cases, which were part of the cargo), but in reality to use them, and distribute them at need, and at a given word he told them; that, among other devices, was the device of presenting Atufal, his right hand man, as chained, though in a moment the chains could be dropped; that in every particular he informed the deponent what part he was expected to enact in every device, and what story he was to tell on every occasion, always threatening him with instant death if he varied in the least: that, conscious that many of the negroes would be turbulent, the negro Babo appointed the four aged negroes, who were calkers, to keep what domestic order they could on the decks; that again and again he harangued the Spaniards and his companions, informing them of his intent, and of his devices, and of the invented story that this deponent was to tell; charging them lest any of them varied from that story; that these arrangements were made and matured during the interval of two or three hours, between their first sighting the ship and the arrival on board of Captain Amasa Delano; that this happened about half-past seven o'clock in the morning, Captain Amasa Delano coming in his boat, and all gladly receiving him; that the deponent, as well as he could force himself, acting then the part of principal owner, and a free captain of the ship, told Captain Amasa Delano, when called upon, that he came from Buenos Ayres, bound to Lima, with three hundred negroes; that off Cape Horn, and in a subsequent fever, many negroes had died; that also, by similar casualties, all the sea officers and the greatest part of the crew had died.

[133] Henchmen.

* * * * * * * * *

[And so the deposition goes on, circumstantially recounting the fictitious story dictated to the deponent by Babo, and through the deponent imposed upon Captain Delano; and also recounting the friendly offers of Captain Delano, with other things, but all of which is here omitted. After the fictitious story, etc. the deposition proceeds:]

* * * * * * * * *

—that the generous Captain Amasa Delano remained on board all the day, till he left the ship anchored at six o'clock in the evening, deponent speaking to him always of his pretended misfortunes, under the fore-mentioned principles, without having had it in his power to tell a single word, or give him the least hint, that he might know the truth and state of things; because the negro Babo, performing the office of an officious servant with all the appearance of submission of the humble slave, did not leave the deponent one moment; that this was in order to observe the deponent's actions and words, for the negro Babo understands well the Spanish; and besides, there were thereabout some others who were constantly on the watch, and likewise understood the Spanish;

* * * that upon one occasion, while deponent was standing on the deck conversing with Amasa Delano, by a secret sign the negro Babo drew him (the deponent) aside, the act appearing as if originating with the deponent; that then, he being drawn aside, the negro Babo proposed to him to gain from Amasa Delano full particulars about his ship, and crew, and arms; that the deponent asked "For what?" that the negro Babo answered he might conceive; that, grieved at the prospect of what might overtake the generous Captain Amasa Delano, the deponent at first refused to ask the desired questions, and used every argument to induce the negro Babo to give up this new design: that the negro Babo showed the point of his dagger; that, after the information had been obtained the negro Babo again drew him aside, telling him that that very night he (the deponent) would be captain of two ships, instead of one, for that, great part of the American's ship's crew being to be absent fishing, the six Ashantees, without any one else, would easily take it; that at this time he said other things to the same purpose; that no entreaties availed; that, before Amasa Delano's coming on board, no hint had been given touching the capture of the American ship: that to prevent this project the deponent was powerless; * * *—that in some things his memory is confused, he cannot distinctly recall every event; * * *—that as soon as they had cast anchor at six of the clock in the evening, as has before been stated, the American Captain took leave, to return to his vessel; that upon a sudden impulse, which the deponent believes to have come from God and his angels, he, after the farewell had been said, followed the generous Captain Amasa Delano as far as the gunwale,[134] where he stayed, under pretense of taking leave, until Amasa Delano should have been seated in his boat; that on shoving off, the deponent sprang from the gunwale into the boat, and fell into it, he knows not how, God guarding him; that—

* * * * * * * * *

[Here, in the original, follows the account of what further happened at the escape, and how the San Dominick was retaken, and of the passage to the coast; including in the recital many expressions of "eternal gratitude" to the "generous Captain Amasa Delano." The deposition then proceeds with recapitulatory remarks, and a partial renumeration of the negroes, making record of their individ-

---

[134] The upper edge of the side of a ship.

ual part in the past events, with a view to furnishing, according to command of the court, the data whereon to found the criminal sentences to be pronounced. From this portion is the following;]

—That he believes that all the negroes, though not in the first place knowing to the design of revolt, when it was accomplished, approved it. * * * That the negro, José, eighteen years old, and in the personal service of Don Alexandro, was the one who communicated the information to the negro Babo, about the state of things in the cabin, before the revolt; that this is known, because, in the preceding midnight, he used to come from his berth, which was under his master's, in the cabin, to the deck where the ringleader and his associates were, and had secret conversations with the negro Babo, in which he was several times seen by the mate; that, one night, the mate drove him away twice; * * * that this same negro José was the one who, without being commanded to do so by the negro Babo, as Lecbe and Martinqui were, stabbed his master, Don Alexandro, after he had been dragged half-lifeless to the deck; * * * that the mulatto steward, Francesco, was of the first band of revolters, that he was, in all things, the creature and tool of the negro Babo; that, to make his court, he, just before a repast in the cabin, proposed, to the negro Babo, poisoning a dish for the generous Captain Amasa Delano; this is known and believed, because the negroes have said it; but that the negro Babo, having another design, forbade Francesco; * * * that the Ashantee Lecbe was one of the worst of them; for that, on the day the ship was retaken, he assisted in the defense of her, with a hatchet in each hand, with one of which he wounded, in the breast, the chief mate of Amasa Delano, in the first act of boarding; this all knew; that, in sight of the deponent, Lecbe struck, with a hatchet, Don Francisco Masa, when, by the negro Babo's orders, he was carrying him to throw him overboard, alive, beside participating in the murder, before mentioned, of Don Alexandro Aranda, and others of the cabin-passengers; that, owing to the fury with which the Ashantees fought in the engagement with the boats, but this Lecbe and Yan survived; that Yan was bad as Lecbe; that Yan was the man who, by Babo's command, willingly prepared the skeleton of Don Alexandro, in a way the negroes afterwards told the deponent, but which he, so long as reason is left him, can never divulge; that Yan and Lecbe were the two who, in a calm by night, riveted the skeleton to the bow; this also the negroes told him; that the negro Babo was he who traced the inscription below it; that the negro Babo was the plotter from first to last; he ordered every murder, and was the helm and keel of the revolt; that Atufal was his lieutenant in all; but Atufal, with his own hand, committed no murder; nor did the negro Babo; * * * that Atufal was shot, being killed in the fight with the boats, ere boarding, * * * that the negresses, of age, were knowing to the revolt, and testified themselves satisfied at the death of their master, Don Alexandro; that, had the negroes not restrained them, they would have tortured to death, instead of simply killing, the Spaniards slain by command of the negro Babo; that the negresses used their utmost influence to have the deponent made away with; that, in the various acts of murder, they sang songs and danced—not gaily, but solemnly; and before the engagement with the boats, as well as during the action, they sang melancholy songs to the negroes, and that this melancholy tone was more inflaming than a different one would have been, and was so intended; that all this is believed, because the negroes have said it.

—that of the thirty-six men of the crew, exclusive of the passengers (all of whom are now dead), which the deponent had knowledge of, six only remained alive, with four cabin-boys and ship-boys, not included with the crew; * * * —that the negroes broke an arm of one of the cabin-boys and gave him strokes with hatchets.

[Then follow various random disclosures referring to various periods of time. The following are extracted;]

—That during the presence of Captain Amasa Delano on board, some attempts were made by the sailors, and one by Hermenegildo Gandix, to convey hints to him of the true state of affairs; but that these attempts were ineffectual, owing to fear of incurring death, and, furthermore, owing to the devices which offered contradictions to the true state of affairs, as well as owing to the generosity and piety of Amasa Delano incapable of sounding such wickedness; * * * that Luys Galgo, a sailor about sixty years of age, and formerly of the king's navy, was one of those who sought to convey tokens to Captain Amasa Delano; but his intent, though undiscovered, being suspected, he was, on a pretense, made to retire out of sight, and at last into the hold, and there was made away with. This the negroes have since said; * * * that one of the ship-boys feeling, from Captain Amasa Delano's presence, some hopes of release, and not having enough prudence, dropped some chance-word respecting his expectations, which being overheard and understood by a slave-boy with whom he was eating at the time, the latter struck him on the head with a knife, inflicting a bad wound, but of which the boy is now healing; that likewise, not long before the ship was brought to anchor, one of the seamen, steering at the time, endangered himself by letting the blacks remark some expression in his countenance, arising from a cause similar to the above; but this sailor, by his heedful after conduct, escaped; * * * that these statements are made to show the court that from the beginning to the end of the revolt, it was impossible for the deponent and his men to act otherwise than they did; * * *—that the third clerk, Hermenegildo Gandix, who before had been forced to live among the seamen, wearing a seaman's habit, and in all respects appearing to be one for the time; he, Gandix, was killed by a musket ball fired through mistake from the boats before boarding; having in his fright run up the mizzen-rigging, calling to the boats—"don't board," lest upon their boarding the negroes should kill him; that his inducing the Americans to believe he some way favored the cause of the negroes, they fired two balls at him, so that he fell wounded from the rigging, and was drowned in the sea; * * *—that the young Don Joaquin, Marques de Aramboalaza, like Hermenegildo Gandix, the third clerk, was degraded to the office and appearance of a common seaman; that upon one occasion when Don Joaquin shrank, the negro Babo commanded the Ashantee Lecbe to take tar and heat it, and pour it upon Don Joaquin's hands; * * *—that Don Joaquin was killed owing to another mistake of the Americans, but one impossible to be avoided, as upon the approach of the boats, Don Joaquin, with a hatchet tied edge out and upright to his hand, was made by the negroes to appear on the bulwarks; whereupon, seen with arms in his hands and in a questionable attitude, he was shot for a renegade seaman; * * * —that on the person of Don Joaquin was found secreted a jewel, which, by papers that were discovered, proved to have been meant for the shrine of our Lady of Mercy in Lima; a votive offering, beforehand prepared and guarded, to attest his gratitude, when he should have landed in Peru, his last destination, for the safe conclusion of his entire voyage from Spain; * * * —that the jewel, with the other effects of the late Don Joaquin, is in the custody of the brethren of the Hospital de Sacerdotes, awaiting the disposition of the honorable court; * * * —that, owing to the condition of the deponent, as well as the haste in which the boats departed for the attack, the Americans were not forewarned that there were, among the apparent crew, a passenger and one of the clerks disguised by the negro Babo; * * * —that, beside the negroes killed in the action, some were killed after the capture and re-anchoring at night, when shackled to the ring-bolts on deck; that these deaths were committed by the sailors, ere they could be prevented. That so soon as informed of it, Captain Amasa Delano used all his authority, and, in particular with his own hand, struck down Martinez Gola, who, having found a razor in the pocket of an old jacket of his, which one of the shackled negroes had on, was aiming it at the negro's throat; that the noble Captain Amasa Delano also wrenched from the hand of Bartholomew Barlo a dagger, secreted at the time of the massacre of the whites, with which he was in the act of stabbing a shackled negro, who, the same day, with another negro, had thrown him down and jumped upon him; * * * —that, for all the events, befalling through so long a time, during which the ship was in the hands of the negro Babo, he cannot here give account; but that, what he has said is the most substantial of what occurs to him at present, and is the truth under the oath which he has taken; which declaration he affirmed and ratified, after hearing it read to him.

He said that he is twenty-nine years of age, and broken in body and mind; that when finally dismissed by the court, he shall not return home to Chili, but betake himself to the monastery on Mount Agonia without; and signed with his honor, and crossed himself, and, for the time, departed as he came, in his litter, with the monk Infelez, to the Hospital de Sacerdotes.   BENITO CERENO.

DOCTOR ROZAS.

If the Deposition have served as the key to fit into the lock of the complications which precede it, then, as a vault whose door has been flung back, the San Dominick's hull lies open today.

Hitherto the nature of this narrative, besides rendering the intricacies in the beginning unavoidable, has more or less required that many things, instead of being set down in the order of occurrence, should be retrospectively, or irregularly given; this last is the case with the following passages, which will conclude the account:

During the long, mild voyage to Lima, there was, as before hinted, a period during which the sufferer a little recovered his health, or, at least in some degree, his tranquillity. Ere the decided relapse which came, the two captains had many cordial conversations—their fraternal unreserve in singular contrast with former withdrawments.

Again and again it was repeated, how hard it had been to enact the part forced on the Spaniard by Babo.

"Ah, my dear friend," Don Benito once said, "at those very times when you thought me so morose and ungrateful, nay, when, as you now admit, you half thought me plotting your murder, at those very times my heart was frozen; I could not look at you, thinking of what, both on board this ship and your own, hung, from other hands, over my kind benefactor. And as God lives, Don Amasa, I know not whether desire for my own safety alone could have nerved me to that leap into your boat, had it not been for the thought that, did you, unenlightened, return to your ship, you, my best friend, with all who might be with you, stolen upon, that night, in your hammocks, would never in this world have wakened again. Do but think how you walked this deck, how you sat in this cabin, every inch of ground mined into honey-combs under you. Had I dropped the least hint, made the least advance towards an understanding between us, death, explosive death—yours as mine—would have ended the scene."

"True, true," cried Captain Delano, starting, "you have saved my life, Don Benito, more than I yours; saved it, too, against my knowledge and will."

"Nay, my friend," rejoined the Spaniard, courteous even to the point of religion, "God charmed your life, but you saved mine. To think of some things you did—those smilings and chattings, rash pointings and gesturings. For less than these, they slew my mate, Raneds; but you had the Prince of Heaven's safe-conduct through all ambuscades."

"Yes, all is owing to Providence, I know: but the temper of my mind that morning was more than commonly pleasant, while the sight of so much suffering, more apparent than real, added to my good-nature, compassion, and charity, happily interweaving the three. Had it been otherwise, doubtless, as you hint, some of my interferences might have ended unhappily enough. Besides, those feelings I spoke of enabled me to get the better of momentary distrust, at times when acuteness might have cost me my life, without saving another's. Only at the end did my suspicions get the better of me, and you know how wide of the mark they then proved."

"Wide, indeed," said Don Benito, sadly; "you were with me all day; stood with me, sat with me, talked with me, looked at me, ate with me, drank with me; and yet, your last act was to clutch for a monster, not only an innocent man, but the most pitiable of all men. To such degree may malign machinations and deceptions impose. So far may even the best man err, in judging the conduct of one with the recesses of whose condition he is not acquainted. But you were forced to it; and you were in time undeceived. Would that, in both respects, it was so ever, and with all men."

"You generalize, Don Benito; and mournfully enough. But the past is passed; why moralize on it? Forget it. See, yon bright sun has forgotten it all, and the blue sea, and the blue sky; these have turned over new leaves."

"Because they have no memory," he dejectedly replied; "because they are not human."

"But these mild trades[135] that now fan your cheek, do they not come with a human-like healing to you? Warm friends, steadfast friends are the trades."

"With their steadfastness they but waft me to my tomb, Señor," was the foreboding response.

"You are saved," cried Captain Delano, more and more astonished and pained; "you are saved: what has cast such a shadow upon you?"

"The negro."

There was silence, while the moody man sat, slowly and unconsciously gathering his mantle about him, as if it were a pall.

There was no more conversation that day.

But if the Spaniard's melancholy sometimes ended in muteness upon topics like the above, there were others upon which he never spoke at all; on which, indeed, all his old reserves were piled. Pass over the worst, and, only to elucidate, let an item or two of these be cited. The dress, so precise and costly, worn by him on the day whose events have been narrated, had not willingly been put on. And that

---

[135] Trade winds.

silver-mounted sword, apparent symbol of despotic command, was not, indeed, a sword, but the ghost of one. The scabbard, artificially stiffened, was empty.

As for the black—whose brain, not body, had schemed and led the revolt, with the plot—his slight frame, inadequate to that which it held, had at once yielded to the superior muscular strength of his captor, in the boat. Seeing all was over, he uttered no sound, and could not be forced to. His aspect seemed to say, since I cannot do deeds, I will not speak words. Put in irons in the hold, with the rest, he was carried to Lima. During the passage, Don Benito did not visit him. Nor then, nor at any time after, would he look at him. Before the tribunal he refused. When pressed by the judges he fainted. On the testimony of the sailors alone rested the legal identity of Babo.

Some months after, dragged to the gibbet at the tail of a mule, the black met his voiceless end. The body was burned to ashes; but for many days, the head, that hive of subtlety, fixed on a pole in the Plaza, met, unabashed, the gaze of the whites; and across the Plaza looked towards St. Bartholomew's church, in whose vaults slept then, as now, the recovered bones of Aranda: and across the Rimac bridge looked towards the monastery, on Mount Agonia without; where, three months after being dismissed by the court, Benito Cereno, borne on the bier, did, indeed, follow his leader.

1855

THE PARADISE OF BACHELORS
AND THE TARTARUS OF MAIDS*

I. The Paradise of Bachelors

It lies not far from Temple-Bar.[1]

Going to it, by the usual way, is like stealing from a heated plain into some cool, deep glen, shady among harboring hills.

Sick with the din and soiled with the mud of Fleet Street—where the Benedick[2] tradesmen are hurrying by, with ledger-lines ruled along their brows, thinking upon rise of bread and fall of babies—you adroitly turn a mystic corner—not a street—glide down a dim, monastic way, flanked by dark, sedate, and solemn

---

* First published in *Harper's New Monthly Magazine* in April 1855. It is a single story with two complementary halves, the "Paradise" of Part One set against the "Tartarus" (in Greek myth, the lowest region of the underworld) of Part Two. Melville's visit to London in 1849 provides the basis for the first part. During the weeks he tried to get *White-Jacket* (1850) published, he was treated with great hospitality by several writers and lawyers; impressed by the conversation and comradeship at a magnificent dinner at Elm Court, Temple (London buildings housing esteemed law societies), he named it the Paradise of Bachelors. The second part also has an autobiographical source in Melville's impressions of Carson's Mill in Dalton, Massachusetts, where he traveled in 1851 to buy a sleigh-load of paper. The complications Elizabeth Melville, (1822–1906), his wife, suffered during pregnancies may account for some of the sexual metaphor in this section.

[1] The stone gateway, designed by the architect Christopher Wren (1632–1723), separating Fleet Street (home of London's book trade) from the Strand (a street that runs along the Thames River).

[2] A recently married man who was formerly a confirmed bachelor, after the bachelor Benedick in Shakespeare's *Much Ado About Nothing*.

piles, and still wending on, give the whole care-worn world the slip, and, disentangled, stand beneath the quiet cloisters[3] of the Paradise of Bachelors.

Sweet are the oases in Sahara; charming the isle-groves of August prairies; delectable pure faith amidst a thousand perfidies: but sweeter, still more charming, most delectable, the dreamy Paradise of Bachelors, found in the stony heart of stunning London.

In mild meditation pace the cloisters; take your pleasure, sip your leisure, in the garden waterward; go linger in the ancient library; go worship in the sculptured chapel: but little have you seen, just nothing do you know, not the sweet kernel have you tasted, till you dine among the banded Bachelors, and see their convivial eyes and glasses sparkle. Not dine in bustling commons,[4] during term-time, in the hall; but tranquilly, by private hint, at a private table; some fine Templar's[5] hospitably invited guest.

Templar? That's a romantic name. Let me see. Brian de Bois G[u]ilbert[6] was a Templar, I believe. Do we understand you to insinuate that those famous Templars still survive in modern London? May the ring of their armed heels be heard, and the rattle of their shields, as in mailed prayer the monk-knights kneel before the consecrated Host? Surely a monk-knight were a curious sight picking his way along the Strand, his gleaming corselet and snowy surcoat[7] spattered by an omnibus. Long-bearded, too, according to his order's rule; his face fuzzy as a pard's;[8] how would the grim ghost look among the crop-haired, close-shaven citizens? We know indeed—sad history recounts it—that a moral blight tainted at last this sacred Brotherhood. Though no sworded foe might outskill them in the fence,[9] yet the worm of luxury crawled beneath their guard, gnawing the core of knightly troth, nibbling the monastic vow, till at last the monk's austerity relaxed to wassailing,[10] and the sworn knights-bachelors grew to be but hypocrites and rakes.

But for all this, quite unprepared were we to learn that Knights-Templars (if at all in being) were so entirely secularized as to be reduced from carving out immortal fame in glorious battling for the Holy Land, to the carving of roast-mutton at a dinner-board. Like Anacreon,[11] do these degenerate Templars now think it sweeter far to fall in banquet than in war? Or, indeed, how can there be any survival of that famous order? Templars in modern London! Templars in their red-cross mantles[12] smoking cigars at the Divan![13] Templars crowded in a railway train, till, stacked with steel helmet, spear, and shield, the whole train looks like one elongated locomotive!

No. The genuine Templar is long since departed. Go view the wondrous tombs

[3] London's Inns of Court (Inner Temple, Middle Temple, Lincoln's Inn, and Gray's Inn), buildings occupied by lawyers and law students.

[4] A large (and hence "bustling") dining room.

[5] A member of the Knights Templar, an order of soldier-monks established in the twelfth century to protect the Holy Sepulchre (thought to be the tomb of Jesus) and Christians traveling to the Holy Land. The order grew corrupt and was dissolved in 1312. The London headquarters gradually became a legal center.

[6] In *Ivanhoe* (1819), by Sir Walter Scott (1771–1832), the Knight Templar Brian de Bois-Guilbert was a villain.

[7] His armor and outercoat.   [8] Leopard's.   [9] In fencing.   [10] Drinking, carousing.

[11] A Greek poet of the sixth century B.C., known chiefly for lyrics celebrating love and wine. According to legend he choked to death on a grape seed.

[12] Loose, sleeveless cloaks with a red cross on a white background, worn by Knights Templar.

[13] An oriental council chamber or a smoking room.

in the Temple Church;[14] see there the rigidly-haughty forms stretched out, with crossed arms upon their stilly hearts, in everlasting and undreaming rest. Like the years before the flood,[15] the bold Knights-Templars are no more. Nevertheless, the name remains, and the nominal society, and the ancient grounds, and some of the ancient edifices. But the iron heel is changed to a boot of patent-leather; the long two-handed sword to a one-handed quill; the monk-giver of gratuitous ghostly counsel now counsels for a fee; the defender of the sarcophagus (if in good practice with his weapon) now has more than one case to defend; the vowed opener and clearer of all highways leading to the Holy Sepulchre, now has it in particular charge to check, to clog, to hinder, and embarrass all the courts and avenues of Law; the knight-combatant of the Saracen, breasting spear-points at Acre,[16] now fights law-points in Westminister Hall.[17] The helmet is a wig.[18] Struck by Time's enchanter's wand, the Templar is to-day a Lawyer.

But, like many others tumbled from proud glory's height—like the apple, hard on the bough but mellow on the ground—the Templar's fall has but made him all the finer fellow.

I dare say those old warrior-priests were but gruff and grouty at the best; cased in Birmingham hardware,[19] how could their crimped arms give yours or mine a hearty shake? Their proud, ambitious, monkish souls clasped shut, like horn-book missals;[20] their very faces clapped in bombshells;[21] what sort of genial men were these? But best of comrades, most affable of hosts, capital diner is the modern Templar. His wit and wine are both of sparkling brands.

The church and cloisters, courts and vaults, lanes and passages, banquet-halls, refectories, libraries, terraces, gardens, broad walks, domicils, and dessert-rooms, covering a very large space of ground, and all grouped in central neighborhood, and quite sequestered from the old city's surrounding din; and every thing about the place being kept in most bachelor-like particularity, no part of London offers to a quiet wight so agreeable a refuge.

The Temple is, indeed, a city by itself. A city with all the best appurtenances, as the above enumeration shows. A city with a park to it, and flower-beds, and a river-side—the Thames flowing by as openly, in one part, as by Eden's primal garden flowed the mild Euphrates.[22] In what is now the Temple Garden the old Crusaders used to exercise their steeds and lances; the modern Templars now lounge on the benches beneath the trees, and, switching their patent-leather boots, in gay discourse exercise at repartee.

Long lines of stately portraits in the banquet-halls, show what great men of mark—famous nobles, judges, and Lord Chancellors—have in their time been

---

[14] The Round Church, or Temple Church, built in 1185 and modeled on the Church of the Holy Sepulchre in Jerusalem, belonged to the Inner Temple and the Middle Temple.

[15] The biblical flood in Genesis 7.

[16] A seaport in Palestine that had been defended by the Knights Templar but fell to the Saracens, or Moslems, in 1291.

[17] Used as a court of law in the nineteenth century.

[18] English lawyers, or barristers, wear wigs in court.

[19] Melville pretends that the Templar's armor, or "hardware," came from the modern industrial city of Birmingham, England.

[20] Devotional books with the pages mounted on a board and covered by animal horn.

[21] Helmets worn by knights in armor.

[22] Major river of arid Southwest Asia, believed by some to have run near the Garden of Eden.

Templars. But all Templars are not known to universal fame; though, if the having warm hearts and warmer welcomes, full minds and fuller cellars, and giving good advice and glorious dinners, spiced with rare divertisements of fun and fancy, merit immortal mention, set down, ye muses, the names of R. F. C.[23] and his imperial brother.

Though to be a Templar, in the one true sense, you must needs be a lawyer, or a student at the law, and be ceremoniously enrolled as member of the order, yet as many such, though Templars, do not reside within the Temple's precincts, though they may have their offices there, just so, on the other hand, there are many residents of the hoary old domicils who are not admitted Templars. If being, say, a lounging gentleman and bachelor, or a quiet, unmarried, literary man, charmed with the soft seclusion of the spot, you much desire to pitch your shady tent among the rest in this serene encampment, then you must make some special friend among the order, and procure him to rent, in his name but at your charge, whatever vacant chamber you may find to suit.

Thus, I suppose, did Dr. Johnson,[24] that nominal Benedick and widower but virtual bachelor, when for a space he resided here. So, too, did that undoubted bachelor and rare good soul, Charles Lamb.[25] And hundreds more, of sterling spirits, Brethren of the Order of Celibacy, from time to time have dined, and slept, and tabernacled here. Indeed, the place is all a honeycomb of offices and domicils. Like any cheese, it is quite perforated through and through in all directions with the snug cells of bachelors. Dear, delightful spot! Ah! when I bethink me of the sweet hours there passed, enjoying such genial hospitalities beneath those time-honored roofs, my heart only finds due utterance through poetry; and, with a sigh, I softly sing, "Carry me back to old Virginny!"[26]

Such then, at large, is the Paradise of Bachelors. And such I found it one pleasant afternoon in the smiling month of May, when, sallying from my hotel in Trafalgar Square,[27] I went to keep my dinner-appointment with that fine Barrister, Bachelor, and Bencher,[28] R. F. C. (he *is* the first and second, and *should be* the third; I hereby nominate him), whose card I kept fast pinched between my gloved forefinger and thumb, and every now and then snatched still another look at the pleasant address inscribed beneath the name, "No. —, Elm Court, Temple."

At the core he was a right bluff, care-free, right comfortable, and most companionable Englishman. If on a first acquaintance he seemed reserved, quite icy in his air—patience; this Champagne will thaw. And if it never do, better frozen Champagne than liquid vinegar.

There were nine gentlemen, all bachelors, at the dinner. One was from "No. —, King's Bench Walk, Temple;" a second, third, and fourth, and fifth, from various courts or passages christened with some similarly rich resounding syllables. It was indeed a sort of Senate of the Bachelors, sent to this dinner from widely-scattered districts, to represent the general celibacy of the Temple. Nay it was, by representation, a Grand Parliament of the best Bachelors in universal Lon-

---

[23] Robert Francis Cooke, Melville's host at a bachelor dinner at Elm Court in December 1849.

[24] Samuel Johnson (1709–1784), a leading literary scholar and critic, whose *Dictionary of the English Language* (1755) was the first comprehensive English dictionary.

[25] Lamb (1775–1834) was an English essayist.

[26] A pun about going back to the state of virginity.

[27] A square in London, named after Lord Horatio Nelson's naval victory at Trafalgar, Spain, in 1805; it features a statue of Nelson (1758–1805) erected in 1843.

[28] A judge, a governor of an Inn of Court; R. F. C. is a lawyer, a bachelor, and "*should be*" a judge, according to the narrator.

don; several of those present being from distant quarters of the town, noted imme-morial seats of lawyers and unmarried men—Lincoln's Inn, Furnival's Inn;[29] and one gentleman, upon whom I looked with a sort of collateral awe, hailed from the spot where Lord Verulam[30] once abode a bachelor—Gray's Inn.

The apartment was well up toward heaven. I know not how many strange old stairs I climbed to get to it. But a good dinner, with famous company, should be well earned. No doubt our host had his dining-room so high with a view to secure the prior exercise necessary to the due relishing and digesting of it.

The furniture was wonderfully unpretending, old, and snug. No new shining mahogany, sticky with undried varnish; no uncomfortably luxurious ottomans, and sofas too fine to use, vexed you in this sedate apartment. It is a thing which every sensible American should learn from every sensible Englishman, that glare and glitter, gimcracks and gewgaws, are not indispensable to domestic solace-ment. The American Benedick snatches, down-town, a tough chop in a gilded show-box;[31] the English bachelor leisurely dines at home on that incomparable South Down of his, off a plain deal board.[32]

The ceiling of the room was low. Who wants to dine under the dome of St. Peter's?[33] High ceilings! If that is your demand, and the higher the better, and you be so very tall, then go dine out with the topping giraffe in the open air.

In good time the nine gentlemen sat down to nine covers,[34] and soon were fairly under way.

If I remember right, ox-tail soup inaugurated the affair. Of a rich russet hue, its agreeable flavor dissipated my first confounding of its main ingredient with team-ster's gads and the raw-hides of ushers.[35] (By way of interlude, we here drank a little claret.) Neptune's was the next tribute rendered—turbot[36] coming second; snow-white, flaky, and just gelatinous enough, not too turtleish in its unctuous-ness.

(At this point we refreshed ourselves with a glass of sherry.) After these light skirmishers had vanished, the heavy artillery of the feast marched in, led by that well-known English generalissimo, roast beef. For aid[e]s-de-camp we had a sad-dle of mutton, a fat turkey, a chicken-pie, and endless other savory things; while for avant-couriers came nine silver flagons of humming ale.[37] This heavy ord-nance,[38] having departed on the track of the light skirmishers, a picked brigade of game-fowl encamped upon the board, their camp-fires lit by the ruddiest of de-canters.

Tarts and puddings followed, with innumerable niceties; then cheese and crack-ers. (By way of ceremony, simply, only to keep up good old fashions, we here each drank a glass of good old port.)

The cloth was now removed; and like Blucher's[39] army coming in at the death

---

[29] An Inn of Chancery, later destroyed.

[30] Sir Francis Bacon (1561–1626), an English writer, scientist, and statesman.

[31] A gaudy restaurant.

[32] Mutton, from the South Down breed of sheep, served on a pine board.

[33] St. Peter's Cathedral in Rome, the world's largest church, with a dome 404 feet high.

[34] Place settings.

[35] Goads, or whips made from oxtails, and rawhide whips of assistant teachers.

[36] A highly esteemed flatfish (hence a tribute from Neptune, the Roman sea god).

[37] For the advance guard of an army came nine silver bottles of ale still bubbly enough to hum.

[38] Cannon or artillery.

[39] Gebhard von Blucher (1742–1819), leader of Prussian forces in the defeat of Napoleon at Waterloo in 1815.

on the field of Waterloo, in marched a fresh detachment of bottles, dusty with their hurried march.

All these manœuvrings of the forces were superintended by a surprising old field-marshal (I can not school myself to call him by the inglorious name of waiter), with snowy hair and napkin, and a head like Socrates.[40] Amidst all the hilarity of the feast, intent on important business, he disdained to smile. Venerable man!

I have above endeavored to give some slight schedule of the general plan of operations. But any one knows that a good, genial dinner is a sort of pell-mell, indiscriminate affair, quite baffling to detail in all particulars. Thus, I spoke of taking a glass of claret, and a glass of sherry, and a glass of port, and a mug of ale—all at certain specific periods and times. But those were merely the state bumpers,[41] so to speak. Innumerable impromptu glasses were drained between the periods of those grand imposing ones.

The nine bachelors seemed to have the most tender concern for each other's health. All the time, in flowing wine, they most earnestly expressed their sincerest wishes for the entire well-being and lasting hygiene of the gentlemen on the right and on the left. I noticed that when one of these kind bachelors desired a little more wine (just for his stomach's sake, like Timothy[42]), he would not help himself to it unless some other bachelor would join him. It seemed held something indelicate, selfish, and unfraternal, to be seen taking a lonely, unparticipated glass. Meantime, as the wine ran apace, the spirits of the company grew more and more to perfect genialness and unconstraint. They related all sorts of pleasant stories. Choice experiences in their private lives were now brought out, like choice brands of Moselle or Rhenish,[43] only kept for particular company. One told us how mellowly he lived when a student at Oxford; with various spicy anecdotes of most frank-hearted noble lords, his liberal companions. Another bachelor, a gray-headed man, with a sunny face, who, by his own account, embraced every opportunity of leisure to cross over into the Low Countries,[44] on sudden tours of inspection of the fine old Flemish architecture there—this learned, white-haired, sunny-faced old bachelor, excelled in his descriptions of the elaborate splendors of those old guild-halls, town-halls, and stadthold-houses, to be seen in the land of the ancient Flemings. A third was a great frequenter of the British Museum, and knew all about scores of wonderful antiquities, of Oriental manuscripts, and costly books without a duplicate. A fourth had lately returned from a trip to Old Granada,[45] and, of course, was full of Saracenic scenery. A fifth had a funny case in law to tell. A sixth was erudite in wines. A seventh had a strange characteristic anecdote of the private life of the Iron Duke,[46] never printed, and never before announced in any public or private company. An eighth had lately been amusing his evenings, now and then, with translating a comic poem of Pulci's.[47] He quoted for us the more amusing passages.

---

[40] Socrates (470?–399 B.C.) was an Athenian philosopher and teacher.

[41] Large drinking glasses filled to the brim, here for drinking toasts.

[42] "Drink no longer water, but use a little wine for thy stomach's sake and thine often infirmities," from 1 Timothy 5:23.

[43] Wines from Germany's Moselle or Rhine rivers regions.

[44] The Netherlands, Belgium, and Luxembourg; Melville may be echoing Shakespeare in *A Comedy of Errors* (III.ii), with "Low Countries" suggesting lower parts of the body.

[45] A province in Spain.

[46] The Duke of Wellington (1762–1852), leader of the British forces that defeated Napoleon at Waterloo in 1815.

[47] Luigi Pulci (1432–1484), a Florentine poet known for the epic *Il Morgante Maggiore* (1483).

And so the evening slipped along, the hours told, not by a water-clock, like King Alfred's, but a wine-chronometer.[48] Meantime the table seemed a sort of Epsom Heath;[49] a regular ring, where the decanters galloped round. For fear one decanter should not with sufficient speed reach his destination, another was sent express after him to hurry him; and then a third to hurry the second; and so on with a fourth and fifth. And throughout all this nothing loud, nothing unmannerly, nothing turbulent. I am quite sure, from the scrupulous gravity and austerity of his air, that had Socrates, the field-marshal, perceived aught of indecorum in the company he served, he would have forthwith departed without giving warning. I afterward learned that, during the repast, an invalid bachelor in an adjoining chamber enjoyed his first sound refreshing slumber in three long, weary weeks.

It was the very perfection of quiet absorption of good living, good drinking, good feeling, and good talk. We were a band of brothers. Comfort—fraternal, household comfort, was the grand trait of the affair. Also, you could plainly see that these easy-hearted men had no wives or children to give an anxious thought. Almost all of them were travelers, too; for bachelors alone can travel freely, and without any twinges of their consciences touching desertion of the fire-side.

The thing called pain, the bugbear styled trouble—those two legends seemed preposterous to their bachelor imaginations. How could men of liberal sense, ripe scholarship in the world, and capacious philosophical and convivial understandings—how could they suffer themselves to be imposed upon by such monkish fables? Pain! Trouble! As well talk of Catholic miracles. No such thing.—Pass the sherry, Sir.—Pooh, pooh! Can't be!—The port, Sir, if you please. Nonsense; don't tell me so.—The decanter stops with you, Sir, I believe.

And so it went.

Not long after the cloth was drawn our host glanced significantly upon Socrates, who, solemnly stepping to a stand, returned with an immense convolved horn, a regular Jericho horn,[50] mounted with polished silver, and otherwise chased[51] and curiously enriched; not omitting two life-like goat's heads, with four more horns of solid silver, projecting from opposite sides of the mouth of the noble main horn.

Not having heard that our host was a performer on the bugle, I was surprised to see him lift this horn from the table, as if he were about to blow an inspiring blast. But I was relieved from this, and set quite right as touching the purposes of the horn, by his now inserting his thumb and forefinger into its mouth; whereupon a slight aroma was stirred up, and my nostrils were greeted with the smell of some choice Rappee.[52] It was a mull of snuff. It went the rounds. Capital idea this, thought I, of taking snuff about this juncture. This goodly fashion must be introduced among my countrymen at home, further ruminated I.

The remarkable decorum of the nine bachelors—a decorum not to be affected by any quantity of wine—a decorum unassailable by any degree of mirthfulness—this was again set in a forcible light to me, by now observing that, though they took snuff very freely, yet not a man so far violated the proprieties, or so far molested the invalid bachelor in the adjoining room as to indulge himself in a

---

[48] Alfred the Great (849–899), king of Wessex, England, from 871 to 899, reportedly designed a clepsydra, or clock that measures time by the flow of water. Melville is saying that time at this festive dinner should be measured by the flow of wine.

[49] A famous racetrack in Epsom, Surrey, England.

[50] In Joshua 6:1–20 seven Israelite priests circled the city of Jericho while they blew trumpets of rams' horns; on the seventh day the walls fell, and Joshua took the city.

[51] Embossed.   [52] A pungent snuff, kept in a mull, or small box.

sneeze. The snuff was snuffed silently, as if it had been some fine innoxious[53] powder brushed off the wings of butterflies.

But fine though they be, bachelors' dinners, like bachelors' lives, can not endure forever. The time came for breaking up. One by one the bachelors took their hats, and two by two, and arm-in-arm they descended, still conversing, to the flagging of the court; some going to their neighboring chambers to turn over the Decameron[54] ere retiring for the night; some to smoke a cigar, promenading in the garden on the cool river-side; some to make for the street, call a hack, and be driven snugly to their distant lodgings.

I was the last lingerer.

"Well," said my smiling host, "what do you think of the Temple here, and the sort of life we bachelors make out to live in it?"

"Sir," said I, with a burst of admiring candor—"Sir, this is the very Paradise of Bachelors!"

II. The Tartarus of Maids

It lies not far from Woedolor Mountain in New England. Turning to the east, right out from among bright farms and sunny meadows, nodding in early June with odorous grasses, you enter ascendingly among bleak hills. These gradually close in upon a dusky pass, which, from the violent Gulf Stream of air unceasingly driving between its cloven walls of haggard rock, as well as from the tradition of a crazy spinster's hut having long ago stood somewhere hereabouts, is called the Mad Maid's Bellows'-pipe.

Winding along at the bottom of the gorge is a dangerously narrow wheel-road, occupying the bed of a former torrent. Following this road to its highest point, you stand as within a Dantean gateway.[1] From the steepness of the walls here, their strangely ebon hue, and the sudden contraction of the gorge, this particular point is called the Black Notch. The ravine now expandingly descends into a great, purple, hopper-shaped[2] hollow, far sunk among many Plutonian,[3] shaggy-wooded mountains. By the country people this hollow is called the Devil's Dungeon. Sounds of torrents fall on all sides upon the ear. These rapid waters unite at last in one turbid brick-colored stream, boiling through a flume among enormous boulders. They call this strange-colored torrent Blood River. Gaining a dark precipice it wheels suddenly to the west, and makes one maniac spring of sixty feet into the arms of a stunted wood of gray-haired pines, between which it thence eddies on its further way down to the invisible lowlands.

Conspicuously crowning a rocky bluff high to one side, at the cataract's verge, is the ruin of an old saw-mill, built in those primitive times when vast pines and hemlocks superabounded throughout the neighboring region. The black-mossed bulk of those immense, rough-hewn, and spike-knotted logs, here and there tumbled all together, in long abandonment and decay, or left in solitary, perilous

---

[53] Harmless (not noxious).

[54] A group of one hundred tales, many of them bawdy, by the Italian writer Giovanni Boccaccio (1313–1375).

[1] In his *Inferno* the Italian poet Dante (1265–1321) describes the entrance to Hell; over the entrance is the statement "Abandon all hope, ye who enter here." This description contrasts with that of the Christopher Wren gateway, Temple Bar, at the outset of "The Paradise of Bachelors."

[2] Shaped like a funnel.   [3] Of Hades, the underworld in Greek myth.

projection over the cataract's gloomy brink, impart to this rude wooden ruin not only much of the aspect of one of rough-quarried stone, but also a sort of feudal, Rhineland, and Thurmberg[4] look, derived from the pinnacled wildness of the neighboring scenery.

Not far from the bottom of the Dungeon stands a large white-washed building, relieved, like some great whited sepulchre,[5] against the sullen background of mountain-side firs, and other hardy evergreens, inaccessibly rising in grim terraces for some two thousand feet.

The building is a paper-mill.

Having embarked on a large scale in the seedsman's business (so extensively and broadcast, indeed, that at length my seeds were distributed through all the Eastern and Northern States, and even fell into the far soil of Missouri and the Carolinas), the demand for paper at my place became so great, that the expenditure soon amounted to a most important item in the general account. It need hardly be hinted how paper comes into use with seedsmen, as envelopes. These are mostly made of yellowish paper, folded square; and when filled, are all but flat, and being stamped, and superscribed with the nature of the seeds contained, assume not a little the appearance of business-letters ready for the mail. Of these small envelopes I used an incredible quantity—several hundreds of thousands in a year. For a time I had purchased my paper from the wholesale dealers in a neighboring town. For economy's sake, and partly for the adventure of the trip, I now resolved to cross the mountains, some sixty miles, and order my future paper at the Devil's Dungeon paper-mill.

The sleighing being uncommonly fine toward the end of January, and promising to hold so for no small period, in spite of the bitter cold I started one gray Friday noon in my pung,[6] well fitted with buffalo and wolf robes; and, spending one night on the road, next noon came in sight of Woedolor Mountain.

The far summit fairly smoked with frost; white vapors curled up from its white-wooded top, as from a chimney. The intense congelation made the whole country look like one petrifaction.[7] The steel shoes of my pung craunched and gritted over the vitreous, chippy snow, as if it had been broken glass. The forests here and there skirting the route, feeling the same all-stiffening influence, their inmost fibres penetrated with the cold, strangely groaned—not in the swaying branches merely, but likewise in the vertical trunk—as the fitful gusts remorselessly swept through them. Brittle with excessive frost, many colossal tough-grained maples, snapped in twain like pipe-stems, cumbered the unfeeling earth.

Flaked all over with frozen sweat, white as a milky ram, his nostrils at each breath sending forth two horn-shaped shoots of heated respiration, Black, my good horse, but six years old, started at a sudden turn, where, right across the track—not ten minutes fallen—an old distorted hemlock lay, darkly undulatory as an anaconda.

Gaining the Bellows'-pipe, the violent blast, dead from behind, all but shoved by high-backed pung up-hill. The gust shrieked through the shivered pass, as if

---

[4] A fourteenth-century fortified castle on the Rhine River in Germany.

[5] In Matthew 23:27 Jesus depicts the Scribes and Pharisees as "whited sepulchres [tombs], which indeed appear beautiful outward, but are within full of dead men's bones, and of all uncleanness." The contrasting allusion in "The Paradise of Bachelors" is to the Church of the Holy Sepulcher in Jerusalem (the presumed site of the tomb of Jesus).

[6] A one-horse sleigh on runners.

[7] The scene is congealing as if it is petrified (turned to stone).

laden with lost spirits bound to the unhappy world. Ere gaining the summit, Black, my horse, as if exasperated by the cutting wind, slung out with his strong hind legs, tore the light pung straight up-hill, and sweeping grazingly through the narrow notch, sped downward madly past the ruined saw-mill. Into the Devil's Dungeon horse and cataract rushed together.

With might and main, quitting my seat and robes, and standing backward, with one foot braced against the dash-board, I rasped and churned the bit, and stopped him just in time to avoid collision, at a turn, with the bleak nozzle of a rock, couchant[8] like a lion in the way—a road-side rock.

At first I could not discover the paper-mill.

The whole hollow gleamed with the white, except, here and there, where a pinnacle of granite showed one wind-swept angle bare. The mountains stood pinned in shrouds—a pass of Alpine corpses. Where stands the mill? Suddenly a whirling, humming sound broke upon my ear. I looked, and there, like an arrested avalanche, lay the large white-washed factory. It was subordinately surrounded by a cluster of other and smaller buildings, some of which, from their cheap, blank air, great length, gregarious windows, and comfortless expression, no doubt were boarding-houses of the operatives.[9] A snow-white hamlet amidst the snows. Various rude, irregular squares and courts resulted from the somewhat picturesque clusterings of these buildings, owing to the broken, rocky nature of the ground, which forbade all method in their relative arrangement. Several narrow lanes and alleys, too, partly blocked with snow fallen from the roof, cut up the hamlet in all directions.

When, turning from the traveled highway, jingling with bells of numerous farmers—who, availing themselves of the fine sleighing, were dragging their wood to market—and frequently diversified with swift cutters dashing from inn to inn of the scattered villages—when, I say, turning from that bustling main-road, I by degrees wound into the Mad Maid's Bellows'-pipe, and saw the grim Black Notch beyond, then something latent, as well as something obvious in the time and scene, strangely brought back to my mind my first sight of dark and grimy Temple-Bar. And when Black, my horse, went darting through the Notch, perilously grazing its rocky wall, I remembered being in a runaway London Omnibus, which in much the same sort of style, though by no means at an equal rate, dashed through the ancient arch of Wren.[10] Though the two objects did by no means completely correspond, yet this partial inadequacy but served to tinge the similitude not less with the vividness than the disorder of a dream. So that, when upon reining up at the protruding rock I at last caught sight of the quaint groupings of the factory-buildings, and with the traveled highway and the Notch behind, found myself all alone, silently and privily stealing through deep-cloven passages into this sequestered spot, and saw the long, high-gabled main factory edifice, with a rude tower—for hoisting heavy boxes—at one end, standing among its crowded outbuildings and boarding-houses, as the Temple Church amidst the surrounding offices and dormitories, and when the marvelous retirement of this mysterious mountain nook fastened its whole spell upon me, then, what memory lacked, all tributary imagination furnished, and I said to myself, "This is the very counterpart of the Paradise of Bachelors, but snowed upon, and frost-painted to a sepulchre."

---

[8] Crouching.   [9] Factory workers.
[10] The gateway designed by Christopher Wren at Temple Bar, described at the outset of "The Paradise of Bachelors."

Dismounting, and warily picking my way down the dangerous declivity—horse and man both sliding now and then upon the icy ledges—at length I drove, or the blast drove me, into the largest square, before one side of the main edifice. Piercingly and shrilly the shotted blast blew by the corner; and redly and demoniacally boiled Blood River at one side. A long wood-pile, of many scores of cords, all glittering in mail of crusted ice, stood crosswise in the square. A row of horse-posts, their north sides plastered with adhesive snow, flanked the factory wall. The bleak frost packed and paved the square as with some ringing metal.

The inverted similitude recurred—"The sweet, tranquil Temple garden, with the Thames bordering its green beds," strangely meditated I.

But where are the gay bachelors?

Then, as I and my horse stood shivering in the wind-spray, a girl ran from a neighboring dormitory door, and throwing her thin apron over her bare head, made for the opposite building.

"One moment, my girl; is there no shed hereabouts which I may drive into?"

Pausing, she turned upon me a face pale with work, and blue with cold; an eye supernatural with unrelated misery.

"Nay," faltered I. "I mistook you. Go on; I want nothing."

Leading my horse close to the door from which she had come, I knocked. Another pale, blue girl appeared, shivering in the doorway as, to prevent the blast, she jealously held the door ajar.

"Nay, I mistake again. In God's name shut the door. But hold, is there no man about?"

That moment a dark-complexioned well-wrapped personage passed, making for the factory door, and spying him coming, the girl rapidly closed the other one.

"Is there no horse-shed here, Sir?"

"Yonder, to the wood-shed," he replied, and disappeared inside the factory.

With much ado I managed to wedge in horse and pung between the scattered piles of wood all sawn and split. Then, blanketing my horse, and piling my buffalo on the blanket's top, and tucking in its edges well around the breast-band and breeching, so that the wind might not strip him bare, I tied him fast, and ran lamely for the factory door, stiff with frost, and cumbered with my driver's dreadnaught.[11]

Immediately I found myself standing in a spacious place, intolerably lighted by long rows of windows, focusing inward the snowy scene without.

At rows of blank-looking counters sat rows of blank-looking girls, with blank, white folders in their blank hands, all blankly folding blank paper.

In one corner stood some huge frame of ponderous iron, with a vertical thing like a piston periodically rising and falling upon a heavy wooden block. Before it—its tame minister—stood a tall girl, feeding the iron animal with half-quires[12] of rose-hued note paper, which, at every downward dab of the piston-like machine, received in the corner the impress of a wreath of roses. I looked from the rosy paper to the pallid cheek, but said nothing.

Seated before a long apparatus, strung with long, slender strings like any harp, another girl was feeding it with foolscap sheets,[13] which, so soon as they curiously traveled from her on the cords, were withdrawn at the opposite end of the

---

[11] A thick woolen coat.   [12] Twelve sheets of paper.

[13] Paper sheets measuring approximately 13 x 16 or 17 inches, so called because of the conical design impressed on them by papermakers.

machine by a second girl. They came to the first girl blank; they went to the second girl ruled.

I looked upon the first girl's brow, and saw it was young and fair; I looked upon the second girl's brow, and saw it was ruled and wrinkled. Then, as I still looked, the two—for some small variety to the monotony—changed places; and where had stood the young, fair brow, now stood the ruled and wrinkled one.

Perched high upon a narrow platform, and still higher upon a high stool crowning it, sat another figure serving some other iron animal; while below the platform sat her mate in some sort of reciprocal attendance.

Not a syllable was breathed. Nothing was heard but the low, steady, overruling hum of the iron animals. The human voice was banished from the spot. Machinery—that vaunted slave of humanity—here stood menially served by human beings, who served mutely and cringingly as the slave serves the Sultan. The girls did not so much seem accessory wheels to the general machinery as mere cogs to the wheels.

All this scene around me was instantaneously taken in at one sweeping glance—even before I had proceeded to unwind the heavy fur tippet[14] from around my neck. But as soon as this fell from me the dark-complexioned man, standing close by, raised a sudden cry, and seizing my arm, dragged me out into the open air, and without pausing for a word instantly caught up some congealed snow and began rubbing both my cheeks.

"Two white spots like the whites of your eyes," he said; "man, your cheeks are frozen."

"That may well be," muttered I; " 'tis some wonder the frost of the Devil's Dungeon strikes in no deeper. Rub away."

Soon a horrible, tearing pain caught at my reviving cheeks. Two gaunt bloodhounds, one on each side, seemed mumbling them. I seemed Actæon.[15]

Presently, when all was over, I re-entered the factory, made known my business, concluded it satisfactorily, and then begged to be conducted throughout the place to view it.

"Cupid is the boy for that," said the dark-complexioned man. "Cupid!" and by this odd fancy-name calling a dimpled, red-cheeked, spirited-looking, forward little fellow, who was rather impudently, I thought, gliding about among the passive-looking girls—like a gold fish through hueless waves—yet doing nothing in particular that I could see, the man bade him lead the stranger through the edifice.

"Come first and see the water-wheel," said this lively lad, with the air of boyishly-brisk importance.

Quitting the folding-room, we crossed some damp, cold boards, and stood beneath a great wet shed, incessantly showering with foam, like the green barnacled bow of some East Indiaman[16] in a gale. Round and round here went the enormous revolutions of the dark colossal water-wheel, grim with its one immutable purpose.

"This sets our whole machinery a-going, Sir; in every part of all these buildings; where the girls work and all."

I looked, and saw that the turbid waters of Blood River had not changed their hue by coming under the use of man.

---

[14] A scarf.

[15] According to Greek myth, Artemis, the goddess of the hunt, changed Actaeon into a stag because he watched her bathing, and he was torn to pieces by his own dogs.

[16] A large sailing ship used in trade with India (the East Indies).

"You make only blank paper; no printing of any sort, I suppose? All blank paper, don't you?"

"Certainly; what else should a paper-factory make?"

The lad here looked at me as if suspicious of my common-sense.

"Oh, to be sure!" said I, confused and stammering; "it only struck me as so strange that red waters should turn out pale chee—paper, I mean."

He took me up a wet and rickety stair to a great light room, furnished with no visible thing but rude, manger-like receptacles running all round its sides; and up to these mangers, like so many mares haltered to the rack, stood rows of girls. Before each was vertically thrust up a long, glittering scythe, immovably fixed at bottom to the manger-edge. The curve of the scythe, and its having no snath[17] to it, made it look exactly like a sword. To and fro, across the sharp edge, the girls forever dragged long strips of rags, washed white, picked from baskets at one side; thus ripping asunder every seam, and converting the tatters almost into lint. The air swam with the fine, poisonous particles, which from all sides darted, sub-tilely, as motes in sun-beams, into the lungs.

"This is the rag-room," coughed the boy.

"You find it rather stifling here," coughed I, in answer; "but the girls don't cough."

"Oh, they are used to it."

"Where do you get such hosts of rags?" picking up a handful from a basket.

"Some from the country round about; some from far over sea—Leghorn[18] and London."

" 'Tis not unlikely, then," murmured I, "that among these heaps of rags there may be some old shirts, gathered from the dormitories of the Paradise of Bache-lors. But the buttons are all dropped off. Pray, my lad, do you ever find any bachelor's buttons hereabouts?"

"None grow in this part of the country. The Devil's Dungeon is no place for flowers."

"Oh! you mean the *flowers* so called—the Bachelor's Buttons?"

"And was not that what you asked about? Or did you mean the gold bosom-buttons of our boss, Old Bach,[19] as our whispering girls all call him?"

"The man, then, I saw below is a bachelor, is he?"

"Oh, yes, he's a Bach."

"The edges of those swords, they are turned outward from the girls, if I see right; but their rags and fingers fly so, I can not distinctly see."

"Turned outward."

Yes, murmured I to myself; I see it now; turned outward; and each erected sword is so borne, edge-outward, before each girl. If my reading fails me not, just so, of old, condemned state-prisoners went from the hall of judgment to their doom: an officer before, bearing a sword, its edge turned outward in significance of their fatal sentence. So, through consumptive pallors[20] of this blank, raggy life, go these white girls to death.

"Those scythes look very sharp," again turning toward the boy.

"Yes; they have to keep them so. Look!"

That moment two of the girls, dropping their rags, plied each a whet-stone up

---

[17] Handle.   [18] Livorno, an Italian port on the Mediterranean Sea.
[19] Bachelor (pronounced *batch*).   [20] The paleness that accompanies consumption or tuberculosis.

and down the sword-blade. My unaccustomed blood curdled at the sharp shriek of the tormented steel.

Their own executioners; themselves whetting the very swords that slay them; meditated I.

"What makes those girls so sheet-white, my lad?"

"Why"—with a roguish twinkle, pure ignorant drollery, not knowing heartlessness—"I suppose the handling of such white bits of sheets all the time makes them so sheety."

"Let us leave the rag-room now, my lad."

More tragical and more inscrutably mysterious than any mystic sight, human or machine, throughout the factory, was the strange innocence of cruel-heartedness in this usage-hardened boy.

"And now," said he, cheerily, "I suppose you want to see our great machine, which cost us twelve thousand dollars only last autumn. That's the machine that makes the paper, too. This way, Sir."

Following him, I crossed a large, bespattered place, with two great round vats in it, full of a white, wet, woolly-looking stuff, not unlike the albuminous part of an egg, soft-boiled.

"There," said Cupid, tapping the vats carelessly, "these are the first beginnings of the paper; this white pulp you see. Look how it swims bubbling round and round, moved by the paddle here. From hence it pours from both vats into that one common channel yonder; and so goes, mixed up and leisurely, to the great machine. And now for that."

He led me into a room, stifling with a strange, blood-like, abdominal heat, as if here, true enough, were being finally developed the germinous particles lately seen.

Before me, rolled out like some long Eastern manuscript, lay stretched one continuous length of iron frame-work—multitudinous and mystical, with all sorts of rollers, wheels, and cylinders, in slowly-measured and unceasing motion.

"Here first comes the pulp now," said Cupid, pointing to the nighest end of the machine. "See; first it pours out and spreads itself upon this wide, sloping board; and then—look—slides, thin and quivering, beneath the first roller there. Follow on now, and see it as it slides from under that to the next cylinder. There; see how it has become just a very little less pulpy now. One step more, and it grows still more to some slight consistence. Still another cylinder, and it is so knitted—though as yet mere dragon-fly wing—that it forms an air-bridge here, like a suspended cobweb, between two more separated rollers; and flowing over the last one, and under again, and doubling about there out of sight for a minute among all those mixed cylinders you indistinctly see, it reappears here, looking now at last a little less like pulp and more like paper, but still quite delicate and defective yet awhile. But—a little further onward, Sir, if you please—here now, at this further point, it puts on something of a real look, as if it might turn out to be something you might possibly handle in the end. But it's not yet done, Sir. Good way to travel yet, and plenty more of cylinders must roll it."

"Bless my soul!" said I, amazed at the elongation, interminable convolutions, and deliberate slowness of the machine; "it must take a long time for the pulp to pass from end to end, and come out paper."

"Oh! not so long," smiled the precocious lad, with a superior and patronizing air; "only nine minutes. But look; you may try it for yourself. Have you a bit of paper? Ah! here's a bit on the floor. Now mark that with any word you please, and let me dab it on here, and we'll see how long before it comes out at the other end."

"Well, let me see," said I, taking out my pencil; "come, I'll mark it with your name."

Bidding me take out my watch, Cupid adroitly dropped the inscribed slip on an exposed part of the incipient mass.

Instantly my eye marked the second-hand on my dial-plate.

Slowly I followed the slip, inch by inch; sometimes pausing for full half a minute as it disappeared beneath inscrutable groups of the lower cylinders, but only gradually to emerge again; and so, on, and on, and on—inch by inch; now in open sight, sliding along like a freckle on the quivering sheet; and then again wholly vanished; and so, on, and on, and on—inch by inch; all the time the main sheet growing more and more to final firmness—when, suddenly, I saw a sort of paper-fall, not wholly unlike a water-fall; a scissory sound smote my ear, as of some cord being snapped; and down dropped an unfolded sheet of perfect foolscap, with my "Cupid" half faded out of it, and still moist and warm.

My travels were at an end, for here was the end of the machine.

"Well, how long was it?" said Cupid.

"Nine minutes to a second," replied I, watch in hand.

"I told you so."

For a moment a curious emotion filled me, not wholly unlike that which one might experience at the fulfillment of some mysterious prophecy. But how absurd, thought I again; the thing is a mere machine, the essence of which is unvarying punctuality and precision.

Previously absorbed by the wheels and cylinders, my attention was now directed to a sad-looking woman standing by.

"That is rather an elderly person so silently tending the machine-end here. She would not seem wholly used to it either."

"Oh," knowingly whispered Cupid, through the din, "she only came last week. She was a nurse formerly. But the business is poor in these parts, and she's left it. But look at the paper she is piling there."

"Ay, foolscap," handling the piles of moist, warm sheets, which continually were being delivered into the woman's waiting hands. "Don't you turn out any thing but foolscap at this machine?"

"Oh, sometimes, but not often, we turn out finer work—cream-laid and royal sheets, we call them. But foolscap being in chief demand, we turn out foolscap most."

It was very curious. Looking at that blank paper continually dropping, dropping, dropping, my mind ran on in wonderings of those strange uses to which those thousand sheets eventually would be put. All sorts of writings would be writ on those now vacant things—sermons, lawyers' briefs, physicians' prescriptions, love-letters, marriage certificates, bills of divorce, registers of births, death-warrants, and so on, without end. Then recurring back to them as they here lay all blank, I could not but bethink me of that celebrated comparison of John Locke,[21] who, in demonstration of his theory that man had no innate ideas, compared the human mind at birth to a sheet of blank paper; something destined to be scribbled on, but what sort of characters no soul might tell.

---

[21] Locke (1632–1704) was an English philosopher who compared the mind of a newborn infant to a blank page, or *tabula rasa*, in *Essay Concerning Human Understanding* (1690).

Pacing slowing to and fro along the involved machine, still humming with its play, I was struck as well by the inevitability as the evolvement-power in all its motions.

"Does that thin cobweb there," said I, pointing to the sheet in its more imperfect stage, "does that never tear or break? It is marvelous fragile, and yet this machine it passes through is so mighty."

"It never is known to tear a hair's point."

"Does it never stop—get clogged?"

"No, It *must* go. The machinery makes it go just *so;* just that very way, and at that very pace you there plainly *see* it go. The pulp can't help going."

Something of awe now stole over me, as I gazed upon this inflexible iron animal. Always, more or less, machinery of this ponderous, elaborate sort strikes, in some moods, strange dread into the human heart, as some living, panting Behemoth might. But what made the thing I saw so specially terrible to me was the metallic necessity, the unbudging fatality which governed it. Though, here and there, I could not follow the thin, gauzy vail of pulp in the course of its more mysterious or entirely invisible advance, yet it was indubitable that, at those points where it eluded me, it still marched on in unvarying docility to the autocratic cunning of the machine. A fascination fastened on me. I stood spell-bound and wandering in my soul. Before my eyes—there, passing in slow procession along the wheeling cylinders, I seemed to see, glued to the pallid incipience of the pulp, the yet more pallid faces of all the pallid girls I had eyed that heavy day. Slowly, mournfully, beseechingly, yet unresistingly, they gleamed along, their agony dimly outlined on the imperfect paper, like the print of the tormented face on the handkerchief of Saint Veronica.[22]

"Halloa! the heat of the room is too much for you," cried Cupid, staring at me.

"No—I am rather chill, if any thing."

"Come out, Sir—out—out," and, with the protecting air of a careful father, the precocious lad hurried me outside.

In a few moments, feeling revived a little, I went into the folding-room—the first room I had entered, and where the desk for transacting business stood, surrounded by the blank counters and blank girls engaged at them.

"Cupid here has led me a strange tour," said I to the dark-complexioned man before mentioned, whom I had ere this discovered not only to be an old bachelor, but also the principal proprietor. "Yours is a most wonderful factory. Your great machine is a miracle of inscrutable intricacy."

"Yes, all our visitors think it so. But we don't have many. We are in a very out-of-the-way corner here. Few inhabitants, too. Most of our girls come from far-off villages."

"The girls," echoed I, glancing round at their silent forms. "Why is it, Sir, that in most factories, female operatives, of whatever age, are indiscriminately called girls, never women?"

"Oh! as to that—why, I suppose, the fact of their being generally unmarried— that's the reason, I should think. But it never struck me before. For our factory here, we will not have married women; they are apt to be off-and-on too much. We want none but steady workers: twelve hours to the day, day after day, through the three hundred and sixty-five days, excepting Sundays, Thanksgiving, and

---

[22] According to legend, Veronica wiped the bleeding face of Jesus as he carried the cross to his crucifixion, and found her handkerchief imprinted with his image.

Fast-days. That's our rule. And so, having no married women, what females we have are rightly enough called girls."

"Then these are all maids," said I, while some pained homage to their pale virginity made me involuntarily bow.

"All maids."

Again the strange emotion filled me.

"Your cheeks look whitish yet, Sir." said the man, gazing at me narrowly. "You must be careful going home. Do they pain you at all now? It's a bad sign, if they do."

"No doubt, Sir," answered I, "when once I have got out of the Devil's Dungeon, I shall feel them mending."

"Ah, yes; the winter air in valleys, or gorges, or any sunken place, is far colder and more bitter than elsewhere. You would hardly believe it now, but it is colder here than at the top of Woedolor Mountain."

"I dare say it is, Sir. But time presses me; I must depart."

With that, remuffling myself in dread-naught and tippet, thrusting my hands into my huge seal-skin mittens, I sallied out into the nipping air, and found poor Black, my horse, all cringing and doubled up with the cold.

Soon, wrapped in furs and meditations, I ascended from the Devil's Dungeon.

At the Black Notch I paused, and once more bethought me of Temple-Bar. Then, shooting through the pass, all alone with inscrutable nature, I exclaimed—Oh! Paradise of Bachelors! and oh! Tartarus of Maids!

1855

*BILLY BUDD, SAILOR**

(An Inside Narrative)[1]

JACK CHASE[2]
Wherever that great heart may now be
Here on Earth or harbored in Paradise

Captain of the Maintop
in the year 1843
in the U.S. Frigate
United States

---

* Melville began writing *Billy Budd* in late 1885 or early 1886 and continued working on the manuscript until his death in September 1891; it was not published until 1924. Harrison Hayford and Merton M. Sealts, Jr. did extraordinary research on the text and on the genesis of the tale in Melville's mind for their 1962 edition. Although *Billy Budd* takes place in 1797, during the aftermath of a famous mutiny in the British Navy, the action may also reflect the ambiguity surrounding a mutiny on the American naval ship *Somers* in 1842.

[1] This enigmatic phrase has been interpreted as a portrait of Melville's brooding inner life, as a retelling of the *Somers* affair from an imaginative and inside perspective, and as Melville's method of saying that *Billy Budd* is not merely a series of adventures but a narrative that will take the reader "inside" to confront human and moral considerations.

[2] Melville's shipmate on the naval vessel *United States*. Chase was a major character in Melville's novel *White-Jacket* (1850).

I

In the time before steamships, or then more frequently than now, a stroller along the docks on any considerable seaport would occasionally have his attention arrested by a group of bronzed mariners, man-of-war's men or merchant sailors in holiday attire, ashore on liberty. In certain instances they would flank, or like a bodyguard quite surround, some superior figure of their own class, moving along with them like Aldebaran[3] among the lesser lights of his constellation. That signal object was the "Handsome Sailor" of the less prosaic time alike of the military and merchant navies. With no perceptible trace of the vain-glorious about him, rather with the offhand unaffectedness of natural regality, he seemed to accept the spontaneous homage of his shipmates.

A somewhat remarkable instance recurs to me. In Liverpool, now half a century ago, I saw under the shadow of the great dingy street-wall of Prince's Dock (an obstruction long since removed) a common sailor so intensely black that he must needs have been a native African of the unadulterate blood of Ham[4]—a symmetric figure much above the average height. The two ends of a gay silk handerchief thrown loose about the neck danced upon the displayed ebony of his chest, in his ears were big hoops of gold, and a Highland bonnet with a tartan band set off his shapely head. It was a hot noon in July; and his face, lustrous with perspiration, beamed with barbaric good humor. In jovial sallies right and left, his white teeth flashing into view, he rollicked along, the center of a company of his shipmates. These were made up of such an assortment of tribes and complexions as would have well fitted them to be marched up by Anacharsis Cloots[5] before the bar of the first French Assembly as Representatives of the Human Race. At each spontaneous tribute rendered by the wayfarers to this black pagod[6] of a fellow— the tribute of a pause and stare, and less frequently an exclamation—the motley retinue showed that they took that sort of pride in the evoker of it which the Assyrian priests doubtless showed for their grand sculptured Bull when the faithful prostrated themselves.

To return. If in some cases a bit of a nautical Murat[7] in setting forth his person ashore, the Handsome Sailor of the period in question evinced nothing of the dandified Billy-be-Dam, an amusing character all but extinct now, but occasionally to be encountered, and in a form yet more amusing than the original, at the tiller of the boats on the tempestuous Erie Canal[8] or, more likely, vaporing in the groggeries[9] along the towpath. Invariably a proficient in his perilous calling, he was also more or less of a mighty boxer or wrestler. It was strength and beauty. Tales of his prowess were recited. Ashore he was the champion; afloat the spokesman; on every suitable occasion always foremost. Close-reefing[10] topsails in a

---

[3] The brightest star and "eye" of the constellation Taurus the Bull.

[4] Noah's son, who was cursed by his father for mocking him (see Genesis 9:22–25); the curse has been assumed to be black skin.

[5] The Baron de Cloots (1755–1794, a Prussian revolutionary who led men of different classes and nationalities before the French National Assembly in 1790 to show the variety and unity of mankind. Melville knew of Cloots from Thomas Carlyle's *The French Revolution* (1837).

[6] An idol.

[7] A dandy, like Joachim Murat (1767–1815), whom Napoleon made king of Naples (1808–1815).

[8] A quick bit of irony, since this manmade canal is generally calm.

[9] Boasting in the bars.   [10] Fastening.

gale, there he was, astride the weather yardarm-end, foot in the Flemish horse as stirrup, both hands tugging at the earing[11] as at a bridle in very much the attitude of young Alexander curbing the fiery Bucephalus.[12] A superb figure, tossed up as by the horns of Taurus against the thunderous sky, cheerily hallooing to the strenuous file along the spar.

The moral nature was seldom out of keeping with the physical make. Indeed, except as toned by the former, the comeliness and power, always attractive in masculine conjunction, hardly could have drawn the sort of honest homage the Handsome Sailor in some examples received from his less gifted associates.

Such a cynosure,[13] at least in aspect, and something such too in nature, though with important variations made apparent as the story proceeds, was welkin-eyed[14] Billy Budd—or Baby Budd, as more familiarly, under circumstances hereafter to be given, he at last came to be called—aged twenty-one, a foretopman[15] of the British fleet toward the close of the last decade of the eighteenth century. It was not very long prior to the time of the narration that follows that he had entered the King's service, having been impressed on the Narrow Seas[16] from a homeward-bound English merchantman into a seventy-four outward bound, H.M.S. *Belliponte;*[17] which ship, as was not unusual in those hurried days, having been obliged to put to sea short of her proper complement of men. Plump upon Billy at first sight in the gangway the boarding officer, Lieutenant Ratcliffe, pounced, even before the merchantman's crew was formally mustered on the quarter-deck for his deliberate inspection. And him only he elected. For whether it was because the other men when ranged before him showed to ill advantage after Billy, or whether he had some scruples in view of the merchantman's being rather short-handed, however it might be, the officer contented himself with his first spontaneous choice. To the surprise of the ship's company, though much to the lieutenant's satisfaction, Billy made no demur. But, indeed, any demur would have been as idle as the protest of a goldfinch popped into a cage.

Noting this uncomplaining acquiescence, all but cheerful, one might say, the shipmaster turned a surprised glance of silent reproach at the sailor. The shipmaster[18] was one of those worthy mortals found in every vocation, even the humbler ones—the sort of person whom everybody agrees in calling "a respectable man." And—nor so strange to report as it may appear to be—though a ploughman of the troubled waters, lifelong contending with the intractable elements, there was nothing this honest soul at heart loved better than simple peace and quiet. For the rest, he was fifty or thereabouts, a little inclined to corpulence, a prepossessing face, unwhiskered, and of an agreeable color—a rather full face, humanely intelligent in expression. On a fair day with a fair wind and all going well, a certain musical chime in his voice seemed to be the veritable unobstructed outcome of the innermost man. He had much prudence, much conscientiousness, and there were occa-

---

[11] He was using the footrope at the end of the yardarm on the windward side as a brace and tugging at another rope.

[12] The fierce horse, with a head resembling a bull's, who was tamed by Alexander the Great (356–323 B.C.).

[13] A center of attention.   [14] Blue-eyed.   [15] A crewman at the top of a ship's foremast.

[16] Forced into naval service on the English and St. George's Channels.

[17] A merchant ship and a warship carrying seventy-four guns; Melville had originally named this ship the *Indomitable* but changed it to *Bellipotent* ("potent in war").

[18] The captain.

sions when these virtues were the cause of overmuch disquietude in him. On a passage, so long as his craft was in any proximity to land, no sleep for Captain Graveling. He took to heart those serious responsibilities not so heavily borne by some shipmasters.

Now while Billy Budd was down in the forecastle[19] getting his kit together, the *Bellipotent's* lieutenant, burly and bluff, nowise disconcerted by Captain Graveling's omitting to proffer the customary hospitalities on an occasion so unwelcome to him, an omission simply caused by preoccupation of thought, unceremoniously invited himself into the cabin, and also to a flask from the spirit locker, a receptacle which his experienced eye instantly discovered. In fact he was one of those sea dogs in whom all the hardship and peril of naval life in the great prolonged wars of his time never impaired the natural instinct for sensuous enjoyment. His duty he always faithfully did; but duty is sometimes a dry obligation, and he was for irrigating its aridity, whensoever possible, with a fertilizing decoction of strong waters. For the cabin's proprietor there was nothing left but to play the part of the enforced host with whatever grace and alacrity were practicable. As necessary adjuncts to the flask, he silently placed tumbler and water jug before the irrepressible guest. But excusing himself from partaking just then, he dismally watched the unembarrassed officer deliberately diluting his grog a little, then tossing it off in three swallows, pushing the empty tumbler away, yet not so far as to be beyond easy reach, at the same time settling himself in his seat and smacking his lips with high satisfaction, looking straight at the host.

These proceedings over, the master broke the silence; and there lurked a rueful reproach in the tone of his voice: "Lieutenant, you are going to take my best man from me, the jewel of 'em."

"Yes, I know," rejoined the other, immediately drawing back the tumbler preliminary to a replenishing. "Yes, I know. Sorry."

"Beg pardon, but you don't understand, Lieutenant. See here, now. Before I shipped that young fellow, my forecastle was a rat-pit of quarrels. It was black times, I tell you, aboard the *Rights* here. I was worried to that degree my pipe had no comfort for me. But Billy came; and it was like a Catholic priest striking peace in an Irish shindy.[20] Not that he preached to them or said or did anything in particular; but a virtue went out of him, sugaring the sour ones. They took to him like hornets to treacle; all but the buffer[21] of the gang, the big shaggy chap with the fire-red whiskers. He indeed, out of envy, perhaps, of the newcomer, and thinking such a "sweet and pleasant fellow," as he mockingly designated him to the others, could hardly have the spirit of a gamecock, must needs bestir himself in trying to get up an ugly row with him. Billy forbore with him and reasoned with him in a pleasant way—he is something like myself, Lieutenant, to whom aught like a quarrel is hateful—but nothing served. So, in the second dogwatch[22] one day, the Red Whiskers in presence of the others, under pretense of showing Billy just whence a sirloin steak was cut—for the fellow had once been a butcher—insultingly gave him a dig under the ribs. Quick as lightning Billy let fly his arm. I dare say he never meant to do quite as much as he did, but anyhow he gave the burly fool a terrible drubbing. It took about half a minute, I should think. And, lord bless you, the lubber was astonished at the celerity. And will you believe it,

[19] The forward part of a ship's upper deck.   [20] A row, brawl.   [21] The bully.
[22] One of two two-hour watches between 4 P.M. and 8 P.M.

Lieutenant, the Red Whiskers now really loves Billy—loves him, or is the biggest hypocrite that ever I heard of. But they all love him. Some of 'em do his washing, darn his old trousers for him; the carpenter is at odd times making a pretty little chest of drawers for him. Anybody will do anything for Billy Budd; and it's the happy family here. But now, Lieutenant, if that young fellow goes—I know how it will be aboard the *Rights*. Not again very soon shall I, coming up from dinner, lean over the capstan smoking a quiet pipe—no, not very soon again, I think. Ay, Lieutenant, you are going to take away the jewel of 'em; you are going to take away my peacemaker!" And with that the good soul had really some ado in checking a rising sob.

"Well," said the lieutenant, who had listened with amused interest to all this and now was waxing merry with his tipple; "well, blessed are the peacemakers, especially the fighting peacemakers. And such are the seventy-four beauties some of which you see poking their noses out of the portholes of yonder warship lying to for me," pointing through the cabin window at the *Bellipotent*. "But courage! Don't look so downhearted, man. Why, I pledge you in advance the royal approbation. Rest assured that His Majesty will be delighted to know that in a time when his hardtack[23] is not sought for by sailors with such avidity as should be, a time also when some shipmasters privily resent the borrowing from them a tar or two for the service; His Majesty, I say, will be delighted to learn that *one* shipmaster at least cheerfully surrenders to the King the flower of his flock, a sailor who with equal loyalty makes no dissent.—But where's my beauty? Ah," looking through the cabin's open door, "here he comes; and, by Jove, lugging along his chest—Apollo with his portmanteau!—My man," stepping out to him, "you can't take that big box aboard a warship. The boxes there are mostly shot boxes. Put your duds in a bag, lad. Boot and saddle for the cavalryman, bag and hammock for the man-of-war's man."

The transfer from chest to bag was made. And, after seeing his man into the cutter and then following him down, the lieutenant pushed off from the *Rights-of-Man*.[24] That was the merchant ship's name, though by her master and crew abbreviated in sailor fashion into the *Rights*. The hardheaded Dundee[25] owner was a staunch admirer of Thomas Paine, whose book in rejoinder to Burke's arraignment of the French Revolution had then been published for some time and had gone everywhere. In christening his vessel after the title of Paine's volume the man of Dundee was something like his contemporary shipowner, Stephen Girard[26] of Philadelphia, whose sympathies, alike with his native land and its liberal philosphers, he envinced by naming his ships after Voltaire, Diderot, and so forth.

But now, when the boat swept under the merchantman's stern, and officer and oarsmen were noting—some bitterly and others with a grin—the name emblazoned there; just then it was that the new recruit jumped up from the bow where the cox-swain[27] had directed him to sit, and waving hat to his silent shipmates

---

[23] A large, hard wafer.

[24] In *The Rights of Man* (1791–1792) Thomas Paine argues for natural human rights in reply to Edmund Burke's *Reflections on the Revolution in France* (1790), which claims that rights are safeguarded by society and its institutions. In *Billy Budd* Melville confronts these opposing doctrines.

[25] From the seaport of Dundee, Scotland.

[26] Girard (1750–1831) was a shipowner, merchant, and student of French philosophical writers such as Voltaire (1694–1778) and Denis Diderot (1713–1784).

[27] Steersman.

sorrowfully looking over at him from the taffrail,[28] bade the lads a genial good-bye. Then, making a salutation as to the ship herself, "And good-bye to you too, old *Rights-of-Man*."

"Down, sir!" roared the lieutenant, instantly assuming all the rigor of his rank, though with difficulty repressing a smile.

To be sure, Billy's action was a terrible breach of naval decorum. But in that decorum he had never been instructed; in consideration of which the lieutenant would hardly have been so energetic in reproof but for the concluding farewell to the ship. This he rather took as meant to convey a covert sally on the new recruit's part, a sly slur at impressment in general, and that of himself in especial. And yet, more likely, if satire it was in effect, it was hardly so by intention, for Billy, though happily endowed with the gaiety of high health, youth, and a free heart, was yet by no means of a satirical turn. The will to it and the sinister dexterity were alike wanting. To deal in double meanings and insinuations of any sort was quite foreign to his nature.

As to his enforced enlistment, that he seemed to take pretty much as he was wont to take any vicissitude of weather. Like the animals, though no philosopher, he was, without knowing it, practically a fatalist. And it may be that he rather liked this adventurous turn in his affairs, which promised an opening into novel scenes and martial excitements.

Aboard the *Bellipotent* our merchant sailor was forthwith rated as an able seaman and assigned to the starboard watch of the foretop.[29] He was soon at home in the service, not at all disliked for his unpretentious good looks and a sort of genial happy-go-lucky air. No merrier man in his mess;[30] in marked contrast to certain other individuals included like himself among the impressed portion of the ship's company; for these when not actively employed were sometimes, and more particularly in the last dogwatch when the drawing near of twilight induced revery, apt to fall into a saddish mood which in some partook of sullenness. But they were not so young as our foretopman, and no few of them must have known a hearth of some sort, others may have had wives and children left, too probably, in uncertain circumstances, and hardly any but must have had acknowledged kith and kin, while for Billy, as will shortly be seen, his entire family was pratically invested in himself.

2

Though our new-made foretopman was well received in the top and on the gun decks, hardly here was he that cynosure he had previously been among those minor ship's companies of the merchant marine, with which companies only had he hitherto consorted.

He was young; and despite his all but fully developed frame, in aspect looked even younger than he really was, owing to a lingering adolescent expression in the as yet smooth face all but feminine in purity of natural complexion but where, thanks to his seagoing, the lily was quite suppressed and the rose had some ado visibly to flush through the tan.

---

[28] A rail at ship's stern.

[29] The right-side watch of the platform atop the foremost; that Budd was assigned as foretopman and rated as able-bodied seaman indicate that he is a skilled sailor.

[30] A group that eats together regularly.

To one essentially such a novice in the complexities of factitious life, the abrupt transition from his former and simpler sphere to the ampler and more knowing world of a great warship; this might well have abashed him had there been any conceit or vanity in his composition. Among her miscellaneous multitude, the *Bellipotent* mustered several individuals who however inferior in grade were of no common natural stamp, sailors more signally susceptive of that air which continuous martial discipline and repeated presence in battle can in some degree impart even to the average man. As the Handsome Sailor, Billy Budd's position aboard the seventy-four was something analogous to that of a rustic beauty transplanted from the provinces and brought into competition with the highborn dames of the court. But this change of circumstances he scarce noted. As little did he observe that something about him provoked an ambiguous smile in one or two harder faces among the bluejackets. Nor less unaware was he of the peculiar favorable effect his person and demeanor had upon the more intelligent gentlemen of the quarterdeck.[1] Nor could this well have been otherwise. Cast in a mold peculiar to the finest physical examples of those Englishmen in whom the Saxon strain would seem not at all to partake of any Norman or other admixture, he showed in face that humane look of reposeful good nature which the Greek sculptor in some instances gave to his heroic strong man, Hercules. But this again was subtly modified by another and pervasive quality. The ear, small and shapely, the arch of the foot, the curve in mouth and nostril, even the indurated hand dyed to the orange-tawny of the coucan's[2] bill, a hand telling alike of the halyards[3] and tar bucket; but, above all, something in the mobile expression, and every chance attitude and movement, something suggestive of a mother eminently favored by Love and the Graces;[4] all this strangely indicated a lineage in direct contradiction to his lot. The mysteriousness here became less mysterious through a matter of fact elicited when Billy at the capstan[5] was being formally mustered into the service. Asked by the officer, a small, brisk little gentleman as it chanced, among other questions, his place of birth, he replied, "Please, sir, I don't know."

"Don't know where you were born? Who was your father?"

"God knows, sir."

Struck by the straightforward simplicity of these replies, the officer next asked, "Do you know anything about your beginning?"

"No, sir. But I have heard that I was found in a pretty silk-lined basket hanging one morning from the knocker of a good man's door in Bristol."[6]

"*Found*, say you? Well," throwing back his head and looking up and down the new recruit; "well, it turns out to have been a pretty good find. Hope they'll find some more like you, my man; the fleet sadly needs them."

Yes, Billy Budd was a foundling, a presumable by-blow,[7] and, evidently, no ignoble one. Noble descent was as evident in him as in a blood horse.

For the rest, with little or no sharpness of faculty or any trace of the wisdom of the serpent, nor yet quite a dove,[8] he possessed that kind and degree of intelli-

---

[1] The rear section of the main deck, reserved for officers.
[2] A fruit-eating bird of tropical America with a large, colorful beak.
[3] Ropes or tackle for hoisting or lowering sails.
[4] According to Greek myth, three sisters who control human pleasure, charm, and beauty.
[5] A drum around which cables are wound to hoist weights such as anchors.
[6] A seaport in southwest England.   [7] A bastard; here, a child born of a casual encounter.
[8] In Matthew 10:16 Christ informs his disciples, "Behold, I send you forth as sheep in the midst of wolves: be ye therefore wise as serpents, and harmless as doves."

gence going along with the unconventional rectitude of a sound human creature, one to whom not yet has been proffered the questionable apple of knowledge. He was illiterate; he could not read, but he could sing, and like the illiterate nightingale was sometimes the composer of his own song.

Of self-consciousness he seemed to have little or none, or about as much as we may reasonably impute to a dog of Saint Bernard's breed.

Habitually living with the elements and knowing little more of the land than as a beach, or, rather, that portion of the terraqueous globe providentially set apart for dance-houses, doxies, and tapsters,[9] in short what sailors call a "fiddler's green," his simple nature remained unsophisticated by those moral obliquities which are not in every case incompatible with that manufacturable thing known as respectability. But are sailors, frequenters of fiddlers' greens, without vices? No; but less often than with landsmen do their vices, so called, partake of crookedness of heart, seeming less to proceed from viciousness than exuberance of vitality after long constraint: frank manifestations in accordance with natural law. By his original constitution aided by the co-operating influences of his lot, Billy in many respects was little more than a sort of upright barbarian, much such perhaps as Adam presumably might have been ere the urbane Serpent wriggled himself into his company.

And here be it submitted that apparently going to corroborate the doctrine of man's Fall,[10] a doctrine now popularly ignored, it is observable that where certain pristine and unadulterate peculiarly characterize anybody in the external uniform of civilization, they will upon scrutiny seem not to be derived from custom or convention, but rather to be out of keeping with these, as if indeed exceptionally transmitted from a period prior to Cain's city[11] and citified man. The character marked by such qualities has to be an unvitiated tasted an untampered-with flavor like that of berries, while the man thoroughly civilized, even in a fair specimen of the breed, has to the same moral palate a questionable smack as of a compounded wine. To any stray inheritor of these primitive qualities found, like Caspar Hauser,[12] wandering dazed in any Christian capital of our time, the good-natured poet's famous invocation, near two thousand years ago, of the good rustic out of his latitude in the Rome of the Caesars, still appropriately holds:

> Honest and poor, faithful in word and thought,
> What hath thee, Fabian, to the city brought?[13]

Though our Handsome Sailor had as much of masculine beauty as one can expect anywhere to see; nevertheless, like the beautiful woman in one of Hawthorne's minor tales,[14] there was just one thing amiss in him. No visible blemish

[9] Whores and bartenders, making it a sailor's paradise.

[10] Adam's sin of yielding to temptation, and his subsequent loss of grace.

[11] After killing his brother, Abel, Cain "went out from the presence of the Lord . . . And he builded a city," from Genesis 4: 16–17. Melville's emphasis on Budd's innocence and "man's Fall" points to the fundamental supposition of the story—that Original Sin exists, with troubling consequences for a world in which that doctrine is unfashionable.

[12] Hauser (1812?–1833) was a German youth, perhaps a victim of amnesia, who appeared in Nuremberg in 1828 claiming to have been held captive in a hole. Supposedly he was of noble birth and an innocent.

[13] From the *Epigrams* of the Roman poet Martial (40?–A.D. 104?)

[14] Hawthorne's shorter tales: "The Birth-Mark" (1843), another story generated by the conviction that to be is to be imperfect.

indeed, as with the lady; no, but an occasional liability to a vocal defect. Though in the hour of elemental uproar or peril he was everything that a sailor should be, yet under sudden provocation of strong heart-feeling his voice, otherwise singularly musical, as if expressive of the harmony within, was apt to develop an organic hesitancy, in fact more or less of a stutter or even worse. In this particular Billy was a striking instance that the arch interferer, the envious marplot of Eden,[15] still has more or less to do with every human consignment to this planet of Earth. In every case, one way or another he is sure to slip in his little card, as much as to remind us—I too have a hand here.

The avowal of such an imperfection in the Handsome Sailor should be evidence not alone that he is not presented as a conventional hero, but also that the story in which he is the main figure is no romance.

3

At the time of Billy Budd's arbitrary enlistment into the *Bellipotent* that ship was on her way to join the Mediterranean fleet. No long time elapsed before the junction was effected. As one of that fleet the seventy-four participated in its movements, though at time on account of her superior sailing qualities, in the absence of frigates, dispatched on separate duty as a scout and at times on less temporary service. But with all this the story has little concernment, restricted as it is to the inner life of one particular ship and the career of an individual sailor.

It was the summer of 1797. In the April of that year had occurred the commotion at Spithead followed in May by a second and yet more serious outbreak in the fleet at the Nore.[1] The latter is known, and without exaggeration in the epithet, as "the Great Mutiny." It was indeed a demonstration more menacing to England than the contemporary manifestoes and conquering and proselyting armies of the French Directory.[2] To the British Empire the Nore Mutiny was what a strike in the fire brigade would be to London threatened by general arson. In a crisis when the kingdom might well have anticipated the famous signal that some years later published along the naval line of battle what it was that upon occasion England expected of Englishmen;[3] *that* was the time when at the mastheads of the three-deckers and seventy-fours moored in her own roadstead—a fleet the right arm of a Power then all but the sole free conservative one of the Old World—the bluejackets, to be numbered by thousands, ran up with huzzas the British colors with the union and cross wiped out; by that cancellation transmuting the flag of founded law and freedom defined, into the enemy's red meteor of unbridled and unbounded revolt. Reasonable discontent growing out of practical grievances in the fleet had been ignited into irrational combustion as by live cinders blown across the Channel from France in flames.[4]

The event converted into irony for a time those spirited strains of Dibdin[5]—as a

---

[15] Satan.

[1] The action of *Billy Budd* takes place in the aftermath of the mutinies at Spithead (a roadstead, or protected anchorage, in the English Channel) and Nore (at the mouth of the Thames River).

[2] A governing body of five that ruled France from 1795 to 1799, after the French Revolution.

[3] Lord Horatio Nelson's (1758–1805) message to his British fleet before the Battle of Trafalgar in 1805: "England expects every man to do his duty."

[4] During and after the French Revolution.

[5] Charles Dibdin (1745–1814), an English dramatist known for his patriotic songs.

song-writer no mean auxiliary to the English government at that European con-
juncture—strains celebrating, among other things the patriotic devotion of the British tar: "And as for my life, 'tis the King's!"

Such an episode in the Island's grand naval story her naval historians naturally
abridge, one of them (William James[6]) candidly acknowledging that fain would he
pass it over did not "impartiality forbid fastidiousness." And yet his mention is
less a narration than a reference, having to do hardly at all with details. Nor are
these readily to be found in the libraries. Like some other events in every age
befalling states everywhere, including America, the Great Mutiny was of such
character that national pride along with views of policy would fain shade it off into
the historical background. Such events cannot be ignored, but there is a considerate way of historically treating them. If a well-constituted individual refrains from
blazoning aught amiss or calamitous in his family, a nation in the like circumstance may without reproach be equally discreet.

Though after parleyings between government and the ringleaders, and concessions by the former as to some glaring abuses, the first uprising—that at
Spithead—with difficulty was put down, or matters for the time pacified; yet at
the Nore the unforeseen renewal of insurrection on a yet larger scale, and emphasized in the conferences that ensued by demands deemed by the authorities not
only inadmissible but aggressively insolent, indicated—if the Red Flag[7] did not
sufficiently do so—what was the spirit animating the men. Final suppression,
however, there was; but only made possible perhaps by the unswerving loyalty of
the marine corps[8] and a voluntary resumption of loyalty among influential sections
of the crews.

To some extent the Nore Mutiny may be regarded as analogous to the distem-
pering irruption of contagious fever in a frame constitutionally sound, and which
anon throws it off.

At all events, of these thousands of mutineers were some of the tars who not so
very long afterwards—whether wholly prompted thereto by patriotism, or pugna-
cious instinct, or by both—helped to win a coronet for Nelson at the Nile, and the
naval crown of crowns for him at Trafalgar.[9] To the mutineers, those battles and
especially Trafalgar were a plenary absolution and a grand one. For all that does to
make up scenic naval display and heroic magnificence in arms, those battles, especially Trafalgar, stand unmatched in human annals.

4

In this matter of writing, resolve as one may to keep to the main road, some
bypaths have an enticement not readily to be withstood. I am going to err into
such a bypath. If the reader will keep me company I shall be glad. At the least, we
can promise ourselves that pleasure which is wickedly said to be in sinning, for a
literal sin the divergence will be.

Very likely it is no new remark that the inventions of our time have at last

---

[6] James (?–1827) was a British historian, author of *Naval History of Great Britain* (1822–1824).

[7] The traditional banner of revolution.

[8] Marines served as security guards on warships and were encouraged to have a "healthy" antagonism
with the sailors.

[9] Nelson was made a baron after his victory over the French fleet at the Battle of the Nile in 1798; his
death during the defeat of the combined French and Spanish navies at the battle of Trafalgar in 1805
won for him "the naval crown of crowns."

brought about a change in sea warfare in degree corresponding to the revolution in all warfare effected by the original introduction from China into Europe of gunpowder. The first European firearm, a clumsy contrivance, was, as is well known, scouted[1] by no few of the knights as a base implement, good enough peradventure for weavers too craven to stand up crossing steel with steel in frank fight. But as ashore knightly valor, though shorn of its blazonry, did not cease with the knights, neither on the seas—though nowadays in encounters there a certain kind of displayed gallantry be fallen out of date as hardly applicable under changed circumstances—did the nobler qualities of such naval magnates as Don John of Austria, Doria, Van Tromp, Jean Bart, the long line of British admirals, and the American Decaturs of 1812[2] become obsolete with their wooden walls.

Nevertheless, to anybody who can hold the Present at its worth without being inappreciative of the Past, it may be foregiven, if to such an one the solitary old hulk at Portsmouth, Nelson's *Victory*,[3] seems to float there, not alone as the decaying monument of a fame incorruptible, but also as a poetic reproach, softened by its picturesqueness, to the *Monitors*[4] and yet mightier hulls of the European ironclads. And this not altogether because such craft are unsightly, unavoidably lacking the symmetry and grand lines of the old battleships, but equally for other reasons.

There are some, perhaps, who while not altogether inaccessible to that poetic reproach just alluded to, may yet on behalf of the new order be disposed to parry it; and this to the extent of iconoclasm, if need be. For example, prompted by the sight of the star inserted in the *Victory*'s quarter-deck designating the spot where the Great Sailor fell, these martial utilitarians may suggest considerations implying that Nelson's ornate publication of his person in battle[5] was not only unnecessary, but not military, nay, savored of foolhardiness and vanity. They may add, too, that at Trafalgar it was in effect nothing less than a challenge to death; and death came; and that but for his bravado the victorious admiral might possibly have survived the battle, and so, instead of having his sagacious dying injuctions overruled by his immediate successor in command, he himself when the contest was decided might have brought his shattered fleet to anchor, a proceeding which might have averted the deplorable loss of life by shipwreck in the elemental tempest that followed the martial one.

Well, should we set aside the more than disputable point whether for various reasons it was possible to anchor the fleet, then plausibly enough the Benthamites[6] of war may urge the above. But the *might-have-been* is but boggy ground to build

---

[1] Scoffed at.

[2] Don John of Austria (1547–1578) led ships of the Holy League to a victory over the Turks at Lepanto off Greece (1571); Andrea Doria (1468?–1560) commanded the Genoese fleet against the Turks; Maarten Tromp (1597–1653) led Dutch fleets against the Spanish and English; Jean Bart (1651?–1702) commanded French privateers against the Dutch; Stephen Decatur (1779–1820) led American ships against the Tripoli pirates (1803–1804) and later against the British in the War of 1812.

[3] Nelson's flagship at the Battle of Trafalgar; Melville saw it in a museum in Portsmouth, England, in 1849.

[4] During the Civil War, the Union ironclad *Monitor* engaged in battle with the Confederate ironclad *Merrimack* at Hampton Roads, off Virginia, in 1862. Melville wrote about this engagement in his poem "A Utilitarian View of the Monitor's Fight" (1866).

[5] Hayford and Sealts present evidence suggesting that at the Battle of Trafalgar the conspicuous uniform (complete with medals) of Nelson, the "Great Sailor," may have made him a target for riflemen aboard the French ships.

[6] Followers of Jeremy Bentham (1748–1832), an English philospher and political theorist who advocated utilitarianism, or usefulness, as the proper guide to action.

on. And, certainly, in foresight as to the larger issue of an encounter, and anxious preparations for it—buoying the deadly way and mapping it out, as at Copenhagen[7]—few commanders have been so painstakingly circumspect as this same reckless declarer of his person in fight.

Personal prudence, even when dictated by quite other than selfish considerations, surely is no special virtue in a military man; while an excessive love of glory, impassioning a less burning impulse, the honest sense of duty, is the first. If the name *Wellington* is not so much of a trumpet to the blood as the simpler name *Nelson*, the reason for this may perhaps be inferred from the above. Alfred[8] in his funeral ode on the victor of Waterloo ventures not to call him the greatest soldier of all time, though in the same ode he invokes Nelson as "the greatest sailor since our world began."

At Trafalgar Nelson on the brink of opening the fight sat down and wrote his last brief will and testament. If under the presentiment of the most magnificent of all victories to be crowned by his own glorious death, a sort of priestly motive led him to dress his person in the jewelled vouchers of his own shining deeds; if thus to have adorned himself for the altar and the sacrifice were indeed vainglory, then affectation and fustian is each more heroic line in the great epics and dramas, since in such lines the poet but embodies in verse those exaltations of sentiment that a nature like Nelson, the opportunity being given, vitalizes into acts.

5

Yes, the outbreak at the Nore was put down. But not every grievance was redressed. If the contractors, for example, were no longer permitted to ply some practices peculiar to their tribe everywhere, such as providing shoddy cloth, rations not sound, or false in the measure; not the less impressment, for one thing, went on. By custom sanctioned for centuries, and judicially maintained by a Lord Chancellor as late as Mansfield,[1] that mode of manning the fleet, a mode now fallen into a sort of abeyance but never formally renounced, it was not practicable to give up in those years. Its abrogation would have crippled the indispensable fleet, one wholly under canvas, no steam power, its innumerable sails and thousands of cannon, everything in short, worked by muscle alone; a fleet the more insatiate in demand for men, because then multiplying its ships of all grades against contingencies present and to come of the convulsed Continent.

Discontent foreran the Two Mutinies,[2] and more or less it lurkingly survived them. Hence it was not unreasonable to apprehend some return of trouble sporadic or general. One instance of such apprehensions: In the same year with this story, Nelson, then Rear Admiral Sir Horatio, being with the fleet off the Spanish coast, was directed by the admiral in command to shift his pennant[3] from the *Captain* to the *Theseus;* and for this reason: that the latter ship having newly arrived on the

---

[7] In 1801 the Danes removed the buoys marking the channel leading to the port of Copenhagen to make navigation virtually impossiible; but Nelson took soundings, replaced the markers, and defeated the Danish fleet.

[8] Alfred, Lord Tennyson (1809–1892), whose "Ode on the Death of the Duke of Wellington" (1852) pays tribute to the victory of Wellington, or Arthur Wellesley (1769–1852), over Napoleon at Waterloo (1815).

[1] William Murray (1705–1793), earl of Mansfield, who authorized the use of impressment to obtain sailors for the British navy while he was Lord Chief Justice (1756–1788).

[2] At Spithead and at Nore.   [3] To shift his command ship and the flag that identified it.

station from home, where it had taken part in the Great Mutiny, danger was apprehended from the temper of the men; and it was thought that an officer like Nelson was the one, not indeed to terrorize the crew into base subjection, but to win them, by force of his mere presence and heroic personality, back to an allegiance if not as enthusiastic as his own yet as true.

So it was that for a time, on more than one quarter-deck, anxiety did exist. At sea, precautionary vigilance was strained against relapse. At short notice an engagement might come one. When it did, the lieutenants assigned to batteries felt it incumbent on them, in some instances, to stand with drawn swords behind the men working the guns.

6

But on board the seventy-four in which Billy now swung his hammock, very little in the manner of the men and nothing obvious in the demeanor of the officers would have suggested to an ordinary observer that the Great Mutiny was a recent event. In their general bearing and conduct the commissioned officers of a warship naturally take their tone from the commander, that is if he have that ascendancy of character that ought to be his.

Captain the Honorable Edward Fairfax Vere, to give his full title, was a bachelor of forty or thereabouts, a sailor of distinction even in a time prolific of renowned seamen. Though allied to the higher nobility, his advancement had not been altogether owing to influences connected with that circumstance. He had seen much service, been in various engagments, always acquitting himself as an officer mindful of the welfare of his men, but never tolerating an infraction of discipline; thoroughly versed in the science of his profession, and intrepid to the verge of temerity, though never injudiciously so. For his gallantry in the West Indian waters as flag lieutenant under Rodney[1] in that admiral's crowning victory over De Grasse, he was made a post captain.

Ashore, in the garb of a civilian, scarce anyone would have taken him for a sailor, more especially that he never garnished unprofessional talk with nautical terms, and grave in his bearing, evinced little appreciation of mere humor. It was not out of keeping with these traits that on a passage when nothing demanded his paramount action, he was the most undemonstrative of men. Any landsman observing this gentleman not conspicuous by his stature and wearing no pronounced insignia, emerging from his cabin to the open deck, and noting the silent deference of the officers retiring to leeward, might have taken him for the King's guest, a civilian aboard the King's ship, some highly honorable discreet envoy on his way to an important post. But in fact this unobtrusiveness of demeanor may have proceeded from a certain unaffected modesty of manhood sometimes accompanying a resolute nature, a modesty evinced at all times not calling for pronounced action, which shown in any rank of life suggests a virtue aristocratic in kind. As with some others engaged in various departments of the world's more heroic activities, Captain Vere though practical enough upon occasion would at times betray a certain dreaminess of mood. Standing alone on the weather side of the

---

[1] George Brydges (1719–1792), Baron Rodney, the British admiral who defeated the French admiral François de Grasse (1723–1788) near the West Indian island of Dominica in 1782. For his fictional part in this real battle, Melville's Vere is made a captain of permanent rank.

quarter-deck, one hand holding by the rigging, he would absently gaze off at the blank sea. At the presentation to him then of some minor matter interruputing the current of his thoughts, he would show more or less irascibility; but instantly he would control it.

In the navy he was popularly known by the appellation "Starry Vere." How such a designation happened to fall upon one who whatever his sterling qualities was without any brilliant ones, was in this wise: A favorite kinsman, Lord Denton, a freehearted fellow, had been the first to meet and congratulate him upon his return to England from his West Indian cruise; and but the day previous turning over a copy of Andrew Marvell's[2] poems had lighted, not for the first time, however, upon the lines entitled "Appleton House," the name of one of the seats of their common ancestor, a hero in the German wars of the seventeenth century, in which poem occur the lines:

> This 'tis to have been from the first
> In a domestic heaven nursed,
> Under the discipline severe
> Of Fairfax and the starry Vere.[3]

And so, upon embracing his cousing fresh from Rodney's great victory wherein he had played so gallant a part, brimming over with just family pride in the sailor of their house, he exuberantly exclaimed, "Give ye joy, Ed; give ye joy, my starry Vere!" This got currency, and the novel prefix serving in familiar parlance readily to distinguish the *Bellipotent*'s captain from another Vere his senior, a distant relative, an officer of like rank in the navy, it remained permanently attached to the surname.

7

In view of the part that the commander of the *Bellipotent* plays in scenes shortly to follow, it may be well to fill out that sketch of him outlined in the previous chapter.

Aside from his qualities as a sea officer Captain Vere was an exceptional character. Unlike no few of England's renowned sailors, long and arduous service with signal devotion to it had not resulted in absorbing and *salting* the entire man. He had a marked leaning toward everything intellectual. He loved books, never going to sea without a newly replenished library, compact but of the best. The isolated leisure, in some cases so wearisome, falling at intervals to commanders even during a war cruise, never was tedious to Captain Vere. With nothing of that literary taste which less heeds the thing conveyed than the vehicle, his bias was toward those books to which every serious mind of superior order occupying any active post of authority in the world naturally inclines: books treating of actual men and events no matter of what era—history, biography, and unconventional writers like Montaigne,[1] who, free from cant and convention, honestly and in the

---

[2] Marvell (1621–1678) was an English poet; Melville's reference to Lord Denton comes from Marvell's poem "Upon Appleton House, to My Lord Fairfax," which mentions the Fairfax estate, Denton.

[3] Anne Vere (?–1665), wife of Thomas, Lord Fairfax (1612–1671), owner of Appleton House.

[1] Michel de Montaigne (1553–1592), a French political theorist and writer.

spirit of common sense philosophize upon realities. In this line of reading he found confirmation of his own more reserved thoughts—confirmation which he had vainly sought in social converse, so that as touching most fundamental topics, there had got to be established in him some positive convictions which he forefelt would abide in him essentially unmodified so long as his intelligent part remained unimpaired. In view of the troubled period in which his lot was cast, this was well for him. His settled convictions were as a dike against those invading waters of novel opinion social, political, and otherwise, which carried away as in a torrent no few minds in those days, minds by nature not inferior to his own. While other members of that aristocracy to which by birth he belonged were incensed at the innovators mainly because their theories were inimical to the privileged classes, Captain Vere disinterestedly opposed them not alone because they seemed to him insusceptible of embodiment in lasting institutions, but at war with the peace of the world and the true welfare of mankind.

With minds less stored than his and less earnest, some officers of his rank, with whom at times he would necessarily consort, found him lacking in the companionable quality, a dry and bookish gentleman, as they deemed. Upon any chance withdrawal from their company one would be apt to say to another something like this: "Vere is a noble fellow, Starry Vere. 'Spite the gazettes,[2] Sir Horatio" (meaning him who became Lord Nelson) "is at bottom scarce a better seaman or fighter. But between you and me now, don't you think there is a queer streak of the pedantic running through him? Yes, like the King's yarn[3] in a coil of navy rope?"

Some apparent ground there was for this sort of confidential criticism; since not only did the captain's discourse never fall into the jocosely familiar, but in illustrating of any point touching the stirring personages and events of the time he would be as apt to cite some historic character or incident of antiquity as he would be to cite from the moderns. He seemed unmindful of the circumstance that to his bluff company such remote allusions, however pertinent they might really be, were altogether alien to men whose reading was mainly confined to the journals.[4] But considerateness in such matters is not easy to natures constituted like Captain Vere's. Their honesty prescribes to them directness, sometimes far-reaching like that of a migratory fowl that in its flight never heeds when it crosses a frontier.

8

The lieutenants and other commissioned gentlemen forming Captain Vere's staff it is not necessary here to particularize, nor needs it to make any mention of any of the warrant officers. But among the petty[1] officers was one who, having much to do with the story, may as well be forthwith introduced. His portrait I essay, but shall never hit it. This was John Claggart, the master-at-arms. But that sea title may to landsmen seem somewhat equivocal. Originally, doubtless, that petty officer's function was the instruction of the men in the use of arms, sword or cutlass. But very long ago, owing to the advance in gunnery making hand-to-hand encounters less frequent and giving to niter[2] and sulphur the pre-eminence over steel, that function ceased; the master-at-arms of a great warship becoming a sort

---

[2] Despite newspaper reports.   [3] A thread that is distinctive.   [4] Newspapers.
[1] Noncommissioned.
[2] Potassium nitrate, which, when mixed with charcoal and sulphur, forms gunpowder.

of chief of police charged among other matters with the duty of preserving order on the populous lower gun decks.

Claggart was a man about five-and-thirty, somewhat spare and tall, yet of no ill figure upon the whole. His hand was too small and shapely to have been accustomed to hard toil. The face was a notable one, the features all except the chin cleanly cut as those on a Greek medallion; yet the chin, beardless as Tecumseh's,[3] had something of strange protuberant broadness in its make that recalled the prints of the Reverend Dr. Titus Oates,[4] the historic deponent with the clerical drawl in the time of Charles II and the fraud of the alleged Popish Plot. It served Claggart in his office that his eye could cast a tutoring glance. His brow was of the sort phrenologically[5] associated with more than average intellect; silken jet curls partly clustering over it, making a foil to the pallor below, a pallor tinged with a faint shade of amber akin to the hue of time-tinted marbles of old. This complexion, singularly contrasting with the red or deeply bronzed visages of the sailors, and in part the result of his official seclusion from the sunlight, though it was not exactly displeasing, nevertheless seemed to hint of something defective or abnormal in the constitution and blood. But his general aspect and manner were so suggestive of an education and career incongruous with this naval function that when not actively engaged in it he looked like a man of high quality, social and moral, who for reasons of his own was keeping incog.[6] Nothing was known of his former life. It might be that he was an Englishman; and yet there lurked a bit of accent in his speech suggesting that possibly he was not such by birth, but through naturalization in early childhood. Among certain grizzled sea gossips of the gun decks and forecastle went a rumor perdue[7] that the master-at-arms was a *chevalier*[8] who had volunteered into the King's navy by way of compounding for some mysterious swindle whereof he had been arraigned at the King's Bench.[9] The fact that nobody could substantiate this report was, of course, nothing against its secret currency. Such a rumor once started on the gun decks in reference to almost anyone below the rank of a commissioned officer would, during the period assigned to this narrative, have seemed not altogether wanting in credibility to the tarry old wiseacres of a man-of-war crew. And indeed a man of Claggart's accomplishments, without prior nautical experience entering the navy at mature life, as he did, and necessarily allotted at the start to the lowest grade in it; a man too who never made allusion to his previous life ashore; these were circumstances which in the dearth of exact knowledge as to his true antecedents opened to the invidious a vague field for unfavorable surmise.

But the sailors' dogwatch gossip concerning him derived a vague plausibility from the fact that now for some period the British navy could so little afford to be squeamish in the matter of keeping up the muster rolls,[10] that not only were press gangs[11] notoriously abroad both afloat and ashore, but there was little or no secret

---

[3] A Shawnee chief (1768?–1813) who tried to unite Native-American tribes against the whites and fought with the British in the War of 1812.

[4] Oates (1649–1705) was an informer and convicted perjurer who accused Catholics of plotting to massacre English Protestants, assassinate King Charles II, and burn London in the so-called Popish Plot (1678).

[5] The pseudoscience of phrenology taught that features of the skull indicate traits of character and intelligence.

[6] Incognito.   [7] Concealed, hidden.

[8] "Knight," (French); here, a swindler (who had "volunteered" for service in the navy to avoid imprisonment).

[9] Court of law.   [10] Registers of a ship's personnel.

[11] Gangs authorized to seize and kidnap men for impressment.

about another matter, namely, that the London police were at liberty to capture any able-bodied suspect, any questionable fellow at large, and summarily ship him to the dockyard or fleet. Furthermore, even among voluntary enlistments there were instances where the motive thereto partook neither of patriotic impulse nor yet of a random desire to experience a bit of sea life and martial adventure. Insolvent debtors of minor grade, together with the promiscuous lame ducks of morality, found in the navy a convenient and secure refuge, secure because, once enlisted aboard a King's ship, they were as much in sanctuary as the transgressor of the Middle Ages harboring himself under the shadow of the altar. Such sanctioned irregularities, which for obvious reasons the governement would hardly think to parade at the time and which consequently, and as affecting the least influential class of mankind, have all but dropped into oblivion, lend color to something for the truth whereof I do not vouch, and hence have some scruple in stating; something I remember having seen in print though the book I cannot recall; but the same thing was personally communicated to me now more than forty years ago by an old pensioner in a cocked hat with whom I had a most interesting talk on the terrace at Greenwich,[12] a Baltimore Negro, a Trafalgar man.[13] It was to this effect: In the case of a warship short of hands whose speedy sailing was imperative, the deficient quota, in lack of any other way of making it good, would be eked out by drafts culled direct from the jails. For reasons previously suggested it would not perhaps be easy at the present day directly to prove or disprove the allegation. But allowed as a verity, how significant would it be of England's straits at the time confronted by those wars[14] which like a flight of harpies[15] rose shrieking from the din and dust of the fallen bastille.[16] That era appears measurably clear to us who look back at it, and but read of it. But to the grandfathers of us graybears, the more thoughtful of them, the genius of it presented an aspect like that of Camoëns'[17] Spirit of the Cape, an eclipsing menace mysterious and prodigious. Not America was exempt from apprehension. At the height of Napoleon's unexampled conquests, there were Americans who had fought at Bunker Hill[18] who looked forward to the possibility that the Atlantic might prove no barrier against the ultimate schemes of this French portentous upstart from the revolutionary chaos who seemed in act of fulfilling judgment prefigure in the Apocalypse.[19]

But the less credence was to be given to the gun-deck talk touching Claggart, seeing that no man holding his office in a man-of-war can ever hope to be popular with the crew. Besides, in derogatory comments upon anyone against whom they have a grudge, or for any reason or no reason mislike, sailors are much like landsmen: they are apt to exaggerate or romance it.

About as much was really known to the *Bellipotent*'s tars of the master-at-arms' career before entering the service as an astronomer knows about a comet's travels prior to its first observable appearance in the sky. The verdict of the sea quidnuncs[20] has been cited only by way of showing what sort of moral impression

[12] Greenwich Hospital, near London.

[13] A veteran of the 1805 Battle of Trafalgar.   [14] The Napoleonic Wars (1796–1815).

[15] According to Greek myth, fierce birds with the faces of demonic women.

[16] A prison in Paris, stormed by citizens at the outbreak of the French Revolution in 1789.

[17] Luiz de Camoëns (1524–1580), a Portuguese poet; in his epic *Lusiads* (1572) the heroic Vasco da Gama is threatened by the Spirit of natural forces as he rounds Africa at the Cape of Good Hope on his way to India.

[18] The site of a Revolutionary War battle (1775) near Boston, in which the British defeated colonists who had run out of gunpowder. Melville means that some veterans of this battle feared that Napoleon might reach across the Atlantic.

[19] The New Testament Book of Revelation.   [20] Gossips.

the man made upon rude uncultivated natures whose conceptions of human wickedness were necessarily of the narrowest, limited to ideas of vulgar rascality—a thief among the swinging hammocks during a night watch, or the man-brokers and land-sharks[21] of the seaports.

It was no gossip, however, but fact that though, as before hinted, Claggart upon his entrance into the navy was, as a novice, assigned to the least honorable section of a man-of-war's crew, embracing the drudgery, he did not long remain there. The superior capacity he immediately evinced, his constitutional sobriety, an ingratiating deference to superiors, together with a peculiar ferreting genius manifested on a singular occasion; all this, capped by certain austere patriotism, abruptly advanced him to the position of master-at-arms.

Of this maritime chief of police the ship's corporals, so called, were the immediate subordinates, and compliant ones; and this, as is to be noted in some business departments ashore, almost to a degree inconsistent with entire moral volition. His place put various converging wires of underground influence under the chief's control, capable when astutely worked through his understrappers[22] of operating to the mysterious discomfort, if nothing worse, of any of the sea commonalty.

9

Life in the foretop well agreed with Billy Budd. There, when not actually engaged on the yards yet higher aloft, the topmen, who as such had been picked out for youth and activity, constituted an aerial club lounging at ease against the smaller stun'sails rolled up into cushions, spinning yarns like the lazy gods, and frequently amused with what was going on in the busy world of the decks below. No wonder then that a young fellow of Billy's disposition was well content in such society. Giving no cause of offense to anybody, he was always alert at a call. So in the merchant service it had been with him. But now such a punctiliousness in duty was shown that his topmates would sometimes good-naturedly laugh at him for it. This heightened alacrity had its cause, namely, the impression made upon him by the first formal gangway-punishment he had ever witnessed, which befell the day following his impressment. It had been incurred by a little fellow, young, a novice afterguardsman[1] absent from his assigned post when the ship was being put about; a dereliction resulting in a rather serious hitch to that maneuver, one demanding instantaneous promptitude in letting go and making fast. When Billy saw the culprit's naked back under the scourge,[2] gridironed with red welts and worse, when he marked the dire expression in the liberated man's face as with his woolen shirt flung over him by the executioner he rushed forward from the spot to bury himself in the crowd, Billy was horrified. He resolved that never through remissness would he make himself liable to such a visitation or do or omit aught that might merit even verbal reproof. What then was his surprise and concern when ultimately he found himself getting into petty trouble occasionally about such matters as the stowage of his bag or something amiss in his hammock, matters under the police oversight of the ship's corporals of the lower decks, and which brought down on him a vague threat from one of them.

---

[21] Those paid to impress sailors and landsmen who cheat sailors.   [22] Subordinates.
[1] A crew member responsible for the sails at a ship's stern; the relatively easy job was usually given to inexperienced sailors.
[2] The whip.

So heedful in all things as he was, how could this be? He could not understand it, and it more than vexed him. When he spoke to his young topmates about it they were either lightly incredulous or found something comical in his unconcealed anxiety. "Is it your bag, Billy?" said one. "Well, sew yourself up in it, bully boy, and then you'll be sure to know if anybody meddles with it."

Now there was a veteran aboard who because his years began to disqualify him for more active work had been recently assigned duty as mainmastman in his watch, looking to the gear belayed at the rail roundabout that great spar near the deck. At off-times the foretopman had picked up some acquaintance with him, and now in his trouble it occurred to him that he might be the sort of person to go to for wise counsel. He was an old Dansker long anglicized in the service,[3] of few words, many wrinkles, and some honorable scars. His wizened face, time-tinted and weather-stained to the complexion of an antique parchment, was here and there peppered blue by the chance explosion of a gun cartridge in action.

He was an *Agamemnon* man, some two years prior to the time of this story having served under Nelson when still captain in that ship immortal in naval memory, which dismantled and in part broken up to her bare ribs is seen a grand skeleton in Haden's etching.[4] As one of a boarding party from the *Agamemnon* he had received a cut slantwise along one temple and cheek leaving a long pale scar like a streak of dawn's light falling athwart the dark visage. It was on account of that scar and the affair in which it was known that he had received it, as well as from his blue-peppered complexion, that the Dansker went among the *Bellipotent*'s crew by the name of "Board-Her-in-the-Smoke."

Now the first time that his small weasel eyes happened to light on Billy Budd, a certain grim internal merriment set all his ancient wrinkles into antic play. Was it that his eccentric unsentimental old sapience, primitive in its kind, saw or thought it saw something which in contrast with the warship's environment looked oddly incongruous in the Handsome Sailor? But after slyly studying him at intervals, the old Merlin's[5] equivocal merriment was modified; for now when the twain would meet, it would start in his face a quizzing sort of look, but it would be but momentary and sometimes replaced by an expression of speculative query as to what might eventually befall a nature like that, dropped into a world not without some mantraps and against whose subtleties simple courage lacking experience and address, and without any touch of defensive ugliness, is of little avail; and where such innocence as man is capable of does yet in a moral emergency not always sharpen the faculties or enlighten the will.

However it was, the Dansker in his ascetic way rather took to Billy. Nor was this only because of a certain philosophic interest in such a character. There was another cause. While the old man's eccentricities, sometimes bordering on the ursine,[6] repelled the juniors, Billy, undeterred thereby, revering him as a salt hero, would make advances, never passing the old *Agamemnon* man without a salutation marked by that respect which is seldom lost on the aged, however crabbed at times or whatever their station in life.

There was a vein of dry humor, or what not, in the mastman; and, whether in freak of patriarchal irony touching Billy's youth and athletic frame, or for some other and more recondite reason, from the first in addressing him he always sub-

---

[3] A Dane who had picked up English ways during his years in the navy.
[4] "The Breaking Up of the *Agamemnon*" (1870), by the English artist Sir Francis Seymour Haden (1818–1910).
[5] The seer and magician in the legends of King Arthur.   [6] Bearlike.

stituted *Baby* for Billy, the Dansker in fact being the originator of the name by which the foretopman eventually became known aboard ship.

Well then, in his mysterious little difficulty going in quest of the wrinkled one, Billy found him off duty in a dogwatch ruminating by himself, seated on a shot box of the upper gun deck, now and then surveying with a somewhat cynical regard certain of the more swaggering promenaders there. Billy recounted his trouble, again wondering how it all happened. The salt seer attentively listened, accompanying the foretopman's recital with queer twitchings of his wrinkles and problematical little sparkles of his small ferret eyes. Making an end of his story, the foretopman asked, "And now, Dansker, do tell me what you think of it."

The old man, shoving up the front of his tarpaulin[7] and deliberately rubbing the long slant scar at the point where it entered the thin hair, laconically said, "Baby Budd, *Jemmy Legs*" (meaning the master-at-arms) "is down on you."

"*Jemmy Legs!*" ejaculated Billy, his welkin eyes expanding. "What for? Why, he calls me 'the sweet and pleasant young fellow,' they tell me."

"Does he so?" grinned the grizzled one; then said, "Ay, Baby lad, a sweet voice has Jemmy Legs."

"No, not always. But to me he has. I seldom pass him but there comes a pleasant word."

"And that's because he's down upon you. Baby Budd."

Such reiteration, along with the manner of it, incomprehensible to a novice, disturbed Billy almost as much as the mystery for which he had sought explanation. Something less unpleasingly oracular he tried to extract; but the old sea Chiron,[8] thinking perhaps that for the nonce he had sufficiently instructed his young Achilles, pursed his lips, gathered all his wrinkles together, and would commit himself to nothing further.

Years, and those experiences which befall certain shrewder men subordinated lifelong to the will of superiors, all this had developed in the Dansker the pithy guarded cynicism that was his leading characteristic.

10

The next day an incident served to confirm Billy Budd in his incredulity as to the Dansker's strange summing up of the case submitted. The ship at noon, going large before the wind, was rolling[1] on her course, and he below at dinner and engaged in some sportful talk with the members of his mess, chanced in a sudden lurch to spill the entire contents of his soup pan upon the new-scrubbed deck. Claggart, the master-at-arms, official rattan[2] in hand, happened to be passing along the battery in a bay of which the mess was lodged, and the greasy liquid streamed just across his path. Stepping over it, he was proceeding on his way without comment, since the matter was nothing to take notice of under the circumstances, when he happened to observe who it was that had done the spilling. His countenance changed. Pausing, he was about to ejaculate something hasty at the sailor, but checked himself, and pointing down to the streaming soup, playfully tapped him from behind with his rattan, saying in a low musical voice peculiar to him at times, "Handsomely done, my lad! And handsome is as handsome did it,

---

[7] A waterproof hat.
[8] According to Greek myth, the centaur (half-man, half-horse) who tutored the warrior Achilles.
[1] Making good time with the wind behind her.   [2] Cane.

too!" And with that passed on. Not noted by Billy as not coming within his view was the involuntary smile, or rather grimace, that accompanied Claggart's equivocal words. Aridly it drew down the thin corners of his shapely mouth. But everybody taking his remark as meant for humorous, and at which therefore as coming from a superior they were bound to laugh "with counterfeited glee,"[3] acted accordingly; and Billy, tickled, it may be, by the allusion to his being the Handsome Sailor, merrily joined in; then addressing his messmates exclaimed, "There now, who says that Jemmy Legs is down on me!"

"And who said he was, Beauty?" demanded one Donald with some surprise. Whereat the foretopman looked a little foolish, recalling that it was only one person, Board-Her-in-the-Smoke, who had suggested what to him was the smoky idea that this master-at-arms was in any peculiar way hostile to him. Meantime that functionary, resuming his path, must have momentarily worn some expression less guarded than that of the bitter smile, usurping the face from the heart—some distorting expression perhaps, for a drummer-boy heedlessly frolicking along from the opposite direction and chancing to come into light collision with his person was strangely disconcerted by his aspect. Nor was the impression lessened when the official, impetuously giving him a sharp cut with the rattan, vehemently exclaimed, "Look where you go!"

11

What was the matter with the master-at-arms? And, be the matter what it might, how could it have direct relation to Billy Budd, with whom prior to the affair of the spilled soup he had never come into any special contact official or otherwise? What indeed could the trouble have to do with one so little inclined to give offense as the merchant-ship's "peacemaker," even him who in Claggart's own phrase was "the sweet and pleasant young fellow"? Yes, why should Jemmy Legs, to borrow the Dansker's expression, be "down" on the Handsome Sailor? But, at heart and not for nothing, as the late chance encounter may indicate to the discerning, down on him, secretly down on him, he assuredly was.

Now to invent something touching the more private career of Claggart, something involving Billy Budd, of which something the latter should be wholly ignorant, some romantic incident implying that Claggart's knowledge of the young bluejacket began at some period anterior to catching sight of him on board the seventy-four—all this, not so difficult to do, might avail in a way more or less interesting to account for whatever of enigma may appear to lurk in the case. But in fact there was nothing of the sort. And yet the cause necessarily to be assumed as the sole one assignable is in its very realism as much charged with that prime element of Radcliffian[1] romance, the mysterious, as any that the ingenuity of the author of *The Mysteries of Udolpho* could devise. For what can more partake of the mysterious than an antipathy spontaneous and profound such as is evoked in certain exceptional mortals by the mere aspect of some other mortal, however harmless he may be, if not called forth by this very harmlessness itself?

Now there can exist no irritating juxtaposition of dissimilar personalities com-

---

[3] In the poem "The Deserted Village" (1770), by Oliver Goldsmith (1730–1774), frightened pupils laugh "with counterfeited glee" at the jokes of their tyrannical schoolmaster.

[1] Ann Radcliffe (1764–1823) was the author of *The Mysteries of Udolpho* (1794) and other Gothic fiction.

parable to that which is possible aboard a great warship fully manned and at sea. There, every day among all ranks, almost every man comes into more or less of contact with almost every other man. Wholly there to avoid even the sight of an aggravating object one must needs give it Jonah's toss[2] or jump overboard himself. Imagine how all this might eventually operate on some peculiar human creature the direct reverse of a saint!

But for the adequate comprehending of Claggart by a normal nature these hints are insufficient. To pass from a normal nature to him one must cross "the deadly space between." And this is best done by indirection.

Long ago an honest scholar, my senior, said to me in reference to one who like himself is now no more, a man so unimpeachably respectable that against him nothing was ever openly said though among the few something was whispered, "Yes, X—— is a nut not to be cracked by the tap of a lady's fan. You are aware that I am the adherent of no organized religion, much less of any philosophy built into a system. Well, for all that, I think that to try and get into X——, enter his labyrinth and get out again, without a clue derived from some source other than what is known as 'knowledge of the world'—that were hardly possible, at least for me."

"Why," said I, "X——, however singular a study to some, is yet human, and knowledge of the world assuredly implies the knowledge of human nature, and in most of its varieties."

"Yes, but a superficial knowledge of it, serving ordinary purposes. But for anything deeper, I am not certain whether to know the world and to know human nature be not two distinct branches of knowledge, which while they may coexist in the same heart, yet either may exist with little or nothing of the other. Nay, in an average man of the world, his constant rubbing with it blunts that finer spiritual insight indispensable to the understanding of the essential in certain exceptional characters, whether evil ones or good. In a matter of some importance I have seen a girl wind an old lawyer about her little finger. Nor was it the dotage of senile love. Nothing of the sort. But he knew law better than he knew the girl's heart. Coke and Blackstone[3] hardly shed so much light into obscure spiritual places as the Hebrew prophets. And who were they? Mostly recluses."

At the time, my inexperience was such that I did not quite see the drift of all this. It may be that I see it now. And, indeed, if that lexicon which is based on Holy Writ were any longer popular, one might with less difficulty define and denominate certain phenomenal men. As it is, one must turn to some authority not liable to the charge of being tinctured with the biblical element.

In a list of definitions included in the authentic translation of Plato, a list attributed to him, occurs this: "Natural Depravity: a depravity according to nature,"[4] a definition which, though savoring of Calvinism, by no means involves Calvin's dogma as to total mankind. Evidently its intent makes it applicable but to individuals. Not many are the examples of this depravity which the gallows and jail supply. At any rate, for notable instances, since these have no vulgar alloy of the

---

[2] Toss it overboard; in Jonah 1:15 sailors cast the disobedient Jonah "into the sea."

[3] Sir Edward Coke (1552–1634) and Sir William Blackstone (1723–1780), prominent British jurists and students of the law.

[4] Hayford and Sealts suggest that the "authentic translation" to which Melville refers is the six-volume Bohn edition of Plato's work (1848–1854). The definition is given in Volume VI; Melville contrasts it with the doctrine of John Calvin (1509–1564), that humans are born totally depraved and doomed.

brute in them, but invariably are dominated by intellectuality, one must go else-where. Civilization, especially if of the austerer sort, is auspicious to it. It folds itself in the mantle of respectablility. It has its certain negative virtues serving as silent auxiliaries. It never allows wine to get within its guard. It is not going too far to say that it is without vices or small sins. There is a phenomenal pride in it that excludes them. It is never mercenary or avaricious. In short, the depravity here meant partakes nothing of the sordid or sensual. It is serious, but free from acerbity. Though no flatterer of mankind it never speaks ill of it.

But the thing which in eminent instances signalizes so exceptional a nature is this: Though the man's even temper and discreet bearing would seem to intimate a mind peculiarly subject to the law of reason, not the less in heart he would seem to riot in complete exemption from that law, having apparently little to do with rea-son further than to employ it as an ambidexter implement for effecting the irra-tional. That is to say: Toward the accomplishment of an aim which in wantonness of atrocity would seem to partake of the insane, he will direct a cool judgment sagacious and sound. These men are madmen, and of the most dangerous sort, for their lunacy is not continuous, but occasional, evoked by some special object; it is protectively secretive, which is as much as to say it is self-contained, so that when, moreover, most active it is to the average mind not distinguishable from sanity, and for the reason above suggested: that whatever its aims may be—and the aim is never declared—the method and the outward proceeding are always perfectly rational.

Now something such as one was Claggart, in whom was the mania of an evil nature, not engendered by vicious training or corrupting books or licentious liv-ing, but born with him and innate, in short "a depravity according to nature."

Dark sayings are these, some will say, But why? Is it because they somewhat savor of Holy Writ in its phrase "mystery of iniquity"?[5] If they do, such savor was far enough from being intended, for little will it commend these pages to many a reader of today.

The point of the present story turning on the hidden nature of the master-at-arms has necessitated this chapter. With an added hint or two in connection with the incident at the mess, the resumed narrative must be left to vindicate, as it may, its own credibility.

12

That Claggart's figure was not amiss, and his face, save the chin, well molded, has already been said. Of these favorable points he seemed not insensible, for he was not only neat but careful in his dress. But the form of Billy Budd was heroic; and if his face was without the intellectual look of the pallid Claggart's, not the less was it lit, like his, from within, though from a different source. The bonfire in his heart made luminous the rose-tan in his cheek.

In view of the marked contrast between the persons of the twain, it is more than probable that when the master-at-arms in the scene last given applied to the sailor the proverb "Handsome is as handsome does," he there let escape an ironic ink-ling, not caught by the young sailors who heard it, as to what it was that had first moved him against Billy, namely, his significant personal beauty.

[5] "For the mystery of iniquity doth already work," from II Thessalonians 2:7.

Now envy and antipathy, passions irreconcilable in reason, nevertheless in fact may spring conjoined like Chang and Eng[1] in one birth. Is Envy then such a monster? Well, though many an arraigned mortal has in hopes of mitigated penalty pleaded guilty to horrible actions, did ever anybody seriously confess to envy? Something there is in it universally felt to be more shameful than even felonious crime. And not only does everybody disown it, but the better sort are inclined to incredulity when it is in earnest imputed to an intelligent man. But since its lodgment is in the heart not the brain, no degree of intellect supplies a guarantee against it. But Claggart's was no vulgar form of the passion. Nor, as directed toward Billy Budd, did it partake of that streak of apprehensive jealously that marred Saul's visage perturbedly brooding on the comely young David.[2] Claggart's envy struck deeper. If askance he eyed the good looks, cheery health, and frank enjoyment of young life in Billy Budd, it was because these went along with a nature that, as Claggart magnetically felt, had in its simplicity never willed malice or experienced the reactionary bite of that serpent. To him, the spirit lodged within Billy, and looking out from his welkin eyes as from windows, that ineffability it was which made the dimple in his dyed cheek, suppled his joints, and dancing in his yellow curls made him pre-eminently the Handsome Sailor. One person excepted, the master-at-arms was perhaps the only man in the ship intellectually capable of adequately appreciating the moral phenomenon presented in Billy Budd. And the insight but intensified his passion, which assuming various secret forms within him, at times assumed that of cynic disdain, disdain of innocence—to be nothing more than innocent! Yet in an aesthetic way he saw the charm of it, the courageous free-and-easy temper of it, and fain would have shared it, but he despaired of it.

With no power to annul the elemental evil in him, though readily enough he could hide it; apprehending the good, but powerless to be it; a nature like Claggart's, surcharged with energy as such natures almost invariably are, what recourse is left to it but to recoil upon itself and, like the scorpion for which the Creator alone is responsible, act out to the end the part allotted it.

13

Passion, and passion in its profoundest, is not a thing demanding a palatial stage whereon to play its part. Down among the groundlings, among the beggars and rakers of the garbage, profound passion is enacted. And the circumstances that provoke it, however trivial or mean, are no measure of its power. In the present instance the stage is a scrubbed gun deck, and one of the external provocations a man-of-war's man's spilled soup.

Now when the master-at-arms noticed whence came that greasy fluid streaming before his feet, he must have taken it—to some extent wilfully, perhaps—not for the mere accident it assuredly was, but for the sly escape of a spontaneous feeling on Billy's part more or less answering to the antipathy on his own. In effect a foolish demonstration, he must have thought, and very harmless, like the futile kick of a heifer, which yet were the heifer a shod stallion would not be so harmless. Even so was it that into the gall of Claggart's envy he infused the vitriol of

---

[1] Famous Siamese twins (1811–1874) exhibited as freaks in the United States by P. T. Barnum (1810–1891). Their show visited Pittsfield, Massachusetts, in 1853 while Melville lived there.

[2] In I Samuel 16: 18 Saul, the first king of Israel, is jealous of his ultimate successor, the "comely" and popular David.

his contempt. But the incident confirmed to him certain telltale reports purveyed to his ear by "Squeak," one of his more cunning corporals, a grizzled little man, so nicknamed by the sailors on account of his squeaky voice and sharp visage ferreting about the dark corners of the lower decks after interlopers, satirically suggesting to them the idea of a rat in a cellar.

From his chief's employing him as an implicit tool in laying little traps for the worriment of the foretopman—for it was from the master-at-arms that the petty persecutions heretofore adverted to had proceeded—the corporal, having naturally enough concluded that his master could have no love for the sailor, made it his business, faithful understrapper that he was, to foment the ill blood by perverting to his chief certain innocent frolics of the good-natured foretopman, besides inventing for his mouth sundry contumelious epithets he claimed to have overheard him let fall. The master-at-arms never suspected the veracity of these reports, more especially as to the epithets, for he well knew how secretly unpopular may become a master-at-arms, at least a master-at-arms of those days, zealous in his function, and how the bluejackets shoot at him in private their raillery and wit; the nickname by which he goes among them (Jemmy Legs) implying under the form of merriment their cherished disrespect and dislike. But in view of the greediness of hate for pabulum[1] it hardly needed a purveyor to feed Claggart's passion.

An uncommon prudence is habitual with the subtler depravity, for it has everything to hide. And in case of an injury but suspected, its secretiveness voluntarily cuts it off from enlightenment or disillusion; and, not unreluctantly, action is taken upon surmise as upon certainty. And the retaliation is apt to be in monstrous disproportion to the supposed offense; for when in anybody was revenge in its exactions aught else but an inordinate usurer? But how with Claggart's conscience? For though consciences are unlike as foreheads, every intelligence, not excluding the scriptural devils who "believe and tremble,"[2] has one. But Claggart's conscience being but the lawyer to his will, made ogres of trifles, probably arguing that the motive imputed to Billy in spilling the soup just when he did, together with the epithets alleged, these, if nothing more, made a strong case against him; nay, justified animosity into a sort of retributive righteousness. The Pharisee is the Guy Fawkes[3] prowling in the hid chambers underlying some natures like Claggart's. And they can really form no conception of an unreciprocated malice. Probably the master-at-arms' clandestine persecution of Billy was started to try the temper of the man; but it had not developed any quality in him that enmity could make official use of or even pervert into plausible self-justification; so that the occurrence at the mess, petty if it were, was a welcome one to that peculiar conscience assigned to be the private mentor of Claggart; and, for the rest, not improbably it put him upon new experiments.

14

Not many days after the last incident narrated, something befell Billy Budd that more graveled him than aught that had previously occurred.

---

[1] Nourishment.

[2] "Thou believest that there is one God; . . . the devils also believe, and tremble," from James 2:19.

[3] Guy Fawkes (1570–1606), here the model of a Pharisee (or religious hypocrite who conspired against Christ), was a Catholic conspirator in the Gunpowder Plot to blow up the Parliament building in London in 1605.

It was a warm night for the latitude; and the foretopman, whose watch at the time was properly below, was dozing on the uppermost deck wither he had ascended from his hot hammock, one of hundreds suspended so closely wedged together over a lower gun deck that there was little or no swing to them. He lay as in the shadow of a hillside, stretched under the lee of the booms,[1] a piled ridge of spare spars amidships between foremast and mainmast among which the ship's largest boat, the launch, was stowed. Alongside of three other slumberers from below, he lay near that end of the booms which approaches the foremast; his station aloft on duty as a foretopman being just over the deck-station of the forecastlemen, entitling him according to usage to make himself more or less at home in that neighborhood.

Presently he was stirred into semiconsciousness by somebody, who must have previously sounded the sleep of the others, touching his shoulder, and then, as the foretopman raised his head, breathing into his ear in quick whisper, "Slip into the lee forechains, Billy; there is something in the wind. Don't speak. Quick, I will meet you there," and disappearing.

Now Billy, like sundry other essentially good-natured ones, had some of the weaknesses inseparable from essential good nature; and among these was a reluctance, almost an incapacity of plumply saying *no* to an abrupt proposition not obviously absurd on the face of it, nor obviously unfriendly, nor iniquitous. And being of warm blood, he had not the phlegm[2] tacitly to negative any proposition by unresponsive inaction. Like his sense of fear, his apprehension as to aught outside of the honest and natural was seldom very quick. Besides, upon the present occasion, the drowse from his sleep still hung upon him.

However it was, he mechanically rose and, sleepily wondering what could be in the wind, betook himself to the designated place, a narrow platform, one of six, outside of the high bulwarks and screened by the great deadeyes[3] and multiple columned lanyards of the shrouds and backstays; and, in a great warship of that time, of dimensions commensurate to the hull's magnitude; a tarry balcony[4] in short, overhanging the sea, and so secluded that one mariner of the *Bellipotent*, a Nonconformist[5] old tar of a serious turn, made it even in daytime his private oratory.[6]

In this retired nook the stranger soon joined Billy Budd. There was no moon as yet; a haze obscured the starlight. He could not distinctly see the stranger's face. Yet from something in the outline and carriage, Billy took him, and correctly, for one of the afterguard.

"Hist! Billy," said the man, in the same quick cautionary whisper as before. "You were impressed, weren't you? Well, so was I"; and he paused, as to mark the effect. But Billy, not knowing exactly what to make of this, said nothing. Then the other: "We are not the only impressed ones, Billy. There's a gang of us.—Couldn't you—help—at a pinch?"

"What do you mean?" demanded Billy, here thoroughly shaking off his drowse.

---

[1] The sheltered side (out of the wind) of the spars that extend the bottoms of sails.
[2] Sluggishness or calmness of temperament.
[3] Flat wooden blocks with holes for the lanyards, or ropes used to fasten the shrouds and backstays (ropes that support masts).
[4] A platform on a mast.
[5] A Protestant dissenter who disdained the religious services of the Anglican church.
[6] A chapel for private prayer.

"Hist, hist!" the hurried whisper now growing husky. "See here," and the man held up two small objects faintly twinkling in the night-light; "see, they are yours, Billy, if you'll only——"

But Billy broke in, and in his resentful eagerness to deliver himself his vocal infirmity somewhat intruded. "D—d—damme, I don't know what you are d—d—driving at, or what you mean, but you had better g—g—go where you belong!" For the moment the fellow, as confounded, did not stir; and Billy, springing to his feet, said, "If you d—don't start, I'll t—t—toss you back over the r—rail!" There was no mistaking this, and the mysterious emissary decamped, disappearing in the direction of the mainmast in the shadow of the booms.

"Hallo, what's the matter?" here came growling from a forecastleman awakened from his deck-doze by Billy's raised voice. And as the foretopman reappeared and was recognized by him: "Ah, Beauty, is it you? Well, something must have been the matter, for you st—st—stuttered."

"Oh," rejoined Billy, now mastering the impediment, "I found an afterguardsman in our part of the ship here, and I bid him be off where he belongs."

"And is that all you did about it, Foretopman?" gruffly demanded another, an irascible old fellow of brick-colored visage and hair who was known to his associate forecastlemen as "Red Pepper." "Such sneaks I should like to marry to the gunner's daughter!"—by that expression meaning that he would like to subject them to disciplinary castigation over a gun.[7]

However, Billy's rendering of the matter satisfactorily accounted to these inquirers for the brief commotion, since of all the sections of a ship's company the forecastlemen, veterans for the most part and bigoted in their sea prejudices, are the most jealous in resenting territorial encroachments, especially on the part of any of the afterguard, of whom they have but a sorry opinion—chiefly landsmen, never going aloft except to reef or furl the mainsail, and in no wise competent to handle a marlinspike[8] or turn in a deadeye, say.

15

This incident sorely puzzled Billy Budd. It was an entirely new experience, the first time in his life that he had ever been personally approached in underhand intriguing fashion. Prior to this encounter he had known nothing of the afterguardsman, the two men being stationed wide apart, one forward and aloft during his watch, the other on deck and aft.

What could it mean? And could they really be guineas,[1] those two glittering objects the interloper had held up to his (Billy's) eyes? Where could the fellow get guineas? Why, even spare buttons are not so plentiful at sea. The more he turned the matter over, the more he was nonplussed, and made uneasy and discomfited. In his disgustful recoil from an overture which, though he but ill comprehended, he instinctively knew must involve evil of some sort, Billy Budd was like a young horse fresh from the pasture suddenly inhaling a vile whiff from some chemical factory, and by repeated snortings trying to get it out of his nostrils and lungs.

---

[7] Flogging; men were lashed to the "gunner's daughter," a gun, for punishment.
[8] A tool for splicing rope.
[1] Gold coins worth a pound and a shilling.

This frame of mind barred all desire of holding further parley with the fellow, even were it but for the purpose of gaining some enlightenment as to his design in approaching him. And yet he was not without natural curiosity to see how such a visitor in the dark would look in broad day.

He espied him the following afternoon in his first dogwatch below, one of the smokers on that forward part of the upper gun deck allotted to the pipe.[2] He recognized him by his general cut and build more than by his round freckled face and glassy eyes of pale blue, veiled with lashes all but white. And yet Billy was a bit uncertain whether indeed it were he—yonder chap about his own age chatting and laughing in freehearted way, leaning against a gun; a genial young fellow enough to look at, and something of a rattlebrain, to all appearance. Rather chubby too for a sailor, even an afterguardsman. In short, the last man in the world, one would think, to be overburdened with thoughts, especially those perilous thoughts that must needs belong to a conspirator in any serious project, or even to the underling of such a conspirator.

Although Billy was not aware of it, the fellow, with a side long watchful glance, had perceived Billy first, and then noting that Billy was looking at him, thereupon nodded a familiar sort of friendly recognition as to an old acquaintance, without interrupting the talk he was engaged in with the group of smokers. A day or two afterwards, chancing in the evening promenade on a gun deck to pass Billy, he offered a flying word of good-fellowship, as it were, which by its unexpectedness, and equivocalness under the circumstances, so embarrassed Billy that he knew not how to respond to it, and let it go unnoticed.

Billy was now left more at a loss than before. The ineffectual speculations into which he was led were so disturbingly alien to him that he did his best to smother them. It never entered his mind that here was a matter which, from its extreme questionableness, it was his duty as a loyal bluejacket to report in the proper quarter. And, probably, had such a step been suggested to him, he would have been deterred from taking it by the thought, one of novice magnanimity, that it would savor overmuch of the dirty work of a telltale. He kept the thing to himself. Yet upon one occasion he could not forbear a little disburdening himself to the old Dansker, tempted thereto perhaps by the influence of a balmy night when the ship lay becalmed; the twain, silent for the most part, sitting together on deck, their heads propped against the bulwarks. But it was only a partial and anonymous account that Billy gave, the unfounded scruples above referred to preventing full disclosure to anybody. Upon hearing Billy's version, the sage Dansker seemed to divine more than he was told; and after a little meditation, during which his wrinkles were pursed as into a point, quite effacing for the time that quizzing expression his face sometimes wore: "Didn't I say so, Baby Budd?"

"Say what?" demanded Billy.

"Why, *Jemmy Legs* is *down* on you."

"And what," rejoined Billy in amazement, "has *Jemmy Legs* to do with that cracked afterguardsman?"

"Ho, it was an afterguardsman, then. A cat's-paw, a cat's-paw!" And with that exclamation, whether it had reference to a light puff of air just then coming over the calm sea, or a subtler relation to the afterguardsman, there is no telling, the old Merlin gave a twisting wrench with his black teeth at his plug of tobacco, vouch-

---

[2] Where smoking was permitted.

safing no reply to Billy's impetuous question, though now repeated, for it was his wont to relapse into grim silence when interrogated in skeptical sort as to any of his sententious oracles, not always very clear ones, rather partaking of that obscurity which invests most Delphic deliverances[3] from any quarter.

Long experience had very likely brought this old man to that bitter prudence which never interferes in aught and never gives advice.

<h1 style="text-align:center">16</h1>

Yes, despite the Dansker's pithy insistence as to the master-at-arms being at the bottom of these strange experiences of Billy on board the *Bellipotent,* the young sailor was ready to ascribe them to almost anybody but the man who, to use Billy's own expression, "always had a pleasant word for him." This is to be wondered at. Yet no so much to be wondered at. In certain matters, some sailors even in mature life remain unsophisticated enough. But a young seafarer of the disposition of our athletic foretopman is much of a child-man. And yet a child's utter innocence is but its blank ignorance, and the innocence more or less wanes as intelligence waxes. But in Billy Budd intelligence, such as it was, had advanced while yet his simple-mindedness remained for the most part unaffected. Experience is a teacher indeed; yet did Billy's years make his experience small. Besides, he had none of that intuitive knowledge of the bad which in natures not good or incompletely so foreruns experience, and therefore may pertain, as in some instances it too clearly does pertain, even to youth.

And what could Billy know of man except of man as a mere sailor? And the old-fashioned sailor, the veritable man before the mast, the sailor from boyhood up, he, though indeed of the same species as a landsman, is in some respects singularly distinct from him. The sailor is frankness, the landsman is finesse. Life is not a game with the sailor, demanding the long head[1]—no intricate game of chess where few moves are made in straight-forwardness and ends are attained by indirection, an oblique, tedious, barren game hardly worth that poor candle burnt out in playing it.

Yes, as a class, sailors are in character a juvenile race. Even their deviations are marked by juvenility, this more especially holding true with the sailors of Billy's time. Then too, certain things which apply to all sailors do more pointedly operate here and there upon the junior one. Every sailor, too, is accustomed to obey orders without debating them; his life afloat is externally ruled for him; he is not brought into that promiscuous commerce with mankind where unobstructed free agency on equal terms—equal superficially, at least—soon teaches one that unless upon occasion he exercise a distrust keen in proportion to the fairness of the appearance, some foul turn may be served him. A ruled undemonstrative distrustfulness is so habitual, not with businessmen so much as with men who know their kind in less shallow relations than business, namely, certain men of the world, that they come at last to employ it all but unconsciously; and some of them would very likely feel real surprise at being charged with it as one of their general characteristics.

---

[3] According to Greek myth, the cryptic, obscure prophecies of the oracle at Delphi.
[1] Foresight and careful planning.

17

But after the little matter at the mess Billy Budd no more found himself in strange trouble at times about his hammock or his clothes bag or what not. As to that smile that occasionally sunned him, and the pleasant passing word, these were, if not more frequent, yet if anything more pronounced than before.

But for all that, there were certain other demonstrations now. When Claggart's unobserved glance happened to light on belted Billy rolling[1] along the upper gun deck in the leisure of the second dogwatch, exchanging passing broadsides of fun with other young promenaders in the crowd, that glance would follow the cheerful sea Hyperion[2] with a settled meditative and melancholy expression, his eyes strangely suffused with incipient feverish tears. Then would Claggart look like the man of sorrows.[3] Yes, and sometimes the melancholy expression would have in it a touch of soft yearning, as if Claggart could even have loved Billy but for fate and ban. But this was an evanescence, and quickly repented of, as it were, by an immitigable look, pinching and shriveling the visage into the momentary semblance of a wrinkled walnut. But sometimes catching sight in advance of the foretopman coming in his direction, he would, upon their nearing, step aside a little to let him pass, dwelling upon Billy for the moment with the glittering dental satire of a Guise.[4] But upon any abrupt unforeseen encounter a red light would flash forth from his eye like a spark from an anvil in a dusk smithy. That quick, fierce light was a strange one, darted from orbs which in repose were of a color nearest approaching a deeper violet, the softest of shades.

Though some of these caprices of the pit could not but be observed by their object, yet were they beyond the construing of such a nature. And the thews[5] of Billy were hardly compatible with that sort of sensitive spiritual organization which in some cases instinctively conveys to ignorant innocence an admonition of the proximity of the malign. He thought the master-at-arms acted in a manner rather queer at times. That was all. But the occasional frank air and pleasant word went for what they purported to be, the young sailor never having heard as yet of the "too fair-spoken man."

Had the foretopman been conscious of having done or said anything to provoke the ill will of the official, it would have been different with him, and his sight might have been purged if not sharpened. As it was, innocence was his blinder.

So was it with him in yet another matter. Two minor officers, the armorer and captain of the hold,[6] with whom he had never exchanged a word, his position in the ship not bringing him into contact with them, these men now for the first began to cast upon Billy, when they chanced to encounter him, that peculiar glance which evidences that the man from whom it comes has been some way tampered with, and to the prejudice of him upon whom the glance lights. Never did it occur to Billy as a thing to be noted or a thing suspicious, though he well knew the fact, that the armorer and captain of the hold, with the ship's yeoman,

---

[1] Billy walking, with a rolling gait, as though he were a nobleman wearing the belt distinguishing his rank.

[2] According to Greek myth, a Titan (or giant) identified with Apollo, the sun god and epitome of manly beauty.

[3] In Isaiah 53:3 the servant of the Lord is said to be "a man of sorrows, and acquainted with grief."

[4] A sixteenth-century French noble family known for treachery and smiling hypocrisy.

[5] Muscles, sinews.

[6] Petty officers responsible for the ship's arms and for the ship's interior, below the deck.

apothecary, and others of that grade, were by naval usage messmates of the master-at-arms, men with ears convenient to his confidential tongue.

But the general popularity that came from our Handsome Sailor's manly forwardness upon occasion and irrestible good nature, indicating no mental superiority tending to excite an invidious feeling, this good will on the part of most of his shipmates made him the less to concern himself about such mute aspects toward him as those whereto allusion has just been made, aspects he could not so fathom as to infer their whole import.

As to the afterguardsman, though Billy for reasons already given necessarily saw little of him, yet when the two did happen to meet, invariably came the fellow's offhand cheerful recognition, sometimes accompanied by a passing pleasant word or two. Whatever that equivocal young person's original design may really have been, or the design of which he might have been the deputy, certain it was from his manner upon these occasions that he had wholly dropped it.

It was as if his precocity of crookedness (and every vulgar villain is precocious) had for once deceived him, and the man he had sought to entrap as a simpleton had through his very simplicity ignominiously baffled him.

But shrewd ones may opine that it was hardly possible for Billy to refrain from going up to the afterguardsman and bluntly demanding to know his purpose in the initial interview so abruptly closed in the forechains. Shrewd ones may also think it but natural in Billy to set about sounding some of the other impressed men of the ship in order to discover what basis, if any, there was for the emissary's obscure suggestions as to plotting disaffection aboard. Yes, shrewd ones may so think. But something more, or rather something else than mere shrewdness is perhaps needful for the due understanding of such a character as Billy Budd's.

As to Claggart, the monomania in the man—if that indeed it were—as involuntarily disclosed by starts in the manifestations detailed, yet in general covered over by his self-contained and rational demeanor; this, like a subterranean fire, was eating its way deeper and deeper in him. Something decisive must come of it.

18

After the mysterious interview in the forechains, the one so abruptly ended there by Billy, nothing especially germane to the story occurred until the events now about to be narrated.

Elsewhere it has been said that in the lack of frigates (of course better sailors than line-of-battle ships) in the English squadron up the Straits[1] at that period, the *Bellipotent 74* was occasionally employed not only as an available substitute for a scout, but at times on detached service of more important kind. This was not alone because of her sailing qualities, not common in a ship of her rate, but quite as much, probably, that the character of her commander, it was thought, specially adapted him for any duty where under unforeseen difficulties a prompt initiative might have to be taken in some matter demanding knowledge and ability in addition to those qualities implied in good seamanship. It was on an expedition of the latter sort, a somewhat distant one, and when the *Bellipotent* was almost at her furthest remove from the fleet, that in the latter part of an afternoon watch she unexpectedly came in sight of a ship of the enemy. It proved to be a frigate. The

[1] The Straits of Gibraltar, into the Mediterranean.

latter, perceiving through the glass that the weight of men and metal would be heavily against her, invoking her light heels crowded sail to get away. After a chase urged almost against hope and lasting until about the middle of the first dogwatch, she signally succeeded in effecting her escape.

Not long after the pursuit had been given up, and ere the excitement incident thereto had altogether waned away, the master-at-arms, ascending from his cavernous sphere, made his appearance cap in hand by the mainmast respectfully waiting the notice of Captain Vere, then solitary walking the weather side of the quarter-deck, doubtless somewhat chafed at the failure of the pursuit. The spot where Claggart stood was the place allotted to men of lesser grades seeking some more particular interview either with the officer of the deck or the captain himself. But from the latter it was not often that a sailor or petty officer of those days would seek a hearing; only some exceptional cause would, according to established custom, have warranted that.

Presently, just as the commander, absorbed in his reflections, was on the point of turning aft in his promenade, he became sensible of Claggart's presence, and saw the doffed cap held in deferential expectancy. Here be it said that Captain Vere's personal knowledge of this petty officer had only begun at the time of the ship's last sailing from home, Claggart then for the first, in transfer from a ship detained for repairs, supplying on board the *Bellipotent* the place of a previous master-at-arms disabled and ashore.

No sooner did the commander observe who it was that now deferentially stood awaiting his notice than a peculiar expression came over him. It was not unlike that which uncontrollably will flit across the countenance of one at unawares encountering a person who, though known to him indeed, has hardly been long enough known for thorough knowledge, but something in whose aspect nevertheless now for the first provokes a vaguely repellent distaste. But coming to a stand and resuming much of his wonted official manner, save that a sort of impatience lurked in the intonation of the opening word, he said "Well? What is it, Master-at-arms?"

With the air of a subordinate grieved at the necessity of being a messenger of ill tidings, and while conscientiously determined to be frank yet equally resolved upon shunning overstatement, Claggart at this invitation, or rather summons to disburden, spoke up. What he said, conveyed in the language of no uneducated man, was to the effect following, if not altogether in these words, namely, that during the chase and preparations for the possible encounter he had seen enough to convince him that at least one sailor aboard was a dangerous character in a ship mustering some who not only had taken a guilty part in the late serious troubles, but others also who, like the man in question, had entered His Majesty's service under another form than enlistment.

At this point Captain Vere with some impatience interrupted him: "Be direct, man; say *impressed men*."

Claggart made a gesture of subservience, and proceeded. Quite lately he (Claggart) had begun to suspect that on the gun decks some sort of movement prompted by the sailor in question was covertly going on, but he had not thought himself warranted in reporting the suspicion so long as it remained indistinct. But from what he had that afternoon observed in the man referred to, the suspicion of something clandestine going on had advanced to a point less removed from certainty. He deeply felt, he added, the serious responsibility assumed in making a report involving such possible consequences to the individual mainly concerned, besides tending to augment those natural anxieties which every naval commander must feel in view of extraordinary outbreaks so recent as those which, he sorrowfully said it, it needed not to name.

Now at the first broaching of the matter Captain Vere, taken by surprise, could not wholly dissemble his disquietude. But as Claggart went on, the former's aspect changed into restiveness under something in the testifier's manner in giving his testimony. However, he refrained from interrupting him. And Claggart, continuing, concluded with this: "God forbid, your honor, that the *Bellipotent*'s should be the experience of the—"

"Never mind that!" here peremptorily broke in the superior, his face altering with anger, instinctively divining the ship that the other was about to name, one in which the Nore Mutiny had assumed a singularly tragical character that for a time jeopardized the life of its commander. Under the circumstances he was indignant at the purposed allusion. When the commissioned officers themselves were on all occasions very heedful how they referred to the recent events in the fleet, for a petty officer unnecessarily to allude to them in the presence of his captain, this struck him as a most immodest presumption. Besides, to his quick sense of self-respect it even looked under the circumstances something like an attempt to alarm him. Nor at first was he without some surprise that one who so far as he had hitherto come under his notice had shown considerable tact in his function should in this particular evince such lack of it.

But these thoughts and kindred dubious ones flitting across his mind were suddenly replaced by an intuitional surmise which, though as yet obscure in form, served practically to affect his reception of the ill tidings. Certain it is that, long versed in everything pertaining to the complicated gun-deck life, which like every other form of life has its secret mines and dubious side, the side popularly disclaimed, Captain Vere did not permit himself to be unduly disturbed by the general tenor of his subordinate's report.

Furthermore, if in view of recent events prompt action should be taken at the first palpable sign of recurring insubordination, for all that, not judicious would it be, he thought, to keep the idea of lingering disaffection alive by undue forwardness in crediting an informer, even if his own subordinate and charged among other things with police surveillance of the crew. This feeling would not perhaps have so prevailed with him were it not that upon a prior occasion the patriotic zeal officially evinced by Claggart had somewhat irritated him as appearing rather supersensible and strained. Furthermore, something even in the official's self-possessed and somewhat ostentatious manner in making his specification strangely reminded him of a bandsman,[2] a perjurious witness in a capital case before a court-martial ashore of which when a lieutenant he (Captain Vere) had been a member.

Now the peremptory check given to Claggart in the matter of the arrested allusion was quickly followed up by this: "You say that there is at least one dangerous man aboard. Name him."

"William Budd, a foretopman, your honor."

"William Budd!" repeated Captain Vere with unfeigned astonishment. "And mean you the man that Lieutenant Ratcliffe took from the merchantman not very long ago, the young fellow who seems to be so popular with the men—Billy, the Handsome Sailor, as they call him?"

"The same, your honor; but for all his youth and good looks, a deep one. Not

---

[2] A hoist operator.

for nothing does he insinuate himself into the good will of his shipmates, since at the least they will at a pinch say—all hands will—a good word for him, and at all hazards. Did Lieutenant Ratcliffe happen to tell your honor of that adroit fling of Budd's, jumping up in the cutter's bow under the merchantman's stern when he was being taken off? It is even masked by that sort of good-humored air that at heart he resents his impressment. You have but noted his fair cheek. A mantrap may be under the ruddy-tipped daisies."

Now the Handsome Sailor as a signal figure among the crew had naturally enough attracted the captain's attention from the first. Though in general not very demonstrative to his officers, he had congratulated Lieutenant Ratcliffe upon his good fortune in lighting on such a fine specimen of the *genus homo*,[3] who in the nude might have posed for a statue of young Adam before the Fall. As to Billy's adieu to the ship *Rights-of-Man*, which the boarding lieutenant had indeed reported to him, but, in a deferential way, more as a good story than aught else, Captain Vere, though mistakenly understanding it as a satiric sally, had but thought so much the better of the impressed man for it; as a military sailor, admiring the spirit that could take an arbitrary enlistment so merrily and sensibly. The foretopman's conduct, too, so far as it had fallen under the captain's notice, had confirmed the first happy augury, while the new recruit's qualities as a "sailor-man" seemed to be such that he had thought of recommending him to the executive officer for promotion to a place that would more frequently bring him under his own observation, namely, the captaincy of the mizzentop,[4] replacing there in the starboard watch a man not so young whom partly for that reason he deemed less fitted for the post. Be it parenthesized here that since the mizzentopment have not to handle such breadths of heavy canvas as the lower sails on the mainmast and foremast, a young man if of the right stuff not only seems best adapted to duty there, but in fact is generally selected for the captaincy of that top, and the company under him are light hands and often but striplings. In sum, Captain Vere had from the beginning deemed Billy Budd to be what in the naval parlance of the time was called a "King's bargain": that is to say, for His Britannic Majesty's navy a capital investment at small outlay or none at all.

After a brief pause, during which the reminiscences above mentioned passed vividly through his mind and he weighed the import of Claggart's last suggestion conveyed in the phrase "mantrap under the daisies," and the more he weighed it the less reliance he felt in the informer's good faith, suddenly he turned upon him and in a low voice demanded: "Do you come to me, Master-at-arms, with so foggy a tale? As to Budd, cite me an act or spoken word of his confirmatory of what you in general charge against him. Stay," drawing nearer to him; "heed what you speak. Just now, and in a case like this, there is a yardarm-end for the false witness."[5]

"Ah, your honor!" sighed Claggart, mildly shaking his shapely head as in sad deprecation of such unmerited severity of tone. Then, bridling—erecting himself as in virtuous self-assertion—he circumstantially alleged certain words and acts which collectively, if credited, led to presumptions mortally inculpating Budd. And for some of these averments, he added, substantiating proof was not far.

With gray eyes impatient and distrustful essaying to fathom to the bottom Claggart's calm violet ones, Captain Vere again heard him out; then for the moment stood ruminating. The mood he evinced, Claggart—himself for the time liberated

---

[3] The human race.   [4] The head of the watch assigned to the rear (mizzen) mast.
[5] You will hang at the end of a yardarm for perjury.

from the other's scrutiny—steadily regarded with a look difficult to render: a look curious of the operation of his tactics, a look such as might have been that of the spokesman of the envious children of Jacob deceptively imposing upon the troubled patriarch the blood-dyed coat of young Joseph.[6]

Though something exceptional in the moral quality of Captain Vere made him, in earnest encounter with a fellow man, a veritable touchstone of that man's essential nature, yet now as to Claggart and what was really going on in him his feeling partook less of intuitional conviction than of strong suspicion clogged by strange dubieties. The perplexity he evinced proceeded less from aught touching the man informed against—as Claggart doubtless opined—than from considerations how best to act in regard to the informer. At first, indeed, he was naturally for summoning that substantiation of his allegations which Claggart said was at hand. But such a proceeding would result in the matter at once getting abroad, which in the present stage of it, he thought, might undesirably affect the ship's company. If Claggart was a false witness—that closed the affair. And therefore, before trying the accusation, he would first practically test the accuser; and he thought this could be done in a quiet, undemonstrative way.

The measure he determined upon involved a shifting of the scene, a transfer to a place less exposed to observation than the broad quarter-deck. For although the few gun-room officers there at the time had, in due observance of naval etiquette, withdrawn to leeward the moment Captain Vere had begun his promenade on the deck's weather side; and though during the colloquy with Claggart they of course ventured not to diminish the distance; and though throughout the interview Captain Vere's voice was far from high, and Claggart's silvery and low; and the wind in the cordage and the wash of the sea helped the more to put them beyond earshot; nevertheless, the interview's continuance already had attracted observation from some topmen aloft and other sailors in the waist or further forward.

Having determined upon his measures, Captain Vere forthwith took action. Abruptly turning to Claggart, he asked, "Master-at-arms, is it now Budd's watch aloft?"

"No, your honor."

Whereupon, "Mr. Wilkes!" summoning the nearest midshipman. "Tell Albert to come to me." Albert was the captain's hammock-boy, a sort of sea valet in whose discretion and fidelity his master had much confidence. The lad appeared.

"You know Budd, the foretopman?"

"I do, sir."

"Go find him. It is his watch off. Manage to tell him out of earshot that he is wanted aft. Contrive it that he speaks to nobody. Keep him in talk yourself. And not till you get well aft here, not till then let him know that the place where he is wanted is my cabin. You understand. Go.—Master-at-arms, show yourself on the decks below, and when you think it time for Albert to be coming with his man, stand by quietly to follow the sailor in."

19

Now when the foretopman found himself in the cabin, closeted there, as it were, with the captain and Claggart, he was surprised enough. But it was a surprise

---

[6] In Genesis 37:31–33, after selling Joseph into bondage, his brothers stained his coat with blood to convince their father, Jacob, of Joseph's death.

unaccompanied by apprehension or distrust. To an immature nature essentially honest and humane, forewarning intimations of subtler danger from one's kind come tardily if at all. The only thing that took shape in the young sailor's mind was this: Yes, the captain, I have always thought, looks kindly upon me. Wonder if he's going to make me his coxswain. I should like that. And may be now he is going to ask the master-at-arms about me.

"Shut the door there, sentry," said the commander; "stand without, and let nobody come in.—Now, Master-at-arms, tell this man to his face what you told of him to me," and stood prepared to scrutinize the mutually confronting visages.

With the measured step and calm collected air of an asylum physician approaching in the public hall some patient beginning to show indications of a coming paroxysm, Claggart deliberately advanced within short range of Billy, and mesmerically looking him in the eye, briefly recapitulated the accusation.

Not at first did Billy take it in. When he did, the rose-tan of his cheek looked struck as by white leprosy. He stood like one impaled and gagged. Meanwhile the accuser's eyes, removing not as yet from the blue dilated ones, underwent a phenomenal change, their wonted rich violet color blurring into a muddy purple. Those lights of human intelligence, losing human expression, were gelidly[1] protruding like the alien eyes of certain uncatalogued creatures of the deep. The first mesmeristic glance was one of serpent fascination; the last was as the paralyzing lurch of the torpedo fish.[2]

"Speak, man!" said Captain Vere to the transfixed one, struck by his aspect even more than by Claggart's. "Speak! Defend yourself!" Which appeal caused but a strange dumb gesturing and gurgling in Billy; amazement at such an accusation so suddenly sprung on inexperience nonage;[3] this, and, it may be, horror of the accuser's eyes, serving to bring out his lurking defect and in this instance for the time intensifying it into a colvulsed tongue-tie; while the intent head and entire form straining forward in an agony of ineffectual eagerness to obey the injunction to speak and defend himself, gave an expression to the face like that of a condemned vestal priestess in the moment of being buried alive,[4] and in the first struggle against suffocation.

Though at the time Captain Vere was quite ignorant of Billy's liability to vocal impediment, he now immediately divined it, since vividly Billy's aspect recalled to him that of a bright young schoolmate of his whom he had once seen struck by much the same startling impotence in the act of eagerly rising in the class to be foremost in response to a testing question put to it by the master. Going close up to the young sailor, and laying a soothing hand on his shoulder, he said, "There is no hurry, my boy. Take your time, take your time." Contrary to the effect intended, these words so fatherly in tone, doubtless touching Billy's heart to the quick, prompted yet more violent efforts at utterance—efforts soon ending for the time in confirming the paralysis, and bringing to his face an expression which was as a crucifixion to behold. The next instant, quick as the flame from a discharged cannon at night, his right arm shot out, and Claggart dropped to the deck. Whether intentionally or but owing to the young athlete's superior height, the blow had taken effect full upon the forehead, so shapely and intellectual-looking a feature in the master-at-arms; so that the body fell over lengthwise, like a heavy plank tilted from erectness. A gasp or two, and he lay motionless.

---

[1] Frozenly.   [2] A fish that paralyzes its prey by electric shock.   [3] Youth.
[4] Priestesses of the Roman goddess Vesta were buried alive if found guilty of unchastity.

"Fated boy," breathed Captain Vere in tone so low as to be almost a whisper, "what have you done! But here, help me."

The twain raised the felled one from the loins up into a sitting position. The spare form flexibly acquiesced, but inertly. It was like handling a dead snake. They lowered it back. Regaining erectness, Captain Vere with one hand covering his face stood to all appearance as impassive as the object at his feet. Was he absorbed in taking in all the bearings of the event and what was best not only now at once to be done, but also in the sequel? Slowly he uncovered his face; and the effect was as if the moon emerging from eclipse should reappear with quite another aspect than that which had gone into hiding. The father in him, manifested towards Billy thus far in the scene, was replaced by the military disciplinarian. In his official tone he bade the foretopman retire to a stateroom aft (pointing it out), and there remain till thence summoned. This order Billy in silence mechanically obeyed. Then going to the cabin door where it opened on the quarter-deck, Captain Vere said to the sentry without, "Tell somebody to send Albert here." When the lad appeared, his master so contrived it that he should not catch sight of the prone one. "Albert," he said to him, "tell the surgeon I wish to see him. You need not come back till called."

When the surgeon entered—a self-poised character of that grave sense and experience that hardly anything could take him aback—Captain Vere advanced to meet him, thus unconsciously intercepting his view of Claggart, and, interrupting the other's wonted ceremonious salutation, said, "Nay. Tell me how it is with yonder man," directing his attention to the prostrate one.

The surgeon looked, and for all his self-command somewhat started at the abrupt revelation. On Claggart's always pallid complexion, thick black blood was now oozing from nostril and ear. To the gazer's professional eye it was unmistakably no living man that he saw.

"Is it so, then?" said Captain Vere, intently watching him. "I thought it. But verify it." Whereupon the customary tests confirmed the surgeon's first glance, who now, looking up in unfeigned concern, cast a look of intense inquisitiveness upon his superior. But Captain Vere, with one hand to his brow, was standing motionless. Suddenly, catching the surgeon's arm convulsively, he exclaimed, pointing down to the body, "It is the divine judgment on Ananias![5] Look!"

Disturbed by the excited manner he had never before observed in the *Bellipotent*'s captain, and as yet wholly ignorant of the affair, the prudent surgeon nevertheless held his peace, only again looking an earnest interrogatory as to what it was that had resulted in such a tragedy.

But Captain Vere was now again motionless, standing absorbed in thought. Again starting, he vehemently exclaimed, "Struck dead by an angel of God! Yet the angel must hang!"

At these passionate interjections, mere incoherences to the listener as yet unapprised of the antecedents, the surgeon was profoundly discomposed. But now, as recollecting himself, Captain Vere in less passionate tone briefly related the circumstances leading up to the event. "But come; we must dispatch," he added. "Help me to remove him" (meaning the body) "to yonder compartment," designating one opposite that where the foretopman remained immured. Anew disturbed by a request that, as implying a desire for secrecy, seemed unaccountably strange to him, there was nothing for the subordinate to do but comply.

---

[5] In Acts 5:3–5 Ananias falls dead when the Apostle Peter says he has not lied to men but to God.

"Go now," said Captain Vere with something of his wonted manner. "Go now. I presently shall call a drumhead court.[6] Tell the lieutenants what has happened, and tell Mr. Mordant" (meaning the captain of marines), "and charge them to keep the matter to themselves."

20

Full of disquietude and misgiving, the surgeon left the cabin. Was Captain Vere suddenly affected in his mind, or was it but a transient excitement, brought about by so strange and extraordinary a tragedy? As to the drumhead court, it struck the surgeon as impolitic, if nothing more. The thing to do, he thought, was to place Billy Budd in confinement, and in a way dictated by usage, and postpone further action in so extraordinary a case to such time as they should rejoin the squadron, and then refer it to the admiral. He recalled the unwonted agitation of Captain Vere and his excited exclamations, so at variance with his normal manner. Was he unhinged?

But assuming that he is, it is not so susceptible of proof. What then can the surgeon do? No more trying situation is conceivable than that of an officer subordinate under a captain whom he suspects to be not mad, indeed, but yet not quite unaffected in his intellects. To argue his order to him would be insolence. To resist him would be mutiny.

In obedience to Captain Vere, he communicated what had happened to the lieutenants and captain of marines, saying nothing as to the captain's state. They fully shared his own surprise and concern. Like him too, they seemed to think that such a matter should be referred to the admiral.

21

Who in the rainbow can draw the line where the violet tint ends and the orange tint begins? Distinctly we see the difference of the colors, but where exactly does the one first blendingly enter into the other? So with sanity and insanity. In pronounced cases there is no question about them. But in some supposed cases, in various degrees supposedly less pronounced, to draw the exact line of demarcation few will undertake, though for a fee becoming considerate some professional experts will. There is nothing namable but that some men will, or undertake to, do it for pay.

Whether Captain Vere, as the surgeon professionally and privately surmised, was really the sudden victim of any degree of aberration, every one must determine for himself by such light as this narrative may afford.

That the unhappy event which has been narrated could not have happened at a worse juncture was but too true. For it was close on the heel of the suppressed insurrections, an aftertime very critical to naval authority, demanding from every English sea commander two qualities not readily interfusable—prudence and rigor. Moreover, there was something crucial in the case.

In the jugglery of circumstances preceding and attending the event on board the

---

[6] An emergency court-martial at sea or in the field (named for the practice of using a drum for a table at the proceedings).

Bellipotent, and in the light of that martial code whereby it was formally to be judged, innocence and guilt personified in Claggart and Budd in effect changed places. In a legal view the apparent victim of the tragedy was he who had sought to victimize a man blameless; and the indisputable deed of the latter, navally regarded, constituted the most heinous of military crimes. Yet more. The essential right and wrong involved in the matter, the clearer that might be, so much the worse for the responsibility of a loyal sea commander, inasmuch as he was not authorized to determine the matter on that primitive basis.

Small wonder then that the *Bellipotent's* captain, though in general a man of rapid decision, felt that circumspectness not less than promptitude was necessary. Until he could decide upon his course, and in each detail; and not only so, but until the concluding measure was upon the point of being enacted, he deemed it advisable, in view of all the circumstances, to guard as much as possible against publicity. Here he may or may not have erred. Certain it is, however, that subsequently in the confidential talk of more than one or two gun rooms and cabins he was not a little criticized by some officers, a fact imputed by his friends and vehemently by his cousin Jack Denton to professional jealousy of Starry Vere. Some imaginative ground for invidious comment there was. The maintenance of secrecy in the matter, the confining all knowledge of it for a time to the place where the homicide occurred, the quarterdeck cabin; in these particulars lurked some resemblance to the policy adopted in those tragedies of the palace which have occurred more than once in the capital founded by Peter the Barbarian.[1]

The case indeed was such that fain would the *Bellipotent's* captain have deferred taking any action whatever respecting it further than to keep the foretopman a close prisoner till the ship rejoined the squadron and then submitting the matter to the judgment of his admiral.

But a true military officer is in one particular like a true monk. Not with more of self-abnegation will the latter keep his vows of monastic obedience than the former his vows of allegiance to martial duty.

Feeling that unless quick action was taken on it, the deed of the foretopman, so soon as it should be known on the gun decks, would tend to awaken any slumbering embers of the Nore among the crew, a sense of the urgency of the case overruled in Captain Vere every other consideration. But though a conscientious disciplinarian, he was no lover of authority for mere authority's sake. Very far was he from embracing opportunities for monopolizing to himself the perils of moral responsibility, none at least that could properly be referred to an official superior or shared with him by his official equals or even subordinates. So thinking, he was glad it would not be at variance with usage to turn the matter over to a summary court of his own officers, reserving to himself, as the one on whom the ultimate accountability would rest, the right of maintaining a supervision of it, or formally or informally interposing at need. Accordingly a drumhead court was summarily convened, he electing the individuals composing it: the first lieutenant, the captain of marines, and the sailing master.[2]

In associating an officer of marines with the sea lieutenant and the sailing master in a case having to do with a sailor, the commander perhaps deviated from general custom. He was prompted thereto by the circumstance that he took that soldier to be a judicious person, thoughtful, and not altogether incapable of grap-

[1] Peter the Great (1672–1725, who founded St. Petersburg (now Leningrad) in 1703.
[2] The ship's navigator.

pling with a difficult case unprecedented in his prior experience. Yet even as to him he was not without some latent misgiving, for withal he was an extremely good-natured man, an enjoyer of his dinner, a sound sleeper, and inclined to obesity—a man who though he would always maintain his manhood in battle might not prove altogether reliable in a moral dilemma involving aught of the tragic. As to the first lieutenant and the sailing master, Captain Vere could not but be aware that though honest natures, of approved gallantry upon occasion, their intelligence was mostly confined to the matter of active seamanship and the fighting demands of their profession.

The court was held in the same cabin where the unfortunate affair had taken place. This cabin, the commander's, embraced the entire area under the poop deck. Aft, and on either side, was a small stateroom, the one now temporarily a jail and the other a dead-house,[3] and a yet smaller compartment, leaving a space between expanding forward into a goodly oblong of length coinciding with the ship's beam.[4] A skylight of moderate dimension was overhead, and at each end of the oblong space were two sashed porthole windows easily convertible back into embrasures for short carronades.[5]

All being quickly in readiness, Billy Budd was arraigned, Captain Vere necessarily appearing as the sole witness in the case, and as such temporarily sinking his rank, though singularly maintaining it in a matter apparently trivial, namely, that he testified from the ship's weather side, with that object having caused the court to sit on the lee side.[6] Concisely he narrated all that had led up to the catastrophe, omitting nothing in Claggart's accusation and deposing as to the manner in which the prisoner had received it. At this testimony the three officers glanced with no little surprise at Billy Budd, the last man they would have suspected either of the mutinous design alleged by Claggart or the undeniable deed he himself had done. The first lieutenant, taking judicial primacy and turning toward the prisoner, said, "Captain Vere has spoken. Is it or is it not as Captain Vere says?"

In response came syllables not so much impeded in the utterance as might have been anticipated. They were these: "Captain Vere tells the truth. It is just as Captain Vere says, but it is not as the master-at-arms said. I have eaten the King's bread and I am true to the King."

"I believe you, my man," said the witness, his voice indicating a suppressed emotion not otherwise betrayed.

"God will bless you for that, your honor!" not without stammering said Billy, and all but broke down. But immediately he was recalled to self-control by another question, to which with the same emotional difficulty of utterance he said, "No, there was no malice between us. I never bore malice against the master-at-arms. I am sorry that he is dead. I did not mean to kill him. Could I have used my tongue I would not have struck him. But he foully lied to my face and in presence of my captain, and I had to say something, and I could only say it with a blow, God help me!"

In the impulsive aboveboard manner of the frank one the court saw confirmed all that was implied in words that just previously had perplexed them, coming as

---

[3] A temporary morgue.   [4] Wildest point.   [5] Light cannons from Carron, Scotland.
[6] Vere's testimony is given from the ship's weather, or higher, side, thus, he sits above the level of the court.

they did from the testifier to the tragedy and promptly following Billy's impassioned disclaimer of mutinous intent—Captain Vere's words, "I believe you, my man."

Next it was asked of him whether he knew of or suspected aught savoring of incipient trouble (meaning mutiny, though the explicit term was avoided) going on in any section of the ship's company.

The reply lingered. This was naturally imputed by the court to the same vocal embarrassment which had retarded or obstructed previous answers. But in main it was otherwise here, the question immediately recalling to Billy's mind the interview with the afterguardsman in the forechains. But an innate repugnance to playing a part at all approaching that of an informer against one's own shipmates—the same erring sense of uninstructed honor which had stood in the way of his reporting the matter at the time, though as a loyal man-of-war's man it was incumbent on him, and failure so to do, if charged against him and proven, would have subjected him to the heaviest of penalties; this, with the blind feeling now his that nothing really was being hatched, prevailed with him. When the answer came it was a negative.

"One question more," said the officer of marines, now first speaking and with a troubled earnestness. "You tell us that what the master-at-arms said against you was a lie. Now why should he have so lied, so maliciously lied, since you declare there was no malice between you?"

At that question, unintentionally touching on a spiritual sphere wholly obscure to Billy's thoughts, he was nonplussed, evincing a confusion indeed that some observers, such as can readily be imagined, would have construed into involuntary evidence of hidden guilt. Nevertheless, he strove some way to answer, but all at once relinquished the vain endeavor, at the same time turning an appealing glance towards Captain Vere as deeming him his best helper and friend. Captain Vere, who had been seated for a time, rose to his feet, addressing the interrogator. "The question you put to him comes naturally enough. But how can he rightly answer it?—or anybody else, unless indeed it be he who lies within there," designating the compartment where lay the corpse. "But the prone one there will not rise to our summons. In effect, though, as it seems to me, the point you make is hardly material. Quite aside from any conceivable motive actuating the master-at-arms, and irrespective of the provocation to the blow, a martial court must needs in the present case confine its attention to the blow's consequence, which consequence justly is to be deemed not otherwise than as the striker's deed."

This utterance, the full significance of which it was not at all likely that Billy took in, nevertheless caused him to turn a wistful interrogative look toward the speaker, a look in its dumb expressiveness not unlike that which a dog of generous breed might turn upon his master, seeking in his face some elucidation of a previous gesture ambiguous to the canine intelligence. Nor was the same utterance without marked effect upon the three officers, more especially the soldier. Couched in it seemed to them a meaning unanticipated, involving a prejudgment on the speaker's part. It served to augment a mental disturbance previously evident enough.

The soldier once more spoke, in a tone of suggestive dubiety addressing at once his associates and Captain Vere: "Nobody is present—none of the ship's company, I mean—who might shed lateral light, if any is to be had, upon what remains mysterious in this matter."

"That is thoughtfully put," said Captain Vere; "I see your drift. Ay, there is a mystery; but, to use a scriptural phrase, it is a 'mystery of iniquity,' a matter for psychologic theologians to discuss. But what has a military court to do with it? Not to add that for us any possible investigation of it is cut off by the lasting tongue-tie of—him—in yonder," again designating the mortuary stateroom. "The prisoner's deed—with that alone we have to do."

To this, and particularly the closing reiteration, the marine soldier, knowing not how aptly to reply, sadly abstained from saying aught. The first lieutenant, who at the outset had not unnaturally assumed primacy in the court, now overrulingly instructed by a glance from Captain Vere, a glance more effective than words, resumed that primacy. Turning to the prisoner, "Budd," he said, and scarce in equable tones, "Budd, if you have aught further to say for yourself, say it now."

Upon this the young sailor turned another quick glance toward Captain Vere; then, as taking a hint from that aspect, a hint confirming his own instinct that silence was now best, replied to the lieutenant, "I have said all, sir."

The marine—the same who had been the sentinel without the cabin door at the time that the foretopman, followed by the master-at-arms, entered it—he, standing by the sailor throughout these judicial proceedings, was now directed to take him back to the after compartment originally assigned to the prisoner and his custodian. As the twain disappeared from view, the three officers, as partially liberated from some inward constraint associated with Billy's mere presence, simultaneously stirred in their seats. They exchanged looks of troubled indecision, yet feeling that decide they must and without long delay. For Captain Vere, he for the time stood—unconsciously with his back toward them, apparently in one of his absent fits—gazing out from a sashed porthole to windward upon the monotonous blank of the twilight sea. But the court's silence continuing, broken only at moments by brief consultations, in low earnest tones, this served to arouse him and energize him. Turning, he to-and-fro paced the cabin athwart; in the returning ascent to windward climbing the slant deck in the ship's lee roll,[7] without knowing it symbolizing thus in his action a mind resolute to surmount difficulties even if against primitive instinct strong as the wind and the sea. Presently he came to a stand before the three. After scanning their faces he stood less as mustering his thoughts for expression than as one inly deliberating how best to put them to well-meaning men not intellectually mature, men with whom it was necessary to demonstrate certain principles that were axioms to himself. Similar impatience as to talking is perhaps one reason that deters some minds from addressing any popular assemblies.

When speak he did, something, both in the substance of what he said and his manner of saying it, showed the influence of unshared studies modifying and tempering the practical training of an active career. This, along with his phraseology, now and then was suggestive of the grounds whereon rested that imputation of a certain pedantry socially alleged against him by certain naval men of wholly practical cast, captains who nevertheless would frankly concede that His Majesty's navy mustered no more efficient officer of their grade than Starry Vere.

What he said was to this effect: "Hitherto I have been but the witness, little

---

[7] Walking up the slanted deck as the ship rolls away from the wind.

more; and I should hardly think now to take another tone, that of your coadjutor for the time, did I not perceive in you—at the crisis too—a troubled hesitancy, proceeding, I doubt not, from the clash of military duty with moral scruple— scruple vitalized by compassion. For the compassion, how can I otherwise than share it? But, mindful of paramount obligations, I strive against scruples that may tend to enervate decision. Not, gentlemen, that I hide from myself that the case is an exceptional one. Speculatively regarded, it well might be referred to a jury of casuists.[8] But for us here, acting not as casuists or moralists, it is a case practical, and under martial law practically to be dealt with.

"But your scruples: do they move as in a dusk? Challenge them. Make them advance and declare themselves. Come now; do they import something like this: If, mindless of palliating circumstances, we are bound to regard the death of the master-at-arms as the prisoner's deed, then does that deed constitute a capital crime whereof the penalty is a mortal one. But in natural justice is nothing but the prisoner's overt act to be considered? How can we adjudge to summary and shameful death a fellow creature innocent before God, and whom we feel to be so?—Does that state it aright? You sign sad assent. Well, I too feel that, the full force of that. It is Nature. But do these buttons that we wear attest that our allegiance is to Nature? No, to the King. Though the ocean, which is inviolate Nature primeval, though this be the element where we move and have our being as sailors, yet as the King's officers lies our duty in a sphere correspondingly natural? So little is that true, that in receiving our commissions we in the most important regards ceased to be natural free agents. When war is declared are we the commissioned fighters previously consulted? We fight at command. If our judgments approve the war, that is but coincidence. So in other particulars. So now. For suppose condemnation to follow these present proceedings. Would it be so much we ourselves that would condemn as it would be martial law operating through us? For that law and the rigor of it, we are not responsible. Our vowed responsibility is in this: That however pitilessly that law may operate in any instances, we nevertheless adhere to it and administer it.

"But the exceptional in the matter moves the hearts within you. Even so too is mine moved. But let not warm hearts betray heads that should be cool. Ashore in a criminal case, will an upright judge allow himself off the bench to be waylaid by some tender kinswoman of the accused seeking to touch him with her tearful plea? Well, the heart here, sometimes the feminine in man, is as that piteous woman, and hard though it be, she must here be ruled out."

He paused, earnestly studying them for a moment; then resumed.

"But something in your aspect seems to urge that it is not solely the heart that moves in you, but also the conscience, the private conscience. But tell me whether or not, occupying the position we do, private conscience should not yield to that imperial one formulated in the code under which alone we officially proceed?"

Here the three men moved in their seats, less convinced than agitated by the course of an argument troubling but the more the spontaneous conflict within.

Perceiving which, the speaker paused for a moment; then abruptly changing his tone, went on.

"To steady us a bit, let us recur to the facts.—In wartime at sea a man-of-war's

---

[8] Those who decide matters by overly sophisticated, hairsplitting arguments.

man strikes his superior in grade, and the blow kills. Apart from its effect the blow itself is, according to the Articles of War, a capital crime. Furthermore——"

"Ay, sir," emotionally broke in the officer of marines, "in one sense it was. But surely Budd purposed neither mutiny nor homicide."

"Surely not, my good man. And before a court less arbitrary and more merciful than a martial one, that plea would largely extenuate. At the Last Assizes[9] it shall acquit. But how here? We proceed under the law of the Mutiny Act. In feature no child can resemble his father more than that Act resembles in spirit the thing from which it derives—War. In His Majesty's service—in this ship, indeed—there are Englishmen forced to fight for the King against their will. Against their conscience, for aught we know. Though as their fellow creatures some of us may appreciate their position, yet as navy officers what reck[10] we of it? Still less recks the enemy. Our impressed men he would fain cut down in the same swath with our volunteer. As regards the enemy's naval conscripts, some of whom may even share our own abhorrence of the regicidal French Directory, it is the same on our side. War looks but to the frontage, the appearance. And the Mutiny Act, War's child, takes after the father. Budd's intent or non-intent is nothing to the purpose.

"But while, put to it by those anxieties in you which I cannot but respect, I only repeat myself—while thus strangely we prolong proceedings that should be summary—the enemy may be sighted and an engagement result. We must do; and one of two things must we do—condemn or let go."

"Can we not convict and yet mitigate the penalty?" asked the sailing master, here speaking, and falteringly, for the first.

"Gentlemen, were that clearly lawful for us under the circumstances, consider the consequences of such clemency. The people" (meaning the ship's company) "have native sense; most of them are familiar with our naval usage and tradition; and how would they take it? Even could you explain to them—which our official position forbids—they, long molded by arbitrary discipline, have not that kind of intelligent responsiveness that might qualify them to comprehend and discriminate. No, to the people the fortopman's deed, however it be worded in the announcement, will be plain homicide committed in a flagrant act of mutiny. What penalty for that should follow, they know. But it does not follow. *Why?* they will ruminate. You know what sailors are. Will they not revert to the recent outbreak at the Nore? Ay. They know the well-founded alarm—the panic it struck throughout England. Your clement sentence they would account pusillanimous. They would think that we flinch, that we are afraid of them—afraid of practicing a lawful rigor singularly demanded at this juncture, lest it should provoke new troubles. What shame to us such a conjecture on their part, and how deadly to discipline. You see then, whither, prompted by duty and the law, I steadfastly drive. But I beseech you, my friends, do not take me amiss. I feel as you do for this unfortunate boy. But did he know our hearts, I take him to be of that generous nature that he would feel even for us on whom in this military necessity so heavy a compulsion is laid."

With that, crossing the deck he resumed his place by the sashed porthole, tacitly leaving the three to come to a decision. On the cabin's opposite side the troubled court sat silent. Loyal lieges, plain and practical, though at bottom they dissented from some points Captain Vere had put to them, they were without the

[9] On Judgment Day.   [10] Care.

faculty, hardly had the inclination, to gainsay one whom they felt to be an earnest man, one too not less their superior in mind than in naval rank. But it is not improbable that even such of his words as were not without influence over them, less came home to them than his closing appeal to their instinct as sea officers: in the forethought he threw out as to the practical consequences to discipline, considering the unconfirmed tone of the fleet at the time, should a man-of-war's man's violent killing at sea of a superior in grade be allowed to pass for aught else than a capital crime demanding prompt infliction of the penalty.

Not unlikely they were brought to something more or less akin to that harassed frame of mind which in the year 1842 actuated the commander of the U.S. brig-of-war *Somers* to resolve, under the so-called Articles of War, Articles modeled upon the English Mutiny Act, to resolve upon the execution at sea of a midshipman and two sailors as mutineers designing the seizure of the brig.[11] Which resolution was carried out though in a time of peace and within not many days' sail of home. An act vindicated by a naval court of inquiry subsequently convened ashore. History, and here cited without comment. True, the circumstances on board the *Somers* were different from those on board the *Bellipotent*. But the urgency felt, well-warranted or otherwise, was much the same.

Says a writer whom few know,[12] "Forty years after a battle it is easy for a noncombatant to reason about how it ought to have been fought. It is another thing personally and under fire to have to direct the fighting while involved in the obscuring smoke of it. Much so with respect to other emergencies involved considerations both practical and moral, and when it is imperative promptly to act. The greater the fog the more it imperils the steamer, and speed is put on though at the hazard of running somebody down. Little ween[13] the snug card players in the cabin of the responsibilities of the sleepless man on the bridge."

In brief, Billy Budd was formally convicted and sentenced to be hung at the yardarm in the early morning watch, it being now night. Otherwise, as is customary in such cases, the sentence would forthwith have been carried out. In wartime on the field or in the fleet, a mortal punishment decreed by a drumhead court—on the field sometimes decreed by but a nod from the general—follows without delay on the heel of conviction, without appeal.

22

It was Captain Vere himself who of his own motion communicated the finding of the court to the prisoner, for that purpose going to the compartment where he was in custody and bidding the marine there to withdraw for the time.

Beyond the communication of the sentence, what took place at this interview was never known. But in view of the character of the twain briefly closeted in that stateroom, each radically sharing in the rarer qualities of our nature—so rare indeed as to be all but incredible to average minds however much cultivated—some conjectures may be ventured.

---

[11] Melville had a deep interest in the alleged mutiny aboard the *Somers:* his cousin Guert Gansevoort was the executive officer aboard the ship and presided over the court that found Midshipman Philip Spencer guilty.

[12] Very likely Melville himself.   [13] Think.

It would have been in consonance with the spirit of Captain Vere should he on this occasion have concealed nothing from the condemned one—should he indeed have frankly disclosed to him the part he himself had played in bringing about the decision, at the same time revealing his actuating motives. On Billy's side it is not improbable that such a confession would have been received in much the same spirit that prompted it. Not without a sort of joy, indeed, he might have appreciated the brave opinion of him implied in his captain's making such a confidant of him. Nor, as to the sentence itself, could he have been insensible that it was imparted to him as to one not afraid to die. Even more may have been. Captain Vere in end may have developed the passion sometimes latent under an exterior stoical or indifferent. He was old enough to have been Billy's father. The austere devotee of military duty, letting himself melt back into what remains primeval in our formalized humanity, may in end have caught Billy to his heart, even as Abraham may have caught young Issac on the brink of resolutely offering him up in obedience to the exacting behest.[1] But there is no telling the sacrament, seldom if in any case revealed to the gadding world, wherever under circumstances at all akin to those here attempted to be set forth two of great Nature's nobler order embrace. There is privacy at the time, inviolable to the survivor; and holy oblivion, the sequel to each diviner magnamimity, providentially covers all at last.

The first to encounter Captain Vere in act of leaving the compartment was the senior lieutenant. The face he beheld, for the moment one expressive of the agony of the strong, was to that officer, though a man of fifty, a startling revelation. That the condemned one suffered less than he who mainly had effected the condemnation was apparently indicated by the former's exclamation in the scene soon perforce to be touched upon.

23

Of a series of incidents within a brief term rapidly following each other, the adequate narration may take up a term less brief, especially if explanation or comment here and there seem requisite to the better understanding of such incidents. Between the entrance into the cabin of him who never left it alive, and him who when he did leave it left it as one condemned to die; between this and the closeted interview just given, less than an hour and a half had elapsed. It was an interval long enough, however, to awaken speculations among no few of the ship's company as to what it was that could be detaining in the cabin the master-at-arms and the sailor; for a rumor that both of them had been seen to enter it and neither of them had been seen to emerge, this rumor had got abroad upon the gun decks, and in the tops, the people of a great warship being in one respect like villagers, taking microscopic note of every outward movement or non-movement going on. When therefore, in weather not at all tempestuous, all hands were called in the second dogwatch, a summons under such circumstances not usual in those hours, the crew were not wholly unprepared for some announcement extraordinary, one having connection too with the continued absence of the two men from their wonted haunts.

There was a moderate sea at the time; and the moon, newly risen and near to

---

[1] In Genesis 22:1–18 the Lord tested Abraham's obedience by commanding him to sacrifice his only son, Isaac, then withdrew the command when Abraham began to obey.

being at its full, silvered the white spar deck wherever not blotted by the clear-cut shadows horizontally thrown of fixtures and moving men. On either side the quarterdeck the marine guard under arms was drawn up; and Captain Vere, standing in his place surrounded by all the wardroom[1] officers, addressed his men. In so doing, his manner showed neither more nor less than that properly pertaining to his supreme position aboard his own ship. In clear terms and concise he told them what had taken place in the cabin: that the master-at-arms was dead, that he who had killed him had been already tried by a summary court and condemned to death, and that the execution would take place in the early morning watch. The word *mutiny* was not named in what he said. He refrained too from making the occasion an opportunity for any preachment as to the maintenance of discipline, thinking perhaps that under existing circumstances in the navy the consequence of violating discipline should be made to speak for itself.

Their captain's announcement was listened to by the throng of standing sailors in a dumbness like that of a seated congregation of believers in hell listening to the clergyman's announcement of his Calvinistic text.

At the close, however, a confused murmur went up. It began to wax. All but instantly, then, at a sign, it was pierced and suppressed by shrill whistles of the boatswain and his mates. The word was given to about ship.

To be prepared for burial Claggart's body was delivered to certain petty officers of his mess. And here, not to clog the sequel with lateral matters, it may be added that at a suitable hour, the master-at-arms was committed to the sea with every funeral honor properly belonging to his naval grade.

In this proceeding as in every public one growing out of the tragedy strict adherence to usage was observed. Nor in any point could it have been at all deviated from, either with respect to Claggart or Billy Budd, without begetting undesirable speculations in the ship's company, sailors, and more particularly men-of-war's men, being of all men the greatest sticklers for usage. For similar cause, all communication between Captain Vere and the condemned one ended with the closeted interview already given, the latter being now surrendered to the ordinary routine preliminary to the end. His transfer under guard from the captain's quarters was effected without unusual precautions—at least no visible ones. If possible, not to let the men so much as surmise that their officers anticipate aught amiss from them is the tacit rule in a military ship. And the more that some sort of trouble should really be apprehended, the more do the officers keep that apprehension to themselves, though not the less unostentatious vigilance may be augmented. In the present instance, the sentry placed over the prisoner had strict orders to let no one have communication with him but the chaplain. And certain unobtrusive measures were taken absolutely to insure this point.

24

In a seventy-four of the old order the deck known as the upper gun deck was the one covered over by the spar deck, which last, though not without its armament, was for the most part exposed to the weather. In general it was at all hours free from hammocks; those of the crew swinging on the lower gun deck and berth deck, the latter being not only a dormitory but also the place for the stowing of the

---

[1] The messroom for all commissioned officers but the captain.

sailors' bags, and on both sides lined with the large chests or movable pantries of the many messes of the men.

On the starboard side of the *Bellipotent's* upper gun deck, behold Billy Budd under sentry lying prone in irons in one of the bays formed by the regular spacing of the guns comprising the batteries on either side. All these pieces were of the heavier caliber of that period. Mounted on lumbering wooden carriages, they were hampered with cumbersome harness of breeching and strong side-tackles for running them out. Guns and carriages, together with the long rammers and shorter linstocks[1] lodged in loops overhead—all these, as customary, were painted black; and the heavy hempen breechings, tarred to the same tint, wore the like livery of the undertakers. In contrast with the funereal hue of these surroundings, the prone sailor's exterior apparel, white jumper and white duck trousers, each more or less soiled, dimly glimmered in the obscure light of the bay like a patch of discolored snow in early April lingering at some upland cave's black mouth. In effect he is already in his shroud, or the garments that shall serve him in lieu of one. Over him but scarce illuminating him, two battle lanterns swing from two massive beams of the deck above. Fed with the oil supplied by the war contractors (whose gains, honest or otherwise, are in every land an anticipated portion of the harvest of death), with flickering splashes of dirty yellow light they pollute the pale moonshine all but ineffectually struggling in obstructed flecks through the open ports from which the tampioned[2] cannon protrude. Other lanterns at intervals serve but to bring out somewhat the obscurer bays which, like small confessionals or side-chapels in a cathedral, branch from the long dim-vistaed broad aisle between the two batteries of that covered tier.

Such was the deck where now lay the Handsome Sailor. Through the rose-tan of his complexion no pallor could have shown. It would have taken days of sequestration from the winds and the sun to have brought about the effacement of that. But the skeleton in the cheekbone at the point of its angle was just beginning delicately to be defined under the warm-tinted skin. In fervid hearts self-contained, some brief experiences devour our human tissue as secret fire in a ship's hold consumes cotton in the bale.

But now lying between the two guns, as nipped in the vice of fate, Billy's agony, mainly proceeding from a generous young heart's virgin experience of the diabolical incarnate and effective in some men—the tension of that agony was over now. It survived not the something healing in the closeted interview with Captain Vere. Without movement, he lay as in a trance, that adolescent expression previously noted as his taking on something akin to the look of a slumbering child in the cradle when the warm hearth-glow of the still chamber at night plays on the dimples that at whiles mysteriously form in the cheek, silently coming and going there. For now and then in the gyved[3] one's trance a serene happy light born of some wandering reminiscence or dream would diffuse itself over his face, and then wane away only anew to return.

The chaplain, coming to see him and finding him thus, and perceiving no sign that he was conscious of his presence, attentively regarded him for a space, then slipping aside, withdrew for the time, peradventure feeling that even he, the minister of Christ though receiving his stipend from Mars,[4] had no consolation to proffer which could result in a peace transcending that which he beheld. But in the

---

[1] Sticks into which matches are inserted for firing cannons.   [2] Plugged.   [3] Shackled.
[4] The chaplain receives his wages from the navy, an institution of Mars, the Roman god of war.

small hours he came again. And the prisoner, now awake to his surroundings, noticed his approach, and civilly, all but cheerfully, welcomed him. But it was to little purpose that in the interview following, the good man sought to bring Billy Budd to some godly understanding that he must die, and at dawn. True, Billy himself freely referred to his death as a thing close at hand; but it was something in the way that children will refer to death in general, who yet among their other sports will play a funeral with hearse and mourners.

Not that like children Billy was incapable of conceiving what death really is. No, but he was wholly without irrational fear of it, a fear more prevalent in highly civilized communities than those so-called barbarous ones which in all respects stand nearer to unadulterate Nature. And, as elsewhere said, a barbarian Billy radically was—as much so, for all the costume, as his countrymen the British captives, living trophies, made to march in the Roman triumph of Germanicus.[5] Quite as much so as those later barbarians, young men probably, and picked specimens among the earlier British converts to Christianity, at least nominally such, taken to Rome (as today converts from lesser isles of the sea may be taken to London), of whom the Pope of that time,[6] admiring the strangness of their personal beauty so unlike the Italian stamp, their clear ruddy complexion and curled flaxen locks, exclaimed, "Angles" (meaning *English,* the modern derivative), "Angles, do you call them? And is it because they look so like angels?" Had it been later in time, one would think that the Pope had in mind Fra Angelico's[7] seraphs, some of whom, plucking apples in gardens of the Hesperides,[8] have the faint rosebud complexion of the more beautiful English girls.

If in vain the good chaplain sought to impress the young barbarian with ideas of death akin to those conveyed in the skull, dial, and crossbones on old tombstones, equally futile to all appearance were his efforts to bring home to him the thought of salvation and a Savior. Billy listened, but less out of awe or reverence, perhaps, than from a certain natural politeness, doubtless at bottom regarding all that in much the same way that most mariners of his class take any discourse abstract or out of the common tone of the workaday world. And this sailor way of taking clerical discourse is not wholly unlike the way in which the primer of Christianity, full of transcendent miracles, was received long ago on tropic isles by any superior *savage,* so called—a Tahitian, say, of Captain Cook's[9] time or shortly after that time. Out of natural courtesy he received, but did not appropriate. It was like a gift placed in the palm of an outreached hand upon which the fingers do not close.

But the *Bellipotent's* chaplain was a discreet man possessing the good sense of a good heart. So he insisted not in his vocation here. At the instance of Captain Vere, a lieutenant had apprised him of pretty much everything as to Billy; and since he felt that innocence was even a better thing than religion wherewith to go to Judgment, he reluctantly withdrew; but in his emotion not without first performing an act strange enough in an Englishman, and under the circumstances yet more so in any regular priest. Stooping over, he kissed on the fair cheek his fellow

---

[5] Germanicus Caesar (15 B.C.–A.D. 19), a Roman general whose victories over Germanic tribes were celebrated in Rome in A.D. 17.

[6] Gregory I (540–604), or Gregory the Great, who served as pope from 590 to 604; however, the incident to which Melville refers occurred before Gregory became pope.

[7] Giovanni da Fiesole (1387–1455), a Florentine painter of angels.

[8] According to Greek myth, islands where golden apples grew.

[9] James Cook (1728–1779), an English explorer who first visited Tahiti in 1769.

man, a felon in martial law, one whom though on the confines of death he felt he could never convert to a dogma; nor for all that did he fear for his future.

Marvel not that having been made acquainted with the young sailor's essential innocence the worthy man lifted not a finger to avert the doom of such a martyr to martial discipline. So to do would not only have been as idle as invoking the desert, but would also have been an audacious transgression of the bounds of his function, one as exactly prescribed to him by military law as that of the boatswain or any other naval officer. Bluntly put, a chaplain is the minister of the Prince of Peace serving in the host of the God of War—Mars. As such, he is as incongruous as a musket would be on the altar at Christmas. Why, then, is he there? Because he indirectly subserves the purpose attested by the cannon; because too he lends the sanction of the religion of the meek to that which practically is the abrogation of everything but brute Force.

25

The night so luminous on the spar deck, but otherwise on the cavernous ones below, levels so like the tiered galleries in a coal mine—the luminous night passed away. But like the prophet in the chariot disappearing in heaven and dropping his mantle to Elisha,[1] the withdrawing night transferred its pale robe to the breaking day. A meek, shy light appeared in the East, where stretched a diaphanous fleece of white furrowed vapor. That light slowly waxed. Suddenly *eight bells* was struck aft, responded to by one louder metallic stroke from forward, It was four o'clock in the morning. Instantly the silver whistles were heard summoning all hands to witness punishment. Up through the great hatchways rimmed with racks of heavy shot the watch below came pouring, overspreading with the watch already on deck the space between the mainmast and foremast including that occupied by the capacious launch and the black booms tiered on either side of it, boat and booms making a summit of observation for the powder-boys[2] and younger tars. A different group comprising one watch of topmen leaned over the rail of that sea balcony, no small one in a seventy-four, looking down on the crowd below. Man or boy, none spake but in whisper, and few spake at all. Captain Vere—as before, the central figure among the assembled commissioned officers—stood nigh the break of the poop deck facing forward. Just below him on the quarter-deck the marines in full equipment were drawn up much as at the scene of the promulgated sentence.

At sea in the old time, the execution by halter[3] of a military sailor was generally from the foreyard. In the present instance, for special reasons the mainyard was assigned. Under an arm of that yard the prisoner was presently brought up, the chaplain attending him. It was noted at the time, and remarked upon afterwards, that in this final scene the good man evinced little or nothing of the perfunctory. Brief speech indeed he had with the condemned one, but the genuine Gospel was less on his tongue than in his aspect and manner towards him. The final preparations personal to the latter being speedily brought to an end by two boatswain's mates, the consummation impended. Billy stood facing aft. At the

---

[1] In II Kings 2:9–15 the prophet Elijah drops his mantle as he is transported to Heaven in a chariot of fire; the cloak is picked up by his disciple Elisha.
[2] Boys who carried gunpowder.   [3] Hangman's noose.

penultimate moment, his words, his only ones, words wholly unobstructed in the utterance, were these: "God bless Captain Vere!" Syllables so unanticipated coming from one with the ignominious hemp about his neck—a conventional felon's benediction directed aft towards the quarters of honor; syllables too delivered in the clear melody of a singing bird on the point of launching from the twig—had a phenomenal effect, not unenhanced by the rare personal beauty of the young sailor, spiritualized now through late experiences so poignantly profound.

Without volition, as it were, as if indeed the ship's populace were but the vehicles of some vocal current electric, with one voice from alow and aloft came a resonant sympathic echo: "God bless Captain Vere!" And yet at that instant Billy alone must have been in their hearts, even as in their eyes.

At the pronounced words and the spontaneous echo that voluminously rebounded them, Captain Vere, either through stoic self-control or a sort of momentary paralysis induced by emotional shock, stood erectly rigid as a musket in the shiparmorer's rack.

The hull, deliberately recovering from the periodic roll to leeward, was just regaining an even keel when the last signal, a preconcerted dumb[4] one, was given. At the same moment it chanced that the vapory fleece hanging low in the East was shot through with a soft glory as of the fleece of the Lamb of God seen in mystical vision,[5] and simultaneously therewith, watched by the wedged mass of upturned faces, Billy ascended; and, ascending, took the full rose of the dawn.

In the pinioned figure arrived at the yard-end, to the wonder of all no motion was apparent, none save that created by the slow roll of the hull in moderate weather, so majestic in a great ship ponderously cannoned.

26

When some days afterwards, in reference to the singularity just mentioned, the purser,[1] a rather ruddy, rotund person more accurate as an accountant than profound as a philosopher, said at mess to the surgeon, "What testimony to the force lodged in will power," the latter, saturnine, spare, and tall, one in whom a discreet causticity went along with a manner less genial than polite, replied, "Your pardon, Mr. Purser. In a hanging scientifically conducted—and under special orders I myself directed how Budd's was to be effected—any movement following the completed suspension and originating in the body suspended, such movement indicates mechanical spasm in the muscular system. Hence the absence of that is no more attributable to will power, as you call it, than to horsepower—begging your pardon."

"But this muscular spasm you speak of, is not that in a degree more or less invariable in these cases?"

"Assuredly so, Mr. Purser."

"How then, my good sir, do you account for its absence in this instance?"

"Mr. Purser, it is clear that your sense of the singularity in this matter equals not mine. You account for it by what you call will power—a term not yet included in the lexicon of science. For me, I do not, with my present knowledge, pretend to account for it at all. Even should we assume the hypothesis that at the first touch

---

[4] A prearranged silent.   [5] Christ seen in a vision like that in Revelation 1:10–14.
[1] A ship's pay officer (the one who holds the purse).

of the halyards the action of Budd's heart, intensified by extraordinary emotion at its climax, abruptly stopped—much like a watch when in carelessly winding it up you strain at the finish, thus snapping the chain—even under that hypothesis how account for the phenomenon that followed?"

"You admit, then, that the absence of spasmodic movement was phenomenal."

"It was phenomenal, Mr. Purser, in the sense that it was an appearance the cause of which is not immediately to be assigned."

"But tell me, my dear sir," pertinaciously continued the other, "was the man's death effected by the halter, or was it a species of euthanasia?"[2]

"*Euthanasia,* Mr. Purser, is something like your *will power:* I doubt its authenticity as a scientific term—begging your pardon again. It is at once imaginative and metaphysical—in short, Greek.—But," abruptly changing his tone, "there is a case in the sick bay that I do not care to leave to my assistants. Beg your pardon, but excuse me." And rising from the mess he formally withdrew.

27

The silence at the moment of execution and for a moment or two continuing thereafter, a silence but emphasized by the regular wash of the sea against the hull or the flutter of a sail caused by the helmsman's eyes being tempted astray, this emphasized silence was gradually distrubed by a sound not easily to be verbally rendered. Whoever has heard the freshet-wave of a torrent suddenly swelled by pouring showers in tropical mountains, showers not shared by the plain; whoever has heard the first muffled murmur of its sloping advance through precipitous woods may form some conception of the sound now heard. The seeming remoteness of its source was because of its murmurous indistinctness, since it came from close by, even from the men massed on the ship's open deck. Being inarticulate, it was dubious in significance further than it seemed to indicate some capricious revulsion of thought or feeling such as mobs ashore are liable to, in the present instance possible implying a sullen revocation on the men's part of their involuntary echoing of Billy's benediction. But ere the murmur had time to wax into clamor it was met by a strategic command, the more telling that it came with abrupt unexpectedness: "Pipe down the starboard watch, Boatswain, and see that they go."

Shrill as the shriek of the sea hawk, the silver whistles of the boatswain and his mates pierced that ominous low sound, dissipating it; and yielding to the mechanism of discipline the throng was thinned by one-half. For the remainder, most of them were set to temporary employments connected with trimming the yards and so forth, business readily to be got up to serve occasion by any officer of the deck.

Now each proceeding that follows a mortal sentence pronounced at sea by a drumhead court is characterized by promptitude not perceptibly merging into hurry, though bordering that. The hammock, the one which had been Billy's bed when alive, having already been ballasted with shot and otherwise prepared to serve for his canvas coffin, the last offices of the sea undertakers, the sailmaker's mates, were now speedily completed. When everything was in readiness a second

---

[2] Here, probably a death painless because of innocence, as in the definition given by the German philosopher Arthur Schopenhauer (1788–1860): "an easy death, not ushered in by disease, and free from all pain and struggle"; or, in the Greek sense, patriotic self-sacrifice.

call for all hands, made necessary by the strategic movement before mentioned, was sounded, now to witness burial.

The details of this closing formality it needs not to give. But when the tilted plank let slide its freight into the sea, a second strange human murmur was heard, blended now with another inarticulate sound proceeding from certain larger sea-fowl who, their attention having been attracted by the peculiar commotion in the water resulting from the heavy sloped dive of the shotted hammock into the sea, flew screaming to the spot. So near the hull did they come, that the stridor or bony creak of their gaunt double-jointed pinions was audible. As the ship under light airs passed on, leaving the burial spot astern, they still kept circling it low down with the moving shadow of their outstretched wings and the croaked requiem of their cries.

Upon sailors as superstitious as those of the age preceding ours, men-of-war's men too who had just beheld the prodigy of repose in the form suspended in air, and now foundering in the deeps; to such mariners the action of the seafowl, though dictated by mere animal greed for prey, was big with no prosaic significance. An uncertain movement began among them, in which some encroachment was made. It was tolerated but for a moment. For suddenly the drum beat to quarters,[1] which familiar sound happening at least twice every day, had upon the present occasion a signal peremptoriness in it. True martial discipline long continued superinduces in average man a sort of impulse whose operation at the official word of command much resembles in its promptitude the effect of an instinct.

The drumbeat dissolved the multitude, distributing most of them along the batteries of the two covered gun decks. There, as wonted, the guns' crews stood by their respective cannon erect and silent. In due course the first officer, sword under arm and standing in his place on the quarter-deck, formally received the successive reports of the sworded lieutenants commanding the sections of batteries below; the last of which reports being made, the summed report he delivered with the customary salute to the commander. All this occupied time, which in the present case was the object in beating to quarters at an hour prior to the customary one. That such variance from usage was authorized by an officer like Captain Vere, a martinet as some deemed him, was evidence of the necessity for unusual action implied in what he deemed to be temporarily the mood of his men. "With mankind," he would say, "forms, measured forms, are everything; and that is the import couched in the story of Orpheus[2] with his lyre spellbinding the wild denizens of the wood." And this he once applied to the disruption of forms going on across the Channel and the consequences thereof.

At this unwonted muster at quarters, all proceeded as at the regular hour. The band on the quarter-deck played a sacred air, after which the chaplain went through the customary morning service. That done, the drum beat the retreat; and toned by music and religious rites subserving the discipline and purposes of war, the men in their wonted orderly manner dispersed to the places allotted them when not at the guns.

And now it was full day. The fleece of low-hanging vapor had vanished, licked up by the sun that late had so glorified it. And the circumambient air in the clearness of its serenity was like smooth white marble in the polished block not yet removed from the marble-dealer's yard.

---

[1] To assemble the crew.
[2] According to Greek myth, a poet who held wild beasts spellbound by his wondrous lyre playing.

28

The symmetry of form attainable in pure fiction cannot so readily be achieved in a narration essentially having less to do with fable than with fact. Truth uncompromisingly told will always have its ragged edges; hence the conclusion of such a narration is apt to be less finished than an architectural finial.[1]

How it fared with the Handsome Sailor during the year of the Great Mutiny has been faithfully given. But though properly the story ends with his life, something in way of sequel will not be amiss. Three brief chapters will suffice.

In the general rechristening under the Directory of the craft originally forming the navy of the French monarchy, the *St. Louis* line-of-battle ship was named the *Athée* (the *Atheist*). Such a name, like some other substituted ones in the Revolutionary fleet, while proclaiming the infidel audacity of the ruling power, was yet, though not so intended to be, the aptest name, if one consider it, ever given to a warship; far more so indeed than the *Devastation,* the *Erebus* (the *Hell*), and similar names bestowed upon fighting ships.

On the return passage to the English fleet from the detached cruise during which occurred the events already recorded, the *Bellipotent* fell in with the *Athée*. An engagement ensued, during which Captain Vere, in the act of putting his ship alongside the enemy with a view of throwing his boarders across her bulwarks, was hit by a musket ball from a porthole of the enemy's main cabin. More than disabled, he dropped to the deck and was carried below to the same cockpit where some of his men already lay. The senior lieutenant took command. Under him the enemy was finally captured, and though much crippled was by rare good fortune successfully taken into Gibraltar, an English port not very distant from the scene of the fight. There, Captain Vere with the rest of the wounded was put ashore. He lingered for some days, but the end came. Unhappily he was cut off too early for the Nile and Trafalgar.[2] The spirit that 'spite its philosophic austerity may yet have indulged in the most secret of all passions, ambition, never attained to the fulness of fame.

Not long before death, while lying under the influence of that magical drug[3] which, soothing the physical frame, mysteriously operates on the subtler element in man, he was heard to murmur words inexplicable to his attendant: "Billy, Budd, Billy Budd." That these were not the accents of remorse would seem clear from what the attendant said to the *Bellipotent's* senior officer of marines, who, as the most reluctant to condemn of the members of the drumhead court, too well knew, though here he kept the knowledge to himself, who Billy Budd was.

29

Some few weeks after the execution, among other matters under the head of "News from the Mediterranean," there appeared in a naval chronicle of the time, an authorized weekly publication, an account of the affair. It was doubtless for the most part written in good faith, though the medium, partly rumor, through which the facts must have reached the writer served to deflect and in part falsify them. The account was as follows:

"On the tenth of the last month a deplorable occurrence took place on board

---

[1] An ornament crowning or concluding a monument.
[2] Vere died before the Battles of the Nile (1798) and Trafalgar (1805).   [3] Probably opium.

H.M.S. *Bellipotent*. John Claggart, the ship's master-at-arms, discovering that some sort of plot was incipient among an inferior section of the ship's company, and that the ringleader was one William Budd; he, Claggart, in the act of arraigning the man before the captain, was vindictively stabbed to the heart by the suddenly drawn sheath knife of Budd.

"The deed and the implement employed sufficiently suggest that though mustered into the service under an English name the assassin was no Englishman, but one of those aliens adopting English cognomens whom the present extraordinary necessities of the service have caused to be admitted into it in considerable numbers.

"The enormity of the crime and the extreme depravity of the criminal appear the greater in view of the character of the victim, a middle-aged man respectable and discreet, belonging to that minor official grade, the petty officers, upon whom, as none know better than the commissioned gentlemen, the efficiency of His Majesty's navy so largely depends. His function was a responsible one, at once onerous and thankless; and his fidelity in it the greater because of his strong patriotic impulse. In this instance as in so many other instances in these days, the character of this unfortunate man signally refutes, if refutation were needed, that peevish saying attributed to the late Dr. Johnson,[1] that patriotism is the last refuge of a scoundrel.

"The criminal paid the penalty of his crime. The promptitude of the punishment has proved salutary. Nothing amiss is now apprehended aboard H.M.S. *Bellipotent*."

The above, appearing in a publication now long ago superannuated and forgotten, is all that hitherto has stood in human record to attest what manner of men respectively were John Claggart and Billy Budd.

30

Everything is for a term venerated in navies. Any tangible object associated with some striking incident of the service is converted into a monument. The spar from which the foretopman was suspended was for some few years kept trace of by the bluejackets. Their knowledges followed it from ship to dockyard and again from dockyard to ship, still pursuing it even when at last reduced to a mere dockyard boom. To them a chip of it was as a piece of the Cross. Ignorant though they were of the secret facts of the tragedy, and not thinking but that the penalty was somehow unavoidably inflicted from the naval point of view, for all that, they instinctively felt that Billy was a sort of man as incapable of mutiny as of wilful murder. They recalled the fresh young image of the Handsome Sailor, that face never deformed by a sneer or subtler vile freak of the heart within. This impression of him was doubtless deepened by the fact that he was gone, and in a measure mysteriously gone. On the gun decks of the *Bellipotent* the general estimate of his nature and its unconscious simplicity eventually found rude utterance from another foretopman, one of his own watch, gifted, as some sailors are, with an artless *poetic* temperament. The tarry hand made some lines which, after circulating among the shipboard crews for a while, finally got rudely printed at Portsmouth as a ballad. The title given to it was the sailor's.

[1] Samuel Johnson (1709–1784), whose saying is reported by his biographer James Boswell (1740–1795) in *Life of Johnson* (1791) as a "pronouncement" made on April 7, 1775.

BILLY IN THE DARBIES[1]

Good of the chaplain to enter Lone Bay
And down on his marrowbones[2] here and pray
For the likes just o' me, Billy Budd. . . . But, look:
Through the port comes the moonshine astray!
It tips the guard's cutlass and silvers this nook;
But 'twill die in the dawning of Billy's last day.
A jewel-block[3] they'll make of me tomorrow,
Pendant pearl from the yardarm-end
Like the eardrop I gave to Bristol Molly . . .
O, 'tis me, not the sentence they'll suspend.   10
Ay, ay, all is up; and I must up too,
Early in the morning, aloft from alow.
On an empty stomach now never it would do.
They'll give me a nibble . . . bit o' biscuit ere I go.
Sure, a messmate will reach me the last parting cup;
But, turning heads away from the hoist and the belay,[4]
Heaven knows who will have the running of me up!
No pipe to those halyards. . . . But aren't it all sham?
A blur's in my eyes; it is dreaming that I am.
A hatchet to my hawser? All adrift to go?   20
The drum roll to grog, and Billy never know?
But Donald he has promised to stand by the plank;
So I'll shake a friendly hand ere I sink.
But . . . no! It is dead then I'll be, come to think.
I remember Taff the Welshman when he sank.
And his cheek it was like the budding pink.
But me they'll lash in hammock, drop me deep.
Fathoms down, fathoms down, how I'll dream fast asleep.
I fell it stealing now. Sentry, are you there?
Just ease these darbies at the wrist,   30
And roll me over fair!
I am sleepy, and the oozy weeds about me twist.

1886?–1891, 1924

from BATTLE-PIECES AND ASPECTS OF THE WAR

THE PORTENT*

(1859)

Hanging from the beam,
Slowly swaying (such the law),

---

[1] Manacles.   [2] Knees.   [3] A pulley at the end of a yardarm.
[4] The hoisting of the body and securing of the rope.
* This poem, the first in *Battle-Pieces and Aspects of the War* (1866), presents the slave rebellion led

Gaunt the shadow on your green,
    Shenandoah![1]
The cut is on the crown[2]
(Lo, John Brown),
And the stabs shall heal no more.

Hidden in the cap[3]
    Is the anguish none can draw
So your future veils its face,   10
    Shenandoah!
But the streaming beard is shown[4]
(Weird[5] John Brown),
The meteor of the war.

1866

THE MARCH INTO VIRGINIA

ENDING IN THE FIRST MANASSAS*

(July 1861)

Did all the lets[1] and bars appear
    To every just or larger end,
Whence should come the trust and cheer?
    Youth must its ignorant impulse lend . . .
Age finds place in the rear.
    All wars are boyish, and are fought by boys,
The champions and enthusiasts of the state:
    Turbid ardours and vain joys
        Not barrenly abate . . .
    Stimulants to the power mature,   10
        Preparatives of fate.

Who here forecasteth the event?
What heart but spurns at precedent
And warnings of the wise,
Contemned foreclosures of surprise?

---

by the abolitionist John Brown (1800–1859) at Harper's Ferry, then in Virginia, in October 1859 as a portent of the Civil War, which began in 1861.
  [1] Brown was hanged in the Shenandoah Valley, at Charlestown, Virginia (now Charles Town, West Virginia), in December 1859.
  [2] Brown had received a head wound, when he was captured.
  [3] The hood placed over the head of a condemned person.
  [4] His beard can be seen beneath the cap.   [5] Uncanny, fantastic.
  * On July 21, 1861, Confederate troops defeated Union forces at Bull Run, a stream near Manassas, Virginia. Melville portrays the Union soldiers as "boyish" and tragically light-hearted as they go into this first major battle of the Civil War.
  [1] Obstacles.

The banners play, the bugles call,
The air is blue and prodigal.
　　No berrying party, pleasure-wooed,
No picnic party in the May,
Ever went less loth than they   20
　　Into that leafy neighbourhood.
In Bacchic glee[2] they file toward Fate,
Moloch's[3] uninitiate;
Expectancy, and glad surmise
Of battle's unknown mysteries.

All they feel is this: 'tis glory,
A rapture sharp, though transitory,
Yet lasting in belaurelled story.
So they gaily go to fight,
Chatting left and laughing right.   30

But some who this blithe mood present,
　　As on in lightsome files they fare,
Shall die experienced ere three days are spent . . .
　　Perish, enlightened by the volleyed glare;
Or shame survive, and, like to adamant,[4]
　　The throe of Second Manassas[5] share.

1866

A UTILITARIAN VIEW OF THE MONITOR'S FIGHT*

Plain be the phrase, yet apt the verse,
　　More ponderous than nimble;
For since grimed War here laid aside
His Orient pomp, 'twould ill befit
　　　　Overmuch to ply
　　The rhyme's barbaric cymbal.

Hail to victory without the gaud[1]
　　Of glory; zeal that needs no fans
Of banners; plain mechanic power
Plied cogently in War now placed . . .   10
　　　　Where War belongs . . .
　　Among the trades and artisans.

---

[2] In revelry; Bacchus was the Roman god of wine.
[3] An ancient Semitic god of fire to whom children were offered in sacrifice.
[4] An imaginary stone of impenetrable hardness.
[5] In the Second Battle of Manassas, on August 30, 1862, Union forces met defeat by Generals Robert
E. Lee and Thomas "Stonewall" Jackson's troops.
　* Two ironclad ships, the Union *Monitor* and the Confederate *Merrimack,* met in combat at Hampton Roads, off Virginia, on May 9, 1862. Because of their heavy armor, neither ship could defeat the other. A utilitarian view is a view based on usefulness.
[1] The gaudiness.

Yet this was battle, and intense . . .
   Beyond the strife of fleets heroic;
Deadlier, closer, calm 'mid storm;
No passion; all went on by crank,
     Pivot, and screw,
   And calculations of caloric.[2]

Needless to dwell; the story's known.
   The ringing of those plates on plates   20
Still ringeth round the world[3] . . .
The clangour of that blacksmiths' fray.
     The anvil-din
   Resounds this message from the Fates:

War shall yet be, and to the end;
   But war-paint shows the streaks of weather;
War yet shall be, but warriors
Are now but operatives;[4] War's made
     Less grand than Peace,
   And a singe runs through lace and feather.   30

1866

SHILOH*

A REQUIEM

(April 1862)

Skimming lightly, wheeling still,
   The swallows fly low
Over the field in clouded days,
   The forest-field of Shiloh—
Over the field where April rain
Solaced the parched one stretched in pain
Through the pause of night
That followed the Sunday fight
   Around the church of Shiloh[1]—
The church so lone, the log-built one,   10

---

[2] Heat.

[3] An echo of line 4 in Ralph Waldo Emerson's "Concord Hymn" (1837) announcing that the colonists who began the Revolutionary War "fired the shot heard round the world"; here, the sounds of cannon-balls bouncing off the armor of the two ships, in its own way a revolutionary development in naval warfare.

[4] Factory workers.

* This poem commemorates the soldiers (of both sides) who died during the Confederate victory at Shiloh, in western Tennessee, in early April 1862.

[1] Much of the fighting took place around the Shiloh Baptist church. Ironically, in this "Sunday fight" human beings were killing each other rather than worshiping in brotherhood.

That echoed to many a parting groan
 And natural prayer
Of dying foemen mingled there—
Foemen at morn, but friends at eve—
 Fame or country least their care:
(What like a bullet can undeceive!)
 But now they lie low,
While over them the swallows skim
 And all is hushed at Shiloh.

             1866

MALVERN HILL*

(July 1862)

Ye elms that wave on Malvern Hill
 In prime of morn and May,
Recall ye how McClellan's men
  Here stood at bay?
While deep within yon forest dim
 Our rigid comrades lay . . .
Some with the cartridge in their mouth,[1]
Others with fixed arms lifted South[2] . . .
  Invoking so
The cypress glades? Ah wilds of woe!   10

The spires of Richmond, late beheld
 Through rifts in musket-haze,
Were closed from view in clouds of dust
  On leaf-walled ways,
Where streamed our wagons in caravan;
 And the Seven Nights and Days
Of march and fast, retreat and fight,
Pinched our grimed faces to ghastly plight . . .
  Does the elm wood
Recall the haggard beards of blood?   20

The battle-smoked flag, with stars eclipsed,
 We followed (it never fell!) . . .
In silence husbanded our strength . . .
  Received their yell;

---

 * At the end of the brutal Seven Days' Battle at Malvern Hill, Virginia, in July 1862, Union forces under General George McClellan repelled attacking Confederate troops under General Robert E. Lee.
 [1] With Civil War muzzle-loading rifles, a soldier would hold a gunpowder-filled cartridge in his mouth until his rifle was prepared for loading.
 [2] Rifles loaded and aimed toward the South.

Till on this slope we patient turned
   With cannon ordered well;

Reverse we proved was not defeat;
But ah, the sod what thousands meet! . . .
     Does Malvern Wood
Bethink itself, and muse and brood?   30

We elms of Malvern Hill
   Remember everything;
But sap the twig will fill:
Wag the world how it will,
   Leaves must be green in spring.[3]

                                   1866

THE COLLEGE COLONEL*

He rides at their head;
   A crutch by his saddle just slants in view,
One slung arm is in splints, you see,[1]
   Yet he guides his strong steed . . . how coldly too.

He brings his regiment home . . .
   Not as they filed two years before,
But a remnant half-tattered, and battered, and worn,
Like castaway sailors, who . . . stunned
     By the surf's loud roar,
   Their mates dragged back and seen no more . . .   10
Again and again breast the surge,
   And at last crawl, spent, to shore.

A still rigidity and pale . . .
   An Indian aloofness lones his brow;
He has lived a thousand years
Compressed in battle's pains and prayers,
   Marches and watches slow.

There are welcoming shouts, and flags;
   Old men off hat to the Boy,
Wreaths from gay balconies fall at his feet,   20
   But to *him* . . . there comes alloy.[2]

---

[3] The elm trees that stand on Malvern Hill remember the scenes of death even as they reaffirm life.

* William Francis Bartlett, a Harvard University student who enlisted in the Union army and rose to the rank of colonel; Melville was living in Pittsfield, Massachusetts, when the town honored Colonel Bartlett with a homecoming celebration.

[1] In battle, Bartlett had lost a leg, and one of his arms was maimed.

[2] A private mood that cuts in on the public celebration.

It is not that a leg is lost,
    It is not that an arm is maimed,
It is not that the fever has racked . . .
    Self he has long disclaimed.

But all through the Seven Days' Fight,[3]
    And deep in the Wilderness[4] grim,
And in the field-hospital tent,
    And Petersburg crater,[5] and dim
Lean brooding in Libby,[6] there came . . .   30
    Ah heaven! . . . what *truth* to him.

                                                          1866

THE MARTYR*

INDICATIVE OF THE PASSION OF THE PEOPLE ON THE 15TH OF APRIL 1865[1]

Good Friday was the day
    Of the prodigy[2] and crime,
When they[3] killed him in his pity,
    When they killed him in his prime
Of clemency and calm . . .
        When with yearning he was filled
        To redeem the evil-willed,
And, though conqueror, be kind;
    But they killed him in his kindness,
    In their madness and their blindness,   10
And they killed him from behind.

There is sobbing of the strong,
    And a pall upon the land;
But the People in their weeping
    Bare the iron hand:
Beware the People weeping
    When they bare the iron hand.

---

[3] The Seven Days' Battle at Malvern Hill, Virginia, in July 1862.
[4] The Battle of the Wilderness in Virginia in May 1864.
[5] The siege of Petersburg, Virginia, which was followed by the Battle of the Crater in July 1864.
[6] Bartlett, captured in Petersburg, was incarcerated in the Confederate Libby Prison in Richmond, Virginia.
* Abraham Lincoln.
[1] President Lincoln was shot by John Wilkes Booth on Good Friday, April 14, 1865 and died on April 15.
[2] An extraordinary and in this case horrendous occurrence.
[3] Lincoln is seen a martyr, one who died for a cause, for refusing to sacrifice principle; "the people" see his assassination not as the act of one man but as something "they," radical opponents of Lincoln's policies and principles, did. Thus, in the next stanza the people weep, but they "Bare the iron hand."

He lieth in his blood . . .
   The father in his face;[4]
They have killed him, the Forgiver . . .   20
   The Avenger[5] takes his place,
The Avenger wisely stern,
     Who in righteousness shall do
     What the heavens call him to,
And the parricides remand;
   For they killed him in his kindness
   In their madness and their blindness,
And his blood is on their hand.

There is sobbing of the strong,
   And a pall upon the land;   30
But the People in their weeping
     Bare the iron hand:
Beware the People weeping
   When they bare the iron hand.

1866

from   *JOHN MARR AND OTHER SAILORS*

THE MALDIVE SHARK*

About the Shark, phlegmatical[1] one,
Pale sot of the Maldive sea,[2]
The sleek little pilot-fish,[3] azure and slim,
How alert in attendance be.
From his saw-pit of mouth, from his charnel of maw,
They have nothing of harm to dread,
But liquidly glide on his ghastly flank
Or before his Gorgonian head;[4]
Or lurk in the port of serrated teeth
In white triple tiers of glittering gates,   10
And there find a haven when peril's abroad.
An asylum in jaws of the Fates![5]

---

[4] With the mention of "parricides" (murderers of a parent) below, this line probably signifies that Lincoln has the face of a father, the father of his nation.

[5] Probably not Andrew Johnson (who succeeded Lincoln as president); with the Forgiver dead, the "passion of the people" takes the form of an Avenger who will perform a heavenly duty and "remand," or place into custody, the parricides.

* The Maldive Islands lie off the southernmost tip of India.   [1] Sluggish.

[2] "Drunkard," or slow-moving animal, of the part of the Indian Ocean around the Maldive Islands.

[3] Small fish that hover near sharks and seem to guide them.

[4] According to Greek myth, the Gorgons were three sisters, with snakes for hair, who could turn beholders to stone.

[5] According to myth, three goddesses who control human destiny.

They are friends; and friendly they guide him to prey,
Yet never partake of the treat . . .
Eyes and brains to the dotard[6] lethargic and dull,
Pale ravener of horrible meat.

1888

THE BERG

A DREAM

I saw a ship of martial[1] build
(Her standards[2] set, her brave apparel on)
Directed as by madness mere
Against a stolid iceberg steer,
Nor budge it, though the infatuate[3] ship went down.
The impact made huge ice-cubes fall
Sullen, in tons that crashed the deck;
But that one avalanche was all . . .
No other movement save the foundering wreck.

Along the spurs of ridges pale,   10
Not any slenderest shaft and frail,
A prism over glass-green gorges lone,
Toppled; nor lace of traceries fine,
Nor pendant drops in grot[4] or mine
Were jarred, when the stunned ship went down.
Nor sole the gulls in cloud that wheeled
Circling one snow-flanked peak afar,
But nearer fowl the floes that skimmed
And crystal beaches, felt no jar.
No thrill[5] transmitted stirred the lock   20
Of jack-straw needle-ice at base;
Towers undermined by waves . . . the block
Atilt impending . . . kept their place.
Seals, dozing sleek on sliddery[6] ledges
Slipt never, when by loftier edges
Through very inertia overthrown,
The impetuous ship in bafflement went down.

Hard Berg (methought), so cold, so vast,
With mortal damps self-overcast;
Exhaling still thy dankish breath . . .   30

---

[6] In a state of dotage or senility; in this poem the pilot-fish are the "eyes and brains" of the sluggish and senile shark.
    [1] Warlike.   [2] Banners, flags.   [3] Foolish, deprived of sound judgment.   [4] Grotto.
    [5] Tremor, vibration.   [6] Slippery.

Adrift dissolving, bound for death;
Though lumpish thou, a lumbering one . . .
A lumbering lubbard loitering slow,
Impingers rue thee and go down,
Sounding thy precipice below,
Nor stir the slimy slug that sprawls
Along thy dead indifference of walls.

1888

from   TIMOLEON

MONODY*

To have known him, to have loved him
    After loneness long;
And then to be estranged in life,[1]
    And neither in the wrong;
And now for death to set his seal . . .
Ease me, a little ease, my song!

By wintry hills his hermit-mound
    The sheeted snow-drifts drape,
And houseless there the snow-bird flits
    Beneath the fir-trees' crape:
Glazed now with ice the cloistral vine[2]   10
    That hid the shyest grape.

1891

ART

In placid hours well pleased we dream
Of many a brave unbodied scheme.
But form to lend, pulsed life create,
What unlike things must meet and mate:
A flame to melt . . . a wind to freeze;
Sad patience . . . joyous energies;
Humility . . . yet pride and scorn;
Instinct and study; love and hate;

---

  * A poem in which a single mourner laments, this monody is thought to be a lament for Nathaniel Hawthorne, who died in 1864.
  [1] There is no evidence that Melville and Hawthorne were ever "estranged," although their lives went different ways in the early 1850s after they had been neighbors in western Massachusetts.
  [2] In his book-length poem, *Clarel* (1876), Melville seems to have portrayed Vine, a shy character, from his memories of Hawthorne.

Audacity . . . reverence. These must mate
And fuse with Jacob's[1] mystic heart,   10
To wrestle with the angel . . . Art.

1891

from HAWTHORNE AND HIS MOSSES*

By A Virginian Spending July In Vermont

It is curious how a man may travel along a country road, and yet miss the grandest or sweetest of prospects by reason of an intervening hedge, so like all other hedges, as in no way to hint of the wide landscape beyond. So has it been with me concerning the enchanting landscape in the soul of this Hawthorne, this most excellent Man of Mosses. His Old Manse has been written now four years, but I never read it till a day or two since. I had seen it in the book-stores—heard of it often—even had it recommended to me by a tasteful friend, as a rare, quiet book, perhaps too deserving of popularity to be popular. . . .

* * *

. . . Where Hawthorne is known, he seems to be deemed a pleasant writer, with a pleasant style,—a sequestered, harmless man, from whom any deep and weighty thing would hardly be anticipated—a man who means no meanings. But there is no man, in whom humour and love, like mountain peaks, soar to such a rapt height as to receive the irradiations of the upper skies;—there is no man in whom humour and love are developed in that high form called genius; no such man can exist without also possessing, as the indispensable complement of these, a great, deep intellect, which drops down into the universe like a plummet. . . .

How profound, nay, appalling, is the moral evolved by the *Earth's Holocaust;*[1] where—beginning with the hollow follies and affectations of the world,—all vanities and empty theories and forms are, one after another, and by an admirably graduated, growing comprehensiveness, thrown into the allegorical fire, till, at length, nothing is left but the all-engendering heart of man; which remaining still unconsumed, the great conflagration is naught.

Of a piece with this, is the *Intelligence Office,* a wondrous symbolising of the secret workings in men's souls. There are other sketches still more charged with ponderous import.

The Christmas Banquet, and *The Bosom Serpent,* would be fine subjects for a curious and elaborate analysis, touching the conjectural parts of the mind that produced them. For spite of all the Indian-summer sunlight on the hither side of Hawthorne's soul, the other side—like the dark half of the physical sphere—is

---

[1] In Genesis 32:24–30 Jacob wrestles with an angel who, at the end of the struggle, blesses him.

* Although Hawthorne's *Mosses From an Old Manse* was published in 1846, Melville reportedly did not read it until 1850. This review first appeared anonymously (hence the subtitle) in the New York *Literary World* on August 17 and 24, 1850, shortly after Melville and Hawthorne first met.

[1] From *Mosses From an Old Manse.* Melville singles out for special praise a number of Hawthorne's tales and sketches.

shrouded in a blackness, ten times black. But this darkness but gives more effect to the ever-moving dawn, that forever advances through it, and circumnavigates his world. Whether Hawthorne has simply availed himself of this mystical blackness as a means to the wondrous effects he makes it to produce in his lights and shades; or whether there really lurks in him, perhaps unknown to himself, a touch of Puritanic gloom,—this, I cannot altogether tell. Certain it is, however, that this great power of blackness in him derives its force from its appeals to that Calvinistic sense of Innate Depravity and Original Sin, from whose visitations, in some shape or other, no deeply thinking mind is always and wholly free. For, in certain moods, no man can weigh this world without throwing in something, somehow like Original Sin, to strike the uneven balance. At all events, perhaps no writer has ever wielded this terrific thought with greater terror than this same harmless Hawthorne. Still more: this black conceit pervades him through and through. You may be witched by his sunlight—transported by the bright gildings in the skies he builds over you; but there is the blackness of darkness beyond; and even his bright gildings but fringe and play upon the edges of thunderclouds. In one word, the world is mistaken in this Nathaniel Hawthorne. He himself must often have smiled at its absurd misconception of him. He is immeasurably deeper than the plummet of the mere critic. For it is not the brain that can test such a man; it is only the heart. You cannot come to know greatness by inspecting it; there is no glimpse to be caught of it, except by intuition; you need not ring it,[2] you but touch it, and you find it is gold.

Now, it is that blackness in Hawthorne, of which I have spoken, that so fixes and fascinates me. It may be, nevertheless, that it is too largely developed in him. Perhaps he does not give us a ray of light for every shade of his dark. But however this may be, this blackness it is that furnishes the infinite obscure of his background,—that background, against which Shakespeare plays his grandest conceits, the things that have made for Shakespeare his loftiest but most circumscribed renown, as the profoundest of thinkers. For by philosophers Shakespeare is not adored, as the great man of tragedy and comedy:—'Off with his head; so much for Buckingham!'[3] This sort of rant interlined by another hand, brings down the house,—those mistaken souls, who dream of Shakespeare as a mere man of Richard the Third humps and Macbeth daggers. But it is those deep far-away things in him; those occasional flashings-forth of the intuitive Truth in him; those short, quick probings at the very axis of reality;—these are the things that make Shakespeare, Shakespeare. Through the mouths of the dark characters of Hamlet, Timon, Lear, and Iago, he craftily says, or sometimes insinuates the things which we feel to be so terrifically true, that it were all but madness for any good man, in his own proper character, to utter, or even hint of them. Tormented into desperation, Lear, the frantic king, tears off the mask, and speaks the same madness of vital truth. But, as I before said, it is the least part of genius that attracts admiration. And so, much of the blind, unbridled admiration that has been heaped upon Shakespeare, has been lavished upon the least part of him. And few of his endless commentators and critics seem to have remembered, or even perceived, that the immediate products of a great mind are not so great as that undeveloped and sometimes undevelopable yet dimly-discernible greatness, to which those immediate

---

[2] Test it for sound.

[3] A line inserted into Shakespeare's *Richard III* by the English dramatist Colley Cibber (1671–1757) in his melodramatic revision of the play in 1700.

products are but the infallible indices. In Shakespeare's tomb lies infinitely more than Shakespeare ever wrote. And if I magnify Shakespeare, it is not so much for what he did do as for what he did not do, or refrained from doing. For in this world of lies, Truth is forced to fly like a scared white doe in the woodlands; and only by cunning glimpses will she reveal herself, as in Shakespeare and other masters of the great Art of Telling the Truth,—even though it be covertly and by snatches.

* * *

Some may start to read of Shakespeare and Hawthorne on the same page. They may say, that if an illustration were needed, a lesser light might have sufficed to elucidate this Hawthorne, this small man of yesterday. But I am not willingly one of those who, as touching Shakespeare at least, exemplify the maxim of Rochefoucauld,[4] that 'we exalt the reputation of some, in order to depress that of others';—who, to teach all noble-souled aspirants that there is no hope for them, pronounce Shakespeare absolutely unapproachable. But Shakespeare has been approached. There are minds that have gone as far as Shakespeare into the universe. And hardly a mortal man, who, at some time or other, has not felt as great thoughts in him as any you will find in Hamlet. We must not inferentially malign mankind for the sake of any one man, whoever he may be. This is too cheap a purchase of contentment for conscious mediocrity to make. Besides, this absolute and unconditional adoration of Shakespeare has grown to be a part of our Anglo-Saxon superstitions. The Thirty-Nine Articles[5] are now forty. Intolerance has come to exist in this matter. You must believe in Shakespeare's unapproachability, or quit the country. But what sort of a belief is this for an American, a man who is bound to carry republican progressiveness into Literature as well as into Life? Believe me, my friends, that men not very much inferior to Shakespeare are this day being born on the banks of the Ohio. And the day will come when you shall say, Who reads a book by an Englishman that is a modern?[6] The great mistake seems to be, that even with those Americans who look forward to the coming of a great literary genius among us, they somehow fancy he will come in the costume of Queen Elizabeth's day; be a writer of dramas founded upon old English history or the tales of Boccaccio.[7] Whereas, great geniuses are parts of the times, they themselves are the times, and possess a corresponding colouring. It is of a piece with the Jews, who, while their Shiloh[8] was meekly walking in their streets, were still praying for his magnificent coming; looking for him in a chariot, who was already among them on an ass. Nor must we forget that, in his own lifetime, Shakespeare was not Shakespeare, but only Master William Shakespeare of the shrewd, thriving, business firm of Condell,[9] Shakespeare and Co., proprietors of the Globe Theatre in London; and by a courtly author, of the name of Chettle,[10] was looked at as an 'upstart crow,' beautified 'with other birds' feath-

---

[4] François de la Rochefoucauld (1613–1680), a French moralist and writer.

[5] The doctrines of the Church of England, comically expanded here to include "the unconditional adoration" of Shakespeare.

[6] An ironic echo of the remark made by the Scottish critic Sydney Smith: "In the four quarters of the globe, who reads an American book?" (*Edinburgh Review*, January 1820).

[7] Giovanni Boccaccio (1313–1375), author of the hundred tales gathered in *The Decameron* (1353).

[8] Messiah.   [9] Henry Condell, who helped publish the first folio edition of Shakespeare's work.

[10] It was Robert Greene and not Henry Chettle who made these disparaging remarks about Shakespeare, in *Groatsworth of Wit Bought With a Million of Repentance* (1592).

ers.' For, mark it well, imitation is often the first charge brought against original-ity. Why this is so, there is not space to set forth here. You must have plenty of sea-room to tell the Truth in; especially when it seems to have an aspect of new-ness, as America did in 1492, though it was then just as old, and perhaps older than Asia, only those sagacious philosophers, the common sailors, had never seen it before, swearing it was all water and moonshine there.

Now I do not say that Nathaniel of Salem is a greater man than William of Avon,[11] or as great. But the difference between the two men is by no means immeasurable. No a very great deal more, and Nathaniel were verily William.

This, too, I mean, that if Shakespeare has not been equalled, give the world time, and he is sure to be surpassed in one hemisphere or the other. Nor will it at all do to say that the world is getting gray and grizzled now, and has lost that fresh charm which she wore of old, and by virtue of which the great poets of past times made themselves what we esteem them to be. Not so. The world is as young to-day as when it was created; and this Vermont morning dew is as wet to my feet, as Eden's dew to Adam's. Nor has nature been all over ransacked by our progeni-tors, so that no new charms and mysteries remain for this latter generation to find. Far from it. The trillionth part has not yet been said; and all that has been said, but multiplies the avenues to what remains to be said. It is not so much paucity as superabundance of material that seems to incapacitate modern authors.

Let America, then, prize and cherish her writers; yea, let her glorify them. They are not so many in number as to exhaust her goodwill. And while she has good kith and kin of her own to take to her bosom, let her not lavish her embraces upon the household of an alien. For believe it or not, England after all, is in many things an alien to us. China has more bonds of real love for us than she. But even were there no strong literary individualities among us, as there are some dozens at least, nevertheless, let America first praise mediocrity even, in her children, be-fore she praises (for everywhere, merit demands acknowledgment from every one) the best excellence in the children of any other land. Let her own authors, I say, have the priority of appreciation. I was much pleased with a hot-headed Carolina cousin of mine, who once said,—'If there were no other American to stand by, in literature, why, then, I would stand by Pop Emmons[12] and his *Fredoniad,* and till a better epic came along, swear it was not very far behind the *Iliad*.' Take away the words, and in spirit he was sound.

* * *

And now, my countrymen, as an excellent author of your own flesh and blood—an unimitating, and, perhaps, in his way, an inimitable man—whom bet-ter can I commend to you, in the first place, than Nathaniel Hawthorne. He is one of the new, and far better generation of your writers. The smell of young beeches and hemlocks is upon him; your own broad prairies are in his soul; and if you travel away inland into his deep and noble nature, you will hear the far roar of his Niagara. Give not over to future generations the glad duty of acknowledging him for what he is. Take that joy to yourself, in your own generation; and so shall he feel those grateful impulses on him, that may possibly prompt him to the full flower of some still greater achievement in your eyes. And by confessing him you

[11] Shakespeare, the "Bard of Avon."

[12] Richard Emmons (1788–1840), whose *Fredoniad: Or, Independence Preserved—An Epic Poem of the War of 1812* (1827) Melville sees as a pathetic effort with a patriotic spirit.

thereby confess others; you brace the whole brotherhood. For genius, all over the world, stands hand in hand, and one shock of recognition runs the whole circle round.

In treating of Hawthorne, or rather of Hawthorne in his writings (for I never saw the man; and in the chances of a quiet plantation life, remote from his haunts, perhaps never shall); in treating of his works, I say, I have thus far omitted all mention of his *Twice Told Tales,* and *Scarlet Letter.*[13] Both are excellent, but full of such manifold, strange, and diffusive beauties, that time would all but fail me to point the half of them out. But there are things in those two books, which, had they been written in England a century ago, Nathaniel Hawthorne had utterly displaced many of the bright names we now revere on authority. But I am content to leave Hawthorne to himself, and to the infallible finding of posterity; and however great may be the praise I have bestowed upon him, I feel that in so doing I have served and honoured myself, rather than him. For, at bottom, great excellence is praise enough to itself; but the feeling of a sincere and appreciative love and admiration toward it, this is relieved by utterance, and warm, honest praise ever leaves a pleasant flavour in the mouth; and it is an honourable thing to confess to what is honourable in others.

* * *

Twenty-four hours have elapsed since writing the foregoing. I have just returned from the haymow, charged more and more with love and admiration of Hawthorne. For I have just been gleaning through the Mosses, picking up many things here and there that had previously escaped me. And I found that but to glean after this man, is better than to be in at the harvest of others. To be frank (though, perhaps, rather foolish), notwithstanding what I wrote yesterday of these Mosses, I had not then culled them all; but had, nevertheless, been sufficiently sensible of the subtle essence in them, as to write as I did. To what infinite height of loving wonder and admiration I may yet be borne, when by repeatedly banqueting on these Mosses I shall have thoroughly incorporated their whole stuff into my being—that, I cannot tell. But already I feel that this Hawthorne has dropped germinous seeds into my soul. He expands and deepens down, the more I contemplate him; and further and further, shoots his strong New England roots into the hot soil in my Southern soul.

By careful reference to the table of contents, I now find that I have gone through all the sketches; but that when I yesterday wrote, I had not at all read two particular pieces, to which I now desire to call special attention—*A Select Party* and *Young Goodman Brown.* Here, be it said to all those whom this poor fugitive scrawl of mine may tempt to the perusal of the Mosses, that they must on no account suffer themselves to be trifled with, disappointed, or deceived by the triviality of many of the titles to these sketches. For in more than one instance, the title utterly belies the piece. It is as if rustic demijohns containing the very best and costliest of Falernian and Tokay, were labelled 'Cider,' 'Perry,' and 'Elderberry wine.' The truth seems to be, that like many other geniuses, this Man of Mosses takes great delight in hoodwinking the world,—at least, with respect to himself. Personally, I doubt not that he rather prefers to be generally esteemed but a so-so sort of author; being willing to reserve the thorough and acute appreciation of what he is, to that party most qualified to judge—that is, to himself. Besides, at

---

[13] Hawthorne's *Twice-Told Tales* was published in 1837 and *The Scarlet Letter* in 1850, the same year as Melville's review.

the bottom of their natures, men like Hawthorne, in many things, deem the plaudits of the public such strong presumptive evidence of mediocrity in the object of
them, that it would in some degree render them doubtful of their own powers, did
they hear much and vociferous braying concerning them in the public pastures.
True, I have been braying myself (if you please to be witty enough to have it so),
but then I claim to be the first that has so brayed in this particular matter; and,
therefore, while pleading guilty to the charge, still claim all the merit due to originality.

But with whatever motive, playful or profound, Nathaniel Hawthorne has chosen to entitle his pieces in the manner he has, it is certain that some of them are
directly calculated to deceive—egregiously deceive, the superficial skimmer of
pages. To be downright and candid once more, let me cheerfully say, that two of
these titles did dolefully dupe no less an eager-eyed reader than myself; and that,
too, after I had been impressed with a sense of the great depth and breadth of this
American man. 'Who in the name of thunder' (as the country people say in this
neighbourhood), 'who in the name of thunder, would anticipate any marvel in a
piece entitled *Young Goodman Brown?*' You would of course suppose that it was
a simple little tale, intended as a supplement to *Goody Two Shoes*. Whereas, it is
deep as Dante; nor can you finish it, without addressing the author in his own
words—'It shall be yours to penetrate, in every bosom, the deep mystery of
sin.' . . . And with Young Goodman, too, in allegorical pursuit of his Puritan
wife, you cry out in your anguish:—

'"Faith!" shouted Goodman Brown, in a voice of agony and desperation; and the
echoes of the forest mocked him, crying, "Faith! Faith!" as if bewildered wretches
were seeking her all through the wilderness.'

Now this same piece entitled *Young Goodman Brown*, is one of the two that I
had not all read yesterday; and I allude to it now, because it is, in itself, such a
strong positive illustration of the blackness in Hawthorne, which I had assumed
from the mere occasional shadows of it, as revealed in several of the other
sketches. But had I previously perused *Young Goodman Brown*, I should have
been at no pains to draw the conclusion, which I came to at a time when I was
ignorant that the book contained one such direct and unqualified manifestation
of it.

The other piece of the two referred to, is entitled *A Select Party*, which, in my
first simplicity upon originally taking hold of the book, I fancied must treat of
some pumpkin-pie party in old Salem; or some chowder party on Cape Cod.
Whereas, by all the gods of Peedee,[14] it is the sweetest and sublimest thing that
has been written since Spenser wrote. Nay, there is nothing in Spenser that surpasses it, perhaps nothing that equals it. And the test is this. Read any canto in
The Faerie Queene and then read *A Select Party*, and decide which pleases you
most, that is, if you are qualified to judge. Do not be frightened at this; for when
Spenser was alive, he was thought of very much as Hawthorne is now,—was
generally accounted just such a 'gentle' harmless man. . . .

* * *

[14] A river, also called the Yadkin River, running from North Carolina to South Carolina, used for
baptisms.

. . . Gainsay it who will, as I now write, I am Posterity speaking by proxy—and after-times will make it more than good, when I declare, that the American who up to the present day has evinced, in literature, the largest brain with the largest heart, that man is Nathaniel Hawthorne. Moreover, that whatever Nathaniel Hawthorne may hereafter write, *Mosses from an Old Manse* will be ultimately accounted his masterpiece. For there is a sure, though secret sign in some works which proves the culmination of the powers (only the developable ones, however) that produced them. But I am by no means desirous of the glory of a prophet. I pray Heaven that Hawthorne may yet prove me an impostor in this prediction. Especially, as I somehow cling to the strange fancy, that, in all men, hiddenly reside certain wondrous, occult properties—as in some plants and minerals—which by some happy but very rare accident (as bronze was discovered by the melting of the iron and brass at the burning of Corinth) may chance to be called forth here on earth; not entirely waiting for their better discovery in the more congenial, blessed atmosphere of heaven.

Once more—for it is hard to be finite upon an infinite subject, and all subjects are infinite. By some people this entire scrawl of mine may be esteemed altogether unnecessary, inasmuch 'as years ago' (they may say) 'we found out the rich and rare stuff in this Hawthorne, who you now parade forth, as if only you *yourself* were the discoverer of this Portuguese diamond[15] in your literature.' But even granting all this—and adding to it, the assumption that the books of Hawthorne have sold by the five thousand—what does that signify? They should be sold by the hundred thousand; and read by the million; and admired by every one who is capable of admiration.

1850

LETTER TO NATHANIEL HAWTHORNE*

[*29 January? 1851*]

Pittsfield, Wednesday,

That side-blow thro' Mrs. Hawthorne will not do.[1] I am not to be charmed out of my promised pleasure by any of that lady's syrenisims [*sic*]. *You,* Sir, I hold accountable, & the visit (in all its original integrity) must be made.—What! *spend the day,* only with us?—A Greenlander might as well talk of spending the day with a friend, when the day is only half an inch long.

As I said before, my best travelling chariot on runners, will be at your door, & provision made not only for the accommodation of all your family, but also for any quantity of *baggage.*

---

[15] A diamond of intricate design.

* This is the first of the surviving letters from Melville to Hawthorne; it shows the imaginative vitality Melville felt at the idea of having Hawthorne for a friend. Melville was notorious for his misspellings, which have been preserved in Howth's Northwestern-Newberry edition.

[1] A visit of the Hawthornes to the Melvilles had apparently been agreed upon a week earlier, but Sophia Hawthorne rather than Hawthorne himself had written to beg out of the invitation. (Footnote information from Northwestern-Newberry edition.) Hence, with the wind as his metaphor, Melville refers to a "side-blow" bringing the news; had Hawthorne written, the wind bringing the news would have blown directly.

Fear not that you will cause the slightest trouble to us. Your bed is already made, & the wood marked for your fire. But a moment ago, I looked into the eyes of two fowls, whose tail feathers have been notched, as destined victims for the table. I keep the word "Welcome" all the time in my mouth, so as to be ready on the instant when you cross the threshold.

(By the way the old Romans you know had a *Salve*[2] carved in *their* thresholds)

Another thing, Mr Hawthorne—Do not think you are coming to any prim non-sensical house—that is nonsensical in the ordinary way. You wont be much bored with punctilios.[3] You may do what you please—say or say *not* what you please. And if you feel any inclination for that sort of thing—you may spend the period of your visit *in bed,* if you like—every hour of your visit.

Mark—There is some excellent Montado Sherry awaiting you & some most potent Port. We will have mulled wine with wisdom, & buttered toast with story-telling & crack jokes & bottles from morning till night.

Come—no nonsense. If you dont—I will send Constables after you.

On *Wednesday* then—weather & sleighing permitting I will be down for you about eleven o'clock A. M.

By the way—should Mrs Hawthorne for any reason conclude that *she,* for one, can not stay overnight with us—then *you* must—& the children, if you please.

H. Melville.

1851, 1960

from   LETTER TO EVERT A. DUYCKINCK*

[*12 February 1851*]

Pittsfield, Wednesday, 1851.

My Dear Duyckinck,

"A dash of salt spray"!—where am I to get salt spray here in inland Pittsfield?[1] I shall have to import it from foreign parts. All I now have to do with salt, is when I salt my horse & cow—not *salt them down*—I dont mean that (tho' indeed I have before now dined on "salt-horse"[2]) but when I give them their weekly salt, by way of seasoning all their week's meals in one prospective lump.

How shall a man go about refusing a man?—Best be roundabout, or plumb on the mark?—I can not write the thing you want. I am in the humor to lend a hand to a friend, if I can;—but I am not in the humor to write the kind of thing you

---

[2] Hail, welcome.   [3] Ceremonies, formal observances.

* Evert Augustus Duyckinck (1816–1878), a friend of Melville's and, with his brother George (1823–1863), editor of the New York *Literary World* from 1847 to 1853. Later the Duyckincks published the *Cyclopaedia of American Literature* (1855, 1866), a comprehensive work about American writers.

[1] Melville is apparently declining an invitation from Evert Duyckinck to contribute an article or story to *Holden's Dollar Magazine,* which the Duyckinck brothers edited later in 1851. (Footnote information from Northwestern-Newberry edition.) Because Melville was known for writing about the sea, the request was probably for "a dash of salt spray."

[2] Salted horse meat.

need—and I am not in the humor to write for Holden's Magazine. If I were to go on to give you all my reasons—you would pronounce [?] me a bore, so I will not do that. You must be content to beleive [sic] that I *have* reasons, or else I would not refuse so small a thing.—As for the Daguerreotype[3] (I spell the word right from your sheet) that's what I can not send you, because I have none. And if I had, I would not send it for such a purpose, even to you.—Pshaw! you cry—& so cry I.—"This is intensified vanity, not true modesty or anything of that sort!"— Again, I say so too. But if it be so, how can I help it. The fact is, almost every- body is having his "mug" engraved nowadays; so that this test of distinction is getting to be reversed; and therefore, to see one's "mug" in a magazine, is pre- sumptive evidence that he's a nobody. So being as vain a man as ever lived; & beleiving that my illustrious name is famous throughout the world—I respectfully decline being oblivionated by a Daguerretype (what a devel [sic] of an unspellable word?)

We are all queer customers, Mr Duyckinck, you, I, & every body else in the world. So if I here seem queer to you, be sure, I am not alone in my queerness, tho' it present itself at a different port, perhaps, from other people, since every one has his own distinct peculiarity. But I trust you take me aright. If you dont' I shall be sorry—that's all.

After a long procrastination, I drove down to see Mr Hawthorne a couple of weeks ago. I found him, of course, buried in snow; & the delightful scenery about him, all wrapped up & tucked away under a napkin, as it were. He was to have made me a day's visit, & I had promised myself much pleasure in getting him up in my snug room here, & discussing the Universe with a bottle of brandy & ci- gars. But he has not been able to come, owing to sickness in his family.—or else, he's up to the lips in the *Universe* again.

By the way, I have recently read his "Twice Told Tales"[4] (I had not read but a few of them before) I think they far exceed the "Mosses"—they are, I fancy, an earlier vintage from his vine. Some of those sketches are wonderfully subtle. Their deeper meanings are worthy of a Brahmin.[5] Still there is something lack- ing—a good deal lacking—to the plump sphericity of the man. What is that?—He does'nt patronise the butcher—he needs roast-beef, done rare.—Nevertheless, for one, I regard Hawthorne (in his books) as evincing a quality of genius, immensely loftier, & more profound, too, than any other American has shown hitherto in the printed form. Irving[6] is a grasshopper to him—putting the *souls* of the two men together, I mean.—But I must close. Enclosed is a note from the "Sad One."[7]

With remembrances to your brother, I am

Truly Yours
H Melville
1851, 1938

---

[3] An early variety of photograph, produced on a silver plate. The process was named for its inventor, Louis Jacques Mande Daguerre (1789–1851). The Duyckincks were planning a series of articles on contemporary American writers, with daguerreotypes.

[4] Nathaniel Hawthorne's *Twice-Told Tales* was published in 1837; when Melville reviewed *Mosses From an Old Manse* (1846) in 1850, he pronounced that collection to be Hawthorne's "masterpiece."

[5] A cultured, upper-class person.   [6] Washington Irving (1783–1859).

[7] Augusta Melville (1821–1876), Melville's sister and a good friend of Duyckinck's.

LETTER TO NATHANIEL HAWTHORNE

[*17? November 1851*]

Pittsfield, Monday afternoon.

My Dear Hawthorne,—People think that if a man has undergone any hardship, he should have a reward; but for my part, if I have done the hardest possible day's work, and then come to sit down in a corner and eat my supper comfortably— why, then I don't think I deserve any reward for my hard day's work—for am I not now at peace? Is not my supper good? My peace and my supper are my re- ward, my dear Hawthorne. So your joy-giving and exultation-breeding letter is not my reward for my ditcher's work[1] with that book, but is the good goddess's bonus over and above what was stipulated for—for not one man in five cycles, who is wise, will expect appreciative recognition from his fellows, or any one of them. Appreciation! Recognition! Is Jove[2] appreciated? Why, ever since Adam, who has got to the meaning of his great allegory— the world? Then we pygmies must be content to have our paper allegories but ill comprehended. I say your appreciation is my glorious gratuity. In my proud, humble way,—a shepherd- king,—I was lord of a little vale in the solitary Crimea;[3] but you have now given me the crown of India. But on trying it on my head, I found it fell down on my ears, notwithstanding their asinine length—for it's only such ears that sustain such crowns.

Your letter was handed me last night on the road going to Mr. Morewood's,[4] and I read it there. Had I been at home, I would have sat down at once and answered it. In me divine maganimities [*sic*] are spontaneous and instantaneous— catch them while you can. The world goes round, and the other side comes up. So now I can't write what I felt. But I felt pantheistic then—your heart beat in my ribs and mine in yours, and both in God's. A sense of unspeakable security is in me this moment, on account of your having understood the book. I have written a wicked book, and feel spotless as the lamb. Ineffable socialities are in me. I would sit down and dine with you and all the gods in old Rome's Pantheon. It is a strange feeling—no hopefulness is in it, no despair. Content—that is it; and irre- sponsibility; but without licentious inclination. I speak now of my profoundest sense of being, not of an incidental feeling.

Whence come you, Hawthorne? By what right do you drink from my flagon of life? And when I put it to my lips—lo, they are yours and not mine. I feel that the Godhead is broken up like the bread at the Supper,[5] and that we are the pieces. Hence this infinite fraternity of feeling. Now, sympathizing with the paper, my angel turns over another page. You did not care a penny for the book. But, now and then as you read, you understood the pervading thought that impelled the book—and that you praised. Was it not so? You were archangel enough to despise

---

[1] Ditchdigging.   [2] Jupiter, the chief deity of Roman myth.
[3] A peninsula in southwestern Russia.   [4] A neighbor whose son married one of Melville's nieces.
[5] The Last Supper (see John 13–15).

the imperfect body, and embrace the soul. Once you hugged the ugly Socrates[6] because you saw the flame in the mouth, and heard the rushing of the demon,—the familiar,—and recognized the sound; for you have heard it in your own solitudes.

My dear Hawthorne, the atmospheric skepticisms steal into me now, and make me doubtful of my sanity in writing you thus. But, believe me, I am not mad, most noble Festus![7] But truth is ever incoherent, and when the big hearts strike together, the concussion is a little stunning. Farewell. Don't write a word about the book. That would be robbing me of my miserly delight. I am heartily sorry I ever wrote anything about you—it was paltry.[8] Lord, when shall we be done growing? As long as we have anything more to do, we have done nothing. So, now, let us add Moby Dick to our blessing, and step from that. Leviathan is not the biggest fish;—I have heard of Krakens.[9]

This is a long letter, but you are not at all bound to answer it. Possibly, if you do answer it, and direct it to Herman Melville, you will missend it—for the very fingers that now guide this pen are not precisely the same that just took it up and put it on this paper. Lord, when shall we be done changing? Ah! it's a long stage, and no inn in sight, and night coming, and the body cold. But with you for a passenger, I am content and can be happy. I shall leave the world, I feel, with more satisfaction for having come to know you. Knowing you persuades me more than the Bible of our immortality.

What a pity, that, for your plain, bluff letter, you should get such gibberish! Mention me to Mrs. Hawthorne and to the children, and so, good-by to you, with my blessing.

Herman.[10]

P.S. I can't stop yet. If the world was entirely made up of Magians,[11] I'll tell you what I should do. I should have a paper-mill established at one end of the house, and so have an endless riband of foolscap rolling in upon my desk; and upon that endless riband I should write a thousand—a million—billion thoughts, all under the form of a letter to you. The divine magnet is on you, and my magnet responds. Which is the biggest? A foolish question—they are *One*.   H.

P.P.S. Don't think that by writing a letter, you shall always be bored with an immediate reply to it—and so keep both of us delving over a writing-desk eternally. No such thing! I sh'n't always answer your letters, and you may do just as you please.

1851, 1898

---

[6] Socrates (470?–399 B.C.), an eminent Greek philosopher, was reportedly a model of ugliness as well as a model of wisdom.

[7] In Acts 26:24–25 the Apostle Paul said, "I am not mad, most noble Festus [the Roman governor]; but speak forth the words of truth and soberness."

[8] Melville's review "Hawthorne and His Mosses," which appeared in the *Literary World* in 1850, contains extremely high praise of Hawthorne.

[9] According to Norwegian myth, sea monsters.

[10] This is the only letter (except for those to his family) that Melville signed with just his first name. (Footnote information from Northwestern-Newberry edition.)

[11] Magi, or wise men: a priestly caste in ancient Media and Persia.

Harriet Beecher Stowe
(1811–1896)

One of the most popular writers in nineteenth-century America, Harriet Beecher Stowe produced a number of domestic works based on rural New England but is best known as the author of *Uncle Tom's Cabin* (1852). Rather than questing for self-realization, Stowe's female characters are notable for self-sacrifice in the service of a noble cause. Through such characters Stowe shared her concerns about a variety of social problems. She presented the evils of slavery through Little Eva in *Uncle Tom's Cabin,* for example, and challenged patriarchy through her idealized depictions of maternal life. Stowe's understanding of Calvinism led her to distinguish between God as stern father and God as loving mother. Ann Douglas, a critic, observes that Stowe identified religious institutions with male power; thus her female characters sometimes appear to wage a quasi-feminist battle against institutions of the church.

Harriet Beecher was born into a respected family of fifteen in Litchfield, Connecticut, in 1811. Her parents were Lyman Beecher, a prominent clergyman, and Roxana Foote; one of her brothers, Henry Ward, was a celebrated preacher; and her sister Catharine was a pioneer in women's education. In Hartford Catharine founded a women's seminary, which Harriet attended. In 1832 Harriet moved with her family to Cincinnati when her father became president of Lane Theological Seminary. Four years later she married Rev. Calvin Ellis Stowe, a professor of biblical literature there; the couple had seven children together. Her eighteen years in Cincinnati, directly across the Ohio River from Kentucky, gave her a close-up view of slavery.

Stowe moved to Brunswick, Maine, in 1850 when her husband was appointed to a post at Bowdoin College. The Fugitive Slave Act, announced the same year, inspired her to begin *Uncle Tom's Cabin: Or, Life Among the Lowly,* which was serialized in the *National Era* (1851–1852) and published shortly thereafter. The book brought her instant fame (350,000 copies were sold during the first year) and made a vital contribution to the abolitionist cause. Stowe claimed that it was not she, but God, who wrote the work. A year later she brought out *A Key to Uncle Tom's Cabin*—a compilation of facts drawn from court records, newspapers, and private letters—to defend herself against charges of inaccuracy. In 1853 she produced another antislavery novel, *Dred: A Tale of the Great Dismal Swamp,* which treats slavery's demoralizing influence upon whites. At the height of her fame in 1853, Stowe traveled through England and met several literary figures, including Charles Dickens, George Eliot, and Lady Byron, the poet's widow. Out of her friendship with Lady Byron came a controversial book, *Lady Byron Vindicated* (1870), which charged that Lord Byron had had incestuous relations with his sister. Rev. Stowe died in 1886, and despite the great fame she had achieved, Stowe spent her later years in virtual solitude and senility. She died in Hartford in 1896.

The phenomenal success of *Uncle Tom's Cabin* makes it easy to forget that Stowe wrote more than twenty-five novels, essays, poems, and stories, many set in her native

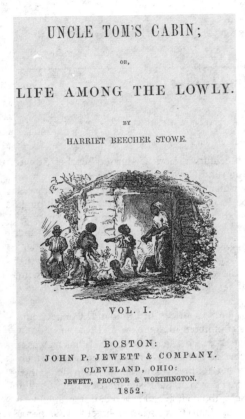

The title page of the first edition (in book form) of Harriet Beecher Stowe's Uncle Tom's Cabin.

New England. The novel *The Minister's Wooing* (1859) is a romance that attacks the injustice of Calvinism. *The Pearl of Orr's Island* (1862) and *Oldtown Folks* (1869) are local-color narratives: the former a depiction of rural Maine, the latter of domestic life in Massachusetts. In the fictional essays *My Wife and I* (1871) and *We and Our Neighbors* (1874), Stowe advocates women's rights and satirizes male sentimentalists. Although her romantic and local-color fiction never achieved wide popularity, it nevertheless had a positive influence on the work of emerging writers such as Sarah Orne Jewett and Mary E. Wilkins Freeman.

Suggested Readings: *The Writings of Harriet Beecher Stowe*, 16 vols., 1896. *Collected Poems*, ed. J. M. Moran, Jr., 1967. R. F. Wilson, *Crusader in Crinoline: The Life of Harriet Beecher Stowe*, 1941. C. H. Foster, *The Rungless Ladder: Harriet Beecher Stowe and New England Puritanism*, 1954. A. C. Crozier, *The Novels of Harriet Beecher Stowe*, 1969. E. Moers, *Harriet Beecher Stowe and American Literature*, 1978. E. Ammons, ed., *Critical Essays on Harriet Beecher Stowe*, 1980. G. Kimball, *The Religious Ideas of Harriet Beecher Stowe*, 1982. T. R. Hovet, *The Master Narrative: Harriet Beecher Stowe's Subversive Story of Slavery in "Uncle Tom's Cabin" and "Dred"*, 1989.

Text Used: *Novels and Stories by Harriet Beecher Stowe: Uncle Tom's Cabin: Or, Life Among the Lowly*, 1899.

from   *UNCLE TOM'S CABIN: OR, LIFE AMONG THE LOWLY**

CHAPTER VII: THE MOTHER'S STRUGGLE[1]

It is impossible to conceive of a human creature more wholly desolate and forlorn than Eliza, when she turned her footsteps from Uncle Tom's cabin.

Her husband's suffering and dangers, and the danger of her child, all blended in her mind, with a confused and stunning sense of the risk she was running, in leaving the only home she had ever known, and cutting loose from the protection of a friend whom she loved and revered. Then there was the parting from every familiar object,—the place where she had grown up, the trees under which she had played, the groves where she had walked many an evening in happier days, by the side of her young husband,—everything, as it lay in the clear, frosty star-light, seemed to speak reproachfully to her, and ask her whither she could go from a home like that?

But stronger than all was maternal love, wrought into a paroxysm of frenzy by the near approach of a fearful danger. Her boy was old enough to have walked by her side, and, in an indifferent case, she would only have led him by the hand; but now the bare thought of putting him out of her arms made her shudder, and she strained him to her bosom with a convulsive grasp, as she went rapidly forward.

The frosty ground creaked beneath her feet, and she trembled at the sound; every quaking leaf and fluttering shadow sent the blood backward to her heart, and quickened her footsteps. She wondered within herself at the strength that seemed to be come upon her; for she felt the weight of her boy as if it had been a feather, and every flutter of fear seemed to increase the supernatural power that bore her on, while from her pale lips burst forth, in frequent ejaculations, the prayer to a Friend above,—"Lord help! Lord, save me!"

If it were *your* Harry, mother, or your Willie, that were going to be torn from you by a brutal trader, to-morrow morning,—if you had seen the man, and heard that the papers were signed and delivered, and you had only from twelve o'clock till morning to make good your escape,—how fast could *you* walk? How many miles could you make in those few brief hours, with the darling at your bosom,—the little sleepy head on your shoulder,—the small, soft arms trustingly holding on to your neck?

For the child slept. At first, the novelty and alarm kept him waking; but his mother so hurriedly repressed every breath or sound, and so assured him that if he were only still she would certainly save him, that he clung quietly round her neck, only asking, as he found himself sinking to sleep,—

"Mother, I don't need to keep awake, do I?"

"No, my darling; sleep, if you want to."

---

* First published serially in the *National Era* from 1851 to 1852. Chapter VII appeared in 1851, Chapter XXX in 1852.

[1] The preceding chapters have introduced the characters, slaves and slave owners, and described the lives and attitudes of Eliza, Uncle Tom, and the Shelbys. At this point Mr. Shelby has sold Uncle Tom and Harry (Eliza's son) to the slave trader Dan Haley. Tom accepts his fate with humility and the prayer that he may someday return to his home in Kentucky. Eliza, however, takes her son and flees across the Ohio River. (Her husband had already decided to run away from his master.)

"But, mother, if I do get asleep, you won't let him get me?"

"No! so may God help me!" said his mother, with a paler cheek and a brighter light in her large, dark eyes.

"You're *sure,* an't you, mother?"

"Yes, *sure!*" said the mother, in a voice that startled herself; for it seemed to her to come from a spirit within, that was no part of her; and the boy dropped his little weary head on her shoulder and was soon asleep. How the touch of those warm arms, and gentle breathings that came in her neck, seemed to add fire and spirit to her movements. It seemed to her as if strength poured into her in electric streams, from every gentle touch and movement of the sleeping, confiding child. Sublime is the dominion of the mind over the body, that, for a time, can make flesh and nerve impregnable, and string the sinews like steel, so that the weak become so mighty.

The boundaries of the farm, the grove, the wood-lot, passed by her dizzily, as she walked on; and still she went, leaving one familiar object after another, slacking not, pausing not, till reddening daylight found her many a long mile from all traces of any familiar objects upon the open highway.

She had often been, with her mistress, to visit some connections, in the little village of T———, not far from the Ohio River, and knew the road well. To go thither, to escape across the Ohio River, were the first hurried outlines of her plan of escape; beyond that, she could only hope in God.

When horses and vehicles began to move along the highway, with that alert perception peculiar to a state of excitement, and which seems to be a sort of inspiration, she became aware that her headlong pace and distracted air might bring on her remark and suspicion. She therefore put the boy on the ground, and, adjusting her dress and bonnet, she walked on at as rapid a pace as she thought consistent with the preservation of appearances. In her little bundle she had provided a store of cakes and apples, which she used as expedients for quickening the speed of the child, rolling the apple some yards before them, when the boy would run with all his might after it; and this ruse, often repeated, carried them over many a half-mile.

After a while, they came to a thick patch of woodland, through which murmured a clear brook. As the child complained of hunger and thirst, she climbed over the fence with him; and sitting down behind a large rock which concealed them from the road, she gave him a breakfast out of her little package. The boy wondered and grieved that she could not eat; and when, putting his arms round her neck, he tried to wedge some of his cake into her mouth, it seemd to her that the rising in her throat would choke her.

"No, no, Harry darling! mother can't eat till you are safe! We must go on,—on,—till we come to the river!" And she hurried again into the road, and again constrained herself to walk regularly and composedly forward.

She was many miles past any neighborhood where she was personally known. If she should chance to meet any who knew her, she reflected that the well-known kindness of the family would be of itself a blind to suspicion, as making it an unlikely supposition that she could be a fugitive. As she was also so white as not to be known as of colored lineage, without a critical survey, and her child was white also, it was much easier for her to pass on unsuspected.

On this presumption, she stopped at noon at a neat farmhouse, to rest herself, and buy some dinner for her child and self; for, as the danger decreased with the distance, the supernatural tension of the nervous system lessened, and she found herself both weary and hungry.

The good woman, kindly and gossiping, seemed rather pleased than otherwise with having somebody come in to talk with; and accepted, without examination, Eliza's statement, that she "was going on a little piece, to spend a week with her friends,"—all which she hoped in her heart might prove strictly true.

An hour before sunset, she entered the villate of T———, by the Ohio River, weary and footsore, but still strong in heart. Her first glance was at the river, which lay, like Jordan,[2] between her and the Canaan of liberty on the other side.

It was now early spring, and the river was swollen and turbulent; great cakes of floating ice were swinging heavily to and fro in the turbid waters. Owing to the peculiar form of the shore on the Kentucky side, the land bending far out into the water, the ice had been lodged and detained in great quantities, and the narrow channel which swept round the bend was full of ice, piled one cake over another, thus forming a temporary barrier to the descending ice, which lodged, and formed a great, undulating raft, filling up the whole river, and extending almost to the Kentucky shore.

Eliza stood, for a moment, contemplating this unfavorable aspect of things, which she saw at once must prevent the usual ferry-boat from running, and then turned into a small public house on the bank, to make a few inquiries.

The hostess, who was busy in various fizzing and stewing operations over the fire, preparatory to the evening meal, stopped, with a fork in her hand, as Eliza's sweet and plaintive voice arrested her.

"What is it?" she said.

"Isn't there any ferry or boat, that takes people over to B———, now?" she said.

"No, indeed!" said the woman; "the boats has stopped running."

Eliza's look of dismay and disappointment struck the woman, and she said, inquiringly,—

"May be you're wanting to get over?—anybody sick? Ye seem mighty anxious?"

"I've got a child that's very dangerous," said Eliza. "I never heard of it till last night, and I've walked quite a piece to-day, in hopes to get to the ferry."

"Well, now, that's onlucky," said the woman, whose motherly sympathies were much aroused; "I'm re'lly consarned for ye. Solomon!" she called, from the window, towards a small back building. A man, in leather apron and very dirty hands, appeared at the door.

"I say, Sol," said the woman, "is that ar man going to tote them bar'ls over to-night?"

"He said he should try, if't was any way prudent," said the man.

"There's a man a piece down here, that's going over with some truck this evening, if he durs' to;[3] he'll be in here to supper to-night, so you'd better set down and wait. That's a sweet little fellow," added the woman, offering him a cake.

But the child, wholly exhausted, cried with weariness.

---

[2] In Exodus 3:17 the Israelites cross the Jordan River to reach Canaan, the Promised Land, after forty years in the desert.

[3] The man a little ways down the riverbank will take some goods ("truck") across the river tonight, if he dares to.

"Poor fellow! he isn't used to walking, and I've hurried him on so," said Eliza.

"Well, take him into this room," said the woman, opening into a small bed-room, where stood a comfortable bed. Eliza laid the weary boy upon it, and held his hands in hers till he was fast asleep. For her there was no rest. As a fire in her bones, the thought of the pursuer urged her on; and she gazed with longing eyes on the sullen, surging waters that lay between her and liberty.

Here we must take our leave of her for the present, to follow the course of her pursuers.

Though Mrs. Shelby had promised that the dinner should be hurried on table, yet it was soon seen, as the thing has often been seen before, that it required more than one to make a bargain. So, although the order was fairly given out in Haley's hearing, and carried to Aunt Chloe[4] by at least half a dozen juvenile messengers, that dignitary only gave certain very gruff snorts, and tosses of her head, and went on with every operation in an unusually leisurely and circumstantial manner.

For some singular reason, an impression seemed to reign among the servants generally that Missis would not be particularly disobliged by delay; and it was wonderful what a number of counter accidents occurred constantly, to retard the course of things. One luckless wight[5] contrived to upset the gravy; and then gravy had to be got up *de novo,*[6] with due care and formality, Aunt Chloe watching and stirring with dogged precision, answering shortly, to all suggestions of haste, that she "warn't a going to have raw gravy on the table, to help nobody's catchings."[7] One tumbled down with the water, and had to go to the spring for more; and another precipitated the butter into the path of events; and there was from time to time giggling news brought into the kitchen that "Mas'r Haley was might oneasy, and that he couldn't sit in his cheer[8] no ways, but was walkin' and stalkin' to the winders and through the porch."

"Sarves him right!" said Aunt Chloe, indignantly. "He'll get wus nor oneasy, one of these days, if he don't mend his ways. *His* master'll be sending for him, and then see how he'll look!"

"He'll go to torment, and no mistake," said little Jake.

"He deserves it!" said Aunt Chloe, grimly; "he's broke a many, many, many hearts,—I tell ye all!" she said, stopping, with a fork uplifted in her hands, "it's like what Mas'r George[9] reads in Ravelations,—souls a callin' under the altar! and a callin' on the Lord for vengeance on sich!—and by and by the Lord he'll hear 'em.—so he will!"[10]

Aunt Chloe, who was much revered in the kitchen, was listened to with open mouth; and, the dinner being now fairly sent in, the whole kitchen was at leisure to gossip with her and to listen to her remarks.

"Sich'll be burnt up forever, and no mistake; won't ther?" said Andy.

"I'd be glad to see it, I'll be boun'," said little Jake.

"Chil'en!" said a voice, that made them all start. It was Uncle Tom, who had come in, and stood listening to the conversation at the door.

---

[4] Uncle Tom's wife, the Shelbys' cook.   [5] Serving person, slave.

[6] "From nothing" (Latin); all over again, from scratch.

[7] She will not hurry the gravy so that Eliza and Harry can be caught.

[8] Chair.   [9] George Shelby.

[10] "I saw under the altar the souls of them that were slain for the word of God, and for the testimony which they held: And they cried with a loud voice, saying, How long, O Lord, holy and true, dost thou not judge and avenge our blood on them that dwell on the earth?" from Revelation 6:9–10.

"Chil'en!" he said, "I'm afeard you don't know what ye're sayin'. Forever is a *dre'ful* word, chil'en; it's awful to think on't. You oughtenter wish that ar to any human crittur."

"We wouldn't to anybody but the soul-drivers,"[11] said Andy; "nobody can help wishing it to them, they's so awful wicked."

"Don't natur herself kinder cry out on 'em?" said Aunt Chloe. "Don't dey tear der suckin' baby right off his mother's breast, and sell him, and der little children as is crying and holding on by her clothes,—don't dey pull 'em off and sells 'em? Don't dey tear wife and husband apart?" said Aunt Chloe, beginning to cry, "when it's jest takin' the very life on 'em?—and all the while does they feel one bit,—don't dey drink and smoke, and take it oncommon easy? Lor', if the devil don't get them, what's he good for?" And Aunt Chloe covered her face with her checked apron, and began to sob in good earnest.

"Pray for them that 'spitefully use you, the good book says,"[12] says Tom.

"Pray for 'em!" said Aunt Chloe; "Lor, it's too tough! I can't pray for 'em."

"It's natur, Chloe, and natur's strong," said Tom, "but the Lord's grace is stronger; besides, you oughter think what an awful state a poor crittur's soul's in that'll do them ar things,—you oughter thank God that you an't *like* him, Chloe. I'm sure I'd rather be sold, ten thousand times over, than to have all that ar poor crittur's got to answer for."

"So'd I, a heap," said Jake. "Lor, *shouldn't* we cotch it, Andy?"

Andy shrugged his shoulders, and gave an acquiescent whistle.

"I'm glad Mas'r didn't go off this morning, as he looked to," said Tom; "that ar hurt me more than sellin', it did. Mebbe it might have been natural for him, but 't would have come desp't hard on me, as has known him from a baby; but I've seen Mas'r, and I begin ter feel sort o' reconciled to the Lord's will now. Mas'r couldn't help hisself; he did right, but I'm feared things will be kinder goin' to rack, when I'm gone. Mas'r can't be spected to be a pryin' round everywhar, as I've done, a keepin' up all the ends. The boys all means well, but they's powerful car'less. That ar troubles me."

The bell here rang, and Tom was summoned to the parlor.

"Tom," said his master, kindly, "I want you to notice that I give this gentleman bonds to forfeit a thousand dollars if you are not on the spot when he wants you, he's going to-day to look after his other business, and you can have the day to yourself. Go anywhere you like, boy."

"Thank you, Mas'r," said Tom.

"And mind yerself," said the trader, "and don't come it over your master with any o' yer nigger tricks; for I'll take every cent out of him, if you an't thar. If he'd hear to me he wouldn't trust any on ye,—slippery as eels!"

"Mas'r," said Tom,—and he stood very straight,—"I was jist eight years old when ole Missis put you into my arms, and you wasn't a year old. 'Thar,' says she, 'Tom, that's to be *your* young Mas'r; take good care on him,' says she. And now I jist ask you, Mas'r, have I ever broke word to you, or gone contrary to you, 'specially since I was a Christian?"

Mr. Shelby was fairly overcome, and the tears rose to his eyes.

"My good boy," said he, "the Lord knows you say but the truth; and if I was able to help it, all the world shouldn't buy you."

"And sure as I am a Christian woman," said Mrs. Shelby, "you shall be re-

---

[11] Slave traders.

[12] "Pray for them which despitefully use you, and persecute you," from Matthew 5:44.

deemed as soon as I can any way bring together means. Sir," she said to Haley, "take good account of whom you sell him to, and let me know."

"Lor, yes, for that matter," said the trader, "I may bring him up in a year, not much the wuss for wear, and trade him back."

"I'll trade with you then, and make it for your advantage," said Mrs. Shelby.

"Of course," said the trader, "all's equal with me; li'ves trade 'em up as down, so I does a good business. All I want is a livin', you know, ma'am; that's all any on us wants, I s'pose."

Mr. and Mrs. Shelby both felt annoyed and degraded by the familiar impudence of the trader, and yet both saw the absolute necessity of putting a constraint on their feelings. The more hopelessly sordid and insensible he appeared, the greater became Mrs. Shelby's dread of his succeeding in recapturing Eliza and her child, and of course the greater her motive for detaining him by every female artifice. She therefore graciously smiled, assented, chatted familiarly, and did all she could to make time pass imperceptibly.

At two o'clock Sam and Andy brought the horses up to the posts, apparently greatly refreshed and invigorated by the scamper of the morning.

Sam was there new oiled from dinner, with an abundance of zealous and ready officiousness. As Haley approached, he was boasting, in flourishing style, to Andy, of the evident and eminent success of the operation, now that he had "farly come to it."

"Your master, I s'pose, don't keep no dogs," said Haley, thoughtfully, as he prepared to mount.

"Heaps on 'em," said Sam, triumphantly; "thar's Bruno,—he's a roarer! and, besides that, 'bout every nigger of us keeps a pup of some natur or uther."

"Poh!" said Haley,—and he said something else, too, with regard to the said dogs, at which Sam muttered,—

"I don't see no use cussin' on 'em, no way."

"But your master don't keep no dogs (I pretty much know he don't) for trackin' out niggers."

Sam knew exactly what he meant, but he kept on a look of earnest and desperate simplicity.

"Our dogs all smells round consid'able sharp. I spect they's the kind, though they han't never had no practice. They's *far* dogs, though, at most anything, if you'd get 'em started. Here, Bruno," he called, whistling to the lumbering Newfoundland, who came pitching tumultuously toward them.

"You go hang!" said Haley, getting up. "Come, tumble[13] up now."

Sam tumbled up accordingly, dexterously contriving to tickle Andy as he did so, which occasioned Andy to split out into a laugh, greatly to Haley's indignation, who made a cut at him with his riding-whip.

"I's 'stonished at yer, Andy," said Sam, with awful gravity. "This yer's a seris bisness, Andy. Yer mustn't be a makin' game. This yer an't no way to help Mas'r."

"I shall take the straight road to the river," said Haley, decidedly, after they had come to the boundaries of the estate. "I know the way of all of 'em,—they makes tracks for the underground."[14]

"Sartin," said Sam, "dat's de idee. Mas'r Haley hits de thing right in de mid-

---

[13] Mount.

[14] The Underground Railroad, the group that helped slaves escape to the North or to Canada, frequently hiding the runaways in their homes, or "stations."

dle. Now, der's two roads to de river,—de dirt road and der pike,—which Mas'r mean to take?"

Andy looked up innocently at Sam, surprised at hearing this new geographical fact, but instantly confirmed what he said by a vehement reiteration.

"Cause," said Sam, "I'd rather be 'clined to 'magine that Lizy'd take de dirt road, bein' it's the least travelled."

Haley, notwithstanding that he was a very old bird, and naturally inclined to be suspicious of chaff, was rather brought up by this view of the case.

"If yer warn't both on yer such cussed liars, now!" he said, contemplatively, as he pondered a moment.

The pensive, reflective tone in which this was spoken appeared to amuse Andy prodigiously, and he drew a little behind, and shook so as apparently to run a great risk of falling off his horse, while Sam's face was immovably composed into the most doleful gravity.

"Course," said Sam, "Mas'r can do as he'd ruther; go de straight road, if Mas'r thinks best,—it's all one to us. Now, when I study 'pon it, I think the straight road de best, *deridedly*."

"She would naturally go a lonesome way," said Haley, thinking aloud, and not minding Sam's remark.

"Dar an't no sayin'," said Sam; "gals is pecular; they never does nothin' ye thinks they will; mose gen'lly the contrar. Gals is nat'lly made contrary; and so, if you thinks they've gone one road, it is sartin you'd better go t' other, and then you'll be sure to find 'em. Now, my private 'pinion is, Lizy took der dirt road; so I think we'd better take de straight one."

This profound generic view of the female sex did not seem to dispose Haley particularly to the straight road; and he announced decidedly that he should go the other, and asked Sam when they should come to it.

"A little piece ahead," said Sam, giving a wink to Andy with the eye which was on Andy's side of the head; and he added, gravely, "but I've studded on de matter, and I'm quite clar we ought not to go dat ar way. I nebber been over it no way. It's despit lonesome, and we might lose our way,—whar we'd come to, de Lord only knows."

"Nevertheless," said Haley, "I shall go that way."

"Now I think on't, I think I hearn 'em tell that dat ar road was all fenced up and down by der creek, and thar, an't it, Andy?"

Andy wasn't certain; he'd only "hearn tell" about that road, but never been over it. In short, he was strictly noncommittal.

Haley, accustomed to strike the balance of probabilities between lies of greater or lesser magnitude, thought that it lay in favor of the dirt road aforesaid. The mention of the thing he thought he perceived was involuntary on Sam's part at first, and his confused attempts to dissuade him he set down to a desperate lying on second thoughts, as being unwilling to implicate Eliza.

When, therefore, Sam indicated the road, Haley plunged briskly into it, followed by Sam and Andy.

Now, the road, in fact, was an old one, that had formerly been a thoroughfare to the river, but abandoned for many years after the laying of the new pike. It was open for about an hour's ride, and after that it was cut across by various farms and fences. Sam knew this fact perfectly well,—indeed, the road had been so long closed up, that Andy had never heard of it. He therefore rode along with an air of dutiful submission, only groaning and vociferating occasionally that 't was "desp't rough, and bad for Jerry's foot."

"Now, I jest give yer warning," said Haley, "I know yer; yer won't get me to turn off this yer road, with all yer fussin',—so you shet up!"

"Mas'r will go his own way!" said Sam, with rueful submission, at the same time winking most portentously to Andy, whose delight was now very near the explosive point.

Sam was in wonderful spirits,—professed to keep a very brisk lookout,—at one time exclaiming that he saw "a gal's bonnet" on the top of some distant eminence, or calling to Andy, "if that thar wasn't 'Lizy' down in the hollow;" always making these exclamations in some rough or craggy part of the road, where the sudden quickening of speed was a special inconvenience to all parties concerned, and thus keeping Haley in a state of constant commotion.

After riding about an hour in this way, the whole party made a precipitate and tumultuous descent into a barnyard belonging to a large farming establishment. Not a soul was in sight, all the hands being employed in the fields; but, as the barn stood conspicuously and plainly square across the road, it was evident that their journey in that direction had reached a decided finale.

"Warn't dat ar what I telled Mas'r?" said Sam, with an air of injured innocence. "How does strange gentleman spect to know more about a country dan de natives born and raised?"

"You rascal!" said Haley, "you knew all about this."

"Did n't I tell yer I *know'd,* and yer would n't believe me? I telled Mas'r 't was all shet up, and fenced up, and I did n't spect we could get through,—Andy heard me."

It was all too true to be disputed, and the unlucky man had to pocket his wrath with the best grace he was able, and all three faced to the right about, and took up their line of march for the highway.

In consequence of all the various delays, it was about three quarters of an hour after Eliza had laid her child to sleep in the village tavern that the party came riding into the same place. Eliza was standing by the window, looking out in another direction, when Sam's quick eye caught a glimpse of her. Haley and Andy were two yards behind. At this crisis, Sam contrived to have his hat blown off, and uttered a loud and characteristic ejaculation, which startled her at once; she drew suddenly back; the whole train swept by the window, round to the front door.

A thousand lives seemed to be concentrated in that one moment to Eliza. Her room opened by a side door to the river. She caught her child, and sprang down the steps towards it. The trader caught a full glimpse of her, just as she was disappearing down the bank; and throwing himself from his horse, and calling loudly on Sam and Andy, he was after her like a hound after a deer. In that dizzy moment her feet to her scarce seemed to touch the ground, and a moment brought her to the water's edge. Right on behind they came; and, nerved with strength such as God gives only to the desperate, with one wild cry and flying leap, she vaulted sheer over the turbid current by the shore, on to the raft of ice beyond. It was a desperate leap,—impossible to anything but madness and despair; and Haley, Sam, and Andy instinctively cried out, and lifted up their hands, as she did it.

The huge green fragment of ice on which she alighted pitched and creaked as her weight came on it, but she stayed there not a moment. With wild cries and desperate energy she leaped to another and still another cake;—stumbling,—leaping,—slipping,—springing upwards again! Her shoes are gone,—her stockings cut from her feet,—while blood marked every step; but she saw nothing, felt nothing, till dimly, as in a dream, she saw the Ohio side, and a man helping her up the bank.

"Yer a brave gal, now, whoever ye ar!" said the man, with an oath.

Eliza recognized the voice and face of a man who owned a farm not far from her old home.

"Oh, Mr. Symmes!—save me,—do save me,—do hide me!" said Eliza.

"Why, what's this?" said the man. "Why, if 't an't Shelby's gal!"

"My child!—this boy!—he'd sold him! There is his Mas'r," said she, pointing to the Kentucky shore. "Oh, Mr. Symmes, you've got a little boy!"

"So I have," said the man, as he roughly, but kindly, drew her up the steep bank. "Besides, you're a right brave gal. I like grit, wherever I see it."

When they had gained the top of the bank, the man paused, "I'd be glad to do something for ye," said he; "but then there's nowhar I could take ye. The best I can do is to tell ye to go *thar*," said he, pointing to a large white house which stood by itself, off the main street of the village. "Go thar; they're kind folks. Thar's no kind o' danger but they'll help you,—they're up to all that sort o' thing."

"The Lord bless you!" said Eliza earnestly.

"No, 'casion, no 'casion in the world," said the man. "What I've done's of no 'count."

"And oh, surely, sir, you won't tell any one!"

"Go to thunder, gal! What do you take a feller for? In course not," said the man. "Come, now, go along like a likely, sensible gal, as you are. You've arnt your liberty, and you shall have it, for all me."

The woman folded her child to her bosom, and walked firmly and swiftly away. The man stood and looked after her.

"Shelby, now, mebbe won't think this yer the most neighborly thing in the world; but what's a feller to do? If he catches one of my gals in the same fix, he's welcome to pay back. Somehow I never could see no kind o' crittur a strivin' and pantin', and trying to clar theirselves, with the dogs arter 'em, and go agin 'em. Besides, I don't see no kind of 'casion for me to be hunter and catcher for other folks, neither."

So spoke this poor heathenish Kentuckian, who had not been instructed in his constitutional relations, and consequently was betrayed into acting in a sort of Christianized manner, which, if he had been better situated and more enlightened, he would not have been left to do.[15]

Haley had stood a perfectly amazed spectator of the scene, till Eliza had disappeared up the bank, when he turned a blank, inquiring look on Sam and Andy.

"That ar was a tolable fair stroke of business," said Sam.

"The gal's got seven devils in her, I believe!" said Haley. "How like a wildcat she jumped!"

"Wal, now," said Sam, scratching his head, "I hope Mas'r'll scuse us tryin' dat ar road. Don't think I feel spry enough for dat ar, no way!" and Sam gave a hoarse chuckle.

"*You* laugh!" said the trader, with a growl.

"Lord bless you, Mas'r, I could n't help it, now," said Sam, giving way to the

---

[15] The tone of this paragraph is deftly ironic: rather than act like a law-abiding citizen of his state, Mr. Symmes acts in a human and "Christianized" manner and is therefore "heathenish" and unenlightened.

long pent-up delight of his soul. "She looked so curi's a leapin' and springin'—
ice a crackin'—and only to hear her,—plump! ker chunk! ker splash! Spring!
Lord! how she goes it!" and Sam and Andy laughed till the tears rolled down their
cheeks.

"I'll make yer laugh t' other side yer mouths!" said the trader, laying about
their heads with his riding-whip.

Both ducked, and ran shouting up the bank, and were on their horses before he
was up.

"Good evening, Mas'r!" said Sam, with much gravity. "I berry much spect
Missis be anxious 'bout Jerry. Mas'r Haley won't want us no longer. Missis
would n't hear of our ridin' the critters over Lizy's bridge to-night;" and with a
facetious poke into Andy's ribs, he started off, followed by the latter, at full
speed,—their shouts of laughter coming faintly on the wind.

Chapter XXX: The Slave Warehouse[1]

A slave warehouse! Perhaps some of my readers conjure up horrible visions of
such a place. They fancy some foul, obscure den, some horrible *Tartarus "in-
formis, ingens, cui lumen ademptum."*[2] But no, innocent friend; in these days men
have learned the art of sinning expertly and genteelly, so as not to shock the eyes
and senses of respectable society. Human property is high in the market; and is,
therefore, well fed, well cleaned, tended, and looked after, that it may come to
sale sleek, and strong, and shining. A slave warehouse in New Orleans is a house
externally not much unlike many others, kept with neatness; and where every day
you may see arranged, under a sort of shed along the outside, rows of men and
women, who stand there as a sign of the property sold within.

Then you shall be courteously entreated to call and examine, and shall find an
abundance of husbands, wives, brothers, sisters, fathers, mothers, and young children, to be "sold separately, or in lots, to suit the convenience of the purchaser;"
and that soul immortal, once bought with blood and anguish by the Son of God,
when the earth shook, and the rocks were rent, and the graves were opened, can
be sold, leased, mortgaged, exchanged for groceries or dry goods, to suit the
phases of trade, or the fancy of the purchaser.

It was a day or two after the conversation between Marie and Miss Ophelia,
that Tom, Adolph, and half a dozen others of the St. Clare estate, were turned
over to the loving kindness of Mr. Skeggs, the keeper of a depot on ———— street,
to await the auction next day.

Tom had with him quite a sizable trunk full of clothing, as had most others of
them. They were ushered, for the night, into a long room, where many other men,
of all ages, sizes, and shades of complexion, were assembled, and from which
roars of laughter and unthinking merriment were proceeding.

"Ah, ha! that's right. Go it, boys,—go it!" said Mr. Skeggs, the keeper. "My
people are always so merry! Sambo, I see!" he said, speaking approvingly to a

---

[1] Primarily a set-piece, a dramatic essay on the inhumanity of large warehouses in which slaves were
kept and sold regardless of family ties, this chapter also tells of Tom's sale to the infamous Simon
Legree.

[2] Some horrible hell, "grotesque, vast, deprived of light" (Latin); according to Greek myth, Tartarus
was an infernal abyss beneath Hades.

burly negro who was performing tricks of low buffoonery, which occasioned the shouts which Tom had heard.

As might be imagined, Tom was in no humor to join these proceedings; and, therefore, setting his trunk as far as possible from the noisy group, he sat down on it, and leaned his face against the wall.

The dealers in the human article make scrupulous and systematic efforts to promote noisy mirth among them, as a means of drowning reflection, and rendering them insensible to their condition. The whole object of the training to which the negro is put, from the time he is sold in the northern market till he arrives south, is systematically directed towards making him callous, unthinking, and brutal. The slave-dealer collects his gang in Virginia or Kentucky, and drives them to some convenient, healthy place,—often a watering-place,—to be fattened.[3] Here they are fed full daily; and, because some incline to pine, a fiddle is kept commonly going among them, and they are made to dance daily; and he who refuses to be merry—in whose soul thoughts of wife, or child, or home, are too strong for him to be gay—is marked as sullen and dangerous, and subjected to all the evils which the ill-will of an utterly irresponsible and hardened man can inflict upon him. Briskness, alertness, and cheerfulness of appearance, especially before observers, are constantly enforced upon them, both by the hope of thereby getting a good master, and the fear of all that the driver may bring upon them, if they prove unsalable.

"What dat ar nigger doin' here?" said Sambo, coming up to Tom, after Mr. Skeggs had left the room. Sambo was a full black, of great size, very lively, voluble, and full of trick and grimace.

"What you doin' here?" said Sambo, coming up to Tom, and poking him facetiously in the side. "Meditatin', eh?"

"I am to be sold at the auction, to-morrow!" said Tom, quietly.

"Sold at auction,—haw! haw! boys, an't this yer fun? I wish't I was gwine that ar way!—tell ye, wouldn't I make 'em laugh? But how is it,—dis yer whole lot gwine to-morrow?" said Sambo, laying his hand freely on Adolph's shoulder.

"Please to let me alone!" said Adolph, fiercely, straightening himself up, with extreme disgust.

"Law, now, boys! dis yer's one o' yer white niggers,—kind o' cream-color, ye know, scented!" said he, coming up to Adolph and snuffing. "O Lor! he'd do for a tobaccer-shop; they could keep him to scent snuff! Lor, he'd keep a whole shop agwine,—he would!"

"I say, keep off, can't you?" said Adolph, enraged.

"Lor, now, how touchy we is,—we white niggers! Look at us, now!" and Sambo gave a ludicrous imitation of Adolph's manner; "here's de airs and graces. We's been in a good family, I specs."

"Yes," said Adolph; "I had a master that could have bought you all for old truck!"

"Laws, now, only think," said Sambo, "the gentlemens that we is!"

"I belonged to the St. Clare family," said Adolph, proudly.

"Lor, you did! Be hanged if they ar'n't lucky to get shet of ye. Spects they's gwine to trade ye off with a lot o' cracked teapots and sich like!" said Sambo, with a provoking grin.

---

[3] Analogies with the treatment of cattle here emphasize that human beings are regarded as property.

Adolph, enraged at this taunt, flew furiously at his adversary, swearing and striking on every side of him. The rest laughed and shouted, and the uproar brought the keeper to the door.

"What now, boys? Order,—order!" he said, coming in and flourishing a large whip.

All fled in different directions, except Sambo, who, presuming on the favor which the keeper had to him as a licensed wag, stood his ground, ducking his head with a facetious grin, whenever the master made a dive at him.

"Lor, Mas'r, 't an't us,—we's reg'lar stiddy,—it's these yer new hands; they 's real aggravatin',—kinder pickin' at us all time!"

The keeper, at this, turned upon Tom and Adolph, and distributing a few kicks and cuffs without much inquiry, and leaving general orders for all to be good boys and go to sleep, left the apartment.

While this scene was going on in the men's sleeping-room, the reader may be curious to take a peep at the corresponding apartment allotted to the women. Stretched out in various attitudes over the floor, he may see numberless sleeping forms of every shade of complexion, from the purest ebony to white, and of all years, from childhood to old age, lying now asleep. Here is a fine bright girl, of ten years, whose mother was sold out yesterday, and who to-night cried herself to sleep when nobody was looking at her. Here, a worn old negress, whose thin arms and callous fingers tell of hard toil, waiting to be sold to-morrow, as a cast-off article, for what can be got for her; and some forty or fifty others, with heads variously enveloped in blankets or articles of clothing, lie stretched around them. But, in a corner, sitting apart from the rest, are two females of a more interesting appearance than common. One of these is a respectably dressed mulatto woman between forty and fifty, with soft eyes and a gentle and pleasing physiognomy. She has on her head a high-raised turban, made of a gray red Madras handkerchief, of the first quality, and her dress is neatly fitted, and of good material, showing that she has been provided for with a careful hand. By her side, and nestling closely to her, is a young girl of fifteen,—her daughter. She is a quadroon,[4] as may be seen from her fairer complexion, though her likeness to her mother is quite discernible. She has the same soft, dark eye, with longer lashes, and her curling hair is of a luxuriant brown. She also is dressed with great neatness, and her white, delicate hands betray very little acquaintance with servile toil. These two are to be sold to-morrow, in the same lot with the St. Clare servants; and the gentleman to whom they belong, and to whom the money for their sale is to be transmitted, is a member of a Christian church in New York, who will receive the money, and go thereafter to the sacrament of his Lord and theirs, and think no more of it.

These two, whom we shall call Susan and Emmeline, had been the personal attendants of an amiable and pious lady of New Orleans, by whom they had been carefully and piously instructed and trained. They had been taught to read and write, diligently instructed in the truths of religion, and their lot had been as happy as one as in their condition it was possible to be. But the only son of their protectress had the management of her property; and, by carelessness and extravagance, involved it to a large amount, and at last failed. One of the largest creditors was the respectable firm of B. & Co., in New York. B. & Co. wrote to their lawyer in New Orleans, who attached the real estate (these two articles and a lot of planta-

---

[4]A person with one black grandparent; therefore, the child of a mulatto and a white.

tion hands formed the most valuable part of it[5]), and wrote word to that effect to New York. Brother B., being, as we have said, a Christian man, and a resident in a free state, felt some uneasiness on the subject. He didn't like trading in slaves and souls of men,—of course, he didn't; but, then, there were thirty thousand dollars in the case, and that was rather too much money to be lost for a principle; and so, after much considering, and asking advice from those that he knew would advise to suit him, Brother B. wrote to his lawyer to dispose of the business in the way that seemed to him the most suitable, and remit the proceeds.

The day after the letter arrived in New Orleans, Susan and Emmeline were attached, and sent to the depot to await a general auction on the following morning; and as they glimmer faintly upon us in the moonlight which steals through the grated window, we may listen to their conversation. Both are weeping, but each quietly, that the other may not hear.

"Mother, just lay your head on my lap, and see if you can't sleep a little," says the girl, trying to appear calm.

"I haven't any heart to sleep, Em; I can't; it's the last night we may be to-gether!"

"Oh, mother, don't say so! perhaps we shall get sold together,—who knows?"

"If 't was anybody's else case, I should say so, too, Em," said the woman; "but I'm so 'feard of losin' you that I don't see anything but the danger."

"Why, mother, the man said we were both likely, and would sell well."

Susan remembered the man's looks and words. With a deadly sickness at her heart, she remembered how he had looked at Emmeline's hands, and lifted up her curly hair, and pronounced her a first-rate article.[6] Susan had been trained as a Christian, brought up in the daily reading of the Bible, and had the same horror of her child's being sold to a life of shame that any other Christian mother might have; but she had no hope,—no protection.

"Mother, I think we might do first-rate, if you could get a place as cook, and I as chambermaid or seamstress, in some family. I dare say we shall. Let's both look as bright and lively as we can, and tell all we can do, and perhaps we shall," said Emmeline.

"I want you to brush your hair all back straight, to-morrow," said Susan.

"What for, mother? I don't look near so well, that way."

"Yes, but you'll sell better so."

"I don't see why!" said the child.

"Respectable families would be more apt to buy you, if they saw you looked plain and decent, as if you wasn't trying to look handsome. I know their ways better'n you do," said Susan.

"Well, mother, then I will."

"And, Emmeline, if we shouldn't ever see each other again, after to-morrow,—if I'm sold way up on a plantation somewhere, and you somewhere else,—always remember how you've been brought up, and all Missis has told you; take your Bible with you, and your hymn-book; and if you're faithful to the Lord, he'll be faithful to you."

So speaks the poor soul, in sore discouragement; for she knows that to-morrow any man, however vile and brutal, however godless and merciless, if he only has money to pay for her, may become owner of her daughter, body and soul; and

---

[5] Here, human beings are "real estate," to be bought and sold.
[6] Here, a young woman becomes an "article" for probable sexual exploitation.

then, how is the child to be faithful? She thinks of all this, as she holds her daughter in her arms, and wishes that she were not handsome and attractive. It seems almost an aggravation to her to remember how purely and piously, how much above the ordinary lot, she has been brought up. But she has no resort but to *pray;* and many such prayers to God have gone up from those same trim, neatly arranged, respectable slave-prisons,—prayers which God has not forgotten, as a coming day shall show; for it is written, "Whoso causeth one of these little ones to offend, it were better for him that a mill-stone were hanged about his neck, and that he were drowned in the depths of the sea."[7]

The soft, earnest, quiet moonbeam looks in fixedly, marking the bars of the grated windows on the prostrate, sleeping forms. The mother and daughter are singing together a wild and melancholy dirge, common as a funeral hymn among the slaves:—

> "Oh, where is weeping Mary?
> Oh, where is weeping Mary?
>   'Rived in the goodly land.
> She is dead and gone to heaven;
> She is dead and gone to heaven;
>   'Rived in the goodly land."

These words, sung by voices of a peculiar and melancholy sweetness, in an air which seemed like the sighing of earthly despair after heavenly hope, floated through the dark prison-rooms with a pathetic cadence, as verse after verse was breathed out,—

> "Oh, where are Paul and Silas?
> Oh, where are Paul and Silas?
>   Gone to the goodly land.
> They are dead and gone to heaven;
> They are dead and gone to heaven;
>   'Rived in the goodly land."

Sing on, poor souls! The night is short, and the morning will part you forever!

But now it is morning, and everybody is astir; and the worthy Mr. Skeggs is busy and bright, for a lot of goods is to be fitted out for auction. There is a brisk lookout on the toilet; injunctions passed around to every one to put on their best face and be spry; and now all are arranged in a circle for a last review, before they are marched up to the Bourse.[8]

Mr. Skeggs, with his palmetto[9] on and his cigar in his mouth, walks around to put farewell touches on his wares.

"How's this?" he said, stepping in front of Susan and Emmeline. "Where's your curls, gal?"

The girl looked timidly at her mother, who, with the smooth adroitness common among her class, answers,—

"I was telling her, last night, to put up her hair smooth and neat, and not havin' it flying about in curls; looks more respectable so."

---

[7] From Matthew 18:5–6.   [8] The Paris stock exchange; here, the "stock" is human.
[9] A stylish hat made of woven palm leaves.

"Bother!" said the man, peremptorily, turning to the girl; "you go right along, and curl yourself real smart!" He added, giving a crack to a rattan[10] he held in his hand, "And be back in quick time, too!"

"You go and help her," he added, to the mother. "Them curls may make a hundred dollars difference in the sale of her."

Beneath a splendid dome were men of all nations, moving to and fro, over the marble pave. On every side of the circular area were little tribunes, or stations, for the use of speakers and auctioneers. Two of these, on opposite sides of the area, were now occupied by brilliant and talented gentlemen, enthusiastically forcing up, in English and French commingled, the bids of connoisseurs in their various wares. A third one, on the other side, still unoccupied, was surrounded by a group, waiting the moment of sale to begin. And here we may recognize the St. Clare servants,—Tom, Adolph, and others; and there, too, Susan and Emmeline, awaiting their turn with anxious and dejected faces. Various spectators, intending to purchase, or not intending, as the case might be, gathered around the group, handling, examining, and commenting on their various points and faces with the same freedom that a set of jockeys discuss the merits of a horse.

"Hulloa, Alf! what brings you here?" said a young exquisite, slapping the shoulder of a sprucely dressed young man, who was examining Adolph through an eye-glass.

"Well, I was wanting a valet, and I heard that St. Clare's lot was going. I thought I'd just look at his"—

"Catch me ever buying any of St. Clare's people! Spoilt niggers, every one. Impudent as the devil!" said the other.

"Never fear that!" said the first. "If I get 'em, I'll soon have their airs out of them; they'll soon find that they've another kind of master to deal with than Monsieur St. Clare. 'Pon my word, I'll buy that fellow. I like the shape of him."

"You'll find it'll take all you've got to keep him. He's deucedly extravagant!"

"Yes, but my lord will find that he *can't* be extravagant with *me*. Just let him be sent to the calaboose[11] a few times, and thoroughly dressed down! I'll tell you if it don't bring him to a sense of his ways! Oh, I'll reform him, up hill and down,—you'll see. I buy him, that's flat!"

Tom had been standing wistfully examining the multitude of faces thronging around him, for one whom he would wish to call master. And if you should ever be under the necessity, sir, of selecting, out of two hundred men, one who was to become your absolute owner and disposer, you would, perhaps, realize, just as Tom did, how few there were that you would feel at all comfortable in being made over to. Tom saw abundance of men,—great, burly, gruff men; little, chirping, dried men; long-favored, lank, hard men; and every variety of stubbed-looking, commonplace men, who pick up their fellow-men as one picks up chips, putting them into the fire or a basket with equal unconcern, according to their convenience; but he saw no St. Clare.

A little before the sale commenced, a short, broad, muscular man, in a checked shirt considerably open at the bosom, and pantaloons much the worse for dirt and wear, elbowed his way through the crowd, like one who is going actively into a business; and, coming up to the group, began to examine them systematically. From the moment that Tom saw him approaching, he felt an immediate and re-

---

[10] A cane or switch.   [11] Prison.

volting horror at him, that increased as he came near. He was evidently, though short, of gigantic strength. His round, bullet-head, large, light-gray eyes, with their shaggy, sandy eyebrows, and stiff, wiry, sunburned hair, were rather unprepossessing items, it is to be confessed; his large, coarse mouth was distended with tobacco, the juice of which, from time to time, he ejected from him with great decision and explosive force; his hands were immensely large, hairy, sunburned, freckled, and very dirty, and garnished with long nails, in a very foul condition. This man proceeded to a very free personal examination of the lot. He seized Tom by the jaw, and pulled open his mouth to inspect his teeth; made him strip up his sleeve, to show his muscle; turned him round, made him jump and spring, to show his paces.

"Where was you raised?" he added, briefly, to these investigations.

"In Kintuck, Mas'r," said Tom, looking about, as if for deliverance.

"What have you done?"

"Had care of Mas'r's farm," said Tom.

"Likely story!" said the other, shortly, as he passed on. He paused a moment before Dolph; then spitting a discharge of tobacco-juice on his well-blacked boots, and giving a contemptuous umph, he walked on. Again he stopped before Susan and Emmeline. He put out his heavy, dirty hand, and drew the girl towards him; passed it over her neck and bust, felt her arms, looked at her teeth, and then pushed her back against her mother, whose patient face showed the suffering she had been going through at every motion of the hideous stranger.

The girl was frightened, and began to cry.

"Stop that, you minx!" said the salesman; "no whimpering here,—the sale is going to begin." And accordingly the sale began.

Adolph was knocked off, at a good sum, to the young gentleman who had previously stated his intention of buying him; and the other servants of the St. Clare lot went to various bidders.

"Now, up with you, boy! d'ye hear?" said the auctioneer to Tom.

Tom stepped upon the block, gave a few anxious looks round: all seemed mingled in a common, indistinct noise,—the clatter of the salesman crying off his qualifications in French and English, the quick fire of French and English bids; and almost in a moment came the final thump of the hammer, and the clear ring on the last syllable of the word *"dollars,"* as the auctioneer announced his price, and Tom was made over.—He had a master.

He was pushed from the block; the short, bullet-headed man, seizing him roughly by the shoulder, pushed him to one side, saying, in a harsh voice, "Stand there, *you!"*

Tom hardly realized anything; but still the bidding went on,—rattling, clattering, now French, now English. Down goes the hammer again,—Susan is sold! She goes down from the block, stops, looks wistfully back,—her daughter stretches her hands towards her. She looks with agony in the face of the man who has bought her,—a respectable, middle-aged man, of benevolent countenance.

"Oh, Mas'r, please do buy my daughter!"

"I'd like to, but I'm afraid I can't afford it!" said the gentleman, looking, with painful interest, as the young girl mounted the block, and looked around her with a frightened and timid glance.

The blood flushes painfully in her otherwise colorless cheek, her eye has a feverish fire, and her mother groans to see that she looks more beautiful than she ever saw her before. The auctioneer sees his advantage, and expatiates volubly in mingled French and English, and bids rise in rapid succession.

"I'll do anything in reason," said the benevolent-looking gentleman, pressing in and joining the bids. In a few moments they have run beyond his purse. He is silent; the auctioneer grows warmer; but bids gradually drop off. It lies now between an aristocratic old citizen and our bullet-headed acquaintance. The citizen bids for a few turns, contemptuously measuring his opponent; but the bullet-head has the advantage over him, both in obstinacy and concealed length of purse, and the controversy lasts but a moment; the hammer falls,—he has got the girl, body and soul, unless God help her.

Her master is Mr. Legree,[12] who owns a cotton plantation on the Red River. She is pushed along into the same lot with Tom and two other men, and goes off, weeping as she goes.

The benevolent gentleman is sorry; but, then, the thing happens every day! One sees girls and mothers crying, at these sales, *always!* it can't be helped, etc.; and he walks off, with his acquisition, in another direction.

Two days after, the lawyer of the Christian firm of B. & Co., New York, sent on their money to them. On the reverse of that draft, so obtained, let them write these words of the great Paymaster, to whom they shall make up their account in a future day; *"When he maketh inquisition for blood, he forgetteth not the cry of the humble!"*[13]

1851–1852

Louisa May Alcott
(1832–1888)

A careful look at Louisa May Alcott's career makes her popular image as a writer of domestic and children's fiction seem curiously misleading. In books such as *Moods* (1865), *Work* (1873), and *Diana & Persis* (written in 1879 but not published until 1978), Alcott showed an eloquent potential for appraising adult male/female relationships in a social context. Born in Germantown, Pennsylvania, in 1832 and educated primarily by her notoriously impractical father, the philosopher and educator Amos Bronson Alcott, she reconstructed her childhood through the character Jo March in *Little Women* (1868). Like Jo, Alcott was a tomboy. Unlike Jo, however, Alcott never married, feeling that women could not combine marriage and a career as men could. She was representative as a female writer involved in a conflict between what she believed and what she was forced to accept. On the surface her works present sentimental love stories or instructional stories for adolescents; underneath lurk challenges to the existing social system.

After serving as a nurse during the Civil War and recording her experiences in *Hospital Sketches* (1863), Alcott wrote her first novel, *Moods*, a triangular love story about a young woman relatively uninhibited for her time and place. Partly because of the criticism *Moods* received, novels such as *Little Women, An Old-Fashioned Girl* (1870), *Rose in Bloom*

---

[12] Simon Legree, who later kills Tom—but never recovers from Tom's dying act of forgiveness.

[13] "When he maketh inquisition for blood, he remembereth them: he forgetteth not the cry of the humble," from Psalm 9:12.

(1876), and *Jack and Jill* (1886) tended to subordinate emotional involvement and emphasize didactic concerns. Although the success of these books enabled her to enjoy popularity and meet financial demands at home, some critics feel that Alcott did not entirely believe in what she wrote, that in yielding to the public taste for fiction with marriages and domestic lessons, she nonetheless harbored feminist attitudes which can be detected in her description of gender roles.

Aware that she could not change the structure of society, Alcott frequently returned her intelligent and independent heroines to traditional female roles. *Work* exemplifies her conflict as a writer. Begun as an adult novel, it was put aside for twelve years until Alcott had a solid reputation as a writer. When she returned to the narrative, she made it something of a love story, didactic in manner, and qualified the image of the enterprising heroine. Perhaps the most unusual products of Alcott's imagination are her suspense thrillers—erotic, violent, and passionate tales typically full of female revenge and ambition. Published anonymously or pseudonymously, these stories were collected by the author Madeleine Stern in *Behind a Mask* (1975) and *Plots and Counterplots* (1976). It is true that Alcott wrote thrillers in order to make money; yet, as Stern observes, these tales of violence may have been cathartic to a writer whose public efforts went into the fashioning of domestic and moralistic fiction.

Louisa May Alcott died in Concord, Massachusetts, in 1888. Although she always remained within conventional limits as a female writer, she did explore with a caustic eye the social relationships of men and women. She represents a generation of mid-nineteenth-century female writers whose imaginations were uncomfortably indentured to society's standards and restrictions.

Suggested Readings: *Hospital Sketches*, 1863. *Little Women*, 1868–1869. *Behind a Mask: The Unknown Thrillers of Louisa May Alcott*, ed. M. Stern, 1975. *Plots and Counterplots: More Unknown Thrillers of Louisa May Alcott*, ed. M. Stern, 1976. M. B. Stern, *Louisa May Alcott*, 1950. C. Meigs, *Invincible Louisa May: The Story of the Author of "Little Women,"* 1968. M. Saxton, *Louisa May: A Modern Biography of Louisa May Alcott*, 1977. R. K. MacDonald, *Louisa May Alcott*, 1983. S. Elbert, *A Hunger for Home: Louisa May Alcott's Place in American Culture*, 1987.

Text Used: *Work: A Story of Experience*, 1873.

from *WORK: A STORY OF EXPERIENCE*

CHAPTER I: CHRISTIE

"Aunt Betsey, there's going to be a new Declaration of Independence."

"Bless and save us, what do you mean, child?" And the startled old lady precipitated a pie into the oven with destructive haste.[1]

"I mean that, being of age, I'm going to take care of myself, and not be a burden any longer. Uncle wishes me out of the way; thinks I ought to go, and, sooner or later, will tell me so. I don't intend to wait for that, but, like the people in fairy tales, travel away into the world and seek my fortune. I know I can find it."

Christie emphasized her speech by energetic demonstrations in the bread-

---

[1] Alcott's novel begins with a contrast between generations: in the opening sentence Christie Devon announces a new Declaration of Independence, while Aunt Betsey puts a pie in the oven.

trough, kneading the dough as if it was her destiny, and she was shaping it to suit herself; while Aunt Betsey stood listening, with uplifted pie-fork, and as much astonishment as her placid face was capable of expressing. As the girl paused, with a decided thump, the old lady exclaimed:

"What crazy idee you got into your head now?"

"A very sane and sensible one that's got to be worked out, so please listen to it, ma'am. I've had it a good while, I've thought it over thoroughly, and I'm sure it's the right thing for me to do. I'm old enough to take care of myself; and if I'd been a boy, I should have been told to do it long ago. I hate to be dependent; and now there's no need of it, I can't bear it any longer. If you were poor, I wouldn't leave you; for I never forget how kind *you* have been to me. But Uncle doesn't love or understand me; I *am* a burden to him, and I must go where I can take care of myself. I can't be happy till I do, for there's nothing here for me. I'm sick of this dull town, where the one idea is eat, drink, and get rich; I don't find any friends to help me as I want to be helped, or any work that I can do well; so let me go, Aunty, and find my place, wherever it is."

"But I do need you, deary; and you mustn't think Uncle don't like you. He does, only he don't show it; and when your odd ways fret him, he ain't pleasant, I know. I don't see why you can't be contented; I've lived here all my days, and never found the place lonesome, or the folks unneighborly." And Aunt Betsey looked perplexed by the new idea.

"You and I are very different, ma'am. There was more yeast put into my composition, I guess; and, after standing quiet in a warm corner so long, I begin to ferment, and ought to be kneaded up in time, so that I may turn out a wholesome loaf. You can't do this; so let me go where it can be done, else I shall turn sour and good for nothing. Does that make the matter any clearer?" And Christie's serious face relaxed into a smile as her aunt's eye went from her to the nicely moulded loaf offered as an illustration.

"I see what you mean, Kitty; but I never thought on 't before. You be better riz[2] than me; though, let me tell you, too much emptins makes bread poor stuff, like baker's trash; and too much workin' up makes it hard and dry. Now fly 'round, for the big oven is most het, and this cake takes a sight of time in the mixin'."

"You haven't said I might go, Aunty," began the girl, after a long pause devoted by the old lady to the preparation of some compound which seemed to require great nicety of measurement in its ingredients; for when she replied, Aunt Betsey curiously interlarded her speech with audible directions to herself from the receipt-book before her.

"I ain't no right to keep you, dear, ef you choose to take (a pinch of salt). I'm sorry you ain't happy, and think you might be ef you'd only (beat six eggs, yolks and whites together). But ef you can't, and feel that you need (two cups of sugar), only speak to Uncle, and ef he says (a squeeze of fresh lemon), go, my dear, and take my blessin' with you (not forgettin' to cover with a piece of paper)."

Christie's laugh echoed through the kitchen; and the old lady smiled benignly, quite unconscious of the cause of the girl's merriment.

"I shall ask Uncle to-night, and I know he won't object. Then I shall write to see if Mrs. Flint has a room for me, where I can stay till I get something to do. There is plenty of work in the world, and I'm not afraid of it; so you'll soon hear good news of me. Don't look sad, for you know I never could forget *you*, even if

[2] Risen, "nicely moulded."

I should become the greatest lady in the land." And Christie left the prints of two floury but affectionate hands on the old lady's shoulders, as she kissed the wrinkled face that had never worn a frown to her.

Full of hopeful fancies, Christie salted the pans and buttered the dough in pleasant forgetfulness of all mundane affairs, and the ludicrous dismay of Aunt Betsey, who followed her about rectifying her mistakes, and watching over her as if this sudden absence of mind had roused suspicions of her sanity.

"Uncle, I want to go away, and get my own living, if you please," was Christie's abrupt beginning, as they sat round the evening fire.

"Hey! what's that?" said Uncle Enos, rousing from the doze he was enjoying, with a candle in perilous proximity to his newspaper and his nose.

Christie repeated her request, and was much relieved, when, after a meditative stare, the old man briefly answered:

"Wal, go ahead."

"I was afraid you might think it rash or silly, sir."

"I think it's the best thing you could do; and I like your good sense in pupposin' on't."[3]

"Then I may really go?"

"Soon's ever you like. Don't pester me about it till you're ready; then I'll give you a little suthing to start off with." And Uncle Enos returned to "The Farmer's Friend," as if cattle were more interesting than kindred.

Christie was accustomed to his curt speech and careless manner; had expected nothing more cordial; and, turning to her aunt, said, rather bitterly:

"Didn't I tell you he'd be glad to have me go? No matter! When I've done something to be proud of, he will be as glad to see me back again." Then her voice changed, her eyes kindled, and the firm lips softened with a smile. "Yes, I'll try my experiment; then I'll get rich; found a home for girls like myself; or, better still, be a Mrs. Fry, a Florence Nightingale,[4] or"—

"How are you on 't for stockin's, dear?"

Christie's castles in the air vanished at the prosaic question; but, after a blank look, she answered pleasantly:

"Thank you for bringing me down to my feet again, when I was soaring away too far and too fast. I'm poorly off, ma'am; but if you are knitting these for me, I shall certainly start on a firm foundation." And, leaning on Aunt Betsey's knee, she patiently discussed the wardrobe question from hose to head-gear.

"Don't you think you could be contented any way, Christie, ef I make the work lighter, and leave you more time for your books and things?" asked the old lady, loth to lose the one youthful element in her quiet life.

"No, ma'am, for I can't find what I want here," was the decided answer.

"What *do* you want, child?"

"Look in the fire, and I'll try to show you."

The old lady obediently turned her spectacles that way; and Christie said in a tone half serious, half playful:

"Do you see those two logs? Well that one smouldering dismally away in the corner is what my life is now; the other blazing and singing is what I want my life to be."

[3] Purposing on it: planning it out.

[4] Elizabeth Gurney Fry (1780–1845), an English prison reformer who founded soup kitchens in London; Florence Nightingale (1820–1920), a legendary English nurse noted for her work with the wounded during the Crimean War (1854–1856).

"Bless me, what an idee! They are both a-burnin' where they are put, and both will be ashes to-morrow; so what difference *doos* it make?"

Christie smiled at the literal old lady; but, following the fancy that pleased her, she added earnestly:

"I know the end is the same; but it *does* make a difference *how* they turn to ashes, and *how* I spend my life. That log, with its one dull spot of fire, gives neither light or warmth, but lies sizzling despondently among the cinders. But the other glows from end to end with cheerful little flames that go singing up the chimney with a pleasant sound. Its light fills the room and shines out into the dark; its warmth draws us nearer, making the hearth the cosiest place in the house, and we shall all miss the friendly blaze when it dies. "Yes," she added, as if to herself, "I hope my life may be like that, so that, whether it be long or short, it will be useful and cheerful while it lasts, will be missed when it ends, and leave something behind besides ashes."

Though she only half understood them, the girl's words touched the kind old lady, and made her look anxiously at the eager young face gazing so wistfully into the fire.

"A good smart blowin' up with the belluses[5] would make the green stick burn most as well as the dry one after a spell. I guess contentedness is the best bellus for young folks, ef they would only think so."

"I dare say you are right, Aunty; but I want to try for myself; and if I fail, I'll come back and follow your advice. Young folks always have discontented fits, you know. Didn't you when you were a girl?"

"Shouldn't wonder ef I did; but Enos came along, and I forgot 'em."

"My Enos has not come along yet, and never may; so I'm not going to sit and wait for any man to give me independence, if I can earn it for myself." And a quick glance at the gruff, gray old man in the corner plainly betrayed that, in Christie's opinion, Aunt Betsey made a bad bargain when she exchanged her girlish aspirations for a man whose soul was in his pocket.[6]

"Jest like her mother, full of hifalutin notions, discontented, and sot in her own idees. Poor capital to start a fortin'[7] on."

Christie's eye met that of her uncle peering over the top of his paper with an expression that always tried her patience. Now it was like a dash of cold water on her enthusiasm, and her face fell as she asked quickly:

"How do you mean, sir?"

"I mean that you are startin' all wrong; your redic'lus notions about independence and self-cultur won't come to nothin' in the long run, and you'll make as bad a failure of your life as your mother did of her'n."

"Please, don't say that to me; I can't bear it, for *I* shall never think her life a failure, because she tried to help herself, and married a good man in spite of poverty, when she loved him! You call that folly; but I'll do the same if I can; and I'd rather have what my father and mother left me, than all the money you are piling up, just for the pleasure of being richer than your neighbors."

"Never mind, dear, he don't mean no harm!" whispered Aunt Betsey, fearing a storm.

But though Christie's eyes had kindled and her color deepened, her voice was low and steady, and her indignation was of the inward sort.

---

[5] Bellows, a device for blowing air on fires to improve burning.
[6] Pocketbook or wallet: Uncle Enos's soul is where his money is.   [7] A fortune.

"Uncle likes to try me by saying such things, and this is one reason why I want to go away before I get sharp and bitter and distrustful as he is. I don't suppose I can make you understand my feeling, but I'd like to try, and then I'll never speak of it again;" and, carefully controlling voice and face, Christie slowly added, with a look that would have been pathetically eloquent to one who could have understood the instincts of a strong nature for light and freedom: "You say I am discontented, proud and ambitious; that's true, and I'm glad of it. I am discontented, because I can't help feeling that there is a better sort of life than this dull one made up of everlasting work, with no object but money. I can't starve my soul for the sake of my body, and I mean to get out of the treadmill if I can. I'm proud, as you call it, because I hate dependence where there isn't any love to make it bearable. You don't say so in words, but I know you begrudge me a home, though you will call me ungrateful when I'm gone. I'm willing to work, but I want work that I can put my heart into, and feel that it does me good, no matter how hard it is. I only ask for a chance to be a useful, happy woman, and I don't think that is a bad ambition. Even if I only do what my dear mother did, earn my living honestly and happily, and leave a beautiful example behind me, to help one other woman as hers helps me, I shall be satisfied."

Christie's voice faltered over the last words, for the thoughts and feelings which had been working within her during the last few days had stirred her deeply, and the resolution to cut loose from the old life had not been lightly made. Mr. Devon had listened behind his paper to this unusual outpouring with a sense of discomfort which was new to him. But though the words reproached and annoyed, they did not soften him, and when Christie paused with tearful eyes, her uncle rose, saying, slowly, as he lighted his candle:

"Ef I'd refused to let you go before, I'd agree to it now; for you need breakin' in, my girl, and you are goin' where you'll get it, so the sooner you're off the better for all on us. Come, Betsey, we may as wal leave, for we can't understand the wants of her higher nater,[8] as Christie calls it, and we've had lecterin' enough for one night." And with a grim laugh the old man quitted the field, worsted but in good order.

"There, there, dear, hev a good cry, and forget all about it!" purred Aunt Betsey, as the heavy footsteps creaked away, for the good soul had a most old-fashioned and dutiful awe of her lord and master.

"I shan't cry but act; for it is high time I *was* off. I've stayed for your sake; now I'm more trouble than comfort, and away I go. Good-night, my dear old Aunty, and don't look troubled, for I'll be a lamb while I stay."

Having kissed the old lady, Christie swept her work away, and sat down to write the letter which was the first step toward freedom. When it was done, she drew nearer to her friendly *confidante* the fire, and till late into the night sat thinking tenderly of the past, bravely of the present, hopefully of the future. Twenty-one to-morrow, and her inheritance a head, a heart, a pair of hands; also the dower[9] of most New England girls, intelligence, courage, and common sense, many practical gifts, and, hidden under the reserve that soon melts in a genial atmosphere, much romance and enthusiasm, and the spirit which can rise to heroism when the great moment comes.

Christie was one of that large class of women who, moderately endowed with talents, earnest and truehearted, are driven by necessity, temperament, or princi-

---

[8] Nature.   [9] Dowry: Christie has as her "dowry" the fine traits of "most New England girls."

ple out into the world to find support, happiness, and homes for themselves. Many turn back discouraged; more accept shadow for substance, and discover their mistake too late; the weakest lose their purpose and themselves; but the strongest struggle on, and, after danger and defeat, earn at last the best success this world can give us, the possession of a brave and cheerful spirit, rich in self-knowledge, self-control, self-help. This was the real desire of Christie's heart; this was to be her lesson and reward, and to this happy end she was slowly yet surely brought by the long discipline of life and labor.

Sitting alone there in the night, she tried to strengthen herself with all the good and helpful memories she could recall, before she went away to find her place in the great unknown world. She thought of her mother, so like herself, who had borne the commonplace life of home till she could bear it no longer. Then had gone away to teach, as most country girls are forced to do. Had met, loved, and married a poor gentleman, and, after a few years of genuine happiness, untroubled even by much care and poverty, had followed him out of the world, leaving her little child to the protection of her brother.

Christie looked back over the long, lonely years she had spent in the old farmhouse, plodding to school and church, and doing her tasks with kind Aunt Betsey while a child; and slowly growing into girlhood, with a world of romance locked up in a heart hungry for love and a larger, nobler life.

She had tried to appease this hunger in many ways, but found little help. Her father's old books were all she could command, and these she wore out with much reading. Inheriting his refined tastes, she found nothing to attract her in the society of the commonplace and often coarse people about her. She tried to like the buxom girls whose one ambition was to "get married," and whose only subjects of conversation were "smart bonnets" and "nice dresses." She tried to believe that the admiration and regard of the bluff young farmers was worth striving for; but when one well-to-do neighbor laid his acres at her feet,[10] she found it impossible to accept for her life's companion a man whose soul was wrapped up in prize cattle and big turnips.

Uncle Enos never could forgive her for this piece of folly, and Christie plainly saw that one of three things would surely happen, if she lived on there with no vent for her full heart and busy mind. She would either marry Joe Butterfield in sheer desperation, and become a farmer's household drudge; settle down into a sour spinster, content to make butter, gossip, and lay up money all her days; or do what poor Matty Stone had done, try to crush and curb her needs and aspirations till the struggle grew too hard, and then in a fit of despair end her life, and leave a tragic story to haunt their quiet river.

To escape these fates but one way appeared: to break loose from this narrow life, go out into the world and see what she could do for herself. This idea was full of enchantment to the eager girl, and, after much earnest thought, she had resolved to try it.

"If I fail, I can come back," she said to herself, even while she scorned the thought of failure, for with all her shy pride she was both brave and ardent, and her dreams were of the rosiest sort.

"I won't marry Joe; I won't wear myself out in a district-school for the mean sum[11] they give a woman; I won't delve away here where I'm not wanted; and I

---

[10] A young farmer, Joe Butterfield, proposed marriage to Christie and pledged his land as proof he could care for her financially.

[11] Pitiful salary.

won't end my life like a coward, because it is dull and hard. I'll try my fate as mother did, and perhaps I may succeed as well." And Christie's thoughts went wandering away into the dim, sweet past when she, a happy child, lived with loving parents in a different world from that.

Lost in these tender memories, she sat till the old moon-faced clock behind the door struck twelve, then the visions vanished, leaving their benison[12] behind them.

As she glanced backward at the smouldering fire, a slender spire of flame shot up from the log that had blazed so cheerily, and shone upon her as she went. A good omen, gratefully accepted then, and remembered often in the years to come.

from   CHAPTER XX: AT FORTY[1]

"Nearly twenty years since I set out to seek my fortune. It has been a long search, but I think I have found it at last. I only asked to be a useful, happy woman, and my wish is granted: for, I believe I *am* useful; I *know* I am happy."

Christie looked so as she sat alone in the flowery parlor one September afternoon, thinking over her life with a grateful, cheerful spirit. Forty to-day, and pausing at that half-way house between youth and age, she looked back into the past without bitter regret or unsubmissive grief, and forward into the future with courageous patience; for three good angels attended her, and with faith, hope, and charity to brighten life, no woman need lament lost youth or fear approaching age. Christie did not, and though her eyes filled with quiet tears as they were raised to the faded cap and sheathed sword[2] hanging on the wall, none fell; and in a moment tender sorrow changed to still tenderer joy as her glance wandered to rosy little Ruth playing hospital with her dollies in the porch. Then they shone with genuine satisfaction as they went from the letters and papers on her table to the garden, where several young women were at work with a healthful color in the cheeks that had been very pale and thin in the spring.

"I think David is satisfied with me; for I have given all my heart and strength to his work, and it prospers well," she said to herself, and then her face grew thoughtful, as she recalled a late event which seemed to have opened a new field of labor for her if she chose to enter it.

A few evenings before she had gone to one of the many meetings of working-women, which had made some stir of late. Not a first visit, for she was much interested in the subject and full of sympathy for this class of workers.

There were speeches of course, and of the most unparliamentary sort, for the meeting was composed almost entirely of women, each eager to tell her special grievance or theory. Any one who chose got up and spoke; and whether wisely or foolishly each proved how great was the ferment now going on, and how difficult it was for the two classes[3] to meet and help one another in spite of the utmost need

---

[12] Blessing.

[1] Christie was twenty-one in Chapter I; now she is forty. There we witnessed a contrast between generations; here we see a contrast between social classes. Since Chapter I she has been a governess, an actress, and a Civil War nurse (as, briefly, was Louisa May Alcott). She has married David Sterling, given birth to a child (Ruth), and been widowed.

[2] Pictures (probably daguerreotypes) of her mother and father.

[3] The working women and the "ladies" who pity them, fail to understand them, and bore them with well-meaning talk.

on one side and the sincerest good-will on the other. The workers poured out their wrongs and hardships passionately or plaintively, demanding or imploring justice, sympathy, and help; displaying the ignorance, incapacity, and prejudice, which make their need all the more pitiful, their relief all the more imperative.

The ladies did their part with kindliness, patience, and often unconscious condescension, showing in their turn how little they knew of the real trials of the women whom they longed to serve, how very narrow a sphere of usefulness they were fitted for in spite of culture and intelligence, and how rich they were in generous theories, how poor in practical methods of relief.

One accomplished creature with learning radiating from every pore, delivered a charming little essay on the strong-minded women of antiquity; then, taking labor into the region of art, painted delightful pictures of the time when all would work harmoniously together in an Ideal Republic, where each did the task she liked, and was paid for it in liberty, equality, and fraternity.[4]

Unfortunately she talked over the heads of her audience, and it was like telling fairy tales to hungry children to describe Aspasia[5] discussing Greek politics with Pericles and Plato reposing upon ivory couches, or Hypatia[6] modestly delivering philosophical lectures to young men behind a Tyrian[7] purple curtain; and the Ideal Republic met with little favor from anxious seamstresses, type-setters, and shop-girls, who said ungratefully among themselves, "That's all very pretty, but I don't see how it's going to better wages among us *now*."

Another eloquent sister gave them a political oration which fired the revolutionary blood in their veins, and made them eager to rush to the State-house *en masse*, and demand the ballot before one-half of them were quite clear what it meant, and the other half were as unfit for it as any ignorant Patrick[8] bribed with a dollar and a sup of whiskey.

A third well-wisher quenched their ardor like a wet blanket, by reading reports of sundry labor reforms in foreign parts; most interesting, but made entirely futile by differences of climate, needs, and customs. She closed with a cheerful budget of statistics, giving the exact number of needle-women who had starved, gone mad, or committed suicide during the past year; the enormous profits wrung by capitalists from the blood and muscles of their employés; and the alarming increase in the cost of living, which was about to plunge the nation into debt and famine, if not destruction generally.

When she sat down despair was visible on many countenances, and immediate starvation seemed to be waiting at the door to clutch them as they went out; for the impressible creatures believed every word and saw no salvation anywhere.

Christie had listened intently to all this; had admired, regretted, or condemned as each spoke; and felt a steadily increasing sympathy for all, and a strong desire to bring the helpers and the helped into truer relations with each other.

The dear ladies were so earnest, so hopeful, and so unpractically benevolent,

---

[4] The rally cry of the French Revolution, something far more radical than this speaker would dream of; the "Ideal Republic" might echo the name of Plato's *Republic*, but the two utopias bear little resemblance to each other. Alcott's scene is loaded with irony.

[5] Aspasia (5th century B.C.) was an accomplished and celebrated woman from Miletus and the lifelong companion of the Athenian statesman Pericles (500–429 B.C.). By law, citizens of Athens could marry only Athenians; Pericles was thus prohibited from marrying Aspasia.

[6] Hypatia (?–A.D. 415) was an eminent female member of the Neoplatonic school of philosophy; she was murdered in Alexandria.

[7] From Tyre (now in Lebanon), noted for its purple dyes.   [8] The stereotypical Irishman.

that it grieved her to see so much breath wasted, so much good-will astray; while the expectant, despondent, or excited faces of the work-women touched her heart; for well she knew how much they needed help, how eager they were for light, how ready to be led if some one would only show a possible way.

As the statistical extinguisher retired, beaming with satisfaction at having added her mite to the good cause, a sudden and uncontrollable impulse moved Christie to rise in her place and ask leave to speak. It was readily granted, and a little stir of interest greeted her; for she was known to many as Mr. Power's[9] friend, David Sterling's wife, or an army nurse who had done well. Whispers circulated quickly, and faces brightened as they turned toward her; for she had a helpful look, and her first words pleased them. When the president invited her to the platform she paused on the lowest step, saying with an expressive look and gesture:

"I am better here, thank you; for I have been and mean to be a working-woman all my life."

"Hear! hear!" cried a stout matron in a gay bonnet, and the rest indorsed the sentiment with a hearty round. Then they were very still, and then in a clear, steady voice, with the sympathetic undertone to it that is so magical in its effect, Christie made her first speech in public since she left the stage.

That early training stood her in good stead now, giving her self-possession, power of voice, and ease of gesture; while the purpose at her heart lent her the sort of simple eloquence that touches, persuades, and convinces better than logic, flattery, or oratory.

What she said she hardly knew: words came faster than she could utter them, thoughts pressed upon her, and all the lessons of her life rose vividly before her to give weight to her arguments, value to her counsel, and the force of truth to every sentence she uttered. She had known so many of the same trials, troubles, and temptations that she could speak understandingly of them; and, better still, she had conquered or outlived so many of them, that she could not only pity but help others to do as she had done. Having found in labor her best teacher, comforter, and friend, she could tell those who listened that, no matter how hard or humble the task at the beginning, if faithfully and bravely performed, it would surely prove a stepping-stone to something better, and with each honest effort they were fitting themselves for the nobler labor, and larger liberty God meant them to enjoy.

The women felt that this speaker was one of them; for the same lines were on her face that they saw on their own, her hands were no fine lady's hands, her dress plainer than some of theirs, her speech simple enough for all to understand; cheerful, comforting, and full of practical suggestion, illustrations out of their own experience, and a spirit of companionship that uplifted their despondent hearts.

Yet more impressive than any thing she said was the subtle magnetism of character, for that has a universal language which all can understand. They saw and felt that a genuine woman stood down there among them like a sister, ready with head, heart, and hand to help them help themselves; not offering pity as an alms, but justice as a right. Hardship and sorrow, long effort and late-won reward had been hers they knew; wifehood, motherhood, and widowhood brought her very near to them; and behind her was the background of an earnest life, against which

---

[9] A benevolent man who has befriended Christie and her daughter.

this figure with health on the cheeks, hope in the eyes, courage on the lips, and the ardor of a wide benevolence warming the whole countenance stood out full of unconscious dignity and beauty; an example to comfort, touch, and inspire them.

It was not a long speech, and in it there was no learning, no statistics, and no politics; yet it was the speech of the evening, and when it was over no one else seemed to have any thing to say. As the meeting broke up Christie's hand was shaken by many roughened by the needle, stained with printer's ink, or hard with humbler toil; many faces smiled gratefully at her, and many voices thanked her heartily. But sweeter than any applause were the words of one woman who grasped her hand, and whispered with wet eyes:

"I knew your blessed husband; he was very good to me, and I've been thanking the Lord he had such a wife for his reward!"

Christie was thinking of all this as she sat alone that day, and asking herself if she should go on; for the ladies had been as grateful as the women; had begged her to come and speak again, saying they needed just such a mediator to bridge across the space that now divided them from those they wished to serve. She certainly seemed fitted to act as interpreter between the two classes; for, from the gentleman her father she had inherited the fine instincts, gracious manners, and unblemished name of an old and honorable race; from the farmer's daughter, her mother, came the equally valuable dower of practical virtues, a sturdy love of independence, and great respect for the skill and courage that can win it.

Such women were much needed and are not always easy to find; for even in democratic America the hand that earns its daily bread must wear some talent, name, or honor as an ornament, before it is very cordially shaken by those that wear white gloves.

"Perhaps this is the task my life has been fitting me for," she said. "A great and noble one which I should be proud to accept and help accomplish if I can. Others have finished the emancipation work[10] and done it splendidly, even at the cost of all this blood and sorrow. I came too late to do any thing but give my husband and behold the glorious end. This new task seems to offer me the chance of being among the pioneers, to do the hard work, share the persecution, and help lay the foundation of a new emancipation[11] whose happy success I may never see. Yet I had rather be remembered as those brave beginners are, though many of them missed the triumph, than as the late comers will be, who only beat the drums and wave the banners when the victory is won."

* * *

With an impulsive gesture Christie stretched her hands to the friends about her, and with one accord they laid theirs on hers, a loving league of sisters, old and young, black and white, rich and poor, each ready to do her part to hasten the coming of the happy end.

"Me too!" cried little Ruth, and spread her chubby hand above the rest: a hopeful omen, seeming to promise that the coming generation of women will not only receive but deserve their liberty, by learning that the greatest of God's gifts to us is the privilege of sharing His great work.

1873

---

[10] The emancipation of slaves.   [11] The emancipation of women.

Mary Lyon, the founder of Mount Holyoke College (1837), the first women's college in the United States.

Rebecca Harding Davis
(1831–1910)

Rebecca Harding Davis, one of America's earliest practitioners of realism, began her career as a sharp and shocking critic of American society. Her early works "Life in the Iron-Mills" (1861) and *Margaret Howth: A Story of Today* (1862) startled the reading public by displaying in a particularly harsh light some of the tragic consequences of industrialism. Later, however, Davis's writings lost their freshness and power and became didactic, domestic, and conventional.

Rebecca Blaine Harding was born in Washington, Pennsylvania, in 1831 but lived most of her early life in nearby Wheeling, Virginia (now West Virginia). The author Tillie Olsen writes in her edition of *Life in the Iron-Mills and Other Stories* (1973) that as a young woman Harding witnessed the ugly side of industrialization right across the street from her room. The pitiful individuals she saw through her windows were eventually fictionalized in "Life in the Iron-Mills," which appeared anonymously in the *Atlantic Monthly* in 1861. Her intent, Olsen writes, was "to dig into this commonplace, this vulgar American life," and see what was in it. What Harding found was so depressing that her

An illustration from the first edition of Rebecca Davis's Waiting for the Verdict *(1868).*

editor, James T. Fields, requested that she make it less severe. Even though she softened the ending of "Iron-Mills" for publication, the story became a sensation because of its starkly realistic portrayal of the lives of industrial workers. Her second work, *Margaret Howth,* concerns the misfortunes of an African-American peddler girl who is barely recognized as a human being. The novel is also based on the life the author observed in Wheeling, which, because of its geographical location in a slave state sandwiched between the free states Pennsylvania and Ohio, exemplified the tragedies of a country divided by slavery.

The success of her first two works brought excitement into what Harding saw as her dull existence in Wheeling. Invited to Boston by Fields in 1862, she was introduced to a number of writers, including Ralph Waldo Emerson, Nathaniel Hawthorne, and Oliver Wendell Holmes. In Philadelphia, on her way home, she met L. Clarke Davis, a young apprentice lawyer four years her junior, who admired "Life in the Iron-Mills" and had asked Harding to meet him. They married the next year, but their life was not easy: Clarke's lack of regular employment forced the young couple to live with relatives in Philadelphia, and the ill health of Rebecca Davis's father required her to make frequent trips to Wheeling. The distress she felt at this time is evident in "The Wife's Story" (1864), which portrays the struggles of a married woman to resolve the conflicting claims of work and family. When the story appeared, Davis was already pregnant with the first of her three children (one of whom, Richard Harding Davis, became a well-known journalist).

Davis continued her exploration of contemporary issues in *Waiting for the Verdict* (1868), which deals with racial bias, and *John Andross* (1874), which discusses corruption in politics. However, family and home took precedence over her career. To raise necessary money, she wrote formula fiction for *Peterson's Magazine,* a popular journal for which her husband worked. In *Silhouettes of American Life* (1892) she showed flashes of her original brilliance along with a patterned sentimentality, but this volume of previously published stories did little to restore her reputation as a writer. Eventually, the uneven quality of such work reduced her following, and well before her death in 1910 Davis had lapsed into obscurity. Only recently has she regained some of her deserved reputation as a critic of nineteenth-century industrialism, racism, and politics.

Suggested Readings: *Margaret Howth: A Story of Today*, 1862. *Waiting for the Verdict*, 1868. *Life in the Iron-Mills and Other Stories*, 1985. W. Hesford, "Literary Contexts of 'Life in the Iron Mills,'" *American Literature*, 1977, 49:70–85. R. J. Strahl, "A Finessing of Form: The Sentimental and the Realistic in the Fiction of Rebecca Harding Davis, John DeForest, and William Dean Howells," Ph.D. diss., Indiana University, 1981. J. Fetterley, "Rebecca Harding Davis," in *Provisions: A Reader From 19th-Century American Women*, 1985. T. Olsen, "A Biographical Interpretation," in *Life in the Iron-Mills and Other Stories*, 1985.

Text Used: "Life in the Iron-Mills," *Atlantic Monthly*, VII:XLII, April 1861.

LIFE IN THE IRON-MILLS*

> *"Is this the end?*
> *O Life, as futile, then, as frail!*
> *What hope of answer or redress?"* [1]

A cloudy day: do you know what that is in a town[2] of iron-works? The sky sank down before dawn, muddy, flat, immovable. The air is thick, clammy with the breath of crowded human beings. It stifles me. I open the window, and, looking out, can scarcely see through the rain the grocer's shop opposite, where a crowd of drunken Irishmen are puffing Lynchburg tobacco[3] in their pipes. I can detect the scent through all the foul smells ranging loose in the air.

The idiosyncrasy of this town is smoke. It rolls sullenly in slow folds from the great chimneys of the iron-foundries, and settles down in black, slimy pools on the muddy streets. Smoke on the wharves, smoke on the dingy boats, on the yellow river,—clinging in a coating of greasy soot to the house-front, the two faded poplars, the faces of the passers-by. The long train of mules, dragging masses of pig-iron[4] through the narrow street, have a foul vapor hanging to their reeking sides. Here, inside, is a little broken figure of an angel pointing upward from the mantel-shelf; but even its wings are covered with smoke, clotted and black. Smoke everywhere! A dirty canary chirps desolately in a cage beside me. Its dream of green fields and sunshine is a very old dream,—almost worn out, I think.

From the back-window I can see a narrow brick-yard sloping down to the riverside, strewed with rain-butts[5] and tubs. The river, dull and tawny-colored, (*la*

---

* First published in the *Atlantic Monthly* in 1861.
[1] An adaptation of lines from Sections XII and LVI of *In Memoriam A. H. H.* (1850), by Alfred, Lord Tennyson (1809–1892).
[2] Harding does not name the town, but in atmosphere and setting it resembles her hometown of Wheeling, Virginia (now West Virginia).
[3] Cheap tobacco from Lynchburg, Virginia.   [4] Crude iron directly from the blast furnace.
[5] Large wooden casks used to catch rainwater.

belle rivière![6]) drags itself sluggishly along, tired of the heavy weight of boats and coal-barges. What wonder? When I was a child, I used to fancy a look of weary, dumb appeal upon the face of the negro-like river slavishly bearing its burden day after day. Something of the same idle notion comes to me to-day, when from the street-window I look on the slow stream of human life creeping past, night and morning, to the great mills. Masses of men, with dull, besotted faces bent to the ground, sharpened here and there by pain or cunning; skin and muscle and flesh begrimed with smoke and ashes; stooping all night over boiling caldrons of metal, laired by day in dens of drunkenness and infamy; breathing from infancy to death an air saturated with fog and grease and soot, vileness for soul and body. What do you make of a case like that, amateur psychologist? You call it an altogether serious thing to be alive: to these men it is a drunken jest, a joke,—horrible to angels perhaps, to them commonplace enough. My fancy about the river was an idle one: it is no type of such a life. What if it be stagnant and slimy here? It knows that beyond there waits for it odorous sunlight,—quaint old gardens, dusky with soft, green foliage of apple-trees, and flushing crimson with roses,—air, and fields, and mountains. The future of the Welsh puddler[7] passing just now is not so pleasant. To be stowed away, after his grimy work is done, in a hole in the muddy graveyard, and after that,————*not* air, nor green fields, nor curious roses.

Can you see how foggy the day is? As I stand here, idly tapping the window-pane, and looking out through the rain at the dirty back-yard and the coalboats below, fragments of an old story float up before me,—a story of this old house into which I happened to come today. You may think it a tiresome story enough, as foggy as the day, sharpened by no sudden flashes of pain or pleasure.—I know: only the outline of a dull life, that long since, with thousands of dull lives like its own, was vainly lived and lost: thousands of them,—massed, vile, slimy lives, like those of the torpid lizards in yonder stagnant water-butt.—Lost? There is a curious point for you to settle, my friend, who study psychology in a lazy, *dilettante*[8] way. Stop a moment. I am going to be honest. This is what I want you to do. I want you to hide your disgust, take no heed to your clean clothes, and come right down with me,—here, into the thickest of the fog and mud and foul effluvia. I want you to hear this story. There is a secret down here, in this nightmare fog, that has lain dumb for centuries: I want to make it a real thing to you. You, Egoist, or Pantheist, or Arminian,[9] busy in making straight paths for your feet on the hills, do not see it clearly,—this terrible question which men here have gone mad and died trying to answer. I dare not put this secret into words. I told you it was dumb. These men, going by with drunken faces and brains full of unawakened power,[10] do not ask it of Society or of God. Their lives ask it; their deaths ask it. There is no reply. I will tell you plainly that I have a great hope; and I bring it to you to be tested. It is this: that this terrible dumb question is its own reply; that it is not the sentence of death we think it, but, from the very extremity of its darkness,

---

[6] "The beautiful river" (French); the phrase is used with a combination of irony and nostalgia for the Ohio River as seen by the early French fur traders.

[7] A worker who stirs oxides into molten pig-iron, turning it into wrought iron.

[8] A person who studies in a superficial way.

[9] Anyone who follows philosophical or theological abstractions and does not face the questions posed by real life: an Egoist is committed to self-interest as the most profitable way of living; a Pantheist believes that God and nature are one; an Arminian (following the ideas of the Dutch theologian Jacob Arminius [1560–1607]) opposes the Calvinistic doctrine of predestination.

[10] Throughout the story there is a sense of potential untapped, unawakened, going to waste.

the most solemn prophecy which the world has known of the Hope to come. I dare make my meaning no clearer, but will only tell my story. It will, perhaps, seem to you as foul and dark as this thick vapor about us, and as pregnant with death; but if your eyes are free as mine are to look deeper, no perfume-tinted dawn will be so fair with promise of the day that shall surely come.

My story is very simple,—only what I remember of the life of one of these men,—a furnace-tender in one of Kirby & John's rolling-mills,—Hugh Wolfe. You know the mills? They took the great order for the Lower Virginia railroads there last winter; run usually with about a thousand men. I cannot tell why I choose the half-forgotten story of this Wolfe more than that of myriads of these furnace-hands. Perhaps because there is a secret underlying sympathy between that story and this day with its impure fog and thwarted sunshine,—or perhaps simply for the reason that this house is the one where the Wolfes lived. There were the father and son,—both hands, as I said, in one of Kirby & John's mills for making railroad-iron,—and Deborah, their cousin, a picker,[11] in some of the cotton-mills. The house was rented then to half a dozen families. The Wolfes had two of the cellar-rooms. The old man, like many of the puddlers and feeders[12] of the mills, was Welsh,—had spent half of his life in the Cornish[13] tin-mines. You may pick the Welsh emigrants, Cornish miners, out of the throng passing the windows, any day. They are a trifle more filthy; their muscles are not so brawny; they stoop more. When they are drunk, they neither yell, nor shout, nor stagger, but skulk along like beaten hounds. A pure, unmixed blood, I fancy: shows itself in the slight angular bodies and sharply-cut facial lines. It is nearly thirty years since the Wolfes lived here. Their lives were like those of their class: incessant labor, sleeping in kennel-like rooms, eating rank pork and molasses, drinking— God and the distillers only know what; with an occasional night in jail, to atone for some drunken excess. Is that all of their lives?—of the portion given to them and these their duplicates swarming the streets to-day?—nothing beneath?—all? So many a political reformer will tell you,—and many a private reformer, too, who has gone among them with a heart tender with Christ's charity, and come out outraged, hardened.

One rainy night, about eleven o'clock, a crowd of half-clothed women stopped outside of the cellar-door. They were going home from the cotton-mill.

"Good-night, Deb," said one, a mulatto, steadying herself against the gas-post. She needed the post to steady her. So did more than one of them.

"Dah 's a ball to Miss Potts' to-night. Ye 'd best come."

"Inteet, Deb, if hur 'll come, hur 'll hef fun," said a shrill Welsh voice in the crowd.

Two or three dirty hands were thrust out to catch the gown of the woman, who was groping for the latch of the door.

"No."

"No? Where 's Kit Small, then?"

"Begorra![14] on the spools. Alleys behint, though we helped her, we dud. An wid ye! Let Deb alone! It's ondacent[15] frettin' a quite body. Be the powers, an'

---

[11] A worker who separates cotton fibers by machine in a cotton mill.
[12] A worker who feeds molten iron into casting forms, so that it will cool (without bubbles) into desired shapes.
[13] Of Cornwall, England.
[14] An Irish expression equivalent of "by golly" or "by gosh" (mild forms of "by God").
[15] Indecent.

we'll have a night of it! there'll be lashin's o' drink,—the Vargent[16] be blessed and praised for 't!"

They went on, the mulatto inclining for a moment to show fight, and drag the woman Wolfe off with them; but, being pacified, she staggered away.

Deborah groped her way into the cellar, and, after considerable stumbling, kindled a match, and lighted a tallow dip, that sent a yellow glimmer over the room. It was low, damp,—the earthen floor covered with a green, slimy moss,—a fetid air smothering the breath. Old Wolfe lay asleep on a heap of straw, wrapped in a torn horse-blanket. He was a pale, meek little man, with a white face and red rabbit-eyes. The woman Deborah was like him; only her face was even more ghastly, her lips bluer, her eyes more watery. She wore a faded cotton gown and a slouching bonnet. When she walked, one could see that she was deformed, almost a hunchback. She trod softly, so as not to waken him, and went through into the room beyond. There she found by the half-extinguished fire an iron saucepan filled with cold boiled potatoes, which she put upon a broken chair with a pint-cup of ale. Placing the old candlestick beside this dainty repast, she untied her bonnet, which hung limp and wet over her face, and prepared to eat her supper. It was the first food that had touched her lips since morning. There was enough of it, however: there is not always. She was hungry,—one could see that easily enough,—and not drunk, as most of her companions would have been found at this hour. She did not drink, this woman,—her face told that, too,—nothing stronger than ale. Perhaps the weak, flaccid wretch had some stimulant in her pale life to keep her up,—some love or hope, it might be, or urgent need. When that stimulant was gone, she would take to whiskey. Man cannot live by work alone. While she was skinning the potatoes, and munching them, a noise behind her made her stop.

"Janey!" she called, lifting the candle and peering into the darkness. "Janey, are you there?"

A heap of ragged coats was heaved up, and the face of a young girl emerged, staring sleepily at the woman.

"Deborah," she said, at last, "I'm here the night."

"Yes, child. Hur 's welcome," she said, quietly eating on.

The girl's face was haggard and sickly; her eyes were heavy with sleep and hunger: real Milesian[17] eyes they were, dark, delicate blue, glooming out from black shadows with a pitiful fright.

"I was alone," she said, timidly.

"Where's the father?" asked Deborah, holding out a potato, which the girl greedily seized.

"He's beyant,—wid Haley,—in the stone house." (Did you ever hear the word *jail* from an Irish mouth?) "I came here. Hugh told me never to stay me-lone."

"Hugh?"

"Yes."

A vexed frown crossed her face. The girl saw it, and added quickly,—

"I have not seen Hugh the day, Deb. The old man says his watch[18] lasts till the mornin'."

The woman sprang up, and hastily began to arrange some bread and flitch[19] in

---

[16] The Virgin Mary.

[17] Irish; the Milesians were the people of the legendary Spanish King Mil, whose ancestors supposedly invaded Ireland around 1300 B.C.

[18] Shift.   [19] A substandard grade of salt pork.

a tin pail, and to pour her own measure of ale into a bottle. Tying on her bonnet, she blew out the candle.

"Lay ye down, Janey dear," she said, gently, covering her with the old rags. "Hur can eat the potatoes, if hur 's hungry."

"Where are ye goin', Deb? The rain 's sharp."

"To the mill, with Hugh's supper."

"Let him bide till th' morn. Sit ye down."

"No, no,"—sharply pushing her off. "The boy'll starve."

She hurried from the cellar, while the child wearily coiled herself up for sleep. The rain was falling heavily, as the woman, pail in hand, emerged from the mouth of the alley, and turned down the narrow street, that stretched out, long and black, miles before her. Here and there a flicker of gas lighted an uncertain space of muddy footwalk and gutter; the long rows of houses, except an occasional lager-bier shop, were closed; now and then she met a band of mill-hands skulking to or from their work.

Not many even of the inhabitants of a manufacturing town know the vast machinery of system by which the bodies of workmen are governed, that goes on unceasingly from year to year. The hands of each mill are divided into watches that relieve each other as regularly as the sentinels of an army. By night and day the work goes on, the unsleeping engines groan and shriek, the fiery pools of metal boil and surge. Only for a day in the week, in half-courtesy to public censure, the fires are partially veiled; but as soon as the clock strikes midnight, the great furnaces break forth with renewed fury, the clamor begins with fresh, breathless vigor, the engines sob and shriek like "gods in pain."

As Deborah hurried down through the heavy rain, the noise of these thousand engines sounded through the sleep and shadow of the city like far-off thunder. The mill to which she was going lay on the river a mile below the city-limits. It was far, and she was weak, aching from standing twelve hours at the spools. Yet it was her almost nightly walk to take this man his supper, though at every square she sat down to rest, and she knew she should receive small word of thanks.

Perhaps, if she had possessed an artist's eye, the picturesque oddity of the scene might have made her step stagger less, and the path seem shorter; but to her the mills were only "summat deilish[20] to look at by night."

The road leading to the mills had been quarried from the solid rock, which rose abrupt and bare on one side of the cinder-covered road, while the river, sluggish and black, crept past on the other. The mills for rolling iron[21] are simply immense tent-like roofs, covering acres of ground, open on every side. Beneath these roofs Deborah looked in on a city of fires, that burned hot and fiercely in the night. Fire in every horrible form: pits of flame waving in the wind; liquid metal-flames writhing in tortuous streams through the sand; wide caldrons filled with boiling fire, over which bent ghastly wretches stirring the strange brewing; and through all, crowds of half-clad men, looking like revengeful ghosts in the red light, hurried, throwing masses of glittering fire. It was like a street in Hell. Even Deborah muttered, as she crept through, " 'T looks like t' Devil's place!" It did,—in more ways than one.

She found the man she was looking for, at last, heaping coal on a furnace. He had not time to eat his supper; so she went behind the furnace, and waited. Only a

---

[20] Somewhat devilish.   [21] Flattening iron ingots for industrial purposes.

few men were with him, and they noticed her only by a "Hyur comes t' hunch-back, Wolfe."

Deborah was stupid with sleep; her back pained her sharply; and her teeth chattered with cold, with the rain that soaked her clothes and dripped from her at every step. She stood, however, patiently holding the pail, and waiting.

"Hout, woman! ye look like a drowned cat. Come near to the fire,"—said one of the men, approaching to scrape away the ashes.

She shook her head. Wolfe had forgotten her. He turned, hearing the man, and came closer.

"I did no' think; gi' me my supper, woman."

She watched him eat with a painful eagerness. With a woman's quick instinct, she saw that he was not hungry,—was eating to please her. Her pale, watery eyes began to gather a strange light.

"Is 't good, Hugh? T' ale was a bit sour, I feared."

"No, good enough." He hesitated a moment. "Ye 're tired, poor lass! Bide here till I go. Lay down there on that heap of ash, and go to sleep."

He threw her an old coat for a pillow, and turned to his work. The heap was the refuse of the burnt iron, and was not a hard bed; the half-smothered warmth, too, penetrated her limbs, dulling their pain and cold shiver.

Miserable enough she looked, lying there on the ashes like a limp, dirty rag,—yet not an unfitting figure to crown the scene of hopeless discomfort and veiled crime: more fitting, if one looked deeper into the heart of things,—at her thwarted woman's form, her colorless life, her waking stupor that smothered pain and hunger,—even more fit to be a type of her class. Deeper yet if one could look, was there nothing worth reading in this wet, faded thing, half-covered with ashes? no story of a soul filled with groping passionate love, heroic unselfishness, fierce jealousy? of years of weary trying to please the one human being whom she loved, to gain one look of real heart-kindness from him? If anything like this were hidden beneath the pale, bleared eyes, and dull, washed-out-looking face, no one had ever taken the trouble to read its faint signs: not the half-clothed furnace-tender, Wolfe, certainly. Yet he was kind to her: it was his nature to be kind, even to the very rats that swarmed in the cellar: kind to her in just the same way. She knew that. And it might be that very knowledge had given to her face its apathy and vacancy more than her low, torpid life. One sees that dead, vacant look steal sometimes over the rarest, finest of women's faces,—in the very midst, it may be, of their warmest summer's day; and then one can guess at the secret of intolerable solitude that lies hid beneath the delicate laces and brilliant smile. There was no warmth, no brilliancy, no summer for this woman; so the stupor and vacancy had time to gnaw into her face perpetually. She was young, too, though no one guessed it; so the gnawing was the fiercer.

She lay quiet in the dark corner, listening, through the monotonous din and uncertain glare of the works, to the dull plash of the rain in the far distance,—shrinking back whenever the man Wolfe happened to look towards her. She knew, in spite of all his kindness, that there was that in her face and form which made him loathe the sight of her. She felt by instinct, although she could not comprehend it, the finer nature of the man, which made him among his fellow-workmen something unique, set apart. She knew, that, down under all the vileness and coarseness of his life, there was a groping passion for whatever was beautiful and pure,—that his soul sickened with disgust at her deformity, even when his words were kindest. Through this dull consciousness, which never left her, came, like a sting, the recollection of the dark blue eyes and lithe figure of the little Irish girl she had left in the cellar. The recollection struck through even her stupid intellect with a vivid glow of beauty and of grace. Little Janey, timid, helpless, clinging to Hugh as her only friend: that was the sharp thought, the bitter thought, that drove into the glazed eyes a fierce light of pain. You laugh at it? Are pain and jealousy less savage realities down here in this place I am taking you to than in your own house or your own heart,—your heart, which they clutch at sometimes? The note is the same, I fancy, be the octave high or low.

If you could go into this mill where Deborah lay, and drag out from the hearts of these men the terrible tragedy of their lives, taking it as a symptom of the disease of their class, no ghost Horror would terrify you more. A reality of soul-starvation, of living death, that meets you every day under the besotted faces on the street,—I can paint nothing of this, only give you the outside outlines of a night, a crisis in the life of one man: whatever muddy depth of soul-history lies beneath you can read according to the eyes God has given you.

Wolfe, while Deborah watched him as a spaniel its master, bent over the furnace with his iron pole, unconscious of her scrutiny, only stopping to receive orders. Physically, Nature had promised the man but little. He had already lost the strength and instinct vigor of a man, his muscles were thin, his nerves weak, his face (a meek, woman's face) haggard, yellow with consumption. In the mill he was known as one of the girl-men: "Molly Wolfe" was his *sobriquet*.[22] He was never seen in the cockpit,[23] did not own a terrier, drank but seldom; when he did, desperately. He fought sometimes, but was always thrashed, pommelled to a jelly. The man was game enough, when his blood was up: but he was no favorite in the mill; he had the taint of school-learning on him,—not to a dangerous extent, only a quarter or so in the free-school in fact, but enough to ruin him as a good hand in a fight.

For other reasons, too, he was not popular. Not one of themselves, they felt that, though outwardly as filthy and ash-covered; silent, with foreign thoughts and longings breaking out through his quietness in innumerable curious ways: this one, for instance. In the neighboring furnace-buildings lay great heaps of the refuse from the ore after the pig-metal is run. *Korl* we call it here: a light, porous substance, of a delicate, waxen, flesh-colored tinge. Out of the blocks of this korl, Wolfe, in his off-hours from the furnace, had a habit of chipping and moulding figures,—hideous, fantastic enough, but sometimes strangely beautiful: even the mill-men saw that, while they jeered at him. It was a curious fancy in the man, almost a passion. The few hours for rest he spent hewing and hacking with his blunt knife, never speaking, until his watch came again,—working at one figure for months, and, when it was finished, breaking it to pieces perhaps, in a fit of disappointment. A morbid, gloomy man, untaught, unled, left to feed his soul in grossness and crime, and hard, grinding labor.

I want you to come down and look at this Wolfe, standing there among the lowest of his kind, and see him just as he is, that you may judge him justly when you hear the story of this night. I want you to look back, as he does every day, at

[22] Nickname.

[23] A pit in which fighting cocks with pointed spurs attached to their legs battle each other until one is disabled or dead; money goes to the victor's owner and to those who bet on the winner. Terriers were bred for hunting.

his birth in vice, his starved infancy; to remember the heavy years he has groped through as boy and man,—the slow, heavy years of constant, hot work. So long ago he began, that he thinks sometimes he has worked there for ages. There is no hope that it will ever end. Think that God put into this man's soul a fierce thirst for beauty,—to know it, to create it; to *be*—something, he knows not what,—other than he is. There are moments when a passing cloud, the sun glinting on the purple thistles, a kindly smile, a child's face, will rouse him to a passion of pain,—when his nature starts up with a mad cry of rage against God, man, whoever it is that has forced this vile, slimy life upon him. With all this groping, this mad desire, a great blind intellect stumbling through wrong, a loving poet's heart, the man was by habit only a coarse, vulgar laborer, familiar with sights and words you would blush to name. Be just: when I tell you about this night, see him as he is. Be just,—not like man's law, which seizes on one isolated fact, but like God's judging angel, whose clear, sad eye saw all the countless cankering days of this man's life, all the countless nights, when, sick with starving, his soul fainted in him, before it judged him for this night, the saddest of all.

I called this night the crisis of his life. If it was, it stole on him unawares. These great turning-days of life cast no shadow before, slip by unconsciously. Only a trifle, a little turn of the rudder, and the ship goes to heaven or hell.

Wolfe, while Deborah watched him, dug into the furnace of melting iron with his pole, dully thinking only how many rails the lump would yield. It was late,—nearly Sunday morning; another hour, and the heavy work would be done,—only the furnaces to replenish and cover for the next day. The workmen were growing more noisy, shouting, as they had to do, to be heard over the deep clamor of the mills. Suddenly they grew less boisterous,—at the far end, entirely silent. Something unusual had happened. After a moment, the silence came nearer; the men stopped their jeers and drunken choruses. Deborah, stupidly lifting up her head, saw the cause of the quiet. A group of five or six men were slowly approaching, stopping to examine each furnace as they came. Visitors often came to see the mills after night: except by growing less noisy, the men took no notice of them. The furnace where Wolfe worked was near the bounds of the works; they halted there hot and tired: a walk over one of these great foundries is no trifling task. The woman, drawing out of sight, turned over to sleep. Wolfe, seeing them stop, suddenly roused from his indifferent stupor, and watched them keenly. He knew some of them: the overseer, Clarke,—a son of Kirby, one of the mill-owners,—and a Doctor May, one of the town-physicians. The other two were strangers. Wolfe came closer. He seized eagerly every chance that brought him into contact with this mysterious class that shone down on him perpetually with the glamour of another order of being. What made the difference between them? That was the mystery of his life. He had a vague notion that perhaps to-night he could find it out. One of the strangers sat down on a pile of bricks, and beckoned young Kirby to his side.

"This *is* hot, with a vengeance. A match, please?"—lighting his cigar. "But the walk is worth the trouble. If it were not that you must have heard it so often, Kirby, I would tell you that your works look like Dante's Inferno."[24]

Kirby laughed.

---

[24] The vision of Hell given in the first section of *The Divine Comedy*, by the Italian poet Dante Alighieri (1265–1321).

"Yes. Yonder is Farinata[25] himself in the burning tomb,"—pointing to some figure in the shimmering shadows.

"Judging from some of the faces of your men," said the other, "they bid fair to try the reality of Dante's vision, some day."[26]

Young Kirby looked curiously around, as if seeing the faces of his hands for the first time.

"They 're bad enough, that 's true. A desperate set, I fancy. Eh, Clarke?"

The overseer did not hear him. He was talking of net profits just then,—giving, in fact, a schedule of the annual business of the firm to a sharp peering little Yankee, who jotted down notes on a paper laid on the crown of his hat: a reporter for one of the city-papers, getting up a series of reviews of the leading manufactories. The other gentlemen had accompanied them merely for amusement. They were silent until the notes were finished, drying their feet at the furnaces, and sheltering their faces from the intolerable heat. At last the overseer concluded with—

"I believe that is a pretty fair estimate, Captain."

"Here, some of you men!" said Kirby, "bring up those boards. We may as well sit down, gentlemen, until the rain is over. It cannot last much longer at this rate."

"Pig-metal,"—mumbled the reporter,—"um!—coal facilities,—um!—hands employed, twelve hundred,—bitumen,[27]—um!—all right, I believe, Mr. Clarke;—sinking-fund,[28]—what did you say was your sinking-fund?"

"Twelve hundred hands?" said the stranger, the young man who had first spoken. "Do you control their votes, Kirby?"

"Control? No." The young man smiled complacently. "But my father brought seven hundred votes to the polls for his candidate last November. No force-work, you understand,—only a speech or two, a hint to form themselves into a society, and a bit of red and blue bunting to make them a flag. The Invincible Roughs,—I believe that is their name. I forget the motto: 'Our country's hope,' I think."

There was a laugh. The young man talking to Kirby sat, with an amused light in his cool gray eye, surveying critically the half-clothed figures of the puddlers, and the slow swing of their brawny muscles. He was a stranger in the city,—spending a couple of months in the borders of a Slave State,[29] to study the institutions of the South,—a brother-in-law of Kirby's—Mitchell. He was an amateur gymnast,—hence his anatomical eye; a patron, in a *blasé* way, of the prize-ring; a man who sucked the essence out of science or philosophy in an indifferent, gentlemanly way; who took Kant, Novalis, Humboldt,[30] for what they were worth in his own scales; accepting all, despising nothing, in heaven, earth, or hell, but one-idea men;[31] with a temper yielding and brilliant as summer water, until his Self

---

[25] In Canto 10 of Dante's *Inferno*, Farinata degli Uberti is immersed in a burning tomb as a punishment for heresy. Such an allusion differentiates the visitors from the workers: for the visitors, the scene before them is like an epic poem; for the workers, it is life.

[26] "They look as if they might be going to Hell, some day."

[27] A tarlike residue of coal distillation.   [28] Money set aside for future obligations.

[29] Set in the narrow finger of West Virginia that runs halfway up Ohio to the west, Wheeling in 1861 was in the slave state of Virginia, north of the Mason-Dixon line and west of the Appalachian Mountains. It would have been a dubious place to study southern institutions.

[30] Immanuel Kant (1724–1804), a German philosopher; Novalis: the pseudonym of Friedrich von Hardenberg (1772–1801), a German romantic writer; Alexander von Humboldt (1769–1859), a German scientist and explorer. Mitchell has chosen excellent people to study but seems less a scholar than a dabbler and dilettante.

[31] Men of one idea.

was touched, when it was ice, though brilliant still. Such men are not rare in the States.

As he knocked the ashes from his cigar, Wolfe caught with a quick pleasure the contour of the white hand, the bloodglow of a red ring he wore. His voice, too, and that of Kirby's, touched him like music,—low, even, with chording cadences. About this man Mitchell hung the impalpable atmosphere belonging to the thorough-bred gentleman. Wolfe, scraping away the ashes beside him, was conscious of it, did obeisance to it with his artist sense, unconscious that he did so.

The rain did not cease. Clarke and the reporter left the mills; the others, comfortably seated near the furnace, lingered, smoking and talking in a desultory way. Greek would not have been more unintelligible to the furnace-tenders, whose presence they soon forgot entirely. Kirby drew out a newspaper from his pocket and read aloud some article, which they discussed eagerly. At every sentence, Wolfe listened more and more like a dumb, hopeless animal, with a duller, more stolid look creeping over his face, glancing now and then at Mitchell, marking acutely every smallest sign of refinement, then back to himself, seeing as in a mirror his filthy body, his more stained soul.

Never! He had no words for such a thought, but he knew now, in all the sharpness of the bitter certainty, that between them there was a great gulf[32] never to be passed. Never!

The bell of the mills rang for midnight. Sunday morning had dawned. Whatever hidden message lay in the tolling bells floated past these men unknown. Yet it was there. Veiled in the solemn music ushering the risen Saviour was a key-note to solve the darkest secrets of a world gone wrong,—even this social riddle which the brain of the grimy puddler grappled with madly to-night.

The men began to withdraw the metal from the caldrons. The mills were deserted on Sundays, except by the hands who fed the fires, and those who had no lodgings and slept usually on the ash-heaps. The three strangers sat still during the next hour, watching the men cover the furnaces, laughing now and then at some jest of Kirby's.

"Do you know," said Mitchell, "I like this view of the works better than when the glare was fiercest? These heavy shadows and the amphitheatre of smothered fires are ghostly, unreal. One could fancy these red smouldering lights to be the half-shut eyes of wild beasts, and the spectral figures their victims in the den."

Kirby laughed. "You are fanciful. Come, let us get out of the den. The spectral figures, as you call them, are a little too real for me to fancy a close proximity in the darkness,—unarmed, too."

The others rose, buttoning their overcoats, and lighting cigars.

"Raining, still," said Doctor May, "and hard. Where did we leave the coach, Mitchell?"

"At the other side of the works.—Kirby, what's that?"

Mitchell started back, half-frightened, as, suddenly turning a corner, the white figure of a woman faced him in the darkness,—a woman, white, of giant proportions, crouching on the ground, her arms flung out in some wild gesture of warning.

"Stop! Make that fire burn there!" cried Kirby, stopping short.

The flame burst out, flashing the gaunt figure into bold relief.

---

[32] "And beside all this, between us and you there is a great gulf fixed," from Luke 16:26, a parable about the beggar Lazarus, in Heaven, and a rich man, in Hell.

Mitchell drew a long breath.

"I thought it was alive," he said, going up curiously.

The others followed.

"Not marble, eh?" asked Kirby, touching it.

One of the lower overseers stopped.

"Korl, Sir."

"Who did it?"

"Can't say. Some of the hands; chipped it out in off-hours."

"Chipped to some purpose, I should say. What a flesh-tint the stuff has! Do you see, Mitchell?"

"I see."

He had stepped aside where the light fell boldest on the figure, looking at it in silence. There was not one line of beauty or grace in it: a nude woman's form, muscular, grown coarse with labor, the powerful limbs instinct with some one poignant longing. One idea: there it was in the tense, rigid muscles, the clutching hands, the wild, eager face, like that of a starving wolf's. Kirby and Doctor May walked around it, critical, curious. Mitchell stood aloof, silent. The figure touched him strangely.

"Not badly done," said Doctor May.

"Where did the fellow learn that sweep of the muscles in the arm and hand? Look at them! They are groping,—do you see?—clutching: the peculiar action of a man dying of thirst."

"They have ample facilities for studying anatomy," sneered Kirby, glancing at the half-naked figures.

"Look," continued the Doctor, "at this bony wrist, and the strained sinews of the instep! A working-woman,—the very type of her class."

"God forbid!" muttered Mitchell.

"Why?" demanded May. "What does the fellow intend by the figure? I cannot catch the meaning."

"Ask him," said the other, dryly. "There he stands,"—pointing to Wolfe, who stood with a group of men, leaning on his ash-rake.

The Doctor beckoned him with the affable smile which kind-hearted men put on, when talking to these people.

"Mr. Mitchell has picked you out as the man who did this,—I'm sure I don't know why. But what did you mean by it?"

"She be hungry."

Wolfe's eyes answered Mitchell, not the Doctor.

"Oh-h! But what a mistake you have made, my fine fellow! You have given no sign of starvation to the body. It is strong,—terribly strong. It has the mad, half-despairing gesture of drowning."

Wolfe stammered, glanced appealingly at Mitchell, who saw the soul of the thing, he knew. But the cool, probing eyes were turned on himself now,—mocking, cruel, relentless.

"Not hungry for meat," the furnace-tender said at last.

"What then? Whiskey?" jeered Kirby, with a coarse laugh.

Wolfe was silent a moment, thinking.

"I dunno," he said, with a bewildered look. "It mebbe. Summat to make her live, I think,—like you. Whiskey ull do it, in a way."

The young man laughed again. Mitchell flashed a look of disgust somewhere,—not at Wolfe.

"May," he broke out impatiently, "are you blind? Look at that woman's face! It asks questions of God, and says, 'I have a right to know.' Good God, how hungry it is!"

They looked a moment; then May turned to the mill-owner:—

"Have you many such hands as this? What are you going to do with them? Keep them at puddling iron?"

Kirby shrugged his shoulders. Mitchell's look had irritated him.

"Ce n'est pas mon affaire."[33] I have no fancy for nursing infant geniuses. I suppose there are some stray gleams of mind and soul among these wretches. The Lord will take care of his own; or else they can work out their own salvation. I have heard you call our American system a ladder which any man can scale. Do you doubt it? Or perhaps you want to banish all social ladders, and put us all on a flat table-land,—eh, May?"

The Doctor looked vexed, puzzled. Some terrible problem lay hid in this woman's face, and troubled these men. Kirby waited for an answer, and, receiving none, went on, warming with his subject.

"I tell you, there's something wrong that no talk of '*Liberté*' or '*Egalité*'[34] will do away. If I had the making of men, these men who do the lowest part of the world's work should be machines,—nothing more,—hands. It would be kindness. God help them! What are taste, reason, to creatures who must live such lives as that?" He pointed to Deborah, sleeping on the ash-heap. "So many nerves to sting them to pain. What if God had put your brain, with all its agony of touch, into your fingers, and bid you work and strike with that?"

"You think you could govern the world better?" laughed the Doctor.

"I do not think at all."

"That is true philosophy. Drift with the stream, because you cannot dive deep enough to find bottom, eh?"

"Exactly," rejoined Kirby. "I do not think. I wash my hands of all social problems,—slavery, caste, white or black. My duty to my operatives[35] has a narrow limit,—the pay-hour on Saturday night. Outside of that, if they cut korl, or cut each other's throats, (the more popular amusement of the two,) I am not responsible."

The Doctor sighed,—a good honest sigh, from the depths of his stomach.

"God help us! Who is responsible?"

"Not I, I tell you," said Kirby, testily. "What has the man who pays them money to do with their souls' concerns, more than the grocer or butcher who takes it?"

"And yet," said Mitchell's cynical voice, "look at her! How hungry she is!"

Kirby tapped his boot with his cane. No one spoke. Only the dumb face of the rough image looking into their faces with the awful question, "What shall we do to be saved?"[36] Only Wolfe's face, with its heavy weight of brain, its weak, uncertain mouth, its desperate eyes, out of which looked the soul of his class,—only

---

[33] "It's not my affair" (French). Adding to the dimensions of the story are biblical overtones relating to Pontius Pilate, the Roman governor who condemned Christ to be crucified, and incidents in the life of Christ.

[34] *Liberté, Egalité*, and *Fraternité* ("Liberty," "Equality," and "Fraternity") were the rallying cries of the French Revolution.

[35] Workers.

[36] In Acts 16:30 the prison-keeper in Philippi asks, "What must I do to be saved?" after an earthquake had made it possible for the prisoners to escape.

Wolfe's face turned towards Kirby's. Mitchell laughed,—a cool, musical laugh.

"Money has spoken!" he said, seating himself lightly on a stone with the air of an amused spectator at a play. "Are you answered?"—turning to Wolfe his clear, magnetic face.

Bright and deep and cold as Arctic air, the soul of the man lay tranquil beneath. He looked at the furnace-tender as he had looked at a rare mosaic in the morning; only the man was the more amusing study of the two.

"Are you answered? Why, May, look at him! *'De profundis clamavi.'*[37] Or, to quote in English, 'Hungry and thirsty, his soul faints in him.' And so Money sends back its answer into the depths through you, Kirby! Very clear the answer, too!—I think I remember reading the same words somewhere:—washing your hands in Eau de Cologne, and saying, 'I am innocent of the blood of this man. See ye to it!'"[38]

Kirby flushed angrily.

"You quote Scripture freely."

"Do I not quote correctly? I think I remember another line, which may amend my meaning: 'Inasmuch as ye did it unto one of the least of these, ye did it unto me.'[39] Deist? Bless you, man, I was raised on the milk of the Word.[40] Now, Doctor, the pocket of the world having uttered its voice, what has the heart to say? You are a philanthropist, in a small way,—*n'est ce pas?*[41] Here, boy, this gentleman can show you how to cut korl better,—or your destiny. Go on, May!"

"I think a mocking devil possesses you to-night," rejoined the Doctor, seriously.

He went to Wolfe and put his hand kindly on his arm. Something of a vague idea possessed the Doctor's brain that much good was to be done here by a friendly word or two; a latent genius to be warmed into life by a waited-for sunbeam. Here it was: he had brought it. So he went on complacently:—

"Do you know, boy, you have it in you to be a great sculptor, a great man?—do you understand?" (talking down to the capacity of his hearer: it is a way people have with children, and men like Wolfe,)—"to live a better, stronger life than I, or Mr. Kirby here? A man may make himself anything he chooses. God has given you stronger powers than many men,—me, for instance."

May stopped, heated, glowing with his own magnanimity. And it was magnanimous. The puddler had drunk in every word, looking through the Doctor's flurry, and generous heat, and self-approval, into his will, with those slow, absorbing eyes of his.

"Make yourself what you will. It is your right."

"I know," quietly. "Will you help me?"

Mitchell laughed again. The Doctor turned now, in a passion,—

"You know, Mitchell, I have not the means. You know, if I had, it is in my heart to take this boy and educate him for"—

"The glory of God, and the glory of John May."

---

[37] "Out of the depths have I cried unto thee," from the Latin text of Psalm 130:1.

[38] As Pontius Pilate washed his hands of responsibility for what was about to happen to Christ, he said "I am innocent of the blood of this just man: see ye to it," from Matthew 27:24.

[39] Christ's words in Matthew 25:40: "Verily I say unto you, Inasmuch as ye have done it unto one of the least of these my brethren, ye have done it unto me."

[40] A deist believes that God created the world but is not involved in its later workings; the "Milk of the Word" is the teachings of Christ.

[41] "Isn't that so?" (French).

May did not speak for a moment; then, controlled, he said,—

"Why should one be raised, when myriads are left?—I have not the money, boy," to Wolfe, shortly.

"Money?" He said it over slowly, as one repeats the guessed answer to a riddle, doubtfully. "That is it? Money?"

"Yes, money,—that is it," said Mitchell, rising, and drawing his furred coat about him. "You've found the cure for all the world's diseases.—Come, May, find your good-humor, and come home. This damp wind chills my very bones. Come and preach your Saint-Simonian[42] doctrines to-morrow to Kirby's hands. Let them have a clear idea of the rights of the soul, and I'll venture next week they'll strike for higher wages. That will be the end of it."

"Will you sent the coach-driver to this side of the mills?" asked Kirby, turning to Wolfe.

He spoke kindly: it was his habit to do so. Deborah, seeing the puddler go, crept after him. The three men waited outside. Doctor May walked up and down, chafed. Suddenly he stopped.

"Go back, Mitchell! You say the pocket and the heart of the world speak without meaning to these people. What has its head to say? Taste, culture, refinement? Go!"

Mitchell was leaning against a brick wall. He turned his head indolently, and looked into the mills. There hung about the place a thick, unclean odor. The slightest motion of his hand marked that he perceived it, and his insufferable disgust. That was all. May said nothing, only quickened his angry tramp.

"Besides," added Mitchell, giving a corollary to his answer, "it would be of no use. I am not one of them."

"You do not mean"—said May, facing him.

"Yes, I mean just that. Reform is born of need, not pity. No vital movement of the people's has worked down, for good or evil; fermented, instead, carried up the heaving, cloggy mass. Think back through history, and you will know it. What will this lowest deep—thieves, Magdalens,[43] negroes—do with the light filtered through ponderous Church creeds, Baconian theories, Goethe schemes?[44] Some day, out of their bitter need will be thrown up their own light-bringer,—their Jean Paul, their Cromwell,[45] their Messiah."

"Bah!" was the Doctor's inward criticism. However, in practice, he adopted the theory; for, when, night and morning, afterwards, he prayed that power might be given these degraded souls to rise, he glowed at heart, recognizing an accomplished duty.

Wolfe and the woman had stood in the shadow of the works as the coach drove off. The Doctor had held out his hand in a frank, generous way, telling him to "take care of himself, and to remember it was his right to rise." Mitchell had simply touched his hat, as an equal, with a quiet look of thorough recognition. Kirby had thrown Deborah some money, which she found, and clutched eagerly

---

[42] The Comte de Saint-Simon (1760–1825), whose works, including *The New Christianity* (1825), influenced socialist thought.

[43] Prostitutes (from the biblical Mary Magdalene).

[44] Truth coming from above, from theories such as those of the English essayist Francis Bacon (1561–1624) or the German writer Johann Wolfgang von Goethe (1749–1832), will not help the workers.

[45] Jean Paul Richter (1763–1825), a German novelist; Oliver Cromwell (1599–1658), a religious and political commander of England.

enough. They were gone now, all of them. The man sat down on the cinder-road, looking up into the murky sky.

"'T be late, Hugh. Wunnot hur come?"

He shook his head doggedly, and the woman crouched out of his sight against the wall. Do you remember rare moments when a sudden light flashed over your-self, your world, God? when you stood on a mountain-peak, seeing your life as it might have been, as it is? one quick instant, when custom lost its force and every-day usage? when your friend, wife, brother, stood in a new light? your soul was bared, and the grave,—a fore-taste of the nakedness of the Judgment-Day? So it came before him, his life, that night. The slow tides of pain he had borne gathered themselves up and surged against his soul. His squalid daily life, the brutal coarse-ness eating into his brain, as the ashes into his skin: before, these things had been a dull aching into his consciousness; to-night, they were reality. He gripped the filthy red shirt that clung, stiff with soot, about him, and tore it savagely from his arm. The flesh beneath was muddy with grease and ashes,—and the heart beneath that! And the soul? God knows.

Then flashed before his vivid poetic sense the man who had left him,—the pure face, the delicate, sinewy limbs, in harmony with all he knew of beauty or truth. In his cloudy fancy he had pictured a Something like this. He had found it in this Mitchell, even when he idly scoffed at his pain: a Man all-knowing, all-seeing, crowned by Nature, reigning,—the keen glance of his eye falling like a sceptre on other men. And yet his instinct taught him that he too————He! He looked at himself with sudden loathing, sick, wrung his hands with a cry, and then was silent. With all the phantoms of his heated, ignorant fancy, Wolfe had not been vague in his ambitions. They were practical, slowly built up before him out of his knowledge of what he could do. Through years he had day by day made this hope a real thing to himself,—a clear, projected figure of himself, as he might become.

Able to speak, to know what was best, to raise these men and women working at his side up with him: sometimes he forgot this defined hope in the frantic an-guish to escape,—only to escape,—out of the wet, the pain, the ashes, some-where, anywhere,—only for one moment of free air on a hill-side, to lie down and let his sick soul throb itself out in the sunshine. But to-night he panted for life. The savage strength of his nature was roused; his cry was fierce to God for justice.

"Look at me!" he said to Deborah, with a low, bitter laugh, striking his puny chest savagely. "What am I worth, Deb? Is it my fault that I am no better? My fault? My fault?"

He stopped, stung with a sudden remorse, seeing her hunchback shape writhing with sobs. For Deborah was crying thankless tears, according to the fashion of women.

"God forgi' me, woman! Things go harder wi' you nor me. It's a worse share."

He got up and helped her to rise; and they went doggedly down the muddy street, side by side.

"It's all wrong," he muttered, slowly,—"all wrong! I dunnot understan'. But it'll end some day."

"Come home, Hugh!" she said, coaxingly; for he had stopped, looking around bewildered.

"Home,—and back to the mill!" He went on saying this over to himself, as if he would mutter down every pain in this dull despair.

She followed him through the fog, her blue lips chattering with cold. They reached the cellar at last. Old Wolfe had been drinking since she went out, and had crept nearer the door. The girl Janey slept heavily in the corner. He went up to her, touching softly the worn white arm with his fingers. Some bitterer thought stung him, as he stood there. He wiped the drops from his forehead, and went into the room beyond, livid, trembling. A hope, trifling, perhaps, but very dear, had died just then out of the poor puddler's life, as he looked at the sleeping, innocent girl,—some plan for the future, in which she had borne a part. He gave it up that moment, then and forever. Only a trifle, perhaps, to us: his face grew a shade paler,—that was all. But, somehow, the man's soul, as God and the angels looked down on it, never was the same afterwards.

Deborah followed him into the inner room. She carried a candle, which she placed on the floor, closing the door after her. She had seen the look on his face, as he turned away: her own grew deadly. Yet, as she came up to him, her eyes glowed. He was seated on an old chest, quiet, holding his face in his hands.

"Hugh!" she said, softly.

He did not speak.

"Hugh, did hur hear what the man said,—him with the clear voice? Did hur hear? Money, money,—that it wud do all?"

He pushed her away,—gently, but he was worn out; her rasping tone fretted him.

"Hugh!"

The candle flared a pale yellow light over the cobwebbed brick walls, and the woman standing there. He looked at her. She was young, in deadly earnest; her faded eyes, and wet, ragged figure caught from their frantic eagerness a power akin to beauty.

"Hugh, it is true! Money ull do it! Oh, Hugh, boy, listen till me! He said it true! It is money!"

"I know. Go back! I do not want you here."

"Hugh, it is t' last time. I'll never worrit hur again."

There were tears in her voice now, but she choked them back.

"Hear till me only to-night! If one of t' witch people wud come, them we heard of t' home, and gif hur all hur wants, what then? Say, Hugh!"

"What do you mean?"

"I mean money."

Her whisper shrilled through his brain.

"If one of t' witch dwarfs wud come from t' lane moors to-night, and gif hur money, to go out,—*out*, I say,—out, lad, where t' sun shines, and t' heath grows, and t' ladies walk in silken gownds, and God stays all t' time,—where t' man lives that talked to us to-night,—Hugh knows,—Hugh could walk there like a king!"

He thought the woman mad, tried to check her, but she went on, fierce in her eager haste.

"If *I* were t' witch dwarf, if I had t' money, wud hur thank me? Wud hur take me out o' this place wid hur and Janey? I wud not come into the gran' house hur wud build, to vex hur wid t' hunch,—only at night, when t' shadows were dark, stand far off to see hur."

Mad? Yes! Are many of us mad in this way?

"Poor Deb! poor Deb!" he said, soothingly.

"It is here," she said, suddenly jerking into his hand a small roll. "I took it! I did it! Me, me!—not hur! I shall be hanged, I shall be burnt in hell, if anybody knows I took it! Out of his pocket, as he leaned against t' bricks. Hur knows?"

She thrust it into his hand, and then, her errand done, began to gather chips together to make a fire, choking down hysteric sobs.

"Has it come to this?"

That was all he said. The Welsh Wolfe blood was honest. The roll was a small green pocket-book containing one or two gold pieces, and a check for an incredible amount, as it seemed to the poor puddler. He laid it down, hiding his face again in his hands.

"Hugh, don't by angry wud me! It 's only poor Deb,—hur knows?"

He took the long skinny fingers kindly in his.

"Angry? God help me, no! Let me sleep. I am tired."

He threw himself heavily down on the wooden bench, stunned with pain and weariness. She brought some old rags to cover him.

It was late on Sunday evening before he awoke. I tell God's truth, when I say he had then no thought of keeping this money. Deborah had hid it in his pocket. He found it there. She watched him eagerly, as he took it out.

"I must gif it to him," he said, reading her face.

"Hur knows," she said with a bitter sigh of disappointment. "But it is hur right to keep it."

His right! The word struck him. Doctor May had used the same. He washed himself, and went out to find this man Mitchell. His right! Why did this chance word cling to him so obstinately? Do you hear the fierce devils whisper in his ear, as he went slowly down the darkening street?

The evening came on, slow and calm. He seated himself at the end of an alley leading into one of the larger streets. His brain was clear to-night, keen, intent, mastering. It would not start back, cowardly, from any hellish temptation, but meet it face to face. Therefore the great temptation of his life came to him veiled by no sophistry,[46] but bold, defiant, owning its own vile name, trusting to one bold blow for victory.

He did not deceive himself. Theft! That was it. At first the word sickened him; then he grappled with it. Sitting there on a broken cart-wheel, the fading day, the noisy groups, the church-bells' tolling passed before him like a panorama,[47] while the sharp struggle went on within. This money! He took it out, and looked at it. If he gave it back, what then? He was going to be cool about it.

People going by to church saw only a sickly mill-boy watching them quietly at the alley's mouth. They did not know that he was mad, or they would not have gone by so quietly: mad with hunger; stretching out his hands to the world, that had given so much to them, for leave to live the life God meant him to live. His soul within him was smothering to death; he wanted so much, thought so much, and *knew*—nothing. There was nothing of which he was certain, except the mill and things there. Of God and heaven he had heard so little, that they were to him what fairy-land is to a child: something real, but not here; very far off. His brain, greedy, dwarfed, full of thwarted energy and unused powers, questioned these men and women going by, coldly, bitterly, that night. Was it not his right to live as they,—a pure life, a good, true-hearted life, full of beauty and kind words? He only wanted to know how to use the strength within him. His heart warmed as he thought of it. He suffered himself to think of it longer. If he took the money?

Then he saw himself as he might be, strong, helpful, kindly. The night crept

---

[46] Clever arguments.

[47] A continuous series of scenes painted on canvas and rolled before an audience.

on, as this one image slowly evolved itself from the crowd of other thoughts and stood triumphant. He looked at it. As he might be! What wonder, if it blinded him to delirium,—the madness that underlies all revolution, all progress, and all fall?

You laugh at the shallow temptation? You see the error underlying its argument so clearly,—that to him a true life was one of full development rather than self-restraint? that he was deaf to the higher tone in a cry of voluntary suffering for truth's sake than in the fullest flow of spontaneous harmony? I do not plead his cause. I only want to show you the mote[48] in my brother's eye: then you can see clearly to take it out.[49]

The money,—there it lay on his knee, a little blotted slip of paper, nothing in itself, used to raise him out of the pit; something straight from God's hand. A thief! Well, what was it to be a thief? He met the question at last, face to face, wiping the clammy drops of sweat from his forehead. God made this money—the fresh air, too—for his children's use. He never made the difference between poor and rich. The Something who looked down on him that moment through the cool gray sky had a kindly face, he knew,—loved his children alike. Oh, he knew that!

There were times when the soft floods of color in the crimson and purple flames, or the clear depth of amber in the water below the bridge, had somehow given him a glimpse of another world than this,—of an infinite depth of beauty and of quiet somewhere,—somewhere,—a depth of quiet and rest and love. Looking up now, it became strangely real. The sun had sunk quite below the hills, but his last rays struck upward, touching the zenith. The fog had risen, and the town and river were steeped in its thick, gray damp; but overhead, the sun-touched smoke-clouds opened like a cleft ocean,—shifting, rolling seas of crimson mist, waves of billowy silver veined with blood-scarlet, inner depths unfathomable of glancing light. Wolfe's artist-eye grew drunk with color. The gates of that other world! Fading, flashing before him now! What, in that world of Beauty, Content, and Right, were the petty laws, the mine and thine, of mill-owners and mill-hands?

A consciousness of power stirred within him. He stood up. A man,—he thought, stretching out his hands,—free to work, to live, to love! Free! His right! He folded the scrap of paper in his hand. As his nervous fingers took it in, limp and blotted, so his soul took in the mean temptation, lapped it in fancied rights, in dreams of improved existences, drifting and endless as the cloud-seas of color. Clutching it, as if the tightness of his hold would strengthen his sense of possession, he went aimlessly down the street. It was his watch at the mill. He need not go, need never go again, thank God!—shaking off the thought with unspeakable loathing.

Shall I go over the history of the hours of that night? how the man wandered from one to another of his old haunts, with a half-consciousness of bidding them farewell,—lanes and alleys and backyards where the mill-hands lodged,—noting, with a new eagerness, the filth and drunkenness, the pig-pens, the ash-heaps covered with potato-skins, the bloated, pimpled women at the doors,—with a new disgust, a new sense of sudden triumph, and, under all, a new, vague dread, unknown before, smothered down, kept under, but still there? It left him but once

---

[48] Speck of dust.

[49] From Christ's words in the Sermon on the Mount, "And why beholdest thou the mote that is in thy brother's eye, but considerest not the beam that is in thine own eye?" from Matthew 7:3–4 (here, a beam is a wooden roof-support).

during the night, when, for the second time in his life, he entered a church. It was a sombre Gothic pile, where the stained light lost itself in far-retreating arches; built to meet the requirements and sympathies of a far other class than Wolfe's. Yet it touched, moved him uncontrollably. The distances, the shadows, the still, marble figures, the mass of silent kneeling worshippers, the mysterious music, thrilled, lifted his soul with a wonderful pain. Wolfe forgot himself, forgot the new life he was going to live, the mean terror gnawing underneath. The voice of the speaker strengthened the charm; it was clear, feeling, full, strong. An old man, who had lived much, suffered much; whose brain was keenly alive, dominant; whose heart was summer-warm with charity. He taught it to-night. He held up Humanity in its grand total; showed the great world-cancer to his people. Who could show it better? He was a Christian reformer; he had studied the age thoroughly; his outlook at man had been free, world-wide, over all time. His faith stood sublime upon the Rock of Ages; his fiery zeal guided vast schemes by which the gospel was to be preached to all nations. How did he preach it to-night? In burning, light-laden words he painted the incarnate Life, Love, the universal Man: words that became reality in the lives of these people,—that lived again in beautiful words and actions, trifling, but heroic. Sin, as he defied it, was a real foe to them; their trials, temptations, were his. His words passed far over the furnace-tender's grasp, toned to suit another class of culture; they sounded in his ears a very pleasant song in an unknown tongue. He meant to cure this world-cancer with a steady eye that had never glared with hunger, and a hand that neither poverty nor strychnine-whiskey[50] had taught to shake. In this morbid, distorted heart of the Welsh puddler he had failed.

Wolfe rose at last, and turned from the church down the street. He looked up; the night had come on foggy, damp; the golden mists had vanished, and the sky lay dull and ash-colored. He wandered again aimlessly down the street, idly wondering what had become of the cloud-sea of crimson and scarlet. The trial-day of this man's life was over, and he had lost the victory. What followed was mere drifting circumstance,—a quicker walking over the path,—that was all. Do you want to hear the end of it? You wish me to make a tragic story out of it? Why, in the police-reports of the morning paper you can find a dozen such tragedies: hints of shipwrecks unlike any that ever befell on the high seas; hints that here a power was lost to heaven,—that there a soul went down where no tide can ebb or flow. Commonplace enough the hints are,—jocose sometimes, done up in rhyme.

Doctor May, a month after the night I have told you of, was reading to his wife at breakfast from this fourth column of the morning-paper: an unusual thing,— these police-reports not being, in general, choice reading for ladies; but it was only one item he read.

"Oh, my dear! You remember that man I told you of, that we saw at Kirby's mill?—that was arrested for robbing Mitchell? Here he is; just listen:—'Circuit Court. Judge Day. Hugh Wolfe, operative in Kirby & John's Loudon Mills. Charge, grand larceny. Sentence, nineteen years hard labor in penitentiary.'— Scoundrel! Serves him right! After all our kindness that night! Picking Mitchell's pocket at the very time!"

His wife said something about the ingratitude of that kind of people, and then they began to talk of something else.

---

[50] Cheap, impure whiskey that could cause nervous system damage or death.

Nineteen years! How easy that was to read! What a simple word for Judge Day to utter! Nineteen years! Half a lifetime!

Hugh Wolfe sat on the window-ledge of his cell, looking out. His ankles were ironed. Not usual in such cases; but he had made two desperate efforts to escape. "Well," as Haley, the jailer, said, "small blame to him! Nineteen years' imprisonment was not a pleasant thing to look forward to." Haley was very good-natured about it, though Wolfe had fought him savagely.

"When he was first caught," the jailer said afterwards, in telling the story, "before the trial, the fellow was cut down at once,—laid there on that pallet like a dead man, with his hands over his eyes. Never saw a man so cut down in my life. Time of the trial, too, came the queerest dodge of any customer I ever had. Would choose no lawyer. Judge gave him one, of course. Gibson it was. He tried to prove the fellow crazy; but it wouldn't go. Thing was plain as daylight: money found on him. 'T was a hard sentence,—all the law allows; but it was for 'xample's sake. These mill-hands are gettin onbearable. When the sentence was read, he just looked up, and said the money was his by rights, and that all the world had gone wrong. That night, after the trial, a gentleman came to see him here, name of Mitchell,—him as he stole from. Talked to him for an hour. Thought he came for curiosity, like. After he was gone, thought Wolfe was remarkable quiet, and went into his cell. Found him very low; bed all bloody. Doctor said he had been bleeding at the lungs. He was as weak as a cat; yet, if ye 'll b'lieve me, he tried to get a-past me and get out. I just carried him like a baby, and threw him on the pallet. Three days after, he tried it again: that time reached the wall. Lord help you! he fought like a tiger,—giv' some terrible blows. Fightin' for life, you see; for he can't live long, shut up in the stone crib down yonder. Got a death-cough now. 'T took two of us to bring him down that day; so I just put the irons on his feet. There he sits, in there. Goin' to-morrow, with a batch more of 'em. That woman, hunchback, tried with him,—you remember?—she's only got three years. 'Complice. But *she's* a woman, you know. He 's been quiet ever since I put on irons: giv' up, I suppose. Looks white, sick-lookin'. It acts different on 'em, bein' sentenced. Most of 'em gets reckless, devilish-like. Some prays awful, and sings them vile songs of the mills, all in a breath. That woman, now, she 's desper't'. Been beggin' to see Hugh, as she calls him, for three days. I'm a-goin' to let her in. She don't go with him. Here she is in this next cell. I'm a-goin' now to let her in."

He let her in. Wolfe did not see her. She crept into a corner of the cell, and stood watching him. He was scratching the iron bars of the window with a piece of tin which he had picked up, with an idle, uncertain, vacant stare, just as a child or idiot would do.

"Tryin' to get out, old boy?" laughed Haley. "Them irons will need a crowbar beside your tin, before you can open 'em."

Wolfe laughed, too, in a senseless way.

"I think I'll get out," he said.

"I believe his brain's touched," said Haley, when he came out.

The puddler scraped away with the tin for half an hour. Still Deborah did not speak. At last she ventured nearer, and touched his arm.

"Blood?" she said, looking at some spots on his coat with a shudder.

He looked up at her. "Why, Deb!" he said, smiling,—such a bright, boyish smile, that it went to poor Deborah's heart directly, and she sobbed and cried out loud.

"Oh, Hugh, lad! Hugh! dunnot look at me, when it wur my fault! To think I brought hur to it! And I loved hur so! Oh, lad, I dud!"

The confession, even in this wretch, came with the woman's blush through the sharp cry.

He did not seem to hear her,—scraping away diligently at the bars with the bit of tin.

Was he going mad? She peered closely into his face. Something she saw there made her draw suddenly back,—something which Haley had not seen, that lay beneath the pinched, vacant look it had caught since the trial, or the curious gray shadow that rested on it. That gray shadow,—yes, she knew what that meant. She had often seen it creeping over women's faces for months, who died at last of slow hunger or consumption. That meant death, distant, lingering: but this——

Whatever it was the woman saw, or thought she saw, used as she was to crime and misery, seemed to make her sick with a new horror. Forgetting her fear of him, she caught his shoulders, and looked keenly, steadily, into his eyes.

"Hugh!" she cried, in a desperate whisper,—"oh, boy, not that! for God's sake, not *that!*"

The vacant laugh went off his face, and he answered her in a muttered word or two that drove her away. Yet the words were kindly enough. Sitting there on his pallet, she cried silently a hopeless sort of tears, but did not speak again. The man looked up furtively at her now and then. Whatever his own trouble was, her distress vexed him with a momentary sting.

It was market-day. The narrow window of the jail looked down directly on the carts and wagons drawn up in a long line, where they had unloaded. He could see, too, and hear distinctly the clink of money as it changed hands, the busy crowd of whites and blacks shoving, pushing one another, and the chaffering and swearing at the stalls. Somehow, the sound, more than anything else had done, wakened him up,—made the whole real to him. He was done with the world and the business of it. He let the tin fall, and looked out, pressing his face close to the rusty bars. How they crowded and pushed! And he,—he should never walk that pavement again! There came Neff Sanders, one of the feeders at the mill, with a basket on his arm. Sure enough, Neff was married the other week. He whistled, hoping he would look up; but he did not. He wondered if Neff remembered he was there,—if any of the boys thought of him up there, and thought that he never was to go down that old cinder-road again. Never again! He had not quite understood it before; but now he did. Not for days or years, but never!—that was it.

How clear the light fell on that stall in front of the market! and how like a picture it was, the dark-green heaps of corn, and the crimson beets, and golden melons! There was another with game: how the light flickered on that pheasant's breast, with the purplish blood dripping over the brown feathers! He could see the red shining of the drops, it was so near. In one minute he could be down there. It was just a step. So easy, as it seemed, so natural to go! Yet it could never be—not in all the thousands of years to come—that he should put his foot on that street again! He thought of himself with a sorrowful pity, as of some one else. There was a dog down in the market, walking after his master with such a stately, grave look!—only a dog, yet he could go backwards and forwards just as he pleased: he had good luck! Why, the very vilest cur, yelping there in the gutter, had not lived his life, had been free to act out whatever thought God had put into his brain; while he—No, he would not think of that! He tried to put the thought away, and to listen to a dispute between a countryman and a woman about some meat; but it would come back. He, what had he done to bear this?

Then came the sudden picture of what might have been, and now. He knew what it was to be in the penitentiary,—how it went with men there. He knew how in these long years he should slowly die, but not until soul and body had become corrupt and rotten,—how, when he came out, if he lived to come, even the lowest of the mill-hands would jeer him,—how his hands would be weak, and his brain senseless and stupid. He believed he was almost that now. He put his hand to his head, with a puzzled, weary look. It ached, his head, with thinking. He tried to quiet himself. It was only right, perhaps; he had done wrong. But was there right or wrong for such as he? What was right? And who had ever taught him? He thrust the whole matter away. A dark, cold quiet crept through his brain. It was all wrong; but let it be! It was nothing to him more than the others. Let it be!

The door grated, as Haley opened it.

"Come, my woman! Must lock up for t' night. Come, stir yerself!"

She went up and took Hugh's hand.

"Good-night, Deb," he said, carelessly.

She had not hoped he would say more; but the tired pain on her mouth just then was bitterer than death. She took his passive hand and kissed it.

"Hur 'll never see Deb again!" she ventured, her lips growing colder and more bloodless.

What did she say that for? Did he not know it? Yet he would not be impatient with poor old Deb. She had trouble of her own, as well as he.

"No, never again," he said, trying to be cheerful.

She stood just a moment, looking at him. Do you laugh at her, standing there, with her hunchback, her rags, her bleared, withered face, and the great despised love tugging at her heart?

"Come, you!" called Haley, impatiently.

She did not move.

"Hugh!" she whispered.

It was to be her last word. What was it?

"Hugh, boy, not THAT!"

He did not answer. She wrung her hands, trying to be silent, looking in his face in an agony of entreaty. He smiled again, kindly.

"It is best, Deb. I cannot bear to be hurted any more."

"Hur knows," she said, humbly.

"Tell my father good-bye; and—and kiss little Janey."

She nodded, saying nothing, looked in his face again, and went out of the door. As she went, she staggered.

"Drinkin' to-day?" broke out Haley, pushing her before him. "Where the Devil did you get it? Here, in with ye!" and he shoved her into her cell, next to Wolfe's, and shut the door.

Along the wall of her cell there was a crack low down by the floor, through which she could see the light from Wolfe's. She had discovered it days before. She hurried in now, and, kneeling down by it, listened, hoping to hear some sound. Nothing but the rasping of the tin on the bars. He was at his old amusement again. Something in the noise jarred on her ear, for she shivered as she heard it. Hugh rasped away at the bars. A dull old bit of tin, not fit to cut korl with.

He looked out of the window again. People were leaving the market now. A tall mulatto girl, following her mistress, her basket on her head, crossed the street just below, and looked up. She was laughing; but, when she caught sight of the haggard face peering out through the bars, suddenly grew grave, and hurried by. A free, firm step, a clear-cut olive face, with a scarlet turban tied on one side, dark, shining eyes, and on the head the basket poised, filled with fruit and flowers, under which the scarlet turban and bright eyes looked out half-shadowed. The picture caught his eye. It was good to see a face like that. He would try to-morrow, and cut one like it. *To-morrow!* He threw down the tin, trembling, and covered his face with his hands. When he looked up again, the daylight was gone.

Deborah, crouching near by on the other side of the wall, heard no noise. He sat on the side of the low pallet, thinking. Whatever was the mystery which the woman had seen on his face, it came out now slowly, in the dark there, and became fixed,—a something never seen on his face before. The evening was darkening fast. The market had been over for an hour; the rumbling of the carts over the pavement grew more infrequent: he listened to each, as it passed, because he thought it was to be for the last time. For the same reason, it was, I suppose, that he strained his eyes to catch a glimpse of each passer-by, wondering who they were, what kind of homes they were going to, if they had children,—listening eagerly to every chance word in the street, as if—(God be merciful to the man! what strange fancy was this?)—as if he never should hear human voices again.

It was quite dark at last. The street was a lonely one. The last passenger, he thought, was gone. No,—there was a quick step: Joe Hill, lighting the lamps. Joe was a good old chap; never passed a fellow without some joke or other. He remembered once seeing the place where he lived with his wife. "Granny Hill" the boys called her. Bedridden she was; but so kind as Joe was to her! kept the room so clean!—and the old woman, when he was there, was laughing at "some of t' lad's foolishness." The step was far down the street; but he could see him place the ladder, run up, and light the gas. A longing seized him to be spoken to once more.

"Joe!" he called, out of the grating. "Good-bye, Joe!"

The old man stopped a moment, listening uncertainly; then hurried on. The prisoner thrust his hand out of the window, and called again, louder; but Joe was too far down the street. It was a little thing; but it hurt him,—this disappointment.

"Good-bye Joe!" he called, sorrowfully enough.

"Be quiet!" said one of the jailers, passing the door, striking on it with his club.

Oh, that was the last, was it?

There was an inexpressible bitterness on his face, as he lay down on the bed, taking the bit of tin, which he had rasped to a tolerable degree of sharpness, in his hand,—to play with, it may be. He bared his arms, looking intently at their corded veins and sinews. Deborah, listening in the next cell, heard a slight clicking sound, often repeated. She shut her lips tightly, that she might not scream; the cold drops of sweat broke over her, in her dumb agony.

"Hur knows best," she muttered at last, fiercely clutching the boards where she lay.

If she could have seen Wolfe, there was nothing about him to frighten her. He lay quite still, his arms outstretched, looking at the pearly stream of moonlight coming into the window. I think in that one hour that came then he lived back over all the years that had gone before. I think that all the low, vile life, all his wrongs, all his starved hopes, came then, and stung him with a farewell poison that made him sick unto death. He made neither moan nor cry, only turned his worn face now and then to the pure light, that seemed so far off, as one that said, "How long, O Lord? how long?"

The hour was over at last. The moon, passing over her nightly path, slowly came nearer, and threw the light across his bed on his feet. He watched it steadily, as it crept up, inch by inch, slowly. It seemed to him to carry with it a great silence. He had been so hot and tired there always in the mills! The years had been so fierce and cruel! There was coming now quiet and coolness and sleep. His tense limbs relaxed, and settled in a calm languor. The blood ran fainter and slow from his heart. He did not think now with a savage anger of what might be and was not; he was conscious only of deep stillness creeping over him. At first he saw a sea of faces: the mill-men,—women he had known, drunken and bloated,—Janeys timid and pitiful,—poor old Debs: then they floated together like a mist, and faded away, leaving only the clear, pearly moonlight.

Whether, as the pure light crept up the stretched-out figure, it brought with it calm and peace, who shall say? His dumb soul was alone with God in judgment. A Voice may have spoken for it from far-off Calvary, "Father, forgive them, for they know not what they do!"[51] Who dare say? Fainter and fainter the heart rose and fell, slower and slower the moon floated from behind a cloud, until, when at last its full tide of white splendor swept over the cell, it seemed to wrap and fold into a deeper stillness the dead figure that never should move again. Silence deeper than the Night! Nothing that moved, save the black, nauseous stream of blood dripping slowly from the pallet to the floor!

There was outcry and crowd enough in the cell the next day. The coroner and his jury, the local editors, Kirby himself, and boys with their hands thrust knowingly into their pockets and heads on one side, jammed into the corners. Coming and going all day. Only one woman. She came late, and outstayed them all. A Quaker, or Friend, as they call themselves. I think this woman was known by that name in heaven. A homely body, coarsely dressed in gray and white. Deborah (for Haley had let her in) took notice of her. She watched them all—sitting on the end of the pallet, holding his head in her arms—with the ferocity of a watch-dog, if any of them touched the body. There was no meekness, no sorrow, in her face; the stuff out of which murderers are made, instead. All the time Haley and the woman were laying straight the limbs and cleaning the cell, Deborah sat still, keenly watching the Quaker's face. Of all the crowd there that day, this woman alone had not spoken to her,—only once or twice had put some cordial to her lips. After they all were gone, the woman, in the same still, gentle way, brought a vase of wood-leaves and berries, and placed it by the pallet, then opened the narrow window. The fresh air blew in, and swept the woody fragrance over the dead face. Deborah looked up with a quick wonder.

"Did hur know my boy wud like it? Did hur know Hugh?"

"I know Hugh now."

The white fingers passed in a slow, pitiful way over the dead, worn face. There was a heavy shadow in the quiet eyes.

"Did hur know where they 'll bury Hugh?" said Deborah in a shrill tone, catching her arm.

This had been the question hanging on her lips all day.

"In t' town-yard? Under t' mud and ash? T' lad'll smother, woman! He wur

[51] Christ's words from the cross: "Father, forgive them: for they know not what they do," from Luke 23:24; Calvary was the site of the crucifixion.

born on t' lane moor, where t' air is frick[52] and strong. Take hur out, for God's sake, take hur out where t' air blows!"

The Quaker hesitated, but only for a moment. She put her strong arm around Deborah and led her to the window.

"Thee sees the hills, friend, over the river? Thee sees how the light lies warm there, and the winds of God blow all the day? I live there,—where the blue smoke is, by the trees. Look at me." She turned Deborah's face to her own, clear and earnest. "Thee will believe me? I will take Hugh and bury him there to-morrow."

Deborah did not doubt her. As the evening wore on, she leaned against the iron bars, looking at the hills that rose far off, through the thick sodden clouds, like a bright, unattainable calm. As she looked, a shadow of their solemn repose fell on her face: its fierce discontent faded into a pitiful, humble quiet. Slow, solemn tears gathered in her eyes: the poor weak eyes turned so hopelessly to the place where Hugh was to rest, the grave heights looking higher and brighter and more solemn than ever before. The Quaker watched her keenly. She came to her at last, and touched her arm.

"When thee comes back," she said, in a low, sorrowful tone, like one who speaks from a strong heart deeply moved with remorse or pity, "thee shall begin thy life again.—there on the hills. I came too late; but not for thee,—by God's help, it may be."

Not too late. Three years after, the Quaker began her work. I end my story here. At evening-time it was light. There is no need to tire you with the long years of sunshine, and fresh air, and slow, patient Christ-love, needed to make healthy and hopeful this impure body and soul. There is a homely pine house, on one of these hills, whose windows overlook broad, wooded slopes and clover-crimsoned meadows,—niched into the very place where the light is warmest, the air freest. It is the Friends' meeting-house.[53] Once a week they sit there, in their grave, earnest way, waiting for the Spirit of Love to speak, opening their simple hearts to receive His words. There is a woman, old, deformed, who takes a humble place among them: waiting like them: in her gray dress, her worn face, pure and meek, turned now and then to the sky. A woman much loved by these silent, restful people; more silent than they, more humble, more loving. Waiting: with her eyes turned to hills higher and purer than these on which she lives,—dim and far off now, but to be reached some day. There may be in her heart some latent hope to meet there the love denied her here,—that she shall find him whom she lost, and that then she will not be all-unworthy. Who blames her? Something is lost in the passage of every soul from one eternity to the other,—something pure and beautiful, which might have been and was not: a hope, a talent, a love, over which the soul mourns, like Esau deprived of his birthright.[54] What blame to the meek Quaker, if she took her lost hope to make the hills of heaven more fair?

Nothing remains to tell that the poor Welsh puddler once lived, but this figure of the mill-woman cut in korl. I have it here in a corner of my library. I keep it hid behind a curtain,—it is such a rough, ungainly thing. Yet there are about it touches, grand sweeps of outline, that show a master's hand. Sometimes,—to-night, for instance,—the curtain is accidentally drawn back, and I see a bare arm stretched out imploringly in the darkness, and an eager, wolfish face watching mine: a wan, woful face, through which the spirit of the dead korl-cutter looks

---

[52] Fresh.   [53] A Quaker place of worship.
[54] In Genesis 25: 27 Esau sold his birthright to his twin brother, Jacob.

out, with its thwarted life, its mighty hunger, its unfinished work. Its pale, vague lips seem to tremble with a terrible question. "Is this the End?" they say,—"nothing beyond?—no more?" Why, you tell me you have seen that look in the eyes of dumb brutes,—horses dying under the lash. I know.

The deep of the night is passing while I write. The gas-light wakens from the shadows here and there the objects which lie scattered through the room: only faintly, though; for they belong to the open sunlight. As I glance at them, they each recall some task or pleasure of the coming day. A half-moulded child's head; Aphrodite;[55] a bough of forest-leaves; music; work; homely fragments, in which lie the secrets of all eternal truth and beauty. Prophetic all! Only this dumb, woful face seems to belong to and end with the night. I turn to look at it. Has the power of its desperate need commanded the darkness away? While the room is yet steeped in heavy shadow, a cool, gray light suddenly touches its head like a blessing hand, and its groping arm points through the broken cloud to the far East, where, in the flickering, nebulous crimson, God has set the promise of the Dawn.

1861

EARLY TO MIDDLE 19TH-CENTURY NONFICTION PROSE

The emphasis of nonfiction prose in eighteenth-century America was, as would be expected, on political independence. The seminal piece of writing was the Declaration of Independence. Closely allied works were *The Federalist* papers (1787–1788) of Alexander Hamilton, James Madison, and John Jay; Thomas Paine's *Common Sense* (1776); and scores of political pamphlets. The writers of these works were attempting to carve out the ideas that would define a new nation. In the nineteenth century the concerns of writers of nonfiction prose broadened. Margaret Fuller, Elizabeth Cady Stanton, and other feminists wrote about women's rights. Frederick Douglass, Harriet Jacobs, and others produced accounts of their horrifying lives as slaves. Noah Webster published his two-volume *American Dictionary of the English Language* in 1828. Historians such as Francis Parkman, George Bancroft, and William Hickling Prescott began to write the history of the new country. And an untold number of men and women promoted abolitionism, advocated antiwar positions, and produced a vast amount of travel writing in the newspapers and magazines that proliferated in the early nineteenth century.

If, however, there is one central emphasis in nonfiction prose of the first half of the nineteenth-century, it is the unfolding of the self. The romanticism that developed in Europe at the beginning of the nineteenth century was fundamentally an assertion of the self. For the early romantics Johann Wolfgang von Goethe, Jean Jacques Rousseau, William Wordsworth, and Samuel Taylor Coleridge, personal autonomy and individual distinctiveness—perhaps best exemplified by Rousseau in *Confessions* (1781, 1788)—had become the cornerstones of human identity. And the romantics had a pronounced effect on America's writers. The Ralph Waldo Emerson who returned to the United States in 1833 after meeting

---

[55] According to Greek myth, the goddess of love.

This early photograph shows how pioneers formed wagon trains, to protect against Native-American attacks and against the elements, as they proceeded in the great westward migration.

Wordsworth, Coleridge, and Thomas Carlyle, among others, was fired with a romantic belief in the power of human intuition. Those nonfiction writers in America who argued on behalf of women's rights and abolitionism, who celebrated the natural beauty of native landscapes and bemoaned the corrupting influences of civilization, and who conceived of transcendentalism were inspired by the ideals of romanticism.

The transcendentalists are perhaps the most clearly romantic of American writers of nonfiction prose. Emerson says "trust thyself," and Henry David Thoreau encourages us to explore ourselves. Margaret Fuller, for two years editor of *The Dial,* the transcendentalist magazine, spent a career urging women to assert themselves. This expansion of the idea of self led naturally and logically to a conflict between the individual and society. We see it in Fuller's feminism. It is even more obvious in Thoreau's work, most notably in his essay "Resistance to Civil Government" (1849). That central document of American literature inspired the Indian nationalist Mahatma Gandhi and Martin Luther King, Jr., among others. "Resistance to Civil Government" was the result of Thoreau's being jailed overnight by Concord, Massachusetts, officials for his refusal to pay a poll tax to a government that tolerated slavery. He believed that an individual has, and must insist upon, the right to refuse to sanction a government if he or she strongly disagrees with the actions of that government. Private morality is, for Thoreau the principled romantic, a sacred area upon which government has no right to intrude.

The subject of slavery was, as we might imagine, central to mid-nineteenth-century discourse. Much of the nonfiction prose of the time—from newspaper articles to political oratory to the writings of abolitionists, including Thoreau, Lydia Maria Child, and the politician Wendell Phillips—engaged this heated subject. Even poets such as John Greenleaf Whittier attacked slavery. Slaves themselves, however, offered the most moving indictments of this demeaning institution. Beginning in the early eighteenth century, more than six thousand accounts of slaves' lives in captivity were produced. Unlike the earlier captivity narratives such as Mary Rowlandson's, which recount one white person's plight after abduction by a band of Native Americans and tend to end with an escape perceived as a triumph of the individual's religious faith, slave narratives are communal tales in which the captive stands for his or her collective race. Olaudah Equiano's *Narrative* (1789) was the prototype of this genre.

In the middle of the nineteenth century, two classic slave narratives appeared: Harriet Jacobs's *Incidents in the Life of a Slave Girl* (1861) and Frederick Douglass's *Narrative* (1845). Jacobs's harrowing autobiography tells a story of such brutality and degradation that its very credibility was questioned until the well-known abolitionist Lydia Maria Child agreed to "edit" and write a brief introduction to it. Douglass's *Narrative* was also introduced by a well-known white abolitionist, the newspaper editor William Lloyd Garrison. It is revealing of nineteenth-century attitudes toward blacks that these works had to be sanctioned by a white establishment figure in order to be fully accepted by a supposedly sympathetic audience.

Douglass's *Narrative* is a skillful literary document that appropriates both the artistic strategies and the language of the white middle class and of Christianity to indict the intertwined evils of racism and slavery. Douglass's search for his role in the world once he is a free man is recognizable as a romanticist's attempt to name, or identify, a self. Read this way, the *Narrative* is an exemplary tale that owes much not only to the genre that it epitomizes, but also to the larger historical moment during which its author lived. In other words, Douglass shares a literary relationship not only with Harriet Jacobs, but also with Emerson and Thoreau. Moreover, this *Narrative* is a clear literary antecedent of such twentieth-century attempts to delineate an African-American self as Ralph Ellison's *Invisible Man* (1952).

After gaining his freedom Douglass devoted much of his energies to lecturing on what he called the "great work" of abolitionism. Doing so, he joined a lecture circuit that offered both a living and a testing ground for many of his contemporaries. Many of Emerson's essays were the revised products of orations that he gave during the winters he spent traveling America's burgeoning lecture circuit. Oratory was, in an age before the advent of the audio and video media, a popular communications medium. In the middle nineteenth century a large and eager audience might come out to hear Emerson exhort them to be self-reliant, to hear (and see) Douglass talk about the horrors of slave life, to see the latest English literary giant—Charles Dickens, for instance—read from his or her works, or to see and listen to political oratory of a vehemence and flamboyance that is all but lost.

The Emancipation Proclamation

In fighting the Civil War, President Abraham Lincoln's primary goal was to preserve the Union—with or without slavery. During the second year of fighting, he began to feel that an emancipation policy, which would take the collective strength of African Americans from the Confederacy and give it to the Union, might strengthen rather than weaken the Union cause. On September 22, 1862, Lincoln proclaimed emancipation as a war measure. As such, the policy could be applied only to Confederate states still in rebellion, not to border states loyal to the Union or to already conquered parts of the South. The provisions of the document, from which the excerpt below was taken, went into effect New Year's Day, 1863.

Final Proclamation of Emancipation

That on the 1st day of January, A.D. 1863, all persons held as slaves within any State or designated part of a State the people whereof shall then be in rebellion against the United States shall be then, thenceforward, and forever free; and the executive government of the United States including the military and naval authority thereof, will recognize and maintain the freedom of such persons and will do no act or acts to repress such persons, or any of them, in any efforts they may make for their actual freedom.

That the executive will on the 1st day of January aforesaid, by proclamation, designate the States and parts of States, if any, in which the people thereof, respectively, shall then be in rebellion against the United States; and the fact that any State or the people thereof shall on that day be in good faith represented in the Congress of the United States by members chosen thereto at elections wherein a majority of the qualified voters of such States shall have participated shall, in the absence of strong countervailing testimony, be deemed conclusive evidence that such State and the people thereof are not then in rebellion against the United States.

Abraham Lincoln, 1862

An especially memorable orator was Abraham Lincoln, who spoke simply and colloquially and whose humor owed much to the southwestern tall tale. The simplicity and clarity of Lincoln's nonfiction prose style (he used no speechwriter but wrote his own material) is evident in the Gettysburg Address (1863). Walt Whitman called Lincoln the writer an "idiomatic western genius."

The nonfiction prose produced by women in the early nineteenth century centered, as did the writings of slaves, around a potent social issue. Women such as Margaret Fuller, Fanny Fern, and Elizabeth Cady Stanton called attention to the inequality of women in a supposedly democratic society. Fern was the most popular of these authors, producing work that was often dismissed for sentimentality by the same readers who revered Charles Dickens's novels. Fuller and Stanton were more consciously militant writers. In her best-known work, *Woman in the Nineteenth Century* (1845), Fuller calls for equal opportunities for women as she castigates the hypocrisy of white males who championed freedom for blacks while restricting the rights of their own wives and daughters.

It was Stanton, however, who called the hypocrisy of white males's into clearest focus. In the 1848 Declaration of Sentiments she and her colleagues used the language of the Declaration of Independence itself to call for women's rights. The second paragraph of the Declaration of Sentiments begins "We hold these truths to be self-evident: that all men and women are created equal." The declaration commences a list of tyrannous "facts" with "The history of mankind is a history of repeated injustices and usurpations on the part of man toward woman."

In the militant writings of women and of slaves we recognize assertions of the self that are as powerful as the famous pronouncements of the transcendentalists. The central emphasis in the rich and varied accomplishments of America's early to middle nineteenth-century writers of nonfiction prose is a romantic call for the primacy of the self in the face of an increasingly conformist and intolerant society. America's nonfiction writers remind us—in their newspaper articles, orations, autobiographies, personal essays, and propaganda pieces—of the significance of the human "I" in a democracy.

Lydia Maria Child
(1802–1880)

In her forties Lydia Maria Child recalled that her childhood had been "cold, shaded, and uncongenial." She was born Lydia Maria Francis in Medford, Massachusetts, in 1802 to Susannah Rand and David Convers Francis. Her father disapproved of her reading, and when her mother died Lydia, age twelve, was sent to live with a sister in isolated Norridgewock, Maine. If her father hoped Lydia would give up her intellectual interests, he was disappointed: she continued to read widely and to correspond with her Harvard-educated brother, Convers, about Homer and John Milton. Out of the experience of patriarchal repression she wrote her first novel when she was twenty-two. Set in Puritan times and featuring the heroine's rebellious marriage to a Native American, *Hobomok* (1824) is both an attack on patriarchal authority and one of the first historical novels to make use of American materials.

During the next few years Lydia Francis pursued a busy literary career; she established the *Juvenile Miscellany* (the first successful children's magazine), wrote another historical novel (*The Rebels* [1825]), and compiled *The Frugal Housewife* (1829), a popular collection of household advice and traditional remedies. In 1828 she married David Lee Child—an idealistic lawyer and abolitionist but an incompetent provider—and, moving to a farm in Weyland, Massachusetts, undertook to support them with her writing. By 1832 she was a highly regarded author, one of only two women granted membership in the Boston Athenaeum. But her success was checked by the publication of the pamphlet *An Appeal in*

Favor of That Class of Americans Called Africans (1833), which called for immediate emancipation and—most upsetting to conventional minds—argued against antimiscegenation laws, laws banning interracial marriage. Public reaction was swift and devastating: a Boston politician threw the *Appeal* out the window with tongs, the *Juvenile Miscellany* lost most of its subscribers, and Child's membership in the Boston Athenaeum was revoked.

Retracting nothing, Child continued to write essays and fiction for the abolitionist cause and on behalf of Native Americans. Moreover, she extended her concern to the plight of the elderly, Chinese immigrants, and the insane. In 1841 she moved to New York City, where she edited the abolitionist William Lloyd Garrison's newspaper *The National Anti-Slavery Standard*. Her wide-ranging newspaper sketches were collected as *Letters From New York* in 1843 and 1845. In 1861 she edited Harriet Jacobs's *Incidents in the Life of a Slave Girl*, and after the Civil War Child published *The Freedman's Book* (1865), a collection of essays directed to newly emancipated slaves. Never a radical feminist, she nonetheless worked for woment's rights with her biography of the writer Madame de Baronne de Staël, her novels *Philothea* (1836) and *A Romance of the Republic* (1867), and historical works such as *The History of the Condition of Women, in Various Ages and Nations* (1835), which documents the variety of women's roles in world history.

Although Child's *Philothea* can be considered one of the few transcendentalist novels, she had little sympathy for abstractions. For Child, as for Herman Melville, literature was concerned with "the great Art of Telling the Truth" (from Melville's "Hawthorne and His Mosses" [1850]), but her truths were practical, social, and political rather than transcendental. After receiving a copy of the just-published *Essays: Second Series* from her friend Ralph Waldo Emerson in 1844, she wrote to Augusta King that she objected to the idea that "everything is 'scene-painting and counterfeit'; . . . my being is so alive and earnest, that it resists and abhors these alluding spectres." Her writing powerfully attests to this vital and earnest concern.

Suggested Readings: *A Romance of the Republic*, 1867, 1969. *Selected Letters, 1817–1880*, ed. M. Meltzer, P. G. Holland, and F. Krasno, 1982. H. G. Baer, *The Heart Is Like Heaven: The Life of Lydia Maria Child*, 1964. M. Meltzer, *Tongue of Flame: The Life of Lydia Maria Child*, 1965. W. S. Osborne, *Lydia Maria Child*, 1980. J. F. Yellin, *Women and Sisters: The Antislavery Feminists in American Culture*, 1989.

Texts Used: *The American Frugal Housewife, Dedicated to Those Who Are Not Ashamed of Economy*, 1836. "Chocorua's Curse": *Hobomok and Other Writings on Indians*, ed. C. L. Karcher, 1986. *The Freedmen's Book*, 1865.

from THE FRUGAL HOUSEWIFE*

GENERAL MAXIMS FOR HEALTH

Rise early. Eat simple food. Take plenty of exercise. Never fear a little fatigue. Let not children be dressed in tight clothes; it is necessary their limbs and muscles should have full play, if you wish for either health or beauty.

---

* First published in 1829, this little volume of strikingly modern tips on health, housekeeping, cooking, and raising children was retitled *The American Frugal Housewife* and went through thirty-three American editions and twenty-one European editions.

Avoid the necessity of a physician, if you can, by careful attention to your diet. Eat what best agrees with your system, and resolutely abstain from what hurts you, however well you may like it. A few days' abstinence, and cold water for a beverage, has driven off many an approaching disease.

If you find yourself really ill, send for a good physician. Have nothing to do with quacks; and do not tamper with quack medicines. You do not know what they are; and what security have you that they know what they are?

Wear shoes that are large enough. It not only produces corns, but makes the feet misshapen, to cramp them.

Wash very often, and rub the skin thoroughly with a hard brush.

Let those who love to be invalids drink strong green tea, eat pickles, preserves, and rich pastry. As far as possible, eat and sleep at regular hours.

Wash the eyes thoroughly in cold water every morning. Do not read or sew at twilight, or by too dazzling a light. If far-sighted, read with rather less light, and with the book somewhat nearer to the eye, than you desire. If near-sighted, read with a book as far as possible. Both these imperfections may be diminished in this way.

Clean teeth in pure water two or three times a day; but, above all, be sure to have them clean before you go to bed.[1]

Have your bed-chamber well aired; and have fresh bed linen every week. Never have the wind blowing directly upon you from open windows during the night. It is *not* healthy to sleep in heated rooms.

Let children have their bread and milk before they have been long up. Cold water and a run in the fresh air before breakfast.

Too frequent use of an ivory comb injures the hair. Thorough combing, washing in suds, or N. E. rum,[2] and thorough brushing, will keep it in order; and the washing does not injure the hair, as is generally supposed. Keep children's hair cut close until ten or twelve years old; it is better for health and the beauty of the hair. Do not sleep with hair frizzled, or braided. Do not make children cross-eyed, by having hair hang down about their foreheads, where they see it continually.

1829

from   HINTS TO PERSONS OF MODERATE FORTUNE

Education of Daughters

There is no subject so much connected with individual happiness and national prosperity as the education of daughters. It is a true, and therefore an old remark, that the situation and prospects of a country may be justly estimated by the character of its women; and we all know how hard it is to engraft upon a woman's character habits and principles to which she was unaccustomed in her girlish days. It is always extremely difficult, and sometimes utterly impossible. Is the present education of young ladies likely to contribute to their own ultimate happiness, or to the welfare of the country? There are many honorable exceptions; but we do think the general tone of female education is bad. The greatest and most universal

---

[1] Dental hygiene was in its infancy at this time; tooth loss was common.
[2] Rum and water, a traditional drink in New England.

error is, teaching girls to exaggerate the importance of getting married; and of course to place an undue importance upon the polite attentions of gentlemen. It was but a few days since, I heard a pretty and sensible girl say, "Did you ever see a man so ridiculously fond of his daughters as Mr.———? He is all the time with them. The other night, at the party, I went and took Anna away by mere force; for I knew she must feel dreadfully to have her father waiting upon her all the time, while the other girls were talking with the beaux." And another young friend of mine said, with an air most laughably serious, "I don't think Harriet and Julia enjoyed themselves at all last night. Don't you think, nobody but their *brother* offered to hand them to[1] the supper-room?"

That a mother should wish to see her daughters happily married, is natural and proper; that a young lady should be pleased with polite attentions is likewise natural and innocent; but this undue anxiety, this foolish excitement about showing off the attentions of somebody, no matter whom, is attended with consequences seriously injurious. It promotes envy and rivalship; it leads our young girls to spend their time between the public streets, the ball room, and the toilet; and, worst of all, it leads them to contract engagements, without any knowledge of their own hearts, merely for the sake of being married as soon as their companions. When married, they find themselves ignorant of the important duties of domestic life; and its quiet pleasures soon grow tiresome to minds worn out by frivolous excitements. If they remain unmarried, their disappointment and discontent are, of course, in proportion to their exaggerated idea of the eclat[2] attendant upon having a lover.[3] The evil increases in a startling ratio; for these girls, so injudiciously educated, will, nine times out of ten, make injudicious mothers, aunts, and friends; thus follies will be accumulated unto the third and fourth generation. Young ladies should be taught that usefulness is happiness, and that all other things are but incidental. With regard to matrimonial speculations, they should be taught nothing! Leave the affections to nature and to truth, and all will end well. How many can I at this moment recollect, who have made themselves unhappy by marrying for the sake of the *name* of being married! How many do I know, who have been instructed to such watchfulness in the game, that they have lost it by trumping their own tricks!

One great cause of the vanity, extravagance and idleness that are so fast growing upon our young ladies, is the absence of *domestic education*. By domestic education, I do not mean the sending daughters into the kitchen some half dozen times, to weary the patience of the cook, and to boast of it the next day in the parlor. I mean two or three years spent with a mother, assisting her in her duties, instructing brothers and sisters, and taking care of their own clothes. This is the way to make them happy, as well as good wives; for, being early accustomed to the duties of life, they will sit lightly as well as gracefully upon them.

But what time do modern girls have for the formation of quiet, domestic habits? Until sixteen they go to school; sometimes these years are judiciously spent, and sometimes they are half wasted; too often they are spent in acquiring the *elements* of a thousand sciences, without being thoroughly acquainted with any; or in a variety of accomplishments of very doubtful value to people of moderate fortune. As soon as they leave school, (and sometimes before,) they begin a round of balls and parties, and staying with gay young friends. Dress and flattery take up

---

[1] Escort them into.   [2] Acclaim.   [3] A suitor.

all their thoughts. What time have they to learn to be useful? What time have they to cultivate the still and gentle affections, which must, in every situation of life, have such an important effect on a woman's character and happiness?

As far as parents can judge what will be a daughter's station, education should be adapted to it; but it is well to remember that it is always easy to know how to spend riches, and always safe to know how to bear poverty.

A superficial acquaintance with such accomplishments as music and drawing is useless and undesirable. They should not be attempted unless there is taste, talent, and time enough to attain excellence. I have frequently heard young women of moderate fortune say, "I have not opened my piano these five years. I wish I had the money expended upon it. If I had employed as much time in learning useful things, I should have been better fitted for the cares of my family."

By these remarks I do not mean to discourage an attention to the graces of life. Gentility and taste are always lovely in all situations. But good things, carried to excess, are often productive of bad consequences. When accomplishments and dress interfere with the duties and permanent happiness of life, they are unjustifiable and displeasing; but where there is a solid foundation in mind and heart, all those elegancies are but becoming ornaments.

Some are likely to have more use for them than others; and they are justified in spending more time and money upon them. But no one should be taught to consider them valuable for mere parade and attraction. Making the education of girls such a series of "man-traps," makes the whole system unhealthy, by poisoning the motive.

1829

CHOCORUA'S CURSE*

The rocky county of Strafford, New-Hampshire, is remarkable for its wild and broken scenery. Ranges of hills towering one above another, as if eager to look upon the beautiful country, which afar off lies sleeping in the embrace of heaven; precipices, from which the young eagles take their flight to the sun; dells rugged and tangled as the dominions of Roderick Vich Alpine, and ravines dark and deep enough for the death scene of a bandit, form the magnificent characteristics of this picturesque region.

A high precipice, called Chocorua's Cliff, is rendered peculiarly interesting by a legend which tradition has scarcely saved from utter oblivion. Had it been in Scotland, perhaps the genius of Sir Walter[1] would have hallowed it, and Americans would have crowded there to kindle fancy on the altar of memory. Being in the midst of our own romantic scenery, it is little known, and less visited; for the vicinity is as yet untraversed by railroads or canals, and no "Mountain House," perched on these tremendous battlements, allures the traveller hither to mock the

---

* First published in the *Token* in 1830. Set in a real county in New Hampshire, Child's story invokes elements of legend (young eagles flying to the sun, the mountainous dominions of Roderick Vich Alpine) to develop an American parable concerning red men and white, nature and civilization.

[1] Sir Walter Scott (1771–1832), a Scottish novelist and poet whose storytelling imbued history and setting with the aura of romance.

majesty of nature with the insipidities of fashion. Our distinguished artist, Mr. Cole,[2] found the sunshine and the winds sleeping upon it in solitude and secresy; and his pencil has brought it before us in its stern repose.

In olden times, when Goffe and Whalley[3] passed for wizards and mountain spirits among the superstitious, the vicinity of the spot we have been describing was occupied by a very small colony, which, either from discontent or enterprise, had retired into this remote part of New-Hampshire. Most of them were ordinary men, led to this independent mode of life from an impatience of restraint, which as frequently accompanies vulgar obstinacy as generous pride. But there was one master spirit among them, who was capable of a higher destiny than he ever fulfilled. The consciousness of this had stamped something of proud humility on the face of Cornelius Campbell; something of a haughty spirit, strongly curbed by circumstances he could not control, and at which he scorned to murmur. He assumed no superiority; but unconsciously he threw around him the spell of intellect, and his companions felt, they knew not why, that he was "among them, but not of them." His stature was gigantic, and he had the bold, quick, tread of one who had wandered frequently and fearlessly among the terrible hiding-places of nature. His voice was harsh, but his whole countenance possessed singular capabilities for tenderness of expression; and sometimes, under the gentle influence of domestic excitement, his hard features would be rapidly lighted up, seeming like the sunshine flying over the shaded fields in an April day.

His companion was one peculiarly calculated to excite and retain the deep, strong energies of manly love. She had possessed extraordinary beauty; and had, in the full maturity of an excellent judgment, relinquished several splendid alliances, and incurred her father's displeasure, for the sake of Cornelius Campbell. Had political circumstances proved favourable, his talents and ambition would unquestionably have worked out a path to emolument and fame; but he had been a zealous and active enemy of the Stuarts, and the restoration of Charles the Second was the death-warrant of his hopes. Immediate flight became necessary, and America was the chosen place of refuge. His adherence to Cromwell's party[4] was not occasioned by religious sympathy, but by political views, too liberal and philosophical for the state of the people; therefore Cornelius Campbell was no favourite with our forefathers, and being of a proud nature, he withdrew with his family to the solitary place we have mentioned.

It seemed a hard fate for one who had from childhood been accustomed to indulgence and admiration, yet Mrs. Campbell enjoyed more than she had done in her days of splendour; so much deeper are the sources of happiness than those of gaiety. Even her face had suffered little from time and hardship. The bloom on her cheek, which in youth had been like the sweet-pea blossom, that most feminine of all flowers, had, it is true, somewhat faded; but her rich, intellectual expression, did but receive additional majesty from years; and the exercise of quiet domestic

[2] Thomas Cole (1801–1848), an English-born painter famous for his landscapes of the Hudson River. Child refers to a Cole painting used as an illustration for this story in the *Token* in 1830.
[3] William Goffe (1605–1679) and his father-in-law, Edward Whalley (?–1675?), were members of the court that signed the death warrant of King Charles I, or Charles Stuart (1600–1649), in 1649. Following the restoration of Charles II (1630–1685) to the throne of England in 1660, they fled to New England and lived in hiding near Hadley, Massachusetts.
[4] Oliver Cromwell (1599–1658), a Puritan leader and Lord Protector of England from 1653 to 1658, who demanded execution at Charles I's trial in 1649. Because Child's character Cornelius Campbell sympathizes with Cromwell on political and not religious grounds, he is unpopular with American Puritans.

love, which, where it is suffered to exist, always deepens and brightens with time, had given a bland and placid expression, which might well have atoned for the absence of more striking beauty. To such a woman as Caroline Campbell, of what use would have been some modern doctrines of equality and independence?

With a mind sufficiently cultivated to appreciate and enjoy her husband's intellectual energies, she had a heart that could not have found another home. The bird will drop into its nest though the treasures of earth and sky are open. To have proved marriage a tyranny, and the cares of domestic life a thraldom, would have affected Caroline Campbell as little, as to be told that the pure, sweet atmosphere she breathed, was pressing upon her so many pounds to every square inch! Over such a heart, and such a soul, external circumstances have little power; all worldly interest was concentrated in her husband and babes, and her spirit was satisfied with that inexhaustible fountain of joy which nature gives, and God has blessed.

A very small settlement, in such a remote place, was of course subject to inconvenience and occasional suffering. From the Indians they received neither injury nor insult. No cause of quarrel had ever arisen; and, although their frequent visits were sometimes troublesome, they never had given indications of jealousy or malice. Chocorua was a prophet among them, and as such an object of peculiar respect. He had a mind which education and motive would have nerved with giant strength; but growing up in savage freedom, it wasted itself in dark, fierce, ungovernable passions. There was something fearful in the quiet haughtiness of his lip—it seemed so like slumbering power, too proud to be lightly roused, and too implacable to sleep again. In his small, black, fiery eye, expression lay coiled up like a beautiful snake. The white people knew that his hatred would be terrible; but they had never provoked it, and even the children became too much accustomed to him to fear him.

Chocorua had a son, about nine or ten years old, to whom Caroline Campbell had occasionally made such gaudy presents as were likely to attract his savage fancy. This won the child's affections, so that he became a familiar visitant, almost an inmate of their dwelling; and being unrestrained by the courtesies of civilized life, he would inspect everything, and taste of everything which came in his way. Some poison, prepared for a mischievous fox, which had long troubled the little settlement, was discovered and drunk by the Indian boy; and he went home to his father to sicken and die.[5] From that moment jealousy and hatred took possession of Chocorua's soul. He never told his suspicions—he brooded over them in secret, to nourish the deadly revenge he contemplated against Cornelius Campbell.

The story of Indian animosity is always the same. Cornelius Campbell left his hut for the fields early one bright, balmy morning in June. Still a lover, though ten years a husband, his last look was turned towards his wife, answering her parting smile—his last action a kiss for each of his children. When he returned to dinner, they were dead—all dead! and their disfigured bodies too cruelly showed that an Indian's hand had done the work!

In such a mind grief, like all other emotions, was tempestuous. Home had been to him the only verdant spot in the wide desert of life. In his wife and children he had garnered up all his heart; and now they were torn from him, the remembrance of their love clung to him like the death-grapple of a drowning man, sinking him

---

[5] Child does not belabor the point, but enmity and escalating violence in this story come from the poisoning of the environment by white settlers.

down, down, into darkness and death. This was followed by a calm a thousand times more terrible—the creeping agony of despair, that brings with it no power of resistance.

> "It was as if the dead could feel
> The icy worm around him steal."

Such, for many days, was the state of Cornelius Campbell. Those who knew and reverenced him, feared that the spark of reason was forever extinguished. But it rekindled again, and with it came a wild, demoniac spirit of revenge. The death-groan of Chocorua would make him smile in his dreams; and when he waked, death seemed too pitiful a vengeance for the anguish that was eating into his very soul.

Chocorua's brethren were absent on a hunting expedition at the time he committed the murder; and those who watched his movements observed that he frequently climbed the high precipice, which afterward took his name, probably looking out for indications of their return.

Here Cornelius Campbell resolved to effect his daily purpose. A party was formed under his guidance, to cut off all chance of retreat, and the dark-minded prophet was to be hunted like a wild beast to his lair.

The morning sun had scarce cleared away the fogs when Chocorua started at a loud voice from beneath the precipice, commanding him to throw himself into the deep abyss below. He knew the voice of his enemy, and replied with an Indian's calmness, "The Great Spirit gave life to Chocorua; and Chocorua will not throw it away at the command of a white man." "Then hear the Great Spirit speak in the white man's thunder!" exclaimed Cornelius Campbell, as he pointed his gun to the precipice. Chocorua, though fierce and fearless as a panther, had never overcome his dread of fire-arms. He placed his hand upon his ears to shut out the stunning report; the next moment the blood bubbled from his neck, and he reeled fearfully on the edge of the precipice. But he recovered himself, and, raising himself on his hands, he spoke in a loud voice, that grew more terrific as its huskiness increased, "A curse upon ye, white men! May the Great Spirit curse ye when he speaks in the clouds, and his words are fire! Chocorua had a son—and ye killed him while his eye still loved to look on the bright sun, and the green earth! The Evil Spirit breathe death upon your cattle! Your graves lie in the war path of the Indian! Panthers howl, and wolves fatten over your bones! Chocorua goes to the Great Spirit—his curse stays with the white men!"

The prophet sunk upon the ground, still uttering inaudible curses—and they left his bones to whiten in the sun. But his curse rested on the settlement. The tomahawk and scalping knife were busy among them, the winds tore up the trees and hurled them at their dwellings, their crops were blasted, their cattle died, and sickness came upon their strongest men. At last the remnant of them departed from the fatal spot to mingle with more populous and prosperous colonies. Cornelius Campbell became a hermit, seldom seeking or seeing his fellow men; and two years after he was found dead in his hut.

To this day the town of Burton,[6] in New-Hampshire, is remarkable for a pestilence which infects its cattle; and the superstitious think that Chocorua's spirit still sits enthroned upon his precipice, breathing a curse upon them.

1830

---

[6] A fictional town.

from **THE FREEDMEN'S BOOK***

TO THE FREEDMEN[1]

I have prepared this book expressly for you, with the hope that those of you who can read will read it aloud to others, and that all of you will derive fresh strength and courage from this true record of what colored men have accomplished, under great disadvantages.

I have written all the biographies over again, in order to give you as much information as possible in the fewest words. I take nothing for my services; and the book is sold to you at the cost of paper, printing, and binding. Whatever money you pay for any of the volumes will be immediately invested in other volumes to be sent to freedmen in various parts of the country, on the same terms; and whatever money remains in my hands, when the book ceases to sell, will be given to the Freedmen's Aid Association, to be expended in schools for you and your children.

Your old friend,

L. MARIA CHILD.

PHILLIS WHEATLEY[2]

Phillis Wheatley was born in Africa, and brought to Boston, Massachusetts, in the year 1761,—a little more than a hundred years ago. At that time the people in Massachusetts held slaves.[3] The wife[4] of Mr. John Wheatley of Boston had several slaves; but they were getting too old to be very active, and she wanted to purchase a young girl, whom she could train up in such a manner as to make her a good domestic. She went to the slave-market for that purpose, and there she saw a little girl with no other clothing than a piece of dirty, ragged carpeting tied round her. She looked as if her health was feeble,—probably owing to her sufferings in the slave-ship, and to the fact of her having no one to care for her after she landed. Mrs. Wheatley was a kind, religious woman; and though she considered the sickly look of the child an objection, there was something so gentle and modest in the expression of her dark countenance, that her heart was drawn toward her, and she bought her in preference to several others who looked more robust. She took her home in her chaise, put her in a bath, and dressed her in clean clothes. They could not at first understand her; for she spoke an African dialect, sprinkled with a few words of broken English; and when she could not make herself understood, she resorted to a variety of gestures and signs. She did not know her own age, but, from her shedding her front teeth at that time, she was supposed to be about seven years old. She could not tell how long it was since the slave-traders tore her from her parents, nor where she had been since that time. The poor little orphan had

---

* Long active in the cause of abolition, Child published this collection of biographical sketches and poems specifically for freed slaves in 1869.
[1] The author's preface.
[2] Wheatley (1753?–1784) was a slave who earned recognition as a poet. Throughout this book, Child adapts her style and diction to an audience with an elementary knowledge of English and of the achievements of other African Americans.
[3] Slavery was abolished in Massachusetts in 1783.   [4] Susannah Wheatley.

probably gone through so much suffering and terror, and been so unable to make herself understood by anybody, that her mind had become bewildered concerning the past. She soon learned to speak English; but she could remember nothing about Africa, except that she used to see her mother pour out water before the rising sun. Almost all of the ancient nations of the world supposed that a Great Spirit had his dwelling in the sun, and they worshipped that Spirit in various forms. One of the most common modes of worship was to pour out water, or wine, at the rising of the sun, and to utter a brief prayer to the Spirit of that glorious luminary. Probably this ancient custom had been handed down, age after age, in Africa, and in that fashion the untaught mother of little Phillis continued to worship the god of her ancestors. The sight of the great splendid orb, coming she knew not whence, rising apparently out of the hills to make the whole world glorious with light, and the devout reverence with which her mother hailed its return every morning, might naturally impress the child's imagination so deeply, that she remembered it after she had forgotten everything else about her native land.

A wonderful change took place in the little forlorn stranger in the course of a year and a half. She not only learned to speak English correctly, but she was able to read fluently in any part of the Bible. She evidently possessed uncommon intelligence and a great desire for knowledge. She was often found trying to make letters with charcoal on the walls and fences. Mrs. Wheatley's daughter, perceiving her eagerness to learn, undertook to teach her to read and write. She found this an easy task, for her pupil learned with astonishing quickness. At the same time she showed such an amiable, affectionate disposition, that all members of the family became much attached to her. Her gratitude to her kind, motherly mistress was unbounded, and her greatest delight was to do anything to please her.

When she was about fourteen years old, she began to write poetry; and it was pretty good poetry, too. Owing to these uncommon manifestations of intelligence, and to the delicacy of her health, she was never put to hard household work, as was intended at the time of her purchase. She was kept constantly with Mrs. Wheatley and her daughter, employed in light and easy services for them. Her poetry attracted attention, and Mrs. Wheatley's friends lent her books, which she read with great eagerness. She soon acquired a good knowledge of geography, history, and English poetry; of the last she was particularly fond. After a while, they found she was trying to learn Latin, which she so far mastered as to be able to read it understandingly. There was no law in Massachusetts against slaves learning to read and write, as there have been in many of the States; and her mistress, so far from trying to hinder her, did everything to encourage her love of learning. She always called her affectionately, "My Phillis," and seemed to be as proud of her attainments as if she had been her own daughter. She even allowed her to have a fire and light in her own chamber in the evening, that she might study and write down her thoughts whenever they came to her.

Phillis was of a very religious turn of mind, and when she was about sixteen she joined the Orthodox Church, that worshipped in the Old-South Meeting-house in Boston. Her character and deportment were such that she was considered an ornament to the church. Clergymen and other literary persons who visited Mrs. Wheatley's took a good deal of notice of her. Her poems were brought forward to be read to the company, and were often much praised. She was not unfrequently invited to the houses of wealthy and distinguished people, who liked to show her off as a kind of wonder. Most young girls would have had their heads completely turned by so much flattery and attention; but seriousness and humility seemed to be natural to Phillis. She always retained the same gentle, modest deportment that had won Mrs. Wheatley's heart when she first saw her in the slave-market. Sometimes, when she went abroad,[5] she was invited to sit at table with other guests; but she always modestly declined, and requested that a plate might be placed for her on a side-table. Being well aware of the common prejudice against her complexion, she feared that some one might be offended by her company at their meals. By pursuing this course she manifested a natural politeness, which proved her to be more truly refined than any person could be who objected to sit beside her on account of her color.

Although she was tenderly cared for, and not required to do any fatiguing work, her constitution never recovered from the shock it had received in early childhood. When she was about nineteen years old,[6] her health failed so rapidly that physicians said it was necessary for her to take a sea-voyage. A son of Mr. Wheatley's was going to England on commercial business, and his mother proposed that Phillis should go with him.

In England she received even more attention than had been bestowed upon her at home. Several of the nobility invited her to their houses; and her poems were published in a volume, with an engraved likeness of the author.[7] In this picture she looks gentle and thoughtful, and the shape of her head denotes intellect. One of the engravings was sent to Mrs. Wheatley, who was delighted with it. When one of her relatives called, she pointed it out to her, and said, "Look at my Phillis! Does she not seem as if she would speak to me?"

Still the young poetess was not spoiled by flattery. One of the relatives of Mrs. Wheatley informs us, that "not all the attention she received, nor all the honors that were heaped upon her, had the slightest influence upon her temper and deportment. She was still the same single-hearted, unsophisticated being."

She addressed a poem to the Earl of Dartmouth,[8] who was very kind to her during her visit to England. Having expressed a hope for the overthrow of tyranny, she says:—

> "Should you, my Lord, while you peruse my song,
> Wonder from whence my love of Freedom sprung,—
> Whence flow these wishes for the common good,
> By feeling hearts alone best understood,—
> I, young in life, by seeming cruel fate,
> Was snatched from Afric's fancied happy state.
> What pangs excruciating must molest,
> What sorrows labor in my parent's breast!
> Steeled was that soul, and by no misery moved,
> That from a father seized his babe beloved.
> Such was my case; and can I then but pray
> Others may never feel tyrannic sway."

The English friends of Phillis wished to present her to their king, George the Third,[9] who was soon expected in London. But letters from America informed her

---

[5] Accompanied the Wheatleys on visits to friends.   [6] In 1773.

[7] With the cooperation of the countess of Huntingdon (Selina Hastings [1707–1791]), Susannah Wheatley arranged to have a volume of Phillis's poems published in London in 1773 under the title *Poems*.

[8] William Legge (1753–1801).

[9] George III (1738–1820), king of England during the American Revolution, reigned from 1760 to 1820.

that her beloved benefactress, Mrs. Wheatley, was in declining health, and greatly desired to see her. No honors could divert her mind from the friend of her childhood. She returned to Boston immediately. The good lady died soon after; Mr. Wheatley soon followed; and the daughter, the kind instructress of her youth, did not long survive. The son married and settled in England. For a short time Phillis stayed with a friend of her deceased benefactress; then she hired a room and lived by herself. It was a sad change for her.

The war of the American Revolution broke out. In the autumn of 1776 General Washington had his headquarters at Cambridge, Massachusetts; and the spirit moved Phillis to address some complimentary verses to him.[10] In reply, he sent her the following courteous note:—

"I thank you most sincerely for your polite notice of me in the elegant lines you enclosed. However undeserving I may be of such encomium,[11] the style and manner exhibit a striking proof of your poetical talents. In honor of which, and as a tribute justly due to you, I would have published the poem, had I not been apprehensive that, while I only meant to give the world this new instance of your genius, I might have incurred the imputation of vanity. This, and nothing else, determined me not to give it a place in the public prints.

"If you should ever come to Cambridge, or near headquarters, I shall be happy to see a person so favored by the Muses,[12] and to whom Nature had been so liberal and beneficient in her dispensations.

"I am, with great respect,

"Your obedient, humble servant,

"GEORGE WASHINGTON."

The early friends of Phillis were dead, or scattered abroad, and she felt alone in the world. She formed an acquaintance with a colored man by the name of Peters,[13] who kept a grocery shop. He was more than commonly intelligent, spoke fluently, wrote easily, dressed well, and was handsome in his person. He offered marriage, and in an evil hour she accepted him. He proved to be lazy, proud, and harsh-tempered. He neglected his business, failed; and became very poor. Though unwilling to do hard work himself, he wanted to make a drudge of his wife. Her constitution was frail, she had been unaccustomed to hardship, and she was the mother of three little children, with no one to help her in her household labors and cares. He had no pity on her, and instead of trying to lighten her load, he made it heavier by his bad temper. The little ones sickened and died, and their gentle mother was completely broken down by toil and sorrow. Some of the descendants of her lamented mistress at last heard of her illness and went to see her. They found her in a forlorn situation, suffering for the common comforts of life. The Revolutionary war was still raging. Everybody was mourning for sons and husbands slain in battle. The country was very poor. The currency was so deranged that a goose cost forty dollars, and other articles in proportion. In such a state of things, people were too anxious and troubled to think about the African poetess, whom they had once delighted to honor; or if they transiently remembered her,

[10] "To His Excellency General Washington," which was dated October 26, 1775, not 1776.

[11] High praise.

[12] Child's note: "The ancient Greeks supposed that nine goddesses, whom they named Muses, inspired people to write various kinds of poetry."

[13] John Peters, a freed man in Boston, whom Phillis married in 1778.

they took it for granted that her husband provided for her. And so it happened that the gifted woman who had been patronized by wealthy Bostonians, and who had rolled through London in the splendid carriages of the English nobility, lay dying alone, in a cold, dirty, comfortless room. It was a mournful reverse of fortune; but she was patient and resigned. She made no complaint of her unfeeling husband; but the neighbors said that when a load of wood was sent to her, he felt himself too much a gentleman to saw it, though his wife was shivering with cold. The descendants of Mrs. Wheatley did what they could to relieve her wants, after they discovered her extremely destitute condition; but, fortunately for her, she soon went "where the wicked cease from troubling, and where the weary are at rest."

Her husband was so generally disliked, that people never called her Mrs. Peters. She was always called Phillis Wheatley, the name bestowed upon her when she first entered the service of her benefactress, and by which she had become known as a poetess.

1869

Ralph Waldo Emerson
(1803–1882)

Born in Boston, Massachusetts, in 1803, Ralph Waldo Emerson was the son of William Emerson, a descendant of a long line of New England clergymen, and Ruth Haskins, whose mercantile family had flourished in the distillery business. As Unitarian pastor of the First Church in Boston, William Emerson worked steadily at his sermons and at church business, never free from a concern about financial stability. His death when Ralph was eight years old left the family in straitened circumstances. The boy was raised by his mother, who went to work managing a series of boardinghouses, and his pious, sardonic, and talented Aunt Mary Moody Emerson. At the Boston Latin school Emerson received the kind of basic education that prepared him to enter Harvard College in 1817.

During these years the reigning philosophy at Harvard (and at most American colleges) was that of John Locke and the eighteenth-century Scottish "Common Sense" realists. Emerson dutifully studied the Scots under several professors, among them Levi Frisbie, who also came to Harvard in 1817 and began to expound theories on the development of the moral sense that he derived from the Common Sense philosophy of Thomas Reid and Dugald Stewart. In his senior year Emerson received a prize for his "Dissertation on the Present State of Ethical Philosophy," a thirty-four-page effort that emphasizes the importance of Reid and Stewart and shows little interest in the new German philosophical thought. Despite what this award might seem to signify, Emerson did not excel in his studies at Harvard. In 1821 he graduated in the middle of his class of fifty-nine students. But at Harvard he began the habit of keeping a journal, in which he recorded ideas, attitudes, and responses to books and authors. Over the years his journals, rich in concept and detail, became a register of the life of a mind; they provided the seeds and verbal patterns for many of Emerson's essays, lectures, and poems and served as a storehouse for the type of allusion that brought a characteristic texture to his oral and written work.

After his graduation Emerson taught intermittently and without commitment at his brother's Boston school for young ladies and lived for some months with his family near the Shaker village at Canterbury, New Hampshire. In 1825 he enrolled in the Harvard Divinity School. Although he showed no special zeal for the ministry even during his studies, he was approved to preach in October 1826 and made junior pastor at the Old Second Church in Boston, where such resolute Puritans as Increase Mather and Cotton Mather had once held office. Now it was Unitarian territory, and the liberal movement that rejected Calvinist orthodoxy and emphasized the individual's capacity for moral improvement became the context in which Emerson's doubts and convictions about personal and institutionalized faith came to fruition.

During the third year of his ministry, and with the unsolicited approval of his Aunt Mary (who was never reluctant to offer an opinion), Emerson married Ellen Tucker of Concord, New Hampshire. With this aspiring young poet he shared an all-too-brief period of happiness that temporarily subordinated the issue of religious doubt. But Ellen died of tuberculosis in 1831 when she was nineteen. A year later, with the feeling of being imprisoned in a diminishing faith, Emerson resigned his pastorate because he no longer believed in the validity of the Lord's Supper, the sacrament of communion. Such a move was inevitable: as a minister Emerson lacked the commitment of one whose faith was alive and ever-deepening; he was more interested in moral rectitude and virtuous living than in the revealed truths of the Bible. Indeed, the first inklings of an Emersonian emphasis on the "self" can be seen in his sermons. Increasingly, he felt it necessary to discern the origins of the self, to trace them to their source. When he concluded that the origins were in an Infinite Being, the foundation for his impressive work of the 1830s and 1840s was set.

On Christmas Day, 1832, Emerson sailed to Europe, where he visited Italy, France, and England. He saw the English writer and poet Walter Savage Landor in Florence and was deeply impressed by a tour of the Jardin des Plantes in Paris, which suggested to Emerson the concept of a unity among all living things. In England he visited Samuel Taylor Coleridge, whose ideas later helped him merge conceptually the philosophies of Neoplatonism and transcendental idealism. Emerson also called on Thomas Carlyle in Scotland at Craigenputtock and began a lasting friendship based on mutual perspectives and intellectual respect. Although Emerson made other trips to England and France between 1847 and 1848 and in 1872, this first visit released his thinking in a formative way.

Once back in the United States Emerson settled in Concord, Massachusetts. The following year, 1835, he married Lydia Jackson, who had heard him speak both in Boston and in her hometown of Plymouth, Massachusetts, and felt very much attuned to the developing tenor of his mind. With a legacy of $1,200 a year from his first wife and money earned by lecturing on the lyceum, or public lecture hall, circuit, Emerson and Lydian (as he called her) settled into a Concord life that provided generous opportunities for intellectual ferment. Beginning with the publication of *Nature* in 1836, Emerson established a reputation for originality of mind that expanded, not always to unqualified applause, over the next decade. Only two weeks after the publication of this eloquent manifesto, the Transcendental Club held the first of its informal meetings. With a membership that included the poet Jones Very, the abolitionist Theodore Parker, and the reformer George Ripley, who founded Brook Farm in 1841, as well as Emerson, this group of speculative thinkers (who called themselves the Symposium, in honor of Plato) met irregularly for more than six years, examining such matters as the basis of faith and the integrity of philosophical idealism. For Emerson the years marked a period of vibrant growth.

In *Nature* Emerson invokes the relation of the individual and the infinite, as he had done in his early sermons, but in this context to explain the possibility of creative human expression: defining "proper creation" as "the working of the Original Cause through the

Christopher Pearse Cranch's caricature of lines from Ralph Waldo Emerson's Nature.

"Standing on the bare ground, — my head bathed by the blithe air, & uplifted into infinite space, — all mean egotism vanishes. I become a transparent Eyeball." *Nature, p. 13.*

instruments he has already made," Emerson extends the miracle of Creation to the inspired words of poets and other transcendentally directed persons. Out of this belief in divine inspiration (by its very nature individual, noninstitutional, even preinstitutional) came the moral imperatives of Emerson's best-known essays. The nationalism of his "American Scholar" address delivered at Harvard in 1837 has an edge, an assurance, because of Emerson's commitment to the originating self. In his appreciative study of Emerson in 1885, Oliver Wendell Holmes looked back on that speech as "Our intellectual Declaration of Independence." At Harvard in 1838 Emerson gave "The Divinity School Ad-dress," the product of ideas that had percolated in his mind for a decade; on that occasion he spoke explicitly for intuitive spiritual experience and against formal religious institutions. As a result, he was not invited to speak at Harvard again for thirty years.

Emerson's life and work in the late 1830s thus promoted him into prominence. And with the publication of *Essays* (1841) and *Essays, Second Series* (1844), Emerson became a major force in American intellectual and cultural life. Such essays as "Self-Reliance" and "The Over-Soul" (from *Essays*) and "The Poet" (from *Second Series*) testify to the accumulating vitality of his ideas. There were those who objected to the non-Christian cast of Emerson's thought: as Ralph L. Rusk reports in his detailed biography of Emerson (1949), Mary Moody Emerson was not alone in calling "Self-Reliance" a "strange medley of atheism and false independence." But the formidable nature of Emerson's writing and lecturing was apparent to a variety of audiences. During these years he continued speaking on lyceum programs. And his involvement with the Transcendental Club brought him to serve as editor of *The Dial* from 1842 to 1844.

By the mid 1840s the radical thrust of Emerson's thinking could extend no farther. Even before that time the weight of experience and personal grief had begun to temper the buoyant perspective of such essays as "Self-Reliance" and "The Over-Soul." For Emerson was no stranger to loss: the death of his first wife in 1831 had been followed by the death of two brothers—Edward in 1834 (following seven years of mental instability) and Charles in 1836. And in 1842 the death of his son Waldo, not yet six years old, from scarlet fever affected him and Lydian deeply. Emerson's grief found expression both in the perplexed essay "Experience" (1844), where he confesses surprise at all he did not feel at this time of sorrow, and in the tender lines of the poem "Threnody" (1847), which portray Waldo as "the wondrous child," "the darling who shall not return." The reserved Emerson, who frequently expressed concern about his austerity of demeanor, is at his human best in this song of lamentation. In a marginal comment scrawled in his copy of the *Essays,* Herman Melville referred to "this Plato who talks thro' his nose" (with reference to Emerson's New England accent). In "Threnody," as Melville would have been the first to admit, Emerson is a father who writes from his heart.

With the publication of *Poems* in 1847, Emerson revealed a poetic impulse different in style and substance from that of such popular and accomplished writers as William Cullen Bryant and Henry Wadsworth Longfellow. Emerson was absorbed by a need to articulate. Elliptical in phasing, such poems as "The Problem" (1840) and "Ode, Inscribed to W. H. Channing" (1847) are demanding in argument, strikingly modern in line and image. The "Ode," particularly, shows an Emerson responsive to social issues of the day, just as his journals and letters testify to his deep moral concern over slavery, the Mexican War, and the removal of the Cherokee nation from the Southeast in the late 1830s. With their inability to be more than relentless efforts, Emerson's poems have an endearing vulnerability lacking in some of his more flinty prose.

In 1850 Emerson published *Representative Men,* a volume of seven essays based on lectures given in Boston in 1845 and 1846 and in England in 1847. Each of the essays is devoted to an individual who exemplifies, in Emerson's view, the best of humankind, who is an originator, a creator of possibility. Among these individuals are Plato, "the philosopher," Shakespeare, "the poet," and the Swedish theologian Emanuel Swedenborg, "the mystic." Six years later Emerson published *English Traits,* a series of incisive and perceptive observations derived from his lectures on England, given after his visit of 1847 to 1848. Two other volumes, *The Conduct of Life* (1860) and *Society and Solitude* (1870), register modifications in Emerson's attitude toward the individual in society. Based on materials from lyceum lectures, such essays as "Fate" and "Illusions" (in *Conduct*) offer a pessimistic and even sardonic view of human destiny, a view only partly offset by Emerson's refusal to be nihilistic. In the title essay "Society and Solitude," a more commonsense Emerson preaches the necessity for balance between the human need for solitude and that for social contact.

Contributing to the making of Emerson's ideas was an assortment of writers from different eras and nations, many of the important ones related by mystical tendencies and the romantic idea of organic form. Coleridge, Carlyle, and expounders of German idealism, for example, blended with Plato, Plotinus, and other Neoplatonic philosophers who sought to reconcile aspects of classical philosophy and Christianity; the ideas of Swedenborg and the experiences of the German mystic Jakob Böhme were linked in Emerson's mind and journals by the wisdom of sacred Eastern books such as the Hindu *Vedas* and the *Bhagavad-Gita.* The concern for the self no doubt came from the Puritan habit of inspecting the soul. But it was the forge of his own genius and temperament that took all these "influences" and produced Emerson's work.

In his later years Emerson suffered a gradual decline of his mental abilities. The writer who had lamented the manner in which we are enslaved by memory had finally no memory to encumber him. Gazing into the casket of his old friend Henry Wadsworth Longfellow in March 1882, Emerson asked who he was looking at, then retired in embarrassment when told. After almost a decade of senility, he died in April 1882 in Concord, the village in which his father had been born, and was buried in Sleepy Hollow Cemetary near the graves of Henry David Thoreau and Nathaniel Hawthorne.

Suggested Readings: *The Letters of Ralph Waldo Emerson*, ed. R. L. Rusk, 1939. *The Early Lectures of Ralph Waldo Emerson*, 3 vols., ed. S. Whicher, R. E. Spiller, and W.E. Williams, 1959–1972. *The Journals and Miscellaneous Notebooks of Ralph Waldo Emerson*, 16 vols., ed. W. Gilman et al., 1960–1986. *The Correspondence of Emerson and Carlyle*, ed. J. Slater, 1964. R. L. Rusk, *The Life of Ralph Waldo Emerson*, 1949. S. E. Whicher, *Freedom and Fate: An Inner Life of Ralph Waldo Emerson*, 1953. J. Porte, *Representative Man: Ralph Waldo Emerson in His Time*, 1979. J. Loving, *Emerson, Whitman, and the American Muse*, 1982. B. L. Packer, *Emerson's Fall: A New Interpretation of the Major Essays*, 1982. D. Van Leer, *Emerson's Epistemology: The Argument of the Essays*, 1986. M. Gonnaud, *An Uneasy Solitude: Individual and Society in the Work of Ralph Waldo Emerson*, 1987. M. K. Cayton, *Emerson's Emergence: Self and Society in the Transformation of New England, 1800–1845*, 1989. A. D. Holder, *Emerson's Rhetoric of Revelation: Nature, the Reader, and the Apocalypse Within*, 1989. J. Michael, *Emerson and Skepticism: The Cipher of the World*, 1989.

Texts Used: *Nature* and "The American Scholar": *The Collected Works of Ralph Waldo Emerson*, Vol. I, ed. A. R. Ferguson, 1971. "Self-Reliance" and "Circles": *The Collected Works*, Vol. II, ed. A. R. Ferguson and J. F. Carr, 1979. "The Poet": *The Collected Works*, Vol. III, ed. A. R. Ferguson, J. F. Carr, and D. E. Wilson, 1983. "Fate": *The Works of Ralph Waldo Emerson: The Conduct of Life*, 1888. "Thoreau": *Lectures and Biographical Sketches*, 1904. Poems: *Poems*, 1918. Journal entries from 1840: *The Journals and Miscellaneous Notebooks of Ralph Waldo Emerson*, Vol. VII: 1838–1842, ed. A. W. Plumstead and H. Hayford, 1969. From 1842: *The Journals*, Vol. VIII: 1841–1843, ed. W. H. Gilman and J. E. Parsons, 1970. From 1864: *The Journals*, Vol. XV: 1860–1866, ed. L. Allardt, D. W. Hill, and R. H. Bennett, 1982. Emerson to Whitman, 1855: W. Whitman, *Leaves of Grass*, ed. H. W. Blodgett and S. Bradley, 1965.

NATURE*

A subtle chain of countless rings
The next unto the farthest brings;
The eye reads omens where it goes,
And speaks all languages the rose;
And, striving to be man, the worm
Mounts through all the spires of form.[1]

INTRODUCTION

Our age is retrospective. It builds the sepulchres of the fathers. It writes biographies, histories, and criticism. The foregoing generations beheld God and nature face to face; we, through their eyes. Why should not we also enjoy an original relation to the universe? Why should not we have a poetry and philosophy of insight and not of tradition, and a religion by revelation to us, and not the history

---

* First published anonymously in 1836 at Emerson's expense, *Nature* was a major statement of ideas fundamental to New England transcendentalism.

[1] The epigraph for the first edition was the quotation "Nature is but an image or imitation of wisdom, the last thing of the soul; nature being a thing which doth only do, but not know," from the Roman Neoplatonic philosopher Plotinus (A.D. 205?–270). In the 1849 edition Emerson substituted his own lines of poetry, here.

of theirs? Embosomed for a season in nature, whose floods of life stream around and through us, and invite us by the powers they supply, to action proportioned to nature, why should we grope among the dry bones of the past, or put the living generation into masquerade out of its faded wardrobe? The sun shines to-day also. There is more wool and flax in the fields. There are new lands, new men, new thoughts. Let us demand our own works and laws and worship.

Undoubtedly we have no questions to ask which are unanswerable. We must trust the perfection of the creation so far, as to believe that whatever curiosity the order of things has awakened in our minds, the order of things can satisfy. Every man's condition is a solution in hieroglyphic to those inquiries he would put. He acts it as life, before he apprehends it as truth. In like manner, nature is already, in its forms and tendencies, describing its own design. Let us interrogate the great apparition, that shines so peacefully around us. Let us inquire, to what end is nature?

All science has one aim, namely, to find a theory of nature. We have theories of races and of functions, but scarcely yet a remote approach to an idea of creation. We are now so far from the road to truth, that religious teachers dispute and hate each other, and speculative men are esteemed unsound and frivolous. But to a sound judgment, the most abstract truth is the most practical. Whenever a true theory appears, it will be its own evidence. Its test is, that it will explain all phenomena. Now many are thought not only unexplained but inexplicable; as language, sleep, madness, dreams, beasts, sex.

Philosophically considered, the universe is composed of Nature and the Soul. Strictly speaking, therefore, all that is separate from us, all which Philosophy distinguishes as the NOT ME,[2] that is, both nature and art, all other men and my own body, must be ranked under this name, NATURE. In enumerating the values of nature and casting up their sum, I shall use the word in both senses;—in its common and in its philosophical import. In inquiries so general as our present one, the inaccuracy is not material; no confusion of thought will occur. *Nature,* in the common sense, refers to essences unchanged by man; space, the air, the river, the leaf. *Art* is applied to the mixture of his will with the same things, as in a house, a canal, a statue, a picture. But his operations taken together are so insignificant, a little chipping, baking, patching, and washing, that in an impression so grand as that of the world on the human mind, they do not vary the result.

CHAPTER I: NATURE

To go into solitude, a man needs to retire as much from his chamber as from society. I am not solitary whilst I read and write, though nobody is with me. But if a man would be alone, let him look at the stars. The rays that come from those heavenly worlds, will separate between him and vulgar things. One might think the atmosphere was made transparent with this design, to give man, in the heavenly bodies, the perpetual presence of the sublime. Seen in the streets of cities, how great they are! If the stars should appear one night in a thousand years, how would men believe and adore; and preserve for many generations the remembrance of the city of God which had been shown! But every night come out these envoys of beauty, and light the universe with their admonishing smile.

[2] A term used in *Sartor Resartus* (1833–1834), by Thomas Carlyle (1795–1881).

The stars awaken a certain reverence, because though always present, they are always inaccessible; but all natural objects make a kindred impression, when the mind is open to their influence. Nature never wears a mean appearance. Neither does the wisest man extort all her secret, and lose his curiosity by finding out all her perfection. Nature never became a toy to a wise spirit. The flowers, the animals, the mountains, reflected all the wisdom of his best hour, as much as they had delighted the simplicity of his childhood.

When we speak of nature in this manner, we have a distinct but most poetical sense in the mind. We mean the integrity of impression made by manifold natural objects. It is this which distinguishes the stick of timber of the wood-cutter, from the tree of the poet. The charming landscape which I saw this morning, is indubitably made up of some twenty or thirty farms. Miller owns this field, Locke that, and Manning the woodland beyond. But none of them owns the landscape. There is a property in the horizon which no man has but he whose eye can integrate all the parts, that is, the poet. This is the best part of these men's farms, yet to this their warranty-deeds give no title.

To speak truly, few adult persons can see nature. Most persons do not see the sun. At least they have a very superficial seeing. The sun illuminates only the eye of the man, but shines into the eye and the heart of the child. The lover of nature is he whose inward and outward senses are still truly adjusted to each other; who has retained the spirit of infancy even into the era of manhood. His intercourse with heaven and earth, becomes part of his daily food. In the presence of nature, a wild delight runs through the man, in spite of real sorrows. Nature says,—he is my creature, and maugre[3] all his impertinent griefs, he shall be glad with me. Not the sun or the summer alone, but every hour and season yields its tribute of delight; for every hour and change corresponds to and authorizes a different state of the mind, from breathless noon to grimmest midnight. Nature is a setting that fits equally well a comic or a mourning piece. In good health, the air is a cordial of incredibly virtue. Crossing a bare common, in snow puddles, at twilight, under a clouded sky, without having in my thoughts any occurrence of special good fortune, I have enjoyed a perfect exhilaration. Almost I fear to think how glad I am. In the woods too, a man casts off his years, as the snake his slough, and at what period soever of life, is always a child. In the woods, is perpetual youth. Within these plantations of God, a decorum and sanctity reign, a perennial festival is dressed, and the guest sees not how he should tire of them in a thousand years. In the woods, we return to reason and faith. There I feel that nothing can befal me in life,—no disgrace, no calamity, (leaving me my eyes,) which nature cannot repair. Standing on the bare ground,—my head bathed by the blithe air, and uplifted into infinite space,—all mean egotism vanishes. I become a transparent eye-ball. I am nothing. I see all. The currents of the Universal Being circulate through me; I am part or particle of God.[4] The name of the nearest friend sounds then foreign and accidental. To be brothers, to be acquaintances,—master or servant, is then a trifle and a disturbance. I am the lover of uncontained and immortal beauty. In the wilderness, I find something more dear and connate[5] than in streets or villages. In

---

[3] Despite.

[4] This famous "transparent eye-ball" passage ends on a mystical note, with the speaker not simply a creature of God but "part or particle of God." For Emerson, this sense of wholeness, oneness, is the very condition of spiritual health.

[5] Related, innate.

the tranquil landscape, and especially in the distant line of the horizon, man beholds somewhat as beautiful as his own nature.

The greatest delight which the fields and woods minister, is the suggestion of an occult relation between man and the vegetable. I am not alone and unacknowledged. They nod to me and I to them. The waving of the boughs in the storm, is new to me and old. It takes me by surprise, and yet is not unknown. Its effect is like that of a higher thought or a better emotion coming over me, when I deemed I was thinking justly or doing right.

Yet it is certain that the power to produce this delight, does not reside in nature, but in man, or in a harmony of both. It is necessary to use these pleasures with great temperance. For, nature is not always tricked[6] in holiday attire, but the same scene which yesterday breathed perfume and glittered as for the frolic of the nymphs, is overspread with melancholy today. Nature always wears the colors of the spirit. To a man laboring under calamity, the heat of his own fire hath sadness in it. Then, there is a kind of contempt of the landscape felt by him who has just lost by death a dear friend. The sky is less grand as it shuts down over less worth in the population.

Chapter II: Commodity[7]

Whoever considers the final cause[8] of the world, will discern a multitude of uses that enter as parts into that result. They all admit of being thrown into one of the following classes: Commodity; Beauty; Language; and Discipline.

Under the general name of Commodity, I rank all those advantages which our senses owe to nature. This, of course, is a benefit which is temporary and mediate,[9] not ultimate, like its service to the soul. Yet although low, it is perfect in its kind, and is the only use of nature which all men apprehend. The misery of man appears like childish petulance, when we explore the steady and prodigal provision that has been made for his support and delight on this green ball which floats him through the heavens. What angels invented these splendid ornaments, these rich conveniences, this ocean of air above, this ocean of water beneath, this firmament of earth between? this zodiac of lights, this tent of dropping clouds, this striped coat of climates, this fourfold year? Beasts, fire, water, stones, and corn serve him. The field is at once his floor, his work-yard, his play-ground, his garden, and his bed.

> "More servants wait on man
> Than he'll take notice of."———[10]

Nature, in its ministry to man, is not only the material, but is also the process and the result. All the parts incessantly work into each other's hands for the profit of man. The wind sows the seed; the sun evaporates the sea; the wind blows the vapor to the field; the ice, on the other side of the planet, condenses rain on this;

---

[6] Dressed. [7] Usefulness. [8] Purpose.
[9] In the middle (of our lives, experiences, daily affairs).
[10] From "Man" (1633), by the English poet George Herbert (1593–1633). Emerson quotes from this poem at length in Chapter 8.

the rain feeds the plant; the plant feeds the animal; and thus the endless circulations of the divine charity nourish man.

The useful arts are but reproductions or new combinations by the wit of man, of the same natural benefactors. He no longer waits for favoring gales, but by means of steam, he realizes the fable of Æolus's bag,[11] and carries the two and thirty winds in the boiler of his boat. To diminish friction, he paves the road with iron bars,[12] and, mounting a coach with a ship-load of men, animals, and merchandise behind him, he darts through the country, from town to town, like an eagle or a swallow through the air. By the aggregate of these aids, how is the face of the world changed, from the era of Noah to that of Napoleon! The private poor man hath cities, ships, canals, bridges, built for him. He goes to the post-office, and the human race run on his errands; to the book-shop, and the human race read and write of all that happens, for him; to the court-house, and nations repair his wrongs. He sets his house upon the road, and the human race go forth every morning, and shovel out the snow, and cut a path for him.

But there is no need of specifying particulars in this class of uses. The catalogue is endless, and the examples so obvious, that I shall leave them to the reader's reflection, with the general remark, that this mercenary benefit is one which has respect to a farther good. A man is fed, not that he may be fed, but that he may work.

Chapter III: Beauty

A nobler want of man is served by nature, namely, the love of Beauty.

The ancient Greeks called the world κόσμοδ,[13] beauty. Such is the constitution of all things, or such the plastic power of the human eye, that the primary forms, as the sky, the mountain, the tree, the animal, give us a delight *in and for themselves;* a pleasure arising from outline, color, motion, and grouping. This seems partly owing to the eye itself. The eye is the best of artists. By the mutual action of its structure and of the laws of light, perspective is produced, which integrates every mass of objects, of what character soever, into a well colored and shaded globe, so that where the particular objects are mean and unaffecting, the landscape which they compose, is round and symmetrical. And as the eye is the best composer, so light is the first of painters. There is no object so foul that intense light will not make beautiful. And the stimulus it affords to the sense, and a sort of infinitude which it hath, like space and time, make all matter gay. Even the corpse hath its own beauty. But beside this general grace diffused over nature, almost all the individual forms are agreeable to the eye, as is proved by our endless imitations of some of them, as the acorn, the grape, the pine-cone, the wheat-ear, the egg, the wings and forms of most birds, the lion's claw, the serpent, the butterfly, sea-shells, flames, clouds, buds, leaves, and the forms of many trees, as the palm.

For better consideration, we may distribute the aspects of Beauty in a threefold manner.

1. First, the simple perception of natural forms is a delight. The influence of

---

[11] In Book 10 of Homer's *Odyssey,* the Greek wind god Aeolus gives Odysseus a bag of winds to blow his ship homeward from Troy.
[12] Railroad tracks.   [13] "Cosmos": order, and hence the beauty of wholeness.

the forms and actions in nature, is so needful to man, that, in its lowest functions, it seems to lie on the confines of commodity and beauty. To the body and mind which have been cramped by noxious work or company, nature is medicinal and restores their tone. The tradesman, the attorney comes out of the din and craft[14] of the street, and sees the sky and the woods, and is a man again. In their eternal calm, he finds himself. The health of the eye seems to demand a horizon. We are never tired, so long as we can see far enough.

But in other hours, Nature satisfies the soul purely by its loveliness, and without any mixture of corporeal benefit. I have seen the spectacle of morning from the hill-top over against my house, from day-break to sun-rise, with emotions which an angel might share. The long slender bars of cloud float like fishes in the sea of crimson light. From the earth, as a shore, I look out into that silent sea. I seem to partake its rapid transformations: the active enchantment reaches my dust, and I dilate and conspire[15] with the morning wind. How does Nature deify us with a few and cheap elements! Give me health and a day, and I will make the pomp of emperors ridiculous. The dawn is my Assyria;[16] the sun-set and moon-rise my Paphos,[17] and unimaginable realms of faerie; broad noon shall be my England of the senses and the understanding; the night shall be my Germany of mystic philosophy and dreams.[18]

Not less excellent, except for our less susceptibility in the afternoon, was the charm, last evening, of a January sunset. The western clouds divided and subdivided themselves into pink flakes modulated with tints of unspeakable softness; and the air had so much life and sweetness, that it was a pain to come within doors. What was it that nature would say? Was there no meaning in the live repose of the valley behind the mill, and which Homer or Shakespeare could not re-form for me in words? The leafless trees become spires of flame in the sunset, with the blue east for their background, and the stars of the dead calices[19] of flowers, and every withered stem and stubble rimed with frost, contribute something to the mute music.

The inhabitants of cities suppose that the country landscape is pleasant only half the year. I please myself with observing the graces of the winter scenery, and believe that we are as much touched by it as by the genial influences of summer. To the attentive eye, each moment of the year has its own beauty, and in the same field, it beholds, every hour, a picture which was never seen before, and which shall never be seen again. The heavens change every moment, and reflect their glory or gloom on the plains beneath. The state of the crop in the surrounding farms alters the expression of the earth from week to week. The succession of native plants in the pastures and road-sides, which make the silent clock by which time tells the summer hours, will make even the divisions of the day sensible to a keen observer. The tribes of birds and insects, like the plants punctual to their time, follow each other, and the year has room for all. By water-courses, the variety is greater. In July, the blue pontederia or pickerel-weed blooms in large

---

[14] Craftiness, scheming.   [15] Breathe.

[16] An ancient Near Eastern empire legendary for its wealth.

[17] An ancient city on the island of Cyprus known for its worship of the Greek love goddess Aphrodite.

[18] The English philosophers Emerson read tended to be rational empiricists, whereas the German philosophers were idealists.

[19] Calyxes, the cuplike outer coverings at the base of flowers.

beds in the shallow parts of our pleasant river,[20] and swarms with yellow butter-flies in continual motion. Art cannot rival this pomp of purple and gold. Indeed the river is a perpetual gala, and boasts each month a new ornament.

But this beauty of Nature which is seen and felt as beauty, is the least part. The shows of day, the dewy morning, the rainbow, mountains, orchards in blossom, stars, moonlight, shadows in still water, and the like, if too eagerly hunted, be-come shows merely, and mock us with their unreality. Go out of the house to see the moon, and 't is mere tinsel; it will not please as when its light shines upon your necessary journey. The beauty that shimmers in the yellow afternoons of October, who ever could clutch it? Go forth to find it, and it is gone: 't is only a mirage as you look from the windows of diligence.

2. The presence of a higher, namely, of the spiritual element is essential to its perfection. The high and divine beauty which can be loved without effeminacy, is that which is found in combination with the human will, and never separate. Beauty is the mark God sets upon virtue. Every natural action is graceful. Every heroic act is also decent,[21] and causes the place and the bystanders to shine. We are taught by great actions that the universe is the property of every individual in it. Every rational creature has all nature for his dowry and estate. It is his, if he will. He may divest himself of it; he may creep into a corner, and abdicate his kingdom, as most men do, but he is entitled to the world by his constitution. In proportion to the energy of thought and will, he takes up the world into himself. "All those things for which men plough, build, or sail, obey virtue;" said an an-cient historian.[22] "The winds and waves," said Gibbon,[23] "are always on the side of the ablest navigators." So are the sun and moon and all the stars of heaven. When a noble act is done,—perchance in a scene of great natural beauty; when Leonidas[24] and his three hundred martyrs consume one day in dying, and the sun and moon come each and look at them once in the steep defile of Thermopylæ; when Arnold Winkelried,[25] in the high Alps, under the shadow of the avalanche, gathers in his side a sheaf of Austrian spears to break the line for his comrades; are not these heroes entitled to add the beauty of the scene to the beauty of the deed? When the bark of Columbus nears the shore of America;—before it, the beach lined with savages, fleeing out of all their huts of cane; the sea behind; and the purple mountains of the Indian Archipelago around, can we separate the man from the living picture? Does not the New World clothe his form with her palm-groves and savannahs as fit drapery? Ever does natural beauty steal in like air, and enve-lope great actions. When Sir Harry Vane[26] was dragged up the Tower-hill, sitting on a sled, to suffer death, as the champion of the English laws, one of the multi-tude cried out to him, "You never sate on so glorious a seat." Charles II, to intimi-date the citizens of London, caused the patriot Lord Russell[27] to be drawn in an

[20] The Concord River, near Emerson's home in Concord, Massachusetts.

[21] Honorable, suitably elegant.

[22] Gaius Sallustius Crispus, or Sallust (86–35 B.C.), a Roman historian; from one of Sallust's mono-graphs, *The Conspiracy of Catiline*.

[23] Edward Gibbon (1737–1794), an English historian; from *The Decline and Fall of the Roman Em-pire* (1788).

[24] King Leonidas (?–480 B.C.) of Sparta, commander of the Greek forces at Thermopylae, who was killed while defending the pass against the Persian army led by Xerxes.

[25] Winkelried (?–1386) was a Swiss hero killed in the Battle of Sempach against the Austrians.

[26] Vane (1613–1662), Puritan colonial governor of Massachusetts from 1636 to 1637, was executed for treason when Charles II was restored to the throne of England.

open coach, through the principal streets of the city, on his way to the scaffold. "But," to use the simple narrative of his biographer, "the multitude imagined they saw liberty and virtue sitting by his side." In private places, among sordid objects, an act of truth or heroism seems at once to draw to itself the sky as its temple, the sun as its candle. Nature stretcheth out her arms to embrace man, only let his thoughts be of equal greatness. Willingly does she follow his steps with the rose and the violet, and bend her lines of grandeur and grace to the decoration of her darling child. Only let his thoughts be of equal scope, and the frame will suit the picture. A virtuous man is in unison with her works, and makes the central figure of the visible sphere. Homer, Pindar, Socrates, Phocion,[28] associate themselves fitly in our memory with the whole geography and climate of Greece. The visible heavens and earth sympathize with Jesus. And in common life, whosoever has seen a person of powerful character and happy genius, will have remarked how easily he took all things along with him,—the persons, the opinions, and the day, and nature became ancillary to a man.

3. There is still another aspect under which the beauty of the world may be viewed, namely, as it becomes an object of the intellect. Beside the relation of things to virtue, they have a relation to thought. The intellect searches out the absolute order of things as they stand in the mind of God, and without the colors of affection. The intellectual and the active powers seem to succeed each other in man, and the exclusive activity of the one, generates the exclusive activity of the other. There is something unfriendly in each to the other, but they are like the alternate periods of feeding and working in animals; each prepares and certainly will be followed by the other. Therefore does beauty, which, in relation to actions, as we have seen, comes unsought, and comes because it is unsought, remain for the apprehension and pursuit of the intellect; and then again, in its turn, of the active power. Nothing divine dies. All good is eternally reproductive. The beauty of nature reforms itself in the mind, and not for barren contemplation, but for new creation.

All men are in some degree impressed by the face of the world; some men even to delight. This love of beauty is Taste. Others have the same love in such excess, that, not content with admiring, they seek to embody it in new forms. The creation of beauty is Art.

The production of a work of art throws a light upon the mystery of humanity. A work of art is an abstract or epitome of the world. It is the result or expression of nature, in miniature. For although the works of nature are innumerable and all different, the result or the expression of them all is similar and single. Nature is a sea of forms radically alike and even unique. A leaf, a sun-beam, a landscape, the ocean, make an analogous impression on the mind. What is common to them all,—that perfectness and harmony, is beauty. Therefore the standard of beauty is the entire circuit of natural forms,—the totality of nature; which the Italians expressed by defining beauty "il piu nell' uno."[29] Nothing is quite beautiful alone; nothing but is beautiful in the whole. A single object is only so far beautiful as it

---

[27] William Russell (1639–1683), executed for plotting to overthrow Charles II.

[28] Homer was the eighth- or the ninth-century B.C. Greek epic poet who wrote *The Iliad* and *The Odyssey;* Pindar (522?–438? B.C.), a Greek lyric poet, was renowned for his odes; Socrates (469–399 B.C.) was the famed Athenian philosopher who was Plato's mentor; Phocion (402?–318 B.C.) was an Athenian general and statesman as well as a popular and effective orator.

[29] "The many in one" (Italian). In his poem "Each and All" (1839), Emerson expresses this idea in the lines, "All are needed by each one; / Nothing is fair or good alone."

suggests this universal grace. The poet, the painter, the sculptor, the musician, the architect, seek each to concentrate this radiance of the world on one point, and each in his several work to satisfy the love of beauty which stimulates him to produce. Thus is Art, a nature passed through the alembic[30] of man. Thus in art, does nature work through the will of a man filled with the beauty of her first works.

The world thus exists to the soul to satisfy the desire of beauty. Extend this element to the uttermost, and I call it an ultimate end. No reason can be asked or given why the soul seeks beauty. Beauty, in its largest and profoundest sense, is one expression for the universe. God is the all-fair. Truth, and goodness, and beauty, are but different faces of the same All. But beauty in nature is not ultimate. It is the herald of inward and eternal beauty, and is not alone a solid and satisfactory good. It must therefore stand as a part and not as yet the last or highest expression of the final cause of Nature.

Chapter IV: Language

A third use which Nature subserves to man is that of Language. Nature is the vehicle of thought, and in a simple, double, and three-fold degree.

  1. Words are signs of natural facts.
  2. Particular natural facts are symbols of particular spiritual facts.
  3. Nature is the symbol of spirit.

  1. Words are signs of natural facts. The use of natural history is to give us aid in supernatural history. The use of the outer creation is to give us language for the beings and changes of the inward creation. Every word which is used to express a moral or intellectual fact, if traced to its root, is found to be borrowed from some material appearance. *Right* originally means *straight; wrong* means *twisted. Spirit* primarily means *wind; transgression,* the crossing of a *line; supercilious,* the *raising of the eye-brow.* We say the *heart* to express emotion, the *head* to denote thought; and *thought* and *emotion* are, in their turn, words borrowed from sensible things, and now appropriated to spiritual nature. Most of the process by which this transformation is made, is hidden from us in the remote time when language was framed; but the same tendency may be daily observed in children. Children and savages use only nouns or names of things, which they continually convert into verbs, and apply to analogous mental acts.

  2. But this origin of all words that convey a spiritual import,—so conspicuous a fact in the history of language,—is our least debt to nature. It is not words only that are emblematic; it is things which are emblematic. Every natural fact is a symbol of some spiritual fact. Every appearance in nature corresponds to some state of the mind, and that state of the mind can only be described by presenting that natural appearance as its picture. An enraged man is a lion, a cunning man is a fox, a firm man is a rock, a learned man is a torch. A lamb is innocence; a snake is subtle spite; flowers express to us the delicate affections. Light and darkness are our familiar expression for knowledge and ignorance; and heat for love. Visible distance behind and before us, is respectively our image of memory and hope.

  Who looks upon a river in a meditative hour, and is not reminded of the flux of

---

[30] An apparatus for distilling or refining.

all things? Throw a stone into the stream, and the circles that propagate themselves are the beautiful type of all influence. Man is conscious of a universal soul within or behind his individual life, wherein, as in a firmament, the natures of Justice, Truth, Love. Freedom, arise and shine. This universal soul, he calls Reason:[31] it is not mine or thine or his, but we are its; we are its property and men. And the blue sky in which the private earth is buried, the sky with its eternal calm, and full of everlasting orbs, is the type of Reason. That which, intellectually considered, we call Reason, considered in relation to nature, we call Spirit. Spirit is the Creator. Spirit hath life in itself. And man in all ages and countries, embodies it in his language, as the FATHER.

It is easily seen that there is nothing lucky or capricious in these analogies, but that they are constant, and pervade nature. These are not the dreams of a few poets, here and there, but man is an analogist, and studies relations in all objects. He is placed in the centre of beings, and a ray of relation passes from every other being to him. And neither can man be understood without these objects, nor these objects without man. All the facts in natural history taken by themselves, have no value, but are barren like a single sex. But marry it to human history, and it is full of life. Whole Floras, all Linnæus' and Buffon's[32] volumes, are but dry catalogues of facts; but the most trivial of these facts, the habit of a plant, the organs, or work, or noise of an insect, applied to the illustration of a fact in intellectual philosophy, or, in any way associated to human nature, affects us in the most lively and agreeable manner. The seed of a plant,—to what affecting analogies in the nature of man, is that little fruit made use of, in all discourse, up to the voice of Paul, who calls the human corpse a seed,—"It is sown a natural body; it is raised a spiritual body."[33] The motion of the earth round its axis, and round the sun, makes the day, and the year. These are certain amounts of brute light and heat. But is there no intent of an analogy between man's life and the seasons? And do the seasons gain no grandeur or pathos from that analogy? The instincts of the ant are very unimportant considered as the ant's; but the moment a ray of relation is seen to extend from it to man, and the little drudge is seen to be a monitor, a little body with a mighty heart, then all its habits, even that said to be recently observed, that it never sleeps, become sublime.

Because of this radical[34] correspondence between visible things and human thoughts, savages, who have only what is necessary, converse in figures. As we go back in history, language becomes more picturesque, until its infancy, when it is all poetry; or, all spiritual facts are represented by natural symbols. The same symbols are found to make the original elements of all languages. It has moreover been observed, that the idioms of all languages approach each other in passages of the greatest eloquence and power. And as this is the first language, so is it the last. This immediate dependence of language upon nature, this conversion of an outward phenomenon into a type of somewhat in human life, never loses its power to affect us. It is this which gives that piquancy to the conversation of a strong-natured farmer or back-woodsman, which all men relish.

---

[31] By "Reason" Emerson means an intuitive power within, which is bestowed by the "universal soul." He uses the term "Understanding" to signify the rational powers of the human being.

[32] Carolus Linnaeus, or Carl von Linné (1707–1778), a Swedish botanist and taxonomist; Comte de Buffon (1707–1788), a French naturalist. Both men devised elaborate classification schemes for plants ("Floras").

[33] The Apostle Paul, from I Corinthians 15:44.

[34] Root.

Thus is nature an interpreter, by whose means man converses with his fellow men. A man's power to connect his thought with its proper symbol, and so to utter it, depends on the simplicity of his character, that is, upon his love of truth and his desire to communicate it without loss. The corruption of man is followed by the corruption of langauge. When simplicity of character and the sovereignty of ideas is broken up by the prevalence of secondary desires, the desire of riches, the desire of pleasure, the desire of power, the desire of praise,—and duplicity and falsehood take place of simplicity and truth, the power over nature as an inter-preter of the will, is in a degree lost; new imagery ceases to be created, and old words are perverted to stand for things which are not; a paper currency is em-ployed when there is no bullion in the vaults. In due time, the fraud is manifest, and words lose all power to stimulate the understanding or the affections. Hun-dreds of writers may be found in every long-civilized nation, who for a short time believe, and make others believe, that they see and utter truths, who do not of themselves clothe one thought in its natural garment, but who feed unconsciously upon the language created by the primary writers of the country, those, namely, who hold primarily on nature.

But wise men pierce this rotten diction and fasten words again to visible things: so that picturesque language is at once a commanding certificate that he who em-ploys it, is a man in alliance with truth and God. The moment our discourse rises above the ground line of familiar facts, and is inflamed with passion or exalted by thought, it clothes itself in images. A man conversing in earnest, if he watch his intellectual processes, will find that always a material image, more or less lumi-nous, arises in his mind, cotemporaneous with every thought, which furnishes the vestment of the thought. Hence, good writing and brilliant discourse are perpetual allegories. This imagery is spontaneous. It is the blending of experience with the present action of the mind. It is proper creation. It is the working of the Original Cause through the instruments he has already made.

These facts may suggest the advantage which the country-life possesses for a powerful mind, over the artificial and curtailed life of cities. We know more from nature than we can at will communicate. Its light flows into the mind evermore, and we forget its presence. The poet, the orator, bred in the woods, whose senses have been nourished by their fair and appeasing changes, year after year, without design and without heed,—shall not lose their lesson altogether, in the roar of cities or the broil of politics. Long hereafter, amidst agitation and terror in national councils,—in the hour of revolution,—these solemn images shall reappear in their morning lustre, as fit symbols and words of the thoughts which the passing events shall awaken. At the call of a noble sentiment, again the woods wave, the pines murmur, the river rolls and shines, and the cattle low upon the mountains, as he saw and heard them in his infancy. And with these forms, the spells of persuasion, the keys of power are put into his hands.

3. We are thus assisted by natural objects in the expression of particular mean-ings. But how great a language to convey such peppercorn[35] informations! Did it need such noble races of creatures, this profusion of forms, this host of orbs in heaven, to furnish man with the dictionary and grammar of his municipal[36] speech? Whilst we use this grand cipher to expedite the affairs of our pot and kettle, we feel that we have not yet put it to its use, neither are able. We are like travellers using the cinders of a volcano to roast their eggs. Whilst we see that it

[35] Trifling.   [36] Local, ordinary.

always stands ready to clothe what we would say, we cannot avoid the question, whether the characters are not significant of themselves. Have mountains, and waves, and skies, no significance but what we consciously give them, when we employ them as emblems of our thoughts? The world is emblematic. Parts of speech are metaphors because the whole of nature is a metaphor of the human mind. The laws of moral nature answer to those of matter as face to face in a glass. "The visible world and the relation of its parts, is the dial plate of the invisible."[37] The axioms of physics translate the laws of ethics. Thus, "the whole is greater than its part;" "reaction is equal to action;" "the smallest weight may be made to lift the greatest, the difference of weight being compensated by time;" and many the like propositions, which have an ethical as well as physical sense. These propositions have a much more extensive and universal sense when applied to human life, than when confined to technical use.

In like manner, the memorable words of history, and the proverbs of nations, consist usually of a natural fact, selected as a picture or parable of a moral truth. Thus; A rolling stone gathers no moss; A bird in the hand is worth two in the bush; A cripple in the right way, will beat a racer in the wrong; Make hay whilst the sun shines; 'T is hard to carry a full cup even; Vinegar is the son of wine; The last ounce broke the camel's back; Long-lived trees make roots first;—and the like. In their primary sense these are trivial facts, but we repeat them for the value of their analogical import. What is true of proverbs, is true of all fables, parables, and allegories.

This relation between the mind and matter is not fancied by some poet, but stands in the will of God, and so is free to be known by all men. It appears to men, or it does not appear. When in fortunate hours we ponder this miracle, the wise man doubts, if, at all other times, he is not blind and deaf;

> ——"Can these things be,
> And overcome us like a summer's cloud,
> Without our special wonder?"[38]

for the universe becomes transparent, and the light of higher laws than its own, shines through it. It is the standing problem which has exercised the wonder and the study of every fine genius since the world began; from the era of the Egyptians and the Brahmins,[39] to that of Pythagoras, of Plato, of Bacon, of Leibnitz,[40] of Swedenborg. There sits the Sphinx[41] at the road-side, and from age to age, as each prophet comes by, he tries his fortune at reading her riddle. There seems to be a necessity in spirit to manifest itself in material forms; and day and night, river and

---

[37] From the Swedish theologian and mystic Emanuel Swedenborg (1688–1772), whose ideas of correspondence between the spiritual and the natural world interested Emerson deeply.

[38] From Shakespeare's *Macbeth* (III. iv. 110–112), which actually reads, "Can *such* things be. . . . "

[39] Brahmans, members of a priestly Hindu caste, named after Brahma, the supreme soul of the Hindu universe.

[40] Pythagoras was a sixth-century B.C. Greek philosopher who believed in the transmigration of souls and claimed he could remember his earlier incarnations; Plato (428–347 B.C.) was the most influential source of idealism in Western philosophical thought; Sir Francis Bacon (1561–1626) was an English statesman and philosopher who championed the inductive method; Gottfried Wilhelm Leibnitz (1646–1716) was a German mathematician and idealist philosopher and the founder of symbolic logic.

[41] According to Greek myth, a winged monster who killed all who failed to answer her riddle. (When Oedipus answered the riddle correctly, she killed herself.)

storm, beast and bird, acid and alkali, preëxist in necessary Ideas in the mind of God, and are what they are by virtue of preceding affections,[42] in the world of spirit. A Fact is the end or last issue of spirit. The visible creation is the terminus or the circumference of the invisible world. "Material objects," said a French philosopher,[43] "are necessarily kinds of *scoriæ* of the substantial thoughts of the Creator, which must always preserve an exact relation to their first origin; in other words, visible nature must have a spiritual and moral side."

This doctrine is abstruse, and though the images of "garment," "scoriæ," "mirror," may stimulate the fancy, we must summon the aid of subtler and more vital expositors to make it plain. "Every scripture is to be interpreted by the same spirit which gave it forth,"[44]—is the fundamental law of criticism. A life in harmony with nature, the love of truth and of virtue, will purge the eyes to understand her text. By degrees we may come to know the primitive sense of the permanent objects of nature, so that the world shall be to us an open book, and every form significant of its hidden life and final cause.

A new interest surprises us, whilst, under the view now suggested, we contemplate the fearful extent and multitude of objects; since "every object rightly seen, unlocks a new faculty of the soul."[45] That which was unconscious truth, becomes, when interpreted and defined in an object, a part of the domain of knowledge,—a new weapon in the magazine[46] of power.

CHAPTER V: DISCIPLINE

In view of this significance of nature, we arrive at once at a new fact, that nature is a discipline. This use of the world includes the preceding uses, as parts of itself.

Space, time, society, labor, climate, food, locomotion, the animals, the mechanical forces, give us sincerest lessons, day by day, whose meaning is unlimited. They educate both the Understanding and the Reason. Every property of matter is a school for the understanding,—its solidity or resistance, its inertia, its extension, its figure, its divisibility. The understanding adds, divides, combines, measures, and finds everlasting nutriment and room for its activity in this worthy scene. Meantime, Reason transfers all these lessons into its own world of thought, by perceiving the analogy that marries Matter and Mind.

1. Nature is a discipline of the understanding in intellectual truths. Our dealing with sensible objects is a constant exercise in the necessary lessons of difference, of likeness, of order, of being and seeming, of progressive arrangement; of ascent from particular to general; of combination to one end of manifold forces. Proportioned to the importance of the organ to be formed, is the extreme care with which its tuition[47] is provided,—a care pretermitted[48] in no single case. What tedious training, day after day, year after year, never ending, to form the common sense; what continual reproduction of annoyances, inconveniences, dilemmas; what rejoicing over us of little men; what disputing of prices, what reckonings of in-

---

[42] All things preexist in the mind of God and exist in the world of spirit before they exist in the world of fact.

[43] Guillaume Oegger, in *The True Messiah* (1829); *scoriae* means slag or refuse from melting metals.

[44] From George Fox (1624–1691), an English mystic and founder of the Society of Friends (Quakers) in 1668.

[45] From *Aids to Reflection* (1825), by Samuel Taylor Coleridge (1772–1834).   [46] A storehouse.

[47] Care, guardianship.   [48] Omitted, neglected.

terest,—and all to form the Hand of the mind;—to instruct us that "good thoughts are no better than good dreams, unless they be executed!"[49]

The same good office is performed by Property and its filial systems of debt and credit. Debt, grinding debt, whose iron face the widow, the orphan, and the sons of genius fear and hate;—debt, which consumes so much time, which so cripples and disheartens a great spirit with cares that seem so base, is a preceptor whose lessons cannot be foregone, and is needed most by those who suffer from it most. Moreover, property, which has been well compared to snow,—"if it fall level to-day, it will be blown into drifts to-morrow,"—is merely the surface action of internal machinery, like the index on the face of a clock. Whilst now it is the gymnastics of the understanding, it is hiving in the foresight of the spirit, experience in profounder laws.

The whole character and fortune of the individual are affected by the least inequalities in the culture of the understanding; for example, in the perception of differences. Therefore is Space, and therefore Time, that man may know that things are not huddled and lumped, but sundered and individual. A bell and a plough have each their use, and neither can do the office of the other. Water is good to drink, coal to burn, wool to wear; but wool cannot be drunk, nor water spun, nor coal eaten. The wise man shows his wisdom in separation, in gradation, and his scale of creatures and of merits, is as wide as nature. The foolish have no range in their scale, but suppose every man is as every other man. What is not good they call the worst, and what is not hateful, they call the best.

In like manner, what good heed, nature forms in us! She pardons no mistakes. Her yea is yea, and her nay, nay.

The first steps in Agriculture, Astronomy, Zoölogy, (those first steps which the farmer, the hunter, and the sailor take,) teach that nature's dice are always loaded; that in her heaps and rubbish are concealed sure and useful results.

How calmly and genially the mind apprehends one after another the laws of physics! What noble emotions dilate the mortal as he enters into the counsels of the creation, and feels by knowledge the privilege to BE! His insight refines him. The beauty of nature shines in his own breast. Man is greater that he can see this, and the universe less, because Time and Space relations vanish as laws are known.

Here again we are impressed and even daunted by the immense Universe to be explored. 'What we know, is a point to what we do not know.'[50] Open any recent journal of science, and weigh the problems suggested concerning Light, Heat, Electricity, Magnetism, Physiology, Geology, and judge whether the interest of natural science is likely to be soon exhausted.

Passing by many particulars of the discipline of nature we must not omit to specify two.

The exercise of the Will or the lesson of power is taught in every event. From the child's successive possession of his several senses up to the hour when he saith, "thy will be done!"[51] he is learning the secret, that he can reduce under his will, not only particular events, but great classes, nay the whole series of events, and so conform all facts to his character. Nature is thoroughly mediate. It is made

[49] Paraphrased from the essay "Of Great Place" in Francis Bacon's *Essays* (1625).

[50] An aphorism variously attributed to the English moralist Bishop Joseph Butler (1692–1752) in the British novel *Tremaine* (1825), by Robert P. Ward, and to the English mathematician and physicist Sir Isaac Newton (1642–1727). The idea has undoubtedly occurred to many other people.

[51] From the Lord's Prayer (Matthew 6:10, 26:42).

to serve. It receives the dominion of man as meekly as the ass on which the Saviour rode.[52] It offers all its kingdoms to man as the raw material which he may mould into what is useful. Man is never weary of working it up. He forges the subtile and delicate air into wise and melodious words, and gives them wing as angles of persuasion and command. More and more, with every thought, does his kingdom stretch over things, until the world becomes, at last, only a realized will,—the double of the man.

2. Sensible objects conform to the premonitions of Reason and reflect the conscience. All things are moral; and in their boundless changes have an unceasing reference to spiritual nature. Therefore is nature glorious with form, color, and motion, that every globe in the remotest heaven; every chemical change from the rudest crystal up to the laws of life; every change of vegetation from the first principle of growth in the eye of a leaf, to the tropical forest and antediluvian[53] coal-mine; every animal function from the sponge up to Hercules,[54] shall hint or thunder to man the laws of right and wrong, and echo the Ten Commandments. Therefore is nature ever the ally of Religion: lends all her pomp and riches to the religious sentiment. Prophet and priest, David, Isaiah,[55] Jesus, have drawn deeply from this source.

This ethical character so penetrates the bone and marrow of nature, as to seem the end for which it was made. Whatever private purpose is answered by any member or part, this is its public and universal function, and is never omitted. Nothing in nature is exhausted in its first use. When a thing has served an end to the uttermost, it is wholly new for an ulterior service. In God, every end is converted into a new means. Thus the use of Commodity, regarded by itself, is mean and squalid. But it is to the mind an education in the great doctrine of Use, namely, that a thing is good only so far as it serves; that a conspiring of parts and efforts to the production of an end, is essential to any being. The first and gross manifestation of this truth, is our inevitable and hated training in values and wants, in corn and meat.

It has already been illustrated, in treating of the significance of material things, that every natural process is but a version of a moral sentence. The moral law lies at the centre of nature and radiates to the circumference. It is the pith and marrow of every substance, every relation, and every process. All things with which we deal, preach to us. What is a farm but a mute gospel? The chaff and the wheat, weeds and plants, blight, rain, insects, sun,—it is a sacred emblem from the first furrow of spring to the last stack which the snow of winter overtakes in the fields. But the sailor, the shepherd, the miner, the merchant, in their several resorts, have each an experience precisely parallel and leading to the same conclusion: because all organizations are radically alike. Nor can it be doubted that this moral sentiment which thus scents the air, and grows in the grain, and impregnates the waters of the world, is caught by man and sinks into his soul. The moral influence of nature upon every individual is that amount of truth which it illustrates to him. Who can estimate this? Who can guess how much firmness the sea-beaten rock has taught the fisherman? how much tranquillity has been reflected to man from

---

[52] "Behold, thy King cometh unto thee, meek, and sitting upon an ass," from Matthew 21:5.
[53] Before the biblical Flood, in Genesis 6:9 the Flood destroyed all creatures not on Noah's Ark.
[54] According to Greek myth, a hero renowned for feats of strength. Here Emerson is saying that ethics applies to life from the simplest animal to the most developed human being.
[55] The second king of Israel, and an Old Testament prophet.

the azure sky, over whose unspotted deeps the winds forevermore drive flocks of stormy clouds, and leave no wrinkle or stain? how much industry and providence and affection we have caught from the pantomine of brutes? What a searching preacher of self-command is the varying phenomenon of Health!

Herein is especially apprehended the Unity of Nature,—the Unity in Variety,—which meets us everywhere. All the endless variety of things make a unique, an identical impression. Xenophanes[56] complained in his old age, that, look where he would, all things hastened back to Unity. He was weary of seeing the same entity in the tedious variety of forms. The fable of Proteus[57] has a cordial truth. Every particular in nature, a leaf, a drop, a crystal, a moment of time is related to the whole, and partakes of the perfection of the whole. Each particle is a microcosm, and faithfully renders the likeness of the world.

Not only resemblances exist in things whose analogy is obvious, as when we detect the type of the human hand in the flipper of the fossil saurus,[58] but also in objects wherein there is great superficial unlikeness. Thus architecture is called "frozen music," by De Stael and Goethe.[59] Vitruvius[60] thought an architect should be a musician. "A Gothic church," said Coleridge, "is a petrified religion."[61] Michael Angelo maintained, that, to an architect, a knowledge of anatomy is essential.[62] In Haydn's oratorios,[63] the notes present to the imagination not only motions, as, of the snake, the stag, and the elephant, but colors also; as the green grass. The law of harmonic sounds reappears in the harmonic colors. The granite is differenced in its laws only by the more or less of heat, from the river that wears it away. The river, as it flows, resembles the air that flows over it; the air resembles the light which traverses it with more subtile currents; the light resembles the heat which rides with it through Space. Each creature is only a modification of the other; the likeness in them is more than the difference, and their radical law is one and the same. Hence it is, that a rule of one art, or a law of one organization, holds true throughout nature. So intimate is this Unity, that, it is easily seen, it lies under the undermost garment of nature, and betrays its source in universal Spirit. For, it pervades Thought also. Every universal truth which we express in words, implies or supposes every other truth. *Omne verum vero consonat.*[64] It is like a great circle on a sphere, comprising all possible circles; which, however, may be drawn, and comprise it, in like manner. Every such truth is the absolute Ens[65] seen from one side. But it has innumerable sides.

The same central Unity is still more conspicuous in actions. Words are finite organs of the infinite mind. They cannot cover the dimensions of what is in truth. They break, chop, and impoverish it. An action is the perfection and publication

---

[56] Xenophanes (570–480 B.C.) was a Greek philosopher who taught that God is single and eternal.
[57] According to Greek myth, a sea god who could assume various shapes.
[58] Fossils of extinct reptiles.
[59] The French writer Anne Louise Germaine (1766–1817), or Mme. de Staël; the German poet and novelist Johann Wolfgang von Goethe (1749–1832).
[60] Vitruvius Pollio (50?–26 B.C.), a Roman writer on architecture.
[61] From Coleridge's "Lecture on the General Character of the Gothic Mind in the Middle Ages" (1836).
[62] In Volume V of his *Journals and Miscellaneous Notebooks* (1966), Emerson records this statement from the sketch of Michelangelo in *Lives of Eminent Persons* (1833), published in London under the auspices of the Society for the Diffusion of Useful Knowledge.
[63] Choral music of the Austrian composer Franz Joseph Haydn (1732–1809).
[64] "Every truth is consonant [agrees] with every other truth" (Latin).
[65] "Abstract being" (Latin).

of thought. A right action seems to fill the eye, and to be related to all nature. "The wise man, in doing one thing, does all; or, in the one thing he does rightly, he sees the likeness of all which is done rightly."[66]

Words and actions are not the attributes of mute and brute nature. They introduce us to the human form, of which all other organizations appear to be degradations. When this organization appears among so many that surround it, the spirit prefers it to all others. It says, 'From such as this, have I drawn joy and knowledge. In such as this, have I found and beheld myself. I will speak to it. It can speak again. It can yield me thought already formed and alive.' In fact, the eye,— the mine,—is always accompanied by these forms, male and female; and these are incomparably the richest informations of the power and order that lie at the heart of things. Unfortunately, every one of them bears the marks as of some injury; is marred and superficially defective. Nevertheless, far different from the deaf and dumb nature around them, these all rest like fountain-pipes on the unfathomed sea of thought and virtue whereto they alone, of all organizations, are the entrances.

It were a pleasant inquiry to follow into detail their ministry to our education, but where would it stop? We are associated in adolescent and adult life with some friends, who, like skies and waters, are coextensive with our idea; who, answering each to a certain affection of the soul, satisfy our desire on that side; whom we lack power to put at such focal distance from us, that we can mend or even analayze them. We cannot chuse but love them. When much intercourse with a friend has supplied us with a standard of exellence, and has increased our respect for the resources of God who thus sends a real person to outgo our ideal; when he has, moreover, become an object of thought, and, whilst his character retains all its unconscious effect, is converted in the mind into solid and sweet wisdom,—it is a sign to us that his office is closing, and he is commonly withdrawn from our sight in a short time.

CHAPTER VI: IDEALISM

Thus is the unspeakable but intelligible and practicable meaning of the world conveyed to man, the immortal pupil, in every object of sense. To this one end of Discipline, all parts of nature conspire.

A noble doubt perpetually suggests itself, whether this end be not the Final Cause of the Universe; and whether nature outwardly exists.[67] It is a sufficient account of that Appearance we call the World, that God will teach a human mind, and so makes it the receiver of a certain number of congruent sensations, which we call sun and moon, man and woman, house and trade. In my utter impotence to test the authenticity of the report of my senses, to know whether the impressions they make on me correspond with outlying objects, what difference does it make, whether Orion[68] is up there in heaven, or some god paints the image in the firmament of the soul? The relations of parts and the end of the whole remaining the same, what is the difference, whether land and sea interact, and worlds revolve and intermingle without number of end,—deep yawning under deep, and

---

[66] From Goethe's *Wilhelm Meister's Travels* (1821–1829).
[67] This is the crucial question of philosophical idealism (what Emerson calls "the Ideal theory" in his next paragraph).
[68] The hunter, a constellation seen near the equator.

galaxy balancing galaxy, throughout absolute space, or, whether, without relations of time and space, the same appearances are inscribed in the constant faith of
man? Whether nature enjoy a substantial existence without, or is only in the apocalypse[69] of the mind, it is alike useful and alike venerable to me. Be it what it
may, it is ideal to me, so long as I cannot try the accuracy of my senses.

The frivolous make themselves merry with the Ideal theory, as if its consequences were burlesque; as if it affected the stability of nature. It surely does not.
God never jests with us, and will not compromise the end of nature, by permitting
any inconsequence in its procession. Any distrust of the permanence of laws,
would paralyze the faculties of man. Their permanence is sacredly respected, and
his faith therein is perfect. The wheels and springs of man are all set to the hypothesis of the permanence of nature. We are not built like a ship to be tossed, but like
a house to stand. It is a natural consequence of this structure, that, so long as the
active powers predominate over the reflective, we resist with indignation any hint
that nature is more short-lived or mutable than spirit. The broker, the wheelwright, the carpenter, the toll-man, are much displeased at the intimation.

But whilst we acquiesce entirely in the permanence of natural laws, the question of the absolute existence of nature, still remains open. It is the uniform effect
of culture on the human mind, not to shake our faith in the stability of particular
phenomena, as of heat, water, azote;[70] but to lead us to regard nature as a phenomenon, not a substance; to attribute necessary existence to spirit; to esteem
nature as an accident and an effect.

To the senses and the unrenewed understanding, belongs a sort of instinctive
belief in the absolute existence of nature. In their view, man and nature are indissolubly joined. Things are ultimates, and they never look beyond their sphere.
The presence of Reason mars this faith. The first effort of thought tends to relax
this despotism of the senses, which binds us to nature as if we were a part of it,
and shows us nature aloof, and, as it were, afloat. Until this higher agency inter-
vened, the animal eye sees, with wonderful accuracy, sharp outlines and colored
surfaces. When the eye of Reason opens, to outline and surface are at once added,
grace and expression. These proceed from imagination and affection, and abate
somewhat of the angular distinctness of objects. If the Reason be stimulated to
more earnest vision, outlines and surfaces become transparent, and are no longer
seen; causes and spirits are seen through them. The best, the happiest moments of
life, are these delicious awakenings of the higher powers, and the reverential withdrawing of nature before its God.

Let us proceed to indicate the effects of culture. 1. Our first institution[71] in the
Ideal philosophy is a hint from nature herself.

Nature is made to conspire with spirit to emancipate us. Certain mechanical
changes, a small alteration in our local position apprizes us of a dualism. We are
strangely affected by seeing the shore from a moving ship, from a balloon, or
through the tints of an unusual sky. The least change in our point of view, gives
the whole world a pictorial air. A man who seldom rides, needs only to get into a
coach and traverse his own town, to turn the street into a puppetshow. The men,
the women,—talking, running, bartering, fighting,—the earnest mechanic,[72] the
lounger, the beggar, the boys, the dogs, are unrealized[73] at once, or, at least,
wholly detached from all relation to the observer, and seen as apparent, not substantial beings. What new thoughts are suggested by seeing a face of country quite

[69] Revelation.   [70] Nitrogen.   [71] Lesson.
[72] Manual worker.   [73] No longer seen (realized) as what they are.

familiar, in the rapid movement of the rail-road car! Nay, the most wonted objects, (make a very slight change in the point of vision,) please us most. In a camera obscura,[74] the butcher's cart, and the figure of one of our own family amuse us. So a portrait of a well-known face gratifies us. Turn the eyes upside down, by looking at the landscape through your legs, and how agreeable is the picture, though you have seen it any time these twenty years!

In these cases, by mechanical means, is suggested the difference between the observer and the spectacle,—between man and nature. Hence arises a pleasure mixed with awe; I may say, a low degree of the sublime is felt from the fact, probably, that man is hereby apprized, that, whilst the world is a spectacle, something in himself is stable.

2. In a higher manner, the poet communicates the same pleasure. By a few strokes he delineates, as on air, the sun, the mountain, the camp, the city, the hero, the maiden, not different from what we know them, but only lifted from the ground and afloat before the eye. He unfixes the land and the sea, makes them revolve around the axis of his primary thought, and disposes them anew. Possessed himself by a heroic passion, he uses matter as symbols of it. The sensual man conforms thoughts to things; the poet conforms things to his thoughts. The one esteems nature as rooted and fast; the other, as fluid, and impresses his being thereon. To him, the refractory world is ductile and flexible; he invests dust and stones with humanity, and makes them the words of the Reason. The imagination may be defined to be, the use which the Reason makes of the material world. Shakespeare possesses the power of subordinating nature for the purposes of expression, beyond all poets. His imperial muse tosses the creation like a bauble from hand to hand, and uses it to embody any capricious shade of thought that is uppermost in his mind. The remotest spaces of nature are visited, and the farthest sundered things are brought together, by a subtle spiritual connexion. We are made aware that magnitude of material things is merely relative, and all objects shrink and expand to serve the passion of the poet. Thus, in his sonnets, the lays of birds, the scents and dyes of flowers, he finds to be the *shadow* of his beloved; time, which keeps her from him, is his *chest;* the suspicion she has awakened, is her *ornament;*[75]

> The ornament of beauty is Suspect,
> A crow which flies in heaven's sweetest air.[76]

His passion is not the fruit of chance; it swells, as he speaks, to a city, or a state.

> No, it was builded far from accident;
> It suffers not in smiling pomp, nor falls
> Under the brow of thralling discontent;
> It fears not policy, that heretic,
> That works on leases of short numbered hours,
> But all alone stands hugely politic.[77]

---

[74] A small chamber or box that reflects an image on a wall; an early version of the camera.
[75] Emerson refers to Shakespeare's Sonnets 98 and 65.   [76] From Shakespeare's Sonnet 70.
[77] From Shakespeare's Sonnet 124.

In the strength of his constancy, the Pyramids seem to him recent and transitory.[78] And the freshness of youth and love dazzles him with its resemblance to
morning.

> Take those lips away
> Which so sweetly were forsworn;
> And those eyes,—the break of day,
> Lights that do mislead the morn.[79]

The wild beauty of this hyperbole, I may say, in passing, it would not be easy
to match in literature.

This transfiguration which all material objects undergo through the passion of
the poet,—this power which he exerts, at any moment, to magnify the small, to
micrify[80] the great,—might be illustrated by a thousand examples from his Plays.
I have before me the Tempest, and will cite only these few lines.

> ARIEL. The strong based promontory
> Have I made shake, and by the spurs plucked up
> The pine and cedar.

Prospero calls for music to sooth the frantic Alonzo, and his companions;

> A solemn air, and the best comforter
> To an unsettled fancy, cure thy brains
> Now useless, boiled within thy skull.

Again;

> The charm dissolves apace
> And, as the morning steals upon the night,
> Melting the darkness, so their rising senses
> Begin to chase the ignorant fumes that mantle
> Their clearer reason.
>   Their understanding
> Begins to swell: and the approaching tide
> Will shortly fill the reasonable shores
> That now lie foul and muddy.[81]

The perception of real affinities between events, that is to say, of *ideal* affinities, for those only are real, enables the poet thus to make free with the most
imposing forms and phenomena of the world, and to assert the predominance of
the soul.

3. Whilst thus the poet delights us by animating nature like a creator, with his
own thoughts, he differs from the philosopher only herein, that the one proposes
Beauty as his main end; the other Truth. But, the philosopher, not less than the

---

[78] "Thy pyramids built up with newer might / To me are nothing novel, nothing strange," from
Shakespeare's Sonnet 123.
[79] From Shakespeare's *Measure for Measure* (IV. i. 1–4).   [80] To make small or insignificant.
[81] From Shakespeare's *The Tempest* (V. i. 46–48, 58–60, 64–68, 79–82). Lines 46–48 are spoken by
Prospero, not by Ariel.

poet, postpones the apparent order and relations of things to the empire of thought. "The problem of philosophy," according to Plato, "is, for all that exists conditionally, to find a ground unconditioned and absolute."[82] It proceeds on the faith that a law determines all phenomena, which being known, the phenomena can be predicted. That law, when in the mind, is an idea. Its beauty is infinite. The true philosopher and the true poet are one, and a beauty, which is truth, and a truth, which is beauty, is the aim of both. Is not the charm of one of Plato's or Aristotle's definitions, strictly like that of the Antigone of Sophocles?[83] It is, in both cases, that a spiritual life has been imparted to nature; that the solid seeming block of matter has been pervaded and dissolved by a thought; that this feeble human being has penetrated the vast masses of nature with an informing soul, and recognised itself in their harmony, that is, seized their law. In physics, when this is attained, the memory disburthens itself of its cumbrous catalogues of particulars, and carries centuries of observation in a single formula.

Thus even in physics, the material is ever degraded before the spiritual. The astronomer, the geometer, rely on their irrefragable analysis, and disdain the results of observation. The sublime remark of Euler[84] on his law of arches, "This will be found contrary to all experience, yet is true;" had already transferred nature into the mind, and left matter like an outcast corpse.

4. Intellectual science has been observed to beget invariably a doubt of the existence of matter. Turgot[85] said, "He that has never doubted the existence of matter, may be assured he has no aptitude for metaphysical inquiries." It fastens the attention upon immortal necessary uncreated natures, that is, upon Ideas; and in their beautiful and majestic presence, we feel that our outward being is a dream and a shade. Whilst we wait in this Olympus of gods, we think of nature as an appendix to the soul. We ascend into their region, and know that these are the thoughts of the Supreme Being. "These are they who were set up from everlasting, from the beginning, or ever the earth was. When he prepared the heavens, they were there; when he established the clouds above, when he strengthened the fountains of the deep. Then they were by him, as one brought up with him. Of them took he counsel."[86]

Their influence is proportionate. As objects of science, they are accessible to few men. Yet all men are capable of being raised by piety or by passion, into their region. And no man touches these divine natures, without becoming, in some degree, himself divine. Like a new soul, they renew the body. We become physically nimble and lightsome; we tread on air; life is no longer irksome, and we think it will never be so. No man fears age or misfortune or death, in their serene company, for he is transported out of the district of change. Whilst we behold unveiled the nature of Justice and Truth, we learn the difference between the absolute and the conditional or relative. We apprehend the absolute. As it were, for the first time, *we exist*. We become immortal, for we learn that time and space are relations of matter; that, with a perception of truth, or a virtuous will, they have no affinity.

5. Finally, religion and ethics, which may be fitly called,—the practice of

---

[82] From Plato's *Republic*, Book V; Emerson took the quotation from Coleridge's *The Friend* (1818).

[83] Aristotle (384–322 B.C.) was an eminent Greek philosopher and a student of Plato; Sophocles (496–406 B.C.) was a Greek dramatist: in his tragedy *Antigone* (441 B.C.), the heroine chooses death rather than compromise sacred principle.

[84] Leonhard Euler (1707–1783), a Swiss mathematician.

[85] Anne Robert Jacques Turgot (1727–1781), a French economist and statesman.

[86] A paraphrase of Proverbs 8:23–30.

ideas, or the introduction of ideas into life,—have an analogous effect with all lower culture, in degrading nature and suggesting its dependence on spirit. Ethics and religion differ herein; that the one is the system of human duties commencing from man; the other, from God. Religion includes the personality of God; Ethics does not. They are one to our present design. They both put nature under foot. The first and last lesson of religion is, "The things that are seen, are temporal; the things that are unseen are eternal."[87] It puts an affront upon nature. It does that for the unschooled, which philosophy does for Berkeley and Viasa.[88] The uniform language that may be heard in the churches of the most ignorant sects, is,—'Contemn the unsubstantial shows of the world; they are vanities, dreams, shadows, unrealities; seek the realities of religion.' The devotee flouts nature. Some theosophists[89] have arrived at a certain hostility and indignation towards matter, as the Manichean[90] and Plotinus. They distrusted in themselves any looking back to these flesh-pots of Egypt.[91] Plotinus was ashamed of his body.[92] In short, they might all better say of matter, what Michael Angelo said of external beauty, "it is the frail and weary weed, in which God dresses the soul, which he has called into time."[93]

It appears that motion, poetry, physical and intellectual science, and religion, all tend to affect our convictions of the reality of the external world. But I own there is something ungrateful in expanding too curiously the particulars of the general proposition, that all culture tends to imbue us with idealism. I have no hostility to nature, but a child's love to it. I expand and live in the warm day like corn and melons. Let us speak her fair. I do not wish to fling stones at my beautiful mother, nor soil my gentle nest. I only wish to indicate the true position of nature in regard to man, wherein to establish man, all right education tends; as the ground which to attain is the object of human life, that is, of man's connexion with nature. Culture inverts the vulgar views of nature, and brings the mind to call that apparent, which it uses to call real, and that real, which it uses to call visionary. Children, it is true, believe in the external world. The belief that it appears only, is an afterthought, but with culture, this faith will as surely arise on the mind as did the first.

The advantage of the ideal theory over the popular faith, is this, that it presents the world in precisely that view which is most desirable to the mind. It is, in fact, the view which Reason, both speculative and practical, that is, philosophy and virtue, take. For, seen in the light of thought, the world always is phenomenal; and virtue subordinates it to the mind. Idealism sees the world in God. It beholds the whole circle of persons and things, of actions and events, of country and religion, not as painfully accumulated, atom after atom, act after act, in an aged creeping Past, but as one vast picture, which God paints on the instant eternity, for the contemplation of the soul. Therefore the soul holds itself off from a too trivial and microscopic study of the universal tablet. It respects the end too much, to

---

[87] From II Corinthians 4:18.

[88] Bishop George Berkeley (1685–1753), an English promoter of philosophical idealism; Vyāsa, a legendary Hindu philosopher and author of the Mahābhārata (200? B.C.).

[89] Those who claim direct mystical insight of a supreme being.

[90] A follower of Manes, a third-century Christian mystic who taught that there was a principle of good and a principle of evil in the universe.

[91] In Exodus 16:2–3 the Israelites in the wilderness yearned for the fleshpots, or luxuries, of Egypt.

[92] Plotinus expressed remorse that the eternal soul was trapped in a perishable body.

[93] From Michelangelo's Sonnet 51; here, "weed" means garment.

immerse itself in the means. It sees something more important in Christianity, than the scandals of ecclesiastical history or the niceties of criticism; and, very incurious concerning persons or miracles, and not at all disturbed by chasms of historical evidence, it accepts from God the phenomenon, as it finds it, as the pure and awful form of religion in the world. It is not hot and passionate at the appearance of what it calls its own good or bad fortune, at the union or opposition of other persons. No man is its enemy. It accepts whatsoever befals, as part of its lesson. It is a watcher more than a doer, and it is a doer, only that it may the better watch.

CHAPTER VII: SPIRIT

It is essential to a true theory of nature and of man, that it should contain somewhat[94] progressive. Uses that are exhausted or that may be, and facts that end in the statement, cannot be all that is true of this brave lodging wherein man is harbored, and wherein all his faculties find appropriate and endless exercise. And all the uses of nature admit of being summed in one, which yields the activity of man an infinite scope. Through all its kingdoms, to the suburbs and outskirts of things, it is faithful to the cause whence it had its origin. It always speaks of Spirit. It suggests the absolute. It is a perpetual effect. It is a great shadow pointing always to the sun behind us.

The aspect of nature is devout. Like the figure of Jesus, she stands with bended head, and hands folded upon the breast. The happiest man is he who learns from nature the lesson of worship.

Of that ineffable essence which we call Spirit, he that thinks most, will say least. We can foresee God in the course and, as it were, distant phenomena of matter; but when we try to define and describe himself, both language and thought desert us, and we are as helpless as fools and savages. That essence refuses to be recorded in propositions, but when man has worshipped him intellectually, the noblest ministry of nature is to stand as the apparition of God. It is the great organ through which the universal spirit speaks to the individual, and strives to lead back the individual to it.

When we consider Spirit, we see that the views already presented do not include the whole circumference of man. We must add some related thoughts.

Three problems are put by nature to the mind; What is matter? Whence is it? and Whereto? The first of these questions only, the ideal theory answers. Idealism saith: matter is a phenomenon, not a substance. Idealism acquaints us with the total disparity between the evidence of our own being, and the evidence of the world's being. The one is perfect; the other, incapable of any assurance; the mind is a part of the nature of things; the world is a divine dream, from which we may presently awake to the glories and certainties of day. Idealism is a hypothesis to account for nature by other principles than those of carpentry and chemistry. Yet, if it only deny the existence of matter, it does not satisfy the demands of the spirit. It leaves God out of me. It leaves me in the splendid labyrinth of my perceptions, to wander without end. Then the heart resists it, because it baulks the affections in denying substantive being to men and women. Nature is so pervaded with human life, that there is something of humanity in all, and in every particular. But this

---

[94] Something; Emerson regularly uses the older form "somewhat" for "something."

theory makes nature foreign to me, and does not account for that consanguinity which we acknowledge to it.

Let it stand then, in the present state of our knowledge, merely as a useful introductory hypothesis, serving to apprize us of the eternal distinction between the soul and the world.

But when, following the invisible steps of thought, we come to inquire, Whence is matter? and Whereto? many truths arise to us out of the recesses of consciousness. We learn that the highest is present to the soul of man, that the dread universal essence, which is not wisdom, or love, or beauty, or power, but all in one, and each entirely, is that for which all things exist, and that by which they are; that spirit creates; that behind nature, throughout nature, spirit is present; that spirit is one and not compound; that spirit does not act upon us from without, that is, in space and time, but spiritually, or through ourselves. Therefore, that spirit, that is, the Supreme Being, does not build up nature around us, but puts it forth through us, as the life of the tree puts forth new branches and leaves through the pores of the old. As a plant upon the earth, so a man rests upon the bosom of God; he is nourished by unfailing fountains, and draws, at his need, inexhaustible power. Who can set bounds to the possibilities of man? Once inhale the upper air, being admitted to behold the absolute natures of justice and truth, and we learn that man has access to the entire mind of the Creator, is himself the creator in the finite. This view, which admonishes me where the sources of wisdom and power lie, and points to virtue as to

> "The golden key
> Which opes the palace of eternity,"[95]

carries upon its face the highest certificate of truth, because it animates me to create my own world through the purification of my soul.

The world proceeds from the same spirit as the body of man. It is a remoter and inferior incarnation of God, a projection of God in the unconscious. But it differs from the body in one important respect. It is not, like that, now subjected to the human will. Its serene order is inviolable by us. It is therefore, to us, the present expositor of the divine mind. It is a fixed point whereby we may measure our departure. As we degenerate, the contrast between us and our house is more evident. We are as much strangers in nature, as we are aliens from God. We do not understand the notes of birds. The fox and the deer run away from us; the bear and tiger rend us. We do not know the uses of more than a few plants, as corn and the apple, the potato and the vine. Is not the landscape, every glimpse of which hath a grandeur, a face of him? Yet this may show us what discord is between man and nature, for you cannot freely admire a noble landscape, if laborers are digging in the field hard by. The poet finds something ridiculous in his delight, until he is out of the sight of men.

CHAPTER VIII: PROSPECTS

In inquiries respecting the laws of the world and the frame of things, the highest reason is always the truest. That which seems faintly possible—it is so refined, is often faint and dim because it is deepest seated in the mind among the eternal

---

[95] From *Comus* (1634), lines 13–14, by John Milton (1608–1674).

verities. Empirical science is apt to cloud the sight, and, by the very knowledge of functions and processes, to bereave the student of the manly contemplation of the whole. The savant[96] becomes unpoetic. But the best read naturalist who lends an entire and devout attention to truth, will see that there remains much to learn of his relation to the world, and that it is not to be learned by any addition or subtraction or other comparison of known quantities, but is arrived at by untaught sallies of the spirit, by a continual self-recovery, and by entire humility. He will perceive that there are far more excellent qualities in the student than preciseness and infallibility; that a guess is often more fruitful than an indisputable affirmation, and that a dream may let us deeper into the secret of nature than a hundred concerted experiments.

For, the problems to be solved are precisely those which the physiologist and the naturalist omit to state. It is not so pertinent to man to know all the individuals of the animal kingdom, as it is to know whence and whereto is this tyrannizing unity in his constitution, which evermore separates and classifies things, endeavoring to reduce the most diverse to one form. When I behold a rich landscape, it is less to my purpose to recite correctly the order and superposition of the strata, than to know why all thought of multitude is lost in a tranquil sense of unity. I cannot greatly honor minuteness in details, so long as there is no hint to explain the relation between things and thoughts; no ray upon the *metaphysics* of conchology,[97] of botany, of the arts, to show the relation of the forms of flowers, shells, animals, architecture, to the mind, and build science upon ideas. In a cabinet of natural history,[98] we become sensible of a certain occult recognition and sympathy in regard to the most unwieldy and eccentric forms of beast, fish, and insect. The American who has been confined, in his own country, to the sight of buildings designed after foreign models, is surprised on entering York Minister or St. Peter's[99] at Rome, by the feeling that these structures are imitations also,—faint copies of an invisible archetype. Nor has science sufficient humanity, so long as the naturalist overlooks that wonderful congruity which subsists between man and the world; of which he is lord, not because he is the most subtile inhabitant, but because he is its head and heart, and finds something of himself in every great and small thing, in every mountain stratum, in every new law of color, fact of astronomy, or atmospheric influence which observation or analysis lay open. A perception of this mystery inspires the muse of George Herbert,[100] the beautiful psalmist of the seventeenth century. The following lines are part of his little poem on Man.

> "Man is all symmetry,
> Full of proportions, one limb to another,
> And to all the world besides.
> Each part may call the farthest, brother;
> For head with foot hath private amity,
> And both with moons and tides.
>
> "Nothing hath got so far
> But man hath caught and kept it as his prey;
> His eyes dismount the highest star;

---

[96] Learned person.
[97] The study of seashells (conchs).   [98] A display case of specimens from nature.
[99] The cathedral at York, England, and St. Peter's Cathedral.
[100] Herbert (1593–1633) was an English metaphysical poet; Emerson quotes stanzas 1–4 and 6 of Herbert's poem "Man."

He is in little all the sphere.
Herbs gladly cure our flesh, because that they
Find their acquaintance there.

"For us, the winds do blow,
The earth doth rest, heaven move, and fountains flow;
Nothing we see, but means our good,
As our delight, or as our treasure;
The whole is either our cupboard of food,
Or cabinet of pleasure.

"The stars have us to bed:
Night draws the curtain; which the sun withdraws.
Music and light attend our head.
All things unto our flesh are kind,
In their descent and being; to our mind,
In their ascent and cause.

"More servants wait on man
Than he'll take notice of. In every path,
He treads down that which doth befriend him
When sickness makes him pale and wan.
Oh mighty love! Man is one world, and hath
Another to attend him."

The perception of this class of truths makes the eternal attraction which draws men to science, but the end is lost sight of in attention to the means. In view of this half-sight of science, we accept the sentence of Plato, that, "poetry comes nearer to vital truth than history." Every surmise and vaticination[101] of the mind is entitled to a certain respect, and we learn to prefer imperfect theories, and sentences, which contain glimpses of truth, to digested systems which have no one valuable suggestion. A wise writer will feel that the ends of study and composition are best answered by announcing undiscovered regions of thought, and so communicating, through hope, new activity to the torpid spirit.

I shall therefore conclude this essay with some traditions of man and nature, which a certain poet[102] sang to me; and which, as they have always been in the world, and perhaps reappear to every bard, may be both history and prophecy.

'The foundations of man are not in matter, but in spirit. But the element of spirit is eternity. To it, therefore, the longest series of events, the oldest chronologies are young and recent. In the cycle of the universal man, from whom the known individuals proceed, centuries are points, and all history is but the epoch of one degradation.

'We distrust and deny inwardly our sympathy with nature. We own and disown our relation to it, by turns. We are, like Nebuchadnezzar,[103] dethroned, bereft of reason, and eating grass like an ox. But who can set limits to the remedial force of spirit?

[101] Prophecy.
[102] Probably Emerson himself; most of the following passages come from his journals.
[103] Nebuchadnezzar (?–562 B.C.), a Babylonian king, lost his reason and "was driven from men, and did eat grass as oxen," from Daniel 4:33.

'A man is a god in ruins. When men are innocent, life shall be longer, and shall pass into the immortal, as gently as we awake from dreams. Now, the world would be insane and rabid, if these disorganizations should last for hundreds of years. It is kept in check by death and infancy. Infancy is the perpetual Messiah, which comes into the arms of fallen men, and pleads with them to return to paradise.

'Man is the dwarf of himself. Once he was permeated and dissolved by spirit. He filled nature with his overflowing currents. Out from him sprang the sun and moon; from man, the sun; from woman, the moon. The laws of his mind, the periods of his actions externized themselves into day and night, into the year and the seasons. But, having made for himself this huge shell, his waters retired; he no longer fills the veins and veinlets; he is shrunk to a drop. He sees, that the structure still fits him, but fits him colossally. Say, rather, once it fitted him, now it corresponds to him from far and on high. He adores timidly his own work. Now is man the follower of the sun, and the woman the follower of the moon. Yet sometimes he starts in his slumber, and wonders at himself and his house, and muses strangely at the resemblance betwixt him and it. He perceives that if his law is still paramount, if still he have elemental power, "if his word is sterling yet in nature," it is not conscious power, it is not inferior but superior to his will. It is Instinct,' Thus my Orphic[104] poet sang.

At present, man applies to nature but half his force. He works on the world with his understanding alone. He lives in it, and masters it by a penny-wisdom; and he that works most in it, is but a half-man, and whilst his arms are strong and his digestion good, his mind is imbruted and he is a selfish savage. His relation to nature, his power over it, is through the understanding; as by manure; the economic use of fire, wind, water, and the mariner's needle; steam, coal, chemical agriculture; the repairs of the human body by the dentist and the surgeon. This is such a resumption of power, as if a banished king should buy his territories inch by inch, instead of vaulting at once into his throne. Meantime, in the thick darkness, there are not wanting gleams of a better light,—occasional examples of the action of man upon nature with his entire force,—with reason as well as understanding. Such examples are; the traditions of miracles in the earliest antiquity of all nations; the history of Jesus Christ; the achievements of a principle, as in religious and political revolutions, and in the abolition of the Slave-trade; the miracles of enthusiasm,[105] as those reported of Swedenborg, Hohenlohe, and the Shakers;[106] many obscure and yet contested facts, now arranged under the name of Animal Magnetism;[107] prayer; eloquence; self-healing; and the wisdom of children. These are examples of Reason's momentary grasp of the sceptre; the exertions of a power which exists not in time or space, but an instantaneous in-streaming causing power. The difference between the actual and the ideal force of man is happily figured by the schoolmen,[108] in saying, that the knowledge of man is an

---

[104] Mystic or oracular after Orpheus, a mythical Greek poet; Emerson's most "orphic" friend was Bronson Alcott (1799–1888), a philosopher and education reformer who published *Orphic Sayings* in 1840. To apply the term "my Orphic poet" to Alcott, however, is to follow a false lead.

[105] Divine ecstacy.

[106] Leopold Franz Emmerich (1794–1849), a German Prince of Hohenlohe-Waldenberg-Schillingfurst, said to have been responsible for miracle cures; and members of the Millennial Church, founded in England in 1747, who were known for their ecstatic dancing and revelations.

[107] Hypnotism.

[108] Scholastic philosophers of the Middle Ages, chief among them Thomas Aquinas (1225–1274).

evening knowledge, *vespertina cognitio,* but that of God is a morning knowledge, *matutina cognitio.*

The problem of restoring to the world original and eternal beauty, is solved by the redemption of the soul. The ruin or the blank, that we see when we look at nature, is in our own eye. The axis of vision is not coincident with the axis of things, and so they appear not transparent but opake. The reason why the world lacks unity, and lies broken and in heaps, is, because man is disunited with himself. He cannot be a naturalist, until he satisfies all the demands of the spirit. Love is as much its demand, as perception. Indeed, neither can be perfect without the other. In the uttermost meaning of the words, thought is devout, and devotion is thought. Deep calls unto deep.[109] But in actual life, the marriage is not celebrated. There are innocent men who worship God after the tradition of their fathers, but their sense of duty has not yet extended to the use of all their faculties. And there are patient naturalists, but they freeze their subject under the wintry light of the understanding. Is not prayer also a study of truth,—a sally of the soul into the unfound infinite? No man ever prayed heartily, without learning something. But when a faithful thinker, resolute to detach every object from personal relations, and see it in the light of thought, shall, at the same time, kindle science with the fire of the holiest affections, then will God go forth anew into the creation.

It will not need, when the mind is prepared for study, to search for objects. The invariable mark of wisdom is to see the miraculous in the common. What is a day? What is a year? What is summer? What is woman? What is a child? What is sleep? To our blindness, these things seem unaffecting. We make fables to hide the baldness of the fact and conform it, as we say, to the higher law of the mind. But when the fact is seen under the light of an idea, the gaudy fable fades and shrivels. We behold the real higher law. To the wise, therefore, a fact is true poetry, and the most beautiful of fables. These wonders are brought to our own door. You also are a man. Man and woman, and their social life, poverty, labor, sleep, fear, fortune, are known to you. Learn that none of these things is superficial, but that each phenomenon hath its roots in the faculties and affections of the mind. Whilst the abstract question occupies your intellect, nature brings it in the concrete to be solved by your hands. It were a wise inquiry for the closet,[110] to compare, point by point, especially at remarkable crises in life, our daily history, with the rise and progress of ideas in the mind.

So shall we come to look at the world with new eyes. It shall answer the endless inquiry of the intellect,—What is truth? and of the affections,—What is good? by yielding itself passive to the educated Will. Then shall come to pass what my poet said; 'Nature is not fixed but fluid. Spirit alters, moulds, makes it. The immobility or bruteness of nature, is the absence of spirit; to pure spirit, it is fluid, it is volatile, it is obedient. Every spirit builds itself a house; and beyond its house, a world; and beyond its world, a heaven. Know then, that the world exists for you. For you is the phenomenon perfect. What we are, that only can we see. All that Adam had, all that Cæsar could, you have and can do. Adam called his house, heaven and earth; Cæsar called his house, Rome; you perhaps call yours, a cobler's trade; a hundred acres of ploughed land; or a scholar's garret. Yet line for line and point for point, your dominion is as great as theirs, though without fine

---

[109] "Deep calleth unto deep at the noise of thy waterspouts: all thy waves and thy billows are gone over me," from Psalm 42:7.

[110] A small, private room; here, a study.

names. Build, therefore, your own world. As fast as you conform your life to the pure idea in your mind, that will unfold its great proportions. A correspondent revolution in things will attend the influx of the spirit. So fast will disagreeable appearances, swine, spiders, snakes, pests, mad-houses, prisons, enemies, vanish; they are temporary and shall be no more seen. The sordor[111] and filths of nature, the sun shall dry up, and the wind exhale. As when the summer comes from the south, the snow-banks melt, and the face of the earth becomes green before it, so shall the advancing spirit create its ornaments along its path, and carry with it the beauty it visits, and the song which enchants it; it shall draw beautiful faces, and warm hearts, and wise discourse, and heroic acts, around its way, until evil is no more seen. The kingdom of man over nature, which cometh not with observation,[112]—a dominion such as now is beyond his dream of God,— he shall enter without more wonder than the blind man feels who is gradually restored to perfect sight.'

1836

THE AMERICAN SCHOLAR*

An Oration Delivered Before the Phi Beta Kappa Society, at Cambridge, August 31, 1837

MR. PRESIDENT, AND GENTLEMEN,

I greet you on the re-commencement of our literary year.[1] Our anniversary is one of hope, and, perhaps, not enough of labor. We do not meet for games of strength or skill, for the recitaton of histories, tragedies and odes, like the ancient Greeks; for parliaments of love and poesy, like the Troubadours;[2] nor for the advancement of science, like our contemporaries in the British and European capitals. Thus far, our holiday has been simply a friendly sign of the survival of the love of letters amongst a people too busy to give to letters any more. As such, it is precious as the sign of an indestructible instinct. Perhaps the time is already come, when it ought to be, and will be something else; when the sluggard intellect of this continent will look from under its iron lids and fill the postponed expectation of the world with something better than the exertions of mechanical skill. Our day of dependence, our long apprenticeship to the learning of other lands, draws to a close. The millions that around us are rushing into life, cannot always be fed on the sere remains of foreign harvests. Events, actions arise, that must be sung, that will sing themselves. Who can doubt that poetry will revive and lead in a new age,

---

[111] Sordidness, squalor.

[112] "And when he was [asked] . . . , when the kingdom of God should come, he answered . . . , The kingdom of God cometh not with observation," from Luke 17:20.

* First published as a pamphlet in 1837, with the subtitle serving as the title. In *Nature, Addresses, and Lectures* (1849) Emerson changed the title to "The American Scholar," thereby addressing all persons devoted to independence of mind.

[1] The academic year, traditionally beginning in September.

[2] Eleventh-through thirteenth-century poets and musicians of southern France who celebrated courtly love.

as the star in the constellation Harp[3] which now flames in our zenith, astronomers announce, shall one day be the pole-star[4] for a thousand years?

In the light of this hope, I accept the topic which not only usage, but the nature of our association, seem to prescribe to this day,—the AMERICAN SCHOLAR. Year by year, we come up hither to read one more chapter of his biography. Let us inquire what light new days and events have thrown on his character, his duties and his hopes.

It is one of those fables,[5] which out of an unknown antiquity, convey an un-looked-for wisdom, that the gods, in the beginning, divided Man into men, that he might be more helpful to himself; just as the hand was divided into fingers, the better to answer its end.

The old fable covers a doctrine ever new and sublime; that there is One Man,—present to all particular men only partially, or through one faculty; and that you must take the whole society to find the whole man. Man is not a farmer, or a professor, or an engineer, but he is all. Man is priest, and scholar, and statesman, and producer, and soldier. In the *divided* or social state, these functions are par-celled out to individuals, each of whom aims to do his stint of the joint work, whilst each other performs his. The fable implies that the individual to possess himself, must sometimes return from his own labor to embrace all the other labor-ers. But unfortunately, this original unit, this fountain of power, has been so dis-tributed to multitudes, has been so minutely subdivided and peddled out, that it is spilled into drops, and cannot be gathered. The state of society is one in which the members have suffered amputation from the trunk, and strut about so many walk-ing monsters,—a good finger, a neck, a stomach, an elbow, but never a man.

Man is thus metamorphosed into a thing, into many things. The planter, who is Man sent out into the field to gather food, is seldom cheered by any idea of the true dignity of his ministry. He sees his bushel and his cart, and nothing beyond, and sinks into the farmer, instead of Man on the farm. The tradesman scarcely ever gives an ideal worth to his work, but is ridden by the routine of his craft, and the soul is subject to dollars. The priest becomes a form; the attorney, a statute-book; the mechanic, a machine; the sailor, a rope of a ship.

In this distribution of functions, the scholar is the delegated intellect. In the right state, he is, *Man Thinking*. In degenerate state, when the victim of society, he tends to become a mere thinker, or, still worse, the parrot of other men's think-ing.

In this view of him, as Man Thinking, the whole theory of his office[6] is con-tained. Him nature solicits, with all her placid, all her monitory pictures. Him the past instructs. Him the future invites. Is not, indeed, every man a student, and do not all things exist for the student's behoof? And, finally, is not the true scholar the only true master? But, as the old oracle said, "All things have two handles. Beware of the wrong one."[7] In life, too often, the scholar errs with mankind and forfeits his privilege. Let us see him in his school, and consider him in reference to the main influences he receives.

I. The first in time and the first in importance of the influences upon the mind is that of nature. Every day, the sun; and, after sunset, night and her stars. Ever the

---

[3] Vega, the bright star in the northern constellation Lyra (shaped like a lyre or harp.)
[4] The North Star, the star closest to the North celestial pole.
[5] *Symposium*, by the Greek philosopher Plato (427?–347? B.C.) includes a version of this fable.
[6] Function, duty.   [7] From the Greek philosopher Epictetus (A.D. 50?–135?).

winds blow; ever the grass grows. Every day, men and women, conversing, beholding and beholden. The scholar must needs stand wistful and admiring before this great spectacle. He must settle its value in his mind. What is nature to him? There is never a beginning, there is never an end to the inexpicable continuity of this web of God, but always circular power returning into itself. Therein it resembles his own spirit, whose beginning, whose ending he never can find—so entire, so boundless. Far, too, as her splendors shine, system on system shooting like rays, upward, downward, without centre, without circumference,—in the mass and in the particle nature hastens to render account of herself to the mind. Classification begins. To the young mind, every thing is individual, stands by itself. By and by, it finds how to join two things, and see in them one nature; then three, then three thousand; and so, tyrannized over by its own unifying instinct, it goes on tying things together, diminishing anomalies, discovering roots running under ground, whereby contrary and remote things cohere, and flower out from one stem. It presently learns, that, since the dawn of history, there has been a constant accumulation and classifying of facts. But what is classification but the perceiving that these objects are not chaotic, and are not foreign, but have a law which is also a law of the human mind? The astronomer discovers that geometry, a pure abstraction of the human mind, is the measure of planetary motion. The chemist finds proportions and intelligible method throughout matter: and science is nothing but the finding of analogy, identity in the most remote parts. The ambitious soul sits down before each refractory fact; one after another, reduces all strange constitutions, all new powers, to their class and their law, and goes on forever to animate the last fibre of organization, the outskirts of nature, by insight.

Thus to him, to this school-boy under the bending dome of day, is suggested, that he and it proceed from one root; one is leaf and one is flower; relation, sympathy, stirring in every vein. And what is that Root? Is not that the soul of his soul?—A thought too bold—a dream too wild. Yet when this spiritual light shall have revealed the law of more earthly natures,—when he has learned to worship the soul, and to see that the natural philosophy that now is, is only the first gropings of its gigantic hand, he shall look forward to an ever expanding knowledge as to a becoming creator. He shall see that nature is the opposite of the soul, answering to it part for part. One is seal, and one is print. Its beauty is the beauty of his own mind. Its laws are the laws of his own mind. Nature then becomes to him the measure of his attainments. So much of nature as he is ignorant of, so much of his own mind does he not yet possess. And, in fine, the ancient precept, "Know thyself," and the modern precept, "Study nature," become at last one maxim.

II. The next great influence[8] into the spirit of the scholar, is, the mind of the Past,—in whatever form, whether of literature, of art, of institutions, that mind is inscribed. Books are the best type of the influence of the past, and perhaps we shall get at the truth—learn the amount of this influence more conveniently—by considering their value alone.

The theory of books is noble. The scholar of the first age received into him the world around; brooded thereon; gave it the new arrangement of his own mind, and uttered it again. It came into him—-life; it went out from him—truth. It came to him—short-lived actions; it went out from him—immortal thoughts. It came to him—business; it went from him—poetry. It was—dead fact; now, it is quick[9] thought. It can stand, and it can go. It now endures, it now flies, it now inspires.[10]

[8] Inflowing.   [9] Living.   [10] Breathes in.

Precisely in proportion to the depth of mind from which it issued, so high does it soar, so long does it sing.

Or, I might say, it depends on how far the process had gone, of transmuting life into truth. In proportion to the completeness of the distillation, so will the purity and imperishableness of the product be. But none is quite perfect. As no air-pump can by any means make a perfect vacuum, so neither can any artist entirely exclude the conventional, the local, the perishable from his book, or write a book of pure thought that shall be as efficient, in all respects, to a remote posterity, as to cotemporaries, or rather to the second age. Each age, it is found, must write its own books; or rather, each generation for the next succeeding. The books of an older period will not fit this.

Yet hence arises a grave mischief. The sacredness which attaches to the act of creation,—the act of thought,—is instantly transferred to the record. The poet chanting, was felt to be a divine man. Henceforth the chant is divine also. The writer was a just and wise spirit. Henceforward it is settled, the book is perfect; as love of the hero corrupts into worship of his statue. Instantly, the book becomes noxious. The guide is a tyrant. We sought a brother, and lo, a governor. The sluggish and perverted mind of the multitude, always slow to open to the incursions of Reason, having once so opened, having once received this book, stands upon it, and makes an outcry, if it is disparaged. Colleges are built on it. Books are written on it by thinkers, not by Man Thinking; by men of talent, that is, who start wrong, who set out from accepted dogmas, not from their own sight of principles. Meek young men grow up in libraries, believing it their duty to accept the views which Cicero, which Locke, which Bacon[11] have given, forgetful that Cicero, Locke and Bacon were only young men in libraries when they wrote these books.

Hence, instead of Man Thinking, we have the bookworm. Hence, the book-learned class, who value books, as such; not as related to nature and the human constitution, but as making a sort of Third Estate[12] with the world and the soul. Hence, the restorers of readings, the emendators, the bibliomaniacs[13] of all degrees.

This is bad; this is worse than it seems. Books are the best of things, well used; abused, among the worst. What is the right use? What is the one end which all means go to effect? They are for nothing but to inspire. I had better never see a book than to be warped by its attraction clean out of my own orbit, and made a satellite instead of a system. The one thing in the world of value, is, the active soul,—the soul, free, sovereign, active. This every man is entitled to; this every man contains within him, although in almost all men, obstructed, and as yet unborn. The soul active sees absolute truth; and utters truth, or creates. In this action, it is genius; not the privilege of here and there a favorite, but the sound estate of every man. In its essence, it is progressive. The book, the college, the school of art, the institution of any kind, stop with some past utterance of genius. This is good, say they,—let us hold by this. They pin me down. They look backward and

[11] The noted orator and Roman statesman Marcus Tullius Cicero (106–43 B.C.); the English philosopher and political theorist John Locke (1632–1704); the English statesman and philosopher Sir Francis Bacon (1561–1626), an early proponent of the inductive method.

[12] The three "estates," or classes, recognized by feudal Europe were the clergy, the nobility, and the commoners. Emerson's analogy criticizes those who value books as objects rather than as manifestations of the world and the spirit.

[13] Those who edit texts, and those obsessed with books.

not forward. But genius always looks forward. The eyes of man are set in his forehead, not in his hindhead. Man hopes. Genius creates. To create,—to create,—is the proof of a divine presence. Whatever talents may be, if the man create not, the pure efflux[14] of the Diety is not his:—cinders and smoke, there may be, but not yet flame. There are creative manners, there are creative actions, and creative words; manners, actions, words, that is, indicative of no custom or authority, but springing spontaneous from the mind's own sense of good and fair.

On the other part, instead of being its own seer, let it receive always from another mind its truth, though it were in torrents of light, without periods of solitude, inquest and self-recovery, and a fatal disservice is done. Genius is always sufficiently the enemy of genius by over-influence. The literature of every nation bear me witness. The English dramatic poets have Shakspearized now for two hundred years.

Undoubtedly there is a right way of reading,—so it be sternly subordinated. Man Thinking must not be subdued by his instruments. Books are for the scholar's idle times. When he can read God directly, the hour is too precious to be wasted in other men's transcripts of their readings. But when the intervals of darkness come, as come they must,—when the soul seeth not, when the sun is hid, and the stars withdraw their shining,—we repair to the lamps which were kindled by their ray to guide our steps to the East again, where the dawn is. We hear that we may speak. The Arabian proverb says, "A fig tree looking on a fig tree, becometh fruitful."

It is remarkable, the character of the pleasure we derive from the best books. They impress us ever with the conviction that one nature wrote and the same reads. We read the verses of one of the great English poets, of Chaucer, of Marvell, of Dryden,[15] with the most modern joy,—with pleasure, I mean, which is in great part caused by the abstraction of all *time* from their verses. There is some awe mixed with the joy of our surprise, when this poet, who lived in some past world, two or three hundred years ago, says that which lies close to my own soul, that which I also had well-nigh thought and said. But for the evidence thence afforded to the philosophical doctrine of the identity of all minds, we should suppose some pre-established harmony, some foresight of souls that were to be, and some preparation of stores for their future wants, like the fact observed in insects, who lay up food before death for the young grub they shall never see.

I would not be hurried by any love of system, by any exaggeration of instincts, to underrate the Book. We all know, that as the human body can be nourished on any food, though it were boiled grass and the broth of shoes, so the human mind can be fed by any knowledge. And great and heroic men have existed, who had almost no other information than by the printed page. I only would say, that it needs a strong head to bear that diet. One must be an inventor to read well. As the proverb says, "He that would bring home the wealth of the Indies, must carry out the wealth of the Indies." There is then creative reading, as well as creative writing. When the mind is braced by labor and invention, the page of whatever book we read becomes luminous with manifold allusion. Every sentence is doubly significant, and the sense of our author is as broad as the world. We then see, what is always true, that as the seer's hour of vision is short and rare among heavy days

[14] Outflowing, emanation.
[15] The English writers Geoffrey Chaucer (1340–1400), Andrew Marvell (1621–1678), and John Dryden (1631–1700).

and months, so is its record, perchance, the least part of his volume. The discerning will read in his Plato or Shakspeare, only that least part,—only the authentic utterances of the oracle,—and all the rest he rejects, were it never so many times Plato's and Shakspeare's.

Of course, there is a portion of reading quite indispensable to a wise man. History and exact science he must learn by laborious reading. Colleges, in like manner, have their indispensable office,—to teach elements. But they can only highly serve us, when they aim not to drill, but to create; when they gather from far every ray of various genius to their hospitable halls, and, by the concentrated fires, set the hearts of their youth on flame. Thought and knowledge are natures in which apparatus and pretension avail nothing. Gowns, and pecuniary foundations,[16] though of towns of gold, can never countervail the least sentence or syllable of wit.[17] Forget this, and our American colleges will recede in their public importance whilst they grow richer every year.

III. There goes in the world a notion that the scholar should be a recluse, a valetudinarian,[18]—as unfit for any handiwork or public labor, as a penknife for an axe. The so-called "practical men" sneer at speculative men, as if, because they speculate or *see,* they could do nothing. I have heard it said that the clergy,—who are always more universally than any other class, the scholars of their day,—are addressed as women: that the rough, spontaneous conversation of men they do not hear, but only a mincing and diluted speech. They are often virtually disfranchised; and, indeed, there are advocates for their celibacy. As far as this is true of the studious classes, it is not just and wise. Action is with the scholar subordinate, but it is essential. Without it, he is not yet man. Without it, thought can never ripen into truth. Whilst the world hangs before the eye as a cloud of beauty, we cannot even see its beauty. Inaction is cowardice, but there can be no scholar without the heroic mind. The preamble of thought, the transition through which it passes from the unconscious to the conscious, is action. Only so much do I know, as I have lived. Instantly we know whose words are loaded with life, and whose not.

The world,—this shadow of the soul, or *other me,* lies wide around. Its attractions are the keys which unlock my thoughts and make me acquainted with myself. I run eagerly into this resounding tumult. I grasp the hands of those next me, and take my place in the ring to suffer and to work, taught by an instinct that so shall the dumb abyss be vocal with speech. I pierce its order; I dissipate its fear; I dispose of it within the circuit of my expanding life. So much only of life as I know by experience, so much of the wilderness have I vanquished and planted, or so far have I extended my being, my dominion. I do not see how any man can afford, for the sake of his nerves and his nap, to spare any action in which he can partake. It is pearls and rubies to his discourse. Drudgery, calamity, exasperation, want, are instructers in eloquence and wisdom. The true scholar grudges every opportunity of action past by, as a loss of power.

It is the raw material out of which the intellect moulds her splendid products. A strange process too, this, by which experience is converted into thought, as a mulberry leaf is converted into satin.[19] The manufacture goes forward at all hours.

The actions and events of our childhood and youth are now matters of calmest observation. They lie like fair pictures in the air. Not so with our recent actions,—

---

[16] Academic robes, and financial foundations.   [17] Intellectual quality.   [18] An invalid.
[19] Satin made from silk, which is produced by silkworms that feed on mulberry leaves.

with the business which we now have in hand. On this we are quite unable to speculate. Our affections as yet circulate through it. We no more feel or know it, than we feel the feet, or the hand, or the brain of our body. The new deed is yet part of life,—remains for a time immersed in our unconscious life. In some contemplative hour, it detaches itself from the life like a ripe fruit, to become a thought of the mind. Instantly, it is raised, transfigured; the corruptible has put on incorruption.[20] Always now it is an object of beauty, however base its origin and neighborhood. Observe, too, the impossibility of antedating this act. In its grub state, it cannot fly, it cannot shine,—it is a dull grub. But suddenly, without observation, the selfsame thing unfurls beautiful wings, and is an angel of wisdom. So is there no fact, no event, in our private history, which shall not, sooner or late, lose its adhesive inert form, and astonish us by soaring from our body into the empyrean.[21] Cradle and infancy, school and playground, the fear of boys, and dogs, and ferules,[22] the love of little maids and berries, and many another fact that once filled the whole sky, are gone already; friend and relative, profession and party, town and country, nation and world, must also soar and sing.

Of course, he who has put forth his total strength in fit actions, has the richest return of wisdom. I will not shut myself out of this globe of action and transplant an oak into a flower pot, there to hunger and pine; nor trust the revenue of some single faculty, and exhaust one vein of thought, much like those Savoyards,[23] who, getting their livelihood by carving shepherds, shepherdesses, and smoking Dutchmen,[24] for all Europe, went out one day to the mountain to find stock, and discovered that they had whittled up the last of their pine trees. Authors we have in numbers, who have written out their vein, and who, moved by a commendable prudence, sail for Greece or Palestine, follow the trapper into the prairie, or ramble round Algiers to replenish their merchantable stock.

If it were only for a vocabulary the scholar would be covetous of action. Life is our dictionary. Years are well spent in country labors; in town—in the insight into trades and manufactures; in frank intercourse with many men and women; in science; in art; to the one end of mastering in all their facts a language, by which to illustrate and embody our perceptions. I learn immediately from any speaker how much he has already lived, through the poverty or the splendor of his speech. Life lies behind us as the quarry from whence we get tiles and copestones for the masonry of to-day. This is the way to learn grammar. Colleges and books only copy the language which the field and the work-yard made.

But the final value of action, like that of books, and better than books, is, that it is a resource. That great principle of Undulation in nature, that shows itself in the inspiring and expiring of the breath; in desire and satiety; in the ebb and flow of the sea, in day and night, in heat and cold, and as yet more deeply ingrained in every atom and every fluid, is known to us under the name of Polarity,—these "fits of easy transmission and reflection," as Newton[25] called them, are the law of nature because they are the law of spirit.

The mind now thinks; now acts; and each fit reproduces the other. When the artist has exhausted his materials, when the fancy no longer paints, when thoughts

---

[20] "For this corruptible must put on incorruption, and this mortal must put on immortality," from I Corinthians 15:53.

[21] The highest heaven.   [22] Rods or rulers for disciplining children.

[23] Inhabitants of Savoy, in the French Alps (then part of Italy).   [24] Pipes.

[25] The English mathematician and natural philosopher Sir Issac Newton (1642–1727), in *Optics* (1704).

are no longer apprehended, and books are a weariness—he has always the re-source to *live*. Character is higher than intellect. Thinking is the function. Living is the functionary. The stream retreats to its source. A great soul will be strong to live, as well as strong to think. Does he lack organ or medium to impart his truths? He can still fall back on this elemental force of living them. This is a total act. Thinking is a partial act. Let the grandeur of justice shine in his affairs. Let the beauty of affection cheer his lowly roof. Those "far from fame" who dwell and act with him will feel the force of his constitution in the doings and passages of the day better than it can be measured by any public and designed display. Time shall teach him that the scholar loses no hour which the man lives. Herein he unfolds the sacred germ of his instinct, screened from influence. What is lost in seemliness is gained in strength. Not out of those on whom systems of education have ex-hausted their culture, comes the helpful giant to destroy the old or to build the new, but out of unhandselled[26] savage nature, out of terrible Druids and Ber-serkirs, come at last Alfred and Shakspear[e].[27]

I hear therefore with joy whatever is beginning to be said of the dignity and necessity of labor to every citizen. There is virtue yet in the hoe and the spade, for learned as well as for unlearned hands. And labor is every where welcome; always we are invited to work; only be this limitation observed, that a man shall not for the sake of wider activity sacrifice any opinion to the popular judgments and modes of action.

I have now spoken of the education of the scholar by nature, by books, and by action. It remains to say somewhat of his duties.

They are such as become Man Thinking. They may all be comprised in self-trust. The office of the scholar is to cheer, to raise, and to guide men by showing them facts amidst appearances. He plies the slow, unhonored, and unpaid task of observation. Flamsteed and Herschel,[28] in their glazed observatories, may cata-logue the stars with the praise of all men, and, the results being splendid and useful, honor is sure. But he, in his private observatory, cataloguing obscure and nebulous stars of the human mind, which as yet no man has thought of as such,— watching days and months, sometimes, for a few facts; correcting still his old records;—must relinquish display and immediate fame. In the long period of his preparation, he must betray often an ignorance and shiftlessness in popular arts, incurring the disdain of the able who shoulder him aside. Long he must stammer in his speech; often forego the living for the dead. Worse yet, he must accept— how often! poverty and solitude. For the ease and pleasure of treading the old road, accepting the fashions, the education, the religion of society, he takes the cross of making his own, and, of course, the self-accusation, the faint heart, the frequent uncertainty and loss of time which are the nettles and tangling vines in the way of the self-relying and self-directed; and the state of virtual hostility in which he seems to stand to society, and especially to educated society. For all this loss and scorn, what offset? He is to find consolation in exercising the highest functions of human nature. He is one who raises himself from private considera-

---

[26] Wild, primitive.

[27] The savage times of ancient pagan Celtic priests (Druids) and legendary Norse warriors who bit their shields and foamed at the mouth (Berserkers) finally gave way to the achievements of Alfred (849–901), king of the West Saxons (who established English laws and encouraged literacy).

[28] John Flamsteed (1646–1719), an astronomer who did pioneer work on mapping the Solar System; Sir William Herschel (1738–1822), an astronomer who discovered the planet Uranus in 1781 and conducted seminal research on nebulae and star clusters.

tions, and breathes and lives on public and illustrious thoughts. He is the world's eye. He is the world's heart. He is to resist the vulgar prosperity that retrogrades ever to barbarism, by preserving and communicating heroic sentiments, noble biographies, melodious verse, and the conclusions of history. Whatsoever oracles the human heart in all emergencies, in all solemn hours has uttered as its commentary on the world of actions,—these shall receive and impart. And whatsoever new verdict Reason from her inviolable seat pronounces on the passing men and events of to-day,—this he shall hear and promulgate.

These being his functions, it becomes him to feel all confidence in himself, and to defer never to the popular cry. He and he only knows the world. The world of any moment is the merest appearance. Some great decorum, some fetish of a government, some ephemeral trade, or war, or man, is cried up by half mankind and cried down by the other half, as if all depended on this particular up or down. The odds are that the whole question is not worth the poorest thought which the scholar has lost in listening to the controversy. Let him not quit his belief that a popgun is a popgun, though the ancient and honorable of the earth affirm it to be the crack of doom. In silence, in steadiness, in severe abstraction, let him hold by himself; add observation to observation, patient of neglect, patient of reproach; and bide his own time,—happy enough if he can satisfy himself alone that this day he has seen something truly. Success treads on every right step. For the instinct is sure that prompts him to tell his brother what he thinks. He then learns that in going down into the secrets of his own mind, he has descended into the secrets of all minds. He learns that he who has mastered any law in his private thoughts, is master to that extent of all men whose language he speaks, and of all into whose language his own can be translated. The poet in utter solitude remembering his spontaneous thoughts and recording them, is found to have recorded that which men in crowded cities find true for them also. The orator distrusts at first the fitness of his frank confessions,—his want of knowledge of the persons he addresses,—until he finds that he is the complement of his hearers;—that they drink his words because he fulfils for them their own nature; the deeper he dives into his privatest secretest presentiment,—to his wonder he finds, this is the most acceptable, most public, and universally true. The people delight in it; the better part of every man feels. This is my music; this is myself.

In self-trust, all the virtues are comprehended. Free should the scholar be,—free and brave. Free even to the definition of freedom, "without any hindrance that does not arise out of his own constitution." Brave; for fear is a thing which a scholar by his very function puts behind him. Fear always springs from ignorance. It is a shame to him if his tranquillity, amid dangerous times, arise from the presumption that like children and women, his is a protected class; or if he seek a temporary peace by the diversion of his thoughts from politics or vexed questions, hiding his head like an ostrich in the flowering bushes, peeping into microscopes, and turning rhymes, as a boy whistles to keep his courage up. So is the danger a danger still: so is the fear worse. Manlike let him turn and face it. Let him look into its eye and search its nature, inspect its origin,—see the whelping of this lion,—which lies no great way back; he will then find in himself a perfect comprehension of its nature and extent; he will have made his hands meet on the other side, and can henceforth defy it, and pass on superior. The world is his who can see through its pretension. What deafness, what stone-blind custom, what overgrown error you behold, is there only by sufferance,—by your sufferance. See it to be a lie, and you have already dealt it its mortal blow.

Yes, we are the cowed,—we the trustless. It is a mischievous notion that we are come late into nature; that the world was finished a long time ago. As the world was plastic and fluid in the hands of God, so it is ever to so much of his attributes as we bring to it. To ignorance and sin, it is flint. They adapt themselves to it as they may; but in proportion as a man has anything in him divine, the firmament flows before him, and takes his signet[29] and form. Not he is great who can alter matter, but he who can alter my state of mind. They are the kings of the world who give the color of their present thought to all nature and all art, and persuade men by the cheerful serenity of their carrying the matter, that this thing which they do, is the apple which the ages have desired to pluck, now at last ripe, and inviting nations to the harvest. The great man makes the great thing. Wherever Macdonald sits, there is the head of the table.[30] Linnæus makes botany the most alluring of studies and wins it from the farmer and the herb-woman. Davy, chemistry: and Cuvier, fossils.[31] The day is always his, who works in it with serenity and great aims. The unstable estimates of men crowd to him whose mind is filled with a truth, as the heaped waves of the Atlantic follow the moon.

For this self-trust, the reason is deeper than can be fathomed,—darker than can be enlightened. I might not carry with me the feeling of my audience in stating my own belief. But I have already shown the ground of my hope, in adverting to the doctrine that man is one. I believe man has been wronged: he has wronged himself. He has almost lost the light that can lead him back to his prerogatives. Men are become of no account. Men in history, men in the world of to-day are bugs, are spawn, and are called "the mass" and "the herd." In a century, in a millenium, one or two men; that is to say—one or two approximations to the right state of every man. All the rest behold in the hero or the poet their own green and crude being—ripened; yes, and are content to be less, so *that* may attain to its full stature. What a testimony—full of grandeur, full of pity, is borne to the demands of his own nature, by the poor clansman, the poor partisan, who rejoices in the glory of his chief. The poor and the low find some amends to their immense moral capacity, for their acquiescence in a political and social inferiority. They are content to be brushed like flies from the path of a great person, so that justice shall be done by him to that common nature which it is the dearest desire of all to see enlarged and glorified. They sun themselves in the great man's light, and feel it to be their own element. They cast the dignity of man from their downtrod selves upon the shoulders of a hero, and will perish to add one drop of blood to make that great heart beat, those giant sinews combat and conquer. He lives for us, and we live in him.

Men such as they are, very naturally seek money or power; and power because it is as good as money,—the "spoils," so called, "of office." And why not? for they aspire to the highest, and this, in their sleep-waking, they dream is highest. Wake them, and they shall quit the false good and leap to the true, and leave governments to clerks and desks. This revolution is to be wrought by the gradual domestication of the idea of Culture. The main enterprise of the world for splendor, for extent, is the upbuilding of a man. Here are the materials strown along the ground. The private life of one man shall be more an [word supplied] illustrious

---

[29] Seal, identifying stamp.   [30] From a Scottish proverb about a leader's authority.
[31] Carl von Linné (1707–1778), or Carolus Linnaeus, a Swedish botanist; Sir Humphrey Davy (1778–1829), an English chemist; Georges Cuvier (1769–1832), a French anatomist and paleontologist.

monarchy,—more formidable to its enemy, more sweet and serene in its influence to its friend, than any kingdom in history. For a man, rightly viewed, comprehendeth the particular natures of all men. Each philosopher, each bard, each actor, has only done for me, as by a delegate, what one day I can do for myself. The books which once we valued more than the apple of the eye, we have quite exhausted. What is that but saying that we have come up with the point of view which the universal mind took through the eyes of that one scribe; we have been that man, and have passed on. First, one; then, another; we drain all cisterns, and waxing greater by all these supplies, we crave a better and more abundant food. The man has never lived that can feed us ever. The human mind cannot be enshrined in a person who shall set a barrier on any one side to this unbounded, unboundable empire. It is one central fire which flaming now out of the lips of Etna, lightens the capes of Sicily; and now out of the throat of Vesuvius,[32] illuminates the towers and vineyards of Naples. It is one light which beams out of a thousand stars. It is one soul which animates all men.

But I have dwelt perhaps tediously upon this abstraction of the Scholar. I ought not to delay longer to add what I have to say, of nearer reference to the time and to this country.

Historically, there is thought to be a difference in the ideas which predominate over successive epochs, and there are data for marking the genius of the Classic, of the Romantic, and now of the Reflective or Philosophical age. With the views I have intimated of the oneness or the identity of the mind through all individuals, I do not much dwell on these differences. In fact, I believe each individual passes through all three. The boy is a Greek; the youth, romantic; the adult, reflective. I deny not, however, that a revolution in the leading idea may be distinctly enough traced.

Our age is bewailed as the age of Introversion. Must that needs be evil? We, it seems, are critical. We are embarrassed with second thoughts. We cannot enjoy any thing for hankering to know whereof the pleasure consists. We are lined with eyes. We see with our feet. The time is infected with Hamlet's unhappiness,—

"Sicklied o'er with the pale cast of thought."[33]

Is it so bad then? Sight is the last thing to be pitied. Would we be blind? Do we fear lest we should outsee nature and God, and drink truth dry? I look upon the discontent of the literary class as a mere announcement of the fact that they find themselves not in the state of mind of their fathers, and regret the coming state as untried; as a boy dreads the water before he has learned that he can swim. If there is any period one would desire to be born in,—is it not the age of Revolution; when the old and the new stand side by side, and admit of being compared; when the energies of all men are searched by fear and by hope; when the historic glories of the old, can be compensated by the rich possibilities of the new era? This time, like all times, is a very good one, if we but know what to do with it.

I read with joy some of the auspicious signs of the coming days as they glimmer already through poetry and art, through philosophy and science, through church and state.

One of these signs is the fact that the same movement which effected the eleva-

---

[32] Active volcanoes: Etna, on the East coast of Sicily; Vesuvius, near Naples, Italy.
[33] From Shakespeare's *Hamlet* (III.i.85).

tion of what was called the lowest class in the state, assumed in literature a very marked and as benign an aspect. Instead of the sublime and beautiful, the near, the low, the common, was explored and poetized. That which had been negligently trodden under foot by those who were harnessing and provisioning themselves for long journeys into far countries, is suddenly found to be richer than all foreign parts. The literature of the poor, the feelings of the child, the philosophy of the street, the meaning of household life, are the topics of the time. It is a great stride. It is a sign—is it not? of new vigor, when the extremities are made active, when currents of warm life run into the hands and the feet. I ask not for the great, the remote, the romantic; what is doing in Italy or Arabia; what is Greek art, or Provencal Ministrelsy;[34] I embrace the common, I explore and sit at the feet of the familiar, the low. Give me insight into to-day, and you may have the antique and future worlds. What would we really know the meaning of? The meal in the firkin;[35] the milk in the pan; the ballad in the street; the news of the boat; the glance of the eye; the form and the gait of the body:—show me the ultimate reason of these matters;—show me the sublime presence of the highest spiritual cause lurking, as always it does lurk, in these suburbs and extremities of nature; let me see every trifle bristling with the polarity that ranges it instantly on an eternal law; and the shop, the plough, and the le[d]ger, referred to the like cause by which light undulates and poets sing;—and the world lies no longer a dull miscellany and lumber room,[36] but has form and order; there is no trifle; there is no puzzle; but one design unites and animates the farthest pinnacle and the lowest trench.

This idea has inspired the genius of Goldsmith, Burns, Cowper, and, in a newer time, of Goethe, Wordsworth, and Carlyle.[37] This idea they have differently followed and with various success. In contrast with their writing, the style of Pope, of Johnson, of Gibbon,[38] looks cold and pedantic. This writing is blood-warm. Man is surprised to find that things near are not less beautiful and wondrous than things remote. The near explains the far. The drop is a small ocean. A man is related to all nature. This perception of the worth of the vulgar, is fruitful in discoveries. Goethe, in this very thing the most modern of the moderns, has shown us, as none ever did, the genius of the ancients.

There is one man of genius who has done much for this philosophy of life, whose literary value has never yet been rightly estimated;—I mean Emanuel Swedenborg.[39] The most imaginative of men, yet writing with the precision of a mathematician, he endeavored to engraft a purely philosophical Ethics on the popular Christianity of his time. Such an attempt, of course, must have difficulty which no genius could surmount. But he saw and showed the connexion between nature and the affections of the soul. He pierced the emblematic or spiritual character of the visible, audible, tangible world. Especially did his shade-loving muse

---

[34] The musical entertainment of medieval troubadors, centered in Provence, in southeastern France.
[35] A small wooden tub.   [36] A storeroom.
[37] Preromantic writers Oliver Goldsmith (1730–1794), Robert Burns (1759–1796), and William Cowper (1731–1800); and romantic writers Johann Wolfgang von Goethe (1749–1832), William Wordsworth (1770–1850), and Thomas Carlyle (1795–1881).
[38] The eighteenth-century writers Alexander Pope (1688–1744), Samuel Johnson (1709–1784), and Edward Gibbon (1737–1794).
[39] Swedenborg (1688–1772) was a Swedish theologian and mystic whose idea of correspondence between the spiritual and the natural world virtually made Creation an allegory of the divine mind—a concept that intrigued Emerson.

hover over and interpret the lower parts of nature; he showed the mysterious bond that allies moral evil to the foul material forms, and has given in epical parables a theory of insanity, of beasts, of unclean and fearful things.

Another sign of our times, also marked by an analogous political movement is, the new importance given to the single person. Every thing that tends to insulate the individual,—to surround him with barriers of natural respect, so that each man shall feel the world is his, and man shall treat with man as a sovereign state with a sovereign state;—tends to true union as well as greatness. "I learned," said the melancholy Pestalozzi,[40] "that no man in God's wide earth is either willing or able to help any other man." Help must come from the bosom alone. The scholar is that man who must take up into himself all the ability of the time, all the contributions of the past, all the hopes of the future. He must be an university of knowledges. If there be one lesson more than another which should pierce his ear, it is, The world is nothing, the man is all; in yourself is the law of all nature, and you know not yet how a globule of sap ascends; in yourself slumbers the whole of Reason; it is for you to know all, it is for you to dare all. Mr. President and Gentlemen, this confidence in the unsearched might of man, belongs by all motives, by all prophecy, by all preparation, to the American Scholar. We have listened too long to the courtly muses of Europe. The spirit of the American freeman is already suspected to be timid, imitative, tame. Public and private avarice make the air we breathe thick and fat. The scholar is decent, indolent, complaisant.[41] See already the tragic consequence. The mind of this country taught to aim at low objects, eats upon itself. There is no work for any but decorous and the complaisant. Young men of the fairest promise, who begin life upon our shores, inflated by the mountain winds, shined upon by all the stars of God, find the earth below not in unison with these,—but are hindered from action by the disgust which the principles on which business is managed inspire, and turn drudges, or die of disgust,—some of them suicides. What is the remedy? They did not yet see, and thousands of young men as hopeful now crowding to the barriers for the career, do not yet see, that if the single man plant himself indomitably on his instincts, and there abide, the huge world will come round to him. Patience—patience;—with the shades of all the good and great for company; and for solace, the perspective of your own infinite life; and for work, the study and the communication of principles, the making those instincts prevalent, the conversion of the world. Is it not the chief disgrace in the world, not to be an unit;—not to be reckoned one character;—not to yield that peculiar fruit which each man was created to bear, but to be reckoned in the gross, in the hundred, or the thousand, of the party, the section, to which we belong; and our opinion predicted geographically, as the north, or the south. Not so, brothers and friends,—please God, ours shall not be so. We will walk on our own feet; we will work with our own hands; we will speak our own minds. The study of letters shall be no longer a name for pity, for doubt, and for sensual indulgence. The dread of man and the love of man shall be a wall of defence and a wreath of joy around all. A nation of men will for the first time exist, because each believes himself inspired by the Divine Soul which also inspires all men.

1837

---

[40] Johann Heinrich Pestalozzi (1746–1827), a Swiss educator.   [41] Willing to please.

SELF-RELIANCE*

"Ne te quæsiveris extra."[1]

*"Man is his own star; and the soul that can
Render an honest and a perfect man,
Commands all light, all influence, all fate;
Nothing to him falls early or too late.
Our acts our angels are, or good or ill,
Our fatal shadows that walk by us still."*

Epilogue to Beaumont and Fletcher's *Honest Man's Fortune.*[2]

Cast the bantling[3] on the rocks,
Suckle him with the she-wolf's teat;
Wintered with the hawk and fox,
Power and speed be hands and feet.

I read the other day some verses written by an eminent painter[4] which were original and not conventional. The soul always hears an admonition in such lines, let the subject be what it may. The sentiment they instil is of more value than any thought they may contain. To believe your own thought, to believe that what is true for you in your private heart, is true for all men,—that is genius. Speak your latent conviction and it shall be the universal sense; for the inmost in due time becomes the outmost,—and our first thought is rendered back to us by the trumpets of the Last Judgment. Familiar as the voice of the mind is to each, the highest merit we ascribe to Moses, Plato, and Milton, is that they set at naught books and traditions, and spoke not what men but what they thought. A man should learn to detect and watch that gleam of light which flashes across his mind from within, more than the lustre of the firmament of bards and sages. Yet he dismisses without notice his thought, because it is his. In every work of genius we recognize our own rejected thoughts: they come back to us with a certain alienated majesty. Great works of art have no more affecting lesson for us than this. They teach us to abide by our spontaneous impression with good-humored inflexibility then most when the whole cry of voices is on the other side. Else, tomorrow a stranger will say with masterly good sense precisely what we have thought and felt all the time, and we shall be forced to take with shame our own opinion from another.

There is a time in every man's education when he arrives at the conviction that envy is ignorance; that imitation is suicide; that he must take himself for better, for worse, as his portion; that though the wide universe is full of good, no kernel of nourishing corn can come to him but through his toil bestowed on that plot of ground which is given to him to till. The power which resides in him is new in

---

* First published in *Essays* in 1841. Many of the ideas in this essay are taken from Emerson's journal entries, dating from 1832 to 1840.

[1] "Do not seek outside yourself" (Latin); from the first of six satires by Persius Flaccus (A.D. 34–62), a Roman Stoic writer.

[2] The Elizabethan dramatists Francis Beaumont (1584–1616) and John Fletcher (1579–1625); however, *The Honest Man's Fortune* (1647) is believed to have been written in 1613 by Fletcher and another dramatist, Philip Massinger (1583–1640).

[3] Infant. These four lines were composed by Emerson.

[4] Probably Washington Allston (1779–1843), an American painter and poet. Emerson praises a poem of Allston's in a journal entry for September 20, 1837.

nature, and none but he knows what that is which he can do, nor does he know until he has tried. Not for nothing one face, one character, one fact makes much impression on him, and another none. This sculpture in the memory is not without preëstablished harmony. The eye was placed where one ray should fall, that it might testify of that particular ray. We but half express ourselves, and are ashamed of that divine idea which each of us represents. It may be safely trusted as proportionate and of good issues, so it be faithfully imparted, but God will not have his work made manifest by cowards. A man is relieved and gay when he has put his heart into his work and done his best; but what he has said or done otherwise, shall give him no peace. It is a deliverance which does not deliver. In the attempt his genius deserts him; no muse befriends; no invention, no hope.

Trust thyself: every heart vibrates to that iron string. Accept the place the divine Providence has found for you; the society of your contemporaries, the connexion of events. Great men have always done so and confided themselves childlike to the genius of their age, betraying their perception that the absolutely trustworthy was seated at their heart, working through their hands, predominating in all their being. And we are now men, and must accept in the highest mind the same transcendent destiny; and not minors and invalids in a protected corner, not cowards fleeing before a revolution, but guides, redeemers, and benefactors, obeying the Almighty effort, and advancing on Chaos and the Dark.

What pretty oracles nature yields us on this text in the face and behavior of children, babes and even brutes. That divided and rebel mind, that distrust of a sentiment because our arithmetic has computed the strength and means opposed to our purpose, these have not. Their mind being whole, their eye is as yet unconquered, and when we look in their faces, we are disconcerted. Infancy conforms to nobody; all conform to it, so that one babe commonly makes four or five out of the adults who prattle and play to it. So God has armed youth and puberty and manhood no less with its own piquancy and charm, and made it enviable and gracious and its claims not to be put by, if it will stand by itself. Do not think the youth has no force because he cannot speak to you and me. Hark! in the next room his voice is sufficiently clear and emphatic. It seems he knows how to speak to his contemporaries. Bashful or bold, then, he will know how to make us seniors very unnecessary.

The nonchalance of boys who are sure of a dinner, and would disdain as much as a lord to do or say aught to conciliate one, is the healthy attitude of human nature. A boy is in the parlour what the pit[5] is in the playhouse; independent, irresponsible, looking out from his corner on such people and facts as pass by, he tries and sentences them on their merits, in the swift summary way of boys, as good, bad, interesting, silly, eloquent, troublesome. He cumbers himself never about consequences, about interests: he gives an independent, genuine verdict. You must court him: he does not court you. But the man is, as it were, clapped into jail by his consciousness. As soon as he has once acted or spoken with eclat,[6] he is a committed person, watched by the sympathy or the hatred of hundreds whose affections must now enter into his account. There is no Lethe[7] for this. Ah, that he could pass again into his neutrality! Who can thus avoid all pledges, and

---

[5] The cheapest seats in Elizabethan theaters, where the audience was not restrained by "proper" manners.

[6] "Brilliance of purpose" (French).

[7] According to Greek myth, the river of forgetfulness, in the underworld.

having observed, observe again from the same unaffected, unbiased, unbribable, unaffrighted innocence, must alway be formidable. He would utter opinions on all passing affairs, which being seen to be not private but necessary, would sink like darts into the ear of men, and put them in fear.

These are the voices which we hear in solitude, but they grow faint and inaudible as we enter into the world. Society everywhere is in conspiracy against the manhood of every one of its members. Society is a joint-stock company in which the members agree for the better securing of his bread to each shareholder, to surrender the liberty and culture of the eater. The virtue in most request is conformity. Self-reliance is its aversion. It loves not realities and creators, but names and customs.

Whoso would be a man must be a nonconformist. He who would gather immortal palms[8] must not be hindered by the name of goodness, but must explore if it be goodness. Nothing is at last sacred but the integrity of your own mind. Absolve you to yourself, and you shall have the suffrage of the world. I remember an answer which when quite young I was prompted to make to a valued adviser who was wont to importune me with the dear old doctrines of the church. On my saying, What have I to do with the sacredness of traditions, if I live wholly from within? my friend suggested—"But these impulses may be from below, not from above." I replied, "They do not seem to me to be such; but if I am the Devil's child, I will live then from the Devil." No law can be sacred to me but that of my nature. Good and bad are but names very readily transferable to that or this; the only right is what is after my constitution, the only wrong what is against it. A man is to carry himself in the presence of all opposition as if every thing were titular and ephemeral but he. I am ashamed to think how easily we capitulate to badges and names, to large societies and dead institutions. Every decent and well-spoken individual affects and sways me more than is right. I ought to go upright and vital, and speak the rude truth in all ways. If malice and vanity wear the coat of philanthropy, shall that pass? If an angry bigot assumes this bountiful cause of Abolition, and comes to me with his last news from Barbadoes,[9] why should I not say to him, 'Go love thy infant; love thy woodchopper: be good-natured and modest: have that grace; and never varnish your hard, uncharitable ambition with this incredible tenderness for black folk a thousand miles off. Thy love afar is spite at home.' Rough and graceless would be such greeting, but truth is handsomer than the affectation of love. Your goodness must have some edge to it—else it is none. The doctrine of hatred must be preached as the counteraction of the doctrine of love when that pules[10] and whines. I shun father and mother and wife and brother, when my genius calls me. I would write on the lintels[11] of the door-post, *Whim*. I hope it is somewhat better than whim at last, but we cannot spend the day in explanation. Expect me not to show cause why I seek or why I exclude company. Then, again, do not tell me, as a good man did to-day, of my obligation to put all poor men in good situations. Are they *my* poor? I tell thee, thou foolish philanthropist, that I grudge the dollar, the dime, the cent I give to such men as do not belong to me and to whom I do not belong. There is a class of persons to whom by all spiritual affinity I am bought and sold; for them I will go to prison, if need be;

---

[8] Great honors.

[9] Slavery was abolished on this British West Indian island in 1834.   [10] Whimpers.

[11] Horizontal beams spanning doorways. Emerson equates the obligation to heed his "genius" with the biblical injunction to shun family in order to follow a divine command (see Matthew 10:34–37) and alludes to the Lord's instructions to Moses for marking with blood the doorposts of houses to be spared from punishment (see Exodus 12:21–23).

but your miscellaneous popular charities; the education at college of fools; the building of meeting-houses to the vain end to which many now stand; alms to sots; and the thousandfold Relief Societies;—though I confess with shame I sometimes succumb and give the dollar, it is a wicked dollar which by and by I shall have the manhood to withhold.

Virtues are in the popular estimate rather the exception than the rule. There is the man *and* his virtues. Men do what is called a good action, as some piece of courage or charity, much as they would pay a fine in expiation of daily non-appearance on parade. Their works are done as an apology or extenuation of their living in the world,—as invalids and the insane pay a high board. Their virtues are penances. I do not wish to expiate, but to live. My life is for itself and not for a spectacle. I much prefer that it should be of a lower strain, so it be genuine and equal, than that it should be glittering and unsteady. I wish it to be sound and sweet, and not to need diet and bleeding.[12] I ask primary evidence that you are a man, and refuse this appeal from the man to his actions. I know that for myself it makes no difference whether I do or forbear those actions which are reckoned excellent. I cannot consent to pay for a privilege where I have intrinsic right. Few and mean as my gifts may be, I actually am, and do not need for my own assurance or the assurance of my fellows any secondary testimony.

What I must do, is all that concerns me, not what the people think. This rule, equally arduous in actual and in intellectual life, may serve for the whole distinction between greatness and meanness. It is the harder, because you will always find those who think they know what is your duty better than you know it. It is easy in the world to live after the world's opinion; it is easy in solitude to live after our own; but the great man is he who in the midst of the crowd keeps with perfect sweetness the independence of solitude.

The objection to conforming to usages that have become dead to you, is, that it scatters your force. It loses your time and blurs the impression of your character. If you maintain a dead church, contribute to a dead Bible-Society, vote with a great party either for the Government or against it, spread your table like base housekeepers,—under all these screens, I have difficulty to detect the precise man you are. And, of course, so much force is withdrawn from your proper life. But do your work, and I shall know you. Do your work, and you shall reinforce yourself. A man must consider what a blindman's-buff is this game of conformity. If I know your sect, I anticipate your argument. I hear a preacher announce for his text and topic the expediency of one of the institutions of his church. Do I not know beforehand that not possibly can he say a new and spontaneous word? Do I not know that with all this ostentation of examining the grounds of the institution, he will do no such thing? Do I not know that he is pledged to himself not to look but at one side,—the permitted side, not as a man, but as a parish minister? He is a retained attorney, and these airs of the bench are the emptiest affectation. Well, most men have bound their eyes with one or another handkerchief, and attached themselves to some one of these communities of opinion. This conformity makes them not false in a few particulars, authors of a few lies, but false in all particulars. Their every truth is not quite true. Their two is not the real two, their four not the real four; so that every word they say chagrins us, and we know not where to begin to set them right. Meantime nature is not slow to equip us in the prison-uniform of the party to which we adhere. We come to wear one cut of face and figure, and acquire by degrees the gentlest asinine expression. There is a mortify-

---

[12] Bloodletting, an old medical practice.

ing experience in particular which does not fail to wreak itself also in the general history; I mean "the foolish face of praise,"[13] the forced smile which we put on in company where we do not feel at ease in answer to conversation which does not interest us. The muscles, not spontaneously moved, but moved by a low usurping wilfulness, grow tight about the outline of the face with the most disagreeable sensation.

For nonconformity the world whips you with its displeasure. And therefore a man must know how to estimate a sour face. The bystanders look askance on him in the public street or in the friend's parlor. If this aversation had its origin in contempt and resistance like his own, he might well go home with a sad countenance; but the sour faces of the multitude, like their sweet faces, have no deep cause, but are put on and off as the wind blows, and a newspaper directs. Yet is the discontent of the multitude more formidable than that of the senate and the college. It is easy enough for a firm man who knows the world to brook the rage of the cultivated classes. Their rage is decorous and prudent, for they are timid as being very vulnerable themselves. But when to their feminine rage the indignation of the people is added, when the ignorant and the poor are aroused, when the unintelligent brute force that lies at the bottom of society is made to growl and mow,[14] it needs the habit of magnanimity and religion to treat it godlike as a trifle of no concernment.

The other terror that scares us from self-trust is our consistency; a reverence for our past act or word, because the eyes of others have no other data for computing our orbit than our past acts, and we are loath to disappoint them.

But why should you keep your head over your shoulder? Why drag about this corpse of your memory, lest you contradict somewhat you have stated in this or that public place? Suppose you should contradict yourself; what then? It seems to be a rule of wisdom never to rely on your memory alone, scarcely even in acts of pure memory, but to bring the past for judgment into the thousand-eyed present, and live ever in a new day. In your metaphysics you have denied personality to the Deity; yet when the devout motions of the soul come, yield to them heart and life, though they should clothe God with shape and color. Leave your theory as Joseph his coat in the hand of the harlot,[15] and flee.

A foolish consistency is the hobgoblin of little minds, adored by little statesmen and philosophers and divines. With consistency a great soul has simply nothing to do. He may as well concern himself with his shadow on the wall. Speak what you think now in hard words, and to-morrow speak what to-morrow thinks in hard words again, though it contradict every thing you said to-day.—'Ah, so you shall be sure to be misunderstood.'—Is it so bad then to be misunderstood? Pythagoras[16] was misunderstood, and Socrates, and Jesus, and Luther, and Copernicus, and Galileo, and Newton,[17] and every pure and wise spirit that ever took flesh. To be great is to be misunderstood.

---

[13] From the ironic poem "Epistle to Dr. Arbuthnot" (1735), by Alexander Pope (1688–1744).

[14] To grimace or mock.

[15] In Genesis 39:12 when Potiphar's wife grabbed Joseph's coat and asked him to sleep with her, "he left his garment in her hand, and fled."

[16] A sixth-century B. C. Greek mathematician and philosopher.

[17] Martin Luther (1483–1546), the German leader of the Protestant Reformation; Nicolaus Copernicus (1473–1543), the Polish astronomer who determined the movements of the solar system; Galileo Galilei (1564–1642), the renowned Italian astronomer and physicist who supported Copernican theories rather than classical Ptolemaic ideas; Sir Issac Newton (1642–1727), the English mathematician and natural philosopher who formulated the laws of gravity and motion.

I suppose no man can violate his nature. All the allies of his will are rounded in by the law of his being as the inequalities of Andes and Himmaleh[18] are insignificant in the curve of the sphere. Nor does it matter how you gauge and try him. A character is like an acrostic or Alexandrian stanza;[19]—read it forward, backward, or across, it still spells the same thing. In this pleasing contrite wood-life which God allows me, let me record day by day my honest thought without prospect or retrospect, and, I cannot doubt, it will be found symmetrical, though I mean it not, and see it not. My book should smell of pines and resound with the hum of insects. The swallow over my window should interweave that thread or straw he carries in his bill into my web also. We pass for what we are. Character teaches above our wills. Men imagine that they communicate their virtue or vice only by overt actions and do not see that virtue or vice emit a breath every moment.

There will be an agreement in whatever variety of actions, so they be each honest and natural in their hour. For of one will, the actions will be harmonious, however unlike they seem. These varieties are lost sight of at a little distance, at a little height of thought. One tendency unites them all. The voyage of the best ship is a zigzag line of a hundred tacks. See the line from a sufficient distance, and it straightens itself to the average tendency. Your genuine action will explain itself and will explain your other genuine actions. Your conformity explains nothing. Act singly, and what you have already done singly, will justify you now. Greatness apppeals to the future. If I can be firm enough to-day to do right and scorn eyes, I must have done so much right before, as to defend me now. Be it how it will, do right now. Always scorn appearances, and you always may. The force of character is cumulative. All the foregone days of virtue work their health into this. What makes the majesty of the heroes of the senate and the field, which so fills the imagination? The consciousness of a train of great days and victories behind. They shed an united light on the advancing actor. He is attended as by a visible escort of angels. That is it which throws thunder into Chatham's[20] voice, and dignity into Washington's port,[21] and America into Adams's[22] eye. Honor is venerable to us because it is no ephemeris. It is always ancient virtue. We worship it to-day, because it is not of to-day. We love it and pay it homage, because it is not a trap for our love and homage, but is self-dependent, self-derived, and therefore of an old immaculate pedigree, even if shown in a young person.

I hope in these days we have heard the last of conformity and consistency. Let the words be gazetted[23] and ridiculous henceforward. Instead of the gong for dinner, let us hear a whistle from the Spartan fife.[24] Let us never bow and apologize more. A great man is coming to eat at my house. I do not wish to please him: I wish that he should wish to please me. I will stand here for humanity, and though I would make it kind, I would make it true. Let us affront and reprimand the smooth mediocrity and squalid contentment of the times, and hurl in the face of custom, and trade, and office, the fact which is the upshot of all history, that there

---

[18] The Himalaya Mountains.

[19] A palindrome, a word or phrase that reads the same forward or backward: "Madam, I'm Adam."

[20] William Pitt (1708–1778), the earl of Chatham, known as "the Great Commoner" for his eloquent insistence on constitutional rights.

[21] George Washington's carriage or bearing.

[22] Samuel Adams (1722–1803), a spokesman for the Revolutionary movement in Massachusetts, or more likely Washington's contemporary John Adams (1735–1826), the second U.S. president, or John Quincy Adams (1767–1848), the sixth U.S. president.

[23] Put in a newspaper and made publicly ridiculous.

[24] The Spartans were known for their rigor and discipline; hence, sober music.

is a great responsible Thinker and Actor working wherever a man works; that a
true man belongs to no other time or place, but is the centre of things. Where he
is, there is nature. He measures you, and all men, and all events. Ordinarily every
body in society reminds us of somewhat else or of some other person. Character,
reality, reminds you of nothing else; it takes place of the whole creation. The man
must be so much that he must make all circumstances indifferent. Every true man
is a cause, a country, and an age; requires infinite spaces and numbers and time
fully to accomplish his design;—and posterity seem to follow his steps as a train
of clients. A man Cæsar is born, and for ages after, we have a Roman Empire.
Christ is born, and millions of minds so grow and cleave to his genius, that he is
confounded with virtue and the possible of man. An institution is the lengthened
shadow of one man; as, Monachism, of the Hermit Antony;[25] the Reformation, of
Luther; Quakerism, of Fox; Methodism, of Wesley; Abolition, of Clarkson.[26]
Scipio,[27] Milton called "the height of Rome;" and all history resolves itself very
easily into the biography of a few stout and earnest persons.

Let a man then know his worth, and keep things under his feet. Let him not
peep or steal, or skulk up and down with the air of a charity-boy, a bastard, or an
interloper, in the world which exists for him. But the man in the street finding no
worth in himself which corresponds to the force which built a tower or sculptured
a marble god, feels poor when he looks on these. To him a palace, a statue, or a
costly book have an alien and forbidding air, much like a gay equipage, and seem
to say like that, 'Who are you, sir?' Yet they are all his, suitors for his notice,
petitioners to his faculties that they will come out and take possession. The picture
waits for my verdict: it is not to command me, but I am to settle its claims to
praise. That popular fable[28] of the sot who was picked up dead drunk in the street,
carried to the duke's house, washed and dressed and laid in the duke's bed, and,
on his waking, treated with all obsequious ceremony like the duke, and assured
that he had been insane, owes its popularity to the fact, that it symbolizes so well
the state of man, who is in the world a sort of sot, but now and then wakes up,
exercises his reason, and finds himself a true prince.

Our reading is mendicant and sycophantic.[29] In history, our imagination plays
us false. Kingdom and lordship, power and estate are a gaudier vocabulary than
private John and Edward in a small house and common day's work: but the things
of life are the same to both: the sum total of both is the same. Why all this deference to Alfred, and Scanderbeg, and Gustavus?[30] Suppose they were virtuous: did
they wear out virtue? As great a stake depends on your private act to-day, as
followed their public and renowned steps. When private men shall act with original views, the lustre will be transferred from the actions of kings to those of gentlemen.

The world has been instructed by its kings, who have so magnetized the eyes of

---

[25] St. Anthony (251?–350?), an Egyptian hermit known as the father of Christian monasticism
("Monachism").

[26] George Fox (1624–1691), founder of the Society of Friends (Quakers); John Wesley (1703–1791),
founder of Methodism; Thomas Clarkson (1760–1846), an English abolitionist.

[27] Scipio Aemilianus (185?–129? B.C.), known as Scipio Africanus, Minor: the destroyer of Carthage
(146 B.C.) and a patron of writers. John Milton (1608–1674) praises him in *Paradise Lost* (IX. 510).

[28] Known from the "Induction" to Shakespeare's *Taming of the Shrew*.

[29] Poverty-stricken and parasitical.

[30] King Alfred the Great (849–899) of England; George Castriota (1403?–1468), an Albanian chieftain; King Gustavus Adolphus (1594–1632) of Sweden.

nations. It has been taught by this colossal symbol the mutual reverence that is due from man to man. The joyful loyalty with which men have everywhere suffered the king, the noble, or the great proprietor to walk among them by a law of his own, make his own scale of men and things, and reverse theirs, pay for benefits not with money but with honor, and represent the Law in his person, was the hieroglyphic by which they obscurely signified their consciousness of their own right and comeliness, the right of every man.

The magnetism which all original action exerts is explained when we inquire the reason of self-trust. Who is the Trustee? What is the aboriginal Self on which a universal reliance may be grounded? What is the nature and power of that science-baffling star, without parallax,[31] without calculable elements, which shoots a ray of beauty even into trivial and impure actions, if the least mark of independence appear? The inquiry leads us to that source, at once the essence of genius, of virtue, and of life, which we call Spontaneity or Instinct. We denote this primary wisdom as Intuition, whilst all later teachings are tuitions. In that deep force, the last fact behind which analysis cannot go, all things find their common origin. For the sense of being which in calm hours rises, we know not how, in the soul, is not diverse from things, from space, from light, from time, from man, but one with them, and proceeds obviously from the same source whence their life and being also proceed. We first share the life by which things exist, and afterwards see them as appearances in nature, and forget that we have shared their cause. Here is the fountain of action and of thought. Here are the lungs of that inspiration which giveth man wisdom, and which cannot be denied without impiety and atheism. We lie in the lap of immense intelligence, which makes us receivers of its truth and organs of its activity. When we discern justice, when we discern truth, we do nothing of ourselves, but allow a passage to its beams. If we ask whence this comes, if we seek to pry into the soul that causes, all philosophy is at fault. Its presence or its absence is all we can affirm. Every man discriminates between the voluntary acts of his mind, and his involuntary perceptions, and knows that to his involuntary perceptions a perfect faith is due. He may err in the expression of them, but he knows that these things are so, like day and night, not to be disputed. My wilful actions and acquisitions are but roving;—the idlest reverie, the faintest native emotion, command my curiosity and respect. Thoughtless people contradict as readily the statement of perceptions as of opinions, or rather much more readily; for, they do not distinguish between perception and notion. They fancy that I choose to see this or that thing. But perception is not whimsical, but fatal. If I see a trait, my children will see it after me, and in course of time, all mankind,—although it may chance that no one has seen it before me. For my perception of it is as much a fact as the sun.

The relations of the soul to the divine spirit are so pure that it is profane to seek to interpose helps. It must be that when God speaketh, he should communicate not one thing, but all things; should fill the world with his voice; should scatter forth light, nature, time, souls, from the centre of the present thought; and new date and new create the whole. Whenever a mind is simple, and receives a divine wisdom, old things pass away,—means, teachers, texts, temples fall; it lives now and absorbs past and future into the present hour. All things are made sacred by relation to it,—one as much as another. All things are dissolved to their centre by their cause, and in the universal miracle petty and particular miracles disappear. If,

---

[31] Without an observable or measurable position.

therefore, a man claims to know and speak of God, and carries you backward to the phraseology of some old mouldered nation in another country, in another world, believe him not. Is the acorn better than the oak which is its fulness and completion? Is the parent better than the child into whom he has cast his ripened being? Whence then this worship of the past? The centuries are conspirators against the sanity and authority of the soul. Time and space are but physiological colors which the eye makes, but the soul is light; where it is, is day; where it was, is night; and history is an impertinence and an injury, if it be anything more than a cheerful apologue or parable of my being and becoming.

Man is timid and apologetic; he is not longer upright; he dares not say 'I think', 'I am,' but quotes some saint or sage. He is ashamed before the blade of grass or the blowing rose. These roses under my window make no reference to former roses or to better ones; they are for what they are; they exist with God to-day. There is no time to them. There is simply the rose; it is perfect in every moment of its existence. Before a leaf-bud has burst, its whole life acts; in the full-blown flower, there is no more; in the leafless root, there is no less. Its nature is satisfied, and it satisfies nature, in all moments alike. But man postpones or remembers; he does not live in the present, but with reverted eye laments the past, or, heedless of the riches that surround him, stands on tiptoe to foresee the future. He cannot be happy and strong until he too lives with nature in the present, above time.

This should be plain enough. Yet see what strong intellects dare not yet hear God himself, unless he speak the phraseology of I know not what David, or Jeremiah, or Paul.[32] We shall not always set so great a price on a few texts, on a few lives. We are like children who repeat by rote the sentences of grandames and tutors, and, as they grow older, of the men of talents and character they chance to see,—painfully recollecting the exact words they spoke; afterwards, when they come into the point of view which those had who uttered these sayings, they understand them, and are willing to let the words go; for, at any time, they can use words as good, when occasion comes. If we live truly, we shall see truly. It is as easy for the strong man to be strong, as it is for the weak to be weak. When we have new perception, we shall gladly disburden the memory of its hoarded treasures as old rubbish. When a man lives with God, his voice shall be as sweet as the murmur of the brook and the rustle of the corn.

And now at last the highest truth on this subject remains unsaid; probably, cannot be said; for all that we say is the far off remembering of the intuition.[33] That thought, by what I can now nearest approach to say it, is this. When good is near you, when you have life in yourself, it is not by any known or accustomed way; you shall not discern the foot-prints of any other; you shall not see the face of man; you shall not hear any name;—the way, the thought, the good shall be wholly strange and new. It shall exclude example and experience. You take the way from man, not to man. All persons that ever existed are its forgotten ministers. Fear and hope are alike beneath it. There is somewhat low even in hope. In the hour of vision, there is nothing that can be called gratitude, nor properly joy. The soul raised over passion beholds identity and eternal causation, perceives the self-existence of Truth and Right, and calms itself with knowing that all things go well. Vast spaces of nature, the Atlantic Ocean, the South Sea,—long intervals of

---

[32] The second king of Israel, reputedly the author of the Book of Psalms; the Hebrew prophet who wrote the Book of Jeremiah; the Apostle known for his letters (New Testament Epistles).

[33] For Emerson *intuition* is knowledge that comes from within, directly from the Holy Spirit (which he later calls the Over-Soul); tuition is knowledge gained by experience or through the senses.

time, years, centuries,—are of no account. This which I think and feel underlay every former state of life and circumstances, as it does underlie my present, and what is called life, and what is called death.

Life only avails, not the having lived. Power ceases in the instant of repose; it resides in the moment of transition from a past to a new state, in the shooting of the gulf, in the darting to an aim. This one fact the world hates, that the soul *becomes;* for, that forever degrades the past, turns all riches to poverty, all reputation to a shame, confounds the saint with the rogue, shoves Jesus and Judas equally aside. Why then do we prate of self-reliance? Inasmuch as the soul is present, there will be power not confident but agent. To talk of reliance, is a poor external way of speaking. Speak rather of that which relies, because it works and is. Who has more obedience than I, masters me, though he should not raise his finger. Round him I must revolve by the gravitation of spirits. We fancy it rhetoric when we speak of eminent virtue. We do not yet see that virtue is Height, and that a man or a company of men plastic and permeable to priniciples, by the law of nature must overpower and ride all cities, nations, kings, rich men, poets, who are not.

This is the ultimate fact which we so quickly reach on this as on every topic, the resolution of all into the ever blessed ONE. Self-existence is the attribute of the Supreme Cause, and it constitutes the measure of good by the degree in which it enters into all lower forms. All things real are so by so much virtue as they contain. Commerce, husbandry, hunting, whaling, war, eloquence, personal weight, are somewhat, and engage my respect as examples of its presence and impure action. I see the same law working in nature for conservation and growth. Power is in nature the essential measure of right. Nature suffers nothing to remain in her kingdoms which cannot help itself. The genesis and maturation of a planet, its poise and orbit, the bended tree recovering itself from the strong wind, the vital resources of every animal and vegetable, are demonstrations of the self-sufficing, and therefore self-relying soul.

Thus all concentrates; let us not rove; let us sit at home with the cause. Let us stun and astonish the intruding rabble of men and books and institutions by a simple declaration of the divine fact. Bid the invaders take the shoes from off their feet, for God is here within.[34] Let our simplicity judge them, and our docility to our own law demonstrate the poverty of nature and fortune beside our native riches.

But now we are a mob. Man does not stand in awe of man, nor is his genius admonished to stay at home, to put itself in communication with the internal ocean, but it goes abroad to beg a cup of water of the urns of other men. We must go alone. I like the silent church before the service begins, better than any preaching. How far off, how cool, how chaste the persons look, begirt each one with a precinct or sanctuary. So let us always sit. Why should we assume the faults of our friend, or wife, or father, or child, because they sit around our hearth, or are said to have the same blood? All men have my blood, and I have all men's. Not for that will I adopt their petulance or folly, even to the extent of being ashamed of it. But your isolation must not be mechanical, but spiritual, that is, must be elevation. At times the whole world seems to be in conspiracy to importune you with emphatic trifles. Friend, client, child, sickness, fear, want, charity, all knock at

[34] In Exodus 3:5 God tells Moses to "put off thy shoes from off they feet, for the place whereon thou standest is holy ground."

once at thy closet door and say,—'Come out unto us.' But keep thy state; come not into their confusion. The power men possess to annoy me. I give them by a weak curiosity. No man can come near me but through my act. "What we love that we have, but by desire we bereave ourselves of the love."[35]

If we cannot at once rise to the sanctities of obedience and faith, let us at least resist our temptations; let us enter into the state of war, and wake Thor and Woden,[36] courage and constancy, in our Saxon breasts. This is to be done in our smooth times by speaking the truth. Check this lying hospitality and lying affection. Live no longer to the expectation of these deceived and deceiving people with whom we converse. Say to them, O father, O mother, O wife, O brother, O friend, I have lived with you after appearances hitherto. Henceforward I am the truth's. Be it known unto you that henceforward I obey no law less than the eternal law. I will have no covenants but proximities. I shall endeavor to nourish my parents, to support my family, to be the chaste husband of one wife,—but these relations I must fill after a new and unprecedented way. I appeal from your customs. I must be myself. I cannot break myself any longer for you, or you. If you can love me for what I am, we shall be the happier. If you cannot, I will seek to deserve that you should. I will not hide my tastes or aversions. I will so trust that what is deep is holy, that I will do strongly before the sun and moon whatever inly rejoices me, and the heart appoints. If you are noble, I will love you; if you are not, I will not hurt you and myself by hypocritical attentions. If you are true, but not in the same truth with me, cleave to your companions; I will seek my own. I do this not selfishly, but humbly and truly. It is alike your interest and mine and all men's, however long we have dwelt in lies, to live in truth. Does this sound harsh to-day? You will soon love what is dictated by your nature as well as mine, and if we follow the truth, it will bring us out safe at last.—But so you may give these friends pain. Yes, but I cannot sell my liberty and my power, to save their sensibility. Besides, all persons have their moments of reason when they look out into the region of absolute truth; then will they justify me and do the same thing.

The populace think that your rejection of popular standards is a rejection of all standard, and mere antinomianism;[37] and the bold sensualist will use the name of philosophy to gild his crimes. But the law of consciousness abides. There are two confessionals, in one or the other of which we must be shriven. You may fulfil your round of duties by clearing yourself in the *direct,* or, in the *reflex* way. Consider whether you have satisfied your relations to father, mother, cousin, neighbor, town, cat, and dog; whether any of these can upbraid you. But I may also neglect this reflex standard, and absolve me to myself. I have my own stern claims and perfect circle. It denies the name of duty to many offices that are called duties. But if I can discharge its debts, it enables me to dispense with the popular code. If any one imagines that this law is lax, let him keep its commandment one day.

And truly it demands something godlike in him who has cast off the common motives of humanity, and has ventured to trust himself for a taskmaster. High be his heart, faithful his will, clear his sight, that he may in good earnest be doctrine, society, law to himself, that a simple purpose may be to him as strong as iron necessity is to others.

---

[35] From the German poet and dramatist Friedrich Schiller (1759–1805).

[36] According to Norse myth, the gods of thunder and of war.

[37] Originally, the belief that faith alone, not obedience to the moral law, is needed for salvation; here, a rejection of moral duties and obligations.

If any man consider the present aspects of what is called by distinction *society,* he will see the need of these ethics. The sinew and heart of man seem to be drawn out, and we are become timorous desponding whimperers. We are afraid of truth, afraid of fortune, afraid of death, and afraid of each other. Our age yields no great and perfect persons. We want men and women who shall renovate life and our social state, but we see that most natures are insolvent, cannot satisfy their own wants, have an ambition out of proportion to their practical force, and do lean and beg day and night continually. Our housekeeping is mendicant, our arts, our occupations, our marriages, our religion we have not chosen, but society has chosen for us. We are parlor soldiers. We shun the rugged battle of fate, where strength is born.

If our young men miscarry in their first enterprizes, they lose all heart. If the young merchant fails, men say he is *ruined.* If the finest genius studies at one of our colleges, and is not installed in an office within one year afterwards in the cities or suburbs of Boston or New York, it seems to his friends and to himself that he is right in being disheartened and in complaining the rest of his life. A sturdy lad from New Hampshire or Vermont, who in turn tries all the professions, who *teams it, farms it, peddles,* keeps a school, preaches, edits a newspaper, goes to Congress, buys a township, and so forth, in successive years, and always, like a cat, falls on his feet, is worth a hundred of these city dolls. He walks abreast with his days, and feels no shame in not 'studying a profession,' for he does not postpone his life, but lives already. He has not one chance, but a hundred chances. Let a Stoic[38] open the resources of man, and tell men they are not leaning willows, but can and must detach themselves; that with the exercise of self-trust, new powers shall appear; that a man is the word made flesh, born to shed healing to the nations,[39] that he should be ashamed of our compassion, and that the moment he acts from himself, tossing the laws, the books, idolatries, and customs out of the window, we pity him no more but thank and revere him,—and that teacher shall restore the life of man to splendor, and make his name dear to all History.

It is easy to see that a greater self-reliance must work a revolution in all the offices and relations of men; in their religion; in their education; in their pursuits; their modes of living; their assocation; in their property; in their speculative views.

1. In what prayers do men allow themselves! That which they call a holy office, is not so much as brave and manly. Prayer looks abroad and asks for some foreign addition to come through some foreign virtue, and loses itself in endless mazes of natural and supernatural, and mediatorial and miraculous. Prayer that craves a particular commodity,—any thing less than all good,—is vicious. Prayer is the contemplation of the facts of life from the highest point of view. It is the soliloquy of a beholding and jubilant soul. It is the spirit of God pronouncing his works good.[40] But prayer as a means to effect a private end, is meanness and theft. It supposes dualism and not unity in nature and consciousness. As soon as the man is at one with God he will not beg. He will then see prayer in all action. The prayer of the farmer kneeling in his field to weed it, the prayer of the rower kneeling with the stroke of his oar, are true prayers heard throughout nature,

---

[38] Stoic philosopher of Greece, from the fourth and third centuries B.C., who advocated detachment and independence from the world.

[39] "The Word was made flesh and dwelt among us . . . ," from John 1:14; "The leaves of the tree were for the healing of the nations," from Revelation 22:2.

[40] "And God saw everything that he had made, and behold, it was very good," from Genesis 1:31.

though for cheap ends. Caratach, in Fletcher's Bonduca,[41] when admonished to inquire the mind of the god Audate, replies,—

"His hidden meaning lies in our endeavors,
Our valors are our best gods."

Another sort of false prayers are our regrets. Discontent is the want of self-reliance: it is infirmity of will. Regret calamities, if you can thereby help the sufferer; if not, attend your own work, and already the evil begins to be repaired. Our sympathy is just as base. We come to them who weep foolishly, and sit down and cry for company, instead of imparting to them truth and health in rough electric shock, putting them once more in communication with their own reason. The secret of fortune is joy in our hands. Welcome evermore to gods and men is the self-helping man. For him all doors are flung wide: him all tongues greet, all honors crown, all eyes follow with desire. Our love goes out to him and embraces him, because he did not need it. We solicitously and apologetically caress and celebrate him, because he held on his way and scorned our disapprobation. The gods love him because men hated him. "To the persevering mortal," said Zoroaster,[42] "the blessed Immortals are swift."

As men's prayers are a disease of the will, so are their creeds a disease of the intellect. They say with those foolish Israelites, 'Let not God speak to us, lest we die. Speak thou, speak any man with us, and we will obey.'[43] Everywhere I am hindered of meeting God in my brother, because he has shut his own temple doors, and recites fables merely of his brother's, or his brother's brother's God. Every new mind is a new classification. If it prove a mind of uncommon activity and power, a Locke, a Lavoisier, a Hutton, a Bentham, a Fourier,[44] it imposes its classification on other men, and lo! a new system. In proportion to the depth of the thought, and so to the number of the objects it touches and brings within reach of the pupil, is his complacency. But chiefly is this apparent in creeds and churches, which are also classifications of some powerful mind acting on the elemental thought of Duty, and man's relation to the Highest. Such is Calvinism, Quakerism, Swedenborgianism.[45] The pupil takes the same delight in subordinating every thing to the new terminology, as a girl who has just learned botany in seeing a new earth and new seasons thereby. It will happen for a time, that the pupil will find his intellectual power has grown by the study of his master's mind. But in all unbalanced minds, the classification is idolized, passes for the end, and not for a speedily exhaustible means, so that the walls of the system blend to their eye in the remote horizon with the walls of the universe; the luminaries of heaven

---

[41] A tragedy by John Fletcher, produced around 1614.

[42] A sixth- or seventh-century B.C. religious teacher and prophet in ancient Persia.

[43] A paraphrase of Exodus 20:19, words spoken by the Israelites to Moses after he brought them the Ten Commandments.

[44] John Locke (1632–1704), an English philosopher who rejected Plato's doctrine of innate ideas; Antoine Laurent Lavoisier (1743–1794), the French chemist whose oxygen theory discredited a popular but currently accepted theory of combustion; James Hutton (1726–1797), a Scottish geologist who formulated controversial but currently accepted theories concerning geologic processes on earth; Jeremy Bentham (1748–1832), an English political scientist who helped reform criminal law and judicial procedures; François Marie Charles Fourier (1772–1837), the French social philosopher whose ideas on the "phalanx" influenced the founding of many utopian communities, including Brook Farm (1841–1847), near West Roxbury, Massachusetts.

[45] The religious doctrine of Emanuel Swedenborg (1688–1772), a Swedish theologian and mystic.

seem to them hung on the arch their master built. They cannot imagine how you aliens have any right to see,—how you can see; 'It must be somehow that you stole the light from us.' They do not yet perceive, that light, unsystematic, indomitable, will break into any cabin, even into theirs. Let them chirp awhile and call it their own. If they are honest and do well, presently their neat new pinfold[46] will be too strait and low, will crack, will lean, will rot and vanish, and the immortal light, all young and joyful, million-orbed, million-colored, will beam over the universe as on the first morning.

2. It is for want of self-culture that the superstition of Travelling, whose idols are Italy, England, Egypt, retains its fascination for all educated Americans. They who made England, Italy, or Greece venerable in the imagination, did so by sticking fast where they were, like an axis of the earth. In manly hours, we feel that duty is our place. The soul is no traveller: the wise man stays at home, and when his necessities, his duties, on any occasion call him from his house, or into foreign lands, he is at home still, and shall make men sensible by the expression of his countenance, that he goes the missionary of wisdom and virtue, and visits cities and men like a sovereign, and not like an interloper or a valet.

I have no churlish objection to the circumnavigation of the globe, for the purposes of art, of study, and benevolence, so that the man is first domesticated, or does not go abroad with the hope of finding somewhat greater than he knows. He who travels to be amused, or to get somewhat which he does not carry, travels away from himself, and grows old even in youth among old things. In Thebes, in Palmyra,[47] his will and mind have become old and dilapidated as they. He carries ruins to ruins.

Travelling is a fool's paradise. Our first journeys discover to us the indifference of places. At home I dream that at Naples, at Rome, I can be intoxicated with beauty, and lose my sadness. I pack my trunk, embrace my friends, embark on the sea, and at last wake up in Naples, and there beside me is the stern Fact, the sad self, unrelenting, identical, that I fled from. I seek the Vatican, and the palaces. I affect to be intoxicated with sights and suggestions, but I am not intoxicated. My giant[48] goes with me wherever I go.

3. But the rage of travelling is a symptom of deeper unsoundness affecting the whole intellectual action. The intellect is vagabond, and our system of education fosters restlessness. Our minds travel when our bodies are forced to stay at home. We imitate; and what is imitation but the travelling of the mind? Our houses are built with foreign taste; our shelves are garnished with foreign ornaments; our opinions, our tastes, our faculties, lean, and follow the Past and the Distant. The soul created the arts wherever they have flourished. It was in his own mind that the artist sought his model. It was an application of his own thought to the thing to be done and the conditions to be observed. And why need we copy the Doric or the Gothic[49] model? Beauty, convenience, grandeur of thought, and quaint expression are as near to us as to any, and if the American artist will study with hope and love the precise thing to be done by him, considering the climate, the soil, the length of the day, the wants of the people, the habit and form of the government, he will create a house in which all these will find themselves fitted, and taste and sentiment will be satisfied also.

Insist on yourself; never imitate. Your own gift you can present every moment

---

[46] An enclosure for animals.   [47] Ruins of ancient Egyptian and Syrian cities.
[48] A person of extraordinary size and power lives within each of us.   [49] Classical or medieval.

with the cumulative force of a whole life's cultivation; but of the adopted talent of another, you have only an extemporaneous, half possession. That which each can do best, none but his Maker can teach him. No man yet knows what it is, nor can, till that person has exhibited it. Where is the master who could have taught Shakspeare? Where is the master who could have instructed Franklin, or Washington, or Bacon,[50] or Newton? Every great man is a unique. The Scipionism of Scipio is precisely that part he could not borrow. Shakspeare will never be made by the study of Shakspeare. Do that which is assigned you, and you cannot hope too much or dare too much. There is at this moment for you an utterance brave and grand as that of the colossal chisel of Phidias,[51] or trowel of the Egyptians, or the pen of Moses, or Dante, but different from all these. Not possibly will the soul all rich, all eloquent, with thousand-cloven tongue, deign to repeat itself; but if you can hear what these patriarchs say, surely you can reply to them in the same pitch of voice: for the ear and the tongue are two organs of one nature. Abide in the simple and noble regions of thy life, obey thy heart, and thou shalt reproduce the Foreworld again.

4. As our Religion, our Education, our Art look abroad, so does our spirit of society. All men plume themselves on the improvement of society, and no man improves.

Society never advances. It recedes as fast on one side as it gains on the other. It undergoes continual changes: it is barbarous, it is civilized, it is christianized, it is rich, it is scientific; but this change is not amelioration. For every thing that is given, something is taken. Society acquires new arts and loses old instincts. What a contrast between the well-clad, reading, writing, thinking American, with a watch, a pencil, and a bill of exchange in his pocket, and the naked New Zealander, whose property is a club, a spear, a mat, and an undivided twentieth of a shed to sleep under. But compare the health of the two men, and you shall see that the white man has lost his aboriginal strength. If the traveller tell us truly, strike the savage with a broad axe, and in a day or two the flesh shall unite and heal as if you struck the blow into soft pitch, and the same blow shall send the white to his grave.

The civilized man has built a coach, but has lost the use of his feet. He is supported on crutches, but lacks so much support of muscle. He has a fine Geneva watch, but he fails of the skill to tell the hour by the sun. A greenwich nautical almanac he has, and so being sure of the information when he wants it, the man in the street does not know a star in the sky. The solstice he does not observe; the equinox he knows as little; and the whole bright calendar of the year is without a dial in his mind. His note-books impair his memory; his libraries overload his wit; the insurance office increases the number of accidents; and it may be a question whether machinery does not encumber; whether we have not lost by refinement some energy, by a christianity entrenched in establishments and forms, some vigor of wild virtue. For every stoic was a stoic; but in Christendom where is the Christian?

There is no more deviation in the moral standard than in the standard of height or bulk. No greater men are now than ever were. A singular equality may be observed between the great men of the first and of the last ages; nor can all the

---

[50] The English philosopher, essayist, and statesman Sir Francis Bacon (1561–1626).
[51] The fifth-century B.C. Greek sculptor who designed the frieze of the Parthenon and a statue of Zeus at Olympia.

science, art, religion and philosophy of the nineteenth century avail to educate greater men than Plutarch's heroes,[52] three or four and twenty centuries ago. Not in time is the race progressive. Phocion, Socrates, Anaxagora, Diogenes,[53] are great men, but they leave no class. He who is really of their class will not be called by their name, but will be his own man, and, in his turn the founder of a sect. The arts and inventions of each period are only its costume, and do not invigorate men. The harm of the improved machinery may compensate its good. Hudson and Behring accomplished so much in their fishing-boats, as to astonish Parry and Franklin,[54] whose equipment exhausted the resources of science and art. Galileo, with an opera-glass, discovered a more splendid series of celestial phenomena than any one since. Columbus found the New World in an undecked boat. It is curious to see the periodical disuse and perishing of means and machinery which were introduced with loud laudation, a few years or centuries before. The great genius returns to essential man. We reckoned the improvements of the art of war among the triumphs of science, and yet Napoleon conquered Europe by the Bivouac,[55] which consisted of falling back on naked valor, and disencumbering it of all aids. The Emperor held it impossible to make a perfect army, says Las Cases,[56] "without abolishing our arms, magazines, commissaries, and carriages, until in imitation of the Roman custom, the soldier should receive his supply of corn, grind it in his hand-mill, and bake his bread himself."

Society is a wave. The wave moves onward, but the water of which it is composed, does not. The same particle does not rise from the valley to the ridge. Its unity is only phenomenal. The persons who make up a nation to-day, next year die, and their experience with them.

And so the reliance on Property, including the reliance on governments which protect it, is the want of self-reliance. Men have looked away from themselves and at things so long, that they have come to esteem the religious, learned, and civil institutions, as guards of property, and they deprecate assaults on these, because they feel them to be assaults on property. They measure their esteem of each other, by what each has, and not by what each is. But a cultivated man becomes ashamed of his property, out of new respect for his nature. Especially he hates what he has, if he see that it is accidental,—came to him by inheritance, or gift, or crime; then he feels that it is not having; it does not belong to him, has not root in him, and merely lies there, because no revolution or no robber takes it away. But that which a man is, does always by necessity acquire, and what the man acquires is living property, which does not wait the beck of rulers, or mobs, or revolutions, or fire, or storm, or bankruptcies, but perpetually renews itself wherever the man breathes. "Thy lot or portion of life," said the Caliph Ali,[57] "is seeking after thee;

---

[52] Plutarch (A. D. 46?–120?) wrote a series of biographies featuring the "parallel lives" of eminent Greeks and Romans.

[53] Phocion (402?–317? B. C.) was an Athenian statesman and general; Socrates (470?–399 B. C.), Anaxagoras (500?–428? B. C.), and Diogenes (412?–323? B. C.) were Greek philosophers.

[54] The findings of early navigators Henry Hudson (?–1611) and Vitus Bering (1680–1741) astounded the later and better-equipped William Edward Parry (1790–1855) and John Franklin (1786–1847), English Arctic explorers.

[55] A temporary encampment without tents or regular means of supply introduced by Napoleon in his victorious campaigns.

[56] Comte Emmanuel Augustin de Las Cases (1766–1842), the French historian who transcribed Napoleon's comments.

[57] Ali ibn-abi-Tālib, the fourth Moslem caliph of Mecca (A. D. 600?–661); Emerson knew this oracular statement from *History of the Saracens* (1708–1757), by Simon Ockley (1678–1720).

therefore be at rest from seeking after it." Our dependence on these foreign goods leads us to our slavish respect for numbers. The political parties meet in numerous conventions; the greater the concourse, and with each new uproar of announcement, The delegation from Essex![58] The Democrats from New Hampshire! The Whigs of Maine! the young patriot feels himself stronger than before by a new thousand of eyes and arms. In like manner the reformers summon conventions, and vote and resolve in multitude. Not so, O friends! will the God deign to enter and inhabit you, but by a method precisely the reverse. It is only as a man puts off all foreign support, and stands alone, that I see him to be strong and to prevail. He is weaker by every recruit to his banner. Is not a man better than a town? Ask nothing of men, and in the endless mutation, thou only firm column must presently appear the upholder of all that surrounds thee. He who knows that power is inborn, that he is weak because he has looked for good out of him and elsewhere, and so perceiving throws himself unhesitatingly on his thought, instantly rights himself, stands in the erect postion, commands his limbs, works miracles; just as a man who stands on his feet is stronger than a man who stands on his head.

So use all that is called Fortune. Most men gamble with her, and gain all, and lose all, as her wheel rolls. But do thou leave as unlawful these winnings, and deal with Cause and Effect, the chancellors of God. In the Will work and acquire, and thou hast chained the wheel of Chance, and shalt sit hereafter out of fear from her rotations. A political victory, a rise of rents, the recovery of your sick, or the return of your absent friend, or some other favorable event, raises your spirits, and you think good days are preparing for you. Do not believe it. Nothing can bring you peace but yourself. Nothing can bring you peace but the triumph of principles.

1841

CIRCLES*

> *Nature centres into balls,*
> *And her proud ephemerals,*
> *Fast to surface and outside,*
> *Scan the profile of the sphere;*
> *Knew they what that signified,*
> *A new genesis were here.*[1]

The eye is the first circle; the horizon which it forms is the second; and throughout nature this primary figure is repeated without end. It is the highest emblem in the cipher of the world. St. Augustine[2] described the nature of God as a circle whose centre was everywhere, and its circumference nowhere. We are all our lifetime reading the copious sense of this first of forms. One moral we have already deduced in considering the circular or compensatory character of every human action. Another analogy we shall now trace; that every action admits of being outdone. Our life is an apprenticeship to the truth, that around every circle another

---

[58] Essex County, Massachusetts.

* First published in *Essays* in 1841.   [1] Emerson added his own lines of poetry in 1847.

[2] Emerson copied this statement from John Norris's *Essay Towards the Theory of the Ideal or Intelligible World* (1701–1704) into his journal along with some other passages Norris quoted from St. Augustine; he mistakenly attributes the statement to Augustine.

can be drawn; that there is no end in nature, but every end is a beginning; that there is always another dawn risen on mid-noon, and under every deep a lower deep opens.

This fact, as far as it symbolizes the moral fact of the Unattainable, the flying Perfect, around which the hands of man can never meet, at once the inspirer and the condemner of every success, may conveniently serve us to connect many illustrations of human power in every department.

There are no fixtures in nature. The universe is fluid and volatile. Permanence is but a word of degrees. Our globe seen by God, is a transparent law, not a mass of facts. The law dissolves the fact and holds it fluid. Our culture is the predominance of an idea which draws after it this train of cities and institutions. Let us rise into another idea: they will disappear. The Greek sculpture is all melted away, as if it had been statues of ice: here and there a solitary figure or fragment remaining, as we see flecks and scraps of snow left in cold dells and mountain clefts, in June and July. For, the genius that created it, creates now somewhat else. The Greek letters last a little longer, but are already passing under the same sentence, and tumbling into the inevitable pit which the creation of new thought opens for all that is old. The new continents are built out of ruins of an old planet: the new races fed out of the decomposition of the foregoing. New arts destroy the old. See the investment of capital in aqueducts, made useless by hydraulics; fortifications, by gunpowder; roads and canals, by railways; sails, by steam; steam by electricity.

You admire this tower of granite, weathering the hurts of so many ages. Yet a little waving hand built this huge wall, and that which builds, is better than that which is built. The hand that built, can topple it down much faster. Better than the hand, and nimbler, was the invisible thought which wrought through it, and thus ever behind the coarse effect, is a fine cause, which, being narrowly seen, is itself the effect of a finer cause. Every thing looks permanent until its secret is known. A rich estate appears to women a firm and lasting fact; to a merchant, one easily created out of any materials, and easily lost. An orchard, good tillage, good grounds, seem a fixture, like a gold mine, or a river, to a citizen; but to a large farmer, not much more fixed than the state of the crop. Nature looks provokingly stable and secular, but it has a cause like all the rest; and when once I comprehend that, will these fields stretch so immovably wide, these leaves hang so individually considerable? Permanence is a word of degrees. Every thing is medial.[3] Moons are no more bounds to spiritual power than bat-balls.

The key to every man is his thought. Sturdy and defying though he look, he has a helm which he obeys, which is, the idea after which all his facts are classified. He can only be reformed by showing him a new idea which commands his own. The life of man is a self-evolving circle, which, from a ring imperceptibly small, rushes on all sides outwards to new and larger circles, and that without end. The extent to which this generation of circles, wheel without wheel will go, depends on the force or truth of the individual soul. For, it is the inert effort of each thought having formed itself into a circular wave of circumstance,—as, for instance, an empire, rules of an art, a local usage, a relgious rite,—to heap itself on that ridge, and to solidify, and hem in the life. But if the soul is quick and strong, it bursts over that boundary on all sides, and expands another orbit on the great deep, which also runs up into a high wave, with attempt again to stop and to bind. But the heart refuses to be imprisoned; in its first and narrowest pulses, it already tends outward with a vast force, and to immense and innumerable expansions.

---

[3] Situated in the middle.

Every ultimate fact is only the first of a new series. Every general law only a particular fact of some more general law presently to disclose itself. There is no outside, no enclosing wall, no circumference to us. The man finishes his story,— how good! how final! how it puts a new face on all things! He fills the sky. Lo! on the other side rises also a man, and draws a circle around the circle we had just pronounced the outline of the sphere. Then already is our first speaker, not man, but only a first speaker. His only redress is forthwith to draw a circle outside of his antagonist. And so men do by themselves. The result of to-day which haunts the mind and cannot be escaped, will presently be abridged into a word, and the principle that seemed to explain nature, will itself be included as one example of a bolder generalization. In the thought of to-morrow there is a power to upheave all thy creed, all the creeds, all the literatures of the nations, and marshal thee to a heaven which no epic dream has yet depicted. Every man is not so much a workman in the world, as he is a suggestion of that he should be. Men walk as prophecies of the next age.

Step by step we scale this mysterious ladder: the steps are actions; the new prospect is power. Every several result is threatened and judged by that which follows. Every one seems to be contradicted by the new; it is only limited by the new. The new statement is always hated by the old, and, to those dwelling in the old, comes like an abyss of skepticism. But the eye soon gets wonted to it, for the eye and it are effects of one cause; then its innocency and benefit appear, and, presently, all its energy spent, it pales and dwindles before the revelation of the new hour.

Fear not the new generalization. Does the fact look crass and material, threatening to degrade thy theory of spirit? Resist it not; it goes to refine and raise thy theory of matter just as much.

There are no fixtures to men, if we appeal to consciousness. Every man supposes himself not to be fully understood; and if there is any truth in him, if he rests at last on the divine soul, I see not how it can be otherwise. The last chamber, the last closet, he must feel, was never opened; there is always a residuum unknown, unanalyzable. That is, every man believes that he has a greater possibility.

Our moods do not believe in each other. To-day, I am full of thoughts, and can write what I please. I see no reason why I should not have the same thought, the same power of expression to-morrow. What I write, whilst I write it, seems the most natural thing in the world: but, yesterday, I saw a dreary vacuity in this direction in which now I see so much; and a month hence, I doubt not, I shall wonder who he was that wrote so many continuous pages. Alas for this infirm faith, this will not strenuous, this vast ebb of a vast flow! I am God in nature; I am a weed by the wall.

The continual effort to raise himself above himself, to work a pitch above his last height, betrays itself in a man's relations. We thirst for approbation, yet cannot forgive the approver. The sweet of nature is love; yet if I have a friend, I am tormented by my imperfections. The love of me accuses the other party. If he were high enough to slight me, then could I love him, and rise by my affection to new heights. A man's growth is seen in the successive choirs of his friends. For every friend whom he loses for truth, he gains a better. I thought, as I walked in the woods and mused on my friends, why should I play with them this game of idolatry? I know and see too well, when not voluntarily blind, the speedy limits of persons called high and worthy. Rich, noble, and great they are by the liberality of our speech, but truth is sad. O blessed Spirit, whom I forsake for these, they are not thou! Every personal consideration that we allow, costs us heavenly state. We sell the thrones of angels for a short and turbulent pleasure.

How often must we learn this lesson? Men cease to interest us when we find their limitations. The only sin is limitation. As soon as you once come up with a man's limitations, it is all over with him. Has he talents? has he enterprises? has he knowledge? it boots not. Infinitely alluring and attractive was he to you yesterday, a great hope, a sea to swim in; now, you have found his shores, found it a pond, and you care not if you never see it again.

Each new step we take in thought reconciles twenty seemingly discordant facts, as expressions of one law. Aristotle and Plato are reckoned the respective heads of two schools. A wise man will see that Aristotle Platonizes. By going one step farther back in thought, discordant opinions are reconciled, by being seen to be two extremes of one principle, and we can never go so far back as to preclude a still higher vision.

Beware when the great God lets loose a thinker on this planet. Then all things are at risk. It is as when a conflagration has broken out in a great city, and no man knows what is safe, or where it will end. There is not a piece of science, but its flank may be turned to-morrow; there is not any literary reputation, not the so-called eternal names of fame, that may not be revised and condemned. The very hopes of man, the thoughts of his heart, the religion of nations, the manners and morals of mankind, are all at the mercy of a new generalization. Generalization is always a new influx of the divinity into the mind. Hence the thrill that attends it.

Valor consists in the power of self-recovery, so that a man cannot have his flank turned, cannot be outgeneralled, but put him where you will, he stands. This can only be by his preferring truth to his past apprehension of truth; and his alert acceptance of it from whatever quarter; the intrepid conviction that his laws, his relations to society, his christianity, his world, may at any time be superseded and decease.

There are degrees in idealism. We learn first to play with it academically, as the magnet was once a toy. Then we see in the heyday of youth and poetry that it may be true, that it is true in gleams and fragments. Then, its countenance waxes stern and grand, and we see that it must be true. It now shows itself ethical and practical. We learn that God IS; that he is in me; and that all things are shadows of him. The idealism of Berkeley[4] is only a crude statement of the idealism of Jesus, and that, again, is a crude statement of the fact that all nature is the rapid efflux of goodness executing and organizing itself. Much more obviously is history and the state of the world at any one time, directly dependent on the intellectual classifcation then existing in the minds of men. The things which are dear to men at this hour, are so on account of the ideas which have emerged on their mental horizon, and which cause the present order of things as a tree bears its apples. A new degree of culture would instantly revolutionize the entire system of human pursuits.

Conversation is a game of circles. In conversation we pluck up the *termini*[5] which bound the common of silence on every side. The parties are not to be judged by the spirit they partake and even express under this Pentecost.[6] To-morrow they will have receded from this high-water mark. To-morrow you shall find

---

[4] George Berkeley (1685–1753), an English philosopher.   [5] "Ends" (Latin).

[6] A Christian feast celebrating the descent of the Holy Spirit on the Apostles. The allusion means that every conversation is a kind of pentecost.

them stooping under the old packsaddles. Yet let us enjoy the cloven flame whilst it glows on our walls. When each new speaker strikes a new light, emancipates us from the oppression of the last speaker, to oppress us with the greatness and exclusiveness of his own thought, then yields us to another redeemer, we seem to recover our rights, to become men. O what truths profound and executable only in ages and orbs, are supposed in the announcement of truth! In common hours, society sits cold and statuesque. We all stand waiting, empty,—knowing, possibly, that we can be full, surrounded by mighty symbols which are not symbols to us, but prose and trivial toys. Then cometh the god, and converts the statues into fiery men, and by a flash of his eye burns up the veil which shrouded all things, and the meaning of the very furniture, of cup and saucer, of chair and clock and tester, is manifest. The facts which loomed so large in the fogs of yesterday,— property, climate, breeding, personal beauty, and the like, have strangely changed their proportions. All that we reckoned settled, shakes and rattles; and literatures, cities, climates, religions, leave their foundations, and dance before our eyes. And yet here again see the swift circumscription. Good as is discourse, silence is better, and shames it. The length of the discourse indicates the distance of thought betwixt the speaker and the hearer. If they were at a perfect understanding in any part, no words would be necessary thereon. If at one in all parts, no words would be suffered.

Literature is a point outside of our hodiernal[7] circle, through which a new one may be described. The use of literature is to afford us a platform whence we may command a view of our present life, a purchase by which we may move it. We fill ourselves with ancient learning; install ourselves the best we can in Greek, in Punic,[8] in Roman houses, only that we may wiselier see French, English, and American houses and modes of living. In like manner, we see literature best from the midst of wild nature, or from the din of affairs, or from a high religion. The field cannot be well seen from within the field. The astronomer must have his diameter of the earth's orbit as a base to find the parallax[9] of any star.

Therefore, we value the poet. All the argument, and all the wisdom, is not in the encyclopedia, or the treatise on metaphysics, or the Body of Divinity, but in the sonnet or the play. In my daily work I incline to repeat my old steps, and do not believe in remedial force, in the power of change and reform. But some Petrarch or Ariosto,[10] filled with the new wine of his imagination, writes me an ode, or a brisk romance, full of daring thought and action. He smites and arouses me with his shrill tones, breaks up my whole chain of habits, and I open my eye on my own possibilities. He claps wings to the sides of all the solid old lumber of the world, and I am capable once more of choosing a straight path in theory and practice.

We have the same need to command a view of the religion of the world. We can never see christianity from the catechism:—from the pastures, from a boat in the pond, from amidst the songs of wood-birds, we possibly may. Cleansed by the elemental light and wind, steeped in the sea of beautiful forms which the field offers us, we may chance to cast a right glance back upon biography. Christianity is rightly dear to the best of mankind; yet was there never a young philosopher whose breeding had fallen into the christian church, by whom that brave text of

---

[7] Belonging to the present day.   [8] Pertaining to ancient Carthage.
[9] The apparent change in position of an object as a result of a change in viewing position.
[10] Francesco Petrarch (1304–1374) and Lodoviso Ariosto (1474–1533), influential Italian poets.

Paul's,[11] was not specially prized:—"Then shall also the Son be subject unto Him who put all things under him, that God may be all in all." Let the claims and virtues of persons be never so great and welcome, the instinct of man presses eagerly onward to the impersonal and illimitable, and gladly arms itself against the dogmatism of bigots with this generous word, out of the book itself.

The natural world may be conceived of as a system of concentric circles, and we now and then detect in nature slight dislocations, which apprize us that this surface on which we now stand, is not fixed, but sliding. These manifold tenacious qualities, this chemistry and vegetation, these metals and animals, which seem to stand there for their own sake, are means and methods only,—are words of God, and as fugitive as other words. Has the naturalist or chemist learned his craft, who has explored the gravity of atoms and the elective affinities, who has not yet discerned the deeper law whereof this is only a partial or approximate statement, namely, that like draws to like; and that the goods which belong to you, gravitate to you, and need not be pursued with pains and cost? Yet is that statement approximate also, and not final. Omnipresence is a higher fact. Not through subtle, subterranean channels, need friend and face be drawn to their counterpart, but, rightly considered, these things proceed from the eternal generation of the soul. Cause and effect are two sides of one fact.

The same law of eternal process ranges all that we call the virtues, and extinguishes each in the light of a better. The great man will not be prudent in the popular sense; all his prudence will be so much deduction from his grandeur. But it behoves each to see when he sacrifices prudence, to what god he devotes it; if to ease and pleasure, he had better be prudent still; if to a great trust, he can well spare his mule and panniers, who has a winged chariot instead. Geoffrey draws on his boots to go through the woods, that his feet may be safer from the bite of snakes; Aaron never thinks of such a peril. In many years, neither is harmed by such an accident. Yet it seems to me that with every precaution you take against such an evil, you put yourself into the power of the evil. I suppose that the highest prudence is the lowest prudence. Is this too sudden a rushing from the centre to the verge of our orbit? Think how many times we shall fall back into pitiful calculations, before we take up our rest in the great sentiment, or make the verge of to-day the new centre. Besides, your bravest sentiment is familiar to the humblest men. The poor and the low have their way of expressing the last facts of philosophy as well as you. "Blessed be nothing," and "the worse things are, the better they are," are proverbs which express the trancendentalism of common life.

One man's justice is another's injustice; one man's beauty, another's ugliness; one man's wisdom, another's folly; as one beholds the same objects from a higher point. One man thinks justice consists in paying debts, and has no measure in his abhorrence of another who is very remiss in this duty, and makes the creditor wait tediously. But that second man has his own way of looking at things; asks himself, which debt must I pay first, the debt to the rich, or the debt to the poor? the debt of money, or the debt of thought to mankind, of genius to nature? For you, O broker, there is no other principle but arithmetic. For me, commerce is of trivial import; love, faith, truth of character, the aspiration of man, these are sacred: nor can I detach one duty, like you, from all other duties, and concentrate my forces mechanically on the payment of moneys. Let me live onward: you shall find that, though slower, the progress of my character will liquidate all these debts without

---

[11] I Corinthians 15:28, by the Apostle Paul.

injustice to higher claims. If a man should dedicate himself to the payment of notes, would not this be injustice? Does he owe no debt but money? And are all claims on him to be postponed to a landlord's or a banker's?

There is no virtue which is final; all are initial. The virtues of society are vices of the saint. The terror of reform is the discovery that we must cast away our virtues, or what we have always esteemed such, into the same pit that has consumed our grosser vices.

> "Forgive his crimes, forgive his virtues too,
> Those smaller faults, half converts to the right."[12]

It is the highest power of divine moments that they abolish our contritions also. I accuse myself of sloth and unprofitableness, day by day; but when these waves of God flow into me, I no longer reckon lost time. I no longer poorly compute my possible achievement by what remains to me of the month or the year; for these moments confer a sort of omnipresence and omnipotence, which asks nothing of duration, but sees that the energy of the mind is commensurate with the work to be done, without time.

And thus, O circular philosopher, I hear some reader exclaim, you have arrived at a fine pyrrhonism,[13] at an equivalence and indifference of all actions, and would fain teach us, that, *if we are true,* forsooth, our crimes may be lively stones out of which we shall construct the temple of the true God.

I am not careful to justify myself. I own I am gladdened by seeing the predominance of the saccharine principle throughout vegetable nature, and not less by beholding in morals that unrestrained inundation of the principle of good into every chink and hole that selfishness has left open, yea, into selfishness and sin itself; so that no evil is pure, nor hell itself without its extreme satisfactions.[14] But lest I should mislead any when I have my own head, and obey my whims, let me remind the reader that I am only an experimenter. Do not set the least value on what I do, or the least discredit on what I do not, as if I pretended to settle anything as true or false. I unsettle all things. No facts are to me sacred; none are profane; I simply experiment, an endless seeker, with no Past at my back.

Yet this incessant movement and progression, which all things partake, could never become sensible to us, but by contrast to some principle of fixture or stability in the soul. Whilst the eternal generation of circles proceeds, the eternal generator abides. That central life is somewhat superior to creation, superior to knowledge and thought, and contains all its circles. Forever it labors to create a life and thought as large and excellent as itself, suggesting to our thought a certain development, as if that which is made, instructs how to make a better.

Thus there is no sleep, no pause, no preservation, but all things renew, germinate, and spring. Why should we import rags and relics into the new hour? Nature abhors the old, and old age seems the only disease: all others run into this one. We

---

[12] From *The Complaint: Or, Night Thoughts on Life, Death, and Immortality* (1742–1745), by the English poet and dramatist Edward Young (1683–1765).

[13] Radical skepticism; the Greek philosopher Pyrrho of Elis (365?–275? B.C.) taught that the proper attitude of the mind is a suspension of judgment about matters of truth and value.

[14] Emerson got this idea from Emanuel Swedenborg (1688–1722), a Swedish theologian and mystic, but toned down some of the more pungent details of the prediction: in *Heaven and Hell* (1758), Swedenborg wrote that those who indulge in earthly pleasures will "love excrementitious things and privies" in the next life.

call it by many names,—fever, intemperance, insanity, stupidity, and crime: they are all forms of old age: they are rest, conservatism, appropriation, inertia, not newness, not the way onward. We grizzle[15] every day. I see no need of it. Whilst we converse with what is above us, we do not grow old, but grow young. Infancy, youth, receptive, aspiring, with religious eye looking upward, counts itself nothing, and abandons itself to the instruction flowing from all sides. But the man and woman of seventy assume to know all, they have outlived their hope, they renounce aspiration, accept the actual for the necessary, and talk down to the young. Let them then become organs of the Holy Ghost; let them be lovers; let them behold truth; and their eyes are uplifted, their wrinkles smoothed, they are perfumed again with hope and power. This old age ought not to creep on a human mind. In nature, every moment is new; the past is always swallowed and forgotten; the coming only is sacred. Nothing is secure but life, transition, the energizing spirit. No love can be bound by oath or covenant to secure it against a higher love. No truth so sublime but it may be trivial tomorrow in the light of new thoughts. People wish to be settled: only as far as they are unsettled, is there any hope for them.

Life is a series of surprises. We do not guess to-day the mood, the pleasure, the power of to-morrow, when we are building up our being. Of lower states,—of acts of routine and sense,—we can tell somewhat; but the masterpieces of God, the total growths and universal movements of the soul, he hideth; they are incalculable. I can know that truth is divine and helpful, but how it shall help me, I can have no guess, for, *so to be* is the sole inlet of *so to know*. The new position of the advancing man has all the powers of the old, yet has them all new. It carries in its bosom all the energies of the past, yet is itself an exhalation of the morning. I cast away in this new moment all my once hoarded knowledge, as vacant and vain. Now, for the first time, seem I to know any thing rightly. The simplest words,— we do not know what they mean, except when we love and aspire.

The difference between talents and character is adroitness to keep the old and trodden round, and power and courage to make a new road to new and better goals. Character makes an overpowering present, a cheerful, determined hour, which fortifies all the company, by making them see that much is possible and excellent, that was not thought of. Character dulls the impression of particular events. When we see the conqueror, we do not think much of any one battle or success. We see that we had exaggerated the difficulty. It was easy to him. The great man is not convulsible or tormentable; events pass over him without much impression. People say sometimes, 'See what I have overcome; see how cheerful I am; see how completely I have triumphed over these black events.' Not if they still remind me of the black event. True conquest is the causing the calamity to fade and disappear as an early cloud of insignificant result in a history so large and advancing.

The one thing which we seek with insatiable desire, is to forget ourselves, to be surprised out of our propriety, to lose our sempiternal memory, and to do something without knowing how or why; in short, to draw a new circle. Nothing great was ever achieved without enthusiasm.[16] The way of life is wonderful: it is by abandonment. The great moments of history are the facilities of performance through the strength of ideas, as the works of genius and religion. "A man," said

---

[15] Age, become gray-haired.
[16] From *The Statesman's Manual* (1816), by Samuel Taylor Coleridge (1772–1834).

Oliver Cromwell, "never rises so high as when he knows not whither he is going."[17] Dreams and drunkenness, the use of opium and alcohol are the semblance and counterfeit of this oracular genius, and hence their dangerous attraction for men. For the like reason, they ask the aid of wild passions, as in gaming and war, to ape in some manner these flames and generosities of the heart.

1841

THE POET*

A moody child and wildly wise
Pursued the game with joyful eyes,
Which chose, like meteors, their way,
And rived the dark with private ray:
They overleapt the horizon's edge,
Searched with Apollo's privilege;
Through man, and woman, and sea, and star,
Saw the dance of nature forward far;
Through worlds, and races, and terms, and times,
Saw musical order, and pairing rhymes.[1]

Olympian bards who sung
Divine ideas below,
Which always find us young,
And always keep us so.[2]

Those who are esteemed umpires of taste, are often persons who have acquired some knowledge of admired pictures or sculptures, and have an inclination for whatever is elegant; but if you inquire whether they are beautiful souls, and whether their own acts are like fair pictures, you learn that they are selfish and sensual. Their cultivation is local, as if you should rub a log of dry wood in one spot to produce fire, all the rest remaining cold. Their knowledge of the fine arts is some study of rules and particulars, or some limited judgment of color or form, which is exercised for amusement or for show. It is a proof of the shallowness of the doctrine of beauty, as it lies in the minds of our amateurs, that men seem to have lost the perception of the instant dependence of form upon soul. There is no doctrine of forms in our philosophy. We were put into our bodies, as fire is put into a pan, to be carried about; but there is no accurate adjustment between the spirit and the organ, much less is the latter the germination of the former. So in regard to other forms, the intellectual men do not believe in any essential dependence of the material world on thought and volition. Theologians think it a pretty air-castle to talk of the spiritual meaning of a ship or a cloud, of a city or a contract, but they prefer to come again to the solid ground of historical evidence; and even the poets are contented with a civil and conformed manner of living, and to

---

[17] Oliver Cromwell (1599–1658), a Puritan leader and Lord Protector of England, reportedly made this remark to the French minister Bellieure.

* First published in *Essays, Second Series* in 1844.

[1] These lines are from an unfinished poem by Emerson, published posthumously as "The Poet" (1883).

[2] These lines are from Emerson's "Ode to Beauty" (1843).

write poems from the fancy, at a safe distance from their own experience. But the highest minds of the world have never ceased to explore the double meaning, or, shall I say, the quadruple, or the centuple, or much more manifold meaning, of every sensuous fact: Orpheus, Empedocles, Heraclitus, Plato, Plutarch, Dante, Swedenborg,[3] and the masters of sculpture, picture, and poetry. For we are not pans and barrows, nor even porters of the fire and torch-bearers, but children of the fire, made of it, and only the same divinity transmuted, and at two or three removes, when we know least about it. And this hidden truth, that the fountains whence all this river of Time, and its creatures, floweth, are intrinsically ideal and beautiful, draws us to the consideration of the nature and functions of the Poet, or the man of Beauty, to the means and materials he uses, and to the general aspect of the art in the present time.

The breadth of the problem is great, for the poet is representative. He stands among partial men for the complete man, and apprises us not of his wealth, but of the commonwealth. The young man reveres men of genius, because, to speak truly, they are more himself than he is. They receive of the soul as he also receives, but they more. Nature enhances her beauty to the eye of loving men, from their belief that the poet is beholding her shows at the same time. He is isolated among his contemporaries, by truth and by his art, but with this consolation in his pursuits, that they will draw all men sooner or later. For all men live by truth, and stand in need of expression. In love, in art, in avarice, in politics, in labor, in games, we study to utter our painful secret. The man is only half himself, the other half is his expression.

Notwithstanding this necessity to be published, adequate expression is rare. I know not how it is that we need an interpreter; but the great majority of men seem to be minors, who have not yet come into possession of their own, or mutes, who cannot report the conversation they have had with nature. There is no man who does not anticipate a supersensual utility in the sun, and stars, earth, and water. These stand and wait to render him a peculiar service. But there is some obstruction, or some excess of phlegm[4] in our constitution, which does not suffer them to yield the due effect. Too feeble fall the impressions of nature on us to make us artists. Every touch should thrill. Every man should be so much an artist, that he could report in conversation what had befallen him. Yet, in our experience, the rays or appulses[5] have sufficient force to arrive at the senses, but not enough to reach the quick, and compel the reproduction of themselves in speech. The poet is the person in whom these powers are in balance, the man without impediment, who sees and handles that which others dream of, traverses the whole scale of experience, and is representative of man, in virtue of being the largest power to receive and to impart.

For the Universe has three children, born at one time, which reappear, under different names, in every system of thought, whether they be called cause, operation, and effect; or, more poetically, Jove, Pluto, Neptune;[6] or, theologically, the Father, the Spirit, and the Son; but which we will call here, the Knower, the Doer,

---

[3] A mythical Greek poet; Greek philosophers of the fifth and fifth to six centuries B.C., respectively; the renowned Greek philosopher Plato (427?–347? B.C.); Plutarch (46?–120? A.D.), a biographer of ancient Greeks and Romans; the medieval Italian poet Dante Alighieri (1265–1321); the theologian and mystic Emanuel Swedenborg (1688–1772).

[4] Sluggishness, apathy.   [5] Energies.

[6] According to Roman myth, the supreme god (Jupiter) and the gods of the underworld and of the sea.

and the Sayer. These stand respectively for the love of truth, for the love of good, and for the love of beauty. These three are equal. Each is that which he is essentially, so that he cannot be surmounted or analyzed, and each of these three has the power of the others latent in him, and his own patent.

The poet is the sayer, the namer, and represents beauty. He is a sovereign, and stands on the centre. For the world is not painted, or adorned, but is from the beginning beautiful; and God has not made some beautiful things, but Beauty is the creator of the universe. Therefore the poet is not any permissive potentate, but is emperor in his own right. Criticism is infested with a cant of materialism, which assumes that manual skill and activity is the first merit of all men, and disparages such as say and do not, overlooking the fact, that some men, namely, poets, are natural sayers, sent into the world to the end of expression, and confounds them with those whose province is action, but who quit it to imitate the sayers. But Homer's words are as costly and admirable to Homer, as Agamemnon's victories are to Agamemnon.[7] The poet does not wait for the hero or the sage, but, as they act and think primarily, so he writes primarily what will and must be spoken, reckoning the others, though primaries also, yet, in respect to him, secondaries and servants; as sitters or models in the studio of a painter, or as assistants who bring building materials to an architect.

For poetry was all written before time was, and whenever we are so finely organized that we can penetrate into that region where the air is music, we hear those primal warblings, and attempt to write them down, but we lose ever and anon a word, or a verse, and substitute something of our own, and thus miswrite the poem. The men of more delicate ear write down these cadences more faithfully, and these transcripts, though imperfect, become the songs of the nations. For nature is as truly beautiful as it is good, or as it is reasonable, and must as much appear, as it must be done, or be known. Words and deeds are quite indifferent modes of the divine energy. Words are also actions, and actions are a kind of words.

The sign and credentials of the poet are, that he announces that which no man foretold. He is the true and only doctor,[8] he knows and tells; he is the only teller of news, for he was present and privy to the appearance which he describes. He is a beholder of ideas, and utterer of the necessary and casual. For we do not speak now of men of poetical talents, or of industry and skill in metre, but of the true poet. I took part in a conversation the other day, concerning a recent writer of lyrics, a man of subtle mind, whose head appeared to be a music-box of delicate tunes and rhythms, and whose skill, and command of language, we could not sufficiently praise. But when the question arose, whether he was not only a lyrist, but a poet, we were obliged to confess that he is plainly a contemporary, not an eternal man. He does not stand out of our low limitations, like a Chimborazo[9] under the line, running up from the torrid base through all the climates of the globe, with belts of the herbage of every latitude on its high and mottled sides; but this genius is the landscape-garden of a modern house, adorned with fountains and statues, with well-bred men and women standing and sitting in the walks and terraces. We hear, through all the varied music, the ground-tone of conventional life. Our poets are men of talents who sing, and not the children of music. The argument is secondary, the finish of the verses is primary.

---

[7] According to Greek myth, the king of Mycenae and commander of the Greek army in the Trojan war, as told in Homer's *Iliad*.
    [8] Teacher.   [9] A mountain in Ecuador, south of the "line" of the equator.

For it is not metres, but a metre-making argument, that makes a poem,—a thought so passionate and alive, that, like the spirit of a plant or an animal, it has an architecture of its own, and adorns nature with a new thing.[10] The thought and the form are equal in the order of time, but in the order of genesis the thought is prior to the form. The poet has a new thought: he has a whole new experience to unfold; he will tell us how it was with him, and all men will be the richer in his fortune. For, the experience of each new age requires a new confession, and the world seems always waiting for its poet. I remember, when I was young, how much I was moved one morning by tidings that genius had appeared in a youth who sat near me at table. He had left his work, and gone rambling none knew whither, and had written hundreds of lines, but could not tell whether that which was in him was therein told: he could tell nothing but that all was changed,—man, beast, heaven, earth, and sea. How gladly we listened! how credulous! Society seemed to be compromised. We sat in the aurora of a sunrise which was to put out all the stars. Boston seemed to be at twice the distance it had the night before, or was much farther than that. Rome,—what was Rome? Plutarch and Shakspeare were in the yellow leaf,[11] and Homer no more should be heard of. It is much to know that poetry has been written this very day, under this very roof, by your side. What! that wonderful spirit has not expired! these stony moments are still sparkling and animated! I had fancied that the oracles were all silent, and nature had spent her fires, and behold! all night, from every pore, these fine auroras have been streaming. Every one has some interest in the advent of the poet, and no one knows how much it may concern him. We know that the secret of the world is profound, but who or what shall be our interpreter, we know not. A mountain ramble, a new style of face, a new person, may put the key into our hands. Of course, the value of genius to us is in the veracity of its report. Talent may frolic and juggle; genius realizes and adds. Mankind, in good earnest, have arrived so far in understanding themselves and their work, that the foremost watchman on the peak announces his news. It is the truest word ever spoken, and the phrase will be the fittest, most musical, and the unerring voice of the world for that time.

All that we call sacred history attests that the birth of a poet is the principal even in chronology. Man, never so often deceived, still watches for the arrival of a brother who can hold him steady to a truth, until he has made it his own. With what joy I begin to read a poem, which I confide in as an inspiration! And now my chains are to be broken; I shall mount about these clouds and opaque airs in which I live,—opaque, though they seem transparent,—and from the heaven of truth I shall see and comprehend my relations. That will reconcile me to life, and renovate nature, to see trifles animated by a tendency, and to know what I am doing. Life will no more be a noise; now I shall see men and women, and know the signs by which they may be discerned from fools and satans. This day shall be better than my birthday; then I became an animal: now I am invited into the science of the real. Such is the hope, but the fruition is postponed. Oftener it falls, that this winged man, who will carry me into the heaven, whirls me into mists, then leaps and frisks about with me as it were from cloud to cloud, still affirming that he is bound heavenward; and I being myself a novice, am slow in perceiving that he does not know the way into the heavens, and is merely bent that I should admire his skill to rise, like a fowl or a flying fish, a little way from the ground or the

---

[10] This sentence expresses the idea of organic form that is basic to the romantic conception of poetry.
[11] Seemed old: "I have lived long enough. My way of life is fallen into the sere, the yellow leaf," from Shakespeare's *Macbeth* (V. iii. 22–23).

water; but the all-piercing, all-feeding, and ocular[12] air of heaven, that man shall never inhabit. I tumble down again soon into my old nooks, and lead the life of exaggerations as before, and have lost some faith in the possiblity of any guide who can lead me thither where I would be.

But leaving these victims of vanity, let us, with new hope, observe how nature, by worthier impulses, has ensured the poet's fidelity to his office of announcement and affirming, namely, by the beauty of things, which becomes a new, and higher beauty, when expressed. Nature offers all her creatures to him as a picture-language. Being used as a type, a second wonderful value appears in the object, far better than its old value, as the carpenter's stretched cord, if you hold your ear close enough, is musical in the breeze. "Things more excellent than every image," says Jamblichus,[13] "are expressed through images." Things admit of being used as symbols, because nature is a symbol, in the whole, and in every part. Every line we can draw in the sand, has expression; and there is no body without its spirit or genius. All form is an effect of character; all condition, of the quality of the life; all harmony, of health; (and, for this reason, a perception of beauty should be sympathetic, or proper only to the good.) The beautiful rests on the foundations of the necessary. The soul makes the body, as the wise Spenser teaches:—

> "So every spirit, as it is most pure,
> And hath in it the more of heavenly light,
> So it the fairer body doth procure
> To habit in, and it more fairly dight,
> With cheerful grace and amiable sight
> For, of the soul, the body form doth take.
> For soul is form, and doth the body make."[14]

Here we find ourselves, suddenly, not in a critical speculation, but in a holy place, and should go very warily and reverently. We stand before the secret of the world, there where Being passes into Appearance, and Unity into Variety.

The Universe is the externization of the soul. Wherever the life is, that bursts into appearance around it. Our science is sensual, and therefore superficial. The earth, and the heavenly bodies, physics, and chemistry, we sensually treat, as if they were self-existent; but these are the retinue of that Being we have. "The mighty heaven," said Proclus,[15] "exhibits, in its transfigurations, clear images of the splendor of intellectual perceptions; being moved in conjunction with the unapparent periods of intellectual natures." Therefore, science always goes abreast with the just elevation of the man, keeping step with religion and metaphysics; or, the state of science is an index of our self-knowledge. Since everything in nature answers to a moral power, if any phenomenon remains brute and dark, it is because the corresponding faculty in the observer is not yet active.

No wonder, then, if these waters be so deep, that we hover over them with a religious regard. The beauty of the fable proves the importance of the sense; to the poet, and to all others; or, if you please, every man is so far a poet as to be susceptible of these enchantments of nature; for all men have the thoughts whereof

---

[12] Visible.   [13] A fourth-century A. D. Neoplatonic philosopher.

[14] From "An Hymn in Honour of Beauty" (1596), by the English poet Edmund Spenser (1552?–1599).

[15] Proclus (410?–485) was a Neoplatonic philosopher who stressed the mystical possibilities of idealist philosophy.

the universe is the celebration. I find that the fascination resides in the symbol. Who loves nature? Who does not? Is it only poets, and men of leisure and cultivation, who live with her? No; but also hunters, farmers, grooms, and butchers, though they express their affection in their choice of life, and not in their choice of words. The writer wonders what the coachman or the hunter values in riding, in horses, and dogs. It is not superficial qualities. When you talk with him, he holds these at as slight a rate as you. His worship is sympathetic; he has no definitions, but he is commanded in nature, by the living power which he feels to be there present. No imitation, or playing of these things, would content him; he loves the earnest of the north wind, of rain, of stone, and wood, and iron. A beauty not explicable, is dearer than a beauty which we can see to the end of. It is nature the symbol, nature certifying the supernatural, body overflowed by life, which he worships, with coarse, but sincere rites.

The inwardness, and mystery, of this attachment, drive men of every class to the use of emblems. The schools of poets, and philosophers, are not more intoxicated with their symbols, than the populace with theirs. In our political parties, compute the power of badges and emblems. See the huge wooden ball rolled by successive ardent crowds from Baltimore to Bunker hill![16] In the political processions, Lowell goes in a loom, and Lynn in a shoe, and Salem in a ship.[17] Witness the cider-barrel, the log-cabin, the hickory-stick, the palmetto,[18] and all the cognizances of party. See the power of national emblems. Some stars, lilies, leopards, a crescent, a lion, an eagle, or other figure, which came into credit God knows how, on an old rag of bunting, blowing in the wind, on a fort, at the ends of the earth, shall make the blood tingle under the rudest, or the most conventional exterior. The people fancy they hate poetry, and they are all poets and mystics!

Beyond this universality of the symbolic language, we are apprised of the divineness of this superior use of things, whereby the world is a temple, whose walls are covered with emblems, pictures, and commandments of the Deity, in this, that there is no fact in nature which does not carry the whole sense of nature; and the distinctions which we make in events, and in affairs, of low and high, honest and base, disappear when nature is used as a symbol. Thought makes everything fit for use. The vocabulary of an omniscient man would embrace words and images excluded from polite conversation. What would be base, or even obscene, to the obscene, becomes illustrious, spoken in a new connexion of thought. The piety of the Hebrew prophets purges their grossness. The circumcision is an example of the power of poetry to raise the low and offensive. Small and mean things serve as well as great symbols. The meaner the type by which a law is expressed, the more pungent it is, and the more lasting in the memories of men: just as we choose the smallest box, or case, in which any needful utensil can be carried. Bare lists of words are found suggestive, to an imaginative and excited mind; as it is related of Lord Chatham, that he was accustomed to read in Bailey's Dictionary,[19] when he was preparing to speak in Parliament. The poorest experi-

---

[16] An allusion to the political slogan "Keep the ball a-rolling," used by the supporters of William Henry Harrison in his 1840 presidential campaign.

[17] Massachusetts towns, each represented in campaign parades by a major industry: Lowell by textiles, Lynn by shoemaking, Salem by shipping.

[18] The cider-barrel and log cabin were part of Harrison's successful "Log Cabin and Hard Cider" campaign against Martin Van Buren in 1840; the palmetto State is South Carolina, which claimed to be the birthplace of Andrew Jackson (known as "Old Hickory").

[19] The English statesman William Pitt (1708–1778), earl of Chatham, celebrated for his oratory; *An Universal Etymological English Dictionary* (1721), compiled by Nathan Bailey (?–1742).

ence is rich enough for all the purposes of expressing thought. Why covet a knowledge of new facts? Day and night, house and garden, a few books, a few actions, serve us as well as would all trades and all spectacles. We are far from having exhausted the significance of the few symbols we use. We can come to use them yet with a terrible simplicity. It does not need that a poem should be long. Every word was once a poem. Every new relation is a new word. Also, we use defects and deformities to a sacred purpose, so expressing our sense that the evils of the world are such only to the evil eye. In the old mythology, mythologists observe, defects are ascribed to divine natures, as lameness to Vulcan, blindness to Cupid, and the like, to signify exuberances.

For, as it is dislocation and detachment from the life of God, that makes things ugly, the poet, who re-attaches things to nature and the Whole,—and re-attaching even artificial things, and violations of nature, to nature, by a deeper insight,— disposes very easily of the most disagreeable facts. Readers of poetry see the factory-village, and the railway, and fancy that the poetry of the landscape is broken up by these: for these works of art are not yet consecrated in their reading; but the poet sees them fall within the great Order not less than the bee-hive, or the spider's geometrical web. Nature adopts them very fast into her vital circles, and the gliding train of cars she loves like her own. Besides, in a centred mind, it signifies nothing how many mechanical inventions you exhibit. Though you add millions, and never so surprising, the fact of mechanics has not gained a grain's weight. The spiritual fact remains unalterable, by many or by few particulars; as no mountain is of any appreciable height to break the curve of the sphere. A shrewd country-boy goes to the city for the first time, and the complacent citizen is not satisfied with his little wonder. It is not that he does not see all the fine houses, and know that he never saw such before, but he disposes of them as easily as the poet finds place for the railway. The chief value of the new fact, is to enhance the great and constant fact of Life, which can dwarf any and every circumstance, and to which the belt of wampum, and the commerce of America, are alike.

The world being thus put under the mind for verb and noun, the poet is he who can articulate it. For, though life is great, and fascinates, and absorbs,—and though all men are intelligent of the symbols through which it is named,—yet they cannot originally use them. We are symbols, and inhabit symbols; workmen, work, and tools, words and things, birth and death, all are emblems; but we sympathize with the symbols, and, being infatuated with the economical uses of things, we do not know that they are thoughts. The poet, by an ulterior intellectual perception, gives them power which makes their old use forgotten, and puts eyes, and a tongue, into every dumb and inanimate object. He perceives the thought's independence of the symbol, the stability of the thought, the accidency and fugacity[20] of the symbol. As the eyes of Lyncæus[21] were said to see through the earth, so the poet turns the world to glass, and shows us all things in their right series and procession. For, through that better perception, he stands one step nearer to things, and sees the flowing or metamorphosis; perceives that thought is multiform; that within the form of every creature is a force impelling it to ascend into a higher form; and, following with his eyes the life, uses the forms which express that life, and so his speech flows with the flowing of nature. All the facts of the animal economy,—sex, nutriment, gestation, birth, growth—are symbols

---

[20] The accidental character and fleetingness or brevity.

[21] According to Greek myth, an Argonaut who sailed with Jason to recover the Golden Fleece; supposedly, he could see through the earth.

of the passage of the world into the soul of man, to suffer there a change, and reappear a new and higher fact. He uses forms according to the life, and not according to the form. This is true science. The poet alone knows astronomy, chemistry, vegetation, and animation, for he does not stop at these facts, but employs them as signs. He knows why the plain, or meadow of space, was strown with these flowers we call suns, and moons, and stars; why the great deep is adorned with animals, with men, and gods; for, in every word he speaks he rides on them as the horses of thought.

By virtue of this science the poet is the Namer, or Language-maker, naming things sometimes after their appearance, sometimes after their essence, and giving to every one its own name and not another's, thereby rejoicing the intellect, which delights in detachment or boundary. The poets made all the words, and therefore language is the archives of history, and, if we must say it, a sort of tomb of the muses. For, though the origin of most of our words is forgotten, each word was at first a stroke of genius, and obtained currency, because for the moment it symbolized the world to the first speaker and to the hearer. The etymologist finds the deadest word to have been once a brilliant picture. Language is fossil poetry. As the limestone of the continent consists of infinite masses of the shells of animalcules, so language is made up of images, or tropes, which now, in their secondary use, have long ceased to remind us of their poetic origin. But the poet names the thing because he sees it, or comes one step nearer to it than any other. This expression, or naming, is not art, but a second nature, grown out of the first, as a leaf out of a tree. What we call nature, is a certain self-regulated motion, or change; and nature does all things by her own hands, and does not leave another to baptize her, but baptizes herself; and this through the metamorphosis again. I remember that a certain poet[22] described it to me thus:

> Genius is the activity which repairs the decays of things, whether wholly or partly of a material and finite kind. Nature, through all her kingdoms, insures herself. Nobody cares for planting the poor fungus: so she shakes down from the gills of one agaric[23] countless spores, any one of which, being preserved, transmits new billions of spores to-morrow or next day. The new agaric of this hour has a chance which the old one had not. This atom of seed is thrown into a new place, not subject to the accidents which destroyed its parent two rods off. She makes a man; and having brought him to ripe age, she will no longer run the risk of losing this wonder at a blow, but she detaches from him a new self, that the kind may be safe from accidents to which the individual is exposed. So when the soul of the poet has come to ripeness of thought, she detaches and sends away from it its poems or songs,—a fearless, sleepless, deathless progeny, which is not exposed to the accidents of the weary kingdom of time: a fearless, vivacious offspring, clad with wings (such was the virtue of the soul out of which they came), which carry them fast and far, and infix them irrecoverably into the hearts of men. These wings are the beauty of the poet's soul. The songs, thus flying immortal from their mortal parent, are pursued by clamorous flights of censures, which swarm in far greater numbers, and threaten to devour them; but these last are not winged. At the end of a very short leap they fall plump down, and rot, having received from the souls out of which they came no beautiful wings. But the melodies of the poet ascend, and leap, and pierce into the deeps of infinite time.

[22] Emerson himself; the passage is from his journal.   [23] A fungus such as a mushroom.

So far the bard taught me, using his freer speech. But nature has a higher end, in the production of new individuals, than security, namely, *ascension,* or, the passage of the soul into higher forms. I knew, in my younger days, the sculptor who made the statue of the youth which stands in the public garden. He was, as I remember, unable to tell, directly, what made him happy, or unhappy, but by wonderful indirections he could tell. He rose one day, according to his habit, before the dawn, and saw the morning break, grand as the eternity out of which it came, and, for many days after, he strove to express this tranquillity, and, lo! his chisel had fashioned out of marble the form of a beautiful youth, Phosphor,[24] whose aspect is such, that, it is said, all persons who look on it become silent. The poet also resigns himself to his mood, and that thought which agitated him is expressed, but *alter idem,*[25] in a manner totally new. The expression is organic, or, the new type which things themselves take when liberated. As, in the sun, objects paint their images on the retina of the eye, so they, sharing the aspiration of the whole universe, tend to paint a far more delicate copy of their essence in his mind. Like the metamorphosis of things into higher organic forms, is their change into melodies. Over everything stands its dæmon, or soul, and, as the form of the thing is reflected by the eye, so the soul of the thing is reflected by a melody. The sea, the mountain-ridge, Niagara, and every flower-bed, pre-exist, or super-exist, in pre-cantations,[26] which sail like odors in the air, and when any man goes by with an ear sufficiently fine, he overhears them, and endeavors to write down the notes, without diluting or depraving them. And herein is the legitimation of criticism, in the mind's faith, that the poems are a corrupt version of some text in nature, with which they ought to be made to tally. A rhyme in one of our sonnets should not be less pleasing than the iterated nodes of a sea-shell, or the resembling difference of a group of flowers. The pairing of the birds is an idyl, not tedious as our idyls are; a tempest is a rough ode without falsehood or rant; a summer, with its harvest sown, reaped, and stored, is an epic song, subordinating how many admirably executed parts. Why should not the symmetry and truth that modulate these, glide into our spirits, and we participate the invention of nature?

This insight, which expresses itself by what is called Imagination, is a very high sort of seeing, which does not come by study, but by the intellect being where and what it sees, by sharing the path, or circuit of things through forms, and so making them translucid to others. The path of things is silent. Will they suffer a speaker to go with them? A spy they will not suffer; a lover, a poet, is the transcendency of their own nature,—him they will suffer. The condition of true naming, on the poet's part, is his resigning himself to the divine *aura* which breathes through forms, and accompanying that.

It is a secret which every intellectual man quickly learns, that beyond the energy of his possessed and conscious intellect, he is capable of a new energy (as of an intellect doubled on itself), by abandonment to the nature of things; that, beside his privacy of power as an individual man, there is a great public power, on which he can draw, by unlocking, at all risks, his human doors, and suffering the ethereal tides to roll and circulate through him: then he is caught up into the life of the Universe, his speech is thunder, his thought is law, and his words are universally intelligible as the plants and animals. The poet knows that he speaks adequately, then only when he speaks somewhat wildly, or, "with the flower of the mind," not

---

[24] According to Greek myth, a god associated with the morning star.
[25] "The same, yet different" (Latin).   [26] Pre-incantations, prophetic incantations.

with the intellect, used as an organ, but with the intellect released from all service, and suffered to take its direction from its celestial life; or, as the ancients were wont to express themselves, not with intellect alone, but with the intellect inebriated by nectar. As the traveller who has lost his way, throws his reins on his horse's neck, and trusts to the instinct of the animal to find his road, so must we do with the divine animal who carries us through this world. For if in any manner we can stimulate this instinct, new passages are opened for us into nature, the mind flows into and through things hardest and highest, and the metamorphosis is possible.

This is the reason why bards love wine, mead,[27] narcotics, coffee, tea, opium, the fumes of sandal-wood and tobacco, or whatever other procurers of animal exhilaration. All men avail themselves of such means as they can, to add this extraordinary power to their normal powers; and to this end they prize conversation, music, pictures, sculpture, dancing, theatres, travelling, war, mobs, fires, gaming, politics, or love, or science, or animal intoxication, which are several coarser or finer *quasi*-mechanical substitutes for the true nectar, which is the ravishment of the intellect by coming nearer to the fact. These are auxiliaries to the centrifugal tendency of a man, to his passage out into free space, and they help him to escape the custody of that body in which he is pent up, and of that jail-yard of individual relations in which he is enclosed. Hence a great number of such as were professionally expressors of Beauty, as painters, poets, musicians, and actors, have been more than others wont to lead a life of pleasure and indulgence; all but the few who received the true nectar; and, as it was a spurious mode of attaining freedom, as it was an emancipation not into the heavens, but into the freedom of baser places, they were punished for that advantage they won, by a dissipation and deterioration. But never can any advantage be taken of nature by a trick. The spirit of the world, the great calm presence of the creator, comes not forth to the sorceries of opium or of wine. The sublime vision comes to the pure and simple soul in a clean and chaste body. That is not an inspiration which we owe to narcotics, but some counterfeit excitement and fury. Milton says, that the lyric poet may drink wine and live generously, but the epic poet, he who shall sing of the gods, and their descent unto men, must drink water out of a wooden bowl.[28] For poetry is not 'Devil's wine,' but God's wine. It is with this as it is with toys. We fill the hands and nurseries of our children with all manner of dolls, drums and horses, withdrawing their eyes from the plain face and sufficing objects of nature, the sun, and moon, the animals, the water, and stones, which should be their toys. So the poet's habit of living should be set on a key so low, that the common influences should delight him. His cheerfulness should be the gift of the sunlight; the air should suffice for his inspiration, and he should be tipsy with water. That spirit which suffices quiet hearts, which seems to come forth to such from every dry knoll of sere grass, from every pine-stump, and half-imbedded stone, on which the dull March sun shines, comes forth to the poor and hungry, and such as are of simple taste. If thou fill thy brain with Boston and New York, with fashion and covetousness, and wilt stimulate thy jaded senses with wine and French coffee, thou shalt find no radiance of wisdom in the lonely waste of the pinewoods.

If the imagination intoxicates the poet, it is not inactive in other men. The metamorphosis excites in the beholder an emotion of joy. The use of symbols has

---

[27] A liquor made of fermented honey and water.
[28] Adapted from John Milton's "Sixth Latin Elegy" (1629).

a certain power of emancipation and exhilaration for all men. We seem to be touched by a wand, which makes us dance and run about happily, like children. We are like persons who come out of a cave or cellar into the open air. This is the effect on us of tropes,[29] fables, oracles, and all poetic forms. Poets are thus liberating gods. Men have really got a new sense, and found within their world, another world, or nest of worlds; for, the metamorphosis once seen, we divine that it does not stop. I will not now consider how much this makes the charm of algebra and the mathematics, which also have their tropes, but it is felt in every definition; as, when Aristotle defines *space* to be an immovable vessel, in which things are contained;—or, when Plato defines a *line* to be a flowing point; or, *figure* to be a bound of solid; and many the like. What a joyful sense of freedom we have, when Vitruvius[30] announces the old opinion of artists, that no architect can build any house well, who does not know something of anatomy. When Socrates, in Charmides,[31] tells us that the soul is cured of its maladies by certain incantations, and that these incantations are beautiful reasons, from which temperance is generated into souls; when Plato calls the world an animal; and Timæus[32] affirms that the plants also are animals; or affirms a man to be a heavenly tree, growing with his root, which is his head, upward; and, as George Chapman, following him, writes,—

> "So in our tree of man, whose nervie root
> Springs in his top;"[33]

when Orpheus speaks of hoariness as "that white flower which marks extreme old age;" when Proclus calls the universe the statue of the intellect; when Chaucer, in his praise of 'Gentilesse,'[34] compares good blood in mean condition to fire, which, though carried to the darkest house betwixt this and the mount of Caucasus, will yet hold its natural office, and burn as bright as if twenty thousand men did it behold; when John saw, in the apocalypse, the ruin of the world through evil, and the stars fall from heaven, as the figtree casteth her untimely fruit,[35] when Æsop reports the whole catalogue of common daily relations through the masquerade of birds, and beasts;[36]—we take the cheerful hint of the immortality of our essence, and its versatile habit and escapes, as when the gypsies say of themselves, "it is in vain to hang them, they cannot die."[37]

The poets are thus liberating gods. The ancient British bards had for the title of their order, "Those who are free throughout the world." They are free, and they make free. An imaginative book renders us much more service at first, by stimulating us through its tropes, than afterward, when we arrive at the precise sense of the author. I think nothing is of any value in books, excepting the transcendental and extraordinary. If a man is inflamed and carried away by his thought, to that degree that he forgets the authors and the public, and heeds only this one dream, which holds him like an insanity, let me read his paper, and you may have all the arguments and histories and criticism. All the value which attaches to Pythagoras,

---

[29] Figures of speech.   [30] Vitruvius Pollio (50?–26 B. C.), a Roman writer on architecture.
[31] One of Plato's dialogues.   [32] The principal speaker in Plato's dialogue "Timaeus."
[33] From the dedication to the translation (1614–1615) of Homer by Chapman (1559?–1634).
[34] Geoffrey Chaucer (1340?–1400), in "The Wife of Bath's Tale."
[35] The Apostle John, author of the Apocalypse, or Book of Revelation; from Revelation 6:13.
[36] In the fables of Aesop, supposedly a Greek of the sixth century B. C.
[37] From *The Zincali* (1841), by the English travel writer and novelist George Borrow (1803–1881).

Paracelsus, Cornelius Agrippa, Cardan, Kepler, Swedenborg, Schelling, Oken,[38] or any other who introduces questionable facts into his cosmogony, as angels, devils, magic, astrology, palmistry, mesmerism, and so on, is the certificate we have of departure from routine, and that here is a new witness. That also is the best success in conversation, the magic of liberty, which puts the world, like a ball, in our hands. How cheap even the liberty then seems; how mean to study, when an emotion communicates to the intellect the power to sap and upheave nature: how great the perspective! nations, times, systems, enter and disappear, like threads in tapestry of large figure and many colors; dream delivers us to dream, and, while the drunkenness lasts, we will sell our bed, our philosophy, our religion, in our opulence.

There is good reason why we should prize this liberation. The fate of the poor shepherd, who, blinded and lost in the snowstorm, perishes in a drift within a few feet of his cottage door, is an emblem of the state of man. On the brink of the waters of life and truth, we are miserably dying. The inaccessibleness of every thought but that we are in, is wonderful. What if you come near to it,—you are as remote, when you are nearest, as when you are farthest. Every thought is also a prison: every heaven is also a prison. Therefore we love the poet, the inventor, who in any form, whether in an ode, or in an action, or in looks and behavior, has yielded us a new thought. He unlocks our chains, and admits us to a new scene.

This emancipation is dear to all men, and the power to impart it, as it must come from greater depth and scope of thought, is a measure of intellect. Therefore all books of the imagination endure, all which ascend to that truth, that the writer sees nature beneath him, and uses it as his exponent.[39] Every verse or sentence, possessing this virtue, will take care of its own immortality. The religions of the world are the ejaculations of a few imaginative men.

But the quality of the imagination is to flow, and not to freeze. The poet did not stop at the color, or the form, but read their meaning; neither may he rest in this meaning, but he makes the same objects exponents of his new thought. Here is the difference betwixt the poet and the mystic, that the last nails a symbol to one sense, which was a true sense for a moment, but soon becomes old and false. For all symbols are fluxional; all language is vehicular and transitive, and is good, as ferries and horses are, for conveyance, not as farms and houses are, for homestead. Mysticism consists in the mistake of an accidental and individual symbol for an universal one. The morning-redness happens to be the favorite meteor to the eyes of Jacob Behmen,[40] and comes to stand to him for truth and faith; and he believes should stand for the same realities to every reader. But the first reader prefers as naturally the symbol of a mother and child, or a gardener and his bulb, or a jeweller polishing a gem. Either of these, or of a myriad more, are equally good to the person to whom they are significant. Only they must be held lightly, and be very willingly translated into the equivalent terms which others use. And the mystic must be steadily told,—All that you say is just as true without the tedious use of that symbol as with it. Let us have a little algebra, instead of this trite rhetoric,—universal signs, instead of these village symbols,—and we shall

---

[38] The sixth-century B.C. Greek mathematician Pythagoras; the Swiss alchemist Philippus Paracelsus (1493–1541); the German physician Cornelius Agrippa (1486?–1535); the Italian mathematician Jerome Cardan (1501–1576); the German astronomer Johannes Kepler (1571–1630); Emanuel Swedenborg; the German philosopher Friedrich von Schelling (1775–1854); the German naturalist Lorenz Oken (1779–1851).

[39] Means of setting forth his principles.   [40] Jakob Böhme (1575–1624), a German mystic.

both be gainers. The history of hierarchies seems to show, that all religious error consisted in making the symbol too stark and solid, and, at last, nothing but an excess of the organ of language.

Swedenborg, of all men in the recent ages, stands eminently for the translator of nature into thought. I do not know the man in history to whom things stood so uniformly for words. Before him the metamorphosis continually plays. Everything on which his eye rests, obeys the impulses of moral nature. The figs become grapes whilst he eats them. When some of his angels affirmed a truth, the laurel twig which they held blossomed in their hands. The noise which, at a distance, appeared like gnashing and thumping, on coming nearer was found to be the voice of disputants. The men, in one of his visions, seen in heavenly light, appeared like dragons, and seemed in darkness; but, to each other, they appeared as men, and, when the light from heaven shone into their cabin, they complained of the darkness, and were compelled to shut the window that they might see.

There was this perception in him, which makes the poet or seer an object of awe and terror, namely, that the same man, or society of men, may wear one aspect to themselves and their companions, and a different aspect to higher intelligences. Certain priests, whom he describes as conversing very learnedly together, appeared to the children, who were at some distance, like dead horses; and many the like misappearances. And instantly the mind inquires, whether these fishes under the bridge, yonder oxen in the pasture, those dogs in the yard, are immutably fishes, oxen, and dogs, or only so appear to me, and perchance to themselves appear upright men; and whether I appear as a man to all eyes. The Bramins[41] and Pythagoras propounded the same question, and if any poet has witnessed the transformation, he doubtless found it in harmony with various experiences. We have all seen changes as considerable in wheat and caterpillars. He is the poet, and shall draw us with love and terror, who sees, through the flowing vest, the firm nature, and can declare it.

I look in vain for the poet whom I describe. We do not, with sufficient plainness, or sufficient profoundness, address ourselves to life, nor dare we chaunt our own times and social circumstance. If we filled the day with bravery, we should not shrink from celebrating it. Time and nature yield us many gifts, but not yet the timely man, the new religion, the reconciler, whom all things await. Dante's praise is, that he dared to write his autobiography in colossal cipher, or into universality. We have yet had no genius in America, with tyrannous eye, which knew the value of our incomparable materials, and saw, in the barbarism and materialism of the times, another carnival of the same gods whose picture he so much admires in Homer; then in the middle age; then in Calvinism. Banks and tariffs, the newspaper and caucus,[42] methodism and unitarianism, are flat and dull to dull people, but rest on the same foundations of wonder as the town of Troy, and the temple of Delphi, and are as swiftly passing away. Our logrolling, our stumps[43] and their politics, our fisheries, our Negroes, and Indians, our boasts, and our repudiations,[44] the wrath of rogues, and the pusillanimity of honest men, the northern trade, the southern planting, the western clearing, Oregon, and Texas, are yet unsung. Yet America is a poem in our eyes; its ample geography dazzles the imagination, and it will not wait long for metres. If I have not found that

---

[41] Brahmans, members of a priestly Hindu caste.   [42] A political meeting.
[43] Our trading political favors, our stump speeches, or impromptu political oratory.
[44] State government refusals to pay off bond issues.

excellent combination of gifts in my countrymen which I seek, neither could I aid myself to fix the idea of the poet by reading now and then in Chalmers's[45] collection of five centuries of English poets. These are wits, more than poets, though there have been poets among them. But when we adhere to the ideal of the poet, we have our difficulties even with Milton and Homer. Milton is too literary, and Homer too literal and historical.

But I am not wise enough for a national criticism, and must use the old largeness a little longer, to discharge my errand from the muse to the poet concerning his art.

Art is the path of the creator to his work. The paths, or methods, are ideal and eternal, though few men ever see them, not the artist himself for years, or for a lifetime, unless he come into the conditions. The painter, the sculptor, the composer, the epic rhapsodist, the orator, all partake one desire, namely, to express themselves symmetrically and abundantly, not dwarfishly and fragmentarily. They found or put themselves in certain conditions, as, the painter and sculptor before some impressive human figures; the orator, into the assembly of the people; and the others, in such scenes as each has found exciting to his intellect; and each presently feels the new desire. He hears a voice, he sees a beckoning. Then he is apprised, with wonder, what herds of dæmons hem him in. He can no more rest; he says, with the old painter, "By God, it is in me, and must go forth of me." He pursues a beauty, half seen, which flies before him. The poet pours out verses in every solitude. Most of the things he says are conventional, no doubt; but by and by he says something which is original and beautiful. That charms him. He would say nothing else but such things. In our way of talking we say, 'That is yours, this is mine;' but the poet knows well that it is not his; that it is as strange and beautiful to him as to you; he would fain hear the like eloquence at length. Once having tasted this immortal ichor,[46] he cannot have enough of it, and, as an admirable creative power exists in these intellections, it is of the last importance that these things get spoken. What a little of all we know is said! What drops of all the sea of our science are baled up! and by what accident it is that these are exposed, when so many secrets sleep in nature! Hence the neccessity of speech and song; hence these throbs and heart-beatings in the orator, at the door of the assembly, to the end, namely, that thought may be ejaculated as Logos, or Word.

Doubt not, O poet, but persist. Say, 'It is in me, and shall out,' Stand there, baulked and dumb, stuttering and stammering, hissed and hooted, stand and strive, until, at last, rage draw out of thee that *dream*-power which every night shows thee is thine own; a power transcending all limit and privacy, and by virtue of which a man is the conductor of the whole river of electricity. Nothing walks, or creeps, or grows, or exists, which must not in turn arise and walk before him as exponent of his meaning. Comes he to that power, his genius is no longer exhaustible. All the creatures, by pairs and by tribes, pour into his mind as into a Noah's ark, to come forth again to people a new world. This is like the stock of air for our respiration, or for the combustion of our fireplace, not a measure of gallons, but the entire atmosphere if wanted. And therefore the rich poets, as Homer, Chaucer, Shakspeare, and Raphael,[47] have obviously no limits to their works, except the

---

[45] Alexander Chalmers (1759–1834) compiled *Works of the English Poets* (1810) in twenty-one volumes.

[46] According to Greek myth, an ethereal fluid that replaced blood in the gods' veins.

[47] Raphael Santi (1483–1520), a majestic painter of the Italian Renaissance.

limits of their lifetime, and resemble a mirror carried through the street, ready to render an image of every created thing.

O poet! a new nobility is conferred in groves and pastures, and not in castles, or by the sword-blade, any longer. The conditions are hard, but equal. Thou shalt leave the world, and know the muse only. Thou shalt not know any longer the times, customs, graces, politics, or opinions of men, but shalt take all from the muse. For the time of towns is tolled from the world by funereal chimes, but in nature the universal hours are counted by succeeding tribes of animals and plants, and by growth of joy on joy. God wills also that thou abdicate a duplex and manifold life, and that thou be content that others speak for thee. Others shall be thy gentlemen, and shall represent all courtesy and worldly life for thee; others shall do the great and resounding actions also. Thou shalt lie close hid with nature, and canst not be afforded to the Capitol or the Exchange.[48] The world is full of renunciations and apprenticeships, and this is thine; thou must pass for a fool and a churl for a long season. This is the screen and sheath in which Pan[49] has protected his well-beloved flower, and thou shalt be known only to thine own, and they shall console thee with tenderest love. And thou shalt not be able to rehearse the names of thy friends in thy verse, for an old shame before the holy ideal. And this is the reward: that the ideal shall be real to thee, and the impressions of the actual world shall fall like summer rain, copious, but not troublesome, to thy invulnerable essence. Thou shalt have the whole land for thy park and manor, the sea for thy bath and navigation, without tax and without envy; the woods and the rivers thou shalt own; and thou shalt possess that wherein others are only tenants and boarders. Thou true land-lord! sea-lord! air-lord! Wherever snow falls, or water flows, or birds fly, wherever day and night meet in twilight, wherever the blue heaven is hung by clouds, or sown with stars, wherever are forms with transparent boundaries, wherever are outlets into celestial space, wherever is danger, and awe, and love, there is Beauty, plenteous as rain, shed for thee, and though thou shouldst walk the world over, thou shalt not be able to find a condition inopportune or ignoble.

1844

FATE*

Delicate omens traced in air
To the lone bard true witness bare;
Birds with auguries on their wings
Chanted undeceiving things
Him to beckon, him to warn;
Well might then the poet scorn
To learn of scribe or courier
Hints writ in vaster character;
And on his mind, at dawn of day,
Soft shadows of the evening lay.

[48] The world of politics or the world of finance.
[49] According to Greek myth, the half-man, half-goat god of fields and woods.
* Presented in December 1851 as part of a lecture series entitled "The Conduct of Life" and first published in *The Conduct of Life* (1860).

For the prevision is allied
Unto the thing so signified;
Or say, the foresight that awaits
Is the same Genius that creates.[1]

It chanced during one winter a few years ago, that our cities were bent on discussing the theory of the Age. By an odd coincidence, four or five noted men were each reading a discourse to the citizens of Boston or New York, on the Spirit of the Times.[2] It so happened that the subject had the same prominence in some remarkable pamphlets and journals issued in London in the same season. To me however the question of the times resolved itself into a practical question of the conduct of life. How shall I live? We are incompetent to solve the times. Our geometry cannot span the huge orbits of the prevailing ideas, behold their return and reconcile their opposition. We can only obey our own polarity. 'T is fine for us to speculate and elect our course, if we must accept an irresistable dictation.

In our first steps to gain our wishes we come upon immovable limitations. We are fired with the hope to reform men. After many experiments we find that we must begin earlier,—at school. But the boys and girls are not docile; we can make nothing of them. We decide that they are not of good stock. We must begin our reform earlier still,—at generation: that is to say there is Fate, or laws of the world.

But if there be irresistible dictation, this dictation understands itself. If we must accept Fate, we are not less compelled to affirm liberty, the significance of the individual, the grandeur of duty, the power of character. This is true, and that other is true. But our geometry cannot span these extreme points and reconcile them. What to do? By obeying each thought frankly, by harping, or, if you will, pounding on each string, we learn at last its power. By the same obedience to other thoughts we learn theirs, and then comes some reasonable hope of harmonizing them. We are sure that, though we know not how, necessity does comport with liberty, the individual with the world, my polarity with the spirit of the times. The riddle of the age has for each a private solution. If one would study his own time, it must be by this method of taking up in turn each of the leading topics which belong to our scheme of human life, and by firmly stating all that is agreeable to experience on one, and doing the same justice to the opposing facts in the others, the true limitations will appear. Any excess of emphasis on one part would be corrected, and a just balance would be made.

But let us honestly state the facts. Our America has a bad name for superficialness. Great men, great nations, have not been boasters and buffoons, but perceivers of the terror of life, and have manned themselves to face it. The Spartan, embodying his religion in his country, dies before its majesty without a question. The Turk, who believes his doom is written on the iron leaf in the moment when he entered the world, rushes on the enemy's sabre with undivided will. The Turk, the Arab, the Persian, accepts the foreordained fate:

"On two days, it steads not to run from thy grave,
    The appointed, and the unappointed day;

---

[1] The epigraphic poem is Emerson's.
[2] Emerson lectured on this subject in New York in January 1851; English writers such as William Hazlitt (1778–1830) and John Stuart Mill (1806–1873) had addressed the theme earlier.

On the first, neither balm nor physician can save,
Nor thee, on the second, the Universe slay."[3]

The Hindoo under the wheel, is as firm. Our Calvinists in the last generation[4] had something of the same dignity. They felt that the weight of the Universe held them down to their place. What could *they* do? Wise men feel that there is something which cannot be talked or voted away,—a strap or belt which girds the world:—

"The Destiny, minister general,
That executeth in the world o'er all,
The purveyance which God hath seen beforne,
So strong it is, that though the world had sworn
The contrary of a thing by yea or nay,
Yet sometime it shall fallen on a day
That falleth not oft in a thousand year;
For, certainly, our appetités here,
Be it of war, or peace, or hate, or love,
All this is ruled by the sight above."

CHAUCER: *The Knighte's Tale*.[5]

The Greek Tragedy expressed the same sense. "Whatever is fated, that will take place. The great immense mind of Jove is not to be transgressed."[6]

Savages cling to a local god of one tribe or town. The broad ethics of Jesus were quickly narrowed to village theologies, which preach an election or favoritism. And now and then an amiable parson, like Jung Stilling or Robert Huntington,[7] believes in a pistareen-Providence,[8] which, whenever the good man wants a dinner, makes that somebody shall knock at his door and leave a half-dollar. But Nature is no sentimentalist,—does not cosset[9] or pamper us. We must see that the world is rough and surly, and will not mind drowning a man or a woman, but swallows your ship like a grain of dust. The cold, inconsiderate of persons, tingles your blood, benumbs your feet, freezes a man like an apple. The diseases, the elements, fortune, gravity, lightning, respect no persons. The way of Providence is a little rude. The habit of snake and spider, the snap of the tiger and other leapers and bloody jumpers, the crackle of the bones of his prey in the coil of the anaconda,—these are in the system, and our habits are like theirs. You have just dined, and however scrupulously the slaughter-house is concealed in the graceful distance of miles, there is complicity, expensive races,—race living at the expense of race. The planet is liable to shocks from comets, perturbations from planets, rendings from earthquake and volcano, alterations of climate, precessions of equinoxes. Rivers dry up by opening of the forest. The sea changes its bed.

---

[3] Emerson translated these lines from a German translation of a Persian poet; in his journal he attributes them to Pindar of Rei in Kuhistan.

[4] Eighteenth-century Calvinists believed that a person's fate is predetermined by God.

[5] A modified version of lines 805–814.

[6] From *The Suppliants* (1047–1049), by the Greek tragic poet Aeschylus (525–456 B.C.); Jove (Jupiter) is the supreme god in Roman myth.

[7] Johann Heinrich Jung-Stilling (1740–1817), a German physician and mystic; actually *William* Huntington (1745–1813), an eccentric English minister.

[8] A Providence consisting of handing out small change to the needy; a pistareen is a Spanish coin of small value.

[9] Pamper.

Towns and counties fall into it. At Lisbon an earthquake killed men like flies.[10] At Naples three years ago ten thousand persons were crushed in a few minutes. The scurvy at sea, the sword of the climate in the west of Africa, at Cayenne, at Panama, at New Orleans, cut off men like a massacre. Our western prairie shakes with fever and ague. The cholera, the small-pox, have proved as mortal to some tribes as a frost to the crickets, which, having filled the summer with noise, are silenced by a fall of the temperature of one night. Without uncovering what does not concern us, or counting how many species of parasites hang on a bombyx,[11] or groping after intestinal parasites or infusory biters,[12] or the obscurities of alternate generation,—the forms of the shark, the *labrus*,[13] the jaw of the seawolf paved with crushing teeth, the weapons of the grampus,[14] and other warriors hidden in the sea, are hints of ferocity in the interiors of nature. Let us not deny it up and down. Providence has a wild, rough, incalculable road to its end, and it is of no use to try to whitewash its huge, mixed instrumentalities, or to dress up that terrific benefactor in a clean shirt and white neckcloth of a student in divinity.

Will you say, the disasters which threaten mankind are exceptional, and one need not lay his account for cataclysms every day? Aye, but what happens once may happen again, and so long as these strokes are not to be parried by us they must be feared.

But these shocks and ruins are less destructive to us than the stealthy power of other laws, which act on us daily. An expense of ends to means is fate;—organization tyrannizing over character. The menagerie, or forms and powers of the spine, is a book of fate; the bill of the bird, the skull of the snake, determines tyrannically its limits. So is the scale of races, of temperaments;[15] so is sex; so is climate; so is the reaction of talents imprisoning the vital power in certain directions. Every spirit makes its house; but afterwards the house confines the spirit.

The gross lines are legible to the dull; the cabman is phrenologist[16] so far, he looks in your face to see if his shilling is sure. A dome of brow denotes one thing, a pot-belly another; a squint, a pugnose, mats of hair, the pigment of the epidermis, betray character. People seem sheathed in their tough organization. Ask Spurzheim, ask the doctors, ask Quetelet[17] if temperaments decide nothing?—or if there be anything they do not decide? Read the description in medical books of the four temperaments and you will think you are reading your own thoughts which you had not yet told. Find the part which black eyes and which blue eyes play severally in the company. How shall a man escape from his ancestors, or draw off from his veins the black drop which he drew from his father's or his mother's life? It often appears in a family as if all the qualities of the progenitors were potted in several jars,—some ruling quality in each son or daughter of the house; and sometimes the unmixed temperament, the rank unmitigated elixir, the family vice, is drawn off in a separate individual and the others are proportionally relieved. We sometimes see a change of expression in our companion and say his

---

[10] The catastrophic Lisbon earthquake of 1775; the Naples disaster occured in 1857.

[11] A silkworm moth.   [12] Microscopic marine organisms.

[13] A heavy-lipped predatory fish.   [14] The killer whale.

[15] In ancient and medieval physiology, the mixture of four "humors" (blood, phlegm, choler, and melancholy) was believed to determine a person's temperament.

[16] According to the pseudo-science of phrenology, the conformation of the skull indicates mental abilities. Here, Emerson's cab driver seems more of a physiognomist, who predicts character from facial features.

[17] Johann Spurzheim (1776–1832), a German physician who popularized phrenology; Lambert Quételet (1796–1874), a Belgian mathematician who perfected the science of statistics.

father or his mother comes to the windows of his eyes, and sometimes a remote relative. In different hours a man represents each of several of his ancestors, as if there were seven or eight of us rolled up in each man's skin,—seven or eight ancestors at least; and they constitute the variety of notes for that new piece of music which his life is. At the corner of the street you read the possibility of each passenger in the facial angle, in the complexion, in the depth of his eye. His parentage determines it. Men are what their mothers made them. You may as well ask a loom which weaves huckaback[18] why it does not make cashmere, as expect poetry from this engineer, or a chemical discovery from that jobber. Ask the digger in the ditch to explain Newton's laws; the fine organs of his brain have been pinched by overwork and squalid poverty from father to son for a hundred years. When each comes forth from his mother's womb, the gate of gifts closes behind him. Let him value his hands and feet, he has but one pair. So he has but one future, and that is already predetermined in his lobes and described in that little fatty face, pig-eye, and squat form. All the privilege and all the legislation of the world cannot meddle or help to make a poet or a prince of him.

Jesus said, "When he looketh on her, he hath commited adultery."[19] But he is an adulterer before he has yet looked on the woman, by the superfluity of animal and the defect of thought in his constitution. Who meets him, or who meets her, in the street, sees that they are ripe to be each other's victim.

In certain men digestion and sex absorb the vital force, and the stronger these are, the individual is so much weaker. The more of these drones perish, the better for the hive. If, later, they give birth to some superior individual, with force enough to add to this animal a new aim and a complete apparatus to work it out, all the ancestors are gladly forgotten. Most men and most women are merely one couple more. Now and then one has a new cell or camarilla[20] opened in his brain,—an architectural, a musical, or a philological[21] knack; some stray taste or talent for flowers, or chemistry, or pigments, or story-telling; a good hand for drawing, a good foot for dancing, an athletic frame for wide journeying, etc.— which skill nowise alters rank in the scale of nature, but serves to pass the time; the life of sensation going on as before. At last these hints and tendencies are fixed in one or in a succession. Each absorbs so much food and force as to become itself a new centre. The new talent draws off so rapidly the vital force that not enough remains for the animal functions, hardly enough for health; so that in the second generation, if the like genius appear, the health is visibly deteriorated and the generative force impaired.

People are born with the moral or with the material bias;—uterine brothers with this diverging destination; and I suppose, with high magnifiers, Mr. Frauenhofer or Dr. Carpenter[22] might come to distinguish in the embryo, at the fourth day,— this is a Whig, and that a Free-soiler.[23]

It was a poetic attempt to lift this mountain of Fate, to reconcile this despotism of race with liberty, which led the Hindoos to say, "Fate is nothing but the deeds

---

[18] A strong linen fabric used for towels.

[19] " . . . whosoever looketh on a woman to lust after her hath committed adultery with her already in his heart," from Matthew 5:28.

[20] A small room, chamber.   [21] Literary.

[22] The German optician Joseph von Frauenhofer (1787–1826), who improved the telescope; the English physiologist William B. Carpenter (1813–1885), who wrote a treatise about the microscope.

[23] In 1851 "Whig" signified the Anti-Democratic party, and "Free-Soiler," the antislavery wing of the Democratic party.

committed in a prior state of existence."[24] I find the coincidence of the extremes of Eastern and Western speculation in the daring statement of Schelling,[25] "There is in every man a certain feeling that he has been what he is from all eternity, and by no means became such in time." To say it less sublimely,—in the history of the individual is always an account of his condition, and he knows himself to be a party to his present estate.

A good deal of our politics is physiological. Now and then a man of wealth in the heyday of youth adopts the tenet of broadest freedom. In England there is always some man of wealth and large connection, planting himself, during all his years of health, on the side of progress, who, as soon as he begins to die, checks his forward play, calls in his troops and becomes conservative. All conservatives are such from personal defects. They have been effeminated by position or nature, born halt and blind, through luxury of their parents, and can only, like invalids, act on the defensive. But strong natures, backwoodsmen, New Hampshire giants, Napoleons, Burkes, Broughams, Websters, Kossuths,[26] are inevitable patriots, until their life ebbs and their defects and gout, palsy and money, warp them.

The strongest idea incarnates itself in majorities and nations, in the healthiest and strongest. Probably the election goes by avoirdupois weight, and if you could weigh bodily the tonnage of any hundred of the Whig and the Democratic party in a town on the Dearborn balance,[27] as they passed the hay-scales, you could predict with certainty which party would carry it. On the whole it would be rather the speediest way of deciding the vote, to put the selectmen or the mayor and aldermen at the hay-scales.

In science we have to consider two things; power and circumstance. All we know of the egg, from each successive discovery, is, *another vesicle*;[28] and if, after five hundred years you get a better observer or a better glass, he finds, within the last observed, another. In vegetable and animal tissue it is just alike, and all that the primary power or spasm operates is still vesicles, vesicles. Yes,—but the tyrannical Circumstance! A vesicle in new circumstances, a vesicle lodged in the darkness, Oken[29] thought, became animal; in light, a plant. Lodged in the parent animal, it suffers changes which end in unsheathing miraculous capability in the unaltered vesicle, and it unlocks itself to fish, bird, or quadruped, head and foot, eye and claw. The Circumstance is Nature. Nature is what you may do. There is much you may not. We have two things,—the circumstance, and the life. Once we thought positive power was all. Now we learn that negative power, or circumstance, is half. Nature is the tyrannous circumstance, the thick skull, the sheathed snake, the ponderous, rock-like jaw; necessitated activity; violent direction; the conditions of a tool, like the locomotive, strong enough on its track, but which can do nothing but mischief off of it; or skates, which are wings on the ice but fetters on the ground.

---

[24] Probably not taken from one source, the quotation expresses the idea of karma.

[25] Friedrich Wilhelm Joseph von Schelling (1775–1854), a German philosopher whose work bridged German philosophical idealism and romanticism.

[26] Edmund Burke (1729–1797), an English statesman; Henry Peter Brougham (1778–1868), an English parliamentary leader; Daniel Webster (1782–1852), a statesman and leader of the Whig party; Lajos Kossuth (1802–1894), leader of the Hungarian fight for freedom in 1848. During Kossuth's 1851 to 1852 visit to the United States, Emerson welcomed him to Concord.

[27] A spring balance, or scale.   [28] A bladderlike vessel or sac.

[29] Lorenz Oken (1779–1851), a German naturalist who taught that all organisms are produced from cells.

The book of Nature is the book of Fate. She turns the gigantic pages,—leaf after leaf,—never re-turning one. One leaf she lays down, a floor of granite; then a thousand ages, and a bed of slate; a thousand ages, and a measure of coal; a thousand ages, and a layer of marl and mud: vegetable forms appear; her first misshapen animals, zoöphyte, trilobium, fish; then, saurians,[30]—rude forms, in which she has only blocked her future statue, concealing under these unwieldly monsters the fine type of her coming king. The face of the planet cools and dries, the races meliorate, and man is born. But when a race has lived its term, it comes no more again.

The population of the world is a conditional population; not the best, but the best that could live now; and the scale of tribes, and the steadiness with which victory adheres to one tribe and defeat to another, is as uniform as the superposition of strata. We know in history what weight belongs to race. We see the English, French, and Germans planting themselves on every shore and market of America and Australia, and monopolizing the commerce of these countries. We like the nervous and victorious habit of our own branch of the family. We follow the step of the Jew, of the Indian, of the Negro. We see how much will has been expended to extinguish the Jew, in vain. Look at the unpalatable conclusions of Knox,[31] in his "Fragment of Races;"—a rash and unsatisfactory writer, but charged with pungent and unforgetable truths. "Nature respects race, and not hybrids." "Every race has its own *habitat*." "Detach a colony from the race, and it deteriorates to the crab."[32] See the shades of the picture. The German and Irish millions, like the Negro, have a great deal of guano[33] in their destiny. They are ferried over the Atlantic and carted over America, to ditch and to drudge, to make corn cheap and then to lie down prematurely to make a spot of green grass on the prairie.

One more fagot of these adamantine bandages[34] is the new science of Statistics. It is a rule that the most casual and extraordinary events, if the basis of population is broad enough, become matter of fixed calculation. It would not be safe to say when a captain like Bonaparte, a singer like Jenny Lind, or a navigator like Bowditch[35] would be born in Boston; but, on a population of twenty or two hundred millions, something like accuracy may be had.[36]

'T is frivolous to fix pedantically the date of particular inventions. They have all been invented over and over fifty times. Man is the arch machine of which all these shifts drawn from himself are toy models. He helps himself on each emergency by copying or duplicating his own structure, just so far as the need is. 'T is hard to find the right Homer, Zoroaster, or Menu; harder still to find the Tubal

---

[30] An animal that appears to be a plant, trilobites, fish; then lizards.

[31] Robert Knox (1791–1862), a Scottish anatomist and ethnologist, who sought to justify racial prejudice scientifically in *The Races of Men: A Fragment* (1850).

[32] The supposed degeneration of apple trees to crabapples when not cultivated; Knox applied this analogy to colonies of people detached from the mother country.

[33] The manure of sea birds, used as fertilizer.

[34] One more bundle of these impenetrable explanations.

[35] Jenny Lind (1820–1887), a popular British coloratura soprano; Nathaniel Bowditch (1773–1838), an American mathematician and astronomer, whose *New American Practical Navigator* (1802) was widely used.

[36] Emerson's note: " 'Everything which pertains to the human species, considered as a whole, belongs to the order of physical facts. The greater the number of individuals, the more does the influence of the individual will disappear, leaving predominance to a series of general facts dependent on causes by which society exists, and is preserved.'—Quetelet."

Cain, or Vulcan, or Cadmus, or Copernicus, or Fust, or Fulton;[37] the indisputable inventor. There are scores and centuries of them. "The air is full of men." This kind of talent so abounds, this constructive tool-making efficiency, as if it adhered to the chemic atoms; as if the air he breathes were made of Vaucansons, Franklins, and Watts.[38]

Doubtless in every million there will be an astronomer, a mathematician, a comic poet, a mystic. No one can read the history of astronomy without perceiving that Copernicus, Newton, Laplace, are not new men, or a new kind of men, but that Thales, Anaximenes, Hipparchus, Empedocles, Aristarchus, Pythagoras, Œnipodes,[39] had anticipated them; each had the same tense geometrical brain, apt for the same vigorous computation and logic; a mind parallel to the movement of the world. The Roman mile probably rested on a measure of a degree of the meridian. Mahometan[40] and Chinese know what we know of leap-year, of the Gregorian calendar,[41] and of the precession of the equinoxes. As in every barrel of cowries brought to New Bedford there shall be one *orangia*,[42] so there will, in a dozen millions of Malays and Mahometans, be one or two astronomical skulls.[43] In a large city, the most casual things, and things whose beauty lies in their casualty, are produced as punctually and to order as the baker's muffin for breakfast. Punch[44] makes exactly one capital joke a week; and the journals contrive to furnish one good piece of news every day.

And not less work the laws of repression, the penalties of violated functions. Famine, typhus, frost, war, suicide and effete races must be reckoned calculable parts of the system of the world.

These are pebbles from the mountain, hints of the terms by which our life is walled up, and which show a kind of mechanical exactness, as of a loom or mill, in what we call casual or fortuitous events.

---

[37] Zoroaster (6th or 7th century B.C.) was a Persian religious seer; Manu, said to be the author of the Hindu *Laws of Manu;* Tubal-Cain, "an instructor of every artificer in brass and iron," from Genesis 4:22; Vulcan, the Roman god of fire and metalworking; Cadmus, a legendary Phoenician prince who slew a dragon and saw an army spring up from its teeth, which he had scattered on the ground; Nicolaus Copernicus (1473–1543), the Polish astronomer who determined the movements of the solar system; Johann Fust (1400?–1466?), a German printer associated with the invention of movable type; Robert Fulton (1765–1815), the American inventor who designed steamboats.

[38] Jacques de Vaucanson (1709–1782), a French mathematician and inventor of self-moving machines (automatons); the American inventor, statesman, and writer Benjamin Franklin (1706–1790); James Watt (1736–1819), the Scottish engineer who invented the modern steam engine.

[39] Sir Isaac Newton (1642–1727), the English mathematician and physicist who formulated the theory of gravity; Pierre Simon (1749–1827), marquis de Laplace, a French mathematician and astronomer; the Greek philosophers Thales (640?–546 B.C.), who taught that the earth is round and that the moon reflects light from the sun and predicted a solar eclipse, and Anaximenes of Miletus (6th century B.C.), who claimed that all substances are derived from air; Hipparchus (2d century B.C.), a Greek astronomer who discovered the precession of the equinoxes; Empedocles (5th century B.C.), a Greek philosopher and statesman who claimed to have prophetic powers; Aristarchus of Samos (3d century B.C.), a Greek astronomer who explained that the earth revolves around the sun and on its own axis; Pythagoras (6th century B.C.), a renowned Greek mathematician and philosopher; Oenopides of Chios (5th century B.C.), a Greek astronomer and mathematician who "anticipated" Pythagoras with his knowledge of the obliquity of the ecliptic.

[40] Mohammedan.

[41] The modern calendar, in use since 1582 (adopted in America in 1752), was named for Pope Gregory XIII (1502–1585).

[42] A particularly bright type of cowrie shell.

[43] Skulls with brains equipped for astronomical study.

[44] A British satirical weekly magazine; Emerson is droll about its humor.

The force with which we resist these torrents of tendency looks so ridiculously inadequate that it amounts to little more than a criticism or a protest made by a minority of one, under compulsion of millions. I seemed in the height of a tempest to see men overboard struggling in the waves, and driven about here and there. They glanced intelligently at each other, but 't was little they could do for one another; 't was much if each could keep afloat alone. Well, they had a right to their eyebeams, and all the rest was Fate.

We cannot trifle with this reality, this cropping-out in our planted gardens of the core of the world. No picture of life can have any veracity that does not admit the odious facts. A man's power is hooped in by a necessity which, by many experiments, he touches on every side until he learns its arc.

The element running through entire nature, which we popularly call Fate, is known to us as limitation. Whatever limits us we call Fate. If we are brute and barbarous, the fate takes a brute and dreadful shape. As we refine, our cheeks become finer. If we rise to spiritual culture, the antagonism takes a spiritual form. In the Hindoo fables, Vishnu follows Maya[45] through all her ascending changes, from insect and crawfish up to elephant; whatever form she took, he took the male form of that kind, until she became at last woman and goddess, and he a man and a god. The limitations refine as the soul purifies, but the ring of necessity is always perched at the top.

When the gods in the Norse heaven were unable to bind the Fenris Wolf[46] with steel or with weight of mountains,—the one he snapped and the other he spurned with his heel,—they put round his foot a limp band softer than silk or cobweb, and this held him; the more he spurned it the stiffer it drew. So soft and so stanch is the ring of Fate. Neither brandy, nor nectar, nor sulphuric ether, nor hell-fire, nor ichor,[47] nor poetry, nor genius, can get rid of this limp band. For if we give it the high sense in which the poets use it, even thought itself is not above Fate; that too must act according to eternal laws, and all that is wilful and fantastic in it is in opposition to its fundamental essence.

And last of all, high over thought, in the world of morals, Fate appears as vindicator, levelling the high, lifting the low, requiring justice in man, and always striking soon or late when justice is not done. What is useful will last; what is hurtful will sink. "The doer must suffer," said the Greeks; "you would soothe a Deity not to be soothed." "God himself cannot procure good for the wicked," said the Welsh triad. "God may consent, but only for a time," said the bard of Spain.[48] The limitation is impassable by any insight of man. In its last and loftiest ascensions, insight itself and the freedom of the will is one of its obedient members. But we must not run into generalizations too large, but show the natural bounds or essential distinctions, and seek to do justice to the other elements as well.

Thus we trace Fate in matter, mind, and morals; in race, in retardations of strata, and in thought and character as well. It is everywhere bound or limitation. But Fate has its lord; limitation its limits,—is different seen from above and from below, from within and from without. For though Fate is immense, so is Power, which is the other fact in the dual world, immense. If Fate follows and limits

---

[45] In the Hindu trinity, Vishnu is the preserver of human beings; Maya is the goddess of illusion.

[46] According to Norse myth, a monster who was restrained by fragile bonds but whose wrath was ever threatening.

[47] According to Greek myth, an ethereal fluid that replaced blood in the gods' veins.

[48] The source of these maxims has not been identified.

Power, Power attends and antagonizes Fate. We must respect Fate as natural history, but there is more than natural history. For who and what is this criticism that pries into the matter? Man is not order of nature, sack and sack, belly and members,[49] link in a chain, nor any ignominious baggage; but a stupendous antagonism, a dragging together of the poles of the Universe. He betrays his relation to what is below him,—thick-skulled, small-brained, fishy, quadrumanous,[50] quadruped ill-disguised, hardly escaped into biped,—and has paid for the new powers by loss of some of the old ones. But the lightning which explodes and fashions planets, maker of planets, and suns, is in him. On one side elemental order, sandstone and granite, rock-ledges, peat-bog, forest, sea and shore; and on the other part thought, the spirit which composes and decomposes nature,—here they are, side by side, god and devil, mind and matter, king and conspirator, belt and spasm, riding peacefully together in the eye and brain of every man.

Nor can he blink the freewill. To hazard the contradiction,—freedom is necessary. If you please to plant yourself on the side of Fate, and say, Fate is all; then we say, a part of Fate is the freedom of man. Forever wells up the impulse of choosing and acting in the soul. Intellect annuls Fate. So far as a man thinks, he is free. And though nothing is more disgusting than the crowing about liberty by slaves, as most men are, and the flippant mistaking for freedom of some paper preamble like a "Declaration of Independence" or the statute right to vote, by those who have never dared to think or to act,—yet it is wholesome to man to look not at Fate, but the other way: the practical view is the other. His sound relation to these facts is to use and command, not to cringe to them. "Look not on Nature, for her name is fatal," said the oracle. The too much contemplation of these limits induces meanness. They who talk much of destiny, their birth-star, &c., are in a lower dangerous plane, and invite the evils they fear.

I cited the instinctive and heroic races as proud believers in Destiny. They conspire with it; a loving resignation is with the event. But the dogma makes a different impression when it is held by the weak and lazy. 'Tis weak and vicious people who cast the blame on Fate. The right use of Fate is to bring up our conduct to the loftiness of nature. Rude and invincible except by themselves are the elements. So let man be. Let him empty his breast of his windy conceits, and show his lordship by manners and deeds on the scale of nature. Let him hold his purpose as with the tug of gravitation. No power, no persuasion, no bribe shall make him give up his point. A man ought to compare advantageously with a river, an oak, or a mountain. He shall have not less the flow, the expansion, and the resistance of these.

'T is the best use of Fate to teach a fatal courage. Go face the fire at sea, or the cholera in your friend's house, or the burglar in your own, or what danger lies in the way of duty,—knowing you are guarded by the cherubim of Destiny. If you believe in Fate to your harm, believe it at least for your good.

For if Fate is so prevailing, man also is part of it, and can confront fate with fate. If the Universe have these savage accidents, our atoms are as savage in resistance. We should be crushed by the atmosphere, but for the reaction of the air within the body. A tube made of a film of glass can resist the shock of the ocean if filled with the same water. If there be omnipotence in the stroke, there is omnipotence of recoil.

---

[49] The dialogue between the belly and other parts of the body is given by Menenius Agrippa in Shakespeare's *Coriolanus* (I. i. 99–150).
[50] Having all four feet with opposable first digits.

1. But Fate against Fate is only parrying and defence: there are also the noble creative forces. The revelation of Thought takes man out of servitude into freedom. We rightly say of ourselves, we were born and afterward we were born again, and many times. We have successive experiences so important that the new forgets the old, and hence the mythology of the seven or the nine heavens. The day of days, the great day of the feast of life, is that in which the inward eye opens to the Unity in things, to the omnipresence of law:—sees that what is must be and ought to be, or is the best. This beatitude dips from on high down on us and we see. It is not in us so much as we are in it. If the air come to our lungs, we breathe and live; if not, we die. If the light come to our eyes, we see; else not. And if truth come to our mind we suddenly expand to its dimensions, as if we grew to worlds. We are as lawgivers; we speak for Nature; we prophesy and divine.

This insight throws us on the party and interest of the Universe, against all and sundry; against ourselves as much as others. A man speaking from insight affirms of himself what is true of the mind: seeing its immortality, he says, I am immortal; seeing its invincibility, he says, I am strong. It is not in us, but we are in it. It is of the maker, not of what is made. All things are touched and changed by it. This uses and is not used. It distances those who share it from those who share it not. Those who share it not are flocks and herds. It dates from itself; not from former men or better men, gospel, or constitution, or college, or custom. Where it shines, Nature is no longer intrusive, but all things make a musical or pictorial impression. The world of men show like a comedy without laughter: populations, interests, government history; 't is all toy figures in a toy house. It does not overvalue particular truths. We hear eagerly every thought and word quoted from an intellectual man. But in his presence our own mind is roused to activity, and we forget very fast what he says, much more interested in the new play of our own thought than in any thought of his. 'T is the majesty into which we have suddenly mounted, the impersonality, the scorn of egotisms, the sphere of laws, that engage us. Once we were stepping a little this way and a little that way; now we are as men in a balloon, and do not think so much of the point we have left, or the point we would make, as of the liberty and glory of the way.

Just as much intellect as you add, so much organic power. He who sees through the design, presides over it, and must will that which must be. We sit and rule, and, though we sleep, our dream will come to pass. Our thought, though it were only an hour old, affirms an oldest necessity, not to be separated from thought, and not to be separated from will. They must always have coexisted. It apprises us of its sovereignty and godhead, which refuse to be severed from it. It is not mine or thine, but the will of all mind. It is poured into the souls of all men, as the soul itself which constitutes them men. I know not whether there be, as is alleged, in the upper region of our atmosphere, a permanent westerly current which carries with it all atoms which rise to that height, but I see that when souls reach a certain clearness of perception they accept a knowledge and motive above selfishness. A breath of will blows eternally through the universe of souls in the direction of the Right and Necessary. It is the air which all intellects inhale and exhale, and it is the wind which blows the worlds into order and orbit.

Thought dissolves the material universe by carrying the mind up into a sphere where all is plastic. Of two men, each obeying his own thought, he whose thought is deepest will be the strongest character. Always one man more than another represents the will of Divine Providence to the period.

2. If thought makes free, so does the moral sentiment. The mixtures of spiritual chemistry refuse to be analyzed. Yet we can see that with the perception of truth is

joined the desire that it shall prevail; that affection is essential to will. Moreover, when a strong will appears, it usually results from a certain unity of organization, as if the whole energy of body and mind flowed in one direction. All great force is real and elemental. There is no manufacturing a strong will. There must be a pound to balance a pound. Where power is shown in will, it must rest on the universal force. Alaric[51] and Bonaparte must believe they rest on a truth, or their will can be bought or bent. There is a bribe possible for any finite will. But the pure sympathy with universal ends is an infinite force, and cannot be bribed or bent. Whoever has had experience of the moral sentiment cannot choose but believe in unlimited power. Each pulse from that heart is an oath from the Most High. I know not what the word *sublime* means, if it be not the intimations, in this infant, of a terrific force. A text of heroism, a name and anecdote of courage, are not arguments but sallies of freedom. One of these is the verse of the Persian Hafiz,[52] "'T is written on the gate of Heaven, 'Woe unto him who suffers himself to be betrayed by Fate!'" Does the reading of history make us fatalists? What courage does not the opposite opinion show! A little whim of will to be free gallantly contending against the universe of chemistry.

But insight is not will, nor is affection will. Perception is cold, and goodness dies in wishes. As Voltaire[53] said, 't is the misfortune of worthy people that they are cowards; "*un des plus grands malheurs des honnêtes gens c'est qu'ils sont des lâches.*" There must be a fusion of these two to generate the energy of will. There can be no driving force except through the conversion of the man into his will, making him the will, and the will him. And one may say boldly that no man has a right perception of any truth who has not been reacted on by it so as to be ready to be its martyr.

The one serious and formidable thing in nature is a will. Society is servile from want of will, and therefore the world wants saviours and religions. One way is right to go; the hero sees it, and moves on that aim, and has the world under him for root and support. He is to others as the world. His approbation is honor; his dissent, infamy. The glance of his eye has the force of sunbeams. A personal influence towers up in memory only worthy, and we gladly forget numbers, money, climate, gravitation, and the rest of Fate.

We can afford to allow the limitation, if we know it is the meter of the growing man. We stand against Fate, as children stand up against the wall in their father's house and notch their height from year to year. But when the boy grows to man, and is master of the house, he pulls down that wall and builds a new and bigger. 'T is only a question of time. Every brave youth is in training to ride and rule this dragon. His science is to make weapons and wings of these passions and retarding forces. Now whether, seeing these two things, fate and power, we are permitted to believe in unity? The bulk of mankind believe in two gods. They are under one dominion here in the house, as friend and parent, in social circles, in letters, in art, in love, in religion; but in mechanics, in dealing with steam and climate, in trade, in politics, they think they come under another; and that it would be a practical blunder to transfer the method and way of working of one sphere into the other. What good, honest, generous men at home, will be wolves and foxes on 'Change![54] What pious men in the parlor will vote for what reprobates at the polls!

---

[51] Alaric (370?–410) was a Visigoth king who sacked Rome in 410.

[52] Shams ud-din Mohammed (14th century), a Persian lyric poet.

[53] Pen name of the French writer François Marie Arouet (1694–1778); Emerson translates Voltaire's statement, then quotes it in French.

[54] The stock exchange.

To a certain point, they believe themselves the care of a Providence. But in a steamboat, in an epidemic, in war, they believe a malignant energy rules.

But relation and connection are not somewhere and sometimes, but everywhere and always. The divine order does not stop where their sight stops. The friendly power works on the same rules in the next farm and the next planet. But where they have not experience they run against it and hurt themselves. Fate then is a name for facts not yet passed under the fire of thought; for causes which are unpenetrated.

But every jet of chaos which threatens to exterminate us is convertible by intellect into wholesome force. Fate is unpenetrated causes. The water drowns ship and sailor like a grain of dust. But learn to swim, trim your bark,[55] and the wave which drowned it will be cloven by it and carry it like its own foam, a plume and a power. The cold is inconsiderate of persons, tingles your blood, freezes a man like a dew-drop. But learn to skate, and the ice will give you a graceful, sweet, and poetic motion. The cold will brace your limbs and brain to genius, and make you foremost men of time. Cold and sea will train an imperial Saxon race, which nature cannot bear to lose, and after cooping it up for a thousand years in yonder England, gives a hundred Englands, a hundred Mexicos. All the bloods it shall absorb and domineer: and more than Mexicos, the secrets of water and steam, the spasms of electricity, the ductility of metals, the chariot of the air, the ruddered balloon are awaiting you.

The annual slaughter from typhus far exceeds that of war; but right drainage destroys typhus. The plague in the sea-service from scurvy is healed by lemon juice and other diets portable or procurable; the depopulation by cholera and small-pox is ended by drainage and vaccination; and every other pest is not less in the chain of cause and effect, and may be fought off. And whilst art draws out the venom, it commonly extorts some benefit from the vanquished enemy. The mischievous torrent is taught to drudge for man; the wild beasts he makes useful for food, or dress, or labor; the chemic explosions are controlled like his watch. These are now the steeds on which he rides. Man moves in all modes, by legs of horses, by wings of wind, by steam, by gas of balloon, by electricity, and stands on tiptoe threatening to hunt the eagle in his own element. There's nothing he will not make his carrier.

Steam was till the other day the devil which we dreaded. Every pot made by any human potter or brazier[56] had a hole in its cover, to let off the enemy, lest he should lift pot and roof and carry the house away. But the Marquis of Worcester,[57] Watt, and Fulton bethought themselves that where was power was not devil, but was God; that it must be availed of, and not by any means let off and wasted. Could he lift pots and roofs and houses so handily? He was the workman they were in search of. He could be used to lift away, chain and compel other devils far more reluctant and dangerous, namely cubic miles of earth, mountains, weight or resistance of water, machinery, and the labors of all men in the world; and time he shall lengthen, and shorten space.

It has not fared much otherwise with higher kinds of steam. The opinion of the million was the terror of the world, and it was attempted either to dissipate it, by amusing nations, or to pile it over with strata of society,—a layer of soldiers, over

---

[55] Trim the sails of your small sailing ship.   [56] A brassworker.

[57] Edward Somerset (1601–1667), marquis of Worcester and earl of Glamorgan, a precursor of James Watt and Robert Fulton who studied mechanics and wrote *Century of Inventions* (1663), which describes a machine similar to a steam engine.

that a layer of lords, and a king on the top; with clamps and hoops of castles, garrisons, and police. But sometimes the religious principle would get in and burst the hoops and rive every mountain laid on top of it. The Fultons and Watts of politics, believing in unity, saw that it was a power, and by satisfying it (as justice satisfies everybody), through a different disposition of society,—grouping it on a level instead of piling it into a mountain,—they have contrived to make of this terror the most harmless and energetic form of a State.

Very odious, I confess, are the lessons of Fate. Who likes to have a dapper phrenologist pronouncing on his fortunes? Who likes to believe that he has, hidden in his skull, spine, and pelvis, all the vices of a Saxon or Celtic race, which will be sure to pull him down,—with what grandeur of hope and resolve he is fired,—into a selfish, huckstering, servile, dodging animal? A learned physician tells us the fact is invariable with the Neapolitan, that when mature he assumes the forms of the unmistakable scoundrel. That is little overstated,—but may pass.

But these are magazines[58] and arsenals. A man must thank his defects, and stand in some terror of his talents. A transcendent talent draws so largely on his forces as to lame him; a defect pays him revenues on the other side. The sufferance which is the badge of the Jew, has made him, in these days, the ruler of the rulers of the earth.[59] If Fate is ore and quarry, if evil is good in the making, if limitation is power that shall be, if calamities, oppositions, and weights are wings and means,—we are reconciled.

Fate involves the melioration. No statement of the Universe can have any soundness which does not admit its ascending effort. The direction of the whole and of the parts is toward benefit, and in proportion to the health. Behind every individual closes organization; before him opens liberty,—the Better, the Best. The first and worse races are dead. The second and imperfect races are dying out, or remain for the maturing of higher. In the latest race, in man, every generosity, every new perception, the love and praise he extorts from his fellows, are certificates of advance out of fate into freedom. Liberation of the will from the sheaths and clogs of organization which he has outgrown, is the end and aim of this world. Every calamity is a spur and valuable hint: and where his endeavors do not yet fully avail, they tell as tendency. The whole circle of animal life,—tooth against tooth, devouring war, war for food, a yelp of pain and a grunt of triumph, until at last the whole menagerie, the whole chemical mass is mellowed and refined for higher use,—pleases at a sufficient perspective.

But to see how fate slides into freedom and freedom into fate, observe how far the roots of every creature run, or find if you can a point where there is no thread of connection. Our life is consentaneous[60] and far-related. This knot of nature is so well tied that nobody was ever cunning enough to find the two ends. Nature is intricate, over-lapped, interweaved and endless. Christopher Wren[61] said of the beautiful King's College chapel, that "if anybody would tell him where to lay the first stone, he would build such another." But where shall we find the first atom in this house of man, which is all consent, inosculation,[62] and balance of parts?

The web of relation is shown in *habitat,* shown in hibernation. When hibernation was observed, it was found that whilst some animals became torpid in winter, others were torpid in summer: hibernation then was a false name. The *long sleep*

---

[58] Storehouses.   [59] Through financial power and control of dominant banks.
[60] Suitable, lived with a single consent.
[61] The English architect (1632–1723) who designed St. Paul's Cathedral.
[62] Joining or blending to make a whole.

is not an effect of cold, but is regulated by the supply of food proper to the animal. It becomes torpid when the fruit or prey it lives on is not in season, and regains its activity when its food is ready.

Eyes are found in light; ears in auricular[63] air; feet on land; fins in water; wings in the air; and each creature where it was meant to be, with a mutual fitness. Every zone has its own *Fauna*. There is adjustment between the animal and its food, its parasite, its enemy. Balances are kept. It is not allowed to diminish in numbers, nor to exceed. The like adjustments exist for man. His food is cooked when he arrives; his coal in the pit; the house ventilated; the mud of the deluge dried; his companions arrived at the same hour, and awaiting him with love, concert, laughter and tears. These are coarse adjustments, but the invisible are not less. There are more belongings to every creature than his air and his food. His instincts must be met, and he has predisposing power that bends and fits what is near him to his use. He is not possible until the invisible things are right for him, as well as the visible. Of what changes then in sky and earth, and in finer skies and earths, does the appearance of some Dante or Columbus apprise us!

How is this effected? Nature is no spendthrift, but takes the shortest way to her ends. As the general says to his soldiers, "If you want a fort, build a fort," so nature makes every creature do its own work and get its living,—is it planet, animal or tree. The planet makes itself. The animal cell makes itself;—then, what it wants. Every creature, wren or dragon, shall make its own lair. As soon as there is life, there is self-direction and absorbing and using of material. Life is freedom,—life in the direct ratio of its amount. You may be sure the new-born man is not inert. Life works both voluntarily and supernaturally in its neighborhood. Do you suppose he can be estimated by his weight in pounds, or that he is contained in his skin,—this reaching, radiating, jaculating[64] fellow? The smallest candle fills a mile with its rays, and the papillæ[65] of a man run out to every star.

When there is something to be done, the world knows how to get it done. The vegetable eye makes leaf, pericarp,[66] root, bark, or thorn, as the need is; the first cell converts itself into stomach, mouth, nose, or nail, according to the want; the world throws its life into a hero or a shepherd, and puts him where he is wanted. Dante and Columbus were Italians, in their time; they would be Russians or Americans to-day. Things ripen, new men come. The adaptation is not capricious. The ulterior aim, the purpose beyond itself, the correlation by which planets subside and crystallize, then animate beasts and men,—will not stop but will work into finer particulars, and from finer to finest.

The secret of the world is the tie between person and event. Person makes event, and event person. The "times," "the age," what is that but a few profound persons and a few active persons who epitomize the times?—Goethe, Hegel, Metternich, Adams, Calhoun, Guizot, Peel, Cobden, Kossuth, Rothschild, Astor, Brunel,[67] and the rest. The same fitness must be presumed between a man and the

---

[63] Audible.   [64] Throwing, hurling.   [65] Small nipplelike projections.

[66] The walls of a ripened plant ovary.

[67] Johann Wolfgang von Goethe (1749–1832), a German writer; George Wilhelm Friedrich Hegel (1770–1831), a German philosopher; Prince Klemens von Metternich (1773–1859), an Austrian statesman; John Adams (1735–1859), second U.S. president; John C. Calhoun (1782–1850), a southern politician and U.S. vice president from 1825 to 1832; François Guizot (1787–1874), a French statesman; Robert Peel (1788–1850), a British prime minister (1834–1835, 1841–1846); Richard Cobden (1804–1865), a British economist and politician; Lajos Kossuth; Meyer Rothschild (1743–1812), a German-Jewish banker; John Jacob Astor (1763–1848), an American fur trader and financier; Isambard Brunel (1806–1859), designer of the first transatlantic steamship, the *Great Western*.

time and event, as between the sexes, or between a race of animals and the food it eats, or the inferior races it uses. He thinks his fate alien, because the copula is hidden. But the soul contains the event that shall befall it; for the event is only the actualization of its thoughts, and what we pray to ourselves for is always granted. The event is the print of your form. It fits you like your skin. What each does is proper to him. Events are the children of his body and mind. We learn that the soul of Fate is the soul of us, as Hafiz sings,—

> "Alas! till now I had not known,
> My guide and fortune's guide are one."

All the toys that infatuate men and which they play for,—houses, land, money, luxury, power, fame, are the selfsame thing, with a new gauze or two of illusion overlaid. And of all the drums and rattles by which men are made willing to have their heads broke, and are led out solemnly every morning to parade,—the most admirable is this by which we are brought to believe that events are arbitrary and independent of actions. At the conjuror's, we detect the hair by which he moves his puppet, but we have not eyes sharp enough to descry the thread that ties cause and effect.

Nature magically suits the man to his fortunes, by making these the fruit of his character. Ducks take to the water, eagles to the sky, waders to the sea margin, hunters to the forest, clerks to counting-rooms, soldiers to the frontier. Thus events grow on the same stem with persons; are sub-persons. The pleasure of life is according to the man that lives it, and not according to the work or the place. Life is an ecstasy. We know what madness belongs to love,—what power to paint a vile object in hues of heaven. As insane persons are indifferent to their dress, diet, and other accommodations, and as we do in dreams, with equanimity, the most absurd acts, so a drop more of wine in our cup of life will reconcile us to strange company and work. Each creature puts forth from itself its own condition and sphere, as the slug sweats out its slimy house on the pear-leaf, and the wooly aphides on the apple perspire their own bed, and the fish its shell. In youth we clothe ourselves with rainbows and go as brave as the zodiac. In age we put out another sort of perspiration,—gout, fever, rheumatism, caprice, doubt, fretting and avarice.

A man's fortunes are the fruit of his character. A man's friends are his magnetisms. We go to Herodotus and Plutarch[68] for examples of Fate; but we are examples. "*Quisque suos patimur manes.*"[69] The tendency of every man to enact all that is in his constitution is expressed in the old belief that the efforts which we make to escape from our destiny only serve to lead us into it: and I have noticed a man likes better to be complimented on his position, as the proof of the last or total excellence, than on his merits.

A man will see his character emitted in the events that seem to meet, but which exude from and accompany him. Events expand with the character. As once he found himself among toys, so now he plays a part in colossal systems, and his growth is declared in his ambition, his companions and his performance. He looks like a piece of luck, but is a piece of causation; the mosaic, angulated and ground

[68] Herodotus (5th century B.C.), a Greek historian known as the Father of History; Plutarch (A.D. 46?–120?), biographer who featured the "parallel lives" of eminent Greeks and Romans.

[69] "Each person undergoes his special penalty," from Book VI of Virgil's *Aeniad* (spoken to Aeneas by his father).

to fit into the gap he fills. Hence in each town there is some man who is, in his brain and performance, an explanation of the tillage, production, factories, banks, churches, ways of living and society of that town. If you do not chance to meet him, all that you see will leave you a little puzzled; if you see him it will become plain. We know in Massachusetts who built New Bedford, who built Lynn, Lowell, Lawrence, Clinton, Fitchburg, Holyoke, Portland, and many another noisy mart. Each of these men, if they were transparent, would seem to you so much men as walking cities, and wherever you put them they would build one.

History is the action and reaction of these two,—Nature and Thought; two boys pushing each other on the curbstone of the pavement. Everything is pusher or pushed; and matter and mind are in perpetual tilt and balance, so. Whilst the man is weak, the earth takes up him. He plants his brain and affections. By and by he will take up the earth, and have his gardens and vineyards in the beautiful order and productiveness of his thought. Every solid in the universe is ready to become fluid on the approach of the mind, and the power to flux it is the measure of the mind. If the wall remain adamant, it accuses the want of thought. To a subtler force it will stream into new forms, expressive of the character of the mind. What is the city in which we sit here, but an aggregate of incongruous materials which have obeyed the will of some man? The granite was reluctant, but his hands were stronger, and it came. Iron was deep in the ground and well combined with stone, but could not hide from his fires. Wood, lime, stuffs, fruits, gums, were dispersed over the earth and sea, in vain. Here they are, within reach of every man's day-labor,—what he wants of them. The whole world is the flux of matter over the wires of thought to the poles or points where it would build. The races of men rise out of the ground preoccupied with a thought which rules them, and divided into parties ready armed and angry to fight for this metaphysical abstraction. The quality of the thought differences the Egyptian and the Roman, the Austrian and the American. The men who come on the stage at one period are all found to be related to each other. Certain ideas are in the air. We are all impressionable, for we are made of them; all impressionable, but some more than others, and these first express them. This explains the curious contemporaneousness of inventions and discoveries. The truth is in the air, and the most impressionable brain will announce it first, but all will announce it a few minutes later. So women, as most susceptible, are the best index of the coming hour. So the great man, that is, the man most imbued with the spirit of the time, is the impressionable man;—of a fibre irritable and delicate, like iodine to light. He feels the infinitesimal attractions. His mind is righter than others because he yields to a current so feeble as can be felt only by a needle delicately poised.

The correlation is shown in defects. Möller,[70] in his Essay on Architecture, taught that the building which was fitted accurately to answer its end would turn out to be beautiful though beauty had not been intended. I find the like unity in human structures rather virulent and pervasive; that a crudity in the blood will appear in the argument; a hump in the shoulder will appear in the speech and handiwork. If his mind could be seen, the hump would be seen. If a man has a seesaw in his voice, it will run into his sentences, into his poem, into the structure of his fable, into his speculation, into his charity. And as every man is hunted by his own dæmon, vexed by his own disease, this checks all his activity.

---

[70] Georg Möller (1784–1852), a German architect and author of *Essay on the Origin and Progress of Gothic Architecture* (1825).

So each man, like each plant, has his parasites. A strong, astringent, bilious nature has more truculent enemies than the slugs and moths that fret my leaves. Such an one has curculios,[71] borers, knife-worms; a swindler ate him first, then a client, then a quack, then smooth, plausible gentlemen, bitter and selfish as Moloch.[72]

This correlation really existing can be divined. If the threads are there, thought can follow and show them. Especially when a soul is quick and docile, as Chaucer sings;—

> "Or if the soul of proper kind
> Be so perfect as men find,
> That it wot what is to come,
> And that he warneth all and some
> Of every of their aventures,
> By previsions or figures;
> But that our flesh hath not might
> It to understand aright
> For it is warned too darkly."[73]

Some people are made up of rhyme, coincidence, omen, periodicity, and presage; they meet the person they seek; what their companion prepares to say to them, they first say to him; and a hundred signs apprise them of what is about to befall.

Wonderful intricacy in the web, wonderful constancy in the design this vagabond life admits. We wonder how the fly finds its mate, and yet year after year, we find two men, two women, without legal or carnal tie, spend a great part of their best time within a few feet of each other. And the moral is that what we seek we shall find;[74] what we flee from flees from us; as Goethe said, "what we wish for in youth, comes in heaps on us in old age,"[75] too often cursed with the granting of our prayer: and hence the high caution, that since we are sure of having what we wish, we beware to ask only for high things.

One key, one solution to the mysteries of human condition, one solution to the old knots of fate, freedom, and foreknowledge, exists; the propounding, namely, of the double consciousness. A man must ride alternately on the horses of his private and his public nature, as the equestrians in the circus throw themselves nimbly from horse to horse, or plant one foot on the back of one and the other foot on the back of the other. So when a man is the victim of his fate, has sciatica in his loins and cramp in his mind; a club-foot and a club in his wit; a sour face, and a selfish temper; a strut in his gait and a conceit in his affection; or is ground to powder by the vice of his race;—he is to rally on his relation to the Universe, which his ruin benefits. Leaving the dæmon who suffers, he is to take sides with the Deity who secures universal benefit by his pain.

To offset the drag of temperament and race, which pulls down, learn this lesson, namely that by the cunning co-presence of two elements, which is throughout nature, whatever, lames or paralyzes you draws in with it the divinity, in some

---

[71] Snout beetles that harm fruit.

[72] A Canaanite fire god to whom children were offered in sacrifice; worship of Moloch was contrary to Hebrew law and condemned by the prophets.

[73] From Geoffrey Chaucer's *The House of Fame* (43–51).   [74] From Matthew 7:7.

[75] From the epigraph to the second part of Goethe's autobiography, *Poetry and Truth* (1811–1813).

form, to repay. A good intention clothes itself with sudden power. When a god wishes to ride, any chip or pebble will bud and shoot out winged feet and serve him for a horse.

Let us build altars to the Blessed Unity which holds nature and souls in perfect solution, and compels every atom to serve an universal end. I do not wonder at a snow-flake, a shell, a summer landscape, or the glory of the stars; but at the necessity of beauty under which the universe lies; that all is and must be pictorial; that the rainbow and the curve of the horizon and the arch of the blue vault are only results from the organism of the eye. There is no need for foolish amateurs to fetch me to admire a garden of flowers, or a sun-gilt cloud, or a waterfall, when I cannot look without seeing splendor and grace. How idle to choose a random sparkle here or there, when the indwelling necessity plants the rose of beauty on the brow of chaos, and discloses the central intention of Nature to be harmony and joy.

Let us build altars to the Beautiful Necessity. If we thought men were free in the sense that in a single exception one fantastical will could prevail over the law of things, it were all one as if a child's hand could pull down the sun. If in the least particular one could derange the order of nature,—who would accept the gift of life?

Let us build altars to the Beautiful Necessity, which secures that all is made of one piece; that plaintiff and defendant, friend and enemy, animal and planet, food and eater are of one kind. In astronomy is vast space but no foreign system; in geology, vast time but the same laws as to-day. Why should we be afraid of Nature, which is no other than "philosophy and theology embodied"? Why should we fear to be crushed by savage elements, we who are made up of the same elements? Let us build to the Beautiful Necessity, which makes man brave in believing that he cannot shun a danger that is appointed, nor incur one that is not; to the Necessity which rudely or softly educates him to the perception that there are no contingencies; that Law rules throughout existence; a Law which is not intelligent but intelligence;—not personal nor impersonal—it disdains words and passes understanding; it dissolves persons; it vivifies nature; yet solicits the pure in heart to draw on all its omnipotence.

1851, 1860

THOREAU*

Henry David Thoreau was the last male descendant of a French ancestor who came to this country from the Isle of Guernsey.[1] His character exhibited occasional traits drawn from this blood, in singular combination with a very strong Saxon genius.

He was born in Concord, Massachusetts, on the 12th of July, 1817. He was graduated at Harvard College in 1837, but without any literary distinction. An iconoclast in literature, he seldom thanked colleges for their service to him, hold-

---

* At Henry David Thoreau's funeral on May 9, 1862, Emerson delivered an address in memory of his Concord friend; revised and lengthened, it was first published in the *Atlantic Monthly* in August 1862.

[1] An island in the English Channel.

ing them in small esteem, whilst yet his debt to them was important. After leaving the University, he joined his brother in teaching a private school, which he soon renounced. His father was a manufacturer of lead-pencils, and Henry applied himself for a time to this craft, believing he could make a better pencil than was then in use. After completing his experiments, he exhibited his work to chemists and artists in Boston, and having obtained their certificates to its excellence and to its equality with the best London manufacture, he returned home contented. His friends congratulated him that he had now opened his way to fortune. But he replied that he should never make another pencil. "Why should I? I would not do again what I have done once." He resumed his endless walks and miscellaneous studies, making every day some new acquaintance with Nature, though as yet never speaking of zoölogy or botany, since, though very studious of natural facts, he was incurious of technical and textual science.

At this time, a strong, healthy youth, fresh from college, whilst all his companions were choosing their profession, or eager to begin some lucrative employment, it was inevitable that his thoughts should be exercised on the same question, and it required rare decision to refuse all the accustomed paths and keep his solitary freedom at the cost of disappointing the natural expectations of his family and friends: all the more difficult that he had a perfect probity,[2] was exact in securing his own independence, and in holding every man to the like duty. But Thoreau never faltered. He was a born protestant. He declined to give up his large ambition of knowledge and action for any narrow craft or profession, aiming at a much more comprehensive calling, the art of living well. If he slighted and defied the opinions of others, it was only that he was more intent to reconcile his practice with his own belief. Never idle or self-indulgent, he preferred, when he wanted money, earning it by some piece of manual labor agreeable to him, as building a boat or a fence, planting, grafting, surveying or other short work, to any long engagements. With his hardy habits and few wants, his skill in wood-craft, and his powerful arithmetic, he was very competent to live in any part of the world. It would cost him less time to supply his wants than another. He was therefore secure of his leisure.

A natural skill for mensuration,[3] growing out of his mathematical knowledge and his habit of ascertaining the measures and distances of objects which interested him, the size of trees, the depth and extent of ponds and rivers, the height of mountains and the air-line distance of his favorite summits,—this, and his intimate knowledge of the territory about Concord, made him drift into the profession of land-surveyor. It had the advantage for him that it led him continually into new and secluded grounds, and helped his studies of Nature. His accuracy and skill in this work were readily appreciated, and he found all the employment he wanted.

He could easily solve the problems of the surveyor, but he was daily beset with graver questions, which he manfully confronted. He interrogated every custom, and wished to settle all his practice on an ideal foundation. He was a protestant *à outrance*,[4] and few lives contain so many renunciations. He was bred to no profession; he never married; he lived alone; he never went to church; he never voted; he refused to pay a tax to the State; he ate no flesh, he drank no wine, he never knew the use of tobacco; and, though a naturalist, he used neither trap nor gun. He chose, wisely no doubt for himself, to be the bachelor of thought and Nature. He had no talent for wealth, and knew how to be poor without the least hint of squalor

---

[2] Integrity.   [3] The art of measuring.   [4] "To the extreme" (French).

or inelegance.[5] Perhaps he fell into his way of living without forecasting it much, but approved it with later wisdom. "I am often reminded," he wrote in his journal, "that if I had bestowed on me the wealth of Crœsus,[6] my aims must be still the same, and my means essentially the same." He had no temptations to fight against,—no appetites, no passions, no taste for elegant trifles. A fine house, dress, the manners and talk of highly cultivated people were all thrown away on him. He much preferred a good Indian, and considered these refinements as impediments to conversation, wishing to meet his companion on the simplest terms. He declined invitations to dinner-parties, because there each was in every one's way, and he could not meet the individuals to any purpose. "They make their pride," he said, "in making their dinner cost much; I make my pride in making my dinner cost little." When asked at table what dish he preferred, he answered, "The nearest." He did not like the taste of wine, and never had a vice in his life. He said,—"I have a faint recollection of pleasure derived from smoking dried lily-stems, before I was a man. I had commonly a supply of these. I have never smoked anything more noxious."

He chose to be rich by making his wants few, and supplying them himself. In his travels, he used the railroad only to get over so much country as was unimportant to the present purpose, walking hundreds of miles, avoiding taverns, buying a lodging in farmer's and fishermen's houses, as cheaper, and more agreeable to him, and because there he could better find the men and the information he wanted.

There was somewhat[7] military in his nature, not to be subdued, always manly and able, but rarely tender, as if he did not feel himself except in opposition. He wanted a fallacy to expose, a blunder to pillory, I may say required a little sense of victory, a roll of the drum, to call his powers into full exercise. It cost him nothing to say No; indeed he found it much easier than to say Yes. It seemed as if his first instinct on hearing a proposition was to controvert it, so impatient was he of the limitations of our daily thought. This habit, of course, is a little chilling to the social affections; and though the companion would in the end acquit him of any malice or untruth, yet it mars conversation. Hence, no equal companion stood in affectionate relations with one so pure and guileless. "I love Henry," said one of his friends, "but I cannot like him; and as for taking his arm, I should as soon think of taking the arm of an elm-tree."

Yet, hermit and stoic as he was, he was really fond of sympathy, and threw himself heartily and childlike into the company of young people whom he loved, and whom he delighted to entertain, as he only could, with the varied and endless anecdotes of his experiences by field and river: and he was always ready to lead a huckleberry-party or a search for chestnuts or grapes. Talking, one day, of a public discourse, Henry remarked that whatever succeeded with the audience was bad. I said, "Who would not like to write something which all can read, like Robinson Crusoe?[8] and who does not see with regret that his page is not solid with a right materialistic treatment, which delights everybody?" Henry objected, of course, and vaunted the better lectures which reached only a few persons. But, at supper, a young girl, understanding that he was to lecture at the Lyceum,[9] sharply

---

[5] In the original manuscript of this essay, Emerson ended one of the sentences in this negative catalogue with the words, "how near to the old monks in their ascetic religion."

[6] The last king of Lydia (in Asia Minor) from 560 to 546 B.C.; his wealth was proverbial.

[7] In Emerson's time, "somewhat" was regularly used for "something."

[8] The perennially popular novel (1719) by Daniel Defoe (1660?–1731).

[9] A public lecture hall.

asked him, "Whether his lecture would be a nice, interesting story, such as she wished to hear, or whether it was one of those old philosophical things that she did not care about." Henry turned to her, and bethought himself, and, I saw, was trying to believe that he had matter that might fit her and her brother, who were to sit up and go to the lecture, if it was a good one for them.

He was a speaker and actor of the truth, born such, and was ever running into dramatic situations from this cause. In any circumstance it interested all bystanders to know what part Henry would take, and what he would say; and he did not disappoint expectation, but used an original judgment on each emergency. In 1845 he built himself a small framed house on the shores of Walden Pond, and lived there two years alone, a life of labor and study. This action was quite native and fit for him. No one who knew him would tax him with affectation. He was more unlike his neighbors in his thought than in his action. As soon as he had exhausted the advantages of that solitude, he abandoned it. In 1847,[10] not approving some uses to which the public expenditure was applied, he refused to pay his town tax, and was put in jail. A friend paid the tax for him, and he was released. The like annoyance was threatened the next year. But as his friends paid the tax, notwithstanding his protest, I believe he ceased to resist. No opposition or ridicule had any weight with him. He coldly and fully stated his opinion without affecting to believe that it was the opinion of the company. It was of no consequence if every one present held the opposite opinion. On one occasion he went to the University Library to procure some books. The librarian refused to lend them. Mr. Thoreau repaired to the President, who stated to him the rules and usages, which permitted the loan of books to resident graduates, to clergymen who were alumni, and to some others resident within a circle of ten miles' radius from the College. Mr. Thoreau explained to the President that the railroad had destroyed the old scale of distances,—that the library was useless, yes, and President and College useless, on the terms of his rules,—that the one benefit he owed to the College was its library,—that, at this moment, not only his want of books was imperative, but he wanted a large number of books, and assured him that he, Thoreau, and not the librarian, was the proper custodian of these. In short, the President found the petitioner so formidable, and the rules getting to look so ridiculous, that he ended by giving him a privilege which in his hands proved unlimited thereafter.

No truer American existed than Thoreau. His preference of his country and condition was genuine, and his aversion from English and European manners and tastes almost reached contempt. He listened impatiently to news or *bonmots*[11] gleaned from London circles; and though he tried to be civil, these anecdotes fatigued him. The men were all imitating each other, and on a small mould. Why can they not live as far apart as possible, and each be a man by himself? What he sought was the most energetic nature; and he wished to go to Oregon, not to London. "In every part of Great Britain," he wrote in his diary, "are discovered traces of the Romans, their funereal urns, their camps, their roads, their dwellings. But New England, at least, is not based on any Roman ruins. We have not to lay the foundations of our houses on the ashes of a former civilization."

But idealist as he was, standing for abolition of slavery, abolition of tariffs, almost for abolition of government, it is needless to say he found himself not only unrepresented in actual politics, but almost equally opposed to every class of reformers. Yet he paid the tribute of his uniform respect to the Anti-Slavery party.

---

[10] Actually 1846; the friend's identity is not known for certain.
[11] *Bons mots,* "witty remarks" (French).

One man, whose personal acquaintance he had formed, he honored with exceptional regard. Before the first friendly word had been spoken for Captain John Brown,[12] he sent notices to most houses in Concord that he would speak in a public hall on the condition and character of John Brown, on Sunday evening, and invited all people to come. The Republican Committee, the Abolitionist Committee, sent him word that it was premature and not advisable. He replied,—"I did not send to you for advice, but to announce that I am to speak." The hall was filled at an early hour by people of all parties, and his earnest eulogy of the hero was heard by all respectfully, by many with a sympathy that surprised themselves.

It was said of Plotinus[13] that he was ashamed of his body, and 't is very likely he had good reason for it,—that his body was a bad servant, and he had not skill in dealing with the material world, as happens often to men of abstract intellect. But Mr. Thoreau was equipped with a most adapted and serviceable body. He was of short stature, firmly built, of light complexion, with strong, serious blue eyes, and a grave aspect,—his face covered in the late years with a becoming beard. His senses were acute, his frame well-knit and hardy, his hands strong and skilful in the use of tools. And there was a wonderful fitness of body and mind. He could pace sixteen rods more accurately than another man could measure them with rod and chain. He could find his path in the woods at night, he said, better by his feet than his eyes. He could estimate the measure of a tree very well by his eye; he could estimate the weight of a calf or a pig, like a dealer. From a box containing a bushel or more of loose pencils, he could take up with his hands fast enough just a dozen pencils at every grasp. He was a good swimmer, runner, skater, boatman, and would probably outwalk most countrymen in a day's journey. And the relation of body to mind was still finer than we have indicated. He said he wanted every stride his legs made. The length of his walk uniformly made the length of his writing. If shut up in the house he did not write at all.

He had a strong common sense, like that which Rose Flammock,[14] the weaver's daughter in Scott's romance, commends in her father, as resembling a yardstick, which, whilst it measures dowlas[15] and diaper, can equally well measure tapestry and cloth of gold. He had always a new resource. When I was planting forest trees, and had procured half a peck of acorns, he said that only a small portion of them would be sound, and proceeded to examine them and select the sound ones. But finding this took time, he said, "I think if you put them all into water the good ones will sink;" which experiment we tried with success. He could plan a garden or a house or a barn; would have been competent to lead a "Pacific Exploring Expedition;" could give judicious counsel in the gravest private or public affairs.

He lived for the day, not cumbered and mortified by his memory. If he brought you yesterday a new proposition, he would bring you to-day another not less revolutionary. A very industrious man, and setting, like all highly organized men, a high value on his time, he seemed the only man of leisure in town, always ready

[12] Brown (1800–1859) was an antislavery activist; with twenty-one followers he captured the U.S. arsenal at Harpers Ferry, Virginia (now West Virginia), in October 1859. He was later executed for his act.

[13] Plotinus (A.D. 205–270) was a Roman Neoplatonist philosopher who believed it a shame to have an eternal soul housed in a perishable body; Emerson reported virtually the same thing about Plotinus twenty-six years earlier in *Nature*.

[14] A character in *The Betrothed* (1825), by Sir Walter Scott (1771–1832).   [15] Coarse cloths.

for any excursion that promised well, or for conversation prolonged into late hours. His trenchant sense was never stopped by his rules of daily prudence, but was always up to the new occasion. He liked and used the simplest food, yet, when some one urged a vegetable diet, Thoreau thought all diets a very small matter, saying that "the man who shoots the buffalo lives better than the man who boards at Graham House."[16] He said,—"You can sleep near the railroad, and never be disturbed: Nature knows very well what sounds are worth attending to, and has made up her mind not to hear the railroad-whistle. But things respect the devout mind, and a mental ecstasy was never interrupted." He noted what repeatedly befell him, that, after receiving from a distance a rare plant, he would presently find the same in his own haunts. And those pieces of luck which happen only to good players happened to him. One day, walking with a stranger, who inquired where Indian arrow-heads could be found, he replied, "Everywhere," and, stooping forward, picked one on the instant from the ground. At Mount Washington,[17] in Tuckerman's Ravine, Thoreau had a bad fall, and sprained his foot. As he was in the act of getting up from his fall, he saw for the first time the leaves of the *Arnica mollis*.[18]

His robust common sense, armed with stout hands, keen perceptions and strong will, cannot yet account for the superiority which shone in his simple and hidden life. I must add the cardinal fact, that there was an excellent wisdom in him, proper to a rare class of men, which showed him the material world as a means and symbol. This discovery, which sometimes yields to poets a certain casual and interrupted light, serving for the ornament of their writing, was in him an unsleeping insight; and whatever faults or obstructions of temperament might cloud it, he was not disobedient to the heavenly vision. In his youth, he said, one day, "The other world is all my art; my pencils will draw no other; my jack-knife will cut nothing else; I do not use it as a means." This was the muse and genius that ruled his opinions, conversation, studies, work and course of life. This made him a searching judge of men. At first glance he measured his companion, and, though insensible to some fine traits of culture, could very well report his weight and calibre. And this made the impression of genius which his conversation sometimes gave.

He understood the matter in hand at a glance, and saw the limitations and poverty of those he talked with, so that nothing seemed concealed from such terrible eyes. I have repeatedly known young men of sensibility converted in a moment to the belief that this was the man they were in search of, the man of men, who could tell them all they should do. His own dealing with them was never affectionate, but superior, didactic, scorning their petty ways,—very slowly conceding, or not conceding at all, the promise of his society at their houses, or even at his own. "Would he not walk with them?" "He did not know. There was nothing so important to him as his walk; he had no walks to throw away on company." Visits were offered him from respectful parties, but he declined them. Admiring friends offered to carry him at their own cost to the Yellowstone River,—to the West Indies,—to South America. But though nothing could be more grave or considered than his refusals, they remind one, in quite new relations, of that fop Brum-

---

[16] A Boston boardinghouse that used the dietary system of Dr. Sylvester Graham (1794–1851), from whom we get "graham flour," made from whole kernels of wheat, and the "graham cracker."
[17] In New Hampshire.   [18] An herb of the aster family, used medicinally.

mel's[19] reply to the gentleman who offered him his carriage in a shower, "But where will *you* ride, then?"—and what accusing silences, and what searching and irresistible speeches, battering down all defences, his companions can remember!

Mr. Thoreau dedicated his genius with such entire love to the fields, hills, and waters of his native town, that he made them known and interesting to all reading Americans, and to people over the sea. The river on whose banks he was born and died he knew from its springs to its confluence with the Merrimack. He had made summer and winter observations on it for many years, and at every hour of the day and night. The result of the recent survey of the Water Commissioners appointed by the State of Massachusetts he had reached by his private experiments, several years earlier. Every fact which occurs in the bed, on the banks or in the air over it; the fishes, and their spawning and nests, their manners, their food; the shad-flies which fill the air on a certain evening once a year, and which are snapped at by the fishes so ravenously that many of these die of repletion; the conical heaps of small stones on the river-shallows, the huge nests of small fishes, one of which will sometimes overfill a cart; the birds which frequent the stream, heron, duck, sheldrake, loon, osprey; the snake, the muskrat, otter, woodchuck and fox, on the banks; the turtle, frog, hyla and cricket, which make the banks vocal,—were all known to him, and, as it were, townsmen and fellow creatures; so that he felt an absurdity or violence in any narrative of one of these by itself apart, and still more of its dimensions on an inch-rule, or in the exhibition of its skeleton, or the specimen of a squirrel or a bird in brandy. He liked to speak of the manners of the river, as itself a lawful creature, yet with exactness, and always to an observed fact. As he knew the river, so the ponds in this region.

One of the weapons he used, more important to him than microscope or alcohol-receiver to other investigators, was a whim which grew on him by indulgence, yet appeared in gravest statement, namely, of extolling his own town and neighborhood as the most favored centre for natural observation. He remarked that the Flora of Massachusetts embraced almost all the important plants of America,—most of the oaks, most of the willows, the best pines, the ash, the maple, the beech, the nuts. He returned Kane's[20] Arctic Voyage to a friend of whom he had borrowed it, with the remark, that "Most of the phenomena noted might be observed in Concord." He seemed a little envious of the Pole, for the coincident sunrise and sunset, or five minutes' day after six months: a splendid fact, which Annursnuc[21] had never afforded him. He found red snow in one of his walks, and told me that he expected to find yet the *Victoria regia*[22] in Concord. He was the attorney of the indigenous plants, and owned to a preference of the weeds to the imported plants, as of the Indian to the civilized man, and noticed, with pleasure, that the willow bean-poles of his neighbor had grown more than his beans. "See these weeds," he said, "which have been hoed at by a million farmers all spring and summer, and yet have prevailed, and just now come out triumphant over all lanes, pastures, fields and gardens, such is their vigor. We have insulted them with low names, too,—as Pigweed, Wormwood, Chickweed, Shad-blossom." He says, "They have brave names, too,—Ambrosia, Stellaria, Amelanchier, Amaranth,[23] etc."

---

[19] George Bryan Brummel (1778–1840), a British dandy generally called "Beau."
[20] Elisha Kent Kane (1820–1857), an American naval officer who explored a route to the North Pole.
[21] A hill in Concord.   [22] The South American water lily.
[23] "Food for the gods," "starlike," "happy," "unfading."

I think his fancy for referring everything to the meridian of Concord did not grow out of any ignorance or depreciation of other longitudes or latitudes, but was rather a playful expression of his conviction of the indifferency of all places, and that the best place for each is where he stands. He expressed it once in this wise: "I think nothing is to be hoped from you, if this bit of mould under your feet is not sweeter to you to eat than any other in this world, or in any world."

The other weapon with which he conquered all obstacles in science was patience. He knew how to sit immovable, a part of the rock he rested on, until the bird, the reptile, the fish, which had retired from him, should come back and resume its habits, nay, moved by curiosity, should come to him and watch him.

It was a pleasure and a privilege to walk with him. He knew the country like a fox or a bird, and passed through it as freely by paths of his own. He knew every track in the snow or on the ground, and what creature had taken this path before him. One must submit abjectly to such a guide, and the reward was great. Under his arm he carried an old music-book to press plants; in his pocket, his diary and pencil, a spy-glass for birds, microscope, jack-knife and twine. He wore a straw hat, stout shoes, strong gray trousers, to brave scrub-oaks and smilax,[24] and to climb a tree for a hawk's or a squirrel's nest. He waded into the pool for the water-plants, and his strong legs were no insignificant part of his armor. On the day I speak of he looked for the Menyanthes,[25] detected it across the wide pool, and, on examination of the florets, decided that it had been in flower five days. He drew out of his breast-pocket his diary, and read the names of all the plants that should bloom on this day, whereof he kept account as a banker when his notes fall due. The Cypripedium[26] not due till to-morrow. He thought that, if waked up from a trance, in this swamp, he could tell by the plants what time of the year it was within two days. The redstart was flying about, and presently the fine grosbeaks, whose brilliant scarlet "makes the rash gazer wipe his eye," and whose fine clear note Thoreau compared to that of a tanager which has got rid of its hoarseness. Presently he heard a note which he called that of the night-warbler, a bird he had never identified, had been in search of twelve years, which always, when he saw it, was in the act of diving down into a tree or bush, and which it was vain to seek; the only bird which sings indifferently by night and by day. I told him he must beware of finding and booking it, lest life should have nothing more to show him. He said, "What you seek in vain for, half your life, one day you come full upon, all the family at dinner. You seek it like a dream, and as soon as you find it you become its prey."

His interest in the flower or the bird lay very deep in his mind, was connected with Nature,—and the meaning of Nature was never attempted to be defined by him. He would not offer a memoir of his observations to the Natural History Society. "Why should I? To detach the description from its connections in my mind would make it no longer true or valuable to me: and they do not wish what belongs to it." His power of observation seemed to indicate additional senses. He saw as with microscope, heard as with ear-trumpet, and his memory was a photographic register of all he saw and heard. And yet none knew better than he that it is not the fact that imports, but the impression or effect of the fact on your mind. Every fact lay in glory in his mind, a type of the order and beauty of the whole.

His determination on Natural History was organic. He confessed that he some-

---

[24] Greenbrier.   [25] The bogbean, or buckbean, which lives in bogs.
[26] A plant of leafy-stemmed orchids, including the lady's slipper.

times felt like a hound or a panther, and, if born among Indians, would have been a fell hunter. But, restrained by his Massachusetts culture, he played out the game in this mild form of botany and ichthyology. His intimacy with animals suggested what Thomas Fuller records of Butler the apiologist, that "either he had told the bees things or the bees had told him." Snakes coiled round his legs; the fishes swam into his hand, and he took them out of the water; he pulled the woodchuck out of its hole by the tail, and took the foxes under his protection from the hunters. Our naturalist had perfect magnanimity; he had no secrets: he would carry you to the heron's haunt, or even to his most prized botanical swamp,—possibly knowing that you could never find it again, yet willing to take his risks.

No college ever offered him a diploma, or a professor's chair; no academy made him its corresponding secretary, its discoverer or even its member. Perhaps these learned bodies feared the satire of his presence. Yet so much knowledge of Nature's secret and genius few others possessed; none in a more large and religious synthesis. For not a particle of respect had he to the opinions of any man or body of men, but homage solely to the truth itself; and as he discovered everywhere among doctors some leaning of courtesy, it discredited them. He grew to be revered and admired by his townsmen, who had at first known him only as an oddity. The farmers who employed him as a surveyor soon discovered his rare accuracy and skill, his knowledge of their lands, of trees, of birds, of Indian remains and the like, which enabled him to tell every farmer more than he knew before of his own farm; so that he began to feel a little as if Mr. Thoreau had better rights in his land than he. They felt, too, the superiority of character which addressed all men with a native authority.

Indian relics abound in Concord,—arrow-heads, stone chisels, pestles and fragments of pottery; and on the river-bank, large heaps of clam-shells and ashes mark spots which the savages frequented. These, and every circumstance touching the Indian, were important in his eyes. His visits to Maine were chiefly for love of the Indian. He had the satisfaction of seeing the manufacture of the bark canoe, as well as of trying his hand in its management on the rapids. He was inquisitive about the making of the stone arrow-head, and in his last days charged a youth setting out for the Rocky Mountains to find an Indian who could tell him that: "It was well worth a visit to California to learn it." Occasionally, a small party of Penobscot Indians would visit Concord, and pitch their tents for a few weeks in summer on the river-bank. He failed not to make acquaintance with the best of them; though he well knew that asking questions of Indians is like catechizing beavers and rabbits. In his last visit to Maine he had great satisfaction from Joseph Polis,[27] an intelligent Indian of Oldtown, who was his guide for some weeks.

He was equally interested in every natural fact. The depth of his perception found likeness of law throughout Nature, and I know not any genius who so swiftly inferred universal law from the single fact. He was no pedant of a department. His eye was open to beauty, and his ear to music. He found these, not in rare conditions, but wheresoever he went. He thought the best of music was in single strains; and he found poetic suggestion in the humming of the telegraph-wire.

His poetry might be bad or good; he no doubt wanted a lyric facility and technical skill, but he had the source of poetry in his spiritual perception. He was a good

---

[27] Thoreau writes extensively about Joseph Polis in *The Maine Woods*, published posthumously in 1864.

reader and critic, and his judgment on poetry was to the ground of it. He could not be deceived as to the presence or absence of the poetic element in any composition, and his thirst for this made him negligent and perhaps scornful of superficial graces. He would pass by many delicate rhythms, but he would have detected every live stanza or line in a volume and knew very well where to find an equal poetic charm in prose. He was so enamoured of the spiritual beauty that he held all actual written poems in very light esteem in the comparison. He admired Æschylus and Pindar;[28] but when some one was commending them, he said that Æschylus and the Greeks, in describing Apollo and Orpheus,[29] had given no song, or no good one. "They ought not to have moved trees, but to have chanted to the gods such a hymn as would have sung all their old ideas out of their heads, and new ones in." His own verses are often rude and defective. The gold does not yet run pure, is drossy and crude. The thyme and marjoram are not yet honey. But if he want lyric fineness and technical merits, if he have not the poetic temperament, he never lacks the causal thought, showing that his genius was better than his talent. He knew the worth of the Imagination for the uplifting and consolation of human life, and liked to throw every thought into a symbol. The fact you tell is of no value, but only the impression. For this reason his presence was poetic, always piqued the curiosity to know more deeply the secrets of his mind. He had many reserves, an unwillingness to exhibit to profane eyes what was still sacred in his own, and knew well how to throw a poetic veil over his experience. All readers of Walden will remember his mythical record of his disappointments:—

"I long ago lost a hound, a bay horse and a turtle-dove, and am still on their trail. Many are the travellers I have spoken concerning them, describing their tracks, and what calls they answered to. I have met one or two who have heard the hound, and the tramp of the horse, and even seen the dove disappear behind a cloud; and they seemed as anxious to recover them as if they had lost them themselves."

His riddles were worth the reading, and I confide that if at any time I do not understand the expression, it is yet just. Such was the wealth of his truth that it was not worth his while to use words in vain. His poem entitled "Sympathy" reveals the tenderness under that triple steel of stoicism, and the intellectual subtility it could animate. His classic poem on "Smoke" suggests Simonides,[30] but is better than any poem of Simonides. His biography is in his verses. His habitual thought makes all his poetry a hymn to the Cause of causes, the Spirit which vivifies and controls his own:—

> "I hearing get, who had but ears,
> And sight, who had but eyes before;
> I moments live, who lived but years,
> And truth discern, who knew but learning's lore."

And still more in these religious lines:—

[28] Aeschylus (525–456 B.C.) was regarded as the founder of Greek tragedy; Pindar (522?–422? B.C.) was a Greek lyric poet, master of the ode.

[29] According to Greek myth, Apollo was the god of light, music, and the arts, and Orpheus was a legendary poet who could play the lyre so wondrously that his music held wild beasts spellbound.

[30] Either Simonides of Amorgos (7th century B.C.) or Simonides of Ceos (5th–6th centuries B.C.), both Greek lyric poets.

> "Now chiefly is my natal hour,
> And only now my prime of life;
> I will not doubt the love untold,
> Which not my worth nor want have bought,
> Which wooed me young, and wooes me old,
> And to this evening hath me brought."[31]

Whilst he used in his writings a certain petulance of remark in reference to churches or churchmen, he was a person of a rare, tender and absolute religion, a person incapable of any profanation, by act or by thought. Of course, the same isolation which belonged to his original thinking and living detached him from the social religious forms. This is neither to be censured nor regretted. Aristotle long ago explained it, when he said, "One who surpasses his fellow citizens in virtue is no longer a part of the city. Their law is not for him, since he is a law to himself."[32]

Thoreau was sincerity itself, and might fortify the convictions of prophets in the ethical laws by his holy living. It was an affirmative experience which refused to be set aside. A truth-speaker he, capable of the most deep and strict conversation; a physician to the wounds of any soul; a friend, knowing not only the secret of friendship, but almost worshipped by those few persons who resorted to him as their confessor and prophet, and knew the deep value of his mind and great heart. He thought that without religion or devotion of some kind nothing great was ever accomplished: and he thought that the bigoted sectarian had better bear this in mind.

His virtues, of course, sometimes ran into extremes. It was easy to trace to the inexorable demand on all for exact truth that austerity which made this willing hermit more solitary even than he wished. Himself of a perfect probity, he required not less of others. He had a disgust at crime, and no worldly success would cover it. He detected paltering as readily in dignified and prosperous persons as in beggars, and with equal scorn. Such dangerous frankness was in his dealing that his admirers called him "that terrible Thoreau," as if he spoke when silent, and was still present when he had departed. I think the severity of his ideal interfered to deprive him of a healthy sufficiency of human society.

The habit of a realist to find things the reverse of their appearance inclined him to put every statement in a paradox. A certain habit of antagonism defaced his earlier writings,—a trick of rhetoric not quite outgrown in his later, of substituting for the obvious word and thought its diametrical opposite. He praised wild mountains and winter forests for their domestic air, in snow and ice he would find sultriness, and commended the wilderness for resembling Rome and Paris. "It was so dry, that you might call it wet."

The tendency to magnify the moment, to read all the laws of Nature in the one object or one combination under your eye, is of course comic to those who do not share the philosopher's perception of identity. To him there was no such thing as size. The pond was a small ocean; the Atlantic, a large Walden Pond. He referred every minute fact to cosmical laws. Though he meant to be just, he seemed haunted by a certain chronic assumption that the science of the day pretended

---

[31] Both from Thoreau's poem "Inspiration," in *A Week on the Concord and Merrimack Rivers* (1849).
[32] From an unknown source.

completeness, and he had just found out that the *savans*[33] had neglected to discriminate a particular botanical variety, had failed to describe the seeds or count the sepals. "That is to say," we replied, "the blockheads were not born in Concord; but who said they were? It was their unspeakable misfortune to be born in London, or Paris, or Rome; but, poor fellows, they did what they could, considering that they never saw Bateman's Pond, or Nine-Acre Corner, or Becky Stow's Swamp; besides, what were you sent into the world for, but to add this observation?"

Had his genius been only contemplative, he had been fitted to his life, but with his energy and practical ability he seemed born for great enterprise and for command; and I so much regret the loss of his rare powers of action, that I cannot help counting it a fault in him that he had no ambition. Wanting this, instead of engineering for all America, he was the captain of a huckleberry-party. Pounding beans is good to the end of pounding empires one of these days; but if, at the end of years, it is still only beans!

But these foibles, real or apparent, were fast vanishing in the incessant growth of a spirit so robust and wise, and which effaced its defeats with new triumphs. His study of Nature was a perpetual ornament to him, and inspired his friends with curiosity to see the world through his eyes, and to hear his adventures. They possessed every kind of interest.

He had many elegancies of his own, whilst he scoffed at conventional elegance. Thus, he could not bear to hear the sound of his own steps, the grit of gravel; and therefore never willingly walked in the road, but in the grass, on mountains and in woods. His senses were acute, and he remarked that by night every dwelling-house gives out bad air, like a slaughter-house. He liked the pure fragrance of melilot.[34] He honored certain plants with special regard, and, over all, the pond-lily,—then, the gentian, and the *Mikania scandens*,[35] and "life-everlasting," and a basstree which he visited every year when it bloomed, in the middle of July. He thought the scent a more oracular inquisition than the sight,—more oracular and trustworthy. The scent, of course, reveals what is concealed from the other senses. By it he detected earthiness. He delighted in echoes, and said they were almost the only kind of kindred voices that he heard. He loved Nature so well, was so happy in her solitude, that he became very jealous of cities and the sad work which their refinements and artifices made with man and his dwelling. The axe was always destroying his forest. "Thank God," he said, "they cannot cut down the clouds!" "All kinds of figures are drawn on the blue ground with this fibrous white paint."

I subjoin a few sentences taken from his unpublished manuscripts, not only as records of his thought and feeling, but for their power of description and literary excellence:—

"Some circumstantial evidence is very strong, as when you find a trout in the milk."

"The chub is a soft fish, and tastes like boiled brown paper salted."

"The youth gets together his materials to build a bridge to the moon, or, perchance, a palace or temple on the earth, and, at length the middle-aged man concludes to build a wood-shed with them."

"The locust z-ing."

---

[33] *Savants*, "learned persons" (French).   [34] Sweet clover.   [35] Climbing hempweed.

"Devil's-needles zigzagging along the Nut-Meadow brook."

"Sugar is not so sweet to the palate as sound to the healthy ear."

"I put on some hemlock-boughs, and the rich salt crackling of their leaves was like mustard to the ear, the crackling of uncountable regiments. Dead trees love the fire."

"The bluebird carries the sky on his back."

"The tanager flies through the green foliage as if it would ignite the leaves."

"If I wish for a horse-hair for my compass-sight I must go to the stable; but the hair-bird, with her sharp eyes, goes to the road."

"Immortal water, alive even to the superficies."

"Fire is the most tolerable third party."

"Nature made ferns for pure leaves, to show what she could do in that line."

"No tree has so fair a bole and so handsome an instep as the beech."

"How did these beautiful rainbow-tints get into the shell of the fresh-water clam, buried in the mud at the bottom of our dark river?"

"Hard are the times when the infant's shoes are second-foot."

"We are strictly confined to our men to whom we give liberty."

"Nothing is so much to be feared as fear. Atheism may comparatively be popular with God himself."

"Of what significance the things you can forget? A little thought is sexton[36] to all the world."

"How can we expect a harvest of thought who have not had a seed-time of character?"

"Only he can be trusted with gifts who can present a face of bronze to expectations."

"I ask to be melted. You can only ask of the metals that they be tender to the fire that melts them. To nought else can they be tender."

There is a flower known to botanists, one of the same genus with our summer plant called "Life-Everlasting," a *Gnaphalium* like that, which grows on the most inaccessible cliffs of the Tyrolese mountains, where the chamois dare hardly venture, and which the hunter, tempted by its beauty, and by his love (for it is immensely valued by the Swiss maidens), climbs the cliffs to gather, and is sometimes found dead at the foot, with the flower in his hand. It is called by botanists the *Gnaphalium leontopodium,* but by the Swiss *Edelweisse,* which signifies *Noble Purity.* Thoreau seemed to me living in the hope to gather this plant, which belonged to him of right. The scale on which his studies proceeded was so large as to require longevity, and we were the less prepared for his sudden disappearance. The country knows not yet, or in the least part, how great a son it has lost. It seems an injury that he should leave in the midst his broken task which none else can finish, a kind of indignity to so noble a soul that he should depart out of Nature before yet he has been really shown to his peers for what he is. But he, at least, is content. His soul was made for the noblest society; he had in a short life exhausted the capabilities of this world; wherever there is knowledge, wherever there is virtue, wherever there is beauty, he will find a home.

1862

---

[36] A church caretaker, belltoller, and gravedigger.

CONCORD HYMN*

SUNG AT THE COMPLETION OF THE BATTLE MONUMENT,
JULY 4, 1837

By the rude bridge that arched the flood,
　　Their flag to April's breeze unfurled,
Here once the embattled farmers stood
　　And fired the shot heard round the world.

The foe long since in silence slept;
　　Alike the conqueror silent sleeps;
And Time the ruined bridge has swept
　　Down the dark stream which seaward creeps.

On this green bank, by this soft stream,
　　We set to-day a votive stone;[1]
That memory may their deed redeem,
　　When, like our sires, our sons are gone.

Spirit, that made those heroes dare
　　To die, and leave their children free,
Bid Time and Nature gently spare
　　The shaft we raise to them and thee.

1837

EACH AND ALL*

Little thinks, in the field, yon red-cloaked clown[1]
Of thee from the hill-top looking down;
The heifer that lows in the upland farm,
Far-heard, lows not thine ear to charm;
The sexton,[2] tolling his bell at noon,
Deems not that great Napoleon
Stops his horse, and lists with delight,
Whilst his files sweep round yon Alpine height;
Nor knowest thou what argument
Thy life to thy neighbor's creed has lent.
All are needed by each one;
Nothing is fair or good alone.

---

* First printed as a leaflet and distributed at the dedication of the monument commemorating the Revolutionary War battles of Lexington and Concord (April 19, 1775).
[1] A stone offering made to fulfill a vow or promise.
* First published in the *Western Messenger* in 1839.
[1] A rustic person, peasant.　[2] Church caretaker, belltoller, and gravedigger.

I thought the sparrow's note from heaven,
Singing at dawn on the alder bough;
I brought him home, in his nest, at even;
He sings the song, but it cheers not now,
For I did not bring home the river and sky;—
He sang to my ear,—they sang to my eye.
The delicate shells lay on the shore;
The bubbles of the latest wave   20
Fresh pearls to their enamel gave,
And the bellowing of the savage sea
Greeted their safe escape to me.
I wiped away the weeds and foam,
I fetched my sea-born treasures home;
But the poor, unsightly, noisome things
Had left their beauty on the shore
With the sun and the sand and the wild uproar.
The lover watched his graceful maid,
As 'mid the virgin train she strayed,   30
Nor knew her beauty's best attire
Was woven still by the snow-white choir.
At last she came to his hermitage,
Like the bird from the woodlands to the cage;—
The gay enchantment was undone,
A gentle wife, but fairy none.
Then I said, 'I covet truth;
Beauty is unripe childhood's cheat;
I leave it behind with the games of youth:'—
As I spoke, beneath my feet   40
The ground-pine curled its pretty wreath,
Running over the club-moss burrs;
I inhaled the violet's breath;
Around me stood the oaks and firs;
Pine-cones and acorns lay on the ground;
Over me soared the eternal sky,
Full of light and of deity;
Again I saw, again I heard,
The rolling river, the morning bird;—
Beauty through my senses stole;   50
I yielded myself to the perfect whole.

1839

THE PROBLEM*

I like a church; I like a cowl;[1]
I love a prophet of the soul;

---

* First published in *The Dial* in 1840; the manuscript bears the date "10 November, 1839" and an earlier title, "The Priest."
[1] A monk's hood.

And on my heart monastic aisles
Fall like sweet strains, or pensive smiles;
Yet not for all his faith can see
Would I that cowlèd churchman be.

Why should the vest[2] on him allure,
Which I could not on me endure?

Not from a vain or shallow thought
His awful Jove young Phidias[3] brought;   10
Never from lips of cunning fell
The thrilling Delphic oracle;[4]
Out from the heart of nature rolled
The burdens of the Bible old;
The litanies of nations came,
Like the volcano's tongue of flame,
Up from the burning core below,—
The canticles of love and woe:
The hand that rounded Peter's dome[5]
And groined the aisles of Christian Rome   20
Wrought in a sad sincerity;
Himself from God he could not free;
He builded better than he knew;—
The conscious stone to beauty grew.

Know'st thou what wove yon woodbird's nest
Of leaves, and feathers from her breast?
Or how the fish outbuilt her shell,
Painting with morn each annual cell?
Or how the sacred pine-tree adds
To her old leaves new myriads?   30
Such and so grew these holy piles,
Whilst love and terror laid the tiles.
Earth proudly wears the Parthenon,
As the best gem upon her zone,[6]
And Morning opes with haste her lids
To gaze upon the Pyramids;
O'er England's abbeys bends the sky,
As on its friends, with kindred eye;
For out of Thought's interior sphere
These wonders rose to upper air;   40
And Nature gladly gave them place,
Adopted them into her race,

---

[2] Vestments.
[3] A 5th-century B.C. Greek sculptor who wrought the ivory and gold statue of Zeus (Jove) at Olympia and supervised construction of the Parthenon, the temple of Athena Parthenos ("the maiden") in Athens.
[4] The prophetess at the shrine of the Greek god Apollo at Delphi, Greece.
[5] The Italian artist Michelangelo (1475–1564), chief architect of St. Peter's Cathedral in Rome.
[6] Encircling band, belt.

And granted them an equal date
With Andes and with Ararat.[7]

These temples grew as grows the grass;
Art might obey, but not surpass.
The passive Master lent his hand
To the vast soul that o'er him planned;
And the same power that reared the shrine
Bestrode the tribes that knelt within.   50
Ever the fiery Pentecost[8]
Girds with one flame the countless host,
Trances the heart through chanting choirs,
And through the priest the mind inspires.
The word unto the prophet spoken
Was writ on tables yet unbroken;[9]
The word by seers or sibyls[10] told,
In groves of oak, or fanes[11] of gold,
Still floats upon the morning wind,
Still whispers to the willing mind.   60
One accent of the Holy Ghost
The heedless world hath never lost.
I know what say the fathers wise,—
The Book itself before me lies,
Old *Chrysostom*, best Augustine,[12]
And he who blent both in his line,
The younger *Golden Lips* or mines,
Taylor,[13] the Shakespeare of divines.
His words are music in my ear.
I see his cowlèd portrait dear;   70
And yet, for all his faith could see,
I would not the good bishop be.

1839, 1840

THE SNOW-STORM*

Announced by all the trumpets of the sky,
Arrives the snow, and, driving o'er the fields,

---

[7] The Andes Mountains in South America; Mount Ararat in Asia Minor, where Noah's Ark supposedly landed after the Flood (see Genesis 8:4).

[8] The descent of the Holy Spirit upon the Apostles, described in Acts 2.

[9] In Exodus 32:1–20, when Moses saw the Israelites worshipping the golden idol, he broke the stone tablets ("tables") on which the Ten Commandments were written.

[10] Prophetesses.   [11] Temples.

[12] The eloquent preacher St. John of Antioch (A.D. 347–407), named "Chrysostom," or "Golden Lips," by an ecumenical council two hundred years after his death; St. Augustine (354–430), bishop of Hippo, in Africa, and author of *Confessions* and *The City of God*.

[13] Jeremy Taylor (1613–1667), an English theologian, here called the Shakespeare of clergymen ("divines") because of his eloquence.

* First published in *The Dial* in 1841.

Seems nowhere to alight: the whited air
Hides hills and woods, the river, and the heaven,
And veils the farm-house at the garden's end.
The sled and traveller stopped, the courier's feet
Delayed, all friends shut out, the housemates sit
Around the radiant fireplace, enclosed
In a tumultuous privacy of storm.

Come see the north wind's masonry.   10
Out of an unseen quarry evermore
Furnished with tile, the fierce artificer
Curves his white bastions with projected roof
Round every windward stake, or tree, or door.
Speeding, the myriad-handed, his wild work
So fanciful, so savage, nought cares he
For number or proportion. Mockingly,
On coop or kennel he hangs Parian[1] wreaths;
A swan-like form invests the hidden thorn;
Fills up the farmer's lane from wall to wall,   20
Maugre[2] the farmer's sighs; and at the gate
A tapering turret overtops the work.
And when his hours are numbered, and the world
Is all his own, retiring, as he were not,
Leaves, when the sun appears, astonished Art
To mimic in slow structures, stone by stone,
Built in an age, the mad wind's night-work,
The frolic architecture of the snow.

1835, 1841

URIEL*

It fell in the ancient periods
    Which the brooding soul surveys,
Or ever the wild Time coined itself
    Into calendar months and days.

This was the lapse of Uriel,
Which in Paradise befell.
Once, among the Pleiads[1] walking,
Seyd[2] overheard the young gods talking;
And the treason, too long pent,
To his ears was evident.   10

---

[1] Of white snow, like the marble quarried on the island of Paros for the sculptors of ancient Greece.
[2] Despite.
* First published in *Poems* (1847), though Emerson seems to have written at least some of these lines in 1845. Uriel is the Light of God, an archangel, in John Milton's *Paradise Lost* (1667).
[1] The Pleiades, a cluster of seven stars named for the daughters of Atlas and Pleione of Greek myth.
[2] Saadi (1184?–1291), a Persian poet.

The young deities discussed
Laws of form, and metre just,
Orb, quintessence, and sunbeams,
What subsisteth, and what seems.
One, with low tones that decide,
And doubt and reverend use defied,
With a look that solved the sphere,
And stirred the devils everywhere,
Gave his sentiment divine
Against the being of a line.   20
"Line in nature is not found;
Unit and universe are round;
In vain produced, all rays return;
Evil will bless, and ice will burn."
As Uriel spoke with piercing eye,
A shudder ran around the sky;
The stern old war-gods shook their heads,
The seraphs frowned from myrtle-beds;
Seemed to the holy festival
The rash word boded ill to all;   30
The balance-beam of Fate was bent;
The bounds of good and ill were rent;
Strong Hades[3] could not keep his own,
But all slid to confusion.
A sad self-knowledge, withering, fell
On the beauty of Uriel;
In heaven once eminent, the god
Withdrew, that hour, into his cloud;
Whether doomed to long gyration
In the sea of generation,   40
Or by knowledge grown too bright
To hit the nerve of feebler sight.
Straightway, a forgetting wind
Stole over the celestial kind,
And their lips the secret kept,
If in ashes the fire-seed slept.
But now and then, truth-speaking things
Shamed the angels' veiling wings;
And, shrilling from the solar course,
Or from fruit of chemic force,   50
Procession of a soul in matter,
Or the speeding change of water,
Or out of the good of evil born,
Came Uriel's voice of cherub scorn,
And a blush tinged the upper sky,
And the gods shook, they knew not why.

1845, 1847

---

[3] According to Greek myth, the god of the underworld.

MERLIN*

I

Thy trivial harp will never please
Or fill my craving ear;
Its chords should ring as blows the breeze,
Free, peremptory, clear.
No jingling serenader's art,
Nor tinkle of piano strings,
Can make the wild blood start
In its mystic springs.
The kingly bard
Must smite the chords rudely and hard,   10
As with hammer or with mace;
That they may render back
Artful thunder, which conveys
Secrets of the solar track,
Sparks of the supersolar blaze.
Merlin's blows are strokes of fate,
Chiming with the forest tone,
When boughs buffet boughs in the wood;
Chiming with the gasp and moan
Of the ice-imprisoned flood;   20
With the pulse of manly hearts;
With the voice of orators;
With the din of city arts;
With the cannonade of wars;
With the marches of the brave;
And prayers of might from martyrs' cave.

Great is the art,
Great be the manners, of the bard.
He shall not his brain encumber
With the coil of rhythm and number;   30
But, leaving rule and pale forethought,
He shall aye¹ climb
For his rhyme.
"Pass in, pass in," the angels say,
"In to the upper doors,
Nor count compartments of the floors,
But mount to paradise
By the stairway of surprise."

Blameless master of the games,
King of sport that never shames,   40

---

* First published in *Poems* (1847); the title refers to a legendary Welsh bard and not to the magician of Arthurian romance.
¹ Always.

He shall daily joy dispense
Hid in song's sweet influence.
Forms more cheerly live and go,
What time the subtle mind
Sings aloud the tune whereto
Their pulses beat,
And march their feet,
And their members are combined.

By Sybarites[2] beguiled,   50
He shall no task decline;
Merlin's mighty line
Extremes of nature reconciled,—
Bereaved a tyrant of his will,
And made the lion mild.
Songs can the tempest still,
Scattered on the stormy air,
Mould the year to fair increase,
And bring in poetic peace.

He shall not seek to weave,
In weak, unhappy times,   60
Efficacious rhymes;
Wait his returning strength.
Bird that from the nadir's floor
To the zenith's top can soar,—
The soaring orbit of the muse exceeds that
          journey's length.
Nor profane affect to hit
Or compass that, by meddling wit,
Which only the propitious mind
Publishes when 't is inclined.
There are open hours   70
When the God's will sallies free,
And the dull idiot might see
The flowing fortunes of a thousand years;—
Sudden, at unawares,
Self-moved, fly-to the doors,
Nor sword of angels could reveal
What they conceal.

                          II
The rhyme of the poet
Modulates the king's affairs;
Balance-loving Nature   80
Made all things in pairs.

---

[2] People known for a hedonistic life style; from the inhabitants of Sybaris, a Greek city in Italy known for wealth and self-indulgence (destroyed in 510 B.C.).

To every foot its antipode;[3]
Each color with its counter glowed;
To every tone beat answering tones,
Higher or graver;
Flavor gladly blends with flavor;
Leaf answers leaf upon the bough;
And match the paired cotyledons.[4]
Hands to hands, and feet to feet,
In one body grooms and brides;   90
Eldest rite, two married sides
In every mortal meet.
Light's far furnace shines,
Smelting balls and bars,
Forging double stars,
Glittering twins and trines.[5]
The animals are sick with love,
Lovesick with rhyme;
Each with all propitious Time
Into chorus wove.   100

Like the dancers' ordered band,
Thoughts come also hand in hand;
In equal couples mated,
Or else alternated;
Adding by their mutual gage,
One to other, health and age.
Solitary fancies go
Short-lived wandering to and fro,
Most like to bachelors,
Or an ungiven maid,   110
Not ancestors,
With no posterity to make the lie afraid,
Or keep truth undecayed.
Perfect-paired as eagle's wings,
Justice is the rhyme of things;
Trade and counting use
The self-same tuneful muse;
And Nemesis,[6]
Who with even matches odd,
Who athwart space redresses   120
The partial wrong,
Fills the just period,
And finishes the song.

Subtle rhymes, with ruin rife,
Murmur in the house of life,

---

[3] Exact opposite.   [4] A plant's first leaves.   [5] Groups of three.
[6] According to Greek myth, the goddess of fate.

Sung by the Sisters[7] as they spin;
In perfect time and measure they
Build and unbuild our echoing clay,
As the two twilights of the day
Fold us music-drunken in.   130

                                        1846, 1847

ODE, INSCRIBED TO W. H. CHANNING*

Though loath to grieve
The evil time's sole patriot,
I cannot leave
My honied thought
For the priest's cant,
Or statesman's rant.

If I refuse
My study for their politique,
Which at the best is trick,
The angry Muse   10
Puts confusion in my brain.

But who is he that prates
Of the culture of mankind,
Of better arts and life?
Go, blindworm, go,
Behold the famous States
Harrying Mexico[1]
With rifle and with knife!

Or who, with accent bolder,
Dare praise the freedom-loving mountaineer?   20
I found by thee, O rushing Contoocook![2]
And in thy valleys, Agiochook![3]
The jackals of the negro-holder.[4]
The God who made New Hampshire

---

[7] According to classical myth, the Fates, three sisters who determine human destiny.

* First published in *Poems* (1847), dedicated to the prominent abolitionist and clergyman William Henry Channing (1810–1884), nephew of the Unitarian leader William Ellery Channing (1780–1842).

[1] In the Mexican War (1846–1848), which Emerson opposed as an effort to enlarge slaveholding territories.

[2] A Native-American name for a river in New Hampshire.

[3] A Native-American name for the White Mountains of New Hampshire.

[4] Those who hunt runaway slaves for bounty. Because New Hampshire had voted Democratic, thus aligning itself with proslavery advocates, Emerson contrasts the state's natural grandeur with its citizens of his day.

Taunted the lofty land
With little men;—
Small bat and wren
House in the oak:—
If earth-fire cleave
The upheaved land, and bury the folk,   30
The southern crocodile would grieve.[5]
Virtue palters; Right is hence;
Freedom praised, but hid;
Funeral eloquence
Rattles the coffin-lid.

What boots[6] thy zeal,
O glowing friend,
That would indignant rend
The northland from the south?
Wherefore? to what good end?   40
Boston Bay and Bunker Hill
Would serve things still;[7]—
Things are of the snake.

The horseman serves the horse,
The neatherd serves the neat,[8]
The merchant serves the purse,
The eater serves his meat;
'T is the day of the chattel,[9]
Web to weave, and corn to grind;
Things are in the saddle,   50
And ride mankind.

There are two laws discrete,
Not reconciled,—
Law for man, and law for thing;
The last builds town and fleet,
But it runs wild,
And doth the man unking.

'T is fit the forest fall,
The steep be graded,
The mountain tunnelled,   60
The sand shaded,
The orchard planted,
The glebe[10] tilled,
The prairie granted,
The steamer built.

---

[5] The slaveholding South would grieve to lose their allies in New Hampshire.
[6] Remedies, profits.
[7] The heroic actions of Revolutionary War days do not save Massachusetts from compromising principle for commercial gain, from serving "things."
[8] The cowherd serves the cow.   [9] Slave.   [10] Field.

Let man serve law for man;
Live for friendship, live for love,
For truth's and harmony's behoof;
The state may follow how it can,
As Olympus follows Jove.[11]   70

    Yet do not I implore
The wrinkled shopman to my sounding woods,
Nor bid the unwilling senator
Ask votes of thrushes in the solitudes.
Every one to his chosen work;—
Foolish hands may mix and mar;
Wise and sure the issues are.
Round they roll till dark is light,
Sex to sex, and even to odd;—
The over-god   80
Who marries Right to Might,
Who peoples, unpeoples,—
He who exterminates
Races by stronger races,
Black by white faces,—
Knows to bring honey
Out of the lion;[12]
Grafts gentlest scion
On pirate and Turk.

The Cossack eats Poland,[13]   90
Like stolen fruit;
Her last noble is ruined,
Her last poet mute:
Straight, into double band
The victors divide;
Half for freedom strike and stand;—
The astonished Muse finds thousands at her side.

           1847

HAMATREYA*

Bulkeley, Hunt, Willard, Hosmer, Meriam, Flint,[1]
Possessed the land which rendered to their toil

---

[11] As the minor deities on Mount Olympus follow Jove (Zeus), the supreme god in Greek myth.

[12] In Judges 14:8 Samson, the Israelite judge known for his strength, discovered honey "in the carcass of a lion."

[13] Poland had been partitioned three times in the late eighteenth century, with Russia ("the Cossack") taking the largest portion.

* First published in *Poems* (1847); this poem is a version of "Maitreya," which Emerson recorded in his journal in 1845, and is an adaptation of a passage in the Hindu scripture *Vishnu Purana* (Bk. IV), which includes the character Maitreya (a variant of Hamatreya).

[1] The first settlers of Concord, Massachusetts, including Rev. Peter Bulkeley, Emerson's ancestor seven generations back.

Hay, corn, roots, hemp, flax, apples, wool and wood.
Each of these landlords walked amidst his farm,
Saying, "'T is mine, my children's and my name's.
How sweet the west wind sounds in my own trees!
How graceful climb those shadows on my hill!
I fancy these pure waters and the flags[2]
Know me, as does my dog: we sympathize;
And, I affirm, my actions smack of the soil."   10

Where are these men? Asleep beneath their grounds:
And strangers, fond[3] as they, their furrows plough.
Earth laughs in flowers, to see her boastful boys
Earth-proud, proud of the earth which is not theirs;
Who steer the plough, but cannot steer their feet
Clear of the grave.
They added ridge to valley, brook to pond,
And sighed for all that bounded their domain;
"This suits me for a pasture; that's my park;
We must have clay, lime, gravel, granite-ledge,   20
And misty lowland, where to go for peat.
The land is well,—lies fairly to the south.
'T is good, when you have crossed the sea and back,
To find the sitfast acres where you left them."
Ah! the hot owner sees not Death, who adds
Him to his land, a lump of mould the more.
Hear what the Earth says:—

EARTH-SONG

"Mine and yours;
Mine, not yours.
Earth endures;   30
Stars abide—
Shine down in the old sea;
Old are the shores;
But where are old men?
I who have seen much,
Such have I never seen.

"The lawyer's deed
Ran sure,
In tail,[4]
To them, and to their heirs   40
Who shall succeed,
Without fail,
Forevermore.

---

[2] Wild irises.   [3] Naïve.
[4] "Entail," the legal method of designating inheritance to specific descendants.

"Here is the land,
Shaggy with wood,
With its old valley,
Mound and flood.
But the heritors?—
Fled like the flood's foam.
The lawyer, and the laws,
And the kingdom,
Clean swept herefrom.

"They called me theirs,
Who so controlled me;
Yet every one
Wished to stay, and is gone,
How am I theirs,
If they cannot hold me,
But I hold them?"

When I heard the Earth-song   60
I was no longer brave;
My avarice cooled
Like lust in the chill of the grave.

1847

DAYS*

Daughters of Time, the hypocritic Days,
Muffled and dumb like barefoot dervishes,[1]
And marching single in an endless file,
Bring diadems and fagots[2] in their hands.
To each they offer gifts after his will,
Bread, kingdoms, stars, and sky that holds them
        all.
I, in my pleached[3] garden, watched the pomp,
Forgot my morning wishes, hastily
Took a few herbs and apples, and the Day
Turned and departed silent. I, too late,   10
Under her solemn fillet[4] saw the scorn.

1857

---

* First published in the inaugural issue of the *Atlantic Monthly* in 1857; collected in *May-Day and Other Pieces* (1867).
[1] Members of Moslem religious orders who take vows of poverty and austerity and wander as friars.
[2] Crowns and bundles of sticks.   [3] Shaded with plaited or interlaced branches.   [4] Headband.

BRAHMA*

If the red slayer[1] think he slays,
   Or if the slain think he is slain,
They know not well the subtle ways
   I keep, and pass, and turn again.

Far or forgot to me is near;
   Shadow and sunlight are the same;
The vanished gods to me appear;
   And one to me are shame and fame.

They reckon ill who leave me out;
   When me they fly, I am the wings;   10
I am the doubter and the doubt,
   And I the hymn the Brahmin[2] sings.

The strong gods pine for my abode,[3]
   And pine in vain the sacred Seven;[4]
But thou, meek lover of the good!
   Find me, and turn thy back on heaven.

                                    1856, 1857

TERMINUS*

It is time to be old,
To take in sail:—
The god of bounds,
Who sets to seas a shore,
Came to me in his fatal rounds,
And said: "No more!
No farther shoot
Thy broad ambitious branches, and thy root.
Fancy departs: no more invent;
Contract thy firmament   10
To compass of a tent.
There's not enough for this and that,
Make thy option which of two;

---

* First published in the inaugural issue of the *Atlantic Monthly* in 1857 and collected in *May-Day and Other Pieces* (1867). In Hindu theology, Brahma is the supreme spirit of the universe.
[1] Death.   [2] A Brahman, a member of the Hindu priestly caste.
[3] The Hindu gods Yama (god of death), Agni (god of fire), and Indra (god of the sky) yearn for oneness with Brahma.
[4] The high saints of Hinduism.
* First published in the *Atlantic Monthly* in 1867 and collected in *May-Day and Other Pieces* (1867). According to Roman myth, the god of boundaries and landmarks.

Economize the failing river,
Not the less revere the Giver,
Leave the many and hold the few.
Timely wise accept the terms,
Soften the fall with wary foot;
A little while
Still plan and smile,   20
And,—fault of novel germs,—
Mature the unfallen fruit.
Curse, if thou wilt, thy sires,
Bad husbands of their fires,
Who, when they gave thee breath,
Failed to bequeath
The needful sinew stark as once,
The Baresark[1] marrow to thy bones,
But left a legacy of ebbing veins,
Inconstant heat and nerveless reins,—   30
Amid the Muses,[2] left thee deaf and dumb,
Amid the gladiators, halt and numb."

   As the bird trims her to the gale,
I trim myself to the storm of time,
I man the rudder, reef the sail,
Obey the voice at eve obeyed at prime:
"Lowly faithful, banish fear,
Right onward drive unharmed;
The port, well worth the cruise, is near,
And every wave is charmed."   40

1867

---

from   JOURNALS

[On Language of the Street: June 24, 1840]

The language of the street is always strong. What can describe the folly & emptiness of scolding like the word *jawing*? I feel too the force of the double negative,
though clean contrary to our grammar rules. And I confess to some pleasure from
the stinging rhetoric of a rattling oath in the mouth of truckmen & teamsters. How
laconic & brisk it is by the side of a page of the North American Review.[1] Cut
these words & they would bleed; they are vascular & alive; they walk & run.
Moreover they who speak them have this elegancy, that they do not trip in their

---

[1] Tough, courageous; from Berserkers, fierce Norse warriors who fought without armor.
[2] According to Greek myth, nine goddesses who presided over literature, the arts, and science.
[1] A leading nineteenth-century cultural and intellectual magazine, founded in Boston in 1815 and
closely affiliated with New England writers. Among its contributors were Emerson, Henry Wadsworth Longfellow, and the historian Francis Parkman (1823–1893).

speech. It is a shower of bullets, whilst Cambridge[2] men & Yale men correct themselves & begin again at every half sentence. I know nobody among my contemporaries except Carlyle[3] who writes with any sinew & vivacity comparable to Plutarch & Montaigne.[4] Yet always this profane swearing & bar-room wit has salt & fire in it. I cannot now read Webster's[5] speeches. Fuller & Brown & Milton[6] are quick, but the list is soon ended. Goethe[7] seems to be well alive, no pedant. Luther[8] too. *Guts* is a stronger word than intestines.

[*On Plans for Brook Farm: October 17, 1840*]

Yesterday George & Sophia Ripley, Margaret Fuller & Alcott[9] discussed here the new social plans. I wished to be convinced, to be thawed, to be made nobly mad by the kindlings before my eye of a new dawn piety. But this scheme was arithmetic & comfort; this was a hint borrowed from the Tremont House & U.S. Hotel;[10] a rage in our poverty & politics to live rich & gentlemanlike, an anchor to leeward against a change of weather; a prudent forecast on the probable issue of the great questions of pauperism & property. And not once could I be inflamed,—but sat aloof & thoughtless, my voice faltered & fell. It was not the cave of persecution which is the palace of spiritual power, but only a room in the Astor House[11] hired for the Transcendentalists. I do not wish to remove from my present prison to a prison a little larger. I wish to break all prisons. I have not yet conquered my own house. It irks & repents me. Shall I raise the siege of this hencoop & march baffled away to a pretended siege of Babylon?[12] It seems to me that to do so were to dodge the problem I am set to solve, & to hide my impotency in the thick of a crowd. I can see too afar that I should not find myself more than now,—no, not so much, in that select, but not by me selected, fraternity. Moreover to join this body would be to traverse all my long trumpeted theory, and the instinct which spoke from it, that one man is a counterpoise to a city,—that a man is stronger than a city, that his solitude is more prevalent & beneficent than the concert of crowds.

[2] Harvard.

[3] The English writer Thomas Carlyle (1795–1881), Emerson's long-time friend and correspondent.

[4] Plutarch (A.D. 46?–120?), a Greek biographer who featured the "parallel lives" of eminent Greeks and Romans; Michel de Montaigne (1553–1592), an incisive French political theorist and writer.

[5] Daniel Webster (1782–1852), whom Emerson and others reviled when Webster championed the Compromise of 1850 (permitting slavery in some states and prohibiting it in others) and gave his famous Seventh of March speech in the U.S. Senate (sacrificing antislavery principles as a way of defending the Union).

[6] Thomas Fuller (1608–1661), an English clergyman and writer; Sir Thomas Browne (1605–1682), an English medical doctor and influential writer; the eminent English poet John Milton (1608–1674), author of *Paradise Lost* (1667).

[7] Johann Wolfgang von Goethe (1749–1832), a German poet and novelist.

[8] Martin Luther (1483–1546), the German leader of the Protestant Reformation.

[9] George Ripley (1802–1880) and his wife, Sophia Dana Ripley, were both transcendentalists and reformers; Fuller (1810–1850) was a leading transcendentalist writer and feminist; Bronson Alcott (1799–1888), an educator and progressive reformer (and father of Louisa May Alcott). The "plans" were for the founding of the Brook Farm Institute of Agriculture and Education, a utopian community established in 1841 near West Roxbury, Massachusetts, with George Ripley as president.

[10] The Tremont House, which opened in 1829, and the U.S. Hotel, which opened in 1840, were deluxe hotels in Boston.

[11] An elegant hotel in New York City that opened in 1836.

[12] An ancient city in Mesopotamia, famous for its luxury; here, any opulent establishment.

[*On the Death of Emerson's Son: January 28, 1842*]

Yesterday night at 15 minutes after eight my little Waldo[13] ended his life.

[*January 30, 1842*]

What he looked upon is better, what he looked not upon is insignificant. The morning of Friday I woke at 3 oclock, & every cock in every barnyard was shrilling with the most unnecessary noise. The sun went up the morning sky with all his light, but the landscape was dishonored by this loss. For this boy in whose remembrance I have both slept & waked so oft, decorated for me the morning star, & the evening cloud, how much more all the particulars of daily economy; for he had touched with his lively curiosity every trivial fact & circumstance in the household[:] the hard coal & the soft coal which I put into my stove; the wood of which he brought his little quota for grandmothers fire, the hammer, the pincers, & file, he was so eager to use; the microscope, the magnet, the little globe, & every trinket & instrument in the study; the loads of gravel on the meadow the nests in the henhouse and many & many a little visit to the doghouse and to the barn,—For every thing he had his own name & way of thinking[,] his own pronunciation & manner. And every word came mended from that tongue. A boy of early wisdom, of a grave & even majestic deportment, of a perfect gentleness

Every tramper that ever tramped is abroad but the little feet are still

He gave up his little innocent breath like a bird.

* * *

The boy had his full swing in the world[.] Never I think did a child enjoy more[;] he had been thoroughly respected by his parents & those around him & not interfered with; and he had been the most fortunate in respect to the influences near him for his Aunt Elizabeth[14] had adopted him from his infancy & treated him ever with that plain & wise love which belongs to her and, as she boasted, had never given him sugar plums.[15] So he was won to her & always signalized her arrival as a visit to him & left playmates playthings & all to go to her. Then Mary Russell[16] had been his friend & teacher for two summers with true love & wisdom. Then Henry Thoreau had been one of the family for the last year, & charmed Waldo by the variety of toys whistles boats popguns & all kinds of instruments which he could make & mend; & possessed his love & respect by the gentle firmness with which he always treated him. Margaret Fuller & Caroline Sturgis[17] had also marked the boy & caressed & conversed with him whenever they were here. . . .

* * *

[13] Waldo (1836–1842), Emerson's son, who died of scarlet fever.
[14] Elizabeth Hoar, who had been engaged to Emerson's brother Charles before Charles's death in 1836.
[15] Had never spoiled him.   [16] A private teacher and governness hired by the Emersons.
[17] A transcendentalist and close friend of the Emerson family.

It seems as if I ought to call upon the winds to describe my boy, my fast receding boy, a child of so large & generous a nature that I cannot paint him by specialties, as I might another.

[On Hawthorn: May 24, 1864]

Yesterday, 23 May, we buried Hawthorne in Sleepy Hollow,[18] in a pomp of sunshine & verdure, & gentle winds. James F. Clarke[19] read the service in the Church & at the grave. Longfellow, Lowell, Holmes, Agassiz, Hoar, Dwight, Whipple, Norton, Alcott, Hillard, Fields, Judge Thomas,[20] & I, attended the hearse as pall bearers. Franklin Pierce[21] was with the family. The church was copiously decorated with white flowers delicately arranged. The corpse was unwillingly shown,—only a few moments to this company of his friends. But i[t] was noble & serene in its aspect,—nothing amiss,—a calm & powerful head. A large company filled the church, & the grounds of the cemetery. All was so bright & quiet, that pain or mourning was hardly suggested, & Holmes said to me, that it looked like a happy meeting.

Clarke in the church said, that, Hawthorne had done more justice than any other to the shades of life, shown a sympathy with the crime in our nature, &, like Jesus, was the friend of sinners.

I thought there was a tragic element in the event, that might be more fully rendered—in the painful solitude of the man,—which, I suppose, could not longer be endured, & he died of it.

I have found in his death a surprise & disappointment. I thought him a greater man than any of his works betray, & that there was still a great deal of work in him, & that he might one day show a purer power.

Moreover I have felt sure . . . that I could well wait his time,—his unwillingness & caprice,—and might one day conquer a friendship. It would have been a happiness, doubtless to both of us, to have come into habits of unreserved intercourse. It was easy to talk with him,—there were no barriers;—only, he said so little, that I talked to[o] much, & stopped only because,—as he gave no indications,—I feared to exceed. He showed no egotism or self-assertion, rather a humility, &, at one time, a fear that he had written himself out.— One day, when I found him on the top of his hill, in the woods, he paced back the path to his house,

[18] Sleepy Hollow Cemetery outside Concord, where Thoreau was buried and where Emerson would be buried.

[19] James Freeman Clarke (1810–1888), the Unitarian minister who had officiated at the wedding of Nathaniel Hawthorne and Sophia Peabody in 1842.

[20] The poets Henry Wadsworth Longfellow, James Russell Lowell, and Oliver Wendell Holmes; Louis Agassiz (1807–1873), a Swiss immigrant and renowned geologist at Harvard; Judge Ebenezer Hoar (1816–1895), brother of Charles Emerson's fiancée, Elizabeth Hoar; John S. Dwight (1813–1893), a music critic who was active at Brook Farm; Edwin Percy Whipple (1819–1886), a lecturer and literary critic; Charles Eliot Norton (1827–1908), a Harvard professor and writer; Bronson Alcott; George Hillard (1808–1879), a lawyer and writer; James T. Fields (1817–1881), Hawthorne's publisher; Benjamin Franklin Thomas (1813–1878), a Massachusetts Supreme Court judge. All (including Emerson) but Alcott, Hillard, and Thomas were members of the Saturday Club, which met at Boston's Parker House hotel for informal socializing the last Saturday of every month.

[21] Pierce (1804–1869), Hawthorne's friend since college days at Bowdoin and former U.S. president (1853–1857).

& said, *"this path is the only remembrance of me that will remain."* Now it appears that I waited too long.

Lately, he had removed himself the more by the indignation his perverse politics & unfortunate friendship for that paltry Franklin Pierce awaked,—though it rather moved pity for Hawthorne, & the assured belief that he would outlive it, & come right at last.[22]

1824–1866?, 1909–1914

LETTER TO WALT WHITMAN*

Concord, Massachusetts, 21 July, 1855.

Dear Sir—I am not blind to the worth of the wonderful gift of "Leaves of Grass." I find it the most extraordinary piece of wit and wisdom that America has yet contributed. I am very happy in reading it, as great power makes us happy. It meets the demand I am always making of what seemed the sterile and stingy nature, as if too much handiwork, or too much lymph[1] in the temperament, were making our western wits fat and mean.[2]

I give you joy of your free and brave thought. I have great joy in it. I find incomparable things said incomparably well, as they must be. I find the courage of treatment which so delights us, and which large perception only can inspire.

I greet you at the beginning of a great career, which yet must have had a long foreground somewhere, for such a start. I rubbed my eyes a little, to see if this sunbeam were no illusion; but the solid sense of the book is a sober certainty. It has the best merits, namely, of fortifying and encouraging.

I did not know until I last night saw the book advertised in a newspaper that I could trust the name as real and available for a post-office.[3] I wish to see my benefactor, and have felt much like striking my tasks, and visiting New York to pay you my respects.

R.W. EMERSON
1855

Henry David Thoreau
(1817–1862)

Early in his essay "Thoreau" (1862), Ralph Waldo Emerson emphasizes the "renunciations" that characterized the life of his Concord friend and neighbor. "He was bred to no profession," Emerson writes; "he never married; he lived alone; he never went to church;

---

[22] Emerson heartily disapproved of Pierce's politically expedient and irresolute position on slavery.
* A response to a copy of *Leaves of Grass* (1855) that Walt Whitman sent to Emerson.
[1] Sluggishness.   [2] Small, petty.
[3] Emerson is referring to getting Whitman's name and address: the first (1855) edition of *Leaves of Grass* was published anonymously.

he never voted, he refused to pay a tax to the State; he ate no flesh, he drank no wine, he never knew the use of tobacco; and, though a naturalist, he used neither trap nor gun." The man Emerson eulogizes is thus defined by negation ("No college" offered him honors, "no academy" made him a member), stripped down to what he was not. Several paragraphs later, Emerson informs us bluntly that "No truer American existed than Thoreau."

Emerson's barrage of negatives corresponds in provocative ways with the chorus of negative descriptions of the United States in its early years of national existence. In *Letters From an American Farmer* (1782), for example, Michel-Guillaume Jean de Crèvecoeur depicts a new nation with "no aristocratical families, no courts, no kings, no bishops, no ecclesiastical dominion, no invisible power giving to the few a very visible one." Looking back to the years of colonial emigration, a character in Sylvester Judd's *Margaret* (1845) rejoices that much of "the Old World on its passage to the New was lost overboard," leaving our ancestors "considerably cleansed by the dashing waters of the Atlantic." The analogy is apparent: as the first Americans cast off the trappings of Europe, Thoreau casts off the paraphernalia of modern life. Emerson's arresting statement that "no truer American existed" is a tacit recognition of Thoreau's alignment with the pristine and revolutionary image of the early nation. Thoreau's admirable and abrasive power lay in the fact that he was a true indicator of what his nation originally hoped to be, the self-discovered man who prized what he was not and frequently blamed his neighbors for what they were.

Born in July 1817 in Concord, Massachusetts, Henry David Thoreau was the third child of Cynthia Dunbar and John Thoreau—his outgoing mother a descendant of a sturdy line of Scotch ancestors, his unassuming father a descendant of French Protestants. Henry's sister Helen, five years his senior, became a teacher; his brother, John, older by two years, became Henry's co-worker and closest friend; Sophia, two years younger than Henry, cared for him during his final illness and edited some of his work posthumously. Thoreau was sent to the Concord Academy, then to Harvard College (with financial assistance from Helen), graduating in 1837 without having distinguished himself academically. But he had developed an appetite for languages that began with his introduction to Greek literature by the visionary poet Jones Very (a tutor of Greek at Harvard) and continued during his temporary residence in 1835 with the maverick thinker Orestes Brownson, from whom Thoreau learned German. His wide reading in world literature is evident in the allusive style of his work.

Following his graduation from Harvard, Thoreau returned to Concord and taught briefly at a local academy. Then, in 1838, Thoreau and his brother John founded a progressive and successful school. While running this educational venture, Henry and John fell in love with the same girl, Ellen Sewall, the daughter of a Unitarian minister in Scituate, Massachusetts, whose younger brother, Edmund, was a favorite in the Thoreaus' school and whose aunt had long boarded in the Thoreau home. Each of the brothers proposed to her in 1840, first John (whom she refused) and then Henry. But Ellen's conservative father thought of Henry as a radical and ordered her to decline the proposal. Once Henry was rejected, conventional romance was no longer a part of his life. Although the school continued to prosper, John's ill health made the brothers decide to close it in 1841.

That same year Thoreau went to live and work as a handyman in the home of Ralph Waldo Emerson, whom he had come to know after his return to Concord in 1837. Through Emerson he became acquainted with such leading transcendentalist figures as Margaret Fuller, Bronson Alcott, Theodore Parker, and William Ellery Channing. Early in 1842 the death of John Thoreau from tetanus and, two weeks later, of Emerson's young son from scarlet fever doubtless brought the two men together in mutual grief. And a decision for Thoreau to range beyond Concord led him to take a position as tutor for the sons of Emerson's brother William on Staten Island in 1843.

The move was not a happy one for Thoreau, although he did meet the influential editor

Horace Greeley, who would help him place his work in the years to come. Homesickness brought him back to Concord in 1844; several months later he decided to begin an experiment at Walden Pond, two miles from Concord. Emerson had purchased several acres bordering the pond, and he gave permission for Thoreau to clear the land and build a cabin. On July 4, 1845, Independence Day now made personal, Thoreau completed his cabin and began what would be twenty-six months of residence at Walden. He was now living out his experiment: seeing what was essential to life in this freedom, stripping away things extraneous to living. Biographers have shown that he did not live as a hermit; he visited with neighbors and walked into Concord frequently. But at Walden Thoreau did cultivate solitude as the condition of self-exploration. And he also wrote the first of his two books, *A Week on the Concord and Merrimack Rivers*, the conglomerate record of a two-week trip with his brother John in 1839, replete with poems, observations on nature, translations from Greek epics, and essays on such topics as fishing, Scripture, canal boats, the Concord Cattle Show, and friendship, all arranged according to the days of a single week. It is a meandering book, a journey through a writer's bountiful consciousness. Thoreau completed the manuscript in 1846, then revised and expanded it each time it was rejected by publishers—until he published an edition of one thousand copies at his own expense in 1849. Praised by friends such as George Ripley, the founder of Brook Farm, *A Week* was a commercial flop, selling approximately two hundred copies (with seventy-five other copies given away). When the publisher returned the unsold books, Thoreau wrote in his journal, "I have now a library of nearly nine hundred volumes, over seven hundred of which I wrote myself."

By this time Thoreau had not only "travelled a good deal in Concord," as he says in the opening chapter of *Walden*, but had published more than thirty items in the transcendental periodical, *The Dial*, founded in 1840 and edited at different times during its four year existence by Margaret Fuller and by Emerson. At Emerson's request, Thoreau edited the April 1843 issue. The friendship of Emerson and Thoreau went through periods of coolness in these years and later, perhaps because Thoreau never liked being considered an Emerson clone, perhaps because Emerson did not like Thoreau's stubborn independence, perhaps because Thoreau did not live up to Emerson's expectations (or anyone else's). Even near the end of his essay on Thoreau, in a eulogizing context of admiration and respect, Emerson files a complaint by negation when he says that his friend had "no ambition."

The Mexican War broke out during Thoreau's second summer at Walden. Refusing to pay his poll tax to support what he saw as a bullying war to extend slavery, Thoreau was arrested and jailed for one night; although the evidence is inconclusive, his aunt Maria may have been the person who paid the tax to free him. He had lectured first at the Concord Lyceum in 1838 and in various small towns near Concord during the following years, at times drawing with subtle humor on his knowledge of the woods, at times developing with caustic wit the idea that most people's lives lack purpose. Now he began to speak with the sense of urgency and principle that informs an essay such as "Resistance to Civil Government" (delivered as a lecture in 1848 and published in 1849) and escalates to moral outrage in "Slavery in Massachusetts" (1854), occasioned by the return of two escaped slaves to their southern owners under the terms of the Fugitive Slave Act of 1850.

What Thoreau confronts in these essays is the question of which should take precedence: individual conscience or duly enacted law, the moral sphere or the legal. He argues that human beings owe allegiance to a higher law and thus must oppose any government whose laws violate the conscience. With unrelenting logic he advocates the radical strategy of passive resistance, something not for the faint of heart or for those afraid of losing their property, as he admits, but the ultimate weapon against tyranny. Adapted by Mahatma Gandhi in his opposition to British imperialism in India and by Martin Luther King, Jr., in

WALDEN;

OR,

LIFE IN THE WOODS.

By HENRY D. THOREAU,

AUTHOR OF "A WEEK ON THE CONCORD AND MERRIMACK RIVERS."

I do not propose to write an ode to dejection, but to brag as lustily as chanticleer in the morning, standing on his roost, if only to wake my neighbors up. — Page 92.

BOSTON:

TICKNOR AND FIELDS.

M DCCC LIV.

The title page of the first edition of Walden, *by Henry David Thoreau.*

his struggle for civil rights in the United States, Thoreau's doctrine of passive resistance has transcended time and place to rewrite history in the twentieth century. A growing passion for justice also led Thoreau to speak in defense of the abolitionist John Brown after Brown had been captured for his October 1859 raid on Harper's Ferry, Virginia. Thoreau had met Brown in Concord in 1857 and again in 1859. In Thoreau's lecture "A Plea for Captain John Brown" (1859), he portrays the militant Brown as a martyr to freedom.

Thoreau left Walden in September 1847 and began to write his second book while he worked in his father's pencil factory to get money to publish his first. Completed in 1849, the initial draft of *Walden* found no favor with publishers who had witnessed the dismal failure of *A Week* earlier that year. Thoreau found ready employment as a carpenter, a day-laborer, and a surveyor during the next few years, all the while perfecting the manuscript of *Walden,* which was finally published in 1854.

Walden personifies Thoreau, informing us that material possessions are burdens, bidding us to simplify life as the condition of knowing what it is, exhorting us to dramatic self-discovery: "Be a Columbus to whole new continents and worlds within you." Shaping the experience of his twenty-six months at Walden Pond into the cycle of a year, Thoreau enlists the seasons as the structuring principle of his book. And, as always, he prizes origins, the pristine quality of beginnings: "The poem of creation is uninterrupted; but few are the ears that hear it." In *Walden* Thoreau may lecture and admonish; but with reverence and nostalgic detachment he asks that we listen to the "poem of creation."

In the late 1840s and throughout the 1850s, Thoreau's excursions (as he called them) to the Maine woods and to Cape Cod took him to various New England settings that provided material for his journal and for later essays. His journal, begun in 1837 at Emerson's suggestion, developed over the years into a remarkable testimony of observation and of inner growth that scholars have begun to see as crucial to an understanding of Thoreau's life and work. His later essays, published in various periodicals and collected posthumously in *Excursions* (1863), *The Maine Woods* (1864), and *Cape Cod* (1865), show a writer probing for truth and simplicity with sporadic grace and vision. In 1850 Thoreau toured Quebec for twelve unhappy days with Ellery Channing; on this trip (remembered in *A Yankee in Canada* [1866]) he was a tourist with a bad cold—impatient, provincial, unwilling to appreciate the Canadian past or present. On a brief visit to New York City in 1856, he met Walt Whitman and once again saw his friend Horace Greeley. Plagued by bronchitis and chronic respiratory illness in the final years of life, Thoreau traveled to Minnesota in 1861, hoping to improve his health. But his physical decline was not to be arrested. Tended in his final months by his sister Sophia, who arranged his papers and correspondence according to his wishes, Thoreau died of tuberculosis in May 1862. (That disease had taken his sister Helen's life in 1848.) Buried in the lot belonging to his mother's family in the New Burying Ground outside Concord, his body was later interred in Concord's Sleepy Hollow Cemetery near the graves of Emerson, Nathaniel Hawthorne, and Bronson Alcott.

Suggested Readings: *The Writings of Henry David Thoreau*, 20 vols., 1906. *Consciousness in Concord: Thoreau's Lost Journal (1840-1841)*, ed. P. Miller, 1958. *The Writings of Henry David Thoreau*, (Princeton Edition), 25 vols. projected, 1971– . S. Paul, *The Shores of America: Thoreau's Inward Exploration*, 1958. W. Harding, *The Days of Henry David Thoreau: A Biography*, 1965. J. Porte, *Emerson and Thoreau: Transcendentalists in Conflict*, 1966. W. Glick, ed., *The Recognition of Henry Thoreau*, 1969. F. Garber, *Thoreau's Redemptive Imagination*, 1977. R. F. Sayre, *Thoreau and the American Indians*, 1977. W. Harding and M. Meyer, eds., *The New Thoreau Handbook*, 1980. S. Cavell, *The Senses of Walden*, 1981. W. Howarth, *The Book of Concord*, 1982. R. D. Richardson, *Henry Thoreau: A Life of the Mind*, 1986. R. Sattelmeyer, *Thoreau's Reading: A Study in Intellectual History*, 1988.

Texts Used: "Resistance to Civil Government" and "Slavery in Massachusetts": *The Writings of Henry D. Thoreau: Reform Papers*, ed. W. Glick, 1973. *Walden: The Writings: Walden*, ed. J. Lyndon Shanley, 1971. Journal entry from 1841: *The Writings: Journal*, Vol. I: 1837–1844, ed. E. H. Witherell et al., 1981. Entries from 1845 and 1846: *The Writings: Journal*, Vol. II: 1842–1848, ed. R. Sattelmeyer, 1984. Entry from 1851: *The Journal of Henry D. Thoreau*, Vol. II: 1850–Sept. 15, 1851, ed. B. Torrey and F. H. Allen, 1949 Entry from 1852: *The Journal*, Vol. III: Sept 16, 1851–Apr. 30, 1852. Entry from 1853: *The Journal*, Vol. V: Mar. 5, 1853–Nov. 30, 1853. All else: *The Journal*, Vol. X: Aug. 8, 1857–June 29, 1858.

RESISTANCE TO CIVIL GOVERNMENT*

I heartily accept the motto,—"That government is best which governs least;"[1] and I should like to see it acted up to more rapidly and systematically. Carried out, it finally amounts to this, which also I believe,—"That government is best which governs not at all;" and when men are prepared for it, that will be the kind of

---

* First published in *Aesthetic Papers*, edited by Elizabeth Peabody (Nathaniel Hawthorne's sister-in-law), in 1849. After Thoreau's death the essay was reprinted in *A Yankee in Canada, With Anti-Slavery and Reform Papers* (1866) with the widely known title "Civil Disobedience." Thoreau's ideas of passive resistance have found expression in Mahatma Gandhi's struggle for India's independence and Martin Luther King's advocacy of civil rights in America.

[1] Words once ascribed to Thomas Jefferson (because they capture the spirit of Jeffersonianism) but

government which they will have. Government is at best but an expedient; but most governments are usually, and all governments are sometimes, inexpedient. The objections which have been brought against a standing army, and they are many and weighty, and deserve to prevail, may also at last be brought against a standing government. The standing army is only an arm of the standing government. The government itself, which is only the mode which the people have chosen to execute their will, is equally liable to be abused and perverted before the people can act through it. Witness the present Mexican war,[2] the work of comparatively a few individuals using the standing government as their tool; for, in the outset, the people would not have consented to this measure.

This American government,—what is it but a tradition, though a recent one, endeavoring to transmit itself unimpaired to posterity, but each instant losing some of its integrity? It has not the vitality and force of a single living man; for a single man can bend it to his will. It is a sort of wooden gun to the people themselves; and, if ever they should use it in earnest as a real one against each other, it will surely split. But it is not the less necessary for this; for the people must have some complicated machinery or other, and hear its din, to satisfy that idea of government which they have. Governments show thus how successfully men can be imposed on, even impose on themselves, for their own advantage. It is excellent, we must all allow; yet this government never of itself furthered any enterprise, but by the alacrity with which it got out of its way. *It* does not keep the country free. *It* does not settle the West. *It* does not educate. The character inherent in the American people has done all that has been accomplished; and it would have done somewhat more, if the government had not sometimes got in its way. For government is an expedient by which men would fain succeed in letting one another alone; and, as has been said, when it is most expedient, the governed are most let alone by it. Trade and commerce, if they were not made of India rubber, would never manage to bounce over the obstacles which legislators are continually putting in their way; and, if one were to judge these men wholly by the effects of their actions, and not partly by their intentions, they would deserve to be classed and punished with those mischievous persons who put obstructions on the railroads.

But, to speak practically and as a citizen, unlike those who call themselves no-government men, I ask for, not at once no government, but *at once* a better government. Let every man make known what kind of government would command his respect, and that will be one step toward obtaining it.

After all, the practical reason why, when the power is once in the hands of the people, a majority are permitted, and for a long period continue, to rule, is not because they are most likely to be in the right, nor because this seems fairest to the minority, but because they are physically the strongest. But a government in which the majority rule in all cases cannot be based on justice, even as far as men understand it. Can there not be a government in which majorities do not virtually decide right and wrong, but conscience?—in which majorities decide only those questions to which the rule of expediency is applicable? Must the citizen ever for a

---

adapted from a motto that appeared on the cover of the *United States Magazine and Democratic Review* (1837–1849): "The best government is that which governs least."

[2] Thoreau presented this essay as a lecture at the Concord Lyceum (a community forum that sponsored an annual lecture series), apparently both in January and February 1848, during and just after the controversy over the Mexican War (1846–1848), which many New Englanders saw as a plan to extend slave territory to the West. His profound opposition to the war arises from his belief that human law must be subject to conscience.

moment, or in the least degree, resign his conscience to the legislator? Why has every man a conscience, then? I think that we should be men first, and subjects afterward. It is not desirable to cultivate a respect for the law, so much as for the right. The only obligation which I have a right to assume, is to do at any time what I think right. It is truly enough said, that a corporation has no conscience;[3] but a corporation of conscientious men is a corporation *with* a conscience. Law never made men a whit more just; and, by means of their respect for it, even the well-disposed are daily made the agents of injustice. A common and natural result of an undue respect for law is, that you may see a file of soldiers, colonel, captain, corporal, privates, powder-monkeys[4] and all, marching in admirable order over hill and dale to the wars, against their wills, aye, against their common sense and consciences, which makes it very steep marching indeed, and produces a palpitation of the heart. They have no doubt that it is a damnable business in which they are concerned; they are all peaceably inclined. Now, what are they? Men at all? or small moveable forts and magazines, at the service of some unscrupulous man in power? Visit the Navy Yard, and behold a marine, such a man as an American government can make, or such as it can make a man with its black arts, a mere shadow and reminiscence of humanity, a man laid out alive and standing, and already, as one may say, buried under arms with funeral accompaniments, though it may be

> "Not a drum was heard, not a funeral note,
>   As his corpse to the rampart we hurried;
> Not a soldier discharged his farewell shot
>   O'er the grave where our hero we buried."[5]

The mass of men serve the State thus, not as men mainly, but as machines, with their bodies. They are the standing army, and the militia, jailers, constable, *posse comitatus,*[6] etc. In most cases there is no free exercise whatever of the judgment or of the moral sense; but they put themselves on a level with wood and earth and stones, and wooden men can perhaps be manufactured that will serve the purpose as well. Such command no more respect than men of straw, or a lump of dirt. They have the same sort of worth only as horses and dogs. Yet such as these even are commonly esteemed good citizens. Others, as most legislators, politicians, lawyers, ministers, and office-holders, serve the State chiefly with their heads; and, as they rarely make any moral distinctions, they are as likely to serve the devil, without intending it, as God. A very few, as heroes, patriots, martyrs, reformers in the great sense, and *men,* serve the State with their consciences also, and so necessarily resist it for the most part; and they are commonly treated by it as enemies. A wise man will only be useful as a man, and will not submit to be "clay," and "stop a hole to keep the wind away,"[7] but leave that office to his dust at least:—

> "I am too high-born to be propertied,
>   To be a secondary at control,

---

[3] The formulation of the English jurist Sir Edward Coke (1552–1634) in a landmark legal decision.
  [4] Draftees who carry gunpowder to cannons. The sentence is arranged in descending order of military rank.
  [5] From "The Burial of Sir John Moore at Corunna" (1817), by the Irish poet Charles Wolfe (1791–1823).
  [6] "Sheriff's posse" (Latin).   [7] From Shakespeare's *Hamlet* (V.i.236–237).

> Or useful serving-man and instrument
> To any sovereign state throughout the world."[8]

He who gives himself entirely to his fellow-men appears to them useless and selfish; but he who gives himself partially to them is pronounced a benefactor and philanthropist.

How does it become a man to behave toward this American government to-day? I answer that he cannot without disgrace be associated with it. I cannot for an instant recognize that political organization as *my* government which is the *slave's* government also.

All men recognize the right of revolution; that is, the right to refuse allegiance to and to resist the government, when its tyranny or its inefficiency are great and unendurable. But almost all say that such is not the case now. But such was the case, they think, in the Revolution of '75.[9] If one were to tell me that this was a bad government because it taxed certain foreign commodities brought to its ports, it is most probable that I should not make an ado about it, for I can do without them: all machines have their friction; and possibly this does enough good to counter-balance the evil. At any rate, it is a great evil to make a stir about it. But when the friction comes to have its machine, and oppression and robbery are organized, I say, let us not have such a machine any longer. In other words, when a sixth of the population of a nation which has undertaken to be the refuge of liberty are slaves, and a whole country [10] is unjustly overrun and conquered by a foreign army, and subjected to military law, I think that it is not too soon for honest men to rebel and revolutionize. What makes this duty the more urgent is the fact, that the country so overrun is not our own, but ours is the invading army.

Paley, a common authority with many on moral questions, in his chapter on the "Duty of Submission to Civil Government,"[11] resolves all civil obligation into expediency; and he proceeds to say, "that so long as the interest of the whole society requires it, that is, so long as the established government cannot be resisted or changed without public inconveniency, it is the will of God that the established government be obeyed, and no longer." . . . "This principle being admitted, the justice of every particular case of resistance is reduced to a computation of the quantity of the danger and grievance on the one side, and of the probability and expense of redressing it on the other." Of this, he says, every man shall judge for himself. But Paley appears never to have contemplated those cases to which the rule of expediency does not apply, in which a people, as well as an individual, must do justice, cost what it may. If I have unjustly wrested a plank from a drowning man, I must restore it to him though I drown myself. This, according to Paley, would be inconvenient. But he that would save his life, in such a case, shall lose it.[12] This people must cease to hold slaves, and to make war on Mexico, though it cost them their existence as a people.

In their practice, nations agree with Paley; but does any one think that Massachusetts does exactly what is right at the present crisis?

---

[8] From Shakespeare's *King John* (V.ii. 79–82).   [9] The American Revolution (1775–1783).
[10] Mexico, "overrun" in the Mexican War.
[11] The full title of this chapter in *Principles of Moral and Political Philosophy* (1785), by William Paley (1743–1805), is "The Duty of Submission to Civil Government Explained." The theological utilitarianism taught by the English moralist Paley is diametrically opposed to what Thoreau advocates here.
[12] "Whosoever will save his life shall lose it: but whosoever will lose his life for my sake, the same shall save it," from Luke 9:24.

> "A drab of state, a cloth-o'-silver slut,
> To have her train borne up, and her soul trail in the dirt."[13]

Practically speaking, the opponents to a reform in Massachusetts are not a hundred thousand politicians at the South, but a hundred thousand merchants and farmers here, who are more interested in commerce and agriculture than they are in humanity, and are not prepared to do justice to the slave and to Mexico, *cost what it may*. I quarrel not with far-off foes, but with those who, near at home, co-operate with, and do the bidding of those far away, and without whom the latter would be harmless. We are accustomed to say, that the mass of men are unprepared; but improvement is slow, because the few are not materially wiser or better than the many. It is not so important that many should be as good as you, as that there be some absolute goodness somewhere; for that will leaven the whole lump.[14] There are thousands who are *in opinion* opposed to slavery and to the war, who yet in effect do nothing to put an end to them; who, esteeming themselves children of Washington and Franklin, sit down with their hands in their pockets,[15] and say that they know not what to do, and do nothing; who even postpone the question of freedom to the question of free-trade, and quietly read the prices-current along with the latest advices[16] from Mexico, after dinner, and, it may be, fall asleep over them both. What is the price-current of an honest man and patriot to-day? They hesitate, and they regret, and sometimes they petition; but they do nothing in earnest and with effect. They will wait, well-disposed, for others to remedy the evil, that they may no longer have it to regret. At most, they give only a cheap vote, and a feeble countenance and God-speed, to the right, as it goes by them. There are nine hundred and ninety-nine patrons of virtue to one virtuous man; but it is easier to deal with the real possessor of a thing than with the temporary guardian of it.

All voting is a sort of gaming, like chequers or backgammon, with a slight moral tinge to it, a playing with right and wrong, with moral questions; and betting naturally accompanies it. The character of the voters is not staked. I cast my vote, perchance, as I think right; but I am not vitally concerned that that right should prevail. I am willing to leave it to the majority. Its obligation, therefore, never exceeds that of expediency. Even voting *for the right* is *doing* nothing for it. It is only expressing to men feebly your desire that it should prevail. A wise man will not leave the right to the mercy of chance, nor wish it to prevail through the power of the majority. There is but little virtue in the action of masses of men. When the majority shall at length vote for the abolition of slavery, it will because they are indifferent to slavery, or because there is but little slavery left to be abolished by their vote. *They* will then be the only slaves. Only *his* vote can hasten the abolition of slavery who asserts his own freedom by his vote.

I hear of a convention to be held at Baltimore,[17] or elsewhere, for the selection of a candidate for the Presidency, made up chiefly of editors, and men who are politicians by profession; but I think, what is it to any independent, intelligent, and respectable man what decision they may come to, shall we not have the ad-

---

[13] From *The Revenger's Tragedy* (1607)(IV.iv. 70–72), attributed to the English dramatist Cyril Tourneur (1575?–1626).

[14] "Know ye not that a little leaven leaveneth the whole lump?" from I Corinthians 5:6.

[15] Who think they are the heirs of such heroes as George Washington and Benjamin Franklin and need do nothing on their own.

[16] News dispatches.   [17] The Democratic Convention, held in Baltimore in May 1848.

vantage of his wisdom and honesty, nevertheless? Can we not count upon some independent votes? Are there not many individuals in the country who do not attend conventions? But no: I find that the respectable man, so called, has immediately drifted from his position, and despairs of his country, when his country has more reason to despair of him. He forthwith adopts one of the candidates thus selected as the only *available* one, thus proving that he is himself *available* for any purposes of the demagogue. His vote is of no more worth than that of any unprincipled foreigner or hireling native, who may have been bought. Oh for a man who is a *man,* and, as my neighbor says, has a bone in his back which you cannot pass your hand through! Our statistics are at fault: the population has been returned too large. How many *men* are there to a square thousand miles in this country? Hardly one. Does not America offer any inducement for men to settle here? The American has dwindled into an Odd Fellow,[18]—one who may be known by the development of his organ of gregariousness,[19] and a manifest lack of intellect and cheerful self-reliance; whose first and chief concern, on coming into the world, is to see that the alms-houses are in good repair; and, before yet he has lawfully donned the virile garb,[20] to collect a fund for the support of the widows and orphans that may be; who, in short, ventures to live only by the aid of the mutual insurance company, which has promised to bury him decently.

It is not a man's duty, as a matter of course, to devote himself to the eradication of any, even the enormous wrong; he may still properly have other concerns to engage him; but it is his duty, at least, to wash his hands of it, and, if he gives it no thought longer, not to give it practically his support. If I devote myself to other pursuits and contemplations, I must first see, at least, that I do not pursue them sitting upon another man's shoulders. I must get off him first, that he may pursue his contemplations too. See what gross inconsistency is tolerated. I have heard some of my townsmen say, "I should like to have them order me out to help put down an insurrection of the slaves, or to march to Mexico,—see if I would go;" and yet these very men have each, directly by their allegiance, and so indirectly, at least, by their money, furnished a substitute. The soldier is applauded who refuses to serve in an unjust war by those who do not refuse to sustain the unjust government which makes the war; is applauded by those whose own act and authority he disregards and sets at nought; as if the State were penitent to that degree that it hired one to scourge it while it sinned, but not to that degree that it left off sinning for a moment. Thus, under the name of order and civil government, we are all made at last to pay homage to and support our own meanness. After the first blush of sin, comes its indifference and from immoral it becomes, as it were, *un*moral, and not quite unnecessary to that life which we have made.

The broadest and most prevalent error requires the most disinterested virtue to sustain it. The slight reproach to which the virtue of patriotism is commonly liable, the noble are most likely to incur. Those who, while they disapprove of the character and measures of a government, yield to it their allegiance and support, are undoubtedly its most conscientious supporters, and so frequently the most serious obstacles to reform. Some are petitioning the State to dissolve the Union, to

---

[18] The Independent Order of Odd Fellows, a benevolent fraternal organization established in 1819, adapted to Thoreau's satiric purposes as a way of saying that too many Americans are conformists.

[19] A term from the pseudoscience of phrenology (judging character from contours of the head), indicating one who loves company.

[20] Clothing that signified a Roman boy of fourteen had reached manhood.

disregard the requisitions of the President.[21] Why do they not dissolve it them-selves,—the union between themselves and the State,—and refuse to pay their quota into its treasury?[22] Do not they stand in the same relation to the State, that the State does to the Union? And have not the same reasons prevented the State from resisting the Union, which have prevented them from resisting the State?

How can a man be satisfied to entertain an opinion merely, and enjoy *it?* Is there any enjoyment in it, if his opinion is that he is aggrieved? If you are cheated out of a single dollar by your neighbor, you do not rest satisfied with knowing that you are cheated, or with saying that you are cheated, or even with petitioning him to pay you your due; but you take effectual steps at once to obtain the full amount, and see that you are never cheated again. Action from principle,—the perception and the performance of right,—changes things and relations; it is essentially revo-lutionary, and does not consist wholly with any thing which was. It not only di-vides states and churches, it divides families; aye, it divides the *individual,* sepa-rating the diabolical in him from the divine.

Unjust laws exist: shall we be content to obey them, or shall we endeavor to amend them, and obey them until we have succeeded, or shall we transgress them at once? Men generally, under such a government as this, think that they ought to wait until they have persuaded the majority to alter them. They think that, if they should resist, the remedy would be worse than the evil. But it is the fault of the government itself that the remedy *is* worse than the evil. *It* makes it worse. Why is it not more apt to anticipate and provide for reform? Why does it not cherish its wise minority? Why does it cry and resist before it is hurt? Why does it not en-courage its citizens to be on the alert to point out its faults, and *do* better than it would have them? Why does it always crucify Christ, and excommunicate Coper-nicus and Luther, and pronounce Washington and Franklin rebels?[23]

One would think, that a deliberate and practical denial of its authority was the only offence never contemplated by government; else, why has it not assigned its definite, its suitable and proportionate penalty? If a man who has no property refuses but once to earn nine shillings[24] for the State, he is put in prison for a period unlimited by any law that I know, and determined only by the discretion of those who placed him there; but if he should steal ninety times nine shillings from the State, he is soon permitted to go at large again.

If the injustice is part of the necessary friction of the machine of government, let it go, let it go: perchance it will wear smooth,—certainly the machine will wear out. If the injustice has a spring, or a pulley, or a rope, or a crank, exclu-sively for itself, then perhaps you may consider whether the remedy will not be worse than the evil; but if it is of such a nature that it requires you to be the agent of injustice to another, then, I say, break the law. Let your life be a counter fric-

---

[21] While James K. Polk, U.S. president from 1845 to 1849, sought troops and money for the war with Mexico, radical abolitionists in Massachusetts proposed leaving the Union, as they believed the conflict would expand slaveholding territory.

[22] Thoreau suggests that an individual can on principle secede from a state and refuse to pay taxes to the state treasury (and he later did just that).

[23] Thoreau expands the notion of government to all governing bodies: the Polish astronomer Nicolaus Copernicus (1473–1543) died before he could be excommunicated by the church for maintaining that the earth is not the center of the universe; Martin Luther (1483–1546), the German leader of the Protestant Reformation, was excommunicated for his religious principles; George Washington and Benjamin Franklin were considered rebels by the British government.

[24] The $1.50 that Thoreau had refused to pay as a poll tax (a tax levied on all male citizens between ages twenty and seventy); "shilling" was then a common monetary term in New England, although there was no American coin or bill of that name.

tion[25] to stop the machine. What I have to do is to see, at any rate, that I do not lend myself to the wrong which I condemn.

As for adopting the ways which the State has provided for remedying the evil, I know not of such ways. They take too much time, and a man's life will be gone. I have other affairs to attend to. I came into this world, not chiefly to make this a good place to live in, but to live in it, be it good or bad. A man has not every thing to do, but something; and because he cannot do *every thing*, it is not necessary that he should do *something* wrong. It is not my business to be petitioning the governor or the legislature any more than it is theirs to petition me; and, if they should not hear my petition, what should I do then? But in this case the State has provided no way: its very Constitution is the evil. This may seem to be harsh and stubborn and unconciliatory; but it is to treat with the utmost kindness and consideration the only spirit that can appreciate or deserves it. So is all change for the better, like birth and death which convulse the body.

I do not hesitate to say, that those who call themselves abolitionists should at once effectually withdraw their support, both in person and property, from the government of Massachusetts, and not wait till they constitute a majority of one, before they suffer the right to prevail through them. I think that it is enough if they have God on their side, without waiting for that other one. Moreover, any man more right than his neighbors, constitutes a majority of one already.

I meet this American government, or its representative the State government, directly, and face to face, once a year, no more, in the person of its tax-gatherer; this is the only mode in which a man situated as I am necessarily meets it; and it then says distinctly, Recognize me; and the simplest, the most effectual, and, in the present posture of affairs, the indispensablest mode of treating with it on this head, of expressing your little satisfaction with and love for it, is to deny it then. My civil neighbor, the tax-gather,[26] is the very man I have to deal with,—for it is, after all, with men and not with parchment that I quarrel,—and he has voluntarily chosen to be an agent of the government. How shall he ever know well what he is and does as an officer of the government, or as a man, until he is obliged to consider whether he shall treat me, his neighbor, for whom he has respect, as a neighbor and well-disposed man, or as a maniac and disturber of the peace, and see if he can get over this obstruction to his neighborliness without a ruder and more impetuous thought or speech corresponding with his action? I know this well, that if one thousand, if one hundred, if ten men whom I could name,—if ten *honest* men only,—aye, if *one* HONEST man, in this State of Massachusetts, *ceasing to hold slaves,* were actually to withdraw from this copartnership, and be locked up in the county jail therefor, it would be the abolition of slavery in America. For it matters not how small the beginning may seem to be: what is once well done is done for ever. But we love better to talk about it: that we say is our mission. Reform keeps many scores of newspapers in its service, but not one man. If my esteemed neighbor, the State's ambassador, who will devote his days to the settlement of the question of human rights in the Council Chamber, instead of being threatened with the prisons of Carolina,[27] were to sit down the prisoner of Massachusetts, that State which is so anxious to foist the sin of slavery upon her sister,—though at present she can discover only an act of inhospitality to be the

---

[25] A device that slows moving parts by friction.

[26] Sam Staples, Thoreau's friend and neighbor in Concord.

[27] Samuel Hoar (1778–1856), a Massachusetts senator from Concord, was sent to South Carolina in 1844 to aid African-American seamen from Massachusetts who had been imprisoned in the port of Charleston; he was expelled from Charleston by legal action.

ground of a quarrel with her,—the Legislature would not wholly waive the subject the following winter.

Under a government which imprisons any unjustly, the true place for a just man is also a prison. The proper place to-day, the only place which Massachusetts has provided for her freer and less desponding spirits, is in her prisons, to be put out and locked out of the State by her own act, as they have already put themselves out by their principles. It is there that the fugitive slave, and the Mexican prisoner on parole, and the Indian come to plead the wrongs of his race, should find them; on that separate, but more free and honorable ground, where the State places those who are not *with* her but *against* her,—the only house in a slave-state in which a free man can abide with honor. If any think that their influence would be lost there, and their voices no longer afflict the ear of the State, that they would not be as an enemy within its walls, they do not know by how much truth is stronger than error, nor how much more eloquently and effectively he can combat injustice who has experienced a little in his own person. Cast your whole vote, not a strip of paper merely, but your whole influence. A minority is powerless while it conforms to the majority; it is not even a minority then; but it is irresistible when it clogs by its whole weight. If the alternative is to keep all just men in prison, or give up war and slavery, the State will not hesitate which to choose. If a thousand men were not to pay their tax-bills this year, that would not be a violent and bloody measure, as it would be to pay them, and enable the State to commit violence and shed innocent blood. This is, in fact, the definition of a peaceable revolution, if any such is possible. If the tax-gatherer, or any other public officer, asks me, as one has done, "But what shall I do?" my answer is, "If you really wish to do any thing, resign your office." When the subject has refused allegiance, and the officer has resigned his office, then the revolution is accomplished. But even suppose blood should flow. Is there not a sort of blood shed when the conscience is wounded? Through this wound a man's real manhood and immortality flow out, and he bleeds to an everlasting death. I see this blood flowing now.

I have contemplated the imprisonment of the offender, rather than the seizure of his goods,—though both will serve the same purpose,—because they who assert the purest right, and consequently are most dangerous to a corrupt State, commonly have not spent much time in accumulating property. To such the State renders comparatively small service, and a slight tax is wont to appear exorbitant, particularly if they are obliged to earn it by special labor with their hands. If there were one who lived wholly without the use of money, the State itself would hesitate to demand it of him. But the rich man—not to make any invidious comparison—is always sold to the institution which makes him rich. Absolutely speaking, the more money, the less virtue; for money comes between a man and his objects, and obtains them for him; and it was certainly no great virtue to obtain it. It puts to rest many questions which he would otherwise be taxed to answer; while the only new question which it puts is the hard but superfluous one, how to spend it. Thus his moral ground is taken from under his feet. The opportunities of living are diminished in proportion as what are called the "means" are increased. The best thing a man can do for his culture when he is rich is to endeavour to carry out those schemes which he entertained when he was poor. Christ answered the Herodians[28] according to their condition. "Show me the tribute-money," said

[28] Officials of Herod, a king of Judea, who were used in an attempt to trick Jesus into defying the law.

he;—and one took a penny out of his pocket;—if you use money which has the image of Cæsar on it, and which he has made current and valuable, that is, *if you are men of the State,* and gladly enjoy the advantages of Cæsar's government, then pay him back some of his own when he demands it; "Render therefore to Cæsar that which is Cæsar's, and to God those things which are God's,"[29]— leaving them no wiser than before as to which was which; for they did not wish to know.

When I converse with the freest of my neighbors, I perceive that, whatever they may say about the magnitude and seriousness of the question, and their regard for the public tranquility, the long and the short of the matter is, that they cannot spare the protection of the existing government, and they dread the consequences of disobedience to it to their property and families. For my own part, I should not like to think that I ever rely on the protection of the State. But, if I deny the authority of the State when it presents its tax-bill, it will soon take and waste all my property, and so harass me and my children without end. This is hard. This makes it impossible for a man to live honestly and at the same time comfortably in outward respects. It will not be worth the while to accumulate property; that would be sure to go again. You must hire[30] or squat somewhere, and raise but a small crop, and eat that soon. You must live within yourself, and depend upon yourself, always tucked up and ready for a start, and not have many affairs. A man may grow rich in Turkey even, if he will be in all respects a good subject of the Turkish government. Confucius said,—"If a State is governed by the principles of reason, poverty and misery are subjects of shame; if a State is not governed by the principles of reason, riches and honors are the subjects of shame."[31] No: until I want the protection of Massachusetts to be extended to me in some distant southern port, where my liberty is endangered, or until I am bent solely on building up an estate at home by peaceful enterprise, I can afford to refuse allegiance to Massachusetts, and her right to my property and life. It costs me less in every sense to incur the penalty of disobedience to the State, than it would to obey. I should feel as if I were worth less in that case.

Some years ago, the State met me in behalf of the church, and commanded me to pay a certain sum toward the support of a clergyman whose preaching my father attended, but never I myself.[32] "Pay it," it said, "or be locked up in the jail." I declined to pay. But, unfortunately, another man saw fit to pay it. I did not see why the schoolmaster should be taxed to support the priest, and not the priest the schoolmaster; for I was not the State's schoolmaster, but I supported myself by voluntary subscription. I did not see why the lyceum[33] should not present its tax-bill, and have the State to back its demand, as well as the church. However, at the request of the selectmen, I condescended to make some such statement as this in writing:—"Know all men by these presents, that I, Henry Thoreau, do not wish to be regarded as a member of any incorporated society which I have not joined." This I gave to the town-clerk; and he has it. The State, having thus learned that I did not wish to be regarded as a member of that church, has never made a like demand on me since; though it said that it must adhere to its original presumption that time. If I had know how to name them, I should then have signed off in detail

---

[29] From Matthew 22:16–21.   [30] Rent.
[31] From the *Analects* (Bk. 13, Ch. 8) of the Chinese philosopher Confucius (551–479? B.C.).
[32] At the time in Massachusetts, local governments collected taxes for churches.
[33] The Concord Lyceum.

from all the societies which I never signed on to; but I did not know where to find a complete list.

I have paid no poll-tax for six years. I was put into a jail once on this account, for one night;[34] and, as I stood considering the walls of solid stone, two or three feet thick, the door of wood and iron, a foot thick, and the iron grating which strained the light, I could not help being struck with the foolishness of that institution which treated me as if I were mere flesh and blood and bones, to be locked up. I wondered that it should have concluded at length that this was the best use it could put me to, and had never thought to avail itself of my services in some way. I saw that, if there was a wall of stone between me and my townsmen, there was a still more difficult one to climb or break through, before they could get to be as free as I was. I did not for a moment feel confined, and the walls seemed a great waste of stone and mortar. I felt as if I alone of all my townsmen had paid my tax. They plainly did not know how to treat me, but behaved like persons who are underbred. In every threat and in every compliment there was a blunder; for they thought that my chief desire was to stand the other side of that stone wall. I could not but smile to see how industriously they locked the door on my meditations, which followed them out again without let or hinderance, and *they* were really all that was dangerous. As they could not reach me, they had resolved to punish my body; just as boys, if they cannot come at some person against whom they have a spite, will abuse his dog. I saw that the State was half-witted, that it was timid as a lone woman with her silver spoons, and that it did not know its friends from its foes, and I lost all my remaining respect for it, and pitied it.

Thus the State never intentionally confronts a man's sense, intellectual or moral, but only his body, his senses. It is not armed with superior wit or honesty, but with superior physical strength. I was not born to be forced. I will breathe after my own fashion. Let us see who is the strongest. What force has a multitude? They only can force me who obey a higher law than I. They force me to become like themselves. I do not hear of *men* being *forced* to live this way or that by masses of men. What sort of life were that to live? When I meet a government which says to me, "Your money or your life," why should I be in haste to give it my money? It may be in a great strait, and not know what to do: I cannot help that. It must help itself; do as I do. It is not worth the while to snivel about it. I am not responsible for the successful working of the machinery of society. I am not the son of the engineer. I perceive that, when an acorn and a chestnut fall side by side, the one does not remain inert to make way for the other, but both obey their own laws, and spring and grow and flourish as best they can, till one, perchance, overshadows and destroys the other. If a plant cannot live according to its nature, it dies; and so a man.

The night in prison was novel and interesting enough. The prisoners in their shirt-sleeves were enjoying a chat and the evening air in the door-way, when I entered. But the jailer[35] said, "Come, boys, it is time to lock up;" and so they dispersed, and I heard the sound of their steps returning into the hollow apartments. My room-mate was introduced to me by the jailer, as "a first-rate fellow and a clever[36] man." When the door was locked, he showed me where to hang my hat, and how he managed matters there. The rooms were whitewashed once a month; and this one, at least,

---

[34] On July 23 or 24, 1846, Thoreau spent a night in the Middlesex County jail in Concord.
[35] Sam Staples.   [36] Honest.

was the whitest, most simply furnished, and probably the neatest apartment in the town. He naturally wanted to know where I came from, and what brought me there; and, when I had told him, I asked him in my turn how he came there, presuming him to be an honest man, of course; and, as the world goes, I believe he was. "Why," said he, "they accused me of burning a barn; but I never did it." As near as I could discover, he had probably gone to bed in a barn when drunk, and smoked his pipe there; and so a barn was burnt. He had the reputation of being a clever man, had been there some three months waiting for his trial to come on, and would have to wait as much longer; but he was quite domesticated and contented, since he got his board for nothing, and thought that he was well treated.

He occupied one window, and I the other; and I saw, that, if one stayed there long, his principal business would be to look out the window. I had soon read all the tracts that were left there, and examined where former prisoners had broken out, and where a grate had been sawed off, and heard the history of the various occupants of that room; for I found that even here there was a history and a gossip which never circulated beyond the walls of the jail. Probably this is the only house in the town where verses are composed, which are afterward printed in a circular form, but not published. I was shown quite a long list of verses which were composed by some young men who had been detected in an attempt to escape, who avenged themselves by singing them.

I pumped my fellow-prisoner as dry as I could, for fear I should never see him again; but at length he showed me which was my bed, and left me to blow out the lamp.

It was like travelling into a far country, such as I had never expected to behold, to lie there for one night. It seemed to me that I never had heard the town-clock strike before, nor the evening sounds of the village; for we slept with the windows open, which were inside the grating. It was to see my native village in the light of the middle ages, and our Concord was turned into a Rhine stream, and visions of knights and castles passed before me. They were the voices of old burghers that I heard in the streets. I was an involuntary spectator and auditor of whatever was done and said in the kitchen of the adjacent village-inn,—a wholly new and rare experience to me. It was a closer view of my native town. I was fairly inside of it. I never had seen its institutions before. This is one of its peculiar institutions; for it is a shire town.[37] I began to comprehend what its inhabitants were about.

In the morning, our breakfasts were put through the hole in the door, in small oblong-square tin pans, made to fit, and holding a pint of chocolate, with brown bread, and an iron spoon. When they called for the vessels again, I was green enough to return what bread I had left; but my comrade seized it, and said that I should lay that up for lunch or dinner. Soon after, he was let out to work at haying in a neighboring field, whither he went every day, and would not be back till noon; so he bade me good-day, saying that he doubted if he should see me again.

When I came out of prison,—for some one interfered, and paid the tax,[38]—I did not perceive that great changes had taken place on the common, such as he observed who went in a youth, and emerged a tottering and gray-headed man; and yet a change had to my eyes come over the scene,—the town, and State, and country,—greater than any that mere time could effect. I saw yet more distinctly the State in which I lived. I saw to what extent the people among whom I lived could be trusted

---

[37] A county seat.

[38] It is not know for certain who paid Thoreau's tax, but his aunt Maria has been suggested.

as good neighbors and friends; that their friendship was for summer weather only; that they did not greatly purpose to do right; that they were a distinct race from me by their prejudices and superstitions, as the Chinamen and Malays are; that, in their sacrifices to humanity, they ran no risks, not even to their property; that, after all, they were not so noble but they treated the thief as he had treated them, and hoped, by a certain outward observance and a few prayers, and by walking in a particular straight though useless path from time to time, to save their souls. This may be to judge my neighbors harshly; for I believe that most of them are not aware that they have such an institution as the jail in their village.

It was formerly the custom in our village, when a poor debtor came out of jail, for his acquaintances to salute him, looking through their fingers, which were crossed to represent the grating of a jail window, "How do ye do?" My neighbors did not thus salute me, but first looked at me, and then at one another, as if I had returned from a long journey. I was put into jail as I was going to the shoemaker's to get a shoe which was mended. When I was let out the next morning, I proceeded to finish my errand, and, having put on my mended shoe, joined a huckleberry party, who were impatient to put themselves under my conduct; and in half an hour,—for the horse was soon tackled,[39]—was in the midst of a huckleberry field, on one of our highest hills, two miles off; and then the State was nowhere to be seen.

This is the whole history of "My Prisons."[40]

I have never declined paying the highway tax, because I am as desirous of being a good neighbor as I am of being a bad subject; and, as for supporting schools, I am doing my part to educate my fellow-countrymen now. It is for no particular item in the tax-bill that I refuse to pay it. I simply wish to refuse allegiance to the State, to withdraw and stand aloof from it effectually. I do not care to trace the course of my dollar, if I could, till it buys a man, or a musket to shoot one with,—the dollar is innocent,—but I am concerned to trace the effects of my allegiance. In fact, I quietly declare war with the State, after my fashion, though I will still make what use and get what advantage of her I can, as is usual in such cases.

If others pay the tax which is demanded of me, from a sympathy with the State, they do but what they have already done in their own case, or rather they abet injustice to a greater extent than the State requires. If they pay the tax from a mistaken interest in the individual taxed, to save his property or prevent his going to jail, it is because they have not considered wisely how far they let their private feelings interfere with the public good.

This, then, is my position at present. But one cannot be too much on his guard in such a case, lest his action be biassed by obstinacy, or an undue regard for the opinions of men. Let him see that he does only what belongs to himself and to the hour.

I think sometimes, Why, this people mean well; they are only ignorant; they would do better if they knew how: why give your neighbors this pain to treat you as they are not inclined to? But I think, again, this is no reason why I should do as they do, or permit others to suffer much greater pain of a different kind. Again, I sometimes say to myself, When many millions of men, without heat, without

---

[39] Harnessed.

[40] A droll reference to the autobiography (1832) of the Italian poet Silvio Pellico (1789–1854), who spent years in Austrian prisons for fighting against the Austrian occupation of Italy.

ill-will, without personal feeling of any kind, demand of you a few shillings only, without the possibility, such is their constitution, of retracting or altering their present demand, and without the possibility, on your side, of appeal to any other millions, why expose yourself to this overwhelming brute force? You do not resist cold and hunger, the winds and the waves, thus obstinately; you quietly submit to a thousand similar necessities. You do not put your head into the fire. But just in proportion as I regard this as not wholly a brute force, but partly a human force, and consider that I have relations to those millions as to so many millions of men, and not of mere brute or inanimate things, I see that appeal is possible, first and instantaneously, from them to the Maker of them, and, secondly, from them to themselves. But, if I put my head deliberately into the fire, there is no appeal to fire or to the Maker of fire, and I have only myself to blame. If I could convince myself that I have any right to be satisfied with men as they are, and to treat them accordingly, and not according, in some respects, to my requisitions and expectations of what they and I ought to be, then, like a good Mussulman[41] and fatalist, I should endeavor to be satisfied with things as they are, and say it is the will of God. And, above all, there is this difference between resisting this and a purely brute or natural force, that I can resist this with some effect; but I cannot expect, like Orpheus,[42] to change the nature of the rocks and trees and beasts.

I do not wish to quarrel with any man or nation. I do not wish to split hairs, to make fine distinctions, or set myself up as better than my neighbors. I seek rather, I may say, even an excuse for conforming to the laws of the land. I am but too ready to conform to them. Indeed I have reason to suspect myself on this head;[43] and each year, as the tax-gatherer comes round, I find myself disposed to review the acts and position of the general and state governments, and the spirit of the people, to discover a pretext for conformity. I believe that the State will soon be able to take all my work of this sort out of my hands, and then I shall be no better a patriot than my fellow-countrymen. Seen from a lower point of view, the Constitution, with all its faults, is very good; the law and the courts are very respectable; even this State and this American government are, in many respects, very admirable and rare things, to be thankful for, such as a great many have described them; but seen from a point of view a little higher, they are what I have described them; seen from a higher still, and the highest, who shall say what they are, or that they are worth looking at or thinking of at all?

However, the government does not concern me much, and I shall bestow the fewest possible thoughts on it. It is not many moments that I live under a government, even in this world. If a man is thought-free, fancy-free, imagination-free, that which *is not* never for a long time appearing *to be* to him, unwise rulers or reformers cannot fatally interrupt him.

I know that most men think differently from myself; but those whose lives are by profession devoted to the study of these or kindred subjects, content me as little as any. Statesmen and legislators, standing so completely within the institution, never distinctly and nakedly behold it. They speak of moving society, but have no resting-place without it. They may be men of a certain experience and discrimination, and have no doubt invented ingenious and even useful systems, for which we sincerely thank them; but all their wit and usefulness lie within certain not very

[41] Moslem.

[42] According to Greek myth, a musician who played the lyre so wondrously that animate things and inanimate objects were charmed and changed.

[43] Point.

wide limits. They are wont to forget that the world is not governed by policy and expediency. Webster[44] never goes behind government, and so cannot speak with authority about it. His words are wisdom to those legislators who contemplate no essential reform in the existing government; but for thinkers, and those who legislate for all time, he never once glances at the subject. I know of those whose serene and wise speculations on this theme would soon reveal the limits of his mind's range and hospitality. Yet, compared with the cheap professions of most reformers, and the still cheaper wisdom and eloquence of politicians in general, his are almost the only sensible and valuable words, and we thank Heaven for him. Comparatively, he is always strong, original, and, above all, practical. Still his quality is not wisdom, but prudence. The lawyer's truth is not Truth, but consistency, or a consistent expediency. Truth is always in harmony with herself, and is not concerned chiefly to reveal the justice that may consist with wrong-doing. He well deserves to be called, as he has been called, the Defender of the Constitution. There are really no blows to be given by him but defensive ones. He is not a leader, but a follower. His leaders are the men of '87.[45] "I have never made an effort," he says, "and never propose to make an effort; I have never countenanced an effort, and never mean to countenance an effort, to disturb the arrangement as originally made, by which the various States came into the Union."[46] Still thinking of the sanction which the Constitution gives to slavery, he says, "Because it was a part of the original compact,—let it stand." Notwithstanding his special acuteness and ability, he is unable to take a fact out of its merely political relations, and behold it as it lies absolutely to be disposed of by the intellect,—what, for instance, it beho[o]ves a man to do here in America to-day with regard to slavery,—but ventures, or is driven, to make some such desperate answer as the following, while professing to speak absolutely, and as a private man,—from which what new and singular code of social duties might be inferred?—"The manner," says he, "in which the governments of those States where slavery exists are to regulate it, is for their own consideration, under their responsibility to their constituents, to the general laws of propriety, humanity, and justice, and to God. Associations formed elsewhere, springing from a feeling of humanity, or any other cause, have nothing whatever to do with it. They have never received any encouragement from me, and they never will."[47]

They who know of no purer sources of truth, who have traced up its stream no higher, stand, and wisely stand, by the Bible and the Constitution, and drink at it there with reverence and humility; but they who behold where it comes trickling into this lake or that pool, gird up their loins once more, and continue their pilgrimage toward its fountain-head.

No man with a genius for legislation has appeared in America. They are rare in the history of the world. There are orators, politicians, and eloquent men, by the thousand; but the speaker has not yet opened his mouth to speak, who is capable of settling the much-vexed questions of the day. We love eloquence for its own

[44] Daniel Webster (1782–1852), a U.S. senator from Massachusetts who angered abolitionists with his support of the Fugitive Slave Act, which required the return of escaped slaves. Here Thoreau bemoans the fact that Webster considers the American Constitution to be the ultimate authority even on moral issues.

[45] The drafters of the Constitution in 1787.

[46] From Webster's speech on "The Admission of Texas" (December 22, 1845).

[47] Thoreau's note: "These extracts have been inserted since the Lecture was read." Thoreau quotes from speeches given by Webster in 1845 and 1848.

sake, and not for any truth which it may utter, or any heroism it may inspire. Our legislators have not yet learned the comparative value of free-trade and of freedom, of union, and of rectitude, to a nation. They have no genius or talent for comparatively humble questions of taxation and finance, commerce and manufactures and agriculture. If we were left solely to the wordy wit of legislators in Congress for our guidance, uncorrected by the seasonable experience and the effectual complaints of the people, America would not long retain her rank among the nations. For eighteen hundred years, though perchance I have no right to say it, the New Testament has been written; yet where is the legislator who has wisdom and practical talent enough to avail himself of the light which it sheds on the science of legislation?

The authority of government, even such as I am willing to submit to,—for I will cheerfully obey those who know and can do better than I, and in many things even those who neither know nor can do so well,—is still an impure one: to be strictly just, it must have the sanction and consent of the governed. It can have no pure right over my person and property but what I concede to it. The progress from an absolute to a limited monarchy, from a limited monarchy to a democracy, is a progress toward a true respect for the individual. Is a democracy, such as we know it, the last improvement possible in government? Is it not possible to take a step further towards recognizing and organizing the rights of man? There will never be a really free and enlightened State, until the State comes to recognize the individual as a higher and independent power, from which all its own power and authority are derived, and treats him accordingly. I please myself with imagining a State at last which can afford to be just to all men, and to treat the individual with respect as a neighbor; which even would not think it inconsistent with its own repose, if a few were to live aloof from it, not meddling with it, nor embraced by it, who fulfilled all the duties of neighbors and fellow-men. A State which bore this kind of fruit, and suffered it to drop off as fast as it ripened, would prepare the way for a still more perfect and glorious State, which also I have imagined, but not yet anywhere seen.

1849

WALDEN*

I: ECONOMY

When I wrote the following pages, or rather the bulk of them, I lived alone, in the woods, a mile from any neighbor, in a house which I had built myself, on the shore of Walden Pond, in Concord, Massachusetts, and earned my living by the labor of my hands only. I lived there two years and two months. At present I am a sojourner in civilized life again.

* First published in 1854 as *Walden, or Life in the Woods,* with Thoreau's epigraph: "I do not propose to write an ode to dejection, but to brag as lustily as chanticleer [the rooster in the medieval epic *Reynard the Fox*] in the morning, standing on his roost, if only to wake my neighbors up." While living at Walden Pond, near Concord, Massachusetts, from July 4, 1845, to September 6, 1847, Thoreau wrote *A Week on the Concord and Merrimack Rivers* (1849) and a substantial part of *Walden,* which he revised and completed between 1849 and 1854.

I should not obtrude my affairs so much on the notice of my readers if very particular inquiries had not been made by my townsmen concerning my mode of life, which some would call impertinent, though they do not appear to me at all impertinent, but, considering the circumstances, very natural and pertinent. Some have asked what I got to eat; if I did not feel lonesome; if I was not afraid; and the like. Others have been curious to learn what portion of my income I devoted to charitable purposes; and some, who have large families, how many poor children I maintained. I will therefore ask those of my readers who feel no particular interest in me to pardon me if I undertake to answer some of these questions in this book. In most books, the *I*, or first person, is omitted; in this it will be retained; that, in respect to egotism, is the main difference. We commonly do not remember that it is, after all, always the first person that is speaking. I should not talk so much about myself if there were any body else whom I knew as well. Unfortunately, I am confined to this theme by the narrowness of my experience. Moreover, I, on my side, require of every writer, first or last, a simple and sincere account of his own life, and not merely what he has heard of other men's lives; some such account as he would send to his kindred from a distant land; for if he has lived sincerely, it must have been in a distant land to me. Perhaps these pages are more particularly addressed to poor students. As for the rest of my readers, they will accept such portions as apply to them. I trust that none will stretch the seams in putting on the coat, for it may do good service to him whom it fits.

I would fain say something, not so much concerning the Chinese and Sandwich Islanders[1] as you who read these pages, who are said to live in New England; something about your condition, especially your outward condition or circumstances in this world, in this town, what it is, whether it is necessary that it be as bad as it is, whether it cannot be improved as well as not. I have travelled a good deal in Concord; and every where, in shops, and offices, and fields, the inhabitants have appeared to me to be doing penance in a thousand remarkable ways. What I have heard of Brahmins[2] sitting exposed to four fires and looking in the face of the sun; or hanging suspended, with their heads downward, over flames; or looking at the heavens over their shoulders "until it becomes impossible for them to resume their natural position, while from the twist of the neck nothing but liquids can pass into the stomach;" or dwelling, chained for life, at the foot of a tree; or measuring with their bodies, like caterpillars, the breadth of vast empires; or standing on one leg on the tops of pillars,—even these forms of conscious penance are hardly more incredible and astonishing than the scenes which I daily witness. The twelve labors of Hercules[3] were trifling in comparison with those which my neighbors have undertaken; for they were only twelve, and had an end; but I could never see that these men slew or captured any monster or finished any labor. They have no friend Iolas to burn with a hot iron the root of the hydra's head, but as soon as one head is crushed, two spring up.

I see young men, my townsmen, whose misfortune it is to have inherited farms, houses, barns, cattle, and farming tools; for these are more easily acquired than got rid of. Better if they had been born in the open pasture and suckled by a

[1] Hawaiians.

[2] Members of the highest Hindu caste; the source of Thoreau's information has not been identified.

[3] According to Greek myth, Hercules was assigned twelve purifying labors; one was to slay the nine-headed monster Hydra, which he did with his friend Iolas: as Hercules cut off each head, Iolas seared the stump so a new head could not grow back.

wolf,[4] that they might have seen with clearer eyes what field they were called to labor in. Who made them serfs of the soil? Why should they eat their sixty acres, when man is condemned to eat only his peck of dirt? Why should they begin digging their graves as soon as they are born? They have got to live a man's life, pushing all these things before them, and get on as well as they can. How many a poor immortal soul have I met well nigh crushed and smothered under its load, creeping down the road of life, pushing before it a barn seventy-five feet by forty, its Augean stables[5] never cleansed, and one hundred acres of land, tillage, mowing, pasture and wood-lot! The portionless, who struggle with no such unnecessary inherited encumbrances, find it labor enough to subdue and cultivate a few cubic feet of flesh.

But men labor under a mistake. The better part of the man is soon ploughed into the soil for compost. By a seeming fate, commonly called necessity, they are employed, as it says in an old book,[6] laying up treasures which moth and rust will corrupt and thieves break through and steal. It is a fool's life, as they will find when they get to the end of it, if not before. It is said that Deucalion and Pyrrha[7] created men by throwing stones over their heads behind them:—

> Inde genus durum sumus, experiensque laborum,
> Et documenta damus quâ simus origine nati.

Or, as Raleigh rhymes it in his sonorous way,—

> "From thence our kind hard-hearted is, enduring
>   pain and care,
> Approving that our bodies of a stony nature are."[8]

So much for a blind obedience to a blundering oracle, throwing the stones over their heads behind them, and not seeing where they fell.

Most men, even in this comparatively free country, through mere ignorance and mistake, are so occupied with the factitious cares and superfluously coarse labors of life that its finer fruits cannot be plucked by them. Their fingers, from excessive toil, are too clumsy and tremble too much for that. Actually, the laboring man has not leisure for a true integrity day by day; he cannot afford to sustain the manliest relations to men; his labor would be depreciated in the market. He has no time to be any thing but a machine. How can he remember well his ignorance—which his growth requires—who has so often to use his knowledge? We should feed and clothe him gratuitously sometimes, and recruit him with our cor-

---

[4] According to Roman myth, Romulus and Remus, the founders of Rome, were suckled by a she-wolf.

[5] One of Hercules' labors was to clean in one day the stables in which three thousand oxen had been kept for thirty years by King Augeas (Hercules diverted two rivers through the stables).

[6] The Bible; Thoreau then paraphrases Matthew 6:19.

[7] According to Greek myth, Deucalion and his wife, Pyrrha, survived a great flood sent by Zeus, the supreme god; to repeople the earth, they threw stones over their shoulders: the stones thrown by Deucalion became men, and those thrown by Pyrrha became women.

[8] From the *Metamorphoses* of the Roman poet Ovid (43 B.C.–A.D. 18); translated from Latin in *The History of the World* (1614), by Sir Walter Raleigh (1554?–1618), an English soldier, courtier, and man of letters.

dials,[9] before we judge of him. The finest qualities of our nature, like the bloom on fruits, can be preserved only by the most delicate handling. Yet we do not treat ourselves nor one another thus tenderly.

Some of you, we all know, are poor, find it hard to live, are sometimes, as it were, gasping for breath. I have no doubt that some of you who read this book are unable to pay for all the dinners which you have actually eaten, or for the coats and shoes which are fast wearing or are already worn out, and have come to this page to spend borrowed or stolen time, robbing your creditors of an hour. It is very evident what mean and sneaking lives many of you live, for my sight has been whetted by experience; always on the limits, trying to get into business and trying to get out of debt, a very ancient slough, called by the Latins, *æs alienum,* another's brass,[10] for some of their coins were made of brass; still living, and dying, and buried by this other's brass; always promising to pay, promising to pay, to-morrow, and dying to-day, insolvent; seeking to curry favor, to get custom,[11] by how many modes, only not state-prison offences; lying, flattering, voting, contracting yourselves into a nutshell of civility, or dilating into an atmosphere of thin and vaporous generosity, that you may persuade your neighbor to let you make his shoes, or his hat, or his coat, or his carriage, or import his groceries for him; making yourselves sick, that you may lay up something against a sick day, something to be tucked away in an old chest, or in a stocking behind the plastering, or, more safely, in the brick bank; no matter where, no matter how much or how little.

I sometimes wonder that we can be so frivolous, I may almost say, as to attend to the gross but somewhat foreign form of servitude called Negro Slavery, there are so many keen and subtle masters that enslave both north and south. It is hard to have a southern overseer; it is worse to have a northern one; but worst of all when you are the slave-driver of yourself. Talk of a divinity in man! Look at the teamster on the highway, wending to market by day or night; does any divinity stir within him? His highest duty to fodder and water his horses! What is his destiny to him compared with the shipping interests? Does not he drive for Squire Make-a-stir?[12] How godlike, how immortal, is he? See how he cowers and sneaks, how vaguely all the day he fears, not being immortal nor divine, but the slave and prisoner of his own opinion of himself, a fame won by his own deeds. Public opinion is a weak tyrant compared with our own private opinion. What a man thinks of himself, that it is which determines, or rather indicates, his fate. Self-emancipation even in the West Indian provinces of the fancy and imagaination,—what Wilberforce,[13] is there to bring that about? Think, also, of the ladies of the land weaving toilet cushions,[14] against the last day, not to betray too green an interest in their fates! As if you could kill time without injuring eternity.

The mass of men lead lives of quiet desperation. What is called resignation is confirmed desperation. From the desperate city you go into the desperate country, and have to console yourself with the bravery of minks and muskrats. A stereotyped but unconscious despair is concealed even under what are called the games

---

[9] Invigorate him with our medicines and liqueurs.   [10] Somebody else's money (Latin).

[11] Business.   [12] An allegorical name.

[13] William Wilberforce (1759–1833), a British statesman and humanitarian instrumental in outlawing the slave trade (1807) and in abolishing slavery in the British Empire (1833). Thoreau's habit of internalizing geography is apparent here.

[14] Embroidered cushions used in ladies' dressing rooms.

and amusements of mankind. There is no play in them, for this comes after work. But it is a characteristic of wisdom not to do desperate things.

When we consider what, to use the words of the catechism,[15] is the chief end of man, and what are the true necessaries and means of life, it appears as if men had deliberately chosen the common mode of living because they preferred it to any other. Yet they honestly think there is no choice left. But alert and healthy natures remember that the sun rose clear. It is never too late to give up our prejudices. No way of thinking or doing, however ancient, can be trusted without proof. What every body echoes or in silence passes by as true to-day may turn out to be false-hood to-morrow, mere smoke of opinion, which some had trusted for a cloud that would sprinkle fertilizing rain on their fields. What old people say you cannot do you try and find that you can. Old deeds for old people, and new deeds for new. Old people did not know enough once, perchance, to fetch fresh fuel to keep the fire a-going; new people put a little dry wood under a pot,[16] and are whirled round the globe with the speed of birds, in a way to kill old people, as the phrase is. Age is no better, hardly so well, qualified for an instructor as youth, for it has not profited so much as it has lost. One may almost doubt if the wisest man has learned any thing of absolute value by living. Practically, the old have no very important advice to give the young, their own experience has been so partial, and their lives have been such miserable failures, for private reasons, as they must believe; and it may be that they have some faith left which belies that experience, and they are only less young than they were. I have lived some thirty years on this planet, and I have yet to hear the first syllable of valuable or even earnest advice from my seniors. They have told me nothing, and probably cannot tell me any thing, to the purpose. Here is life, an experiment to a great extent untried by me; but it does not avail me that they have tried it. If I have any experience which I think valuable, I am sure to reflect that this my Mentors[17] said nothing about.

One farmer says to me, "You cannot live on vegetable food solely, for it fur-nishes nothing to make bones with;" and so he religiously devotes a part of his day to supplying his system with the raw material of bones; walking all the while he talks behind his oxen, which, with vegetable-made bones, jerk him and his lum-bering plough along in spite of every obstacle. Some things are really necessaries of life in some circles, the most helpless and diseased, which in others are luxuries merely, and in others still are entirely unknown.

The whole ground of human life seems to some to have been gone over by their predecessors, both the heights and the valleys, and all things to have been cared for. According to Evelyn,[18] "the wise Solomon prescribed ordinances for the very distances of trees; and the Roman prætors have decided how often you may go into your neighbor's land to gather the acorns which fall on it without trespass, and what share belongs to that neighbor." Hippocrates[19] has even left directions how we should cut our nails; that is, even with the ends of the fingers, neither

---

[15] The Westminster Catechism in the *New England Primer* taught colonial children that the "chief end of man . . . is to glorify God and to enjoy him forever."

[16] Under the boiler of a steam engine.

[17] Derived from Mentor, the teacher of Odysseus's son, Telemachus, in Homer's *Odyssey*.

[18] John Evelyn (1620–1706), a noted English diarist and author of *Sylva* (1644), a book on growing trees. Praetors were Roman officials with judicial duties.

[19] Hippocrates (460?–377? B.C.) was a renowned Greek physician whose treatises include "Air, Earth, and Locality," which deals with the effect of environment on health.

shorter nor longer. Undoubtedly the very tedium and ennui which presume to have exhausted the variety and the joys of life are as old as Adam. But man's capacities have never been measured; nor are we to judge of what he can do by any precedents, so little has been tried. Whatever have been thy failures hitherto, "be not afflicted, my child, for who shall. . .assign to thee what thou hast left undone?"[20]

We might try our lives by a thousand simple tests; as, for instance, that the same sun which ripens my beans illumines at once a system of earths like ours. If I had remembered this it would have prevented some mistakes. This was not the light in which I hoed them. The stars are the apexes of what wonderful triangles! What distant and different beings in the various mansions of the universe are contemplating the same one at the same moment! Nature and human life are as various as our several constitutions. Who shall say what prospect life offers to another? Could a greater miracle take place than for us to look through each other's eyes for an instant? We should live in all the ages of the world in an hour; ay, in all the worlds of the ages. History, Poetry, Mythology!—I know of no reading of another's experience so startling and informing as this would be.

The greater part of what my neighbors call good I believe in my soul to be bad, and if I repent of any thing, it is very likely to be my good behavior. What demon possessed me that I behaved so well? You may say the wisest thing you can old man,—you who have lived seventy years, not without honor of a kind,—I hear an irresistible voice which invites me away from all that. One generation abandons the enterprises of another like stranded vessels.

I think that we may safely trust a good deal more than we do. We may waive just so much care of ourselves as we honestly bestow elsewhere. Nature is as well adapted to our weakness as to our strength. The incessant anxiety and strain of some is a well nigh incurable form of disease. We are made to exaggerate the importance of what work we do; and yet how much is not done by us! or, what if we had been taken sick? How vigilant we are! determined not to live by faith if we can avoid it; all the day long on the alert, at night we unwillingly say our prayers and commit ourselves to uncertainties. So thoroughly and sincerely are we compelled to live, reverencing our life, and denying the possibility of change. This is the only way, we say; but there are as many ways as there can be drawn radii from one centre. All change is a miracle to contemplate; but it is a miracle which is taking place every instant. Confucius said, "To know that we know what we know, and that we do not know what we do not know, that is true knowledge."[21] When one man has reduced a fact of the imagination to be a fact to his understanding, I foresee that all men will at length establish their lives on that basis.

Let us consider for a moment what most of the trouble and anxiety which I have referred to is about, and how much it is necessary that we be troubled, or, at least, careful. It would be some advantage to live a primitive and frontier life, though in the midst of an outward civilization, if only to learn what are the gross necessaries of life and what methods have been taken to obtain them; or even to look over the old day-books of the merchants, to see what it was that men most commonly bought at the stores, what they stored, that is, what are the grossest groceries. For the improvements of ages have had but little influence on the essential laws of

[20] From the *Vishnu Purana*, a Hindu religious text.
[21] From the *Analects* (Bk. II, Ch. 17) of the Chinese philosopher Confucius (551?–479 B.C.).

man's existence; as our skeletons, probably, are not to be distinguished from those of our ancestors.

By the words, *necessary of life,* I mean whatever, of all that man obtains by his own exertions, has been from the first, or from long use has become, so important to human life that few, if any, whether from savageness, or poverty, or philosophy, ever attempt to do without it. To many creatures there is in this sense but one necessary of life, Food. To the bison of the prairie it is a few inches of palatable grass, with water to drink; unless he seeks the Shelter of the forest or the mountain's shadow. None of the brute creation requires more than Food and Shelter. The necessaries of life for man in this climate may, accurately enough, be distributed under the several heads of Food, Shelter, Clothing, and Fuel; for not till we have secured these are we prepared to entertain the true problems of life with freedom and a prospect of success. Man has invented, not only houses, but clothes and cooked food; and possibly from the accidental discovery of the warmth of fire, and the consequent use of it, at first a luxury, arose the present necessity to sit by it. We observe cats and dogs acquiring the same second nature. By proper Shelter and Clothing we legitimately retain our own internal heat; but with an excess of these, or of Fuel, that is, with an external heat greater than our own internal, may not cookery properly be said to begin? Darwin, the naturalist, says of the inhabitants of Tierra del Fuego,[22] that while his own party, who were well clothed and sitting close to a fire, were far from too warm, these naked savages, who were farther off, were observed, to his great surprise, "to be streaming with perspiration at undergoing such a roasting." So, we are told, the New Hollander[23] goes naked with impunity, while the European shivers in his clothes. Is it impossible to combine the hardiness of these savages with the intellectualness of the civilized man? According to Liebig,[24] man's body is a stove, and food the fuel which keeps up the internal combustion in the lungs. In cold weather we eat more, in warm less. The animal heat is the result of a slow combustion, and disease and death take place when this is too rapid; or for want of fuel, or from some defect in the draught, the fire goes out. Of course the vital heat is not to be confounded with fire; but so much for analogy. It appears, therefore, from the above list, that the expression, *animal life,* is nearly synonymous with the expression, *animal heat;* for while Food may be regarded as the Fuel which keeps up the fire within us,— and Fuel serves only to prepare that Food or to increase the warmth of our bodies by addition from without,—Shelter and Clothing also serve only to retain the *heat* thus generated and absorbed.

The grand necessity, then, for our bodies, is to keep warm, to keep the vital heat in us. What pains we accordingly take, not only with our Food, and Clothing, and Shelter, but with our beds, which are our night-clothes, robbing the nests and breasts of birds to prepare this shelter within a shelter, as the mole has its bed of grass and leaves at the end of its burrow! The poor man is wont to complain that this is a cold world; and to cold, no less physical than social, we refer directly a great part of our ails. The summer, in some climates, makes possible to man a sort of Elysian[25] life. Fuel, except to cook his Food, is then unnecessary; the sun is his fire, and many of the fruits are sufficiently cooked by its rays; while Food gener-

---

[22] Charles Darwin (1809–1882) describes the inhabitants of Tierra del Fuego, at the southern tip of South America, in his *Journal of Researches* (1839).

[23] An Aboriginal Australian.   [24] Justus von Liebig (1803–1873), a German chemist.

[25] According to Greek myth, the Elysian fields were home to the virtuous dead.

ally is more various, and more easily obtained, and Clothing and Shelter are wholly or half unnecessary. At the present day, and in this country, as I find by my own experience, a few implements, a knife, an axe, a spade, a wheelbarrow, &c., and for the studious, lamplight, stationery, and access to a few books, rank next to necessaries, and can all be obtained at a trifling cost. Yet some, not wise, go to the other side of the globe, to barbarous and unhealthy regions, and devote themselves to trade for ten or twenty years, in order that they may live,—that is, keep comfortably warm,—and die in New England at last. The luxuriously rich are not simply kept comfortably warm, but unnaturally hot; as I implied before, they are cooked, of course *à la mode*.[26]

Most of the luxuries, and many of the so called comforts of life, are not only not indispensable, but positive hinderances to the elevation of mankind. With respect to luxuries and comforts, the wisest have ever lived a more simple and meager life than the poor. The ancient philosophers, Chinese, Hindoo, Persian, and Greek, were a class than which none has been poorer in outward riches, none so rich in inward. We know not much about them. It is remarkable that *we* know so much of them as we do. The same is true of the more modern reformers and benefactors of their race. None can be an impartial or wise observer of human life but from the vantage ground of what *we* should call voluntary poverty. Of a life of luxury the fruit is luxury, whether in agriculture, or commerce, or literature, or art. There are nowadays professors of philosophy, but not philosophers. Yet it is admirable to profess because it was once admirable to live. To be a philosopher is not merely to have subtle thoughts, nor even to found a school, but so to love wisdom as to live according to its dictates, a life of simplicity, independence, magnanimity, and trust. It is to solve some of the problems of life, not only theoretically, but practically. The success of great scholars and thinkers is commonly a courtier-like success, not kingly, not manly. They make shift to live merely by conformity, practically as their fathers did, and are in no sense the progenitors of a nobler race of men. But why do men degenerate ever? What makes families run out? What is the nature of the luxury which enervates and destroys nations? Are we sure that there is none of it in our own lives? The philosopher is in advance of his age even in the outward form of his life. He is not fed, sheltered, clothed, warmed, like his contemporaries. How can a man be a philosopher and not maintain his vital heat by better methods than other men?

When a man is warmed by the several modes which I have described, what does he want next? Surely not more warmth of the same kind, as more and richer food, larger and more splendid houses, finer and more abundant clothing, more numerous incessant and hotter fires, and the like. When he has obtained those things which are necessary to life, there is another alternative than to obtain the superfluities; and that is, to adventure on life now, his vacation from humbler toil having commenced. The soil, it appears, is suited to the seed, for it has sent its radicle[27] downward, and it may now send its shoot upward also with confidence. Why has man rooted himself thus firmly in the earth, but that he may rise in the same proportion into the heavens above?—for the nobler plants are valued for the fruit they bear at last in the air and light, far from the ground, and are not treated like the humbler esculents,[28] which, though they may be biennials, are cultivated

---

[26] In style, according to the fashion (French): by central heating.   [27] Root.   [28] Edibles.

only till they have perfected their root, and often cut down at top for this purpose, so that most would not know them in their flowering season.

I do not mean to prescribe rules to strong and valiant natures, who will mind their own affairs whether in heaven or hell, and perchance build more magnificently and spend more lavishly than the richest, without ever impoverishing themselves, not knowing how they live,—if, indeed, there are any such, as has been dreamed; nor to those who find their encouragement and inspiration in precisely the present condition of things, and cherish it with the fondness and enthusiasm of lovers,—and, to some extent, I reckon myself in this number; I do not speak to those who are well employed, in whatever circumstances, and they know whether they are well employed or not;—but mainly to the mass of men who are discontented, and idly complaining of the hardness of their lot or of the times, when they might improve them. There are some who complain most energetically and inconsolably of any, because they are, as they say, doing their duty. I also have in my mind that seemingly wealthy, but most terribly impoverished class of all, who have accumulated dross,[29] but know not how to use it, or get rid of it, and thus have forged their own golden or silver fetters.

If I should attempt to tell how I have desired to spend my life in years past, it would probably surprise those of my readers who are somewhat acquainted with its actual history; it would certainly astonish those who know nothing about it. I will only hint at some of the enterprises which I have cherished.

In any weather, at any hour of the day or night, I have been anxious to improve the nick of time, and notch it on my stick[30] too; to stand on the meeting of two eternities, the past and future, which is precisely the present moment; to toe that line. You will pardon some obscurities, for there are more secrets in my trade than in most men's, and yet not voluntarily kept, but inseparable from its very nature. I would gladly tell all that I know about it, and never paint "No Admittance" on my gate.

I long ago lost a hound, a bay horse, and a turtle-dove, and am still on their trail.[31] Many are the travellers I have spoken concerning them, describing their tracks and what calls they answered to. I have met one or two who had heard the hound, and the tramp of the horse, and even seen the dove disappear behind a cloud, and they seemed as anxious to recover them as if they had lost them themselves.

To anticipate, not the sunrise and the dawn merely, but, if possible, Nature herself! How many mornings, summer and winter, before yet any neighbor was stirring about his business, have I been about mine! No doubt, many of my townsmen have met me returning from this enterprise, farmers starting for Boston in the twilight, or woodchoppers going to their work. It is true, I never assisted the sun materially in his rising, but, doubt not, it was of the last importance only to be present at it.

So many autumn, ay, and winter days, spent outside the town, trying to hear what was in the wind, to hear and carry it express! I well-nigh sunk all my capital

[29] The scum forming on molten metals.   [30] Make a record of it.

[31] A passage baffling even to Thoreau, who replied to a letter from his admiring friend B. B. Wiley in 1857 that the items mentioned symbolize profound losses in life, "according as I now understand my own words." The paragraph takes on the allegorical quality of a quest for a lost condition in life.

in it, and lost my own breath into the bargain, running in the face of it. If it had concerned either of the political parties, depend upon it, it would have appeared in the Gazette with the earliest intelligence.[32] At other times watching from the observatory of some cliff or tree, to telegraph any new arrival; or waiting at evening on the hill-tops for the sky to fall, that I might catch something, though I never caught much, and that, manna-wise[33] would dissolve again in the sun.

For a long time I was reporter to a journal,[34] of no very wide circulation, whose editor has never yet seen fit to print the bulk of my contributions, and, as is too common with writers, I got only my labor for my pains. However, in this case my pains were their own reward.

For many years I was self-appointed inspector of snow storms and rain storms, and did my duty faithfully; surveyor, if not of highways, then of forest paths and all across-lot routes, keeping them open, and ravines bridged and passable at all seasons, where the public heel had testified to their utility.

I have looked after the wild stock of the town, which give a faithful herdsman a good deal of trouble by leaping fences; and I have had an eye to the unfrequented nooks and corners of the farm; though I did not always know whether Jonas or Solomon worked in a particular field to-day; that was none of my business. I have watered the red huckleberry, the sand cherry and the nettle tree, the red pine and the black ash, the white grape and the yellow violet, which might have withered else in dry seasons.

In short, I went on thus for a long time, I may say it without boasting, faithfully minding my business, till it became more and more evident that my townsmen would not after all admit me into the list of town officers, nor make my place a sinecure with a moderate allowance. My accounts, which I can swear to have kept faithfully, I have, indeed, never got audited, still less accepted, still less paid and settled. However, I have not set my heart on that.

Not long since, a strolling Indian went to sell baskets at the house of a well-known lawyer in my neighborhood. "Do you wish to buy any baskets?" he asked. "No, we do not want any," was the reply. "What!" exclaimed the Indian as he went out the gate, "do you mean to starve us?" Having seen his industrious white neighbors so well off,—that the lawyer had only to weave arguments, and by some magic wealth and standing followed, he had said to himself; I will go into business; I will weave baskets; it is a thing which I can do. Thinking that when he had made the baskets he would have done his part, and then it would be the white man's to buy them. He had not discovered that it was necessary for him to make it worth the other's while to buy them, or at least make him think that it was so, or to make something else which it would be worth his while to buy. I too had woven a kind of basket of a delicate texture, but I had not made it worth any one's while to buy them.[35] Yet not the less, in my case, did I think it worth my while to weave them, and instead of studying how to make it worth men's while to buy my baskets, I studied rather how to avoid the necessity of selling them. The life which men praise and regard as successful is but one kind. Why should we exaggerate any one kind at the expense of the others?

[32] In Concord's weekly newspaper with the earliest news.
[33] In Exodus 16 manna, the food miraculously given to the Israelites on their journey out of Egypt, melted in the sun.
[34] Probably Thoreau's own journal, on which he levied for contributions to various magazines.
[35] A reference to Thoreau's first book, *A Week on the Concord and Merrimack Rivers,* which sold few copies.

Finding that my fellow-citizens were not likely to offer me any room in the court house, or any curacy or living[36] any where else, but I must shift for myself, I turned my face more exclusively than ever to the woods, where I was better known. I determined to go into business at once, and not wait to acquire the usual capital, using such slender means as I had already got. My purpose in going to Walden Pond was not to live cheaply nor to live dearly there, but to transact some private business with the fewest obstacles; to be hindered from accomplishing which for want of a little common sense, a little enterprise and business talent, appeared not so sad as foolish.

I have always endeavored to acquire strict business habits; they are indispensable to every man. If your trade is with the Celestial Empire,[37] then some small counting house on the coast, in some Salem harbor, will be fixture enough. You will export such articles as the country affords, purely native products, much ice and pine timber and a little granite, always in native bottoms.[38] These will be good ventures. To oversee all the details yourself in person; to be at once pilot and captain, and owner and underwriter; to buy and sell and keep the accounts; to read every letter received, and write or read every letter sent; to superintend the discharge of imports night and day; to be upon many parts of the coast almost at the same time;—often the richest freight will be discharged upon a Jersey shore;[39]— to be your own telegraph, unweariedly sweeping the horizon, speaking all passing vessels bound coastwise; to keep up a steady despatch of commodities, for the supply of such a distant and exorbitant market; to keep yourself informed of the state of the markets, prospects of war and peace every where, and anticipate the tendencies of trade and civilization,—taking advantage of the results of all exploring expeditions, using new passages and all improvements in navigation;— charts to be studied, the position of reefs and new lights and buoys to be ascertained, and ever, and ever, the logarithmic tables to be corrected, for by the error of some calculator the vessel often splits upon a rock that should have reached a friendly pier,—there is the untold fate of La Perouse;[40]—universal science to be kept pace with, studying the lives of all great discoverers and navigators, great adventurers and merchants, from Hanno and the Phœnicians[41] down to our day; in fine, account of stock to be taken from time to time, to know how you stand. It is a labor to task the faculties of a man,—such problems of profit and loss, of interest, of tare and tret,[42] and gauging of all kinds in it, as demand a universal knowledge.

I have thought that Walden Pond would be a good place for business, not solely on account of the railroad and the ice trade; it offers advantages which it may not be good policy to divulge; it is a good port and a good foundation. No Neva[43] marshes to be filled; though you must every where build on piles of your own driving. It is said that a flood-tide, with a westerly wind, and ice in the Neva, would sweep St. Petersburg from the face of the earth.

---

[36] Any appointment as a county official, or any appointment as a clergyman, or income from a church office.

[37] China, so named because its emperors were thought to be sons of Heaven.   [38] Ships.

[39] Shipwrecked on the New Jersey coast.

[40] Jean François de Galaup (1741–1788?), count de la Perouse, a French explorer who disappeared after being shipwrecked in the New Hebrides, in the South Pacific.

[41] The Phoenicians and the Carthaginian navigator Hanno (6th–5th centuries B.C.) were noted for exploration and navigational skill.

[42] Commercial calculations of weight and of allowance for waste or spoilage.

[43] A river in Russia, near St. Petersburg (now Leningrad).

As this business was to be entered into without the usual capital, it may not be easy to conjecture where those means, that will still be indispensable to every such undertaking, were to be obtained. As for Clothing, to come at once to the practical part of the question, perhaps we are led oftener by the love of novelty, and a regard for the opinions of men, in procuring it, than by a true utility. Let him who has work to do recollect that the object of clothing is, first, to retain the vital heat, and secondly, in this state of society, to cover nakedness, and he may judge how much of any necessary or important work may be accomplished without adding to his wardrobe. Kings and queens who wear a suit but once, though made by some tailor or dress-maker to their majesties, cannot know the comfort of wearing a suit that fits. They are no better than wooden horses to hang the clean clothes on. Every day our garments become more assimilated to ourselves, receiving the impress of the wearer's character, until we hesitate to lay them aside, without such delay and medical appliances and some such solemnity even as our bodies. No man ever stood the lower in my estimation for having a patch in his clothes; yet I am sure that there is greater anxiety, commonly, to have fashionable, or at least clean and unpatched clothes, than to have a sound conscience. But even if the rent[44] is not mended, perhaps the worst vice betrayed is improvidence. I sometimes try my acquaintances by such tests as this;—who could wear a patch, or two extra seams only, over the knee? Most behave as if they believed that their prospects for life would be ruined if they should do it. It would be easier for them to hobble to town with a broken leg than with a broken pantaloon. Often if an accident happens to a gentleman's legs, they can be mended; but if a similar accident happens to the legs of his pantaloons, there is no help for it; for he considers, not what is truly respectable, but what is respected. We know but few men, a great many coats and breeches. Dress a scarecrow in your last shift, you standing shiftless by, who would not soonest salute the scarecrow? Passing a cornfield the other day, close by a hat and coat on a stake, I recognized the owner of the farm. He was only a little more weather-beaten than when I saw him last. I have heard of a dog that barked at every stranger who approached his master's premises with clothes on, but was easily quieted by a naked thief. It is an interesting question how far men would retain their relative rank if they were divested of their clothes. Could you, in such a case, tell surely of any company of civilized men, which belonged to the most respected class? When Madam Pfeiffer,[45] in her adventurous travels round the world, from east to west, had got so near home as Asiatic Russia, she says that she felt the necessity of wearing other than a travelling dress, when she went to meet the authorities, for she "was now in a civilized country, where—"people are judged of by their clothes." Even in our democratic New England towns the accidental possession of wealth, and its manifestation in dress and equipage alone, obtain for the possessor almost universal respect. But they who yield such respect, numerous as they are, are so far heathen, and need to have a missionary sent to them. Beside, clothes introduced sewing, a kind of work which you may call endless; a woman's dress, at least is never done.[46]

A man who has at length found something to do will not need to get a new suit to do it in; for him the old will do, that has lain dusty in the garret for an indeterminate period. Old shoes will serve a hero longer than they have served his

---

[44] The rip or tear.

[45] Ida Reyer Pfeiffer (1797–1858), an Austrian traveler and writer, author of *A Lady's Journey Round the World* (1852).

[46] A variant of the saying "A man works from sun to sun, but a woman's work is never done."

valet,—if a hero ever has a valet,—bare feet are older than shoes, and he can make them do. Only they who go to soirées and legislative halls must have new coats, coats to change as often as the man changes in them. But if my jacket and trousers, my hat and shoes, are fit to worship God in, they will do; will they not? Who ever saw his old clothes,—his old coat, actually worn out, resolved into its primitive elements, so that it was not a deed of charity to bestow it on some poor boy, by him perchance to be bestowed on some poorer still, or shall we say richer, who could do with less? I say, beware of all enterprises that require new clothes, and not rather a new wearer of clothes. If there is not a new man, how can the new clothes be made to fit? If you have any enterprise before you, try it in your old clothes. All men want, not something to *do with,* but something to *do,* or rather something to *be.* Perhaps we should never procure a new suit, however ragged or dirty the old, until we have so conducted, so enterprised or sailed in some way, that we feel like new men in the old, and that to retain it would be like keeping new wine in old bottles.[47] Our moulting season, like that of the fowls, must be a crisis in our lives. The loon retires to solitary ponds to spend it. Thus also the snake casts its slough, and the caterpillar its wormy coat, by an internal industry and expansion; for clothes are but our outmost cuticle and mortal coil. Otherwise we shall be found sailing under false colors, and be inevitably cashiered[48] at last by our own opinion, as well as that of mankind.

We don garment after garment, as if we grew like exogenous plants[49] by addition without. Our outside and often thin and fanciful clothes are our epidermis or false skin, which partakes not of our life, and may be stripped off here and there without fatal injury; our thicker garments, constantly worn, are our cellular integument, or cortex;[50] but our shirts are our liber or true bark, which cannot be removed without girdling and so destroying the man. I believe that all races at some seasons wear something equivalent to the shirt. It is desirable that a man be clad so simply that he can lay his hands on himself in the dark, and that he live in all respects so compactly and preparedly, that, if an enemy take the town, he can, like the old philosopher, walk out the gate empty-handed without anxiety. While one thick garment is, for most purposes, as good as three thin ones, and cheap clothing can be obtained at prices really to suit customers; while a thick coat can be bought for five dollars, which will last as many years, thick pantaloons for two dollars, cowhide boots for a dollar and a half a pair, a summer hat for a quarter of a dollar, and a winter cap for sixty-two and a half cents, or a better be made at home at a nominal cost, where is he so poor that, clad in such a suit, *of his own earning,* there will not be found wise men to do him reverence?

When I ask for a garment of a particular form, my tailoress tells me gravely, "They do not make them so now," not emphasizing the "They" at all, as if she quoted an authority as impersonal as the Fates,[51] and I find it difficult to get made what I want, simply because she cannot believe that I mean what I say, that I am so rash. When I hear this oracular sentence, I am for a moment absorbed in thought, emphasizing to myself each word separately that I may come at the meaning of it, that I may find out by what degree of consanguinity *They* are related to *me,* and what authority they may have in an affair which affects me so

---

[47] "Neither do men put new wine into old bottles: else the bottles break . . . but they put new wine into new bottles, and both are preserved," from Matthew 9:17.
[48] Dismissed, fired.   [49] Plants that grow by adding exterior layers.
[50] The skin of a cell, or the outer layer; here, inner bark.
[51] According to classical myth, three goddesses who determine human destiny.

nearly; and, finally, I am inclined to answer her with equal mystery, and without any more emphasis of the "they,"—"It is true, they did not make them so recently, but they do now." Of what use this measuring of me if she does not measure my character, but only the breadth of my shoulders, as it were a peg to hang the coat on? We worship not the Graces, nor the Parcæ,[52] but Fashion. She spins and weaves and cuts with full authority. The head monkey at Paris puts on a traveller's cap, and all the monkeys in America do the same. I sometimes despair of getting any thing quite simple and honest done in this world by the help of men. They would have to be passed through a powerful press first, to squeeze their old notions out of them, so that they would not soon get upon their legs again, and then there would be some one in the company with a maggot in his head, hatched from an egg deposited there nobody knows when, for not even fire kills these things, and you would have lost your labor. Nevertheless, we will not forget that some Egyptian wheat is said to have been handed down to us by a mummy.[53]

On the whole, I think that it cannot be maintained that dressing has in this or any country risen to the dignity of an art. At present men make shift to wear what they can get. Like shipwrecked sailors, they put on what they can find on the beach, and at a little distance, whether of space or time, laugh at each other's masquerade. Every generation laughs at the old fashions, but follows religiously the new. We are amused at beholding the costume of Henry VIII, or Queen Elizabeth,[54] as much as if it was that of the King and Queen of the Cannibal Islands. All costume off a man is pitiful or grotesque. It is only the serious eye peering from and the sincere life passed within it, which restrain laughter and consecrate the costume of any people. Let Harlequin,[55] be taken with a fit of the colic and his trappings will have to serve that mood too. When the soldier is hit by a cannon ball rags are as becoming as purple.[56]

The childish and savage taste of men and women for new patterns keeps how many shaking and squinting through kaleidoscopes that they may discover the particular figure which this generation requires to-day. The manufacturers have learned that this taste is merely whimsical. Of two patterns which differ only by a few threads more or less of a particular color, the one will be sold readily, the other lie on the shelf, though it frequently happens that after the lapse of a season the latter becomes the most fashionable. Comparatively, tattooing is not the hideous custom which it is called. It is not barbarous merely because the printing is skin-deep and unalterable.

I cannot believe that our factory system is the best mode by which men may get clothing. The condition of the operatives[57] is becoming every day more like that of the English; and it cannot be wondered at, since, as far as I have heard or observed, the principal object is, not that mankind may be well and honestly clad, but, unquestionably, that the corporations may be enriched. In the long run men hit only what they aim at. Therefore, though they should fail immediately, they had better aim at something high.

---

[52] According to Greek myth, the Graces were three goddesses who control pleasure, charm, and beauty; Parcae, or "birth-spirits," is a Roman name for the Fates.

[53] The notion that wheat would grow from seeds sealed in ancient Egyptian tombs was popular in the nineteenth century.

[54] The king (1509–1547) and queen (1558–1603) of England.

[55] A character in comedy and pantomime, with masked face, multicolored tights, and frequently a shaved head.

[56] The traditional color of royalty.   [57] Factory workers.

As for a Shelter, I will not deny that this is now a necessary of life, though there are instances of men having done without it for long periods in colder countries than this. Samuel Laing[58] says that "The Laplander in his skin dress, and in a skin bag which he puts over his head and shoulders, will sleep night after night on the snow—in a degree of cold which would extinguish the life of one exposed to it in any woollen clothing." He had seen them alseep thus. Yet he adds, "They are not hardier than other people." But, probably, man did not live long on the earth without discovering the convenience which there is in a house, the domestic comforts, which phrase may have originally signified the satisfactions of the house more than of the family; though these must be extremely partial and occasional in those climates where the house is associated in our thoughts with winter or the rainy season chiefly, and two thirds of the year, except for a parasol, is unnecessary. In our climate, in the summer, it was formerly almost solely a covering at night. In the Indian gazettes[59] a wigwam was the symbol of a day's march, and a row of them cut or painted on the bark of a tree signified that so many times they had camped. Man was not made so large limbed and robust but that he must seek to narrow his world, and wall in a space such as fitted him. He was at first bare and out of doors; but though this was pleasant enough in serene and warm weather, by daylight, the rainy season and the winter, to say nothing of the torrid sun, would perhaps have nipped his race in the bud if he had not made haste to clothe himself with the shelter of a house. Adam and Eve, according to the fable,[60] wore the bower before other clothes. Man wanted a home, a place of warmth, or comfort, first of physical warmth, then the warmth of the affections.

We may imagine a time when, in the infancy of the human race, some enterprising mortal crept into a hollow in a rock for shelter. Every child begins the world again, to some extent, and loves to stay out doors, even in wet and cold. It plays house, as well as horse, having an instinct for it. Who does not remember the interest with which when young he looked at shelving rocks, or any approach to a cave? It was the natural yearning of that portion of our most primitive ancestor which still survived in us. From the cave we have advanced to roofs of palm leaves, of bark and boughs, of linen woven and stretched, of grass and straw, of boards and shingles, of stones and tiles. At last, we know not what it is to live in the open air, and our lives are domestic in more senses than we think. From the hearth to the field is a great distance. It would be well perhaps if we were to spend more of our days and nights without any obstruction between us and the celestial bodies, if the poet did not speak so much from under a roof, or the saint dwell there so long. Birds do not sing in caves, nor do doves cherish their innocence in dovecots.[61]

However, if one designs to construct a dwelling house, it behooves him to exercise a little Yankee shrewdness, lest after all he find himself in a workhouse, a labyrinth without a clew, a museum, an almshouse, a prison, or a splendid mausoleum instead. Consider first how slight a shelter is absolutely necessary. I have seen Penobscot Indians,[62] in this town, living in tents of thin cotton cloth, while the snow was nearly a foot deep around them, and I thought that they would be glad to have it deeper to keep out the wind. Formerly, when how to get my living

---

[58] Laing (1780–1868), an English writer, wrote *Journal of a Residence in Norway* (1837).
[59] According to Indian sign languages.
[60] Calling the biblical story of Adam and Eve a "fable" did not endear Thoreau to orthodox readers.
[61] Dovecotes, boxes for nesting birds.   [62] A tribe from northern Maine.

honestly, with freedom left for my proper pursuits, was a question which vexed me even more than it does now, for unfortunately I am become somewhat callous, I used to see a large box by the railroad, six feet long by three wide, in which the laborers locked up their tools at night, and it suggested to me that every man who was hard pushed might get such a one for a dollar, and, having bored a few auger holes in it, to admit the air at least, get into it when it rained and at night, and hook down the lid, and so have freedom in his love, and in his soul be free. This did not appear the worst, nor by any means a despicable alternative. You could sit up as late as you pleased, and, whenever you got up, got abroad without any landlord or house-lord dogging you for rent. Many a man is harassed to death to pay the rent of a larger and more luxurious box who would not have frozen to death in such a box as this. I am far from jesting. Economy is a subject which admits of being treated with levity, but it cannot so be disposed of. A comfortable house for a rude and hardy race, that lived mostly out of doors, was once made here almost entirely of such materials as Nature furnished ready to their hands. Gookin,[63] who was superintendent of the Indians subject to the Massachusetts Colony, writing in 1674, says, "The best of their houses are covered very neatly, tight and warm, with barks of trees, slipped from their bodies at those seasons when the sap is up, and made into great flakes, with pressure of weighty timber, when they are green. . . . The meaner sort are covered with mats which they make of a kind of bulrush, and are also indifferently tight and warm, but not so good as the former. . . . Some I have seen, sixty or a hundred feet long and thirty feet broad. . . . I have often lodged in their wigwams, and found them as warm as the best English houses." He adds, that they were commonly carpeted and lined within with well-wrought embroidered mats, and were furnished with various utensils. The Indians had advanced so far as to regulate the effect of the wind by a mat suspended over the hole in the roof and moved by a string. Such a lodge was in the first instance constructed in a day or two at most, and taken down and put up in a few hours; and every family owned one, or its apartment in one.

In the savage state every family owns a shelter as good as the best, and sufficient for its coarser and simpler wants; but I think that I speak within bounds when I say that, though the birds of the air have their nests, and the foxes their holes,[64] and the savages their wigwams, in modern civilized society not more than one half the families own a shelter. In the large towns and cities, where civilization especially prevails, the number of those who own a shelter is a very small fraction of the whole. The rest pay an annual tax for this outside garment of all, become indispensable summer and winter, which would buy a village of Indian wigwams, but now helps to keep them poor as long as they live. I do not mean to insist here on the disadvantage of hiring compared with owning, but it is evident that the savage owns his shelter because it costs so little, while the civilized man hires his commonly because he cannot afford to own it; nor can he, in the long run, any better afford to hire. But, answers one, by merely paying this tax the poor civilized man secures an abode which is a palace compared with the savage's. An annual rent of from twenty-five to a hundred dollars, these are the country rates,

[63] Daniel Gookin (1612–1687), from his *Historical Collections of the Indians in New England* (1792) (Ch. III).

[64] "The foxes have holes, and the birds of the air have nests; but the Son of man hath not where to lay his head," from Matthew 8:20.

entitles him to the benefit of the improvements of centuries, spacious apartments, clean paint and paper, Rumford fireplace, back plastering,[65] Venetian blinds, copper pump, spring lock, a commodious cellar, and many other things. But how happens it that he who is said to enjoy these things is so commonly a *poor* civilized man, while the savage, who has them not, is rich as a savage? If it is asserted that civilization is a real advance in the condition of man,—and I think that it is, though only the wise improve their advantages,—it must be shown that it has produced better dwellings without making them more costly; and the cost of a thing is the amount of what I will call life which is required to be exchanged for it, immediately or in the long run. An average house in this neighborhood costs perhaps eight hundred dollars, and to lay up this sum will take from ten to fifteen years of the laborer's life, even if he is not encumbered with a family;—estimating the pecuniary value of every man's labor at one dollar a day, for if some receive more, others receive less;—so that he must have spent more than half his life commonly before *his* wigwam will be earned. If we suppose him to pay a rent instead, this is but a doubtful choice of evils. Would the savage have been wise to exchange his wigwam for a palace on these terms?

It may be guessed that I reduce almost the whole advantage of holding this superfluous property as a fund in store against the future, so far as the individual is concerned, mainly to the defraying of funeral expenses. But perhaps a man is not required to bury himself. Nevertheless this points to an important distinction between the civilized man and the savage; and, no doubt, they have designs on us for our benefit, in making the life of a civilized people an *institution,* in which the life of the individual is to a great extent absorbed, in order to preserve and perfect that of the race. But I wish to show at what a sacrifice this advantage is at present obtained, and to suggest that we may possibly so live as to secure all the advantage without suffering any of the disadvantage. What mean ye by saying that the poor ye have always with you, or that the fathers have eaten sour grapes, and the children's teeth are set on edge?[66]

"As I live, saith the Lord God, ye shall not have occasion any more to use this proverb in Israel."

"Behold all souls are mine; as the soul of the father, so also the soul of the son is mine: the soul that sinneth it shall die."

When I consider my neighbors, the farmers of Concord, who are at least as well off as the other classes, I find that for the most part they have been toiling twenty, thirty, or forty years, that they may become the real owners of their farms, which commonly they have inherited with encumbrances, or else bought with hired money,—and we may regard one third of that toil as the cost of their houses,—but commonly they have not paid for them yet. It is true, the encumbrances sometimes outweigh the value of the farm, so that the farm itself becomes one great encumbrance, and still a man is found to inherit it, being well acquainted with it, as he says. On applying to the assessors, I am surprised to learn that they cannot at once name a dozen in the town who own their farms free and

---

[65] A smokeless stove invented by Benjamin Thompson (1753–1814), Count Rumford; insulation.

[66] Thoreau takes exception to the words "For ye have the poor always with you," from Matthew 26:11, and to the proverb "The fathers have eaten . . .," from Ezekiel 18:2. As cryptic as they are here, the following two quotations, from Ezekiel 18:3–4, advance the idea that each person is born fresh in the Lord.

clear. If you would know the history of these homesteads, inquire at the bank where they are mortgaged. The man who has actually paid for his farm with labor on it is so rare that every neighbor can point to him. I doubt if there are three such men in Concord. What has been said of the merchants, that a very large majority, even ninety-seven in a hundred, are sure to fail, is equally true of the farmers. With regard to the merchants, however, one of them says pertinently that a great part of their failures are not genuine pecuniary failures, but merely failures to fulfil their engagements, because it is inconvenient; that is, it is the moral character that breaks down. But this puts an infinitely worse face on the matter, and suggests, beside, that probably not even the other three succeed in saving their souls, but are perchance bankrupt in a worse sense than they who fail honestly. Bankruptcy and repudiation are the spring-boards from which much of our civilization vaults and turns its somersets, but the savage stands on the unelastic plank of famine. Yet the Middlesex Cattle Show goes off here with *éclat*[67] annually, as if all the joints of the agricultural machine were suent.[68]

The farmer is endeavoring to solve the problem of a livelihood by a formula more complicated than the problem itself. To get his shoestrings he speculates in herds of cattle. With consummate skill he has set his trap with a hair spring[69] to catch comfort and independence, and then, as he turned away, got his own leg into it. This is the reason he is poor; and for a similar reason we are all poor in respect to a thousand savage comforts, though surrounded by luxuries. As Chapman[70] sings,—

> "The false society of men—
> —for earthly greatness
> All heavenly comforts rarefies to air."

And when the farmer has got his house, he may not be the richer but the poorer for it, and it be the house that has got him. As I understand it, that was a valid objection urged by Momus against the house which Minerva[71] made, that she "had not made it movable, by which means a bad neighborhood might be avoided;" and it may still be urged, for our houses are such unwieldly property that we are often imprisoned rather than housed in them; and the bad neighborhood to be avoided is our own scurvy selves. I know one or two families, at least, in this town, who, for nearly a generation, have been wishing to sell their houses in the outskirts and move into the village, but have not been able to accomplish it, and only death will set them free.

Granted that the *majority* are able at last either to own or hire the modern house with all its improvements. While civilization has been improving our houses, it has not equally improved the men who are to inhabit them. It has created palaces, but it was not so easy to create noblemen and kings. And *if the civilized man's pursuits are no worthier than the savage's, if he is employed the greater part of his life in obtaining gross necessaries and comforts merely, why should he have a better dwelling than the former?*

---

[67] An agricultural country fair held in Concord, each September, with *éclat*, or "brilliantly" (French).   [68] Working well.   [69] A trap adjusted so carefully that a hair would spring it.
[70] George Chapman (1559?–1634), an English poet and dramatist, from *Caesar and Pompey* (1631) (V. ii).
[71] According to Greek myth, Momus was the god of mockery, criticism, and faultfinding; Minerva was the goddess of handicrafts (and of wisdom).

But how do the poor *minority* fare? Perhaps it will be found, that just in proportion as some have been placed in outward circumstances above the savage, others have been degraded below him. The luxury of one class is counterbalanced by the indigence of another. On the one side is the palace, on the other are the almshouse and "silent poor".[72] The myriads who built the pyramids to be the tombs of the Pharaohs were fed on garlic,[73] and it may be were not decently buried themselves. The mason who finishes the cornice of the palace returns at night perchance to a hut not so good as a wigwam. It is a mistake to suppose that, in a country where the usual evidences of civilization exist, the condition of a very large body of the inhabitants may not be as degraded as that of savages. I refer to the degraded poor, not now to the degraded rich. To know this I should not need to look farther than to the shanties which every where border our railroads, that last improvement in civilization; where I see in my daily walks human beings living in sties, and all winter with an open door, for the sake of light, without any visible, often imaginable, wood pile, and the forms of both old and young are permanently contracted by the long habit of shrinking from cold and misery, and the development of all their limbs and faculties is checked. It certainly is fair to look at that class by whose labor the works which distinguish this generation are accomplished. Such too, to a greater or less extent, is the condition of the operatives of every denomination in England, which is the great workhouse of the world. Or I could refer you to Ireland,[74] which is marked as one of the white or enlightened spots on the map. Contrast the physical condition of the Irish with that of the North American Indian, or the South Sea Islander, or any other savage race before it was degraded by contact with the civilized man. Yet I have no doubt that that people's rulers are as wise as the average of civilized rulers. Their condition only proves what squalidness may consist with civilization. I hardly need refer now to the laborers in our Southern States who produce the staple exports of this country, and are themselves a staple production of the South.[75] But to confine myself to those who are said to be in *moderate* circumstances.

Most men appear never to have considered what a house is, and are actually though needlessly poor all their lives because they think that they must have such a one as their neighbors have. As if one were to wear any sort of coat which the tailor might cut out for him, or, gradually leaving off palmleaf hat or cap of woodchuck skin, complain of hard times because he could not afford to buy him a crown! It is possible to invent a house still more convenient and luxurious than we have, which yet all would admit that man could not afford to pay for. Shall we always study to obtain more of these things, and not sometimes to be content with less? Shall the respectable citizen thus gravely teach, by precept and example, the necessity of the young man's providing a certain number of superfluous glow-shoes,[76] and umbrellas, and empty guest chambers for empty guests, before he dies? Why should not our furniture be as simple as the Arab's or the Indian's? When I think of the benefactors of the race, whom we have apotheosized as messengers from heaven, bearers of divine gifts to man, I do not see in my mind any

---

[72] Those who conceal their poverty to stay out of the poorhouse.

[73] The Greek historian Herodotus (480?–425? B.C.) mentions that onions and garlic were supplied to those who worked on the Egyptian pyramids.

[74] The potato famine in the 1840s brought widespread hardship to Ireland, which appears as a "white" spot on the map because some early mapmakers used white to indicate settled lands and dark colors to signify unexplored terrain.

[75] Of slave breeders in the South.   [76] Galoshes.

retinue at their heels, any car-load of fashionable furniture. Or what if I were to allow—would it not be a singular allowance?—that our furniture should be more complex than the Arab's, in proportion as we are morally and intellectually his superiors! At present our houses are cluttered and defiled with it, and a good housewife would sweep out the greater part into the dust hole, and not leave her morning's work undone. Morning work! By the blushes of Aurora and the music of Memnon,[77] what should be man's *morning work* in this world? I had three pieces of limestone on my desk, but I was terrified to find that they required to be dusted daily, when the furniture of my mind was all undusted still, and I threw them out the window in disgust. How, then, could I have a furnished house? I would rather sit in the open air, for no dust gathers on the grass, unless where man has broken ground.

It is the luxurious and dissipated who set the fashions which the herd so diligently follow. The traveller who stops at the best houses, so called, soon discovers this, for the publicans,[78] presume him to be a Sardanapalus,[79] and if he resigned himself to their tender mercies he would soon be completely emasculated. I think that in the railroad car we are inclined to spend more on luxury than on safety and convenience, and it threatens without attaining these to become no better than a modern drawing room, with its divans, and ottomans, and sunshades, and a hundred other oriental things, which we are taking west with us, invented for the ladies of the harem and the effeminate natives of the Celestial Empire, which Jonathan[80] should be ashamed to know the names of. I would rather sit on a pumpkin and have it all to myself, than be crowded on a velvet cushion. I would rather ride on earth in an ox cart with a free circulation, than go to heaven in the fancy car of an excursion train and breathe a *malaria* all the way.[81]

The very simplicity and nakedness of man's life in the primitive ages imply this advantage at least, that they left him still but a sojourner in nature. When he was refreshed with food and sleep he contemplated his journey again. He dwelt, as it were, in a tent in this world, and was either threading the valleys, or crossing the plains, or climbing the mountain tops. But lo! men have become the tools of their tools. The man who independently plucked the fruits when he was hungry is become a farmer; and he who stood under a tree for shelter, a housekeeper. We now no longer camp as for a night, but have settled down on earth and forgotten heaven. We have adopted Christianity merely as an improved method of *agri-*culture. We have built for this world a family mansion, and for the next a family tomb. The best works of art are the expression of man's struggle to free himself from this condition, but the effect of our art is merely to make this low state comfortable and that higher state to be forgotten. There is actually no place in this village for a work of *fine* art, if any had come down to us, to stand, for our lives, our houses and streets, furnish no proper pedestal for it. There is not a nail to hang a picture on, nor a shelf to receive the bust of a hero or a saint. When I consider how our houses are built and paid for, or not paid for, and their internal economy managed and sustained, I wonder that the floor does not give way under the visitor while he is admiring the gewgaws upon the mantel-piece, and let him through into

[77] The Roman goddess of the dawn, and the music of the king of ancient Egypt, whose statue supposedly sounded musical vibrations when struck by the first rays of the sun.

[78] Innkeepers.   [79] A decadent and self-indulgent ninth-century B.C. ruler of Assyria.

[80] A nickname for a Yankee or an American.

[81] An illusion to Nathaniel Hawthorne's satire on transcendentalism and liberal religion, "The Celestial Railroad" (1846); "malaria" literally means "bad air."

the cellar, to some solid and honest though earthy foundation. I cannot but perceive that this so called rich and refined life is a thing jumped at, and I do not get on in the enjoyment of the *fine* arts which adorn it, my attention being wholly occupied with the jump; for I remember that the greatest genuine leap, due to human muscles alone, on record, is that of certain wandering Arabs, who are said to have cleared twenty-five feet on level ground. Without factitious[82] support, man is sure to come to earth again beyond that distance. The first question which I am tempted to put to the proprietor of such great impropriety is, Who bolsters you? Are you one of the ninety-seven who fail? or of the three who succeed? Answer me these questions, and then perhaps I may look at your bawbles and find them ornamental. The cart before the horse is neither beautiful nor useful. Before we can adorn our houses with beautiful objects the walls must be stripped, and our lives must be stripped, and beautiful housekeeping and beautiful living be laid for a foundation: now, a taste for the beautiful is most cultivated out of doors, where there is no house and no housekeeper.

Old Johnson,[83] in his "Wonder-Working Providence," speaking of the first settlers of this town, with whom he was contemporary, tells us that "they burrow themselves in the earth for their first shelter under some hillside, and, casting the soil aloft upon timber, they make a smoky fire against the earth, at the highest side." They did not "provide them houses," says he, "till the earth, by the Lord's blessing, brought forth bread to feed them," and the first year's crop was so light that "they were forced to cut their bread very thin for a long season." The secretary of the Province of New Netherland,[84] writing in Dutch, in 1650, for the information of those who wished to take up land there, states more particularly, that "those in New Netherland, and especially in New England, who have no means to build farm houses at first according to their wishes, dig a square pit in the ground, cellar fashion, six or seven feet deep, as long and as broad as they think proper, case the earth inside with wood all round the wall, and line the wood with the bark of trees or something else to prevent the caving in of the earth; floor this cellar with plank, and wainscot it overhead for a ceiling, raise a roof of spars clear up, and cover the spars with bark or green sods, so that they can live dry and warm in these houses with their entire families for two, three, and four years, it being understood that partitions are run through those cellars which are adapted to the size of the family. The wealthy and principal men in New England, in the beginning of the colonies, commenced their first dwelling houses in this fashion for two reasons; firstly, in order not to waste time in building, and not to want food the next season; secondly, in order not to discourage poor laboring people whom they brought over in numbers from Fatherland. In the course of three or four years, when the country became adapted to agriculture, they built themselves handsome houses, spending on them several thousands."

In this course which our ancestors took there was a show of prudence at least, as if their principle were to satisfy the more pressing wants first. But are the more pressing wants satisfied now? When I think of acquiring for myself one of our luxurious dwellings, I am deterred, for, so to speak, the country is not yet adapted

---

[82] Artificial.

[83] Edward Johnson (1598–1672), author of *Wonder-Working Providence of Sion's Saviour In New England* (1654), a history of New England settlement from 1628 to 1652.

[84] Later, the colony and then the state of New York. The Dutch provincial secretary, Cornelis van Tienhoven, is quoted from *Documentary History of the State of New-York* (1851), edited by Edmund Bailey O'Callaghan.

to *human* culture, and we are still forced to cut our *spiritual* bread far thinner than our forefathers did their wheaten. Not that all architectural ornament is to be neglected even in the rudest periods; but let our houses first be lined with beauty, where they come in contact with our lives, like the tenement of the shellfish, and not overlaid with it. But, alas! I have been inside one or two of them, and know what they are lined with.

Though we are not so degenerate but that we might possibly live in a cave or a wigwam or wear skins to-day, it certainly is better to accept the advantages, though so dearly bought, which the invention and industry of mankind offer. In such a neighborhood as this, boards and shingles, lime and bricks, are cheaper and more easily obtained than suitable caves, or whole logs, or bark in sufficient quantities, or even well-tempered clay of flat stones. I speak understandingly on this subject, for I have made myself acquainted with it both theoretically and practically. With a little more wit we might use these materials so as to become richer than the richest now are, and make our civilization a blessing. The civilized man is a more experienced and wiser savage. But to make haste to my own experiment.

Near the end of March, 1845, I borrowed an axe and went down to the woods by Walden Pond, nearest to where I intended to build my house, and began to cut down some tall arrowy white pines, still in their youth, for timber. It is difficult to begin without borrowing, but perhaps it is the most generous course thus to permit your fellow-men to have an interest in your enterprise. The owner of the axe, as he released his hold on it, said that it was the apple of his eye; but I returned it sharper than I received it. It was a pleasant hillside where I worked, covered with pine woods, through which I looked out on the pond, and a small open field in the woods where pines and hickories were springing up. The ice in the pond was not yet dissolved, though there were some open spaces, and it was all dark colored and saturated with water. There were some slight flurries of snow during the days that I worked there; but for the most part when I came out on to the railroad, on my way home, its yellow sand heap stretched away gleaming in the hazy atmosphere, and the rails shone in the spring sun, and I heard the lark and pewee and other birds already come to commence another year with us. They were pleasant spring days, in which the winter of man's discontent[85] was thawing as well as the earth, and the life that had lain torpid began to stretch itself. One day, when my axe had come off,[86] and I had cut a green hickory for a wedge, driving it with a stone, and had placed the whole to soak in a pond hole in order to swell the wood, I saw a striped snake run into the water, and he lay on the bottom, apparently without inconvenience, as long as I staid there, or more than a quarter of an hour; perhaps because he had not yet fairly come out of the torpid state. It appeared to me that for a like reason men remain in their present low and primitive condition; but if they should feel the influence of the spring of springs arousing them, they would of necessity rise to a higher and more ethereal life. I had previously seen the snakes in frosty mornings in my path with portions of their bodies still numb and inflexible, waiting for the sun to thaw them. On the 1st of April it rained and melted the ice, and in the early part of the day, which was very foggy, I heard a stray goose groping about over the pond and cackling as if lost, or like the spirit of the fog.

---

[85] Adapted from the opening line of Shakespeare's *Richard III*.
[86] When the axe-head had come off the handle.

So I went on for some days cutting and hewing thimber, and also studs and rafters, all with my narrow axe, not having many communicable or scholar-like thoughts, singing to myself,—

> Men say they know many things;
> Bu lo! they have taken wings,—
> The arts and sciences,
> And a thousand appliances;
> The wind that blows
> Is all that any body knows.[87]

I hewed the main timbers six inches square, most of the studs on two sides only, and the rafters and floor timbers on one side, leaving the rest of the bark on, so that they were just as straight and much stronger than sawed ones. Each stick was carefully mortised or tenoned by its stump, for I had borrowed other tools by this time. My days in the woods were not very long ones; yet I usually carried my dinner of bread and butter, and read the newspaper in which it was wrapped, at noon, sitting amid the green pine boughs which I had cut off, and to my bread was imparted some of their fragrance, for my hands were covered with a thick coat of pitch. Before I had done I was more the friend than the foe of the pine tree, though I had cut down some of them, having become better acquainted with it. Sometimes a rambler in the wood was attracted by the sound of my axe, and we chatted pleasantly over the chips which I had made.

By the middle of April, for I made no haste in my work, but rather made the most of it, my house was framed and ready for the raising. I had already bought the shanty of James Collins, an Irishman who worked on the Fitchburg Railroad, for boards. James Collins' shanty was considered an uncommonly fine one. When I called to see it he was not at home. I walked about the outside, at first unobserved from within, the window was so deep and high. It was of small dimensions, with a peaked cottage roof, and not much else to be seen, the dirt being raised five feet all around as if it were a compost heap. The roof was the soundest part, though a good deal warped and made brittle by the sun. Door-sill there was none, but a perennial passage for the hens under the board. Mrs. C. came to the door and asked me to view it from the inside. The hens were driven in by my approach. It was dark, and had a dirt floor for the most part, dank, clammy, and aguish, only here a board and there a board which would not bear removal. She lighted a lamp to show me the inside of the roof and the walls, and also that the board floor extended under the bed, warning me not to step into the cellar, a sort of dust hole two feet deep. In her own words, they were "good boards overhead, good boards all around, and a good window,"—of two whole squares originally, only the cat had passed out that way lately. There was a stove, a bed, and a place to sit, an infant in the house where it was born, a silk parasol, gilt-framed looking-glass, and a patent new coffee mill nailed to an oak sapling, all told. The bargain was soon concluded, for James had in the mean while returned. I to pay four dollars and twenty-five cents to-night, he to vacate at five to-morrow morning, selling to nobody else meanwhile: I to take possession at six. It were well, he said, to be there early, and anticipate certain indistinct but wholly unjust claims on the score of ground rent and fuel. This he assured me was the only encumbrance. At

---

[87] Throughout *Walden*, the poetry not appearing in quotation marks is Thoreau's.

six I passed him and his family on the road. One large bundle held their all,—bed, coffee-mill, looking-glass, hens —all but the cat, she took to the woods and became a wild cat, and, as I learned afterward, trod in a trap set for woodchucks, and so became a dead cat at last.

I took down this dwelling the same morning, drawing the nails, and removed it to the pond side by small cartloads, spreading the boards on the grass there to bleach and warp back again in the sun. One early thrush gave me a note or two as I drove along the woodland path. I was informed treacherously by a young Patrick[88] that neighbor Seeley, an Irishman, in the intervals of the carting, transferred the still tolerable, straight, and drivable nails, staples, and spikes to his pocket, and then stood when I came back to pass the time of day, and look freshly up, unconcerned, with spring thoughts, at the devastation; there being a dearth of work, as he said. He was there to represent spectatordom, and help make this seemingly insignificant event one with the removal of the gods of Troy.[89]

I dug my cellar in the side of a hill sloping to the south, where a woodchuck had formerly dug his burrow, down through sumach and blackberry roots, and the lowest stain of vegetation, six feet square by seven deep, to a fine sand where potatoes would not freeze in any winter. The sides were left shelving, and not stoned; but the sun having never shone on them, the sand still keeps its place. It was but two hours' work. I took particular pleasure in this breaking of ground, for in almost all latitudes men dig into the earth for an equable temperature. Under the most splendid house in the city is still to be found the cellar where they store their roots as of old, and long after the superstructure has disappeared posterity remark its dent in the earth. The house is still but a sort of porch at the entrance of a burrow.

At length, in the beginning of May, with the help of some of my acquaintances, rather to improve so good an occasion for neighborliness than for any necessity, I set up the frame of my house. No man was ever more honored in the character of his raisers[90] than I. They are destined, I trust, to assist at the raising of loftier structures one day. I began to occupy my house on the 4th of July, as soon as it was boarded and roofed, for the boards were carefully feather-edged and lapped,[91] so that it was perfectly impervious to rain; but before boarding I laid the foundation of a chimney at one end, bringing two cartloads of stones up the hill from the pond in my arms. I built the chimney after my hoeing in the fall, before a fire became necessary for warmth, doing my cooking in the mean while out of doors on the ground, early in the morning: which mode I still think is in some respects more convenient and agreeable than the usual one. When it stormed before my bread was baked, I fixed a few boards over the fire, and sat under them to watch my loaf, and passed some pleasant hours in that way. In those days, when my hands were much employed, I read but little, but the least scraps of paper which lay on the ground, my holder, or tablecloth, afforded me as much entertainment, in fact answered the same purpose as the Iliad.[92]

---

[88] Irishman; Thoreau uses "treacherously" (in mock-seriousness) because one Irishman is informing on another.

[89] According to Greek myth, the city of Troy could not be conquered so long as the statue of the goddess Pallas Athena remained in the temple; the theft of the statue by the Greeks during the Trojan War thus made their conquest possible.

[90] Among the acquaintances who helped Thoreau "raise" the frame of his small house were Ralph Waldo Emerson, the educator and reformer Bronson Alcott (1799–1888), the poet William Ellery Channing (1818–1901), and the Concord farmer Edward Hosmer and his three sons.

[91] Cut, nailed, and overlapped to shed rain.

[92] Homer's epic poem about the Trojan War and the Greek victory at Troy.

It would be worth the while to build still more deliberately than I did, considering, for instance, what foundation a door, a window, a cellar, a garret, have in the nature of man, and perchance never raising any superstructure until we found a better reason for it than our temporal necessities even. There is some of the same fitness in a man's building his own house that there is in a bird's building its own nest. Who knows but if men constructed their dwellings with their own hands, and provided food the themselves and families simply and honestly enough, the poetic faculty would be universally developed, as birds universally sing when they are so engaged? But alas! we do like cowbirds and cuckoos, which lay their eggs in nests which other birds have built, and cheer no traveller with their chattering and unmusical notes. Shall we forever resign the pleasure of construction to the carpenter? What does architecture amount to in the experience of the mass of men? I never in all my walks came across a man engaged in so simple and natural an occupation as building his house. We belong to the community. It is not the tailor alone who is the ninth part of a man;[93] it is as much the preacher, and the merchant, and the farmer. Where is this division of labor to end? and what object does it finally serve? No doubt another *may* also think for me; but it is not therefore desirable that he should do so to the exclusion of my thinking for myself.

True, there are architects so called in this country, and I have heard of one[94] at least possessed with the idea of making architectural ornaments have a core of truth, a necessity, and hence a beauty, as if it were a revelation to him. All very well perhaps from his point of view, but only a little better than the common dilettantism. A sentimental reformer in architecture, he began at the cornice, not at the foundation. It was only how to put a core of truth within the ornaments, that every sugar plum in fact might have an almond or caraway seed in it,—though I hold that almonds are most wholesome without the sugar,—and not how the inhabitant, the indweller, might build truly within and without, and let the ornaments take care of themselves. What reasonable man ever supposed that ornaments were something outward and in the skin merely,—that the tortoise got his spotted shell, or the shellfish its mother-o'-pearl tints, by such a contract as the inhabitants of Broadway their Trinity Church?[95] But a man has no more to do with the style of architecture of his house than a tortoise with that of its shell: nor need the soldier be so idle as to try to paint the precise *color* of his virtue on his standard. The enemy will find it out. He may turn pale when the trial comes. This man seemed to me to lean over the cornice and timidly whisper his half truth to the rude occupants who really knew it better than he. What of architectural beauty I now see, I know has gradually grown from within outward, out of the necessities and character of the indweller, who is the only builder,—out of some unconscious truthfulness, and nobleness, without ever a thought for the appearance; and whatever additional beauty of this kind is destined to be produced will be preceded by a like unconscious beauty of life. The most interesting dwellings in this country, as the painter knows, are the most unpretending, humble log huts and cottages of the poor commonly; it is the life of the inhabitants whose shells they are, and not any peculiarity in their surfaces merely, which makes them *picturesque;* and equally interesting will be the citizen's suburban box, when his life shall be as simple and as agreeable to the imagination, and there is as little straining after effect in the style of his dwelling. A great proportion of architectural ornaments are literally

[93] A play on the proverb "Nine tailors make a man."

[94] According to Thoreau's *Journal* (January 11, 1852), this "architect" was the sculptor Horatio Greenough (1805–1852); Thoreau knew Greenough's ideas imperfectly and indirectly.

[95] A New York City church, constructed in an ornamented, Gothic style (1839–1846).

hollow, and a September gale would strip them off, like borrowed plumes, without injury to the substantials. They can do without *architecture* who have no olives nor wines in the cellar.[96] What if an equal ado were made about the ornaments of style in literature, and the architects of our bibles spent as much time about their cornices as the architects of our churches do? So are made the *belles-lettres* and the *beaux-arts* and their professors.[97] Much it concerns a man, forsooth, how a few sticks are slanted over him or under him, and what colors are daubed upon his box. It would signify somewhat, if, in any earnest sense, *he* slanted them and daubed it; but the spirit having departed out of the tenant, it is of a piece with constructing his own coffin,—the architecture of the grave, and "carpenter" is but another name for "coffin-maker." One man says, in his despair or indifference to life, take up a handful of the earth at your feet, and paint your house that color. Is he thinking of his last and narrow house?[98] Toss up a copper[99] for it as well. What an abundance of leisure he must have! Why do you take up a handful of dirt? Better paint your house your own complexion; let it turn pale or blush for you. An enterprise to improve the style of cottage architecture! When you have got my ornaments ready I will wear them.

Before winter I built a chimney, and shingled the sides of my house, which were already impervious to rain, with imperfect and sappy shingles made of the first slice of the log, whose edges I was obliged to straighten with a plane.

I have thus a tight shingled and plastered house, ten feet wide by fifteen long, and eight-feet posts, with a garret and a closet, a large window on each side, two trap doors, one door at the end, and a brick fireplace opposite. The exact cost of my house, paying the usual price for such materials as I used, but not counting the work, all of which was done by myself, was as follows; and I give the details because very few are able to tell exactly what their houses cost, and fewer still, if any, the separate cost of the various materials which compose them:—

Boards,	$8 03½,	mostly shanty boards.
Refuse shingles for roof and sides,	4 00	
Laths,	1 25	
Two second-hand windows with glass,	2 43	
One thousand old brick,	4 00	
Two casks of lime,	2 40	That was high.
Hair,	0 31	More than I needed
Mantle-tree iron,	0 15	
Nails,	3 90	
Hinges and screws,	0 14	
Latch,	0 10	
Chalk,	0 01	
		I carried a good part
Transportation,	1 40}	on my back.
In all,	$28 12½	

---

[96] Who own nothing valuable: olives and wine were expensive imports then.
[97] "Fine literature," "fine arts" (French), and those who make a living talking about them.
[98] The grave or coffin.
[99] A coin with which to pay Charon, the ferryman of the dead crossing the river Styx of Greek myth.

These are all the materials excepting the timber stones and sand, which I claimed by squatter's right. I have also a small wood-shed adjoining, made chiefly of the stuff which was left after building the house.

I intend to build me a house which will surpass any on the main street in Concord in grandeur and luxury, as soon as it pleases me as much and will cost me no more than my present one.

I thus found that the student who wishes for a shelter can obtain one for a lifetime at an expense not greater than the rent which he now pays annually. If I seem to boast more than is becoming, my excuse is that I brag for humanity rather than for myself; and my shortcomings and inconsistencies do not affect the truth of my statement. Notwithstanding much cant and hypocrisy,—chaff which I find it difficult to separate from my wheat, but for which I am as sorry as any man,—I will breathe freely and stretch myself in this respect, it is such a relief to both the moral and physical system; and I am resolved that I will not through humility become the devil's attorney. I will endeavor to speak a good word for the truth. At Cambridge College[100] the mere rent of a student's room, which is only a little larger than my own, is thirty dollars each year, though the corporation had the advantage of building thirty-two side by side and under one roof, and the occupant suffers the inconvenience of many and noisy neighbors, and perhaps a residence in the fourth story. I cannot but think that if we had more true wisdom in these respects, not only less education would be needed, because, forsooth, more would already have been acquired, but the pecuniary expense of getting an education would in a great measure vanish. Those conveniences which the student requires at Cambridge or elsehwere cost him or somebody else ten times as great a sacrifice of life as they would with proper management on both sides. Those things for which the most money is demanded are never the things which the student most wants. Tuition, for instance, is an important item in the term bill, while for the far more valuable education which he gets by associating with the most cultivated of his contemporaries no charge is made. The mode of founding a college is, commonly, to get up a subscription of dollars and cents, and then following blindly the principles of a division of labor to its extreme, a principle which should never be followed but with circumspection,—to call in a contractor who makes this a subject of speculation, and he employs Irishmen or other operatives actually to lay the foundations, while the students that are to be are said to be fitting themselves for it; and for these oversights successive generations have to pay. I think that it would be *better than this,* for the students, or those who desire to be benefited by it, even to lay the foundation themselves. The student who secures his coveted leisure and retirement by systematically shirking any labor necessary to man obtains but an ignoble and unprofitable leisure, defrauding himself of the experience which alone can make leisure fruitful. "But," says one, "you do not mean that the students should go to work with their hands instead of their heads?" I do not mean that exactly, but I mean something which he might think a good deal like that; I mean that they should not *play* life, or *study* it merely, while the community supports them at this expensive game, but earnestly *live* it from beginning to end. How could youths better learn to live than by at once trying the experiment of living? Methinks that would exercise their minds as much as mathematics. If I wished a boy to know something about the arts and sciences, for instance, I would not pursue the common course, which is merely to send him into the neighbor-

[100] Harvard College in Cambridge, Massachusetts; Thoreau graduated there in 1837.

hood of some professor, where any thing is professed and practised but the art of life;—to survey the world through a telescope or a microscope, and never with his natural eye; to study chemistry, and not learn how his bread is made, or mechanics, and not learn how it is earned; to discover new satellites to Neptune, and not detect the motes in his eyes, or to what vagabond he is a satellite himself; or to be devoured by the monsters that swarm all around him, while contemplating the monsters in a drop of vinegar. Which would have advanced the most at the end of a month,—the boy who made his own jack-knife from the ore which he had dug and smelted, reading as much as would be necessary for this,—or the boy who had attended the lectures on metallurgy at the Institute in the mean while, and had received a Rodgers' penknife[101] from his father? Which would be most likely to cut his fingers?—To my astonishment I was informed on leaving college that I had studied navigation!—why, if I had taken one turn down the harbor I should have known more about it. Even the *poor* student studies and is taught only *political* economy, while that economy of living which is synonymous with philosophy is not even sincerely professed in our colleges. The consequence is, that while he is reading Adam Smith, Ricardo, and Say,[102] he runs his father in debt irretrievably.

As with our colleges, so with a hundred "modern improvements"; there is an illusion about them; there is not always a positive advance. The devil goes on exacting compound interest to the last for his early share and numerous succeeding investments in them. Our inventions are wont to be pretty toys, which distract our attention from serious things. They are but improved means to an unimproved end, an end which it was already but too easy to arrive at; as railroads lead to Boston or New York. We are in great haste to construct a magnetic telegraph from Maine to Texas; but Maine and Texas, it may be, have nothing important to communicate. Either is in such a predicament as the man who was earnest to be introduced to a distinguished deaf woman, but when he was presented, and one end of her ear trumpet was put into his hand, had nothing to say. As if the main object were to talk fast and not to talk sensibly. We are eager to tunnel under the Atlantic and bring the old world some weeks nearer to the new; but perchance the first news that will leak through into the broad, flapping American ear will be that the Princess Adelaide[103] has the whooping cough. After all, the man whose horse trots a mile in a minute does not carry the most important message; he is not an evangelist, nor does he come round eating locusts and wild honey.[104] I doubt if Flying Childers[105] ever carried a peck of corn to mill.

One says to me, "I wonder that you do not lay up money; you love to travel; you might take the cars and go to Fitchburg[106] to-day and see the country." But I am wiser than that. I have learned that the swiftest traveller is he that goes afoot. I say to my friend, Suppose we try who will get there first. The distance is thirty miles; the fare ninety cents. That is almost a day's wages. I remember when

---

[101] A knife produced by the English cutlery firm of Joseph Rodgers and Sons.

[102] Classical economists: the Scottish Adam Smith (1723–1790), the English David Ricardo (1772–1823), and the French Jean Baptiste Say (1767–1832).

[103] Princess Adelaide of Orleans (1771–1847), sister of Louis-Philippe, king of France from 1830 to 1848.

[104] In Matthew 3:4 John the Baptist subsisted on locusts and wild honey while he lived in the wilderness.

[105] A famous English racehorse.

[106] Fitchburg (near Concord), Massachusetts, a small town at the end of the railroad line that ran by Walden Pond.

wages were sixty cents a day for laborers on this very road. Well, I start now on foot, and get there before night; I have travelled at that rate by the week together. You will in the mean while have earned your fare, and arrive there some time to-morrow, or possibly this evening, if you are lucky enough to get a job in season. Instead of going to Fitchburg, you will be working here the greater part of the day. And so, if the railroad reached round the world, I think that I should keep ahead of you; and as for seeing the country and getting experience of that kind, I should have to cut your acquaintance altogether.

Such is the universal law, which no man can ever outwit, and with regard to the railroad even we may say it is as broad as it is long. To make a railroad round the world available to all mankind is equivalent to grading the whole surface of the planet. Men have an indistinct notion that if they keep up this activity of joint stocks and spades[107] long enough all will at length ride somewhere, in next to no time, and for nothing; but though a crowd rushes to the depot, and the conductor shouts "All aboard!" when the smoke is blown away and the vapor condensed, it will be perceived that a few are riding, but the rest are run over,—and it will be called, and will be "A melancholy accident." No doubt they can ride at last who shall have earned their fare, that is, if they survive so long, but they will probably have lost their elasticity and desire to travel by that time. This spending of the best part of one's life earning money in order to enjoy a questionable liberty, during the least valuable part of it, reminds me of the Englishman who went to India to make a fortune first, in order that he might return to England and live the life of a poet. He should have gone up garret at once. "What!" exclaim a million Irishmen starting up from all the shanties in the land, "is not this railroad which we have built a good thing?" Yes, I answer, *comparatively* good, that is, you might have done worse; but I wish, as you are brothers of mine, that you could have spent your time better than digging in this dirt.

Before I finished my house, wishing to earn ten or twelve dollars by some honest and agreeable method, in order to meet my unusual expenses, I planted about two acres and a half of light and sandy soil near it chiefly with beans, but also a small part with potatoes, corn, peas, and turnips. The whole lot contains eleven acres, mostly growing up to pines and hickories, and was sold the preceding season for eight dollars and eight cents an acre. One farmer said that it was "good for nothing but to raise cheeping squirrels on." I put no manure on this land, not being the owner, but merely a squatter, and not expecting to cultivate so much again, and I did not quite hoe it all once. I got out several cords of stumps in ploughing, which supplied me with fuel for a long time, and left small circles of virgin mould, easily distinguishable through the summer by the greater luxuriance of the beans there. The dead and for the most part unmerchantable wood behind my house, and the driftwood from the pond, have supplied the remainder of my fuel. I was obliged to hire a team and a man for the ploughing, though I held the plough myself. My farm outgoes for the first season were, for implements, seeds, work, etc., $14 72 1/2. The seed corn was given me. This never costs any thing to speak of, unless you plant more than enough. I got twelve bushels of beans, and eighteen bushels of potatoes, beside some peas and sweet corn. The yellow corn and turnips were too late to come to any thing. My whole income from the farm was

---

[107] Organizing corporations and building railroads.

$23 44.

Deducting the outgoes, ... 14 72½

there are left, ...$ 8 71½.

beside produce consumed and on hand at the time this estimate was made of the value of $4 50,—the amount on hand much more than balancing a little grass which I did not raise. All things considered, that is, considering the importance of a man's soul and of to-day, notwithstanding the short time occupied by my experiment, nay, partly even because of its transient character, I believe that that was doing better than any farmer in Concord did that year.

The next year I did better still, for I spaded up all the land which I required, about a third of an acre, and I learned from the experience of both years, not being in the least awed by many celebrated works on husbandry, Arthur Young,[108] among the rest, that if one would live simply and eat only the crop which he raised, and raise no more than he ate, and not exchange it for an insufficient quantity of more luxurious and expensive things, he would need to cultivate only a few rods of ground, and that it would be cheaper to spade up that than to use oxen to plough it, and to select a fresh spot from time to time than to manure the old, and he could do all his necessary farm work as it were with his left hand at odd hours in the summer; and thus he would not be tied to an ox, or horse, or cow, or pig, as at present. I desire to speak impartially on this point, and as one not interested in the success or failure of the present economical and social arrangements. I was more independent than any farmer in Concord, for I was not anchored to a house or farm, but could follow the bent of my genius, which is a very crooked one, every moment. Beside being better off than they already, if my house had been burned or my crops had failed, I should have been nearly as well off as before.

I am wont to think that men are not so much the keepers of herds as herds are the keepers of men, the former are so much the freer. Men and oxen exchange work; but if we consider necessary work only, the oxen will be seen to have greatly the advantage, their farm is so much the larger. Man does some of his part of the exchange work in his six weeks of haying, and it is no boy's play. Certainly no nation that lived simply in all respects, that is, no nation of philosophers, would commit so great a blunder as to use the labor of animals. True, there never was and is not likely soon to be a nation of philosophers, nor am I certain it is desirable that there should be. However, *I* should never have broken a horse or bull and taken him to board for any work he might do for me, for fear I should become a horse-man or a herds-man merely; and if society seems to be the gainer by so doing, are we certain that what is one man's gain is not another's loss, and that the stable-boy has equal cause with his master to be satisfied? Granted that some public works would not have been constructed without this aid, and let man share the glory of such with the ox and horse; does it follow that he could not have accomplished works yet more worthy of himself in that case? When men begin to do, not merely unnecessary or artistic, but luxurious and idle work, with their assistance, it is inevitable that a few do all the exchange work with the oxen, or, in other words, become the slaves of the strongest. Man thus not only works for the animal within him, but, for a symbol of this, he works for the animal without him. Though we have many substantial houses of brick or stone, the prosperity of the

[108] Young (1741–1820) was an English writer of practical books on farming.

farmer is still measured by the degree to which the barn overshadows the house. This town is said to have the largest houses for oxen cows and horses hereabouts, and it is not behindhand in its public buildings; but there are very few halls for free worship or free speech in this county. It should not be by their architecture, but why not even by their power of abstract thought, that nations should seek to commemorate themselves? How much more admirable the Bhagvat-Geeta[109] than all the ruins of the East! Towers and temples are the luxury of princes. A simple and independent mind does not toil at the bidding of any prince. Genius is not a retainer to any emperor, nor is its material silver, or gold, or marble, except to a trifling extent. To what end, pray, is so much stone hammered? In Arcadia,[110] when I was there, I did not see any hammering stone. Nations are possessed with an insane ambition to perpetuate the memory of themselves by the amount of hammered stone they leave. What if equal pains were taken to smooth and polish their manners? One piece of good sense would be more memorable than a monument as high as the moon. I love better to see stones in place. The grandeur of Thebes[111] was a vulgar grandeur. More sensible is a rod[112] of stone wall that bounds an honest man's field than a hundred-gated Thebes that has wandered farther from the true end of life. The religion and civilization which are barbaric and heathenish build splendid temples; but what you might call Christianity does not. Most of the stone a nation hammers goes toward its tomb only. It buries itself alive. As for the Pyramids, there is nothing to wonder at in them so much as the fact that so many men could be found degraded enough to spend their lives constructing a tomb for some ambitious booby, whom it would have been wiser and manlier to have drowned in the Nile, and then given his body to the dogs. I might possibly invent some excuse for them and him, but I have no time for it. As for the religion and love of art of the builders, it is much the same all the world over, whether the building be an Egyptian temple or the United States Bank. It costs more than it comes to. The mainspring is vanity, assisted by a love of garlic and bread and butter. Mr. Balcom, a promising young architect, designs it on the back of his Vitruvius,[113] with hard pencil and ruler, and the job is let out to Dobson & Sons, stonecutters. When the thirty centuries begin to look down on it, mankind begin to look up at it. As for your high towers and monuments, there was a crazy fellow once in this town who undertook to dig through to China, and he got so far that, as he said, he heard the Chinese pots and kettles rattle; but I think that I shall not go out of my way to admire the hole which he made. Many are concerned about the monuments of the West and the East,—to know who built them. For my part, I should like to know who in those days did not build them,—who were above such trifling. But to proceed with my statistics.

By surveying, carpentry, and day-labor of various other kinds in the village in the mean while, for I have as many trades as fingers, I had earned $13 34. The expense of food for eight months, namely, from July 4th to March 1st, the time when these estimates were made, though I lived there more than two years,—not counting potatoes, a little green corn, and some peas, which I had raised, nor considering the value of what was on hand at the last date, was

[109] The *Bhagavad-Gītā*, a sacred Hindu text.

[110] According to Greek myth, a place of pastoral simplicity and happiness; Thoreau imagined going there.

[111] A major city in ancient Egypt; Homer describes it in *The Iliad* as "hundred-gated."

[112] A measurement equivalent to sixteen and a half feet.

[113] Marcus Vitruvius Pollio (1st century B.C.), a Roman architect; Thoreau makes up the other names in this sentence to illustrate his point about vanity.

Rice,	$1	73½	
Molasses,	1	73	Cheapest form of the saccharine.
Rye meal,	1	04¾	
Indian meal,	0	99¾	Cheaper than rye.
Pork,	0	22	
Flour,	0	88	Costs more than Indian meal, both money and trouble.
Sugar,	0	80	
Lard,	0	65	
Apples,	0	25	
Dried apple,	0	22	
Sweet potatoes,	0	10	
One pumpkin,	0	6	
One watermelon,	0	2	
Salt,	0	3	

All experiments which failed.

Yes, I did eat $8 74, all told; but I should not thus unblushingly publish my guilt, if I did not know that most of my readers were equally guilty with myself, and that their deeds would look no better in print. The next year I sometimes caught a mess of fish for my dinner, and once I went so far as to slaughter a woodchuck which ravaged my bean-field,—effect his transmigration, as a Tarter[114] would say,—and devour him, partly for experiment's sake; but though it afforded me a momentary enjoyment, notwithstanding a musky flavor, I saw that the longest use would not make that a good practice, however it might seem to have your woodchucks ready dressed by the village butcher.

Clothing and some incidental expenses within the same dates, though little can be inferred from this item, amounted to

	$8 40¾
Oil and some household utensils, ...	2 00

So that all the pecuniary outgoes, excepting for washing and mending, which for the most part were done out of the house, and their bills have not yet been received,—and these are all and more than all the ways by which money necessarily goes out in this part of the world,—were

House, ...	$28 12½
Farm one year, ...	14 72½
Food eight months, ...	8 74
Clothing, etc., eight months, ...	8 40¾
Oil, etc., eight months, ...	2 00
In all, ...	$61 99¾

I address myself now to those of my readers who have a living to get. And to meet this I have for farm produce sold

	$23 44
Earned by day-labor, ...	13 34
In all, ...	$36 78,

[114] A tribesman of Russian Asia who believed souls pass into other bodies (transmigrate) after death.

which subtracted from the sum of the outgoes leaves a balance of $25 21¾ on the one side,—this being very nearly the means with which I started, and the measure of expenses to be incurred,—and on the other, beside the leisure and independence and health thus secured, a comfortable house for me as long as I choose to occupy it.

These statistics, however accidental and therefore uninstructive they may appear, as they have a certain completeness, have a certain value also. Nothing was given me of which I have not rendered some account. It appears from the above estimate, that my food alone cost me in money about twenty-seven cents a week. It was, for nearly two years after this, rye and Indian meal without yeast, potatoes, rice, a very little salt pork, molasses, and salt, and my drink water. It was fit that I should live on rice, mainly, who loved so well the philosophy of India. To meet the objections of some inveterate cavillers, I may as well state, that if I dined out occasionally, as I always had done, and I trust shall have opportunities to do again, it was frequently to the detriment of my domestic arrangements. But the dining out, being, as I have stated, a constant element, does not in the least affect a comparative statement like this.

I learned from my two years' experience that it would cost incredibly little trouble to obtain one's necessary food, even in this latitude; that a man may use as simple a diet as the animals, and yet retain health and strength. I have made a satisfactory dinner, satisfactory on several accounts, simply off a dish of purslane (*Portulaca oleracea*)[115] which I gathered in my cornfield, boiled and salted. I give the Latin on account of the savoriness of the trivial name. And pray what more can a reasonable man desire, in peaceful times, in ordinary noons, than a sufficient number of ears of green sweet-corn boiled, with the addition of salt? Even the little variety which I used was a yielding to the demands of appetite, and not of health. Yet men have come to such a pass that they frequently starve, not for want of necessaries, but for want of luxuries; and I know a good woman who thinks that her son lost his life because he took to drinking water only.

The reader will perceive that I am treating the subject rather from an economic than a dietetic point of view, and he will not venture to put my abstemiousness to the test unless he has a well-stocked larder.

Bread I at first made of pure Indian meal and salt, genuine hoe-cakes,[116] which I baked before my fire out of doors on a shingle or the end of a stick of timber sawed off in building my house; but it was wont to get smoked and to have a piny flavor. I tried flour also; but have at last found a mixture of rye and Indian meal most convenient and agreeable. In cold weather it was no little amusement to bake several small loaves of this in succession, tending and turning them as carefully as an Egyptian his hatching eggs.[117] They were a real cereal fruit which I ripened, and they had to my senses a fragrance like that of other noble fruits, which I kept in as long as possible by wrapping them in cloths. I made a study of the ancient and indispensable art of bread-making, consulting such authorities as offered, going back to the primitive days and first invention of the unleavened kind, when from the wildness of nuts and meats men first reached the mildness and refinement of this diet, and travelling gradually down in my studies through that accidental souring of the dough which, it is supposed, taught the leavening process, and through the various fermentations thereafter, till I came to "good, sweet, whole-

---

[115] A flowering weed used in salads.
[116] Thin breads made of cornmeal, originally baked on a hoe.
[117] Ancient Egyptians were the first to hatch eggs in incubators.

some bread," the staff of life. Leaven, which some deem the soul of bread, the *spiritus*[118] which fills its cellular tissue, which is religiously preserved like the vestal fire,[119]—some precious bottle-full, I suppose, first brought over in the Mayflower, did the business for America, and its influence is still rising, swelling, spreading, in cerealian[120] billows over the land,—this seed I regularly and faith-fully procured from the village, till at length one morning I forgot the rules, and scalded my yeast; by which accident I discovered that even this was not indispen-sable,—for my discoveries were not by the synthetic but analytic process,—and I have gladly omitted it since, though most housewives earnestly assured me that safe and wholesome bread without yeast might not be, and elderly people prophe-sied a speedy decay of the vital forces. Yet I find it not to be an essential ingredi-ent, and after going without it for a year am still in the land of the living; and I am glad to escape the trivialness of carrying a bottle-full in my pocket, which would sometimes pop and discharge its contents to my discomfiture. It is simpler and more respectable to omit it. Man is an animal who more than any other can adapt himself to all climates and circumstances. Neither did I put any sal soda, or other acid or alkali, into my bread. It would seem that I made it according to the recipe which Marcus Porcius Cato[121] gave about two centuries before Christ. "Panem depsticium sic facito. Manus mortariumque bene lavato. Farinam in mortarium indito, aquæ paulatim addito, subigitoque pulchre. Ubi bene subegeris, defingito, coquitoque sub testu." Which I take to mean—"Make kneaded bread thus. Wash your hands and trough well. Put the meal into the trough, add water gradually, and knead it thoroughly. When you have kneaded it well, mould it, and bake it under a cover," that is, in a baking-kettle. Not a word about leaven. But I did not always use this staff of life. At one time, owing to the emptiness of my purse, I saw none of it for more than a month.

Every New Englander might easily raise all his own breadstuffs in this land of rye and Indian corn, and not depend on distant and fluctuating markets for them. Yet so far are we from simplicity and independence that, in Concord, fresh and sweet meal is rarely sold in the shops, and hominy and corn in a still coarser form are hardly used by any. For the most part the farmer gives to his cattle and hogs the grain of his own producing, and buys flour, which is at least no more whole-some, at a greater cost, at the store. I saw that I could easily raise my bushel or two of rye and Indian corn, for the former will grow on the poorest land, and the latter does not require the best, and grind them in a hand-mill, and so do without rice and pork; and if I must have some concentrated sweet, I found by experiment that I could make a very good molasses either of pumpkins or beets, and I knew that I needed only to set out a few maples to obtain it more easily still, and while these were growing I could use various substitutes beside those which I have named, "For," as the Forefathers sang,—

> "we can make liquor to sweeten our lips
> Of pumpkins and parsnips and walnut-tree chips."[122]

---

[118] "Breath of life" (Latin).   [119] The sacred fire of the ancient Romans.

[120] A pun on the word "cerulean" (blue).

[121] Cato (234–149 B.C.) was a Roman statesman who advocated a return to the simplicity of an agri-cultural state; the recipe is from his *De Agricultura,* which also contains recipes for curing hams and making cheesecake.

[122] From an untitled poem in *Historical Collections* (1839), by John Warner Barber (1798–1885).

Finally, as for salt, that grossest of groceries, to obtain this might be a fit occasion for a visit to the seashore, or, if I did without it altogether, I should probably drink the less water. I do not learn that the Indians ever troubled themselves to go after it.

Thus I could avoid all trade and barter, so far as my food was concerned, and having a shelter already, it would only remain to get clothing and fuel. The pantaloons which I now wear were woven in a farmer's family,—thank Heaven there is so much virtue still in man; for I think the fall from the farmer to the operative as great and memorable as that from the man to the farmer;—and in a new country fuel is an encumbrance. As for a habitat, if I were not permitted still to squat, I might purchase one acre at the same price for which the land I cultivated was sold—namely, eight dollars and eight cents. But as it was, I considered that I enhanced the value of the land by squatting on it.

There is a certain class of unbelievers who sometimes ask me such questions as, if I think that I can live on vegetable food alone; and to strike at the root of the matter at once,—for the root is faith,—I am accustomed to answer such, that I can live on board nails. If they cannot understand that, they cannot understand much that I have to say. For my part, I am glad to hear of experiments of this kind being tried; as that a young man tried for a fortnight to live on hard, raw corn on the ear, using his teeth for all mortar. The squirrel tribe tried the same and succeeded. The human race is interested in these experiments, though a few old women who are incapacitated for them, or who own their thirds in mills,[123] may be alarmed.

My furniture, part of which I made myself, and the rest cost me nothing of which I have not rendered an account, consisted of a bed, a table, a desk, three chairs, a looking-glass three inches in diameter, a pair of tongs and andirons, a kettle, a skillet, and a frying-pan, a dipper, a wash-bowl, two knives and forks, three plates, one cup, one spoon, a jug for oil, a jug for molasses, and a japanned[124] lamp. None is so poor that he need sit on a pumpkin. That is shiftlessness. There is a plenty of such chairs as I like best in the village garrets to be had for taking them away. Furniture! Thank God, I can sit and I can stand without the aid of a furniture warehouse. What man but a philosopher would not be ashamed to see his furniture packed in a cart and going up country exposed to the light of heaven and the eyes of men, a beggarly account of empty boxes? That is Spaulding's[125] furniture. I could never tell from inspecting such a load whether it belonged to a so called rich man or a poor one; the owner always seemed poverty-stricken. Indeed, the more you have of such things the poorer you are. Each load looks as if it contained the contents of a dozen shanties; and if one shanty is poor, this is a dozen times as poor. Pray, for what do we *move* ever but to get rid of our furniture, our *exuviæ;*[126] at last to go from this world to another newly furnished, and leave this to be burned? It is the same as if all these traps were buckled to a man's belt, and he could not move over the rough country where our lines are cast without dragging them,—dragging his trap. He was a lucky fox that left his tail in the trap. The muskrat will gnaw his third leg off to be free. No wonder man has lost his elasticity. How often he is at a dead set![127] "Sir, if I may be so bold, what

---

[123] The women who are "incapacitated" here are toothless; the others inherited the traditional third of a husband's estate and invested in mills that grind the corn for them.

[124] Decorated and lacquered in a Japanese style.   [125] Reference unidentified.

[126] "Things that can be discarded" (Latin).   [127] At a dead end.

do you mean by a dead set?" If you are a seer, whenever you meet a man you will see all that he owns, ay, and much that he pretends to disown, behind him, even to his kitchen furniture and all the trumpery which he saves and will not burn, and he will appear to be harnessed to it and making what headway he can. I think that the man is at a dead set who has got through a knot hole or gateway where his sledge load of furniture cannot follow him. I cannot but feel compassion when I hear some trig,[128] compact-looking man, seemingly free, all girded and ready, speak of his "furniture," as whether it is insured or not. "But what shall I do with my furniture?" My gay butterfly is entangled in a spider's web then. Even those who seem for a long while not to have any, if you inquire more narrowly you will find have some stored in somebody's barn. I look upon England to-day as an old gentleman who is travelling with a great deal of baggage, trumpery which has accumulated from long housekeeping, which he has not the courage to burn; great trunk, little trunk, bandbox and bundle. Throw away the first three at least. It would surpass the powers of a well man nowadays to take up his bed and walk,[129] and I should certainly advise a sick one to lay down his bed and run. When I have met an immigrant tottering under a bundle which contained his all,—looking like an enormous wen[130] which had grown out of the nape of his neck,—I have pitied him, not because that was his all, but because he had all *that* to carry. If I have got to drag my trap, I will take care that it be a light one and do not nip me in a vital part. But perchance it would be wisest never to put one's paw into it.

I would observe, by the way, that it costs me nothing for curtains, for I have no gazers to shut out but the sun and moon, and I am willing that they should look in. The moon will not sour milk nor taint meat of mine, nor will the sun injure my furniture or fade my carpet, and if he is sometimes too warm a friend, I find it still better economy to retreat behind some curtain which nature has provided, than to add a single item to the details of housekeeping. A lady once offered me a mat, but as I had no room to spare within the house, nor time to spare within or without to shake it, I declined it, preferring to wipe my feet on the sod before my door. It is best to avoid the beginnings of evil.

Not long since I was present at the auction of a deacon's effects, for his life had not been ineffectual:—

"The evil that men do lives after them."[131]

As usual, a great proportion was trumpery which had begun to accumulate in his father's day. Among the rest was a dried tapeworm. And now, after lying half a century in his garret and other dust holes, these things were not burned; instead of a *bonfire,* or purifying destruction of them, there was an *auction,* or increasing of them.[132] The neighbors eagerly collected to view them, bought them all, and carefully transported them to their garrets and dust holes, to lie there till their estates are settled, when they will start again. When a man dies he kicks the dust.

The customs of some savage nations might, perchance, be profitably imitated by us, for they at least go through the semblance of casting their slough annually; they have the idea of the thing, whether they have the reality or not. Would it not

---

[128] Trim.

[129] In Matthew 9:6 Jesus said to a man afflicted of palsy, "Arise, take up thy bed, and go unto thine house."

[130] A cyst.   [131] From Shakespeare's *Julius Caesar* (III.ii.81).

[132] The Latin *auctio* means "to increase"; auctioneers seek to increase the price.

be well if we were to celebrate such a "busk," or "feast of first fruits," as Bartram[133] describes to have been the custom of the Mucclasse Indians? "When a town celebrates the busk," says he, "having previously provided themselves with new clothes, new pots, pans, and other household utensils and furniture, they collect all their worn out clothes and other despicable things, sweep and cleanse their houses, squares, and the whole town, of their filth, which with all the remaining grain and other old provisions they cast together into one common heap, and consume it with fire. After having taken medicine, and fasted for three days, all the fire in the town is extinguished. During this fast they abstain from the gratification of every appetite and passion whatever. A general amnesty is proclaimed; all malefactors may return to their town.—"

"On the fourth morning, the high priest, by rubbing dry wood together, produces new fire in the public square, from whence very habitation in the town is supplied with the new and pure flame."

They then feast on the new corn and fruits and dance and sing for three days, "and the four following days they receive visits and rejoice with their friends from neighboring towns who have in like manner purified and prepared themselves."

The Mexicans also practised a similar purification at the end of every fifty-two years, in the belief that it was time for the world to come to an end.

I have scarcely heard of a truer sacrament, that is, as the dictionary defines it, "outward and visible sign of an inward and spiritual grace," than this, and I have no doubt that they were originally inspired directly from Heaven to do thus, though they have no biblical record of the revelation.

For more than five years I maintained myself thus solely by the labor of my hands, and I found, that by working about six weeks in a year, I could meet all the expenses of living. The whole of my winters, as well as most of my summers, I had free and clear for study. I have thoroughly tried school-keeping, and found that my expenses were in proportion, or rather out of proportion, to my income, for I was obliged to dress and train, not to say think and believe, accordingly, and I lost my time into the bargain. As I did not teach for the good of my fellow-men, but simply for a livelihood, this was a failure. I have tried trade; but I found that it would take ten years to get under way in that, and that then I should probably be on my way to the devil. I was actually afraid that I might by that time be doing what is called a good business. When formerly I was looking about to see what I could do for a living, some sad experience in conforming to the wishes of friends being fresh in my mind to tax my ingenuity, I thought often and seriously of picking huckleberries; that surely I could do, and its small profits might suffice,— for my greatest skill has been to want but little,—so little capital it required, so little distraction from my wonted moods, I foolishly thought. While my acquaintances went unhesitatingly into trade or the professions, I contemplated this occupation as most like theirs; ranging the hills all summer to pick the berries which came in my way, and thereafter carelessly dispose of them; so, to keep the flocks of Admetus.[134] I also dreamed that I might gather the wild herbs, or carry evergreens to such villagers as loved to be reminded of the woods, even to the city, by hay-cart loads. But I have since learned that trade curses every thing it handles;

---

[133] William Bartram (1739–1823), an American naturalist, in *Travels Through North and South Carolina* (1791).

[134] According to Greek myth, during a period of banishment from Mt. Olympus, the sun god Apollo tended the flocks of King Admetus.

and though you trade in messages from heaven, the whole curse of trade attaches to the business.

As I preferred some things to others, and especially valued my freedom, as I could fare hard and yet succeed well, I did not wish to spend my time in earning rich carpets or other fine furniture, or delicate cookery, or a house in the Grecian or the Gothic style just yet. If there are any to whom it is no interruption to acquire these things, and who know how to use them when acquired, I relinquish to them the pursuit. Some are "industrious," and appear to love labor for its own sake, or perhaps because it keeps them out of worse mischief; to such I have at present nothing to say. Those who would not know what to do with more leisure than they now enjoy, I might advise to work twice as hard as they do,—work till they pay for themselves, and get their free papers.[135] For myself I found that the occupation of a day-laborer was the most independent of any, especially as it required only thirty or forty days in a year to support one. The laborer's day ends with the going down of the sun, and he is then free to devote himself to his chosen pursuit, independent of his labor; but his employer, who speculates from month to month, has no respite from one end of the year to the other.

In short, I am convinced, both by faith and experience, that to maintain one's self on this earth is not a hardship but a pastime, if we will live simply and wisely;[136] as the pursuits of the simpler nations are still the sports of the more artificial. It is not necessary that a man should earn his living by the sweat of his brow, unless he sweats easier than I do.

One young man of my acquaintance, who has inherited some acres, told me that he thought he should live as I did, *if he had the means*. I would not have any one adopt *my* mode of living on any account; for, beside that before he has fairly learned it I may have found out another for myself, I desire that there may be as many different persons in the world as possible; but I would have each one be very careful to find out and pursue *his own* way, and not his father's or his mother's or his neighbor's instead. The youth may build or plant or sail, only let him not be hindered from doing that which he tells me he would like to do. It is by a mathematical point only that we are wise, as the sailor or the fugitive slave keeps the polestar[137] in his eye; but that is sufficient guidance for all our life. We may not arrive at our port within a calculable period, but we would preserve the true course.

Undoubtedly, in this case, what is true for one is truer still for a thousand, as a large house is not more expensive than a small one in proportion to its size, since one roof may cover, one cellar underlie, and one wall separate several apartments. But for my part, I preferred the solitary dwelling. Moreover, it will commonly be cheaper to build the whole yourself than to convince another of the advantage of the common wall; and when you have done this, the common partition, to be much cheaper, must be a thin one, and that other may prove a bad neighbor, and also not keep his side in repair. The only coöperation which is commonly possible is exceedingly partial and superficial; and what little true coöperation there is, is as if it were not, being a harmony inaudible to men. If a man has faith he will coöperate with equal faith every where; if he has not faith, he will continue to live like the rest of the world, whatever company he is joined to. To coöperate, in the highest as well as the lowest sense, means *to get our living together*. I heard it

---

[135] To work off their debts as did indentured servants.

[136] A theory of Charles Fourier (1772–1837), a French social reformer and founder of agrarian cooperatives; the Brook Farm transcendentalist community used his ideas.

[137] The North Star, which gives the sailor direction and guides the escaped slave toward freedom.

proposed lately that two young men should travel together over the world, the one without money, earning his means as he went, before the mast and behind the plough, the other carrying a bill of exchange in his pocket. It was easy to see that they could not long be companions or coöperate, since one would not *operate* at all. They would part at the first interesting crisis in their adventures. Above all, as I have implied, the man who goes alone can start today; but he who travels with another must wait till that other is ready, and it may be a long time before they get off.

But all this is very selfish, I have heard some of my townsmen say. I confess that I have hitherto indulged very little in philanthropic enterprises. I have made some sacrifices to a sense of duty, and among others have sacrificed this pleasure also. There are those who have used all their arts to persuade me to undertake the support of some poor family in the town; and if I had nothing to do,—for the devil finds employment for the idle,[138]—I might try my hand at some such pastime as that. However, when I have thought to indulge myself in this respect, and lay their Heaven under an obligation by maintaining certain poor persons in all respects as comfortably as I maintain myself, and have even ventured so far as to make them the offer, they have one and all unhesitatingly preferred to remain poor. While my townsmen and women are devoted in so many ways to the good of their fellows, I trust that one at least may be spared to other and less humane pursuits. You must have a genius for charity as well as for any thing else. As for Doing-good, that is one of the professions which are full. Moreover, I have tried it fairly, and, strange as it may seem, am satisfied that it does not agree with my constitution. Probably I should not consciously and deliberately forsake my particular calling to do the good which society demands of me, to save the universe from annihilation; and I believe that a like but infinitely greater steadfastness elsewhere is all that now preserves it. But I would not stand between any man and his genius; and to him who does this work, which I decline, with his whole heart and soul and life, I would say, Persevere, even if the world call it doing evil, as it is most likely they will.

I am far from supposing that my case is a peculiar one; no doubt many of my readers would make a similar defence. At doing something,—I will not engage that my neighbors shall pronounce it good,—I do not hesitate to say that I should be a capital fellow to hire; but what that is, it is for my employer to find out. What *good* I do, in the common sense of that word, must be aside from my main path, and for the most part wholly unintended. Men say, practically, Begin where you are and such as you are, without aiming mainly to become of more worth, and with kindness aforethought go about doing good. If I were to preach at all in this strain, I should say rather, Set about being good. As if the sun should stop when he had kindled his fires up to the splendor of a moon or a star of the sixth magnitude, and go about like a Robin Goodfellow,[139] peeping in at every cottage window, inspiring lunatics, and tainting meats, and making darkness visible, instead of steadily increasing his genial heat and beneficence till he is of such brightness that no mortal can look him in the face, and then, and in the mean while too, going about the world in his own orbit, doing it good, or rather, as a truer philosophy has discovered, the world going about him getting good. When Phaeton,[140]

[138] A popular proverb in Thoreau's time.
[139] A mischievous elf in folklore; personified as Puck in Shakespeare's *A Midsummer Night's Dream*.
[140] According to Greek myth, the son of Apollo who attempted to drive his father's sun chariot.

wishing to prove his heavenly birth by his beneficence, had the sun's chariot but one day, and drove out of the beaten track, he burned several blocks of houses in the lower streets of heaven, and scorched the surface of the earth, and dried up every spring, and made the great desert of Sahara, till at length Jupiter hurled him headlong to the earth with a thunderbolt, and the sun, through grief at his death, did not shine for a year.

There is no odor so bad as that which arises from goodness tainted. It is human, it is divine, carrion. If I knew for a certainty that a man was coming to my house with the conscious design of doing me good, I should run for my life, as from that dry and parching wind of the African deserts called the simoom, which fills the mouth and nose and ears and eyes with dust till you are suffocated, for fear that I should get some of his good done to me,—some of its virus mingled with my blood. No,—in this case I would rather suffer evil the natural way. A man is not a good *man* to me because he will feed me if I should be starving, or warm me if I should be freezing, or pull me out of a ditch if I should ever fall into one. I can find you a Newfoundland dog that will do as much. Philanthropy is not love for one's fellow-man in the broadest sense. Howard[141] was no doubt an exceedingly kind and worthy man in his way, and has his reward; but, comparatively speaking, what are a hundred Howards to *us,* if their philanthropy do not help *us* in our best estate, when we are most worthy to be helped? I never heard of a philanthropic meeting in which it was sincerely proposed to do any good to me, or the like of me.

The Jesuits[142] were quite balked by those Indians who, being burned at the stake, suggested new modes of torture to their tormentors. Being superior to physical suffering, it sometimes chanced that they were superior to any consolation which the missionaries could offer; and the law to do as you would be done by fell with less persuasiveness on the ears of those, who, for their part, did not care how they were done by, who loved their enemies after a new fashion, and came very near freely forgiving them all they did.

Be sure that you give the poor the aid they most need, though it be your example which leaves them far behind. If you give money, spend yourself with it, and do not merely abandon it to them. We make curious mistakes sometimes. Often the poor man is not so cold and hungry as he is dirty and ragged and gross. It is partly his taste, and not merely his misfortune. If you give him money, he will perhaps buy more rags with it. I was wont to pity the clumsy Irish laborers who cut ice on the pond, in such mean and ragged clothes, while I shivered in my more tidy and somewhat more fashionable garments, till, one bitter cold day, one who had slipped into the water came to my house to warm him, and I saw him strip off three pairs of pants and two pairs of stockings ere he got down to the skin, though they were dirty and ragged enough, it is true, and that he could afford to refuse the *extra* garments which I offered him, he had so many *intra*[143] ones. This ducking was the very thing he needed. Then I began to pity myself, and I saw that it would be a greater charity to bestow on me a flannel shirt than a whole slop-shop[144] on him. There are a thousand hacking at the branches of evil to one who is striking at the root, and it may be that he who bestows the largest amount of time and money on the needy is doing the most by his mode of life to produce that misery which he strives in vain to relieve. It is the pious slave-breeder devoting the proceeds of

---

[141] John Howard (1726?–1790), an English philanthropist and prison reformer.

[142] Missionaries of the Society of Jesus, a Roman Catholic religious order, who sought converts to Christianity among American Indians.

[143] *Extra* means "outer," and *intra,* "inner" (Latin).   [144] A shop for cheap clothing.

every tenth slave[145] to buy a Sunday's liberty for the rest. Some show their kindness to the poor by employing them in their kitchens. Would they not be kinder if they employed themselves there? You boast of spending a tenth part of your income in charity; may be you should spend the nine tenths so, and done with it. Society recovers only a tenth part of the property then. Is this owing to the generosity of him in whose possession it is found, or to the remissness of the officers of justice?

Philanthropy is almost the only virtue which is sufficiently appreciated by mankind. Nay, it is greatly overrated; and it is our selfishness which overrates it. A robust poor man, one sunny day here in Concord, praised a fellow-townsman to me, because, as he said, he was kind to the poor; meaning himself. The kind uncles and aunts of the race are more esteemed than its true spiritual fathers and mothers. I once heard a reverend lecturer on England, a man of learning and intelligence, after enumerating her scientific, literary, and political worthies, Shakspeare, Bacon, Cromwell, Milton, Newton,[146] and others, speak next of her Christian heroes, whom, as if his profession required it of him, he elevated to a place far above all the rest, as the greatest of the great. They were Penn, Howard, and Mrs. Fry.[147] Every one must feel the falsehood and cant of this. The last were not England's best men and women; only, perhaps, her best philanthropists.

I would not subtract any thing from the praise that is due to philanthropy, but merely demand justice for all who by their lives and works are a blessing to mankind. I do not value chiefly a man's uprightness and benevolence, which are, as it were, his stem and leaves. Those plants of whose greenness withered we make herb tea for the sick, serve but a humble use, and are most employed by quacks. I want the flower and fruit of a man; that some fragrance be wafted over from him to me, and some ripeness flavor our intercourse. His goodness must not be a partial and transitory act, but a constant superfluity, which costs him nothing and of which he is unconscious. This is a charity that hides a multitude of sins.[148] The philanthropist too often surrounds mankind with the remembrance of his own cast-off griefs as an atmosphere, and calls it sympathy. We should impart our courage, and not our despair, our health and ease, and not our disease, and take care that this does not spread by contagion. From what southern plains comes up the voice of wailing?[149] Under what latitudes reside the heathen to whom we would send light? Who is that intemperate and brutal man whom we would redeem? If any thing ail a man, so that he does not perform his functions, if he have a pain in his bowels even,—for that is the seat of sympathy,[150]—he forthwith sets about reforming—the world. Being a microcosm himself, he discovers, and it is a true discovery, and he is the man to make it,—that the world has been eating green apples; to his eyes, in fact, the globe itself is a great green apple, which there is danger awful to think of that the children of men will nibble before it is ripe; and straightway his drastic philanthropy seeks out the Esquimaux and the Patagonian,[151] and embraces the populous Indian and Chinese villages; and thus, by a

[145] In the custom of tithing, one-tenth of a parishioner's income is given to support the church.

[146] The philosopher, essayist, and statesman Sir Francis Bacon (1561–1626); the revolutionary leader and Lord Protector of the Commonwealth Oliver Cromwell (1599–1658); the poet John Milton (1608–1674); the mathematician and natural philosopher Sir Isaac Newton (1642–1727).

[147] The American Quaker William Penn (1644–1718), John Howard, and the English Quaker Elizabeth Fry (1780–1845) were active in social reform.

[148] " . . . charity shall cover the multitude of sins," from I Peter 4:8.

[149] "*Our* southern plains," or slave states.

[150] An old idea held that the bowels are the source of sympathy.

[151] The Eskimo and the inhabitant of Patagonia, in southern South America.

few years of philanthropic activity, the powers in the mean while using him for their own ends, no doubt, he cures himself of his dyspepsia, the globe acquires a faint blush on one or both of its cheeks, as if it were beginning to be ripe, and life loses its crudity and is once more sweet and wholesome to live. I never dreamed of any enormity greater than I have committed. I never knew, and never shall know, a worse man than myself.

I believe that what so saddens the reformer is not his sympathy with his fellows in distress, but, though he be the holiest son of God, is his private ail. Let this be righted, let the spring come to him, the morning rise over his couch, and he will forsake his generous companions without apology. My excuse for not lecturing against the use of tobacco is, that I never chewed it; that is a penalty which reformed tobacco-chewers have to pay; though there are things enough I have chewed, which I could lecture against. If you should ever be betrayed into any of these philanthropies, do not let your left hand know what your right hand does,[152] for it is not worth knowing. Rescue the drowning and tie your shoe-strings. Take your time, and set about some free labor.

Our manners have been corrupted by communication with the saints. Our hymn-books resound with a melodious cursing of God and enduring him forever. One would say that even the prophets and redeemers had rather consoled the fears than confirmed the hopes of man. There is nowhere recorded a simple and irrepressible satisfaction with the gift of life, any memorable praise of God. All health and success does me good, however far off and withdrawn it may appear; all disease and failure helps to make me sad and does me evil, however much sympathy it may have with me or I with it. If, then, we would indeed restore mankind by truly Indian, botanic, magnetic, or natural means, let us first be as simple and well as Nature ourselves, dispel the clouds which hang over our own brows, and take up a little life into our pores. Do not stay to be an overseer of the poor, but endeavor to become one of the worthies of the world.

I read in the Gulistan, or Flower Garden, of Sheik Sadi of Shiraz,[153] that "They asked a wise man, saying; Of the many celebrated trees which the Most High God has created lofty and umbrageous, they call none azad, or free, excepting the cypress, which bears no fruit; what mystery is there in this? He replied; Each has its appropriate produce, and appointed season, during the continuance of which it is fresh and blooming, and during their absence dry and withered; to neither of which states is the cypress exposed, being always flourishing; and of this nature are the azads, or religious independents.—Fix not thy heart on that which is transitory; for the Dijlah, or Tigris, will continue to flow through Bagdad after the race of caliphs[154] is extinct: if thy hand has plenty, be liberal as the date tree; but if it affords nothing to give away, be an azad, or free man, like the cypress."

COMPLEMENTAL VERSES[155]
THE PRETENSIONS OF POVERTY

"Thou dost presume too much, poor needy wretch,
To claim a station in the firmament,

---

[152] "But when thou doest alms, let not thy left hand know what thy right hand doeth," from Matthew 6:3.

[153] Muslih-ud-Din (1184?–1291), or Saadi, a Persian poet, in *Gulistān*, (1258), or *"Rose Garden."*

[154] Heads of Islam.

[155] From *Coelum Britannicum* (1661), by the English poet Thomas Carew (1595?–1645?); Thoreau offered the lines, complete with his own title, as a tongue-in-cheek rebuttal to the idea set forth in "Economy."

Because thy humble cottage, or thy tub,
Nurses some lazy or pedantic virtue
In the cheap sunshine or by shady springs,
With roots and pot-herbs; where thy right hand,
Tearing those humane passions from the mind,
Upon whose stocks fair blooming virtues flourish,
Degradeth nature, and benumbeth sense,
And, Gorgon-like,[156] turns active men to stone.
We not require the dull society
Of your necessitated temperance,
Or that unnatural stupidity
That knows nor joy nor sorrow; nor your forc'd
Falsely exalted passive fortitude
Above the active. This low abject brood,
That fix their seats in mediocrity,
Become your servile minds; but we advance
Such virtues only as admit excess,
Brave, bounteous acts, regal magnificence,
All-seeing prudence, magnanimity
That knows no bound, and that heroic virtue
For which antiquity hath left no name,
But patterns only, such as Hercules,
Achilles, Theseus.[157] Back to thy loath'd cell;
And when thou seest the new enlightened sphere,
Study to know but what those worthies were."

T. Carew

II: Where I Lived, and What I Lived For

At a certain season of our life we are accustomed to consider every spot as the possible site of a house. I have thus surveyed the country on every side within a dozen miles of where I live. In imagination I have bought all the farms in succession, for all were to be bought, and I knew their price. I walked over each farmer's premises, tasted his wild apples, discoursed on husbandry with him, took his farm at his price, at any price, mortgaging it to him in my mind; even put a higher price on it,—took every thing but a deed of it,—took his word for his deed, for I dearly love to talk,—cultivated it, and him too to some extent, I trust, and withdrew when I had enjoyed it long enough, leaving him to carry it on. This experience entitled me to be regarded as a sort of real-estate broker by my friends. Wherever I sat, there I might live, and the landscape radiated from me accordingly. What is a house but a *sedes,* a seat?—better if a country seat. I discovered many a site for a house not likely to be soon improved, which some might have thought too far from the village, but to my eyes the village was too far from it. Well, there I might live, I said; and there I did live, for an hour, a summer and a winter life; saw how I could let the years run off, buffet the winter through, and see the spring come in. The future inhabitants of this region, wherever they may

---

[156] According to Greek myth, three sisters with hideous faces and glaring eyes, who turned to stone all who met their gaze.
[157] According to Greek myth, heroes: Achilles, known for leading the Trojan War and for his one vulnerable spot, his heel; Theseus, known for killing the Minotaur, a monster with the head of a bull.

place their houses, may be sure that they have been anticipated. An afternoon sufficed to lay out the land into orchard woodlot and pasture, and to decide what fine oaks or pines should be left to stand before the door, and whence each blasted tree could be seen to the best advantage; and then I let it lie, fallow perchance, for a man is rich in proportion to the number of things which he can afford to let alone.

My imagination carried me so far that I even had the refusal of several farms,—the refusal was all I wanted,—but I never got my fingers burned by actual possession. The nearest that I came to actual possession was when I bought the Hollowell Place,[1] and had begun to sort my seeds, and collected materials with which to make a wheelbarrow to carry it on or off with; but before the owner gave me a deed of it, his wife—every man has such a wife—changed her mind and wished to keep it, and he offered me ten dollars to release him. Now, to speak the truth, I had but ten cents in the world, and it surpassed my arithmetic to tell, if I was that man who had ten cents, or who had a farm, or ten dollars, or all together. However, I let him keep the ten dollars and the farm too, for I had carried it far enough; or rather, to be generous, I sold him the farm for just what I gave for it, and, as he was not a rich man, made him a present of ten dollars, and still had my ten cents, and seeds, and materials for a wheelbarrow left. I found thus that I had been a rich man without any damage to my poverty. But I retained the landscape, and I have since annually carried off what it yielded without a wheelbarrow. With respect to landscapes,—

> "I am monarch of all I *survey,*
> My right there is none to dispute."[2]

I have frequently seen a poet withdraw, having enjoyed the most valuable part of a farm, while the crusty farmer supposed that he had got a few wild apples only. Why, the owner does not know it for many years when a poet has put his farm in rhyme, the most admirable kind of invisible fence, has fairly impounded it, milked it, skimmed it, and got all the cream, and left the farmer only the skimmed milk.

The real attractions of the Hollowell farm, to me, were; its complete retirement, being about two miles from the village, half a mile from the nearest neighbor, and separated from the highway by a broad field; its bounding on the river, which the owner said protected it by its fogs from frosts in the spring, though that was nothing to me; the gray color and ruinous state of the house and barn, and the dilapidated fences, which put such an interval between me and the last occupant; the hollow and lichen-covered appled trees, gnawed by rabbits, showing what kind of neighbors I should have; but above all; the recollection I had of it from my earliest voyages up the river, when the house was concealed behind a dense grove of red maples, through which I heard the house-dog bark. I was in haste to buy it, before the proprietor finished getting out some rocks, cutting down the hollow apple trees, and grubbing up some young birches which had sprung up in the pasture, or, in short, had made any more of his improvements. To enjoy these advantages I

---

[1] A farm on the Sudbury River near Concord.
[2] From "Verses Supposed to be Written by Alexander Selkirk," by the English poet William Cowper (1731–1800). Selkirk (1676–1721) was a Scottish sailor after whom Daniel Defoe's Robinson Crusoe was modeled. Thoreau, who worked occasionally as a surveyor, plays on the word "survey."

was ready to carry it on; like Atlas[3] to take the world on my shoulders,—I never heard what compensation he received for that,—and do all those things which had no other motive or excuse but that I might pay for it and be unmolested in my possession of it; for I knew all the while that it would yield the most abundant crop of the kind I wanted if I could only afford to let it alone. But it turned out as I have said.

All that I could say, then, with respect to farming on a large scale, (I have always cultivated a garden,) was, that I had had my seeds ready. Many think that seeds improve with age. I have no doubt that time discriminates between the good and the bad; and when at last I shall plant, I shall be less likely to be disappointed. But I would say to my fellows, once for all, As long as possible live free and uncommitted. It makes but little difference whether you are committed to a farm or the county jail.

Old Cato,[4] whose "De Re Rustica" is my "Cultivator," says, and the only translation I have seen makes sheer nonsense of the passage, "When you think of getting a farm, turn it thus in your mind, not to buy greedily; nor spare your pains to look at it, and do not think it enough to go round it once. The oftener you go there the more it will please you if it is good." I think I shall not buy greedily, but go round and round it as long as I live, and be buried in it first, that it may please me the more at last.

The present was my next experiment of this kind, which I purpose to describe more at length; for convenience, putting the experience of two years into one. As I have said, I do not propose to write an ode to dejection, but to brag as lustily as chanticleer in the morning, standing on his roost, if only to wake my neighbors up.

When first I took up my abode in the woods, that is, began to spend my nights as well as days there, which, by accident, was on Independence Day, or the fourth of July, 1845, my house was not finished for winter, but was merely a defence against the rain, without plastering or chimney, the walls being of rough weather-stained boards, with wide chinks, which made it cool at night. The upright white hewn studs and freshly planed door and window casings gave it a clean and airy look, especially in the morning, when its timbers were saturated with dew, so that I fancied by noon some sweet gum would exude from them. To my imagination it retained throughout the day more or less of this auroral[5] character, reminding me of a certain house on a mountain which I had visited the year before. This was an airy and unplastered cabin, fit to entertain a travelling god, and where a goddess might trail her garments. The winds which passed over my dwelling were such as sweep over the ridges of mountains, bearing the broken strains, or celestial parts only, of terrestrial music. The morning wind forever blows, the poem of creation is uninterrupted; but few are the ears that hear it. Olympus[6] is but the outside of the earth every where.

The only house I had been the owner of before, if I except a boat, was a tent, which I used occasionally when making excursions in the summer, and this is still

---

[3] According to Greek myth, a Titan, or giant god, who was forced to support the heavens on his shoulders.

[4] Cato's *De Agricultura* was also known as *De Re Rustica;* two farming magazines named "Cultivator" were published in Thoreau's time.

[5] Morning.   [6] Mt. Olympus, home of the gods in Greek myth.

rolled up in my garret; but the boat,[7] after passing from hand to hand, has gone down the stream of time. With this more substantial shelter about me, I had made some progress toward settling in the world. This frame, so slightly clad, was a sort of crystallization around me, and reacted on the builder. It was suggestive somewhat as a picture in outlines. I did not need to go out doors to take the air, for the atmosphere within had lost none of its freshness. It was not so much within doors as behind a door where I sat, even in the rainiest weather. The Harivansa[8] says, "An abode without birds is like a meat without seasoning." Such was not my abode, for I found my self suddenly neighbor to the birds; not by having imprisoned one, but having caged myself near them. I was not only nearer to some of those which commonly frequent the garden and the orchard, but to those wilder and more thrilling songsters of the forest which never, or rarely, serenade a villager,—the wood-thrush, the veery, the scarlet tanager, the field-sparrow, the whippoorwill, and many others.

I was seated by the shore of a small pond, about a mile and a half south of the village of Concord and somewhat higher than it, in the midst of an extensive wood between that town and Lincoln, and about two miles south of that our only field known to fame, Concord Battle Ground;[9] but I was so low in the woods that the opposite shore, half a mile off, like the rest, covered with wood, was my most distant horizon. For the first week, whenever I looked out on the pond it impressed me like a tarn[10] high up on the side of a mountain, its bottom far above the surface of other lakes, and, as the sun arose, I saw it throwing off its nightly clothing of mist, and here and there, by degrees, its soft ripples or its smooth reflecting surface was revealed, while the mists, like ghosts, were stealthily withdrawing in every direction into the woods, as at the breaking up of some nocturnal conventicle. The very dew seemed to hang upon the trees later into the day than usual, as on the sides of mountains.

This small lake was of most value as a neighbor in the intervals of a gentle rain storm in August, when, both air and water being perfectly still, but the sky overcast, mid-afternoon had all the serenity of evening, and the wood-thrush sang around, and was heard from shore to shore. A lake like this is never smoother than at such a time; and the clear portion of the air above it being shallow and darkened by clouds, the water, full of light and reflections, becomes a lower heaven itself so much the more important. From a hill top near by, where the wood had been recently cut off, there was a pleasing vista southward across the pond, through a wide indentation in the hills which form the shore there, where their opposite sides sloping toward each other suggested a stream flowing out in that direction through a wooded valley, but stream there was none. That way I looked between and over the near green hills to some distant and higher ones in the horizon, tinged with blue. Indeed, by standing on tiptoe I could catch a glimpse of some of the peaks of the still bluer and more distant mountain ranges in the north-west, those true-blue coins from heaven's own mint, and also of some portion of the village. But in other directions, even from this point, I could not see over or beyond the woods which surrounded me. It is well to have some water in your neighborhood, to give buoyancy to and float the earth. One value even of the smallest well is, that when

---

[7] Built by Thoreau, used for excursions on the Concord and Merrimack rivers, and sold to Nathaniel Hawthorne for seven dollars. Hawthorne later gave it to the poet William Ellery Channing.

[8] A Hindu religious epic of the fifth century.

[9] The site of a battle at the outset of the American Revolution, April 19, 1775.

[10] A small mountain lake.

you look into it you see that the earth is not continent but insular. This is as important as that it keeps butter cool. When I looked across the pond from this peak toward the Sudbury meadows, which in time of flood I distinguished elevated perhaps by a mirage in their seething valley, like a coin in a basin, all the earth beyond the pond appeared like a thin crust insulated and floated even by this small sheet of intervening water, and I was reminded that this on which I dwelt was but *dry land*.

Though the view from my door was still more contracted, I did not feel crowded or confined in the least. There was pasture enough for my imagination. The low shrub-oak plateau to which the opposite shore arose, stretched away toward the prairies of the West and the steppes of Tartary,[11] affording ample room for all the roving families of men. "There are none happy in the world but beings who enjoy freely a vast horizon,"—said Damodara,[12] when his herds required new and larger pastures.

Both place and time were changed, and I dwelt nearer to those parts of the universe and to those eras in history which had most attracted me. Where I lived was as far off as many a region viewed nightly by astronomers. We are wont to imagine rare and delectable places in some remote and more celestial corner of the system, behind the constellation of Cassiopeia's Chair, far from noise and disturbance. I discovered that my house actually had its site in such a withdrawn, but forever new and unprofaned, part of the universe. If it were worth the while to settle in those parts near to the Pleiades of the Hyades, to Aldebaran or Altair,[13] then I was really there, or at an equal remoteness from the life which I had left behind, dwindled and twinkling with as fine a ray to my nearest neighbor, and to be seen only in moonless nights by him. Such was that part of creation where I had squatted;-

> "There was a shepherd that did live,
> And held his thoughts as high
> As were the mounts whereon his flocks
> Did hourly feed him by."[14]

What should we think of the shepherd's life if his flocks always wandered to higher pastures than his thoughts?

Every morning was a cheerful invitation to make my life of equal simplicity, and I may say innocence, with Nature herself. I have been as sincere a worshipper of Aurora as the Greeks.[15] I got up early and bathed in the pond; that was a religious exercise, and one of the best things which I did. They say that characters were engraven on the bathing tub of king Tching-thang[16] to this effect: "Renew thyself completely each day; do it again, and again, and forever again." I can understand that. Morning brings back the heroic ages. I was as much affected by the faint hum of a mosquito making its invisible and unimaginable tour through my apartment at earliest dawn, when I was sitting with door and windows open, as

---

[11] The ascending plains of Russian Asia, home of the Tartars.

[12] The Hindu god Krishna in the *Harivansa*.   [13]*Constellations and stars*.

[14] Anonymous lines set to music by Robert Jones in 1611 and printed in Thomas Evans's *Old Ballads* (1810).

[15] Actually, the Roman goddess of the dawn was named Eos by the Greeks.

[16] Founder of China's Shang dynasty (1766–1122 B.C.); the injunction to renew the self is from Confucius, *The Great Learning* (Ch. 1).

I could be by any trumpet that ever sang of fame. It was Homer's requiem; itself an Iliad and Odyssey in the air, singing its own wrath and wanderings. There was something cosmical about it; a standing advertisement, till forbidden,[17] of the everlasting vigor and fertility of the world. The morning, which is the most memorable season of the day, is the awakening hour. Then there is least somnolence in us; and for an hour, at least, some part of us awakes which slumbers all the rest of the day and night. Little is to be expected of that day, if it can be called a day, to which we are not awakened by our Genius,[18] but by the mechanical nudgings of some servitor, are not awakened by our own newly-acquired force and aspirations from within, accompanied by the undulations of celestial music, instead of factory bells, and a fragrance filling the air—to a higher life than we fell asleep from; and thus the darkness bear its fruit, and prove itself to be good, no less than the light. That man who does not believe that each day contains an earlier, more sacred, and auroral hour than he has yet profaned, has despaired of life, and is pursuing a descending and darkening way. After a partial cessation of his sensuous life, the soul of man, or its organs rather, are reinvigorated each day, and his Genius tries again what noble life it can make. All memorable events, I should say, transpire in morning time and in morning atmosphere. The Vedas[19] say, "All intelligences awake with the morning." Poetry and art, and the fairest and most memorable of the actions of men, date from such an hour. All poets and heroes, like Memnon, are the children of Aurora, and emit their music at sunrise. To him whose elastic and vigorous thought keeps pace with the sun, the day is a perpetual morning. It matters not what the clocks say or the attitudes and labors of men. Morning is when I am awake and there is a dawn in me. Moral reform is the effort to throw off sleep. Why is it that men give so poor an account of their day if they have not been slumbering? They are not such poor calculators. If they had not been overcome with drowsiness they would have performed something. The millions are awake enough for physical labor; but only one in a million is awake enough for effective intellectual exertion, only one in a hundred millions to a poetic or divine life. To be awake is to be alive. I have never yet met a man who was quite awake. How could I have looked him in the face?

We must learn to reawaken and keep ourselves awake, not by mechanical aids, but by an infinite expectation of the dawn, which does not forsake us in our soundest sleep. I know of no more encouraging fact than the unquestionable ability of man to elevate his life by a conscious endeavor. It is something to be able to paint a particular picture, or to carve a statue, and so to make a few objects beautiful; but it is far more glorious to carve and paint the very atmosphere and medium through which we look, which morally we can do. To affect the quality of the day, that is the highest of arts. Every man is tasked to make his life, even in its details, worthy of the contemplation of his most elevated and critical hour. If we refused, or rather used up, such paltry information as we get, the oracles would distinctly inform us how this might be done.

I went to the woods because I wished to live deliberately, to front only the essential facts of life, and see if I could not learn what it had to teach, and not, when I came to die, discover that I had not lived. I did not wish to live what was not life, living is so dear; nor did I wish to practise resignation, unless it was quite necessary. I wanted to live deep and suck out all the marrow of life, to live so

---

[17] The letters "TF" directed a newspaper to run an advertisement until canceled.   [18] Guardian spirit.
[19] Ancient sacred Hindu scriptures.

sturdily and Spartan-like[20] as to put to rout all that was not life, to cut a broad swath and shave close, to drive life into a corner, and reduce it to its lowest terms, and, if it proved to be mean, why then to get the whole and genuine meanness of it, and publish its meanness to the world; or if it were sublime, to know it by experience, and be able to give a true account of it in my next excursion. For most men, it appears to me, are in a strange uncertainty about it, whether it is of the devil or of God, and have *somewhat hastily* concluded that it is the chief end of man here to "glorify God and enjoy him forever."[21]

Still we live meanly, like ants; though the fable tells us that we were long ago changed into men; like pygmies we fight with cranes;[22] it is error upon error, and clout upon clout, and our best virtue has for its occasion a superfluous and evitable wretchedness. Our life is frittered away by detail. An honest man has hardly need to count more than his ten fingers, or in extreme cases he may add his ten toes, and lump the rest. Simplicity, simplicity, simplicity! I say, let your affairs be as two or three, and not a hundred or a thousand; instead of a million count half a dozen, and keep your accounts on your thumb nail. In the midst of this chopping sea of civilized life, such are the clouds and storms and quicksands and thousand-and-one items to be allowed for, that a man has to live, if he would not founder and go to the bottom and not make his port at all, by dead reckoning, and he must be a great calculator indeed who succeeds. Simplify, simplify. Instead of three meals a day, if it be necessary eat but one; instead of a hundred dishes, five; and reduce other things in proportion. Our life is like a German Confederacy,[23] made up of petty states, with its boundary forever fluctuating, so that even a German cannot tell you how it is bounded at any moment. The nation itself, with all its so called internal improvements, which, by the way, are all external and superficial, is just such an unwieldy and overgrown establishment, cluttered with furniture and tripped up by its own traps, ruined by luxury and heedless expense, by want of calculation and a worthy aim, as the million households in the land; and the only cure for it as for them is in a rigid economy, a stern and more than Spartan simplicity of life and elevation of purpose. It lives too fast. Men think that it is essential that the *Nation* have commerce, and export ice, and talk through a telegraph, and ride thirty miles an hour, without a doubt, whether *they* do or not; but whether we should live like baboons or like men, is a little uncertain. If we do not get out sleepers,[24] and forge rails, and devote days and nights to the work, but go to tinkering upon our *lives* to improve *them,* who will build railroads? And if railroads are not built, how shall we get to heaven in season? But if we stay at home and mind our business, who will want railroads? We do not ride on the railroad; it rides upon us. Did you ever think what those sleepers are that underlie the railroad? Each one is a man, an Irish-man, or a Yankee man. The rails are laid on them, and they are covered with sand, and the cars run smoothly over them. They are sound sleepers, I assure you. And every few years a new lot is laid down and

---

[20] With discipline and courage.

[21] Adapted from the opening lines of the "Shorter Catechism" in the *New England Primer:* "Man's chief End is to Glorify God, and to Enjoy Him for ever." *"Somewhat hastily"* puts an ironic bite to the message.

[22] According to Greek myth, the supreme god Zeus turned ants into humans to repopulate a plague-ravaged kingdom; Homer's *Iliad* (Bk. III) compares the Trojans to cranes fighting with pygmies.

[23] Until Germany was unified in 1871 by Prince Otto von Bismarck (1815–1898), it was an assemblage of minor states.

[24] Wooden railroad ties (also, we must wake people from their lives of sleep).

run over; so that, if some have the pleasure of riding on a rail, others have the misfortune to be ridden upon. And when they run over a man that is walking in his sleep, a supernumerary sleeper in the wrong position, and wake him up, they suddenly stop the cars, and make a hue and cry about it, as if this were an exception. I am glad to know that it takes a gang of men for every five miles to keep the sleepers down and level in their beds as it is, for this is a sign that they may sometime get up again.

Why should we live with such hurry and waste of life? We are determined to be starved before we are hungry. Men say that a stitch in time saves nine, and so they take a thousand stitches to-day to save nine to-morrow. As for *work,* we haven't any of any consequence. We have the Saint Vitus' dance,[25] and cannot possibly keep our heads still. If I should only give a few pulls at the parish bell-rope, as for a fire, that is, without setting the bell,[26] there is hardly a man on his farm in the outskirts of Concord, notwithstanding that press of engagements which was his excuse so many times this morning, nor a boy, nor a woman, I might almost say, but would forsake all and follow that sound, not mainly to save property from the flames, but, if we will confess the truth, much more to see it burn, since burn it must, and we, be it known, did not set it on fire,—or to see it put out, and have a hand in it, if that is done as handsomely; yes, even if it were the parish church itself. Hardly a man takes a half hour's nap after dinner, but when he wakes he holds up his head and asks, "What's the news?" as if the rest of mankind had stood his sentinels. Some give directions to be waked every half hour, doubtless for no other purpose; and then, to pay for it, they tell what they have dreamed. After a night's sleep the news is as indispensable as the breakfast. "Pray tell me any thing new that has happened to a man any where on this globe",—and he reads it over his coffee and rolls, that a man has had his eyes gouged out this morning on the Wachito River;[27] never dreaming the while that he lives in the dark unfathomed mammoth cave[28] of this world, and has but the rudiment of an eye himself.

For my part, I could easily do without the post-office. I think that there are very few important communications made through it. To speak critically, I never received more than one or two letters in my life—I wrote this some years ago—that were worth the postage. The penny-post is, commonly, an institution through which you seriously offer a man that penny for his thoughts which is so often safely offered in jest. And I am sure that I never read any memorable news in a newspaper. If we read of one man robbed, or murdered, or killed by accident, or one house burned, or one vessel wrecked, or one steamboat blown up, or one cow run over on the Western Railroad,[29] or one mad dog killed, or one lot of grasshoppers in the winter,—we never need read of another. One is enough. If you are acquainted with the principle, what do you care for a myriad instances and applications? To a philosopher all *news,* as it is called, is gossip, and they who edit and read it are old women over their tea. Yet not a few are greedy after this gossip. There was such a rush, as I hear, the other day at one of the offices to learn the foreign news by the last arrival, that several large squares of plate glass belonging to the establishment were broken by the pressure,—news which I seriously think a ready wit might write a twelvemonth or twelve years beforehand with sufficient

---

[25] Chorea, a nervous disorder characterized by spasmodic twitchings.
[26] Pulling the bell rope so hard that the bell inverts.   [27] Arkansas's Ouachita River.
[28] Mammoth Cave in Kentucky, a deep cave in which blind fish had been seen.
[29] From Worcester, Massachusetts, to Albany, New York.

accuracy. As for Spain, for instance, if you know how to throw in Don Carlos and the Infanta, and Don Pedro[30] and Seville and Granada, from time to time in the right proportions,—they may have changed the names a little since I saw the papers,—and serve up a bull-fight when other entertainments fail, it will be true to the letter, and give us as good an idea of the exact state or ruin of things in Spain as the most succinct and lucid reports under this head in the newspapers: and as for England, almost the last significant scrap of news from that quarter was the revolution of 1649;[31] and if you have learned the history of her crops for an average year, you never need attend to that thing again, unless your speculations are of a merely pecuniary character. If one may judge who rarely looks into the newspapers, nothing new does ever happen in foreign parts, a French revolution not excepted.

What news! how much more important to know what that is which was never old! "Kieou-pe-yu (great dignitary of the state of Wei) sent a man to Khoung-tseu[32] to know his news. Khoung-tseu caused the messenger to be seated near him, and questioned him in these terms: What is your master doing? The messenger answered with respect: My master desires to diminish the number of his faults, but he cannot accomplish it. The messenger being gone, the philosopher remarked: What a worthy messenger! What a worthy messenger!" The preacher, instead of vexing the ears of drowsy farmers on their day of rest at the end of the week,—for Sunday is the fit conclusion of an ill-spent week, and not the fresh and brave beginning of a new one,—with this one other draggle-tail of a sermon, should shout with thundering voice,—"Pause! Avast! Why so seeming fast, but deadly slow?"

Shams and delusions are esteemed for soundest truths, while reality is fabulous. If men would steadily observe realities only, and not allow themselves to be deluded, life, to compare it with such things as we know, would be like a fairy tale and the Arabian Nights' Entertainments.[33] If we respected only what is inevitable and has a right to be, music and poetry would resound along the streets. When we are unhurried and wise, we perceive that only great and worthy things have any permanent and absolute existence,—that petty fears and petty pleasures are but the shadow of the reality. This is always exhilarating and sublime. By closing the eyes and slumbering, and consenting to be deceived by shows, men establish and confirm their daily life of routine and habit every where, which still is built on purely illusory foundations. Children, who play life, discern its true law and relations more clearly than men, who fail to live it worthily, but who think that they are wiser by experience, that is, by failure. I have read in a Hindoo book, that "there was a king's son, who, being expelled in infancy from his native city, was brought up by a forester, and, growing up to maturity in that state, imagined himself to belong to the barbarous race with which he lived. One of his father's ministers having discovered him, revealed to him what he was, and the misconception of his character was removed, and he knew himself to be a prince. So soul," continues the Hindoo philosopher, "from the circumstances in which it is placed, mistakes its own character, until the truth is revealed to it by some holy

---

[30] Don Carlos de Borbón (1788–1855) revolted when his niece Isabella II (1830–1904), the Infanta, was named to the throne of Spain; Dom Pedro de Alcántara Bourbón (1798–1834) of Portugal overthrew his usurping brother, Dom Miguel, and established a constitutional monarchy.

[31] When the Puritan Commonwealth supplanted the English monarchy.

[32] Confucius; the episode is related in the *Analects* (Bk. XIV, Ch. 26).

[33] *The Thousand and One Nights,* a collection of ancient Oriental and Middle Eastern tales.

teacher, and then it knows itself to be *Brahme*."[34] I perceive that we inhabitants of New England live this mean life that we do because our vision does not penetrate the surface of things. We think that that *is* which *appears* to be. If a man should walk through this town and see only the reality, where, think you, would the "Mill-dam"[35] go to? If he should give us an account of the realities he beheld there, we should not recognize the place in his description. Look at a meeting-house, or a court-house, or a jail, or a shop, or a dwelling-house, and say what that thing really is before a true gaze, and they would all go to pieces in your account of them. Men esteem truth remote, in the outskirts of the system, behind the farthest star, before Adam and after the last man. In eternity there is indeed something true and sublime. But all these times and places and occasions are now and here. God himself culminates in the present moment, and will never be more divine in the lapse of all the ages. And we are enabled to apprehend at all what is sublime and noble only by the perpetual instilling and drenching of the reality which surrounds us. The universe constantly and obediently answers to our conceptions; whether we travel fast or slow, the track is laid for us. Let us spend our lives in conceiving then. The poet or the artist never yet had so fair and noble a design but some of his posterity at least could accomplish it.

Let us spend one day as deliberately as Nature, and not be thrown off the track by every nutshell and mosquito's wing that falls on the rails. Let us rise early and fast, or break fast, gently and without perturbation; let company come and let company go, let the bells ring and the children cry,—determined to make a day of it. Why should we knock under and go with the stream? Let us not be upset and overwhelmed in that terrible rapid and whirlpool called a dinner, situated in the meridian shallows. Weather this danger and you are safe, for the rest of the way is down hill. With unrelaxed nerves, with morning vigor, sail by it, looking another way, tied to the mast like Ulysses.[36] If the engine whistles, let it whistle till it is hoarse for its pains. If the bell rings, why should we run? We will consider what kind of music they are like. Let us settle ourselves, and work and wedge our feet downward through the mud and slush of opinion, and prejudice, and tradition, and delusion, and appearance, that alluvion[37] which covers the globe, through Paris and London, through New York and Boston and Concord, through church and state, through poetry and philosophy and religion, till we come to a hard bottom and rocks in place, which we can call *reality*, and say, This is, and no mistake; and then begin, having a *point d'appui*,[38] below freshet and frost and fire, a place where you might found a wall or a state, or set a lamp-post safely, or perhaps a gauge, not a Nilometer,[39] but a Realometer, that future ages might know how deep a freshet of shams and appearances had gathered from time to time. If you stand right fronting and face to face to a fact, you will see the sun glimmer on both its surfaces, as if it were a cimeter,[40] and feel its sweet edge dividing you through the heart and marrow, and so you will happily conclude your mortal career. Be it life or death, we crave only reality. If we are really dying, let

---

[34] In Hindu theology, Brahma, the chief member of the trinity and creator of the universe.

[35] The commercial center of Concord.

[36] In Homer's *Odyssey*, Ulysses (Odysseus) has himself tied to his ship's mast so he can hear the seductive song of the Sirens and not be lured to destruction.

[37] Alluvium, sediment deposited by flowing water.

[38] "Point of support" (French), or base of operations.

[39] A gauge used by Egyptians to measure the depth of the Nile River.

[40] A scimitar, a sword with a curved blade.

us hear the rattle in our throats and feel cold in the extremities; if we are alive, let us go about our business.

Time is but the stream I go a-fishing in. I drink at it; but while I drink I see the sandy bottom and detect how shallow it is. Its thin current slides away but eternity remains. I would drink deeper; fish in the sky, whose bottom is pebbly with stars. I cannot count one. I know not the first letter of the alphabet. I have always been regretting that I was not as wise as the day I was born. The intellect is a cleaver; it discerns and rifts its way into the secret of things. I do not wish to be any more busy with my hands than is necessary. My head is hands and feet. I feel all my best faculties concentrated in it. My instinct tells me that my head is an organ for burrowing, as some creatures use their snout and fore-paws, and with it I would mine and burrow my way through these hills. I think that the richest vein is somewhere hereabouts; so by the divining rod and thin rising vapors[41] I judge; and here I will begin to mine.

III: READING

With a little more deliberation in the choice of their pursuits, all men would perhaps become essentially students and observers, for certainly their nature and destiny are interesting to all alike. In accumulating property for ourselves or our posterity, in founding a family or a state, or acquiring fame even, we are mortal; but in dealing with truth we are immortal, and need fear no change nor accident. The oldest Egyptian or Hindoo philosopher raised a corner of the veil from the statue of the divinity; and still the trembling robe remains raised, and I gaze upon as fresh a glory as he did, since it was I in him that was then so bold, and it is he in me that now reviews the vision. No dust has settled on that robe; no time has elapsed since that divinity was revealed. That time which we really improve, or which is improvable, is neither past, present, nor future.

My residence was more favorable, not only to thought, but to serious reading, than a university; and though I was beyond the range of the ordinary circulating library, I had more than ever come within the influence of those books which circulate round the world, whose sentences were first written on bark, and are now merely copied from time to time on to linen paper. Says the poet Mîr Camar Uddîn Mast,[1] "Being seated to run through the region of the spiritual world; I have had this advantage in books. To be intoxicated by a single glass of wine; I have experienced this pleasure when I have drunk the liquor of the esoteric doctrines." I kept Homer's Iliad on my table through the summer, though I looked at his page only now and then. Incessant labor with my hands, at first, for I had my house to finish and my beans to hoe at the same time, made more study impossible. Yet I sustained myself by the prospect of such reading in future. I read one or two shallow books of travel in the intervals of my work, till that employment made me ashamed of myself, and I asked where it was then that *I* lived.

The student may read Homer or Æschylus[2] in the Greek without danger of dissipation or luxuriousness, for it implies that he in some measure emulate their

---

[41] In superstition, aids in locating water or precious metals underground.

[1] An eighteenth-century Persian poet whose work Thoreau knew from the 1839 translation of Garcin de Tassy (1794–1878).

[2] The dramatist Aeschylus (525–456 B.C.) was the father of Greek tragedy.

heroes, and consecrate morning hours to their pages. The heroic books, even if printed in the character of our mother tongue, will always be in a language dead to degenerate times; and we must laboriously seek the meaning of each word and line, conjecturing a larger sense than common use permits out of what wisdom and valor and generosity we have. The modern cheap and fertile press, with all its translations, has done little to bring us nearer to the heroic writers of antiquity. They seem as solitary, and the letter in which they are printed as rare and curious, as ever. It is worth the expense of youthful days and costly hours, if you learn only some words of an ancient language, which are raised out of the trivialness of the street, to be perpetual suggestions and provocations. It is not in vain that the farmer remembers and repeats the few Latin words which he had heard. Men sometimes speak as if the study of the classics would at length make way for more modern and practical studies; but the adventurous student will always study classics, in whatever language they may be written and however ancient they may be. For what are the classics but the noblest recorded thoughts of man? They are the only oracles which are not decayed, and there are such answers to the most modern inquiry in them as Delphi and Dodona[3] never gave. We might as well omit to study Nature because she is old. To read well, that is, to read true books in a true spirit, is a noble exercise, and one that will task the reader more than any exercise which the customs of the day esteem. It requires a training such as the athletes underwent, the steady intention almost of the whole life to this object. Books must be read as deliberately and reservedly as they were written. It is not enough even to be able to speak the language of that nation by which they are written, for there is a memorable interval between the spoken and the written language, the language heard and the language read. The one is commonly transitory, a sound, a tongue, a dialect merely, almost brutish, and we learn it unconsciously, like the brutes, of our mothers. The other is the maturity and experience of that; if that is our mother tongue, this is our father tongue, a reserved and select expression, too significant to be heard by the ear, which we must be born again in order to speak. The crowds of men who merely *spoke* the Greek and Latin tongues in the middle ages were not entitled by the accident of birth to *read* the works of genius written in those languages; for these were not written in that Greek or Latin which they knew, but in the select language of literature. They had not learned the nobler dialects of Greece and Rome, but the very materials on which they were written were waste paper to them, and they prized instead a cheap contemporary literature. But when the several nations of Europe had acquired distinct though rude written languages of their own, sufficient for the purposes of their rising literatures, then first learning revived, and scholars were enabled to discern from that remoteness the treasures of antiquity. What the Roman and Grecian multitude could not *hear*, after the lapse of ages a few scholars *read*, and a few scholars only are still reading it.

However much we may admire the orator's occasional bursts of eloquence, the noblest written words are commonly as far behind or above the fleeting spoken language as the firmament with its stars is behind the clouds. *There* are the stars, and they who can may read them. The astronomers forever comment on and observe them. They are not exhalations like our daily colloquies and vaporous breath. What is called eloquence in the forum is commonly found to be rhetoric in the study. The orator yields to the inspiration of a transient occasion, and speaks

---

[3] The locations of ancient Greek shrines built to honor Apollo and Zeus, respectively.

to the mob before him, to those who can *hear* him; but the writer, whose more equable life is his occasion, and who would be distracted by the event and the crowd which inspire the orator, speaks to the intellect and heart of mankind, to all in any age who can *understand* him.

No wonder that Alexander[4] carried the Iliad with him on his expeditions in a precious casket. A written word is the choicest of relics. It is something at once more intimate with us and more universal than any other work of art. It is the work of art nearest to life itself. It may be translated into every language, and not only be read but actually breathed from all human lips;—not be represented on canvas or in marble only, but be carved out of the breath of life itself. The symbol of an ancient man's thought becomes a modern man's speech. Two thousand summers have imparted to the monuments of Grecian literature, as to her marbles, only a maturer golden and autumnal tint, for they have carried their own serene and celestial atmosphere into all lands to protect them against the corrosion of time. Books are the treasured wealth of the world and the fit inheritance of generations and nations. Books, the oldest and the best, stand naturally and rightfully on the shelves of every cottage. They have no cause of their own to plead, but while they enlighten and sustain the reader his common sense will not refuse them. Their authors are a natural and irresistible aristocracy in every society, and, more than kings or emperors, exert an influence on mankind. When the illiterate and perhaps scornful trader has earned by enterprise and industry his coveted leisure and independence, and is admitted to the circles of wealth and fashion, he turns inevitably at last to those still higher but yet inaccessible circles of intellect and genius, and is sensible only of the imperfection of his culture and the vanity and insufficiency of all his riches, and further proves his good sense by the pains which he takes to secure for his children that intellectual culture whose want he so keenly feels; and thus it is that he becomes the founder of a family.

Those who have not learned to read the ancient classics in the language in which they were written must have a very imperfect knowledge of the history of the human race; for it is remarkable that no transcript of them has ever been made into any modern tongue, unless our civilization itself may be regarded as such a transcript. Homer has never yet been printed in English,[5] nor Æschylus, nor Virgil even,—works as refined, as solidly done, and as beautiful almost as the morning itself; for later writers, say what we will of their genius, have rarely, if ever, equalled the elaborate beauty and finish and the lifelong and heroic literary labors of the ancients. They only talk of forgetting them who never knew them. It will be soon enough to forget them when we have the learning and the genius which will enable us to attend to and appreciate them. That age will be rich indeed when those relics which we call Classics, and the still older and more than classic but even less known Scriptures of the nations, shall have still further accumulated, when the Vaticans[6] shall be filled with Vedas and Zendavestas[7] and Bibles, with Homers and Dantes and Shakspeares, and all the centuries to come shall have successively deposited their trophies in the forum of the world. By such a pile we may hope to scale heaven at last.

---

[4] Alexander the Great (356–323 B.C.), the celebrated general and king of Macedon who in his youth was tutored by Aristotle.

[5] Translated into good, effective English; the Greek tragedian Aeschylus (525?–456 B.C.); the Roman poet Publius Vergillius Maro (70–19 B.C.), or Virgil, author of *The Aeniad*.

[6] Libraries with treasured holdings, such as those of the Vatican in Rome.

[7] Sacred texts of the Zoroastrian religion in ancient Persia.

The works of the great poets have never yet been read by mankind, for only great poets can read them. They have only been read as the multitude read the stars, at most astrologically, not astronomically. Most men have learned to read to serve a paltry convenience, as they have learned to cipher in order to keep accounts and not be cheated in trade; but of reading as a noble intellectual exercise they know little or nothing; yet this only is reading, in a high sense, not that which lulls us as a luxury and suffers the nobler faculties to sleep the while, but what we have to stand on tiptoe to read and devote our most alert and wakeful hours to.

I think that having learned our letters we should read the best that is in literature, and not be forever repeating our a b abs, and words of one syllable, in the fourth or fifth classes, sitting on the lowest and foremost form[8] all our lives. Most men are satisfied if they read or hear read, and perchance have been convicted[9] by the wisdom of one good book, the Bible, and for the rest of their lives vegetate and dissipate their faculties in what is called easy reading. There is a work in several volumes in our Circulating Library entitled Little Reading,[10] which I thought referred to a town of that name which I had not been to. There are those who, like cormorants and ostriches, can digest all sorts of this, even after the fullest dinner of meats and vegetables, for they suffer nothing to be wasted. If others are the machines to provide this provender, they are the machines to read it. They read the nine thousandth tale about Zebulon and Sephronia,[11] and how they loved as none had ever loved before, and neither did the course of their true love run smooth,—at any rate, how it did run and stumble, and get up again and go on! how some poor unfortunate got up onto a steeple, who had better never have gone up as far as the belfry; and then, having needlessly got him up there, the happy novelist rings the bell for all the world to come together and hear, O dear! how he did get down again! For my part, I think that they had better metamorphose all such aspiring heroes of universal noveldom into man weathercocks, as they used to put heroes among the constellations, and let them swing round there till they are rusty, and not come down at all to bother honest men with their pranks. The next time the novelist rings the bell I will not stir though the meeting-house burn down. "The Skip of the Tip-Toe-Hop, a Romance of the Middle Ages, by the celebrated author of 'Tittle-Tol-Tan,' to appear in monthly parts;[12] a great rush; don't all come together." All this they read with saucer eyes, and erect and primitive curiosity, and with unwearied gizzard, whose corrugations even yet need no sharpening, just as some little four-year-old bencher[13] his two-cent gilt-covered edition of Cinderella,—without any improvement, that I can see, in the pronunciation, or accent, or emphasis, or any more skill in extracting or inserting the moral. The result is dulness of sight, a stagnation of the vital circulations, and a general deliquium[14] and sloughing off of all the intellectual faculties. This sort of gingerbread is baked daily and more sedulously than pure wheat or rye-and-Indian in almost every oven, and finds a surer market.

The best books are not read even by those who are called good readers. What does our Concord culture amount to? There is in this town, with a very few excep-

---

[8] We should not be forever learning the alphabet and sitting on the low children's benches (forms) at the front of a one-room schoolhouse.

[9] Convinced, given convictions.

[10] The 1836 *Catalogue of Concord Social Library* lists a book called *Much Instruction From Little Reading.*

[11] Made-up names of characters in the stale plots of popular novels.   [12] Installments: serially.

[13] A child too young to be seated at a desk.   [14] Melting away.

tions, no taste for the best or for very good books even in English literature, whose words all can read and spell. Even the college-bred and so called liberally educated men here and elsewhere have really little or no acquaintance with the English classics; and as for the recorded wisdom of mankind, the ancient classics and Bibles, which are accessible to all who will know of them, there are the feeblest efforts any where made to become acquainted with them. I know a woodchopper, of middle age, who takes a French paper, not for news as he says, for he is above that, but to "keep himself in practice," he being a Canadian by birth; and when I ask him what he considers the best thing he can do in this world, he says, beside this, to keep up and add to his English. This is about as much as the college bred generally do or aspire to do, and they take an English paper for the purpose. One who has just come from reading perhaps one of the best English books will find how many with whom he can converse about it? Or suppose he comes from reading a Greek or Latin classic in the original, whose praises are familiar even to the so called illiterate; he will find nobody at all to speak to, but must keep silence about it. Indeed, there is hardly the professor in our colleges, who, if he has mastered the difficulties of the language, has proportionally mastered the difficulties of the wit and poetry of a Greek poet, and has any sympathy to impart to the alert and heroic reader; and as for the sacred Scriptures, or Bibles of mankind, who in this town can tell me even their titles? Most men do not know that any nation but the Hebrews have had a scripture. A man, any man, will go considerably out of his way to pick up a silver dollar; but here are golden words, which the wisest men of antiquity have uttered, and whose worth the wise of every succeeding age have assured us of;—and yet we learn to read only as far as Easy Reading, the primers and class-books, and when we leave school, the "Little Reading," and story books, which are for boys and beginners; and our reading, our conversation and thinking, are all on a very low level, worthy only of pygmies and manikins.

I aspire to be acquainted with wiser men than this our Concord soil has produced, whose names are hardly known here. Or shall I hear the name of Plato and never read his book? As if Plato[15] were my townsman and I never saw him,—my next neighbor and I never heard him speak or attended to the wisdom of his words. But how actually is it? His Dialogues, which contain what was immortal in him, lie on the next shelf, and yet I never read them. We are under-bred and low-lived and illiterate; and in this respect I confess I do not make any very broad distinction between the illiterateness of my townsman who cannot read at all, and the illiterateness of him who has learned to read only what is for children and feeble intellects. We should be as good as the worthies of antiquity, but partly by first knowing how good they were. We are a race of tit-men,[16] and soar but little higher in our intellectual flights than the columns of the daily paper.

It is not all books that are as dull as their readers. There are probably words addressed to our condition exactly, which, if we could really hear and understand, would be more salutary than the morning or the spring to our lives, and possibly put a new aspect on the face of things for us. How many a man has dated a new era in his life from the reading of a book. The book exists for us perchance which will explain our miracles and reveal new ones. The at present unutterable things we may find somewhere uttered. These same questions that disturb and puzzle and confound us have in their turn occurred to all the wise men; not one has been

---

[15] Plato (427?–347 B.C.) was a renowned Greek philosopher and student of Socrates.
[16] We are small, like the titbird.

omitted; and each has answered them, according to his ability, by his words and his life. Moreover, with wisdom we shall learn liberality. The solitary hired man on a farm in the outskirts of Concord, who has had his second birth and peculiar religious experience, and is driven as he believes into silent gravity and exclusiveness by his faith, may think it is not true; but Zoroaster, thousands of years ago, travelled the same road and had the same experience; but he, being wise, knew it to be universal, and treated his neighbors accordingly, and is even said to have invented and established worship among men. Let him humbly commune with Zoroaster then, and, through the liberalizing influence of all the worthies, with Jesus Christ himself, and let "our church" go by the board.

We boast that we belong to the nineteenth century and are making the most rapid strides of any nation. But consider how little this village does for its own culture. I do not wish to flatter my townsmen, nor to be flattered by them, for that will not advance either of us. We need to be provoked,—goaded like oxen, as we are, into a trot. We have a comparatively decent system of common schools, schools for infants only; but excepting the half-starved Lyceum[17] in the winter, and latterly the puny beginning of a library suggested by the state, no school for ourselves. We spend more on almost any article of bodily aliment or ailment than on our mental aliment. It is time that we had uncommon schools, that we did not leave off our education when we begin to be men and women. It is time that villages were universities, and their elder inhabitants the fellows of universities, with leisure—if they are indeed so well off—to pursue liberal studies the rest of their lives. Shall the world be confined to one Paris or one Oxford forever? Cannot students be boarded here and get a liberal education under the skies of Concord? Can we not hire some Abelard[18] to lecture to us? Alas! what with foddering the cattle and tending the store, we are kept from school too long, and our education is sadly neglected. In this country, the village should in some respects take the place of the nobleman of Europe. It should be the patron of the fine arts. It is rich enough. It wants only the magnanimity and refinement. It can spend money enough on such things as farmers and traders value, but it is thought Utopian to propose spending money for things which more intelligent men know to be of far more worth. This town has spent seventeen thousand dollars on a town-house,[19] thank fortune or politics, but probably it will not spend so much on living wit, the true meat to put into that shell, in a hundred years. The one hundred and twenty-five dollars annually subscribed for a Lyceum in the winter is better spent than any other equal sum raised in the town. If we live in the nineteenth century, why should we not enjoy the advantages which the nineteenth century offers? Why should our life be in any respect provincial? If we will read newspapers, why not skip the gossip of Boston and take the best newspaper in the world at once?—not be sucking the pap of "neutral family" papers, or browsing "Olive Branches"[20] here in New England. Let the reports of all the learned societies come to us, and we will see if they know any thing. Why should we leave it to Harper & Brothers and Redding & Co.[21] to select our reading? As the nobleman of cultivated taste surrounds himself with whatever conduces to his culture,—genius—learning—wit—books—paintings—statuary—music—philosophical instruments, and the

---

[17] The Concord Lyceum, a community forum that sponsored an annual lecture series, with tickets sold by subscription; Thoreau was active in arranging the series.

[18] Peter Abélard (1079–1142), a French theologian and teacher who espoused controversial views.

[19] A courthouse.   [20] A Methodist weekly paper published in Boston.

[21] A New York publisher and a Boston bookseller.

like; so let the village do,—not stop short at a pedagogue, a parson, a sexton, a parish library, and three selectmen, because our pilgrim forefathers got through a cold winter once on a bleak rock with these. To act collectively is according to the spirit of our institutions; and I am confident that, as our circumstances are more flourishing, our means are greater than the nobleman's. New England can hire all the wise men in the world to come and teach her, and board them round the while, and not be provincial at all. That is the *uncommon* school we want. Instead of noblemen, let us have noble villages of men. If it is necessary, omit one bridge over the river, go round a little there, and throw one arch at least over the darker gulf of ignorance which surrounds us.

IV: SOUNDS

But while we are confined to books, though the most select and classic, and read only particular written languages, which are themselves but dialects and provincial, we are in danger of forgetting the language which all things and events speak without metaphor, which alone is copious and standard. Much is published, but little printed. The rays which stream through the shutter will be no longer remembered when the shutter is wholly removed. No method nor discipline can supersede the necessity of being forever on the alert. What is a course of history, or philosophy, or poetry, no matter how well selected, or the best society, or the most admirable routine of life, compared with the discipline of looking always at what is to be seen? Will you be a reader, a student merely, or a seer? Read your fate, see what is before you, and walk on into futurity.

I did not read books the first summer; I hoed beans. Nay, I often did better than this. There were times when I could not afford to sacrifice the bloom of the present moment to any work, whether of the head or hands. I love a broad margin to my life. Sometimes, in a summer morning, having taken my accustomed bath, I sat in my sunny doorway from sunrise till noon, rapt in a revery, amidst the pines and hickories and sumachs, in undisturbed solitude and stillness, while the birds sang around or flitted noiseless through the house, until by the sun falling in at my west window, or the noise of some traveller's wagon on the distant highway, I was reminded of the lapse of time. I grew in those seasons like corn in the night, and they were far better than any work of the hands would have been. They were not time subtracted from my life, but so much over and above my usual allowance. I realized what the Orientals mean by contemplation and the forsaking of works. For the most part, I minded not how the hours went. The day advanced as if to light some work of mine; it was morning, and lo, now it is evening, and nothing memorable is accomplished. Instead of singing like the birds, I silently smiled at my incessant good fortune. As the sparrow had its trill, sitting on the hickory before my door, so had I my chuckle or suppressed warble which he might hear out of my nest. My days were not days of the week, bearing the stamp of any heathen deity,[1] nor were they minced into hours and fretted by the ticking of a clock; for I lived like the Puri Indians,[2] of whom it is said that "for yesterday,

---

[1] The names of ancient gods from Norse and Roman mythology, such as Wednesday (Woden's Day), Thursday (Thor's Day), and Saturday (Saturn's Day).
[2] Natives of eastern Brazil; from Ida Pfieffer's *A Lady's Voyage Round the World.*

to-day, and to-morrow they have only one word, and they express the variety of meaning by pointing backward for yesterday, forward for to-morrow, and over-head for the passing day." This was sheer idleness to my fellow-townsmen, no doubt; but if the birds and flowers had tried me by their standard, I should not have been found wanting. A man must find his occasions in himself, it is true. The natural day is very calm, and will hardly reprove his indolence.

I had this advantage, at least, in my mode of life, over those who were obliged to look abroad for amusement, to society and the theatre, that my life itself was become my amusement and never ceased to be novel. It was a drama of many scenes and without an end. If we were always indeed getting our living, and regu-lating our lives according to the last and best mode we had learned, we should never be troubled with ennui. Follow your genius closely enough, and it will not fail to show you a fresh prospect every hour. Housework was a pleasant pastime. When my floor was dirty, I rose early, and, setting all my furniture out of doors on the grass, bed and bedstead making but one budget,[3] dashed water on the floor, and sprinkled white sand from the pond on it, and then with a broom scrubbed it clean and white; and by the time the villagers had broken their fast the morning sun had dried my house sufficiently to allow me to move in again, and my medita-tions were almost uninterrupted. It was pleasant to see my whole household ef-fects out on the grass, making a little pile like a gypsy's pack, and my three-legged table, from which I did not remove the books and pen and ink, standing amid the pines and hickories. They seemed glad to get out themselves, and as if unwilling to be brought in. I was sometimes tempted to stretch an awning over them and take my seat there. It was worth the while to see the sun shine on these things, and hear the free wind blow on them; so much more interesting most fa-miliar objects look out of doors than in the house. A bird sits on the next bough, life-everlasting grows under the table, and blackberry vines run round its legs; pine cones, chestnut burs, and strawberry leaves are strewn about. It looked as if this was the way these forms came to be transferred to our furniture, to tables, chairs, and bedsteads,—because they once stood in their midst.

My house was on the side of a hill, immediately on the edge of the larger wood, in the midst of a young forest of pitch pines and hickories, and half a dozen rods from the pond, to which a narrow footpath led down the hill. In my front yard grew the strawberry, blackberry, and life-everlasting, johnswort and golden-rod, shrub-oaks and sand-cherry, blueberry and ground-nut. Near the end of May, the sand-cherry, *Cerasus pumila,* adorned the sides of the path with its delicate flowers arranged in umbels cylindrically about its short stems, which last, in the fall, weighed down with good sized and handsome cherries, fell over in wreaths like rays on every side. I tasted them out of compliment to Nature, though they were scarcely palatable. The sumach, *Rhus glabra,* grew luxuriantly about the house, pushing up through the embankment which I had made, and growing five or six feet the first season. Its broad pinnate tropical leaf was pleasant though strange to look on. The large buds, suddenly pushing out late in the spring from dry sticks which had seemed to be dead, developed themselves as by magic into graceful green and tender boughs, an inch in diameter; and sometimes, as I sat at my window, so heedlessly did they grow and tax their weak joints, I heard a fresh and tender bough suddenly fall like a fan to the ground, when there was not a breath of air stirring, broken off by its own weight. In August, the large masses of

[3] Grouping.

berries, which, when in flower, had attracted many wild bees, gradually assumed their bright velvety crimson hue, and by their weight again bent down and broke the tender limbs.

As I sit at my window this summer afternoon, hawks are circling about my clearing; the tantivy[4] of wild pigeons, flying by twos and threes athwart my view, or perching restless on the white-pine boughs behind my house, gives a voice to the air; a fishhawk dimples the glassy surface of the pond and brings up a fish; a mink steals out of the marsh before my door and seizes a frog by the shore; the sedge is bending under the weight of the reed-birds flitting hither and thither; and for the last half hour I have heard the rattle of railroad cars, now dying away and then reviving like the beat of a partridge, conveying travelers from Boston to the country. For I did not live so out of the world as that boy, who, as I hear, was put out to a farmer in the east part of the town, but ere long ran away and came home again, quite down at the heel and homesick. He had never seen such a dull and out-of-the-way place; the folks were all gone off; why, you couldn't even hear the whistle! I doubt if there is such a place in Massachusetts now:—

> "In truth, our village has become a butt
> For one of those fleet railroad shafts, and o'er
> Our peaceful plain its soothing sound is—Concord."[5]

The Fitchburg Railroad touches the pond about a hundred rods south of where I dwell. I usually go to the village along its causeway, and am, as it were, related to society by this link. The men on the freight trains, who go over the whole length of the road, bow to me as to an old acquaintance, they pass me so often, and apparently they take me for an employee; and so I am. I too would fain be a track-repairer somewhere in the orbit of the earth.

The whistle of the locomotive penetrates my woods summer and winter, sounding like the scream of a hawk sailing over some farmer's yard, informing me that many restless city merchants are arriving within the circle of the town, or adventurous country traders from the other side. As they come under one horizon, they shout their warning to get off the track to the other, heard sometimes through the circles of two towns. Here come your groceries, country; your rations, countrymen! Nor is there any man so independent on his farm that he can say them nay. And here's your pay for them! screams the countryman's whistle; timber like long battering rams going twenty miles an hour against the city's walls, and chairs enough to seat all the weary and heavy laden that dwell within them. With such huge and lumbering civility the country hands a chair to the city. All the Indian huckleberry hills are stripped, all the cranberry meadows are raked into the city. Up comes the cotton, down goes the woven cloth; up comes the silk, down goes the woollen; up come the books, but down goes the wit that writes them.

When I meet the engine with its train of cars moving off with planetary motion,—or, rather, like a comet, for the beholder knows not if with that velocity and with that direction it will ever revisit this system, since its orbit does not look like a returning curve,—with its steam cloud like a banner streaming behind in golden and silver wreaths, like many a downy cloud which I have seen, high in the heavens, unfolding its masses to the light,—as if this travelling demigod, this

---

[4] Impetuous rush.   [5] From "Walden Spring" (1849), by the poet William Ellery Channing.

cloud-compeller, would ere long take the sunset sky for the livery of his train; when I hear the iron horse make the hills echo with his snort like thunder, shaking the earth with his feet, and breathing fire and smoke from his nostrils, (what kind of winged horse or fiery dragon they will put into the new Mythology I don't know,) it seems as if the earth had got a race now worthy to inhabit it. If all were as it seems, and men made the elements their servants for noble ends! If the cloud that hangs over the engine were the perspiration of heroic deeds, or as beneficent to men as that which floats over the farmer's fields, then the elements and Nature herself would cheerfully accompany men on their errands and be their escort.

I watch the passage of the morning cars with the same feeling that I do the rising of the sun, which is hardly more regular. Their train of clouds stretching far behind and rising higher and higher, going to heaven while the cars are going to Boston, conceals the sun for a minute and casts my distant field into the shade, a celestial train beside which the petty train of cars which hugs the earth is but the barb of the spear. The stabler of the iron horse was up early this winter morning by the light of the stars amid the mountains, to fodder and harness his steed. Fire, too, was awakened thus early to put the vital heat in him and get him off. If the enterprise were as innocent as it is early! If the snow lies deep, they strap on his snow-shoes, and with the giant plow, plow a furrow from the mountains to the seaboard, in which the cars, like a following drill-barrow,[6] sprinkle all the restless men and floating merchandise in the country for seed. All day the fire-steed flies over the country, stopping only that his master may rest, and I am awakened by his tramp and defiant snort at midnight, when in some remote glen in the woods he fronts the elements incased in ice and snow; and he will reach his stall only with the morning star, to start once more on his travels without rest or slumber. Or perchance, at evening, I hear him in his stable blowing off the superfluous energy of the day, that he may calm his nerves and cool his liver and brain for a few hours of iron slumber. If the enterprise were as heroic and commanding as it is protracted and unwearied!

Far through unfrequented woods on the confines of towns, where once only the hunter penetrated by day, in the darkest night dart these bright saloons without the knowledge of their inhabitants; this moment stopping at some brilliant station-house in town or city, where a social crowd is gathered, the next in the Dismal Swamp,[7] scaring the owl and fox. The startings and arrivals of the cars are now the epochs in the village day. They go and come with such regularity and precision, and their whistle can be heard so far, that the farmers set their clocks by them, and thus one well conducted institution regulates a whole country. Have not men improved somewhat in punctuality since the railroad was invented? Do they not talk and think faster in the depot than they did in the stage-office? There is something electrifying in the atmosphere of the former place. I have been astonished at the miracles it has wrought; that some of my neighbors, who, I should have prophesied, once for all, would never get to Boston by so prompt a conveyance, were on hand when the bell rang. To do things "railroad fashion" is now the by-word; and it is worth the while to be warned so often and so sincerely by any power to get off its track. There is no stopping to read the riot act, no firing over the heads of the mob, in this case. We have constructed a fate, an *Atropos*,[8] that never turns aside. (Let that be the name of your engine.) Men are advertised that

---

[6] A machine for planting seeds.
[7] In the deep woods; the Dismal Swamp is in North Carolina and Virginia.
[8] According to Greek myth, one of the three Fates; she cut the thread of human life.

at a certain hour and minute these bolts will be shot toward particular points of the compass; yet it interferes with no man's business, and the children go to school on the other track. We live the steadier for it. We are all educated thus to be sons of Tell.[9] The air is full of invisible bolts. Every path but your own is the path of fate. Keep on your own track, then.

What recommends commerce to me is its enterprise and bravery. It does not clasp its hands and pray to Jupiter. I see these men every day go about their business with more or less courage and content, doing more even than they suspect, and perchance better employed than they could have consciously devised. I am less affected by their heroism who stood up for half an hour in the front line at Buena Vista,[10] than by the steady and cheerful valor of the men who inhabit the snow-plough for their winter quarters; who have not merely the three-o'-clock in the morning courage, which Bonaparte[11] thought was the rarest, but whose courage does not go to rest so early, who go to sleep only when the storm sleeps or the sinews of their iron steed are frozen. On this morning of the Great Snow, perchance, which is still raging and chilling men's blood, I hear the muffled tone of their engine bell from out the fog bank of their chilled breath, which announces that the cars *are coming,* without long delay, notwithstanding the veto of a New England north-east snow storm,[12] and I behold the ploughmen covered with snow and rime, their heads peering above the mould-board[13] which is turning down other than daisies and the nests of field-mice, like bowlders of the Sierra Nevada,[14] that occupy an outside place in the universe.

Commerce is unexpectedly confident and serene, alert, adventurous, and unwearied. It is very natural in its methods withal, far more so than many fantastic enterprises and sentimental experiments, and hence its singular success. I am refreshed and expanded when the freight train rattles past me, and I smell the stores which go dispensing their odors all the way from Long Wharf to Lake Champlain,[15] reminding me of foreign parts, of coral reefs, and Indian oceans, and tropical climes, and the extent of the globe. I feel more like a citizen of the world at the sight of the palm-leaf[16] which will cover so many flaxen New England heads the next summer, the Manilla hemp and cocoa-nut husks, the old junk, gunny bags, scrap iron, and rusty nails. This car-load of torn sails is more legible and interesting now than if they should be wrought into paper and printed books. Who can write so graphically the history of the storms they have weathered as these rents have done? They are proof-sheets which need no correction. Here goes lumber from the Maine woods, which did not go out to sea in the last freshet, risen four dollars on the thousand because of what did go out or was split up; pine,

---

[9] William Tell, the thirteenth-century Swiss patriot who reportedly shot an apple off his son's head, then set off a revolt against foreign oppression when he killed the Austrian tyrant who commanded him to do it.

[10] A battle (1847) in which superior American forces defeated Mexican forces during the Mexican War (1846–1848). Thoreau does not hail the courage of American soldiers in this battle because he opposed the war as a strategy for extending slave territory.

[11] Napoleon Bonaparte (1769–1821), the military leader and emperor of France (1804–1815). "Three-o'-clock in the morning courage" is spontaneous, instinctive in a brave soldier suddenly awakened to face peril.

[12] Probably the great snowstorm of February 1717, noted as a bit of New England lore in Thoreau's journal; "rime" is frost.

[13] Snowplow.

[14] The California mountain range that must have seemed an "outside place" to a stay-at-home traveler like Thoreau.

[15] From Boston harbor to Lake Champlain, on the border of New York and Vermont.

[16] Hats woven of palm leaves.

spruce, cedar,—first, second, third and fourth qualities, so lately all of one quality, to wave over the bear, and moose, and caribou. Next rolls Thomaston lime,[17] a prime lot, which will get far among the hills before it gets slacked. These rags in bales, of all hues and qualities, the lowest condition to which cotton and linen descend, the final result of dress,—of patterns which are now no longer cried up, unless it be in Milwaukie,[18] as those splendid articles, English, French, or American prints, ginghams, muslins, etc., gathered from all quarters of both fashion and poverty, going to become paper of one color or a few shades only, on which forsooth will be written tales of real life, high and low, and founded on fact! This closed car smells of salt fish, the strong New England and commercial scent, reminding me of the Grand Banks[19] and the fisheries. Who has not seen a salt fish, thoroughly cured for this world, so that nothing can spoil it, and putting the perseverance of the saints to the blush? with which you may sweep or pave the streets, and split your kindlings, and the teamster shelter himself and his lading against sun wind and rain behind it,—and the trader, as a Concord trader once did, hang it up by his door for a sign when he commences business, until at last his oldest customer cannot tell surely whether it be animal, vegetable, or mineral, and yet it shall be as pure as a snowflake, and if it be put into a pot and boiled, will come out an excellent dun[20] fish for a Saturday's dinner. Next Spanish hides, with the tails still preserving their twist and the angle of elevation they had when the oxen that wore them were careering over the pampas of the Spanish main,[21]— a type of all obstinacy, and evincing how almost hopeless and incurable are all constitutional vices. I confess, that practically speaking, when I have learned a man's real disposition, I have no hopes of changing it for the better or worse in this state of existence. As the Orientals say, "A cur's tail may be warmed, and pressed, and bound round with ligatures, and after a twelve years' labor bestowed upon it, still it will retain its natural form."[22] The only effectual cure for such inveteracies as these tails exhibit is to make glue of them, which I believe is what is usually done with them, and then they will stay put and stick. Here is a hogshead of molasses or of brandy directed to John Smith, Cuttingsville, Vermont, some trader among the green Mountains, who imports for the farmers near his clearing, and now perchance stands over his bulk-head and thinks of the last arrivals on the coast, how they may affect the price for him, telling his customers this moment, as he has told them twenty times before this morning, that he expects some by the next train of prime quality. It is advertised in the Cuttingsville Times.

While these things go up other things come down. Warned by the whizzing sound, I look up from my book and see some tall pine, hewn on far northern hills, which has winged its way over the green Mountains and the Connecticut,[23] shot like an arrow through the township within ten minutes, and scarce another eye beholds it; going

---

[17] Lime from Thomaston, Maine, which will be slaked ("slacked") with water to produce calcium hydroxide for farming.

[18] A bit of snobbery: the patterns are no longer sought after, "unless it be in Milwaukie."

[19] Fishing banks off the Newfoundland coast.

[20] Salted and dried, then aged in hay or manure. Thoreau puns on the dun color of such a "done" fish.

[21] The grasslands of the Spanish-owned portion of South America.

[22] From "The Lion and the Rabbit," in *Fables and Proverbs From the Sanskrit*, translated by Charles Wilkins (1749?–1836).

[23] The Connecticut River.

> "to be the mast
> Of some great ammiral."[24]

And hark! here comes the cattle-train bearing the cattle of a thousand hills, sheepcots, stables, and cow-yards in the air, drovers with their sticks, and shepherd boys in the midst of their flocks, all but the mountain pastures, whirled along like leaves blown from the mountains by the September gales. The air is filled with the bleating of calves and sheep, and the hustling of oxen, as if a pastoral valley were going by. When the old bell-wether[25] at the head rattles his bell, the mountains do indeed skip like rams and the little hills like lambs.[26] A car-load of drovers, too, in the midst, on a level with their droves now, their vocation gone, but still clinging to their useless sticks as their badge of office. But their dogs, where are they? It is a stampede to them; they are quite thrown out; they have lost the scent. Methinks I hear them barking behind the Peterboro' Hills,[27] or panting up the western slope of the Green Mountains. They will not be in at the death. Their vocation, too, is gone. Their fidelity and sagacity are below par now. They will slink back to their kennels in disgrace, or perchance run wild and strike a league with the wolf and the fox. So is your pastoral life whirled past and away. But the bell rings, and I must get off the track and let the cars go by;—

> What's the railroad to me?
> I never go to see
> Where it ends.
> If fills a few hollows,
> And makes banks for the swallows,
> It sets the sand a-blowing,
> And the blackberries a-growing,

but I cross it like a cart-path in the woods. I will not have my eyes put out and my ears spoiled by its smoke and steam and hissing.

Now that the cars are gone by, and all the restless world with them, and the fishes in the pond no longer feel their rumbling, I am more alone than ever. For the rest of the long afternoon, perhaps, my meditations are interrupted only by the faint rattle of a carriage or team along the distant highway.

Sometimes, on Sundays, I heard the bells, the Lincoln, Acton, Bedford,[28] or Concord bell, when the wind was favorable, a faint, sweet, and, as it were, natural melody, worth importing into the wilderness. At a sufficient distance over the woods this sound acquires a certain vibratory hum, as if the pine needles in the horizon were the strings of a harp which it swept. All sound heard at the greatest possible distance produces one and the same effect, a vibration of the universal lyre, just as the intervening atmosphere makes a distant ridge of earth interesting to our eyes by the azure tint it imparts to it. There came to me in this case a

---

[24] Admiral; from John Milton's *Paradise Lost* (I.293–294).
[25] A male sheep that leads the flock, with a bell attached to his neck.
[26] In fear of the Lord, "the mountains skipped like rams, and the little hills like lambs" from Psalm 114:4.
[27] In southern New Hampshire.   [28] Towns near Concord.

melody which the air had strained, and which had conversed with every leaf and needle of the wood, that portion of the sound which the elements had taken up and modulated and echoed from vale to vale. The echo is, to some extent, an original sound, and therein is the magic and charm of it. It is not merely a repetition of what was worth repeating in the bell, but partly the voice of the wood; the same trivial words and notes sung by a wood-nymph.

At evening, the distant lowing of some cow in the horizon beyond the woods sounded sweet and melodious, and at first I would mistake it for the voices of certain minstrels by whom I was sometimes serenaded, who might be straying over hill and dale; but soon I was not unpleasantly disappointed when it was prolonged into the cheap and natural music of the cow. I do not mean to be satirical, but to express my appreciation of those youths' singing, when I state that I perceived clearly that it was akin to the music of the cow, and they were at length one articulation of Nature.

Regularly at half past seven, in one part of the summer, after the evening train had gone by, the whippoorwills chanted their vespers for half an hour, sitting on a stump by my door, or upon the ridge pole of the house. They would begin to sing almost with as much precision as a clock, within five minutes of a particular time, referred to the setting of the sun, every evening. I had a rare opportunity to become acquainted with their habits. Sometimes I heard four or five at once in different parts of the wood, by accident one a bar behind another, and so near me that I distinguished not only the cluck after each note, but often that singular buzzing sound like a fly in a spider's web, only proportionally louder. Sometimes one would circle round and round me in the woods a few feet distant as if tethered by a string, when probably I was near its eggs. They sang at intervals throughout the night, and were again as musical as ever just before and about dawn.

When other birds are still the screech owls take up the strain, like mourning women their ancient u-lu-lu. Their dismal scream is truly Ben Jonsonian.[29] Wise midnight hags! It is no honest and blunt tu-whit tu-who of the poets, but, without jesting, a most solemn graveyard ditty, the mutual consolations of suicide lovers remembering the pangs and the delights of supernal love in the infernal groves. Yet I love to hear their wailing, their doleful responses, trilled along the woodside, reminding me sometimes of music and singing birds; as if it were the dark and tearful side of music, the regrets and sighs that would fain be sung. They are the spirits, the low spirits and melancholy forebodings, of fallen souls that once in human shape night-walked the earth and did the deeds of darkness, now expiating their sins with their wailing hymns or threnodies[30] in the scenery of their transgressions. They give me a new sense of the variety and capacity of that nature which is our common dwelling. *Oh-o-o-o-o that I never had been bor-r-r-r-n!* sighs one on this side of the pond, and circles with the restlessness of despair to some new perch on the gray oaks. Then—*that I never had been bor-r-r-r-n!* echoes another on the farther side with tremulous sincerity, and—*bor-r-r-r-n!* comes faintly from far in the Lincoln woods.

I was also serenaded by a hooting owl. Near at hand you could fancy it the most melancholy sound in Nature, as if she meant by this to stereotype and make permanent in her choir the dying moans of a human being,—some poor weak relic

---

[29] Of Ben Jonson (1572–1637), an Elizabethan dramatist, whose work was more tragic and comic than "dismal."

[30] Dirges, lamentations for the dead.

of mortality who has left hope behind, and howls like an animal, yet with human sobs, on entering the dark valley, made more awful by a certain gurgling melodiousness,—I find myself beginning with the letters gl when I try to imitate it,—expressive of a mind which has reached the gelatinous mildewy stage in the mortification of all healthy and courageous thought. It reminded me of ghouls and idiots and insane howlings. But now one answers from far woods in a strain made really melodious by distance,—*Hoo hoo hoo, hoorer hoo;* and indeed for the most part it suggested only pleasing associations, whether heard by day or night, summer or winter.

I rejoice that there are owls. Let them do the idiotic and maniacal hooting for men. It is a sound admirably suited to swamps and twilight woods which no day illustrates, suggesting a vast and undeveloped nature which men have not recognized. They represent the stark twilight and unsatisfied thoughts which all have. All day the sun has shone on the surface of some savage swamp, where the double spruce stands hung with usnea lichens,[31] and small hawks circulate above, and the chicadee lisps amid the evergreens, and the partridge and rabbit skulk beneath; but now a more dismal and fitting day dawns, and a different race of creatures awakes to express the meaning of Nature there.

Late in the evening I heard the distant rumbling of wagons over bridges,—a sound heard farther than almost any other at night,—the baying of dogs, and sometimes again the lowing of some disconsolate cow in a distant barn-yard. In the mean while all the shore rang with the trump of bullfrogs, the sturdy spirits of ancient wine-bibbers and wassailers, still unrepentant, trying to sing a catch in their Stygian lake,[32]—if the Walden nymphs will pardon the comparison, for though there are almost no weeds, there are frogs there,—who would fain keep up the hilarious rules of their old festal tables, though their voices have waxed hoarse and solemnly grave, mocking at mirth, and the wine has lost its flavor, and become only liquor to distend their paunches, and sweet intoxication never comes to drown the memory of the past, but mere saturation and waterloggedness and distention. The most aldermanic,[33] with his chin upon a heart-leaf, which serves for a napkin to his drooling chaps, under this northern shore quaffs a deep draught of the once scorned water, and passes round the cup with the ejaculation *tr-r-r-oonk, tr-r-r-oonk, tr-r-r-oonk!* and straightway comes over the water from some distant cove the same password repeated, where the next in seniority and girth has gulped down to his mark;[34] and when this observance has made the circuit of the shores, then ejaculates the master of ceremonies, with satisfaction, *tr-r-r-oonk!* and each in his turn repeats the same down to the least distended, leakiest, and flabbiest paunched, that there be no mistake; and then the bowl goes round again and again, until the sun disperses the morning mist, and only the patriarch is not under the pond,[35] but vainly bellowing *troonk* from time to time, and pausing for a reply.

I am not sure that I ever heard the sound of cock-crowing from my clearing, and I thought that it might be worth the while to keep a cockerel for his music merely, as a singing bird. The note of this once wild Indian pheasant is certainly the most remarkable of any bird's, and if they could be naturalized without being

---

[31] A hanging form of an algae/fungus combination.

[32] Singing successive parts in a round in their lake like the river Styx of the Underworld.

[33] Like a fat political leader.

[34] The large, collective cups of drinking societies were traditionally marked to designate each person's share.

[35] Under the table, or drunk.

domesticated, it would soon become the most famous sound in our woods, surpassing the clangor of the goose and the hooting of the owl; and then imagine the cackling of the hens to fill the pauses when their lords' clarions rested! No wonder that man added this bird to his tame stock,—to say nothing of the eggs and drumsticks. To walk in a winter morning in a wood where these birds abounded, their native woods, and hear the wild cockerels crow on the trees, clear and shrill for miles over the resounding earth, drowning the feebler notes of other birds,—think of it! It would put nations on the alert. Who would not be early to rise, and rise earlier and earlier every successive day of his life, till he became unspeakably healthy, wealthy, and wise? This foreign bird's note is celebrated by the poets of all countries along with the notes of their native songsters. All climates agree with brave Chanticleer. He is more indigenous even than the natives. His health is ever good, his lungs are sound, his spirits never flag. Even the sailor on the Atlantic and Pacific is awakened by his voice;[36] but its shrill sound never roused me from my slumbers. I kept neither dog, cat, cow, pig, nor hens, so that you would have said there was a deficiency of domestic sounds; neither the churn, nor the spinning wheel, nor even the singing of the kettle, nor the hissing of the urn, nor children crying, to comfort one. An old-fashioned man would have lost his senses or died of ennui before this. Not even rats in the wall, for they were starved out, or rather were never baited in,—only squirrels on the roof and under the floor, a whippoorwill on the ridge pole, a blue-jay screaming beneath the window, a hare or woodchuck under the house, a screech-owl or a cat-owl behind it, a flock of wild geese or a laughing loon on the pond, and a fox to bark in the night. Not even a lark or an oriole, those mild plantation birds, ever visited my clearing. No cockerels to crow nor hens to cackle in the yard. No yard! but unfenced Nature reaching up to your very sills. A young forest growing up under your windows, and wild sumachs and blackberry vines breaking through into your cellar; sturdy pitch-pines rubbing and creaking against the shingles for want of room, their roots reaching quite under the house. Instead of a scuttle or a blind blown off in the gale,—a pine tree snapped off or torn up by the roots behind your house for fuel. Instead of no path to the front-yard gate in the great Snow,—no gate,—no front-yard,—and no path to the civilized world!

V: Solitude

This is a delicious evening, when the whole body is one sense, and imbibes delight through every pore. I go and come with a strange liberty in Nature, a part of herself.[1] As I walk along the stony shore of the pond in my shirt sleeves, though it is cool as well as cloudy and windy, and I see nothing special to attract me, all the elements are unusually congenial to me. The bullfrogs trump to usher in the night, and the note of the whippoorwill is borne on the rippling wind from over the water. Sympathy with the fluttering alder and poplar leaves almost takes away my breath; yet, like the lake, my serenity is rippled but not ruffled. These small waves raised by the evening wind are as remote from storm as the smooth reflecting surface. Though it is now dark, the wind still blows and roars in the wood, the

---

[36] Fowl were taken on ocean voyages to provide eggs and meat.

[1] The first large pattern of *Walden* culminates in this chapter: Thoreau has moved from the society of his neighbors to the society of books, then (withdrawing further) from the sounds of commerce and nature to solitude and a sense of communion with nature.

waves still dash, and some creatures lull the rest with their notes. The repose is never complete. The wildest animals do not repose, but seek their prey now; the fox, and skunk, and rabbit, now roam the fields and woods without fear. They are Nature's watchmen,—links which connect the days of animated life.

When I return to my house I find that visitors have been there and left their cards, either a bunch of flowers, or a wreath of evergreen, or a name in pencil on a yellow walnut leaf or a chip. They who come rarely to the woods take some little piece of the forest into their hands to play with by the way, which they leave, either intentionally or accidentally. One has peeled a willow wand, woven it into a ring, and dropped it on my table. I could always tell if visitors had called in my absence, either by the bended twigs or grass, or the print of their shoes, and generally of what sex or age or quality they were by some slight trace left, as a flower dropped, or a bunch of grass plucked and thrown away, even as far off as the railroad, half a mile distant, or by the lingering odor of a cigar or pipe. Nay, I was frequently notified of the passage of a traveller along the highway sixty rods off by the scent of his pipe.

There is commonly sufficient space about us. Our horizon is never quite at our elbows. The thick wood is not just at our door, nor the pond, but somewhat is always clearing, familiar and worn by us, appropriated and fenced in some way, and reclaimed from Nature. For what reason have I this vast range and circuit, some square miles of unfrequented forest, for my privacy, abandoned to me by men? My nearest neighbor is a mile distant, and no house is visible from any place but the hill-tops within half a mile of my own. I have my horizon bounded by woods all to myself; a distant view of the railroad where it touches the pond on the one hand, and of the fence which skirts the woodland road on the other. But for the most part it is as solitary where I live as on the prairies. It is as much Asia or Africa as New England. I have, as it were, my own sun and moon and stars, and a little world all to myself. At night there was never a traveller passed my house, or knocked at my door, more than if I were the first or last man; unless it were in the spring, when at long intervals some came from the village to fish for pouts,—they plainly fished much more in the Walden Pond of their own natures, and baited their hooks with darkness,—but they soon retreated, usually with light baskets, and left "the world to darkness and to me,"[2] and the black kernel of the night was never profaned by any human neighborhood. I believe that men are generally still a little afraid of the dark, though the witches are all hung, and Christianity and candles have been introduced.

Yet I experienced sometimes that the most sweet and tender, the most innocent and encouraging society may be found in any natural object, even for the poor misanthrope and most melancholy man. There can be no very black melancholy to him who lives in the mist of Nature and has his senses still. There was never yet such a storm but it was Æolian music[3] to a healthy and innocent ear. Nothing can rightly compel a simple and brave man to a vulgar sadness. While I enjoy the friendship of the seasons I trust that nothing can make life a burden to me. The gentle rain which waters my beans and keeps me in the house to-day is not drear and melancholy, but good for me too. Though it prevents my hoeing them, it is of far more worth than my hoeing. If it should continue so long as to cause the seeds

[2] From "Elegy Written in a Country Churchyard" (1751), by the English poet Thomas Gray (1716–1771).

[3] Music from the Aeolian harp (named for Aeolus, keeper of the winds in Greek myth) was caused by breezes passing over its strings.

to rot in the ground and destroy the potatoes in the low lands, it would still be good for the grass on the uplands, and, being good for the grass, it would be good for me. Sometimes, when I compare myself with other men, it seems as if I were more favored by the gods than they, beyond any deserts that I am conscious of; as if I had a warrant and surety at their hands which my fellows have not, and were especially guided and guarded. I do not flatter myself, but if it be possible they flatter me. I have never felt lonesome, or in the least oppressed by a sense of solitude, but once, and that was a few weeks after I came to the woods, when, for an hour, I doubted if the near neighborhood of man was not essential to a serene and healthy life. To be alone was something unpleasant. But I was at the same time conscious of a slight insanity in my mood, and seemed to foresee my recovery. In the midst of a gentle rain while these thoughts prevailed, I was suddenly sensible of such sweet and beneficent society in Nature, in the very pattering of the drops, and in every sound and sight around my house, an infinite and unaccountable friendliness all at once like an atmosphere sustaining me, as made the fancied advantages of human neighborhood insignificant, and I have never thought of them since. Every little pine needle expanded and swelled with sympathy and befriended me. I was so distinctly made aware of the presence of something kindred to me, even in scenes which we are accustomed to call wild and dreary, and also that the nearest of blood to me and humanest was not a person nor a villager, that I thought no place could ever be strange to me again.—

> "Mourning untimely consumes the sad;
> Few are their days in the land of the living,
> Beautiful daughter of Toscar."[4]

Some of my pleasantest hours were during the long rain storms in the spring or fall, which confined me to the house for the afternoon as well as the forenoon, soothed by their ceaseless roar and pelting; when an early twilight ushered in a long evening in which many thoughts had time to take root and unfold themselves. In those driving north-east rains which tried the village houses so, when the maids stood ready with mop and pail in front entries to keep the deluge out, I sat behind my door in my little house, which was all entry, and thoroughly enjoyed its protection. In one heavy thunder shower the lightning struck a large pitch-pine across the pond, making a very conspicuous and perfectly regular spiral groove from top to bottom, an inch or more deep, and four or five inches wide, as you would groove a walking-stick. I passed it again the other day, and was struck with awe on looking up and beholding that mark, now more distinct than ever, where a terrific and resistless bolt came down out of the harmless sky eight years ago. Men frequently say to me, "I should think you would feel lonesome down there, and want to be nearer to folks, rainy and snowy days and nights especially." I am tempted to reply to such,—This whole earth which we inhabit is but a point in space. How far apart, think you, dwell the two most distant inhabitants of yonder star, the breadth of whose disk cannot be appreciated by our instruments? Why should I feel lonely? is not our planet in the Milky Way? This which you put seems to me not to be the most important questions. What sort of space is that which separates a man from his fellows and makes him solitary? I have found that no exertion of the legs can bring two minds much nearer to one another. What do

---

[4] From *Ossian* (1762), by the Scottish poet James McPherson (1735–1796).

we want most to dwell near to? Not to many men surely, the depot, the post-office, the bar-room, the meeting-house, the school-house, the grocery, Beacon Hill, or the Five Points,[5] where men most congregate, but to the perennial source of our life, whence in all our experience we have found that to issue; as the willow stands near the water and sends out its roots in that direction. This will vary with different natures, but this is the place where a wise man will dig his cellar . . . I one evening overtook one of my townsmen, who has accumulated what is called "a handsome property",—though I never got a *fair* view of it,—on the Walden road, driving a pair of cattle to market, who inquired of me how I could bring my mind to give up so many of the comforts of life. I answered that I was very sure I liked it passably well; I was not joking. And so I went home to my bed, and left him to pick his way through the darkness and the mud to Brighton,[6]—or Bright-town,—which place he would reach some time in the morning.

Any prospect of awakening or coming to life to a dead man makes indifferent all times and places. The place where that may occur is always the same and indescribably pleasant to all our senses. For the most part we allow only outlying and transient circumstances to make our occasions. They are, in fact, the cause of our distraction. Nearest to all things is that power which fashions their being. *Next* to us the grandest laws are continually being executed. *Next* to us is not the work-man whom we have hired, with whom we love so well to talk, but the workman whose work we are.

"How vast and profound is the influence of the subtile powers of Heaven and of Earth!"

"We seek to perceive them, and we do not see them, we seek to hear them, and we do not hear them; identified with the substance of things, they cannot be separated from them."

"They cause that in all the universe men purify and sanctify their hearts, and clothe themselves in their holiday garments to offer sacrifices and oblations to their ancestors. It is an ocean of subtile intelligences. They are every where, above us, on our left, on our right; they environ us on all sides."[7]

We are the subjects of an experiment which is not a little interesting to me. Can we not do without the society of our gossips a little while under these circumstances,—have our own thoughts to cheer us? Confucius says truly, "Virtue does not remain as an abandoned orphan; it must of necessity have neighbors."[8]

With thinking we may be beside ourselves in a sane sense. By a conscious effort of the mind we can stand aloof from actions and their consequences; and all things, good and bad, go by us like a torrent. We are not wholly involved in Nature. I may be either the drift-wood in the stream, or Indra[9] in the sky looking down on it. I *may* be affected by a theatrical exhibition; on the other hand, I *may not* be affected by an actual event which appears to concern me much more. I only know myself as a human entity; the scene, so to speak, of thoughts and affections; and am sensible of a certain doubleness by which I can stand as remote from myself as from another. However intense my experience, I am conscious of the presence and criticism of a part of me, which, as it were, is not a part of me, but spectator, sharing no experience, but taking note of it; and that is no more I than it

---

[5] Beacon Hill was a fashionable section in Boston; Five Points, a poor and crime-ridden area in lower Manhattan.

[6] The site of slaughterhouses in Boston; "Bright" means "ox."

[7] All from Confucius, *The Doctrine of the Mean* (Ch. 16).

[8] From *the Analects* (Bk. IV, Ch. 25).   [9] The Hindu god of the sky.

is you. When the play, it may be the tragedy, of life is over, the spectator goes his way. It was a kind of fiction, a work of the imagination only, so far as he was concerned. This doubleness may easily make us poor neighbors and friends sometimes.

I find it wholesome to be alone the greater part of the time. To be in company, even with the best, is soon wearisome and dissipating. I love to be alone. I never found the companion that was so companionable as solitude. We are for the most part more lonely when we go abroad among men than when we stay in our chambers. A man thinking or working is always alone, let him be where he will. Solitude is not measured by the miles of space that intervene between a man and his fellows. The really diligent student in one of the crowded hives of Cambridge College is as solitary as a dervish[10] in the desert. The farmer can work alone in the field or the woods all day, hoeing or chopping, and not feel lonesome, because he is employed; but when he comes home at night he cannot sit down in a room alone, at the mercy of his thoughts, but must be where he can "see the folks," and recreate, and as he thinks remunerate himself for his day's solitude; and hence he wonders how the student can sit alone in the house all night and most of the day without ennui and "the blues;" but he does not realize that the student, though in the house, is still at work in *his* field, and chopping in *his* woods, as the farmer in his, and in turn seeks the same recreation and society that the latter does, though it may be a more condensed form of it.

Society is commonly too cheap. We meet at very short intervals, not having had time to acquire any new value for each other. We meet at meals three times a day, and give each other a new taste of that old musty cheese that we are. We have had to agree on a certain set of rules, called etiquette and politeness, to make this frequent meeting tolerable, and that we need not come to open war. We meet at the post-office, and at the sociable, and about the fireside every night; we live thick and are in each other's way, and stumble over one another, and I think that we thus lose some respect for one another. Certainly less frequency would suffice for all important and hearty communications. Consider the girls in a factory,— never alone, hardly in their dreams.[11] It would be better if there were but one inhabitant to a square mile, as where I live. The value of a man is not in his skin, that we should touch him.

I have heard of a man lost in the woods and dying of famine and exhaustion at the foot of a tree, whose loneliness was relieved by the grotesque visions with which, owing to bodily weakness, his diseased imagination surrounded him, and which he believed to be real. So also, owing to bodily and mental health and strength, we may be continually cheered by a like but more normal and natural society, and come to know that we are never alone.

I have a great deal of company in my house; especially in the morning, when nobody calls. Let me suggest a few comparisons, that some one may convey an idea of my situation. I am no more lonely than the loon in the pond that laughs so loud, or than Walden Pond itself. What company has that lonely lake, I pray? And yet it has not the blue devils,[12] but the blue angels in it, in the azure tint of its waters. The sun is alone, except in thick weather, when there sometimes appear to

---

[10] A member of a Moslem religious order who takes vows of poverty and austerity and wanders as a friar.

[11] Some young women working in New England factories were required to live in company-owned dormitories.

[12] The blues, depression.

be two, but one is a mock sun. God is alone,—but the devil, he is far from being alone; he sees a great deal of company; he is legion. I am no more lonely than a single mullein or dandelion in a pasture, or a bean leaf, or sorrel, or a horse-fly, or a humble-bee. I am no more lonely than the Mill Brook,[13] or a weathercock, or the northstar, or the south wind, or an April shower, or a January thaw, or the first spider in a new house.

I have occasional visits in the long winter evenings, when the snow falls fast and the wind howls in the wood, from an old settler and original proprietor,[14] who is reported to have dug Walden Pond, and stoned it, and fringed it with pine woods; who tells me stories of old time and of new eternity; and between us we manage to pass a cheerful evening with social mirth and pleasant views of things, even without apples or cider,—a most wise and humorous friend, whom I love much, who keeps himself more secret than ever did Goffe or Whalley;[15] and though he is thought to be dead, none can show where he is buried. An elderly dame,[16] too, dwells in my neighborhood, invisible to most persons, in whose odorous herb garden I love to stroll sometimes, gathering simples[17] and listening to her fables; for she has a genius of unequalled fertility, and her memory runs back farther than mythology, and she can tell me the original of every fable, and on what fact every one is founded, for the incidents occurred when she was young. A ruddy and lusty old dame, who delights in all weathers and seasons, and is likely to outlive all her children yet.

The indescribable innocence and beneficence of Nature,—of sun and wind and rain, of summer and winter,—such health, such cheer, they afford forever! and such sympathy have they ever with our race, that all Nature would be affected, and the sun's brightness fade, and the winds would sigh humanely, and the clouds rain tears, and the woods shed their leaves and put on mourning in midsummer, if any man should ever for a just cause grieve. Shall I not have intelligence with the earth? Am I not partly leaves and vegetable mould myself?

What is the pill which will keep us well, serene, contented? Not my or thy great-grandfather's, but our great-grandmother Nature's universal, vegetable, botanic medicines, by which she has kept herself young always, outlived so many old Parrs[18] in her day, and fed her health with their decaying fatness. For my panacea, instead of one of those quack vials of a mixture dipped from Acheron and the Dead Sea,[19] which come out of those long shallow black-schooner looking wagons which we sometimes see made to carry bottles, let me have a draught of undiluted morning air. Morning air! If men will not drink of this at the fountainhead of the day, why, then, we must even bottle up some and sell it in the shops, for the benefit of those who have lost their subscription ticket to morning time in this world. But remember, it will not keep quite till noon-day even in the coolest cellar, but drive out the stopples[20] long ere that and follow westward the steps of

---

[13] A brook running through the center of Concord.
[14] A visionary spirit who enriches Thoreau's solitude.
[15] The English Puritans William Goffe (1605?–1679) and his father-in-law Edward Whalley (1615?–1675), who signed the death warrant of King Charles I (1600–1649) of England. Following the restoration of Charles II (1630–1685) to the throne of England in 1660, they fled to New England and lived in hiding near Hadley, Massachusetts.
[16] Mother Nature.   [17] Herbs.
[18] The Englishman Thomas Parr, who died in England in 1635, reportedly at the age of 152 years.
[19] The river Styx and the salt lake between Israel and Jordan, then thought to contain no living organisms.
[20] Stoppers, plugs.

Aurora. I am no worshipper of Hygeia,[21] who was the daughter of that old herb-doctor Æsculapius, and who is represented on monuments holding a serpent in one hand, and in the other a cup out of which the serpent sometimes drinks; but rather of Hebe,[22] cupbearer to Jupiter, who was the daughter of Juno and wild lettuce, and who had the power of restoring gods and men to the vigor of youth. She was probably the only thoroughly sound-conditioned, healthy, and robust young lady that ever walked the globe, and wherever she came it was spring.

VI: Visitors

I think that I love society as much as most,[1] and am ready enough to fasten myself like a bloodsucker for the time to any full-blooded man that comes in my way. I am naturally no hermit, but might possibly sit out the sturdiest frequenter of the bar-room, if my business called me thither.

I had three chairs in my house; one for solitude, two for friendship, three for society. When visitors came in larger and unexpected numbers there was but the third chair for them all, but they generally economized the room by standing up. It is surprising how many great men and women a small house will contain. I have had twenty-five or thirty souls, with their bodies, at once under my roof, and yet we often parted without being aware that we had come very near to one another. Many of our houses, both public and private, with their almost innumerable apartments, their huge halls and their cellars for the storage of wines and other munitions of peace, appear to me extravagantly large for their inhabitants. They are so vast and magnificent that the latter seem to be only vermin which infest them. I am surprised when the herald blows his summons before some Tremont or Astor or Middlesex House,[2] to see come creeping out over the piazza for all inhabitants a ridiculous mouse, which soon again slinks into some hole in the pavement.

One inconvenience I sometimes experienced in so small a house, the difficulty of getting to a sufficient distance from my guest when we began to utter the big thoughts in big words. You want room for your thoughts to get into sailing trim and run a course or two before they make their port. The bullet of your thought must have overcome its lateral and ricochet motion and fallen into its last and steady course before it reaches the ear of the hearer, else it may plough out again through the side of his head. Also, our sentences wanted room to unfold and form their columns in the interval. Individuals, like nations, must have suitable broad and natural boundaries, even a considerable neutral ground, between them. I have found it a singular luxury to talk across the pond to a companion on the opposite side. In my house we were so near that we could not begin to hear,—we could not speak low enough to be heard; as when you throw two stones into calm water so near that they break each other's undulations. If we are merely loquacious and loud

---

[21] According to Greek myth, the goddess of health (hence the word "hygiene"), daughter of Aesculapius, the god of medicine, whose token was a serpent shedding its skin (symbolic of the renewal of life).

[22] According to Greek myth, the goddess of youth, who served Jupiter (Zeus) and was supposedly conceived when Juno (Hera) ate wild lettuce.

[1] Emerging from an established solitude, Thoreau begins to incorporate the outer world into his vision: first society and agricultural activities, then, with an ever-deepening focus, nature as an example for human life.

[2] Fashionable hotels in Boston, New York, and Concord.

talkers, then we can afford to stand very near together, cheek by jowl, and feel each other's breath; but if we speak reservedly and thoughtfully, we want to be farther apart, that all animal heat and moisture may have a chance to evaporate. If we would enjoy the most intimate society with that in each of us which is without, or above, being spoken to, we must not only be silent, but commonly so far apart bodily that we cannot possibly hear each other's voice in any case. Referred to this standard, speech is for the convenience of those who are hard of hearing; but there are many fine things which we cannot say if we have to shout. As the conversation began to assume a loftier and grander tone, we gradually shoved our chairs farther apart till they touched the wall in opposite corners, and then commonly there was not room enough.

My "best" room, however, my withdrawing room, always ready for company, on whose carpet the sun rarely fell, was the pine wood behind my house. Thither in summer days, when distinguished guests came, I took them, and a priceless domestic swept the floor and dusted the furniture and kept the things in order.

If one guest came he sometimes partook of my frugal meal, and it was no interruption to conversation to be stirring a hasty-pudding,[3] or watching the rising and maturing of a loaf of bread in the ashes, in the mean while. But if twenty came and sat in my house there was nothing said about dinner, though there might be bread enough for two, more than if eating were a forsaken habit; but we naturally practised abstinence; and this was never felt to be an offence against hospitality, but the most proper and considerate course. The waste and decay of physical life, which so often needs repair, seemed miraculously retarded in such a case, and the vital vigor stood its ground. I could entertain thus a thousand as well as twenty; and if any ever went away disappointed or hungry from my house when they found me at home, they may depend upon it that I sympathized with them at least. So easy is it, though many housekeepers doubt it, to establish new and better customs in the place of the old. You need not rest your reputation on the dinners you give. For my own part, I was never so effectually deterred from frequenting a man's house, by any kind of Cerberus[4] whatever, as by the parade one made about dining me, which I took to be a very polite and roundabout hint never to trouble him so again. I think I shall never revisit those scenes. I should be proud to have for the motto of my cabin those lines of Spenser which one of my visitors inscribed on a yellow walnut leaf for a card:—

> "Arrivéd there, the little house they fill,
>   Ne looke for entertainment where none was;
> Rest is their feast, and all things at their will:
>   The noblest mind the best contentment has."[5]

When Winslow,[6] afterward governor of the Plymouth Colony, went with a companion on a visit of ceremony to Massassoit[7] on foot through the woods, and arrived tired and hungry at his lodge, they were well received by the king, but nothing was said about eating that day. When the night arrived, to quote their own

---

[3] Cornmeal mush.

[4] According to Greek myth, a three-headed dog guarding the entrance of Hades.

[5] From *The Faerie Queene* (1590) (I.i.35), by the English poet Edmund Spenser (1552?–1599).

[6] Edward Winslow (1595–1655), a founder of the Plymouth Colony, and its governor in 1633, 1636, and 1644.

[7] Massasoit (1580?–1661) was a Wampanoag chief who befriended the colonists.

words,—"He laid us on the bed with himself and his wife, they at the one end and we at the other, it being only plank, laid a foot from the ground, and a thin mat upon them. Two more of his chief men, for want of room, pressed by and upon us; so that we were worse weary of our lodging than of our journey." At one o'clock the next day Massassoit "brought two fishes that he had shot," about thrice as big as a bream; "these being boiled, there were at least forty looked for a share in them. The most ate of them. This meal only we had in two nights and a day; and had not one of us bought a partridge, we had taken our journey fasting." Fearing that they would be light-headed for want of food and also sleep, owing to "the savages' barbarous singing, (for they used to sing themselves asleep,)" and that they might get home while they had strength to travel, they departed. As for lodging, it is true they were but poorly entertained, though what they found an inconvenience was no doubt intended for an honor; but as far as eating was concerned, I do not see how the Indians could have done better. They had nothing to eat themselves, and they were wiser than to think that apologies could supply the place of food to their guests; so they drew their belts tighter and said nothing about it. Another time when Winslow visited them, it being a season of plenty with them, there was no deficiency in this respect.

As for men, they will hardly fail one any where. I had more visitors while I lived in the woods than at any other period of my life; I mean that I had some. I met several there under more favorable circumstances than I could any where else. But fewer came to see me upon trivial business. In this respect, my company was winnowed by my mere distance from town. I had withdrawn so far within the great ocean of solitude, into which the rivers of society empty, that for the most part, so far as my needs were concerned, only the finest sediment was deposited around me. Beside, there were wafted to me evidences of unexplored and uncultivated continents on the other side.

Who should come to my lodge this morning but a true Homeric or Paphlagonian[8] man,—he had so suitable and poetic a name that I am sorry I cannot print it here,—a Canadian, a wood-chopper and post-maker, who can hole fifty posts in a day, who made his last supper on a woodchuck which his dog caught. He, too, has heard of Homer, and, "if it were not for books," would "not know what to do rainy days," though perhaps he has not read one wholly through for many rainy seasons. Some priest who could pronounce the Greek itself taught him to read his verse in the testament in his native parish far away; and now I must translate to him, while he holds the book, Achilles' reproof to Patroclus[9] for his sad countenance.—"Why are you in tears, Patroclus, like a young girl?"—

> "Or have you alone heard some news from Phthia?
> They say that Mencœtius lives yet, son of Actor,
> And Peleus lives, son of Æacus, among the Myrmidons,
> Either of whom having died, we should greatly grieve."

He says, "That's good." He has a great bundle of white-oak bark[10] under his arm for a sick man, gathered this Sunday morning. "I suppose there's no harm in

---

[8] From a mountainous region in Asia minor whose inhabitants were thought to be rugged and uncivilized; the visitor was Alek Therien, a Concord resident.
[9] The noble friend of the hero Achilles, from the *Iliad* (Bk. XVI).
[10] Used to brew medicine.

going after such a thing to-day," says he. To him Homer was a great writer, though what this writing was about he did not know. A more simple and natural man it would be hard to find. Vice and disease, which cast such a sombre moral hue over the world, seemed to have hardly any existence for him. He was about twenty-eight years old, and had left Canada and his father's house a dozen years before to work in the States, and earn money to buy a farm with at last, perhaps in his native country. He was cast in the coarsest mould; a stout but sluggish body, yet gracefully carried, with a thick sunburnt neck, dark bushy hair, and dull sleepy blue eyes, which were occasionally lit up with expression. He wore a flat gray cloth cap, a dingy wool-colored greatcoat, and cowhide boots. He was a great consumer of meat, usually carrying his dinner to his work a couple of miles past my house,—for he chopped all summer,—in a tin pail; cold meats, often cold woodchucks, and coffee in a stone bottle which dangled by a string from his belt; and sometimes he offered me a drink. He came along early, crossing my bean-field, though without anxiety or haste to get to his work, such as Yankees exhibit. He wasn't a-going to hurt himself. He didn't care if he only earned his board. Frequently he would leave his dinner in the bushes, when his dog had caught a woodchuck by the way, and go back a mile and a half to dress it and leave it in the cellar of the house where he boarded, after deliberating first for half an hour whether he could not sink it in the pond safely till nightfall,—loving to dwell long upon these themes. He would say, as he went by in the morning, "How thick the pigeons are! If working every day were not my trade, I could get all the meat I should want by hunting,—pigeons, woodchucks, rabbits, partridges,—by gosh! I could get all I should want for a week in one day."

He was a skilful chopper, and indulged in some flourishes and ornaments in his art. He cut his trees level and close to the ground, that the sprouts which came up afterward might be more vigorous and a sled might slide over the stumps; and instead of leaving a whole tree to support his corded wood, he would pare it away to a slender stake or splinter which you could break off with your hand at last.

He interested me because he was so quiet and solitary and so happy withal; a well of good humor and contentment which overflowed at his eyes. His mirth was without alloy. Sometimes I saw him at his work in the woods, felling trees, and he would greet me with a laugh of inexpressible satisfaction, and a salutation in Canadian French, though he spoke English as well. When I approached him he would suspend his work, and with half-suppressed mirth lie along the trunk of a pine which he had felled, and, peeling off the inner bark, roll it up into a ball and chew it while he laughed and talked. Such an exuberance of animal spirits had he that he sometimes tumbled down and rolled on the ground with laughter at any thing which made him think and tickled him. Looking round upon the trees he would exclaim,—"By George! I can enjoy myself well enough here chopping; I want no better sport." Sometimes, when at leisure, he amused himself all day in the woods with a pocket pistol, firing salutes to himself at regular intervals as he walked. In the winter he had a fire by which at noon he warmed his coffee in a kettle; and as he sat on a log to eat his dinner the chickadees would sometimes come round and alight on his arm and peck at the potato in his fingers; and he said that he "liked to have the little *fellers* about him."

In him the animal man chiefly was developed. In physical endurance and contentment he was cousin to the pine and the rock. I asked him once if he was not sometimes tired at night, after working all day; and he answered, with a sincere and serious look, "Gorrappit, I never was tired in my life." But the intellectual and what is called spiritual man in him were slumbering as in an infant. He had been instructed only in that innocent and ineffectual way in which the Catholic priests teach the aborigines, by which the pupil is never educated to the degree of consciousness, but only to the degree of trust and reverence, and a child is not made a man, but kept a child. When Nature made him, she gave him a strong body and contentment for his portion, and propped him on every side with reverence and reliance, that he might live out his threescore years and ten a child. He was so genuine and unsophisticated than no introduction would serve to introduce him, more than if you introduced a woodchuck to your neighbor. He had got to find him out as you did. He would not play any part. Men paid him wages for work, and so helped to feed and clothe him; but he never exchanged opinions with them. He was so simply and naturally humble—if he can be called humble who never aspires—that humility was no distinct quality in him, nor could he conceive of it. Wiser men were demi-gods to him. If you told him that such a one was coming, he did as if he thought that any thing so grand would expect nothing of himself, but take all the responsibility on itself, and let him be forgotten still. He never heard the sound of praise. He particularly reverenced the writer and the preacher. Their performances were miracles. When I told him that I wrote considerably, he thought for a long time that it was merely the handwriting which I meant, for he could write a remarkably good hand himself. I sometimes found the name of his native parish handsomely written in the snow by the highway, with the proper French accent, and knew that he had passed. I asked him if he ever wished to write his thoughts. He said that he had read and written letters for those who could not, but he never tried to write thoughts,—no, he could not, he could not tell what to put first, it would kill him, and then there was spelling to be attended to at the same time!

I heard that a distinguished wise man and reformer asked him if he did not want the world to be changed; but he answered with a chuckle of surprise in his Canadian accent, not knowing that the question had ever been entertained before, "No, I like it well enough." It would have suggested many things to a philosopher to have dealings with him. To a stranger he appeared to know nothing of things in general; yet I sometimes saw in him a man whom I had not seen before, and I did not know whether he was as wise as Shakspeare or as simply ignorant as a child, whether to suspect him of a fine poetic consciousness or of stupidity. A townsman told me that when he met him sauntering through the village in his small close-fitting cap, and whistling to himself, he reminded him of a prince in disguise.

His only books were an almanac and an arithmetic, in which last he was considerably expert. The former was a sort of cyclopædia to him, which he supposed to contain an abstract of human knowledge, as indeed it does to a considerable extent. I loved to sound him on the various reforms of the day, and he never failed to look at them in the most simple and practical light. He had never heard of such things before. Could he do without factories? I asked. He had worn the home-made Vermont gray,[11] he said, and that was good. Could he dispense with tea and coffee? Did this country afford any beverage beside water? He had soaked hemlock leaves in water and drank it, and thought that was better than water in warm weather. When I asked him if he could do without money, he showed the conven-

---

[11] Homespun clothing.

ience of money in such a way as to suggest and coincide with the most philosophical accounts of the origin of this institution, and the very derivation of the word
pecunia.[12] If an ox were his property, and he wished to get needles and thread at
the store, he thought it would be inconvenient and impossible soon to go on mortgaging some portion of the creature each time to that amount. He could defend
many institutions better than any philosopher, because, in describing them as they
concerned him, he gave the true reason for their prevalence, and speculation had
not suggested to him any other. At another time, hearing Plato's definition of a
man,—a biped without feathers,—and that one[13] exhibited a cock plucked and
called it Plato's man, he thought it an important difference that the *knees* bent the
wrong way. He would sometimes exclaim, "How I love to talk! By George, I
could talk all day!" I asked him once, when I had not seen him for many months,
if he had got a new idea this summer. "Good Lord," said he, "a man that has to
work as I do, if he does not forget the ideas he has had, he will do well. May be
the man you hoe with is inclined to race; then, by gorry, your mind must be there;
you think of weeds." He would sometimes ask me first on such occasions, if I had
made any improvement. One winter day I asked him if he was always satisfied
with himself, wishing to suggest a substitute within him for the priest without, and
some higher motive for living. "Satisfied!" said he; "some men are satisfied with
one thing, and some with another. One man, perhaps, if he has got enough, will
be satisfied to sit all day with his back to the fire and his belly to the table, by
George!" Yet I never, by any manœuvring, could get him to take the spiritual
view of things; the highest that he appeared to conceive of was a simple expediency, such as you might expect an animal to appreciate; and this, practically, is
true of most men. If I suggested any improvement in his mode of life, he merely
answered, without expressing any regret, that it was too late. Yet he thoroughly
believed in honesty and the like virtues.

There was a certain positive originality, however slight, to be detected in him,
and I occasionally observed that he was thinking for himself and expressing his
own opinion, a phenomenon so rare that I would any day walk ten miles to observe it, and it amounted to the re-origination of many of the institutions of society. Though he hesitated, and perhaps failed to express himself distinctly, he always had a presentable thought behind. Yet his thinking was so primitive and
immersed in his animal life, that, though more promising than a merely learned
man's, it rarely ripened to any thing which can be reported. He suggested that
there might be men of genius in the lowest grades of life, however permanently
humble and illiterate, who take their own view always, or do not pretend to see at
all; who are as bottomless even as Walden Pond was thought to be, though they
may be dark and muddy.

Many a traveller came out of his way to see me and the inside of my house,
and, as an excuse for calling, asked for a glass of water. I told them that I drank at
the pond, and pointed thither, offering to lend them a dipper. Far off as I lived, I
was not exempted from that annual visitation which occurs, methinks, about the
first of April, when every body is on the move; and I had my share of good luck,

---

[12] "Money" (Latin), originally meaning "property in cattle," from *pecus*, cattle.
[13] Diogenes (412?–323 B.C.), a Greek philosopher who showed the limitation of Plato's definition,
just as Alek Therien's point about knee-joints suggests something overlooked by Diogenes.

though there were some curious specimens among my visitors. Half-witted men from the almshouse and elsewhere came to see me; but I endeavored to make them exercise all the wit they had, and make their confessions to me; in such cases making wit the theme of our conversation; and so was compensated. Indeed, I found some of them to be wiser than the so called *overseers* of the poor and selectmen of the town, and thought it was time that the tables were turned. With respect to wit, I learned that there was not much difference between the half and the whole. One day, in particular, an inoffensive, simple-minded pauper, whom with others I had often seen used as fencing stuff, standing or sitting on a bushel in the fields to keep cattle and himself from straying, visited me, and expressed a wish to live as I did. He told me, with the utmost simplicity and truth, quite superior, or rather *inferior,* to any thing that is called humility, that he was "deficient in intellect." These were his words. The Lord had made him so, yet he supposed the Lord cared as much for him as for another. "I have always been so," said he. "from my childhood; I never had much mind; I was not like other children; I am weak in the head. It was the Lord's will, I suppose." And there he was to prove the truth of his words. He was a metaphysical puzzle to me. I have rarely met a fellow-man on such promising ground.—it was so simple and sincere and so true all that he said. And, true enough, in proportion as he appeared to humble himself was he exalted.[14] I did not know at first but it was the result of a wise policy. It seemed that from such a basis of truth and frankness as the poor weak-headed pauper had laid, our intercourse might go forward to something better than the intercourse of sages.

I had some guests from those not reckoned commonly among the town's poor, but who should be; who are among the world's poor, at any rate; guests who appeal, not to your hospitality, but to your *hospitalality;* who earnestly wish to be helped, and preface their appeal with the information that they are resolved, for one thing, never to help themselves. I require of a visitor that he be not actually starving, though he may have the very best appetite in the world, however he got it. Objects of charity are not guests. Men who did not know when their visit had terminated, though I went about my business again, answering them from greater and greater remoteness. Men of almost every degree of wit called on me in the migrating season. Some who had more wits than they knew what to do with; runaway slaves[15] with plantation manners, who listened from time to time, like the fox in the fable, as if they heard the hounds a-baying on their track, and looked at me beseechingly, as much as to say,—

"O Christian, will you send me back?"[16]

One real runaway slave, among the rest, whom I helped to forward toward the northstar. Men of one idea, like a hen with one chicken, and that a duckling; men of a thousand ideas, and unkempt heads, like those hens which are made to take charge of a hundred chickens, all in pursuit of one bug, a score of them lost in every morning's dew,—and become frizzled and mangy in consequence; men of ideas instead of legs, a sort of intellectual centipede that made you crawl all over.

---

[14] "Whosoever shall exalt himself shall be abased; and he that shall humble himself shall be exalted," from Matthew 23:12.

[15] Thoreau's cabin was a stop on the Underground Railroad, which aided escaped slaves on their way North.

[16] Source unidentified.

One man proposed a book in which visitors should write their names, as at the White Mountains; but, alas! I have too good a memory to make that necessary.

I could not but notice some of the peculiarities of my visitors. Girls and boys and young women generally seemed glad to be in the woods. They looked in the pond and at the flowers, and improved their time. Men of business, even farmers, thought only of solitude and employment, and of the great distance at which I dwelt from something or other; and though they said that they loved a ramble in the woods occasionally, it was obvious that they did not. Restless committed men, whose time was all taken up in getting a living or keeping it; ministers who spoke of God as if they enjoyed a monopoly of the subject, who could not bear all kinds of opinions; doctors, lawyers, uneasy housekeepers who pried into my cupboard and bed when I was out,—how came Mrs.——to know that my sheets were not as clean as hers?—young men who had ceased to be young, and had concluded that it was safest to follow the beaten track of the professions,—all these generally said that it was not possible to do so much good in my position. Ay! there was the rub.[17] The old and infirm and the timid, of whatever age or sex, thought most of sickness, and sudden accident and death; to them life seemed full of danger,— what danger is there if you don't think of any?—and they thought that a prudent man would carefully select the safest position, where Dr. B.[18] might be on hand at a moment's warning. To them the village was literally a *com-munity*, a league for mutual defence, and you would suppose that they would not go a-huckleberrying without a medicine chest. The amount of it is, if a man is alive, there is always *danger* that he may die, though the danger must be allowed to be less in proportion as he is dead-and-alive to begin with. A man sits as many risks as he runs. Finally, there were the self-styled reformers, the greatest bores of all, who thought that I was forever singing,—

> This is the house that I built;
> This is the man that lives in the house that I built;[19]

but they did not know that the third line was,—

> These are the folks that worry the man
> That lives in the house that I built.

I did not fear the hen-harriers,[20] for I kept no chickens; but I feared the men-harriers rather.

I had more cheering visitors than the last. Children come a-berrying, railroad men taking a Sunday morning walk in clean shirts, fishermen and hunters, poets and philosophers, in short, all honest pilgrims, who came out to the woods for freedom's sake, and really left the village behind, I was ready to greet with,— "Welcome, Englishmen! welcome, Englishmen!"[21] for I had had communication with that race.

---

[17] "Ay, there's the rub," from Shakespeare's *Hamlet* (III. i. 66).

[18] Josiah Bartlett, a Concord physician.

[19] A parody of the nursery rhyme, "This is the house that Jack built"; Thoreau shows his displeasure with the "self-styled reformers."

[20] Hawks; "men-harriers" are these visitors who constantly annoy Thoreau.

[21] Words supposedly spoken by the Native-American chief Samoset to the Pilgrims landing at Plymouth in 1620.

VII: The Bean-Field

Meanwhile my beans, the length of whose rows, added together, was seven miles already planted, were impatient to be hoed, for the earliest had grown considerably before the latest were in the ground; indeed they were not easily to be put off. What was the meaning of this so steady and self-respecting, this small Herculean labor, I knew not. I came to love my rows, my beans, though so many more than I wanted. They attached me to the earth, and so I got strength like Antæus.[1] But why should I raise them? Only Heaven knows. This was my curious labor all summer,—to make this portion of the earth's surface, which had yielded only cinquefoil, blackberries, johnswort, and the like, before, sweet wild fruits and pleasant flowers, produce instead this pulse. What shall I learn of beans or beans of me? I cherish them, I hoe them, early and late I have an eye to them; and this is my day's work. It is a fine broad leaf to look on. My auxiliaries are the dews and rains which water this dry soil, and what fertility is in the soil itself, which for the most part is lean and effete. My enemies are worms, cool days, and most of all woodchucks. The last have nibbled for me a quarter of an acre clean. But what right had I to oust johnswort and the rest, and break up their ancient herb garden? Soon, however, the remaining beans will be too tough for them, and go forward to meet new foes.

When I was four years old, as I well remember, I was brought from Boston to this my native town, through these very woods and this field, to the pond. It is one of the oldest scenes stamped on my memory. And now to-night my flute has waked the echoes over that very water. The pines still stand here older than I; or, if some have fallen, I have cooked my supper with their stumps, and a new growth is rising all around, preparing another aspect for new infant eyes. Almost the same johnswort springs from the same perennial root in this pasture, and even I have at length helped to clothe that fabulous landscape of my infant dreams, and one of the results of my presence and influence is seen in these bean leaves, corn blades, and potato vines.

I planted about two acres and a half of upland; and as it was only about fifteen years since the land was cleared, and I myself had got out two or three cords of stumps, I did not give it any manure; but in the course of the summer it appeared by the arrow-heads which I turned up in hoeing, that an extinct nation had anciently dwelt here and planted corn and beans ere white men came to clear the land, and so, to some extent, had exhausted the soil for this very crop.

Before yet any woodchuck or squirrel had run across the road, or the sun had got above the shrub-oaks, while all the dew was on, though the farmers warned me against it,—I would advise you to do all your work if possible while the dew is on,—I began to level the ranks of haughty weeds in my bean-field and throw dust upon their heads. Early in the morning I worked barefooted, dabbling like a plastic artist in the dewy and crumbling sand, but later in the day the sun blistered my feet. There the sun lighted me to hoe beans, pacing slowly backward and forward over that yellow gravelly upland, between the long green rows, fifteen rods, the one end terminating in a shrub oak copse where I could rest in the shade, the other in a blackberry field where the green berries deepened their tints by the time I had made another bout. Removing the weeds, putting fresh soil about the bean stems, and encouraging this weed which I had sown, making the yellow soil

---

[1] According to Greek myth, the giant who drew strength from touching the earth, his mother; in deadly combat, Hercules held him aloft and crushed him.

express its summer thought in bean leaves and blossoms rather than in wormwood and piper and millet grass, making the earth say beans instead of grass,—this was my daily work. As I had little aid from horses or cattle, or hired men or boys, or improved implements of husbandry, I was much slower, and became much more intimate with my beans than usual. But labor of the hands, even when pursued to the verge of drudgery, is perhaps never the worst form of idleness. It has a constant and imperishable moral, and to the scholar it yields a classic result. A very *agricola laboriosus*[2] was I to travellers bound westward through Lincoln and Wayland[3] to nobody knows where; they sitting at their ease in gigs,[4] with elbows on knees, and reins loosely hanging in festoons; I the home-staying, laborious native of the soil. But soon my homestead was out of their sight and thought. It was the only open and cultivated field for a great distance on either side of the road; so they made the most of it; and sometimes the man in the field heard more of travellers' gossip and comment than was meant for his ear: "Beans so late! peas so late!"—for I continued to plant when others had begun to hoe,—the ministerial husbandman had not suspected it. "Corn, my boy, for fodder; corn for fodder." "Does he *live* there?" asks the black bonnet of the gray coat; and the hard-featured farmer reins up his grateful dobbin to inquire what you are doing where he sees no manure in the furrow, and recommends a little chip dirt,[5] or any little waste stuff, or it may be ashes or plaster. But here were two acres and a half of furrows, and only a hoe for cart and two hands to draw it,—there being an aversion to other carts and horses,—and chip dirt far away. Fellow-travellers as they rattled by compared it aloud with the fields which they had passed, so that I came to know how I stood in the agricultural world. This was one field not in Mr. Colman's report.[6] And, by the way, who estimates the value of the crop which Nature yields in the still wilder fields unimproved by man? The crop of *English* hay is carefully weighed, the moisture calculated, the silicates and the potash; but in all dells and pond holes in the woods and pastures and swamps grows a rich and various crop only unreaped by man. Mine was, as it were, the connecting link between wild and cultivated fields; as some states are civilized, and others half-civilized, and others savage or barbarous, so my field was, though not in a bad sense, a half-cultivated field. They were beans cheerfully returning to their wild and primitive state that I cultivated, and my hoe played the *Ranz des Vaches*[7] for them.

Near at hand, upon the topmost spray of a birch, sings the brown-thrasher—or red mavis, as some love to call him—all the morning, glad of your society, that would find out another farmer's field if yours were not here. While you are planting the seed, he cries,—"Drop it, drop it,—cover it up, cover it up,—pull it up, pull it up, pull it up." But this was not corn, and so it was safe from such enemies as he. You may wonder what his rigmarole, his amateur Paganini[8] performances on one string or on twenty, have to do with your planting, and yet prefer it to leached ashes or plaster. It was a cheap sort of top dressing in which I had entire faith.

As I drew a still fresher soil about the rows with my hoe, I disturbed the ashes

---

[2] "Hardworking farmer" (Latin).   [3] Towns near Concord.
[4] Small horse-drawn carriages with two wheels.
[5] Fertilizer made from dried manure; Thoreau farmed without the aid of chemical fertilizers.
[6] Henry Colman (1785–1849), compiler of statistical reports on Massachusetts agriculture between 1838 and 1841.
[7] The song of the Swiss herdsman in the drama *William Tell* (1804), by the German writer Friedrich von Schiller (1759–1805).
[8] Nicolò Paganini (1782–1840), an Italian violin virtuoso and composer.

of unchronicled nations who in primeval years lived under these heavens, and their small implements of war and hunting were brought to the light of this modern day. They lay mingled with other natural stones, some of which bore the marks of having been burned by Indian fires, and some by the sun, and also bits of pottery and glass brought hither by the recent cultivators of the soil. When my hoe tinkled against the stones, that music echoed to the woods and the sky, and was an accompaniment to my labor which yielded an instant and immeasurable crop. It was no longer beans that I hoed, nor I that hoed beans; and I remembered with as much pity as pride, if I remembered at all, my acquaintances who had gone to the city to attend the oratorios. The night-hawk circled overhead in the sunny afternoons—for I sometimes made a day of it—like a mote in the eye, or in heaven's eye, falling from time to time with a swoop and a sound as if the heavens were rent, torn at last to very rags and tatters, and yet a seamless cope[9] remained; small imps that fill the air and lay their eggs on the ground on bare sand or rocks on the tops of hills, where few have found them; graceful and slender like ripples caught up from the pond, as leaves are raised by the wind to float in the heavens; such kindredship is in Nature. The hawk is aerial brother of the wave which he sails over and surveys, those his perfect air-inflated wings answering to the elemental unfledged pinions of the sea. Or sometimes I watched a pair of hen-hawks circling high in the sky, alternately soaring and descending, approaching and leaving one another, as if they were the imbodiment of my own thoughts. Or I was attracted by the passage of wild pigeons from this wood to that, with a slight quivering winnowing sound and carrier haste; or from under a rotten stump my hoe turned up a sluggish portentous and outlandish spotted salamander, a trace of Egypt and the Nile, yet our contemporary. When I paused to lean on my hoe, these sounds and sights I heard and saw any where in the row, a part of the inexhaustible entertainment which the country offers.

On gala days the town fires its great guns, which echo like popguns to these woods, and some waifs of martial music occasionally penetrate thus far. To me, away there in my bean-field at the other end of the town, the big guns sounded as if a puff ball[10] had burst; and when there was a military turnout of which I was ignorant, I have sometimes had a vague sense all the day of some sort of itching and disease in the horizon, as if some eruption would break out there soon, either scarlatina or canker-rash,[11] until at length some more favorable puff of wind, making haste over the fields and up the Wayland road, brought me information of the "trainers."[12] It seemed by the distant hum as if somebody's bees had swarmed, and that the neighbors, according to Virgil's advice, by a faint *tintinnabulum*[13] upon the most sonorous of their domestic utensils, were endeavoring to call them down into the hive again. And when the sound died quite away, and the hum had ceased, and the most favorable breezes told no tale, I knew that they had got the last drone of them all safely into the Middlesex hive, and that now their minds were bent on the honey with which it was smeared.

I felt proud to know that the liberties of Massachusetts and of our fatherland were in such safe keeping; and as I turned to my hoeing again I was filled with an inexpressible confidence, and pursued my labor cheerfully with a calm trust in the future.

When there were several bands of musicians, it sounded as if all the village was

---

[9] A cape or canopy.   [10] A fungus that bursts when mature, releasing spores.
[11] Scarlet fever and cold-sores.   [12] The local militia.
[13] A tinkling of bells; Virgil suggests in the *Georgics* that bees may be made to swarm by the gentle ringing of bells.

a vast bellows, and all the buildings expanded and collapsed alternately with a din. But sometimes it was a really noble and inspiring strain that reached these woods, and the trumpet that sings of fame, and I felt as if I could spit[14] a Mexican with a good relish,—for why should we always stand for trifles?—and looked round for a woodchuck or a skunk to exercise my chivalry upon. These martial strains seemed as far away as Palestine, and reminded me of a march of crusaders in the horizon, with a slight tantivy and tremulous motion of the elm-tree tops which overhang the village. This was one of the *great* days; though the sky had from my clearing only the same everlastingly great look that it wears daily, and I saw no difference in it.

It was a singular experience that long acquaintance which I cultivated with beans, what with planting, and hoeing, and harvesting, and threshing, and picking over, and selling them,—the last was the hardest of all, —I might add eating, for I did taste. I was determined to know beans. When they were growing, I used to hoe from five o'clock in the morning till noon, and commonly spent the rest of the day about other affairs. Consider the intimate and curious acquaintance one makes with various kinds of weeds,—it will bear some iteration in the account, for there was no little iteration in the labor,—disturbing their delicate organizations so ruthlessly, and making such invidious distinctions with his hoe, levelling whole ranks of one species, and sedulously cultivating another. That's Roman wormwood,—that's pigweed,—that's sorrel,—that's piper-grass,—have at him, chop him up, turn his roots upward to the sun, don't let him have a fibre in the shade, if you do he'll turn himself t'other side up and be as green as a leek in two days. A long war, not with cranes, but with weeds, those Trojans who had sun and rain and dews on their side. Daily the beans saw me come to their rescue armed with a hoe, and thin the ranks of their enemies, filling up the trenches with weedy dead. Many a lusty crest-waving Hector,[15] that towered a whole foot above his crowding comrades, fell before my weapon and rolled in the dust.

Those summer days which some of my contemporaries devoted to the fine arts in Boston or Rome, and others to contemplation in India, and others to trade in London or New York, I thus, with the other farmers of New England, devoted to husbandry. Not that I wanted beans to eat, for I am by nature a Pythagorean,[16] so far as beans are concerned, whether they mean porridge or voting, and exchanged them for rice; but, perchance, as some must work in fields if only for the sake of tropes[17] and expression, to serve a parable-maker one day. It was on the whole a rare amusement, which, continued too long, might have become a dissipation. Thought I gave them no manure, and did not hoe them all once, I hoed them unusually well as far as I went, and was paid for it in the end, "there being in truth," as Evelyn[18] says, "no compost or lætation whatsoever comparable to this continual motion, repastination, and turning of the mould with the spade." "The

---

[14] Stab through, impale. Here Thoreau jokes about the Mexican War, a subject he ordinarily treats with moral seriousness.

[15] In *The Iliad,* a Trojan hero during the Greek seige of Troy; Homer presents him as a valiant opponent, noble in defeat. Siding with the Greeks (and the beans), Thoreau fells this heroic weed with his hoe.

[16] Followers of the Greek philosopher and mathematician Pythagoras (6th century B.C.), who practiced a rigid asceticism in matters of food, including an opposition to the eating of beans, perhaps because beans cause flatulence. In ancient times beans were sometimes used to tally votes.

[17] Figures of speech.

[18] John Evelyn, from *Terra: A Philosophical Discourse of Earth* (1729). Laetation is a method of spreading fertilizer around a plant in a leftward movement; repastination means re-digging, re-hoeing.

earth," he adds elsewhere, "especially if fresh, has a certain magnetism in it, by which it attracts the salt, power, or virtue (call it either) which gives it life, and is the logic of all the labor and stir we keep about it, to sustain us; all dungings and other sordid temperings being but the vicars succedaneous[19] to this improvement." Moreover, this being one of those "worn-out and exhausted lay fields which enjoy their sabbath," had perchance, as Sir Kenelm Digby[20] thinks likely, attracted "vital spirits" from the air. I harvested twelve bushels of beans.

But to be more particular; for it is complained that Mr. Colman has reported chiefly the expensive experiments of gentlemen farmers; my outgoes were,—

For a hoe,	$0 54
Ploughing, harrowing, and furrowing,	7 50, Too much.
Beans for seed,	3 12½
Potatoes "	1 33
Peas "	0 40
Turnip seed,	0 06
White line for crow fence,[21]	0 02
Horse cultivator and boy three hours,	1 00
Horse and cart to get crop,	0 75
In all,	$14 72½

My income was, (patrem familias vendacem, non emacem esse oportet,[22]) from

Nine bushels and twelve quarts of beans sold,	$16 94
Five " large potatoes,	2 50
Nine " small "	2 25
Grass,	1 00
Stalks,	0 75
In all,	$23 44

Leaving a pecuniary profit, as I have elsewhere said, of $8 71½.

This is the result of my experience in raising beans. Plant the common small white bush bean about the first of June, in rows three feet by eighteen inches apart, being careful to select fresh round and unmixed seed. First look out for worms, and supply vacancies by planting anew. Then look out for woodchucks, if it is an exposed place, for they will nibble off the earliest tender leaves almost clean as they go; and again, when the young tendrils make their appearance, they have notice of it, and will shear them off with both buds and young pods, sitting erect like a squirrel. But above all harvest as early as possible, if you would escape frosts and have a fair and saleable crop; you may save much loss by this means.

This further experience also I gained. I said to myself, I will not plant beans

---

[19] Substitutes.

[20] Digby (1603–1665) was a versatile English writer who produced works on science, plants, and the occult. Here Thoreau says that his beans drew nutrients from the earth and maybe even from the air.

[21] Defense.

[22] "The head of the household should be a seller, not a buyer" (Latin), from Cato's *De Agricultura*.

and corn with so much industry another summer, but such seeds, if the seed is not lost, as sincerity, truth, simplicity, faith, innocence, and the like, and see if they will not grow in this soil, even with less toil and manurance, and sustain me, for surely it has not been exhausted for these crops. Alas! I said this to myself; but now another summer is gone, and another, and another, and I am obliged to say to you, Reader, that the seeds which I planted, if indeed they *were* the seeds of those virtues, were wormeaten or had lost their vitality, and so did not come up. Commonly men will only be brave as their fathers were brave, or timid. This generation is very sure to plant corn and beans each new year precisely as the Indians did centuries ago and taught the first settlers to do, as if there were a fate in it. I saw an old man the other day, to my astonishment, making the holes with a hoe for the seventieth time at least, and not for himself to lie down in! But why should not the New Englander try new adventures, and not lay so much stress on his grain, his potato and grass crop, and his orchards?—raise other crops than these? Why concern ourselves so much about our beans for seed, and not be concerned at all about a new generation of men? We should really be fed and cheered if when we met a man we were sure to see that some of the qualities which I have named, which we all prize more than those other productions, but which are for the most part broadcast and floating in the air, had taken root and grown in him. Here comes such a subtile and ineffable quality, for instance, as truth or justice, though the slightest amount or new variety of it, along the road. Our ambassadors should be instructed to send home such seeds as these, and Congress help to distribute them over all the land. We should never stand upon ceremony with sincerity. We should never cheat and insult and banish one another by our meanness, if there were present the kernel of worth and friendliness. We should not meet thus in haste. Most men I do not meet at all, for they seem not to have time; they are busy about their beans. We would not deal with a man thus plodding ever, leaning on a hoe or a spade as a staff between his work, not as a mushroom, but partially risen out of the earth, something more than erect, like swallows alighted and walking on the ground.—

> "And as he spake, his wings would now and then
> Spread, as he meant to fly, then close again,"[23]

so that we should suspect that we might be conversing with an angel. Bread may not always nourish us; but it always does us good, it even takes stiffness out of our joints, and makes us supple and buoyant, when we knew not what ailed us, to recognize any generosity in man or Nature, to share any unmixed and heroic joy.

Ancient poetry and mythology suggest, at least, that husbandry was once a sacred art; but it is pursued with irreverent haste and heedlessness by us, our object being to have large farms and large crops merely. We have no festival, nor procession, nor ceremony, not excepting our Cattle-shows and so called Thanksgivings, by which the farmer expresses a sense of the sacredness of his calling, or is reminded of its sacred origin. It is the premium and the feast which tempt him. He sacrifices not to Ceres and the Terrestrial Jove, but to the infernal Plutus[24] rather. By avarice and selfishness, and a grovelling habit, from which none of us

---

[23] From "The Shepheard's Oracles," by Francis Quarles (1592–1644).

[24] According to Roman myth, the goddess of agriculture (for whom "cereal" is named); Jupiter, the supreme god; a combination of the Roman and Greek Pluto, god of the underworld and the source of wealth, and the Greek Plutus, the blind god of wealth.

is free, of regarding the soil as property, or the means of acquiring property chiefly, the landscape is deformed, husbandry is degraded with us, and the farmer leads the meanest of lives. He knows Nature but as a robber. Cato says that the profits of agriculture are particularly pious or just, (*maximeque pius quæstus,*) and according to Varro[25] the old Romans "called the same earth Mother and Ceres, and thought that they who cultivated it led a pious and useful life, and that they alone were left of the race of King Saturn."[26]

We are wont to forget that the sun looks on our cultivated fields and on the prairies and forests without distinction. They all reflect and absorb his rays alike, and the former make but a small part of the glorious picture which he beholds in his daily course. In his view the earth is all equally cultivated like a garden. Therefore we should receive the benefit of his light and heat with a corresponding trust and magnanimity. What though I value the seed of these beans, and harvest that in the fall of the year? This broad field which I have looked at so long looks not to me as the principal cultivator, but away from me to influences more genial to it, which water and make it green. These beans have results which are not harvested by me. Do they not grow for woodchucks partly? The ear of wheat, (in Latin *spica,* obsoletely *speca,* from *spe,* hope,) should not be the only hope of the husbandman; its kernel or grain (*granum,* from *gerendo,* bearing,) is not all that it bears. How, then, can our harvest fail? Shall I not rejoice also at the abundance of the weeds whose seeds are the granary of the birds? It matters little comparatively whether the fields fill the farmer's barns. The true husbandman will cease from anxiety, as the squirrels manifest no concern whether the woods will bear chestnuts this year or not, and finish his labor with every day, relinquishing all claim to the produce of his fields, and sacrificing in his mind not only his first but his last fruits also.

VIII: The Village

After hoeing, or perhaps reading and writing, in the forenoon, I usually bathed again in the pond, swimming across one of its coves for a stint, and washed the dust of labor from my person, or smoothed out the last wrinkle which study had made, and for the afternoon was absolutely free. Every day or two I strolled to the village to hear some of the gossip which is incessantly going on there, circulating either from mouth to mouth, or from newspaper to newspaper, and which, taken in homœopathic doses,[1] was really as refreshing in its way as the rustle of leaves and the peeping of frogs. As I walked in the woods to see the birds and squirrels, so I walked in the village to see the men and boys; instead of the wind among the pines I heard the carts rattle. In one direction from my house there was a colony of muskrats in the river meadows; under the grove of elms and buttonwoods in the other horizon was a village of busy men, as curious to me as if they had been prairie dogs, each sitting at the mouth of its burrow, or running over to a neighbor's to gossip. I went there frequently to observe their habits. The village appeared to me a great news room; and on one side, to support it, as once at Redding & Company's on State Street,[2] they kept nuts and raisins, or salt and meal and

---

[25] Marcus Terentius Varro (116–27 B.C.), a Roman poet, satirist, geographer, and scientist, from his *Rerum Rusticarum.*
[26] According to Roman myth, the god of agriculture (the Latin "Saturnus" means "the sower").
[1] Very small amounts.   [2] In Boston.

other groceries. Some have such a vast appetite for the former commodity, that is, the news, and such sound digestive organs, that they can sit forever in public avenues without stirring, and let it simmer and whisper through them like the Etesian winds,[3] or as if inhaling ether, it only producing numbness and insensibility to pain,—otherwise it would often be painful to hear,—without affecting the consciousness. I hardly ever failed, when I rambled through the village, to see a row of such worthies, either sitting on a ladder sunning themselves, with their bodies inclined forward and their eyes glancing along the line this way and that, from time to time, with a voluptuous expression, or else leaning against a barn with their hands in their pockets, like caryatides[4], as if to prop it up. They, being commonly out of doors, heard whatever was in the wind. These are the coarsest mills, in which all gossip is first rudely digested or cracked up before it is emptied into finer and more delicate hoppers within doors. I observed that the vitals of the village were the grocery, the bar-room, the post-office, and the bank; and, as a necessary part of the machinery, they kept a bell, a big gun, and a fire-engine, at convenient places; and the houses were so arranged as to make the most of mankind, in lanes and fronting one another, so that every traveller had to run the gantlet, and every man, woman, and child might get a lick at him. Of course, those who were stationed nearest to the head of the line, where they could most see and be seen, and have the first blow at him, paid the highest prices for their places; and the few straggling inhabitants in the outskirts, where long gaps in the line began to occur, and the traveller could get over walls or turn aside into cow paths, and so escape, paid a very slight ground or window tax.[5] Signs were hung out on all sides to allure him; some to catch him by the appetite, as the tavern and victualling cellar; some by the fancy, as the dry goods store and the jeweller's; and others by the hair or the feet or the skirts, as the barber, the shoemaker, or the tailor. Besides, there was a still more terrible standing invitation to call at every one of these houses, and company expected about these times. For the most part I escaped wonderfully from these dangers, either by proceeding at once boldly and without deliberation to the goal, as is recommended to those who run the gantlet, or by keeping my thoughts on high things, like Orpheus, who, "loudly singing the praises of the gods to his lyre, drowned the voices of the Sirens, and kept out of danger."[6] Sometimes I bolted suddenly, and nobody could tell my whereabouts, for I did not stand much about gracefulness, and never hesitated at a gap in a fence. I was even accustomed to make an irruption into some houses, where I was well entertained, and after learning the kernels and the very last sieve-ful of news, what had subsided, the prospects of war and peace, and whether the world was likely to hold together much longer, I was let out through the rear avenues, and so escaped to the woods again.

It was very pleasant, when I staid late in town, to launch myself into the night, especially if it was dark and tempestuous, and set sail from some bright village parlor or lecture room, with a bag of rye or Indian meal upon my shoulder, for my snug harbor in the woods, having made all tight without and withdrawn under hatches with a merry crew of thoughts, leaving only my outer man at the helm, or even tying up the helm when it was plain sailing. I had many a genial thought by

---

[3] Summer winds on the Mediterranean Sea.

[4] Draped female figures supporting a wall or the upper story of a building.

[5] A tax based on the amount of ground owned or on the number of windows in a house.

[6] Apparently, Thoreau's own translation from *De Sapientia Veterum* (1609), a collection of fables assembled by Sir Francis Bacon.

the cabin fire "as I sailed." I was never cast away nor distressed in any weather, though I encountered some severe storms. It is darker in the woods, even in common nights, than most suppose. I frequently had to look up at the opening between the trees above the path in order to learn my route, and, where there was no cart-path, to feel with my feet the faint track which I had worn, or steer by the known relation of particular trees which I felt with my hands, passing between two pines for instance, not more than eighteen inches apart, in the midst of the woods, invariably, in the darkest night. Sometimes, after coming home thus late in a dark and muggy night, when my feet felt the path which my eyes could not see, dreaming and absent-minded all the way, until I was aroused by having to raise my hand to lift the latch, I have not been able to recall a single step of my walk, and I have thought that perhaps my body would find its way home if its master should forsake it, as the hand finds its way to the mouth without assistance. Several times, when a visitor chanced to stay into evening, and it proved a dark night, I was obliged to conduct him to the cart-path in the rear of the house, and then point out to him the direction he was to pursue, and in keeping which he was to be guided rather by his feet than his eyes. One very dark night I directed thus on their way two young men who had been fishing in the pond. They lived about a mile off through the woods, and were quite used to the route. A day or two after one of them told me that they wandered about the greater part of the night, close by their own premises, and did not get home till toward morning, by which time, as there had been several heavy showers in the mean while, and the leaves were very wet, they were drenched to their skins. I have heard of many going astray even in the village streets, when the darkness was so thick that you could cut it with a knife, as the saying is. Some who live in the outskirts, having come to town a-shopping in their wagons, have been obliged to put up for the night; and gentlemen and ladies making a call have gone half a mile out of their way, feeling the sidewalk only with their feet, and not knowing when they turned. It is a surprising and memorable, as well as valuable experience, to be lost in the woods any time. Often in a snow storm, even by day, one will come out upon a well-known road, and yet find it impossible to tell which way leads to the village. Though he knows that he has travelled it a thousand times, he cannot recognize a feature in it, but it is as strange to him as if it were a road in Siberia. By night, of course, the perplexity is infinitely greater. In our most trivial walks, we are constantly, though unconsciously, steering like pilots by certain well-known beacons and headlands, and if we go beyond our usual course we still carry in our minds the bearing of some neighboring cape; and not till we are completely lost, or turned round,—for a man needs only to be turned round once with his eyes shut in this world to be lost,—do we appreciate the vastness and strangeness of Nature. Every man has to learn the points of compass again as often as he awakes, whether from sleep or any abstraction. Not till we are lost, in other words, not till we have lost the world, do we begin to find ourselves, and realize where we are and the infinite extent of our relations.

One afternoon, near the end of the first summer, when I went to the village to get a shoe from the cobbler's, I was seized and put into jail, because, as I have elsewhere related,[7] I did not pay a tax to, or recognize the authority of, the state which buys and sells men, women, and children, like cattle at the door of its senate-house. I had gone down to the woods for other purposes. But, wherever a

---

[7] In "Resistance to Civil Government" (1849).

man goes, men will pursue and paw him with their dirty institutions, and, if they can, constrain him to belong to their desperate odd-fellow society. It is true, I might have resisted forcibly with more or less effect, might have run "amok" against society; but I preferred that society should run "amok" against me, it being the desperate party. However, I was released the next day, obtained my mended shoe, and returned to the woods in season to get my dinner of huckleberries on Fair-Haven Hill. I was never molested by any person but those who represented the state. I had no lock nor bolt but for the desk which held my papers, not even a nail to put over my latch or windows. I never fastened my door night or day, though I was to be absent several days; not even when the next fall I spent a fortnight[8] in the woods of Maine. And yet my house was more respected than if it had been surrounded by a file of soldiers. The tired rambler could rest and warm himself by my fire, the literary amuse himself with the few books on my table, or the curious, by opening my closet door, see what was left of my dinner, and what prospect I had of a supper. Yet, though many people of every class came this way to the pond, I suffered no serious inconvenience from these sources, and I never missed any thing but one small book, a volume of Homer, which perhaps was improperly gilded, and this I trust a soldier of our camp has found by this time.[9] I am convinced, that if all men were to live as simply as I then did, thieving and robbery would be unknown. These take place only in communities where some have got more than is sufficient while others have not enough. The Pope's Homers[10] would soon get properly distributed.—

> "*Nec bella fuerunt,*
> *Faginus astabat dum scyphus ante dapes.*"

> "Nor wars did men molest,
> When only beechen bowls were in request."[11]

"You who govern public affairs, what need have you to employ punishments? Love virtue, and the people will be virtuous. The virtues of a superior man are like the wind; the virtues of a common man are like the grass; the grass, when the wind passes over it, bends."[12]

IX: The Ponds

Sometimes, having had a surfeit of human society and gossip, and worn out all my village friends, I rambled still farther westward than I habitually dwell, into yet more unfrequented parts of the town, "to fresh woods and pastures new,"[1] or, while the sun was setting, made my supper of huckleberries and blueberries on

---

[8] In September 1846.

[9] Thoreau used these words in a translation of Confucius he published in *The Dial* in 1843: someone of similar loyalties or tastes has found the missing article and will put it to good use.

[10] Homer's *Iliad* and *Odyssey*, translated by Alexander Pope (1688–1744). The first volume of Pope's translation of *The Iliad* was the book taken from Thoreau's cabin.

[11] From the *Elegies* of the Roman poet Albius Tibullus (54?–18? B.C.).

[12] From *The Analects* (Bk. XII, Ch. 19) of Confucius.

[1] From the final line of John Milton's elegiac poem "Lycidas" (1637).

Fair Haven Hill, and laid up a store for several days. The fruits do not yield their true flavor to the purchaser of them, nor to him who raises them for the market. There is but one way to obtain it, yet few take that way. If you would know the flavor of huckleberries, ask the cow-boy[2] or the partridge. It is a vulgar error[3] to suppose that you have tasted huckleberries who never plucked them. A huckleberry never reaches Boston; they have not been known there since they grew on her three hills. The ambrosial and essential part of the fruit is lost with the bloom which is rubbed off in the market cart, and they become mere provender. As long as Eternal Justice reigns, not one innocent huckleberry can be transported thither from the country's hills.

Occasionally, after my hoeing was done for the day, I joined some impatient companion who had been fishing on the pond since morning, as silent and motionless as a duck or a floating leaf, and, after practising various kinds of philosophy, had concluded commonly, by the time I arrived, that he belonged to the ancient sect of Cœnobites.[4] There was one older man, an excellent fisher and skilled in all kinds of woodcraft, who was pleased to look upon my house as a building erected for the convenience of fishermen; and I was equally pleased when he sat in my doorway to arrange his lines. Once in a while we sat together on the pond, he at one end of the boat, and I at the other; but not many words passed between us, for he had grown deaf in later years, but he occasionally hummed a psalm, which harmonized well enough with my philosophy. Our intercourse was thus altogether one of unbroken harmony, far more pleasing to remember than if it had been carried on by speech. When, as was commonly the case, I had none to commune with, I used to raise the echoes by striking with a paddle on the side of my boat, filling the surrounding woods with circling and dilating sound, stirring them up as the keeper of a menagerie his wild beasts, until I elicited a growl from every wooded vale and hill-side.

In warm evenings I frequently sat in the boat playing the flute, and saw the perch, which I seemed to have charmed, hovering around me, and the moon travelling over the ribbed bottom, which was strewed with the wrecks of the forest. Formerly I had come to this pond adventurously, from time to time, in dark summer nights, with a companion, and making a fire close to the water's edge, which we thought attracted the fishes, we caught pouts with a bunch of worms strung on a thread; and when we had done, far in the night, threw the burning brands high into the air like skyrockets, which, coming down into the pond, were quenched with a loud hissing, and we were suddenly groping in total darkness. Through this, whistling a tune, we took our way to the haunts of men again. But now I had made my home by the shore.

Sometimes, after staying in a village parlor till the family had all retired, I have returned to the woods, and, partly with a view to the next day's dinner, spent the hours of midnight fishing from a boat by moonlight, serenaded by owls and foxes, and hearing, from time to time, the creaking note of some unknown bird close at hand. These experiences were very memorable and valuable to me,—anchored in forty feet of water, and twenty or thirty rods from the shore, surrounded sometimes by thousands of small perch and shiners, dimpling the surface with their tails in the moonlight, and communicating by a long flaxen line with mysterious

---

[2] The boy who herds the cows.   [3] A common error, made by the general public.

[4] A member of a religious order who lives in a monastery or convent; here, a pun on the sound of the word, "see no bites."

nocturnal fishes which had their dwelling forty feet below, or sometimes dragging sixty feet of line about the pond as I drifted in the gentle night breeze, now and then feeling a slight vibration along it, indicative of some life prowling about its extremity, of dull uncertain blundering purpose there, and slow to make up its mind. At length you slowly raise, pulling hand over hand, some horned pout squeaking and squirming to the upper air. It was very queer, especially in dark nights, when your thoughts had wandered to vast and cosmogonal themes in other spheres, to feel this faint jerk, which came to interrupt your dreams and link you to Nature again. It seemed as if I might next cast my line upward into the air, as well as downward into this element which was scarcely more dense. Thus I caught two fishes as it were with one hook.

The scenery of Walden is on a humble scale, and, though very beautiful, does not approach to grandeur, nor can it much concern one who has not long frequented it or lived by its shore; yet this pond is so remarkable for its depth and purity as to merit a particular description. It is a clear and deep green well, half a mile long and a mile and three quarters in circumference, and contains about sixty-one and a half acres; a perennial spring in the midst of pine and oak woods, without any visible inlet or outlet except by the clouds and evaporation. The surrounding hills rise abruptly from the water to the height of forty to eighty feet, though on the south-east and east they attain to about one hundred and one hundred and fifty feet respectively, within a quarter and a third of a mile. They are exclusively woodland. All our Concord waters have two colors at least, one when viewed at a distance, and another, more proper, close at hand. The first depends more on the light, and follows the sky. In clear weather, in summer, they appear blue at a little distance, especially if agitated, and at a great distance all appear alike. In stormy weather they are sometimes of a dark slate color. The sea, however, is said to be blue one day and green another without any perceptible change in the atmosphere. I have seen our river, when, the landscape being covered with snow, both water and ice were almost as green as grass. Some consider blue "to be the color of pure water, whether liquid or solid."[5] But, looking directly down into our waters from a boat, they are seen to be of very different colors. Walden is blue at one time and green at another, even from the same point of view. Lying between the earth and the heavens, it partakes of the color of both. Viewed from a hill-top it reflects the color of the sky, but near at hand it is of a yellowish tint next the shore where you can see the sand, then a light green, which gradually deepens to a uniform dark green in the body of the pond. In some lights, viewed even from a hill-top, it is of a vivid green next the shore. Some have referred this to the reflection of the verdure; but it is equally green there against the railroad sandbank, and in the spring, before the leaves are expanded, and it may be simply the result of the prevailing blue mixed with the yellow of the sand. Such is the color of its iris. This is that portion, also, where in the spring, the ice being warmed by the heat of the sun reflected from the bottom, and also transmitted through the earth, melts first and forms a narrow canal about the still frozen middle. Like the rest of our waters, when much agitated, in clear weather, so that the surface of the waves may reflect the sky at the right angle, or because there is more light mixed with it, it appears at a little distance of a darker blue than the sky itself; and

[5] An opinion set forth by the Scottish scientist James D. Forbes (1809–1868) in *Travels Through the Alps of Savoy* (1843).

at such a time, being on its surface, and looking with divided vision, so as to see the reflection, I have discerned a matchless and indescribable light blue, such as watered or changeable silks and sword blades suggest, more cerulean than the sky itself, alternating with the original dark green on the opposite sides of the waves, which last appeared but muddy in comparison. It is a vitreous greenish blue, as I remember it, like those patches of the winter sky seen through cloud vistas in the west before sundown. Yet a single glass of its water held up to the light is as colorless as an equal quantity of air. It is well known that a large plate of glass will have a green tint, owing, as the makers say, to its "body," but a small piece of the same will be colorless. How large a body of Walden water would be required to reflect a green tint I have never proved. The water of our river is black or a very dark brown to one looking directly down on it, and, like that of most ponds, imparts to the body of one bathing in it a yellowish tinge; but this water is of such crystalline purity that the body of the bather appears of an alabaster whiteness, still more unnatural, which, as the limbs are magnified and distorted withal, produces a monstrous effect, making fit studies for a Michael Angelo.[6]

The water is so transparent that the bottom can easily be discerned at the depth of twenty-five or thirty feet. Paddling over it, you may see many feet beneath the surface the schools of perch and shiners, perhaps only an inch long, yet the former easily distinguished by their transverse bars, and you think that they must be ascetic fish that find a subsistence there. Once, in the winter, many years ago, when I had been cutting holes through the ice in order to catch pickerel, as I stepped ashore I tossed my axe back on to the ice, but, as if some evil genius had directed it, it slid four or five rods directly into one of the holes, where the water was twenty-five feet deep. Out of curiosity, I lay down on the ice and looked through the hole, until I saw the axe a little on one side, standing on its head, with its helve erect and gently swaying to and fro with the pulse of the pond; and there it might have stood erect and swaying till in the course of time the handle rotted off, if I had not disturbed it. Making another hole directly over it with an ice chisel which I had, and cutting down the longest birch which I could find in the neighborhood with my knife, I made a slip-noose, which I attached to its end, and, letting it down carefully, passed it over the knob of the handle, and drew it by a line along the birch, and so pulled the axe out again.

The shore is composed of a belt of smooth rounded white stones like paving stones, excepting one or two short sand beaches, and is so steep that in many places a single leap will carry you into water over your head; and were it not for its remarkable transparency, that would be the last to be seen of its bottom till it rose on the opposite side. Some think it is bottomless. It is nowhere muddy, and a casual observer would say that there were no weeds at all in it; and of noticeable plants, except in the little meadows recently overflowed, which do not properly belong to it, a closer scrutiny does not detect a flag nor a bulrush, nor even a lily, yellow or white, but only a few small heart-leaves and potamogetons, and perhaps a water-target[7] or two; all which however a bather might not perceive; and these plants are clean and bright like the element they grow in. The stones extend a rod or two into the water, and then the bottom is pure sand, except in the deepest parts, where there is usually a little sediment, probably from the decay of the

---

[6] Michelangelo (1475–1564), Italian artist, sculptor, and chief architect of St. Peter's Cathedral in Rome.
[7] Small pond weeds and an oval water plant.

leaves which have been wafted on to it so many successive falls, and a bright green weed is brought up on anchors even in midwinter.

We have one other pond just like this, White Pond in Nine Acre Corner, about two and a half miles westerly; but, though I am acquainted with most of the ponds within a dozen miles of this centre, I do not know a third of this pure and well-like character. Successive nations perchance have drank at, admired, and fathomed it, and passed away, and still its water is green and pellucid as ever. Not an intermitting spring! Perhaps on that spring morning when Adam and Eve were driven out of Eden Walden Pond was already in existence, and even then breaking up in a gentle spring rain accompanied with mist and a southerly wind, and covered with myriads of ducks and geese, which had not heard of the fall, when still such pure lakes sufficed them. Even then it had commenced to rise and fall, and had clarified its waters and colored them of the hue they now wear, and obtained a patent of heaven to be the only Walden Pond in the world and distiller of celestial dews. Who knows in how many unremembered nations' literatures this has been the Castalian Fountain?[8] or what nymphs presided over it in the Golden Age?[9] It is a gem of the first water which Concord wears in her coronet.

Yet perchance the first who came to this well have left some trace of their footsteps. I have been surprised to detect encircling the pond, even where a thick wood has just been cut down on the shore, a narrow shelf-like path in the steep hill-side, alternately rising and falling, approaching and receding from the water's edge, as old probably as the race of man here, worn by the feet of aboriginal hunters, and still from time to time unwittingly trodden by the present occupants of the land. This is particularly distinct to one standing on the middle of the pond in winter, just after a light snow has fallen, appearing as a clear undulating white line, unobscured by weeds and twigs, and very obvious a quarter of a mile off in many places where in summer it is hardly distinguishable close at hand. The snow reprints it, as it were, in clear white type alto-relievo.[10] The ornamented grounds of villas which will one day be built here may still preserve some trace of this.

The pond rises and falls, but whether regularly or not, and within what period, nobody knows, though, as usual, many pretend to know. It is commonly higher in the winter and lower in the summer, though not corresponding to the general wet and dryness. I can remember when it was a foot or two lower, and also when it was a least five feet higher, than when I lived by it. There is a narrow sand-bar running into it, with very deep water on one side, on which I helped boil a kettle of chowder, some six rods from the main shore, about the year 1824, which it has not been possible to do for twenty-five years; and on the other hand, my friends used to listen with incredulity when I told them, that a few years later I was accustomed to fish from a boat in a secluded cove in the woods, fifteen rods from the only shore they knew, which place was long since converted into a meadow. But the pond has risen steadily for two years, and now, in the summer of '52, is just five feet higher than when I lived there,[11] or as high as it was thirty years ago, and fishing goes on again in the meadow. This makes a difference of level, at the outside, of six or seven feet; and yet the water shed by the surrounding hills is

---

[8] According to Greek myth, a sacred spring on Mt. Parnassus, named for the nymph Castalia, who threw herself into it. Like Walden Pond this spring is fed by subterranean sources.

[9] The world in its pristine original state. The high value Thoreau puts on phenomena that carry with them the purity of an unspoiled beginning is apparent here.

[10] Raised to stand out boldly, in high relief, from a background.

[11] Evidence that Thoreau was working on this part of his manuscript in summer 1852.

insignificant in amount, and this overflow must be referred to causes which affect the deep springs. This same summer the pond has begun to fall again. It is remarkable that this fluctuation, whether periodical or not, appears thus to require many years for its accomplishment. I have observed one rise and a part of two falls, and I expect that a dozen or fifteen years hence the water will again be as low as I have ever known it. Flint's Pond, a mile eastward, allowing for the disturbance occasioned by its inlets and outlets, and the smaller intermediate ponds also, sympathize with Walden, and recently attained their greatest height at the same time with the latter. The same is true, as far as my observation goes, of White Pond.

This rise and fall of Walden at long intervals serves this use at least; the water standing at this great height for a year or more, though it makes it difficult to walk round it, kills the shrubs and trees which have sprung up about its edge since the last rise, pitch-pines, birches, alders, aspens, and others, and, falling again, leaves an unobstructed shore; for, unlike many ponds and all waters which are subject to a daily tide, its shore is cleanest when the water is lowest. On the side of the pond next my house, a row of pitch pines fifteen feet high has been killed and tipped over as if by a lever, and thus a stop put to their encroachments; and their size indicates how many years have elapsed since the last rise to this height. By this fluctuation the pond asserts its title to a shore, and thus the *shore* is *shorn,* and the trees cannot hold it by right of possession. These are the lips of the lake on which no beard grows. It licks its chaps from time to time. When the water is at its height, the alders, willows, and maples send forth a mass of fibrous red roots several feet long from all sides of their stems in the water, and to the height of three or four feet from the ground, in the effort to maintain themselves; and I have known the high-blueberry bushes about the shore, which commonly produce no fruit, bear an abundant crop under these circumstances.

Some have been puzzled to tell how the shore became so regularly paved. My townsmen have all heard the tradition, the oldest people tell me that they heard it in their youth, that anciently the Indians were holding a pow-wow upon a hill here, which rose as high into the heavens as the pond now sinks deep into the earth, and they used much profanity, as the story goes, though this vice is one of which the Indians were never guilty, and while they were thus engaged the hill shook and suddenly sank, and only one old squaw, named Walden, escaped, and from her the pond was named. It has been conjectured that when the hill shook these stones rolled down its side and became the present shore. It is very certain, at any rate, that once there was no pond here, and now there is one; and this Indian fable does not in any respect conflict with the account of that ancient settler whom I have mentioned, who remembers so well when he first came here with his divining rod, saw a thin vapor rising from the sward, and the hazel pointed steadily downward, and he concluded to dig a well here. As for the stones, many still think that they are hardly to be accounted for by the action of the waves on these hills; but I observe that the surrounding hills are remarkably full of the same kind of stones, so that they have been obliged to pile them up in walls on both sides of the railroad cut nearest the pond; and, moreover, there are most stones where the shore is most abrupt; so that, unfortunately, it is no longer a mystery to me. I detect the paver.[12] If the name was not derived from that of some English locality,—Saffron Walden,[13] for instance,—one might suppose that it was called, originally, *Walled-in* Pond.

---

[12] The result of glacial movement.   [13] A village near London.

The pond was my well ready dug. For four months in the year its water is as cold as it is pure at all times; and I think that it is then as good as any, if not the best, in the town. In the winter, all water which is exposed to the air is colder than springs and wells which are protected from it. The temperature of the pond water which had stood in the room where I sat from five o'clock in the afternoon till noon the next day, the sixth of March, 1846, the thermometer having been up to 65° or 70° some of the time, owing partly to the sun on the roof, was 42°, or one degree colder than the water of one of the coldest wells in the village just drawn. The temperature of the Boiling Spring[14] the same day was 45°, or the warmest of any water tried, though it is the coldest that I know of in summer, when, beside, shallow and stagnant surface water is not mingled with it. Moreover, in summer, Walden never becomes so warm as most water which is exposed to the sun, on account of its depth. In the warmest weather I usually placed a pailful in my cellar, where it became cool in the night, and remained so during the day; though I also resorted to a spring in the neighborhood. It was as good when a week old as the day it was dipped, and had no taste of the pump. Whoever camps for a week in summer by the shore of a pond, needs only bury a pail of water a few feet deep in the shade of his camp to be independent on the luxury of ice.

There have been caught in Walden, pickerel, one weighing seven pounds, to say nothing of another which carried off a reel with great velocity, which the fisherman safely set down at eight pounds because he did not see him, perch and pouts, some of each weighing over two pounds, shiners, chivins or roach, (*Leuciscus pulchellus,*) a very few breams, (*Pomotis obesus,*) and a couple of eels, one weighing four pounds,—I am thus particular because the weight of a fish is commonly its only title to fame, and these are the only eels I have heard of here;—also, I have a faint recollection of a little fish some five inches long, with silvery sides and a greenish back, somewhat dace-like[15] in its character, which I mention here chiefly to link my facts to fable. Nevertheless, this pond is not very fertile in fish. Its pickerel, though not abundant, are its chief boast. I have seen at one time lying on the ice pickerel of at least three different kinds; a long and shallow one, steel-colored, most like those caught in the river; a bright golden kind, with greenish reflections and remarkably deep, which is the most common here; and another, golden-colored, and shaped like the last, but peppered on the sides with small dark brown or black spots, intermixed with a few faint blood-red ones, very much like a trout. The specific name *reticulatus*[16] would not apply to this; it should be *guttatus*[17] rather. These are all very firm fish, and weigh more than their size promises. The shiners, pouts, and perch also, and indeed all the fishes which inhabit this pond, are much cleaner, handsomer, and firmer fleshed than those in the river and most other ponds, as the water is purer, and they can easily be distinguished from them. Probably many ichthyologists[18] would make new varieties of some of them. There are also a clean race of frogs and tortoises, and a few muscles in it; muskrats and minks leave their traces about it, and occasionally a travelling mud-turtle visits it. Sometimes, when I pushed off my boat in the morning, I disturbed a great mud-turtle which had secreted himself under the boat in the night. Ducks and geese frequent it in the spring and fall, the white-bellied swallows (*Hirundo bicolor*) skim over it, kingfishers dart away from its

---

[14] A bubbling spring (not a hot spring) west of Walden Pond.
[15] Like a small freshwater fish of the carp family.   [16] Netlike.   [17] Speckled.
[18] Zoologists who specialize in the study of fish.

coves, and the peetweets (*Totanus macularius*) "teter" along its stony shores all summer. I have sometimes disturbed a fishhawk sitting on a white-pine over the water; but I doubt if it is ever profaned by the wing of a gull, like Fair Haven.[19] At most, it tolerates one annual loon. These are all the animals of consequence which frequent it now.

You may see from a boat, in calm weather, near the sandy eastern shore, where the water is eight or ten feet deep, and also in some other parts of the pond; some circular heaps half a dozen feet in diameter by a foot in height, consisting of small stones less than a hen's egg in size, where all around is bare sand. At first you wonder if the Indians could have formed them on the ice for any purpose, and so, when the ice melted, they sank to the bottom; but they are too regular and some of them plainly too fresh for that. They are similar to those found in rivers; but as there are no suckers nor lampreys here, I know not by what fish they could be made. Perhaps they are the nests of the chivin.[20] These lend a pleasing mystery to the bottom.

The shore is irregular enough not to be monotonous. I have in my mind's eye the western indented with deep bays, the bolder northern, and the beautifully scolloped southern shore, where successive capes overlap each other and suggest unexplored coves between. The forest has never so good a setting, nor is so distinctly beautiful, as when seen from the middle of a small lake amid hills which rise from the water's edge; for the water in which it is reflected not only makes the best foreground in such a case, but, with its winding shore, the most natural and agreeable boundary to it. There is no rawness nor imperfection in its edge there, as where the axe has cleared a part, or a cultivated field abuts on it. The trees have ample room to expand on the water side, and each sends forth its most vigorous branch in that direction. There Nature has woven a natural selvage, and the eye rises by just gradations from the low shrubs of the shore to the highest trees. There are few traces of man's hand to be seen. The water laves the shore as it did a thousand years ago.

A lake is the landscape's most beautiful and expressive feature. It is earth's eye; looking into which the beholder measures the depth of his own nature. The fluviatile trees next the shore are the slender eyelashes which fringe it, and the wooded hills and cliffs around are its overhanging brows.

Standing on the smooth sandy beach at the east end of the pond, in a calm September afternoon, when a slight haze makes the opposite shore line indistinct, I have seen whence came the expression, "the glassy surface of a lake." When you invert your head,[21] it looks like a thread of finest gossamer stretched across the valley, and gleaming against the distant pine woods, separating one stratum of the atmosphere from another. You would think that you could walk dry under it to the opposite hills, and that the swallows which skim over might perch on it. Indeed, they sometimes dive below the line, as it were by mistake, and are undeceived. As you look over the pond westward you are obliged to employ both your hands to defend your eyes against the reflected as well as the true sun, for they are equally bright; and if, between the two, you survey its surface critically, it is literally as smooth as glass, except where the skater insects, at equal intervals

---

[19] Where the Sudbury widens into a bay southwest of Walden Pond.

[20] In his variorum edition of *Walden* (1962), Walter Harding reports that Thoreau's hunch has been confirmed by later research: the heaps were made by chivin, nest-building fish.

[21] Bend over and look through your legs, to get a different perspective on nature.

scattered over its whole extent, by their motions in the sun produce the finest imaginable sparkle on it, or, perchance, a duck plumes itself, or, as I have said, a swallow skims so low as to touch it. It may be that in the distance a fish describes an arc of three or four feet in the air, and there is one bright flash where it emerges, and another where it strikes the water; sometimes the whole silvery arc is revealed; or here and there, perhaps, is a thistle-down floating on its surface, which the fishes dart at and so dimple it again. It is like molten glass cooled but not congealed, and the few motes in it are pure and beautiful like the imperfections in glass. You may often detect a yet smoother and darker water, separated from the rest as if by an invisible cobweb, boom of the water nymphs, resting on it. From a hill-top you can see a fish leap in almost any part; for not a pickerel or shiner picks an insect from this smooth surface but it manifestly disturbs the equilibrium of the whole lake. It is wonderful with what elaborateness this simple fact is advertised,—this piscine murder will out,—and from my distant perch I distinguish the circling undulations when they are half a dozen rods in diameter. You can even detect a water-bug (*Gyrinus*) ceaselessly progressing over the smooth surface a quarter of a mile off; for they furrow the water slightly, making a conspicuous ripple bounded by two diverging lines, but the skaters glide over it without rippling it perceptibly. When the surface is considerably agitated there are no skaters nor water-bugs on it, but apparently, in calm days, they leave their havens and adventurously glide forth from the shore by short impulses till they completely cover it. It is a soothing employment, on one of those fine days in the fall when all the warmth of the sun is fully appreciated, to sit on a stump on such a height as this, overlooking the pond, and study the dimpling circles which are incessantly inscribed on its otherwise invisible surface amid the reflected skies and trees. Over this great expanse there is no disturbance but it is thus at once gently smoothed away and assuaged, as, when a vase of water is jarred, the trembling circles seek the shore and all is smooth again. Not a fish can leap or an insect fall on the pond but it is thus reported in circling dimples, in lines of beauty, as it were the constant welling up of its fountain, the gentle pulsing of its life, the heaving of its breast. The thrills of joy and thrills of pain are undistinguishable. How peaceful the phenomena of the lake! Again the works of man shine as in the spring. Ay, every leaf and twig and stone and cobweb sparkles now at mid-afternoon as when covered with dew in a spring morning. Every motion of an oar or an insect produces a flash of light; and if an oar falls, how sweet the echo!

In such a day, in September or October, Walden is a perfect forest mirror, set round with stones as precious to my eye as if fewer or rarer. Nothing so fair, so pure, and at the same time so large, as a lake, perchance, lies on the surface of the earth. Sky water. It needs no fence. Nations come and go without defiling it. It is a mirror which no stone can crack, whose quicksilver will never wear off, whose gilding Nature continually repairs; no storms, no dust, can dim its surface ever fresh;—a mirror in which all impurity presented to it sinks, swept and dusted by the sun's hazy brush,—this the light dust-cloth,—which retains no breath that is breathed on it, but sends its own to float as clouds high above its surface, and be reflected in its bosom still.

A field of water betrays the spirit that is in the air. It is continually receiving new life and motion from above. It is intermediate in its nature between land and sky. On land only the grass and trees wave, but the water itself is rippled by the wind. I see where the breeze dashes across it by the streaks or flakes of light. It is remarkable that we can look down on its surface. We shall, perhaps, look down thus on the surface of air at length, and mark where a still subtler spirit sweeps over it.

The skaters and water-bugs finally disappear in the latter part of October, when the severe frosts have come; and then and in November, usually, in a calm day, there is absolutely nothing to ripple the surface. One November afternoon, in the calm at the end of a rain storm of several days' duration, when the sky was still completely overcast and the air was full of mist, I observed that the pond was remarkably smooth, so that it was difficult to distinguish its surface; though it no longer reflected the bright tints of October, but the sombre November colors of the surrounding hills. Though I passed over it as gently as possible, the slight undulations produced by my boat extended almost as far as I could see, and gave a ribbed appearance to the reflections. But, as I was looking over the surface, I saw here and there at a distance a faint glimmer, as if some skater insects which had escaped the frosts might be collected there, or, perchance, the surface, being so smooth, betrayed where a spring welled up from the bottom. Paddling gently to one of these places, I was surprised to find myself surrounded by myriads of small perch, about five inches long, of a rich bronze color in the green water, sporting there and constantly rising to the surface and dimpling it, sometimes leaving bubbles on it. In such transparent and seemingly bottomless water, reflecting the clouds, I seemed to be floating through the air as in a balloon, and their swimming impressed me as a kind of flight or hovering, as if they were a compact flock of birds passing just beneath my level on the right or left, their fins, like sails, set all around them. There were many such schools in the pond, apparently improving the short season before winter would draw an icy shutter over their broad skylight, sometimes giving to the surface an appearance as if a slight breeze struck it, or a few rain-drops fell there. When I approached carelessly and alarmed them, they made a sudden plash and rippling with their tails, as if one had struck the water with a brushy bough, and instantly took refuge in the depths. At length the wind rose, the mist increased, and the waves began to run, and the perch leaped much higher than before, half out of water, a hundred black points, three inches long, at once above the surface. Even as late as the fifth of December, one year, I saw some dimples on the surface, and thinking it was going to rain hard immediately, the air being full of mist, I made haste to take my place at the oars and row homeward; already the rain seemed rapidly increasing, though I felt none on my cheek, and I anticipated a thorough soaking. But suddenly the dimples ceased, for they were produced by the perch, which the noise of my oars had scared into the depths, and I saw their schools dimly disappearing; so I spent a dry afternoon after all.

An old man who used to frequent this pond nearly sixty years ago, when it was dark with surrounding forests, tells me that in those days he sometimes saw it all alive with ducks and other water fowl, and that there were many eagles about it. He came here a-fishing, and used an old log canoe which he found on the shore. It was made of two white-pine logs dug out and pinned together, and was cut off square at the ends. It was very clumsy, but lasted a great many years before it became water-logged and perhaps sank to the bottom. He did not know whose it was; it belonged to the pond. He used to make a cable for his anchor of strips of hickory bark tied together. An old man, a potter, who lived by the pond before the Revolution, told him once that there was an iron chest at the bottom, and that he had seen it. Sometimes it would come floating up to the shore; but when you went toward it, it would go back into deep water and disappear. I was pleased to hear of the old log canoe, which took the place of an Indian one of the same material but more graceful construction, which perchance had first been a tree on the bank, and then, as it were, fell into the water, to float there for a generation, the most proper vessel for the lake. I remember that when I first looked into these depths there were many large trunks to be seen indistinctly lying on the bottom, which had either been blown over formerly, or left on the ice at the last cutting, when wood was cheaper; but now they have mostly disappeared.

When I first paddled a boat on Walden, it was completely surrounded by thick and lofty pine and oak woods, and in some of its coves grape vines had run over the trees next the water and formed bowers under which a boat could pass. The hills which form its shores are so steep, and the woods on them were then so high, that, as you looked down from the west end, it had the appearance of an amphitheatre for some kind of sylvan spectacle. I have spent many an hour, when I was younger, floating over its surface as the zephyr willed, having paddled my boat to the middle, and lying on my back across the seats, in a summer forenoon, dreaming awake, until I was aroused by the boat touching the sand, and I arose to see what shore my fates had impelled me to; days when idleness was the most attractive and productive industry. Many a forenoon have I stolen away, preferring to spend thus the most valued part of the day; for I was rich, if not in money, in sunny hours and summer days, and spent them lavishly; nor do I regret that I did not waste more of them in the workshop or the teacher's desk. But since I left those shores the woodchoppers have still further laid them waste, and now for many a year there will be no more rambling through the aisles of the wood, with occasional vistas through which you see the water. My Muse may be excused if she is silent henceforth. How can you expect the birds to sing when their groves are cut down?

Now the trunks of trees on the bottom, and the old log canoe, and the dark surrounding woods, are gone, and the villagers, who scarcely know where it lies, instead of going to the pond to bathe or drink, are thinking to bring its water, which should be as sacred as the Ganges[22] at least, to the village in a pipe, to wash their dishes with!—to earn their Walden by the turning of a cock or drawing of a plug! That devilish Iron Horse, whose ear-rending neigh is heard throughout the town, has muddied the Boiling Spring with his foot, and he it is that has browsed off all the woods on Walden shore; that Trojan horse,[23] with a thousand men in his belly, introduced by mercenary Greeks! Where is the country's champion, the Moore[24] of Moore Hall, to meet him at the Deep Cut[25] and thrust an avenging lance between the ribs of the bloated pest?

Nevertheless, of all the characters I have known, perhaps Walden wears best, and best preserves its purity. Many men have been likened to it, but few deserve that honor. Though the woodchoppers have laid bare first this shore and then that, and the Irish have built their sties by it, and the railroad has infringed on its border, and the ice-men have skimmed it once, it is itself unchanged, the same water which my youthful eyes fell on; all the change is in me. It has not acquired one permanent wrinkle after all its ripples. It is perennially young, and I may stand

[22] The principal river in India, considered sacred by Hindus.

[23] Allusion to the strategy that allowed the Greeks to enter Troy and conquer their foes in the Trojan War.

[24] A dragon slayer in "The Dragon of Wantley," collected in *Reliques of Ancient English Poetry* (1765), by Thomas Percy (1729–1811).

[25] A railroad cut near Walden Pond.

and see a swallow dip apparently to pick an insect from its surface as of yore. It struck me again to-night, as if I had not seen it almost daily for more than twenty years,—Why, here is Walden, the same woodland lake that I discovered so many years ago; where a forest was cut down last winter another is springing up by its shore as lustily as ever; the same thought is welling up to its surface that was then; it is the same liquid joy and happiness to itself and its Maker, ay, and it *may* be to me. It is the work of a brave man surely, in whom there was no guile! He rounded this water with his hand, deepened and clarified it in his thought, and in his will bequeathed it to Concord. I see by its face that it is visited by the same reflection; and I can almost say, Walden, is it you?

> It is no dream of mine,
> To ornament a line;
> I cannot come nearer to God and Heaven
> Than I live to Walden even.
> I am its stony shore,
> And the breeze that passes o'er;
> In the hollow of my hand
> Are its water and its sand,
> And its deepest resort
> Lies high in my thought.

The cars never pause to look at it; yet I fancy that the engineers and firemen and brakemen, and those passengers who have a season ticket and see it often, are better men for the sight. The engineer does not forget at night, or his nature does not, that he has beheld this vision of serenity and purity once at least during the day. Though seen but once, it helps to wash out State-street[26] and the engine's soot. One proposes that it be called "God's Drop."[27]

I have said that Walden has no visible inlet nor outlet, but it is on the one hand distantly and indirectly related to Flint's Pond, which is more elevated, by a chain of small ponds coming from that quarter, and on the other directly and manifestly to Concord River, which is lower, by a similar chain of ponds through which in some other geological period it may have flowed, and by a little digging, which God forbid, it can be made to flow thither again. If by living thus reserved and austere, like a hermit in the woods, so long, it has acquired such wonderful purity, who would not regret that the comparatively impure waters of Flint's Pond should be mingled with it, or itself should ever go to waste its sweetness in the ocean wave?

Flint's, or Sandy Pond, in Lincoln, our greatest lake and inland sea, lies about a mile east of Walden. It is much larger, being said to contain one hundred and ninety-seven acres, and is more fertile in fish; but it is comparatively shallow, and not remarkably pure. A walk through the woods thither was often my recreation. It was worth the while, if only to feel the wind blow on your cheek freely, and see the waves run, and remember the life of mariners. I went a-chestnutting there in the fall, on windy days, when the nuts were dropping into the water and were washed to my feet; and one day, as I crept along its sedgy shore, the fresh spray

---

[26] The center of commercial and financial activities in Boston.
[27] God's eyedropper to wash out the commerce and soot of the world.

blowing in my face, I came upon the mouldering wreck of a boat, the sides gone, and hardly more than the impression of its flat bottom left amid the rushes; yet its model was sharply defined, as if it were a large decayed pad, with its veins. It was as impressive a wreck as one could imagine on the sea-shore, and had as good a moral. It is by this time mere vegetable mould and undistinguishable pond shore, through which rushes and flags have pushed up. I used to admire the ripple marks on the sandy bottom, at the north end of this pond, made firm and hard to the feet of the wader by the pressure of the water, and the rushes which grew in Indian file, in waving lines, corresponding to these marks, rank behind rank, as if the waves had planted them. There also I have found, in considerable quantities, curious balls, composed apparently of fine grass or roots, of pipewort perhaps, from half an inch to four inches in diameter, and perfectly spherical. These wash back and forth in shallow water on a sandy bottom, and are sometimes cast on the shore. They are either solid grass, or have a little sand in the middle. At first you would say that they were formed by the action of the waves, like a pebble; yet the smallest are made of equally coarse materials, half an inch long, and they are produced only at one season of the year. Moreover, the waves, I suspect, do not so much construct as wear down a material which has already acquired consistency. They preserve their form when dry for an indefinite period.

Flint's Pond! Such is the poverty of our nomenclature. What right had the unclean and stupid farmer, whose farm abutted on this sky water, whose shores he has ruthlessly laid bare, to give his name to it? Some skin-flint, who loved better the reflecting surface of a dollar, or a bright cent, in which he could see his own brazen face; who regarded even the wild ducks which settled in it as trespassers; his fingers grown into crooked and horny talons from the long habit of grasping harpy-like;[28]—so it is not named for me. I go not there to see him nor to hear of him; who never *saw* it, who never bathed in it, who never loved it, who never protected it, who never spoke a good word for it, nor thanked God that he had made it. Rather let it be named from the fishes that swim in it, the wild fowl or quadrupeds which frequent it, the wild flowers which grow by its shores, or some wild man or child the thread of whose history is interwoven with its own; not from him who could show no title to it but the deed which a like-minded neighbor or legislature gave him,—him who thought only of its money value; whose presence perchance cursed all the shore; who exhausted the land around it, and would fain have exhausted the waters within it; who regretted only that it was not English hay or cranberry meadow,—there was nothing to redeem it, forsooth, in his eyes,— and would have drained and sold it for the mud at its bottom. It did not turn his mill, and it was no *privilege* to him to behold it. I respect not his labors, his farm where every thing has its price; who would carry the landscape, who would carry his God, to market, if he could get any thing for him; who goes to market *for* his god as it is; on whose farm nothing grows free, whose fields bear no crops, whose meadows no flowers, whose trees no fruits, but dollars; who loves not the beauty of his fruits, whose fruits are not ripe for him till they are turned to dollars. Give me the poverty that enjoys true wealth. Farmers are respectable and interesting to me in proportion as they are poor,—poor farmers. A model farm! where the house stands like a fungus in a muck-heap, chambers for men, horses, oxen, and swine, cleansed and uncleansed, all contiguous to one another! Stocked with men! A

---

[28] According to Greek myth, harpies, with the bodies of birds and the faces of women, were monsters who carry away the soul at the moment of death.

great grease-spot, redolent of manures and buttermilk! Under a high state of cultivation, being manured with the hearts and brains of men! As if you were to raise your potatoes in the church-yard! Such is a model farm.

No, no; if the fairest features of the landscape are to be named after men, let them be the noblest and worthiest men alone. Let our lakes receive as true names at least as the Icarian Sea, where "still the shore" a "brave attempt resounds."[29]

Goose Pond, of small extent, is on my way to Flint's; Fair-Haven, an expansion of Concord River, said to contain some seventy acres, is a mile south-west; and White Pond, of about forty acres, is a mile and a half beyond Fair-Haven. This is my lake country.[30] These, with Concord River, are my water privileges; and night and day, year in year out, they grind such grist as I carry to them.

Since the woodcutters, and the railroad, and I myself have profaned Walden, perhaps the most attractive, if not the most beautiful, of all our lakes, the gem of the woods, is White Pond;—a poor name from its commonness, whether derived from the remarkable purity of its waters or the color of its sands. In these as in other respects, however, it is a lesser twin of Walden. They are so much alike that you would say they must be connected under ground. It has the same stony shore, and its waters are of the same hue. As at Walden, in sultry dog-day weather, looking down through the woods on some of its bays which are not so deep but that the reflection from the bottom tinges them, its waters are of a misty bluish-green or glaucous color. Many years since I used to go there to collect the sand by cart-loads, to make sand-paper with, and I have continued to visit it ever since. One who frequents it proposes to call it Virid Lake.[31] Perhaps it might be called Yellow-Pine Lake, from the following circumstance. About fifteen years ago you could see the top of a pitch-pine, of the kind called yellow-pine hereabouts, though it is not a distinct species, projecting above the surface in deep water, many rods from the shore. It was even supposed by some that the pond had sunk, and this was one of the primitive forest that formerly stood there. I find that even so long ago as 1792, in a "Topographical Description of the Town of Concord," by one of its citizens, in the Collections of the Massachusetts Historical Society, the author, after speaking of Walden and White Ponds, adds: "In the middle of the latter may be seen, when the water is very low, a tree which appears as if it grew in the place where it now stands, although the roots are fifty feet below the surface of the water; the top of this tree is broken off, and at that place measures fourteen inches in diameter."[32] In the spring of '49 I talked with the man who lives nearest the pond in Sudbury, who told me that it was he who got out this tree ten or fifteen years before. As near as he could remember, it stood twelve or fifteen rods from the shore, where the water was thirty or forty feet deep. It was in the winter, and he had been getting out ice in the forenoon, and had resolved that in the afternoon, with the aid of his neighbors, he would take out the old yellow-pine. He sawed a

---

[29] From "Icarus" by the Scottish poet William Drummond (1585–1649) of Hawthornden; according to Greek myth, Icarus, with waxen wings made by his father, Daedalus, flew too near the sun and fell to his death in the part of the Aegean Sea that bears his name.

[30] The local equivalent of the Lake Country in England, made famous by William Wordsworth and other romantic writers.

[31] Green Lake, with the connotation of greenness, freshness.

[32] From William Jones's "Topographical Description of Concord," in the *Massachusetts Historical Society Collections* (1792), Vol. I. Walter Harding identifies the man who took the tree out as "a Mr. Haynes."

channel in the ice toward the shore, and hauled it over and along and out on to the ice with oxen; but, before he had gone far in his work, he was surprised to find that it was wrong end upward, with the stumps of the branches pointing down, and the small end firmly fastened in the sandy bottom. It was about a foot in diameter at the big end, and he had expected to get a good saw-log, but it was so rotten as to be fit only for fuel, if for that. He had some of it in his shed then. There were marks of an axe and of woodpeckers on the but. He thought that it might have been a dead tree on the shore, but was finally blown over into the pond, and after the top had become waterlogged, while the but-end was still dry and light, had drifted out and sunk wrong end up. His father, eighty years old, could not remember when it was not there. Several pretty large logs may still be seen lying on the bottom, where, owing to the undulation of the surface, they look like huge water snakes in motion.

This pond has rarely been profaned by a boat, for there is little in it to tempt a fisherman. Instead of the white lily, which requires mud, or the common sweet flag, the blue flag (*Iris versicolor*) grows thinly in the pure water, rising from the stony bottom all around the shore, where it is visited by humming birds in June, and the color both of its bluish blades and its flowers, and especially their reflections, are in singular harmony with the glaucous water.

White Pond and Walden are great crystals on the surface of the earth, Lakes of Light. If they were permanently congealed, and small enough to be clutched, they would, perchance, be carried off by slaves, like precious stones, to adorn the heads of emperors; but being liquid, and ample, and secured to us and our successors forever, we disregard them, and run after the diamond of Kohinoor.[33] They are too pure to have a market value; they contain no muck. How much more beautiful than our lives, how much more transparent than our characters, are they! We never learned meanness of them. How much fairer than the pool before the farmer's door, in which his ducks swim! Hither the clean wild ducks come. Nature has no human inhabitant who appreciates her. The birds with their plumage and their notes are in harmony with the flowers, but what youth or maiden conspires with the wild luxuriant beauty of Nature? She flourishes most alone, far from the towns where they reside. Talk of heaven! ye disgrace earth.

X: BAKER FARM

Sometimes I rambled to pine groves, standing like temples, or like fleets at sea, full-rigged, with wavy boughs, and rippling with light, so soft and green and shady that the Druids[1] would have forsaken their oaks to worship in them; or to the cedar wood beyond Flint's Pond, where the trees, covered with hoary blue berries, spiring higher and higher, are fit to stand before Valhalla,[2] and the creeping juniper covers the ground with wreaths full of fruit; or to swamps where the usnea lichen hangs in festoons from the black-spruce trees, and toad-stools, round tables of the swamp gods, cover the ground, and more beautiful fungi adorn the stumps, like butterflies or shells, vegetable winkles;[3] where the swamp-pink and

[33] An immense diamond discovered in India in the eighteenth century and made part of the British crown jewels when the Punjab area was annexed in 1849 (when Thoreau was writing *Walden*).

[1] Pagan priests of ancient Britain to whom oak groves were sacred.

[2] According to Norse myth, the hall of the mighty god Odin, in which he receives the souls of heroes slain in battle.

[3] Snails.

dogwood grow, the red alder-berry glows like eyes of imps, the waxwork grooves and crushes the hardest woods in its folds, and the wild-holly berries make the beholder forget his home with their beauty, and he is dazzled and tempted by nameless other wild forbidden fruits, too fair for mortal taste. Instead of calling on some scholar, I paid many a visit to particular trees, of kinds which are rare in this neighborhood, standing far away in the middle of some pasture, or in the depths of a wood or swamp, or on a hill-top; such as the black-birch, of which we have some handsome specimens two feet in diameter; its cousin the yellow-birch, with its loose golden vest, perfumed like the first; the beech, which has so neat a bole[4] and beautifully lichen-painted, perfect in all its details, of which, excepting scattered specimens, I know but one small grove of sizeable trees left in the township, supposed by some to have been planted by the pigeons that were once baited with beech nuts near by; it is worth the while to see the silver grain sparkle when you split this wood; the bass; the hornbeam; the *Celtis occidentalis,* or false elm, of which we have but one well-grown; some taller mast of a pine, a shingle tree, or a more perfect hemlock than usual, standing like a pagoda in the midst of the woods; and many others I could mention. These were the shrines I visited both summer and winter.

Once it chanced that I stood in the very abutment of a rainbow's arch, which filled the lower stratum of the atmosphere, tinging the grass and leaves around, and dazzling me as if I looked through colored crystal. It was a lake of rainbow light, in which, for a short while, I lived like a dolphin. If it had lasted longer it might have tinged my employments and life. As I walked on the railroad causeway, I used to wonder at the halo of light around my shadow, and would fain fancy myself one of the elect.[5] One who visited me declared that the shadows of some Irishmen before him had no halo about them, that it was only natives that were so distinguished. Benvenuto Cellini[6] tells us in his memoirs, that, after a certain terrible dream or vision which he had during his confinement in the castle of St. Angelo, a resplendent light appeared over the shadow of his head at morning and evening, whether he was in Italy or France, and it was particularly conspicuous when the grass was moist with dew. This was probably the same phenomenon to which I have referred, which is especially observed in the morning, but also at other times, and even by moonlight. Though a constant one, it is not commonly noticed, and, in the case of an excitable imagination like Cellini's, it would be basis enough for superstition. Beside, he tells us that he showed it to very few. But are they not indeed distinguished who are conscious that they are regarded at all?

I set out one afternoon to go a-fishing to Fair-Haven, through the woods, to eke out my scanty fare of vegetables. My way led through Pleasant Meadow, an adjunct of the Baker Farm, that retreat of which a poet[7] has since sung, beginning,—

> "Thy entry is a pleasant field,
> Which some mossy fruit trees yield
> Partly to a ruddy brook,

[4] Trunk.   [5] In Calvinist theology, those predestined for salvation.

[6] Cellini (1500–1571), an Italian metalsmith and sculptor, in Ch. 26 of the *Autobiography of Benvenuto Cellini* (written 1558–1562); he was imprisoned briefly in the castle of St. Angelo in Rome.

[7] The younger William Ellery Channing; all the poetry in this chapter is by Channing.

By gliding musquash[8] undertook,
And mercurial trout,
Darting about."

I thought of living there before I went to Walden. I "hooked" the apples, leaped the brook, and scared the musquash and the trout. It was one of those afternoons which seem indefinitely long before one, in which many events may happen, a large portion of our natural life, though it was already half spent when I started. By the way there came up a shower, which compelled me to stand half an hour under a pine, piling boughs over my head, and wearing my handkerchief for a shed; and when at length I had made one cast over the pickerel-weed, standing up to my middle in water, I found myself suddenly in the shadow of a cloud, and the thunder began to rumble with such emphasis that I could do no more than listen to it. The gods must be proud, thought I, with such forked flashes to rout a poor unarmed fisherman. So I made haste for shelter to the nearest hut, which stood half a mile from any road, but so much the nearer to the pond, and had long been uninhabited:—

"And here a poet builded,
In the completed years,
For behold a trivial cabin
That to destruction steers."

So the Muse fables. But therein, as I found, dwelt now John Field, an Irishman, and his wife, and several children, from the broad-faced boy who assisted his father at his work, and now came running by his side from the bog to escape the rain, to the wrinkled, sibyl-like, cone-headed infant[9] that sat upon its father's knee as in the palaces of nobles, and looked out from its home in the midst of wet and hunger inquisitively upon the stranger, with the privilege of infancy, not knowing but it was the last of a noble line, and the hope and cynosure of the world, instead of John Field's poor starveling brat. There we sat together under that part of the roof which leaked the least, while it showered and thundered without. I had sat there many times of old before the ship was built that floated this family to America. An honest, hard-working, but shiftless man plainly was John Field; and his wife, she too was brave to cook so many successive dinners in the recesses of that lofty stove; with round greasy face and bare breast,[10] still thinking to improve her condition one day; with the never absent mop in one hand, and yet no effects of it visible any where. The chickens, which had also taken shelter here from the rain, stalked about the room like members of the family, too humanized methought to roast well. They stood and looked in my eye or pecked at my shoe significantly. Meanwhile my host told me his story, how hard he worked "bogging" for a neighboring farmer, turning up a meadow with a spade or bog hoe at the rate of ten dollars an acre and the use of the land with manure for one year, and his little broad-faced son worked cheerfully at his father's side the while, not knowing how

---

[8] Muskrat.

[9] According to Greek myth, Sibyl was granted her wish of as many years of life as she had grains of sand in her hand; because she forgot to ask for perennial youth, she grew incredibly wrinkled in advanced age.

[10] With more of her chest uncovered than Thoreau was accustomed to seeing.

poor a bargain the latter had made. I tried to help him with my experience, telling him that he was one of my nearest neighbors, and that I too, who came a-fishing here, and looked like a loafer, was getting my living like himself; that I lived in a tight light and clean house, which hardly cost more than the annual rent of such a ruin as his commonly amounts to; and how, if he chose, he might in a month or two build himself a palace of his own; that I did not use tea, nor coffee, nor butter, nor milk, nor fresh meat, and so did not have to work to get them; again, as I did not work hard, I did not have to eat hard, and it cost me but a trifle for my food; but as he began with tea, and coffee, and butter, and milk, and beef, he had to work hard to pay for them, and when he had worked hard he had to eat hard again to repair the waste of his system,—and so it was as broad as it was long, indeed it was broader than it was long, for he was discontented and wasted his life into the bargain; and yet he had rated it as a gain in coming to America, that here you could get tea, and coffee, and meat every day. But the only true America is that country where you are at liberty to pursue such a mode of life as may enable you to do without these, and where the state does not endeavor to compel you to sustain the slavery and war and other superfluous expenses which directly or indirectly result from the use of such things. For I purposely talked to him as if he were a philosopher, or desired to be one. I should be glad if all the meadows on the earth were left in a wild state, if that were the consequence of men's beginning to redeem themselves. A man will not need to study history to find out what is best for his own culture. But alas! the culture of an Irishman is an enterprise to be undertaken with a sort of moral bog hoe. I told him, that as he worked so hard at bogging, he required thick boots and stout clothing, which yet were soon soiled and worn out, but I wore light shoes and thin clothing, which cost not half so much, though he might think that I was dressed like a gentleman, (which, however, was not the case,) and in an hour or two, without labor, but as a recreation, I could, if I wished, catch as many fish as I should want for two days, or earn enough money to support me a week. If he and his family would live simply, they might all go a-huckleberrying in the summer for their amusement. John heaved a sigh at this, and his wife stared with arms a-kimbo, and both appeared to be wondering if they had capital enough to begin such a course with, or arithmetic enough to carry it through. It was sailing by dead reckoning to them, and they saw not clearly how to make their port so; therefore I suppose they still take life bravely, after their fashion, face to face, giving it tooth and nail, not having skill to split its massive columns with any fine entering wedge, and rout it in detail;— thinking to deal with it roughly, as one should handle a thistle. But they fight at an overwhelming disadvantage,—living, John Field, alas! without arithmetic, and failing so.

"Do you ever fish?" I asked. "Oh yes, I catch a mess now and then when I am lying by; good perch I catch." "What's your bait?" "I catch shiners with fishworms, and bait the perch with them." "You'd better go now, John," said his wife with glistening and hopeful face; but John demurred.

The shower was now over, and a rainbow above the eastern woods promised a fair evening; so I took my departure. When I had got without I asked for a drink, hoping to get a sight of the well bottom, to complete my survey of the premises; but there, alas! are shallows and quicksands, and rope broken withal, and bucket irrecoverable. Meanwhile the right culinary vessel was selected, water was seemingly distilled, and after consultation and long delay passed out to the thirsty one,—not yet suffered to cool, not yet to settle. Such gruel sustains life here, I thought; so, shutting my eyes, and excluding the motes by a skilfully directed under-current,[11] I drank to genuine hospitality the heartiest draught I could. I am not squeamish in such cases when manners are concerned.

As I was leaving the Irishman's roof after the rain, bending my steps again to the pond, my haste to catch pickerel, wading in retired meadows, in sloughs and bog-holes, in forlorn and savage places, appeared for an instant trivial to me who had been sent to school and college; but as I ran down the hill toward the reddening west, with the rainbow over my shoulder, and some faint tinkling sounds borne to my ear through the cleansed air, from I know not what quarter, my Good Genius seemed to say,—Go fish and hunt far and wide day by day,—farther and wider,—and rest thee by many brooks and hearth-sides without misgiving. Remember thy Creator in the days of thy youth.[12] Rise free from care before the dawn, and seek adventures. Let the noon find thee by other lakes, and the night overtake thee every where at home. There are no larger fields than these, no worthier games than may here be played. Grow wild according to thy nature, like these sedges and brakes, which will never become English hay. Let the thunder rumble; what if it threaten ruin to farmers' crops? that is not its errand to thee. Take shelter under the cloud, while they flee to carts and sheds. Let not to get a living be thy trade, but thy sport. Enjoy the land, but own it not. Through want of enterprise and faith men are where they are, buying and selling, and spending their lives like serfs.

O Baker Farm!

> "Landscape where the richest element
> Is a little sunshine innocent." * *[13]

> "No one runs to revel
> On thy rail-fenced lea." * *

> "Debate with no man hast thou,
>   With questions art never perplexed,
> As tame at the first sight as now,
>   In thy plain russet gabardine dressed." * *

> "Come ye who love,
>   And ye who hate,
> Children of the Holy Dove,
>   And Guy Faux[14] of the state,
> And hang conspiracies
> From the tough rafters of the trees!"

Men come tamely home at night only from the next field or street, where their household echoes haunt, and their life pines because it breathes its own breath over again; their shadows morning and evening reach farther than their daily

[11] Drinking carefully to avoid the particles of dirt or dust in the water.

[12] "Remember now thy creator in the days of thy youth. . . ," from Ecclesiastes 12:1.

[13] The asterisks are Thoreau's.

[14] Guy Fawkes (1570–1606), a Catholic conspirator executed for his part in the Gunpowder Plot to blow up the English House of Lords and King James I on November 5, 1605, the opening day of Parliament.

steps. We should come home from far, from adventures, and perils, and discoveries every day, with new experience and character.

Before I had reached the pond some fresh impulse had brought out John Field, with altered mind, letting go "bogging" ere this sunset. But he, poor man, disturbed only a couple of fins while I was catching a fair string, and he said it was his luck; but when we changed seats in the boat luck changed seats too. Poor John Field!—I trust he does not read this, unless he will improve by it,—thinking to live by some derivative old country mode in this primitive new country,—to catch perch with shiners. It is good bait sometimes, I allow. With his horizon all his own, yet he a poor man, born to be poor, with his inherited Irish poverty or poor life, his Adam's grandmother and boggy ways, not to rise in this world, he nor his posterity, till their wading webbed bog-trotting feet get *talaria*[15] to their heels.

XI: Higher Laws

As I came home through the woods with my string of fish, trailing my pole, it being now quite dark, I caught a glimpse of a woodchuck stealing across my path, and felt a strange thrill of savage delight, and was strongly tempted to seize and devour him raw; not that I was hungry then, except for that wildness which he represented. Once or twice, however, while I lived at the pond, I found myself ranging the woods, like a half-starved hound, with a strange abandonment, seeking some kind of venison which I might devour, and no morsel could have been too savage for me. The wildest scenes had become unaccountably familiar. I found in myself, and still find, an instinct toward a higher, or, as it is named, spiritual life, as do most men, and another toward a primitive rank and savage one, and I reverence them both. I love the wild not less than the good. The wildness and adventure that are in fishing still recommended it to me. I like sometimes to take rank hold on life and spend my day more as the animals do. Perhaps I have owed to this employment and to hunting, when quite young, my closest acquaintance with Nature. They early introduce us to and detain us in scenery with which otherwise, at that age, we should have little acquaintance. Fishermen, hunters, woodchoppers, and others, spending their lives in the fields and woods, in a peculiar sense a part of Nature themselves, are often in a more favorable mood for observing her, in the intervals of their pursuits, than philosophers or poets even, who approach her with expectation. She is not afraid to exhibit herself to them. The traveller on the prairie is naturally a hunter, on the head waters of the Missouri and Columbia a trapper, and at the Falls of St. Mary[1] a fisherman. He who is only a traveller learns things at second-hand and by the halves, and is poor authority. We are most interested when science reports what those men already know practically or instinctively, for that alone is a true *humanity*, or account of human experience.

They mistake who assert that the Yankee has few amusements, because he has not so many public holidays, and men and boys do not play so many games as they do in England, for here the more primitive but solitary amusements of hunting fishing and the like have not yet given place to the former. Almost every New England boy among my contemporaries shouldered a fowling piece between the

---

[15] According to Greek myth, the winged heels of the gods.
[1] The falls of the St. Mary's River between Lake Superior and Lake Huron.

ages of ten and fourteen; and his hunting and fishing grounds were not limited like the preserves of an English nobleman, but were more boundless even than those of a savage. No wonder, then, that he did not oftener stay to play on the common. But already a change is taking place, owing, not to an increased humanity, but to an increased scarcity of game, for perhaps the hunter is the greatest friend of the animals hunted, not excepting the Humane Society.

Moreover, when at the pond, I wished sometimes to add fish to may fare for variety. I have actually fished from the same kind of necessity that the first fishers did. Whatever humanity I might conjure up against it was all factitious, and concerned my philosophy more than my feelings. I speak of fishing only now, for I had long felt differently about fowling, and sold my gun before I went to the woods. Not that I am less humane than others, but I did not perceive that my feelings were much affected. I did not pity the fishes nor the worms. This was habit. As for fowling, during the last years that I carried a gun my excuse was that I was studying ornithology, and sought only new or rare birds. But I confess that I am now inclined to think that there is a finer way of studying ornithology than this. It requires so much closer attention to the habits of the birds, that, if for that reason only, I have been willing to omit the gun. Yet notwithstanding the objection on the score of humanity, I am compelled to doubt if equally valuable sports are ever substituted for these; and when some of my friends have asked me anxiously about their boys, whether they should let them hunt, I have answered, yes,—remembering that it was one of the best parts of my education,—*make* them hunters, though sportsmen only at first, if possible, mighty hunters at last, so that they shall not find game large enough for them in this or any vegetable wilderness,—hunters as well as fishers of men.[2] Thus far I am of the opinion of Chaucer's nun, who

> "yave not of the text a pulled hen
> That saith that hunters ben not holy men."[3]

There is a period in the history of the individual, as of the race, when the hunters are the "best men," as the Algonquins called them. We cannot but pity the boy who has never fired a gun; he is no more humane, while his education has been sadly neglected. This was my answer with respect to those youths who were bent on this pursuit, trusting that they would soon outgrow it. No humane being, past the thoughtless age of boyhood, will wantonly murder any creature, which holds its life by the same tenure that he does. The hare in its extremity cries like a child. I warn you, mothers, that my sympathies do not always make the usual phil-*anthropic*[4] distinctions.

Such is oftenest the young man's introduction to the forest, and the most original part of himself. He goes thither at first as a hunter and fisher, until at last, if he has the seeds of a better life in him, he distinguishes his proper objects, as a poet or naturalist it may be, and leaves the gun and fish-pole behind. The mass of men

---

[2] Jesus' words to the fishermen Simon and Andrew: "Come ye after me, and I will make you to become fishers of men," from Mark 1:17.

[3] Said of the monk, not the nun, in Geoffrey Chaucer's prologue to *The Canterbury Tales:* he gave not a plucked hen for the text that says hunters are not holy men.

[4] Philanthropy means a love for *humankind;* Thoreau does not always distinguish between human beings and other living creatures.

are still and always young in this respect. In some countries a hunting parson is no uncommon sight. Such a one might make a good shepherd's dog, but is far from being the Good Shepherd. I have been surprised to consider that the only obvious employment, except wood-chopping, ice-cutting, or the like business, which ever to my knowledge detained at Walden Pond for a whole half day any of my fellow-citizens, whether fathers or children of the town, with just one exception, was fishing. Commonly they did not think that they were lucky, or well paid for their time, unless they got a long string of fish, though they had the opportunity of seeing the pond all the while. They might go there a thousand times before the sediment of fishing would sink to the bottom and leave their purpose pure; but no doubt such a clarifying process would be going on all the while. The governor and his council faintly remember the pond, for they went a-fishing there when they were boys; but now they are too old and dignified to go a-fishing, and so they know it no more forever. Yet even they expect to go to heaven at last. If the legislature regards it, it is chiefly to regulate the number of hooks to be used there; but they know nothing about the hook of hooks with which to angle for the pond itself, impaling the legislature for a bait. Thus, even in civilized communities, the embryo man passes through the hunter stage of development.

I have found repeatedly, of late years, that I cannot fish without falling a little in self-respect. I have tried it again and again. I have skill at it, and, like many of my fellows, a certain instinct for it, which revives from time to time, but always when I have done I feel that it would have been better if I had not fished. I think that I do not mistake. It is a faint intimation, yet so are the first streaks of morning. There is unquestionably this instinct in me which belongs to the lower orders of creation; yet with every year I am less a fisherman, though without more humanity or even wisdom; at present I am no fisherman at all. But I see that if I were to live in a wilderness I should again be tempted to become a fisher and hunter in earnest. Beside, there is something essentially unclean about this diet and all flesh, and I began to see where housework commences, and whence the endeavor, which costs so much, to wear a tidy and respectable appearance each day, to keep the house sweet and free from all ill odors and sights. Having been my own butcher and scullion and cook, as well as the gentleman for whom the dishes were served up, I can speak from an unusually complete experience. The practical objection to animal food in my case was its uncleanness; and, besides, when I had caught and cleaned and cooked and eaten my fish, they seemed not to have fed me essentially. It was insignificant and unnecessary, and cost more than it came to. A little bread or a few potatoes would have done as well, with less trouble and filth. Like many of my contemporaries, I had rarely for many years used animal food, or tea, or coffee, etc.; not so much because of any ill effects which I had traced to them, as because they were not agreeable to my imagination. The repugnance to animal food is not the effect of experience, but is an instinct. It appeared more beautiful to live low and fare hard in many respects; and though I never did so, I went far enough to please my imagination. I believe that every man who has ever been earnest to preserve his higher or poetic faculties in the best condition has been particularly inclined to abstain from animal food, and from much food of any kind. It is a significant fact, stated by entomologists, I find it in Kirby and Spence,[5] that "some insects in their perfect state, though furnished with organs of feeding, make no use of them;" and they lay it down as "a general rule, that

[5] *An Introduction to Entomology* (1846), by William Kirby and William Spence.

almost all insects in this state eat much less than in that of larvæ. The voracious caterpillar when transformed into a butterfly," . . "and the gluttonous maggot when become a fly," content themselves with a drop or two of honey or some other sweet liquid. The abdomen under the wings of the butterfly still represents the larva. This is the tid-bit which tempts his insectivorous fate. The gross feeder is a man in the larva state; and there are whole nations in that condition, nations without fancy or imagination, whose vast abdomens betray them.

It is hard to provide and cook so simple and clean a diet as will not offend the imagination; but this, I think, is to be fed when we feed the body; they should both sit down at the same table. Yet perhaps this may be done. The fruits eaten temperately need not make us ashamed of our appetites, nor interrupt the worthiest pursuits. But put an extra condiment into your dish, and it will poison you. It is not worth the while to live by rich cookery. Most men would feel shame if caught preparing with their own hands precisely such a dinner, whether of animal or vegetable food, as is every day prepared for them by others. Yet till this is otherwise we are not civilized, and, if gentlemen and ladies, are not true men and women. This certainly suggests what change is to be made. It may be vain to ask why the imagination will not be reconciled to flesh and fat. I am satisfied that it is not. Is it not a reproach that man is a carnivorous animal? True, he can and does live, in a great measure, by preying on other animals; but this is a miserable way,—as any one who will go to snaring rabbits, or slaughtering lambs, may learn,—and he will be regarded as a benefactor of his race who shall teach man to confine himself to a more innocent and wholesome diet. Whatever my own practice may be, I have no doubt that it is a part of the destiny of the human race, in its gradual improvement, to leave off eating animals, as surely as the savage tribes have left off eating each other when they came in contact with the more civilized.

If one listens to the faintest but constant suggestions of his genius, which are certainly true, he sees not to what extremes, or even insanity, it may lead him; and yet that way, as he grows more resolute and faithful, his road lies. The faintest assured objection which one healthy man feels will at length prevail over the arguments and customs of mankind. No man ever followed his genius till it misled him. Though the result were bodily weakness, yet perhaps no one can say that the consequences were to be regretted, for these were a life in conformity to higher principles. If the day and the night are such that you greet them with joy, and life emits a fragrance like flowers and sweet-scented herbs, is more elastic, more starry, more immortal,—that is your success. All nature is your congratulation, and you have cause momentarily to bless yourself. The greatest gains and values are farthest from being appreciated. We easily come to doubt if they exist. We soon forget them. They are the highest reality. Perhaps the facts most astounding and most real are never communicated by man to man. The true harvest of my daily life is somewhat as intangible and indescribable as the tints of morning or evening. It is a little star-dust caught, a segment of the rainbow which I have clutched.

Yet, for my part, I was never unusually squeamish; I could sometimes eat a fried rat with a good relish, if it were necessary. I am glad to have drunk water so long, for the same reason that I prefer the natural sky to an opium-eater's heaven. I would fain keep sober always; and there are infinite degrees of drunkenness. I believe that water is the only drink for a wise man; wine is not so noble a liquor; and think of dashing the hopes of a morning with a cup of warm coffee, or of an evening with a dish of tea! Ah, how low I fall when I am tempted by them! Even music may be intoxicating. Such apparently slight causes destroyed Greece and Rome, and will destroy England and America. Of all ebriosity,[6] who does not prefer to be intoxicated by the air he breathes? I have found it to be the most serious objection to coarse labors long continued, that they compelled me to eat and drink coarsely also. But to tell the truth, I find myself at present somewhat less particular in these respects. I carry less religion to the table, ask no blessing; not because I am wiser than I was, but, I am obliged to confess, because, however much it is to be regretted, with years I have grown more coarse and indifferent. Perhaps these questions are entertained only in youth, as most believe of poetry. My practice is "nowhere," my opinion is here. Nevertheless I am far from regarding myself as one of those privileged ones to whom the Ved[7] refers when it says, that "he who has true faith in the Omnipresent Supreme Being may eat all that exists," that is, is not bound to inquire what is his food, or who prepares it; and even in their case it is to be observed, as a Hindoo commentator has remarked, that the Vedant limits this privilege to "the time of distress."[8]

Who has not sometimes derived an inexpressible satisfaction from his food in which appetite had no share? I have been thrilled to think that I owed a mental perception to the commonly gross sense of taste, that I have been inspired through the palate, that some berries which I had eaten on a hill-side had fed my genius. "The soul not being mistress of herself," says Thseng-tseu,[9] "one looks, and one does not see; one listens, and one does not hear; one eats, and one does not know the savor of food." He who distinguishes the true savor of his food can never be a glutton; he who does not cannot be otherwise. A puritan may go to his brown-bread crust with as gross an appetite as ever an alderman to his turtle. Not that food which entereth into the mouth defileth a man, but the appetite with which it is eaten.[10] It is neither the quality nor the quantity, but the devotion to sensual savors; when that which is eaten is not a viand to sustain our animal, or inspire our spiritual life, but food for the worms that possess us. If the hunter has a taste for mud-turtles, muskrats, and other such savage tid-bits, the fine lady indulges a taste for jelly made of a calf's foot, or for sardines from over the sea, and they are even. He goes to the mill-pond, she to her preserve-pot. The wonder is how they, how you and I, can live this slimy beastly life, eating and drinking.

Our whole life is startlingly moral. There is never an instant's truce between virtue and vice. Goodness is the only investment that never fails. In the music of the harp which trembles round the world it is the insisting on this which thrills us. The harp is the travelling patterer for the Universe's Insurance Company, recommending its laws, and our little goodness is all the assessment that we pay. Though the youth at last grows indifferent, the laws of the universe are not indifferent, but are forever on the side of the most sensitive. Listen to every zephyr for some reproof, for it is surely there, and he is unfortunate who does not hear it. We cannot touch a string or move a stop but the charming moral transfixes us. Many an irksome noise, go a long way off, is heard as music, a proud sweet satire on the meanness of our lives.

We are conscious of an animal in us, which awakens in proportion as our

---

[6] Intoxication.   [7] One of the Vedas.

[8] From Rajah Rammohun Roy's translation (1832) of the Vedas.

[9] A disciple of Confucius; used in Confucius's *The Great Learning* (Ch. 7).

[10] "Not that which goeth into the mouth defileth a man; but that which cometh out of the mouth, this defileth a man," from Matthew 15:11.

higher nature slumbers. It is reptile and sensual, and perhaps cannot be wholly expelled; like the worms which, even in life and health, occupy our bodies. Possibly we may withdraw from it, but never change its nature. I fear that it may enjoy a certain health of its own; that we may be well, yet not pure. The other day I picked up the lower jaw of a hog, with white and sound teeth and tusks, which suggested that there was an animal health and vigor distinct from the spiritual. This creature succeeded by other means than temperance and purity. "That in which men differ from brute beasts," says Mencius,[11] "is a thing very inconsiderable; the common herd lose it very soon; superior men preserve it carefully." Who knows what sort of life would result if we had attained to purity? If I knew so wise a man as could teach me purity I would go to seek him forthwith. "A command over our passions, and over the external senses of the body, and good acts, are declared by the Ved to be indispensable in the mind's approximation to God."[12] Yet the spirit can for the time pervade and control every member and function of the body, and transmute what in form is the grossest sensuality into purity and devotion. The generative energy, which, when we are loose, dissipates and makes us unclean, when we are continent invigorates and inspires us. Chastity is the flowering of man; and what are called Genius, Heroism, Holiness, and the like, are but various fruits which succeed it. Man flows at once to God when the channel of purity is open. By turns our purity inspires and our impurity casts us down. He is blessed who is assured that the animal is dying out in him day by day, and the divine being established. Perhaps there is none but has cause for shame on account of the inferior and brutish nature to which he is allied. I fear that we are such gods or demigods only as fauns and satyrs,[13] the divine allied to beasts, the creatures of appetite, and that, to some extent, our very life is our disgrace.—

> "How happy's he who hath due place assigned
> To his beasts and disaforested his mind!

> * * *

> Can use his horse, goat, wolf, and ev'ry beast,
> And is not ass himself to all the rest!
> Else man not only is the herd of swine,
> But he's those devils too which did incline
> Them to a headlong rage, and made them worse."[14]

All sensuality is one, though it takes many forms; all purity is one. It is the same whether a man eat, or drink, or cohabit, or sleep sensually. They are but one appetite, and we only need to see a person do any one of these things to know how great a sensualist he is. The impure can neither stand nor sit with purity. When the reptile is attacked at one mouth of his burrow, he shows himself at another. If you would be chaste, you must be temperate. What is chastity? How shall a man know if he is chaste? He shall not know it. We have heard of this virtue, but we know

---

[11] Mencius (372?–289? B.C.) was a Chinese philosopher; from the *Works of Mencius* (IV. 19).
[12] From Rajah Rammohun Roy's translation of the Vedas.
[13] According to Greek myth, sylvan demigods, half man and half goat or horse.
[14] From "To Sir Edward Herbert, at Julyers," by the English poet John Donne (1573–1631).

not what it is. We speak conformably to the rumor which we have heard. From exertion come wisdom and purity; from sloth ignorance and sensuality. In the student sensuality is a sluggish habit of mind. An unclean person is universally a slothful one, one who sits by a stove, whom the sun shines on prostrate, who reposes without being fatigued. If you would avoid uncleanness, and all the sins, work earnestly, though it be at cleaning a stable. Nature is hard to be overcome, but she must be overcome. What avails it that you are Christian, if you are not purer than the heathen, if you deny yourself no more, if you are not more religious? I know of many systems of religion esteemed heathenish whose precepts fill the reader with shame, and provoke him to new endeavors, though it be to the performance of rites merely.

I hesitate to say these things, but it is not because of the subject,—I care not how obscene my *words* are,—but because I cannot speak of them without betraying my impurity. We discourse freely without shame of one form of sensuality, and are silent about another. We are so degraded that we cannot speak simply of the necessary functions of human nature. In earlier ages, in some countries, every function was reverently spoken of and regulated by law. Nothing was too trivial for the Hindoo lawgiver, however offensive it may be to modern taste. He teaches how to eat, drink, cohabit, void excrement and urine, and the like, elevating what is mean, and does not falsely excuse himself by calling these things trifles.

Every man is the builder of a temple, called his body,[15] to the god he worships, after a style purely his own, nor can he get off by hammering marble instead. We are all sculptors and painters, and our material is our own flesh and blood and bones. Any nobleness begins at once to refine a man's features, any meanness or sensuality to imbrute them.

John Farmer[16] sat at his door one September evening, after a hard day's work, his mind still running on his labor more or less. Having bathed he sat down to recreate his intellectual man. It was a rather cool evening, and some of his neighbors were apprehending a frost. He had not attended to the train of his thoughts long when he heard some one playing on a flute, and that sound harmonized with his mood. Still he thought of his work; but the burden of his thought was, that though this kept running in his head, and he found himself planning and contriving it against his will, yet it concerned him very little. It was no more than the scurf[17] of his skin, which was constantly shuffled off. But the notes of the flute came home to his ears out of a different sphere from that he worked in, and suggested work for certain faculties which slumbered in him. They gently did away with the street, and the village, and the state in which he lived. A voice said to him,—Why do you stay here and live this mean moiling life, when a glorious existence is possible for you? Those same stars twinkle over other fields than these.—But how to come out of this condition and actually migrate thither? All that he could think of was to practise some new austerity, to let his mind descend into his body and redeem it, and treat himself with ever increasing respect.

---

[15] "Ye are the temple of God," from I Corinthians 3:16.

[16] A generic name for the single character in this brief drama between the habits that keep people in a rut and the higher instincts that call some to a creative life of beauty. Thoreau himself played the flute.

[17] The outer scales; the notes of the flute go much deeper.

XII: BRUTE NEIGHBORS

Sometimes I had a companion[1] in my fishing, who came through the village to my house from the other side of the town, and the catching of the dinner was as much a social exercise as the eating of it.

Hermit. I wonder what the world is doing now. I have not heard so much as a locust over the sweet-fern these three hours. The pigeons are all asleep upon their roosts,—no flutter from them. Was that a farmer's noon horn which sounded from beyond the woods just now? The hands are coming in to boiled salt beef and cider and Indian bread. Why will men worry themselves so? He that does not eat need not work. I wonder how much they have reaped. Who would live there where a body can never think for the barking of Bose?[2] And O, the housekeeping! to keep bright the devil's door-knobs, and scour his tubs this bright day! Better not keep a house. Say, some hollow tree; and then for morning calls and dinner-parties! Only a woodpecker tapping. O, they swarm; the sun is too warm there; they are born too far into life for me. I have water from the spring, and a loaf of brown bread on the shelf.—Hark! I hear a rustling of the leaves. Is it some ill-fed village hound yielding to the instinct of the chase? or the lost pig which is said to be in these woods, whose tracks I saw after the rain? It comes on apace; my sumachs and sweet-briars tremble.—Eh, Mr. Poet, is it you? How do you like the world to-day?

Poet. See those clouds; how they hang! That's the greatest thing I have seen to-day. There's nothing like it in old paintings, nothing like it in foreign lands,—unless when we were off the coast of Spain. That's a true Mediterranean sky. I thought, as I have my living to get, and have not eaten to-day, that I might go a-fishing. That's the true industry for poets. It is the only trade I have learned. Come, let's along.

Hermit. I cannot resist. My brown bread will soon be gone. I will go with you gladly soon, but I am just concluding a serious meditation. I think that I am near the end of it. Leave me alone, then, for a while. But that we may not be delayed, you shall be digging the bait meanwhile. Angle-worms are rarely to be met with in these parts, where the soil was never fattened with manure; the race is nearly extinct. The sport of digging the bait is nearly equal to that of catching the fish, when one's appetite is not too keen; and this you may have all to yourself to-day. I would advise you to set in the spade down yonder among the ground-nuts, where you see the johnswort waving. I think that I may warrant you one worm to every three sods you turn up, if you look well in among the roots of the grass, as if you were weeding. Or, if you choose to go farther, it will not be unwise, for I have found the increase of fair bait to be very nearly as the squares of the distances.

Hermit alone. Let me see; where was I? Methinks I was nearly in this frame of mind; the world lay about at this angle. Shall I go to heaven or a-fishing? If I should soon bring this meditation to an end, would another so sweet occasion be likely to offer? I was as near being resolved into the essence of things as ever I

---

[1] The younger William Ellery Channing, the "Poet" in the following dialogue with the "Hermit" (Thoreau).

[2] Then a common name for a dog.

was in my life. I fear my thoughts will not come back to me. If it would do any good, I would whistle for them. When they make us an offer, is it wise to say, We will think of it? My thoughts have left no track, and I cannot find the path again. What was it that I was thinking of? It was a very hazy day. I will just try these three sentences of Con-fut-see;[3] they may fetch that state about again. I know not whether it was the dumps or a budding ecstasy. Mem.[4] There never is but one opportunity of a kind.

Poet. How now, Hermit, is it too soon? I have got just thirteen whole ones, beside several which are imperfect or undersized; but they will do for the smaller fry; they do not cover up the hook so much. Those village worms are quite too large; a shiner may make a meal off one without finding the skewer.

Hermit. Well, then, let's be off. Shall we to the Concord? There's good sport there if the water be not too high.

Why do precisely these objects which we behold make a world? Why has man just these species of animals for his neighbors; as if nothing but a mouse could have filled this crevice? I suspect that Pilpay & Co.[5] have put animals to their best use, for they are all beasts of burden, in a sense, made to carry some portion of our thoughts.

The mice which haunted my house were not the common ones, which are said to have been introduced into the country, but a wild native kind (*Mus leucopus*) not found in the village. I sent one to a distinguished naturalist,[6] and it interested him much. When I was building, one of these had its nest underneath the house, and before I had laid the second floor, and swept out the shavings, would come out regularly at lunch time and pick up the crumbs at my feet. It probably had never seen a man before; and it soon became quite familiar, and would run over my shoes and up my clothes. It could readily ascend the sides of the room by short impulses, like a squirrel, which it resembled in its motions. At length, as I leaned with my elbow on the bench one day, it ran up my clothes, and along my sleeve, and round and round the paper which held my dinner, while I kept the latter close, and dodged and played at bo-peep with it; and when at last I held still a piece of cheese between my thumb and finger, it came and nibbled it, sitting in my hand, and afterward cleaned its face and paws, like a fly, and walked away.

A phœbe soon built in my shed, and a robin for protection in a pine which grew against the house. In June the partridge, (*Tetrao umbellus,*) which is so shy a bird, led her brood past my windows, from the woods in the rear to the front of my house, clucking and calling to them like a hen, and in all her behavior proving herself the hen of the woods. The young suddenly disperse on your approach, at a signal from the mother, as if a whirlwind had swept them away, and they so exactly resemble the dried leaves and twigs that many a traveller has placed his foot in the midst of a brood, and heard the whir of the old bird as she flew off, and her anxious calls and mewing, or seen her trail her wings to attract his attention, without suspecting their neighborhood. The parent will sometimes roll and spin

---

[3] Confucius.   [4] Memorandum.

[5] Pilpay was the supposed author of a collection of Sanskrit animal fables; "& Co." refers to others who relate such fables.

[6] Louis Agassiz (1807–1873), a Swiss zoologist and geologist who came to America in 1846 and began teaching at Harvard in 1848.

round before you in such a dishabille, that you cannot, for a few moments, detect what kind of creature it is. The young squat still and flat, often running their heads under a leaf, and mind only their mother's directions given from a distance, nor will your approach make them run again and betray themselves. You may even tread on them, or have your eyes on them for a minute, without discovering them. I have held them in my open hand at such a time, and still their only care, obedient to their mother and their instinct, was to squat there without fear or trembling. So perfect is this instinct, that once, when I had laid them on the leaves again, and one accidentally fell on its side, it was found with the rest in exactly the same position ten minutes afterward. They are not callow like the young of most birds, but more perfectly developed and precocious even than chickens. The remarkably adult yet innocent expression of their open and serene eyes is very memorable. All intelligence seems reflected in them. They suggest not merely the purity of infancy, but a wisdom clarified by experience. Such an eye was not born when the bird was, but is coeval with the sky it reflects. The woods do not yield another such a gem. The traveller does not often look into such a limpid well. The ignorant or reckless sportsman often shoots the parent at such a time, and leaves these innocents to fall a prey to some prowling beast or bird, or gradually mingle with the decaying leaves which they so much resemble. It is said that when hatched by a hen they will directly disperse on some alarm, and so are lost, for they never hear the mother's call which gathers them again. These were my hens and chickens.

It is remarkable how many creatures live wild and free though secret in the woods, and still sustain themselves in the neighborhood of towns, suspected by hunters only. How retired the otter manages to live here! He grows to be four feet long, as big as a small boy, perhaps without any human being getting a glimpse of him. I formerly saw the raccoon in the woods behind where my house is built, and probably still heard their whinnering at night. Commonly I rested an hour or two in the shade at noon, after planting, and ate my lunch, and read a little by a spring which was the source of a swamp and of a brook, oozing from under Brister's Hill, half a mile from my field. The approach to this was through a succession of descending grassy hollows, full of young pitch-pines, into a larger wood about the swamp. There, in a very secluded and shaded spot, under a spreading white-pine, there was yet a clean firm sward to sit on. I had dug out the spring and made a well of clear gray water, where I could dip up a pailful without roiling it, and thither I went for this purpose almost every day in midsummer, when the pond was warmest. Thither too the wood-cock led her brood, to probe the mud for worms, flying but a foot above them down the bank, while they ran in a troop beneath; but at last, spying me, she would leave her young and circle round and round me, nearer and nearer, till within four or five feet, pretending broken wings and legs, to attract my attention and get off her young, who would already have taken up their march, with faint wiry peep, single file through the swamp, as she directed. Or I heard the peep of the young when I could not see the parent bird. There too the turtle-doves sat over the spring, or fluttered from bough to bough of the soft white-pines over my head; or the red squirrel, coursing down the nearest bough, was particularly familiar and inquisitive. You only need sit still long enough in some attractive spot in the woods that all its inhabitants may exhibit themselves to you by turns.

I was witness to events of a less peaceful character. One day when I went out to my wood-pile, or rather my pile of stumps, I observed two large ants, the one red, the other much larger, nearly half an inch long, and black, fiercely contending with one another. Having once got hold they never let go, but struggled and wrestled and rolled on the chips incessantly. Looking farther, I was surprised to find that the chips were covered with such combatants, that it was not a *duellum,* but a *bellum,*[7] a war between two races of ants, the red always pitted against the black, and frequently two red ones to one black. The legions of these Myrmidons[8] covered all the hills and vales in my wood-yard, and the ground was already strewn with the dead and dying, both red and black. It was the only battle which I have ever witnessed, the only battle-field I ever trod while the battle was raging; internecine war; the red republicans on the one hand, and the black imperialists on the other. On every side they were engaged in deadly combat, yet without any noise that I could hear, and human soldiers never fought so resolutely. I watched a couple that were fast locked in each other's embraces, in a little sunny valley amid the chips, now at noon-day prepared to fight till the sun went down, or life went out. The smaller red champion had fastened himself like a vice to his adversary's front, and through all the tumblings on that field never for an instant ceased to gnaw at one of his feelers near the root, having already caused the other to go by the board; while the stronger black one dashed him from side to side, and, as I saw on looking nearer, had already divested him of several of his members. They fought with more pertinacity than bull-dogs. Neither manifested the least disposition to retreat. It was evident that their battle-cry was Conquer or die. In the mean while there came along a single red ant on the hillside of this valley, evidently full of excitement, who either had despatched his foe, or had not yet taken part in the battle; probably the latter, for he had lost none of his limbs; whose mother had charged him to return with his shield or upon it.[9] Or perchance he was some Achilles, who had nourished his wrath apart, and had now come to avenge or rescue his Patroclus.[10] He saw this unequal combat from afar,—for the blacks were nearly twice the size of the red,—he drew near with rapid pace till he stood on his guard within half an inch of the combatants; then, watching his opportunity, he sprang upon the black warrior, and commenced his operations near the root of his right fore-leg, leaving the foe to select among his own members; and so there were three united for life, as if a new kind of attraction had been invented which put all other locks and cements to shame. I should not have wondered by this time to find that they had their respective musical bands stationed on some eminent chip, and playing their national airs the while, to excite the slow and cheer the dying combatants. I was myself excited somewhat even as if they had been men. The more you think of it, the less the difference. And certainly there is not the fight recorded in Concord history, at least, if in the history of America, that will bear a moment's comparison with this, whether for the numbers engaged in it, or for the patriotism and heroism displayed. For numbers and for carnage it

---

[7] Not a duel but a war.

[8] As related in Homer's *Iliad,* the Myrmidons were the troops who fought under the Greek hero Achilles in the Trojan War; because *myrmex* is the Greek word for "ant," Thoreau mock-heroically connects the battle of the ants with the epic struggle of Greeks and Trojans.

[9] Supposedly, the exhortation of a Spartan mother to her son, as reported in *Sayings of Spartan Women,* by the Greek biographer Plutarch (A.D.46?–120?).

[10] After a quarrel with the Greek leader Agamemnon during the Trojan War, the temperamental Achilles sulked in his tent until the death of his friend Patroclus brought him fiercely into battle.

was an Austerlitz or Dresden.[11] Concord Fight! Two killed on the patriots' side, and Luther Blanchard wounded! Why here every ant was a Buttrick,—"Fire! for God's sake fire!"—and thousands shared the fate of Davis and Hosmer.[12] There was not one hireling[13] there. I have no doubt that it was a principle they fought for, as much as our ancestors, and not to avoid a three-penny tax on their tea; and the results of this battle will be as important and memorable to those whom it concerns as those of the battle of Bunker Hill, at least.

I took up the chip on which the three I have particularly described were struggling, carried it into my house, and placed it under a tumbler on my window-sill, in order to see the issue. Holding a microscope[14] to the first-mentioned red ant, I saw that, though he was assiduously gnawing at the near fore-leg of his enemy, having severed his remaining feeler, his own breast was all torn away, exposing what vitals he had there to the jaws of the black warrior, whose breast-plate was apparently too thick for him to pierce; and the dark carbuncles of the sufferer's eyes shone with ferocity such as war only could excite. They struggled half an hour longer under the tumbler, and when I looked again the black soldier had severed the heads of his foes from their bodies, and the still living heads were hanging on either side of him like ghastly trophies at his saddle-bow, still apparently as firmly fastened as ever, and he was endeavoring with feeble struggles, being without feelers and with only the remnant of a leg, and I know not how many other wounds, to divest himself of them; which at length, after half an hour more, he accomplished. I raised the glass, and he went off over the window-sill in that crippled state. Whether he finally survived that combat, and spent the remainder of his days in some Hotel des Invalides,[15] I do not know; but I thought that his industry would not be worth much thereafter. I never learned which party was victorious, nor the cause of the war; but I felt for the rest of that day as if I had had my feelings excited and harrowed by witnessing the struggle, the ferocity and carnage, of a human battle before my door.

Kirby and Spence tell us that the battles of ants have long been celebrated and the date of them recorded, though they say that Huber[16] is the only modern author who appears to have witnessed them. "Æneas Sylvius,"[17] say they, "after giving a very circumstantial account of one contested with great obstinacy by a great and small species on the trunk of a pear tree," adds that "'This action was fought in the pontificate of Eugenius the Fourth,[18] in the presence of Nicholas Pistoriensis, an eminent lawyer, who related the whole history of the battle with the greatest fidelity.' A similar engagement between great and small ants is recorded by Olaus Magnus,[19] in which the small ones, being victorious, are said to have buried the bodies of their own soldiers, but left those of their giant enemies a prey to the

---

[11] Battles fought during the Napoleonic Wars in the first decade of the nineteenth century.

[12] Davis and Hosmer were the only colonists killed at the American Revolutionary War battle of Concord on April 19, 1775; Blanchard and Buttrick were active in the battle. The cry "Fire! for God's sake fire!" was reportedly sounded at the outset of the battle.

[13] A mercenary soldier.   [14] A magnifying glass.

[15] At one time the soldiers' hospital in Paris; now the site of Napoleon's tomb.

[16] Pierre Huber (1777–1840), an entomologist whose *The Natural History of Ants* (1810) includes a description of ants fighting that was incorporated in Kirby and Spence's *Introduction to Entomology*.

[17] The pen name of Enea Silvio Piccolomini (1405–1464), a noted humanist scholar who became Pope Pius II (1458–1464).

[18] Gabriele Condulmer (1383–1447), a Venetian who served as Pope Eugene IV from 1431 to 1447.

[19] Magnus (1490–1557) was a Swedish bishop and historian.

birds. This event happened previous to the expulsion of the tyrant Christiern the Second[20] from Sweden." The battle which I witnessed took place in the Presidency of Polk, five years before the passage of Webster's Fugitive-Slave Bill.[21]

Many a village Bose, fit only to course[22] a mud-turtle in a victualling cellar, sported his heavy quarters in the woods, without the knowledge of his master, and ineffectually smelled at old fox burrows and woodchucks' holes; led perchance by some slight cur which nimbly threaded the wood, and might still inspire a natural terror in its denizens;—now far behind his guide, barking like a canine bull toward some small squirrel which had treed itself for scrutiny, then, cantering off, bending the bushes with his weight, imagining that he is on the track of some stray member of the gerbille family. Once I was surprised to see a cat walking along the stony shore of the pond, for they rarely wander so far from home. The surprise was mutual. Nevertheless the most domestic cat, which has lain on a rug all her days, appears quite at home in the woods, and, by her sly and stealthy behavior, proves herself more native there than the regular inhabitants. Once, when berrying, I met with a cat with young kittens in the woods, quite wild, and they all, like their mother, had their backs up and were fiercely spitting at me. A few years before I lived in the woods there was what was called a "winged cat" in one of the farm-houses in Lincoln nearest the pond, Mr. Gilian Baker's. When I called to see her in June, 1842, she was gone a-hunting in the woods, as was her wont, (I am not sure whether it was a male or female, and so use the more common pronoun,) but her mistress told me that she came into the neighborhood a little more than a year before, in April, and was finally taken into their house; that she was of dark brownish-gray color, with a white spot on her throat, and white feet, and had a large bushy tail like a fox; that in the winter the fur grew thick and flatted out along her sides, forming strips ten or twelve inches long by two and a half wide, and under her chin like a muff, the upper side loose, the under matted like felt, and in the spring these appendages cropped off. They gave me a pair of her "wings," which I keep still. There is no appearance of a membrane about them. Some thought it was part flying-squirrel or some other wild animal, which is not impossible, for, according to naturalists, prolific hybrids have been produced by the union of the marten and domestic cat. This would have been the right kind of cat for me to keep, if I had kept any; for why should not a poet's cat be winged as well as his horse?[23]

In the fall the loon (*Colymbus glacialis*) came, as usual, to moult and bathe in the pond, making the woods ring with his wild laughter before I had risen. At rumor of his arrival all the Mill-dam sportsmen are on the alert, in gigs and on foot, two by two and three by three, with patent rifles and conical balls[24] and spy-glasses. They come rustling through the woods like autumn leaves, at least ten men to one loon. Some station themselves on this side of the pond, some on that, for the poor bird cannot be omnipresent; if he dive here he must come up there.

---

[20] Christian II (1481–1559), king of Denmark and Norway (1513–1523), who conducted a massacre of Swedish nobles during his reign as king of Sweden (1520–1523). Deposed in 1523, he was imprisoned for life in 1532.

[21] In 1845: here Thoreau again criticizes Daniel Webster, senator from Massachusetts, who supported the Compromise of 1850, which strengthened the Fugitive Slave Act. James K. Polk, eleventh U.S. president (1845–1849) did not formally leave office until March, as was the custom then.

[22] Chase.

[23] According to Greek myth, the winged horse Pegasus represented the poet's inspiration.

[24] Special rifles and bullets.

But now the kind October wind rises, rustling the leaves and rippling the surface of the water, so that no loon can be heard or seen, though his foes sweep the pond with spy-glasses, and make the woods resound with their discharges. The waves generously rise and dash angrily, taking sides with all waterfowl, and our sportsmen must beat a retreat to town and shop and unfinished jobs. But they were too often successful. When I went to get a pail of water early in the morning I frequently saw this stately bird sailing out of my cove within a few rods. If I endeavored to overtake him in a boat, in order to see how he would manœuvre, he would dive and be completely lost, so that I did not discover him again, sometimes, till the latter part of the day. But I was more than a match for him on the surface. He commonly went off in a rain.

As I was paddling along the north shore one very calm October afternoon, for such days especially they settle on to the lakes, like the milkweed down, having looked in vain over the pond for a loon, suddenly one, sailing out from the shore toward the middle a few rods in front of me, set up his wild laugh and betrayed himself. I pursued with a paddle and he dived, but when he came up I was nearer than before. He dived again, but I miscalculated the direction he would take, and we were fifty rods apart when he came to the surface this time, for I had helped to widen the interval; and again he laughed long and loud, and with more reason than before. He manœuvred so cunningly that I could not get within half a dozen rods of him. Each time, when he came to the surface, turning his head this way and that, he coolly surveyed the water and the land, and apparently chose his course so that he might come up where there was the widest expanse of water and at the greatest distance from the boat. It was surprising how quickly he made up his mind and put his resolve into execution. He led me at once to the widest part of the pond, and could not be driven from it. While he was thinking one thing in his brain, I was endeavoring to divine his thought in mine. It was a pretty game, played on the smooth surface of the pond, a man against a loon. Suddenly your adversary's checker disappears beneath the board, and the problem is to place yours nearest to where his will appear again. Sometimes he would come up unexpectedly on the opposite side of me, having apparently passed directly under the boat. So long-winded was he and so unweariable, that when he had swum farthest he would immediately plunge again, nevertheless; and then no wit could divine where in the deep pond, beneath the smooth surface, he might be speeding his way like a fish, for he had time and ability to visit the bottom of the pond in its deepest part. It is said that loons have been caught in the New York lakes eighty feet beneath the surface, with hooks set for trout,—though Walden is deeper than that. How surprised must the fishes be to see this ungainly visitor from another sphere speeding his way amid their schools! Yet he appeared to know his course as surely under water as on the surface, and swam much faster there. Once or twice I saw a ripple where he approached the surface, just put his head out to reconnoitre, and instantly dived again. I found that it was as well for me to rest on my oars and wait his reappearing as to endeavor to calculate where he would rise; for again and again, when I was straining my eyes over the surface one way, I would suddenly be startled by his unearthly laugh behind me. But why, after displaying so much cunning, did he invariably betray himself the moment he came up by that loud laugh? Did not his white breast enough betray him? He was indeed a silly loon, I thought. I could commonly hear the plash of the water when he came up, and so also detected him. But after an hour he seemed as fresh as ever, dived as willingly and swam yet farther than at first. It was surprising to see how serenely he sailed off with unruffled breast when he came to the surface, doing all the work with his webbed feet beneath. His usual note was this demoniac laughter, yet somewhat like that of a water-fowl; but occasionally, when he had balked me most successfully and come up a long way off, he uttered a long-drawn unearthly howl, probably more like that of a wolf than any bird; as when a beast puts his muzzle to the ground and deliberately howls. This was his looning,—perhaps the wildest sound that is ever heard here, making the woods ring far and wide. I concluded that he laughed in derision of my efforts, confident of his own resources. Though the sky was by this time overcast, the pond was so smooth that I could see where he broke the surface when I did not hear him. His white breast, the stillness of the air, and the smoothness of the water were all against him. At length, having come up fifty rods off, he uttered one of those prolonged howls, as if calling on the god of loons to aid him, and immediately there came a wind from the east and rippled the surface, and filled the whole air with misty rain, and I was impressed as if it were the prayer of the loon answered, and his god was angry with me; and so I left him disappearing far away on the tumultuous surface.

For hours, in fall days, I watched the ducks cunningly tack and veer and hold the middle of the pond, far from the sportsman; tricks which they will have less need to practise in Louisiana bayous. When compelled to rise they would sometimes circle round and round and over the pond at a considerable height, from which they could easily see to other ponds and the river, like black motes in the sky; and, when I thought they had gone off thither long since, they would settle down by a slanting flight of a quarter of a mile on to a distant part which was left free; but what beside safety they got by sailing in the middle of Walden I do not know, unless they love its water for the same reason that I do.

XIII: HOUSE-WARMING

In October I went a-graping to the river meadows, and loaded myself with clusters more precious for their beauty and fragrance than for food. There too I admired, though I did not gather, the cranberries, small waxen gems, pendants of the meadow grass, pearly and red, which the farmer plucks with an ugly rake, leaving the smooth meadow in a snarl, heedlessly measuring them by the bushel and the dollar only, and sells the spoils of the meads to Boston and New York; destined to be *jammed*,[1] to satisfy the tastes of lovers of Nature there. So butchers rake the tongues of bison out of the prairie grass,[2] regardless of the torn and drooping plant. The barberry's brilliant fruit was likewise food for my eyes merely; but I collected a small store of wild apples for coddling, which the proprietor and travellers had overlooked. When chestnuts were ripe I laid up half a bushel for winter. It was very exciting at that season to roam the then boundless chestnut woods of Lincoln,—they now sleep their long sleep under the railroad,—with a bag on my shoulder, and a stick to open burrs with in my hand, for I did not always wait for the frost, amid the rustling of leaves and the loud reproofs of the red-squirrels and the jays, whose half-consumed nuts I sometimes stole, for the burrs which they had selected were sure to contain sound ones. Occasionally I climbed and shook the trees. They grew also behind my house, and one large tree which almost overshadowed it, was, when in flower, a bouquet which scented the whole neighborhood, but the squirrels and the jays got most of its fruit; the last coming in flocks

---

[1] Made into jam.   [2] Buffalo were killed simply for their tongues, considered by some a delicacy.

early in the morning and picking the nuts out of the burrs before they fell. I relinquished these trees to them and visited the more distant woods composed wholly of chestnut. These nuts, as far as they went, were a good substitute for bread. Many other substitutes might, perhaps, be found. Digging one day for fish-worms I discovered the ground-nut (*Apios tuberosa*) on its string, the potato of the aborigines, a sort of fabulous fruit, which I had begun to doubt if I had ever dug and eaten in childhood, as I had told, and had not dreamed it. I had often since seen its crimpled red velvety blossom supported by the stems of other plants without knowing it to be the same. Cultivation has well nigh exterminated it. It has a sweetish taste, much like that of a frostbitten potato, and I found it better boiled than roasted. This tuber seemed like a faint promise of Nature to rear her own children and feed them simply here at some future period. In these days of fatted cattle and waving grain-fields, this humble root, which was once the *totem* of an Indian tribe, is quite forgotten, or known only by its flowering vine; but let wild Nature reign here once more, and the tender and luxurious English grains will probably disappear before a myriad of foes, and without the care of man the crow may carry back even the last seed of corn to the great corn-field of the Indian's God in the south-west, whence he is said to have brought it; but the now almost exterminated ground-nut will perhaps revive and flourish in spite of frosts and wildness, prove itself indigenous, and resume its ancient importance and dignity as the diet of the hunter tribe. Some Indian Ceres or Minerva[3] must have been the inventor and bestower of it; and when the reign of poetry commences here, its leaves and string of nuts may be represented on our works of art.

Already, by the first of September, I had seen two or three small maples turned scarlet across the pond, beneath where the white stems of three aspens diverged, at the point of a promontory, next the water. Ah, many a tale their color told! And gradually from week to week the character of each tree came out, and it admired itself reflected in the smooth mirror of the lake. Each morning the manager of this gallery substituted some new picture, distinguished by more brilliant or harmonious coloring, for the old upon the walls.

The wasps came by thousands to my lodge in October, as to winter quarters, and settled on my windows within and on the walls over-head, sometimes deterring visitors from entering. Each morning, when they were numbed with cold, I swept some of them out, but I did not trouble myself much to get rid of them; I even felt complimented by their regarding my house as a desirable shelter. They never molested me seriously, though they bedded with me; and they gradually disappeared, into what crevices I do not know, avoiding winter and unspeakable cold.

Like the wasps, before I finally went into winter quarters in November, I used to resort to the north-east side of Walden, which the sun, reflected from the pitch-pine woods and the stony shore, made the fire-side of the pond; it is so much pleasanter and wholesomer to be warmed by the sun while you can be, than by an artificial fire. I thus warmed myself by the still glowing embers which the summer, like a departed hunter, had left.

When I came to build my chimney I studied masonry. My bricks being second-hand ones required to be cleaned with a trowel, so that I learned more than usual of the qualities of bricks and trowels. The mortar on them was fifty years old, and

---

[3] According to Roman myth, the goddess of agriculture and the goddess of wisdom.

was said to be still growing harder; but this is one of those sayings which men love to repeat whether they are true or not. Such sayings themselves grow harder and adhere more firmly with age, and it would take many blows with a trowel to clean an old wiseacre of them. Many of the villages of Mesopotamia are built of second-hand bricks of a very good quality, obtained from the ruins of Babylon, and the cement on them is older and probably harder still. However that may be, I was struck by the peculiar toughness of the steel which bore so many violent blows without being worn out. As my bricks had been in a chimney before, though I did not read the name of Nebuchadnezzar[4] on them, I picked out as many fire-place bricks as I could find, to save work and waste, and I filled the spaces between the bricks about the fire-place with stones from the pond shore, and also made my mortar with the white sand from the same place. I lingered most about the fire-place, as the most vital part of the house. Indeed, I worked so deliberately, that though I commenced at the ground in the morning, a course of bricks raised a few inches above the floor served for my pillow at night; yet I did not get a stiff neck for it that I remember; my stiff neck is of older date. I took a poet[5] to board for a fortnight about those times, which caused me to be put to it for room. He brought his own knife, though I had two, and we used to scour them by thrusting them into the earth. He shared with me the labors of cooking. I was pleased to see my work rising so square and solid by degrees, and reflected, that, if it proceeded slowly, it was calculated to endure a long time. The chimney is to some extent an independent structure, standing on the ground and rising through the house to the heavens; even after the house is burned it still stands sometimes, and its importance and independence are apparent. This was toward the end of summer. It was now November.

The north wind had already begun to cool the pond, though it took many weeks of steady blowing to accomplish it, it is so deep. When I began to have a fire at evening, before I plastered my house, the chimney carried smoke particularly well, because of the numerous chinks between the boards. Yet I passed some cheerful evenings in that cool and airy apartment, surrounded by the rough brown boards full of knots, and rafters with the bark on high over-head. My house never pleased my eye so much after it was plastered, though I was obliged to confess that it was more comfortable. Should not every apartment in which man dwells be lofty enough to create some obscurity over-head, where flickering shadows may play at evening about the rafters? These forms are more agreeable to the fancy and imagination than fresco paintings or other the most expensive furniture. I now first began to inhabit my house, I may say, when I began to use it for warmth as well as shelter. I had got a couple of old fire-dogs[6] to keep the wood from the hearth, and it did me good to see the soot form on the back of the chimney which I had built, and I poked the fire with more right and more satisfaction than usual. My dwelling was small, and I could hardly entertain an echo in it; but it seemed larger for being a single apartment and remote from neighbors. All the attractions of a house were concentrated in one room; it was kitchen, chamber, parlor, and keeping-room;[7] and whatever satisfaction parent or child, master or servant, derive

---

[4] King Nebuchadnezzar (605–552 B.C.) of Babylon, who had his name stamped on the bricks used in his palace.
[5] The younger William Ellery Channing.   [6] Andirons.   [7] Living room.

from living in a house, I enjoyed it all. Cato says, the master of a family (*patremfamilias*) must have in his rustic villa "cellam oleariam, vinariam, dolia multa, uti lubeat caritatem expectare, et rei, et virtuti, et gloriæ erit," that is, "an oil and wine cellar, many casks, so that it may be pleasant to expect hard times; it will be for his advantage, and virtue, and glory."[8] I had in my cellar a firkin of potatoes, about two quarts of peas with the weevil in them, and on my shelf a little rice, a jug of molasses, and of rye and Indian meal a peck each.

I sometimes dream of a larger and more populous house, standing in a golden age, of enduring materials, and without ginger-bread work, which shall still consist of only one room, a vast, rude, substantial, primitive hall, without ceiling or plastering, with bare rafters and purlins supporting a sort of lower heaven over one's head,—useful to keep off rain and snow; where the king and queen posts[9] stand out to receive your homage, when you have done reverence to the prostrate Saturn of an older dynasty[10] on stepping over the sill; a cavernous house, wherein you must reach up a torch upon a pole to see the roof; where some may live in the fire-place, some in the recess of a window, and some on settles, some at one end of the hall, some at another, and some aloft on rafters with the spiders, if they choose; a house which you have got into when you have opened the outside door, and the ceremony is over; where the weary traveller may wash, and eat, and converse, and sleep, without further journey; such a shelter as you would be glad to reach in a tempestuous night, containing all the essentials of a house, and nothing for house-keeping; where you can see all the treasures of the house at one view, and every thing hangs upon its peg that a man should use; at once kitchen, pantry, parlor, chamber, store-house, and garret; where you can see so necessary a thing as a barrel or a ladder, so convenient a thing as a cupboard, and hear the pot boil, and pay your respects to the fire that cooks your dinner and the oven that bakes your bread, and the necessary furniture and utensils are the chief ornaments; where the washing is not put out, nor the fire, nor the mistress, and perhaps you are sometimes requested to move from off the trap-door, when the cook would descend into the cellar, and so learn whether the ground is solid or hollow beneath you without stamping. A house whose inside is as open and manifest as a bird's nest, and you cannot go in at the front door and out at the back without seeing some of its inhabitants; where to be a guest is to be presented with the freedom of the house, and not to be carefully excluded from seven eighths of it, shut up in a particular cell, and told to make yourself at home there,—in solitary confinement. Nowadays the host does not admit you to *his* hearth, but has got the mason to build one for yourself somewhere in his alley, and hospitality is the art of *keeping* you at the greatest distance. There is as much secrecy about the cooking as if he had a design to poison you. I am aware that I have been on many a man's premises, and might have been legally ordered off, but I am not aware that I have been in many men's houses. I might visit in my old clothes a king and queen who lived simply in such a house as I have described, if I were going their way; but backing out of a modern palace will be all that I shall desire to learn, if ever I am caught in one.

---

[8] From Cato's *De Agricultura* (III.2); Thoreau's stock of supplies is much more meager than what Cato recommends.

[9] Purlins are horizontal beams that support rafters; king and queen posts are vertical roof beams.

[10] According to Roman myth, the god Saturn was overthrown by Jupiter, hence the reference to "an older dynasty"; those who worshipped at the temple of Saturn bared their heads to show respect.

It would seem as if the very language of our parlors would lose all its nerve and degenerate into *palaver*[11] wholly, our lives pass at such remoteness from its symbols, and its metaphors and tropes are necessarily so far fetched, through slides and dumb-waiters, as it were; in other words, the parlor is so far from the kitchen and workshop. The dinner even is only the parable of a dinner, commonly. As if only the savage dwelt near enough to Nature and Truth to borrow a trope from them. How can the scholar, who dwells away in the North West Territory or the Isle of Man,[12] tell what is parliamentary in the kitchen?

However, only one or two of my guests were ever bold enough to stay and eat a hasty-pudding with me; but when they saw that crisis approaching they beat a hasty retreat rather, as if it would shake the house to its foundations. Nevertheless, it stood through a great many hasty-puddings.

I did not plaster till it was freezing weather. I brought over some whiter and cleaner sand for this purpose from the opposite shore of the pond in a boat, a sort of conveyance which would have tempted me to go much farther if necessary. My house had in the mean while been shingled down to the ground on every side. In lathing I was pleased to be able to send home each nail with a single blow of the hammer, and it was my ambition to transfer the plaster from the board to the wall neatly and rapidly. I remembered the story of a conceited fellow, who, in fine clothes, was wont to lounge about the village once, giving advice to workmen. Venturing one day to substitute deeds for words, he turned up his cuffs, seized a plasterer's board, and having loaded his trowel without mishap, with a complacent look toward the lathing overhead, made a bold gesture thitherward; and straightway, to his complete discomfiture, received the whole contents in his ruffled bosom. I admired anew the economy and convenience of plastering, which so effectually shuts out the cold and takes a handsome finish, and I learned the various casualties to which the plasterer is liable. I was surprised to see how thirsty the bricks were which drank up all the moisture in my plaster before I had smoothed it, and how many pailfuls of water it takes to christen a new hearth. I had the previous winter made a small quantity of lime by burning the shells of the *Unio fluviatilis*,[13] which our river affords, for the sake of the experiment; so that I knew where my materials came from. I might have got good limestone within a mile or two and burned it myself, if I had cared to do so.

The pond had in the mean while skimmed over[14] in the shadiest and shallowest coves, some days or even weeks before the general freezing. The first ice is especially interesting and perfect, being hard, dark, and transparent, and affords the best opportunity that ever offers for examining the bottom where it is shallow; for you can lie at your length on ice only an inch thick, like a skater insect on the surface of the water, and study the bottom at your leisure, only two or three inches distant, like a picture behind a glass, and the water is necessarily always smooth then. There are many furrows in the sand where some creature has travelled about and doubled on its tracks; and, for wrecks, it is strewn with the cases of cadis worms made of minute grains of white quartz. Perhaps these have creased it, for you find some of their cases in the furrows, though they are deep and broad for

---

[11] Profuse and idle talk.

[12] The original Northwest Territory became the states Ohio, Indiana, Michigan, Illinois, Wisconsin, and Minnesota; The Isle of Man is in the Irish Sea between England and Ireland.

[13] Freshwater clam.   [14] Began to freeze.

them to make. But the ice itself is the object of most interest, though you must improve the earliest opportunity to study it. If you examine it closely the morning after it freezes, you find that the greater part of the bubbles, which at first appeared to be within it, are against its under surface, and that more are continually rising from the bottom; while the ice is as yet comparatively solid and dark, that is, you see the water through it. These bubbles are from an eightieth to an eighth of an inch in diameter, very clear and beautiful, and you see your face reflected in them through the ice. There may be thirty or forty of them to a square inch. There are also already within the ice narrow oblong perpendicular bubbles about half an inch long, sharp cones with the apex upward; or oftener, if the ice is quite fresh, minute spherical bubbles one directly above another, like a string of beads. But these within the ice are not so numerous nor obvious as those beneath. I sometimes used to cast on stones to try the strength of the ice, and those which broke through carried in air with them, which formed very large and conspicuous white bubbles beneath. One day when I came to the same place forty-eight hours afterward, I found that those large bubbles were still perfect, though an inch more of ice had formed, as I could see distinctly by the seam in the edge of a cake. But as the last two days had been very warm, like an Indian summer, the ice was not now transparent, showing the dark green color of the water, and the bottom, but opaque and whitish or gray, and though twice as thick was hardly stronger than before, for the air bubbles had greatly expanded under this heat and run together, and lost their regularity; they were no longer one directly over another, but often like silvery coins poured from a bag, one overlapping another, or in thin flakes, as if occupying slight cleavages. The beauty of the ice was gone, and it was too late to study the bottom. Being curious to know what position my great bubbles occupied with regard to the new ice, I broke out a cake containing a middling sized one, and turned it bottom upward. The new ice had formed around and under the bubble, so that it was included between the two ices. It was wholly in the lower ice, but close against the upper, and was flattish, or perhaps slightly lenticular, with a rounded edge, a quarter of an inch deep by four inches in diameter; and I was surprised to find that directly under the bubble the ice was melted with great regularity in the form of a saucer reversed, to the height of five eighths of an inch in the middle, leaving a thin partition there between the water and the bubble, hardly an eighth of an inch thick; and in many places the small bubbles in this partition had burst out downward, and probably there was no ice at all under the largest bubbles, which were a foot in diameter. I inferred that the infinite number of minute bubbles which I had first seen against the under surface of the ice were now frozen in likewise, and that each, in its degree, had operated like a burning glass on the ice beneath to melt and rot it. These are the little air-guns which contribute to make the ice crack and whoop.

At length the winter set in in good earnest, just as I had finished plastering, and the wind began to howl around the house as if it had not had permission to do so till then. Night after night the geese came lumbering in in the dark with a clangor and a whistling of wings, even after the ground was covered with snow, some to alight in Walden, and some flying low over the woods toward Fair Haven, bound for Mexico. Several times, when returning from the village at ten or eleven o'clock at night, I heard the tread of a flock of geese, or else ducks, on the dry leaves in the woods by a pond-hole behind my dwelling, where they had come up to feed, and the faint honk or quack of their leader as they hurried off. In 1845

Walden froze entirely over for the first time on the night of the 22d of December, Flint's and other shallower ponds and the river having been frozen ten days or more; in '46, the 16th; in '49, about the 31st; and in '50, about the 27th of December; in '52, the 5th of January; in '53, the 31st of December. The snow had already covered the ground since the 25th of November, and surrounded me suddenly with the scenery of winter. I withdrew yet farther into my shell, and endeavored to keep a bright fire both within my house and within my breast. My employment out of doors now was to collect the dead wood in the forest, bringing it in my hands or on my shoulders, or sometimes trailing a dead pine tree under each arm to my shed. An old forest fence which had seen its best days was a great haul for me. I sacrificed it to Vulcan, for it was past serving the god Terminus.[15] How much more interesting an event is that man's supper who has just been forth in the snow to hunt, nay, you might say, steal, the fuel to cook it with! His bread and meat are sweet. There are enough fagots and waste wood of all kinds in the forests of most of our towns to support many fires, but which at present warm none, and, some think, hinder the growth of the young wood. There was also the drift-wood of the pond. In the course of the summer I had discovered a raft of pitch-pine logs with the bark on, pinned together by the Irish when the railroad was built. This I hauled up partly on the shore. After soaking two years and then lying high six months it was perfectly sound, though waterlogged past drying. I amused myself one winter day with sliding this piecemeal across the pond, nearly half a mile, skating behind with one end of a log fifteen feet long on my shoulder, and the other on the ice; or I tied several logs together with a birch withe, and then, with a longer birch or alder which had a hook at the end, dragged them across. Though completely waterlogged and almost as heavy as lead, they not only burned long, but made a very hot fire; nay, I thought that they burned better for the soaking, as if the pitch, being confined by the water, burned longer as in a lamp.

Gilpin,[16] in his account of the forest borderers of England, says that "the encroachments of trespassers, and the houses and fences thus raised on the borders of the forest," were "considered as great nuisances by the old forest law, and were severely punished under the name of *purprestures,* as tending *ad terrorem ferarum-ad nocumentum forestæ, etc.*," to the frightening of the game and the detriment of the forest. But I was interested in the preservation of the venison and the vert[17] more than the hunters or wood-choppers, and as much as though I had been the Lord Warden[18] himself; and if any part was burned, though I burned it myself by accident, I grieved with a grief that lasted longer and was more inconsolable than that of the proprietors; nay, I grieved when it was cut down by the proprietors themselves. I would that our farmers when they cut down a forest felt some of that awe which the old Romans did when they came to thin, or let in the light to, a consecrated grove, (*lucum conlucare,*) that is, would believe that it is sacred to some god. The Roman made an expiatory offering, and prayed, Whatever god or goddess thou art to whom this grove is sacred, be propitious to me, my family, and children, etc.

---

[15] According to Roman myth, the god of fire and the god of boundaries. Thoreau sacrificed the fence to Vulcan by burning it because it was too battered to serve Terminus as a boundary.

[16] From *Remarks on Forest Scenery* (1834), by the English student of nature William Gilpin (1724–1804).

[17] The deer and the green vegetation.

[18] The British official responsible for protecting forests and wildlife.

It is remarkable what a value is still put upon wood even in this age and in this new country, a value more permanent and universal than that of gold. After all our discoveries and inventions no man will go by a pile of wood. It is as precious to us as it was to our Saxon and Norman ancestors. If they made their bows of it, we make our gun-stocks of it. Michaux,[19] more than thirty years ago, says that the price of wood for fuel in New York and Philadelphia "nearly equals, and sometimes exceeds, that of the best wood in Paris, though this immense capital annually requires more than three hundred thousand cords, and is surrounded to the distance of three hundred miles by cultivated plains." In this town the price of wood rises almost steadily, and the only question is, how much higher it is to be this year than it was the last. Mechanics and tradesmen who come in person to the forest on no other errand, are sure to attend the wood auction, and even pay a high price for the privilege of gleaning after the wood-chopper. It is now many years that men have resorted to the forest for fuel and the materials of the arts; the New Englander and the New Hollander, the Parisian and the Celt, the farmer and Robinhood, Goody Blake and Harry Gill,[20] in most parts of the world the prince and the peasant, the scholar and the savage, equally require still a few sticks from the forest to warm them and cook their food. Neither could I do without them.

Every man looks at his wood-pile with a kind of affection. I loved to have mine before my window, and the more chips the better to remind me of my pleasing work. I had an old axe which nobody claimed, with which by spells in winter days, on the sunny side of the house, I played about the stumps which I had got out of my bean-field. As my driver prophesied when I was ploughing, they warmed me twice, once while I was splitting them, and again when they were on the fire, so that no fuel could give out more heat. As for the axe, I was advised to get the village blacksmith to "jump" it;[21] but I jumped him, and putting a hickory helve from the woods into it, made it do. If it was dull, it was at least hung true.

A few pieces of fat pine[22] were a great treasure. It is interesting to remember how much of this food for fire is still concealed in the bowels of the earth. In previous years I had often gone "prospecting" over some bare hill-side, where a pitch-pine wood had formerly stood, and got out the fat pine roots. They are almost indestructible. Stumps thirty or forty years old, at least, will still be sound at the core, though the sapwood has all become vegetable mould, as appears by the scales of the thick bark forming a ring level with the earth four or five inches distant from the heart. With axe and shovel you explore this mine, and follow the marrowy store, yellow as beef tallow, or as if you had struck on a vein of gold, deep into the earth. But commonly I kindled my fire with the dry leaves of the forest, which I had stored up in my shed before the snow came. Green hickory finely split makes the woodchopper's kindlings, when he has a camp in the woods. Once in a while I got a little of this. When the villagers were lighting their fires beyond the horizon, I too gave notice to the various wild inhabitants of Walden vale, by a smoky streamer from my chimney, that I was awake.—

[19] F. Andre Michaux (1746–1802), a French botanist and author of *North American Sylva* (first American ed. 1818), which Thoreau cites frequently in his journals.

[20] William Wordsworth's poem "Goody Blake and Harry Gill" (1798), in which the landowner Gill denies firewood to Blake, whereupon God answers her prayer that Gill "never more be warm."

[21] Sharpen it; instead of getting his axe sharpened, Thoreau fitted it with a new handle ("hickory helve").

[22] Pine rich with tars; still sold as "fatwood" to kindle fires.

Light-winged Smoke, Icarian bird,
Melting thy pinions in thy upward flight,
Lark without song, and messenger of dawn,
Circling above the hamlets as thy nest;
Or else, departing dream, and shadowy form
Of midnight vision, gathering up thy skirts;
By night star-veiling, and by day
Darkening the light and blotting out the sun;
Go thou my incense upward from this hearth,
And ask the gods to pardon this clear flame.

Hard green wood just cut, though I used but little of that, answered my purpose better than any other. I sometimes left a good fire when I went to take a walk in a winter afternoon; and when I returned, three or four hours afterward, it would be still alive and glowing. My house was not empty though I was gone. It was as if I had left a cheerful housekeeper behind. It was I and Fire that lived there; and commonly my housekeeper proved trustworthy. One day, however, as I was splitting wood, I though that I would just look in at the window and see if the house was not on fire; it was the only time I remember to have been particularly anxious on this score; so I looked and saw that a spark had caught my bed, and I went in and extinguished it when it had burned a place as big as my hand. But my house occupied so sunny and sheltered a position, and its roof was so low, that I could afford to let the fire go out in the middle of almost any winter day.

The moles nested in my cellar, nibbling every third potato, and making a snug bed even there of some hair left after plastering and of brown paper; for even the wildest animals love comfort and warmth as well as man, and they survive the winter only because they are so careful to secure them. Some of my friends spoke as if I was coming to the woods on purpose to freeze myself. The animal merely makes a bed, which he warms with his body in a sheltered place; but man, having discovered fire, boxes up some air in a spacious apartment, and warms that, instead of robbing himself, makes that his bed, in which he can move about divested of more cumbrous clothing, maintain a kind of summer in the midst of winter, and by means of windows even admit the light, and with a lamp lengthen out the day. Thus he goes a step or two beyond instinct, and saves a little time for the fine arts. Though, when I had been exposed to the rudest blasts a long time, my whole body began to grow torpid, when I reached the genial atmosphere of my house I soon recovered my faculties and prolonged my life. But the most luxuriously housed has little to boast of in this respect, nor need we trouble ourselves to speculate how the human race may be at last destroyed. It would be easy to cut their threads any time with a little sharper blast from the north. We go on dating from Cold Fridays and Great Snows; but a little colder Friday, or greater snow, would put a period to man's existence on the globe.

The next winter I used a small cooking-stove for economy, since I did not own the forest; but it did not keep fire so well as the open fire-place. Cooking was then, for the most part, no longer a poetic, but merely a chemic process. It will soon be forgotten, in these days of stoves, that we used to roast potatoes in the ashes, after the Indian fashion. The stove not only took up room and scented the house, but it concealed the fire, and I felt as if I had lost a companion. You can always see a face in the fire. The laborer, looking into it at evening, purifies his thoughts of the dross and earthiness which they have accumulated during the day. But I could no longer sit and look into the fire, and the pertinent words of a poet recurred to me with new force.—

"Never, bright flame, may be denied to me
Thy dear, life imaging, close sympathy.
What but my hopes shot upward e'er so bright?
What but my fortunes sunk so low in night?

Why art thou banished from our hearth and hall,
Thou who art welcomed and beloved by all?
Was thy existence then too fanciful
For our life's common light, who are so dull?

Did thy bright gleam mysterious converse hold
With our congenial souls? secrets too bold?
Well, we are safe and strong, for now we sit
Beside a hearth where no dim shadows flit,
Where nothing cheers nor saddens, but a fire
Warms feet and hands—nor does to more aspire;
By whose compact utilitarian heap
The present may sit down and go to sleep,
Nor fear the ghosts who from the dim past walked,
And with us by the unequal light of the old wood
     fire talked."

MRS. HOOPER[23]

XIV: Former Inhabitants; and Winter Visitors

I weathered some merry snow storms, and spent some cheerful winter evenings by my fire-side, while the snow whirled wildly without, and even the hooting of the owl was hushed. For many weeks I met no one in my walks but those who came occasionally to cut wood and sled it to the village. The elements, however, abetted me in making a path through the deepest snow in the woods, for when I had once gone through the wind blew the oak leaves into my tracks, where they lodged, and by absorbing the rays of the sun melted the snow, and so not only made a dry bed for my feet, but in the night their dark line was my guide. For human society I was obliged to conjure up the former occupants of these woods. Within the memory of many of my townsmen the road near which my house stands resounded with the laugh and gossip of inhabitants, and the woods which border it were notched and dotted here and there with their little gardens and dwellings, though it was then much more shut in by the forest than now. In some places, within my own remembrance, the pines would scrape both sides of a chaise at once, and women and children who were compelled to go this way to Lincoln alone and on foot did it with fear, and often ran a good part of the distance. Though mainly but a humble route to neighboring villages, or for the woodman's team, it once amused the

[23] From "The Wood-Fire" (published in the transcendentalist periodical, *The Dial*, in 1840), by Ellen Hooper (1812–1848).

traveller more than now by its variety, and lingered longer in his memory. Where now firm open fields stretch from the village to the woods, it then ran through a maple swamp on a foundation of logs,[1] the remnants of which, doubtless, still underlie the present dusty highway, from the Stratton, now the Alms House, Farm, to Brister's Hill.

East of my bean-field, across the road, lived Cato Ingraham, slave of Duncan Ingraham, Esquire, gentleman of Concord village; who built his slave a house, and gave him permission to live in Walden Woods;—Cato, not Uticensis, but Concordiensis.[2] Some say that he was a Guinea Negro. There are a few who remember his little patch among the walnuts, which he let grow up till he should be old and need them; but a younger and whiter speculator got them at last. He too, however, occupies an equally narrow house[3] at present. Cato's half-obliterated cellar hole still remains, though known to few, being concealed from the traveller by a fringe of pines. It is now filled with the smooth sumach, *(Rhus glabra,)* and one of the earliest species of golden-rod *(Solidago stricta)* grows there luxuriantly.

Here, by the very corner of my field, still nearer to town, Zilpha, a colored woman, had her little house, where she spun linen for the townsfolk, making the Walden Woods ring with her shrill singing, for she had a loud and notable voice. At length, in the war of 1812, her dwelling was set on fire by English soldiers, prisoners on parole, when she was away, and her cat and dog and hens were all burned up together. She led a hard life, and somewhat inhumane. One old frequenter of these woods remembers, that as he passed her house one noon he heard her muttering to herself over her gurgling pot,—"Ye are all bones, bones!" I have seen bricks amid the oak copse there.

Down the road, on the right hand, on Brister's Hill, lived Brister Freeman, "a handy Negro," slave of Squire Cummings once,—there where grow still the apple-trees which Brister planted and tended; large old trees now, but their fruit still wild and ciderish to my taste. Not long since I read his epitaph in the old Lincoln burying-ground, a little on one side, near the unmarked graves of some British grenadiers who fell in the retreat from Concord,[4]—where he is styled "Sippio Brister,"—Scipio Africanus[5] he had some title to be called,—"a man of color," as if he were discolored. It also told me, with staring emphasis, when he died; which was but an indirect way of informing me that he ever lived. With him dwelt Fenda, his hospitable wife, who told fortunes, yet pleasantly,—large, round, and black, blacker than any of the children of night, such a dusky orb as never rose on Concord before or since.

Farther down the hill, on the left, on the old road in the woods, are marks of some homestead of the Stratton family; whose orchard once covered all the slope of Brister's Hill, but was long since killed out by pitch-pines, excepting a few stumps, whose old roots furnish still the wild stocks of many a thrifty village tree.

Nearer yet to town, you come to Breed's location, on the other side of the way, just on the edge of the wood; ground famous for the pranks of a demon not distinctly named in old mythology, who has acted a prominent and astounding part in our New England life, and deserves, as much as any mythological character, to

---

[1] A so-called corduroy road, made of logs laid side by side.
[2] Not Cato of Utica but Cato of Concord.   [3] A grave.
[4] The Battle of Concord in 1775, at the beginning of the American Revolution.
[5] Either Scipio Africanus Major (234?–183 B.C.), who defeated Hannibal at Zama in Africa in 202 B.C., or Scipio Africanus Minor (185?–129 B.C.), who destroyed Carthage in Africa in 146 B.C.

have his biography written one day; who first comes in the guise of a friend or hired man, and then robs and murders the whole family,—New England Rum. But history must not yet tell the tragedies enacted here; let time intervene in some measure to assuage and lend an azure tint to them. Here the most indistinct and dubious tradition says that once a tavern stood; the well the same, which tempered the traveller's beverage and refreshed his steed. Here then men saluted one another, and heard and told the news, and went their ways again.

Breed's hut was standing only a dozen years ago, though it had long been unoccupied. It was about the size of mine. It was set on fire by mischievous boys, one Election night, if I do not mistake. I lived on the edge of the village then, and had just lost myself over Davenant's Gondibert,[6] that winter that I labored with a lethargy,—which, by the way, I never knew whether to regard as a family complaint, having an uncle who goes to sleep shaving himself, and is obliged to sprout potatoes in a cellar Sundays, in order to keep awake and keep the Sabbath, or as the consequence of my attempt to read Chalmer's collection of English poetry[7] without skipping. It fairly overcame my Nervii. I had just sunk my head on this when the bells rung fire, and in hot haste the engines rolled that way, led by a straggling troop of men and boys, and I among the foremost, for I had leaped the brook. We thought it was far south over the woods,—we who had run to fires before,—barn, shop, or dwelling-house, or all together. "It's Baker's barn," cried one. "It is the Codman Place," affirmed another. And then fresh sparks went up above the wood, as if the roof fell in, and we all shouted "Concord to the rescue!" Wagons shot past with furious speed and crushing loads, bearing, perchance, among the rest, the agent of the Insurance Company, who was bound to go however far; and ever and anon the engine bell tinkled behind, more slow and sure, and rearmost of all, as it was afterward whispered, came they who set the fire and gave the alarm. Thus we kept on like true idealists, rejecting the evidence of our senses, until at a turn in the road we heard the crackling and actually felt the heat of the fire from over the wall, and realized, alas! that we were there. The very nearness of the fire but cooled our ardor. At first we thought to throw a frog-pond on to it; but concluded to let it burn, it was so far gone and so worthless. So we stood round our engine, jostled one another, expressed our sentiments through speaking trumpets, or in lower tone referred to the great conflagrations which the world has witnessed, including Bascom's shop, and, between ourselves, we thought that, were we there in season with our "tub",[8] and a full frog-pond by, we could turn that threatened last and universal one into another flood. We finally retreated without doing any mischief,—returned to sleep and Gondibert. But as for Gondibert, I would except that passage in the preface about wit being the soul's powder,—"but most of mankind are strangers to wit, as Indians are to powder."

It chanced that I walked that way across the fields the following night, about the same hour, and hearing a low moaning at this spot, I drew near in the dark, and discovered the only survivor of the family that I know, the heir of both its virtues and its vices, who alone was interested in this burning, lying on his stom-

[6] A romantic epic by the English dramatist William D'Avenant (1606–1668), published in 1661 but never finished because the author grew bored with it. The poem affected Thoreau in a similar way.

[7] Alexander Chalmers (1759–1834) edited a twenty-one-volume collection of English poetry in 1810. Reading through it "without skipping" would get on anyone's "Nervii," or nerves: the Nervii were a European tribe conquered by Julius Caesar.

[8] Water pump.

ach and looking over the cellar wall at the still smouldering cinders beneath, muttering to himself, as is his wont. He had been working far off in the river meadows all day, and had improved the first moments that he could call his own to visit the home of his fathers and his youth. He gazed into the cellar from all sides and points of view by turns, always lying down to it, as if there was some treasure, which he remembered, concealed between the stones, where there was absolutely nothing but a heap of bricks and ashes. The house being gone, he looked at what there was left. He was soothed by the sympathy which my mere presence implied, and showed me, as well as the darkness permitted, where the well was covered up; which, thank Heaven, could never be burned; and he groped long about the wall to find the well-sweep[9] which his father had cut and mounted, feeling for the iron hook or staple by which a burden had been fastened to the heavy end,—all that he could now cling to,—to convince me that it was no common "rider."[10] I felt it, and still remark it almost daily in my walks, for by it hangs the history of a family.

Once more, on the left, where are seen the well and lilac bushes by the wall, in the now open field, lived Nutting and Le Grosse. But to return toward Lincoln.

Farther in the woods than any of these, where the road approaches nearest to the pond, Wyman the potter squatted, and furnished his townsmen with earthen ware, and left descendants to succeed him. Neither were they rich in worldly goods, holding the land by sufferance while they lived; and there often the sheriff came in vain to collect the taxes, and "attached a chip,"[11] for form's sake, as I have read in his accounts, there being nothing else that he could lay his hands on. One day in midsummer, when I was hoeing, a man who was carrying a load of pottery to market stopped his horse against my field and inquired concerning Wyman the younger. He had long ago bought a potter's wheel of him, and wished to know what had become of him. I had read of the potter's clay and wheel in Scripture,[12] but it had never occurred to me that the pots we use were not such as had come down unbroken from those days, or grown on trees like gourds somewhere, and I was pleased to hear that so fictile an art was ever practised in my neighborhood.

The last inhabitant of these woods before me was an Irishman, Hugh Quoil, (if I have spelt his name with coil[13] enough,) who occupied Wyman's tenement,— Col. Quoil, he was called. Rumor said that he had been a soldier at Waterloo. If he had lived I should have made him fight his battles over again. His trade here was that of a ditcher. Napoleon went to St. Helena;[14] Quoil came to Walden Woods. All I know of him is tragic. He was a man of manners, like one who had seen the world, and was capable of more civil speech than you could well attend to. He wore a great coat in mid-summer, being affected with the trembling delirium, and his face was the color of carmine.[15] He died in the road at the foot of Brister's Hill shortly after I came to the woods, so that I have not remembered him as a neighbor. Before his house was pulled down, when his comrades avoided it as "an unlucky castle," I visited it. There lay his old clothes curled up by use, as if they were himself, upon his raised plank bed. His pipe lay broken on the hearth,

---

[9] Pole used to lift a bucket from a well.   [10] Fence rail.

[11] Seized an insignificant item so that a legal record could be made of the action.

[12] In Romans 9:21 or perhaps Isaiah 64:8.

[13] As Harding points out in the variorum *Walden*, the name was spelled "Coyle" in a death notice run by the *Concord Freeman* in 1845.

[14] The island to which Napoleon was sent in exile after his defeat at Waterloo in 1815.   [15] Scarlet.

instead of a bowl broken at the fountain. The last could never have been the symbol of his death, for he confessed to me that, though he had heard of Brister's Spring, he had never seen it; and soiled cards, kings of diamonds spades and hearts, were scattered over the floor. One black chicken which the administrator could not catch, black as night and as silent, not even croaking, awaiting Reynard,[16] still went to roost in the next apartment. In the rear there was the dim outline of a garden, which had been planted but had never received its first hoeing, owing to those terrible shaking fits, though it was now harvest time. It was overrun with Roman wormwood and beggar-ticks, which last stuck to my clothes for all fruit. The skin of a woodchuck was freshly stretched upon the back of the house, a trophy of his last Waterloo; but no warm cap or mittens would he want more.

Now only a dent in the earth marks the site of these dwellings, with buried cellar stones, and strawberries, raspberries, thimble-berries, hazel-bushes, and sumachs growing in the sunny sward there; some pitch-pine or gnarled oak occupies what was the chimney nook, and a sweet-scented black-birch, perhaps, waves where the door-stone was. Sometimes the well dent is visible, where once a spring oozed; now dry and tearless grass; or it was covered deep,—not to be discovered till some late day,—with a flat stone under the sod, when the last of the race departed. What a sorrowful act must that be,—the covering up of wells! coincident with the opening of wells of tears. These cellar dents, like deserted fox burrows, old holes, are all that is left where once were the stir and bustle of human life, and "fate, free-will, foreknowledge absolute,"[17] in some form and dialect or other were by turns discussed. But all I can learn of their conclusions amounts to just this, that "Cato and Brister pulled wool;"[18] which is about as edifying as the history of more famous schools of philosophy.

Still grows the vivacious lilac a generation after the door and lintel and the sill are gone, unfolding its sweet-scented flowers each spring, to be plucked by the musing traveller; planted and tended once by children's hands, in front-yard plots,—now standing by wall-sides in retired pastures, and giving place to new-rising forests;—the last of that stirp, sole survivor of that family. Little did the dusky children think that the puny slip with its two eyes only, which they stuck in the ground in the shadow of the house and daily watered, would root itself so, and outlive them and house itself in the rear that shaded it, and grown man's garden and orchard, and tell their story faintly to the lone wanderer a half century after they had grown up and died,—blossoming as fair, and smelling as sweet, as in that first spring. I mark its still tender, civil, cheerful, lilac colors.

But this small village, germ of something more, why did it fail while Concord keeps its ground? Were there no natural advantages,—no water privileges, forsooth? Ay, the deep Walden Pond and cool Brister's Spring,—privilege to drink long and healthy draughts at these, all unimproved by these men but to dilute their glass. They were universally a thirsty race. Might not the basket, stable-broom, mat-making, corn-parching, linen-spinning, and pottery business have thrived here, making the wilderness to blossom like the rose, and a numerous posterity have inherited the land of their fathers? The sterile soil would at least have been proof against a low-land degeneracy. Alas! how little does the memory of these

---

[16] A fox, from the fable *Reynard the Fox*.   [17] From John Milton's *Paradise Lost* (II. 560).
[18] Cleaned animal skins.

human inhabitants enhance the beauty of the landscape! Again, perhaps Nature will try, with me for a first settler, and my house raised last spring to be the oldest in the hamlet.

I am not aware that any man has ever built on the spot which I occupy. Deliver me from a city built on the site of a more ancient city, whose materials are ruins, whose gardens cemeteries. The soil is blanched and accursed there, and before that becomes necessary the earth itself will be destroyed. With such reminiscences I repeopled the woods and lulled myself asleep.

At this season I seldom had a visitor. When the snow lay deepest no wanderer ventured near my house for a week or fortnight at a time, but there I lived as snug as a meadow mouse, or as cattle and poultry which are said to have survived for a long time buried in drifts, even without food; or like that early settler's family in the town of Sutton, in this state, whose cottage was completely covered by the great snow of 1717 when he was absent, and an Indian found it only by the hole which the chimney's breath made in the drift, and so relieved the family. But no friendly Indian concerned himself about me; nor needed he, for the master of the house was at home. The Great Snow! How cheerful it is to hear of! When the farmers could not get to the woods and swamps with their teams, and were obliged to cut down the shade trees before their houses, and when the crust was harder cut off the trees in the swamps ten feet from the ground, as it appeared the next spring.

In the deepest snows, the path which I used from the highway to my house, about half a mile long, might have been represented by a meandering dotted line, with wide intervals between the dots. For a week of even weather I took exactly the same number of steps, and of the same length, coming and going, stepping deliberately and with the precision of a pair of dividers in my own deep tracks,— to such routine the winter reduces us,—yet often they were filled with heaven's own blue. But no weather interfered fatally with my walks, or rather my going abroad, for I frequently tramped eight or ten miles through the deepest snow to keep an appointment with a beech-tree, or a yellow-birch, or an old acquaintance among the pines; when the ice and snow causing their limbs to droop, and so sharpening their tops, had changed the pines into fir-trees; wading to the tops of the highest hills when the snow was nearly two feet deep on a level, and shaking down another snow-storm on my head at every step; or sometimes creeping and floundering thither on my hands and knees, when the hunters had gone into winter quarters. One afternoon I amused myself by watching a barred owl (*Strix nebulosa*) sitting on one of the lower dead limbs of a white-pine, close to the trunk, in broad daylight, I standing within a rod of him. He could hear me when I moved and cronched the snow with my feet, but could not plainly see me. When I made most noise he would stretch out his neck, and erect his neck feathers, and open his eyes wide; but their lids soon fell again, and he began to nod. I too felt a slumberous influence after watching him half an hour, as he sat thus with his eyes half open, like a cat, winged brother of the cat. There was only a narrow slit left between their lids, by which he preserved a peninsular relation to me; thus, with half-shut eyes, looking out from the land of dreams, and endeavoring to realize me, vague object or mote that interrupted his visions. At length, on some louder noise or my nearer approach, he would grow uneasy and sluggishly turn about on his perch, as if impatient at having his dreams disturbed; and when he launched himself off and flapped through the pines, spreading his wings to unexpected breadth, I could not hear the slightest sound from them. Thus, guided amid the pine boughs rather by a delicate sense of their neighborhood than by sight, feeling his twilight way as it were with his sensitive pinions, he found a new perch, where he might in peace await the dawning of his day.

As I walked over the long causeway made for the railroad through the meadows, I encountered many a blustering and nipping wind, for nowhere has it freer play; and when the frost had smitten me on one cheek, heathen as I was, I turned to it the other also.[19] Nor was it much better by the carriage road from Brister's Hill. For I came to town still, like a friendly Indian, when the contents of the broad open fields were all piled up between the walls of the Walden road, and half an hour sufficed to obliterate the tracks of the last traveller. And when I returned new drifts would have formed, through which I floundered, where the busy northwest wind had been depositing the powdery snow round a sharp angle in the road, and not a rabbit's track, nor even the fine print, the small type, of a deer mouse was to be seen. Yet I rarely failed to find, even in mid-winter, some warm and springy swamp where the grass and the skunk-cabbage still put forth with perennial verdure, and some hardier bird occasionally awaited the return of spring.

Sometimes, notwithstanding the snow, when I returned from my walk at evening I crossed the deep tracks of a woodchopper leading from my door, and found his pile of whittlings on the hearth, and my house filled with the odor of his pipe. Or on a Sunday afternoon, if I chanced to be at home, I heard the cronching of the snow made by the step of a long-headed farmer, who from far through the woods sought my house, to have a social "crack;" one of the few of his vocation who are "men on their farms;"[20] who donned a frock instead of a professor's gown, and is as ready to extract the moral out of church or state as to haul a load of manure from his barn-yard. We talked of rude and simple times, when men sat about large fires in cold bracing weather, with clear heads; and when other dessert failed, we tried our teeth on many a nut which wise squirrels have long since abandoned, for those which have the thickest shells are commonly empty.

The one who came from farthest to my lodge, through deepest snows and most dismal tempests, was a poet.[21] A farmer, a hunter, a soldier, a reporter, even a philosopher, may be daunted; but nothing can deter a poet, for he is actuated by pure love. Who can predict his comings and goings? His business calls him out at all hours, evern when doctors sleep. We made that small house ring with boisterous mirth and resound with the murmur of such sober talk, making amends then to Walden vale for the long silences. Broadway was still and deserted in comparison. At suitable intervals there were regular salutes of laughter, which might have been referred indifferently to the last uttered or the forth-coming jest. We made many a "bran new" theory of life over a thin dish of gruel, which combined the advantages of conviviality with the clear-headedness which philosophy requires.

I should not forget that during my last winter at the pond there was another welcome visitor,[22] who at one time came through the village, through snow and rain and darkness, till he saw my lamp through the trees, and shared with me some long winter evenings. One of the last of the philosophers,—Connecticut gave him

---

[19] From the injunction about turning the other cheek in Matthew 5:39.

[20] An application of Emerson's dictum in *The American Scholar* to be whole human beings first rather than somebody identified and measured by a job.

[21] William Ellery Channing.

[22] Bronson Alcott (1799–1888), a philosophical optimist and educational reformer, much admired by Concord transcendentalists; as Thoreau correctly says, "He has no venture in the present."

to the world,—he peddled first her wares, afterwards, as he declares, his brains. These he peddles still, prompting God and disgracing man, bearing for fruit his brain only, like the nut its kernel. I think that he must be the man of the most faith of any alive. His words and attitude always suppose a better state of things than other men are acquainted with, and he will be the last man to be disappointed as the ages revolve. He has no venture in the present. But though comparatively disregarded now, when his day comes, laws unsuspected by most will take effect, and masters of families and rulers will come to him for advice.—

"How blind that cannot see serenity!"[23]

A true friend of man; almost the only friend of human progress. An Old Mortality,[24] say rather an Immortality, with unwearied patience and faith making plain the image engraven in men's bodies, the God of whom they are but defaced and leaning monuments. With his hospitable intellect he embraces children, beggars, insane, and scholars, and entertains the thought of all, adding to it commonly some breadth and elegance. I think that he should keep a caravansary on the world's highway, where philosophers of all nations might put up, and on his sign should be printed, "Entertainment for man, but not for his beast. Enter ye that have leisure and a quiet mind, who earnestly seek the right road." He is perhaps the sanest man and has the fewest crotchets of any I chance to know; the same yesterday and tomorrow. Of yore we had sauntered and talked, and effectually put the world behind us; for he was pledged to no institution in it, freeborn, *ingenuus*.[25] Whichever way we turned, it seemed that the heavens and the earth had met together, since he enhanced the beauty of the landscape. A blue-robed man, whose fittest roof is the overarching sky which reflects his serenity. I do not see how he can ever die; Nature cannot spare him.

Having each some shingles of thought well dried, we sat and whittled them, trying our knives, and admiring the clear yellowish grain of the pumpkin pine. We waded so gently and reverently, or we pulled together so smoothly, that the fishes of thought were not scared from the stream, nor feared any angler on the bank, but came and went grandly, like the clouds which float through the western sky, and the mother-o'-pearl flocks[26] which sometimes form and dissolve there. There we worked, revising mythology, rounding a fable here and there, and building castles in the air for which earth offered no worthy foundation. Great Looker! Great Expecter! to converse with whom was a New England Night's Entertainment. Ah! such discourse we had, hermit and philosopher, and the old settler I have spoken of,—we three,—it expanded and racked my little house; I should not dare to say how many pounds' weight there was above the atmospheric pressure on every circular inch; it opened its seams so that they had to be calked with much dulness thereafter to stop the consequent leak;—but I had enough of that kind of oakum already picked.

There was one other[27] with whom I had "solid seasons," long to be remembered, at his house in the village, and who looked in upon me from time to time; but I had no more for society there.

---

[23] From *The Life and Death of Thomas Woolsey, Cardinal* (1599), by the English biographer Thomas Storer (1571–1604).
[24] The title character in a novel (1816) by Sir Walter Scott (1771–1832).
[25] Fresh, noble of character (but also naïve). [26] Clouds that look like the white wool of sheep.
[27] Ralph Waldo Emerson.

There too, as every where, I sometimes expected the Visitor who never comes.[28] The Vishnu Purana says, "The house-holder is to remain at eventide in his court-yard as long as it takes to milk a cow, or longer if he pleases, to await the arrival of a guest."[29] I often performed this duty of hospitality, waited long enough to milk a whole herd of cows, but did not see the man approaching from the town.

XV: WINTER ANIMALS

When the ponds were firmly frozen, they afforded not only new and shorter routes to many points, but new views from their surfaces of the familiar landscape around them. When I crossed Flint's Pond, after it was covered with snow, though I had often paddled about and skated over it, it was so unexpectedly wide and so strange that I could think of nothing but Baffin's Bay.[1] The Lincoln hills rose up around me at the extremity of a snowy plain, in which I did not remember to have stood before; and the fishermen, at an indeterminable distance over the ice, moving slowly about with their wolfish dogs, passed for sealers or Esquimaux, or in misty weather loomed like fabulous creatures, and I did not know whether they were giants or pygmies. I took this course when I went to lecture in Lincoln[2] in the evening, travelling in no road and passing no house between my own hut and the lecture room. In Goose Pond, which lay in my way, a colony of muskrats dwelt, and raised their cabins high above the ice, though none could be seen abroad when I crossed it. Walden, being like the rest usually bare of snow, or with only shallow and interrupted drifts on it, was my yard, where I could walk freely when the snow was nearly two feet deep on a level elsewhere and the villagers were confined to their streets. There, far from the village street, and except at very long intervals, from the jingle of sleigh-bells, I slid and skated, as in a vast moose-yard well trodden, overhung by oak woods and solemn pines bent down with snow or bristling with icicles.

For sounds in winter nights, and often in winter days, I heard the forlorn but melodious note of a hooting owl indefinitely far; such a sound as the frozen earth would yield if struck with a suitable plectrum,[3] the very *lingua vernacula*[4] of Walden Wood, and quite familiar to me at last, though I never saw the bird while it was making it. I seldom opened my door in a winter evening without hearing it; *Hoo hoo hoo, hoorer hoo,* sounded sonorously, and the first three syllables accented somewhat like *how der do;* or sometimes *hoo hoo* only. One night in the beginning of winter, before the pond froze over, about nine o'clock, I was startled by the loud honking of a goose, and, stepping to the door, heard the sound of their wings like a tempest in the woods as they flew low over my house. They passed over the pond toward Fair Haven, seemingly deterred from settling by my light, their commodore honking all the while with a regular beat. Suddenly an unmistakable cat-owl from very near me, with the most harsh and tremendous voice I ever

---

[28] Thoreau is not waiting for a specific person but for some kind of revelation, of some Ultimate Truth or Answer To Life; hence, the vague mysterious tone of the paragraph.

[29] From H. H. Wilson's translation of the Hindu scripture *Vishnu Purana* (1840).

[1] In the Arctic Ocean near Greenland; now Baffin Bay.

[2] Thoreau continued to lecture in Lincoln and other nearby villages during his stay at Walden Pond.

[3] A piece of ivory or metal used to pluck stringed instruments.

[4] "Vernacular speech" (Latin), ordinary language.

heard from any inhabitant of the woods, responded at regular intervals to the goose, as if determined to expose and disgrace this intruder from Hudson's Bay by exhibiting a greater compass and volume of voice in a native, and *boo-hoo* him out of Concord horizon. What do you mean by alarming the citadel at this time of night consecrated to me? Do you think I am ever caught napping at such an hour, and that I have not got lungs and a larynx as well as yourself? *Boo-hoo, boo-hoo, boo-hoo!* It was one of the most thrilling discords I ever heard. And yet, if you had a discriminating ear, there were in it the elements of a concord such as these plains never saw nor heard.

I also heard the whooping of the ice in the pond,[5] my great bed-fellow in that part of Concord, as if it were restless in its bed and would fain turn over, were troubled with flatulency and bad dreams; or I was waked by the cracking of the ground by the frost, as if some one had driven a team against my door, and in the morning would find a crack in the earth a quarter of a mile long and a third of an inch wide.

Sometimes I heard the foxes as they ranged over the snow crust, in moonlight nights, in search of a partridge or other game, barking raggedly and demoniacally like forest dogs, as if laboring with some anxiety, or seeking expression, struggling for light and to be dogs outright and run freely in the streets; for if we take the ages into our account, may there not be a civilization going on among brutes as well as men? They seemed to me to be rudimental, burrowing men, still standing on their defence, awaiting for transformation. Sometimes one came near to my window, attracted by my light, barked a vulpine[6] curse at me, and then retreated.

Usually the red squirrel (*Sciurus Hudsonius*) waked me in the dawn, coursing over the roof and up and down the sides of the house, as if sent out of the woods for this purpose. In the course of the winter I threw out half a bushel of ears of sweet-corn, which had not got ripe, on to the snow crust by my door, and was amused by watching the motions of the various animals which were baited by it. In the twilight and the night the rabbits came regularly and made a hearty meal. All day long the red squirrels came and went, and afforded me much entertainment by their manœuvres. One would approach at first warily through the shrub-oaks, running over the snow crust by fits and starts like a leaf blown by the wind, now a few paces this way, with wonderful speed and waste of energy, making inconceivable haste with his "trotters," as if it were for a wager, and now as many paces that way, but never getting on more than half a rod at a time; and then suddenly pausing with a ludicrous expression and a gratuitous somerset,[7] as if all the eyes in the universe were fixed on him,—for all the motions of a squirrel, even in the most solitary recesses of the forest, imply spectators as much as those of a dancing girl,—wasting more time in delay and circumspection than would have sufficed to walk the whole distance,—I never saw one walk,—and then suddenly, before you could say Jack Robinson, he would be in the top of a young pitch-pine, winding up his clock and chiding all imaginary spectators, soliloquizing and talking to all the universe at the same time,—for no reason that I could ever detect, or he himself was aware of, I suspect. At length he would reach the corn, and selecting a suitable ear, frisk about in the same uncertain trigonometrical way to the top-most stick of my wood-pile, before my window, where he looked me in the face, and there sit for hours, supplying himself with a new ear from time

---

[5] Sounds caused by the ice expanding and contracting.   [6] Foxlike.   [7] A somersault.

to time, nibbling at first voraciously and throwing the half-naked cobs about; till at length he grew more dainty still and played with his food, tasting only the inside of the kernel, and the ear, which was held balanced over the stick by one paw, slipped from his careless grasp and fell to the ground, when he would look over at it with a ludicrous expression of uncertainty, as if suspecting that it had life, with a mind not made up whether to get it again, or a new one, or be off; now thinking of corn, then listening to hear what was in the wind. So the little impudent fellow would waste many an ear in a forenoon; till at last, seizing some longer and plumper one, considerably bigger than himself, and skilfully balancing it, he would set out with it to the woods, like a tiger with a buffalo, by the same zig-zag course and frequent pauses, scratching along with it as if it were too heavy for him and falling all the while, making its fall a diagonal between a perpendicular and horizontal, being determined to put it through at any rate;—a singularly frivolous and whimsical fellow;—and so he would get off with it to where he lived, perhaps carry it to the top of a pine tree forty or fifty rods distant, and I would afterwards find the cobs strewn about the woods in various directions.

At length the jays arrive, whose discordant screams were heard long before, as they were warily making their approach an eighth of a mile off, and in a stealthy and sneaking manner they flit from tree to tree, nearer and nearer, and pick up the kernels which the squirrels have dropped. Then, sitting on a pitch-pine bough, they attempt to swallow in their haste a kernel which is too big for their throats and chokes them; and after great labor they disgorge it, and spend an hour in the endeavor to crack it by repeated blows with their bills. They were manifestly thieves, and I had not much respect for them; but the squirrels, though at first shy, went to work as if they were taking what was their own.

Meanwhile also came the chicadees in flocks, which picking up the crumbs the squirrels had dropped, flew to the nearest twig, and placing them under their claws, hammered away at them with their little bills, as if it were an insect in the bark, till they were sufficiently reduced for their slender throats. A little flock of these tit-mice came daily to pick a dinner out of my wood-pile, or the crumbs at my door, with faint flitting lisping notes, like the tinkling of icicles in the grass, or else with sprightly *day day day* or more rarely, in spring-like days, a wiry summery *phe-be* from the wood-side. They were so familiar that at length one alighted on an armful of wood which I was carrying in, and pecked at the sticks without fear. I once had a sparrow alight upon my shoulder for a moment while I was hoeing in a village garden, and I felt that I was more distinguished by that circumstance than I should have been by any epaulet I could have worn. The squirrels also grew at last to be quite familiar, and occasionally stepped upon my shoe, when that was the nearest way.

When the ground was not yet quite covered, and again near the end of winter, when the snow was melted on my south hill-side and about my wood-pile, the partridges came out of the woods morning and evening to feed there. Whichever side you walk in the woods the partridge bursts away on whirring wings, jarring the snow from the dry leaves and twigs on high, which comes sifting down in the sun-beams like golden dust; for this brave bird is not to be scared by winter. It is frequently covered up by drifts, and, it is said, "sometimes plunges from on wing into the soft snow, where it remains concealed for a day or two."[8] I used to start them in the open land also, where they had come out of the woods at sunset to

---

[8] Source unidentified.

"bud" the wild apple-trees. They will come regularly every evening to particular trees, where the cunning sportsman lies in wait for them, and the distant orchards next the woods suffer thus not a little. I am glad that the partridge gets fed, at any rate. It is Nature's own bird which lives on buds and diet-drink.[9]

In dark winter mornings, or in short winter afternoons, I sometimes heard a pack of hounds threading all the woods with hounding cry and yelp, unable to resist the instinct of the chase, and the note of the hunting horn at intervals, proving that man was in the rear. The woods ring again, and yet no fox bursts forth on to the open level of the pond, nor following pack pursuing their Actæon.[10] And perhaps at evening I see the hunters returning with a single brush[11] trailing from their sleigh for a trophy, seeking their inn. They tell me that if the fox would remain in the bosom of the frozen earth he would be safe, or if he would run in a straight line away no fox-hound could overtake him; but, having left his pursuers far behind, he stops to rest and listen till they come up, and when he runs he circles round to his old haunts, where the hunters await him. Sometimes, however, he will run upon a wall many rods, and then leap off far to one side, and he appears to know that water will not retain his scent. A hunter told me that he once saw a fox pursued by hounds burst out on to Walden when the ice was covered with shallow puddles, run part way across, and then return to the same shore. Ere long the hounds arrived, but here they lost the scent. Sometimes a pack hunting by themselves would pass my door, and circle round my house, and yelp and hound[12] without regarding me, as if afflicted by a species of madness, so that nothing could divert them from the pursuit. Thus they circle until they fall upon the recent trail of a fox, for a wise hound will forsake every thing else for this. One day a man came to my hut from Lexington to inquire after his hound that made a large track, and had been hunting for a week by himself. But I fear that he was not the wiser for all I told him, for every time I attempted to answer his questions he interrupted me by asking, "What do you do here?" He had lost a dog, but found a man.

One old hunter who has a dry tongue, who used to come to bathe in Walden once every year when the water was warmest, and at such times looked in upon me, told me, that many years ago he took his gun one afternoon and went out for a cruise[13] in Walden Wood; and as he walked the Wayland road he heard the cry of hounds approaching, and ere long a fox leaped the wall into the road, and as quick as thought leaped the other wall out of the road, and his swift bullet had not touched him. Some way behind came an old hound and her three pups in full pursuit, hunting on their own account, and disappeared again in the woods. Late in the afternoon, as he was resting in the thick woods south of Walden, he heard the voice of the hounds far over toward Fair Haven still pursuing the fox; and on they came, their hounding cry which made all the woods ring sounding nearer and nearer, now from Well-Meadow, now from the Baker Farm. For a long time he stood still and listened to their music, so sweet to a hunter's ear, when suddenly the fox appeared, threading the solemn aisles with an easy coursing pace, whose sound was concealed by a sympathetic rustle of the leaves, swift and still, keeping the ground, leaving his pursuers far behind; and, leaping upon a rock amid the woods, he sat erect and listening, with his back to the hunter. For a moment

---

[9] Water.

[10] According to Greek myth, a famous hunter whom Artemis changed into a stag when he saw her bathing; he was then torn to pieces by his own hounds.

[11] Tail.   [12] Howl.   [13] To look for wood he could sell.

compassion restrained the latter's arm; but that was a short-lived mood, and as quick as thought can follow thought his piece was levelled, and *whang!*—the fox rolling over the rock lay dead on the ground. The hunter still kept his place and listened to the hounds. Still on they came, and now the near woods resounded through all their aisles with their demoniac cry. At length the old hound burst into view with muzzle to the ground, and snapping the air as if possessed, and ran directly to the rock; but spying the dead fox she suddenly ceased her hounding, as if struck dumb with amazement, and walked round and round him in silence; and one by one her pups arrived, and, like their mother, were sobered into silence by the mystery. Then the hunter came forward and stood in their midst, and the mystery was solved. They waited in silence while he skinned the fox, then followed the brush a while, and at length turned off into the woods again. That evening a Weston Squire[14] came to the Concord hunter's cottage to inquire for his hounds, and told how for a week they had been hunting on their own account from Weston woods. The Concord hunter told him what he knew and offered him the skin; but the other declined it and departed. He did not find his hounds that night, but the next day learned that they had crossed the river and put up at a farm-house for the night, whence, having been well fed, they took their departure early in the morning.

The hunter who told me this could remember one Sam Nutting, who used to hunt bears on Fair Haven Ledges, and exchange their skins for rum in Concord village; who told him, even, that he had seen a moose there. Nutting had a famous fox-hound named Burgoyne,[15]—he pronounced it Bugine,—which my informant used to borrow. In the "Wast Book"[16] of an old trader of this town, who was also a captain, town-clerk, and representative, I find the following entry. Jan 18th, 1742—3, "John Melven Cr. by 1 Grey Fox 0-2-3;" they are not found here; and in his ledger, Feb. 7th, 1743, Hezekiah Stratton has credit "by 1/2 a Catt skin 0-1-4 1/2;" of course, a wild-cat, for Stratton was a sergeant in the old French war, and would not have got credit for hunting less noble game. Credit is given for deer skins also, and they were daily sold. One man still preserves the horns of the last deer that was killed in this vicinity, and another has told me the particulars of the hunt in which his uncle was engaged. The hunters were formerly a numerous and merry crew here. I remember well one gaunt Nimrod[17] who would catch up a leaf by the road-side and play a strain on it wilder and more melodious, if my memory serves me, than any hunting horn.

At midnight, when there was a moon, I sometimes met with hounds in my path prowling about the woods, which would skulk out of my way, as if afraid, and stand silent amid the bushes till I had passed.

Squirrels and wild mice disputed for my store of nuts. There were scores of pitch-pines around my house, from one to four inches in diameter, which had been gnawed by mice the previous winter,—a Norwegian winter for them, for the snow lay long and deep, and they were obliged to mix a large proportion of pine

---

[14] A gentleman from the town of Weston. With his (rare) use of the word "Squire," Thoreau puns on the name of Squire Western in the novel *Tom Jones* (1749), by the English novelist Henry Fielding (1707–1754).

[15] Probably named after the British general John Burgoyne (1722–1792), a hero in the Seven Years War (1756–1763) against France, who led the British in the Battle of Saratoga during the American Revolution and surrendered in October 1777.

[16] A type of portable diary in which to record business transactions.

[17] A "mighty hunter before the Lord," mentioned in Genesis 10:9.

bark with their other diet. These trees were alive and apparently flourishing at mid-summer, and many of them had grown a foot, though completely girdled; but after another winter such were without exception dead. It is remarkable that a single mouse should thus be allowed a whole pine tree for its dinner, gnawing round instead of up and down it; but perhaps it is necessary in order to thin these trees, which are wont to grow up densely.

The hares (*Lepus Americanus*) were very familiar. One had her form under my house all winter, separated from me only by the flooring, and she startled me each morning by her hasty departure when I began to stir,—thump, thump, thump, striking her head against the floor timbers in her hurry. They used to come round my door at dusk to nibble the potato parings which I had thrown out, and were so nearly the color of the ground that they could hardly by distinguished when still. Sometimes in the twilight I alternately lost and recovered sight of one sitting motionless under my window. When I opened my door in the evening, off they would go with a squeak and a bounce. Near at hand they only excited my pity. One evening one sat by my door two paces from me, at first trembling with fear, yet unwilling to move; a poor wee thing, lean and bony, with ragged ears and sharp nose, scant tail and slender paws. It looked as if Nature no longer contained the breed of nobler bloods, but stood on her last toes. Its large eyes appeared young and unhealthy, almost dropsical. I took a step, and lo, away it scud with an elastic spring over the snow crust, straightening its body and its limbs into graceful length, and soon put the forest between me and itself,—the wild free venison, asserting its vigor and the dignity of Nature. Not without reason was its slenderness. Such then was its nature. (*Lepus, levipes,* light-foot, some think.)

What is a country without rabbits and partridges? They are among the most simple and indigenous animal products; ancient and venerable families known to antiquity as to modern times; of the very hue and substance of Nature, nearest allied to leaves and to the ground,—and to one another; it is either winged or it is legged. It is hardly as if you had seen a wild creature when a rabbit or a partridge bursts away, only a natural one, as much to be expected as rustling leaves. The partridge and the rabbit are still sure to thrive, like true natives of the soil, whatever revolutions occur. If the forest is cut off, the sprouts and bushes which spring up afford them concealment, and they become more numerous than ever. That must be a poor country indeed that does not support a hare. Our woods teem with them both, and around every swamp may be seen the partridge or rabbit walk, beset with twiggy fences[18] and horse-hair snares, which some cow-boy tends.

XVI: The Pond in Winter

After a still winter night I awoke with the impression that some question had been put to me, which I had been endeavoring in vain to answer in my sleep, as what-how-when-where? But there was dawning Nature, in whom all creatures live, looking in at my broad windows with serene and satisfied face, and no question on *her* lips. I awoke to an answered question, to Nature and daylight. The snow lying deep on the earth dotted with young pines, and the very slope of the hill on which my house is placed, seemed to say, Forward! Nature puts no question and answers none which we mortals ask. She has long ago taken her resolution. "O Prince, our

---

[18] Small fences made of twigs to divert rabbits and small game into traps.

eyes contemplate with admiration and transmit to the soul the wonderful and varied spectacle of this universe. The night veils without doubt a part of this glorious creation; but day comes to reveal to us this great work, which extends from earth even into the plains of the ether."[1]

Then to my morning work. First I take an axe and pail and go in search of water, if that be not a dream. After a cold and snowy night it needed a divining rod to find it. Every winter the liquid and trembling surface of the pond, which was so sensitive to every breath, and reflected every light and shadow, becomes solid to the depth of a foot or a foot and a half, so that it will support the heaviest teams, and perchance the snow covers it to an equal depth, and it is not to be distinguished from any level field. Like the marmots in the surrounding hills, it closes its eye-lids and becomes dormant for three months or more. Standing on the snow-covered plain, as if in a pasture amid the hills, I cut my way first through a foot of snow, and then a foot of ice, and open a window under my feet, where, kneeling to drink, I look down into the quiet parlor of the fishes, pervaded by a softened light as through a window of ground glass, with its bright sanded floor the same as in summer; there a perennial waveless serenity reigns as in the amber twilight sky, corresponding to the cool and even temperament of the inhabitants. Heaven is under our feet as well as over our heads.

Early in the morning, while all things are crisp with frost, men come with fishing reels and slender lunch, and let down their fine lines through the snowy field to take pickerel and perch; wild men, who instinctively follow other fashions and trust other authorities than their townsmen, and by their goings and comings stitch towns together in parts where else they would be ripped. They sit and eat their luncheon in stout fear-naughts[2] on the dry oak leaves on the shore, as wise in natural lore as the citizen is in artificial. They never consulted with books, and know and can tell much less than they have done. The things which they practise are said not yet to be known. Here is one fishing for pickerel with grown perch for bait. You look into his pail with wonder as into a summer pond, as if he kept summer locked up at home, or knew where she had retreated. How, pray, did he get these in mid-winter? O, he got worms out of rotten logs since the ground froze, and so he caught them. His life itself passes deeper in Nature than the studies of the naturalist penetrate; himself a subject for the naturalist. The latter raises the moss and bark gently with his knife in search of insects; the former lays open logs to their core with his axe, and moss and bark fly far and wide. He gets his living by barking trees. Such a man has some right to fish, and I love to see Nature carried out in him. The perch swallows the grub-worm, the pickerel swallows the perch, and the fisherman swallows the pickerel; and so all the chinks in the scale of being are filled.

When I strolled around the pond in misty weather I was sometimes amused by the primitive mode which some ruder fisherman had adopted. He would perhaps have placed alder branches over the narrow holes in the ice, which were four or five rods apart and an equal distance from the shore, and having fastened the end of the line to a stick to prevent its being pulled through, have passed the slack line over a twig of the alder, a foot or more above the ice, and tied a dry oak leaf to it, which, being pulled down, would show when he had a bite. These alders loomed through the mist at regular intervals as you walked half way round the pond.

---

[1] Thoreau's translation from a French edition of the *Harivansa,* a sacred Hindu text.
[2] Heavy woolen coats in which to "fear-naught" (nothing) from the weather.

Ah, the pickerel of Walden! when I see them lying on the ice, or in the well which the fisherman cuts in the ice, making a little hole to admit the water, I am always surprised by their rare beauty, as if they were fabulous fishes, they are so foreign to the streets, even to the woods, foreign as Arabia to our Concord life. They possess a quite dazzling and transcendent beauty which separates them by a wide interval from the cadaverous cod and haddock whose fame is trumpeted in our streets. They are not green like the pines, nor gray like the stones, nor blue like the sky; but they have, to my eyes, if possible, yet rarer colors, like flowers and precious stones, as if they were the pearls, the animalized *nuclei* or crystals of the Walden water. They, of course, are Walden all over and all through; are themselves small Waldens in the animal kingdom, Waldenses.[3] It is surprising that they are caught here,—that in this deep and capacious spring, far beneath the rattling teams and chaises and tinkling sleighs that travel the Walden road, this great gold and emerald fish swims. I never chanced to see its kind in any market; it would be the cynosure of all eyes there. Easily, with a few convulsive quirks, they give up their watery ghosts, like a mortal translated before his time to the thin air of heaven.

As I was desirous to recover the long lost bottom of Walden Pond, I surveyed it carefully, before the ice broke up, early in '46, with compass and chain and sounding line. There have been many stories told about the bottom, or rather no bottom, of this pond, which certainly had no foundation for themselves. It is remarkable how long men will believe in the bottomlessness of a pond without taking the trouble to sound it. I have visited two such Bottomless Ponds in one walk in this neighborhood. Many have believed that Walden reached quite through to the other side of the globe. Some who have lain flat on the ice for a long time, looking down through the illusive medium, perchance with watery eyes into the bargain, and driven to hasty conclusions by the fear of catching cold in their breasts, have seen vast holes "into which a load of hay might be driven," if there were any body to drive it, the undoubted source of the Styx and entrance to the Infernal Regions from these parts. Others have gone down from the village with a "fifty-six"[4] and a wagon load of inch rope, but yet have failed to find any bottom; for while the "fifty-six" was resting by the way, they were paying out the rope in the vain attempt to fathom their truly immeasurable capacity for marvellousness. But I can assure my readers that Walden has a reasonably tight bottom at a not unreasonable, though at an unusual, depth. I fathomed it easily with a cod-line and a stone weighing about a pound and a half, and could tell accurately when the stone left the bottom, by having to pull so much harder before the water got underneath to help me. The greatest depth was exactly one hundred and two feet; to which may be added the five feet which it has risen since, making one hundred and seven. This is a remarkable depth for so small an area; yet not an inch of it can be spared by the imagination. What if all ponds were shallow? Would it not react on the minds of men? I am thankful that this pond was made deep and pure for a symbol. While men believe in the infinite some ponds will be thought to be bottomless.

A factory owner, hearing what depth I had found, thought that it could not be true, for, judging from his acquaintance with dams, sand would not lie at so steep an angle. But the deepest ponds are not so deep in proportion to their area as most

[3] A sect of French Protestant dissidents in the twelfth century; also called Waldensians.
[4] A fifty-six-pound weight.

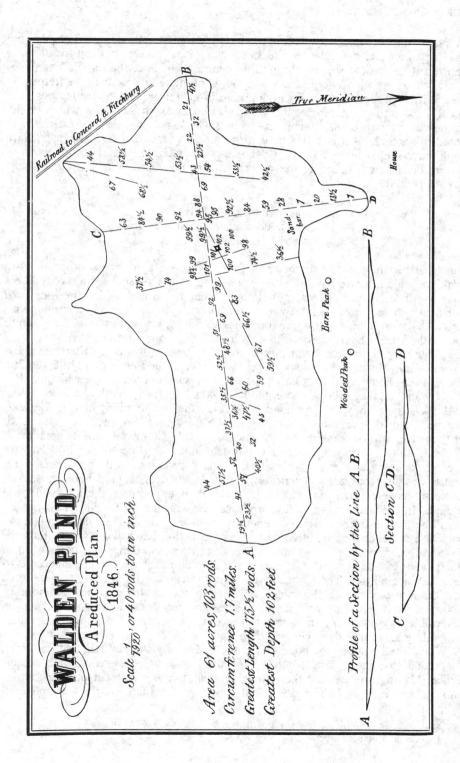

WALDEN POND.
A reduced Plan.
1846.

Scale $\frac{1}{7920}$, or 40 rods to an inch.

Area 61 acres, 103 rods.
Circumference 1.7 miles.
Greatest Length 175½ rods. A
Greatest Depth 102 feet.

Railroad to Concord & Fitchburg

True Meridian

House

Sand-bar.

Bare Peak ○

Wooded Peak ○

Profile of a Section by the Line A.B.

Section C.D.

suppose, and, if drained, would not leave very remarkable valleys. They are not like cups between the hills; for this one, which is so unusually deep for its area, appears in a vertical section through its centre not deeper than a shallow plate. Most ponds, emptied, would leave a meadow no more hollow than we frequently see. William Gilpin,[5] who is so admirable in all that relates to landscapes, and usually so correct, standing at the head of Loch Fyne, in Scotland, which he describes as "a bay of salt water, sixty or seventy fathoms deep, four miles in breadth," and about fifty miles long, surrounded by mountains, observes, "If we could have seen it immediately after the diluvian crash, or whatever convulsion of Nature occasioned it, before the waters gushed in, what a horrid chasm it must have appeared!

> So high as heaved the tumid hills, so low
> Down sunk a hollow bottom, broad, and deep,
> Capacious bed of waters—."[6]

But if, using the shortest diameter of Loch Fyne, we apply these proportions to Walden, which, as we have seen, appears already in a vertical section only like a shallow plate, it will appear four times as shallow. So much for the *increased* horrors of the chasm of Loch Fyne when emptied. No doubt many a smiling valley with its stretching cornfields occupies exactly such a "horrid chasm," from which the waters have receded, though it requires the insight and the far sight of the geologist to convince the unsuspecting inhabitants of this fact. Often an inquisitive eye may detect the shores of a primitive lake in the low horizon hills, and no subsequent elevation of the plain has been necessary to conceal their history. But it is easiest, as they who work on the highways know, to find the hollows by the puddles after a shower. The amount of it is, the imagination, give it the least license, dives deeper and soars higher than Nature goes. So, probably, the depth of the ocean will be found to be very inconsiderable compared with its breadth.

As I sounded through the ice I could determine the shape of the bottom with greater accuracy than is possible in surveying harbors which do not freeze over, and I was surprised at its general regularity. In the deepest part there are several acres more level than almost any field which is exposed to the sun wind and plough. In one instance, on a line arbitrarily chosen, the depth did not vary more than one foot in thirty rods; and generally, near the middle, I could calculate the variation for each one hundred feet in any direction beforehand within three or four inches. Some are accustomed to speak of deep and dangerous holes even in quiet sandy ponds like this, but the effect of water under these circumstances is to level all inequalities. The regularity of the bottom and its conformity to the shores and the range of the neighboring hills were so perfect that a distant promontory betrayed itself in the soundings quite across the pond, and its direction could be determined by observing the opposite shore. Cape becomes bar, and plain shoal, and valley and gorge deep water and channel.

When I had mapped the pond by the scale of ten rods to an inch, and put down the soundings, more than a hundred in all, I observed this remarkable coincidence. Having noticed that the number indicating the greatest depth was apparently in the centre of the map, I laid a rule on the map lengthwise, and then

---

[5] From *Observations on the Highlands of Scotland* (1808), by William Gilpin.
[6] From John Milton's *Paradise Lost* (VII. 288–290).

breadthwise, and found, to my surprise, that the line of greatest length intersected the line of greatest breadth *exactly* at the point of greatest depth, notwithstanding that the middle is so nearly level, the outline of the pond far from regular, and the extreme length and breadth were got by measuring into the coves; and I said to myself, Who knows but this hint would conduct to the deepest part of the ocean as well as of a pond or puddle? Is not this the rule also for the height of mountains, regarded as the opposite of valleys? We know that a hill is not highest at its narrowest part.

Of five coves, three, or all which had been sounded, were observed to have a bar quite across their mouths and deeper water within, so that the bay tended to be an expansion of water within the land not only horizontally but vertically, and to form a basin or independent pond, the direction of the two capes showing the course of the bar. Every harbor on the sea-coast, also, has its bar at its entrance. In proportion as the mouth of the cove was wider compared with its length, the water over the bar was deeper compared with that in the basin. Given, then, the length and breadth of the cove, and the character of the surrounding shore, and you have almost elements enough to make out a formula for all cases.

In order to see how nearly I could guess, with this experience, at the deepest point in a pond, by observing the outlines of its surface and the character of its shores alone, I made a plan of White Pond, which contains about forty-one acres, and, like this, has no island in it, nor any visible inlet or outlet; and as the line of greatest breadth fell very near the line of least breadth, where two opposite capes approached each other and two opposite bays receded, I ventured to mark a point a short distance from the latter line, but still on the line of greatest length, as the deepest. The deepest part was found to be within one hundred feet of this, still farther in the direction to which I had inclined, and was only one foot deeper, namely, sixty feet. Of course, a stream running through, or an island in the pond, would make the problem much more complicated.

If we knew all the laws of Nature, we should need only one fact, or the description of one actual phenomenon, to infer all the particular results at that point. Now we know only a few laws, and our result is vitiated, not of course, by any confusion or irregularity in Nature, but by our ignorance of essential elements in the calculation. Our notions of law and harmony are commonly confined to those instances which we detect; but the harmony which results from a far greater number of seemingly conflicting, but really concurring, laws, which we have not detected, is still more wonderful. The particular laws are as our points of view, as, to the traveller, a mountain outline varies with every step, and it has an infinite number of profiles, though absolutely but one form. Even when cleft or bored through it is not comprehended in its entireness.

What I have observed of the pond is no less true in ethics. It is the law of average. Such a rule of the two diameters not only guides us toward the sun in the system and the heart in man, but draw lines through the length and breadth of the aggregate of a man's particular daily behaviors and waves of life into his coves and inlets, and where they intersect will be the height or depth of his character. Perhaps we need only to know how his shores trend and his adjacent country or circumstances, to infer his depth and concealed bottom. If he is surrounded by mountainous circumstances, an Achillean[7] shore, whose peaks overshadow and are reflected in his bosom, they suggest a corresponding depth in him. But a low

[7] Like the rocky and mountainous shore of Thessaly, home of Achilles.

and smooth shore proves him shallow on that side. In our bodies, a bold projecting brow falls off to and indicates a corresponding depth of thought. Also there is
a bar across the entrance of our every cove, or particular inclination; each is our
harbor for a season, in which we are detained and partially land-locked. These
inclinations are not whimsical usually, but their form, size, and direction are determined by the promontories of the shore, the ancient axes of elevation. When
this bar is gradually increased by storms, tides, or currents, or there is a subsi-
dence of the waters, so that it reaches to the surface, that which was at first but an
inclination in the shore in which a thought was harbored becomes an individual
lake, cut off from the ocean, wherein the thought secures its own conditions,
changes, perhaps, from salt to fresh, becomes a sweet sea, dead sea, or a marsh.
At the advent of each individual into this life, may we not suppose that such a bar
has risen to the surface somewhere? It is true, we are such poor navigators that our
thoughts, for the most part, stand off and on upon a harborless coast, are conversant only with the bights[8] of the bays of poesy, or steer for the public ports of
entry, and go into the dry docks of science, where they merely refit for this world,
and no natural currents concur to individualize them.

As for the inlet or outlet of Walden, I have not discovered any but rain and
snow and evaporation, though perhaps, with a thermometer and a line, such
places may be found, for where the water flows into the pond it will probably be
coldest in the summer and warmest in winter. When the ice-men were at work
here in '46–7, the cakes sent to the shore were one day rejected by those who
were stacking them up there, not being thick enough to lie side by side with the
rest; and the cutters thus discovered that the ice over a small space was two or
three inches thinner than elsewhere, which made them think that there was an inlet
there. They also showed me in another place what they thought was a "leach
hole," through which the pond leaked out under a hill into a neighboring meadow,
pushing me out on a cake of ice to see it. It was a small cavity under ten feet of
water; but I think that I can warrant the pond not to need soldering till they find a
worse leak than that. One has suggested, that if such a "leach hole" should be
found, its connection with the meadow, if any existed, might be proved by conveying some colored powder or sawdust to the mouth of the hole, and then putting
a strainer over the spring in the meadow, which would catch some of the particles
carried through by the current.

While I was surveying, the ice, which was sixteen inches thick, undulated
under a slight wind like water. It is well known that a level cannot be used on ice.
At one rod from the shore its greatest fluctuation, when observed by means of a
level on land directed toward a graduated staff on the ice, was three quarters of an
inch, though the ice appeared firmly attached to the shore. It was probably greater
in the middle. Who knows but if our instruments were delicate enough we might
detect an undulation in the crust of the earth? When two legs of my level were on
the shore and the third on the ice, and the sights were directed over the latter, a
rise or fall of the ice of an almost infinitesimal amount made a difference of several feet on a tree across the pond. When I began to cut holes for sounding, there
were three or four inches of water on the ice under a deep snow which had sunk it
thus far; but the water began immediately to run into these holes, and continued to
run for two days in deep streams, which wore away the ice on every side, and

---

[8] Bends or curves, generally with reference to waters; here, the rhythm and flow of poetry.

contributed essentially, if not mainly, to dry the surface of the pond; for, as the water ran in, it raised and floated the ice. This was somewhat like cutting a hole in the bottom of a ship to let the water out. When such holes freeze, and a rain succeeds, and finally a new freezing forms a fresh smooth ice over all, it is beautifully mottled internally by dark figures, shaped somewhat like a spider's web, what you may call ice rosettes, produced by the channels worn by the water flowing from all sides to a centre. Sometimes, also, when the ice was covered with shallow puddles, I saw a double shadow of myself, one standing on the head of the other, one on the ice, the other on the trees or hillside.

While yet it is cold January, and snow and ice are thick and solid, the prudent landlord comes from the village to get ice to cool his summer drink; impressively, even pathetically wise, to foresee the heat and thirst of July now in January,—wearing a thick coat and mittens! when so many things are not provided for. It may be that he lays up no treasures in this world[9] which will cool his summer drink in the next. He cuts and saws the solid pond, unroofs the house of fishes, and carts off their very element and air, held fast by chains and stakes like corded wood, through the favoring winter air, to wintry cellars, to underlie the summer there. It looks like solidified azure, as, far off, it is drawn through the streets. These ice-cutters are a merry race, full of jest and sport, and when I went among them they were wont to invite me to saw pit-fashion with them, I standing underneath.

In the winter of '46–7 there came a hundred men of Hyperborean[10] extraction swoop down on to our pond one morning, with many car-loads of ungainly-looking farming tools, sleds, ploughs, drill-barrows, turf-knives, spades, saws, rakes, and each man was armed with a double-pointed pike-staff, such as is not described in the New-England Farmer or the Cultivator.[11] I did not know whether they had come to sow a crop of winter rye, or some other kind of grain recently introduced from Iceland. As I saw no manure, I judged that they meant to skim the land, as I had done, thinking the soil was deep and had lain fallow long enough. They said that a gentleman farmer, who was behind the scenes, wanted to double his money, which, as I understood, amounted to half a million already; but in order to cover each one of his dollars with another, he took off the only coat, ay, the skin itself, of Walden Pond in the midst of a hard winter. They went to work at once, ploughing, harrowing, rolling, furrowing, in admirable order, as if they were bent on making this a model farm; but when I was looking sharp to see what kind of seed they dropped into the furrow, a gang of fellows by my side suddenly began to hook up the virgin mould itself, with a peculiar jerk, clean down to the sand, or rather the water,—for it was a very springy soil,—indeed all the *terra firma* there was, and haul it away on sleds, and then I guessed that they must be cutting peat in a bog. So they came and went every day, with a peculiar shriek from the locomotive, from and to some point of the polar regions, as it seemed to me, like a flock of arctic snow-birds. But sometimes Squaw Walden had her revenge, and a hired man, walking behind his team, slipped through a crack in the ground down

---

[9] "Lay not up for yourselves treasures upon earth, where moth and rust doth corrupt, and where thieves break through and steal," from Matthew 6:19.

[10] According to Greek myth, invaders from the North (literally, "from beyond the north wind"); these "hundred men" are Irish.

[11] Farm journals.

toward Tartarus,[12] and he who was so brave suddenly became but the ninth part of a man, almost gave up his animal heat, and was glad to take refuge in my house, and acknowledged that there was some virtue in a stove; or sometimes the frozen soil took a piece of steel out of a ploughshare, or a plough got set in the furrow and had to be cut out.

To speak literally, a hundred Irishmen, with Yankee overseers, came from Cambridge every day to get out the ice. They divided it into cakes by methods too well known to require description, and these, being sledded to the shore, were rapidly hauled off on to an ice platform, and raised by grappling irons and block and tackle, worked by horses, on to a stack, as surely as so many barrels of flour, and there placed evenly side by side, and row upon row, as if they formed the solid base of an obelisk designed to pierce the clouds. They told me that in a good day they could get out a thousand tons, which was the yield of about one acre. Deep ruts and "cradle holes" were worn in the ice, as on *terra firma,* by the passage of the sleds over the same track, and the horses invariably ate their oats out of cakes of ice hollowed out like buckets. They stacked up the cakes thus in the open air in a pile thirty-five feet high on one side and six or seven rods square, putting hay between the outside layers to exclude the air; for when the wind, though never so cold, finds a passage through, it will wear large cavities, leaving slight supports or studs only here and there, and finally topple it down. At first it looked like a vast blue fort or Valhalla; but when they began to tuck the coarse meadow hay into the crevices, and this became covered with rime and icicles, it looked like a venerable moss-grown and hoary ruin, built of azure-tinted marble, the abode of Winter, that old man we see in the almanac,—his shanty, as if he had a design to estivate[13] with us. They calculated that not twenty-five per cent. of this would reach its destination, and that two or three per cent. would be wasted in the cars. However, a still greater part of this heap had a different destiny from what was intended; for, either because the ice was found not to keep so well as was expected, containing more air than usual, or for some other reason, it never got to market. This heap, made in the winter of '46–7 and estimated to contain ten thousand tons, was finally covered with hay and boards; and though it was unroofed the following July, and a part of it carried off, the rest remaining exposed to the sun, it stood over that summer and the next winter, and was not quite melted till September 1848. Thus the pond recovered the greater part.

Like the water, the Walden ice, seen near at hand, has a green tint, but at a distance is beautifully blue, and you can easily tell it from the white ice of the river, or the merely greenish ice of some ponds, a quarter of a mile off. Sometimes one of those great cakes slips from the ice-man's sled into the village street, and lies there for a week like a great emerald, an object of interest to all passers. I have noticed that a portion of Walden which in the state of water was green will often, when frozen, appear from the same point of view blue. So the hollows about this pond will, sometimes, in the winter, be filled with a greenish water somewhat like its own, but the next day will have frozen blue. Perhaps the blue color of water and ice is due to the light and air they contain, and the most transparent is the bluest. Ice is an interesting subject for contemplation. They told me that they had some in the ice-houses at Fresh Pond five years old which was as

---

[12] According to Greek myth, a part of the underworld where souls suffer punishment for their misdeeds on earth.

[13] To pass the summer, perhaps drowsily.

good as ever. Why is it that a bucket of water soon becomes putrid, but frozen remains sweet forever? It is commonly said that this is the difference between the affections and the intellect.

Thus for sixteen days I saw from my window a hundred men at work like husbandmen, with teams and horses and apparently all the implements of farming, such a picture as we see on the first page of the almanac; and as often as I looked out I was reminded of the fable of the lark and the reapers, or the parable of the sower,[14] and the like; and now they are all gone, and in thirty days more, probably, I shall look from the same window on the pure sea-green Walden water there, reflecting the clouds and the trees, and sending up its evaporations in solitude, and no traces will appear that a man has ever stood there. Perhaps I shall hear a solitary loon laugh as he dives and plumes himself, or shall see a lonely fisher in his boat, like a floating leaf, beholding his form reflected in the waves, where lately a hundred men securely labored.

Thus it appears that the sweltering inhabitants of Charleston and New Orleans, of Madras and Bombay and Calcutta, drink at my well. In the morning I bathe my intellect in the stupendous and cosmogonal[15] philosophy of the Bhagvat Geeta, since whose composition years of the gods have elapsed, and in comparison with which our modern world and its literature seem puny and trivial; and I doubt if that philosophy is not to be referred to a previous state of existence, so remote is its sublimity from our conceptions. I lay down the book and go to my well for water, and lo! there I meet the servant of the Brahmin, priest of Brahma and Vishnu and Indra,[16] who still sits in his temple on the Ganges reading the Vedas, or dwells at the root of a tree with his crust and water jug. I meet his servant come to draw water for his master, and our buckets as it were grate together in the same well. The pure Walden water is mingled with the sacred water of the Ganges. With favoring winds it is wafted past the site of the fabulous islands of Atlantis and the Hesperides,[17] makes the periplus of Hanno,[18] and, floating by Ternate and Tidore[19] and the mouth of the Persian Gulf, melts in the tropic gales of the Indian seas, and is landed in ports of which Alexander[20] only heard the names.

XVII: SPRING

The opening of large tracts by the ice-cutters commonly causes a pond to break up earlier; for the water, agitated by the wind, even in cold weather, wears away the surrounding ice. But such was not the effect on Walden that year, for she had soon got a thick new garment to take the place of the old.[1] This pond never breaks up so soon as the others in this neighborhood, on account both of its greater depth and

[14] Aesop's fable of the meadowlark who protects her young from men who are reaping a field; and Matthew 13:3–43.

[15] Cosmology is the branch of philosophy that studies, and formulates theories about, the creation of the universe.

[16] Hindu deities.   [17] According to classical myth, islands at the western end of the world.

[18] To sail out of the Mediterranean Sea, around the west coast of Africa, and into the Indian Ocean; the Carthaginian navigator Hanno supposedly made this journey in 480 B.C.

[19] Indonesian islands.

[20] Alexander the Great, king of Macedon, traveled widely in his military campaigns.

[1] Literally and metaphorically, the coming of spring marks the final movement of *Walden;* the renewal of life celebrated here leads into the powerful injunctions to self-discovery pervading Thoreau's "Conclusion."

its having no stream passing through it to melt or wear away the ice. I never knew it to open in the course of a winter, not excepting that of '52–3, which gave the ponds so severe a trial. It commonly opens about the first of April, a week or ten days later than Flint's Pond and Fair-Haven, beginning to melt on the north side and in the shallower parts where it began to freeze. It indicates better than any water hereabouts the absolute progress of the season, being least affected by transient changes of temperature. A severe cold of a few days' duration in March may very much retard the opening of the former ponds, while the temperature of Walden increases almost uninterruptedly. A thermometer thrust into the middle of Walden on the 6th of March, 1847, stood at 32°, or freezing point; near the shore at 33°; in the middle of Flint's Pond, the same day, at 32 1/2°; at a dozen rods from the shore, in shallow water, under ice a foot thick, at 36°. This difference of three and a half degrees between the temperature of the deep water and the shallow in the latter pond, and the fact that a great proportion of it is comparatively shallow, show why it should break up so much sooner than Walden. The ice in the shallowest part was at this time several inches thinner than in the middle. In midwinter the middle had been the warmest and the ice thinnest there. So, also, every one who has waded about the shores of a pond in summer must have perceived how much warmer the water is close to the shore, where only three or four inches deep, than a little distance out, and on the surface where it is deep, than near the bottom. In spring the sun not only exerts an influence through the increased temperature of the air and earth, but its heat passes through ice a foot or more thick, and is reflected from the bottom in shallow water, and so also warms the water and melts the under side of the ice, at the same time that it is melting it more directly above, making it uneven, and causing the air bubbles which it contains to extend themselves upward and downward until it is completely honey-combed, and at last disappears suddenly in a single spring rain. Ice has its grain as well as wood, and when a cake begins to rot or "comb," that is, assume the appearance of honey-comb, whatever may be its position, the air cells are at right angles with what was the water surface. Where there is a rock or a log rising near to the surface the ice over it is much thinner, and is frequently quite dissolved by this reflected heat; and I have been told that in the experiment at Cambridge to freeze water in a shallow wooden pond, though the cold air circulated underneath, and so had access to both sides, the reflection of the sun from the bottom more than counterbalanced this advantage. When a warm rain in the middle of the winter melts off the snow-ice from Walden, and leaves a hard dark or transparent ice on the middle, there will be a strip of rotten though thicker white ice, a rod or more wide, about the shores, created by this reflected heat. Also, as I have said, the bubbles themselves within the ice operate as burning glasses to melt the ice beneath.

The phenomena of the year take place every day in a pond on a small scale. Every morning, generally speaking, the shallow water is being warmed more rapidly than the deep, though it may not be made so warm after all, and every evening it is being cooled more rapidly until the morning. The day is an epitome of the year. The night is the winter, the morning and evening are the spring and fall, and the noon is the summer. The cracking and booming of the ice indicate a change of temperature. One pleasant morning after a cold night, February 24th, 1850, having gone to Flint's Pond to spend the day, I noticed with surprise, that when I struck the ice with the head of my axe, it resounded like a gong for many rods around, or as if I had struck on a tight drum-head. The pond began to boom about an hour after sunrise, when it felt the influence of the sun's rays slanted upon it from over the hills; it stretched itself and yawned like a waking man with a gradually increasing tumult, which was kept up three or four hours. It took a short siesta at noon, and boomed once more toward night, as the sun was withdrawing his influence. In the right stage of the weather a pond fires its evening gun with great regularity. But in the middle of the day, being full of cracks, and the air also being less elastic, it had completely lost its resonance, and probably fishes and muskrats could not then have been stunned by a blow on it.[2] The fishermen say that the "thundering of the pond" scares the fishes and prevents their biting. The pond does not thunder every evening, and I cannot tell surely when to expect its thundering; but though I may perceive no difference in the weather, it does. Who would have suspected so large and cold and thick-skinned a thing to be so sensitive? Yet it has its law to which it thunders obedience when it should as surely as the buds expand in the spring. The earth is all alive and covered with papillæ. The largest pond is as sensitive to atmospheric changes as the globule of mercury in its tube.

One attraction in coming to the woods to live was that I should have leisure and opportunity to see the spring come in. The ice in the pond at length begins to be honey-combed, and I can set my heel in it as I walk. Fogs and rains and warmer suns are gradually melting the snow; the days have grown sensibly longer; and I see how I shall get through the winter without adding to my wood-pile, for large fires are no longer necessary. I am on the alert for the first signs of spring, to hear the chance note of some arriving bird, or the striped squirrel's chirp, for his stores must be now nearly exhausted, or see the woodchuck venture out of his winter quarters. On the 13th of March, after I had heard the bluebird, song-sparrow, and red-wing, the ice was still nearly a foot thick. As the weather grew warmer, it was not sensibly worn away by the water, nor broken up and floated off as in rivers, but, though it was completely melted for half a rod in width about the shore, the middle was merely honey-combed and saturated with water, so that you could put your foot through it when six inches thick; but by the next day evening, perhaps, after a warm rain followed by fog, it would have wholly disappeared, all gone off with the fog, spirited away. One year I went across the middle only five days before it disappeared entirely. In 1845 Walden was first completely open on the 1st of April; in '46, the 25th of March; in '47, the 8th of April; in '51, the 28th of March; in '52, the 18th of April; in '53, the 23d of March; in '54, about the 7th of April.

Every incident connected with the breaking up of the rivers and ponds and the settling of the weather is particularly interesting to us who live in a climate of so great extremes. When the warmer days come, they who dwell near the river hear the ice crack at night with a startling whoop as loud as artillery, as if its icy fetters were rent from end to end, and within a few days see it rapidly going out. So the alligator comes out of the mud with quakings of the earth. One old man, who has been a close observer of Nature, and seems as thoroughly wise in regard to all her operations as if she had been put upon the stocks when he was a boy, and he had

---

[2] Fishermen sometimes smack the ice hard hoping to stun the fish below and make them easier to catch.

helped to lay her keel,—who has come to his growth, and can hardly acquire more of natural lore if he should live to the age of Methuselah,[3]—told me, and I was surprised to hear him express wonder at any of Nature's operations, for I thought that there were no secrets between them, that one spring day he took his gun and boat, and thought that he would have a little sport with the ducks. There was ice still on the meadows, but it was all gone out of the river, and he dropped down without obstruction from Sudbury, where he lived, to Fair-Haven Pond, which he found, unexpectedly, covered for the most part with a firm field of ice. It was a warm day, and he was surprised to see so great a body of ice remaining. Not seeing any ducks, he hid his boat on the north or back side of an island in the pond, and then concealed himself in the bushes on the south side, to await them. The ice was melted for three or four rods from the shore, and there was a smooth and warm sheet of water, with a muddy bottom, such as the ducks love, within, and he thought it likely that some would be along pretty soon. After he had lain still there about an hour he heard a low and seemingly very distant sound, but singularly grand and impressive, unlike any thing he had ever heard, gradually swelling and increasing as if it would have a universal and memorable ending, a sullen rush and roar, which seemed to him all at once like the sound of a vast body of fowl coming in to settle there, and, seizing his gun, he started up in haste and excited; but he found, to his surprise, that the whole body of the ice had started while he lay there, and drifted in to the shore, and the sound he had heard was made by its edge grating on the shore,—at first gently nibbled and crumbled off, but at length heaving up and scattering its wrecks along the island to a considerable height before it came to a stand still.

At length the sun's rays have attained the right angle, and warm winds blow up mist and rain and melt the snow banks, and the sun dispersing the mist smiles on a checkered landscape of russet and white smoking with incense, through which the traveller picks his way from islet to islet, cheered by the music of a thousand tinkling rills and rivulets whose veins are filled with the blood of winter which they are bearing off.

Few phenomena gave me more delight than to observe the forms which thawing sand and clay assume in flowing down the sides of a deep cut on the railroad through which I passed on my way to the village, a phenomenon not very common on so large a scale, though the number of freshly exposed banks of the right material must have been greatly multiplied since railroads were invented. The material was sand of every degree of fineness and of various rich colors, commonly mixed with a little clay. When the frost comes out in the spring, and even in a thawing day in the winter, the sand begins to flow down the slopes like lava, sometimes bursting out through the snow and overflowing it where no sand was to be seen before. Innumerable little streams overlap and interlace one with another, exhibiting a sort of hybrid product, which obeys half way the law of currents, and half way that of vegetation. As it flows it takes the forms of sappy leaves or vines, making heaps of pulpy sprays a foot or more in depth, and resembling, as you look down on them, the laciniated lobed and imbricated thalluses[4] of some lichens; or you are reminded of coral, of leopards' paws or birds' feet, of brains or lungs or bowels, and excrements of all kinds. It is a truly *grotesque* vegetation,

---

[3] In Genesis 5:27, 969 years.
[4] Young shoots that grow with both "laciniated" (deep, irregular) and "imbricated" (lapped over, patterned) lobes.

whose forms and color we see imitated in bronze, a sort of architectural foliage more ancient and typical than acanthus, chiccory, ivy, vine, or any vegetable leaves; destined perhaps, under some circumstances, to become a puzzle to future geologists. The whole cut impressed me as if it were a cave with its stalactites laid open to the light. The various shades of the sand are singularly rich and agreeable, embracing the different iron colors, brown, gray, yellowish, and reddish. When the flowing mass reaches the drain at the foot of the bank it spreads out flatter into *strands,* the separate streams losing their semi-cylindrical form and gradually becoming more flat and broad, running together as they are more moist, till they form an almost flat *sand,* still variously and beautifully shaded, but in which you can trace the original forms of vegetation; till at length, in the water itself, they are converted into *banks,* like those formed off the mouths of rivers, and the forms of vegetation are lost in the ripple marks on the bottom.

The whole bank, which is from twenty to forty feet high, is sometimes overlaid with a mass of this kind of foliage, or sandy rupture, for a quarter of a mile on one or both sides, the produce of one spring day. What makes this sand foliage remarkable is its springing into existence thus suddenly. When I see on the one side the inert bank,—for the sun acts on one side first,—and on the other this luxuriant foliage, the creation of an hour, I am affected as if in a peculiar sense I stood in the laboratory of the Artist who made the world and me,—had come to where he was still at work, sporting on this bank, and with excess of energy strewing his fresh designs about. I feel as if I were nearer to the vitals of the globe, for this sandy overflow is something such a foliaceous[5] mass as the vitals of the animal body. You find thus in the very sands an anticipation of the vegetable leaf. No wonder that the earth expresses itself outwardly in leaves, it so labors with the idea inwardly. The atoms have already learned this law, and are pregnant by it. The overhanging leaf sees here its prototype. *Internally,* whether in the globe or animal body, it is a moist thick *lobe,* a word especially applicable to the liver and lungs and the *leaves* of fat, ($\lambda\epsilon\iota\beta\omega$, *labor, lapsus,* to flow or slip downward, a lapsing; $\lambda o\beta o\delta$, *globus,* lobe, globe; also lap, flap, and many other words,) *externally* a dry thin *leaf,* even as the *f* and *v* are pressed and dried *b.* The radicals of lobe are *lb,* the soft mass of the *b* (single lobed, or B, double lobed,) with a liquid *l* behind it pressing it forward. In globe, *glb,* the guttural *g* adds to the meaning the capacity of the throat. The feathers and wings of birds are still drier and thinner leaves. Thus, also, you pass from the lumpish grub in the earth to the airy and fluttering butterfly. The very globe continually transcends and translates itself, and becomes winged in its orbit. Even ice begins with delicate crystal leaves, as if it had flowed into moulds which the fronds of water plants have impressed on the watery mirror. The whole tree itself is but one leaf, and rivers are still vaster leaves whose pulp is intervening earth, and towns and cities are the ova of insects in their axils.[6]

When the sun withdraws the sand ceases to flow, but in the morning the streams will start once more and branch and branch again into a myriad of others. You here see perchance how blood vessels are formed. If you look closely you observe that first there pushes forward from the thawing mass a stream of softened sand with a drop-like point, like the ball of the finger, feeling its way slowly and

---

[5] Like a mass of foliage.

[6] The angle between a branch or leaf and the stem out of which it grows, from the Latin *axilla,* or "armpit."

blindly downward, until at last with more heat and moisture, as the sun gets higher, the most fluid portion, in its effort to obey the law to which the most inert also yields, separates from the latter and forms for itself a meandering channel or artery within that, in which is seen a little silvery stream glancing like lightning from one stage of pulpy leaves or branches to another, and ever and anon swallowed up in the sand. It is wonderful how rapidly yet perfectly the sand organizes itself as it flows, using the best material its mass affords to form the sharp edges of its channel. Such are the sources of rivers. In the silicious matter which the water deposits is perhaps the bony system, and in the still finer soil and organic matter the fleshy fibre or cellular tissue. What is man but a mass of thawing clay? The ball of the human finger is but a drop congealed. The fingers and toes flow to their extent from the thawing mass of the body. Who knows what the human body would expand and flow out to under a more genial heaven? Is not the hand a spreading *palm* leaf with its lobes and veins? The ear may be regarded, fancifully, as a lichen, *umbilicaria*, on the side of the head, with its lobe or drop. The lip (*labium* from *labor* (?)) laps or lapses from the sides of the cavernous mouth. The nose is a manifest congealed drop or stalactite. The chin is a still larger drop, the confluent dripping of the face. The cheeks are a slide from the brows into the valley of the face, opposed and diffused by the cheek bones. Each rounded lobe of the vegetable leaf, too, is a thick and now loitering drop, larger or smaller; the lobes are the fingers of the leaf; and as many lobes as it has, in so many directions it tends to flow, and more heat or other genial influences would have caused it to flow yet farther.

Thus it seemed that this one hillside illustrated the principle of all the operations of Nature. The Maker of this earth but patented a leaf. What Champollion[7] will decipher this hieroglyphic for us, that we may turn over a new leaf at last? This phenomenon is more exhilarating to me than the luxuriance and fertility of vineyards. True, it is somewhat excrementitious in its character, and there is no end to the heaps of liver lights[8] and bowels, as if the globe were turned wrong side outward; but this suggests at least that Nature has some bowels, and there again is mother of humanity. This is the frost coming out of the ground; this is Spring. It precedes the green and flowery spring, as mythology precedes regular poetry. I know of nothing more purgative of winter fumes and indigestions. It convinces me that Earth is still in her swaddling clothes, and stretches forth baby fingers on every side. Fresh curls spring from the baldest brow. There is nothing inorganic. These foliaceous heaps lie along the bank like the slag of a furnace, showing that Nature is "in full blast" within. The earth is not a mere fragment of dead history, stratum upon stratum like the leaves of a book, to be studied by geologists and antiquaries chiefly, but living poetry like the leaves of a tree, which precede flowers and fruit,—not a fossil earth, but a living earth; compared with whose great central life all animal and vegetable life is merely parasitic. Its throes will heave our exuviæ from their graves. You may melt your metals and cast them into the most beautiful moulds you can; they will never excite me like the forms which this molten earth flows out into. And not only it, but the institutions upon it, are plastic like clay in the hands of the potter.

---

[7] Jean François Champollion (1790–1832), the French archeologist who deciphered the hieroglyphics on the Rosetta Stone (found in 1799 by Napoleon's troops near the Egyptian city of Rosetta) and thereby made it possible for scholars to learn about ancient Egyptian culture.

[8] Lungs. Many editors put a comma after "liver" to indicate the liver, the lungs, and the bowels. Immediately below, Thoreau makes use of the old belief that the bowels were the seat of compassion.

Ere long, not only on these banks, but on every hill and plain and in every hollow, the frost comes out of the ground like a dormant quadruped from its burrow, and seeks the sea with music, or migrates to other climes in clouds. Thaw with his gentle persuasion is more powerful than Thor[9] with his hammer. The one melts, the other but breaks in pieces.

When the ground was partially bare of snow, and a few warm days had dried its surface somewhat, it was pleasant to compare the first tender signs of the infant year just peeping forth with stately beauty of the withered vegetation which had withstood the winter,—life-everlasting, golden-rods, pinweeds, and graceful wild grasses, more obvious and interesting frequently than in summer even, as if their beauty was not ripe till then; even cotton-grass, cat-tails, mulleins, johnswort, hard-hack, meadow-sweet, and other strong stemmed plants, those unexhausted granaries which entertain the earliest birds,—decent weeds,[10] at least, which widowed Nature wears. I am particularly attracted by the arching and sheaf-like top of the wool-grass; it brings back the summer to our winter memories, and is among the forms which art loves to copy, and which, in the vegetable kingdom, have the same relation to types already in the mind of man that astronomy has. It is an antique style older than Greek or Egyptian. Many of the phenomena of Winter are suggestive of an inexpressible tenderness and fragile delicacy. We are accustomed to hear this king described as a rude and boisterous tyrant; but with the gentleness of a lover he adorns the tresses of Summer.

At the approach of spring the red-squirrels got under my house, two at a time, directly under my feet as I sat reading or writing, and kept up the queerest chuckling and chirruping and vocal pirouetting and gurgling sounds that ever were heard; and when I stamped they only chirruped the louder, as if past all fear and respect in their mad pranks, defying humanity to stop them. No you don't—chickaree—chickaree. They were wholly deaf to my arguments, or failed to perceive their force, and fell into a strain of invective that was irresistible.

The first sparrow of spring! The year beginning with younger hope than ever! The faint silvery warblings heard over the partially bare and moist fields from the blue-bird, the song-sparrow, and the red-wing, as if the last flakes of winter tinkled as they fell! What at such a time are histories, chronologies, traditions, and all written revelations? The brooks sing carols and glees to the spring. The marsh-hawk sailing low over the meadow is already seeking the first slimy life that awakes. The sinking sound of melting snow is heard in all dells, and the ice dissolves apace in the ponds. The grass flames up on the hillsides like a spring fire,—"et primitus oritur herba imbribus primoribus evocata,"[11]—as if the earth sent forth an inward heat to greet the returning sun; not yellow but green is the color of its flame;—the symbol of perpetual youth, the grass-blade, like a long green ribbon, streams from the sod into the summer, checked indeed by the frost, but anon pushing on again, lifting its spear of last year's hay with the fresh life below. It grows as steadily as the rill oozes out of the ground. It is almost identical with that, for in the growing days of June, when the rills are dry, the grass blades are their channels, and from year to year the herds drink at this perennial green

[9] According to Norse myth, the god of thunder. As pronounced with a New England accent, "thaw" and "Thor" would sound much the same.

[10] Proper attire for mourning.

[11] "And the first grass begins to grow, evoked by the first rains" (Latin), from Varro's *Rerum Rusticarum* (II.2).

stream, and the mower draws from it betimes their winter supply. So our human life but dies down to its root, and still puts forth its green blade to eternity.

Walden is melting apace. There is a canal two rods wide along the northerly and westerly sides, and wider still at the east end. A great field of ice has cracked off from the main body. I hear a song-sparrow singing from the bushes on the shore,—*olit, olit, olit,—chip, chip, chip, che char,—che wiss, wiss, wiss.* He too is helping to crack it. How handsome the great sweeping curves in the edge of the ice, answering somewhat to those of the shore, but more regular! It is unusually hard, owing to the recent severe but transient cold, and all watered or waved like a palace floor. But the wind slides eastward over its opaque surface in vain, till it reaches the living surface beyond. It is glorious to behold this ribbon of water sparkling in the sun, the bare face of the pond full of glee and youth, as if it spoke the joy of the fishes within it, and of the sands on its shore,—a silvery sheen as from the scales of a *leuciscus*,[12] as it were all one active fish. Such is the contrast between winter and spring. Walden was dead and is alive again.[13] But this spring it broke up more steadily, as I have said.

The change from storm and winter to serene and mild weather, from dark and sluggish hours to bright and elastic ones, is a memorable crisis which all things proclaim. It is seemingly instantaneous at last. Suddenly an influx of light filled my house, though the evening was at hand, and the clouds of winter still overhung it, and the eaves were dripping with sleety rain. I looked out the window, and lo! where yesterday was cold gray ice there lay the transparent pond already calm and full of hope as on a summer evening, reflecting a summer evening sky in its bosom, though none was visible overhead, as if it had intelligence with some remote horizon. I heard a robin in the distance, the first I had heard for many a thousand years, methought, whose note I shall not forget for many a thousand more,—the same sweet and powerful song of yore. O the evening robin, at the end of a New England summer day! If I could ever find the twig he sits upon! I mean *he;* I mean *the twig.* This at least is not the *Turdus migratorius*.[14] The pitch-pines and shrub-oaks about my house, which had so long drooped, suddenly resumed their several characters, looked brighter, greener, and more erect and alive, as if effectually cleansed and restored by the rain. I knew that it would not rain any more. You may tell by looking at any twig of the forest, ay, at your very wood-pile, whether its winter is past or not. As it grew darker, I was startled by the *honking* of geese flying low over the woods, like weary travellers getting in late from southern lakes, and indulging at last in unrestrained complaint and mutual consolation. Standing at my door, I could hear the rush of their wings; when, driving toward my house, they suddenly spied my light, and with hushed clamor wheeled and settled in the pond. So I came in, and shut the door, and passed my first spring night in the woods.

In the morning I watched the geese from the door through the mist, sailing in the middle of the pond, fifty rods off, so large and tumultuous that Walden appeared like an artificial pond for their amusement. But when I stood on the shore they at once rose up with a great flapping of wings at the signal of their commander, and when they had got into rank circled about over my head, twenty-nine of them, and then steered straight to Canada, with a regular *honk* from the leader at intervals, trusting to break their fast in muddier pools. A "plump" of ducks rose

---

[12] Freshwater fish.   [13] "For this my son was dead, and is alive again," from Luke 15:24.
[14] American robin.

at the same time and took the route to the north in the wake of their noisier cousins.

For a week, I heard the circling groping clangor of some solitary goose in the foggy mornings, seeking its companion, and still peopling the woods with the sound of a larger life than they could sustain. In April the pigeons were seen again flying express in small flocks, and in due time I heard the martins twittering over my clearing, though it had not seemed that the township contained so many that it could afford me any, and I fancied that they were peculiarly of the ancient race that dwelt in hollow trees ere white men came. In almost all climes the tortoise and the frog are among the precursors and heralds of this season, and birds fly with song and glancing plumage, and plants spring and bloom, and winds blow, to correct this slight oscillation of the poles and preserve the equilibrium of Nature.

As every season seems best to us in its turn, so the coming in of spring is like the creation of Cosmos out of Chaos and the realization of the Golden Age.—

"Eurus ad Auroram, Nabathæaque regna recessit,
Persidaque, et radiis juga subdita matutinis."

"The East-Wind withdrew to Aurora and the Nabathæan kingdom,
And the Persian, and the ridges placed under the morning rays.

* * *

Man was born. Whether that Artificer of things,
The origin of a better world, made him from the divine seed;
Or the earth being recent and lately sundered from the high
Ether, retained some seeds of cognate heaven."[15]

A single gentle rain makes the grass many shades greener. So our prospects brighten on the influx of better thoughts. We should be blessed if we lived in the present always, and took advantage of every accident that befell us, like the grass which confesses the influence of the slightest dew that falls on it; and did not spend our time in atoning for the neglect of past opportunities, which we call doing our duty. We loiter in winter while it is already spring. In a pleasant spring morning all men's sins are forgiven. Such a day is a truce to vice. While such a sun holds out to burn, the vilest sinner may return. Through our own recovered innocence we discern the innocence of our neighbors. You may have known your neighbor yesterday for a thief, a drunkard, or a sensualist, and merely pitied or despised him, and despaired of the world; but the sun shines bright and warm this first spring morning, re-creating the world, and you meet him at some serene work, and see how his exhausted and debauched veins expand with still joy and bless the new day, feel the spring influence with the innocence of infancy, and all his faults are forgotten. There is not only an atmosphere of good will about him, but even a savor of holiness groping for expression, blindly and ineffectually perhaps, like a new-born instinct, and for a short hour the south hill-side echoes to no vulgar jest. You see some innocent fair shoots preparing to burst from his gnarled

[15] From the *Metamorphoses* (Bk. I), of the Latin poet Ovid (43 B.C.–A.D. 18).

rind and try another year's life, tender and fresh as the youngest plant. Even he has entered into the joy of his Lord. Why the jailer does not leave open his prison doors,—why the judge does not dismiss his case,—why the preacher does not dismiss his congregation! It is because they do not obey the hint which God gives them, nor accept the pardon which he freely offers to all.

"A return to goodness produced each day in the tranquil and beneficent breath of the morning, causes that in respect to the love of virtue and the hatred of vice, one approaches a little the primitive nature of man, as the sprouts of the forest which has been felled. In like manner the evil which one does in the interval of a day prevents the germs of virtues which began to spring up again from developing themselves and destroys them.

"After the germs of virtue have thus been prevented many times from developing themselves, then the beneficent breath of evening does not suffice to preserve them. As soon as the breath of evening does not suffice longer to preserve them, then the nature of man does not differ much from that of the brute. Men seeing the nature of this man like that of the brute, think that he has never possessed the innate faculty of reason. Are those the true and natural sentiments of man?"[16]

> "The Golden Age was first created, which without any avenger
> Spontaneously without law cherished fidelity and rectitude.
> Punishment and fear were not; nor were threatening words read
> On suspended brass; nor did the suppliant crowd fear
> The words of their judge; but were safe without an avenger.
> Not yet the pine felled on its mountains had descended
> To the liquid waves that it might see a foreign world,
> And mortals knew no shores but their own.
>
> * * *
>
> There was eternal spring, and placid zephyrs with warm
> Blasts soothed the flowers born without seed."[17]

On the 29th of April, as I was fishing from the bank of the river near the Nine-Acre-Corner bridge, standing on the quaking grass and willow roots, where the muskrats lurk, I heard a singular rattling sound, somewhat like that of the sticks which boys play with their fingers, when, looking up, I observed a very slight and graceful hawk, like a night-hawk, alternately soaring like a ripple and tumbling a rod or two over and over, showing the underside of its wings, which gleamed like a satin ribbon in the sun, or like the pearly inside of a shell. This sight reminded me of falconry and what nobleness and poetry are associated with that sport. The Merlin it seemed to me it might be called: but I care not for its name. It was the most ethereal flight I had ever witnessed. It did not simply flutter like a butterfly, nor soar like the larger hawks, but it sported with proud reliance in the fields of air; mounting again and again with its strange chuckle, it repeated its free and beautiful fall, turning over and over like a kite, and then recovering from its lofty tumbling, as if it had never set its foot on *terra firma*. It appeared to have no companion in the universe,—sporting there alone,—and to need none but the morning and the ether with which it played. It was not lonely, but made all the

---

[16] From the *Book of Mencius* (VI.1).   [17] From Ovid's *Metamorphoses*, Bk. I.

earth lonely beneath it. Where was the parent which hatched it, its kindred, and its father in the heavens? The tenant of the air, it seemed related to the earth but by an egg hatched some time in the crevice of a crag;—or was its native nest made in the angle of a cloud, woven of the rainbow's trimmings and the sunset sky, and lined with some soft midsummer haze caught up from earth? Its eyry[18] now some cliffy cloud.

Beside this I got a rare mess of golden and silver and bright cupreous[19] fishes, which looked like a string of jewels. Ah! I have penetrated to those meadows on the morning of many a first spring day, jumping from hummock to hummock, from willow root to willow root, when the wild river valley and the woods were bathed in so pure and bright a light as would have waked the dead, if they had been slumbering in their graves, as some suppose. There needs no stronger proof of immortality. All things must live in such a light. O Death, where was thy sting? O Grave, where was thy victory, then?[20]

Our village life would stagnate if it were not for the unexplored forests and meadows which surround it. We need the tonic of wilderness,—to wade sometimes in marshes where the bittern and the meadow-hen lurk, and hear the booming of the snipe; to smell the whispering sedge where only some wilder and more solitary fowl builds her nest, and the mink crawls with its belly close to the ground. At the same time that we are earnest to explore and learn all things, we require that all things be mysterious and unexplorable, that land and sea be infinitely wild, unsurveyed and unfathomed by us because unfathomable. We can never have enough of Nature. We must be refreshed by the sight of inexhaustible vigor, vast and Titanic features, the sea-coast with its wrecks, the wilderness with its living and its decaying trees, the thunder cloud, and the rain which lasts three weeks and produces freshets. We need to witness our own limits transgressed, and some life pasturing freely where we never wander. We are cheered when we observe the vulture feeding on the carrion which disgusts and disheartens us and deriving health and strength from the repast. There was a dead horse in the hollow by the path to my house, which compelled me sometimes to go out of my way, especially in the night when the air was heavy, but the assurance it gave me of the strong appetite and inviolable health of Nature was my compensation for this. I love to see that Nature is so rife with life that myriads can be afforded to be sacrificed and suffered to prey on one another; that tender organizations can be so serenely squashed out of existence like pulp,—tadpoles which herons gobble up, and tortoises and toads run over in the road; and that sometimes it has rained flesh and blood! With the liability to accident, we must see how little account is to be made of it. The impression made on a wise man is that of universal innocence. Poison is not poisonous after all, nor are any wounds fatal. Compassion is a very untenable ground. It must be expeditious. Its pleadings will not bear to be stereotyped.

Early in May, the oaks, hickories, maples, and other trees, just putting out amidst the pine woods around the pond, imparted a brightness like sunshine to the landscape, especially in cloudy days, as if the sun were breaking through mists and shining faintly on the hill-sides here and there. On the third or fourth of May I saw a loon in the pond, and during the first week of the month I heard the whippoorwill, the brown-thrasher, the veery, the wood-pewee, the chewink, and

---

[18] Aerie, or bird's nest.   [19] Copper-colored.

[20] "O death, where is thy sting? O grave, where is thy victory?" from I Corinthians 15:55.

other birds. I had heard the wood-thrush long before. The phœbe had already come once more and looked in at my door and window, to see if my house was cavern-like enough for her, sustaining herself on humming wings with clinched talons, as if she held by the air, while she surveyed the premises. The sulphur-like pollen of the pitch-pine soon covered the pond and the stones and rotten wood along the shore, so that you could have collected a barrel-ful. This is the "sulphur showers" we hear of. Even in Calidas' drama of Sacontala,[21] we read of "rills dyed yellow with the golden dust of the lotus." And so the seasons went rolling on into summer, as one rambles into higher and higher grass.

Thus was my first year's life in the woods completed; and the second year was similar to it.[22] I finally left Walden September 6th, 1847.

XVIII: Conclusion

To the sick the doctors wisely recommend a change of air and scenery. Thank Heaven, here is not all the world. The buck-eye does not grow in New England, and the mocking-bird is rarely heard here. The wild-goose is more of a cosmopolite than we; he breaks his fast in Canada, takes a luncheon in the Ohio, and plumes himself for the night in a southern bayou. Even the bison, to some extent, keeps pace with the seasons, cropping the pastures of the Colorado only till a greener and sweeter grass awaits him by the Yellowstone. Yet we think that if rail-fences are pulled down, and stone-walls piled up on our farms, bounds are henceforth set to our lives and our fates decided. If you are chosen town-clerk, forsooth, you cannot go to Tierra del Fuego[1] this summer: but you may go to the land of infernal fire nevertheless. The universe is wider than our views of it.

Yet we should oftener look over the tafferel[2] of our craft, like curious passengers, and not make the voyage like stupid sailors picking oakum.[3] The other side of the globe is but the home of our correspondent. Our voyaging is only great-circle sailing,[4] and the doctors prescribe for diseases of the skin merely. One hastens to Southern Africa to chase the giraffe; but surely that is not the game he would be after. How long, pray, would a man hunt giraffes if he could? Snipes and woodcocks also may afford rare sport; but I trust it would be nobler game to shoot one's self.—

> "Direct your eye sight inward, and you'll find
> A thousand regions in your mind
> Yet undiscovered. Travel them, and be
> Expert in home-cosmography."[5]

---

[21] The Sanskrit drama *Sacontalá*, by the fifth-century Hindu writer Cálidás. Thoreau knew this work in a translation by Sir William Jones (1746–1794), a British expert on Sanskrit.

[22] A reminder that Thoreau has shaped the experience of twenty-six months into one year.

[1] At the southernmost tip of South America; its translation from Spanish, "Land of Fire," can be juxtaposed with "the land of infernal fire," below.

[2] Rail at the ship's stern ("taffrail").

[3] Picking old rope apart so that it can be tarred and used for caulking.

[4] Sailing by the most direct route.

[5] From "To My Honoured Friend, Sir Ed. P. Knight," by the English poet William Habington (1605–1664).

What does Africa,—what does the West stand for? Is not our own interior white on the chart?[6] black though it may prove, like the coast, when discovered. Is it the source of the Nile, or the Niger, or the Mississippi, or a North-West Passage around this continent, that we would find? Are these the problems which most concern mankind? Is Franklin[7] the only man who is lost, that his wife should be so earnest to find him? Does Mr. Grinnell[8] know where he himself is? Be rather the Mungo Park, the Lewis and Clarke and Frobisher,[9] of your own streams and oceans; explore your own higher latitudes,—with shiploads of preserved meats to support you, if they be necessary; and pile the empty cans sky-high for a sign.[10] Were preserved meats invented to preserve meat merely? Nay, be a Columbus to whole new continents and worlds within you, opening new channels, not of trade, but of thought. Every man is the lord of a realm beside which the earthly empire of the Czar[11] is but a petty state, a hummock left by the ice. Yet some can be patriotic who have no *self*-respect, and sacrifice the greater to the less. They love the soil which makes their graves, but have no sympathy with the spirit which may still animate their clay. Patriotism is a maggot in their heads. What was the meaning of that South-Sea Exploring Expedition,[12] with all its parade and expense, but an indirect recognition of the fact, that there are continents and seas in the moral world, to which every man is an isthmus or an inlet, yet unexplored by him, but that it is easier to sail many thousand miles through cold and storm and cannibals, in a government ship, with five hundred men and boys to assist one, than it is to explore the private sea, the Atlantic and Pacific Ocean of one's being alone.—

> "Erret, et extremos alter scrutetur Iberos.
> Plus habet hic vitæ, plus habet ille viæ."

> Let them wander and scrutinize the outlandish Australians.
> I have more of God, they more of the road.[13]

It is not worth the while to go round the world to count the cats in Zanzibar.[14] Yet do this even till you can do better, and you may perhaps find some "Symmes' Hole"[15] by which to get at the inside at last. England and France, Spain and Portu-

---

[6] Unexplored.

[7] Sir John Franklin (1786–1847), a British explorer lost while searching for an Arctic passage from the Atlantic to the Pacific.

[8] Henry Grinnell (1799–1874), a whale-oil merchant from New York, who sponsored two attempts to find Franklin.

[9] Mungo Park (1771–1806), a Scottish explorer of Africa and author of *Travels in the Interior Districts of Africa* (1799); Meriwether Lewis (1774–1809) and William Clark (1770–1838), explorers of the American Northwest (1804–1806); Sir Martin Frobisher (1535?–1594), an English explorer of Canada.

[10] One trace of the lost Franklin expedition was a pile of empty cans that had held tinned meat.

[11] During Thoreau's lifetime, czarist Russia was the largest nation in the world.

[12] The American expedition to the Antarctic (1838–1842) led by the naval officer Charles Wilkes (1798–1877).

[13] From the idyll "Old Man of Verona," by the Roman poet Claudian (4th–5th centuries B.C.); Thoreau substitutes "Australians" for "Spaniards," adds the word "outlandish" (perhaps in honor of the Australian outback), and inserts "of God" for "of life."

[14] In his variorum *Walden,* Harding reports that Thoreau had read Charles Pickering's *The Races of Man* (1851), which includes an account of domestic cats in Zanzibar.

[15] In 1818 Captain John Symmes (1780–1829) advanced the theory that the earth is hollow, with openings at the North and South Poles.

gal, Gold Coast and Slave Coast, all front on this private sea; but no bark from them has ventured out of sight of land, though it is without doubt the direct way to India. If you would learn to speak all tongues and conform to the customs of all nations, if you would travel farther than all travellers, be naturalized in all climes, and cause the Sphinx to dash her head against a stone,[16] even obey the precept of the old philosopher, and Explore thyself. Herein are demanded the eye and the nerve. Only the defeated and deserters go to the wars, cowards that run away and enlist. Start now on that farthest western way, which does not pause at the Mississippi or the Pacific, nor conduct toward a worn-out China or Japan, but leads on direct a tangent to this sphere, summer and winter, day and night, sun down, moon down, and at last earth down too.

It is said that Mirabeau[17] took to highway robbery "to ascertain what degree of resolution was necessary in order to place one's self in formal opposition to the most sacred laws of society." He declared that "a soldier who fights in the ranks does not require half so much courage as a foot-pad,"[18]—"that honor and religion have never stood in the way of a well-considered and a firm resolve." This was manly, as the world goes; and yet it was idle, if not desperate. A saner man would have found himself often enough "in formal opposition" to what are deemed "the most sacred laws of society," through obedience to yet more sacred laws, and so have tested his resolution without going out of his way. It is not for a man to put himself in such an attitude to society, but to maintain himself in whatever attitude he find himself through obedience to the laws of his being, which will never be one of opposition to a just government, if he should chance to meet with such.

I left the woods for as good a reason as I went there. Perhaps it seemed to me that I had several more lives to live, and could not spare any more time for that one. It is remarkable how easily and insensibly we fall into a particular route, and make a beaten track for ourselves. I had not lived there a week before my feet wore a path from my door to the pond-side; and though it is five or six years since I trod it, it is still quite distinct. It is true, I fear that others may have fallen into it, and so helped to keep it open. The surface of the earth is soft and impressible by the feet of men; and so with the paths which the mind travels. How worn and dusty, then, must be the highways of the world, how deep the ruts of tradition and conformity! I did not wish to take a cabin passage, but rather to go before the mast on the deck of the world, for there I could best see the moonlight amid the mountains. I do not wish to go below now.

I learned this, at least, by my experiment; that if one advances confidently in the direction of his dreams, and endeavors to live the life which he has imagined, he will meet with a success unexpected in common hours. He will put some things behind, will pass an invisible boundary; new, universal, and more liberal laws will begin to establish themselves around and within him; or the old laws be expanded, and interpreted in his favor in a more liberal sense, and he will live with the license of a higher order of beings. In proportion as he simplifies his life, the laws of the universe will appear less complex, and solitude will not be solitude, nor poverty poverty, nor weakness weakness. If you have built castles in the air, your work need not be lost; that is where they should be. Now put the foundations under them.

[16] The Sphinx killed herself in this way when Oedipus solved her riddle.
[17] Count de Mirabeau (1749–1791), a French statesman; from a passage in *Harper's New Monthly Magazine* in 1850.
[18] A robber.

It is a ridiculous demand which England and America make, that you shall speak so that they can understand you. Neither men nor toad-stools grow so. As if that were important, and there were not enough to understand you without them. As if Nature could support but one order of understandings, could not sustain birds as well as quadrupeds, flying as well as creeping things, and *hush* and *who,* which Bright[19] can understand, were the best English. As if there were safety in stupidity alone. I fear chiefly lest my expression may not be *extra- vagant* enough, may not wander far enough beyond the narrow limits of my daily experience, so as to be adequate to the truth of which I have been convinced. *Extra vagance!* it depends on how you are yarded. The migrating buffalo, which seeks new pastures in another latitude, is not extravagant like the cow which kicks over the pail, leaps the cow-yard fence, and runs after her calf, in milking time. I desire to speak somewhere *without* bounds; like a man in a waking moment, to men in their waking moments; for I am convinced that I cannot exaggerate enough even to lay the foundation of a true expression. Who that has heard a strain of music feared then lest he should speak extravagantly any more forever? In view of the future or possible, we should live quite laxly and undefined in front, our outlines dim and misty on that side; as our shadows reveal an insensible perspiration toward the sun. The volatile truth of our words should continually betray the inadequacy of the residual statement. Their truth is instantly *translated;* its literal monument alone remains. The words which express our faith and piety are not definite; yet they are significant and fragrant like frankincense to superior natures.

Why level downward to our dullest perception always, and praise that as common sense? The commonest sense is the sense of men asleep, which they express by snoring. Sometimes we are inclined to class those who are once-and-a-half witted with the half-witted, because we appreciate only a third part of their wit. Some would find fault with the morning-red, if they ever got up early enough. "They pretend," as I hear, "that the verses of Kabir[20] have four different senses; illusion, spirit, intellect, and the exoteric doctrine of the Vedas;" but in this part of the world it is considered a ground for complaint if a man's writings admit of more than one interpretation. While England endeavors to cure the potato-rot, will not any endeavor to cure the brain-rot, which prevails so much more widely and fatally?

I do not suppose that I have attained to obscurity, but I should be proud if no more fatal fault were found with my pages on this score than was found with the Walden ice. Southern customers objected to its blue color, which is the evidence of its purity, as if it were muddy, and preferred the Cambridge ice, which is white, but tastes of weeds. The purity men love is like the mists which envelop the earth, and not like the azure ether beyond.

Some are dinning in our ears that we Americans, and moderns generally, are intellectual dwarfs compared with the ancients, or even the Elizabethan men. But what is that to the purpose? A living dog is better than a dead lion.[21] Shall a man go and hang himself because he belongs to the race of pygmies, and not be the biggest pygmy that he can? Let every one mind his own business, and endeavor to be what he was made.

---

[19] An ox; *hush* and *who* are commands for "go" and "stop."

[20] A Hindu mystic; the quotation, apparently translated by Thoreau, is from *Histoire de la Littérature Hindoue* (1839), by Garcin de Tassy.

[21] From Ecclesiastes 9:4.

Why should we be in such desperate haste to succeed, and in such desperate enterprises? If a man does not keep pace with his companions, perhaps it is because he hears a different drummer. Let him step to the music which he hears, however measured or far away. It is not important that he should mature as soon as an apple-tree or an oak. Shall he turn his spring into summer? If the condition of things which we were made for is not yet, what were any reality which we can substitute? We will not be shipwrecked on a vain reality. Shall we with pains erect a heaven of blue glass over ourselves, though when it is done we shall be sure to gaze still at the true ethereal heaven far above, as if the former were not?

There was an artist in the city of Kouroo[22] who was disposed to strive after perfection. One day it came into his mind to make a staff. Having considered that in an imperfect work time is an ingredient, but into a perfect work time does not enter, he said to himself, It shall be perfect in all respects, though I should do nothing else in my life. He proceeded instantly to the forest for wood, being resolved that it should not be made of unsuitable material; and as he searched for and rejected stick after stick, his friends gradually deserted him, for they grew old in their works and died, but he grew not older by a moment. His singleness of purpose and resolution, and his elevated piety, endowed him, without his knowledge, with perennial youth. As he made no compromise with Time, Time kept out of his way, and only sighed at a distance because he could not overcome him. Before he had found a stock in all respects suitable the city of Kouroo was a hoary ruin, and he sat on one of its mounds to peel the stick. Before he had given it the proper shape the dynasty of the Candahars was at an end, and with the point of the stick he wrote the name of the last of that race in the sand, and then resumed his work. By the time he had smoothed and polished the staff Kalpa was no longer the pole-star; and ere he had put on the ferrule and the head adorned with precious stones, Brahma had awoke and slumbered many times. But why do I stay to mention these things? When the finishing stroke was put to his work, it suddenly expanded before the eyes of the astonished artist into the fairest of all the creations of Brahma. He had made a new system in making a staff, a world with full and fair proportions; in which, though the old cities and dynasties had passed away, fairer and more glorious ones had taken their places. And now he saw by the heap of shavings still fresh at his feet, that, for him and his work, the former lapse of time had been an illusion, and that no more time had elapsed than is required for a single scintillation from the brain of Brahma to fall on and inflame the tinder of a mortal brain. The material was pure, and his art was pure; how could the result be other than wonderful?

No face which we can give to a matter will stead us so well at last as the truth. This alone wears well. For the most part, we are not where we are, but in a false position. Through an infirmity of our natures, we suppose a case, and put ourselves into it, and hence are in two cases at the same time, and it is doubly difficult to get out. In sane moments we regard only the facts, the case that is. Say what you have to say, not what you ought. Any truth is better than make-believe. Tom Hyde, the tinker,[23] standing on the gallows, was asked if he had any thing to say. "Tell the tailors," said he, "to remember to make a knot in their thread before they take the first stitch." His companion's prayer is forgotten.

However mean your life is, meet it and live it; do not shun it and call it hard

---

[22] Thoreau's own fable, with a message that the true quest for perfection sets time aside and results in a pure creation.

[23] A mender of pots and pans, who is implicitly praised for his matter-of-fact words to the tailors who will sew his shroud.

names. It is not so bad as you are. It looks poorest when you are richest. The fault-finder will find faults even in paradise. Love your life, poor as it is. You may perhaps have some pleasant, thrilling, glorious hours, even in a poor-house. The setting sun is reflected from the windows of the alms-house as brightly as from the rich man's abode; the snow melts before its door as early in the spring. I do not see but a quiet mind may live as contentedly there, and have as cheering thoughts, as in a palace. The town's poor seem to me often to live the most independent lives of any. May be they are simply great enough to receive without misgiving. Most think that they are above being supported by the town; but it oftener happens that they are not above supporting themselves by dishonest means, which should be more disreputable. Cultivate property like a garden herb, like sage. Do not trouble yourself much to get new things, whether clothes or friends. Turn the old; return to them. Things do not change; we change. Sell your clothes and keep your thoughts. God will see that you do not want society. If I were confined to a corner of a garret all my days, like a spider, the world would be just as large to me while I had my thoughts about me. The philosopher said: "From an army of three divisions one can take away its general, and put it in disorder; from the man the most abject and vulgar one cannot take away his thought."[24] Do not seek so anxiously to be developed, to subject yourself to many influences to be played on; it is all dissipation. Humility like darkness reveals the heavenly lights. The shadows of poverty and meanness gather around us, "and lo! creation widens to our view."[25] We are often reminded that if there were bestowed on us the wealth of Crœsus,[26] our aims must still be the same, and our means essentially the same. Moreover, if you are restricted in your range by poverty, if you cannot buy books and newspapers, for instance, you are but confined to the most significant and vital experiences; you are compelled to deal with the material which yields the most sugar and the most starch. It is life near the bone where it is sweetest. You are defended from being a trifler. No man loses ever on a lower level by magnanimity on a higher. Superfluous wealth can buy superfluities only. Money is not required to buy one necessary of the soul.

I live in the angle of a leaden wall, into whose composition was poured a little alloy of bell metal. Often, in the repose of my mid-day, there reaches my ears a confused *tintinnabulum*[27] from without. It is the noise of my contemporaries. My neighbors tell me of their adventures with famous gentlemen and ladies, what notabilities they met at the dinner-table; but I am no more interested in such things than in the contents of the Daily Times. The interest and the conversation are about costume and manners chiefly; but a goose is a goose still, dress it as you will. They tell me of California and Texas, of England and the Indies, of the Hon. Mr. ——————— of Georgia or of Massachusetts, all transient and fleeting phenomena, till I am ready to leap from their court-yard like the Mameluke bey.[28] I delight to come to my bearings,—not walk in procession with pomp and parade, in a conspicuous place, but to walk even with the Builder of the universe, if I may,—not to live in this restless, nervous, bustling, trivial Nineteenth Century, but stand or sit thoughtfully while it goes by. What are men celebrating? They are

---

[24] From the *Analects* (IX.25) of Confucius.

[25] From "Sonnet to Night" (1828), by the British theological writer Joseph Blanco White (1775–1841).

[26] The last King of Lydia, from 560 to 546 B.C., supposedly the richest man on earth.

[27] Tinkling of bells.

[28] One of the Mamelukes, an Egyptian military caste, who escaped a massacre of the entire caste in 1811 by leaping from a wall onto his horse.

all on a committee of arrangements, and hourly expect a speech from somebody. God is only the president of the day, and Webster[29] is his orator. I love to weigh, to settle, to gravitate toward that which most strongly and rightfully attracts me;— not hang by the beam of the scale and try to weigh less,—not suppose a case, but take the case that is; to travel the only path I can, and that on which no power can resist me. It affords me no satisfaction to commence to spring an arch before I have got a solid foundation. Let us not play at kittly-benders.[30] There is a solid bottom every where. We read that the traveller asked the boy if the swamp before him had a hard bottom. The boy replied that it had. But presently the traveller's horse sank in up to the girths, and he observed to the boy, "I thought you said that this bog had a hard bottom." "So it has," answered the latter, "but you have not got half way to it yet." So it is with the bogs and quicksands of society; but he is an old boy that knows it. Only what is thought said or done at a certain rare coincidence is good. I would not be one of those who will foolishly drive a nail into mere lath and plastering; such a deed would keep me awake nights. Give me a hammer, and let me feel for the furring.[31] Do not depend on the putty. Drive a nail home and clinch it so faithfully that you can wake up in the night and think of your work with satisfaction,—a work at which you would not be ashamed to invoke the Muse. So will help you God, and so only. Every nail driven should be as another rivet in the machine of the universe, you carrying on the work.

Rather than love, than money, than fame, give me truth. I sat at a table where were rich food and wine in abundance, and obsequious attendance, but sincerity and truth were not; and I went away hungry from the inhospitable board. The hospitality was as cold as the ices. I thought that there was no need of ice to freeze them. They talked to me of the age of the wine and the fame of the vintage; but I thought of an older, a newer, and purer wine, of a more glorious vintage, which they had not got, and could not buy. The style, the house and grounds and "entertainment" pass for nothing with me. I called on the king, but he made me wait in his hall, and conducted like a man incapacitated for hospitality. There was a man in my neighborhood who lived in a hollow tree. His manners were truly regal. I should have done better had I called on him.

How long shall we sit in our porticoes practising idle and musty virtues, which any work would make impertinent? As if one were to begin the day with long-suffering, and hire a man to hoe his potatoes; and in the afternoon go forth to practise Christian meekness and charity with goodness aforethought! Consider the China pride[32] and stagnant self-complacency of mankind. This generation reclines a little to congratulate itself on being the last of an illustrious line; and in Boston and London and Paris and Rome, thinking of its long descent, it speaks of its progress in art and science and literature with satisfaction. There are the Records of the Philosophical Societies, and the public Eulogies of *Great Men!* It is the good Adam contemplating his own virtue. "Yes, we have done great deeds, and sung divine songs, which shall never die,"—that is, as long as *we* can remember them. The learned societies and great men of Assyria,—where are they? What youthful philosophers and experimentalists we are! There is not one of my readers who has yet lived a whole human life. These may be but the spring months in the life of the race. If we have had the seven-years' itch, we have not seen the seventeen-year locust yet in Concord. We are acquainted with a mere pellicle[33] of the

---

[29] Daniel Webster; the statement is ironic because of Thoreau's dislike for him.
[30] Skating or sliding over thin ice.   [31] Wall studs.
[32] An idea gleaned from China's isolationist position in the nineteenth century.
[33] A thin skin or film.

globe on which we live. Most have not delved six feet beneath the surface, nor leaped as many above it. We know not where we are. Beside, we are sound asleep nearly half our time. Yet we esteem ourselves wise, and have an established order on the surface. Truly, we are deep thinkers, we are ambitious spirits! As I stand over the insect crawling amid the pine needles on the forest floor, and endeavoring to conceal itself from my sight, and ask myself why it will cherish those humble thoughts, and hide its head from me who might perhaps be its benefactor, and impart to its race some cheering information, I am reminded of the greater Benefactor and Intelligence that stands over me the human insect.

There is an incessant influx of novelty into the world, and yet we tolerate incredible dulness. I need only suggest what kind of sermons are still listened to in the most enlightened countries. There are such words as joy and sorrow, but they are only the burden of a psalm, sung with a nasal twang, while we believe in the ordinary and mean. We think that we can change our clothes only. It is said that the British Empire is very large and respectable, and that the United States are a first-rate power. We do not believe that a tide rises and falls behind every man which can float the British Empire like a chip, if he should ever harbor it in his mind. Who knows what sort of seventeen-year locust will next come out of the ground? The government of the world I live in was not framed, like that of Britain, in after-dinner conversations over the wire.

The life in us is like the water in the river. It may rise this year higher than man has ever known it, and flood the parched uplands; even this may be the eventful year, which will drown out all our muskrats. It was not always dry land where we dwell. I see far inland the banks which the stream anciently washed, before science began to record its freshets. Every one has heard the story which has gone the rounds of New England, of a strong and beautiful bug which came out of the dry leaf of an old table of apple-tree wood, which had stood in a farmer's kitchen for sixty years, first in Connecticut, and afterward in Massachusetts,—from an egg deposited in the living tree many years earlier still, as appeared by counting the annual layers beyond it; which was heard gnawing out for several weeks, hatched perchance by the heat of an urn.[34] Who does not feel his faith in a resurrection and immortality strengthened by hearing of this? Who knows what beautiful and winged life, whose egg has been buried for ages under many concentric layers of woodenness in the dead dry life of society, deposited at first in the alburnum[35] of the green and living tree, which has been gradually converted into the semblance of its well-seasoned tomb,—heard perchance gnawing out now for years by the astonished family of man, as they sat round the festive board,—may unexpectedly come forth from amidst society's most trivial and handselled furniture,[36] to enjoy its perfect summer life at last!

I do not say that John or Jonathan[37] will realize all this; but such is the character of that morrow which mere lapse of time can never make to dawn. The light which puts out our eyes is darkness to us. Only that day dawns to which we are awake. There is more day to dawn. The sun is but a morning star.

THE END

1846–1854, 1854

---

[34] The story is related in several places, among them Timothy Dwight's *Travels in New England and New York* (1821).

[35] The young, soft wood of a stem. [36] "Trivial" furniture that has been given away.

[37] John Bull, a common term for a Britisher, or Brother Jonathan, a common term for an American.

SLAVERY IN MASSACHUSETTS*

I lately attended a meeting of the citizens of Concord, expecting, as one among many, to speak on the subject of slavery in Massachusetts; but I was surprised and disappointed to find that what had called my townsmen together was the destiny of Nebraska,[1] and not of Massachusetts, and that what I had to say would be entirely out of order. I had thought that the house was on fire, and not the prairie; but though several of the citizens of Massachusetts are now in prison for attempting to rescue a slave from her own clutches,[2] not one of the speakers at that meeting expressed regret for it, not one even referred to it. It was only the disposition of some wild lands a thousand miles off, which appeared to concern them. The inhabitants of Concord are not prepared to stand by one of their own bridges,[3] but talk only of taking up a position on the highlands beyond the Yellowstone river. Our Buttricks, and Davises, and Hosmers are retreating thither, and I fear that they will have no Lexington Common between them and the enemy. There is not one slave in Nebraska; there are perhaps a million slaves in Massachusetts.

They who have been bred in the school of politics fail now and always to face the facts. Their measures are half measures and make-shifts, merely. They put off the day of settlement indefinitely, and meanwhile, the debt accumulates. Though the Fugitive Slave Law had not been the subject of discussion on that occasion, it was at length faintly resolved by my townsmen, at an adjourned meeting, as I learn, that the compromise compact of 1820[4] having been repudiated by one of the parties, "Therefore, . . . the Fugitive Slave Law must be repealed." But this is not the reason why an iniquitous law should be repealed. The fact which the politician faces is merely, that there is less honor among thieves than was supposed, and not the fact that they are thieves.

As I had no opportunity to express my thoughts at that meeting, will you allow me to do so here?

Again[5] it happens that the Boston Court House is full of armed men, holding prisoner and trying a MAN, to find out if he is not really a SLAVE. Does any one think that Justice or God awaits Mr. Loring's[6] decision? For him to sit there deciding still, when this question is already decided from eternity to eternity, and the unlettered slave himself, and the multitude around, have long since heard and

---

* First printed in *The Liberator,* a weekly paper edited by the abolitionist William Lloyd Garrison (1805–1879), on July 21, 1854. Parts of the essay were delivered on July 4, 1854, at an antislavery celebration in Framingham, Massachusetts, during which Garrison burned a copy of the Constitution because it did not prohibit slavery.

[1] Thoreau was angered at the passage of the 1854 Kansas-Nebraska Act, which substituted the policy of "squatter sovereignty" (allowing voters to bring slavery to their states) for earlier provisions barring slavery from the new territories; he was even more incensed at the Massachusetts citizens who transferred their concerns to the West and ignored injustice at home.

[2] On May 25, 1854, nine men were arrested in Boston for attempting to free Anthony Burns, a runaway slave held under the Fugitive Slave Law for return to his master in Virginia.

[3] Thoreau contrasts the present-day inhabitants of Concord with those who fought bravely in the Battle of Concord at the outset of the Revolutionary War in 1775. Buttrick took part in that battle; Davis and Hosmer were killed.

[4] The Missouri Compromise; by its terms, Maine was admitted to the Union as a free state and Missouri as a slave state, and slavery was prohibited in any new states north of 36°30′ N. The Kansas-Nebraska Act of 1854 repealed the Missouri Compromise.

[5] A similar case in 1851 had resulted in the return of the escaped slave Thomas Simms to Georgia under the Fugitive Slave Act.

[6] Judge Edward G. Loring, whose ruling under the Fugitive Slave Act remanded Anthony Burns to Virginia.

assented to the decision, is simply to make himself ridiculous. We may be tempted to ask from whom he received his commission, and who he is that received it; what novel statutes he obeys, and what precedents are to him of authority. Such an arbiter's very existence is an impertinence. We do not ask him to make up his mind, but to make up his pack.

I listen to hear the voice of a Governor, Commander-in-Chief of the forces of Massachusetts. I hear only the creaking of crickets and the hum of insects which now fill the summer air. The Governor's exploit is to review the troops on muster days. I have seen him on horseback, with his hat off, listening to a chaplain's prayer. It chances that is all I have ever seen of a Governor. I think that I could manage to get along without one. If *he* is not of the least use to prevent my being kidnapped, pray of what important use is he likely to be to me? When freedom is most endangered, he dwells in the deepest obscurity. A distinguished clergyman told me that he chose the profession of a clergyman, because it afforded the most leisure for literary pursuits. I would recommend to him the profession of a Governor.

Three years ago, also, when the Simm's tragedy was acted, I said to myself, there is such an officer, if not such a man, as the Governor of Massachusetts,— what has he been about the last fortnight? Has he had as much as he could to do keep on the fence during this moral earthquake? It seemed to me that no keener satire could have been aimed at, no more cutting insult have been offered to that man, than just what happened—the absence of all inquiry after him in that crisis. The worst and the most I chance to know of him is, that he did not improve that opportunity to make himself known, and worthily known. He could at least have *resigned* himself into fame. It appeared to be forgotten that there was such a man, or such an office. Yet no doubt he was endeavoring to fill the gubernatorial chair all the while. He was no Governor of mine. He did not govern me.

But at last, in the present case, the Governor was heard from. After he and the United States Government had perfectly succeeded in robbing a poor innocent black man of his liberty for life, and, as far as they could, of his Creator's likeness in his breast, he made a speech to his accomplices, at a congratulatory supper!

I have read a recent law of this State, making it penal for "any officer of the Commonwealth" to "detain, or aid in the . . . detention," any where within its limits, "of any person, for the reason that he is claimed as a fugitive slave."[7] Also, it was a matter of notoriety that a writ of replevin[8] to take the fugitive out of the custody of the United States Marshal could not be served, for want of sufficient force to aid the officer.

I had thought that the Governor was in some sense the executive officer of the State; that it was his business, as a Governor, to see that the laws of the State were executed; while, as a man, he took care that he did not, by so doing, break the laws of humanity; but when there is any special important use for him, he is useless, or worse than useless, and permits the laws of the State to go unexecuted. Perhaps I do not know what are the duties of a Governor; but if to be a Governor requires to subject one's self to so much ignominy without remedy, if it is to put a restraint upon my manhood, I shall take care never to be Governor of Massachusetts. I have not read far in the statutes of this Commonwealth. It is not profitable reading. They do not always say what is true; and they do not always mean what

---

[7] Massachusetts enacted (unidentified) legislation nullifying the Fugitive Slave Law in that state, but the next paragraph makes clear that this legislation was not enforced.

[8] The writ by which property (here, a slave) is recovered.

they say. What I am concerned to know is, that that man's influence and authority were on the side of the slaveholder, and not of the slave—of the guilty, and not of the innocent—of injustice, and not of justice. I never saw him of whom I speak; indeed, I did not know that he was Governor until this event occurred. I heard of him and Anthony Burns at the same time, and thus, undoubtedly, most will hear of him. So far am I from being governed by him. I do not mean that it was any thing to his discredit that I had not heard of him, only that I heard what I did. The worst I shall say of him is, that he proved no better than the majority of his constituents would be likely to prove. In my opinion, he was not equal to the occasion.

The whole military force of the State is at the service of a Mr. Suttle,[9] a slaveholder from Virginia, to enable him to catch a man whom he calls his property; but not a soldier is offered to save a citizen of Massachusetts from being kidnapped! Is this what all these soldiers, all this *training* has been for these seventy-nine years past?[10] Have they been trained merely to rob Mexico, and carry back fugitive slaves to their masters?

These very nights, I heard the sound of a drum in our streets. There were men *training* still; and for what? I could with an effort pardon the cockerels of Concord for crowing still, for they, perchance, had not been beaten that morning; but I could not excuse this rub-a-dub of the "trainers."[11] The slave was carried back by exactly such as these, i.e., by the soldier, of whom the best you can say in this connection is, that he is a fool made conspicuous by a painted coat.

Three years ago, also, just a week after the authorities of Boston assembled to carry back a perfectly innocent man, and one whom they knew to be innocent, into slavery, the inhabitants of Concord caused the bells to be rung and the cannons to be fired, to celebrate their liberty—and the courage and love of liberty of their ancestors who fought at the bridge.[12] As if *those* three millions had fought for the right to be free themselves, but to hold in slavery three million others. Now-a-days, men wear a fool's cap, and call it a liberty cap.[13] I do not know but there are some, who, if they were tied to a whipping-post, and could but get one hand free, would use it to ring the bells and fire the cannons, to celebrate *their* liberty. So some of my townsmen took the liberty to ring and fire; that was the extent of their freedom; and when the sound of the bells died away, their liberty died away also; when the powder was all expended, their liberty went off with the smoke.

The joke could be no broader, if the inmates of the prisons were to subscribe for all the powder to be used in such salutes, and hire the jailers to do the firing and ringing for them, while they enjoyed it through the grating.

This is what I thought about my neighbors.

Every humane and intelligent inhabitant of Concord, when he or she heard those bells and those cannons, thought not with pride of the events of the 19th of

---

[9] The legal owner of Anthony Burns.

[10] The years since 1775, when Revolutionary War soldiers fought in the patriotic Battles of Concord and Lexington.

[11] The young roosters of Concord can be pardoned for crowing because they have not been drummed to order (beaten down by regimen); but the drumlike clamor ("rub-a-dub") of the soldiers ("'trainers'") is inexcusable.

[12] Another reference to the case of Thomas Simms; ironically, the citizens of Concord celebrated Independence Day, July 4th, one week later and included a tribute to their ancestors who fought for liberty at the Battle of Concord.

[13] The close-fitting cap first worn by slaves freed by the Romans, later adopted by partisans of the American and French Revolutions.

April, 1775, but with shame of the events of the 12th of April, 1851.[14] But now we have half buried that old shame under a new one.

Massachusetts sat waiting Mr. Loring's decision, as if it could in any way affect her own criminality. Her crime, the most conspicuous and fatal crime of all, was permitting him to be the umpire in such a case. It was really the trial of Massachusetts. Every moment that she hesitated to set this man free—every moment that she now hesitates to atone for her crime, she is convicted. The Commissioner on her case is God; not Edward G. God, but simple God.

I wish my countrymen to consider, that whatever the human law may be, neither an individual nor a nation can ever commit the least act of injustice against the obscurest individual, without having to pay the penalty for it. A government which deliberately enacts injustice, and persists in it, will at length ever become the laughing-stock of the world.

Much has been said about American slavery, but I think that we do not even yet realize what slavery is. If I were seriously to propose to Congress to make mankind into sausages, I have no doubt that most of the members would smile at my proposition, and if any believed me to be in earnest, they would think that I proposed something much worse than Congress had ever done. But if any of them will tell me that to make a man into a sausage would be much worse,—would be any worse, than to make him into a slave,—than it was to enact the Fugitive Slave Law, I will accuse him of foolishness, of intellectual incapacity, of making a distinction without a difference. The one is just as sensible a proposition as the other.

I hear a good deal said about trampling this law under foot. Why, one need not go out of his way to do that. This law rises not to the level of the head or the reason; its natural habitat is in the dirt. It was born and bred, and has its life only in the dust and mire, on a level with the feet, and he who walks with freedom, and does not with Hindoo mercy avoid treading on every venomous reptile, will inevitably tread on it, and so trample it under foot,—and Webster,[15] its maker, with it, like the dirt-bug and its ball.

Recent events will be valuable as a criticism on the administration of justice in our midst, or, rather, as showing what are the true resources of justice in any community. It has come to this, that the friends of liberty, the friends of the slave, have shuddered when they have understood that his fate was left to the legal tribunals of the country to be decided. Free men have no faith that justice will be awarded in such a case; the judge may decide this way or that; it is a kind of accident, at best. It is evident that he is not a competent authority in so important a case. It is no time, then, to be judging according to his precedents, but to establish a precedent for the future. I would much rather trust to the sentiment of the people. In their vote, you would get something of some value, at least, however small; but, in the other case, only the trammelled judgment of an individual, of no significance, be it which way it might.

It is to some extent fatal to the courts, when the people are compelled to go behind them. I do not wish to believe that the courts were made for fair weather, and for very civil cases merely,—but think of leaving it to any court in the land to

---

[14] Before dawn that morning nearly three hundred armed men put Simms on a ship that sailed for the South.

[15] Daniel Webster (1782–1852), a U.S. senator from Massachusetts, whose support of the Compromise of 1850, with its acceptance of the Fugitive Slave Law, angered many voters and diminished his political influence. A dirt-bug is a beetle that forms masses of dung in which it lays its eggs.

decide whether more than three millions of people, in this case, a sixth part of a nation, have a right to be freemen or not! But it has been left to the courts of *justice,* so-called—to the Supreme Court of the land—and, as you all know, recognizing no authority but the Constitution, it has decided that the three millions are, and shall continue to be, slaves. Such judges as these are merely the inspectors of a pick-lock and murderer's tools, to tell him whether they are in working order or not, and there they think that their responsibility ends. There was a prior case on the docket, which they, as judges appointed by God, had no right to skip; which having been justly settled, they would have been saved from this humiliation. It was the case of the murderer himself.

The law will never make men free; it is men who have got to make the law free. They are the lovers of law and order, who observe the law when the government breaks it.

Among human beings, the judge whose words seal the fate of a man furthest into eternity, is not he who merely pronounces the verdict of the law, but he, whoever he may be, who, from a love of truth, and unprejudiced by any custom or enactment of men, utters a true opinion or *sentence* concerning him. He it is that *sentences* him. Whoever has discerned truth, has received his commission from a higher source than the chiefest justice in the world, who can discern only law. He finds himself constituted judge of the judge.—Strange that it should be necessary to state such simple truths.

I am more and more convinced that, with reference to any public question, it is more important to know what the country thinks of it, than what the city thinks. The city does not *think* much. On any moral question, I would rather have the opinion of Boxboro[16] than of Boston and New York put together. When the former speaks, I feel as if somebody *had* spoken, as if *humanity* was yet, and a reasonable being had asserted its rights,—as if some unprejudiced men among the country's hills had at length turned their attention to the subject, and by a few sensible words redeemed the reputation of the race. When, in some obscure country town, the farmers come together to a special town meeting, to express their opinion on some subject which is vexing the land, that, I think, is the true Congress, and the most respectable one that is ever assembled in the United States.

It is evident that there are, in this Commonwealth, at least, two parties, becoming more and more distinct—the party of the city, and the party of the country. I know that the country is mean enough, but I am glad to believe that there is a slight difference in her favor. But as yet, she has few, if any organs, through which to express herself. The editorials which she reads, like the news, come from the sea-board. Let us, the inhabitants of the country, cultivate self-respect. Let us now send to the city for aught more essential than our broadcloths and groceries, or, if we read the opinions of the city, let us entertain opinions of our own.

Among measures to be adopted, I would suggest to make as earnest and vigorous an assault on the Press as has already been made, and with effect, on the Church. The Church has much improved within a few years; but the Press is almost, without exception, corrupt. I believe that, in this country, the press exerts a greater and a more pernicious influence than the Church did in its worst period. We are not a religious people, but we are a nation of politicians. We do not care for the Bible, but we do care for the newspaper. At any meeting of politicians,—

---

[16] Thoreau's name for a typical small town.

like that at Concord the other evening, for instance,—how impertinent it would be to quote from the Bible! how pertinent to quote from a newspaper or from the Constitution! The newspaper is a Bible which we read every morning and every afternoon, standing and sitting, riding and walking. It is a Bible which every man carries in his pocket, which lies on every table and counter, and which the mail, and thousands of missionaries, are continually dispensing. It is, in short, the only book which America has printed, and which America reads. So wide is its influence. The editor is a preacher whom you voluntarily support. Your tax is commonly once cent daily, and it costs nothing for pew hire.[17] But how many of these preachers preach the truth? I repeat the testimony of many an intelligent foreigner, as well as my own convictions, when I say, that probably no country was ever ruled by so mean a class of tyrants as, with a few noble exceptions, are the editors of the periodical press in *this* country. And as they live and rule only by their servility, and appealing to the worst, and not the better nature of man, the people who read them are in the condition of the dog that returns to his vomit.

The *Liberator* and the *Commonwealth*[18] were the only papers in Boston, as far as I know, which made themselves heard in condemnation of the cowardice and meanness of the authorities of that city, as exhibited in '51. The other journals, almost without exception, by their manner of referring to and speaking of the Fugitive Slave Law, and the carrying back of the slave Simms, insulted the common sense of the country, at least. And, for the most part, they did this, one would say, because they thought so to secure the approbation of their patrons, not being aware that a sounder sentiment prevailed to any extent in the heart of the Commonwealth. I am told that some of them have improved of late; but they are still eminently time-serving. Such is the character they have won.

But, thank fortune, this preacher can be even more easily reached by the weapons of the reformer than could the recreant priest. The free men of New England have only to refrain from purchasing and reading these sheets, have only to withhold their cents, to kill a score of them at once. One whom I respect told me that he purchased Mitchell's *Citizen* in the cars,[19] and then threw it out the window. But would not his contempt have been more fatally expressed, if he had not bought it?

Are they Americans? are they New Englanders? are they inhabitants of Lexington, and Concord, and Framingham, who read and support the Boston *Post, Mail, Journal, Advertiser, Courier,* and *Times?*[20] Are these the Flags of our Union? I am not a newspaper reader, and may omit to name the worst.

Could slavery suggest a more complete servility than some of these journals exhibit? Is there any dust which their conduct does not lick, and make fouler still with its slime? I do not know whether the Boston *Herald* is still in existence, but I remember to have seen it about the streets when Simms was carried off. Did it not act its part well—serve its master faithfully? How could it have gone lower on its belly? How can a man stoop lower than he is low? do more than put his extremities in the place of the head he has? than make his head his lower extremity? When I have taken up this paper with my cuffs turned up, I have heard the gurgling of

[17] An annual fee for an assigned church pew.

[18] Along with Garrison's *Liberator*, the Boston *Commonwealth*, edited by the teacher and biographer Franklin Benjamin Sanborn (1831–1917) was a staunch abolitionist paper.

[19] Bought a copy of this Boston newspaper on the train.

[20] New England newspapers that were conservative in policy; the nationally prominent *Daily Advertiser*, for example, was identified with the monied interests.

the sewer through every column. I have felt that I was handling a paper picked out of the public gutters, a lead from the gospel of the gambling-house, the groggery and the brothel, harmonizing with the gospel of the Merchants' Exchange.[21]

The majority of the men of the North, and of the South, and East, and West, are not men of principle. If they vote, they do not send men to Congress on errands of humanity, but while their brothers and sisters are being scourged and hung for loving liberty, while———I might here insert all that slavery implies and is,———it is the mismanagement of wood and iron and stone and gold which concerns them. Do what you will, O Government! with my wife and children, my mother and brother, my father and sister, I will obey your commands to the letter. It will indeed grieve me if you hurt them, if you deliver them to overseers to be hunted by hounds or to be whipped to death; but nevertheless, I will preaceably pursue my chosen calling on this fair earth, until perchance, one day, when I have put on mourning for them dead, I shall have persuaded you to relent. Such is the attitude, such are the words of Massachusetts.

Rather than do thus, I need not say what match I would touch, what system endeavor to blow up,—but as I love my life, I would side with the light, and let the dark earth roll from under me, calling my mother and my brother to follow.

I would remind my countrymen, that they are to be men first, and Americans only at a late and convenient hour. No matter how valuable law may be to protect your property, even to keep soul and body together, if it do not keep you and humanity together.

I am sorry to say, that I doubt if there is a judge in Massachusetts who is prepared to resign his office, and get his living innocently, whenever it is required of him to pass sentence under a law which is merely contrary to the law of God. I am compelled to see that they put themselves, or rather, are by character, in this respect, exactly on a level with the marine who discharges his musket in any direction he is ordered to. They are just as much tools and as little men. Certainly, they are not the more to be respected, because their master enslaves their understandings and consciences, instead of their bodies.

The judges and lawyers,—simply as such, I mean,—and all men of expediency, try this case by a very low and incompetent standard. They consider, not whether the Fugitive Slave Law is right, but whether it is what they call *constitutional*. Is virtue constitutional, or vice? Is equity constitutional, or iniquity? In important moral and vital questions like this, it is just as impertinent to ask whether a law is constitutional or not, as to ask whether it is profitable or not. They persist in being the servants of the worst of men, and not the servants of humanity. The question is not whether you or your grandfather, seventy years ago, did not enter into an agreement to serve the devil, and that service is not accordingly now due; but whether you will not now, for once and at last, serve God,—in spite of your own past recreancy, or that of your ancestor,—by obeying that eternal and only just CONSTITUTION, which He, and not any Jefferson or Adams, has written in your being.[22]

The amount of it[23] is, if the majority vote the devil to be God, the minority will

---

[21] The financial center.

[22] The law of conscience, God's law, is deeper and more primary than the traditions of such great statesmen as Thomas Jefferson, third U.S. president (1801–1809), and John Adams, second U.S. president (1797–1801).

[23] What it all adds up to.

live and behave accordingly, and obey the successful candidate, trusting that some time or other, by some Speaker's casting vote, perhaps, they may reinstate God. This is the highest principle I can get out of or invent for my neighbors. These men act as if they believed that they could safely slide down hill a little way—or a good way—and would surely come to a place, by and by, where they could begin to slide up again. This is expediency, or choosing that course which offer the slightest obstacles to the feet, that is, a down-hill one. But there is no such thing as accomplishing a righteous reform by the use of "expediency." There is no such thing as sliding up hill. In morals, the only sliders are backsliders.

Thus we steadily worship Mammon,[24] both School, and State, and Church, and the Seventh Day curse God with a tintamar[25] from one end of the Union to the other.

Will mankind never learn that policy is not morality—that it never secures any moral right, but considers merely what is expedient? chooses the available candidate, who is invariably the devil,—and what right have his constituents to be surprised, because the devil does not behave like an angel of light? What is wanted is men, not of policy, but of probity—who recognize a higher law than the Constitution, or the decision of the majority. The fate of the country does not depend on how you vote at the polls—the worst man is as strong as the best at that game; it does not depend on what kind of paper you drop into the ballot-box once a year, but on what kind of man you drop from your chamber into the street every morning.

What should concern Massachusetts is not the Nebraska Bill, nor the Fugitive Slave Bill, but her own slaveholding and servility. Let the State dissolve her union with the slaveholder. She may wriggle and hesitate, and ask leave to read the Constitution once more; but she can find no respectable law or precedent which sanctions the continuance of such a Union for an instant.

Let each inhabitant of the State dissolve his union with her, as long as she delays to do her duty.

The events of the past month teach me to distrust Fame. I see that she does not finely discriminate, but coarsely hurrahs. She considers not the simple heroism of an action, but only as it is connected with its apparent consequences. She praises till she is hoarse the easy exploit of the Boston tea party,[26] but will be comparatively silent about the braver and more disinterestedly heroic attack on the Boston Court-House, simply because it was unsuccessful!

Covered with disgrace, the State has sat down cooly to try for their lives and liberties the men who attempted to do its duty for it. And this is called *justice!* They who have shown that they can behave particularly well may perchance be put under bonds for *their good behavior*. They whom truth requires at present to plead guilty, are of all the inhabitants of the State, pre-eminently innocent. While the Governor, and the Mayor, and countless officers of the Commonwealth, are at large, the champions of liberty are imprisoned.

Only they are guiltless, who commit the crime of contempt of such a Court. It behoves every man to see that his influence is on the side of justice, and let the courts make their own characters. My sympathies in this case are wholly with the

[24] One of the fallen angels in John Milton's *Paradise Lost* (1667); here, our own material interests.

[25] A ringing of bells. The ironic logic of the passage is that if materialism pervades our lives, we cannot praise God on Sunday.

[26] The famous dumping of tea into Boston harbor in 1773 as a protest against British taxes.

accused, and wholly against the accusers and their judges. Justice is sweet and musical; but injustice is harsh and discordant. The judge still sits grinding at his organ, but it yields no music, and we hear only the sound of the handle, and the crowd toss him their coppers the same as before.

Do you suppose that that Massachusetts which is now doing these things,—which hesitates to crown these men, some of whose lawyers, and even judges, perchance, may be driven to take refuge in some poor quibble, that they may not wholly outrage their instinctive sense of justice,—do you suppose that she is any thing but base and servile? that she is the champion of liberty?

Show me a free State, and a court truly of justice, and I will fight for them, if need be; but show me Massachusetts, and I refuse her my allegiance, and express contempt for her courts.

The effect of a good government is to make life more valuable,—of a bad one, to make it less valuable. We can afford that railroad, and all merely material stock, should lose some of its value, for that only compels us to live more simply and economically; but suppose that the value of life itself should be diminished! How can we make a less demand on man and nature, how live more economically in respect to virtue and all noble qualities, than we do? I have lived for the last month,—and I think that every man in Massachusetts capable of the sentiment of patriotism must have had a similar experience,—with the sense of having suffered a vast and indefinite loss. I did not know at first what ailed me. At last it occurred to me that what I had lost was a country. I had never respected the Government near to which I had lived, but I had foolishly thought that I might manage to live here, minding my private affairs, and forget it. For my part, my old and worthiest pursuits have lost I cannot say how much of their attraction, and I feel that my investment in life here is worth many per cent. less since Massachusetts last deliberately sent back an innocent man, Anthony Burns, to slavery. I dwelt before, perhaps, in the illusion that my life passed somewhere only *between* heaven and hell, but now I cannot persuade myself that I do not dwell *wholly within* hell. The site of that political organization called Massachusetts is to me morally covered with volcanic scoriæ[27] and cinders, such as Milton describes in the infernal regions. If there is any hell more unprincipled than our rulers, and we, the ruled, I feel curious to see it. Life itself being worth less, all things with it, which minister to it, are worth less. Suppose you have a small library, with pictures to adorn the walls—a garden laid out around—and contemplate scientific and literary pursuits, etc., and discover all at once that your villa, with all its contents, is located in hell, and that the justice of the peace has a cloven foot and a forked tail[28]—do not these things suddenly lose their value in your eyes?

I feel that, to some extent, the State has fatally interfered with my lawful business. It has not only interrupted me in my passage through Court street on errands of trade, but it has interrupted me and every man on his onward and upward path, on which he had trusted soon to leave Court street far behind. What right had it to remind me of Court street? I have found that hollow which even I had relied on for solid.

I am surprised to see men going about their business as if nothing had hap-

---

[27] Lava; in Book I of Milton's *Paradise Lost,* Satan and the fallen angels lie on the burning lake of Hell.
[28] Conventional tokens of Satan.

pened. I say to myself—Unfortunates! they have not heard the news. I am surprised that the man whom I just met on horseback should be so earnest to overtake his newly-bought cows running away—since all property is insecure—and if they do not run away again, they may be taken away from him when he gets them. Fool! does he not know that his seed-corn is worth less this year—that all beneficent harvests fail as you approach the empire of hell? No prudent man will build a stone house under these circumstances, or engage in any peaceful enterprise which it requires a long time to accomplish. Art is as long as ever, but life is more interrupted and less available for a man's proper pursuits. It is not an era of repose. We have used up all our inherited freedom. If we would save our lives, we must fight for them.

I walk toward one of our ponds, but what signifies the beauty of nature when men are base? We walk to lakes to see our serenity reflected in them; when we are not serene, we go not to them. Who can be serene in a country where both the rulers and the ruled are without principle? The remembrance of my country spoils my walk. My thoughts are murder to the State, and involuntarily go plotting against her.

But it chanced the other day that I scented a white water-lily, and a season I had waited for had arrived. It is the emblem of purity. It bursts up so pure and fair to the eye, and so sweet to the scent, as if to show us that purity and sweetness reside in, and can be extracted from, the slime and muck of earth. I think I have plucked the first one that has opened for a mile. What confirmation of our hopes is in the fragrance of this flower! I shall not so soon despair of the world for it, notwithstanding slavery, and the cowardice and want of principle of Northern men. It suggests what kind of laws have prevailed longest and widest, and still prevail, and that the time may come when man's deeds will smell as sweet. Such is the odor which the plant emits. If Nature can compound this fragrance still annually, I shall believe her still young and full of vigor, her integrity and genius unimpaired, and that there is virtue even in man, too, who is fitted to perceive and love it. It reminds me that Nature has been partner to no Missouri Compromise. I scent no compromise in the fragrance of the water-lily. It is not a *Nymphœa Douglassii.*[29] In it, the sweet, and pure, and innocent, are wholly sundered from the obscene and baleful. I do not scent in this the time-serving irresolution of a Massachusetts Governor, nor of a Boston Mayor. So behave that the odor of your actions may enhance the general sweetness of the atmosphere, that when we behold or scent a flower, we may not be reminded how inconsistent your deeds are with it; for all odor is but one form of advertisement of a moral quality, and if fair actions had not been performed, the lily would not smell sweet. The foul slime stands for the sloth and vice of man, the decay of humanity; the fragrant flower that springs from it, for the purity and courage which are immortal.

Slavery and servility have produced no sweet-scented flower annually, to charm the senses of men, for they have no real life: they are merely a decaying and a death, offensive to all healthy nostrils. We do not complain that they *live,* but that they do not *get buried.* Let the living bury them; even they are good for manure.

1854

[29] A pun on the name of Stephen A. Douglas (1813–1861), the senator from Illinois who incorporated "squatter sovereignty" into the Compromise of 1850 and the Kansas-Nebraska Act in 1854.

from   JOURNAL*

[*Purpose of the Journal: February 8, 1841*]

My Journal is that of me which would else spill over and run to waste.—gleanings from the field which in action I reap. I must not live for it, but in it for the gods— They are my correspondent to whom daily I send off this sheet post-paid. I am clerk in their counting room and at evening transfer the account from day-book to ledger.

It is as a leaf which hangs over my head in the path—I bend the twig and write my prayers on it then letting it go the bough springs up and shows the scrawl to heaven. As if it were not kept shut in my desk—but were as public a leaf as any in nature—it is papyrus by the river side—it is vellum in the pastures—it is parchment on the hills—I find it every where as free as the leaves which troop along the lanes in autumn—The crow—the goose—the eagle—carry my quill—and the wind blows the leaves—as far as I go—Or if my imagination does not soar, but gropes in slime and mud—then I write with a reed.

[*The Beginning at Walden: July 5, 1845*]

Walden Sat. July 5th–45

Yesterday I came here to live.[1] My house makes me think of some mountain houses I have seen, which seemed to have a fresher auroral atmosphere about them as I fancy of the halls of Olympus.[2] I lodged at the house of a saw-miller last summer, on the Caatskills mountains,[3] high up as Pine orchard in the blue-berry & raspberry region, where the quiet and cleanliness & coolness seemed to be all one, which had this ambrosial character. He was the miller of the Kaaterskill Falls,[4] They were a clean & wholesome family inside and out—like their house. The latter was not plastered—only lathed and the inner doors were not hung. The house seemed high placed, airy, and perfumed, fit to entertain a travelling God. It was so high indeed that all the music, the broken strains, the waifs & accompaniments of tunes, that swept over the ridge of the Caatskills, passed through its aisles. Could not man be man in such an abode? And would he ever find out this grovelling life?

It was the very light & atmosphere in which the works of Grecian art were composed, and in which they rest. They have appropriated to themselves a loftier hall than mortals ever occupy, at least on a level with the mountain brows of the world.

There was wanting a little of the glare of the lower vales and in its place a pure twilight as became the precincts of heaven Yet so equable and calm was the sea-

---

* Thoreau's massive journal has only begun to be studied in ways that will yield a sense of its contours and evolutionary relevance to his life. Begun in 1837 and kept until his death in 1862, the journal (amounting to more than 2 million words) is the record of Thoreau's imaginative, spiritual, and day-to-day observations about the world in which he lived and the world which he strove to create. Many of his lectures and essays came from passages in the journal, as did numerous passages in *A Week on the Concord and Merrimack Rivers* (1849) and *Walden* (1854).

[1] Thoreau moved into his cabin at Walden Pond on July 4, 1845.

[2] According to Greek myth, the summit of Mt. Olympus was the abode of the gods.

[3] The Catskill Mountains, part of the Appalachian system in New York state.   [4] In the Catskills.

son there that you could not tell whether it was morning or noon or evening.
Always there was the sound of the morning cricket

[*Emancipation of the Mind: July 6, 1845*]

July 6th
I wish to meet the facts of life—the vital facts, which where the phenomena or
actuality the Gods meant to show us,—face to face, And so I came down here.[5]
Life! who knows what it is—what it does? If I am not quite right here I am less
wrong than before—and now let us see what they will have. The preacher, instead
of vexing the ears of drowsy farmers on their day of rest, at the end of the week,
(for sunday always seemed to me like a fit conclusion of an ill spent week and not
the fresh and brave beginning of a new one) with this one other draggletail and
postponed affair of a sermon, from thirdly to 15thly, should teach them with a
thundering voice—pause & simplicity.
    stop—Avast—Why so fast? In all studies we go not forward but rather back-
ward with redoubled pauses, we always study *antiques*—with silence and *reflection*. Even time has a depth, and below its surface the waves do not lapse and roar.
I wonder men can be so frivolous almost as to attend to the gross form of negro
slavery—there are so many keen and subtle masters, who subject us both.[6] Self-
emancipation[7] in the West Indies of a man's thinking and imagining provinces,
which should be more than his island territory One emancipated heart & intellect—It would knock off the fetters from a million slaves.

[*On Emerson: Winter 1845–1846*]

Emerson again is a critic poet philosopher—with talent not so conspicuous—not
so adequate to his task——Lives a far more intense life—seeks to realize a divine
life—his affections and intellect equally developed.—has advanced farther and a
new heaven opens to him—Love & Friendship—Religion—Poetry—The Holy
are familiar to him The life of an Artist—move variegated—more observing—
finer perception—not so robust—elastic—practical enough in his own field—
faithful—a judge of men
    There is no such general critic of men & things—no such trustworthy & faith-
ful man.—More of the divine realized in him than in any.
    A poetic-critic—reserving the unqualified nouns for the gods

* * *

Emerson has special talents unequalled—The divine in man has had no more
easy methodically distinct expression.
    His personal influence upon young persons greater than any man's
    In his world every man would be a poet—Love would reign—Beauty would
take place—Man & nature would harmonize—

---

[5] To Walden.
    [6] How can anyone take part in the "gross" institution of slavery when all human beings are slaves to
"subtle" masters as a part of life?
    [7] True self-emancipation would precipitate a general emancipation.

[*The Fugitive Slave Law: April 1851*]

In '75 two or three hundred of the inhabitants of Concord[8] assembled at one of the bridges with arms in their hands to assert the right of three millions to tax themselves, to have a voice in governing themselves. About a week ago the authorities of Boston, having the sympathy of many of the inhabitants of Concord, assembled in the gray of the dawn, assisted by a still larger armed force, to send back a perfectly innocent man, and one whom they knew to be innocent, into a slavery as complete as the world ever knew.[9] Of course it makes not the least difference—I wish you to consider this—who the man was,—whether he was Jesus Christ or another,—for inasmuch as ye did it unto the least of these his brethren ye did it unto him.[10] Do you think *he* would have stayed here in liberty and let the black man go into slavery in his stead? They sent him back, I say, to live in slavery with other three millions—mark that—whom the same slave power, or slavish power, North and South, holds in that condition,—three millions who do not, like the first mentioned, assert the right to govern themselves but simply to run away and stay away from their prison.

Just a week afterward, those inhabitants of this town who especially sympathize with the authorities of Boston in this their deed caused the bells to be rung and the cannon to be fired to celebrate the courage and the love of liberty of those men who assembled at the bridge. As if *those* three millions had fought for the right to be free themselves, but to hold in slavery three million others. Why, gentlemen,[11] even consistency, though it is much abused, is sometimes a virtue. Every humane and intelligent inhabitant of Concord, when he or she heard those bells and those cannon, thought not so much of the events of the 19th of April, 1775, as of the event of the 12th of April, 1851.

I wish my townsmen to consider that, whatever the human law may be, neither an individual nor a nation can ever deliberately commit the least act of injustice without having to pay the penalty for it. A government which deliberately enacts injustice, and persists in it!—it will become the laughing-stock of the world.

Much as has been said about American slavery, I think that commonly we do not yet realize what slavery is. If I were seriously to propose to Congress to make mankind into sausages, I have no doubt that most would smile at my proposition and, if any believed me to be in earnest, they would think that I proposed something much worse than Congress had ever done. But, gentlemen, if any of you will tell me that to make a man into a sausage would be much worse—would be any worse—than to make him into a slave,—than it was then to enact the fugitive slave law,—I shall here accuse him of foolishness, of intellectual incapacity, of making a distinction without a difference. The one is just as sensible a proposition as the other.

When I read the account of the carrying back of the fugitive into slavery, which was read last Sunday evening, and read also what was not read here, that the man

---

[8] In the Battle of Concord at the outset of the American Revolution in 1775.

[9] On the morning of April 19, 1851, approximately three hundred armed men put the slave Thomas Simms on a ship in Boston harbor to be returned to his "owner" in Georgia under the conditions of the Fugitive Slave Law.

[10] "Inasmuch as ye have done it unto one of the least of these my brethren, ye have done it unto me," from Matthew 25:40.

[11] As the style of this entry suggests, Thoreau was readying remarks that would publicly express his moral outrage. Much of what he says here (including the sausages example below) appears in "Slavery in Massachusetts," given as a lecture in Framington, Massachusetts, on July 4, 1854, and published in William Lloyd Garrison's *The Liberator* three weeks later.

who made the prayer on the wharf was Daniel Foster[12] of *Concord,* I could not help feeling a slight degree of pride because, of all the towns in the Commonwealth, Concord was the only one distinctly named as being represented in that new tea-party, and, as she had a place in the first, so would have a place in this, the last and perhaps next most important chapter of the History of Massachusetts. But my second feeling, when I reflected how short a time that gentleman has resided in this town, was one of doubt and shame, because the *men* of Concord in recent times have done nothing to entitle them to the honor of having their town named in such a connection.

I hear a good deal said about trampling this law under foot. Why, one need not go out of his way to do that. This law lies not at the level of the head or the reason. Its natural habitat is in the dirt. It was bred and has its life only in the dust and mire, on a level with the feet; and he who walks with freedom, unless, with a sort of quibbling and Hindoo mercy,[13] he avoids treading on every venomous reptile, will inevitably tread on it, and so trample it under foot.

[The California Gold Rush: February 1, 1852]

The recent rush to California[14] and the attitude of the world, even of its philosophers and prophets, in relation to it appears to me to reflect the greatest disgrace on mankind. That so many are ready to get their living by the lottery of gold-digging without contributing any value to society, and that the great majority who stay at home justify them in this both by precept and example! It matches the infatuation of the Hindoos who have cast themselves under the car of Juggernaut.[15] I know of no more startling development of the morality of trade and all the modes of getting a living than the rush to California affords. Of what significance the philosophy, or poetry, or religion of a world that will rush to the lottery of California gold-digging on the receipt of the first news, to live by luck, to get the means of commanding the labor of others less lucky, *i.e.* of slaveholding, without contributing any value to society? And that is called enterprise, and the devil is only a little more enterprising! The philosophy and poetry and religion of such a mankind are not worth the dust of a puffball.[16] The hog that *roots* his own living, and so makes manure, would be ashamed of such company. If I could command the wealth of all the worlds by lifting my finger, I would not pay such a price for it. It makes God to be a moneyed gentleman who scatters a handful of pennies in order to see mankind scramble for them. Going to California. It is only three thousand miles nearer to hell. I will resign my life sooner than live by luck. The world's raffle. A subsistence in the domains of nature a thing to be raffled for! No wonder that they gamble there. I never heard that they did anything else there. What a comment, what a satire, on our institutions! The conclusion will be that mankind will hang itself upon a tree. And who would interfere to cut it down. And have all the precepts in all the bibles taught men only this? and is the last and most admirable invention of the Yankee race only an improved muck-rake?— patented too! If one came hither to sell lottery tickets, bringing satisfactory cre-

---

[12] A fellow townsman of Thoreau's. The irony is heavy here.

[13] Mercy dictated by equivocation or by religious belief.   [14] The California Gold Rush of 1849.

[15] A form of the Hindu god Vishnu, whose idol so excited worshipers when it was hauled by car that they threw themselves under the wheels out of blind devotion; here, the mindless acclaim for those who rush to California in search of gold.

[16] A fungus that releases its spores in a smokelike cloud ("dust") when struck.

dentials, and the prizes were seats in heaven, this world would buy them with a rush.

Did God direct us so to get our living, digging where we never planted,—and He would perchance reward us with lumps of gold? It is a text, oh! for the Jonahs[17] of this generation, and yet the pulpits are as silent as immortal Greece, silent, some of them, because the preacher is gone to California himself. The gold of California is a touchstone which has betrayed the rottenness, the baseness, of mankind. Satan, from one of his elevations, showed mankind the kingdom of California, and they entered into a compact with him at once.

[*The Return of the* Week: *October 28, 1853*]

For a year or two past, my *publisher,*[18] falsely so called, has been writing from time to time to ask what disposition should be made of the copies of "A Week on the Concord and Merrimack Rivers" still on hand, and at last suggesting that he had use for the room they occupied in his cellar. So I had them all sent to me here, and they have arrived to-day by express, filling the man's wagon,—706 copies out of an edition of 1000 which I bought of Munroe four years ago and have been ever since paying for, and have not quite paid for yet. The wares are sent to me at last, and I have an opportunity to examine my purchase. They are something more substantial than fame, as my back knows, which has borne them up two flights of stairs to a place similar to that to which they trace their origin. Of the remaining two hundred and ninety and odd, seventy-five were given away, the rest sold. I have now a library of nearly nine hundred volumes, over seven hundred of which I wrote myself. Is it not well that the author should behold the fruits of his labor? My works are piled up on one side of my chamber half as high as my head, my *opera omnia.*[19] This is authorship; these are the work of my brain. . . .

[*The Facts of a Poet's Life: October 27, 1857*]

The real facts of a poet's life would be of more value to us than any work of art. I mean that the very scheme and form of his poetry (so called) is adopted at a sacrifice of vital truth and poetry.[20] Shakespeare has left us his fancies and imaginings, but the truth of his life, with its becoming circumstances, we know nothing about. The writer is reported, the liver not at all. Shakespeare's house! how hollow it is! No man can conceive of Shakespeare in that house. But we want the basis of fact, of an actual life, to complete our Shakespeare, as much as a statue wants its pedestal. A poet's life with this broad actual basis would be as superior to Shakespeare's as a lichen,[21] with its base or thallus, is superior in the order of being to a fungus.

---

[17] A Hebrew prophet thrown overboard in a storm sent because he disobeyed God, swallowed by a fish, and cast ashore unharmed; a person whose presence brings bad luck.

[18] James Munroe of Boston, whom Thoreau had paid to publish 1000 copies of *A Week on the Concord and Merrimack Rivers* in 1849.

[19] "Complete works" (Latin).

[20] Thoreau deeply believed that the lives of artists are greater than their works (which, as artifacts made for the public, lack the full reality of life).

[21] A mosslike combination of fungi and algae that derives its moisture chiefly from the air; a thallus is the body or base of the lichen.

[*Defacers of Mountain-Tops: June 2, 1858*]

Notwithstanding the newspaper and egg-shell left by visitors, these parts of nature are still peculiarly unhandselled[22] and untracked. The natural terraces of rock are the steps of this temple, and it is the same whether it rises above the desert or a New England village. Even the inscribed rocks are as solemn as most ancient gravestones, and nature reclaims them with bog and lichens. . . . These sculptors seemed to me to court such alliance with the grave as they who put their names over tombstones along the highway. One, who was probably a blacksmith, had sculptured the emblems of his craft, an anvil and hammer, beneath his name. Apparently a part of the regular outfit of mountain-climbers is a hammer and cold-chisel, and perhaps they allow themselves a supply of garlic[23] also. Certainly you could not hire a stone-cutter to do so much engraving for less than several thousand dollars. But no Old Mortality[24] will ever be caught renewing these epitaphs. It reminds what kinds of steeps do climb the false pretenders to fame, whose chief exploit is the carriage of the tools with which to inscribe their names. For speaking epitaphs they are, and the mere name is a sufficient revelation of the character. They are all of one trade,—stonecutters, defacers of mountain-tops. "Charles & Lizzie!" Charles carried the sledge-hammer, and Lizzie the cold-chisel. Some have carried up a paint-pot, and painted their names on the rocks.

1837–1859, 1906

Margaret Fuller
(1810–1850)

Almost a century and a half after the tragedy of Margaret Fuller's death, we are beginning to acknowledge the extraordinary nature of her achievement. Fuller enjoyed international celebrity in her own day, both as a writer and as a personality; following her death in 1850, however, her reputation was obscured by a neglect condoned by most of her contemporaries. Long considered a rather bizarre figure on the periphery of American transcendentalism, Fuller has come to assume a position of significance in the history of American literature.

Sarah Margaret Fuller, the oldest of eight children, was born in Cambridgeport, Massachusetts, in 1810. Fuller's childhood was marked by imposing family responsibility (her mother, Margaret Crane, was sickly) and a precocious devotion to study. Her father, the lawyer Timothy Fuller, was a Jeffersonian democrat whose energy and discipline shaped his daughter's life as it had his own. He undertook her home education with all of the nineteenth-century vigor usually directed toward an oldest son; at age five she received a thorough grounding in Latin, for example. Although she was a remarkably intelligent child, her exhaustive education apparently provoked the nightmares and headaches from

---

[22] Literally, ungiven: wild, not yet involved in human transactions.
[23] Probably added to suggest that these "Sculptors" and litterers have bad breath.
[24] The title character in the novel *Old Mortality* (1816), by Sir Walter Scott (1771–1832); Old Mortality wanders around Scotland repairing the tombs of religious dissenters.

which she constantly suffered, and she later came to perceive her childhood as "unnatural." As the physical health of her mother flagged under the burdens of housekeeping and childbearing, Fuller was increasingly called upon to help with the monotonous chores that constituted nineteenth-century women's work. She tutored her younger brothers and sisters while maintaining a daunting personal schedule of study, and so passed an adolescence that formed habits of single-minded concentration and fervent dedication to intellectual pursuits.

The Fuller family moved to Cambridge proper in 1826, and Margaret entered the intellectual arena she would occupy for the rest of her life. The cultivated community of Cambridge figured nationally as the birthplace of Unitarianism and as the setting for debate over such new ideas as socialism, abolitionism, and feminism. Fuller thrived in this bracing atmosphere and soon acquired a local reputation for her intelligence and her broad range of knowledge. She and her friend Lydia Maria Child took Madame de Baronne de Staël, a revolutionary French writer, for their model, and there are interesting parallels between Fuller's life and that of de Staël, including their precocious intellectual development and informed conversation. Always tall for her age, Fuller was apparently what Victorian novelists would call "rather plain." She learned to carry herself well, however, and paid great attention to her dress; like de Staël, as Fuller grew into womanhood she became a striking, if not conventionally beautiful, figure. In addition to her imposing carriage, her odd habit of closing her eyes while she spoke at any length was often noted. Her appearance as well as her intellectual pursuits contributed to her reputation as something of an eccentric.

During this period in Cambridge Fuller's cousin James Freeman Clarke introduced her to Johann Wolfgang von Goethe's writing. German romanticism offered an appealing alternative to the rational pall with which Unitarianism cloaked New England's intellectual life. To Fuller, Goethe posed an ideal of the artist and thinker as public figure, a concept akin to Roman public virtue, with which she was familiar through her reading of Latin literature. She was planning to write a biography of Goethe when Timothy Fuller moved his family to a gentlemanly farm in Groton, Massachusetts, in 1833. She sorely missed the stimulating community of Cambridge; her experience of bucolic Groton may have accounted for her tepid response to the Brook Farm transcendentalist community outside Boston. In 1835 she toured New York state with friends and met the English author Harriet Martineau. When Fuller's father died suddenly of cholera in October 1835, she assumed financial responsibility for the family.

Fuller met Ralph Waldo Emerson in 1836 and shortly thereafter joined the Transcendental Club. She was always to enjoy a profound friendship with Emerson; she had great respect for him as the dominant intellect of his age. Their acquaintance was founded on such a degree of mutual admiration that it has been analyzed as a subconscious love of which Emerson's wife, Lydia, was jealous. But it is a mistake to relegate Margaret Fuller to the adulatory role of Emerson's student: she was a complex and dynamic person, able to assess Emerson's strengths and weaknesses. Not content to follow Emerson as a teacher, Fuller prevailed upon him to read Goethe and other German romantic writers and steadfastly defended the value of Italian painting in the face of Emerson's inability to appreciate art.

Always under the pressure of providing financial support for her family, Fuller taught at Bronson Alcott's radical Temple School for a brief time in 1836 and then taught for two years (1837–1839) at the progressive Green Street School. Both positions were congenial, and she earned a handsome salary at the Green Street School. But she found teaching emotionally exhausting and was discouraged that it left her little time for writing. She managed to publish an English translation of Johann Peter Eckermann's *Conversations with Goethe* in 1839, but the biography of Goethe remained unfinished. From 1839 to 1844 she conducted "conversations " for women in Boston. The conversation format, used by other speakers of the time (notably Bronson Alcott), was related to the Socratic method of teaching, in which the responsibility for learning was shared by the student, who engaged in direct discussion of the topic at hand. Fuller believed that conventional education provided only exercises in rote, especially for women, and it was her ambition to encourage women to allow their minds to range freely over a variety of subjects that had no apparent relevance to their domestic lives. Fuller's intellectual superiority and even arrogance were on display during these sessions, but she made several deep and lasting friendships among the women who paid to attend.

Emerson persuaded Fuller to assume the editorship of the newly founded transcendental journal, *The Dial,* for which she also wrote a substantial portion of the contents from 1840 to 1842. From this period comes "The Great Lawsuit," later reprinted as "Woman in the Nineteenth Century" (1845). In 1844 Fuller moved to New York City to write a regular column of literary criticism for Horace Greeley's *Tribune.* She achieved considerable influence as a critic, insisting upon the need for an original American literature and discerning the talent of Edgar Allan Poe, Nathaniel Hawthorne, and Herman Melville while they were relatively unknown. She also acquainted her audience with European literature in an effort to dispel the parochialism that she felt characterized American intellectual life. In 1846 Fuller published *Papers on Literature and Art,* a collection of her essays and reviews, and in August of that year embarked on a tour of Europe as a correspondent for the *Tribune.*

Fuller first visited England, where she met with William Wordsworth and Thomas Carlyle and Giuseppe Mazzini, an Italian patriot and revolutionary. In Paris she met the French novelist George Sand and became friendly with the Polish patriot Adam Mickiewicz. Excited by the political involvement of Mazzini and Mickiewicz, she went to Italy in spring 1847, continuing to produce copy for the *Tribune.* While there, she fell in love with the young aristocrat Marchese d'Ossoli (Giovanni Angelo Ossoli), who seemed to her to personify the romantic virtues of natural spontaneity and sympathetic feeling. She refused his early proposal of marriage, but they became lovers, and in September 1848 she gave birth to a son. This stay in Italy during the Risorgimento (the movement for Italian unification, led by Giuseppi Garibaldi) confirmed her republican sympathies, and she determined to write a history of the Italian revolution. After directing a military hospital during Garibaldi's struggle against the French in 1849, she and Ossoli left Rome for Florence, where they lived with their son while Margaret finished her manuscript. Financial difficulties made them determine to settle temporarily in the United States, where Margaret hoped to earn an income from her writing.

At this time, apparently, Ossoli and Fuller were married, possibly in anticipation of the stern reception they, as unmarried parents, would otherwise have gotten in New England. All three perished when their ship sank off Fire Island, New York, during the last hours of their voyage to America in July 1850. Fuller's body and her last manuscript were never found.

Margaret Fuller's reputation has undergone a critical change. She was probably known better in her own day as a conversationalist than as a writer, and many of her contemporaries were disappointed that the brilliance of her conversation was not adequately reflected in her prose. Her eccentricities, too, were sufficiently disconcerting to make such friends as Emerson and Hawthorne agree (rather smugly) that an early death might have been a blessing for such an unconventional figure. Her journals and correspondence were heavily edited for publication by Emerson, in compliance with his bland expectations of American womanhood. It has thus taken some time to recognize that Fuller was not merely Emerson's handmaiden, a paragon among New England blue-stockings—that she was in every way the intellectual equal of the gifted people with whom she associated in Cambridge, Concord, New York, and Europe. In her writing and in her life, she transcends her own time as a model of activism and intellectualism.

Suggested Readings: *Summer on the Lakes,* 1843. *Woman in the Nineteenth Century,* 1845. *The Letters of Margaret Fuller,* 4 vols., ed. R. N. Hudspeth, 1983– . W. H. Channing, J. F. Clarke, and R. W. Emerson, eds., *Memoirs of Margaret Fuller Ossoli,* 1852. B. G. Chevigny, *The Woman and the Myth: Margaret Fuller's Life and Writings,* 1976. P. Blanchard, *Margaret Fuller: From Transcendentalism to Revolution,* 1987. J. Myerson, ed., *Margaret Fuller: Essays on American Life and Letters,* 1978. M. V. Allen, *The Achievement of Margaret Fuller,* 1979.

Texts Used: "The Great Lawsuit": *The Dial,* July 1843, IV (1): 1–47. "American Literature": *Papers on Literature and Art,* Pt. II, 1846. *At Home and Abroad,* ed. A. B. Fuller, 1856.

THE GREAT LAWSUIT*

Man versus Men. Woman versus Women.

This great suit has now been carried on through many ages, with various results. The decisions have been numerous, but always followed by appeals to still higher courts. How can it be otherwise, when the law itself is the subject of frequent elucidation, constant revision? Man has, now and then, enjoyed a clear, triumphant hour, when some irresistible conviction warmed and purified the atmosphere of his planet. But, presently, he sought repose after his labors, when the crowd of pigmy adversaries bound him in his sleep. Long years of inglorious imprisonment followed, while his enemies revelled in his spoils, and no counsel could be found to plead his cause, in the absence of that all-promising glance, which had, at times, kindled the poetic soul to revelation of his claims, of his rights.

Yet a foundation for the largest claim is now established. It is known that his inheritance consists in no partial sway, no exclusive possession, such as his adversaries desire. For they, not content that the universe is rich, would, each one for himself, appropriate treasure; but in vain! The many-colored garment, which clothed with honor an elected son, when rent asunder for the many, is a worthless spoil. A band of robbers cannot live princely in the prince's castle; nor would he,

---

* First published in *The Dial* in July 1843. With additions that expanded the size but not the message of the essay, it was reprinted in 1844 as *Woman in the Nineteenth Century* due, according to Fuller's preliminary footnote, to objections to the ambiguity of the first title. With considerable eloquence she says that she prefers the original title "partly for the reason others do not like it,—that is, that it requires some thought to see what it means, and might thus prepare the reader to meet me on my own ground. Besides, it offers a larger scope, and is, in that way, more just to my desire. I meant by that title to intimate the fact that, while it is the destiny of Man, in the course of the ages, to ascertain and fulfill the law of his being, so that his wife shall be seen, as a whole, to be that of an angel or messenger, the actions of prejudices and passions which attend, in the day, the growth of the individual, is continually obstructing the holy work that is to make earth a part of heaven. By Man I mean both man and woman; these are the two halves of one thought. I lay no especial stress on the welfare of either. I believe that the welfare of the one cannot be effected without that of the other. My highest wish is that this truth should be distinctly and rationally apprehended, and the conditions of life and freedom recognized as the same for the daughter and sons of time; twin exponents of a divine thought."

like them, be content with less than all, though he would not, like them, seek it as fuel for riotous enjoyment, but as his principality, to administer and guard for the use of all living things therein. He cannot be satisfied with any one gift of the earth, any one department of knowledge, or telescopic peep at the heavens. He feels himself called to understand and aid nature, that she may, through his intelligence, be raised and interpreted; to be a student of, and servant to, the universe-spirit; and only king of his planet, that, as an angelic minister, he may bring it into conscious harmony with the law of that spirit.

Such is the inheritance of the orphan prince, and the illegitimate children of his family will not always be able to keep it from him, for, from the fields which they sow with dragon's teeth, and water with blood, rise monsters, which he alone has power to drive away.

But it is not the purpose now to sing the prophecy of his jubilee. We have said that, in clear triumphant moments, this has many, many times been made manifest, and those moments, though past in time, have been translated into eternity by thought. The bright signs they left hang in the heavens, as single stars or constellations, and, already, a thickly-sown radiance consoles the wanderer in the darkest night. Heroes have filled the zodiac of beneficent labors, and then given up their mortal part[1] to the fire without a murmur. Sages and lawgivers have bent their whole nature to the search for truth, and thought themselves happy if they could buy, with the sacrifice of all temporal ease and pleasure, one seed for the future Eden. Poets and priests have strung the lyre with heart-strings, poured out their best blood upon the altar which, reared anew from age to age, shall at last sustain the flame which rises to highest heaven. What shall we say of those who, if not so directly, or so consciously, in connection with the central truth, yet, led and fashioned by a divine instinct, serve no less to develop and interpret the open secret of love passing into life, the divine energy creating for the purpose of happiness;—of the artist, whose hand, drawn by a preëxistent harmony to a certain medium, moulds it to expressions of life more highly and completely organized than are seen elsewhere, and, by carrying out the intention of nature, reveals her meaning to those who are not yet sufficiently matured to divine it; of the philosopher, who listens steadily for causes, and, from those obvious, infers those yet unknown; of the historian, who, in faith that all events must have their reason and their aim, records them, and lays up archives from which the youth of prophets may be fed. The man of science dissects the statement, verifies the facts, and demonstrates connection even where he cannot its purpose.

Lives, too, which bear none of these names, have yielded tones of no less significance. The candlestick, set in a low place, has given light as faithfully, where it was needed, as that upon the hill.[2] In close alleys, in dismal nooks, the Word has been read as distinctly, as when shown by angels to holy men in the dark prison. Those who till a spot of earth, scarcely larger than is wanted for a grave, have deserved that the sun should shine upon its sod till violets answer.

So great has been, from time to time, the promise, that, in all ages, men have

---

[1] Fuller's note: "Ovid, Apotheosis of Hercules, translated into clumsy English by Mr. Gay, as follows. 'Jove said, / Be all your fears forborne, / Th' Œtean fires do thou, great hero, scorn; / Who vanquished all things, shall subdue the flame; / The part alone of gross *maternal* frame, / Fire shall devour, while that from me he drew / Shall live immortal, and its force renew; / That, when he's dead, I'll raise to realms above, / May all the powers the righteous act approve. / If any God dissent, and judge too great / The sacred honors of the heavenly seat, / Even he shall own his deeds deserve the sky, / Even he, reluctant, shall at length comply. / Th' assembled powers assent.'"

[2] Source unidentified.

said the Gods themselves came down to dwell with them; that the All-Creating wandered on the earth to taste in a limited nature the sweetness of virtue, that the All-Sustaining incarnated himself, to guard, in space and time, the destinies of his world; that heavenly genius dwelt among the shepherds, to sing to them and teach them how to sing. Indeed,

> "Der stets den Hirten gnädig sich bewies."

> "He has constantly shown himself favorable to shepherds."

And these dwellers in green pastures and natural students of the stars, were selected to hail, first of all, the holy child, whose life and death presented the type of excellence, which has sustained the heart of so large a portion of mankind in these later generations.

Such marks have been left by the footsteps of man, whenever he has made his way through the wilderness of men. And whenever the pigmies stepped in one of these, they felt dilate within the breast somewhat that promised larger stature and purer blood. They were tempted to forsake their evil ways, to forsake the side of selfish personal existence, of decrepit skepticism, and covetousness of corruptible possessions. Conviction flowed in upon them. They, too, raised the cry; God is living, all is his, and all created beings are brothers, for they are his children. These were the triumphant moments; but, as we have said, man slept and selfishness awoke.

Thus he is still kept out of his inheritance, still a pleader, still a pilgrim. But his reinstatement is sure. And now, no mere glimmering consciousness, but a certainty, is felt and spoken, that the highest ideal man can form of his own capabilities is that which he is destined to attain. Whatever the soul knows how to seek, it must attain. Knock, and it shall be opened; seek, and ye shall find.[3] It is demonstrated, it is a maxim. He no longer paints his proper nature in some peculiar form and says, "Prometheus had it," but "Man must have it."[4] However disputed by many, however ignorantly used, or falsified, by those who do receive it, the fact of an universal, unceasing revelation, has been too clearly stated in words, to be lost sight of in thought, and sermons preached from the text, "Be ye perfect,"[5] are the only sermons of a pervasive and deep-searching influence.

But among those who meditate upon this text, there is great difference of view, as to the way in which perfection shall be sought.

Through the intellect, say some; Gather from every growth of life its seed of thought; look behind every symbol for its law. If thou canst *see* clearly, the rest will follow.

Through the life, say others; Do the best thou knowest to-day. Shrink not from incessant error, in this gradual, fragmentary state. Follow thy light for as much as it will show thee, be faithful as far as thou canst, in hope that faith presently will lead to sight. Help others, without blame that they need thy help. Love much, and be forgiven.

It needs not intellect, needs not experience, says a third. If you took the true way, these would be evolved in purity. You would not learn through them, but express through them a higher knowledge. In quietness, yield thy soul to the

---

[3] From Matthew 7:7–9.

[4] According to Greek myth, Prometheus gave the stolen gift of fire to the human race and was punished by the supreme god, Zeus.

[5] From Matthew 5:48.

causal soul. Do not disturb its teachings by methods of thine own. Be still, seek not, but wait in obedience. Thy commission will be given.

Could we, indeed, say what we want, could we give a description of the child that is lost, he would be found. As soon as the soul can say clearly, that a certain demonstration is wanted, it is at hand. When the Jewish prophet described the Lamb, as the expression of what was required by the coming era, the time drew nigh.[6] But we say not, see not, as yet, clearly, what we would. Those who call for a more triumphant expression of love, a love that cannot be crucified, show not a perfect sense of what has already been expressed. Love has already been expressed, that made all things new, that gave the worm its ministry as well as the eagle; a love, to which it was alike to descend into the depths of hell, or to sit at the right hand of the Father.[7]

Yet, no doubt, a new manifestation is at hand, a new hour in the day of man. We cannot expect to see him a completed being, when the mass of men lie so entangled in the sod, or use the freedom of their limbs only with wolfish energy. The tree cannot come to flower till its root be freed from the cankering worm, and its whole growth open to air and light. Yet something new shall presently be shown of the life of man, for hearts crave it now, if minds do not know how to ask it.

Among the strains of prophecy, the following, by an earnest mind of a foreign land, written some thirty years ago, is not yet outgrown; and it has the merit of being a positive appeal from the heart, instead of a critical declaration what man shall *not* do.

"The ministry of man implies, that he must be filled from the divine fountains which are being engendered through all eternity, so that, at the mere name of his Master, he may be able to cast all his enemies into the abyss; that he may deliver all parts of nature from the barriers that imprison them; that he may purge the terrestrial atmosphere from the poisons that infect it; that he may preserve the bodies of men from the corrupt influences that surround, and the maladies that afflict them; still more, that he may keep their souls pure from the malignant insinuations which pollute, and the gloomy images that obscure them; that we may restore its serenity to the Word, which false words of men fill with mourning and sadness; that he may satisfy the desires of the angels, who await from him the development of the marvels of nature; that, in fine, his world may be filled with God, as eternity is."[8]

Another attempt we will give, by an obscure observer of our own day and country, to draw some lines of the desired image. It was suggested by seeing the design of Crawford's Orpheus,[9] and connecting with the circumstance of the American, in his garret at Rome, making choice of this subject, that of Americans here at home, showing such ambition to represent the character, by calling their

---

[6] In Isaiah 7:10–15, the Lord announces the coming of Jesus to Ahaz.

[7] In Mark 16, after Jesus rose from the dead and appeared to his disciples, he "was taken up into heaven and sitteth on the right hand of God."

[8] Fuller's note: "St. Martin." The passage is from *The Ministry of Man and Spirit* (1802), by the French philosopher Louis Claude de Saint-Martin (1743–1803).

[9] According to Greek myth, Orpheus could play the lyre so wondrously that his music charmed wild beasts. At the Allston Gallery in Boston in 1839 Fuller saw the statue of Orpheus by the American sculptor Thomas Crawford (1813–1857), then living in Rome; as a tribute to its evocative beauty she wrote the lines in the following paragraph.

prose and verse, Orphic sayings,[10] Orphics. Orpheus was a lawgiver by theocratic commission. He understood nature, and made all her forms move to his music. He told her secrets in the form of hymns, nature as seen in the mind of God. Then it is the prediction, that to learn and to do, all men must be lovers, and Orpheus was, in a high sense, a lover. His soul went forth towards all beings, yet could remain sternly faithful to a chosen type of excellence. Seeking what he loved, he feared not death nor hell, neither could any presence daunt his faith in the power of the celestial harmony that filled his soul.

It seemed significant of the state of things in this country, that the sculptor should have chosen the attitude of shading his eyes. When we have the statue here, it will give lessons in reverence.

> Each Orpheus must to the depths descend,
> For only thus the poet can be wise,
> Must make the sad Persephone[11] his friend,
> And buried love to second life arise;
> Again his love must lose through too much love,
> Must lose his life by living life too true,
> For what he sought below is passed above,
> Already done is all that he would do;
> Must tune all being with his single lyre,
> Must melt all rocks free from their primal pain,
> Must search all nature with his one soul's fire,
> Must bind anew all forms in heavenly chain.
> If he already sees what he must do,
> Well may he shade his eyes from the far-shining view.

Meanwhile, not a few believe, and men themselves have expressed the opinion, that the time is come when Euridice is to call for an Orpheus, rather than Orpheus for Euridice; that the idea of man, however imperfectly brought out, has been far more so than that of woman, and that an improvement in the daughters will best aid the reformation of the sons of this age.

It is worthy of remark, that, as the principle of liberty is better understood and more nobly interpreted, a broader protest is made in behalf of woman. As men become aware that all men have not had their fair chance, they are inclined to say that no women have had a fair chance. The French revolution, that strangely disguised angel, bore witness in favor of woman, but interpreted her claims no less ignorantly than those of man. Its idea of happiness did not rise beyond outward enjoyment, unobstructed by the tyranny of others. The title it gave was Citoyen, Citoyenne,[12] and it is not unimportant to woman that even this species of equality was awarded her. Before, she could be condemned to perish on the scaffold for treason, but not as a citizen, but a subject. The right, with which this title then invested a human being, was that of bloodshed and license. The Goddess of Liberty was impure. Yet truth was prophesied in the ravings of that hideous fever

---

[10] Bronson Alcott (1799–1888), the most quixotic and mystical of the Concord transcendentalists, published "Orphic Sayings" in *The Dial* (edited by Fuller) in 1840 and 1841.

[11] According to Greek myth, the queen of Hades; so powerfully did Orpheus hold Hades spellbound by his music that he almost made "buried love to second life arise" by resurrecting his dead wife, Eurydice.

[12] Both words mean "citizen," the first male, the second female, equal under the law.

induced by long ignorance and abuse. Europe is conning a valued lesson from the blood-stained page. The same tendencies, farther unfolded, will bear good fruit in this country.

Yet, in this country, as by the Jews, when Moses was leading them to the promised land,[13] everything has been done that inherited depravity could, to hinder the promise of heaven from its fulfilment. The cross, here as elsewhere, has been planted only to be blasphemed by cruelty and fraud. The name of the Prince of Peace has been profaned by all kinds of injustice towards the Gentile whom he said he came to save. But I need not speak of what has been done towards the red man, the black man. These deeds are the scoff of the world; and they have been accompanied by such pious words, that the gentlest would not dare to intercede with, "Father forgive them, for they know not what they do."[14]

Here, as elsewhere, the gain of creation consists always in the growth of individual minds, which live and aspire, as flowers bloom and birds sing, in the midst of morasses; and in the continual development of that thought, the thought of human destiny, which is given to eternity to fulfil, and which ages of failure only seemingly impede. Only seemingly, and whatever seems to the contrary, this country is as surely destined to elucidate a great moral law, as Europe was to promote the mental culture of man.

Though the national independence be blurred by the servility of individuals; though freedom and equality have been proclaimed only to leave room for a monstrous display of slave dealing, and slave keeping; though the free American so often feels himself free, like the Roman, only to pamper his appetites and his indolence through the misery of his fellow beings, still it is not in vain, that the verbal statement has been made, "All men are born free and equal."[15] There it stands, a golden certainty, wherewith to encourage the good, to shame the bad. The new world may be called clearly to perceive that it incurs the utmost penalty, if it reject the sorrowful brother. And if men are deaf, the angels hear. But men cannot be deaf. It is inevitable that an external freedom, such as has been achieved for the nation, should be so also for every member of it. That, which has once been clearly conceived in the intelligence, must be acted out. It has become a law, as irrevocable as that of the Medes in their ancient dominion.[16] Men will privately sin against it, but the law so clearly expressed by a leading mind of the age,

> "Tutti fatti a sembianza d' un Solo;
> Figli tutti d' un solo riscatto,
> In qual ora, in qual parte del suolo
> Trascorriamo quest' aura vital,
> Siam fratelli, siam stretti ad un patto:
> Maladetto colui che lo infrange,
> Che s' innalza sul fiacco che piange,
> Che contrista uno spirto immortal."[17]

[13] Fuller suggests the paradox of Moses leading the Israelites out of bondage to the Promised Land while establishing a demeaning role for Israelite women.

[14] From Luke 23:34, Jesus' reference to the Roman soldiers who nailed him to the cross.

[15] Adaptation of "all men are created equal," from the Declaration of Independence.

[16] Ancient Media was forcibly annexed to Persia around 550 B.C.; its former territory is now in West Iran and South Azerbaijan.

[17] Fuller's note: "Manzoni." Alessandro Manzoni (1785–1873), an Italian novelist, poet, and dramatist.

"All made in the likeness of the One,
All children of one ransom,
In whatever hour, in whatever part of the soil
We draw this vital air,
We are brothers, we must be bound by one compact,
Accursed he who infringes it,
Who raises himself upon the weak who weep,
Who saddens an immortal spirit."

cannot fail of universal recognition.

We sicken no less at the pomp than the strife of words. We feel that never were lungs so puffed with the wind of declamation, on moral and religious subjects, as now. We are tempted to implore these "word-heroes," these word-Catos, word-Christs,[18] to beware of cant above all things; to remember that hypocrisy is the most hopeless as well as the meanest of crimes, and that those must surely be polluted by it, who do not keep a little of all this morality and religion for private use.[19] We feel that the mind may "grow black and rancid in the smoke" even of altars. We start up from the harangue to go into our closet and shut the door. But, when it has been shut long enough, we remember that where there is so much smoke, there must be some fire; with so much talk about virtue and freedom must be mingled some desire for them; that it cannot be in vain that such have become the common topics of conversation among men; that the very newspapers should proclaim themselves Pilgrims, Puritans, Heralds of Holiness.[20] The king that maintains so costly a retinue cannot be a mere Count of Carabbas[21] fiction. We have waited here long in the dust; we are tired and hungry, but the triumphal procession must appear at last.

Of all its banners, none has been more steadily upheld, and under none has more valor and willingness for real sacrifices been shown, than that of the champions of the enslaved African.[22] And this band it is, which, partly in consequence of a natural following out of principles, partly because many women have been prominent in that cause, makes, just now, the warmest appeal in behalf of woman.

Though there has been a growing liberality on this point, yet society at large is not so prepared for the demands of this party, but that they are, and will be for some time, coldly regarded as the Jacobins[23] of their day.

"Is it not enough," cries the sorrowful trader, "that you have done all you could to break up the national Union, and thus destroy the prosperity of our country, but now you must be trying to break up family union, to take my wife away from the cradle, and the kitchen hearth, to vote at polls, and preach from a pulpit? Of course, if she does such things, she cannot attend to those of her own sphere. She is happy enough as she is. She has more leisure than I have, every means of improvement, every indulgence."

[18] People who talk like the heroic Roman Marcus Porcius Cato (95–46 B.C.), called "the conscience of Rome," or like Jesus—but who do nothing but talk.

[19] Fuller's note: "Dr. Johnson's one piece of advice should be written on every door; 'Clear your mind of cant.' But Byron, to whom it was so acceptable, in clearing away the noxious vine, shook down the building too. Stirling's emendation is note-worthy, 'Realize your cant, not cast it off.'"

[20] Common names for newspapers then.

[21] A character in *Le Chat Botté* (*Puss in Boots*), the embodiment of pride and pretension, by Charles Perrault (1628–1703).

[22] Abolitionists.

[23] A political group founded in Paris in 1789 at the outset of the French Revolution; by 1793 under Maximillian Robespierre (1758–1794) it had become a radical faction.

"Have you asked her whether she was satisfied with these indulgences?"

"No, but I know she is. She is too amiable to wish what would make me unhappy, and too judicious to wish to step beyond the sphere of her sex. I will never consent to have our peace disturbed by any such discussions."

"'Consent'—you? it is not consent from you that is in question, it is assent from your wife."

"Am not I the head of my house?"

"You are not the head of your wife. God has given her a mind of her own."

"I am the head and she the heart."

"God grant you play true to one another then. If the head represses no natural pulse of the heart, there can be no question as to your giving your consent. Both will be of one accord, and there needs but to present any question to get a full and true answer. There is no need of precaution, of indulgence, or consent. But our doubt is whether the heart consents with the head, or only acquiesces in its decree; and it is to ascertain the truth on this point, that we propose some liberating measures."

Thus vaguely are these questions proposed and discussed at present. But their being proposed at all implies much thought, and suggests more. Many women are considering within themselves what they need that they have not, and what they can have, if they find they need it. Many men are considering whether women are capable of being and having more than they are and have, and whether, if they are, it will be best to consent to improvement in their condition.

The numerous party, whose opinions are already labelled and adjusted too much to their mind to admit of any new light, strive, by lectures on some model-woman of bridal-like beauty and gentleness, by writing or lending little treatises, to mark out with due precision the limits of woman's sphere, and woman's mission, and to prevent other than the rightful shepherd from climbing the wall, or the flock from using any chance gap to run astray.

Without enrolling ourselves at once on either side, let us look upon the subject from that point of view which to-day offers. No better, it is to be feared, than a high house-top. A high hill-top, or at least a cathedral spire, would be desirable.

It is not surprising that it should be the Anti-Slavery party that pleads for woman, when we consider merely that she does not hold property on equal terms with men; so that, if a husband dies without a will, the wife, instead of stepping at once into his place as head of the family, inherits only a part of his fortune, as if she were a child, or ward only, not an equal partner.

We will not speak of the innumerable instances, in which profligate or idle men live upon the earnings of industrious wives; or if the wives leave them and take with them the children, to perform the double duty of mother and father, follow from place to place, and threaten to rob them of the children, if deprived of the rights of a husband, as they call them, planting themselves in their poor lodgings, frightening them into paying tribute by taking from them the children, running into debt at the expense of these otherwise so overtasked helots.[24] Though such instances abound, the public opinion of his own sex is against the man, and when cases of extreme tyranny are made known, there is private action in the wife's favor. But if woman be, indeed, the weaker party, she ought to have legal protection, which would make such oppression impossible.

And, knowing that there exists, in the world of men, a tone of feeling towards women as towards slaves, such as is expressed in the common phrase, "Tell that

[24] Serfs, the lowest class of serfs in ancient Sparta.

to women and children;" that the infinite soul can only work through them in already ascertained limits; that the prerogative of reason, man's highest portion, is allotted to them in a much lower degree; that it is better for them to be engaged in active labor, which is to be furnished and directed by those better able to think, etc., etc., we need not go further, for who can review the experience of last week, without recalling words which imply, whether in jest or earnest, these views, and views like these? Knowing this, can we wonder that many reformers think that measures are not likely to be taken in behalf of women, unless their wishes could be publicly represented by women?

That can never be necessary, cry the other side. All men are privately influenced by women; each has his wife, sister, or female friends, and is too much biassed by these relations to fail of representing their interests. And if this is not enough, let them propose and enforce their wishes with the pen. The beauty of home would be destroyed, the delicacy of the sex be violated, the dignity of halls of legislation destroyed, by an attempt to introduce them there. Such duties are inconsistent with those of a mother; and then we have ludicrous pictures of ladies in hysterics at the polls, and senate chambers filled with cradles.

But if, in reply, we admit as truth that woman seems destined by nature rather to the inner circle, we must add that the arrangements of civilized life had not been as yet such as to secure it to her. Her circle, if the duller, is not the quieter. If kept from excitement, she is not from drudgery. Not only the Indian carries the burdens of the camp, but the favorites of Louis the Fourteenth[25] accompany him in his journeys, and the washerwoman stands at her tub and carries home her work at all seasons, and in all states of health.

As to the use of the pen, there was quite as much opposition to woman's possessing herself of that help to free-agency as there is now to her seizing on the rostrum or the desk; and she is likely to draw, from a permission to plead her cause that way, opposite inferences to what might be wished by those who now grant it.

As to the possibility of her filling, with grace and dignity, any such position, we should think those who had seen the great actresses, and heard the Quaker preachers of modern times, would not doubt, that woman can express publicly the fulness of thought and emotion, without losing any of the peculiar beauty of her sex.

As to her home, she is not likely to leave it more than she now does for balls, theatres, meetings for promoting missions, revival meetings, and others to which she flies, in hope of an animation for her existence, commensurate with what she sees enjoyed by men. Governors of Ladies' Fairs are no less engrossed by such a charge, than the Governor of the State by his; presidents of Washingtonian societies,[26] no less away from home than presidents of conventions. If men look straitly to it, they will find that, unless their own lives are domestic, those of the women will not be. The female Greek, of our day, is as much in the street as the male, to cry, What news? We doubt not it was the same in Athens of old. The women, shut out from the market-place, made up for it at the religious festivals. For human beings are not so constituted, that they can live without expansion; and if they do not get it one way, must another, or perish.

And, as to men's representing women fairly, at present, while we hear from

[25] Courtesans, who are enslaved as much as are squaws or washerwomen.
[26] Organizations similar to the busy Daughters of the American Revolution.

men who owe to their wives not only all that is comfortable and graceful, but all that is wise in the arrangement of their lives, the frequent remark, "You cannot reason with a woman," when from those of delicacy, nobleness, and poetic culture, the contemptuous phrase, "Women and children," and that in no light sally of the hour, but in works intended to give a permanent statement of the best experiences, when not one man in the million, shall I say, no, not in the hundred million, can rise above the view that woman was made *for man,* when such traits as these are daily forced upon the attention, can we feel that man will always do justice to the interests of woman? Can we think that he takes a sufficiently discerning and religious view of her office and destiny, ever to do her justice, except when prompted by sentiment; accidentally or transiently, that is, for his sentiment will vary according to the relations in which he is placed. The lover, the poet, the artist, are likely to view her nobly. The father and the philosopher have some chance of liberality; the man of the world, the legislator for expediency, none.

Under these circumstances, without attaching importance in themselves to the changes demanded by the champions of woman, we hail them as signs of the times. We would have every arbitrary barrier thrown down. We would have every path laid open to woman as freely as to man. Were this done, and a slight temporary fermentation allowed to subside, we believe that the Divine would ascend into nature to a height unknown in the history of past ages, and nature, thus instructed, would regulate the spheres not only so as to avoid collision, but to bring forth ravishing harmony.

Yet then, and only then, will human beings be ripe for this, when inward and outward freedom for woman, as much as for man, shall be acknowledged as a right, not yielded as a concession. As the friend of the negro assumes that one man cannot, by right, hold another in bondage, so should the friend of woman assume that man cannot, by right, lay even well-meant restrictions on woman. If the negro be a soul, if the woman be a soul, apparelled in flesh, to one master only are they accountable. There is but one law for all souls, and, if there is to be an interpreter of it, he comes not as man, or son of man, but as Son of God.

Were thought and feeling once so far elevated that man should esteem himself the brother and friend, but nowise the lord and tutor of woman, were he really bound with her in equal worship, arrangements as to function and employment would be of no consequence. What woman needs is not as a woman to act or rule, but as a nature to grow, as an intellect to discern, as a soul to live freely, and unimpeded to unfold such powers as were given her when we left our common home. If fewer talents were given her, yet, if allowed the free and full employment of these, so that she may render back to the giver his own with usury, she will not complain, nay, I dare to say she will bless and rejoice in her earthly birth-place, her earthly lot.

Let us consider what obstructions impede this good era, and what signs give reason to hope that it draws near.

I was talking on this subject with Miranda,[27] a woman, who, if any in the world, might speak without heat or bitterness of the position of her sex. Her father was a man who cherished no sentimental reverence for woman, but a firm belief in the equality of the sexes. She was his eldest child, and came to him at an age when he needed a companion. From the time she could speak and go alone, he addressed her not as a plaything, but as a living mind. Among the few verses he ever

[27] The character "Miranda" reflects Fuller's experiences.

wrote were a copy addressed to this child, when the first locks were cut from her head, and the reverence expressed on this occasion for that cherished head he never belied. It was to him the temple of immortal intellect. He respected his child, however, too much to be an indulgent parent. He called on her for clear judgment, for courage, for honor and fidelity, in short for such virtues as he knew. In so far as he possessed the keys to the wonders of this universe, he allowed free use of them to her, and by the incentive of a high expectation he forbade, as far as possible, that she should let the privilege lie idle.

Thus this child was early led to feel herself a child of the spirit. She took her place easily, not only in the world of organized being, but in the world of mind. A dignified sense of self-dependence was given as all her portion, and she found it a sure anchor. Herself securely anchored, her relations with others were established with equal security. She was fortunate, in a total absence of those charms which might have drawn to her bewildering flatteries, and of a strong electric nature, which repelled those who did not belong to her, and attracted those who did. With men and women her relations were noble; affectionate without passion, intellectual without coldness. The world was free to her, and she lived freely in it. Outward adversity came, and inward conflict, but that faith and self-respect had early been awakened, which must always lead at last to an outward serenity, and an inward peace.

Of Miranda I had always thought as an example, that the restraints upon the sex were insuperable only to those who think them so, or who noisily strive to break them. She had taken a course of her own, and no man stood in her way. Many of her acts had been unusual, but excited no uproar. Few helped, but none checked her; and the many men, who knew her mind and her life, showed to her confidence as to a brother, gentleness as to a sister. And not only refined, but very coarse men approved one in whom they saw resolution and clearness of design. Her mind was often the leading one, always effective.

When I talked with her upon these matters, and had said very much what I have written, she smilingly replied, And yet we must admit that I have been fortunate, and this should not be. My good father's early trust gave the first bias, and the rest followed of course. It is true that I have had less outward aid, in after years, than most women, but that is of little consequence. Religion was early awakened in my soul, a sense that what the soul is capable to ask it must attain, and that, though I might be aided by others, I must depend on myself as the only constant friend. This self-dependence, which was honored in me, is deprecated as a fault in most women. They are taught to learn their rule from without, not to unfold it from within.

This is the fault of man, who is still vain, and wishes to be more important to woman than by right he should be.

Men have not shown this disposition towards you, I said.

No, because the position I early was enabled to take, was one of self-reliance. And were all women as sure of their wants as I was, the result would be the same. The difficulty is to get them to the point where they shall naturally develop self-respect, the question how it is to be done.

Once I thought that men would help on this state of things more than I do now. I saw so many of them wretched in the connections they had formed in weakness and vanity. They seemed so glad to esteem women whenever they could!

But early I perceived that men never, in any extreme of despair, wished to be women. Where they admired any woman they were inclined to speak of her as above her sex. Silently I observed this, and feared it argued a rooted skepticism, which for ages had been fastening on the heart, and which only an age of miracles could eradicate.

Ever I have been treated with great sincerity; and I look upon it as a most signal instance of this, that an intimate friend of the other sex said in a fervent moment, that I deserved in some star to be a man. Another used as highest praise, in speaking of a character in literature, the words "a manly woman."

It is well known that of every strong woman they say she has a masculine mind.[28]

This by no means argues a willing want of generosity towards woman. Man is as generous towards her, as he knows how to be.

Wherever she has herself arisen in national or private history, and nobly shone forth in any ideal of excellence, men have received her, not only willingly, but with triumph. Their encomiums indeed are always in some sense mortifying, they show too much surprise.

In every-day life the feelings of the many are stained with vanity. Each wishes to be lord in a little world, to be superior at least over one; and he does not feel strong enough to retain a life-long ascendant over a strong nature. Only a Brutus would rejoice in a Portia.[29] Only Theseus could conquer before he wed the Amazonian Queen.[30] Hercules wished rather to rest from his labors with Dejanira,[31] and received the poisoned robe, as a fit guerdon. The tale should be interpreted to all those who seek repose with the weak.

But not only is man vain and fond of power, but the same want[32] of development, which thus affects him morally in the intellect, prevents his discerning the destiny of woman. The boy wants no woman, but only a girl to play ball with him, and mark his pocket handkerchief.

Thus in Schiller's Dignity of Woman,[33] beautiful as the poem is, there is no "grave and perfect man," but only a great boy to be softened and restrained by the influence of girls. Poets, the elder brothers of their race, have usually seen further; but what can you expect of every-day men, if Schiller was not more prophetic as to what women must be? Even with Richter[34] one foremost thought about a wife was that she would "cook him something good."

The sexes should not only correspond to and appreciate one another, but prophesy to one another. In individual instances this happens. Two persons love in one another the future good which they aid one another to unfold. This is very imperfectly done as yet in the general life. Man has gone but little way, now he is waiting to see whether woman can keep step with him, but instead of calling out

---

[28] In *The Dial* Fuller gives no indication where Miranda's voice stops, but in the 1844 version this is clearly her last statement.

[29] The unfortunate wife of Brutus in Shakespeare's *Julius Caesar*.

[30] According to Greek myth, Theseus was a hero who (among other things) defeated an invasion of the Amazons and married the Amazonian queen, Hippolyte. Fuller seems to offer this mythic episode as an example of male domination.

[31] To win back the love of the wandering Hercules, Dejanira followed the advice given years before by Nessus and sent her husband a robe permeated with a supposed love potion that turned out to be deadly poison. Fuller telescopes the details of this complex story to make it a warning against choosing an apparently docile wife. "Guerdon" means reward.

[32] Lack.

[33] A poem by Friedrich von Schiller (1759–1805), a German dramatist, poet, and historian.

[34] Jean Paul Richter (1763–1825), a German novelist whose *Levana: Or, The Doctrine of Education* (1807) exemplifies Fuller's point.

like a good brother; You can do it if you only think so, or impersonally; Any one can do what he tries to do, he often discourages with school-boy brag; Girls cant do that, girls cant play ball. But let any one defy their taunts, break through, and be brave and secure, they rend the air with shouts.

No! man is not willingly ungenerous. He wants faith and love, because he is not yet himself an elevated being. He cries with sneering skepticism; Give us a sign. But if the sign appears, his eyes glisten, and he offers not merely approval, but homage.

The severe nation[35] which taught that the happiness of the race was forfeited through the fault of a woman, and showed its thought of what sort of regard man owed her, by making him accuse her on the first question to his God, who gave her to the patriarch as a handmaid, and, by the Mosaical law, bound her to allegiance like a serf, even they greeted, with solemn rapture, all great and holy women as heroines, prophetesses, nay judges in Israel; and, if they made Eve listen to the serpent, gave Mary to the Holy Spirit. In other nations it has been the same down to our day. To the woman, who could conquer, a triumph was awarded. And not only those whose strength was recommended to the heart by association with goodness and beauty, but those who were bad, if they were steadfast and strong, had their claims allowed. In any age a Semiramis, an Elizabeth of England, a Catharine of Russia[36] makes her place good, whether in a large or small circle.

How has a little wit, a little genius, always been celebrated in a woman! What an intellectual triumph was that of the lonely Aspasia,[37] and how heartily acknowledged! She, indeed, met a Pericles. But what annalist, the rudest of men, the most plebeian of husbands, will spare from his page one of the few anecdotes of Roman women?—Sappho, Eloisa![38] The names are of thread-bare celebrity. The man habitually most narrow towards women will be flushed, as by the worst assault on Christianity, if you say it has made no improvement in her condition. Indeed, those most opposed to new acts in her favor are jealous of the reputation of those which have been done.

We will not speak of the enthusiasm excited by actresses, improvisatrici,[39] female singers, for here mingles the charm of beauty and grace, but female authors, even learned women, if not insufferably ugly and slovenly, from the Italian professor's daughter, who taught behind the curtain, down to Mrs. Carter and Madame Dacier,[40] are sure of an admiring audience, if they can once get a platform on which to stand.

But how to get this platform, or how to make it of reasonably easy access is the difficulty. Plants of great vigor will almost always struggle into blossom, despite

---

[35] The Israelites.

[36] Semiramis (9th century B.C.) was an Assyrian princess and the reputed founder of Babylon; Elizabeth I (1533–1603), queen of England from 1558 to 1603, Catherine II (1729–1796), empress of Russia from 1762 to 1796.

[37] Aspasia (470?–410 B.C.) was a celebrated woman from Miletus, in Greece, who became the lifelong *hetaera*, or courtesan, of the great Athenian statesman Pericles. (Athenian men could marry only the daughters of other Athenian men.)

[38] Sappho (7th century B.C.) was a Greek lyric poet; Eloisa, more frequently Heloïse (1101–1164), was a French abbess known for her marriage to, and romantic relationship with, the French theologian Peter Abelard (1079–1142).

[39] Female dancers who improvise.

[40] Elizabeth Carter (1717–1806), a British essayist who translated the works of the Greek philosopher Epictetus (1758); Anne LeFevre Dacier (1654–1720), a French writer who translated the classics.

impediments. But there should be encouragement, and a free, genial atmosphere for those of more timid sort, fair play for each in its own kind. Some are like the little, delicate flowers, which love to hide in the dripping mosses by the sides of mountain torrents, or in the shade of tall trees. But others require an open field, a rich and loosened soil, or they never show their proper hues.

It may be said man does not have his fair play either; his energies are repressed and distorted by the interposition of artificial obstacles. Aye, but he himself has put them there; they have grown out of his own imperfections. If there *is* a misfortune in woman's lot, it is in obstacles being interposed by men, which do *not* mark her state, and if they express her past ignorance, do not her present needs. As every man is of woman born, she has slow but sure means of redress, yet the sooner a general justness of thought makes smooth the path, the better.

Man is of woman born, and her face bends over him in infancy with an expression he can never quite forget. Eminent men have delighted to pay tribute to this image, and it is a hacknied observation, that most men of genius boast some remarkable development in the mother. The rudest tar brushes off a tear with his coat-sleeve at the hallowed name. The other day I met a decrepit old man of seventy, on a journey, who challenged the stage-company to guess where he was going. They guessed aright, "To see your mother." "Yes," said he, "she is ninety-two, but has good eye-sight still, they say. I've not seen her these forty years, and I thought I could not die in peace without." I should have liked his picture painted as a companion piece to that of a boisterous little boy, whom I saw attempt to declaim at a school exhibition.

> "O that those lips had language! Life has passed
> With me but roughly since I heard thee last."[41]

He got but very little way before sudden tears shamed him from the stage.

Some gleams of the same expression which shone down upon his infancy, angelically pure and benign, visit man again with hopes of pure love, of a holy marriage. Or if not before, in the eyes of the mother of his child they again are seen, and dim fancies pass before his mind, that woman may not have been born for him alone, but have come from heaven, a commissioned soul, a messenger of truth and love.

In gleams, in dim fancies, this thought visits the mind of common men. It is soon obscured by the mists of sensuality, the dust of routine, and he thinks it was only some meteor or ignis fatuus[42] that shone. But, as a Rosicrucian lamp,[43] it burns unwearied, though condemned to the solitude of tombs. And, to its permanent life, as to every truth, each age has, in some form, borne witness. For the truths, which visit the minds of careless men only in fitful gleams, shine with radiant clearness into those of the poet, the priest, and the artist.

Whatever may have been the domestic manners of the ancient nations, the idea of woman was nobly manifested in their mythologies and poems, where she ap-

---

[41] From "On the Receipt of My Mother's Picture," by the English poet William Cowper (1731–1800).

[42] "Foolish fire" (Latin), from its tendency to mislead travelers: a light that appears over marshy ground in the night, supposedly caused by the combustion of marsh gas; popularly, will-o'-the-wisp.

[43] Prominent in the seventeenth and eighteenth centuries, the Rosicrucians were a society of philosophers claiming to have a secret knowledge of nature; it was their custom to have an eternally lighted lamp.

peared as Sita in the Ramayana, a form of tender purity, in the Egyptian Isis,[44] of divine wisdom never yet surpassed. In Egypt, too, the Sphynx,[45] walking the earth with lion tread, looked out upon its marvels in the calm, inscrutable beauty of a virgin's face, and the Greek could only add wings to the great emblem. In Greece, Ceres and Proserpine,[46] significantly termed "the great goddesses," were seen seated, side by side. They needed not to rise for any worshipper or any change; they were prepared for all things, as those initiated to their mysteries knew. More obvious is the meaning of those three forms, the Diana, Minerva, and Vesta.[47] Unlike in the expression of their beauty, but alike in this,—that each was self-sufficing. Other forms were only accessories and illustrations, none the complement to one like these. Another might indeed be the companion, and the Apollo and Diana set off one another's beauty. Of the Vesta, it is to be observed, that not only deep-eyed, deep-discerning Greece, but ruder Rome, who represents the only form of good man (the always busy warrior) that could be indifferent to woman, confided the permanence of its glory to a tutelary goddess, and her wisest legislator spoke of Meditation as a nymph.

In Sparta, thought, in this respect as all others, was expressed in the characters of real life, and the women of Sparta were as much Spartans as the men. The Citoyen, Citoyenne, of France; was here actualized. Was not the calm equality they enjoyed well worth the honors of chivalry? They intelligently shared the ideal life of their nation.

Generally, we are told of these nations, that women occupied there a very subordinate position in actual life. It is difficult to believe this, when we see such range and dignity of thought on the subject in the mythologies, and find the poets producing such ideals as Cassandra, Iphigenia, Antigone, Macaria,[48] (though it is not unlike our own day, that men should revere those heroines of their great princely houses at theatres, from which their women were excluded,) where Sibylline priestesses[49] told the oracle of the highest god, and he could not be content to reign with a court of less than nine Muses.[50] Even Victory[51] wore a female form.

But whatever were the facts of daily life, I cannot complain of the age and nation, which represents its thought by such a symbol as I see before me at this moment. It is a zodiac of the busts of gods and goddesses, arranged in pairs. The circle breathes the music of a heavenly order. Male and female heads are distinct in expression, but equal in beauty, strength, and calmness. Each male head is that

---

[44] In the *Ramayana* (300? B.C.), a Sanskrit epic poem detailing the adventures of the Hindu god Ramachandra (the seventh incarnation of Vishnu), Sita is kidnapped, then rescued by Ramachandra; according to Egyptian myth, Isis is the goddess of fertility.

[45] According to Greek myth, a monster with a lion's body, wings, and the head and bust of a woman.

[46] According to Roman myth, the goddesses of agriculture and of the Underworld, respectively; their Greek counterparts were Demeter and Persephone.

[47] According to Roman myth, the goddesses of the moon (worshipped especially by women), of handicrafts and war, and of home and hearth.

[48] According to Greek myth, Cassandra, daughter of Priam and Hecuba, prophesied the doom of Troy but was not believed; Iphigenia, daughter of Agamemnon and Clytemnestra, was rescued by the goddess Artemis when Agamemnon was about to sacrifice her to get a fair wind for sailing to war; Antigone, daughter of Oedipus and Jocasta, was put to death because she buried her brother's corpse against the order of her uncle, Creon; Macaria, daughter of Heracles and Deianura, sacrificed herself to save Athens.

[49] Servants of Apollo who delivered divine messages to the oracle at Delphi.

[50] According to Greek myth, goddesses who control literature and the arts and sciences.

[51] One of the greatest Greek sculptures, a representation of the Greek goddess of victory (Nike) entitled *Winged Victory*, or *Victory at Samothrace* (an island in the northeastern Aegean Sea).

of a brother and a king, each female of a sister and a queen. Could the thought, thus expressed, be lived out, there would be nothing more to be desired. There would be unison in variety, congeniality in difference.

Coming nearer our own time, we find religion and poetry no less true in their revelations. The rude man, but just disengaged from the sod, the Adam, accuses woman to his God, and records her disgrace to their posterity. He is not ashamed to write that he could be drawn from heaven by one beneath him. But in the same nation, educated by time, instructed by successive prophets, we find woman in as high a position as she has ever occupied. And no figure, that has ever arisen to greet our eyes, has been received with more fervent reverence than that of the Madonna. Heine calls her the Dame du Comptoir of the Catholic Church, and this jeer well expresses a serious truth.[52]

And not only this holy and significant image was worshipped by the pilgrim, and the favorite subject of the artist, but it exercised an immediate influence on the destiny of the sex. The empresses, who embraced the cross, converted sons and husbands.[53] Whole calendars of female saints, heroic dames of chivalry, binding the emblem of faith on the heart of the best-beloved, and wasting the bloom of youth in separation and loneliness, for the sake of duties they thought it religion to assume, with innumerable forms of poesy, trace their lineage to this one. Nor, however imperfect may be the action, in our day, of the faith thus expressed, and though we can scarcely think it nearer this ideal than that of India or Greece was near their ideal, is it in vain that the truth has been recognised, that woman is not only a part of man, bone of his bone and flesh of his flesh, born that men might not be lonely, but in themselves possessors of and possessed by immortal souls. This truth undoubtedly received a greater outward stability from the belief of the church, that the earthly parent of the Saviour of souls was a woman.

The Assumption of the Virgin, as painted by sublime artists, Petrarch's Hymn to the Madonna,[54] cannot have spoken to the world wholly without result, yet oftentimes those who had ears heard not.

Thus, the Idea of woman has not failed to be often and forcibly represented. So many instances throng on the mind, that we must stop here, lest the catalogue be swelled beyond the reader's patience.

Neither can she complain that she has not had her share of power. This, in all ranks of society, except the lowest, has been hers to the extent that vanity could crave, far beyond what wisdom would accept. In the very lowest, where man, pressed by poverty, sees in woman only the partner of toils and cares, and cannot hope, scarcely has an idea of a comfortable home, he maltreats her, often, and is less influenced by her. In all ranks, those who are amiable and uncomplaining, suffer much. They suffer long, and are kind; verily, they have their reward. But wherever man is sufficiently raised above extreme poverty, or brutal stupidity, to care for the comforts of the fireside, or the bloom and ornament of life, woman has always power enough, if she chooses to exert it, and is usually disposed to do so in proportion to her ignorance and childish vanity. Unacquainted with the im-

[52] The "jeer," "Lady of the Counter," or "Counting House," comes from Heinrich Heine (1797–1856), a German poet and satirist.

[53] One such figure was St. Helena (A.D. 248?–328), who converted to Christianity in A.D. 313; mother of the Roman emperor Constantine the Great (A.D. 280?–337), she supposedly discovered the True Cross and the Holy Sepulchre in Jerusalem.

[54] According to Catholic doctrine, the Virgin Mary was taken into Heaven, body and soul; the Italian poet Francesco Petrarca (1304–1374) was a Renaissance writer of great influence.

portance of life and its purposes, trained to a selfish coquetry and love of petty power, she does not look beyond the pleasure of making herself felt at the moment, and governments are shaken and commerce broken up to gratify the pique of a female favorite. The English shopkeeper's wife does not vote, but it is for her interest that the politician canvasses by the coarsest flattery. France suffers no woman on her throne, but her proud nobles kiss the dust at the feet of Pompadour and Dubarry,[55] for such flare in the lighted foreground where a Roland[56] would modestly aid in the closet. Spain shuts up her women in the care of duennas,[57] and allows them no book but the Breviary;[58] but the ruin follows only the more surely from the worthless favorite of a worthless queen.

It is not the transient breath of poetic incense, that women want; each can receive that from a lover. It is not life-long sway; it needs but to become a coquette, a shrew, or a good cook, to be sure of that. It is not money, nor notoriety, nor the badges of authority, that men have appropriated to themselves. If demands made in their behalf lay stress on any of these particulars, those who make them have not searched deeply into the need. It is for that which at once includes all these and precludes them; which would not be forbidden power, lest there be temptation to steal and misuse it; which would not have the mind perverted by flattery from a worthiness of esteem. It is for that which is the birthright of every being capable to receive it,—the freedom, the religious, the intelligent freedom of the universe, to use its means, to learn its secret as far as nature has enabled them, with God alone for their guide and their judge.

Ye cannot believe it, men; but the only reason why women ever assume what is more appropriate to you, is because you prevent them from finding out what is fit for themselves. Were they free, were they wise fully to develop the strength and beauty of woman, they would never wish to be men, or manlike. The well-instructed moon flies not from her orbit to seize on the glories of her partner. No; for she knows that one law rules, one heaven contains, one universe replies to them alike. It is with women as with the slave.

> "Vor dem Sklaven, wenn er die Kette bricht,
> Vor dem freien Menschen erzittert nicht."[59]

Tremble not before the free man, but before the slave who has chains to break.

In slavery, acknowledged slavery, women are on a par with men. Each is a work-tool, an article of property,—no more! In perfect freedom, such as is painted in Olympus, in Swedenborg's angelic state,[60] in the heaven where there is no marrying nor giving in marriage,[61] each is a purified intelligence, an enfranchised soul,—no less!

---

[55] Jeanne Antoinette Poisson (1721–1764), Marquise de Pompadour, mistress of Louis XV of France from 1745 to 1750 or 1751 and his confidante until her death; Jeanne Bécu (1743–1793), comtesse du Barry, mistress of Louis XV, guillotined during the French Revolution.

[56] Marie Jeanne Roland (1754–1793), a Jacobin activist guillotined during the French Revolution, after which her husband, Jean Roland (1734–1793), committed suicide.

[57] Older women who act as escorts and chaperones.

[58] A prayer book with specified devotional readings.

[59] Source unidentified; the translation is apparently Fuller's.

[60] Emanuel Swedenborg (1688–1772), a Swedish philosopher and mystic, portrayed the "angelic state" in his visionary book *Heaven and Hell* (1758).

[61] "For in the resurrection they neither marry, nor are given in marriage, but are as angels of God in heaven," from Matthew 22:30.

> Jene himmlische Gestalten
> Sie fragen nicht nach Mann und Weib,
> Und keine Kleider, keine Falten
> Umgeben den verklärten Leib.[62]

The child who sang this was a prophetic form, expressive of the longing for a state of perfect freedom, pure love. She could not remain here, but was transplanted to another air. And it may be that the air of this earth will never be so tempered, that such can bear it long. But, while they stay, they must bear testimony to the truth they are constituted to demand.

That an era approaches which shall approximate nearer to such a temper than any has yet done, there are many tokens, indeed so many that only a few of the most prominent can here be enumerated.

The reigns of Elizabeth of England and Isabella of Castile[63] foreboded this era. They expressed the beginning of the new state, while they forwarded its progress. These were strong characters, and in harmony with the wants of their time. One showed that this strength did not unfit a woman for the duties of a wife and mother; the other, that it could enable her to live and die alone. Elizabeth is certainly no pleasing example. In rising above the weakness, she did not lay aside the weaknesses ascribed to her sex; but her strength must be respected now, as it was in her own time.

We may accept it as an omen for ourselves, that it was Isabella who furnished Columbus with the means of coming hither. This land must pay back its debt to woman, without whose aid it would not have been brought into alliance with the civilized world.

The influence of Elizabeth on literature was real, though, by sympathy with its finer productions, she was no more entitled to give name to an era than Queen Anne.[64] It was simply that the fact of having a female sovereign on the throne affected the course of a writer's thoughts. In this sense, the presence of a woman on the throne always makes its mark. Life is lived before the eyes of all men, and their imaginations are stimulated as to the possibilities of woman. "We will die for our King, Maria Theresa,"[65] cry the wild warriors, clashing their swords, and the sounds vibrate through the poems of that generation. The range of female character in Spenser alone might content us for one period. Britomart and Belphoebe have as much room in the canvass as Florimel; and where this is the case, the haughtiest Amazon will not murmur that Una should be felt to be the highest type.[66]

Unlike as was the English Queen to a fairy queen, we may yet conceive that it was the image of *a* queen before the poet's mind, that called up this splendid court of women.

---

[62] From *The Apprenticeship of Wilhelm Meister* (1796), by Johann Wolfgang von Goethe (1749–1832); looking into the next world shortly before her death, young Mignon sings, "Yonder heavenly forms inquire not if one is man or woman; no clothing or costume encloses the transfigured body."

[63] Isabella I (1451–1504), queen of Castile, Spain (1474–1504).

[64] Anne (1665–1714), queen of Great Britain and Ireland (1702–1714).

[65] Maria Theresa (1717–1780) was an Austrian archduchess, queen of Bohemia and Hungary (1740–1780), and consort of the Holy Roman emperor Francis I.

[66] In the allegorical poem *The Faerie Queene* (1590, 1596), by the English writer Edmund Spenser (1552–1599), Britomart, a female knight, represents chastity; Belphoebe, a huntress, resembles the reigning Queen Elizabeth; Florimel is a witch, and Una the personification of truth.

Shakspeare's range is also great, but he has left out the heroic characters, such as the Macaria of Greece, the Britomart of Spenser. Ford and Massinger[67] have, in this respect, shown a higher flight of feeling than he. It was the holy and heroic woman they most loved, and if they could not paint an Imogen, a Desdemona, a Rosalind, yet in those of a stronger mould, they showed a higher ideal, though with so much less poetic power to represent it, than we see in Portia or Isabella. The simple truth of Cordelia,[68] indeed, is of this sort. The beauty of Cordelia is neither male nor female; it is the beauty of virtue.

The ideal of love and marriage rose high in the mind of all the Christian nations who were capable of grave and deep feeling. We may take as examples of its English aspect, the lines,

> "I could not love thee, dear, so much,
> Loved I not honor more."[69]

The address of the Commonwealth's man to his wife as she looked out from the Tower window to see him for the last time on his way to execution. "He stood up in the cart, waved his hat, and cried, 'To Heaven, my love, to Heaven! and leave you in the storm!'"

Such was the love of faith and honor, a love which stopped, like Colonel Hutchinson's, "on this side idolatry," because it was religious.[70] The meeting of two such souls Donne describes as giving birth to an "abler soul."[71]

Lord Herbert wrote to his love,

> "Were not our souls immortal made,
> Our equal loves can make them such."[72]

In Spain the same thought is arrayed in a sublimity, which belongs to the sombre and passionate genius of the nation. Calderon's Justina[73] resists all the temptation of the Demon, and raises her lover with her above the sweet lures of mere temporal happiness. Their marriage is vowed at the stake, their souls are liberated together by the martyr flame into "a purer state of sensation and existence."

In Italy, the great poets wove into their lives an ideal love which answered to

[67] English dramatists: among the plays of John Ford (1586–1640?) that show respect for a 'holy and heroic woman" are *Love's Sacrifice* (1633) and *Perkin Warbeck* (1634); such plays by Philip Massinger (1583–1640) include *The Duke of Milan* (1623) and *The Maid of Honour* (1632).

[68] Female characters in Shakespeare's plays: Imogen in *Cymbeline;* Desdemona in *Othello;* Rosalind in *As You Like It;* Portia in *The Merchant of Venice* or in *Julius Caesar;* Isabella in *Measure for Measure;* Cordelia in *King Lear.*

[69] The final two lines of the lyric "To Lucasta, Going to the Wars" (1649), one of the poems to "Lucasta" (Lucy Sacheverell) by the English writer Richard Lovelace (1618–1658).

[70] John Hutchinson (1615–1664) was one of the men who signed the death warrant of King Charles I; saved from death at the time of the Restoration, Hutchinson was imprisoned for life; in *The Memoirs of the Life of Colonel Hutchinson* (1809), his wife, Lucy Apsley (1620–1680?), writes of their deep love. But it was the English dramatist Ben Jonson (1572–1637) who wrote of Shakespeare, "I loved the man, and do honor his memory (on this side idolatry) as much as any," in his *Timber: Or, Discoveries Made Upon Men and Matters* (1640).

[71] From "The Ecstasy" (1633) by the English cleric and poet John Donne (1572–1631).

[72] From "An Ode Upon a Question Moved Whether Love Should Continue Forever," by the English historian and poet Edward Herbert, (1583–1648), baron of Cherbury.

[73] A major character in *El Magico Prodigioso* ("*The Mighty Magician*"), by the Spanish dramatist Pedro Calderón de la Barca (1600–1681).

the highest wants. It included those of the intellect and the affections, for it was a love of spirit for spirit. It was not ascetic and superhuman, but interpreting all things, gave their proper beauty to details of the common life, the common day; the poet spoke of his love not as a flower to place in his bosom, or hold carelessly in his hand, but as a light towards which he must find wings to fly, or "a stair to heaven." He delighted to speak of her not only as the bride of his heart, but the mother of his soul, for he saw that, in cases where the right direction has been taken, the greater delicacy of her frame, and stillness of her life, left her more open to spiritual influx than man is. So he did not look upon her as betwixt him and earth, to serve his temporal needs, but rather betwixt him and heaven, to purify his affections and lead him to wisdom through her pure love. He sought in her not so much the Eve as the Madonna.

In these minds the thought, which glitters in all the legends of chivalry, shines in broad intellectual effulgence, not to be misinterpreted. And their thought is reverenced by the world, though it lies so far from them as yet, so far, that it seems as though a gulf of Death lay between.

Even with such men, the practice was often widely different from the mental faith. I say mental, for if the heart were thoroughly alive with it, the practice could not be dissonant. Lord Herbert's was a marriage of convention, made for him at fifteen; he was not discontented with it, but looked only to the advantages it brought of perpetuating his family on the basis of a great fortune. He paid, in act, what he considered a dutiful attention to the bond; his thoughts travelled elsewhere, and, while forming a high ideal of the companionship of minds in marriage, he seems never to have doubted that its realization must be postponed to some other stage of being. Dante, almost immediately after the death of Beatrice,[74] married a lady chosen for him by his friends.

Centuries have passed since, but civilized Europe is still in a transition state about marriage, not only in practice, but in thought. A great majority of societies and individuals are still doubtful whether earthly marriage is to be a union of souls, or merely a contract of convenience and utility. Were woman established in the rights of an immortal being, this could not be. She would not in some countries be given away by her father, with scarcely more respect for her own feelings than is shown by the Indian chief, who sells his daughter for a horse, and beats her if she runs away from her new home. Nor, in societies where her choice is left free, would she be perverted, by the current of opinion that seizes her, into the belief that she must marry, if it be only to find a protector, and a home of her own.

Neither would man, if he thought that the connection was of permanent importance, enter upon it so lightly. He would not deem it a trifle, that he was to enter into the closest relations with another soul, which, if not eternal in themselves, must eternally affect his growth.

Neither, did he believe woman capable of friendship, would he, by rash haste, lose the chance of finding a friend in the person who might, probably, live half a century by his side. Did love to his mind partake of infinity, he would not miss his chance of its revelations, that he might the sooner rest from his weariness by a bright fireside, and have a sweet and graceful attendant, "devoted to him alone." Were he a step higher, he would not carelessly enter into a relation, where he

---

[74] Beatrice Portinari (1266–1290), the ideal love of the Italian poet Dante Alighieri (1265–1321) and the model for the Beatrice who guides the pilgrim Dante through Paradise in Dante's *The Divine Comedy*.

might not be able to do the duty of a friend, as well as a protector from external ill, to the other party, and have a being in his power pining for sympathy, intelligence, and aid, that he could not give.

Where the thought of equality has become pervasive, it shows itself in four kinds.

The household partnership. In our country the woman looks for a "smart but kind" husband, the man for a "capable, sweet-tempered" wife.

The man furnishes the house, the woman regulates it. Their relation is one of mutual esteem, mutual dependence. Their talk is of business, their affection shows itself by practical kindness. They know that life goes more smoothly and cheerfully to each for the other's aid; they are grateful and content. The wife praises her husband as a "good provider," the husband in return compliments her as a "capital housekeeper." This relation is good as far as it goes.

Next comes a closer tie which takes the two forms, either of intellectual companionship, or mutual idolatry. The last, we suppose, is to no one a pleasing subject of contemplation. The parties weaken and narrow one another; they lock the gate against all the glories of the universe that they may live in a cell together. To themselves they seem the only wise, to all others steeped in infatuation, the gods smile as they look forward to the crisis of cure, to men the woman seems an unlovely syren, to women the man an effeminate boy.

The other form, of intellectual companionship, has become more and more frequent. Men engaged in public life, literary men, and artists have often found in their wives companions and confidants in thought no less than in feeling. And, as in the course of things the intellectual development of woman has spread wider and risen higher, they have, not unfrequently, shared the same employment. As in the case of Roland and his wife, who were friends in the household and the nation's councils, read together, regulated home affairs, or prepared public documents together indifferently.

It is very pleasant, in letters begun by Roland and finished by his wife, to see the harmony of mind and the difference of nature, one thought, but various ways of treating it.

This is one of the best instances of a marriage of friendship. It was only a friendship, whose basis was esteem; probably neither party knew love, except by name.

Roland was a good man, worthy to esteem and be esteemed, his wife as deserving of admiration as able to do without it. Madame Roland is the fairest specimen we have yet of her class, as clear to discern her aim, as valiant to pursue it, as Spenser's Britomart, austerely set apart from all that did not belong to her, whether as woman or as mind. She is an antetype of a class to which the coming time will afford a field, the Spartan matron, brought by the culture of a book-furnishing age to intellectual consciousness and expansion.

Self-sufficing strength and clear-sightedness were in her combined with a power of deep and calm affection. The page of her life is one of unsullied dignity.

Her appeal to posterity is one against the injustice of those who committed such crimes in the name of liberty. She makes it in behalf of herself and her husband. I would put beside it on the shelf a little volume, containing a similar appeal from the verdict of contemporaries to that of mankind, that of Godwin in behalf of his wife, the celebrated, the by most men detested Mary Wolstonecraft.[75] In his view

[75] *Memoirs of the Author of "A Vindication of the Rights of Women"* (1798), by William Godwin (1756–1836); the author Mary Wollstonecraft (1759–1797) and Godwin were married shortly before her death in childbirth.

it was an appeal from the injustice of those who did such wrong in the name of virtue.

Were this little book interesting for no other cause, it would be so for the generous affection evinced under the peculiar circumstances. This man had courage to love and honor this woman in the face of the world's verdict, and of all that was repulsive in her own past history. He believed he saw of what soul she was, and that the thoughts she had struggled to act out were noble. He loved her and he defended her for the meaning and tendency of her inner life. It was a good fact.

Mary Wolstonecraft, like Madame Dudevant[76] (commonly known as George Sand) in our day, was a woman whose existence better proved the need of some new interpretation of woman's rights, than anything she wrote. Such women as these, rich in genius, of most tender sympathies, and capable of high virtue and a chastened harmony, ought not to find themselves by birth in a place so narrow, that in breaking bonds they became outlaws. Were there as much room in the world for such, as in Spenser's poem for Britomart, they would not run their heads so wildly against its laws. They find their way at last to purer air, but the world will not take off the brand it has set upon them. The champion of the rights of woman found in Godwin one who plead her own cause like a brother. George Sand smokes, wears male attire, wishes to be addressed as Mon frère;[77] perhaps, if she found those who were as brothers indeed, she would not care whether she were brother or sister.

We rejoice to see that she, who expresses such a painful contempt for men in most of her works, as shows she must have known great wrong from them, in La Roche Mauprat,[78] depicting one raised, by the workings of love, from the depths of savage sensualism to a moral and intellectual life. It was love for a pure object, for a steadfast woman, one of those who, the Italian said, could make the stair to heaven.

Women like Sand will speak now, and cannot be silenced; their characters and their eloquence alike foretell an era when such as they shall easier learn to lead true lives. But though such forebode, not such shall be the parents of it. Those who would reform the world must show that they do not speak in the heat of wild impulse; their lives must be unstained by passionate error; they must be severe lawgivers to themselves. As to their transgressions and opinions, it may be observed, that the resolve of Eloisa to be only the mistress of Abelard, was that of one who saw the contract of marriage a seal of degradation.[79] Wherever abuses of this sort are seen, the timid will suffer, the bold protest. But society is in the right to outlaw them till she has revised her law, and she must be taught to do so, by one who speaks with authority, not in anger and haste.

If Godwin's choice of the calumniated authoress of the "Rights of Woman," for his honored wife, be a sign of a new era, no less so is an article of great learning and eloquence, published several years since in an English review, where the writer, in doing full justice to Eloisa, shows his bitter regret that she lives not now

---

[76] Amandine Aurore Lucie Dupin (1804–1876), Baronne Dudevant, a prolific French novelist who used the pen name George Sand; her unconventional behavior shocked many but evoked admiration from those concerned with the liberation of women.

[77] "My brother" (French); here, my "fellow" or my "comrade."

[78] An 1837 drama by George Sand.

[79] As the romantic story goes, Eloisa (Heloïse) refused to marry Peter Abelard because marriage would force him to stop teaching theology within the church. Actually, the two had married secretly when she was his student, but her uncle, Canon Fulbert of Notre Dame Cathedral in Paris, ended that union by hiring men to attack and emasculate Abelard, who then became a monk.

to love him, who might have known better how to prize her love than did the egotistical Abelard.

These marriages, these characters, with all their imperfections, express an onward tendency. They speak of aspiration of soul, of energy of mind, seeking clearness and freedom. Of a like promise are the tracts now publishing by Goodwin Barmby[80] (the European Pariah as he calls himself) and his wife Catharine. Whatever we may think of their measures, we see in them wedlock, the two minds are wed by the only contract that can permanently avail, of a common faith, and a common purpose.

We might mention instances, nearer home, of minds, partners in work and in life, sharing together, on equal terms, public and private interests, and which have not on any side that aspect of offence which characterizes the attitude of the last named; persons who steer straight onward, and in our freer life have not been obliged to run their heads against any wall. But the principles which guide them might, under petrified or oppressive institutions, have made them warlike, paradoxical, or, in some sense, Pariahs. The phenomenon is different, the law the same, in all these cases. Men and women have been obliged to build their house from the very foundation. If they found stone ready in the quarry, they took it peaceably, otherwise they alarmed the country by pulling down old towers to get materials.

These are all instances of marriage as intellectual companionship. The parties meet mind to mind, and a mutual trust is excited which can buckler them against a million. They work together for a common purpose, and, in all these instances, with the same implement, the pen.

A pleasing expression in this kind is afforded by the union in the names of the Howitts. William and Mary Howitt[81] we heard named together for years, supposing them to be brother and sister; the equality of labors and reputation, even so, was auspicious, more so, now we find them man and wife. In his late work on Germany, Howitt mentions his wife with pride, as one among the constellation of distinguished English women; and in a graceful, simple manner.

In naming these instances we do not mean to imply that community of employment is an essential to union of this sort, more than to the union of friendship. Harmony exists in difference no less than in likeness, if only the same key-note govern both parts. Woman the poem, man the poet; woman the heart, man the head; such divisions are only important when they are never to be transcended. If nature is never bound down, nor the voice of inspiration stifled, that is enough. We are pleased that women should write and speak, if they feel the need of it, from having something to tell; but silence for a hundred years would be as well, if that silence be from divine command, and not from man's tradition.

While Goetz von Berlichingen[82] rides to battle, his wife is busy in the kitchen; but difference of occupation does not prevent that community of life, that perfect esteem, with which he says,

"Whom God loves, to him gives he such a wife!"

Manzoni thus dedicates his Adelchi.[83]

---

[80] A minor British publisher.
[81] William Howitt (1792–1879) and Mary Howitt (1799–1888), British writers and translators.
[82] Berlichingen (1481–1562) was a German knight featured in Goethe's play *Götz von Berlichingen* (1773).
[83] The tragedy *Adelchi* (1822), by Manzoni.

"To his beloved and venerated wife, Enrichetta Luigia Blondel, who, with conjugal affections and maternal wisdom, has preserved a virgin mind, the author dedicates this Adelchi, grieving that he could not, by a more splendid and more durable monument, honor the dear name and the memory of so many virtues."

The relation could not be fairer, nor more equal, if she too had written poems. Yet the position of the parties might have been the reverse as well; the woman might have sung the deeds, given voice to the life of the man, and beauty would have been the result, as we see in pictures of Arcadia[84] the nymph singing to the shepherds, or the shepherd with his pipe allures the nymphs, either makes a good picture. The sounding lyre requires not muscular strength, but energy of soul to animate the hand which can control it. Nature seems to delight in varying her arrangements, as if to show that she will be fettered by no rule, and we must admit the same varieties that she admits.

I have not spoken of the higher grade of marriage union, the religious, which may be expressed as pilgrimage towards a common shrine. This includes the others; home sympathies, and household wisdom, for these pilgrims must know how to assist one another to carry their burdens along the dusty way; intellectual communion, for how sad it would be on such a journey to have a companion to whom you could not communicate thoughts and aspirations, as they sprang to life, who would have no feeling for the more and more glorious prospects that open as we advance, who would never see the flowers that may be gathered by the most industrious traveller. It must include all these. Such a fellow pilgrim Count Zinzendorf[85] seems to have found in his countess of whom he thus writes.

"Twenty-five years' experience has shown me that just the help-mate whom I have is the only one that could suit my vocation. Who else could have so carried through my family affairs? Who lived so spotlessly before the world? Who so wisely aided me in my rejection of a dry morality? Who so clearly set aside the Pharisaism[86] which, as years passed, threatened to creep in among us? Who so deeply discerned as to the spirits of delusion which sought to bewilder us? Who would have governed my whole economy so wisely, richly, and hospitably when circumstances commanded? Who have taken indifferently the part of servant or mistress, without on the one side affecting an especial spirituality, on the other being sullied by any worldly pride? Who, in a community where all ranks are eager to be on a level, would, from wise and real causes, have known how to maintain inward and outward distinctions? Who, without a murmur, have seen her husband encounter such dangers by land and sea? Who undertaken with him and sustained such astonishing pilgrimages? Who amid such difficulties always held up her head, and supported me? Who found so many hundred thousands and acquitted them on her own credit? And, finally, who, of all human beings, would so well understand and interpret to others my inner and outer being as this one, of such nobleness in her way of thinking, such great intellectual capacity, and free from the theological perplexities that enveloped me?"

[84] A pastoral region in Greece, celebrated in poetry for its simplicity and rustic charm.

[85] Nikolas Ludwig (1700–1760), Count von Zinzendorf, was a German churchman and bishop of the Moravian church, which had been founded in 1467 in Bohemia; in the United States from 1841 to 1843, he helped to found congregations in eastern Pennsylvania, notably in Bethlehem.

[86] The Pharisees were a strict Jewish sect, the hypocritical members of which Jesus denounced as "whited sepulchres" in Matthew 23:27.

An observer[87] adds this testimony.

"We may in many marriages regard it as the best arrangement, if the man has so much advantage over his wife that she can, without much thought of her own, be, by him, led and directed, as by a father. But it was not so with the Count and his consort. She was not made to be a copy; she was an original; and, while she loved and honored him, she thought for herself on all subjects with so much intelligence, that he could and did look on her as sister and friend also."

Such a woman is the sister and friend of all beings, as the worthy man is their brother and helper.

Another sign of the time is furnished by the triumphs of female authorship. These have been great and constantly increasing. They have taken possession of so many provinces for which men had pronounced them unfit, that though these still declare there are some inaccessible to them, it is difficult to say just *where* they must stop.

The shining names of famous women have cast light upon the path of the sex, and many obstructions have been removed. When a Montague[88] could learn better than her brother, and use her lore to such purpose afterwards as an observer, it seemed amiss to hinder women from preparing themselves to see, or from seeing all they could when prepared. Since Somerville[89] has achieved so much, will any young girl be prevented from attaining a knowledge of the physical sciences, if she wishes it? De Staël's[90] name was not so clear of offence; she could not forget the woman in the thought; while she was instructing you as a mind, she wished to be admired as a woman; sentimental tears often dimmed the eagle glance. Her intellect, too, with all its splendor, trained in a drawing room, fed on flattery, was tainted and flawed; yet its beams make the obscurest school house in New England warmer and lighter to the little rugged girls, who are gathered together on its wooden bench. They may never through life hear her name, but she is not the less their benefactress.

This influence has been such that the aim certainly is, how, in arranging school instruction for girls, to give them as fair a field as boys. These arrangements are made as yet with little judgment or intelligence, just as the tutors of Jane Grey,[91] and the other famous women of her time, taught them Latin and Greek, because they knew nothing else themselves, so now the improvement in the education of girls is made by giving them gentlemen as teachers, who only teach what has been taught themselves at college, while methods and topics need revision for those new cases, which could better be made by those who had experienced the same wants. Women are often at the head of these institutions, but they have as yet

[87] Fuller's note: "Spangenberg." August Gotlieb Spangenberg (1704–1792), who succeeded Count Von Zinzendorf as bishop of the Moravian church.

[88] Lady Mary Wortley Montagu (1689–1762), who helped establish letterwriting as a virtual genre in eighteenth-century English literature and introduced the practice of inoculation against smallpox in England.

[89] Mary Somerville (1789–1872), a British writer on science.

[90] Germaine de Staël (1766–1817), a French-Swiss critic, novelist, and leading figure in literary/political salons, whose study *On Germany* (1810) had a profound effect on the European appreciation of romanticism.

[91] Lady Jane Grey (1537–1554), grandniece of Henry VIII, queen of England for nine days in 1553 before a fierce political rebellion removed her from the throne; first imprisoned, she was beheaded when she was seventeen.

seldom been thinking women, capable to organize a new whole for the wants of the time, and choose persons to officiate in the departments. And when some portion of education is got of a good sort from the school, the tone of society, the much larger proportion received from the world, contradicts its purport. Yet books have not been furnished, and a little elementary instruction been given in vain. Women are better aware how large and rich the universe is, not so easily blinded by the narrowness and partial views of a home circle.

Whether much or little has or will be done, whether women will add to the talent of narration, the power of systematizing, whether they will carve marble as well as draw, is not important. But that it should be acknowledged that they have intellect which needs developing, that they should not be considered complete, if beings of affection and habit alone, is important.

Yet even this acknowledgment, rather obtained by woman than proffered by man, has been sullied by the usual selfishness. So much is said of women being better educated that they may be better companions and mothers *of men!* They should be fit for such companionship, and we have mentioned with satisfaction instances where it has been established. Earth knows no fairer, holier relation than that of a mother. But a being of infinite scope must not be treated with an exclusive view to any one relation. Give the soul free course, let the organization be freely developed, and the being will be fit for any and every relation to which it may be called. The intellect, no more than the sense of hearing, is to be cultivated, that she may be a more valuable companion to man, but because the Power who gave a power by its mere existence signifies that it must be brought out towards perfection.

In this regard, of self-dependence and a greater simplicity and fulness of being, we must hail as a preliminary the increase of the class contemptuously designated as old maids.

We cannot wonder at the aversion with which old bachelors and old maids have been regarded. Marriage is the natural means of forming a sphere, of taking root on the earth: it requires more strength to do this without such an opening, very many have failed of this, and their imperfections have been in every one's way. They have been more partial, more harsh, more officious and impertinent than others. Those, who have a complete experience of the human instincts, have a distrust as to whether they can be thoroughly human and humane, such as is hinted at in the saying, "Old maids' and bachelors' children are well cared for," which derides at once their ignorance and their presumption.

Yet the business of society has become so complex, that it could now scarcely be carried on without the presence of these despised auxiliaries, and detachments from the army of aunts and uncles are wanted to stop gaps in every hedge. They rove about, mental and moral Ishmaelites,[92] pitching their tents amid the fixed and ornamental habitations of men.

They thus gain a wider, if not so deep, experience. They are not so intimate with others, but thrown more upon themselves, and if they do not there find peace and incessant life, there is none to flatter them that they are not very poor and very mean.

A position, which so constantly admonishes, may be of inestimable benefit. The person may gain, undistracted by other relationships, a closer communion with the One. Such a use is made of it by saints and sibyls. Or she may be one of

---

[92] Wanderers, from the Hebrew descendants of Ishmael in Genesis.

the lay sisters of charity, or more humbly only the useful drudge of all men, or the intellectual interpreter of the varied life she sees.

Or she may combine all these. Not "needing to care that she may please a husband," a frail and limited being, all her thoughts may turn to the centre, and by steadfast contemplation enter into the secret of truth and love, use it for the use of all men, instead of a chosen few, and interpret through it all the forms of life.

Saints and geniuses have often chosen a lonely position, in the faith that, if undisturbed by the pressure of near ties they could give themselves up to the inspiring spirit, it would enable them to understand and reproduce life better than actual experience could.

How many old maids take this high stand, we cannot say; it is an unhappy fact that too many of those who come before the eye are gossips rather, and not always good-natured gossips. But, if these abuse, and none make the best of their vocation, yet, it has not failed to produce some good fruit. It has been seen by others, if not by themselves, that beings likely to be left alone need to be fortified and furnished within themselves, and education and thought have tended more and more to regard beings as related to absolute Being, as well as to other men. It has been seen that as the loss of no bond ought to destroy a human being, so ought the missing of none to hinder him from growing. And thus a circumstance of the time has helped to put woman on the true platform. Perhaps the next generation will look deeper into this matter, and find that contempt is put on old maids, or old women at all, merely because they do not use the elixir which will keep the soul always young. No one thinks of Michael Angelo's Persican Sibyl, or St. Theresa, or Tasso's Leonora, or the Greek Electra[93] as an old maid, though all had reached the period in life's course appointed to take that degree.

Even among the North American Indians, a race of men as completely engaged in mere instinctive life as almost any in the world, and where each chief, keeping many wives as useful servants, of course looks with no kind eye on celibacy in woman, it was excused in the following instance mentioned by Mrs. Jameson.[94] A woman dreamt in youth that she was betrothed to the sun. She built her a wigwam apart, filled it with emblems of her alliance and means of an independent life. There she passed her days, sustained by her own exertions, and true to her supposed engagement.

In any tribe, we believe, a woman, who lived as if she was betrothed to the sun, would be tolerated, and the rays which made her youth blossom sweetly would crown her with a halo in age.

There is on this subject a nobler view than heretofore, if not the noblest, and we greet improvement here, as much as on the subject of marriage. Both are fertile themes, but time permits not here to explore them.

If larger intellectual resources begin to be deemed necessary to woman, still more is a spiritual dignity in her, or even the mere assumption of it listened to with respect. Joanna Southcote, and Mother Anne Lee are sure of a band of disciples;

---

[93] One of the classical sibyls, or prophetesses, painted by Michelangelo on the ceiling of the Sistine Chapel in Rome; St. Theresa of Avila (1515–1582), a Spanish Carmelite nun and renowned mystic; Leonora d'Este, who cared for the Italian tragic poet Torquato Tasso (1544–1595) after an accidental blow to the head in 1575 left him intermittently insane; the title character in the Greek tragedy *Electra*, by Sophocles (496–406 B.C.); together with her brother, Orestes, she avenges the murder of her father.

[94] Anna Brownell Jameson (1794–1860), an English author of critical works on art and literature, including *Shakespeare's Heroine's* (1832).

Ecstatica, Dolorosa,[95] of enraptured believers who will visit them in their lowly huts, and wait for hours to revere them in their trances. The foreign noble traverses land and sea to hear a few words from the lips of the lowly peasant girl, whom he believes especially visited by the Most High. Very beautiful in this way was the influence of the invalid of St. Petersburg, as described by De Maistre.[96]

To this region, however misunderstood, and ill-developed, belong the phenomena of Magnetism, or Mesmerism, as it is now often called, where the trance of the Ecstatica purports to be produced by the agency of one human being on another, instead of, as in her case, direct from the spirit.

The worldling has his sneer here as about the services of religion. "The churches can always be filled with women." "Show me a man in one of your magnetic states, and I will believe."

Women are indeed the easy victims of priestcraft, or self-delusion, but this might not be, if the intellect was developed in proportion to the other powers. They would then have a regulator and be in better equipoise, yet must retain the same nervous susceptibility, while their physical structure is such as it is.

It is with just that hope, that we welcome everything that tends to strengthen the fibre and develop the nature on more sides. When the intellect and affections are in harmony, when intellectual consciousness is calm and deep, inspiration will not be confounded with fancy.

The electrical, the magnetic element in woman has not been fairly developed at any period. Everything might be expected from it; she has far more of it than man. This is commonly expressed by saying, that her intuitions are more rapid and more correct.

But I cannot enlarge upon this here, except to say that on this side is highest promise. Should I speak of it fully, my title should be Cassandra, my topic the Seeress of Prevorst, the first, or the best observed subject of magnetism in our times, and who, like her ancestresses at Delphos, was roused to ecstasy or phrenzy by the touch of the laurel.[97]

In such cases worldlings sneer, but reverent men learn wondrous news, either from the person observed, or by the thoughts caused in themselves by the observation. Fenelon learns from Guyon,[98] Kerner from his Seeress what we fain would know. But to appreciate such disclosures one must be a child, and here the phrase, "women and children," may perhaps be interpreted aright, that only little children shall enter into the kingdom of heaven.[99]

All these motions of the time, tides that betoken a waxing moon, overflow upon our own land. The world at large is readier to let woman learn and manifest the capacities of her nature than it ever was before, and here is a less encumbered

---

[95] Joanna Southcote (1750–1814), an English religious reformer; Mother Anne Lee (1736–1784), founder of the Shakers in England (1747), who moved to the United States in 1774 and founded communities in New York and New England; Ecstatica and Dolorosa are generic names for religious enthusiasts.

[96] Joseph De Maistre (1753–1821), a French philosopher and author of *Les Soirées de Saint Pétersbourg* (1821).

[97] In *Summer on the Lakes* (1843) Fuller reports her interest in Justinus Kerner's German study of the clairvoyant Seeress of Prevorst; the priestesses of the oracle at Delphi used laurel leaves to predict the future.

[98] The French Archbishop François Fenelon (1651–1715) learned about the dimensions of self-effacing spirituality from the mystic Jeanne Guyon (1648–1717).

[99] "Suffer little children to come unto me . . . ; for of such is the kingdom of God," from Mark 10:14–15.

field, and freer air than anywhere else. And it ought to be so; we ought to pay for Isabella's jewels.[100]

The names of nations are feminine. Religion, Virtue, and Victory are feminine. To those who have a superstition as to outward signs, it is not without significance that the name of the Queen of our mother-land should at this crisis be Victoria. Victoria the First. Perhaps to us it may be given to disclose the era there outwardly presaged.

Women here are much better situated than men. Good books are allowed with more time to read them. They are not so early forced into the bustle of life, nor so weighed down by demands for outward success. The perpetual changes, incident to our society, make the blood circulate freely through the body politic, and, if not favorable at present to the grace and bloom of life, they are so to activity, resource, and would be to reflection but for a low materialist tendency, from which the women are generally exempt.

They have time to think, and no traditions chain them, and few conventionalities compared with what must be met in other nations. There is no reason why the fact of a constant revelation should be hid from them, and when the mind once is awakened by that, it will not be restrained by the past, but fly to seek the seeds of a heavenly future.

Their employments are more favorable to the inward life than those of the men.

Woman is not addressed religiously here, more than elsewhere. She is told to be worthy to be the mother of a Washington, or the companion of some good man. But in many, many instances, she has already learnt that all bribes have the same flaw; that truth and good are to be sought for themselves alone. And already an ideal sweetness floats over many forms, shines in many eyes.

Already deep questions are put by young girls on the great theme, What shall I do to inherit eternal life?

Men are very courteous to them. They praise them often, check them seldom. There is some chivalry in the feeling towards "the ladies," which gives them the best seats in the stage-coach, frequent admission not only to lectures of all sorts, but to courts of justice, halls of legislature, reform conventions. The newspaper editor "would be better pleased that the Lady's Book[101] were filled up exclusively by ladies. It would then, indeed, be a true gem, worthy to be presented by young men to the mistresses of their affections." Can gallantry go farther?

In this country is venerated, wherever seen, the character which Goethe spoke of as an Ideal. "The excellent woman is she, who, if the husband dies, can be a father to the children." And this, if rightly read, tells a great deal.

Women who speak in public, if they have a moral power, such as has been felt from Angelina Grimke and Abby Kelly,[102] that is, if they speak for conscience' sake, to serve a cause which they hold sacred, invariably subdue the prejudices of their hearers, and excite an interest proportionate to the aversion with which it had been the purpose to regard them.

A passage in a private letter so happily illlustrates this, that I take the liberty to

[100] According to some reports, Queen Isabella sold her jewels to finance the first voyage of Christopher Columbus.

[101] *Godey's Lady's Book* (1830–1898) was a popular monthly magazine founded in Philadelphia and edited from 1837 to 1877 by Sarah J. Hale (1788–1879), the author of "Mary had a little lamb."

[102] Prominent Quaker abolitionists: Grimke (1805–1879), originally from South Carolina, was the author of *An Appeal to the Christian Women of the South* (1836); Kelly (1811–1887) was the first woman to lecture on abolition to audiences of men and women.

make use of it, though there is not opportunity to ask leave either of the writer or owner of the letter. I think they will pardon me when they see it in print; it is so good, that as many as possible should have the benefit of it.

Abby Kelly in the Town-House of ———

"The scene was not unheroic,—to see that woman, true to humanity and her own nature, a centre of rude eyes and tongues, even gentlemen feeling licensed to make part of a species of mob around a female out of her sphere. As she took her seat in the desk amid the great noise, and in the throng full, like a wave, of something to ensue, I saw her humanity in a gentleness and unpretension, tenderly open to the sphere around her, and, had she not been supported by the power of the will of genuineness and principle, she would have failed. It led her to prayer, which, in woman especially, is childlike; sensibility and will going to the side of God and looking up to him; and humanity was poured out in aspiration.

"She acted like a gentle hero, with her mild decision and womanly calmness. All heroism is mild and quiet and gentle, for it is life and possession, and combativeness and firmness show a want of actualness. She is as earnest, fresh, and simple as when she first entered the crusade. I think she did much good, more than the men in her place could do, for woman feels more as being and reproducing; this brings the subject more into home relations. Men speak through and mostly from intellect, and this addresses itself in others, which creates and is combative."

Not easily shall we find elsewhere, or before this time, any written observations on the same subject, so delicate and profound.

The late Dr. Channing,[103] whose enlarged and tender and religious nature shared every onward impulse of his time, though his thoughts followed his wishes with a deliberative caution, which belonged to his habits and temperament, was greatly interested in these expectations for women. His own treatment of them was absolutely and thoroughly religious. He regarded them as souls, each of which had a destiny of its own, incalculable to other minds, and whose leading it must follow, guided by the light of a private conscience. He had sentiment, delicacy, kindness, taste, but they were all pervaded and ruled by this one thought, that all beings had souls, and must vindicate their own inheritance. Thus all beings were treated by him with an equal, and sweet, though solemn courtesy. The young and unknown, the woman and child, all felt themselves regarded with an infinite expectation, from which there was no reaction to vulgar prejudice. He demanded of all he met, to use his favorite phrase, "great truths."

His memory, every way dear and reverend, is by many especially cherished for this intercourse of unbroken respect.

At one time when the progress of Harriet Martineau through this country, Angelina Grimke's appearance in public, and the visit of Mrs. Jameson[104] had turned his thoughts to this subject, he expressed high hopes as to what the coming era would bring to woman. He had been much pleased with the dignified courage of Mrs. Jameson in taking up the defence of her sex, in a way from which women usually shrink, because, if they express themselves on such subjects with suffi-

---

[103] William Ellery Channing (1780–1842), a religious reformer and a major force in the founding of Unitarianism.

[104] Harriet Martineau (1802–1876), a British journalist and advocate of social reform, toured in the United States in 1835; Angelina Grimke lectured in the late 1830s; Anna Brownell Jameson traveled through New England in 1836.

cient force and clearness to do any good, they are exposed to assaults whose vulgarity makes them painful. In intercourse with such a woman, he had shared her indignation at the base injustice, in many respects, and in many regions done to the sex; and been led to think of it far more than ever before. He seemed to think that he might some time write upon the subject. That his aid is withdrawn from the cause is a subject of great regret, for on this question, as on others, he would have known how to sum up the evidence and take, in the noblest spirit, middle ground. He always furnished a platform on which opposing parties could stand, and look at one another under the influence of his mildness and enlightened candor.

Two younger thinkers, men both, have uttered noble prophecies, auspicious for woman. Kinmont, all whose thoughts tended towards the establishment of the reign of love and peace, thought that the inevitable means of this would be an increased predominance given to the idea of woman. Had he lived longer to see the growth of the peace party, the reforms in life and medical practice which seek to substitute water for wine and drugs, pulse for animal food, he would have been confirmed in his view of the way in which the desired changes are to be effected.

In this connection I must mention Shelley,[105] who, like all men of genius, shared the feminine development, and, unlike many, knew it. His life was one of the first pulsebeats in the present reform-growth. He, too, abhorred blood and heat, and, by his system and his song, tended to reinstate a plant-like gentleness in the development of energy. In harmony with this his ideas of marriage were lofty, and of course no less so of woman, her nature, and destiny.

For woman, if by a sympathy as to outward condition, she is led to aid the enfranchisement of the slave, must no less so, by inward tendency, to favor measures which promise to bring the world more thoroughly and deeply into harmony with her nature. When the lamb takes place of the lion as the emblem of nations, both women and men will be as children of one spirit, perpetual learners of the word and doers thereof, not hearers only.

A writer in a late number of the New York Pathfinder, in two articles headed "Femality," has uttered a still more pregnant word than any we have named. He views woman truly from the soul, and not from society, and the depth and leading of his thoughts is proportionally remarkable. He views the feminine nature as a harmonizer of the vehement elements, and this has often been hinted elsewhere; but what he expresses most forcibly is the lyrical, the inspiring and inspired apprehensiveness of her being.

Had I room to dwell upon this topic, I could not say anything so precise, so near the heart of the matter, as may be found in that article; but, as it is, I can only indicate, not declare, my view.

There are two aspects of woman's nature, expressed by the ancients as Muse and Minerva. It is the former to which the writer in the Pathfinder looks. It is the latter which Wordsworth has in mind, when he says,

"With a placid brow,
Which woman ne'er should forfeit, keep thy vow."[106]

The especial genius of woman I believe to be electrical in movement, intuitive in function, spiritual in tendency.[107] She is great not so easily in classification, or

---

[105] The English romantic poet Percy Bysshe Shelley (1792–1822).

[106] Adapted from "Liberty: Sequel to the Preceding" (1835), by the English romantic poet William Wordsworth (1770–1850).

[107] Sparklike, quick.

re-creation, as in an instinctive seizure of causes, and a simple breathing out of what she receives that has the singleness of life, rather than the selecting or energizing of art.

More native to her is it to be the living model of the artist, than to set apart from herself any one form in objective reality; more native to inspire and receive the poem than to create it. In so far as soul is in her completely developed, all soul is the same; but as far as it is modified in her as woman, it flows, it breathes, it sings, rather than deposits soil, or finishes work, and that which is especially feminine flushes in blossom the face of earth, and pervades like air and water all this seeming solid globe, daily renewing and purifying its life. Such may be the especially feminine element, spoken of as Femality. But it is no more the order of nature that it should be incarnated pure in any form, than that the masculine energy should exist unmingled with it in any form.

Male and female represent the two sides of the great radical dualism. But, in fact, they are perpetually passing into one another. Fluid hardens to solid, solid rushes to fluid. There is no wholly masculine man, no purely feminine woman.

History jeers at the attempts of physiologists to bind great original laws by the forms which flow from them. They make a rule; they say from observation, what can and cannot be. In vain! Nature provides exceptions to every rule: She sends women to battle, and sets Hercules spinning;[108] she enables women to bear immense burdens, cold, and frost; she enables the man, who feels maternal love, to nourish his infant like a mother. Of late she plays still gayer pranks. Not only she deprives organizations, but organs, of a necessary end. She enables people to read with the top of the head, and see with the pit of the stomach. Presently she will make a female Newton, and a male Syren.[109]

Man partakes of the feminine in the Apollo, woman of the masculine as Minerva.

Let us be wise and not impede the soul. Let her work as she will. Let us have one creative energy, one incessant revelation. Let it take what form it will, and let us not bind it by the past to man or woman, black or white. Jove sprang from Rhea, Pallas from Jove.[110] So let it be.

If it has been the tendency of the past remarks to call woman rather to the Minerva side,—if I, unlike the more generous writer, have spoken from society no less than the soul,—let it be pardoned. It is love that has caused this, love for many incarcerated souls, that might be freed could the idea of religious self-dependence be established in them, could the weakening habit of dependence on others be broken up.

Every relation, every gradation of nature, is incalculably precious, but only to the soul which is poised upon itself, and to whom no loss, no change, can bring dull discord, for it is in harmony with the central soul.

If any individual live too much in relations, so that he becomes a stranger to the resources of his own nature, he falls after a while into a distraction, or imbecility, from which he can only be cured by a time of isolation, which gives the renovating fountains time to rise up. With a society it is the same. Many minds, deprived of the traditionary or instinctive means of passing a cheerful existence, must find

[108] Among nature's tricks or "exceptions": women, supposedly weak, go to war, while the strongest men (like Hercules) do domestic work.

[109] The English mathematician and physicist Sir Isaac Newton (1642–1727); according to Greek myth, sirens were women who sang seductive songs to lure sailors to shipwreck on their island.

[110] Fuller mixes the Greek and Roman names for deities, but she means that the female Rhea bore the male Jove; the female Pallas Athena sprang from Jove's head, fully grown and fully armed.

help in self-impulse or perish. It is therefore that while any elevation, in the view of union, is to be hailed with joy, we shall not decline celibacy as the great fact of the time. It is one from which no vow, no arrangement, can at present save a thinking mind. For now the rowers are pausing on their oars, they wait a change before they can pull together. All tends to illustrate the thought of a wise contemporary. Union is only possible to those who are units. To be fit for relations in time, souls, whether of man or woman, must be able to do without them in the spirit.

It is therefore that I would have woman lay aside all thought, such as she habitually cherishes, of being taught and led by men. I would have her, like the Indian girl, dedicate herself to the Sun, the Sun of Truth, and go no where if his beams did not make clear the path. I would have her free from compromise, from complaisance, from helplessness, because I would have her good enough and strong enough to love one and all beings, from the fulness, not he poverty of being.

Men, as at present instructed, will not help this work, because they also are under the slavery of habit. I have seen with delight their poetic impulses. A sister is the fairest ideal, and how nobly Wordsworth, and even Byron, have written of a sister.[111]

There is no sweeter sight than to see a father with his little daughter. Very vulgar men become refined to the eye when leading a little girl by the hand. At that moment the right relation between the sexes seems established, and you feel as if the man would aid in the noblest purpose, if you ask him in behalf of his little daughter. Once two fine figures stood before me, thus. The father of very intellectual aspect, his falcon eye softened by affection as he looked down on his fair child, she the image of himself, only more graceful and brilliant in expression. I was reminded of Southey's Kehama,[112] when lo, the dream was rudely broken. They were talking of education, and he said,

"I shall not have Maria brought too forward. If she knows too much, she will never find a husband; superior women hardly ever can."

"Surely," said the wife, with a blush, "you wish Maria to be as good and wise as she can, whether it will help her to marriage or not."

"No," he persisted, "I want her to have a sphere and a home, and some one to protect her when I am gone."

It was a trifling incident, but made a deep impression. I felt that the holiest relations fail to instruct the unprepared and perverted mind. If this man, indeed, would have looked at it on the other side, he was the last that would have been willing to have been taken himself for the home and protection he could give, but would have been much more likely to repeat the tale of Alcibiades with his phials.

But men do *not* look at both sides, and women must leave off asking them and being influenced by them, but retire within themselves, and explore the groundwork of being till they find their peculiar secret. Then when they come forth again, renovated and baptized, they will know how to turn all dross to gold, and will be rich and free though they live in a hut, tranquil, if in a crowd. Then their sweet singing shall not be from passionate impulse, but the lyrical overflow of a divine rapture, and a new music shall be elucidated from this many-chorded world.

[111] A tribute to the literary honors paid by Wordsworth to his sister Dorothy and by Byron to his half-sister Augusta Leigh. Not until later in the century did evidence point to Byron's incest with Augusta; and only in the twentieth century was the possibility raised that Wordsworth and Dorothy might have committed incest.

[112] *The Curse of Kehama* (1810), a narrative poem by Robert Southey (1774–1843).

Grant her then for a while the armor and the javelin.[113] Let her put from her the press of other minds and meditate in virgin loneliness. The same idea shall reappear in due time as Muse, or Ceres, the all-kindly, patient Earth-Spirit.

I tire every one with my Goethean illustrations. But it cannot be helped.

Goethe, the great mind which gave itself absolutely to the leadings of truth, and let rise through him the waves which are still advancing through the century, was its intellectual prophet. Those who know him, see, daily, his thought fulfilled more and more, and they must speak of it, till his name weary and even nauseate, as all great names have in their time. And I cannot spare the reader, if such there be, his wonderful sight as to the prospects and wants of women.

As his Wilhelm[114] grows in life and advances in wisdom, he becomes acquainted with women of more and more character, rising from Mariana to Macaria.

Macaria, bound with the heavenly bodies in fixed revolutions, the centre of all relations, herself unrelated, expresses the Minerva side.

Mignon, the electrical, inspired lyrical nature.

All these women, though we see them in relations, we can think of as unrelated. They all are very individual, yet seem nowhere restrained. They satisfy for the present, yet arouse an infinite expectation.

The economist Theresa, the benevolent Natalia, the fair Saint, have chosen a path, but their thoughts are not narrowed to it. The functions of life to them are not ends, but suggestions.

Thus to them all things are important, because none is necessary. Their different characters have fair play, and each is beautiful in its minute indications, for nothing is enforced or conventional, but everything, however slight, grows from the essential life of the being.

Mignon and Theresa wear male attire when they like, and it is graceful for them to do so, while Macaria is confined to her arm chair behind the green curtain, and the Fair Saint could not bear a speck of dust on her robe.

All things are in their places in this little world because all is natural and free, just as "there is room for everything out of doors." Yet all is rounded in by natural harmony which will always arise where Truth and Love are sought in the light of freedom.

Goethe's book bodes an era of freedom like its own, of "extraordinary generous seeking," and new revelations. New individualities shall be developed in the actual world, which shall advance upon it as gently as the figures come out upon his canvass.

A profound thinker has said "no married woman can represent the female world, for she belongs to her husband. The idea of woman must be represented by a virgin."

But that is the very fault of marriage, and of the present relation between the sexes, that the woman does belong to the man, instead of forming a whole with him. Were it otherwise there would be no such limitation to the thought.

Woman, self-centred, would never be absorbed by any relation; it would be only an experience to her as to man. It is a vulgar error that love, *a* love to woman is her whole existence; she also is born for Truth and Love in their universal energy. Would she but assume her inheritance, Mary would not be the only Virgin

---

[113] Traditional weapons of Athena, the Greek goddess of wisdom.

[114] Goethe's *The Apprenticeship of Wilhelm Meister* (1796); the names in the following paragraphs are those of female characters in this prototypical novel.

Mother. Not Manzoni[115] alone would celebrate in his wife the virgin mind with the maternal wisdom and conjugal affections. The soul is ever young, ever virgin.

And will not she soon appear? The woman who shall vindicate their birthright for all women; who shall teach them what to claim, and how to use what they obtain? Shall not her name be for her era Victoria, for her country and her life Virginia?[116] Yet predictions are rash; she herself must teach us to give her the fitting name.

1843

from PAPERS ON LITERATURE AND ART

from AMERICAN LITERATURE

Its Position in the Present Time and Prospects for the Future

Some thinkers may object to this essay, that we are about to write of that which has, as yet, no existence.

For it does not follow because many books are written by persons born in America that there exists an American literature. Books which imitate or represent the thoughts and life of Europe do not constitute an American literature. Before such can exist, an original idea must animate this nation and fresh currents of life must call into life fresh thoughts along its shores.

We have no sympathy with national vanity. We are not anxious to prove that there is as yet much American literature. Of those who think and write among us in the methods and of the thoughts of Europe, we are not impatient; if their minds are still best adapted to such food and such action. If their books express life of mind and character in graceful forms, they are good and we like them. We consider them as colonists and useful schoolmasters to our people in a transition state; which lasts rather longer than is occupied in passing, bodily, the ocean which separates the new from the old world.

We have been accused of an undue attachment to foreign continental literature, and, it is true, that in childhood, we had well nigh "forgotten our English," while constantly reading in other languages. Still, what we loved in the literature of continental Europe was the range and force of ideal manifestation in forms of national and individual greatness. A model was before us in the great Latins of simple masculine minds seizing upon life with unbroken power. The stamp both of nationality and individuality was very strong upon them; their lives and thoughts stood out in clear and bold relief. The English character has the iron force of the Latins, but not the frankness and expansion. Like their fruits, they need a summer sky to give them more sweetness and a richer flavour. This does not apply to Shakspeare, who has all the fine side of English genius, with the rich colouring, and more fluent life, of the Catholic countries. Other poets, of England also, are expansive more or less, and soar freely to seek the blue sky, but take it as

---

[115] Manzoni's *Adelchi*.   [116] Shall she not be the model of authority and of purity?

a whole, there is in English literature, as in English character, a reminiscence of walls and ceilings, a tendency to the arbitrary and conventional that repels a mind trained in admiration of the antique spirit. It is only in later days that we are learning to prize the peculiar greatness which a thousand times outweighs this fault, and which has enabled English genius to go forth from its insular position and conquer such vast dominion in the realms both of matter and of mind.

Yet there is, often, between child and parent, a reaction from excessive influence having been exerted, and such an one we have experienced, in behalf of our country, against England. We use her language, and receive, in torrents, the influence of her thought, yet it is, in many respects, uncongenial and injurious to our constitution. What suits Great Britain, with her insular position and consequent need to concentrate and intensify her life, her limited monarchy, and spirit of trade, does not suit a mixed race, continually enriched with new blood from other stocks the most unlike that of our first descent, with ample field and verge enough to range in and leave every impulse free, and abundant opportunity to develope a genius, wide and full as our rivers, flowery, luxuriant and impassioned as our vast prairies, rooted in strength as the rocks on which the Puritan fathers landed.

That such a genius is to rise and work in this hemisphere we are confident; equally so that scarce the first faint streaks of that day's dawn are yet visible. It is sad for those that foresee, to know they may not live to share its glories, yet it is sweet, too, to know that every act and word, uttered in the light of that foresight, may tend to hasten or ennoble its fulfilment.

That day will not rise till the fusion of races among us is more complete. It will not rise till this nation shall attain sufficient moral and intellectual dignity to prize moral and intellectual, no less highly than political, freedom, not till, the physical resources of the country being explored, all its regions studded with towns, broken by the plow, netted together by railways and telegraph lines, talent shall be left at leisure to turn its energies upon the higher department of man's existence. Nor then shall it be seen till from the leisurely and yearning soul of that riper time national ideas shall take birth, ideas craving to be clothed in a thousand fresh and original forms.

Without such ideas all attempts to construct a national literature must end in abortions like the monster of Frankenstein,[1] things with forms, and the instincts of forms, but soulless, and therefore revolting. We cannot have expression till there is something to be expressed.

The symptoms of such a birth may be seen in a longing felt here and there for the sustenance of such ideas. At present, it shows itself, where felt, in sympathy with the prevalent tone of society, by attempts at external action, such as are classed under the head of social reform. But it needs to go deeper, before we can have poets, needs to penetrate beneath the springs of action, to stir and remake the soil as by the action of fire.

Another symptom is the need felt by individuals of being even sternly sincere. This is the one great means by which alone progress can be essentially furthered. Truth is the nursing mother of genius. No man can be absolutely true to himself, eschewing cant, compromise, servile imitation, and complaisance, without becoming original, for there is in every creature a fountain of life which, if not choked back by stones and other dead rubbish, will create a fresh atmosphere,

---

[1] The monster in *Frankenstein, or the Modern Prometheus* (1818), by the British writer Mary Wollstonecraft Shelley (1797–1851).

and bring to life fresh beauty. And it is the same with the nation as with the individual man.

The best work we do for the future is by such truth. By use of that, in whatever way, we harrow the soil and lay it open to the sun and air. The winds from all quarters of the globe bring seed enough, and there is nothing wanting but preparation of the soil, and freedom in the atmosphere, for ripening of a new and golden harvest.

* * *

Under present circumstances the amount of talent and labour given to writing ought to surprise us. Literature is in this dim and struggling state, and its pecuniary results exceedingly pitiful. From many well known causes it is impossible for ninety-nine out of the hundred, who wish to use the pen, to ransom, by its use, the time they need. This state of things will have to be changed in some way. No man of genius writes for money; but it is essential to the free use of his powers, that he should be able to disembarrass his life from care and perplexity. This is very difficult here; and the state of things gets worse and worse, as less and less is offered in pecuniary meed for works demanding great devotion of time and labour (to say nothing of the ether engaged) and the publisher, obliged to regard the transaction as a matter of business, demands of the author to give him only what will find an immediate market, for he cannot afford to take any thing else. This will not do! When an immortal poet was secure only of a few copyists to circulate his works, there were princes and nobles to patronize literature and the arts. Here is only the public, and the public must learn how to cherish the nobler and rarer plants, and to plant the aloe, able to wait a hundred years for its bloom, or its garden will contain, presently, nothing but potatoes and pot-herbs. We shall have, in the course of the next two or three years, a convention of authors to inquire into the causes of this state of things and propose measures for its remedy. Some have already been thought of that look promising, but we shall not announce them till the time be ripe; that date is not distant, for the difficulties increase from day to day, in consequence of the system of cheap publication, on a great scale.

The ranks that led the way in the first half century of this republic were far better situated than we, in this respect. The country was not so deluged with the dingy page, reprinted from Europe, and patriotic vanity was on the alert to answer the question, "Who reads an American book?"[2] And many were the books written, worthy to be read, as any out of the first class in England. They were, most of them, except in their subject matter, English books.

The list is large, and, in making some cursory comments, we do not wish to be understood as designating *all* who are worthy of notice, but only those who present themselves to our minds with some special claims. In history there has been nothing done to which the world at large has not been eager to award the full meed of its deserts. Mr. Prescott,[3] for instance, has been greeted with as much warmth abroad as here. We are not disposed to undervalue his industry and power of clear and elegant arrangement. The richness and freshness of his materials is such that a sense of enchantment must be felt in their contemplation. We must regret, however, that they should have been first presented to the public by one who possesses

---

[2] The question asked sardonically by Sydney Smith (1771–1845), an English critic, clergyman, and essayist, in the *Edinburgh Review* (1820).

[3] William Hickling Prescott (1796–1859), author of *History of the Conquest of Mexico* (1843).

nothing of the higher powers of the historian, great leading views, or discernment as to the motives of action and the spirit of an era. Considering the splendour of the materials the books are wonderfully tame, and every one must feel that having once passed through them and got the sketch in the mind, there is nothing else to which it will recur. The absence of thought, as to that great picture of Mexican life, with its heroisms, its terrible but deeply significant superstitions, its admirable civic refinement, seems to be quite unbroken.

Mr. Bancroft[4] is a far more vivid writer; he has great resources and great command of them, and leading thoughts by whose aid he groups his facts. But we cannot speak fully of his historical works, which we have only read and referred to here and there.

In the department of ethics and philosophy, we may inscribe two names as likely to live and be blessed and honoured in the later time. These are the names of Channing and of Emerson.

Dr. Channing[5] had several leading thoughts which corresponded with the wants of his time, and have made him in it a father of thought. His leading idea of "the dignity of human nature" is one of vast results, and the peculiar form in which he advocated it had a great work to do in this new world. The spiritual beauty of his writings is very great; they are all distinguished for sweetness, elevation, candour, and a severe devotion to truth. On great questions, he took middle ground, and sought a panoramic view; he wished also to stand high, yet never forgot what was above more than what was around and beneath him. He was not well acquainted with man on the impulsive and passionate side of his nature, so that his view of character was sometimes narrow, but it was always noble. He exercised an expansive and purifying power on the atmosphere, and stands a godfather at the baptism of this country.

The Sage of Concord[6] has a very different mind, in every thing except that he has the same disinterestedness and dignity of purpose, the same purity of spirit. He is a profound thinker. He is a man of ideas, and deals with causes rather than effects. His ideas are illustrated from a wide range of literary culture and refined observation, and embodied in a style whose melody and subtle fragrance enchant those who stand stupified before the thoughts themselves, because their utmost depths do not enable them to sound his shallows. His influence does not yet extend over a wide space; he is too far beyond his place and his time, to be felt at once or in full, but it searches deep, and yearly widens its circles. He is a harbinger of the better day. His beautiful elocution has been a great aid to him in opening the way for the reception of his written word.

In that large department of literature which includes descriptive sketches, whether of character or scenery, we are already rich. Irving, a genial and fair nature, just what he ought to be, and would have been, at any time of the world, has drawn the scenes amid which his youth was spent in their primitive lineaments, with all the charms of his graceful jocund humour. He has his niche and need never be deposed; it is not one that another could occupy.

The first enthusiasm about Cooper[7] having subsided, we remember more his faults than his merits. His ready resentment and way of showing it in cases which

---

[4] George Bancroft (1800–1891), author of a memorable *History of the United States* (1834–1876), published in ten volumes that were later revised to six.

[5] William Ellery Channing (1780–1842), a Unitarian religious leader.

[6] Fuller's name for Ralph Waldo Emerson (1803–1882), who lived in Concord, Massachusetts.

[7] James Fenimore Cooper (1789–1851), author of sea fiction and of wilderness novels.

it is the wont of gentlemen to pass by in silence, or meet with a good humoured smile, have caused unpleasant associations with his name, and his fellow citizens, in danger of being tormented by suits for libel, if they spoke freely of him, have ceased to speak of him at all. But neither these causes, nor the baldness of his plots, shallowness of thought, and poverty in the presentation of character, should make us forget the grandeur and originality of his sea-sketches, nor the redemption from oblivion of our forest-scenery, and the noble romance of the hunter-pioneer's life. Already, but for him, this fine page of life's romance would be almost forgotten. He has done much to redeem these irrevocable beauties from the corrosive acid of a semi-civilized invasion.

Miss Sedgwick[8] and others have portrayed, with skill and feeling, scenes and personages from the revolutionary time. Such have a permanent value in proportion as their subject is fleeting. The same charm attends the spirited delineations of Mrs. Kirkland,[9] and that amusing book, "A New Purchase." The features of Hoosier, Sucker, and Wolverine[10] life are worth fixing; they are peculiar to the soil, and indicate its hidden treasures; they have, also, that charm which simple life, lived for its own sake, always has, even in rude and all but brutal forms.

What shall we say of the poets? The list is scanty; amazingly so, for there is nothing in the causes that paralyze other kinds of literature that could affect lyrical and narrative poetry. Men's hearts beat, hope, and suffer always, and they must crave such means to vent them; yet of the myriad leaves garnished with smooth stereotyped rhymes that issue yearly from our press, you will not find, one time in a million, a little piece written from any such impulse, or with the least sincerity or sweetness of tone. They are written for the press, in the spirit of imitation or vanity, the paltriest offspring of the human brain, for the heart disclaims, as the ear is shut against them. This is the kind of verse which is cherished by the magazines as a correspondent to the tawdry pictures of smiling milliners' dolls in the frontispiece. Like these they are only a fashion, a fashion based on no reality of love or beauty. The inducement to write them consists in a little money, or more frequently the charm of seeing an anonymous name printed at the top in capitals.

We must here, in passing, advert also to the style of story current in the magazines, flimsy beyond any texture that was ever spun or even dreamed of by the mind of man, in any other age and country. They are said to be "written for the seamstresses," but we believe that every way injured class could relish and digest better fare even at the end of long days of exhausting labour. There are exceptions to this censure; stories by Mrs. Child[11] have been published in the magazines, and now and then good ones by Mrs. Stephens[12] and others; but, take them generally, they are calculated to do a positive injury to the public mind, acting as an opiate, and of an adulterated kind, too.

But to return to the poets. At their head Mr. Bryant[13] stands alone. His range is

---

[8] Catharine Maria Sedgwick (1789–1867), whose novels include *Hope Leslie: Or, Early Times in the Massachusetts* (1827) and *Married or Single?* (1857).

[9] Caroline Stansbury Kirkland (1801–1864), whose *A New Home—Who'll Follow* (1839) describes her life in the frontier settlement of Pinckney, Michigan.

[10] Nicknames for the states Indiana, Illinois, and Michigan, respectively.

[11] Lydia Maria Child (1802–1880), an abolitionist and advocate of women's rights, whose fiction includes *Hobomok* (1824) and "Chocorua's Curse" (1830).

[12] Ann Sophia Stephens (1810–1886), a prolific writer of stories and historical novels, including *Alice Copley: A Tale of Queen Mary's Time* (1844) and *Malaeska: The Indian Wife of the White Hunter* (1860).

[13] William Cullen Bryant (1794–1878), a highly respected poet and critic known for didactic verse about nature.

not great, nor his genius fertile. But his poetry is purely the language of his inmost nature, and the simple lovely garb in which his thoughts are arranged, a direct gift from the Muse. He has written nothing that is not excellent, and the atmosphere of his verse refreshes and composes the mind, like leaving the highway to enter some green, lovely, fragrant wood.

* * *

Longfellow[14] is artificial and imitative. He borrows incessantly, and mixes what he borrows, so that it does not appear to the best advantage. He is very faulty in using broken or mixed metaphors. The ethical part of his writing has a hollow, second-hand sound. He has, however, elegance, a love of the beautiful, and a fancy for what is large and manly, if not a full sympathy with it. His verse breathes at times much sweetness; and, if not allowed to supersede what is better may promote a taste for good poetry. Though imitative, he is not mechanical.

We cannot say as much for Lowell,[15] who, we must declare it, though to the grief of some friends, and the disgust of more, is absolutely wanting in the true spirit and tone of poesy. His interest in the moral questions of the day has supplied the want of vitality in himself; his great facility at versification has enabled him to fill the ear with a copious stream of pleasant sound. But his verse is stereotyped; his thought sounds no depth, and posterity will not remember him.

R. W. Emerson, in melody, in subtle beauty of thought and expression, takes the highest rank upon this list. But his poems are mostly philosophical, which is not the truest kind of poetry. They want the simple force of nature and passion, and, while they charm the ear and interest the mind, fail to wake far-off echoes in the heart. The imagery wears a symbolical air, and serves rather as illustration, than to delight us by fresh and glowing forms of life.

* * *

We see we have omitted honoured names in this essay. We have not spoken of Brown,[16] as a novelist by far our first in point of genius and instruction as to the soul of things. Yet his works have fallen almost out of print. It is their dark, deep gloom that prevents their being popular, for their very beauties are grave and sad. But we see that Ormond is being republished at this moment. The picture of Roman character, of the life and resources of a single noble creature, of Constantia alone, should make that book an object of reverence. All these novels should be republished; if not favorites, they should at least not be lost sight of, for there will always be some who find in such powers of mental analysis the only response to their desires.

We have not spoken of Hawthorne,[17] the best writer of the day, in a similar range with Irving, only touching many more points and discerning far more deeply. But we have omitted many things in this slight sketch, for the subject, even in this stage, lies as a volume in our mind, and cannot be unrolled in completeness unless time and space were more abundant. Our object was to show that

[14] Henry Wadsworth Longfellow (1807–1882), probably the most popular and revered poet in the nineteenth century; Fuller's assessment anticipates more recent judgments of his work.

[15] James Russell Lowell (1819–1891), author of witty and satirical verse.

[16] Charles Brockden Brown (1771–1810), author of Gothic romances including *Arthur Mervyn* (1799) and *Ormond* (1799); Constantia is a character in *Ormond*.

[17] Nathaniel Hawthorne (1804–1864), here, before the publication of his novels; Washington Irving (1783–1859), a writer of tales and histories that made him well known in the 1840s.

although by a thousand signs, the existence is foreshown of those forces which are to animate an American literature, that faith, those hopes are not yet alive which shall usher it into a homogeneous or fully organized state of being. The future is glorious with certainties for those who do their duty in the present, and, lark-like, seeking the sun, challenge its eagles to an earthward flight, where their nests may be built in our mountains, and their young raise their cry of triumph, unchecked by dullness in the echoes.

REVIEW OF NATHANIEL HAWTHORNE'S *MOSSES FROM AN OLD MANSE**

We have been seated here the last ten minutes, pen in hand, thinking what we can possibly say about this book that will not be either superfluous or impertinent.

Superfluous, because the attractions of Hawthorne's writings cannot fail of one and the same effect on all persons who possess the common sympathies of men. To all who are still happy in some groundwork of unperverted Nature, the delicate, simple, human tenderness, unsought, unbought and therefore precious morality, the tranquil elegance and playfulness, the humour which never breaks the impression of sweetness and dignity, do an inevitable message which requires no comment of the critic to make its meaning clear. Impertinent, because the influence of this mind, like that of some loveliest aspects of Nature, is to induce silence from a feeling of repose. We do not think of any thing particularly worth saying about this that has been so fitly and pleasantly said.

Yet is seems *un*fit that we, in our office of chronicler of intellectual advents and apparitions, should omit to render open and audible honour to one whom we have long delighted to honour. It may be, too, that this slight notice of ours may awaken the attention of those distant or busy who might not otherwise search for the volume, which comes betimes in the leafy month of June.

So we will give a slight account of it, even if we cannot say much of value. Though Hawthorne has now a standard reputation, both for the qualities we have mentioned and the beauty of the style in which they are embodied, yet we believe he has not been very widely read. This is only because his works have not been published in the way to ensure extensive circulation in this new, hurrying world of ours. The immense extent of country over which the reading (still very small in proportion to the mere working) community is scattered, the rushing and pushing of our life at this electrical stage of development, leave no work a chance to be speedily and largely known that is not trumpeted and placarded. And, odious as are the features of a forced and artificial circulation, it must be considered that it does no harm in the end. Bad books will not be read if they are bought instead of good, while the good have an abiding life in the log-cabin settlements and Red River steamboat landings, to which they would in no other way penetrate. Under the auspices of Wiley and Putnam,[1] Hawthorne will have a chance to collect all

---

* First appeared in the New York *Tribune* in 1846, shortly before Fuller left for Europe; *Mosses From an Old Manse* was published in 1846.

[1] The publishers of *Mosses*.

his own public about him, and that be felt as a presence which before was only a rumor.

The volume before us shares the charms of Hawthorne's earlier tales; the only difference being that his range of subjects is a little wider. There is the same gentle and sincere companionship with Nature, the same delicate but fearless scrutiny of the secrets of the heart, the same serene independence of petty and artificial restrictions, whether on opinions or conduct, the same familiar, yet pensive sense of the spiritual or demoniacal influences that haunt the palpable life and common walks of men, not by many apprehended except in results. We have here to regret that Hawthorne, at this stage of his mind's life, lays no more decisive hand upon the apparition—brings it no nearer than in former days. We had hoped that we should see, no more as in a glass darkly, but face to face. Still, still brood over his page the genius of revery and the nonchalance of Nature, rather than the ardent earnestness of the human soul which feels itself born not only to see and disclose, but to understand and interpret such things. Hawthorne intimates and suggests, but he does not lay bare the mysteries of our being.

The introduction to the "Mosses,"[2] in which the old manse, its inhabitants and visitants are portrayed, is written with even more than his usual charm of placid grace and many strokes of his admirable good sense. Those who are not, like ourselves, familiar with the scene and its denizens, will still perceive how true that picture must be; those of us who are thus familiar will best know how to prize the record of objects and influences unique in our country and time.

"The Birth Mark" and "Rapaccini's Daughter," embody truths of profound importance in shapes of aerial elegance. In these, as here and there in all these pieces, shines the loveliest ideal of love, and the beauty of feminine purity (by which we mean no mere acts or abstinences, but perfect single truth felt and done in gentleness) which is its root.

"The Celestial Railroad," for its wit, wisdom, and the graceful adroitness with which the natural and material objects are interwoven with the allegories, has already won its meed of admiration. "Fire-worship" is a most charming essay for its domestic sweetness and thoughtful life. "Goodman Brown" is one of those disclosures we have spoken of, of the secrets of the breast. Who has not known such a trial that is capable indeed of sincere aspiration toward that only good, that infinite essence, which men call God. Who has not known the hour when even that best beloved image cherished as the one precious symbol left, in the range of human nature, believed to be still pure gold when all the rest have turned to clay, shows, in severe ordeal, the symptoms of alloy. Oh, hour of anguish, when the old familiar faces grow dark and dim in the lurid light—when the gods of the hearth, honoured in childhood, adored in youth, crumble, and nothing, nothing is left which the daily earthly feelings can embrace—can cherish with unbroken faith! Yet some survive that trial more happily than young Goodman Brown. They are those who have not sought it—have never of their own accord walked forth with the Tempter into the dim shades of Doubt. Mrs. Bull-Frog is an excellent humourous picture of what is called to be "content at last with substantial realities!!" The "Artist of the Beautiful" presents in a form that is, indeed, beautiful, the opposite view as to what *are* the substantial realities of life. Let each man choose between them according to his kind. Had Hawthorne written "Roger Malvin's Burial"

---

[2] The introductory sketch in *Mosses;* the titles that follow are of stories in that collection.

alone, we should be pervaded with the sense of the poetry and religion of his soul.

As a critic, the style of Hawthorne, faithful to his mind, shows repose, a great reserve of strength, a slow secure movement. Though a very refined, he is also a very clear writer, showing, as we said before, a placid grace, and an indolent command of language.

And now, beside the full, calm yet romantic stream of his mind, we will rest. It has refreshment for the weary, islets of fascination no less than dark recesses and shadows for the imaginative, pure reflections for the pure of heart and eye, and like the Concord he so well describes, many exquisite lilies for him who knows how to get at them.

REVIEW OF CHARLES BROCKDEN BROWN'S *ORMOND* AND *WIELAND**

We rejoice to see these reprints of Brown's novels, as we have long been ashamed that one who ought to be the pride of the country, and who is, in the higher qualities of the mind, so far in advance of our other novelists, should have become almost inaccessible to the public.

It has been the custom to liken Brown to Godwin.[1] But there was no imitation, no second-hand in the matter. They were congenial natures, and whichever had come first might have lent an impulse to the other. Either mind might have been conscious of the possession of that peculiar vein of ore without thinking of working it for the mint of the world, till the other, led by accident, or overflow of feeling, showed him how easy it was to put the reveries of his solitary hours into words and upon paper for the benefit of his fellow men.

> "My mind to me a kingdom is."[2]

Such a man as Brown or Godwin has a right to say that. It is no scanty, turbid rill, requiring to be daily fed from a thousand others or from the clouds! Its plenteous source rushes from a high mountain between bulwarks of stone. Its course, even and full, keeps ever green its banks, and affords the means of life and joy to a million gliding shapes, that fill its deep waters, and twinkle above its golden sands.

Life and Joy! Yes, Joy! These two have been called the dark masters, because they disclose the twilight recesses of the human heart. Yet their gravest page is joy compared with the mixed, shallow, uncertain pleasures of vulgar minds. Joy! because they were all alive and fulfilled the purposes of being. No sham, no imitation, no convention deformed or veiled their native lineaments, checked the use of

---

* First appeared in the New York *Tribune* in 1846; *Ormond* was published in 1799 and *Wieland* in 1798.

[1] William Godwin (1756–1836), an English political philosopher, father of Mary Wollstonecraft Shelley (who wrote *Frankenstein* [1818]) and author of the Gothic novel *The Adventures of Caleb Williams* (1794).

[2] Source unidentified.

their natural force. All alive themselves, they understood that there is no joy without truth, no perception of joy without real life. Unlike most men, existence was to them not a tissue of words and seemings, but a substantial possession.

Born Hegelians,[3] without the pretensions of science, they sought God in their own consciousness, and found him. The heart, because it saw itself so fearfully and wonderfully made, did not disown its Maker. With the highest idea of the dignity, power and beauty of which human nature is capable, they had courage to see by what an oblique course it proceeds, yet never lose faith that it would reach its destined aim. Thus their darkest disclosures are not hobgoblin shows, but precious revelations.

Brown is great as ever human writer was in showing the self-sustaining force of which a lonely mind is capable. He takes one person, makes him brood like the bee, and extract from the common life before him all its sweetness, its bitterness, and its nourishment.

We say makes *him,* but it increases our own interest in Brown that, a prophet in this respect of a better era, he has usually placed this thinking royal mind in the body of a woman. This personage too is always feminine, both in her character and circumstances, but a conclusive proof that the term *feminine* is not a synonym for *weak.* Constantia, Clara Wieland,[4] have loving hearts, graceful and plastic natures, but they have also noble thinking minds, full of resource, constancy, courage. The Marguerite of Godwin, no less, is all refinement, and the purest tenderness, but she is also the soul of honour, capable of deep discernment and of acting in conformity with the inferences she draws. The man of Brown and Godwin has not eaten of the fruit of the tree of knowledge and been driven to sustain himself by sweat of his brow for nothing, but has learned the structure and laws of things, and become a being, rational, benignant, various, and desirous of supplying the loss of innocence by the attainment of virtue. So his women need not be quite so weak as Eve, the slave of feeling or of flattery: she also has learned to guide her helm amid the storm across the troubled waters.

The horrors which mysteriously beset these persons, and against which, so far as outward facts go, they often strive in vain, are but a representation of those powers permitted to work in the same way throughout the affairs of this world. Their demoniacal attributes only represent a morbid state of the intellect, gone to excess from want of balance with the other powers. There is an intellectual as well as a physical drunkenness, and which no less impels to crime. Carwin, urged on to use his ventriloquism, till the presence of such a strange agent wakened the seeds of fanaticism in the breast of Wieland, is in a state no more foreign to nature than that of the wretch executed last week, who felt himself drawn as by a spell to murder his victim because he had thought of her money and the pleasures it might bring him, till the feeling possessed his brain that hurls the gamester to ruin. The victims of such agency are like the soldier of the Rio Grande, who, both legs shot off and his life-blood rushing out with every pulse, replied serenely to his pitying comrades that "he had now that for which the soldier enlisted." The end of the drama is not in this world, and the fiction which rounds off the whole to harmony and felicity before the curtain falls, sins against truth, and deludes the reader. The

---

[3] Born in tune with the dialectical ideas of the German philosopher Georg Wilhelm Friedrich Hegel (1770–1831).

[4] The names in this and the following paragraph are characters in the works of Brown and of Godwin.

Nelsons[5] of the human race are all the more exposed to the assaults of fate that they are decorated with the badges of well-earned glory. Who, but feels as they fall in death, or rise again to a mutilated existence, that the end is not yet? Who, that thinks, but must feel that the recompense is, where Brown places it, in the accumulation of mental treasure, in the severe assay by fire that leaves the gold pure to be used sometime—somewhere.

Brown, man of the brooding eye, the teeming brain, the deep and fervent heart; if thy country prize thee not and has almost lost thee out of sight, it is that her heart is made shallow and cold, her eye dim, by the pomp of circumstance, the love of gross outward gain. She cannot long continue thus, for it takes a great deal of soul to keep a huge body from disease and dissolution. As there is more soul thou wilt be more sought, and many will yet sit down with thy Constantia to the meal and water on which she sustained her full and thoughtful existence, who could not endure the ennui of aldermanic dinners, or find any relish in the imitation of French cookery. To-day many will read the words, and some have a cup large enough to receive the spirit, before it is lost in the sand on which their feet are planted.

Brown's high standard of the delights of intellectual communion and of friendship correspond with the fondest hopes of early days. But in the relations of real life, at present, there is rarely more than one of the parties ready for such intercourse as he describes. On the one side there will be dryness, want of perception or variety, a stupidity unable to appreciate life's richest boon when offered to its grasp, and the finer nature is doomed to retrace its steps, unhappy as those who having force to raise a spirit cannot retain or make it substantial, and stretch out their arms only to bring them back empty to the breast.

1846

from AT HOME AND ABROAD*

[Italy and America: 1847]

. . . In many ways Italy is of kin to us; she is the country of Columbus, of Amerigo, of Cabot.[1] It would please me much to see a cannon here bought by the contributions of Americans, at whose head should stand the name of Cabot, to be used by the Guard for salutes on festive occasions, if they should be so happy as to have no more serious need. In Tuscany they are casting one to be called the "Gioberti," from a writer who has given a great impulse to the present movement. I should like the gift of America to be called the AMERIGO, the COLUMBO, or the

---

[5] Horatio Viscount Nelson (1758–1805), hero of the British naval victory at Trafalgar (1805); during the battle he wore a conspicuous uniform (complete with medals) that may have made him the target of riflemen aboard the French ships.

* Entries written by Fuller during her stay in Italy from 1846 to 1850, first published posthumously in *At Home and Abroad* (1856), and edited by Arthur B. Fuller, the writer's brother.

[1] Three Italian explorers of what the Europeans thought of as the New World: Christopher Columbus (1451–1506), from Genoa; Amerigo Vespucci (1454–1512), from Florence; John Cabot (1461?–1498), probably from Genoa.

WASHINGTON. Please think of this, some of my friends, who still care for the eagle, the Fourth of July, and the old cries of hope and honor. See if there are any objections that I do not think of, and do something if it is well and brotherly. Ah! America, with all thy rich boons, thou hast a heavy account to render for the talent given; see in every way that thou be not found wanting.

[*Mrs. Trollope: 1847*]

. . . Can anything be more sadly expressive of times out of joint than the fact that Mrs. Trollope[2] is a resident in Italy? Yes! she is fixed permanently in Florence, as I am told, pensioned at the rate of two thousand pounds a year to trail her slime over the fruit of Italy. She is here in Rome this winter, and, after having violated the virgin beauty of America, will have for many a year her chance to sully the imperial matron of the civilized world. What must the English public be, if it wishes to pay two thousand pounds a year to get Italy Trollopified?

[*Present Conditions in the United States: 1848*]

. . . My friends write to urge my return; they talk of our country as the land of the future. It is so, but that spirit which made it all it is of value in my eyes, which gave all hope with which I can sympathize for that future, is more alive here at present[3] than in America. My country is at present spoiled by prosperity, stupid with the lust of gain, soiled by crime in its willing perpetuation of slavery, shamed by an unjust war, noble sentiment much forgotten even by individuals, the aims of politicians selfish or petty, the literature frivolous and venal. In Europe, amid the teachings of adversity, a nobler spirit is struggling,—a spirit which cheers and animates mine. I hear earnest words of pure faith and love. I see deeds of brotherhood. This is what makes *my* America. I do not deeply distrust my country. She is not dead, but in my time she sleepeth, and the spirit of our fathers flames no more, but lies hid beneath the ashes. It will not be so long; bodies cannot live when the soul gets too overgrown with gluttony and falsehood. But it is not the making a President out of the Mexican war[4] that would make me wish to come back. Here things are before my eyes worth recording, and, if I cannot help this work, I would gladly be its historian.

[*George Washington: 1849*]

At home one gets callous about the character of Washington, from a long experience of Fourth of July bombast in his praise. But seeing the struggles of other

---

[2] Frances Trollope (1780–1863), who resided in Cincinnati from 1827 to 1830, disliked much that she saw in the United States, and wrote her famous book of observations, *Domestic Manners of the Americans* (1832).

[3] Fuller was abroad during a period of nationalism and political activism that led to the unification of Italy; she saw it as an exciting time of questing for liberty.

[4] In America's war with Mexico, General Winfield Scott (1786–1866) led the American forces on a victorious campaign from Vera Cruz to Mexico City in 1847; a national hero, he was a candidate for president in 1852.

nations, and the deficiencies of the leaders who try to sustain them, the heart is again stimulated, and puts forth buds of praise. One appreciates the wonderful combination of events and influences that gave our independence so healthy a birth, and the almost miraculous merits of the men who tended its first motions. In the combination of excellences needed at such a period with the purity and modesty which dignify the private man in the humblest station, Washington as yet stands alone. No country has ever had such a good future; no other is so happy as to have a pattern of spotless worth which will remain in her latest day venerable as now.

1856

CONTEXTS

Women's Rights in the 1830s

The involvement of women in the reform movements of the 1830s made women more aware of their own lack of rights. Although the editor and abolitionist leader William Lloyd Garrison encouraged equal participation of women in the fight for emancipation, social convention frowned on women speaking in public, and many reform organizations would not accept women as members. In 1839 numerous members of the American Anti-Slavery Society issued a public statement opposing the complete integration of women in the society's work. The reasoning of the petitioners, as published in the May 31, 1839, issue of the *Liberator,* closely resembles a common argument of slaveholders for depriving African Americans of their constitutional rights:

Protest

We the undersigned, members and delegates of the American Anti-Slavery Society, as a duty, and therefore a right, hereby protest against the principle, assumed by a majority of persons representing said Society at its present meeting, that women have the right of originating, debating, and voting on questions which come before said Society, and are eligible to its various offices:—and we protest against the assumption of said principle for the following, among other reasons, viz:

1. Because it is contrary to the expectation, design, and spirit of the Constitution of said Society, as clearly indicated by the proceedings of the framers of that instrument, at the commencement, in the progress, and at the completion of the work.

2. Because it is at variance with the construction of said instrument, as made known by the constant usage of the Society from its first to its present meeting.

3. Because it is repugnant to the wishes, the wisdom, or the moral sense of many of the early and present members of said Society, and devoted friends to the cause for which that Society was organized.

4. Because, though assumed by a majority of persons representing said Society in its present meeting, we believe it to be wide from the expression of the general sense of the abolitionists of this country of either sex, and, if not objected to in this formal manner, might seem to be the unqualified and unlimited sanction of the friends of the slave and the asserter of his rights.

Abolitionists against women's participation in the American Anti-Slavery Society, 1839

Declaration of Sentiments
(1848)

The Declaration of Sentiments of the Woman's Rights Convention at Seneca Falls, New York, on July 19 and 20, 1848, is the first extensive expression of the principles and grievances underlying feminists' dispute with male-dominated society. The document is at once the product of a historical moment and a voice in an evolving political dialogue. Because women's history was virtually unrecorded, the authors of the declaration knew little of the tradition they had joined. When Mary Ann McClintock, Lucretia Mott, Elizabeth Cady Stanton, and Martha C. Wright drafted the declaration, however, they commanded other valuable resources, some the common property of an age that sought a "true" social system. Karl Marx and Friedrich Engels had recently envisioned all history as class struggle; American utopianism had flourished in the 1840s, fostering such experiments as the transcendentalist cooperative community Brook Farm (1841–1847), near Boston, and the religious Oneida Community (1848–1880), in Oneida, New York. The authors understood, too, that changes in the social order were affecting women's lives in the workplace and in education. Moreover, the state of New York had recently supplanted common law with the first statute guaranteeing the property rights of married women— probably because wealthy farmers feared the spendthrift habits of sons-in-laws.

But the Declaration of Sentiments derives most immediately from its authors' experience in organized reform. Before adopting the Declaration of Independence as the model most commensurate with their ideas, they considered statements of the temperance and antislavery movements, which they knew well. Abolitionism offered particularly rich soil for the early women's movement. Along with such abolitionist women as Sarah and Angelina Grimké, Sojourner Truth, and Frances Wright, the authors had sharpened their political skills on the issue of slavery. Indeed, the Seneca Falls convention may be said to have had its inception in London in 1840, when the World Anti-Slavery Convention refused to seat American women delegates, including Stanton and Mott, who had to sit behind a curtain throughout the ten-day convention and resolved then to work for women's rights. Many men who supported the early women's movement also came from the antislavery movement, among them William Lloyd Garrison (who refused his seat at the London convention when the women were rejected) and Frederick Douglass (who signed the Declaration of Sentiments and defended women's rights in the *North Star*).

The Seneca Falls convention adopted the declaration with amendments and approved eleven of twelve resolutions unanimously. Many delegates feared that the resolution concerning the right to vote would bring ridicule on the whole endeavor, but it was narrowly sustained by the efforts of Stanton and Douglass, who argued that the vote was the only guarantee for other rights. One hundred people signed the document. Although the convention and the declaration were immediately belittled, particularly by the pulpit and the press, two weeks later a larger convention met at Rochester, New York, to reaffirm and extend the claims of the original document. The Seneca Falls declaration now stands as a landmark of the "old" feminism, the pursuit of women's political rights that extended from the American Revolution through the ratification of the Nineteenth Amendment in 1920. It serves likewise as an expression of issues central to the "new" feminism, including women's economic, social, and marital status.

Suggested Readings: *Proceedings of the Woman's Rights Conventions Held at Seneca Falls & Rochester, N. Y., July & August, 1848,* 1870, rpt. as *Woman's Rights Conventions, Seneca Falls &*

This 1870 lithograph by Louis Prang & Co. shows the leading women suffragists of the mid-nineteenth century (clockwise from top): Lucretia Mott, Elizabeth Cady Stanton, Mary A. Livermore, Lydia Maria Child, Susan B. Anthony, and Grace Greenwood; Anna E. Dickinson is in the center.

Rochester, 1848, 1969. E. C. Stanton, *Eighty Years & More, 1815–1897*, 1898, rpt. 1971. E. Flexner, *Century of Struggle: The Woman's Rights Movement in the United States*, 1975. M. Gurko, *The Ladies of Seneca Falls: The Birth of the Woman's Rights Movement*, 1976. M. H. Bacon, *Valiant Friend: The Life of Lucretia Mott*, 1980. L. W. Banner, *Elizabeth Cady Stanton: A Radical for Woman's Rights*, 1980. E. Griffith, *In Her Own Right: The Life of Elizabeth Cady Stanton*, 1984.

Text Used: *Report of the Woman's Rights Convention, Held At Seneca Falls, N. Y., July 19th & 20th, 1848*, 1848.

DECLARATION OF SENTIMENTS

When, in the course of human events, it becomes necessary for one portion of the family of man to assume among the people of the earth a position different from that which they have hitherto occupied, but one to which the laws of nature and of nature's God entitle them, a decent respect to the opinions of mankind requires that they should declare the causes that impel them to such a course.

We hold these truths to be self-evident: that all men and women are created equal; that they are endowed by their Creator with certain inalienable rights, that among these are life, liberty, and the pursuit of happiness; that to secure these rights governments are instituted, deriving their just powers from the consent of the governed[.] Whenever any form of government becomes destructive of these ends, it is the right of those who suffer from it to refuse allegiance to it, and to insist upon the institution of a new government, laying its foundation on such principles, and organizing its powers in such form as to them shall seem most likely to effect their safety and happiness. Prudence, indeed, will dictate that governments long established should not be changed for light and transient causes; and accordingly, all experience hath shown that mankind are more disposed to suffer, while evils are sufferable, than to right themselves by abolishing the forms to which they were accustomed. But when a long train of abuses and usurpations, pursuing invariably the same object evinces a design to reduce them under absolute despotism, it is their duty to throw off such government, and to provide new guards for their future security. Such has been the patient sufferance of the women under this government, and such is now the necessity which constrains them to demand the equal station to which they are entitled.

The history of mankind is a history of repeated injuries and usurpations on the part of man toward woman, having in direct object the establishment of an absolute tyranny over her. To prove this, let facts be submitted to a candid world.

He has never permitted her to exercise her inalienable right to the elective franchise.

He has compelled her to submit to laws, in the formation of which she had no voice.

He has withheld from her rights which are given to the most ignorant and degraded men—both natives and foreigners.

Having deprived her of this first right of a citizen, the elective franchise, thereby leaving her without representation in the halls of legislation, he has oppressed her on all sides.

He has made her, if married, in the eye of the law, civilly dead.

He has taken from her all right in property, even to the wages she earns.

He has made her, morally, an irresponsible being, as she can commit many crimes with impunity, provided they be done in the presence of her husband. In the covenant of marriage, she is compelled to promise obedience to her husband, he becoming, to all intents and purposes, her master—the law giving him power to deprive her of her liberty, and to administer chastisement.

He has so framed the laws of divorce, as to what shall be the proper causes of divorce; in case of separation, to whom the guardianship of the children shall be given; as to be wholly regardless of the happiness of women—the law, in all cases, going upon a false supposition of the supremacy of man, and giving all power into his hands.

After depriving her of all rights as a married woman, if single and the owner of property, he has taxed her to support a government which recognizes her only when her property can be made profitable to it.

He has monopolized nearly all the profitable employments, and from those she is permitted to follow, she receives but a scanty remuneration.

He closes against her all the avenues to wealth and distinction, which he considers most honorable to himself. As a teacher of theology, medicine, or law, she is not known.

He has denied her the facilities for obtaining a thorough education—all colleges being closed against her.

He allows her in Church, as well as State, but a subordinate position, claiming Apostolic authority for her exclusion from the ministry, and, with some exceptions, from any public participation in the affairs of the Church.

He has created a false public sentiment, by giving to the world a different code of morals for men and women, by which moral delinquencies which exclude women from society, are not only tolerated but deemed of little account in man.

He has usurped the prerogative of Jehovah himself, claiming it as his right to assign for her a sphere of action, when that belongs to her conscience and to her God.

He has endeavored, in every way that he could, to destroy her confidence in her own powers, to lessen her self-respect, and to make her willing to lead a dependent and abject life.

Now, in view of this entire disfranchisement of one-half of the people of this country, their social and religious degradation,—in view of the unjust laws above mentioned, and because women do feel themselves aggrieved, oppressed, and fraudulently deprived of their most sacred rights, we insist that they have immediate admission to all the rights and privileges which belong to them as citizens of the United States.

In entering upon the great work before us, we anticipate no small amount of misconception, misrepresentation, and ridicule; but we shall use every instrumentality within our power to effect our object. We shall employ agents, circulate tracts, petition the state and national legislatures, and endeavor to enlist the pulpit and the press in our behalf. We hope this Convention will be followed by a series of Conventions, embracing every part of the country.

Firmly relying upon the final triumph of the Right and the True, we do this day affix our signatures to this declaration.

[Signatures]

RESOLUTIONS

Whereas the great precept of nature is conceded to be, "that man shall pursue his own true and substantial happiness." Blackstone, in his Commentaries, remarks, that this law of Nature being coeval with mankind, and dictated by God himself, is of course superior in obligation to any other. It is binding over all the globe, in all countries, and at all times; no human laws are of any validity if contrary to this, and such of them as are valid, derive all their force, and all their validity, and all their authority, mediately and immediately, from this original; therefore,

Resolved, That such laws as conflict, in any way, with the true and substantial happiness of woman, are contrary to the great precept of nature, and of no validity; for this is "superior in obligation to any other."

Resolved, That all laws which prevent woman from occupying such a station in society as her conscience shall dictate, or which place her in a position inferior to that of man, are contrary to the great precept of nature, and therefore of no force or authority.

Resolved, That woman is man's equal—was intended to be so by the Creator, and the highest good of the race demands that she should be recognized as such.

Resolved, That the women of this country ought to be enlightened in regard to the laws under which they live, that they may no longer publish their degradation, by declaring themselves satisfied with their present position, nor their ignorance, by asserting that they have all the rights they want.

Resolved, That inasmuch as man, while claiming for himself intellectual superiority, does [] accord to woman moral superiority, it is pre-eminently his duty to encourage her to speak, and teach, as she has an opportunity, in all religious assemblies.

Resolved, That the same amount of virtue, delicacy, and refinement of behavior, that is required of woman in the social state, should also be required of man, and the same transgressions should be visited with equal severity on both man and woman.

Resolved, That the objection of indelicacy and impropriety, which is so often brought against woman when she addresses a public audience, comes with a very ill-grace from those who encourage, by their attendance, her appearance on the stage, in the concert, or in feats of the circus.

Resolved, That woman has too long rested satisfied in the circumscribed limits which corrupt customs and a perverted application of the Scriptures have marked out for her, and that it is time she should move in the enlarged sphere which her great Creator has assigned her.

Resolved, That it is the duty of the women of this country to secure to themselves their sacred right to the elective franchise.

Resolved, That the equality of human rights results necessarily from the fact of the identity of the race in capabilities and responsibilities.

Resolved, therefore, That, being invested by the Creator with the same capabilities, and the same consciousness of responsibility for their exercise, it is demonstrably the right and duty of woman, equally with man, to promote every righteous cause, by every righteous means; and especially in regard to the great subjects of morals and religion, it is self-evidently her right to participate with her brother in teaching them, both in private and in public, by writing and by speaking, by any instrumentalities proper to be used, and in any assemblies proper to be held; and this being a self-evident truth, growing out of the divinely implanted principles of human nature, any custom or authority adverse to it, whether modern or wearing the hoary sanction of antiquity, is to be regarded as a self-evident falsehood, and at war with mankind.

Resolved, That the speedy success of our cause depends upon the zealous and untiring efforts of both men and women, for the overthrow of the monopoly of the pulpit, and for the securing to woman an equal participation with men in the various trades, professions and commerce.

1848

Fanny Fern (Sara Payson Willis)
(1811–1872)

Fanny Fern was one of the first and most popular female columnists, an innovative prose stylist admired for her social commentary and biting satire. Born Sara Payson Willis in Portland, Maine, in 1811, she briefly attended Catharine Beecher's Female Seminary, where her school compositions were sought after by the local newspaper editor. Willis began writing professionally, however, only when a series of personal disasters left her virtually destitute. Her happy first marriage, to the bank cashier Charles Eldredge in 1837, ended with Eldredge's death in 1846, just a short while after the death of her mother, sister, and firstborn daughter. Left with two children and no means of support, Willis, under pressure from her father, contracted a frustrating marriage of convenience to the merchant Samuel Farrington in 1849. Because she soon left Farrington, she was eventually divorced for desertion. Unable to support herself in the traditional women's vocations of teaching and sewing, she began to write as Fanny Fern, selling her first column for fifty cents in 1851; four years later she was paid one hundred dollars a column by the New York *Ledger*. In 1856 she married the editor and biographer James Parton, eleven years her junior, who had once resigned an editorial position rather than assent to canceling her sometimes controversial columns.

The pseudonym Fanny Fern both mimics and subtly parodies the names of popular contemporary writers such as Grace Greenwood, Fanny Foxglove, and Harriet Honeysuckle. Although she published numerous sentimental pieces, Fern also satirized sentimentality, and her essays on topics such as prostitution and prison reform are biting and acute. Her most common subject, however, was the condition of women; indeed, a persistent concern with women, minorities, and social issues places her firmly in the tradition of the reform-minded writers Lydia Maria Child and Margaret Fuller. Not surprisingly, the outspoken quality of Fern's writing caused her (like Fuller) to be deemed "unnatural" and "unfeminine." Despite such criticism, she continued to speak her mind on the foibles of society.

Fern also wrote several novels, the best of which is the autobiographical *Ruth Hall* (1854), dubbed "Ruthless Hall" by some readers. Modeled on her own career, the narrative tells the story of a woman's rise from widowhood and poverty to wealth and power as a popular columnist. The novel shocked readers accustomed to less assertive heroines but drew praise from Nathaniel Hawthorne (no lover of women's fiction), who remarked to his publisher, William Ticknor, in 1855 that Fern "writes as if the devil was in her; and that is the only condition under which a woman ever writes anything worth reading." Published before the secret of the Fern pseudonym was known, *Ruth Hall* contained scathing and easily recognized portraits of acquaintances—including one of her brother, the critic and publisher N. P. Willis, who had actively tried to thwart her writing career. The novel intensified accusations that Fern was an "unnatural" woman, but the criticism seemed not to bother the author: over the span of a long career, lasting until her death in 1872, Sara Payson Willis never doubted that women could write as well as—and typically more trenchantly than—men could.

Suggested Readings: *Hidden Hands: An Anthology of American Women Writers, 1790–1870*, ed. L. M. Freibert and B. A. White, 1985. J. Fetterley, *Provisions: A Reader From 19th-Century American Women*, 1985. J. W. Warren, "Introduction" to *Ruth Hall and Other Writings*, 1986.

Text Used: *Ruth Hall and Other Writings*, ed. J. W. Warren, 1986.

from HAVE WE ANY MEN AMONG US?*

Walking along the street the other day, my eye fell upon this placard,—

> MEN WANTED

Well; they have been "wanted" for some time; but the article is not in the market, although there are plenty of spurious imitations. Time was, when a lady could decline writing for a newspaper without subjecting herself to paragraphic attacks from the editor, invading the sanctity of her private life. Time was, when she could decline writing without the editor's revenging himself, by asserting falsely that "he had often refused her offered contributions?" Time was, when if an editor heard a vague rumor affecting a lady's reputation, he did not endorse it by republication, and then meanly screen himself from responsibility by adding, "we presume, however, that this is only an *on dit!*"[1] Time was, when a lady could be a successful authoress, without being obliged to give an account to the dear public of the manner in which she appropriated the proceeds of her honest labors. Time was, when whiskered braggadocios in railroad cars and steamboats did not assert, (in blissful ignorance that they were looking the lady authoress straight in the face!) that they were "on the most intimate terms of friendship with her!" Time was, when *milk-and-water husbands and relatives* did not force a defamed woman to unsex herself in the manner stated in the following paragraph:

> "MAN SHOT BY A YOUNG WOMAN,—One day last week, a young lady of good character, daughter of Col.——, having been calumniated by a young man, called upon him, armed with a revolver. The slanderer could not, or did not deny his allegations; whereupon she fired, inflicting a dangerous if not a fatal wound in his throat."

Yes; it is very true that there are "MEN wanted." Wonder how many 1854 will furnish?

1853

from "LEAVES OF GRASS"†

Well Baptized: fresh, hardy, and grown for the masses. Not more welcome is their natural type to the winter-bound, bed-ridden, and spring-emancipated invalid. "Leaves of Grass" thou art unspeakably delicious, after the forced, stiff, Parnassian exotics for which our admiration has been vainly challenged.

Walt Whitman, the effeminate world needed thee. The timidest soul whose wings ever drooped with discouragement, could not choose but rise on thy strong pinions.

---

* First published in the *Musical World and Times,* September 24, 1853.
[1] "One says" (French); corresponds to the vague "they say."
† First published in the *New York Ledger,* May 10, 1856. Fern was the first woman to write favorably about Walt Whitman's *Leaves of Grass* (1855), the second edition of which was published in 1856. Fern and her husband, James Parton, knew Whitman personally, but a squabble over a debt in 1857 ended their friendship.

> "Undrape—you are not guilty to me, nor stale nor discarded;
> I see through the broadcloth and gingham whether or no. . . .
>
> O despairer, here is my neck,
> You shall *not* go down! Hang your whole weight upon me."

Walt Whitman, the world needed a "Native American" of thorough, out-and-out breed—enamored of *women* not *ladies, men* not *gentlemen;* something beside a mere Catholic-hating Know-Nothing;[1] it needed a man who dared speak out his strong, honest thoughts, in the face of pusillanimous, toadeying, republican aristocracy; dictionary-men, hypocrites, cliques and creeds; it needed a large-hearted, untainted, self-reliant, fearless son of the Stars and Stripes, who disdains to sell his birthright for a mess of pottage; who does

> "Not call one greater or one smaller,
> That which fills its period and place being equal to any;"

who will

> "Accept nothing which all cannot have their counterpart of
>   on the same terms."

Fresh "Leaves of Grass"! not submitted by the self-reliant author to the fingering of any publisher's critic, to be arranged, re-arranged and disarranged to his circumscribed liking, till they hung limp, tame, spirit-less, and scentless. No. It were a spectacle worth seeing, this glorious Native American, who, when the daily labor of chisel and plane was over, himself, with toil-hardened fingers, handled the types to print the pages which wise and good men have since delighted to endorse and to honor. Small critics, whose contracted vision could see no beauty, strength, or grace, in these "Leaves," have long ago repented that they so hastily wrote themselves down shallow by such a premature confession. Where an Emerson, and a Howitt[2] have commended, my woman's voice of praise may not avail; but happiness was born a twin, and so I would fain share with others the unmingled delight which these "Leaves" have given me.

I say unmingled; I am not unaware that the charge of coarseness and sensuality has been affixed to them.[3] My moral constitution may be hopelessly tainted—or too sound to be tainted, as the critic wills—but I confess that I extract no poison from these "Leaves"—to me they have brought only healing. Let him who can do so, shroud the eyes of the nursing babe lest it should see its mother's breast. Let him look carefully between the gilded covers of books, backed by high-sounding names, and endorsed by parson and priest, lying unrebuked upon his own family

---

[1] The influx of Catholic immigrants into America in the 1840s and 1850s evoked the formation of secret "nativist" societies whose members answered "I know nothing" to questions about their activities. The Native American party came to be known as the "Know-Nothings"; in the election of 1854 it won seventy-five seats in Congress, largely on an anti-immigrant and anti-Catholic platform. The issure of slavery split the party soon afterward.

[2] Both Ralph Waldo Emerson and the British reviewer and writer William Howitt (1792–1879) praised *Leaves of Grass,* the first in a letter to Whitman, the second in a review in *Life Illustrated* in 1856.

[3] Many readers criticized the vulgarity and sexual frankness of *Leaves of Grass.* The poet John Greenleaf Whittier, for example, considered the book shocking and threw his gift copy into the fireplace.

table; where the asp of sensuality lies coiled amid rhetorical flowers. Let him examine well the paper dropped weekly at his door, in which virtue and religion are rendered disgusting, save when they walk in satin slippers, or, clothed in purple and fine linen, kneel on a damask *"prie-dieu."*[4]

Sensual! No—the moral assassin looks you not boldly in the eye by broad daylight; but Borgia-like[5] takes you treacherously by the hand, while from the glittering ring on his finger he distils through your veins the subtle and deadly poison.

Sensual? The artist who would inflame, paints you not nude Nature, but stealing Virtue's veil, with artful artlessness now conceals, now exposes, the ripe and swelling proportions.

Sensual? Let him who would affix this stigma upon "Leaves of Grass," write upon his heart, in letters of fire, these noble words of its author:

> "In woman I see the bearer of the great fruit, which is immortality
> . . . the good thereof is not tasted by *roues,* and never can be. . . .
> Who degrades or defiles the living human body is cursed,
> Who degrades or defiles the body of the dead is not more cursed."[6]

* * *

I close the extracts from these "Leaves," which it were easy to multiply, for one is more puzzled what to leave unculled, than what to gather, with the following sentiments; for which, and for all the good things included between the covers of his book, Mr. Whitman will please accept the cordial grasp of a woman's hand:

> "The wife—and she is not one jot less than the husband,
> The daughter—and she is just as good as the son,
> The mother—and she is every bit as much as the father."[7]

1856

MALE CRITICISM ON LADIES BOOKS*

"Courtship and marriage, servants and children, these are the great objects of a woman's thoughts, and they necessarily form the staple topics of their writings and their conversation. We have no right to expect anything else in a woman's book."—N.Y. Times

Is it in feminine novels *only* that courtship, marriage, servants and children are the staple? Is not this true of all novels?—of Dickens, of Thackery, of Bulwer[1] and a host of others? Is it peculiar to feminine pens, most astute and liberal of critics?

---

[4] A frame with a lower ledge for kneeling in prayer and an upper ledge for holding a book (French).

[5] The Borgias were an Italian family of the late fifteenth and early sixteenth centuries noted for political and religious intrigue.

[6] None of the twelve poems in the 1855 edition of *Leaves of Grass* had a title, and Whitman revised most of them in later editions. Here Fern cites lines from the untitled poem that became "I Sing the Body Electric," but these lines are not present in the revised poem with this title.

[7] From the untitled poem in the 1855 edition that became "A Song for Occupations."

* First published in the *New York Ledger,* May 23, 1857.

[1] Nineteenth-century British novelists: Charles Dickens (1812–1870); William Makepeace Thackeray (1811–1863); Edward George Bulwer-Lytton (1803–1873).

Would a novel be a novel if it did not treat of courtship and marriage? and if it could be so recognized, would it find readers? When I see such a narrow, snarling criticism as the above, I always say to myself, the writer is some unhappy man, who has come up without the refining influence of mother, or sister, or reputable female friends; who has divided his migratory life between boarding-houses, restaurants, and the outskirts of editorial sanctums; and who knows as much about reviewing a woman's book, as I do about navigating a ship, or engineering an omnibus from the South Ferry, through Broadway, to Union Park.[2] I think I see him writing that paragraph in a fit of spleen—of *male* spleen—in his small boarding-house upper chamber, by the cheerful light of a solitary candle, flickering alternately on cobwebbed walls, dusty wash-stand, begrimed bowl and pitcher, refuse cigar stumps, boot-jacks, old hats, buttonless coats, muddy trousers, and all the wretched accompaniments of solitary, selfish male existence, not to speak of his own puckered, unkissable face; perhaps, in addition, his boots hurt, his cravat-bow persists in slipping under his ear for want of a pin, and a wife to pin it (poor wretch!) or he has been refused by some pretty girl, as he deserved to be (narrow-minded old vinegar-cruet!) or snubbed by some lady authoress; or, more trying than all to the male constitution, has had a weak cup of coffee for that morning's breakfast.

But seriously—we have had quite enough of this shallow criticism (?) on lady-books. Whether the book which called forth the remark above quoted, was a good book or a bad one, I know not: I should be inclined to think the *former* from the dispraise of such a pen. Whether ladies can write novels or not, is a question I do not intend to discuss; but that some of them have no difficulty in finding either publishers or readers is a matter of history; and that gentlemen often write over feminine signatures would seem also to argue that feminine literature is, after all, in good odor with the reading public. Granted that lady-novels are not all that they should be—is such shallow, unfair, wholesale, sneering criticism (?) the way to reform them? Would it not be better and more manly to point out a better way kindly, justly, *and above all, respectfully?* or—what would be a much harder task for such critics—write a better book!

1857

THE "COMING" WOMAN*

Men often say, "When *I* marry, my wife must be this, that and the other," enumerating all physical, mental, and moral perfections. One cannot but smile to look at the men who say these things; smile to think of the equivalent they will bring for all the amiability, beauty, health, intellectuality, domesticity, and faithfulness they so modestly require; smile to think of the perforated hearts, damaged morals, broken-down constitutions, and irritable tempers, which the bright, pure, innocent girl is to receive with her wedding ring. If one half the girls knew the previous life of the men they marry, the list of old maids would be wonderfully increased.

Doubted? Well, if there is room for a doubt now, thank God the "coming" woman's Alpha and Omega[1] will not be matrimony. *She* will not of necessity sour

---

[2] In New York City.

* First published in the *New York Ledger*, February 12, 1859.

[1] The first and last letters of the Greek alphabet; hence, "beginning and end."

into a pink-nosed old maid, or throw herself at any rickety old shell of humanity, whose clothes are as much out of repair as his morals. No, the future man will have to "step lively;" *this* wife is not to be had for the whistling. He will have a long canter round the pasture for her, and then she will leap the fence and leave him limping on the ground. Thick-soled boots and skating are coming in, and "nerves," novels and sentiment (by consequence) are going out. The coming woman, as I see her, is not to throw aside her needle; neither is she to sit embroidering worsted dogs and cats, or singing doubtful love ditties, and rolling up her eyes to "the chaste moon."

Heaven forbid she should stamp round with a cigar in her mouth, elbowing her fellows, and puffing smoke in their faces; or stand on the free-love platform, *public or private—call it by what specious name you will*—wooing men who, low as they may have sunk in their own self-respect, would die before they would introduce her to the unsullied sister who shared their cradle.

Heaven forbid the coming woman should not have warm blood in her veins, quick to rush to her cheek, or tingle at her fingers' ends when her heart is astir. No, the coming woman shall be no cold, angular, flat-chested, narrow-shouldered, skimpy sharp-visaged Betsey,[2] but she shall be a bright-eyed, full-chested, broad-shouldered, large-souled, intellectual being; able to walk, able to eat, able to fulfill her maternal destiny, and able—if it so please God—to go to her grave happy, self-poised and serene, though unwedded.

1859

FASHIONABLE INVALIDISM*

I hope to live to see the time when it will be considered a *disgrace* to be sick. When people with flat chests and stooping shoulders, will creep round the back way, like other violators of known laws. Those who *inherit* sickly constitutions have my sincerest pity. I only request one favor of them, that they cease perpetuating themselves till they are physically on a sound basis. But a woman who laces so tightly that she breathes only by a rare accident; who vibrates constantly between the confectioner's shop and the dentist's office; who has ball-robes and jewels in plenty, but who owns neither an umbrella, nor a water-proof cloak, nor a pair of thick boots; who lies in bed till noon, never exercises, and complains of "total want of appetite," save for pastry and pickles, is simply a disgusting nuisance. Sentiment is all very nice; but, were I a man, I would beware of a woman who "couldn't eat." Why don't she take care of herself? Why don't she take a nice little bit of beefsteak with her breakfast, and a nice *walk*—not *ride*—after it? Why don't she stop munching sweet stuff between meals? Why don't she go to bed at a decent time, and lead a clean, healthy life? The doctors and confectioners have ridden in their carriages long enough; let the butchers and shoemakers take a turn at it. A man or woman who "can't eat" is never sound on any question. It is waste breath to converse with them. They take hold of everything by the wrong handle. Of course it makes them very angry to whisper pityingly, "dyspepsia,"[1] when they

---

[2] A made-up name to represent a type.

* First published in the *New York Ledger*, July 27, 1867.

[1] Indigestion; the fashionable invalid would rather have a more complicated problem than indigestion.

advance some distorted opinion; but I always do it. They are not going to muddle my brain with their theories, because their internal works are in a state of physical disorganization. Let them go into a Lunatic Asylum and be properly treated till they can learn how they are put together, and how to manage themselves sensibly.

How I *rejoice* in a man or woman with a chest; who can look the sun in the eye, and step off as if they had not wooden legs. It is a rare sight. If a woman now has an errand round the corner, she must have a carriage to go there; and the men, more dead than alive, so lethargic are they with constant smoking, creep into cars and omnibuses, and curl up in a corner, dreading nothing so much as a little wholesome exertion. The more "tired" they are, the more diligently they smoke, like the women who drink perpetual *tea* "to keep them up."

Keep them up! Heavens! I am fifty-five, and I feel half the time as if I were just made. To be sure I was born in Maine, where the timber and the human race last; but I do not eat pastry, nor candy, nor ice-cream. I do not drink tea! I walk, not ride. I own stout boots—pretty ones, too! I have a water-proof cloak, and no diamonds. I like a nice bit of beefsteak and a glass of ale, and anybody else who wants it may eat pap.[2] I go to bed at ten, and get up a six. I dash out in the rain, because it feels good on my face. I don't care for my clothes, but I *will* be well; and after I am buried, I warn you, don't let any fresh air or sunlight down on my coffin, if you don't want me to get up.

1867

THE WORKING-GIRLS OF NEW YORK*

Nowhere more than in New York does the contest between squalor and splendor so sharply present itself. This is the first reflection of the observing stranger who walks its streets. Particularly is this noticeable with regard to its women. Jostling on the same pavement with the dainty fashionist is the care-worn working-girl. Looking at both these women, the question arises, which lives the more miserable life—she whom the world styles "fortunate," whose husband belongs to three clubs, and whose only meal with his family is an occasional breakfast, from year's end to year's end; who is as much a stranger to his own children as to the reader; whose young son of seventeen has already a detective on his track employed by his father to ascertain where and how he spends his nights and his father's money; swift retribution for that father who finds food, raiment, shelter, equipages for his household; but love, sympathy, companionship—never? Or she—this other woman—with a heart quite as hungry and unappeased, who also faces day by day the same appalling question: *Is this all life has for me?*

A great book is yet unwritten about women. Michelet[1] has aired his wax-doll theories regarding them. The defender of "woman's rights" has given us her views. Authors and authoresses of little, and big repute, have expressed themselves on this subject, and none of them as yet have begun to grasp it: men—

---

[2] Soft food for infants or invalids.

* Published in *Folly As It Flies* (1868); the critic and editor Joyce W. Warren has found that some of Fern's columns have been cut out of the only remaining copy of the *New York Ledger;* this may have been one of them.

[1] Jules Michelet (1798–1894), a French historian, whose study *La Femme* (1859) portrays the ideal woman as pliant, submissive, and naïve. In the following sentence Fern may be speaking generically of "the defender" of woman's rights; no specific person has been identified.

because they lack spirituality, rightly and justly to interpret women; women—because they dare not, or will not tell us that which most interests us to know. Who shall write this bold, frank, truthful book remains to be seen. Meanwhile woman's millennium is yet a great way off; and while it slowly progresses, conservatism and indifference gaze through their spectacles at the seething elements of to-day, and wonder "what ails all our women?"

Let me tell you what ails the working-girls. While yet your breakfast is progressing, and your toilet unmade, comes forth through Chatham Street and the Bowery, a long procession of them by twos and threes to their daily labor. Their breakfast, so called, has been hastily swallowed in a tenement house, where two of them share, in a small room, the same miserable bed. Of its quality you may better judge, when you know that each of these girls pays but three dollars a week for board, to the working man and his wife where they lodge.

The room they occupy is close and unventilated, with no accommodations for personal cleanliness, and so near to the little Flinegans that their Celtic night-cries[2] are distinctly heard. They have risen unrefreshed, as a matter of course, and their ill-cooked breakfast does not mend the matter. They emerge from the doorway where their passage is obstructed by "nanny goats" and ragged children rooting together in the dirt, and pass out into the street. They shiver as the sharp wind of early morning strikes their temples. There is no look of youth on their faces; hard lines appear there. Their brows are knit; their eyes are sunken; their dress is flimsy, and foolish, and tawdry; always a hat, and feather or soiled artificial flower upon it; the hair dressed with an abortive attempt at style; a soiled petticoat; a greasy dress, a well-worn sacque or shawl, and a gilt breast-pin and earrings.

Now follow them to the large, black-looking building, where several hundred of them are manufacturing hoop-skirts. If you are a woman you have worn plenty; but you little thought what passed in the heads of these girls as their busy fingers glazed the wire, or prepared the spools for covering them, or secured the tapes which held them in their places. *You* could not stay five minutes in that room, where the noise of the machinery used is so deafening, that only by the motion of the lips could you comprehend a person speaking.

Five minutes! Why, these young creatures bear it, from seven in the morning till six in the evening; week after week, month after month, with only half an hour at midday to eat their dinner of a slice of bread and butter or an apple, which they usually eat in the building, some of them having come a long distance. As I said, the roar of machinery in that room is like the roar of Niagara. Observe them as you enter. Not one lifts her head. They might as well be machines, for any interest or curiosity they show, save always to know *what o'clock it is*. Pitiful! pitiful, you almost sob to yourself, as you look at these young girls. *Young?* Alas! it is only in years that they are young.

1868

THE HISTORY OF OUR LATE WAR*

Many able works have already appeared on this subject, and many more will doubtless follow. But *my* History of the War is yet to be written; not indeed *by*

---

[2] The crying of babies in a sterotyped Irish family, which lives close to the working-girls in this scenario.

* First published in the *New York Ledger*, February 15, 1868.

me, but *for* me. A history which shall record, not the deeds of our Commanders and Generals, noble and great as they were, because these will scarcely fail of historical record and prominence; but *my* history shall preserve for the descendants of those who fought for our flag, the noble deeds of our *privates*, who shared the danger but missed the glory. Scattered far and wide in our remote villages—hidden away amid our mountains—struggling for daily bread in our swarming cities, are these unrecognized heroes. Travelling through our land, one meets them everywhere; but only as accident, or chance, leads to conversation with them, does the plain man by your side become transfigured in your eyes, till you feel like uncovering your head in his presence, as when one stands upon holy ground. Not only because they were brave upon the battle-field, but for their sublime self-abnegation under circumstances when the best of us might be forgiven our selfishness; in the tortures of the ambulance and hospital—quivering through the laggard hours, that might or might not bring peace and rest and health. Oh! what a book might be written upon the noble unselfishness *there* displayed; not only towards those who fought *for* our flag; but *against* it. The coveted drop of water, handed by one dying man to another, whose sufferings seemed the greater. The simple request to the physician to pass *his* wounds by, till those of another, whose existence was unknown to him a moment before, should have been alleviated. Who shall embalm us these?

Last summer, when I was away in the country, I was accustomed to row every evening at sunset on a lovely lake near by. The boatman who went with me was a sunburnt, pleasant-faced young man, whose stroke at the oar it was poetry to see. He made no conversation unless addressed, save occasionally to little Bright-Eyes, who sometimes accompanied me. One evening, as the sun set gloriously and the moon rose, and the aurora borealis was sending up flashes of rose and silver, I said, "Oh, this is too beautiful to leave. I *must* cross the lake again." I made some remark about the brilliance of the North Star, when he remaked simply, "That star was a good friend to me in the war." "Were you in the war?" asked I; "and all these evenings you have rowed a loyal woman like me about this lake, and I knew nothing of it!" Then, at my request, came the story of Andersonville,[1] and its horrors, told simply, and without a revengeful word; then the thrilling attempt at escape, through a country absolutely unknown, and swarming with danger, during which the North Star, of which I had just spoken, was his only guide. Then came a dark night, when the friendly star, alas! disappeared. But a watch, which he had saved his money to obtain, had a compass on the back of it. Still of what use was that without a light? Our boatman was a Yankee. He caught a glow-worm and pinched it. It flashed light sufficient for him to see that he was heading for one of our camps, where, after many hours of travel, he at last found safety, sinking down insensible from fatigue and hunger, as soon as he reached it. So ravenously did he eat, when food was brought, that a raging fever followed; and when he was carried, a mere skeleton, to his home on the borders of the lovely lake where we were rowing, whose peaceful flow had mocked him in dreams in that seething, noisome prison pen, he did not even recognize it. For months his mother watched his sick-bed, till reason and partial health returned—till by degrees he became what he then was.

When he had finished, I said, "Give me your hand—*both of 'em*—and God

---

[1] A notorious Confederate prisoner of war camp in Georgia where more than eight thousand men died of malnutrition and other illnesses in 1864; Major Henry Wirtz, commander at Andersonville, was the only Confederate soldier executed for criminal conduct after the Civil War.

bless you!"—and—then I *mentioned* his jailers! Not a word of bitterness passed his lips—only this: "I used to gasp in the foul air at Andersonville, and think of this quiet, smooth lake, and our little house with the trees near it, and long so to see them again, and row my little boat here. But," he added, quietly, "*they* thought they were as right as we, and they *did* fight well!"

I swallowed a big lump in my throat—as our boat neared the shore, and he handed me out—and said, penitently, "Well, if *you* can forgive them, I am sure I ought to; but it will be the hardest work I ever did."—"Well, it is strange," said he: "I have often noticed it, since my return, that you who stayed at home feel more bitter about it, than we who came so near dying there of foul air and starvation."

1868

THE MODERN OLD MAID*

She don't shuffle round in "skimpt" raiment,[1] and awkward shoes, and cotton gloves, with horn side-combs fastening six hairs to her temples; nor has she a sharp nose, and angular jaw, and hollow cheeks, and only two front teeth. She don't read "Law's Serious Call,"[2] or keep a cat, or a snuff-box, or go to bed at dark, save on vestry-meeting nights, nor scowl at little children, or gather catnip, or apply a broomstick to astonished dogs.

Not a bit of it. The modern "old maid" is round and jolly, and has her full complement of hair and teeth, and two dimples in her cheek, and has a laugh as musical as a bobolink's song. She wears pretty, nicely fitting dresses too, and cunning little ornaments around her plump throat, and becoming bits of color in her hair, and at her breast, in the shape of little knots and bows; and her waist is shapely, and her hands have sparkling rings, and no knuckles;[3] and her foot is cunning, and is prisoned in a bewildering boot; and she goes to concerts and parties and suppers and lectures and matinees, and she don't go alone either; and she lives in a nice house, earned by herself, and gives jolly little teas in it. She don't care whether she is married or not, nor need she. She can afford to wait, as men often do, till they have "seen life," and when their bones are full of aches, and their blood tamed down to water, and they have done going out, and want somebody to swear at and to nurse them—then marry!

Ah! the modern old maid has her eye-teeth cut.[4] She takes care of herself, instead of her sister's nine children, through mumps, and measles, and croup, and chicken-pox, and lung fever and leprosy, and what not.

She don't work that way for no wages and bare toleration, day and night. No, sir! If she has no money, she teaches, or she lectures, or she writes books or poems, or she is a book-keeper, or she sets types, or she does anything but hang on to the skirts of somebody else's husband, and she feels well and independent in

---

* First published in the *New York Ledger*, June 5, 1869.
[1] Old-fashioned attire, lacking in style.
[2] *A Serious Call to a Devout and Holy Life* (1728), by the English religious writer William Law (1686–1761). Reading this book, having a cat and a snuffbox, and going to bed early are offered here as typical occupations of the traditional old maid.
[3] No red and swollen knuckles from years of household drudgery.   [4] She is no longer naïve.

consequence, and holds up her head with the best, and asks no favors, and "*Woman's Rights*" has done it!

That awful bugbear, "Woman's Rights"! which small souled men, and, I am sorry to say, narrow *women* too, burlesque and ridicule, and won't believe in, till the Juggernaut of Progress[5] knocks them down and rides over them, because they will neither climb up on it, nor get out of the way.

The fact is, the *Modern* Old Maid is as good as the Modern Young Maid, and a great deal better, to those who have outgrown bread and butter. She has sense as well as freshness, and conversation and repartee as well as dimples and curves.

She carries a dainty parasol, and a natty little umbrella, and wears killing bonnets, and has live poets and sages and philosophers in her train, and knows how to use her eyes, and don't care if she never sees a cat, and couldn't tell a snuff-box from a patent reaper,[6] and has a bank-book and dividends; yes, sir! and her name is Phœbe or Alice; and Woman's Rights has done it.

1869

HOW I LOOK*

A correspondent inquires how I look? Am I tall? have I dark, or light complexion? and what color are my eyes?

I should be very happy to answer these questions, did I know myself. I proceed to explain why I cannot tell whether "I be I."

First—one evening I was seated at the opera, waiting patiently for the performances to begin. In two orchestra chairs, directly in front of me, sat a lady and gentleman, both utter strangers to me. Said the *gentleman* to his companion, "Do you see the lady who has just entered yonder box?" pointing, as he did so, to the gallery; "well, that is Fanny Fern."—"You know her, then?" asked the lady.— "Intimately," replied this strange gentleman—"*intimately*. Observe how expensively she is dressed. See those diamonds, and that lace! Well, I assure you, that every cent she has ever earned by her writings goes straightway upon her back."[1] Naturally desiring to know how I did look, I used my opera-glass. The lady was tall, handsome, graceful, and beautifully dressed. The gentleman who accompanied me began to grow red in the face, at the statement of my *intimate* acquaintance, and insisted on a word with him; but the fun was too good to be spoiled, and the game too insignificant to hunt; so, in hope of farther revelations, I laughingly observed my "double" during the evening, who looked as I have just described, for your benefit.

Again—in a list of pictures announced to be sold lately, was one labelled "Fanny Fern." Having lost curiosity concerning that lady myself, I did not go on a tour of inspection; but a gentleman friend of mine who did, came back in high glee at the manner in which the purchaser thereof, if any should be found, would be swindled—as "I was *not* I" in that case either.

Some time ago "Fanny Fern" was peddled round California, or at least, so I

---

[5] In Hindu theology Juggernaut, a form of the god Vishnu, signifies a call for blind devotion or sacrifice; here, unstoppable progress.

[6] Any patented machine for reaping grain. "Phoebe" and "Alice" signify the modern old maid.

* First published in the *New York Ledger*, April 9, 1870.   [1] All her money goes into clothes.

was informed by letter. In this instance they had given her, by way of variety, black eyes and hair, and a brunette complexion. I think she was also taken smiling. A friend, moreover, informed me that he had seen me, with an angelic expression, seated upon a rosy cloud, with wings at my back. This last fact touched me. Wings are what I sigh for. It was too cruel a mockery.

You will see from the above, how impossible it is, for such a chameleon female, to describe herself, even to one "who likes my writings." If it will throw any light on the subject, however, I will inform you that a man who got into my parlor under cover of "New-Year's calls," after breathlessly inspecting me, remarked, "Well, now, I *am* agreeably disappointed! I thought from the way you *writ,* that you were a great six-footer of a woman, with snapping black eyes and a big waist, and I *am* pleased to find you looking so soft and so femi-*nine!*"

I would have preferred, had I been consulted, that he should have omitted the word "soft;" but after the experiences narrated above, this was a trifle.

1870

Frederick Douglass
(1818?–1895)

Among the many American books that concern themselves with the struggle for identity and liberty, one of the most powerful is Frederick Douglass's *Narrative of the Life of Frederick Douglass, an American Slave, Written by Himself* (1845). The fundamental structure of the *Narrative* is instructive: the fact that Douglass was a black man telling of his escape from slavery informs the fact that Douglass is an American who, like Benjamin Franklin, was compelled to tell his life story as a model of American individuality and initiative. Douglass focuses on those qualities of persistence, honesty, and social responsiblity that have been present in American writing since John Winthrop's speech "Model of Christian Charity" (1630). But the *Narrative* is specifically and crucially the story of a slave and his struggle for freedom. And among other important slave narratives of the antebellum period, including those of Harriet Jacobs, Solomon Northup, and Moses Roper, it has endured as the most influential and important. Douglass's astute use of irony, his avoidance of indulgent literary and polemic techniques, and his powerful effect on later African-American writers have made an enduring place for the *Narrative* in the history of American letters.

Douglass was born a slave on the eastern coast of Maryland in 1817 or 1818 with the given name Frederick Bailey. His mother, Harriet Bailey, was a slave; his white father, as he came to believe, was superintendent of the plantation on which young Frederick grew up. When he was eight Bailey was sent to work for the family of Thomas Auld in Baltimore. Despite Auld's steadfast opposition, Bailey laid the groundwork for his future success by teaching himself to read and to write. When he was sixteen, he was hired out as a field hand for Edward Covey, an overseer known for brutality and for "breaking" slaves under his authority. For the first time in Bailey's life he was whipped, made to crawl, made to doubt his strength of spirit. As related in the 1845 *Narrative,* his decision to defy

Covey physically, to challenge him as one man to another, was a turning point in Bailey's life as a slave and as a human being.

With the help of Anna Murray, a free African-American woman from Baltimore, Bailey escaped from slavery in 1838. In New York City he and Anna were married; shortly afterwards they moved to New Bedford, Massachusetts, where over the next three years Bailey established himself as a leader in the abolitionist movement. By 1841 he was publicly acclaimed for his commitment to the cause of freedom and for his ability as a speaker. Shortly after he arrived in the North, he had renamed himself, replacing "Frederick Bailey" with the name of the protagonist of Sir Walter Scott's *The Lady of the Lake* (1810). It was thus as Frederick Douglass, a self-named man, that he established his authority as lecturer and writer.

Much of the detail concerning Douglass's early life and career comes from the 1845 *Narrative*. The man and the book make each other possible and reinforce a single identity, that of a writer capable of irony and nuance, aware of what his audience considers important. Douglass demonstrates a particular awareness of prominent and value-laden ideas by applying moral precepts to the crisis of slavery. His profound adherence to the laws of conscience as opposed to the laws of the land places his voice among those of Roger Williams, Thomas Jefferson, and Henry David Thoreau. Douglass's moral self-reliance is particularly evident in the crucial tenth chapter of the *Narrative:* "My long crushed spirit rose, cowardice departed, bold defiance took its place; and I now resolved that, however long I remained a slave in form, the day had passed when I would be a slave in fact." Like Thoreau in "Resistance to Civil Government" (1849), Douglass demonstrates a dominant commitment to what is *right* as opposed to what is legal in an effort to maintain the liberty of the soul in the face of the body's imprisonment.

Douglass maintains the integrity of the *Narrative* by eschewing the use of sentimental and personal stratagems to manipulate his audience. He refuses, for example, to divulge the particulars of his escape from a Baltimore shipyard in 1838 for fear of exposing the individuals who helped him and the methods he used—which he hopes may be duplicated. As a result the *Narrative* does not exploit melodramatic sequences and facile emotionalism (although it contains enough compelling detail to have made Douglass fear recapture as a slave).

Douglass's developing prominence can be measured by his ability to inspire later writers who have addressed the issue of race in American society. Charles W. Chesnutt and Booker T. Washington contributed biographies, and homage to Douglass has come from African-American writers from W. E. B. DuBois to Martin Luther King, Jr. A more profound literary influence can be found on the textual level: both the act of naming oneself as an assertion of identity and the ritual of self-actualization through violence (as we see in Douglass's fight with Edward Covey) are decisive to such novels as Richard Wright's *Black Boy* (1945), Ralph Ellison's *Invisible Man* (1952), and Toni Morrison's *Song of Solomon* (1977).

The *Narrative* of 1845 was only the beginning of Douglass's career as a writer and nationally recognized spokesman for African Americans. As Walt Whitman did with his *Leaves of Grass* (1855), Douglass spent much of his career rewriting, revising, and updating his autobiographical work. The second version of his story, *My Bondage and My Freedom*, appeared in 1855, and the third, *Life and Times of Frederick Douglass*, was published in 1881 and revised again in 1892; it reached a final length of almost eight hundred pages. However, the three later versions of Douglass's life story never achieved the authority and forthrightness of the original *Narrative*. The results of the critic Michael Meyer's comparison of specific parallel passages leave little doubt that the later versions lack the punch and immediacy of the original.

In the *Narrative* Douglass reconstructs the story of his life and the impact of his experience as a slave on a consciousness still in the making, coming in the final chapters to his self-conscious debut as a public speaker. The power of his style as a writer is apparent by contrast with the prefatory letters from the abolitionists William Lloyd Garrison and Wendell Phillips in this first edition. Whereas these letters are self-consciously didactic, almost heavy-handed in their assumption of authority, Douglass relieves the reader from the weight of instruction with the idiom of a man rather than that of a cause: "I was born in Tuckahoe, near Hillsborough, and about twelve miles from Easton, in Talbot County, Maryland." His straightforward style reveals a writer at one with his text and effectively recreates the significant details of his life.

Douglass was also a noted journalist, activist, diplomat, and novelist. His one novel, *The Heroic Slave* (1853), was loosely autobiographical and expanded his antislavery agenda. The hero, who has killed to free himself, prophetically describes the public discourse justifying the Civil War: "We struck for freedom, and if a true heart be in you, you will honor us for that deed." Douglass's recognition of the unfortunate necessity of violence and political activity within the Constitution eventually distanced him from the militant separatism of Garrison. As a journalist Douglass continued his polemic efforts on behalf of abolition; additionally, he endorsed the cause of temperance and women's rights in conjunction with Margaret Fuller, who had initially championed the *Narrative* when other abolitionists feared its intensity. Douglass's career as an editor began with the *North Star* (1847–1851); continued with the *Liberty Party Paper*, which was renamed *Frederick Douglass' Paper* (1851–1860); and concluded with *Douglass' Monthly* (1861–1863). Although he had counseled against the abolitionist John Brown's raid on the Harper's Ferry arsenal in 1859, Douglass's acquaintance with, and positive comments following, the attack placed him under suspicion of conspiracy and forced his escape to Canada. When his accusers publicly recanted, Douglass was vindicated.

Following the Civil War Douglass expanded his activities to include international diplomacy and other issues of broad political importance. From 1877 until 1886 he served as marshal and recorder of deeds for the District of Columbia. Additionally, he focused on the plight of the black race in the Caribbean as a member of the Santo Domingo commission (1871) and as U.S. consul general to Haiti (1889–1891). Upon his return to the United States, he completed the final revision of his autobiography, which now included the full story of his sojourn in England and Ireland following his initial escape from slavery nearly a half century earlier.

After Douglass's death in 1895, his authority among African Americans was recognized to a degree that perhaps no other individual has achieved. When African-American leaders became divided between the parties of assimilation and resistance, the first championed by Booker T. Washington, the second by W. E. B. Du Bois, both claimed the ideological paternity of Douglass. Douglass's importance to writers has been equally vital. His spirit informs the work of Harlem Renaissance writers as well as the current explosion of African-American literature. Perhaps no other figure in American letters is so responsible for both the public and private discourse of his people and his nation.

Suggested Readings: P. F. Foner, ed., *The Life and Writing of Frederick Douglass*, 5 vols., 1971. J. W. Blassinggame, ed., *The Frederick Douglass Papers*, 2 vols., 1979–1982. C. W. Chesnutt, *Frederick Douglass*, 1899. P. F. Foner, *Frederick Douglass: A Biography*, 1964. N. I. Huggins, *Slave and Citizen: The Life of Frederick Douglass*, 1980. W. E. Martin, Jr., *The Mind of Frederick Douglass*, 1984. H. Bloom, ed., *Narrative of the Life of Frederick Douglas: Modern Critical Interpretations*, 1988. D. W. Blight, *Frederick Douglass' Civil War: Keeping Faith in Jubilee*, 1989.

Text Used: *Narrative of the Life of Frederick Douglass, an American Slave*, 1845.

NARRATIVE OF THE LIFE OF FREDERICK DOUGLASS*

PREFACE[1]

In the month of August, 1841, I attended an anti-slavery convention in Nantucket, at which it was my happiness to become acquainted with Frederick Douglass, the writer of the following Narrative. He was a stranger to nearly every member of that body; but, having recently made his escape from the southern prison-house of bondage,[2] and feeling his curiosity excited to ascertain the principles and measures of the abolitionists,—of whom he had heard a somewhat vague description while he was a slave,—he was induced to give his attendance, on the occasion alluded to, though at that time a resident in New Bedford.

Fortunate, most fortunate occurrence!—fortunate for the millions of his manacled brethren, yet panting for deliverance from their awful thraldom!—fortunate for the cause of negro emancipation, and of universal liberty!—fortunate for the land of his birth, which he has already done so much to save and bless!—fortunate for a large circle of friends and acquaintances, whose sympathy and affection he has strongly secured by the many sufferings he has endured, by his virtuous traits of character, by his ever-abiding remembrance of those who are in bonds, as being bound with them!—fortunate for the multitudes, in various parts of our republic, whose minds he has enlightened on the subject of slavery, and who have been melted to tears by his pathos, or roused to virtuous indignation by his stirring eloquence against the enslavers of men!—fortunate for himself, as it at once brought him into the field of public usefulness, "gave the world assurance of a MAN," quickened the slumbering energies of his soul, and consecrated him to the great work of breaking the rod of the oppressor, and letting the oppressed go free!

I shall never forget his first speech at the convention—the extraordinary emotion it excited in my own mind—the powerful impression it created upon a crowded auditory, completely taken by surprise—the applause which followed from the beginning to the end of his felicitous remarks. I think I never hated slavery so intensely as at that moment; certainly, my perception of the enormous outrage which is inflicted by it, on the godlike nature of its victims, was rendered far more clear than ever. There stood one, in physical proportion and stature commanding and exact—in intellect richly endowed—in natural eloquence a prodigy—in soul manifestly "created but a little lower than the angels"[3]—yet a slave, ay, a fugitive slave,—trembling for his safety, hardly daring to believe that on the American soil, a single white person could be found who would befriend him at all hazards, for the love of God and humanity! Capable of high attainments as an intellectual and moral being—needing nothing but a comparatively small amount of cultivation to make him an ornament to society and a blessing to his race—by

---

* First printed in May 1845 by the Anti-Slavery Office in Boston, the source of the present text.
[1] Written by William Lloyd Garrison (1805–1879), a journalist, reformer, and militant spokesman for the abolitionist movement in America.
[2] Douglass escaped from the home of Hugh Auld in 1838; after settling in New Bedford, Massachusetts, he gradually became active among local abolitionists.
[3] "Thou hast made him [man] "a little lower than the angels," from Psalm 8:5.

the law of the land, by the voice of the people, by the terms of the slave code, he was only a piece of property, a beast of burden, a chattel personal, nevertheless!

A beloved friend[4] from New Bedford prevailed on Mr. Douglass to address the convention. He came forward to the platform with a hesitancy and embarrassment, necessarily the attendants of a sensitive mind in such a novel position. After apologizing for his ignorance, and reminding the audience that slavery was a poor school for the human intellect and heart, he proceeded to narrate some of the facts in his own history as a slave, and in the course of his speech gave utterance to many noble thoughts and thrilling reflections. As soon as he had taken his seat, filled with hope and admiration, I rose, and declared that Patrick Henry,[5] of revolutionary fame, never made a speech more eloquent in the cause of liberty, than the one we had just listened to from the lips of that hunted fugitive. So I believed at that time—such is my belief now. I reminded the audience of the peril which surrounded this self-emancipated young man at the North,—even in Massachusetts, on the soil of the Pilgrim Fathers, among the descendants of revolutionary sires; and I appealed to them, whether they would ever allow him to be carried back into slavery,—law or no law, constitution or no constitution. The response was unanimous and in thunder-tones—"NO!" "Will you succor and protect him as a brother-man—a resident of the old Bay State?"[6] "YES!" shouted the whole mass, with an energy so startling, that the ruthless tyrants south of Mason and Dixon's line[7] might almost have heard the mighty burst of feeling, and recognized it as the pledge of an invincible determination, on the part of those who gave it, never to betray him that wanders, but to hide the outcast, and firmly to abide the consequences.

It was at once deeply impressed upon my mind, that, if Mr. Douglass could be persuaded to consecrate his time and talents to the promotion of the anti-slavery enterprise, a powerful impetus would be given to it, and a stunning blow at the same time inflicted on northern prejudice against a colored complexion. I therefore endeavored to instil hope and courage into his mind, in order that he might dare to engage in a vocation so anomalous and responsible for a person in his situation; and I was seconded in this effort by warm-hearted friends, especially by the late General Agent of the Massachusetts Anti-Slavery Society, Mr. John A. Collins, whose judgment in this instance entirely coincided with my own. At first, he could give no encouragement; with unfeigned diffidence, he expressed his conviction that he was not adequate to the performance of so great a task; the path marked out was wholly an untrodden one; he was sincerely apprehensive that he should do more harm than good. After much deliberation, however, he consented to make a trial; and ever since that period, he has acted as a lecturing agent, under the asupices either of the American or the Massachusetts Anti-Slavery Society. In labors he has been most abundant; and his success in combating prejudice, in gaining proselytes, in agitating the public mind, has far surpassed the most sanguine expectations that were raised at the commencement of his brilliant career.

[4] William C. Coffin, a prominent abolitionist in New Bedford.

[5] Henry (1736–1799), the statesman famous for his words to the Virginia House of Delegates in 1775: "I know not what course others may take, but as for me, give me liberty or give me death."

[6] Massachusetts.

[7] The Mason-Dixon line was surveyed by the English astronomers Charles Mason and Jeremiah Dixon between 1763 and 1767 to establish the boundary between Pennsylvania and Maryland; in 1779 it was extended to present-day West Virginia. Prior to the Civil War it was the boundary between slave states and free states.

He has borne himself with gentleness and meekness, yet with true manliness of character. As a public speaker, he excels in pathos, wit, comparison, imitation, strength of reasoning, and fluency of language. There is in him that union of head and heart, which is indispensable to an enlightenment of the heads and a winning of the hearts of others. May his strength continue to be equal to his day! May he continue to "grow in grace, and in the knowledge of God," that he may be increasingly serviceable in the cause of bleeding humanity, whether at home or abroad!

It is certainly a very remarkable fact, that one of the most efficient advocates of the slave population, now before the public, is a fugitive slave, in the person of Frederick Douglass; and that the free colored population of the United States are as ably represented by one of their own number, in the person of Charles Lenox Remond,[8] whose eloquent appeals have extorted the highest applause of multitudes on both sides of the Atlantic. Let the calumniators of the colored race despise themselves for their baseness and illiberality of spirit, and henceforth cease to talk of the natural inferiority of those who require nothing but time and opportunity to attain to the highest point of human excellence.

It may, perhaps, be fairly questioned, whether any other portion of the population of the earth could have endured the privations, sufferings and horrors of slavery, without having become more degraded in the scale of humanity than the slaves of African descent. Nothing has been left undone to cripple their intellects, darken their minds, debase their moral nature, obliterate all traces of their relationship to mankind; and yet how wonderfully they have sustained the mighty load of a most frightful bondage, under which they have been groaning for centuries! To illustrate the effect of slavery on the white man,—to show that he has no powers of endurance, in such a condition, superior to those of his black brother,—Daniel O'Connell,[9] the distinguished advocate of universal emancipation, and the mightiest champion of prostrate but not conquered Ireland, relates the following anecdote in a speech delivered by him in the Conciliation Hall, Dublin, before the Loyal National Repeal Association, March 31, 1845. "No matter," said Mr. O'Connell, "under what specious term it may disguise itself, slavery is still hideous. *It has a natural, an inevitable tendency to brutalize every noble faculty of man.* An American sailor, who was cast away on the shore of Africa, where he was kept in slavery for three years, was, at the expiration of that period, found to be imbruted and stultified—he had lost all reasoning power; and having forgotten his native language, could only utter some savage gibberish between Arabic and English, which nobody could understand, and which even he himself found difficulty in pronouncing. So much for the humanizing influence of THE DOMESTIC INSTITUTION!" Admitting this to have been an extraordinary case of mental deterioration, it proves at least that the white slave can sink as low in the scale of humanity as the black one.

Mr. Douglass has very properly chosen to write his own Narrative, in his own style, and according to the best of his ability, rather than to employ some one else. It is, therefore, entirely his own production; and, considering how long and dark was the career he had to run as a slave,—how few have been his opportunities to improve his mind since he broke his iron fetters,—it is, in my judgment, highly

---

[8] Remond (1810–1873), a free-born African American and one of the first abolitionist lecturers of his race, returned from Great Britain and Ireland in 1842; under the auspices of the Massachusetts Anti-Slavery Society, he and Douglass spoke throughout the state in 1842.

[9] O'Connell (1775–1847), a leader in the struggle for Catholic emancipation and Irish independence and frequently hailed as the "Liberator."

effects of slavery, let him go to Colonel Lloyd's plantation, and, on allowance-day, place himself in the deep pine woods, and there let him, in silence, analyze the sounds that shall pass through the chambers of his soul,—and if he is not thus impressed, it will only be because "there is no flesh in his obdurate heart."

I have often been utterly astonished, since I came to the north, to find persons who could speak of the singing, among slaves, as evidence of their contentment and happiness. It is impossible to conceive of a greater mistake. Slaves sing most when they are most unhappy. The songs of the slave represent the sorrows of his heart; and he is relieved by them, only as an aching heart is relieved by its tears. At least, such is my experience. I have often sung to drown my sorrow, but seldom to express my happiness. Crying for joy, and singing for joy, were alike uncommon to me while in the jaws of slavery. The singing of a man cast away upon a desolate island might be as appropriately considered as evidence of contentment and happiness, as the singing of a slave; the songs of the one and of the other are prompted by the same emotion.

Chapter III

Colonel Lloyd kept a large and finely cultivated garden, which afforded almost constant employment for four men, besides the chief gardener, (Mr. M'Durmond.) This garden was probably the greatest attraction of the place. During the summer months, people came from far and near—from Baltimore, Easton, and Annapolis—to see it. It abounded in fruits of almost every description, from the hardy apple of the north to the delicate orange of the south. This garden was not the least source of trouble on the plantation. Its excellent fruit was quite a temptation to the hungry swarms of boys, as well as the older slaves, belonging to the colonel, few of whom had the virtue or the vice to resist it. Scarcely a day passed, during the summer, but that some slave had to take the lash for stealing fruit. The colonel had to resort to all kinds of stratagems to keep his slaves out of the garden. The last and most successful one was that of tarring his fence all around; after which, if a slave was caught with any tar upon his person, it was deemed sufficient proof that he had either been into the garden, or had tried to get in. In either case, he was severely whipped by the chief gardener. This plan worked well; the slaves became as fearful of tar as of the lash. They seemed to realize the impossibility of touching *tar* without being defiled.

The colonel also kept a splendid riding equipage. His stable and carriage-house presented the appearance of some of our large city livery establishments. His horses were of the finest form and noblest blood. His carriage-house contained three splendid coaches, three or four gigs, besides dearborns and barouches[16] of the most fashionable style.

This establishment was under the care of two slaves—old Barney and young Barney—father and son. To attend to this establishment was their sole work. But it was by no means an easy employment; for in nothing was Colonel Lloyd more particular than in the management of his horses. The slightest inattention to these was unpardonable, and was visited upon those, under whose care they were placed, with the severest punishment; no excuse could shield them, if the colonel only suspected any want of attention to his horses—a supposition which he fre-

---

[16] Horse-drawn carriages with two or four wheels.

So profoundly ignorant of the nature of slavery are many persons, that they are stubbornly incredulous whenever they read or listen to any recital of the cruelties which are daily inflicted on its victims. They do not deny that the slaves are held as property; but that terrible fact seems to convey to their minds no idea of injustice, exposure to outrage, or savage barbarity. Tell them of cruel scourgings, of mutilations and brandings, of scenes of pollution and blood, of the banishment of all light and knowledge, and they affect to be greatly indignant at such enormous exaggerations, such wholesale misstatements, such abominable libels on the character of the southern planters! As if all these direful outrages were not the natural results of slavery! As if it were less cruel to reduce a human being to the condition of a thing, than to give him a severe flagellation, or to deprive him of necessary food and clothing! As if whips, chains, thumb-screws, paddles, bloodhounds, overseers, drivers, patrols, were not all indispensable to keep the slaves down, and to give protection to their ruthless oppressors! As if, when the marriage institution is abolished, concubinage, adultery, and incest, must not necessarily abound; when all the rights of humanity are annihilated, any barrier remains to protect the victim from the fury of the spoiler; when absolute power is assumed over life and liberty, it will not be wielded with destructive sway! Skeptics of this character abound in society. In some few instances, their incredulity arises from a want of reflection; but, generally, it indicates a hatred of the light, a desire to shield slavery from the assaults of its foes, a contempt of the colored race, whether bond or free. Such will try to discredit the shocking tales of slaveholding cruelty which are recorded in this truthful Narrative; but they will labor in vain. Mr. Douglass has frankly disclosed the place of his birth, the names of those who claimed ownership in his body and soul, and the names also of those who committed the crimes which he has alleged against them. His statements, therefore, may easily be disproved, if they are untrue.

In the course of his Narrative, he relates two instances of murderous cruelty,— in one of which a planter deliberately shot a slave belonging to a neighboring plantation, who had unintentionally gotten within his lordly domain in quest of fish; and in the other, an overseer blew out the brains of a slave who had fled to a stream of water to escape a bloody scourging. Mr. Douglass states that in neither of these instances was any thing done by way of legal arrest or judicial investigation. The Baltimore American, of March 17, 1845, relates a similar case of atrocity, perpetrated with similar impunity—as follows:—"*Shooting a Slave.*—We learn, upon the authority of a letter from Charles county, Maryland, received by a gentleman of this city, that a young man, named Matthews, a nephew of General Matthews, and whose father, it is believed, holds an office at Washington, killed one of the slaves upon his father's farm by shooting him. The letter states that young Matthews had been left in charge of the farm; that he gave an order to the servant, which was disobeyed, when he proceeded to the house, *obtained a gun, and, returning, shot the servant*. He immediately, the letter continues, fled to his father's residence, where he still remains unmolested."—Let it never be forgotten, that no slaveholder or overseer can be convicted of any outrage perpetrated on the person of a slave, however diabolical it may be, on the testimony of colored witnesses, whether bond or free. By the slave code, they are adjudged to be as incompetent to testify against a white man, as though they were indeed a part of the brute creation. Hence, there is no legal protection in fact, whatever there may be in form, for the slave population; and any amount of cruelty may be inflicted on them with impunity. Is it possible for the human mind to conceive of a more horrible state of society?

The effect of a religious profession on the conduct of southern masters is vividly described in the following Narrative, and shown to be any thing but salutary. In the nature of the case, it must be in the highest degree pernicious. The testimony of Mr. Douglass, on this point, is sustained by a cloud of witnesses, whose veracity is unimpeachable. "A slaveholder's profession of Christianity is a palpable imposture. He is a felon of the highest grade. He is a man-stealer. It is of no importance what you put in the other scale."

Reader! are you with the man-stealers in sympathy and purpose, or on the side of their down-trodden victims? If with the former, then are you the foe of God and man. If with the latter, what are you prepared to do and dare in their behalf? Be faithful, be vigilant, be untiring in your efforts to break every yoke, and let the oppressed go free. Come what may—cost what it may—inscribe on the banner which you unfurl to the breeze, as your religious and political motto—"No Compromise with Slavery! No Union with Slaveholders!"

Wm. Lloyd Garrison.

Boston, May 1, 1845.

Letter from Wendell Phillips, Esq.[12]

Boston, April 22, 1845.

My Dear Friend:

You remember the old fable of "The Man and the Lion," where the lion complained that he should not be so misrepresented "when the lions wrote history."

I am glad the time has come when the "lions write history." We have been left long enough to gather the character of slavery from the involuntary evidence of the masters. One might, indeed, rest sufficiently satisfied with what, it is evident, must be, in general, the results of such a relation, without seeking farther to find whether they have followed in every instance. Indeed, those who stare at the half-peck of corn a week, and love to count the lashes on the slave's back, are seldom the "stuff" out of which reformers and abolitionists are to be made. I remember that, in 1838 many were waiting for the results of the West India experiment,[13] before they could come into our ranks. Those "results" have come long ago; but, alas! few of that number have come with them, as converts. A man must be disposed to judge of emancipation by other tests than whether it has increased the produce of sugar,—and to hate slavery for other reasons than because it starves men and whips women,—before he is ready to lay the first stone of his anti-slavery life.

I was glad to learn, in your story, how early the most neglected of God's children waken to a sense of their rights, and of the injustice done them. Experience is a keen teacher; and long before you had mastered your A B C, or knew where the "white sails" of the Chesapeake were bound, you began, I see, to gauge the wretchedness of the slave, not by his hunger and want, not by his lashes and toil, but by the cruel and blighting death which gathers over his soul.

In connection with this, there is one circumstance which makes your recollectioins peculiarly valuable, and renders your early insight the more remarkable.

---

[12] Phillips (1811–1884) was a Boston-born lawyer who joined the Anti-Slavery Society in 1835 (after seeing Garrison mobbed by proslavery sympathizers) and became a powerful abolitionist speaker.

[13] Slavery in the British West Indies was ended in 1834; four years later, abolitionists were watching the consequences of that "experiment."

You come from that part of the country where we are told slavery appears with its fairest features. Let us hear, then, what it is at its best estate—gaze on its bright side, if it has one; and then imagination may task her powers to add dark lines to the picture, as she travels southward to that (for the colored man) Valley of the Shadow of Death, where the Mississippi sweeps along.

Again, we have known you long, and can put the most entire confidence in your truth, candor, and sincerity. Every one who has heard you speak has felt, and, I am confident, every one who reads your book will feel, persuaded that you give them a fair specimen of the whole truth. No one-sided portrait,—no wholesale complaints,—but strict justice done, whenever individual kindliness has neutralized, for a moment, the deadly system with which it was strangely allied. You have been with us, too, some years, and can fairly compare the twilight of rights, which your race enjoy at the North, with that "noon of night" under which they labor south of Mason and Dixon's line. Tell us whether, after all, the half-free colored man of Massachusetts is worse off than the pampered slave of the rice swamps!

In reading your life, no one can say that we have unfairly picked out some rare specimens of cruelty. We know that the bitter drops, which even you have drained from the cup, are no incidental aggravations, no individual ills, but such as must mingle always and necessarily in the lot of every slave. They are the essential ingredients, not the occasional results, of the system.

After all, I shall read your book with trembling for you. Some years ago, when you were beginning to tell me your real name and birthplace, you may remember I stopped you, and preferred to remain ignorant of all. With the exception of a vague description, so I continued, till the other day, when you read me your memoirs. I hardly knew, at the time, whether to thank you or not for the sight of them, when I reflected that it was still dangerous, in Massachusetts, for honest men to tell their names! They say the fathers, in 1776, signed the Declaration of Independence with the halter about their necks. You, too, publish your declaration of freedom with danger compassing you around. In all the broad lands which the Constitution of the United States overshadows, there is no single spot,—however narrow or desolate,—where a fugitive slave can plant himself and say, "I am safe." The whole armory of Northern Law has no shield for you. I am free to say that, in your place, I should throw the MS. into the fire.

You, perhaps, may tell your story in safety, endeared as you are to so many warm hearts by rare gifts, and a still rarer devotion of them to the service of others. But it will be owing only to your labors, and the fearless efforts of those who, trampling the laws and Constitution of the country under their feet, are determined that they will "hide the outcast," and that their hearts shall be, spite of the law, an asylum for the oppressed, if, some time or other, the humblest may stand in our streets, and bear witness in safety against the cruelties of which he has been the victim.

Yet it is sad to think, that these very throbbing hearts which welcome your story, and form your best safeguard in telling it, are all beating contrary to the "statute in such case made and provided." Go on, my dear friend, till you, and those who, like you, have been saved, so as by fire, from the dark prison-house, shall stereotype these free, illegal pulses into statutes; and New England, cutting loose from a blood-stained Union, shall glory in being the house of refuge for the oppressed;—till we no longer merely "*hide* the outcast," or make a merit of standing idly by while he is hunted in our midst; but, consecrating anew the soil of the Pilgrims as an asylum for the oppressed, proclaim our *welcome* to the slave so loudly, that the tones shall reach every hut in the Carolinas, and make the broken-hearted bondman leap up at the thought of old Massachusetts.

God speed the day!

Till then, and ever,

Yours truly,

Wendell Phillips.

Chapter I

I was born in Tuckahoe, near Hillsborough, and about twelve miles from Easton, in Talbot county, Maryland. I have no accurate knowledge of my age, never having seen any authentic record containing it. By far the larger part of the slaves know as little of their ages as horses know of theirs, and it is the wish of most masters within my knowledge to keep their slaves thus ignorant. I do not remember to have ever met a slave who could tell of his birthday. They seldom come nearer to it than planting-time, harvest-time, cherry-time, spring-time, or fall-time. A want of information concerning my own was a source of unhappiness to me even during childhood. The white children could tell their ages. I could not tell why I ought to be deprived of the same privilege. I was not allowed to make any inquiries of my master concerning it. He deemed all such inquiries on the part of a slave improper and impertinent, and evidence of a restless spirit. The nearest estimate I can give makes me now between twenty-seven and twenty-eight years of age. I come to this, from hearing my master say, some time during 1835, I was about seventeen years old.

My mother was named Harriet Bailey. She was the daughter of Isaac and Betsey Bailey, both colored, and quite dark. My mother was of a darker complexion than either my grandmother or grandfather.

My father was a white man. He was admitted to be such by all I ever heard speak of my parentage. The opinion was also whispered that my master was my father; but of the correctness of this opinion, I know nothing; the means of knowing was withheld from me. My mother and I were separated when I was but an infant—before I knew her as my mother. It is a common custom, in the part of Maryland from which I ran away, to part children from their mothers at a very early age. Frequently, before the child has reached its twelfth month, its mother is taken from it, and hired out on some farm a considerable distance off, and the child is placed under the care of an old woman, too old for field labor. For what this separation is done, I do not know, unless it be to hinder the development of the child's affection toward its mother, and to blunt and destroy the natural affection of the mother for the child. This is the inevitable result.

I never saw my mother, to know her as such, more than four or five times in my life; and each of these times was very short in duration, and at night. She was hired by a Mr. Stewart, who lived about twelve miles from my home. She made her journeys to see me in the night, travelling the whole distance on foot, after the performance of her day's work. She was a field hand, and a whipping is the penalty of not being in the field at sunrise, unless a slave has special permission from his or her master to the contrary—a permission which they seldom get, and one that gives to him that gives it the proud name of being a kind master. I do not recollect of ever seeing my mother by the light of day. She was with me in the night. She would lie down with me, and get me to sleep, but long before I waked she was gone. Very little communication ever took place between us. Death soon ended what little we could have while she lived, and with it her hardships and suffering. She died when I was about seven years old, on one of my master's farms, near Lee's Mill. I was not allowed to be present during her illness, at her death, or burial. She was gone long before I knew any thing about it. Never having enjoyed, to any considerable extent, her soothing presence, her tender and watchful care, I received the tidings of her death with much the same emotions I should have probably felt at the death of a stranger.

Called thus suddenly away, she left me without the slightest intimation of who my father was. The whisper that my master was my father, may or may not be true; and, true or false, it is of but little consequence to my purpose whilst the fact remains, in all its glaring odiousness, that slaveholders have ordained, and by law established, that the children of slave women shall in all cases follow the condition of their mothers; and this is done too obviously to administer to their own lusts, and made a gratification of their wicked desires profitable as well as pleasurable; for by this cunning arrangement, the slaveholder, in cases not a few, sustains to his slaves the double relation of master and father.

I know of such cases; and it is worthy of remark that such slaves invariably suffer greater hardships, and have more to contend with, than others. They are, in the first place, a constant offence to their mistress. She is ever disposed to find fault with them; they can seldom do any thing to please her; she is never better pleased than when she sees them under the lash, especially when she suspects her husband of showing to his mulatto children favors which he withholds from his black slaves. The master is frequently compelled to sell this class of his slaves, out of deference to the feelings of his white wife; and, cruel as the deed may strike any one to be, for a man to sell his own children to human flesh-mongers, it is often the dictate of humanity for him to do so; for, unless he does this, he must not only whip them himself, but must stand by and see one white son tie up his brother, of but few shades darker complexion than himself, and ply the gory lash to his naked back; and if he lisp one word of disapproval, it is set down to his parental partiality, and only makes a bad matter worse, both for himself and the slave whom he would protect and defend.

Every year brings with it multitudes of this class of slaves. It was doubtless in consequence of a knowledge of this fact, that one great statesman of the south predicted the downfall of slavery by the inevitable laws of population. Whether this prophecy is ever fulfilled or not, it is nevertheless plain that a very different-looking class of people are springing up at the south, and are now held in slavery, from those originally brought to this country from Africa; and if their increase will do no other good, it will do away the force of the argument, that God cursed Ham, and therefore American slavery is right.[14] If the lineal descendants of Ham are alone to be scripturally enslaved, it is certain that slavery at the south must soon become unscriptural; for thousands are ushered into the world, annually, who,

---

[14] In Genesis 9:20–27 the biblical patriarch Noah curses his son Ham and commits him to bondage to his brothers; the passage was interpreted as scriptural authority for slavery.

like myself, owe their existence to white fathers, and those fathers most frequently their own masters.

I have had two masters. My first master's name was Anthony. I do not remember his first name. He was generally called Captain Anthony—a title which, I presume, he acquired by sailing a craft on the Chesapeake Bay. He was not considered a rich slaveholder. He owned two or three farms, and about thirty slaves. His farms and slaves were under the care of an overseer. The overseer's name was Plummer. Mr. Plummer was a miserable drunkard, a profane swearer, and a savage monster. He always went armed with a cowskin[15] and a heavy cudgel. I have known him to cut and slash the women's heads so horribly, that even master would be enraged at his cruelty, and would threaten to whip him if he did not mind himself. Master, however, was not a humane slaveholder. It required extraordinary barbarity on the part of an overseer to affect him. He was a cruel man, hardened by a long life of slaveholding. He would at times seem to take great pleasure in whipping a slave. I have often been awakened at the dawn of day by the most heart-rending shrieks of an own aunt of mine, whom he used to tie up to a joist, and whip upon her naked back till she was literally covered with blood. No words, no tears, no prayers, from his gory victim, seemed to move his iron heart from its bloody purpose. The louder she screamed, the harder he whipped; and where the blood ran fastest, there he whipped longest. He would whip her to make her scream, and whip her to make her hush; and not until overcome by fatigue, would he cease to swing the blood-clotted cowskin. I remember the first time I ever witnessed this horrible exhibition. I was quite a child, but I well remember it. I never shall forget it whilst I remember any thing. It was the first of a long series of such outrages, of which I was doomed to be a witness and a participant. It struck me with awful force. It was the blood-stained gate, the entrance to the hell of slavery, through which I was about to pass. It was a most terrible spectacle. I wish I could commit to paper the feelings with which I beheld it.

This occurrence took place very soon after I went to live with my old master, and under the following circumstances. Aunt Hester went out one night,—where or for what I do not know,—and happened to be absent when my master desired her presence. He had ordered her not to go out evenings, and warned her that she must never let him catch her in company with a young man, who was paying attention to her belonging to Colonel Lloyd. The young man's name was Ned Roberts, generally called Lloyd's Ned. Why master was so careful of her, may be safely left to conjecture. She was a woman of noble form, and of graceful proportions, having very few equals, and fewer superiors, in personal appearance, among the colored or white women of our neighborhood.

Aunt Hester had not only disobeyed his orders in going out, but had been found in company with Lloyd's Ned; which circumstance, I found, from what he said while whipping her, was the chief offence. Had he been a man of pure morals himself, he might have been thought interested in protecting the innocence of my aunt; but those who knew him will not suspect him of any such virtue. Before he commenced whipping Aunt Hester, he took her into the kitchen, and stripped her from neck to waist, leaving her neck, shoulders, and back, entirely naked. He then told her to cross her hands, calling her at the same time a d— —d b— —h. After crossing her hands, he tied them with a strong rope, and led her to a stool under a large hook in the joist, put in for the purpose. He made her get upon the

---

[15] A whip made of cowhide.

stool, and tied her hands to the hook. She now stood fair for his infernal purpose. Her arms were stretched up at their full length, so that she stood upon the ends of her toes. He then said to her, "Now, you d— —d b— —h, I'll learn you how to disobey my orders!" and after rolling up his sleeves, he commenced to lay on the heavy cowskin, and soon the warm, red blood (amid heart-rending shrieks from her, and horrid oaths from him) came dripping to the floor. I was so terrified and horror-stricken at the sight, that I hid myself in a closet, and dared not venture out till long after the bloody transaction was over. I expected it would be my turn next. It was all new to me. I had never seen any thing like it before. I had always lived with my grandmother on the outskirts of the plantation, where she was put to raise the children of the younger women. I had therefore been, until now, out of the way of the bloody scenes that often occurred on the plantation.

Chapter II

My master's family consisted of two sons, Andrew and Richard; one daughter, Lucretia, and her husband, Captain Thomas Auld. They lived in one house, upon the home plantation of Colonel Edward Lloyd. My master was Colonel Lloyd's clerk and superintendent. He was what might be called the overseer of the overseers. I spent two years of childhood on this plantation in my old master's family. It was there that I witnessed the bloody transaction recorded in the first chapter; and as I received my first impressions of slavery on this plantation, I will give some description of it, and of slavery as it there existed. The plantation is about twelve miles north of Easton, in Talbot county, and is situated on the border of Miles River. The principal products raised upon it were tobacco, corn, and wheat. These were raised in great abundance; so that, with the products of this and the other farms belonging to him, he was able to keep in almost constant employment a large sloop, in carrying them to market at Baltimore. This sloop was named Sally Lloyd, in honor of one of the colonel's daughters. My master's son-in-law, Captain Auld, was master of the vessel; she was otherwise manned by the colonel's own slaves. Their names were Peter, Isaac, Rich, and Jake. These were esteemed very highly by the other slaves, and looked upon as the privileged ones of the plantation; for it was no small affair, in the eyes of the slaves, to be allowed to see Baltimore.

Colonel Lloyd kept from three to four hundred slaves on his home plantation, and owned a large number more on the neighboring farms belonging to him. The names of the farms nearest to the home plantation were Wye Town and New Design. "Wye Town" was under the overseership of a man named Noah Willis. New Design was under the overseership of a Mr. Townsend. The overseers of these, and all the rest of the farms, numbering over twenty, received advice and direction from the managers of the home plantation. This was the great business place. It was the seat of government for the whole twenty farms. All disputes among the overseers were settled here. If a slave was convicted of any high misdemeanor, became unmanagable, or evinced a determination to run away, he was brought immediately here, severely whipped, put on board the sloop, carried to Baltimore, and sold to Austin Woolfolk, or some other slave-trader, as a warning to the slaves remaining.

Here, too, the slaves of all the other farms received their monthly allowance of food, and their yearly clothing. The men and women slaves received, as their monthly allowance of food, eight pounds of pork, or its equivalent in fish, and one bushel of corn meal. Their yearly clothing consisted of two coarse linen shirts, one pair of linen trousers, like the shirts, one jacket, one pair of trousers for winter, made of coarse negro cloth, one pair of stockings, and one pair of shoes; the whole of which could not have cost more than seven dollars. The allowance of the slave children was given to their mothers, or the old women having the care of them. The children unable to work in the field had neither shoes, stockings, jackets, nor trousers, given to them; their clothing consisted of two coarse linen shirts per year. When these failed them, they went naked until the next allowance-day. Children from seven to ten years old, of both sexes, almost naked, might be seen at all seasons of the year.

There were no beds given the slaves, unless one coarse blanket be considered such, and none but the men and women had these. This, however, is not considered a very great privation. They find less difficulty from the want of beds, than from the want of time to sleep; for when their day's work in the field is done, the most of them having their washing, mending, and cooking to do, and having few or none of the ordinary facilities for doing either of these, very many of their sleeping hours are consumed in preparing for the field the coming day; and when this is done, old and young, male and female, married and single, drop down side by side, on one common bed,—the cold, damp floor,—each covering himself or herself with their miserable blankets; and here they sleep till they are summoned to the field by the driver's horn. At the sound of this, all must rise, and be off to the field. There must be no halting; every one must be at his or her post; and woe betides them who hear not this morning summons to the field; for if they are not awakened by the sense of hearing, they are by the sense of feeling: no age nor sex finds any favor. Mr. Severe, the overseer, used to stand by the door of the quarter, armed with a large hickory stick and heavy cowskin, ready to whip any one who was so unfortunate as not to hear, or, from any other cause, was prevented from being ready to start for the field at the sound of the horn.

Mr. Severe was rightly named: he was a cruel man. I have seen him whip a woman, causing the blood to run half an hour at the time; and this, too, in the midst of her crying children, pleading for their mother's release. He seemed to take pleasure in manifesting his fiendish barbarity. Added to his cruelty, he was a profane swearer. It was enough to chill the blood and stiffen the hair of an ordinary man to hear him talk. Scarce a sentence escaped him but that was commenced or concluded by some horrid oath. The field was the place to witness his cruelty and profanity. His presence made it both the field of blood and of blasphemy. From the rising till the going down of the sun, he was cursing, raving, cutting, and slashing among the slaves of the field, in the most frightful manner. His career was short. He died very soon after I went to Colonel Lloyd's; and he died as he lived, uttering, with his dying groans, bitter curses and horrid oaths. His death was regarded by the slaves as the result of a merciful providence.

Mr. Severe's place was filled by a Mr. Hopkins. He was a very different man. He was less cruel, less profane, and made less noise, than Mr. Severe. His course was characterized by no extraordinary demonstrations of cruelty. He whipped, but seemed to take no pleasure in it. He was called by the slaves a good overseer.

The home plantation of Colonel Lloyd wore the appearance of a country village. All the mechanical operations for all the farms were performed here. The shoemaking and mending, the blacksmithing, cartwrighting, coopering, weaving, and grain-grinding, were all performed by the slaves on the home plantation. The whole place wore a business-like aspect very unlike the neighboring farms. The number of houses, too, conspired to give it advantage over the neighboring farms. It was called by the slaves the *Great House Farm*. Few privileges were esteemed higher, by the slaves of the out-farms, than that of being selected to do errands at the Great House Farm. It was associated in their minds with greatness. A representative could not be prouder of his election to a seat in the American Congress, than a slave on one of the out-farms would be of his election to do errands at the Great House Farm. They regarded it as evidence of great confidence reposed in them by their overseers; and it was on this account, as well as a constant desire to be out of the field from under the driver's lash, that they esteemed it a high privilege, one worth careful living for. He was called the smartest and most trusty fellow, who had this honor conferred upon him the most frequently. The competitors for this office sought as diligently to please their overseers, as the office-seekers in the political parties seek to please and deceive the people. The same traits of character might be seen in Colonel Lloyd's slaves, as are seen in the slaves of the political parties.

The slaves selected to go to the Great House Farm, for the monthly allowance for themselves and their fellow-slaves, were peculiarly enthusiastic. While on their way, they would make the dense old woods, for miles around, reverberate with their wild songs, revealing at once the highest joy and the deepest sadness. They would compose and sing as they went along, consulting neither time or tune. The thought that came up, came out—if not in the word, in the sound;—and as frequently in the one as in the other. They would sometimes sing the most pathetic sentiment in the most rapturous tone, and the most rapturous sentiment in the most pathetic tone. Into all of their songs they would manage to weave something of the Great House Farm. Especially would they do this, when leaving home. They would then sing most exultingly the following words:—

> "I am going away to the Great House Farm!
> O, yea! O, yea! O!"

This they would sing, as a chorus, to words which to many would seem unmeaning jargon, but which, nevertheless, were full of meaning to themselves. I have sometimes thought that the mere hearing of those songs would do more to impress some minds with the horrible character of slavery, than the reading of whole volumes of philosophy on the subject could do.

I did not, when a slave, understand the deep meaning of those rude and apparently incoherent songs. I was myself within the circle; so that I neither saw nor heard as those without might see and hear. They told a tale of woe which was then altogether beyond my feeble comprehension; they were tones loud, long, and deep; they breathed the prayer and complaint of souls boiling over with the bitterest anguish. Every tone was a testimony against slavery, and a prayer to God for deliverance from chains. The hearing of those wild notes always depressed my spirit, and filled me with ineffable sadness. I have frequently found myself in tears while hearing them. The mere recurrence to those songs, even now, afflicts me; and while I am writing these lines, an expression of feeling has already found its way down my cheek. To those songs I trace my first glimmering conception of the dehumanizing character of slavery. I can never get rid of that conception. Those songs still follow me, to deepen my hatred of slavery, and quicken my sympathies for my brethren in bonds. If any one wishes to be impressed with the soul-killing effects of slavery, let him go to Colonel Lloyd's plantation, and, on allowance-day, place himself in the deep pine woods, and there let him, in silence, analyze the sounds that shall pass through the chambers of his soul,—and if he is not thus impressed, it will only be because "there is no flesh in his obdurate heart."

I have often been utterly astonished, since I came to the north, to find persons who could speak of the singing, among slaves, as evidence of their contentment and happiness. It is impossible to conceive of a greater mistake. Slaves sing most when they are most unhappy. The songs of the slave represent the sorrows of his heart; and he is relieved by them, only as an aching heart is relieved by its tears. At least, such is my experience. I have often sung to drown my sorrow, but seldom to express my happiness. Crying for joy, and singing for joy, were alike uncommon to me while in the jaws of slavery. The singing of a man cast away upon a desolate island might be as appropriately considered as evidence of contentment and happiness, as the singing of a slave; the songs of the one and of the other are prompted by the same emotion.

CHAPTER III

Colonel Lloyd kept a large and finely cultivated garden, which afforded almost constant employment for four men, besides the chief gardener, (Mr. M'Durmond.) This garden was probably the greatest attraction of the place. During the summer months, people came from far and near—from Baltimore, Easton, and Annapolis—to see it. It abounded in fruits of almost every description, from the hardy apple of the north to the delicate orange of the south. This garden was not the least source of trouble on the plantation. Its excellent fruit was quite a temptation to the hungry swarms of boys, as well as the older slaves, belonging to the colonel, few of whom had the virtue or the vice to resist it. Scarcely a day passed, during the summer, but that some slave had to take the lash for stealing fruit. The colonel had to resort to all kinds of stratagems to keep his slaves out of the garden. The last and most successful one was that of tarring his fence all around; after which, if a slave was caught with any tar upon his person, it was deemed sufficient proof that he had either been into the garden, or had tried to get in. In either case, he was severely whipped by the chief gardener. This plan worked well; the slaves became as fearful of tar as of the lash. They seemed to realize the impossibility of touching *tar* without being defiled.

The colonel also kept a splendid riding equipage. His stable and carriage-house presented the appearance of some of our large city livery establishments. His horses were of the finest form and noblest blood. His carriage-house contained three splendid coaches, three or four gigs, besides dearborns and barouches[16] of the most fashionable style.

This establishment was under the care of two slaves—old Barney and young Barney—father and son. To attend to this establishment was their sole work. But it was by no means an easy employment; for in nothing was Colonel Lloyd more particular than in the management of his horses. The slightest inattention to these was unpardonable, and was visited upon those, under whose care they were placed, with the severest punishment; no excuse could shield them, if the colonel only suspected any want of attention to his horses—a supposition which he fre-

---

[16] Horse-drawn carriages with two or four wheels.

quently indulged, and one which, of course, made the office of old and young Barney a very trying one. They never knew when they were safe from punishment. They were frequently whipped when least deserving, and escaped whipping when most deserving it. Every thing depended upon the looks of the horses, and the state of Colonel Lloyd's own mind when his horses were brought to him for use. If a horse did not move fast enough, or hold his head high enough, it was owing to some fault of his keepers. It was painful to stand near the stable-door, and hear the various complaints against the keepers when a horse was taken out for use. "This horse has not had proper attention. He has not been sufficiently rubbed and curried, or he has not been properly fed; his food was too wet or too dry; he got it too soon or too late; he was too hot or too cold; he had too much hay, and not enough of grain; or he had too much grain, and not enough of hay; instead of old Barney's attending to the horse, he had very improperly left it to his son." To all these complaints, no matter how unjust, the slave must answer never a word. Colonel Lloyd could not brook any contradiction from a slave. When he spoke, a slave must stand, listen, and tremble; and such was literally the case. I have seen Colonel Lloyd make old Barney, a man between fifty and sixty years of age, uncover his bald head, kneel down upon the cold, damp ground, and receive upon his naked and toil-worn shoulders more than thirty lashes at the time. Colonel Lloyd had three sons—Edward, Murray, and Daniel,—and three sons-in-law, Mr. Winder, Mr. Nicholson, and Mr. Lowndes. All of these lived at the Great House Farm, and enjoyed the luxury of whipping the servants when they pleased, from old Barney down to William Wilkes, the coach-driver. I have seen Winder make one of the house-servants stand off from him a suitable distance to be touched with the end of his whip, and at every stroke raise great ridges upon his back.

To describe the wealth of Colonel Lloyd would be almost equal to describing the riches of Job.[17] He kept from ten to fifteen house-servants. He was said to own a thousand slaves, and I think this estimate quite within the truth. Colonel Lloyd owned so many that he did not know them when he saw them; nor did all the slaves of the out-farms know him. It is reported of him, that, while riding along the road one day, he met a colored man, and addressed him in the usual manner of speaking to colored people on the public highways of the south: "Well, boy, whom do you belong to?" "To Colonel Lloyd," replied the slave. "Well, does the colonel treat you well?" "No, sir," was the ready reply. "What, does he work you too hard?" "Yes, sir." "Well, don't he give you enough to eat?" "Yes, sir, he gives me enough, such as it is."

The colonel, after ascertaining where the slave belonged, rode on; the man also went on about his business, not dreaming that he had been conversing with his master. He thought, said, and heard nothing more of the matter, until two or three weeks afterwards. The poor man was then informed by his overseer that, for having found fault with his master, he was now to be sold to a Georgia trader. He was immediately chained and handcuffed; and thus, without a moment's warning, he was snatched away, and forever sundered, from his family and friends, by a hand more unrelenting than death. This is the penalty of telling the truth, of telling the simple truth, in answer to a series of plain questions.

It is partly in consequence of such facts, that slaves, when inquired of as to their condition and the character of their masters, almost universally say they are

[17] The biblical figure who was extremely wealthy before being tested with misfortune, despite which he retained his faith.

contented, and that their masters are kind. The slaveholders have been known to send in spies among their slaves, to ascertain their views and feelings in regard to their condition. The frequency of this has had the effect to establish among the slaves the maxim, that a still tongue makes a wise head. They suppress the truth rather than take the consequences of telling it, and in so doing prove themselves a part of the human family. If they have any thing to say of their masters, it is generally in their masters' favor, especially when speaking to an untried man. I have been frequently asked, when a slave, if I had a kind master, and do not remember ever to have given a negative answer; nor did I, in pursuing this course, consider myself as uttering what was absolutely false; for I always measured the kindness of my master by the standard of kindness set up among slaveholders around us. Moreover, slaves are like other people, and imbibe prejudices quite common to others. They think their own better than that of others. Many, under the influence of this prejudice, think their own masters are better than the masters of other slaves; and this, too, in some cases, when the very reverse is true. Indeed, it is not uncommon for slaves even to fall out and quarrel among themselves about the relative goodness of their masters, each contending for the superior goodness of his own over that of the others. At the very same time, they mutually execrate their masters when viewed separately. It was so on our plantation. When Colonel Lloyd's slaves met the slaves of Jacob Jepson, they seldom parted without a quarrel about their masters; Colonel Lloyd's slaves contending that he was the richest, and Mr. Jepson's slaves that he was the smartest, and most of a man. Colonel Lloyd's slaves would boast his ability to buy and sell Jacob Jepson. Mr. Jepson's slaves would boast his ability to whip Colonel Lloyd. These quarrels would almost always end in a fight between the parties, and those that whipped were supposed to have gained the point at issue. They seemed to think that the greatness of their masters was transferable to themselves. It was considered as being bad enough to be a slave; but to be a poor man's slave was deemed a disgrace indeed!

CHAPTER IV

Mr. Hopkins remained but a short time in the office of overseer. Why his career was so short, I do not know, but suppose he lacked the necessary severity to suit Colonel Lloyd. Mr. Hopkins was succeeded by Mr. Austin Gore, a man possessing, in an eminent degree, all those traits of character indispensable to what is called a first-rate overseer. Mr. Gore had served Colonel Lloyd, in the capacity of overseer, upon one of the out-farms, and had shown himself worthy of the high station of overseer upon the home or Great House Farm.

Mr. Gore was proud, ambitious, and persevering. He was artful, cruel, and obdurate. He was just the man for such a place, and it was just the place for such a man. It afforded scope for the full exercise of all his powers, and he seemed to be perfectly at home in it. He was one of those who could torture the slightest look, word, or gesture, on the part of the slave, into impudence, and would treat it accordingly. There must be no answering back to him; no explanation was allowed a slave, showing himself to have been wrongfully accused. Mr. Gore acted fully up to the maxim laid down by slaveholders,—"It is better that a dozen slaves suffer under the lash, than that the overseer should be convicted, in the presence of the slaves, of having been at fault." No matter how innocent a slave might be—it availed him nothing, when accused by Mr. Gore of any misdemeanor. To be accused was to be convicted, and to be convicted was to be punished; the one always following the other with immutable certainty. To escape punishment was to escape accusation; and few slaves had the fortune to do either, under the overseership of Mr. Gore. He was just proud enough to demand the most debasing homage of the slave, and quite servile enough to crouch, himself, at the feet of the master. He was ambitious enough to be contented with nothing short of the highest rank of overseers, and persevering enough to reach the height of his ambition. He was cruel enough to inflict the severest punishment, artful enough to descend to the lowest trickery, and obdurate enough to be insensible to the voice of a reproving conscience. He was, of all the overseers, the most dreaded by the slaves. His presence was painful; his eye flashed confusion; and seldom was his sharp, shrill voice heard, without producing horror and trembling in their ranks.

Mr. Gore was a grave man, and, though a young man, he indulged in no jokes, said no funny words, seldom smiled. His words were in perfect keeping with his looks, and his looks were in perfect keeping with his words. Overseers will sometimes indulge in a witty word, even with the slaves; not so with Mr. Gore. He spoke but to command, and commanded but to be obeyed; he dealt sparingly with his words, and bountifully with his whip, never using the former where the latter would answer as well. When he whipped, he seemed to do so from a sense of duty, and feared no consequences. He did nothing reluctantly, no matter how disagreeable; always at his post, never inconsistent. He never promised but to fulfil. He was, in a word, a man of the most inflexible firmness and stone-like coolness.

His savage barbarity was equalled only by the consummate coolness with which he committed the grossest and most savage deeds upon the slaves under his charge. Mr. Gore once undertook to whip one of Colonel Lloyd's slaves, by the name of Demby. He had given Demby but few stripes, when, to get rid of the scourging, he ran and plunged himself into a creek, and stood there at the depth of his shoulders, refusing to come out. Mr. Gore told him that he would give him three calls, and that, if he did not come out at the third call, he would shoot him. The first call was given. Demby made no response, but stood his ground. The second and third calls were given with the same result. Mr. Gore then, without consultation or deliberation with any one, not even giving Demby an additional call, raised his musket to his face, taking deadly aim at his standing victim, and in an instant poor Demby was no more. His mangled body sank out of sight, and blood and brains marked the water where he had stood.

A thrill of horror flashed through every soul upon the plantation, excepting Mr. Gore. He alone seemed cool and collected. He was asked by Colonel Lloyd and my old master, why he resorted to this extraordinary expedient. His reply was, (as well as I can remember,) that Demby had become unmanageable. He was setting a dangerous example to the other slaves,—one which, if suffered to pass without some such demonstration on his part, would finally lead to the total subversion of all rule and order upon the plantation. He argued that if one slave refused to be corrected, and escaped with his life, the other slaves would soon copy the example; the result of which would be, the freedom of the slaves, and the enslavement of the whites. Mr. Gore's defence was satisfactory. He was continued in his station as overseer upon the home plantation. His fame as an overseer went abroad. His horrid crime was not even submitted to judicial investigation. It was committed in the presence of slaves, and they of course could neither institute a suit, nor testify against him; and thus the guilty perpetrator of one of the bloodiest and most foul murders goes unwhipped of justice, and uncensured by the community in which he lives. Mr. Gore lived in St. Michael's, Talbot county, Maryland, when I left there; and if he is still alive, he very probably lives there now; and if so, he is now, as he was then, as highly esteemed and as much respected as though his guilty soul had not been stained with his brother's blood.

I speak advisedly when I say this,—that killing a slave, or any colored person, in Talbot county, Maryland, is not treated as a crime, either by the courts or the community. Mr. Thomas Lanman, of St. Michael's, killed two slaves, one of whom he killed with a hatchet, by knocking his brains out. He used to boast of the commission of the awful and bloody deed. I have heard him do so laughingly, saying, among other things, that he was the only benefactor of his country in the company, and that when others would do as much as he had done, we should be relieved of "the d——d niggers."

The wife of Mr. Giles Hick, living but a short distance from where I used to live, murdered my wife's cousin, a young girl between fifteen and sixteen years of age, mangling her person in the most horrible manner, breaking her nose and breastbone with a stick, so that the poor girl expired in a few hours afterward. She was immediately buried, but had not been in her untimely grave but a few hours before she was taken up and examined by the coroner, who decided that she had come to her death by severe beating. The offence for which this girl was thus murdered was this:—She had been set that night to mind Mrs. Hick's baby, and during the night she fell asleep, and the baby cried. She, having lost her rest for several nights previous, did not hear the crying. They were both in the room with Mrs. Hicks. Mrs. Hicks, finding the girl slow to move, jumped from her bed, seized an oak stick of wood by the fireplace, and with it broke the girl's nose and breastbone, and thus ended her life. I will not say that this most horrid murder produced no sensation in the community. It did produce sensation, but not enough to bring the murderess to punishment. There was a warrant issued for her arrest, but it was never served. Thus she escaped not only punishment, but even the pain of being arraigned before a court for her horrid crime.

Whilst I am detailing bloody deeds which took place during my stay on Colonel Lloyd's plantation, I will briefly narrate another, which occurred about the same time as the murder of Demby by Mr. Gore.

Colonel Lloyd's slaves were in the habit of spending a part of their nights and Sundays in fishing for oysters, and in this way made up the deficiency of their scanty allowance. An old man belonging to Colonel Lloyd, while thus engaged, happened to get beyond the limits of Colonel Lloyd's, and on the premises of Mr. Beal Bondly. At this trespass, Mr. Bondly took offence, and with his musket came down to the shore, and blew its deadly contents into the poor old man.

Mr. Bondly came over to see Colonel Lloyd the next day, whether to pay him for his property, or to justify himself in what he had done, I know not. At any rate, this whole fiendish transaction was soon hushed up. There was very little said about it at all, and nothing done. It was a common saying, even among little white boys, that it was worth a half-cent to kill a "nigger," and a half-cent to bury one.

CHAPTER V

As to my own treatment while I lived on Colonel Lloyd's plantation, it was very similar to that of the other slave children. I was not old enough to work in the field, and there being little else than field work to do, I had a great deal of leisure time. The most I had to do was to drive up the cows at evening, keep the fowls out of the garden, keep the front yard clean, and run of errands for my old master's daughter, Mrs. Lucretia Auld. The most of my leisure time I spent in helping Master Daniel Lloyd in finding his birds, after he had shot them. My connection with Master Daniel was of some advantage to me. He became quite attached to me, and was a sort of protector of me. He would not allow the older boys to impose upon me, and would divide his cakes with me.

I was seldom whipped by my old master, and suffered little from any thing else than hunger and cold. I suffered much from hunger, but much more from cold. In hottest summer and coldest winter, I was kept almost naked—no shoes, no stockings, no jacket, no trousers, nothing on but a coarse tow linen shirt, reaching only to my knees. I had no bed. I must have perished with cold, but that, the coldest nights, I used to steal a bag which was used for carrying corn to the mill. I would crawl into this bag, and there sleep on the cold, damp, clay floor, with my head in and feet out. My feet have been so cracked with the frost, that the pen with which I am writing might be laid in the gashes.

We were not regularly allowanced. Our food was coarse corn meal boiled. This was called *mush*. It was put into a large wooden tray or trough, and set down upon the ground. The children were then called, like so many pigs, and like so many pigs they would come and devour the mush; some with oyster-shells, others with pieces of shingle, some with naked hands, and none with spoons. He that ate fastest got most; he that was strongest secured the best place; and few left the trough satisfied.

I was probably between seven and eight years old when I left Colonel Lloyd's plantation. I left it with joy. I shall never forget the ecstasy with which I received the intelligence that my old master (Anthony) had determined to let me go to Baltimore, to live with Mr. Hugh Auld, brother to my old master's son-in-law, Captain Thomas Auld. I received this information about three days before my departure. They were three of the happiest days I ever enjoyed. I spent the most part of all these three days in the creek, washing off the plantation scurf, and preparing myself for my departure.

The pride of appearance which this would indicate was not my own. I spent the time in washing, not so much because I wished to, but becaue Mrs. Lucretia had told me I must get all the dead skin off my feet and knees before I could go to Baltimore; for the people in Baltimore were very cleanly, and would laugh at me if I looked dirty. Besides, she was going to give me a pair of trousers, which I should not put on unless I got all the dirt off me. The thought of owning a pair of trousers was great indeed! It was almost a sufficient motive, not only to make me take off what would be called by pig-drovers the mange, but the skin itself. I went at it in good earnest, working for the first time with the hope of reward.

The ties that ordinarily bind children to their homes were all suspended in my case. I found no severe trial in my departure. My home was charmless; it was not home to me; on parting from it, I could not feel that I was leaving any thing which I could have enjoyed by staying. My mother was dead, my grandmother lived far off, so that I seldom saw her. I had two sisters and one brother, that lived in the same house with me; but the early separation of us from our mother had well nigh blotted the fact of our relationship from our memories. I looked for home elsewhere, and was confident of finding none which I should relish less than the one which I was leaving. If, however, I found in my new home hardship, hunger, whipping, and nakedness, I had the consolation that I should not have escaped any one of them by staying. Having already had more than a taste of them in the house of my old master, and having endured them there, I very naturally inferred my ability to endure them elsewhere, and especially at Baltimore; for I had something of the feeling about Baltimore that is expressed in the proverb, that "being hanged in England is preferable to dying a natural death in Ireland." I had the strongest desire to see Baltimore. Cousin Tom, though not fluent in speech, had inspired me with that desire by his eloquent description of the place. I could never point out any thing at the Great House, no matter how beautiful or powerful, but that he had seen something at Baltimore far exceeding, both in beauty and strength, the object which I pointed out to him. Even the Great House itself, with all its pictures, was far inferior to many buildings in Baltimore. So strong was my desire, that I thought a gratification of it would fully compensate for whatever loss of comforts I should sustain by the exchange. I left without a regret, and with the highest hopes of future happiness.

We sailed out of Miles River for Baltimore on a Saturday morning. I remember only the day of the week, for at that time I had no knowledge of the days of the month, nor the months of the year. On setting sail, I walked aft, and gave to Colonel Lloyd's plantation what I hoped would be the last look. I then placed myself in the bows of the sloop, and there spent the remainder of the day in looking ahead, interesting myself in what was in the distance rather than in things near by or behind.

In the afternoon of that day, we reached Annapolis, the capital of the State. We stopped but a few moments, so that I had no time to go on shore. It was the first large town that I had ever seen, and though it would look small compared with some of our New England factory villages, I thought it a wonderful place for its size—more imposing even than the Great House Farm!

We arrived at Baltimore early on Sunday morning, landing at Smith's Wharf, not far from Bowley's Wharf. We had on board the sloop a large flock of sheep; and after aiding in driving them to the slaughter-house of Mr. Curtis on Louden Slater's Hill, I was conducted by Rich, one of the hands belonging on board of the sloop, to my new home in Alliciana Street, near Mr. Gardner's ship-yard, on Fells Point.

Mr. and Mrs. Auld were both at home, and met me at the door with their little son Thomas, to take care of whom I had been given. And here I saw what I had never seen before; it was a white face beaming with the most kindly emotions; it was the face of my new mistress, Sophia Auld. I wish I could describe the rapture that flashed through my soul as I beheld it. It was a new and strange sight to me, brightening up my pathway with the light of happiness. Little Thomas was told, there was his Freddy,—and I was told to take care of little Thomas; and thus I entered upon the duties of my new home with the most cheering prospect ahead.

I look upon my departure from Colonel Lloyd's plantation as one of the most interesting events of my life. It is possible, and even quite probable, that but for the mere circumstances of being removed from that plantation to Baltimore, I should have to-day, instead of being here seated by my own table, in the enjoyment of freedom and the happiness of home, writing this Narrative, been confined in the galling chains of slavery. Going to live at Baltimore laid the foundation, and opened the gateway, to all my subsequent prosperity. I have ever regarded it as the first plain manifestation of that kind providence which has ever since attended me, and marked my life with so many favors. I regarded the selection of myself as being somewhat remarkable. There were a number of slave children that might have been sent from the plantation to Baltimore. There were those younger, those older, and those of the same age. I was chosen from among them all, and was the first, last, and only choice.

I may be deemed superstitious, and even egotistical, in regarding this event as a special interposition of divine Providence in my favor. But I should be false to the earliest sentiments of my soul, if I suppressed the opinion. I prefer to be true to myself, even at the hazard of incurring the ridicule of others, rather than to be false, and incur my own abhorrence. From my earliest recollection, I date the entertainment of a deep conviction that slavery would not always be able to hold me within its foul embrace; and in the darkest hours of my career in slavery, this living word of faith and spirit of hope departed not from me, but remained like ministering angels to cheer me through the gloom. This good spirit was from God, and to him I offer thanksgiving and praise.

Chapter VI

My new mistress proved to be all she appeared when I first met her at the door,— a woman of the kindest heart and finest feelings. She had never had a slave under her control previously to myself, and prior to her marriage she had been dependent upon her own industry for a living. She was by trade a weaver; and by constant application to her business, she had been in a good degree preserved from the blighting and dehumanizing effects of slavery. I was utterly astonished at her goodness. I scarcely knew how to behave towards her. She was entirely unlike any other white woman I had ever seen. I could not approach her as I was accustomed to approach other white ladies. My early instruction was all out of place. The crouching servility, usually so acceptable a quality in a slave, did not answer when manifested toward her. Her favor was not gained by it; she seemed to be disturbed by it. She did not deem it impudent or unmannerly for a slave to look her in the face. The meanest slave was put fully at ease in her presence, and none left without feeling better for having seen her. Her face was made of heavenly smiles, and her voice of tranquil music.

But, alas! this kind heart had but a short time to remain such. The fatal poison of irresponsible power was already in her hands, and soon commenced its infernal work. That cheerful eye, under the influence of slavery, soon became red with rage; that voice, made all of sweet accord, changed to one of harsh and horrid discord; and that angelic face gave place to that of a demon.

Very soon after I went to live with Mr. and Mrs. Auld, she very kindly commenced to teach me the A, B, C. After I had learned this, she assisted me in learning to spell words of three or four letters. Just at this point of my progress, Mr. Auld found out what was going on, and at once forbade Mrs. Auld to instruct me further, telling her, among other things, that it was unlawful, as well as unsafe, to teach a slave to read.[18] To use his own words, further, he said, "If you give a nigger an inch, he will take an ell. A nigger should know nothing but to obey his master—to do as he is told to do. Learning would *spoil* the best nigger in the world. Now," said he, "if you teach that nigger (speaking of myself) how to read, there would be no keeping him. It would forever unfit him to be a slave. He would at once become unmanageable, and of no value to his master. As to himself, it could do him no good, but a great deal of harm. It would make him discon-

---

[18] In some southern states it was illegal to teach a slave to read or write.

tented and unhappy." These words sank deep into my heart, stirred up sentiments within that lay slumbering, and called into existence an entirely new train of thought. It was a new and special revelation, explaining dark and mysterious things, with which my youthful understanding had struggled, but struggled in vain. I now understood what had been to me a most perplexing difficulty—to wit, the white man's power to enslave the black man. It was a grand achievement, and I prized it highly. From that moment, I understood the pathway from slavery to freedom. It was just what I wanted, and I got it at a time when I the least expected it. Whilst I was saddened by the thought of losing the aid of my kind mistress, I was gladdened by the invaluable instruction which, by the merest accident, I had gained from my master. Though conscious of the difficulty of learning without a teacher, I set out with high hope, and a fixed purpose, at whatever cost of trouble, to learn how to read. The very decided manner with which he spoke, and strove to impress his wife with the evil consequences of giving me instruction, served to convince me that he was deeply sensible of the truths he was uttering. It gave me the best assurance that I might rely with the utmost confidence on the results which, he said, would flow from teaching me to read. What he most dreaded, that I most desired. What he most loved, that I most hated. That which to him was a great evil, to be carefully shunned, was to me a great good, to be diligently sought; and the argument which he so warmly urged, against my learning to read, only served to inspire me with a desire and determination to learn. In learning to read, I owe almost as much to the bitter opposition of my master, as to the kindly aid of my mistress. I acknowledge the benefit of both.

I had resided but a short time in Baltimore before I observed a marked difference, in the treatment of slaves, from that which I had witnessed in the country. A city slave is almost a freeman, compared with a slave on the plantation. He is much better fed and clothed, and enjoys privileges altogether unknown to the slave on the plantation. There is a vestige of decency, a sense of shame, that does much to curb and check those outbreaks of atrocious cruelty so commonly enacted upon the plantation. He is a desperate slaveholder, who will shock the humanity of his nonslaveholding neighbors with the cries of his lacerated slave. Few are willing to incur the odium attaching to the reputation of being a cruel master; and above all things, they would not be known as not giving a slave enough to eat. Every city slaveholder is anxious to have it known of him, that he feeds his slaves well; and it is due to them to say, that most of them do give their slaves enough to eat. There are, however, some painful exceptions to this rule. Directly opposite to us, on Philpot Street, lived Mr. Thomas Hamilton. He owned two slaves. Their names were Henrietta and Mary. Henrietta was about twenty-two years of age, Mary was about fourteen; and of all the mangled and emaciated creatures I ever looked upon, these two were the most so. His heart must be harder than stone, that could look upon these unmoved. The head, neck, and shoulders of Mary were literally cut to pieces. I have frequently felt her head, and found it nearly covered with festering sores, caused by the lash of her cruel mistress. I do not know that her master ever whipped her, but I have been an eye-witness to the cruelty of Mrs. Hamilton. I used to be in Mr. Hamilton's house nearly every day. Mrs. Hamilton used to sit in a large chair in the middle of the room, with a heavy cowskin always by her side, and scarce an hour passed during the day but was marked by the blood of one of these slaves. The girls seldom passed her without her saying, "Move faster, you *black gip!*" at the same time giving them a blow with the cowskin over the head or shoulders, often drawing the blood. She would then say,

"Take that, you *black gip!*"—continuing, "If you don't move faster, I'll move you!" Added to the cruel lashings to which these slaves were subjected, they were kept nearly half-starved. They seldom knew what it was to eat a full meal. I have seen Mary contending with the pigs for the offal thrown into the street. So much was Mary kicked and cut to pieces, that she was oftener called *"pecked"* [19] than by her name.

CHAPTER VII

I lived in Master Hugh's family about seven years. During this time, I succeeded in learning to read and write. In accomplishing this, I was compelled to resort to various stratagems. I had no regular teacher. My mistress, who had kindly commenced to instruct me, had, in compliance with the advice and direction of her husband, not only ceased to instruct, but had set her face against my being instructed by any one else. It is due, however, to my mistress to say of her, that she did not adopt this course of treatment immediately. She at first lacked the depravity indispensable to shutting me up in mental darkness. It was at least necessary for her to have some training in the exercise of irresponsible power, to make her equal to the task of treating me as though I were a brute.

My mistress was, as I have said, a kind and tender-hearted woman; and in the simplicity of her soul she commenced, when I first went to live with her, to treat me as she supposed one human being ought to treat another. In entering upon the duties of a slaveholder, she did not seem to perceive that I sustained to her the relation of a mere chattel, and that for her to treat me as a human being was not only wrong, but dangerously so. Slavery proved as injurious to her as it did to me. When I went there, she was a pious, warm, and tender-hearted woman. There was no sorrow or suffering for which she had not a tear. She had bread for the hungry, clothes for the naked, and comfort for every mourner that came within her reach. Slavery soon proved its ability to divest her of these heavenly qualities. Under its influence, the tender heart became stone, and the lamblike disposition gave way to one of tiger-like fierceness. The first step in her downward course was in her ceasing to instruct me. She now commenced to practise her husband's precepts. She finally became even more violent in her opposition than her husband himself. She was not satisfied with simply doing as well as he had commanded; she seemed anxious to do better. Nothing seemed to make her more angry than to see me with a newspaper. She seemed to think that here lay the danger. I have had her rush at me with a face made all up of fury, and snatch from me a newspaper, in a manner that fully revealed her apprehension. She was an apt woman; and a little experience soon demonstrated, to her satisfaction, that education and slavery were incompatible with each other.

From this time I was most narrowly watched. If I was in a separate room any considerable length of time, I was sure to be suspected of having a book, and was at once called to give an account of myself. All this, however, was too late. The first step had been taken. Mistress, in teaching me the alphabet, had given me the *inch,* and no precaution could prevent me from taking the *ell.*

The plan which I adopted, and the one by which I was most successful, was that of making friends of all the little white boys whom I met in the street. As

---

[19] As if she had been brutally pecked by a chicken.

many of these as I could, I converted into teachers. With their kindly aid, obtained at different times and in different places, I finally succeeded in learning to read. When I was sent of errands, I always took my book with me, and by going one part of my errand quickly, I found time to get a lesson before my return. I used also to carry bread with me, enough of which was always in the house, and to which I was always welcome; for I was much better off in this regard than many of the poor white children in our neighborhood. This bread I used to bestow upon the hungry little urchins, who, in return, would give me that more valuable bread of knowledge. I am strongly tempted to give the names of two or three of those little boys, as a testimonial of the gratitude and affection I bear them; but prudence forbids;—not that it would injure me, but it might embarrass them; for it is almost an unpardonable offence to teach slaves to read in this Christian country. It is enough to say of the dear little fellows, that they lived on Philpot Street, very near Durgin and Bailey's ship-yard. I used to talk this matter of slavery over with them. I would sometimes say to them, I wished I could be as free as they would be when they got to be men. "You will be free as soon as you are twenty-one, *but I am a slave for life!* Have not I as good a right to be free as you have?" These words used to trouble them; they would express for me the liveliest sympathy, and console me with the hope that something would occur by which I might be free.

I was now about twelve years old, and the thought of being *a slave for life* began to bear heavily upon my heart. Just about this time, I got hold of a book entitled "The Columbian Orator."[20] Every opportunity I got, I used to read this book. Among much of other interesting matter, I found in it a dialogue between a master and his slave. The slave was represented as having run away from his master three times. The dialogue represented the conversation which took place between them, when the slave was retaken the third time. In this dialogue, the whole argument in behalf of slavery was brought forward by the master, all of which was disposed of by the slave. The slave was made to say some very smart as well as impressive things in reply to his master—things which had the desired though unexpected effect; for the conversation resulted in the voluntary emancipation of the slave on the part of the master.

In the same book, I met with one of Sheridan's[21] mighty speeches on and in behalf of Catholic emancipation. These were choice documents to me. I read them over and over again with unabated interest. They gave tongue to interesting thoughts of my own soul, which had frequently flashed through my mind, and died away for want of utterance. The moral which I gained from the dialogue was the power of truth over the conscience of even a slaveholder. What I got from Sheridan was a bold denunciation of slavery, and a powerful vindication of human rights. The reading of these documents enabled me to utter my thoughts, and to meet the arguments brought forward to sustain slavery; but while they relieved me of one difficulty, they brought on another even more painful than the one of which I was relieved. The more I read, the more I was led to abhor and detest my enslavers. I could regard them in no other light than a band of successful robbers, who had left their homes, and gone to Africa, and stolen us from our homes, and in a strange land reduced us to slavery. I loathed them as being the meanest as well as the most wicked of men. As I read and contemplated the subject, behold! that very

---

[20] A popular collection of poems, speeches, dialogues, and plays.
[21] Richard Brinsley Sheridan (1751–1816), an Irish-born dramatist and political figure who spoke in favor of Catholic emancipation as a member of the British Parliament.

discontentment which Master Hugh had predicted would follow my learning to read had already come, to torment and sting my sould to unutterable anguish. As I writhed under it, I would at times feel that learning to read had been a curse rather than a blessing. It had given me a view of my wretched condition, without the remedy. It opened my eyes to the horrible pit, but to no ladder upon which to get out. In moments of agony, I envied my fellow-slaves for their stupidity. I have often wished myself a beast. I preferred the condition of the meanest reptile to my own. Any thing, no matter what, to get rid of thinking! It was this everlasting thinking of my condition that tormented me. There was no getting rid of it. It was pressed upon me by every object within sight or hearing, animate or inanimate. The silver trump of freedom had roused my soul to eternal wakefulness. Freedom now appeared, to disappear no more forever. It was heard in every sound, and seen in every thing. It was ever present to torment me with a sense of my wretched condition. I saw nothing without seeing it, I heard nothing without hearing it, and felt nothing without feeling it. It looked from every star, it smiled in every calm, breathed in every wind, and moved in every storm.

I often found myself regretting my own existence, and wishing myself dead; and but for the hope of being free, I have no doubt but that I should have killed myself, or done something for which I should have been killed. While in this state of mind, I was eager to hear any one speak of slavery. I was a ready listener. Every little while, I could hear something about the abolitionists. It was some time before I found what the word meant. It was always used in such connections as to make it an interesting word to me. If a slave ran away and succeeded in getting clear, or if a slave killed his master, set fire to a barn, or did any thing very wrong in the mind of a slaveholder, it was spoken of as the fruit of *abolition*. Hearing the word in this connection very often, I set about learning what it meant. The diction-ary afforded me little or no help. I found it was "the act of abolishing;" but then I did not know what was to be abolished. Here I was perplexed. I did not dare to ask any one about its meaning, for I was satisfied that it was something they wanted me to know very little about. After a patient waiting, I got one of our city papers, containing an account of the number of petitions from the north, praying for the abolition of slavery in the District of Columbia, and of the slave trade between the States. From this time I understood the words *abolition* and *abolition-ist*, and always drew near when that word was spoken, expecting to hear some-thing of importance to myself and fellow-slaves. The light broke in upon me by degrees. I went one day down on the wharf of Mr. Waters; and seeing two Irish-men unloading a scow of stone, I went, unasked, and helped them. When we had finished, one of them came to me and asked me if I were a slave. I told him I was. He asked, "Are ye a slave for life?" I told him that I was. The good Irishman seemed to be deeply affected by the statement. He said to the other that it was a pity so fine a little fellow as myself should be a slave for life. He said it was a shame to hold me. They both advised me to run away to the north; that I should find friends there, and that I should be free. I pretended not to be interested in what they said, and treated them as if I did not understand them; for I feared they might be treacherous. White men have been known to encourage slaves to escape, and then, to get the reward, catch them and return them to their masters. I was afraid that these seemingly good men might use me so; but I nevertheless remem-bered their advice, and from that time I resolved to run away. I looked forward to a time at which it would be safe for me to escape. I was too young to think of doing so immediately; besides, I wished to learn how to write, as I might have occasion to write my own pass. I consoled myself with the hope that I should one day find a good chance. Meanwhile, I would learn to write.

The idea as to how I might learn to write was suggested to me by being in Durgin and Bailey's ship-yard, and frequently seeing the ship carpenters, after hewing, and getting a piece of timber ready for use, write on the timber the name of that part of the ship for which it was intended. When a piece of timber was intended for the larboard side, it would be marked thus—"L." When a piece was for the starboard side, it would be marked thus—"S." A piece for the larboard side forward, would be marked thus—"L. F." When a piece was for starboard side forward, it would be marked thus—"S. F." For larboard aft, it would be marked thus—"L. A." For starboard aft, it would be marked thus—"S. A." I soon learned the names of these letters, and for what they were intended when placed upon a piece of timber in the ship-yard. I immediately commenced copying them, and in a short time was able to make the four letters named. After that, when I met with any boy who I knew could write, I would tell him I could write as well as he. The next word would be, "I don't believe you. Let me see you try it." I would then make the letters which I had been so fortunate as to learn, and ask him to beat that. In this way I got a good many lessons in writing, which it is quite possible I should never have gotten in any other way. During this time, my copy-book was the board fence, brick wall, and pavement; my pen and ink was a lump of chalk. With these, I learned mainly how to write. I then commenced and continued copying the Italics in Webster's Spelling Book,[22] until I could make them all without looking on the book. By this time, my little Master Thomas had gone to school, and learned how to write, and had written over a number of copy-books. These had been brought home, and shown to some of our near neighbors, and then laid aside. My mistress used to go to class meeting at the Wilk Street meeting-house every Monday afternoon, and leave me to take care of the house. When left thus, I used to spend the time in writing in the spaces left in Master Thomas's copy-book, copying what he had written. I continued to do this until I could write a hand very similar to that of Master Thomas. Thus, after a long, tedious effort for years, I finally succeeded in learning how to write.

CHAPTER VIII

In a very short time after I went to live at Baltimore, my old master's youngest son Richard died; and in about three years and six months after his death, my old master, Captain Anthony, died, leaving only his son, Andrew, and daughter, Lucretia, to share his estate. He died while on a visit to see his daughter at Hillsborough. Cut off thus unexpectedly, he left no will as to the disposal of his property. It was therefore necessary to have a valuation of the property, that it might be equally divided between Mrs. Lucretia and Master Andrew. I was immediately sent for, to be valued with the other property. Here again my feelings rose up in detestation of slavery. I had now a new conception of my degraded condition. Prior to this, I had become, if not insensible to my lot, at least partly so. I left Baltimore with a young heart overborne with sadness, and a soul full of apprehen-

[22] The famous *Spelling Book* (1783) devised by Noah Webster (1758–1843) from the first part of his *Grammatical Institute of the English Language* (1783–1785); used in American schools throughout the nineteenth century.

sion. I took passage with Captain Rowe, in the schooner Wild Cat, and, after a sail of about twenty-four hours, I found myself near the place of my birth. I had now been absent from it almost, if not quite, five years. I, however, remembered the place very well. I was only about five years old when I left it, to go and live with my old master on Colonel Lloyd's plantation; so that I was now between ten and eleven years old.

We were all ranked together at the valuation. Men and women, old and young, married and single, were ranked with horses, sheep, and swine. There were horses and men, cattle and women, pigs and children, all holding the same rank in the scale of being, and were all subjected to the same narrow examination. Silvery-headed age and sprightly youth, maids and matrons, had to undergo the same indelicate inspection. At this moment, I saw more clearly than ever the brutalizing effects of slavery upon both slave and slaveholder.

After the valuation, then came the division. I have no language to express the high excitement and deep anxiety which were felt among us poor slaves during this time. Our fate for life was now to be decided. We had no more voice in that decision than the brutes among whom we were ranked. A single word from the white men was enough—against all our wishes, prayers, and entreaties—to sunder forever the dearest friends, dearest kindred, and strongest ties known to human beings. In addition to the pain of separation, there was the horrid dread of falling into the hands of Master Andrew. He was known to us all as being a most cruel wretch,—a common drunkard, who had, by his reckless mismanagement and profligate dissipation, already wasted a large portion of his father's property. We all felt that we might as well be sold at once to the Georgia traders, as to pass into his hands; for we knew that that would be our inevitable condition,—a condition held by us all in the utmost horror and dread.

I suffered more anxiety than most of my fellowslaves. I had known what it was to be kindly treated; they had known nothing of the kind. They had seen little or nothing of the world. They were in very deed men and women of sorrow, and acquainted with grief. Their backs had been made familiar with the bloody lash, so that they had become callous; mine was yet tender; for while at Baltimore I got few whippings, and few slaves could boast of a kinder master and mistress than myself; and the thought of passing out of their hands into those of Master Andrew—a man who, but a few days before, to give me a sample of his bloody disposition, took my little brother by the throat, threw him on the ground, and with the heel of his boot stamped upon his head till the blood gushed from his nose and ears—was well calculated to make me anxious as to my fate. After he had committed this savage outrage upon my brother, he turned to me, and said that was the way he meant to serve me one of these days,—meaning, I suppose, when I came into his possession.

Thanks to a kind Providence, I fell to the portion of Mrs. Lucretia, and was sent immediately back to Baltimore, to live again in the family of Master Hugh. Their joy at my return equalled their sorrow at my departure. It was a glad day to me. I had escaped a worse than lion's jaws. I was absent from Baltimore, for the purpose of valuation and division, just about one month, and it seemed to have been six.

Very soon after my return to Baltimore, my mistress, Lucretia, died, leaving her husband and one child, Amanda; and in a very short time after her death, Master Andrew died. Now all the property of my old master, slaves included, was in the hands of strangers,—strangers who had had nothing to do with accumulating it. Not a slave was left free. All remained slaves, from the youngest to the oldest. If any one thing in my experience, more than another, served to deepen my conviction of the infernal character of slavery, and to fill me with unutterable loathing of slaveholders, it was their base ingratitude to my poor old grandmother. She had served my old master faithfully from youth to old age. She had been the source of all his wealth; she had peopled his plantation with slaves; she had become a great grandmother in his service. She had rocked him in infancy, attended him in childhood, served him through life, and at his death wiped from his icy brow the cold death-sweat, and closed his eyes forever. She was nevertheless left a slave—a slave for life—a slave in the hands of strangers; and in their hands she saw her children, her grandchildren, and her great-grandchildren, divided, like so many sheep, without being gratified with the small privilege of a single word, as to their or her own destiny. And, to cap the climax of their base ingratitude and fiendish barbarity, my grandmother, who was now very old, having outlived my old master and all his children, having seen the beginning and end of all of them, and her present owners finding she was of but little value, her frame already racked with the pains of old age, and complete helplessness fast stealing over her once active limbs, they took her to the woods, built her a little hut, put up a little mud-chimney, and then made her welcome to the privilege of supporting herself there in perfect loneliness; thus virtually turning her out to die! If my poor old grandmother now lives, she lives to suffer in utter loneliness; she lives to remember and mourn over the loss of children, the loss of grandchildren, and the loss of great-grandchildren. They are, in the language of the slave's poet, Whittier,[23]—

> "Gone, gone, sold and gone
> To the rice swamp dank and lone,
> Where the slave-whip ceaseless swings,
> Where the noisome insect stings,
> Where the fever-demon strews
> Poison with the falling dews,
> Where the sickly sunbeams glare
> Through the hot and misty air:—
>   Gone, gone, sold and gone
>   To the rice swamp dank and lone,
>   From Virginia hills and waters—
>   Woe is me, my stolen daughters!"

The hearth is desolate. The children, the unconscious children, who once sang and danced in her presence, are gone. She gropes her way, in the darkness of age, for a drink of water. Instead of the voices of her children, she hears by day the moans of the dove, and by night the screams of the hideous owl. All is gloom. The grave is at the door. And now, when weighed down by the pains and aches of old age, when the head inclines to the feet, when the beginning and ending of human existence meet, and helpless infancy and painful old age combine together—at this time, this most needful time, the time for the exercise of that tenderness and affection which children only can exercise towards a declining parent—my poor old grandmother, the devoted mother of twelve children, is left all

[23] John Greenleaf Whittier (1807–1892), the Massachusetts poet and abolitionist, in "The Farewell: Of a Virginia Slave Mother to Her Daughter Sold Into Southern Bondage" (1838).

alone, in yonder little hut, before a few dim embers. She stands—she sits—she staggers—she falls—she groans—she dies—and there are none of her children or grandchildren present, to wipe from her wrinkled brow the cold sweat of death, or to place beneath the sod her fallen remains. Will not a righteous God visit for these things?

In about two years after the death of Mrs. Lucretia, Master Thomas married his second wife. Her name was Rowena Hamilton. She was the eldest daughter of Mr. William Hamilton. Master now lived in St. Michael's. Not long after his marriage, a misunderstanding took place between himself and Master Hugh; and as a means of punishing his brother, he took me from him to live with himself at St. Michael's. Here I underwent another most painful separation. It, however, was not so severe as the one I dreaded at the division of property; for, during this interval, a great change had taken place in Master Hugh and his once kind and affectionate wife. The influence of brandy upon him, and of slavery upon her, had effected a disastrous change in the characters of both; so that, as far as they were concerned, I thought I had little to lose by the change. But it was not to them that I was attached. It was to those little Baltimore boys that I felt the strongest attachment. I had received many good lessons from them, and was still receiving them, and the thought of leaving them was painful indeed. I was leaving, too, without the hope of ever being allowed to return. Master Thomas had said he would never let me return again. The barrier betwixt himself and brother he considered impassable.

I then had to regret that I did not at least make the attempt to carry out my resolution to run away; for the chances of success are tenfold greater from the city than from the country.

I sailed from Baltimore for St. Michael's in the sloop Amanda, Captain Edward Dodson. On my passage, I paid particular attention to the direction which the steamboats took to go to Philadelphia. I found, instead of going down, on reaching North Point they went up the bay, in a north-easterly direction. I deemed this knowledge of the utmost importance. My determination to run away was again revived. I resolved to wait only so long as the offering of a favorable opportunity. When that came, I was determined to be off.

Chapter IX

I have now reached a period of my life when I can give dates. I left Baltimore, and went to live with Master Thomas Auld, at St. Michael's, in March, 1832. It was now more than seven years since I lived with him in the family of my old master, on Colonel Lloyd's plantation. We of course were now almost entire strangers to each other. He was to me a new master, and I to him a new slave. I was ignorant of his temper and disposition; he was equally so of mine. A very short time, however, brought us into full acquaintance with each other. I was made acquainted with his wife not less than with himself. They were well matched, being equally mean and cruel. I was now, for the first time during a space of more than seven years, made to feel the painful gnawings of hunger—a something which I had not experienced before since I left Colonel Lloyd's plantation. It went hard enough with me then, when I could look back to no period at which I had enjoyed a sufficiency. It was tenfold harder after living in Master Hugh's family, where I had always had enough to eat, and of that which was good. I have said Master

Thomas was a mean man. He was so. Not to give a slave enough to eat, is regarded as the most aggravated development of meanness even among slaveholders. The rule is, no matter how coarse the food, only let there be enough of it. This is the theory; and in the part of Maryland from which I came, it is the general practice,—though there are many exceptions. Master Thomas gave us enough of neither coarse nor fine food. There were four slaves of us in the kitchen—my sister Eliza, my aunt Priscilla, Henny, and myself; and we were allowed less than a half of a bushel of corn-meal per week, and very little else, either in the shape of meat or vegetables. It was not enough for us to subsist upon. We were therefore reduced to the wretched necessity of living at the expense of our neighbors. This we did by begging and stealing, whichever came handy in the time of need, the one being considered as legitimate as the other. A great many times have we poor creatures been nearly perishing with hunger, when food in abundance lay mouldering in the safe and smoke-house,[24] and our pious mistress was aware of the fact; and yet that mistress and her husband would kneel every morning, and pray that God would bless them in basket and store!

Bad as all slaveholders are, we seldom meet one destitute of every element of character commanding respect. My master was one of this rare sort. I do not know of one single noble act ever performed by him. The leading trait in his character was meanness; and if there were any other element in his nature, it was made subject to this. He was mean; and, like most other mean men, he lacked the ability to conceal his meanness. Captain Auld was not born a slaveholder. He had been a poor man, master only of a Bay craft. He came into possession of all his slaves by marriage; and of all men, adopted slaveholders are the worst. He was cruel, but cowardly. He commanded without firmness. In the enforcement of his rules, he was at times rigid, and at times lax. At times, he spoke to his slaves with the firmness of Napoleon and the fury of a demon; at other times, he might well be mistaken for an inquirer who had lost his way. He did nothing of himself. He might have passed for a lion, but for his ears.[25] In all things noble which he attempted, his own meanness shone most conspicuous. His airs, words, and actions, were the airs, words, and actions of born slaveholders, and, being assumed, were awkward enough. He was not even a good imitator. He possessed all the disposition to deceive, but wanted the power. Having no resources within himself, he was compelled to be the copyist of many, and being such, he was forever the victim of inconsistency; and of consequence he was an object of contempt, and was held as such even by his slaves. The luxury of having slaves of his own to wait upon him was something new and unprepared for. He was a slaveholder without the ability to hold slaves. He found himself incapable of managing his slaves either by force, fear, or fraud. We seldom called him "master;" we generally called him "Captain Auld," and were hardly disposed to title him at all. I doubt not that our conduct had much to do with making him appear awkward, and of consequence fretful. Our want of reverence for him must have perplexed him greatly. He wished to have us call him master, but lacked the firmness necessary to command us to do so. His wife used to insist upon our calling him so, but to no purpose. In August, 1832, my master attended a Methodist camp-meeting held in the Bay-side, Talbot county, and there experienced religion. I indulged a faint

---

[24] A place to cure meat and fish by smoking, after which it could be stored and preserved in a meat safe.

[25] Probably, that his ears made him look like a jackass; he was not as powerful as he professed to be.

hope that his conversion would lead him to emancipate his slaves, and that, if he did not do this, it would, at any rate, make him more kind and humane. I was disappointed in both these respects. It neither made him to be humane to his slaves, nor to emancipate them. If it had any effect on his character, it made him more cruel and hateful in all his ways; for I believe him to have been a much worse man after his conversion than before. Prior to his conversion, he relied upon his own depravity to shield and sustain him in his savage barbarity; but after his conversion, he found religious sanction and support for his slaveholding cruelty. He made the greatest pretensions to piety. His house was the house of prayer. He prayed morning, noon, and night. He very soon distinguished himself among his brethren, and was soon made a class-leader and exhorter. His activity in revivals was great, and he proved himself an instrument in the hands of the church in converting many souls. His house was the preachers' home. They used to take great pleasure in coming there to put up; for while he starved us, he stuffed them. We have had three or four preachers there at a time. The names of those who used to come most frequently while I lived there, were Mr. Storks, Mr. Ewery, Mr. Humphry, and Mr. Hickey. I have also seen Mr. George Cookman at our house. We slaves loved Mr. Cookman. We believed him to be a good man. We thought him instrumental in getting Mr. Samuel Harrison, a very rich slaveholder, to emancipate his slaves; and by some means got the impression that he was laboring to effect the emancipation of all the slaves. When he was at our house, we were sure to be called in to prayers. When the others were there, we were sometimes called in and sometimes not. Mr. Cookman took more notice of us than either of the other ministers. He could not come among us without betraying his sympathy for us, and, stupid as we were, we had the sagacity to see it.

While I lived with my master in St. Michael's, there was a white young man, a Mr. Wilson, who proposed to keep a Sabbath school for the instruction of such slaves as might be disposed to learn to read the New Testament. We met but three times, when Mr. West and Mr. Fairbanks, both class-leaders, with many others, came upon us with sticks and other missiles, drove us off, and forbade us to meet again. Thus ended our little Sabbath school in the pious town of St. Michael's.

I have said my master found religious sanction for his cruelty. As an example, I will state one of many facts going to prove the charge. I have seen him tie up a lame young woman, and whip her with a heavy cowskin upon her naked shoulders, causing the warm red blood to drip; and, in justification of the bloody deed, he would quote this passage of Scripture—"He that knoweth his master's will, and doeth it not, shall be beaten with many stripes."[26]

Master would keep this lacerated young woman tied up in this horrid situation four or five hours at a time. I have known him to tie her up early in the morning, and whip her before breakfast; leave her, go to his store, return at dinner, and whip her again, cutting her in the places already made raw with his cruel lash. The secret of master's cruelty toward "Henny" is found in the fact of her being almost helpless. When quite a child, she fell into the fire, and burned herself horribly. Her hands were so burnt that she never got the use of them. She could do very little but bear heavy burdens. She was to master a bill of expense; and as he was a mean man, she was a constant offence to him. He seemed desirous of getting the poor girl out of existence. He gave her away once to his sister; but, being a poor gift, she was not disposed to keep her. Finally, my benevolent master, to use his

---

[26] From Luke 12:47, wrenched out of context and woefully misapplied.

own words, "set her adrift to take care of herself." Here was a recently-converted man, holding on upon the mother, and at the same time turning out her helpless child, to starve and die! Master Thomas was one of the many pious slaveholders who hold slaves for the very charitable purpose of taking care of them.

My master and myself had quite a number of differences. He found me unsuitable to his purpose. My city life, he said, had had a very pernicious effect upon me. It had almost ruined me for every good purpose, and fitted me for every thing which was bad. One of my greatest faults was that of letting his horse run away, and go down to his father-in-law's farm, which was about five miles from St. Michael's. I would then have to go after it. My reason for this kind of carelessness, or carefulness, was, that I could always get something to eat when I went there. Master William Hamilton, my master's father-in-law, always gave his slaves enought to eat. I never left there hungry, no matter how great the need of my speedy return. Master Thomas at length said he would stand it no longer. I had lived with him nine months, during which time he had given me a number of severe whippings, all to no good purpose. He resolved to put me out, as he said, to be broken; and, for this purpose, he let me for one year to a man named Edward Covey. Mr. Covey was a poor man, a farm-renter. He rented the place upon which he lived, as also the hands with which he tilled it. Mr. Covey had acquired a very high reputation for breaking young slaves, and this reputation was of immense value to him. It enabled him to get his farm tilled with much less expense to himself than he could have had it done without such a reputation. Some slaveholders thought it not much loss to allow Mr. Covey to have their slaves one year, for the sake of the training to which they were subjected, without any other compensation. He could hire young help with great ease, in consequence of this reputation. Added to the natural good qualities of Mr. Covey, he was a professor of religion—a pious soul—a member and a class-leader in the Methodist church. All of this added weight to his reputation as a "nigger-breaker." I was aware of all the facts, having been made acquainted with them by a young man who had lived there. I nevertheless made the change gladly; for I was sure of getting enough to eat, which is not the smallest consideration to a hungry man.

CHAPTER X

I left Master Thomas's house, and went to live with Mr. Covey, on the 1st of January, 1833. I was now, for the first time in my life, a field hand. In my new employment, I found myself even more awkward than a country boy appeared to be in a large city. I had been at my new home but one week before Mr. Covey gave me a very severe whipping, cutting my back, causing the blood to run, and raising ridges on my flesh as large as my little finger. The details of this affair are as follows: Mr. Covey sent me, very early in the morning of one of our coldest days in the month of January, to the woods, to get a load of wood. He gave me a team of unbroken oxen. He told me which was the in-hand ox, and which the off-hand one.[27] He then tied the end of a large rope around the horns of the in-hand ox, and gave me the other end of it, and told me, if the oxen started to run, that I must hold on upon the rope. I had never driven oxen before, and of course I was very awkward. I, however, succeeded in getting to the edge of the woods

---

[27] The "in-hand" ox is the one to the driver's right, the "off-hand" ox to the left.

with little difficulty; but I had got a very few rods into the woods, when the oxen took fright, and started full tilt, carrying the cart against trees, and over stumps, in the most frightful manner. I expected every moment that my brains would be dashed out against the trees. After running thus for a considerable distance, they finally upset the cart, dashing it with great force against a tree, and threw themselves into a dense thicket. How I escaped death, I do not know. There I was, entirely alone, in a thick wood, in a place new to me. My cart was upset and shattered, my oxen were entangled among the young trees, and there was none to help me. After a long spell of effort, I succeeded in getting my cart righted, my oxen disentangled, and again yoked to the cart. I now proceeded with my team to the place where I had, the day before, been chopping wood, and loaded my cart pretty heavily, thinking in this way to tame my oxen. I then proceeded on my way home. I had now consumed one half of the day. I got out of the woods safely, and now felt out of danger. I stopped my oxen to open the woods gate; and just as I did so, before I could get hold of my ox-rope, the oxen again started, rushed through the gate, catching it between the wheel and the body of the cart, tearing it to pieces, and coming within a few inches of crushing me against the gate-post. Thus twice, in one short day, I escaped death by the merest chance. On my return, I told Mr. Covey what had happened, and how it happened. He ordered me to return to the woods again immediately. I did so, and he followed on after me. Just as I got into the woods, he came up and told me to stop my cart, and that he would teach me how to trifle away my time, and break gates. He then went to a large gum-tree, and with his axe cut three large switches, and, after trimming them up neatly with his pocket-knife, he ordered me to take off my clothes. I made him no answer, but stood with my clothes on. He repeated his order. I still made him no answer, nor did I move to strip myself. Upon this he rushed at me with the fierceness of a tiger, tore off my clothes, and lashed me till he had worn out his switches, cutting me so savagely as to leave the marks visible for a long time after. This whipping was the first of a number just like it, and for similar offences.

I lived with Mr. Covey one year. During the first six months, of that year, scarce a week passed without his whipping me. I was seldom free from a sore back. My awkwardness was almost always his excuse for whipping me. We were worked fully up to the point of endurance. Long before day we were up, our horses fed, and by the first approach of day we were off to the field with our hoes and ploughing teams. Mr. Covey gave us enough to eat, but scarce time to eat it. We were often less than five minutes taking our meals. We were often in the field from the first approach of day till its last lingering ray had left us; and at saving-fodder time,[28] midnight often caught us in the field binding blades.

Covey would be out with us. The way he used to stand it, was this. He would spend the most of his afternoons in bed. He would then come out fresh in the evening, ready to urge us on with his words, example, and frequently with the whip. Mr. Covey was one of the few slaveholders who could and did work with his hands. He was a hard-working man. He knew by himself just what a man or a boy could do. There was no deceiving him. His work went on in his absence almost as well as in his presence; and he had the faculty of making us feel that he was ever present with us. This he did by surprising us. He seldom approached the spot where we were at work openly, if he could do it secretly. He always aimed at taking us by surprise. Such was his cunning, that we used to call him, among

---

[28] Harvesting time; blades are the leaves of plants.

ourselves, "the snake." When we were at work in the cornfield, he would sometimes crawl on his hands and knees to avoid detection, and all at once he would
rise nearly in our midst, and scream out, "Ha, ha! Come, come! Dash on, dash
on!" This being his mode of attack, it was never safe to stop a single minute. His
comings were like a thief in the night. He appeared to us as being ever at hand. He
was under every tree, behind every stump, in every bush, and at every window,
on the plantation. He would sometimes mount his horse, as if bound to St. Michael's, a distance of seven miles, and in half an hour afterwards you would see
him coiled up in the corner of the wood-fence, watching every motion of the
slaves. He would, for this purpose, leave his horse tied up in the woods. Again,
he would sometimes walk up to us, and give us orders as though he was upon the
point of starting on a long journey, turn his back upon us, and make as though he
was going to the house to get ready; and, before he would get half way thither, he
would turn short and crawl into a fence-corner, or behind some tree, and there
watch us till the going down of the sun.

Mr. Covey's *forte*[29] consisted in his power to deceive. His life was devoted to
planning and perpetrating the grossest deceptions. Every thing he possessed in the
shape of learning or religion, he made conform to his disposition to deceive. He
seemed to think himself equal to deceiving the Almighty. He would make a short
prayer in the morning, and a long prayer at night; and, strange as it may seem, few
men would at times appear more devotional than he. The exercises of his family
devotions were always commenced with singing; and, as he was a very poor
singer himself, the duty of raising the hymn generally came upon me. He would
read his hymn, and nod at me to commence. I would at times do so; at others, I
would not. My non-compliance would almost always produce much confusion.
To show himself independent of me, he would start and stagger through with his
hymn in the most discordant manner. In this state of mind, he prayed with more
than ordinary spirit. Poor man! such was his disposition, and success at deceiving,
I do verily believe that he sometimes deceived himself into the solemn belief, that
he was a sincere worshipper of the most high God; and this, too, at a time when he
may be said to have been guilty of compelling his woman slave to commit the sin
of adultery. The facts in the case are these: Mr. Covey was a poor man; he was
just commencing in life; he was only able to buy one slave; and, shocking as is the
fact, he bought her, as he said, for *a breeder*. This woman was named Caroline.
Mr. Covey bought her from Mr. Thomas Lowe, about six miles from St. Michael's. She was a large, able-bodied woman, about twenty years old. She had
already given birth to one child, which proved her to be just what he wanted.
After buying her, he hired a married man of Mr. Samuel Harrison, to live with
him one year; and him he used to fasten up with her every night! The result was,
that, at the end of the year, the miserable woman gave birth to twins. At this result
Mr. Covey seemed to be highly pleased, both with the man and the wretched
woman. Such was his joy, and that of his wife, that nothing they could do for
Caroline during her confinement was too good, or too hard, to be done. The children were regarded as being quite an addition to his wealth.

If at any one time of my life more than another, I was made to drink the bitterest dregs of slavery, that time was during the first six months of my stay with Mr.
Covey. We were worked in all weathers. It was never too hot or too cold; it could
never rain, blow, hail, or snow, too hard for us to work in the field. Work, work,

[29] Specialty.

work, was scarcely more the order of the day than of the night. The longest days were too short for him, and the shortest nights too long for him. I was somewhat unmanageable when I first went there, but a few months of this discipline tamed me. Mr. Covey succeeded in breaking me. I was broken in body, soul, and spirit. My natural elasticity was crushed, my intellect languished, the disposition to read departed, the cheerful spark that lingered about my eye died; the dark night of slavery closed in upon me; and behold a man transformed into a brute!

Sunday was my only leisure time. I spent this in a sort of beast-like stupor, between sleep and wake, under some large tree. At times I would rise up, a flash of energetic freedom would dart through my soul, accompanied with a faint beam of hope, that flickered for a moment, and then vanished. I sank down again, mourning over my wretched condition. I was sometimes prompted to take my life, and that of Covey, but was prevented by a combination of hope and fear. My sufferings on this plantation seem now like a dream rather than a stern reality.

Our house stood within a few rods of the Chesapeake Bay, whose broad bosom was ever white with sails from every quarter of the habitable globe. Those beautiful vessels, robed in purest white, so delightful to the eye of freemen, were to me so many shrouded ghosts, to terrify and torment me with thoughts of my wretched condition. I have often, in the deep stillness of a summer's Sabbath, stood all alone upon the lofty banks of that noble bay, and traced, with saddened heart and tearful eye, the countless number of sails moving off to the mighty ocean. The sight of these always affected me powerfully. My thoughts would compel utterance; and there, with no audience but the Almighty, I would pour out my soul's complaint, in my rude way, with an apostrophe to the moving multitude of ships:—

"You are loosed from your moorings, and are free; I am fast in my chains, and am a slave! You move merrily before the gentle gale, and I sadly before the bloody whip! You are freedom's swift-winged angels, that fly round the world; I am confined in bands of iron! O that I were free! O, that I were on one of your gallant decks, and under your protecting wing– Alas! betwixt me and you, the turbid waters roll. Go on, go on. O that I could also go! Could I but swim! If I could fly! O, why was I born a man, of whom to make a brute! The glad ship is gone; she hides in the dim distance. I am left in the hottest hell of unending slavery. O God, save me! God, deliver me! Let me be free! Is there any God? Why am I a slave? I will run away. I will not stand it. Get caught, or get clear, I'll try it. I had as well die with ague as the fever. I have only one life to lose. I had as well be killed running as die standing. Only think of it; one hundred miles straight north, and I am free! Try it? Yes! God helping me, I will. It cannot be that I shall live and die a slave. I will take to the water. This very bay shall yet bear me into freedom. The steamboats steered in a north-east course from North Point. I will do the same; and when I get to the head of the bay, I will turn my canoe adrift, and walk straight through Delaware into Pennyslvania. When I get there, I shall not be required to have a pass; I can travel without being disturbed. Let but the first opportunity offer, and, come what will, I am off. Meanwhile, I will try to bear up under the yoke. I am not the only slave in the world. Why should I fret? I can bear as much as any of them. Besides, I am but a boy, and all boys are bound to some one. It may be that my misery in slavery will only increase my happiness when I get free. There is a better day coming."

Thus I used to think, and thus I used to speak to myself; goaded almost to madness at one moment, and at the next reconciling myself to my wretched lot.

I have already intimated that my condition was much worse, during the first six months of my stay at Mr. Covey's, than in the last six. The circumstances leading to the change in Mr. Covey's course toward me form an epoch in my humble history. You have seen how a man was made a slave; you shall see how a slave was made a man. On one of the hottest days of the month of August, 1833, Bill Smith, William Hughes, a slave named Eli, and myself, were engaged in fanning wheat.[30] Hughes was clearing the fanned wheat from before the fan, Eli was turning, Smith was feeding, and I was carrying wheat to the fan. The work was simple, requiring strength rather than intellect; yet, to one entirely unused to such work, it came very hard. About three o'clock of that day, I broke down; my strength failed me; I was seized with a violent aching of the head, attended with extreme dizziness; I trembled in every limb. Finding what was coming, I nerved myself up, feeling it would never do to stop work. I stood as long as I could stagger to the hopper with grain. When I could stand no longer, I fell, and felt as if held down by an immense weight. The fan of course stopped; every one had his own work to do; and no one could do the work of the other, and have his own go on at the same time.

Mr. Covey was at the house, about one hundred yards from the treading-yard where we were fanning. On hearing the fan stop, he left immediately, and came to the spot where we were. He hastily inquired what the matter was. Bill answered that I was sick, and there was no one to bring wheat to the fan. I had by this time crawled away under the side of the post and rail-fence by which the yard was enclosed, hoping to find relief by getting out of the sun. He then asked where I was. He was told by one of the hands. He came to the spot, and, after looking at me awhile, asked me what was the matter. I told him as well as I could, for I scarce had strength to speak. He then gave me a savage kick in the side, and told me to get up. I tried to do so, but fell back in the attempt. He gave me another kick, and again told me to rise. I again tried, and succeeded in gaining my feet; but, stooping to get the tub with which I was feeding the fan, I again staggered and fell. While down in this situation, Mr. Covey took up the hickory slat with which Hughes had been striking off the half-bushel measure, and with it gave me a heavy blow upon the head, making a large wound, and the blood ran freely; and with this again told me to get up. I made no effort to comply, having now made up my mind to let him do his worst. In a short time after receiving this blow, my head grew better. Mr. Covey had now left me to my fate. At this moment I resolved, for the first time, to go to my master, enter a complaint, and ask his protection. In order to this, I must that afternoon walk seven miles; and this, under the circumstances, was truly a severe undertaking. I was exceedingly feeble; made so as much by the kicks and blows which I received, as by the severe fit of sickness to which I had been subjected. I, however, watched my chance, while Covey was looking in an opposite direction, and started for St. Michael's. I succeeded in getting a considerable distance on my way to the woods, when Covey discovered me, and called after me to come back, threatening what he would do if I did not come. I disregarded both his calls and his threats, and made my way to the woods as fast as my feeble state would allow; and thinking I might be overhauled by him if I kept the road, I walked through the woods, keeping far enough from the road to avoid detection, and near enough to prevent losing my way I had not gone far before my little strength again failed me. I could go no farther. I fell down, and

[30] Separating the wheat from the chaff.

lay for a considerable time. The blood was yet oozing from the wound on my head. For a time I thought I should bleed to death; and think now that I should have done so, but that the blood so matted my hair as to stop the wound. After lying there about three quarters of an hour, I nerved myself up again, and started on my way, through bogs and briers, barefooted and bare-headed, tearing my feet sometimes at nearly every step; and after a journey of about seven miles, occupying some five hours to perform it, I arrived at master's store. I then presented an appearance enough to affect any but a heart of iron. From the crown of my head to my feet, I was covered with blood. My hair was all clotted with dust and blood; my shirt was stiff with blood. My legs and feet were torn in sundry places with briers and thorns, and were also covered with blood. I suppose I looked like a man who had escaped a den of wild beasts, and barely escaped them. In this state, I appeared before my master, humbly entreating him to interpose his authority for my protection. I told him all the circumstances as well as I could, and it seemed, as I spoke, at times to affect him. He would then walk the floor, and seek to justify Covey by saying he expected I deserved it. He asked me what I wanted. I told him, to let me get a new home; that as sure as I lived with Mr. Covey again, I should live with but to die with him; that Covey would surely kill me; he was in a fair way for it. Master Thomas ridiculed the idea that there was any danger of Mr. Covey's killing me, and said that he knew Mr. Covey; that he was a good man, and that he could not think of taking me from him; that, should he do so, he would lose the whole year's wages; that I belonged to Mr. Covey for one year, and that I must go back to him, come what might; and that I must not trouble him with any more stories, or that he would himself *get hold of me.* After threatening me thus, he gave me a very large dose of salts, telling me that I might remain in St. Michael's that night, (it being quite late,) but that I must be off back to Mr. Covey's early in the morning; and that if I did not, he would *get hold of me,* which meant that he would whip me. I remained all night, and, according to his orders, I started off to Covey's in the morning, (Saturday morning,) wearied in body and broken in spirit. I got no supper that night, or breakfast that morning. I reached Covey's about nine o'clock; and just as I was getting over the fence that divided Mrs. Kemp's fields from ours, out ran Covey with his cowskin, to give me another whipping. Before he could reach me, I succeeded in getting to the cornfield; and as the corn was very high, it afforded me the means of hiding. He seemed very angry, and searched for me a long time. My behavior was altogether unaccountable. He finally gave up the chase, thinking, I suppose, that I must come home for something to eat; he would give himself no further trouble in looking for me. I spent that day mostly in the woods, having the alternative before me,—to go home and be whipped to death, or stay in the woods and be starved to death. That night, I fell in with Sandy Jenkins, a slave with whom I was somewhat acquainted. Sandy had a free wife[31] who lived about four miles from Mr. Covey's; and it being Saturday, he was on his way to see her. I told him my circumstances, and he very kindly invited me to go home with him. I went home with him, and talked this whole matter over, and got his advice as to what course it was best for me to pursue. I found Sandy an old adviser. He told me, with great solemnity, I must go back to Covey; but that before I went, I must go with him into another part of the woods, where there was a certain *root,* which, if I would take some of it with me, carrying it *always on my right side,* would render it impossible for Mr.

---

[31] A wife who had been freed legally and was not a slave.

Covey, or any other white man, to whip me. He said he had carried it for years; and since he had done so, he had never received a blow, and never expected to while he carried it. I at first rejected the idea, that the simple carrying of a root in my pocket would have any such effect as he had said, and was not disposed to take it; but Sandy impressed the necessity with much earnestness, telling me it could do no harm, if it did no good. To please him, I at length took the root, and, according to his direction, carried it upon my right side. This was Sunday morning. I immediately started for home; and upon entering the yard gate, out came Mr. Covey on his way to meeting. He spoke to me very kindly, bade me drive the pigs from a lot near by, and passed on towards the church. Now, this singular conduct of Mr. Covey really made me begin to think that there was something in the *root* which Sandy had given me; and had it been on any other day than Sunday, I could have attributed the conduct to no other cause than the influence of that root; and as it was, I was half inclined to think the *root* to be something more than I at first had taken it to be. All went well till Monday morning. On this morning, the virtue of the *root* was fully tested. Long before daylight, I was called to go and rub, curry, and feed, the horses. I obeyed, and was glad to obey. But whilst thus engaged, whilst in the act of throwing down some blades from the loft, Mr. Covey entered the stable with a long rope; and just as I was half out of the loft, he caught hold of my legs, and was about tying me. As soon as I found what he was up to, I gave a sudden spring, and as I did so, he holding to my legs, I was brought sprawling on the stable floor. Mr. Covey seemed now to think he had me, and could do what he pleased; but at this moment—from whence came the spirit I don't know—I resolved to fight; and, suiting my action to the resolution, I seized Covey hard by the throat; and as I did so, I rose. He held on to me, and I to him. My resistance was so entirely unexpected, that Covey seemed taken all aback. He trembled like a leaf. This gave me assurance, and I held him uneasy, causing the blood to run where I touched him with the ends of my fingers. Mr. Covey soon called out to Hughes for help. Hughes came, and, while Covey held me, attempted to tie my right hand. While he was in the act of doing so, I watched my chance, and gave him a heavy kick close under the ribs. This kick fairly sickened Hughes, so that he left me in the hands of Mr. Covey. This kick had the effect of not only weakening Hughes, but Covey also. When he saw Hughes bending over with pain, his courage quailed. He asked me if I meant to persist in my resistance. I told him I did, come what might; that he had used me like a brute for six months, and that I was determined to be used so no longer. With that, he strove to drag me to a stick that was lying just out of the stable door. He meant to knock me down. But just as he was leaning over to get the stick, I seized him with both hands by his collar, and brought him by a sudden snatch to the ground. By this time, Bill came. Covey called upon him for assistance. Bill wanted to know what he could do. Covey said, "Take hold of him, take hold of him!" Bill said his master hired him out to work, and not to help to whip me; so he left Covey and myself to fight our own battle out. We were at it for nearly two hours. Covey at length let me go, puffing and blowing at a great rate, saying that if I had not resisted, he would not have whipped me half so much. The truth was, that he had not whipped me at all. I considered him as getting entirely the worst end of the bargain; for he had drawn no blood from me, but I had from him. The whole six months afterwards, that I spent with Mr. Covey, he never laid the weight of his finger upon me in anger. He would occasionally say, he didn't want to get hold of me again. "No," thought I, "you need not; for you will come off worse than you did before."

The battle with Mr. Covey was the turning-point in my career as a slave. It rekindled the few expiring embers of freedom, and revived within me a sense of my own manhood. It recalled the departed self-confidence, and inspired me again with a determination to be free. The gratification afforded by the triumph was a full compensation for whatever else might follow, even death itself. He only can understand the deep satisfaction which I experienced, who has himself repelled by force the bloody arm of slavery. I felt as I never felt before. It was a glorious resurrection, from the tomb of slavery, to the heaven of freedom. My long-crushed spirit rose, cowardice departed, bold defiance took its place; and I now resolved that, however long I might remain a slave in form, the day had passed forever when I could be a slave in fact. I did not hesitate to let it be known of me, that the white man who expected to succeed in whipping, must also succeed in killing me.

From this time I was never again what might be called fairly whipped, though I remained a slave four years afterwards. I had several fights, but was never whipped.

It was for a long time a matter of surprise to me why Mr. Covey did not immediately have me taken by the constable to the whipping-post, and there regularly whipped for the crime of raising my hand against a white man in defence of myself. And the only explanation I can now think of does not entirely satisfy me; but such as it is, I will give it. Mr. Covey enjoyed the most unbounded reputation for being a first-rate overseer and negro-breaker. It was of considerable importance to him. That reputation was at stake; and had he sent me—a boy about sixteen years old—to the public whipping-post, his reputation would have been lost; so, to save his reputation, he suffered me to go unpunished.

My term of actual service to Mr. Edward Covey ended on Christmas day, 1833. The days between Christmas and New Year's day are allowed as holidays; and, accordingly, we were not required to perform any labor, more than to feed and take care of the stock. This time we regarded as our own, by the grace of our masters; and we therefore used or abused it nearly as we pleased. Those of us who had families at a distance, were generally allowed to spend the whole six days in their society. This time, however, was spent in various ways. The staid, sober, thinking and industrious ones of our number would employ themselves in making corn-brooms, mats, horse-collars, and baskets; and another class of us would spend the time in hunting opossums, hares, and coons. But by far the larger part engaged in such sports and merriments as playing ball, wrestling, running foot-races, fiddling, dancing, and drinking whisky; and this latter mode of spending the time was by far the most agreeable to the feelings of our masters. A slave who would work during the holidays was considered by our masters as scarcely deserving them. He was regarded as one who rejected the favor of his master. It was deemed a disgrace not to get drunk at Christmas; and he was regarded as lazy indeed, who had not provided himself with the necessary means, during the year, to get whisky enough to last him through Christmas.

From what I know of the effect of these holidays upon the slave, I believe them to be among the most effective means in the hands of the slaveholder in keeping down the spirit of insurrection. Were the slaveholders at once to abandon this practice, I have not the slightest doubt it would lead to an immediate insurrection among the slaves. These holidays serve as conductors, or safety-valves, to carry off the rebellious spirit of enslaved humanity. But for these, the slave would be forced up to the wildest desperation; and woe betide the slaveholder, the day he ventures to remove or hinder the operation of those conductors! I warn him that, in such an event, a spirit will go forth in their midst, more to be dreaded than the most appalling earthquake.

The holidays are part and parcel of the gross fraud, wrong, and inhumanity of slavery. They are professedly a custom established by the benevolence of the slaveholders; but I undertake to say, it is the result of selfishness, and one of the grossest frauds committed upon the down-trodden slave. They do not give the slaves this time because they would not like to have their work during its continuance, but because they know it would be unsafe to deprive them of it. This will be seen by the fact, that the slaveholders like to have their slaves spend those days just in such a manner as to make them as glad of their ending as of their beginning. Their object seems to be, to disgust their slaves with freedom, by plunging them into the lowest depths of dissipation. For instance, the slaveholders not only like to see the slave drink of his own accord, but will adopt various plans to make him drunk. One plan is, to make bets on their slaves, as to who can drink the whisky without getting drunk; and in this way they succeed in getting whole multitudes to drink to excess. Thus, when the slave asks for virtuous freedom, the cunning slaveholder, knowing his ignorance, cheats him with a dose of vicious dissipation, artfully labelled with the name of liberty. The most of us used to drink it down, and the result was just what might be supposed: many of us were led to think that there was little to choose between liberty and slavery. We felt, and very properly too, that we had almost as well be slaves to man as to rum. So, when the holidays ended, we staggered up from the filth of our wallowing, took a long breath, and marched to the field,—feeling, upon the whole, rather glad to go, from what our master had deceived us into a belief was freedom, back to the arms of slavery.

I have said that this mode of treatment is a part of the whole system of fraud and inhumanity of slavery. It is so. The mode here adopted to disgust the slave with freedom, by allowing him to see only the abuse of it, is carried out in other things. For instance, a slave loves molasses; he steals some. His master, in many cases, goes off to town, and buys a large quantity; he returns, takes his whip, and commands the slave to eat the molasses, until the poor fellow is made sick at the very mention of it. The same mode is sometimes adopted to make the slaves refrain from asking for more food than their regular allowance. A slave runs through his allowance, and applies for more. His master is enraged at him; but, not willing to send him off without food, gives him more than is necessary, and compels him to eat it within a given time. Then, if he complains that he cannot eat it, he is said to be satisfied neither full nor fasting, and is whipped for being hard to please! I have an abundance of such illustrations of the same principle, drawn from my own observation, but think the cases I have cited sufficient. The practice is a very common one.

On the first of January, 1834, I left Mr. Covey, and went to live with Mr. William Freeland, who lived about three miles from St. Michael's. I soon found Mr. Freeland a very different man from Mr. Covey. Though not rich, he was what would be called an educated southern gentleman. Mr. Covey, as I have shown, was a well-trained negro-breaker and slave-driver. The former (slaveholder though he was) seemed to possess some regard for honor, some reverence for justice, and some respect for humanity. The latter seemed totally insensible to all such sentiments. Mr. Freeland had many of the faults peculiar to slave-holders, such as being very passionate and fretful; but I must do him the justice to say, that he was exceedingly free from those degrading vices to which Mr. Covey was constantly addicted. The one was open and frank, and we always knew where to find him. The other was a most artful deceiver, and could be understood only by such as were skilful enough to detect his cunningly-devised frauds. Another advantage I gained in my new master was, he made no pretensions to, or profession of, religion; and this, in my opinion, was truly a great advantage. I assert most unhesitatingly, that the religion of the south is a mere covering for the most horrid crimes,—a justifier of the most appalling barbarity,—a sanctifier of the most hateful frauds,—and a dark shelter under, which the darkest, foulest, grossest, and most infernal deeds of slaveholders find the strongest protection. Were I to be again reduced to the chains of slavery, next to that enslavement, I should regard being the slave of a religious master the greatest calamity that could befall me. (For of all slaveholders with whom I have ever met, religious slaveholders are the worst. I have ever found them the meanest and basest, the most cruel and cowardly, of all others.) It was my unhappy lot not only to belong to a religious slaveholder, but to live in a community of such religionists. Very near Mr. Freeland lived the Rev. Daniel Weeden, and in the same neighborhood lived the Rev. Rigby Hopkins. These were members and ministers in the Reformed Methodist Church. Mr. Weeden owned, among others, a woman slave, whose name I have forgotten. This woman's back, for weeks, was kept literally raw, made so by the lash of this merciless, *religious* wretch. He used to hire hands. His maxim was, Behave well or behave ill, it is the duty of a master occasionally to whip a slave, to remind him of his master's authority. Such was his theory, and such his practice.

Mr. Hopkins was even worse than Mr. Weeden. His chief boast was his ability to manage slaves. The peculiar feature of his government was that of whipping slaves in advance of deserving it. He always managed to have one or more of his slaves to whip every Monday morning. He did this to alarm their fears, and strike terror into those who escaped. His plan was to whip for the smallest offences, to prevent the commission of large ones. Mr. Hopkins could always find some excuse for whipping a slave. It would astonish one, unaccustomed to a slaveholding life, to see with what wonderful ease a slaveholder can find things, of which to make occasion to whip a slave. A mere look, word, or motion,—a mistake, accident, or want of power,—are all matters for which a slave may be whipped at any time. Does a slave look dissatisfied? It is said, he has the devil in him, and it must be whipped out. Does he speak loudly when spoken to by his master? Then he is getting high-minded, and should be taken down a button-hole lower. Does he forget to pull off his hat at the approach of a white person? Then he is wanting in reverence, and should be whipped for it. Does he ever venture to vindicate his conduct, when censured for it? Then he is guilty of impudence,—one of the greatest crimes of which a slave can be guilty. Does he ever venture to suggest a different mode of doing things from that pointed out by his master? He is indeed presumptuous, and getting above himself; and nothing less than a flogging will do for him. Does he, while ploughing, break a plough,—or, while hoeing, break a hoe? It is owing to his carelessness, and for it a slave must always be whipped. Mr. Hopkins could always find something of this sort to justify the use of the lash, and he seldom failed to embrace such opportunities. There was not a man in the whole county, with whom the slaves who had the getting their own home, would not prefer to live, rather than with this Rev. Mr. Hopkins. And yet there was not a man any where round, who made higher professions of religion, or was more active in revivals,—more attentive to the class, love-feast, prayer and preaching meetings, or more devotional in his family,—that prayed earlier, later, louder, and longer,—than this same reverend slave-driver, Rigby Hopkins.

But to return to Mr. Freeland, and to my experience while in his employment. He, like Mr. Covey, gave us enough to eat; but, unlike Mr. Covey, he also gave us sufficient time to take our meals. He worked us hard, but always between sunrise and sunset. He required a good deal of work to be done, but gave us good tools with which to work. His farm was large, but he employed hands enough to work it, and with ease, compared with many of his neighbors. My treatment, while in his employment, was heavenly, compared with what I experienced at the hands of Mr. Edward Covey.

Mr. Freeland was himself the owner of but two slaves. Their names were Henry Harris and John Harris. The rest of his hands he hired. These consisted of myself, Sandy Jenkins,[32] and Handy Caldwell. Henry and John were quite intelligent, and in a very little while after I went there, I succeeded in creating in them a strong desire to learn how to read. This desire soon sprang up in the others also. They very soon mustered up some old spelling-books, and nothing would do but that I must keep a Sabbath school. I agreed to do so, and accordingly devoted my Sundays to teaching these my loved fellow-slaves how to read. Neither of them knew his letters when I went there. Some of the slaves of the neighboring farms found what was going on, and also availed themselves of this little opportunity to learn to read. It was understood, among all who came, that there must be as little display about it as possible. It was necessary to keep our religious masters at St. Michael's unacquainted with the fact, that, instead of spending the Sabbath in wrestling, boxing, and drinking whisky, we were trying to learn how to read the will of God; for they had much rather see us engaged in those degrading sports, than to see us behaving like intellectual, moral, and accountable beings. My blood boils as I think of the bloody manner in which Messrs. Wright Fairbanks and Garrison West, both class-leaders, in connection with many others, rushed in upon us with sticks and stones, and broke up our virtuous little Sabbath school, at St. Michael's—all calling themselves Christians! humble followers of the Lord Jesus Christ! But I am again disgressing.

I held my Sabbath school at the house of a free colored man, whose name I deem it imprudent to mention; for should it be known, it might embarrass him greatly, though the crime of holding the school was committed ten years ago. I had at one time over forty scholars, and those of the right sort, ardently desiring to learn. They were of all ages, though mostly men and women. I look back to those Sundays with an amount of pleasure not to be expressed. They were great days to my soul. The work of instructing my dear fellow-slaves was the sweetest engagement with which I was ever blessed. We loved each other, and to leave them at the close of the Sabbath was a severe cross indeed. When I think that these precious souls are to-day shut up in the prison-house of slavery, my feelings overcome me, and I am almost ready to ask, "Does a righteous God govern the universe? and for what does he hold the thunders in his right hand, if not to smite the oppressor, and deliver the spoiled out of the hand of the spoiler?" These dear souls came not to

---

[32] Douglass's note: "This is the same man who gave me the roots to prevent my being whipped by Mr. Covey. He was 'a clever soul.' We used frequently to talk about the fight with Covey, and as often as we did so, he would claim my success as the result of the roots which he gave me. This superstition is very common among the more ignorant slaves. A slave seldom dies but that his death is attributed to trickery."

Sabbath school because it was popular to do so, nor did I teach them because it was reputable to be thus engaged. Every moment they spent in that school, they were liable to be taken up, and given thirty-nine lashes. They came because they wished to learn. Their minds had been starved by their cruel masters. They had been shut up in mental darkness. I taught them, because it was the delight of my soul to be doing something that looked like bettering the condition of my race. I kept up my school nearly the whole year I lived with Mr. Freeland; and, beside my Sabbath school, I devoted three evenings in the week, during the winter, to teaching the slaves at home. And I have the happiness to know, that several of those who came to Sabbath school learned how to read; and that one, at least, is now free through my agency.

The year passed off smoothly. It seemed only about half as long as the year which preceded it. I went through it without receiving a single blow. I will give Mr. Freeland the credit of being the best master I ever had, *till I became my own master.* For the ease with which I passed the year, I was, however, somewhat indebted to the society of my fellow-slaves. They were noble souls; they not only possessed loving hearts, but brave ones. We were linked and interlinked with each other. I loved them with a love stronger than any thing I have experienced since. It is sometimes said that we slaves do not love and confide in each other. In answer to this assertion, I can say, I never loved any or confided in any people more than my fellow-slaves, and especially those with whom I lived at Mr. Freeland's. I believe we would have died for each other. We never undertook to do any thing, of any importance, without a mutual consultation. We never moved separately. We were one; and as much so by our tempers and dispositions, as by the mutual hardships to which we were necessarily subjected by our condition as slaves.

At the close of the year 1834, Mr. Freeland again hired me of my master, for the year 1835. But, by this time, I began to want to live *upon free land* as well as *with Freeland;* and I was no longer content, therefore, to live with him or any other slaveholder. I began, with the commencement of the year, to prepare myself for a final struggle, which should decide my fate one way or the other. My tendency was upward. I was fast approaching manhood, and year after year had passed, and I was still a slave. These thoughts roused me—I must do something. I therefore resolved that 1835 should not pass without witnessing an attempt, on my part, to secure my liberty. But I was not willing to cherish this determination alone. My fellow-slaves were dear to me. I was anxious to have them participate with me in this, my life-giving determination. I therefore, though with great prudence, commenced early to ascertain their views and feelings in regard to their condition, and to imbue their minds with thoughts of freedom. I bent myself to devising ways and means for our escape, and meanwhile strove, on all fitting occasions, to impress them with the gross fraud and inhumanity of slavery. I went first to Henry, next to John, then to the others. I found, in them all, warm hearts and noble spirits. They were ready to hear, and ready to act when a feasible plan should be proposed. This was what I wanted. I talked to them of our want of manhood, if we submitted to our enslavement without at least one noble effort to be free. We met often, and consulted frequently, and told our hopes and fears, recounted the difficulties, real and imagined, which we should be called on to meet. At times we were almost disposed to give up, and try to content ourselves with our wretched lot; at others, we were firm and unbending in our determination to go. Whenever we suggested any plan, there was shrinking—the odds were fearful. Our path was beset with the greatest obstacles; and if we succeeded in gaining the end of it, our right to be free was yet questionable—we were yet liable to be returned to bondage. We could see no spot, this side of the ocean, where we could be free. We knew nothing about Canada. Our knowledge of the north did not extend farther than New York; and to go there, and be forever harassed with the frightful liability of being returned to slavery—with the certainty of being treated tenfold worse than before—the thought was truly a horrible one, and one which it was not easy to overcome. The case sometimes stood thus: At every gate through which we were to pass, we saw a watchman—at every ferry a guard—on every bridge a sentinel—and in every wood a patrol. We were hemmed in upon every side. Here were the difficulties, real or imagined—the good to be sought, and the evil to be shunned. On the one hand, there stood slavery, a stern reality, glaring frightfully upon us,—its robes already crimsoned with the blood of millions, and even now feasting itself greedily upon our own flesh. On the other hand, away back in the dim distance, under the flickering light of the north star, behind some craggy hill or snow-covered mountain, stood a doubtful freedom— half frozen—beckoning us to come and share its hospitality. This in itself was sometimes enough to stagger us; but when we permitted ourselves to survey the road, we were frequently appalled. Upon either side we saw grim death, assuming the most horrid shapes. Now it was starvation, causing us to eat our own flesh;— now we were contending with the waves, and were drowned;—now we were overtaken, and torn to pieces by the fangs of the terrible bloodhound. We were stung by scorpions, chased by wild beasts, bitten by snakes, and finally, after having nearly reached the desired spot,—after swimming rivers, encountering wild beasts, sleeping in the woods, suffering hunger and nakedness,—we were overtaken by our pursuers, and, in our resistance, we were shot dead upon the spot! I say, this picture sometimes appalled us, and made us

> "rather bear those ills we had,
> Than fly to others, that we knew not of."[33]

In coming to a fixed determination to run away, we did more than Patrick Henry, when he resolved upon liberty or death. With us it was a doubtful liberty at most, and almost certain death if we failed. For my part, I should prefer death to hopeless bondage.

Sandy, one of our number, gave up the notion, but still encouraged us. Our company then consisted of Henry Harris, John Harris, Henry Bailey, Charles Roberts, and myself. Henry Bailey was my uncle, and belonged to my master. Charles married my aunt: he belonged to my master's father-in-law, Mr. William Hamilton.

The plan we finally concluded upon was, to get a large canoe belonging to Mr. Hamilton, and upon the Saturday night previous to Easter holidays, paddle directly up the Chesapeake Bay. On our arrival at the head of the bay, a distance of seventy or eighty miles from where we lived, it was our purpose to turn our canoe adrift, and follow the guidance of the north star till we got beyond the limits of Maryland. Our reason for taking the water route was, that we were less liable to be suspected as runaways; we hoped to be regarded as fishermen; whereas, if we should take the land route, we should be subjected to interruptions of almost every

---

[33] Shakespeare's *Hamlet* (III.i.81–82).

kind. Any one having a white face, and being so disposed, could stop us, and subject us to examination.

The week before our intended start, I wrote several protections, one for each of us. As well as I can remember, they were in the following words, to wit:—

> "This is to certify that I, the undersigned, have given the bearer, my servant, full liberty to go to Baltimore, and spend the Easter holidays. Written with mine own hand, etc., 1835.
> "WILLIAM HAMILTON,
> "Near St. Michael's, in Talbot county, Maryland."

We were not going to Baltimore; but, in going up the bay, we went toward Baltimore, and these protections were only intended to protect us while on the bay.

As the time drew near for our departure, our anxiety became more and more intense. It was truly a matter of life and death with us. The strength of our determination was about to be fully tested. At this time, I was very active in explaining every difficulty, removing every doubt, dispelling every fear, and inspiring all with the firmness indispensable to success in our undertaking; assuring them that half was gained the instant we made the move; we had talked long enough; we were now ready to move; if not now, we never should be; and if we did not intend to move now, we had as well fold our arms, sit down, and acknowledge ourselves fit only to be slaves. This, none of us were prepared to acknowledge. Every man stood firm; and at our last meeting, we pledged ourselves afresh, in the most solemn manner, that, at the time appointed, we would certainly start in pursuit of freedom. This was in the middle of the week, at the end of which we were to be off. We went, as usual, to our several fields of labor, but with bosoms highly agitated with thoughts of our truly hazardous undertaking. We tried to conceal our feelings as much as possible; and I think we succeeded very well.

After a painful waiting, the Saturday morning, whose night was to witness our departure, came. I hailed it with joy, bring what of sadness it might. Friday night was a sleepless one for me. I probably felt more anxious than the rest, because I was, by common consent, at the head of the whole affair. The responsibility of success or failure lay heavily upon me. The glory of the one, and the confusion of the other, were alike mine. The first two hours of that morning were such as I never experienced before, and hope never to again. Early in the morning, we went, as usual, to the field. We were spreading manure; and all at once, while thus engaged, I was overwhelmed with an indescribable feeling, in the fulness of which I turned to Sandy, who was near by, and said, "We are betrayed!" "Well," said he, "that thought has this moment struck me." We said no more. I was never more certain of any thing.

The horn was blown as usual, and we went up from the field to the house for breakfast. I went for the form, more than for want of any thing to eat that morning. Just as I got to the house, in looking out at the lane gate, I saw four white men, with two colored men. The white men were on horseback, and the colored ones were walking behind, as if tied. I watched them a few moments till they got up to our lane gate. Here they halted, and tied the colored men to the gate-post. I was not yet certain as to what the matter was. In a few moments, in rode Mr. Hamilton, with a speed betokening great excitement. He came to the door, and inquired if Master William was in. He was told he was at the barn. Mr. Hamilton, without dismounting, rode up to the barn with extraordinary speed. In a few moments, he and Mr. Freeland returned to the house. By this time, the three consta-bles rode up, and in great haste dismounted, tied their horses, and met Master William and Mr. Hamilton returning from the barn; and after talking awhile, they all walked up to the kitchen door. There was no one in the kitchen but myself and John. Henry and Sandy were up at the barn. Mr. Freeland put his head in at the door, and called me by name, saying there were some gentlemen at the door who wished to see me. I stepped to the door, and inquired what they wanted. They at once seized me, and, without giving me any satisfaction, tied me—lashing my hands closely together. I insisted upon knowing what the matter was. They at length said, that they had learned I had been in a "scrape," and that I was to be examined before my master; and if their information proved false, I should not be hurt.

In a few moments, they succeeded in tying John. They then turned to Henry, who had by this time returned, and commanded him to cross his hands. "I won't!" said Henry, in a firm tone, indicating his readiness to meet the consequences of his refusal. "Won't you?" said Tom Graham, the constable. "No, I won't!" said Henry, in a still stronger tone. With this, two of the constables pulled out their shining pistols, and swore, by their Creator, that they would make him cross his hands or kill him. Each cocked his pistol, and, with fingers on the trigger, walked up to Henry, saying, at the same time, if he did not cross his hands, they would blow his damned heart out. "Shoot me, shoot me!" said Henry; "you can't kill me but once. Shoot, shoot,—and be damned! *I won't be tied!*" This he said in a tone of loud defiance; and at the same time, with a motion as quick as lightning, he with one single stroke dashed the pistols from the hand of each constable. As he did this, all hands fell upon him, and, after beating him some time, they finally overpowered him, and got him tied.

During the scuffle, I managed, I know not how, to get my pass out, and, with-out being discovered, put it into the fire. We were all now tied; and just as we were to leave for Easton jail, Betsy Freeland, mother of William Freeland, came to the door with her hands full of biscuits, and divided them between Henry and John. She then delivered herself of a speech, to the following effect:—addressing herself to me, she said, "*You devil! You yellow devil!* it was you that put it into the heads of Henry and John to run away. But for you, you long-legged mulatto devil! Henry nor John would never have thought of such a thing." I made no reply, and was immediately hurried off towards St. Michael's. Just a moment previous to the scuffle with Henry, Mr. Hamilton suggested the propriety of making a search for the protections which he had understood Frederick had written for himself and the rest. But, just at the moment he was about carrying his proposal into effect, his aid was needed in helping to tie Henry; and the excitement attending the scuffle caused them either to forget, or to deem it unsafe, under the circumstances, to search. So we were not yet convicted of the intention to run away.

When we got about half way to St. Michael's, while the constables having us in charge were looking ahead, Henry inquired of me what he should do with his pass. I told him to eat it with his biscuit, and own nothing; and we passed the word around, "*Own nothing*;" and "*Own nothing*!" said we all. Our confidence in each other was unshaken. We were resolved to succeed or fail together, after the calamity had befallen us as much as before. We were now prepared for any thing. We were to be dragged that morning fifteen miles behind horses, and then to be placed in the Easton jail. When we reached St. Michael's, we underwent a sort of examination. We all denied that we ever intended to run away. We did this more to bring out the evidence against us, than from any hope of getting clear of being sold; for, as I have said, we were ready for that. The fact was, we cared but little where we went, so we went together. Our greatest concern was about separation. We dreaded that more than any thing this side of death. We found the evidence against us to be the testimony of one person; our master would not tell who it was; but we came to a unanimous decision among ourselves as to who their informant was. We were sent off to the jail at Easton. When we got there, we were delivered up to the sheriff, Mr. Joseph Graham, and by him placed in jail. Henry, John, and myself, were placed in one room together—Charles, and Henry Bailey, in another. Their object in separating us was to hinder concert.

We had been in jail scarcely twenty minutes, when a swarm of slave traders, and agents for slave traders, flocked into jail to look at us, and to ascertain if we were for sale. Such a set of beings I never saw before! I felt myself surrounded by so many fiends from perdition. A band of pirates never looked more like their father, the devil. They laughed and grinned over us, saying, "Ah, my boys! we have got you, haven't we?" And after taunting us in various ways, they one by one went into an examination of us, with intent to ascertain our value. They would impudently ask us if we would not like to have them for our masters. We would make them no answer, and leave them to find out as best they could. Then they would curse and swear at us, telling us that they could take the devil out of us in a very little while, if we were only in their hands.

While in jail, we found ourselves in much more comfortable quarters than we expected when we went there. We did not get much to eat, nor that which was very good; but we had a good clean room, from the windows of which we could see what was going on in the street, which was very much better than though we had been placed in one of the dark, damp cells. Upon the whole, we got along very well, so far as the jail and its keeper were concerned. Immediately after the holidays were over, contrary to all our expectations, Mr. Hamilton and Mr. Freeland came up to Easton, and took Charles, the two Henrys, and John, out of jail, and carried them home, leaving me alone. I regarded this separation as a final one. It caused me more pain than any thing else in the whole transaction. I was ready for any thing rather than separation. I supposed that they had consulted together, and had decided that, as I was the whole cause of the intention of the others to run away, it was hard to make the innocent suffer with the guilty; and that they had, therefore, concluded to take the others home, and sell me, as a warning to the others that remained. It is due to the noble Henry to say, he seemed almost as reluctant at leaving the prison as at leaving home to come to the prison. But we knew we should, in all probability, be separated, if we were sold; and since he was in their hands, he concluded to go peaceably home.

I was now left to my fate. I was all alone, and within the walls of a stone prison. But a few days before, and I was full of hope. I expected to have been safe in a land of freedom; but now I was covered with gloom, sunk down to the utmost despair. I thought the possibility of freedom was gone. I was kept in this way about one week, at the end of which, Captain Auld, my master, to my surprise and utter astonishment, came up, and took me out, with the intention of sending me, with a gentleman of his acquaintance, into Alabama. But, from some cause or other, he did not send me to Alabama, but concluded to send me back to Baltimore, to live again with his brother Hugh, and to learn a trade.

Thus, after an absence of three years and one month, I was once more permitted to return to my old home at Baltimore. My master sent me away, because there existed against me a very great prejudice in the community, and he feared I might be killed.

In a few weeks after I went to Baltimore, Master Hugh hired me to Mr. William Gardner, an extensive ship-builder, on Fell's Point. I was put there to learn how to calk. It, however, proved a very unfavorable place for the accomplishment of this object. Mr. Gardner was engaged that spring in building two large man-of-war brigs, professedly for the Mexican government. The vessels were to be launched in the July of that year, and in failure thereof, Mr. Gardner was to lose a considerable sum; so that when I entered, all was hurry. There was no time to learn any thing. Every man had to do that which he knew how to do. In entering the ship-yard, my orders from Mr. Gardner were, to do whatever the carpenters commanded me to do. This was placing me at the beck and call of about seventy-five men. I was to regard all these as masters. Their word was to be my law. My situation was a most trying one. At times I needed a dozen pair of hands. I was called a dozen ways in the space of a single minute. Three or four voices would strike my ear at the same moment. It was—"Fred., come help me to cant this timber here."—"Fred., come carry this timber yonder."—"Fred., bring that roller here."—"Fred., go get a fresh can of water."—"Fred., come help saw off the end of this timber."—"Fred., go quick, and get the crowbar."—"Fred., hold on the end of this fall."[34]—"Fred., go to the blacksmith's shop, and get a new punch."—"Hurra, Fred.! run and bring me a cold chisel."—"I say, Fred., bear a hand, and get up a fire as quick as lightning under that steam-box."—"Halloo, nigger! come, turn this grindstone."—"Come, come! move, move! and *bowse*[35] this timber forward."—"I say, darky, blast your eyes, why don't you heat up some pitch?"—"Halloo! halloo! halloo!" (Three voices at the same time.) "Come here!—Go there!——Hold on where you are! Damn you, if you move, I'll knock your brains out!"

This was my school for eight months; and I might have remained there longer, but for a most horrid fight I had with four of the white apprentices, in which my left eye was nearly knocked out, and I was horribly mangled in other respects. The facts in the case were these: Until a very little while after I went there, white and black ship-carpenters worked side by side, and no one seemed to see any impropriety in it. All hands seemed to be very well satisfied. Many of the black carpenters were freemen. Things seemed to be going on very well. All at once, the white carpenters knocked off, and said they would not work with free-colored workmen. Their reason for this, as alleged, was, that if free colored carpenters were encouraged, they would soon take the trade into their own hands, and poor white men would be thrown out of employment. They therefore felt called upon at once to put a stop to it. And, taking advantage of Mr. Gardner's necessities, they broke off, swearing they would work no longer, unless he would discharge his black carpenters. Now, though this did not extend to me in form, it did reach me in fact. My fellow-apprentices very soon began to feel it degrading to them to work with me. They began to put on airs, and talk about the "niggers" taking the country, saying we all ought to be killed; and, being encouraged by the journey-men, they commenced making my condition as hard as they could, by hectoring me around, and sometimes striking me. I, of course, kept the vow I made after the fight with Mr. Covey, and struck back again, regardless of consequences; and while I kept them from combining, I succeeded very well; for I could whip the

---

[34] The end of a rope or tackle.   [35] Haul.

whole of them, taking them separately. They, however, at length combined, and came upon me, armed with sticks, stones, and heavy handspikes. One came in front with a half brick. There was one at each side of me, and one behind me. While I was attending to those in front, and on either side, the one behind ran up with the handspike, and struck me a heavy blow upon the head. It stunned me. I fell, and with this they all ran upon me, and fell to beating me with their fists. I let them lay on for a while, gathering strength. In an instant, I gave a sudden surge, and rose to my hands and knees. Just as I did that, one of the number gave me, with his heavy boot, a powerful kick in the left eye. My eyeball seemed to have burst. When they saw my eye closed, and badly swollen, they left me. With this I seized the handspike, and for a time pursued them. But here the carpenters interfered, and I thought I might as well give it up. It was impossible to stand my hand against so many. All this took place in sight of not less than fifty white ship-carpenters, and not one interposed a friendly word; but some cried, "Kill the damned nigger! Kill him! kill him! He struck a white person." I found my only chance for life was in flight. I succeeded in getting away without an additional blow, and barely so; for to strike a white man is death by Lynch law,[36]—and that was the law in Mr. Gardner's ship-yard; nor is there much of any other out of Mr. Gardner's ship-yard.

I went directly home, and told the story of my wrongs to Master Hugh; and I am happy to say of him, irreligious as he was, his conduct was heavenly, compared with that of his brother Thomas under similar circumstances. He listened attentively to my narration of the circumstances leading to the savage outrage, and gave many proofs of his strong indignation at it. The heart of my once overkind mistress was again melted into pity. My puffed-out eye and blood-covered face moved her to tears. She took a chair by me, washed the blood from my face, and, with a mother's tenderness, bound up my head, covering the wounded eye with a lean piece of fresh beef. It was almost compensation for my suffering to witness, once more, a manifestation of kindness from this, my once affectionate old mistress. Master Hugh was very much enraged. He gave expression to his feelings by pouring out curses upon the heads of those who did the deed. As soon as I got a little the better of my bruises, he took me with him to Esquire Watson's, on Bond Street, to see what could be done about the matter. Mr. Watson inquired who saw the assault committed. Master Hugh told him it was done in Mr. Gardner's ship-yard, at mid-day, where there were a large company of men at work. "As to that," he said, "the deed was done, and there was no question as to who did it." His answer was, he could do nothing in the case, unless some white man would come forward and testify. He could issue no warrant on my word. If I had been killed in the presence of a thousand colored people, their testimony combined would have been insufficient to have arrested one of the murderers. Master Hugh, for once, was compelled to say this state of things was too bad. Of course, it was impossible to get any white man to volunteer his testimony in my behalf, and against the white young men. Even those who may have sympathized with me were not prepared to do this. It required a degree of courage unknown to them to do so; for just at that time, the slightest manifestation of humanity toward a colored person was denounced as abolitionism, and that name subjected its bearer to frightful liabili-

---

[36] To be lynched without benefit of legal procedures. Originally, the term was "Lynch's law," probably after justice of the peace Charles Lynch (1736–1796), who used unconventional methods of trial and punishment.

ties. The watchwords of the bloody-minded in that region, and in those days, were, "Damn the abolitionists!" and "Damn the niggers!" There was nothing done, and probably nothing would have been done if I had been killed. Such was, and such remains, the state of things in the Christian city of Baltimore.

Master Hugh, finding he could get no redress, refused to let me go back again to Mr. Gardner. He kept me himself, and his wife dressed my wound till I was again restored to health. He then took me into the ship-yard of which he was foreman, in the employment of Mr. Walter Price. There I was immediately set to calking, and very soon learned the art of using my mallet and irons. In the course of one year from the time I left Mr. Gardner's, I was able to command the highest wages given to the most experienced calkers. I was now of some importance to my master. I was bringing him from six to seven dollars per week. I sometimes brought him nine dollars per week: my wages were a dollar and a half a day. After learning how to calk, I sought my own employment, made my own contracts, and collected the money which I earned. My pathway became much more smooth than before; my condition was now much more comfortable. When I could get no calking to do, I did nothing. During these leisure times, those old notions about freedom would steal over me again. When in Mr. Gardner's employment, I was kept in such a perpetual whirl of excitement, I could think of nothing, scarcely, but my life; and in thinking of my life, I almost forgot my liberty. I have observed this in my experience of slavery,—that whenever my condition was improved, instead of its increasing my contentment, it only increased my desire to be free, and set me to thinking of plans to gain my freedom. I have found that, to make a contented slave, it is necessary to make a thoughtless one. It is necessary to darken his moral and mental vision, and, as far as possible, to annihilate the power of reason. He must be able to detect no inconsistencies in slavery; he must be made to feel that slavery is right; and he can be brought to that only when he ceases to be a man.

I was now getting, as I have said, one dollar and fifty cents per day. I contracted for it; I earned it; it was paid to me; it was rightfully my own; yet, upon each returning Saturday night, I was compelled to deliver every cent of that money to Master Hugh. And why? Not because he earned it,—not because he had any hand in earning it,—not because I owed it to him,—nor because he possessed the slightest shadow of a right to it; but solely because he had the power to compel me to give it up. The right of the grim-visaged pirate upon the high seas is exactly the same.

CHAPTER XI

I now come to that part of my life during which I planned, and finally succeeded in making, my escape from slavery. But before narrating any of the peculiar circumstances, I deem it proper to make known my intention not to state all the facts connected with the transaction. My reasons for pursuing this course may be understood from the following: First, were I to give a minute statement of all the facts, it is not only possible, but quite probable, that others would thereby be involved in the most embarrassing difficulties. Secondly, such a statement would most undoubtedly induce greater vigilance on the part of slaveholders than has existed heretofore among them; which would, of course, be the means of guarding a door whereby some dear brother bondman might escape his galling chains. I deeply regret the necessity that impels me to suppress any thing of importance connected with my experience in slavery. It would afford me great pleasure indeed, as well as materially add to the interest of my narrative, were I at liberty to gratify a curiosity, which I know exists in the minds of many, by an accurate statement of all the facts pertaining to my most fortunate escape. But I must deprive myself of this pleasure, and the curious of the gratification which such a statement would afford. I would allow myself to suffer under the greatest imputations which evil-minded men might suggest, rather than exculpate myself, and thereby run the hazard of closing the slightest avenue by which a brother slave might clear himself of the chains and fetters of slavery.

I have never approved of the very public manner in which some of our western friends have conducted what they call the *underground railroad*,[37] but which, I think, by their open declarations, has been made most emphatically the *upper-ground railroad*. I honor those good men and women for their noble daring, and applaud them for willingly subjecting themselves to bloody persecution, by openly avowing their participation in the escape of slaves. I, however, can see very little good resulting from such a course, either to themselves or the slaves escaping; while, upon the other hand, I see and feel assured that those open declarations are a positive evil to the slaves remaining, who are seeking to escape. They do nothing towards enlightening the slave, whilst they do much towards enlightening the master. They stimulate him to greater watchfulness, and enhance his power to capture his slave. We owe something to the slaves south of the line as well as to those north of it; and in aiding the latter on their way to freedom, we should be careful to do nothing which would be likely to hinder the former from escaping from slavery. I would keep the merciless slaveholder profoundly ignorant of the means of flight adopted by the slave. I would leave him to imagine himself surrounded by myriads of invisible tormentors, ever ready to snatch from his infernal grasp his trembling prey. Let him be left to feel his way in the dark; let darkness commensurate with his crime hover over him; and let him feel that at every step he takes, in pursuit of the flying bondman, he is running the frightful risk of having his hot brains dashed out by an invisible agency. Let us render the tyrant no aid; let us not hold the light by which he can trace the footprints of our flying brother. But enough of this. I will now proceed to the statement of those facts, connected with my escape, for which I am alone responsible, and for which no one can be made to suffer but myself.

In the early part of the year 1838, I became quite restless. I could see no reason why I should, at the end of each week, pour the reward of my toil into the purse of my master. When I carried to him my weekly wages, he would, after counting the money, look me in the face with a robber-like fierceness, and ask, "Is this all?" He was satisfied with nothing less than the last cent. He would, however, when I made him six dollars, sometimes give me six cents, to encourage me. It had the opposite effect. I regarded it as a sort of admission of my right to the whole. The fact that he gave me any part of my wages was proof, to my mind, that he believed me entitled to the whole of them. I always felt worse for having received any thing; for I feared that the giving me a few cents would ease his conscience, and make him feel himself to be a pretty honorable sort of robber. My discontent grew upon me. I was ever on the look-out for means of escape; and, finding no

---

[37] The method by which many slaves traveled to freedom: moving northward from designated house to designated house and from friend to friend, supposedly in great secrecy. Douglass has some understandable reservations about advertising the procedure.

direct means, I determined to try to hire my time, with a view of getting money with which to make my escape. In the spring of 1838, when Master Thomas came to Baltimore to purchase his spring goods, I got an opportunity, and applied to him to allow me to hire my time. He unhesitatingly refused my request, and told me this was another stratagem by which to escape. He told me I could go nowhere but that he could get me; and that, in the event of my running away, he should spare no pains in his efforts to catch me. He exhorted me to content myself, and be obedient. He told me, if I would be happy, I must lay out no plans for the future. He said, if I behaved myself properly, he would take care of me. Indeed, he advised me to complete thoughtlessness of the future, and taught me to depend solely upon him for happiness. He seemed to see fully the pressing necessity of setting aside my intellectual nature, in order to contentment in slavery. But in spite of him, and even in spite of myself, I continued to think, and to think about the injustice of my enslavement, and the means of escape.

About two months after this, I applied to Master Hugh for the privilege of hiring my time. He was not acquainted with the fact that I had applied to Master Thomas, and had been refused. He too, at first, seemed disposed to refuse; but, after some reflection, he granted me the privilege, and proposed the following terms: I was to be allowed all my time, make all contracts with those for whom I worked, and find my own employment; and, in return for this liberty, I was to pay him three dollars at the end of each week; find myself in calking tools, and in board and clothing. My board was two dollars and a half per week. This, with the wear and tear of clothing and calking tools, made my regular expenses about six dollars per week. This amount I was compelled to make up, or relinquish the privilege of hiring my time. Rain or shine, work or no work, at the end of each week the money must be forthcoming, or I must give up my privilege. This arrangement, it will be perceived, was decidedly in my master's favor. It relieved him of all need of looking after me. His money was sure. He received all the benefits of slaveholding without its evils; while I endured all the evils of a slave, and suffered all the care and anxiety of a freeman. I found it a hard bargain. But, hard as it was, I thought it better than the old mode of getting along. It was a step towards freedom to be allowed to bear the responsibilities of a freeman, and I was determined to hold on upon it. I bent myself to the work of making money. I was ready to work at night as well as day, and by the most untiring perseverance and industry, I made enough to meet my expenses, and lay up a little money every week. I went on thus from May till August. Master Hugh then refused to allow me to hire my time longer. The ground for his refusal was a failure on my part, one Saturday night, to pay him for my week's time. This failure was occasioned by my attending a camp meeting about ten miles from Baltimore. During the week, I had entered into an engagement with a number of young friends to start from Baltimore to the camp ground early Saturday evening; and being detained by my employer, I was unable to get down to Master Hugh's without disappointing the company. I knew that Master Hugh was in no special need of the money that night. I therefore decided to go to camp meeting, and upon my return pay him the three dollars. I staid at the camp meeting one day longer than I intended when I left. But as soon as I returned, I called upon him to pay what he considered his due. I found him very angry; he could scarce restrain his wrath. He said he had a great mind to give me a severe whipping. He wished to know how I dared go out of the city without asking his permission. I told him I hired my time, and while I paid him the price which he asked for it, I did not know that I was bound to ask him when and where I should go. This reply troubled him; and, after reflecting a few moments, he turned to me, and said I should hire my time no longer; that the next thing he should know of, I would be running away. Upon the same plea, he told me to bring my tools and clothing home forthwith. I did so; but instead of seeking work, as I had been accustomed to do previously to hiring my time, I spent the whole week without the performance of a single stroke of work. I did this in retaliation. Saturday night, he called upon me as usual for my week's wages. I told him I had no wages; I had done no work that week. Here we were upon the point of coming to blows. He raved, and swore his determination to get hold of me. I did not allow myself a single word; but was resolved, if he laid the weight of his hand upon me, it should be blow for blow. He did not strike me, but told me that he would find me in constant employment in future. I thought the matter over during the next day, Sunday, and finally resolved upon the third day of September, as the day upon which I would make a second attempt to secure my freedom. I now had three weeks during which to prepare for my journey. Early on Monday morning, before Master Hugh had time to make any engagement for me, I went out and got employment of Mr. Butler, at his ship-yard near the draw-bridge, upon what is called the City Block, thus making it unnecessary for him to seek employment for me. At the end of the week, I brought him between eight and nine dollars. He seemed very well pleased, and asked me why I did not do the same the week before. He little knew what my plans were. My object in working steadily was to remove any suspicion he might entertain of my intent to run away; and in this I succeeded admirably. I suppose he thought I was never better satisfied with my condition than at the very time during which I was planning my escape. The second week passed, and again I carried him my full wages; and so well pleased was he, that he gave me twenty-five cents, (quite a large sum for a slaveholder to give a slave,) and bade me to make a good use of it. I told him I would.

Things went on without very smoothly indeed, but within there was trouble. It is impossible for me to describe my feelings as the time of my contemplated start drew near. I had a number of warm-hearted friends in Baltimore,—friends that I loved almost as I did my life,—and the thought of being separated from them forever was painful beyond expression. It is my opinion that thousands would escape from slavery, who now remain, but for the strong cords of affection that bind them to their friends. The thought of leaving my friends was decidedly the most painful thought with which I had to contend. The love of them was my tender point, and shook my decision more than all things else. Besides the pain of separation, the dream and apprehension of a failure exceeded what I had experienced at my first attempt. The appalling defeat I then sustained returned to torment me. I felt assured that, if I failed in this attempt, my case would be a hopeless one—it would seal my fate as a slave forever. I could not hope to get off with any thing less than the severest punishment, and being placed beyond the means of escape. It required no very vivid imagination to depict the most frightful scenes through which I should have to pass, in case I failed. The wretchedness of slavery, and the blessedness of freedom, were perpetually before me. It was life and death with me. But I remained firm, and, according to my resolution, on the third day of September, 1838, I left my chains, and succeeded in reaching New York without the slightest interruption of any kind. How I did so,—what means I adopted,—what direction I travelled, and by what mode of conveyance,—I must leave unexplained, for the reasons before mentioned.

I have been frequently asked how I felt when I found myself in a free State. I have never been able to answer the question with any satisfaction to myself. It was a moment of the highest excitement I ever experienced. I suppose I felt as one may imagine the unarmed mariner to feel when he is rescued by a friendly man-of-war from the pursuit of a pirate. In writing to a dear friend, immediately after my arrival at New York, I said I felt like one who had escaped a den of hungry lions. This state of mind, however, very soon subsided; and I was again seized with a feeling of great insecurity and loneliness. I was yet liable to be taken back, and subjected to all the tortures of slavery. This in itself was enough to damp the ardor of my enthusiasm. But the loneliness overcame me. There I was in the midst of thousands, and yet a perfect stranger; without home and without friends, in the midst of thousands of my own brethren—children of a common Father, and yet I dared not to unfold to any one of them my sad condition. I was afraid to speak to any one for fear of speaking to the wrong one, and thereby falling into the hands of money-loving kidnappers, whose business it was to lie in wait for the panting fugitive, as the ferocious beasts of the forest lie in wait for their prey. The motto which I adopted when I started from slavery was this—"Trust no man!" I saw in every white man an enemy, and in almost every colored man cause for distrust. It was a most painful situation; and, to understand it, one must needs experience it, or imagine himself in similar circumstances. Let him be a fugitive slave in a strange land—a land given up to be the hunting-ground for slaveholders—whose inhabitants are legalized kidnappers—where he is every moment subjected to the terrible liability of being seized upon by his fellow-men, as the hideous crocodile seizes upon his prey!—I say, let him place himself in my situation—without home or friends—without money or credit—wanting shelter, and no one to give it—wanting bread, and no money to buy it,—and at the same time let him feel that he is pursued by merciless men-hunters, and in total darkness as to what to do, where to go, or where to stay,—perfectly helpless both as to the means of defence and means of escape,—in the midst of plenty, yet suffering the terrible gnawings of hunger,—in the midst of houses, yet having no home,—among fellow-men, yet feeling as if in the midst of wild beasts, whose greediness to swallow up the trembling and half-famished fugitive is only equalled by that with which the monsters of the deep swallow up the helpless fish upon which they subsist,—I say, let him be placed in this most trying situation,—the situation in which I was placed,—then, and not till then, will he fully appreciate the hardships of, and know how to sympathize with, the toil-worn and whip-scarred fugitive slave.

Thank Heaven, I remained but a short time in this distressed situation. I was relieved from it by the humane hand of Mr. David Ruggles,[38] whose vigilance, kindness, and perseverance, I shall never forget. I am glad of an opportunity to express, as far as words can, the love and gratitude I bear him. Mr. Ruggles is now afflicted with blindness, and is himself in need of the same kind offices which he was once so forward in the performance of toward others. I had been in New York but a few days, when Mr. Ruggles sought me out, and very kindly took me to his boarding-house at the corner of Church and Lespenard Streets. Mr.

[38] Ruggles (1810–1849), an African-American journalist and abolitionist, aided Douglass in his escape from Maryland in 1838, took him into his home, and made arrangements for his wedding before Douglass and his wife went on to New Bedford. Ruggles was also involved in a legal proceeding involving John P. Darg (1771–1852), a slaveowner who was trying to reclaim escaped slaves.

Ruggles was then very deeply engaged in the memorable *Darg* case, as well as attending to a number of other fugitive slaves, devising ways and means for their successful escape; and, though watched and hemmed in on almost every side, he seemed to be more than a match for his enemies.

Very soon after I went to Mr. Ruggles, he wished to know of me where I wanted to go; as he deemed it unsafe for me to remain in New York. I told him I was a calker, and should like to go where I could get work. I thought of going to Canada; but he decided against it, and in favor of my going to New Bedford, thinking I should be able to get work there at my trade. At this time, Anna,[39] my intended wife, came on; for I wrote to her immediately after my arrival at New York, (notwithstanding my homeless, houseless, and helpless condition,) informing her of my successful flight, and wishing her to come on forthwith. In a few days after her arrival, Mr. Ruggles called in the Rev. J. W. C. Pennington, who, in the presence of Mr. Ruggles, Mrs. Michaels, and two or three others, performed the marriage ceremony, and gave us a certificate, of which the following is an exact copy:—

"THIS may certify, that I joined together in holy matrimony Frederick Johnson[40] and Anna Murray, as man and wife, in the presence of Mr. David Ruggles and Mrs. Michaels.
"JAMES W. C. PENNINGTON.
"New York, Sept. 15, 1838."

Upon receiving this certificate, and a five-dollar bill from Mr. Ruggles, I shouldered one part of our baggage, and Anna took up the other, and we set out forthwith to take passage on board of the steamboat John W. Richmond for Newport, on our way to New Bedford. Mr. Ruggles gave me a letter to a Mr. Shaw in Newport, and told me, in case my money did not serve me to New Bedford, to stop in Newport and obtain further assistance; but upon our arrival at Newport, we were so anxious to get to a place of safety, that, notwithstanding we lacked the necessary money to pay our fare, we decided to take seats in the stage, and promise to pay when we got to New Bedford. We were encouraged to do this by two excellent gentlemen, residents of New Bedford, whose names I afterward ascertained to be Joseph Ricketson and William C. Taber. They seemed at once to understand our circumstances, and gave us such assurance of their friendliness as put us fully at ease in their presence. It was good indeed to meet with such friends, at such a time. Upon reaching New Bedford, we were directed to the house of Mr. Nathan Johnson, by whom we were kindly received, and hospitably provided for. Both Mr. and Mrs. Johnson took a deep and lively interest in our welfare. They proved themselves quite worthy of the name of abolitionists. When the stagedriver found us unable to pay our fare, he held on upon our baggage as security for the debt. I had but to mention the fact to Mr. Johnson, and he forthwith advanced the money.

We now began to feel a degree of safety, and to prepare ourselves for the duties and responsibilities of a life of freedom. On the morning after our arrival at New Bedford, while at the breakfast-table, the question arose as to what name I should be called by. The name given me by my mother, was "Frederick Augustus Wash-

---

[39] Douglass's note: "She was free."
[40] Douglass's note: "I had changed my name from Frederick *Bailey* to that of *Johnson*."

ington Bailey." I, however, had dispensed with the two middle names long before I left Maryland so that I was generally known by the name of "Frederick Bailey." I started from Baltimore bearing the name of "Stanley." When I got to New York, I again changed my name to "Frederick Johnson," and thought that would be the last change. But when I got to New Bedford, I found it necessary again to change my name. The reason of this necessity was, that there were so many Johnsons in New Bedford, it was already quite difficult to distinguish between them. I gave Mr. Johnson the privilege of choosing me a name, but told him he must not take from me the name of "Frederick." I must hold on to that, to preserve a sense of my identity. Mr. Johnson had just been reading the "Lady of the Lake," and at once suggested that my name be "Douglass."[41] From that time until now I have been called "Frederick Douglass;" and as I am more widely known by that name than by either of the others, I shall continue to use it as my own.

I was quite disappointed at the general appearance of things in New Bedford. The impression which I had received respecting the character and condition of the people of the north, I found to be singularly erroneous. I had very strangely supposed, while in slavery, that few of the comforts, and scarcely any of the luxuries, of life were enjoyed at the north, compared with what were enjoyed by the slaveholders of the south. I probably came to this conclusion from the fact that northern people owned no slaves. I supposed that they were about upon a level with the non-slaveholding population of the south. I knew *they* were exceedingly poor, and I had been accustomed to regard their poverty as the necessary consequence of their being non-slaveholders. I had somehow imbibed the opinion that, in the absence of slaves, there could be no wealth, and very little refinement. And upon coming to the north, I expected to meet with a rough, hard-handed, and uncultivated population, living in the most Spartan-like simplicity, knowing nothing of the ease, luxury, pomp, and grandeur of southern slaveholders. Such being my conjectures, any one acquainted with the appearance of New Bedford may very readily infer how palpably I must have seen my mistake.

In the afternoon of the day when I reached New Bedford, I visited the wharves, to take a view of the shipping. Here I found myself surrounded with the strongest proofs of wealth. Lying at the wharves, and riding in the stream, I saw many ships of the finest model, in the best order, and of the largest size. Upon the right and left, I was walled in by granite warehouses of the widest dimensions, stowed to their utmost capacity with the necessaries and comforts of life. Added to this, almost every body seemed to be at work, but noiselessly so, compared with what I had been accustomed to in Baltimore. There were no loud songs heard from those engaged in loading and unloading ships. I heard no deep oaths or horrid curses on the laborer. I saw no whipping of men; but all seemed to go smoothly on. Every man appeared to understand his work, and went at it with a sober, yet cheerful earnestness, which betokened the deep interest which he felt in what he was doing, as well as a sense of his own dignity as a man. To me this looked exceedingly strange. From the wharves I strolled around and over the town, gazing with wonder and admiration at the splendid churches, beautiful dwellings, and finely-cultivated gardens; evincing an amount of wealth, comfort, taste, and refinement, such as I had never seen in any part of slaveholding Maryland.

Every thing looked clean, new, and beautiful. I saw few or no dilapidated

---

[41] A central character in the narrative poem *The Lady of the Lake* (1810), by the British poet and novelist Sir Walter Scott (1771–1832).

houses, with poverty-stricken inmates; no half-naked children and barefooted women, such as I had been accustomed to see in Hillsborough, Easton, St. Michael's, and Baltimore. The people looked more able, stronger, healthier, and happier, than those of Maryland. I was for once made glad by a view of extreme wealth, without being saddened by seeing extreme poverty. But the most astonishing as well as the most interesting thing to me was the condition of the colored people, a great many of whom, like myself, had escaped thither as a refuge from the hunters of men. I found many, who had not been seven years out of their chains, living in finer houses, and evidently enjoying more of the comforts of life, than the average of slaveholders in Maryland. I will venture to assert that my friend Mr. Nathan Johnson (of whom I can say with a grateful heart, "I was hungry, and he gave me meat; I was thirsty, and he gave me drink; I was a stranger, and he took me in"[42]) lived in a neater house; dined at a better table; took, paid for, and read, more newspapers; better understood the moral, religious, and political character of the nation,—than nine tenths of the slaveholders in Talbot county Maryland. Yet Mr. Johnson was a working man. His hands were hardened by toil, and not his alone, but those also of Mrs. Johnson. I found the colored people much more spirited than I had supposed they would be. I found among them a determination to protect each other from the blood-thirsty kidnapper, at all hazards. Soon after my arrival, I was told of a circumstance which illustrated their spirit. A colored man and a fugitive slave were on unfriendly terms. The former was heard to threaten the latter with informing his master of his whereabouts. Straightway a meeting was called among the colored people, under the stereotyped notice, "Business of importance!" The betrayer was invited to attend. The people came at the appointed hour, and organized the meeting by appointing a very religious old gentleman as president, who, I believe, made a prayer, after which he addressed the meeting as follows: *"Friends, we have got him here, and I would recommend that you young men just take him outside the door, and kill him!"* With this, a number of them bolted at him; but they were intercepted by some more timid than themselves, and the betrayer escaped their vengeance, and has not been seen in New Bedford since. I believe there have been no more such threats, and should there be hereafter, I doubt not that death would be the consequence.

I found employment, the third day after my arrival, in stowing a sloop with a load of oil. It was new, dirty, and hard work for me; but I went at it with a glad heart and a willing hand. I was now my own master. It was a happy moment, the rapture of which can be understood only by those who have been slaves. It was the first work, the reward of which was to be entirely my own. There was no Master Hugh standing ready, the moment I earned the money, to rob me of it. I worked that day with a pleasure I had never before experienced. I was at work for myself and newly-married wife. It was to me the starting-point of a new existence. When I got through with that job, I went in pursuit of a job of calking; but such was the strength of prejudice against color, among the white calkers, that they refused to work with me, and of course I could get no employment.[43] Finding my trade of no immediate benefit, I threw off my calking habiliments, and prepared myself to do any kind of work I could get to do. Mr. Johnson kindly let me have his wood-

---

[42] From Matthew 25:35.
[43] Douglass's note: "I am told that colored persons can now get employment at calking in New Bedford—a result of anti-slavery effort."

horse and saw, and I very soon found myself a plenty of work. There was no work too hard—none too dirty. I was ready to saw wood, shovel coal, carry the hod, sweep the chimney, or roll oil casks,—all of which I did for nearly three years in New Bedford, before I became known to the anti-slavery world.

In about four months after I went to New Bedford, there came a young man to me, and inquired if I did not wish to take the "Liberator."[44] I told him I did; but, just having made my escape from slavery, I remarked that I was unable to pay for it then. I, however, finally became a subscriber to it. The paper came, and I read it from week to week with such feelings as it would be quite idle for me to attempt to describe. The paper became my meat and my drink. My soul was set all on fire. Its sympathy for my brethren in bonds—its scathing denunciations of slaveholders—its faithful exposures of slavery—and its powerful attacks upon the upholders of the institution—sent a thrill of joy through my soul, such as I had never felt before!

I had not long been a reader of the "Liberator," before I got a pretty correct idea of the principles, measures and spirit of the anti-slavery reform. I took right hold of the cause. I could do but little; but what I could, I did with a joyful heart, and never felt happier than when in an anti-slavery meeting. I seldom had much to say at the meetings, because what I wanted to say was said so much better by others. But, while attending an anti-slavery convention at Nantucket, on the 11th of August, 1841, I felt strongly moved to speak, and was at the same time much urged to do so by Mr. William C. Coffin, a gentleman who had heard me speak in the colored people's meeting at New Bedford. It was a severe cross, and I took it up reluctantly. The truth was, I felt myself a slave, and the idea of speaking to white people weighed me down. I spoke but a few moments, when I felt a degree of freedom, and said what I desired with considerable ease. From that time until now, I have been engaged in pleading the cause of my brethren—with what success, and with what devotion, I leave those acquainted with my labors to decide.

APPENDIX

I find, since reading over the foregoing Narrative that I have, in several instances, spoken in such a tone and manner, respecting religion, as may possibly lead those unacquainted with my religious views to suppose me an opponent of all religion. To remove the liability of such misapprehension, I deem it proper to append the following brief explanation. What I have said respecting and against religion, I mean strictly to apply to the *slaveholding religion* of this land, and with no possible reference to Christianity proper; for, between the Christianity of this land, and the Christianity of Christ, I recognize the widest possible difference—so wide, that to receive the one as good, pure, and holy, is of necessity to reject the other as bad, corrupt, and wicked. To be the friend of the one, is of necessity to be the enemy of the other. I love the pure, peaceable, and impartial Christianity of Christ: I therefore hate the corrupt, slaveholding, women-whipping, cradle-plundering, partial and hypocritical Christianity of this land. Indeed, I can see no rea-

---

[44] The best-known publication of the abolitionist movement, *The Liberator* first appeared in January 1831; in 1838 it had a circulation of about 1500 (including many African Americans) that grew to approximately 3000 in the 1850s. The last issue was published upon the ratification of the Thirteenth Amendment in 1865.

son, but the most deceitful one, for calling the religion of this land Christianity. I look upon it as the climax of all misnomers, the boldest of all frauds, and the grossest of all libels. Never was there a clearer case of "stealing the livery of the court of heaven to serve the devil in." I am filled with unutterable loathing when I contemplate the religious pomp and show, together with the horrible inconsistencies, which every where surround me. We have men-stealers for ministers, women-whippers for missionaries, and cradle-plunderers for church members. The man who wields the blood-clotted cowskin during the week fills the pulpit on Sunday, and claims to be a minister of the meek and lowly Jesus. The man who robs me of my earnings at the end of each week meets me as a class-leader on Sunday morning, to show me the way of life, and the path of salvation. He who sells my sister, for purposes of prostitution, stands forth as the pious advocate of purity. He who proclaims it a religious duty to read the Bible denies me the right of learning to read the name of the God who made me. He who is the religious advocate of marriage robs whole millions of its sacred influence, and leaves them to the ravages of wholesale pollution. The warm defender of the sacredness of the family relation is the same that scatters whole families,—sundering husbands and wives, parents and children, sisters and brothers,—leaving the hut vacant, and the hearth desolate. We see the thief preaching against theft, and the adulterer against adultery. We have men sold to build churches, women sold to support the gospel, and babes sold to purchase Bibles for the *poor heathen! all for the glory of God and the good of souls!* The slave auctioneer's bell and the church-going bell chime in with each other, and the bitter cries of the heart-broken slave are drowned in the religious shouts of his pious master. Revivals of religion and revivals in the slave-trade go hand in hand together. The slave prison and the church stand near each other. The clanking of fetters and the rattling of chains in the prison, and the pious psalm and solemn prayer in the church, may be heard at the same time. The dealers in the bodies and souls of men erect their stand in the presence of the pulpit, and they mutually help each other. The dealer gives his blood-stained gold to support the pulpit, and the pulpit, in return, covers his infernal business with the garb of Christianity. Here we have religion and robbery the allies of each other— devils dressed in angels' robes, and hell presenting the semblance of paradise.

"Just God! and these are they,
    Who minister at thine altar, God of right!
Men who their hands, with prayer and blessing, lay
    On Israel's ark of light.[45]

"What! preach, and kidnap men?
    Give thanks, and rob thy own afflicted poor?
Talk of thy glorious liberty, and then
    Bolt hard the captive's door?

"What! servants of thy own
    Merciful Son, who came to seek and save
The homeless and the outcast, fettering down
    The tasked and plundered slave!

[45] The ark of the covenant, which is said to contain the word of God, the Torah.

"Pilate and Herod[46] friends!
Chief priests and rulers, as of old, combine!
Just God and holy! is that church which lends
Strength to the spoiler thine?"[47]

The Christianity of America is a Christianity, of whose votaries it may be as truly said, as it was of the ancient scribes and Pharisees,[48] "They bind heavy burdens, and grievous to be borne, and lay them on men's shoulders, but they themselves will not move them with one of their fingers. All their works they do for to be seen of men.——They love the uppermost rooms at feasts, and the chief seats in the synagogues, ... and to be called of men, Rabbi, Rabbi.—— But woe unto you, scribes and Pharisees, hypocrites! for ye shut up the kingdom of heaven against men; for ye neither go in yourselves, neither suffer ye them that are entering to go in. Ye devour widows' houses, and for a pretence make long prayers; therefore ye shall receive the greater damnation. Ye compass sea and land to make one proselyte, and when he is made, ye make him twofold more the child of hell than yourselves.——Woe unto you, scribes and Pharisees, hypocrites! for ye pay tithe of mint, and anise, and cumin, and have omitted the weightier matters of the law, judgment, mercy, and faith; these ought ye to have done, and not to leave the other undone. Ye blind guides! which strain at a gnat, and swallow a camel. Woe unto you, scribes and Pharisees, hypocrites! for ye make clean the outside of the cup and of the platter; but within, they are full of extortion and excess.——Woe unto you, scribes and Pharisees, hypocrites! for ye are like unto whited sepulchres, which indeed appear beautiful outward, but are within full of dead men's bones and of all uncleanness. Even so ye also outwardly appear righteous unto men, but within ye are full of hypocrisy and iniquity."[49]

Dark and terrible as is this picture, I hold it to be strictly true of the overwhelming mass of professed Christians in America. They strain at a gnat, and swallow a camel. Could any thing be more true of our churches? They would be shocked at the proposition of fellowshipping a *sheep*-stealer; and at the same time they hug to their communion a *man*-stealer, and brand me with being an infidel, if I find fault with them for it. They attend with Pharisaical strictness to the outward forms of religion, and at the same time neglect the weightier matters of the law, judgment, mercy, and faith. They are always ready to sacrifice, but seldom to show mercy. They are they who are represented as professing to love God whom they have not seen, whilst they hate their brother whom they have seen. They love the heathen on the other side of the globe. They can pray for him, pay money to have the Bible put into his hand, and missionaries to instruct him; while they despise and totally neglect the heathen at their own doors.

Such is, very briefly, my view of the religion of this land; and to avoid any misunderstanding, growing out of the use of general terms, I mean, by the religion of this land, that which is revealed in the words, deeds, and actions, of those

---

[46] Pontius Pilate, the Roman procurator of Judea who gave Jesus up to be crucified; Herod Antipater, the local ruler of Galilee who had the head of John the Baptist brought on a platter to his stepdaughter, Salome.

[47] From John Greenleaf Whittier's poem "Clerical Oppressors" (1835?).

[48] Biblical scholars who taught Jewish law and edited and interpreted the Bible, and members of an influential Jewish sect who prided themselves on strict observance of traditional religious laws.

[49] From Matthew 23, Jesus' denunciation of the hypocrisy of the scribes and Pharisees.

bodies, north and south, calling themselves Christian churches, and yet in union with slaveholders. It is against religion, as presented by these bodies, that I have felt it my duty to testify.

I conclude these remarks by copying the following portrait of the religion of the south, (which is, by communion and fellowship, the religion of the north,) which I soberly affirm is "true to the life," and without caricature or the slightest exaggeration. It is said to have been drawn, several years before the present anti-slavery agitation began, by a northern Methodist preacher, who, while residing at the south, had an opportunity to see slaveholding morals, manners, and piety, with his own eyes. "Shall I not visit for these things? said the Lord. Shall not my soul be avenged on such a nation as this?"[50]

"A PARODY"[51]

"Come, saints and sinners, hear me tell
How pious priests whip Jack and Nell,
And women buy and children sell,
And preach all sinners down to hell,
    And sing of heavenly union.

"They'll bleat and baa, dona like goats,
Gorge down black sheep, and strain at motes,
Array their backs in fine black coats,
Then seize their negroes by their throats
    And choke, for heavenly union.

"They'll church you if you sip a dram,
And damn you if you steal a lamb;
Yet rob old Tony, Doll, and Sam,
Of human rights, and bread and ham;
    Kidnapper's heavenly union.

"They'll loudly talk of Christ's reward,
And bind his image with a cord,
And scold, and swing the lash abhorred,
And sell their brother in the Lord
    To handcuffed heavenly union.

"They'll read and sing a sacred song,
And make a prayer both loud and long,
And teach the right and do the wrong,
Hailing the brother, sister throng,
    With words of heavenly union.

"We wonder how such saints can sing,
Or praise the Lord upon the wing,
Who roar, and scold, and whip, and sting,

---

[50] From Jeremiah 5:9.
[51] Douglass's parody of "Heavenly Union," a hymn popular in many southern churches at the time.

And to their slaves and mammon cling,
  In guilty conscience union.

"They'll raise tobacco, corn, and rye,
And drive, and thieve, and cheat, and lie,
And lay up treasures in the sky,
By making switch and cowskin fly,
  In hope of heavenly union.

"They'll crack old Tony on the skull,
And preach and roar like Bashan bull,[52]
Or braying ass, of mischief full,
Then seize old Jacob by the wool,
  And pull for heavenly union.

"A roaring, ranting, sleek man-thief,
Who lived on mutton, veal, and beef,
Yet never would afford relief
To needy, sable sons of grief,
  Was big with heavenly union.

"'Love not the world,' the preacher said,
And winked his eye, and shook his head;
He seized on Tom, and Dick, and Ned,
Cut short their meat, and clothes, and bread,
  Yet still loved heavenly union.

"Another preacher whining spoke
Of One whose heart for sinners broke:
He tied old Nanny to an oak,
And drew the blood at every stroke,
  And prayed for heavenly union.

"Two others oped their iron jaws,
And waved their children-stealing paws;
There sat their children in gewgaws;
By stinting negroes' backs and maws,
  They kept up heavenly union.

"All good from Jack another takes,
And entertains their flirts and rakes,
Who dress as sleek as glossy snakes,
And cram their mouths with sweetened cakes;
  And this goes down for union."

Sincerely and earnestly hoping that this little book may do something toward throwing light on the American slave system, and hastening the glad day of deliv-

---

[52] Powerful bulls mentioned in the Old Testament.

erance to the millions of my brethren in bonds—faithfully relying upon the power of truth, love, and justice, for success in my humble efforts—and solemnly pledging my self anew to the sacred cause,—I subscribe myself,

FREDERICK DOUGLASS.

1845

—Lynn, Mass., April 28, 1845.

An 1862 photograph by Henry P. Moore showing slaves planting sweet potatoes in South Carolina. Southern plantations were dependent on the forced labor of African Americans.

Harriet Jacobs
(1813–1897)

Harriet Ann Jacobs's *Incidents in the Life of a Slave Girl: Written by Herself* (1861) is a rare narrative that explores what it was to be a black female slave in an American society dominated by white males. The first edition—with an author's preface signed by Linda

Brent, Jacobs's persona, and an editor's introduction by Lydia Maria Child, the well-known abolitionist—was published without attribution to Jacobs. Earlier, Jacobs had tried to publish the work herself, without success; it appeared only with the help of Child.

Jacobs was born a slave in Edenton, North Carolina, in 1813. Orphaned as a child, she later became the property of three-year-old Matilda Norcom, whose father, James Norcom, was a physician with licentious propensities. To protect herself from his advances, Jacobs became sexually involved with a young white lawyer, Samuel Tredwell Sawyer, when she was sixteen and gave birth to two children. Her attempts to avoid victimization, however, only stoked the sexual desires of Dr. Norcom, whose wife became increasingly jealous of the attention he paid to the young slave. In desperation Jacobs was driven to hide in a boxlike crawlspace in the attic of her grandmother's house, where she stayed for seven years. She emerged only occasionally, spending most of her time reading and sewing, and finding solace in watching her children, who had been sold to their father, grow. When she fled to the North in 1842 and laid claim to her children, Dr. Norcom still posed a threat until Jacobs's freedom was purchased by the woman for whom she worked as a babysitter, Cornelia Grinnell Willis (the second Mrs. Nathaniel Willis), in 1852. Several years earlier Jacobs had met the Quaker reformer Amy Post, whose encouragement gradually led Jacobs to overcome a feeling of shame and to make her experience as a slave woman public. The resulting book, *Incidents,* brought Jacobs recognition and security. She then worked for the poor as a representative of Quakers from Philadelphia and New York and organized nursing homes and orphanages for African Americans in Savannah, Georgia. She returned North in 1868, living with her daughter until Jacobs's death in 1897.

Jacobs's persona in *Incidents,* Linda Brent, is an African-American woman struggling for freedom. Like Jacobs she proves her spirit and integrity by refusing to be seduced by a powerful and persistent master, Dr. Flint. Not only does she defy her tormentor from her coffinlike cell—she defeats him. The cell, which suggests woman's immobility, contrasts sharply with the image of running prevalent in male slave narratives. Linked with the book's main concern of freedom are issues of motherhood, domesticity, and female community. In other words, whereas *Incidents* is a slave narrative, it is also a sentimental novel clearly intended for a female audience. Its appeal lies in its depiction of male tyranny corrupting domestic values—an evil that threatens all women, not just slaves. As the editor Jean Fagan Yellin has observed, *Incidents* not only condemns American racism but challenges the patriarchy that generates it. And it does so in the voice of a woman who, by publicizing her painful experience, brought a hitherto forbidden topic—the sexual abuse of slave women—into public discussions of slavery.

Suggested Readings: *Incidents in the Life of a Slave Girl. Told by Herself,* ed. L. M. Child, 1861. J. F. Yellin, ed., *Incidents in the Life of a Slave Girl. Written by Herself,* 1987. J. Fetterley, "Harriet Jacobs," in *Provisions: A Reader From 19th-Century American Women,* 1985. W. L. Andrews, *To Tell a Free Story: The First Century of Afro-American Autobiography, 1760–1865,* 1986. H. Carby, *Reconstructing Womanhood,* 1987. V. Smith. *Self-Discovery and Authority in Afro-American Narrative,* 1988.

Test Used: *Incidents in the Life of a Slave Girl,* intro. by V. Smith, 1988.

from INCIDENTS IN THE LIFE OF A SLAVE GIRL*

Written by Herself

PREFACE BY THE AUTHOR

Reader, be assured this narrative is no fiction. I am aware that some of my adventures may seem incredible; but they are, nevertheless, strictly true. I have not exaggerated the wrongs inflicted by Slavery; on the contrary, my descriptions fall far short of the facts. I have concealed the names of places, and given persons fictitious names. I had no motive for secrecy on my own account, but I deemed it kind and considerate towards others to pursue this course.

I wish I were more competent to the task I have undertaken. But I trust my readers will excuse deficiencies in consideration of circumstances. I was born and reared in Slavery; and I remained in a Slave State[1] twenty-seven years. Since I have been at the North it has been necessary for me to work diligently for my own support, and the education of my children. This has not left me much leisure to make up for the loss of early opportunities to improve myself; and it has compelled me to write these pages at irregular intervals, whenever I could snatch an hour from household duties.

When I first arrived in Philadelphia, Bishop Paine[2] advised me to publish a sketch of my life, but I told him I was altogether incompetent to such an undertaking. Though I have improved my mind somewhat since that time, I still remain of the same opinion; but I trust my motives will excuse what might otherwise seem presumptuous. I have not written my experiences in order to attract attention to myself; on the contrary, it would have been more pleasant to me to have been silent about my own history. Neither do I care to excite sympathy for my own sufferings. But I do earnestly desire to arouse the women of the North to a realizing sense of the condition of two millions of women at the South, still in bondage, suffering what I suffered, and most of them far worse. I want to add my testimony to that of abler pens to convince the people of the Free States what Slavery really is. Only by experience can any one realize how deep, and dark, and foul is that pit of abominations.[3] May the blessing of God rest on this imperfect effort in behalf of my persecuted people!

LINDA BRENT[4]

---

* An autobiographical narrative, first published privately in 1861.   [1] North Carolina.
[2] Daniel A. Payne (1811–1893), elected bishop of the African Methodist Episcopal church in 1852 and later president of Wilberforce University in Ohio; he met Jacobs in 1842.
[3] "He brought me . . . out of an horrible pit, out of the miry clay, and set my feet upon a rock . . . ," from Psalm 40:2.
[4] Jacobs's persona in this narrative, an enabling literary strategy that made the telling of the story possible.

Introduction by the Editor*

The author of the following autobiography is personally known to me, and her conversation and manners inspire me with confidence. During the last seventeen years, she has lived the greater part of the time with a distinguished family in New York,[1] and has so deported herself as to be highly esteemed by them. This fact is sufficient, without further credentials of her character. I believe those who know her will not be disposed to doubt her veracity, though some incidents in her story are more romantic than fiction.

At her request, I have revised her manuscript; but such changes as I have made have been mainly for purposes of condensation and orderly arrangement. I have not added any thing to the incidents, or changed the import of her very pertinent remarks. With trifling exceptions, both the ideas and the language are her own. I pruned excrescences a little, but otherwise I had no reason for changing her lively and dramatic way of telling her own story. The names of both persons and places are known to me; but for good reasons I suppress them.

It will naturally excite surprise that a woman reared in Slavery should be able to write so well. But circumstances will explain this. In the first place, nature endowed her with quick perceptions. Secondly, the mistress, with whom she lived till she was twelve years old, was a kind, considerate friend, who taught her to read and spell. Thirdly, she was placed in favorable circumstances after she came to the North; having frequent intercourse with intelligent persons, who felt a friendly interest in her welfare, and were disposed to give her opportunities for self-improvement.

I am well aware that many will accuse me of indecorum for presenting these pages to the public; for the experiences of this intelligent and much-injured woman belong to a class which some call delicate subjects, and others indelicate. This peculiar phase of Slavery has generally been kept veiled; but the public ought to be made acquainted with its monstrous features, and I willingly take the responsibility of presenting them with the veil withdrawn. I do this for the sake of my sisters in bondage, who are suffering wrongs so foul, that our ears are too delicate to listen to them. I do it with the hope of arousing conscientious and reflecting women at the North to a sense of their duty in the exertion of moral influence on the question of Slavery, on all possible occasions. I do it with the hope that every man who reads this narrative will swear solemnly before God that, so far as he has power to prevent it, no fugitive from Slavery shall ever be sent back to suffer in that loathsome den of corruption and cruelty.

L. Maria Child.

---

* Lydia Maria Child (1802–1880), an author, reformer, and editor who met Jacobs in 1860; she agreed to write this introduction as a way of getting Jacobs's story published, lending her well-known name to the work of an unknown writer. But the publisher who set this condition went out of business, and *Incidents* was privately published with Child's introduction in 1861.

[1] The family of Nathaniel P. Willis (1806–1867), an editor, critic, and writer and the brother of Sara Payson Willis (better known as Fanny Fern), and Cornelia Grinnell Willis, who purchased Jacobs's freedom in 1852 for $300 to make sure she would no longer be harassed by her former owners.

I: CHILDHOOD

I was born a slave; but I never knew it till six years of happy childhood had passed away. My father[1] was a carpenter, and considered so intelligent and skilful in his trade, that, when buildings out of the common line were to be erected, he was sent for from long distances, to be head workman. On condition of paying his mistress two hundred dollars a year, and supporting himself, he was allowed to work at his trade, and manage his own affairs. His strongest wish was to purchase his children; but, though he several times offered his hard earnings for that purpose, he never succeeded. In complexion my parents were a light shade of brownish yellow, and were termed mulattoes. They lived together in a comfortable home; and, though we were all slaves, I was so fondly shielded that I never dreamed I was a piece of merchandise, trusted to them for safe keeping, and liable to be demanded of them at any moment. I had one brother, William, who was two years younger than myself—a bright, affectionate child. I had also a great treasure in my maternal grandmother,[2] who was a remarkable woman in many respects. She was the daughter of a planter in South Carolina, who, at his death, left her mother and his three children free, with money to go to St. Augustine, where they had relatives. It was during the Revolutionary War; and they were captured on their passage, carried back, and sold to different purchasers. Such was the story my grandmother used to tell me; but I do not remember all the particulars. She was a little girl when she was captured and sold to the keeper of a large hotel. I have often heard her tell how hard she fared during childhood. But as she grew older she evinced so much intelligence, and was so faithful, that her master and mistress could not help seeing it was for their interest to take care of such a valuable piece of property. She became an indispensable personage in the household, officiating in all capacities, from cook and wet nurse to seamstress. She was much praised for her cooking; and her nice crackers became so famous in the neighborhood that many people were desirous of obtaining them. In consequence of numerous requests of this kind, she asked permission of her mistress to bake crackers at night, after all the household work was done; and she obtained leave to do it, provided she would clothe herself and her children from the profits. Upon these terms, after working hard all day for her mistress, she began her midnight bakings, assisted by her two oldest children. The business proved profitable; and each year she laid by a little, which was saved for a fund to purchase her children. Her master died, and the property was divided among his heirs. The widow had her dower in the hotel, which she continued to keep open. My grandmother remained in her service as a slave; but her children were divided among her master's children. As she had five, Benjamin, the youngest one, was sold, in order that each heir might have an equal portion dollars and cents. There was so little difference in our ages that he seemed more like my brother than my uncle. He was a bright, handsome lad, nearly white; for he inherited the complexion my grandmother had derived from Anglo-Saxon ancestors. Though only ten years old, seven hundred and twenty dollars were paid for him. His sale was a terrible blow to my grand-

---

[1] Daniel Jacobs (?–1826?); in writing her life story as if it were fiction, Jacobs gives Linda Brent the same (unnamed) relatives she herself had.
[2] Molly Horniblow (1771?–1853).

mother; but she was naturally hopeful, and she went to work with renewed energy, trusting in time to be able to purchase some of her children. She had laid up three hundred dollars, which her mistress one day begged as a loan, promising to pay her soon. The reader probably knows that no promise or writing given to a slave is legally binding; for, according to Southern laws, a slave, *being* property, can *hold* no property. When my grandmother lent her hard earnings to her mistress, she trusted solely to her honor. The honor of a slaveholder to a slave!

To this good grandmother I was indebted for many comforts. My brother Willie and I often received portions of the crackers, cakes, and preserves, she made to sell; and after we ceased to be children we were indebted to her for many more important services.

Such were the unusually fortunate circumstances of my early childhood. When I was six years old, my mother[3] died; and then, for the first time, I learned, by the talk around me, that I was a slave. My mother's mistress was the daughter of my grandmother's mistress. She was the foster sister of my mother; they were both nourished at my grandmother's breast. In fact, my mother had been weaned at three months old, that the babe of the mistress might obtain sufficient food. They played together as children; and, when they became women, my mother was a most faithful servant to her whiter foster sister. On her death-bed her mistress promised that her children should never suffer for any thing; and during her lifetime she kept her word. They all spoke kindly of my dead mother, who had been a slave merely in name, but in nature was noble and womanly. I grieved for her, and my young mind was troubled with the thought who would now take care of me and my little brother. I was told that my home was now to be with her mistress; and I found it a happy one. No toilsome or disagreeable duties were imposed upon me. My mistress was so kind to me that I was always glad to do her bidding, and proud to labor for her as much as my young years would permit. I would sit by her side for hours, sewing diligently, with a heart as free from care as that of any free-born white child. When she thought I was tired, she would send me out to run and jump; and away I bounded, to gather berries or flowers to decorate her room. Those were happy days—too happy to last. The slave child had no thought for the morrow; but there came that blight, which too surely waits on every human being born to be a chattel.

When I was nearly twelve years old, my kind mistress[4] sickened and died. As I saw the cheek grow paler, and the eye more glassy, how earnestly I prayed in my heart that she might live! I loved her; for she had been almost like a mother to me. My prayers were not answered. She died, and they buried her in the little churchyard, where, day after day, my tears fell upon her grave.

I was sent to spend a week with my grandmother. I was now old enough to begin to think of the future; and again and again I asked myself what they would do with me. I felt sure I should never find another mistress so kind as the one who was gone. She had promised my dying mother that her children should never suffer for any thing; and when I remembered that, and recalled her many proofs of attachment to me, I could not help having some hopes that she had left me free. My friends were almost certain it would be so. They thought she would be sure to

---

[3] Delilah Jacobs (?–1820), Molly Horniblow's daughter.
[4] Margaret Horniblow (1797–1825); the slave Molly was given the family name.

do it, on account of my mother's love and faithful service. But, alas! we all know that the memory of a faithful slave does not avail much to save her children from the auction block.

After a brief period of suspense, the will of my mistress was read, and we learned that she had bequeathed me to her sister's daughter,[5] a child of five years old. So vanished our hopes. My mistress had taught me the precepts of God's Word: "Thou shalt love thy neighbor as thyself." "Whatsoever ye would that men should do unto you, do ye even so unto them."[6] But I was her slave, and I suppose she did not recognize me as her neighbor. I would give much to blot out from my memory that one great wrong. As a child, I loved my mistress; and, looking back on the happy days I spent with her, I try to think with less bitterness of this act of injustice. While I was with her, she taught me to read and spell; and for this privilege, which so rarely falls to the lot of a slave, I bless her memory.

She possessed but few slaves; and at her death those were all distributed among her relatives. Five of them were my grandmother's children, and had shared the same milk that nourished her mother's children. Notwithstanding my grandmother's long and faithful service to her owners, not one of her children escaped the auction block. These God-breathing machines are no more, in the sight of their masters, than the cotton they plant, or the horses they tend.

VI: THE JEALOUS MISTRESS

I would ten thousand times rather that my children should be the half-starved paupers of Ireland than to be the most pampered among the slaves of America.[1] I would rather drudge out my life on a cotton plantation, till the grave opened to give me rest, than to live with an unprincipled master and a jealous mistress. The felon's home in a penitentiary is preferable. He may repent, and turn from the error of his ways, and so find peace; but it is not so with a favorite slave. She is not allowed to have any pride of character. It is deemed a crime in her to wish to be virtuous.

Mrs. Flint[2] possessed the key to her husband's character before I was born. She might have used this knowledge to counsel and to screen the young and the innocent among her slaves; but for them she had no sympathy. They were the objects of her constant suspicion and malevolence. She watched her husband with unceasing vigilance; but he was well practised in means to evade it. What he could not find opportunity to say in words he manifested in signs. He invented more than were ever thought of in a deaf and dumb asylum. I let them pass, as if I did not understand what he meant; and many were the curses and threats bestowed on me for my stupidity. One day he caught me teaching myself to write.[3] He frowned, as if he was not well pleased; but I suppose he came to the conclusion that such an

---

[5] Mary Matilda Norcom (1822–?), who is named Emily Flint here.

[6] From Mark 12:31 and from Matthew 7:12, respectively.

[1] The numerous references to the potato famine in Ireland, and in some cases to Irish enslavement by the British, show an awareness of mutual hardship on the part of abolitionist writers.

[2] Linda Brent is now living in the Flint household (just as Harriet Jacobs lived in the home of Dr. and Mrs. Norcom).

[3] Ordinarily, slaves were not allowed to learn how to read and write.

accomplishment might help to advance his favorite scheme. Before long, notes were often slipped into my hand. I would return them, say, "I can't read them, sir." "Can't you?" he replied; "then I must read them to you." He always finished the reading by asking, "Do you understand?" Sometimes he would complain of the heat of the tea room, and order his supper to be placed on a small table in the piazza. He would seat himself there with a well-satisfied smile, and tell me to stand by and brush away the flies. He would eat very slowly, pausing between the mouthfuls. These intervals were employed in describing the happiness I was so foolishly throwing away, and in threatening me with the penalty that finally awaited my stubborn disobedience. He boasted much of the forbearance he had exercised towards me, and reminded me that there was a limit to his patience. When I succeeded in avoiding opportunities for him to talk to me at home, I was ordered to come to his office, to do some errand. When there, I was obliged to stand and listen to such language as he saw fit to address to me. Sometimes I so openly expressed my contempt for him that he would become violently enraged, and I wondered why he did not strike me. Circumstanced as he was, he probably thought it was better policy to be forbearing. But the state of things grew worse and worse daily. In desperation I told him that I must and would apply to my grandmother for protection. He threatened me with death, and worse than death, if I made any complaint to her. Strange to say, I did not despair. I was naturally of a buoyant disposition, and always I had a hope of somehow getting out of his clutches. Like many a poor, simple slave before me, I trusted that some threads of joy would yet be woven into my dark destiny.

I had entered my sixteenth year, and every day it became more apparent that my presence was intolerable to Mrs. Flint. Angry words frequently passed between her and her husband. He had never punished me himself, and he would not allow any body else to punish me. In that respect, she was never satisfied; but, in her angry moods, no terms were too vile for her to bestow upon me. Yet I, whom she detested so bitterly, had far more pity for her than he had, whose duty it was to make her life happy. I never wronged her, or wished to wrong her; and one word of kindness from her would have brought me to her feet.

After repeated quarrels between the doctor and his wife, he announced his intention to take his youngest daughter, then four years old, to sleep in his apartment. It was necessary that a servant should sleep in the same room, to be on hand if the child stirred. I was selected for that office, and informed for what purpose that arrangement had been made. By managing to keep within sight of people, as much as possible, during the day time, I had hitherto succeeded in eluding my master, though a razor was often held to my throat to force me to change this line of policy. At night I slept by the side of my great aunt, where I felt safe. He was too prudent to come into her room. She was an old woman and had been in the family many years. Moreover, as a married man, and a professional man, he deemed it necessary to save appearances in some degree. But he resolved to remove the obstacle in the way of his scheme; and he thought he had planned it so that he should evade suspicion. He was well aware how much I prized my refuge by the side of my old aunt, and he determined to dispossess me of it. The first night the doctor had the little child in his room alone. The next morning, I was ordered to take my station as nurse the following night. A kind Providence interposed in my favor. During the day Mrs. Flint heard of this new arrangement, and a storm followed. I rejoiced to hear it rage.

After a while my mistress sent for me to come to her room. Her first question was, "Did you know you were to sleep in the doctor's room?"

"Yes, ma'am."

"Who told you?"

"My master."

"Will you answer truly all the questions I ask?"

"Yes, ma'am."

"Tell me, then, as you hope to be forgiven, are you innocent of what I have accused you?"

"I am."

She handed me a Bible, and said, "Lay your hand on your heart, kiss this holy book, and swear before God that you tell me the truth."

I took the oath she required, and I did it with a clear conscience.

"You have taken God's holy word to testify your innocence," said she. "If you have deceived me, beware! Now take this stool, sit down, look me directly in the face, and tell me all that has passed between your master and you."

I did as she ordered. As I went on with my account her color changed frequently, she wept, and sometimes groaned. She spoke in tones so sad, that I was touched by her grief. The tears came to my eyes; but I was soon convinced that her emotions arose from anger and wounded pride. She felt that her marriage vows were desecrated, her dignity insulted; but she had no compassion for the poor victim of her husband's perfidy. She pitied herself as a martyr; but she was incapable of feeling for the condition of shame and misery in which her unfortunate, helpless slave was placed.

Yet perhaps she had some touch of feeling for me; for when the conference was ended, she spoke kindly, and promised to protect me. I should have been much comforted by this assurance if I could have had confidence in it; but my experiences in slavery had filled me with distrust. She was not a very refined woman, and had not much control over her passions. I was an object of her jealousy, and, consequently, of her hatred; and I knew I could not expect kindness or confidence from her under the circumstances in which I was placed. I could not blame her. Slave-holders' wives feel as other women would under similar circumstances. The fire of her temper kindled from small sparks, and now the flame became so intense that the doctor was obliged to give up his intended arrangement.

I knew I had ignited the torch, and I expected to suffer for it afterwards; but I felt too thankful to my mistress for the timely aid she rendered me to care much about that. She now took me to sleep in a room adjoining her own. There I was an object of her especial care, though not of her especial comfort, for she spent many a sleepless night to watch over me. Sometimes I woke up, and found her bending over me. At other times she whispered in my ear, as though it was her husband who was speaking to me, and listened to hear what I would answer. If she startled me, on such occasions, she would glide stealthily away; and the next morning she would tell me I had been talking in my sleep, and ask who I was talking to. At last, I began to be fearful for my life. It had been often threatened; and you can imagine, better than I can describe, what an unpleasant sensation it must produce to wake up in the dead of night and find a jealous woman bending over you. Terrible as this experience was, I had fears that it would give place to one more terrible.

My mistress grew weary of her vigils; they did not prove satisfactory. She changed her tactics. She now tried the trick of accusing my master of crime, in my presence, and gave my name as the author of the accusation. To my utter astonishment, he replied, "I don't believe it; but if she did acknowledge it, you tortured her into exposing me." Tortured into exposing him! Truly, Satan had no difficulty in distinguishing the color of his soul! I understood his object in making this false representation. It was to show me that I gained nothing by seeking the protection of my mistress; that the power was still all in his own hands. I pitied Mrs. Flint. She was a second wife, many years the junior of her husband; and the hoary-headed[4] miscreant was enough to try the patience of a wiser and better woman. She was completely foiled, and knew not how to proceed. She would gladly have had me flogged for my supposed false oath; but, as I have already stated, the doctor never allowed any one to whip me. The old sinner was politic. The application of the lash might have led to remarks that would have exposed him in the eyes of his children and grandchildren. How often did I rejoice that I lived in a town where all the inhabitants knew each other! If I had been on a remote plantation, or lost among the multitude of a crowded city, I should not be a living woman at this day.

The secrets of slavery are concealed like those of the Inquisition. My master was, to my knowledge, the father of eleven slaves. But did the mothers dare to tell who was the father of their children? Did the other slaves dare to allude to it, except in whispers among themselves? No, indeed! They knew too well the terrible consequences.

My grandmother could not avoid seeing things which excited her suspicions. She was uneasy about me, and tried various ways to buy me; but the never-changing answer was always repeated: "Linda does not belong to *me*. She is my daughter's property, and I have no legal right to sell her." The conscientious man! He was too scrupulous to *sell* me; but he had no scruples whatever about committing a much greater wrong against the helpless young girl placed under his guardianship, as his daughter's property. Sometimes my persecutor would ask me whether I would like to be sold. I told him I would rather be sold to any body than to lead such a life as I did. On such occasions he would assume the air of a very injured individual, and reproach me for my ingratitude. "Did I not take you into the house, and make you the companion of my own children?" he would say. "Have I ever treated you like a negro? I have never allowed you to be punished, not even to please your mistress. And this is the recompense I get, you ungrateful girl!" I answered that he had reasons of his own for screening me from punishment, and that the course he pursued made my mistress hate me and persecute me. If I wept, he would say, "Poor child! Don't cry! don't cry! I will make peace for you with your mistress. Only let me arrange matters in my own way. Poor, foolish girl! you don't know what is for your own good. I would cherish you. I would make a lady of you. Now go, and think of all I have promised you."

I did think of it.

Reader, I draw no imaginary pictures of southern homes. I am telling you the plain truth. Yet when victims make their escape from this wild beast of Slavery, northerners consent to act the part of blood-hounds, and hunt the poor fugitive back into his den, "full of dead men's bones, and all uncleanness."[5] Nay, more, they are not only willing, but proud, to give their daughters in marriage to

---

[4] Ancient.

[5] "Woe unto you, scribes and Pharisees, hypocrites! for ye are like unto whited sepulchres, which indeed appear beautiful outward, but are within full of dead men's bones, and of all uncleanness," from Matthew 23:27.

slaveholders. The poor girls have romantic notions of a sunny clime, and of the flowering vines that all the year round shade a happy home. To what disappointments are they destined! The young wife soon learns that the husband in whose hands she has placed her happiness pays no regard to his marriage vows. Children of every shade of complexion play with her own fair babies, and too well she knows that they are born unto him of his own household. Jealousy and hatred enter the flowery home, and it is ravaged of its loveliness.

Southern women often marry a man knowing that he is the father of many little slaves. They do not trouble themselves about it. They regard such children as property, as marketable as the pigs on the plantation; and it is seldom that they do not make them aware of this by passing them into the slave-trader's hands as soon as possible, and thus getting them out of their sight. I am glad to say there are some honorable exceptions.

I have myself known two southern wives who exhorted their husbands to free those slaves towards whom they stood in a "parental relation;" and their request was granted. These husbands blushed before the superior nobleness of their wives' natures. Though they had only counselled them to do that which it was their duty to do, it commanded their respect, and rendered their conduct more exemplary. Concealment was at an end, and confidence took the place of distrust.

Though this bad institution deadens the moral sense, even in white women, to a fearful extent, it is not altogether extinct. I have heard southern ladies say of Mr. Such a one, "He not only thinks it no disgrace to be the father of those little niggers, but he is not ashamed to call himself their master. I declare, such things ought not to be tolerated in any decent society!"

VII: The Lover

Why does the slave ever love? Why allow the tendrils of the heart to twine around objects which may at any moment be wrenched away by the hand of violence? When separations come by the hand of death, the pious soul can bow in resignation, and say, "Not my will, but thine be done, O Lord!"[1] But when the ruthless hand of man strikes the blow, regardless of the misery he causes, it is hard to be submissive. I did not reason thus when I was a young girl. Youth will be youth. I loved, and I indulged the hope that the dark clouds around me would turn out a bright lining. I forgot that in the land of my birth the shadows are too dense for light to penetrate. A land

> "Where laughter is not mirth; nor thought the mind;
> Nor words a language; nor e'en men mankind.
> Where cries reply to curses, shrieks to blows,
> And each is tortured in his separate hell."[2]

There was in the neighborhood a young colored carpenter; a free born man. We had been well acquainted in childhood, and frequently met together afterwards. We became mutually attached, and he proposed to marry me. I loved him with all

---

[1] From Matthew 26:39.
[2] From "The Lament of Tasso" (1817), by the English romantic poet George Gordon (1788–1824), Lord Byron; the poem, a soliloquy, expresses the speaker's wish for his lover as he lies in prison.

the ardor of a young girl's first love. But when I reflected that I was a slave, and that the laws gave no sanction to the marriage of such, my heart sank within me. My lover wanted to buy me; but I knew that Dr. Flint was too wilful and arbitrary a man to consent to that arrangement. From him, I was sure of experiencing all sorts of opposition, and I had nothing to hope from my mistress. She would have been delighted to have got rid of me, but not in that way. It would have relieved her mind of a burden if she could have seen me sold to some distant state, but if I was married near home I should be just as much in her husband's power as I had previously been,—for the husband of a slave has no power to protect her. Moreover, my mistress, like many others, seemed to think that slaves had no right to any family ties of their own; that they were created merely to wait upon the family of the mistress. I once heard her abuse a young slave girl, who told her that a colored man wanted to make her his wife. "I will have you peeled and pickled,[3] my lady," said she, "if I ever hear you mention that subject again. Do you suppose that I will have you tending *my* children with the children of that nigger?" The girl to whom she said this had a mulatto child, of course not acknowledged by its father. The poor black man who loved her would have been proud to acknowledge his helpless offspring.

Many and anxious were the thoughts I revolved in my mind. I was at a loss what to do. Above all things, I was desirous to spare my lover the insults that had cut so deeply into my own soul. I talked with my grandmother about it, and partly told her my fears. I did not dare to tell her the worst. She had long suspected all was not right, and if I confirmed her suspicions I knew a storm would rise that would prove the overthrow of all my hopes.

This love-dream had been my support through many trials; and I could not bear to run the risk of having it suddenly dissipated. There was a lady in the neighborhood, a particular friend of Dr. Flint's who often visited the house. I had a great respect for her, and she had always manifested a friendly interest in me. Grandmother thought she would have great influence with the doctor. I went to this lady, and told her my story. I told her I was aware that my lover's being a freeborn man would prove a great objection; but he wanted to buy me; and if Dr. Flint would consent to that arrangement, I felt sure he would be willing to pay any reasonable price. She knew that Mrs. Flint disliked me; therefore, I ventured to suggest that perhaps my mistress would approve of my being sold, as that would rid her of me. The lady listened with kindly sympathy, and promised to do her utmost to promote my wishes. She had an interview with the doctor, and I believe she pleaded my cause earnestly; but it was all to no purpose.

How I dreaded my master now! Every minute I expected to be summoned to his presence; but the day passed, and I heard nothing from him. The next morning, a message was brought to me: "Master wants you in his study." I found the door ajar, and I stood a moment gazing at the hateful man who claimed a right to rule me, body and soul. I entered, and tried to appear calm. I did not want him to know how my heart was bleeding. He looked fixedly at me, with an expression which seemed to say, "I have half a mind to kill you on the spot." At last he broke the silence, and that was a relief to both of us.

"So you want to be married, do you?" said he, "and to a free nigger."

"Yes, sir."

"Well, I'll soon convince you whether I am your master, or the nigger fellow

---

[3] Whipped and then rinsed with brine.

you honor so highly. If you *must* have a husband, you may take up with one of my slaves."

What a situation I should be in, as the wife of one of *his* slaves, even if my heart had been interested!

I replied, "Don't you suppose, sir, that a slave can have some preference about marrying? Do you suppose that all men are alike to her?"

"Do you love this nigger?" said he, abruptly.

"Yes, sir."

"How dare you tell me so!" he exclaimed, in great wrath. After a slight pause, he added, "I supposed you thought more of yourself; that you felt above the insults of such puppies."

"I replied, "If he is a puppy I am a puppy, for we are both of the negro race. It is right and honorable for us to love each other. The man you call a puppy never insulted me, sir; and he would not love me if he did not believe me to be a virtuous woman."

He sprang upon me like a tiger, and gave me a stunning blow. It was the first time he had ever struck me; and fear did not enable me to control my anger. When I had recovered a little from the effects, I exclaimed, "You have struck me for answering you honestly. How I despise you!"

There was silence for some minutes. Perhaps he was deciding what should be my punishment; or, perhaps, he wanted to give me time to reflect on what I had said, and to whom I had said it. Finally, he asked, "Do you know what you have said?"

"Yes, sir; but your treatment drove me to it."

"Do you know that I have a right to do as I like with you,—that I can kill you, if I please?"

"You have tried to kill me, and I wish you had; but you have no right to do as you like with me."

"Silence!" he exclaimed, in a thundering voice. "By heavens, girl, you forget yourself too far! Are you mad? If you are, I will soon bring you to your senses. Do you think any other master would bear what I have borne from you this morning? Many masters would have killed you on the spot. How would you like to be sent to jail for your insolence?"

"I know I have been disrespectful, sir," I replied; "but you drove me to it; I couldn't help it. As for the jail, there would be more peace for me there than there is here."

"You deserve to go there," said he, "and to be under such treatment, that you would forget the meaning of the word *peace*. It would do you good. It would take some of your high notions out of you. But I am not ready to send you there yet, notwithstanding your ingratitude for all my kindness and forbearance. You have been the plague of my life. I have wanted to make you happy, and I have been repaid with the basest ingratitude; but though you have proved yourself incapable of appreciating my kindness, I will be lenient towards you, Linda. I will give you one more chance to redeem your character. If you behave yourself and do as I require, I will forgive you and treat you as I always have done; but if you disobey me, I will punish you as I would the meanest slave on my plantation. Never let me hear that fellow's name mentioned again. If I ever know of your speaking to him, I will cowhide you both; and if I catch him lurking about my premises, I will shoot him as soon as I would a dog. Do you hear what I say? I'll teach you a lesson about marriage and free niggers! Now go, and let this be the last time I have occasion to speak to you on this subject."

Reader, did you ever hate? I hope not. I never did but once; and I trust I never shall again. Somebody has called it "the atmosphere of hell;" and I believe it is so.

For a fortnight the doctor did not speak to me. He thought to mortify me; to make me feel that I had disgraced myself by receiving the honorable addresses of a respectable colored man, in preference to the base proposals of a white man. But though his lips disdained to address me, his eyes were very loquacious. No animal ever watched its prey more narrowly than he watched me. He knew that I could write, though he had failed to make me read his letters; and he was now troubled lest I should exchange letters with another man. After a while he became weary of silence; and I was sorry for it. One morning, as he passed through the hall, to leave the house, he contrived to thrust a note into my hand. I thought I had better read it, and spare myself the vexation of having him read it to me. It expressed regret for the blow he had given me, and reminded me that I myself was wholly to blame for it. He hoped I had become convinced of the injury I was doing myself by incurring his displeasure. He wrote that he had made up his mind to go to Louisiana; that he should take several slaves with him, and intended I should be one of the number. My mistress would remain where she was; therefore I should have nothing to fear from that quarter. If I merited kindness from him, he assured me that it would be lavishly bestowed. He begged me to think over the matter, and answer the following day.

The next morning I was called to carry a pair of scissors to his room. I laid them on the table, with the letter beside them. He thought it was my answer, and did not call me back. I went as usual to attend my young mistress to and from school. He met me in the street, and ordered me to stop at his office on my way back. When I entered, he showed me his letter, and asked me why I had not answered it. I replied, "I am your daughter's property, and it is in your power to send me, or take me, wherever you please." He said he was very glad to find me so willing to go, and that we should start early in the autumn. He had a large practice in the town, and I rather thought he had made up the story merely to frighten me. However that might be, I was determined that I would never go to Louisiana with him.

Summer passed away, and early in the autumn Dr. Flint's eldest son was sent to Louisiana to examine the country, with a view to emigrating. That news did not disturb me. I knew very well that I should not be sent with *him*. That I had not been taken to the plantation before this time, was owing to the fact that his son was there. He was jealous of his son; and jealousy of the overseer had kept him from punishing me by sending me into the fields to work. Is it strange that I was not proud of these protectors? As for the overseer, he was a man for whom I had less respect than I had for a bloodhound.

Young Mr. Flint did not bring back a favorable report of Louisiana, and I heard no more of that scheme. Soon after this, my lover met me at the corner of the street, and I stopped to speak to him. Looking up, I saw my master watching us from his window. I hurried home, trembling with fear. I was sent for, immediately, to go to his room. He met me with a blow. "When is mistress to be married?" said he, in a sneering tone. A shower of oaths and imprecations followed. How thankful I was that my lover was a free man! that my tyrant had no power to flog him for speaking to me in the street!

Again and again I revolved in my mind how all this would end. There was no hope that the doctor would consent to sell me on any terms. He had an iron will, and was determined to keep me, and to conquer me. My lover was an intelligent and religious man. Even if he could have obtained permission to marry me while I was a slave, the marriage would give him no power to protect me from my master. It would have made him miserable to witness the insults I should have been subjected to. And then, if we had children, I knew they must "follow the condition of the mother." What a terrible blight that would be on the heart of a free, intelligent father! For *his* sake, I felt that I ought not to link his fate with my own unhappy destiny. He was going to Savannah to see about a little property left him by an uncle; and hard as it was to bring my feelings to it, I earnestly entreated him not to come back. I advised him to go to the Free States, where his tongue would not be tied, and where his intelligence would be of more avail to him. He left me, still hoping the day would come when I could be bought. With me the lamp of hope had gone out. The dream of my girlhood was over. I felt lonely and desolate.

Still I was not stripped of all. I still had my good grandmother, and my affectionate brother. When he put his arms round my neck, and looked into my eyes, as if to read there the troubles I dared not tell, I felt that I still had something to love. But even that pleasant emotion was chilled by the reflection that he might be torn from me at any moment, by some sudden freak of my master. If he had known how we loved each other, I think he would have exulted in separating us. We often planned together how we could get to the north. But, as William remarked, such things are easier said than done. My movements were very closely watched, and we had no means of getting any money to defray our expenses. As for grandmother, she was strongly opposed to her children's undertaking any such project. She had not forgotten poor Benjamin's sufferings, and she was afraid that if another child tried to escape, he would have a similar or a worse fate. To me, nothing seemed more dreadful than my present life. I said to myself, "William *must* be free. He shall go to the north, and I will follow him." Many a slave sister has formed the same plans.

XII. Fear of Insurrection

Not far from this time Nat Turner's insurrection broke out;[1] and the news threw our town into great commotion. Strange that they should be alarmed, when their slaves were so "contented and happy"! But so it was.

It was always the custom to have a muster every year. On that occasion every white man shouldered his musket. The citizens and the so-called country gentlemen wore military uniforms. The poor whites took their places in the ranks in every-day dress, some without shoes, some without hats. This grand occasion had already passed; and when the slaves were told there was to be another muster, they were surprised and rejoiced. Poor creatures! They thought it was going to be a holiday. I was informed of the true state of affairs, and imparted it to the few I could trust. Most gladly would I have proclaimed it to every slave; but I dared not. All could not be relied on. Mighty is the power of the torturing lash.

By sunrise, people were pouring in from every quarter within twenty miles of the town. I knew the houses were to be searched; and I expected it would be done by country bullies and the poor whites. I knew nothing annoyed them so much as to see colored people living in comfort and respectability; so I made arrangements

---

[1] In August 1831 Nat Turner and his followers massacred fifty-five whites in Southampton County, Virginia; the shuddering consequences of that event were felt throughout the South. Linda Brent's story moves now to 1831, incorporates the news of the insurrection, and tells of its effect on people in the area. Meanwhile, Linda has had a son by her lover (later she has a daughter). Thrown out of the house by Mrs. Flint, she now lives with her grandmother.

for them with especial care. I arranged every thing in my grandmother's house as neatly as possible. I put white quilts on the beds, and decorated some of the rooms with flowers. When all was arranged, I sat down at the window to watch. Far as my eye could reach, it rested on a motley crowd of soldiers. Drums and fifes were discoursing martial music. The men were divided into companies of sixteen, each headed by a captain. Orders were given, and the wild scouts rushed in every direction, wherever a colored face was to be found.

It was a grand opportunity for the low whites, who had no negroes of their own to scourge. They exulted in such a chance to exercise a little brief authority, and show their subserviency to the slaveholders; not reflecting that the power which trampled on the colored people also kept themselves in poverty, ignorance, and moral degradation. Those who never witnessed such scenes can hardly believe what I know was inflicted at this time on innocent men, women, and children, against whom there was not the slightest ground for suspicion. Colored people and slaves who lived in remote parts of the town suffered in an especial manner. In some cases the searchers scattered powder and shot among their clothes, and then sent other parties to find them, and bring them forward as proof that they were plotting insurrection. Every where men, women, and children were whipped till the blood stood in puddles at their feet. Some received five hundred lashes; others were tied hands and feet, and tortured with a bucking paddle, which blisters the skin terribly. The dwellings of the colored people, unless they happened to be protected by some influential white person, who was nigh at hand, were robbed of clothing and every thing else the marauders thought worth carrying away. All day long these unfeeling wretches went round, like a troop of demons, terrifying and tormenting the helpless. At night, they formed themselves into patrol bands, and went wherever they chose among the colored people, acting out their brutal will. Many women hid themselves in woods and swamps, to keep out of their way. If any of the husbands or fathers told of these outrages, they were tied up to the public whipping post, and cruelly scourged for telling lies about white men. The consternation was universal. No two people that had the slightest tinge of color in their faces dared to be seen talking together.

I entertained no positive fears about our household, because we were in the midst of white families who would protect us. We were ready to receive the soldiers whenever they came. It was not long before we heard the tramp of feet and the sound of voices. The door was rudely pushed open; and in they tumbled, like a pack of hungry wolves. They snatched at every thing within their reach. Every box, trunk, closet, and corner underwent a thorough examination. A box in one of the drawers containing some silver change was eagerly pounced upon. When I stepped forward to take it from them, one of the solders turned and said angrily, "What d'ye foller us fur? D'ye s'pose white folks is come to steal?"

I replied, "You have come to search; but you have searched that box, and I will take it, if you please."

At that moment I saw a white gentleman who was friendly to us; and I called to him, and asked him to have the goodness to come in and stay till the search was over. He readily complied. His entrance into the house brought in the captain of the company, whose business it was to guard the outside of the house, and see that none of the inmates left it. This officer was Mr. Litch, the wealthy slaveholder whom I mentioned,[2] in the account of neighboring planters, as being notorious for his cruelty. He felt above soiling his hands with the search. He merely gave or-

[2] An account given in Ch. IX: "Sketches of Neighboring Slaveholders."

ders; and, if a bit of writing was discovered, it was carried to him by his ignorant followers, who were unable to read.

My grandmother had a large trunk of bedding and table cloths. When that was opened, there was a great shout of surprise; and one exclaimed, "Where'd the damned niggers git all dis sheet an' table clarf?"

My grandmother, emboldened by the presence of our white protector, said, "You may be sure we didn't pilfer 'em from *your* houses."

"Look here, mammy," said a grim-looking fellow without any coat, "you seem to feel mighty gran' 'cause you got all them 'ere fixens. White folks oughter have 'em all."

His remarks were interrupted by a chorus of voices shouting, "We's got 'em! We's got 'em! Dis 'ere yaller gal's got letters!"

There was a general rush for the supposed letter, which, upon examination, proved to be some verses written to me by a friend. In packing away my things, I had overlooked them. When their captain informed them of their contents, they seemed much disappointed. He inquired of me who wrote them. I told him it was one of my friends. "Can you read them?" he asked. When I told him I could, he swore, and raved, and tore the paper into bits. "Bring me all your letters!" said he, in a commanding tone. I told him I had none. "Don't be afraid," he continued, in an insinuating way. "Bring them all to me. Nobody shall do you any harm." Seeing I did not move to obey him, his pleasant tone changed to oaths and threats. "Who writes to you? half free niggers?" inquired he. I replied, "O, no; most of my letters are from white people. Some request me to burn them after they are read, and some I destroy without reading."

An exclamation of surprise from some of the company put a stop to our conversation. Some silver spoons which ornamented an old-fashioned buffet had just been discovered. My grandmother was in the habit of preserving fruit for many ladies in the town, and of preparing suppers for parties; consequently she had many jars of preserves. The closet that contained these was next invaded, and the contents tasted. One of them, who was helping himself freely, tapped his neighbor on the shoulder, and said, "Wal done! Don't wonder de niggers want to kill all de white folks, when dey live on 'sarves" [meaning preserves]. I stretched out my hand to take the jar, saying, "You were not sent here to search for sweetmeats."

"And what *were* we sent for?" said the captain, bristling up to me. I evaded the question.

The search of the house was completed, and nothing found to condemn us. They next proceeded to the garden, and knocked about every bush and vine, with no better success. The captain called his men together, and, after a short consultation, the order to march was given. As they passed out of the gate, the captain turned back, and pronounced a malediction on the house. He said it ought to be burned to the ground, and each of its inmates receive thirty-nine lashes. We came out of this affair very fortunately; not losing any thing except some wearing apparel.

Towards evening the turbulence increased. The soldiers, stimulated by drink, committed still greater cruelties. Shrieks and shouts continually rent the air. Not daring to go to the door, I peeped under the window curtain. I saw a mob dragging along a number of colored people, each white man, with his musket upraised, threatening instant death if they did not stop their shrieks. Among the prisoners was a respectable old colored minister. They had found a few parcels of shot in his house, which his wife had for years used to balance her scales. For this they were going to shoot him on Court House Green. What a spectacle was that for a civilized country! A rabble, staggering under intoxication, assuming to be the administrators of justice!

The better class of the community exerted their influence to save the innocent, persecuted people; and in several instances they succeeded, by keeping them shut up in jail till the excitement abated. At last the white citizens found that their own property was not safe from the lawless rabble they had summoned to protect them. They rallied the drunken swarm, drove them back into the country, and set a guard over the town.

The next day, the town patrols were commissioned to search colored people that lived out of the city; and the most shocking outrages were committed with perfect impunity. Every day for a fortnight, if I looked out, I saw horsemen with some poor panting negro tied to their saddles, and compelled by the lash to keep up with their speed, till they arrived at the jail yard. Those who had been whipped too unmercifully to walk were washed with brine, tossed into a cart, and carried to jail. One black man, who had not fortitude to endure scourging, promised to give information about the conspiracy. But it turned out that he knew nothing at all. He had not even heard the name of Nat Turner. The poor fellow had, however, made up a story, which augmented his own sufferings and those of the colored people.

The day patrol continued for some weeks, and at sundown a night guard was substituted. Nothing at all was proved against the colored people, bond or free. The wrath of the slaveholders was somewhat appeased by the capture of Nat Turner. The imprisoned were released. The slaves were sent to their masters, and the free were permitted to return to their ravaged homes. Visiting was strictly forbidden on the plantations. The slaves begged the privilege of again meeting at their little church in the woods, with their burying ground around it. It was built by the colored people, and they had no higher happiness than to meet there and sing hymns together, and pour out their hearts in spontaneous prayer. Their request was denied, and the church was demolished. They were permitted to attend the white churches, a certain portion of the galleries being appropriated to their use. There, when every body else had partaken of the communion, and the benediction had been pronounced, the minister said, "Come down, now, my colored friends." They obeyed the summons, and partook of the bread and wine, in commemoration of the meek and lowly Jesus, who said, "God is your Father, and all ye are brethren."[3]

XXI: THE LOOPHOLE OF RETREAT*

A small shed had been added to my grandmother's house years ago. Some boards were laid across the joists at the top, and between these boards and the roof was a very small garret, never occupied by any thing but rats and mice. It was a pent roof, covered with nothing but shingles, according to the southern custom for such buildings. The garret was only nine feet long and seven wide. The highest part

---

[3] "For one is your master, even Christ; and all ye are brethren," from Matthew 23:8.

* This title comes from the mock-heroic and didactic poem "The Task" (1785), by the British writer William Cowper (1731–1800). Having again refused Dr. Flint's sexual overtures, Linda Brent was sent to work on the plantation for the first time in her life. Worry over her fate and that of her children led her to run away (with the hope of rescuing the children later) and finally to hide in a small room in her grandmother's house, the "garret" she describes here.

was three feet high, and sloped down abruptly to the loose board floor. There was no admission for either light or air. My uncle Philip, who was a carpenter, had very skilfully made a concealed trap-door, which communicated with the storeroom. He had been doing this while I was waiting in the swamp. The storeroom opened upon a piazza. To this hole I was conveyed as soon as I entered the house. The air was stifling; the darkness total. A bed had been spread on the floor. I could sleep quite comfortably on one side; but the slope was so sudden that I could not turn on the other without hitting the roof. The rats and mice ran over my bed; but I was weary, and I slept such sleep as the wretched may, when a tempest has passed over them. Morning came. I knew it only by the noises I heard; for in my small den day and night were all the same. I suffered for air even more than for light. But I was not comfortless. I heard the voices of my children. There was joy and there was sadness in the sound. It made my tears flow. How I longed to speak to them! I was eager to look on their faces; but there was no hole, no crack, through which I could peep. This continued darkness was oppressive. It seemed horrible to sit or lie in a cramped position day after day, without one gleam of light. Yet I would have chosen this, rather than my lot as a slave, though white people considered it an easy one; and it was so compared with the fate of others. I was never cruelly over-worked; I was never lacerated with the whip from head to foot; I was never so beaten and bruised that I could not turn from one side to the other; I never had my heel-strings cut to prevent my running away; I was never chained to a log and forced to drag it about, while I toiled in the fields from morning till night; I was never branded with hot iron, or torn by bloodhounds. On the contrary, I had always been kindly treated, and tenderly cared for, until I came into the hands of Dr. Flint. I had never wished for freedom till then. But though my life in slavery was comparatively devoid of hardships, God pity the woman who is compelled to lead such a life!

My food was passed up to me through the trap-door my uncle had contrived; and my grandmother, my uncle Phillip, and aunt Nancy would seize such opportunities as they could, to mount up there and chat with me at the opening. But of course this was not safe in the daytime. It must all be done in darkness. It was impossible for me to move in an erect position, but I crawled about my den for exercise. One day I hit my head against something, and found it was a gimlet. My uncle had left it sticking there when he made the trap-door. I was as rejoiced as Robinson Crusoe[1] could have been at finding such a treasure. It put a lucky thought into my head. I said to myself, "Now I will have some light. Now I will see my children." I did not dare to begin my work during the daytime, for fear of attracting attention. But I groped round; and having found the side next the street, where I could frequently see my children, I stuck the gimlet in and waited for evening. I bored three rows of holes, one above another; then I bored out the interstices between. I thus succeeded in making one hole about an inch long and an inch broad. I sat by it till late into the night, to enjoy the little whiff of air that floated in. In the morning I watched for my children. The first person I saw in the street was Dr. Flint. I had a shuddering, superstitious feeling that it was a bad omen. Several familiar faces passed by. At last I heard the merry laugh of children, and presently two sweet little faces were looking up at me, as though they

---

[1] The well-known title character in *The Life and Strange Surprising Adventures of Robinson Crusoe* (1719), by the English novelist Daniel Defoe (1660–1731).

knew I was there, and were conscious of the joy they imparted. How I longed to *tell* them I was there!

My condition was now a little improved. But for weeks I was tormented by hundreds of little red insects, fine as a needle's point, that pierced through my skin, and produced an intolerable burning. The good grandmother gave me herb teas and cooling medicines, and finally I got rid of them. The heat of my den was intense, for nothing but thin shingles protected me from the scorching summer's sun. But I had my consolations. Through my peeping-hole I could watch the children, and when they were near enough, I could hear their talk. Aunt Nancy brought me all the news she would hear at Dr. Flint's. From her I learned that the doctor had written to New York to a colored woman, who had been born and raised in our neighborhood, and had breathed his contaminating atmosphere. He offered her a reward if she could find out any thing about me. I know not what was the nature of her reply; but he soon after started for New York in haste, saying to his family that he had business of importance to transact. I peeped at him as he passed on his way to the steamboat. It was a satisfaction to have miles of land and water between us, even for a little while; and it was a still greater satisfaction to know that he believed me to be in the Free States. My little den seemed less dreary than it had done. He returned, as he did from his former journey to New York, without obtaining any satisfactory information. When he passed our house next morning, Benny was standing at the gate. He had heard them say that he had gone to find me, and he called out, "Dr. Flint, did you bring my mother home? I want to see her." The doctor stamped his foot at him in a rage, and exclaimed, "Get out of the way, you little damned rascal! If you don't, I'll cut off your head."

Benny ran terrified into the house, saying, "You can't put me in jail again. I don't belong to you now." It was well that the wind carried the words away from the doctor's ear. I told my grandmother of it, when we had our next conference at the trap-door; and begged of her not to allow the children to be impertinent to the irascible old man.

Autumn came, with a pleasant abatement of heat. My eyes had become accustomed to the dim light, and by holding my book or work in a certain position near the aperture I contrived to read and sew. That was a great relief to the tedious monotony of my life. But when winter came, the cold penetrated through the thin shingle roof, and I was dreadfully chilled. The winters there are not so long, or so severe, as in northern latitudes; but the houses are not built to shelter from cold, and my little den was peculiarly comfortless. The kind grandmother brought me bed-clothes and warm drinks. Often I was obliged to lie in bed all day to keep comfortable; but with all my precautions, my shoulders and feet were frostbitten. O, those long, gloomy days, with no object for my eye to rest upon, and no thoughts to occupy my mind, except the dreary past and the uncertain future! I was thankful when there came a day sufficiently mild for me to wrap myself up and sit at the loophole to watch the passers by. Southerners have the habit of stopping and talking in the streets, and I heard many conversations not intended to meet my ears. I heard slave-hunters planning how to catch some poor fugitive. Several times I heard allusions to Dr. Flint, myself, and the history of my children, who, perhaps, were playing near the gate. One would say, "I wouldn't move my little finger to catch her, as old Flint's property." Another would say, "I'll catch *any* nigger for the reward. A man ought to have what belongs to him, if he *is* a damned brute." The opinion was often expressed that I was in the Free

States. Very rarely did any one suggest that I might be in the vicinity. Had the least suspicion rested on my grandmother's house, it would have been burned to the ground. But it was the last place they thought of. Yet there was no place, where slavery existed, that could have afforded me so good a place of concealment.

Dr. Flint and his family repeatedly tried to coax and bribe my children to tell something they had heard said about me. One day the doctor took them into a shop, and offered them some bright little silver pieces and gay handkerchiefs if they would tell where their mother was. Ellen shrank away from him, and would not speak; but Benny spoke up, and said, "Dr. Flint, I don't know where my mother is. I guess she's in New York; and when you go there again, I wish you'd ask her to come home, for I want to see her; but if you put her in jail, or tell her you'll cut her head off, I'll tell her to go right back."

XXII: Christmas Festivities

Christmas was approaching. Grandmother brought me materials, and I busied myself making some new garments and little playthings for my children. Were it not that hiring day is near at hand, and many families are fearfully looking forward to the probability of separation in a few days, Christmas might be a happy season for the poor slaves. Even slave mothers try to gladden the hearts of their little ones on that occasion. Benny and Ellen had their Christmas stockings filled. Their imprisoned mother could not have the privilege of witnessing their surprise and joy. But I had the pleasure of peeping at them as they went into the street with their new suits on. I heard Benny ask a little playmate whether Santa Claus brought him any thing. "Yes" replied the boy; "but Santa Claus ain't a real man. It's the children's mothers that put things into the stockings." "No, that can't be," replied Benny, "for Santa Claus brought Ellen and me these new clothes, and my mother has been gone this long time."

How I longed to tell him that his mother made those garments, and that many a tear fell on them while she worked!

Every child rises early on Christmas morning to see the Johnkannaus.[1] Without them, Christmas would be shorn of its greatest attraction. They consist of companies of slaves from the plantations, generally of the lower class. Two athletic men, in calico wrappers, have a net thrown over them, covered with all manner of bright-colored stripes. Cows' tails are fastened to their backs, and their heads are decorated with horns. A box, covered with sheepskin, is called the gumbo box. A dozen beat on this, while others strike triangles and jawbones, to which bands of dancers keep time. For a month previous they are composing songs, which are sung on this occasion. These companies, of a hundred each, turn out early in the morning, and are allowed to go round till twelve o'clock, begging for contributions. Not a door is left unvisited where there is the least chance of obtaining a penny or a glass of rum. They do not drink while they are out, but carry the rum home in jugs, to have a carousal. These Christmas donations frequently amount to twenty or thirty dollars. It is seldom that any white man or child refuses to give them a trifle. If he does, they regale his ears with the following song:—

---

[1] Sometimes called the "John Canoe" or "John Connor" festival, consisting of a blend of masquerade traditions as described by Jacobs.

> "Poor massa, so dey say;
> Down in de heel, so dey say:
> Got no money, so dey say;
> Not one shillin, so dey say;
> God A'mighty bress you, so dey say."

Christmas is a day of feasting, both with white and colored people. Slaves, who are lucky enough to have a few shillings, are sure to spend them for good eating; and many a turkey and pig is captured, without saying, "By your leave, sir." Those who cannot obtain these, cook a 'possum, or a raccoon, from which savory dishes can be made. My grandmother raised poultry and pigs for sale; and it was her established custom to have both a turkey and a pig roasted for Christmas dinner.

On this occasion, I was warned to keep extremely quiet, because two guests had been invited. One was the town constable, and the other was a free colored man, who tried to pass himself off for white, and who was always ready to do any mean work for the sake of currying favor with white people. My grandmother had a motive for inviting them. She managed to take them all over the house. All the rooms on the lower floor were thrown open for them to pass in and out; and after dinner, they were invited up stairs to look at a fine mocking bird my uncle had just brought home. There, too, the rooms were all thrown open, that they might look in. When I heard them talking on the piazza, my heart almost stood still. I knew this colored man had spent many nights hunting for me. Every body knew he had the blood of a slave father in his veins; but for the sake of passing himself off for white, he was ready to kiss the slaveholders' feet. How I despised him! As for the constable, he wore no false colors. The duties of his office were despicable, but he was superior to his companion, inasmuch as he did not pretend to be what he was not. Any white man, who could raise money enough to buy a slave, would have considered himself degraded by being a constable; but the office enabled its possessor to exercise authority. If he found any slave out after nine o'clock, he could whip him as much as he liked; and that was a privilege to be coveted. When the guests were ready to depart, my grandmother gave each of them some of her nice pudding, as a present for their wives. Through my peep-hole I saw them go out of the gate, and I was glad when it closed after them. So passed the first Christmas in my den.

XLI: Free at Last*

Mrs. Bruce, and every member of her family, were exceedingly kind to me. I was thankful for the blessings of my lot, yet I could not always wear a cheerful countenance. I was doing harm to no one; on the contrary, I was doing all the good I could in my small way; yet I could never go out to breathe God's free air without trepidation at my heart. This seemed hard; and I could not think it was a right state of things in any civilized country.

From time to time I received news from my good old grandmother. She could

---

* After years of hiding in her grandmother's "garret," Linda Brent escaped to the North and was soon after reunited with her son and daughter. Although she found work with the Bruce family, her safety and that of her children was in doubt because of the passage of the Fugitive Slave Act of 1850, which sanctioned the return of escaped slaves to their owners in the South.

not write; but she employed others to write for her. The following is an extract from one of her last letters:—

"Dear Daughter: I cannot hope to see you again on earth; but I pray to God to unite us above, where pain will no more rack this feeble body of mine; where sorrow and parting from my children will be no more.[1] God has promised these things if we are faithful unto the end. My age and feeble health deprive me of going to church now; but God is with me here at home. Thank your brother for his kindness. Give much love to him, and tell him to remember the Creator in the days of his youth,[2] and strive to meet me in the Father's kingdom. Love to Ellen and Benjamin. Don't neglect him. Tell him for me, to be a good boy. Strive, my child; to train them for God's children. May he protect and provide for you, is the prayer of your loving old mother."

These letters both cheered and saddened me. I was always glad to have tidings from the kind, faithful old friend of my unhappy youth; but her messages of love made my heart yearn to see her before she died, and I mourned over the fact that it was impossible. Some months after I returned from my flight to New England, I received a letter from her, in which she wrote, "Dr. Flint is dead. He has left a distressed family. Poor old man! I hope he made his peace with God."

I remembered how he had defrauded my grandmother of the hard earnings she had loaned; how he had tried to cheat her out of the freedom her mistress had promised her, and how he had persecuted her children; and I thought to myself that she was a better Christian than I was, if she could entirely forgive him. I cannot say, with truth, that the news of my old master's death softened my feelings towards him. There are wrongs which even the grave does not bury. The man was odious to me while he lived, and his memory is odious now.

His departure from this world did not diminish my danger. He had threatened my grandmother that his heirs should hold me in slavery after he was gone; that I never should be free so long as a child of his survived. As for Mrs. Flint, I had seen her in deeper afflictions than I supposed the loss of her husband would be, for she had buried several children; yet I never saw any signs of softening in her heart. The doctor had died in embarrassed circumstances, and had little to will to his heirs, except such property as he was unable to grasp. I was well aware what I had to expect from the family of Flints; and my fears were confirmed by a letter from the south, warning me to be on my guard, because Mrs. Flint openly declared that her daughter could not afford to lose so valuable a slave as I was.

I kept close watch of the newspapers for arrivals; but one Saturday night, being much occupied, I forgot to examine the Evening Express as usual. I went down into the parlor for it, early in the morning, and found the boy about to kindle a fire with it. I took it from him and examined the list of arrivals. Reader, if you have never been a slave, you cannot imagine the acute sensation of suffering at my heart, when I read the names of Mr. and Mrs. Dodge, at a hotel in Courtland Street. It was a third-rate hotel, and that circumstance convinced me of the truth of what I had heard, that they were short of funds and had need of my value, as *they* valued me; and that was by dollars and cents. I hastened with the paper to Mrs. Bruce. Her heart and hand were always open to every one in distress, and she

---

[1] " . . . and there shall be no more . . . sorrow, nor crying, neither shall there be any more pain . . . ," from Revelation 21:4.

[2] "Remember now thy Creator in the days of thy youth, while the evil days come not, nor the years draw nigh, when thou shalt say, I have no pleasure in them," from Ecclesiastes 12:1.

always warmly sympathized with mine. It was impossible to tell how near the enemy was. He might have passed and repassed the house while we were sleeping. He might at that moment be waiting to pounce upon me if I ventured out of doors. I had never seen the husband of my young mistress, and therefore I could not distinguish him from any other stranger. A carriage was hastily ordered; and, closely veiled, I followed Mrs. Bruce, taking the baby again with me into exile. After various turnings and crossings, and returnings, the carriage stopped at the house of one of Mrs. Bruce's friends, where I was kindly received. Mrs. Bruce returned immediately, to instruct the domestics what to say if any one came to inquire for me.

It was lucky for me that the evening paper was not burned up before I had a chance to examine the list of arrivals. It was not long after Mrs. Bruce's return to her house, before several people came to inquire for me. One inquired for me, another asked for my daughter Ellen, and another said he had a letter from my grandmother, which he was requested to deliver in person.

They were told, "She *has* lived here, but she has left."

"How long ago?"

"I don't know, sir."

"Do you know where she went?"

"I do not, sir." And the door was closed.

This Mr. Dodge, who claimed me as his property, was originally a Yankee pedler in the south; then he became a merchant, and finally a slaveholder. He managed to get introduced into what was called the first society, and married Miss Emily Flint. A quarrel arose between him and her brother, and the brother cowhided him. This led to a family feud, and he proposed to remove to Virginia. Dr. Flint left him no property, and his own means had become circumscribed, while a wife and children depended upon him for support. Under these circumstances, it was very natural that he should make an effort to put me into his pocket.

I had a colored friend, a man from my native place, in whom I had the most implicit confidence. I sent for him, and told him that Mr. and Mrs. Dodge had arrived in New York. I proposed that he should call upon them to make inquiries about his friends at the south, with whom Dr. Flint's family were well acquainted. He thought there was no impropriety in his doing so, and he consented. He went to the hotel, and knocked at the door of Mr. Dodge's room, which was opened by the gentleman himself, who gruffly inquired, "What brought you here? How came you to know I was in the city?"

"Your arrival was published in the evening papers, sir; and I called to ask Mrs. Dodge about my friends at home. I didn't suppose it would give any offence."

"Where's that negro girl, that belongs to my wife?"

"What girl, sir?"

"You know well enough. I mean Linda, that ran away from Dr. Flint's plantation, some years ago. I dare say you've seen her, and know where she is."

"Yes, sir, I've seen her, and know where she is. She is out of your reach, sir."

"Tell me where she is, or bring her to me, and I will give her a chance to buy her freedom."

"I don't think it would be of any use, sir. I have heard her say she would go to the ends of the earth, rather than pay any man or woman for her freedom, because she thinks she has a right to it. Besides, she couldn't do it, if she would, for she has spent her earnings to educate her children."

This made Mr. Dodge very angry, and some high words passed between them.

My friend was afraid to come where I was; but in the course of the day I received a note from him. I supposed they had not come from the south, in the winter, for a pleasure excursion; and now the nature of their business was very plain.

Mrs. Bruce came to me and entreated me to leave the city the next morning. She said her house was watched, and it was possible that some clew to me might be obtained. I refused to take her advice. She pleaded with an earnest tenderness, that ought to have moved me; but I was in a bitter, disheartened mood. I was weary of flying from pillar to post. I had been chased during half my life, and it seemed as if the chase was never to end. There I sat, in that great city, guiltless of crime, yet not daring to worship God in any of the churches. I heard the bells ringing for afternoon service, and, with contemptuous sarcasm, I said, "Will the preachers take for their text, 'Proclaim liberty to the captive, and the opening of prison doors to them that are bound'? or will they preach from the text, 'Do unto others as ye would they should do unto you'?"[3] Oppressed Poles and Hungarians could find a safe refuge in that city; John Mitchell[4] was free to proclaim in the City Hall his desire for "a plantation well stocked with slaves;" but there I sat, an oppressed American, not daring to show my face. God forgive the black and bitter thoughts I indulged on that Sabbath day! The Scripture says, "Oppression makes even a wise man mad;"[5] and I was not wise.

I had been told that Mr. Dodge said his wife had never signed away her right to my children, and if he could not get me, he would take them. This it was, more than any thing else, that roused such a tempest in my soul. Benjamin was with his uncle William in California, but my innocent young daughter had come to spend a vacation with me. I thought of what I had suffered in slavery at her age, and my heart was like a tiger's when a hunter tries to seize her young.

Dear Mrs. Bruce! I seem to see the expression of her face, as she turned away discouraged by my obstinate mood. Finding her expostulations unavailing, she sent Ellen to entreat me. When ten o'clock in the evening arrived and Ellen had not returned, this watchful and unwearied friend became anxious. She came to us in a carriage, bringing a well-filled trunk for my journey—trusting that by this time I would listen to reason. I yielded to her, as I ought to have done before.

The next day, baby and I set out in a heavy snow storm, bound for New England again. I received letters from the City of Iniquity,[6] addressed to me under an assumed name. In a few days one came from Mrs. Bruce, informing me that my new master was still searching for me, and that she intended to put an end to this persecution by buying my freedom. I felt grateful for the kindness that prompted this offer, but the idea was not so pleasant to me as might have been expected. The more my mind had become enlightened, the more difficult it was for me to consider myself an article of property; and to pay money to those who had so grievously oppressed me seemed like taking from my sufferings the glory of triumph. I wrote to Mrs. Bruce, thanking her, but saying that being sold from one owner to another seemed too much like slavery; that such a great obligation could not be easily cancelled; and that I preferred to go to my brother in California.

Without my knowledge, Mrs. Bruce employed a gentleman in New York to enter into negotiations with Mr. Dodge. He proposed to pay three hundred dollars down, if Mr. Dodge would sell me, and enter into obligations to relinquish all

---

[3] From Isaiah 61:1 and from Matthew 7:12, respectively.

[4] Mitchell (1815–1875) founded *The Citizen,* a New York proslavery newspaper.

[5] "Surely oppression maketh a wise man mad; and a gift destroyeth the heart," from Ecclesiastes 7:7.

[6] New York, a city of fear and danger for Linda Brent at this time.

claim to me or my children forever after. He who called himself my master said he scorned so small an offer for such a valuable servant. The gentleman replied, "You can do as you choose, sir. If you reject this offer you will never get any thing; for the woman has friends who will convey her and her children out of the country."

Mr. Dodge concluded that "half a loaf was better than no bread," and he agreed to the proffered terms. By the next mail I received this brief letter from Mrs. Bruce: "I am rejoiced to tell you that the money for your freedom has been paid to Mr. Dodge. Come home to-morrow. I long to see you and my sweet babe."

My brain reeled as I read these lines. A gentleman near me said, "It's true; I have seen the bill of sale." "The bill of sale!" Those words struck me like a blow. So I was *sold* at last! A human being *sold* in the free city of New York! The bill of sale is on record, and future generations will learn from it that women were articles of traffic in New York, late in the nineteenth century of the Christian religion. It may hereafter prove a useful document to antiquaries, who are seeking to measure the progress of civilization in the United States. I well know the value of that bit of paper; but much as I love freedom, I do not like to look upon it. I am deeply grateful to the generous friend who procured it, but I despise the miscreant who demanded payment for what never rightfully belonged to him or his.

I had objected to having my freedom bought, yet I must confess that when it was done I felt as if a heavy load had been lifted from my weary shoulders. When I rode home in the cars I was no longer afraid to unveil my face and look at people as they passed. I should have been glad to have met Daniel Dodge himself; to have had him seen me and known me, that he might have mourned over the untoward circumstances which compelled him to sell me for three hundred dollars.

When I reached home, the arms of my benefactress were thrown round me, and our tears mingled. As soon as she could speak, she said, "O Linda, I'm *so* glad it's all over! You wrote to me as if you thought you were going to be transferred from one owner to another. But I did not buy you for your services. I should have done just the same, if you had been going to sail for California to-morrow. I should, at least, have the satisfaction of knowing that you left me a free woman."

My heart was exceedingly full. I remembered how my poor father had tried to buy me, when I was a small child, and how he had been disappointed. I hoped his spirit was rejoicing over me now. I remembered how my good old grandmother had laid up her earnings to purchase me in later years, and how often her plans had been frustrated. How that faithful, loving old heart would leap for joy, if she could look on me and my children now that we were free! My relatives had been foiled in all their efforts, but God had raised me up a friend among strangers, who had bestowed on me the precious, long-desired boon. Friend! It is a common word, often lightly used. Like other good and beautiful things, it may be tarnished by careless handling; but when I speak of Mrs. Bruce as my friend, the word is sacred.

My grandmother lived to rejoice in my freedom; but not long after, a letter came with a black seal. She had gone "where the wicked cease from troubling, and the weary are at rest."[7]

Time passed on, and a paper came to me from the south, containing an obituary notice of my uncle Phillip. It was the only case I ever knew of such an honor conferred upon a colored person. It was written by one of his friends, and con-

[7] From Job 3:17.

tained these words: "Now that death has laid him low, they call him a good man and a useful citizen; but what are eulogies to the black man, when the world has faded from his vision? It does not require man's praise to obtain rest in God's kingdom." So they called a colored man a *citizen!* Strange words to be uttered in that region!

Reader, my story ends with freedom; not in the usual way, with marriage.[8] I and my children are now free! We are as free from the power of slaveholders as are the white people of the north; and though that, according to my ideas, is not saying a great deal, it is a vast improvement in *my* condition. The dream of my life is not yet realized. I do not sit with my children in a home of my own. I still long for a hearthstone of my own, however humble. I wish it for my children's sake far more than for my own. But God so orders circumstances as to keep me with my friend Mrs. Bruce. Love, duty, gratitude, also bind me to her side. It is a privilege to serve her who pities my oppressed people, and who has bestowed the inestimable boon of freedom on me and my children.

It has been painful to me, in many ways, to recall the dreary years I passed in bondage. I would gladly forget them if I could. Yet the retrospection is not altogether without solace; for with those gloomy recollections come tender memories of my good old grandmother, like light fleecy clouds floating over a dark and troubled sea.

1861

Abraham Lincoln
(1809–1865)

As all American schoolchildren learn, Abraham Lincoln was born in a Hardin County, Kentucky, log cabin in 1809, spent his boyhood in Indiana, and later moved to Illinois, where he split fence rails before taking up politics and law. But Lincoln was not a child of the frontier. With the exception of a brief stay in Indiana in 1816 (months before it became a state), he never lived in a territory that had not reached statehood; moreover, he spent virtually all of his adult life in towns and cities and faced resolutely toward the centers of state and national political power. Students of Lincoln thus face a double task: to discover the man as he was and to trace the myth-making that has transmuted a canny politician into the exemplar of democracy. To seek beyond the aura of heroism and martyrdom, however, is not to diminish Lincoln or his admirers; his achievements are remarkable in their own right, and many elements of the Lincoln myth spring from qualities of the man himself. His literary achievements tend to be overlooked; his authority comes from his grace as a writer.

Lincoln was largely self-educated, both in his youth, when he had little formal schooling, and as an adult, when he taught himself the law. In 1834, four years after moving to Illinois, he was elected as a Whig to the state legislature. Two years later he passed the bar

---

[8] As many nineteenth-century novels did.

exam and began to establish himself as a shrewd advocate and skilled speaker; in 1842 he married the well-to-do Mary Todd. Elected to Congress in 1846, he served one term, during which he opposed the Mexican War as a proslavery venture, a position that alienated most of his constituents. In 1855 he ran unsuccessfully for the Senate.

Shortly afterward Lincoln joined the new Republican party and opposed Stephen Douglas for the Senate. Again he was defeated, but the campaign debates drew national attention to Lincoln and his cautious antislavery position. Rebutting Douglas at Ottawa, Illinois, Lincoln invoked the Declaration of Independence in support of the right of African Americans to "life, liberty, and the pursuit of happiness" but carefully distinguished between these "enumerated" rights and full racial equality. Judiciously and pragmatically, he shaped a politically tenable position on slavery and emerged as a leading presidential candidate. In 1860 he won a clear electoral victory as the Republican nominee, although he did not win a majority of the popular vote.

The Civil War severely tested both Lincoln and the presidency. Much of the burden of directing the war effort fell on the president. In this emergency, Lincoln assumed extraordinary executive powers, governing in part by proclamation, suspending habeas corpus, and extending military authority into civil domains. Such actions brought allegations that he had exceeded his constitutional authority.

Lincoln was assassinated by John Wilkes Booth on Good Friday, 1865, five days after the surrender of General Robert E. Lee's Confederate troops. Almost immediately, Lincoln's image was transformed from politician to redeemer and healer. Crowds of citizens mourned at his funeral train, and within weeks Walt Whitman had elegized "the sweetest, wisest soul of all my days and lands" in the poignant poem "When Lilacs Last in the Dooryard Bloom'd" (1865). As Lincoln's reputation flourished in the century and a half since his death, he has become a frequent subject of American poetry, drama, and historical fiction. His biographers include William Dean Howells, Edgar Lee Masters, and Carl Sandburg.

Suggested Readings: *The Collected Works of Abraham Lincoln*, 10 vols., ed. R. P. Basler et al., 1974. *Abraham Lincoln: A Documentary Portrait Through His Speeches and Writings*, ed. D. E. Fehrenbacher, 1977. J. G. Nicolay and J. Hay, *Abraham Lincoln*, 10 vols., 1886. W. H. Herndon and J. W. Weik, *Abraham Lincoln*, 1892. C. Sandburg, *Abraham Lincoln*, 6 vols., 1939. V. Searcher, *Lincoln Today*, 1969. C. B. Strozier, *Lincoln's Quest for Union: Public and Private Meanings*, 1987.

Text Used: *Documents of American History*, ed. H. S. Commager, 1948.

THE GETTYSBURG ADDRESS

Address Delivered at the Dedication of the Cemetery at Gettysburg November 19, 1863

Four score and seven years[1] ago our fathers brought forth on this continent, a new nation, conceived in Liberty, and dedicated to the proposition that all men are created equal.

[1] In 1776, the year in which the Declaration of Independence was signed.

Now we are engaged in a great civil war, testing whether that nation or any nation so conceived and so dedicated, can long endure. We are met on a great battle-field of that war. We have come to dedicate a portion of that field, as a final resting place for those who here gave their lives that that nation might live. It is altogether fitting and proper that we should do this.

But, in a larger sense, we can not dedicate—we can not consecrate—we can not hallow—this ground. The brave men, living and dead, who struggled here, have consecrated it, far above our poor power to add or detract. The world will little note, nor long remember what we say here, but it can never forget what they did here. It is for us the living, rather, to be dedicated here to the unfinished work which they who fought here have thus far so nobly advanced. It is rather for us to be here dedicated to the great task remaining before us—that from these honored dead we take increased devotion to that cause for which they gave the last full measure of devotion—that we here highly resolve that these dead shall not have died in vain—that this nation, under God, shall have a new birth of freedom—and that government of the people, by the people, for the people, shall not perish from the earth.

1863

SECOND INAUGURAL ADDRESS

March 4, 1865

Fellow-Countrymen:—At this second appearing to take the oath of the presidential office there is less occasion for an extended address than there was at the first. Then a statement somewhat in detail of a course to be pursued seemed fitting and proper. Now, at the expiration of four years, during which public declarations have been constantly called forth on every point and phase of the great contest which still absorbs the attention and engrosses the energies of the nation, little that is new could be presented. The progress of our arms, upon which all else chiefly depends, is as well known to the public as to myself, and it is, I trust, reasonably satisfactory and encouraging to all. With high hope for the future, no prediction in regard to it is ventured.

On the occasion corresponding to this four years ago all thoughts were anxiously directed to an impending civil war. All dreaded it, all sought to avert it. While the inaugural address was being delivered from this place, devoted altogether to *saving* the Union without war, insurgent agents were in the city seeking to *destroy* it without war—seeking to dissolve the Union and divide effects by negotiation. Both parties deprecated war, but one of them would *make* war rather than let the nation survive, and the other would *accept* war rather than let it perish, and the war came.

One eighth of the whole population was colored slaves, not distributed generally over the Union, but localized in the southern part of it. These slaves constituted a peculiar and powerful interest. All knew that this interest was somehow the cause of the war. To strengthen, perpetuate, and extend this interest was the object for which the insurgents would rend the Union even by war, while the Government claimed no right to do more than to restrict the territorial enlargement of it.

Neither party expected for the war the magnitude or the duration which it has already attained. Neither anticipated that the *cause* of the conflict might cease with or even before the conflict itself should cease. Each looked for an easier triumph, and a result less fundamental and astounding. Both read the same Bible and pray to the same God, and each invokes His aid against the other. It may seem strange that any men should dare to ask a just God's assistance in wringing their bread from the sweat of other men's faces, but let us judge not, that we be not judged.[1] The prayers of both could not be answered. That of neither has been answered fully. The Almighty has His own purposes. "Woe unto the world because of offenses: for it must needs be that offenses come, but woe to that man by whom the offense cometh."[2] If we shall suppose that American slavery is one of those offenses which, in the providence of God, must needs come, but which, having continued through His appointed time, He now wills to remove, and that He gives to both North and South this terrible war, as the woe due to those by whom the offense came, shall we discern therein any departure from those divine attributes which the believers in a living God always ascribe to Him? Fondly do we hope, fervently do we pray, that this mighty scourge of war may speedily pass away. Yet, if God wills that it continue until all the wealth piled by the bondsman's two hundred and fifty years of unrequited toil shall be sunk, and until every drop of blood drawn with the lash shall be paid by another drawn with the sword, as was said three thousand years ago, so still it must be said, "The judgments of the Lord are true and righteous altogether."[3]

With malice toward none, with charity for all, with firmness in the right as God gives us to see the right, let us strive on to finish the work we are in, to bind up the nation's wounds, to care for him who shall have borne the battle and for his widow and his orphan, to do all which may achieve and cherish a just and lasting peace among ourselves and with all nations.

1865

EARLY TO MIDDLE 19TH-CENTURY POETRY

In 1820 the English critic Sydney Smith provoked indignation in the United States with a barrage of questions in the *Edinburgh Review* that began "who reads an American book?" He swirled on to ask who ("in the four quarters of the globe") admires American art, learns from American medicine, looks through American telescopes, or "drinks out of American glasses? or eats from American plates?" The most elaborate response to Smith's scornful attack came not from artists, physicians, or dishmakers but from the editor Samuel Kettell. Out of a conviction that American poetry had begun to demonstrate "a national spirit," Kettell issued his three-volume *Specimens of American Poetry* (1829), which includes the work of 189 writers, most of them contemporary. It was a decidedly uneven collection of verse. Many of Kettell's poets wrote dismal romantic stuff: a mawkish hymn to the ocean, a tearful tribute to parting, an indulgent consideration of beauty refined

---

[1] "Judge ye not, that ye be not judged," from Matthew 7:1; the biblical cadences here enhance the solemnity and compassion of Lincoln's words.
[2] From Matthew 18:7.   [3] From Psalm 19:9.

by consumption. Some of them addressed American topics—the monument at Bunker Hill, the Indian maiden Pocahontas—and thus pointed, however feebly, toward materials that might go into the making of a national poetry. But three of the younger writers—William Cullen Bryant, Henry Wadsworth Longfellow, and John Greenleaf Whittier—would become admired American poets in the nineteenth century. It is to Kettell's credit that he recognized their youthful promise.

Despite the limitations of quality in Kettell's anthology, the collection does suggest the role of poetry in a nation still testing the dimensions of its independence. Kettell's parade of patriotic poems, for example, is both understandable and amusing. His assessment of Bryant brings us to see something of deeper import: the appeal of conservative and didactic verse in the first half of the nineteenth century. After noting Bryant's "propriety" and love of nature, Kettell praises this model poet for upholding "a pure and classical standard in an age" that tends "toward lawless fanaticism and wildness." These last words may seem surprising to anyone who thinks the late twentieth century has a monopoly on "wildness"— and they may be exaggerated to make a point. But Kettell's description of the "age" was echoed in many newspapers and magazines throughout the 1820s and 1830s, and it provides a social backdrop against which we can measure the attraction of poetry that was comforting in its values and manner.

As a lawyer, newspaper editor, and literary critic, William Cullen Bryant understood the adjunct role of the poet in a utilitarian America and thus anticipated the practice and stance of the (younger) "Fireside Poets," so-named because families commonly read their works around the fireside: Longfellow, Whittier, Oliver

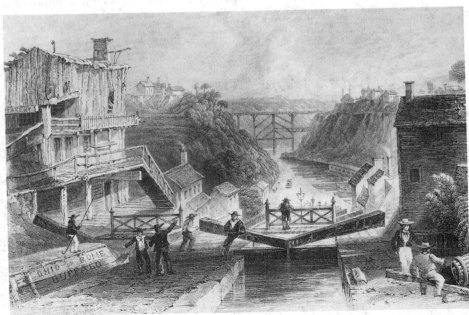

The Erie Canal, as seen in this 1838 engraving, opened a major route to the West when it was completed in 1825 and helped further the nation's romantic expansionism.

Wendell Holmes, and James Russell Lowell, all of whom made important contributions to other professions. Much of Bryant's poetry offered readers a romantic sensibility familiar from the work of William Wordsworth and Samuel Taylor Coleridge. Pervading this romanticism, however, and giving it an American bias is Bryant's appreciation of native landscapes and his comforting belief that nature is a gentle and wise teacher. "To a Waterfowl" (1818) and "The Prairies" (1833) illustrate the two main articles of Bryant's poetic faith—the first with its didactic reassurance that a benign power guides us through life, the second with its celebration of a setting "for which the speech of England has no name."

In the hands of Bryant and the Fireside Poets, American poetry came to affirm and validate social norms. The poetry they wrote could criticize social practice from a moral perspective. If Bryant's decorous work asserted a reformist faith in the benevolence of progress, that of the Fireside Poets frequently confronted social and political issues even as it proclaimed the importance of domestic values. Whittier, for example, expressed his deep abolitionist feelings in poems such as "Massachusetts to Virginia" (1843) and "Ichabod" (1850) but produced the classic memory-poem of the nineteenth century in *Snowbound* (1866), a paean to the richness of domestic harmony—nostalgic, triumphant in its recollections. Lowell used dialect and a facade of naïveté in *The Biglow Papers* (1848, 1867) to protest the Mexican War and the expansion of slavery, but he also wrote light verse and the witty *Fable for Critics* (1848) which pictures the composed Bryant in "supreme iceolation" and describes Poe as "three-fifths . . . genius and two-fifths sheer fudge." And Longfellow, the most popular poet of the century, made epic poems from the fabric of American history in such narratives as *Evangeline* (1847) and *The Song of Hiawatha* (1855), although he remained the champion of domestic piety in his best-known verse.

Bryant and the Fireside Poets produced work that incorporated American topics through the lens of a temperate romanticism. In a variety of ways they taught and affirmed traditional values, took up political causes with idealistic passion, and ranged in form from the sonnet to the epic. They personified the image of the poet as public figure, someone available for political discourse or for ceremonial occasions. In a deep and real sense, they were part of the society for which they wrote.

Although the Fireside Poets made American poetry seem chiefly a New England enterprise, a number of southern poets reminded the nation of the distinctiveness of their region in the mid-nineteenth century. *Russell's Magazine*, founded in 1857 by Paul Hamilton Hayne, provided a ready outlet for a number of poets—including Hayne, Henry Timrod, and William John Grayson—who made up the informal "Russell's Bookstore Group" in Charleston, South Carolina. The early work of both Hayne and Timrod celebrates the beauty of nature in the American South. Some of this southern poetry defends the institution of slavery: Grayson's *The Hireling and the Slave* (1854), for example, presents an idyllic portrait of slavery in contrast to the harsh life of European laborers.

Juxtaposed with such a view is the poetic vision of Frances E. W. Harper, the most notable African-American poet in the years between Phillis Wheatley (in the eighteenth century) and Paul Laurence Dunbar (at the end of the nineteenth). Many of Harper's poems portray oppression and the abuses of slavery, with dramatic eloquence. "The Slave Mother: A Tale of the Ohio" (1874) anticipates the fateful plot of Toni Morrison's *Beloved* (1987) in relating starkly the story of a mother who sacrifices her baby's life so as not to condemn the child to a life of slavery. Harper's poetry shows us the experience of oppression from the inside. Her voice authenticates pain and degradation, just as the voices of the abolitionists articulate principle.

=CONTEXTS=

The Abolition Movement

In the 1830s America experienced a resurgence of antislavery sentiment, largely due to three factors: the debates over slavery in conventions called for the purpose of rewriting state constitutions; Nat Turner's Rebellion in Virginia in 1831; and the publication of the *Liberator*, a radical abolitionist newspaper by William Lloyd Garrison (1805–1879) calling for the immediate, unconditional emancipation of all slaves in America. Garrison's weekly was launched on January 1, 1831, and continued publication for thirty-four years, folding its doors only after slavery had been abolished by the Thirteenth Amendment to the Constitution. (Garrison was the first editor to print the poems of John Greenleaf Whittier, a fellow abolitionist and a founder of the American Anti-Slavery Society.) Garrison's statement of his aims and purposes, reprinted below from the first issue, alarmed northern moderates, outraged southerners, and caused a split between those who called for the gradual end of slavery and those who wanted its immediate end.

Commencement of the *Liberator*

Assenting to the "self-evident truth" maintained in the American Declaration of Independence, "that all men are created equal, and endowed by their Creator with certain inalienable rights—among which are life, liberty, and the pursuit of happiness," I shall strenuously contend for the immediate enfranchisement of our slave population. In Park Street Church, on the Fourth of July, 1829, in an address on slavery, I unreflectingly assented to the popular but pernicious doctrine of gradual abolition. I seize this opportunity to make a full and unequivocal recantation, and thus publicly to ask pardon of my God, of my country, and of my brethren, the poor slaves, for having uttered a sentiment so full of timidity, injustice and absurdity. A similar recantation, from my pen, was published in the *Genius of Universal Emancipation*, at Baltimore, in September, 1829. My conscience is now satisfied.

I am aware, that many object to the severity of my language; but is there not cause for severity? I will be as harsh as truth, and as uncompromising as justice. On this subject, I do not wish to think, or speak, or write, with moderation. No! no! Tell a man, whose house is on fire, to give a moderate alarm; tell him to moderately rescue his wife from the hands of the ravisher; tell the mother to gradually extricate her babe from the fire into which it has fallen; but urge me not to use moderation in a cause like the present! I am in earnest. I will not equivocate—I will not excuse—I will not retreat a single inch—AND I WILL BE HEARD. The apathy of the people is enough to make every statue leap from its pedestal, and to hasten the resurrection of the dead.

William Lloyd Garrison, 1831

Two major formulations of poetic theory in this period came from Edgar Allan Poe and Ralph Waldo Emerson, both poets of considerable talent. Romantic that he was in defining *beauty* as the province of the poem, Poe nonetheless stressed the importance of *form* in poetry; to him the poet was a craftsman who introduced such considerations as rhyme and meter, of tone and even length, into the making of a poem. Militantly opposed to what he called "the heresy of *The Didactic*" (and thus to the practice of the honored writers of New England), Poe defines poetry in his essay "The Poetic Principle" (1850) as *"The Rhythmical Creation of Beauty."* To Emerson, conversely, the poet is a seer or prophet who releases us from the prison of our own little worlds. In his essay "The Poet" (1844) Emerson asserts the priority of "thought" in the genesis of a poem; "it is not metres but a metre-making argument, that makes a poem, a thought so passionate and alive, that, like the spirit of a thought or an animal, it has an architecture of its own, and adorns nature with a new thing." The form of a poem is thus organic, expressive, profoundly liberating.

Poe and Emerson visualized the possibilities of poetry in diametrically opposed ways, Poe in a way that intrigued the French symbolists and some modernist poets, Emerson in a way that appealed to any number of romantic poets but principally and dramatically to his contemporary, Walt Whitman. In "The Poet," Emerson laments the fact that the United States had not yet produced a writer who realized "the value of our incomparable materials." He called for a poet who could exalt the details of American life: such things as political caucuses, logrolling, and western clearing "are flat and dull to dull people," he argues, but they "rest on the same foundations of wonder as the town of Troy, and the temple of Delphos." Emerson admits that he is not the poet to celebrate these "unsung" aspects of American life, but he asserts that "America is a poem in our eyes," that "its ample geography dazzles the imagination." A decade later Walt Whitman began to write this vast poem. With egocentric grace he remarked to the journalist J. T. Trowbridge, "I had been simmering, simmering, simmering; Emerson brought me to a boil."

What Whitman extracted from Emerson and from the democratic nation that had grown awkwardly through the first half of the nineteenth century was the crucial idea of "self." The first edition of *Leaves of Grass* appeared in 1855 and evoked strong reactions from other writers: Whittier threw his gift copy into the fireplace, Lowell reportedly refused to read it, and Emerson praised it warmly. Notwithstanding the small sales of the book, Whitman published a second edition in 1856 and a third in 1860 (there were nine in all). Each edition grew, adjusting and rearranging its vision, absorbing the experience of the nation into the democratic and collective self at the center. Radically different in form and substance from any previous poetry, Whitman's *Leaves* celebrates the self as encompassing, expansive, boastfully inclusive in its vision. No longer is it necessary to have history and legend to forge an epic: as Whitman makes clear in the remarkable preface to the 1855 edition of *Leaves* and in that volume's "Song of Myself," the human being, body and soul (which are one), becomes epic in importance, deserving of epic treatment in a land of epic proportions.

Devastating and crippling, the Civil War gave American poets a tragic subject of their own, a gathering event for the expression of grief. From different perspectives Whitman, Herman Melville, and Henry Timrod wrote poems about individual battles and individual soldiers dead or broken in body. Tempered in assertion, solemn in tone, the poems in Whitman's *Drum-Taps* (1865) display a haunting sorrow, the consequence of a shattered optimism that found deepest expression in his tribute to Abraham Lincoln, "When Lilacs Last in the Dooryard Bloom'd." By comparison with these meditations on death, the poems in Melville's *Battle-Pieces* (1866) seem distanced, almost frozen with commemorative pride in the heroism and suffering of the war. Even the delicate portrait of "The College Colonel" is restrained, mannered, austere in its reckoning of pain.

Whereas Whitman and Melville write about the consequences of battle from fixed perspectives after-the-fact, three poems by Timrod frame the Civil War from developing points of view in Charleston, South Carolina. *Ethnogenesis,* written in 1861 during sessions of the Confederate Congress (but not published until 1873), is not so much a war poem as a founding statement that hails the Confederacy, congratulates the South for its character and climate, and predicts victory over the North. "Charleston" (1862) portrays that southern city in portentous calm, awaiting the clash of arms that will bring "triumph or the tomb." And the "Ode" (1867) to the Confederate dead buried at Magnolia Cemetery honors the "martyrs of a fallen cause" whose "defeated valor" hallows the earth forever.

Among American poets only Whitman emerged from the trauma of the Civil War with hope for the future. His optimism was qualified, his flagrant boasting about America a thing of the past. Yet, so great was his faith in democracy, so firm was his commitment to the future, that Whitman in *Democratic Vistas* (1871) came to see the war years as "the years of parturition," the years of the birth of the country. In April 1865 Bryant published "Abraham Lincoln," honoring the president who had seen the nation through four years of strife. It is a polished and accomplished poem, deserving of the praise Samuel Kettell gave Bryant's work in 1829. But to read that poem alongside Whitman's "When Lilacs Last in the Dooryard Bloom'd," written in the same year, is to see that a revolution had occurred in American poetry, radical beyond Bryant's powers, encompassing beyond what Kettell could have foreseen. With Walt Whitman's "barbaric yawp" (as he termed it in *Song of Myself*), poetry in America became American poetry.

William Cullen Bryant
(1794–1878)

William Cullen Bryant, lawyer, journalist, literary critic, and romantic nature poet, was one of the most dominant literary figures of his age. A member of the Knickerbocker group and other literary societies, he spent his life close to the arts. He was among the first to call for a truly American literature and the first American poet to achieve international acclaim. The son of a physician father and a mother who was a descendant of the Puritan John Alden, Bryant was born in 1794 in Cummington, Massachusetts, and educated early at the hands of country Calvinist ministers. When he was thirteen, he published *The Embargo* (1808), a satire in verse on the political policies of Thomas Jefferson. He entered Williams College in 1810 but left after less than a year and embarked on the study of law. Admitted to the bar in 1814, he established a law practice in Great Barrington, Massachusetts, and married Fanny Fairchild in 1821.

Bryant gave up his legal work to pursue a career in journalism. In 1825 he moved to New York City and began editing the *New York Review*. A year later he became an assistant editor of the New York *Evening Post,* and in 1829 he assumed the editorship of this prestigious journal, a position he held until his death in 1878. Bryant occupies a central place in the history of American journalism.

Bryant's poetry is important as a transition between the neoclassical tendencies of the early republic and the American romanticism that would follow. Bryant published his first

Pictured in Kindred Spirits *(1849), by Asher Durand, are William Cullen Bryant, poet, and Thomas Cole, landscape painter, in a setting that exemplifies the romantic ideal of harmony between nature and people.*

collection of poetry, *Poems,* in 1821; it includes "Thanatopsis," perhaps his most famous poem, originally drafted around 1811. As a forerunner of the romantic movement in America, he led the literary revolt against neoclassicism in part by stressing the use of American materials, including the American landscape. Bryant claimed from his earliest childhood to be "a delighted observer of external nature," and his poetry is filled with images drawn from his youth in the Berkshires of Massachusetts. The major themes in his work include nature, mutability, death, the past, and poetry itself. Insistently didactic, his poetry repeatedly suggests the moral and spiritual perfection to be found in the contemplation of nature. Many of his best poems are meditative and describe the goodness of nature in detail.

In keeping with Bryant's romantic inclinations, his poetry also shows remarkable range in terms of metrical freedom and experimentation. A meticulous craftsman, Bryant became a master of poetic forms; during the final decade of his life he translated Homer's the *Iliad* (1870) and the *Odyssey* (1871–1872) into simple and effective blank verse. As his work demonstrates, Bryant was interested in scientific progress and perhaps even more so in politics—advocating the rights of labor unions, free trade, and a free press. His concern for human rights is evident in his stand against slavery and in his interest in the traditions of Native Americans. An exceptionally prominent figure in his own time, Bryant continued writing and publishing until his death. His limited reputation today seems scant appreciation for a lifetime of measured but definite achievement.

Suggested Readings: *The Letters of William Cullen Bryant,* ed. W. C. Bryant II and T. G. Voss, 4 vols., 1975–1984. C. S. Johnson, *Politics and a Bellyful: The Journalistic Career of William Cullen Bryant,* 1962. H. H. Peckham, *Gotham Yankee: A Biography of William Cullen Bryant,* 1971. C. H. Brown, *William Cullen Bryant,* 1972. J. T. Phair, *A Bibliography of William Cullen Bryant and His Critics, 1808-1972,* 1975.

Text Used: "The Poet" and "Abraham Lincoln": *The Poetical Works of William Cullen Bryant,* ed. P. Godwin, Vol. II, 1883, rpt. 1967. All else: *The Poetical Works,* Vol. I.

THANATOPSIS*

To him who in the love of Nature holds
Communion with her visible forms, she speaks
A various language; for his gayer hours
She has a voice of gladness, and a smile
And eloquence of beauty, and she glides
Into his darker musings, with a mild
And healing sympathy, that steals away
Their sharpness, ere he is aware. When thoughts
Of the last bitter hour come like a blight
Over thy spirit, and sad images   10
Of the stern agony, and shroud, and pall,
And breathless darkness, and the narrow house,
Make thee to shudder, and grow sick at heart;—
Go forth, under the open sky, and list

* First published in part in the *North American Review* (1817) and revised into the present form for publication in Bryant's *Poems* (1821). The Greek word "thanatopsis" means "meditation on death."

To Nature's teachings, while from all around—
Earth and her waters, and the depths of air—
Comes a still voice.—[1]

                   Yet a few days, and thee
The all-beholding sun shall see no more
In all his course; nor yet in the cold ground,
Where thy pale form was laid, with many tears,   20
Nor in the embrace of ocean, shall exist
Thy image. Earth, that nourished thee, shall claim
Thy growth, to be resolved to earth again,
And, lost each human trace, surrendering up
Thine individual being, shalt thou go
To mix for ever with the elements,
To be a brother to the insensible rock
And to the sluggish clod, which the rude swain[2]
Turns with his share,[3] and treads upon. The oak
Shall send his roots abroad, and pierce thy mould.   30

    Yet not to thine eternal resting-place
Shalt thou retire alone, nor couldst thou wish
Couch more magnificent. Thou shalt lie down
With patriarchs of the infant world—with kings,
The powerful of the earth—the wise, the good,
Fair forms, and hoary seers of ages past,
All in one mighty sepulchre. The hills
Rock-ribbed and ancient as the sun,—the vales
Stretching in pensive quietness between;
The venerable woods—rivers that move   40
In majesty, and the complaining brooks
That make the meadows green; and, poured round
    all,
Old Ocean's gray and melancholy waste,—
Are but the solemn decorations all
Of the great tomb of man. The golden sun,
The planets, all the infinite host of heaven,
Are shining on the sad abodes of death,
Through the still lapse of ages. All that tread
The globe are but a handful to the tribes
That slumber in its bosom.—Take the wings   50
Of morning, pierce the Barcan wilderness,[4]
Or lose thyself in the continuous woods
Where rolls the Oregon,[5] and hears no sound,
Save his own dashings—yet the dead are there:
And millions in those solitudes, since first

---

[1] From this point to the end of the poem, nature in its entirety speaks in "a still voice" of stoic authority.
[2] Farmer.   [3] Plowshare.   [4] The Libyan desert of Barca.
[5] The Native-American name for Oregon's Columbia River.

The flight of years began, have laid them down
In their last sleep—the dead reign there alone.
So shalt thou rest, and what if thou withdraw
In silence from the living, and no friend
Take note of thy departure? All that breathe   60
Will share thy destiny. The gay will laugh
When thou art gone, the solemn brood of care
Plod on, and each one as before will chase
His favorite phantom; yet all these shall leave
Their mirth and their employments, and shall come
And make their bed with thee. As the long train
Of ages glides away, the sons of men,
The youth in life's fresh spring, and he who goes
In the full strength of years, matron and maid,
The speechless babe, and the gray-headed man—   70
Shall one by one be gathered to thy side,
By those, who in their turn shall follow them.
    So live, that when thy summons comes to join
The innumerable caravan, which moves
To that mysterious realm, where each shall take
His chamber in the silent halls of death,
Thou go not, like the quarry-slave at night,
Scourged to his dungeon, but, sustained and soothed
By an unfaltering trust, approach thy grave,
Like one who wraps the drapery of his couch   80
About him, and lies down to pleasant dreams.

                              1811?, 1817

TO A WATERFOWL*

Whither, midst falling dew,
While glow the heavens with the last steps of day,
Far, through their rosy depths, dost thou pursue
Thy solitary way?

Vainly the fowler's eye
Might mark thy distant flight to do thee wrong,
As, darkly painted on the crimson sky,
Thy figure floats along.

Seek'st thou the plashy[1] brink
Of weedy lake, or marge of river wide,   10
Or where the rocking billows rise and sink
On the chafed ocean-side?

* First published in the *North American Review* (1818).   [1] Marshy.

There is a Power whose care
Teaches thy way along that pathless coast—
The desert and illimitable air—
Lone wandering, but not lost.

All day thy wings have fanned,
At that far height, the cold, thin atmosphere,
Yet stoop not, weary, to the welcome land,
Though the dark night is near.   20

And soon that toil shall end;
Soon shalt thou find a summer home, and rest,
And scream among thy fellows; reeds shall bend,
Soon, o'er thy sheltered nest.

Thou'rt gone, the abyss of heaven
Hath swallowed up thy form; yet, on my heart
Deeply has sunk the lesson thou hast given,
And shall not soon depart.

He who, from zone to zone,
Guides through the boundless sky thy certain flight,   30
In the long way that I must tread alone,
Will lead my steps aright.

1815, 1818

THE MURDERED TRAVELLER*

When Spring, to woods and wastes around,
Brought bloom and joy again,
The murdered traveller's bones were found,
Far down a narrow glen.

The fragrant birch, above him, hung
Her tassels in the sky;
And many a vernal blossom sprung,
And nodded careless by.[1]

The red-bird warbled, as he wrought
His hanging nest o'erhead,   10
And fearless, near the fatal spot,
Her young the partridge led.

---

* First published in the *United States Literary Gazette* (1825).
[1] This neglected poem shows an aspect of Bryant's poetic vision that is fascinating and uncharacteristic: nature here is not in sympathy with the tragic human spectacle; it bursts out in springtime flower and song, life unaware of death.

But there was weeping far away,
And gentle eyes, for him,
With watching many an anxious day,
Were sorrowful and dim.

They little knew, who loved him so,
The fearful death he met,
When shouting o'er the desert snow,
Unarmed, and hard beset;[2]—   20

Nor how, when round the frosty pole
The northern dawn was red,
The mountain-wolf and wild-cat stole
To banquet on the dead;[3]—

Nor how, when strangers found his bones,
They dressed the hasty bier,[4]
And marked his grave with nameless stones,
Unmoistened by a tear.

But long they looked, and feared, and wept,
Within his distant home;   30
And dreamed, and started as they slept,
For joy that he was come.

Long, long they looked—but never spied
His welcome step again,
Nor knew the fearful death he died
Far down that narrow glen.

1824, 1825

THE AFRICAN CHIEF*

Chained in the market-place he stood,
A man of giant frame,
Amid the gathering multitude
That shrunk to hear his name[1]—
All stern of look and strong of limb,
His dark eye on the ground:—
And silently they gazed on him,
As on a lion bound.

---

[2] Strenuously attacked.
[3] A gory picture for any poet to draw, particularly the well-mannered Bryant.
[4] The litter, or hastily made coffin, on which bones were carried to a grave.
* First published in the *United States Review* (1826).
[1] The scene is a marketplace in Africa where this mighty chief stands to be sold to slave traders; apparently his name is well known, for the multitude shrinks back when they hear it.

Vainly, but well that chief had fought,
He was a captive now,   10
Yet pride, that fortune humbles not,
Was written on his brow.
The scars his dark broad bosom wore
Showed warrior true and brave;
A prince among his tribe before,
He could not be a slave.[2]

Then to his conqueror he spake:
"My brother is a king;
Undo this necklace from my neck,
And take this bracelet ring,   20
And send me where my brother reigns,
And I will fill thy hands
With store of ivory from the plains,
And gold-dust from the sands."

"Not for thy ivory nor thy gold
Will I unbind thy chain;
That bloody hand shall never hold
The battle-spear again.
A price that nation never gave[3]
Shall yet be paid for thee;   30
For thou shalt be the Christian's slave,
In lands beyond the sea."

Then wept the warrior chief, and bade[4]
To shred his locks away;
And one by one, each heavy braid
Before the victor lay.
Thick were the platted locks, and long,
And closely hidden there
Shone many a wedge of gold among
The dark and crisped hair.   40

"Look, feast thy greedy eye with gold
Long kept for sorest need;
Take it—thou askest sums untold—
And say that I am freed.

Take it—my wife, the long, long day,
Weeps by the cocoa-tree,
And my young children leave their play,
And ask in vain for me."

---

[2] Meant literally and forcefully, this line anticipates the poem's tragic ending.
[3] A price beyond what anyone ever paid will be "paid for thee."   [4] Told them to.

"I take thy gold, but, I have made
Thy fetters fast and strong,
And ween[5] that by the cocoa-shade
Thy wife will wait thee long."
Strong was the agony that shook
The captive's frame to hear,
And the proud meaning of his look
Was changed to mortal fear.

His heart was broken—crazed his brain:
At once his eye grew wild;
He struggled fiercely with his chain,
Whispered, and wept, and smiled;
Yet wore not long those fatal bands,
And once, at shut of day,
They drew him forth upon the sands,
The foul hyena's prey.[6]

$$1825, 1826$$

THE POET*

Thou, who wouldst wear the name
Of poet mid thy brethren of mankind,
And clothe in words of flame
Thoughts that shall live within the general mind!
Deem not the framing of a deathless lay
The pastime of a drowsy summer day.

But gather all thy powers,
And wreak them[1] on the verse that thou dost weave,
And in thy lonely hours,
At silent morning or at wakeful eve,
While the warm current tingles through thy veins,
Set forth the burning words in fluent strains.

No smooth array of phrase,
Artfully sought and ordered though it be,
Which the cold rhymer lays

---

[5] Know.

[6] The ending is suggested not only by line 16 but by the fact that the chief smiles after experiencing fear and wildness: he is so attuned to his surroundings that nature, in the form of a savage hyena, takes away his life before he can be sold into bondage. Bryant's stance against slavery was strong, although his best-known poems would hardly attest to the fact.

* First published in *Thirty Poems* (1864).   [1] Release them, apply them fully.

Upon his page with languid industry,
Can wake the listless pulse to livelier speed,
Or fill with sudden tears the eyes that read.

The secret wouldst thou know
To touch the heart or fire the blood at will?   20
Let thine own eyes o'erflow;
Let thy lips quiver with the passionate thrill;
Seize the great thought, ere yet its power be past,
And bind, in words, the fleet emotion fast.

Then, should thy verse appear
Halting and harsh, and all unaptly wrought,
Touch the crude line with fear,
Save in the moment of impassioned thought;
Then summon back the original glow, and mend
The strain with rapture that with fire was penned.   30

Yet let no empty gust
Of passion find a utterance in thy lay,
A blast that whirls the dust
Along the howling street and dies away;
But feelings of calm power and mighty sweep,
Like currents journeying through the windless deep.

Seek'st thou, in living lays,
To limn[2] the beauty of the earth and sky?
Before thine inner gaze
Let all that beauty in clear vision lie;   40
Look on it with exceeding love, and write
The words inspired by wonder and delight.

Of tempests wouldst thou sing,
Or tell of battles—make thyself a part
Of the great tumult; cling
To the tossed wreck with terror in thy heart;
Scale, with the assaulting host, the rampart's height,
And strike and struggle in the thickest fight.

So shalt thou frame a lay[3]
That haply may endure from age to age,   50
And they who read shall say:
"What witchery hangs upon this poet's page!
What art is his the written spells to find
That sway from mood to mood the willing mind!"

1863, 1864

---

[2] Paint, portray.   [3] A song or poem.

ABRAHAM LINCOLN*

Oh, slow to smite and swift to spare,
Gentle and merciful and just!
Who, in the fear of God, didst bear
The sword of power, a nation's trust!

In sorrow by thy bier we stand,
Amid the awe that hushes all,
And speak the anguish of a land
That shook with horror at thy fall.

Thy task is done; the bond[1] are free:
We bear thee to an honored grave.
Whose proudest monument shall be   10
The broken fetters[2] of the slave.

Pure was thy life; its bloody close
Hath placed thee with the sons of light,
Among the noble host of those
Who perished in the cause of Right.

1865

Henry Wadsworth Longfellow
(1807–1882)

Henry Wadsworth Longfellow was the most widely read American poet in the nineteenth
century. The sales of his poems suggest his immense popularity: his first collection, *Voices
of the Night* (1839), sold 43,000 copies; *The Song of Hiawatha* (1855) sold 30,000 copies
within six months; and *The Courtship of Miles Standish* (1858) sold an astonishing 15,000
copies on its first day of publication. So great was his fame in England that he was the first
American to have his bust preserved in Poet's Corner of Westminster Abbey after his

---

* First published in the New York *Evening Post,* April 26, 1865. The poem was written at the request
of the Committee on Arrangements and read to a gathering of mourners on April 24, 1865, when
Lincoln's funeral procession passed through New York City. Lincoln had been assassinated on April
24, 1865.
[1] Slaves.   [2] Shackles.

death in 1882. With James Russell Lowell, John Greenleaf Whittier, and Oliver Wendell Holmes, Longfellow was one of the culturally approved "Fireside Poets," whose works became standard educational fare throughout the nation. Master of a wide range of verse forms, Longfellow was particularly adept as a writer of ballads, sonnets, and narrative poems.

Longfellow was born in 1807 in Portland, Maine, then a part of Massachusetts, into a long-established family that could trace its ancestry back to the *Mayflower*. He attended Portland Academy and later Bowdoin College, where he was a classmate of Nathaniel Hawthorne. Upon graduation in 1825, Longfellow accepted a professorship in modern languages at Bowdoin, and the college sent him to Europe for three years of preparatory study in Europe. In 1829 he assumed his post at Bowdoin. Longfellow held positions in the field of modern foreign language at Harvard University as well. In 1835 he returned to Europe for intense language study, particularly German, in preparation for his Harvard appointment. On the journey, however, his wife since 1831, Mary Potter, died after a miscarriage. From 1836 to 1854 he was chairman of modern languages at Harvard; during that time he met and married the heiress Frances Appleton. After eighteen years of marriage, during which she bore three daughters and two sons, she was killed in a house fire in 1861.

Given his training in foreign languages, and his immersion in foreign culture, it is not surprising that Longfellow remained interested in foreign literature and the classics throughout his long career, from his collection of European poetry in *Poets and Poetry of Europe* (1845) to his *Tales of a Wayside Inn* (1863) and his translation of Dante's *Divine Comedy* (1867). Although his knowledge of other literary traditions, particularly Germanic and Scandinavian, allowed him to borrow from a virtual storehouse of poetry, Longfellow demonstrated great versatility in his use of prosody and poetic forms. And like William Cullen Bryant and other writers concerned to create an American literature, Longfellow used his talents to explore American history, legends, and folklore. Works such as *Evangeline* (1847), *Hiawatha,* and *The Courtship of Miles Standish* attest to this considerable effort.

Longfellow was a deeply traditional writer, a poet of assurance whose commitment to the values of domesticity endeared him to a wide audience. By considering that *Hiawatha* and the first edition of Walt Whitman's *Leaves of Grass* were published in the same year, 1855, we get a sense of American poetry at a crossroads—Longfellow offering the public what it wanted, Whitman offering the same public what it had to have. Because the twentieth century has come to prefer Whitman, we have tended to neglect the work of our public poet par excellence—along with that of the other Fireside Poets. Yet, even from our perspective, many of Longfellow's shorter lyrics, and especially the more personal of his sonnets, command respect and admiration.

Suggested Readings: *Kavanagh, A Tale,* ed. J. Downey, 1965. *The Poetical Works of Longfellow,* 1893, rpt. 1975. *The Letters of Henry Wadsworth Longfellow,* 6 vols., ed. A. Hilen, 1966–1982. S. Longfellow, *The Life of Henry Wadsworth Longfellow,* 3 vols., 1886, rpt. 1969. N. Arvin, *Longfellow: His Life and Work,* 1963. C. B. Williams, *Henry Wadsworth Longfellow,* 1964. L. R. Thompson, *Young Longfellow (1807–1843),* 1969. E. Wagenknecht, *Henry Wadsworth Longfellow, His Poetry and Prose,* 1986.

Text Used: *The Complete Poetical Works of Henry Wadsworth Longfellow,* 1922.

A portrait of Longfellow's three daughters.

A PSALM OF LIFE*

What the Heart of the Young Man Said to the Psalmist

Tell me not, in mournful numbers,[1]
Life is but an empty dream!—

---

* First published in the *Knickerbocker of New-York Monthly Magazine* (1838).
[1] Meters, poetic rhythms.

For the soul is dead that slumbers,
　And things are not what they seem.

Life is real! Life is earnest!
　And the grave is not its goal;
Dust thou art, to dust returnest,[2]
　Was not spoken of the soul.

Not enjoyment, and not sorrow,
　Is our destined end or way;
But to act, that each to-morrow   10
　Find us farther than to-day.

Art is long, and Time is fleeting,[3]
　And our hearts, though stout and brave,
Still, like muffled drums, are beating
　Funeral marches to the grave.

In the world's broad field of battle,
　In the bivouac of Life,
Be not like dumb, driven cattle!
　Be a hero in the strife!   20

Trust no Future, howe'er pleasant!
　Let the dead Past bury its dead!
Act,—act in the living Present!
　Heart within, and God o'erhead!

Lives of great men all remind us
　We can make our lives sublime,
And, departing, leave behind us
　Footprints on the sands of time;

Footprints, that perhaps another,
　Sailing o'er life's solemn main,   30
A forlorn and shipwrecked brother,
　Seeing, shall take heart again.

Let us, then, be up and doing,
　With a heart for any fate;
Still achieving, still pursuing,
　Learn to labor and to wait.

1838

---

[2] " . . . for dust you are and unto dust you shall return," from Genesis 3:19.

[3] Scholars have carefully traced this idea to the Greek physician Hippocrates (460?–377 B.C.), to the Roman philosopher Seneca (4? B.C.–A.D. 65), to the English poet Geoffrey Chaucer (1343?–1400), and to the German poet and novelist Johann Wolfgang von Goethe (1749–1832).

MEZZO CAMMIN*

Written at Boppard on the Rhine, August 25, 1842, just before leaving for home.

Half of my life is gone, and I have let
    The years slip from me and have not fulfilled
The aspiration of my youth, to build
    Some tower of song with lofty parapet.
Not indolence, nor pleasure, nor the fret
    Of restless passions that would not be stilled,
    But sorrow, and a care that almost killed,[1]
    Kept me from what I may accomplish yet;
Though, half-way up the hill, I see the Past
    Lying beneath me with its sounds and sights,—   10
    A city in the twilight dim and vast,
With smoking roofs, soft bells, and gleaming lights,—
    And hear above me on the autumnal blast
    The cataract of Death far thundering from the heights.

                        1842, 1886

THE JEWISH CEMETERY AT NEWPORT†

How strange it seems! These Hebrews in their graves,
    Close by the street of this fair seaport town,
Silent beside the never-silent waves,
    At rest in all this moving up and down!

The trees are white with dust, that o'er their sleep
    Wave their broad curtains in the south-wind's breath,
While underneath these leafy tents they keep
    The long, mysterious Exodus[1] of Death.

And these sepulchral stones, so old and brown,
    That pave with level flags[2] their burial-place,   10

---

    * First published posthumously in the *Life of Henry Wadsworth Longfellow* (1886), edited by Samuel Longfellow (1819–1892), Henry's brother. The title is taken from the opening line of Dante's *Divine Comedy, "Nel mezzo del cammin di nostra vita"* ("Midway along the path of life"); Longfellow wrote the poem when he was thirty-five, half of the biblical allotment of threescore and ten years (Psalm 89:10).

    [1] The death of Longfellow's first wife, Mary Potter, in 1835.

    † First published in *Putnam's Monthly Magazine* in 1854. Newport is a seaport town in Rhode Island.

    [1] A journey; the biblical book of Exodus tells of the journey of the Israelites from Egypt.

    [2] Flagstones; the stones in this extant cemetery are flat with the ground.

Seem like the tablets of the Law, thrown down
　　And broken by Moses at the mountain's base.[3]

The very names recorded here are strange,
　　Of foreign accent, and of different climes;
Alvares and Rivera[4] interchange
　　With Abraham and Jacob[5] of old times.

"Blessed by God, for he created Death!"
　　The mourners said, "and Death is rest and peace;"
Then added, in the certainty of faith,
　　"And giveth Life that nevermore shall cease."   20

Closed are the portals of their Synagogue.
　　No Psalms of David now the silence break,
No Rabbi reads the ancient Decalogue[6]
　　In the grand dialect the Prophets spake.

Gone are the living, but the dead remain,
　　And not neglected; for a hand unseen,
Scattering its bounty, like a summer rain,
　　Still keeps their graves and their remembrance green.

How came they here? What burst of Christian hate,
　　What persecution, merciless and blind,   30
Drove o'er the sea—that desert desolate—
　　These Ishmaels and Hagars[7] of mankind?

They lived in narrow streets and lanes obscure,
　　Ghetto and Judenstrass,[8] in mirk and mire;
Taught in the school of patience to endure
　　The life of anguish and the death of fire.

All their lives long, with the unleavened bread
　　And bitter herbs of exile and its fears,
The wasting famine of the heart they fed,
　　And slaked its thirst with marah[9] of their tears.   40

Anathema maranatha![10] was the cry
　　That rang from town to town, from street to street:

---

[3] In Exodus 32:1–19, when Moses came down from the mountain and saw the Israelites worshipping an idol, he broke the stone tablets inscribed with the Ten Commandments.
　　[4] Names (on the gravestones) of Jews who had come from Portugal and Spain.
　　[5] Old Testament patriarchs.　　[6] The Ten Commandments.
　　[7] Outcasts and pariahs (see Genesis 16 and 21).　　[8] "Street of Jews" (German).
　　[9] "Bitterness" (Hebrew).
　　[10] "If any man does not love the Lord Jesus Christ, let him be anathema. Maranatha," from I Corinthians 16:22–23: this cry rang after the Jews.

At every gate the accursed Mordecai[11]
    Was mocked and jeered, and spurned by Christian feet.

Pride and humiliation hand in hand
    Walked with them through the world where'er they went;
Trampled and beaten were they as the sand,
    And yet unshaken as the continent.

For in the background figures vague and vast
    Of patriarchs and of prophets rose sublime,   50
And all the great traditions of the Past
    They saw reflected in the coming time.

And thus forever with reverted look
    The mystic volume of the world they read,
Spelling it backward, like a Hebrew book,[12]
    Till life became a Legend of the Dead.

But ah! what once has been shall be no more!
    The groaning earth in travail and in pain
Brings forth its races, but does not restore,
    And the dead nations never rise again.   60

                                                    1852, 1854

DIVINA COMMEDIA*

I

Oft have I seen at some cathedral door
    A laborer, pausing in the dust and heat,
    Lay down his burden, and with reverent feet
    Enter, and cross himself, and on the floor
Kneel to repeat his paternoster[1] o'er;
    Far off the noises of the world retreat;
    The loud vociferations of the street
    Become an undistinguishable roar.
So, as I enter here from day to day,
    And leave my burden at this minster gate,[2]   10
    Kneeling in prayer, and not ashamed to pray,

---

[11] In Esther 5–7, a Jewish leader reviled by the Persians.
[12] Hebrew is read from right to left.
    * Six sonnets first published in Longfellow's 1865 to 1867 translation of the *Divine Comedy*, by Dante Alighieri (1265–1321), the first two placed before the *Inferno*, the next two before the *Purgatorio*, and the final two before the *Paradiso*. They evidence Longfellow's increasing mastery of the sonnet form.
    [1] "Our father" (Latin), the first words of the Lord's Prayer.   [2] At the door of the church.

The tumult of the time[3] disconsolate
   To inarticulate murmurs dies away,
   While the eternal ages watch and wait.

II

How strange the sculptures that adorn these towers!
   This crowd of statues, in whose folded sleeves
   Birds build their nests; while canopied with leaves
   Parvis[4] and portal bloom like trellised bowers,
And the vast minster seems a cross of flowers!
   But fiends and dragons on the gargoyled eaves[5]   20
   Watch the dead Christ between the living thieves,
   And, underneath, the traitor Judas lowers!
Ah! from what agonies of heart and brain,
   What exultations trampling on despair,
   What tenderness, what tears, what hate of wrong,
What passionate outcry of a soul in pain,
   Uprose this poem of the earth and air,
   This mediæval miracle of song!

III

I enter, and I see thee in the gloom
   Of the long aisles, O poet saturnine![6]   30
   And strive to make my steps keep pace with thine.
   The air is filled with some unknown perfume;
The congregation of the dead make room
   For thee to pass; the votive tapers[7] shine;
   Like rooks[8] that haunt Ravenna's groves of pine[9]
   The hovering echoes fly from tomb to tomb.
From the confessionals I hear arise
   Rehearsals[10] of forgotten tragedies,
   And lamentations from the crypts below;
And then a voice celestial that begins   40
   With the pathetic words, "Although your sins
   As scarlet be," and ends with "as the snow."[11]

[3] Longfellow began these sonnets while the Civil War was still in progress.
[4] An enclosed courtyard in front of a church.
[5] Gutter spouts carved in grotesque designs projecting from the roofs of Gothic churches, here portraying the dead Christ between the two thieves at Calvary while Judas, Jesus' betrayer, looks on, scowling.
[6] Dante; "saturnine" means grave, somber.   [7] Small devotional candles, also called vigil lights.
[8] Ravens.
[9] Dante is buried in Ravenna, Italy; "groves of pine" signifies that his memory is ever green.
[10] Retellings.
[11] "Though your sins be as scarlet, they shall be as white as snow," from Isaiah 1:18.

IV

With snow-white veil and garments as of flame,
   She[12] stands before thee, who so long ago
   Filled thy young heart with passion and the woe
   From which thy song and all its splendors came;
And while with stern rebuke she speaks thy name,
   The ice about thy heart melts as the snow
   On mountain heights, and in swift overflow
   Comes gushing from thy lips in sobs of shame.   50
Thou makest full confession; and a gleam,
   As of the dawn on some dark forest cast,
   Seems on thy lifted forehead to increase;
Lethe and Eunoë[13]—the remembered dream
   And the forgotten sorrow—bring at last
   That perfect pardon which is perfect peace.

V

I lift mine eyes, and all the windows blaze
   With forms of Saints and holy men who died,
   Here martyred and hereafter glorified;
   And the great Rose upon its leaves displays   60
Christ's Triumph, and the angelic roundelays,[14]
   With splendor upon splendor multiplied;
   And Beatrice again at Dante's side
   No more rebukes, but smiles her words of praise.
And then the organ sounds, and unseen choirs
   Sing the old Latin hymns of peace and love
   And benedictions of the Holy Ghost;
And the melodious bells among the spires
   O'er all the house-tops and through heaven above
   Proclaim the elevation of the Host![15]   70

VI

O star of morning and of liberty!
   O bringer of the light, whose splendor shines
   Above the darkness of the Apennines,[16]
   Forerunner of the day that is to be![17]
The voices of the city and the sea,

[12] Dante's idealized love, Beatrice. Even at this time Longfellow was blending the image of Dante's Beatrice from the *Divine Comedy* with that of his second wife, Frances Appleton, who was burned to death in 1861.

[13] Rivers in classical legend: Lethe, of forgetfulness; Eunoe, of pleasant memories.

[14] Of a stained-glass window portraying the risen Christ with a choir of angels singing; in the *Paradiso*, Canto 30, Dante is granted a vision of the Trinity and the souls in Heaven in the form of a rose.

[15] By custom, church bells were rung at the consecration of the Mass when the Host or Communion wafer, was raised by the priest.

[16] Mountains in Italy.   [17] All of these tributes are to Dante.

The voices of the mountains and the pines,
   Repeat thy song, till the familiar lines
   Are footpaths for the thought of Italy!
Thy flame is blown abroad from all the heights,
   Through all the nations, and a sound is heard,   80
   As of a mighty wind, and men devout,
Strangers of Rome,[18] and the new proselytes,
   In their own language hear thy wondrous word,
   And many are amazed and many doubt.

1865–1867

MILTON*

I pace the sounding sea-beach and behold
   How the voluminous billows roll and run,
   Upheaving and subsiding, while the sun
   Shines through their sheeted emerald far unrolled,
And the ninth wave,[1] slow gathering fold by fold
   All its loose-flowing garments into one,
   Plunges upon the shore, and floods the dun
   Pale reach of sands, and changes them to gold.
So majestic cadence rise and fall
   The mighty undulations of thy song,
   O sightless bard, England's Mæonides![2]   10
And ever and anon, high over all
   Uplifted, a ninth wave superb and strong,
   Floods all the soul with its melodious seas.

1873?, 1875

KEATS†

The young Endymion[1] sleeps Endymion's sleep;
   The shepherd-boy whose tale was left half told!
   The solemn grove uplifts its shield of gold
   To the red rising moon, and loud and deep

---

[18] All people, even those who are not members of the Roman Catholic Church, listen to Dante's epic poem.

* First published in the *Atlantic Monthly* in 1875, this sonnet is a tribute to the English poet John Milton (1608–1674), author of the epic poem *Paradise Lost* (1667).

[1] Supposedly the strongest in a series of waves.

[2] The Greek epic poet Homer, said to have been blind, like Milton.

† First published in the *Atlantic Monthly* in 1875, this sonnet pays tribute to the British romantic poet John Keats (1795–1821).

[1] Keats is here identified with the protagonist of his poem "Endymion" (1818), who, like his prototype in Greek myth, was cast into perpetual sleep.

The nightingale is singing from the steep;
  It is midsummer, but the air is cold;
  Can it be death? Alas, beside the fold
A shepherd's pipe lies shattered near his sheep.
Lo! in the moonlight gleams a marble white,
  On which I read: "Here lieth one whose name   10
  Was writ in water."[2] And was this the meed[3]
Of his sweet singing? Rather let me write:
  "The smoking flax before it burst to flame
  Was quenched by death, and broken the bruised reed."[4]

1875

NATURE*

As a fond mother, when the day is o'er,
  Leads by the hand her little child to bed,
  Half willing, half reluctant to be led,
And leave his broken playthings on the floor,
Still gazing at them through the open door,
  Nor wholly reassured and comforted
  By promises of others in their stead,
Which, though more splendid, may not please him more:
So Nature deals with us, and takes away
  Our playthings one by one, and by the hand   10
  Leads us to rest so gently, that we go
Scarce knowing if we wish to go or stay,
  Being too full of sleep to understand
  How far the unknown transcends the what we know.

1874, 1875

THE CROSS OF SNOW†

In the long, sleepless watches of the night,
  A gentle face—the face of one long dead—
  Looks at me from the wall, where round its head
The night-lamp casts a halo of pale light.

---

[2] Adapted form of the epitaph on Keats's tombstone.   [3] Reward.
[4] "A bruised reed he shall not break, and a smoldering wick he shall not quench, until he establishes justice on the earth . . .", from Isaiah 42:3–4.
  * First published in the *Atlantic Monthly* in 1875.
  † First published posthumously in the *Life of Henry Wadsworth Longfellow* (1886), edited by Samuel Longfellow (1819–1892), Henry's brother. Like "Mezzo Cammin," this poem is deeply personal, a meditation on the enduring grief Longfellow carried with him after the tragic death of his second wife by fire. It is interesting that these two poems, among Longfellow's most accomplished, were considered too private to share with his public. His almost stereotyped image as a public poet does not reflect all of his abilities.

Here in this room she died; and soul more white
   Never through martyrdom of fire was led
   To its repose; nor can in books be read
   The legend of a life more benedight.[1]
There is a mountain in the distant West
   That, sun-defying, in its deep ravines   10
   Displays a cross of snow upon its side.
Such is the cross I wear upon my breast
   These eighteen years, through all the changing scenes
   And seasons, changeless since the day she died.

                        1879, 1886

John Greenleaf Whittier
(1807–1892)

Born on a farm north of Boston near Haverhill, Massachusetts, in 1807, John Greenleaf Whittier received a relatively scant education at the area's District School, followed by a brief two-term stint at Haverhill Academy. In contrast to his contemporary Henry Wadsworth Longfellow, for whom poetry seemed to come naturally, Whittier conscientiously learned his craft, modeling his early work on that of the Scottish poet Robert Burns. Before he turned twenty-five Whittier had produced many amateurish poems that can be seen as workshop experiences, preludes to his later successes. His first published piece was printed in 1826 in the Newburyport, Massachusetts, *Free Press,* a newspaper run by William Lloyd Garrison, who encouraged Whittier to pursue writing as a career and became his lifelong friend and associate in abolitionist and other reform causes.

Whittier was raised as a Quaker, and the tenets of that religion influenced his life and his work. His great cause was abolitionism, which he began to champion as early as the 1830s. Valuing the virtue of direct communication, he used his talent as a writer of poetry and of newspaper editorials to raise public awareness of the slavery issue. In 1833 he published *Justice and Expediency,* an abolitionist pamphlet that brought him into the public eye and coincided with his election as a delegate to the National Anti-Slavery Convention in Philadelphia. In 1835 he was elected to a term in the Massachusetts legislature and was active in the Whig party. Later, in 1839, he helped to found the Liberty party, which had its basis in abolitionism. For much of his life Whittier edited various reform journals, including *The Pennsylvania Freeman* in Philadelphia and the *National Era* in Washington, D.C. He paid for his principles in these years by being mobbed and stoned and made the target of gunfire.

Whittier wrote one lengthy work of fiction, *Leaves From Margaret Smith's Journal in the Province of Massachusetts Bay* (1849), which explores the temper of the Puritan mind prior to the Salem witchcraft trials of 1692. During this middle period of his career, however, much of his creative energy went into the writing of antislavery poems ("Massachu-

---

[1] Blessed.

Etching of John Brown leaving jail, on his way to be executed, by Thomas Hoovenden (1885). Courtesy of the New-York Historical Society.

setts to Virginia" among them), which were collected in *Voices of Freedom* (1846); together with the later "Ichabod" (1850) and "Laus Deo!" (1865), these poems stand as examples of the writer's deep commitment to human justice. Yet, Whittier's reputation does not rest exclusively on political verse: he was considered one of the "Fireside Poets" and much of his poetry is rooted in the traditions of New England country life. After the Civil War he celebrated the values of that life in his "winter idyl," *Snow-Bound* (1866). In that poem Whittier portrays rural New England with compelling authority, carefully depicting the virtues of domesticity in a time gone by. *Snow-Bound* is a masterful triumph of nostalgia, with its implicit contrast between the safety and simple pleasures of the past, and the turmoil and complexity of the present.

In ill health, Whittier spent his later years in the family home he had inherited in Amesbury, Massachusetts, and in nearby Danvers. He died of a stroke in Hampton Falls, New Hampshire, in 1892. Poet of the conscience and poet of the hearth, Whittier's work continues to speak to the issues of a later day as it spoke to those of his own.

Suggested Readings: *Whittier on Writers and Writing: The Uncollected Critical Writings of John Greenleaf Whittier,* ed. E. H. Cady and H. H. Clark, 1950. *Letters of John Greenleaf Whittier,* 3 vols., ed. J. B. Pickard, 1975. E. Wagenknecht, *John Greenleaf Whittier: A Portrait in Paradox,*

1967. J. A. Pollard, *John Greenleaf Whittier, Friend of Man*, 1969. R. P. Warren, *John Greenleaf Whittier's Poetry: An Appraisal and a Selection*, 1971. J. K. Kribbs, ed., *Critical Essays on John Greenleaf Whittier*, 1980. R. H. Woodwell, *John Greenleaf Whittier: A Biography*, 1985.

Texts Used: "Massachusetts to Virginia," "Proem," and "Ichabod!": *The Poetical Works of John Greenleaf Whittier*, Vol. I, 1884. "Brown of Ossawatomie": *The Poetical Works*, Vol. II. All else: *The Poetical Works*, Vol. III.

MASSACHUSETTS TO VIRGINIA*

The blast from Freedom's Northern hills, upon its Southern way,
Bears greetings to Virginia from Massachusetts Bay:—
No word of haughty challenging, nor battle bugle's peal,
Nor steady tread of marching files, nor clang of horsemen's steel.

No trains of deep-mouthed cannon along our highways go,—
Around our silent arsenals untrodden lies the snow;
And to the land-breeze of our ports, upon their errands far,
A thousand sails of commerce swell, but none are spread for war.

We hear thy threats, Virginia! thy stormy words and high,
Swell harshly on the Southern winds which melt along our sky;   10
Yet, not one brown, hard hand foregoes its honest labor here,—
No hewer of our mountain oaks suspends his axe in fear.

Wild are the waves which lash the reefs along St. George's bank,—[1]
Cold on the shore of Labrador the fog lies white and dank;
Through storm and wave and blinding mist stout are the hearts which man
The fishing-smacks of Marblehead, the sea-boats of Cape Ann.[2]

The cold north light and wintry sun glare on their icy forms,
Bent grimly o'er their straining lines or wrestling with the storms;
Free as the winds they drive before, rough as the waves they roam,
They laugh to scorn the slaver's threat against their rocky home.   20

What means the Old Dominion?[3] Hath she forgot the day
When o'er her conquered valleys swept the Briton's steel array?
How side by side, with sons of hers, the Massachusetts men
Encountered Tarleton's charge of fire, and stout Cornwallis,[4] then?

* Read at the Essex County Anti-Slavery Convention on January 2, 1843, and published that month in *The Liberator*. Whittier's note: "Written on reading an account of the proceedings of the citizens of Norfolk, Va., in reference to George Latimer, the alleged fugitive slave, who was seized in Boston without warrant at the request of James B. Grey, of Norfolk, claiming to be his master. The case caused great excitement North and South, and led to the presentation of a petition to Congress, signed by more than fifty thousand citizens of Massachusetts, calling for such laws and proposed amendments to the Constitution as should relieve the Commonwealth from all further participation in the crime of oppression. George Latimer himself was finally given his free papers for the sum of four hundred dollars."

[1] Off the coast of Newfoundland.   [2] On the Massachusetts coast.   [3] Virginia.
[4] British generals who commanded troops in Virginia during the American Revolution.

Forgets she how the Bay State,[5] in answer to the call
Of her old House of Burgesses, spoke out from Faneuil Hall?[6]
When, echoing back her Henry's[7] cry, came pulsing on each breath
Of Northern winds, the thrilling sounds of "LIBERTY OR DEATH!"

What asks the Old Dominion? If now her sons have proved
False to their fathers' memory,—false to the faith they loved,   30
If she can scoff at Freedom, and its great charter[8] spurn,
Must we of Massachusetts from truth and duty turn?

We hunt your bondmen,[9] flying from Slavery's hateful hell,—
Our voices, at your bidding, take up the bloodhound's yell,—
We gather, at your summons, above our fathers' graves,
From Freedom's holy altar-horns[10] to tear your wretched slaves!

Thank God! not yet so vilely can Massachusetts bow;
The spirit of her early time is with her even now;
Dream not because her Pilgrim blood moves slow and calm and cool,
She thus can stoop her chainless neck, a sister's slave and tool!   40

All that a *sister* State should do, all that a *free* State may,
Heart, hand, and purse we proffer, as in our early day;
But that one dark loathsome burden ye must stagger with alone,
And reap the bitter harvest which ye yourselves have sown!

Hold, while ye may, your struggling slaves, and burden God's free air
With woman's shriek beneath the lash, and manhood's wild despair;
Cling closer to the "cleaving curse"[11] that writes upon your plains
The blasting of Almighty wrath against a land of chains.

Still shame your gallant ancestry, the cavaliers of old,
By watching round the shambles[12] where human flesh is sold,—   50
Gloat o'er the new-born child, and count his market value, when
The maddened mother's cry of woe shall pierce the slaver's den!
Lower than plummet[13] soundeth, sink the Virginia name;
Plant, if ye will, your fathers' graves with rankest weeds of shame;
Be, if ye will, the scandal of God's fair universe,—
We wash our hands forever of your sin and shame and curse.

---

[5] Massachusetts.
[6] The lower house in Virginia's colonial legislature; the famous meeting hall in Boston.
[7] The Virginia statesman Patrick Henry (1736–1799).   [8] The Declaration of Independence.
[9] Slaves. Fugitive Slave Laws required northern states to return runaway slaves to the South; later, with the Compromise of 1850, the situation grew worse.
[10] In I Kings 1:50–53 and 2:28, outcasts seeking asylum could grasp horns protruding from the altars of Israelites.
[11] See Deuteronomy 13:12–17.
[12] Slaughterhouse for animals, where slave markets were set up.
[13] A lead weight for "sounding" or measuring water depth.

A voice from lips whereon the coal from Freedom's shrine hath been,[14]
Thrilled, as but yesterday, the hearts of Berkshire's mountain men:[15]
The echoes of that solemn voice are sadly lingering still
In all our sunny valleys, on every wind-swept hill.   60

And when the prowling man-thief[16] came hunting for his prey
Beneath the very shadow of Bunker's shaft[17] of gray,
How, through the free lips of the son, the father's warning spoke;
How, from its bonds of trade and sect, the Pilgrim city[18] broke!

A hundred thousand right arms were lifted up on high,—
A hundred thousand voices sent back their loud reply;
Through the thronged towns of Essex[19] the startling summons rang,
And up from bench and loom and wheel her young mechanics sprang!

The voice of free, broad Middlesex,—of thousands as of one,—
The shaft of Bunker calling to that of Lexington,—   70
From Norfolk's ancient villages, from Plymouth's rocky bound
To where Nantucket[20] feels the arms of ocean close her round;—
From rich and rural Worcester, where through the calm repose
Of cultured vales and fringing woods the gentle Nashua[21] flows,
To where Wachuset's[22] wintry blasts the mountain larches stir,
Swelled up to Heaven the thrilling cry of "God save Latimer!"

And sandy Barnstable rose up, wet with the salt sea spray,—
And Bristol sent her answering shout down Narragansett Bay![23]
Along the broad Connecticut[24] old Hampden felt the thrill,
And the cheer of Hampshire's woodmen swept down from Holyoke Hill.   80

The voice of Massachusetts! Of her free sons and daughters,—
Deep calling unto deep aloud,[25]—the sound of many waters!
Against the burden of that voice what tyrant power shall stand?
No fetters in the Bay State! No slave upon her land!

Look to it well, Virginians! In calmness we have borne,
In answer to our faith and trust, your insult and your scorn;

---

[14] "Then flew one of the seraphims unto me, having a live coal . . . from off the altar: And he laid it upon my mouth, and said, Lo, . . . thine iniquity is taken away, and thy sin purged," from Isaiah 6:6–7.

[15] Men from the Berkshire Mountains of western Massachusetts.   [16] Slave hunter.

[17] The Bunker Hill monument on the site of the early Revolutionary War battle.   [18] Boston.

[19] Whittier's home county; the following stanzas name other counties in Massachusetts (Middlesex, Norfolk, Plymouth, Worcester, Barnstable, Bristol, Hampden, and Hampshire) to suggest the wide opposition to George Latimer's arrest.

[20] An island off the Massachusetts coast.   [21] A river in Massachusetts.

[22] A mountain in Massachusetts.   [23] The bay off Rhode Island and Massachusetts.

[24] The Connecticut River.

[25] "Deep calleth unto deep at the noise of thy waterspouts: all thy waves and thy billows are gone over me," from Psalm 42:7.

You've spurned our kindest counsels,—you've hunted for our lives,—
And shaken round our hearths and homes your manacles and gyves![26]
We wage no war,—we lift no arm,—we fling no torch within
The fire-damps[27] of the quaking mine beneath your soil of sin;   90
We leave ye with your bondmen, to wrestle, while ye can,
With the strong upward tendencies and godlike soul of man!

But for us and for our children, the vow which we have given
For freedom and humanity is registered in heaven;
No slave-hunt in our borders,—no pirate on our strand!
No fetters in the Bay State,—no slave upon our land!

                                                                        1843

PROEM*

    I love the old melodious lays
Which softly melt the ages through,
    The songs of Spenser's[1] golden days,
    Arcadian Sidney's[2] silvery phrase,
Sprinkling our noon of time with freshest morning dew.

    Yet, vainly in my quiet hours
To breathe their marvellous notes I try;
    I feel them, as the leaves and flowers
    In silence feel the dewy showers,
And drink with glad still lips the blessing of the sky.   10

    The rigor of a frozen clime,
The harshness of an untaught ear,
    The jarring words of one whose rhyme
    Beat often Labor's hurried time,
Or Duty's rugged march through storm and strife, are here.

    Of mystic beauty, dreamy grace,
No rounded art the lack supplies;
    Unskilled the subtle lines to trace,
    Or softer shades of Nature's face,
I view her common forms with unanointed eyes.   20

    Nor mine the seer-like power to show[3]
The secrets of the heart and mind;
    To drop the plummet-line below

---

[26] Leg chains.   [27] The methane-gas mixture found in underground mines.
* First published as a preface in *Poems* (published in 1848 but dated 1849).
[1] The English poet Edmund Spenser (1552–1599), author of *The Faerie Queene* (1589, 1596).
[2] Sir Philip Sidney (1554–1586), an English poet who wrote the prose romance *The Arcadia* (1590).
[3] This stanza illustrates the lack of pretension characteristic of Whittier as a poet.

Our common world of joy and woe,
A more intense despair of brighter hope to find.

Yet here at least an earnest sense
Of human right and weal is shown;
A hate of tyranny intense,
And hearty in its vehemence,
As if my brother's pain and sorrow were my own.   30

O Freedom! if to me belong
Nor mighty Milton's gift divine,
Nor Marvell's wit and graceful song,
Still with a love as deep and strong
As theirs, I lay, like them, my best gifts on thy shrine!

1848

ICHABOD!*

So fallen! so lost! the light withdrawn
    Which once he wore!
The glory from his gray hairs gone
    Forevermore!

Revile him not,—the Tempter hath
    A snare for all;
And pitying tears, not scorn and wrath,
    Befit his fall!

O, dumb be passion's stormy rage,
    When he who might   10
Have lighted up and led his age,
    Falls back in night.

Scorn! would the angels laugh, to mark
    A bright soul driven,
Fiend-goaded, down the endless dark,
    From hope and heaven!

Let not the land once proud of him
    Insult him now,
Nor brand with deeper shame his dim,
    Dishonored brow.   20

* First published in *Songs of Labor, and Other Poems* (1850). The title is from I Samuel 4:21: "And she named the child Ichabod, saying, The glory is departed from Israel." The poem is a castigation of Daniel Webster (1782–1852), U.S. senator from Massachusetts who championed the Compromise of 1850 and thus helped to strengthen the provisions of the Fugitive Slave Act.

But let its humbled sons, instead,
    From sea to lake,
A long lament, as for the dead,
    In sadness make.

Of all we loved and honored, naught
    Save power remains,—
A fallen angel's pride of thought,
    Still strong in chains.

All else is gone; from those great eyes
    The soul has fled: 30
When faith is lost, when honor dies,
    The man is dead!

Then, pay the reverence of old days
    To his dead fame;
Walk backward, with averted gaze,[1]
    And hide the shame!

1850

BROWN OF OSSAWATOMIE*

John Brown of Ossawatomie spake on his dying day:
"I will not have to shrive my soul a priest in Slavery's pay.[1]
But let some poor slave-mother whom I have striven to free,
With her children, from the gallows-stair put up a prayer for me!"

John Brown of Ossawatomie, they led him out to die;
And lo! a poor slave-mother with her little child pressed nigh.
Then the bold, blue eye grew tender, and the old harsh face grew mild,
As he stooped between the jeering ranks and kissed the negro's child!

The shadows of his stormy life that moment fell apart;
And they who blamed the bloody hand forgave the loving heart.   10
That kiss from all its guilty means redeemed the good intent,
And round the grisly fighter's hair the martyr's aureole[2] bent!

---

[1] As did Noah's children, to avoid the sight of their father lying drunk and naked in his tent, in Genesis 9:20–23.

* First published in *The Independent* in 1859. Ossawatomie is a town in Kansas to which the abolitionist John Brown (1800–1859) had moved with his five sons in 1855. His murder of five proslavery neighbors made him known as "Brown of Ossawatomie." In October 1859 Brown and twenty-one followers captured the U.S. Armory at Harper's Ferry, Virginia, intending to establish a base for freeing slaves; the next day marines under the command of Robert E. Lee retook the Armory. Brown was captured, found guilty, and executed on December 2, 1859.

[1] "I will not confess to a priest whose wages are paid by slaveowners."   [2] Halo.

Perish with him the folly that seeks through evil good!
Long live the generous purpose unstained with human blood!
Not the raid of midnight terror, but the thought which underlies;
Not the borderer's pride of daring, but the Christian's sacrifice.

Nevermore may yon Blue Ridges[3] the Northern rifle hear,
Nor see the light of blazing homes flash on the negro's spear.
But let the free-winged angel Truth their guarded passes scale,
To teach that right is more than might, and justice more than mail!   20

So vainly shall Virginia set her battle in array;
In vain her trampling squadrons knead the winter snow with clay.
She may strike the pouncing eagle, but she dares not harm the dove;
And every gate she bars to Hate shall open wide to Love!

1859

LAUS DEO!*

On Hearing the Bells Ring on the Passage of the Constitutional Amendment Abolishing Slavery[1]

It is done!
Clang of bell and roar of gun
Send the tidings up and down.
How the belfries rock and reel!
How the great guns, peal on peal,
Fling the joy from town to town!

Ring, O bells!
Every stroke exulting tells
Of the burial hour of crime.
Loud and long, that all may hear,   10
Ring for every listening ear
Of Eternity and Time!

Let us kneel:
God's own voice is in that peal,
And this spot is holy ground.[2]
Lord, forgive us! What are we,
That our eyes this glory see,
That our ears have heard the sound!

---

[3] The Blue Ridge Mountains of Virginia.

* First published in *The Independent* in 1865. The Latin title means "Praise God."

[1] Ratification of the Thirteenth Amendment to the U.S. Constitution was announced on December 18, 1865.

[2] Adapted from the Lord's words to Moses in Exodus 3:3–5; biblical phrases pervade this poem of thanksgiving.

For the Lord
On the whirlwind is abroad;   20
In the earthquake he has spoken;
He has smitten with his thunder[3]
The iron walls asunder,
And the gates of brass are broken!

Loud and long
Lift the old exulting song;
Sing with Miriam by the sea
He has cast the mighty down;
Horse and rider sink and drown;
"He hath triumphed gloriously!"[4]   30

Did we dare,
In our agony of prayer,[5]
Ask for more than He has done?
When was ever his right hand
Over any time or land
Stretched as now beneath the sun?[6]

How they pale,
Ancient myth and song and tale,
In this wonder of our days,
When the cruel rod of war   40
Blossoms white with righteous law,[7]
And the wrath of man is praise!

Blotted out!
All within and all about
Shall a fresher life begin;
Freer breathe the universe
As it rolls its heavy curse
On the dead and buried sin!

It is done!
In the circuit of the sun   50
Shall the sound thereof go forth.
It shall bid the sad rejoice,
It shall give the dumb a voice,[8]
It shall belt with joy the earth!

---

[3] "After it a voice roareth: he thundereth with the voice of his excellency. . . . God thundereth marvellously with his voice; great things doeth he . . ." from Job 37:4–5.

[4] From Exodus 15:21.

[5] "And being in agony he prayed more earnestly . . . " from Luke 22:44.

[6] "His hand is stretched out still" (showing the mercy of the Lord after human transgressions), from Isaiah 5:25.

[7] Reference both to Aaron's rod of war (see Exodus 7:9–17) and to his rod of law (see Numbers 17:8–10).

[8] " . . . behold, your God . . . will come and save you. . . . Then shall . . . the tongue of the dumb sing . . .", from Isaiah 35:4–6.

Ring and swing,
Bells of joy! On morning's wing
Send the song of praise abroad!
With a sound of broken chains
Tell the nations that He reigns,
Who alone is Lord and God!   60

1865

SNOW-BOUND*

A Winter Idyl

*"As the Spirits of Darkness be stronger in the dark, so Good Spirits which be
Angels of Light are augmented not only by the Divine light of the Sun, but also by
our common Wood Fire: and as the celestial Fire drives away dark spirits, so also
this our Fire of Wood doth the same."*

COR. AGRIPPA, *Occult Philosophy*, Book I. chap. v.[1]

*"Announced by all the trumpets of the sky,
Arrives the snow; and, driving o'er the fields,
Seems nowhere to alight; the whited air
Hides hills and woods, the river and the heaven,
And veils the farm-house at the garden's end.
The sled and traveller stopped, the courier's feet
Delayed, all friends shut out, the housemates sit
Around the radiant fireplace, enclosed
In a tumultuous privacy of storm."*[2]

EMERSON

The sun that brief December day
Rose cheerless over hills of gray,
And, darkly circled, gave at noon
A sadder light than waning moon.
Slow tracing down the thickening sky
Its mute and ominous prophecy,
A portent seeming less than threat,

---

* Written in 1865 and 1866 and first published as a small volume in 1866. In a prefatory note inserted in the 1891 edition, Whittier mentions that storytelling was a major "resource" during long winter evenings in the family farmhouse when he was a boy, and dedicates his poem to the memory of that household. Members of the "Whittier homestead" (all mentioned in the poem) were his mother and father, his brother and two sisters, an aunt and uncle ("both unmarried"), and the district schoolmaster, who was then boarding with them. And a volatile young woman, Whittier goes on to say, was included in the snow-bound circle: Harriet Livermore, then boarding about two miles away, who spent much of her life traveling in Europe and Asia preaching the Second Coming of Christ. As an old woman she was found "wandering in Syria with a tribe of Arabs, who with the Oriental notion that madness is inspiration, accepted her as their prophetess and leader." It is small wonder that Whittier describes Livermore in the poem as a "not unfeared, half-welcome guest."

[1] Heinrich Cornelius Agrippa (1486–1525), a German physician and student of occult science.
[2] From Ralph Waldo Emerson's "The Snow-Storm" (1841).

It sank from sight before it set.
A chill no coat, however stout,
Of homespun stuff could quite shut out,   10
A hard, dull bitterness of cold,
    That checked, mid-vein, the circling race
    Of life-blood in the sharpened face,
The coming of the snow-storm told.
The wind blew east:[3] we heard the roar
Of Ocean on his wintry shore,
And felt the strong pulse throbbing there
Beat with low rhythm our inland air.

Meanwhile we did our nightly chores,—
Brought in the wood from out of doors,   20
Littered[4] the stalls, and from the mows[5]
Raked down the herd's-grass for the cows:
Heard the horse whinnying for his corn;
And, sharply clashing horn on horn,
Impatient down the stanchion[6] rows
The cattle shake their walnut bows;
While, peering from his early perch
Upon the scaffold's pole of birch,
The cock his crested helmet bent
And down his querulous challenge sent.   30

Unwarmed by any sunset light
The gray day darkened into night,
A night made hoary with the swarm
And whirl-dance of the blinding storm,
As zigzag wavering to and fro
Crossed and recrossed the wingéd snow:
And ere the early bedtime came
The white drift piled the window-frame,
And through the glass the clothes-line posts
Looked in like tall and sheeted ghosts.   40

So all night long the storm roared on:
The morning broke without a sun;
In tiny spherule[7] traced with lines
Of Nature's geometric signs,
In starry flake, and pellicle,[8]
All day the hoary[9] meteor fell;
And, when the second morning shone,
We looked upon a world unknown,
On nothing we could call our own.

---

[3] From the East, so they could hear the "roar" of the Atlantic Ocean.
[4] Put down straw for bedding.   [5] Haymows.
[6] Adjustable braces fixed to posts that hold an animal's neck in place during feeding or milking; they are shaped like bows and made of walnut.
[7] A small spherical body.   [8] A thin crust of crystals.   [9] Ancient.

Around the glistening wonder bent   50
The blue walls of the firmament,
No cloud above, no earth below,—
A universe of sky and snow!
The old familiar sights of ours
Took marvellous shapes; strange domes and towers
Rose up where sty or corn-crib stood,
Or garden wall, or belt of wood;
A smooth white mound the brush-pile showed,
A fenceless drift what once was road;
The bridle-post an old man sat   60
With loose-flung coat and high cocked hat;
The well-curb had a Chinese roof;
And even the long sweep,[10] high aloof,
In its slant splendor, seemed to tell
Of Pisa's leaning miracle.[11]

A prompt, decisive man, no breath
Our father wasted: "Boys, a path!"
Well pleased, (for when did farmer boy
Count such a summons less than joy?)
Our buskins[12] on our feet we drew;   70
    With mittened hands, and caps drawn low,
    To guard our necks and ears from snow
We cut the solid whiteness through.
And, where the drift was deepest, made
A tunnel walled and overlaid
With dazzling crystal: we had read
Of rare Aladdin's wondrous cave,
And to our own his name we gave,
With many a wish the luck were ours
To test his lamp's supernal powers.   80
We reached the barn with merry din,
And roused the prisoned brutes within.
The old horse thrust his long head out,
And grave with wonder gazed about;
The cock his lusty greeting said,
And forth his speckled harem led;
The oxen lashed their tails, and hooked,[13]
And mild reproach of hunger looked;
The hornéd patriarch of the sheep,
Like Egypt's Amun[14] roused from sleep,   90
Shook his sage head with gesture mute,
And emphasized with stamp of foot.

All day the gusty north-wind bore
The loosening drift its breath before;

---

[10] Well-sweep, a pole used to raise the well bucket.   [11] The leaning tower of Pisa in Italy.
[12] Boots.   [13] Hooked their horns: bent their heads sideways.
[14] According to Egyptian myth, a god with a ram's head.

Low circling round its southern zone,
The sun through dazzling snow-mist shone.
No church-bell lent its Christian tone
To the savage air, no social smoke
Curled over woods of snow-hung oak.
A solitude made more intense   100
By dreary-voicéd elements,
The shrieking of the mindless wind,
The moaning tree-boughs swaying blind,
And on the glass the unmeaning beat
Of ghostly finger-tips of sleet.
Beyond the circle of our hearth
No welcome sound of toil or mirth
Unbound the spell, and testified
Of human life and thought outside.
We minded that the sharpest ear   110
The buried brooklet could not hear,
The music of whose liquid lip
Had been to us companionship,
And, in our lonely life, had grown
To have an almost human tone.

As night drew on, and, from the crest
Of wooded knolls that ridged the west,
The sun, a snow-blown traveller, sank
From sight beneath the smothering bank,
We piled, with care, our nightly stack   120
Of wood against the chimney-back,—
The oaken log, green, huge, and thick,
And on its top the stout back-stick;
The knotty forestick laid apart,
And filled between with curious art
The ragged brush; then, hovering near,
We watched the first red blaze appear,
Heard the sharp crackle, caught the gleam
On whitewashed wall and sagging beam,
Until the old, rude-furnished room   130
Burst, flower-like, into rosy bloom;
While radiant with a mimic flame
Outside the sparkling drift became,
And through the bare-boughed lilac-tree
Our own warm hearth seemed blazing free.
The crane and pendent trammels[15] showed,
The Turks' heads[16] on the andirons glowed;
While childish fancy, prompt to tell
The meaning of the miracle,
Whispered the old rhyme: "*Under the tree,*   140
When fire outdoors burns merrily,
There the witches are making tea."

---

[15] Pothooks.   [16] Turbanlike designs.

The moon above the eastern wood
Shone at its full; the hill-range stood
Transfigured in the silver flood,
Its blown snows flashing cold and keen,
Dead white, save where some sharp ravine
Took shadow, or the sombre green
Of hemlocks turned to pitchy black
Against the whiteness at their back.   150
For such a world and such a night
Most fitting that unwarming light,
Which only seemed where'er it fell
To make the coldness visible.

Shut in from all the world without,
We sat the clean-winged hearth about,
Content to let the north-wind roar
In baffled rage at pane and door,
While the red logs before us beat
The frost-line back with tropic heat;   160
And ever, when a louder blast
Shook beam and rafter as it passed,
The merrier up its roaring draught
The great throat of the chimney laughed,
The house-dog on his paws outspread
Laid to the fire his drowsy head,
The cat's dark silhouette on the wall
A couchant[17] tiger's seemed to fall;
And, for the winter fireside meet,
Between the andirons' straddling feet,   170
The mug of cider simmered slow,
The apples sputtered in a row,
And, close at hand, the basket stood
With nuts from brown October's wood.

What matter how the night behaved?
What matter how the north-wind raved?
Blow high, blow low, not all its snow
Could quench our hearth-fire's ruddy glow.
O Time and Change!—with hair as gray
As was my sire's that winter day,   180
How strange it seems, with so much gone
Of life and love, to still live on!
Ah, brother![18] only I and thou
Are left of all that circle now,—
The dear home faces whereupon
That fitful firelight paled and shone.
Henceforward, listen as we will,
The voices of that hearth are still;
Look where we may, the wide earth o'er,

---

[17] Lying down with head raised.   [18] Matthew Whittier (1812–1883).

Those lighted faces smile no more.   190
We tread the paths their feet have worn,
  We sit beneath their orchard-trees,
  We hear, like them, the hum of bees
And rustle of the bladed corn;
We turn the pages that they read,
  Their written words we linger o'er,
But in the sun they cast no shade,
No voice is heard, no sign is made,
  No step is on the conscious floor!
Yet Love will dream, and Faith will trust,   200
(Since He who knows our need is just,)
That somehow, somewhere, meet we must.
Alas for him who never sees
The stars shine through his cypress-trees!
Who, hopeless, lays his dead away,
Nor looks to see the breaking day
Across the mournful marbles[19] play!
Who hath not learned, in hours of faith,
  The truth to flesh and sense unknown,
That Life is ever lord of Death,   210
  And Love can never lose its own!

We sped the time with stories old,
Wrought puzzles out, and riddles told,
Or stammered from our school-book lore
"The Chief of Gambia's golden shore."[20]
How often since, when all the land
Was clay in Slavery's shaping hand,
As if a trumpet called, I've heard
Dame Mercy Warren's[21] rousing word:
"Does not the voice of reason cry,   220
  Claim the first right which Nature gave,
From the red scourge of bondage fly,
  Nor deign to live a burdened slave!"
Our father rode again his ride
On Memphremagog's[22] wooded side;
Sat down again to moose and samp[23]
In trapper's hut and Indian camp;
Lived o'er the old idyllic ease
Beneath St. François'[24] hemlock-trees;
Again for him the moonlight shone   230

[19] Tombstones of marble.
[20] From "The African Chief," an antislavery poem by Sarah Wentworth Morton (1759–1846).
[21] Mercy Otis Warren (1728–1814), whose *History of the Rise, Progress, and Termination of the American Revolution* (1805) is valuable as a contemporary record of events; however, the poem quoted is by Sarah Wentworth Morton.
[22] A lake between Vermont and Quebec. As Whittier says in his 1891 preface, his father told stories of travels in Canada.
[23] Sat down to eat moose and cornmeal mush.   [24] A village north of Lake Memphremagog.

On Norman cap and bodiced zone;[25]
Again he heard the violin play
Which led the village dance away,
And mingled in its merry whirl
The grandam and the laughing girl.
Or, nearer home, our steps he led
Where Salisbury's[26] level marshes spread
   Mile-wide as flies the laden bee;
Where merry mowers, hale and strong,
Swept, scythe on scythe, their swaths along   240
   The low green prairies of the sea.
We shared the fishing off Boar's Head,[27]
   And round the rocky Isles of Shoals[28]
   The hake-broil[29] on the drift-wood coals;
The chowder on the sand-beach made,
Dipped by the hungry, steaming hot,
With spoons of clam-shell from the pot.
We heard the tales of witchcraft old,
And dream and sign and marvel told
To sleepy listeners as they lay   250
Stretched idly on the salted hay,
   Adrift along the winding shores,
When favoring breezes deigned to blow
The square sail of the gundelow[30]
   And idle lay the useless oars.

Our mother, while she turned her wheel
Or run the new-knit stocking-heel,
Told how the Indian hordes came down
At midnight on Cocheco town,[31]
And how her own great-uncle bore   260
His cruel scalp-mark to fourscore.
Recalling, in her fitting phrase,
   So rich and picturesque and free,
   (The common unrhymed poetry
Of simple life and country ways,)
The story of her early days,—
She made us welcome to her home;
Old hearths grew wide to give us room;
We stole with her a frightened look
At the gray wizard's conjuring-book,[32]   270
The fame whereof went far and wide

[25] Whittier's father remembers the dress of French-Canadian women, the cap like those worn in Normandy, France, and the bodices around their waists.
[26] A town in northeast Massachusetts.   [27] A headland on the New England coast.
[28] Off the New Hampshire coast.
[29] A variety of cod, commonly broiled over an open fire.   [30] Flat-bottomed boat.
[31] A village near Dover, New Hampshire, on the Cocheco River; in his 1891 preface Whittier says his mother knew of "strange people" who lived on the Piscataqua and Cocheco rivers.
[32] Agrippa's *Occult Philosophy*.

Through all the simple country side;
We heard the hawks at twilight play,
The boat-horn on Piscataqua,
The loon's weird laughter far away;
We fished her little trout-brook, knew
What flowers in wood and meadow grew,
What sunny hillsides autumn-brown
She climbed to shake the ripe nuts down,
Saw where in sheltered cove and bay   280
The ducks' black squadron anchored lay,
And heard the wild-geese calling loud
Beneath the gray November cloud.

Then, haply, with a look more grave,
And soberer tone, some tale she gave
From painful Sewell's ancient tome,[33]
Beloved in every Quaker home,
Of faith fire-winged by martyrdom,
Or Chalkley's Journal,[34] old and quaint,—
Gentlest of skippers, rare sea-saint!—   290
Who, when the dreary calms prevailed,
And water-butt and bread-cask failed,
And cruel, hungry eyes pursued
His portly presence mad for food,
With dark hints muttered under breath
Of casting lots for life or death,
Offered, if Heaven withheld supplies,
To be himself the sacrifice.
Then, suddenly, as if to save
The good man from his living grave,   300
A ripple on the water grew,
A school of porpoise flashed in view.
"Take, eat,"[35] he said, "and be content;
These fishes in my stead are sent
By Him who gave the tangled ram
To spare the child of Abraham."[36]

Our uncle, innocent of books,
Was rich in lore of fields and brooks,
The ancient teachers never dumb
Of Nature's unhoused lyceum.[37]   310

---

[33] William Sewell or Sewal (1650–1725), whose *History of the Quakers* (1725) detailed the persecutions the Quakers suffered at the hands of the Puritans in the seventeenth century. Whittier, a Quaker, owned a copy of the book.

[34] The sea-going Quaker Thomas Chalkley (1675–1741) published his *Journal* in 1747.

[35] Christ's words to the Apostles: "Take, eat; this is my body," from Matthew 26:26.

[36] In Genesis 22:8–13, Abraham was willing to obey God by sacrificing his son Isaac; a ram was given in Isaac's place.

[37] Public lecture hall. "My uncle," Whittier writes in his 1891 preface, "had many stories of hunting and fishing and some of witchcraft and superstition."

In moons and tides and weather wise,
He read the clouds as prophecies,
And foul or fair could well divine,
By many an occult hint and sign,
Holding the cunning-warded keys[38]
To all the woodcraft mysteries;
Himself to Nature's heart so near
That all her voices in his ear
Of beast or bird had meanings clear,
Like Apollonius[39] of old,   320
Who knew the tales the sparrows told,
Or Hermes,[40] who interpreted
What the sage cranes of Nilus said;
A simple, guileless, childlike man,
Content to live where life began;
Strong only on his native grounds,
The little world of sights and sounds
Whose girdle was the parish bounds,
Whereof his fondly partial pride
The common features magnified,   330
As Surrey hills to mountains grew
In White of Selborne's[41] loving view,—
He told how teal and loon he shot,
And how the eagle's eggs he got,
The feats on pond and river done,
The prodigies of rod and gun;
Till, warming with the tales he told,
Forgotten was the outside cold,
The bitter wind unheeded blew,
From ripening corn the pigeons flew,   340
The partridge drummed i' the wood, the mink
Went fishing down the river-brink.
In fields with bean or clover gay,
The woodchuck, like a hermit gray,
    Peered from the doorway of his cell;
The muskrat plied the mason's trade,
And tier by tier his mud-walls laid;
And from the shagbark overhead
    The grizzled squirrel dropped his shell.

Next, the dear aunt, whose smile of cheer   350
And voice in dreams I see and hear,—
The sweetest woman ever Fate

[38] Keys with intricate notches; hence, keys to "woodcraft mysteries."

[39] Appollonius of Tyana (1st century B.C.), a Greek philosopher and mystic who supposedly had miraculous powers.

[40] Hermes Trismegistus, legendary Egyptian author of books on magic; here he is said to have interpreted motions of cranes along the Nile ("Nilus") River.

[41] *The Natural History and Antiquities of Selborne* (1789), by Gilbert White (1720–1793) of Surrey, England.

Perverse denied a household mate,
Who, lonely, homeless, not the less
Found peace in love's unselfishness,
And welcome wheresoe'er she went,
A calm and gracious element,
Whose presence seemed the sweet income
And womanly atmosphere of home,—
Called up her girlhood memories,   360
The huskings and the apple-bees,
The sleigh-rides and the summer sails,
Weaving through all the poor details
And homespun warp of circumstance
A golden woof-thread of romance.
For well she kept her genial mood
And simple faith of maidenhood;
Before her still a cloud-land lay,
The mirage loomed across her way;
The morning dew, that dries so soon   370
With others, glistened at her noon;
Through years of toil and soil and care,
From glossy tress to thin gray hair,
All unprofaned she held apart
The virgin fancies of the heart.
Be shame to him of woman born
Who hath for such but thought of scorn.

There, too, our elder sister plied
Her evening task the stand beside;
A full, rich nature, free to trust,   380
Truthful and almost sternly just,
Impulsive, earnest, prompt to act,
And make her generous thought a fact,
Keeping with many a light disguise
The secret of self-sacrifice.
O heart sore-tried! thou hast the best
That Heaven itself could give thee,—rest,
Rest from all bitter thoughts and things!
    How many a poor one's blessing went
    With thee beneath the low green tent   390
Whose curtain never outward swings!

As one who held herself a part
Of all she saw, and let her heart
    Against the household bosom lean,
Upon the motley-braided mat
Our youngest and our dearest sat,
Lifting her large, sweet, asking eyes,
    Now bathed within the eternal green
And holy peace of Paradise.
O, looking from some heavenly hill,   400

Or from the shade of saintly palms,
  Or silver reach of river calms,
Do those large eyes behold me still?
With me one little year ago:—
The chill weight of the winter snow
  For months upon her grave has lain;
And now, when summer south-winds blow
  And brier and harebell bloom again,
I tread the pleasant paths we trod,
I see the violet-sprinkled sod   410
Whereon she leaned, too frail and weak
The hillside flowers she loved to seek,
Yet following me where'er I went
With dark eyes full of love's content.
The birds are glad; the brier-rose fills
The air with sweetness; all the hills
Stretch green to June's unclouded sky;
But still I wait with ear and eye
For something gone which should be nigh,
A loss in all familiar things,   420
In flower that blooms and bird that sings.
And yet, dear heart! remembering thee,
  Am I not richer than of old?
Safe in thy immortality,
  What change can reach the wealth I hold?
  What chance can mar the pearl and gold
Thy love hath left in trust with me?
And while in life's late afternoon,
  Where cool and long the shadows grow,
I walk to meet the night that soon   430
  Shall shape and shadow overflow,
I cannot feel that thou art far,
Since near at need the angels are;
And when the sunset gates unbar,
  Shall I not see thee waiting stand,
And, white against the evening star,
  The welcome of thy beckoning hand?

Brisk wielder of the birch and rule,
The master of the district school
Held at the fire his favored place,   440
Its warm glow lit a laughing face
Fresh-hued and fair, where scarce appeared
The uncertain prophecy of beard.
He teased the mitten-blinded cat,
Played cross-pins on my uncle's hat,
Sang songs, and told us what befalls
In classic Dartmouth's college halls.
Born the wild Northern hills among,
From whence his yeoman father wrung

By patient toil subsistence scant,   450
Not competence and yet not want,
He early gained the power to pay
His cheerful, self-reliant way;
Could doff at ease his scholar's gown
To peddle wares from town to town;
Or through the long vacation's reach
In lonely lowland districts teach,
Where all the droll experience found
At stranger hearths in boarding round,
The moonlit skater's keen delight,   460
The sleigh-drive through the frosty night,
The rustic party, with its rough
Accompaniment of blind-man's-buff,
And whirling plate,[42] and forfeits paid,
His winter task a pastime made.
Happy the snow-locked homes wherein
He tuned his merry violin,
Or played the athlete in the barn,
Or held the good dame's winding-yarn,
Or mirth-provoking versions told   470
Of classic legends rare and old,
Wherein the scenes of Greece and Rome
Had all the commonplace of home,
And little seemed at best the odds
'Twixt Yankee pedlers and old gods;
Where Pindus-born Aracthus[43] took
The guise of any grist-mill brook,
And dread Olympus[44] at his will
Became a huckleberry hill.

A careless boy that night he seemed;   480
    But at his desk he had the look
And air of one who wisely schemed,
    And hostage from the future took
    In trainéd thought and lore of book.
Large-brained, clear-eyed,—of such as he
Shall Freedom's young apostles be,
Who, following in War's bloody trail,[45]
Shall every lingering wrong assail;
All chains from limb and spirit strike,
Uplift the black and white alike;   490
Scatter before their swift advance
The darkness and the ignorance,

[42] A children's game of spinning a pewter plate on its edge longer than others can, with the losers paying a penalty.

[43] A river in Greece originating in the Pindus Mountains.

[44] According to Greek myth, Mt. Olympus was the abode of the gods.

[45] In the classroom, the schoolmaster follows the progress of the Civil War in the context of its moral issues.

The pride, the lust, the squalid sloth,
Which nurtured Treason's monstrous growth,
Made murder pastime, and the hell
Of prison-torture possible;
The cruel lie of caste refute,
Old forms remould, and substitute
For Slavery's lash the freeman's will,
For blind routine, wise-handed skill;   500
A school-house plant on every hill,
Stretching in radiate nerve-lines thence
The quick wires of intelligence;[46]
Till North and South together brought
Shall own the same electric thought,
In peace a common flag salute,
And, side by side in labor's free
And unresentful rivalry,
Harvest the fields wherein they fought.

                                                                     510
Another guest[47] that winter night
Flashed back from lustrous eyes the light.
Unmarked by time, and yet not young,
The honeyed music of her tongue
And words of meekness scarcely told
A nature passionate and bold,
Strong, self-concentred, spurning guide,
Its milder features dwarfed beside
Her unbent will's majestic pride.
She sat among us, at the best,   520
A not unfeared, half-welcome guest,
Rebuking with her cultured phrase
Our homeliness of words and ways.
A certain pard-like,[48] treacherous grace
   Swayed the lithe limbs and drooped the lash,
   Lent the white teeth their dazzling flash;
   And under low brows, black with night,
   Rayed out at times a dangerous light;
The sharp heat-lightnings of her face
Presaging ill to him whom Fate   530
Condemned to share her love or hate.
A woman tropical, intense
In thought and act, in soul and sense,
She blended in a like degree
The vixen and the devotee,
Revealing with each freak or feint
   The temper of Petruchio's Kate,[49]
The raptures of Siena's saint.[50]
Her tapering hand and rounded wrist

---

[46] Communication by telegraph.   [47] Harriet Livermore.   [48] Leopardlike.
[49] The explosive heroine tamed by Petruchio in Shakespeare's *Taming of the Shrew*.
[50] St. Catherine (1347–1380) of Siena, Italy.

Had facile power to form a fist;
The warm, dark languish of her eyes   540
Was never safe from wrath's surprise.
Brows saintly calm and lips devout
Knew every change of scowl and pout;
And the sweet voice had notes more high
And shrill for social battle-cry.

Since then what old cathedral town
Has missed her pilgrim staff and gown,
What convent-gate has held its lock
Against the challenge of her knock!
Through Smyrna's[51] plague-hushed thoroughfares,   550
Up sea-set Malta's[52] rocky stairs,
Gray olive slopes of hills that hem
Thy tombs and shrines, Jerusalem,
Or startling on her desert throne
The crazy Queen of Lebanon[53]
With claims fantastic as her own,
Her tireless feet have held their way;
And still, unrestful, bowed, and gray,
She watches under Eastern skies,
    With hope each day renewed and fresh,   560
    The Lord's quick coming in the flesh,
Whereof she dreams and prophesies!

Where'er her troubled path may be,
    The Lord's sweet pity with her go!
The outward wayward life we see,
    The hidden springs we may not know.
Nor is it given us to discern
    What threads the fatal sisters spun,[54]
    Through what ancestral years has run
The sorrow with the woman born,   570
What forged her cruel chain of moods,
What set her feet in solitudes,
    And held the love within her mute,
What mingled madness in the blood,
    A life-long discord and annoy,
    Water of tears with oil of joy,
And hid within the folded bud
    Perversities of flower and fruit.
It is not ours to separate
The tangled skein of will and fate,   580

---

[51] Now Izmir in Turkey.   [52] A mountainous island in the Mediterranean Sea, south of Sicily.
[53] Lady Hester Stanhope (1776–1839), an eccentric Englishwoman who settled in Lebanon in 1810 and ruled despotically over a small area of the land. Harriet Livermore lived with her for a while before the two quarreled about accompanying Christ into Jerusalem at the time of the Second Coming.
[54] The three Fates of Greek myth, who spin the thread of life, measure it, and cut it off.

To show what metes and bounds should stand
Upon the soul's debatable land,
And between choice and Providence
Divide the circle of events;
   But He who knows our frame is just,
Merciful and compassionate,
And full of sweet assurances
And hope for all the language is.
   That He remembereth we are dust![55]

At last the great logs, crumbling low,   590
Sent out a dull and duller glow,
The bull's-eye watch[56] that hung in view,
Ticking its weary circuit through,
Pointed with mutely-warning sign
Its black hand to the hour of nine.
That sign the pleasant circle broke:
My uncle ceased his pipe to smoke,
Knocked from its bowl the refuse gray
And laid it tenderly away,
Then roused himself to safely cover   600
The dull red brands with ashes over.
And while, with care, our mother laid
The work aside, her steps she stayed
One moment, seeking to express
Her grateful sense of happiness
For food and shelter, warmth and health,
And love's contentment more than wealth,
With simple wishes (not the weak,
Vain prayers which no fulfilment seek,
But such as warm the generous heart,   610
O'er-prompt to do with Heaven its part)
That none might lack, that bitter night,
For bread and clothing, warmth and light.

Within our beds awhile we heard
The wind that round the gables roared,
With now and then a ruder shock,
Which made our very bedsteads rock.
We heard the loosened clapboards tost,
The board-nails snapping in the frost;
And on us, through the unplastered wall,   620
Felt the light sifted snow-flakes fall.
But sleep stole on, as sleep will do
When hearts are light and life is new;
Faint and more faint the murmurs grew,
Till in the summer-land of dreams

---

[55] "For he knoweth our frame; he remembereth that we are dust," from Psalm 103:14.
[56] A globe-shaped watch, with thick glass facing; not for the wrist.

They softened to the sound of streams,
Low stir of leaves, and dip of oars,
And lapsing waves on quiet shores.

Next morn we wakened with the shout
   Of merry voices high and clear;   630
   And saw the teamsters[57] drawing near
To break the drifted highways out.
Down the long hillside treading slow
We saw the half-buried oxen go,
Shaking the snow from heads uptost,
Their straining nostrils white with frost.
Before our door the straggling train
Drew up, an added team to gain.
The elders threshed their hands a-cold,
   Passed, with the cider-mug, their jokes   640
   From lip to lip; the younger folks
Down the loose snow-banks, wrestling, rolled,
Then toiled again the cavalcade
   O'er windy hill, through clogged ravine,
   And woodland paths that wound between
Low drooping pine-boughs winter-weighed.
From every barn a team afoot,
At every house a new recruit,
Where, drawn by Nature's subtlest law,
Haply the watchful young men saw   650
Sweet doorway pictures of the curls
And curious eyes of merry girls,
Lifting their hands in mock defence
Against the snow-ball's compliments,
And reading in each missive tost
The charm with Eden never lost.

We heard once more the sleigh-bells' sound;
   And, following where the teamsters led,
The wise old Doctor went his round,
Just pausing at our door to say,   660
In the brief autocratic way
Of one who, prompt at Duty's call,
Was free to urge her claim on all,
   That some poor neighbor sick abed
At night our mother's aid would need.
For, one in generous thought and deed,
   What mattered in the sufferer's sight
   The Quaker matron's inward light,
The Doctor's mail[58] of Calvin's creed?

---

[57] Those in the business of hauling with a team of horses; here, plowing drifted snow.
[58] Whittier questions the importance of the difference between his mother's "inward light" (the Quaker center of belief) and the doctor's armorlike Calvinist creed of predestination when the two people are together "in generous thought and deed."

All hearts confess the saints elect   670
   Who, twain in faith, in love agree,
And melt not in an acid sect
   The Christian pearl of charity!

So days went on: a week had passed
Since the great world was heard from last.
The Almanac was studied o'er,
Read and reread our little store,
Of books and pamphlets, scarce a score;
One harmless novel, mostly hid
From younger eyes, a book forbid,   680
And poetry, (or good or bad,
A single book was all we had,)
Where Ellwood's[59] meek, drab-skirted Muse,
   A stranger to the heathen Nine,
   Sang, with a somewhat nasal whine,
The wars of David and the Jews.
At last the floundering carrier bore
The village paper to our door.
Lo! broadening outward as we read,
To warmer zones the horizon spread;   690
In panoramic length unrolled
We saw the marvels that it told.
Before us passed the painted Creeks,[60]
   And daft McGregor on his raids
   In Costa Rica's everglades.
And up Taygetos winding slow
Rode Ypsilanti's Mainote Greeks,
A Turk's head at each saddle-bow![61]
Welcome to us its week-old news,
Its corner for the rustic Muse,   700
   Its monthly gauge of snow and rain,
Its record, mingling in a breath
The wedding knell and dirge of death;
Jest, anecdote, and love-lorn tale,
The latest culprit sent to jail;
Its hue and cry of stolen and lost,
Its vendue[62] sales and goods at cost,
   And traffic calling loud for gain.
We felt the stir of hall and street,
The pulse of life that round us beat;   710

[59] The English Quaker Thomas Ellwood (1639–1714), who wrote the poem *Davideis* (1712), epic in length but not, according to Whittier, in inspiration; Ellwood's "drab-skirted Muse" knows nothing of the Muses of Greek mythology and brings him to write boringly of biblical themes.

[60] The newspaper broadens their horizons with news of the Creek Indians, defeated in the Creek War of 1813 to 1814 (and then moved from their homes in Georgia and Alabama to what is now Oklahoma) and news of the Scottish adventurer Gregor MacGregor (who failed in an attempt to colonize Costa Rica in 1819) and of the Greek revolutionary patriot Alexander Ypsilanti (who defeated the Turks at Mt. Taygetos in 1820). All this news was probably not in one issue.

[61] The defeated Turks were decapitated, and their heads mounted on saddles as trophies of victory.

[62] Auction.

The chill embargo of the snow
Was melted in the genial glow;
Wide swung again our ice-locked door,
And all the world was ours once more!

Clasp, Angel of the backward look
 And folded wings of ashen gray
 And voice of echoes far away,
The brazen covers of thy book;
The weird palimpsest[63] old and vast,
Wherein thou hid'st the spectral past;   720
Where, closely mingling, pale and glow
The characters of joy and woe;
The monographs of outlived years,
Or smile-illumed or dim with tears,
 Green hills of life that slope to death,
And haunts of home, whose vistaed trees
Shade off to mournful cypresses
 With the white amaranths[64] underneath.
Even while I look, I can but heed
 The restless sands' incessant fall,   730
Importunate hours that hours succeed,
Each clamorous with its own sharp need,
 And duty keeping pace with all.
Shut down and clasp the heavy lids;
I hear again the voice that bids
The dreamer leave his dream midway
For larger hopes and graver fears:
Life greatens in these later years,
The century's aloe[65] flowers to-day!

Yet, haply, in some lull of life,   740
Some Truce of God which breaks its strife,
The worldling's eyes shall gather dew,
 Dreaming in throngful city ways
Of winter joys his boyhood knew;
And dear and early friends—the few
Who yet remain—shall pause to view
 These Flemish pictures of old days;[66]
Sit with me by the homestead hearth,
And stretch the hands of memory forth
 To warm them at the wood-fire's blaze!   750
And thanks untraced to lips unknown
Shall greet me like the odors blown
From unseen meadows newly mown,
Or lilies floating in some pond,

[63] Parchment with original writing faintly visible beneath later writing.
[64] Legendary unfading flowers.   [65] A fabled plant said to bloom only once each century.
[66] Seventeenth-century Flemish painters were known for the realistic detail with which they depicted domestic scenes.

Wood-fringed, the wayside gaze beyond;
The traveller owns the grateful sense
Of sweetness near, he knows not whence,
And, pausing, takes with forehead bare
The benediction of the air.

1865–1866, 1866

CHICAGO*

Men said at vespers: "All is well!"
In one wild night the city fell;[1]
Fell shrines of prayer and marts of gain
Before the fiery hurricane.

On threescore spires had sunset shone,
Where ghastly sunrise looked on none:
Men clasped each other's hands, and said:
"The City of the West is dead!"

Brave hearts who fought, in slow retreat,
The fiends of fire from street to street,   10
Turned, powerless, to the blinding glare,
The dumb defiance of despair.

A sudden impulse thrilled each wire
That signalled round that sea of fire;
Swift words of cheer, warm heart-throbs came;
In tears of pity died the flame!

From East, from West, from South and North,
The messages of hope shot forth,
And, underneath the severing wave,
The world, full-handed, reached to save   20

Fair seemed the old; but fairer still
The new, the dreary void shall fill
With dearer homes than those o'erthrown,
For love shall lay each corner-stone.

Rise, stricken city!—from thee throw
The ashen sackcloth of thy woe;
And build, as to Amphion's strain,[2]
To songs of cheer thy walls again!

---

* First published in the *Atlantic Monthly* in 1872.   [1] The night of October 8, 1871.
[2] Amphion's music: according to Greek myth, Amphion and his twin brother, Zethus, built the walls
of Thebes; Amphion was a harpist of such skill that his music drew the stones into place.

How shrivelled in thy hot distress
The primal sin of selfishness!   30
How instant rose, to take thy part,
The angel in the human heart!

Ah! not in vain the flames that tossed
Above thy dreadful holocaust;
The Christ again has preached through thee
The Gospel of Humanity!

Then lift once more thy towers on high,
And fret with spires the western sky,
To tell that God is yet with us,
And love is still miraculous!   40

1872

Oliver Wendell Holmes
(1809–1894)

Born into an honored family in Cambridge, Massachusetts, in 1809, Oliver Wendell
Holmes spent virtually his entire life in the Boston area, which he called with playful
seriousness "the hub of the solar system." A descendant of Anne Bradstreet, America's
first published poet, Holmes was educated at Phillips and Andover Academies and Harvard University. He studied medicine in Boston and Paris and received an M.D. degree
from Harvard Medical School in 1836, afterward serving as professor of anatomy for two
years at Dartmouth College and for more than forty years at Harvard. For six of these
years Holmes was dean of the Harvard Medical School. During his long and distinguished
career in the field of medical education, Holmes made noteworthy contributions to the
battle against infectious diseases; especially important is his study *The Contagiousness of
Puerperal Fever* (1843), a disease associated with childhood mortality.

In his literary endeavors Holmes gracefully represented what he termed the "Brahmin
Caste" in New England, a social aristocracy both "harmless" and "inoffensive." His verse
is characteristically light and occasional, limited by its avocational nature yet marked by a
beguiling playfulness, wit, and neoclassical charm. His early patriotic ballad, "Old Iron-
sides" (1830), is commonly credited with (unintentionally) saving the U.S.S. *Constitution*,
a Boston-built warship, from demolition. In 1836 Holmes published his first volume,
Poems, which was followed by a number of expanded books of poetry over the years. A
gentle sentimentality informs much of this "Fireside Poet's" verse, but his humorous depiction of the breakdown of the "one-hoss shay" (or one-horse carriage) in "The Deacon's
Masterpiece" (1858) uses science to satirize and reject the Calvinist heritage of his father,
the Reverend Abiel Holmes. And Holmes's most serious poem, "The Chambered Nautilus" (1858), reflects the scientific rationalism that gave a durable edge to his conservative
intelligence.

Holmes named and helped to found the *Atlantic Monthly* in 1857. His series of essays entitled "The Autocrat of the Breakfast Table," begun over twenty-five years earlier, was published in the *New England Magazine* and collected into a volume in 1858. In the years that followed, Holmes wrote three "medicated" novels, as he called them—*Elsie Venner: A Romance of Destiny* (1861), *The Guardian Angel* (1867), and *A Moral Antipathy* (1885). Informally organized and lacking effective narrative structure, these novels combine social commentary and abnormal case histories, suggesting rational rather than teleological or deterministic explanations for human behavior. In *Elsie Venner,* for example, a pregnant woman bitten by a rattlesnake eventually gives birth to a child who shows alarming evidence of that prenatal influence.

Holmes died at age eighty-five in his beloved Boston in 1894. His achievements were larger and more encompassing than the few poems and essays we might read today can suggest. Popularly regarded as "the most intelligent man in New England," he commanded respect and admiration as writer and speaker, as doctor and humanitarian—as a dedicated and accomplished human being.

Suggested Readings: *The Autocrat of the Breakfast-Table,* 1858. *Elsie Venner: A Romance of Destiny,* 1861. *The Poetical Works of Oliver Wendell Holmes,* ed. E. M. Tilton, 1975. J. T. Morse, Jr., *Life and Letters of Oliver Wendell Holmes,* 2 vols., 1896. M. A. de Wolfe Howe, *Holmes of the Breakfast-Table,* 1939, rpt. 1972. E. M. Tilton, *Amiable Autocrat: A Biography of Dr. Oliver Wendell Holmes,* 1947. E. P. Hoyt, *The Improper Bostonian: Dr. Oliver Wendell Holmes,* 1979.

Text Used: *The Poetical Works of Oliver Wendell Holmes,* 1890.

THE HEIGHT OF THE RIDICULOUS*

I wrote some lines once on a time
   In wondrous merry mood,
And thought, as usual, men would say
   They were exceeding good.

They were so queer, so very queer,
   I laughed as I would die;
Albeit, in the general way,
   A sober man am I.

I called my servant, and he came;
   How kind it was of him   10
To mind a slender man like me,
   He of the mighty limb!

"These to the printer," I exclaimed,
   And, in my humorous way,
I added, (as a trifling jest,)
   "There'll be the devil to pay."

* First published in *The Collegian* in 1830.

He took the paper, and I watched,
    And saw him peep within;
At the first line he read, his face
    Was all upon the grin.   20

He read the next; the grin grew broad,
    And shot from ear to ear;
He read the third; a chuckling noise
    I now began to hear.

The fourth; he broke into a roar;
    The fifth; his waistband split;
The sixth; he burst five buttons off,
    And tumbled in a fit.

Ten days and nights, with sleepless eye,
    I watched that wretched man,   30
And since, I never dare to write
    As funny as I can.

                                                    1830

MY AUNT*

My aunt! my dear unmarried aunt!
    Long years have o'er her flown;
Yet still she strains the aching clasp
    That binds her virgin zone;[1]
I know it hurts her,—though she looks
    As cheerful as she can;
Her waist is ampler than her life,
    For life is but a span.[2]

My aunt! my poor deluded aunt!
    Her hair is almost gray;   10
Why will she train that winter curl
    In such a spring-like way?
How can she lay her glasses down,
    And say she reads as well,
When, through a double convex lens,
    She just makes out to spell?

Her father—grandpapa! forgive
    This erring lip its smiles—
Vowed she should make the finest girl
    Within a hundred miles;

* First published in the *New England Magazine* in 1831.
[1] The "clasp" or buckle on the waistband or belt traditionally worn by unmarried young women.
[2] Pun on "span" to mean distance (nine inches) and time, as in Psalm 90:10: "The days of our years are threescore years and ten."

He sent her to a stylish school; 20
   'T was in her thirteenth June;
And with her, as the rules required,
   "Two towels and a spoon."

They braced my aunt against a board,
   To make her straight and tall;
They laced her up, they starved her down,
   To make her light and small;
They pinched her feet, they singed her hair,
   They screwed it up with pins;—
O never mortal suffered more 30
   In penance for her sins.

So, when my precious aunt was done,
   My grandsire brought her back;
(By daylight, lest some rabid youth
   Might follow on the track;)
"Ah!" said my grandsire, as he shook
   Some powder in his pan,[3]
"What could this lovely creature do
   Against a desperate man!"

40
Alas! nor chariot, nor barouche,[4]
   Nor bandit cavalcade,
Tore from the trembling father's arms
   His all-accomplished maid.
For her how happy had it been!
   And Heaven had spared to me
To see one sad, ungathered rose
   On my ancestral tree.

1831

THE CHAMBERED NAUTILUS*

This is the ship of pearl, which, poets feign,[1]
   Sails the unshadowed main,—
   The venturous bark[2] that flings
On the sweet summer wind its purpled wings
In gulfs enchanted, where the Siren[3] sings,
   And coral reefs lie bare,
Where the cold sea-maids[4] rise to sun their streaming hair.

---

[3] To get his gun ready for action.   [4] Four-wheeled carriage.

* First published in the *Atlantic Monthly* in 1858. The pearly nautilus is a mollusk native to the South Pacific and Indian Oceans; it builds a spiral shell by growing a larger shell compartment each year. The Greeks thought it could move over the water, using a membrane as a sail.

[1] Make believe, pretend.   [2] Ship.

[3] According to Greek myth, a nymph whose singing lured sailors to destruction.   [4] Mermaids.

Its webs of living gauze no more unfurl;
   Wrecked is the ship of pearl!
    And every chambered cell,   10
Where its dim dreaming life was wont to dwell,
As the frail tenant shaped his growing shell,
    Before thee lies revealed,—
Its irised[5] ceiling rent, its sunless crypt unsealed!

Year after year beheld the silent toil
   That spread his lustrous coil;
    Still, as the spiral grew,
He left the past year's dwelling for the new,
Stole with soft step its shining archway through,
    Built up its idle door,   20
Stretched in his last-found home, and knew the old no more.

Thanks for the heavenly message brought by thee,
   Child of the wandering sea,
    Cast from her lap,[6] forlorn!
From thy dead lips a clearer note is born
Than ever Triton[7] blew from wreathéd horn!
    While on mine ear it rings,
Through the deep caves of thought I hear a voice that sings:—

Build thee more stately mansions, O my soul,
   As the swift seasons roll!   30
    Leave thy low-vaulted past!
Let each new temple, nobler than the last,
Shut thee from heaven with a dome more vast,
    Till thou at length art free,
Leaving thine outgrown shell by life's unresting sea!

1858

THE DEACON'S MASTERPIECE*

OR, THE WONDERFUL "ONE-HOSS SHAY"[1]

A Logical Story

Have you heard of the wonderful one-hoss shay,
That was built in such a logical way
It ran a hundred years to a day,
And then, of a sudden, it—ah, but stay,

---

[5] Rainbow colored; according to Greek myth, Iris was the goddess of the rainbow.
[6] Thrown up on the beach.
[7] According to Greek myth, a seagod who regulated the waves by blowing on a conch shell.
* First published in the *Atlantic Monthly* (1858).
[1] A chaise, a two-wheeled carriage drawn by a single horse.

I'll tell you what happened without delay,
Scaring the parson into fits,
Frightening people out of their wits,—
Have you ever heard of that, I say?

Seventeen hundred and fifty-five.
Georgius Secundus[2] was then alive,—   10
Snuffy old drone from the German hive.
That was the year when Lisbon-town
Saw the earth open and gulp her down,[3]
And Braddock's[4] army was done so brown,
Left without a scalp to its crown.
It was on the terrible Earthquake-day
That the Deacon finished the one-hoss shay.

Now in building of chaises, I tell you what,
There is always *somewhere* a weakest spot,—
In hub, tire, felloe,[5] in spring or thill,[6]   20
In panel, or crossbar, or floor, or sill,
In screw, bolt, thoroughbrace,[7]—lurking still,
Find it somewhere you must and will,—
Above or below, or within or without,—
And that's the reason, beyond a doubt,
That a chaise *breaks down,* but does n't *wear out.*

But the Deacon swore, (as Deacons do,
With an "I dew vum,"[8] or an "I tell *yeou*",)
He would build one shay to beat the taown
'n' the keounty 'n' all the kentry raoun';   30
It should be so built that it *couldn'* break daown:
—"Fur," said the Deacon, "'t's mighty plain
Thut the weakes' place mus' stan' the strain;
'n' the way t' fix it, uz I maintain,
    Is only jest
T' make that place uz strong uz the rest."

So the Deacon inquired of the village folk
Where he could find the strongest oak,
That could n't be split nor bent nor broke,—
That was for spokes and floor and sills;   40
He sent for lancewood to make the thills;
The crossbars were ash, from the straightest trees,
The panels of white-wood, that cuts like cheese,
But lasts like iron for things like these;

[2] George II (1683–1760), or George Augustus of the House of Hanover, a German-born King of England (1727–1760).
[3] The disastrous Lisbon earthquake of 1755.
[4] General Edward Braddock (1695–1755), killed along with many of his troops when the French and Native Americans ambushed the British in 1755.
[5] The wheel's rim.   [6] The shafts harnessing the horse.
[7] A strap connecting the body of the carriage to the springs.   [8] "I do vow."

The hubs of logs from the "Settler's ellum,"[9]—
Last of its timber,—they could n't sell 'em,
Never an axe had seen their chips,
And the wedges flew from between their lips,
Their blunt ends frizzled like celery-tips;
Step and prop-iron, bolt and screw,   50
Spring, tire, axle, and linchpin[10] too,
Steel of the finest, bright and blue;
Thoroughbrace bison-skin, thick and wide;
Boot, top, dasher,[11] from tough old hide
Found in the pit when the tanner died.
That was the way he "put her through."—
"There!" said the Deacon, "naow she'll dew!"

Do! I tell you, I rather guess
She was a wonder, and nothing less!
Colts grew horses, beards turned gray,   60
Deacon and deaconess dropped away,
Children and grandchildren—where were they?
But there stood the stout old one-hoss shay
As fresh as on Lisbon-earthquake-day!

EIGHTEEN HUNDRED;—it came and found
The Deacon's masterpiece strong and sound.
Eighteen hundred increased by ten;—
"Hahnsum kerridge" they called it then.
Eighteen hundred and twenty came;—
Running as usual; much the same.   70
Thirty and forty at last arrive,
And then come fifty, and FIFTY-FIVE.

Little of all we value here
Wakes on the morn of its hundredth year
Without both feeling and looking queer.
In fact, there's nothing that keeps its youth,
So far as I know, but a tree and truth.
(This is a moral that runs at large;
Take it.—You're welcome.—No extra charge.)
FIRST OF NOVEMBER,—the Earthquake-day—[12]   80
There are traces of age in the one-hoss shay,
A general flavor of mild decay,
But nothing local, as one may say.
There could n't be,—for the Deacon's art
Had made it so like in every part
That there was n't a chance for one to start.
For the wheels were just as strong as the thills,
And the floor was just as strong as the sills,

---

[9] Either an elm tree standing when the first settler came to the area, or the elm planted by the first settler.
[10] A pin attaching the wheel to the axle.   [11] Dashboard.
[12] The date of the 1755 Lisbon earthquake.

And the panels just as strong as the floor,
And the whipple-tree[13] neither less nor more,   90
And the back-crossbar as strong as the fore,
And spring and axle and hub *encore.*
And yet, *as a whole,* it is past a doubt
In another hour it will be *worn out!*

First of November, 'Fifty-five!
This morning the parson takes a drive.
Now, small boys, get out of the way!
Here comes the wonderful one-hoss shay,
Drawn by a rat-tailed, ewe-necked bay.[14]
"Huddup!" said the parson.—Off went they.   100
The parson was working his Sunday's text,—
Had got to *fifthly,* and stopped perplexed
At what the—Moses—was coming next.
All at once the horse stood still,
Close by the meet'n'-house on the hill.
—First a shiver, and then a thrill,
Then something decidedly like a spill,—
And the parson was sitting upon a rock,
At half past nine by the meet'n'-house clock,—
Just the hour of the Earthquake shock![15]   110
—What do you think the parson found,
When he got up and stared around?
The poor old chaise in a heap or mound,
As if it had been to the mill and ground!
You see, of course, if you're not a dunce,
How it went to pieces all at once,—
All at once, and nothing first,—
Just as bubbles do when they burst.

End of the wonderful one-hoss shay.
Logic is logic. That's all I say.   120

                                    1858

James Russell Lowell
(1819–1891)

Like the other "Fireside Poets," James Russell Lowell was a man of many talents who became one of America's most distinguished men of letters. Both his poetry and his essays

[13] A wooden bar attaching a carriage to a horse's harness.
[14] A reddish-brown horse with a thin neck and a ratlike tail.
[15] The climax of the poem is timed to coincide not only with the year and the day but the hour of the Lisbon earthquake.

were representative of the cultured society from which he sprang. Born in 1819 in Cambridge, Massachusetts, into a family that could trace its New England roots back to the 1630s, Lowell was the son of a clergyman. Lowell graduated from Harvard University as class poet in 1838 and went on to complete his studies at Harvard Law School in 1840—but he did not find the practice of law rewarding. In 1844 he married Maria White, under whose influence he became a vocal advocate of such causes as temperance, women's rights, and abolitionism. The topical nature of his *Poems* (1844) demonstrates the concerns he shared with Maria and marks a sharp departure from the romantic melancholy of his first volume of poems, *A Year's Life* (1841). The year 1848 marked the high point of Lowell's career as poet and knowing satirist. During that year he published the verse satires *The Biglow Papers* (first series) and *A Fable for Critics,* a two-volume set of *Poems,* and the verse parable *The Vision of Sir Launfal.*

After Maria Lowell's death in 1853 (by which time three of their four children had died), Lowell gradually adopted the mantle of conservatism that was his by tradition and training. Unable to make a living by literary endeavor, he succeeded Henry Wadsworth Longfellow as Smith Professor of Modern Languages at Harvard in 1856 and remained in this post for thirty years. Lowell married his surviving child's governess, Frances Dunlap, in 1857. He also served as the first editor of the *Atlantic Monthly* from 1857 to 1861 and co-edited the *North American Review* from 1863 to 1872. Lowell became active in Republican politics as a convention delegate and presidential elector and was later named American ambassador to Spain (1877–1880) and to England (1880–1885).

The study of James Russell Lowell at Elmwood, in Cambridge, Massachusetts.

As a member of what Oliver Wendell Holmes termed the Brahmin caste and as a founder of the literary circle called the Saturday Club, Lowell had close associations with writers such as Longfellow, Ralph Waldo Emerson, Nathaniel Hawthorne, and John Greenleaf Whittier. Perhaps because of this independent company, Lowell continued to comment on social and political issues. With crackerbarrel wit and a Down East dialect, the first series of *The Biglow Papers* had been directed against American imperialism and the Mexican War, which Lowell saw as a means of extending the evil of slavery. A second series of these papers, equally trenchant and folksy, was published in 1867 and supported the northern cause in the Civil War. Different in tone and purpose, in the voice of the public poet, Lowell's "Ode Recited at the Harvard Commemoration" (1865) honored the Harvard students and graduates who died in the Civil War.

Lowell returned to Massachusetts after Frances Lowell's death in 1885. He died of cancer at his childhood home in Cambridge in 1891. Whether Lowell was assessing his contemporaries (and himself) in *A Fable for Critics*, lampooning political expediency in *The Biglow Papers*, or appraising the fortunes of his country in the later *Political Essays* (1888), his talent for satire came from his learning and his concern for the moral equilibrium of the nation. Along with that of other Fireside Poets, his work embodies values that many nineteenth-century Americans held dear.

Suggested Readings: *Letters of James Russell Lowell*, 3 vols., ed. C. E. Norton, 1894. *Literary Criticism of James Russell Lowell*, ed. H. F. Smith, 1969. *The Biglow Papers, First Series*, ed. T. Wortham, 1977. *The Poetical Works of James Russell Lowell*, rev. ed., 1978. M. Duberman, *James Russell Lowell*, 1966. L. Howard, *Victorian Knight-Errant: The Early Literary Career of James Russell Lowell*, 1971. E. Wagenknecht, *James Russell Lowell: A Portrait of a Many-Sided Man*, 1976. C. D. Heymann, *American Aristocracy: The Life and Times of James Russell, Amy, and Robert Lowell*, 1980.

Text Used: *The Poetical Works of James Russell Lowell*, Vol. IV, 1904.

from A FABLE FOR CRITICS*

[*Ralph Waldo Emerson*]

"There comes Emerson first, whose rich words, every one,
Are like gold nails in temples to hang trophies on,
Whose prose is grand verse, while his verse, the Lord knows,
Is some of it pr— No, 't is not even prose;
I'm speaking of metres; some poems have welled
From those rare depths of soul that have ne'er been excelled;
They're not epics, but that does n't matter a pin,
In creating, the only hard thing's to begin;
A grass-blade's no easier to make than an oak;
If you've once found the way, you've achieved the grand stroke;   10
In the worst of his poems are mines of rich matter,

---

* Lowell's comic manner and musical-comedy rhymes in this assessment of American writers should not eclipse the quality of his critical perception, which is often incisive and provocative. The manner and the matter are those of a man who puts the literary gossip of the day in the service of his judgment.

But thrown in a heap with a crash and a clatter;
Now it is not one thing nor another alone
Makes a poem, but rather the general tone,
The something pervading, uniting the whole,
The before unconceived, unconceivable soul,
So that just in removing this trifle or that, you
Take away, as it were, a chief limb of the statue;
Roots, wood, bark, and leaves singly perfect may be,
But, clapt hodge-podge together, they don't make a tree.   20

"But, to come back to Emerson (whom, by the way,
I believe we left waiting),—his is, we may say,
A Greek head on right Yankee shoulders, whose range
Has Olympus for one pole, for t'other the Exchange;[1]
He seems, to my thinking (although I'm afraid
The comparison must, long ere this, have been made),
A Plotinus-Montaigne, where the Egyptian's gold mist
And the Gascon's[2] shrewd wit cheek-by-jowl co-exist;
All admire, and yet scarcely six converts he's got
To I don't (nor they either) exactly know what;   30
For though he builds glorious temples, 't is odd
He leaves never a doorway to get in a god.
'T is refreshing to old-fashioned people like me
To meet such a primitive Pagan as he,
In whose mind all creation is duly respected
As parts of himself—just a little projected;
And who's willing to worship the stars and the sun,
A convert to—nothing but Emerson.
So perfect a balance there is in his head,
That he talks of things sometimes as if they were dead;   40
Life, nature, love, God, and affairs of that sort,
He looks at as merely ideas; in short,
As if they were fossils stuck round in a cabinet,
Of such vast extent that our earth's a mere dab in it;
Composed just as he is inclined to conjecture her,
Namely, one part pure earth, ninety-nine parts pure lecturer;
You are filled with delight at his clear demonstration,
Each figure, word, gesture, just fits the occasion,
With the quiet precision of science he'll sort 'em,
But you can't help suspecting the whole a *post mortem*.   50

"There are persons, mole-blind to the soul's make and style,
Who insist on a likeness 'twixt him and Carlyle;[3]

---

[1] Stock market. Here Lowell notes the blend of idealism and practicality in Emerson, which makes him a combination of the Greek Neoplatonist Plotinus (A.D. 205?–270?) and the rationalist French thinker Michel de Montaigne (1533–1592).

[2] Plotinus was born in Egypt, Montaigne in Gascony, France.

[3] Thomas Carlyle (1795–1871), a Scottish writer, many of whose ideas coincided with those of his American friend Emerson; the two enjoyed a stimulating and significant correspondence over the years. The Greek philopopher Plato (427–347 B.C.) is the fountainhead of western philosophical idealism.

To compare him with Plato would be vastly fairer,
Carlyle's the more burly, but E. is the rarer;
He sees a fewer objects, but clearlier, truelier,
If C.'s as original, E.'s more peculiar. . . .

* * *

[*William Cullen Bryant*]

"There is Bryant, as quiet, as cool, and as dignified,
As a smooth, silent iceberg, that never is ignified,
Save when by reflection 't is kindled o' nights
With a semblance of flame by the chill Northern Lights.   60
He may rank (Griswold[4] says so) first bard of your nation
(There's no doubt that he stands in supreme ice-olation),
Your topmost Parnassus[5] he may set his heel on,
But no warm applauses come, peal following peal on,—
He's too smooth and too polished to hang any zeal on:
Unqualified merits, I'll grant, if you choose, he has 'em,
But he lacks the one merit of kindling enthusiasm;
If he stir you at all, it is just, on my soul,
Like being stirred up with the very North Pole.

"He is very nice reading in summer, but *inter*   70
Nos,[6] we don't want *extra* freezing in winter;
Take him up in the depth of July, my advice is,
When you feel an Egyptian devotion to ices.[7]
But, deduct all you can, there's enough that's right good in him,
He has a true soul for field, river, and wood in him;
And his heart, in the midst of brick walls, or where'er it is,
Glows, softens, and thrills with the tenderest charities—
To you mortals that delve in this trade-ridden planet?
No, to old Berkshire's hills, with their limestone and granite.
If you're one who *in loco* (add *foco* here) *desipis*,[8]   80
You will get of his outermost heart (as I guess) a piece;
But you'd get deeper down if you came as a precipice,
And would break the last seal of its inwardest fountain,
If you only could palm yourself off for a mountain.
Mr. Quivis,[9] or somebody quite as discerning,
Some scholar who's hourly expecting his learning,

[4] Rufus Griswold (1815–1857), editor of *The Poets and Poetry of America* (1842) and *The Female Poets of America* (1849), best remembered for his malevolent criticism of Edgar Allan Poe following Poe's death.
[5] According to Greek myth, a mountain sacred to the Muses (the goddesses controlling literature and the arts) and to the sun god Apollo.
[6] "Between us" (Latin).
[7] Pun on "Isis," the Egyptian goddess of fertility.
[8] Latin word play: *in loco desipis* means "to act silly at times"; *loco foco* signifies the Locofocos, a group of liberal Democrats in the 1830s who carried on a meeting when their opponents turned out the lights by lighting "locofocos," the then-new friction matches.
[9] Mr. Whoever.

Calls B. the American Wordsworth;[10] but Wordsworth
May be rated at more than your whole tuneful herd's worth.
No, don't be absurd, he's an excellent Bryant;
But, my friends, you'll endanger the life of your client,   90
By attempting to stretch him up into a giant:
If you choose to compare him, I think there are two per-
-sons fit for a parallel—Thompson and Cowper;[11]
I don't mean exactly,—there's something of each,
There's T.'s love of nature, C.'s penchant to preach;
Just mix up their minds so that C.'s spice of craziness
Shall balance and neutralize T.'s turn for laziness,
And it gives you a brain cool, quite frictionless, quiet,
Whose internal police nips the buds of all riot,—   100
A brain like a permanent strait-jacket put on
The heart that strives vainly to burst off a button,—
A brain which, without being slow or mechanic,
Does more than a larger less drilled, more volcanic;
He's a Cowper condensed, with no craziness bitten,
And the advantage that Wordsworth before him had written.

"But, my dear little bardlings, don't prick up your ears
Nor suppose I would rank you and Bryant as peers;
If I call him an iceberg, I don't mean to say
There is nothing in that which is grand in its way;   110
He is almost the one of your poets that knows
How much grace, strength, and dignity lie in Repose;
If he sometimes fall short, he is too wise to mar
His thought's modest fulness by going too far;
'T would be well if your authors should all make a trial
Of what virtue there is in severe self-denial,
And measure their writings by Hesiod's staff,[12]
Which teaches that all has less value than half.

* * *

[Nathaniel Hawthorne]

"There is Hawthorne, with genius so shrinking and rare
That you hardly at first see the strength that is there;   120
A frame so robust, with a nature so sweet,
So earnest, so graceful, so lithe and so fleet,
Is worth a descent from Olympus to meet;
'T is as if a rough oak that for ages had stood,
With his gnarled bony branches like ribs of the wood,

---

[10] The English romantic poet William Wordsworth (1770–1850).
[11] James Thomson (1700–1748), a Scottish poet, author of *The Seasons* (1730); William Cowper (1731–1800), an English writer, author of the pastoral and didactic poem "The Task" (1784).
[12] By the criteria established by Hesiod (8th century B.C.), a Greek poet who advocates compression in language.

Should bloom, after cycles of struggle and scathe,
With a single anemone trembly and rathe;[13]
His strength is so tender, his wildness so meek,
That a suitable parallel sets one to seek,—
He's a John Bunyan Fouqué, a Puritan Tieck;[14]   130
When Nature was shaping him, clay was not granted
For making so full-sized a man as she wanted,
So, to fill out her model, a little she spared
From some finer-grained stuff for a woman prepared,
And she could not have hit a more excellent plan
For making him fully and perfectly man.

* * *

[*James Fenimore Cooper*]

"Here's Cooper, who's written six volumes to show
He's as good as a lord: well, let's grant that he's so;
If a person prefer that description of praise,
Why, a coronet's certainly cheaper than bays;[15]   140
But he need take no pains to convince us he's not
(As his enemies say) the American Scott.[16]
Choose any twelve men, and let C. read aloud
That one of his novels of which he's most proud,
And I'd lay any bet that, without ever quitting
Their box,[17] they'd be all, to a man, for acquitting.
He has drawn you one character, though, that is new,
One wildflower he's plucked that is wet with the dew
Of this fresh Western world, and, the thing not to mince,
He has done naught but copy it ill ever since;   150
His Indians, with proper respect be it said,
Are just Natty Bumppo,[18] daubed over with red,
And his very Long Toms[19] are the same useful Nat,
Rigged up in duck pants and a sou'wester hat
(Though once in a Coffin, a good chance was found
To have slipped the old fellow away under ground).
All his other men-figures are clothes upon sticks,
The *dernière chemise*[20] of a man in a fix

[13] Lowell reaches out for this rhyme: "scathe" means misfortune; "rathe," early in the season.

[14] According to Lowell, Hawthorne blends the didacticism of the English nonconformist churchman John Bunyan (1628–1688), who wrote *Pilgrim's Progress* (1678), and the imagination of Friedrich Fouqué (1777–1843), a German writer of fanciful tales, and is a Puritan version of the German romantic writer Ludwig Tieck (1773–1853).

[15] A small crown designating a rank below royalty is cheaper than a garland bestowed for victory.

[16] Sir Walter Scott (1771–1832), the Scottish novelist whose work was frequently cited as a paradigm for Cooper's fiction.

[17] Jury box.   [18] The hero of Cooper's five Leather-Stocking Tales.

[19] Long Tom Coffin, the experienced sailor in Cooper's novel *The Pilot* (1823); Lowell then puns on his surname.

[20] "Last shirt" (French); here, last resort.

(As a captain besieged, when his garrison's small,
Sets up caps upon poles to be seen o'er the wall); 160
And the women he draws from one model don't vary,
All sappy as maples and flat as a prairie.
When a character's wanted, he goes to the task
As a cooper would do in composing a cask;
He picks out the staves, of their qualities heedful,
Just hoops them together as tight as is needful,
And, if the best fortune should crown the attempt, he
Has made at the most something wooden and empty.

"Don't suppose I would underrate Cooper's abilities;
If I thought you'd do that, I should feel very ill at ease; 170
The men who have given to *one* character life
And objective existence are not very rife;
You may number them all, both prose-writers and singers,
Without overrunning the bounds of your fingers,
And Natty won't go to oblivion quicker
Than Adams the parson or Primrose the vicar.[21]

"There is one thing in Cooper I like, too, and that is
That on manners he lectures his countrymen gratis;[22]
Not precisely so either, because, for a rarity,
He is paid for his tickets in unpopularity. 180
Now he may overcharge his American pictures,
But you'll grant there's a good deal of truth in his strictures;
And I honor the man who is willing to sink
Half his present repute for the freedom to think,
And when he has thought, be his cause strong or weak,
Will risk t'other half for the freedom to speak,
Caring naught for what vengeance the mob has in store,
Let that mob be the upper ten thousand or lower.

* * *

[Edgar Allan Poe]

"There comes Poe, with his raven, like Barnaby Rudge,[23]
Three fifths of him genius and two fifths sheer fudge, 190
Who talks like a book of iambs and pentameters,
In a way to make people of common sense damn metres,

---

[21] Parson Adams in the novel *Joseph Andrews* (1742), by the English novelist Henry Fielding (1707–1754); Dr. Primrose in *The Vicar of Wakefield* (1766), by the English poet and novelist Oliver Goldsmith (1730–1774).

[22] "Free" (Latin); after his return from a lengthy stay in Europe in the 1830s, Cooper admonished his countrymen on a number of their democratic "excesses."

[23] Edgar Allan Poe's "The Raven" (1845); the title character of Charles Dickens's novel *Barnaby Rudge* (1841), who owned a raven.

Who has written some things quite the best of their kind,
But the heart somehow seems all squeezed out by the mind,
Who— But hey-day! What's this? Messieurs Mathews[24] and Poe,
You must n't fling mud-balls at Longfellow so,
Does it make a man worse that his character's such
As to make his friends love him (as you think) too much?
Why, there is not a bard at this moment alive
More willing than he that his fellows should thrive;   200
While you are abusing him thus, even now
He would help either one of you out of a slough;
You may say that he's smooth and all that till you're hoarse,
But remember that elegance also is force;
After polishing granite as much as you will,
The heart keeps its tough old persistency still;
Deduct all you can, *that* still keeps you at bay;
Why, he'll live till men weary of Collins and Gray.[25]
I'm not over-fond of Greek metres in English,[26]
To me rhyme's a gain, so it be not too jinglish,   210
And your modern hexameter verses are no more
Like Greek ones than sleek Mr. Pope is like Homer;[27]
As the roar of the sea to the coo of a pigeon is,
So, compared to your moderns, sounds old Melesigenes;[28]
I may be too partial, the reason, perhaps, o't is
That I've heard the old blind man recite his own rhapsodies,
And my ear with that music impregnate may be,
Like the poor exiled shell with the soul of the sea,
Or as one can't bear Strauss when his nature is cloven
To its deeps within deeps by the stroke of Beethoven;[29]   220
But, set that aside, and 't is truth that I speak,
Had Theocritus[30] written in English, not Greek,
I believe that his exquisite sense would scarce change a line
In that rare, tender, virgin-like pastoral Evangeline.
That's not ancient nor modern, its place is apart
Where time has no sway, in the realm of pure Art,
'T is a shrine of retreat from Earth's hubbub and strife
As quiet and chaste as the author's own life.

* * *

[24] Cornelius Mathews (1817–1889), a New York editor, critic, and poet who attacked Longfellow's poetry (as did Poe).

[25] William Collins (1721–1759), an English lyric poet; Thomas Gray (1716–1771), an English poet, author of "Elegy Written in a Country Churchyard" (1751).

[26] Longfellow adapted the hexameters of Greek epic poetry for his American epic poem *Evangeline* (1847).

[27] Alexander Pope (1688–1744), the English poet who translated Homer's *Iliad* and *Odyssey* into heroic couplets.

[28] Lowell coins this Greek work signifying "Melos-born"; he has read Homer (who was reputedly blind) in the original.

[29] When the lilting waltzes of the Viennese composer Johann Strauss show the graver tones of symphonies written by the German composer Ludwig van Beethoven.

[30] Theocritus (3d century B.C.) was a Greek pastoral poet.

[*Washington Irving*]

"What! Irving? thrice welcome, warm heart and fine brain,
You bring back the happiest spirit from Spain,[31]   230
And the gravest sweet humor, that ever were there
Since Cervantes[32] met death in his gentle despair;
Nay, don't be embarrassed, nor look so beseeching,
I shan't run directly against my own preaching,
And, having just laughed at their Raphaels and Dantes,[33]
Go to setting you up beside matchless Cervantes;
But allow me to speak what I honestly feel,—
To a true poet-heart add the fun of Dick Steele,[34]
Throw in all of Addison, *minus* the chill,
With the whole of that partnership's stock and good-will,   240
Mix well, and while stirring, hum o'er, as a spell,
The fine *old* English Gentleman,[35] simmer it well,
Sweeten just to your own private liking, then strain,
That only the finest and clearest remain,
Let it stand out of doors till a soul it receives
From the warm lazy sun loitering down through green leaves,
And you'll find a choice nature, not wholly deserving
A name either English or Yankee,—just Irving.

* * *

[*Oliver Wendell Holmes*]

"There's Holmes, who is matchless among you for wit;
A Leyden-jar[36] always full-charged, from which flit   250
The electrical tingles of hit after hit;

---

[31] Washington Irving served as U.S. minister to Spain from 1842 to 1845; he had written *A Chronicle of the Conquest of Granada* (1829) and *Legends of the Alhambra* (1832).

[32] Miguel de Cervantes Saavedra (1547–1616), the Spanish novelist who wrote the influential *Don Quixote de la Mancha* (1605, 1615).

[33] Feeling that the work of American writers and artists was being neglected, members of the informal Young America movement (among them the editor Evert A. Duyckinck [1816–1878] and Herman Melville) promoted American talent in the 1840s. Here, with typical exaggeration, Lowell laughs at those being touted as the equal of the Italian masters Raphael Santi (1483–1520), a Renaissance painter, and Dante Alighieri (1265–1321), author of *The Divine Comedy*.

[34] The English writers Richard Steele (1672–1729) and Joseph Addison (1672–1719) collaborated on a famous series of essays in the periodical *The Spectator*; their prose style was admired by Irving, Benjamin Franklin, and many other authors.

[35] In the essay "*The English Country Gentleman*" in Irving's *Bracebridge Hall* (1822).

[36] An electrical condenser that has a glass jar coated with tinfoil inside and out and a brass knob on top that connects to the inner coating.

In long poems 't is painful sometimes, and invites
A thought of the way the new Telegraph[37] writes,
Which pricks down its little sharp sentences spitefully
As if you got more than you'd title to rightfully,
And you find yourself hoping its wild father Lightning
Would flame in for a second and give you a fright'ning.
He has perfect sway of what *I* call a sham metre,
But many admire it, the English pentameter,
And Campbell,[38] I think, wrote most commonly worse,   260
With less nerve, swing, and fire in the same kind of verse,
Nor e'er achieved aught in't so worthy of praise
As the tribute of Holmes to the grand *Marseillaise*.[39]
You went crazy last year over Bulwer's New Timon;[40]—
Why, if B., to the day of his dying, should rhyme on,
Heaping verses on verses and tomes upon tomes,
He could ne'er reach the best point and vigor of Holmes.
His are just the fine hands, too, to weave you a lyric
Full of fancy, fun, feeling, or spiced with satiric
In a measure so kindly, you doubt if the toes   270
That are trodden upon are your own or your foes'.

[*James Russell Lowell*]

"There is Lowell, who's striving Parnassus to climb
With a whole bale of *isms* tied together with rhyme,
He might get on alone, spite of brambles and boulders,
But he can't with that bundle he has on his shoulders,
The top of the hill he will ne'er come nigh reaching
Till he learns the distinction 'twixt singing and preaching;
His lyre has some chords that would ring pretty well,
But he'd rather by half make a drum of the shell,
And rattle away till he's old as Methusalem,[41]   280
At the head of a march to the last new Jerusalem.[42]

1848

---

[37] Recently invented by Samuel F. B. Morse (1791–1872), in 1844.

[38] Thomas Campbell (1777–1844), a Scottish poet known for his war songs.

[39] The French national anthem, whose stirring rhythms Holmes praises in "Poetry: A Metrical Essay" (1836).

[40] *The New Timon: A Romance of London* (1846), by the British novelist Edward Bulwer-Lytton (1803–1873).

[41] Methuselah, who lived 969 years, according to Genesis 5:27.

[42] The latest reform movement to cure the ills of the world.

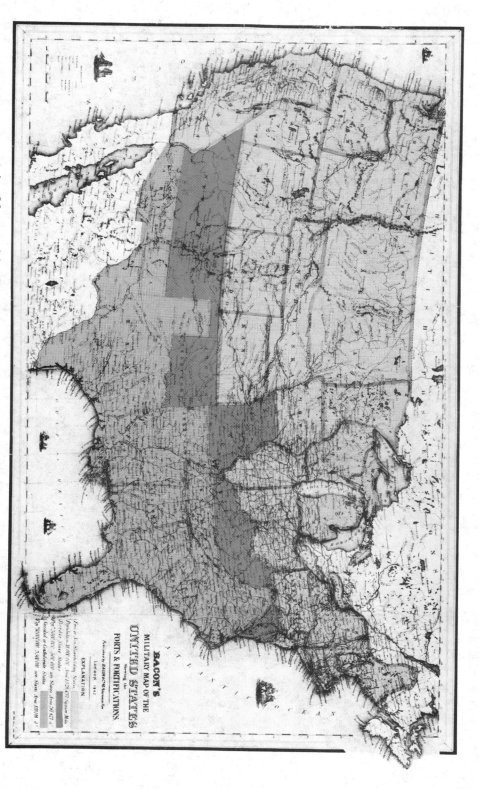

An 1862 map of the United States showing: light area, the free or nonslaveholding states; dark area, the border slave states; medium area, the seceded or Confederate states.

Frances E. W. Harper
(1825–1911)

A brilliant speaker, a writer of essays, short fiction, and a novel, Frances E. W. Harper is best known today for her stirring oratorical poetry. During her lifetime she was probably the most popular African-American poet. Born in 1825 to free parents in Baltimore—in the slave state of Maryland—Frances Ellen Watkins was orphaned at age three and raised by an aunt and uncle. She attended a school for free African Americans, conducted by her uncle in Baltimore. In 1850 she moved to the North and obtained a teaching position at Union Seminary (later Wilberforce University), near Columbus, Ohio. Morally drawn to the antislavery cause, she worked actively for the Underground Railroad and began to lecture widely on abolition. She delivered her first abolitionist speech in 1854 in New Bedford, Massachusetts, and was later employed as a lecturer by the Anti-Slavery Society of Maine. In 1860 she married Fenton Harper, a widowed father, and ceased her public work for a time, settling on a farm in Ohio and giving birth to a daughter. After her husband died in 1863, Harper moved to Philadelphia and resumed her career as a lecturer. Nearly fifty years passed until her death of heart disease in 1911.

The four volumes of poetry for which Harper is known reflect her commitment to the causes of abolition and women's rights. Her most famous collection, *Poems on Miscellaneous Subjects,* was published in 1854 and went through numerous editions. The ambitious *Moses: A Story of the Nile* (1869) has deep historical resonance, though its allegorical flourishes make it unfashionably abstract for many readers. A volume entitled *Poems* (1871), however, draws poignantly on Harper's experience in the South during the years of Reconstruction. Her last significant book of poetry, *Sketches of Southern Life* (1872), provides an emotional picture of the conditions Harper had found in her travels. By means of a central character named Aunt Chloe, Harper explores the divergence between the dream of equality and the stark reality of discrimination.

Dedicated to Harper's daughter, *Iola Leroy: Or, Shadows Uplifted* (1892) is an ambitious novel split curiously in two parts, the first focused on historical settings and issues (the Civil War and Reconstruction), the second on Iola's search for her mother and for happiness in marriage. Along with a number of nineteenth-century writers, including Samuel Woodworth in *The Mysterious Chief* (1816), James Fenimore Cooper in *The Spy* (1821), and John William DeForest in *Miss Ravenel's Conversion From Secession to Loyalty* (1867), Harper found it difficult to merge historical and personal narrative into unified form. Yet, the themes of *Iola Leroy* and Harper's skill at characterization mark the novel as a provocative achievement.

Confident of her talents as a speaker, Harper made major contributions to the traditions of oral poetry. As Maryemma Graham, an editor of Harper's work, has observed, informing that work was a deep sense of piety fostered by the Bible and by the specific example of John Greenleaf Whittier and of Henry Wadsworth Longfellow. Not only do Harper's best poems bring piety and passion to an engagement with social issues, but they dramatize the importance of a convincing poetic voice—thereby remaining vital.

Suggested Readings: *Poems on Miscellaneous Subjects,* 1854, rpt. 1969. *Iola Leroy: Or, Shadows Uplifted,* 1892, rpt. 1988. *Idylls of the Bible,* 1901, rpt. 1975. M. H. Washington, *Invented Lives,* 1985. H. V. Carby, *Reconstructing Womanhood,* 1987. M. Graham, "Introduction," in *Complete Poems of Frances E. W. Harper,* 1988.

Text Used: *Complete Poems of Frances E. W. Harper,* ed. M. Graham, 1988.

THE SLAVE AUCTION*

The sale began—young girls were there,
　　Defenceless in their wretchedness,
Whose stifled sobs of deep despair
　　Revealed their anguish and distress.

And mothers stood with streaming eyes,
　　And saw their dearest children sold;
Unheeded rose their bitter cries,
　　While tyrants bartered them for gold.

And woman, with her love and truth—
　　For these in sable forms may dwell—　　　　　　　　10
Gaz'd on the husband of her youth,
　　With anguish none may paint or tell.

And men, whose sole crime was their hue,
　　The impress of their Maker's hand,
And frail and shrinking children, too,
　　Were gathered in that mournful band.

Ye who have laid your love to rest,
　　And wept above their lifeless clay,
Know not the anguish of that breast,
　　Whose lov'd are rudely torn away.　　　　　　　　20

Ye may not know how desolate
　　Are bosoms rudely forced to part,
And how a dull and heavy weight
　　Will press the life-drops from the heart.

1854

BURY ME IN A FREE LAND†

Make me a grave where'er you will,
In a lowly plain, or a lofty hill,
Make it among earth's humblest graves.
But not in a land where men are slaves.

I could not rest if around my grave
I heard the steps of a trembling slave;
His shadow above my silent tomb
Would make it a place of fearful gloom.

---

* First published in *Poems on Miscellaneous Subjects* (1854).
　† First published in *The Liberator*, William Lloyd Garrison's abolitionist weekly, in 1864; included in *Poems* (1871).

I could not rest if I heard the tread
Of a coffie gang to the shambles led,[1]   10
And the mother's shriek of wild despair
Rise like a curse on the trembling air.

I could not sleep if I saw the lash
Drinking her blood at each fearful gash,
And I saw her babes torn from her breast,
Like trembling doves from their parent nest.

I'd shudder and start if I heard the bay
Of blood-hounds seizing their human prey,
And I heard the captive plead in vain
As they bound afresh his galling chain.   20

If I saw young girls from their mother's arms
Bartered and sold for their youthful charms,
My eye would flash with a mournful flame,
My death-paled cheek grow red with shame.

I would sleep, dear friends, where bloated might
Can rob no man of his dearest right;
My rest shall be calm in any grave
Where none can call his brother a slave.

I ask no monument, proud and high
To arrest the gaze of the passers-by;   30
All that my yearning spirit craves,
Is bury me not in a land of slaves.

1864

FIFTEENTH AMENDMENT*

Beneath the burden of our joy
    Tremble, O wires,[1] from East to West!
Fashion with words your tongues of fire,
    To tell the nation's high behest.[2]

Outstrip the winds, and leave behind
    The murmur of the restless waves;
Nor tarry with your glorious news,
    Amid the ocean's coral caves.

---

[1] A train of men or women bound together like beasts (a slave caravan) led to a place for slaughtering animals for meat.

* First published in *Poems* (1871); ratified on March 30, 1870, the Fifteenth Amendment to the U.S. Constitution gave former slaves the right to vote.

[1] Telegraph wires that would carry the good news.   [2] Command, mandate.

Ring out! ring out! your sweetest chimes,
    Ye bells, that call to praise;   10
Let every heart with gladness thrill,
    And songs of joyful triumph raise.

Shake off the dust, O rising race!
    Crowned as a brother and a man;
Justice to-day asserts her claim,
    And from thy brow fades out the ban.

With freedom's chrism[3] upon thy head,
    Her precious ensign[4] in thy hand,
Go place thy once despised name
    Amid the noblest of the land.   20

A ransomed race! give God the praise,
    Who let thee through a crimson sea,
And 'mid the storm of fire and blood,
    Turned out the war-cloud's light to thee.

1871

THE SLAVE MOTHER*

A Tale of the Ohio[1]

I have but four, the treasures of my soul,
    They lay like doves around my heart;
I tremble lest some cruel hand
    Should tear my household wreaths apart.

My baby girl, with childish glance,
    Looks curious in my anxious eye,
She little knows that for her sake
    Deep shadows round my spirit lie.

My playful boys could I forget,
    My home might seem a joyous spot,   10
But with their sunshine mirth I blend
    The darkness of their future lot.

And thou my babe, my darling one,
    My last, my loved, my precious child,
Oh! when I think upon thy doom
    My heart grows faint and then throbs wild.

---

[3] Holy oil used in baptism.   [4] Banner.
* First published in the twentieth edition of *Poems on Miscellaneous Subjects* (1874).
[1] The Ohio River.

The Ohio's bridged and spanned with ice,
   The northern star is shining bright,
I'll take the nestlings of my heart
   And search for freedom by its light.   20

Winter and night were on the earth,
   And feebly moaned the shivering trees,
A sigh of winter seemed to run
   Through every murmur of the breeze.

She fled,[2] and with her children all,
   She reached the stream and crossed it o'er,
Bright visions of deliverance came
   Like dreams of plenty to the poor.

Dreams! vain dreams, heroic mother,
   Give all thy hopes and struggles o'er,   30
The pursuer is on thy track,
   And the hunter at thy door.

Judea's[3] refuge cities had power
   To shelter, shield and save,
E'en Rome[4] had altars, 'neath whose shade
   Might crouch the wan and weary slave.

But Ohio had no sacred fane,[5]
   To human rights so consecrated,
Where thou may'st shield thy hapless ones
   From their darkly gathering fate.   40

Then, said the mournful mother,
   If Ohio cannot save,
I will do a deed for freedom,
   Shalt find each child a grave.

I will save my precious children
   From their darkly threatened doom,
I will hew their path to freedom
   Through the portals of the tomb.

A moment in the sunlight,
   She held a glimmering knife,   50
The next moment she had bathed it
   In the crimson fount of life.

---

[2] Here the point of view changes from first person to that of an omniscient spectator, giving an added perspective to the plight of the slave mother. The two points of view alternate throughout the remainder of the poem.

[3] A division of Palestine under the Romans; the cities of Judea could offer protection to outcasts.

[4] The altar would afford asylum to the slave.   [5] Temple or church.

They snatched away the fatal knife,
　　Her boys shrieked wild with dread;
The baby girl was pale and cold,
　　They raised it up, the child was dead.

Sends this deed of fearful daring
　　Through my country's heart no thrill,
Do the icy hands of slavery
　　Every pure emotion chill?　　　　　　　　　　　60

Oh! if there is any honor,
　　Truth or justice in the land,
Will ye not, us men and Christians,
　　On the side of freedom stand?

　　　　　　　　　　　　　　　　　　　　　　1874

Henry Timrod
(1828–1867)

Henry Timrod was born in Charleston, South Carolina, in 1828. During his youth he studied at several schools in Charleston and went on to enroll at Franklin College (now the
University of Georgia) in Athens in 1845. A year later, short of money and plagued by ill
health, he returned to Charleston to study law. There he developed friendships with several
men in Charleston's active literary community, among them Paul Hamilton Hayne (with
whom Timrod founded *Russell's Magazine* in 1857), the scholar Basil Gildersleeve, and
the novelist William Gilmore Simms. Timrod soon gave up the study of law and turned to
the classics, hoping for a college professorship. But he was forced to settle for various
positions as a tutor on plantations. Meanwhile, he spent holidays with his literary friends
in Charleston and wrote poetry (as he had since his days in college), which was published
in newspapers and, under the pseudonym Aglaus, in the *Southern Literary Messenger*. In
1860 his small volume *Poems* was published by the Boston firm of Ticknor and Fields and
brought him national, albeit fleeting, praise.

　　Like many southern writers of the time, Timrod found his life and his poetry changed
by the Civil War. For several months he served as clerk in the Confederate Army, but his
perilous health foreclosed any career as a soldier. Instead, he wrote poems in support of
the southern cause, transforming his interest in nature poetry to poems of war—its glory
and ultimate tragedy. Timrod's early war poems, such as "Ethnogenesis" (1861), reveal
his enthusiasm for, and confidence in, the Confederacy. As the war dragged on and his
health failed, however, the problematic outcome of the military struggle generated the kind
of ambivalent vision he explored stoically in "Charleston" (1862). Later poems, including
"Ode Sung at the Occasion of Decorating the Graves of the Confederate Dead" (1867),
mourn the fate of "martyrs of a fallen cause." During the final years of the war, Timrod
moved to Columbia, South Carolina, as an editor of the *South Carolinian* daily newspaper.
He married Kate S. Goodwin (to whom his poem *Katie* [1884] is dedicated) in 1864 and

had a son the following year. But events proved devastating for him: not only did he witness the burning of Columbia in February 1865, but his son died later that year. Following the war, Timrod's health continued to deteriorate while he worked at a series of low-paying jobs. He died of tuberculosis aggravated by poor nutrition in 1867.

Known as the "Laureate of the Confederacy," Timrod expressed the range of emotions associated with the South during the Civil War. With its elevated diction and conventional anthems of praise, his poetry has seemed cloying to some modern readers. Nevertheless, as Edd Winfield Parks, a biographer, has observed, the spiritual history of the Confederacy can be traced in Timrod's work. What Timrod gives us is the emotional genesis of a lost-cause mentality that would later haunt (and serve) southern writers as diverse as Margaret Mitchell, William Faulkner, and Walker Percy.

Suggested Readings: P. H. Hayne, ed., *The Poems of Henry Timrod*, 1872, rpt. 1972. G. A. Cardwell, Jr., *The Uncollected Poems of Henry Timrod*, 1942. E. W. Parks and A. W. Parks, eds., *Collected Poems: A Variorum Edition*, 1965. J. B. Hubbell, *The Last Years of Henry Timrod*, 1941. E. W. Parks, *Henry Timrod*, 1964.

Text Used: *Poems of Henry Timrod*, 1901.

CHARLESTON*

> Calm as that second summer which precedes
>   The first fall of the snow,
> In the broad sunlight of heroic deeds,
>   The City bides the foe.
>
> As yet, behind their ramparts stern and proud,
>   Her bolted thunders sleep—
> Dark Sumter,[1] like a battlemented cloud,
>   Looms o'er the solemn deep.
>
> No Calpe[2] frowns from lofty cliff or scar
>   To guard the holy strand;
> But Moultrie[3] holds in leash her dogs of war
>   Above the level sand.
>
> And down the dunes a thousand guns lie couched,
>   Unseen, beside the flood—
> Like tigers in some Orient jungle crouched
>   That wait and watch for blood.
>
> Meanwhile, through streets still echoing with trade,
>   Walk grave and thoughtful men,

10

---

* First published in the December 13, 1862, issue of the Charleston *Mercury*.

[1] Fort Sumter, at the entrance to Charleston harbor, was the scene of the first incident of the Civil War: advocates of secession fired on the fort.

[2] Rock of Gibraltar.

[3] The fort on Sullivan's Island off Charleston, named for the Revolutionary War general William Moultrie (1730–1805).

Whose hands may one day wield the patriot's blade
   As lightly as the pen.   20

And maidens, with such eyes as would grow dim
   Over a bleeding hound,
Seem each one to have caught the strength of him
   Whose sword she sadly bound.

Thus girt without and garrisoned at home,
   Day patient following day,
Old Charleston looks from roof, and spire, and dome,
   Across her tranquil bay.

Ships, through a hundred foes, from Saxon lands
   And spicy Indian ports.[4]   30
Bring Saxon steel and iron to her hands,
   And Summer to her courts.[5]

But still, along yon dim Atlantic line,
   The only hostile smoke
Creeps like a harmless mist above the brine,
   From some frail, floating oak.

Shall the Spring dawn, and she still clad in smiles,
   And with an unscathed brow,
Rest in the strong arms of her palm-crowned isles,[6]
   As fair and free as now?   40

We know not; in the temple of the Fates
   God has inscribed her doom;
And, all untroubled in her faith, she waits
   The triumph or the tomb.

1862

ODE*

*Sung on the Occasion of Decorating the Graves of the Confederate Dead,
at Magnolia Cemetery, Charleston, S. C., 1867*

I

Sleep sweetly in your humble graves,
   Sleep, martyrs of a fallen cause;
Though yet no marble column craves
   The pilgrim here to pause.

[4] From England and northern Europe and from ports in the West Indies.
[5] Courtyards, where happiness is still possible.
[6] The islands off the South Carolina coast, which have palm trees.
* Sung on Decoration Day (Memorial Day) at the Magnolia Cemetery in Charleston on June 16,
1866, and first printed in the *Charleston Courier* on June 18, 1866.

II

In seeds of laurel in the earth
        The blossom of your fame is blown,
And somewhere, waiting for its birth,
        The shaft is in the stone!

III

Meanwhile, behalf the tardy years
        Which keep in trust your storied tombs,
Behold! your sisters bring their tears,
        And these memorial blooms.

IV

Small tributes! but your shades[1] will smile
        More proudly on these wreaths today,
Than when some cannon-moulded pile
        Shall overlook this bay.

V

Stoop, angels, hither from the skies!
        There is no holier spot of ground
Than where defeated valor lies,
        By mourning beauty crowned!

1866

Walt Whitman
(1819–1892)

Walt Whitman owes his considerable prominence in American literary history to a single volume of poetry, *Leaves of Grass,* which he first published in 1855 and continued to rework through eight subsequent editions until his death in 1892. Whitman's poetry is marked by startling innovations in style and content that not only reflect the contemporary transition from romanticism to realism, but that signal the liberation of American literature from its European parentage and from the domination of the New England intellectual establishment. A politicized and self-conscious writer, Whitman adapted the romantic concept of the poet as national bard, developing and enacting the role of the American poet as a personification of the democratic ideal: the preeminently common man. In his poetry he celebrates his own vigor as a poet and a man and the dynamic diversity that characterized mid-nineteenth-century America.

Walter Whitman, Jr., the second of eight surviving children, was born on May 31, 1819, in rural West Hills, Long Island. His mother, Louisa Van Velsor, was an energetic

---

[1] Spirits.

woman of Dutch extraction to whom he was devoted. His father had farmed a share of the large tract of land on eastern Long Island that had been owned by the Whitmans since the seventeenth century, but he moved his family to Brooklyn to work as a carpenter when Walt was just four. A noticeable strain of instability ran through the family: Whitman's father was probably an alcoholic; a feeble-minded brother required lifelong care; another died, syphilitic, in a mental institution; and a sister suffered from neurologic problems and depression. A penchant for solitude earned young Walt a reputation for eccentricity.

Whitman's father was a friend of Thomas Paine and an avid reader of political literature. Discourse in the Whitman household was thus imbued with eighteenth-century liberalism, and the individualistic and egalitarian premise of the senior Whitman's politics remained a permanent influence. The family also supported the views of the Scottish feminist Fanny Wright and subscribed to her radical newspaper, *The Free Enquirer*. As a youth Walt looked to the leaders of the American Revolution, especially George Washington, as heroes, and one of Whitman's most important childhood memories centered on seeing the Marquis de Lafayette at an Independence Day ceremony.

Whitman's liberal political beliefs were matched by a nonsectarian religious outlook, an outlook associated with the tolerance that had historically characterized the Dutch of his maternal ancestry. His family was familiar with eighteenth-century deism and was much influenced by the Quaker preacher Elias Hicks, whose earthbound religious philosophy bore some resemblance to Ralph Waldo Emerson's. Throughout his life Whitman valued the quiet introspection and the humanitarianism that are fundamental to Quaker belief.

Despite the senior Whitman's political and philosophical interests, the family did not represent the learned tradition of, say, a Henry Adams; nevertheless, Whitman was well read, and many of the classics of western literature were available to him. In addition to his father's political pamphlets, he read at an early age the novels of Sir Walter Scott, Charles Dickens, and George Sand. Whitman knew the Bible well and had read Greek drama and the writings of Homer, Epicurus, and Lucretius, as well as the work of Shakespeare, Dante, John Milton, and the English romantic poets. The thread of mysticism running through Whitman's poetry may owe something to his reading of Indian literature, especially the Hindu *Bhagavad-Gita* and the Vedic Upanishads.

One of the most important elements of Whitman's thought is his glorification of the experiences of the common man. His own life was composed of such experiences. He left school when he was twelve to become a printer's apprentice, and by nineteen he was editing the weekly *Long Islander*. He taught school in rural Long Island from 1836 to 1841 and then took up his journalistic career once again, editing and writing for newspapers in Brooklyn, New York City, and New Orleans. In 1842 he published *Franklin Evans: Or, the Inebriate*, a formula-ridden and forgettable temperance novel. During these years Whitman developed a camaraderie with stagecoach drivers and with other working-class men, thus demonstrating an egalitarian politics even in his social life. He also became an avid theatergoer and enthusiast of Italian opera. He continued doing newspaper work into the 1850s, writing political editorials and sentimental poems and stories.

In 1855 Whitman published (at his own expense) *Leaves of Grass*, a curious, slim volume of twelve untitled poems prefaced by nine pages of rambling prose and an engraved daguerreotype of the anonymous author. This portrait of the artist as a relaxed young man, casually clothed, one hand resting on his hip, conveys the essence of Whitman's concept of himself as poet: "one of the roughs," he called himself, a man of the quotidian world, curious, confident, and aware. Whitman sent a gift copy of *Leaves of Grass* to Ralph Waldo Emerson, who responded in a now-famous letter greeting the author "at the beginning of a great career" and congratulating him on having produced "the most extraordinary bit of wit and wisdom that America has yet contributed." Despite Emerson's

The frontispiece and title page of the first edition of Walt Whitman's Leaves of Grass.

acclaim, this first edition of Whitman's poetry knew little critical success, except for some anonymous and positive reviews written by Whitman himself.

The 1855 preface, which did not appear in subsequent editions of *Leaves of Grass,* is now regarded as an American literary manifesto on the order of Emerson's *American Scholar* (1837) and "The Poet" (1844), to which it is indebted. In it Whitman foreshadows a countercultural poetics that neglects ordinary conventions of versification to exploit the "brawny" richness of Americanized English, "the dialect of common sense." He defines "the greatest poet" as one who "says to the past, Rise and walk before me that I may realize you," as someone connected realistically with his own time and place yet transcending it to "glow for a moment on the extremist verge." The style of the preface is eccentric, punctuated by numerous ellipses and characterized by the declamatory tone of a voice crying in the wilderness; it is the sound of a new voice calling attention to itself. Whitman sings of the beauty of America that coexists with the spiritual beauty of the American people. He hails his country as the ultimate democracy in which citizens can enjoy "the President's taking off his hat to them not they to him."

"Song of Myself" (untitled until 1881) is probably the best known and most significant of the twelve poems in this first edition. In this poem of 1346 lines, the poet celebrates his individuality, the authenticity of his own experiences in nature and in American society, and the diversity of the American population with whom he identifies. Whitman's style here reflects his rejection of nineteenth-century poetic convention and draws its strength from structural and rhythmic patterns similar to the language of biblical texts. Much critical notice has been given to the "chanting" voice of "Song of Myself"; the primitive power of the poem originates partly in the cumulative effect of Whitman's descriptive catalogues, which build in force to a mythic authority.

During the year following the first edition of *Leaves of Grass,* Whitman continued to do newspaper work and promoted the sale of his book. He flaunted Emerson's personal letter of congratulation in newspaper advertisements and on the spine of the second edition, a bit of self-promotion that many (but apparently not Emerson) found offensive. Whitman's preoccupation with personal image (evident even in the studied insouciance of the first edition daguerreotype), is part of his chosen subject, the dignity of the individual human being; yet, there remains a quality of self-interest in his search for identity that allows some to dismiss him as insincere and affected. Certainly, it can be said that one literary tradition in which Whitman participated fully was the age-old quest for fame. He seemed to have achieved some measure of it in 1855 and 1856, when he was visited by Emerson, Henry David Thoreau, and Bronson Alcott. In 1856 Whitman published a second edition of *Leaves of Grass*, which contains the important addition of the "Sun-Down Poem" (later called "Crossing Brooklyn Ferry"). At this time he worked as an editor at the Brooklyn *Times* and began working on the group of homoerotic poems known as the "Calamus" poems. In 1860 he published a third edition of *Leaves of Grass*, which includes the sexually frank "Enfans d'Adam" (later titled "Children of Adam") and "Calamus" poems as well as the important metaphorical account of the poet's assumption of his vocation, "A Word Out of the Sea" (later titled "Out of the Cradle Endlessly Rocking"). Whitman was always concerned about the sexually explicit nature of some of his work, and Emerson had tried, to no avail, to persuade him not to publish "Enfans d'Adam." Upon the publication of this third edition, the doors of Boston's literary elite were slammed in Whitman's face, in smarting contrast to the effusive reception that had earlier greeted him. The 1860 edition is considered critically important, however, because it marks the conclusion of Whitman's interest in the creative and procreative aspect of his poetic role; henceforth, Whitman's poetry would convey an emphasis on the poet as cultural prophet.

In 1862 Whitman traveled to Washington, D.C., to care for his brother George, who had been wounded in the Civil War. Whitman had always visited the sick among his Brooklyn acquaintances, and he now found himself performing that same humanitarian service among his brother's many wounded comrades. He was greatly appreciated as a cheering presence and worked arduously as a hospital attendant, sometimes assisting during medical procedures. These experiences and his general political interest in Abraham Lincoln's presidential election and in the Civil War provide the subject for *Drum-Taps*, a group of poems published in 1865. The volume was subsequently issued as a "sequel" with the addition of the magnificent elegy of Lincoln, "When Lilacs Last in the Dooryard Bloom'd," and was incorporated, with the *Passage to India* (1871) poems, in the 1872 edition of *Leaves of Grass*.

In Washington in 1865 Whitman worked for six months in the Army Paymaster's Office but lost his job when the supervisor discovered the erotic nature of his poetry. Whitman was given a new job in the Attorney General's office, however, by William O'Connor, a friend who wrote the appreciative biography *The Good Gray Poet* (1866). In 1871 Whitman published *Democratic Vistas*, a prose pamphlet that explores the cultural possibilities of democracy. In 1873 he suffered a paralytic stroke, after which he was moved to the Camden, New Jersey, home of his brother George to recuperate.

Whitman's poetic power, many feel, diminished after the 1860 edition of *Leaves of Grass*. When he had recovered physically from the events of 1873, he did not produce anything of substance, with the exception of *Specimen Days*, a volume of prose published in 1882. But his popular reputation grew in these later years, and he came to be lionized in Camden in much the same way Emerson had been in Concord. Whitman issued subsequent editions of *Leaves of Grass* in 1876, 1881, and 1891 to 1892 despite continuing threats of suppression because of the candid quality of his poetry. He died in Camden on March 26, 1892. A century later Whitman's celebration of democracy, diversity, and his own vitality remains for us the quintessential expression of the American artist.

Suggested Readings: *Leaves of Grass,* 1860 edition, ed. R. H. Pearce, 1961. *Walt Whitman: The Correspondence,* 6 vols., ed. E. H. Miller, 1961–1977. *The Collected Writings of Walt Whitman,* ed. G. W. Allen and S. Bradley, 1961– . H. Traubel, *With Walt Whitman in Camden,* 6 vols., 1906. G. W. Allen, *The Solitary Singer: A Critical Biography of Walt Whitman,* 1955, rpt. 1985. R. Asselineau, *The Evolution of Walt Whitman,* 1962. J. C. Smuts, *Walt Whitman: A Study in the Evolution of a Personality,* 1973. J. Woodress, ed., *Critical Essays on Walt Whitman,* 1983. G. W. Allen, *The New Walt Whitman Handbook,* 1986. G. Hutchinson, *The Ecstatic Whitman: Literary Shamanism and the Crisis of the Union,* 1986. M. W. Thomas, *The Lunar Light of Whitman's Poetry,* 1987. K. C. Larson, *Whitman's Drama of Consensus,* 1988. B. Erkkila, *Whitman the Political Poet,* 1989. E. H. Miller, *Walt Whitman's "Song of Myself"; A Mosaic of Interpretations,* 1989. K. M. Price, *Whitman and Tradition,* 1990.

Texts Used: "Preface," poems, and "A Backward Glance O'er Travel'd Roads": *Leaves of Grass,* ed. H. W. Blodgett and S. Bradley, 1965. "My Tribute to Four Poets" and "Boston Common": *The Complete Prose Works of Walt Whitman,* Vol. II, 1902. All else: *The Complete Prose Works,* Vol. I.

from   *LEAVES OF GRASS*

PREFACE TO THE 1855 EDITION*

America does not repel the past or what it has produced under its forms or amid other politics or the idea of castes or the old religions. . . . accepts the lesson with calmness . . . is not so impatient as has been supposed that the slough[1] still sticks to opinions and manners and literature while the life which served its requirements has passed into the new life of the new forms . . . perceives that the corpse is slowly borne from the eating and sleeping rooms of the house . . . perceives that it waits a little while in the door . . . that it was fittest for its days . . . that its action has descended to the stalwart and wellshaped heir who approaches . . . and that he shall be fittest for his days.

The Americans of all nations at any time upon the earth have probably the fullest poetical nature. The United States themselves are essentially the greatest poem. In the history of the earth hitherto the largest and most stirring appear tame and orderly to their ampler largeness and stir. Here at last is something in the doings of man that corresponds with the broadcast doings of the day and night. Here is not merely a nation but a teeming nation of nations. Here is action untied from strings necessarily blind to particulars and details magnificently moving in vast masses. Here is the hospitality which forever indicates heroes. . . . Here are the roughs and beards and space and ruggedness and nonchalance that the soul loves. Here the performance disdaining the trivial unapproached in the tremendous audacity of its crowds and groupings and the push of its perspective spreads with crampless and flowing breadth and showers its prolific and splendid extravagance. One sees it must indeed own the riches of the summer and winter, and need never be bankrupt while corn grows from the ground or the orchards drop apples or the bays contain fish or men beget children upon women.

Other states indicate themselves in their deputies. . . . but the genius of the United States is not best or most in its executives or legislatures, nor in its ambas-

---

* Omitted from later editions, although much of the preface material is retained in the poems added to those editions. The ellipses and idiosyncratic spellings are Whitman's.
[1] The outer, discarded skin of a snake.

sadors or authors or colleges or churches or parlors, nor even in its newspapers or inventors . . . but always most in the common people. Their manners speech dress friendships—the freshness and candor of their physiognomy—the picturesque looseness of their carriage . . . their deathless attachment to freedom—their aversion to anything indecorous or soft or mean—the practical acknowledgment of the citizens of one state by the citizens of all other states—the fierceness of their roused resentment—their curiosity and welcome of novelty—their self-esteem and wonderful sympathy—their susceptibility to a slight—the air they have of persons who never knew how it felt to stand in the presence of superiors—the fluency of their speech—their delight in music, the sure symptom of manly tenderness and native elegance of soul . . . their good temper and openhandedness—the terrible significance of their elections—the President's taking off his hat to them not they to him—these too are unrhymed poetry. It awaits the gigantic and generous treatment worthy of it.

The largeness of nature or the nation were monstrous without a corresponding largeness and generosity of the spirit of the citizen. Not nature nor swarming states nor streets and steamships nor prosperous business nor farms nor capital nor learning may suffice for the ideal of man . . . nor suffice the poet. No reminiscences may suffice either. A live nation can always cut a deep mark and can have the best authority the cheapest . . . namely from its own soul. This is the sum of the profitable uses of individuals or states and of present action and grandeur and of the subjects of poets.—As if it were necessary to trot back generation after generation to the eastern records! As if the beauty and sacredness of the demonstrable must fall behind that of the mythical! As if men do not make their mark out of any times! As if the opening of the western continent by discovery and what has transpired since in North and South America were less than the small theatre of the antique or the aimless sleep-walking of the middle ages! The pride of the United States leaves the wealth and finesse of the cities and all returns of commerce and agriculture and all the magnitude of geography or shows of exterior victory to enjoy the breed of fullsized men or one fullsized man unconquerable and simple.

The American poets are to enclose old and new for America is the race of races. Of them a bard[2] is to be commensurate with a people. To him the other continents arrive as contributions . . . he gives them reception for their sake and his own sake. His spirit responds to his country's spirit. . . . he incarnates its geography and natural life and rivers and lakes. Mississippi with annual freshets and changing chutes, Missouri and Columbia and Ohio and Saint Lawrence with the falls and beautiful masculine Hudson, do not embouchure[3] where they spend themselves more than they embouchure into him. The blue breadth over the inland sea of Virginia and Maryland and the sea off Massachusetts and Maine and over Manhattan bay and over Champlain and Erie and over Ontario and Huron and Michigan and Superior, and over the Texan and Mexican and Floridian and Cuban seas and over the seas off California and Oregon, is not tallied by the blue breadth of the waters below more than the breadth of above and below is tallied by him. When the long Atlantic coast stretches longer and the Pacific coast stretches longer he easily stretches with them north or south. He spans between them also from east to west and reflects what is between them. On him rise solid growths that offset the growths of pine and cedar and hemlock and liveoak and locust and

---

[2] A national or tribal poet, traditionally in the epic or heroic vein; one who sustained and continued the oral tradition of the people.

[3] Pour out.

chestnut and cypress and hickory and limetree and cottonwood and tuliptree and cactus and wildvine and tamarind and persimmon. . . . and tangles as tangled as any canebrake or swamp. . . . and forests coated with transparent ice and icicles hanging from the boughs and crackling in the wind. . . . and sides and peaks of mountains. . . . and pasturage sweet and free as savannah or upland or prairie. . . . with flights and songs and screams that answer those of the wildpigeon and highhold[4] and orchard oriole and coot and surf-duck and redshouldered-hawk and fish-hawk and white-ibis and indian-hen and cat-owl and water-pheasant and qua-bird and pied-sheldrake and blackbird and mockingbird and buzzard and condor and night-heron and eagle. To him the hereditary countenance descends both mother's and father's. To him enter the essences of the real things and past and present events—of the enormous diversity of temperature and agriculture and mines—the tribes of red aborigines—the weatherbeaten vessels entering new ports or making landings on rocky coasts—the first settlements north or south— the rapid stature and muscle—the haughty defiance of '76,[5] and the war and peace and formation of the constitution. . . . the union always surrounded by blatherers and always calm and impregnable—the perpetual coming of immigrants—the wharf hem'd cities and superior marine[6]—the unsurveyed interior—the loghouses and clearings and wild animals and hunters and trappers. . . . the free commerce—the fisheries and whaling and golddigging—the endless gestation of new states—the convening of Congress every December,[7] the members duly coming up from all climates and the uttermost parts. . . . the noble character of the young mechanics[8] and of all free American workmen and workwomen. . . . the general ardor and friendliness and enterprise—the perfect equality of the female with the male. . . . the large amativeness[9]—the fluid movement of the population— the factories and mercantile life and laborsaving machinery—the Yankee swap[10]—the New-York firemen and the target excursion[11]—the southern plantation life—the character of the northeast and of the northwest and southwest— slavery and the tremulous spreading of hands to protect it, and the stern opposition to it which shall never cease till it ceases or the speaking of tongues and the moving of lips cease. For such the expression of the American poet is to be transcendant and new. It is to be indirect and not direct or descriptive or epic. Its quality goes through these to much more. Let the age and wars of other nations be chanted and their eras and characters be illustrated and that finish the verse. Not so the great psalm of the republic. Here the theme is creative and has vista. Here comes one among the wellbeloved stonecutters and plans with decision and science and sees the solid and beautiful forms of the future where there are now no solid forms.

Of all nations the United States with veins full of poetical stuff most need poets and will doubtless have the greatest and use them the greatest. Their Presidents shall not be their common referee so much as their poets shall. Of all mankind the great poet is the equable man. Not in him but off from him things are grotesque or eccentric or fail of their sanity. Nothing out of its place is good and nothing in its place is bad. He bestows on every object or quality its fit proportions neither more nor less. He is the arbiter of the diverse and he is the key. He is the equalizer of

---

[4] Woodpecker.　　[5] The Declaration of Independence.
[6] Maritime industry.　　[7] Before 1933 Congress convened on the first Monday in December.
[8] Manual laborers.　　[9] Amorousness.
[10] A shrewd deal, from the reputation of New Englanders (Yankees) for hard bargaining.
[11] The outing to a shooting match.

his age and land. . . . he supplies what wants supplying and checks what wants checking. If peace is the routine out of him speaks the spirit of peace, large, rich, thrifty, building vast and populous cities, encouraging agriculture and the arts and commerce—lighting the study of man, the soul, immortality—federal, state or municipal government, marriage, health, freetrade, intertravel by land and sea. . . . nothing too close, nothing too far off . . . the stars not too far off. In war he is the most deadly force of the war. Who recruits him recruits horse and foot[12] . . . he fetches parks of artillery[13] the best that engineer ever knew. If the time becomes slothful and heavy he knows how to arouse it . . . he can make every word he speaks draw blood. Whatever stagnates in the flat[14] of custom or obedience or legislation he never stagnates. Obedience does not master him, he masters it. High up out of reach he stands turning a concentrated light . . . he turns the pivot with his finger . . . he baffles the swiftest runners as he stands and easily overtakes and envelops them. The time straying toward infidelity and confections and persiflage he withholds by his steady faith . . . he spreads out his dishes . . . he offers the sweet firmfibred meat that grows men and women. His brain is the ultimate brain. He is no arguer . . . he is judgment. He judges not as the judge judges but as the sun falling around a helpless thing. As he sees the farthest he has the most faith. His thoughts are the hymns of the praise of things. In the talk on the soul and eternity and God off of his equal plane he is silent. He sees eternity less like a play with a prologue and denouement. . . . he sees eternity in men and women . . . he does not see men and women as dreams or dots. Faith is the antiseptic of the soul . . . it pervades the common people and preserves them . . . they never give up believing and expecting and trusting. There is that indescribable freshness and unconsciousness about an illiterate person that humbles and mocks the power of the noblest expressive genius. The poet sees for a certainty how one not a great artist may be just as sacred and perfect as the greatest artist. . . . The power to destroy or remould is freely used by him but never the power of attack. What is past is past. If he does not expose superior models and prove himself by every step he takes he is not what is wanted. The presence of the greatest poet conquers . . . not parleying or struggling or any prepared attempts. Now he has passed that way see after him! there is not left any vestige of despair or misanthropy or cunning or exclusiveness or the ignominy of a nativity or color or delusion of hell or the necessity of hell. . . . and no man thenceforward shall be degraded for ignorance or weakness or sin.

The greatest poet hardly knows pettiness or triviality. If he breathes into any thing that was before thought small it dilates with the grandeur and life of the universe. He is a seer. . . . he is individual . . . he is complete in himself . . . . the others are as good as he, only he sees it and they do not. He is not one of the chorus. . . . he does not stop for any regulation . . . he is the president of regulation. What the eyesight does to the rest he does to the rest. Who knows the curious mystery of the eyesight? The other senses corroborate themselves, but this is removed from any proof but its own and foreruns the identities of the spiritual world. A single glance of it mocks all the investigations of man and all the instruments and books of the earth and all reasoning. What is marvellous? what is unlikely? what is impossible or baseless or vague? after you have once just opened the space of a peachpit and given audience to far and near and to the sunset and

---

[12] Cavalry and infantry.
[13] Local militias commonly drilled in city parks, which in times of need became supply depots.
[14] Low, marshy land.

had all things enter with electric swiftness softly and duly without confusion or jostling or jam.

The land and sea, the animals fishes and birds, the sky of heaven and the orbs, the forests mountains and rivers, are not small themes . . . but folks expect of the poet to indicate more than the beauty and dignity which always attach to dumb real objects . . . . they expect him to indicate the path between reality and their souls. Men and women perceive the beauty well enough. .probably as well as he. The passionate tenacity of hunters, woodmen, early risers, cultivators of gardens and orchards and fields, the love of healthy women for the manly form, seafaring persons, drivers of horses, the passion for light and the open air, all is an old varied sign of the unfailing perception of beauty and of a residence of the poetic in outdoor people. They can never be assisted by poets to perceive . . . some may but they never can. The poetic quality is not marshalled in rhyme or uniformity or abstract addresses to things nor in melancholy complaints or good precepts, but is the life of these and much else and is in the soul. The profit of rhyme is that it drops seeds of a sweeter and more luxuriant rhyme, and of uniformity that it conveys itself into its own roots in the ground out of sight. The rhyme and uniformity of perfect poems show the free growth of metrical laws and bud from them as unerringly and loosely as lilacs or roses on a bush, and take shapes as compact as the shapes of chestnuts and oranges and melons and pears, and shed the perfume impalpable to form. The fluency and ornaments of the finest poems or music or orations or recitations are not independent but dependent. All beauty comes from beautiful blood and a beautiful brain. If the greatnesses are in conjunction in a man or woman it is enough . . . . the fact will prevail through the universe . . . . but the gaggery[15] and gilt of a million years will not prevail. Who troubles himself about his ornaments or fluency is lost. This is what you shall do: Love the earth and sun and the animals, despise riches, give alms to every one that asks, stand up for the stupid and crazy, devote your income and labor to others, hate tyrants, argue not concerning God, have patience and indulgence toward the people, take off your hat to nothing known or unknown or to any man or number of men, go freely with powerful uneducated persons and with the young and with the mothers of families, read these leaves in the open air every season of every year of your life, re-examine all you have been told at school or church or in any book, dismiss whatever insults your own soul, and your very flesh shall be a great poem and have the richest fluency not only in its words but in the silent lines of its lips and face and between the lashes of your eyes and in every motion and joint of your body. . . . . The poet shall not spend his time in unneeded work. He shall know that the ground is always ready ploughed and manured . . . . others may not know it but he shall. He shall go directly to the creation. His trust shall master the trust of everything he touches . . . . and shall master all attachment.

The known universe has one complete lover and that is the greatest poet. He consumes an eternal passion and is indifferent which chance happens and which possible contingency of fortune or misfortune and persuades daily and hourly his delicious pay. What balks or breaks others is fuel for his burning progress to contact and amorous joy. Other proportions of the reception of pleasure dwindle to nothing to his proportions. All expected from heaven or from the highest he is rapport with in the sight of the daybreak or a scene of the winter woods or the presence of children playing or with his arm round the neck of a man or woman.

---

[15] Falseness.

His love above all love has leisure and expanse . . . . he leaves room ahead of himself. He is no irresolute or suspicious lover . . . he is sure . . . he scorns intervals. His experience and the showers and thrills are not for nothing. Nothing can jar him . . . . suffering and darkness cannot—death and fear cannot. To him complaint and jealousy and envy are corpses buried and rotten in the earth . . . . he saw them buried. The sea is not surer of the shore or the shore of the sea than he is of the fruition of his love and of all perfection and beauty.

The fruition of beauty is no chance of hit or miss . . . it is inevitable as life . . . . it is exact and plumb as gravitation. From the eyesight proceeds another eyesight and from the hearing proceeds another hearing and from the voice proceeds another voice eternally curious of the harmony of things with man. To these respond perfections not only in the committees that were supposed to stand for the rest but in the rest themselves just the same. These understand the law of perfection in masses and floods . . . that its finish is to each for itself and onward from itself . . . that it is profuse and impartial . . . that there is not a minute of the light or dark nor an acre of the earth or sea without it—nor any direction of the sky nor any trade or employment nor any turn of events. This is the reason that about the proper expression of beauty there is precision and balance . . . one part does not need to be thrust above another. The best singer is not the one who has the most lithe and powerful organ . . . the pleasure of poems is not in them that take the handsomest measure and similes and sound.

Without effort and without exposing in the least how it is done the greatest poet brings the spirit of any or all events and passions and scenes and persons some more and some less to bear on your individual character as you hear or read. To do this well is to compete with the laws that pursue and follow time. What is the purpose must surely be there and the clue of it must be there . . . . and the faintest indication is the indication of the best and then becomes the clearest indication. Past and present and future are not disjoined but joined. The greatest poet forms the consistence of what is to be from what has been and is. He drags the dead out of their coffins and stands them again on their feet . . . . he says to the past, Rise and walk before me that I may realize you. He learns the lesson. . . . he places himself where the future becomes present. The greatest poet does not only dazzle his rays over character and scenes and passions . . . he finally ascends and finishes all . . . he exhibits the pinnacles that no man can tell what they are for or what is beyond . . . . he glows a moment on the extremest verge. He is most wonderful in his last half-hidden smile or frown . . . by that flash of the moment of parting the one that sees it shall be encouraged or terrified afterward for many years. The greatest poet does not moralize or make applications of morals . . . he knows the soul. The soul has that measureless pride which consists in never acknowledging any lessons but its own. But it has sympathy as measureless as its pride and the one balances the other and neither can stretch too far while it stretches in company with the other. The inmost secrets of art sleep with the twain. The greatest poet has lain close betwixt both and they are vital in his style and thoughts.

The art of art, the glory of expression and the sunshine of the light of letters is simplicity. Nothing is better than simplicity . . . . nothing can make up for excess or for the lack of definiteness. To carry on the heave of impulse and pierce intellectual depths and give all subjects their articulations are powers neither common nor very uncommon. But to speak in literature with the perfect rectitude and insousiance[16] of the movements of animals and the unimpeachableness of the sentiment of trees in the woods and grass by the roadside is the flawless triumph of art. If you have looked on him who has achieved it you have looked on one of the masters of the artists of all nations and times. You shall not contemplate the flight of the graygull over the bay or the mettlesome action of the blood horse or the tall leaning of sunflowers on their stalk or the appearance of the sun journeying through heaven or the appearance of the moon afterward with any more satisfaction than you shall contemplate him. The greatest poet has less a marked style and is more the channel of thoughts and things without increase or diminution, and is the free channel of himself. He swears to his art, I will not be meddlesome, I will not have in my writing any elegance or effect or originality to hang in the way between me and the rest like curtains. I will have nothing hang in the way, not the richest curtains. What I tell I tell for precisely what it is. Let who may exalt or startle or fascinate or sooth I will have purposes as health or heat or snow has and be as regardless of observation. What I experience or portray shall go from my composition without a shred of my composition. You shall stand by my side and look in the mirror with me.

The old red blood and stainless gentility of great poets will be proved by their unconstraint. A heroic person walks at his ease through and out of that custom or precedent or authority that suits him not. Of the traits of the brotherhood of writers savans[17] musicians inventors and artists nothing is finer than silent defiance advancing from new free forms. In the need of poems philosophy politics mechanism science behaviour, the craft of art, an appropriate native grand-opera, shipcraft, or any craft, he is greatest forever and forever who contributes the greatest original practical example. The cleanest expression is that which finds no sphere worthy of itself and makes one.

The messages of great poets to each man and woman are, Come to us on equal terms, Only then can you understand us, We are no better than you, What we enclose you enclose, What we enjoy you may enjoy. Did you suppose there could be only one Supreme? We affirm there can be unnumbered Supremes, and that one does not countervail another any more than one eyesight countervails another . . and that men can be good orgrand only of the consciousness of their supremacy within them. What do you think is the grandeur of storms and dismemberments and the deadliest battles and wrecks and the wildest fury of the elements and the power of the sea and the motion of nature and of the throes of human desires and dignity and hate and love? It is that something in the soul which says, Rage on, Whirl on, I tread master here and everywhere, Master of the spasms of the sky and of the shatter of the sea, Master of nature and passion and death, And of all terror and all pain.

The American bards shall be marked for generosity and affection and for encouraging competitors . . They shall be kosmos . . without monopoly or secresy . . glad to pass any thing to any one . . hungry for equals night and day. They shall not be careful of riches and privilege . . . . they shall be riches and privilege . . . . they shall perceive who the most affluent man is. The most affluent man is he that confronts all the shows he sees by equivalents out of the stronger wealth of himself. The American bard shall delineate no class of persons nor one or two out of the strata of interests nor love most nor truth most nor the

---

[16] Indifference.   [17] Savants, or learned men.

soul most nor the body most . . . . and not be for the eastern states more than the western or the northern states more than the southern.

Exact science and its practical movements are no checks on the greatest poet but always his encouragement and support. The outset and remembrance are there . . there the arms that lifted him first and brace him best. . . . there he returns after all his goings and comings. The sailor and traveler . . the anatomist, chemist, astronomer, geologist, phrenologist, spiritualist, mathematician, historian and lexicographer are not poets, but they are the lawgivers of poets and their construction underlies the structure of every perfect poem. No matter what rises or is uttered they sent the seed of the conception of it . . . of them and by them stand the visible proofs of souls . . . . . always of their fatherstuff must be begotten the sinewy races of bards. If there shall be love and content between the father and the son and if the greatness of the son is the exuding of the greatness of the father there shall be love between the poet and the man of demonstrable science. In the beauty of poems are the tuft and final applause of science.

Great is the faith of the flush of knowledge and of the investigation of the depths of qualities and things. Cleaving and circling here swells the soul of the poet yet it president of itself always. The depths are fathomless and therefore calm. The innocence and nakedness are resumed . . . they are neither modest nor immodest. The whole theory of the special and supernatural and all that was twined with it or educed[18] out of it departs as a dream. What has ever happened . . . . what happens and whatever may or shall happen, the vital laws enclose all . . . . they are sufficent for any case and for all cases . . . none to be hurried or retarded . . . . any miracle of affairs or persons inadmissible in the vast clear scheme where every motion and every spear of grass and the frames and spirits of men and women and all that concerns them are unspeakably perfect miracles all referring to all and each distinct and in its place. It is also not consistent with the reality of the soul to admit that there is anything in the known universe more divine than men and women.

Men and women and the earth and all upon it are simply to be taken as they are, and the investigation of their past and present and future shall be unintermitted and shall be done with perfect candor. Upon this basis philosophy speculates ever looking toward the poet, ever regarding the eternal tendencies of all toward happiness never inconsistent with what is clear to the senses and to the soul. For the eternal tendencies of all toward happiness make the only point of sane philosophy. Whatever comprehends less than that . . . whatever is less than the laws of light and of astronomical motion . . . or less than the laws that follow the thief the liar the glutton and the drunkard through this life and doubtless afterward . . . . . . or less than vast stretches of time or the slow formation of density or the patient upheaving of strata—is of no account. Whatever would put God in a poem or system of philosophy as contending against some being or influence is also of no account. Sanity and ensemble characterise the great master . . . spoilt in one principle all is spoilt. The great master has nothing to do with miracles. He sees health for himself in being one of the mass . . . . he sees the hiatus in singular eminence. To the perfect shape comes common ground. To be under the general law is great for that is to correspond with it. The master knows that he is unspeakably great and that all are unspeakably great. . . . that nothing for in-

---

[18] Drawn forth.

stance is greater than to conceive children and bring them up well . . . that to be is just as great as to perceive or tell.

In the make of the great masters the idea of political liberty is indispensible. Liberty takes the adherence of heroes wherever men and women exist . . . . but never takes any adherence or welcome from the rest more than from poets. They are the voice and exposition of liberty. They out of ages are worthy the grand idea . . . . to them it is confided and they must sustain it. Nothing has precedence of it and nothing can warp or degrade it. The attitude of great poets is to cheer up slaves and horrify despots. The turn of their necks, the sound of their feet, the motions of their wrists, are full of hazard to the one and hope to the other. Come nigh them awhile and though they neither speak or advise you shall learn the faithful American lesson. Liberty is poorly served by men whose good intent is quelled from one failure or two failures or any number of failures, or from the casual indifference or ingratitude of the people, or from the sharp show of the tushes[19] of power, or the bringing to bear soldiers and cannon or any penal statutes. Liberty relies upon itself, invites no one, promises nothing, sits in calmness and light, is positive and composed, and knows no discouragement. The battle rages with many a loud alarm and frequent advance and retreat . . . . the enemy triumphs . . . . the prison, the handcuffs, the iron necklace and anklet, the scaffold, garrote and leadballs do their work . . . . the cause is asleep . . . . the strong throats are choked with their own blood . . . . the young men drop their eyelashes toward the ground when they pass each other . . . . and is liberty gone out of that place? No never. When liberty goes it is not the first to go nor the second or third to go . . it waits for all the rest to go . . it is the last. . . When the memories of the old martyrs are faded utterly away . . . . when the large names of patriots are laughed at in the public halls from the lips of the orators . . . . when the boys are no more christened after the same but christened after tyrants and traitors instead . . . . when the laws of the free are grudgingly permitted and laws for informers and bloodmoney are sweet to the taste of the people . . . . when I and you walk abroad upon the earth stung with compassion at the sight of numberless brothers answering our equal friendship and calling no man master— and when we are elated with noble joy at the sight of slaves . . . . when the soul retires in the cool communion of the night and surveys its experience and has much extasy over the word and deed that put back a helpless innocent person into the gripe of the gripers or into any cruel inferiority . . . . when those in all parts of these states who could easier realize the true American character but do not yet—when the swarms of cringers, suckers, doughfaces,[20] lice of politics, planners of sly involutions for their own preferment to city offices or state legislatures or the judiciary or congress or the presidency, obtain a response of love and natural deference from the people whether they get the offices or no . . . . when it is better to be a bound booby[21] and rogue in office at a high salary than the poorest free mechanic or farmer with his hat unmoved from his head and firm eyes and a candid and generous heart . . . . and when servility by town or state or the federal government or any oppression on a large scale or small scale can be tried on without its own punishment following duly after in exact proportion against the smallest chance of escape . . . . or rather when all life and all the souls of men

---

[19] Tusks.   [20] Swindlers; changeable, unscrupulous people.   [21] A political fool who owes favors.

and women are discharged from any part of the earth—then only shall the instinct of liberty be discharged from that part of the earth.

As the attributes of the poets of the kosmos concentre in the real body and soul and in the pleasure of things they possess the superiority of genuineness over all fiction and romance. As they emit themselves facts are showered over with light . . . . the daylight is lit with more volatile light . . . . also the deep between the setting and rising sun goes deeper many fold. Each precise object or condition or combination or process exhibits a beauty . . . . the multiplication table its—old age its—the carpenter's trade its—the grand-opera its . . . . the hugehulled clean-shaped New-York clipper at sea under steam or full sail gleams with unmatched beauty . . . . the American circles and large harmonies of government gleam with theirs . . . . and the commonest definite intentions and actions with theirs. The poets of the kosmos advance through all interpositions and coverings and turmoils and stratagems to first principles. They are of use . . . . they dissolve poverty from its need and riches from its conceit. You large proprietor they say shall not realize or perceive more than any one else. The owner of the library is not he who holds a legal title to it having bought and paid for it. Any one and every one is owner of the library who can read the same through all the varieties of tongues and subjects and styles, and in whom they enter with ease and take residence and force toward paternity and maternity, and make supple and powerful and rich and large. . . . . These American states strong and healthy and accomplished shall receive no pleasure from violations of natural models and must not permit them. In paintings or mouldings or carvings in mineral or wood, or in the illustrations of books or newspapers, or in any comic or tragic prints, or in the patterns of woven stuffs or any thing to beautify rooms or furniture or costumes, or to put upon cornices or monuments or on the prows of sterns of ships, or to put anywhere before the human eye indoors or out, that which distorts honest shapes or which creates unearthly beings or places or contingencies is a nuisance and revolt. Of the human form especially it is so great it must never be made ridiculous. Of ornaments to a work nothing outre[22] can be allowed . . but those ornaments can be allowed that conform to the perfect facts of the open air and that flow out of the nature of the work and come irrepressibly from it and are necessary to the completion of the work. Most works are most beautiful without ornament. . . Exaggerations will be revenged in human physiology. Clean and vigorous children are jetted[23] and conceived only in those communities where the models of natural forms are public every day. . . . . . Great genius and the people of these states must never be demeaned to romances. As soon as histories are properly told there is no more need of romances.

The great poets are also to be known by the absence in them of tricks and by the justification of perfect personal candor. Then folks echo a new cheap joy and a divine voice leaping from their brains: How beautiful is candor! All faults may be forgiven of him who has perfect candor. Henceforth let no man of us lie, for we have seen that openness wins the inner and outer world and that there is no single exception, and that never since our earth gathered itself in a mass have deceit or subterfuge or prevarication attracted its smallest particle or the faintest tinge of a shade—and that through the enveloping wealth and rank of a state or the whole republic of states a sneak or sly person shall be discovered and despised . . . . and that the soul has never been once fooled and never can be fooled . . . . and thrift

[22] Extravagant, improper.   [23] Ejaculated.

without the loving nod of the soul is only a fœtid puff . . . . and there never grew up in any of the continents of the globe nor upon any planet or satellite or star, nor upon the asteroids, nor in any part of ethereal space, nor in the midst of density, nor under the fluid wet of the sea, nor in that condition which precedes the birth of babes, nor at any time during the changes of life, nor in that condition that follows what we term death, nor in any stretch of abeyance or action afterward of vitality, nor in any process of formation or reformation anywhere, a being whose instinct hated the truth.

Extreme caution or prudence, the soundest organic health, large hope and comparison and fondness for women and children, large alimentiveness[24] and destructiveness and causality, with a perfect sense of the oneness of nature and the propriety of the same spirit applied to human affairs . . these are called up of the float[25] of the brain of the world to be parts of the greatest poet from his birth out of his mother's womb and from her birth out of her mother's. Caution seldom goes far enough. It has been thought that the prudent citizen was the citizen who applied himself to solid gains and did well for himself and his family and completed a lawful life without debt or crime. The greatest poet sees and admits these economies as he sees the economies of food and sleep, but has higher notions of prudence than to think he gives much when he gives a few slight attentions at the latch of the gate. The premises of the prudence of life are not the hospitality of it or the ripeness and harvest of it. Beyond the independence of a little sum laid aside for burial-money, and of a few clapboards around and shingles overhead on a lot of American soil owned, and the easy dollars that supply the year's plain clothing and meals, the melancholy prudence of the abandonment of such a great being as a man is to the toss and pallor of years of moneymaking with all their scorching days and icy nights and all their stifling deceits and underhanded dodgings, or infinitessimals of parlors, or shameless stuffing while others starve . . and all the loss of the bloom and odor of the earth and of the flowers and atmosphere and of the sea and of the true taste of the women and men you pass or have to do with in youth or middle age, and the issuing sickness and desperate revolt at the close of a life without elevation or naivete, and the ghastly chatter of a death without serenity or majesty, is the great fraud upon modern civilization and forethought, blotching the surface and system which civilization undeniably drafts, and moistening with tears the immense features it spreads and spreads with such velocity before the reached kisses of the soul. . . Still the right explanation remains to be made about prudence. The prudence of the mere wealth and respectability of the most esteemed life appears too faint for the eye to observe at all when little and large alike drop quietly aside at the thought of the prudence suitable for immortality. What is wisdom that fills the thinness of a year or seventy or eighty years to wisdom spaced out by ages and coming back at a certain time with strong reinforcements and rich presents and the clear faces of wedding-guests as far as you can look in every direction running gaily toward you? Only the soul is of itself . . . . all else has reference to what ensues. All that a person does or thinks is of consequence. Not a move can a man or woman make that affects him or her in a day or a month or any part of the direct lifetime or the hour of death but the same affects him or her onward afterward through the indirect lifetime. The indirect is always as great and real as the direct. The spirit receives from the body just as much as it gives to the body. Not one name of word or deed . . not of venereal

---

[24] Love of food.   [25] Buoyancy.

sores or discolorations . . not the privacy of the onanist[26] . . not of the putrid veins of gluttons or rumdrinkers . . . not peculation[27] or cunning or betrayal or murder . . no serpentine poison of those that seduce women . . not the foolish yielding of women . . not prostitution . . not of any depravity of young men . . not of the attainment of gain by discreditable means . . not any nastiness of appetite . . not any harshness of officers to men or judges to prisoners or fathers to sons or sons to fathers or of husbands to wives or bosses to their boys . . not of greedy looks or malignant wishes . . . nor any of the wiles practised by people upon themselves . . . ever is or ever can be stamped on the programme but it is duly realized and returned, and that returned in further performances . . . and they returned again. Nor can the push of charity or personal force ever be any thing else than the profoundest reason, whether it bring arguments to hand or no. No specification is necessary . . to add or subtract or divide is in vain. Little or big, learned or unlearned, white or black, legal or illegal, sick or well, from the first inspiration down the windpipe to the last expiration out of it, all that a male or female does that is vigorous and benevolent and clean is so much sure profit to him or her in the unshakable order of the universe and through the whole scope of it forever. If the savage or felon is wise it is well. . . . if the greatest poet or savan is wise it is simply the same . . if the President or chief justice is wise it is the same . . if the young mechanic or farmer is wise it is no more or less . . if the prostitute is wise it is no more nor less. The interest will come round . . all will come round. All the best actions of war and peace . . . all help given to relatives and strangers and the poor and old and sorrowful and young children and widows and the sick, and to all shunned persons . . all furtherance of fugitives and of the escape of slaves . . all the self-denial that stood steady and aloof on wrecks and saw others take the seats of the boats . . . all offering of substance or life for the good old cause, or for a friend's sake or opinion's sake . . . all pains of enthusiasts scoffed at by their neighbors . . all the vast sweet love and precious suffering of mothers . . . all honest men baffled in strifes recorded or unrecorded . . . . all the grandeur and good of the few ancient nations whose fragments of annals we inherit . . and all the good of the hundreds of far mightier and more ancient nations unknown to us by name or date or location. . . . all that was ever manfully begun, whether it succeeded or no. . . . all that has at any time been well suggested out of the divine heart of man or by the divinity of his mouth or by the shaping of his great hands . . and all that is well thought or done this day on any part of the surface of the globe . . or on any of the wandering stars or fixed stars by those there as we are here . . or that is henceforth to be well thought or done by you whoever you are, or by any one—these singly and wholly inured at their time and inure now and will inure always to the identities from which they sprung or shall spring . . . Did you guess any of them lived only its moment? The world does not so exist . . no parts palpable or impalpable so exist . . . no result exists now without being from its long antecedent result, and that from its antecedent, and so backward without the farthest mentionable spot coming a bit nearer the beginning than any other spot. . . . . Whatever satisfies the soul is truth. The prudence of the greatest poet answers at last the craving and glut of the soul, is not contemptuous of less ways of prudence if they conform to its ways, puts off nothing, permits no let-up for its own case or any case, has no particular sabbath or judgment-day, divides not the living from the dead or the righteous from the un-

---

[26] Masturbator, after Onan, the son of Judah, in Genesis 38:9.   [27] Embezzlement.

righteous, is satisfied with the present, matches every thought or act by its correlative, knows no possible forgiveness or deputed atonement . . knows that the young man who composedly periled his life and lost it has done exceeding well for himself, while the man who has not periled his life and retains it to old age in riches and ease has perhaps achieved nothing for himself worth mentioning . . and that only that person has no great prudence to learn who has learnt to prefer real longlived things, and favors body and soul the same, and perceives the indirect assuredly following the direct, and what evil or good he does leaping onward and waiting to meet him again—and who in his spirit in any emergency whatever neither hurries or avoids death.

The direct trial of him who would be the greatest poet is today. If he does not flood himself with the immediate age as with vast oceanic tides . . . . . and if he does not attract his own land body and soul to himself and hang on its neck with incomparable love and plunge his semitic muscle[28] into its merits and demerits . . . and if he be not himself the age transfigured . . . . and if to him is not opened the eternity which gives similitude to all periods and locations and processes and animate and inanimate forms, and which is the bond of time, and rises up from its inconceivable vagueness and infiniteness in the swimming shape of today, and is held by the ductile anchors of life, and makes the present spot the passage from what was to what shall be, and commits itself to the representation of this wave of an hour and this one of the sixty beautiful children of the wave— let him merge in the general run and wait his development. . . . . Still the final test of poems or any character or work remains. The prescient poet projects himself centuries ahead and judges performer or performance after the changes of time. Does it live through them? Does it still hold on untired? Will the same style and the direction of genius to similar points be satisfactory now? Has no new discovery in science or arrival at superior planes of thought and judgment and behaviour fixed him or his so that either can be looked down upon? Have the marches of tens and hundreds and thousands of years made willing detours to the right hand and the left hand for his sake? Is he beloved long and long after he is buried? Does the young man think often of him? and the young woman think often of him? and do the middleaged and the old think of him?

A great poem is for ages and ages in common and for all degrees and complexions and all departments and sects and for a woman as much as a man and a man as much as a woman. A great poem is no finish to a man or woman but rather a beginning. Has any one fancied he could sit at last under some due authority and rest satisfied with explanations and realize and be content and full? To no such terminus does the greatest poet bring . . . he brings neither cessation or sheltered fatness and ease. The touch of him tells in action. Whom he takes he takes with firm sure grasp into live regions previously unattained . . . . thenceforward is no rest . . . . they see the space and ineffable sheen that turn the old spots and lights into dead vacuums. The companion of him beholds the birth and progress of stars and learns one of the meanings. Now there shall be a man cohered out of tumult and chaos . . . . the elder encourages the younger and shows him how . . . they two shall launch off fearlessly together till the new world fits an orbit for itself and looks unabashed on the lesser orbits of the stars and sweeps through the ceaseless rings and shall never be quiet again.

There will soon be no more priests. Their work is done. They may wait

---

[28] Whitman's euphemism for penis.

awhile . . perhaps a generation or two . . dropping off by degrees. A superior breed shall take their place. . . . the gangs of kosmos and prophets en masse shall take their place. A new order shall arise and they shall be the priests of man, and every man shall be his own priest. The churches built under their umbrage[29] shall be the churches of men and women. Through the divinity of themselves shall the kosmos and the new breed of poets be interpreters of men and women and of all events and things. They shall find their inspiration in real objects today, symptoms of the past and future . . . . They shall not deign to defend immortality or God or the perfection of things or liberty or the exquisite beauty and reality of the soul. They shall arise in America and be responded to from the remainder of the earth.

The English language befriends the grand American expression. . . . it is brawny enough and limber and full enough. On the tough stock of a race who through all change of circumstance was never without the idea of political liberty, which is the animus of all liberty, it has attracted the terms of daintier and gayer and subtler and more elegant tongues. It is the powerful language of resistance . . . it is the dialect of common sense. It is the speech of the proud and melancholy races and of all who aspire. It is the chosen tongue to express growth faith self-esteem freedom justice equality friendliness amplitude prudence decision and courage. It is the medium that shall well nigh express the inexpressible.

No great literature nor any like style of behaviour or oratory or social intercourse or household arrangements or public institutions or the treatment by bosses of employed people, nor executive detail of the army or navy, nor spirit of legislation or courts or police or tuition or architecture or songs or amusements or the costumes of young men, can long elude the jealous and passionate instinct of American standards. Whether or no the sign appears from the mouths of the people, it throbs a live interrogation in every freeman's and freewoman's heart after that which passes by, or this built to remain. Is it uniform with my country? Are its disposals without ignominious distinctions? Is it for the evergrowing communes of brothers and lovers, large, well-united, proud beyond the old models, generous beyond all models? Is it something grown fresh out of the fields or drawn from the sea for use to me today here? I know that what answers for me an American must answer for any individual or nation that serves for a part of my materials. Does this answer? or is it without reference to universal needs? or sprung of the needs of the less developed society of special ranks? or old needs of pleasure overlaid by modern science and form? Does this acknowledge liberty with audible and absolute acknowledgment, and set slavery at nought for life and death? Will it help breed one goodshaped and wellhung man, and a woman to be his perfect and independent mate? Does it improve manners? Is it for the nursing of the young of the republic? Does it solve[30] readily with the sweet milk of the nipples of the breasts of the mother of many children? Has it too the old ever-fresh forbearance and impartiality? Does it look with the same love on the last born and on those hardening toward stature, and on the errant, and on those who disdain all strength of assault outside of their own?

The poems distilled from other poems will probably pass away. The coward will surely pass away. The expectation of the vital and great can only be satisfied by the demeanor of the vital and great. The swarms of the polished deprecating and reflectors and the polite float off and leave no remembrance. America prepares with composure and goodwill for the visitors that have sent word. It is

---

[29] Shade, shelter.   [30] Dissolve.

not intellect that is to be their warrant and welcome. The talented, the artist, the ingenious, the editor, the statesman, the erudite . . they are not unappreciated . . they fall in their place and do their work. The soul of the nation also does its work. No disguise can pass on it . . no disguise can conceal from it. It rejects none, it permits all. Only toward as good as itself and toward the like of itself will it advance half-way. An individual is as superb as a nation when he has the qualities which make a superb nation. The soul of the largest and wealthiest and proudest nation may well go half-way to meet that of its poets. The signs are effectual. There is no fear of mistake. If the one is true the other is true. The proof of a poet is that his country absorbs him as affectionately as he has absorbed it.

1855

from INSCRIPTIONS*

ONE'S-SELF I SING

One's-Self I sing, a simple separate person,
Yet utter the word Democratic, the word En-Masse.

Of physiology from top to toe I sing,
Not physiognomy[1] alone nor brain alone is worthy for the Muse, I say the
    Form complete is worthier far,
The Female equally with the Male I sing.

Of Life immense in passion, pulse, and power,
Cheerful, for freest action form'd under the laws divine,
The Modern Man I sing.

1867

BEGINNING MY STUDIES†

Beginning my studies the first step pleas'd me so much,
The mere fact consciousness, these forms, the power of motion,
The least insect or animal, the senses, eyesight, love,
The first step I say awed me and pleas'd me so much,
I have hardly gone and hardly wish'd to go any farther,
But stop and loiter all the time to sing it in ecstatic songs.

1865

---

* Group title for the opening nine poems of the 1871 edition of *Leaves of Grass*, increased to include twenty-four poems in 1881.
[1] The art of judging human character from physical characteristics, especially facial features.
† First appeared in *Drum-Taps* (1865) and added to "Inscriptions" in 1871.

SHUT NOT YOUR DOORS*

Shut not your doors to me proud libraries,
For that which was lacking on all your well-fill'd shelves, yet needed most,
   I bring,
Forth from the war emerging, a book I have made,
The words of my book nothing, the drift of it every thing,
A book separate, not link'd with the rest nor felt by the intellect,
But you ye untold latencies will thrill to every page.

1865

POETS TO COME**

Poets to come! orators, singers, musicians to come!
Not to-day is to justify me and answer what I am for,
But you, a new brood, native, athletic, continental, greater than before known,
Arouse! for you must justify me.

I myself but write one or two indicative words for the future,
I but advance a moment only to wheel and hurry back in the darkness.

I am a man who, sauntering along without fully stopping, turns a casual look upon
   you and then averts his face,
Leaving it to you to prove and define it,
Expecting the main things from you.

1860

SONG OF MYSELF†

I

I celebrate myself, and sing myself,
And what I assume you shall assume,
For every atom belonging to me as good belongs to you.

I loafe and invite my soul,
I lean and loafe at my ease observing a spear of summer grass.

---

* First appeared in *Drum-Taps* (1865), revised, and added to "Inscriptions" in 1881.
** First appeared in "Chants Democratic" of the 1860 edition of *Leaves of Grass,* revised, and eventually added to "Inscriptions" in 1881.
† Appeared in the 1855 edition of *Leaves of Grass* untitled and without subdivisions. In the 1856 edition it was titled "Poem of Walt Whitman, an American," and in 1860 and later editions, "Walt Whitman." Not until 1881 did it appear as "Song of Myself."

My tongue, every atom of my blood, form'd from this soil, this air,
Born here of parents born here from parents the same, and their parents
  the same,
I, now thirty-seven years old in perfect health begin,
Hoping to cease not till death.

Creeds and schools in abeyance,
Retiring back a while sufficed at what they are, but never forgotten,
I harbor for good or bad, I permit to speak at every hazard,
Nature without check with original energy.

10

2

Houses and rooms are full of perfumes, the shelves are crowded with
  perfumes,
I breathe the fragrance myself and know it and like it,
The distillation would intoxicate me also, but I shall not let it.

The atmosphere is not a perfume, it has no taste of the distillation, it is
  odorless,
It is for my mouth forever, I am in love with it,
I will go to the bank by the wood and become undisguised and naked,
I am mad for it to be in contact with me.
The smoke of my own breath,

20

Echoes, ripples, buzz'd whispers, love-root, silk-thread, crotch and vine,
My respiration and inspiration, the beating of my heart, the passing of
  blood and air through my lungs,
The sniff of green leaves and dry leaves, and of the shore and dark-color'd
  sea-rocks, and of hay in the barn,
The sound of the belch'd words of my voice loos'd to the eddies of the wind,
A few light kisses, a few embraces, a reaching around of arms,
The play of shine and shade on the trees as the supple boughs wag,
The delight alone or in the rush of the streets, or along the fields and
  hill-sides,
The feeling of health, the full-noon trill, the song of me rising from bed
  and meeting the sun.

Have you reckon'd a thousand acres much? have you reckon'd the
  earth much?
Have you practis'd so long to learn to read?
Have you felt so proud to get at the meaning of poems?

30

Stop this day and night with me and you shall possess the origin of
  all poems,
You shall possess the good of the earth and sun, (there are millions of suns
  left,)
You shall no longer take things at second or third hand, nor look through
  the eyes of the dead, nor feed on the spectres in books,
You shall not look through my eyes either, nor take things from me,
You shall listen to all sides and filter them from yourself.

3

I have heard what the talkers were talking, the talk of the beginning
    and the end,
But I do not talk of the beginning or the end.

There was never any more inception than there is now,   40
Nor any more youth or age than there is now,
And will never be any more perfection than there is now,
Nor any more heaven or hell than there is now.

Urge and urge and urge,
Always the procreant urge of the world.

Out of the dimness opposite equals advance, always substance and
    increase, always sex,
Always a knit of identity, always distinction, always a breed of life.

To elaborate is no avail, learn'd and unlearn'd feel that it is so.

Sure as the most certain sure, plumb in the uprights, well entretied,[1]
    braced in the beams,
Stout as a horse, affectionate, haughty, electrical,
I and this mystery here we stand.   50

Clear and sweet is my soul, and clear and sweet is all that is not my soul.

Lack one lacks both, and the unseen is proved by the seen,
Till that becomes unseen and receives proof in its turn.

Showing the best and dividing it from the worst, age vexes age,
Knowing the perfect fitness and equanimity of things, while they discuss
    I am silent, and go bathe and admire myself.

Welcome is every organ and attribute of me, and of any man hearty
    and clean,
Not an inch nor a particle of an inch is vile, and none shall be less familiar
    than the rest.

I am satisfied—I see, dance, laugh, sing;
As the hugging and loving bed-fellow[2] sleeps at my side through the
    night, and withdraws at the peep of the day with stealthy tread,   60
Leaving me baskets cover'd with white towels swelling the house with
    their plenty,
Shall I postpone my acceptation and realization and scream at my eyes,
That they turn from gazing after and down the road,
And forthwith cipher[3] and show me to a cent,
Exactly the value of one and exactly the value of two, and which
    is ahead?

---

[1] Cross-braced or supported.
[2] In the 1855 version, God is the "loving bed-fellow."   [3] Calculate.

4

Trippers and askers[4] surround me,
People I meet, the effect upon me of my early life or the ward and city I
 live in, or the nation,
The latest dates, discoveries, inventions, societies, authors old and new,
My dinner, dress, associates, looks, compliments, dues,
The real or fancied indifference of some man or woman I love,   70
The sickness of one of my folks or of myself, or ill-doing or loss or lack
 of money, or depressions or exaltations,
Battles, the horrors of fratricidal war, the fever of doubtful news, the
 fitful events;
These come to me days and nights and go from me again,
But they are not the Me myself.

Apart from the pulling and hauling stands what I am,
Stands amused, complacent, compassionating, idle, unitary,
Looks down, is erect, or bends an arm on an impalpable certain rest,
Looking with side-curved head curious what will come next,
Both in and out of the game and watching and wondering at it.

Backward I see in my own days where I sweated through fog with
 linguists and contenders,   80
I have no mockings or arguments, I witness and wait.

5

I believe in you my soul, the other I am must not abase itself to you,
And you must not be abased to the other.

Loafe with me on the grass, loose the stop from your throat,
Not words, not music or rhyme I want, not custom or lecture, not even
 the best,
Only the lull I like, the hum of your valvèd voice.

I mind how once we lay such a transparent summer morning,
How you settled your head athwart my hips and gently turn'd over
 upon me.
And parted the shirt from my bosom-bone, and plunged your tongue to
 my bare-stript heart,
And reach'd till you felt my beard, and reach'd till you held my feet.   90

Swiftly arose and spread around me the peace and knowledge that pass
 all the argument of the earth,
And I know that the hand of God is the promise of my own,
And I know that the spirit of God is the brother of my own,
And that all the men ever born are also my brothers, and the women my
 sisters and lovers,
And that a kelson[5] of the creation is love,
And limitless are leaves stiff or drooping in the fields,

---

[4] Travelers and solicitors.   [5] Keelson, or timbers that brace a ship's keel.

And brown ants in the little wells beneath them,
And mossy scabs of the worm fence,[6] heap'd stones, elder, mullein and
    poke-weed.

6

A child said *What is the grass?* fetching it to me with full hands;
How could I answer the child? I do not know what it is any more
    than he.   100

I guess it must be the flag of my disposition, out of hopeful green
    stuff woven.

Or I guess it is the handkerchief of the Lord,
A scented gift and remembrancer designedly dropt,
Bearing the owner's name someway in the corners, that we may see and
    remark, and say *Whose?*

Or I guess the grass is itself a child, the produced babe of the vegetation.

Or I guess it is a uniform hieroglyphic,
And it means, Sprouting alike in broad zones and narrow zones,
Growing among black folks as among white,
Kanuck, Tuckahoe,[7] Congressman, Cuff,[8] I give them the same, I
    receive them the same.

And now it seems to me the beautiful uncut hair of graves.   110

Tenderly will I use you curling grass,
It may be you transpire from the breasts of young men,
It may be if I had known them I would have loved them,
It may be you are from old people, or from offspring taken soon out of
    their mothers' laps,
And here you are the mothers' laps.

This grass is very dark to be from the white heads of old mothers,
Darker than the colorless beards of old men,
Dark to come from under the faint red roofs of mouths.

O I perceive after all so many uttering tongues,
And I perceive they do not come from the roofs of mouths for nothing.   120

I wish I could translate the hints about the dead young men and women,
And the hints about old men and mothers, and the offspring taken soon
    out of their laps.

What do you think has become of the young and old men?
And what do you think has become of the women and children?

---

[6] An undulating or zigzag fence of split rails.
[7] A French-Canadian; a native of Tidewater Virginia.   [8] An African American.

They are alive and well somewhere,
The smallest sprout shows there is really no death,
And if ever there was it led forward life, and does not wait at the end to
   arrest it,
And ceas'd the moment life appear'd.

All goes onward and outward, nothing collapses,
And to die is different from what any one supposed, and luckier.   130

7

Has any one supposed it lucky to be born?
I hasten to inform him or her it is just as lucky to die, and I know it.

I pass death with the dying and birth with the new-wash'd babe, and am
   not contain'd between my hat and boots,
And peruse manifold objects, no two alike and every one good,
The earth good and the stars good, and their adjuncts all good.

I am not an earth nor an adjunct of an earth,
I am the mate and companion of people, all just as immortal and
   fathomless as myself,
(They do not know how immortal, but I know.)

Every kind for itself and its own, for me mine male and female,
For me those that have been boys and that love women,
For me the man that is proud and feels how it stings to be slighted,   140
For me the sweet-heart and the old maid, for me mothers and the mothers
   of mothers,
For me lips that have smiled, eyes that have shed tears,
For me children and the begetters of children.

Undrape! you are not guilty to me, nor stale nor discarded,
I see through the broadcloth and gingham whether or no,
And am around, tenacious, acquisitive, tireless, and cannot be
   shaken away.

8

The little one sleeps in its cradle,
I lift the gauze and look a long time, and silently brush away flies with
   my hand.

The youngster and the red-faced girl turn aside up the busy hill,   150
I peeringly view them from the top.

The suicide sprawls on the bloody floor of the bedroom,
I witness the corpse with its dabbled hair, I note where the pistol
   has fallen.

The blab of the pave,[9] tires of carts, sluff of boot-soles, talk of
    the promenaders,
The heavy omnibus, the driver with his interrogating thumb, the clank of
    the shod horses on the granite floor,
The snow-sleighs, clinking, shouted jokes, pelts of snow-balls,
The hurrahs for popular favorites, the fury of rous'd mobs,
The flap of the curtain'd litter, a sick man inside borne to the hospital,
The meeting of enemies, the sudden oath, the blows and fall,
The excited crowd, the policeman with his star quickly working his
    passage to the centre of the crowd,   160
The impassive stones that receive and return so many echoes,
What groans of over-fed or half-starv'd who fall sunstruck or in fits,
What exclamations of women taken suddenly who hurry home and give
    birth to babes,
What living and buried speech is always vibrating here, what howls
    restrain'd by decorum,
Arrests of criminals, slights, adulterous offers made, acceptances,
    rejections with convex lips,
I mind them or the show or resonance of them—I come and I depart.

9

The big doors of the country barn stand open and ready,
The dried grass of the harvest-time loads the slow-drawn wagon,
The clear light plays on the brown gray and green intertinged,
The armfuls are pack'd to the sagging mow.   170

I am there, I help, I came stretch'd atop of the load,
I felt its soft jolts, one leg reclined on the other,
I jump from the cross-beams and seize the clover and timothy,
And roll head over heels and tangle my hair full of wisps.

10

Alone far in the wilds and mountains I hunt,
Wandering amazed at my own lightness and glee,
In the late afternoon choosing a safe spot to pass the night,
Kindling a fire and broiling the fresh-kill'd game,
Falling asleep on the gather'd leaves with my dog and gun by my side.

The Yankee clipper is under her sky-sails,[10] she cuts the sparkle
    and scud,   180
My eyes settle the land, I bend at her prow or shout joyously from
    the deck.

The boatmen and clam-diggers arose early and stopt for me,
I tuck'd my trowser-ends in my boots and went and had a good time;
You should have been with us that day round the chowder-kettle.

I saw the marriage of the trapper in the open air in the far west, the bride
    was a red girl,

---

[9] Street talk.   [10] Top sails; scud is sea foam.

Her father and his friends sat near cross-legged and dumbly smoking,
    they had moccasins to their feet and large thick blankets hanging from
    their shoulders,
On a bank lounged the trapper, he was drest mostly in skins, his
    luxuriant beard and curls protected his neck, he held his bride by
    the hand,
She had long eyelashes, her head was bare, her coarse straight locks
    descended upon her voluptuous limbs and reach'd to her feet.[11]

The runaway slave came to my house and stopt outside,
I heard his motions crackling the twigs of the woodpile,   190
Through the swung half-door of the kitchen I saw him limpsy and weak,
And went where he sat on a log and led him in and assured him,
And brought water and fill'd a tub for his sweated body and bruis'd feet,
And gave him a room that enter'd from my own, and gave him some
    coarse clean clothes,
And remember perfectly well his revolving eyes and his awkwardness,
And remember putting plasters on the galls of his neck and ankles;
He staid with me a week before he was recuperated and pass'd north,
I had him sit next me at table, my fire-lock[12] lean'd in the corner.

11

Twenty-eight young men bathe by the shore,
Twenty-eight young men and all so friendly;
Twenty-eight years of womanly life and all so lonesome.   200

She owns the fine house by the rise of the bank,
She hides handsome and richly drest aft the blinds of the window.

Which of the young men does she like the best?
Ah the homeliest of them is beautiful to her.

Where are you off to, lady? for I see you,
You splash in the water there, yet stay stock still in your room.

Dancing and laughing along the beach came the twenty-ninth bather,
The rest did not see her, but she saw them and loved them.

The beards of the young men glisten'd with wet, it ran from their
    long hair,   210
Little streams pass'd all over their bodies.

An unseen hand also pass'd over their bodies,
It descended tremblingly from their temples and ribs.

The young men float on their backs, their white bellies bulge to the sun,
    they do not ask who seizes fast to them,

[11] This stanza is based on the painting *The Trapper's Bride*, by Alfred Jacob Miller (1810–1874).
[12] Gun.

They do not know who puffs and declines with pendant and
    bending arch,
They do not think whom they souse with spray.

12

The butcher-boy puts off his killing-clothes, or sharpens his knife at the
    stall in the market,
I loiter enjoying his repartee and his shuffle and break-down.[13]

Blacksmiths with grimed and hairy chests environ the anvil,
Each has his main-sledge, they are all out, there is a great heat in
    the fire.   220

From the cinder-strew'd threshold I follow their movements,
The lithe sheer[14] of their waists plays even with their massive arms,
Overhand the hammers swing, overhand so slow, overhand so sure,
They do no hasten, each man hits in his place.

13

The negro holds firmly the reins of his four horses, the block swags
    underneath on its tied-over chain,
The negro that drives the long dray[15] of the stone-yard, steady and tall he
    stands pois'd on one leg on the string piece,[16]
His blue shirt exposes his ample neck and breast and loosens over his
    hip-band,
His glance is calm and commanding, he tosses the slouch of his hat away
    from his forehead,
The sun falls on his crispy hair and mustache, falls on the black of his
    polish'd and perfect limbs.

I behold the picturesque giant and love him, and I do not stop there,   230
I go with the team also.

In me the caresser of life wherever moving, backward as well as
    forward sluing,[17]
To niches aside and junior[18] bending, not a person or object missing,
Absorbing all to myself and for this song.

Oxen that rattle the yoke and chain or halt in the leafy shade, what is that
    you express in your eyes?
It seems to me more than all the print I have read in my life.

My tread scares the wood-drake and wood-duck on my distant and day-
    long ramble,
They rise together, they slowly circle around.

---

[13] Two popular minstrel-show steps: the shuffle, a sliding, slow step; the break-down, faster and
uninhibited.
    [14] Upward curve.   [15] A low, heavy cart for haulage.
    [16] A heavy timber used to shore up construction or to brace a load.   [17] Twisting.   [18] Lesser.

I believe in those wing'd purposes,
And acknowledge red, yellow, white, playing within me,   240
And consider green and violet and the tufted crown intentional,
And do not call the tortoise unworthy because she is not something else,
And the jay in the woods never studied the gamut,[19] yet trills pretty
    well to me,
And the look of the bay mare shames silliness out of me.

14

The wild gander leads his flock through the cool night,
Ya-honk he says, and sounds it down to me like an invitation,
The pert[20] may suppose it meaningless, but I listening close,
Find its purpose and place up there toward the wintry sky.

The sharp-hoof'd moose of the north, the cat on the house-sill, the
    chickadee, the prairie dog,
The litter of the grunting sow as they tug at her teats,   250
The brood of the turkey-hen and she with her half-spread wings,
I see in them and myself the same old law.

The press of my foot to the earth springs a hundred affections,
They scorn the best I can do to relate them.
I am enamour'd of growing out-doors,
Of men that live among cattle or taste of the ocean or woods,
Of the builders and steerers of ships and the wielders of axes and mauls,
    and the drivers of horses,
I can eat and sleep with them week in and week out.

What is commonest, cheapest, nearest, easiest, is Me,
Me going in for my chances, spending for vast returns,   260
Adorning myself to bestow myself on the first that will take me,
Not asking the sky to come down to my good will,
Scattering it freely forever.

15

The pure contralto sings in the organ loft,
The carpenter dresses his plank, the tongue of his foreplane whistles its
    wild ascending lisp,
The married and unmarried children ride home to their Thanksgiving
    dinner,
The pilot seizes the king-pin,[21] he heaves down with a strong arm,
The mate stands braced in the whale-boat, lance and harpoon are ready,
The duck-shooter walks by silent and cautious stretches,
The deacons are ordain'd with cross'd hands at the altar,   270
The spinning-girl retreats and advances to the hum of the big wheel,
The farmer stops by the bars[22] as he walks on a First-day loafe[23] and
    looks at the oats and rye,

---

[19] Never practiced musical scales.   [20] The bold.
[21] The extended spoke of the pilot wheel.   [22] Fence rails.
[23] The Quaker designation for the first day of the week: Sunday, a day of leisure.

The lunatic is carried at last to the asylum a confirm'd case,
(He will never sleep any more as he did in the cot in his mother's
  bed-room;)
The jour printer[24] with gray head and gaunt jaws works at his case,
He turns his quid of tobacco while his eyes blurr with the manuscript;
The malform'd limbs are tied to the surgeon's table,
What is removed drops horribly in a pail;
The quadroon[25] girl is sold at the auction-stand,the drunkard nods by the
  bar-room stove,
The machinist rolls up his sleeves, the policeman travels his beat, the
  gate-keeper marks who pass,   280
The young fellow drives the express-wagon, (I love him, though I do not
  know him;)
The half-breed straps on his light boots to compete in the race,
The western turkey-shooting draws old and young, some lean on their
  rifles, some sit on logs,
Out from the crowd steps the marksman, takes his position, levels
  his piece;
The groups of newly-come immigrants cover the wharf or levee,
As the woolly-pates[26] hoe in the sugar-field, the overseer views them
  from his saddle,
The bugle calls in the ball-room, the gentlemen run for their partners, the
  dancers bow to each other,
The youth lies awake in the cedar-roof'd garret and harks to the
  musical rain,
The Wolverine[27] sets traps on the creek that helps fill the Huron,
The squaw wrapt in her yellow-hemm'd cloth is offering moccasins and
  bead-bags for sale,   290
The connoisseur peers along the exhibition-gallery with half-shut eyes
  bent sideways,
As the deck-hands make fast the steamboat the plank is thrown for the
  shore-going passengers,
The young sister holds out the skein while the elder sister winds it off in
  a ball, and stops now and then for the knots,
The one-year wife is recovering and happy having a week ago borne her
  first child,
The clean-hair'd Yankee girl works with her sewing-machine or in the
  factory or mill,
The paving-man leans on his two-handed rammer, the reporter's lead
  flies swiftly over the note-book, the sign-painter is lettering with blue
  and gold,
The canal boy trots on the tow-path,[28] the book-keeper counts at his
  desk, the shoemaker waxes his thread,
The conductor beats time for the band and all the performers follow him,
The child is baptized, the convert is making his first professions,
The regatta is spread on the bay, the race is begun, (how the white
  sails sparkle!)   300

---

[24] Journeyman printer, working out his case of typefaces.
[25] One-quarter black (with one black grandparent).   [26] African-American slaves.
[27] Michigan resident.   [28] A path along which draft animals tow canal barges.

The drover watching his drove sings out to them that would stray,
The pedler sweats with his pack on his back, (the purchaser higgling
    about the odd cent;)
The bride unrumples her white dress, the minute-hand of the clock
    moves slowly,
The opium-eater reclines with rigid head and just-open'd lips,
The prostitute draggles her shawl, her bonnet bobs on her tipsy and
    pimpled neck,
The crowd laugh at her blackguard oaths, the men jeer and wink to
    each other,
(Miserable! I do not laugh at your oaths nor jeer you;)
The President holding a cabinet council is surrounded by the
    great Secretaries,
On the piazza walk three matrons stately and friendly with
    twined arms,
The crew of the fish-smack pack repeated layers of halibut in the hold,   310
The Missourian crosses the plains toting his wares and his cattle,
As the fare-collector goes through the train he gives notice by the
    jingling of loose change,
The floor-men are laying the floor, the tinners are tinning[29] the roof, the
    masons are calling for mortar,
In single file each shouldering his nod pass onward the laborers;
Seasons pursuing each other the indescribable crowd is gather'd, it is the
    fourth of Seventh-month,[30] (what salutes of cannon and small arms!)
Seasons pursuing each other the plougher ploughs, the mower mows,
    and the winter-grain falls in the ground;
Off on the lakes the pike-fisher watches and waits by the hole in the
    frozen surface,
The stumps stand thick round the clearing, the squatter strikes deep with
    his axe,
Flatboatmen make fast towards dusk near the cotton-wood or
    pecan-trees,
Coon-seekers[31] go through the regions of the Red river or through those
    drain'd by the Tennessee, or through those of the Arkansas,   320
Torches shine in the dark that hangs on the Chattahooche
    or Altamahaw,[32]
Patriarchs sit at supper with sons and grandsons and great-grandsons
    around them,
In walls of adobie, in canvas tents, rest hunters and trappers after their
    day's sport,
The city sleeps and the country sleeps,
The living sleep for their time, the dead sleep for their time,
The old husband sleeps by his wife and the young husband sleeps by
    his wife;
And these tend inward to me, and I tend outward to them,
And such as it is to be of these more or less I am,
And of these one and all I weave the song of myself.

---

[29] Repairing a sheet-metal roof.   [30] The Quaker designation for the Fourth of July.
[31] Racoon hunters; the Red River borders Texas and Oklahoma.
[32] Rivers in Alabama and Louisiana.

16

I am of old and young, of the foolish as much as the wise,   330
Regardless of others, ever regardful of others,
Maternal as well as paternal, a child as well as a man,
Stuff'd with the stuff that is coarse and stuff'd with the stuff that is fine,
One of the Nation of many nations, the smallest the same and the largest
    the same,
A Southerner soon as a Northerner, a planter nonchalant and hospitable
    down by the Oconee[33] I live,
A Yankee bound my own way ready for trade, my joints the limberest
    joints on earth and the sternest joints on earth,
A Kentuckian walking the vale of the Elkhorn[34] in my deer-skin leggings,
    a Louisianian or Georgian,
A boatman over lakes or bays or along coasts, a Hoosier, Badger,
    Buckeye;[35]
At home on Kanadian snow-shoes or up in the bush, or with fishermen
    off Newfoundland,
At home in the fleet of ice-boats, sailing with the rest and tacking,   340
At home on the hills of Vermont or in the woods of Maine, or the
    Texan ranch,
Comrade of Californians, comrade of free North-Westerners, (loving
    their big proportions,)
Comrade of raftsmen and coalmen, comrade of all who shake hands and
    welcome to drink and meat,
A learner with the simplest, a teacher of the thoughtfullest,
A novice beginning yet experient of myriads of seasons,
Of every hue and caste am I, of every rank and religion,
A farmer, mechanic, artist, gentleman, sailor, quaker,
Prisoner, fancy-man,[36] rowdy, lawyer, physician, priest.

I resist any thing better than my own diversity,
Breathe the air but leave plenty after me,   350
And am not stuck up, and am in my place.

(The moth and the fish-eggs are in their place,
The bright suns I see and the dark suns I cannot see are in their place,
The palpable is in its place and the impalpable is in its place.)

17

These are really the thoughts of all men in all ages and lands, they are
    not original with me,
If they are not yours as much as mine they are nothing, or next to nothing,
If they are not the riddle and the untying of the riddle they are nothing,
If they are not just as close as they are distant they are nothing.

This is the grass that grows wherever the land is and the water is,
This the common air that bathes the globe.   360

---

[33] A river in Georgia.   [34] A river in Nebraska.
[35] An inhabitant of Indiana, Wisconsin, and Ohio, respectively.   [36] A pimp.

18

With music strong I come, with my cornets and my drums,
I play not marches for accepted victors only, I play marches for
    conquer'd and slain persons.

Have you heard that it was good to gain the day?
I also say it is good to fall, battles are lost in the same spirit in which
    they are won.

I beat and pound for the dead,
I blow through my embouchures[37] my loudest and gayest for them.

Vivas to those who have fail'd!
And to those whose war-vessels sank in the sea!
And to those themselves who sank in the sea!
And to all generals that lost engagements, and all overcome heroes!   370
And the numberless unknown heroes equal to the greatest heroes known!

19

This is the meal equally set, this the meat for natural hunger,
It is for the wicked just the same as the righteous, I make appointments
    with all,
I will not have a single person slighted or left away,
The kept-woman, sponger, thief, are hereby invited,
The heavy-lipp'd slave is invited, the venerealee[38] is invited;
There shall be no difference between them and the rest.

This is the press of a bashful hand, this the float and odor of hair,
This the touch of my lips to yours, this the murmur of yearning,
This the far-off depth and height reflecting my own face,   380
This the thoughtful merge of myself, and the outlet again.

Do you guess I have some intricate purpose?
Well I have, for the Fourth-month[39] showers have, and the mica on the
    side of a rock has.

Do you take it I would astonish?
Does the daylight astonish? does the early redstart twittering through
    the woods?
Do I astonish more than they?

This hour I tell things in confidence,
I might not tell everybody, but I will tell you.

20

Who goes there? hankering, gross, mystical, nude;
How is it I extract strength from the beef I eat?   390

---

[37] Mouthpieces of wind and brass instruments.
[38] One infected with a venereal disease or obsessed with sexual desire.   [39] April.

What is a man anyhow? what am I? what are you?

All I mark as my own you shall offset it with your own,
Else it were time lost listening to me.

I do not snivel that snivel the world over,
That months are vacuums and the ground but wallow and filth.

Whimpering and truckling fold with powders for invalids,[40] conformity,
    goes to the fourth-remov'd,[41]
I wear my hat as I please indoors or out.

Why should I pray? why should I venerate and be ceremonious?

Having pried through the strata, analyzed to a hair, counsel'd with
    doctors and calculated close,
I find no sweeter fat than sticks to my own bones.   400

In all people I see myself, none more and not one a barley-corn less,
And the good or bad I say of myself I say of them.

I know I am solid and sound,
To me the converging objects of the universe perpetually flow,
All are written to me, and I must get what the writing means.

I know I am deathless,
I know this orbit of mine cannot be swept by a carpenter's compass,
I know I shall not pass like a child's carlacue[42] cut with a burnt stick
    at night.

I know I am august,
I do not trouble my spirit to vindicate itself or be understood,   410
I see that the elementary laws never apologize,
(I reckon I behave no prouder than the level I plant my house by,
    after all.)

I exist as I am, that is enough,
If no other in the world be aware I sit content,
And if each and all be aware I sit content.

One world is aware and by far the largest to me, and that is myself,
And whether I come to my own to-day or in ten thousand or ten
    million years,
I can cheerfully take it now, or with equal cheerfulness I can wait.
My foothold is tenon'd and mortis'd[43] in granite,

---

[40] Whimpering and yielding are appropriate medicines to be combined with the other powders administered to invalids.
[41] Those removed from society.
[42] A curlicue, here a brief pattern of light "cut" in the darkness by the glowing end of a burning stick.
[43] Joined with interlocking pieces.

I laugh at what you call dissolution,   420
And I know the amplitude of time.

21

I am the poet of the Body and I am the poet of the Soul,
The pleasures of heaven are with me and the pains of hell are with me,
The first I graft and increase upon myself, the latter I translate into a
   new tongue.

I am the poet of the woman the same as the man,
And I say it is as great to be a woman as to be a man,
And I say there is nothing greater than the mother of men.

I chant the chant of dilation or pride,
We have had ducking and deprecating about enough,
I show that size is only development.   430

Have you outstript the rest? are you the President?
It is a trifle, they will more than arrive there every one, and still pass on.

I am he that walks with the tender and growing night,
I call to the earth and sea half-held by the night.

Press close bare-bosom'd night—press close magnetic nourishing night!
Night of south winds—night of the large few stars!
Still nodding night—mad naked summer night.

Smile O voluptuous cool-breath'd earth!
Earth of the slumbering and liquid trees!
Earth of departed sunset—earth of the mountains misty-topt!
Earth of the vitreous[44] pour of the full moon just tinged with blue!   440
Earth of shine and dark mottling the tide of the river!
Earth of the limpid gray of clouds brighter and clearer for my sake!
Far-swooping elbow'd earth—rich apple blossom'd earth!
Smile, for your lover comes.

Prodigal, you have given me love—therefore I to you give love!
O unspeakable passionate love.

22

You sea! I resign myself to you also—I guess what you mean,
I behold from the beach your crooked inviting fingers,
I believe you refuse to go back without feeling of me,   450
We must have a turn together, I undress, hurry me out of sight of
   the land,
Cushion me soft, rock me in billowy drowse,
Dash me with amorous wet, I can repay you.

[44] Glasslike.

Sea of stretch'd ground-swells,
Sea breathing broad and convulsive breaths,
Sea of the brine of life and of unshovell'd yet always-ready graves,
Howler and scooper of storms, capricious and dainty sea,
I am integral with you, I too am of one phase and of all phases.

Partaker of influx and efflux, I, extoller of hate and conciliation,
Extoller of amies[45] and those that sleep in each others' arms.   460

I am he attesting sympathy,
(Shall I make my list of things in the house and skip the house that
    supports them?)

I am not the poet of goodness only, I do not decline to be the poet of
    wickedness also.

What blurt is this about virtue and about vice?
Evil propels me and reform of evil propels me, I stand indifferent,
My gait is no fault-finder's or rejecter's gait,
I moisten the roots of all that has grown.

Did you fear some scrofula[46] out of the unflagging pregnancy?
Did you guess the celestial laws are yet to be work'd over and rectified?

I find one side a balance and the antipodal side a balance,   470
Soft doctrine as steady help as stable doctrine,
Thoughts and deeds of the present our rouse and early start.

This minute that comes to me over the past decillions,[47]
There is no better than it and now.

What behaved well in the past or behaves well to-day is not such
    a wonder,
The wonder is always and always how there can be a mean man or
    an infidel.

23

Endless unfolding of words of ages!
And mine a word of the modern, the word En-Masse.

A word of the faith that never balks,
Here or henceforward it is all the same to me, I accept Time
    absolutely.   480

It alone is without flaw, it alone rounds and completes all,
That mystic baffling wonder alone completes all.

---

[45] "Friends" or "lovers" (French).
[46] A form of tuberculosis involving swelling of the lymph glands and inflammation of the joints;
"scrofulous" carries a connotation of moral degeneracy.
[47] Many years: one followed by thirty-three zeros.

I accept Reality and dare not question it,
Materialism first and last imbuing.

Hurrah for positive science! long live exact demonstration!
Fetch stonecrop[48] mixt with cedar and branches of lilac,
This is the lexicographer, this the chemist, this made a grammar of the
    old cartouches,[49]
These mariners put the ship through dangerous unknown seas,
This is the geologist, this works with the scalpel, and this is a
    mathematician.

Gentlemen, to you the first honors always!   490
Your facts are useful, and yet they are not my dwelling,
I but enter by them to an area of my dwelling.

Less the reminders of properties told my words,
And more the reminders they of life untold, and of freedom and
    extrication,
And make short account of neuters and geldings, and favor men and
    women fully equipt,
And beat the gong of revolt, and stop with fugitives and them that plot
    and conspire.

24

Walt Whitman, a kosmos, of Manhattan the son,
Turbulent, fleshy, sensual, eating, drinking and breeding,
No sentimentalist, no stander above men and women or apart
    from them,
No more modest than immodest.   500

Unscrew the locks from the doors!
Unscrew the doors themselves from their jambs!

Whoever degrades another degrades me,
And whatever is done or said returns at last to me.

Through me the afflatus[50] surging and surging, through me the current
    and index.

I speak the pass-word primeval, I give the sign of democracy,
By God! I will accept nothing which all cannot have their counterpart
    of on the same terms.

Through me many long dumb voices,
Voices of the interminable generations of prisoners and slaves,
Voices of the diseas'd and despairing and of thieves and dwarfs,   510

[48] A plant used as a medicinal herb.
[49] Deciphered the Egyptian hieroglyphs carved in oblong or oval figures.
[50] A divine wind, communicating knowledge or inspiration.

Voices of cycles of preparation and accretion,
And of the threads that connect the stars, and of wombs and of the
    father-stuff,
And of the rights of them the others are down upon,
Of the deform'd, trivial, flat, foolish, despised,
Fog in the air, beetles rolling balls of dung.

Through me forbidden voices,
Voices of sexes and lusts, voices veil'd and I remove the veil,
Voices indecent by me clarified and transfigur'd.

I do not press my fingers across my mouth,
I keep as delicate around the bowels as around the head and heart,   520
Copulation is no more rank to me than death is.

I believe in the flesh and the appetites,
Seeing, hearing, feeling, are miracles, and each part and tag of me is a
    miracle.

Divine am I inside and out, and I make holy whatever I touch or am
    touch'd from,
The scent of these arm-pits aroma finer than prayer,
This head more than churches, bibles, and all the creeds.

If I worship one thing more than another it shall be the spread of my
    own body, or any part of it,
Translucent mould of me it shall be you!
Shaded ledges and rests it shall be you!
Firm masculine colter[51] it shall be you!   530
Whatever goes to the tilth[52] of me it shall be you!
You my rich blood! your milky stream pale strippings of my life!
Breast that presses against other breasts it shall be you!
My brain it shall be your occult convolutions!
Root of wash'd sweet-flag![53] timorous pond-snipe! nest of guarded
    duplicate eggs! it shall be you!
Mix'd tussled hay of head, beard, brawn, it shall be you!
Trickling sap of maple, fibre of manly wheat, it shall be you!
Sun so generous it shall be you!
Vapors lighting and shading my face it shall be you!
You sweaty brooks and dews it shall be you!   540
Winds whose soft-tickling genitals rub against me it shall be you!
Broad muscular fields, branches of live oak, loving lounger in my
    winding paths, it shall be you!
Hands I have taken, face I have kiss'd, mortal I have ever touch'd, it
    shall be you.

I dote on myself, there is that lot of me and all so luscious,
Each moment and whatever happens thrills me with joy,

---

[51] A sharp blade that cuts the ground in front of a plowshare.   [52] Cultivation.
[53] The aromatic root of the calamus plant.

I cannot tell how my ankles bend, nor whence the cause of my
    faintest wish,
Nor the cause of the friendship I emit, nor the cause of the friendship I
    take again.

That I walk up my stoop, I pause to consider if it really be,
A morning-glory at my window satisfies me more than the
    metaphysics of books.

To behold the day-break!   550
The little light fades the immense and diaphanous shadows,
The air tastes good to my palate.

Hefts[54] of the moving world at innocent gambols silently rising freshly
    exuding,
Scooting obliquely high and low.

Something I cannot see puts upward libidinous prongs,
Seas of bright juice suffuse heaven.

The earth by the sky staid with, the daily close of their junction,
The heav'd challenge from the east that moment over my head,
The mocking taunt, See then whether you shall be master!

25

Dazzling and tremendous how quick the sun-rise would kill me,   560
If I could not now and always send sun-rise out of me.

We also ascend dazzling and tremendous as the sun,
We found our own O my soul in the calm and cool of the daybreak.

My voice goes after what my eyes cannot reach,
With the twirl of my tongue I encompass worlds and volumes of worlds.

Speech is the twin of my vision, it is unequal to measure itself,
It provokes me forever, it says sarcastically,
Walt you contain enough, why don't you let it out then?

Come now I will not be tantalized, you conceive too much of
    articulation,
Do you not know O speech how the buds beneath you are folded?   570
Waiting in gloom, protected by frost,
The dirt receding before my prophetical screams,
I underlying causes to balance them at last,
My knowledge my live parts, it keeping tally with the meaning of all
    things,
Happiness, (which whoever hears me let him or her set out in search of
    this day.)

---

[54] The most massive parts.

My final merit I refuse you, I refuse putting from me what I really am,
Encompass worlds, but never try to encompass me,
I crowd your sleekest and best by simply looking toward you.

Writing and talk do not prove me,
I carry the plenum[55] of proof and every thing else in my face,   580
With the hush of my lips I wholly confound the skeptic.

26

Now I will do nothing but listen,
To accrue what I hear into this song, to let sounds contribute toward it.

I hear bravuras of birds, bustle of growing wheat, gossip of flames, clack
   of sticks cooking my meals,
I hear the sound I love, the sound of the human voice,
I hear all sounds running together, combined, fused or following,
Sounds of the city and sounds out of the city, sounds of the day and night,
Talkative young ones to those that like them, the loud laugh of work-
   people at their meals,
The angry base[56] of disjointed friendship, the faint tones of the sick,
The judge with hands tight to the desk, his pallid lips pronouncing a
   death-sentence,   590
The heave'e'yo of stevedores unlading ships by the wharves, the refrain
   of the anchor-lifters,
The ring of alarm-bells, the cry of fire, the whirr of swift-streaking
   engines and hose-carts with premonitory tinkles and color'd lights,
The steam-whistle, the solid roll of the train of approaching cars,
The slow march play'd at the head of the association marching two
   and two,
(They go to guard some corpse, the flag-tops are draped with black
   muslin.)

I hear the violoncello, ('tis the young man's heart's complaint,)
I hear the key'd cornet, it glides quickly in through my ears,
It shakes mad-sweet pangs through my belly and breast.

I hear the chorus, it is a grand opera,
Ah this indeed is music—this suits me.   600

A tenor large and fresh as the creation fills me,
The orbic flex of his mouth is pouring and filling me full.

I hear the train'd soprano (what work with hers is this?)
The orchestra whirls me wider than Uranus[57] flies,
It wrenches such ardors from me I did not know I possess'd them,
It sails me, I dab with bare feet, they are lick'd by the indolent waves,

---

[55] Fullness.   [56] Bass.
[57] Then thought to be the most remote planet; it orbits the sun at a mean distance of nearly 2 million
miles.

I am cut by bitter and angry hail, I lose my breath,
Steep'd amid honey'd morphine, my windpipe throttled in fakes[58]
   of death,
At length let up again to feel the puzzle of puzzles,
And that we call Being.   610

27

To be in any form, what is that?
(Round and round we go, all of us, and ever come back thither,)
If nothing lay more develop'd the quahaug[59] in its callous shell were
   enough.

Mine is no callous shell,
I have instant conductors all over me whether I pass or stop,
They seize every object and lead it harmlessly through me.

I merely stir, press, feel with my fingers, and am happy,
To touch my person to some one else's is about as much as I can stand.

28

Is this then a touch? quivering me to a new identity,
Flames and ether making a rush for my veins,   620
Treacherous tip of me reaching and crowing to help them,
My flesh and blood playing out lightning to strike what is hardly
   different from myself,
On all sides prurient provokers stiffening my limbs,
Straining the udder of my heart for its withheld drip,
Behaving licentious toward me, taking no denial,
Depriving me of my best as for a purpose,
Unbuttoning my clothes, holding me by the bare waist,
Deluding my confusion with the calm of the sunlight and pasture-fields,
Immodestly sliding the fellow-senses away,
They bribed to swap off with touch and go and graze at the edges of me,   630
No consideration, no regard for my draining strength or my anger,
Fetching the rest of the herd around to enjoy them a while,
Then all uniting to stand on a headland and worry me.

The sentries desert every other part of me,
They have left me helpless to a red marauder,
They all come to the headland to witness and assist against me.

I am given up by traitors,
I talk wildly, I have lost my wits, I and nobody else am the greatest
   traitor,
I went myself first to the headland, my own hands carried me there.

You villain touch! what are you doing? my breath is tight in its throat,   640
Unclench your floodgates, you are too much for me.

---

[58] Coils of rope.   [59] Quahog, an edible Atlantic clam.

29

Blind loving wrestling touch, sheath'd hooded sharp-tooth'd touch!
Did it make you ache so, leaving me?

Parting track'd by arriving, perpetual payment of perpetual loan,
Rich showering rain, and recompense richer afterward.

Sprouts take and accumulate, stand by the curb prolific and vital,
Landscapes projected masculine, full-sized and golden.

30

All truths wait in all things,
They neither hasten their own delivery nor resist it,
They do not need the obstetric forceps of the surgeon,   650
The insignificant is as big to me as any,
(What is less or more than a touch?)

Logic and sermons never convince,
The damp of the night drives deeper into my soul.

(Only what proves itself to every man and woman is so,
Only what nobody denies is so.)

A minute and a drop of me settle my brain,
I believe the soggy clods shall become lovers and lamps,
And a compend[60] of compends is the meat of a man or woman,
And a summit and flower there is the feeling they have for each other,   660
And they are to branch boundlessly out of that lesson until it becomes
     omnific,
And until one and all shall delight us, and we them.

31

I believe a leaf of grass is no less than the journey-work of the stars,
And the pismire[61] is equally perfect, and a grain of sand, and the egg of
     the wren,
And the tree-toad is a chef-d'œuvre[62] for the highest,
And the running blackberry would adorn the parlors of heaven,
And the narrowest hinge in my hand puts to scorn all machinery,
And the cow crunching with depress'd head surpasses any statue,
And a mouse is miracle enough to stagger sextillions[63] of infidels.

I find I incorporate gneiss,[64] coal, long-threaded moss, fruits, grains,
     esculent roots,   670
And am stucco'd with quadrupeds and birds all over,
And have distanced what is behind me for good reasons,
But call any thing back again when I desire it.

---

[60] A compendium or short summary, especially of a very broad subject.   [61] Ant.
[62] A masterpiece (French).   [63] A large number: one followed by twenty-one zeros.
[64] Layered, coarse-grained metamorphic rock.

In vain the speeding or shyness,
In vain the plutonic rocks[65] send their old heat against my approach,
In vain the mastodon retreats beneath its own powder'd bones,
In vain objects stand leagues off and assume manifold shapes,
In vain the ocean settling in hollows and the great monsters lying low,
In vain the buzzard houses herself with the sky,
In vain the snake slides through the creepers and logs,   680
In vain the elk takes to the inner passes of the woods,
In vain the razor-bill'd auk sails far north to Labrador,
I follow quickly, I ascend to the nest in the fissure of the cliff.

32

I think I could turn and live with animals, they are so placid and self-
  contain'd,
I stand and look at them long and long.

They do not sweat and whine about their condition,
They do not lie awake in the dark and weep for their sins,
They do not make me sick discussing their duty to God,
Not one is dissatisfied, not one is demented with the mania of owning
  things,
Not one kneels to another, nor to his kind that lived thousands of
  years ago,   690
Not one is respectable or unhappy over the whole earth.

So they show their relations to me and I accept them,
They bring me tokens of myself, they evince them plainly in their
  possession.

I wonder where they get those tokens,
Did I pass that way huge times ago and negligently drop them?

Myself moving forward then and now and forever,
Gathering and showing more always and with velocity,
Infinite and omnigenous,[66] and the like of these among them,
Not too exclusive toward the reachers of my remembrancers,
Picking out here one that I love, and now go with him on brotherly
  terms.   700

A gigantic beauty of a stallion, fresh and responsive to my caresses,
Head high in the forehead, wide between the ears,
Limbs glossy and supple, tail dusting the ground,
Eyes full of sparkling wickedness, ears finely cut, flexibly moving.

His nostrils dilate as my heels embrace him,
His well-built limbs tremble with pleasure as we race around and return.

---

[65] Rock formed from molten material beneath the earth's crust; from the Roman god Pluto, the ruler
of the Underworld.
[66] Of all forms.

I but use you a minute, then I resign you, stallion,
Why do I need your paces when I myself out-gallop them?
Even as I stand or sit passing faster than you.

33

Space and Time! now I see it is true, what I guess'd at,   710
What I guess'd when I loaf'd on the grass,
What I guess'd while I lay alone in my bed,
And again as I walk'd the beach under the paling stars of the morning.

My ties and ballasts leave me, my elbows rest in sea-gaps,[67]
I skirt sierras, my palms cover continents,
I am afoot with my vision.

By the city's quadrangular houses—in log huts, camping with
    lumbermen,
Along the ruts of the turnpike, along the dry gulch and rivulet bed,
Weeding my onion-patch or hoeing rows of carrots and parsnips,
    crossing savannas, trailing in forests,
Prospecting, gold-digging, girdling the trees of a new purchase,   720
Scorch'd ankle-deep by the hot sand, hauling by boat down the shallow
    river,
Where the panther walks to and fro on a limb overhead, where the buck
    turns furiously at the hunter,
Where the rattlesnake suns his flabby length on a rock, where the otter is
    feeding on fish,
Where the alligator in his tough pimples sleeps by the bayou,
Where the black bear is searching for roots or honey, where the beaver
    pats the mud with his paddle-shaped tail;
Over the growing sugar, over the yellow-flower'd cotton plant, over the
    rice in its low moist field,
Over the sharp-peak'd farm house, with its scallop'd scum and slender
    shoots from the gutters,[68]
Over the western persimmon, over the long-leav'd corn, over the
    delicate blue-flower flax,
Over the white and brown buckwheat, a hummer and buzzer[69] there with
    the rest,
Over the dusky green of the rye as it ripples and shades in the breeze;   730
Scaling mountains, pulling myself cautiously up, holding on by low
    scragged[70] limbs,
Walking the path worn in the grass and beat through the leaves of the
    brush,
Where the quail is whistling betwixt the woods and the wheat-lot,
Where the bat flies in the Seventh-month eve, where the great goldbug[71]
    drops through the dark,

---

[67] Estuaries, inlets.
[68] Patterns of sediment washed down from the roof peaks, and shoots of plants that have colonized the sediment deposited in the rain-gutters.
[69] A hummingbird and a bee.   [70] Low-growing.   [71] A beetle.

Where the brook puts out of the roots of the old tree and flows to the
    meadow,
Where cattle stand and shake away flies with the tremulous shuddering
    of their hides,
Where the cheese-cloth hangs in the kitchen, where andirons straddle the
    hearth-slab, where cobwebs fall in festoons from the rafters;
Where trip-hammers crash, where the press is whirling its cylinders,
Wherever the human heart beats with terrible throes under its ribs,
Where the pear-shaped balloon is floating aloft, (floating in it myself
    and looking composedly down,)   740
Where the life-car[72] is drawn on the slip-noose, where the heat hatches
    pale-green eggs in the dented sand,
Where the she-whale swims with her calf and never forsakes it,
Where the steam-ship trails hind-ways its long pennant of smoke,
Where the fin of the shark cuts like a black chip out of the water,
Where the half-burn'd brig[73] is riding on unknown currents,
Where shells grow to her slimy deck, where the dead are corrupting
    below;
Where the dense-starr'd flag is borne at the head of the regiments,
Approaching Manhattan up by the long-stretching island,
Under Niagara, the cataract[74] falling like a veil over my countenance,
Upon a door-step, upon the horse-block[75] of hard wood outside,   750
Upon the race-course, or enjoying picnics or jibs or a good game of
    baseball,
At he-festivals, with blackguard gibes, ironical license, bull-dances,[76]
    drinking, laughter,
At the cider-mill tasting the sweets of the brown mash, sucking the
    juice through a straw,
At apple-peelings wanting kisses for all the red fruit I find,
At musters,[77] beach-parties, friendly bees, huskings,[78] house-raisings;
Where the mocking-bird sounds his delicious gurgles, cackles, screams,
    weeps,
Where the hay-rick[79] stands in the barn-yard, where the dry-stalks are
    scatter'd, where the brood-cow waits in the hovel,
Where the bull advances to do his masculine work, where the stud to the
    mare, where the cock is treading the hen,
Where the heifers browse, where geese nip their food with short jerks,
Where sun-down shadows lengthen over the limitless and lonesome
    prairie,   760
Where herds of buffalo make a crawling spread of the square miles far
    and near,
Where the humming-bird shimmers, where the neck of the long-lived
    swan is curving and winding,

[72] A watertight "car" that moves on ropes, used to evacuate ships.
[73] A brigantine, or two-masted ship.   [74] Large waterfall.   [75] A step to aid in mounting horses.
[76] Country dances in which men danced with men, due to a shortage of women.
[77] Military assemblies or community gatherings.
[78] Social events for the completion of a labor-intensive task such as quilting or preserving; corn-husking.
[79] Hayracks, from which livestock eat hay.

Where the laughing-gull scoots by the shore, where she laughs her near-
  human laugh,
Where bee-hives range on a gray bench in the garden half hid by the high
  weeds,
Where band-neck'd partridges roost in a ring on the ground with their
  heads out,
Where burial coaches enter the arch'd gates of a cemetery,
Where winter wolves bark amid wastes of snow and icicled trees,
Where the yellow-crown'd heron comes to the edge of the marsh at night
  and feeds upon small crabs,
Where the splash of swimmers and divers cools the warm noon,
Where the katy-did works her chromatic reed[80] on the walnut-tree over
  the well,   770
Through patches of citrons[81] and cucumbers with silver-wired leaves,
Through the salt-lick or orange glade, or under conical firs,
Through the gymnasium, through the curtain'd saloon, through the
  office or public hall;
Pleas'd with the native and pleas'd with the foreign, pleas'd with the
  new and old,
Pleas'd with the homely woman as well as the handsome,
Pleas'd with the quakeress as she puts off her bonnet and talks
  melodiously,
Pleas'd with the tune of the choir of the whitewash'd church,
Pleas'd with the earnest words of the sweating Methodist preacher,
  impress'd seriously at the camp-meeting;
Looking in at the shop windows of Broadway the whole forenoon,
  flatting the flesh of my nose on the thick plate glass,
Wandering the same afternoon with my face turn'd up to the clouds, or
  down a lane or along the beach,   780
My right and left arms round the sides of two friends, and I in the
  middle;
Coming home with the silent and dark-cheek'd bush-boy, (behind me he
  rides at the drape[82] of the day,)
Far from the settlements studying the print of animals' feet, or the
  moccasin print,
By the cot in the hospital reaching lemonade to a feverish patient,
Nigh the coffin'd corpse when all is still, examining with a candle;
Voyaging to every port to dicker and adventure,
Hurrying with the modern crowd as eager and fickle as any,
Hot toward one I hate, ready in my madness to knife him,
Solitary at midnight in my back yard, my thoughts gone from me a
  long while,
Walking the old hills of Judæa with the beautiful gentle God by
  my side,   790
Speeding through space, speeding through heaven and the stars,
Speeding amid the seven satellites and the broad ring,[83] and the
  diameter of eighty thousand miles,

---

[80] Colorful harmony.   [81] An edible type of watermelon.   [82] Close.
[83] The seven planets then known and the rings of Saturn.

Speeding with tail'd meteors, throwing fire-balls like the rest,
Carrying the crescent child that carries its own full mother in its belly,[84]
Storming, enjoying, planning, loving, cautioning,
Backing and filling, appearing and disappearing,
I tread day and night such roads.

I visit the orchards of spheres and look at the product,
And look at quintillions[85] ripen'd and look at quintillions green.

I fly those flights of a fluid and swallowing soul,   800
My course runs below the soundings of plummets.

I help myself to material and immaterial,
No guard can shut me off, no law prevent me.

I anchor my ship for a little while only,
My messengers continually cruise away or bring their returns to me.

I go hunting polar furs and the seal, leaping chasms with a pike-pointed
    staff, clinging to topples[86] of brittle and blue.

I ascend to the foretruck,[87]
I take my place late at night in the crow's-nest,
We sail the arctic sea, it is plenty light enough,
Through the clear atmosphere I stretch around on the wonderful beauty,   810
The enormous masses of ice pass me and I pass them, the scenery is
    plain in all directions,
The white-topt mountains show in the distance, I fling out my fancies
    toward them,
We are approaching some great battle-field in which we are soon to be
    engaged,
We pass the colossal outposts of the encampment, we pass with still feet
    and caution,
Or we are entering by the suburbs some vast and ruin'd city,
The blocks and fallen architecture more than all the living cities of
    the globe.

I am a free companion, I bivouac by invading watchfires,
I turn the bridegroom out of bed and stay with the bride myself,
I tighten her all night to my thighs and lips.

My voice is the wife's voice, the screech by the rail of the stairs,   820
They fetch my man's body up dripping and drown'd.

I understand the large hearts of heroes,
The courage of present times and all times,

[84] A crescent moon, with the full moon palely visible.   [85] Many: one followed by eighteen zeros.
[86] Fallen, or "toppled" chunks of ice.   [87] The platform of a foremast.

How the skipper saw the crowded and rudderless wreck of the steam-
    ship, and Death chasing it up and down the storm,
How he knuckled tight and gave not back an inch, and was faithful of
    days and faithful of nights,
And chalk'd in large letters on a board, *Be of good cheer, we will not
    desert you;*
How he follow'd with them and tack'd with them three days and would
    not give it up,
How he saved the drifting company at last,
How the lank loose-gown'd women look'd when boated from the side of
    their prepared graves,
How the silent old-faced infants and the lifted sick, and the sharp-lipp'd
    unshaved men;   830
All this I swallow, it tastes good, I like it well, it becomes mine,
I am the man, I suffer'd, I was there.[88]

The disdain and calmness of martyrs,
The mother of old, condemn'd for a witch, burnt with dry wood, her
    children gazing on,
The hounded slave that flags in the race, leans by the fence, blowing,
    cover'd with sweat,
The twinges that sting like needles his legs and neck, the murderous
    buckshot and the bullets,
All these I feel or am.

I am the hounded slave, I wince at the bite of the dogs,
Hell and despair are upon me, crack and again crack the marksmen,
I clutch the rails of the fence, my gore dribs,[89] thinn'd with the ooze of
    my skin,   840
I fall on the weeds and stones,
The riders spur their unwilling horses, haul close,
Taunt my dizzy ears and beat me violently over the head with whip-
    stocks.

Agonies are one of my changes of garments,
I do not ask the wounded person how he feels, I myself become the
    wounded person,
My hurts turn livid upon me as I lean on a cane and observe.

I am the mash'd fireman with breast-bone broken,
Tumbling walls buried me in their debris,
Heat and smoke I inspired,[90] I heard the yelling shouts of my comrades,
I heard the distant click of their picks and shovels,   850
They have clear'd the beams away, they tenderly lift me forth.

I lie in the night air in my red shirt, the pervading hush is for my sake,
Painless after all I lie exhausted but not so unhappy,

---

[88] At the wreck of the *San Francisco*, caught in a storm only one day out from New York. The ship drifted in high seas from December 23, 1853 to January 5, 1854.
[89] Drips.   [90] Inhaled.

White and beautiful are the faces around me, the heads are bared of
    their fire-caps,
The kneeling crowd fades with the light of the torches.

Distant and dead resuscitate,
They show as the dial or move as the hands of me, I am the
    clock myself.

I am an old artillerist, I tell of my fort's bombardment,
I am there again.

Again the long roll of the drummers,   860
Again the attacking cannon, mortars,
Again to my listening ears the cannon responsive.

I take part, I see and hear the whole,
The cries, curses, roar, the plaudits for well-aim'd shots,
The ambulanza slowly passing trailing its red drip,
Workmen searching after damages, making indispensable repairs,
The fall of grenades through the rent roof, the fan-shaped explosion,
The whizz of limbs, heads, stone, wood, iron, high in the air.

Again gurgles the mouth of my dying general, he furiously waves with
    his hand,
He gasps through the clot *Mind not me—mind—the entrenchments.*   870

34

Now I tell what I knew in Texas in my early youth,
(I tell not the fall of Alamo,
Not one escaped to tell the fall of Alamo,
The hundred and fifty are dumb yet at Alamo,)
'Tis the tale of the murder in cold blood of four hundred and twelve
    young men.[91]

Retreating they had form'd in a hollow square with their baggage for
    breastworks,
Nine hundred lives out of the surrounding enemy's, nine times their
    number, was the price they took in advance,
Their colonel was wounded and their ammunition gone,
They treated for an honorable capitulation, receiv'd writing and seal,
    gave up their arms and march'd back prisoners of war.

They were the glory of the race of rangers,   880
Matchless with horse, rifle, song, supper, courtship,
Large, turbulent generous, handsome, proud, and affectionate,
Bearded, sunburnt, drest in the free costume of hunters,
Not a single one over thirty years of age.

---

[91] A massacre near what is now Goliad, Texas, in March 1836; Whitman had never been in Texas.

The second First-day morning they were brought out in squads and
    massacred, it was beautiful early summer,
The work commenced about five o'clock and was over by eight.

None obey'd the command to kneel,
Some made a mad and helpless rush, some stood stark and straight,
A few fell at once, shot in the temple or heart, the living and dead lay
    together,
The maim'd and mangled dug in the dirt, the new-comers saw
    them there,   890
Some half-kill'd attempted to crawl away,
These were despatch'd with bayonets or batter'd with the blunts of
    muskets,
A youth not seventeen years old seiz'd his assassin till two more came to
    release him,
The three were all torn and cover'd with the boy's blood.

At eleven o'clock began the burning of the bodies;
That is the tale of the murder of the four hundred and twelve young men.

35

Would you hear of an old-time-sea-fight?[92]
Would you learn who won by the light of the moon and stars?
List to the yarn, as my grandmother's father the sailor told it to me.

Our foe was no skulk in his ship I tell you, (said he,)   900
His was the surly English pluck, and there is no tougher or truer, and
    never was, and never will be;
Along the lower'd eve he came horribly raking[93] us.

We closed with him, the yards entangled, the cannon touch'd,
My captain lash'd fast[94] with his own hands.

We had receiv'd some eighteen pound shots under the water,
On our lower-gun-deck two large pieces had burst at the first fire, killing
    all around and blowing up overhead.

Fighting at sun-down, fighting at dark,
Ten o'clock at night, the full moon well up, our leaks on the gain, and
    five feet of water reported,[95]
The master-at-arms loosing the prisoners confined in the after-hold to
    give them a chance for themselves.

The transit to and from the magazine[96] is now stopt by the sentinels,   910
They see so many strange faces they do not know whom to trust.

---

[92] The sea battle between the American ship *Bonhomme Richard*, commanded by John Paul Jones, and the British ship *Serapis* on September 23, 1779; in this battle Jones uttered the famous words, "I have not yet begun to fight."
[93] Aiming heavy gunfire along the length of.   [94] Lashed the two ships fast to one another.
[95] Jones reported that the *Bonhomme Richard* took on five feet of water during the battle.
[96] Ammunition storeroom.

Our frigate takes fire,
The other asks if we demand quarter[97]?
If our colors are struck and the fighting done?[98]

Now I laugh content, for I hear the voice of my little captain,
We have not struck, he composedly cries, *we have just begun our*
    part of the fighting.

Only three guns are in use,
One is directed by the captain himself against the enemy's mainmast,
Two well serv'd with grape and canister[99] silence his musketry and
    clear his decks.

The tops[100] alone second the fire of this little battery, especially the
    main-top,   920
The hold out bravely during the whole of the action.

Not a moment's cease,
The leaks gain fast on the pumps, the fire eats toward the powder-
    magazine.

One of the pumps has been shot away, it is generally thought we are
    sinking.

Serene stands the little captain,
He is not hurried, his voice is neither high nor low,
His eyes give more light to us than our battle-lanterns.

Toward twelve there in the beams of the moon they surrender to us.

36

Stretch'd and still lies the midnight,
Two great hulls motionless on the breast of the darkness,   930
Our vessel riddled and slowly sinking, preparations to pass to the one
    we have conquer'd,
The captain on the quarter-deck coldly giving his orders through a
    countenance white as a sheet,
Near by the corpse of the child that serv'd in the cabin,
The dead face of an old salt with long white hair and carefully curl'd
    whiskers,
The flames spite of all that can be done flickering aloft and below,
The husky voices of the two or three officers yet fit for duty,
Formless stacks of bodies and bodies by themselves, dabs of flesh upon
    the masts and spars,
Cut of cordage, dangle of rigging, slight shock of the soothe of waves,
Black and impassive guns, litter of powder-parcels, strong scent,
A few large stars overhead, silent and mournful shining,   940

[97] Mercy.
[98] The British thought the Americans, whose flag had been shot away, were surrendering.
[99] Grape-size and smaller iron balls fired from the cannon.
[100] Marksmen firing from platforms on the ship's masts.

Delicate sniffs of sea-breeze, smells of sedgy grass and fields by the
    shore, death-messages given in charge to survivors,
The hiss of the surgeon's knife, the gnawing teeth of this saw,
Wheeze, cluck, swash of falling blood, short wild scream, and long,
    dull, tapering groan,
These so, these irretrievable.

37

You laggards there on guard! look to your arms!
In at the conquer'd doors they crowd! I am possess'd!
Embody all presences outlaw'd or suffering,
See myself in prison shaped like another man,
And feel the dull unintermitted pain.

For me the keepers of convicts shoulder their carbines and keep watch,   950
It is I let out in the morning and barr'd at night.

Not a mutineer walks handcuff'd to jail but I am handcuff'd to him and
    walk by his side,
(I am less the jolly one there, and more the silent one with sweat on my
    twitching lips.)

Not a youngster is taken for larceny but I go up too, and am tried and
    sentenced.

Not a cholera patient lies at the last gasp but I also lie at the last gasp,
My face is ash-color'd, my sinews gnarl, away from me people retreat.

Askers embody themselves in me and I am embodied in them,
I project my hat,[101] sit shame-faced, and beg.

38

Enough! enough! enough!
Somehow I have been stunn'd. Stand back!   960
Give me a little time beyond my cuff'd head, slumbers, dreams, gaping,
I discover myself on the verge of a usual mistake.

That I could forget the mockers and insults!
That I could forget the trickling tears and the blows of the bludgeons
    and hammers!
That I could look with a separate look on my own crucifixion and bloody
    crowning.

I remember now,
I resume the overstaid fraction,
The grave of rock multiplies what has been confided to it, or to any
    graves,
Corpses rise, gashes heal, fastenings roll from me.

[101] Extend my hat (as though to beg for money).

I troop forth replenish'd with supreme power, one of an average
    unending procession, 970
Inland and sea-coast we go, and pass all boundary lines,
Our swift ordinances on their way over the whole earth,
The blossoms we wear in our hats the growth of thousands of years.

Eleves,[102] I salute you! come forward!
Continue your annotations, continue your questionings.

39

The friendly and flowing savage, who is he?
Is he waiting for civilization, or past it and mastering it?

Is he some Southwesterner rais'd out-doors? is he Kanadian?
Is he from the Mississippi country? Iowa, Oregon, California?
The mountains? prairie-life, bush-life? or sailor from the sea? 980

Wherever he goes men and women accept and desire him,
They desire he should like them, touch them, speak to them, stay
    with them.

Behavior lawless as snow-flakes, words simple as grass, uncomb'd head,
    laughter, and naiveté,
Slow-stepping feet, common features, common modes and emanations,
They descend in new forms from the tips of his fingers,
They are wafted with the odor of his body or breath, they fly out of the
    glance of his eyes.

40

Flaunt of the sunshine I need not your bask—lie over!
You light surfaces only, I force surfaces and depths also.

Earth! you seem to look for something at my hands,
Say, old top-knot,[103] what do you want? 990

Man or woman, I might tell how I like you, but cannot,
And might tell what it is in me and what it is in you, but cannot,
And might tell that pining I have, that pulse of my nights and days.

Behold, I do not give lectures or a little charity,
When I give I give myself.

You there, impotent, loose in the knees,
Open your scarf'd chops[104] till I blow grit[105] within you,
Spread your palms and lift the flaps of your pockets,

---

[102] "Students" or "disciples" (French).
[103] "Indian": Certain tribes of Native Americans wore an ornament or tuft of hair on the top of the head.
[104] Lined and weathered jaws.   [105] Breathe courage.

I am not to be denied, I compel, I have stores plenty and to spare,
And any thing I have I bestow.   1000

I do not ask who you are, that is not important to me,
You can do nothing and be nothing but what I will infold you.

To cotton-field drudge or cleaner of privies I lean,
On his right cheek I put the family kiss,
And in my soul I swear I never will deny him.

On women fit for conception I start bigger and nimbler babes,
(This day I am jetting the stuff of far more arrogant republics.)

To any one dying, thither I speed and twist the knob of the door,
Turn the bed-clothes toward the foot of the bed,
Let the physician and the priest go home.   1010

I seize the descending man and raise him with resistless will,
O despairer, here is my neck,
By God, you shall not go down! hang your whole weight upon me.

I dilate you with tremendous breath, I buoy you up,
Every room of the house do I fill with an arm'd force,
Lovers of me, bafflers of graves.

Sleep—I and they keep guard all night,
Not doubt, not decease shall dare to lay finger upon you,
I have embraced you, and henceforth possess you to myself,
And when you rise in the morning you will find what I tell you is so.   1020

41

I am he bringing help for the sick as they pant on their backs,
And for strong upright men I bring yet more needed help.

I heard what was said of the universe,
Heard it and heard it of several thousand years;
It is middling well as far as it goes—but is that all?

Magnifying and applying come I,
Outbidding at the start the old cautious hucksters,
Taking myself the exact dimensions of Jehovah,[106]
Lithographing Kronos, Zeus his son, and Hercules his grandson,
Buying drafts of Osiris, Isis, Belus, Brahma, Buddha,   1030
In my portfolio placing Manito loose, Allah on a leaf, the crucifix
    engraved,

---

[106] The Judeo-Christian God.

With Odin and the hideous-faced Mexitli[107] and every idol and image,
Taking them all for what they are worth and not a cent more,
Admitting they were alive and did the work of their days,
(They bore mites as for unfledg'd birds who have now to rise and fly and
    sing for themselves,)
Accepting the rough deific sketches to fill out better in myself,
    bestowing them freely on each man and woman I see,
Discovering as much or more in a framer framing a house,
Putting higher claims for him there with his roll'd-up sleeves driving the
    mallet and chisel,
Not objecting to special revelations, considering a curl of smoke or a
    hair on the back of my hand just as curious as any revelation,
Lads ahold of fire-engines and hook-and-ladder ropes no less to me than
    the gods of the antique wars,   1040
Minding their voices peal through the crash of destruction,
Their brawny limbs passing safe over charr'd laths, their white foreheads
    whole and unhurt out of the flames;
By the mechanic's wife with her babe at her nipple interceding for every
    person born,
Three scythes at harvest whizzing in a row from three lusty angels with
    shirts bagg'd out at their waists,
The snag-tooth'd hostler[108] with red hair redeeming sins past and to
    come,
Selling all he possesses, traveling on foot to fee lawyers for his brother
    and sit by him while he is tried for forgery;
What was strewn in the amplest strewing the square rod about me, and
    not filling the square rod then,
The bull and the bug[109] never worshipp'd half enough,
Dung and dirt more admirable than was dream'd,
The supernatural of no account, myself waiting my time to be one of
    the supremes,   1050
The day getting ready for me when I shall do as much good as the best,
    and be as prodigious;
By my life-lumps![110] becoming already a creator,
Putting myself here and now to the ambush'd womb of the shadows.

42

A call in the midst of the crowd,
My own voice, orotund sweeping and final.

[107] The Titan, or giant god, Kronos (or Cronus) was the supreme god in Greek myth until he was
overthrown by his son Zeus; Hercules, the son of Zeus and Alcmene, was known for his strength;
Osiris and Isis, the Egyptian god and goddess of fertility; Belus, an Assyrian god-king; Brahma, the
supreme Hindu god; Buddha, Siddhartha Gautama (6th century B.C.), founder of Buddhism; Manito,
the Algonquian Indian god of nature; Allah, the Muslim God; Odin, the supreme Norse god; Mexitli,
an Aztec war god.
[108] Stableman.   [109] The bull was worshipped by Greeks, Egyptians, and Moslems; the beetle, by
Egyptians.
[110] Testicles.

Come my children,
Come my boys and girls, my women, household and intimates,
Now the performer launches his nerve, he has pass'd his prelude on the
    reeds within.

Easily written loose-finger'd chords—I feel the thrum of your climax
    and close.

My head slues round on my neck,   1060
Music rolls, but not from the organ,
Folks are around me, but they are no household of mind.

Ever the hard unsunk ground,
Ever the eaters and drinkers, ever the upward and downward sun, ever
    the air and the ceaseless tides,
Ever myself and my neighbors, refreshing, wicked, real,
Ever the old inexplicable query, ever that thorn'd thumb, that breath of
    itches and thirsts,
Ever the vexer's *hoot! hoot!* till we find where the sly one hides and
    bring him forth,
Ever love, ever the sobbing liquid of life,
Ever the bandage under the chin, ever the trestles[111] of death.

Here and there with dimes on the eyes walking,[112]   1070
To feed the greed of the belly the brains liberally spooning,
Tickets buying, taking, selling, but in to the feast never once going,
Many sweating, ploughing, thrashing, and then the chaff for payment
    receiving,
A few idly owning, and they the wheat continually claiming.

This is the city and I am one of the citizens,
Whatever interests the rest interests me, politics, wars, markets,
    newspapers, schools,
The mayor and councils, banks, tariffs, steamships, factories, stocks,
    stores, real estate and personal estate.

The little plentiful manikins skipping around in collars and tail'd coats,
I am aware who they are, (they are positively not worms or fleas,)
I acknowledge the duplicates of myself, the weakest and shallowest is
    deathless with me,   1080
What I do and say the same waits for them,
Every thought that flounders in me the same flounders in them.

I know perfectly well my own egotism,
Know my omnivorous lines and must not write any less,
And would fetch you whoever you are flush with myself.

---

[111] Sawhorses or other supports for a coffin.
[112] Coins placed on the eyes of the dead; also, the greedy.

Not words of routine this song of mine,
But abruptly to question, to leap beyond yet nearer bring;
This printed and bound book—but the printer and the printing-office
   boy?
The well-taken photographs—but your wife or friend close and solid in
   your arms?
The black ship mail'd with iron, her mighty guns in her turrets—but the
   pluck of the captain and engineers?   1090
In the houses the dishes and fare and furniture—but the host and hostess,
   and the look out of their eyes?
The sky up there—yet here or next door, or across the way?
The saints and sages in history—but you yourself?
Sermons, creeds, theology—but the fathomless human brain,
And what is reason? and what is love? and what is life?

                                  43
I do not despise you priests, all time, the world over,
My faith is the greatest of faiths and the least of faiths,
Enclosing worship ancient and modern and all between ancient and
   modern,
Believing I shall come again upon the earth after five thousand years,
Waiting responses from oracles, honoring the gods, saluting the sun,   1100
Making a fetich[113] of the first rock or stump, powowing with sticks in the
   circle of obis,[114]
Helping the llama or brahmin[115] as he trims the lamps of the idols,
Dancing yet through the streets in a phallic procession, rapt and austere
   in the woods a gymnosophist,[116]
Drinking mead[117] from the skull-cup, to Shastas and Vedas[118] admirant,
   minding the Koran,
Walking the teokallis,[119] spotted with gore from the stone and knife,
   beating the serpent-skin drum,
Accepting the Gospels, accepting him that was crucified, knowing
   assuredly that he is divine,
To the mass kneeling or the puritan's prayer rising, or sitting patiently in
   a pew,
Ranting and frothing in my insane crisis, or waiting dead-like till my
   spirit arouses me,
Looking forth on pavement and land, or outside of pavement and land,
Belonging to the winders of the circuit of circuits.   1110

One of that centripetal and centrifugal gang I turn and talk like a man
   leaving charges before a journey.

---

[113] A fetish, or primitive object of worship.   [114] Charms used in sorcery, of African origin.
[115] Lama (or Tibetan high priest) or member of the highest Hindu caste.
[116] Member of an ascetic Hindu sect.
[117] An alcoholic beverage made from fermented honey and water.
[118] Books of Hindu law (Shastras) and Hindu sacred writings, respectively.
[119] An Aztec temple where human sacrifice was conducted.

Down-hearted doubters dull and excluded,
Frivolous, sullen, moping, angry, affected, dishearten'd, atheistical,
I know every one of you, I know the sea of torment, doubt, despair and
    unbelief.

How the flukes splash!
How they contort rapid as lightning, with spasms and spouts of blood!

Be at peace bloody flukes[120] of doubters and sullen mopers,
I take my place among you as much as among any,
The past is the push of you, me, all, precisely the same,
And what is yet untried and afterward is for you, me, all, precisely
    the same.   1120

I do not know what is untried and afterward,
But I know it will in its turn prove sufficient, and cannot fail.

Each who passes is consider'd, each who stops is consider'd, not a single
    one can it fail.

It cannot fail the young man who died and was buried,
Nor the young woman who died and was put by his side,
Nor the little child that peep'd in at the door, and then drew back and
    was never seen again,
Nor the old man who has lived without purpose, and feels it with
    bitterness worse than gall,
Nor him in the poor house tubercled by rum and the bad disorder,[121]
Nor the numberless slaughter'd and wreck'd, nor the brutish koboo
    call'd the ordure[122] of humanity,
Nor the sacs merely floating with open mouths for food to slip in,   1130
Nor any thing in the earth, or down in the oldest graves of the earth,
Nor any thing in the myriads of spheres, nor the myriads of myriads that
    inhabit them,
Nor the present, nor the least wisp that is known.

44

It is time to explain myself—let us stand up.

What is known I strip away,
I launch all men and women forward with me into the Unknown.

The clock indicates the moment—but what does eternity indicate?

We have thus far exhausted trillions of winters and summers,
There are trillions ahead, and trillions ahead of them.

Births have brought us richness and variety,   1140
And other births will bring us richness and variety.

---

[120] The tail fins of stricken whales.   [121] Syphilis.   [122] Native of Sumatra; excrement.

I do not call one greater and one smaller,
That which fills its period and place is equal to any.

Were mankind murderous or jealous upon you, my brother, my sister?
I am sorry for you, they are not murderous or jealous upon me,
All has been gentle with me, I keep no account with lamentation,
(What have I to do with lamentation?)

I am an acme of things accomplish'd, and I am encloser of things to be.

My feet strike an apex of the apices of the stairs,
On every step bunches of ages, and larger bunches between the steps,   1150
All below duly travel'd, and still I mount and mount.

Rise after rise bow the phantoms behind me,
Afar down I see the huge first Nothing, I know I was even there,
I waited unseen and always, and slept through the lethargic mist,
And took my time, and took no hurt from the fetid carbon.

Long I was hugg'd close—long and long.

Immense have been the preparations for me,
Faithful and friendly the arms that have help'd me.

Cycles ferried my cradle, rowing and rowing like cheerful boatmen,
For room to me stars kept aside in their own rings,   1160
They sent influences to look after what was to hold me.

Before I was born out of my mother generations guided me,
My embryo has never been torpid, nothing could overlay it.

For it the nebula cohered to an orb,
The long slow strata piled to rest it on,
Vast vegetables gave it sustenance,
Monstrous sauroids[123] transported it in their mouths and deposited it
    with care.

All forces have been steadily employ'd to complete and delight me,
Now on this spot I stand with my robust soul.

45

O span of youth! ever-push'd elasticity!
O manhood, balanced, florid and full.   1170

My lovers suffocate me,
Crowding my lips, thick in the pores of my skin,
Jostling me through streets and public halls, coming naked to me at
    night,

---

[123] Lizardlike reptiles; here, dinosaurs.

Crying by day *Ahoy!* from the rocks of the river, swinging and chirping
    over my head,
Calling my name from flower-beds, vines, tangled underbrush,
Lighting on every moment of my life,
Bussing[124] my body with soft balsamic busses,
Noiselessly passing handfuls out of their hearts and giving them to
    be mine.

Old age superbly rising! O welcome, ineffable grace of dying days!   1180

Every condition promulges[125] not only itself, it promulges what grows
    after and out of itself,
And the dark hush promulges as much as any.

I open my scuttle[126] at night and see the far-sprinkled systems,
And all I see multiplied as high as I can cipher edge but the rim of the
    farther systems.

Wider and wider they spread, expanding, always expanding,
Outward and outward and forever outward.

My sun has his sun and round him obediently wheels,
He joins with his partners a group of superior circuit,
And greater sets follow, making specks of the greatest inside them.

There is no stoppage and never can be stoppage,   1190
If I, you, and the worlds, and all beneath or upon their surfaces, were
    this moment reduced back to a pallid float,[127] it would not avail in
    the long run,
We should surely bring up again where we now stand,
And surely go as much farther, and then farther and farther.

A few quadrillions of eras, a few octillions[128] of cubic leagues, do not
    hazard the span or make it impatient,
They are but parts, any thing is but a part.

See ever so far, there is limitless space outside of that,
Count ever so much, there is limitless time around that.

My rendezvous is appointed, it is certain,
The Lord will be there and wait till I come on perfect terms,
The great Camerado,[129] the lover true for whom I pine will be there.   1200

46

I know I have the best of time and space, and was never measured and
    never will be measured.

---

[124] Kissing.
[125] Promulgates or publicly advocates.   [126] Roof hatch.   [127] Returned to a primordial soup.
[128] One followed by twenty-seven zeros.   [129] Comrade.

I tramp a perpetual journey, (come listen all!)
My signs are a rain-proof coat, good shoes, and a staff cut from the
    woods,
No friend of mine takes his ease in my chair,
I have no chair, no church, no philosophy,
I lead no man to a dinner-table, library, exchange,[130]
But each man and each woman of you I lead upon a knoll,
My left hand hooking you round the waist,
My right hand pointing to landscapes of continents and the public road.

Not I, not any one else can travel that road for you,   1210
You must travel it for yourself.
It is not far, it is within reach,
Perhaps you have been on it since you were born and did not know,
Perhaps it is everywhere on water and on land.

Shoulder your duds dear son, and I will mine, and let us hasten forth,
Wonderful cities and free nations we shall fetch[131] as we go.

If you tire, give me both burdens, and rest the chuff[132] of your hand on
    my hip,
And in due time you shall repay the same service to me,
For after we start we never lie by again.

This day before dawn I ascended a hill and look'd at the crowded
    heaven,   1220
And I said to my spirit *When we become the enfolders of those orbs,
    and the pleasure and knowledge of every thing in them, shall we be
    fill'd and satisfied then?*
And my spirit said *No, we but level that lift*[133] *to pass and continue
    beyond.*

You are also asking me questions and I hear you,
I answer that I cannot answer, you must find out for yourself.

Sit a while dear son,
Here are biscuits to eat and here is milk to drink,
But as soon as you sleep and renew yourself in sweet clothes, I kiss you
    with a good-by kiss and open the gate for your egress hence.

Long enough have you dream'd contemptible dreams,
Now I wash the gum from your eyes,
You must habit yourself to the dazzle of the light and of every moment
    of your life.   1230

Long have you timidly waded holding a plank by the shore,
Now I will you to be a bold swimmer,

---

[130] Stock exchange.   [131] Reach.   [132] The fleshy part of the palm.   [133] Elevation.

To jump off in the midst of the sea, rise again, nod to me, shout, and
    laughingly dash with your hair.

47

I am the teacher of athletes,
He that by me spreads a wider breast than my own proves the width of
    my own,
He most honors my style who learns under it to destroy the teacher.

The boy I love, the same becomes a man not through derived power, but
    in his own right,
Wicked rather than virtuous out of conformity or fear,
Fond of his sweetheart, relishing well his steak,
Unrequited love or a slight cutting him worse than sharp steel cuts,   1240
First-rate to ride, to fight, to hit the bull's eye, to sail a skiff, to sing a
    song or play on the banjo,
Preferring scars and the beard and faces pitted with small-pox over all
    latherers,
And those well-tann'd to those that keep out of the sun.

I teach straying from me, yet who can stray from me?
I follow you whoever you are from the present hour,
My words itch at your ears till you understand them.

I do not say these things for a dollar or to fill up the time while I wait
    for a boat,
(It is you talking just as much as myself, I act as the tongue of you,
Tied in your mouth, in mine it begins to be loosen'd.)

I swear I will never again mention love or death inside a house,   1250
And I swear I will never translate myself at all, only to him or her who
    privately stays with me in the open air.

If you would understand me go to the heights or water-shore,
The nearest gnat is an explanation, and a drop or motion of waves a key,
The maul, the oar, the hand-saw, second my words.

No shutter'd room or school can commune with me,
But roughs and little children better than they.

The young mechanic is closest to me, he knows me well,
The woodman that takes his axe and jug with him shall take me with him
    all day,
The farm-boy ploughing in the field feels good at the sound of my voice,
In vessels that sail my words sail, I go with fishermen and seamen and
    love them.   1260

The soldier camp'd or upon the march is mine,
On the night ere the pending battle many seek me, and I do not fail them,
On that solemn night (it may be their last) those that know me seek me.

My face rubs to the hunter's face when he lies down alone in his blanket,
The driver thinking of me does not mind the jolt of his wagon,
The young mother and old mother comprehend me,
The girl and the wife rest the needle a moment and forget where they are,
They and all would resume what I have told them.

48

I have said that the soul is not more than the body,
And I have said that the body is not more than the soul,   1270
And nothing, not God, is greater to one than one's self is,
And whoever walks a furlong without sympathy walks to his own funeral
    drest in his shroud,
And I or you pocketless of a dime may purchase the pick of the earth,
And to glance with an eye or show a bean in its pod confounds the
    learning of all times,
And there is no trade or employment but the young man following it
    may become a hero,
And there is no object so soft but it makes a hub for the wheel'd
    universe,
And I say to any man or woman, Let your soul stand cool and composed
    before a million universes.

And I say to mankind, Be not curious about God,
For I who am curious about each am not curious about God,
(No array of terms can say how much I am at peace about God
    and about death.)   1280

I hear and behold God in every object, yet understand God not in the
    least,
Nor do I understand who there can be more wonderful than myself.

Why should I wish to see God better than this day?
I see something of God each hour of the twenty-four, and each moment
    then,
In the faces of men and women I see God, and in my own face in the
    glass,
I find letters from God dropt in the street, and every one is sign'd by
    God's name,
And I leave them where they are, for I know that wheresoe'er I go,
Others will punctually come for ever and ever.

49

And as to you Death, and you bitter hug of mortality, it is idle to try to
    alarm me.

To his work without flinching the accoucheur[134] comes,   1290
I see the elder-hand pressing receiving supporting,

---

[134] Midwife or obstetrician.

I recline by the sills of the exquisite flexible doors,
And mark the outlet, and mark the relief and escape.

And as to you Corpse I think you are good manure, but that does not
    offend me,
I smell the white roses sweet-scented and growing,
I reach to the leafy lips, I reach to the polish'd breasts of melons.

And as to you Life I reckon you are the leavings of many deaths,
(No doubt I have died myself ten thousand times before.)

I hear you whispering there O stars of heaven,
O suns—O grass of graves—O perpetual transfers and promotions,   1300
If you do not say any thing how can I say any thing?

Of the turbid pool that lies in the autumn forest,
Of the moon that descends the steeps of the soughing[135] twilight,
Toss, sparkles of day and dusk—toss on the black stems that decay in
    the muck,
Toss to the moaning gibberish of the dry limbs.

I ascend from the moon, I ascend from the night,
I perceive that the ghastly glimmer is noonday sunbeams reflected,
And debouch[136] to the steady and central from the offspring great
    or small.

50
There is that in me—I do not know what it is—but I know it is in me.

Wrench'd and sweaty—calm and cool then my body becomes,   1310
I sleep—I sleep long.

I do not know it—it is without name—it is a word unsaid,
It is not in any dictionary, utterance, symbol.

Something it swings on more than the earth I swing on,
To it the creation is the friend whose embracing awakes me.

Perhaps I might tell more. Outlines! I plead for my brothers and sisters.

Do you see O my brothers and sisters?
It is not chaos or death—it is form, union, plan—it is eternal life—it
    is Happiness.

51
The past and present wilt—I have fill'd them, emptied them,
And proceed to fill my next fold of the future.   1320

---

[135] Murmuring.   [136] Emerge, or flow outward from a narrow place into open country.

Listener up there! what have you to confide to me?
Look in my face while I snuff the sidle of evening,[137]
(Talk honestly, no one else hears you, and I stay only a minute longer.)

Do I contradict myself?
Very well then I contradict myself,
(I am large, I contain multitudes.)

I concentrate toward them that are nigh, I wait on the door-slab.

Who has done his day's work? who will soonest be through with his
    supper?
Who wishes to walk with me?

Will you speak before I am gone? will you prove already too late?   1330

52

The spotten hawk swoops by and accuses me, he complains of my gab
    and my loitering.

I too am not a bit tamed, I too am untranslatable,
I sound my barbaric yawp over the roofs of the world.

The last scud[138] of day holds back for me,
It flings my likeness after the rest and true as any on the
    shadow'd wilds,
It coaxes me to the vapor and the dusk.

I depart as air, I shake my white locks at the runaway sun,
I effuse[139] my flesh in eddies, and drift it in lacy jags.

I bequeath myself to the dirt to grow from the grass I love,
If you want me again look for me under your boot-soles.   1340

You will hardly know who I am or what I mean,
But I shall be good health to you nevertheless,
And filter and fibre your blood.

Failing to fetch me at first keep encouraged,
Missing me one place search another,
I stop somewhere waiting for you.

1855

---

[137] The fading twilight.   [138] Mist.   [139] Pour forth.

from CHILDREN OF ADAM*

FROM PENT-UP ACHING RIVERS[1]

From pent-up aching rivers,
From that of myself without which I were nothing,
From what I am determin'd to make illustrious, even if I stand
    sole among men,
From my own voice resonant, singing the phallus,
Singing the song of procreation,
Singing the need of superb children and therein superb grown people,
Singing the muscular urge and the blending,
Singing the bedfellow's song, (O resistless yearning!
O for any and each the body correlative attracting!
O for you whoever you are your correlative body! O it, more than
    all else, you delighting!)   10
From the hungry gnaw that eats me night and day,
From native moments, from bashful pains, singing them,
Seeking something yet unfound though I have diligently sought it
    many a long year,
Singing the true song of the soul fitful at random,
Renascent with grossest Nature or among animals,
Of that, of them and what goes with them my poems informing,
Of the smell of apples and lemons, of the pairing of birds,
Of the wet of woods, of the lapping of waves,
Of the mad pushes of waves upon the land, I them chanting,
The overture lighty sounding, the strain anticipating,   20
The welcome nearness, the sight of the perfect body,
The swimmer swimming naked in the bath, or motionless on his
    back lying and floating,
The female form approaching, I pensive, love-flesh tremulous aching,
The divine list for myself or you or for any one making,
The face, the limbs, the index from head to foot, and what it arouses,
The mystic deliria, the madness amorous, the utter abandonment,
(Hark close and still what I now whisper to you,
I love you, O you entirely possess me,
O that you and I escape from the rest and go utterly off, free and lawless,
Two hawks in the air, two fishes swimming in the sea not more
    lawless than we;)   30
The furious storm through me careering, I passionately trembling,
The oath of the inseparableness of two together, of the woman that
    loves me and whom I love more than my life, that oath swearing,
(O I willingly stake all for you,
O let me be lost if it must be so!

---

* Fifteen poems were included in the group "Enfans d'Adam" in the 1860 edition of *Leaves of Grass;* by 1871 sixteen poems comprised "Children of Adam."
[1] Originally untitled; first appeared with this title in the 1867 edition of *Leaves of Grass.*

O you and I! what is it to us what the rest do or think?
What is all else to us? only that we enjoy each other and exhaust
    each other if it must be so;)
From the master, the pilot I yield the vessel to,
The general commanding me, commanding all, from him permission
    taking,
From time the programme hastening, (I have loiter'd too long as it is,)
From sex, from the warp and from the woof,[2]   40
From privacy, from frequent repinings alone,
From plenty of persons near and yet the right person not near,
From the soft sliding of hands over me and thrusting of fingers
    through my hair and beard,
From the long sustain'd kiss upon the mouth or bosom,
From the close pressure that makes me or any man drunk, fainting
    with excess,
From what the divine husband knows, from the work of fatherhood,
From exultation, victory and relief, from the bedfellow's embrace
    in the night,
From the act-poems of eyes, hands, hips and bosoms,
From the cling of the trembling arm,
From the bending curve and the clinch,   50
From side by side the pliant coverlet off-throwing,
From the one so unwilling to have me leave, and me just as unwilling
    to leave,
(Yet a moment O tender waiter, and I return,)
From the hour of shining stars and dropping dews,
From the night a moment I emerging flitting out,
Celebrate you act divine and you children prepared for,
And you stalwart loins.

                                                1860

ONCE I PASS'D THROUGH A POPULOUS CITY

Once I pass'd through a populous city imprinting my brain for future
    use with its shows, architecture, customs, traditions,
Yet now of all that city I remember only a woman I casually met
    there who detain'd me for love of me,
Day by day and night by night we were together—all else has
    long been forgotten by me,
I remember I say only that woman who passionately clung to me,
Again we wander, we love, we separate again,
Again she holds me by the hand, I must not go.
I see her close beside me with silent lips sad and tremulous.

                                              1860

---

[2] From the lengthwise threads in fabric and from the threads woven horizontally between them.

FACING WEST FROM CALIFORNIA'S SHORES*

Facing west from California's shores,
Inquiring, tireless, seeking what is yet unfound.
I, a child, very old, over waves, towards the house of maternity,[1]
   the land of migrations, look afar,
Look off the shores of my Western sea, the circle almost circled;
For starting westward from Hindustan,[2] from the vales of Kashmere,[3]
From Asia, from the north, from the God, the sage, and the hero,
From the south, from the flowery peninsulas and the spice islands,[4]
Long having wander'd since, round the earth having wander'd
Now I face home again, very pleas'd and joyous,
(But where is what I started for so long ago?
And why is it yet unfound?)

1860

AS ADAM EARLY IN THE MORNING

As Adam early in the morning,
Walking forth from the bower refresh'd with sleep,
Behold me where I pass, hear my voice, approach,
Touch me, touch the palm of your hand to my body as I pass,
Be not afraid of my body.

1861

from   CALAMUS†

IN PATHS UNTRODDEN[1]

In paths untrodden,
In the growth by margins of pond-waters,
Escaped from the life that exhibits itself,
From all the standards hitherto publish'd, from the pleasure,
   profits, conformities,
Which too long I was offering to feed my soul,
Clear to me now standards not yet publish'd, clear to me that my soul,

---

* Originally untitled; first appeared with this title in the 1867 edition of *Leaves of Grass*.
[1] Asia, believed to be the birthplace of civilization.   [2] India.
[3] Kashmire, a mountainous region adjacent to India, Pakistan, and Tibet.   [4] Indonesia.
† Forty-five poems were included in this group in the 1860 edition of *Leaves of Grass;* by the 1881 edition, there were thirty-nine. Whitman defined calamus as "the very large & aromatic grass, or rush, growing about water-ponds in the valleys—spears about three feet high—often called 'sweet flag'—grows all over the Northern and Middle States. . . . "
[1] First appeared with this title in the 1867 edition of *Leaves of Grass*.

Here by myself away from the clank of the world,
Tallying and talk'd to here by tongues aromatic,
No longer abash'd, (for in this secluded spot I can respond as I
    would not dare elsewhere,)   10
Strong upon me the life that does not exhibit itself, yet contains
    all the rest,
Resolv'd to sing no songs to-day but those of manly attachment,
Projecting them along that substantial life,
Bequeathing hence types of athletic love,
Afternoon this delicious Ninth-month in my forty-first year,[2]
I proceed for all who are or have been young men,
To tell the secret of my nights and days,
To celebrate the need of comrades.

1860

RECORDERS AGES HENCE*

Recorders ages hence,
Come, I will take you down underneath this impassive[1] exterior, I
    will tell you what to say to me,
Publish my name and hang up my picture as that of the tenderest lover,
The friend the lover's portrait, of whom his friend his lover was fondest,
Who was not proud of his songs, but of the measureless ocean of
    love within him, and freely pour'd it forth,
Who often walk'd lonesome walks thinking of his dear friends,
    his lovers,
Who pensive away from one he lov'd often lay sleepless and
    dissatisfied at night,
Who knew too well the sick, sick dread lest the one he lov'd
    might secretly be indifferent to him,
Whose happiest days were far away through fields, in woods, on
    hills, he and another wandering hand in hand, they twain
    apart from other men,
Who oft as he saunter'd the streets curv'd with his arm the shoulder
    of his friend, while the arm of his friend rested upon him also.   10

1860

I SAW IN LOUISIANA A LIVE-OAK GROWING†

I saw in Louisiana a live-oak growing,
All alone stood it and the moss hung down from the branches,
Without any companion it grew there uttering joyous leaves of
    dark greed,

---

[2] September 1859, from the Quaker numerical designations for months.
* First appeared with this title in 1867.   [1] Unemotional.
† First appeared with this title in the 1867 edition of *Leaves of Grass*.

And its look, rude, unbending, lusty, made me think of myself,
But I wonder'd how it could utter joyous leaves standing alone
   there without its friend near, for I knew I could not,
And I broke off a twig with a certain number of leaves upon it,
   and twined around it a little moss,
And brought it away, and I have placed it in sight in my room,
It is not needed to remind me as of my own dear friends,
(For I believe lately I think of little else than of them,)
Yet it remains to me a curious token, it makes me think of manly love;   10
For all that, and though the live-oak glistens there in Louisiana
   solitary in a wide flat space,
Uttering joyous leaves all its life without a friend a lover near,
I know very well I could not.

                                           1860

I HEAR IT WAS CHARGED AGAINST ME*

I hear it was charged against me that I sought to destroy institutions,
But really I am neither for nor against institutions,
(What indeed have I in common with them? or what with the
   destruction of them?)
Only I will establish in the Mannahatta and in every city of these
   States inland and seaboard,
And in the fields and woods, and above every keel little or large
   that dents the water,
Without edifices or rules or trustees or any argument,
The institution of the dear love of comrades.

                                           1860

HERE THE FRAILEST LEAVES OF ME**

Here the frailest leaves of me and yet my strongest lasting,
Here I shade and hide my thoughts, I myself do not expose them,
And yet they expose me more than all my other poems.

                                         1860

FULL OF LIFE NOW†

Full of life now, compact, visible,
I, forty years old the eighty-third year of the States,

---

* First appeared with this title in the 1867 edition of *Leaves of Grass.*
** First appeared with this title in the 1867 edition of *Leaves of Grass.*
† First appeared with this title in the 1867 edition of *Leaves of Grass.*

To one a century hence or any number of centuries hence,
To you yet unborn these, seeking you.

When you read these I that was visible am become invisible,
Now it is you, compact, visible, realizing my poems, seeking me,
Fancying how happy you were if I could be with you and become
  your comrade;
Be it as if I were with you. (Be not too certain but I am now with you.)

1857, 1860

CROSSING BROOKLYN FERRY*

I

Flood-tide below me! I see you face to face!
Clouds of the west—sun there half an hour high—I see you
  also face to face.

Crowds of men and women attired in the usual costumes, how
  curious you are to me!
On the ferry-boats the hundreds and hundreds that cross, returning
  home, are more curious to me than you suppose,
And you that shall cross from shore to shore years hence are more
  to me, and more in my meditations, than you might suppose.

2

The impalpable sustenance of me from all things at all hours of
  the day,
The simple, compact, well-join'd scheme, myself disintegrated,
  every one disintegrated yet part of the scheme,
The similitudes of the past and those of the future,
The glories strung like beads on my smallest sights and hearings,
  on the walk in the street and the passage over the river,
The current rushing so swiftly and swimming with me far away,   10
The others that are to follow me, the ties between me and them,
The certainty of others, the life, love, sight, hearing of others.

Others will enter the gates of the ferry and cross from shore to shore,
Others will watch the run of the flood-tide,
Others will see the shipping of Manhattan north and west, and the
  heights of Brooklyn to the south and east,
Others will see the islands large and small;
Fifty years hence, others will see them as they cross, the sun half
  an hour high,
A hundred years hence, or ever so many hundred years hence,
  others will see them,

---

* Titled "Sun-Down Poem" in the 1856 edition of *Leaves of Grass;* first appeared with this title in the
1860 edition.

Will enjoy the sunset, the pouring-in of the flood-tide, the falling-
   back to the sea of the ebb-tide.

3

It avails not, time nor place—distance avails not,   20
I am with you, you men and women of a generation, or ever so
   many generations hence,
Just as you feel when you look on the river and sky, so I felt,
Just as any of you is one of a living crowd, I was one of a crowd,
Just as you are refresh'd by the gladness of the river and the bright
   flow, I was refresh'd,
Just as you stand and lean on the rail, yet hurry with the swift
   current, I stood yet was hurried,
Just as you look on the numberless masts of ships and the thick-
   stemm'd pipes of steamboats, I look'd.

I too many and many a time cross'd the river of old,
Watched the Twelfth-month[1] sea-gulls, saw them high in the air
   floating with motionless wings, oscillating their bodies,
Saw how the glistening yellow lit up parts of their bodies and left the
   rest in strong shadow,
Saw the slow-wheeling circles and the gradual edging toward the south,   30
Saw the reflection of the summer sky in the water,
Had my eyes dazzled by the shimmering track of beams,
Look'd at the fine centrifugal spokes of light round the shape of my
   head in the sunlit water,
Look'd on the haze on the hills southward and south-westward,
Look'd on the vapor as it flew in fleeces tinged with violet,
Look'd toward the lower bay to notice the vessels arriving,
Saw their approach, saw aboard those that were near me,
Saw the white sails of schooners and sloops, saw the ships at anchor,
The sailors at work in the rigging or out astride the spars,
The round masts, the swinging motion of the hulls, the slender
   serpentine pennants,   40
The large and small steamers in motion, the pilots in their pilot-
   houses,
The white wake left by the passage, the quick tremulous whirl of
   the wheels,
The flags of all nations, the falling of them at sunset,
The scallop-edged waves in the twilight, the ladled cups, the
   frolicsome crests and glistening,
The stretch afar growing dimmer and dimmer, the gray walls of
   the granite storehouses by the docks,
On the river the shadowy group, the big steam-tug closely flank'd
   on each side by the barges, the hay-boat, the belated lighter,[2]
On the neighboring shore the fires from the foundry chimneys
   burning high and glaringly into the night,
Casting their flicker of black contrasted with wild red and yellow light
   over the tops of houses, and down into the clefts of streets.

[1] December, from the Quaker numerical designations for months.
[2] A barge used to load or to lighten (unload) cargo ships.

4

These and all else were to me the same as they are to you,
I loved well those cities, loved well the stately and rapid river,   50
The men and women I saw were all near to me,
Others the same—others who look back on me because I look'd
    forward to them,
(The time will come, though I stop here to-day and to-night.)

5

What is it then between us?
What is the count of the scores or hundreds of years between us?

Whatever it is, it avails not—distance avails not, and place avails not,
I too lived, Brooklyn of ample hills was mine,
I too walk'd the streets of Manhattan island, and bathed in the waters
    around it,
I too felt the curious abrupt questionings stir within me,
In the day among crowds of people sometimes they came upon me,   60
In my walks home late at night or as I lay in my bed they came upon me,
I too had been struck from the float forever held in solution,
I too had receiv'd identity by my body,
That I was I knew was of my body, and what I should be I knew I
    should be of my body.

6

It is not upon you alone the dark patches fall,
The dark threw its patches down upon me also,
The best I had done seem'd to me blank and suspicious,
My great thoughts as I supposed them, were they not in reality meagre?
Nor is it you alone who know what it is to be evil,
I am he who knew what it was to be evil,   70
I too knitted the old knot of contrariety,
Blabb'd, blush'd, resented, lied, stole, grudg'd,
Had guile, anger, lust, hot wishes I dared not speak,
Was wayward, vain, greedy, shallow, sly, cowardly, malignant,
The wolf, the snake, the hog, not wanting[3] in me,
The cheating look, the frivolous word, the adulterous wish, not
    wanting,
Refusals, hates, postponements, meanness, laziness, none of these
    wanting,
Was one with the rest, the days, and haps[4] of the rest,
Was call'd by my nighest[5] name by clear loud voices of young men
    as they saw me approaching or passing,
Felt their arms on my neck as I stood, or the negligent leaning of
    their flesh against me as I sat,   80
Saw many I loved in the street or ferry-boat or public assembly, yet
    never told them a word,
Lived the same life with the rest, the same old laughing, gnawing,
    sleeping,

---

[3] Lacking.   [4] Chance happenings.   [5] Nearest, most familiar.

Play'd the part that still looks back on the actor or actress,
The same old role, the role that is what we make it, as great as we like,
Or as small as we like, or both great and small.

7

Closer yet I approach you,
What thought you have of me now, I had as much of you—I laid in
    my stores in advance,
I consider'd long and seriously of you before you were born.

Who was to know what should come home to me?
Who knows but I am enjoying this?   90
Who knows, for all the distance, but I am as good as looking at
    you now, for all you cannot see me?

8

Ah, what can ever be more stately and admirable to me than mast-
    hemm'd Manhattan?
River and sunset and scallop-edg'd waves of flood-tide?
The sea-gulls oscillating their bodies, the hay-boat in the twilight,
    and the belated lighter?
What gods can exceed these that clasp me by the hand, and with
    voices I love call me promptly and loudly by my nighest
    name as I approach?
What is more subtle than this which ties me to the woman or man that
    looks in my face?
Which fuses me into you now, and pours my meaning into you?

We understand then do we not?
What I promis'd without mentioning it, have you not accepted?
What the study could not teach—what the preaching could not
    accomplish is accomplish'd, is it not?   100

9

Flow on, river! flow with the flood-tide, and ebb with the ebb-tide!
Frolic on, crested and scallop-edg'd waves!
Gorgeous clouds of the sunset! drench with your splendor me, or the
    men and women generations after me!
Cross from shore to shore, countless crowds of passengers!
Stand up, tall masts of Mannahatta! stand up, beautiful hills of Brooklyn!
Throb, baffled and curious brain! throw out questions and answers!
Suspend here and everywhere, eternal float of solution!
Gaze, loving and thirsting eyes, in the house or street or public
    assembly!
Sound out, voices of young men! loudly and musically call me by
    my nighest name!
Live, old life! play the part that looks back on the actor or actress!   110
Play the old role, the role that is great or small according as one
    makes it!
Consider, you who peruse me, whether I may not in unknown ways
    be looking upon you;

Be firm, rail over the river, to support those who lean idly, yet
   haste with the hasting current;
Fly on, sea-birds! fly sideways, or wheel in large circles high in
   the air;
Receive the summer sky, you water, and faithfully hold it till all
   downcast eyes have time to take it from you!
Diverge, fine spokes of light, from the shape of my head, or any
   one's head, in the sunlit water!
Come on, ships from the lower bay! pass up or down, white-sail'd
   schooners, sloops, lighters!
Flaunt away, flags of all nations! be duly lower'd at sunset!
Burn high your fires, foundry chimneys! cast black shadows at
   nightfall! cast red and yellow light over the tops of the
   houses!
Appearances, now or henceforth, indicate what you are,   120
You necessary film, continue to envelop the soul,
About my body for me, and your body for you, be hung our
   divinest aromas,
Thrive, cities—bring your freight, bring your shows, ample and
   sufficient rivers,
Expand, being than which none else is perhaps more spiritual,
Keep your places, objects than which none else is more lasting.

You have waited, you always wait, you dumb, beautiful ministers,
We receive you with free sense at last, and are insatiate henceforward,
Not you any more shall be able to foil us, or withhold yourselves from us,
We use you, and do not cast you aside—we plant you permanently
   within us,
We fathom you not—we love you—there is perfection in you also,   130
You furnish your parts toward eternity,
Great or small, you furnish your parts toward the soul.

                                     1856

from   SEA-DRIFT*

OUT OF THE CRADLE ENDLESSLY ROCKING[1]

Out of the cradle endlessly rocking,
Out of the mocking-bird's throat, the musical shuttle,
Out of the Ninth-month[2] midnight,
Over the sterile sands and the fields beyond, where the child leaving
   his bed wander'd alone, bareheaded, barefoot,

---

* Eleven poems compiled in the 1881 edition of *Leaves of Grass*.
[1] First appeared as "A Child's Reminiscence" in the December 24, 1859 issue of the New York *Saturday Press* and with this title in the 1871 edition of *Leaves of Grass*.
[2] September, from the Quaker numerical designations for months; perhaps reflective of the nine-month-long human gestational cycle.

Down from the shower'd halo,
Up from the mystic play of shadows twining and twisting as if they
    were alive,
Out from the patches of briers and blackberries,
From the memories of the bird that chanted to me,
From your memories sad brother, from the fitful risings and fallings
    I heard,
From under that yellow half-moon late-risen and swollen as if with tears,   10
From those beginning notes of yearning and love there in the mist,
From the thousand responses of my heart never to cease,
From the myriad thence-arous'd words,
From the word stronger and more delicious than any,
From such as now they start the scene revisiting,
As a flock, twittering, rising, or overhead passing,
Borne hither, ere all eludes me, hurriedly,
A man, yet by these tears a little boy again,
Throwing myself on the sand, confronting the waves,
I, chanter of pains and joys, uniter of here and hereafter,   20
Taking all hints to use them, but swiftly leaping beyond them,
A reminiscence sing.

Once Paumanok,[3]
When the lilac-scent was in the air and Fifth-month[4] grass was
    growing,
Up this seashore in some briers,
Two feather'd guests from Alabama, two together,
And their nest, and four light-green eggs spotted with brown,
And every day the he-bird to and fro near at hand,
And every day the she-bird crouch'd on her nest, silent, with
    bright eyes,
And every day I, a curious boy, never too close, never disturbing
    them,   30
Cautiously peering, absorbing, translating.

Shine! shine! shine!
Pour down your warmth, great sun!
While we bask, we two together.

Two together!
Winds blow south, or winds blow north,
Day come white, or night come black,
Home, or rivers and mountains from home,
Singing all time, minding no time,
While we two keep together.   40

Till of a sudden,
May-be kill'd, unknown to her mate,
One forenoon the she-bird crouch'd not on the nest,

---

[3] A Native-American name for Long Island.   [4] May.

Nor return'd that afternoon, nor the next,
Nor ever appear'd again.

And thenceforward all summer in the sound of the sea,
And at night under the full of the moon in calmer weather,
Over the hoarse surging of the sea,
Or flitting from brier to brier by day,
I saw, I heard at intervals the remaining one, the he-bird,   50
The solitary guest from Alabama.

Blow! blow! blow!
Blow up sea-winds along Paumanok's shore;
I wait and I wait till you blow my mate to me.

Yes, when the stars glisten'd,
All night long on the prong of a moss-scallop'd stake,
Down almost amid the slapping waves,
Sat the lone singer wonderful causing tears.

He call'd on his mate,
He pour'd forth the meanings which I of all men know.   60

Yes my brother I know,
The rest might not, but I have treasur'd every note,
For more than once dimly down to the beach gliding,
Silent, avoiding the moonbeams, blending myself with the shadow,
Recalling now the obscure shapes, the echoes, the sounds and
     sights after their sorts,
The white arms out in the breakers tirelessly tossing,
I, with bare feet, a child, the wind wafting my hair,
Listen'd long and long.

Listen'd to keep, to sing, now translating the notes,
Following you my brother,   70

Soothe! soothe! soothe!
Close on its wave soothes the wave behind,
And again another behind embracing and lapping, every one close,
But my love soothes not me, not me.

Low hangs the moon, it rose late,
It is lagging—O I think it is heavy with love, with love.

O madly the sea pushes upon the land,
With love, with love.

O night! do I not see my love fluttering out among the breakers?
What is that little black thing I see there in the white?   80

Loud! loud! loud!
Loud I call to you, my love!

High and clear I shoot my voice over the waves,
Surely you must know who is here, is here,
You must know who I am, my love.

Low-hanging moon!
What is that dusky spot in your brown yellow?
O it is the shape, the shape of my mate!
O moon do not keep her from me any longer.

Land! land! O land!   90
Whichever way I turn, O I think you could give me my mate back
*   again if you only would,*
For I am almost sure I see her dimly whichever way I look.

O rising stars!
Perhaps the one I want so much will rise, will rise with some of you.

O throat! O trembling throat!
Sound clearer through the atmosphere!
Pierce the woods, the earth,
Somewhere listening to catch you must be the one I want.

Shake out carols!
Solitary here, the night's carols!   100
Carols of lonesome love! death's carols!
Carols under that lagging, yellow, waning moon!
O under that moon where she droops almost down into the sea!
O reckless despairing carols.

But soft! sink low!
Soft! let me just murmur,
And do you wait a moment you husky-nois'd sea,
For somewhere I believe I heard my mate responding to me,
So faint, I must be still, be still to listen,
But not altogether still, for then she might not come immediately
*   to me.*   110

Hither my love!
Here I am! here!
With this just-sustain'd note I announce myself to you,
This gentle call is for you my love, for you.

Do not be decoy'd elsewhere,
That is the whistle of the wind, it is not my voice,
That is the fluttering, the fluttering of the spray,
Those are the shadows of leaves.

O darkness! O in vain!
O I am very sick and sorrowful.   120

O brown halo in the sky near the moon, drooping upon the sea!
O troubled reflection in the sea!
O throat! O throbbing heart!
And I singing uselessly, uselessly all the night.

O past! O happy life! O songs of joy!
In the air, in the woods, over fields,
Loved! loved! loved! loved! loved!
But my mate no more, no more with me!
We two together no more.

The aria sinking,   130
All else continuing, the stars shining,
The winds blowing, the notes of the bird continuous echoing,
With angry moans the fierce old mother incessantly moaning,
On the sands of Paumanok's shore gray and rustling,
The yellow half-moon enlarged, sagging down, drooping, the face
    of the sea almost touching,
The boy ecstatic, with his bare feet the waves, with his hair the
    atmosphere dallying,
The love in the heart long pent, now loose, now at last tumultuously
    bursting,
The aria's meaning, the ears, the soul, swiftly depositing,
The strange tears down the cheeks coursing,
The colloquy there, the trio, each uttering,   140
The undertone, the savage old mother incessantly crying,
To the boy's soul's questions sullenly timing, some drown'd secret
    hissing,
To the outsetting bard.

Demon or bird! (said the boy's soul,)
Is it indeed toward your mate you sing? or is it really to me?
For I, that was a child, my tongue's use sleeping, now I have
    heard you,
Now in a moment I know what I am for, I awake,
And already a thousand singers, a thousand songs, clearer, louder
    and more sorrowful than yours,
A thousand warbling echoes have started to life within me, never
    to die.

O you singer solitary, singing by yourself, projecting me,   150
O solitary me listening, never more shall I cease perpetuating you,
Never more shall I escape, never more the reverberations,
Never more the cries of unsatisfied love be absent from me,
Never again leave me to be the peaceful child I was before what there
    in the night,

By the sea under the yellow and sagging moon,
The messenger there arous'd, the fire, the sweet hell within,
The unknown want, the destiny of me.

O give me the clew! (it lurks in the night here somewhere,)
O if I am to have so much, let me have more!

A word then, (for I will conquer it,)   160
The word final, superior to all,
Subtle, sent up—what is it?—I listen;
Are you whispering it, and have been all the time, you sea-waves?
Is that it from your liquid rims, and wet sands?

Whereto answering, the sea,
Delaying not, hurrying not,
Whisper'd me through the night, and very plainly before day-break,
Lisp'd to me the low and delicious word death,
And again death, death, death, death,
Hissing melodious, neither like the bird nor like my arous'd child's
    heart,   170
But edging near as privately for me rustling at my feet,
Creeping thence steadily up to my ears and laving me softly all over,
Death, death, death, death, death.

Which I do not forget,
But fuse the song of my dusky demon and brother,
That he sang to me in the moonlight on Paumanok's gray beach,
With the thousand responsive songs at random,
My own songs awaked from that hour,
And with them the key, the word up from the waves,
The word of the sweetest song and all songs,   180
That strong and delicious word which, creeping to my feet,
(Or like some old crone rocking the cradle, swathed in sweet
    garments, bending aside,)
The sea whisper'd me.

                                                                 1859

AS I EBB'D WITH THE OCEAN OF LIFE*

I

As I ebb'd with the ocean of life,
As I wended the shores I know,
As I walk'd where the ripples continually wash you Paumanok,[1]
Where they rustle up hoarse and sibilant,
Where the fierce old mother endlessly cries for her castaways,

---

* First published as "Bardic Symbols" in the April 1860 issue of the *Atlantic Monthly* and with this
title in the 1881 edition of *Leaves of Grass*.
[1] A Native-American name for Long Island.

I musing late in the autumn day, gazing off southward,
Held by this electric self out of the pride of which I utter poems,
Was seiz'd by the spirit that trails in the lines underfoot,
The rim, the sediment that stands for all the water and all the land
  of the globe.

Fascinated, my eyes reverting from the south, dropt, to follow those
  slender windrows,[2]
Chaff, straw, splinters of wood, weeds, and the sea-gluten,   10
Scum, scales from shining rocks, leaves of salt-lettuce, left by the tide,
Miles walking, the sound of breaking waves the other side of me,
Paumanok there and then as I thought the old thought of likenesses,[3]
These you presented to me you fish-shaped island,
As I wended the shores I know,
As I walk'd with that electric self seeking types.

2

As I wend to the shores I know not,
As I list to the dirge, the voices of men and women wreck'd,
As I inhale the impalpable breezes that set in upon me,   20
As the ocean so mysterious rolls toward me closer and closer,
I too but signify at the utmost a little wash'd-up drift.
A few sands and dead leaves to gather,
Gather, and merge myself as part of the sands and drift.

O baffled, balk'd, bent to the very earth,
Oppress'd with myself that I have dared to open my mouth,
Aware now that amid all that blab whose echoes recoil upon me I
  have not once had the least idea who or what I am,
But that before all my arrogant poems the real Me stands yet
  untouch'd, untold, altogether unreach'd,
Withdrawn far, mocking me with mock-congratulatory signs and bows,
With peals of distant ironical laughter at every word I have written,   30
Pointing in silence to these songs, and then to the sand beneath.

I perceive I have not really understood any thing, not a single
  object, and that no man ever can,
Nature here in sight of the sea taking advantage of me to dart
  upon me and sting me,
Because I have dared to open my mouth to sing at all.

3

You oceans both, I close with you,
We murmur alike reproachfully rolling sands and drift, knowing
  not why,
These little shreds indeed standing for you and me and all.

---

[2] Rows of waves formed by the wind.
[3] In transcendental terms, the correspondence between the "wash'd-up drift" and the poet.

You friable[4] shore with trails of debris,
You fish-shaped island, I take what is underfoot,
What is yours is mine my father.   40

I too Paumanok,
I too have bubbled up, floated the measureless float, and been
    wash'd on your shores,
I too am but a trail of drift and debris,
I too leave little wrecks upon you, you fish-shaped island.

I throw myself upon your breast my father,[5]
I cling to you so that you cannot unloose me,
I hold you so firm till you answer me something.

Kiss me my father,
Touch me with your lips as I touch those I love,
Breathe to me while I hold you close the secret of the murmuring
    I envy.   50

4

Ebb, ocean of life, (the flow will return,)
Cease not your moaning you fierce old mother,
Endlessly cry for your castaways, but fear not, deny not me,
Rustle not up so hoarse and angry against my feet as I touch you
    or gather from you.

I mean tenderly by you and all,
I gather for myself and for this phantom looking down where we
    lead, and following me and mine.
Me and mine, loose windrows, little corpses,
Froth, snowy white, and bubbles,
(See, from my dead lips the ooze exuding at last,
See, the prismatic colors glistening and rolling,)   60
Tufts of straw, sands, fragments,
Buoy'd hither from many moods, one contradicting another,
From the storm, the long calm, the darkness, the swell,
Musing, pondering, a breath, a briny tear, a dab of liquid or soil,
Up just as much out of fathomless workings fermented and thrown,
A limp blossom or two, torn, just as much over waves floating, drifted
    at random,
Just as much for us that sobbing dirge of Nature,
Just as much whence we come that blare of the cloud-trumpets,
We, capricious, brought hither we know not whence, spread out
    before you,
You up there walking or sitting,   70
Whoever you are, we too lie in drifts at your feet.

1859?, 1860

---

[4] Crumbling.   [5] Paumanok, his native land; the ocean is his "fierce old mother."

from   By the Roadside*

A HAND-MIRROR[1]

Hold it up sternly—see this it sends back, (who is it? is it you?)
Outside fair costume, within ashes and filth,
No more a flashing eye, no more a sonorous voice or springy step,
Now some slave's eye, voice, hands, step,
A drunkard's breath, unwholesome eater's face, venerealee's flesh,
Lungs rotting away piecemeal, stomach sour and cankerous,
Joints rheumatic, bowels clogged with abomination,
Blood circulating dark and poisonous streams,
Words babble, hearing and touch callous,
No brain, no heart left, no magnetism of sex;   10
Such from one look in this looking-glass ere you go hence,
Such a result so soon—and from such a beginning!

1860

WHEN I HEARD THE LEARN'D ASTRONOMER**

When I heard the learn'd astronomer,
When the proofs, the figures, were ranged in columns before me,
When I was shown the charts and diagrams, to add, divide, and
    measure them,
When I sitting heard the astronomer where he lectured with much
    applause in the lecture-room,
How soon unaccountable I became tired and sick,
Till rising and gliding out I wander'd off by myself,
In the mystical moist night-air, and from time to time,
Look'd up in perfect silence at the stars.

1865

TO A PRESIDENT†

All you are doing and saying is to America dangled mirages,
You have not learn'd of Nature—of the politics of Nature you
    have not learn'd the great amplitude, rectitude, impartiality,

---

* Twenty-nine poems that appeared in various sections of *Leaves of Grass* and *Drum-Taps* (1865)
until grouped with this title in the 1881 edition of *Leaves.*
    [1] First appeared with this title in the 1860 edition of *Leaves.*
    ** First published in *Drum-Taps* (1865) and eventually added to "By the Roadside" in the 1881
edition of *Leaves of Grass.*
    † Whitman's criticism is aimed at James Buchanan (1791–1868), the fifteenth U.S. president (1857–
1861), who failed to take a firm stand against slavery.

You have not seen that only such as they are for these States,
And that what is less than they must sooner or later lift off from
  these States.

1860

THE DALLIANCE OF THE EAGLES*

Skirting the river road, (my forenoon walk, my rest,)
Skyward in air a sudden muffled sound, the dalliance of the eagles,
The rushing amorous contact high in space together,
The clinching interlocking claws, a living, fierce, gyrating wheel,
Four beating wings, two beaks, a swirling mass tight grappling,
In tumbling turning clustering loops, straight downward falling,
Till o'er the river pois'd, the twain yet one, a moment's lull,
A motionless still balance in the air, then parting, talons loosing,
Upward again on slow-firm pinions slanting, their separate diverse flight,
She hers, he his, pursuing.   10

1880

THE RUNNER

On a flat road runs the well-train'd runner,
He is lean and sinewy with muscular legs,
He is thinly clothed, he leans forward as he runs,
With lightly closed fists and arms partially rais'd.

1867

from DRUM-TAPS†

BEAT! BEAT! DRUMS!¹

Beat! beat! drums!—blow! bugles! blow!
Through the windows—through doors—burst like a ruthless force,
Into the solemn church, and scatter the congregation,
Into the school where the scholar is studying;
Leave not the bridegroom quiet—no happiness must he have now
  with his bride,

---

* First appeared in *Cope's Tobacco Plant* in November 1880; added to the 1881 edition of *Leaves of Grass*. Here, "dalliance" refers to mating.
† First published separately with fifty-three poems in 1865; revised with eighteen new poems as "Sequel to Drum-Taps" (1865–1866)—a volume that received unenthusiastic reviews—and added to the 1867 edition of *Leaves of Grass*, ultimately as a group of forty-three poems in the 1881 edition.
¹ First published simultaneously in *Harper's Weekly* and the New York *Ledger* on September 28, 1861.

Nor the peaceful farmer any peace, ploughing his field or gathering
   his grain,
So fierce you whirr and pound you drums—so shrill you bugles blow.

Beat! beat! drums!—blow! bugles! blow!
Over the traffic of cities—over the rumble of wheels in the streets;
Are beds prepared for sleepers at night in the houses? no sleepers
   must sleep in those beds,   10
No bargainers' bargains by day—no brokers or speculators—would
   they continue?
Would the talkers be talking? would the singer attempt to sing?
Would the lawyer rise in the court to state his case before the judge?
Beat! beat! drums!—blow! bugles! blow!
Then rattle quicker, heavier drums—you bugles wilder blow.
Make no parley—stop for no expostulation,
Mind not the timid—mind not the weeper or prayer,
Mind not the old man beseeching the young man,
Let not the child's voice be heard, nor the mother's entreaties,
Make even the trestles to shake the dead where they lie awaiting
   the hearses,   20
So strong you thump O terrible drums—so loud you bugles blow.

1861

CAVALRY CROSSING A FORD

A line in long array where they wind betwixt green islands,
They take a serpentine course, their arms flash in the sun—hark
   to the musical clank,
Behold the silvery river, in it the splashing horses loitering stop to drink,
Behold the brown-faced men, each group, each person a picture, the
   negligent rest on the saddles,
Some emerge on the opposite bank, others are just entering the
   ford—while,
Scarlet and blue and snowy white,
The guidon flags[1] flutter gayly in the wind.

1865

VIGIL STRANGE I KEPT ON THE FIELD ONE NIGHT

Vigil strange I kept on the field one night;
When you my son and my comrade dropt at my side that day,
One look I but gave which your dear eyes return'd with a look I
   shall never forget,

---

[1] Military flags or pennants for identification and signaling.

One touch of your hand to mine O boy, reach'd up as you lay
    on the ground,
Then onward I sped in the battle, the even-contested battle,
Till late in the night reliev'd to the place at last again I made my way,
Found you in death so cold dear comrade, found your body son
    of responding kisses, (never again on earth responding,)
Bared your face in the starlight, curious the scene, cool blew the
    moderate night-wind,
Long there and then in vigil I stood, dimly around me the battle-
    field spreading,
Vigil wondrous and vigil sweet there in the fragrant silent night,   10
But not a tear fell, not even a long-drawn sigh, long, long I gazed,
Then on the earth partially reclining sat by your side leaning my chin
    in my hands,
Passing sweet hours, immortal and mystic hours with you dearest
    comrade—not a tear, not a word,
Vigil of silence, love and death, vigil for you my son and my soldier,
As onward silently stars aloft, eastward new ones upward stole,
Vigil final for you brave boy, (I could not save you, swift was your
    death,
I faithfully loved you and cared for you living, I think we shall surely
    meet again,)
Till at latest lingering of the night, indeed just as the dawn appear'd,
My comrade I wrapt in his blanket, envelop'd well his form,
Folded the blanket well, tucking it carefully over head and carefully
    under feet,   20
And there and then and bathed by the rising sun, my son in his
    grave, in his rude-dug grave I deposited,
Ending my vigil strange with that, vigil of night and battle-field dim,
Vigil for boy of responding kisses, (never again on earth responding,)
Vigil for comrade swiftly slain, vigil I never forget, how as day
    brighten'd,
I rose from the chill ground and folded my soldier well in his blanket,
And buried him where he fell.

1865

A MARCH IN THE RANKS HARD-PREST, AND
THE ROAD UNKNOWN

A march in the ranks hard-prest, and the road unknown,
A route through a heavy wood with muffled steps in the darkness,
Our army foil'd with loss severe, and the sullen remnant retreating,
Till after midnight glimmer upon us the lights of a dim-lighted building,
We come to an open space in the woods, and halt by the dim-lighted
    building,
'Tis a large old church at the crossing roads, now an impromptu hospital,
Entering but for a minute I see a sight beyond all the pictures and
    poems ever made,

Shadows of deepest, deepest black, just lit by moving candles and lamps,
And by one great pitchy torch stationary with wild red flame and clouds
  of smoke,
By these, crowds, groups of forms vaguely I see on the floor, some
  in the pews laid down,
At my feet more distinctly a soldier, a mere lad, in danger of bleeding
  to death, (he is shot in the abdomen,)
I stanch the blood temporarily, (the youngster's face is white as a lily,)
Then before I depart I sweep my eyes o'er the scene fain to absorb it all,
Faces, varieties, postures beyond description, most in obscurity,
  some of them dead,
Surgeons operating, attendants holding lights, the smell of ether,
  the odor of blood,
The crowd, O the crowd of the bloody forms, the yard outside also fill'd,
Some on the bare ground, some on planks or stretchers, some in the
  death-spasm sweating,
An occasional scream or cry, the doctor's shouted orders or calls,
The glisten of the little steel instruments catching the glint of the
  torches,
These I resume as I chant, I see again the forms, I smell the odor,
Then hear outside the orders given, *Fall in, my men, fall in;*
But first I bend to the dying lad, his eyes open, a half-smile gives
  he me,
Then the eyes close, calmly close, and I speed forth to the darkness,
Resuming, marching, ever in darkness marching, on in the ranks,
The unknown road still marching.

1865

A SIGHT IN CAMP IN THE DAYBREAK GRAY AND DIM

A sight in camp in the daybreak gray and dim,
As from my tent I emerge so early sleepless,
As slow I walk in the cool fresh air the path near by the hospital tent,
Three forms I see on stretchers lying, brought out there untended lying,
Over each the blanket spread, ample brownish woolen blanket,
Gray and heavy blanket, folding, covering all.

Curious I halt and silent stand,
Then with light fingers I from the face of the nearest the first just lift
  the blanket;
Who are you elderly man so gaunt and grim, with well-gray'd hair,
  and flesh all sunken about the eyes?
Who are you my dear comrade?
Then to the second I step—and who are you my child and darling?
Who are you sweet boy with cheeks yet blooming?

Then to the third—a face nor child nor old, very calm, as of beautiful
  yellow-white ivory;

Young man I think I know you—I think this face is the face of the
   Christ himself,
Dead and divine and brother of all, and here again he lies.

1865

THE WOUND-DRESSER*

I

An old man bending I come among new faces,
Years looking backward resuming in answer to children,
Come tell us old man, as from young men and maidens that love me,
(Arous'd and angry, I'd thought to beat the alarum, and urge
   relentless war,
But soon my fingers fail'd me, my face droop'd and I resign'd myself,
To sit by the wounded and soothe them, or silently watch the dead;)
Years hence of these scenes, of these furious passions, these chances,
Of unsurpass'd heroes, (was one side so brave? the other was
   equally brave;)
Now be witness again, paint the mightiest armies of earth,
Of those armies so rapid so wondrous what saw you to tell us?   10
What stays with you latest and deepest? of curious panics,
Of hard-fought engagements or sieges tremendous what deepest
   remains?

2

O maidens and young men I love and that love me,
What you ask of my days those the strangest and sudden your
   talking recalls,
Soldier alert I arrive after a long march covr'd with sweat and dust,
In the nick of time I come, plunge in the fight, loudly shout in the
   rush of successful charge,
Enter the captur'd works[1]—yet lo, like a swift-running river they fade,
Pass and are gone they fade—I dwell not on soldiers' perils or
   soldiers' joys,
(Both I remember well—many the hardships, few the joys, yet I
   was content.)

But in silence, in dreams' projections,   20
While the world of gain and appearance and mirth goes on,
So soon what is over forgotten, and waves wash the imprints off
   the sand,
With hinged knees returning I enter the doors, (while for you up there,
Whoever you are, follow without noise and be of strong heart.)

---

  * First appeared as "The Dresser" in the 1865 edition of *Leaves of Grass* and with this title in the
1876 edition.
  [1] Breastworks, fortifications.

Bearing the bandages, water and sponge,
Straight and swift to my wounded I go,
Where they lie on the ground after the battle brought in,
Where their priceless blood reddens the grass the ground,
Or to the rows of the hospital tent, or under the roof'd hospital,
To the long rows of cots up and down each side I return,   30
To each and all one after another I draw near, not one do I miss,
An attendant follows holding a tray, he carries a refuse pail,
Soon to be fill'd with clotted rags and blood, emptied, and fill'd again.

I onward go, I stop,
With hinged knees and steady hand to dress wounds,
I am firm with each, the pangs are sharp yet unavoidable,
One turns to me his appealing eyes—poor boy! I never knew you,
Yet I think I could not refuse this moment to die for you, if that
    would save you.

                              3
On, on I go, (open doors of time! open hospital doors!)
The crush'd head I dress, (poor crazed hand tear not the bandage away,)   40
The neck of the cavalry-man with the bullet through and through
    I examine,
Hard the breathing rattles, quite glazed already the eye, yet life
    struggles hard,
(Come sweet death! be persuaded O beautiful death!
In mercy come quickly.)

From the stump of the arm, the amputated hand,
I undo the clotted lint, remove the slough, wash off the matter
    and blood,
Back on his pillow the soldier bends with curv'd neck and side-
    falling head,
His eyes are closed, his face is pale, he dares not look on the
    bloody stump,
And has not yet look'd on it.

I dress a wound in the side, deep, deep,   50
But a day or two more, for see the frame all wasted and sinking,
And the yellow-blue countenance see.

I dress the perforated shoulder, the foot with the bullet-wound,
Cleanse the one with a gnawing and putrid gangrene, so sickening,
    so offensive,
While the attendant stands behind aside me holding the tray and pail.

I am faithful, I do not give out,
The fractur'd thigh, the knee, the wound in the abdomen,
These and more I dress with impassive hand, (yet deep in my
    breast a fire, a burning flame.)

4

Thus in silence in dreams' projections,
Returning, resuming, I thread my way through the hospitals, 60
The hurt and wounded I pacify with soothing hand,
I sit by the restless all the dark night, some are so young,
Some suffer so much, I recall the experience sweet and sad,
(Many a soldier's loving arms about this neck have cross'd and rested,
Many a soldier's kiss dwells on these bearded lips.)

1865

DIRGE FOR TWO VETERANS*

The last sunbeam
Lightly falls from the finish'd Sabbath,
On the pavement here, and there beyond it is looking,
Down a new-made double grave.

Lo, the moon ascending,
Up from the east the silvery round moon,
Beautiful over the house-tops, ghastly, phantom moon,
Immense and silent moon.

I see a sad procession,
And I hear the sound of coming full-key'd bugles, 10
All the channels of the city streets they're flooding,
As with voices and with tears.

I hear the great drums pounding,
And the small drums steady whirring,
And every blow of the great convulsive drums,
Strikes me through and through.

For the son is brought with the father,
(In the foremost ranks of the fierce assault they fell,
Two veterans son and father dropt together,
And the double grave awaits them.) 20

Now nearer blow the bugles,
And the drums strike more convulsive,
And the daylight o'er the pavement quite has faded,
And the strong dead-march enwraps me.

In the eastern sky up-buoying,
The sorrowful vast phantom moves illumin'd,
('Tis some mother's large transparent face,
In heaven brighter growing.)

* First appeared in the "Sequel to Drum-Taps" (1865–1866).

O strong dead-march you please me!
O moon immense with your silvery face you soothe me!   30
O my soldiers twain! O my veterans passing to burial!
    What I have I also give you.

The moon gives you light,
And the bugles and the drums give you music,
And my heart, O my soldiers, my veterans,
    My heart gives you love.

1865–1866

THE ARTILLERYMAN'S VISION*

While my wife at my side lies slumbering, and the wars are over long,
And my head on the pillow rests at home, and the vacant midnight passes,
And through the stillness, through the dark, I hear, just hear, the
    breath of my infant,
There in the room as I wake from sleep this vision presses upon me;
The engagement opens there and then in fantasy unreal,
The skirmishers begin, they crawl cautiously ahead, I hear the
    irregular snap! snap!
I hear the sounds of the different missiles, the short *t-h-t! t-h-t!* of
    the rifle-balls,
I see the shells exploding leaving small white clouds, I hear the great
    shells shrieking as they pass,
The grape like the hum and whirr of wind through the trees,
    (tumultuous now the contest rages,)
All the scenes at the batteries rise in detail before me again,   10
The crashing and smoking, the pride of the men in their pieces,
The chief-gunner ranges and sights his piece and selects a fuse of the
    right time,
After firing I see him lean aside and look eagerly off to note the effect;
Elsewhere I hear the cry of a regiment charging, (the young colonel
    leads himself this time with brandish'd sword,)
I see the gaps cut by the enemy's volleys, (quickly fill'd up, no delay,)
I breathe the suffocating smoke, then the flat clouds hover low
    concealing all;
Now a strange lull for a few seconds, not a shot fired on either side,
Then resumed the chaos louder than ever, with eager calls and orders
    of officers,
While from some distant part of the field the wind wafts to my ears
    a shout of applause, (some special success,)
And ever the sound of the cannon far or near, (rousing even in
    dreams a devilish exultation and all the old mad joy
    in the depths of my soul,)   20

---

* First published as "The Veteran's Vision" in the 1865 edition of *Leaves of Grass* and with this title
in the 1871 edition.

And ever the hastening of infantry shifting positions, batteries,
    cavalry, moving hither and thither,
(The falling, dying, I heed not, the wounded dripping and red I heed
    not, some to the rear are hobbling,)
Grime, heat, rush, aide-de-camps galloping by or on a full run,
With the patter of small arms, the warning *s-s-t* of the rifles, (these in
    my vision I hear or see,)
And bombs bursting in air, and at night the vari-color'd rockets.

                                                                    1865

RECONCILIATION*

Word over all, beautiful as the sky,
Beautiful that war and all its deeds of carnage must in time be utterly lost,
That the hands of the sisters Death and Night incessantly softly wash again,
    and ever again, this soil'd world;
For my enemy is dead, a man divine as myself is dead,
I look where he lies white-faced and still in the coffin—I draw near,
Bend down and touch lightly with my lips the white face in the coffin.

                                                                    1865–1866

from   MEMORIES OF PRESIDENT LINCOLN†

WHEN LILACS LAST IN THE DOORYARD BLOOM'D¹

1

When lilacs last in the dooryard bloom'd,
And the great star² early droop'd in the western sky in the night,
I mourn'd, and yet shall mourn with ever-returning spring.

Ever-returning spring, trinity sure to me you bring,
Lilac blooming perennial and drooping star in the west,
And thought of him I love.

2

O powerful western fallen star!
O shades of night—O moody, tearful night!
O great star disappear'd—O the black murk that hides the star!

---

* First appeared in the "Sequel to Drum-Taps" (1865–1866).
† Four poems first grouped as "President Lincoln's Burial Hymn" in the 1871 edition of *Leaves of Grass* and with this title in the 1881 edition.
¹ First appeared in the "Sequel to Drum-Taps"(1865–1866).
² Venus.

O cruel hands that hold me powerless—O helpless soul of me!   10
O harsh surrounding cloud that will not free my soul.

                                    3
In the dooryard fronting an old farm-house near the white-wash'd palings,
Stands the lilac-bush tall-growing with heart-shaped leaves of rich green,
With many a pointed blossom rising delicate, with the perfume strong
    I love,
With every leaf a miracle—and from this bush in the dooryard,
With delicate-color'd blossoms and heart-shaped leaves of rich green,
A sprig with its flower I break.

                                    4
In the swamp in secluded recesses,
A shy and hidden bird is warbling a song.

Solitary the thrush,   20
The hermit withdrawn to himself, avoiding the settlements,
Sings by himself a song.

Song of the bleeding throat,
Death's outlet song of life, (for well dear brother I know,
If thou wast not granted to sing thou would'st surely die.)

                                    5
Over the breast of the spring, the land, amid cities,
Amid lanes and through old woods, where lately the violets peep'd
    from the ground, spotting the gray debris,
Amid the grass in the fields each side of the lanes, passing the endless
    grass,
Passing the yellow-spear'd wheat, every grain from its shroud in the
    dark-brown fields uprisen,
Passing the apple-tree blows³ of white and pink in the orchards,   30
Carrying a corpse to where it shall rest in the grave,
Night and day journeys a coffin.⁴

                                    6
Coffin that passes through lanes and streets,
Through day and night with the great cloud darkening the land,
With the pomp of the inloop'd flags with the cities draped in black,
With the show of the States themselves as of crape-veil'd women standing,
With processions long and winding and the flambeaus⁵ of the night,
With the countless torches lit, with the silent sea of faces and the
    unbared heads,
With the waiting depot, the arriving coffin, and the sombre faces,

---

³ Blossoms.
⁴ Lincoln's body was transported by train from Washington, D.C., to Springfield, Illinois, for burial
after he was assassinated in April 1865.
⁵ Torches or candles.

With dirges through the night, with the thousand voices rising strong
    and solemn,   40
With all the mournful voices of the dirges pour'd around the coffin,
The dim-lit churches and the shuddering organs—where amid these
    you journey,
With the tolling tolling bells' perpetual clang,
Here, coffin that slowly passes,
I give you my sprig of lilac.

7

(Nor for you, for one alone,
Blossoms and branches green to coffins all I bring,
For fresh as the morning, thus would I chant a song for you O sane
    and sacred death.

All over bouquets of roses,
O death, I cover you over with roses and early lilies,   50
But mostly and now the lilac that blooms the first,
Copious I break, I break the sprigs from the bushes,
With loaded arms I come, pouring for you,
For you and the coffins all of you O death.)

8

O western orb sailing the heaven,
Now I know what you must have meant as a month since I walk'd,
As I walk'd in silence the transparent shadowy night,
As I saw you had something to tell as you bent to me night after night,
As you droop'd from the sky low down as if to my side, (while the
    other stars all look'd on,)
As we wander'd together the solemn night, (for something I know not
    what kept me from sleep,)   60
As the night advanced, and I saw on the rim of the west how full you
    were of woe,
As I stood on the rising ground in the breeze in the cool transparent night,
As I watch'd where you pass'd and was lost in the netherward black of
    the night,
As my soul in its trouble dissatisfied sank, as where you sad orb,
Concluded, dropt in the night, and was gone.

9

Sing on there in the swamp,
O singer bashful and tender, I hear your notes, I hear your call,
I hear, I come presently, I understand you,
But a moment I linger, for the lustrous star has detain'd me,
The star my departing comrade holds and detains me.   70

10

O how shall I warble myself for the dead one there I loved?
And how shall I deck my song for the large sweet soul that has gone?
And what shall my perfume be for the grave of him I love?

Sea-winds blown from east and west,
Blown from the Eastern sea and blown from the Western sea, till
   there on the prairies meeting,
These and with these and the breath of my chant,
I'll perfume the grave of him I love.

11

O what shall I hang on the chamber walls?
And what shall the pictures be that I hang on the walls,
To adorn the burial-house of him I love?   80

Pictures of growing spring and farms and homes,
With the Fourth-month[6] eve at sundown, and the gray smoke lucid
   and bright,
With floods of the yellow gold of the gorgeous, indolent, sinking
   sun, burning, expanding the air,
With the fresh sweet herbage under foot, and the pale green leaves of
   the trees prolific,
In the distance the flowing glaze, the breast of the river, with a
   wind-dapple here and there,
With ranging hills on the banks, with many a line against the sky, and
   shadows,
And the city at hand with dwellings so dense, and stacks of chimneys,
And all the scenes of life and the workshops, and the workmen homeward
   returning.

12

Lo, body and soul—this land,
My own Manhattan with spires, and the sparkling and hurrying tides,
   and the ships,   90
The varied and ample land, the South and the North in the light, Ohio's
   shores and flashing Missouri,
And ever the far-spreading prairies cover'd with grass and corn.

Lo, the most excellent sun so calm and haughty,
The violet and purple morn with just-felt breezes,
The gentle soft-born measureless light
The miracle spreading bathing all, the fulfill'd noon,
The coming eve delicious, the welcome night and the stars,
Over my cities shining all, enveloping man and land.

13

Sing on, sing on you gray-brown bird,
Sing from the swamps, the recesses, pour your chant from the bushes,   100
Limitless out of the dusk, out of the cedars and pines.

Sing on dearest brother, warble your reedy song,
Loud human song, with voice of uttermost woe.

---

[6] April, from the Quaker numerical designations for months.

O liquid and free and tender!
O wild and loose to my soul—O wondrous singer!
You only I hear—yet the star holds me, (but will soon depart,)
Yet the lilac with mastering odor holds me.

14

Now while I sat in the day and look'd forth,
In the close of the day with its light and the fields of spring, and
    the farmers preparing their crops,
In the large unconscious scenery of my land with its lakes and forests,   110
In the heavenly aerial beauty, (after the perturb'd winds and the storms,)
Under the arching heavens of the afternoon swift passing, and the voices
    of children and women,
The many-moving sea-tides, and I saw the ships how they sail'd,
And the summer approaching with richness, and the fields all busy
    with labor,
And the infinite separate houses, how they all went on, each with
    its meals and minutia of daily usages,
And the streets how their throbbings throbb'd, and the cities pent—lo,
    then and there,
Falling upon them all and among them all, enveloping me with the rest,
Appear'd the cloud, appear'd the long black trail,
And I knew death, its thought, and the sacred knowledge of death.

Then with the knowledge of death as walking one side of me,   120
And the thought of death close-walking the other side of me,
And I in the middle as with companions, and as holding the hands
    of companions,
I fled forth to the hiding receiving night that talks not,
Down to the shores of the water, the path by the swamp in the dimness,
To the solemn shadowy cedars and ghostly pines so still.

And the singer so shy to the rest receiv'd me,
The gray-brown bird I know receiv'd us comrades three,
And he sang the carol of death, and a verse for him I love.

From deep secluded recesses,
From the fragrant cedars and the ghostly pines so still,   130
Came the carol of the bird.

And the charm of the carol rapt me,
As I held as if by their hands my comrades in the night,
And the voice of my spirit tallied the song of the bird.

Come lovely and soothing death,
Undulate round the world, serenely arriving, arriving,
In the day, in the night, to all, to each,
Sooner or later delicate death.

Prais'd be the fathomless universe,
For life and joy, and for objects and knowledge curious,   140
And for love, sweet love—but praise! praise! praise!
For the sure-enwinding arms of cool-enfolding death.

Dark mother always gliding near with soft feet,
Have none chanted for thee a chant of fullest welcome?
Then I chant it for thee, I glorify thee above all,
I bring thee a song that when thou must indeed come, come unfalteringly.

Approach strong deliveress,
When it is so, when thou hast taken them I joyously sing the dead,
Lost in the loving floating ocean of thee,
Laved in the flood of thy bliss O death.   150

From me to thee glad serenades,
Dances for thee I propose saluting thee, adornments and feastings
    for thee,
And the sights of the open landscape and the high-spread sky are fitting,
And life and the fields, and the huge and thoughtful night.

The night in silence under many a star,
The ocean shore and the husky whispering wave whose voice I know,
And the soul turning to thee O vast and well-veil'd death,
And the body gratefully nestling close to thee.

Over the tree-tops I float thee a song,
Over the rising and sinking waves, over the myriad fields and the
    prairies wide,
Over the dense-pack'd cities all and the teeming wharves and ways,   160
I float this carol with joy, with joy to thee O death.

15

To the tally of my soul,
Loud and strong kept up the gray-brown bird,
With pure deliberate notes spreading filling the night.

Loud in the pines and cedars dim,
Clear in the freshness moist and the swamp-perfume,
And I with my comrades there in the night.

While my sight that was bound in my eyes unclosed,
As to long panoramas of visions.   170

And I saw askant[7] the armies,
I saw as in noiseless dreams hundreds of battle-flags,

---

[7] From the corner of the eye, obliquely.

Borne through the smoke of the battles and pierc'd with missiles I
   saw them,
And carried hither and yon through the smoke, and torn and bloody,
And at last but a few shreds left on the staffs, (and all in silence,)
And the staffs all splinter'd and broken.

I saw battle-corpses, myriads of them,
And the white skeletons of young men, I saw them,
I saw the debris and debris of all the slain soldiers of the war,
But I saw they were not as was thought,   180
They themselves were fully at rest, they suffer'd not,
The living remain'd and suffer'd, the mother suffer'd,
And the wife and the child and the musing comrade suffer'd,
And the armies that remain'd suffer'd.

16

Passing the visions, passing the night,
Passing, unloosing the hold of my comrades' hands,
Passing the song of the hermit bird and the tallying song of my soul,
Victorious song, death's outlet song, yet varying ever-altering song,
As low and wailing, yet clear the notes, rising and falling, flooding
   the night,
Sadly sinking and fainting, as warning and warning, and yet again
   bursting with joy,   190
Covering the earth and filling the spread of the heaven,
As that powerful psalm in the night I heard from recesses,
Passing, I leave thee lilac with heart-shaped leaves,
I leave thee there in the door-yard, blooming, returning with spring.

I cease from my song for thee,
From my gaze on thee in the west, fronting the west, communing with thee,
O comrade lustrous with silver face in the night.

Yet each to keep and all, retrievements out of the night,
The song, the wondrous chant of the gray-brown bird,
And the tallying chant, the echo arous'd in my soul,   200
With the lustrous and drooping star with the countenance full of woe,
With the holders holding my hand nearing the call of the bird,
Comrades mine and I in the midst, and their memory ever to keep,
   for the dead I loved so well,
For the sweetest, wisest soul of all my days and lands—and this for his
   dear sake,
Lilac and star and bird twined with the chant of my soul,
There in the fragrant pines and the cedars dusk and dim.

1865–1866

from   AUTUMN RIVULETS*

THERE WAS A CHILD WENT FORTH[1]

There was a child went forth every day,
And the first object he look'd upon, that object he became,
And that object became part of him for the day or a certain part of
   the day,
Or for many years or stretching cycles of years.

The early lilacs became part of this child,
And grass and white and red morning-glories, and white and red clover,
   and the song of the phœbe-bird,
And the Third-month lambs and the sow's pink-faint litter, and the
   mare's foal and the cow's calf,
And the noisy brood of the barnyard or by the mire of the pond-side,
And the fish suspending themselves so curiously below there, and the
   beautiful curious liquid,
And the water-plants with their graceful flat heads, all became part
   of him.   10

The field-sprouts of Fourth-month and Fifth-month became part of him,
Winter-grain sprouts and those of the light-yellow corn, and the
   esculent roots of the garden,
And the apple-trees cover'd with blossoms and the fruit afterward,
   and wood-berries, and the commonest weeds by the road,
And the old drunkard staggering home from the outhouse of the tavern
   whence he had lately risen,
And the schoolmistress that pass'd on her way to the school,
And the friendly boys that pass'd, and the quarrelsome boys,
And the tidy and fresh-cheek'd girls, and the barefoot negro boy and girl,
And all the changes of city and country wherever he went.

His own parents, he that had father'd him and she that had conceiv'd
   him in her womb and birth'd him,
They gave this child more of themselves than that,   20
They gave him afterward every day, they became part of him.

The mother at home quietly placing the dishes on the supper-table,
The mother with mild words, clean her cap and gown, a wholesome
   odor falling off her person and clothes as she walks by,
The father, strong, self-sufficient, manly, mean, anger'd, unjust,

---

* Thirty-eight poems first grouped with this title in the 1881 edition of *Leaves of Grass*.
[1] Originally untitled, published as "Poem of the Child That Went Forth, and Always Goes Forth,
Forever and Forever" in the 1856 edition of *Leaves* and ultimately with this title in the 1871 edition.

The blow, the quick loud word, the tight bargain, the crafty lure,
The family usages, the language, the company, the furniture, the
    yearning and swelling heart,
Affection that will not be gainsay'd, the sense of what is real, the
    thought if after all it should prove unreal,
The doubts of day-time and the doubts of night-time, the curious
    whether and how,
Whether that which appears so is so, or is it all flashes and specks?
Men and women crowding fast in the streets, if they are not flashes
    and specks what are they?   30
The streets themselves and the façades of houses, and goods in the
    windows,
Vehicles, teams, the heavy-plank'd wharves, the huge crossing at
    the ferries,
The village on the highland seen from afar at sunset, the river between,
Shadows, aureola and mist, the light falling on roofs and gables of
    white or brown two miles off,
The schooner near by sleepily dropping down the tide, the little boat
    slack-tow'd astern,
The hurrying tumbling waves, quick-broken crests, slapping,
The strata of color'd clouds, the long bar of maroon-tint away solitary
    by itself, the spread of purity it lies motionless in,
The horizon's edge, the flying sea-crow, the fragrance of salt marsh
    and shore mud,
These became part of that child who went forth every day, and who
    now goes, and will always go forth every day.

1855

TO A COMMON PROSTITUTE

Be composed—be at ease with me—I am Walt Whitman, liberal
    and lusty as Nature,
Not till the sun excludes you do I exclude you,
Not till the waters refuse to glisten for you and the leaves to rustle for
    you, do my words refuse to glisten and rustle for you.

My girl I appoint with you an appointment, and I charge you that you make
preparation to be worthy to meet me,
And I charge you that you be patient and perfect till I come.

Till then I salute you with a significant look that you do not forget me.

1860

PASSAGE TO INDIA*

I

Singing my days,
Singing the great achievements of the present,
Singing the strong light works of engineers,
Our modern wonders, (the antique ponderous Seven[1] outvied,)
In the Old World the east the Suez canal,[2]
The New by its mighty railroad spann'd,[3]
The seas inlaid with eloquent gentle wires;[4]
Yet first to sound, and ever sound, the cry with thee O soul,
The Past! the Past! the Past!

The Past—the dark unfathom'd retrospect!   10
The teeming gulf—the sleepers and the shadows!
The past—the infinite greatness of the past!
For what is the present after all but a growth out of the past?
(As a projectile form'd, impell'd, passing a certain line, still keeps on,
So the present, utterly form'd, impell'd by the past.)

2

Passage O soul to India!
Eclaircise[5] the myths Asiatic, the primitive fables.

Not you alone proud truths of the world,
Nor you alone ye facts of modern science,
But myths and fables of eld,[6] Asia's, Africa's fables,   20
The far-darting beams of the spirit, the unloos'd dreams,
The deep diving bibles and legends,
The daring plots of the poets, the elder religions;
O you temples fairer than lilies pour'd over by the rising sun!
O you fables spurning the known, eluding the hold of the known,
     mounting to heaven!
You lofty and dazzling towers, pinnacled, red as roses, burnish'd with
     gold!
Towers of fables immortal fashion'd from mortal dreams!
You too I welcome and fully the same as the rest!
You too with joy I sing.

---

* First published as the title poem of a volume of seventy-five poems in 1871 and in the 1871 edition of *Leaves of Grass.*
[1] The Seven Wonders of the Ancient World: the pyramids of Egypt; the Temple of Artemis at Ephesus, in Asia Minor; the hanging gardens of Babylon; the Mausoleum at Halicarnassus, in Asia Minor; the Pharos, or lighthouse, at Alexandria, Egypt; the statue of Zeus at Olympia, Greece; and the Colossus of Rhodes.
[2] Begun in April 1859 and completed in November 1869.
[3] The Union Pacific and Central Pacific railroads, joined at Promontory, Utah, in May 1869.
[4] The Trans-Atlantic cable, completed in 1866.
[5] Make clear, explain; from *éclair,* "a flash of illumination" (French).   [6] Old, or antiquity.

Passage to India!
Lo, soul, seest thou not God's purpose from the first?
The earth to be spann'd, connected by network,
The races, neighbors, to marry and be given in marriage,
The oceans to be cross'd, the distant brought near,
The lands to be welded together.

A worship new I sing,
You captains, voyagers, explorers, yours,
You engineers, you architects, machinists, yours,
You, not for trade or transportation only,
But in God's name, and for thy sake O soul.   40

3

Passage to India!
Lo soul for thee of tableaus twain,
I see in one the Suez canal initiated, open'd,
I see the procession of steamships, the Empress Eugenie's[7] leading
    the van,
I mark from on deck the strange landscape, the pure sky, the level
    sand in the distance,
I pass swiftly the picturesque groups, the workmen gather'd,
The gigantic dredging machines.

In one again, different, (yet thine, all thine, O soul, the same,)
I see over my own continent the Pacific railroad surmounting every
    barrier,[8]
I see continual trains of cars winding along the Platte carrying freight
    and passengers,   50
I hear the locomotives rushing and roaring, and the shrill steam-whistle,
I hear the echoes reverberate through the grandest scenery in the world,
I cross the Laramie plains, I note the rocks in grotesque shapes, the buttes,
I see the plentiful larkspur and wild onions, the barren, colorless,
    sage-deserts,
I see in glimpses afar or towering immediately above me the great
    mountains, I see the Wind river and the Wahsatch mountains,
I see the Monument mountain and the Eagle's Nest, I pass the
    Promontory, I ascend the Nevadas,
I scan the noble Elk mountain and wind around its base,
I see the Humboldt range, I thread the valley and cross the river,
I see the clear waters of Lake Tahoe, I see forests of majestic pines,
Or crossing the great desert, the alkaline plains, I behold enchanting
    mirages of waters and meadows,   60
Marking through these and after all, in duplicate slender lines,
Bridging the three or four thousand miles of land travel,
Tying the Eastern to the Western sea,
The road between Europe and Asia.

[7] Eugénie de Guzmán (1853–1920), wife of Napoleon III and empress of France (1853–1871).
[8] Along the route from Omaha to San Francisco.

(Ah Genoese[9] thy dream! thy dream!
Centuries after thou art laid in thy grave,
The shore thou foundest verifies thy dream.)

4

Passage to India!
Struggles of many a captain, tales of many a sailor dead,
Over my mood stealing and spreading they come,   70
Like clouds and cloudlets in the unreach'd sky.

Along all history, down the slopes,
As a rivulet running, sinking now, and now again to the surface rising,
A ceaseless thought, a varied train—lo, soul, to thee, thy sight, they rise,
The plans, the voyages again, the expeditions;
Again Vasco de Gama[10] sails forth,
Again the knowledge gain'd, the mariner's compass,
Lands found and nations born, thou born America,
For purpose vast, man's long probation fill'd,
Thou rondure[11] of the world at last accomplish'd.   80

5

O vast Rondure, swimming in space,
Cover'd all over with visible power and beauty,
Alternate light and day and the teeming spiritual darkness,
Unspeakable high processions of sun and moon and countless stars above,
Below, the manifold grass and waters, animals, mountains, trees,
With inscrutable purpose, some hidden prophetic intention,
Now first it seems my thought begins to span thee.

Down from the gardens of Asia descending radiating,
Adam and Eve appear, then their myriad progeny after them,
Wandering, yearning, curious, with restless explorations,   90
With questionings, baffled, formless, feverish, with never-happy hearts,
With that sad incessant refrain, *Wherefore unsatisfied soul?* and *Whither
    O mocking life?*

Ah who shall soothe these feverish children?
Who justify these restless explorations?
Who speak the secret of impassive earth?
Who bind it to us? what is this separate Nature so unnatural?
What is this earth to our affections? (unloving earth, without a throb
    to answer ours,
Cold earth, the place of graves.)

[9] Christopher Columbus, a native of Genoa, Italy.
[10] Da Gama (1469?–1524), a Portuguese navigator, was the first European to sail around southern
Africa to India.
[11] Encirclement.

Yet soul be sure the first intent remains, and shall be carried out,
Perhaps even how the time has arrived.   100

After the seas are all cross'd, (as they seem already cross'd,)
After the great captains and engineers have accomplish'd their work,
After the noble inventors, after the scientists, the chemist, the
    geologist, ethnologist,
Finally shall come the poet worthy that name,
The true son of God shall come singing his songs.

Then not your deeds only O voyagers, O scientists and inventors, shall
    be justified,
All these hearts as of fretted children shall be sooth'd,
All affection shall be fully responded to, the secret shall be told,
All these separations and gaps shall be taken up and hook'd and link'd
    together,
The whole earth, this cold, impassive, voiceless earth, shall be
    completely justified,   110
Trinitas[12] divine shall be gloriously accomplish'd and compacted by
    the true son of God, the poet,
(He shall indeed pass the straits and conquer the mountains,
He shall double the cape of Good Hope to some purpose,)
Nature and Man shall be disjoin'd and diffused no more,
The true son of God shall absolutely fuse them.

6

Year at whose wide-flung door I sing!
Year of the purpose accomplish'd!
Year of the marriage of continents, climates and oceans!
(No mere doge of Venice[13] now wedding the Adriatic,)
I see O year in you the vast terraqueous globe given and giving all,   120
Europe to Asia, Africa join'd, and they to the New World,
The lands, geographies, dancing before you, holding a festival garland,
As brides and bridegrooms hand in hand.

Passage to India!
Cooling airs from Caucasus[14] far, soothing cradle of man,
The river Euphrates[15] flowing, the past lit up again.

Lo soul, the retrospect brought forward,
The old, most populous, wealthiest of earth's lands,
The streams of the Indus and the Ganges[16] and their many affluents,
(I my shores of America walking to-day behold, resuming all,)   130

---

[12] The Holy Trinity (an attempt at Spanish).

[13] The doge, or chief magistrate, each year cast a ring into the sea to symbolize the marriage of the Adriatic Sea and the city-state of Venice.

[14] The mountainous region in Russia between the Black and Caspian Seas.

[15] A river originating in Turkey and flowing into the Persian Gulf, one of four rivers said to flow from the Garden of Eden; the Euphrates Valley was considered the cradle of Western civilization.

[16] Great rivers of India.

The tale of Alexander[17] on his warlike marches suddenly dying,
On one side China and on the other side Persia and Arabia,
To the south the great seas and the bay of Bengal,
The flowing literatures, tremendous epics, religions, castes,
Old occult Brahma interminably far back, the tender and junior Buddha,[18]
Central and southern empires and all their belongings, possessors,
The wars of Tamerlane, the reign of Aurungzebe,[19]
The traders, rulers, explorers, Moslems, Venetians, Byzantium, the
    Arabs, Portuguese,
The first travelers famous yet, Marco Polo, Batouta the Moor,[20]
Doubts to be solv'd, the map incognita,[21] blanks to be fill'd,   140
The foot of man unstay'd, the hands never at rest,
Thyself O soul that will not brook a challenge.

The mediæval navigators rise before me,
The world of 1492, with its awaken'd enterprise,
Something swelling in humanity now like the sap of the earth in spring,
The sunset splendor of chivalry declining.

And who art thou sad shade?
Gigantic, visionary, thyself a visionary,
With majestic limbs and pious beaming eyes,
Spreading around with every look of thine a golden world,   150
Enhuing it with gorgeous hues.

As the chief histrion,[22]
Down to the footlights walks in some great scena,
Dominating the rest I see the Admiral[23] himself,
(History's type of courage, action, faith,)
Behold him sail from Palos[24] leading his little fleet,
His voyage behold, his return, his great fame,
His misfortunes, calumniators, behold him a prisoner, chain'd,
Behold his dejection, poverty, death.

(Curious in time I stand, noting the efforts of heroes,   160
Is the deferment long? bitter the slander, poverty, death?
Lies the seed unreck'd[25] for centuries in the ground? lo, to God's
    due occasion,
Uprising in the night, its sprouts, blooms,
And fills the earth with use and beauty.)

[17] Alexander III (356–323 B.C.), or Alexander the Great, king of Macedon (336–323 B.C.), who extended his empire as far as the Indus River and died on his return from an invasion of India.
   [18] Brahma was the supreme Hindu god; Buddha, or Siddhartha Gautama (6th century B.C.) founder of Buddhism.
   [19] Tamerlane (1336?–1405) was the Mongol conqueror of southern and western Asia; Aurungzebe (1618–1707) was the self-proclaimed " Conquerer of the World."
   [20] Polo (1254–1324), the famed Venetian traveler, was in China from 1271 to 1295; Batouta (1303–1377) was an explorer of Asia and Africa.
   [21] Unknown.   [22] Actor.   [23] Columbus.
   [24] The Spanish port from which Columbus sailed in August 1492.   [25] Unnoticed or disregarded.

7

Passage indeed O soul to primal thought,
Not lands and seas alone, thy own clear freshness,
The young maturity of brood and bloom,
To realms of budding bibles.

O soul, repressless, I with thee and thou with me,
Thy circumnavigation of the world begin,   170
Of man, the voyage of his mind's return,
To reason's early paradise,
Back, back to wisdom's birth, to innocent intuitions,
Again with fair creation.

8

O we can wait no longer,
We too take ship O soul,
Joyous we too launch out on trackless seas,
Fearless for unknown shores on waves of ecstasy to sail,
Amid the wafting winds, (thou pressing me to thee, I thee to me, O soul,)
Caroling free, singing our song of God,   180
Chanting our chant of pleasant exploration.

With laugh and many a kiss,
(Let others deprecate, let others weep for sin, remorse, humiliation,)
O soul thou pleasest me, I thee.

Ah more than any priest O soul we too believe in God,
But with the mystery of God we dare not dally.

O soul thou pleasest me, I thee,
Sailing these seas or on the hills, or waking in the night,
Thoughts, silent thoughts, of Time and Space and Death, like waters
    flowing,
Bear me indeed as through the regions infinite,   190
Whose air I breathe, whose ripples hear, lave me all over,
Bathe me O God in thee, mounting to thee,
I and my soul to range in range of thee.

O Thou transcendent,
Nameless, the fibre and the breath,
Light of the the light, shedding forth universes, thou centre of them,
Thou mightier centre of the true, the good, the loving,
Thou moral, spiritual fountain—affection's source—thou reservoir,
(O pensive soul of me—O thirst unsatisfied—waitest not there?
Waitest not haply for us somewhere there the Comrade perfect?)   200
Thou pulse—thou motive of the stars, suns, systems,
That, circling, move in order, safe, harmonious,
Athwart the shapeless vastnesses of space,
How should I think, how breathe a single breath, how speak, if, out
    of myself,
I could not launch, to those, superior universes?

Swiftly I shrivel at the thought of God,
At Nature and its wonders, Time and Space and Death,
But that I, turning, call to thee O soul, thou actual Me,
And lo, thou gently masterest the orbs,
Thou matest Time, smilest content at Death,
And fillest, swellest full the vastnesses of Space.   210

Greater than stars or suns,
Bounding O soul thou journeyest forth;
What love than thine and ours could wider amplify?
What aspirations, wishes, outvie thine and ours O soul?
What dreams of the ideal? what plans of purity, perfection, strength?
What cheerful willingness for others' sake to give up all?
For others' sake to suffer all?

Reckoning ahead O soul, when thou, the time achiev'd,
The seas all cross'd, weather'd the capes, the voyage done,   220
Surrounded, copest, frontest God, yieldest, the aim attain'd,
As fill'd with friendship, love complete, the Elder Brother found,
The Younger melts in fondness in his arms.

9

Passage to more than India!
Are thy wings plumed indeed for such far flights?
O soul, voyagest thou indeed on voyages like those?
Disportest thou on waters such as those?
Soundest below the Sanscrit and the Vedas?[26]
Then have thy bent[27] unleash'd.

Passage to you, your shores, ye aged fierce enigmas!   230
Passage to you, to mastership of you, ye strangling problems!
You, strew'd with the wrecks of skeletons, that, living, never
    reach'd you.

Passage to more than India!
O secret of the earth and sky!
Of you O waters of the sea! O winding creeks and rivers!
Of you O woods and fields! of you strong mountains of my land!
Of you O prairies! of you gray rocks!
O morning red! O clouds! O rain and snows!
O day and night, passage to you!

O sun and moon and all your stars! Sirius and Jupiter!   240
Passage to you!

Passage, immediate passage! the blood burns in my veins!
Away O soul! hoist instantly the anchor!
Cut the hawsers—haul out—shake out every sail!
Have we not stood here like trees in the ground long enough?

[26] Ancient Hindu scriptures written in Sanskrit.   [27] Energy.

Have we not grovel'd here long enough, eating and drinking like
 mere brutes?
Have we not darken'd and dazed ourselves with books long enough?

Sail forth—steer for the deep waters only,
Reckless O soul, exploring, I with thee, and thou with me,
For we are bound where mariner has not yet dared to go,   250
And we will risk the ship, ourselves and all.

O my brave soul!
O farther farther sail!
O daring joy, but safe! are they not all the seas of God?
O farther, farther, farther sail!

1871

THE SLEEPERS*

I

I wander all night in my vision,
Stepping with light feet, swiftly and noiselessly stepping and stopping,
Bending with open eyes over the shut eyes of sleepers,
Wandering and confused, lost to myself, ill-assorted, contradictory,
Pausing, gazing, bending, and stopping.

How solemnly they look there, stretch'd and still,
How quiet they breathe, the little children in their cradles.

The wretched features of ennuyés,[1] the white features of corpses, the livid
 faces of drunkards, the sick-gray faces of onanists,[2]
The gash'd bodies on battle-fields, the insane in their strong-door'd
 rooms, the sacred idiots, the new-born emerging from gates,
 and the dying emerging from gates,
The night pervades them and infolds them.   10

The married couple sleep calmly in their bed, he with his palm on the
 hip of the wife, and she with her palm on the hip of the husband,
The sisters sleep lovingly side by side in their bed,
The men sleep lovingly side by side in theirs,
And the mother sleeps with her little child carefully wrapt.

The blind sleep, and the deaf and dumb sleep,
The prisoner sleeps well in the prison, the runaway son sleeps,

---

* Originally untitled; published as "Night Poem" in the 1856 edition of *Leaves of Grass*, as "Sleep-
Chasings" in the 1860 edition, and with this title in the 1871 edition.
[1] Bored people, from *ennui*, "boredom" (French).
[2] Masturbators, after Onan, the son of Judah, in Genesis 38:9.

The murderer that is to be hung next day, how does he sleep?
And the murder'd person, how does he sleep?

The female that loves unrequited sleeps,
And the male that loves unrequited sleeps,
The head of the money-maker that plotted all day sleeps,   20
And the enraged and treacherous dispositions, all, all sleep.

I stand in the dark with drooping eyes by the worst-suffering and the
     most restless,
I pass my hands soothingly to and fro a few inches from them,
The restless sink in their beds, they fitfully sleep.

Now I pierce the darkness, new beings appear,
The earth recedes from me into the night,
I saw that it was beautiful, and I see that what is not the earth is beautiful.

I go from bedside to bedside, I sleep close with the other sleepers each
     in turn,
I dream in my dream all the dreams of the other dreamers,   30
And I become the other dreamers.

I am a dance—play up there! the fit is whirling me fast!

I am the ever-laughing—it is new moon and twilight,
I see the hiding of douceurs,[3] I see nimble ghosts whichever way I look,
Cache[4] and cache again deep in the ground and sea, and where it is
     neither ground nor sea.

Well do they do their jobs those journeymen divine,
Only from me can they hide nothing, and would not if they could,
I reckon I am their boss and they make me a pet besides,
And surround me and lead me and run ahead when I walk,
To lift their cunning covers to signify[5] me with stretch'd arms, and
     resume the way;
Onward we move, a gay gang of blackguards! with mirth-shouting   40
     music and wild-flapping pennants of joy!

I am the actor, the actress, the voter, the politician,
The emigrant and the exile, the criminal that stood in the box,[6]
He who has been famous and he who shall be famous after to-day,
The stammerer, the well-form'd person, the wasted or feeble person.

I am she who adorn'd herself and folded her hair expectantly,
My truant lover has come, and it is dark.

---

[3] "Delights" or "pleasures" (French).   [4] Hide.
[5] Their knowing covers to signal.   [6] The courtroom box in which the accused stands.

Double yourself and receive me darkness,
Receive me and my lover too, he will not let me go without him.

I roll myself upon you as upon a bed, I resign myself to the dusk.   50

He whom I call answers me and takes the place of my lover,
He rises with me silently from the bed.

Darkness, you are gentler than my lover, his flesh was sweaty and panting,
I feel the hot moisture yet that he left me.

My hands are spread forth, I pass them in all directions,
I would sound up the shadowy shore to which you are journeying.

Be careful darkness! already what was it touch'd me?
I thought my lover had gone, else darkness and he are one,
I hear the heart-beat, I follow, I fade away.

2

I descend my western course,[7] my sinews are flaccid,   60
Perfume and youth course through me and I am their wake.

It is my face yellow and wrinkled instead of the old woman's,
I sit low in a straw-bottom chair and carefully darn my grandson's
    stockings.

It is I too, the sleepless widow looking out on the winter midnight,
I see the sparkles of starshine on the icy and pallid earth.

A shroud I see and I am the shroud, I wrap a body and lie in the coffin,
It is dark here under ground, it is not evil or pain here, it is blank here,
    for reasons.

(It seems to me that every thing in the light and air ought to be happy,
Whoever is not in his coffin and the dark grave let him know he
    has enough.)

3

I see a beautiful gigantic swimmer swimming naked through the eddies
    of the sea,   70
His brown hair lies close and even to his head, he strikes out with
    courageous arms, he urges himself with his legs,
I see his white body, I see his undaunted eyes,
I hate the swift-running eddies that would dash him head-foremost on
    the rocks.

What are you doing you ruffianly red-trickled waves?
Will you kill the courageous giant? will you kill him in the prime of his
    middle age?

[7] Age.

Steady and long he struggles,
He is baffled, bang'd, bruis'd, he holds out while his strength holds out,
The slapping eddies are spotted with his blood, they bear him away,
   they roll him, swing him, turn him,
His beautiful body is borne in the circling eddies, it is continually
   bruis'd on rocks,
Swiftly and out of sight is borne the brave corpse.   80

4

I turn but do not extricate myself,
Confused, a past-reading, another, but with darkness yet.

The beach is cut by the razory ice-wind, the wreck-guns[8] sound,
The tempest lulls, the moon comes floundering through the drifts.

I look where the ship helplessly heads end on, I hear the burst as she
   strikes, I hear the howls of dismay, they grow fainter and fainter.

I cannot aid with my wringing fingers,
I can but rush to the surf and let it drench me and freeze upon me.

I search with the crowd, not one of the company is wash'd to us alive,
In the morning I help pick up the dead and lay them in rows in a barn.

5

Now of the older war-days, the defeat at Brooklyn,[9]   90
Washington stands inside the lines, he stands on the intrench'd hills amid
   a crowd of officers,
His face is cold and damp, he cannot repress the weeping drops,
He lifts the glass perpetually to his eye, the color is blanch'd from
   his cheeks,
He sees the slaughter of the southern braves confided to him by
   their parents.

The same at last and at last when peace is declared,
He stands in the room of the old tavern, the well-belov'd soldiers all pass
   through,
The officers speechless and slow draw near in their turns,
The chief encircles their necks with his arm and kisses them on the
   cheek,
He kisses lightly the wet cheeks one after another, he shakes hands and
   bids good-by to the army.

6

Now what my mother told me one day as we sat at dinner together,   100
Of when she was a nearly grown girl living home with her parents
   on the old homestead.

---

[8] Guns that fire a life line to ships in distress.
[9] The British defeated American forces at the Battle of Brooklyn Heights on August 27, 1776; Washington was able to ferry his troops to New York City.

A red squaw came one breakfast-time to the old homestead,
On her back she carried a bundle of rushes for rush-bottoming chairs,
Her hair, straight, shiny, coarse, black, profuse, half-envelop'd her face,
Her step was free and elastic, and her voice sounded exquisitely as
    she spoke.

My mother look'd in delight and amazement at the stranger,
She look'd at the freshness of her tall-borne face and full and pliant limbs,
The more she look'd upon her she loved her,
Never before had she seen such wonderful beauty and purity,
She made her sit on a bench by the jamb of the fireplace, she cook'd
    food for her,   110
She had no work to give her, but she gave her remembrance and fondness.

The red squaw staid all the forenoon, and toward the middle of the
    afternoon she went away,
O my mother was loth to have her go away,
All the week she thought of her, she watch'd for her many a month,
She remember'd her many a winter and many a summer,
But the red squaw never came nor was heard of there again.

7

A show of the summer softness—a contact of something unseen—an
    amour of the light and air,
I am jealous and overwhelm'd with friendliness,
And will go gallivant with the light and air myself.

O love and summer, you are in the dreams and in me,   120
Autumn and winter are in the dreams, the farmer goes with his thrift,
The droves[10] and crops increase, the barns are well-fill'd.

Elements merge in the night, ships make tacks in the dreams,
The sailor sails, the exile returns home,
The fugitive returns unharm'd, the immigrant is back beyond months
    and years,
The poor Irishman lives in the simple house of his childhood with the
    well-known neighbors and faces,
They warmly welcome him, he is barefoot again, he forgets he is well off,
The Dutchman voyages home, and the Scotchman and Welshman
    voyage home, and the native of the Mediterranean voyages home,
To every port of England, France, Spain, enter well-fill'd ships,
The Swiss foots it toward his hills, the Prussian goes his way, the
    Hungarian his way, and the Pole his way,   130
The Swede returns, and the Dane and Norwegian return.

---

[10] Of animals.

The homeward bound and the outward bound,
The beautiful lost swimmer, the ennuyé, the onanist, the female that
    loves unrequited, the money-maker,
The actor and actress, those through with their parts and those waiting
    to commence,
The affectionate boy, the husband and wife, the voter, the nominee that
    is chosen and the nominee that has fail'd,
The great already known and the great any time after to-day,
The stammerer, the sick, the perfect-form'd, the homely,
The criminal that stood in the box, the judge that sat and sentenced him,
    the fluent lawyers, the jury, the audience,
The laugher and weeper, the dancer, the midnight widow, the red squaw,
The consumptive, the erysipalite,[11] the idiot, he that is wrong'd,   140
The antipodes,[12] and every one between this and them in the dark,
I swear they are averaged now—one is no better than the other,
The night and sleep have liken'd them and restored them.

I swear they are all beautiful,
Every one that sleeps is beautiful, every thing in the dim light is
    beautiful,
The wildest and bloodiest is over, and all is peace.

Peace is always beautiful,
The myth of heaven indicates peace and night.

The myth of heaven indicates the soul,
The soul is always beautiful, it appears more or it appears less, it comes
    or it lags behind,   150
It comes from its embower'd garden and looks pleasantly on itself
    and encloses the world,
Perfect and clean the genitals previously jetting, and perfect and clean
    the womb cohering,
The head well-grown proportion'd and plumb, and the bowels and joints
    proportion'd and plumb.

The soul is always beautiful,
The universe is duly in order, every thing is in its place,
What has arrived is in its place and what waits shall be in its place,
The twisted skull waits, the watery or rotten blood waits,
The child of the glutton or venerealee waits long, and the child
    of the drunkard waits long, and the drunkard himself waits long,
The sleepers that lived and died wait, the far advanced are to go on in
    their turns, and the far behind are to come on in their turns,
The diverse shall be no less diverse, but they shall flow and unite—
    they unite now.   160

---

[11] One who suffers from erysipelas, a bacterial infection of the skin.
[12] Points on opposite sides of the earth; here, those who live on the other side of the earth.

8

The sleepers are very beautiful as they lie unclothed,
They flow hand in hand over the whole earth from east to west as
  they lie unclothed,
The Asiatic and African are hand in hand, the European and American
  are hand in hand,
Learn'd and unlearn'd are hand in hand, and male and female are hand
  in hand,
The bare arm of the girl crosses the bare breast of her lover, they
  press close without lust, his lips press her neck,
The father holds his grown or ungrown son in his arms with measureless
  love, and the son holds the father in his arms with measureless love,
The white hair of the mother shines on the white wrist of the daughter,
The breath of the boy goes with the breath of the man, friend is inarm'd
  by friend,
The scholar kisses the teacher and the teacher kisses the scholar, the
  wrong'd is made right,
The call of the slave is one with the master's call, and the master
  salutes the slave,   170
The felon steps forth from the prison, the insane becomes sane, the
  suffering of sick persons is reliev'd,
The sweatings and fevers stop, the throat that was unsound is sound, the
  lungs of the consumptive are resumed, the poor distress'd head is free,
The joints of the rheumatic move as smoothly as ever, and smoother
  than ever,
Stiflings and passages open, the paralyzed become supple,
The swell'd and convuls'd and congested awake to themselves in
  condition,
They pass the invigoration of the night and the chemistry of the night,
  and awake.

I too pass from the night,
I stay a while away O night, but I return to you again and love you.

Why should I be afraid to trust myself to you?
I am not afraid, I have been well brought forward by you,   180
I love the rich running day, but I do not desert her in whom I lay so long,
I know not how I came of you and I know not where I go with you, but
  I know I came well and shall go well.

I will stop only a time with the night, and rise betimes,
I will duly pass the day O my mother, and duly return to you.

1855

from   WHISPERS OF HEAVENLY DEATH*

CHANTING THE SQUARE DEIFIC[1]

I

Chanting the square deific, out of the One advancing, out of the sides,
Out of the old and new, out of the square entirely divine,
Solid, four-sided, (all the sides needed,) from this side Jehovah[2] am I,
Old Brahm I, and I Saturnius[3] am;
Not Time affects me—I am Time, old, modern as any,
Unpersuadable, relentless, executing righteous judgments,
As the Earth, the Father, the brown old Kronos,[4] with laws,
Aged beyond computation, yet ever new, ever with those mighty laws
    rolling,
Relentless I forgive no man—whoever sins dies—I will have that
    man's life;
Therefore let none expect mercy—have the seasons, gravitation, the
    appointed days, mercy? no more have I,   10
But as the seasons and gravitation, and as all the appointed days that
    forgive not,
I dispense from this side judgments inexorable without the least remorse.

2

Consolator most mild, the promis'd one advancing,
With gentle hand extended, the mightier God am I,
Foretold by prophets and poets in their most rapt prophecies and poems,
From this side, lo! the Lord Christ gazes—lo! Hermes[5] I—lo! mine is
    Hercules'[6] face,
All sorrow, labor, suffering, I, tallying it, absorb in myself,
Many times have I been rejected, taunted, put in prison, and crucified,
    and many times shall be again,
All the world have I given up for my dear brothers' and sisters' sake,
    for the soul's sake,
Wending my way through the homes of men, rich or poor, with the kiss
    of affection,   20

---

* Thirteen poems that first appeared in *Passage to India* (1871); published as a group of eighteen
poems in the 1881 edition of *Leaves of Grass*.
  [1] First printed in "Sequel to Drum-Taps" (1856–1866), then in *Passage to India* (1871); added to the
1881 edition of *Leaves*.
  [2] The Judeo-Christian God.
  [3] Brahma, the supreme god of Hindu theology; Saturn, the Titan, or giant god, who preceded Jupiter
as the supreme god of Roman myth.
  [4] The equivalent of Saturn; Chronus, associated with time.
  [5] According to Greek myth, the winged messenger of the gods.
  [6] According to Greek myth, a hero known for his strength.

For I am affection, I am the cheer-bringing God, with hope and
    all-enclosing charity,
With indulgent words as to children, with fresh and sane words,
    mine only,
Young and strong I pass knowing well I am destin'd myself to an
    early death;
But my charity has no death—my wisdom dies not, neither early nor late,
And my sweet love bequeath'd here and elsewhere never dies.

3

Aloof, dissatisfied, plotting revolt,
Comrade of criminals, brother of slaves,
Crafty, despised, a drudge, ignorant,
With sudra[7] face and worn brow, black, but in the depths of my heart,
    proud as any,
Lifted now and always against whoever scorning assumes to rule me,   30
Morose, full of guile, full of reminiscences, brooding, with many wiles,
(Though it was thought I was baffled and dispel'd, and my wiles done,
    but that will never be,)
Defiant, I, Satan, still live, still utter words, in new lands duly appearing,
    (and old ones also,)
Permanent here from my side, warlike, equal with any, real as any,
Nor time nor change shall ever change me or my words.

4

Santa Spirita,[8] breather, life,
Beyond the light, lighter than light,
Beyond the flames of hell, joyous, leaping easily above hell,
Beyond Paradise, perfumed solely with mine own perfume,
Including all life on earth, touching, including God, including Saviour
    and Satan,   40
Ethereal, pervading all, (for without me what were all? what were God?)
Essence of forms, life of the real identities, permanent, positive,
    (namely the unseen,)
Life of the great round world, the sun and stars, and of man, I, the
    general soul,
Here the square finishing, the solid, I the most solid,
Breathe my breath also through these songs.

1865–1866

A NOISELESS PATIENT SPIDER*

A noiseless patient spider,
I mark'd where on a little promontory it stood isolated,

---

[7] The lowest Hindu caste.   [8] The Holy Spirit.
* First appeared in London's *Broadway Magazine* in October 1868.

Mark'd how to explore the vacant vast surrounding,
It launch'd forth filament, filament, filament, out of itself,
Ever unreeling them, ever tirelessly speeding them.

And you O my soul where you stand,
Surrounded, detached, in measureless oceans of space,
Ceaselessly musing, venturing, throwing, seeking the spheres to
    connect them,
Till the bridge you will need be form'd, till the ductile anchor hold,
Till the gossamer thread you fling catch somewhere, O my soul.   10

1868

from   FROM NOON TO STARRY NIGHT*

TO A LOCOMOTIVE IN WINTER[1]

Thee for my recitative,[2]
Thee in the driving storm even as now, the snow, the winter-day declining,
Thee in thy panoply,[3] thy measur'd dual throbbing and thy beat convulsive,
Thy black cylindric body, golden brass and silvery steel,
Thy ponderous side-bars, parallel and connecting rods, gyrating, shuttling
    at thy sides,
Thy metrical, now swelling pant and roar, now tapering in the distance,
Thy great protruding head-light fix'd in front,
Thy long, pale, floating vapor-pennants, tinged with delicate purple,
The dense and murky clouds out-belching from thy smoke-stack,
Thy knitted frame, thy springs and valves, the tremulous twinkle of
    thy wheels,   10
Thy train of cars behind, obedient, merrily following,
Through gale or calm, now swift, now slack, yet steadily careering;
Type of the modern—emblem of motion and power—pulse of the
    continent,
For once come serve the Muse and merge in verse, even as here I see thee,
With storm and buffeting gusts of wind and falling snow,
By day thy warning ringing bell to sound its notes,
By night thy silent signal lamps to swing.

Fierce-throated beauty!
Roll through my chant with all thy lawless music, thy swinging lamps
    at night,

---

* Twenty-two poems that first appeared in the 1881 edition of *Leaves of Grass*.
[1] First published in the New York *Daily Tribune* on February 19, 1876.
[2] In musical terminology, an intermediate form between speaking and singing: a particularly apt mode of address for Whitman, who is both conversational and celebratory.
[3] Armor.

Thy madly-whistled laughter, echoing, rumbling like an earthquake,
    rousing all,   20
Law of thyself complete, thine own track firmly holding,
(No sweetness debonair of tearful harp or glib piano thine,)
Thy trills of shrieks by rocks and hills return'd,
Launch'd o'er the prairies wide, across the lakes,
To the free skies unpent and glad and strong.

1876

from   SONGS OF PARTING*

CAMPS OF GREEN[1]

Not alone those camps of white, old comrades of the wars,
When as order'd forward, after a long march,
Footsore and weary, soon as the light lessens we halt for the night,
Some of us so fatigued carrying the gun and knapsack, dropping asleep
    in our tracks,
Others pitching the little tents, and the fires lit up begin to sparkle,
Outposts of pickets posted surrounding alert through the dark,
And a word provided for countersign, careful for safety,
Till to the call of the drummers at daybreak loudly beating the drums,
We rise up refresh'd, the night and sleep pass'd over, and resume our
    journey,
Or proceed to battle.   10

Lo, the camps of the tents of green,
Which the days of peace keep filling, and the days of war keep filling,
With a mystic army, (is it too order'd forward? is it too only halting awhile,
Till night and sleep pass over?)

Now in those camps of green, in their tents dotting the world,
In the parents, children, husbands, wives, in them, in the old and young,
Sleeping under the sunlight, sleeping under the moonlight, content and
    silent there at last,
Behold the mighty bivouac-field and waiting-camp of all,
Of the corps and generals all, and the President over the corps and
    generals all,
And of each of us O soldiers, and of each and all in the ranks we fought,   20
(There without hatred we all, all meet.)

For presently O soldiers, we too camp in our place in the bivouac-
    camps of green,

* Seventeen poems from five different editions, first collected with this title in the 1881 edition of
Leaves of Grass.
[1] First appeared in *Drum-Taps* (1865); added to the 1867 edition of *Leaves.*

But we need not provide for outposts, nor word for the countersign,
Nor drummer to beat the morning drum.

1865

AS THEY DRAW TO A CLOSE*

As they draw to a close,
Of what underlies the precedent songs—of my aims in them,
Of the seed I have sought to plant in them,
Of joy, sweet joy, through many a year, in them,
(For them, for them have I lived, in them my work is done,)
Of many an aspiration fond, of many a dream and plan;
Through Space and Time fused in a chant, and the flowing eternal identity,
To Nature encompassing these, encompassing God—to the joyous,
    electric all,
To the sense of Death, and accepting exulting in Death in its turn the
    same as life,
The entrance of man to sing;   10
To compact you, ye parted, diverse lives,
To put rapport the mountains and rocks and streams,
And the winds of the north, and the forests of oak and pine,
With you O soul.

1871

from   FIRST ANNEX: SANDS AT SEVENTY†

DEATH OF GENERAL GRANT[1]

As one by one withdraw the lofty actors,
From that great play on history's stage eterne,
That lurid, partial act of war and peace—of old and new contending,
Fought out through wrath, fears, dark dismays, and many a long suspense;
All past—and since, in countless graves receding, mellowing,
Victor's and vanquish'd—Lincoln's and Lee's[2]—now thou with them,
Man of the mighty days—and equal to the days!

---

* First published in *Passage to India* (1871) as "Thought" and with this title in the 1881 edition of
Leaves of Grass.
† First published with prose pieces in *November Boughs* (1888); added to the 1884 reprint of *Leaves
of Grass*.
[1] First appeared in *Harper's Weekly* on May 16, 1885, although Ulysses S. Grant (1822–1885),
eighteenth U.S. president (1869–1877), did not die until July 23, 1885.
[2] Abraham Lincoln and Robert E. Lee.

Thou from the prairies!—tangled and many-vein'd and hard has been
   thy part,
To admiration has it been enacted!

1885

from   SECOND ANNEX: GOOD-BYE MY FANCY*

OSCEOLA[1]

*[When I was nearly grown to manhood in Brooklyn, New York, (middle of 1838,) I met
one of the return'd U. S. Marines from Fort Moultrie, S. C., and had long talks with
him—learn'd the occurrence below described—death of Osceola. The latter was a young,
brave, leading Seminole in the Florida war of that time—was surrender'd to our troops,
imprison'd and literally died of "a broken heart," at Fort Moultrie. He sicken'd of his
confinement—the doctor and officers made every allowance and kindness possible for
him; then the close:]*

When his hour for death had come,
He slowly rais'd himself from the bed on the floor,
Drew on his war-dress, shirt, leggings, and girdled the belt around his waist,
Call'd for vermilion paint (his looking-glass was held before him,)
Painted half his face and neck, his wrists, and back-hands.
Put the scalp-knife carefully in his belt—then lying down, resting a moment,
Rose again, half sitting, smiled, gave in silence his extended hand to each
   and all,
Sank faintly low to the floor (tightly grasping the tomahawk handle,)
Fix'd his look on wife and little children—the last:

(And here a line in memory of his name and death.)

1890

L. OF G. 'S PURPORT†

Not to exclude or demarcate, or pick out evils from their formidable
   masses (even to expose them,)
But add, fuse, complete, extend—and celebrate the immortal and
   the good.

Haughty this song, its words and scope,
To span vast realms of space and time,
Evolution—the cumulative—growths and generations.

* Thirty-one poems and prose pieces added to the 1891–1892 edition of *Leaves of Grass*.
[1] First published in *Monson's Illustrated World* in April 1890. Osceola (?–1838) was a brave leader
in the second Seminole War (1835–1837) who was seized and imprisoned while working toward a
truce; he died after four months in captivity. The bracketed note is Whitman's.
† A statement of Whitman's intent in writing *Leaves of Grass*.

Begun in ripen'd youth and steadily pursued,
Wandering, peering, dallying with all—war, peace, day, and night
   absorbing,
Never even for one brief hour abandoning my task,
I end it here in sickness, poverty, and old age.

I sing of life, yet mind me well of death: 10
To-day shadowy Death dogs my steps, my seated shape, and has for years—
Draws sometimes close to me, as face to face.

                                            1891

GOOD-BYE MY FANCY!

Good-bye my Fancy!
Farewell dear mate, dear love!
I'm going away, I know not where,
Or to what fortune, or whether I may ever see you again,
So Good-bye my Fancy.
Now for my last—let me look back a moment;
The slower fainter ticking of the clock is in me,
Exit, nightfall, and soon the heart-thud stopping.

Long have we lived, joy'd, caress'd together;
Delightful!—now separation—Good-bye my Fancy.   10

Yet let me not be too hasty,
Long indeed have we lived, slept, filter'd, become really blended
   into one;
Then if we die we die together, (yes, we'll remain one,)
If we go anywhere we'll go together to meet what happens,
May-be we'll be better off and blither, and learn something,
May-be it is yourself now really ushering me to the true songs,
   (who knows?)
May-be it is you the mortal knob really undoing, turning—so now
   finally,
Good-bye—and hail! my Fancy.

                                            1891

from   A BACKWARD GLANCE O'ER TRAVEL'D ROADS*

Perhaps the best of songs heard, or of any and all true love, or life's fairest episodes, or sailors', soldiers' trying scenes on land or sea, is the *résumé* of them, or
any of them, long afterwards, looking at the actualities away back past, with all

* First appeared as the introduction to *November Boughs* (1888) and added to the 1889 edition of
Leaves of Grass.

their practical excitations gone. How the soul loves to float amid such reminiscences!

So here I sit gossiping in the early candle-light of old age—I and my book—casting backward glances over our travel'd road. After completing, as it were, the journey—(a varied jaunt of years, with many halts and gaps of intervals—or some lengthen'd ship-voyage, where in more than once the last hour had apparently arrived, and we seem'd certainly going down—yet reaching port in a sufficient way through all discomfitures at last)—After completing my poems, I am curious to review them in the light of their own (at the time unconscious, or mostly unconscious) intentions, with certain unfoldings of the thirty years they seek to embody. These lines, therefore, will probably blend the weft of first purposes and speculations, with the warp of that experience afterwards, always bringing strange developments.

Result of seven or eight stages and struggles extending through nearly thirty years, (as I nigh my three-score-and-ten[1] I live largely on memory,) I look upon "Leaves of Grass," now finish'd to the end of its opportunities and powers, as my definitive *carte visite*[2] to the coming generations of the New World,[3] if I may assume to say so. That I have not gain'd the acceptance of my own time, but have fallen back on fond dreams of the future—anticipations—("still lives the song, though Regnar dies"[4])—That from a worldly and business point of view "Leaves of Grass" has been worse than a failure—that public criticism on the book and myself as author of it yet shows mark'd anger and contempt more than anything else—("I find a solid line of enemies to you everywhere,"—letter from W. S. K.,[5] Boston, May 28, 1884)—And that solely for publishing it I have been the object of two or three pretty serious special official buffetings—is all probably no more than I ought to have expected.[6] I had my choice when I commmenc'd. I bid neither for soft eulogies, big money returns, nor the approbation of existing schools and conventions. As fulfill'd, or partially fulfill'd, the best comfort of the whole business (after a small band of the dearest friends and upholders ever vouchsafed to man or cause—doubtless all the more faithful and uncompromising—this little phalanx!—for being so few) is that, unstopp'd and unwarp'd by any influence outside the soul within me, I have had my say entirely my own way, and put it unerringly on record—the value thereof to be decided by time.

In calculating that decision, William O'Connor and Dr. Bucke[7] are far more peremptory than I am. Behind all else that can be said, I consider "Leaves of Grass" and its theory experimental—as, in the deepest sense, I consider our American republic itself to be, with its theory. (I think I have at least enough philosophy not to be too absolutely certain of any thing, or any results.) In the second place, the volume is a *sortie*—whether to prove triumphant, and conquer

---

[1] The biblical "allotment" of years for human life, in Psalm 89:10.

[2] "Calling card" (French).

[3] From the ballad "Alfred the Harper" (14.1.3), by John Sterling (1806–1844); Regnar was a British hero slaughtered by the Danes.

[4] Whitman's note: "When Champollion, on his death-bed, handed to the printer the revised proof of his 'Egyptian Grammer,' he said gayly, 'Be careful of this—it is my *carte de visite* to posterity.' " Jean François Champollion (1790–1832) was a French Egyptologist.

[5] William Sloane Kennedy (1850–1929), a critic and Whitman biographer.

[6] Whitman was in fact fired from his Department of the Interior post in 1865.

[7] O'Connor (1832–1929), a journalist, wrote a vindication of Whitman (*The Good Gray Poet* [1866]); Richard Maurice Bucke (1837–1902), a Canadian physician, wrote a biographical study of the poet (*Walt Whitman* [1883]). Both men were close friends and disciples of Whitman.

its field of aim and escape and construction, nothing less than a hundred years from now can fully answer. I consider the point that I have positively gain'd a hearing, to far more than make up for any and all other lacks and withholdings. Essentially, *that* was from the first, and has remain'd throughout, the main object. Now it seems to be achiev'd, I am certainly contented to waive any otherwise momentous drawbacks, as of little account. Candidly and dispassionately reviewing all my intentions, I feel that they were creditable—and I accept the result, whatever it may be.

After continued personal ambition and effort, as a young fellow, to enter with the rest into competition for the usual rewards, business, political, literary, etc.— to take part in the great *mêlée,* both for victory's prize itself and to do some good—After years of those aims and pursuits, I found myself remaining possess'd, at the age of thirty-one to thirty-three, with a special desire and conviction. Or rather, to be quite exact, a desire that had been flitting through my previous life, or hovering on the flanks, mostly indefinite hitherto, had steadily advanced to the front, defined itself, and finally dominated everything else. This was a feeling or ambition to articulate and faithfully express in literary or poetic form, and uncompromisingly, my own physical, emotional, moral, intellectual, and æsthetic Personality, in the midst of, and tallying, the momentous spirit and facts of its immediate days, and of current America—and to exploit that Personality, identified with place and date, in a far more candid and comprehensive sense than any hitherto poem or book.

Perhaps this is in brief, or suggests, all I have sought to do. Given the Nineteenth Century, with the United States, and what they furnish as area and points of view, "Leaves of Grass" is, or seeks to be, simply a faithful and doubtless self-will'd record. In the midst of all, it gives one man's—the author's—identity, ardors, observations, faiths, and thoughts, color'd hardly at all with any decided coloring from other faiths or other identities. Plenty of songs had been sung— beautiful, matchless songs—adjusted to other lands than these—another spirit and stage of evolution; but I would sing, and leave out or put in, quite solely with reference to America and to-day. Modern science and democracy seem'd to be throwing out their challenge to poetry to put them in its statements in contradistinction to the songs and myths of the past. As I see it now (perhaps too late,) I have unwittingly taken up that challenge and made an attempt at such statements—which I certainly would not assume to do now, knowing more clearly what it means.

For grounds for "Leaves of Grass," as a poem, I abandon'd the conventional themes, which do not appear in it: none of the stock ornamentation, or choice plots of love or war, or high, exceptional personages of Old-World song; nothing, as I may say, for beauty's sake—no legend, or myth, or romance, nor euphemism, nor rhyme. But the broadest average of humanity and its identities in the now ripening Nineteenth Century, and especially in each of their countless examples and practical occupations in the United States to-day.

One main contrast of the ideas behind every page of my verses, compared with establish'd poems, is their different relative attitude towards God, towards the objective universe, and still more (by reflection, confession, assumption, etc.) the quite changed attitude of the ego, the one chanting or talking, towards himself and towards his fellow-humanity. It is certainly time for America, above all, to begin this readjustment in the scope and basic point of view of verse; for everything else has changed. As I write, I see in an article on Wordsworth, in one of the current

English magazines, the lines, "A few weeks ago an eminent French critic said that, owing to the special tendency to science and to its all-devouring force, poetry would cease to be read in fifty years." But I anticipate the very contrary. Only a firmer, vastly broader, new area begins to exist—nay, is already form'd—to which the poetic genius must emigrate. Whatever may have been the case in years gone by, the true use for the imaginative faculty of modern times is to give ultimate vivification to facts, to science, and to common lives, endowing them with the glows and glories and final illustriousness which belong to every real thing, and to real things only. Without that ultimate vivification—which the poet or other artist alone can give—reality would seem incomplete, and science, democracy, and life itself, finally in vain.

Few appreciate the moral revolutions, our age, which have been profounder far than the material or inventive or war-produced ones. The Nineteenth Century, now well towards its close (and ripening into fruit the seeds of the two preceding centuries[8])—the uprisings of national masses and shiftings of boundary-lines—the historical and other prominent facts of the United States—the war of attempted Secession—the stormy rush and haste of nebulous forces—never can future years witness more excitement and din of action—never completer change of army front along the whole line, the whole civilized world. For all these new and evolutionary facts, meanings, purposes, new poetic messages, new forms and expressions, are inevitable.

My Book and I—what a period we have presumed to span! those thirty years from 1850 to '80—and America in them! Proud, proud indeed may we be, if we have cull'd enough of that period in its own spirit to worthily waft a few live breaths of it to the future!

Let me not dare, here or anywhere, for my own purposes, or any purposes, to attempt the definition of Poetry, nor answer the question what it is. Like Religion, Love, Nature, while those terms are indispensable, and we all give a sufficiently accurate meaning to them, in my opinion no definition that has ever been made sufficiently encloses the name Poetry; nor can any rule or convention ever so absolutely obtain but some great exception may arise and disregard and overturn it.

Also it must be carefully remember'd that first-class literature does not shine by any luminosity of its own; nor do its poems. They grow of circumstances, and are evolutionary. The actual living light is always curiously from elsewhere—follows unaccountable sources, and is lunar and relative at the best. There are, I know, certain controling themes that seem endlessly appropriated to the poets—as war, in the past—in the Bible, religious rapture and adoration—always love, beauty, some fine plot, or pensive or other emotion. But, strange as it may sound at first, I will say there is something striking far deeper and towering far higher than those themes for the best elements of modern song.

Just as all the old imaginative works rest, after their kind, on long trains of presuppositions, often entirely unmention'd by themselves, yet supplying the most important bases of them, and without which they could have had no reason for being, so "Leaves of Grass," before a line was written, presupposed something different from any other, and, as it stands, is the result of such presupposition. I should say, indeed, it were useless to attempt reading the book without first carefully tallying that preparatory background and quality in the mind. Think of the

---

[8] Whitman's note: "The ferment and germination even of the United States to-day, dating back to, and in my opinion mainly founded on, the Elizabethan age in English history, the age of Francis Bacon and Shakspere. Indeed, when we pursue it, what growth or advent is there that does not date back, back, until lost—perhaps its most tantalizing clues lost—in the receded horizons of the past?"

United States to-day—the facts of these thirty-eight or forty empires solder'd in one—sixty or seventy millions of equals, with their lives, their passions, their future—these incalculable, modern, American, seething multitudes around us, of which we are inseparable parts! Think, in comparison, of the petty environage and limited area of the poets of past or present Europe, no matter how great their genius. Think of the absence and ignorance, in all cases hitherto, of the multitudinousness, vitality, and the unprecedented stimulants of to-day and here. It almost seems as if a poetry with cosmic and dynamic features of magnitude and limitlessness suitable to the human soul, were never possible before. It is certain that a poetry of absolute faith and equality for the use of the democratic masses never was.

In estimating first-class song, a sufficient Nationality, or, on the other hand, what may be call'd the negative and lack of it, (as in Goethe's case, it sometimes seems to me,) is often, if not always, the first element. One needs only a little penetration to see, at more or less removes, the material facts of their country and radius, with the coloring of the moods of humanity at the time, and its gloomy or hopeful prospects, behind all poets and each poet, and forming their birth-marks. I know very well that my "Leaves" could not possibly have emerged or been fashion'd or completed, from any other era than the latter half of the Nineteenth Century, nor any other land than democratic America, and from the absolute triumph of the National Union arms.

And whether my friend claim it for me or not, I know well enough, too, that in respect to pictorial talent, dramatic situations, and especially in verbal melody and all the conventional technique of poetry, not only the divine works that to-day stand ahead in the world's reading, but dozens more, transcend (some of them immeasurably transcend) all I have done, or could do. But it seem'd to me, as the objects in Nature, the themes of æstheticism, and all special exploitations of the mind and soul, involve not only their own inherent quality, but the quality, just as inherent and important, of *their point of view*,[9] the time had come to reflect all themes and things, old and new, in the lights thrown on them by the advent of America and democracy—to chant those themes through the utterance of one, not only the grateful and reverent legatee of the past, but the born child of the New World—to illustrate all through the genesis and ensemble of to-day; and that such illustration and ensemble are the chief demands of America's prospective imaginative literature. Not to carry out, in the approved style, some choice plot of fortune or misfortune, or fancy, or fine thoughts, or incidents, or courtesies—all of which has been done overwhelmingly and well, probably never to be excell'd—but that while in such æsthetic presentation of objects, passions, plots, thoughts, etc., our lands and days do not want, and probably will never have, anything better than they already possess from the bequests of the past, it still remains to be said that there is even towards all those a subjective and contemporary point of view appropriate to ourselves alone, and to our new genius and environments, different from anything hitherto; and that such conception of current or gone-by life and art is for us the only means of their assimilation consistent with the Western world.

Indeed, and anyhow, to put it specifically, has not the time arrived when, (if it must be plainly said, for democratic America's sake, if for no other) there must imperatively come a readjustment of the whole theory and nature of Poetry? The

---

[9] Whitman's note: "According to Immanuel Kant, the last essential reality, giving shape and significance to all the rest." Kant (1724–1804) was a German metaphysician and transcendental philosopher.

question is important, and I may turn the argument over and repeat it: Does not the best thought of our day and Republic conceive of a birth and spirit of song superior to anything past or present? To the effectual and moral consolidation of our lands (already, as materially establish'd, the greatest factors in known history, and far, far greater through what they prelude and necessitate, and are to be in future)—to conform with and build on the concrete realities and theories of the universe furnish'd by science, and henceforth the only irrefragable basis for anything, verse included—to root both influences in the emotional and imaginative action of the modern time, and dominate all that precedes or opposes them—is not either a radical advance and step forward, or a new verteber[10] of the best song indispensable?

The New World receives with joy the poems of the antique, with European feudalism's rich fund of epics, plays, ballads—seeks not in the least to deaden or displace those voices from our ear and area—holds them indeed as indispensable studies, influences, records, comparisons. But though the dawn-dazzle of the sun of literature is in those poems for us of to-day—though perhaps the best parts of current character in nations, social groups, or any man's or woman's individuality, Old World or New, are from them—and though if I were ask'd to name the most precious bequest to current American civilization from all the hitherto ages, I am not sure but I would name those old and less old songs ferried hither from east and west—some serious words and debits remain; some acrid considerations demand a hearing. Of the great poems receiv'd from abroad and from the ages, and to-day enveloping and penetrating America, is there one that is consistent with these United States, or essentially applicable to them as they are and are to be? Is there one whose underlying basis is not a denial and insult to democracy? What a comment it forms, anyhow, on this era of literary fulfilment, with the splendid day-rise of science and resuscitation of history, that our chief religious and poetical works are not our own, nor adapted to our light, but have been furnish'd by far-back ages out of their arriere[11] and darkness, or, at most, twilight dimness! What is there in those works that so imperiously and scornfully dominates all our advanced civilization, and culture?

Even Shakespere, who so suffuses current letters and art (which indeed have in most degrees grown out of him,) belongs essentially to the buried past. Only he holds the proud distinction for certain important phases of that past, of being the loftiest of the singers life has yet given voice to. All, however, relate to and rest upon conditions, standards, politics, sociologies, ranges of belief, that have been quite eliminated from the Eastern hemisphere, and never existed at all in the Western. As authoritative types of song they belong in America just about as much as the persons and institutes they depict. True, it may be said, the emotional, moral, and æsthetic natures of humanity have not radically changed—that in these the old poems apply to our times and all times, irrespective of date; and that they are of incalculable value as pictures of the past. I willingly make those admissions, and to their fullest extent; then advance the points herewith as of serious, even paramount importance.

I have indeed put on record elsewhere my reverence and eulogy for those never-to-be-excell'd poetic bequests, and their indescribable preciousness as heirlooms for America. Another and separate point must now be candidly stated. If I had not stood before those poems with uncover'd head, fully aware of their colossal grandeur and beauty of form and spirit, I could not have written "Leaves of

---

[10] Vertebra.   [11] "Backward," "behind the times" (French).

Grass." My verdict and conclusions as illustrated in its pages are arrived at through the temper and inculcation of the old works as much as through anything else—perhaps more than through anything else. As America fully and fairly construed is the legitimate result and evolutionary outcome of the past, so I would dare to claim for my verse. Without stopping to qualify the averment, the Old World has had the poems of myths, fictions, feudalism, conquest, caste, dynastic wars, and splendid exceptional characters and affairs, which have been great; but the New World needs the poems of realities and science and of the democratic average and basic equality, which shall be greater. In the centre of all, and object of all, stands the Human Being, towards whose heroic and spiritual evolution poems and everything directly or indirectly tend, Old World or New.

Continuing the subject, my friends have more than once suggested—or may be the garrulity of advancing age is possessing me—some further embryonic facts of "Leaves of Grass," and especially how I enter'd upon them. Dr. Bucke has, in his volume, already fully and fairly described the preparation of my poetic field, with the particular and general plowing, planting, seeding, and occupation of the ground, till everything was fertilized, rooted, and ready to start its own way for good or bad. Not till after all this, did I attempt any serious acquaintance with poetic literature. Along in my sixteenth year I had become possessor of a stout, well-cramm'd one thousand page octavo volume (I have it yet,) containing Walter Scott's poetry entire—an inexhaustible mine and treasury of poetic forage (especially the endless forests and jungles of notes)—has been so to me for fifty years, and remains so to this day.[12]

Later, at intervals, summers and falls, I used to go off, sometimes for a week at a stretch, down in the country, or to Long Island's seashores—there, in the presence of outdoor influences, I went over thoroughly the Old and New Testaments, and absorb'd (probably to better advantage for me than in any library or indoor room—it makes such difference *where* you read,) Shakespere, Ossian,[13] the best translated versions I could get of Homer, Eschylus, Sophocles,[14] the old German Nibelungen,[15] the ancient Hindoo poems, and one or two other masterpieces, Dante's[16] among them. As it happen'd, I read the latter mostly in an old wood. The Iliad (Buckley's prose version,) I read first thoroughly on the peninsula of Orient, northeast end of Long Island, in a shelter'd hollow of rocks and sand, with the sea on each side. (I have wonder'd since why I was not overwhelm'd by those mighty masters. Likely because I read them, as described, in the full presence of

---

[12] Whitman's note: "Sir Walter Scott's COMPLETE POEMS; especially including BORDER MINSTRELSY; then Sir Tristrem; Lay of the Last Minstrel; Ballads from the German; Marmion; Lady of the Lake; Vision of Don Roderick; Lord of the Isles; Rokeby; Bridal of Triermain; Field of Waterloo; Harold the Dauntless; all the Dramas; various Introductions, endless interesting Notes, and Essays on Poetry, Romance, etc.

Lockhart's 1833 (or '34) edition with Scott's latest and copious revisions and annotations. (All the poems were thoroughly read by me, but the ballads of the Border Minstrelsy over and over again.)"

[13] A third-century Gaelic poet whose epic poems were translated by James Macpherson (1736–1796), a Scottish poet; many of the poems presented by Macpherson as close translations from the Gaelic were largely Macpherson's own work. Even after the hoax was exposed, the poems remained very popular.

[14] The eighth-century B.C. Greek epic poet, author of the *Iliad* and the *Odyssey*; Aeschylus (525–456 B.C.) and Sophocles (496?–406 B.C.) were Greek tragic dramatists who wrote *Oedipus the King* and *Agamemnon*, respectively.

[15] The *Nibelungen*, or *Nibelungenlied* (early 13th century) is the German epic about the legendary Siegfried, and is the subject of Richard Wagner's four-part opera, *Der Ring des Nibelungen* (1876).

[16] Dante Alighieri (1265–1321), the Italian poet whose masterpiece was *The Divine Comedy*.

Nature, under the sun, with the far-spreading landscape and vistas, or the sea rolling in.)

Toward the last I had among much else look'd over Edgar Poe's poems—of which I was not an admirer, tho' I always saw that beyond their limited range of melody (like perpetual chimes of music bells, ringing from lower *b* flat up to *g*) they were melodious expressions, and perhaps never excell'd ones, of certain pronounc'd phases of human morbidity. (The Poetic area is very spacious—has room for all—has so many mansions!) But I was repaid in Poe's prose by the idea that (at any rate for our occasions, our day) there can be no such thing as a long poem. The same thought had been haunting my mind before, but Poe's argument, though short, work'd the sum out and proved it to me.

Another point had an early settlement, clearing the ground greatly. I saw from the time my enterprise and questionings positively shaped themselves (how best can I express my own distinctive era and surroundings, America, Democracy?) that the trunk and centre whence the answer was to radiate, and to which all should return from straying however far a distance, must be an identical body and soul, a personality—which personality, after many considerations and ponderings I deliberately settled should be myself—indeed could not be any other. I also felt strongly (whether I have shown it or not) that to the true and full estimate of the Present both the Past and the Future are main considerations.

These, however, and much more might have gone on and come to naught (almost positively would have come to naught,) if a sudden, vast, terrible, direct and indirect stimulus for new and national declamatory expression had not been given to me. It is certain, I say, that, although I had made a start before, only from the occurrence of the Secession War, and what it show'd me as by flashes of lightning, with the emotional depths it sounded and arous'd (of course, I don't mean in my heart only, I saw it just as plainly in others, in millions)—that only from the strong flare and provocation of that war's sights and scenes the final reasons-for-being of an autochthonic[17] and passionate song definitely came forth.

I went down to the war fields in Virginia (end of 1862), lived thenceforward in camp—saw great battles and the days and nights afterward—partook of all the fluctuations, gloom, despair, hopes again arous'd, courage evoked—death readily risk'd—*the cause,* too—along and filling those agonistic and lurid following years, 1863-'64-'65—the real parturition years (more than 1776-'83) of this henceforth homogeneous Union. Without those three or four years and the experiences they gave, "Leaves of Grass" would not now be existing.

1888

from *DEMOCRATIC VISTAS**

[American Literature]

America, filling the present with greatest deeds and problems, cheerfully accepting the past, including feudalism (as, indeed, the present is but the legitimate birth

[17] Indigenous; here, a peculiarly American song.

* First appeared in the *Galaxy* in December 1867 as "Democracy"; incorporated in *Democratic Vistas* with the essays "Personalism" and "Literature" in 1871. In 1867 Thomas Carlyle (1795–1881) published the essay "Shooting Niagara," in which he offered a scathing critique of American democracy. *Democratic Vistas* is Whitman's response.

of the past, including feudalism), counts, as I reckon, for her justification and success (for who, as yet, dare claim success?) almost entirely on the future. Nor is that hope unwarranted. To-day, ahead, though dimly yet, we see, in vistas, a copious, sane, gigantic offspring. For our New World I consider far less important for what it has done, or what it is, than for results to come. Sole among nationalities, these States have assumed the task to put in forms of lasting power and practicality, on areas of amplitude rivaling the operations of the physical kosmos, the moral political speculations of ages, long, long deferr'd, the democratic republican principle, and the theory of development and perfection by voluntary standards, and self-reliance. Who else, indeed, except the United States, in history, so far, have accepted in unwitting faith, and, as we now see, stand, act upon, and go security for, these things?

* * *

Before proceeding further, it were perhaps well to discriminate on certain points. Literature tills its crops in many fields, and some may flourish, while others lag. What I say in these Vistas has its main bearing on imaginative literature, especially poetry, the stock of all. In the department of science, and the specialty of journalism, there appear, in these States, promises, perhaps fulfilments, of highest earnestness, reality, and life. These, of course, are modern. But in the region of imaginative, spinal and essential attributes, something equivalent to creation is, for our age and lands, imperatively demanded. For not only is it not enough that the new blood, new frame of democracy shall be vivified[1] and held together merely by political means, superficial suffrage, legislation, etc., but it is clear to me that, unless it goes deeper, gets at least as firm and as warm a hold in men's hearts, emotions and belief, as, in their days, feudalism or ecclesiasticism, and inaugurates its own perennial sources, welling from the centre forever, its strength will be defective, its growth doubtful, and its main charm wanting. I suggest, therefore, the possibility, should some two or three really original American poets (perhaps artists or lecturers), arise, mounting the horizon like planets, stars of the first magnitude, that, from their eminence, fusing contributions, races, far localities, etc., together, they would give more compaction and more moral identity (the quality to-day most needed), to these States, than all its Constitutions, legislative and judicial ties, and all its hitherto political, warlike, or materialistic experiences.

* * *

It may be claim'd (and I admit the weight of the claim) that common and general worldly prosperity and a populace well to do, and with all life's material comforts, is the main thing, and is enough. It may be argued that our republic is, in performance, really enacting to-day the grandest arts, poems, etc., by beating up the wilderness into fertile farms, and in her railroads, ships, machinery, etc. And it may be ask'd, Are these not better, indeed, for America, than any utterances even of greatest rhapsode,[2] artist, or literatus?

I too hail those achievements with pride and joy: then answer that the soul of man will not with such only—nay, not with such at all—be finally satisfied; but needs what (standing on these and on all things, as the feet stand on the ground) is address'd to the loftiest, to itself alone.

---

[1] Brought to life.   [2] Rhapsodist: in ancient Greece, a traveling singer of heroic songs.

Out of such considerations, such truths, arises for treatment in these Vistas the important question of character, of an American stock-personality, with literatures and arts for outlets and return-expressions, and, of course, to correspond, within outlines common to all. To these, the main affair, the thinkers of the United States, in general so acute, have either given feeblest attention, or have remain'd, and remain, in a state of somnolence.[3]

For my part, I would alarm and caution even the political and business reader, and to the utmost extent, against the prevailing delusion that the establishment of free political institutions, and plentiful intellectual smartness, with general good order, physical plenty, industry, etc. (desirable and precious advantages as they all are), do, of themselves, determine and yield to our experiment of democracy the fruitage of success. With such advantages at present fully, or almost fully, possess'd—the Union just issued, victorious, from the struggle[4] with the only foes it need ever fear (namely, those within itself, the interior ones), and with unprecedented materialistic advancement—society, in these States, is canker'd, crude, superstitious, and rotten. Political, or law-made society is, and private, or voluntary society, is also. In any vigor, the element of the moral conscience, the most important, the verteber[5] to State or man, seems to me either entirely lacking, or seriously enfeebled or ungrown.

I say we had best look our times and lands searchingly in the face, like a physician diagnosing some deep disease. Never was there, perhaps, more hollowness at heart than at present, and here in the United States. Genuine belief seems to have left us. The underlying principles of the States are not honestly believ'd in (for all this hectic glow, and these melodramatic screamings), nor is humanity itself believ'd in. What penetrating eye does not everywhere see through the mask? The spectacle is appaling.[6] We live in an atmosphere of hypocrisy throughout. The men believe not in the women, nor the women in the men. A scornful superciliousness rules in literature. The aim of all the *littérateurs*[7] is to find something to make fun of. A lot of churches, sects, etc., the most dismal phantasms I know, usurp the name of religion. Conversation is a mass of badinage.

* * *

. . . Today, in books, in the rivalry of writers, especially novelists, success (so-call'd), is for him or her who strikes the mean flat, average, the sensational appetite for stimulus, incident, persiflage,[8] etc., and depicts, to the common calibre, sensual, exterior life. To such, or the luckiest of them, as we see the audiences are limitless and profitable; but they cease presently. While this day, or any day, to workmen portraying interior or spiritual life, the audiences were limited, and often laggard—but they last forever.

Compared with the past, our modern science soars, and our journals serve—but ideal and even ordinary romantic literature, does not, I think, substantially advance. Behold the prolific brood of the contemporary novel, magazine-tale, theatre-play, etc. The same endless thread of tangled and superalative love-story, inherited, apparently from the Amadises and Palmerins[9] of the 13th, 14th, and 15th centuries over there in Europe. The costumes and associations brought down

---

[3] Sleep.   [4] The Civil War.   [5] Vertebrae.
[6] Appalling: literally, causing a person to turn pale.   [7] "Literary men" (French).   [8] Playful banter.
[9] Amadis de Gaul and Palmerin were heroes of chivalric romance.

to date, the seasoning hotter and more varied, the dragons and ogres left out—but the *thing,* I should say, has not advanced—is just as sensational, just as strain'd—remains about the same, nor more, nor less.

* * *

. . . America demands a poetry that is bold, modern, and all-surrounding and kosmical, as she is herself. It must in no respect ignore science or the modern, but inspire itself with sciennce and the modern. It must bend its vision toward the future, more than the past. Like America, it must extricate itself from even the greatest models of the past, and, while courteous to them, must have entire faith in itself, and the products of its own democratic spirit only. Like her, it must place in the van, and hold up at all hazards, the banner of the divine pride of man in himself (the radical foundation of the new religion). Long enough have the People been listening to poems in which common humanity, deferential, bends low, humiliated, acknowledging superiors. But America listens to no such poems. Erect, inflated, and fully self-esteeming be the chant; and then America will listen with pleased ears.

1867

from *SPECIMEN DAYS**

ABRAHAM LINCOLN

August 12th.[1863]—I see the President almost every day, as I happen to live where he passes to or from his lodgings out of town. He never sleeps at the White House during the hot season, but has quarters at a healthy location some three miles north of the city, the Soldiers' Home, a United States military establishment. I saw him this morning about 8 1/2 coming in to business, riding on Vermont Avenue, near L Street. He always has a company of twenty-five or thirty cavalry, with sabres drawn and held upright over their shoulders. They say this guard was against his personal wish, but he let his counselors have their way. The party makes no great show in uniform or horses. Mr. Lincoln on the saddle generally rides a good-sized, easy-going gray horse, is dress'd in plain black, somewhat rusty and dusty, wears a black stiff hat, and looks about as ordinary in attire, etc., as the commonest man. A lieutenant, with yellow straps, rides at his left, and following behind, two by two, come the cavalry men, in their yellow-striped jackets. They are generally going at a slow trot, as that is the pace set them by the one they wait upon. The sabres and accoutrements[1] clank, and the entirely unornamental *cortège*[2] as it trots towards Lafayette Square arouses no sensation, only some

---

* *Specimen Days and Collect* (1882) is Whitman's autobiographical narrative consisting of prefaces and essays.

[1] Miscellaneous equipment of a soldier.

[2] "Retinue" (French), ceremonial procession.

curious stranger stops and gazes. I see very plainly Abraham Lincoln's dark brown face, with the deep-cut lines, the eyes, always to me with a deep latent sadness in the expression. We have got so that we exchange bows, and very cordial ones. Sometimes the President goes and comes in an open barouche.[3] The cavalry always accompany him, with drawn sabres. Often I notice as he goes out evenings—and sometimes in the morning, when he returns early—he turns off and halts at the large and handsome residence of the Secretary of War, on K Street, and holds conference there. If in his barouche, I can see from my window he does not alight, but sits in his vehicle, and Mr. Stanton[4] comes out to attend him. Sometimes one of his sons, a boy of ten or twelve, accompanies him, riding at his right on a pony. Earlier in the summer I occasionally saw the President and his wife, toward the latter part of the afternoon, out in a barouche, on a pleasure ride through the city. Mrs. Lincoln was dress'd in complete black, with a long crape veil. The equipage is of the plainest kind, only two horses, and they nothing extra. They pass'd me once very close, and I saw the President in the face fully, as they were moving slowly, and his look, though abstracted, happen'd to be directed steadily in my eye. He bow'd and smiled, but far beneath his smile I noticed well the expression I have alluded to. None of the artists or pictures has caught the deep, though subtle and indirect expression of this man's face. There is something else there. One of the great portrait painters of two or three centuries ago is needed.

Two Brothers, One South, One North

May 28–9. [1865]—I staid to-night a long time by the bedside of a new patient, a young Baltimorean, aged about 19 years, W. S. P., (2d Maryland, southern,) very feeble, right leg amputated, can't sleep hardly at all—has taken a great deal of morphine, which, as usual, is costing more than it comes to. Evidently very intelligent and well bred—very affectionate—held on to my hand, and put it by his face, not willing to let me leave. As I was lingering, soothing him in his pain, he says to me suddenly, "I hardly think you know who I am—I don't wish to impose upon you—I am a rebel soldier." I said I did not know that, but it made no difference. Visiting him daily for about two weeks after that, while he lived, (death had mark'd him, and he was quite alone,) I loved him much, always kiss'd him, and he did me. In an adjoining ward I found his brother, an officer of rank, a Union soldier, a brave and religious man, (Col. Clifton K. Prentiss, sixth Maryland infantry, Sixth corps, wounded in one of the engagements at Petersburg, April 2—linger'd, suffer'd much, died in Brooklyn, Aug. 20, '65).[1] It was in the same battle both were hit. One was a strong Unionist, the other Secesh;[2] both fought on their respective sides, both badly wounded, and both brought together here after a separation of four years. Each died for his cause.

---

[3] A four-wheeled carriage with an outside seat for the driver and a top that could be raised to cover the back seat.

[4] Edwin Masters Stanton (1814–1869), U.S. secretary of war from 1862 to 1868.

[1] This information was added after the essay was first written.   [2] A secessionist.

THE MILLION DEAD, TOO, SUMM'D UP

The dead in this war—there they lie, strewing the fields and woods and valleys and battle-fields of the South—Virginia, the Peninsula—Malvern Hill and Fair Oaks—the banks of the Chickahominy—the terraces of Fredericksburg—Antietam bridge—the grisly ravines of Manassas—the bloody promenade of the Wilderness[1]—the varieties of the *strayed* dead, (the estimate of the War Department is 25,000 national soldiers kill'd in battle and never buried at all, 5,000 drown'd—15,000 inhumed[2] by strangers, or on the march in haste, in hitherto unfound localities—2,000 graves cover'd by sand and mud by Mississippi freshets,[3] 3,000 carried away by caving-in of banks, etc.,)—Gettysburg, the West, Southwest—Vicksburg—Chattanooga—the trenches of Petersburg[4]—the numberless battles, camps, hospitals everywhere—the crop reap'd by the mighty reapers, typhoid, dysentery, inflammations—and blackest and loathsomest of all, the dead and living burial-pits, the prison-pens of Andersonville, Salisbury, Belle Isle, etc., (not Dante's pictured hell[5] and all its woes, its degradations, filthy torments, excell'd those prisons)—the dead, the dead, the dead—*our* dead—or South or North, ours all, (all, all, all, finally dear to me)—or East or West—Atlantic coast or Mississippi valley—somewhere they crawl'd to die, alone, in bushes, low gullies, or on the sides of hills—(there, in secluded spots, their skeletons, bleach'd bones, tufts of hair, buttons, fragments of clothing, are occasionally found yet)—our young men once so handsome and so joyous, taken from us—the son from the mother, the husband from the wife, the dear friend from the dear friend—the clusters of camp graves, in Georgia, the Carolinas, and in Tennessee—the single graves left in the woods or by the roadside, (hundreds, thousands, obliterated)—the corpses floated down the rivers, and caught and lodged, (dozens, scores, floated down the upper Potomac, after the cavalry engagements, the pursuit of Lee, following Gettysburg)—some lie at the bottom of the sea—the general million, and the special cemeteries in almost all the States—the infinite dead—(the land entire saturated, perfumed with their impalpable ashes' exhalation in Nature's chemistry distill'd, and shall be so forever, in every future grain of wheat and ear of corn, and every flower that grows, and every breath we draw)—not only Northern dead leavening[6] Southern soil—thousands, aye tens of thousands, of Southerners, crumble to-day in Northern earth.

And everywhere among those countless graves—everywhere in the many soldier Cemeteries of the Nation, (there are now, I believe, over seventy of them)—as at the time in the vast trenches, the depositories of the slain, Northern and Southern, after the great battles—not only where the scathing trail passed those years, but radiating since in all the peaceful quarters of the land—we see, and ages yet may see, on monuments and gravestones, singly or in masses, to thousands or tens of thousands, the significant word *Unknown.*

(In some of the cemeteries nearly *all* the dead are unknown. At Salisbury, N. C., for instance, the known are only 85, while the unknown are 12,027, and

---

[1] The scenes of Civil War battles in Virginia.　　[2] Buried.
[3] A rush of fresh water flowing into a salt sea.
[4] The scenes of Civil War battles in Pennsylvania, Mississippi, Tennessee, and Virginia.
[5] In *The Divine Comedy* by Dante Alighieri (1265–1321).
[6] Fermenting; permeating with an influence that changes the original material. This image complements that of "Nature's chemistry distill'd."

11,700 of these are buried in trenches. A national monument has been put up here, by order of Congress, to mark the spot—but what visible, material monument can ever fittingly commemorate that spot?)

MY TRIBUTE TO FOUR POETS*

April 16. [1881]—A short but pleasant visit to Longfellow. I am not one of the calling kind, but as the author of *Evangeline* kindly took the trouble to come and see me three years ago in Camden,[1] where I was ill, I felt not only the impulse of my own pleasure on that occasion, but a duty. He was the only particular eminence I called on in Boston, and I shall not soon forget his lit-up face and glowing warmth and courtesy, in the modes of what is called the old school.

And now just here I feel the impulse to interpolate something about the mighty four who stamp this first American century with its birth-marks of poetic literature. In a late magazine one of my reviewers, who ought to know better, speaks of my "attitude of contempt and scorn and intolerance" toward the leading poets—of my "deriding" them, and preaching their "uselessness." If anybody cares to know what I think—and have long thought and avow'd—about them, I am entirely willing to propound. I can't imagine any better luck befalling these States for a poetical beginning and initiation than has come from Emerson, Longfellow, Bryant, and Whittier. Emerson, to me, stands unmistakably at the head, but for the others I am at a loss where to give any precedence. Each illustrious, each rounded, each distinctive. Emerson for his sweet, vital-tasting melody, rhym'd philosophy, and poems as amber-clear as the honey of the wild bee he loves to sing. Longfellow for rich color, graceful forms and incidents—all that makes life beautiful and love refined—competing with the singers of Europe on their own ground, and, with one exception,[2] better and finer work than that of any of them. Bryant pulsing the first interior verse-throbs of a mighty world—bard of the river and the wood, ever conveying a taste of open air, with scents as from hayfields, grapes, birch-borders—always lurkingly fond of threnodies[3]—beginning and ending his long career with chants of death, with here and there through all, poems, or passages of poems, touching the highest universal truths, enthusiasms, duties—morals as grim and eternal, if not as stormy and fateful, as anything in Eschylus.[4] While in Whittier, with his special themes—(his outcropping love of heroism and war, for all his Quakerdom, his verses at times like the measur'd step of Cromwell's old vererans[5])—in Whittier lives the zeal, the moral energy, that founded New England—the splendid rectitude and ardor of Luther, Milton, George Fox[6]—I must not, dare not, say the wilfulness and narrowness—though

---

* Ralph Waldo Emerson (1803–1882), Henry Wadsworth Longfellow (1807–1882), William Cullen Bryant (1794–1878), and John Greenleaf Whittier (1819–1892).

[1] Camden, New Jersey, where Whitman spent his last nineteen years.

[2] Alfred, Lord Tennyson (1809–1892), the British poet laureate from 1850 to 1892, is the obvious choice.

[3] Funereal songs or poems.

[4] Aeschylus (525-456 B.C.), a Greek tragedian.

[5] Veterans; Oliver Cromwell (1599–1658), revolutionary leader and Lord protector of England from 1653 to 1658, known for imposing strict discipline on his troops.

[6] Martin Luther (1483–1546), German leader of the Protestant Reformation; the English poet John Milton (1608–1674), author of *Paradise Lost* (1667); Fox (1624–1691), the English founder of the Society of Friends, or Quakers. Whitman had a profound respect for the Quakers, as is evident in this comparison of Fox to a great reformer and a great poet.

doubtless the world needs now, and always will need, almost above all, just such narrowness and wilfulness.[7]

BOSTON COMMON—MORE OF EMERSON*

Oct. 10–13. [1881]—I spend a good deal of time on the Common, these delicious days and nights—every mid-day from 11.30 to about 1—and almost every sunset another hour. I know all the big trees, especially the old elms along Tremont and Beacon streets,[1] and have come to a sociable-silent understanding with most of them, in the sunlit air (yet crispy-cool enough), as I saunter along the wide unpaved walks. Up and down this breadth by Beacon Street, between these same old elms, I walk'd for two hours, of a bright sharp February mid-day twenty-one years ago, with Emerson, then in his prime, keen, physically and morally magnetic, arm'd at every point, and when he chose, wielding the emotional just as well as the intellectual. During those two hours he was the talker and I the listener. It was an argument-statement, reconnoitring, review, attack, and pressing home (like an army corps in order, artillery, cavalry, infantry), of all that could be said against that part (and a main part) in the construction of my poems, "Children of Adam."[2] More precious than gold to me that dissertation—it afforded me, ever after, this strange and paradoxical lesson: each point of E.'s statement was unanswerable, no judge's charge ever more complete or convincing, I could never hear the points better put—and then I felt down in my soul the clear and unmistakable conviction to disobey all, and pursue my own way. "What have you to say then to such things?" said E., pausing in conclusion. "Only that while I can't answer them at all, I feel more settled than ever to adhere to my own theory, and exemplify it," was my candid response. Whereupon we went and had a good dinner at the American House. And thenceforward I never waver'd or was touch'd with qualms (as I confess I had been two or three times before).

1863–1882, 1882

---

[7] The "narrowness and wilfulness" of Luther, Milton, and Fox would be narrowness of concentration and wilfulness of purpose; while Whitman offers tribute to the artistic talents of the four poets, he stops just short of crediting them with the attributes of the three great men just named.

* The Common is a public park in central Boston; Ralph Waldo Emerson (1803–1882). In this more personal form of writing, Whitman does not employ the Quaker numerical designations for days and months that he uses in his poems.

[1] Boston streets.

[2] A group of poems first published in the 1860 edition of *Leaves of Grass* as "Enfans d'Adam" and in the 1867 edition with this title.

Writing About Literature

To read literature is to enter a conversation—a dialogue, really—with the author and other readers, to respond to their interpretations of the human situation with comments of your own. Writing about great literature may at first be intimidating—you may think "I can't say anything *new* about Mark Twain" or "I don't know as much about Black America as James Baldwin does." But if literature *doesn't* provoke you to respond, then the author hasn't done the job.

To provoke a response is why your instructor asks you to write about the works you read: to make you think, to make you take part in the conversation, even if your thoughts, discoveries, and "lines" in the dialogue have all been uttered before. You, too, have a right to take part in the ongoing discussion about American literature and to convey your response to your readers.

The nature of that response will vary from reader to reader and from situation to situation. You may react to a work differently in a short-answer exam question than you would in a ten-page paper, or differently if you particularly like a work than if you are particularly offended by it. Some readers are fascinated by works about the areas where they grew up, whereas others prefer the lure of faraway places and exotic situations. But all readers will create their interpretations based on several similar principles: the nature of their own readers, the kind of response for which they are asked, and the angle of their approach.

In literature classes you may be asked to construct your interpretation of a particular text, based only on the materials in this book and on your class discussions. Or your instructor may send you to outside sources to give you other perspectives as a way of shaping your response. We will discuss the procedures and pitfalls of both methods. But first we need to make some important observations about reading literature.

READING LITERATURE TO WRITE ABOUT IT

You can read a work of literature in two ways: *precritically* and *critically*. A *precritical reading* is a surface reading: you read to find out what goes on where, what happens, who says what about whatever. You do not look very deeply; you just go from the first line to the last. The dangers of such reading to writing about the work are many: you can write only about the obvious things. You can recount the plot and explain the obvious symbols and devices the author uses, but not in any great depth. The only audiences interested in this kind of writing are people who have not read the work—and you instructor does not fit into this group. A surface reading alone generally guarantees a disastrous paper.

A *critical reading* involves slow, careful, close reading and *rereading* of the text. You read "between the lines," trying to figure out what is really going on, what the author expects of you. You should take notes; ask questions; jot down your ideas, responses, perplexities. This careful process of reading and rereading will help you unfold a text's possibilities. You will write about *how* things happen in the work; you can assume that your readers already know what happens in the work and are interested in exploring beneath the surface with you.

FINDING A SUBJECT: THINKING ABOUT YOUR READERS

You need to remember a special factor of taking part in the conversation about literature: the readers with whom you are conversing. You must consciously imagine *someone* reading your paper. Generally, your reader will be your instructor, who will have special expectations regarding your response. Your instructor will want to see how clear an understanding of the work you have developed, how well you can express your response, and how strong a case you can make. The instructor typically does not want you to recount the plot in great detail: he or she has also read the work! (Think of conversations you have had in which someone repeated a story everyone else in the group already knew well. How interested were you in hearing that story?)

You do not want your readers to say "So what?" about your paper. You do not want to bore them with vague, uninteresting statements. A thesis like "There are many references to homemade items in 'Everyday Use'" will probably elicit the "so what?" response; who cares? But saying "Alice Walker uses domestic objects to emphasize values that readers might not consider otherwise" makes readers say "Really? Tell me how." That is the response you want.

USING ONLY A PRIMARY SOURCE

When you start to write about a work of literature, first ask yourself "What in this work might catch my readers' interest?" Some elements are so obvious that most readers understand their use the first time they read a work; these probably are not good elements to discuss. Go back to the notes you made in your critical reading. Look for an element that you had to think about for a while before you really understood it. Chances are that such an element will lead you to an interesting paper. These interesting elements tend to fall into three categories—*construction, language,* and *context*—within which you can usually find an angle of attack for your paper.

Writing About Construction

If you are writing about a work without referring to secondary sources such as journal articles or critical books, the work's construction is one of the best places to start: its plot (what happens), setting (when and where it happens), and its characters (to whom it happens, or who makes it happen). Each of these building blocks contributes to the overall structure of the work. The following list of questions can help you think about these elements. Not all the questions will apply to all works, but some will certainly apply to the work you are studying.

Plot. Does the work have a plot? (Some poems, for instance, do not.) What is the sequence of events? Did the author put them in chronological order or not, and why? Are key events omitted or just hinted at and why? Does the work have a particular pace or rhythm? Does the action seem to speed up or slow down? Where does the action happen, and why? Does the story seem to reach a climax, and where does that occur?

Setting. When and where does the work take place? In what ways would the work be different if it took place somewhere else? Does the choice of setting influence the action in different ways? (For instance, if the work were set upon a ship rather than in a large city, what would have to be left out of the plot?) How are the people and events in the work influenced by the setting?

Characters. Who are they? Do they actually appear in the work? (For instance, Miss Emily's father and fianceé are dead before William Faulkner's "A Rose for Emily" begins.) What sorts of elements in the work tell us about the characters: what they do, what they say, how they dress, what other people say about them, etc.? Who tells us about these characters: themselves, other characters, a narrator? Do the characters seem real (traditionally called "round" characters), or do they seem more like cartoon stereotypes ("flat" characters)?

Writing About Language

Few words in a work of literature are there accidentally; authors choose each word for precise reasons. Paying attention to what things are called, how they are described, and what those words bring to mind may lead to interesting angles for your "conversation" about the work. Here are some suggestions you can use to focus your attention on literary language.

Metaphor is a general term for language that has enriched meanings and a specific term for literary comparison. In general, metaphoric language is loaded with multiple meanings and connotations. In particular, a metaphor is an equation of two unlike objects:

> My life had stood — a Loaded Gun —
> In Corners —   (Emily Dickinson)

In this equation, the abstract concept "life" suddenly becomes the physical object "a Loaded Gun—In Corners." The comparison surprises us: women do not typically compare themselves to "masculine" items such as guns or see themselves as weapons to guard their homes and loved ones. Dickinson challenges her readers to see the implications of this comparison. The more oblique and nonstereotyped the comparison of objects being equated, the better—the deeper readers must explore to see the ramifications, and the richer the possibilities for writing.

Simile is a type of metaphorical language that compares two unrelated concepts, using the words "like" or "as" to emphasize the relationships. Unlike metaphor, which says one thing *is* another, simile suggests comparisons less forcefully:

> Like travelers with exotic destinations on their minds, the graduates were remarkably forgetful.   (Maya Angelou)

This example compares eighth-graders contemplating high school to travelers about to undertake some extraordinary journey; a little humor is implied in the comparison. Examining similes allows you to write about some of the most subtle effects an author creates.

Symbols are images that have literal as well as deeper meanings. By recognizing a symbol, readers can understand some of a work's deep implications. Some symbols have generalized meanings: a cross calls up Christian images; the American flag, patriotic images; a pillared mansion, images of the South and the Civil War. Other symbols have particular meanings in the work where they appear: Faith's pink hair ribbons in Nathaniel Hawthorne's "Young Goodman Brown," the quilts in "Everyday Use," the Mississippi River in Mark Twain's *Huckleberry Finn*. Writing about a symbol or set of symbols allows you to show your readers another level of meaning in the works you examine.

Tone is the author's attitude to the people and events described in a work: comic, ironic, satiric, sentimental, and so forth. Many things contribute to tone, including the narrator's point of view, the way things are described (for instance, journalistically, overstatedly, understatedly), the reactions of other characters in the work, and the types of sentences and vocabulary the author uses. Tone is sometimes hard to pin down, but writing about it is typically rewarding for both you and your readers because it requires you to look at how many elements work together to create an overall effect.

Writing About Context

Literature does not just happen in a vacuum. Writers are part of their times and part of literary history. When they create a work of literature, they draw on what they know of their own and of past times, the ideas and controversies that were important in their world, as well as the many things they have read. Examining one of these elements may give you an angle from which to approach your paper.

The writer's biography can play an important part in your discussion. The headnotes and introductions in this anthology may help you to understand what a writer has experienced in creating a particular work; for instance, knowing about

Anne Bradstreet's family tragedies may give you insight into some of her poems, and knowing about life in New Orleans can help you better understand Kate Chopin's stories. Knowing about Whitman's service as a nurse to wounded Civil War soldiers and his devotion to Abraham Lincoln lets you see new depths in "When Lilacs Last in the Dooryard Bloom'd." Knowing about Adrienne Rich's involvement in feminism helps you interpret "Snapshots of a Daughter-in-Law." Be careful, though, not to force correspondences: an author cannot control history but *does* control how history enters a particular work. The fickle women in Ernest Hemingway's war novels are not the actual nurse who jilted him, though that experience probably contributed to his development of those female characters.

Political and philosophical movements also contribute greatly to works. The introductions and nonfiction prose selections in this anthology show you how much literature is influenced by the ideas to which authors are exposed. Benjamin Franklin, Thomas Jefferson, John Adams, Thomas Paine, Alexander Hamilton, and James Madison, for instance, wrote in an era when revolution, democracy, and representative government were being widely discussed. Middle nineteenth-century writers were heavily influenced by the emancipation and women's rights movements. Late twentieth-century writers react to the civil rights movement, feminism, and the Vietnam War. A literary work interpreted in light of these movements can yield an interesting paper.

Allusion allows a writer to connect his or her work to other works of literature. In "The Jolly Corner" when Henry James refers to Penelope and Ulysses, James is suggesting that readers connect the long separation of his heroine and protagonist with those figures from Homer's *Odyssey*. In "The Jacob's Ladder" Denise Levertov is referring to a familiar episode in the Old Testament. The challenge in writing about allusions is for you to show readers *how* thinking about these suggested comparisons expands your understanding of the work in which they occur.

USING SECONDARY SOURCES

When your instructor asks you to use secondary sources, such as books and journal articles to help you write about literature, you are *not* being asked to summarize what everyone else thinks about a work, but to support *your* interpretation of a work with what other people have written. You are like a lawyer presenting a case: you make the arguments to the jury and call witnesses (the secondary sources) to provide evidence for your case. You have three tasks when you use secondary sources in writing a paper. First, you must find an angle of attack, just as you do when you write from a primary source only. Second, you must find supporting evidence in the works of other writers. And third, you must present that supporting evidence in correct fashion. We have already reviewed the first task, so let us look at what the other two involve.

Finding Secondary Sources

Libraries are full of secondary sources: biographies, collections of letters and diaries, critical interpretations, collections, and the like. You may wish to begin by looking in the card catalog and scanning the shelves for books that may apply. Skim the introductions, conclusions, tables of contents, and indexes to see if the work you are studying is covered in those books. You can use reference books and computer sources such as *Book Review Digest* or the *MLA International Bibliography* to find articles and reviews. (You can also check the suggested readings and texts used in this anthology). The sources you choose will depend on the author you are studying and your angle of approach.

Citing Sources in Your Paper

Every discipline has its own conventions for format and citing secondary sources. In literature those conventions are established by the Modern Language Association and set out in two books: the *MLA Handbook for Writers of Research Papers* (1988) and *the MLA Style Manual* (1985). These books cover in great detail the fine points we will summarize here; your instructor or reference librarian can help you find the books if you have questions not answered here.

Paper Format

In general, put your name and identification number, instructor's name, course name, and date in the top left corner of the first page, with a one-inch margin all around. Doublespace down and input the title, underlining only the names of complete works (see below). Put your last name and the page number in the upper right corner of every page after the first, and staple or clip the pages together firmly in the upper left corner. *Doublespace* the entire paper, including quotations and your list of Works Cited. Do not use a separate cover page or folder unless your instructor calls for it.

Working Quotations Into Your Text

Cite sources within your text through parenthetical references to sources you quote, paraphrase, or summarize. If the material you quote, paraphrase, or summarize takes up less than four typed lines, place a page reference in parentheses *after* the quotation marks and *before* the next major punctuation mark:

    M. Wynn Thomas calls this lecture "astonishing" (243).

OR:

    Richard F. Adams has found seven of the traditional seventeen

    elements of pastoral elegy in "When Lilacs Last in the

    Dooryard Bloom'd" (479-487).

(The end punctuation goes inside the quotation marks only when the line ends with a question mark or exclamation point, or when there is no parenthetical reference.) Drama is cited by act, scene, and line number rather than page number: (3.1.74). When making a first reference to a text not named in your introduction to the quote, briefly identify it with the parenthetical page reference: (Wright 564) or ("Lilacs" 23).

If a direct quote consists of more than four typed lines of prose or dialogue or more than two typed lines of poetry, end the introductory material with whatever punctuation mark is appropriate (or none, if none is required). Then doublespace, indent ten spaces from the left margin, and doublespace the long quotation (with no opening quotation marks, unless they appear in the original text). End the quote with the punctuation the original text uses, move two spaces to the right, and put the quote's page numbers in parentheses. No punctuation follows the parentheses. Then doublespace and return to your text. If continuing the same paragraph, return to the left margin; if starting a new paragraph, indent the usual five spaces.

Fine Points. If the original text has unusual spelling, punctuation, capitalization, or spacing, do your best to reproduce it on your page. If you begin quoting from poetry in the middle of a line, indent that line the number of spaces missing to indicate this positioning. Underline only the titles of complete works (such as novels, plays, long poems, and collections); names of newspapers, journals, magazines, movies, TV programs, records, and works of art; and unfamiliar foreign words and phrases. Use quotation marks around the titles of poems, articles in journals or magazines, and essays, introductions, forewords, and the like not published separately. (Follow these rules in the text, your title, and your list of Works Cited.)

If you leave words or sentences out of a quotation in your paper, use ellipsis marks, the spaced sets of three or four dots, to show readers where you have trimmed the original text. Three spaced dots indicate words or phrases are omitted; four spaced dots indicate that the omission includes the end of one or more sentences. (Omissions of one or more paragraphs may be indicated by three spaced asterisks.) If you need to tailor a quote to match your sentence grammar, include your alterations in square brackets to show your editorial changes. If there is a mistake, such as a typographical error, in your source, copy the mistake exactly and follow it with the Latin term "*sic*" in square brackets to tell your readers you recognize the mistake. To call attention to particular words, underline them to italicize them. (If you underline words in a direct quote, add the phrase *emphasis mine* to the cited page numbers to point out the change.)

Citing Sources at the End of Your Text

A bibliography, called a list of Works Cited, starts on a new page following your paper, with the title *Works Cited* centered one inch from the top of the page. Works you quoted, summarized, or paraphrased in your essay are listed here in alphabetical order by author. If a source has no author, list it alphabetically by the first word of its title (excepting "a," "an," and "the").

In accordance with recently adopted MLA guidelines, for every work cited give (1) the author's name (if applicable), last name first; (2) the full title (underlined or in quotations; use single quotation marks for a quotation within a quotation), followed by the edition number, if any; (3) the source in which the work appears (if appropriate), underlined; (4) the city (and state, if the city is not well known) of publication, followed by a colon; (5) the publisher (abbreviating "University" to "U" and "Press" to "P"), followed by a comma; and (6) the year or years published. For sources that appear in other bound volumes (such as articles in a journal or essays in a collection), include (7) the beginning and ending page numbers. Each of these seven elements, except for the place of publication and publisher, is separated from the others by a period and two spaces. Begin each reference at the left margin and indent continuation lines five spaces.

Works Cited entries can take hundreds of forms. Here are examples of the most common; you can find examples of other forms in the *MLA Handbook*.

A BOOK

Thomas, M. Wynn. The Lunar Light of Whitman's Poetry. Cambridge:

    Harvard UP, 1987.

A LITERARY WORK IN A BOOK

Adams, Richard P. " 'Lilacs' as Pastoral Elegy." Critics on

    Walt Whitman: Readings in Literary Criticism. Ed. Richard

    H. Rupp. Coral Gables: U Miami P, 1972. 69–76.

AN EDITED TEXT

This form draws attention to the author:

Whitman, Walt. "When Lilacs Last in the Dooryard Bloom'd."

    Leaves of Grass: A Textual Variorum of the Printed Poems.

    Ed. Sculley Bradley, Harold W. Blodgett, Arthur Golden, and

    William White. New York: New York UP, 1980. 2:529–539.

This form draws attention to the editors:

Bradley, Sculley, Harold W. Blodgett, Arthur Golden, and William

    White, eds. "When Lilacs Last in the Dooryard Bloom'd."

    By Walt Whitman. Leaves of Grass: A Textual Variorum of

    the Printed Poems. New York: New York UP, 1980. 2:529–539.

AN ARTICLE APPEARING IN A JOURNAL

Wright, George T. "The Lyric Present: Simple Present Verbs in

    English Poems." PMLA 89 (1974): 563–579.

A BOOK REVIEW

Kakutani, Michiko. Rev. of Sweet Desserts, by Lucy Ellmann.

    New York Times 6 June 1989: B6.

Avoiding Plagiarism

Plagiarism is one of the worst of scholarly crimes. When you plagiarize, you present another writer's thoughts or words or concepts as if they were yours. Plagiarism not only denies writers true credit for their work, but it blurs the distinctions between your own arguments and the supporting evidence. You can suffer many penalties for plagiarism: an "F" on the paper or in the course, probation, suspension, even expulsion. It is important to indicate which ideas in your paper are yours and which come from your sources, in order to avoid committing this serious offense.

To avoid plagiarism, follow four simple rules. One, *keep accurate notes*. When making notes from a book or journal, use quotations marks to indicate words you have copied directly from your sources. Use underlining or highlighting pen to indicate information and ideas you have paraphrased or summarized. Anything that comes from your source must be documented in your paper.

Two, *provide an introduction* to all source material you use in your paper. This attribution can be as simple as "According to Gay Wilson Allen," "Feidelson argues that," or "Critics such as Allen (1970) and Thomas (1987) suggest." By introducing your sources, you signal to your reader that secondary material follows; you are providing expert evidence to back up your contentions, showing your audience that other readers agree with your interpretations. Attributions make your paper seem better integrated, not just a collection of notecards and photocopies cut and pasted together to form an essay.

Three, *include parenthetical references* to the sources of your evidence. These page or line references tell your readers specifically where you got your evidence, so that they can find it easily if they become interested in further exploring your topic. The sample student paper below shows you several skillful ways of incorporating these references to give the information without interrupting the prose.

Four, *provide a list of Works Cited*. This bibliography helps the interested reader find the sources of your evidence. It also provides continuity to the "conversation" by showing where in the discussion of a particular work you place yourself in that conversation. If you provide all four of these elements, you should produce a carefully documented paper that lets your readers easily see what your arguments are and how the evidence in secondary sources supports your positions.

Sample Student Paper

On the following pages you will find a sample student paper based on a student's reading of Whitman's poem "When Lilacs Last in the Dooryard Bloom'd." We point out her thesis and supporting arguments to show how she constructed her paper; we also provide annotations to show you some of the technical aspects of presentation. Following the paper is a paragraph from another paper on "Lilacs," this one using secondary sources to support the argument. These examples should help you see how a written response to literature is assembled.

1   Susanna Jones (8583432)

Dr. Tarvers

Principles of Literary Study

October 14, 19--

A Time to Mourn

Funerals and memorial services are for the living,

the cliché goes. They are an organized way to express

grief and put it behind us, a way to stop thinking

about the past ("Remember when . . .?") and the future

("She could have been . . . .") and return to the

2   present in which we must live. In "When Lilacs Last

in the Dooryard Bloom'd," Walt Whitman conducts such

a memorial service, forcing both himself and his

readers to cease grieving for Abraham Lincoln and to

move toward a future worthy of Lincoln's efforts, as

a way of keeping Lincoln's memory perpetually present.

Whitman reinforces this determination to leave the past

3   behind by repeatedly manipulating verb tenses through-

out the poem.

1. Leave one-inch margins all around.
2. Titles of works not published are placed separately in quotation marks.
3. Thesis of the student's paper.

Jones 2   **4**

The poem begins in the sad past of 1865, when
lilacs "bloom'd," Venus "droop'd," and the narrator
"mourn'd" for the fallen president ("Lilacs" 1-3).   **5, 6**

7 Immediately Whitman uses tense to force his readers to
leave the past behind by reminding us that "Ever-
returning spring" brings a "trinity sure" to mind: the
lilac, the star, and the memory of Lincoln. Moreover,
like the Holy Trinity of Christian symbolism, this
trinity exists in the present, always the same, always
true, always with us. The symbol representing the truth
is described in the present tense: ". . . near the   **8**
white-wash'd palings, / <u>Stands</u> the lilac-bush" (12-13;   **9**

10 emphasis mine). And, in affirmation of the present,
the narrator tells us that "a sprig with its flower
I break" (17) at the same time that the hidden hermit
thrush "sings by himself a song" (22). In choosing
the present tense to describe these eternal symbols,
Whitman reminds us that truth and love are timeless.

4. From page 2 on, put your last name and the page number in the right corner,
one-half inch from the top.

5. Use a short title for the first citation of the work.

6. Indicate line numbers without using the abbreviation *ll.*

7. One of the student's supporting arguments.

8. Ellipsis marks show the omission of words.

9. Poetry quotes of fewer than three lines are run into the text, separated by a
slash with one space on either side.

10. "Emphasis mine" shows that underlining was added by the student.

Jones 3

The lilac and birdsong prompt the narrator to
remember Lincoln's funeral procession, with a grief
so real that past events seem to become real in the
present. Amid positive images of birth-budding
violets, sprouting grain, and blooming trees, "night
and day journeys a coffin" (32). The narrator's
present-tense report makes this stark contrast
seem as if he had just now observed it: the coffin
"passes," it "journey[s]," and he "give[s]" it the
spray of lilac (Stanza 6). His memory keeps these
past actions alive.

                                                   7

                                                 11

Again the narrator gathers his composure and
forces his attention back to the present by choosing
the present tense. He assures us that he does not
mourn for Lincoln alone but for everyone who has died
in the past: "Blossoms and branches green to all coffins
I bring" (47); ". . . I cover you with roses and early
lilies, / ... I break the sprigs from the bushes"
(50, 52). But his grasp on the present is still weak,
and his memories again draw him back, as he turns to
address the evening star: "Now I know what you must

---

11. The student's editorial changes for smooth grammar are enclosed in brackets.

Jones 4

have meant as a month since I walk'd" (56). He tells
the thrush "I hear, I come presently . . ." (68), "But
a moment I linger, for the lustrous star has detain'd
me" (69). Memories of the fallen president, "the dead
one there I loved" (71), make the future without
Lincoln seem overwhelming; the poet shifts into the
future tense as he wrestles with the impossibility of
finding a suitable way to mourn his lost leader
(Stanza 10).

Whitman's solution to this dilemma is to escape
out of time entirely. He poses the question "how
shall I warble for the dead one there I loved?" (71)
and answers in phrases without verb tense--fragments
that use present participles to construct a timeless
picture of the vital, growing America that was Lincoln's
dream and will be his best monument: "growing spring
and farms and homes," "the fresh sweet herbage under
foot," and, above all,

7

12

    the city at hand with dwellings so

   dense, and stacks of chimneys,

And all the scenes of life and the workshops,

and the workmen homeward returning. . . .

12. Poetry quotes of three lines or more are treated as excerpts, indented ten spaces, and doublespaced. Extra indention of the first line shows that this quote begins in mid-line. Turnovers (continuation lines) are also indented.

Jones 5

The varied and ample land, the South and the
    North in the light, Ohio's shores and
    flashing Missouri . . . .
The miracle spreading bathing all, the
    fulfill'd noon,
The coming eve delicious, the welcome night
    and the stars,
Over my cities shining all, enveloping man
    and land. (87-98)

13

7   To celebrate this escape out of time, the poet
returns to the present tense and encourages the thrush
to sing on. The thrush's carol uses present tense to
remind us that death is always with us, just as are
life and joy, the objects of human curiosity, day and
night. But the song's calm acceptance of death sends
Whitman's memory back to the past one last time, to a
month before Lincoln's death and a night when Whitman
found himself at the edge of a marsh, listening to
another thrush, smelling lilacs, and watching the
evening star. That night Whitman had thought the
thrush "sang the carol of death, and a verse for him I
love" (128) in memory of the soldiers who died during
the Civil War--the men whom Whitman had nursed and whose
sufferings he describes so graphically (171-184).

14

13. Line reference numbers follow the punctuation in the last line of the excerpt.
14. Reference to summarized material.

Jones 6

This memory, underscored by the thrush's song,
"sadly sinking and fainting . . . and yet again
bursting with joy" (190), is transformed, just as
Whitman would later claim Lincoln's death had been,
into one of "those climax moments on the stage of
universal Time . . . suddenly ringing down the curtain"
(<u>Prose</u> 2:508). At last, through the agency of the
thrush's carol, Whitman passes from the grief of the
past into the determination of the present and future:

15   }   **7**

> As that powerful psalm in the night I <u>heard</u>
> from recesses,
>
> Passing, I <u>leave</u> thee lilac with heart-shaped
> leaves,
>
> I <u>leave</u> thee there in the dooryard, blooming,
> returning with spring. (192-194, emphasis
> mine)

10

His grief has been mastered. From here on, he will
live and write about Lincoln in the present tense, and,
in doing so, will keep the memories of Lincoln, his
fallen soldiers, the lilac, the star, and the thrush
ever alive, ever well, ever present. The funeral is
over; life can go on.

15. Reference to another work by Whitman; the reference indicates Volume 2, followed by a colon and the page number.

Jones 7

16

Works Cited

Whitman, Walt. "When Lilacs Last in the Dooryard

Bloom'd." <u>American Literature</u>: <u>A Prentice Hall</u>

<u>Anthology</u>. Ed. Emory Elliott, Linda Kerber,

A. Walton Litz, and Terence Martin. Englewood

Cliffs: Prentice Hall, 1991. 1:2014-2020.

—————. "The Death of Abraham Lincoln." <u>Prose</u>   **17**

<u>Works</u>. Ed. Floyd Stovall. New York: New York U,

1963-1964. 2:497-509.

Sample Paragraph From a Paper With Secondary Sources

Although critics such as Feidelson (1956), Adams

(1957), Allen (1970), and Thomas (1987) have explored   **18**

the classical elements of mourning in this poem, few

other than George T. Wright have given weight to the

Christian religious imagery Whitman incorporates into

his elegy. This incorporation is subtle, handled mostly

through vocabulary and grammar. Every action is consid-

ered carefully, performed deliberately, and reinforced

by the poet's choice of the present tense, as in a

religious service. Wright (1974) calls this tense the   **19**

16. The Works Cited list begins on a new page.
17. Reference to a second work by the same author is indicated by typing ten hyphens followed by a period.
18. Attribution to secondary sources: author's last name and date.
19. First reference to an article: author's last name and date.

"lyric present," and notes that it "characteristically convey[s] a sense of elevation and, often, of solemnity which seems appropriate to visionary experience." Citing Whitman's "here, coffin, that slowly passes, / I <u>give</u> you my sprig of lilac" (emphasis his), Wright argues that the poet is acting as if he were the minister conducting Lincoln's funeral (568). This impression is reinforced by Whitman's references to the "trinity" of symbols and by his descriptions of dirges, processions, chants, miracles, souls, and powerful psalms in the poem.

20. Shows that the emphasis was added by the source, not the student.

21. Placing the parenthetical reference at the end of several sentences with attribution shows that everything between the first attribution and this reference comes from the same source.

Glossary

Allegory: a narrative in which the persons, things, concepts, or events signify a hidden or symbolic meaning; an extension of **metaphor.**

Alliteration: the repetition of a (generally initial) consonant sound within a line or phrase.

Allusion: an explicit or indirect reference in a work to something outside the work itself.

Apron: in theater, the part of the stage in front of the **proscenium arch.**

Archetype: themes, images, character types, or narrative designs that seem to be identifiable in a wide array of literature as well as in myths and dreams. Examples of archetypes are death and rebirth and Paradise versus Hell.

Assonance: the repetition of a vowel sound within a line, stanza, or sentence.

Ballad: a narrative poem, originally of folk origin and meant to be sung, that tends to focus upon a climactic episode and is told without comment.

Beat poetics: an often impassioned poetry of the 1950s and 1960s distinguished by its celebration of freedom, rejection of social mores, and frequent use of colloquial language, as exemplified by the work of such poets as Allen Ginsberg, Lawrence Ferlinghetti, and Leonard Cohen. "Beat" suggests the beat of the bongo drum, which often accompanied readings of beat poetry, as well as "beatniks," with whom the beat poets were associated.

Bildungsroman: a German term for a novel of development, which recounts a protagonist's life experience and typically involves a crisis of conscience.

Blank verse: lines of unrhymed iambic pentameter (see **meter**) in verse paragraphs rather than stanzas.

Burlesque: a form of satire that attempts to ridicule a serious literary work by means of an amusing imitation. Two classes of burlesque are *parody,* which imitates the serious materials and style of a work and applies them to a lowly subject, and *travesty,* which mocks a work by treating its lofty subject in a jocular and undignified manner.

Canto: a major division of a long poem; originally a singing or chanting section of a poem.

Closed form: a form of poetry in which the thought and grammar are complete within a couplet.

Dénouement: a French term for the final outcome or unraveling of a plot.

Deus ex machina: a Latin term (meaning "god from a machine") for any unlikely plot contrivance.

Didactic: intended to be instructive, educational, or moralistic.

Dramatic irony: an ironic situation in which a reader or the audience is aware of things of which a character is not, or in which a character's speech and actions reveal that character to differ from his or her self-image.

Elegy: a poem lamenting the death of a particular person, or a meditative poem concerning mortality.

Epic: a long narrative poem of elevated diction, typically recounting history, legend, or the deeds of a national hero.

Epistolary: written in, or conducted by, letters.

Foot: the basic metrical unit in poetry, generally containing one stressed syllable and one or two unstressed syllables.

Free verse: poetry free of traditional metrical, rhyming, and stanzaic patterns, although not necessarily free of a patterning device such as **alliteration** or a visual repetition of line length.

Genre: a French term for a literary form, such as **epic** poem, captivity narrative, or western novel.

Heroic couplet: a rhyming couplet of lines of ten syllables, so called because it was originally used for heroic, or **epic** poetry.

Homilitic: like a homily, or sermon.

Hudibrastic: in the style of Samuel Butler's *Hudibras* (1663–1678), a **mock-epic** satirical poem that ridiculed the Puritans.

Hyperbole: an overstatement or exaggeration.

Idiom: the language or dialect of a group or class, or a language unit of a group or class that differs from the norm in syntax or meaning.

Imagism: a poetic movement that flourished in England and America between about 1909 and 1917 as a reaction to **romanticism** and called for poetry that renders the poet's response to a visual object or scene as exactly and tersely as possible without abstraction. Influenced by T. E. Hulme's aesthetic philosophy and by the Japanese haiku, the movement's leaders included Ezra Pound, Amy Lowell, and Hilda Doolittle.

Irony: an expression in which the intended meaning is different from, or opposite to, the literal meaning.

"Little" magazine: a literary magazine, commonly avant-garde, with a small readership and generally a small page size.

Local color: writing that emphasizes the setting, dialect, ways of thinking and feeling, dress, and custom characteristic of a specific region; used most often in connection with the local-color movement in American literature from 1870 to 1890.

Lyric poetry: originally, ancient Greek poetry accompanied by a lyre; now, a relatively short nonnarrative poem expressing the poet's thoughts or feelings.

Masque: a short, elaborately staged court drama with actors and dancers usually masked.

Melodrama: a form of drama, especially popular in the nineteenth century, full of tragic elements but with a happy ending; the characters are flat types: the hero and heroine epitomize virtue, and the villain is Satan incarnate.

Metaphor: a figure of speech in which one thing is equated to another, normally unrelated thing, without the use of a word of comparison, such as "like" or "as"; for example, "Her wrinkles are love's graves."

Meter: a measure of poetic rhythm, determined by the type and number of **feet** in a **poetic line.** The four standard meters of verse in English are *iambic* (an unstressed syllable followed by a stressed), *anapestic* (two unstressed syllables followed by a stressed), *trochaic* (a stressed syllable followed by an unstressed), and *dactylic* (a stressed syllable followed by two unstressed). The number of feet in a line determines the type of verse: trimeter for a line with three feet, tetrameter for four feet, pentameter for five feet, and so on.

Metonymy: a figure of speech in which a closely related term is substituted for what is actually meant: for example, "the White House denies any wrongdoing" for "the president denies any wrongdoing."

Mock epic: a poem in **epic** form and manner, ludicrously elevating some trivial subject to epic grandeur (also known as mock heroic).

Modernism: a trend in literature of the first half of the twentieth century toward radical experimentation, such as the use of **stream-of-consciousness** narration and of **myth** as a structural principle. Cultural relativism, discontinuity, and alienation are the driving forces behind much modernist literature, which was promoted by such writers as T. S. Eliot, Ezra Pound, James Joyce, Virginia Woolf, and William Faulkner.

Motif: a frequently recurring literary element, such as a word, an image, or a symbol. A *leitmotif* is a recurrent element in a single work or in the work of a single author.

Myth: an ancient story dealing with fabulous deeds of gods or heroes, or an imaginary world in which fictitious characters and events are faithful to moral, philosophical, and/or aesthetic "truths" rather than to scientific truths.

Naturalism: a literary philosophy by which human beings are seen as part of the natural order, unconnected to a spiritual world outside nature, and as such are victims of blind external or biological forces. It evolved in the nineteenth century from **realism** and was influenced by the evolutionary principles of Charles Darwin and by scientific determinism.

Neoclassicism: an artistic and literary movement that began around 1660 in France and lasted until the age of **romanticism,** at the end of the eighteenth century. Neoclassicist writers, such as John Dryden and Alexander Pope, are distinguished by their interest in order, decorum, dialectical reasoning, and a return to classical aesthetic principles.

New Criticism: a methodology for interpreting literature, made popular in America by the work of Cleanth Brooks and Robert Penn Warren, which predominated in the 1940s and 1950s. New Critics are concerned with the autonomous nature of a text and with the interplay of meaning and structure rather than with biographical or historical considerations.

Ode: a serious poem on an exalted subject, generally in an elevated style.

Onomatopoeia: words that sound like their meaning, such as "buzz," "bark," and "hiss." Sound patterns that reinforce meaning over one or more lines may also be onomatopoeic.

Open form: a form of poetry in which the sense of the second line of a couplet is completed in the next couplet.

Organic form: the way in which structure may seem to develop inherently within a text as it unifies and stabilizes the work as a whole.

Oxymoron: the juxtaposition of terms or ideas that are literally contradictory, such as "living death," "howling stillness."

Paradox: a statement that seems self-contradictory but is somehow true.

Persona: a Latin term for "mask"; the projected speaker or narrator of a text, a mask for the author.

Personification: the attribution of human qualities to nature, animals, or objects.

Picaresque: a type of fiction, generally satiric, that deals with the adventures of a roguish hero.

Poetic line: a structural unit of measurement in verse; unlike a line of prose, a poetic line need not make sense as a unit. In *metrical verse,* the length of a line is determined by the number of **feet** it contains and by the **meter** used; in *accentual verse,* by the number of accented syllables; in *syllabic verse,* by a syllable count; and in **free verse,** by units of conversational rhythm, of syntax, of breath, or of thought, or by rhetorical units.

Point of view: the perspective through which a literary work is given. With a *first-person* point of view, the narrator identifies himself or herself as "I" and is commonly the main character. With a *third-person* point of view, the narrator is outside the story and refers to characters as "he," "she," and "they." With an *omniscient* point of view, the third-person narrator knows all, can be everywhere, and can enter characters' minds.

Postmodernism: a literary and artistic philosophy that rejects all formal constraints, following the **modernism** of the early twentieth century. The postmodern artist tends to accept the world as fragmented and incoherent and to represent those characteristics in art, typically in a comic and self-reflexive style.

Proscenium arch: an arch over the front of a stage. The arch, from which a curtain typically is hung, separates the audience from the action.

Prosody: the analysis of versification, including description of **meters** and of **stanzaic forms.**

Quatrain: a stanza consisting of four lines with some pattern of rhyme; it is the most common **stanzaic form** in English.

Realism: a nineteenth-century literary philosophy that attempted to represent "real life" faithfully as the common reader might know it, partly in reaction to **romanticism.** Realism also refers to a recurrent style of writing typified by the nineteenth-century realists.

Romanticism: a wide-ranging artistic and literary movement inspired politically, by the revolutions in America and in France, and intellectually, as a reaction to the Enlightenment. Romantic works are known for their rejection of classical models, the privileging of individual experience, the celebration of imagination, and a marked interest in the artist as a hero and prophet aspiring beyond human limitation.

Satire: literature that ridicules social institutions or vices and follies.

Sestina: a complicated verse form, invented by twelfth-century French troubadours, that consists of six stanzas of six lines each and a concluding tercet, or grouping of three lines. The terminal words of the first stanza are repeated as terminal words in the succeeding stanzas, as in the tercets, in a strict but varying order.

Socratic irony: an ironic situation in which a character feigns ignorance and a desire to be enlightened by opinions that turn out to be erroneous.

Soliloquy: in drama, a speech given by a character generally alone on stage, expressing thoughts aloud.

Sonnet: a poem of fourteen lines in *iambic pentameter* (see **meter**) with a rhyme scheme.

Stanzaic form: in poetry, a structure consisting of stanzas (groupings of verse / lines), generally marked by a recurrent rhyme scheme. Typical stanzaic forms are the *couplet,* a pair of rhymed lines; the *tercet,* or *triplet,* three lines with a single rhyme; and the **quatrain,** a four-line stanza.

Stream of consciousness: a narrative technique that attempts to reproduce the uninterrupted flow of a character's mental processes; ideas and sense impressions may intermingle without logical progression.

Synecdoche: a figure of speech in which a part is substituted for the whole, or vice-versa, such as "wheels" for "car" or "copper" for "penny."

Synesthesia: the description of one type of sensory experience in terms of another: for example, sound might be described in terms of color, as in "the trumpet's red blare."

Tone: the author's attitude—playful, serious, somber, ironic, and so on—revealed through language, atmosphere, and mood.

Transcendentalism: in American literature, a nonsystematic nineteenth-century philosophy that holds that all of creation is spiritual in nature and is best known through the intuitive rather than the rational mind. Largely developed by Ralph Waldo Emerson and derived from the work of Immanuel Kant and of Thomas Carlyle, among others, it was seen by many as a threat to traditional Christianity because of its pantheistic strain.

Unity: the sense that the aspects of a play form a unified entity: the *"three unities,"* as defined by Aristotle, are *unity of time* (the play's action occurring in one day), *unity of place* (in one setting), and *unity of action* (in an orderly manner leading toward the plot's resolution).

Vorticism: an artistic movement, begun in the early twentieth century, that relates art forms to the machine and to modern industrial civilization. Regarding lifelike representation as unnecessary, it insists upon an imaginative reconstruction of nature in mechanistic designs, aligning it with cubism and futurism.

Acknowledgments

Abigail Adams: Reprinted by permission of the publishers from *The Book of Abigail and John,* edited by L. H. Butterfield, Marc Friedlander, and Mary-Jo Kline, Cambridge, Mass.: Harvard University Press, Copyright © 1975 by The Massachusetts Historical Society.

John Adams: From *The Adams-Jefferson Letters: The Complete Correspondence Between Thomas Jefferson and Abigail and John Adams,* edited by Lester J. Cappon. Copyright © 1959, 1988 The University of North Carolina Press. Published for the Institute of Early American History and Culture in Williamsburg, VA. Reprinted by permission.

Joel Barlow: From *A Yankee Odyssey: The Life of Joel Barlow* by James Woodress. Copyright © 1958 by James Woodress, copyright renewed 1986. Reprinted by permission of Harper & Row, Publishers, Inc. From *Joel Barlow and Napoleon* by Leon Howard, Huntington Library Quarterly, Vol. II, October 1938. Reprinted with the permission of The Henry E. Huntington Library.

William Bartram: From *The Travels of William Bartram,* Naturalist's Edition, edited by Francis Harper. Yale University Press, 1958.

Robert Beverley: From *The History and the Present State of Virginia,* edited with an Introduction by Louis B. Wright. The University of North Carolina Press.

William Bradford: From *Of Plymouth Plantation* by William Bradford, edited by Samuel Eliot Morison. Copyright 1952 by Samuel Eliot Morison and renewed © 1980 by Emily M. Beck. Reprinted by permission of Alfred A. Knopf, Inc.

Anne Bradstreet: Reprinted by permission of the publishers from *Works of Anne Bradstreet,* edited by Jeannine Hensely, Cambridge, Mass.: Harvard University Press, Copyright © 1967 by the President and Fellows of Harvard College. All rights reserved.

Charles Brockden Brown: Reprinted with permission of the publishers from *The Novels and Related Works of Charles Brockden Brown.* Bicentennial Edition. C.S.E. Edition, Vol. III: Arthur Mervyn: or Memoirs of the Year 1793, edited by Sydney J. Krause and S. W. Reid, The Kent State University Press, 1980. From *Wieland and "Memoirs of Carwin"* by Charles Brockden Brown, edited by Sydney J. Krause and S. W. Reid. C.S.E. Edition. The Kent State University Press, 1977.

William Cullen Bryant: From *Poetical Works of William Cullen Bryant,* 2 vols., edited by Park Godwin (New York: Russell & Russell, 1967).

William Byrd II: Reprinted by permission of the publishers from *The Prose of William Byrd of Westover,* edited by Louis B. Wright, Cambridge, Mass.: The Belknap Press of Harvard University Press, Copyright © 1966 by the President and Fellows of Harvard College.

Lydia Maria Child: From *The American Frugal Housewife* by Lydia Maria Child. Reprinted by permission of Alice M. Geffen, 1972. From *Hobomok & Other Writings on Indians by Lydia Maria Child* by Carolyn L. Karcher. Copyright © 1986 by Rutgers, The State University. Reprinted by permission of Rutgers University Press.

Christopher Columbus: From the *Journals and Other Documents on the Life and Voyages of Christopher Columbus,* trans. and edited by Samuel Eliot Morison, 1963. By permission of Emily Morison Beck.

Jonathan Edwards: From *The Great Awakening,* edited by C. C. Goen. Reprinted with permission from Yale University Press. Copyright © 1972 Yale University Press.

Ralph Waldo Emerson: Reprinted by permission of the publishers from *The Collected Works of Ralph Waldo Emerson,* edited by Alfred R. Ferguson; Vol. I, Introduction and Notes by Robert E. Spiller; Vols. II & III, Introduction and Notes by Joseph Slater; Cambridge, Mass.: The Belknap Press of Harvard University Press, Copyright © 1971, 1979 and 1983 by the President and Fellows of Harvard College. Reprinted by permission of the publishers from *The Journals and Miscellaneous Notebooks of Ralph Waldo Emerson;* Vol. VII, Plumstead and Hayford, eds.; Vol. VIII, Gilman and Parsons, eds.; Vol. XV, Allardt and Hill, eds.; Cambridge, Mass.: The Belknap Press of Harvard University Press, Copyright © 1969, 1979, and 1982 by the President and Fellows of Harvard College. Letter to Walt Whitman reprinted by permission of New York University Press from *Walt Whitman: Leaves of Grass, Reader's Comprehensive Edition,* edited by Harold W. Blodgett and Sculley Bradley. Copyright © 1965 by New York University.

The Federalist: Reprinted by permission of the publishers from *The Federalist* by Alexander Hamilton, James Madison, and John Jay, edited by Benjamin Hitch Wright, Cambridge, Mass.: The Belknap Press of Harvard University Press, Copyright © 1961 by the President and Fellows of Harvard College.

Fannie Fern: From *Ruth Hall and Other Writings* by Fanny Fern, edited by Joyce W. Warren. Copyright © 1986 by Rutgers, The State University. Reprinted by permission of Rutgers University Press.

Hannah Webster Foster: From *The Coquette* by Hannah W. Foster, edited by Cathy N. Davidson. Copyright © 1987 by Cathy N. Davidson. Reprinted by permission of Oxford University Press, Inc.

Benjamin Franklin: From *The Papers of Benjamin Franklin,* Copyright © 1963 by the American Philosophical Society and Yale University. All rights reserved. From *The Autobiography of Benjamin Franklin,* Copyright © 1964 by the American Philosophical Society and Yale University.

Philip Freneau: From *The Last Poems of Philip Freneau,* edited by Lewis Leary. Copyright 1945 by the Trustees of Rutgers College in New Jersey. Reprinted by permission of Rutgers University Press. From *The Poems of Philip Freneau,* Vol. II, edited by Fred Lewis Pattee (New York: Russell & Russell, 1963). From *Poems of Freneau,* edited by Harry Hayden Clark (New York: Hafner Press, 1960).

Frances E. W. Harper: From *Complete Poems of Frances E. W. Harper,* edited by Maryemma Graham. Copyright © 1988 by Oxford University Press, Inc. Reprinted by permission.

George Washington Harris: From *Humor of the Old Southwest,* edited by Hennig Cohen and William B. Dillingham. Copyright © 1964, 1975, the University of Georgia Press.

Nathaniel Hawthorne: Copyright © 1965, 1972, 1974 by The Ohio State University Press. The text of *The Scarlet Letter* is that of the Centenary Edition of *The Works of Nathaniel Hawthorne* and is reprinted by permission. Copyright © 1962 by The Ohio State University.

Washington Irving: From *The Sketch-Book of Geoffrey Crayon, Gent.* by Washington Irving. Copyright © 1978 and reprinted with the permission of Twayne Publishers, a division of G. K. Hall & Co., Boston.

Harriet Jacobs: From *Incidents in the Life of a Slave Girl* by Harriet Jacobs, edited by Valerie Smith. The Schomburg Library of Nineteenth-Century Black Women Writers, Copyright © 1988 by Oxford University Press, Inc. Reprinted by permission.

Thomas Jefferson: From *The Notes on the State of Virginia* by Thomas Jefferson. The University of North Carolina Press, 1954.

Augustus Baldwin Longstreet: From *Humor of the Old Southwest,* edited by Hennig Cohen and William B. Dillingham. Copyright © 1964, 1975, the University of Georgia Press.

Cotton Mather: Reprinted by permission of the publishers from *Bonifacius: An Essay Upon the Good,* edited by David Levin, Cambridge, Mass.: The Belknap Press of Harvard University Press, Copyright © 1966 by the President and Fellows of Harvard College.

Herman Melville: From *Correspondence: The Writings of Herman Melville,* the Northwestern-Newberry Edition, Volume XIV, edited by Lynn Horth. Revised and augmented version of the Davis-Gilman edition of *Letters* (Yale University Press, 1960). The Northwestern University Press and The Newberry Library, Evanston and Chicago, 1991. "Billy Budd, Sailor" reprinted with permission of The University of Chicago Press. Edited from the manuscript with Introduction and Notes by Harrison Hayford and Merton M. Sealts, Jr. Copyright © 1962 by The University of Chicago Press.

Native-American Literature: From The Book of *Chilam Balam of Chumayel,* trans. by Ralph L. Roys, with an Introduction by J. Eric S. Thompson. New edition copyright © 1967 by the University of Oklahoma Press. From *Singing for Power: The Song Magic of the Papago Indians of Southern Arizona,* by Ruth Murray Underhill, pp. 68-70. Copyright 1938, © 1966 by Ruth Murray Underhill. Reprinted with permission of The University of California Press. From *Told in Tlingit* by George R. Betts. Transcribed in Tlingit by Constance Naish and Gillian Story. Translated into English by Nora Marks Dauenhauer. Reprinted from *Haa Shuka, Our Ancestors: Tlingit Oral Narratives,* edited by Nora Marks Dauenhauer and Richard Dauenhauer, © 1987 by Sealaska Heritage Foundation. Seattle: University of Washington Press.

Thomas Paine: From *The Writings of Thomas Paine,* edited by Moncure Daniel Conway, Vol. IV, 1967. Courtesy of AMS Press, Inc.

Susanna Haswell Rowson: From *Charlotte Temple* by Susanna Rowson, edited by Cathy N. Davidson. Copyright © 1987 by Cathy N. Davidson. Reprinted by permission of Oxford University Press, Inc.

Samuel Sewall: Excerpts from *The Diary of Samuel Sewall,* edited by M. Halsey Thomas. Copyright © 1973 by Farrar, Straus & Giroux, Inc. Reprinted by permission of Farrar, Straus & Giroux, Inc.

Edward Taylor: From *Poems of Edward Taylor,* edited by Donald E. Stanford. Copyright © 1960 by Donald E. Stanford; renewed 1988. Reprinted by permission.

Henry David Thoreau: From *Walden: Writings of Henry D. Thoreau.* Copyright © 1971, 1989 Princeton University Press. Complete text, pp. 3-333 reprinted with permission of Princeton University Press. From *Writings of Henry D. Thoreau: Reform Papers.* Copyright © 1973 Princeton University Press. Excerpt, pp. 63-109 reprinted with permission of Princeton University Press.

Thomas Bangs Thorpe: From *Humor of the Old Southwest,* edited by Hennig Cohen and William B. Dillingham. Copyright © 1964, 1975, the University of Georgia Press.

Royall Tyler: From *The Contrast* by Royall Tyler, 1970. Courtesy of AMS Press, Inc.

Mercy Otis Warren: From *The Plays and Poems of Mercy Otis Warren,* 1980. Reprinted by permission of Scholars' Facsimiles & Reprints.

Phillis Wheatley: From *The Poems of Phillis Wheatley,* Revised and Enlarged Edition, edited by Julian D. Mason. Copyright © 1989 The University of North Carolina Press. Reprinted by permission.

Walt Whitman: Reprinted by permission of New York University Press from *Walt Whitman: Leaves of Grass, Reader's Comprehensive Edition,* edited by Harold W. Blodgett and Sculley Bradley. Copyright © 1965 by New York University Press.

John Woolman: From *The Journal and Major Essays of John Woolman,* edited by Phillips P. Moulton. Copyright © 1971 by Phillips P. Moulton. Published by Oxford University Press.

From *The European Discovery of America: The Southern Voyages 1492–1616* by Samuel Eliot Morison. Copyright © 1974 by Samuel Eliot Morison. Reprinted by permission of Oxford University Press, Inc.

From *The Abolitionists* by Louis Ruchames. Copyright © 1963 by Louis Ruchames. Reprinted by permission of The Putnam Publishing Group.

PHOTOS AND ILLUSTRATIONS

American Antiquarian Society, Worcester, Mass.: p. 532. AP/Wide World Photos: p. 1896. Association of American Railroads, Washington, DC: p. 1326. The Berkshire Museum: p. 838. The Bettmann Archive: pp. 46, 96, 274, 613, 1096, 1925. Boston Athenaeum: p. 1838. Courtesy of the British Museum: p. 15, 521. Brown University Library: p. 761. Culver Pictures: p. 1287. Ewing Galloway, N.Y.: p. 867. Field Museum of National History: p. 423. Historical Society of Pennsylvania: p. 321. By permission of the Houghton Library, Harvard University: p. 1343. Henry E. Huntington Library and Art Gallery: p. 117. Independence National Historical Park, Philadelphia: pp. 454, 657. Thomas Jefferson Memorial Foundation: 427. Keystone View Co. of New York: p. 460. Library of Congress: pp. 115, 185, 186, 273, 545, 1094, 1341, 1477, 1681, 1732, 1746, 1914, 1923. Lilly Library, Indiana University: p. 763. Massachusetts Historical Society: p. 706. Moorland-Spingarn Research Center, Howard University: p. 1915. Courtesy of Mount Holyoke College: p. 1298. Courtesy of Museum of Fine Arts, Boston: pp. 215, 603. National Gallery of Art, Washington, Andrew A. Mellon Collection: p. 709. National Portrait Gallery, Smithsonian Institution: pp. 707, 1474. New England Mutual Life Insurance Co., Boston: p. 83. New York Historical Society: pp. 431, 532, 1812. New York Public Library: pp. 7, 57, 59, 60, 82, 149, 235, 318, 400, 468, 469, 520, 533, 560, 562, 611, 659, 671, 697, 837, 855, 1270, 1298, 1299, 1329, 1847. New York State Historical Association, Cooperstown: p. 746. The Perry Pictures, Boston Edition: p. 1858. Photo © Lamson, Portland: p. 1867. Photo by Sarony, New York: p. 1856. A. J. Telfer, Cooperstown, N.Y.: p. 745. The Valentine Museum, Richmond, Va.: p.1920. Virginia State Library: p. 245. Courtesy of Worcester Art Museum: p. 670.

Index